AIRLINE FLEETS
2015

Edited by Lyn Buttifant, Chris Chatfield, Peter Hillman and Terry Smith

in collaboration with
Tony Beales, Roy Blewett, Paul Compton, Steve Darke, Colin Frost,
Dave Garbett, Peter Gerhardt, Rolf Larsson, Robert Swan,
Barrie Towey, Tony Wheeler and John Wilkinson

Introduction 3
Explanatory Notes... 5
Fleet Lists 7
Jet and turboprop airliners in non-airline use............ 644
Airlines removed since the 2014 edition.................. 665
Airline two-letter IATA designators.......................... 667
Airline three-letter ICAO designators........................ 674
Airport three-letter IATA codes.............................. 686
Nationality index... 695
Operator Index... 697
Airline alliances.. 716

Published by Air-Britain Publishing, part of Air-Britain Trading Limited,
the trading arm of The Air-Britain Trust.

Sales Department   Causeway House, Chiddingstone Causeway,
Tonbridge, Kent TN11 8JP

Membership Enquiries   1 Rose Cottages, 179 Penn Road
Hazlemere,Bucks HP15 7NE

Further information is available on our website: http://www.air-britain.co.uk

PHOTO CAPTIONS

Front cover   Boeing787-8 Dreamliner VT-ANH of Air India about to touch down at London-Heathrow on 16.214 (Marcus Reeves)

Rear cover   Top down: Embraer ERJ-I95 PR-AUB of Brazilian internal low-cost carrier Azul on approach to Rio de Janeiro on 29.9.14 (Helio Salmon); Airbus A319-112 N744P of US Airways wearing retro Piedmont colours at Charlotte-Douglas International, NC on 31.3.14, and Dornier Do.228-201 CS-AYT of Portuguese regional operator Aero Vip about to land at Funchal Airport, Madeira on 30.6.14 (both Brian Nichols)

ISBN I978-0-85130-472-4   ISSN 0262-1657
Printed by Bell & Bain Ltd, Glasgow

INTRODUCTION

Information and Changes for the 2015 Edition

A few minor changes have been made to increase the book's user-friendliness. For example, more of the alternative names used by some operators have been included both in the main text and the operator index. Enhancements introduced in the last five years have been retained, including the separate section re-introduced last year, listing those operators who have been removed from the 2014 edition in the course of compiling this edition, and the reasons for their removal. The summary of the current situation regarding the various airline alliances and their affiliates has been retained. Because it is cheper to print in 32-page units, rather than finish the book with a 24-page unit, there is space for some blank pages at the end of the book for readers' notes.

Please do take the time to look at the section at the end of these notes that details the use of abbreviations and symbols. A clear understanding of these will facilitate your use of the book. For example the ♦ symbol is used to highlight the introduction of a new aircraft to a particular fleet (except in the section devoted to Jet and Turboprop airliners in non-airline use).

Once again this year space has been made available for deliveries expected through the year, although given the ever-continuing fluidity of the market it is doubtful that every potential delivery will have been included; nevertheless the reader should be able to keep the book reasonably updated throughout the year.

The overall prospects for the airline industry have not diminished at all in the last twelve months. There is a continuing feeling of optimism that the commercial aviation sector will be able to sustain its current revenue and earnings growth, reinforced by continuing high production levels at front-end and supply chain providers, driven by the twin forces of obsolete aircraft replacement by more fuel-efficient types, and continued increases in passenger and freight traffic.

Both aircraft orders and production aro oxpoctou lu ilse over the next ten years, so that barring political disruption, commercial aircraft production over this period is still expected to increase by around 25% on existing rates.

The Russian industry continues to find market penetration difficult in the face of well-established Western-built airliners, and most Soviet-era jets have now been taken out of service. The ability of the fledgling Chinese airliner industry to make any serious headway remains questionable, although Its long-awaited CACC C919 170-seat twinjet airliner is about to make its maiden flight.

New-build Twin Otters continue to be sold by Viking Air, RUAG are producing new Dornier 228NGs for Venezuela, Cessna's Caravan continues to sell strongly to both civil and military users, and Pilatus are selling their PC-12 faster than they can satisfy orders. Operators in remote areas are buying the Quest Kodiak, GippsAero Airvan and Pacific Aerospace 750XL – there continues to be little evidence of a global recession amongst either the major aircraft manufacturers, or those who have found niches in which to sell, and who can collectively provide the vital means of transportation that the global economy requires.

Details included

Details are included for approximately 2,500 operators in over 200 countries. As a general guideline, the complete fleets of operators with an IATA two- or three-letter code are included (unless they only operate corporate flights), together with non-IATA-coded operators of regular services where fleets are known. Many of the world's major helicopter fleets down to Bell 206 and Ecureuil/AStar size are included, with the large majority of all twin-engined aircraft and many single-engined aircraft down to Piper Cherokee Six size that are operated on passenger, tourism support or express freight services. A number of emergency medical (EMS) and flight-seeing operators are also ncluded within the same size guidelines.

The larger fleets are shown in type and registration order, with a space separating types. For space-saving reasons, smaller fleets and those with a large number of types but only one or two aircraft of each type are listed in registration order. This format is being developed all the time and has hopefully resulted in as clean a presentation of the data as is possible within sensible boundaries.

Civil-registered jet and turboprop airliners in non-airline use, i.e. those owned and operated by the manufacturers or used in executive or special purpose roles, are again included in this year's edition. This section **does not** include details of the stored ex-airline aircraft.

The component parts of the US majors have again been grouped together under the airline heading and cross-referenced to the individual feeder carriers although this is becoming increasingly difficult as more and more operators provide feeder services to a range of airlines.

Credits

We are indebted to the following for contributions, corrections, assistance and the use of information – Peter Budden, Ian Burnett, Sue Bushell, Dennis Clement, Jeremy Day, David Fidler, Philip Hancock, Norman Hibberd, Dave Partington, Paul Wiggins, all contributors to the Commercial Scene section of Air-Britain News edited by Tony Wheeler; Aviation Letter and the various Air-Britain publications as well as relevant web-sites.

Update Information

For readers who are not already members of Air-Britain, this edition can be kept up-to-date by reading Commercial Scene and other sections in Air-Britain News Details of the many benefits of membership are included at the end of this book.

Where possible, information received up to **15th May 2015** has been incorporated in the main text. Naturally, in a work of this complexity and scope, some errors and omissions will occur, and any reader who can add to, amend or correct the information included in this publication is invited to contact the e-mail address below.

Users are advised that the information in this publication cannot be reproduced, stored in a retrieval system or transmitted in the form in which it appears, by any means electronic, photocopying, recording or otherwise, without the express prior permission of the Copyright owner. Individual items of information may be used in other publications with due acknowledgement to Air-Britain (Historians).

Updates and corrections should be sent to the following address:

airlinefleets@air-britain.co.uk

EXPLANATORY NOTES

1 Noise Regulations

With effect from 01Jan85 FAR Part 36 Stage 2 regulations came into force with respect to four-engined aircraft. These prevented any further civil operations of Boeing 707/720 and DC-8 (except -70 series) aircraft to or from US airports unless they were fitted with hushkits so that they conformed to the new noise standards. Similar regulations applied in the UK from 01Jan88. Stage 3 requirements are now implemented with all non-compliant aircraft required to be hush-kitted or re-engined; this applies to 707s, 727s, 737s (srs-100/200s), DC-8/9s, 1-11s, Tu-134/154s and Il-62/76s. Many of these aircraft are being withdrawn from service as the economic situation makes it uneconomic to undertake the costly conversions (indeed some of the planned hush-kitting schemes have been abandoned). In the main text of the book reference is made, where known, to the type of hush-kit fitted to Boeing 707, 727, early 737s and Douglas DC-8s and 9s and whether it is Stage 2 or Stage 3 compliant. (For example, FedEx 3 means a 727 fitted with a Stage 3 compliant FedEx hush-kit). Stage 4 hush-kits are also available for MD-80 series.

2 Chapter 11

In the US section of this book, reference is sometimes made to 'Chapter 11'. This refers to a section of the US bankruptcy code designed to give a company protection from its creditors while it attempts a financial reorganisation. Plans for such a reorganisation have to be submitted to and approved by the bankruptcy court. A Chapter 11 filing may or may not be accompanied by a cessation of operations. If operations do continue, then it is usually at a very much reduced level. If they are suspended, then it is possible that they may be restarted in some form at a future date. If the reorganisation plan fails, then an application for liquidation under Chapter 7 will be made.

Since a Chapter 11 filing does not automatically result in a permanent cessation of operations, airlines are only deleted from this book if at the time of writing it appears that resumption of operations in the near future is unlikely.

3 Boeing 747 Suffixes

An M suffix after Boeing 747-200s indicates that the aircraft is a Combi (Mixed) version fitted with a Side Cargo Door. While not used officially in national registers, the M suffix convention is used in Boeing official literature and is therefore adopted in this publication. Suffixes SCD and EUD indicate converted Side Cargo Door and Extended Upper Deck versions. SF indicates that the aircraft is a 'Special Freighter' conversion and BCF a Boeing Converted Freighter; BDSF is similar but converted by IAI without Boeing support (for 747-400 passenger to freight conversions).

4 Boeing 737 Test Registrations

Several Boeing 737s complete their first flights from Renton (PAE) to Boeing Field (BFI) with the registration N1786B or other test registration and these are shown when known.

5 Winglets/Sharklets

In the book the suffix /W indicates that the aircraft is fitted with Aviation Partner Boeing winglets. The same suffix is employed for Airbus aircraft fitted with sharklets.

6 German Spellings

German place names appear in anglicised form for operator bases but in the native German spelling for aircraft names (e.g. in the Lufthansa fleet).

7 Description of Entries

Countries are listed in alphabetical order of nationality prefix, with the airlines in each country also in alphabetical order. Fleets are listed in alphabetical order of aircraft manufacturer where five or more of the same type occur, otherwise they are listed in registration order. Aircraft type descriptions generally quote the manufacturer currently considered responsible for producing the aircraft. The immediate previous identity appears after the constructor's number and helps determine the source of newly acquired aircraft.

Each Country is identified in bold and italics and enclosed in a box; followed by airlines in alphabetical order, each again enclosed in a box. The details listed for each airline are its name (and any trading or alternative name where appropriate); airline call-sign; the two-letter IATA designator and three-letter ICAO codes in brackets (where allocated and known); and their main operating base(s), again with the recognised IATA three-letter code in brackets (where allocated).

Each individual entry, from the left, lists current registration (or that known to be reserved and likely to be taken up with that operator in brackets), followed by type. The next column lists the construction number, followed, for Boeing and McDonnell-Douglas types, by the line number separated by a slash (/). There then appears the immediate past identity (where known) followed by any fleet number or name. The final entry indicates any lease arrangements or other comments. Any three-letter designation refers to another airline and these codes are to be found indexed later in the book. Aircraft on order (recognized by o/o against their entry) are listed where either delivery is due in the year following the date of publication or where details of the aircraft are known. Otherwise details of aircraft on order for delivery in subsequent years are listed at the bottom of the aircraft type or airline entry; also listed there are any alliances, franchises or ownership details of interest.

Leased (lsd) aircraft will be found in the owner's fleet as well as that of the leasing airline. Where it is known that an aircraft is due to change operator during the currency of this book, it is shown in both fleets with a suitable note. Aircraft that have been withdrawn from service (wfs) are listed unless they are known to have been broken up or are beyond repair. Likewise, aircraft that have been involved in accidents but not confirmed as written off are still included with their accident date.

8 Abbreviations

Abbreviations and symbols used in the text have the following meanings:

♦	Any entry that is a new delivery, new aircraft in the fleet, addition of winglets, storage or lease.
[xxx]	Any 3-letter code in square brackets indicates the three-letter code of the aircraft's storage location
<	Leased in from
>	Leased out to
c/s	Colour Scheme
FP	Floatplane
Frtr	Freighter
o/o	on order and expected to be delivered before the next edition
SPB	Seaplane Base
wfs	withdrawn from service
WS	Wheels/Skis

AP-   PAKISTAN (Islamic Republic of Pakistan)

AHS AIR INTERNATIONAL   (AHS)   Karachi (KHI)

☐ AP-BIO	Boeing 747-243F	22545/545	ex N545SG	♦
☐ AP-BKS	Boeing 747-281BF	23813/683	ex EK74723	♦

AIRBLUE   Airblue (PA/ABQ)   Karachi (KHI)

☐ AP-EDA	Airbus A320-214	3974	ex F-WWIT	
☐ AP-EDD	Airbus A320-214	1467	ex EI-CVD	
☐ AP-EDG	Airbus A320-214/S	5891	ex F-WWIV	
☐ AP-EDH	Airbus A320-214/S	5943	ex F-WWDR	
☐ UR-WRH	Airbus A321-231	2462	ex G-TTID	<WRC♦
☐ UR-WRJ	Airbus A321-231	1869	ex UR-DAT	<WRC♦
☐ UR-WRO	Airbus A321-211	0781	ex G-OOPH	<WRC♦

AIR INDUS   (I6/MPK)   Karachi (KHI)

☐ A6-ESS	Boeing 737-33A	25011/2012	ex G-STRI	<ESJ
☐ AP-BLE	Boeing 737-322	24672/1915	ex JY-JAO	
☐ AP-BLF	Boeing 737-33A	27469/2864	ex N901AS	
☐ AP-BLG	Boeing 737-33A	27910/2873	ex N902AS	

JS AIR CHARTER   JS Charters (JSJ)   Karachi (KHI)

☐ AP-BJC	Beech 1900C-1	UC-119	ex N119YV	
☐ AP-BJS	Beech 1900C-1	UC-145	ex ZS-PCD	

HAWK AIRLINES

☐ AP-BIY	Britten-Norman BN-2B-21 Islander	2132	ex G-HEBR	
☐ AP-BJJ	Britten-Norman BN-2A-27 Islander	476	ex G-BDJV	

PAKISTAN INTERNATIONAL AIRLINES   Pakistan (PK/PIA)   Karachi (KHI)

☐ AP-BDZ	Airbus A310-308	585	ex F-WWCH		
☐ AP-BEB	Airbus A310-308	587	ex F-WWCT		wfs
☐ AP-BEC	Airbus A310-308	590	ex F-WWCX		
☐ AP-BEG	Airbus A310-308	653	ex F-WWCZ		
☐ AP-BEQ	Airbus A310-308	656	ex F-WWCB		
☐ AP-BEU	Airbus A310-308	691	ex F-WWCD		
☐ AP-BGN	Airbus A310-324ET	676	ex F-WQTG		dam 24Jun14
☐ AP-BGO	Airbus A310-324ET	678	ex F-WQTC		
☐ AP-BGP	Airbus A310-324ET	682	ex F-WQTF		
☐ AP-BGQ	Airbus A310-325ET	660	ex F-OGYT		
☐ AP-BGR	Airbus A310-325ET	687	ex F-OGYU		
☐ AP-BLB	Airbus A320-214	2155	ex B-6016		♦
☐ AP-BLC	Airbus A320-214	2212	ex B-6015		♦
☐ AP-BLD	Airbus A320-214	2274	ex B-6017		♦
☐ AP-BLU	Airbus A320-214	2719	ex OK-LEE		♦
☐ AP-BLV	Airbus A320-214	2758	ex OK-LEF		♦
☐ AP-BLW	Airbus A320-214	2789	ex OK-LEG		♦
☐ AP-BHH	ATR 42-500	645	ex F-WWLE	Gwadar	
☐ AP-BHI	ATR 42-500	653	ex F-WWLK	Ziarat	
☐ AP-BHM	ATR 42-500	659	ex F-WWLQ		
☐ AP-BHN	ATR 42-500	661	ex F-WWLS		
☐ AP-BHO	ATR 42-500	663	ex F-WWLU		
☐ AP-BHP	ATR 42-500	665	ex F-WWLW	Gilgit	
☐ AP-BGJ	Boeing 777-240ER	33775/467			
☐ AP-BGK	Boeing 777-240ER	33776/469			
☐ AP-BGL	Boeing 777-240ER	33777/473			
☐ AP-BGY	Boeing 777-240LR	33781/504	ex N5022E		
☐ AP-BGZ	Boeing 777-240LR	33782/519	ex N6066Z		
☐ AP-BHV	Boeing 777-340ER	33778/601			
☐ AP-BHW	Boeing 777-340ER	33779/611			
☐ AP-BHX	Boeing 777-240ER	35296/613			
☐ AP-BID	Boeing 777-340ER	33780/705			
☐ AP-BFU	Boeing 747-367	23392/634	ex B-HIJ		
☐ AP-BFV	Boeing 747-367	23534/659	ex B-HIK		
☐ AP-BFY	Boeing 747-367	23920/690	ex B-HOM		
☐ AP-BKY	ATR 72-212A	994	ex F-WNUC		♦
☐ AP-BKZ	ATR 72-212A	1029	ex F-WNUE		♦
☐ AP-	ATR 72-212A	1036	ex F-WNUF		o/o♦
☐ AP-	ATR 72-212A	1037	ex F-WNUG		o/o♦

| SHAHEEN AIR CARGO | Shaheen Cargo (SEE) | | Islamabad (ISB) |

Ops freight flights with Boeing 707-320Cs leased from Pakistan AF and Ilyushin Il-76s leased from other operators, as required.

| SHAHEEN AIR INTERNATIONAL | Shaheen Air (NL/SAI) | | Karachi (KHI) |

☐ AP-BLH	Airbus A320-232	0542	ex EI-CUM	
☐ AP-BLI	Airbus A320-232	0877	ex EI-ELG	
☐ AP-BLJ	Airbus A320-232	1497	ex EI-EUS	
☐ AP-BLK	Airbus A320-232	2027	ex EI-EUL	
☐ AP-BLM	Airbus A320-232	3105	ex EI-EYF	
☐ AP-BLN	Airbus A320-232	3270	ex EI-EYG	
☐ AP-BJN	Boeing 737-4H6	26460/2533	ex N829AR	dam 30Dec14♦
☐ AP-BJO	Boeing 737-4H6	27166/2410	ex N146PA	
☐ AP-BJP	Boeing 737-4H8	27167/2419	ex N109PR	
☐ AP-BJQ	Boeing 737-4H6	26449/2491	ex N102KR	
☐ AP-BJR	Boeing 737-4Q8	25164/2447	ex SP-LLL	
☐ AP-BJT	Boeing 737-4Q8	25740/2461	ex SP-LLK	
☐ AP-BJU	Boeing 737-4H6	26465/2362	ex N104HK	[KHI]
☐ AP-BJV	Boeing 737-4H6	27190/2568	ex N112SE	[KHI]
☐ AP-BKF	Boeing 737-430	27004/2344	ex N418BC	[KHI]
☐ AP-BKO	Boeing 737-406	25355/2132	ex N355SM	[KHI]
☐ AP-BHB	Boeing 737-277 (Nordam 3)	22655/872	ex N188AW Chundam	[KHI]
☐ AP-BHC	Boeing 737-291 (Nordam 3)	21509/521	ex EX-040	[KHI]
☐ AP-BIU	Boeing 737-236	21807/710	ex ZS-OKE	[KHI]
☐ AP-BKL	Airbus A330-301	055	ex VQ-BEU	
☐ AP-BKM	Airbus A330-301	070	ex VQ-BCW	
☐ AP-BKN	Airbus A330-301	086	ex VQ-BEQ	
☐ JY-JAG	Boeing 767-204ER	24757/299	ex G-SLVR	<JAV♦

| STAR AIR AVIATION | (6S/URJ) | | Karachi (KHI) |

☐ AP-ESC	Douglas DC-9-32	48150/1014	ex A6-ESC	[RKT]

| VISION AIR INTERNATIONAL | (VIS) | | Karachi (KHI) |

☐ AP-BIA	Boeing 737-2H3	22625/776	ex UP-B3705	
☐ AP-BIV	Boeing 747-246F	22477/494	ex N224JT	
☐ AP-BIZ	Boeing 737-2H3	22624/758	ex UP-B3704	wfs
☐ AP-BKE	Boeing 737-229C	20915/401	ex 5Y-JAP	♦
☐ AP-VAI	Boeing 747-41BF	32804/1312	ex B-2461	o/o♦
☐ AP-VIS	Boeing 747-41BF	32803/1306	ex B-2473	o/o♦

A2-   BOTSWANA (Republic of Botswana)

| AIR BOTSWANA | Botswana (BP/BOT) | | Gaborone (GBE) |

☐ A2-ABD	British Aerospace 146 Srs.100	E1101	ex (G-CBAE)		wfs
☐ A2-ABF	British Aerospace 146 Srs.100	E1160	ex G-BVLJ		wfs
☐ A2-ABG	Avro 146-RJ85	E2303	ex D-AVRP	Gcwihaba	
☐ A2-ABH	Avro 146-RJ85	E2304	ex D-AVRQ	Domboshaba	
☐ A2-ABN	ATR 42-500	507	ex F-WQNG	Chobe	
☐ A2-ABO	ATR 42-500	511	ex F-WQNC	Okavango	
☐ A2-ABP	ATR 42-500	512	ex F-WQNI	Makgadikgadi	
☐ A2-ABR	ATR 72-212A	786	ex F-WWEE		

| BLUE SKY AIRWAYS | | | Gaborone (GBE) |

☐ A2-FMX	Boeing 737-247 (Nordam 3)	23520/1329	ex ZS-SHL	

| AIR CHARTER BOTSWANA | | | |

☐ A2-SPA	Pilatus PC-12	788	

| DELTA AIR | | | Maun (MUB) |

☐ A2-AGR	Cessna U206F Stationair	U20601837	ex ZS-OCC	
☐ A2-AHN	Cessna U206G Stationair 6 II	U20606432	ex ZS-LKX	
☐ A2-AIW	Cessna 210N Centurion II	21064163	ex ZS-MYC	
☐ A2-AJA	Britten-Norman BN-2A Islander	271	ex ZS-LKE	
☐ A2-AJJ	Cessna 210L Centurion II	21061533	ex ZS-KPV	

| KALAHARI AIR SERVICES AND CHARTER | | | Gaborone (GBE) |

☐ A2-AFK	Cessna 210N Centurion II	21064203	ex N5427Y	
☐ A2-AHZ	Beech 200 Super King Air	BB-95	ex ZS-JPD	
☐ A2-DBH	Beech C90 King Air	LJ-988	ex ZS-LUU	
☐ A2-KAB	Beech 1900C-1	UC-150	ex ZS-PCE	

☐ A2-KAS	Beech 200 Super King Air	BB-614	ex ZS-LKA

MACK AIR — Maun (MUB)

☐ A2-AIC	Cessna U206G Stationair 6 II	U20606419	ex N9353Z
☐ A2-AJI	Cessna U206G Stationair 6 II	U20606842	ex ZS-NSS
☐ A2-AKB	Cessna U206F Stationair	U20601889	ex A2-ZHJ
☐ A2-FMD	Cessna U206G Stationair 6 II	U20606005	ex ZS-KSM
☐ A2-ZFF	Cessna U206D Super Skywagon	U206-1263	ex ZS-FPD
☐ A2-AJZ	Gippsland GA-8 Airvan	GA8-04-059	ex VH-CRQ
☐ A2-AKI	Cessna 208B Caravan I	208B0552	ex 5Y-VIJ
☐ A2-BBK	Gippsland GA-8 Airvan	GA8-11-147	
☐ A2-MEG	Cessna 208B Caravan I	208B0944	ex N4085S
☐ A2-NVH	Cessna 208B Caravan I	208B0473	ex ZS-NVH

MAJOR BLUE AIR — Maun (MUB)

☐ A2-MBA	Cessna 208B Caravan I	208B2136	ex N6251V
☐ A2-MBB	Cessna U206H Stationair II	20608276	ex ZS-AAT
☐ A2-MBC	Cessna 172S	172S10112	ex ZS-OHY
☐ A2-MBF	Cessna 172R	17281267	ex ZS-MSP

MOREMI AIR SERVICES — Maun (MUB)

☐ A2-AEI	Cessna U206F Stationair	U20602470	ex ZS-LDJ
☐ A2-LEB	Gippsland GA-8 Airvan	GA8-07-123	
☐ A2-SEB	Gippsland GA-8 Airvan		
☐ A2-TEN	Cessna 210L Centurion II	21061141	ex A2-AIY
☐ A2-UEB	Gippsland GA-8 Airvan		
☐ A2-ZED	Britten-Norman BN-2A-21 Islander	736	ex ZS-XGF

NAC EXECUTIVE CHARTER — Gaborone (GBE)

☐ A2-AJO	Beech 58 Baron	TH-614	ex ZS-OGB
☐ A2-CDC	Beech C90GTI King Air	LJ-1947	
☐ A2-MXI	Beech 200T Super King Air	BT-5	ex N205EC

NORTHERN AIR CHARTER — Maun (MUB)

☐ A2-ADK	Cessna U206G Stationair 6 II	U20606056	ex ZS-KUO
☐ A2-AER	Cessna U206G Stationair 6 II	U20606324	ex ZS-KXE
☐ A2-NAB	Cessna U206G Stationair 6 II	U20605439	ex ZS-KDA

SAFARI AIR — Maun (MUB)

☐ A2-AIX	Cessna U206F Stationair	U20601944	ex ZS-MAD
☐ A2-CEX	Cessna 207 Skywagon	20700154	ex ZS-IDG
☐ A2-SAA	Gippsland GA-8 Airvan	GA8-08-143	
☐ A2-SAF	Gippsland GA-8 Airvan	GA8-08-141	

SEFOFANE AIR CHARTER — Maun (MUB)

☐ A2-AIV	Cessna U206G Stationair 6 II	U20606410	ex ZS-LUA
☐ A2-ANT	Cessna U206G Stationair 6 II	U20606237	ex ZS-ANT
☐ A2-BEE	Cessna U206G Stationair 6 II	U20605665	ex ZS-KUL
☐ A2-JET	Cessna 206H Stationair	20608027	ex ZS-OIA
☐ A2-OWL	Cessna U206G Stationair 6 II	U20606978	ex ZS-NXR
☐ A2-XIG	Cessna U206G Stationair 6 II	U20605528	ex ZS-NSU
☐ A2-BUF	Cessna 208B Caravan I	208B0815	ex ZS-BUF Kwatale
☐ A2-EGL	Cessna 208B Caravan I	208B1158	ex ZS-ABR
☐ A2-HOP	Bell 206B Jet Ranger	2551	ex ZS-HHW
☐ A2-NAS	Cessna 208B Caravan I	208B0704	ex ZS-TSW
☐ 9J-TAU	Cessna 208B Caravan I	208B1262	ex N1239Y

WILDERNESS AIR — Maun (MUB)

☐ A2-BOK	Cessna 206H Stationair	20608029		FP
☐ A2-JKL	Cessna 206H Stationair	20608047	ex N248AS	FP
☐ A2-LEO	Cessna 208B Caravan I	208B0820	ex N1307A	
☐ A2-ZEB	Cessna 208B Caravan I	208B0750	ex A2-AEB	

XUGANA AIR — Maun (MUB)

☐ A2-AKH	Cessna 208 Caravan I	20800288	ex C-FWTK
☐ A2-AKK	Cessna 208B Caravan I	208B0441	ex ZS-OAR
☐ A2-AKO	Cessna 208B Caravan I	208B0736	ex ZS-OWW

A3- TONGA (Kingdom of Tonga)

CHATHAMS PACIFIC			(CP)		Nukuialofa
☐ A3-LYP	Britten-Norman BN-2A-27 Islander	821	ex ZK-LYP		>RLT
☐ ZK-CIC	Swearingen SA227AC Metro III	AC-623B	ex N623AV		>RLT
☐ ZK-CID	Convair 580F	385	ex HZ-SN22		

PEAU VAVA'U AIR			(30/PVU)	Tongatapu-Fua'amotu Intl (TBU)
☐ A3-FEW	Beech 65-80 Queen Air	LC-168	ex DQ-FEW	Queenaire 8800 conversion

REAL TONGA AIRLINES			(RT/RLT)	Tongatapu-Fua'amotu Intl (TBU)
☐ A3-LYP	Britten-Norman BN-2A-27 Islander	821	ex ZK-LYP	<CP
☐ A3-PAS	Britten-Norman BN-2A-26 Islander	1159	ex 5W-JUN	
☐ A3-RTL	AVIC I Y7-MA-60	0940	ex B-1027L	wfs
☐ A3-SAM	British Aerospace Jetstream 3206	982	ex VH-OTF	♦
☐ A3-SPV	Harbin Y-12E	032		♦
☐ YJ-AVS	Harbin Y-12IV	029		<AVN wfs
☐ ZK-CIC	Swearingen SA.227AC Metro III	AC-623B	ex N623AV	<CP

AOC suspended Sep14; ops continue

A4O- OMAN (Sultanate of Oman)

OMAN AIR		Khanjar (WY/OMA)		Muscat-Seeb Intl (MCT)
☐ A4O-DA	Airbus A330-243	1038	ex F-WWYM	
☐ A4O-DB	Airbus A330-343X	1044	ex F-WWKA	
☐ A4O-DC	Airbus A330-243	1049	ex F-WWKL	
☐ A4O-DD	Airbus A330-343X	1063	ex F-WWYN	
☐ A4O-DE	Airbus A330-343X	1093	ex F-WWYM	
☐ A4O-DF	Airbus A330-243	1120	ex F-WWYA	
☐ A4O-DG	Airbus A330-243	1227	ex F-WWYG	
☐ A4O-DH	Airbus A330-343	1572	ex F-WWKP	♦
☐ A4O-DI	Airbus A330-343	1582	ex F-WWKA	♦
☐ A4O-DJ	Airbus A330-343	1599	ex F-WWKY	♦
☐ A4O-BA	Boeing 737-8BK/W	29685/2457	ex N1786B	Fahud	
☐ A4O-BB	Boeing 737-8Q8/W	30721/2255		
☐ A4O-BC	Boeing 737-81M/W	35284/2738	ex N1786B	Ras Al Had
☐ A4O-BD	Boeing 737-81M/W	35287/2804	ex N1786B	
☐ A4O-BE	Boeing 737-81M/W	37161/2919	ex N1786B	
☐ A4O-BF	Boeing 737-8FZ/W	29637/3051		
☐ A4O-BG	Boeing 737-8FZ/W	29664/3060	ex N1787B	
☐ A4O-BH	Boeing 737-81M/W	40066/5104		♦
☐ A4O-BJ	Boeing 737-81M/W	34242/1674		
☐ A4O-BL	Boeing 737-81M/W	40067/5152	ex N1796B	♦
☐ A4O-BM	Boeing 737-8FZ/W	29682/2853		Mirbat
☐ A4O-BP	Boeing 737-8Q8/W	35272/2537	ex N1786B	
☐ A4O-BQ	Boeing 737-81M/W	44421/5189		♦
☐ A4O-BR	Boeing 737-81M/W	33104/1337		
☐ A4O-BU	Boeing 737-81M/W	35108/2554	ex N1786B	
☐ A4O-BV	Boeing 737-81M/W	40068/5160		♦
☐ A4O-BW	Boeing 737-81M/W	44422/5297		♦
☐ A4O-BX	Boeing 737-81M/W	44423/5310	ex N1796B	♦
☐ A4O-AS	ATR 42-500	574	ex VT-ADL	
☐ A4O-AT	ATR 42-500	576	ex VT-ADN	
☐ A4O-BI	Boeing 737-91MER/W	40069/5150		♦
☐ A4O-BK	Boeing 737-91MER/W	40070/5395		o/o♦
☐ A4O-BO	Boeing 737-71M	33103/1154	ex N6066Z	
☐ A4O-BY	Boeing 737-91MER/W	44424/5320	ex N1786B	♦
☐ A4O-BZ	Boeing 737-91MER/W	44425/5419		o/o♦
☐ A4O-EA	Embraer ERJ-175LR	17000323	ex PT-TBT	
☐ A4O-EB	Embraer ERJ-175LR	17000324	ex PT-TCJ	
☐ A4O-EC	Embraer ERJ-175LR	17000349	ex PT-TDY	
☐ A4O-ED	Embraer ERJ-175LR	17000354	ex PT-TGQ	
☐ A4O-	Boeing 787-8	42378/340		o/o♦
☐ A4O-	Boeing 787-8	42379/372		o/o♦

A5- BHUTAN (Kingdom of Bhutan)

BHUTAN AIRLINES/TASHI AIR		(BTN)		Paro (PBH)
☐ A5-BAA	Pilatus PC-12	885	ex G-DAKI	
☐ A5-BAB	Airbus A319-112	1541	ex N361MS	Rimp	♦
☐ A5-BAC	Airbus A319-112	1551	ex N740DB	Dorji	♦

DRUK AIR		**Royal Bhutan (KB/DRK)**			**Paro (PBH)**
☐ A5-JSW	Airbus A319-115/S	6496	ex D-AVYB		◆
☐ A5-RGF	Airbus A319-115	2306	ex D-AVYA		
☐ A5-RGG	Airbus A319-115	2346	ex D-AVWO		
☐ A5-RGH	ATR 42-500	622	ex F-OITQ	Great Lamou	
☐ A5-RGI	Airbus A319-112	3950	ex SX-OAG		

A6- UNITED ARAB EMIRATES (Al Imarat al-Arabiya al-Muttahida)

ABU DHABI AVIATION		**(AXU)**		**Abu Dhabi-Bateen (AZI)**
☐ A6-AWA	AgustaWestland AW139	31044	ex I-EASJ	>Omni
☐ A6-AWB	AgustaWestland AW139	31053		>Omni
☐ A6-AWD	AgustaWestland AW139	31095		>Omni
☐ A6-AWE	AgustaWestland AW139	31106		>Heligo
☐ A6-AWF	AgustaWestland AW139	31118		>Omni
☐ A6-AWG	AgustaWestland AW139	41006		>Omni
☐ A6-AWK	AgustaWestland AW139	31150		
☐ A6-AWO	AgustaWestland AW139	41215	ex N341SH	
☐ A6-AWP	AgustaWestland AW139	31102	ex M-ERIT	VIP
☐ A6-BAM	Bell 212	31165	ex C-GTHQ	
☐ A6-BBC	Bell 212	30777		[AUH]
☐ A6-BBK	Bell 212	30802		
☐ A6-BBL	Bell 212	30822		[AUH]
☐ A6-BBP	Bell 212	30917		
☐ A6-BBQ	Bell 212	30942		
☐ A6-BBS	Bell 212	30977		[AUH]
☐ A6-BBU	Bell 212	31183	ex VH-FTV	
☐ A6-BBZ	Bell 212	32141		[AUH]
☐ A6-	Bell 212	30891	ex C-FRUT	
☐ A6-BAH	Bell 412HP	36119	ex C-GBUP	
☐ A6-BAI	Bell 412HP	36122		
☐ A6-BAL	Bell 412HP	36150		
☐ A6-BAO	Bell 412HP	36152		
☐ A6-BAP	Bell 412HP	36189	ex N52091	
☐ A6-BAQ	Bell 412EP	36190		
☐ A6-BAS	Bell 412EP	36215		
☐ A6-HBN	Bell 412EP	36590	ex N463FB	
☐ A6-HBO	Bell 412EP	36591	ex N463CB	
☐ A6-HBP	Bell 412EP	36592	ex N463EB	
☐ A6-HBQ	Bell 412EP	36593	ex N463HB	
☐ A6-ADA	de Havilland DHC-8Q-202	471	ex C-GLOT	
☐ A6-ADB	de Havilland DHC-8Q-315	650	ex C-FLUJ	
☐ A6-ADC	de Havilland DHC-8Q-202	473	ex C-GFRP	
☐ A6-ADD	de Havilland DHC-8Q-315	627	ex V2-LGL	
☐ A6-ADE	de Havilland DHC-8Q-315	628	ex V2-LGM	
☐ A6-ADG	de Havilland DHC-8Q-315MSA	624	ex V2-LGK	SAR/AEW
☐ A6-ADK	de Havilland DHC-8-402Q	4222	ex C-FTIA	VIP
☐ A6-ADM	de Havilland DHC-8-402Q	4491	ex C-FGUT	◆
☐ A6-BCE	Bell 206B JetRanger III	2185		[AUH]
☐ A6-BCF	Bell 206B JetRanger III	2423		[AUH]
☐ A6-BCK	Bell 206B JetRanger III	2426		[AUH]
☐ A6-BCL	Bell 206B JetRanger III	2720		[AUH]
☐ A6-JAZ	Beech 350 King Air	FL-532	ex N6232E	

AEROGULF DUBAI		**Aerogulf**		**Dubai (DXB)**
☐ A6-ALA	Bell 212	30664	ex N71AL	
☐ A6-ALC	Bell 212	30790	ex N2781A	
☐ A6-ALD	Bell 212	30809	ex N143AL	
☐ A6-ALW	Bell 212	35065	ex N62200	
☐ A6-ALX	Bell 212	30888	ex YV-191CP	
☐ A6-ALM	AgustaWestland AW139	41017	ex A6-AWJ	
☐ A6-ALL	AgustaWestland AW139	31150	ex A6-AWK	
☐ A6-ALO	Bell 206L-3 LongRanger III	51435	ex PT-YBK	
☐ A6-ALP	Bell 206B JetRanger III	2495	ex (A6-BCJ)	

AIR ARABIA		**Arabia (G9/ABY)**		**Sharjah (SHJ)**
☐ A6-ABF	Airbus A320-214	2764	ex SU-AAA	
☐ A6-ABP	Airbus A320-214	3802	ex F-WWBV	wfs
☐ A6-ABR	Airbus A320-214	3925	ex F-WWBP	
☐ A6-ABS	Airbus A320-214	4061	ex F-WWBE	
☐ A6-ABT	Airbus A320-214	4243	ex F-WWDO	

☐ A6-ABU	Airbus A320-214	4310	ex CN-NMD		
☐ A6-ANA	Airbus A320-214	4468	ex D-AXAD		
☐ A6-ANB	Airbus A320-214	4524	ex F-WWDK	10th Anniversary c/s	
☐ A6-ANE	Airbus A320-214	4806	ex D-AVVY		
☐ A6-ANF	Airbus A320-214	4848	ex F-WWIY		
☐ A6-ANG	Airbus A320-214	4890	ex D-AVVF		
☐ A6-ANH	Airbus A320-214	4958	ex D-AXAX		
☐ A6-ANI	Airbus A320-214	5017	ex F-WWIX		
☐ A6-ANL	Airbus A320-214	5276	ex F-WWIM		
☐ A6-ANM	Airbus A320-214	5307	ex F-WWIK		
☐ A6-ANN	Airbus A320-214	5423	ex F-WWDV		
☐ A6-ANO	Airbus A320-214/S	5452	ex F-WWIM		
☐ A6-ANP	Airbus A320-214/S	5502	ex F-WWBR		
☐ A6-ANQ	Airbus A320-214/S	5576	ex F-WWIZ		
☐ A6-ANR	Airbus A320-214/S	5718	ex D-AVVN		
☐ A6-ANS	Airbus A320-214/S	5772	ex D-AVVY		
☐ A6-ANT	Airbus A230-214/S	5889	ex D-AVVK		
☐ A6-ANU	Airbus A320-214/S	5903	ex D-AVVQ		
☐ A6-ANV	Airbus A320-214/S	5984	ex D-AUBP		
☐ A6-ANW	Airbus A320-214/S	6000	ex D-AUBT		
☐ A6-ANX	Airbus A320-214/S	6054	ex F-WWDJ		
☐ A6-ANY	Airbus A320-214/S	6080	ex F-WWBI		
☐ A6-ANZ	Airbus A320-214/S	6166	ex F-WWBP		
☐ A6-AOA	Airbus A320-214/S	6176	ex F-WWBT		♦
☐ A6-AOB	Airbus A320-214/S	6234	ex D-AVVN		♦
☐ A6-AOC	Airbus A320-214/S	6293	cx F WWBE		♦
☐ A6-AOD	Airbus A320-214/S	6365	ex F-WWDH		♦
☐ A6-AOE	Airbus A320-214/S	6430	ex F-WWBB		♦
☐ A6-AOF	Airbus A320-214/S	6444	ex F-WWBZ		♦
☐ A6-AOH	Airbus A320-214/S	6481	ex F-WWBS		♦
☐ A6-AOI	Airbus A320-214/S	6553	ex F-WWIF		♦
☐ A6-	Airbus A320-214/S	6665	ex		o/o♦
☐ A6-	Airbus A320-214/S	6749	ex		o/o♦
☐ A6-	Airbus A320-214/S	6838	ex		o/o♦

AVE.COM	**Phoenix Sharjah (P3/PHW)**			**Sharjah (SHJ)**
☐ A6-PHA	Boeing 737-2T4	23444/1154	ex EX-027	[SHJ]
☐ A6-PHF	Boeing 737-219	21645/535	ex EX-012	

BLUE SKY AVIATION SERVICES				**Sharjah (SHJ)**
☐ A6-SRI	Airbus A300B4-622RF	788	ex N788UK	♦

EASTERN SKYJETS	**(EE/ESJ)**			**Dubai (DXB)**
☐ A6-ESE	Boeing 737-46J	27213/2585	ex N213TH	wfs
☐ A6-ESF	Boeing 737-4Y0	25177/2176	ex EI-EMY	
☐ A6-ESK	British Aerospace Jetstream 41	41090	ex G-CEDS	
☐ A6-ESS	Boeing 737-33A	25011/2012	ex G-STRI	>MPK

EMIRATES	**Emirates (EK/UAE)**			**Dubai (DXB)**
☐ A6-EAE	Airbus A330-243	384	ex F-WWYS	
☐ A6-EAF	Airbus A330-243	392	ex F-WWYX	
☐ A6-EAG	Airbus A330-243	396	ex F-WWKJ	
☐ A6-EAH	Airbus A330-243	409	ex F-WWKT	
☐ A6-EAK	Airbus A330-243	452	ex F-WWKF	
☐ A6-EAM	Airbus A330-243	491	ex F-WWYO	
☐ A6-EAO	Airbus A330-243	509	ex F-WWYX	
☐ A6-EAP	Airbus A330-243	525	ex F-WWKV	
☐ A6-EAQ	Airbus A330-243	518	ex F-WWKT	
☐ A6-EAR	Airbus A330-243	536	ex F-WWYF	
☐ A6-EAS	Airbus A330-243	455	ex F-WWKH	
☐ A6-EKQ	Airbus A330-243	248	ex F-WWYX	
☐ A6-EKR	Airbus A330-243	251	ex F-WWKO	
☐ A6-EKS	Airbus A330-243	283	ex F-WWKH	
☐ A6-EKT	Airbus A330-243	293	ex F-WWKR	
☐ A6-EKU	Airbus A330-243	295	ex F-WWYF	
☐ A6-EKV	Airbus A330-243	314	ex F-WWYR	
☐ A6-EKW	Airbus A330-243	316	ex F-WWYS	
☐ A6-EKX	Airbus A330-243	326	ex F-WWYV	
☐ A6-EKY	Airbus A330-243	328	ex F-WWYX	
☐ A6-EDA	Airbus A380-861	011	ex D-AXXA	
☐ A6-EDB	Airbus A380-861	013	ex D-AXAB	
☐ A6-EDC	Airbus A380-861	016	ex D-AXAC	
☐ A6-EDD	Airbus A380-861	020	ex D-AXAD	
☐ A6-EDE	Airbus A380-861	017	ex D-AXAE	
☐ A6-EDF	Airbus A380-861	007	ex F-WWJB	
☐ A6-EDG	Airbus A380-861	023	ex F-WWST	
☐ A6-EDH	Airbus A380-861	025	ex F-WWSV	

13

Reg	Type	c/n	Notes	Marks
A6-EDI	Airbus A380-861	028	ex F-WWSZ	
A6-EDJ	Airbus A380-861	009	ex F-WWEA	
A6-EDK	Airbus A380-861	030	ex F-WWSD	
A6-EDL	Airbus A380-861	046	ex F-WWAG	
A6-EDM	Airbus A380-861	042	ex F-WWAO	
A6-EDN	Airbus A380-861	056	ex F-WWAR	
A6-EDO	Airbus A380-861	057	ex F-WWAS	
A6-EDP	Airbus A380-861	077	ex F-WWSY	
A6-EDQ	Airbus A380-861	080	ex F-WWSV	
A6-EDR	Airbus A380-861	083	ex F-WWSZ	
A6-EDS	Airbus A380-861	086	ex F-WWSB	
A6-EDT	Airbus A380-861	090	ex F-WWSE	
A6-EDU	Airbus A380-861	098	ex F-WWAB	
A6-EDV	Airbus A380-861	101	ex F-WWAG	
A6-EDW	Airbus A380-861	103	ex F-WWAL	
A6-EDX	Airbus A380-861	105	ex F-WWAK	
A6-EDY	Airbus A380-861	106	ex F-WWAS	
A6-EDZ	Airbus A380-861	107	ex F-WWSD	
A6-EEA	Airbus A380-861	108	ex F-WWSI	
A6-EEB	Airbus A380-861	109	ex F-WWSN	
A6-EEC	Airbus A380-861	110	ex F-WWAE	
A6-EED	Airbus A380-861	111	ex F-WWAQ	
A6-EEE	Airbus A380-861	112	ex F-WWAU Dubai Expo 2020	
A6-EEF	Airbus A380-861	113	ex F-WWSJ	
A6-EEG	Airbus A380-861	116	ex F-WWSS	
A6-EEH	Airbus A380-861	119	ex F-WWSY	
A6-EEI	Airbus A380-861	123	ex F-WWAM	
A6-EEJ	Airbus A380-861	127	ex F-WWAZ	
A6-EEK	Airbus A380-861	132	ex F-WWSF	
A6-EEL	Airbus A380-861	133	ex F-WWSH	
A6-EEM	Airbus A380-861	134	ex F-WWSP	
A6-EEN	Airbus A380-861	135	ex F-WWSR	
A6-EEO	Airbus A380-861	136	ex F-WWAX	
A6-EEP	Airbus A380-861	138	ex F-WWAF	
A6-EEQ	Airbus A380-861	141	ex F-WWAG	
A6-EER	Airbus A380-861	139	ex F-WWSB	
A6-EES	Airbus A380-861	140	ex F-WWAD	
A6-EET	Airbus A380-861	142	ex F-WWAH	
A6-EEU	Airbus A380-861	147	ex F-WWAR	
A6-EEV	Airbus A380-861	150	ex F-WWSA	
A6-EEW	Airbus A380-861	153	ex F-WWAE	
A6-EEX	Airbus A380-861	154	ex F-WWAN	
A6-EEY	Airbus A380-861	157	ex F-WWAV	
A6-EEZ	Airbus A380-861	158	ex F-WWAU	
A6-EOA	Airbus A380-861	159	ex F-WWSE	
A6-EOB	Airbus A380-861	164	ex F-WWSO	
A6-EOC	Airbus A380-861	165	ex F-WWSJ	
A6-EOD	Airbus A380-861	168	ex F-WWSY	
A6-EOE	Airbus A380-861	169	ex F-WWSZ	
A6-EOF	Airbus A380-861	171	ex F-WWAM	♦
A6-EOG	Airbus A380-861	172	ex F-WWAX	♦
A6-EOH	Airbus A380-861	174	ex F-WWSH	♦
A6-EOI	Airbus A380-861	178	ex F-WWAD	♦
A6-EOJ	Airbus A380-861	182	ex F-WWSF	o/o♦
A6-EOK	Airbus A380-861	184	ex F-WWSU	o/o♦
A6-EOL	Airbus A380-861	186	ex F-WWAG	o/o♦
A6-EOM	Airbus A380-861	187	ex F-WWAH	o/o♦
A6-EON	Airbus A380-861	188	ex F-WWAK	o/o♦
A6-EOO	Airbus A380-861	190	ex F-WWAR	o/o♦
A6-EOP	Airbus A380-861	200	ex F-WWSV	o/o♦
A6-EOQ	Airbus A380-861	201	ex F-WWAN	o/o♦
A6-EOR	Airbus A380-861	202	ex F-WW	o/o♦
A6-EOS	Airbus A380-861	203	ex F-WW	o/o♦
A6-	Airbus A380-861	204	ex F-WW	o/o♦
A6-	Airbus A380-861	205	ex F-WW	o/o♦
A6-	Airbus A380-861	206	ex F-WW	o/o♦
A6-	Airbus A380-861	207	ex F-WW	o/o♦
A6-	Airbus A380-861	208	ex F-WW	o/o♦
A6-	Airbus A380-861	209	ex F-WW	o/o♦
A6-	Airbus A380-861	210	ex F-WW	o/o♦
A6-	Airbus A380-861	211	ex F-WW	o/o♦
A6-	Airbus A380-861	213	ex F-WW	o/o♦
A6-	Airbus A380-861	214	ex F-WW	o/o♦
A6-	Airbus A380-861	216	ex F-WW	o/o♦
A6-	Airbus A380-861	217	ex F-WW	o/o♦
A6-	Airbus A380-861	218	ex F-WW	o/o♦
A6-	Airbus A380-861	219	ex F-WW	o/o♦
A6-	Airbus A380-861	220	ex F-WW	o/o♦
A6-EMF	Boeing 777-21H	27249/42		
A6-EMG	Boeing 777-21HER	27252/63	ex N5020K	
A6-EMH	Boeing 777-21HER	27251/54		
A6-EMI	Boeing 777-21HER	27250/47	ex N5028Y	

☐ A6-EMJ	Boeing 777-21HER	27253/91	
☐ A6-EMK	Boeing 777-21HER	29324/171	
☐ A6-EML	Boeing 777-21HER	29325/176	
☐ A6-EWA	Boeing 777-21HLR	35572/654	
☐ A6-EWB	Boeing 777-21HLR	35573/662	ex N5573S
☐ A6-EWC	Boeing 777-21HLR	35576/677	
☐ A6-EWD	Boeing 777-21HLR	35577/688	ex N5017V
☐ A6-EWE	Boeing 777-21HLR	35582/725	
☐ A6-EWF	Boeing 777-21HLR	35586/739	ex N5017V
☐ A6-EWG	Boeing 777-21HLR	35578/741	ex N6018N
☐ A6-EWH	Boeing 777-21HLR	35587/747	
☐ A6-EWI	Boeing 777-21HLR	35589/757	ex N5017V
☐ A6-EWJ	Boeing 777-21HLR	35590/775	ex N5017V
☐ A6-EBA	Boeing 777-31HER	32706/506	
☐ A6-EBB	Boeing 777-36NER	32789/508	
☐ A6-EBC	Boeing 777-36NER	32790/512	
☐ A6-EBD	Boeing 777-31HER	33501/516	ex N5022E
☐ A6-EBE	Boeing 777-36NER	32788/532	
☐ A6-EBF	Boeing 777-31HER	32708/536	
☐ A6-EBG	Boeing 777-36NER	33862/535	
☐ A6-EBH	Boeing 777-31HER	32707/539	
☐ A6-EBI	Boeing 777-36NER	32785/540	
☐ A6-EBJ	Boeing 777-36NER	32787/542	
☐ A6-EBK	Boeing 777-31HER	34481/549	ex N5020K
☐ A6-EBL	Boeing 777-31HER	32709/551	ex N5017V
☐ A6-EBM	Boeing 777-31HER	34482/556	
☐ A6-EBN	Boeing 777-36NER	32791/560	
☐ A6-EBO	Boeing 777-36NER	32792/568	
☐ A6-EBP	Boeing 777-31HER	32710/569	ex N5017V
☐ A6-EBQ	Boeing 777-36NER	33863/576	ex N5017V
☐ A6-EBR	Boeing 777-31HER	34483/578	
☐ A6-EBS	Boeing 777-31HER	32715/582	
☐ A6-EBT	Boeing 777-31HER	32730/585	
☐ A6-EBU	Boeing 777-31HER	34484/590	
☐ A6-EBV	Boeing 777-31HER	32728/594	
☐ A6-EBW	Boeing 777-36NER	32793/598	
☐ A6-EBX	Boeing 777-31HER	32729/619	ex N5017V
☐ A6-EBY	Boeing 777-36NER	33864/622	ex N5017V
☐ A6-EBZ	Boeing 777-31HER	32713/628	
☐ A6-ECA	Boeing 777-36NER	32794/632	ex N5017B
☐ A6-ECB	Boeing 777-31HER	32714/641	ex N5016R
☐ A6-ECC	Boeing 777-36NER	33865/664	ex N5020K
☐ A6-ECD	Boeing 777-36NER	32795/669	ex N5017V
☐ A6-ECE	Boeing 777-31HER	35575/681	
☐ A6-ECF	Boeing 777-31HER	35574/690	
☐ A6-ECG	Boeing 777-31HER	35579/709	
☐ A6-ECH	Boeing 777-31HER	35581/714	
☐ A6-ECI	Boeing 777-31HER	35580/728	ex N1785B
☐ A6-ECJ	Boeing 777-31HER	35583/734	
☐ A6-ECK	Boeing 777-31HER	35584/743	ex N5017V
☐ A6-ECL	Boeing 777-36NER	37704/748	
☐ A6-ECM	Boeing 777-36NER	37703/755	ex N5017V
☐ A6-ECN	Boeing 777-36NER	37705/761	
☐ A6-ECO	Boeing 777-36NER	37706/765	
☐ A6-ECP	Boeing 777-36NER	37707/768	
☐ A6-ECQ	Boeing 777-31HER	35588/779	
☐ A6-ECR	Boeing 777-31HER	35592/794	ex N5017V
☐ A6-ECS	Boeing 777-31HER	38980/803	ex N5017V
☐ A6-ECT	Boeing 777-31HER	35591/808	
☐ A6-ECU	Boeing 777-31HER	35593/817	
☐ A6-ECV	Boeing 777-31HER	35594/824	
☐ A6-ECW	Boeing 777-31HER	38981/828	
☐ A6-ECX	Boeing 777-31HER	38982/830	ex N5017V
☐ A6-ECY	Boeing 777-31HER	35595/840	
☐ A6-ECZ	Boeing 777-31HER	38983/847	
☐ A6-EGA	Boeing 777-31HER	38984/861	ex N5017V
☐ A6-EGB	Boeing 777-31HER	38985/929	
☐ A6-EGC	Boeing 777-31HER	35596/945	
☐ A6-EGD	Boeing 777-31HER	38988/946	
☐ A6-EGE	Boeing 777-31HER	35597/951	
☐ A6-EGF	Boeing 777-31HER	38987/961	
☐ A6-EGG	Boeing 777-31HER	41070/965	
☐ A6-EGH	Boeing 777-31HER	35585/969	
☐ A6-EGI	Boeing 777-31HER	38986/974	
☐ A6-EGJ	Boeing 777-31HER	38989/978	
☐ A6-EGK	Boeing 777-31HER	41071/981	
☐ A6-EGL	Boeing 777-31HER	41072/985	
☐ A6-EGM	Boeing 777-31HER	41073/988	
☐ A6-EGN	Boeing 777-31HER	41074/993	
☐ A6-EGO	Boeing 777-31HER	35598/1000	1,000[th] 777 c/s
☐ A6-EGP	Boeing 777-31HER	35599/1010	
☐ A6-EGQ	Boeing 777-31HER	41076/1014	

☐ A6-EGR	Boeing 777-31HER	41077/1018		
☐ A6-EGS	Boeing 777-31HER	41078/1021		
☐ A6-EGT	Boeing 777-31HER	35600/1024		
☐ A6-EGU	Boeing 777-31HER	41079/1028		
☐ A6-EGV	Boeing 777-31HER	38990/1031		
☐ A6-EGW	Boeing 777-31HER	35601/1034		
☐ A6-EGX	Boeing 777-31HER	35602/1037		
☐ A6-EGY	Boeing 777-31HER	41080/1039		
☐ A6-EGZ	Boeing 777-31HER	41081/1044		
☐ A6-EMM	Boeing 777-31H	29062/256		
☐ A6-EMN	Boeing 777-31H	29063/262		
☐ A6-EMO	Boeing 777-31H	28680/300		
☐ A6-EMP	Boeing 777-31H	29395/326	ex N50281	
☐ A6-EMQ	Boeing 777-31H	32697/396		
☐ A6-EMR	Boeing 777-31H	29396/402		
☐ A6-EMS	Boeing 777-31H	29067/408	ex N50281	
☐ A6-EMT	Boeing 777-31H	32699/414	ex N5014K	
☐ A6-EMU	Boeing 777-31H	29064/418		
☐ A6-EMV	Boeing 777-31H	28687/432		
☐ A6-EMW	Boeing 777-31H	32700/434		
☐ A6-EMX	Boeing 777-31H	32702/444		
☐ A6-ENA	Boeing 777-31HER	41082/1047		
☐ A6-ENB	Boeing 777-31HER	41075/1055	ex N5023Q	
☐ A6-ENC	Boeing 777-31HER	41083/1058		
☐ A6-END	Boeing 777-31HER	41084/1063		
☐ A6-ENE	Boeing 777-31HER	35603/1069		
☐ A6-ENF	Boeing 777-31HER	41085/1073		
☐ A6-ENG	Boeing 777-31HER	35604/1076		
☐ A6-ENH	Boeing 777-31HER	41086/1080		
☐ A6-ENI	Boeing 777-31HER	41087/1087		
☐ A6-ENJ	Boeing 777-31HER	35605/1099		
☐ A6-ENK	Boeing 777-31HER	38991/1116		
☐ A6-ENL	Boeing 777-31HER	41370/1130		
☐ A6-ENM	Boeing 777-31HER	41359/1168		
☐ A6-ENN	Boeing 777-31HER	41360/1177		
☐ A6-ENO	Boeing 777-31HER	41361/1183		
☐ A6-ENP	Boeing 777-31HER	41362/1193		
☐ A6-ENQ	Boeing 777-31HER	41363/1201		
☐ A6-ENR	Boeing 777-31HER	41364/1207		♦
☐ A6-ENS	Boeing 777-31HER	41365/1220	500th B777-300ER delivered	♦
☐ A6-ENT	Boeing 777-31HER	41366/1225		♦
☐ A6-ENU	Boeing 777-31HER	41367/1236		♦
☐ A6-ENV	Boeing 777-31HER	41368/1243		♦
☐ A6-ENW	Boeing 777-31HER	41369/1249		♦
☐ A6-ENX	Boeing 777-31HER	42318/1261		♦
☐ A6-ENY	Boeing 777-31HER	42122/1276		♦
☐ A6-ENZ	Boeing 777-31HER	42319/1289		
☐ A6-EPA	Boeing 777-31HER	42320/1317		o/o♦
☐ A6-EPB	Boeing 777-31HER	42321/1325		o/o♦
☐ A6-EPC	Boeing 777-31HER	42322/1335		o/o♦
☐ A6-EPD	Boeing 777-31HER	42323/1341		o/o♦
☐ A6-EPE	Boeing 777-31HER	42324/1348		o/o♦
☐ A6-	Boeing 777-31HER	41371/		o/o♦
☐ A6-	Boeing 777-31HER	41372/		o/o♦
☐ A6-	Boeing 777-31HER	41373/		o/o♦
☐ A6-EFD	Boeing 777-F1H	35606/766		
☐ A6-EFE	Boeing 777-F1H	35607/788	ex N5017V	
☐ A6-EFF	Boeing 777-F1H	35612/955		
☐ A6-EFG	Boeing 777-F1H	35613/996		
☐ A6-EFH	Boeing 777-F1H	35608/1046		
☐ A6-EFI	Boeing 777-F1H	35609/1060		
☐ A6-EFJ	Boeing 777-F1H	35610/1065		
☐ A6-EFK	Boeing 777-F1H	35611/1088		
☐ A6-EFL	Boeing 777-F1H	42230/1138		
☐ A6-EFM	Boeing 777-F1H	42231/1146		
☐ A6-EFN	Boeing 777-F1H	42232/1212		
☐ A6-EFO	Boeing 777-F1H	42233/1248		♦
☐ A6-EFS	Boeing 777-F1H	42234/1330		o/o♦
☐ A6-CJE	Airbus A319CJ-115	4822	ex F-WHUL	VIP
☐ A6-ERE	Airbus A340-541	572	ex F-WWTV	
☐ A6-ERF	Airbus A340-541	394	ex F-WWTE	[RKT]
☐ A6-ERM	Airbus A340-313X	236	ex D-AIFL	
☐ A6-ERN	Airbus A340-313X	166	ex D-ASIC	
☐ A6-ERO	Airbus A340-313X	163	ex D-ASIB	
☐ A6-ERP	Airbus A340-313X	185	ex D-AGBM	
☐ N415MC	Boeing 747-47UF	32837/1304		<GTI
☐ OO-THC	Boeing 747-4HAERF	35235/1389	ex N50217	<TAY
☐ OO-THD	Boeing 747-4HAERF	35236/1399		<TAY

EMIRATES INTERNATIONAL AIR CARGO

☐ A6-	Boeing 737-476SF	28151/2785	ex N16AQ	o/o♦

ETIHAD AIRWAYS — Etihad (EY/ETD) — Abu Dhabi (AUH)

☐ A6-EIA	Airbus A320-232	1944	ex PH-MPD	>SEY
☐ A6-EIB	Airbus A320-232	1945	ex PH-MPE Abu Dhabi Grand Prix c/s	
☐ A6-EIC	Airbus A320-232	2167	ex PH-MPF	
☐ A6-EIF	Airbus A320-232	3004	ex EI-EAO	
☐ A6-EIG	Airbus A320-232	3050	ex EI-EAN	
☐ A6-EIH	Airbus A320-232	3693	ex F-WWBH	
☐ A6-EII	Airbus A320-232	3713	ex F-WWIX	
☐ A6-EIJ	Airbus A320-232	3902	ex F-WWIA	
☐ A6-EIK	Airbus A320-232	3676	ex VT-INW	
☐ A6-EIL	Airbus A320-232	4066	ex F-WWBH	
☐ A6-EIM	Airbus A320-232	4077	ex F-WWBO	
☐ A6-EIN	Airbus A320-232	4124	ex F-WWIN	
☐ A6-EIP	Airbus A320-232	5095	ex D-AUBN	
☐ A6-EIO	Airbus A320-232	4934	ex F-WWBP	
☐ A6-EIQ	Airbus A320-232	5348	ex D-AUBL	
☐ A6-EIR	Airbus A320-232	5407	ex D-AVVE	
☐ A6-EIS	Airbus A320-232/S	5714	ex F-WWDT	
☐ A6-EIT	Airbus A320-232/S	5791	ex F-WWIH	
☐ A6-EIU	Airbus A320-232/S	5821	ex D-AXAN	
☐ A6-EIV	Airbus A320-232/S	5882	ex F-WWIJ	
☐ A6-EIW	Airbus A320-232/S	5924	ex F-WWIU	
☐ A6-EIX	Airbus A320-232/S	6134	ex F-WWIP	♦
☐ A6-EIY	Airbus A320-232/S	6226	ex F-WWIF	♦
☐ A6-EIZ	Airbus A320-211	0350	ex 9H-AFE	
☐ A6-EJA	Airbus A320-232/S	6527	ex F-WWDC	♦
☐ A6-AEA	Airbus A321-231/S	5836	ex D-AVZL	
☐ A6-AEB	Airbus A321-231/S	6108	ex D-AZAI	♦
☐ A6-AEC	Airbus A321-231/S	6143	ex D-AVXL	♦
☐ A6-AED	Airbus A321-231/S	6382	ex D-AVXT	♦
☐ A6-AEE	Airbus A321-231/S	6534	ex D-AVXE	♦
☐ A6-AEF	Airbus A321-231/S	6554	ex D-AZAL	♦
☐ A6-	Airbus A321-231/S	6731	ex	o/o♦
☐ A6-	Airbus A321-231/S	6760	ex	o/o♦
☐ A6-	Airbus A321-231/S	6790	ex	o/o♦
☐ A6-	Airbus A321-231/S	6818	ex	o/o♦
☐ A6-	Airbus A321-321/S	6821	ex	o/o♦
☐ A6-AGA	Airbus A330-202	825	ex VT-JWF	
☐ A6-AGB	Airbus A330-202	831	ex VT-JWG	
☐ A6-DCA	Airbus A330-243F	1032	ex F-WWKG	
☐ A6-DCB	Airbus A330-243F	1070	ex F-WWYF	
☐ A6-DCC	Airbus A330-243F	1414	ex F-WWTL	
☐ A6-DCD	Airbus A330-243F	1524	ex F-WWKY	♦
☐ A6-EYA	Airbus A330-202	888	ex VT-JWK	
☐ A6-EYC	Airbus A330-202	885	ex VT-JWJ	
☐ A6-EYD	Airbus A330-243	658	ex F-WWYN	
☐ A6-EYE	Airbus A330-243	688	ex F-WWYJ Manchester City FC c/s	
☐ A6-EYF	Airbus A330-243	717	ex F-WWYN	
☐ A6-EYG	Airbus A330-243	724	ex F-WWKN	
☐ A6-EYH	Airbus A330-243	729	ex F-WWKR Expo 2015 c/s	
☐ A6-EYI	Airbus A330-243	730	ex F-WWKS	
☐ A6-EYJ	Airbus A330-243	737	ex F-WWYB	
☐ A6-EYK	Airbus A330-243	788	ex F-WWKM	
☐ A6-EYL	Airbus A330-243	809	ex F-WWYB	
☐ A6-EYM	Airbus A330-243	824	ex F-WWKD	
☐ A6-EYN	Airbus A330-243	832	ex F-WWKN	
☐ A6-EYO	Airbus A330-243	852	ex F-WWKT	
☐ A6-EYP	Airbus A330-243	854	ex F-WWYY	
☐ A6-EYQ	Airbus A330-243	868	ex F-WWYQ	
☐ A6-EYR	Airbus A330-243	975	ex F-WWKS	
☐ A6-EYS	Airbus A330-243	991	ex F-WWKM	
☐ A6-EYT	Airbus A330-243	1486	ex F-WWYN	
☐ A6-EYU	Airbus A330-243	1521	ex F-WWKA	♦
☐ A6-EYY	Airbus A330-243	751	ex VT-EYY Aldabra	opf SEY
☐ A6-EYZ	Airbus A330-243	807	ex VT-JWE	opf SEY
☐ A6-AFA	Airbus A330-343X	1071	ex F-WWYP	
☐ A6-AFB	Airbus A330-343X	1081	ex F-WWYL	
☐ A6-AFC	Airbus A330-343X	1167	ex F-WWYR	
☐ A6-AFD	Airbus A330-343X	1205	ex F-WWKN	
☐ A6-AFE	Airbus A330-343X	1226	ex F-WWKM	
☐ A6-AFF	Airbus A330-343X	1245	ex F-WWKU	
☐ A6-EHE	Airbus A340-642HGW	829	ex F-WWCG	
☐ A6-EHF	Airbus A340-642HGW	837	ex F-WWCB	

☐ A6-EHH	Airbus A340-642HGW	870	ex F-WWCK	
☐ A6-EHI	Airbus A340-642HGW	929	ex F-WWCB	
☐ A6-EHJ	Airbus A340-642HGW	933	ex F-WWCF	
☐ A6-EHK	Airbus A340-642HGW	1030	ex F-WWCX	
☐ A6-EHL	Airbus A340-642HGW	1040	ex F-WWCH	
☐ A6-APA	Airbus A380-861	166	ex F-WWSS	♦
☐ A6-APB	Airbus A380-861	170	ex F-WWAB	♦
☐ A6-APC	Airbus A380-861	176	ex F-WWAY	o/o♦
☐ A6-APD	Airbus A380-861	180	ex F-WWAZ	o/o♦
☐ A6-APE	Airbus A380-861	191	ex F-WWSA	o/o♦
☐ A6-	Airbus A380-861	195	ex F-WW	o/o♦
☐ A6-	Airbus A380-861	198	ex F-WW	o/o♦
☐ A6-	Airbus A380-861	199	ex F-WW	o/o♦
☐ A6-LRA	Boeing 777-237LR	36300/610	ex VT-ALA	
☐ A6-LRB	Boeing 777-237LR	36301/621	ex VT-ALB	
☐ A6-LRC	Boeing 777-237LR	36302/629	ex VT-ALC	
☐ A6-LRD	Boeing 777-237LR	36303/663	ex VT-ALD	♦
☐ A6-LRE	Boeing 777-237LR	36304/698	ex VT-ALE	♦
☐ A6-ETA	Boeing 777-3FXER	34597/538	ex N6018N	
☐ A6-ETB	Boeing 777-3FXER	34598/543	ex N5020K	
☐ A6-ETC	Boeing 777-3FXER	34599/544		
☐ A6-ETD	Boeing 777-3FXER	34600/547		
☐ A6-ETE	Boeing 777-3FXER	34601/548		
☐ A6-ETF	Boeing 777-3FXER	39700/832	ex N1794B	
☐ A6-ETG	Boeing 777-3FXER	39681/932		
☐ A6-ETH	Boeing 777-3FXER	39683/957		
☐ A6-ETI	Boeing 777-3FXER	39684/987		
☐ A6-ETJ	Boeing 777-3FXER	39685/994		
☐ A6-ETK	Boeing 777-3FXER	39686/1019		
☐ A6-ETL	Boeing 777-3FXER	39687/1064		
☐ A6-ETM	Boeing 777-3FXER	39688/1067	ex N6009F	
☐ A6-ETN	Boeing 777-3FXER	39689/1086		
☐ A6-ETO	Boeing 777-3FXER	39690/1105		
☐ A6-ETP	Boeing 777-3FXER	41699/1111		
☐ A6-ETQ	Boeing 777-3FXER	41700/1137		
☐ A6-ETR	Boeing 777-3FXER	41701/1155	ex N5573S	
☐ A6-ETS	Boeing 777-3FXER	44548/1235		♦
☐ A6-JAA	Boeing 777-35RER	35159/650	ex VT-JES	
☐ A6-JAB	Boeing 777-35RER	35160/653	ex VT-JER	
☐ A6-JAC	Boeing 777-35RER	35157/627	ex VT-JEN	♦
☐ A6-JAD	Boeing 777-35RER	35158/637	ex VT-JEP	♦
☐ A6-JAE	Boeing 777-35RER	35163/675	ex VT-JEG	♦
☐ A6-JAF	Boeing 777-35RER	35164/660	ex VT-JEL	♦
☐ A6-BLA	Boeing 787-9	39646/229	ex N1009N	♦
☐ A6-BLB	Boeing 787-9	39647/253		♦
☐ A6-BLC	Boeing 787-9	39648/286		o/o♦
☐ A6-BLD	Boeing 787-9	39649/302		o/o♦
☐ A6-BLE	Boeing 787-9	39650/305		o/o♦
☐ A6-DDA	Boeing 777-FFX	39682/939		
☐ A6-DDB	Boeing 777-FFX	39692/1072		
☐ A6-DDC	Boeing 777-FFX	39691/1100		
☐ A6-EID	Airbus A319-132	1947	ex D-APAA	
☐ A6-EIE	Airbus A319-132	1955	ex D-APAB	
☐ A6-EHA	Airbus A340-541	748	ex F-WWTS	
☐ A6-EHB	Airbus A340-541	757	ex F-WWTU	
☐ A6-EHC	Airbus A340-541	761	ex F-WWTV	
☐ A6-EHD	Airbus A340-541	783	ex F-WWTY	
☐ N476MC	Boeing 747-47UF	29256/1213	ex G-GSSA	<GTI♦
☐ N855GT	Boeing 747-87UF	37567/1476		<GTI

FALCON AVIATION SERVICES — Falcon Aviation (FVS) — Abu Dhabi-Bateen (AZI)

☐ A6-FLA	de Havilland DHC-8Q-402	4454	ex C-GWLV	>SGG♦
☐ A6-FLL	Embraer Legacy 600	14501051	ex PT-SEG	♦
☐ A6-FLO	Embraer Legacy 600	14501096	ex PT-SMF	♦
☐ A6-FLQ	de Havilland DHC-8Q-402	4484	ex C-FFLA	♦
☐ A6-FLR	de Havilland DHC-8-402Q	4486	ex C-FFWY	>IKM♦
☐ A6-HHS	Embraer Lineage 1000	19000296	ex PT-TZK	♦
☐ A6-IGT	Embraer Lineage 1000	19000362	ex PT-TPB	♦
☐ A6-YMA	Embraer Legacy 650	14501190	ex PR-LBO	♦

FAZZA SKY/DUBAI SKYDIVE — Dubai-Palm

☐ DU-SD1	Cessna 208B Caravan I	208B1141	ex D-FAAC	
☐ DU-SD3	de Havilland DHC-6 Twin Otter 300	765	ex ST-AHV	
☐ DU-SD4	de Havilland DHC-6 Twin Otter 200	132	ex F-GKHM	
☐ DU-333	Pilatus PC-8/B2-H4	966	ex HB-FNL	

FLYDUBAI (FZ/FDB) Dubai (DXB)

☐ A6-FDC	Boeing 737-8KN/W	40233/2952	exOO-JDF
☐ A6-FDD	Boeing 737-8KN/W	40234/2966	ex EI-FEB
☐ A6-FDE	Boeing 737-8KN/W	40235/3053	ex EI-FEC
☐ A6-FDF	Boeing 737-8KN/W	40236/3110	ex EI-FED
☐ A6-FDG	Boeing 737-8KN/W	29636/3197	
☐ A6-FDH	Boeing 737-8KN/W	31716/3270	
☐ A6-FDI	Boeing 737-8KN/W	31765/3302	
☐ A6-FDJ	Boeing 737-8KN/W	40237/3356	ex N6046P
☐ A6-FDK	Boeing 737-8KN/W	40238/3391	
☐ A6-FDL	Boeing 737-8KN/W	40239/3460	
☐ A6-FDM	Boeing 737-8KN/W	40240/3485	
☐ A6-FDN	Boeing 737-8KN/W	40241/3517	ex N1786B
☐ A6-FDO	Boeing 737-8KN/W	40242/3540	ex N1786B
☐ A6-FDP	Boeing 737-8KN/W	40243/3582	
☐ A6-FDQ	Boeing 737-8KN/W	40244/3619	ex N1786B
☐ A6-FDR	Boeing 737-8KN/W	40245/3640	
☐ A6-FDS	Boeing 737-8KN/W	40246/3659	
☐ A6-FDT	Boeing 737-8KN/W	40247/3706	
☐ A6-FDU	Boeing 737-8KN/W	40249/3720	
☐ A6-FDV	Boeing 737-8KN/W	40248/3768	
☐ A6-FDW	Boeing 737-8KN/W	40250/3868	
☐ A6-FDX	Boeing 737-8KN/W	40251/3901	
☐ A6-FDY	Boeing 737-8KN/W	40252/3923	
☐ A6-FDZ	Boeing 737-8KN/W	40253/4081	
☐ A6-FEA	Boeing 737-8KN/W	40254/4096	
☐ A6-FEB	Boeing 737-8KN/W	40255/4216	
☐ A6-FEC	Boeing 737-8KN/W	40256/4243	
☐ A6-FED	Boeing 737-8KN/W	40257/4277	ex N1786B
☐ A6-FEE	Boeing 737-8KN/W	40258/4433	ex N1786B
☐ A6-FEF	Boeing 737-8KN/W	40259/4467	
☐ A6-FEG	Boeing 737-8KN/W	40281/4534	
☐ A6-FEH	Boeing 737-8KN/W	40260/4648	
☐ A6-FEI	Boeing 737-8KN/W	40261/4671	
☐ A6-FEJ	Boeing 737-8KN/W	40262/4699	
☐ A6-FEK	Boeing 737-8KN/W	40282/4738	
☐ A6-FEL	Boeing 737-8KN/W	40263/4781	ex N1796B
☐ A6-FEM	Boeing 737-8KN/W	40264/4988	
☐ A6-FEN	Boeing 737-8KN/W	40265/4979	♦
☐ A6-FEO	Boeing 737-8KN/W	40266/5004	♦
☐ A6-FEP	Boeing 737-8KN/W	40269/5083	♦
☐ A6-FEQ	Boeing 737-8KN/W	40267/5117	♦
☐ A6-FER	Boeing 737-8KN/W	40268/5163	♦
☐ A6-FES	Boeing 737-8KN/W	40270/5187	♦
☐ A6-FET	Boeign 737-8KN/W	40271/5241	♦
☐ A6-FEU	Boeing 737-8KN/W	40273/5285	♦
☐ A6-FEV	Boeing 737-8KN/W	40275/5323	♦
☐ A6-FEW	Boeing 737-8KN/W	40276/5364	♦
☐ A6-FEX	Boeing 737-8KN/W	40278/5397	o/o♦
☐ A6-	Boeing 737-8KN/W	40272/	o/o♦
☐ A6-	Boeing 737-8KN/W	40274/	o/o♦
☐ A6-	Boeing 737-8KN/W	40277/	o/o♦

GLOBAL JET AIRLINES (GBG) Dubai (DXB)

☐ A6-JAK	Boeing 737-406	24959/1949	ex N959PR	
☐ A6-JMK	Boeing 737-322	24674/1928	ex N399UA	
☐ A6-PHH	Boeing 737-3Q8	26314/2707	ex G-THOF	♦

HELI DUBAI Dubai (DXB)

☐ A6-WSL	Aérospatiale AS350B3 Ecureuil	4218	ex VH-MDQ

MAXIMUS AIR CARGO Cargo Max (MXU) Abu Dhabi (AUH)

☐ A6-MAC	Lockheed L-382G-44K-30 Hercules	5024	ex 1215	<UAE AF
☐ A6-MAX	Lockheed L-382G-44K-30 Hercules	4895	ex 1216	<UAE AF
☐ A6-MXB	Airbus A300B4-622RF	767	ex TF-ELE	[AUH]
☐ A6-QFY	Lockheed L-382G Hercules	4834	ex 311 UAE AF	
☐ UR-BXQ	Ilyushin Il-76TD	1023410360	ex EX-832	
☐ UR-BXS	Ilyushin Il-76TD	1023411368	ex EX-436	
☐ UR-ZYD	Antonov An-124 Ruslan	19530502843	ex UR-CCX	

MIDEX AIRLINES (MG/MIX) Al Ain (AAN)

☐ A6-MDB	Airbus A300B4-203F	196	ex N372PC	Midex 2	[AUH]
☐ A6-MDC	Airbus A300B4-203F	218	ex N373PC	Midex 3	[SHJ]
☐ A6-MDD	Airbus A300B4-203F	203	ex N473AS	Midex 4	[SHJ]
☐ A6-MDF	Airbus A300B4-203F	134	ex N370PC	Midex 6	[AUH]
☐ A6-MDG	Boeing 747-228F	25266/878	ex PH-MCN	Midex 7	

| ☐ A6-MDH | Boeing 747-228F | 24735/772 | ex F-WCZY | Midex 8 |
| ☐ A6-MDI | Boeing 747-228F | 24879/822 | ex F-WCZX | Midex 9 |

ROTANA JET   (RG/RJD)   Abu Dhabi (AUH)

☐ A6-RRA	Embraer ERJ-145MP	145398	ex F-GUBA	
☐ A6-RRB	Embraer ERJ-145MP	145419	ex F-GUBB	
☐ A6-RRC	Airbus A319-112	1618	ex EI-FDA	
☐ A6-RRD	Embraer ERJ-145MP	145333	ex F-GUBD	♦
☐ A6-RRJ	Airbus A319-115CJ	5277	ex D-AVYW	

SEAWINGS   Dubai-Creek SPB

| ☐ A6-SEA | Cessna 208 Caravan I | 20800118 | ex TF-SEA | FP |
| ☐ A6-SEB | Cessna 208 Caravan I | 20800401 | ex N1000X | FP |

SKYLINK ARABIA   (SKA)   Dubai (DXB)

☐ A6-SKA	Hawker 800XP	258432	ex N809LX	
☐ ER-AZN	Antonov An-24RV	37308801	ex RA-46624	[KIV]
☐ RDPL-34155	Ilyushin Il-76T	073411338	ex ER-IBD	[RKT]
☐ RDPL-34157	Ilyushin Il-76T	093418556	ex ER-IBP	wfs
☐ ZS-IRE	Boeing 727-2Q9F (FedEx 3)	21931/1531	ex N741DH	
☐ ZS-JES	Fokker F.28 Fellowship 4000	11236	ex 5H-MVK	[HLA]
☐ ZS-SKA	Fokker 70	11559	ex PH-ZFT	opf Golden Wings
☐ 4L-FFE	Ilyushin Il-76T	093418548	ex UP-I7611	[RKT]

A7-   QATAR (State of Qatar)

GULF HELICOPTERS   Doha (DOH)

☐ A6-GHM	AgustaWestland AW139	31450		
☐ A7-GHA	AgustaWestland AW139	31132		
☐ A7-GHB	AgustaWestland AW139	31140		
☐ A7-GHC	AgustaWestland AW139	31225		
☐ A7-GHD	AgustaWestland AW139	31233		>United Offshore
☐ A7-GHE	AgustaWestland AW139	31235		>United Offshore
☐ A7-GHF	AgustaWestland AW139	31242		>United Offshore
☐ A7-GHG	AgustaWestland AW139	41222	ex N420SM	
☐ A7-GHH	AgustaWestland AW139	41225	ex N413SM	
☐ A7-GHJ	AgustaWestland AW139	41241	ex N459SM	
☐ A7-GHK	AgustaWestland AW139	41248	ex N460SM	
☐ A7-GHL	AgustaWestland AW139	31381		
☐ A7-GHO	AgustaWestland AW139	31523		♦
☐ A7-GHP	AgustaWestland AW139	31527	ex I-EASS	♦
☐ A7-GHQ	AgustaWestland AW139			♦
☐ A7-GHT	AgustaWestland AW139	31068	ex A7-HBT	♦
☐ A7-	AgustaWestland AW139	31460	ex OY-HHL	

☐ A7-HAV	Bell 412SP	33205	ex D-HHNN	
☐ A7-HAW	Bell 412HP	36046	ex N9142N	
☐ A7-HAY	Bell 412EP	36126	ex N2045S	
☐ A7-HAZ	Bell 412HP	36041	ex N92801	
☐ A7-HBB	Bell 412EP	36259	ex N9026K	
☐ A7-HBC	Bell 412EP	36276	ex N9154J	
☐ A7-HBD	Bell 412EP	36088	ex N4324X	
☐ A7-HBH	Bell 412EP	36326	ex N8067Q	
☐ A7-HBI	Bell 412EP	36270	ex PP-MBE	
☐ A7-HBJ	Bell 412EP	36370	ex N43939	
☐ A7-HBL	Bell 412SP	33117	ex EP-HUC	
☐ A7-HBP	Bell 412SP	36016	ex EP-HUF	
☐ A7-HBQ	Bell 412EP	36412	ex N7512Z	
☐ A7-HBR	Bell 412SP	36017	ex EP-HUG	
☐ A7-HBS	Bell 412SP	33116	ex A7-HBK	
☐ VT-HGF	Bell 412EP	36206	ex A7-HBE	>United Helicharters
☐ VT-UHB	Bell 412EP	36400		>United Helicharters

☐ A7-GAA	AgustaWestland AW189	49009	ex I-RAIL	♦
☐ A7-GAB	AgustaWestland AW189	49010	ex I-PTFJ	♦
☐ A7-GAC	AgustaWestland AW189	49015	ex I-RAIS	♦
☐ A7-HAO	Agusta-Bell 206B JetRanger II	8044	ex A4O-DC	
☐ A7-HBF	Bell 230	23015	ex N236X	
☐ A7-HBN	Bell 212	31130	ex VT-HGE	
☐ A7-HBO	Bell 212	30911	ex EP-HUE	
☐ A7-HHT	Sikorsky S-92A	920031	ex N7113U	

QATAR AIRWAYS   Qatari (QR/QTR)   Doha (DOH)

Member of oneWorld

| ☐ A7-ADA | Airbus A320-232 | 1566 | ex F-WWBG | Al Zubara |

☐ A7-ADB	Airbus A320-232	1648	ex F-WWDU	Dukhan	
☐ A7-ADC	Airbus A320-232	1773	ex F-WWDG	Mesaieed	
☐ A7-ADD	Airbus A320-232	1895	ex F-WWBT	Halul	
☐ A7-ADE	Airbus A320-232	1957	ex F-WWIG	Al Gharafa	
☐ A7-ADF	Airbus A320-232	2097	ex F-WWIP	Al Wukeir	
☐ A7-ADG	Airbus A320-232	2121	ex F-WWIT	Al Ghuweriyah	
☐ A7-ADH	Airbus A320-232	2138	ex F-WWBI	Al Jumeilliyah	
☐ A7-ADI	Airbus A320-232	2161	ex F-WWBK	Al Khuraytiyat	
☐ A7-ADJ	Airbus A320-232	2288	ex F-WWBS	Al Samriya	
☐ A7-AHA	Airbus A320-232	4110	ex F-WWDT		
☐ A7-AHB	Airbus A320-232	4130	ex F-WWIR		
☐ A7-AHC	Airbus A320-232	4183	ex F-WWIB		
☐ A7-AHD	Airbus A320-232	4436	ex D-AVVW		
☐ A7-AHE	Airbus A320-232	4479	ex D-AUBC		
☐ A7-AHF	Airbus A320-232	4496	ex F-WWIJ		
☐ A7-AHG	Airbus A320-232	4615	ex D-AXAV		
☐ A7-AHH	Airbus A320-232	4700	ex F-WWBD		
☐ A7-AHI	Airbus A320-232	4754	ex F-WWDA		
☐ A7-AHJ	Airbus A320-232	4784	ex F-WWDT		
☐ A7-AHL	Airbus A320-232	4802	ex F-WWBC		oneWorld c/s
☐ A7-AHO	Airbus A320-232	4810	ex F-WWDI		oneWorld c/s
☐ A7-AHP	Airbus A320-232	4858	ex F-WWBJ		
☐ A7-AHQ	Airbus A320-232	4930	ex F-WWBI		
☐ A7-AHR	Airbus A320-232	4968	ex F-WWDV		
☐ A7-AHS	Airbus A320-232	5010	ex F-WWDX		
☐ A7-AHT	Airbus A320-232	5078	ex F-WWIC		
☐ A7-AHU	Airbus A320-232	5127	ex F-WWDT		
☐ A7-AHV	Airbus A320-232/S	5182	ex F-WWBG		
☐ A7-AHW	Airbus A320-232/S	5217	ex D-AXAS		
☐ A7-AHX	Airbus A320-232/S	5361	ex F-WWIV		
☐ A7-AHY	Airbus A320-232/S	5395	ex F-WWBJ		
☐ A7-	Airbus A320-232/S	6832	ex		o/o♦
☐ A7-ADK	Airbus A321-231	1487	ex OE-LOS		
☐ A7-ADS	Airbus A321-231	1928	ex D-AVXA	Al Aaliyah	
☐ A7-ADT	Airbus A321-231	2107	ex D-AVXD	Al Saffiyah	
☐ A7-ADV	Airbus A321-231	3274	ex D-AVZM		
☐ A7-AIA	Airbus A321-231	4173	ex D-AZAB		
☐ A7-AIB	Airbus A321-231	4382	ex D-AVZY		
☐ A7-AIC	Airbus A321-231	4406	ex D-AZAD		
☐ A7-AID	Airbus A321-231	4530	ex D-AVZJ		
☐ A7-ACA	Airbus A330-202	473	ex F-WWKR	Al Wajbah	
☐ A7-ACB	Airbus A330-202	489	ex F-WWYN	Al Majida	
☐ A7-ACC	Airbus A330-202	511	ex F-WWKR	Al Shahaniya	
☐ A7-ACD	Airbus A330-202	521	ex F-WWKU	Al Wuseil	
☐ A7-ACE	Airbus A330-202	571	ex F-WWKF	Al Dhakira	
☐ A7-ACF	Airbus A330-202	638	ex F-WWYQ	Al Kara'anah	
☐ A7-ACG	Airbus A330-202	743	ex F-WWKV	Al Wabra	
☐ A7-ACH	Airbus A330-202	441	ex F-WWYK	Al Mafjar	
☐ A7-ACI	Airbus A330-202	746	ex F-WWKV	Muathier	
☐ A7-ACJ	Airbus A330-202	760	ex F-WWYO	Zikreet	
☐ A7-ACK	Airbus A330-202	792	ex F-WWKP		
☐ A7-ACL	Airbus A330-202	820	ex F-WWKA		
☐ A7-ACM	Airbus A330-202	849	ex F-WWKP		
☐ A7-AFL	Airbus A330-202	612	ex F-WWKZ	Al Messila	
☐ A7-AFM	Airbus A330-202	616	ex F-WWKT	Al-Udaid	
☐ A7-AFP	Airbus A330-202	684	ex F-WWYG	Al Shamal	
☐ A7-AFF	Airbus A330-243F	1578	ex F-WWYT		♦
☐ A7-AFG	Airbus A330-243F	1584	ex F-WWKM		♦
☐ A7-AFH	Airbus A330-243F	1594	ex F-WWYH		♦
☐ A7-AFV	Airbus A330-243F	1350	ex F-WXAD		
☐ A7-AFY	Airbus A330-243F	1386	ex F-WWYR		
☐ A7-AFZ	Airbus A330-243F	1406	ex F-WWTS		
☐ A7-	Airbus A330-243F	1688	ex F-WW		o/o♦
☐ A7-AEA	Airbus A330-302	623	ex F-WWYC	Al Muntazah	
☐ A7-AEB	Airbus A330-302	637	ex F-WWYP	Al Sayliyah	
☐ A7-AEC	Airbus A330-302	659	ex F-WWYX	Al Markhiya	
☐ A7-AED	Airbus A330-302	680	ex F-WWYD	Al Nu'uman	
☐ A7-AEE	Airbus A330-302	711	ex F-WWYK	Semaisma	
☐ A7-AEF	Airbus A330-302	721	ex F-WWKJ	Al Rumellah	
☐ A7-AEG	Airbus A330-302	734	ex F-WWYU	Al Duhell	
☐ A7-AEH	Airbus A330-302	789	ex F-WWKN		
☐ A7-AEI	Airbus A330-302	813	ex F-WWYI		
☐ A7-AEJ	Airbus A330-302	826	ex F-WWKF		
☐ A7-AEM	Airbus A330-302	893	ex F-WWYK		
☐ A7-AEN	Airbus A330-302	907	ex F-WWYE		
☐ A7-AEO	Airbus A330-302	918	ex F-WWYQ		
☐ A7-ALA	Airbus A350-941	006	ex F-WZFA	Sudanthel	♦
☐ A7-ALB	Airbus A350-941	007	ex F-WZFB		♦

☐	A7-ALC	Airbus A350-941	009	ex F-WZFD		o/o♦
☐	A7-ALD	Airbus A350-941	010	ex F-WZFE		o/o♦
☐	A7-	Airbus A350-941	008	ex F-WZFC		♦
☐	A7-	Airbus A350-941	011	ex F-WZFF		o/o♦
☐	A7-	Airbus A350-951	012	ex F-WZFG		o/o♦
☐	A7-	Airbus A350-941	021	ex F-WZ		o/o♦
☐	A7-APA	Airbus A380-861	137	ex F-WWST		
☐	A7-APB	Airbus A380-861	143	ex F-WWAJ		
☐	A7-APC	Airbus A380-861	145	ex F-WWAL		
☐	A7-APD	Airbus A380-861	160	ex F-WWSG		o/o
☐	A7-APE	Airbus A380-861	181	ex F-WWSC		o/o♦
☐	A7-APF	Airbus A380-861	189	ex F-WWAO		o/o♦
☐	A7-APG	Airbus A380-861	193	ex F-WWSD		o/o♦
☐	A7-	Airbus A380-861	197	ex F-WW		o/o♦
☐	A7-BBA	Boeing 777-2DZLR	36012/753	ex N1788B	Alhuwaila	
☐	A7-BBB	Boeing 777-2DZLR	36013/762	ex N50281	Gaza	
☐	A7-BBC	Boeing 777-2DZLR	36015/825	ex N5023Q		
☐	A7-BBD	Boeing 777-2DZLR	36016/831	ex N5573S		
☐	A7-BBE	Boeing 777-2DZLR	36017/837			
☐	A7-BBF	Boeing 777-2DZLR	36018/842			
☐	A7-BBG	Boeing 777-2DZLR	36101/883			
☐	A7-BBH	Boeing 777-2DZLR	36102/885		Al Qalail	
☐	A7-BBI	Boeing 777-2DZLR	41061/962		Jaow Alsalam	
☐	A7-BAA	Boeing 777-3DZER	36009/676			oneWorld c/s
☐	A7-BAB	Boeing 777-3DZER	36103/686		Um-Alamad	oneWorld c/s
☐	A7-BAC	Boeing 777-3DZER	36010/731	ex N5016R		
☐	A7-BAE	Boeing 777-3DZER	36104/769		Almas-Habia	FC Barcelona c/s
☐	A7-BAF	Boeing 777-3DZER	37661/815			oneWorld c/s
☐	A7-BAG	Boeing 777-3DZER	36014/819	ex N5017Q	Littoriya	
☐	A7-BAH	Boeing 777-3DZER	37662/849			
☐	A7-BAI	Boeing 777-3DZER	36095/742	ex N5028Y		
☐	A7-BAJ	Boeing 777-3DZER	36096/851		Al Gharia	
☐	A7-BAK	Boeing 777-3DZER	36097/859			
☐	A7-BAL	Boeing 777-3DZER	38244/893	ex N52081		
☐	A7-BAM	Boeing 777-3DZER	38245/922			
☐	A7-BAN	Boeing 777-3DZER	38246/925			
☐	A7-BAO	Boeing 777-3DZER	36011/750			
☐	A7-BAP	Boeing 777-3DZER	38248/958		Al Qattard	
☐	A7-BAQ	Boeing 777-3DZER	38247/910			
☐	A7-BAS	Boeing 777-3DZER	41062/997		Bu Funtas	
☐	A7-BAT	Boeing 777-3DZER	41738/1149			
☐	A7-BAU	Boeing 777-3DZER	41739/1163			
☐	A7-BAV	Boeing 777-3DZER	41740/1179			
☐	A7-BAW	Boeing 777-3DZER	41741/1071			
☐	A7-BAX	Boeing 777-3DZER	41780/1035			
☐	A7-BAY	Boeing 777-3DZER	41778/1078			
☐	A7-BAZ	Boeing 777-3DZER	41781/1093			
☐	A7-BEA	Boeing 777-3DZER	41779/1098			
☐	A7-BEB	Boeing 777-3DZER	43215/1218			♦
☐	A7-BEC	Boeing 777-3DZER	43216/1226			♦
☐	A7-BED	Boeing 777-3DZER	60330/1244			♦
☐	A7-BEE	Boeing 777-3DZER	60331/1314			o/o♦
☐	A7-BEF	Boeing 777-3DZER	60332/			o/o♦
☐	A7-BEG	Boeing 777-3DZER	60333/			o/o♦
☐	A7-BFA	Boeing 777-FDZ	36098/865			
☐	A7-BFB	Boeing 777-FDZ	36100/874		Libseer	
☐	A7-BFC	Boeing 777-FDZ	36099/970		Lbeshairiya	
☐	A7-BFD	Boeing 777-FDZ	41427/1004			
☐	A7-BFE	Boeing 777-FDZ	39644/1110			
☐	A7-BFF	Boeing 777-FDZ	39645/1192			
☐	A7-BFG	Boeing 777-FDZ	42299/1238			♦
☐	A7-BFH	Boeing 777-FDZ	42298/1284			♦
☐	A7-BCA	Boeing 787-8	38319/57			
☐	A7-BCB	Boeing 787-8	38320/58	ex N1003W	Ras Rikin	
☐	A7-BCC	Boeing 787-8	38321/82			
☐	A7-BCD	Boeing 787-8	38322/99			
☐	A7-BCE	Boeing 787-8	38323/103			
☐	A7-BCF	Boeing 787-8	38324/109			
☐	A7-BCG	Boeing 787-8	38325/116			
☐	A7-BCH	Boeing 787-8	38326/129			
☐	A7-BCI	Boeing 787-8	38327/138			
☐	A7-BCJ	Boeing 787-8	38328/144			
☐	A7-BCK	Boeing 787-8	38329/62			
☐	A7-BCL	Boeing 787-8	38330/64			
☐	A7-BCM	Boeing 787-8	38331/150			
☐	A7-BCN	Boeing 787-8	38332/176			♦
☐	A7-BCO	Boeing 787-8	38333/188			♦
☐	A7-BCP	Boeing 787-8	38334/207			♦

☐ A7-BCQ	Boeing 787-8	38335/215			♦
☐ A7-BCR	Boeing 787-8	38336/225	ex N1012N		♦
☐ A7-BCS	Boeing 787-8	38337/261	ex N1791B		♦
☐ A7-BCT	Boeing 787-8	38338/266	ex N10187		♦
☐ A7-BCU	Boeing 787-8	38339/277	ex N1003N		♦
☐ A7-BCV	Boeing 787-8	38340/292			o/o♦
☐ A7-BCW	Boeing 787-8	38341/328			o/o♦
☐ A7-BCX	Boeing 787-8	38342/352			o/o♦
☐ A7-BCY	Boeing 787-8	38343/354			o/o♦
☐ A7-BCZ	Boeing 787-8	38344/384			o/o♦
☐ A7-	Boeing 787-8	38345/394			o/o♦
☐ A7-	Boeing 787-8	38346/410			o/o♦
☐ A7-AGA	Airbus A340-642HGW	740	ex F-WWCP		
☐ A7-AGB	Airbus A340-642HGW	715	ex F-WWCR	Ras Dukhan	
☐ A7-AGC	Airbus A340-642HGW	766	ex F-WWCM	Ras Ushainij	
☐ A7-AGD	Airbus A340-642HGW	798	ex F-WWCL		
☐ A7-CJA	Airbus A319-133LR	1656	ex D-AVYT	Al Hilal	
☐ A7-CJB	Airbus A319-133LR	2341	ex D-AVWK	Al Jasra	
☐ A7-	Airbus A320-271Neo	6772	ex		o/o♦
☐ A7-	Airbus A320-271Neo	6449	ex		o/o♦
☐ A7-	Airbus A320-271Neo	6907	ex		o/o♦
☐ A7-	Airbus A320-271Neo	6946	ex		o/o♦

A9C- BAHRAIN (State of Bahrain)

DHL INTERNATIONAL AVIATION — Dilmun (ES/DHX) — Bahrain (BAH)

☐ A9C-DHC	Boeing 757-225SF	22211/74	ex N314ST		
☐ A9C-DHD	Boeing 757-225SF	22611/75	ex N315ST		wfs
☐ A9C-DHE	Boeing 757-225PCF	22210/42	ex N241AL		
☐ HZ-SNA	Boeing 727-264F (FedEx 3)	20896/1051	ex A9C-SNA	all-white	jt ops with RSE
☐ HZ-SNB	Boeing 727-223F (FedEx 3)	21084/1199	ex EC-HAH	all-white	jt ops with RSE

GULF AIR — Gulf Air (GF/GFA) — Bahrain (BAH)

☐ A9C-CA	Airbus A321-231	5025	ex D-AZAL		
☐ A9C-CB	Airbus A321-231	5074	ex D-AVZN		
☐ A9C-CC	Airbus A321-231	5180	ex D-AVZK		
☐ A9C-CD	Airbus A321-231	5257	ex D-AZAA		VIP
☐ A9C-CE	Airbus A321-231	5321	ex F-WXAF		
☐ A9C-CF	Airbus A321-231	5336	ex F-WXAG		
☐ A9C-AB	Airbus A320-214	4030	ex F-WWIB		
☐ A9C-AC	Airbus A320-214	4059	ex F-WWBD		
☐ A9C-AD	Airbus A320-214	4083	ex F-WWBT		
☐ A9C-AE	Airbus A320-214	4146	ex D-AVVG		
☐ A9C-AF	Airbus A320-214	4158	ex F-WWBQ		
☐ A9C-AG	Airbus A320-214	4188	ex F-WWIG		
☐ A9C-AH	Airbus A320-214	4218	ex F-WWBH		
☐ A9C-AI	Airbus A320-214	4255	ex F-WWIO		
☐ A9C-AJ	Airbus A320-214	4502	ex F-WWIU		
☐ A9C-AK	Airbus A320-214	4541	ex D-AXAM		
☐ A9C-AL	Airbus A320-214	4780	ex F-WWDP		
☐ A9C-AM	Airbus A320-214	4827	ex D-AXAL		
☐ A9C-AN	Airbus A320-214	4865	ex D-AUBP		
☐ A9C-AO	Airbus A320-214	4860	ex F-WWDF		
☐ A9C-AP	Airbus A320-214	5171	ex D-AXAP		
☐ A9C-AQ	Airbus A320-214	5175	ex F-WWDR		
☐ A9C-KA	Airbus A330-243	276	ex A4O-KA	501	
☐ A9C-KB	Airbus A330-243	281	ex A4O-KB	502	
☐ A9C-KC	Airbus A330-243	286	ex A4O-KC	503	
☐ A9C-KD	Airbus A330-243	287	ex A4O-KD	504	
☐ A9C-KE	Airbus A330-243	334	ex A4O-KE	505	
☐ A9C-KF	Airbus A330-243	340	ex A4O-KF	506 Aldafra	

MENA AEROSPACE — (MEN)

☐ A9C-JWC	Boeing 737-3G7F	24711/1843	ex A6-HLH	

TEXEL AIR — (XLR) — Bahrain (BAH)

☐ A9C-JNC	Boeing 737-3G7F	24710/1825	ex N308AW	Samantha	♦
☐ A9C-TXL	Boeing 737-3Q8F	28200/2854	ex N453KA		♦

B- CHINA (People's Republic Of China)

AIR CHINA		Air China (CA/CCA)		Beijing-Capital (PEK)

Member of Star Alliance

☐ B-2364	Airbus A319-115	2499	ex D-AVWB	
☐ B-6004	Airbus A319-115	2508	ex D-AVWO	
☐ B-6014	Airbus A319-115	2525	ex D-AVWE	
☐ B-6034	Airbus A319-115	2237	ex D-AVWL	
☐ B-6035	Airbus A319-115	2269	ex D-AVWX	
☐ B-6036	Airbus A319-115	2285	ex D-AVYS	
☐ B-6037	Airbus A319-115	2293	ex D-AVYY	
☐ B-6038	Airbus A319-115	2298	ex D-AVWF	
☐ B-6044	Airbus A319-115	2532	ex D-AVWL	
☐ B-6046	Airbus A319-115	2545	ex D-AVWW	
☐ B-6047	Airbus A319-115	2551	ex D-AVYJ	
☐ B-6223	Airbus A319-115	2805	ex D-AVWV	
☐ B-6225	Airbus A319-115	2819	ex D-AVXB	
☐ B-6226	Airbus A319-115	2839	ex D-AVYI	
☐ B-6227	Airbus A319-115	2847	ex D-AVXG	
☐ B-6228	Airbus A319-115	2890	ex D-AVYI	
☐ B-6238	Airbus A319-115	3250	ex D-AVWO	
☐ B-6468	Airbus A319-115/S	6514	ex D-AVYC	♦
☐ B-	Airbus A319-115	6603	ex	o/o♦
☐ B-	Airbus A319-115	6699	ex	o/o♦
☐ B-2404	Airbus A319-131	2454	ex D-AVWE	
☐ B-6022	Airbus A319-131	2000	ex D-AVYZ	
☐ B-6023	Airbus A319-131	2007	ex F-WWBJ	
☐ B-6024	Airbus A319-131	2015	ex D-AVWT	
☐ B-6031	Airbus A319-131	2172	ex D-AVWW	
☐ B-6032	Airbus A319-131	2202	ex D-AVYF	
☐ B-6033	Airbus A319-131	2205	ex D-AVYJ	
☐ B-6048	Airbus A319-131	2559	ex D-AVYU	
☐ B-6213	Airbus A319-131	2614	ex D-AVXS	
☐ B-6216	Airbus A319-131	2643	ex D-AVWO	
☐ B-6235	Airbus A319-131	3195	ex D-AVWC	
☐ B-6236	Airbus A319-131	3200	ex D-AVWG	
☐ B-6237	Airbus A319-131	3226	ex D-AVYJ	
☐ B-1852	Airbus A320-214/S	6239	ex B-513L	♦
☐ B-1853	Airbus A320-214	6169	ex B-520L	♦
☐ B-1873	Airbus A320-214/S	6251	ex F-WWDN	♦
☐ B-1875	Airbus A320-214/S	6283	ex B-518L	♦
☐ B-2210	Airbus A320-214	1296	ex F-WWBG	
☐ B-2376	Airbus A320-214	0876	ex F-WWIF	
☐ B-2377	Airbus A320-214	0921	ex F-WWDY	
☐ B-6606	Airbus A320-214	3337	ex B-6350	
☐ B-6607	Airbus A320-214	3461	ex B-6390	
☐ B-6608	Airbus A320-214	3601	ex B-6393	
☐ B-6609	Airbus A320-214	3215	ex B-6336	
☐ B-6610	Airbus A320-214	3221	ex B-6337	
☐ B-6611	Airbus A320-214	3506	ex B-6391	
☐ B-6767	Airbus A320-214	4803	ex D-AVVW	
☐ B-6793	Airbus A320-214	4829	ex F-WWIM	
☐ B-6822	Airbus A320-214	4900	ex D-AVVI	
☐ B-6828	Airbus A320-214	4963	ex F-WWDP	
☐ B-6846	Airbus A320-214	4985	ex F-WWIL	
☐ B-6847	Airbus A320-214	4895	ex B-520L	
☐ B-6881	Airbus A320-214	5174	ex D-AXAQ	
☐ B-6882	Airbus A320-214	4997	ex B-510L	
☐ B-6915	Airbus A320-214	5014	ex B-512L	
☐ B-6916	Airbus A320-214	5032	ex B-514L	
☐ B-6941	Airbus A320-214	5386	ex D-AUBV	
☐ B-6967	Airbus A320-214	5419	ex B-505L	
☐ B-9918	Airbus A320-214	5568	ex B-507L	
☐ B-9923	Airbus A320-214	5664	ex B-517L	
☐ B-9925	Airbus A320-214	5690	ex B-520L	
☐ B-9926	Airbus A320-214	5771	ex B-509L	
☐ B-	Airbus A320-214	6466	ex	o/o♦
☐ B-	Airbus A320-214	6743	ex	o/o♦
☐ B-6676	Airbus A320-232	4317	ex F-WWBR	
☐ B-6677	Airbus A320-232	4348	ex F-WWBU	
☐ B-6731	Airbus A320-232	4473	ex B-501L	
☐ B-6733	Airbus A320-232	4566	ex B-508L	
☐ B-6745	Airbus A320-232	4593	ex B-511L	
☐ B-6773	Airbus A320-232	4775	ex F-WWDJ	
☐ B-6823	Airbus A320-232	4873	ex D-AVZA	
☐ B-6918	Airbus A320-232	5091	ex B-520L	

☐ B-6960	Airbus A320-232	5352	ex B-514L		
☐ B-9922	Airbus A320-232	5600	ex B-510L		
☐ B-1637	Airbus A321-213/S	6579	ex D-AVXG		o/o♦
☐ B-1638	Airbus A321-213/S	6641	ex		o/o♦
☐ B-1639	Airbus A321-213/S	6567	ex D-AZAQ		♦
☐ B-1816	Airbus A321-213	6013	ex D-AVZF		
☐ B-1855	Airbus A321-213	6196	ex D-AZAJ		♦
☐ B-1876	Airbus A321-213/S	6319	ex D-AZAG		♦
☐ B-6326	Airbus A321-213	3329	ex D-AVZX		
☐ B-6327	Airbus A321-213	3307	ex D-AVZT		
☐ B-6361	Airbus A321-213	3523	ex D-AVZX	Beautiful Sichuan c/s	
☐ B-6362	Airbus A321-213	3623	ex D-AVZG		
☐ B-6363	Airbus A321-213	3653	ex D-AVZV		
☐ B-6365	Airbus A321-213	3655	ex D-AVZW		
☐ B-6382	Airbus A321-213	3665	ex D-AVZX		
☐ B-6383	Airbus A321-213	3678	ex D-AZAE		
☐ B-6385	Airbus A321-213	3722	ex D-AZAH		
☐ B-6386	Airbus A321-213	3725	ex D-AZVS		
☐ B-6555	Airbus A321-213	3766	ex D-AZAO		
☐ B-6556	Airbus A321-213	3806	ex D-AVZD		
☐ B-6593	Airbus A321-213	3973	ex D-AVZS		
☐ B-6595	Airbus A321-213	4022	ex D-AVZG		
☐ B-6596	Airbus A321-213	4031	ex D-AVZI		
☐ B 6597	Airbus A321-213	4062	ex D-AVZO		
☐ B-6599	Airbus A321-213	3940	ex D-AZAI		
☐ B-6603	Airbus A321-213	4131	ex D-AZAJ		
☐ B-6605	Airbus A321-213	4091	ex D-AVZX		
☐ B-6631	Airbus A321-213	4180	ex D-AZAM		
☐ B-6632	Airbus A321-213	4221	ex D-AVZJ		
☐ B-6633	Airbus A321-213	4283	ex D-AZAQ		
☐ B-6665	Airbus A321-213	4318	ex D-AVZW		
☐ B-6675	Airbus A321-213	4377	ex D-AZAA		
☐ B-6701	Airbus A321-213	4472	ex D-AVZE		
☐ B-6711	Airbus A321-213	4494	ex D-AVZF		
☐ B-6712	Airbus A321-213	4538	ex D-AVZQ		
☐ B-6961	Airbus A321-213	5435	ex D-AVZW		
☐ B-6973	Airbus A321-213	5573	ex D-AVZR		
☐ B-9919	Airbus A321-213	5743	ex D-AZAJ		
☐ B-1833	Airbus A321-232	6159	ex D-AVXQ		♦
☐ B-1877	Airbus A321-232/S	6273	ex D-AVZQ		♦
☐ B-1878	Airbus A321-232/S	6308	ex D-AVZZ		♦
☐ B-1879	Airbus A321-232/S	6354	ex D-AVXL		♦
☐ B-6741	Airbus A321-232	4617	ex D-AZAN		
☐ B-6742	Airbus A321-232	4719	ex D-AVZE		
☐ B-6791	Airbus A321-232	4771	ex D-AVZK		
☐ B-6792	Airbus A321-232	4834	ex D-AVZU		
☐ B-6823	Airbus A321-232	4873	ex D-AVZA		
☐ B-6825	Airbus A321-232	4949	ex D-AZAD		
☐ B-6848	Airbus A321-232	5054	ex D-AZAR		
☐ B-6883	Airbus A321-232	5124	ex D-AVZA		
☐ B-6885	Airbus A321-232	5199	ex D-AVZR		
☐ B-6917	Airbus A321-232	5265	ex D-AZAB		
☐ B-6919	Airbus A321-232	5346	ex D-AVZA		
☐ B-6942	Airbus A321-232	5432	ex D-AVZT		
☐ B-5918	Airbus A330-243	1396	ex F-WWKJ		
☐ B-5927	Airbus A330-243	1444	ex F-WWKO		
☐ B-5932	Airbus A330-243	1459	ex F-WWCC		
☐ B-5933	Airbus A330-243	1471	ex F-WWYI		
☐ B-6070	Airbus A330-243	750	ex F-WWKA		
☐ B-6071	Airbus A330-243	756	ex F-WWYQ		
☐ B-6072	Airbus A330-243	759	ex F-WWYK		
☐ B-6073	Airbus A330-243	780	ex F-WWYM		
☐ B-6075	Airbus A330-243	785	ex F-WWYY		
☐ B-6076	Airbus A330-243	797	ex F-WWKU		
☐ B-6079	Airbus A330-243	810	ex F-WWYF		
☐ B-6080	Airbus A330-243	815	ex F-WWYL		
☐ B-6081	Airbus A330-243	839	ex F-WWYO		
☐ B-6090	Airbus A330-243	860	ex F-WWYN		
☐ B-6091	Airbus A330-243	867	ex F-WWYP	Star Alliance c/s	
☐ B-6092	Airbus A330-243	873	ex F-WWKV		
☐ B-6093	Airbus A330-243	884	ex F-WWKO	Star Alliance c/s	
☐ B-6113	Airbus A330-243	890	ex F-WWYM		
☐ B-6115	Airbus A330-243	909	ex F-WWYG		
☐ B-6117	Airbus A330-243	903	ex F-WWKR		
☐ B-6130	Airbus A330-243	930	ex F-WWKS		
☐ B-6131	Airbus A330-243	941	ex F-WWKO		
☐ B-6132	Airbus A330-243	944	ex F-WWYT		
☐ B-6505	Airbus A330-243	957	ex F-WWYC		
☐ B-6533	Airbus A330-243	1237	ex F-WWKG		
☐ B-6536	Airbus A330-243	1260	ex F-WWYY		

☐ B-6540	Airbus A330-243	1282	ex F-WWKS	
☐ B-6541	Airbus A330-243	1304	ex F-WWYT	
☐ B-6549	Airbus A330-243	1330	ex F-WWTQ	
☐ B-5901	Airbus A330-343E	1353	ex F-WWCS	
☐ B-5906	Airbus A330-343E	1373	ex F-WWYB	
☐ B-5912	Airbus A330-343E	1493	ex F-WWTM	
☐ B-5913	Airbus A330-343E	1509	ex F-WWKK	
☐ B-5916	Airbus A330-343E	1383	ex F-WWYO	
☐ B-5919	Airbus A330-343E	1413	ex F-WWTJ	
☐ B-5925	Airbus A330-343E	1434	ex F-WWCT	
☐ B-5946	Airbus A330-343E	1525	ex F-WWYG	♦
☐ B-5947	Airbus A330-343E	1538	ex F-WWCO	♦
☐ B-5948	Airbus A330-343E	1541	ex F-WWCR	♦
☐ B-5956	Airbus A330-343E	1563	ex F-WWYV	♦
☐ B-5957	Airbus A330-343E	1570	ex F-WWKN	♦
☐ B-5958	Airbus A330-343E	1587	ex F-WWCE	♦
☐ B-6503	Airbus A330-343E	1333	ex F-WWTU	
☐ B-6511	Airbus A330-343	1110	ex F-WWYG	
☐ B-6512	Airbus A330-343	1087	ex F-WWKD	
☐ B-6513	Airbus A330-343	1130	ex F-WWKN	
☐ B-6523	Airbus A330-343	1187	ex F-WWYP	
☐ B-6525	Airbus A330-343	1199	ex F-WWYU	
☐ B-6530	Airbus A330-343	1216	ex F-WWKP	
☐ B-	Airbus A330-343	1658	ex F-WW	o/o♦
☐ B-	Airbus A330-343	1695	ex F-WW	o/o♦
☐ B-2612	Boeing 737-79L	33411/1538		
☐ B-2613	Boeing 737-79L	33412/1544	ex N1786B	
☐ B-2700	Boeing 737-79L	33413/1560		
☐ B-5043	Boeing 737-79L	33408/1331		
☐ B-5044	Boeing 737-79L	33409/1351		
☐ B-5045	Boeing 737-79L	33410/1354		
☐ B-5201	Boeing 737-79L/W	34023/1795	ex N1786B	
☐ B-5202	Boeing 737-79L/W	34537/1837	ex N1786B	
☐ B-5203	Boeing 737-79L/W	34538/1853		
☐ B-5211	Boeing 737-79L	34019/1749		
☐ B-5213	Boeing 737-79L/W	34020/1769	ex N1786B	
☐ B-5214	Boeing 737-79L/W	34021/1774		
☐ B-5217	Boeing 737-79L/W	34022/1786		
☐ B-5220	Boeing 737-79L/W	34539/1856	ex (B-5204)	
☐ B-5227	Boeing 737-79L/W	34541/1937		
☐ B-5228	Boeing 737-79L/W	34542/1993		
☐ B-5229	Boeing 737-79L/W	34543/2006		
☐ B-5296	Boeing 737-79L/W	41091/4301	ex N1786B	
☐ B-5297	Boeing 737-79L/W	41092/4354		
☐ B-5803	Boeing 737-79L/W	41093/4658	ex N1796B	
☐ B-1738	Boeing 737-89L/W	41325/5186		♦
☐ B-1760	Boeing 737-88L/W	41101/5240	ex N1787B	♦
☐ B-1761	Boeing 737-89L/W	41102/5265		♦
☐ B-1762	Boeing 737-89L/W	41103/5333		♦
☐ B-1763	Boeing 737-89L/W	41104/5381		♦
☐ B-1764	Boeing 737-89L/W	41105/5424		o/o♦
☐ B-1766	Boeing 737-89L/W	41108/5327		♦
☐ B-1767	Boeing 737-89L/W	41109/5230		♦
☐ B-1768	Boeing 737-89L/W	41110/5276		♦
☐ B-1909	Boeing 737-89L/W	40022/4681		
☐ B-1942	Boeing 737-89L/W	40023/4746		
☐ B-1945	Boeing 737-89L/W	41094/4790	ex N1786B	
☐ B-1946	Boeing 737-89L/W	41095/4828		
☐ B-1947	Boeing 737-89L/W	41314/4756		
☐ B-1956	Boeing 737-89L/W	40024/4864		
☐ B-1957	Boeing 737-89L/W	40041/4992		♦
☐ B-1958	Boeing 737-89L/W	40042/5037		♦
☐ B-1959	Boeing 737-89L/W	41321/4982		♦
☐ B-1975	Boeing 737-89L/W	41323/5065		♦
☐ B-1976	Boeing 737-89L/W	41098/5131		♦
☐ B-1977	Boeing 737-88L/W	41099/5181		♦
☐ B-1978	Boeing 737-89L/W	41324/5120	ex N1795B	♦
☐ B-2161	Boeing 737-86N	28655/965	ex N1786B	
☐ B-2509	Boeing 737-8Z0	30072/466	ex N1787B	
☐ B-2510	Boeing 737-8Z0	30071/381	ex N1786B	
☐ B-2511	Boeing 737-8Z0	30073/487	ex N1786B	
☐ B-2641	Boeing 737-89L	29876/337		
☐ B-2642	Boeing 737-89L	29877/359		
☐ B-2643	Boeing 737-89L	29878/379	ex N1786B	
☐ B-2645	Boeing 737-89L	29879/427	ex N1786B	
☐ B-2648	Boeing 737-89L	29880/511	ex N1786B	
☐ B-2649	Boeing 737-89L	30159/572	ex N1784B	
☐ B-2650	Boeing 737-89L	30160/594		
☐ B-2657	Boeing 737-89L	30517/1224		
☐ B-2671	Boeing 737-89L	30515/1165		

☐ B-2672	Boeing 737-89L	30516/1168		
☐ B-2673	Boeing 737-86N	29888/1133	ex N1786B	
☐ B-2690	Boeing 737-86N	29889/1153		
☐ B-5167	Boeing 737-808	34701/1887	ex N1787B	
☐ B-5170	Boeing 737-808	34705/1998		
☐ B-5172	Boeing 737-8Q8	30704/1985		
☐ B-5173	Boeing 737-8Q8	30705/2001		
☐ B-5175	Boeing 737-86N	35209/2067		
☐ B-5176	Boeing 737-86N	34258/2096		special c/s
☐ B-5177	Boeing 737-86N	35210/2127		special c/s
☐ B-5178	Boeing 737-86N	32682/2117	ex N1787B	Peony c/s
☐ B-5179	Boeing 737-86N	35211/2146		
☐ B-5198	Boeing 737-89L/W	36491/2759		
☐ B-5312	Boeing 737-8Q8	29374/2203	ex N1786B	
☐ B-5325	Boeing 737-86N	32692/2275	ex N1786B	
☐ B-5326	Boeing 737-86N	35214/2308		
☐ B-5327	Boeing 737-86N	35219/2371	ex N1779B	
☐ B-5328	Boeing 737-86N	35221/2444	ex N1786B	
☐ B-5329	Boeing 737-86N	35222/2463		
☐ B-5341	Boeing 737-89L/W	36483/2403	ex N1786B	
☐ B-5342	Boeing 737-89L/W	36484/2441	ex N1786B	
☐ B-5343	Boeing 737-89L/W	36485/2470		
☐ B-5387	Boeing 737-89L/W	36492/2828		
☐ B-5390	Boeing 737-89L/W	36486/2606		
☐ B-5391	Boeing 737-89L/W	36487/2664	ex N1786B	
☐ B-5392	Boeing 737-89L/W	36488/2674		
☐ B-5397	Boeing 737-89L/W	36489/2704	ex N1787B	
☐ B-5398	Boeing 737-89L/W	36490/2715		
☐ B-5422	Boeing 737-89L/W	36741/2845	ex N1787B	
☐ B-5423	Boeing 737-89L/W	36742/2877		
☐ B-5425	Boeing 737-89L/W	36743/2896		
☐ B-5426	Boeing 737-89L/W	36744/2969		
☐ B-5431	Boeing 737-86N	36812/2918	ex N1787B	
☐ B-5436	Boeing 737-86N	36813/2976		
☐ B-5437	Boeing 737-86N	36815/3020		
☐ B-5438	Boeing 737-86N	36816/3032		
☐ B-5442	Boeing 737-86N/W	36745/3049		
☐ B-5443	Boeing 737-86N/W	36746/3072	ex N1786B	
☐ B-5447	Boeing 737-89L/W	40015/3509		
☐ B-5477	Boeing 737-89L/W	36755/3387		
☐ B-5485	Boeing 737-89L/W	36747/3124	ex N1796B	
☐ B-5486	Boeing 737-89L/W	36748/3127	ex N1786B	
☐ B-5495	Boeing 737-89L/W	36749/3145	ex N1787B	
☐ B-5496	Boeing 737-89L/W	36750/3155	ex N1787B	
☐ B-5497	Boeing 737-89L/W	36751/3167		
☐ B-5500	Boeing 737-89L/W	36752/3188	ex N1786B	
☐ B-5507	Boeing 737-89L/W	36753/3247	ex N1796B	
☐ B-5508	Boeing 737-86N/W	36545/3275		
☐ B-5509	Boeing 737-86N/W	36547/3300		
☐ B-5510	Boeing 737-86N/W	36548/3312	ex N1795B	
☐ B-5518	Boeing 737-89L/W	36754/3336	ex N1786B	
☐ B-5519	Boeing 737-86N	36802/3350	ex N1787B	
☐ B-5525	Boeing 737-86N	37886/3436		
☐ B-5553	Boeing 737-89L/W	40026/3576		>CCD
☐ B-5570	Boeing 737-89L/W	40032/3608	ex N1786B	
☐ B-5572	Boeing 737-89L/W	40027/3670		
☐ B-5582	Boeing 737-89L/W	40028/3707		
☐ B-5583	Boeing 737-89L/W	40016/3749		
☐ B-5585	Boeing 737-89L/W	40029/3756		
☐ B-5621	Boeing 737-89L/W	40030/3846		
☐ B-5622	Boeing 737-89L/W	40031/3859		
☐ B-5639	Boeing 737-89L/W	40033/4004		>CCD
☐ B-5642	Boeing 737-89L/W	40017/4060		>CCD
☐ B-5679	Boeing 737-89L/W	40034/4117		
☐ B-5680	Boeing 737-89L/W	40035/4149	ex N1786B	
☐ B-5681	Boeing 737-89L/W	40025/4202	ex N1786B	
☐ B-5682	Boeing 737-89L/W	40036/4213		
☐ B-5696	Boeing 737-89L/W	40019/4275		
☐ B-5729	Boeing 737-89L/W	40038/4422		>CCD
☐ B-5793	Boeing 737-89L/W	40021/4595	ex N5515X	
☐ B-5848	Boeing 737-89L/W	41307/4607	ex N1786B	
☐ B-5849	Boeing 737-89L/W	41309/4649	ex N5573B	
☐ B-5851	Boeing 737-89L/W	41313/4725		
☐ B-2443	Boeing 747-4J6	25881/957		
☐ B-2445	Boeing 747-4J6	25882/1021		
☐ B-2447	Boeing 747-4J6	25883/1054		
☐ B-2469	Boeing 747-4J6M	28756/1175		[VCV]
☐ B-2472	Boeing 747-4J6	30158/1243		
☐ B-2479	Boeing 747-89L	41193/1510		♦
☐ B-2480	Boeing 747-89L	41194/1518		o/o♦
☐ B-2481	Boeing 747-89L	41847/1515		♦

☐ B-2482	Boeing 747-89L	44933/1517			o/o♦
☐ B-2485	Boeing 747-89L	41191/1499			♦
☐ B-2486	Boeing 747-89L	41192/1507			♦
☐ B-2487	Boeing 747-89L	44932/1508	ex N5510E		♦
☐ B-2059	Boeing 777-2J6	29153/168			
☐ B-2060	Boeing 777-2J6	29154/173			
☐ B-2061	Boeing 777-2J6	29155/179			
☐ B-2063	Boeing 777-2J6	29156/214			
☐ B-2064	Boeing 777-2J6	29157/240			
☐ B-2065	Boeing 777-2J6	29744/280			
☐ B-2066	Boeing 777-2J6	29745/290			
☐ B-2067	Boeing 777-2J6	29746/338			
☐ B-2068	Boeing 777-2J6	29747/344			
☐ B-2069	Boeing 777-2J6	29748/349			
☐ B-2006	Boeing 777-39LER	44931/1239		Love China c/s	♦
☐ B-2031	Boeing 777-39LER	38670/1017			
☐ B-2032	Boeing 777-39LER	38671/1032		Star Alliance c/s	
☐ B-2033	Boeing 777-39LER	38673/1045			
☐ B-2035	Boeing 777-39LER	38674/1051		Smiling China c/s	
☐ B-2036	Boeing 777-39LER	38676/1066			
☐ B-2037	Boeing 777-39LER	38677/1094			
☐ B-2038	Boeing 777-39LER	38678/1085			
☐ B-2039	Boeing 777-39LER	38679/1114			
☐ B-2040	Boeing 777-39LER	38680/1123			
☐ B-2043	Boeing 777-39LER	41441/1132			
☐ B-2045	Boeing 777-39LER	41443/1187			
☐ B-2046	Boeing 777-39LER	41442/1165			
☐ B-2047	Boeing 777-39LER	60374/1196			
☐ B-2085	Boeing 777-39LER	38666/943			
☐ B-2086	Boeing 777-39LER	38667/966			
☐ B-2087	Boeing 777-39LER	38672/954			
☐ B-2088	Boeing 777-39LER	38668/979			
☐ B-2089	Boeing 777-39LER	38675/990			
☐ B-2090	Boeing 777-39LER	38669/1009			
☐ B-2389	Airbus A340-313X	243	ex F-WWJE		[PEK]
☐ B-2390	Airbus A340-313X	264	ex F-WWJY		[PEK]
☐ B-2535	Boeing 737-3J6	25078/2002			wfs
☐ B-2627	Boeing 737-36E	26315/2706	ex N141LF		wfs
☐ B-2820	Boeing 757-2Z0	25885/476			[CTU]
☐ B-2821	Boeing 757-2Z0	25886/480			[CTU]
☐ B-2947	Boeing 737-33A	25511/2599			wfs
☐ B-2948	Boeing 737-3J6	27361/2631			wfs
☐ B-6188	Airbus A318CJ-112	3617	ex D-AIJO		VIP

AIR CHINA CARGO		**AirChina Freight (CA/CAO)**		**Beijing-Capital (PEK)**	
☐ B-2409	Boeing 747-412SF	26560/1052	ex 9V-SFC		
☐ B-2453	Boeing 747-412BCF	27134/981	ex B-KAH		[MZJ]
☐ B-2457	Boeing 747-412BCF	27067/953	ex B-KAG		[MZJ]
☐ B-2460	Boeing 747-4J6BCF	24348/792			[MZJ]
☐ B-2475	Boeing 747-4FTF	34239/1367			
☐ B-2476	Boeing 747-4FTF	34240/1373			
☐ B-2091	Boeing 777-FFT	44682/1230			♦
☐ B-2092	Boeing 777-FFT	44683/1272			♦
☐ B-2093	Boeing 777-FFT	44684/1316			o/o♦
☐ B-2094	Boeing 777-FFT	44685/1326			o/o♦
☐ B-2095	Boeing 777-FFT	44678/1158			
☐ B-2096	Boeing 777-FFT	44679/1180			
☐ B-2097	Boeing 777-FFT	44680/1188			
☐ B-2098	Boeing 777-FFT	44681/1210			♦
☐ B-2462	Boeing 747-2J6F	24960/814			
☐ B-2836	Boeing 757-2Z0SF	27258/595			♦
☐ B-2841	Boeing 757-2Z0PCF	27367/624			
☐ B-2855	Boeing 757-2Z0F	29792/822			♦
☐ B-2856	Boeing 757-2Z0SF	29793/833			♦

AIR CHINA INNER MONGOLIA		**(CNM)**			
☐ B-2670	Boeing 737-89L	30514/1055			♦
☐ B-5226	Boeing 737-79L/W	34540/1877	ex N1787B		

AMERICA–ASIA TRAVEL AIR					
☐ B-9469	Cessna 208 Caravan I	20800540	ex N20480		

ANYANG GENERAL AVIATION

☐ B-9827	Cessna 208 Caravan I	20800560	ex N8158G	♦

BEIJING AIRLINES (BJN) Beijing-Capital (PEK)

☐ B-3999	Boeing 737-79L/W (BBJ1)	41090/3636	ex N448BJ	VIP
☐ B-8319	Airbus A319CJ-115	4956	ex VP-CGX	VIP

CAPITAL AIRLINES (JD/CBJ) Beijing-Capital (PEK)

☐ B-6169	Airbus A319-112	2985	ex D-AVXJ	[CTU]
☐ B-6177	Airbus A319-112	3285	ex D-AVYY	
☐ B-6198	Airbus A319-112	2617	ex D-AVYI	
☐ B-6199	Airbus A319-112	2644	ex D-AVWP	
☐ B-6210	Airbus A319-115	2557	ex D-AVYK	
☐ B-6211	Airbus A319-115	2561	ex D-AVYO	
☐ B-6215	Airbus A319-112	2611	ex D-AVXR	
☐ B-6222	Airbus A319-112	2733	ex D-AVXL	
☐ B-6178	Airbus A319-132	3548	ex D-AVWK	
☐ B-6179	Airbus A319-132	3561	ex D-AVWR	
☐ B-6180	Airbus A319-132	3578	ex D-AVYA	
☐ B-6181	Airbus A319-132	3580	ex D-AVYB	
☐ B-6182	Airbus A319-132	3520	ex D-AVWA	
☐ B-6192	Airbus A319-132	3768	ex D-AVXG	
☐ B-6193	Airbus A319-133	3849	ex D-AVYV	
☐ B-6245	Airbus A319-133	3851	ex D-AVYW	
☐ B-6400	Airbus A319-132	3638	ex B-502L	
☐ B-6401	Airbus A319-132	3842	ex B-510L	
☐ B-6402	Airbus A319-132	3914	ex B-507L	
☐ B-6403	Airbus A319-132	3958	ex B-509L	
☐ B-6405	Airbus A319-132	3982	ex B-511L	
☐ B-6415	Airbus A319-133	4410	ex B-516L	
☐ B-6416	Airbus A319-133	4529	ex D-AVYK	
☐ B-6417	Airbus A319-133	4522	ex D-AVYJ	
☐ B-6418	Airbus A319CJ-133	4042	ex F-WWDA	VIP
☐ B-6435	Airbus A319CJ-133	4428	ex B-3333	VIP
☐ B-1603	Airbus A320-214	6206	ex B-504L	<CRK♦
☐ B-1809	Airbus A320-214	5848	ex B-520L	
☐ B-1810	Airbus A320-214	5997	ex B-520L	♦
☐ B-1811	Airbus A320-214	6041	ex B-504L	<CRK♦
☐ B-6769	Airbus A320-214	5114	ex F-WWIT	♦
☐ B-6858	Airbus A320-214	5008	ex F-WWDR	♦
☐ B-6859	Airbus A320-214	5072	ex F-WWDK	♦
☐ B-6867	Airbus A320-214	5471	ex B-509L	
☐ B-6869	Airbus A320-214	5630	ex D-AUBP	
☐ B-6952	Airbus A320-214	5331	ex F-WWIO	
☐ B-9961	Airbus A320-214	5722	ex B-503L	
☐ B-9962	Airbus A320-214	5656	ex B-516L	♦
☐ B-	Airbus A320-214	6570	ex	o/o♦
☐ B-	Airbus A320-214	6664	ex	o/o♦
☐ B-	Airbus A320-214	6759	ex	o/o♦
☐ B-	Airbus A320-214	6769	ex	o/o♦
☐ B-	Airbus A320-214	6776	ex	o/o♦
☐ B-1621	Airbus A320-232/S	6198	ex F-WWDF vip.com c/s	♦
☐ B-1622	Airbus A320-232/S	6212	ex F-WWDM	♦
☐ B-1623	Airbus A320-232/S	6229	ex F-WWIJ	♦
☐ B-1642	Airbus A320-232/S	6426	ex F-WWDX	♦
☐ B-1643	Airbus A320-232/S	6480	ex D-AXAV	♦
☐ B-1691	Airbus A320-232/S	6580	ex F-WWDP	♦
☐ B-6709	Airbus A320-232	4412	ex D-AVVH	
☐ B-6710	Airbus A320-232	4440	ex F-WWDT	
☐ B-6723	Airbus A320-232	4483	ex D-AUBE	
☐ B-6725	Airbus A320-232	4471	ex F-WWBZ	
☐ B-6726	Airbus A320-232	4505	ex F-WWBC	
☐ B-6727	Airbus A320-232	4513	ex F-WWBM	
☐ B-6746	Airbus A320-232	4580	ex F-WWIH	
☐ B-6747	Airbus A320-232	4540	ex B-506L	
☐ B-6748	Airbus A320-232	4602	ex B-512L	
☐ B-6795	Airbus A320-232	4677	ex B-518L	
☐ B-6898	Airbus A320-232	5185	ex F-WWDX	
☐ N60FC	Airbus A320CJ-232	4388	ex F-WHUH	VIP
☐ B-8126	Gulfstream V-SP	5349	ex N949GA	
☐ B-8157	Gulfstream V-SP	5342	ex N854GA	
☐ B-8255	Gulfstream V-SP	5352	ex N152GA	
☐ B-8258	Gulfstream V-SP	5360	ex N360GA	
☐ B-8259	Gulfstream V-SP	5357	ex N757GA	

☐ B-8261	Gulfstream V-SP	5364	ex N764GA	
☐ B-8273	Gulfstream V-SP	5399	ex N399GA	
☐ B-8297	Gulfstream V-SP	5423	ex N423GA	
☐ B-8302	Gulfstream V-SP	5437		♦
☐ B-8306	Gulfstream V-SP	5445		♦
☐ B-3902	Hawker 850XP	258858	ex N71958	
☐ B-3907	Hawker 4000	RC-48	ex N6005V	
☐ B-3912	Hawker 900XP	HA-0195	ex N975XP	
☐ B-5266	Boeing 737-7AK/W (BBJ1)	29866/408	ex N720CH	VIP
☐ B-7768	Canadair Challenger 650	5888	ex C-GNEC	
☐ B-8028	Dassault Falcon 7X	101	ex N940EX	
☐ B-8195	Bombardier BD-700 Global 6000	4488	ex C-GMYE	
☐ B-8212	Dassault Falcon 900LX	276	ex F-WWFF	♦
☐ B-8213	Dassault Falcon 7X	105		♦
☐ B-8217	Dassault Falcon 7X	251	ex F-WWNG	♦
☐ B-8265	Gulfstream IV	4258	ex N258GA	
☐ B-8291	Gulfstream IV-X	4272	ex N272GA	♦
☐ B-8295	Gulfstream IVX	4274	ex N274GA	
☐ N712JM	Boeing 737-73W/W (BBJ1)	40116/4465		VIP wfs

CHANG AN AIRLINES		**Changan (2Z/CGN)**		**Xi'an (SIA)**
☐ B-3444	AVIC I Y7-100C	09701		
☐ B-3445	AVIC I Y7-100C	09705		
☐ B-3475	AVIC I Y7-100C	06703		
☐ B-3707	AVIC I Y7-100C	12701		
☐ B-3708	AVIC I Y7-100C	11705		
☐ B-5115	Boeing 737-8FH/W	29640/1649		
☐ B-5116	Boeing 737-8FH/W	29672/1745	ex N1786B	
☐ B-5180	Boeing 737-8FH/W	35089/2042		
☐ B-5181	Boeing 737-8FH/W	35090/2073		

CHENGDU AIRLINES		**(EU/UEA)**		**Chengdu (CTU)**
☐ B-1630	Airbus A320-214/S	6248	ex F-WWDI	♦
☐ B-1631	Airbus A320-214/S	6281	ex F-WWIG	♦
☐ B-1632	Airbus A320-214/S	6292	ex F-WWBC	♦
☐ B-1633	Airbus A320-214/S	6357	ex F-WWBX	♦
☐ B-1856	Airbus A320-214/S	5957	ex OE-LEP	
☐ B-2340	Airbus A320-232	0540	ex F-WWDK	
☐ B-6728	Airbus A320-214	2696	ex D-ABDE	
☐ B-6729	Airbus A320-214	2820	ex D-ABDF	
☐ B-6730	Airbus A320-214	2835	ex D-ABDG	
☐ B-6850	Airbus A320-214	4347	ex OE-IBB	
☐ B-6900	Airbus A320-214	2654	ex D-ABDC	
☐ B-6907	Airbus A320-214	5003	ex OE-LEI	
☐ B-6940	Airbus A320-214	3706	ex OE-IAC	
☐ B-9985	Airbus A320-214	5252	ex D-ABNC	
☐ B-6163	Airbus A319-112	3024	ex D-AVXR	
☐ B-6229	Airbus A319-115	2762	ex B-1136L	
☐ B-6230	Airbus A319-112	2774	ex D-AVYF	

CHINA CARGO AIRLINES		**Cargo King (CK/CKK)**		**Shanghai-Pu Dong Intl (PVG)**
☐ B-2076	Boeing 777-F6N	37711/846	ex N5573S	
☐ B-2077	Boeing 777-F6N	37713/856		
☐ B-2078	Boeing 777-F6N	37714/869		
☐ B-2079	Boeing 777-F6N	37715/876		
☐ B-2082	Boeing 777-F6N	37716/942		
☐ B-2083	Boeing 777-F6N	37717/949		
☐ B-2425	Boeing 747-40BERF	35207/1377		
☐ B-2426	Boeing 747-40BERF	35208/1392		
☐ B-2428	Boeing 747-412F	28263/1094	ex 9V-SFE	
☐ B-2433	Boeing 747-412F	28027/1256	ex 9V-SFI	
☐ B-2809	Boeing 757-26DPCF	24472/235	ex N5573B	

CHINA EASTERN AIRLINES		**China Eastern (MU/CES)**		**Shanghai-Pu Dong Intl (PVG)**
Member of SkyTeam				
☐ B-2317	Airbus A300B4-605R	741	ex F-WWAY	[DRS}
☐ B-2318	Airbus A300B4-605R	707	ex F-WWAU	[DRS]
☐ B-2319	Airbus A300B4-605R	732	ex F-WWAT	[DRS]
☐ B-2324	Airbus A300B4-622R	725	ex F-WWAR	[DRS]
☐ B-2325	Airbus A300B4-605R	746	ex F-WWAA	[DRS]
☐ B-2326	Airbus A300B4-605R	754	ex F-WWAY	[SHA]
☐ B-2330	Airbus A300B4-605R	763	ex F-WWAH	[DRS]

☐ B-2217	Airbus A319-112	1601	ex D-AVWX		
☐ B-2333	Airbus A319-112	1377	ex D-AVWE		
☐ B-6167	Airbus A319-115	3168	ex D-AVWB		
☐ B-6172	Airbus A319-115	3186	ex D-AVYG		
☐ B-6217	Airbus A319-115	2693	ex D-AVXC		
☐ B-6218	Airbus A319-115	2757	ex D-AVWH		
☐ B-6231	Airbus A319-115	2825	ex D-AVXD		
☐ B-6423	Airbus A319-115	5273	ex D-AVYG		
☐ B-6428	Airbus A319-115	5330	ex D-AVWD		
☐ B-6429	Airbus A319-115	5338	ex D-AVWE		
☐ B-6431	Airbus A319-115	5380	ex D-AVWI		
☐ B-6432	Airbus A319-115	5412	ex D-AVWM		
☐ B-6452	Airbus A319-115/S	5886	ex B-504L	Magnificent Qinghai c/s	
☐ B-6458	Airbus A319-115/S	5973	ex B-512L		♦
☐ B-6459	Airbus A319-115/S	6116	ex B-514L		♦
☐ B-6460	Airbus A319-115/S	6144	ex B-517L		♦
☐ B-6461	Airbus A319-115/S	6160	ex B-519L		♦
☐ B-6465	Airbus A319-115/S	6250	ex B-514L		♦
☐ B-6466	Airbus A319-115/S	6269	ex B-516L		♦
☐ B-6469	Airbus A319-115/S	6368	ex B-516L		♦
☐ B-6470	Airbus A319-115/S	6307	ex B-501L		♦
☐ B-6471	Airbus A319-115/S	6453	ex B-503L		
☐ B-6476	Airbus A319-115/S	6469	ex B-506L		♦
☐ B-	Airbus A319-115/S	6519	ex		o/o
☐ B-	Airbus A319-115/S	6836	ex		o/o♦
☐ B-6427	Airbus A319-133	5267	ex D-AVYD		
☐ B-6430	Airbus A319-133	5376	ex D-AVWH		
☐ B-6439	Airbus A319-133	5439	ex B-507L		
☐ B-6446	Airbus A319-133	5623	ex B-512L		
☐ B-6450	Airbus A319-133/S	5700	ex B-501L		
☐ B-6456	Airbus A319-132/S	5920	ex B-507L		
☐ B-6457	Airbus A319-132/S	5826	ex B-513L		
☐ B-6462	Airbus A319-132/S	6052	ex B-511L		♦
☐ B-6463	Airbus A319-132/S	6191	ex B-502L		♦
☐ B-6472	Airbus A319-132/S	6298	ex B-514L		♦
☐ B-	Airbus A319-132/S	6593	ex		o/o♦
☐ B-1609	Airbus A320-214/S	6355	ex F-WWBT	Beautiful Gansu c/s	♦
☐ B-1610	Airbus A320-214/S	6373	ex D-AXAG		♦
☐ B-1611	Airbus A320-214/S	6379	ex D-AXAJ		♦
☐ B-1612	Airbus A320-214/S	6323	ex D-AVVY		♦
☐ B-1613	Airbus A320-214/S	6274	ex B-517L		♦
☐ B-1836	Airbus A320-214/S	6111	ex D-AXAT		♦
☐ B-1860	Airbus A320-214/S	6213	ex D-AVVJ		♦
☐ B-1861	Airbus A320-214/S	6260	ex D-AVVR		♦
☐ B-1862	Airbus A320-214/S	6127	ex B-515L		♦
☐ B-1863	Airbus A320-232/S	6137	ex B-516L		♦
☐ B-1865	Airbus A320-214	6151	ex B-518L		♦
☐ B-2202	Airbus A320-214	0925	ex F-WWID		
☐ B-2205	Airbus A320-214	0984	ex F-WWDI		
☐ B-2206	Airbus A320-214	0986	ex F-WWDJ		wfs
☐ B-2207	Airbus A320-214	1028	ex F-WWDG		
☐ B-2208	Airbus A320-214	1070	ex F-WWBH		
☐ B-2209	Airbus A320-214	1030	ex F-WWDU		
☐ B-2211	Airbus A320-214	1041	ex F-WWID		
☐ B-2212	Airbus A320-214	1316	ex F-WWDG		
☐ B-2213	Airbus A320-214	1345	ex F-WWDX		
☐ B-2228	Airbus A320-214	1906	ex F-WWDK		
☐ B-2229	Airbus A320-214	1911	ex F-WWDT		
☐ B-2335	Airbus A320-214	1312	ex F-WWBZ		
☐ B-2336	Airbus A320-214	1330	ex F-WWDV		
☐ B-2337	Airbus A320-214	1357	ex F-WWBF		
☐ B-2338	Airbus A320-214	1361	ex F-WWBU		
☐ B-2356	Airbus A320-214	0665	ex F-WWBB		
☐ B-2357	Airbus A320-214	0754	ex F-WWIY		
☐ B-2358	Airbus A320-214	0838	ex F-WWBB		
☐ B-2359	Airbus A320-214	0854	ex F-WWBK		
☐ B-2372	Airbus A320-214	0897	ex F-WWDK		
☐ B-2375	Airbus A320-214	0909	ex F-WWDS		
☐ B-2378	Airbus A320-214	0939	ex F-WWIQ		
☐ B-2379	Airbus A320-214	0967	ex F-WWBN		
☐ B-2398	Airbus A320-214	1108	ex F-WWDH		
☐ B-2399	Airbus A320-214	1093	ex F-WWIZ		
☐ B-2413	Airbus A320-214	2493	ex F-WWDZ		
☐ B-2415	Airbus A320-214	2498	ex F-WWIL		
☐ B-6001	Airbus A320-214	1981	ex F-WWDL		
☐ B-6002	Airbus A320-214	2022	ex F-WWDG		
☐ B-6003	Airbus A320-214	2034	ex F-WWIF		
☐ B-6005	Airbus A320-214	2036	ex F-WWIZ		
☐ B-6006	Airbus A320-214	2068	ex F-WWIL		
☐ B-6007	Airbus A320-214	2056	ex F-WWIR		
☐ B-6008	Airbus A320-214	2049	ex F-WWII		

☐	B-6009	Airbus A320-214	2219	ex F-WWDN		
☐	B-6010	Airbus A320-214	2221	ex F-WWIU		
☐	B-6011	Airbus A320-214	2235	ex F-WWBY		
☐	B-6012	Airbus A320-214	2239	ex F-WWDP		
☐	B-6013	Airbus A320-214	2244	ex F-WWIR		
☐	B-6259	Airbus A320-214	2562	ex F-WWIZ		
☐	B-6260	Airbus A320-214	2591	ex F-WWDT		
☐	B-6261	Airbus A320-214	2606	ex F-WWBR	Young Pioneers c/s	
☐	B-6262	Airbus A320-214	2627	ex F-WWDV		
☐	B-6333	Airbus A320-214	3170	ex F-WWIN		
☐	B-6335	Airbus A320-214	3197	ex F-WWIX		
☐	B-6370	Airbus A320-214	3559	ex F-WWBF		
☐	B-6371	Airbus A320-214	3611	ex D-AVVF	Beautiful Gansu	Flying Apsaras c/s
☐	B-6758	Airbus A320-214	4718	ex F-WWBX		
☐	B-6760	Airbus A320-214	4627	ex B-514L		
☐	B-6797	Airbus A320-214	4685	ex B-519L		
☐	B-6798	Airbus A320-214	4702	ex B-520L		
☐	B-6799	Airbus A320-214	4711	ex B-501L		
☐	B-6801	Airbus A320-214	4722	ex B-502L		
☐	B-6802	Airbus A320-214	4729	ex B-503L		
☐	B-6805	Airbus A320-214	4877	ex F-WWDZ		
☐	B-6829	Airbus A320-214	4769	ex B-507L		
☐	B-6830	Airbus A320-214	4776	ex B-508L		
☐	B-6831	Airbus A320-214	4799	ex B-509L		
☐	B-6832	Airbus A320-214	4831	ex B-512L		
☐	B-6870	Airbus A320-214	4844	ex B-515L		
☐	B-6871	Airbus A320-214	4857	ex B-516L		
☐	B-6873	Airbus A320-214	4903	ex B-501L		
☐	B-6878	Airbus A320-214	4938	ex B-505L		
☐	B-6879	Airbus A320-214	4946	ex B-506L		
☐	B-6880	Airbus A320-214	4967	ex B-507L		
☐	B-6928	Airbus A320-214	4987	ex B-509L		
☐	B-9927	Airbus A320-214	5527	ex D-AXAQ		
☐	B-9941	Airbus A320-214/S	5691	ex F-WWDK		
☐	B-9942	Airbus A320-214/S	5710	ex D-AVVK	Magnificent Qinghai c/s	
☐	B-9943	Airbus A320-214/S	5726	ex F-WWBY	Magnificent Qinghai c/s	
☐	B-9946	Airbus A320-214/S	5735	ex D-AVVR		
☐	B-9970	Airbus A320-214/S	5759	ex F-WWIS		
☐	B-	Airbus A320-214	6582	ex		o/o♦
☐	B-	Airbus A320-214	6661	ex		o/o♦
☐	B-1607	Airbus A320-232	6180	ex B-501L		♦
☐	B-1608	Airbus A320-232	6228	ex B-512L		♦
☐	B-1641	Airbus A320-232/S	6340	ex B-504L		♦
☐	B-1655	Airbus A320-232/S	6431	ex B-501L		♦
☐	B-1815	Airbus A320-232/S	5864	ex B-502L		
☐	B-1835	Airbus A320-232/S	5942	ex B-507L		♦
☐	B-1859	Airbus A320-232	6062	ex B-506L		♦
☐	B-1678	Airbus A320-232/S	6578	ex F-WWDN		♦
☐	B-6346	Airbus A320-232	3481	ex F-WWDL		
☐	B-6372	Airbus A320-232	3613	ex F-WWIH		
☐	B-6373	Airbus A320-232	3650	ex F-WWDP		
☐	B-6375	Airbus A320-232	3677	ex F-WWBC		
☐	B-6376	Airbus A320-232	3692	ex F-WWBF		
☐	B-6399	Airbus A320-232	3716	ex F-WWBJ		
☐	B-6558	Airbus A320-232	3793	ex F-WWBH		
☐	B-6559	Airbus A320-232	3904	ex F-WWIB		
☐	B-6560	Airbus A320-232	3937	ex F-WWDQ		
☐	B-6585	Airbus A320-232	3965	ex F-WWIE		
☐	B-6586	Airbus A320-232	3775	ex B-504L		
☐	B-6587	Airbus A320-232	3797	ex B-505L		
☐	B-6600	Airbus A320-232	3870	ex B-506L		
☐	B-6601	Airbus A320-232	4037	ex F-WWIL		
☐	B-6616	Airbus A320-232	3929	ex B-508L		
☐	B-6617	Airbus A320-232	4144	ex D-AVVC		
☐	B-6635	Airbus A320-232	4027	ex B-513L		
☐	B-6636	Airbus A320-232	4043	ex B-514L		
☐	B-6637	Airbus A320-232	4111	ex B-517L		
☐	B-6638	Airbus A320-232	4240	ex F-WWDI		
☐	B-6639	Airbus A320-232	4252	ex F-WWIN		
☐	B-6671	Airbus A320-232	4186	ex B-520L		
☐	B-6672	Airbus A320-232	4220	ex B-502L		
☐	B-6673	Airbus A320-232	4340	ex F-WWBF		
☐	B-6693	Airbus A320-232	4239	ex B-504L		
☐	B-6695	Airbus A320-232	4297	ex B-508L		
☐	B-6696	Airbus A320-232	4309	ex B-509L		
☐	B-6713	Airbus A320-232	4342	ex B-511L		
☐	B-6715	Airbus A320-232	4355	ex B-512L		
☐	B-6716	Airbus A320-232	4423	ex B-517L		
☐	B-6875	Airbus A320-232	5053	ex F-WWBO		
☐	B-6876	Airbus A320-232	5135	ex D-AVVF		
☐	B-6877	Airbus A320-232	5144	ex D-AVVL		
☐	B-6926	Airbus A320-231	5227	ex D-AVZU		

☐ B-6929	Airbus A320-232	5156	ex F-WWDE		
☐ B-6930	Airbus A320-232	5242	ex F-WWBX		
☐ B-6950	Airbus A320-232	5326	ex D-AUBH		
☐ B-6951	Airbus A320-232	5363	ex F-WWDS		
☐ B-9900	Airbus A320-232	5461	ex F-WWBC		
☐ B-9901	Airbus A320-232	5508	ex F-WWDI		
☐ B-9902	Airbus A320-232	5524	ex F-WWIS		
☐ B-9921	Airbus A320-232/S	5516	ex B-513L		
☐ B-9945	Airbus A320-232/S	5628	ex B-513L		
☐ B-9972	Airbus A320-232/S	5823	ex D-AXAO		
☐ B-9973	Airbus A320-232/S	5852	ex D-AVVA		
☐ B-9975	Airbus A320-232/S	5711	ex B-502L		
☐ B-	Airbus A320-232	6624	ex		o/o♦
☐ B-	Airbus A320-232	6668	ex		o/o♦
☐ B-	Airbus A320-232	6688	ex		o/o♦
☐ B-	Airbus A320-232	6752	ex		o/o♦
☐ B-	Airbus A320-232	6792	ex		o/o♦
☐ B-2289	Airbus A321-211	2309	ex D-AVZD		
☐ B-2290	Airbus A321-211	2315	ex D-AVZM		
☐ B-2419	Airbus A321-211	2882	ex D-AVZJ		
☐ B-2420	Airbus A321-211	2895	ex D-AVZA		
☐ B-6329	Airbus A321-211	3233	ex D-AVZH		
☐ B-6330	Airbus A321-211	3247	ex D-AVZK		
☐ B-6331	Airbus A321-211	3249	ex D-AVZO		
☐ B-6332	Airbus A321-211	3262	ex D-AVZB		
☐ B-6345	Airbus A321-211	3471	ex D-AVZV		
☐ B-6367	Airbus A321-211	3612	ex D-AZAD		
☐ B-	Airbus A321-211	6762	ex		o/o♦
☐ B-	Airbus A321-211	6873	ex		o/o♦
☐ B-	Airbus A321-211	6942	ex		o/o♦
☐ B-1615	Airbus A321-231/S	6396	ex D-AVXZ		♦
☐ B-1640	Airbus A321-231/S	6499	ex D-AVZU		♦
☐ B-1679	Airbus A321-231/S	6630	ex D-AVXV		o/o♦
☐ B-1812	Airbus A321-231/S	5998	ex D-AVZA		
☐ B-1813	Airbus A321-231/S	6089	ex D-AZAA		
☐ B-1837	Airbus A321-231/S	6199	ex D-AZAL	SkyTeam c/s	♦
☐ B-1838	Airbus A321-231/S	6203	ex D-AZAN	SkyTeam c/s	♦
☐ B-1858	Airbus A321-231/S	6305	ex D-AVZY		♦
☐ B-6591	Airbus A321-231	3969	ex D-AVVA		
☐ B-6592	Airbus A321-231	4045	ex D-AVZL		
☐ B-6642	Airbus A321-231	4198	ex D-AVZE		
☐ B-6643	Airbus A321-231	4209	ex D-AVZF		
☐ B-6668	Airbus A321-231	4374	ex D-AVZX		
☐ B-6753	Airbus A321-231	4638	ex D-AZAT		
☐ B-6755	Airbus A321-231	4746	ex D-AVZG		
☐ B-6886	Airbus A321-231	5402	ex D-AVZI		
☐ B-6923	Airbus A321-231	5192	ex D-AVZP		
☐ B-6925	Airbus A321-231	5210	ex D-AVZT		
☐ B-6927	Airbus A321-231	5309	ex D-AZAP		
☐ B-9903	Airbus A321-231	5481	ex D-AZAH		
☐ B-9905	Airbus A321-231	5519	ex D-AZAR		
☐ B-9906	Airbus A321-231	5558	ex D-AVZF		
☐ B-9907	Airbus A321-231	5575	ex D-AZAF		
☐ B-9933	Airbus A321-231	5736	ex D-AZAF		
☐ B-9947	Airbus A321-231	5705	ex D-AZAI		
☐ B-9971	Airbus A321-231/S	5770	ex D-AZAU		
☐ B-	Airbus A321-231	6875	ex		o/o♦
☐ B-	Airbus A321-231	6774	ex		o/o♦
☐ B-	Airbus A321-231	6825	ex		o/o♦
☐ B-	Airbus A321-231	6845	ex		o/o♦
☐ B-5902	Airbus A330-243	1324	ex F-WWTK		
☐ B-5903	Airbus A330-243	1331	ex F-WWTR		
☐ B-5908	Airbus A330-243	1372	ex F-WWYA	SkyTeam c/s	
☐ B-5920	Airbus A330-243	1375	ex F-WWYD		
☐ B-5931	Airbus A330-243	1440	ex F-WWKG		
☐ B-5936	Airbus A330-243	1461	ex F-WWCQ		
☐ B-5937	Airbus A330-243	1468	ex F-WWKT		
☐ B-5938	Airbus A330-243	1479	ex F-WWYU		
☐ B-5941	Airbus A330-243	1484	ex F-WWKJ		
☐ B-5942	Airbus A330-243	1500	ex F-WWTU		
☐ B-5943	Airbus A330-243	1520	ex F-WWYJ		
☐ B-5949	Airbus A330-243	1537	ex F-WWCN	SkyTeam c/s	♦
☐ B-5952	Airbus A330-243	1547	ex F-WWCY		♦
☐ B-5961	Airbus A330-243	1569	ex F-WWKK		♦
☐ B-5962	Airbus A330-243	1588	ex F-WWCG		♦
☐ B-5968	Airbus A330-243	1603	ex F-WWCO		♦
☐ B-5973	Airbus A330-243	1617	ex F-WWKV		o/o♦
☐ B-5975	Airbus A330-243	1639	ex F-WWCD		o/o♦
☐ B-6082	Airbus A330-243	821	ex F-WWKB		
☐ B-6099	Airbus A330-243	916	ex F-WWYP		

☐ B-6120	Airbus A330-343	720	ex F-WWYZ		♦
☐ B-6121	Airbus A330-243	728	ex F-WWKQ		
☐ B-6122	Airbus A330-243	732	ex F-WWKT		
☐ B-6123	Airbus A330-243	735	ex F-WWYA		
☐ B-6537	Airbus A330-243	1262	ex F-WWKT		
☐ B-6538	Airbus A330-243	1267	ex F-WWKH	SkyTeam c/s	
☐ B-6543	Airbus A330-243	1280	ex F-WWKM		
☐ B-	Airbus A330-243	1655	ex F-WW		o/o♦
☐ B-	Airbus A330-243	1664	ex F-WW		o/o♦
☐ B-5953	Airbus A330-343E	1551	ex F-WWKT		♦
☐ B-5969	Airbus A330-343E	1595	ex F-WWYJ		♦
☐ B-5976	Airbus A330-343E	1632	ex F-WW		o/o♦
☐ B-6083	Airbus A330-343E	830	ex F-WWKK		
☐ B-6085	Airbus A330-343E	836	ex F-WWYK		
☐ B-6095	Airbus A330-343E	851	ex F-WWKR		
☐ B-6100	Airbus A330-343E	928	ex F-WWKJ		
☐ B-6119	Airbus A330-343	713	ex F-WWYT		♦
☐ B-6125	Airbus A330-343	773	ex F-WWKF		
☐ B-6126	Airbus A330-343	777	ex F-WWKK		
☐ B-6127	Airbus A330-343	781	ex F-WWYT		
☐ B-6128	Airbus A330-343	782	ex F-WWYV	Yunnan Peacock c/s	
☐ B-6129	Airbus A330-343	791	ex F-WWKO		
☐ B-6506	Airbus A330-343E	936	ex F-WWKG		
☐ B-6507	Airbus A330-343E	942	ex F-WWYK		
☐ B-2571	Boeing 737-39P	29410/3053			
☐ B-2572	Boeing 737-39P	29411/3071			
☐ B-2573	Boeing 737-39P	29412/3080	ex N1786B		
☐ B-2969	Boeing 737-36R	30102/3108	ex N1787B		
☐ B-2988	Boeing 737-36R	29087/2970			
☐ B-2682	Boeing 737-79P	33038/1219			
☐ B-2685	Boeing 737-79P	33040/1244			
☐ B-5034	Boeing 737-79P	30036/1336			
☐ B-5209	Boeing 737-79P/W	33042/1947	ex N1779B		
☐ B-5257	Boeing 737-79P/W	33759/2968	ex N1786B		
☐ B-5258	Boeing 737-79P/W	36760/3009			
☐ B-5262	Boeing 737-79P/W	36764/3067	ex N1787B		
☐ B-5276	Boeing 737-79P/W	39719/3741			
☐ B-1722	Boeing 737-89P/W	41513/5174			♦
☐ B-1723	Boeing 737-89P/W	41511/5197	ex N1787B		♦
☐ B-1737	Boeing 737-81B/W	41606/5232			♦
☐ B-1772	Boeing 737-89P/W	41470/5244			♦
☐ B-1773	Boeing 737-89P/W	41504/5378			♦
☐ B-1776	Boeing 737-81B/W	41609/5406			♦
☐ B-1780	Boeing 737-81B/W	41610/5421			o/o♦
☐ B-1789	Boeing 737-89P/W	41472/5365	ex N1795B		♦
☐ B-1910	Boeing 737-89P/W	39932/4680			
☐ B-1933	Boeing 737-89P/W	41514/4893	ex N1787B		
☐ B-1961	Boeing 737-89P/W	39732/4820	ex N5515X		
☐ B-1981	Boeing 737-89P/W	41478/5041		SkyTeam c/s	♦
☐ B-1983	Boeing 737-89P/W	41473/4997			♦
☐ B-1790	Boeing 737-89P/W	41509/5405			♦
☐ B-5085	Boeing 737-89P/W	30691/1702			
☐ B-5086	Boeing 737-89P/W	32800/1681			
☐ B-5087	Boeing 737-89P/W	32802/1725			
☐ B-5100	Boeing 737-89P/W	30681/1645	ex N1786B		
☐ B-5101	Boeing 737-89P/W	30682/1673			
☐ B-5199	Boeing 737-89P/W	36272/2753			
☐ B-5376	Boeing 737-86N/W	35226/2641			
☐ B-5472	Boeing 737-89P/W	36761/3001	ex N1779B		
☐ B-5473	Boeing 737-89P/W	36763/3036	ex N1786B		
☐ B-5475	Boeing 737-89P/W	36765/3065			
☐ B-5492	Boeing 737-89P/W	29661/3083	ex N1787B		
☐ B-5493	Boeing 737-89P/W	29652/3121			
☐ B-5501	Boeing 737-86N/W	39388/3204			
☐ B-5515	Boeing 737-89P/W	36769/3311			
☐ B-5516	Boeing 737-86N/W	39389/3304	ex N1787B		
☐ B-5517	Boeing 737-89P/W	29653/3294	ex N1786B		
☐ B-5530	Boeing 737-89P/W	29655/3351	ex N1786B		
☐ B-5589	Boeing 737-89P/W	40949/4101			
☐ B-5665	Boeing 737-8HX/W	38106/3976			
☐ B-5689	Boeing 737-89P/W	41512/5154			♦
☐ B-5722	Boeing 737-89P/W	41785/4245			
☐ B-5731	Boeing 737-89P/W	40951/4303			
☐ B-5779	Boeing 737-89P/W	39726/4503			
☐ B-5780	Boeing 737-89P/W	39728/4615			
☐ B-5857	Boeing 737-89P/W	39886/4694			
☐ B-5858	Boeing 737-89P/W	39887/4684			
☐ B-	Boeing 737-81B/W	41611/			o/o
☐ B-	Boeing 737-81B/W	41612/			o/o

☐ B-	Boeing 737-81B/W	41613/		o/o
☐ B-	Boeing 737-81B/W	41614/		o/o
☐ B-2001	Boeing 777-39PER	43269/1232		♦
☐ B-2002	Boeing 777-39PER	43288/1247		♦
☐ B-2003	Boeing 777-39PER	43270/1253		♦
☐ B-2005	Boeing 777-39PER	43271/1259		♦
☐ B-2020	Boeing 777-39PER	43272/1285		♦
☐ B-2021	Boeing 777-39PER	43273/1309		o/o♦
☐ B-2022	Boeing 777-39PER	43274/1321		o/o♦
☐ B-2023	Boeing 777-39PER	43275/1324		o/o♦
☐ B-3052	Embraer ERJ-145LI	14500905	ex PT-SOE	wfs
☐ B-3055	Embraer ERJ-145LI	14500921		
☐ B-3056	Embraer ERJ-145LI	14500928		
☐ B-3057	Embraer ERJ-145LI	14500932		
☐ B-3058	Embraer ERJ-145LI	14500958		
☐ B-3059	Embraer ERJ-145LI	14500949		
☐ B-2308	Airbus A300B4-605RF	532	ex F-WWAH	wfs
☐ B-2382	Airbus A340-313X	141	ex F-WWJC	[LDE]
☐ B-6053	Airbus A340-642	577	ex F-WWCM	wfs

CHINA EASTERN AIRLINES JIANGSU · Nanjing (NKG)

☐ B-1635	Airbus A320-214/S	6258	ex B-515L	♦
☐ B-1636	Airbus A320-232/S	6284	ex B-519L	♦
☐ B-2219	Airbus A320-214	1532	ex F-WWIP	
☐ B-2220	Airbus A320-214	1542	ex F-WWIV	
☐ B-2221	Airbus A320-214	1639	ex F-WWDZ	
☐ B-2230	Airbus A320-214	1964	ex F-WWDR	
☐ B-2410	Airbus A320-214	2437	ex F-WWIX	
☐ B-2411	Airbus A320-214	2451	ex F-WWDF	
☐ B-2412	Airbus A320-214	2478	ex F-WWDV	
☐ B-6756	Airbus A320-214	4659	ex D-AXAD	
☐ B-6757	Airbus A320-214	4709	ex F-WWBH	
☐ B-6759	Airbus A320-214	4723	ex F-WWDG	
☐ B-6796	Airbus A320-214	4765	ex F-WWBV	
☐ B-6803	Airbus A320-214	4748	ex B-505L	
☐ B-6872	Airbus A320-214	4886	ex B-519L	
☐ B-6890	Airbus A320-214	5048	ex D-AXAO	
☐ B-6891	Airbus A320-214	5047	ex F-WWDQ	
☐ B-6892	Airbus A320-214	5063	ex F-WWBT	
☐ B-6893	Airbus A320-214	5136	ex D-AVVG	
☐ B-9950	Airbus A320-214/S	5668	ex F-WWBT	
☐ B-2291	Airbus A321-211	2543	ex D-AVZF	
☐ B-2292	Airbus A321-211	2549	ex D-AVZI	
☐ B-6332	Airbus A321-211	3262	ex D-AVZB	
☐ B-6366	Airbus A321-211	3593	ex D-AZAB	
☐ B-6368	Airbus A321-211	3639	ex D-AVZT	
☐ B-6369	Airbus A321-211	3682	ex D-AVZB	
☐ B-3049	Embraer ERJ-145LI	14500839	ex PT-SOA	wfs
☐ B-3050	Embraer ERJ-145LI	14500848	ex PT-SOB	wfs
☐ B-3051	Embraer ERJ-145LI	14500898	ex PT-SOD	wfs
☐ B-3053	Embraer ERJ-145LI	14500882	ex PT-SOC	wfs

CHINA EASTERN YUNNAN (MU)

☐ B-2538	Boeing 737-3W0	25090/2040	
☐ B-2589	Boeing 737-3W0	27127/2377	
☐ B-2594	Boeing 737-341	26853/2275	ex (PP-VPB)
☐ B-2955	Boeing 737-33A	27453/2687	
☐ B-2956	Boeing 737-33A	27907/2690	
☐ B-2958	Boeing 737-3W0	27522/2727	
☐ B-2966	Boeing 737-33A	27462/2765	
☐ B-2981	Boeing 737-3W0	28972/2919	
☐ B-2983	Boeing 737-3W0	28973/2941	
☐ B-2985	Boeing 737-3W0	29068/2945	
☐ B-2986	Boeing 737-3W0	29069/2951	
☐ B-2502	Boeing 737-7W0/W	30075/311	
☐ B-2503	Boeing 737-7W0/W	30074/292	ex N1786B
☐ B-2639	Boeing 737-7W0/W	29912/140	ex N1787B
☐ B-2640	Boeing 737-7W0/W	29913/148	ex N1800B
☐ B-5054	Boeing 737-79P/W	29365/1841	ex N1784B
☐ B-5074	Boeing 737-79P/W	33008/1718	ex N1786B
☐ B-5084	Boeing 737-79P/W	33009/1728	ex N1786B
☐ B-5093	Boeing 737-79P/W	29357/1630	
☐ B-5094	Boeing 737-79P/W	29358/1651	
☐ B-5095	Boeing 737-79P/W	29361/1694	

☐ B-5096	Boeing 737-79P/W	29362/1713			
☐ B-5097	Boeing 737-79P/W	29364/1823	ex N6067E		
☐ B-5225	Boeing 737-79P/W	33045/1999			
☐ B-5231	Boeing 737-79P/W	33046/2034			
☐ B-5242	Boeing 737-79P/W	36269/2357			
☐ B-5243	Boeing 737-79P/W	36270/2398			♦
☐ B-5245	Boeing 737-79P/W	36271/2697			
☐ B-5255	Boeing 737-79P/W	36757/2902	ex N1786B		
☐ B-5256	Boeing 737-79P/W	36758/2949			
☐ B-5259	Boeing 737-79P/W	36762/3046			
☐ B-5263	Boeing 737-79P/W	36766/3086	ex N1796B		
☐ B-5265	Boeing 737-79P/W	36767/3239	ex N1786B		
☐ B-5267	Boeing 737-79P/W	36768/3269			
☐ B-5270	Boeing 737-79P/W	36770/3330			
☐ B-5271	Boeing 737-79P/W	36772/3444	ex N1787B		
☐ B-5282	Boeing 737-79P/W	39720/3840	ex N1786B		
☐ B-5293	Boeing 737-79P/W	39721/4133		Yunnan Peacock orange c/s	♦
☐ B-5295	Boeing 737-79P/W	39723/4258		Yunnan Peacock purple c/s	♦
☐ B-5802	Boeing 737-79P/W	39725/4418		Yunnan Peacock orange c/s	♦
☐ B-5807	Boeing 737-79P/W	39727/4577		Yunnan Peacock orange c/s	♦
☐ B-5809	Boeing 737-79P/W	39729/4677		Yunnan Peacock orange c/s	♦
☐ B-5815	Boeing 737-79P/W	39308/4906		Yunnan Peacock orange c/s	♦
☐ B-5816	Boeing 737-79P/W	39310/4986		Yunnan Peacock orange c/s	♦
☐ B-5817	Boeing 737-79P/W	39739/5121	ex N1786B	Yunnan Peacock orange c/s	♦
☐ B-5819	Boeing 737-79P/W	39731/4806		Yunnan Peacock orange c/s	♦
☐ B-5820	Boeing 737-79P/W	39733/4855	ex N5573K	Yunnan Peacock orange c/s	♦
☐ B-5821	Boeing 737-79P/W	39737/5050		Yunnan Peacock orange c/s	♦
☐ B-5822	Boeing 737-79P/W	39735/4937		Yunnan Peacock orange c/s	♦
☐ B-5828	Boeing 737-79P/W	39741/5306		Yunnan Peacock c/s	♦
☐ B-1702	Boeing 737-89P/W	39738/5073		Yunnan Peacock orange c/s	♦
☐ B-1703	Boeing 737-89P/W	41486/5080	ex N1787B	Yunnan Peacock orange c/s	♦
☐ B-1798	Boeing 737-89P/W	39740/5275		Yunnan Peacock orange c/s	♦
☐ B-1809	Boeing 737-89P/W	41308/4659		Yunnan Peacock orange c/s	♦
☐ B-1907	Boeing 737-89P/W	39730/4721		Yunnan Peacock orange c/s	♦
☐ B-5683	Boeing 737-86N/W	39400/4097		Yunnan Peacock orange c/s	♦
☐ B-5515	Boeing 737-89P/W	36769/3311			
☐ B-5527	Boeing 737-89P/W	36771/3343			
☐ B-5647	Boeing 737-8HX/W	38105/3959	ex N1787B		
☐ B-5701	Boeing 737-89P/W	39722/4198		Yunnan Peacock purple c/s	
☐ B-5756	Boeing 737-89P/W	39724/4383	ex N5515R	Yunnan Peacock purple c/s	
☐ B-5795	Boeing 737-89P/W	41305/4587		Yunnan Peacock orange c/s	♦
☐ B-5796	Boeing 737-89P/W	41306/4599		Yunnan Peacock orange c/s	♦
☐ B-3013	Canadair CRJ-200LR	7571	ex C-FVAZ		[KMG]
☐ B-3019	Canadair CRJ-200LR	7581	ex C-FMMX		[KMG]
☐ B-3021	Canadair CRJ-200LR	7596	ex C-FMNW		[KMG]
☐ B-3070	Canadair CRJ-200LR	7647	ex C-FMLB		[KMG]
☐ B-3071	Canadair CRJ-200LR	7684	ex C-FMMT		[KMG]
☐ B-5921	Airbus A330-243	1402	ex F-WWYF		♦
☐ B-5926	Airbus A330-243	1421	ex F-WWTQ		♦
☐ B-5930	Airbus A330-243	1429	ex F-WWCJ		♦

CHINA EXPRESS AIRLINES		**China Express (G5/HXA)**		**Guiyang (KWE)**

☐ B-3360	Canadair CRJ-900LR	15289	ex C-GIAJ		
☐ B-3361	Canadair CRJ-900LR	15290	ex C-GZQP		
☐ B-3362	Canadair CRJ-900LR	15291	ex C-GZQX		
☐ B-3363	Canadair CRJ-900LR	15312			
☐ B-3366	Canadair CRJ-900LR	15321			♦
☐ B-3368	Canadair CRJ-900LR	15332	ex C-GIAU		♦
☐ B-3369	Canadair CRJ-900LR	15344			♦
☐ B-3371	Canadair CRJ-900LR	15358	ex C-GIAO		♦
☐ B-3372	Canadair CRJ-900LR	15359			♦
☐ B-7691	Canadair CRJ-900LR	15288	ex C-GIAE		
☐ B-7692	Canadair CRJ-900LR	15280	ex C-GPOX		
☐ B-7693	Canadair CRJ-900LR	15281	ex C-GZQT		
☐ B-7760	Canadair CRJ-900LR	15282	ex C-GIAI		
☐ B-7762	Canadair CRJ-900LR	15286	ex C-GHZV		
☐ B-	Canadair CRJ-900LR	15363			♦
☐ B-3001	Canadair CRJ-200LR	7565	ex B-KBJ		wfs
☐ B-3016	Canadair CRJ-200LR	7614	ex C-FMKV		wfs
☐ B-7700	Canadair CRJ-200LR	7704	ex N387DF		wfs

CHINA FLYING DRAGON AVIATION CO		**Feilong (CFA)**		**Harbin - Ping Fang**

☐ B-7420	Aérospatiale AS350B2 Ecureuil	2522	ex F-WYMH	
☐ B-7421	Aérospatiale AS350B2 Ecureuil	2523	ex F-WYMG	
☐ B-7422	Aérospatiale AS350B2 Ecureuil	2534	ex F-WYMB	
☐ B-7423	Aérospatiale AS350B2 Ecureuil	2538	ex F-WYMF	
☐ B-7424	Aérospatiale AS350B2 Ecureuil	2547	ex F-WYME	

☐ B-7425	Aérospatiale AS350B2 Ecureuil	2554	ex F-WYMF	
☐ B-7427	Aérospatiale AS350B2 Ecureuil	2566		
☐ B-3201	AVIC II Y-11B	003		prototype, status?
☐ B-3862	AVIC II Y-11	(11)0407		
☐ B-3863	AVIC II Y-11	(11)0408		
☐ B-3864	AVIC II Y-11	(11)0409		
☐ B-3874	AVIC II Y-11	(11)0102		
☐ B-3875	AVIC II Y-11	(11)0105		
☐ B-3876	AVIC II Y-11	(11)0106		
☐ B-3877	AVIC II Y-11	(11)0107		
☐ B-3878	AVIC II Y-11	(11)0110		
☐ B-3879	AVIC II Y-11	(11)0201		
☐ B-3880	AVIC II Y-11	(11)0202		
☐ B-3881	AVIC II Y-11	(11)0203		
☐ B-3882	AVIC II Y-11	(11)0204		
☐ B-3883	AVIC II Y-11	(11)0205		
☐ B-3884	AVIC II Y-11	(11)0210		
☐ B-3750	Harbin Y-12E	016		
☐ B-3752	Harbin Y-12-IV	050		
☐ B-3753	Harbin Y-12-IV	051		
☐ B-3755	Harbin Y-12E	020		
☐ B-3756	Harbin Y-12E	023		
☐ B-3803	Harbin Y-12 II	0003		Surveyor
☐ B-3804	Harbin Y-12 II	0011		Surveyor
☐ B-3805	Harbin Y-12 II	0005		Surveyor
☐ B-3806	Harbin Y-12 II	0008		Frtr
☐ B-3807	Harbin Y-12 II	0016		opf Maritime Service
☐ B-3808	Harbin Y-12 II	0017		opf Maritime Service
☐ B-3819	Harbin Y-12 II	0004		Frtr
☐ B-3825	Harbin Y-12 IV	007		
☐ B-3830	Harbin Y-12 II	003		
☐ B-3831	Harbin Y-12E	004		
☐ B-3835	Harbin Y-12	009		
☐ B-3837	Harbin Y-12	012		
☐ B-3842	Harbin Y-12 IV	0062	ex 9N-AHQ	
☐ B-3846	Harbin Y-12 IV	013	ex DQ-AFR	
☐ B-3852	Harbin Y-12 IV	036		
☐ B-3855	Harbin Y-12 IV	047		
☐ B-3858	Harbin Y-12 IV	039		
☐ B-3586	Beech B300 King Air	FL-775	ex N81977	
☐ B-3587	Beech B300 King Air	FL-776	ex N80876	♦
☐ B-3588	Beech B300 King Air	FL-768	ex N81486	
☐ B-3659	Beriev Be-103	3503		
☐ B-3660	Beriev Be-103	3504		
☐ B-7109	AVIC II Z-9A Haitun (SA365N)	045		opf Ministry of Forestry
☐ B-7110	AVIC II Z-9A Haitun (SA365N)	047		opf Ministry of Forestry
☐ B-7112	AVIC II Z-9A Haitun (SA365N)			
☐ B-7780	AgustaWestland AW139	31423		
☐ B-7781	AgustaWestland AW139	31445		
☐ B-7802	M.IM-25TC	34001212169		
☐ B-8173	Yunshuji Y-5BCD	1011		
☐ B-8175	Yunshuji Y-5BCD	1012		

CHINA POSTAL AIRLINES	China Post (8Y/CYZ)			Nanjing-Lukou (NKG)
☐ B-3101	AVIC II Y-8F-100	10(08)01		
☐ B-3102	AVIC II Y-8F-100	10(08)02		
☐ B-3103	AVIC II Y-8F-100	10(08)05		
☐ B-3109	AVIC II Y-8F-100	13(08)03		
☐ B-3110	AVIC II Y-8F-100	13(08)04		c/n not confirmed
☐ B-2526	Boeing 737-3Y0SF	25172/2089		
☐ B-2527	Boeing 737-3Y0SF	25173/2097		
☐ B-2528	Boeing 737-3Y0SF	25174/2168		
☐ B-2655	Boeing 737-3Q8SF	26288/2480	ex N339LF	
☐ B-2656	Boeing 737-3Q8SF	26292/2519	ex N141LF	
☐ B-2661	Boeing 737-3Q8SF	26284/2418	ex N379BC	
☐ B-2662	Boeing 737-3Q8SF	24988/2466	ex N441LF	
☐ B-2961	Boeing 737-35NSF	28156/2774		
☐ B-2962	Boeing 737-35NSF	28157/2778		
☐ B-2968	Boeing 737-35NSF	28158/2818		
☐ B-2996	Boeing 737-35NSF	29316/3065	ex N1786B	
☐ B-5071	Boeing 737-341QC	24277/1658	ex N277HE	
☐ B-5072	Boeing 737-341QC	24279/1673	ex N279HE	
☐ B-2135	Boeing 737-45RSF	29035/3046	ex N202BK	
☐ B-2513	Boeing 737-45RSF	29034/3015	ex N653AC	
☐ B-2525	Boeing 737-4Q8SF	26337/2811	ex N271LF	
☐ B-2881	Boeing 737-45RSF	29032/2943	ex N651AC	
☐ B-2882	Boeing 737-45RSF	29033/2963	ex N652AC	

☐ B-2887	Boeing 737-4Q8SF	26335/2793	ex N261LF	
☐ B-2891	Boeing 737-46JSF	28334/2802	ex N212BF	
☐ B-2892	Boeing 737-46JSF	28271/2801	ex N211BF	
☐ B-2970	Boeing 737-4Q8SF	26337/2811	ex N271LF	o/o

CHINA SOUTHERN AIRLINES — China Southern (CZ/CSN) — Guangzhou (CAN)

Member of SkyTeam

☐ B-6183	Airbus A319-115	3828	ex D-AVYK
☐ B-6187	Airbus A319-115	3903	ex D-AVWQ
☐ B-6195	Airbus A319-112	3983	ex D-AVYF
☐ B-6200	Airbus A319-115	2519	ex D-AVYX
☐ B-6201	Airbus A319-115	2541	ex D-AVWV
☐ B-6202	Airbus A319-115	2546	ex D-AVWX
☐ B-6203	Airbus A319-112	2554	ex D-AVYS
☐ B-6208	Airbus A319-112	2555	ex D-AVWU
☐ B-6209	Airbus A319-112	2558	ex D-AVYP
☐ B-6408	Airbus A319-112	4038	ex D-AVYL
☐ B-6409	Airbus A319-112	4071	ex D-AVYU
☐ B-2294	Airbus A319-132	2371	ex D-AVWL
☐ B-2295	Airbus A319-132	2408	ex D-AVWB
☐ B-2296	Airbus A319-132	2426	ex D-AVYZ
☐ B-2297	Airbus A319-132	2435	ex D-AVYH
☐ B-6018	Airbus A319-132	1971	ex D-AVYC
☐ B-6019	Airbus A319-132	1986	ex D-AVYJ
☐ B-6020	Airbus A319-133	2004	ex D-AVWB
☐ B-6021	Airbus A319-133	2008	ex D-AVWN
☐ B-6039	Airbus A319-132	2200	ex D-AVYE
☐ B-6040	Airbus A319-132	2203	ex D-AVYG
☐ B-6041	Airbus A319-132	2232	ex D-AVWI
☐ B-6158	Airbus A319-132	2901	ex D-AVWP
☐ B-6160	Airbus A319-132	2940	ex D-AVWW
☐ B-6161	Airbus A319-132	2948	ex D-AVXB
☐ B-6162	Airbus A319-132	2969	ex D-AVYT
☐ B-6168	Airbus A319-132	3020	ex D-AVXN
☐ B-6190	Airbus A319-132	3860	ex D-AVWC
☐ B-6191	Airbus A319-132	3890	ex D-AVWJ
☐ B-6205	Airbus A319-132	2505	ex D-AVWG
☐ B-6206	Airbus A319-132	2574	ex D-AVXD
☐ B-6207	Airbus A319-132	2579	ex D-AVXF
☐ B-6219	Airbus A319-132	2667	ex D-AVYG
☐ B-6220	Airbus A319-132	2815	ex D-AVWX
☐ B-6239	Airbus A319-132	3144	ex D-AVXT
☐ B-6240	Airbus A319-132	3258	ex D-AVXM
☐ B-6241	Airbus A319-132	3269	ex D-AVYA
☐ B-6242	Airbus A319-132	3311	ex D-AVYR
☐ B-6243	Airbus A319-132	3342	ex D-AVYJ
☐ B-6407	Airbus A319-132	4036	ex D-AVYK
☐ B-1800	Airbus A320-214	5976	ex F-WWBB
☐ B-1803	Airbus A320-214	5945	ex F-WWDU
☐ B-2406	Airbus A320-214	2354	ex F-WWIP
☐ B-2408	Airbus A320-214	2361	ex F-WWBM
☐ B-6251	Airbus A320-214	2484	ex F-WWIO
☐ B-6252	Airbus A320-214	2506	ex F-WWBP
☐ B-6253	Airbus A320-214	2511	ex F-WWIT
☐ B-6255	Airbus A320-214	2637	ex F-WWBX
☐ B-6263	Airbus A320-214	2708	ex F-WWIU
☐ B-6272	Airbus A320-214	2770	ex F-WWDM
☐ B-6281	Airbus A320-214	2796	ex F-WWIC
☐ B-6282	Airbus A320-214	2824	ex F-WWDF
☐ B-6283	Airbus A320-214	2834	ex F-WWBP
☐ B-6287	Airbus A320-214	2899	ex F-WWDB
☐ B-6288	Airbus A320-214	2855	ex F-WWIS
☐ B-6289	Airbus A320-214	2861	ex F-WWIY
☐ B-6290	Airbus A320-214	2877	ex F-WWBK
☐ B-6291	Airbus A320-214	2915	ex F-WWDM
☐ B-6292	Airbus A320-214	2960	ex F-WWBN
☐ B-6293	Airbus A320-214	2986	ex F-WWIG
☐ B-6303	Airbus A320-214	2950	ex F-WWIL
☐ B-6620	Airbus A320-214	4172	ex F-WWDM
☐ B-6623	Airbus A320-214	4205	ex D-AVVZ
☐ B-6656	Airbus A320-214	4322	ex D-AXAN
☐ B-6681	Airbus A320-214	4365	ex F-WWDQ
☐ B-6682	Airbus A320-214	4325	ex B-510L
☐ B-6702	Airbus A320-214	4362	ex B-513L
☐ B-6703	Airbus A320-214	4396	ex B-515L
☐ B-6737	Airbus A320-214	4456	ex B-520L
☐ B-6739	Airbus A320-214	4550	ex B-507L
☐ B-6775	Airbus A320-214	4613	ex D-AXAU
☐ B-6776	Airbus A320-214	4671	ex D-ABFR

☐ B-6782	Airbus A320-214	4794	ex D-ABFV	
☐ B-6783	Airbus A320-214	4808	ex D-ABFW	
☐ B-6785	Airbus A320-214	4854	ex D-AUBN	
☐ B-6815	Airbus A320-214	4928	ex D-AXAC	
☐ B-6817	Airbus A320-214	4880	ex D-AVVA	
☐ B-6827	Airbus A320-214	4982	ex D-AVVQ	
☐ B-9929	Airbus A320-214	5693	ex F-WWDM	
☐ B-9930	Airbus A320-214	5730	ex D-AVVQ	
☐ B-1651	Airbus A320-232/S	6462	ex B-504L	♦
☐ B-1652	Airbus A320-232	6506	ex B-	o/o♦
☐ B-1653	Airbus A320-232	6530	ex	o/o♦
☐ B-1801	Airbus A320-232/S	6018	ex F-WWBX	
☐ B-1802	Airbus A320-232	5837	ex B-519L	
☐ B-1805	Airbus A320-232	5817	ex B-512L	
☐ B-1826	Airbus A320-232	5875	ex B-503L	
☐ B-1827	Airbus A320-232	5930	ex B-508L	
☐ B-1828	Airbus A320-232/S	6078	ex F-WWIQ	
☐ B-1829	Airbus A320-232/S	6106	ex D-AXAR	♦
☐ B-2350	Airbus A320-232	0712	ex F-WWDI	
☐ B-2351	Airbus A320-232	0718	ex F-WWBI	
☐ B-2352	Airbus A320-232	0720	ex F-WWBU	
☐ B-2353	Airbus A320-232	0722	ex F-WWBM	
☐ B-2365	Airbus A320-232	0849	ex F-WWBI	
☐ B-2366	Airbus A320-232	0859	ex F-WWBO	
☐ B-2367	Airbus A320-232	0881	ex F-WWDB	
☐ B-2368	Airbus A320-232	0895	ex F-WWDJ	
☐ B-2369	Airbus A320-232	0900	ex F-WWDM	
☐ B-2391	Airbus A320-232	0950	ex F-WWIZ	
☐ B-2392	Airbus A320-232	0966	ex F-WWBK	
☐ B-2393	Airbus A320-232	1035	ex F-WWDX	
☐ B-2395	Airbus A320-232	1039	ex F-WWDZ	
☐ B-2396	Airbus A320-232	1057	ex F-WWIO	
☐ B-6269	Airbus A320-232	2743	ex F-WWBK	
☐ B-6275	Airbus A320-232	2680	ex F-WWIY	
☐ B-6276	Airbus A320-232	2689	ex F-WWIG	
☐ B-6277	Airbus A320-232	2701	ex F-WWIR	
☐ B-6278	Airbus A320-232	2714	ex F-WWBD	
☐ B-6279	Airbus A320-232	2772	ex F-WWDR	
☐ B-6575	Airbus A320-232	3910	ex F-WWIS	
☐ B-6577	Airbus A320-232	3959	ex F-WWDJ	
☐ B-6582	Airbus A320-232	3999	ex F-WWDK	
☐ B-6583	Airbus A320-232	4003	ex F-WWDP	
☐ B-6588	Airbus A320-232	4017	ex F-WWBX	
☐ B-6627	Airbus A320-232	4225	ex F-WWBO	
☐ B-6641	Airbus A320-232	4140	ex B-518L	
☐ B-6651	Airbus A320-232	4260	ex F-WWBC	
☐ B-6652	Airbus A320-232	4290	ex F-WWIX	
☐ B-6653	Airbus A320-232	4232	ex B-503L	
☐ B-6655	Airbus A320-232	4350	ex D-AXAU	
☐ B-6678	Airbus A320-232	4248	ex B-505L	
☐ B-6679	Airbus A320-232	4370	ex F-WWBJ	
☐ B-6680	Airbus A320-232	4279	ex B-507L	
☐ B-6761	Airbus A320-232	4696	ex F-WWDM	
☐ B-6762	Airbus A320-232	4751	ex D-AVVM	
☐ B-6766	Airbus A320-232	4919	ex B-503L	
☐ B-6786	Airbus A320-232	4782	ex F-WWDS	
☐ B-6812	Airbus A320-232	4883	ex D-AVVD	
☐ B-6813	Airbus A320-232	4864	ex F-WWDG	
☐ B-6816	Airbus A320-232	4912	ex F-WWBQ	
☐ B-6826	Airbus A320-232	4836	ex B-513L	
☐ B-6895	Airbus A320-232	5168	ex F-WWDM	
☐ B-6896	Airbus A320-232	5170	ex D-AXAG	
☐ B-6897	Airbus A320-232	5214	ex D-AVVW	
☐ B-6908	Airbus A320-232	5202	ex F-WWIY	
☐ B-6909	Airbus A320-232	5225	ex F-WWBO	
☐ B-6910	Airbus A320-232	5061	ex B-517L	
☐ B-6911	Airbus A320-232	5268	ex F-WWIC	
☐ B-6945	Airbus A320-232	5151	ex B-506L	
☐ B-6946	Airbus A320-232	5183	ex B-510L	
☐ B-6975	Airbus A320-232	5288	ex B-513L	
☐ B-6976	Airbus A320-232	5410	ex B-518L	
☐ B-6977	Airbus A320-232	5503	ex D-AXAH	
☐ B-9911	Airbus A320-232	5480	ex B-510L	
☐ B-9912	Airbus A320-232	5561	ex B-516L	
☐ B-9913	Airbus A320-232	5484	ex B-511L	
☐ B-9915	Airbus A320-232/S	5506	ex B-512L	
☐ B-9916	Airbus A320-232	5564	ex B-519L	
☐ B-9917	Airbus A320-232	5602	ex F-WWDY	
☐ B-9931	Airbus A320-232	5611	ex B-511L	
☐ B-9932	Airbus A320-232	5579	ex B-508L	
☐ B-9951	Airbus A320-232	5671	ex B-518L	
☐ B-9952	Airbus A320-232	5756	ex F-WWIP	

☐ B-9953	Airbus A320-232	5832	ex D-AXAR	
☐ B-9958	Airbus A320-232	5750	ex B-506L	
☐ B-9959	Airbus A320-232	5797	ex B-510L	
☐ B-	Airbus A320-232	6551	ex	o/o♦
☐ B-	Airbus A320-232	6612	ex	o/o♦
☐ B-	Airbus A320-232	6645	ex	o/o♦
☐ B-	Airbus A320-232	6805	ex	o/o♦
☐ B-1605	Airbus A321-231	6366	ex D-AVXQ	♦
☐ B-1606	Airbus A321-231	6385	ex D-AVXU	♦
☐ B-1616	Airbus A321-231	6440	ex D-AVZA	♦
☐ B-1625	Airbus A321-231	6461	ex D-AVZG	♦
☐ B-1626	Airbus A321-231	6504	ex D-AVZW	♦
☐ B-1650	Airbus A321-231	6556	ex D-AZAM	♦
☐ B-1806	Airbus A321-231/S	5949	ex D-AZAD	
☐ B-1830	Airbus A321-231	6049	ex D-AVZQ	
☐ B-1831	Airbus A321-231	6104	ex D-AZAG	
☐ B-1832	Airbus A321-231	6146	ex D-AVXM	♦
☐ B-1843	Airbus A321-231/S	6186	ex D-AZAD	♦
☐ B-1845	Airbus A321-231	6205	ex D-AZAP	♦
☐ B-1846	Airbus A321-231	6211	ex D-AZAS	♦
☐ B-1847	Airbus A321-231	6233	ex D-AZAT	♦
☐ B-1848	Airbus A321-231	6241	ex D-AVZC	♦
☐ B-1880	Airbus A321-231	6261	ex D-AVZK	♦
☐ B-2280	Airbus A321-231	1596	ex D-AVZL	
☐ B-2281	Airbus A321-231	1614	ex D-AVZA	
☐ B-2282	Airbus A321-231	1776	ex D-AVZC	
☐ B-2283	Airbus A321-231	1788	ex D-AVZE	
☐ B-2284	Airbus A321-231	1974	ex D-AVZN	
☐ B-2285	Airbus A321-231	1995	ex D-AVZZ	
☐ B-2287	Airbus A321-231	2080	ex D-AVZW	
☐ B-2288	Airbus A321-231	2067	ex D-AVZP	
☐ B-2417	Airbus A321-231	2521	ex D-AVZC	
☐ B-2418	Airbus A321-231	2530	ex D-AVZD	
☐ B-6265	Airbus A321-231	2713	ex D-AVZI	
☐ B-6267	Airbus A321-231	2741	ex D-AVZK	
☐ B-6270	Airbus A321-231	2759	ex D-AVZL	
☐ B-6271	Airbus A321-231	2767	ex D-AVZM	
☐ B-6273	Airbus A321-231	2809	ex D-AVZC	
☐ B-6302	Airbus A321-231	2936	ex D-AVZT	
☐ B-6305	Airbus A321-231	2971	ex D-AVZM	
☐ B-6306	Airbus A321-231	3067	ex D-AVZJ	
☐ B-6307	Airbus A321-231	3075	ex D-AVZB	
☐ B-6308	Airbus A321-231	3112	ex D-AVZE	
☐ B-6317	Airbus A321-231	3217	ex D-AVZD	
☐ B-6318	Airbus A321-231	3251	ex D-AVZP	
☐ B-6319	Airbus A321-231	3241	ex D-AVZJ	
☐ B-6339	Airbus A321-231	3507	ex D-AVZJ	
☐ B-6342	Airbus A321-231	3459	ex D-AVZT	
☐ B-6343	Airbus A321-231	3493	ex D-AVZF	
☐ B-6353	Airbus A321-231	3552	ex D-AVZP	
☐ B-6355	Airbus A321-231	3566	ex D-AVZS	
☐ B-6356	Airbus A321-231	3587	ex D-AVZR	
☐ B-6378	Airbus A321-231	3645	ex D-AVZU	
☐ B-6379	Airbus A321-231	3681	ex D-AZAF	
☐ B-6389	Airbus A321-231	3764	ex D-AZAN	
☐ B-6397	Airbus A321-231	3784	ex D-AZAQ	
☐ B-6398	Airbus A321-231	3847	ex D-AVZH	
☐ B-6552	Airbus A321-231	3867	ex D-AVZL	
☐ B-6553	Airbus A321-231	3920	ex D-AVZY	
☐ B-6578	Airbus A321-231	3934	ex D-AZAE	
☐ B-6579	Airbus A321-231	3938	ex D-AZAH	
☐ B-6580	Airbus A321-231	3951	ex D-AZAT	
☐ B-6581	Airbus A321-231	3981	ex D-AZAM	
☐ B-6622	Airbus A321-211	4194	ex D-AVZD	
☐ B-6625	Airbus A321-231	4184	ex D-AZAN	
☐ B-6626	Airbus A321-231	4189	ex D-AVZB	
☐ B-6628	Airbus A321-231	4217	ex D-AVZI	
☐ B-6629	Airbus A321-231	4224	ex D-AVZL	
☐ B-6630	Airbus A321-231	4230	ex D-AVZQ	
☐ B-6657	Airbus A321-231	4266	ex D-AVZH	
☐ B-6658	Airbus A321-231	4271	ex D-AVZR	
☐ B-6659	Airbus A321-231	4292	ex D-AZAV	
☐ B-6660	Airbus A321-231	4299	ex D-AZAX	
☐ B-6661	Airbus A321-231	4341	ex D-AZAS	
☐ B-6662	Airbus A321-211	4274	ex D-AVZT	
☐ B-6663	Airbus A321-211	4338	ex D-AZAR	
☐ B-6683	Airbus A321-231	4369	ex D-AVZS	
☐ B-6685	Airbus A321-231	4416	ex D-AZAE	
☐ B-6686	Airbus A321-231	4387	ex D-AZAC	
☐ B-6687	Airbus A321-231	4430	ex D-AZAI	
☐ B-6912	Airbus A321-231	5279	ex D-AZAF	
☐ B-6913	Airbus A321-231	5237	ex D-AVZO	

☐ B-6978	Airbus A321-231	5534	ex D-AZAX	
☐ B-6979	Airbus A321-231	5655	ex D-AVZU	
☐ B-9960	Airbus A321-231	5890	ex D-AVZX	
☐ B-6135	Airbus A330-223	1096	ex F-WWYT	
☐ B-6515	Airbus A330-223	1116	ex F-WWKJ	
☐ B-6516	Airbus A330-223	1129	ex F-WWKE	
☐ B-6526	Airbus A330-223	1220	ex F-WWKD	
☐ B-6528	Airbus A330-223	1202	ex F-WWYB	SkyTeam c/s
☐ B-6531	Airbus A330-223	1233	ex F-WWYK	
☐ B-6532	Airbus A330-223	1244	ex F-WWYU	
☐ B-6542	Airbus A330-223	1297	ex F-WWYZ	
☐ B-6547	Airbus A330-223	1309	ex F-WWKI	
☐ B-6548	Airbus A330-223	1335	ex F-WWTX	
☐ B-6056	Airbus A330-243	649	ex F-WWKI	
☐ B-6057	Airbus A330-243	652	ex F-WWKL	
☐ B-6058	Airbus A330-243	656	ex F-WWYV	
☐ B-6059	Airbus A330-243	664	ex F-WWKP	
☐ B-6077	Airbus A330-243	818	ex F-WWYQ	
☐ B-6078	Airbus A330-243	840	ex F-WWYS	
☐ B-5917	Airbus A330-323	1392	ex F-WWYY	
☐ B-5922	Airbus A330-323	1425	ex F-WWKM	
☐ B-5928	Airbus A330-323	1430	ex F-WWCL	SkyTeam c/s
☐ B-5939	Airbus A330-323	1494	ex F-WWTN	
☐ B-5940	Airbus A330-323	1519	ex F-WWYE	
☐ B-5951	Airbus A330-323	1536	ex F-WWCL	♦
☐ B-5959	Airbus A330-323	1575	ex F-WWKS	♦
☐ B-5965	Airbus A330-323	1593	ex F-WWYG	♦
☐ B-5966	Airbus A330-323	1625	ex F-WWYU	♦
☐ B-5967	Airbus A330-323	1636	ex F-WW	o/o♦
☐ B-5970	Airbus A330-323	1645	ex F-WWKJ	o/o♦
☐ B-6086	Airbus A330-343E	879	ex F-WWKG	
☐ B-6087	Airbus A330-343E	889	ex F-WWKZ	
☐ B-6098	Airbus A330-343E	908	ex F-WWYF	
☐ B-6111	Airbus A330-343E	935	ex F-WWKF	
☐ B-6112	Airbus A330-343E	937	ex F-WWKI	
☐ B-6500	Airbus A330-343E	954	ex F-WWKT	
☐ B-6501	Airbus A330-343E	964	ex F-WWYK	
☐ B-6502	Airbus A330-343E	958	ex F-WWYD	
☐ B-6136	Airbus A380-841	031	ex F-WWSF	
☐ B-6137	Airbus A380-841	036	ex F-WWAM	
☐ B-6138	Airbus A380-841	054	ex F-WWAX	
☐ B-6139	Airbus A380-841	088	ex F-WWAR	
☐ B-6140	Airbus A380-841	120	ex F-WWSB	
☐ B-2574	Boeing 737-37K	29407/3100	ex N1786B	
☐ B-2575	Boeing 737-37K	29408/3104	ex N1800B	
☐ B-2583	Boeing 737-31B	25897/2554		
☐ B-2920	Boeing 737-3Q8	27271/2523		[TUS]
☐ B-2927	Boeing 737-31B	27290/2595		[MZJ]
☐ B-2931	Boeing 737-31L	27276/2567		[MZJ]
☐ B-2936	Boeing 737-37K	27335/2609		[TUS]
☐ B-2959	Boeing 737-31B	27520/2775		
☐ B-2169	Boeing 737-71B	32936/1531		
☐ B-2620	Boeing 737-71B	32937/1569		
☐ B-2622	Boeing 737-71B	32938/1603		
☐ B-2916	Boeing 737-71B	32939/1607		
☐ B-2917	Boeing 737-71B	32940/1624		
☐ B-5068	Boeing 737-71B	32933/1430		
☐ B-5069	Boeing 737-71B	32934/1465		
☐ B-5070	Boeing 737-71B	32935/1507		
☐ B-5232	Boeing 737-71B	35360/2051		
☐ B-5233	Boeing 737-71B	35361/2077		
☐ B-5235	Boeing 737-71B	29370/2137	ex N1786B	
☐ B-5236	Boeing 737-71B	35362/2102		
☐ B-5237	Boeing 737-71B	29372/2131	ex N1786B	
☐ B-5238	Boeing 737-71B	35363/2066		
☐ B-5239	Boeing 737-71B	35364/2156		
☐ B-5240	Boeing 737-71B	35368/2264		
☐ B-5241	Boeing 737-71B	35372/2291		
☐ B-5247	Boeing 737-71B	35377/2980	ex N1786B	
☐ B-5250	Boeing 737-71B	35378/2346	ex N1786B	
☐ B-5251	Boeing 737-71B	35384/2446		
☐ B-5252	Boeing 737-71B	35382/3034	ex N1786B	
☐ B-5253	Boeing 737-71B	35383/3005		
☐ B-5275	Boeing 737-71B/W	38912/3730		
☐ B-5281	Boeing 737-71B/W	38914/3864		
☐ B-5283	Boeing 737-71B/W	38919/4000		
☐ B-5285	Boeing 737-71B/W	38917/3922		

☐ B-5290	Boeing 737-71B/W	38925/4120			
☐ B-5291	Boeing 737-71B/W	38962/4103			
☐ B-1700	Boeing 737-86N/W	43401/5261	ex N1787B		◆
☐ B-1701	Boeing 737-86N/W	41251/5008			◆
☐ B-1717	Boeing 737-81B/W	38924/5146			◆
☐ B-1718	Boeing 737-81B/W	38934/5203			◆
☐ B-1736	Boeing 737-81B/W	41326/5247	ex N1787B		◆
☐ B-1747	Boeing 737-81B/W	41327/5281			◆
☐ B-1748	Boeing 737-81B/W	41328/5334			◆
☐ B-1916	Boeing 737-81B/W	41315/4750			
☐ B-1917	Boeing 737-81B/W	41316/4803			
☐ B-1918	Boeing 737-81B/W	38915/4831	ex N5573K		
☐ B-1919	Boeing 737-81B/W	38965/4799			
☐ B-1920	Boeing 737-86N/W	41265/4745			
☐ B-1921	Boeing 737-86N/W	41245/4766			
☐ B-1922	Boeing 737-86N/W	41246/4792			
☐ B-1923	Boeing 737-86N/W	35645/4812			
☐ B-1925	Boeing 737-86N/W	41250/4941			◆
☐ B-1950	Boeing 737-81B/W	41317/4880	ex N5573K		
☐ B-1951	Boeing 737-81B/W	38921/4878			
☐ B-1952	Boeing 737-81B/W	41319/4912			◆
☐ B-1953	Boeing 737-81B/W	41320/4946			◆
☐ B-1955	Boeing 737-81B/W	38923/4959			◆
☐ B-1979	Boeing 737-86N/W	41252/5046			◆
☐ B-1980	Boeing 737-86N/W	41268/4993			◆
☐ B-2693	Boeing 737-81B	32921/1187	ex N6065Y		
☐ B-2694	Boeing 737-81B	32922/1199			
☐ B-2695	Boeing 737-81B	32923/1213			
☐ B-2696	Boeing 737-81B	32924/1230			
☐ B-2697	Boeing 737-81B	32925/1250			
☐ B-5020	Boeing 737-81B	32926/1268			
☐ B-5021	Boeing 737-81B	32927/1290			
☐ B-5022	Boeing 737-81B	32928/1323			
☐ B-5040	Boeing 737-81B	32929/1348			
☐ B-5041	Boeing 737-81B	32930/1355			
☐ B-5042	Boeing 737-81B	32931/1362			
☐ B-5067	Boeing 737-81B	32932/1395			
☐ B-5112	Boeing 737-86N	34248/1806			
☐ B-5113	Boeing 737-81B	34250/1784			
☐ B-5120	Boeing 737-83N/W	32580/1024	ex N313TZ		
☐ B-5122	Boeing 737-83N/W	32610/1110	ex N320TZ		
☐ B-5123	Boeing 737-83N/W	32611/1135	ex N322TZ		
☐ B-5128	Boeing 737-83N/W	32882/1163	ex N324TZ		
☐ B-5129	Boeing 737-83N/W	32884/1181	ex N325TZ		
☐ B-5147	Boeing 737-81B	30697/1915	ex N1786B		
☐ B-5149	Boeing 737-81B	30699/1933			
☐ B-5155	Boeing 737-8K5/W	30783/804	ex N307TA		
☐ B-5156	Boeing 737-81Q/W	30786/1138	ex N786TA		
☐ B-5157	Boeing 737-81Q/W	30787/1234	ex N787TM		
☐ B-5163	Boeing 737-81B	30708/2087			
☐ B-5165	Boeing 737-81B	30709/1961			
☐ B-5166	Boeing 737-81B	33006/1983			
☐ B-5189	Boeing 737-81B	35365/2191			
☐ B-5190	Boeing 737-81B	35366/2223			
☐ B-5191	Boeing 737-81B	35367/2237	ex N1786B		
☐ B-5192	Boeing 737-81B	35369/2272			
☐ B-5193	Boeing 737-81B	35370/2299			
☐ B-5195	Boeing 737-81B	35371/2302			
☐ B-5300	Boeing 737-81B	35375/2314			
☐ B-5310	Boeing 737-81B	35376/2329			
☐ B-5339	Boeing 737-81B	35380/2372	ex N1782B		
☐ B-5340	Boeing 737-81B	35381/2402			
☐ B-5356	Boeing 737-81B	35385/2486	ex N1787B		
☐ B-5419	Boeing 737-81B	35379/2957	ex N1787B		
☐ B-5420	Boeing 737-81B	35374/2940			
☐ B-5421	Boeing 737-81B	35373/2881			
☐ B-5445	Boeing 737-81B	35388/3154	ex N1796B		
☐ B-5446	Boeing 737-81B	35389/3144			
☐ B-5468	Boeing 737-81B	35386/3068	ex N1786B		
☐ B-5469	Boeing 737-81B	35387/3041			
☐ B-5586	Boeing 737-86J/W	36878/3631			
☐ B-5587	Boeing 737-81B/W	38966/3650	ex N1786B		
☐ B-5596	Boeing 737-81B/W	38964/3700			
☐ B-5597	Boeing 737-81B/W	38913/3776	ex N1780B		
☐ B-5598	Boeing 737-86J/W	36877/3784			
☐ B-5609	Boeing 737-81B/W	38963/3838			
☐ B-5640	Boeing 737-81B/W	38918/3961			
☐ B-5641	Boeing 737-81B/W	38916/3898			
☐ B-5643	Boeing 737-81B/W	38920/4031			
☐ B-5645	Boeing 737-81B/W	38922/4076			
☐ B-5646	Boeing 737-81B/W	38932/4064			
☐ B-5675	Boeing 737-81B/W	38926/4154	ex N1786B		

☐ B-5676	Boeing 737-81B/W	38927/4138		
☐ B-5677	Boeing 737-81B/W	38928/4178		
☐ B-5678	Boeing 737-81B/W	38929/4165		
☐ B-5697	Boeing 737-81B/W	38931/4207		
☐ B-5698	Boeing 737-81B/W	38933/4244	ex N1787B	
☐ B-5699	Boeing 737-81B/W	38935/4274	ex N1782B	
☐ B-5715	Boeing 737-81B/W	38936/4300		
☐ B-5716	Boeing 737-81B/W	38937/4307		
☐ B-5717	Boeing 737-81B/W	38938/4347		
☐ B-5718	Boeing 737-81B/W	38939/4359		
☐ B-5719	Boeing 737-81B/W	38940/4370	ex N5515X	
☐ B-5720	Boeing 737-81B/W	38941/4379		
☐ B-5721	Boeing 737-81B/W	38942/4388		
☐ B-5738	Boeing 737-81B/W	38930/4443		
☐ B-5739	Boeing 737-81B/W	38943/4427		
☐ B-5740	Boeing 737-81B/W	38944/4409		
☐ B-5741	Boeing 737-81B/W	38945/4464		
☐ B-5742	Boeing 737-81B/W	38946/4454		
☐ B-5743	Boeing 737-81B/W	38947/4492		
☐ B-5745	Boeing 737-81B/W	38948/4498		
☐ B-5746	Boeing 737-81B/W	38952/4505		
☐ B-5747	Boeing 737-81B/W	38961/4485		
☐ B-5748	Boeing 737-81B/W	41302/4415		
☐ B-5749	Boeing 737-81B/W	41303/4439		
☐ B-5759	Boeing 737-81B/W	38949/4541		
☐ B-5760	Boeing 737-81B/W	38957/4533		
☐ B-5761	Boeing 737-81B/W	38958/4527		
☐ B-5762	Boeing 737-81B/W	38950/4548		
☐ B-5766	Boeing 737-81B/W	38951/4570		
☐ B-5767	Boeing 737-81B/W	38959/4576		
☐ B-5768	Boeing 737-81B/W	38960/4585		
☐ B-5769	Boeing 737-81B/W	38953/4617	ex N5573L	
☐ B-5770	Boeing 737-81B/W	38954/4598		
☐ B-5836	Boeing 737-81B/W	38955/4642	ex N5573P	
☐ B-5837	Boeing 737-81B/W	38956/4662		
☐ B-2812	Boeing 757-28S	32341/961		
☐ B-2813	Boeing 757-28S	32342/966		
☐ B-2823	Boeing 757-21B	25888/575		
☐ B-2824	Boeing 757-21B	25889/583		
☐ B-2825	Boeing 757-21B	25890/585		
☐ B-2827	Boeing 757-2Y0	26156/503		[CAN]
☐ B-2830	Boeing 757-28S	32343/1015	ex N60668	
☐ B-2831	Boeing 757-2Y0	26153/482		
☐ B-2835	Boeing 757-236	25598/445	ex N5573P	
☐ B-2838	Boeing 757-2Z0	27260/613		
☐ B-2851	Boeing 757-28S	29215/797		
☐ B-2853	Boeing 757-28S	29216/811		
☐ B-2859	Boeing 757-28S	29217/868		
☐ B-2010	Boeing 777-F1B	41634/1268		♦
☐ B-2026	Boeing 777-F1B	41635/1306		o/o♦
☐ B-2027	Boeing 777-F1B	41636/1308		o/o♦
☐ B-2028	Boeing 777-F1B	41637/1318		o/o♦
☐ B-2041	Boeing 777-F1B	41632/1120		
☐ B-2042	Boeing 777-F1B	41633/1126		
☐ B-2051	Boeing 777-21B	27357/20		Toyota Camry c/s
☐ B-2052	Boeing 777-21B	27358/24	ex N5017V	
☐ B-2053	Boeing 777-21B	27359/46		
☐ B-2054	Boeing 777-21B	27360/48		
☐ B-2071	Boeing 777-F1B	37309/760	ex N447BA	
☐ B-2072	Boeing 777-F1B	37310/770	ex N448BA	
☐ B-2073	Boeing 777-F1B	37311/811	ex N553BA	
☐ B-2075	Boeing 777-F1B	37312/820	ex N554BA	
☐ B-2080	Boeing 777-F1B	37314/983		
☐ B-2081	Boeing 777-F1B	37313/888		
☐ B-2007	Boeing 777-31BER	43221/1223		♦
☐ B-2008	Boeing 777-31BER	43222/1229		♦
☐ B-2009	Boeing 777-31BER	43223/1260		♦
☐ B-2048	Boeing 777-31BER	43220/1219		♦
☐ B-2099	Boeing 777-31BER	43219/1173		
☐ B-	Boeing 777-31BER	43224/1329		o/o♦
☐ B-2725	Boeing 787-8	34923/34		
☐ B-2726	Boeing 787-8	34924/36		
☐ B-2727	Boeing 787-8	34925/43	ex N1014X	
☐ B-2732	Boeing 787-8	34926/93		
☐ B-2733	Boeing 787-8	34927/95		
☐ B-2735	Boeing 787-8	34928/119		
☐ B-2736	Boeing 787-8	34929/100		
☐ B-2737	Boeing 787-8	34930/104		
☐ B-2787	Boeing 787-8	34931/154		

☐ B-2788	Boeing 787-8	34932/172		♦
☐ B-3135	Embraer ERJ-190LR	19000535	ex PT-TUY	
☐ B-3136	Embraer ERJ-190LR	19000513	ex PT-TSR	
☐ B-3137	Embraer ERJ-190LR	19000524	ex PT-TUL	
☐ B-3138	Embraer ERJ-190LR	19000539	ex PT-TZJ	
☐ B-3139	Embraer ERJ-190LR	19000548	ex PT-TBO	
☐ B-3145	Embraer ERJ-190LR	19000529	ex PT-TUR	
☐ B-3146	Embraer ERJ-190LR	19000476	ex PT-TOW	
☐ B-3147	Embraer ERJ-190LR	19000477	ex PT-TOX	
☐ B-3148	Embraer ERJ-190LR	19000483	ex PT-TPI	
☐ B-3149	Embraer ERJ-190LR	19000488	ex PT-TPN	
☐ B-3197	Embraer ERJ-190LR	19000456	ex PT-TNX	
☐ B-3198	Embraer ERJ-190LR	19000465	ex PT-TOI	
☐ B-3199	Embraer ERJ-190LR	19000469	ex PT-TOL	
☐ B-3205	Embraer ERJ-190LR	19000556	ex PT-TDL	
☐ B-3206	Embraer ERJ-190LR	19000560	ex PT-TDP	
☐ B-3209	Embraer ERJ-190LR	19000564	ex PT-TDT	
☐ B-3210	Embraer ERJ-190LR	19000570	ex PT-TES	
☐ B-3216	Embraer ERJ-190LR	19000598	ex PT-TIF	
☐ B-3217	Embraer ERJ-190LR	19000605	ex PT-TJJ	
☐ B-3218	Embraer ERJ-190LR	19000613	ex PT-TJT	
☐ B-7118	Sikorsky S-76C+	760819	ex N819S	
☐ B-7303	Sikorsky S-76A	760289		
☐ B-7304	Sikorsky S-76A	760293		
☐ B-7306	Sikorsky S-76A	760106	ex VH-XHA	
☐ B-7307	Sikorsky S-76C+	760478		
☐ B-7308	Sikorsky S-76C+	760480		
☐ B-7311	Sikorsky S-76C+	760192		
☐ B-7320	Sikorsky S-76C+	760263		
☐ B-7323	Sikorsky S-76C+	760772	ex N772L	
☐ B-7329	Sikorsky S-76C++	760769		
☐ B-7330	Sikorsky S-76C++	760771		
☐ B-7331	Sikorsky S-76C++	760715	ex N2557H	
☐ B-7116	Sikorsky S-92A	920147	ex N2208U	♦
☐ B-7117	Sikorsky S-92A	920156	ex N156F	♦
☐ B-7333	Sikorsky S-92A	920115	ex N115KH	♦
☐ B-7350	Sikorsky S-92A	920188	ex N988R	♦
☐ B-7351	Sikorsky S-92A	920189	ex N189D	♦
☐ N7352	Sikorsky S92A	920230	ex N230Y	♦
☐ B-7353	Sikorsky S-92A	920247		♦
☐ B-2461	Boeing 747-41BF	32804/1312		[PVG]
☐ B-2473	Boeing 747-41BF	32803/1306	ex N1788B	[PVG]
☐ B-3060	Embraer ERJ-145LI	145701	ex PT-SGF	[NNY]

CHINA UNITED AIRLINES — Lianhang (KN/CUA) — Beijing-Nanyuan (NAY)

☐ B-4008	Boeing 737-3T0	23839/1507	ex N19357	opf Govt
☐ B-4009	Boeing 737-3T0	23840/1516	ex N27358	opf Govt
☐ B-4018	Boeing 737-33A	25502/2310		opf Govt
☐ B-4019	Boeing 737-33A	25503/2313		opf Govt
☐ B-4020	Boeing 737-34N	28081/2746		opf Govt
☐ B-4021	Boeing 737-34N	28082/2747		opf Govt
☐ B-4052	Boeing 737-3Q8	24701/1957	ex PK-GWI	opf Govt
☐ B-4053	Boeing 737-3Q8	24702/1994	ex PK-GWJ	opf Govt
☐ B-2681	Boeing 737-79P	33037/1198		
☐ B-2684	Boeing 737-79P	33039/1227		
☐ B-4025	Boeing 737-76D	33470/1334	ex B-5048	opf Govt
☐ B-4026	Boeing 737-76D	33472/1343	ex B-2689	opf Govt
☐ B-5033	Boeing 737-79P	30657/1319		
☐ B-5208	Boeing 737-79P/W	33041/1902	ex N1787B	
☐ B-5210	Boeing 737-79P/W	33043/1976		
☐ B-5223	Boeing 737-79P/W	33044/1987		
☐ B-1523	Boeing 737-89P/W	39742/5349		♦
☐ B-1750	Boeing 737-89P/W	61308/5201		♦
☐ B-1751	Boeing 737-89P/W	61309/5209		♦
☐ B-1752	Boeing 737-89P/W	61310/5211		♦
☐ B-1753	Boeing 737-89P/W	61311/5215		♦
☐ B-1989	Boeing 737-89P/W	39734/4913		♦
☐ B-1990	Boeing 737-89P/W	39736/5007		
☐ B-5183	Boeing 737-8Q8/W	30711/2159	ex N1787B	<CSH
☐ B-5323	Boeing 737-8Q8/W	30725/2292		<CSH
☐ B-5353	Boeing 737-8Q8/W	30728/2386		
☐ B-5399	Boeing 737-86N/W	35224/2617		<CSH
☐ B-5448	Boeing 737-86N/W	38021/3679	ex N1786B	
☐ B-5470	Boeing 737-86D/W	35774/3010	ex N1786B	
☐ B-5471	Boeing 737-86D/W	35775/3098	ex N1796B	
☐ B-5547	Boeing 737-86N/W	36806/3448	ex N1786B	

☐ B-5703	Boeing 737-89P/W	41784/4170		
☐ B-5705	Boeing 737-89P/W	38828/4191		
☐ B-5722	Boeing 737-8Q8/W	41785/4245		
☐ B-5838	Boeing 737-89P/W	40953/4575	ex N5573P	
☐ B-5839	Boeing 737-89P/W	40952/4536		
☐ B-5840	Boeing 737-89P/W	41304/4493		
☐ B-4005	Canadair CRJ-200LR	7138	ex C-FZAT	opf Govt
☐ B-4006	Canadair CRJ-200LR	7149	ex C-FZIS	opf Govt
☐ B-4007	Canadair CRJ-200LR	7180	ex C-GATM	opf Govt
☐ B-4010	Canadair CRJ-200LR	7189	ex C-GATY	opf Govt
☐ B-4011	Canadair CRJ-200LR	7193	ex C-GBFR	opf Govt
☐ B-4701	Canadair CRJ-200LR	7639	ex C-GKAK	opf China Maritime Service
☐ B-4702	Canadair CRJ-200LR	7455	ex C-GHUT	opf China Maritime Service
☐ B-4071	Harbin Y-7G	0201		
☐ B-4072	Harbin Y-7G	0204		
☐ B-4073	Harbin Y-7G	0205		operator unconfirmed
☐ B-4074	Harbin Y-7G	0206		operator unconfirmed
☐ B-4075	Harbin Y-7G	0207		operator unconfirmed
☐ B-4076	Harbin Y-7G	0208		operator unconfirmed
☐ B-4077	Harbin Y-7G	0209		operator unconfirmed
☐ B-4004	Tupolev Tu-154M	71485A714		wfs
☐ B-4012	Yakovlev Yak-42D	4520424914375		opf Chinese Navy
☐ B-4014	Tupolev Tu-154M	84790A847		
☐ B-4028	Tupolev Tu-154M	93A967		VIP
☐ B-4050	Tupolev Tu-154M	73086A730		wfs
☐ B-4061	Canadair CRJ-701ER	10183	ex C-FCRA	opf Chinese AF
☐ B-4062	Canadair CRJ-701ER	10187	ex C-FCRF	opf Chinese AF
☐ B-4063	Canadair CRJ-701ER	10204	ex C-FEHT	opf Chinese AF
☐ B-4064	Canadair CRJ-701ER	10206	ex C-FEHU	opf Chinese AF
☐ B-4090	Airbus A319-115	5023	ex D-AVYJ	opf Govt
☐ B-4091	Airbus A319-115	5088	ex D-AVYP	opf Govt
☐ B-4092	Airbus A319-115	5907	ex D-AVWB	

CHINA WEST AIR		(PN/CHB)		Chongqing (CKG)
☐ B-1629	Airbus A320-232/S	6237	ex F-WWIM	♦
☐ B-1817	Airbus A320-214/S	5912	ex D-AUBA	
☐ B-1897	Airbus A320-232/S	6076	ex (9V-TRP)	♦
☐ B-1898	Airbus A320-232/S	6120	ex F-WWBF	♦
☐ B-6743	Airbus A320-232	4569	ex D-AVVB	
☐ B-6763	Airbus A320-232	4482	ex B-502L	
☐ B-6765	Airbus A320-232	4687	ex D-AUBB	
☐ B-6790	Airbus A320-232	4686	ex F-WWIJ	
☐ B-6811	Airbus A320-232	4644	ex B-515L	
☐ B-9949	Airbus A320-214	5626	ex F-WWBD	
☐ B-9969	Airbus A320-232/S	6023	ex (9V-TRO)	♦
☐ B-9981	Airbus A320-214	5740	ex B-505L	
☐ B-9982	Airbus A320-214	5679	ex B-519L	
☐ B-6412	Airbus A319-132	4262	ex B-506L	
☐ B-6413	Airbus A319-132	4452	ex D-AVYB	
☐ B-6420	Airbus A319-133	5105	ex D-AVYS	♦
☐ B-6421	Airbus A319-133	4995	ex D-AVYF	♦

CHINA XINHUA AIRLINES		Xinhua (XW/CXH)		Tianjin (TSN)
☐ B-5080	Boeing 737-86N	28614/477	ex N614LS	
☐ B-5082	Boeing 737-883	30193/587	ex LN-RCS	
☐ B-5138	Boeing 737-84P/W	32607/1832		<CHH
☐ B-5139	Boeing 737-84P/W	32608/1855		<CHH
☐ B-5141	Boeing 737-84P/W	34030/1800		<CHH
☐ B-5153	Boeing 737-84P/W	34029/1921		<CHH

CHONGQING AIRLINES		Chongqing (OQ/CQN)		Chongqing (CKG)
☐ B-2343	Airbus A320-233	0696	ex F-WWII	
☐ B-2345	Airbus A320-233	0698	ex F-WWBT	
☐ B-2346	Airbus A320-233	0704	ex F-WWDY	
☐ B-2347	Airbus A320-233	0705	ex F-WWIL	
☐ B-6576	Airbus A320-232	3941	ex F-WWDS	
☐ B-9976	Airbus A320-232	5645	ex D-AUBU	
☐ B-9977	Airbus A320-232	5713	ex D-AVVL	
☐ B-5187	Boeing 737-8BK	33828/2124		<CSN
☐ B-6246	Airbus A319-133	3836	ex D-AVYO	
☐ B-6247	Airbus A319-133	3876	ex D-AVWG	
☐ B-6248	Airbus A319-133	3901	ex D-AVWP	

CITIC OFFSHORE HELICOPTERS   China Helicopter (CHC)   Shenzhen Heliport

☐ B-7127	Eurocopter EC225LP	2676		
☐ B-7128	Eurocopter EC225LP	2687		
☐ B-7143	Eurocopter EC225LP	2927		♦
☐ B-7151	Eurocopter EC255LP	2895		
☐ B-7190	Eurocopter EC225LP	2555		
☐ B-7191	Eurocopter EC225LP	2855	ex F-WWOP	
☐ B-7192	Eurocopter EC225LP	2866		
☐ B-7193	Eurocopter EC255LP	2823		
☐ B-7951	Aérospatiale AS332L	2165	ex F-WYMQ	
☐ B-7956	Aérospatiale AS332L1	2356	ex HL9202	
☐ B-7957	Aérospatiale AS332L1	9000		
☐ B-7958	Aérospatiale AS332L1	9001	ex F-WQDT	
☐ B-7959	Aérospatiale AS332L1	2087	ex F-WYMR	
☐ B-7961	Aérospatiale AS332L1	2641		
☐ B-7962	Aérospatiale AS332L1	2644		
☐ B-7101	Aérospatiale AS365N	6012		
☐ B-7102	Aérospatiale AS365N	6013		
☐ B-7103	Aérospatiale AS365N	6041		
☐ B-7105	Aérospatiale AS365N	6046		
☐ B-7106	Aérospatiale AS365N	6047		
☐ B-7107	Aérospatiale AS365N	6027		
☐ B-7005	Eurocopter EC155B	6639		
☐ B-7006	Eurocopter EC155B	6641		
☐ B-7008	Eurocopter EC155B	6623		
☐ B-7120	Eurocopter EC155B1	6717	ex F-WWOU	
☐ B-7132	Eurocopter EC155B1	6904		
☐ B-7133	Eurocopter EC155B1	6912		
☐ B-7135	Eurocopter EC155B1	6915		
☐ B-7141	Eurocopter EC155B1	6941		
☐ B-7152	Eurocopter EC155B1	6980		
☐ B-7187	Eurocopter EC155B1	6950		
☐ B-7189	Eurocopter EC155B1	6954		
☐ B-7190	Eurocopter EC155B1	6957		
☐ B-7007	Eurocopter EC135T2	0246		
☐ B-7305	Sikorsky S-92A	920215	ex N215PW	♦
☐ B-7429	Aérospatiale AS350B3	4627		
☐ B-7772	Agusta A109E Power	11136		
☐ B-7776	Agusta A109S	22132		
☐ B-7778	Agusta A109S	22139		

DALIAN AIRLINES   (CA/CCD)   Dalian Zhoushuizi (DLC)

☐ B-5196	Boeing 737-86N	36810/2699		
☐ B-5197	Boeing 737-86N	36811/2777		
☐ B-5553	Boeing 737-89L/W	40026/3576	ex N1786B	<CCA
☐ B-5639	Boeing 737-89L/W	40033/4004		<CCA
☐ B-5642	Boeing 737-89L/W	40017/4060		<CCA
☐ B-5729	Boeing 737-89L/W	40038/4422		<CCA♦
☐ B-5850	Boeing 737-89L/W	41311/4689		

DONGHAI AIRLINES   Donghai Air (J5/EPA)   Shenzhen Bao'an (SZX)

☐ B-2505	Boeing 737-36QSF	28657/2859	ex N657AG	
☐ B-2517	Boeing 737-3W0SF	23396/1166	ex N5573K	
☐ B-2518	Boeing 737-3W0SF	23397/1193	ex N1791B	
☐ B-2608	Boeing 737-36QSF	28662/659	ex N662AG	
☐ B-2897	Boeing 737-3Y0F	24902/1973	ex N108KH	
☐ B-2898	Boeing 737-3Y0F	24916/2066	ex N106KH	
☐ B-5046	Boeing 737-341SF	24276/1645	ex N276HE	
☐ B-5047	Boeing 737-341SF	24278/1660	ex N278HE	
☐ B-1705	Boeing 737-86J/W	39387/4966	ex N844BA	♦
☐ B-1770	Boeing 737-8Q8/W	41802/5228		♦
☐ B-1771	Boeing 737-8Q8/W	41803/5274		♦
☐ B-5311	Boeing 737-8Q8	29373/2171		
☐ B-5313	Boeing 737-8Q8	30716/2210	ex N1786B	

DONGHUA AIRLINES   Jinjiang (JJN)

☐ B-3889	AVIC II Y-11	(11)0305	

FUZHOU AIRLINES   (FU/FZA)   Fuzhou (FOC)

☐ B-1905	Boeing 737-86J/W	39383/4601	ex N267SC	♦
☐ B-1906	Boeing 737-86J/W	37768/4118	ex N268SC	♦
☐ B-5182	Boeing 737-808/W	34708/2097		♦

☐ B-5430	Boeing 737-84P/W	34032/2827	ex N1787B	◆
☐ B-5503	Boeing 737-84P/W	36782/3186	ex N1796B	◆

GRAND CHINA AIR — Grand China (CN/GDC) — Haikou (HAK)

☐ B-2652	Boeing 737-84P	30475/731	ex N1786B	Jin Sui Piao Xiang special c/s
☐ B-5089	Boeing 737-883	28320/551	ex OY-KKU	
☐ B-5482	Boeing 737-84P/W	35748/2938	ex N1786B	<CHH◆

GUANGDONG PROVINCE GENERAL AVIATION

☐ B-9461	Cessna 208B Caravan I	208B2320	ex N90243
☐ B-9462	Cessna 208B Caravan I	208B2326	ex N9031X
☐ B-9631	Cessna 208B Caravan I	208B2419	ex N95446

GUIZHOU AIRLINES — (CGH) — Guiyang Longdongbao (KWE)

☐ B-5120	Boeing 737-83N/W	32580/1024	ex N313TZ
☐ B-5121	Boeing 737-83N/W	32609/1059	ex N316TZ
☐ B-5125	Boeing 737-83N/W	32612/1184	ex N326TZ
☐ B-5126	Boeing 737-83N/W	32613/1197	ex N327TZ
☐ B-5127	Boeing 737-83N/W	32615/1207	ex N329TZ
☐ B-5221	Boeing 737-71B	29366/1872	ex N1795B
☐ B-5222	Boeing 737-71B	29367/1896	ex N1784B
☐ B-5230	Boeing 737-71B	29371/2064	

GX AIRLINES — (GX/CBG) — Nanning (NNG)

☐ B-3122	Embraer ERJ-190LR	19000186	ex PT-SDU	◆
☐ B-3125	Embraer ERJ-190LR	19000194	ex PT-SGC	◆
☐ B-3165	Embraer ERJ-190LR	19000340	ex PT-TXZ	◆
☐ B-3179	Embraer ERJ-190LR	19000426	ex PT-TCK	◆
☐ B-3215	Embraer ERJ-190LR	19000591	ex PT-THQ	◆

HAINAN AIRLINES — Hainan (HU/CHH) — Haikou (HAK)

☐ B-5955	Airbus A330-243	1558	ex F-WWYM	◆
☐ B-5979	Airbus A330-243	1591	ex F-WWCN	◆
☐ B-5963	Airbus A330-243	1573	ex F-WWKQ	◆
☐ B-6088	Airbus A330-243	906	ex F-WWYD	
☐ B-6089	Airbus A330-243	919	ex F-WWYS	
☐ B-6116	Airbus A330-243	875	ex F-WWKB	
☐ B-6118	Airbus A330-243	881	ex F-WWKI	
☐ B-6133	Airbus A330-243	982	ex F-WWYY	
☐ B-6519	Airbus A330-243	1159	ex F-WWKF	
☐ B-5905	Airbus A330-343X	1325	ex F-WWTL	
☐ B-5910	Airbus A330-343E	1369	ex B-LNN	
☐ B-5935	Airbus A330-343X	1438	ex F-WWKE	
☐ B-5950	Airbus A330-343X	1532	ex F-WWCH	◆
☐ B-5971	Airbus A330-343E	1614	ex F-WWKD	o/o◆
☐ B-5972	Airbus A330-343E	1634	ex F-WWYL	o/o◆
☐ B-6520	Airbus A330-343X	1168	ex F-WWYJ	
☐ B-6527	Airbus A330-343X	1178	ex F-WWKE	
☐ B-6529	Airbus A330-343X	1190	ex F-WWKG	
☐ B-6539	Airbus A330-343X	1255	ex F-WWYM	
☐ B-	Airbus A330-343	1656	ex F-WW	o/o◆
☐ B-	Airbus A330-343	1663	ex F-WW	o/o◆
☐ B-5060	Boeing 737-76N	28582/154	ex N582HE	
☐ B-5062	Boeing 737-76N	28585/173	ex N585HE	
☐ B-5288	Boeing 737-74P/W	39201/4519		
☐ B-5289	Boeing 737-74P/W	39198/4395	ex N1787B	
☐ B-5805	Boeing 737-79P/W	39199/4449		>LKE
☐ B-5806	Boeing 737-79P/W	39200/4483		>LKE
☐ B-5813	Boeing 737-74P/W	39210/4885		
☐ B-1725	Boeing 737-84P/W	38147/5167		◆
☐ B-1726	Boeing 737-84P/W	39217/5155		◆
☐ B-1727	Boeing 737-84P/W	39216/5128		◆
☐ B-1728	Boeing 737-84P/W	39218/5194		◆
☐ B-1729	Boeing 737-84P/W	41377/5175	ex N1795B	◆
☐ B-1733	Boeing 737-86N/W	41254/5132		◆
☐ B-1735	Boeing 737-86N/W	41269/5097		◆
☐ B-1783	Boeing 737-84P/W	39219/5233	ex N1786B	◆
☐ B-1785	Boeing 737-84P/W	41378/5243		◆
☐ B-1786	Boeing 737-84P/W	39220/5268	ex N1796B	◆
☐ B-1787	Boeing 737-84P/W	41379/5277	ex N1796B	◆
☐ B-1793	Boeing 737-86J/W	36122/4391	ex N361AB	◆
☐ B-1795	Boeing 737-84P/W	41568/5308		◆

☐ B-1796	Boeing 737-84P/W	41569/5331	ex N1795B		♦
☐ B-1797	Boeing 737-84P/W	41570/5382			♦
☐ B-1798	Boeing 737-86N/W	43403/5359			♦
☐ B-1799	Boeing 737-84P/W	41381/5418			o/o♦
☐ B-1902	Boeing 737-86J/W	37769/4159	ex N278SC		
☐ B-1903	Boeing 737-86J/W	36872/4209	ex N263SC		
☐ B-1927	Boeing 737-84P/W	39207/4760	ex N5573B		
☐ B-1928	Boeing 737-84P/W	39208/4794	ex N5515X		
☐ B-1929	Boeing 737-84P/W	39209/4838	ex N5515X		
☐ B-1989	Boeing 737-84P/W	39214/5027	ex N1796B		♦
☐ B-1992	Boeing 737-84P/W	41376/4996			♦
☐ B-1995	Boeing 737-84P/W	39213/5006			♦
☐ B-1997	Boeing 737-84P/W	39215/5076			♦
☐ B-2638	Boeing 737-8Q8	28220/212	ex N361LF	special palm c/s	
☐ B-2646	Boeing 737-8Q8	28056/273	ex N371LF	special orchid c/s	
☐ B-2647	Boeing 737-84P	29947/345	ex N1787B	special Happy Sea Wave c/s	
☐ B-2651	Boeing 737-84P	30474/607	ex N1787B		
☐ B-2676	Boeing 737-84P/W	32602/1170			
☐ B-2677	Boeing 737-84P/W	32604/1191			
☐ B-5083	Boeing 737-883	28319/548	ex LN-RCO		
☐ B-5090	Boeing 737-883	28321/577	ex LN-RCR		
☐ B-5135	Boeing 737-84P/W	32603/1766	ex N1786B		
☐ B-5136	Boeing 737-84P/W	32605/1796	ex B-KBE		
☐ B-5137	Boeing 737-84P/W	32606/1805	ex B-KBF		
☐ B-5337	Boeing 737-84P/W	35747/2433			
☐ B-5338	Boeing 737-84P/W	35749/2330			
☐ B-5346	Boeing 737-8BK/W	29673/2373	ex N1786B		
☐ B-5358	Boeing 737-84P/W	35077/2419	ex N1787B		
☐ B-5359	Boeing 737-8FH/W	35101/2459	ex N1786B		
☐ B-5371	Boeing 737-84P/W	35752/2556	ex N1787B		
☐ B-5372	Boeing 737-84P/W	35758/2593			
☐ B-5373	Boeing 737-84P/W	35754/2618	ex N1787B		
☐ B-5375	Boeing 737-84P/W	35762/2648	ex N1786B		
☐ B-5403	Boeing 737-84P/W	35756/2691	ex N1786B		
☐ B-5405	Boeing 737-84P/W	35759/2668			
☐ B-5406	Boeing 737-84P/W	35760/2678			
☐ B-5408	Boeing 737-84P/W	35764/2778	ex N1786B		
☐ B-5416	Boeing 737-84P/W	34031/2801	ex N1780B		
☐ B-5417	Boeing 737-86N/W	35639/2821			
☐ B-5418	Boeing 737-86N/W	36541/2769	ex N1786B		
☐ B-5427	Boeing 737-8Q8/W	35285/2772	ex N1787B		
☐ B-5428	Boeing 737-86N/W	36542/2806	ex N1796B		
☐ B-5429	Boeing 737-86N/W	36543/2831	ex N1796B		
☐ B-5433	Boeing 737-86N/W	36542/2806			
☐ B-5439	Boeing 737-808/W	34707/2046	ex B-KBH		
☐ B-5449	Boeing 737-808/W	34971/2400	ex B-KXH		
☐ B-5462	Boeing 737-84P/W	36780/3095	ex N1796B		
☐ B-5463	Boeing 737-84P/W	35755/3339	ex N1787B		
☐ B-5465	Boeing 737-84P/W	34033/2854	ex N1787B		
☐ B-5466	Boeing 737-84P/W	34034/2912			
☐ B-5467	Boeing 737-84P/W	36779/2885			
☐ B-5478	Boeing 737-84P/W	35751/3038	ex N1786B		
☐ B-5479	Boeing 737-84P/W	35753/3066	ex N1786B		
☐ B-5480	Boeing 737-86N/W	35648/2973			
☐ B-5481	Boeing 737-86N/W	35649/2981			
☐ B-5482	Boeing 737-84P/W	35748/2938	ex N1786B		>GDC
☐ B-5483	Boeing 737-84P/W	35750/3007			
☐ B-5502	Boeing 737-84P/W	35757/3192	ex N1786B		
☐ B-5520	Boeing 737-84P/W	35765/3344			
☐ B-5521	Boeing 737-84P/W	35766/3313			
☐ B-5522	Boeing 737-84P/W	36781/3278	ex N1786B		
☐ B-5538	Boeing 737-84P/W	36783/3382			
☐ B-5539	Boeing 737-84P/W	35763/3378			
☐ B-5540	Boeing 737-84P/W	35761/3392			
☐ B-5579	Boeing 737-84P/W	39223/3610			
☐ B-5580	Boeing 737-84P/W	39224/3647			
☐ B-5581	Boeing 737-84P/W	38143/3713			
☐ B-5611	Boeing 737-84P/W	38145/3783			
☐ B-5620	Boeing 737-84P/W	38144/3733			
☐ B-5623	Boeing 737-84P/W	38148/3865			
☐ B-5625	Boeing 737-84P/W	38146/3812			
☐ B-5636	Boeing 737-84P/W	38149/3889			
☐ B-5637	Boeing 737-84P/W	38150/3937			
☐ B-5638	Boeing 737-84P/W	38151/3951			
☐ B-5661	Boeing 737-84P/W	38152/3995			
☐ B-5662	Boeing 737-84P/W	38153/4036			
☐ B-5663	Boeing 737-84P/W	38154/4063			
☐ B-5685	Boeing 737-84P/W	38155/4115			
☐ B-5686	Boeing 737-84P/W	38156/4147			
☐ B-5687	Boeing 737-84P/W	38157/4171			
☐ B-5709	Boeing 737-808/W	34709/2121	ex B-KBI		
☐ B-5710	Boeing 737-84P/W	35072/2155	ex B-KBK		
☐ B-5711	Boeing 737-84P/W	39195/4304			

48

☐ B-5712	Boeing 737-84P/W	39196/4355				
☐ B-5713	Boeing 737-84P/W	39197/4381				
☐ B-5733	Boeing 737-84P/W	37422/3214	ex B-KBT			
☐ B-5735	Boeing 737-84P/W	37953/3299	ex B-KBU			
☐ B-5763	Boeing 737-808/W	34710/2144	ex B-KXE			
☐ B-5765	Boeing 737-84P/W	35274/2570	ex B-KBQ			
☐ B-5797	Boeing 737-84P/W	39202/4584				
☐ B-5798	Boeing 737-84P/W	39203/4596				
☐ B-5835	Boeing 737-84P/W	35276/2611	ex B-KBR			
☐ B-5852	Boeing 737-84P/W	39204/4651				
☐ B-5853	Boeing 737-84P/W	39205/4678				
☐ B-5855	Boeing 737-84P/W	39206/4716				
☐ B-2722	Boeing 787-8	34939/76				
☐ B-2723	Boeing 787-8	34944/81				
☐ B-2728	Boeing 787-8	34938/73	ex N1006F			
☐ B-2729	Boeing 787-8	34941/79				
☐ B-2730	Boeing 787-8	34943/85				
☐ B-2731	Boeing 787-8	34945/131				
☐ B-2738	Boeing 787-8	34940/151	ex N1014X			
☐ B-2739	Boeing 787-8	38055/171				♦
☐ B-2750	Boeing 787-8	34942/262				♦
☐ B-2759	Boeing 787-8	38056/274	ex N1008S			♦
☐ B-2112	Boeing 737 36NSF	28599/3115	ex EI-DRS			
☐ B-2490	Boeing 767-34PER	33047/889				
☐ B-2491	Boeing 767-34PER	33048/891				
☐ B-2492	Boeing 767-34PER	33049/893				
☐ B-2579	Boeing 737-33A	25505/2342	ex N402AW	Blue Flowers c/s		wfs
☐ B-2989	Boeing 737-46Q	28758/2939				>CXH
☐ B-3000	Boeing 737-36QSF	29326/3020	ex N932HA			>YZR

HAINAN ASIA PACIFIC GENERAL AVIATION

☐ B-9617	Cessna 208B Caravan I	208B2362	ex N95399	

HEBEI AIRLINES (NS/HBH) Shenyang

☐ B-3040	Embraer ERJ-145LR	145317	ex PT-SMI	wfs
☐ B-3041	Embraer ERJ-145LR	145349	ex PT-SNP	wfs
☐ B-3042	Embraer ERJ-145LR	145352	ex PT-SNR	wfs
☐ B-3043	Embraer ERJ-145LR	145377	ex PT-SQB	wfs
☐ B-3045	Embraer ERJ-145LR	145470	ex PT-SVP	wfs
☐ B-3140	Embraer ERJ-190LR	19000625	ex PT-TKN	
☐ B-3187	Embraer ERJ-190LR	19000497	ex PT-TPW	
☐ B-3188	Embraer ERJ-190LR	19000502	ex PT-TRJ	
☐ B-3207	Embraer ERJ-190LR	19000561	ex PT-TDQ	
☐ B-3208	Embraer ERJ-190LR	19000566	ex PT-TDV	
☐ B-1930	Boeing 737-85C/W	39335/4796	ex N5515X	
☐ B-2658	Boeing 737-75C	30512/637	ex N1786B	
☐ B-2998	Boeing 737-75C	29042/73	ex N1786B	
☐ B-5212	Boeing 737-75C	34024/1703		
☐ B-5215	Boeing 737-75C	34025/1724		
☐ B-5456	Boeing 737-85C/W	35054/2914	ex N1786B	
☐ B-5660	Boeing 737-85C/W	38397/4215	ex N1786B	<CXA
☐ B-5753	Boeing 737-85C/W	39331/4402		
☐ B-6170	Airbus A319-132	2396	ex N101LF	

HULUNBEIER AVIC GENERAL AVIATION

☐ B-9807	Cessna 208BEX Caravan I	208B5033	ex N20260	♦
☐ B-9826	Cessna 208BEX Caravan I	208B5091	ex N81576	♦
☐ B-9828	Cessna 208BEX Caravan I	208B5105	ex N8158M	♦

HEBEI AVIC GENERAL AVIATION

☐ B-0406	Cessna 208BEX Caravan I	208B5119	ex N3046L	♦

JIANGNAN UNIVERSAL AVIATION Changzhou-West Suburbs (CZX)

☐ B-3761	Harbin Y-12II	057		
☐ B-3865	AVIC II Y-11	(11)0410		
☐ B-3866	AVIC II Y-11	(11)0104		
☐ B-3867	AVIC II Y-11	(11)0206		
☐ B-3868	AVIC II Y-11	(11)0109		
☐ B-3821	Harbin Y-12 II	0032	ex JU-1019	
☐ B-3823	Harbin Y-12 II	0068	ex JU-1021	

JILIN PROVINCE GENERAL AVIATION

☐ B-3751	Harbin Y-12IV	046

JOY AIR/HAPPY AIRLINES (JR/JOY) Xian-Yanliang (SIA)

☐ B-3430	AVIC MA60	0102	
☐ B-3431	AVIC MA60	0103	
☐ B-3433	AVIC MA60	0715	
☐ B-3451	AVIC MA60	0705	
☐ B-3452	AVIC MA60	0706	
☐ B-3453	AVIC MA60	0707	
☐ B-3455	AVIC MA60	0803	dam 04Feb14
☐ B-3459	AVIC MA60	0804	
☐ B-3476	AVIC MA60	0805	
☐ B-3716	AVIC MA60	1002	
☐ B-3717	AVIC MA60	1003	
☐ B-3718	AVIC MA60	1103	♦

JUNEYAO AIRLINES Air Juneyao (HO/DKH) Shanghai-Hongqiao (SHA)

☐ B-1681	Airbus A320-214/S	6542	ex F-WWDK		♦
☐ B-1870	Airbus A320-214/S	6315	ex F-WWIC		♦
☐ B-1871	Airbus A320-214/S	6392	ex F-WWDQ		♦
☐ B-6298	Airbus A320-214	2975	ex F-WWDO		
☐ B-6311	Airbus A320-214	3027	ex F-WWBM		
☐ B-6338	Airbus A320-214	3368	ex F-WWDE		
☐ B-6340	Airbus A320-214	3234	ex F-WWBH		
☐ B-6341	Airbus A320-214	3268	ex F-WWBU		
☐ B-6381	Airbus A320-214	3485	ex F-WWIG		
☐ B-6395	Airbus A320-214	3596	ex F-WWDI		
☐ B-6396	Airbus A320-214	3605	ex F-WWDN		
☐ B-6572	Airbus A320-214	3967	ex F-WWIF		
☐ B-6602	Airbus A320-214	3984	ex F-WWBJ		
☐ B-6618	Airbus A320-214	4102	ex F-WWDO		
☐ B-6619	Airbus A320-214	4154	ex F-WWBK		
☐ B-6640	Airbus A320-214	4064	ex B-515L		
☐ B-6670	Airbus A320-214	4276	ex F-WWDU		
☐ B-6717	Airbus A320-214	4401	ex F-WWBK		
☐ B-6735	Airbus A320-214	4429	ex B-518L		
☐ B-6736	Airbus A320-214	4573	ex F-WWBT		
☐ B-6768	Airbus A320-214	4833	ex F-WWIV		
☐ B-6787	Airbus A320-214	4587	ex B-510L		
☐ B-6788	Airbus A320-214	4652	ex B-516L		
☐ B-6860	Airbus A320-214	4981	ex D-AVVN		
☐ B-6861	Airbus A320-214	4840	ex B-514L		
☐ B-6901	Airbus A320-214	5070	ex D-AUBG		
☐ B-6921	Airbus A320-214	5013	ex B-511L		
☐ B-6922	Airbus A320-214	5071	ex B-518L		
☐ B-6948	Airbus A320-214	5329	ex F-WWDI		
☐ B-6949	Airbus A320-214	5339	ex F-WWIS		
☐ B-6962	Airbus A320-214	5491	ex F-WXAJ		
☐ B-6963	Airbus A320-214	5455	ex F-WXAI		
☐ B-6965	Airbus A320-214	5226	ex B-512L		
☐ B-6966	Airbus A320-214	5131	ex B-504L		
☐ B-9978	Airbus A320-214	5737	ex F-WWIU		
☐ B-	Airbus A320-214	6765	ex		o/o♦
☐ B-	Airbus A320-214	6794	ex		o/o♦
☐ B-	Airbus A320-214	6808	ex		o/o♦
☐ B-	Airbus A320-214	6815	ex		o/o♦
☐ B-	Airbus A320-214	6843	ex		o/o♦
☐ B-	Airbus A320-214	6854	ex		o/o♦
☐ B-	Airbus A320-214	6865	ex		o/o♦
☐ B-	Airbus A320-214	6882	ex		o/o♦
☐ B-	Airbus A320-214	6906	ex		o/o♦
☐ B-1645	Airbus A321-211/S	6433	ex D-AZAV		♦
☐ B-1646	Airbus A321-211/S	6435	ex D-AZAW		o♦
☐ B-1647	Airbus A321-211/S	6477	ex D-AVZL		♦
☐ B-1808	Airbus A321-211/S	5876	ex D-AVZU		
☐ B-9957	Airbus A321-211	5674	ex D-AVZZ		
☐ B-1857	Airbus A321-211/S	6172	ex D-AVXV		♦
☐ B-1872	Airbus A321-211/S	6221	ex D-AZAX	all red	♦
☐ B-8036	Airbus A321-211/S	6627	ex D-AVXT		o/o♦
☐ B-	Airbus A321-211/S	6701	ex		o/o♦
☐ B-	Airbus A321-211/S	6855	ex		o/o♦

KUNMING AIRLINES (KY/KNA) Kunming (KMG)

☐ B-2635	Boeing 737-79K	29191/127	ex N1786B	♦
☐ B-2666	Boeing 737-78S	30169/631	ex N1786B	♦

☐ B-2668	Boeing 737-78S	30171/681	ex N1786B	♦
☐ B-2678	Boeing 737-76N	32244/895	ex N315ML	♦
☐ B-2679	Boeing 737-76N	29893/710	ex N313ML	♦
☐ B-1507	Boeing 737-87L/W	42050/5407		♦
☐ B-1926	Boeing 737-87L/W	41111/4752		
☐ B-1991	Boeing 737-87L/W	41112/5093		
☐ B-5702	Boeing 737-87L/W	39131/4265	ex N1786B	♦
☐ B-5672	Boeing 737-87L/W	39154/4146		

LIJING HELICOPTERS

☐ B-7366	Sikorsky S-92A	920193	ex N193G

LUCKY AIRLINES — Lucky Air (8L/LKE) — Dali City (DLU)

☐ B-5061	Boeing 737-76N	28583/163	ex N583HE		
☐ B-5246	Boeing 737-7Q8/W	30674/1511	ex N751AL		
☐ B-5248	Boeing 737-790/W	30626/1273	ex N629AS		
☐ B-5249	Boeing 737-790	33011/1291	ex N645AS		
☐ B-5268	Boeing 737-790/W	30662/1382	ex N648AS	Oriental Sea c/s	
☐ B-5272	Boeing 737-790/W	30663/1386	ex N649AS		
☐ B-5292	Boeing 737-7V3/W	30676/1619	ex N171LF		
☐ B-5805	Boeing 737-79P/W	39199/4449			<CHH
☐ B-5806	Boeing 737-79P/W	39200/4483			<CHH
☐ B-5810	Boeing 737-752/W	34299/1829	ex TC-JKN		
☐ B-5823	Boeing 737-74P/W	39211/4904	ex N1787B		♦
☐ B-5825	Boeing 737-74P/W	39212/4940	ex N1787B		♦
☐ B-1825	Airbus A320-214	3240	ex EI-FDK		
☐ B-5407	Boeing 737-808/W	34967/2239	ex B-KXF		
☐ B-5409	Boeing 737-808/W	34968/2265	ex B-KXG		
☐ B-5732	Boeing 737-84P/W	35076/2380	ex B-KBM		
☐ B-6198	Airbus A319-112	2617	ex D-AVYI		
☐ B-6212	Airbus A319-115	2581	ex D-AVXG		
☐ B-6221	Airbus A319-112	2746	ex D-AVYL		
☐ B-6943	Airbus A320-214	5172	ex F-WWDP		♦
☐ B-6947	Airbus A320-214	5220	ex F-WWBK		♦
☐ B-6959	Airbus A320-214	5100	ex B-501L		♦

MEIYA AIRWAYS

☐ B-9466	Cessna 208 Caravan I	20800538	ex N2047F	FP
☐ B-9469	Cessna 208 Caravan I	20800540	ex N20480	FP

9 AIR — Transjade (AQ/JYH) — Guangzhou (CAN)

☐ B-1715	Boeing 737-8GP/W	39819/4968	ex N746DB	♦
☐ B-1716	Boeing 737-8GP/W	39829/5202	ex N387DC	♦
☐ B-1791	Boeing 737-8GP/W	39820/5016	ex N748DB	♦
☐ B-	Boeing 737-86N/W	38041/4516	ex N863TM	o/o♦
☐ B-	Boeing 737-86N/W	41259/4448	ex N864TM	o/o♦

OKAY AIRWAYS — Okayjet (BK/OKA) — Tianjin (TSN)

☐ B-3433	AVIC MA60	0715		
☐ B-3440	AVIC MA60	0714		
☐ B-3705	AVIC MA60	0902		
☐ B-3706	AVIC MA60	0911		
☐ B-3709	AVIC MA60	0509		
☐ B-3710	AVIC MA60	0510	ex B-895L	
☐ B-3711	AVIC MA60	0809		
☐ B-3712	AVIC MA60	0913		
☐ B-3722	AVIC MA60	1004		
☐ B-3713	AVIC MA60	0914		
☐ B-3714	AVIC MA60	0915		
☐ B-3722	AVIC MA60	1004		
☐ B-3723	AVIC MA60	1005		
☐ B-3725	AVIC MA60	1010		♦
☐ B-1732	Boeing 737-86N/W	41255/5161		♦
☐ B-1962	Boeing 737-86N/W	41248/4863	ex N1786B	♦
☐ B-1963	Boeing 737-86N/W	41249/4905		
☐ B-5367	Boeing 737-8Q8/W	30733/2452	ex N1786B	
☐ B-5562	Boeing 737-8HO/W	37934/3491		
☐ B-5571	Boeing 737-86N/W	35643/2884	ex N546MS	
☐ B-5573	Boeing 737-8HO/W	37932/3498		
☐ B-5575	Boeing 737-8AS/W	33554/1418	ex N598MS	
☐ B-5577	Boeing 737-8AS/W	33557/1438	ex N594MS	
☐ B-5578	Boeing 737-8AS/W	33560/1447	ex N328MS	
☐ B-5841	Boeing 737-8Q8/W	41789/4532		

☐ B-5842	Boeing 737-86N/W	41262/4624		
☐ B-5843	Boeing 737-86N/W	38042/4565	ex N1796B	
☐ B-1521	Boeing 737-9KFER/W	41118/5412		o/o♦
☐ B-1739	Boeing 737-9KFER/W	41114/5223	ex N1786B	♦
☐ B-2117	Boeing 737-3Q8SF	24961/2133	ex N141LF	
☐ B-4071	Shaanxi Y-8F-100			
☐ B-4072	Shaanxi Y-8F-100			
☐ B-	Boeing 737-9KFER/W	41119/		o/o♦

QINGDAO AIRLINES (QW/QDA) Qingdao Liuting Intl (TAO)

☐ B-1617	Airbus A320-214/S	6259	ex F-WWDV	♦
☐ B-1648	Airbus A320-214/S	6413	ex F-WWDN	♦
☐ B-1649	Airbus A320-214/S	6547	ex F-WWDQ	♦
☐ B-1693	Airbus A320-214/S	6608	ex F-WWBF	o/o♦
☐ B-9955	Airbus A320-214/S	6061	ex D-AXAJ	
☐ B-9956	Airbus A320-214/S	6102	ex D-AXAQ	
☐ B-	Airbus A320-214	6681	ex	o/o♦
☐ B-	Airbus A320-232	6785	ex	o/o♦
☐ B-	Airbus A320-214	6874	ex	o/o♦

QINGHAI DRAGON GENERAL AVIATION

☐ B-3767	Harbin Y-12E	025		♦

RAINBOW JET Cai Hong (RBW) Jinan (TNA)

☐ B-3630	Cessna 208B Caravan I	208B0883	ex N12285	
☐ B-3631	Cessna 208 Caravan I	20800333	ex N1228V	FP
☐ B-3632	Cessna 208 Caravan I	20800332	ex N1284F	FP
☐ B-3636	Cessna 208 Caravan I	20800338	ex N1321L	FP
☐ B-3639	Cessna 208 Caravan I	20800354	ex N5263U	FP

RUILI AIRLINES (DR/RLH) Kunming-Changshui

☐ B-1960	Boeing 737-86J/W	37786/4732	ex N377AB	
☐ B-5811	Boeing 737-76J/W	36873/3496	ex N873RL	
☐ B-5812	Boeing 737-76J/W	36874/3488	ex N874RL	
☐ B-5829	Boeing 737-7ME/W	60460/5173		♦
☐ B-5830	Boeing 737-7ME/W	60461/5343		♦

SF AIRLINES (O3/CSS) Shenzhen (SZX)

☐ B-2598	Boeing 737-3J6SF	27128/2493		
☐ B-2630	Boeing 737-36ESF	26317/2719	ex N151LF	♦
☐ B-2877	Boeing 737-33VSF	29331/3062	ex G-EZYG	
☐ B-2924	Boeing 737-31BSF	27287/2575		♦
☐ B-2941	Boeing 737-31BSF	27344/2622		
☐ B-2951	Boeing 737-3Z0SF	27373/2658		
☐ B-2817	Boeing 757-21BPCF	25258	ex N852AG	
☐ B-2826	Boeing 757-2Y0SF	26155/495		♦
☐ B-2828	Boeing 757-25CPCF	25899/565		
☐ B-2829	Boeing 757-25CPCF	25900/574		
☐ B-2832	Boeing 757-2Z0PCF	25887/554		
☐ B-2839	Boeing 757-2Z0PCF	27269/615		
☐ B-2840	Boeing 757-2Z0SF	27270/622		
☐ B-2844	Boeing 757-2Z0SF	27511/669		♦
☐ B-2845	Boeing 757-2Z0SF	27512/674		
☐ B-2899	Boeing 757-21BSF	24401/232	ex N401AN	
☐ B-	Boeing 757-2G5	26278/671	ex N167CR	o/o♦
☐ B-	Boeing 757-28A	27621/738	ex N166CR	o/o♦
☐ B-	Boeing 757-25F	30757/928	ex G-JMCD	o/o♦
☐ B-	Boeing 757-25F	30758/932	ex G-JMCE	o/o♦
☐ B-2017	Boeing 737-4K5SF	27102/2394	ex N197SF	
☐ B-2506	Boeing 737-429SF	25226/2104	ex N196SF	
☐ B-2883	Boeing 737-4KFSF	27830/2670	ex N198SF	
☐ B-	Boeing 767-381ERSF	32972/877	ex JA603A	♦

SHAN XI AIRLINES Shanxi (CXI) Taiyuan-Wusu (TYN)

☐ B-3701	AVIC I Y7-100C	12705		[TYN]
☐ B-3702	AVIC I Y7-100C	12707		[TYN]
☐ B-3703	AVIC I Y7-100C	12708		[TYN]

SHANDONG AIRLINES Shandong (SC/CDG) Jinan (TNA)

☐ B-1506	Boeing 737-85N/W	41623/5376		♦
☐ B-1508	Boeing 737-85N/W	41624/5403		♦

☐ B-1730	Boeing 737-89L/W	41100/5205		
☐ B-1731	Boeing 737-85N/W	41619/5139	ex N1787B	◆
☐ B-1743	Boeing 737-85N/W	41620/5256		◆
☐ B-1745	Boeing 737-85N/W	41621/5239		◆
☐ B-1746	Boeing 737-85N/W	41622/5266		◆
☐ B-1931	Boeing 737-85N/W	39935/4789		
☐ B-1932	Boeing 737-85N/W	39937/4823	ex N1786B	
☐ B-1982	Boeing 737-85N/W	41615/5003		◆
☐ B-1983	Boeing 737-85N/W	41616/4980		◆
☐ B-1985	Boeing 737-85N/W	41617/5015		◆
☐ B-1986	Boeing 737-85N/W	41618/5082		◆
☐ B-1987	Boeing 737-89L/W	41096/4994		◆
☐ B-1988	Boeing 737-89L/W	41097/5087		◆
☐ B-5111	Boeing 737-85N/W	33660/1752	ex N1786B	
☐ B-5117	Boeing 737-85N/W	33661/1770		
☐ B-5118	Boeing 737-85N/W	33664/1726		
☐ B-5119	Boeing 737-85N/W	33665/1775	ex N1781B	
☐ B-5321	Boeing 737-8AL/W	35073/2197		
☐ B-5331	Boeing 737-8AL/W	35075/2287		
☐ B-5332	Boeing 737-8FH/W	35095/2295		
☐ B-5333	Boeing 737-8FH/W	35096/2336	ex N1782B	
☐ B-5335	Boeing 737-8FH/W	35097/2345	ex N1787B	
☐ B-5336	Boeing 737-8FH/W	35098/2361		
☐ B-5347	Boeing 737-85N/W	36190/2429		
☐ B-5348	Boeing 737-85N/W	36191/2453	ex N1786B	
☐ B-5349	Boeing 737-85N/W	36192/2642		
☐ B-5350	Boeing 737-85N/W	36193/2669	ex N1786B	
☐ B-5351	Boeing 737-85N/W	36194/2684		
☐ B-5352	Boeing 737-85N/W	36195/2823		
☐ B-5450	Boeing 737-85N/W	36773/2874	ex N1786B	
☐ B-5451	Boeing 737-85N/W	36776/2998		
☐ B-5452	Boeing 737-85N/W	36777/3045	ex N1796B	
☐ B-5453	Boeing 737-85N/W	36778/3277		
☐ B-5490	Boeing 737-85P/W	35493/3594		
☐ B-5491	Boeing 737-85P/W	36584/3626		
☐ B-5513	Boeing 737-86N/W	36546/3293	ex N1784B	
☐ B-5526	Boeing 737-8FZ/W	31717/3237	ex N1796B	
☐ B-5531	Boeing 737-8FZ/W	29659/3280	ex N1787B	
☐ B-5536	Boeing 737-8AL/W	37424/3342	ex N1786B	
☐ B-5537	Boeing 737-8AL/W	37954/3359		
☐ B-5541	Boeing 737-85N/W	40882/3368	ex N1789B	
☐ B-5542	Boeing 737-85N/W	40883/3383	ex N1786B	
☐ B-5543	Boeing 737-86N/W	39392/3447	ex N1786B	
☐ B-5560	Boeing 737-86N/W	38013/3560		
☐ B-5561	Boeing 737-86N/W	38016/3589		
☐ B-5590	Boeing 737-85N/W	39128/3708		
☐ B-5591	Boeing 737-8HX/W	38098/3711		
☐ B-5592	Boeing 737-8HX/W	38099/3757		
☐ B-5593	Boeing 737-85N/W	39115/3742		
☐ B-5626	Boeing 737-8HX/W	38103/3903		
☐ B-5627	Boeing 737-85N/W	38637/3890		
☐ B-5628	Boeing 737-85N/W	39125/3934		
☐ B-5629	Boeing 737-85N/W	38638/3957		
☐ B-5648	Boeing 737-85N/W	38639/4028		
☐ B-5649	Boeing 737-85N/W	38640/4061		
☐ B-5650	Boeing 737-85N/W	38641/4102		
☐ B-5651	Boeing 737-85N/W	38642/4145	ex N6046P	
☐ B-5652	Boeing 737-85N/W	39126/4271	ex N1796B	
☐ B-5723	Boeing 737-8FZ/W	39329/4311		
☐ B-5725	Boeing 737-85N/W	39330/4351		
☐ B-5726	Boeing 737-85N/W	38883/4372		
☐ B-5727	Boeing 737-85N/W	39110/4406		
☐ B-5728	Boeing 737-89L/W	40020/4466		
☐ B-5755	Boeing 737-89L/W	40043/4504		
☐ B-5757	Boeing 737-89L/W	40039/4542		
☐ B-5758	Boeing 737-89L/W	40044/4581		
☐ B-5781	Boeing 737-85N/W	39332/4491		
☐ B-5782	Boeing 737-85N/W	39111/4486		
☐ B-5783	Boeing 737-85N/W	39112/4522		
☐ B-5785	Boeing 737-85N/W	39113/4569		
☐ B-5786	Boeing 737-85N/W	39127/4556		
☐ B-5787	Boeing 737-85N/W	39114/4660	ex N5573B	Expo 2014 c/s
☐ B-5856	Boeing 737-89L/W	40040/4712		
☐ B-3005	Canadair CRJ-200LR	7435	ex C-FMKW	
☐ B-3006	Canadair CRJ-200LR	7443	ex C-FMLV	
☐ B-3007	Canadair CRJ-200LR	7498	ex C-FMLF	
☐ B-3008	Canadair CRJ-200LR	7512	ex B-604L	
☐ B-3009	Canadair CRJ-200LR	7522	ex C-FMMY	
☐ B-3079	Canadair CRJ-701ER	10118		
☐ B-3080	Canadair CRJ-701ER	10120		
☐ B-5066	Boeing 737-36Q	28761/3011	ex N286CH	

☐ B-5205	Boeing 737-75N/W	33654/1790	
☐ B-5206	Boeing 737-75N/W	33666/1742	ex N1779B
☐ B-5207	Boeing 737-75N/W	33663/1838	ex N1787B

SHANDONG GENERAL AVIATION

| ☐ B-9811 | Pacific Aerospace 750XL | 193 | ex ZK-KNL | ♦ |
| ☐ B-9817 | Pacific Aerospace 750XL | 195 | ex ZK-KNN | ♦ |

SHANGHAI AIRLINES — Shanghai Air (FM/CSH) — Shanghai-Hongqiao (SHA)

Member of Star Alliance

☐ B-6096	Airbus A330-343E	862	ex F-WWYG	
☐ B-6097	Airbus A330-343E	866	ex F-WWYL	
☐ B-6127	Airbus A330-343	781	ex F-WWYT	
☐ B-6545	Airbus A330-243	1291	ex F-WWYB	
☐ B-6546	Airbus A330-243	1303	ex F-WWYS	
☐ B-2577	Boeing 737-76D	30168/600	ex N1786B	
☐ B-2913	Boeing 737-76D	30167/550	ex N1786B	
☐ B-5260	Boeing 737-76D/W	35777/3037		
☐ B-5261	Boeing 737-76D/W	35778/3064	ex N1786B	
☐ B-5269	Boeing 737-76D/W	35779/3235		
☐ B-5801	Boeing 737-76D/W	39303/4349	ex N5573P	
☐ B-5808	Boeing 737-76D/W	39305/4597		
☐ B-5826	Boeing 737-76D/W	39313/5272	ex N1796B	♦
☐ B-5827	Boeing 737-76D/W	39315/5356		♦
☐ B-1720	Boeing 737-86D/W	41493/5135		♦
☐ B-1721	Boeing 737-86D/W	41501/5193		♦
☐ B-1740	Boeing 737-86D/W	39312/5259	ex N1786B	♦
☐ B-1741	Boeing 737-86D/W	39314/5312		♦
☐ B-1742	Boeing 737-86D/W	39316/5409		♦
☐ B-1900	Boeing 737-86D/W	39306/4707	ex N5573K	
☐ B-1901	Boeing 737-86D/W	38060/4653		
☐ B-1948	Boeing 737-86D/W	39307/4817		
☐ B-1949	Boeing 737-89P/W	39933/4743		
☐ B-1967	Boeing 737-86D/W	39309/4948		♦
☐ B-1968	Boeing 737-86D/W	39311/5039		♦
☐ B-2153	Boeing 737-8Q8	28242/942	ex N1786B	
☐ B-2167	Boeing 737-8Q8	30631/1047		
☐ B-2168	Boeing 737-8Q8	30632/1086		
☐ B-2686	Boeing 737-8Q8	28251/1200		
☐ B-2688	Boeing 737-86D/W	33471/1192	ex N60668	
☐ B-5076	Boeing 737-86N/W	32739/1434		
☐ B-5077	Boeing 737-86N/W	32742/1464		
☐ B-5130	Boeing 737-8Q8	32801/1666		
☐ B-5131	Boeing 737-8Q8	30686/1704	ex N1784B	
☐ B-5132	Boeing 737-8Q8	30685/1789	special flower c/s	
☐ B-5140	Boeing 737-8Q8	30698/1911		
☐ B-5142	Boeing 737-8Q8	30700/1942	ex N1782B	
☐ B-5145	Boeing 737-8Q8	33007/1986		
☐ B-5185	Boeing 737-8Q8/W	30715/2230		
☐ B-5315	Boeing 737-86D	35767/2316		
☐ B-5316	Boeing 737-86D	35768/2362		
☐ B-5320	Boeing 737-8Q8/W	30718/2251	ex N1786B	
☐ B-5330	Boeing 737-86N/W	35212/2277	ex N1786B	
☐ B-5368	Boeing 737-8Q8	35273/2567		
☐ B-5369	Boeing 737-8Q8/W	35281/2709		
☐ B-5370	Boeing 737-8Q8/W	35271/2551	ex N1786B	
☐ B-5393	Boeing 737-86D/W	35769/2632		
☐ B-5395	Boeing 737-86D/W	35770/2698	ex N1786B	
☐ B-5396	Boeing 737-86D/W	35771/2740	ex N1786B	
☐ B-5460	Boeing 737-86D/W	35772/3047		
☐ B-5461	Boeing 737-86D/W	35773/2939	ex N1787B	
☐ B-5523	Boeing 737-86D/W	35776/3360	ex n1796b	
☐ B-5545	Boeing 737-86N/W	36803/3376		
☐ B-5546	Boeing 737-86N/W	39391/3431	ex N1786B	
☐ B-5548	Boeing 737-86N/W	36807/3479	ex N1795B	
☐ B-5549	Boeing 737-86N/W	37888/3470	ex N1796B	
☐ B-5550	Boeing 737-86N/W	39393/3483		
☐ B-5576	Boeing 737-86N/W	38011/3531		
☐ B-5610	Boeing 737-86N/W	37906/3744	ex N1786B	
☐ B-5691	Boeing 737-86N/W	39402/4177		
☐ B-5692	Boeing 737-8SH/W	41301/4241		
☐ B-5730	Boeing 737-86D/W	39302/4313		
☐ B-5799	Boeing 737-86D/W	39304/4557		<CRK
☐ B-5831	Boeing 737-86D/W	38059/4608		
☐ B-5832	Boeing 737-86D/W	37907/4545		
☐ B-5833	Boeing 737-86D/W	37908/4586		

☐ B-2498	Boeing 767-36D	27684/849		
☐ B-2500	Boeing 767-36DER	35155/946		
☐ B-2563	Boeing 767-36D	27309/546		
☐ B-2566	Boeing 767-36DER	35156/950		
☐ B-2567	Boeing 767-36D	27685/686		
☐ B-2570	Boeing 767-36D	27941/770		
☐ B-2875	Boeing 757-26D	33966/1049	ex N1795B	wfs
☐ B-2880	Boeing 757-26D	33961/1046	ex N1795B	wfs
☐ B-3011	Canadair CRJ-200ER	7556	ex C-FMKZ	[PVG]
☐ B-3018	Canadair CRJ-200ER	7453	ex C-FMNQ	[PVG]
☐ B-3020	Canadair CRJ-200ER	7459	ex C-FMMQ	[PVG]

SHANXI GENERAL AVIATION

☐ B-9816	Cessna 208 Caravan I	20800557	ex N8158A	♦

SHENZHEN AIRLINES　　Shenzhen Air (ZH/CSZ)　　Shenzhen (SZX)

Member of Star Alliance

☐ B-6153	Airbus A319-115	2841	ex D-AVYM	
☐ B-6159	Airbus A319-112	2905	ex D-AVWQ	
☐ B-6165	Airbus A319-112	2935	ex D-AVWM	
☐ B-6196	Airbus A319-115	2672	ex D-AVYK	
☐ B-6197	Airbus A319-115	2684	ex D-AVWM	
☐ B-1683	Airbus A320-214/S	6564	ex F-WWDE	♦
☐ B-6286	Airbus A320-214	2909	ex F-WWDU	
☐ B-6296	Airbus A320-214	2973	ex F-WWDN Star Alliance c/s	
☐ B-6297	Airbus A320-214	2980	ex F-WWBP Star Alliance c/s	
☐ B-6312	Airbus A320-214	3131	ex F-WWBK	
☐ B-6313	Airbus A320-214	3132	ex F-WWBP	
☐ B-6315	Airbus A320-214	3153	ex F-WWBZ	
☐ B-6316	Airbus A320-214	3206	ex F-WWII	
☐ B-6351	Airbus A320-214	3366	ex F-WWIU	
☐ B-6352	Airbus A320-214	3383	ex F-WWDN	
☐ B-6357	Airbus A320-214	3440	ex F-WWDZ	
☐ B-6358	Airbus A320-214	3435	ex F-WWDV	
☐ B-6359	Airbus A320-214	3456	ex D-AVVA	
☐ B-6360	Airbus A320-214	3528	ex F-WWDV	
☐ B-6377	Airbus A320-214	3599	ex F-WWDK	
☐ B-6392	Airbus A320-214	3696	ex D-AVVA	
☐ B-6550	Airbus A320-214	3756	ex F-WWBX	
☐ B-6563	Airbus A320-214	3698	ex B-503L	
☐ B-6565	Airbus A320-214	3971	ex F-WWIO	
☐ B-6566	Airbus A320-214	3855	ex F-WWDK	
☐ B-6567	Airbus A320-214	3887	ex F-WWBS	
☐ B-6568	Airbus A320-214	3898	ex F-WWDN	
☐ B-6569	Airbus A320-214	3848	ex F-WWDE	
☐ B-6570	Airbus A320-214	4010	ex B-512L	
☐ B-6589	Airbus A320-214	4028	ex F-WWIA	
☐ B-6647	Airbus A320-214	4226	ex F-WWBT	
☐ B-6648	Airbus A320-214	4159	ex B-519L	
☐ B-6649	Airbus A320-214	4208	ex B-501L	
☐ B-6855	Airbus A320-214	4876	ex B-518L	
☐ B-6938	Airbus A320-214	5110	ex B-502L	
☐ B-9908	Airbus A320-214	5369	ex B-515L	
☐ B-9909	Airbus A320-214	5521	ex D-AXAN	
☐ B-9910	Airbus A320-214	5550	ex B-515L	
☐ B-9938	Airbus A320-214	5589	ex B-509L	
☐ B-9939	Airbus A320-214	5639	ex B-514L	
☐ B-9979	Airbus A320-214	5731	ex B-504L	
☐ B-9980	Airbus A320-214	5766	ex B-508L	
☐ B-	Airbus A320-214	6704	ex	o/o♦
☐ B-	Airbus A320-214	6724	ex	o/o♦
☐ B-	Airbus A320-214	6742	ex	o/o♦
☐ B-	Airbus A320-214	6878	ex	o/o♦
☐ B-	Airbus A320-214	6893	ex	o/o♦
☐ B-1601	Airbus A320-232/S	6197	ex B-503L	♦
☐ B-1602	Airbus A320-232/S	6217	ex B-511L	♦
☐ B-1841	Airbus A320-232	5986	ex B-519L	♦
☐ B-1842	Airbus A320-232	6019	ex B-502L	♦
☐ B-6571	Airbus A320-232	3935	ex F-WWDO	
☐ B-6613	Airbus A320-232	4176	ex F-WWDY	
☐ B-6615	Airbus A320-232	4214	ex F-WWIM	
☐ B-6650	Airbus A320-232	4300	ex F-WWBQ	
☐ B-6690	Airbus A320-232	4359	ex F-WWDL	
☐ B-6691	Airbus A320-232	4409	ex D-AVVE	
☐ B-6692	Airbus A320-232	4407	ex F-WWDS	
☐ B-6697	Airbus A320-232	4288	ex F-WWIS	

☐ B-6720	Airbus A320-232	4474	ex F-WWDC	
☐ B-6721	Airbus A320-232	4514	ex D-AXAF	
☐ B-6722	Airbus A320-232	4531	ex F-WWDQ	
☐ B-6740	Airbus A320-232	4435	ex B-519L	
☐ B-6749	Airbus A320-232	4633	ex F-WWDU	
☐ B-6750	Airbus A320-232	4666	ex F-WWBC	
☐ B-6780	Airbus A320-232	4726	ex D-AUBL	
☐ B-6781	Airbus A320-232	4620	ex B-513L	
☐ B-6806	Airbus A320-232	4845	ex D-AUBF	
☐ B-6807	Airbus A320-232	4897	ex D-AVVH	
☐ B-6833	Airbus A320-232	4920	ex F-WWIB	
☐ B-6835	Airbus A320-232	4986	ex D-AVVS	
☐ B-6853	Airbus A320-232	4866	ex B-517L	
☐ B-6856	Airbus A320-232	4929	ex B-504L	
☐ B-6857	Airbus A320-232	5002	ex D-AVVW	
☐ B-6935	Airbus A320-232	4977	ex B-508L	
☐ B-6937	Airbus A320-232	5082	ex B-519L	
☐ B-6939	Airbus A320-232	5176	ex B-509L	
☐ B-1710	Boeing 737-87L/W	39158/5182		♦
☐ B-1711	Boeing 737-87L/W	39159/5159		♦
☐ B-1712	Boeing 737-87L/W	39160/5199	ex N1795B	♦
☐ B-1713	Boeing 737-87L/W	39161/5213		♦
☐ B-1755	Boeing 737-87L/W	40822/5236		♦
☐ B-1756	Boeing 737-87L/W	40823/5264		♦
☐ B-1757	Boeing 737-87L/W	40824/5326	ex N1796B	♦
☐ B-1758	Boeing 737-87L/W	40825/5363		♦
☐ B-1759	Boeing 737-87L/W	40826/5425		o/o♦
☐ B-1926	Boeing 737-87L/W	41111/4752		
☐ B-1935	Boeing 737-87L/W	39140/4754	ex N5573K	
☐ B-1936	Boeing 737-87L/W	39141/4797		
☐ B-1937	Boeing 737-87L/W	37619/4804		
☐ B-1938	Boeing 737-87L/W	37618/4834		
☐ B-1939	Boeing 737-87L/W	37621/4869	ex N5573P	
☐ B-1940	Boeing 737-87L/W	37622/4909	ex N1796B	
☐ B-1941	Boeing 737-87L/W	37625/4877	ex N5515X	♦
☐ B-1972	Boeing 737-87L/W	37620/5035		♦
☐ B-1973	Boeing 737-87L/W	37624/5053		♦
☐ B-1993	Boeing 737-87L/W	37623/5010		♦
☐ B-2691	Boeing 737-8Q8	30628/808	ex N802SY	
☐ B-2692	Boeing 737-8Q8	28241/841	ex N803SY	
☐ B-5049	Boeing 737-86N	28639/772	ex N639SH	
☐ B-5050	Boeing 737-86N	28643/828	ex N643SH	
☐ B-5073	Boeing 737-8Q8/W	30680/1402		
☐ B-5075	Boeing 737-8Q8	30692/1410		
☐ B-5078	Boeing 737-8Q8	30690/1414	ex N1779B	
☐ B-5079	Boeing 737-8Q8	30693/1422		
☐ B-5186	Boeing 737-8BK	33020/2103		
☐ B-5187	Boeing 737-8BK	33828/2124		>CQN
☐ B-5317	Boeing 737-86N/W	32686/2175	ex N1781B	
☐ B-5322	Boeing 737-86N/W	32688/2218		
☐ B-5345	Boeing 737-86N/W	35215/2306	ex N1780B	
☐ B-5357	Boeing 737-8AL/W	35081/2519	ex N1787B	
☐ B-5360	Boeing 737-86J/W	30062/485	ex D-ABAW	
☐ B-5361	Boeing 737-86J/W	30063/517	ex D-ABAX	
☐ B-5362	Boeing 737-86J/W	30499/567	ex D-ABAY	
☐ B-5363	Boeing 737-86J/W	30500/593	ex D-ABAZ	
☐ B-5365	Boeing 737-86J/W	30501/619	ex D-ABAC	
☐ B-5377	Boeing 737-8AL/W	35079/2555	ex N1786B	
☐ B-5378	Boeing 737-8AL/W	35085/2563	ex N1787B	
☐ B-5379	Boeing 737-8AL/W	35087/2605	ex N1786B	
☐ B-5380	Boeing 737-87L/W	35527/2616		
☐ B-5381	Boeing 737-87L/W	35528/2631		City of Hohhot
☐ B-5400	Boeing 737-87L/W	35529/2677		
☐ B-5401	Boeing 737-87L/W	35530/2703	ex N1786B	
☐ B-5402	Boeing 737-87L/W	35531/2726	ex N1780B	
☐ B-5410	Boeing 737-8AL/W	35088/2771		
☐ B-5411	Boeing 737-87L/W	35532/2851		
☐ B-5412	Boeing 737-87L/W	35533/2900		
☐ B-5413	Boeing 737-87L/W	35535/2895	ex N1786B	
☐ B-5440	Boeing 737-87L/W	35534/3003		
☐ B-5441	Boeing 737-87L/W	35536/3019	ex N1786B	
☐ B-5606	Boeing 737-87L/W	39143/3624	ex N1787B	
☐ B-5607	Boeing 737-87L/W	39144/3643	ex N1789B	
☐ B-5608	Boeing 737-87L/W	39145/3656	ex N1796B	
☐ B-5612	Boeing 737-87L/W	39146/3698	ex N1787B	
☐ B-5613	Boeing 737-87L/W	39147/3705		
☐ B-5615	Boeing 737-87L/W	39148/3736		
☐ B-5616	Boeing 737-87L/W	39149/3755		
☐ B-5617	Boeing 737-87L/W	39150/3770		
☐ B-5618	Boeing 737-87L/W	39151/3828		
☐ B-5619	Boeing 737-87L/W	39152/3841		
☐ B-5670	Boeing 737-87L/W	39129/4029		

☐ B-5671	Boeing 737-87L/W	39153/4107		
☐ B-5672	Boeing 737-87L/W	39154/4146		>KNA
☐ B-5673	Boeing 737-87L/W	39155/4158		
☐ B-5690	Boeing 737-87L/W	39130/4175		
☐ B-5702	Boeing 737-87L/W	39131/4265		>KNA
☐ B-5736	Boeing 737-87L/W	39132/4470		
☐ B-5737	Boeing 737-87L/W	39133/4488		
☐ B-5771	Boeing 737-87L/W	39134/4550		
☐ B-5772	Boeing 737-87L/W	39135/4554		
☐ B-5773	Boeing 737-87L/W	39156/4566	ex N1786B	
☐ B-5775	Boeing 737-87L/W	39136/4612		
☐ B-5776	Boeing 737-87L/W	39157/4604	ex N5573L	
☐ B-5778	Boeing 737-87L/W	39137/4647		
☐ B-5859	Boeing 737-87L/W	39138/4695		
☐ B-5860	Boeing 737-87L/W	39139/4703		
☐ B-5102	Boeing 737-97L	33644/1750		
☐ B-5103	Boeing 737-97L	33645/1760	ex N1786B	
☐ B-5105	Boeing 737-97L	33646/1764	ex N1784B	
☐ B-5106	Boeing 737-97L	33648/1722		
☐ B-5109	Boeing 737-97L	33649/1755		
☐ B-2633	Boeing 737-79K	29190/110	ex N1786B	
☐ B-2667	Boeing 737-78S	30170/654		
☐ B-2669	Boeing 737-77L	32722/1023	ex N1786B	
☐ B-5025	Boeing 737-7BX	30741/823	ex N366ML	

SHENZHEN GRAND SEA AVIATION

☐ B-9426	Cessna 208B Caravan I	208B2202	ex N2052G

SHUANGYANG AVIATION		Shuangyang (CSY)		Anshun (AOG)
☐ B-3811	Harbin Y-12 II	0012		Combi
☐ B-3813	Harbin Y-12 II	0025		Sprayer
☐ B-3814	Harbin Y-12 II	0026		Sprayer
☐ B-3827	Harbin Y-12 II	0063	ex 9N-ACF	
☐ B-3828	Harbin Y-12 II	0071	ex 9N-ADB	
☐ B-3895	AVIC II Y-11	(11)0401		
☐ B-3896	AVIC II Y-11	(11)0402		
☐ B-3897	AVIC II Y-11	(11)0403		
☐ B-3898	AVIC II Y-11	(11)0404		

SICHUAN AIRLINES		Chuanhang (3U/CSC)		Chengdu (CTU)
☐ B-2298	Airbus A319-133	2534	ex D-AVYM	
☐ B-2299	Airbus A319-133	2597	ex D-AVXN	
☐ B-2300	Airbus A319-133	2639	ex D-AVWK	
☐ B-6043	Airbus A319-133	2313	ex D-AVYI	
☐ B-6045	Airbus A319-133	2348	ex D-AVYH	
☐ B-6054	Airbus A319-133	2510	ex D-AVWC	
☐ B-6170	Airbus A319-132	2396	ex N101LF	
☐ B-6171	Airbus A319-133	2431	ex N112CG	
☐ B-6173	Airbus A319-133	3114	ex D-AYYA	
☐ B-6175	Airbus A319-133	3116	ex D-AYYB	
☐ B-6176	Airbus A319-133	3124	ex D-AYYC	
☐ B-6185	Airbus A319-133	3680	ex D-AVYY	
☐ B-6406	Airbus A319-133	3962	ex D-AVXP	
☐ B-6410	Airbus A319-133	4018	ex D-AVYG	
☐ B-6419	Airbus A319-133	4660	ex B-517L	
☐ B-6422	Airbus A319-133	5208	ex D-AVYU	
☐ B-6433	Airbus A319-133	5286	ex D-AVYZ	
☐ B-6442	Airbus A319-133	5389	ex B-517L	
☐ B-6445	Airbus A319-133	5609	ex D-AVYP	
☐ B-6447	Airbus A319-133	5650	ex B-515L	
☐ B-6448	Airbus A319-133	5765	ex D-AVXD	
☐ B-6449	Airbus A319-133/S	5868	ex D-AVWA	
☐ B-6453	Airbus A319-133/S	5910	ex B-506L	
☐ B-6455	Airbus A319-133/S	5953	ex B-510L	♦
☐ B-1665	Airbus A320-214/S	6540	ex	o/o♦
☐ B-1881	Airbus A320-214/S	6339	ex D-AXAC	♦
☐ B-1882	Airbus A320-214/S	6369	ex D-AXAF	♦
☐ B-1883	Airbus A320-214/S	6367	ex F-WWDJ	♦
☐ B-1885	Airbus A320-214/S	6386	ex F-WWIB	♦
☐ B-1886	Airbus A320-214/S	6397	ex F-WWIN	♦
☐ B-	Airbus A320-214	6654	ex	o/o♦
☐ B-	Airbus A320-214	6677	ex	o/o♦
☐ B-	Airbus A320-214	6710	ex	o/o♦
☐ B-	Airbus A320-214	6713	ex	o/o♦
☐ B-	Airbus A320-214	6732	ex	o/o♦

☐ B-	Airbus A320-214	6847	ex		o/o♦
☐ B-	Airbus A320-214/S	6934	ex		o/o♦
☐ B-1660	Airbus A320-232/S	6402	ex B-519L		♦
☐ B-1661	Airbus A320-232/S	6421	ex B-520L		♦
☐ B-1662	Airbus A320-232/S	6486	ex B-507L		♦
☐ B-1818	Airbus A320-232/S	5964	ex B-511L		
☐ B-1819	Airbus A320-232	5896	ex B-505LL		
☐ B-1820	Airbus A320-232/S	6008	ex B-501L		♦
☐ B-1821	Airbus A320-232/S	5977	ex B-511L		♦
☐ B-1887	Airbus A320-232S	6030	ex B-503L		♦
☐ B-2341	Airbus A320-232	0551	ex F-WWBI		
☐ B-2342	Airbus A320-232	0556	ex F-WWIL		
☐ B-2373	Airbus A320-233	0919	ex F-WWIC		
☐ B-2397	Airbus A320-233	1013	ex F-WWDP		
☐ B-6049	Airbus A320-233	0902	ex (D-ANNI)		
☐ B-6321	Airbus A320-232	3210	ex F-WWIK		
☐ B-6322	Airbus A320-232	3158	ex F-WWDP		
☐ B-6323	Airbus A320-232	3167	ex F-WWIM		
☐ B-6325	Airbus A320-232	3196	ex F-WWIE		
☐ B-6347	Airbus A320-232	3386	ex F-WWDP		
☐ B-6348	Airbus A320-232	3449	ex F-WWIY		
☐ B-6388	Airbus A320-232	3591	ex B-501L		
☐ B-6621	Airbus A320-232	4068	ex F-WWBI		
☐ B-6697	Airbus A320-232	4288	ex F-WWIS		
☐ B-6700	Airbus A320-232	4326	ex F-WWIA		
☐ B-6719	Airbus A320-232	4424	ex F-WWBD		
☐ B-6732	Airbus A320-232	4378	ex B-514L		
☐ B-6770	Airbus A320-232	4642	ex F-WWBU		
☐ B-6771	Airbus A320-232	4619	ex D-AXAW		
☐ B-6772	Airbus A320-232	4525	ex B-505L		
☐ B-6778	Airbus A320-232	4707	ex F-WWBE		
☐ B-6779	Airbus A320-232	4575	ex B-509L		
☐ B-1822	Airbus A320-232/S	5937	ex F-WWIZ		
☐ B-6843	Airbus A320-232	4905	ex D-AVVJ		
☐ B-6905	Airbus A320-232	4911	ex B-502L		
☐ B-6953	Airbus A320-232	5041	ex B-515L		
☐ B-6955	Airbus A320-232	5121	ex B-503L		
☐ B-6956	Airbus A320-232	5141	ex B-505L		
☐ B-9935	Airbus A320-232/S	5646	ex F-WWIM		
☐ B-	Airbus A320-232	6635	ex		o/o♦
☐ B-1663	Airbus A321-231/S	6581	ex D-AVXH		o/o♦
☐ B-1677	Airbus A321-231/S	6475	ex D-AVZK		♦
☐ B-1823	Airbus A321-231/S	6148	ex D-AVXN		♦
☐ B-1890	Airbus A321-231/S	6303	ex D-AVZW		♦
☐ B-1891	Airbus A321-231/S	6316	ex D-AZAF		♦
☐ B-2293	Airbus A321-131	0591	ex N451LF		
☐ B-2370	Airbus A321-231	0878	ex D-AVZF		
☐ B-2371	Airbus A321-231	0915	ex D-AVZM		
☐ B-6387	Airbus A321-231	3583	ex D-AVZE		
☐ B-6551	Airbus A321-231	3730	ex D-AZAI		
☐ B-6590	Airbus A321-231	3893	ex D-AVZV		
☐ B-6598	Airbus A321-231	3996	ex D-AZAQ		
☐ B-6718	Airbus A321-231	4420	ex D-AZAF		
☐ B-6810	Airbus A321-231	4731	ex D-AVZH		
☐ B-6836	Airbus A321-231	4824	ex D-AVZR		
☐ B-6838	Airbus A321-231	4856	ex D-AVZZ		
☐ B-6839	Airbus A321-231	4830	ex D-AVZT		
☐ B-6845	Airbus A321-231	4923	ex D-AVZI		
☐ B-6899	Airbus A321-231	5233	ex D-AVZB		
☐ B-6906	Airbus A321-231	5160	ex D-AVZF		
☐ B-6920	Airbus A321-231	5197	ex D-AVZQ		
☐ B-6957	Airbus A321-231	5303	ex D-AZAN		
☐ B-6968	Airbus A321-231	5543	ex D-AVZB		
☐ B-9936	Airbus A321-231	5670	ex D-AVZY		
☐ B-9937	Airbus A321-231	5647	ex D-AVZT		
☐ B-9967	Airbus A321-231/S	5470	ex D-AZAE		
☐ B-	Airbus A321-231	6703	ex		o/o♦
☐ B-	Airbus A321-231	6945	ex		o/o♦
☐ B-5923	Airbus A330-343E	1397	ex F-WWKL		
☐ B-5929	Airbus A330-343E	1432	ex F-WWCO		
☐ B-5945	Airbus A330-343E	1528	ex F-WWYP		
☐ B-5960	Airbus A330-343E	1579	ex F-WWYZ		♦
☐ B-6517	Airbus A330-243	1138	ex F-WWYZ		
☐ B-6518	Airbus A330-243	1082	ex F-WWYZ		
☐ B-6535	Airbus A330-243	1241	ex F-WWYB		
☐ B-	Airbus A330-243	1662	ex F-WW		o/o♦

SICHUAN WEST GENERAL AVIATION

☐ B-9467	Cessna 208B Caravan I	208B2184	ex N9004G	

SICHUAN AOLIN GENERAL AVIATION — Chengdu (CTU)

☐ B-3637	Cessna 208B Caravan I	208B0919	ex N1294D	
☐ B-3640	Cessna 208B Caravan I	208B0952	ex N1132X	
☐ B-3641	Cessna 208B Caravan I	208B0953	ex N1133B	

SOUTH CHINA SEA RESCUE AVIATION

☐ B-7136	Eurocopter EC225LP	2781	ex F-WJXR	

SPRING AIRLINES — Air Spring (9C/CQH) — Shanghai-Hongqiao (SHA)

☐ B-1627	Airbus A320-214/S	6403	ex F-WWIF	♦
☐ B-1628	Airbus A320-214/S	6410	ex D-AXAN	♦
☐ B-1656	Airbus A320-214/S	6452	ex F-WWIV	♦
☐ B-1657	Airbus A320-214/S	6524	ex F-WWBX	♦
☐ B-1670	Airbus A320-214/S	6329	ex B-503L	♦
☐ B-1671	Airbus A320-214/S	6318	ex B-502L	♦
☐ B-1672	Airbus A320-214/S	6358	ex B-515L	♦
☐ B-1807	Airbus A320-214/S	5816	ex B-511L	
☐ B-1839	Airbus A320-214/S	6073	ex B-513L	♦
☐ B-1840	Airbus A320-214/S	6117	ex D-AXAV	♦
☐ B-1892	Airbus A320-214/S	6216	ex D-AVVK	♦
☐ B-1893	Airbus A320-214/S	6218	ex F-WWDQ	♦
☐ B-1895	Airbus A320-214/S	6220	ex F-WWDS	♦
☐ B-1896	Airbus A320-214/S	6231	ex F-WWIK	♦
☐ B-6301	Airbus A320-214	2939	ex F-WWIO	
☐ B-6309	Airbus A320-214	3014	ex F-WWBO	
☐ B-6310	Airbus A320-214	3023	ex F-WWBZ	
☐ B-6320	Airbus A320-214	1686	ex N686RL	
☐ B-6561	Airbus A320-214	3819	ex F-WWIO	
☐ B-6562	Airbus A320-214	3747	ex F-WWIL	
☐ B-6612	Airbus A320-214	4072	ex F-WWBM	
☐ B-6645	Airbus A320-214	4168	ex D-AVVQ	
☐ B-6646	Airbus A320-214	4093	ex B-516L	
☐ B-6667	Airbus A320-214	4244	ex F-WWDP	
☐ B-6705	Airbus A320-214	4331	ex D-AXAQ	
☐ B-6706	Airbus A320-214	4366	ex D-AXAX	
☐ B-6707	Airbus A320-214	4373	ex F-WWBO	
☐ B-6708	Airbus A320-214	4375	ex D-AVVB	
☐ B-6751	Airbus A320-214	4499	ex B-503L	
☐ B-6752	Airbus A320-214	4586	ex F-WWIP	
☐ B-6820	Airbus A320-214	4738	ex F-WWIP	
☐ B-6821	Airbus A320-214	4750	ex F-WWIV	
☐ B-6837	Airbus A320-214	4809	ex B-511L	♦
☐ B-6840	Airbus A320-214	4760	ex B-506L	
☐ B-6841	Airbus A320-214	4816	ex F-WWDX	
☐ B-6851	Airbus A320-214	4909	ex F-WWBG	
☐ B-6852	Airbus A320-214	4809	ex B-510L	
☐ B-6862	Airbus A320-214	4983	ex F-WWIH	
☐ B-6863	Airbus A320-214	4978	ex F-WWIE	
☐ B-6902	Airbus A320-214	5108	ex F-WWIV	
☐ B-6931	Airbus A320-214	5022	ex B-513L	
☐ B-6932	Airbus A320-214	5051	ex B-516L	
☐ B-6970	Airbus A320-214	5403	ex D-AVVD	
☐ B-6971	Airbus A320-214	5434	ex D-AVVN	
☐ B-6972	Airbus A320-214	5466	ex F-WWBD	
☐ B-8012	Airbus A320-214/S	6591	ex F-WWID	o/o♦
☐ B-9920	Airbus A320-214	5378	ex B-516L	
☐ B-9928	Airbus A320-214/S	5446	ex F-WWIL	
☐ B-9940	Airbus A320-214	5562	ex B-517L	
☐ B-9965	Airbus A320-214/S	5778	ex D-AXAD	
☐ B-9986	Airbus A320-214/S	5911	ex F-WWBQ	
☐ B-	Airbus A320-214	6497	ex	o/o♦
☐ B-	Airbus A320-214	6697	ex	o/o♦
☐ B-	Airbus A320-214	6721	ex	o/o♦
☐ B-	Airbus A320-214	6737	ex	o/o♦
☐ B-	Airbus A320-214	6779	ex	o/o♦
☐ B-	Airbus A320-214	6830	ex	o/o♦
☐ B-	Airbus A320-214	6857	ex	o/o♦
☐ B-	Airbus A320-214	6886	ex	o/o♦
☐ B-	Airbus A320-214	6911	ex	o/o♦

TIANJIN AIRLINES — (GS/GCR) — Tianjin (TSN)

☐ B-1659	Airbus A320-214/S	6348	ex B-514L		♦
☐ B-6865	Airbus A320-214	5006	ex F-WWDM		
☐ B-6903	Airbus A320-214	5117	ex F-WWBH		♦
☐ B-9963	Airbus A320-214	4600	ex OE-ICD	5th East	
☐ B-9983	Airbus A320-214	5799	ex D-AXAH		
☐ B-9987	Airbus A320-214	5760	ex B-507L		

☐ B-1618	Airbus A320-232/S	5835	ex F-WHUK	♦
☐ B-1619	Airbus A320-232/S	5850	ex F-WHUL	♦
☐ B-1620	Airbus A320-232/S	5853	ex F-WHUM	♦
☐ B-1658	Airbus A320-232/S	6449	ex F-WWIU	♦
☐ B-1849	Airbus A320-232/S	5894	ex F-WHUI	♦
☐ B-1850	Airbus A320-232/S	5928	ex F-WHUJ	♦
☐ B-1851	Airbus A320-232/S	5971	ex F-WXAE	♦
☐ B-6789	Airbus A320-232	4739	ex B-504L	♦
☐ B-9948	Airbus A320-232	2475	ex EI-FCF	
☐ B-9989	Airbus A320-232	2338	ex EI-FDN	
☐ B-3873	Dornier 328-310 (328JET)	3201	ex D-BDXO	[SIA]
☐ B-3892	Dornier 328-310 (328JET)	3212	ex N328LM	[TSN]
☐ B-3946	Dornier 328-310 (328JET)	3208	ex D-BDXI	[SIA]
☐ B-3947	Dornier 328-310 (328JET)	3203	ex D-BXXX	[SIA]
☐ B-3948	Dornier 328-310 (328JET)	3204	ex D-BYYY	[SIA]
☐ B-3949	Dornier 328-310 (328JET)	3198	ex N328AB	[SIA]
☐ B-3960	Dornier 328-310 (328JET)	3123	ex D-BDXJ	[TSN]
☐ B-3961	Dornier 328-310 (328JET)	3128	ex D-BDXK	[SIA]
☐ B-3962	Dornier 328-310 (328JET)	3143	ex D-BDXX	[SIA]
☐ B-3963	Dornier 328-310 (328JET)	3138	ex D-BDXT	[TSN]
☐ B-3965	Dornier 328-310 (328JET)	3140	ex D-BDXW	[SIA]
☐ B-3966	Dornier 328-310 (328JET)	3135	ex D-BDXQ	[SIA]
☐ B-3967	Dornier 328-310 (328JET)	3144	ex D-BDXB	[SIA]
☐ B-3968	Dornier 328-310 (328JET)	3148	ex D-BDXE	wfs
☐ B-3969	Dornier 328-310 (328JET)	3153	ex D-BDXN	[SIA]
☐ B-3970	Dornier 328-310 (328JET)	3154	ex D-BDXP	[SIA]
☐ B-3971	Dornier 328-310 (328JET)	3172	ex D-BDXJ	[SIA]
☐ B-3972	Dornier 328-310 (328JET)	3175	ex D-BDXK	[SIA]
☐ B-3973	Dornier 328-310 (328JET)	3158	ex D-BDXQ	[SIA]
☐ B-3975	Dornier 328-310 (328JET)	3159	ex D-BDXU	[TSN]
☐ B-3976	Dornier 328-310 (328JET)	3177	ex D-BDXY	[SIA]
☐ B-3977	Dornier 328-310 (328JET)	3182	ex D-BDXD	[SIA]
☐ B-3978	Dornier 328-310 (328JET)	3187	ex D-BDXP	[TSN]
☐ B-3979	Dornier 328-310 (328JET)	3191	ex D-BDXT	[SIA]
☐ B-3982	Dornier 328-310 (328JET)	3195	ex D-BDXJ	[SIA]
☐ B-3983	Dornier 328-310 (328JET)	3211	ex N328LM	[SIA]
☐ B-3985	Dornier 328-310 (328JET)	3215	ex D-BHUU	[SAI]
☐ B-3986	Dornier 328-310 (328JET)	3217	ex N328FQ	[SIA]
☐ B-3987	Dornier 328-310 (328JET)	3218	ex N328QR	[SIA]
☐ B-3030	Embraer ERJ-145LI	14501009	ex PT-SOX	
☐ B-3031	Embraer ERJ-145LI	14501013	ex PT-SOY	
☐ B-3032	Embraer ERJ-145LI	14501019	ex PT-SOZ	
☐ B-3033	Embraer ERJ-145LI	14501022	ex PT-SZJ	
☐ B-3035	Embraer ERJ-145LI	14500996	ex PT-SOU	
☐ B-3036	Embraer ERJ-145LI	14501000	ex PT-SOV	
☐ B-3037	Embraer ERJ-145LI	14501005	ex PT-SOW	
☐ B-3038	Embraer ERJ-145LI	14501024	ex PT-SZK	
☐ B-3039	Embraer ERJ-145LI	14500992	ex PT-SOT	
☐ B-3067	Embraer ERJ-145LI	14501036	ex PT-SZR	
☐ B-3068	Embraer ERJ-145LI	14501040	ex PT-SZS	
☐ B-3069	Embraer ERJ-145LI	14501043	ex PT-SZT	
☐ B-3081	Embraer ERJ-145LI	14501027	ex PT-SZN	
☐ B-3082	Embraer ERJ-145LI	14501030	ex PT-SZP	
☐ B-3083	Embraer ERJ-145LI	14501033	ex PT-SZQ	
☐ B-3085	Embraer ERJ-145LI	14501047	ex PT-SZU	
☐ B-3086	Embraer ERJ-145LI	14501050	ex PT-SZV	
☐ B-3087	Embraer ERJ-145LI	14501053	ex PT-SZW	
☐ B-3088	Embraer ERJ-145LI	14501056	ex PT-SZX	
☐ B-3090	Embraer ERJ-145LI	14501063	ex PT-TKK	
☐ B-3091	Embraer ERJ-145LI	14501065	ex PT-TKM	
☐ B-3092	Embraer ERJ-145LI	14501068	ex PT-XUQ	
☐ B-3093	Embraer ERJ-145LI	14501070	ex PT-TBU	
☐ B-3095	Embraer ERJ-145LI	14501073	ex PT-TBW	
☐ B-3120	Embraer ERJ-190LR	19000171	ex PT-SDG	
☐ B-3121	Embraer ERJ-190LR	19000181	ex PT-SDP	
☐ B-3123	Embraer ERJ-190LR	19000192	ex PT-SGA	
☐ B-3127	Embraer ERJ-190LR	19000207	ex PT-SGQ	
☐ B-3128	Embraer ERJ-190LR	19000229	ex PT-SIA	
☐ B-3129	Embraer ERJ-190LR	19000246	ex PT-SIR	
☐ B-3150	Embraer ERJ-190LR	19000253	ex PT-SIY	
☐ B-3151	Embraer ERJ-190LR	19000268	ex PT-TLI	
☐ B-3152	Embraer ERJ-190LR	19000274	ex PT-TLO	
☐ B-3153	Embraer ERJ-190LR	19000284	ex PT-TLY	
☐ B-3155	Embraer ERJ-190LR	19000293	ex PT-TZH	
☐ B-3156	Embraer ERJ-190LR	19000299	ex PT-TZN	
☐ B-3157	Embraer ERJ-190LR	19000306	ex PT-TZU	
☐ B-3158	Embraer ERJ-190LR	19000313	ex PT-TXB	
☐ B-3159	Embraer ERJ-190LR	19000318	ex PT-TXG	
☐ B-3160	Embraer ERJ-190LR	19000323	ex PT-TXL	
☐ B-3161	Embraer ERJ-190LR	19000328	ex PT-TXQ	

☐ B-3162	Embraer ERJ-190LR	19000331	ex PT-TXR
☐ B-3163	Embraer ERJ-190LR	19000335	ex PT-TXV
☐ B-3166	Embraer ERJ-190LR	19000348	ex PT-XQO
☐ B-3167	Embraer ERJ-190LR	19000352	ex PT-XQS
☐ B-3168	Embraer ERJ-190LR	19000355	ex PT-XQU
☐ B-3169	Embraer ERJ-190LR	19000369	ex PT-XNH
☐ B-3170	Embraer ERJ-190LR	19000371	ex PT-XNI
☐ B-3171	Embraer ERJ-190LR	19000379	ex PT-XNO
☐ B-3172	Embraer ERJ-190LR	19000385	ex PT-XNT
☐ B-3173	Embraer ERJ-190LR	19000394	ex PT-XUA
☐ B-3175	Embraer ERJ-190LR	19000405	ex PT-TYY
☐ B-3176	Embraer ERJ-190LR	19000406	ex PT-TYZ
☐ B-3177	Embraer ERJ-190LR	19000410	ex PT-TBI
☐ B-3178	Embraer ERJ-190LR	19000417	ex PT-TBO
☐ B-3180	Embraer ERJ-190LR	19000442	ex PT-TIC
☐ B-3181	Embraer ERJ-190LR	19000454	ex PT-TJY
☐ B-3182	Embraer ERJ-190LR	19000459	ex PT-TNZ
☐ B-3183	Embraer ERJ-190LR	19000472	ex PT-TOS
☐ B-3185	Embraer ERJ-190LR	19000480	ex PT-TPF
☐ B-3186	Embraer ERJ-190LR	19000489	ex PT-
☐ B-3189	Embraer ERJ-190LR	19000508	ex PT-TSE
☐ B-3190	Embraer ERJ-190LR	19000517	ex PT-TUE
☐ B-3191	Embraer ERJ-190LR	19000527	ex PT-TUP
☐ B-3192	Embraer ERJ-190LR	19000536	ex PT-TUZ
☐ B-3193	Embraer ERJ-190LR	19000574	ex PT-TFH
☐ B-3195	Embraer ERJ-190LR	19000582	ex PT-TGS
☐ B-3212	Embraer ERJ-190LR	19000567	ex PT-TDX
☐ B-3213	Embraer ERJ-190LR	19000574	ex PT-TEZ

TIBET AIRLINES (TV/TBA) Lhasa Gonggar (LXA)

☐ B-6425	Airbus A319-115	5157	ex B-507L	
☐ B-6426	Airbus A319-115	5256	ex D-AVYB	
☐ B-6436	Airbus A319-115	4766	ex D-AVYH	
☐ B-6437	Airbus A319-115	4801	ex D-AVWA	
☐ B-6438	Airbus A319-115	4846	ex D-AVWQ	
☐ B-6440	Airbus A319-115	5451	ex B-508L	
☐ B-6441	Airbus A319-115	5529	ex B-514L	
☐ B-6443	Airbus A319-115	5563	ex B-518L	
☐ B-6451	Airbus A319-115/S	5855	ex B-501L	
☐ B-6467	Airbus A319-115/S	6404	ex D-AVWW	♦
☐ B-6473	Airbus A319-115/S	6380	ex B-517L	♦
☐ B-6475	Airbus A319-115/S	6391	ex B-518L	♦
☐ B-6480	Airbus A319-115/S	6588	ex D-AVYE	o/o♦
☐ B-	Airbus A319-115	6716	ex	o/o♦
☐ B-	Airbus A320-214	6870	ex	o/o♦

UNI-TOP AIRLINES (UW/UTP)

☐ B-2317	Airbus A300B4-605RF	741	ex F-WWAY	o/o♦
☐ B-2318	Airbus A300B4-605RF	707	ex F-WWAU	o/o♦
☐ B-2319	Airbus A300B4-605RF	732	ex F-WWAT	o/o♦
☐ B-2325	Airbus A300B4-605RF	746	ex F-WWAA	o/o♦
☐ B-2326	Airbus A300B4-605RF	754	ex F-WWAY	o/o♦
☐ B-2330	Airbus A300B4-605RF	763	ex F-WWAH	o/o♦
☐ B-2448	Boeing 747-2J6BSF	23461/628	ex N60668	
☐ B-2450	Boeing 747-2J6BSF	23746/670	ex N6018N	

UNIVERSAL AIRLINES

☐ B-3101	Shaanxi Y-8F-100	100801	ex Chinese AF
☐ B-9457	Cessna 208B Caravan I	208B2224	ex N60214
☐ B-9458	Cessna 208B Caravan I	208B2233	ex N30439
☐ B-9459	Cessna 208B Caravan I	208B2235	ex N30355
☐ B-9460	Cessna 208B Caravan I	208B2237	ex N6023R

URUMQI AIRLINES (UQ/CUH) Urumqi Diwopu Intl (URC)

☐ B-2157	Boeing 737-84P/W	32600/1015	ex N1786B	♦
☐ B-2158	Boeing 737-84P/W	32601/1033		♦
☐ B-2159	Boeing 737-84P/W	32599/972	ex N1787B	♦

WUHAN HELICOPTERS GENERAL AVIATION

☐ B-7455	Eurocopter AS350B3 Ecureuil	7655
☐ B-7456	Eurocopter AS350B3 Ecureuil	7678

XIAMEN AIRLINES   Xiamen Air (MF/CXA)   Xiamen (XMN)

Member of SkyTeam

☐ B-2659	Boeing 737-75C	30513/676			
☐ B-2991	Boeing 737-75C	29085/90			
☐ B-2992	Boeing 737-75C	29086/108	ex N1786B		
☐ B-2999	Boeing 737-75C	29084/86	ex N1796B		
☐ B-5028	Boeing 737-75C	30034/1275			
☐ B-5029	Boeing 737-75C	30634/1229			
☐ B-5038	Boeing 737-7Q8	30656/1304	ex N1787B		
☐ B-5039	Boeing 737-75C	28258/1315			
☐ B-5216	Boeing 737-75C	34026/1733			
☐ B-5218	Boeing 737-75C	34027/1767	ex N1786B		
☐ B-5219	Boeing 737-75C	34028/1771			
☐ B-5277	Boeing 737-75C/W	38381/3697			
☐ B-5278	Boeing 737-75C/W	38383/3734			
☐ B-5279	Boeing 737-75C/W	38384/3721			
☐ B-5280	Boeing 737-75C/W	35385/3752			
☐ B-1706	Boeing 737-85C/W	39905/5066			♦
☐ B-1707	Boeing 737-85C/W	39906/5126			♦
☐ B-1708	Boeing 737-85C/W	39911/5075			♦
☐ B-1709	Boeing 737-85C/W	39912/5212			♦
☐ B-1749	Boeing 737-85C/W	39909/5234			♦
☐ B-1911	Boeing 737-85C/W	39907/4748			
☐ B-1912	Boeing 737-85C/W	39908/4862			
☐ B-1913	Boeing 737-85C/W	39900/4919	ex N1787B		♦
☐ B-1915	Boeing 737-85C/W	39901/4945			♦
☐ B-1969	Boeing 737-85C/W	39902/5005			♦
☐ B-1970	Boeing 737-85C/W	39903/4981			♦
☐ B-1971	Boeing 737-85C/W	39904/5034			♦
☐ B-1966	Boeing 737-85C/W	39910/5321			♦
☐ B-5151	Boeing 737-86N/W	34255/1975			
☐ B-5152	Boeing 737-86N/W	34256/1990			
☐ B-5159	Boeing 737-85C/W	35044/2018	ex N1784B	SkyTeam c/s	
☐ B-5160	Boeing 737-85C/W	35045/2050			
☐ B-5161	Boeing 737-85C/W	35046/2105			
☐ B-5162	Boeing 737-85C/W	35047/2130	ex N1787B		
☐ B-5301	Boeing 737-85C/W	35048/2194			
☐ B-5302	Boeing 737-85C/W	35049/2271			
☐ B-5303	Boeing 737-85C/W	35050/2305	ex N1780B		
☐ B-5305	Boeing 737-85C/W	35051/2364			
☐ B-5306	Boeing 737-85C/W	35052/2418	ex N1786B		
☐ B-5307	Boeing 737-85C/W	35053/2447			
☐ B-5308	Boeing 737-86N/W	32687/2229			
☐ B-5309	Boeing 737-86N/W	32689/2254			
☐ B-5318	Boeing 737-85C/W	30723/2283			
☐ B-5319	Boeing 737-8FH/W	35102/2471	ex N1796B		
☐ B-5355	Boeing 737-8FH/W	35104/2495	ex N1780B		
☐ B-5382	Boeing 737-86N/W	36540/2681			
☐ B-5383	Boeing 737-86N/W	35631/2693			
☐ B-5385	Boeing 737-86N/W	35633/2741			
☐ B-5386	Boeing 737-86N/W	35634/2732			
☐ B-5388	Boeing 737-86N/W	35635/2764			
☐ B-5389	Boeing 737-86N/W	35636/2775	ex N1786B		
☐ B-5432	Boeing 737-86N/W	35641/2852			
☐ B-5433	Boeing 737-86N/W	35642/2855	ex N1796B		
☐ B-5435	Boeing 737-86N/W	35644/2922			
☐ B-5458	Boeing 737-85C/W	35055/3016	ex N1786B		
☐ B-5459	Boeing 737-85C/W	35057/2992	ex N1796B		
☐ B-5476	Boeing 737-85C/W	35056/3091			
☐ B-5487	Boeing 737-85C/W	35058/3150	ex N1786B		
☐ B-5488	Boeing 737-85C/W	37148/3104	ex N1786B		
☐ B-5489	Boeing 737-85C/W	37149/3142	ex N1796B		
☐ B-5498	Boeing 737-85C/W	37574/3160	ex N1796B		
☐ B-5499	Boeing 737-85C/W	37575/3190	ex N1786B		
☐ B-5511	Boeing 737-85C/W	37576/3245	ex N1787B		
☐ B-5512	Boeing 737-85C/W	37577/3255			
☐ B-5528	Boeing 737-85C/W	37578/3332			
☐ B-5529	Boeing 737-85C/W	37150/3386			
☐ B-5532	Boeing 737-85C/W	37151/3397			
☐ B-5533	Boeing 737-85C/W	37152/3403			
☐ B-5535	Boeing 737-85C/W	37579/3424			
☐ B-5551	Boeing 737-84P/W	36697/3443	ex N1786B		
☐ B-5552	Boeing 737-84P/W	37425/3408			
☐ B-5563	Boeing 737-86N/W	38012/3550			
☐ B-5565	Boeing 737-86N/W	38015/3566			
☐ B-5566	Boeing 737-85C/W	37153/3571	ex N1796B		
☐ B-5595	Boeing 737-86N/W	38017/3614	ex N1786B		
☐ B-5601	Boeing 737-86N/W	36823/3712			
☐ B-5602	Boeing 737-86N/W	36824/3703			

☐ B-5603	Boeing 737-86N/W	38020/3638		
☐ B-5605	Boeing 737-86N/W	38022/3672		
☐ B-5630	Boeing 737-85C/W	38386/3897		
☐ B-5631	Boeing 737-85C/W	38387/3929		
☐ B-5632	Boeing 737-85C/W	38388/3973		
☐ B-5633	Boeing 737-85C/W	38389/3987		
☐ B-5635	Boeing 737-85C/W	38390/4012		
☐ B-5653	Boeing 737-85C/W	38391/4112		
☐ B-5655	Boeing 737-85C/W	38392/4121		
☐ B-5656	Boeing 737-85C/W	38393/4135		
☐ B-5657	Boeing 737-85C/W	38394/4153		
☐ B-5658	Boeing 737-85C/W	38395/4173		
☐ B-5659	Boeing 737-85C/W	38396/4187		
☐ B-5660	Boeing 737-85C/W	38397/4215		>HBH
☐ B-5688	Boeing 737-85C/W	41792/4688	100th Boeing c/s	
☐ B-5706	Boeing 737-85C/W	38398/4306		
☐ B-5707	Boeing 737-85C/W	38399/4375		
☐ B-5708	Boeing 737-85C/W	38403/4357		
☐ B-5750	Boeing 737-85C/W	38380/4475		
☐ B-5751	Boeing 737-85C/W	38400/4419		
☐ B-5752	Boeing 737-85C/W	38404/4461		
☐ B-5788	Boeing 737-85C/W	38382/4497		
☐ B-5789	Boeing 737-85C/W	38401/4525		
☐ B-5790	Boeing 737-85C/W	38402/4537		
☐ B 5791	Rneing 737-85C/W	39930/4555		
☐ B-5792	Boeing 737-85C/W	41790/4568		
☐ B-5845	Boeing 737-85C/W	39931/4645		
☐ B-5846	Boeing 737-85C/W	41791/4622	ex N1796B	
☐ B-5847	Boeing 737-85C/W	41793/4709	ex N5573L	
☐ B-2848	Boeing 757-25C	27513/685		
☐ B-2849	Boeing 757-25C	27517/698		
☐ B-2862	Boeing 757-25C	34008/1047		
☐ B-2866	Boeing 757-25C	34009/1048		
☐ B-2868	Boeing 757-25C	32941/993		
☐ B-2869	Boeing 757-25C	32942/1009		
☐ B-2760	Boeing 787-8	41540/270		♦
☐ B-2761	Boeing 787-8	41541/282		♦
☐ B-2762	Boeing 787-8	41542/304		o/o♦
☐ B-2768	Boeing 787-8	41538/201		♦
☐ B-2769	Boeing 787-8	41539/227		♦
☐ B-	Boeing 787-8	41543/343		o/o♦

XINJIANG GENERAL AVIATION (XTH) Shihezi

☐ B-3869	AVIC II Y-11	(11)0501	
☐ B-3870	AVIC II Y-11	(11)0502	
☐ B-3885	AVIC II Y-11	(11)0301	
☐ B-3887	AVIC II Y-11	(11)0303	
☐ B-3888	AVIC II Y-11	(11)0304	
☐ B-3890	AVIC II Y-11	(11)0306	
☐ B-3891	AVIC II Y-11	(11)0307	
☐ B-3894	AVIC II Y-11	(11)0310	
☐ B-3768	Harbin Y-12 IV	062	♦
☐ B-3815	Harbin Y-12 II	0023	Geological survey
☐ B-3817	Harbin Y-12 II	0029	Photographic survey
☐ B-3818	Harbin Y-12 II	0030	Photographic survey
☐ B-3847	Harbin Y-12 IV	045	
☐ B-3849	Harbin Y-12 IV	036	
☐ B-3850	Harbin Y-12 IV	007	
☐ B-9055	Quest Kodiak 100	100-0102	ex N102KQ	♦

YANGTZE RIVER EXPRESS Yangtze River (Y8/YZR) Shanghai-Hongqiao (SHA)

☐ B-2112	Boeing 737-36NSF	28599/3115	ex EI-DRS	
☐ B-2113	Boeing 737-36NSF	28602/3118	ex EI-DRY	
☐ B-2115	Boeing 737-36NSF	28606/3124	ex EI-DRZ	♦
☐ B-2119	Boeing 737-332SF	25998/2510	ex B-LHO	♦
☐ B-2578	Boeing 737-33AF	25603/2333	ex N401AW special flower c/s	
☐ B-2885	Boeing 737-39KSF	27274/2559	ex B-LHN	
☐ B-2908	Boeing 737-341SF	26854/2303	ex PP-VPC	
☐ B-2942	Boeing 737-332SF	25997/2506	ex N304DE	
☐ B-2945	Boeing 737-39KSF	27362/2639		
☐ B-2963	Boeing 737-3Q8SF	26325/2772		
☐ B-3000	Boeing 737-36QSF	29326/3020	ex N932HA	<CHH
☐ B-5053	Boeing 737-322SF	24378/1704	ex N357UA	
☐ B-5055	Boeing 737-330QC	24283/1677	ex N283A	
☐ B-5056	Boeing 737-330QC	23836/1508	ex N836Y	
☐ B-5057	Boeing 737-330QC	23837/1514	ex N837Y	

☐ B-5058	Boeing 737-330QC	23835/1465	ex N835A	
☐ B-5059	Boeing 737-322SF	24362/1696	ex N356UA	
☐ B-2432	Boeing 747-481SF	28283/1142	ex N200FQ	
☐ B-2435	Boeing 747-481SF	28282/1133	ex N483YR	
☐ B-2437	Boeing 747-481F	25207/870	ex N599MS	
☐ B-2501	Boeing 737-44PF	29914/3067	ex N1786B	
☐ B-2576	Boeing 737-44PF	29915/3106	ex N1786B	♦
☐ B-2993	Boeing 737-46QSF	28759/2981		

YING'AN AIRLINES

| ☐ B-3832 | Harbin Y-12E | 011 | |

ZHEJIANG DONGHUA GENERAL AVIATION

| ☐ B-3763 | Harbin Y-12IV | | ♦ |

ZHEJIANG LOONG AIRLINES (GJ/CDC) Hangzhou (HGH)

☐ B-1673	Airbus A320-214/S	6600	ex F-WWBR	o/o♦
☐ B-1866	Airbus A320-214/S	6026	ex F-WWDE	
☐ B-1867	Airbus A320-214/S	6055	ex D-AXAH	♦
☐ B-1868	Airbus A320-214/S	6065	ex D-AXAK	
☐ B-1869	Airbus A320-214/S	6157	ex D-AVVA	
☐ B-	Airbus A320-214/S	6648	ex	o/o♦
☐ B-	Airbus A320-214/S	6671	ex	o/o♦
☐ B-	Airbus A320-214/S	6679	ex	o/o♦
☐ B-	Airbus A320-214/S	6714	ex	o/o♦
☐ B-2584	Boeing 737-3J6SF	25891/2385		
☐ B-2949	Boeing 737-3J6SF	27372/2650		
☐ B-2954	Boeing 737-3J6SF	27518/2768		

ZHONGFEI GENERAL AVIATION Zhongfei (CFZ) Xi'an-Yanliang (SIA)

☐ B-3820	Harbin Y-12 II	0031	
☐ B-3829	Harbin Y-12 II	0031	
☐ B-3856	Harbin Y-12 IV	040	
☐ B-3857	Harbin Y-12 IV	049	
☐ B-3858	Harbin Y-12 IV	039	
☐ B-3266	Cessna 560XLS Citation Excel	560-6176	♦
☐ B-3269	Cessna 560XLS Citation Excel	560-6177	♦

ZHONGSHAN EAGLE

| ☐ B-9327 | Cessna 208B Caravan I | 208B2196 | ex N1035Q | |

ZHOUSHAN AVIC GENERAL AVIATION

| ☐ B-0403 | Cessna 208BEX Caravan I | 208B5137 | ex N30904 | ♦ |
| ☐ B-0405 | Cessna 208BEX Caravan I | 208B5138 | ex N81609 | ♦ |

ZHUHAI GENERAL AVIATION

☐ B-3811	Harbin Y-12II	0012		
☐ B-3812	Harbin Y-12 II	0024		
☐ B-3813	Harbin Y-12 II	0025		
☐ B-9820	Cessna 208B Caravan I	208B5064	ex N564JV	♦
☐ B-9821	Cessna 208B Caravan I	208B5069	ex N569JV	♦

B-H/K/L CHINA - HONG KONG

AIR HONG KONG Air Hong Kong (LD/AHK) Hong Kong (HKG)

☐ B-LDA	Airbus A300F4-605R	855	ex F-WWAN	
☐ B-LDB	Airbus A300F4-605R	856	ex F-WWAP	
☐ B-LDC	Airbus A300F4-605R	857	ex F-WWAQ	
☐ B-LDD	Airbus A300F4-605R	858	ex F-WWAR	
☐ B-LDE	Airbus A300F4-605R	859	ex F-WWAS	
☐ B-LDF	Airbus A300F4-605R	860	ex F-WWAT	
☐ B-LDG	Airbus A300F4-605R	870	ex F-WWAJ	
☐ B-LDH	Airbus A300F4-605R	871	ex F-WWAK	
☐ B-LDM	Airbus A300B4-622RF	683	exEI-OZK	♦
☐ B-LDN	Airbus A300B4-622RF	770	ex EI-OZJ	<ABR♦
☐ B-HOU	Boeing 747-467BCF	24925/834	ex VR-HOU	
☐ B-HUR	Boeing 747-444BCF	24976/827	ex ZS-SAV	
☐ B-HUS	Boeing 747-444BCF	25152/861	ex ZS-SAW	

CATHAY PACIFIC AIRWAYS	**Cathay (CX/CPA)**		**Hong Kong (HKG)**

Member of oneWorld

☐ B-HLD	Airbus A330-342	102	ex VR-HLD	
☐ B-HLF	Airbus A330-342	113	ex VR-HLF	
☐ B-HLH	Airbus A330-342	121	ex VR-HLH	
☐ B-HLJ	Airbus A330-342	012	ex VR-HLJ	
☐ B-HLM	Airbus A330-343X	386	ex F-WWYT	
☐ B-HLN	Airbus A330-343X	389	ex F-WWYV	
☐ B-HLO	Airbus A330-343X	393	ex F-WWYY	
☐ B-HLP	Airbus A330-343X	418	ex F-WWKV	
☐ B-HLQ	Airbus A330-343X	420	ex F-WWYB	
☐ B-HLR	Airbus A330-343X	421	ex F-WWYC	
☐ B-HLS	Airbus A330-343X	423	ex F-WWYD	
☐ B-HLT	Airbus A330-343X	439	ex F-WWYJ	
☐ B-HLU	Airbus A330-343X	539	ex F-WWYG	
☐ B-HLV	Airbus A330-343X	548	ex F-WWYI	
☐ B-HLW	Airbus A330-343X	565	ex F-WWYR	
☐ B-LAC	Airbus A330-342	679	ex F-WWYC	
☐ B-LAD	Airbus A330-342	776	ex F-WWKI	Progress Hong Kong c/s
☐ B-LAE	Airbus A330-342	850	ex F-WWKQ	
☐ B-LAF	Airbus A330-342	855	ex F-WWYC	
☐ B-LAG	Airbus A330-342	895	ex F-WWYV	
☐ B-LAH	Airbus A330-342	915	ex F-WWYN	
☐ B-LAI	Airbus A330-342	959	ex F-WWYE	
☐ B-LAJ	Airbus A330-343E	1163	ex F-WWKR	
☐ B-LAK	Airbus A330-343E	1196	ex F-WWYD	
☐ B-LAL	Airbus A330-343E	1222	ex F-WWYC	
☐ B-LAM	Airbus A330-343E	1239	ex F-WWKL	
☐ B-LAN	Airbus A330-343E	1285	ex F-WWYE	
☐ B-LAO	Airbus A330-343E	1317	ex F-WWKR	
☐ B-LAP	Airbus A330-343E	1343	ex F-WWCH	
☐ B-LAQ	Airbus A330-343E	1349	ex F-WWCO	
☐ B-LAR	Airbus A330-343E	1362	ex F-WWKG	
☐ B-LAX	Airbus A330-343E	1366	ex F-WWKO	
☐ B-LAZ	Airbus A330-343E	1387	ex F-WWYS	
☐ B-LBA	Airbus A330-343E	1409	ex F-WWTV	
☐ B-LBB	Airbus A330-343E	1436	ex F-WWCV	1,000th A330
☐ B-LBC	Airbus A330-343E	1443	ex F-WWKN	
☐ B-LBD	Airbus A330-343E	1503	ex F-WWTY	
☐ B-LBE	Airbus A330-343E	1523	ex F-WWKZ	
☐ B-LBF	Airbus A330-343E	1545	ex F-WWCV	
☐ B-LBG	Airbus A330-343E	1557	ex F-WWYL	♦
☐ B-LBH	Airbus A330-343E	1567	ex F-WW	♦
☐ B-LBI	Airbus A330-343E	1598	ex F-WWKI	♦
☐ B-LBJ	Airbus A330-343E	1618	ex F-WWYA	♦
☐ B-LBK	Airbus A330-343E	1621	ex F-WWKN	♦
☐ B-HXA	Airbus A340-313X	136	ex VR-HXA	
☐ B-HXC	Airbus A340-313X	142	ex VR-HXC	
☐ B-HXD	Airbus A340-313X	147	ex VR-HXD	
☐ B-HXE	Airbus A340-313X	157	ex VR-HXE	
☐ B-HXF	Airbus A340-313X	160	ex VR-HXF	
☐ B-HXG	Airbus A340-313X	208	ex F-WWJC	
☐ B-HXH	Airbus A340-313X	218	ex F-WWJT	
☐ B-HXI	Airbus A340-313X	220	ex F-WWJO	
☐ B-HXJ	Airbus A340-313X	227	ex F-WWJL	
☐ B-HXK	Airbus A340-313X	228	ex F-WWJI	
☐ B-HXM	Airbus A340-313X	123	ex 9V-SJA	[XMN]
☐ B-HKT	Boeing 747-412	27132/955	ex 4X-ELS	
☐ B-HKU	Boeing 747-412	27069/1010	ex 9V-SMV	
☐ B-HKX	Boeing 747-412BCF	26557/1101	ex 9V-SPL	[MZJ]
☐ B-HUI	Boeing 747-467	27230/1033	ex VR-HUI	
☐ B-HUJ	Boeing 747-467	27595/1061	ex VR-HUJ	
☐ B-HUL	Boeing 747-467F	30804/1255		
☐ B-HUO	Boeing 747-467F	32571/1271	ex B-HUM	
☐ B-HUP	Boeing 747-467F	30805/1282	ex (B-HUN)	
☐ B-HUQ	Boeing 747-467F	34150/1356		[MZJ]
☐ B-LIA	Boeing 747-467ERF	37299/1404		
☐ B-LIB	Boeing 747-467ERF	36867/1409	ex N5014K	
☐ B-LIC	Boeing 747-467ERF	36868/1413	ex N5014K	
☐ B-LID	Boeing 747-467ERF	36869/1414		
☐ B-LIE	Boeing 747-467ERF	36870/1415	ex N5022E	
☐ B-LIF	Boeing 747-467ERF	36871/1417		
☐ B-LJA	Boeing 747-867F	39238/1427		Hong Kong Trader c/s
☐ B-LJB	Boeing 747-867F	39239/1428		
☐ B-LJC	Boeing 747-867F	39240/1433		
☐ B-LJD	Boeing 747-867F	39241/1438		
☐ B-LJE	Boeing 747-867F	39242/1441	ex N1785B	

☐	B-LJF	Boeing 747-867F	39243/1447		
☐	B-LJG	Boeing 747-867F	39244/1450		
☐	B-LJH	Boeing 747-867F	39245/1457		
☐	B-LJI	Boeing 747-867F	39247/1460		
☐	B-LJJ	Boeing 747-867F	39246/1464		
☐	B-LJK	Boeing 747-867F	43394/1483		
☐	B-LJL	Boeing 747-867F	43536/1484		
☐	B-LJM	Boeing 747-867F	43825/1486		
☐	B-HNA	Boeing 777-267	27265/14	ex VR-HNA	
☐	B-HNB	Boeing 777-267	27266/18	ex VR-HNB	
☐	B-HNC	Boeing 777-267	27263/28	ex VR-HNC	
☐	B-HND	Boeing 777-267	27264/31	ex VR-HND	
☐	B-HNL	Boeing 777-267	27116/1	ex N7771	
☐	B-HNE	Boeing 777-367	27507/94	ex N5014K	
☐	B-HNF	Boeing 777-367	27506/102	ex N5016R	
☐	B-HNG	Boeing 777-367	27505/118	ex N5017V	
☐	B-HNH	Boeing 777-367	27504/136		
☐	B-HNI	Boeing 777-367	27508/204		
☐	B-HNJ	Boeing 777-367	27509/224		
☐	B-HNK	Boeing 777-367	27510/248		
☐	B-HNM	Boeing 777-367	33702/456		
☐	B-HNN	Boeing 777-367	33703/462		
☐	B-HNO	Boeing 777-367	33704/470		
☐	B-HNP	Boeing 777-367	34243/513		
☐	B-HNQ	Boeing 777-367	34244/567	ex N6009F	
☐	B-KPA	Boeing 777-367ER	36154/661	ex N1788B	
☐	B-KPB	Boeing 777-367ER	35299/670		Spirit of Hong Kong c/s
☐	B-KPC	Boeing 777-367ER	34432/674		
☐	B-KPD	Boeing 777-367ER	36155/680		
☐	B-KPE	Boeing 777-367ER	36156/685		
☐	B-KPF	Boeing 777-367ER	36832/692		
☐	B-KPG	Boeing 777-367ER	35300/700		
☐	B-KPH	Boeing 777-367ER	35301/720	ex N50281	
☐	B-KPI	Boeing 777-367ER	36833/746		
☐	B-KPJ	Boeing 777-367ER	36157/754	ex N5016R	
☐	B-KPK	Boeing 777-367ER	36158/783	ex N5023Q	
☐	B-KPL	Boeing 777-367ER	36161/818		
☐	B-KPM	Boeing 777-367ER	36159/835		
☐	B-KPN	Boeing 777-367ER	36165/839		
☐	B-KPO	Boeing 777-367ER	36160/843	ex N5022E	
☐	B-KPP	Boeing 777-367ER	36164/845	ex N1785B	
☐	B-KPQ	Boeing 777-367ER	36162/860	ex N5016R	
☐	B-KPR	Boeing 777-367ER	36163/877		
☐	B-KPS	Boeing 777-367ER	39232/920		
☐	B-KPT	Boeing 777-367ER	37896/927		
☐	B-KPU	Boeing 777-367ER	39233/934		
☐	B-KPV	Boeing 777-367ER	37901/941		
☐	B-KPW	Boeing 777-367ER	39234/950		
☐	B-KPX	Boeing 777-367ER	37897/956		
☐	B-KPY	Boeing 777-367ER	37899/991		
☐	B-KPZ	Boeing 777-367ER	37900/1003		
☐	B-KQA	Boeing 777-367ER	37898/1008		
☐	B-KQB	Boeing 777-367ER	39235/1012		
☐	B-KQC	Boeing 777-367ER	39236/1040		
☐	B-KQD	Boeing 777-367ER	39237/1077		
☐	B-KQE	Boeing 777-367ER	41432/1089		
☐	B-KQF	Boeing 777-367ER	41428/1101		
☐	B-KQG	Boeing 777-367ER	42142/1127	ex N5014K	
☐	B-KQH	Boeing 777-367ER	42143/1133		
☐	B-KQI	Boeing 777-367ER	41429/1139		
☐	B-KQJ	Boeing 777-367ER	41760/1147		
☐	B-KQK	Boeing 777-367ER	41430/1159		
☐	B-KQL	Boeing 777-367ER	41431/1164		
☐	B-KQM	Boeing 777-367ER	41433/1195		
☐	B-KQN	Boeing 777-367ER	41761/1209		♦
☐	B-KQO	Boeing 777-367ER	41757/1216		♦
☐	B-KQP	Boeing 777-367ER	41758/1224		♦
☐	B-KQQ	Boeing 777-367ER	41762/1231		♦
☐	B-KQR	Boeing 777-367ER	41759/1240		♦
☐	B-KQS	Boeing 777-367ER	42144/1246		♦
☐	B-KQT	Boeing 777-367ER	41766/1255		♦
☐	B-KQU	Boeing 777-367ER	42145/1263		♦
☐	B-KQV	Boeing 777-367ER	41765/1273		♦
☐	B-KQW	Boeing 777-367ER	41763/1282		♦
☐	B-KQX	Boeing 777-367ER	60725/1295		♦
☐	B-KQY	Boeing 777-367ER	41764/1304		o/o♦
☐	B-KQZ	Boeing 777-367ER	60723/1319		o/o♦
☐	B-	Boeing 777-367ER	60724/1333		o/o♦

DRAGONAIR		Dragon (KA/HDA)		Hong Kong (HKG)
☐ B-HSD	Airbus A320-232	0756	ex F-WWBC	
☐ B-HSE	Airbus A320-232	0784	ex F-WWDL	
☐ B-HSG	Airbus A320-232	0812	ex B-22315	
☐ B-HSI	Airbus A320-232	0930	ex F-WWIE	
☐ B-HSJ	Airbus A320-232	1253	ex F-WWIU	
☐ B-HSK	Airbus A320-232	1721	ex F-WWDF	
☐ B-HSL	Airbus A320-232	2229	ex F-WWIE	
☐ B-HSM	Airbus A320-232	2238	ex F-WWDG	
☐ B-HSN	Airbus A320-232	2428	ex F-WWBI	
☐ B-HSO	Airbus A320-232	4023	ex F-WWDN	
☐ B-HSP	Airbus A320-232	4247	ex F-WWDV	
☐ B-HSQ	Airbus A320-232	5024	ex F-WWBD	
☐ B-HSR	Airbus A320-232	5030	ex D-AXAK	
☐ B-HST	Airbus A320-232	5362	ex D-AUBS	
☐ B-HSU	Airbus A320-232	5429	ex D-AVVL	
☐ B-HTD	Airbus A321-231	0993	ex D-AVZF	
☐ B-HTE	Airbus A321-231	1024	ex D-AVZD	
☐ B-HTF	Airbus A321-231	0633	ex G-OZBC	
☐ B-HTG	Airbus A321-231	1695	ex D-AVZA	
☐ B-HTH	Airbus A321-231	1984	ex D-AVZX	
☐ B-HTI	Airbus A321-231	2021	ex D-AVXJ	
☐ B-HTJ	Airbus A321-231	3369	ex A7-ADW	
☐ B-HTK	Airbus A321-231	3669	ex A7-ADZ	♦
☐ B-HLA	Airbus A330-342	071	ex VR-HLA	
☐ B-HLB	Airbus A330-342	083	ex VR-HLB	
☐ B-HLC	Airbus A330-342	099	ex VR-HLC	
☐ B-HLE	Airbus A330-342	109	ex VR-HLE	
☐ B-HLG	Airbus A330-342	118	ex VR-HLG	
☐ B-HLI	Airbus A330-342	155	ex VR-HLI	
☐ B-HLJ	Airbus A330-342	012	ex VR-HLJ	
☐ B-HLK	Airbus A330-342	017	ex VR-HLK	
☐ B-HLL	Airbus A330-342	244	ex F-WWKG	
☐ B-HWM	Airbus A330-343E	1457	ex F-WWYO	
☐ B-HYB	Airbus A330-342	106	ex VR-HYB	
☐ B-HYF	Airbus A330-342	234	ex F-WWKF	
☐ B-HYG	Airbus A330-343	405	ex F-WWKQ	
☐ B-HYI	Airbus A330-343	479	ex F-WWKU	
☐ B-HYJ	Airbus A330-343	512	ex F-WWYR	
☐ B-HYQ	Airbus A330-343	581	ex F-WWKK	
☐ B-LAA	Airbus A330-342	669	ex F-WWKS Asia's World City titles	
☐ B-LAB	Airbus A330-342	673	ex F-WWKZ Asia's World City titles	

HONGKONG AIRLINES		Bauhina (HX/CRK)		Hong Kong (HKG)
☐ B-LPB	Airbus A320-214	4970	ex F-WWID	>HKE
☐ B-LPC	Airbus A320-214	5147	ex F-WWBR	
☐ B-LPD	Airbus A320-214	5189	ex F-WWIE	
☐ B-LPE	Airbus A320-214	5260	ex F-WWDY	
☐ B-LPF	Airbus A320-214	5264	ex F-WWIA	>HKE
☐ B-LPG	Airbus A320-214	5266	ex F-WWIB	>HKE
☐ B-LPH	Airbus A320-214	5341	ex F-WWBR	>HKE
☐ B-LPI	Airbus A320-214	5416	ex D-AVVH	
☐ B-LPJ	Airbus A320-214	5514	ex F-WWDK	
☐ B-LPK	Airbus A320-214	5544	ex F-WWDV	
☐ B-LPL	Airbus A320-214/S	6003	ex D-AUBU	
☐ B-LPM	Airbus A320-214/S	6246	ex F-WWBQ	♦
☐ B-LPN	Airbus A320-214/S	6442	ex B-502L	♦
☐ B-1603	Airbus A320-214	6206	ex B-504L	>CBJ♦
☐ B-1811	Airbus A320-214	6041	ex B-504L	>CBJ♦
☐ B-9983	Airbus A320-214	5799	ex D-AXAH	>GCR
☐ B-	Airbus A320-214	6764	ex	o/o♦
☐ B-LNC	Airbus A330-223	1031	ex F-WJKJ	
☐ B-LND	Airbus A330-223	1042	ex F-WWKK	
☐ B-LNE	Airbus A330-223	1039	ex F-WJKJ	
☐ B-LNF	Airbus A330-223	1059	ex F-WJKF	
☐ B-LNG	Airbus A330-223	1054	ex F-WWYC	
☐ B-LNI	Airbus A330-223	1034	ex B-6521	
☐ B-LNJ	Airbus A330-243	1277	ex F-WWYJ	
☐ B-LNK	Airbus A330-243	1286	ex F-WWYH	
☐ B-LNL	Airbus A330-243	1322	ex F-WWTI	
☐ B-LNV	Airbus A330-243F	1175	ex B-5900	
☐ B-LNW	Airbus A330-243F	1320	ex F-WWKL	
☐ B-LNX	Airbus A330-243F	1115	ex F-WWKO	
☐ B-LNY	Airbus A330-243F	1062	ex F-WWKD	
☐ B-LNZ	Airbus A330-243F	1051	ex F-WWKU	

☐ B-5935	Airbus A330-343X	1438	ex F-WWKE	>CHH
☐ B-LNM	Airbus A330-343E	1358	ex F-WWCY	
☐ B-LNO	Airbus A330-343E	1384	ex F-WWYP	
☐ B-LNP	Airbus A330-343E	1398	ex F-WWKR	
☐ B-	Airbus A330-343E	1677	ex F-WW	o/o♦
☐ B-	Airbus A330-343E	1686	ex F-WW	o/o♦

HONG KONG EXPRESS AIRWAYS   Hong Kong Shuttle (UO/HKE)   Hong Kong (HKG)

☐ B-LCA	Airbus A320-232	2717	ex EI-FER	Sui Maai	
☐ B-LCB	Airbus A320-232	2322	ex EI-FFO	Haa Gaau	♦
☐ B-LCC	Airbus A320-232/S	6142	ex F-WWIY	Cha Siu Baau	♦
☐ B-LCD	Airbus A320-232/S	6302	ex F-WWDL	Ceon Gyun	♦
☐ B-LCE	Airbus A320-232	2299	ex EI-FGD	Chang Fun	♦
☐ B-LPB	Airbus A320-214	4970	ex F-WWID		<CRK
☐ B-LPF	Airbus A320-214	5264	ex F-WWIA		<CRK
☐ B-LPG	Airbus A320-214	5266	ex F-WWIB		<CRK
☐ B-LPH	Airbus A320-214	5341	ex F-WWBR		<CRK

SKY SHUTTLE HELICOPTERS   Heli Hong Kong (UO/HHK)   HK/Macau Heliport

☐ B-KHM	AgustaWestland AW139	31238	
☐ B-KHN	AgustaWestland AW139	31243	
☐ B-MHI	AgustaWestland AW139	31220	
☐ B-MHK	AgustaWestland AW139	31229	
☐ B-MHL	AgustaWestland AW139	31230	

B-M   CHINA - MACAU

AIR MACAU   Air Macau (NX/AMU)   Macau (MFM)

☐ B-MAF	Airbus A321-131	0620	ex CS-MAF	Acores	
☐ B-MAG	Airbus A321-131	0631	ex CS-MAG	Ilha de Coloane	
☐ B-MAJ	Airbus A321-231	0908	ex CS-MAJ	Farol da Guia	
☐ B-MAP	Airbus A321-231	1850	ex D-AVZX	Rio das Perolas	
☐ B-MAQ	Airbus A321-231	1926	ex D-AVZS	Lago Tai	
☐ B-MBA	Airbus A321-231	5459	ex D-AZAA	Synergy	
☐ B-MBB	Airbus A321-231	5523	ex D-AZAU		
☐ B-MBM	Airbus A321-231	6324	ex D-AZAI	Prosperous	Macau welcomes you c/s♦
☐ B-MCA	Airbus A321-231	6517	ex D-AZAA	Flourish	♦
☐ B-M	Airbus A321-231/S	6912	ex		o/o♦
☐ B-M	Airbus A321-231/S	6916	ex		o/o♦
☐ B-MAH	Airbus A320-232	0805	ex CS-MAH	Ilha da Madeira	
☐ B-MAK	Airbus A319-132	1758	ex D-AVYF	Rio Yangtze	
☐ B-MAL	Airbus A319-132	1790	ex D-AVYR	Rio Amarelo	
☐ B-MAN	Airbus A319-132	1912	ex D-AVWZ	Rio Huang Pu	
☐ B-MAO	Airbus A319-132	1962	ex D-AVWU	Rio Yaluzangbu	
☐ B-MAX	Airbus A320-232	0928	ex N928MD		
☐ B-MBC	Airbus A320-232	4197	ex 5B-DCG	Lotus	

B-   CHINA- TAIWAN (Republic of China)

CHINA AIRLINES   China Airlines/Dynasty (CI/CAL)   Taipei-Taoyuan/Sung Shan (TPE/TSA)

Member of SkyTeam

☐ B-18301	Airbus A330-302	602	ex F-WWYM	
☐ B-18302	Airbus A330-302	607	ex F-WWYY	
☐ B-18303	Airbus A330-302	641	ex F-WWYS	
☐ B-18305	Airbus A330-302	671	ex F-WWKN	orchid c/s
☐ B-18306	Airbus A330-302	675	ex F-WWYU	
☐ B-18307	Airbus A330-302	691	ex F-WWYL	
☐ B-18308	Airbus A330-302	699	ex F-WWKA	
☐ B-18309	Airbus A330-302	707	ex F-WWKI	
☐ B-18310	Airbus A330-302	714	ex F-WWYV	
☐ B-18311	Airbus A330-302	752	ex F-WWKZ	SkyTeam c/s
☐ B-18312	Airbus A330-302	769	ex F-WWYS	
☐ B-18315	Airbus A330-302	823	ex F-WWKS	
☐ B-18316	Airbus A330-302	838	ex F-WWYM	
☐ B-18317	Airbus A330-302	861	ex F-WWYA	
☐ B-18351	Airbus A330-302	725	ex F-WWKO	
☐ B-18352	Airbus A330-302	805	ex F-WWYG	
☐ B-18353	Airbus A330-302	920	ex F-WWYU	
☐ B-18355	Airbus A330-302	1177	ex F-WWYI	Welcome to Taiwan c/s
☐ B-18356	Airbus A330-302	1272	ex F-WWKD	
☐ B-18357	Airbus A330-302	1278	ex F-WWYK	
☐ B-18358	Airbus A330-302	1346	ex F-WWCL	
☐ B-18359	Airbus A330-302	1367	ex F-WWKP	
☐ B-18360	Airbus A330-302	1450	ex F-WWYA	

☐ B-18361	Airbus A330-302	1539	ex F-WWCP	Cloud Gate Dance Theatre c/s	♦
☐ B-18801	Airbus A340-313X	402	ex F-WWJC		[VCV]
☐ B-18802	Airbus A340-313X	406	ex F-WWJK		
☐ B-18803	Airbus A340-313X	411	ex F-WWJL		
☐ B-18805	Airbus A340-313X	415	ex F-WWJO		
☐ B-18806	Airbus A340-313X	433	ex F-WWJS		
☐ B-18807	Airbus A340-313X	541	ex F-WWJK		
☐ B-18601	Boeing 737-809/W	28402/113	ex N1787B		
☐ B-18605	Boeing 737-809/W	28404/130	ex N1784B		
☐ B-18606	Boeing 737-809/W	28405/132			
☐ B-18607	Boeing 737-809/W	29104/139			
☐ B-18608	Boeing 737-809/W	28406/141			
☐ B-18609	Boeing 737-809/W	28407/161			
☐ B-18610	Boeing 737-809/W	29105/295	ex N1786B		
☐ B-18612	Boeing 737-809/W	30173/695	ex N1785B		
☐ B-18615	Boeing 737-809/W	30174/1175	ex N6067E		
☐ B-18617	Boeing 737-809/W	29106/302	ex B-18611		
☐ B-18651	Boeing 737-8Q8/W	41786/4417			
☐ B-18652	Boeing 737-8Q8/W	41787/4455			
☐ B-18653	Boeing 737-8Q8/W	41788/4510			
☐ B-18655	Boeing 737-8MA/W	40945/4830			
☐ B-18656	Boeing 737-8MA/W	40946/4916			♦
☐ B-18657	Boeing 737-8FH/W	39943/4944			♦
☐ B-18201	Boeing 747-409	28709/1114			
☐ B-18202	Boeing 747-409	28710/1132		special Jimmy c/s	
☐ B-18203	Boeing 747-409	28711/1136			
☐ B-18205	Boeing 747-409	28712/1137			
☐ B-18206	Boeing 747-409	29030/1145		SkyTeam c/s	
☐ B-18207	Boeing 747-409	29219/1176			
☐ B-18208	Boeing 747-409	29031/1186			
☐ B-18210	Boeing 747-409	33734/1353			
☐ B-18211	Boeing 747-409	33735/1354			
☐ B-18212	Boeing 747-409	33736/1357			
☐ B-18215	Boeing 747-409	33737/1358			
☐ B-18251	Boeing 747-409	27965/1063	ex B-16801		[VCV]
☐ N168CL	Boeing 747-409	29906/1219	ex B-18209		[VCV]
☐ B-18701	Boeing 747-409F	30759/1249			
☐ B-18702	Boeing 747-409F	30760/1252			[VCV]
☐ B-18703	Boeing 747-409F	30761/1254	ex N744CL		[VCV]
☐ B-18705	Boeing 747-409F	30762/1263	ex N705CL		[VCV]
☐ B-18706	Boeing 747-409F	30763/1267			
☐ B-18707	Boeing 747-409F	30764/1269			
☐ B-18708	Boeing 747-409F	30765/1288			
☐ B-18709	Boeing 747-409F	30766/1294			
☐ B-18710	Boeing 747-409F	30767/1300			
☐ B-18711	Boeing 747-409F	30768/1314			
☐ B-18712	Boeing 747-409F	33729/1332			
☐ B-18715	Boeing 747-409F	33731/1334			
☐ B-18716	Boeing 747-409F	33732/1339			
☐ B-18717	Boeing 747-409F	30769/1346			
☐ B-18718	Boeing 747-409F	30770/1348			
☐ B-18719	Boeing 747-409F	33739/1355			
☐ B-18720	Boeing 747-409F	33733/1359			
☐ B-18721	Boeing 747-409F	33738/1362			
☐ B-18722	Boeing 747-409F	34265/1372			
☐ B-18723	Boeing 747-409F	34266/1379			
☐ B-18725	Boeing 747-409F	30771/1385			
☐ B-18001	Boeing 777-309ER	43978/1301			o/o♦
☐ B-18002	Boeing 777-309ER	43980/1307			o/o♦
☐ B-18003	Boeing 777-309ER	43977/1327			o/o♦
☐ B-18051	Boeing 777-36NER	41821/1227			♦
☐ B-18052	Boeing 777-36NER	41822/1245			♦
☐ B-18053	Boeing 777-36NER	41845/1254			♦
☐ B-18055	Boeing 777-36NER	41823/1265			♦

DAILY AIR   Taipei-Sung Shan (TSA)

☐ B-55561	Dornier 228-212	8215	ex B-12253	
☐ B-55563	Dornier 228-212	8224	ex B-12259	
☐ B-55565	Dornier 228-212	8234	ex B-11152	dam 21Dec14
☐ B-55567	Dornier 228-212	8235	ex B-11156	

EVA AIRWAYS   Eva (BR/EVA)   Taipei-Taoyuan (TPE)

Member of Star Alliance

☐ B-16201	Airbus A321-211	5354	ex D-AVZD

☐	B-16202	Airbus A321-211	5328	ex D-AZAT		
☐	B-16203	Airbus A321-211	5377	ex D-AVZH		
☐	B-16205	Airbus A321-211	5485	ex D-AZAI		
☐	B-16206	Airbus A321-211/S	5808	ex D-AVZG	Star Alliance c/s	
☐	B-16207	Airbus A321-211/S	5849	ex D-AVZM		
☐	B-16208	Airbus A321-211/S	6024	ex D-AVZI		
☐	B-16209	Airbus A321-211/S	6042	ex D-AVZP		
☐	B-16210	Airbus A321-211/S	6087	ex D-AVZZ		
☐	B-16211	Airbus A321-211/S	6179	ex D-AVXX		♦
☐	B-16212	Airbus A321-211/S	6276	ex D-AVZR		♦
☐	B-16213	Airbus A321-211/S	6312	ex D-AZAA		♦
☐	B-16215	Airbus A321-211/S	6488	ex D-AVZQ		♦
☐	B-16216	Airbus A321-211/S	6545	ex D-AZAH		♦
☐	B-16217	Airbus A321-211/S	6585	ex D-AVXI		o/o♦
☐	B-	Airbus A321-211/S	6653	ex		o/o♦
☐	B-	Airbus A321-211/S	6707	ex		o/o♦
☐	B-	Airbus A321-211/S	6747	ex		o/o♦
☐	B-16301	Airbus A330-203	530	ex F-WWYA		
☐	B-16302	Airbus A330-203	535	ex F-WWYE		
☐	B-16303	Airbus A330-203	555	ex F-WWYL		
☐	B-16305	Airbus A330-203	573	ex F-WWYP		
☐	B-16306	Airbus A330-203	587	ex F-WWKL		
☐	B-16307	Airbus A330-203	634	ex F-WWYJ		
☐	B-16308	Airbus A330-203	655	ex F-WWYT		
☐	B-16309	Airbus A330-203	661	ex F-WWYY		
☐	B-16310	Airbus A330-203	678	ex F-WWYB		
☐	B-16311	Airbus A330-203	693	ex F-WWYP	Hello Kitty c/s	
☐	B-16312	Airbus A330-203	755	ex F-WWYP		
☐	B-16331	Airbus A330-302	1254	ex F-WWYF		
☐	B-16332	Airbus A330-302	1268	ex F-WWKN		
☐	B-16333	Airbus A330-302	1274	ex F-WWKE		
☐	B-	Airbus A330-302	1684	ex F-WW		o/o♦
☐	B-	Airbus A330-302	1690	ex F-WW		o/o♦
☐	B-16401	Boeing 747-45E	27062/942			
☐	B-16403	Boeing 747-45EM	27141/976	ex N403EV		[VCV]
☐	B-16408	Boeing 747-45EM	28092/1076	ex N408EV		[SBD]
☐	B-16409	Boeing 747-45EM	28093/1077	ex N409EV		wfs
☐	B-16410	Boeing 747-45E	29061/1140			
☐	B-16411	Boeing 747-45E	29111/1151			
☐	B-16412	Boeing 747-45E	29112/1159			
☐	B-16402	Boeing 747-45EBDSF	27063/947			
☐	B-16406	Boeing 747-45EMBDSF	27898/1051	ex N406EV		
☐	B-16407	Boeing 747-45EMSF	27899/1053	ex N407EV		
☐	B-16462	Boeing 747-45EMBDSF	27173/998			
☐	B-16481	Boeing 747-45EF	30607/1251			
☐	B-16482	Boeing 747-45EF	30608/1279			
☐	B-16483	Boeing 747-45EF	30609/1309			
☐	B-16701	Boeing 777-35EER	32639/524		Star Alliance c/s	
☐	B-16702	Boeing 777-35EER	32640/531			
☐	B-16703	Boeing 777-35EER	32643/572		Hello Kitty c/s	
☐	B-16705	Boeing 777-35EER	32645/597	ex N6009F		
☐	B-16706	Boeing 777-35EER	33750/612			
☐	B-16707	Boeing 777-35EER	33751/634			
☐	B-16708	Boeing 777-35EER	33752/658			
☐	B-16709	Boeing 777-35EER	33753/683			
☐	B-16710	Boeing 777-35EER	32641/707			
☐	B-16711	Boeing 777-35EER	33754/721	ex N5028Y		
☐	B-16712	Boeing 777-35EER	33755/735			
☐	B-16713	Boeing 777-35EER	33756/758			
☐	B-16715	Boeing 777-35EER	33757/810			
☐	B-16716	Boeing 777-35EER	32642/822			
☐	B-16717	Boeing 777-35EER	32644/863	ex N559BA		
☐	B-16718	Boeing 777-35EER	43289/1189			
☐	B-16719	Boeing 777-36NER	42103/1202			♦
☐	B-16720	Boeing 777-36NER	41820/1213			♦
☐	B-16721	Boeing 777-35EER	43290/1275			♦
☐	B-16722	Boeing 777-36NER	42107/1302			o/o♦
☐	B-16723	Boeing 777-36NER	42108/1313			o/o♦
☐	B-	Boeing 777-35EER	44554/1349			o/o♦
☐	B-16108	McDonnell-Douglas MD-11F	48778/619			wfs
☐	B-16109	McDonnell-Douglas MD-11F	48779/620			[VCV]
☐	B-16110	McDonnell-Douglas MD-11F	48786/630			[VCV]
☐	B-16111	McDonnell-Douglas MD-11F	48787/631			[VCV]
☐	B-16112	McDonnell-Douglas MD-11F	48789/633	ex N90178		[SBD]
☐	B-16113	McDonnell-Douglas MD-11F	48790/634	ex N9030Q		wfs
☐	B-17917	McDonnell-Douglas MD-90-30ER	53572/2217			<UIA

□ B-17925	McDonnell-Douglas MD-90-30ER	53568/2171	ex B-16902	<UIA
□ B-17926	McDonnell-Douglas MD-90-30ER	53567/2169	ex B-15301	<UIA
□ B-55411	Airbus A318-112CJ	3886	ex B-6411	♦
□ B-77777	Airbus A318-112CJ	3363	ex 9H-AFL	opf Minth Grp
□ N888YF	Boeing 737-7BC/W (BBJ)	33036/1060	ex N110QS	VIP

FAR EASTERN AIR TRANSPORT — *Far Eastern (FE/FEA)* — *Taipei-Sung Shan (TSA)*

□ B-28007	McDonnell-Douglas MD-83	49807/1829		
□ B-28011	McDonnell-Douglas MD-83	53118/1954		
□ B-28017	McDonnell-Douglas MD-83	53166/2052		[TPE]
□ B-28021	McDonnell-Douglas MD-83	53167/2056		
□ B-28025	McDonnell-Douglas MD-83	53602/2214		
□ B-28027	McDonnell-Douglas MD-83	53603/2218		
□ B-28035	McDonnell-Douglas MD-82	53480/2127	ex B-88889	
□ B-28037	McDonnell-Douglas MD-82	53479/2124	ex B-88888	
□ B-27013	Boeing 757-27AEM	29608/835		[TPE]
□ B-27015	Boeing 757-27AEM	29609/876		[TPE]

GREAT WING AIRLINES — *Taichung*

| □ B-69832 | Britten-Norman BN-2A-26 Islander | 2039 | ex B-12232 |

MANDARIN AIRLINES — *Mandarin Air (AE/MDA)* — *Taipei-Sung Shan (TSA)*

□ B-16821	Embraer ERJ-190AR	19000087	ex PT-SNF
□ B-16822	Embraer ERJ-190AR	19000091	ex PT-SNK
□ B-16823	Embraer ERJ-190AR	19000099	ex PT-SNT
□ B-16825	Embraer ERJ-190AR	19000167	ex PT-SAZ
□ B-16826	Embraer ERJ-190AR	19000175	ex PT-SDK
□ B-16827	Embraer ERJ-190AR	19000182	ex PT-SDQ
□ B-16828	Embraer ERJ-190AR	19000190	ex PT-SDY
□ B-16829	Embraer ERJ-190AR	19000302	ex PT-TZQ

ROC AVIATION — *Taipei-Sung Shan (TSA)*

| □ B-68802 | Britten-Norman BN-2B-20 Islander | 2241 | ex G-BSPU |

TIGERAIR TAIWAN — *(IT/TTW)* — *Taipei-Taoyuan (TPE)*

□ B-50001	Airbus A320-232/S	6187	ex F-WWIH	♦
□ B-50003	Airbus A320-232/S	4804	ex 9V-TAW	♦
□ B-50005	Airbus A320-232/S	6522	ex F-WWDH	♦
□ B-50006	Airbus A320-232/S	6604	ex F-WWDG	o/o♦
□ B-	Airbus A320-232	4874	ex 9V-TAY	o/o♦

TRANSASIA AIRWAYS — *Transasia (GE/TNA)* — *Taipei-Sung Shan (TSA)*

□ B-22310	Airbus A320-232	0791	ex F-WWDR	
□ B-22311	Airbus A320-232	0822	ex F-WWBY	
□ B-22312	Airbus A320-232	2914	ex 4R-ABH	
□ B-22316	Airbus A320-232	5055	ex F-WWBS	
□ B-22317	Airbus A320-232	2376	ex EI-FCS	
□ B-22318	Airbus A320-233	3577	ex N681TA	♦
□ B-22605	Airbus A321-131	0606	ex F-WGYY	
□ B-22606	Airbus A321-131	0731	ex F-WQGL	
□ B-22607	Airbus A321-131	0746	ex F-WQGM	
□ B-22610	Airbus A321-231/S	6294	ex D-AVZV	
□ B-	Airbus A321-231/S	6693	ex	♦
□ B-	Airbus A321-231/S	6718	ex	o/o♦
□ B-	Airbus A321-231/S	6757	ex	o/o♦
□ B-22801	ATR 72-212A	517	ex F-WWLK	
□ B-22803	ATR 72-212A	527	ex F-WWLC	
□ B-22805	ATR 72-212A	558	ex F-WQIU	
□ B-22806	ATR 72-212A	560	ex F-WQIY	
□ B-22807	ATR 72-212A	567	ex F-WQIZ	
□ B-22811	ATR 72-212A	749	ex F-WQNC	
□ B-22812	ATR 72-212A	774	ex F-WWEM	
□ B-22815	ATR 72-600	1133	ex F-WWEV	
□ B-22817	ATR 72-600	1145	ex F-WWEJ	♦
□ B-22818	ATR 72-600	1198	ex F-WWEP	♦
□ B-22820	ATR 72-600	1222	ex F-WWEU	♦
□ B-	ATR 72-600	1251	ex F-WWEC	o/o♦
□ B-	ATR 72-600	1261	ex F-WW	o/o♦
□ B-22101	Airbus A330-343E	1357	ex F-WWCX	
□ B-22102	Airbus A330-343E	1378	ex F-WWYH	

UNI AIR		Glory (B7/UIA)		Taipei-Sung Shan (TSA)
☐ B-17001	ATR 72-600	1044	ex F-WWEG	
☐ B-17002	ATR 72-600	1061	ex F-WWEV	
☐ B-17003	ATR 72-600	1078	ex F-WWEO	
☐ B-17005	ATR 72-600	1090	ex F-WWEC	
☐ B-17006	ATR 72-600	1101	ex F-WWEN	
☐ B-17007	ATR 72-600	1111	ex F-WWEX	
☐ B-17008	ATR 72-600	1125	ex F-WWEN	
☐ B-17009	ATR 72-600	1136	ex F-WWEZ	
☐ B-17010	ATR 72-600	1150	ex F-WWEO	♦
☐ B-17011	ATR 72-600	1163	ex F-WWED	♦
☐ B-17012	ATR 72-600	1175	ex F-WWEP	♦
☐ B-17013	ATR 72-600	1183	ex F-WWEX	♦
☐ B-17015	ATR 72-600	1240	ex F-WWEP	♦
☐ B-17917	McDonnell-Douglas MD-90-30ER	53572/2217		>EVA
☐ B-17918	McDonnell-Douglas MD-90-30ER	53571/2193	ex B-16903	
☐ B-17919	McDonnell-Douglas MD-90-30	53569/2173	ex N6206F	
☐ B-17920	McDonnell-Douglas MD-90-30	53574/2186		
☐ B-17925	McDonnell-Douglas MD-90-30ER	53568/2171	ex B-16902	>EVA
☐ B-17926	McDonnell-Douglas MD-90-30ER	53567/2169	ex B-15301	>EVA

V AIR		(ZV/VAX)		Taipei-Taoyuan (TPE)
☐ B-22608	Airbus A321-231/S	6009	ex D-AVZE	♦

C- CANADA

ADLAIR AVIATION			Cambridge Bay, NT/Yellowknife, NT (YCB/YZF)	
☐ C-FCGB	Beech 200 Super King Air	BB-24	ex N80MC	
☐ C-FGYN	de Havilland DHC-2 Beaver	134	ex CF-GYN	FP/WS
☐ C-GBFP	Learjet 25B	25B-167	ex N664CL Ernie Lyall	EMS
☐ C-GCYN	Beech 200 Super King Air	BB-710	ex C-GXHW	
☐ C-GFYN	de Havilland DHC-6 Twin Otter 200	209	ex N915SA	FP/WS

ADVENTURE AIR			Lac du Bonnet, MB (YAX)	
☐ C-FKLR	Cessna 208 Caravan I	20800223	ex N899A	FP
☐ C-FXPC	de Havilland DHC-2 Beaver	1196	ex CF-XPC	FP
☐ C-GAAX	Cessna 208B Caravan I	208B0348	ex N32JA	FP
☐ C-GGRJ	Cessna A185F Skywagon	18502745	ex (N1090F)	FP
☐ C-GKYG	de Havilland DHC-3 Otter	261	ex N2750	FP
☐ C-GRRJ	de Havilland DHC-3 Turbo Otter	296	ex C-FXZD	FP
☐ C-GSUV	de Havilland DHC-3 Otter	376	ex N445FD	FP
☐ C-GUEH	Piper PA-31 Turbo Navajo C	31-7712057	ex N27255	
☐ C-GWQE	Cessna 337F Super Skymaster II	33701459	ex N1859M	
☐ C-GYER	Cessna U206F Stationair	U206-03503		♦

AIR BELLEVUE			St Félicien, QC	
☐ C-GABM	Cessna 208 Caravan I	20800308	ex N12712	

AIR BRAVO			Thunder Bay, ON (YQT)	
☐ C-FKPA	Pilatus PC-12/45	275	ex N275PC	
☐ C-FKSL	Pilatus PC-12/45	324	ex N324PC	
☐ C-FPCI	Pilatus PC-12/45	399	ex N399PB	
☐ C-FPCN	Pilatus PC-12/45	258	ex N258WC	[YTS]
☐ C-FTAB	Pilatus PC-12/45	229	ex C-FMPO	
☐ C-FXAB	Pilatus PC-12/45	239		

AIR CAB			Vancouver-Coal Harbour, BC (CXH)	
☐ C-FOES	de Havilland DHC-2 Turbo Beaver III	1673/TB43	ex CF-OES	
☐ C-FRJG	de Havilland DHC-2 Beaver	1550	ex CF-RJG	FP
☐ C-GAXE	de Havilland DHC-2 Beaver	841	ex 54-1698	FP
☐ C-GJGC	de Havilland DHC-2 Beaver	88	ex CF-GQM	FP
☐ C-GJZE	de Havilland DHC-2 Beaver	1276	ex N87780	FP
☐ C-FBMO	Cessna A185E Skywagon	18501627	ex N1934U	FP
☐ C-FQGZ	Cessna A185E Skywagon	18501691	ex N1967U	FP

AIR CANADA	Air Canada (AC/ACA)		Montreal-Mirabel/Montreal-Trudeau, QC (YMX/YUL)	
Member of Star Alliance				
☐ C-FYJI	Airbus A319-114	0682	ex D-AVYH 258	
☐ C-FYKC	Airbus A319-114	0691	ex D-AVYP 260	

☐ C-FYKR	Airbus A319-114	0693	ex D-AVYQ	261	
☐ C-FZUH	Airbus A319-114	0711	ex D-AVYV	264	TCA retro c/s
☐ C-FZUJ	Airbus A319-114	0719	ex D-AVYW	265	
☐ C-FZUL	Airbus A319-114	0721	ex D-AVYY	266	
☐ C-GAPY	Airbus A319-114	0728	ex D-AVYE	267	
☐ C-GAQL	Airbus A319-114	0732	ex D-AVYX	268	
☐ C-GAQX	Airbus A319-114	0736	ex D-AVYG	269	
☐ C-GAQZ	Airbus A319-114	0740	ex D-AVYH	270	
☐ C-GARG	Airbus A319-114	0742	ex D-AVYM	271	
☐ C-GBHM	Airbus A319-114	0769	ex D-AVYB	274	
☐ C-GBIA	Airbus A319-114	0817	ex D-AVYM	280	
☐ C-GBIP	Airbus A319-114	0546	ex D-AVYV	285	
☐ C-GITP	Airbus A319-112	1562	ex D-AVYR	286	
☐ C-GITR	Airbus A319-112	1577	ex D-AVWR	287	
☐ C-FDCA	Airbus A320-211	0232	ex F-WWIY	405	op by Air Canada Jetz
☐ C-FDQQ	Airbus A320-211	0059	ex F-WWDI	201	
☐ C-FDQV	Airbus A320-211	0068	ex F-WWDO	202	
☐ C-FDRH	Airbus A320-211	0073	ex F-WWDC	203	Star Alliance c/s
☐ C-FDRK	Airbus A320-211	0084	ex F-WWDP	204	Star Alliance c/s
☐ C-FDRP	Airbus A320-211	0122	ex F-WWIP	205	
☐ C-FDSN	Airbus A320-211	0126	ex F-WWIU	206	
☐ C-FDST	Airbus A320-211	0127	ex F-WWIV	207	
☐ C-FDSU	Airbus A320-211	0141	ex F-WWDH	208	
☐ C-FFWI	Airbus A320-211	0149	ex F-WWDP	209	
☐ C-FFWJ	Airbus A320-211	0150	ex F-WWDQ	210	
☐ C-FFWM	Airbus A320-211	0154	ex F-WWDY	211	
☐ C-FFWN	Airbus A320-211	0159	ex F-WWIG	212	
☐ C-FGJI	Airbus A320-214	1787	ex OO-TCJ	241	♦
☐ C-FGKH	Airbus A320-214	1975	ex OO-TCI		♦
☐ C-FGKP	Airbus A321-212	3884	ex F-GTAV		♦
☐ C-FGYL	Airbus A320-211	0254	ex F-WWBF	218	
☐ C-FGYS	Airbus A320-211	0255	ex F-WWBG	219	
☐ C-FKCK	Airbus A320-211	0265	ex 'G-FKCK'	220	
☐ C-FKCO	Airbus A320-211	0277	ex F-WWDX	221	
☐ C-FKCR	Airbus A320-211	0290	ex F-WWBY	222	
☐ C-FKOJ	Airbus A320-211	0330	ex F-WWIB	226	
☐ C-FKPT	Airbus A320-211	0324	ex F-WWDC	225	
☐ C-FLSS	Airbus A320-211	0284	ex F-WWBU	408	
☐ C-FLSU	Airbus A320-211	0309	ex F-WWIJ	411	
☐ C-FMSX	Airbus A320-211	0378	ex 'C-FMSK'	232	
☐ C-FNVU	Airbus A320-211	0403	ex F-WWBO	415	
☐ C-FNVV	Airbus A320-211	0404	ex F-WWDF	416	
☐ C-FPDN	Airbus A320-211	0341	ex F-WWBR	228	
☐ C-FPWD	Airbus A320-211	0231	ex F-WWDV	404	op by Air Canada Jetz
☐ C-FPWE	Airbus A320-211	0175	ex F-WWIN	402	op by Air Canada Jetz
☐ C-FTJO	Airbus A320-211	0183	ex F-WWIX	213	
☐ C-FTJQ	Airbus A320-211	0242	ex F-WWDJ	215	
☐ C-FTJR	Airbus A320-211	0248	ex F-WWDT	216	
☐ C-FTJS	Airbus A320-211	0253	ex F-WWBE	217	
☐ C-FXCD	Airbus A320-214	2018	ex F-WWBV	239	
☐ C-FZQS	Airbus A320-214	2145	ex F-WWDI	240	
☐ C-FZUB	Airbus A320-214	1940	ex F-WWIP	238	
☐ C-GJVT	Airbus A320-214	1719	ex F-WWBC	235	
☐ C-GKOD	Airbus A320-214	1864	ex F-WWIE	236	
☐ C-GKOE	Airbus A320-214	1874	ex F-WWBN	237	
☐ C-GPWG	Airbus A320-214	0174	ex F-WWIM	401	op by Air Canada Jetz
☐ C-GQCA	Airbus A320-211	0210	ex F-WWIC	403	op by Air Canada Jetz
☐ C-FGKN	Airbus A321-212	3051	ex F-GTAN		♦
☐ C-GITU	Airbus A321-211	1602	ex D-AMTA	451	Star Alliance c/s
☐ C-GITY	Airbus A321-211	1611	ex D-AVAV	452	
☐ C-GIUB	Airbus A321-211	1623	ex D-AMTB	453	
☐ C-GIUE	Airbus A321-211	1632	ex D-AMTC	454	
☐ C-GIUF	Airbus A321-211	1638	ex D-AMTD	455	
☐ C-GJVX	Airbus A321-211	1726	ex D-AVXC	456	
☐ C-GJWD	Airbus A321-211	1748	ex D-AVXE	457	
☐ C-GJWI	Airbus A321-211	1772	ex D-AVZA	458	
☐ C-GJWN	Airbus A321-211	1783	ex D-AVZD	459	
☐ C-GJWO	Airbus A321-211	1811	ex D-AVZI	460	
☐ C-GFAF	Airbus A330-343X	277	ex F-WWKO	931	
☐ C-GFAH	Airbus A330-343X	279	ex F-WWYB	932	
☐ C-GFAJ	Airbus A330-343X	284	ex F-WWYA	933	
☐ C-GFUR	Airbus A330-343X	344	ex F-WWYC	934	
☐ C-GHKR	Airbus A330-343X	400	ex F-WWKM	935	
☐ C-GHKW	Airbus A330-343X	408	ex F-WWKS	936	
☐ C-GHKX	Airbus A330-343X	412	ex F-WWKU	937	
☐ C-GHLM	Airbus A330-343X	419	ex F-WWYA	938	Star Alliance c/s
☐ C-FCAB	Boeing 767-375ER	24082/213	ex N6055X	681	
☐ C-FCAE	Boeing 767-375ER	24083/215	ex N6046P	682	
☐ C-FCAF	Boeing 767-375ER	24084/219	ex N6038E	683	

☐ C-FCAG	Boeing 767-375ER	24085/220	ex N6009F	684	
☐ C-FOCA	Boeing 767-375ER	24575/311		640	
☐ C-FPCA	Boeing 767-375ER	24306/258		637	
☐ C-FTCA	Boeing 767-375ER	24307/259		638	
☐ C-FXCA	Boeing 767-375ER	24574/302		639	
☐ C-GBZR	Boeing 767-38EER	25404/411	ex HL7267	645	
☐ C-GDUZ	Boeing 767-38EER	25347/399	ex HL7266	646	
☐ C-GEOQ	Boeing 767-375ER	30112/765		647	
☐ C-GEOU	Boeing 767-375ER	30108/771		648	
☐ C-GHLA	Boeing 767-35HER	26387/445	ex VH-BZL	656	
☐ C-GHLK	Boeing 767-35HER	26388/456	ex VH-BZM	657	
☐ C-GHLV	Boeing 767-333ER	30852/843	ex N6055X	661	
☐ C-GHOZ	Boeing 767-375ER	24087/249	ex N487CT	685	
☐ C-GLCA	Boeing 767-375ER	25120/361		641	
☐ C-GSCA	Boeing 767-375ER	25121/372	ex B-2564	642	
☐ C-FIUA	Boeing 777-233LR	35239/640		701	
☐ C-FIUF	Boeing 777-233LR	35243/651	ex N1788B	702	
☐ C-FIUJ	Boeing 777-233LR	35244/679		703	
☐ C-FIVK	Boeing 777-233LR	35245/689		704	
☐ C-FNND	Boeing 777-233LR	35246/695		705	
☐ C-FNNH	Boeing 777-233LR	35247/699		706	
☐ C-FITL	Boeing 777-333ER	35256/620		731	
☐ C-FITU	Boeing 777-333ER	35254/626		732	
☐ C-FITW	Boeing 777-333ER	35298/638		733	
☐ C-FIUL	Boeing 777-333ER	35255/642		734	
☐ C-FIUR	Boeing 777-333ER	35242/649		735	
☐ C-FIUV	Boeing 777-333ER	35248/702		736	
☐ C-FIUW	Boeing 777-333ER	35249/712		737	
☐ C-FIVM	Boeing 777-333ER	35251/717		738	
☐ C-FIVQ	Boeing 777-333ER	35240/749		740	
☐ C-FIVR	Boeing 777-333ER	35241/763		741	
☐ C-FIVS	Boeing 777-333ER	35784/797		742	
☐ C-FIVW	Boeing 777-333ER	42218/1108		743	
☐ C-FIVX	Boeing 777-333ER	42219/1125		744	
☐ C-FNNQ	Boeing 777-333ER	43251/1154		745	
☐ C-FNNU	Boeing 777-333ER	43249/1161		746	
☐ C-FNNW	Boeing 777-333ER	43250/1174		747	
☐ C-FRAM	Boeing 777-333ER	35250/726		739	
☐ C-GHPQ	Boeing 787-8	35257/160		801	
☐ C-GHPT	Boeing 787-8	35258/170		802	
☐ C-GHPU	Boeing 787-8	35259/174		803	
☐ C-GHPV	Boeing 787-8	35260/220		804	
☐ C-GHPX	Boeing 787-8	35261/230		806	♦
☐ C-GHPY	Boeing 787-8	35262/235		805	♦
☐ C-GHQQ	Boeing 787-8	35263/254	ex N8570Y	807	♦
☐ C-GHQY	Boeing 787-8	35264/265		808	♦
☐ C-FNOE	Boeing 787-9	35265/323		831	o/o♦
☐ C-FN0G	Boeing 787-9	35266/332		832	o/o♦
☐ C-FNOH	Boeing 787-9	35267/366			o/o♦
☐ C-	Boeing 787-9	35268/371			o/o♦
☐ C-	Boeing 787-9	37171/393			o/o♦
☐ C-	Boeing 787-9	37173/405			o/o♦
☐ C-	Boeing 787-9	37174/407			o/o♦
☐ C-	Boeing 787-9	37180/409			o/o♦
☐ C-	Boeing 787-9	35269/395			o/o♦
☐ C-FFYJ	Embraer ERJ-190AR	19000013	ex PT-STM	302	
☐ C-FFYM	Embraer ERJ-190AR	19000015	ex PT-STP	303	
☐ C-FFYT	Embraer ERJ-190AR	19000018	ex PT-STS	304	
☐ C-FGLW	Embraer ERJ-190AR	19000022	ex PT-STW	306	
☐ C-FGLX	Embraer ERJ-190AR	19000024	ex PT-STY	307	
☐ C-FGLY	Embraer ERJ-190AR	19000028	ex PT-SGC	308	
☐ C-FGMF	Embraer ERJ-190AR	19000019	ex PT-STT	305	
☐ C-FHIQ	Embraer ERJ-190AR	19000031	ex PT-SGF	309	
☐ C-FHIS	Embraer ERJ-190AR	19000036	ex PT-SGK	310	
☐ C-FHIU	Embraer ERJ-190AR	19000037	ex PT-SGL	311	
☐ C-FHJJ	Embraer ERJ-190AR	19000041	ex PT-SGQ	312	
☐ C-FHJT	Embraer ERJ-190AR	19000043	ex PT-SGS	313	
☐ C-FHJU	Embraer ERJ-190AR	19000044	ex PT-SGT	314	
☐ C-FHKA	Embraer ERJ-190AR	19000046	ex PT-SGV	315	
☐ C-FHKE	Embraer ERJ-190AR	19000048	ex PT-SGX	316	
☐ C-FHKI	Embraer ERJ-190AR	19000052	ex PT-SIB	317	
☐ C-FHKP	Embraer ERJ-190AR	19000055	ex PT-SIE	318	
☐ C-FHKS	Embraer ERJ-190AR	19000064	ex PT-SJC	319	
☐ C-FHLH	Embraer ERJ-190AR	19000068	ex PT-SJH	320	
☐ C-FHNL	Embraer ERJ-190AR	19000070	ex PT-SJJ	321	
☐ C-FHNP	Embraer ERJ-190AR	19000071	ex PT-SJK	322	
☐ C-FHNV	Embraer ERJ-190AR	19000075	ex PT-SJP	323	
☐ C-FHNW	Embraer ERJ-190AR	19000077	ex PT-SJS	324	

74

☐ C-FHNX	Embraer ERJ-190AR	19000083	ex PT-SNA	325	
☐ C-FHNY	Embraer ERJ-190AR	19000085	ex PT-SND	326	
☐ C-FHON	Embraer ERJ-190AR	19000097	ex PT-SNR	330	
☐ C-FHOS	Embraer ERJ-190AR	19000101	ex PT-SNV	331	
☐ C-FHOY	Embraer ERJ-190AR	19000105	ex PT-SNZ	332	
☐ C-FLWE	Embraer ERJ-190AR	19000092	ex PT-SNL	327	
☐ C-FLWH	Embraer ERJ-190AR	19000094	ex PT-SNO	328	
☐ C-FLWK	Embraer ERJ-190AR	19000096	ex PT-SNQ	329	
☐ C-FMYV	Embraer ERJ-190AR	19000108	ex PT-SQC	333	
☐ C-FMZB	Embraer ERJ-190AR	19000111	ex PT-SQF	334	
☐ C-FMZD	Embraer ERJ-190AR	19000115	ex PT-SQJ	335	
☐ C-FMZR	Embraer ERJ-190AR	19000116	ex PT-SQK	336	
☐ C-FMZU	Embraer ERJ-190AR	19000118	ex PT-SQM	337	
☐ C-FMZW	Embraer ERJ-190AR	19000124	ex PT-SQT	338	
☐ C-FNAI	Embraer ERJ-190AR	19000132	ex PT-SYK	339	
☐ C-FNAJ	Embraer ERJ-190AR	19000134	ex PT-SYM	340	
☐ C-FNAN	Embraer ERJ-190AR	19000136	ex PT-SYO	341	
☐ C-FNAP	Embraer ERJ-190AR	19000142	ex PT-SYU	342	
☐ C-FNAQ	Embraer ERJ-190AR	19000146	ex PT-SYY	343	
☐ C-FNAW	Embraer ERJ-190AR	19000149	ex PT-SAC	344	
☐ C-FNAX	Embraer ERJ-190AR	19000151	ex PT-SAG	345	
☐ C-GWEN	Embraer ERJ-190AR	19000010	ex PT-STJ	301	
☐ CF-TCC	Lockheed L-10A	1116	ex N3749	Trans Canada Airlines c/s	
☐ C-GKOL	Airbus A340-541	445	ex F-WWTH		>TAM

AIR CANADA EXPRESS   Jazz (QK/JZA)

Halifax, NS/Calgary, AB/London, ON/Vancouver, BC (YHZ/YYC/YXU/YVR)

Note: Fleet is being repainted into mainline Air Canada c/s, colours will be replaced.

☐ C-FDJA	Canadair CRJ-200ER	7979	ex C-FMLI	162 green
☐ C-FEJA	Canadair CRJ-200ER	7983	ex C-FMLV	163 yellow
☐ C-FFJA	Canadair CRJ-200ER	7985	ex C-FMNH	164 orange
☐ C-FIJA	Canadair CRJ-200ER	7987	ex C-FMNX	165 red
☐ C-FZJA	Canadair CRJ-200ER	7988	ex C-FMNY	166
☐ C-GGJA	Canadair CRJ-200ER	8002	ex C-FMMY	167 yellow
☐ C-GJZJ	Canadair CRJ-200ER	7553	ex N706BR	157 orange
☐ C-GJZZ	Canadair CRJ-200ER	7978	ex C-FMLF	161 red
☐ C-GKEJ	Canadair CRJ-200ER	7269	ex N577ML	180 red
☐ C-GKEK	Canadair CRJ-200ER	7270	ex N578ML	181 green
☐ C-GKEM	Canadair CRJ-200ER	7277	ex N579ML	182 yellow
☐ C-GKEP	Canadair CRJ-200ER	7303	ex N581ML	183 orange
☐ C-GKER	Canadair CRJ-200ER	7368	ex N588ML	184 red
☐ C-GKEU	Canadair CRJ-200ER	7376	ex N589ML	185 green
☐ C-GKEW	Canadair CRJ-200ER	7385	ex N590ML	186 yellow
☐ C-GKEZ	Canadair CRJ-200ER	7327	ex N583ML	187 orange
☐ C-GKFR	Canadair CRJ-200ER	7330	ex N584ML	188 red
☐ C-GKGC	Canadair CRJ-200ER	7334	ex N585ML	189 green
☐ C-GMJA	Canadair CRJ-200ER	8003	ex C-FMNB	168 orange
☐ C-GNJA	Canadair CRJ-200ER	8004	ex C-FMKV	169
☐ C-GOJA	Canadair CRJ-200ER	8009	ex C-FMLI	170
☐ C-GQJA	Canadair CRJ-200ER	7963	ex C-FCGX	171
☐ C-GTJA	Canadair CRJ-200ER	7966	ex C-FCLV	172
☐ C-GUJA	Canadair CRJ-200ER	8011	ex C-FMLS	173 orange
☐ C-GXJA	Canadair CRJ-200ER	8017	ex C-FMNX	174 yellow
☐ C-GZJA	Canadair CRJ-200ER	8018	ex C-FMNY	175
☐ C-FBJZ	Canadair CRJ-705ER	15037		702 green
☐ C-FCJZ	Canadair CRJ-705ER	15040		703
☐ C-FDJZ	Canadair CRJ-705ER	15041		704
☐ C-FJJZ	Canadair CRJ-705ER	15043		705
☐ C-FKJZ	Canadair CRJ-705ER	15044		706
☐ C-FLJZ	Canadair CRJ-705ER	15045		707
☐ C-FNJZ	Canadair CRJ-705ER	15046		708
☐ C-FTJZ	Canadair CRJ-705ER	15047		709
☐ C-FUJZ	Canadair CRJ-705ER	15048		710
☐ C-GDJZ	Canadair CRJ-705ER	15049		711 green
☐ C-GFJZ	Canadair CRJ-705ER	15050		712
☐ C-GJAZ	Canadair CRJ-705ER	15036		701 red
☐ C-GLJZ	Canadair CRJ-705ER	15051		713 orange
☐ C-GNJZ	Canadair CRJ-705ER	15052		714
☐ C-GOJZ	Canadair CRJ-705ER	15053		715
☐ C-GPJZ	Canadair CRJ-705ER	15055	ex C-FGND	716 red
☐ C-FABA	de Havilland DHC-8-102	092		805 orange
☐ C-FABN	de Havilland DHC-8-102	044		803 red
☐ C-FABT	de Havilland DHC-8-102	049		848 green
☐ C-FABW	de Havilland DHC-8-102	097		806 green
☐ C-FACD	de Havilland DHC-8-102	150		808 yellow
☐ C-FGQK	de Havilland DHC-8-102	193		819 yellow

☐ C-FGRC	de Havilland DHC-8-102	195		821 green	
☐ C-FGRM	de Havilland DHC-8-102	199		820 red	
☐ C-FGRP	de Havilland DHC-8-102	207		822 green	
☐ C-FGRY	de Havilland DHC-8-102	212		844 red	
☐ C-FJMG	de Havilland DHC-8-102A	255		824 orange	
☐ C-FPON	de Havilland DHC-8-102	171		836 orange	
☐ C-GANF	de Havilland DHC-8-102	042		802 orange	
☐ C-GANI	de Havilland DHC-8-102	064		830 green	
☐ C-GANK	de Havilland DHC-8-102	087		831 yellow	
☐ C-GANQ	de Havilland DHC-8-102	096		833 yellow	
☐ C-GANS	de Havilland DHC-8-102	057		828 green	
☐ C-GCTC	de Havilland DHC-8-102	065	ex V2-LEE	846 orange	
☐ C-GION	de Havilland DHC-8-102	127		832 yellow	
☐ C-GJIG	de Havilland DHC-8-102	068		826 orange	
☐ C-GJMI	de Havilland DHC-8-102	077		825 yellow	
☐ C-GJMO	de Havilland DHC-8-102	079		834 yellow	
☐ C-GJSV	de Havilland DHC-8-102	085		814 green	
☐ C-GJSX	de Havilland DHC-8-102	088		835 red	
☐ C-GKON	de Havilland DHC-8-102	130		815 red	
☐ C-GOND	de Havilland DHC-8-102	090		840 red	
☐ C-GONJ	de Havilland DHC-8-102	095		839 orange	
☐ C-GONN	de Havilland DHC-8-102	101		898 yellow	
☐ C-GONO	de Havilland DHC-8-102	102		807 orange	
☐ C-GONR	de Havilland DHC-8-102	109		841 green	
☐ C-GONW	de Havilland DHC-8-102	112		843 green	
☐ C-GONX	de Havilland DHC-8-102	118		829 red	
☐ C-GONY	de Havilland DHC-8-102	115		827 yellow	
☐ C-GTAI	de Havilland DHC-8-102	078		853 yellow	
☐ C-GTBP	de Havilland DHC-8-102	066		855 green	
☐ C-FACF	de Havilland DHC-8-311A	259		308 yellow	
☐ C-FACT	de Havilland DHC-8-311A	262		309 green	
☐ C-FACV	de Havilland DHC-8-311A	278		311 red	
☐ C-FADF	de Havilland DHC-8-311A	272	ex C-FACU	310 red	
☐ C-FJFM	de Havilland DHC-8-311A	240		324 yellow	
☐ C-FJVV	de Havilland DHC-8-311A	271		306 red	
☐ C-FJXZ	de Havilland DHC-8-311A	264	ex C-FTAQ	326 red	
☐ C-FMDW	de Havilland DHC-8-311A	269		305 green	
☐ C-FRUZ	de Havilland DHC-8-311	293	ex N2492B	327 red	
☐ C-FSOU	de Havilland DHC-8-311A	342	ex LN-WFA	328 green	
☐ C-FTAK	de Havilland DHC-8-311A	246		323 red	
☐ C-GABO	de Havilland DHC-8-311A	248		312 orange	
☐ C-GABP	de Havilland DHC-8-311A	257		307 green	
☐ C-GETA	de Havilland DHC-8-301	186		321 red	
☐ C-GEWQ	de Havilland DHC-8-311A	202		325 red	
☐ C-GHTA	de Havilland DHC-8-301	198		316 orange	
☐ C-GKTA	de Havilland DHC-8-301	124		317 green	
☐ C-GLTA	de Havilland DHC-8-301	154		318 green	
☐ C-GMON	de Havilland DHC-8-301	131		301 orange	
☐ C-GMTA	de Havilland DHC-8-301	174		319 yellow	
☐ C-GNON	de Havilland DHC-8-301	137		302 green	
☐ C-GSTA	de Havilland DHC-8-301	182		320 yellow	
☐ C-GTAG	de Havilland DHC-8-301	200		315 orange	
☐ C-GTAQ	de Havilland DHC-8-301	180	ex C-FGVK	313 red	
☐ C-GTAT	de Havilland DHC-8-301	188	ex C-FGVT	314 red	
☐ C-GUON	de Havilland DHC-8-301	143		303 green	
☐ C-GVON	de Havilland DHC-8-301	149		304 orange	
☐ C-GVTA	de Havilland DHC-8-301	190		322 red	
☐ C-GGAH	de Havilland DHC-8-402Q	4432		416	
☐ C-GGBF	de Havilland DHC-8-402Q	4433		417	dam 06Nov14
☐ C-GGCI	de Havilland DHC-8-402Q	4434		418	
☐ C-GGDU	de Havilland DHC-8-402Q	4435		419	
☐ C-GGFJ	de Havilland DHC-8-402Q	4436		420	
☐ C-GGFP	de Havilland DHC-8-402Q	4437		421	
☐ C-GGMI	de Havilland DHC-8-402Q	4413		415	
☐ C-GGMN	de Havilland DHC-8-402Q	4405		414	
☐ C-GGMQ	de Havilland DHC-8-402Q	4403		413	
☐ C-GGMU	de Havilland DHC-8-402Q	4397		411	
☐ C-GGMZ	de Havilland DHC-8-402Q	4399		407	
☐ C-GGND	de Havilland DHC-8-402Q	4394		410	
☐ C-GGNF	de Havilland DHC-8-402Q	4393		409	
☐ C-GGNW	de Havilland DHC-8-402Q	4388		408	
☐ C-GGNY	de Havilland DHC-8-402Q	4386		407	
☐ C-GGNZ	de Havilland DHC-8-402Q	4384		406	
☐ C-GGOF	de Havilland DHC-8-402Q	4383		405	
☐ C-GGOI	de Havilland DHC-8-402Q	4381		404	
☐ C-GGOK	de Havilland DHC-8-402Q	4372		403	
☐ C-GGOY	de Havilland DHC-8-402Q	4365		401	
☐ C-GKUK	de Havilland DHC-8-402Q	4369		402	
☐ C-FRIA	Canadair CRJ-100ER	7045	ex C-FMLQ	101 all white	[YYC]
☐ C-FVMD	Canadair CRJ-100ER	7082		113 orange	[YUL]

| ☐ C-FXMY | Canadair CRJ-100ER | 7124 | 124 yellow | [YYC] |

Ops services in conjunction with Air Georgian, EVAS Air and Sky Regional

AIR CANADA ROUGE (RV/ROU)

☐ C-FYIY	Airbus A319-114	0634	ex D-AVYP	252	
☐ C-FYJE	Airbus A319-114	0656	ex D-AVYZ	255	
☐ C-FYJG	Airbus A319-114	0670	ex D-AVYE	256	
☐ C-FYJH	Airbus A319-114	0672	ex D-AVYF	257	
☐ C-FYJP	Airbus A319-114	0688	ex D-AVYJ	259	
☐ C-FYKW	Airbus A319-114	0695	ex D-AVYS	262	
☐ C-FYNS	Airbus A319-114	0572	ex D-AVYK	251	
☐ C-FZUG	Airbus A319-114	0697	ex D-AVYT	263	
☐ C-GARJ	Airbus A319-114	0752	ex D-AVYP	272	
☐ C-GARO	Airbus A319-114	0757	ex D-AVYQ	273	
☐ C-GBHN	Airbus A319-114	0773	ex D-AVYK	275	
☐ C-GBHO	Airbus A319-114	0779	ex D-AVYT	276	◆
☐ C-GBHR	Airbus A319-114	0785	ex D-AVYU	277	
☐ C-GBHY	Airbus A319-114	0800	ex D-AVYE	278	
☐ C-GBHZ	Airbus A319-114	0813	ex D-AVYG	279	
☐ C-GBIJ	Airbus A319-114	0829	ex D-AVYH	281	
☐ C-GBIK	Airbus A319-114	0831	ex D-AVYI	282	◆
☐ C-GBIM	Airbus A319-114	0840	ex D-AVYQ	283	◆
☐ C-GBIN	Airbus A319-114	0845	ex D-AVYA	284	◆
☐ C-GJVY	Airbus A319 112	1742	ex XA-MXI	292	◆
☐ C-GKOB	Airbus A319-112	1853	ex N571SX	296	◆
☐ C-GSJB	Airbus A319-112	1673	ex XA-MXH	290	
☐ C-FIYE	Boeing 767-33AER/W	33422/892	ex N589HA		◆
☐ C-FJZK	Boeing 767-3Q8ER	29386/831	ex 5Y-KYV		o/o◆
☐ C-FMWP	Boeing 767-333ER/W	25583/508		631	◆
☐ C-FMWQ	Boeing 767-333ER/W	25584/596		632	◆
☐ C-FMWU	Boeing 767-333ER/W	25585/597		633	
☐ C-FMWV	Boeing 767-333ER/W	25586/599		634	
☐ C-FMWY	Boeing 767-333ER/W	25587/604		635	
☐ C-FMXC	Boeing 767-333ER/W	25588/606		636	
☐ C-GHPE	Boeing 767-33AER/W	33423/897	ex N591HA	691	
☐ C-GHPN	Boeing 767-33AER/W	33424/901	ex N593HA	692	
☐ C-GHLQ	Boeing 767-333ER/W	30846/832	ex N6009F	658	◆
☐ C-GHLT	Boeing 767-333ER/W	30850/835	ex N6018N	659	◆
☐ C-GHLU	Boeing 767-333ER	30851/836	ex N6046P	660	◆

AIR CREEBEC Cree (YN/CRQ) Val d'Or, QC / Timmins, ON (YVO/YTS)

☐ C-FCJD	de Havilland DHC-8-102	158	
☐ C-FCLS	de Havilland DHC-8-106	249	ex N841EX
☐ C-FCSK	de Havilland DHC-8-102	122	
☐ C-FCWP	de Havilland DHC-8-102	111	ex N925CA
☐ C-FDWO	de Havilland DHC-8-106	277	ex N880CC
☐ C-GAIS	de Havilland DHC-8-102	138	ex C-FCIZ
☐ C-GJOP	de Havilland DHC-8-102	121	ex N381BC
☐ C-GTCO	de Havilland DHC-8-102	119	
☐ C-GUXF	de Havilland DHC-8-102	173	ex VH-QQE
☐ C-GYWX	de Havilland DHC-8-102	175	ex N283BC
☐ C-GZEW	de Havilland DHC-8-314	393	ex N801SA
☐ C-GZJC	de Havilland DHC-8-103	060	ex OY-RUW
☐ C-FEYP	Beech A100 King Air	B-206	ex N86BM
☐ C-FEYT	Beech A100 King Air	B-210	
☐ C-FHGG	Beech A100 King Air	B-207	ex N727LE
☐ C-FLIY	Hawker Siddeley HS.748 Srs.2A/244	1723	ex SE-LEG	Frtr
☐ C-FPJR	Hawker Siddeley HS.748 Srs.2A/244	1725	ex SE-LEK	Frtr
☐ C-FTQR	Beech 1900D	UE-129	
☐ C-GIZX	Beech A100 King Air	B-172	ex N753DB

AIR-DALE FLYING SERVICE Ranger Lake SPB, ON/Wawa Hawk Junction SPB, ON

| ☐ C-GELP | de Havilland DHC-2 Beaver | 780 | ex N5318G | FP |

AIR GASPESIE Saint-Bruno, PQ

| ☐ C-GFKA | Pilatus PC-12/45 | 182 | ◆ |

AIR GEORGIAN/AIR ALLIANCE Georgian (ZX/GGN) Toronto-Pearson Intl, ON (YYZ)

☐ C-GAAR	Beech 1900D	UE-207	ex N10625	964 Baie-Saint Laurent
☐ C-GAAS	Beech 1900D	UE-209	ex N10659	965 Iles de la Madelaine
☐ C-GAAU	Beech 1900D	UE-232	ex N10705	904 Baie Comeau
☐ C-GAAV	Beech 1900D	UE-235	ex N10708	967
☐ C-GGGA	Beech 1900D	UE-291	ex N20704	951
☐ C-GHGA	Beech 1900D	UE-293	ex N21063	953
☐ C-GMGA	Beech 1900D	UE-315	ex N22890	956 Baie Comeau

□ C-GORA	Beech 1900D	UE-326	ex N23164	957	
□ C-GORC	Beech 1900D	UE-320	ex N22976	959	
□ C-GORF	Beech 1900D	UE-330	ex N23222	958	
□ C-GORN	Beech 1900D	UE-403	ex N330DH	974	
□ C-GVGA	Beech 1900D	UE-292	ex N20707	952	
□ C-GWGA	Beech 1900D	UE-309	ex N22874	955	
□ C-GZGA	Beech 1900D	UE-306	ex N22700	954	
□ C-FSKM	Canadair CRJ-100ER	7071	ex C-FMKZ	100	Air Canada Express c/s♦
□ C-FWJF	Canadair CRJ-100ER	7095		101	
□ C-FWJI	Canadair CRJ-100ER	7096		103	Air Canada Express c/s
□ C-FWRR	Canadair CRJ-100ER	7107		105	Air Canada Express c/s♦
□ C-FWRS	Canadair CRJ-100ER	7112	ex N275AV		♦
□ C-FWRT	Canadair CRJ-100ER	7118		122	Air Canada Express c/s♦
□ C-GUPC	Cessna 680 Citation Sovereign	680-0335	ex N5261R		

AIR INUIT		Air Inuit (3H/AIE)		Kuujjuaq, QC (YVP)
□ C-FAIY	de Havilland DHC-6 Twin Otter 300	362	ex C-FASS	FP/WS
□ C-FJFR	de Havilland DHC-6 Twin Otter 300	784	ex HK-2762	
□ C-FTJJ	de Havilland DHC-6 Twin Otter 300	325	ex 8Q-MAJ	
□ C-GMDC	de Havilland DHC-6 Twin Otter 300	763		dam 01Nov13
□ C-GNDO	de Havilland DHC-6 Twin Otter 300	430		
□ C-GTYX	de Havilland DHC-6 Twin Otter 300	631		
□ C-FAID	de Havilland DHC-8-314	400	ex OE-LTD	
□ C-FEAI	de Havilland DHC-8-314	334	ex G-WOWB	
□ C-FIAI	de Havilland DHC-8-314Q	485	ex OE-LTL	
□ C-FKTM	de Havilland DHC-8-311A	298	ex V2-LGC	♦
□ C-FOAI	de Havilland DHC-8-314Q	466	ex OE-LTI	
□ C-FYAI	de Havilland DHC-8-314	420	ex ZS-NMP	
□ C-GIAB	de Havilland DHC-8-314	296	ex G-WOWA	
□ C-GRAI	de Havilland DHC-8-314Q	483	ex OE-LTK	
□ C-GUAI	de Havilland DHC-8-314	423	ex OE-LTF	
□ C-GXAI	de Havilland DHC-8-314Q	481	ex OE-LTJ	
□ C-FAIO	Beech A100 King Air	B-132	ex C-GXHP	
□ C-FAIP	Beech A100 King Air	B-193	ex F-GXAB	
□ C-FAIV	de Havilland DHC-8-106	235	ex N828EX	
□ C-FDAO	de Havilland DHC-8-102	123		
□ C-FDOX	Hawker Siddeley HS.748 Srs.2A/310LFD	1749	ex TJ-CCD	Frtr
□ C-FGET	Hawker Siddeley HS.748 Srs.2A	1724		Frtr♦
□ C-GAIG	Boeing 737-2S2C	21928/603	ex A6-ZYB	
□ C-GAIK	Beech A100 King Air	B-104	ex C-GCFD	
□ C-GMAI	Boeing 737-2Q2C	21467/515	ex TN-AHW	

AIR IVANHOE			Foleyet-Ivanhoe Lake, ON
□ C-GDVB	Cessna 180H	18052032	FP
□ C-GERE	de Havilland DHC-2 Beaver	352	ex N62784	FP
□ C-GPUS	de Havilland DHC-2 Beaver	624	ex 53-2824	FP

AIR LABRADOR/LABRADOR AIRWAYS	Lab Air (WJ/LAL)		Goose Bay, NL (YYR)
□ C-FCSW	de Havilland DHC-6 Twin Otter 300	355		♦
□ C-FGON	de Havilland DHC-6 Twin Otter 300	369	ex CF-GON	FP/WS
□ C-FOPN	de Havilland DHC-6 Twin Otter 300	291	ex F-BTOO	FP/WS
□ C-GIZF	de Havilland DHC-6 Twin Otter 300	549	ex N61UT	
□ C-GKSN	de Havilland DHC-6 Twin Otter 300	493	ex N148DE	
□ C-GLAI	de Havilland DHC-6 Twin Otter 300	296	ex N5377G	FP/WS
□ C-GNQY	de Havilland DHC-6 Twin Otter 300	450	ex N965HA	FP/WS
□ C-FJEA	Beech A100 King Air	B-107		♦
□ C-FWXL	Beech 1900D	UE-5		♦
□ C-GTMB	Beech 1900D	UE-345	ex N23388	
□ C-GUYR	Cessna 208 Caravan I	20800031	ex N604MA	
□ C-GZUZ	Beech A100 King Air	B-143		

AIR MELANCON			St Anne-du-Lac, QC
□ C-FZVP	de Havilland DHC-2 Beaver	1033	ex N564	FP/WS
□ C-GQXH	de Havilland DHC-2 Beaver	536	ex N1579	FP/WS

AIR MONT-LAURIER			Ste-Veronique, QC
□ C-FQQC	de Havilland DHC-2 Beaver	56	ex CF-QQC	FP
□ C-FSUB	de Havilland DHC-3 Otter	8	ex RCAF 3662	FP
□ C-FTUR	de Havilland DHC-2 Beaver	1529	ex CF-TUR	FP
□ C-GGSC	de Havilland DHC-3 Otter	366	ex N5072F	FP
□ C-GMGP	Cessna A185E Skywagon	18502077	ex N9054F	FP

| ☐ C-GUML | de Havilland DHC-2 Beaver | 307 | ex N1402Z | | FP |
| ☐ C-GVLK | Cessna U206G Stationair 6 II | U20604329 | ex N756SW | | FP |

AIR MONTMAGNY/MONTMAGNY AIR SERVICE

Montmagny, QC

☐ C-GBFU	Britten-Norman BN-2A-27 Islander	535	ex N70JA	
☐ C-GCTM	Cessna U206G Stationair	U20603794	ex N8920G	
☐ C-GGJG	Britten-Norman BN-2B-26 Islander	2219	ex F-ODUP	
☐ C-GOSJ	Partenavia P.68 Observer	241-02		
☐ C-GTMQ	Cessna 206H Stationair	20608038	ex N7255B	

AIR NOOTKA

Gold River, BC

☐ C-FCDT	de Havilland DHC-2 Beaver	390		FP♦
☐ C-FIBR	Cessna 180K Skywagon	18052788		FP
☐ C-GIUR	Cessna A185F Skywagon	18503290	FP	

AIR NORTH

Air North (4N/ANT)

Whitehorse, YT (YXY)

☐ C-FAGI	Hawker Siddeley HS.748 Srs.2A/276	1699	ex G-11-6	
☐ C-FCSE	Hawker Siddeley HS.748 Srs 2A/269	1679	ex G-AYFL	
☐ C-FYDU	Hawker Siddeley HS.748 Srs.2A/273	1694	ex ZK-MCP	wfs
☐ C-FYDY	Hawker Siddeley HS.748 Srs.2A/233	1661	ex ZK-MCJ	[YXY]
☐ C-GANA	Hawker Siddeley HS.748 Srs.2A/234	1758	ex C-GFNW	wfs
☐ C-FANB	Boeing 737-48E	25764/2314	ex N764TA	
☐ C-FANF	Boeing 737-55D	27417/2392	ex N289SC	♦
☐ C-GANH	Boeing 737-505/W	27153/2516	ex VP-BOQ	
☐ C-GANJ	Boeing 737-548	26287/2427	ex N248TR	
☐ C-GANU	Boeing 737-55D	27416/2389	ex N225SC	♦
☐ C-GANV	Boeing 737-2X6C	23122/1036	ex N816AL	

AIR NUNAVUT

Air Baffin (BFF)

Iqaluit, NT (YFB)

☐ C-FCGW	Beech 200 Super King Air	BB-207	ex N111WH	CatPass 200 conversion
☐ C-FFEV	AMD Falcon 10	204	ex XA-UDP	
☐ C-FZNQ	Beech 200 Super King Air	BB-264	ex N465CJ	CatPass 200 conversion
☐ C-FZOP	AMD Falcon 10	44	ex (N90AB)	
☐ C-GSXJ	AMD Falcon 10	100	ex XA-UML	
☐ C-GZYO	Beech 200 Super King Air	BB-383	ex N384DB	

AIR ROBERVAL

(RBV)

Roberval, PQ (YRJ)

☐ C-FNFI	de Havilland DHC-3 Otter	379		FP/WS
☐ C-FNME	Cessna 208 Caravan I	20800318	ex N208JL	
☐ C-FVVY	de Havilland DHC-3 Turbo Otter	410	ex RCAF 9427	FP/WS
☐ C-GLIE	Cessna 208B Caravan I	208B0703	ex N903DP	

AIR SAGUENAY

Lac St-Sebastien, QC

☐ C-FIUS	de Havilland DHC-2 Beaver	901	ex CF-IUS	FP/WS
☐ C-FJAC	de Havilland DHC-2 Beaver	937	ex CF-JAC	FP/WS
☐ C-FJGV	de Havilland DHC-2 Beaver	977	ex CF-JGV	FP/WS
☐ C-FJKI	de Havilland DHC-2 Beaver	992	ex CF-JKI	FP/WS
☐ C-FKRJ	de Havilland DHC-2 Beaver	1210	ex CF-KRJ	FP/WS
☐ C-FOCU	de Havilland DHC-2 Beaver	73	ex CF-OCU	FP/WS
☐ C-FRZL	de Havilland DHC-2 Beaver	1283	ex CF-RZL	FP/WS
☐ C-FUWJ	de Havilland DHC-2 Beaver	453	ex N7691	FP/WS
☐ C-FYYT	de Havilland DHC-2 Beaver	1569	ex VH-IDZ	FP/WS
☐ C-GAEF	de Havilland DHC-2 Beaver	372	ex 51-16830	FP/WS
☐ C-GPUO	de Havilland DHC-2 Beaver	810	ex 54-1677	FP/WS
☐ C-GUJI	de Havilland DHC-2 Beaver	1141	ex N68013	FP/WS
☐ C-GUJU	de Havilland DHC-2 Beaver	1639	ex N4600Y	FP/WS
☐ C-GWAE	de Havilland DHC-2 Beaver	1094	ex N93434	FP/WS
☐ C-FAZW	de Havilland DHC-3 Otter	451	ex JW-9101	FP/WS
☐ C-FSVP	de Havilland DHC-3 Otter	28		FP/WS♦
☐ C-FDAK	de Havilland DHC-3 Otter	157	ex CF-DAK	FP/WS
☐ C-FJZN	de Havilland DHC-3 Otter	205	ex CF-JZN	FP/WS
☐ C-FODT	de Havilland DHC-3 Turbo Otter	218	ex CF-ODT	FP/WS
☐ C-GLCO	de Havilland DHC-3 Turbo Otter	420	ex N17681	FP/WS
☐ C-GLFL	de Havilland DHC-3 Turbo Otter	329	ex 58-1712	FP/WS
☐ C-GLJI	de Havilland DHC-3 Otter	150	ex 55-3297	FP/WS
☐ C-GLMT	de Havilland DHC-3 Turbo Otter	216	ex IM-1716	FP/WS
☐ C-GQDU	de Havilland DHC-3 Turbo Otter	43	ex N94472	FP/WS
☐ C-GUTQ	de Havilland DHC-3 Otter	402	ex HK-3049X	FP/WS
☐ C-GVNX	de Havilland DHC-3 Otter	353	ex N5335G	FP/WS
☐ C-FYAO	Cessna A185E Skywagon	18501472	ex (N2722J)	FP/WS
☐ C-GAYC	Cessna A185F Skywagon	18503999		FP/WS
☐ C-GTBY	Cessna 208 Caravan I	20800261	ex C-GFLN	FP/WS
☐ C-GUBN	Cessna U206F Stationair II	U20602860	ex (N1185Q)	FP/WS

☐ C-GUJQ   Cessna A185F Skywagon   18503048   FP/WS

AIR SPRAY		Air Spray (ASB)		Edmonton-Municipal/Red Deer, AB (YEG/YQF)
☐ CF-CUI	Douglas B-26C Invader	28803	ex N9401Z	12
☐ C-FKBM	Douglas A-26B Invader	27415	ex N8017E	20
☐ C-FPGF	Douglas A-26B Invader	29154	ex 44-35857	1
☐ CF-ZTC	Douglas B-26C Invader	29136	ex N9300R	13 Lucky Jack
☐ C-GHZM	Douglas A-26B Invader	27400	ex N4805E	5 Fire Eater
☐ C-FDTH	Lockheed L-188A Electra	1038	ex C-GKIL	
☐ C-FLJO	Lockheed L-188C Electra	1103	ex N429NA	82
☐ C-FLXT	Lockheed L-188C Electra	1130	ex N308D	
☐ C-FVFH	Lockheed L-188A Electra	1006	ex PK-RLF	89
☐ C-FZCS	Lockheed L-188C Electra	1060	ex HR-SHN	87
☐ C-GHZI	Lockheed L-188C Electra	2007	ex N1968R	84
☐ C-GJTZ	Lockheed L-188C Electra	1133	ex N290F	
☐ C-GNPB	Lockheed L-188A Electra	1028	ex Honduras 555	
☐ C-GOIZ	Lockheed L-188AF Electra	1053	ex N343HA	
☐ C-GYVI	Lockheed L-188CF Electra	1112	ex N360Q	83 [YQF]
☐ C-GZCF	Lockheed L-188CF Electra	1091	ex G-CEXS	90
☐ C-GZVM	Lockheed L-188A Electra	1036	ex N351Q	85
☐ C-GZYH	Lockheed L-188A Electra	1124	ex HR-AMM	[YQF]
☐ C-FAKP	Rockwell 690 Turbo Commander	11040	ex N690DC	56
☐ C-FIIL	Rockwell 690A Turbo Commander	11167	ex N85AB	
☐ C-FMCX	Rockwell 690B Turbo Commander	11446	ex N137BW	
☐ C-FZRQ	Rockwell 690 Turbo Commander	11025	ex N100LS	51
☐ C-GFPP	Rockwell 690 Turbo Commander	11032	ex N349AC	52
☐ C-GJFO	Rockwell 690 Turbo Commander	11035	ex N15VZ	53
☐ C-GKDZ	Rockwell 690 Turbo Commander	11016	ex N428SJ	54
☐ C-GYFG	Rockwell 690A Turbo Commander	11189		
☐ C-GZON	Rockwell 690 Turbo Commander	11020	ex N14CV	55
☐ C-FEHK	Ted Smith Aerostar 600A	60-0400-140	ex N17LH	307
☐ C-FJCF	Ted Smith Aerostar 600A	60-0153-067	ex N37HA	308
☐ C-FNVD	Cessna A185E Skywagon	185-1348		
☐ C-GPBX	Gulfstream 695A	96060	ex FAH-006	
☐ C-GXJP	Cessna 310P	310P0073	ex N101QC	305
☐ C-GXXN	Cessna T310P	310P0002	ex N5702M	306
☐ N907AS	British Aerospace 146-200	E2156	ex OB-1948P	for tanker conversion♦
☐ N908AS	British Aerospace 146-200	E2082	ex N773CS	for tanker conversion♦

AIR TAMARAC				Clova SPB, QC
☐ C-FJNA	Cessa 180A	32841		FP
☐ C-FMMO	de Havilland DHC-2 Beaver	1431	ex CF-MMO	FP
☐ C-FMPT	de Havilland DHC-2 Beaver	1260	ex CF-MPT	FP
☐ C-FZNK	Cessna A185E Skywagon	18501822		FP

AIR TINDI		Air Tindi (8T/TID)		Yellowknife, NT (YZF)
☐ C-FATA	Beech 200 Super King Air	BB-283	ex N283JP	
☐ C-FCGU	Beech 200B Super King Air	BB-301	ex N611SW	CatPass 200 conversion
☐ C-FYKN	Beech B300 Super King Air	FL-36	ex N96KA	
☐ C-GATK	Beech B200GT Super King Air	BY-225		♦
☐ C-GBYN	Beech B200 Super King Air	BB-1232	ex N209CM	
☐ C-GDPB	Beech 200C Super King Air	BL-44	ex N18379	EMS
☐ C-GNHM	Beech 200 Super King Air	BB-188	ex N417RC	
☐ C-GNWT	Beech B200GT Super King Air	BY-215		
☐ C-GTUC	Beech 200 Super King Air	BB-268	ex N565RA	♦
☐ C-GXHF	Beech 200 Super King Air	BB-1343	ex 5Y-ECO	Beech 1300 conversion
☐ C-GYKI	Beech B200GT Super King Air	BY-230		♦
☐ C-FATM	de Havilland DHC-6 Twin Otter 300	265	ex PJ-ATL	FP/WS
☐ C-FATO	de Havilland DHC-6 Twin Otter 300	674	ex A6-MRM	FP/WS
☐ C-FATW	de Havilland DHC-6 Twin Otter 300	525	ex PK-BRA	FP/WS
☐ C-GMAS	de Havilland DHC-6 Twin Otter 300	438	ex N546N	FP/WS
☐ C-GNPS	de Havilland DHC-6 Twin Otter 300	558		FP/WS
☐ C-FWZV	de Havilland DHC-7-103	081	ex P2-ANP	
☐ C-GCEV	de Havilland DHC-7-102	063	ex HB-IVY	
☐ C-GCPY	de Havilland DHC-7-102	101	ex OY-CTC	
☐ C-GFFL	de Havilland DHC-7-102	074	ex HB-IVY	
☐ C-GUAT	de Havilland DHC-7-103	010	ex OY-CBT	
☐ C-FAFG	Cessna 208B Caravan I	208B0724	ex N997Q	
☐ C-FDAU	Canadair CL601 Challenger	3056	ex Germany 1206	
☐ C-FKAY	Cessna 208B Caravan I	208B0470	ex N1294N	dam 20Nov14
☐ C-FXUY	de Havilland DHC-3 Turbo Otter	142	ex N214L	FP/WS
☐ C-FYKN	Beech B300 Super King Air	FL-36	ex N96KA	
☐ C-GATH	Cessna 208B Caravan I	208B1244	ex N5225K	

80

☐ C-GATY	Cessna 208 Caravan I	20800305	ex N52627	FP/WS
☐ C-GJDA	Learjet 35A	35A-505	ex N90PN	
☐ C-GXCB	Learjet 35A	35A-417	ex LX-ONE	

AIR TRANSAT — Transat (TS/TSC) — Montreal-Trudeau, QC (YUL)

☐ C-FDAT	Airbus A310-308	658	ex A6-EKK	305
☐ C-GFAT	Airbus A310-304	545	ex A6-EKG	301
☐ C-GLAT	Airbus A310-308	588	ex A6-EKI	302
☐ C-GPAT	Airbus A310-308	597	ex A6-EKJ	303
☐ C-GSAT	Airbus A310-308	600	ex 5Y-KQM	304
☐ C-GTSF	Airbus A310-304	472	ex CS-TEZ	345
☐ C-GTSH	Airbus A310-308	599	ex D-AIDN	343
☐ C-GTSW	Airbus A310-304	483	ex CS-TEH	348
☐ C-GTSY	Airbus A310-304	447	ex N447DN	344
☐ C-GCTS	Airbus A330-342	177	ex B-HYE	002
☐ C-GGTS	Airbus A330-243	250	ex F-WWKK	101
☐ C-GITS	Airbus A330-243	271	ex F-WWKY	102
☐ C-GKTS	Airbus A330-342	111	ex B-HYC	100
☐ C-GPTS	Airbus A330-243	480	ex F-WWKV	103
☐ C-GTSD	Airbus A330-343	407	ex TC-SGJ	004
☐ C-GTSI	Airbus A330-243	427	ex G-OJMB	105
☐ C-GTSJ	Airbus A330-243	795	ex G-TCXA	203
☐ C-GTSN	Airbus A330-243	369	ex HB-IQZ	104
☐ C-GTSO	Airbus A330-342	132	ex B-HYD	003
☐ C-GTSR	Airbus A330-243	966	ex XA-MXP	201
☐ C-GTSZ	Airbus A330-243	971	ex XA-MXQ	202
☐ C-GTQB	Boeing 737-8Q8/W	30696/1892	ex VT-AXD	401
☐ C-GTQC	Boeing 737-8Q8/W	29368/1910	ex VT-AXE	402 ♦
☐ C-GTQF	Boeing 737-8Q8/W	29369/1939	ex VT-AXF	403 ♦
☐ C-GTQG	Boeing 737-8Q8/W	30701/1946	ex VT-AXG	404 ♦

AIR TUNILIK — Schefferville-Squaw Lake, QC (YKL)

☐ C-FAZX	de Havilland DHC-3 Otter	458		FP/WS♦
☐ C-FLAN	de Havilland DHC-2 Beaver	1140		FP/WS♦
☐ C-FLLX	de Havilland DHC-2 Beaver	1293	ex CF-LLX	FP/WS
☐ C-FSHC	de Havilland DHC-2 Beaver	1261		FP/WS♦

AIRCO AIRCRAFT CHARTERS — Edmonton-Municipal, AB (YXD)

☐ C-FTOQ	Beech 1900D	UE-78	ex ZS-SDH	
☐ C-FTOW	Beech 1900D	UE-130		
☐ C-FWPG	Beech 100 King Air	B-67	ex N26KW	
☐ C-FWYF	Beech 100 King Air	B-89	ex N169RA	
☐ C-FWYN	Beech 100 King Air	B-47	ex C-GNAX	
☐ C-FWYO	Beech 100 King Air	B-28	ex N27JJ	
☐ C-GBMI	Piper PA-31-350 Chieftain	31-8352007	ex N23NP	
☐ C-GZNB	Piper PA-31-350 Navajo Chieftain	31-7752079	ex N6654B	

AIREXPRESS ONTARIO — Oshawa, ON (YOO)

| ☐ C-GBBS | Beech 200 Super King Air | BB-757 | ex N948MB | |

ALBERTA CENTRAL AIRWAYS — Lac la Biche, AB (YLB)

☐ C-FSUG	Beech B200 Super King Air	BB-1699		
☐ C-FWPN	Beech 100 King Air	B-51		
☐ C-GACA	Beech 200 Super King Air	BB-1309	ex N4277C	Beech 1300 conversion
☐ C-GACN	Beech 200 Super King Air	BB-1384	ex N575T	Beech 1300 conversion
☐ C-GSWU	Beech B200 Super King Air	BB-1590	ex N928BW	
☐ C-FTMU	de Havilland DHC-6 Twin Otter 300	782	ex C-FZPQ	
☐ C-FTSU	de Havilland DHC-6 Twin Otter 300	451	ex C-FINM	

ALKAN AIR — Alkan Air (AKN) — Whitehorse, YT (YXY)

☐ C-FAKN	Beech 200 Super King Air	BB-216	ex LN-VIU	
☐ C-FAKW	Beech 300LW Super King Air	FA-183	ex N19NC	
☐ C-FLPC	Beech 300 Super King Air	FL-127	ex N300LS	
☐ C-GMOC	Beech 200 Super King Air	BB-513	ex N513SA	
☐ C-GTEM	Beech B300 King Air	FL-236	ex N2346S	
☐ C-FAKV	Cessna 208B Caravan I	208B1008	ex N916TP	
☐ C-FAKZ	Cessna 208B Caravan I	208B0666	ex N939JL	
☐ C-FCPV	de Havilland DHC-6 Twin Otter 300	371	ex N371SS	
☐ C-FQMO	Cessna U206F Stationair	U20603456		
☐ C-FSKF	Cessna 208B Caravan I	208B0673	ex N5268M	
☐ C-GLCS	de Havilland DHC-3 Turbo Otter	428	ex N17685	
☐ C-GSDT	Piper PA-31-350 Chieftain	31-8152102	ex N120FL	

☐ C-GYTB Cessna U206G Stationair U20603685 ex (N7579N)

ALLEN AIRWAYS Sioux Lookout, ON (YXL)

☐ C-FERZ	Cessna 180K	18053071	ex N2799K	FP
☐ C-FYCK	Cessna A185E Skywagon	185-1478	ex CF-YCK	FP/WS
☐ C-GQDO	Cessna A185F Skywagon	18503745	ex (N8585Q)	FP/WS

ALPINE AVIATION Whitehorse, YT (YXY)

☐ CF-FHZ	de Havilland DHC-2 Beaver	66	ex C-FFHZ	FP
☐ C-FGSI	Cessna U206F Stationair	U20602165	ex CF-GSI	FP
☐ C-GLFW	Cessna 180J Skywagon	18052625		FP

ALPINE HELICOPTERS Kelowna, BC (YLW)

☐ C-FJCH	Bell 206L-1 LongRanger	45737	ex N144JD	
☐ C-FSKR	Bell 206L-1 LongRanger	45607	ex N171KA	
☐ C-GALH	Bell 206L-3 LongRanger III	51297	ex N753HL	
☐ C-GALJ	Bell 206L-3 LongRanger III	51010	ex N22654	
☐ C-GALL	Bell 206L-3 LongRanger III	51015	ex N22660	
☐ C-GRLK	Bell 206L-3 LongRanger III	51028	ex N42814	
☐ C-FAHB	Bell 212	30794	ex A6-BBH	
☐ C-FAHC	Bell 212	31246	ex N212HT	
☐ C-FAHG	Bell 212	30940	ex N8530F	
☐ C-FAHK	Bell 212	30852	ex XA-SSE	
☐ C-FAHL	Bell 212	30588	ex XA-SSJ	
☐ C-FAHR	Bell 212	30789	ex A6-BBI	
☐ C-FALK	Bell 212	30982	ex N212EL	
☐ C-FALV	Bell 212	30816	ex N74AL	
☐ C-FGCO	Bell 212	30933		♦
☐ C-GAHO	Bell 212	30937		
☐ C-GAHV	Bell 212	30699		♦
☐ C-GALI	Bell 212	30525	ex JA9510	
☐ C-GIRZ	Bell 212	30622	ex RP-C1677	
☐ C-GRNR	Bell 212	30999		
☐ C-FAHI	Bell 407	53016	ex N409KA	
☐ C-FALA	Bell 407	53115		
☐ C-FALC	Bell 407	53056	ex C-FZDS	
☐ C-FALF	Bell 407	53271	ex CC-CWS	
☐ C-FALM	Bell 407	53018	ex N409KA	
☐ C-FNOB	Bell 407	53070	ex N57416	
☐ C-GALG	Bell 407	53059	ex N409PH	
☐ C-GAVL	Bell 407	53148		♦
☐ C-GYAA	Bell 407	53152	ex N407RH	
☐ C-FALU	Bell 206B JetRanger III	1072		
☐ C-GALX	Bell 206B JetRanger	1046	ex N58096	
☐ C-GJSL	Bell 206B JetRanger	3557		
☐ C-GLAV	Bell 206L-1 LongRanger	45414		♦

ATIKOKAN AERO SERVICE Atikokan-Municipal, ON (YIB)

☐ CF-IJE	Cessna 180	32066		
☐ CF-IPL	de Havilland DHC-2 Beaver	132		FP/WS
☐ C-GDZH	de Havilland DHC-2 Beaver	356	ex 51-16555	FP/WS

ATLEO RIVER AIR SERVICE Tofino, BC (YTP)

☐ C-GALZ	Bell 206B Jet Ranger	1563		
☐ C-GIYQ	Cessna A185F Skywagon II	18503618	ex (N7582Q)	FP/WS
☐ C-GYJX	Cessna A185F Skywagon	18503187	ex (N93161)	FP

ATLIN AIR CHARTERS Atlin, BC

☐ C-GGEK	Cessna 207A Stationair 8 II	20700731	ex N63AK	
☐ C-GOZR	de Havilland DHC-2 Beaver	800	ex 54-1670	

AVIATION STARLINK Starlink (Q4/TLK) Dorval, QB

☐ C-FDBJ	Dassault Falcon 2000EX	145	ex N47WS	
☐ C-GCAQ	Beech B350 Super King Air	FL-748	ex N748KA	
☐ C-GCCN	British Aerospace Jetstream 3112	704	ex N333PX	
☐ C-GCCZ	British Aerospace Jetstream 3112	712	ex N335PX	
☐ C-GCGT	Hawker 850XP	258828	ex N7128T	
☐ C-GDBJ	Pilatus PC-12/47E	1457	ex N457NX	♦
☐ C-GDFW	British Aerospace Jetstream 3102	720	ex G-HDGS	♦
☐ C-GIRL	Cessna 525 Citation CJ1+	525-0641		♦
☐ C-GLIV	Beech 390 Premiere	RB-259	ex N42LG	♦

☐ C-GOAB	Dassault Falcon 2000EX	90	ex C-GOHB	
☐ C-GOHB	Dassault Falcon 2000EX	232	ex F-WWGX	
☐ C-GOHI	Pilatus PC-12/47E	1297	ex HB-F..	
☐ C-GOHJ	de Havilland DH.125 Srs.700A	25049	ex C-GNOW	
☐ C-GROG	Hawker 850XP	258852	ex N7302P	
☐ C-GTLP	Embraer EMB.500 Phenom 100	50000265	ex PT-MMP	

BAMAJI AIR   Sioux Lookout, ON (YXL)

☐ C-FHEP	de Havilland DHC-2 Beaver	69	ex C-FIOB	FP/WS
☐ C-FKAC	Found FBA-2C1 Bush Hawk XP	42		FP/WS
☐ C-GBKA	Cessna A185F Skywagon	18502375	ex N53099	FP/WS
☐ C-GDYD	de Havilland DHC-2 Beaver	1461	ex VH-IMH	FP/WS
☐ C-GIPR	Cessna 208 Caravan I	20800343		FP/WS
☐ C-GZBS	de Havilland DHC-2 Beaver	975		fp/ws

BAR XH AIR dba Integra Air   Palliser (BXH)   Medicine Hat, AB (YXH)

☐ C-FFIA	British Aerospace Jetstream 3112	779	ex C-FSAS	
☐ C-FPNQ	Beech B200 Super King Air	BB-1645		♦
☐ C-GGIA	British Aerospace Jetstream 3112	778	ex C-FMIP	
☐ C-GNGI	British Aerospace Jetstream 3112	739	ex N855JS	
☐ C-GSIA	Beech 200 Super King Air	BB-373	ex N200FE	
☐ C-GXHR	Beech B200 Super King Air	BB-1305	ex 5Y-EOB	Beech 1300 conversion

BEARSKIN AIRLINES/BEARSKIN LAKE AIR SERVICE

Bearskin (JV/BLS)   Sioux Lookout, ON (YXL)

☐ C-FYAG	Swearingen SA227AC Metro III	AC-670B	ex N670VG	Spirit of Fort Frances
☐ C-FYWG	Swearingen SA227AC Metro III	AC-782B	ex N3000S	Spirit of Winnipeg
☐ C-GYHD	Swearingen SA227AC Metro III	AC-739B	ex N227JH	Spirit of Dryden
☐ C-GYQT	Swearingen SA227AC Metro III	AC-644B	ex N644VG	Spirit of Thunder Bay
☐ C-GYRL	Swearingen SA227AC Metro III	AC-706B	ex G-BUKA	
☐ C-GYXL	Swearingen SA227AC Metro III	AC-725B	ex N227FA	Spirit of Sioux Lookout
☐ C-FXUS	Swearingen SA227CC Metro 23	CC-841B	ex N456LA	
☐ C-GAFQ	Swearingen SA227DC Metro 23	DC-890B	ex N211SA	
☐ C-GJVB	Swearingen SA227DC Metro 23	DC-902B	ex N902WB	
☐ C-GJVC	Swearingen SA227DC Metro 23	DC-885B	ex N885ML	
☐ C-GJVH	Swearingen SA227DC Metro 23	DC-898B	ex N898ML	
☐ C-GJVO	Swearingen SA227AC Metro 23	DC-846B	ex VH-KEU	
☐ C-GJVW	Swearingen SA227DC Metro 23	DC-872B	ex VH-KEX	
☐ C-GSNP	Swearingen SA227DC Metro 23	DC-838B	ex VH-KAN	
☐ C-GSOQ	Swearingen SA227DC Metro 23	DC-837B	ex VH-KDO	
☐ C-GYTL	Swearingen SA227CC Metro 23	CC-829B	ex N30154	Spirit of Big Trout Lake

BEAVER AIR SERVICES   The Pas, MN/Missinippi (YQD/-)

☐ C-FICU	Beech 200 Super King Air	BB-324		♦
☐ C-FTYO	Beech B200 Super King Air	BB-1222	ex N126KA	
☐ C-FWXI	Beech B200 Super King Air	BB-1224	ex C-GTLA	EMS
☐ C-GKHI	Beech B200 Super King Air	BB-1265	ex N544P	
☐ C-GOGT	Beech 200 Super King Air	BB-536		
☐ C-FMCB	Cessna 208B Caravan I	208B1114		
☐ C-FRSP	Cessna 310H	310H0076		
☐ C-GHQF	Piper PA-31-350	31-8052050		
☐ C-GMKO	Piper PA-31-350	31-7952063		
☐ C-GWHW	Piper PA-31-350	31-8052060		

BLACK SHEEP AVIATION   Whitehorse, YT (YXY)

☐ C-FMKP	Cessna 208 Caravan I	20800189	ex N9770F	
☐ C-GCTP	Cessna A185P Skywagon	18504275		FP/WS
☐ C-GDHW	de Havilland DHC-3 Turbo Otter	10	ex C-FGTL	FP/WS
☐ C-GNPO	de Havilland DHC-2 Beaver	773		FP/WS

BLUE WATER AVIATION SERVICES   Silver Falls, MB

☐ C-FIOF	de Havilland DHC-3 Turbo Otter	24	ex LN-SUV	FP/WS
☐ C-FKOA	de Havilland DHC-3 Turbo Otter	130	ex CF-KOA	FP/WS
☐ C-GBTU	de Havilland DHC-3 Turbo Otter	209	ex IM1711	FP/WS
☐ C-GHYB	de Havilland DHC-3 Otter	386	ex UB656	FP/WS
☐ C-GSMG	de Havilland DHC-3 Turbo Otter	363	ex RCAF 9405	FP/WS
☐ C-FCUW	Cessna 337 Super Skymaster	337-0009	ex N2109X	
☐ C-FHWM	Swearingen SA226-T Merlin	T-289		♦
☐ C-FXOQ	Piper PA-31 Navajo	31-440		
☐ C-GFVZ	Cessna A185F Skywagon	18503058	ex (N21451)	FP/WS
☐ C-GGGD	Cessna TU206G Stationair 8	U20605664	ex (N5348X)	FP/WS

BUFFALO AIRWAYS		Buffalo (BFL)		Hay River, NT/Yellowknife (YHY/YZF)	
☐ C-FAYN	Canadair CL215	1105		282	
☐ C-FAYU	Canadair CL215	1106		283	
☐ C-GBPD	Canadair CL215	1084		291	opf NWT Govt
☐ C-GBYU	Canadair CL215	1083	ex C-GKEA	290	opf NWT Govt
☐ C-GCSX	Canadair CL215	1088	ex C-GKEA	295	opf NWT Govt
☐ C-GDHN	Canadair CL215	1089	ex C-GKEE	296	opf NWT Govt
☐ C-GDKW	Canadair CL215	1095		280	
☐ C-GNCS	Canadair CL215	1008	ex N215NC		opf NWT Govt
☐ C-FBAE	Douglas DC-3	12591	ex C-FDTH		[YQF]
☐ C-FCUE	Douglas DC-3	12983	ex NC41407		
☐ C-FDTB	Douglas DC-3	12597	ex CF-TEC		[YQF]
☐ C-FFAY	Douglas DC-3	4785	ex CF-FAY		[YQF]
☐ CF-FTR	Douglas DC-3	32843/16095	ex N142JR		
☐ C-FLFR	Douglas DC-3	13155	ex CF-LFR		
☐ C-FQBC	Douglas DC-3	27026/15581			
☐ C-FROD	Douglas DC-3	13028	ex C-GPNW		
☐ C-GJKM	Douglas DC-3	13580	ex CAF 12946		
☐ C-GPNR	Douglas DC-3	13333	ex CAF 12932		
☐ C-GWIR	Douglas DC-3	9371	ex N18262		
☐ C-GWZS	Douglas DC-3	12327	ex CAF 12913		
☐ C-FBAA	Douglas C-54D-DC	10653	ex N4994H	12 Arctic Expeditor	[YZF]
☐ C-FBAJ	Douglas C-54A-DC	3088	ex N11712	02	[YHY]
☐ C-FBAK	Douglas C-54D-DC	10613	ex N62342		[YHY]
☐ C-FBAM	Douglas C-54G-DC	36009	ex N4958M		[YHY]
☐ C-FBAP	Douglas C-54A-DC	36089	ex N2742G	15	[YHY]
☐ C-FIQM	Douglas C-54G-DC	36088	ex N4218S	57 Arctic Trader	Tanker
☐ C-GBAJ	Douglas C-54A-DC	27328	ex N62297		Tanker
☐ C-GBNV	Douglas C-54G-DC	35988	ex N3303F	56	Tanker
☐ C-GBSK	Douglas C-54G-DC	36049	ex N4989N		
☐ C-GCTF	Douglas C-54E-DC	27281	ex N51819	58	Tanker
☐ C-GPSH	Douglas C-54A-DC	7458	ex N7171H	1 Arctic Distributor	
☐ C-FBAQ	Lockheed L-188AF Electra	1039	ex OE-ILB		
☐ C-FIJV	Lockheed L-188C Electra	1140	ex N4HG		
☐ C-FIJX	Lockheed L-188CF Electra	2010	ex N2RK		
☐ C-GLBA	Lockheed L-188AF Electra	1145	ex OE-ILA		
☐ C-GXFC	Lockheed L-188 AF Electra	1100	ex G-LOFC		
☐ C-GZFE	Lockheed L-188CF Electra	1144	ex G-LOFE		
☐ C-FAVO	Curtiss C-46D Commando	33242	ex N9891Z	Arctic Thunder	
☐ C-FCGH	Beech 65-A90 King Air	LJ-203	ex CF-CGH	Birddog 4	
☐ C-FGWE	Cessna 310Q II	310Q0920	ex (N69686)		
☐ C-FPQM	Consolidated PBY-5A Catalina	CV-425	ex CF-GMS	714	
☐ C-FMWM	Beech 100 King Air	B-59	ex N702JL		
☐ C-FNRM	Rockwell 690C	11692			♦
☐ C-FNRP	Rockwell 690C	11627	ex N88BJ		♦
☐ CF-SAN	Noorduyn Norseman V	N29-29	ex CF-SAN		FP
☐ C-FULX	Beech 95-C55 Baron	TE-147	ex CF-ULX	Birddog 3	
☐ C-FUPT	Cessna A185E Skywagon	185-1075	ex (N4568F)	141	
☐ C-GBAU	Beech 95-D55 Baron	TE-701	ex N7907R	3	
☐ C-GIWJ	Beech 95 Travel Air	TD-32	ex N2707Y		
☐ C-GTFC	Convair 240-27	279	ex N152PA		
☐ C-GTPO	Curtiss C-46 Commando	22556			
☐ C-GTXW	Curtiss C-46A Commando	30386	ex 5Y-TXW		[YZF]
☐ C-GWCB	Beech B95 Travel Air	TD-369	ex N9914R	140	
☐ C-GYFM	Beech 95 Travel Air	TD-202	ex N654Q		
☐ C-	Douglas DC-6BF	44434/515	ex N434TA		

CALM AIR		Calm Air (MO/CAV)		Thompson, MB (YTH)	
☐ C-FAFS	ATR 42-300	298	ex N298DG		
☐ C-FCIJ	ATR 42-300	139	ex ZS-OSN		
☐ C-FECI	ATR 42-320	203	ex F-WNUG		
☐ C-FJYW	ATR 42-300	235	ex N233RM	422	
☐ C-FMAK	ATR 42-300	142	ex N142GP		
☐ C-GDSS	ATR 42-300	329	ex D-BCRN		
☐ C-GKKR	ATR 42-320	197	ex SX-BIC		
☐ C-FAMO	Hawker Siddeley HS.748				
	Srs.2A/258LFD	1669	ex CF-AMO	746	[YTH]
☐ C-FAPU	Dornier 328-310 (328JET)	3145	ex N401FJ		VIP
☐ C-FCRZ	ATR 72-202	357	ex F-WDHA		
☐ C-FJCQ	ATR 72-202QC	311	ex F-GPOC		
☐ C-FULE	ATR 72-202	215	ex F-WNUE		
☐ C-GBEU	Dornier 328-310 (328JET)	3185	ex N424FJ		VIP
☐ C-GHSC	Hawker Siddeley HS.748 Srs.2B/LFD	1790	ex G-BJTL	745	Frtr
☐ C-GPBR	ATR 72-202	237	ex D-ANFC		♦

CAMERON AIR SERVICE			Toronto-City Centre, ON (YTZ)
☐ C-FKCA	Cessna 208 Caravan I	20800211	ex N211PA
☐ C-FXWH	Cessna U206C Super Skywagon	U2061170	ex CF-XWH
☐ C-GCGA	Cessna 208 Caravan I	20800242	ex (A6-CGA)
☐ C-GGSG	Cessna TU206G Stationair 6	U20605852	ex (N6281X)

CANADIAN HELICOPTERS		Canadian (CDN)	Montreal-Les Cedres, QC/Edmonton, AB
☐ C-FCCA	Aérospatiale AS350BA AStar	2900	
☐ C-FCHN	Aérospatiale AS350B2 AStar	2921	
☐ C-FETA	Aérospatiale AS350D AStar	1085	ex N137BH
☐ C-FFBU	Aérospatiale AS350B2 AStar	1215	ex N3605B
☐ C-FHVH	Aérospatiale AS350BA AStar	1256	ex N36075
☐ C-FNCH	Aérospatiale AS350B3 AStar	7225	
☐ C-FNIZ	Aérospatiale AS350B3 AStar	3190	♦
☐ C-FNZU	Aérospatiale AS350B3 AStar	3195	
☐ C-FNZZ	Aérospatiale AS350B3 AStar	7263	
☐ C-FPBA	Aérospatiale AS350B2 AStar	2492	ex JA6091
☐ C-FPER	Aérospatiale AS350B2 AStar	2552	ex F-WYMK
☐ C-FPLJ	Aérospatiale AS350D AStar	1060	ex C-FQNS
☐ C-FQNS	Aérospatiale AS350B2 AStar	1423	ex N5783Y
☐ C-FSHV	Aérospatiale AS350B AStar	1287	ex N5143R
☐ C-FSLB	Aérospatiale AS350B2 AStar	2142	ex JA9786
☐ C-FTNZ	Aérospatiale AS350B2 AStar	2286	♦
☐ C-FVVH	Aérospatiale AS350BA AStar	2612	
☐ C-GAHH	Aérospatiale AS350B AStar	1036	ex XA-
☐ C-GAHI	Aérospatiale AS350B2 AStar	1086	
☐ C-GALD	Aérospatiale AS350BA AStar	1146	
☐ C-GATX	Aérospatiale AS350BA AStar	1221	
☐ C-GAVO	Aérospatiale AS350B3 AStar	3139	
☐ C-GAYX	Aérospatiale AS350BA2 AStar	1179	
☐ C-GBCZ	Aérospatiale AS350B2 AStar	1159	ex N3600W
☐ C-GBPS	Aérospatiale AS350BA AStar	1277	ex N3610R
☐ C-GCEC	Aérospatiale AS350BA AStar	1431	ex N666JK
☐ C-GCHH	Aérospatiale AS350B2 AStar	2461	ex ZK-HND
☐ C-GCKP	Aérospatiale AS350D AStar	1138	ex N140BH
☐ C-GCWD	Aérospatiale AS350BA AStar	2047	ex N844BP
☐ C-GCWW	Aérospatiale AS350B2 AStar	1435	ex N340DF
☐ C-GDKD	Aérospatiale AS350BA AStar	1432	ex N5785H
☐ C-GDSX	Aérospatiale AS350BA AStar	1134	ex N35972
☐ C-GDUF	Aérospatiale AS350BA AStar	1309	
☐ C-GELC	Aérospatiale AS350B AStar	1162	
☐ C-GEPH	Aérospatiale AS350B AStar	1193	ex ZK-HET
☐ C-GEVH	Aérospatiale AS350BA AStar	2620	ex F-WYMN
☐ C-GFHS	Aérospatiale AS350B AStar	1401	
☐ C-GGIE	Aérospatiale AS350B2 AStar	3280	
☐ C-GHVD	Aérospatiale AS350B2 AStar	1236	
☐ C-GLNE	Aérospatiale AS350BA AStar	1128	ex N3599N
☐ C-GLNK	Aérospatiale AS350B2 AStar	1261	ex N3608C
☐ C-GLNM	Aérospatiale AS350B2 AStar	1262	ex N3608D
☐ C-GLNO	Aérospatiale AS350B2 AStar	1264	ex N3608N
☐ C-GMEY	Aérospatiale AS350B AStar	1004	ex N350AS
☐ C-GMIZ	Aérospatiale AS350B2 AStar	1170	
☐ C-GNMN	Aérospatiale AS350BA AStar	1315	ex XA-SNA
☐ C-GNZF	Aérospatiale AS350B2 AStar	4419	
☐ C-GNZM	Aérospatiale AS350B2 AStar	2349	ex ZK-HNK
☐ C-GNZW	Aérospatiale AS350B2 AStar	2073	♦
☐ C-GOVH	Aérospatale AS350BA AStar	1286	
☐ C-GRBT	Aérospatiale AS350B2 AStar	1246	ex N877JM
☐ C-GRGJ	Aérospatiale AS350BA AStar	1171	ex N3600G
☐ C-GRGU	Aérospatiale AS350BA AStar	1213	ex N7172H
☐ C-GSLF	Aérospatiale AS350D AStar	1310	
☐ C-GTPF	Aérospatiale AS350BA AStar	2932	
☐ C-GTVH	Aérospatiale AS350B2 AStar	2611	ex N600CH
☐ C-GZAD	Eurocopter AS350B3 Ecureuil	3491	♦
☐ C-FXIH	Aérospatiale AS355N TwinStar	5740	
☐ C-GHCD	Aérospatiale AS355N TwinStar	5702	ex N441L
☐ C-GNZA	Aérospatiale AS355N TwinStar	5654	
☐ C-GNZB	Aérospatiale AS355N TwinStar	5664	
☐ C-GNZS	Aérospatiale AS355N TwinStar	5666	ex JDFH-28
☐ C-GODG	Aérospatiale AS355N TwinStar	5659	
☐ C-GVHC	Aérospatiale AS355F2 TwinStar	5195	ex N5801T
☐ C-GVHK	Aérospatiale AS355F1 TwinStar	5098	ex N60031
☐ C-FBQH	Bell 206B JetRanger II	745	ex CF-BQH
☐ C-FHTS	Bell 206B JetRanger II	1037	ex CF-HTS
☐ C-FKNX	Bell 206B JetRanger III	2440	ex N5003X
☐ C-FOAN	Bell 206B JetRanger II	791	ex CF-OAN
☐ C-GAHC	Bell 206B JetRanger II	468	ex N2959W
☐ C-GBHE	Bell 206B JetRanger II	1335	

☐	C-GDBA	Bell 206B JetRanger III	2232	ex N16821		
☐	C-GETF	Bell 206B JetRanger III	3036			
☐	C-GFQH	Bell 206B JetRanger II	1090	ex N100JG		
☐	C-GIXS	Bell 206B JetRanger III	2304	ex N272RM		
☐	C-GNLE	Bell 206B JetRanger III	2358	ex N56PH		
☐	C-GNLG	Bell 206B JetRanger III	2360			
☐	C-GNPH	Bell 206B JetRanger III	2352	ex N58148		
☐	C-GOKE	Bell 206B JetRanger III	1830	ex N49655		
☐	C-GSHP	Bell 206B JetRanger II	1259	ex N259CH		
☐	C-GYQH	Bell 206B JetRanger III	1394	ex N111BH		
☐	C-FNYQ	Bell 206L LongRanger	45047	ex N20LT		
☐	C-GGZQ	Bell 206L LongRanger	45006	ex N49637		
☐	C-GLMV	Bell 206L-1 LongRanger II	45430	ex N454CH		
☐	C-GLQY	Bell 206L LongRanger	45146			
☐	C-GMHS	Bell 206L LongRanger	45120			
☐	C-GMHT	Bell 206L LongRanger	45127	ex N16847		
☐	C-GMHY	Bell 206L LongRanger	45145	ex N16924		
☐	C-GNLC	Bell 206L LongRanger	45055	ex N9978K		
☐	C-GNMC	Bell 206L LongRanger	45067			
☐	C-GNZR	Bell 206L LongRanger	45118	ex N16809		
☐	C-GQEZ	Bell 206L LongRanger	45038	ex N9942K		
☐	C-GTLB	Bell 206L LongRanger	45031	ex N9927K		
☐	C-GTOM	Bell 206L LongRanger	45010			
☐	C-GVHX	Bell 206L LongRanger	45138	ex N90AC		
☐	C-FBHF	Bell 212	30509	ex N7072J		
☐	C-FNJJ	Bell 212	30944	ex N2093S		
☐	C-FOKV	Bell 212	30819	ex N16787		
☐	C-GAHD	Bell 212	30570	ex N7034J		
☐	C-GFQP	Bell 212	30578	ex N58120		
☐	C-GHVH	Bell 212	30877	ex N8555V		
☐	C-GKCH	Bell 212	31213	ex N360EH		
☐	C-GOKL	Bell 212	30597	ex N2990W		
☐	C-GOKY	Bell 212	30698	ex (5H-)		
☐	C-GFFJ	Sikorsky S-76A	760138			EMS
☐	C-GIMM	Sikorsky S-76A	760044			EMS
☐	C-GIMN	Sikorsky S-76A	760110	ex G-BIAV		EMS
☐	C-GIMR	Sikorsky S-76A	760079	ex G-BHYB		
☐	C-GLFO	Sikorsky S-76A	760149	ex N76LA		
☐	C-FAVI	Bell 407	53315			
☐	C-FBCH	Eurocopter EC120B	1467			
☐	C-FDCH	Sikorsky S-61N	61773	ex ZS-PWR		
☐	C-FFAB	Eurocopter EC120B	1486			
☐	C-FLCN	Eurocopter EC120B	1055			
☐	C-FOCH	Eurocopter EC120B	1547			
☐	C-GJQG	Sikorsky S-61N	61722	ex HS-HTC		
☐	C-GJQN	Sikorsky S-61N	61815	ex HS-HTA		
☐	C-GZEY	Bell 412EP	36313			♦

CANADIAN NORTH — Norterra (5T/MPE) — Yellowknife, NT (YZF)

☐	C-GCNS	Boeing 737-275	23283/1109	ex C9-BAN	560	
☐	C-GCNV	Boeing 737-232	23074/993	ex N302DL	586	
☐	C-GDPA	Boeing 737-2T2C (AvAero 3)	22056/655		584	Spirit of Yellowknife
☐	C-GKCP	Boeing 737-217 (AvAero 3)	22729/915		523	
☐	C-GNDU	Boeing 737-242C (AvAero 3)	22877/880		562	
☐	C-GOPW	Boeing 737-275C (AvAero 3)	22160/688	ex N8288V	582	Spirit of Nunavut
☐	C-GSPW	Boeing 737-275C (AvAero 3)	22618/813		583	
☐	C-FGCN	Boeing 737-36N	28590/3097	ex N590AG	595	
☐	C-FKCN	Boeing 737-36N	28573/3041	ex N753DB	593	
☐	C-GCNK	Boeing 737-36Q	29189/3057	ex N892AG		
☐	C-GCNO	Boeing 737-36N	28596/3112	ex C-GOKF		CFL logojet c/s♦
☐	C-GCNU	Boeing 737-36Q/W	29140/3013	ex N291AG	592	
☐	C-GCNW	Boeing 737-36Q/W	28760/2989	ex VP-CAK	590	
☐	C-GCNZ	Boeing 737-36Q/W	28664/2940	ex N664AG	591	
☐	C-GICN	Boeing 737-36Q/W	29405/3047	ex N405GT	594	
☐	C-GPNL	Boeing 737-36N	28872/3082	ex G-TOYG	599	Celebrity Cruises c/s♦
☐	C-GZCN	Boeing 737-36NF	28594/3107	ex C-GKFP	596	♦
☐	C-GECN	de Havilland DHC-8-106	324	ex C-FSQY	324	
☐	C-GRGI	de Havilland DHC-8-106	304	ex N829PH	304	
☐	C-GRGO	de Havilland DHC-8-106	258	ex N735AG	258	
☐	C-GXCN	de Havilland DHC-8-106	345	ex RA-67255345		

CANJET — Canjet (C6/CJA) — Halifax-Intl, NS (YHZ)

☐	C-FTCX	Boeing 737-8AS/W	29921/560	ex EI-CSF	801	>TVS
☐	C-FTCZ	Boeing 737-8AS/W	29923/576	ex EI-CSH	802	>TVS

☐ C-FYQN	Boeing 737-8AS/W	29933/1038	ex EI-CST	804		>JAF
☐ C-FYQO	Boeing 737-8AS/W	29934/1050	ex EI-CSV	805		

CAN-WEST CORPORATE AIR CHARTERS — Slave Lake, AB (YZH)

☐ C-FKCW	Beech B200 Super King Air	BB-973	ex C-FEVC		
☐ C-FLBQ	Cessna 560 Citation Ultra	560-0429	ex (N146EC0		◆
☐ C-FOOS	Cessna U206E Stationair	U20601698	ex (N9498G)		
☐ C-FSAO	Beech B200 Super King Air	BB-1610	ex N713TA		
☐ C-FVKC	Beech B300 King Air	FL-273			◆
☐ C-GAYZ	Cessna A185F Skywagon	18504040	ex (N6416E)		
☐ C-GIRG	Cessna A185F SkyWagon II	18504181	ex (N61424)		
☐ C-GJMZ	Partenavia P.68 Observer	369270B			
☐ C-GKZS	Cessna 560 Citation Ultra	560-0460	ex (N163EC)		
☐ C-GLGD	Cessna U206G Stationair 6	U20606261	ex (N6388Z)		
☐ C-GNCW	Beech Baron 58	TH-1313	ex N6138C		
☐ C-GPNB	Beech B200 Super King Air	BB-1921			◆
☐ C-GSAZ	Piper PA-31 Navajo C	31-8112063	ex N4094Y		
☐ C-GXNL	Cessna 210L Centurion II	21060909	ex N5327V		
☐ C-GYDD	Cessna A185F Skywagon	18503124	ex (N80516)		

CARGOJET AIRWAYS — Cargojet (W8/CJT)

Winnipeg-Intl, MB/Toronto-Pearson Intl, QC (YWG/YYZ)

☐ C-FCJF	Boeing 727-223F (FedEx 3)	22011/1653	ex C-GACG		
☐ C-FCJU	Boeing 727-260F (FedEx 3)	22759/1789	ex C-FACM		
☐ C-FCJV	Boeing 727-223F	22469/1769	ex N713AA		
☐ C-GCJB	Boeing 727-225F (FedEx 3)	21855/1535	ex N886MA		
☐ C-GCJD	Boeing 727-231F (FedEx 3)	21988/1586	ex N808MA		
☐ C-GCJK	Boeing 727-223F (FedEx 3)	22015/1666	ex N899AA		
☐ C-GCJN	Boeing 727-225F (FedEx 3)	21451/1310	ex N610PA		
☐ C-GCJQ	Boeing 727-225F (FedEx 3)	22437/1682	ex N806MA		
☐ C-GCJZ	Boeing 727-225F (FedEx 3)	21854/1532	ex N889MA		
☐ C-GUJC	Boeing 727-260F (FedEx 3)	21979/1534	ex C-FACJ		
☐ C-FGKJ	Boeing 757-223F	25298/433	ex N664AA		◆
☐ C-FKAJ	Boeing 757-23APCF	24566/255	ex N720DB		
☐ C-FKCJ	Boeing 757-236F	24792/279	ex SE-DUO		
☐ C-FLAJ	Boeing 757-23APCF	24567/257	ex TF-FID		◆
☐ C-GIAJ	Boeing 757-28APCF	23767/127	ex N767AN		
☐ C-FDIJ	Boeing 767-39HERF	26257/488	ex N760NA		◆
☐ C-FGAJ	Boeing 767-223F	22319/112	ex N317AA		
☐ C-FGSJ	Boeing 767-39HER/W BCF	26256	ex OY-SRS	634	opf Purolator◆
☐ C-FMCJ	Boeing 767-223F	22316/95	ex N313AA		
☐ C-FPIJ	Boeing 767-33AER BDSF	27918/603	ex I-DEIG		◆
☐ C-GCJI	Boeing 767-232SCD	22217/27	ex N742AX		◆
☐ C-GCJO	Boeing 767-223SF	22315/94	ex N312AA		◆
☐ C-GKLY	Boeing 767-223 BDSF	22314/73	ex N714AX		◆
☐ C-GUAJ	Boeing 767-35EERF	26063/434	ex N224CY		◆
☐ C-GVIJ	Boeing 767-328ER BDSF	27212/531	ex N365CM		◆
☐ C-GYAJ	Boeing 767-35EERF	26064/438	ex N225CY		◆

CARSON AIR — Kelowna, BC (YLW)

☐ C-FKTE	Beech B350 King Air	FL-477	ex HB-GJP		
☐ C-FRLD	Beech B350 King Air	FL-33	ex N15WS		
☐ C-GILK	Beech B350 King Air	FL-535	ex HB-GJT		
☐ C-GJLK	Beech B350 King Air	FL-13	ex C-FWXR	EMS, for BC Ambulance Service	
☐ C-GRUU	Beech B350 King Air	FL-301	ex N 4211V		
☐ C-GRXX	Beech B350 King Air	FL-221	ex PT-SFA		
☐ C-FBWQ	Swearingen SA226TC Metro II	TC-379	ex N1011U		
☐ C-FKKR	Swearingen SA226TC Metro II	TC-308	ex N300GL		
☐ C-GCAU	Swearingen SA226TC Metro II	TC-331E	ex N255AM		Frtr
☐ C-GCAW	Swearingen SA226TC Metro II	TC-358	ex N1009R	no titles	
☐ C-GDLK	Swearingen SA226TC Metro II	TC-302	ex N151SA		
☐ C-GKKC	Swearingen SA226TC Metro II	TC-370	ex N125AV		
☐ C-GKLJ	Swearingen SA226TC Metro II	TC-380	ex C-GMET		
☐ C-GKLN	Swearingen SA226TC Metro II	TC-253	ex N328BA		
☐ C-GLSC	Swearingen SA226TC Metro II	TC-325	ex N162SW		
☐ C-FAFR	Swearingen SA227AC Metro III	AC-684B	ex N585MA		
☐ C-FCAV	Piper PA-42 Cheyenne III	42-8001006	ex N131RC		
☐ C-FCAW	Swearingen SA26AT Merlin IIB	T26-172E	ex N135SR		
☐ C-FJKK	Swearingen SA227AC Metro III	AC-713B	ex N2719H		
☐ C-FTJC	Cessna 560 Citation Encore	560-0544	ex N544VP		
☐ C-GAMI	Swearingen SA227AC Metro III	AC-587	ex N3115T		
☐ C-GKLK	Swearingen SA227AC Metro III	AC-741B	ex N41NE		
☐ C-GRFC	Cessna 560 Citation Encore	560-0702	ex N702AM		

| ☐ C-GRUC | Cessna 208 Caravan I | 20800374 | ex N208RB | ♦ |
| ☐ C-GRYC | Cessna 560 Citation Encore+ | 560-0770 | ex EC-KKK | |

CENTRAL MOUNTAIN AIR/NORTHERN THUNDERBIRD AIR (NTA)
Glacier (9M/GLR)   Smithers, BC (YYD)

☐ C-FCMB	Beech 1900D	UE-278		916	(NTA)
☐ C-FCME	Beech 1900D	UE-277		915	(NTA)
☐ C-FCMN	Beech 1900D	UE-276		914	(NTA)
☐ C-FCMO	Beech 1900D	UE-281		917	(NTA)
☐ C-FCMP	Beech 1900D	UE-271	ex N11037	912	(NTA)
☐ C-FCMR	Beech 1900D	UE-283	ex N21872	918	(NTA)
☐ C-FCMU	Beech 1900D	UE-285		919	(NTA)
☐ C-FCMV	Beech 1900D	UE-272	ex N11079	913	(NTA)
☐ C-FDTR	Beech 1900D	UE-76	ex N76ZV		(NTA)
☐ C-GCMA	Beech 1900D	UE-289		920	(NTA)
☐ C-GCML	Beech 1900D	UE-243	ex N10879	925	(NTA)
☐ C-GCMY	Beech 1900D	UE-287		921	(NTA)
☐ C-GFSV	Beech 1900D	UE-346	ex N23424	922	(NTA)
☐ C-GGBY	Beech 1900D	UE-351	ex YV-654C	923	(NTA)

☐ C-FCMG	Dornier 328-110	3055	ex N116JH	♦
☐ C-FDYN	Dornier 328-100	3096	ex "C-FDYW"	
☐ C-FGQN	de Havilland DHC-2 Beaver	96		
☐ C-FHVX	Dornier 328-110	3094	ex D-CMTM	(NTA)
☐ C-FJFW	de Havilland DHC-8-311	315	ex N315SN	
☐ C-GRUR	de Havilland DHC-8-311	256	ex G-WOWE	
☐ C-GWRN	Piper PA-31 Navajo Chieftain	31-7852062		

CGG AVIATION CANADA   Ottawa-Rockcliffe, ON (YRO)

☐ C-FZLK	Cessna 208B Caravan I	208B0569	ex N1210N	Tail magnetometer
☐ C-GDPP	CASA 212-200	CC50-3-265	ex N430CA	Nose & tail magnetometer
☐ C-GGRD	Cessna 208B Caravan I	208B1150	ex N208ML	
☐ C-GGSU	Douglas DC-3C	13439		♦
☐ C-GJPI	de Havilland DHC-7-102	036	ex N702GW	
☐ C-GNCA	Cessna 208B Caravan I	208B0764	ex N208KC	Tail magnetometer

CHAPLEAU AIR SERVICES   Chapleau, ON

☐ C-FJFE	de Havilland DHC-2 Beaver	986		FP♦
☐ C-FOCT	de Havilland DHC-2 Beaver	59	ex CF-OCT	FP
☐ C-GUTS	Cessna 180	32597		FP

CHARTRIGHT AIR   (HRT)   Mississauga, ON

☐ C-FIBQ	Cessna 560 Citation Ultra	560-0486	ex (N168EC)	♦
☐ C-FUBQ	Cessan 560 Citation Ultra	560-0455	ex (N161EC)	♦
☐ C-GJYL	Cessna 560 Citation V	560-0232	ex N502E	♦
☐ C-GKZC	Cessna 560 Citation Ultra	560-0373	ex (N113EC)	♦
☐ C-GKZM	Cessna 560 Citation Ultra	560-0510	ex (N176EC)	♦
☐ C-FBNA	Cessna 650 Citation III	650-0046	ex N650TT	♦
☐ C-FEAG	Beech 200 Super King Air	BB-777		♦
☐ C-FGEP	Agusta AW109SP	22285		♦
☐ C-FGFI	Dassault Falcon 900	138	ex VH-FHR	♦
☐ C-FGGE	Beech B300 King Air	FL-912		♦
☐ C-FJCB	Bombardier BD-100 Challenger 300	20192	ex C-FQOM	♦
☐ C-FLPB	Grumman Gulfstream 200	020	ex N816CC	♦
☐ C-FNMU	Agusta AW119 Mk II	14731		♦
☐ C-FORB	Grumman Gulfstream IV	1336	ex N235LP	♦
☐ C-FREQ	British Aerospace Jetstream 31	ex N733VN		♦
☐ C-FSBC	Cessna 650 Citation VII	650-7092		♦
☐ C-FWUT	Bombardier BD-100 Challenger 300	20246		♦
☐ C-FWWW	Agusta A109S	22119		♦
☐ C-GBBB	Canadair Challenger 604	5556	ex N3736	♦
☐ C-GFLU	Canadair Challenger 604	5410	ex (N410MU)	♦
☐ C-GJCB	Bombardier BD-700 Global 5000	9389	ex C-GCPV	♦
☐ C-GMRO	Learjet 45	45-086	ex N386K	♦
☐ C-GRAD	Beech B100 King Air	BE-24		♦
☐ C-GSJK	Bombardier BD-100A Challenger	20433	ex C-GOXD	♦
☐ C-GSMR	Dassault Falcon 2000	88	ex C-GSCL	♦
☐ C-GTKI	Cessna 650 Citation	650-0037	ex D-CVAI	♦
☐ C-GTUF	Hawker 850XP	258796		♦
☐ C-GVWI	Canadair Challenger 604	5950		♦
☐ C-GWPB	Grumman Gulfstream 200	119		♦
☐ C-GWQR	Canadair CL-605 Challenger	5955		♦

CHC HELICOPTERS INTERNATIONAL (RBD) Vancouver-International, BC (YVR)

☐ C-FRHM	Sikorsky S-76C++	760689	ex N25042	based Bata
☐ C-FUVS	Sikorsky S-76C+	760547	ex ZS-RRX	
☐ C-FUVU	Sikorsky S-76C+	760548	ex ZS-RRY	
☐ C-FXXV	Sikorsky S-76C	760468		
☐ C-FZUY	Sikorsky S-76C++	760765	ex N765L	
☐ C-GHRJ	Sikorsky S-76C	760574	ex 5N-BHP	
☐ C-GHRM	Sikorsky S-76C	760572		
☐ C-GHRU	Sikorsky S-76C	760593	ex 5N-BIJ	
☐ C-GHRX	Sikorsky S-76C+	760589	ex 5N-BIE	
☐ C-GIHO	Sikorsky S-76A++	760015	ex HS-HTO	
☐ C-GIMJ	Sikorsky S-76A++	760009	ex D2-EXZ	
☐ C-GMNB	Sikorsky S-76C+	760490	ex VT-HGH	
☐ C-FBXY	Sikorsky S-92A	920216		♦
☐ C-FBYI	Sikorsky S-92A	920022		♦
☐ C-FCPM	Aérospatiale AS332L	2069	ex G-BUZD	
☐ C-FEAE	Sikorsky S-92A	920229		♦
☐ C-GHYO	Aérospatiale AS332L	2038	ex G-PUMA	
☐ C-GLGB	Aérospatiale AS332L	2107	ex VH-LHK	
☐ C-GRWV	Aérospatiale AS365N2 Dauphin 2	6301		
☐ C-GRWX	Aérospatiale AS365N2 Dauphin 2	6358		
☐ C-GSBA	AgustaWestland AW139	31414	ex G-MGAR	
☐ C-GSBC	AgustaWestland AW139	31418	ex G-LOWC	
☐ C-GSBN	AgustaWestland AW139	31141		
☐ C-GXIK	Aérospatiale AS365N3 Dauphin 2	6423		♦

CHIMO AIR SERVICE (Peter Hagedorn Investments) Red Lake SPB, ON (YRL)

☐ C-FDNZ	Noorduyn Norseman V	55		FP♦
☐ CF-JIN	Noorduyn Norseman V	CCF-55	ex CF-LFR	FP
☐ CF-KAO	Noorduyn Norseman VI	636	ex 44-70371	FP
☐ CF-NPO	Cessna 280D	18051047		FP♦
☐ C-FODQ	de Havilland DHC-3 Otter	111		FP
☐ CF-SMS	Cessna 180C	50833		FP♦
☐ C-GYYS	de Havilland DHC-3 Otter	276	ex N1UW	FP

COCHRANE AIR SERVICES Cochrane-Lillabelle Lake, ON (YCN)

☐ C-FEYQ	de Havilland DHC-2 Beaver	465	ex CF-EYQ	FP
☐ C-FHID	Cessna 180	30582		FP
☐ C-FJPB	de Havilland DHC-2 Beaver	1319	ex N1019T	FP

CONAIR AVIATION Conair Canada (FGD) Abbotsford, BC (YXX)

☐ C-FDHE	Air Tractor AT-802A	802A-0346		
☐ C-FDHK	Air Tractor AT-802A	802A-0198		
☐ C-FDHL	Air Tractor AT-802A	802A-0199		
☐ C-FDHN	Air Tractor AT-802A	802A-0200		
☐ C-FDHO	Air Tractor AT-802A	802A-0351		
☐ C-FDHV	Air Tractor AT-802A	802A-0348		
☐ C-FDHX	Air Tractor AT-802A	802A-0311		
☐ C-FDHZ	Air Tractor AT-802A	802A-0319		
☐ C-FFQR	Air Tractor AT-802A	802A-0586		♦
☐ C-FFQS	Air Tractor AT-802A	802A-0583		♦
☐ C-FLSI	Air Tractor AT-802A	802A-0173		
☐ C-FXVF	Air Tractor AT-802	802-0033		
☐ C-FXVL	Air Tractor AT-802	802-0034		
☐ C-FYFN	Air Tractor AT-802A	802A-0324		
☐ C-GAAG	Air Tractor AT-802A	802A-0174		
☐ C-GBPV	Air Tractor AT-802A	802A-0354		
☐ C-GBPY	Air Tractor AT-802A	802A-0356		♦
☐ C-GSXW	Air Tractor AT-802A	802A-0476		
☐ C-GSYB	Air Tractor AT-802A	802A-0482		
☐ C-GSYF	Air Tractor AT-802A	802A-0488	ex N1001U	
☐ C-GSYK	Air Tractor AT-802A	802A-0491	ex N8521D	
☐ C-GYBF	Air Tractor AT-802A	802A-0393		
☐ C-GXNY	Air Tractor AT-802A	802A-0536		♦
☐ C-GXOB	Air Tractor AT-802A	802A-0542		♦
☐ C-GXOD	Air Tractor AT-802A	802A-0544		♦
☐ C-FAFC	Cessna 208B Caravan I	208B0663	ex N1229A	
☐ C-FDON	Cessna 208B Caravan I	208B2015	ex N5067U	
☐ C-GKJW	Cessna 208B Caravan I	208B2088	ex N88NB	♦
☐ C-GMKW	Cessna 208BEX Caravan I	208B5017		
☐ C-GSDG	Cessna 208B Caravan I	208B0376	ex N1118P	127
☐ C-FEFK	Conair Firecat	G-360/014	ex F-ZBEH	574
☐ C-FEFX	Conair Firecat	G-527/031	ex N425DF	575
☐ C-FJOH	Conair Firecat	G-254/034	ex N424DF	576
☐ C-FOPV	Conair Firecat	DHC-34/006	ex RCN1535	566

☐ C-FOPY	Conair Firecat	DHC-24/019	ex CF-IOF	569	
☐ C-GHDY	Conair Firecat	G-374/029	ex Bu136465	573	
☐ C-GHPJ	Conair Firecat	G-509/022	ex Bu136600	571	
☐ C-GWHK	Conair Firecat	DHC-37/016	ex CAF12138	2	Tanker
☐ C-GWUP	Conair Firecat	DHC-19/012	ex RCN12120	568	
☐ C-FEKF	Convair 580F	80	ex C-GEVB	445	Tanker 45
☐ C-FFKF	Convair 580	179	ex C-GEVC	444	Tanker 44
☐ C-FHKF	Convair 580	374	ex C-GEUZ	455	Tanker 55
☐ C-FJVD	Convair 580	478	ex N8099S		[YXX]
☐ C-FKFA	Convair 580	100	ex C-FLVY	452	Tanker 52
☐ C-FKFB	Convair 580	57	ex N568JA	447	Tanker 47
☐ C-FKFL	Convair 580	465	ex C-FZQS	449	Tanker 49
☐ C-FKFM	Convair 580F	70	ex N73133	454	Tanker 54
☐ C-GKFO	Convair 580F	78	ex N5815	453	Tanker 53
☐ C-GYXC	Convair 580	507	ex VH-PDV		
☐ C-GYXS	Convair 580	501	ex VH-PAL		
☐ C-FNWD	Rockwell 690B Turbo Commander	11497			
☐ C-FYYJ	Lockheed L-188AC Electra	1143	ex G-LOFD		
☐ C-GBQD	Rockwell 690A Turbo Commander	11237			
☐ C-GFSK	Canadair CL215T	1085	ex C-GKDN	201	
☐ C-GFSL	Canadair CL215T	1086	ex C-GKDP	202	
☐ C-GFSM	Canadair CL215T	1098		203	
☐ C-GFSN	Canadair CL215T	1099		204	
☐ C-GOSX	Piper PA-60 Aerostar 600A	60-0863-8161246	ex N3647B	110	
☐ C-GPCT	Cessna 525 Citation	525-0256	ex N196HA		
☐ C-GSYM	Cessna 525 Citation	525-0302	ex N3263		
☐ C-GUSZ	Piper PA-60 Aerostar 600A	60-0894-8161253	ex N6893Q	118	
☐ C-GYCG	Lockheed L-188PF Electra	1138	ex C-FIJR		

CONNECT AIR (CCT) Calgary, AB (YYC)

☐ C-GOIA	SAAB SF.340B	340B-347	ex N347CJ	

CORILAIR CHARTERS Campbell River, BC

☐ C-FEWP	Cessna U206D Skylane	U206-1344	ex CF-EWP	
☐ C-GACK	de Havilland DHC-2 Beaver	711	ex 53-7903	FP
☐ C-GADD	de Havilland DHC-2 Beaver	1153	ex 56-0407	FP
☐ C-GMTM	Cessna A185E Skywagon	18504289		fp
☐ C-GTNE	Cessna A185E Skywagon	18501889	ex CF-QLN	FP

COUGAR HELICOPTERS Cougar (CHI) Halifax-Waterfront Heliport, NS (YWF)

☐ C-GDKN	Sikorsky S-92A	920111	ex N21278	
☐ C-GFCH	Sikorsky S-92A	920242		♦
☐ C-GICH	Sikorsky S-92A	920105	ex PR-JAE	♦
☐ C-GIKN	Sikorsky S-92A	920126	ex N2183N	
☐ C-GKNR	Sikorsky S-92A	920054	ex G-CGZS	
☐ C-GMCH	Sikorsky S-92A	920023	ex N8016B	
☐ C-GQCH	Sikorsky S-92A	920074	ex N2581T	
☐ C-GSCH	Sikorsky S-92A	920010	ex N7108J	
☐ C-GVCH	Sikorsky S-92A	920080	ex N25837	

COULSON AIRCRANE Port Alberni, BC (YPB)

☐ C-FCLM	Sikorsky S-61N	61492	ex N265F		
☐ C-FIRX	Sikorsky S-61N	61257	ex N562EH		
☐ C-FMAY	Sikorsky S-61N	61363	ex N306V		
☐ C-FTNK	Sikorsky S-61N	61473	ex ZS-HSZ		
☐ C-FXEC	Sikorsky S-61N	61821	ex N264P		
☐ C-FIRW	Sikorsky S-76B	760355	ex N7689S		
☐ C-FLYK	Martin JRM-3 Mars	76820	ex Bu76820	Philippine Mars	Tanker
☐ C-FLYL	Martin JRM-3 Mars	76823	ex Bu76823	Hawaii Mars	Tanker
☐ C-GXOH	Bell 206B JetRanger II	865	ex N14844		

COURTESY AIR (947786 Alberta) Buffalo Narrows, SK (YVT)

☐ C-FCAK	Beech A100 King Air	B-96	ex N116RJ	
☐ C-FCAZ	Beech 100 King Air	B-44	ex N440SM	
☐ C-FCBZ	Beech A100 King Air	B-116	ex N601LM	
☐ C-FCOZ	Beech 100 King Air	B-53	ex N153JA	
☐ C-FJKY	Beech A100 King Air	B-202	ex N919JP	
☐ C-FJDF	Beech 1900C	UB-68	ex N68GH	
☐ C-FJMF	Beech C99	U-180	ex OY-PAG	
☐ C-FJTF	Beech 1900C	UB-39	ex N888MX	
☐ C-FLMF	Beech C99	U-189	ex N189AV	
☐ C-GDVD	Beech 58 Baron	TH-668	ex N4557S	
☐ C-GFFH	Beech B60 Duke	P-310		

☐ C-GKLO	Piper PA-31-350 Chieftain	31-8152118	ex N4505N
☐ C-GKNL	Piper PA-31-350 Chieftain	31-7852083	ex N27607
☐ C-GMFV	Cessna U206G Stationair 6 II	U20604714	ex N732RY
☐ C-GMJN	Cessna 550 Citation II	550-0433	ex N7ZU
☐ C-GNRM	Piper PA-31-350 Navajo Chieftain	31-7752145	ex N27315

CUSTOM HELICOPTERS   Winnipeg-St Andrews, MB (YAV)

☐ C-FCHJ	Aérospatiale AS350B2 AStar	2603	ex XC-JAK
☐ C-FCHO	Aérespatiale AS350B2 AStar	2781	ex C-GAVQ
☐ C-GCHX	Aérospatiale AS350BA AStar	2517	ex CP-2335
☐ C-GOGJ	Aérospatiale AS350B2 AStar	2749	
☐ C-GOGQ	Aérospatiale AS350B3 AStar	3196	

☐ C-FJMH	Bell 206B JetRanger II	1331	ex N70711
☐ C-FKBV	Bell 206B JetRanger II	364	ex N465CC
☐ C-FSVG	Bell 206B JetRanger III	2865	ex N1074G
☐ C-FZSJ	Bell 206B JetRanger II	648	ex CF-ZSJ
☐ C-GBWN	Bell 206B JetRanger II	2204	
☐ C-GFIV	Bell 206B JetRanger II	424	ex N1481W
☐ C-GKBU	Bell 206B JetRanger II	386	ex N1448W
☐ C-GPQS	Bell 206B JetRanger II	2382	
☐ C-GQQO	Bell 206B JetRanger II	1096	ex N83182
☐ C-GSHJ	Bell 206B JetRanger II	114	ex N125GW

☐ C-FYHN	Bell 206L LongRanger	45050	ex NG00FB
☐ C-GAVH	Bell 206L-1 LongRanger III	45740	ex N385FP
☐ C-GCHG	Bell 206L-3 LongRanger II	51508	ex N8592X
☐ C-GCHI	Bell 206L-1 LongRanger III	45516	ex N141VG
☐ C-GCHZ	Bell 206L-1 LongRanger III	45314	ex N210AH
☐ C-GIPG	Bell 206L-1 LongRanger II	45592	ex N3895K
☐ C-GOFH	Bell 206L-1 LongRanger III	45359	
☐ C-GOFI	Bell 206L-1 LongRanger III	45342	

☐ C-FCHD	Bell 205A-1	30014	ex N5598M
☐ C-FCHE	Bell 205A-1	30167	ex XA-SSR
☐ C-GRWK	Bell 205A-1	30005	ex N3764U

EAGLE COPTERS   Calgary, AB (YYC)

☐ C-FBHY	Bell 212	31194		
☐ C-FKJX	Bell 212	30766		♦
☐ C-FZXH	Bell 206B JetRanger II	622		
☐ C-GAHM	Bell 205A-1	30215		♦
☐ C-GBHF	Bell 206B JetRanger II	1028		
☐ C-GLGO	Bell 412EP	36399		♦
☐ C-GNTH	Bell 412	33046	ex 5N-BDD	
☐ C-GOEJ	Sikorsky S-76C	760474	ex B-MHF	
☐ C-GOEP	Sikorsky S-76C	760475	ex B-MHG	
☐ C-GOEU	Sikorsky S-76C	760476	ex B-MHH	
☐ C-GQKU	Bell 206B JetRanger II	2173		
☐ C-GQLG	Bell 205A-1	30008		♦
☐ C-GUNW	Bell 412EP	36101	ex XA-SYL	
☐ C-GUOC	Bell 412EP	36051	ex XA-UAR	
☐ C-GUVK	Bell 212	30581	ex N214SJ	
☐ C-GXXH	Bell 407	53197	ex N782FS	

ELBOW RIVER HELICOPTERS   Calgary-Springbank, AB (YBW)

☐ C-GERB	Bell 206L-3 LongRanger III	51008		
☐ C-GERW	Bell 212	30814	ex C-FRWM	
☐ C-GERX	Bell 206L-4 LongRanger IV	52348		
☐ C-GKCA	Bell 206L-3 LongRanger III	51341		
☐ C-GTKE	Bell 212	30704		
☐ C-GYRI	Bell 407	53551	ex N407KW	♦
☐ C-GZAV	Bell 407	53002		
☐ C-GZER	Bell 212	31191		

ELK ISLAND AIR   Tyndall, MN

☐ CF-ESR	Cessna U206A Super Skywagon	U2060630		FP
☐ C-GFIQ	de Havilland DHC-2 Beaver	632	ex N90525	FP♦
☐ C-GPVC	de Havilland DHC-2 Beaver	290	ex N9257Z	FP

ENERJET   (EG/ENJ)   Calgary, AB (YYC)

☐ C-FKEJ	Boeing 737-73A/W	28497/216	ex VQ-BDI	♦
☐ C-FYEJ	Boeing 737-73A/W	28498/775	ex N715DB	
☐ C-GDEJ	Boeing 737-73V	32427/1489	ex G-EZKF	

ENTERLAKE AIR SERVICES · Selkirk, MB

☐ C-FIQC	Cessna 180	18032280		FP/WS
☐ C-FSFH	Beech 3T		ex 43-35481	FP/WS
☐ C-GCKZ	Cessna A185F Skywagon	18502665	ex (N4949C)	FP/WS

EXCELLENT ADVENTURES OUTPOSTS · Ear Falls SPB, ON (YMY)

☐ C-FBEO	de Havilland DHC-3 Otter	373		
☐ C-FSRE	Beech 3N	CA-61		FP♦

EXPLOITS VALLEY AIR SERVICES / EVAS AIR · Gander, NL (YQX)

☐ C-FEVA	Beech 1900D	UE-126	ex N126YV	
☐ C-FPUB	Beech 1900D	UE-55	ex N1550J	♦
☐ C-GAAT	Beech 1900D	UE-217	ex N1564J 963	
☐ C-GERI	Beech 1900D	UE-162	ex N162ZV	
☐ C-GLHO	Beech 1900D	UE-266	ex N10950	
☐ C-GLXV	Beech 1900D	UE-242	ex N242YV	
☐ C-GORI	Beech 1900D	UE-47		♦
☐ C-GORZ	Beech 1900D	UE-134		♦
☐ C-GSNQ	Beech 1900D	UE-139	ex N139ZV	
☐ C-GUPW	Beech 1900D	UE-172	ex N16540	
☐ C-FPQM	Consolidated PBY-5A Catalina	CV-425		
☐ C-GLKT	Piper PA-44-180 Seminole	44-7995218		

EXPRESSAIR · Expressair · Ottawa, ON (YOW)

☐ C-FKAZ	Cessna 208 Caravan I	20800236		FP
☐ C-GAWP	Pilatus PC-12/45	187	ex N187PC	
☐ C-GPOP	Cessna 650 Citation III	650-0042	ex N342AS	

FAST AIR · (PBR) · Winnipeg-Intl, MB (YWG)

☐ C-FDEB	Beech 200 Super King Air	BB-55	ex N200BC	
☐ C-FFAP	Beech 200 Super King Air	BB-257		
☐ C-FFAR	Beech 200 Super King Air	BB-864	ex N847TS	
☐ C-GDHF	Beech B200 Super King Air	BB-1129	ex CS-DDF	CatPass 250 conversion
☐ C-GFAD	Beech B200 Super King Air	BB-1428	ex N660MW	
☐ C-GFAV	Beech 200 Super King Air	BB-492	ex N64DC	
☐ C-GFSB	Beech 200 Super King Air	BB-84		
☐ C-GWGI	Beech B200 Super King Air	BB-1022	ex C-FDGP	
☐ C-FHPB	Beech B300 King Air	FL-34	ex N57SC	
☐ C-FJOJ	IAI Gulfstream 200	143	ex C-GSQE	♦
☐ C-FREE	IAI Gulfstream 150	296		
☐ C-GCGS	British Aerospace 125 Srs.800A	258123	ex N353WG	
☐ C-GDSR	IAI 112A Jet Commander	313	ex N611WV	
☐ C-GNDI	Piper PA-31T Cheyenne	31T-7620036	ex N73TB	
☐ C-GSQE	IAI 1124 Westwind	271	ex XC-FJOJ	
☐ C-GWPK	IAI Gulfstream 150	288	ex N208GA	

FIRST AIR/BRADLEY AIR SERVICES · Firstair (7F/FAB)
Carp, ON/Iqaluit, NT/Yellowknife, NT (YRP/YFB/YZF)

☐ C-FIQR	ATR 42-300QC	133	ex F-WWEE	
☐ C-FIQU	ATR 42-300QC	138	ex F-WWEK	
☐ C-FTCP	ATR 42-300QC	143	ex F-WWEO	
☐ C-FTJB	ATR 42-300QC	119	ex N423TE	
☐ C-GHCP	ATR 42-300QC	123	ex F-WWET	
☐ C-GKLB	ATR 42-310	331	ex G-CDFF	
☐ C-GSRR	ATR 42-300QC	125	ex OY-MUH	
☐ C-GULU	ATR 42-310	155	ex 5R-MJD	
☐ C-GUNO	ATR 42-310	132	ex 5R-MJC	
☐ C-FACP	Boeing 737-2L9 (AvAero 3)	22072/623	ex C2-RN9	
☐ C-FNVK	Boeing 737-2R4C	23130/1040	ex JY-JAF	Frtr
☐ C-FNVT	Boeing 737-248C (AvAero 3)	21011/411	ex F-GKTK	Snowy Owl c/s
☐ C-GCPT	Boeing 737-217 (AvAero 3)	22258/770		Inukshuk tail logo
☐ C-GNDC	Boeing 737-242C (AvAero 3)	21728/580		
☐ C-FFNC	Boeing 737-406	27232/2591	ex PH-BTF	
☐ C-FFNE	Boeing 737-406C	27233/2601	ex PH-BTG	
☐ C-FFNF	Boeing 737-406C	25412/2161	ex PH-BTA	
☐ C-GLHR	ATR 72-212F	423	ex EI-CLB	
☐ C-GRMZ	ATR 72-212	432	ex EI-CLD	
☐ C-GUSI	Lockheed L-328G-31C Hercules	4600	ex ZS-RSI	EARL titles

FLAIR AIRLINES — Flair (FLE) — Kelowna, BC (YLW)

☐ C-FLDX	Boeing 737-408	24804/1851	ex N737DX	
☐ C-FLEJ	Boeing 737-4B3	24751/2107	ex CN-RPB	
☐ C-FLEN	Boeing 737-4K5	24769/1839	ex OK-VGZ	
☐ C-FLER	Boeing 737-46B	24573/1844	ex N41XA	
☐ C-FLHJ	Boeing 737-4Q8	25104/2476	ex N771AS	♦
☐ C-FSCO	Dornier 328-130	3109	ex D-CDXV	opf Shell Canada♦
☐ C-GJRH	Cessna 340	340-0058	ex N340BD	
☐ C-GSCL	Embraer ERJ-175LR	17000241	ex PT-SFR	opf Shell Canada

FORDE LAKE AIR SERVICES — Hornepayne, ON (YHN)

☐ C-FGYP	de Havilland DHC-2 Beaver	145	ex C-FPBJ	FP
☐ C-FLUA	de Havilland DHC-2 Beaver	1318	ex CF-LUA	FP
☐ C-GRAP	de Havilland DHC-2 Beaver	829	ex 54-1690	FP

FOREST PROTECTION — Fredericton, NB

☐ C-FFPL	Air Tractor AT-802	802-0110		
☐ C-FZPV	Air Tractor AT-802	802-0141		
☐ C-GBWF	Air Tractor AT-802A	802A-0303		
☐ C-GJJK	Air Tractor AT-802	802-0120		
☐ C-GJJX	Air Tractor AT-802	802-0121		
☐ C-GZRH	Air Tractor AT-802	802-0143		
☐ C-GZUE	Air Tractor AT-802	802-0147		
☐ C-GJDF	Cessna 337G Super Skymaster	33701516		
☐ C-GLVG	Piper PA-60 Aerostar 600A	60-0695-7961217	ex N6072U	
☐ C-GMGZ	Piper PA-60 Aerostar 600A	60-0708-7961220		
☐ C-GRIK	Piper PA-60 Aerostar 600A	60-0563-7961183		
☐ C-GUHK	Piper PA-60 Aerostar 600	60-0761-8061230		♦
☐ C-GXMA	Cessna 337G Super Skymaster	33701644		

FORT FRANCES SPORTSMEN AIRWAYS — Fort Frances, ON (YAG)

☐ C-GMDG	de Havilland DHC-3 Turbo Otter	302	ex N90575	FP/WS
☐ C-GMLB	de Havilland DHC-3 Turbo Otter	359		FP/WS♦
☐ C-GUTL	de Havilland DHC-3 Turbo Otter	365	ex HK-3048X	FP/WS

GILLAM AIR SERVICES — Gillam, MB (YGX)

☐ C-GPPP	Britten-Norman BN-2A-27 Islander	423	ex (N93JA)	
☐ C-GSAD	Britten-Norman BN-2A-26 Islander	7	ex N32JC	
☐ C-GXQV	Cessna A185F Skywagon	18503375		

GOGAL AIR SERVICES — Snow Lake, MB

☐ CF-ECG	Noorduyn Norseman V	N29-43		FP/WS
☐ CF-JFA	de Havilland DHC-2 Beaver	1581	ex N5563	FP/WS
☐ C-FKCL	Piper PA-31-350 Navajo Chieftain	31-7752134		
☐ C-GCWO	Cessna A185F Skywagon	18503207	ex N93275	FP/WS

GOLDAK AIRBORNE SURVEYS — Saskatoon, SK (YXE)

☐ C-GJBB	Piper PA-31 Turbo Navajo	31-519	ex N310DS	Surveyor
☐ C-GJBG	Piper PA-31 Navajo C	31-7612003	ex N59718	Surveyor
☐ C-GLDX	Cessna 208 Caravan I	20800366	ex C-FFCL	

GOVERNMENT OF QUEBEC — Quebec (QUE) — Quebec, QC (YQB)

☐ C-FASE	Canadair CL215T	1114	ex Greece 1114 238	
☐ C-FAWQ	Canadair CL215T	1115	ex Greece 1115 239	
☐ C-FTXG	Canadair CL215	1014	ex CF-TXG 228	
☐ C-FTXJ	Canadair CL215	1017	ex CF-TXJ 230	
☐ C-FTXK	Canadair CL215	1018	ex CF-TXK 231	
☐ C-GFQB	Canadair CL215	1092	ex C-GKDP 237	
☐ C-GQBA	Canadair CL415	2005	ex C-GKDN 240	
☐ C-GQBC	Canadair CL415	2012	ex C-GKET 241	
☐ C-GQBD	Canadair CL415	2016	ex C-GBPU 242	
☐ C-GQBE	Canadair CL415	2017	ex C-GKEA 243	
☐ C-GQBF	Canadair CL415	2019	ex C-FVKV 244	
☐ C-GQBG	Canadair CL415	2022	ex C-FVLW 245	
☐ C-GQBI	Canadair CL415	2023	ex C-FVLI 246	
☐ C-GQBK	Canadair CL415	2026	ex C-FVLY 247	
☐ C-GBPQ	Bell 206B JetRanger III	2897	ex YU-HLL	
☐ C-GCFG	Canadair Challenger 601	3022	ex C-GLXS	
☐ C-GQBQ	Canadair Challenger 604	5051	ex N300KC	EMS

☐ C-GQBT	de Havilland DHC-8Q-202	470	ex P2-ANL	EMS/VIP
☐ C-GSQA	Bell 206LT TwinRanger	52060		Police
☐ C-GSQL	Bell 412EP	36262	ex N6077U	
☐ C-GURG	Canadair Challenger 601-3R	5165	ex XA-PTR	
☐ C-GURM	de Havilland DHC-8Q-315	609	ex C-FLGJ	

GREEN AIRWAYS   Red Lake, ON (YRL)

☐ C-FLEA	de Havilland DHC-3 Otter	286	ex CF-LEA	FP/WS
☐ C-FLNC	Cessna 180 Skywagon	18032497		FP/WS
☐ C-FOBE	Noorduyn UC-64A Norseman	480	ex 43-35406	FP/WS
☐ C-FODJ	de Havilland DHC-3 Otter	14	ex CF-ODJ	FP/WS

GRONDAIR/GRONDIN TRANSPORT   St Frederic du Beauce, QC

☐ C-FNNM	Cessna TR182RG Skylane	R18200946	ex N738NR
☐ C-FQTA	Cessna R182RG Skylane	R18200324	ex N4107C
☐ C-FQTC	Cessna R182RG Skylane	R18201717	ex N4608T
☐ C-FRGN	Cessna R182RG Skylane	R18200394	ex N9083C
☐ C-FRYF	Cessna R182RG Skylane	R18201001	ex N65ET
☐ C-FRYP	Cessna R182RG Skylane	R18200479	ex N9879C
☐ C-FRZE	Cessna R182RG Skylane	R18200197	ex N2657C
☐ C-GCJA	Cessna R182RG Skylane	R18201219	ex (N757DM)
☐ C-GHVC	Cessna R182RG Skylane	R18201886	ex N5532T
☐ C-GRUA	Cessna R182RG Skylane	R18200077	ex N7325X
☐ C-GSCF	Cessna R182RG Skylane	R18201257	ex N757QM
☐ C-GVCV	Cessna R182RG Skylane	R18200030	ex N7343T
☐ C-GAST	Cessna 310R	310R0730	ex N5009J
☐ C-GAWT	Cessna 310R	310R1600	
☐ C-GBRC	Cessna 310R	310R1284	ex N6116X
☐ C-GJGW	Cessna 310R	310R0960	ex N37200
☐ C-GMCR	Cessna 310R	310R1424	
☐ C-FDOV	Beech A100 King Air	B-117	
☐ C-FINP	Cessna 337G Super Skymaster II	33701523	
☐ C-FONY	Beech A100 King Air	B-154	ex N46JK
☐ C-GIGB	Cessna 337G Super Skymaster II	33701599	ex N72478
☐ C-GMAG	Beech A100 King Air	B-229	ex N100HC
☐ C-GRIR	Beech A100 King Air	B-144	ex N999G
☐ C-GSRW	Piper PA-31 Turbo Navajo	31-262	ex N707FR
☐ C-GUMQ	Piper PA-31 Turbo Navajo	31-84	ex N777GS

HARBOUR AIR SEAPLANES   Harbour Air   Vancouver-Coal Harbour, BC (CXH)

☐ C-FAWA	de Havilland DHC-2 Beaver	1430	ex VH-IDR		FP
☐ C-FAXI	de Havilland DHC-2 Beaver	1514	ex N6535D	205	FP
☐ C-FEBE	de Havilland DHC-2 Beaver	792	ex N9983B		FP
☐ C-FFHQ	de Havilland DHC-2 Beaver	42	ex CF-FHQ	203	FP
☐ C-FIFQ	de Havilland DHC-2 Beaver	825	ex CF-IFQ		FP
☐ C-FJBP	de Havilland DHC-2 Beaver	942	ex CF-JBP		FP
☐ C-FJOS	de Havilland DHC-2 Beaver	1030	ex CF-JOS		FP
☐ C-FOCJ	de Havilland DHC-2 Beaver	39	ex CF-OCJ		FP
☐ C-FOCY	de Havilland DHC-2 Beaver	79	ex CF-OCY	204	FP
☐ C-FWAC	de Havilland DHC-2 Beaver	1356	ex N68089		FP
☐ C-GFDI	de Havilland DHC-2 Beaver	606	ex 53-2810		FP
☐ C-GMKP	de Havilland DHC-2 Beaver	1374	ex N87775		FP
☐ C-GOLC	de Havilland DHC-2 Beaver	1392	ex N62354		FP
☐ C-GTBQ	de Havilland DHC-2 Beaver	1316	ex N9036		FP
☐ C-FHAA	de Havilland DHC-3 Turbo Otter	357	ex C-GIWT	309	FP
☐ C-FHAD	de Havilland DHC-3 Turbo Otter	119	ex N81FW	315	FP
☐ C-FHAJ	de Havilland DHC-3 Turbo Otter	406	ex 9H-AFA		FP
☐ C-FHAS	de Havilland DHC-3 Turbo Otter	382	ex N382BH	310	FP
☐ C-FHAX	de Havilland DHC-3 Turbo Otter	339	ex N41755	313	FP
☐ C-FITF	de Havilland DHC-3 Turbo Otter	89	ex CF-ITF	303	FP
☐ C-FIUZ	de Havilland DHC-3 Turbo Otter	135	ex F-OAKK	306	FP
☐ C-FJHA	de Havilland DHC-3 Turbo Otter	393	ex 4R-ARB		FP
☐ C-FLAP	de Havilland DHC-3 Otter	289	ex CF-LAP		FP
☐ C-FODH	de Havilland DHC-3 Turbo Otter	3	ex CF-ODH	307	FP
☐ C-FRNO	de Havilland DHC-3 Turbo Otter	21	ex N128F	301	FP
☐ C-GEND	de Havilland DHC-3 Turbo Otter	371	ex N83U		FP
☐ C-GHAG	de Havilland DHC-3 Turbo Otter	214	ex 4R-ARA		FP
☐ C-GHAQ	de Havilland DHC-3 Turbo Otter	288	ex DQ-GLL		FP
☐ C-GHAR	de Havilland DHC-3 Turbo Otter	42	ex N234KA	308	FP
☐ C-GHAS	de Havilland DHC-3 Turbo Otter	284	ex N84SF	310	FP
☐ C-GHAZ	de Havilland DHC-3 Turbo Otter	19	ex C-FEYY		FP
☐ C-GLCP	de Havilland DHC-3 Turbo Otter	422	ex N17682		FP
☐ C-GOPP	de Havilland DHC-3 Turbo Otter	355	ex N53KA	305	FP
☐ C-GUTW	de Havilland DHC-3 Turbo Otter	405	ex RCAF 9423	302	FP
☐ C-GVNL	de Havilland DHC-3 Turbo Otter	105	ex N5341G	304	FP

☐ C-GCRE	Cessna A185F Skywagon	18502522	ex (N1807R)	FP

HAWK AIR — Wawa-Hawk Junction, ON (YXZ)

☐ C-FBBG	de Havilland DHC-2 Beaver	358-173	ex N2848D	FP
☐ C-FOUZ	Cessna 180F Skywagon	18051238		FP
☐ C-FQMN	de Havilland DHC-3 Turbo Otter	184	ex N2959W	FP

HAWKAIR AVIATION SERVICE — Hawkair (BH/BHA) — Terrace, BC (YXT)

☐ C-FCJE	de Havilland DHC-8-102	165		
☐ C-FDNG	de Havilland DHC-8-102	166		
☐ C-FIDL	de Havilland DHC-8-311	305	ex V2-LFW	wfs
☐ C-FYDH	de Havilland DHC-8-102	083	ex N809LR	

HEARST AIR SERVICE — Hearst, ON (YHF)

☐ C-FBTU	de Havilland DHC-2 Beaver	1564	ex CF-BTU	FP/WS
☐ C-FDDX	de Havilland DHC-3 Turbo Otter	165	ex CF-DDX	FP/WS
☐ C-FKAE	Cessna 208 Caravan I	20800316	ex C-FKAL	
☐ C-FOEK	de Havilland DHC-2 Turbo Beaver	1650/TB28	ex CF-OEK	FP/WS

HELIEXPRESS — Quebec, QC (YQB)

☐ C-FCCI	Aérospatiale AS350BA AStar	1303	ex N5768Y	
☐ C-GDEH	Aérospatiale AS350BA AStar	1348	ex N905DB	
☐ C-GHEX	Aérospatiale AS350B2 AStar	2867	ex CP-2392	
☐ C-GIMG	Aérospatiale AS350B2 AStar	1382	ex ZK-HZZ	
☐ C-GJPC	Aérospatiale AS350BA AStar	1398	ex N269JM	
☐ C-GRDI	Aérospatiale AS350B2 AStar	2866	ex C-FWAU	
☐ C-GSRQ	Aérospatiale AS350BA AStar	1081		
☐ C-GVEM	Aérospatiale AS350BA AStar	2510	ex N752BH	
☐ C-GADA	Bell 205A-1	30031	ex PK-UHJ	

HELI-LIFT INTERNATIONAL — Yorkton, SK (YQV)

☐ C-GHLE	Bell 205A-1	30195	ex HL9150	
☐ C-GHLJ	Bell 206L-3 LongRanger III	51280	ex N60992	
☐ C-GHLX	Aérospatiale AS350B AStar	1589	ex N85PB	
☐ C-GIYN	Aérospatiale AS350BA AStar	1776	ex JA9368	
☐ C-GMOR	Bell 205A-1	30159	ex LX-HOR	
☐ C-GQCW	Aérospatiale AS350BA AStar	1255	ex N3607T	
☐ C-GSHK	Bell 204B	2067	ex Thai 920	

HELIFOR INDUSTRIES — Campbell River, BC (YBL)

☐ C-FHCN	Boeing Vertol 107 II	404	ex N194CH	
☐ C-GHFF	Boeing Vertol 107 II	406	ex N195CH	<WCO

HELIJET INTERNATIONAL — Helijet (JB/JBA) — Vancouver-Intl, BC (YVR)

☐ C-FZAA	Sikorsky S-76A	760043	ex N348AA	
☐ C-GCHJ	Sikorsky S-76C	760496	ex N397U	
☐ C-GHHJ	Sikorsky S-76C	760500	ex N88CP	
☐ C-GHJJ	Sikorsky S-76A	760235	ex C-GTXJ	
☐ C-GHJL	Sikorsky S-76A II	760214	ex N101PB	EMS
☐ C-GHJP	Sikorsky S-76A II	760065	ex (C-GHJT)	
☐ C-GHJT	Sikorsky S-76B	760299		♦
☐ C-GHJV	Sikorsky S-76A	760167	ex N5426U	
☐ C-GHJW	Sikorsky S-76A II	760074	ex N586C	
☐ C-GIHJ	Sikorsky S-76C	760438	ex N986AH	
☐ C-GIHS	Sikorsky S-76A++	760250	ex HS-HTS	
☐ C-GHJS	Aérospatiale AS350B2 AStar	2479		
☐ C-GHJU	Learjet 31A	31A-120	ex N200TJ	EMS
☐ C-GVIQ	Bell 206L-1 LongRanger III	45492	ex N83MT	
☐ C-GVIZ	Bell 206L-1 LongRanger III	45346	ex N26SH	
☐ C-GXHJ	Bell 206L-1 LongRanger	45741	ex N3174P	

HIGHLAND HELICOPTERS — Vancouver-Intl, BC (YVR)

☐ C-FHHC	Aérospatiale AS350B2 AStar	2569	ex N2PW	
☐ C-FHHU	Aérospatiale AS350B2 AStar	2790	ex C-FSQY	
☐ C-FHHY	Aérospatiale AS350BA AStar	1650	ex C-GSKI	
☐ C-FJHH	Aérospatiale AS350B2 AStar	3279		
☐ C-FKHH	Aérospatiale AS350B2 AStar	2736		
☐ C-FYYA	Aérospatiale AS350BA AStar	2295	ex ZK-HOU	
☐ C-GDHH	Aérospatiale AS350B2 AStar	4103		
☐ C-GGTO	Aérospatiale AS350B2 AStar	4393		
☐ C-GHHH	Aérospatiale AS350B2 AStar	3270		

☐ C-GHHV	Aérospatiale AS350B2 AStar	2918	ex N4034Q	
☐ C-GHHW	Aérospatiale AS350B2 AStar	3039		
☐ C-GHHZ	Aérospatiale AS350B2 AStar	3054		
☐ C-GMVF	Aérospatiale AS350B2 AStar	3327		♦
☐ C-GNHH	Aérospatiale AS350B2 AStar	2737	ex N9446H	
☐ C-GRHH	Aérospatiale AS350B2 AStar	3315	ex N37PT	
☐ C-GRJO	Aérospatiale AS350B2 AStar	4277		
☐ C-GTIA	Aérospatiale AS350B2 AStar	4328	ex F-WWPZ	
☐ C-GXHH	Aérospatiale AS350B2 AStar	4058	ex F-WQDF	
☐ C-FCDL	Bell 206B JetRanger III	3852	ex N93AJ	
☐ C-FCOY	Bell 206B JetRanger III	3280	ex N7023J	
☐ C-FETC	Bell 206B JetRanger III	3515	ex C-GTIA	
☐ C-FHHB	Bell 206B Jetranger	519	ex CF-HHB	
☐ C-FHHI	Bell 206B JetRanger III	2310	ex N101CD	
☐ C-GHHG	Bell 206B JetRanger	1396	ex N918TR	
☐ C-GIZO	Bell 206B JetRanger III	2715		
☐ C-GJMJ	Bell 206B JetRanger	620	ex N7112J	
☐ C-GKDG	Bell 206B JetRanger III	2969		
☐ C-GKJL	Bell 206B JetRanger III	3005		
☐ C-GMDX	Bell 206B JetRanger III	3032		
☐ C-GMZH	Bell 206B JetRanger III	3203		
☐ C-GNLT	Bell 206B JetRanger III	2973		
☐ C-GNSQ	Bell 206B JetRanger III	3274		
☐ C-GOPF	Bell 206B JetRanger III	3227		
☐ C-GOPK	Bell 206B JetRanger III	3247		
☐ C-GAXW	Bell 206L-3 LongRanger III	51395	ex N6501S	
☐ C-GFHH	Bell 206L-3 LongRanger III	51362	ex C-FPCL	

HURON AIR AND OUTFITTERS   Armstrong, ON (YYW)

☐ C-FDPW	de Havilland DHC-2 Beaver	1339	ex 58-2011	FP/WS

HYDRO-QUEBEC (SERVICE TRANSPORT AERIEN)
Hydro (OQ/HYD)   Montreal-Trudeau, QC (YUL)

☐ C-GHQL	de Havilland DHC-8-402Q	4115		op by AIE
☐ C-GHQP	de Havilland DHC-8-402Q	4004	ex C-GIHK	op by AIE
☐ C-GJNL	de Havilland DHC-8-311	422	ex G-BXPZ	op by AIE

ICARUS FLYING SERVICE   Ile de la Madelaine, QC (YGR)

☐ C-GFBF	Britten-Norman BN-2B-27 Islander	2125	ex VP-FBF	
☐ C-GNLX	Piper PA-60-601 Aerostar	61P-0689-7963326		♦

IGNACE AIRWAYS   Ignace/Thunder Bay, ON (ZUC/YQT)

☐ C-FAPR	de Havilland DHC-3 Otter	31	ex LN-LMM	FP
☐ C-FMAM	Noorduyn Norseman V	N29-26		FP
☐ CF-TTL	Cessna U206C Super Skywagon	U206-1062	ex N29088	FP
☐ C-GZBR	de Havilland DHC-2 Beaver	1272	ex N434GR	FP

INLAND AIR CHARTERS   Prince Rupert, BC (YPR)

☐ C-FGQC	de Havilland DHC-2 Beaver	75	ex CF-GQC	FP
☐ C-FJOM	de Havilland DHC-2 Beaver	1024	ex CF-JOM	FP
☐ C-FJPX	de Havilland DHC-2 Beaver	1076	ex CF-JPX	FP
☐ C-FKDC	de Havilland DHC-2 Beaver	1080	ex CF-KDC	FP
☐ C-FOCZ	de Havilland DHC-2 Beaver	100	ex N254BD	FP
☐ C-FOSP	de Havilland DHC-2 Beaver	1501	ex N2961	FP
☐ C-GCYM	de Havilland DHC-2 Beaver	354	ex N63PS	FP

INTEGRA AIR   Lethbridge, AB (YQL)

Assoc with Bar XH Air (qv)

ISLAND EXPRESS AIR   (IAX)   Abbotsford, BC (YXX)

☐ C-FASN	Beech B100 King Air	BE-17		
☐ C-GDFR	Piper PA-31-325 Navajo	31-7812085		
☐ C-GIEA	Piper PA-31-350 Chieftain	31-8052196		
☐ C-GMDL	Piper PA-31-325 Navajo	31-7512033		♦

JACKSON AIR SERVICES   Jackson (JCK)   Flin Flon, MB (YFO)

☐ C-FMAJ	de Havilland DHC-3 Otter	383	ex 4655	FP/WS
☐ C-GISX	Cessna A185F Skywagon II	18503836	ex N4669E	FP/WS
☐ C-GVOQ	Cessna A185F Skywagon	18503790		FP/WS

JOHNNY MAY'S AIR CHARTERS				Kuujjuaq, QC (YVP)

☐ C-GMAY	de Havilland DHC-3 Otter	282	ex C-FCEE	FP/WS

KABEELO AIRWAYS				Confederation Lake, ON (YMY)

☐ C-GDYT	de Havilland DHC-2 Beaver	1109	ex 56-4403	FP
☐ C-GLSA	de Havilland DHC-2 Beaver	1389	ex N94471	FP

KASBA AIR SERVICE/LAKE LODGE				Kasba Lake, NT (YDU)

☐ CF-MAS	de Havilland DHC-2 Beaver	38	ex C-FMAS	FP

KAYAIR SERVICE				Ear Falls, ON (YMY)

☐ CF-KLJ	Cessna 180A	50261		FP
☐ CF-TBH	Beech 3T	6226	43-35671	FP
☐ C-FVYY	Cessna A185E Skywagon	185-1316		FP

KD AIR		Kay Dee (XC/KDC)		Port Alberni, BC (YPB)

☐ C-GPCA	Piper PA-31 Turbo Navajo	31-42	ex N333DG
☐ C-GROJ	Piper PA-31-350 Navajo Chieftain	31-7405249	
☐ C-GXEY	Piper PA-31-350 Navajo Chieftain	31-7305044	ex N74910

KEEWATIN AIR		(FK/KEW)	Churchill, MB/Rankin Inlet, NU (YYQ /YRT)

☐ C-FCGT	Beech 200 Super King Air	BB-159	ex N47FH	EMS
☐ C-FRMV	Beech B200 Super King Air	BB-979	ex N22TP	
☐ C-FSKN	Beech B200 Super King Air	BB-1109	ex F-GLLH	
☐ C-FSKO	Beech B200 Super King Air	BB-1007	ex N514MA	EMS
☐ C-FSKX	Beech B200 Super King Air	BB-1126		♦
☐ C-FZPW	Beech B200 Super King Air	BB-940	ex N519SA	EMS
☐ C-GYGT	Beech B200 Super King Air	BB-1323	ex N4KU	
☐ C-GYSR	Beech B200 Super King Air	BB-1364	ex N660PB	
☐ C-FJXL	Beech 1900C-1	UC-102	ex N15479	
☐ C-FJXO	Beech 1900C	UC-124	ex N124CU	
☐ C-GDJH	Learjet 35A	35A-353	ex N3819G	
☐ C-GFLA	Pilatus PC-12/45	293		EMS
☐ C-GYFB	Learjet 35A	35A-644	ex N893AC	

KENN BOREK AIR		Borek Air (4K/KBA)		
	Calgary-Intl, AB/Edmonton-Intl, AB/ Iqaluit, NT/Resolute Bay, NT (YYC/YEG/YFB/YRB)			

☐ C-FBKB	Basler BT-67	25615/14170		
☐ C-FGCX	Basler BT-67	19446		♦
☐ C-FKAL	Basler BT-67	13840	ex N8187E	op by Cargo North; frtr
☐ C-FMKB	Basler BT-67	47/19560	ex N57NA	Frtr
☐ C-GAWI	Basler BT-67	50/19227	ex N79017 Lidia	>Alfred Wegener Institute
☐ C-GEAJ	Basler BT-67	35/14615/26120	ex N40386	
☐ C-GHGF	Basler BT-67	56/14519/25964	ex N9923S	>Alfred Wegener Institute
☐ C-GJKB	Basler BT-67	28/13383	ex N167BT	
☐ C-GKKB	Basler BT-67	20494	ex N1427	
☐ C-GVKB	Basler BT-67	54/12300	ex N907Z	
☐ C-FBCN	Beech 200 Super King Air	BB-7		
☐ C-FEKB	Beech 200 Super King Air	BB-468	ex N9UT	Beech 1300 conversion
☐ C-FKBI	Beech B200GT Super King Air	BY-93	ex M-ARIE	♦
☐ C-GKBN	Beech 200 Super King Air	BB-404	ex N315MS	
☐ C-GKBP	Beech 200 Super King Air	BB-505	ex HP-1083P	
☐ C-FBBV	de Havilland DHC-6 Twin Otter 300	311	ex C-FMPC	
☐ C-FDHB	de Havilland DHC-6 Twin Otter 300	338	ex CF-DHB	wfs
☐ C-FGOG	de Havilland DHC-6 Twin Otter 300	348	ex CF-GOG	
☐ C-GCKB	de Havilland DHC-6 Twin Otter 300	312	ex C-FMPF	
☐ C-GDHC	de Havilland DHC-6 Twin Otter 300	494		
☐ C-GIKB	de Havilland DHC-6 Twin Otter 100	064	ex 8Q-CSL	[YYC]
☐ C-GKBC	de Havilland DHC-6 Twin Otter 300	650		♦
☐ C-GKBG	de Havilland DHC-6 Twin Otter 300	733		
☐ C-GKBH	de Havilland DHC-6 Twin Otter 300	732	ex 8Q-MAV	
☐ C-GKBO	de Havilland DHC-6 Twin Otter 300	725	ex HP-1273APP	
☐ C-GKBR	de Havilland DHC-6 Twin Otter 300	617	ex 8Q-MAU	
☐ C-GKCS	de Havilland DHC-6 Twin Otter 300	693	ex 8Q-MAA	
☐ C-GKBV	de Havilland DHC-6 Twin Otter 300	287	ex 8Q-MAB	
☐ C-GOKB	de Havilland DHC-6 Twin Otter 300	339		♦
☐ C-GTKB	de Havilland DHC-6 Twin Otter 100	60	ex 8Q-MAC	
☐ C-GXXB	de Havilland DHC-6 Twin Otter 300	426	ex 8Q-MAN	
☐ C-GZVH	de Havilland DHC-6 Twin Otter 300	671		
☐ C-FLKB	Embraer EMB.110P1 Bandeirante	110397	ex N903LE	[YYC]

☐ C-FRKB	Beech 100 King Air	B-72	ex C-GTLF		
☐ C-FTUA	Beech 100 King Air	B-61	ex C-GSYN		
☐ C-GBBR	Embraer EMB.110P1 Bandeirante	110444	ex HP-1177AP		wfs
☐ C-GFKB	Embraer EMB.110P1 Bandeirante	110400	ex 9N-AFF		[YYC]
☐ C-GHUE	Beech 1900D	UE-52			♦
☐ C-GKBZ	Beech 100 King Air	B-85	ex LN-PAJ		
☐ C-GSKB	Beech1900D	UE-182	ex 9N-AHZ		

KENORA AIR SERVICE   Kenora SPB, ON (YQK)

☐ C-FWDB	Cessna A185E Skywagon	185-1250	ex (N4783Q)		FP
☐ C-FWMM	Cessna A185F Skywagon	18502238	ex N4361Q		FP
☐ C-GOTD	Cessna A185F Skywagon	18502445	ex (N1724R)		FP
☐ C-GYJY	Cessna A185F Skywagon	18502468	ex N1748R		FP
☐ C-GYXY	Cessna A185F Skywagon	18503370			FP
☐ CF-CBA	de Havilland DHC-3 Otter	230	ex C-FCBA		FP
☐ C-FFHO	de Havilland DHC-2 Beaver	50	ex CF-FHO		
☐ CF-JEI	de Havilland DHC-2 Beaver	1020			FP
☐ C-FNOT	de Havilland DHC-2 Beaver	1067	ex N4193A		FP
☐ CF-TBX	Beech D18S	A-479	ex N841B		FP
☐ C-GAQJ	de Havilland DHC-2 Beaver	1130	ex 56-4411		FP
☐ C-GEHX	Beech 3NM	CA-112	ex CF-ZNF		FP

KEYSTONE AIR SERVICE   Keystone (KEE)   Swan River, MB (YSE)

☐ C-FAFT	Beech 200 Super King Air	BB-57	ex N121DA	
☐ C-FPCD	Beech B99	U-151	ex C-FBRO	
☐ C-FSPN	Beech 200 Super King Air	BB-745	ex N428P	
☐ C-GBDN	Piper PA-31-350 Navajo Chieftain	31-7652035	ex N59763	
☐ C-GCJH	Piper PA-31-350 Chieftain	31-7952109	ex N42FL	
☐ C-GCTG	Piper PA-31-350 Navajo Chieftain	31-7552087		
☐ C-GFOL	Beech 200 Super King Air	BB-27	ex N120DP	
☐ C-GGQU	Piper PA-31 Turbo Navajo	31-155	ex N9116Y	
☐ C-GOSU	Piper PA-31-350 Navajo Chieftain	31-7752148	ex N27327	

KF CARGO   Flightcraft (KW/KFA)   Kelowna, BC (YLW)

☐ C-GGKF	Boeing 727-223F (FedEx 3)	21523/1467	ex C-FMKF	718	
☐ C-GIKF	Boeing 727-227F (FedEx 3)	20772/982	ex N99763	721	
☐ C-GJKF	Boeing 727-227F (FedEx 3)	21042/1106	ex N10756	722	
☐ C-GKFH	Boeing 727-223F	22460/1746	ex N742JW		
☐ C-GKKF	Boeing 727-227F (FedEx 3)	21043/1113	ex N16758	723	
☐ C-GLKF	Boeing 727-227F (FedEx 3)	21118/1167	ex N14760	724	
☐ C-GMKF	Boeing 727-227F (FedEx 3)	21119/1175	ex N16761	725	
☐ C-GNKF	Boeing 727-227F (FedEx 3)	20839/1031	ex N88770	726	
☐ C-GQKF	Boeing 727-243F (FedEx 3)	21265/1226	ex N17402	720	
☐ C-GTKF	Boeing 727-225F (FedEx 3)	21580/1435	ex N8883Z	728	
☐ C-GWKF	Boeing 727-243F/W (Duganair 3)	21270/1231	ex N17407	719	
☐ C-GXKF	Boeing 727-243F/W (Duganair 3)	21663/1438	ex N17410	716	
☐ N231FL	Boeing 727-22C	19205/438	ex C-FKFP		wfs
☐ C-FKFZ	Convair 580F	151	ex N11151	510	
☐ C-GKFF	Convair 580F	160	ex N9067R	511	
☐ C-GKFG	Convair 580F	22	ex N32KA	516	[YLW]
☐ C-GKFU	Convair 580F	82	ex N90857	501	
☐ C-GKFY	Convair 580F	91	ex N400AB		[YLW]
☐ N538JA	Convair 580F	38	ex N73120		[YLW]
☐ C-FBPL	Beech 390 Premier 1A	RB-150	ex N6150Y		
☐ C-FCTB	Beech 390 Premier 1A	RB-271	ex C-GYMB		
☐ C-GKFA	Douglas DC-10-30F	46921/214	ex N811SL	101	
☐ C-GKFB	Douglas DC-10-30F	46949/179	ex N949PL	102	
☐ C-GKFD	Douglas DC-10-30F	47928/192	ex N304WL	103	
☐ C-GKFT	Douglas DC-10-30F	46917/211	ex N303WL		
☐ C-GKFX	Beech A60 Duke	P-235	ex N60GF		

KIVALLIQ AIR NUNAVUT LIFELINE   Kivalliq   Winnipeg-Intl, MB/Rankin Inlet, NU (YWG/YRT)

☐ C-FJXL	Beech 1900C	UC-102	ex N15479		EMS
☐ C-GFLA	Pilatus PC-12/45	293			EMS♦
Assoc with Keewatin Air (qv)					

KLUANE AIRWAYS   Whitehorse, YT (YXY)

☐ C-FMPS	de Havilland DHC-2 Beaver	1114	ex CF-MPS	FP
☐ C-GIFH	de Havilland DHC-2 Beaver	92		FP♦

L AND A AVIATION   Hay River, NT (YHY)

☐ CF-ZEB	Cessna 337F Super Skymaster	33701428	ex N1828M
☐ C-GHYK	Cessna 337F Super Skymaster	33701352	

☐ C-GHYT	Beech A100 King Air	B-98	ex N998RC	
☐ C-GJEM	Cessna 208 Caravan I	20800152		
☐ C-GJHM	Cessna A185F Skywagon	18504203		

LABRADOR AIR SAFARI — Baie Comeau, QC (YBC)

| ☐ C-FPQC | de Havilland DHC-2 Beaver | 873 | ex CF-IKQ | FP/WS |

LAC LA CROIX QUETICO AIR SERVICE — Lac la Croix, ON/Crane Lake, MB

☐ C-FHAN	de Havilland DHC-2 Beaver	316	ex N11255	FP
☐ C-FVSF	Cessna A185E Skywagon	185-1223	ex CF-VSF	FP
☐ C-GDZD	de Havilland DHC-2 Beaver	496	ex 52-6116	FP
☐ C-GUEC	Cessna A185F Skywagon	18503986	ex N5513E	FP

LAC SEUL AIRWAYS — Ear Falls, ON (YMY)

| ☐ CF-HXY | de Havilland DHC-3 Otter | 67 | | FP |
| ☐ C-GLLO | Cessna U206F Stationair II | U20602913 | ex N1602Q | FP |

LAKELSE AIR — Terrace, BC (YXT)

☐ C-FBCU	Aérospatiale AS350B2 AStar	1206		
☐ C-FLQF	Aérospatiale AS350B2 AStar	3547		♦
☐ C-FLQH	Aérospatiale AS350B2 AStar	2970		♦
☐ C-FLQM	Aérospatiale AS350B2 AStar	2886		♦
☐ C-FLQX	Aérospatiale AS350B2 AStar	2786		♦
☐ C-FNBR	Aérospatiale AS350B2 AStar	2565	ex N60618	
☐ C-FXPM	Aérospatiale AS350BA AStar	1428	ex C-FBHX	
☐ C-GBCN	Aérospatiale AS350B2 AStar	2609	ex F-GLHP	
☐ C-GMNI	Aérospatiale AS350B2 AStar	2896		
☐ C-GPTC	Aérospatiale AS350B2 AStar	2092	ex OY-HDY	
☐ C-GPWL	Aérospatiale AS350B2 AStar	2956		♦
☐ C-GPWV	Aérospatiale AS350B AStar	1637		
☐ C-FHQT	Bell 204B	2024	ex C-GEAV	
☐ C-FLAQ	Aérospatiale AS355N TwinStar	5669		
☐ C-GALU	Bell 206B JetRanger III	2511	ex N50071	
☐ C-GHQW	Bell 206B JetRanger III	1708		
☐ C-GPWH	Bell 206B JetRanger	3131		♦
☐ C-GWHO	Bell 206L LongRanger	45013	ex N3GH	

LAKES DISTRICT AIR SERVICES — Burns Lake, BC (YPZ)

☐ C-FBPB	de Havilland DHC-2 Beaver	1434	ex VH-IDF	FP/WS
☐ C-FFHS	de Havilland DHC-2 Beaver	51	ex CF-HHS	FP/WS
☐ C-FLVN	Cessna 182E	18253755		FP/WS
☐ C-FVXQ	Cessna A185E Skywagon	185-1198	ex CF-XVQ	FP/WS

LAUZON AVIATION — Elliot Lake, ON (YEL)

☐ C-FRUY	de Havilland DHC-2 Beaver	687	ex N74157	FP
☐ C-FSDY	de Havilland DHC-2 Beaver	897	ex N64273	FP
☐ C-FUET	Cessna 180H	18051673		FP

LAWRENCE BAY AIRWAYS — La Ronge, SK (YVC)

☐ C-FQQD	de Havilland DHC-2 Beaver	1580	ex FAP 64-374	FP
☐ C-GUJX	de Havilland DHC-2 Beaver	1132	ex 56-4412	FP
☐ C-GYEC	Cessna 180H	18051579		FP

LEUENBERGER AIR SERVICE — Nakina SPB, ON (YQN)

☐ C-FSOX	de Havilland DHC-3 Turbo Otter	437	ex CF-SOX	FP
☐ C-GLCW	de Havilland DHC-3 Turbo Otter	172	ex 55-3310	FP
☐ C-GYLX	Cessna A185F Skywagon	18503354		FP

LITTLE RED AIR SERVICE — Little Red (LRA) — Fort Vermilion, AB

☐ C-FGWR	Beech B200 Super King Air	BB-1599	ex C-FGWD	
☐ C-FLRD	Beech A100 King Air	B-243	ex PT-OFZ	
☐ C-FPQQ	Beech B200 Super King Air	BB-1304	ex N3173K	
☐ C-FSLR	Cessna U206G Stationair	U206G03712		
☐ C-GGBZ	Cessna U206G Stationair	U206G05637		
☐ C-GGUH	Cessna 208B Caravan I	208B0827	ex N51478	
☐ C-GHJF	Beech B200 Super King Air	BB-1493		
☐ C-GICJ	Cessna U206F Stationair	U20603044	ex N4318Q	
☐ C-GLRR	Piper PA-31-325 Navajo	31-7812044	ex N815CE	
☐ C-GLRT	Cessna 208B Caravan I	208B0963		
☐ C-GWVT	Cessna U206F Stationair	U20602918	ex (N1721Q)	

MANITOBA GOVERNMENT AIR SERVICES · Winnipeg-Intl/Thompson, MB (YWG/YTH)

☐ C-FTUV	Canadair CL215	1020	ex CF-TUV	256
☐ C-FTXI	Canadair CL215	1016	ex CF-TXI	255
☐ C-GBOW	Canadair CL215	1087	ex C-GKDY	253
☐ C-GMAF	Canadair CL215	1044	ex C-GUMW	250
☐ C-GMAK	Canadair CL215	1107		254
☐ C-GUMW	Canadair CL215	1065		251
☐ C-GYJB	Canadair CL215	1068		252

☐ C-FMAX	de Havilland DHC-3 Turbo Otter	267		
☐ C-FMFK	de Havilland DHC-3 Turbo Otter	54		♦
☐ C-FODY	de Havilland DHC-3 Turbo Otter	429		
☐ C-FWAH	de Havilland DHC-6 Twin Otter 300	240	ex CF-WAH	
☐ C-GBEB	de Havilland DHC-6 Twin Otter 300	272		
☐ C-GBNE	Cessna 560 Citation V	560-0244	ex N701NB	
☐ C-GBNX	Cessna 560 Citation V	0074	ex N593MD	EMS
☐ C-GDAT	Cessna 310R	310R1883	ex N315U	
☐ C-GMFW	Canadair CL415	2082		
☐ C-GMFX	Canadair CL415	2083		
☐ C-GMFY	Canadair CL415	2078		
☐ C-GMFZ	Canadair CL415	2086		
☐ C-GMLN	Cessna 310R	310R1884	ex N316U	
☐ C-GRNE	Piper PA-31-350 Chieftain	31-7952224	ex N91834	
☐ C-GYNE	Cessna 310R	310R1367	ex N4086C	

MARITIME AIR CHARTER · Halifax, NS (YHZ)

☐ C-FDOR	Beech A100 King Air	B-103	ex CF-DOR
☐ C-GILS	Britten-Norman BN-2A-21 Islander	0416	ex N92JA
☐ C-GUND	Beech 200 Super King Air	BB-139	ex N810JB
☐ C-GXUG	Piper PA-31 Turbo Navajo	31-665	ex N1GY

MARTINI AVIATION · Fort Langley, BC

☐ C-GMLZ	Agusta A109C	7655		
☐ C-GMNT	de Havilland DHC-2 Turbo Beaver	1653/TB30	ex N4478	FP
☐ C-GPIZ	Cessna 208 Caravan I	20800547		
☐ C-GPLT	Cessna 525B Citation	525B-0268		♦
☐ C-GTMW	de Havilland DHC-3 Turbo Otter	427	ex C-FODX	

MAX AVIATION · Max Aviation (MAX) · Montreal-St Hubert, QC (YHU)

☐ C-FJDQ	Beech B100 King Air	BE-16	ex C-GDFZ
☐ C-FOGP	Beech B100 King Air	BE-134	ex N363EA
☐ C-GMNL	Beech B100 King Air	BE-48	ex N2830S
☐ C-GPJL	Beech B100 King Air	BE-107	ex N3699B
☐ C-GPRU	Beech B100 King Air	BE-26	ex N36WH
☐ C-GSWG	Beech B100 King Air	BE-131	ex N6354H
☐ C-GVIK	Beech A100 King Air	BE-7	ex N57HT
☐ C-GYPA	Beech A100 King Air	BE-32	ex N493DT
☐ C-GCVS	Beech B200C Super King Air	BL-13	ex N817BB

McMURRAY AVIATION · Fort McMurray, AB (YMM)

☐ C-FKEY	Cessna 208 Caravan I	20800307	ex N526KA
☐ F-FXCL	Cessna 208BEX Caravan I	208B5107	♦
☐ C-GHLI	Cessna 208B Caravan I	208B0565	ex N5858J
☐ C-GKOM	Cessna 208 Caravan I	20800365	ex N675TF
☐ C-GWKO	Cessna 208B Caravan I	208B1245	ex N52591
☐ C-GWRK	Cessna 208B Caravan I	208B1229	ex N208LC
☐ C-GHGT	Cessna U206G Stationair	U20605874	
☐ C-GHJB	Cessna U206E Stationair	U20601677	ex N9477G
☐ C-GQPS	Cessna U206G Stationair	U20604346	
☐ C-GRKO	Cessna U206G Stationair	U20606617	ex N9707Z

MINIPI AVIATION · Goose Bay, NL (YYR)

☐ C-FCOO	de Havilland DHC-2 Beaver	314	ex N377JW	FP

MOLSON AIR · Wabowden, MB

☐ C-FBQY	de Havilland DHC-2 Beaver	1496	ex N147Q	FP/WS
☐ C-GYBQ	Cessna A185F Skywagon	18503568	ex N4014Q	FP/WS

MORNINGSTAR AIR EXPRESS · Morningstar (MAL) · Edmonton-Intl, AB (YEG)

☐ C-FMAI	Boeing 757-2B7SF	27199/586	ex N908FD	Giovanna	Lsd fr/opf FDX
☐ C-FMEK	Boeing 757-2B7SF	27123/534	ex N902FD	Hannah	Lsd fr/opf FDX

☐ C-FMEP	Boeing 757-2B7SF	27144/544	ex N904FD	Rachel		Lsd fr/opf FDX
☐ C-FMEU	Boeing 757-2B7SF	27200/589	ex N909FD	Morgan		Lsd fr/opf FDX
☐ C-FMFG	Boeing 757-2B7F	27198/584	ex N907FD	Megan		Lsd fr/opf FDX
☐ C-FEXB	Cessna 208B Caravan I	208B0539	ex N758FX			Lsd fr/opf FDX
☐ C-FEXE	Cessna 208B Caravan I	208B0244	ex N750FE			Lsd fr/opf FDX
☐ C-FEXF	Cessna 208B Caravan I	208B0508	ex N749FX			Lsd fr/opf FDX
☐ C-FEXH	Cessna 208B Caravan I	208B0017	ex N917FE			
☐ C-FEXO	Cessna 208B Caravan I	208B0535	ex N757FX			Lsd fr/opf FDX
☐ C-FEXX	Cessna 208B Caravan I	208B0209	ex (N877FE)			Lsd fr/opf FDX
☐ C-FEXY	Cessna 208B Caravan I	208B0226	ex N896FE			Lsd fr/opf FDX
☐ C-FTAR	ATR 72-202F	217	ex N809FX			Lsd fr/opf FDX

MUSTANG HELICOPTERS · Red Deer, AB (YQF)

☐ C-FAEF	Aérospatiale AS350B2 AStar	2152			♦
☐ C-FAOV	Aérospatiale AS350B2 AStar	9066			
☐ C-FAOX	Aérospatiale AS350B2 AStar	9067			
☐ C-FAOZ	Aérospatiale AS350B2 AStar	9068	ex N68CQ		
☐ C-FHEI	Aérospatiale AS350B2 AStar	2969			♦
☐ C-FHVV	Aérospatiale AS350BA AStar	1225			HI
☐ C-FIFL	Aérospatiale AS350BA AStar	1453			HI
☐ C-FJYL	Aérospatiale AS350BA AStar	2959			HE
☐ C-FLIZ	Aérospatiale AS350BA AStar	2484			HI
☐ C-FMHI	Aérospatiale AS350B2 AStar	9037	ex EI-MYO		HI
☐ C-FMNE	Aérospatiale AS350B2 AStar	9082		poss w/o 25Aug11	
☐ C-FMOZ	Aérospatiale AS350BA AStar	1374	ex F-GHFR		HI
☐ C-FNWE	Aérospatiale AS350B2 AStar	9086			
☐ C-FNYE	Aérospatiale AS350B2 AStar	9091			
☐ C-FNYF	Aérospatiale AS350B2 AStar	9092			
☐ C-FNYG	Aérospatiale AS350B2 AStar	9093			HE
☐ C-FNYK	Aérospatiale AS350B2 AStar	9088			
☐ C-FONZ	Aérospatiale AS350BA AStar	1400	ex HR-ANU		HI
☐ C-FOZT	Aérospatiale AS350BA AStar	2064			♦
☐ C-FPHY	Aérospatiale AS350A AStar	1496			HE
☐ C-FQHC	Aérospatiale AS350BA AStar	1011			♦
☐ C-FSPF	Aérospatiale AS350B2 AStar	2785			♦
☐ C-FVIG	Aérospatiale AS350B2 AStar	2893	ex N333AS		HE
☐ C-FVIT	Aérospatiale AS350B2 AStar	2890	ex N544AS		HE
☐ C-FVRT	Aérospatiale AS350B2 AStar	2849			♦
☐ C-FZXY	Aérospatiale AS350BA AStar	2082	ex N6102E		HI
☐ C-GAWV	Aérospatiale AS350B2 AStar	2998			HI
☐ C-GBKX	Aérospatiale AS350B3 AStar	7512			
☐ C-GBKY	Aérospatiale AS350B3 AStar	7535			
☐ C-GGIS	Aérospatiale AS350BA AStar	1110	ex N40445		HI
☐ C-GIEQ	Aérospatiale AS350B2 AStar	3349			♦
☐ C-GIYJ	Aérospatiale AS350BA AStar	1407			♦
☐ C-GJHC	Aérospatiale AS350B2 AStar	3412			HI
☐ C-GJPA	Aérospatiale AS350BA AStar	1075	ex C-FHAH		HI
☐ C-GMIM	Aérospatiale AS350BA AStar	1257			HI
☐ C-GMQM	Aérospatiale AS350BA AStar	1380	ex N108SH		HI
☐ C-GRYK	Aérospatiale AS350B3 AStar	7331			
☐ C-GVEI	Aérospatiale AS350B2 AStar	2671			♦
☐ C-GVIA	Aérospatiale AS350B2 AStar	2297	ex N442BV		HE
☐ C-GXTH	Aérospatiale AS350B2 AStar	9049			HE
☐ C-GXTO	Aérospatiale AS350B2 AStar	9061	ex N681CC		HI
☐ C-GZGM	Aérospatiale AS350B2 AStar	9056			
☐ C-FBYU	Bell 205A-1	30168			HE
☐ C-FCNV	Bell 205A-1	30288			HI
☐ C-FFHB	Bell 205A-1	30294	ex VH-HHW		
☐ C-FSMI	Bell 205A-1	30263	ex (N205HT)		HI
☐ C-GFHW	Bell 205A-1	30115			HI
☐ C-GFRE	Bell 205A-1	30185	ex EC-FYX		
☐ C-GHUF	Bell 205A-1	30106	ex N687CC		
☐ C-GKVI	Bell 205A-1	30182	ex C-GOLE		
☐ C-GLHE	Bell 205A-1	30092			HE
☐ C-GLHH	Bell 205A-1	30223			HE
☐ C-GLVI	Bell 205A-1	30209	ex C-GPET		
☐ C-GVHP	Bell 205A-1	30119	ex N688CC		
☐ C-GVIE	Bell 205B	30188	ex N394EH		HE
☐ C-FXHA	Aérospatiale AS3552 Twin Star	5426			
☐ C-GARE	Bell 206B JetRanger II	1852			HI
☐ C-GCVI	Bell 407	53854			
☐ C-GFIT	Bell 214B-1	28040			
☐ C-GGVI	Bell 407	53834			HE
☐ C-GHNQ	Bell 206L LongRanger	45014	ex N259MH		HI
☐ C-GJVI	Bell 407	53866			HI
☐ C-GMHO	Aérospatiale AS355NP Twin Star	5787			♦
☐ C-GVIB	Bell 407	53826	ex C-FTLZ		HE
☐ C-GYHZ	Bell 206L LongRanger	45126			HI

☐ C-GZAN	Bell 212	30589
☐ C-GZNF	Bell 212	30580
☐ C-GZNK	Bell 212	30729

Assoc with Heli-Inter (HI) and Heli-Excel (HE)

NAKINA OUTPOST CAMPS AND AIR SERVICE (T2)   Nakina, ON (YQN)

☐ CF-MIQ	de Havilland DHC-3 Turbo Otter	336		FP/WS
☐ C-FMPY	de Havilland DHC-3 Turbo Otter	324	ex CF-MPY	FP/WS
☐ C-FNQB	Cessna 208 Caravan I	20800387	ex N5184N	
☐ C-FTIN	Cessna A185F Skywagon	18503362	ex N7325H	FP/WS
☐ C-FUYC	Cessna 208B Caravan I	208B1204	ex N208DD	
☐ C-FZRJ	Cessna 208B Caravan I	208B0597	ex N52609	
☐ C-GEOW	Pilatus PC-12/45	244	ex HB-FRO	
☐ C-GMVB	Cessna 208B Caravan I	208B0317		
☐ C-GNQZ	Pilatus PC-12/47E	1309	ex N309NG	

NATIONAL HELICOPTERS   Toronto, ON

☐ C-FFUJ	Bell 206B JetRanger III	2982	ex N525W	
☐ C-FLYC	Bell 206L-1 LongRanger II	45478	ex XA-SPN	
☐ C-FNHB	Bell 206L-1 LongRanger	45661		
☐ C-FNHE	MBB Bo105CDN-BS4	S-349		
☐ C-FNHG	Bell 206L-1 LongRanger II	45784	ex N220HC	
☐ C-FOHL	Bell 430	49103		
☐ C-GNHX	Bell 430	49025		♦
☐ C-GTMI	Augsta A109S	22160		

NESTOR FALLS FLY-IN OUTPOSTS   Nestor Falls SPB, ON

☐ C-FMDB	de Havilland DHC-2 Beaver	268	ex N2104X	FP
☐ C-FODK	de Havilland DHC-3 Turbo Otter	13	ex CF-ODK	FP
☐ C-FSOR	de Havilland DHC-3 Turbo Otter	239	ex IM 1725	FP
☐ C-GDWB	Cessna U206G Stationair	U20604460	ex N756YJ	FP
☐ C-GYGL	Cessna A185F Skywagon	18503298	ex (N94269)	FP

NEWFOUNDLAND & LABRADOR AIR SERVICES   St John's, NL (YYT)

☐ C-FDNL	Canadair CL415	2091			♦
☐ C-FIGJ	Canadair CL415	2084			
☐ C-FNJC	Canadair CL415	2077		287	
☐ C-FOFI	Canadair CL415	2081		288	
☐ C-FTXA	Canadair CL215	1006	ex CF-TXA	284	
☐ C-FYWP	Canadair CL215	1002	ex CF-YWP	285	
☐ C-GNLF	Beech B300 Super King Air	FL-591			
☐ C-GNLO	Beech C300 Super King Air	FM-46	ex N81454		

NIIGAANI AIR   Thunder Bay, ON (YQT)

| ☐ C-FCAR | Piper PA-31-360 Navajo Chieftain | 31-7405483 | | |
| ☐ C-GEDE | de Havilland DHC-2 Beaver | 1541 | ex VH-OMO | FP |

NOLINOR AVIATION   Nolinor (NRL)   Montreal-Trudeau, QC (YUL)

☐ C-FAWV	Convair 580F	154	ex C-FMGB	Frtr
☐ C-FHNM	Convair 580F	454	ex N583P	>SKG
☐ C-FTAP	Convair 580	334	ex N580N	
☐ C-GQHB	Convair 580	376	ex ZS-KRX	
☐ C-GRLQ	Convair 580	347	ex N580TA	

☐ C-FVNC	Learjet 31A	31A-187		♦
☐ C-GNLK	Boeing 737-2K2C	20836/354	ex HA-LEW	♦
☐ C-GNLN	Boeing 737-2B6C (Nordam 3)	23050/975	ex CN-RMN	Frtr
☐ C-GNRD	Boeing 737-229C (Nordam 3)	21738/576	ex XA-TWP	
☐ C-GTUK	Boeing 737-2B6C (Nordam 3)	23049/951	ex CN-RMM	Frtr

NOMAD AIR   Whitehorse, YT (YXY)

☐ C-FTBI	Shorts SC.7 Skyvan Srs.3	SH.1847		
☐ C-GTBN	Dornier 228-201	8100	ex PJ-DVA	
☐ C-GTBU	Shorts SC.7 Skyvan Srs.3	SH1844	ex C-FUMC	

NORDPLUS   Schefferville-Squaw Lake, QC (YKL)

| ☐ C-FODG | de Havilland DHC-2 Beaver | 205 | | FP |
| ☐ C-GFUT | de Havilland DHC-3 Otter | 404 | ex CAF9422 | FP |

NORTH CARIBOO AIR/FLYING SERVICE   North Caribou (NCB)   Fort St John, BC (YXJ)

| ☐ C-FCGC | Beech 200 Super King Air | BB-236 | ex N46KA | CatPass 200 conversion |
| ☐ C-FCGM | Beech 200 Super King Air | BB-217 | ex N200CD | CatPass 200 conversion |

☐	C-FNNC	Beech 200 Super King Air	BB-222		
☐	C-FRRQ	Beech 200 Super King Air	BB-560	ex F-GTEF	
☐	C-FZVX	Beech 200 Super King Air	BB-231	ex N200FH	
☐	C-GAEW	Beech B200 Super King Air	BB-1546		
☐	C-GDFN	Beech 200 Super King Air	BB-359	ex N351MA	
☐	C-GDFT	Beech 200 Super King Air	BB-354	ex N221BG	
☐	C-GJJT	Beech 200 Super King Air	BB-828	ex N62GA	
☐	C-GZRX	Beech 200 Super King Air	BB-574	ex N75WL	
☐	C-FMCN	Beech 1900D	UE-20	ex N220CJ	
☐	C-FNCL	Beech 1900D	UE-11	ex C-FSKT	
☐	C-FNCP	Beech 1900D	UE-58	ex C-GSKY	
☐	C-FNSN	Beech 1900D	UE-51	ex ZS-PVN	
☐	C-FNSV	Beech 1900D	UE-179	ex ZS-PPI	
☐	C-FRNC	Beech 1900D	UE-316	ex ZS-PRH	
☐	C-GNCE	Beech 1900D	UE-298	ex YV1367	
☐	C-FDGP	de Havilland DHC-8-402Q	4029	ex D-ADHB	
☐	C-FGNJ	de Havilland DHC-8-402Q	4028	ex D-ADHA	
☐	C-FHNC	de Havilland DHC-8-311	412	ex V2-LES	
☐	C-FLSX	de Havilland DHC-8-106	285	ex N834EX	
☐	C-FNXN	de Havilland DHC-8-311Q	464	ex C-GUPQ	
☐	C-FODL	de Havilland DHC-8-106	294	ex N881CC	
☐	C-GAQN	de Havilland DHC-8-311	548	ex 5N-BHW	
☐	C-GLWN	de Havilland DHC-8-311A	311	ex G-WOWC	
☐	C-GNCF	de Havilland DHC-8-311A	244	ex PH-ADQ	
☐	C-FIDN	Beech 100 King Air	B-3	ex N13303	
☐	C-FMKD	Beech 65-B90 King Air	LJ-376	ex N300RV	
☐	C-FMPC	de Havilland DHC-2 Turbo Beaver	1300	ex S2-ACE	
☐	C-FMXY	Beech 100 King Air	B-40	ex N923K	
☐	C-FPDR	Canadair CL-601-3R Challenger	5155	ex N401RJ	
☐	CF-QSX	Cessna A185F Skywagon	18502116	ex (N70334)	
☐	C-FSUA	Avro 146-RJ100	E3373	ex G-POWF	♦
☐	C-GCFM	Beech 65-C90 King Air	LJ-886	ex N15SL	
☐	C-GLAC	Beech 58 Baron	TH-339	ex N6YC	
☐	C-GMWO	Piper PA-31 Navajo C	31-8112042	ex N4086Y	
☐	C-GRNT	British Aerospace 146-200	E2140	ex G-11-140	[YYC]
☐	C-GSUI	Avro 146-RJ100	E3369	ex G-BZAZ	
☐	C-	Avro 146-RJ85	E2235	ex OY-RCD	for spares use

NORTH STAR AIR   Pickle Lake, ON (YPL)

☐	C-FIXS	Cessna 208B Caravan I	208B1209		
☐	C-FLNB	Cessna 208B Caravan I	208B0799	ex N799B	
☐	C-FVPC	Pilatus PC-12/45	358	ex N358PC	
☐	C-FYZS	Pilatus PC-12/45	227	ex N227PC	
☐	C-GCQA	de Havilland DHC-3 Turbo Otter	77	ex N129JH	FP/WS
☐	C-GKAY	Pilatus PC-12/45	178		♦

NORTH-WRIGHT AIRWAYS   Northwright (HW/NWL)
Norman Wells/Good Hope/Deline, NT (YVQ/YGH/YWJ)

☐	C-FBAX	Cessna 207 Skywagon	20700355	ex N1755U	
☐	C-FKHD	Beech 99	U-11	ex F-BRUN	
☐	C-FNWH	Beech 1900D	UE-112	ex N112ZV	
☐	C-FNWL	de Havilland DHC-6 Twin Otter 300	596	ex N16NG	
☐	C-FVCE	Beech 99A	U-118	ex N918BB	FP
☐	CF-WHP	Cessna 337C Skymaster	3370895		
☐	C-FZIZ	Pilatus PC-6/B1-H2 Turbo Porter	2009		FP
☐	C-GAAP	Pilatus PC-6/B1-H2 Turbo Porter	569	ex N2851T	FP
☐	C-GALF	Cessna 207A Stationair 8 II	20700674	ex N9118M	
☐	C-GDBI	Cessna 207 Skywagon	20700039	ex N91052	
☐	C-GDLC	Cessna 208B Caravan I	208B0767	ex N5151D	
☐	C-GFCV	Cessna U206C Super Skywagon	U206-1213	ex N4345E	
☐	C-GHDT	Helio 295 Super Courier	1401	ex N6327V	
☐	C-GHXR	Cessna U206F Stationair	U20603064		FP
☐	C-GJGZ	Cessna A185F Skywagon II	18503856	ex (N4750E)	
☐	C-GMOK	Cessna 207A Stationair 8 II	20700673	ex N6373D	
☐	C-GNWA	Cessna A185F Skywagon II	18503345	ex C-GFJC	
☐	C-GRDD	de Havilland DHC-6 Twin Otter 100	54	ex N8081N	FP/WS
☐	C-GZGO	Britten-Norman BN-2A-26 Islander	2017	ex N59360	
☐	C-GZIZ	Cessna 208B Caravan I	208B0546	ex N5262W	
☐	C-GZVX	Cessna U206G Stationair 6	U20604110	ex (N756HT)	

NORTHERN AIR CHARTER   Peace River, AB (YPE)

☐	C-GNAB	Beech B200 Super King Air	BB-1941		
☐	C-GNAG	Beech B200 Super King Air	BB-1239		
☐	C-GNAK	Beech B200 Super King Air	BB-1376	ex HK-3990X	Catpass 200 conversion
☐	C-GNAM	Beech B200 Super King Air	BB-1339	ex N252AF	EMS, Beech 1300 conversion
☐	C-GNAX	Beech B200 Super King Air	BB-1419	ex N146SB	

☐ C-GNAC	Piper PA-31 Navajo C	31-7812106	ex N27707
☐ C-GNAP	Piper PA-23-250 Aztec F	27-8054002	ex C-GTGS
☐ C-GNAR	Beech 1900D	UE-252	ex JA017A

NORTHERN AIR SOLUTIONS — Bracebridge, ON

☐ C-FHLG	Cessna 550 Citation	550-0424	ex N435UM
☐ C-GHGV	Pilatus PC-12/45	342	ex N372GT
☐ C-GZGZ	Pilatus PC-12/45	357	ex N7725X

NORTHERN ROCKIES AIR CHARTER — Watson Lake, YT

| ☐ CF-DTW | de Havilland DHC-2 Beaver | 732 | ex N1018H | FP |
| ☐ CF-GWM | Cessna U206F Skywagon | U20601802 | | FP |

NORTHWARD AIR — Dawson Creek, BC (YDQ)

☐ C-FOMF	Cessna A185A Skywagon	185-0423	ex (N1623Z)
☐ CF-SLV	Cessna U206 Super Skywagon	U206-0412	ex N8012Z
☐ C-GGKB	Piper PA-23 Aztec 250	27-3694	
☐ C-GLKM	Helio H-391B Courier	034		FP

NORTHWAY AVIATION — Northway (NAL) — St Andrews, MB

☐ C-FBBA	Cessna 208B Caravan I	208B2366	ex N8117J
☐ C-GNWD	Cessna 208B Caravan I	208B1188	ex N471MC
☐ C-GNWI	Cessna 208 Caravan I	20800391	ex N85EE
☐ C-GNWU	Cessna 208B Caravan I	208B2028	◆
☐ C-GNWV	Cessna 208B Caravan I	208B1115	ex N5093D

NORTHWEST FLYING — Nestor Falls SPB, ON

☐ CF-HZA	Beech D-18S	A-111		FP◆
☐ CF-NKL	Beech C-45H	AF-378	ex N9864Z	FP
☐ C-GEBL	de Havilland DHC-2 Beaver	1068	ex N33466	FP
☐ C-GIUN	Cessna 180K	18052803		FP

NORTHWESTERN AIR — Polaris (J3/PLR) — Fort Smith, NT (YSM)

☐ C-FCPE	British Aerospace Jetstream 3112	825	ex G-31-825
☐ C-FNAA	British Aerospace Jetstream 3112	929	ex C-GINL
☐ C-FNAE	British Aerospace Jetstream 3212	881	ex N431AM
☐ C-FNAF	British Aerospace Jetstream 3112	789	ex N411UE
☐ C-FNAM	British Aerospace Jetstream 3112	767	ex N767JX
☐ C-FNAZ	British Aerospace Jetstream 3212	843	ex C-GEAZ
☐ C-GNAH	British Aerospace Jetstream 3212	874	ex N874CP
☐ C-GNAQ	British Aerospace Jetstream 3212	837	ex C-FZYB
☐ C-GPSN	British Aerospace Jetstream 3112	783	ex C-GHGI
☐ C-FLLL	de Havilland DHC-3 Turbo Otter	292	ex CF-LLL
☐ C-GAIX	Cessna A185F Skymaster	18503890	
☐ C-GIJL	Cessna 210L Centurion	21061226	
☐ C-GNAL	Beech 99	U-57	ex TF-ELD
☐ C-GTPU	Cessna U206G Stationair	U20604749	
☐ C-GWQW	Cessna U206E Stationair	U20601573	

NT AIR/NORTHERN THUNDERBIRD AIR — Thunderbird (NTA) — Prince George/Smithers, BC (YXS/YYD)

☐ C-FNTA	Beech B300 King Air	FL-806	ex N8006R	
☐ C-GCMT	Beech 1900C-1	UC-120	ex N15683	
☐ C-GCMZ	Beech 1900C-1	UC-61	ex N1568L	929
☐ C-GDOX	Cessna 208B Caravan I	208B0541	ex N621BB	
☐ C-GEFA	Beech 1900C-1	UC-94	ex N80346	927
☐ C-GXRX	Beech 100 King Air	B-36		

Assoc with Central Mountain Air (qv)

OCEAN PACIFIC AIR SERVICES — Prince Rupert, BC

☐ C-FTCW	de Havilland DHC-2 Beaver	646		FP◆
☐ C-FWOP	Cessna 180 Skywagon	18032463		FP
☐ C-FWZE	de Havilland DHC-2 Beaver	1214		FP

ONTARIO MINISTRY OF NATURAL RESOURCES AVIATION SERVICES — Trillium (TRI) — Sault Ste Marie, ON (YAM)

☐ C-GOGD	Canadair CL415	2028	ex C-GAOI	270
☐ C-GOGE	Canadair CL415	2031	ex C-GAUR	271
☐ C-GOGF	Canadair CL415	2032	ex C-GBGE	272
☐ C-GOGG	Canadair CL415	2033	ex C-GBFY	273
☐ C-GOGH	Canadair CL415	2034	ex C-GCNO	274
☐ C-GOGW	Canadair CL415	2037	ex C-GBPM	275

☐ C-GOGX	Canadair CL415	2038	ex C-GBPU	276
☐ C-GOGY	Canadair CL415	2040		277
☐ C-GOGZ	Canadair CL415	2043		278
☐ C-FOEH	de Havilland DHC-2 Turbo Beaver	1644/TB24	ex CF-OEH	FP/WS
☐ C-FOER	de Havilland DHC-2 Turbo Beaver	1671/TB41	ex CF-OER	FP/WS
☐ C-FOEU	de Havilland DHC-2 Turbo Beaver	1678/TB46	ex CF-OEU	FP/WS
☐ C-FOEW	de Havilland DHC-2 Turbo Beaver	1682/TB50	ex CF-OEW	FP/WS
☐ C-FOPA	de Havilland DHC-2 Turbo Beaver	1688/TB56	ex CF-OPA	FP/WS
☐ C-FOPG	de Havilland DHC-6 Twin Otter 300	232	ex CF-OPG	FP/WS
☐ C-FOPI	de Havilland DHC-6 Twin Otter 300	243	ex CF-OPI	FP/WS
☐ C-FOPJ	de Havilland DHC-6 Twin Otter 300	344	ex CF-OPJ	FP/WS
☐ C-GOGA	de Havilland DHC-6 Twin Otter 300	739		FP/WS
☐ C-GOGB	de Havilland DHC-6 Twin Otter 300	761		FP/WS
☐ C-GOGC	de Havilland DHC-6 Twin Otter 300	750		FP/WS
☐ C-FATR	Eurocopter EC130B4	3759		
☐ C-FMNR	Eurocopter EC130B4	4391		
☐ C-FONA	Eurocopter EC130B4	4945		
☐ C-FONC	Eurocopter EC130B4	4702		
☐ C-FONM	Eurocopter EC130B4	4566		
☐ C-FONV	Eurocopter EC130B4	7340		
☐ C-GONB	Eurocopter EC130B4	4885		
☐ C-CONT	Eurocopter EC130R4	4423		
☐ C-FOPD	Pilatus PC12/47E	1398		
☐ C-FOPP	Eurocopter EC135P2+	0948		
☐ C-FOPS	Eurocopter EC135P2+	0959		
☐ C-GOGL	Aérospatiale AS350B2 AStar	2738		
☐ C-GOGS	Beech B300 Super King Air	FL-269	ex N3169N	
☐ C-GOIC	Beech B300 Super King Air	FL-272	ex N3172N	
☐ C-GOXY	Cessna T206H Stationair	T20608804		

OPSMOBIL Grande Prairie, AB (YQU)

☐ C-FHAU	Aérospatiale AS350BA AStar	2778		
☐ C-FXAH	Aérospatiale AS350BA AStar	2509	ex N905BK	
☐ C-FXBP	Aérospatiale AS350BA AStar	1553	ex I-VBIT	
☐ C-FXDM	Aérospatiale AS350BA AStar	1548	ex N798JH	
☐ C-FXED	Aérospatiale AS350BA AStar	3087		
☐ C-FXEJ	Aérospatiale AS350BA AStar	1031		
☐ C-FXHP	Aérospatiale AS350BA AStar	3100		
☐ C-GOFX	Aérospatiale AS350BA AStar	2195		
☐ C-GREV	Aérospatiale AS350BA AStar	1039		♦
☐ C-FARQ	Cessna 208B Caravan I	208B0765		♦
☐ C-FHHA	Bell 206L-1 LongRanger	45662		♦
☐ C-FZHG	Piper PA-31 Navajo	31-753		♦
☐ C-GELJ	Bell 206B JetRanger	116		♦
☐ C-GEMK	Eurocopter EC120B	1427		♦
☐ C-GEMU	Eurocopter EC120B	1057		♦
☐ C-GFYK	Cessna U206F Stationair	U206-03350		♦
☐ C-GTEZ	Bell 206B JetRanger	746		♦
☐ C-GTQU	Bell 206B JetRanger	766		♦
☐ C-GXAG	Bell 206B JetRanger	150		♦

ORCA AIRWAYS Richmond, BC (YVR)

☐ C-FFFH	Piper PA-31-350 Navajo Chieftain	31-7552130	ex N54CG	
☐ C-FLRA	Piper PA-31-350 Navajo Chieftain	31-7752091	ex N52MS	
☐ C-GGQM	Piper PA-31-350 Navajo Chieftain	31-7952033	ex TF-EGU	
☐ C-GIKA	Piper PA-31-350 Chieftain	31-7952161		
☐ C-GNAE	Piper PA-31-350 Chieftain	31-7952157		
☐ C-GNAZ	Piper PA-31-350 Navajo Chieftain	31-7752162		
☐ C-GPAK	Piper PA-31-350 Chieftain	31-8052070	ex N3558S	
☐ C-GPAP	Piper PA-31-350 Chieftain	31-8152005		
☐ C-GPMP	Piper PA-31-350 Chieftain	31-7852024	ex C-GWTT	
☐ C-GPWP	Piper PA-31-350 Chieftain	31-7952090	ex N35164	
☐ C-GWXL	Piper PA-31-350 Chieftain	31-7952036	ex C-GLYG	
☐ C-GXHK	Piper PA-31-350 Navajo Chieftain	31-7752108	ex N115SC	
☐ C-GYYK	Piper PA-31-350 Navajo Chieftain	31-7752029		
☐ C-GZBO	Piper PA-31-350 Chieftain	31-8252048	ex N430S	
☐ C-FAXE	Beech 100 King Air	B-41		
☐ C-FIOA	Swearingen SA227AT Merlin IVC	AT-492	ex N8897Y	
☐ C-FIOB	Swearingen SA227AT Metro III	AC-614	ex N614TR	
☐ C-FIOC	Swearingen SA227AC Metro III	AC-632	ex N632TR	
☐ C-GTWL	Learjet 35A	35A-490	ex N502JF	♦

ORNGE GLOBAL AIR — Thunder Bay, ON (YQT)

☐ C-GRXA	Pilatus PC-12/47E	1083	ex N983NG	EMS
☐ C-GRXB	Pilatus PC-12/47E	1094	ex N994NG	EMS
☐ C-GRXD	Pilatus PC-12/47E	1106	ex N106PC	EMS
☐ C-GRXE	Pilatus PC-12/47E	1117	ex N117PZ	EMS
☐ C-GRXH	Pilatus PC-12/47E	1163	ex N163NP	EMS
☐ C-GRXM	Pilatus PC-12/47E	1169	ex N169NP	EMS
☐ C-GRXN	Pilatus PC-12/47E	1224	ex N224NG	EMS
☐ C-GRXO	Pilatus PC-12/47E	1225	ex N225NG	EMS
☐ C-GRXP	Pilatus PC-12/47E	1249	ex N249NG	EMS
☐ C-GRXR	Pilatus PC-12/47E	1255	ex N255NG	EMS

OSNABURGH AIRWAYS — Pickle Lake, ON (YPL)

☐ C-FCZO	de Havilland DHC-3 Otter	71	ex CF-CZO	FP/WS
☐ C-FFQX	Noorduyn Norseman VI	625	ex N51131	FP/WS
☐ C-GMAU	de Havilland DHC-2 Beaver	1134	ex N775E	FP/WS

OSPREY WINGS — La Ronge, SK (YVC)

☐ C-FDGV	de Havilland DHC-6 Twin Otter 200	154		♦
☐ C-FLXP	de Havilland DHC-6 Twin Otter 200	217	ex N201EH	FP/WS
☐ C-FVEG	de Havilland DHC-6 Twin Otter 300	260	ex OH-SLK	FP/WS
☐ C-GIGK	de Havilland DHC-6 Twin Otter 300	492	ex N300BC	
☐ C-GPVQ	de Havilland DHC-6 Twin Otter 100	99	ex N990KD	FP/WS
☐ C-GQOQ	de Havilland DHC-6 Twin Otter 200	155	ex EC-BPE	FP/WS
☐ C-FASZ	de Havilland DHC-3 Turbo Otter	463	ex IM672	FP/WS
☐ C-FBPK	Beech 1900D	UE-128	ex N128EU	
☐ CF-DIZ	de Havilland DHC-3 Turbo Otter	460	ex JW-9107	FP/WS
☐ C-FORN	Cessna 182E Skylane	18254110		FP/WS
☐ C-FTCT	de Havilland DHC-2 Beaver	962	ex FAP-0205	FP/WS
☐ C-FXRI	de Havilland DHC-3 Turbo Otter	258	ex VH-SBT	FP/WS
☐ C-GAIJ	de Havilland DHC-2 Beaver	1373	ex N5334G	FP/WS
☐ C-GCIM	Cessna A185F Skywagon II	18503953	ex (N5308E)	FP/WS
☐ C-GJUM	Piper PA-31T Cheyenne	31T-7520021	ex N31PT	
☐ C-GKJR	Cessna A185F Skywagon	18504232		
☐ C-GPHD	de Havilland DHC-3 Turbo Otter	113	ex 55-3267	FP/WS
☐ C-GQKS	de Havilland DHC-2 Beaver	1096	ex N690	FP/WS
☐ C-GTGP	Beech B200 Super King Air	BB-1292	ex N333TP	
☐ C-GURF	Beech 1900D	UE-279	ex YV1366	
☐ C-GUWL	de Havilland DHC-2 Beaver	1223	ex 67-6140	FP/WS

PACIFIC COASTAL AIRLINES — Pasco (8P/PCO) — Port Hardy, BC (YZT)

☐ C-FPCO	Beech 1900C	UB-52	ex C-GKHB		
☐ C-FPCV	Beech 1900C	UB-9	ex N189GA	302	
☐ C-FPCX	Beech 1900C	UB-66	ex OY-JRF		
☐ C-GBPC	Beech 1900C	UB-43	ex N565M		
☐ C-GCPZ	Beech 1900C	UB-71	ex C-GNPG		
☐ C-GIPC	Beech 1900C-1	UC-110	ex N210CU	Special c/s	
☐ C-GPCY	Beech 1900C	UB-45	ex C-FYZD	301	
☐ C-GPCE	SAAB SF.340A	340A-004	ex N340SZ	Trawler c/s	
☐ C-GPCG	SAAB SF.340A	340A-094	ex N107EA		
☐ C-GPCJ	SAAB SF.340A	340A-006	ex N360SZ	Sailing boat c/s	[YVR]
☐ C-GPCN	SAAB SF.340A	340A-027	ex N27XJ		
☐ C-GPCQ	SAAB SF.340A	340A-043	ex N43SZ		
☐ C-	SAAB SF.340B	340B-338	ex N338CJ		♦
☐ C-FDSG	de Havilland DHC-2 Beaver	892	ex 54-1737		FP
☐ C-FHUZ	Grumman G-21A Goose	B-83	ex BuA37830		
☐ C-FIOL	Grumman G-21A Goose	B-107	ex RCN 397		
☐ C-FITS	de Havilland DHC-3 Turbo Otter	090	ex CF-ITS		FP
☐ C-FMAZ	de Havilland DHC-2 Beaver	1413	ex CF-MAZ		
☐ C-FUAZ	Grumman G-21A Goose	1077	ex N95400		
☐ C-FUVQ	de Havilland DHC-2 Beaver	696			FP
☐ C-GASF	de Havilland DHC-2 Beaver	1202	ex 57-2561		FP
☐ C-GAUI	Beech B200 Super King Air	BB-853	ex C-GADI		
☐ C-GDDJ	Grumman G-21A Goose	1184	ex N1257A		
☐ C-GPCF	Short SD.3-60	SH3620	ex (N366AC)	706	
☐ C-GPCW	Short SD.3-60	SH3622	ex 8Q-OCA	703	

PACIFIC SKY AVIATION — Victoria, BC (YYJ)

☐ C-FHSP	Beech B300C King Air	FM-57	ex N957FM	♦
☐ C-FHTP	Cessna 441	441-0265	ex C-FHSP	♦
☐ C-FNGV	Piper PA-31-350 Chieftain	31-8252013		
☐ C-FPHS	Boeing 737-53A	24970/1977	ex C-GBGL	
☐ C-GDTB	de Havilland DHC-2 Turbo Beaver	16T2/TB42	ex C-GJZX	

☐ C-GODH   de Havilland DHC-2 Turbo Beaver   979

PASCAN AVIATION — Pascan (P6/PSC) — Quebec, QC (YQB)

☐ C-FHSC	Beech B100 King Air	BE-105	ex N87XX		
☐ C-FIDC	Beech B100 King Air	BE-27	ex N87JE		
☐ C-FLKS	Beech B100 King Air	BE-123	ex N827RM		
☐ C-FODC	Beech B100 King Air	BE-59	ex N777DQ		
☐ C-GNSC	Beech B100 King Air	BE-102	ex N57TJ		
☐ C-FFPA	British Aerospace Jetstream 32EP	959	ex N959AE		[MQY]
☐ C-FHQA	British Aerospace Jetstream 3212	876	ex N876CP		wfs
☐ C-FIBA	British Aerospace Jetstream 3212	863	ex N3126		
☐ C-FKQA	British Aerospace Jetstream 3212	877	ex N877CP		wfs
☐ C-FPSC	British Aerospace Jetstream 32EP	930	ex N930AE		
☐ C-FPSI	British Aerospace Jetstream 32EP	963	ex N963AE		
☐ C-FPSJ	British Aerospace Jetstream 32EP	957	ex N957AE		
☐ C-FZVY	British Aerospace Jetstream 3212	833	ex N833JX		
☐ C-GPPS	British Aerospace Jetstream 32EP	961	ex N961AE		
☐ C-GPSK	British Aerospace Jetstream 32EP	958	ex N958AE		
☐ C-GQJT	British Aerospace Jetstream 3212	886	ex N886CP		wfs
☐ C-GUSC	British Aerospace Jetstream 32EP	902	ex N242BM		
☐ C-FAXY	Pilatus PC-12/45	274			
☐ C-FRDN	Piper PA-31-350 Navajo Chieftain	31-7852095			
☐ C-FYUT	Pilatus PC-12/45	254	ex N254PC		
☐ C-GBTL	Pilatus PC-12/45	159	ex N159PB		
☐ C-GPEA	ATR 42-300QC	158	ex D-BCRP		
☐ C-GPEB	ATR 42-300	122	ex D-BCRO		
☐ C-GPEK	ATR 42-310	112	ex OY-CIU		
☐ C-GRDC	Pilatus PC-12/45	214	ex PT-XTG		
☐ C-GVDQ	Piper PA-31-350 Chieftain	31-8152119	ex N40869		

PELICAN NARROWS AIR SERVICES — Pelican Narrows, SK

☐ C-GFZA	Cessna A185F Skywagon	18503084			FP/WS
☐ C-GTBC	de Havilland DHC-2 Beaver	1364	ex 58-2032		FP/WS

PERIMETER AVIATION — Perimeter (PAG) — Winnipeg-Intl, MB (YWG)

☐ C-FOFR	de Havilland DHC-8-106	317	ex N288DH		
☐ C-FPPW	de Havilland DHC-8-106	390	ex N827EX		
☐ C-GJYZ	de Havilland DHC-8-314	368	ex ZS-NMB		<AIE
☐ C-GLKY	de Havilland DHC-8-314	538	ex 9Y-WIP		
☐ C-GWPS	de Havilland DHC-8-102	120	ex N928HA		
☐ C-FBTL	Swearingen SA226TC Metro II	TC-385	ex XA-TGG		
☐ C-FFDB	Swearingen SA226TC Metro II	TC-249	ex N327BA		
☐ C-FIHB	Swearingen SA226TC Metro II	TC-361	ex N166SW		
☐ C-FIHE	Swearingen SA226TC Metro II	TC-373	ex N1010Z		
☐ C-FJNW	Swearingen SA226TC Metro IIA	TC-352	ex N167MA		
☐ C-FSLZ	Swearingen SA226TC Metro II	TC-222EE	ex N104GS		
☐ C-FSWT	Swearingen SA226TC Metro II	TC-382	ex N1011N		
☐ C-FUZY	Swearingen SA226TC Metro II	TC-343	ex VH-UZY		
☐ C-GIQF	Swearingen SA226TC Metro II	TC-279	ex F-GFGE		
☐ C-GIQG	Swearingen SA226TC Metro II	TC-285	ex F-GFGD		
☐ C-GIQK	Swearingen SA226TC Metro II	TC-288	ex F-GFGF		
☐ C-GQAJ	Swearingen SA226TC Metro II	TC-295	ex C-FUIF	Aeromed titles	EMS
☐ C-GQAP	Swearingen SA226TC Metro II	TC-263	ex N103UR		
☐ C-GYRD	Swearingen SA226TC Metro II	TC-278	ex N5493M		jt ops with Dene Cree Air
☐ C-FAMC	Swearingen SA227AC Metro III	AC-719B	ex N436MA		♦
☐ C-FFJM	Swearingen SA227AC Metro III	AC-700	ex N459AM		
☐ C-FJLO	Swearingen SA227AC Metro III	AC-678B	ex (N941BC)		
☐ C-FJTS	Swearingen SA227AC Metro III	AC-696B	ex N227LD		
☐ C-FLRY	Swearingen SA227AC Metro III	AC-756B	ex ZS-SDM		
☐ C-FMAV	Swearingen SA227AC Metro III	AC-616	ex VH-UUF		
☐ C-FTSK	Swearingen SA227AC Metro III	AC-647B	ex C-FAFM		
☐ C-GWVH	Swearingen SA227AC Metro IIIA	AC-714	ex VH-UUQ		
☐ C-FAMF	Swearingen SA226T Merlin IIIA	T-274	ex I-SWAA		
☐ C-FEQK	Beech 95-B55 Baron	TC-1374	ex CF-EQK		
☐ C-FKMZ	Beech E95 Travel Air	TD-708	ex N6223V		
☐ C-FRXO	Beech 95-B55 Baron	TC-870			
☐ C-GFQC	Beech B99	U-120	ex N47156		
☐ C-GPCL	Swearingen SA226AT Merlin IV	AT-017	ex N511M		Frtr

PORTER AIRLINES — (PD/POE) — Toronto-City Centre, ON (YTZ)

☐ C-FLQY	de Havilland DHC-8-402Q	4306	819	
☐ C-GKQA	de Havilland DHC-8-402Q	4357	821	
☐ C-GKQB	de Havilland DHC-8-402Q	4359	822	

☐ C-GKQC	de Havilland DHC-8-402Q	4360	823	
☐ C-GKQD	de Havilland DHC-8-402Q	4361	824	
☐ C-GKQE	de Havilland DHC-8-402Q	4390	825	
☐ C-GKQF	de Havilland DHC-8-402Q	4391	826	
☐ C-GLQB	de Havilland DHC-8-402Q	4130	801	
☐ C-GLQC	de Havilland DHC-8-402Q	4134	802	
☐ C-GLQD	de Havilland DHC-8-402Q	4138	803	
☐ C-GLQE	de Havilland DHC-8-402Q	4140	804	
☐ C-GLQF	de Havilland DHC-8-402Q	4193	805	
☐ C-GLQG	de Havilland DHC-8-402Q	4194	806	
☐ C-GLQH	de Havilland DHC-8-402Q	4225	807	
☐ C-GLQJ	de Havilland DHC-8-402Q	4228	808	
☐ C-GLQK	de Havilland DHC-8-402Q	4247	809	
☐ C-GLQL	de Havilland DHC-8-402Q	4249	810	
☐ C-GLQM	de Havilland DHC-8-402Q	4252	811	
☐ C-GLQN	de Havilland DHC-8-402Q	4254	812	
☐ C-GLQO	de Havilland DHC-8-402Q	4270	813	
☐ C-GLQP	de Havilland DHC-8-402Q	4271	814	
☐ C-GLQQ	de Havilland DHC-8-402Q	4272	815	
☐ C-GLQR	de Havilland DHC-8-402Q	4278	816	
☐ C-GLQV	de Havilland DHC-8-402Q	4279	817	
☐ C-GLQX	de Havilland DHC-8-402Q	4282	818	
☐ C-GLQZ	de Havilland DHC-8-402Q	4308	820	

PROPAIR — Propair (PRO) — Rouyn-Noranda, QC (YUY)

☐ C-FDJX	Beech A100 King Air	B-165	ex N811CU	
☐ C-FDOU	Beech A100 King Air	B-112	ex CF-DOU	
☐ C-FPAJ	Beech A100 King Air	B-151	ex N324B	
☐ C-FWRM	Beech A100 King Air	B-125	ex N89JM	
☐ C-GDPI	Beech A100 King Air	B-156	ex N21RX	
☐ C-GJJF	Beech A100 King Air	B-123	ex N741EB	
☐ C-GJLJ	Beech A100 King Air	B-235	ex N23517	
☐ C-GJLP	Beech A100 King Air	B-148	ex N67V	
☐ C-FAWE	Grumman G.159 Gulfstream 1	188	ex HB-LDT	
☐ C-FOGY	Beech 200 Super King Air	BB-168	ex N10VW	
☐ C-GDSG	Beech 1900D	UE-205		♦
☐ C-GLPJ	Beech 1900C-1	UC-139	ex N253RM	

PROVINCE OF ALBERTA AIR TRANSPORTATION SERVICES — Alberta (GOA) — Edmonton-Municipal, AB (YXD)

☐ C-GFSJ	de Havilland DHC-8-103	017	

PROVINCIAL AIRLINES/PAL AIRLINES — (PB/SPR) — St Johns, NL (YYT)

☐ C-FMGP	Beech B300 Super King Air	FL-783	ex N8043D	
☐ C-FMUN	Beech B300 Super King Air	FL-658		
☐ C-GEHS	Beech 200 Super King Air	BB-227		
☐ C-GGAO	Beech 200 Super King Air	BB-659	ex N77QX	
☐ C-GGJF	Beech B200 Super King Air	BB-939	ex N125KW	
☐ C-GMRS	Beech 200 Super King Air	BB-187	ex N630DB	Maritime Patrol
☐ C-GMWR	Beech 200 Super King Air	BB-68	ex N844N	Maritime Patrol
☐ C-GPGR	Beech 200 Super King Air	BB-403		
☐ C-GTJZ	Beech 200 Super King Air	BB-499	ex N499TT	
☐ C-FWLG	de Havilland DHC-6 Twin Otter 300	731	ex N915MA	
☐ C-GIED	de Havilland DHC-6 Twin Otter 300	600	ex N604NA	
☐ C-GIMK	de Havilland DHC-6 Twin Otter 300	352	ex N300EH	
☐ C-GJDE	de Havilland DHC-6 Twin Otter 300	471	ex C-GMPK	FP/WS
☐ C-GNFZ	de Havilland DHC-6 Twin Otter 300	719	ex 9Q-CEL	
☐ C-FDND	de Havilland DHC-8-102	129		♦
☐ C-FHRC	de Havilland DHC-8-102	209	ex TR-LGL	
☐ C-FPAE	de Havilland DHC-8-315	562	ex EC-ICA	
☐ C-GPAB	de Havilland DHC-8-106MPA	275	ex N827PH	
☐ C-GPAL	de Havilland DHC-8-102	157	ex N824PH	
☐ C-GPAR	de Havilland DHC-8-311	519	ex HP-1625PST	
☐ C-GPAU	de Havilland DHC-8-106	282	ex N833EX	
☐ C-GRNN	de Havilland DHC-8-106MPA	314	ex N830PH	
☐ C-GYCV	de Havilland DHC-8-314	487	ex 9Y-WIT	♦
☐ C-FABF	Cessna S550 Citation II	S550-0101		
☐ C-FJIC	Cessna 750 Citation X	750-0020	ex N8JQ	
☐ C-FPAG	SAAB SF.340A	340A-028	ex N336BE	
☐ C-FPAI	SAAB SF.340A	340A-047	ex N337BE	♦
☐ C-GMEW	Swearingen SA227AC Metro III	AC-668B	ex N668JS	
☐ C-GPAJ	SAAB SF.340B	340B-416	ex N416XJ	
☐ C-GPAO	SAAB SF.340B	340B-407	ex N407XJ	

QUANTUM HELICOPTERS — Terrace, BC (YXT)

☐ C-FFHK	Bell 206B JetRanger	1065	ex CF-FHK	
☐ C-FRCL	Bell 206LR+ LongRanger	45019	ex SE-HUD	
☐ C-GMQH	Bell 206L LongRanger	45103	ex PH-HXH	
☐ C-GSLV	Bell 206B JetRanger III	4199	ex N3202G	
☐ C-GTVL	Bell 206B JetRanger II	2166		
☐ C-FREW	Aérospatiale AS350BA AStar	1289		
☐ C-FSOZ	Aérospatiale AS350B2 AStar	2129	ex N141MB	
☐ C-GEYN	Aérospatiale AS350B2 AStar	2732	ex VP-BBB	
☐ C-GJUP	Aérospatiale AS350B1 AStar	2155		

RAINBOW AIRWAYS — Dunchurch, ON

☐ C-FOCB	de Havilland DHC-2 Beaver	21	ex CF-OCB	FP

RCMP - GRC AIR SERVICES (ROYAL CANADIAN MOUNTED POLICE) — Ottawa, ON

☐ C-FGSB	Aérospatiale AS350B3 AStar	3796	
☐ C-FMPH	Aérospatiale AS350B3 AStar	3683	
☐ C-FMPP	Aérospatiale AS350B3 AStar	4124	
☐ C-FRPQ	Aérospatiale AS350B3 AStar	3636	ex F-WQDZ
☐ C-GMPF	Aérospatiale AS350B3 AStar	4229	
☐ C-GMPK	Aérospatiale AS350B3 AStar	3923	
☐ C-GMPN	Aérospatiale AS350B3 AStar	3072	
☐ C-FDGM	Cessna U206G Stationair	U20606864	
☐ C-FDTM	Cessna T206H Stationair	T20608476	
☐ C-FHGY	Cessna T206H Stationair	T20608583	
☐ C-FSWC	Cessna T206H Stationair	T20608438	
☐ C-GNSE	Cessna T206H Stationair	T20608847	
☐ C-GTJN	Cessna T206H Stationair	T20608443	
☐ C-FGMQ	Pilatus PC-12/47E	1107	ex N107NX
☐ C-FMPA	Pilatus PC-12/47E	1216	ex N216NX
☐ C-FMPB	Pilatus PC-12/45	283	ex N283PC
☐ C-FMPF	Pilatus PC-12/47	768	ex HB-FSY
☐ C-FMPK	Pilatus PC-12/47E	1092	ex N992NG
☐ C-GMPA	Pilatus PC-12/47E	1262	ex N262NX
☐ C-GMPB	Pilatus PC-12/47E	1304	ex N304NX
☐ C-GMPE	Pilatus PC-12/47E	1073	ex N973NG
☐ C-GMPM	Pilatus PC-12/47E	1011	ex N911NG
☐ C-GMPO	Pilatus PC-12/47E	1197	ex N197PE
☐ C-GMPP	Pilatus PC-12/45	374	ex N374PC
☐ C-GMPQ	Pilatus PC-12/47E	1268	ex N268NX
☐ C-GMPV	Pilatus PC-12/47E	1181	ex N181PE
☐ C-GMPW	Pilatus PC-12/47E	1336	ex N336NX
☐ C-GMPX	Pilatus PC-12/47E	1017	ex N917NG
☐ C-GMPY	Pilatus PC-12/45	311	ex N311PB
☐ C-FMPQ	Eurocopter EC120B Colibri	1533	
☐ C-FRPH	Cessna 208B Caravan I	208B0377	ex N1118B
☐ C-FSUJ	Cessna 208B Caravan I	208B0373	ex N973CC
☐ C-GHVP	Cessna 210R Centurion	21064920	
☐ C-GMPI	Quest Kodiak 100	100-0047	ex N496KQ
☐ C-GMPJ	de Havilland DHC-6 Twin Otter 300	534	
☐ C-GMPR	Cessna 208 Caravan I	20800253	ex N208CF
☐ C-GMPT	Eurocopter EC120B Colibri	1355	
☐ C-GTCT	Cessna 210R Centurion	21064949	

RED SUCKER LAKE AIR SERVICES — Red Sucker Lake, MB

☐ C-FTHE	Piper PA-31 Navajo C	31-7512005	ex N121L	
☐ C-GMAM	de Havilland DHC-2 Beaver	1558	ex G-AZLU	FP/WS

RIVER AIR — Kenora/Menaki, ON (YQK/-)

☐ C-FAYM	Cessna U206E Skywagon	U20601541	ex (N9141M)	FP
☐ C-FFYC	Cessna 208 Caravan I	20800111	ex N9647F	FP
☐ C-FMAQ	de Havilland DHC-2 Beaver	14	ex CF-MAQ	FP/WS
☐ C-FRSW	Beech 3NM	CA-105	ex CF-RSW	
☐ C-GHOJ	Cessna 180K Skywagon	18053042		FP
☐ C-GIAT	Cessna A185F Skywagon	18502619	ex N4851C	FP
☐ C-GPDS	de Havilland DHC-2 Beaver	1349	ex N62352	FP
☐ C-GYKO	de Havilland DHC-3 Turbo Otter	287	ex N22UT	FP

R1 AIRLINES — Transcanada (TSH) — Calgary-Intl, AB (YYC)

☐ C-FDXV	de Havilland DHC-8-202	426	ex N988HA	wfs♦
☐ C-FRIB	de Havilland DHC-8-102	114	ex 5Y-BYB	

☐ C-GRGK	de Havilland DHC-8-202Q	522	ex B-17201	
☐ C-GUZX	de Havilland DHC-8-311Q	489	ex 9Y-WIL	
☐ C-GXYA	de Havilland DHC-8-314	414	ex VH-SDE	♦
☐ C-GEXM	Canadair CRJ-200ER	7187	ex N622BR	
☐ C-GRGD	Canadair CRJ-200ER	7572	ex N549MS	
☐ C-GRIA	Canadair CRJ-200ER	7561	ex N127MN	150
☐ C-GVEU	Canadair CRJ-200ER	7644	ex N676BR	

ROSS AIR — Clearwater Lake SPB, ON

☐ C-FOMJ	de Havilland DHC-2 Turbo Beaver	1683-TB51		♦
☐ CF-PFC	Beech C-45H	AF-199	ex N9942Z	
☐ C-GCIZ	Cessna A185F Skywagon	18503316	ex N1614H	FP
☐ C-GDCN	de Havilland DHC-2 Turbo Beaver	1661/TB35	ex N8PE	FP

ROSS AIR SERVICE — Sandy Bay, SK

☐ C-FWXV	Cessna A185E Skywagon	185-1355	ex CF-WXV	FP/WS

RUSTY MYERS FLYING SERVICE — Fort Frances, ON (YAG)

☐ C-FERM	Beech 3N	CA-62	ex CAF 1487	FP
☐ C-FKSJ	Cessna 208 Caravan I	20800035	ex N9382F	FP
☐ C-FOBT	de Havilland DHC-2 Beaver	3	ex CF-OBT	FP
☐ C-FOBY	de Havilland DHC-2 Beaver	13	ex CF-OBY	FP
☐ C-FRPL	Beech 3NM	CA-225	ex CAF 2346	FP
☐ C-FRVL	Beech 3T	7835	ex CAF 1396	FP
☐ CF-ZRI	Beech D18S	A-940	ex N164U	FP
☐ C-GAGK	Cessna 208 Caravan I	20800342	ex N51744	FP

SABOURIN LAKE LODGE — Sabourin Lake, MB

☐ C-FSJX	de Havilland DHC-2 Beaver	1592	ex CF-SJX	FP

SALT SPRING ISLAND AIR — Saltspring Island, BC

☐ C-FAOP	de Havilland DHC-2 Beaver	1249	ex CF-AOP	FP
☐ C-FJFL	de Havilland DHC-2 Beaver	898	ex CF-JFL	FP
☐ CF-ZZJ	de Havilland DHC-2 Beaver	1019	ex 5H-TCP	FP

SALTWATER WEST ENTERPRISES — Smithers, BC (YYD)

☐ CF-TQO	Cessna A185E Skywagon	18501700		FP
☐ C-GFTZ	de Havilland DHC-3 Otter	174	ex N90574	FP
☐ C-GPXG	Cessna U206F Stationair	U20602326		FP

SANDY LAKE SEAPLANE SERVICE — Sandy Lake, ON (ZSI)

☐ C-FBHP	Cessna 207A Skywagon	20700647		FP/WS
☐ C-GBBZ	Cessna U206G Stationair	U20605712	ex (N5396X)	FP/WS
☐ C-GBGJ	Cessna U206G Stationair	U20605249	ex N5368U	FP/WS
☐ C-GEBZ	Cessna 207 Skywagon	20700303	ex N1703U	FP/WS
☐ C-GEOL	Piper PA-31-350 Chieftain	7852114		♦
☐ C-GHKB	Cessna 207 Skywagon	20700228	ex N1628U	FP/WS
☐ C-GTCC	Cessna U206F Stationair	U20602167	ex N7303Q	FP/WS

SAPAWE AIR — Eva Lake, QC

☐ C-FEYR	de Havilland DHC-2 Beaver	497	ex CF-EYR	FP
☐ C-FOCC	de Havilland DHC-2 Beaver	23	ex CF-OOC	FP
☐ C-GKBW	de Havilland DHC-2 Beaver	310	ex N1441Z	FP

SASKATCHEWAN GOVERNMENT NORTHERN AIR OPERATIONS
Saskatchewan (SGS) — La Ronge/Saskatoon, SK (YVC/YXE)

☐ C-GLLS	Beech B200 Super King Air	BB-1601	ex N2303F	
☐ C-GSAE	Beech B200 Super King Air	BB-1748	ex N50848	EMS
☐ C-GSAH	Beech B200 Super King Air	BB-1972	ex N7022F	EMS
☐ C-GSAU	Beech B200 Super King Air	BB-1974	ex N7074N	EMS
☐ C-GSAV	Beech B200 Super King Air	BB-1790	ex N4470T	EMS
☐ C-FAFN	Canadair CL215T	1093	ex C-GKDY	216
☐ C-FAFO	Canadair CL215	1094	ex C-GKBO	217
☐ C-FAFP	Canadair CL215T	1100	ex C-GKEA	218
☐ C-FAFQ	Canadair CL215T	1101	ex C-GKEE	219
☐ C-FYWO	Canadair CL215	1003	ex CF-YWO	214
☐ C-FYXG	Canadair CL215	1009	ex CF-YXG	215
☐ C-FMFP	Rockwell 690A Turbo Commander	11307	ex N690TD	
☐ C-FNAO	Gulfstream Commander 690C	11731	ex N815BC	

☐ CF-SPG	Beech 95-B55 Baron	TC-940			
☐ C-FSPM	Gulfstream Commander 690D	15002	ex N721ML		
☐ C-GEAS	Beech 350 Super King Air	FL-17	ex N56872		
☐ C-GEHP	Grumman CS2F-2 Tracker	DHC-97	ex CAF12198 1		Tanker
☐ C-GEHR	Grumman CS2F-2 Tracker	DHC-51	ex CAF12185 3		Tanker
☐ C-GEQC	Grumman CS2F-2 Tracker	DHC-53	ex CAF12187 4		Tanker
☐ C-GEQE	Grumman CS2F-2 Tracker	DHC-92	ex CAF12193 6		Tanker
☐ C-GOVT	Gulfstream Commander 695A	15020	ex N600CM		
☐ C-GSAO	Beech 95-B55 Baron	TC-2149	ex N4974M		
☐ C-GSKQ	Convair 580	217	ex N723ES	475	Tanker
☐ C-GSKR	Convair 580	509	ex N57RD	471	Tanker
☐ C-GSPG	Beech 95-B55 Baron	TC-2213	ex N2064A		
☐ C-GVSE	Beech 95-B55 Baron	TC-2270	ex N717BC		
☐ C-GVSK	Convair 580	238	ex N43938	473	Tanker
☐ C-GYSK	Convair 580	234	ex N131SF	474	Tanker

SEAIR SEAPLANES · Vancouver-International SPB, BC

☐ C-FJOE	Cessna 208 Caravan I	20800390	ex N5254Y	FP
☐ C-FLAC	Cessna 208 Caravan I	20800357	ex N5267J	FP
☐ C-GIGO	Cessna 208B Caravan I	208B0549		FP
☐ C-GMOW	Cessna 208 Caravan I	20800528	ex N5036Q	FP
☐ C-GSAS	Cessna 208 Caravan I	20800341	ex N5154J	FP
☐ C-GURL	Cessna 208 Caravan I	20800501	ex N52475	FP
☐ C-FDHC	de Havilland DHC-2 Turbo Beaver	1677/TB45	ex N164WC	FP
☐ C-FPCG	de Havilland DHC-2 Beaver	1000	ex N188JM	FP
☐ C-FPMA	de Havilland DHC-2 Turbo Beaver	1625/TB15	ex N1454T	FP
☐ C-GOBC	de Havilland DHC-2 Beaver	1560	ex N159M	FP
☐ C-GTMC	de Havilland DHC-2 Beaver	1171	ex N100HF	FP
☐ C-GYIX	Cessna A185F Skywagon	18503162	ex (N93021)	FP

SHARP WINGS · Williams Lake, BC

☐ C-GKMN	de Havilland DHC-2 Beaver	348	ex N9755Z	FP/WS

SHOWALTER'S FLY-IN SERVICE · Ear Falls SPB, ON (YMY)

☐ C-FAIH	Cessna 180 Skywagon	18051690		FP
☐ C-FXUO	Beech D18S	CA-208	ex RCAF 2329	FP
☐ C-FZNG	Beech D18S	CA-182	ex RCAF 2309	FP
☐ C-FZYE	de Havilland DHC-2 Beaver	192	ex CF-ZYE	FP
☐ C-GESW	Beech C18S	7911	ex N4858V	FP♦

SIFTON AIR YUKON · Haines Junction, YK (YHT)

☐ C-FRKA	Cessna 206 Super Skywagon	206-0200	ex N5200U	FP
☐ C-GVKJ	Cessna 205 (210-5)	205-0092	ex N1892Z	FP

SIMPSON AIR · Commuter Canada (NCS) · Fort Simpson, NT (YFS)

☐ C-FNEQ	Cessna U206G Stationair	U20605036		FP
☐ C-FNML	Piper PA-23-250 Aztec	27-7554075	ex N8VV	
☐ C-GGHU	Cessna U206G Stationair 6 II	U20605723	ex (N5407X)	FP
☐ C-GMGD	de Havilland DHC-2 Beaver	519		FP♦
☐ C-GPMS	Cessna U206G Stationair 6 II	U20604207	ex (N756MU)	FP
☐ C-GVCD	Piper PA-31-350 Navajo Chieftain	31-7405457		♦
☐ C-GWXI	Cessna A185F Skywagon	18502818	ex (N1298F)	FP/WS

SIOUX NARROWS AIRWAYS · Great Bear Lake, NT (DAS)

☐ CF-GTP	Noorduyn UC-64A Norseman	423	ex 43-35349	FP
☐ CF-QHY	Douglas DC-3	26005/14560	ex RCAF 12958	
☐ C-GBDW	de Havilland DHC-2 Beaver	954	ex C9-AGS	FP
☐ C-GMXS	de Havilland DHC-2 Beaver	1213	ex N5382G	FP
☐ C-GUJY	de Havilland DHC-2 Beaver	393	ex C-GVMH	FP

SKY REGIONAL AIRLINES · Sky Regional (RS/SKV) · Toronto-Island (YTZ)

☐ C-FSRJ	de Havilland DHC-8-402Q	4165	ex N501LX	945
☐ C-FSRN	de Havilland DHC-8-402Q	4170	ex N503LX	946
☐ C-FSRW	de Havilland DHC-8-402Q	4172	ex N504LX	947
☐ C-FSRY	de Havilland DHC-8-402Q	4174	ex N505LX	948
☐ C-FSRZ	de Havilland DHC-8-402Q	4176	ex N506LX	949
☐ C-FEIQ	Embraer ERJ-175SU	17000083	ex PT-SZI	371
☐ C-FEIX	Embraer ERJ-175SU	17000085	ex PT-SZK	372
☐ C-FEJB	Embraer ERJ-175SU	17000086	ex PT-SZL	373
☐ C-FEJC	Embraer ERJ-175SU	17000089	ex PT-SZP	374
☐ C-FEJD	Embraer ERJ-175SU	17000090	ex PT-SZQ	375

☐ C-FEJF	Embraer ERJ-175SU	17000091	ex PT-SZR	376
☐ C-FEJL	Embraer ERJ-175SU	17000095	ex PT-SZV	377
☐ C-FEJP	Embraer ERJ-175SU	17000096	ex PT-SZW	378
☐ C-FEJY	Embraer ERJ-175SU	17000097	ex PT-SZX	379
☐ C-FEKD	Embraer ERJ-175SU	17000101	ex PT-SAC	380
☐ C-FEKH	Embraer ERJ-175SU	17000102	ex PT-SAH	381
☐ C-FEKI	Embraer ERJ-175SU	17000103	ex PT-SAI	382
☐ C-FEKJ	Embraer ERJ-175SU	17000109	ex PT-SAR	383
☐ C-FEKS	Embraer ERJ-175SU	17000110	ex PT-SAS	384
☐ C-FFYG	Embraer ERJ-175SU	17000116	ex PT-SDD	385

SKYLINK EXPRESS		**Skylink (SLQ)**		**Charlottetown, PE (YYG)**
☐ C-FKAX	Beech 1900C	UB-67	ex N3067X	Frtr
☐ C-GKGA	Beech 1900C-1	UC-117	ex N117ZR	Frtr
☐ C-GSKA	Beech 1900C	UB-32	ex N317BH	
☐ C-GSKG	Beech 1900C-1	UC-22	ex N19016	
☐ C-GSKM	Beech 1900C	UB-21	ex N61MK	
☐ C-GSKN	Beech 1900C-1	UC-54	ex N31729	
☐ C-GSKU	Beech 1900C	UB-35	ex N735GL	
☐ C-GSKW	Beech 1900C	UB-33	ex N318BH	
☐ C-GTGA	Beech 1900C-1	UC-62	ex N62YV	Frtr
☐ C-FAFJ	Cessba 208B Caravan I	208B0641	ex N52655	
☐ C-FFGA	Cessna 208B Caravan I	208B0662	ex N5264E	026
☐ C-FHGA	Cessna 208B Caravan I	208B0047	ex C-FESH	024
☐ C-GEGA	Cessna 208B Caravan I	208B0379	ex N1119A	
☐ C-GLGA	Cessna 208B Caravan I	208B0350	ex N64AP	
☐ C-GSKS	Cessna 208B Caravan I	208B0762	ex N52623	
☐ C-GSKT	Cessna 208B Caravan I	208B0759	ex N5262W	
☐ C-GSKV	Cessna 208B Caravan I	208B0847		
☐ C-GYYJ	Piper PA-31-350 Navajo Chieftain	31-7652086	ex N59833	

SKYNORTH AIR				**Winnipeg International, MB (YWG)**
☐ C-FHMA	Mitsubishi Mu-2B-60	1523SA	ex N65JG	
☐ C-GBTI	Beech 65-E90 King Air	LW-111		
☐ C-GMUU	Mitsubishi Mu-2B-60	1544SA		♦
☐ C-GSNM	Beech 65-E90 King Air	LW-194		
☐ C-GTZK	Piper PA-31 Turbo Navajo	31-381	ex N9SG	

SKYSERVICE BUSINESS AVIATION		**(SYB)**		**Toronto-Pearson Intl, ON (YYZ)**
☐ C-GMXB	Canadair CRJ-900LR	15175	ex CX-CRC	♦
☐ C-GMXH	Canadair CRJ-900LR	15209	ex CX-CRG	♦
☐ C-GMXJ	Canadair CRJ-900LR	15169	ex CX-CRB	♦

SLATE FALLS AIRWAYS		**(SYJ)**		**Sioux Lookout, ON (YXL)**
☐ C-FCZP	de Havilland DHC-3 Turbo Otter	69	ex CF-CZP	FP/WS
☐ CF-DIN	de Havilland DHC-2 Beaver	68		FP/WS
☐ C-FNWX	de Havilland DHC-3 Turbo Otter	412	ex CF-NWX	FP/WS
☐ C-GGPU	Cessna U206G Stationair 6 II	U20605798		FP/WS
☐ C-GGPW	Cessna U206G Stationair	U20605029		FP/WS
☐ C-GGRW	Cessna U206G Stationair 6 II	U20605689	ex N5373X	FP/WS

SOUTH NAHANNI AIRWAYS				**Whitehorse, YT (YXY)**
☐ C-GNTT	Cessna U206G Stationair	U20604651		FP/WS

SPRUCE AIR				**Pitt Meadows, BC**
☐ C-FEBB	de Havilland DHC-2 Beaver	746	ex N41PS	FP
☐ C-FPVW	Cessna 180G Skywagon	18051403		FP

STRAIT AIR		**Nanuck (NUK)**		**L'Anse au Clair, NL**
☐ C-FVTQ	Piper PA-31-350 Chieftain	31-7853034	ex N300DT	
☐ C-GPXW	Piper PA-31-350 Navajo Chieftain	31-7652134		
☐ C-GQAM	Piper PA-31 Navajo Chieftain	31-7912093		
☐ C-GRFJ	Piper PA-31 Navajo Chieftain	31-7812031		
☐ C-GRYE	Piper PA-31-350 Navajo Chieftain	31-7852155		
☐ C-FJJR	Britten-Norman BN-2A-27 Islander	424	ex OO-TOP	
☐ C-FPLG	Beech A100 King Air	B-224	ex N16SM	
☐ C-GJBQ	Beech A100 King Air	B-191	ex N214CK	
☐ C-GJXF	Beech A100 King Air	B-159	ex C-GLPG	
☐ C-GZBQ	de Havilland DHC-2 Beaver	919		

SUDBURY AVIATION — Whitewater Lake, ON

☐ C-FHVT	de Havilland DHC-2 Beaver I	284	ex VP-PAT	FP/WS
☐ C-FIUU	de Havilland DHC-2 Beaver I	945	ex CF-IUU	FP/WS
☐ C-FVIA	de Havilland DHC-2 Beaver	714		fp/ws♦
☐ C-GQVG	Cessna A185F Skywagon	18503818	ex N4619E	FP/WS

SUMMIT AIR (CHARTERS) — Yellowknife, NT/Atlin, BC/Whitehorse, YT (YZF/YSQ/YXY)

☐ C-FEQW	Dornier 228-202	8103	ex P2-MBQ	
☐ C-FEQX	Dornier 228-202	8101	ex P2-MBP	
☐ C-FPSH	Dornier 228-202	8071	ex N253MC	
☐ C-FUCN	Dornier 228-202	8109	ex N276MC	opf UNHAS
☐ C-GSAX	Dornier 228-202	8153	ex P2-MBV	opf UN
☐ C-FASC	de Havilland DHC-8-102	038	ex C-GJUZ	
☐ C-FASQ	de Havilland DHC-6 Twin Otter 100	78	ex C-FAKM	FP/WS
☐ C-FASV	de Havilland DHC-5A Buffalo	95A	ex 5Y-GBA	
☐ C-FERJ	Avro 146-RJ85	E2290	ex G-CHFR	♦
☐ C-FLRJ	Avro 146-RJ85	E2302	ex G-CHKP	♦
☐ C-FOEV	de Havilland DHC-2 Turbo Beaver III	1680/TB48	ex CF-OEV	FP/WS
☐ C-FOPE	de Havilland DHC-2 Turbo Beaver III	1691/TB59	ex CF-OPE	FP/WS
☐ C-FSWN	Piper PA-31-350 Chieftain	31-7952182	ex C-GREP	
☐ C-FTFX	de Havilland DHC-6 Twin Otter 300	340	ex CF-TFX	FP/WS
☐ C-FTXQ	de Havilland DHC-6 Twin Otter 300	308	ex N776A	
☐ C-GASB	de Havilland DHC-8-102	013	ex N802MX	
☐ C-GKOA	Short SC.7 Skyvan	SH1905	ex N52NS	Frtr
☐ C-GUSA	ATR 72-202F	353	ex SE-MGL	♦

SUMMIT HELICOPTERS — Yellowknife, NT (YZF)

☐ C-FCCK	Bell 412	36009	♦
☐ C-FHPW	Aérospatiale AS355 N Twin Star	5697	♦
☐ C-FTHD	Bell 407	53134	
☐ C-FXFX	Aérospatiale AS355F2 TwinStar	5305	
☐ C-GCCD	Bell 412	33213	
☐ C-GCVJ	Bell 407	53423	
☐ C-GENT	Bell 206L LongRanger	45041	
☐ C-GIML	Sikorsky S-76A	760017	♦
☐ C-GKWS	Sikorsky S-76A	760297	♦
☐ C-GKWT	Sikorsky S-76A	760295	♦
☐ C-GPIH	Bell 407	53426	
☐ C-GTHN	Bell 206L-4 LongRanger IV	52238	
☐ C-GTHU	Bell 407	53333	
☐ C-GTHW	Bell 206L LongRanger	45073	
☐ C-GTHZ	Bell 206L-4 LongRanger IV	52346	
☐ C-GXLI	Sikorsky S-76A	760187	♦

SUNWEST AVIATION — Chinook (CNK) — Calgary-Intl, AB (YYC)

☐ C-FAFF	Beech B350 King Air	FL-112	ex N405J	♦
☐ C-FBOM	Beech 200 Super King Air	BB-693	ex C-GXHN	
☐ C-FDTC	Beech B350 King Air	FL-234	ex N3234K	
☐ C-FPCP	Beech B300 King Air	FL-317	ex N3217V	
☐ C-GHOP	Beech 200 Super King Air	BB-120	ex N6773S	
☐ C-GJFY	Beech 200 Super King Air	BB-812	ex C-GYUI	
☐ C-GHCS	Beech 1900D	UE-353	ex VT-TOI	
☐ C-GROK	Beech 1900D	UE-362	ex N196NW	
☐ C-GSLX	Beech 1900D	UE-264	ex C-GSLB	
☐ C-GSWB	Beech 1900D	UE-386	ex N847CA	
☐ C-GSWV	Beech 1900D	UE-141	ex N17354	all-white
☐ C-GSWX	Beech 1900D	UE-63	ex N166K	
☐ C-GSWZ	Beech 1900D	UE-337	ex N23159	
☐ C-FBXG	de Havilland DHC-8-311Q	443	ex B-15235	♦
☐ C-FNSA	de Havilland DHC-8-315	354	ex ZS-NLZ	♦
☐ C-GBOS	de Havilland DHC-8-315Q	565	ex OY-EDK	
☐ C-GFCD	de Havilland DHC-8-315Q	576	ex EC-IGE	
☐ C-GYUP	de Havilland DHC-8-202	536	ex C-GULN	
☐ C-FDOI	Piper PA-31-350 Chieftain	31-8152150	ex N40901	
☐ C-FVVS	Piper PA-31-350 Chieftain	31-7952199	ex N35347	
☐ C-GMOZ	Piper PA-31-350 Chieftain	31-8052067	ex N3556B	
☐ C-GOHO	Piper PA-31-350 Chieftain	31-8152167	ex N38SL	
☐ C-GRWN	Piper PA-31-350 Chieftain	31-8152044	ex N4076J	
☐ C-GAAF	Swearingen SA227DC Metro 23	DC-891B	ex B-3956	
☐ C-GMWW	Swearingen SA227DC Metro 23	DC-882B	ex N453LA	
☐ C-GSAF	Swearingen SA227DC Metro 23	DC-866B	ex B-3951	♦
☐ C-GSHV	Swearingen SA227DC Metro 23	DC-900B	ex D-CJKO	
☐ C-GSHY	Swearingen SA227DC Metro 23	DC-897B	ex N3051Q	

☐ C-GSHZ	Swearingen SA227DC Metro 23	DC-887B	ex N3007C	
☐ C-FBXG	de Havilland DHC-8-314	443	ex B-15235	♦
☐ C-FGEW	Swearingen SA226TC Metro II	TC-347	ex N330BA	
☐ C-FMIX	Hawker 800XP	258392	ex F-HBOM	
☐ C-FMPI	Bell 206B JetRanger	978		♦
☐ C-FNOC	Cessna 208 Caravan I	20800090	ex N9536F	
☐ C-FNSA	de Havilland DHC-8-315	354	ex ZS-NLZ	♦
☐ C-GGWH	Canadair Challenger 604	5371	ex N371CL	
☐ C-GNGV	Cessna 560 Citation V	560-0053	ex C-FACC	
☐ C-GOAG	Dassault Falcon 900EX	15	ex N914JL	
☐ C-GPDB	Learjet 45	45-041	ex C-GPDQ	
☐ C-GPGF	Beech B350 King Air	FL-572	ex N902CE	
☐ C-GSAF	Swearingen SA227DC Metro 23	DC-866B	ex B-3951	♦
☐ C-GSOC	Cessna 680 Citation Sovereign	680-0195	ex N973AC	
☐ C-GSOE	Cessna 680 Citation Sovereign	680-0223	ex N223SV	
☐ C-GSWK	Swearingen SA227DC Metro II	TC-368	ex F-GEBU	The Spirit of Medicine Hat
☐ C-GSWO	Cessna 208 Caravan I	20800153	ex N1016M	
☐ C-GSWP	Learjet 55	55-019	ex N141SM	
☐ C-GSWQ	Learjet 45	45-022	ex N845RL	
☐ C-GTJL	Learjet 35A	35A-124	ex N8LA	
☐ C-GTJO	Canadair Challenger 604	5489	ex N230LC	
☐ C-GVFX	Canadair Challenger 300	20287	ex N301MB	♦
☐ C-GVVZ	Learjet 45	45-020	ex N45NP	
☐ C-GZCZ	Grumman Gulfstream 150	273	ex N373GA	
☐ C-GZDO	Grumman Gulfstream 150	282	ex C-GPDQ	

SUNWING AIRLINES Sunwing (WG/SWG) Toronto-Pearson Intl, ON (YYZ)

☐ C-FDBD	Boeing 737-8Q8/W	30703/1964	ex 9M-FFA	♦
☐ C-FEAK	Boeing 737-86Q/W	30292/1451	ex N292AG	
☐ C-FFPH	Boeing 737-81D/W	39440/4892		♦
☐ C-FGVK	Boeing 737-86N/W	32740/1444	ex OK-TVK	<TVS
☐ C-FJVE	Boeing 737-8DC/W	34596/1875	ex N740EH	♦
☐ C-FLSW	Boeing 737-8HX/W	36552/2658		
☐ C-FPRP	Boeing 737-8FH/W	39959/5414		o/o♦
☐ C-FTAH	Boeing 737-8Q8/W	29351/1471	ex OK-TVJ	>TVS
☐ C-FTDW	Boeing 737-808/W	34704/1958	ex N1786B	Joan Maria
☐ C-FTJH	Boeing 737-8BK/W	29642/2247	ex N1786B	
☐ C-FTOH	Boeing 737-8HX/W	29647/2865		
☐ C-FWGH	Boeing 737-86J/W	37752/3835	ex D-ABMC	♦
☐ C-FYBG	Boeing 737-8K5/W	35142/2660	ex OO-JBG	<JAF♦
☐ C-FYJD	Boeing 737-8Q8/W	41807/5420		o/o♦
☐ C-FYLC	Boeing 737-8BK/W	33029/1945	ex G-OXLC	
☐ C-GFEH	Boeing 737-8GS/W	41608/5346		♦
☐ C-GKVP	Boeing 737-8K5/W	32907/1117	ex OK-TVP	<QS
☐ C-GNCH	Boeing 737-81D/W	39438/4816		
☐ C-GOFW	Boeing 737-8BK/W	33018/1488	ex LN-NOS	
☐ C-GOWG	Boeing 737-86J/W	37757/3377	ex D-ABKO	
☐ C-GRKB	Boeing 737-86Q/W	30294/1469	ex OK-TVE	<TVS
☐ C-GTVG	Boeing 737-8Q8/W	30719/2257	ex OK-TVG	<TVS♦
☐ C-GVVH	Boeing 737-8Q8/W	35275/2604	ex OK-TVH	<TVS

SUPERIOR AIRWAYS Red Lake, ON (YRL)

☐ C-FAMK	Cessna 208B Caravan I	208B0853		
☐ C-FLIG	Cessna 180B	50470		♦
☐ C-FVWY	Piper PA-31-350 Navajo Chieftain	31-8252063		
☐ C-FYMK	Cessna 208B Caravan I	208B2219	ex N79PF	
☐ C-FYMT	Cessna 208 Caravan I	20800386	ex N991Y	
☐ C-GAGT	Cessna T206H Stationair	t20608158		
☐ C-GAJT	Piper PA-31-350C Chieftain	81-52012		
☐ C-GAJW	Piper PA-31-350C Chieftain	81-52157		
☐ C-GEZU	de Havilland DHC-2 Beaver	647		FP♦
☐ C-GLGQ	Cessna R182 Skylane	R18202039		
☐ C-GXJW	Beech 58 Baron	TH-815		
☐ C-GYUY	Cessna 185F Skywagon	18503731		♦

THUNDER AIRLINES Air Thunder (THU) Thunder Bay, ON (YQT)

☐ C-FASB	Beech A100 King Air	B-163	ex SE-ING	
☐ C-FJJH	Beech A100 King Air	B-146		♦
☐ C-GASI	Beech A100 King Air	B-126	ex N23BW	
☐ C-GKAJ	Beech A100 King Air	B-232	ex N9192S	
☐ C-GNEX	Beech A100 King Air	B-211	ex N9194F	
☐ C-GUPP	Beech A100 King Air	B-157	ex N123CS	
☐ C-GYQK	Beech A100 King Air	B-153	ex N120AS	
☐ C-FFFG	Mitsubishi MU-2L	662	ex N5191B	
☐ C-FFSS	Mitsubishi MU-2B	783SA		
☐ C-FRWK	Mitsubishi MU-2L	1521SA	ex N437MA	
☐ C-GAMC	Mitsubishi MU-2L	785SA	ex N273MA	

☐ C-GGDC	Mitsubishi MU-2B	796SA	
☐ C-GYUA	Mitsubishi MU-2B-60	15535A	ex N479MA
☐ C-GZNS	Mitsubishi MU-2L	1550SA	ex N64WB
☐ C-FWVR	Cessna 208B Caravan I	208B0483	ex N51426

THUNDERBIRD AVIATION — Stony Rapids, SK (YSF)

| ☐ CF-PEM | de Havilland DHC-3 Otter | 438 | | FP |

TINTINA AIR — Whitehorse, YT (YXY)

☐ C-FDUW	de Havilland DHC-2 Beaver	736		FP
☐ C-FFKL	de Havilland DHC-2 Beaver	1343	ex CF-FKL	
☐ C-FSKS	Cessna 208B Caravan I	208B0722		♦
☐ C-GEUA	Piper PA-31 Navajo	31-187		
☐ C-GGBC	Piper PA-32-260 Cherokee Six	32-1161		
☐ C-GJAS	Cessna 208 Caravan I	20800322	ex N51869	FP/WS

TOFINO AIR LINES — Tofino, BC (YTP)

☐ C-FGCY	de Havilland DHC-2 Beaver	216	ex CF-GCY	FP
☐ C-FICK	de Havilland DHC-2 Beaver	796	ex CF-ICK	FP
☐ C-FJIM	de Havilland DHC-2 Beaver	461	ex N66035	FP
☐ C-FMXR	de Havilland DHC-2 Beaver	374	ex N7160C	FP
☐ C-FOCL	de Havilland DHC-2 Beaver	41		FP
☐ C-GFLT	de Havilland DHC-2 Beaver	279	ex N5149G	FP
☐ C-GHBX	Cessna 180J	18052449	ex (N52029)	FP
☐ C-GHZR	Cessna 180J	18052667	ex (N7542K)	FP
☐ C-GIDX	Cessna 180J	18052709	ex (N7716K)	FP
☐ C-GYFO	Cessna 180J	18052759	ex (N7825K)	FP

TRANS CAPITAL AIR — Toronto-City Centre, ON (YTZ)

☐ C-FERO	de Havilland DHC-7-103	106	ex OY-GRF	♦
☐ C-FJHQ	de Havilland DHC-7-103	011	ex PK-TVS	opf UN
☐ C-FPBJ	de Havilland DHC-7-103	009	ex OY-GRD	opf UN
☐ C-FWYU	de Havilland DHC-7-103	012	ex N678MA	opf UN as UN-234
☐ C-GCPP	de Havilland DHC-7-102	087	ex HK-3111W	[YTZ]
☐ C-GGXS	de Havilland DHC-7-102	064	ex 4X-AHB	opf UN
☐ C-GNUY	de Havilland DHC-7-102	033	ex N330KK	[YTZ]
☐ C-GTGO	de Havilland DHC-7-102	106	ex OY-GRE	♦
☐ C-GVPP	de Havilland DHC-7-102	072	ex N272EP	opf UN
☐ C-GVWD	de Havilland DHC-7-102	108	ex HK-3340W	

TRANSPORT CANADA — Transport (TGO) — Various

☐ C-FGXE	Beech 65-C90A King Air	LJ-1179	ex N179RC
☐ C-FGXG	Beech 65-C90A King Air	LJ-1139	ex N212RL
☐ C-FGXH	Beech 65-C90A King Air	LJ-1162	ex N477JA
☐ C-FGXJ	Beech 65-C90A King Air	LJ-1178	ex N357CY
☐ C-FGXL	Beech 65-C90A King Air	LJ-1189	ex N200SL
☐ C-FGXO	Beech 65-C90A King Air	LJ-1200	ex N68TW
☐ C-FGXS	Beech 65-C90A King Air	LJ-1207	ex N207RC
☐ C-FGXT	Beech 65-C90A King Air	LJ-1230	ex N1564P
☐ C-FGXU	Beech 65-C90A King Air	LJ-1140	ex N8841
☐ C-FGXZ	Beech 65-C90A King Air	LJ-1177	ex N479JA
☐ C-FCGK	Bell 206B JetRanger	24	
☐ C-FCGQ	Bell 206B JetRanger	182	
☐ C-FDOC	Bell 206B JetRanger	349	
☐ C-GCHM	Bell 206L LongRanger	45083	
☐ C-GCHR	Bell 206L-1 LongRanger	45220	
☐ C-GCHS	Bell 206L-1 LongRanger	45221	
☐ C-FDOF	Bell 212	30536	
☐ C-FDOP	Bell 212	30567	
☐ C-GCGB	Bell 212	30930	ex N241LG
☐ C-GCHF	Bell 212	30617	
☐ C-GCHT	Bell 212	30910	
☐ C-FJCZ	Cessna 550 Citation II	550-0700	
☐ C-FJWZ	Cessna 550 Citation II	550-0685	
☐ C-FJXN	Cessna 550 Citation II	550-0684	ex N6778L
☐ C-FKCE	Cessna 550 Citation II	550-0686	
☐ C-FKDX	Cessna 550 Citation II	550-0687	ex N6778Y
☐ C-FKEB	Cessna 550 Citation II	550-0688	
☐ C-FKLB	Cessna 550 Citation II	550-0699	
☐ C-FLZA	Cessna 550 Citation II	550-0701	
☐ C-FMFM	Cessna 550 Citation II	550-0702	

☐ C-GCFN	MBB 105CBS-4	S-682		
☐ C-GCFO	MBB 105CBS-4	S-715		
☐ C-GCFQ	MBB 105CBS-4	S-716		
☐ C-GCFS	MBB 105CBS-4	S-725		
☐ C-GCFT	MBB 105CBS-4	S-726		
☐ C-GCFU	MBB 105CBS-4	S-727		
☐ C-GCFV	MBB 105CBS-4	S-728		
☐ C-GCFX	MBB 105CBS-4	S-730		
☐ C-GCFY	MBB 105CBS-4	S-733		
☐ C-GCHU	MBB 105CBS-4	S-696		
☐ C-GCHV	MBB 105CBS-4	S-641		
☐ C-GCHW	MBB 105CBS-4	S-681		
☐ C-GCHY	MBB 105CBS-4	S-729		
☐ C-GGGM	MBB 105CBS-4	S-618		
☐ C-FMOT	Bell 407	53664		
☐ C-GCFJ	de Havilland DHC-8-100	020		
☐ C-GCFR	de Havilland DHC-7-102	102		
☐ C-GDOT	Bell 407	53672		
☐ C-GPND	Bell 407	53833		
☐ C-GSUR	de Havilland DHC-8-102	046	ex C-GJVB	

TRANSWEST AIR Athabaska (ABS) La Ronge/Stony Rapids, SK (YVC/YSF)

☐ C-FGHY	de Havilland DHC-2 Beaver	1344	ex 58-2015	FP/WS
☐ C-FGQD	de Havilland DHC-2 Beaver	76	ex CF-QGD	FP/WS
☐ C-FIFJ	de Havilland DHC-2 Beaver	831	ex CF-IFJ	FP/WS
☐ C-FORC	de Havilland DHC-2 Beaver	1499		FP/WS
☐ C-GMAQ	de Havilland DHC-2 Beaver	234	ex 51-16784	FP/WS
☐ C-FAAF	Piper PA-31-350 Navajo Chieftain	31-7752096	ex N27229	
☐ C-FNVH	Piper PA-31-350 Navajo Chieftain	31-7305098	ex N98BJ	
☐ C-FZPJ	Piper PA-31-350 Navajo Chieftain	31-7752185	ex N27359	
☐ C-GAYY	Piper PA-31-325 Navajo Chieftain	31-8012006		
☐ C-GGIQ	Piper PA-31-350 Navajo Chieftain	31-7552082	ex N59989	
☐ C-GQHV	Piper PA-31-350 Navajo Chieftain	31-7405230	ex N54293	
☐ C-GUNP	Piper PA-31-350 Chieftain	31-8052048	ex N3554D	
☐ C-GWUM	Piper PA-31-350 Navajo Chieftain	31-7405404	ex N66878	
☐ C-FGLF	de Havilland DHC-6 Twin Otter 200	138	ex LV-APT	FP/WS
☐ C-FHPE	de Havilland DHC-3 Turbo Otter	273	ex Burma 4651	FP/WS
☐ C-FJTG	Bell 205A-1	30104	ex N8138J	
☐ C-FJVW	SAAB SF.340B	340B-289	ex ZS-PDP	♦
☐ C-FOHG	Bell 407	53187	ex N478WN	
☐ C-FOKD	Bell 407	53193	ex N407NR	
☐ C-FPGE	de Havilland DHC-6 Twin Otter 200	197	ex CF-PGE	FP/WS
☐ C-FSCA	de Havilland DHC-6 Twin Otter 100	17	ex CF-SCA	FP/WS
☐ C-FSEW	Beech 300LW Super King Air	FA-203	ex XB-RZH	
☐ C-FTMC	Bell 206L-4 LongRanger IV	52223	ex XC-CJS	
☐ C-FVOG	de Havilland DHC-6 Twin Otter 100	35	ex CF-VOG	FP/WS
☐ C-FYHD	Bell 205A-1	30128		♦
☐ C-GALM	Cessna A185F Skywagon	18503711	ex N783A	FP/WS
☐ C-GAON	Cessna 310R II	310R1627	ex N2632Y	
☐ C-GCNC	Bell 206B JetRanger II	1142	ex N58152	
☐ C-GELT	Bell 206B JetRanger III	2994	ex N5744V	
☐ C-GFSG	Beech 200 Super King Air	BB-671		
☐ C-GJHW	Beech A100 King Air	B-175	ex N92DL	dam 25Mar14
☐ C-GKCY	SAAB SF.340A	340A-133	ex SE-ISM	
☐ C-GPDC	Beech B350 Super King Air	FL-114	ex N895CA	
☐ C-GPNO	Beech 95-B55 Baron	TC-734	ex N174E	
☐ C-GSYC	Beech B300 King Air	FL-20	ex N99U	
☐ C-GTJX	SAAB SF.340B	340B-165	ex N586MA	
☐ C-GTWG	Beech 1900D	UE-79	ex N79SK	
☐ C-GTWK	SAAB SF.340B	340B-190	ex XA-TUQ	
☐ C-GVTH	Bell 407	53332		
☐ C-GXZA	Cessna A185F Skywagon	18503019	ex N5211R	FP/WS
☐ C-GYHY	Bell 206B JetRanger III	2317	ex N16825	

TSAYTA AVIATION Fort St James, BC (YXJ)

☐ C-FCNH	Cessna A185E Skywagon	18501944		FP
☐ C-FIAX	de Havilland DHC-2 Beaver	140	ex VH-AAD	FP
☐ C-FMZC	de Havilland DHC-3 Turbo Otter	362	ex N362TT	FP
☐ C-GCXF	Britten-Norman BN-2A-26 Islander	84		♦
☐ C-GDER	Cessna TU206G Stationair	U20605730		FP
☐ C-GKAW	Britten-Norman BN-2A-8 Islander	128	ex N158MA	
☐ C-GMZP	Britten-Norman BN-2A-21 Islander	874	ex N341CC	
☐ C-GWDW	de Havilland DHC-2 Beaver	306	ex N311N	FP
☐ C-GWKX	Cessna A185E Skywagon	18502032	ex N70167	FP/WS

TUDHOPE AIRWAYS — Hudson, ON

| ☐ C-FOCP | de Havilland DHC-2 Beaver | 49 | ex CF-OCP | FP/WS |
| ☐ C-FSDC | Found FBA-2C | 17 | ex CF-SDC | FP/WS |

TWEEDSMUIR AIR SERVICES — Nimpo Lake, BC

| ☐ C-FFHT | de Havilland DHC-2 Beaver | 55 | ex CF-FHT | FP |
| ☐ C-GFRJ | Cessna A185F Skywagon II | 18504011 | | FP |

TYAX AIR SERVICE — Gold Bridge, BC

| ☐ C-GIYV | de Havilland DHC-2 Beaver | 1488 | ex XP823 | FP/WS |

UNIVERSAL HELICOPTERS — Goose Bay, NL (YYR)

☐ C-FAPN	Aérospatiale AS350BA AStar	2201	
☐ C-FEPB	Aérospatiale AS350B3 AStar	7540	
☐ C-FXAL	Aérospatiale AS350B AStar	1816	ex SE-HNP
☐ C-GNAI	Aérospatiale AS350B2 AStar	1685	ex N380NA
☐ C-GPBY	Aérospatiale AS350B2 AStar	2076	ex N165TB
☐ C-FCNG	Bell 206L LongRanger	45149	ex C-GMPT
☐ C-FCWR	Bell 206L LongRanger	45086	ex C-GMPM
☐ C-FLIA	Bell 206L-4 LongRanger IV	52149	ex N9221U
☐ C-FPHO	Bell 206L LongRanger	45147	ex N3247K
☐ C-GAHS	Bell 206LR+ LongRanger	45048	ex D-HMHS
☐ C-GDCA	Bell 206LR+ LongRanger	45021	ex N31DM
☐ C-GIZY	Bell 206LR+ LongRanger	45027	ex N176KH
☐ C-GLSH	Bell 206LR+ LongRanger	45018	
☐ C-GQIX	Bell 206L LongRanger	45008	ex N8EL
☐ C-GVYO	Bell 206LR+ LongRanger	46609	ex N16950
☐ C-FEPR	Bell 407	53888	
☐ C-FTJU	Bell 407	53331	ex C-CEOA
☐ C-FXYF	Bell 407	53022	
☐ C-GOFL	Bell 407	53130	

VAN CITY SEAPLANES — Pitt Meadow, BC

☐ C-FGQZ	de Havilland DHC-2 Beaver	118	ex CF-GQZ	FP
☐ C-FJFQ	de Havilland DHC-2 Beaver	963	ex CF-JFQ	FP
☐ C-FTNI	Cessna 182G Skylane	18255208		FP

VANCOUVER ISLAND AIR — Campbell River, BC (YBL)

☐ C-FCSN	Beech D18S	CA-16	ex RCAF1441	FP
☐ C-FGNR	Beech 3NM	CA-191	ex CF-GNR	FP
☐ C-FIZB	Cessna 180J	18052409	ex N46262	FP
☐ C-FQND	de Havilland DHC-3 Otter	233		
☐ C-FWCA	de Havilland DHC-2 Beaver	1285	ex C-GUDB	FP
☐ C-GAIV	Beech TC-45G	AF-80	ex N711KP	FP
☐ C-GVIX	de Havilland DHC-3 Turbo Otter	97	ex C-GGOR	FP

VIH HELICOPTERS — Victoria, BC (YYJ)

☐ C-FBER	Bell 206B JetRanger III	2648	ex N5018L	
☐ C-FHSO	Bell 206B JetRanger	165	ex CF-HSO	
☐ C-FIGR	Kamov KA-32-IIBC	(31588) 8707/05		
☐ C-FMKV	Kamov Ka-32A-IIBC	(31599) 8809/09		
☐ C-FQNG	Sikorsky S-61N	61032	ex N301Y	
☐ C-GKHL	Kamov Ka-32A-IIBC	(31594) 8801/03	ex RA-31594	dam 04Aug13
☐ C-GURI	Kamov Ka-32A-IIBC	(31600) 8810/10		
☐ C-GVIY	Bell 222UT	47562	ex JA9665	
☐ C-GWGS	Bell 206B JetRanger	447	ex N2230W	

VIKING OUTPOST AIR — Red Lake, ON

☐ C-FBYA	Cessna 180	32621		FP
☐ C-FHVD	Cessna 180	31583		FP
☐ C-FXHA	Cessna A185E Skywagon	1851391		FP
☐ C-GEZW	de Havilland DHC-2 Beaver	1217	ex (N3122F)	FP
☐ C-GGMB	de Havilland DHC-2 Beaver	1263	ex N1440Z	FP

VILLERS AIR SERVICES — Fort Nelson, BC (YYE)

☐ C-FGAQ	Britten-Norman BN-2A-27 Islander	212	ex G-51-212	
☐ C-FJBD	Beech 58 Baron	TH-260	ex N518SW	
☐ C-FTVP	Cessna 208B Caravan I	208B1264	ex N5090Y	
☐ C-GEBH	Cessna U206E Stationair	U20601697	ex N8232Q	

☐ C-GPMV   Piper PA-31 Navajo C   31-7712081   ex N273PE

VOYAGE AIR   Fort McMurray, AB (ZFM)

☐ C-GBNA	de Havilland DHC-3 Turbo Otter	125	ex N5368G	FP/WS
☐ C-GDOB	de Havilland DHC-2 Beaver	774	ex C-GEZR	FP/WS
☐ C-GOLB	Cessna A185F Skywagon	18503188	ex N93173	FP/WS
☐ C-GOZP	Cessna A185F Skywagon	18503258	ex (N93874)	FP/WS
☐ C-GQQJ	de Havilland DHC-2 Beaver	719	ex N202PS	FP/WS
☐ C-GUJW	de Havilland DHC-2 Beaver	1657	ex 305	FP/WS
☐ C-GZSI	de Havilland DHC-2 Beaver	1003	ex N5327	FP/WS

VOYAGEUR AIRWAYS   Voyageur (VC/VAL)   Sudbury/North Bay, ON (YSB/YYB)

☐ C-FEXZ	de Havilland DHC-8-314	319	ex G-BRYJ	
☐ C-FEYG	de Havilland DHC-8-311	320	ex N320BC	opf UN
☐ C-FIQT	de Havilland DHC-8-314	395	ex N342EN	
☐ C-FNCU	de Havilland DHC-8-314	517	ex G-NVSB	
☐ C-GHQZ	de Havilland DHC-8-314	370	ex OE-LLY	opf UN
☐ C-FMCY	Canadair CRJ-100LR	7064	ex D-ACLP	
☐ C-FMUV	Canadair CRJ-100LR	7073	ex D-ACLQ	
☐ C-FWWU	Canadair CRJ-200LR	7299	ex N299BS	opf UN
☐ C-FXHC	Canadair CRJ-200ER	7329	ex N329BS	opf UN
☐ C-FXLH	Canadair CRJ-200LR	7283	ex G-MKSA	
☐ C-GIXR	Canadair CRJ-200LR	7434	ex VT-SAS	opf UN
☐ C-GIXT	Canadair CRJ-200LR	7393	ex VT-SAR	opf UN
☐ C-GMKG	Canadair CRJ-200LR	7191	ex N27191	
☐ C-GUXM	Canadair CRJ-200LR	7228	ex N37228	wfs
☐ C-FAPP	Beech A100 King Air	B-169	ex N305TZ	
☐ C-FBGS	Beech A100 King Air	B-204	ex N108JL	
☐ C-FZKM	de Havilland DHC-7-102	061	ex N903HA	
☐ C-GFOF	de Havilland DHC-7-102	037	ex N67RM	opf UN
☐ C-GGUL	de Havilland DHC-7-102	070	ex N905HA	opf UN
☐ C-GLOL	de Havilland DHC-7-102	039	ex HB-IVW	opf UN

WAASHESHKUN AIRWAYS   Mistissini, QC

☐ C-FDIO	de Havilland DHC-3 Otter	452		FP/WS♦
☐ C-GLPM	de Havilland DHC-3 Turbo Otter	147	ex C-FJFJ	♦

WABAKIMI AIR   Armstrong, ON (YYW)

☐ CF-BJY	de Havilland DHC-2 Beaver	173	ex N47920	FP/WS
☐ C-FBPC	de Havilland DHC-2 Beaver	144	ex VH-AAS	FP/WS
☐ C-FYLZ	de Havilland DHC-3 Turbo Otter	247	ex VH-SBR	FP/WS

WAHKASH CONTRACTING   Campbell River, BC (YBL)

☐ C-FIGF	de Havilland DHC-2 Beaver	834	ex CF-IGF	FP
☐ C-GVHT	de Havilland DHC-2 Beaver	257	ex 51-16797	FP

WAMAIR SERVICE & OUTFITTING   Matheson Island, MB

☐ C-FJQI	Piper PA-31-350 Navajo Chieftain	31-7552065		♦
☐ C-GBAO	Piper PA-31-350 Navajo Chieftain	31-7405234		♦
☐ C-GJPX	Cessna 208 Caravan I	20800302	ex N1284N	FP/WS
☐ C-GYWQ	Cessna U206G Stationair	U20604439		FP/WS

WASAYA AIRWAYS   Wasaya (WT/WSG)   Thunder Bay, ON (YQT)

☐ C-FQWA	Beech 1900D	UE-75	ex N175MH	
☐ C-FWAU	Beech 1900D	UE-164	ex N861CA	
☐ C-FWAX	Beech 1900D	UE-297	ex N21679	
☐ C-FWZK	Beech 1900D	UE-8	ex D-CBSF	
☐ C-GSWA	Beech 1900D	UE-34	ex N83801	
☐ C-GWOV	Beech 1900D	UE-332	ex N535M	
☐ C-GZVJ	Beech 1900D	UE-223	ex N1123J	
☐ C-FKPI	Pilatus PC-12/45	250	ex N250PB	
☐ C-FKRB	Pilatus PC-12/45	233	ex HB-FRD	
☐ C-FWAV	Pilatus PC-12/45	280	ex N280PC	
☐ C-GBJV	Pilatus PC-12/45	237	ex HB-FRH	
☐ C-GGWA	Pilatus PC-12/45	184	ex C-GMPE	
☐ C-FHWA	Cessna 208B Caravan I	208B0967	ex N428FC	
☐ C-FKAD	Cessna 208B Caravan I	208B0327		
☐ C-FKDL	Cessna 208B Caravan I	208B0240	ex (N5127B)	
☐ C-FPCC	Cessna 208B Caravan I	208B0840	ex N52623	
☐ C-FWAW	Cessna 208B Caravan I	208B0895	ex N5265B	

☐ C-FFFS	Hawker Siddeley HS.748				
	Srs.2A/209LFD	1663	ex G-BHCJ	806	Frtr
☐ C-GLTC	Hawker Siddeley HS.748				
	Srs.2A/244LFD	1656	ex N57910	801	Frtr
☐ C-GMAA	Hawker Siddeley HS.748				
	Srs.2A/214LFD	1576	ex TR-LQY	807	Frtr
☐ C-GMWT	de Havilland DHC-8Q-314	442	ex OE-LTH		

WATSON'S SKYWAYS   Wawa-Hawk Junction, ON (YXZ)

☐ C-GIKP	Cessna 208 Caravan I	20800141	ex C-GHGV	FP
☐ C-GOFB	de Havilland DHC-3 Turbo Otter	39		FP

WEAGAMOW AIR   Weagamow-Round Lake, ON (ZRJ)

☐ C-FLIN	Piper PA-31-350 Chieftain	31-8152013		
☐ C-FOCD	de Havilland DHC-2 Beaver	24		FP
☐ C-GNNO	Cessna A185F Skywagon	18502685	ex (N1016F)	FP

WEST CARIBOU AIR SERVICE   Thunder Bay, ON (YQT)

☐ C-FBWP	Cessna 185A Skywagon	1850430		FP
☐ C-FKAS	Noorduyn UC-64A Norseman		ex 43-5376	FP

WEST COAST AIR   (8O)   Vancouver-Coal Harbor, BC (CXH)

☐ C-FGQH	de Havilland DHC-6 Twin Otter 100	106	ex 8Q-MAF	604	FP
☐ C-GQKN	de Havilland DHC-6 Twin Otter 200	94	ex PZ-TAV	606	FP
Assoc with Harbour Air (H3)					

WEST WIND AVIATION/PRONTO AIRWAYS   Westwind (WEW)   Regina, SK (YQR)

☐ C-GLDE	ATR 42-320	374	ex N374AF	
☐ C-GWEA	ATR 42-320	240	ex D2-FLA	
☐ C-GWWC	ATR 42-300	0209	ex N209AT	
☐ C-GWWD	ATR 42-300	0211	ex N213AT	
☐ C-GWWR	ATR 42-300	238	ex G-RHUM	
☐ C-FWWF	Beech 200 Super King Air	BB-374	ex N111UR	
☐ C-FWWQ	Beech 200 Super King Air	BB-667	ex N667NA	
☐ C-GWWN	Beech 200 Super King Air	BB-14	ex N418CS	
☐ C-GWWV	Beech 200 Super King Air	BB-287	ex N498AC	
☐ C-GYDQ	Beech 200 Super King Air	BB-455	ex N900DG	
☐ C-GPRL	Beech 1900C-1	UC-67	ex N192YV	
☐ C-GPRT	Beech 1900C-1	UC-140	ex N140YV	Pronto A/W c/s
☐ C-GPRZ	Beech 1900C-1	UC-76	ex ZS-PJM	
☐ C-GWWX	Beech 1900C-1	UC-44	ex OY-JRI	
☐ C-GWWY	Beech 1900C-1	UC-63	ex ZS-PDI	
☐ C-FCPD	British Aerospace Jetstream 3112	822	ex G-31-822	
☐ C-FZJE	Cessna 401B	401B0032	ex (N7931Q)	
☐ C-GAXR	Cessna 401B	401B0050	ex N1250C	
☐ C-GDCG	Beech 1900D	UE-368	ex C-GWEA	
☐ C-GEUY	Cessna 414 II	414-0821		
☐ C-GGCA	Beech 1900D	UE-359	ex N31559	
☐ C-GGPX	Cessna 402C II	402C0280	ex C-GGSN	
☐ C-GHGK	British Aerospace Jetstream 3112	786	ex N786SC	
☐ C-GRSY	Cessna 401	401-0248	ex N8400F	
☐ C-GSQD	Cessna 401	401-0300		
☐ C-GWEX	British Aerospace Jetstream 3112	796	ex C-GZOS	
☐ C-GWWK	Beech 1900D	UE-395	ex VH-RUI	
☐ C-GWWU	Cessna 560 Citation Ultra	560-0304	ex N401KH	

WESTJET   Westjet (WS/WJA)   Calgary-Intl, AB (YYC)

☐ C-GBWS	Boeing 737-6CT	34288/1931		608
☐ C-GEWJ	Boeing 737-6CT	35571/2045	ex N1786B	615
☐ C-GPWS	Boeing 737-6CT	34284/1759		601
☐ C-GWCQ	Boeing 737-6CT	35111/2004		610
☐ C-GWCT	Boeing 737-6CT	35112/2016		611
☐ C-GWCY	Boeing 737-6CT	35113/2022		612
☐ C-GWJU	Boeing 737-6CT	34289/1956		609
☐ C-GWSB	Boeing 737-6CT	34285/1797	ex N1786B	602
☐ C-GWSI	Boeing 737-6CT	34286/1816		603
☐ C-GWSJ	Boeing 737-6CT	34621/1862		605
☐ C-GWSK	Boeing 737-6CT	34287/1912	ex N1787B	607
☐ C-GWSL	Boeing 737-6CT	34633/1884		606
☐ C-GXWJ	Boeing 737-6CT	35570/2032		613
☐ C-FBWJ	Boeing 737-7CT/W	32767/1629	ex (C-GWSA)	230
☐ C-FBWS	Boeing 737-7CT/W	37088/3080	ex N1786B	255

☐ C-FCWJ	Boeing 737-7CT/W	35086/2613	ex N1786B	250	
☐ C-FEWJ	Boeing 737-7CT/W	32769/1665		232	
☐ C-FGWJ	Boeing 737-7CT/W	32764/1553		226	
☐ C-FIBW	Boeing 737-7CT/W	37956/3649		266	
☐ C-FIWJ	Boeing 737-7CT/W	30712/2185		240	
☐ C-FIWS	Boeing 737-76N/W	32404/851	ex N1786B	001	
☐ C-FJWS	Boeing 737-76N/W	28651/872	ex N1786B	002	
☐ C-FKIW	Boeing 737-7CT/W	37955/3616	ex N1796B	265	
☐ C-FKWS	Boeing 737-76N/W	30134/905	ex N1787B	003	
☐ C-FLWJ	Boeing 737-7CT/W	38096/3520	ex N1786B	262	
☐ C-FMWJ	Boeing 737-7CT/W	32771/1754	ex N1786B	233	
☐ C-FTWJ	Boeing 737-7CT/W	30713/2220	ex N1786B	241	
☐ C-FUWS	Boeing 737-7CT/W	32765/1574		228	
☐ C-FWBX	Boeing 737-7CT/W	32751/1333		210	
☐ C-FWCN	Boeing 737-7CT/W	33698/1346		212	
☐ C-FWSF	Boeing 737-7CT/W	32758/1431		218	
☐ C-FWSI	Boeing 737-7CT/W	36691/2983		253	
☐ C-FWSK	Boeing 737-7CT/W	36420/2671	ex N1786B	251	
☐ C-FWSO	Boeing 737-7CT/W	32759/1445		219	
☐ C-FWSV	Boeing 737-7CT/W	32760/1472		220	
☐ C-FWSX	Boeing 737-7CT/W	32761/1493		221	
☐ C-FWSY	Boeing 737-7CT/W	32762/1501		222	
☐ C-FXWJ	Boeing 737-7CT/W	32768/1648	ex (C-GZWS)	231	
☐ C-FZWS	Boeing 737-76N/W	32731/1044		006	
☐ C-GCWJ	Boeing 737-7CT/W	33970/1556		227	
☐ C-GGWJ	Boeing 737-7CT/W	35503/2334		242	
☐ C-GLWS	Boeing 737-76N/W	32581/1009	ex N1787B	005	
☐ C-GMWJ	Boeing 737-7CT/W	35985/2135	ex N1779B	239	
☐ C-GQWJ	Boeing 737-7CT/W	35505/2436	ex N1786B	246	
☐ C-GRWS	Boeing 737-76N/W	32881/1155		007	
☐ C-GSWJ	Boeing 737-7CT/W	37423/3357	ex N1786B	261	
☐ C-GTWS	Boeing 737-76N/W	32883/1179		008	
☐ C-GUWJ	Boeing 737-7CT/W	36422/2497	ex N1786B	248	
☐ C-GUWS	Boeing 737-76N/W	33378/1206		009	
☐ C-GVWJ	Boeing 737-7CT/W	36421/2484	ex N1786B	247	
☐ C-GWAZ	Boeing 737-7CT/W	32763/1522		223	
☐ C-GWBF	Boeing 737-7CT/W	32757/1370		213	
☐ C-GWBJ	Boeing 737-7CT/W	32754/1385	ex N1787B	215	
☐ C-GWBN	Boeing 737-7CT/W	34155/1772		235	
☐ C-GWBT	Boeing 737-7CT/W	32755/1396		216	
☐ C-GWBX	Boeing 737-7CT/W	34156/1793	ex N1786B	236	
☐ C-GWCM	Boeing 737-7CT/W	32756/1413	ex N1795B	217	
☐ C-GWCN	Boeing 737-7CT/W	34157/1818	ex N1784B	237	
☐ C-GWJE	Boeing 737-7CT/W	35078/2431		245	
☐ C-GWJF	Boeing 737-7CT/W	32766/1599		229	
☐ C-GWJG	Boeing 737-7CT/W	35504/2366	ex N1786B	243	
☐ C-GWJK	Boeing 737-7CT/W	35084/2564	ex N1786B	249	
☐ C-GWJO	Boeing 737-7CT/W	33969/1527		225	
☐ C-GWJT	Boeing 737-7CT/W	40338/3529	ex N1787B	263	
☐ C-GWSE	Boeing 737-76N/W	33379/1216		010	
☐ C-GWSH	Boeing 737-76N/W	29886/1258		011	
☐ C-GWSN	Boeing 737-7CT/W	37089/3090	ex N1796B	256	
☐ C-GWSO	Boeing 737-7CT/W	37090/3092	ex N1796B	257	
☐ C-GWSP	Boeing 737-7CT/W	36693/3108	ex N1787B	258	
☐ C-GWSQ	Boeing 737-7CT/W	37091/3134		259	
☐ C-GWSU	Boeing 737-7CT/W	36689/2860	ex N1787B	252	
☐ C-GWSY	Boeing 737-7CT/W	37421/3184	ex N1786B	260	
☐ C-GYWJ	Boeing 737-7CT/W	32772/1879		238	
☐ C-FAWJ	Boeing 737-8CT/W	35502/2323		807	
☐ C-FBWI	Boeing 737-8CT/W	39090/4364	ex N5573P	822	
☐ C-FCNW	Boeing 737-8CT/W	39092/3580		816	
☐ C-FCSX	Boeing 737-8CT/W	60126/5106		832	♦
☐ C-FDMB	Boeing 737-8CT/W	60127/5188		833	♦
☐ C-FKRF	Boeing 737-8CT/W	60123/5079	ex N60436	829	♦
☐ C-FKWJ	Boeing 737-8CT/W	36435/3469		815	
☐ C-FPLS	Boeing 737-8CT/W	60132/5401	ex (C-FUCD)		♦
☐ C-FRWA	Boeing 737-8CT/W	39085/4293	ex N5515X	821	
☐ C-FUCS	Boeing 737-8CT/W	60129/5296		836	♦
☐ C-FUJR	Boeing 737-8CT/W	60130/5341		837	♦
☐ C-FUMF	Boeing 737-8CT/W	60128/5248		835	♦
☐ C-FUSM	Boeing 737-8CT/W	39081/4702	ex N5573B	826	
☐ C-FWIJ	Boeing 737-8CT/W	39072/4087		819	
☐ C-FWJS	Boeing 737-8CT/W	39076/4953		827	♦
☐ C-FWSE	Boeing 737-8CT/W	36690/2987		811	
☐ C-FWVJ	Boeing 737-8CT/W	37962/3863		817	
☐ C-GAWS	Boeing 737-8CT/W	38880/4268	ex N1781B	820	
☐ C-GDMP	Boeing 737-8CT/W	60131/5367		838	♦
☐ C-GJWS	Boeing 737-8CT/W	34152/1714		802	
☐ C-GJLZ	Boeing 737-8CT/W	60125/5103		831	♦
☐ C-GKWJ	Boeing 737-8CT/W	34151/1684		801	
☐ C-GKWA	Boeing 737-8CT/W	39089/4377		823	
☐ C-GVWA	Boeing 737-8CT/W	39088/4641	ex N1787B	825	

☐ C-GWBL	Boeing 737-8CT/W	34154/1734		806		
☐ C-GWBU	Boeing 737-8CT/W	39075/4970		828		♦
☐ C-GWRG	Boeing 737-8CT/W	39071/3931		818		
☐ C-GWSA	Boeing 737-8CT/W	34153/1731	ex N1786B	805		
☐ C-GWSR	Boeing 737-8CT/W	35288/2802		809		
☐ C-GWSV	Boeing 737-8CT/W	37158/2841		810		
☐ C-GWSX	Boeing 737-8CT/W	36696/3314		813		
☐ C-GWSZ	Boeing 737-8CT/W	37092/3164		812	Walt Disney World c/s	
☐ C-GWUX	Boeing 737-8CT/W	60124/5090	ex N6055X	830		♦
☐ C-GWWJ	Boeing 737-8CT/W	35080/2524	ex N1786B	808		
☐ C-GZWS	Boeing 737-8CT/W	32770/1719		803		
☐ C-FOGJ	Boeing 767-338ER	25274/396	ex N324BC			o/o♦
☐ C-GOGN	Boeing 767-338ER	25576/549	ex N328BC			o/o♦

WESTJET ENCORE — Encore (WR/WEN) — Calgary-Intl, AB (YYC)

☐ C-FENU	de Havilland DHC-8-402Q	4446	403	
☐ C-FENY	de Havilland DHC-8-402Q	4447	404	
☐ C-FHEN	de Havilland DHC-8-402Q	4441	402	
☐ C-FIWE	de Havilland DHC-8-402Q	4466	411	
☐ C-FKWE	de Havilland DHC-8-402Q	4467	412	
☐ C-FNEN	de Havilland DHC-8-402Q	4453	406	
☐ C-FOEN	de Havilland DHC-8-402Q	4440	401	
☐ C-FOWE	de Havilland DHC-8-402Q	4471	413	♦
☐ C-FQWE	de Havilland DHC-8-402Q	4473	415	♦
☐ C-FUWE	de Havilland DHC-8-402Q	4477	416	♦
☐ C-FWEZ	de Havilland DHC-8-402Q	4483	417	♦
☐ C-GENM	de Havilland DHC-8-402Q	4456	407	
☐ C-GJWE	de Havilland DHC-8-402Q	4460	408	
☐ C-GVWE	de Havilland DHC-8-402Q	4485	418	
☐ C-GWEF	de Havilland DHC-8-402Q	4487	419	♦
☐ C-GWEG	de Havilland DHC-8-402Q	4488	420	♦
☐ C-GWEO	de Havilland DHC-8-402Q	4462	409	
☐ C-GWEP	de Havilland DHC-8-402Q	4463	410	
☐ C-GWEQ	de Havilland DHC-8-402Q	4490	421	
☐ C-GWEU	de Havilland DHC-8-402Q	4493	422	♦

WHITE RIVER AIR SERVICES — (WRA) — White River, ON (YWR)

☐ CF-FHR	de Havilland DHC-2 Beaver	46		FP
☐ CF-ODE	de Havilland DHC-2 Beaver	131		FP♦
☐ C-FWRA	de Havilland DHC-3 Turbo Otter	213	ex India IM1714	FP

WHITE RIVER HELICOPTERS — Terrace, BC

☐ C-FAVN	Bell 206L-3 LongRanger	51001	♦
☐ C-FIYM	Aérospatiale AS350B2 AStar	1881	♦
☐ C-FTYI	Aéerospatiale AS350B2 AStar	1960	♦
☐ C-GTMH	Bell 206B JetRanger	175	♦
☐ C-GWRA	Aérospatiale AS350B2 AStar	1059	♦

WILDCAT HELICOPTERS — Kelowna, BC (YLW)

☐ C-FCAD	Bell 212	30923	
☐ C-FCAN	Bell 212	30919	
☐ C-FOHK	Bell 212	30806	
☐ C-GGAT	Bell 212	30846	
☐ C-GSGT	Bell 212	30771	
☐ C-GSRH	Bell 212	30895	
☐ C-FWTK	Bell 412SP	36001	ex N2148K
☐ C-FWTQ	Bell 412SP	36002	ex N2149S
☐ C-FWTY	Bell 412SP	36004	ex N33008
☐ C-GBND	Bell 412SP	36007	ex C-GIWT
☐ C-GTAK	Bell 206B JetRanger	1649	

WILDERNESS AIR — Vermilion Bay, ON (YVG)

☐ C-FGMK	de Havilland DHC-2 Beaver	1329	ex 58-2003	FP
☐ C-FJOF	de Havilland DHC-2 Beaver	1053	ex CF-JOF	FP
☐ C-FODV	de Havilland DHC-3 Otter	411	ex CF-ODV	FP
☐ C-FRXJ	Found FBA-2C	14		FP
☐ C-GFZF	Cessna A185E Skywagon	18502002	ex N70118	FP
☐ C-GLAB	de Havilland DHC-3 Turbo Otter	348	ex 55-2210	FP
☐ C-GNFN	Cessna 208 Caravan I	20800502		FP
☐ C-GNXG	de Havilland DHC-2 Beaver	650		FP

WILDERNESS NORTH AIR — Thunder Bay, ON (YQT)

☐ C-FYCX	de Havilland DHC-3 Turbo Otter	44	ex N10704	FP
☐ C-GNZO	de Havilland DHC-2 Beaver	399		

☐ C-GWNF	Air Tractor AT-802	802-0250		
☐ C-GNWL	Air Tractor AT-802A	802A-0299		
☐ C-GWNO	Cessna A185E Skywagon	185-1387		
☐ C-GNWU	Air Tractor AT-802A	802A-0373		

WINGS OVER KISSISSING/KISSISSING LAKE LODGE   Kississing Lake/Pine Falls, NB

☐ C-FDCL	Cessna U206G Super Skywagon	U20603542	ex N8790Q	FP/WS
☐ C-FENB	Noorduyn UC-64A Norseman	324	ex 43-5384	FP
☐ C-FFVZ	de Havilland DHC-3 Turbo Otter	145	ex N80944	FP/WS
☐ C-FIKP	de Havilland DHC-2 Beaver	890	ex CF-IKP	FP
☐ C-FKIE	Cessna 180A Skywagon	18050180		FP/WS
☐ C-FKIX	Cessna 185A Skywagon	18503794	ex N9866Q	FP
☐ C-FOBR	Noorduyn Norseman V	N29-35	ex CF-OBR	FP
☐ C-FODW	de Havilland DHC-3 Turbo Otter	403	ex CF-ODW	FP/WS
☐ C-FRHW	de Havilland DHC-3 Otter	445	ex 5N-ABN	FP/WS
☐ C-FSAP	Noorduyn Norseman VI	N29-231		FP
☐ C-FSKA	Beech A100 King Air	B-239	ex N154TC	
☐ C-FWEJ	de Havilland DHC-3 Turbo Otter	208	ex IM1710	FP/WS
☐ C-FYMV	de Havilland DHC-2 Beaver	1589	ex CF-YMV	FP
☐ C-GADE	de Havilland DHC-2 Beaver	730	ex 53-7919	FP
☐ C-GBWP	Bell 206B JetRanger	1537		
☐ C-GDLW	Cessna TU206G Super Skywagon	U20606654		FP/WS
☐ C-GEWP	de Havilland DHC-2 Turbo Beaver	1543/TB2	ex ET-AKI	FP/WS
☐ C-GLJV	Beech B100 Super King Air	BB-1345	ex N754SC	♦
☐ C-GMLL	Cessna 337 Skymaster	33700004		
☐ C-GNCV	Beech 100 King Air	B-23	ex N701RJ	
☐ C-GOCN	Cessna 208B Caravan I	208B0780	ex N308KC	FP
☐ C-GPCB	Beech 100 King Air	B-45	ex N704S	
☐ C-GRZI	Noorduyn Norseman VI	175		
☐ C-GTLS	Beech 100 King Air	B-35	ex N178WM	
☐ C-GYOS	Cessna A185F Skywagon	18503269		FP♦

WOLVERINE AIR   Fort Simpson, NT (YFS)

☐ C-FTOE	Piper PA-31 Navajo	31-7401213	ex N180M	
☐ C-FTQB	Cessna A185F Skywagon	18501655	ex (N1948U)	
☐ C-GANE	Cessna TU206G Stationair	U20606764		
☐ C-GIHF	Britten-Norman BN-2A-26 Islander	475	ex G-BDJU	
☐ C-GQOA	Cessna U206G Stationair 6	U20604993	ex (N4600U)	
☐ C-GTUG	Cessna U206G Stationair 6	U20606214		

YELLOWHEAD HELICOPTERS   Valemount, BC

☐ C-FDUB	Aérospatiale AS350B2 AStar	3041	ex N4073S	
☐ C-FIEM	Aérospatiale AS350B3 AStar	7343		♦
☐ C-FXHS	Aérospatiale AS350B2 AStar	2248		
☐ C-GMYH	Aérospatiale AS350B3 AStar	7649		♦
☐ C-GNME	Aérospatiale AS350B2 AStar	2826	ex N351WW	
☐ C-GNMJ	Aérospatiale AS350BA AStar	2829		
☐ C-GOLV	Aérospatiale AS350BA AStar	1108	ex N3595N	
☐ C-GPHM	Aérospatiale AS350B2 AStar	2488		
☐ C-GPHQ	Aérospatiale AS350B1 AStar	2017	ex N855NM	
☐ C-GPHR	Aérospatiale AS350B1 AStar	2268		
☐ C-GPTL	Aérospatiale AS350B2 AStar	2103	ex OY-HEH	
☐ C-FPQX	Bell 206B JetRanger II	1330		
☐ C-GBYH	Bell 206B JetRanger	2240		♦
☐ C-GDGH	Bell 206B JetRanger III	2476		
☐ C-GHQW	Bell 206B JetRanger II	1708		♦
☐ C-GORO	Bell 206B JetRanger	2086	ex N15558	
☐ C-GVYH	Bell 206B JetRanger III	2989		♦
☐ C-GXYH	Bell 206B JetRanger III	2267		
☐ C-GYHL	Bell 206B JetRanger II	1702		
☐ C-GYHR	Bell 206B JetRanger III	2671		
☐ C-GYHT	Bell 206B JetRanger III	4104		
☐ C-FBHW	Bell 205	30286		
☐ C-FGYH	Bell 407	53641		
☐ C-FYHA	Bell 205A-1	30175		
☐ C-FYHL	Bell 427	56020		
☐ C-FYHT	Bell 212	30869	ex C-FCSL	
☐ C-FYHY	Bell 407	53945		
☐ C-GGSM	Bell 212	30741		
☐ C-GGSO	Bell 212	30696	ex N90220	
☐ C-GNYH	Bell 407	53868		
☐ C-GPWX	Bell 212	30535		♦
☐ C-GYHF	Bell 407	53707		
☐ C-GYHP	Bell 206L-1 LongRanger	45400		
☐ C-GYHQ	Bell 206L-1 LongRanger	45419		
☐ C-GYHU	Bell 205A-1	30177		
☐ C-GYHX	Bell 206L-3 LongRanger III	51545		

☐ C-GYLR   Bell 206L-4 LongRanger IV   52219

CC-   CHILE (Republic of Chile)

AEROCARDAL		Cardal (CDA)		Santiago-Benitez Intl (SCL)
☐ CC-AAQ	Dornier 228-202	8119	ex CS-TGO	
☐ CC-ACK	Agusta A109S Grand	22170		
☐ CC-ANZ	Agusta A109S Grand	22085	ex PR-VIN	♦
☐ CC-AOA	IAI Gulfstream G150	237	ex EC-KMS	♦
☐ CC-CWA	MBB 105LSA-3	2006	ex N96LS	
☐ CC-CWC	Dornier 228-202K	8162	ex D-CLEE	
☐ CC-CWE	Cessna 421C	421C0614	ex CC-PJB	
☐ CC-CWI	MBB 105CB-2	S-193	ex C-11	
☐ CC-CWK	IAI Gulfstream G150	219	ex N219GA	
☐ CC-CWW	Cessna S550 Citation II	S550-0002	ex N211VP	
☐ CC-CWX	Dornier 228-101	7027	ex CC-CSA	
☐ CC-CWZ	Cessna S550 Citation S/II	S550-0143	ex N458PE	

AERODESIERTO				Arica (ARI)
☐ CC-ACD	Boeing 737-2K9	23404/1176	ex C9-BAK	[SCL]♦
☐ CC-CVI	Boeing 737-2Q3	22367/706	ex N763AA	♦

AEROSERVICIO				Santiago-Tobalaba (SCT)
☐ CC-CDR	Cessna 208B Caravan 1	208B1202	ex N13194	

AEROVIAS DAP		Dap (DAP)		Punta Arenas (PUQ)
☐ CC-ABD	Boeing 737-2Q3	22736/896	ex N763BA	
☐ CC-AAG	Boeing 737-247	23608/1399	ex LV-BIF	
☐ CC-ACO	British Aerospace 146 Srs.200	E2094	ex OY-RCB	
☐ CC-ACQ	Beech 300LW Super King Air	FA-205	ex N205FA	
☐ CC-AEH	Cessna 404	404-0440	ex CC-ETC	
☐ CC-AJS	Avro 146-RJ85	E2233	ex OY-RCE	<FLI
☐ CC-CHV	de Havilland DHC-6 Twin Otter 300	709	ex (G-BHUY)	
☐ CC-CLV	Cessna 402C	402C0073	ex CC-PQL	
☐ CC-CLY	Beech 100 King Air	B-79	ex CC-PIE	
☐ CC-COV	Cessna 402C	402C0282	ex CC-PQM	
☐ CC-CZP	British Aerospace 146 Srs.200	E2042	ex G-FLTD	

BARRICK SERVICIOS MINEROS				
☐ CC-ACH	de Havilland DHC-6 Twin Otter 300	613	ex C-GGPM	
☐ CC-AMM	de Havilland DHC-6 Twin Otter 400	895	ex C-GVVA	♦
☐ CC-PQQ	de Havilland DHC-6 Twin Otter 300	793	ex C-FWZB	♦

CHILEJET				Santiago-Benitez Intl (SCL)
☐ CC-ADZ	Boeing 737-3G7	24634/1823	ex N307AW	♦

DAP HELICOPTEROS		HeliDap (DHE)		Punta Arenas (PUQ)
☐ CC-ACM	MBB Bo 105CBS-4	S-414	ex EC-HNT	
☐ CC-CHK	MBB Bo 105CB-4-2	S-687	ex H-62	EMS
☐ CC-CHM	MBB Bo 105CB-4-2	S-688	ex H-63	EMS
☐ CC-CHN	MBB Bo 105CB-4-2	S-689	ex H-64	EMS
☐ CC-CHQ	MBB Bo 105CB-4-2	S-708	ex H-65	EMS
☐ CC-CHR	MBB Bo 105CB-4-2	S-710	ex H-66	EMS
☐ CC-AEK	Aérospatiale AS350B3 Ecureuil	4092	ex EC-JTM	
☐ CC-CCA	Eurocopter EC135T1	0122	ex N214TD	
☐ CC-CMV	Aérospatiale AS355F2 Ecureuil 2	5372	ex N225CC	

HELIWORKS		Heliworks (HLW)		Concepcion (CCP)
☐ CC-AQD	Mitsubishi MU-2B-36A	707SA	ex N707AF	
☐ CC-CRE	Piper PA-34-200T Seneca II	34-7770432	ex CC-PTP	
☐ CC-PRI	Piper PA-34-200T Seneca II	34-8070034	ex CC-CCI	

LAN AIRLINES		LAN (LA/LAN)		Santiago-Benitez Intl (SCL)
Member of oneWorld				
☐ CC-BCD	Airbus A319-112	4871	ex D-AVYA	
☐ CC-BCE	Airbus A319-112	5005	ex D-AVYH	
☐ CC-BCF	Airbus A319-112	5097	ex D-AVYQ	
☐ CC-COY	Airbus A319-132	2295	ex D-AVWA	
☐ CC-COZ	Airbus A319-132	2304	ex D-AVWN	

☐ CC-CPJ	Airbus A319-132	2845	ex D-AVYX		
☐ CC-CPL	Airbus A319-132	2858	ex D-AVYB		
☐ CC-CYL	Airbus A319-132	3779	ex D-AVXJ		
☐ CC-BAN	Airbus A320-214	4758	ex F-WWBP		
☐ CC-BAP	Airbus A320-214	4815	ex D-AXAJ		
☐ CC-BAQ	Airbus A320-214	4839	ex D-AXAD		
☐ CC-BAR	Airbus A320-214	4892	ex D-AVVG		
☐ CC-BAS	Airbus A320-214	4896	ex F-WWBO		
☐ CC-BAT	Airbus A320-214	4921	ex D-AXAA		
☐ CC-BAU	Airbus A320-214	4943	ex D-AXAQ		
☐ CC-BAW	Airbus A320-214	5125	ex D-AVVD		
☐ CC-BAX	Airbus A320-214	5178	ex D-AXAR		
☐ CC-BAY	Airbus A320-214	5213	ex D-AVVV		
☐ CC-BAZ	Airbus A320-214	5229	ex D-AUBO		
☐ CC-BFA	Airbus A320-214	5234	ex D-AVVT		
☐ CC-BFB	Airbus A320-214	5263	ex D-AXAK		
☐ CC-BFC	Airbus A320-214	5316	ex D-AUBD		
☐ CC-BFD	Airbus A320-214	5324	ex D-AUBG		
☐ CC-BFE	Airbus A320-214	5364	ex D-AUBT		
☐ CC-BFF	Airbus A320-214	5408	ex F-WWDC		
☐ CC-BFG	Airbus A320-214	5443	ex D-AVVQ		
☐ CC-BFH	Airbus A320-214	5453	ex D-AVVS		
☐ CC-BFI	Airbus A320-214	5483	ex D-AVVZ		
☐ CC-BFJ	Airbus A320-214	5493	ex D-AXAD		
☐ CC-BFK	Airbus A320-214/S	5548	ex D-AXAW		
☐ CC-BFL	Airbus A320-214/S	5554	ex D-AXAY		
☐ CC-BFM	Airbus A320-214/S	5586	ex D-AUBF		
☐ CC-BFN	Airbus A320-214/S	5583	ex F-WWDP		
☐ CC-BFO	Airbus A320-214/S	5686	ex D-AVVE		
☐ CC-BFP	Airbus A320-214/S	5707	ex D-AVVJ		
☐ CC-BFQ	Airbus A320-214/S	5764	ex D-AVVW		
☐ CC-BFR	Airbus A320-214/S	5801	ex D-AXAI		
☐ CC-BFS	Airbus A320-214/S	5818	ex D-AXAM		
☐ CC-BFT	Airbus A320-214/S	5859	ex D-AVVB		
☐ CC-BFU	Airbus A320-214/S	5929	ex D-AUBG		
☐ CC-BFV	Airbus A320-214/S	5965	ex F-WWIR		
☐ CC-BFW	Airbus A320-214/S	6135	ex D-AXAY		♦
☐ CC-BFX	Airbus A320-214/S	6183	ex D-AVVE		♦
☐ CC-BJD	Airbus A320-214/S	5748	ex PR-TYE		
☐ CC-BJE	Airbus A320-214/S	5654	ex PR-TYB		
☐ CC-BJF	Airbus A320-214/S	5666	ex PR-TYC		♦
☐ CC-BAA	Airbus A320-233	4383	ex HC-CLA		♦
☐ CC-BAB	Airbus A320-233	4400	ex HC-CLB		
☐ CC-BAC	Airbus A320-233	4439	ex HC-CLC	oneWorld c/s	♦
☐ CC-BAD	Airbus A320-233	4476	ex HC-CLD		♦
☐ CC-BAE	Airbus A320-233	4509	ex HC-CLE		
☐ CC-BAF	Airbus A320-232	4516	ex D-AXAG		
☐ CC-BAG	Airbus A320-232	4546	ex D-AXAO		
☐ CC-BAH	Airbus A320-232	4549	ex D-AUBQ		
☐ CC-BAJ	Airbus A320-232	4576	ex F-WWBX		
☐ CC-BAK	Airbus A320-232	4597	ex D-AVVH		
☐ CC-BAL	Airbus A320-232	4657	ex D-AXAC		
☐ CC-BAM	Airbus A320-232	4697	ex D-AUBD		
☐ CC-BJB	Airbus A320-232	3264	ex HK-4740		
☐ CC-BJC	Airbus A320-232	3330	ex HK-4738		
☐ CC-COF	Airbus A320-233	1355	ex F-WWBE		
☐ CC-COL	Airbus A320-233	1568	ex LV-CKV		♦
☐ CC-CQM	Airbus A320-233	3280	ex F-WWDM		
☐ CC-CQN	Airbus A320-233	3319	ex F-WWBC		
☐ CC-CQO	Airbus A320-233	3535	ex F-WWDZ		
☐ CC-CQP	Airbus A320-233	3556	ex F-WWBC		
☐ CC-BEA	Airbus A321-211/S	6364	ex D-AVXO		♦
☐ CC-BEB	Airbus A321-211/S	6398	ex D-AZAD		♦
☐ CC-BEC	Airbus A321-211/S	6406	ex D-AZAJ		♦
☐ CC-BED	Airbus A321-211/S	6484	ex D-AVZP		♦
☐ CC-	Airbus A321-211/S	6698	ex		o/o♦
☐ CC-	Airbus A321-211/S	6780	ex		o/o♦
☐ CC-	Airbus A321-211/S	6814	ex		o/o♦
☐ CC-	Airbus A321-211/S	6908	ex		o/o♦
☐ CC-	Airbus A321-211/S	6933	ex		o/o♦
☐ CC-BDA	Boeing 767-316ER/W	40798/1011			
☐ CC-BDB	Boeing 767-316ER/W	40590/1014			
☐ CC-BDC	Boeing 767-316ER/W	40591/1016			
☐ CC-BDD	Boeing 767-316ER/W	40799/1029			
☐ CC-BJA	Boeing 767-316ER/W	26329/641	ex LV-BMR		
☐ CC-CRV	Boeing 767-316ER/W	27615/681	ex LV-BFU		
☐ CC-CWF	Boeing 767-316ER/W	34626/940			
☐ CC-CWH	Boeing 767-316ER/W	34628/945	ex LV-CKU		♦
☐ CC-CWV	Boeing 767-316ER/W	35230/955			

☐ CC-CWY	Boeing 767-316ER/W	35231/961			
☐ CC-CXC	Boeing 767-316ER/W	36710/962			
☐ CC-CXD	Boeing 767-316ER/W	35697/967	ex HC-CJX		
☐ CC-CXE	Boeing 767-316ER/W	35696/968	ex HC-CKY		
☐ CC-CXF	Boeing 767-316ER/W	36711/970	ex HC-CIZ		
☐ CC-CXG	Boeing 767-316ER/W	36712/972	ex N5020K		
☐ CC-CXH	Boeing 767-316ER/W	35698/973	ex HC-CJA		
☐ CC-CXI	Boeing 767-316ER/W	37800/984			
☐ CC-CXJ	Boeing 767-316ER/W	37801/985		oneWorld c/s	
☐ CC-CXK	Boeing 767-316ER/W	37802/987			
☐ CC-CXL	Boeing 767-31BER/W	26265/570	ex LV-BFD		
☐ CC-CZT	Boeing 767-316ER/W	29228/699			
☐ CC-CZU	Boeing 767-316ER/W	29229/729			
☐ CC-BBA	Boeing 787-8	38471/68			
☐ CC-BBB	Boeing 787-8	38466/74			
☐ CC-BBC	Boeing 787-8	38472/80			
☐ CC-BBD	Boeing 787-8	38484/118			
☐ CC-BBE	Boeing 787-8	38473/113			
☐ CC-BBF	Boeing 787-8	38476/185			
☐ CC-BBG	Boeing 787-8	38477/195			♦
☐ CC-BBH	Boeing 787-8	42224/205			♦
☐ CC-BBI	Boeing 787-8	38480/210			♦
☐ CC-BBJ	Boeing 787-8	42225/234			♦
☐ CC-BGA	Boeing 787-9	35317/259			♦
☐ CC-BGB	Boeing 787-9	35318/276			
☐ CC-BGC	Boeing 787-9	35321/309			o/o♦
☐ CC-BGD	Boeing 787-9	35322/327			o/o♦
☐ CC-	Boeing 787-9	38459/386			o/o♦
☐ CC-	Boeing 787-9	38478/341			o/o♦
☐ CC-	Boeing 787-9	38479/350			o/o♦
☐ CC-	Boeing 787-9	38461/382			o/o♦
☐ CC-	Boeing 787-9	38467/403			o/o♦
☐ CC-	Boeing 787-9	38764/399			o/o♦
☐ CC-CQA	Airbus A340-313X	359	ex F-WWJY		wfs
☐ CC-CQC	Airbus A340-313X	363	ex F-WWJZ		
☐ CC-CQF	Airbus A340-313X	442	ex F-WWJY		
☐ CC-	Airbus A350-941	024	ex F-WZ		o/o♦

LAN CARGO — LAN Cargo (UC/LCO) — Santiago-Benitez Intl (SCL)

☐ CC-CZZ	Boeing 767-316F/W	25756/712			
☐ N312LA	Boeing 767-316F	32572/846			>FDX
☐ N418LA	Boeing 767-316F/W	34246/936			>LAE♦
☐ N420LA	Boeing 767-316F/W	34627/948			>MAA
☐ N524LA	Boeing 767-346F	35816/956	ex JA631J		
☐ PR-ABD	Boeing 767-316F/W	34245/935			>TUS
☐ N772LA	Boeing 777-F6N	37708/774			
☐ N774LA	Boeing 777-F6N	37710/782			
☐ N776LA	Boeing 777-F16	38091/1038			
☐ N778LA	Boeing 777-F16	41518/1050			

LAN EXPRESS — Lanex (LU/LXP) — Santiago-Benitez Intl (SCL)

99.4% owned subsidiary of LAN Airlines and ops aircraft leased from the parent

LASSA - LINEA DE AEROSERVICIOS — (LSE) — Santiago-Tobalaba (SCTB)

☐ CC-AEV	Piper PA-31T Cheyenne	31T-7920091	ex N26SL	
☐ CC-ARV	Cessna 551 Citation II SP	551-0059	ex N59DY	
☐ CC-CPR	Piper PA-31T2 Cheyenne	31T-8166070	ex CC-PTA	
☐ CC-PVE	Piper PA-31T2 Cheyenne IIXL	31T-8166038	ex N161TC	♦

LINEA AEREA COSTA NORTE — Costa Norte (NOT) — Iquique (IQQ)

☐ CC-CAJ	Cessna 337H Super Skymaster II	33701860	ex N1368L	
☐ CC-CFU	Rockwell 500S Shrike Commander	3320	ex N348TT	
☐ CC-CFW	Rockwell 500S Shrike Commander	3230	ex N567PT	
☐ CC-CGB	Cessna 337H Super Skymaster II	33701941	ex N123YM	

ONE AIRLINES — (ONS)

☐ CC-AIT	Boeing 737-36N	28554/2835	ex N855CC	♦

SKY AIRLINE — Aerosky (H2/SKU) — Santiago-Benitez Intl (SCL)

☐ CC-AFX	Airbus A319-111	2283	ex G-EZEU
☐ CC-AFY	Airbus A319-111	2129	ex G-EZEC
☐ CC-AFZ	Airbus A319-111	2251	ex G-EZEP

☐ CC-AHC	Airbus A319-111	2119	ex G-EZEA	
☐ CC-AHD	Airbus A319-111	2460	ex D-ALAC	
☐ CC-AHE	Airbus A319-111	2548	ex G-EZIU	
☐ CC-AIB	Airbus A319-111	2378	ex G-EZMS	
☐ CC-AIC	Airbus A319-111	2380	ex G-EJJB	
☐ CC-AID	Airbus A319-111	2436	ex G-EZIC	
☐ CC-AIY	Airbus A319-111	2214	ex VQ-BMO	
☐ CC-AJF	Airbus A319-111	2249	ex VQ-BMN	
☐ CC-AJG	Airbus A319-112	3331	ex VQ-BNF	♦
☐ CC-AMP	Airbus A319-112	3171	ex VQ-BMM	
☐ CC-ABV	Airbus A320-233	1400	ex N470TA	
☐ CC-ABW	Airbus A320-233	1523	ex N484TA	
☐ CC-ADO	Airbus A320-231	0447	ex N447AG	
☐ CC-CTK	Boeing 737-230 (Nordam 3)	22402/744	ex N261LR	[SCL]
☐ CC-CTO	Boeing 737-230	22114/657	ex LV-BBI	[SCL]

TRANSPORTES AEREOS CORPORATIVOS/CORPFLITE — Santiago-Tobalaba

☐ CC-AAI	Dornier 228-202K	8156	ex LN-MOL	
☐ CC-AGR	Cessna 650 Citation III	650-0003	ex N411SL	
☐ CC-ARG	Dornier 228-100	7005	ex D-ILKA	♦
☐ CC-CIW	Piper PA-31T Cheyenne II	31T-7820018	ex N35RT	

CN- MOROCCO (Kingdom of Morocco)

AIR ARABIA MAROC — Nawras (3O/MAC) — Casablanca-Mohamed V (CMN)

☐ CN-NMF	Airbus A320-214	4539	ex A6-ANC	
☐ CN-NMG	Airbus A320-214	4568	ex A6-AND	
☐ CN-NMH	Airbus A320-214	5143	ex A6-ANJ	
☐ CN-NMI	Airbus A320-214	5206	ex A6-ANK	♦

ALFA AIR — (ALM)

| ☐ CN-TMK | British Aerospace Jetstream 32 | 943 | ex C-FIBD | |

HELICONIA OFFSHORE HELICOPTERS — Marrakech

☐ CN-HBA	Aérospatiale AS350BA Ecureuil	1200	ex F-GCFQ	♦
☐ CN-HCE	Aérospatiale AS350B3 Ecureuil	5000	ex F-HJCE	♦
☐ F-HOGP	AgustaWestland AW139	31565	ex I-PTFR	♦
☐ F-HOIL	AgustaWestland AW139	31566		♦

REGIONAL AIR LINES — Maroc Regional (FN/RGL) — Casablanca-Anfa (CAS)

☐ CN-RBS	Hawker 900XP	HA-0091	ex N61391	
☐ CN-RLA	Beech 1900D	UE-259	ex N10863	
☐ CN-RLG	ATR 42-320	366	ex F-WQNM	wfs

ROYAL AIR MAROC — Royalair Maroc (AT/RAM) — Casablanca-Mohamed V (CMN)

☐ EC-KUL	ATR 72-212A	809	ex F-WWET	<SWT♦
☐ EC-KVI	ATR 72-212A	824	ex F-WWEM	<AEA♦
☐ EC-LST	ATR 72-201F	234	ex SP-OLL	<SWT
☐ EC-LYB	ATR 72-212A	550	ex N550LL	<SWT♦
☐ EC-MAF	ATR 72-212A	568	ex OY-CIN	<SWT♦
☐ CN-COE	ATR 72-600	960	ex F-WWLP	Royal Air Maroc Express
☐ CN-COF	ATR 72-600	958	ex F-WWLO	Royal Air Maroc Express
☐ CN-COG	ATR 72-600	1035	ex F-WWET	Royal Air Maroc Express
☐ CN-COH	ATR 72-600	1034	ex F-WWES	Royal Air Maroc Express
☐ CN-COI	ATR 72-600	1143	ex F-WWEH	Royal Air Maroc Express♦
☐ CN-RNL	Boeing 737-7B6/W	28982/236	ex N1786B	
☐ CN-RNM	Boeing 737-7B6/W	28984/294	ex N1786B	
☐ CN-RNQ	Boeing 737-7B6/W	28985/501	ex N1786B	
☐ CN-RNR	Boeing 737-7B6/W	28986/519	ex N1787B	
☐ CN-RNV	Boeing 737-7B6/W	28988/1261		
☐ CN-ROD	Boeing 737-7B6/W	33062/1883		
☐ CN-RGE	Boeing 737-86N/W	36822/3746		
☐ CN-RGF	Boeing 737-86N/W	36826/3773		
☐ CN-RGG	Boeing 737-86N/W	36829/3815		
☐ CN-RGH	Boeing 737-86N/W	36828/3850		
☐ CN-RGI	Boeing 737-86N/W	36831/3858		
☐ CN-RGJ	Boeing 737-8B6/W	33072/3949		
☐ CN-RGK	Boeing 737-8B6/W	33073/3970		
☐ CN-RGM	Boeing 737-8B6/W	33074/4365	ex N5515R	
☐ CN-RGN	Boeing 737-8B6/W	33075/4378		

☐ CN-RNJ	Boeing 737-8B6/W	28980/55		
☐ CN-RNK	Boeing 737-8B6/W	28981/60		
☐ CN-RNP	Boeing 737-8B6/W	28983/492	ex N1786B	
☐ CN-RNU	Boeing 737-8B6/W	28987/1095		
☐ CN-RNW	Boeing 737-8B6/W	33057/1347	ex N1787B	
☐ CN-RNZ	Boeing 737-8B6/W	33058/1432		
☐ CN-ROA	Boeing 737-8B6/W	33059/1457		
☐ CN-ROB	Boeing 737-8B6/W	33060/1646		
☐ CN-ROC	Boeing 737-8B6/W	33061/1661		
☐ CN-ROE	Boeing 737-8B6/W	33063/1913	ex N1781B	
☐ CN-ROH	Boeing 737-85P/W	33978/1957		
☐ CN-ROJ	Boeing 737-85P/W	33979/1963		
☐ CN-ROK	Boeing 737-8B6/W	33064/2180	ex N1786B	
☐ CN-ROL	Boeing 737-8B6/W	33065/2206	ex N1787B	
☐ CN-ROP	Boeing 737-8B6/W	33066/2506	ex N1782B	
☐ CN-ROR	Boeing 737-8B6/W	33067/2527	ex N1786B	
☐ CN-ROS	Boeing 737-8B6/W	37718/2773		
☐ CN-ROT	Boeing 737-8B6/W	33068/2883		
☐ CN-ROU	Boeing 737-8B6/W	33069/2911		
☐ CN-ROY	Boeing 737-8B6/W	33070/3233		
☐ CN-ROZ	Boeing 737-8B6/W	33071/3258	ex N1786B	
☐ CN-CDF	Beech 200 Super King Air	BB-577		Trainer
☐ CN-CDN	Beech 200 Super King Air	BB-713	ex N36741	Trainer
☐ CN-RGA	Boeing 747-428	25629/956	ex F-OGTG	
☐ CN-RGB	Boeing 787-8	43817/248		♦
☐ CN-RGC	Boeing 787-8	43818/285		♦
☐ CN-RGO	Embraer ERJ-190AR	19000680	ex PR-EIC	♦
☐ CN-RGP	Embraer ERJ-190AR	19000681	ex PR-EID	♦
☐ CN-RGQ	Embraer ERJ-190AR	19000682	ex PR-EIE	♦
☐ CN-RGR	Embraer ERJ-190AR	19000684	ex PR-EIO	♦
☐ CN-RNS	Boeing 767-36NER	30115/863		
☐ CN-RNT	Boeing 767-36NER	30843/867		
☐ CN-ROV	Boeing 767-3Q8ER	27686/793	ex N201LF	
☐ CN-ROW	Boeing 767-343ER	30008/743	ex N768MT	
☐ CN-ROX	Boeing 737-3M8F	24020/1614	ex N240MT	
☐ CS-TQW	Airbus A330-223	262	ex VN-A370	<HFY♦

CP- BOLIVIA (Republic of Bolivia)

AEROCON   *Aerocon (A4/AEK)*   **Trinidad (TDD)**

☐ CP-2176	Dornier 228-202K	8163	ex D-CIKI	
☐ CP-2393	LET L-410UVP-E3	872020	ex YV-869CP	
☐ CP-2477	Swearingen SA227DC Metro 23	DC-830B	ex N1119K	
☐ CP-2485	Swearingen SA227DC Metro 23	DC-817B	ex VH-UUD	
☐ CP-2527	Swearingen SA227DC Metro 23	DC-824B	ex N471Z	
☐ CP-2563	Swearingen SA227BC Metro III	BC-783B	ex N783ML	
☐ CP-2602	Swearingen SA227BC Metro III	BC-780B	ex N780A	
☐ CP-2725	Swearingen SA227AC Metro III	AC-664	ex N26974	[TDD]

Ops suspended Feb15; to restart

AEROESTE   *Este Bolivia (ROE)*   **Santa Cruz-El Trompillo (SRZ)**

☐ CP-2266	Rockwell 690B Turbo Commander	11395	ex N816PC	
☐ CP-2328	LET L-410UVP-E20	912536	ex S9-TAY	
☐ CP-2673	Beech 1900D	UE-344	ex YV-1371	

AMAZONAS TRANSPORTES AEREOS   Amazonas (Z8/AZN)   **La Paz (LPB)**

☐ CP-2715	Canadair CRJ-200LR	7218	ex N37218	
☐ CP-2733	Canadair CRJ-200LR	7217	ex N17217	
☐ CP-2742	Canadair CRJ-200LR	7195	ex N77195	
☐ CP-2762	Canadair CRJ-200LR	7173	ex N27173	
☐ CP-2856	Canadair CRJ-200LR	7226	ex N720AV	
☐ CP-2867	Canadair CRJ-200LR	7612	ex N465SM	
☐ CP-2908	Canadair CRJ-200LR	7247	ex N335MS	♦
☐ CP-2969	Canadair CRJ-200LR	7209	ex N571ML	♦
☐ CP-2459	Swearingen SA227DC Metro 23	DC-847B	ex N847LS	
☐ CP-2473	Swearingen SA227DC Metro 23	CC-842B	ex N510FS	

BOLIVIANA DE AVIACION   *(OB/BOV)*   **La Paz (LPB)**

☐ CP-2550	Boeing 737-33A	25118/2065	ex N401LF	
☐ CP-2551	Boeing 737-382	24449/1857	ex N449AN	
☐ CP-2552	Boeing 737-3M8	25041/2024	ex D-ADIJ	
☐ CP-2640	Boeing 737-382	24366/1699	ex N934PG	
☐ CP-2684	Boeing 737-33A	27455/2709	ex N455AN	
☐ CP-2716	Boeing 737-3Q8	26309/2674	ex PR-WJP	
☐ CP-2718	Boeing 737-33A	25057/2046	ex N706DB	

☐ CP-2815	Boeing 737-3U3	28738/2988	ex ZK-SJC	
☐ CP-2920	Boeing 737-37N	28548/2961	ex N285CL	♦
☐ CP-2921	Boeing 737-33R	28868/2881	ex N886CL	♦

☐ CP-2717	Boeing 737-53A	24788/1921	ex LV-BIX	
☐ CP-2880	Boeing 767-33AER	27376/560	ex PT-MSU	♦
☐ CP-2881	Boeing 767-33AER	27377/561	ex N368MS	♦
☐ CP-2923	Boeing 737-7Q8/W	30642/1097	ex VQ-BIB	♦
☐ CP-2924	Boeing 737-7Q8	30037/1449	ex N330AR	♦

ECO EXPRESS				**La Paz (LPB)**
☐ CP-2026	Convair 340-70	249	ex 53-7797	

ECOJET		**(ECO)**		**Cochabamba (CBB)**
☐ CP-2788	Avro 146-RJ85	E2278	ex D-AVRK	
☐ CP-2814	Avro 146-RJ85	E2317	ex D-AVRR	
☐ CP-2850	Avro 146-RJ85	E2277	ex D-AVRJ	
☐ CP-2889	Avro 146-RJ85	E2269	ex G-CGXS	♦

LINEAS AEREAS CANEDO		**(LCN)**		**Cochabamba (CBB)**
☐ CP-744	Aero Commander 680	680341-34	ex OB-M-573 Juan Salvador Gaviota	
☐ CP-896	Aero Commander 680	680-548-216	ex N316E Jose Fernando Gaviota	
☐ CP-973	Curtiss C-46C Commando	32941	ex N32227	
☐ CP-1080	Curtiss C-46A Commando	26771	ex TAM61	[LPB]
☐ CP-1093	Aero Commander 680F	680F-1035-51	ex N6197X	
☐ CP-1128	Douglas DC-3D	1998	ex N15M	on rebuild [CBB]
☐ CP-1960	Douglas DC-3C	18993	ex PT-KVN	[TDD]
☐ CP-2421	Douglas C-117D	12979/43365	ex N545CT	>RSU

TAB CARGO/TRANSPORTES AEREOS BOLIVIANOS		**Bol (2L/BOL)**		**La Paz (LPB)**
☐ CP-1376	Lockheed 382C-72D Hercules	4759	ex TAM-91	
☐ CP-2184	Lockheed 182A-2A Hercules	3228	ex TAM-69	
☐ CP-2555	Douglas DC-10-30F	46937/152	ex N833LA	wfs
☐ CP-2791	McDonnell-Douglas MD-10-30F	48312/442	ex N314FE	

TAM - TRANSPORTES AEREO MILITAR				**La Paz (LPB)**
☐ FAB-112	Boeing 737-2Q3	23117/1033	ex CC-CTD Gral Pablo Zarate Willka	
☐ FAB-113	Boeing 737-2Q3	23481/1241	ex CC-CTB	
☐ FAB-114	Boeing 737-230	22135/781	ex CC-CRQ Gral Div Aé Walter Arze Rojas	♦
☐ FAB-115	Boeing 737-322	24653/1810	ex N378UA	
☐ FAB-116	Boeing 737-230 (Nordam 3)	22122/721	ex CC-CTF	
☐ FAB-117	Boeing 737-230	22636/808	ex CC-CTH	♦
☐ FAB-118	Boeing 737-230	22139/791	ex CC-CTM	♦
☐ FAB-100	British Aerospace 146 Srs.200	E2080	ex N290UE	[CBB]
☐ FAB-101	British Aerospace 146 Srs.200	E2041	ex OY-RCZ	[LPB]
☐ FAB-102	British Aerospace 146 Srs.200	E2023	ex G-CLHD	[LPB]
☐ FAB-103	British Aerospace 146 Srs.200	E2040	ex EI-DJJ	[LPB]
☐ FAB-105	British Aerospace 146 Srs.200	E2022	ex N140CA	
☐ FAB-106	British Aerospace 146 Srs.200	E2048	ex N147FF	
☐ FAB-61	Lockheed 282-1B Hercules	3549	ex 58-0750	
☐ FAB-65	Lockheed 282-1B Hercules	3588	ex 59-1536	
☐ FAB-66	Lockheed 282-1B Hercules	3560	ex 59-1524	
☐ FAB-86	CASA C212-100	AV2-2-70	ex T.12C-44	
☐ FAB-87	CASA C212-100	AA1-13-110	ex T.12B-57	
☐ FAB-90	Fokker F.27M Troopship 400M	10578	ex TAM-90	
☐ FAB-97	CAIC MA60	0412	ex B-858L	
☐ FAB-111	Boeing 727-224 (FedEx 3)	22449/1756	ex CP-2499 Tupac Katari	
☐ TAM-85	CASA C212-100	A7-3-90	ex Nicaragua 221	

CS- PORTUGAL (Republic of Portugal)

AERO VIP		**Aerovip (WV/RVP)**		**Cascais-Tires**
☐ CS-AYT	Dornier 228-200	8084	ex VP-FBK	
☐ CS-TGG	Dornier 228-202K	8160	ex D-CORA	>AUR
☐ CS-TLJ	Short SD.3-60	SH3692	ex OY-MUD	wfs
☐ CS-	British Aerospace Jetstream 32EP	857	ex SE-LHG	♦

EUROATLANTIC AIRWAYS		**EuroAtlantic (YU/MMZ)**		**Lisbon (LIS)**
☐ CS-TFT	Boeing 767-3Y0ER	26208/505	ex S9-DBY	
☐ CS-TKS	Boeing 767-36NER	30841/841	ex EI-FKI	♦
☐ CS-TKT	Boeing 767-36NER	30853/837	ex EI-FKJ	o/o♦

☐ CS-TLO	Boeing 767-383ER	24318/257	ex N318SR	>CUB
☐ CS-TLZ	Boeing 767-375ERF	24086/248	ex N240LD	
☐ CS-TRN	Boeing 767-33AER	25535/491	ex N535AW	
☐ CS-TRW	Boeing 767-35DER	24865/322	ex SP-LPA	♦
☐ CS-TFM	Boeing 777-212ER	28513/144	ex 9V-SRA	
☐ CS-TQU	Boeing 737-8K2/W	30646/1122	ex PH-HZY	>CND

HELIPORTUGAL — Heliportugal (HPL) — Cascais-Tires

☐ CS-HFI	Aérospatiale AS350B2 Ecureuil	1216	ex PT-YJC
☐ CS-HFO	Aérospatiale AS350B2 Ecureuil	1824	ex F-GFDL
☐ CS-HFX	Aérospatiale AS350B2 Ecureuil	4081	ex F-WWXD
☐ CS-HGG	Aérospatiale AS350B2 Ecureuil	9085	ex F-WQEH
☐ CS-HGO	Aérospatiale AS350B3 Ecureuil	4521	
☐ CS-HHO	Aérospatiale AS350B3 Ecureuil	4888	
☐ CS-HFV	Aérospatiale SA365N1 Dauphin 2	6338	ex N661ME
☐ CS-HGA	Aérospatiale SA365N1 Dauphin 2	6336	ex JA9978
☐ CS-HGV	Aérospatiale SA365N3 Dauphin 2	6829	
☐ CS-HGW	Aérospatiale SA365N3 Dauphin 2	6830	
☐ CS-HGX	Aérospatiale SA365N1 Dauphin 2	6138	ex 5N-BIK
☐ CS-HHF	Aérospatiale AS365N1 Dauphin 2	6128	ex CS-HGN
☐ CS-HHI	Aérospatiale SA365N Dauphin 2	6089	ex F-OIBJ
☐ CS-HHR	Aérospatiale AS365N3 Dauphin 2	6841	ex F-OJTU
☐ CS-HFQ	Eurocopter EC130B4	4033	ex HB-ZEY
☐ CS-HGH	AgustaWestland AW139	31115	ex I-EASH
☐ CS-HGQ	AgustaWestland AW139	31057	ex N915DH
☐ CS-HGU	AgustaWestland AW139	31143	

HI FLY — (5K/HFY) — Lisbon (LIS)

☐ CS-TFZ	Airbus A330-243	1008	ex F-WWYD	
☐ CS-TMT	Airbus A330-322	096	ex F-WQSA	
☐ CS-TQP	Airbus A330-202	211	ex N272LF	
☐ CS-TQW	Airbus A330-223	262	ex VN-A370	>RAM
☐ CS-TRI	Airbus A330-322	127	ex D-AERQ	
☐ CS-	Airbus A330-243	437	ex F-WJKF	o/o♦
☐ CS-	Airbus A330-243	451	ex F-WJKG	o/o♦
☐ CS-TFW	Airbus A340-541	910	ex F-WJKH	<ARA
☐ CS-TFX	Airbus A340-541	912	ex F-WJKI	<ARA
☐ CS-TQM	Airbus A340-313X	117	ex A6-EYC	
☐ CS-TQY	Airbus A340-313X	190	ex A6-ERQ	
☐ CS-TQZ	Airbus A340-313X	202	ex A6-ERR	
☐ CS-TRJ	Airbus A321-231	1004	ex EI-FDP	opf Belgian AF

LEASE FLY — (LZF) — Cascais-Tires

☐ CS-DTO	ATR 42-320	095	ex F-GKYN	
☐ CS-DVF	ATR 72-202	350	ex SE-MGM	<Afrijet Business Service
☐ CS-DVL	ATR 42-320	333	ex F-HBCS	opf PGA♦
☐ CS-DVO	ATR 42-320	337	ex HR-AXA	♦

OMNI - AVIACAO E TECNOLOGIA — Omni (OAV) — Cascais-Tires

☐ CS-DTI	Beech 200 Super King Air	BB-681	ex F-GGPR		
☐ CS-HDS	Bell 222	47028	ex G-META		EMS
☐ CS-TFR	Learjet 45XP	45-382	ex N40073		
☐ CS-TFV	Canadair Challenger 300	20252	ex C-FWRE		
☐ CS-TLU	Airbus A319-133CJ	1256	ex F-GSVU		>WHT
☐ CS-TLW	Learjet 45XR	45-144	ex D-CEMM		
☐ CS-TMU	Beech 1900D	UE-335	ex N23269	Castor	opf LIS
☐ CS-TMV	Beech 1900D	UE-341	ex N23309	Esquilio	opf LIS

ORBEST — Orbest (4O/OBS) — Lisbon (LIS)

☐ CS-TRH	Airbus A330-343	833	ex EC-KCP	>EVE
☐ CS-TRL	Airbus A320-214	3758	ex EC-KYZ	
☐ CS-TRX	Airbus A330-223	802	ex EI-EZL	♦

PGA EXPRESS — (OC/OAC) — Lisbon (LIS)

☐ CS-TMU	Beech 1900D	UE-335	ex N23269	Castor	op by OAV
☐ CS-TMV	Beech 1900D	UE-341	ex N23309	Esquilio	op by OAV

PORTUGALIA AIRLINES		**Portugalia (NI/PGA)**			**Lisbon (LIS)**
☐ CS-TPG	Embraer ERJ-145EP	145014	ex PT-SYK	Melro	
☐ CS-TPH	Embraer ERJ-145EP	145017	ex PT-SYN	Pardal	
☐ CS-TPI	Embraer ERJ-145EP	145031	ex PT-SYZ	Cuco	
☐ CS-TPJ	Embraer ERJ-145EP	145036	ex PT-SZC	Chapim	
☐ CS-TPK	Embraer ERJ-145EP	145041	ex PT-SZG	Gaio	
☐ CS-TPL	Embraer ERJ-145EP	145051	ex PT-SZQ	Pisco	
☐ CS-TPM	Embraer ERJ-145EP	145095	ex PT-SBR	Rola	
☐ CS-TPN	Embraer ERJ-145EP	145099	ex PT-SBV	Brigao	
☐ CS-TPA	Fokker 100	11257	ex PH-LMF	Albatroz	
☐ CS-TPB	Fokker 100	11262	ex PH-EZE	Pelicano	
☐ CS-TPC	Fokker 100	11287	ex PH-LML	Flamingo	
☐ CS-TPD	Fokker 100	11317	ex EP-IDK	Condor	
☐ CS-TPE	Fokker 100	11342	ex PH-LNJ	Gaviao	
☐ CS-TPF	Fokker 100	11258	ex PH-EZD	Grifo	
☐ CS-DVL	ATR 42-320	333	ex F-HBCS		opb LZF♦
☐ CS-TRU	ATR 42-600	1011	ex F-WNUB		<WHT♦
☐ CS-TRV	ATR 42-600	1016	ex F-WWLZ		<WHT♦

SATA AIR ACORES		**SATA (SP/SAT)**			**Ponta Delgada (PDL)**
☐ CS-TRB	de Havilland DHC-8-202Q	476	ex C-FXBX	Graciosa	
☐ CS-TRC	de Havilland DHC-8-202Q	480	ex C-FXBZ	Faial	
☐ CS-TRD	de Havilland DHC-8-402Q	4291	ex C-GAUA	Manuel de Arriaga	
☐ CS-TRE	de Havilland DHC-8-402Q	4295	ex C-GBIY	Teofilo Braga	
☐ CS-TRF	de Havilland DHC-8-402Q	4297	ex C-GBJE	Flores	
☐ CS-TRG	de Havilland DHC-8-402Q	4298	ex C-GBJF		

SATA INTERNATIONAL		**Air Azores (S4/RZO)**			**Ponta Delgada (PDL)**
☐ CS-TGU	Airbus A310-304	571	ex F-GJKQ	Terceira	
☐ CS-TGV	Airbus A310-304	651	ex F-WQKR	Sao Miguel	
☐ CS-TKJ	Airbus A320-212	0795	ex C-FTDA	Pico	
☐ CS-TKK	Airbus A320-214	2390	ex F-WWII	Corvo	
☐ CS-TKM	Airbus A310-304	661	ex JY-AGL	Autonomia	[MZJ]
☐ CS-TKN	Airbus A310-325ET	624	ex TF-ELR	Macaronesia	
☐ CS-TKO	Airbus A320-214	3891	ex F-WWDC	Diaspora	
☐ CS-TKP	Airbus A320-214	2011	ex EC-INZ	S Jorge	

To be renamed Azores Airlines

TAP AIR PORTUGAL		**Air Portugal (TP/TAP)**			**Lisbon (LIS)**
Member of Star Alliance					
☐ CS-TTA	Airbus A319-111	0750	ex D-AVYO	Vieira da Silva	
☐ CS-TTB	Airbus A319-111	0755	ex D-AVYJ	Gago Coutinho	
☐ CS-TTC	Airbus A319-111	0763	ex D-AVYS	Fernando Pessoa	
☐ CS-TTD	Airbus A319-111	0790	ex D-AVYC	Amadeo de Souza-Cardoso	
☐ CS-TTE	Airbus A319-111	0821	ex D-AVYN	Francisco d'Ollanda	
☐ CS-TTF	Airbus A319-111	0837	ex D-AVYL	Calouste Gulbenkian	
☐ CS-TTG	Airbus A319-111	0906	ex D-AVYN	Humberto Delgado	
☐ CS-TTH	Airbus A319-111	0917	ex D-AVYJ	Antonio Sergio	
☐ CS-TTI	Airbus A319-111	0933	ex D-AVYP	Eça de Queirós	
☐ CS-TTJ	Airbus A319-111	0979	ex D-AVYM	Eusébio	
☐ CS-TTK	Airbus A319-111	1034	ex D-AVYL	Miguel Torga	
☐ CS-TTL	Airbus A319-111	1100	ex D-AVYX	Almeida Garrett	
☐ CS-TTM	Airbus A319-111	1106	ex D-AVWR	Alexandre Herculano	
☐ CS-TTN	Airbus A319-111	1120	ex D-AVYI	Camilo Castelo Branco	
☐ CS-TTO	Airbus A319-111	1127	ex D-AVYH	Antero de Quental	
☐ CS-TTP	Airbus A319-111	1165	ex D-AVWV	Josefa d'Obidos	
☐ CS-TTQ	Airbus A319-112	0629	ex SU-LBF	Agostinho da Silva	
☐ CS-TTR	Airbus A319-112	1756	ex C-GJWE	Soares dos Reis	
☐ CS-TTS	Airbus A319-112	1765	ex C-GJWF	Guilhermina Suggia	
☐ CS-TTU	Airbus A319-112	1668	ex VT-SCD	Sophia de Meillo Breyner	
☐ CS-TTV	Airbus A319-112	1718	ex VT-SCE	Aristides de Sousa Mendes	
☐ CS-TMW	Airbus A320-214	1667	ex F-WWII	Luisa Todi	
☐ CS-TNG	Airbus A320-214	0945	ex F-WWIX	Mouzinho da Silveira	
☐ CS-TNH	Airbus A320-214	0960	ex F-WWBH	Almada Negreiros	
☐ CS-TNI	Airbus A320-214	0982	ex F-WWDF	Aquilino Ribeiro	
☐ CS-TNJ	Airbus A320-214	1181	ex F-WWDS	Florbela Espanca	
☐ CS-TNK	Airbus A320-214	1206	ex F-WWIL	Teofilo Braga	
☐ CS-TNL	Airbus A320-214	1231	ex F-WWIJ	Vitorino Nemésio	
☐ CS-TNM	Airbus A320-214	1799	ex F-WWIF	Natalia Correia	
☐ CS-TNN	Airbus A320-214	1816	ex F-WWID	Gil Vicente	
☐ CS-TNP	Airbus A320-214	2178	ex 9H-AER	Alexandre O'Neill	
☐ CS-TNQ	Airbus A320-214	3769	ex F-WWDQ	Jose Regio	
☐ CS-TNR	Airbus A320-214	3883	ex F-WWIU	Luis De Freitas Branco	
☐ CS-TNS	Airbus A320-214	4021	ex F-WWDM	D Afonso Henriques	

☐ CS-TNT	Airbus A320-214	4095	ex F-WWDI	Rafael Bordalo Pinheiro	
☐ CS-TNU	Airbus A320-214	4106	ex F-WWDR	Columbano Bordalo Pinheiro	
☐ CS-TNV	Airbus A320-214	4145	ex F-WWIY	Grao Vasco	
☐ CS-TNW	Airbus A320-214	2792	ex 9K-CAC	José Saramago	
☐ CS-TNX	Airbus A320-214	2822	ex 9K-CAD	Malangatana	
☐ CS-TQD	Airbus A320-214	0870	ex HB-IJT	Eugénio de Andrade	
☐ CS-TOM	Airbus A330-202	899	ex F-WWKN	Vasco da Gama	
☐ CS-TON	Airbus A330-202	904	ex F-WWKT	Joao XXI	
☐ CS-TOO	Airbus A330-202	914	ex F-WWYL	Fernao de Magalhaes	
☐ CS-TOP	Airbus A330-202	934	ex F-WWKZ	Pedro Nunes	
☐ CS-TOQ	Airbus A330-203	477	ex PT-MVH	Pedro Teixeira	
☐ CS-TOR	Airbus A330-203	486	ex PT-MVK	Bartolomeu Dias	
☐ CS-TOE	Airbus A330-223	305	ex D-AXEL	Pedro Alvares Cabral	
☐ CS-TOF	Airbus A330-223	308	ex D-ARND	Infante D Henrique	
☐ CS-TOG	Airbus A330-223	312	ex D-ARNO	Bartolomeu de Gusmão	
☐ CS-TOH	Airbus A330-223	181	ex OE-LAO	Nuno Gonçalves	Star Alliance c/s
☐ CS-TOI	Airbus A330-223	195	ex OE-LAN	Damião de Góis	
☐ CS-TOJ	Airbus A330-223	223	ex OE-LAM	D João II 'O Príncipe Perfeito'	
☐ CS-TOK	Airbus A330-223	317	ex OE-LAP	Padre António Vieira	
☐ CS-TOL	Airbus A330-223	877	ex F-WWKF	Joao Goncalves Zarco	
☐ CS-TJE	Airbus A321-211	1307	ex D-AVZM	Pero Vaz de Caminha	
☐ CS-TJF	Airbus A321-211	1399	ex D-AVZI	Luis Vaz de Camões	
☐ CS-TJG	Airbus A321-211	1713	ex D-AVZS	Amalia Rodrigues	
☐ CS-TOA	Airbus A340-312	041	ex F-WWJB	Fernao Mendes Pinto	
☐ CS-TOB	Airbus A340-312	044	ex F-WWJN	D. Joao de Castro	
☐ CS-TOC	Airbus A340-312	079	ex F-WWJS	Wenceslau de Moraes	
☐ CS-TOD	Airbus A340-312	091	ex F-WWJA	D. Francisco de Almeida	

WHITE AIRWAYS   *Whitejet (WI/WHT)*   *Lisbon (LIS)*

☐ CS-FAF	Boeing 737-8FB/W	41159/4973		Mbasogo	opf CEL♦
☐ CS-TFU	Airbus A319CJ-115	2440	ex I-ECJA		
☐ CS-TLU	Airbus A319CJ-133	1256	ex F-GSVU		
☐ CS-TQJ	Airbus A319CJ-115	2675	ex VP-BEY		
☐ CS-TQV	Airbus A310-304	494	ex PR-WTA		
☐ CS-TQX	Boeing 777-2FBLR	40668/937	ex 3C-LLS	Djibloho	opf CEL
☐ CS-TRO	Airbus A320-214	0548	ex PR-WTB		
☐ CS-TRU	ATR 42-600	1011	ex F-WNUB		>PGA♦
☐ CS-TRV	ATR 42-600	1016	ex F-WWLZ		>PGA♦

CU- CUBA (Republic of Cuba)

AEROCARIBBEAN   *AeroCaribbean (CRN)*   *Havana (HAV)*

☐ CU-T1509	ATR 42-300	009	ex CU-T1296	
☐ CU-T1512	ATR 42-300	136	ex CU-T1298	
☐ CU-C1515	Ilyushin Il-18GrM	188010805	ex CU-C132	Frtr
☐ CU-T1537	Yakovlev Yak-40	9021360	ex CU-T1450	
☐ CU-T1538	Yakovlev Yak-40	9021260	ex CU-T1449	
☐ CU-T1540	Embraer EMB.110C Bandeirante	110091	ex CU-T1108	
☐ CU-T1541	Embraer EMB.110C Bandeirante	110116	ex CU-T1109	
☐ CU-T1544	ATR 72-212	472	ex F-WQNG	
☐ CU-T1545	ATR 72-212	473	ex F-WQNI	
☐ CU-T1547	ATR 72-212	485	ex F-WQNB	
☐ CU-T1548	ATR 72-212	453	ex F-WQNQ	
☐ CU-T1550	ATR 42-300	014	ex PP-PTE	
☐ CU-T1551	Embraer EMB.110P1 Bandeirante	110132	ex PT-GKV	
☐ CU-T1552	Embraer EMB.110P Bandeirante	110111	ex PT-GKM	

AEROGAVIOTA   *Gaviota (KG/GTV)*   *Havana (HAV)*

☐ CU-T1228	Antonov An-26	12604	
☐ CU-T1238	Antonov An-26	7803	
☐ CU-T1239	Antonov An-26	7907	
☐ CU-T1240	Antonov An-26	11210	
☐ CU-T1241	Antonov An-26	11301	
☐ CU-T1402	Antonov An-26B	12605	ex 14-02
☐ CU-T1403	Antonov An-26B	12905	ex 14-03
☐ CU-T1406	Antonov An-26B	13502	ex 14-06
☐ CU-T1408	Antonov An-26	6903	ex 14-28
☐ CU-T1417	Antonov An-26		
☐ CU-T1420	Antonov An-26	87036607	ex 14-20
☐ CU-T1421	Antonov An-26	6610	ex 14-21
☐ CU-T1423	Antonov An-26	3806	
☐ CU-T1425	Antonov An-26	6904	ex 14-25
☐ CU-T1426	Antonov An-26	5603	ex 14-26
☐ CU-T1428	Antonov An-26B	11303	ex 14-28
☐ CU-T1429	Antonov An-26	7006	ex 14-29

☐ CU-T1432	Antonov An-26	7306	ex 14-32	
☐ CU-T1433	Antonov An-26	7309	ex 14-33	
☐ CU-T1434	Antonov An-26	7701	ex 14-34	
☐ CU-T1435	Antonov An-26	7702	ex 14-35	

Status of this fleet is uncertain

☐ CU-H1423	Mil Mi-8T			
☐ CU-H1424	Mil Mi-8P			
☐ CU-H1427	Mil Mi-8PS			
☐ CU-H1431	Mil Mi-8P			
☐ CU-H1436	Mil Mi-8T			

☐ CU-T1240	ATR 42-500	617	ex F-WWLB	
☐ CU-H1429	Mil Mi-17 (Mi-8MTV-1)			
☐ CU-H1430	Mil Mi-17 (Mi-8MTV-1)			
☐ CU-T1454	ATR 42-500	616	ex F-WWLA	
☐ CU-T1455	ATR 42-500	618	ex F-WWLC	
☐ CU-T1456	ATR 42-500	619	ex F-WWLD	
☐ CU-T1463	Antonov An-24RV	47309405	ex CU-T1223	♦
☐ CU-T1464	Antonov An-24RV			♦

AEROTAXI   Havana (HAV)

☐ CU-T1195	LET L-410UVP-E			
☐ CU-T1196	LET L-410UVP-E			
☐ CU-T1542	Embraer EMB.110C Bandeirante	110136	ex PT-GKY	

CUBANA DE AVIACION   Cubana (CU/CUB)   Havana (HAV)

☐ CU-T1214	Antonov An-24RV	47309404	ex CU-T923	
☐ CU-T1237	Antonov An-24RV	37308909	ex RA-46641	status uncertain
☐ CU-T1244	Antonov An-24RV	57310301	ex JU-1011	status uncertain
☐ CU-T1260	Antonov An-24RV	57310307	ex CCCP-47307 La Pinta	status uncertain
☐ CU-T1706	Antonov An-24RV	67310701	ex RDPL-34151	

☐ CU-T1710	Antonov An-158	201-01		
☐ CU-T1711	Antonov An-158	201-02		
☐ CU-T1712	Antonov An-158	201-03	ex UR-EXC	
☐ CU-T1714	Antonov An-158	201-04		♦
☐ CU-T1715	Antonov An-158	201-05		♦

☐ CS-TLO	Boeing 767-383ER	24318/257	ex N318SR	<MMZ♦
☐ CU-T1228	Antonov An-26	12604	ex CU-T1401	
☐ CU-T1229	Antonov An-26	13501	ex CU-T1405	
☐ CU-C1700	Tupolev Tu-204-100SE	1450744664036	ex RA-64036	
☐ CU-C1703	Tupolev Tu-204-100SE	1450744764037		
☐ CU-T1230	Antonov An-26	14306	ex CU-T1407	
☐ CU-T1250	Ilyushin Il-96-300	74393202015		
☐ CU-T1251	Ilyushin Il-96-300	74393202016		
☐ CU-T1254	Ilyushin Il-96-300	74393202017		
☐ CU-T1282	Ilyushin Il-62M	2052456		wfs
☐ CU-T1701	Tupolev Tu-204-100E	1450744664035	) P/ls may be reversed	
☐ CU-T1702	Tupolev Tu-204-100E	1450743764042	)	
☐ CU-T1716	Antonov An-158	20506		♦
☐ CU-T1717	Ilyushin Il-96-300	74393201005	ex RA-96008	♦
☐ LY-COM	Airbus A320-212	0528	ex VP-BRB	<NVD
☐ LY-VEQ	Airbus A320-214	0709	ex B-2459	<NVD♦
☐ LY-VEV	Airbus A320-211	0211	ex G-YRGW	<NVD♦
☐ LY-VEW	Airbus A320-214	1005	ex N115MT	<NVD♦

CX-   URUGUAY (Republic of Uruguay)

AEROMAS   Aeromas Express (MSM)   Montevideo-Carrasco (MVD)

☐ CX-BDI	Piper PA-23-250 Aztec B	27-2265	ex N5217Y	
☐ CX-BRM	Beech A80 Queen Air	LD-200	ex N326JB	Excalibur Queenaire conv	[MVD]
☐ CX-MAS	Embraer EMB.110P1 Bandeirante	110393	ex N91DA	
☐ CX-MAX	Cessna 208A Caravan I	208A00042	ex ZP-TYT	

AIR CLASS/AERO VIP   Aola (VZ/QCL)   Montevideo-Carrasco (MVD)

☐ CX-CAR	Boeing 727-214F (FedEx 3)	21958/1533	ex N788AT	
☐ CX-CLA	Swearingen SA227AC Metro III	AC-736	ex N339LC	opf DHL
☐ CX-CLS	Swearingen SA227AC Metro III	AC-755B	ex N27465	
☐ CX-CSS	Swearingen SA227AC Metro III	AC-642	ex N821BC	
☐ N227DD	Boeing 727-227F (FedEx 3)	21996/1571	ex YV236T	♦

ALAS URUGUAY   (ALY)   Montevideo-Carrasco (MVD)

| ☐ CX-OAA | Boeing 737-36N/W | 28569/2996 | ex UR-GAN | [POA]♦ |
| ☐ CX-OAB | Boeing 737-33R/W | 28869/2887 | ex UR-GAQ | [POA]♦ |

BQB LINEAS AÉREAS		(5Q/BQB)		Montevideo-Carrasco (MVD)
☐ CX-JCL	ATR 72-212A	805	ex F-WWEQ	Jean Mermoz	[MVD]
☐ CX-JPL	ATR 72-212A	816	ex F-WWEF	Antoine de Saint-Exupery	[MVD]
☐ CX-POS	ATR 72-212A	636	ex EI-FCE	Obdulio Jacinto Varela	[MVD]
To restart ops May15				

SERVICIOS AEREOS DEL SUR/SAS TAXI AEREO			
☐ CX-STA	Beech C90 King Air	LJ-990	ex N1836H

C2- NAURU (Republic of Nauru)

NAURU AIRLINES		(ON/RON)		Brisbane, QLD (BNE)
☐ VH-INU	Boeing 737-3Y0	23684/1353	ex N323AW	[ASP]
☐ VH-NLK	Boeing 737-33A	23635/1436	ex N635AN	
☐ VH-ONU	Boeing 737-3U3	28732/2966	ex ZK-NGD	♦
☐ VH-PNI	Boeing 737-36N	28555/2846	ex N325MS	
☐ VH-VLI	Boeing 737-3H6SF	27125/2415	ex F-GIXR	
☐ VH-YNU	Boeing 737-319	25607/3126	ex ZK-NGH	♦

C3- ANDORRA (Principality of Andorra)

HELITRANS	Grau Roig Heliport

Leases Aérospatiale Ecureuil helicopters from Heliswiss Iberica when required

C5- GAMBIA (Republic of The Gambia)

AEOLUS AIR		Aeolus (AAZ)		
☐ C5-AAF	Airbus A320-231	0373	ex EY-624	>AFG♦
☐ C5-AAN	Boeing 737-522	26687/2402	ex 4L-AJE	>TRQ
☐ C5-AAO	Airbus A320-231	0368	ex N368MX	
☐ C5-AAR	Airbus A320-231	0424	ex F-WTDF	

C6- BAHAMAS (Commonwealth of the Bahamas)

ABACO AIR			Marsh Harbour (MHH)
☐ C6-BAA	Britten-Norman BN-2A-21 Islander	214	ex N214TL
☐ C6-BFR	Aero Commander 500	825	ex N846VK
☐ C6-BFS	Aero Commander 500	685	ex N6285B
☐ C6-BHH	Britten-Norman BN-2B-26 Islander	2021	ex N599MS
☐ C6-BHY	Aero Commander 500	834	ex N521SQ

ANGEL AIR			
☐ C6-DOC	Beech C99	U-231	ex C6-RRM

BAHAMASAIR		Bahamas (UP/BHS)		Nassau (NAS)
☐ C6-BFG	de Havilland DHC-8-311A	288	ex C-GESR	
☐ C6-BFH	de Havilland DHC-8-311A	291	ex C-GFOD	
☐ C6-BFJ	de Havilland DHC-8-311Q	323	ex N583DS	
☐ C6-BFO	de Havilland DHC-8-301	164	ex N802XV	
☐ C6-BFP	de Havilland DHC-8-311Q	309	ex N994DC	
☐ C6-BFC	Boeing 737-505	27631/2866	ex LN-BUG	
☐ C6-BFD	Boeing 737-5H6	26448/2484	ex LV-BAX	
☐ C6-BFE	Boeing 737-528	26450/2503	ex LV-BAR	
☐ C6-	Boeing 737-505	27627/2800	ex N653AC	o/o♦

CAT ISLAND AIR		(CIS)		Nassau (NAS)
☐ C6-CAH	Embraer EMB.110P1 Bandeirante	110249	ex C6-BHA	[NAS]
☐ C6-CAP	Embraer EMB.110P1 Bandeirante	110304	ex J8-VAZ	
☐ C6-CAT	Piper PA-23-250 Aztec E	27-7554083	ex N54779	

CHEROKEE AIR			Marsh Harbour (MHH)
☐ C6-BGS	Piper PA-23-250 Aztec F	27-7854067	ex N17MR
☐ C6-SBH	Cessna 208B Caravan I	208B0822	ex N822SA

133

LEAIR CHARTER SERVICES				Nassau (NAS)
☐ C6-CAB	Embraer EMB.110P1 Bandeirante	110198	ex G-ONEW	
☐ C6-LEE	Piper PA-23-250 Aztec F	27-7654049	ex N62568	
☐ C6-PDX	Embraer EMB.110P1 Bandeirante	110299		[OPF]

PINEAPPLE AIR		Pineapple (PNP)		Nassau (NAS)
☐ C6-HAN	Beech C99	U-165	ex N42517	
☐ C6-KMC	Embraer EMB.110P1 Bandeirante	110259	ex C-FYRH	
☐ C6-MIC	Embraer EMB.110P1 Bandeirante	110407	ex C-FZSN	
☐ N157PA	Beech 1900C	UB-56	ex N505RH	
☐ N381CR	Beech 1900C	UB-69	ex N331CR	
☐ N800MX	Beech 1900C	UB-48		

REGIONAL AIR		Regional Bahamas (RGB)		Nassau (NAS)
☐ C6-RAS	Cessna 208B Caravan I	208B0693	ex N90HE	

SALAMIS AVIATION				Nassau (NAS)
☐ N75X	Swearingen SA227TT Merlin IIIC	TT-421	ex N90BJ	
☐ N81WS	Swearingen SA227TT Merlin IIIC	TT-480	ex N500DB	

SEAIR AIRWAYS		Seair (DYL)		Nassau (NAS)
☐ C6-BGT	Piper PA-23-250 Aztec E	27-7305051	ex N89BB	
☐ C6-BUS	Britten-Norman BN-2A-26 Islander	2040	ex N23US	

SKY BAHAMAS		Sky Bahamas (Q7/SBM)		Nassau (NAS)
☐ C6-SBD	SAAB SF.340A	340A-021	ex N776SB	wfs
☐ C6-SBF	Beech 1900D	UE-2	ex N2YV	
☐ C6-SBG	SAAB SF.340A	340A-110	ex N110XJ	
☐ C6-SBK	SAAB SF.340B	340B-196	ex N196CJ	
☐ C6-SBL	SAAB SF.340A	340A-131	ex LV-BTP	♦

SOUTHERN AIR CHARTERS		(PL)		Nassau (NAS)
☐ C6-BGY	Piper PA-23-250 Aztec E	27-7554044	ex N166PG	
☐ N376SA	Beech 1900C	UB-72	ex N504RH	
☐ N378SA	Beech 1900C	UB-31	ex N196GA	

VISION AIR				Freeport (FPO)
☐ N800MX	Beech 1900C	UB-48	ex N896FM	

WESTERN AIR		Western Bahamas (WST)		Freeport (FPO)
☐ C6-HBW	SAAB SF.340A	340A-067	ex N712MG	
☐ C6-JAY	SAAB SF.340A	340A-120	ex N418MW	
☐ C6-LSR	SAAB SF.340A	340A-122	ex C6-CAA	
☐ C6-RMW	SAAB SF.340A	340A-121	ex N121CQ	
☐ C6-VIP	SAAB SF.340A	340A-098	ex N98XJ	♦
☐ C6-ASD	Swearingen SA227AC Metro III	AC-749B	ex 86-0457	
☐ C6-JER	Swearingen SA227AC Metro III	AC-588		
☐ C6-SAR	Swearingen SA227AC Metro III	AC-598		
☐ C6-WAL	Piper PA-31-350 Navajo Chieftain	31-7652129	ex N70FS	

C9- MOZAMBIQUE (Republic of Mozambique)

KAYA AIRLINES		Kamoz (IK/KYY)		Maputo/Beira (MPM/BEW)
☐ C9-AUQ	Embraer EMB.120ER Brasilia	120139	ex 3D-BCI	
☐ C9-AUU	Embraer EMB.120RT Brasilia	120200	ex ZS-OEN	wfs
☐ 3D-NVA	LET L-410UVP-E3	882035	ex 3D-ZZM	
☐ 3D-NVC	LET L-410UVP	831033	ex 5Y-BLC Sluffy	

LAM - LINHAS AEREAS DE MOCAMBIQUE		Mozambique (TM/LAM)		Maputo (MPM)
☐ C9-AUL	de Havilland DHC-8-402Q	4019	ex LN-RDC	>MXE
☐ C9-AUM	de Havilland DHC-8-402Q	4020	ex LN-RDE	>MXE
☐ C9-BAP	Boeing 737-53S	29074/3086	ex N614SC Zalala	
☐ C9-BAQ	Boeing 737-752/W	33792/1571	ex N855AM Poelela	
☐ C9-EMA	Embraer ERJ-190AR	19000301	ex PT-TZP Cobue	
☐ C9-EMB	Embraer ERJ-190AR	19000309	ex PT-TZX Chiloane	
☐ ZS-VDP	Boeing 737-31L	27346/2636	ex N346TP	<BRH♦

MAKOND AIR-LINK

☐ C9-HAV	Bell 206L-3 Long Ranger	51213	ex ZS-HGA	♦
☐ C9-HMK	Bell 206L-3 Long Ranger	45502	ex ZS-RSH	♦

MOCAMBIQUE EXPRESSO — Mozambique Express (MXE) — Maputo/Beira (MPM/BEW)

☐ C9-AUL	de Havilland DHC-8-402Q	4019	ex LN-RDC	<LAM
☐ C9-AUM	de Havilland DHC-8-402Q	4020	ex LN-RDE	<LAM
☐ C9-AUY	de Havilland DHC-8-402Q	4021	ex G-ECOW	
☐ C9-MEH	Embraer ERJ-145MP	145294	ex F-GUPT	
☐ C9-MEI	Embraer EMB.120RT Brasilia	120228	ex ZS-AAB	
☐ C9-MEJ	Embraer EMB.120ER Brasilia	120252	ex ZS-AAG	opb Sahara African Avn♦
☐ C9-MEX	Embraer ERJ-145MP	145266	ex F-GUAM	

STA - SOCIEDADE DE TRANSPORTS AÉREOS — Maputo (MPM)

Ops services with Islanders leased from sister company TTA and other aircraft as required

TTA – SOCIEDADE DE TRANSPORTE E TRABALHO AEREO
Kanimanbo (2Z/TTA) — Maputo (MPM)

☐ C9-AMH	Piper PA-32-300 Cherokee Six C	32-40682	ex ZS-IGO	[MPM]
☐ C9-AOV	Britten-Norman BN-2A-3 Islander	624	ex G-AYJF	
☐ C9-APD	Britten-Norman BN-2A-9 Islander	683	ex G-AZXO	

D-   GERMANY (Federal Republic of Germany)

ADVANCED AVIATION — Bad Saulgau/Bangui (-/BGF)

☐ D-CAAL	Dornier 228-202K	8152	ex CS-TGH	>SCD Avn
☐ D-FLIP	Cessna 208B Caravan I	208B0331	ex N3331	based Memmingen

AEROLINE — Sylt-Air (7E/AWU) — Westerland (GWT)

☐ D-GFPG	Partenavia P.68B	170		
☐ D-IOLB	Cessna 404 Titan II	404-0691	ex SE-IVG	

AEROLOGIC — German Cargo (3S/BOX) — Leipzig-Halle (LEJ)

☐ D-AALA	Boeing 777-FZN	36001/780		
☐ D-AALB	Boeing 777-FZN	36002/799	ex N5017Q	
☐ D-AALC	Boeing 777-FZN	36003/836		
☐ D-AALD	Boeing 777-FZN	36004/838		
☐ D-AALE	Boeing 777-FZN	36198/872		
☐ D-AALF	Boeing 777-FZN	36201/881		
☐ D-AALG	Boeing 777-FZN	36199/894		
☐ D-AALH	Boeing 777-FZN	36200/904		

AIR HAMBURG — Air Hamburg (AHO) — Hamburg (HAM)

☐ D-AFUN	Embraer Legacy 650	14501168	ex N650EE	♦
☐ D-AJET	Embraer Legacy 650	14501166	ex PT-TFK	
☐ D-AVIB	Embraer Legacy 600	14501109	ex PT-TKG	
☐ D-CAHO	Cessna 560XLS+ Citation	560-6165		♦
☐ D-CGAA	Cessna 560XLS+ Citation	560-6173		
☐ D-IAEB	Britten-Norman BN-2A-6 Islander	218	ex OH-BNB	
☐ D-ISKY	Beech B200 Super King Air	BB-2014	ex N6394Y	

AIR SERVICE BERLIN — Berlin-Treptow SPB

☐ D-EGUF	Cessna U206G Stationair	U20603596	ex SE-GUF	Robertson STOL	FP
☐ D-FWJC	Antonov An-2T	1G8650	ex DDR-WJC		based Gransee
☐ D-CXXX	Douglas DC-3C	26735/15290	ex G-AMRA		

AIR SERVICE WILDGRUBER — Friedrichshafen-Loewental (FDH)

☐ D-FOXY	Cessnn 208 Caravan I	20800303	ex I-SEAA	FP
☐ D-IEXE	Beech 99	U-46	ex (N99LM)	

AIRBERLIN — AirBerlin (AB/BER) — Berlin-Tegel (TXL)

Member of oneWorld

☐ D-ABDB	Airbus A320-214	2619	ex SP-IAH	
☐ D-ABDO	Airbus A320-214	3055	ex HB-IOW	
☐ D-ABDQ	Airbus A320-214	3121	ex F-WWBD	

☐	D-ABDU	Airbus A320-214	3516	ex D-AVVC	
☐	D-ABDW	Airbus A320-214	3945	ex F-WWDX	
☐	D-ABDX	Airbus A320-214	3995	ex F-WWDG	>VLG
☐	D-ABDY	Airbus A320-214	4013	ex F-WWIG	
☐	D-ABFA	Airbus A320-214	4101	ex D-AVVK	
☐	D-ABFB	Airbus A320-214	4128	ex F-WWIQ	>VLG
☐	D-ABFC	Airbus A320-214	4161	ex D-AVVP	
☐	D-ABFE	Airbus A320-214	4269	ex D-AXAE	
☐	D-ABFF	Airbus A320-214	4329	ex D-AXAP	
☐	D-ABFG	Airbus A320-214	4291	ex D-AXAG	
☐	D-ABFK	Airbus A320-214	4433	ex D-AVVQ	
☐	D-ABFN	Airbus A320-214	4510	ex F-WWBK	
☐	D-ABFO	Airbus A320-214	4565	ex D-AVVA	
☐	D-ABFP	Airbus A320-214	4606	ex D-AXAS	
☐	D-ABFU	Airbus A320-214	4743	ex D-AVVJ	
☐	D-ABFZ	Airbus A320-214	4988	ex D-AVVT	
☐	D-ABNA	Airbus A320-214	5191	ex D-AVVC	
☐	D-ABNE	Airbus A320-214	2003	ex G-KKAZ	
☐	D-ABNF	Airbus A320-214	1961	ex G-SUEW	
☐	D-ABNH	Airbus A320-214	1775	ex OE-IDF	♦
☐	D-ABNI	Airbus A320-214	1717	ex OE-IDE	♦
☐	D-ABNJ	Airbus A320-214/S	5522	ex OE-LER	♦
☐	D-ABNK	Airbus A320-214	1769	ex F-WTDO	♦
☐	D-ABNL	Airbus A320-214	1852	ex F-WTDP	♦
☐	D-ABNN	Airbus A320-214	1889	ex OY-VKM	♦
☐	D-ABZA	Airbus A320-216	3532	ex EI-DST	♦
☐	D-ABZB	Airbus A320-216	3515	ex EI-DSS	♦
☐	D-ABZC	Airbus A320-216	3502	ex EI-DSR	♦
☐	D-ABZD	Airbus A320-216	3412	ex EI-DSN	o/o♦
☐	D-ABZE	Airbus A320-216	3464	ex EI-DSO	o/o♦
☐	D-ABZF	Airbus A320-216	3482	ex EI-DSP	o/o♦
☐	D-ABZG	Airbus A320-216	3362	ex EI-DSM	o/o♦
☐	D-ABZH	Airbus A320-216	3343	ex EI-DSL	o/o♦
☐	D-ABZI	Airbus A320-216	3328	ex EI-DSK	♦
☐	D-ABZJ	Airbus A320-216	3295	ex EI-DSJ	o/o♦
☐	D-ABZK	Airbus A320-216	3213	ex EI-DSI	o/o♦
☐	D-ABZL	Airbus A320-216	3178	ex EI-DSH	♦
☐	D-ABZM	Airbus A320-216	3115	ex EI-DSG	o/o♦
☐	D-ABZN	Airbus A320-216	3080	ex EI-DSF	o/o♦
☐	D-	Airbus A320-214/S	6877	ex	o/o♦
☐	D-	Airbus A320-214	6902	ex	o/o♦
☐	D-ABCA	Airbus A321-211	3708	ex D-AVZO	
☐	D-ABCB	Airbus A321-211	3749	ex D-AVZC	
☐	D-ABCC	Airbus A321-211	4334	ex D-AZAK	
☐	D-ABCF	Airbus A321-211	1966	ex N221LF	
☐	D-ABCG	Airbus A321-211	1988	ex N341LF	
☐	D-ABCH	Airbus A321-211	4728	ex D-AVZF	
☐	D-ABCI	Airbus A321-211	5038	ex D-AZAO	
☐	D-ABCJ	Airbus A321-211	5126	ex D-AVZC	
☐	D-ABCK	Airbus A321-211	5133	ex D-AVZD	
☐	D-ABCL	Airbus A321-211/S	6168	ex D-AVXU	♦
☐	D-ABCM	Airbus A321-211/S	6432	ex D-AZAU	♦
☐	D-ABCN	Airbus A321-211/S	6454	ex D-AVZE	♦
☐	D-ABCO	Airbus A321-211/S	6501	ex D-AVZV	♦
☐	D-ABCP	Airbus A321-211/S	6629	ex	o/o♦
☐	D-ABCQ	Airbus A321-211/S	6639	ex D-AVXY	o/o♦
☐	D-ABCR	Airbus A321-211/S	6719	ex	o/o♦
☐	D-ALSA	Airbus A321-211	1629	ex D-AVZC	
☐	D-ALSB	Airbus A321-211	1994	ex D-AVZR	
☐	D-ALSC	Airbus A321-211	2005	ex D-AVXI	
☐	D-ABXA	Airbus A330-223	288	ex HB-IQH	
☐	D-ABXB	Airbus A330-223	322	ex HB-IQQ	
☐	D-ABXC	Airbus A330-223	665	ex I-EEZJ	
☐	D-ABXD	Airbus A330-223	822	ex EI-EZJ	
☐	D-ALPA	Airbus A330-223	403	ex F-WWKO	
☐	D-ALPB	Airbus A330-223	432	ex F-WWYG	
☐	D-ALPC	Airbus A330-223	444	ex F-WWKD	
☐	D-ALPD	Airbus A330-223	454	ex F-WWKG	
☐	D-ALPE	Airbus A330-223	469	ex F-WWKO	
☐	D-ALPF	Airbus A330-223	476	ex F-WWKT	
☐	D-ALPG	Airbus A330-223	493	ex F-WWKI	
☐	D-ALPH	Airbus A330-223	739	ex F-WWYD	
☐	D-ALPI	Airbus A330-223	828	ex F-WWKI	
☐	D-ALPJ	Airbus A330-223	911	ex F-WWYA	
☐	D-ABAF	Boeing 737-86J/W	30878/844	ex N1787B	[NWI]
☐	D-ABAG	Boeing 737-86J/W	30879/871	ex N1786B	
☐	D-ABBD	Boeing 737-86J/W	30880/1043	ex TC-IZF	
☐	D-ABBK	Boeing 737-8BK/W	33013/1317		
☐	D-ABKA	Boeing 737-82R/W	29329/224	ex TC-APG	
☐	D-ABKD	Boeing 737-86J/W	37742/2796		

☐ D-ABKG	Boeing 737-86J/W	37746/3109	ex N1786B	>PGT
☐ D-ABKJ	Boeing 737-86J/W	37749/3176	ex N1786B	
☐ D-ABKK	Boeing 737-86J/W	37753/3261	ex N1787B	
☐ D-ABKM	Boeing 737-86J/W	37755/3349	ex N1769B	
☐ D-ABKN	Boeing 737-86J/W	37756/3371		
☐ D-ABKP	Boeing 737-86J/W	37758/3439	ex N1787B	
☐ D-ABKQ	Boeing 737-86J/W	37760/3545		
☐ D-ABKS	Boeing 737-86J/W	36880/3685		
☐ D-ABKT	Boeing 737-86J/W	36881/3671		
☐ D-ABMB	Boeing 737-86J/W	36121/3853		
☐ D-ABMD	Boeing 737-86J/W	37761/3887		
☐ D-ABME	Boeing 737-86J/W	37766/4049		
☐ D-ABMF	Boeing 737-86J/W	37767/4065	ex N60436	
☐ D-ABMI	Boeing 737-86J/W	37770/4184		
☐ D-ABMK	Boeing 737-86J/W	37772/4264		
☐ D-ABML	Boeing 737-86J/W	37773/4281		
☐ D-ABMP	Boeing 737-86J/W	37779/4472		
☐ D-ABMQ	Boeing 737-86J/W	37780/4500	ex N1786B	
☐ D-ABMR	Boeing 737-86J/W	37781/4535	ex N5515X	
☐ D-ABMS	Boeing 737-86J/W	37782/4564		
☐ D-ABMU	Boeing 737-86J/W	39384/4663		
☐ D-ABMV	Boeing 737-86J/W	37785/4698		
☐ D-ABMY	Boeing 737-86J/W	37750/5314		♦
☐ D-ABMZ	Boeing 737-86J/W	36875/5353		♦
☐ D-ABQA	de Havilland DHC-8-402Q	4223	ex C-FTID	opb LGW
☐ D-ABQB	de Havilland DHC-8-402Q	4226	ex C-FTUM	opb LGW
☐ D-ABQC	de Havilland DHC-8-402Q	4231	ex C-FUCI	opb LGW
☐ D-ABQD	de Havilland DHC-8-402Q	4234	ex C-FUCS	opb LGW
☐ D-ABQE	de Havilland DHC-8-402Q	4239	ex C-FURQ	opb LGW
☐ D-ABQF	de Havilland DHC-8-402Q	4245	ex C-FVGV	opb LGW
☐ D-ABQG	de Havilland DHC-8-402Q	4250	ex C-FVUN	opb LGW
☐ D-ABQH	de Havilland DHC-8-402Q	4256	ex C-FWGO	opb LGW
☐ D-ABQI	de Havilland DHC-8-402Q	4264	ex C-FXIW	opb LGW
☐ D-ABQJ	de Havilland DHC-8-402Q	4274	ex C-FYGN	opb LGW
☐ D-ABQK	de Havilland DHC-8-402Q	4265	ex HB-JIK	opb LGW♦
☐ D-ABQL	de Havilland DHC-8-402Q	4198	ex HB-JIJ	opb LGW♦
☐ D-ABQM	de Havilland DHC-8-402Q	4119	ex N419KA	opb LGW♦
☐ D-ABQN	de Havilland DHC-8-402Q	4124	ex C-FEUF	opb LGW♦
☐ D-ABQO	de Havilland DHC-8-402Q	4129	ex N129KA	opb LGW♦
☐ D-ABQP	de Havilland DHC-8-402Q	4137	ex C-FDLO	opb LGW♦
☐ D-ABQQ	de Havilland DHC-8-402Q	4198	ex HB-JGA	opb LGW♦
☐ D-ABGQ	Airbus A319-112	3700	ex D-AVWM	>VLG
☐ D-ABGR	Airbus A319-112	3704	ex D-AVWJ	>VLG
☐ D-ABGS	Airbus A319-112	3865	ex SP-IBA	
☐ D-ABLC	Boeing 737-76J/W	36116/2730		
☐ D-ABLD	Boeing 737-76J/W	36117/2776	ex N1787B	
☐ D-AGEC	Boeing 737-76J/W	36118/2832	ex (D-ABLE)	
☐ D-ASTX	Airbus A319-112	3202	ex HB-IOY	<GMI

ARCUS AIR LOGISTIC		**Arcus Air (AZE)**		**Mannheim (MHG)**
☐ D-CAAL	Dornier 228-212	8155	ex D-CAAZ	♦
☐ D-CAAM	Dornier 228-212	8205	ex D-CBDH	
☐ D-CAAR	Dornier 228-212	8211	ex 57+02	

AVANTI AIR		**Avanti Air (ATV)**		**Frankfurt (FRA)**
☐ D-ANFC	ATR 72-202	237	ex F-WWEG	wfs
☐ D-ANFE	ATR 72-202	272	ex SP-LFC	>BPA
☐ D-AOLG	Fokker 100	11452	ex PH-RRN	♦

BIN AIR		**Binair (BID)**		**Munich (MUC)**
☐ D-CAVA	Swearingen SA227AC Metro III	AC-758B	ex F-GPSN	
☐ D-CBIN	Swearingen SA227AT Merlin IVC	AT-440B	ex I-FSAD	
☐ D-CCCC	Swearingen SA227AT Merlin IVC	AT-511	ex N600N	
☐ D-CKPP	Swearingen SA227DC Metro 23	DC-805B	ex N715MQ	
☐ D-CNAF	Swearingen SA227AC Metro III	AC-505B	ex TF-BBG	
☐ D-CNAY	Swearingen SA227AT Merlin IVC	AT-493	ex PH-RAX	
☐ D-CPSW	Swearingen SA227AC Metro III	AC-757B	ex F-GJPN	
☐ D-CSAL	Swearingen SA227AC Metro III	AC-601	ex I-FSAH	

BUSINESSWINGS/AEROTRANS FLUGCHARTER		**(JMP)**		**Kassel-Calden (KSF)**
☐ D-CULT	Dornier 228-212	8192	ex LN-BER	
☐ D-FALK	Cessna 208 Caravan I	20800023	ex N9354F	
☐ D-FAST	Cessna 208 Caravan I	20800207	ex N208MC	
☐ D-IROL	Dornier 228-100	7003	ex SE-KHL	
☐ D-IVER	de Havilland DHC-6 Twin Otter 300	411	ex SE-IYP	

CONDOR		Condor (DE/CFG)				Frankfurt (FRA)
□ D-AICA	Airbus A320-212	0774	ex F-WWDN	Hans		retro 1960s Condor c/s
□ D-AICC	Airbus A320-212	0809	ex F-WWIE			
□ D-AICD	Airbus A320-212	0884	ex F-WWDE			
□ D-AICE	Airbus A320-212	0894	ex F-WWDI			
□ D-AICF	Airbus A320-212	0905	ex F-WWDP			
□ D-AICG	Airbus A320-212	0957	ex F-WWBE			
□ D-AICH	Airbus A320-212	0971	ex F-WWBY			
□ D-AICI	Airbus A320-212	1381	ex F-WWIP			
□ D-AICK	Airbus A320-212	1416	ex F-WWDZ			
□ D-AICL	Airbus A320-212	1437	ex F-WWBG			
□ LY-VEL	Airbus A320-232	1998	ex EI-EUB			<NVD♦
□ D-AIAA	Airbus A321-211	1607	ex D-ALSD			
□ D-AIAC	Airbus A321-211/S	5969	ex D-AZAN			
□ D-AIAD	Airbus A321-211/S	6053	ex D-AVZR			
□ D-AIAE	Airbus A321-211/S	6376	ex D-AVXS			♦
□ D-AIAF	Airbus A321-211/S	6459	ex D-AVZF			♦
□ D-AIAG	Airbus A321-211/S	6590	ex D-AVXJ			♦
□ D-AIAH	Airbus A321-211/S	6615	ex D-AVXP			o/o♦
□ D-ABOA	Boeing 757-330/W	29016/804	ex N757X			
□ D-ABOB	Boeing 757-330/W	29017/810	ex N6067B			
□ D-ABOC	Boeing 757-330/W	29015/818	ex N6069B			
□ D-ABOE	Boeing 757-330/W	29012/839	ex N1012N			
□ D-ABOF	Boeing 757-330/W	29013/846				
□ D-ABOG	Boeing 757-330/W	29014/849				
□ D-ABOH	Boeing 757-330/W	30030/855	ex N1787B			
□ D-ABOI	Boeing 757-330/W	29018/909	ex N1002R			
□ D-ABOJ	Boeing 757-330/W	29019/915				
□ D-ABOK	Boeing 757-330/W	29020/918	ex N1795B			
□ D-ABOL	Boeing 757-330/W	29021/923				
□ D-ABOM	Boeing 757-330/W	29022/926				
□ D-ABON	Boeing 757-330/W	29023/929	ex N1003M	Wir lieben fliegen c/s		
□ D-ABUA	Boeing 767-330ER/W	26991/455				
□ D-ABUB	Boeing 767-330ER/W	26987/466				
□ D-ABUC	Boeing 767-330ER/W	26992/470				
□ D-ABUD	Boeing 767-330ER/W	26983/471				
□ D-ABUE	Boeing 767-330ER/W	26984/518	ex N1788B			
□ D-ABUF	Boeing 767-330ER/W	26985/537				
□ D-ABUH	Boeing 767-330ER/W	26986/553	ex N6046P			
□ D-ABUI	Boeing 767-330ER/W	26988/562				
□ D-ABUK	Boeing 767-343ER/W	30009/746	ex EI-CRM			
□ D-ABUL	Boeing 767-31BER/W	26259/534	ex EI-CRD			
□ D-ABUM	Boeing 767-31BER/W	25170/542	ex EI-CRF	retro 1980s Condor c/s		
□ D-ABUS	Boeing 767-38EER/W	30840/829	ex OO-JAP			♦
□ D-ABUZ	Boeing 767-330ER/W	25209/382	ex (N634TW)			
□ D-ASXD	Boeing 737-8AS/W	33562/1466	ex EI-DCD			<SXD♦

EAT LEIPZIG		EuroTrans (QY/BCS)			Leipzig-Halle (LEJ)
□ D-AEAB	Airbus A300B4-622RF	837	ex A6-HAZ		
□ D-AEAC	Airbus A300B4-622RF	602	ex N4602	DHL c/s	
□ D-AEAD	Airbus A300B4-622RF	617	ex N2617	DHL c/s	
□ D-AEAE	Airbus A300B4-622RF	753	ex N4753		
□ D-AEAF	Airbus A300B4-622RF	836	ex A6-SUL	DHL c/s	
□ D-AEAG	Airbus A300B4-622RF	621	ex N2621		
□ D-AEAH	Airbus A300B4-622RF	783	ex N5783	DHL c/s	
□ D-AEAI	Airbus A300B4-622RF	637	ex N3740	DHL c/s	
□ D-AEAJ	Airbus A300B4-622RF	641	ex N5641	DHL c/s	
□ D-AEAK	Airbus A300B4-622RF	670	ex N2670		
□ D-AEAL	Airbus A300B4-622RF	679	ex N4679		
□ D-AEAM	Airbus A300B4-622RF	797	ex A6-NIN	DHL c/s	
□ D-AEAN	Airbus A300B4-622RF	703	ex N4703		
□ D-AEAO	Airbus A300B4-622RF	711	ex N7151		
□ D-AEAP	Airbus A300B4-622RF	724	ex N1724		
□ D-AEAQ	Airbus A300B4-622RF	729	ex N3729		
□ D-AEAR	Airbus A300B4-622RF	730	ex N4730	DHL c/s	
□ D-AEAS	Airbus A300B4-622RF	737	ex N4737		
□ D-AEAT	Airbus A300B4-622RF	740	ex N3637		
□ D-AZMO	Airbus A300B4-622RF	872	ex N140MN		♦
□ EI-EXR	Airbus A300B4-622RF	677	ex (TC-ACM)		♦
□ D-ALEA	Boeing 757-236SF	22172/9	ex OO-DLN		
□ D-ALEB	Boeing 757-236SF	22173/10	ex OO-DPF		
□ D-ALEC	Boeing 757-236SF	22175/13	ex OO-DLQ		
□ D-ALED	Boeing 757-236SF	22179/24	ex OO-DLP		
□ D-ALEE	Boeing 757-236SF	22183/32	ex OO-DPB		
□ D-ALEF	Boeing 757-236SF	22189/58	ex OO-DPM		

□ D-ALEG	Boeing 757-236SF	23398/77	ex OO-DPO	
□ D-ALEH	Boeing 757-236SF	23492/89	ex OO-DPK	
□ D-ALEI	Boeing 757-236SF	23493/90	ex OO-DPJ	
□ D-ALEJ	Boeing 757-23APF	24971/340	ex OO-DLJ	
□ D-ALEK	Boeing 757-236SF	23533/93	ex OO-DPN	
□ VH-TCA	Boeing 757-236PCF	25620/449	exg-CSVS	>YMN

EUROWINGS
Eurowings (EW/EWG) — Dortmund/Nuremberg (DTM/NUE)

□ D-AIZQ	Airbus A320-214/S	5497	ex D-AXAE	♦
□ D-AIZR	Airbus A320-214/S	5525	ex D-AXAP	♦
□ D-AIZS	Airbus A320-214/S	5557	ex D-AXAZ	♦
□ D-AIZT	Airbus A320-214/S	5601	ex D-AUBL	♦
□ D-AIZU	Airbus A320-214/S	5635	ex D-AUBR	♦
□ D-AIZV	Airbus A320-214/S	5658	ex D-AUBY	o/o♦
□ D-ACNF	Canadair CRJ-900NG	15243	ex C-GIAU	>GWI
□ D-ACNG	Canadair CRJ-900NG	15245	ex C-GZQF	
□ D-ACNH	Canadair CRJ-900NG	15247	ex C-GZQK	>GWI
□ D-ACNI	Canadair CRJ-900NG	15248	ex C-GHZV	>GWI
□ D-ACNJ	Canadair CRJ-900NG	15249	ex C-GZQX	
□ D-ACNK	Canadair CRJ-900NG	15251	ex C-GIBL	>GWI
□ D-ACNL	Canadair CRJ-900NG	15252	ex C-GZQA	>GWI
□ D-ACNM	Canadair CRJ-900NG	15253	ex C-GHZZ	
□ D-ACNN	Canadair CRJ-900NG	15254	ex C-GIAH	>GWI
□ D-ACNO	Canadair CRJ-900NG	15255	ex C-GIBN	
□ D-ACNP	Canadair CRJ-900NG	15259	ex C-GZQV	>GWI
□ D-ACNQ	Canadair CRJ-900NG	15260	ex C-GIBG	
□ D-ACNR	Canadair CRJ-900NG	15263		
□ D-ACNT	Canadair CRJ-900NG	15264	ex C-GICB	
□ D-ACNU	Canadair CRJ-900NG	15267	ex C-GICP	
□ D-ACNV	Canadair CRJ-900NG	15268	ex C-GIAR	>GWI
□ D-ACNW	Canadair CRJ-900NG	15269	ex C-GIAU	
□ D-ACNX	Canadair CRJ-900NG	15270	ex C-GIAW	

EXCELLENT AIR
Excellent Air (GZA) — Münster-Osnabruck

| □ D-IICE | Beech 200 Super King Air | BB-269 | ex N269D | EMS |

FLM AVIATION
Kiel Air FLM (FKI) — Hamburg/Kiel/Parchim (HAM/KEL/-)

□ D-CMNX	Dornier 228-202K	8065	ex TF-VMG	
□ D-CNAG	Swearingen SA227DC Metro 23	DC-893B	ex N3032A	
□ D-GBRD	Partenavia P.68B	14	ex OY-DZR	
□ D-ILKA	Dornier 228-100	7005	ex LN-HTB	

FRISIA LUFTVERKEHR
Norden-Norddeich (NOE)

| □ D-IFKU | Britten-Norman BN-2B-20 Islander | 2290 | ex G-BVXY | Norderney |
| □ D-IFTI | Britten-Norman BN-2B-20 Islander | 2299 | ex G-BWYY | Norddeich |

GERMANIA
Germania (ST/GMI) — Cologne (CGN)

□ D-ASTA	Airbus A319-112	4663	ex D-AVYF	Dr Heinrich Bischoff
□ D-ASTB	Airbus A319-112	4691	ex D-AVYO	
□ D-ASTC	Airbus A319-112	5085	ex D-AVYO	
□ D-ASTT	Airbus A319-112	3560	ex D-AHHB	
□ D-ASTU	Airbus A319-112	3533	ex D-AHHA	
□ D-ASTX	Airbus A319-112	3202	ex HB-IOY	>BER
□ D-ASTY	Airbus A319-112	3407	ex OE-LED	
□ D-ASTZ	Airbus A319-112	3019	ex OE-LEK	
□ D-ABLA	Boeing 737-76J/W	36114/2421	ex N1786B	♦
□ D-ABLB	Boeing 737-76J/W	36115/2692		
□ D-AGEL	Boeing 737-75B/W	28110/5	ex N1791B	
□ D-AGEN	Boeing 737-75B/W	28100/16	ex N1789B	
□ D-AGEP	Boeing 737-75B/W	28102/18	ex N5573B	
□ D-AGEQ	Boeing 737-75B/W	28103/23	ex N1787B	
□ D-AGER	Boeing 737-75B	28107/27	ex N1002R	
□ D-AGES	Boeing 737-75B/W	28108/28		
□ D-AGET	Boeing 737-75B/W	28109/31		
□ D-AGEU	Boeing 737-75B/W	28104/39		
□ D-ASTD	Airbus A321-211/S	5843	ex D-AVZO	
□ D-ASTE	Airbus A321-211/S	6005	ex D-AVZD	
□ D-ASTP	Airbus A321-211	0684	ex UR-WRP	♦
□ D-ASTV	Airbus A321-211	0995	ex TS-IQB	
□ D-ASTW	Airbus A321-211	0970	ex TS-IQA	

GERMANWINGS	German Wings (4U/GWI)			Berlin-Tegel (TXL)

☐ D-AKNF	Airbus A319-112	0646	ex D-AVYB	
☐ D-AKNG	Airbus A319-112	0654	ex D-AVYX	
☐ D-AKNI	Airbus A319-112	1016	ex D-AVYK	
☐ D-AKNJ	Airbus A319-112	1172	ex D-AVWF	
☐ D-AKNK	Airbus A319-112	1077	ex N718UW	
☐ D-AKNL	Airbus A319-112	1084	ex N719US	
☐ D-AKNM	Airbus A319-112	1089	ex N720US	
☐ D-AKNN	Airbus A319-112	1136	ex N726US	
☐ D-AKNO	Airbus A319-112	1147	ex N727UW	
☐ D-AKNP	Airbus A319-112	1155	ex N728UW	
☐ D-AKNQ	Airbus A319-112	1170	ex N729US	
☐ D-AKNR	Airbus A319-112	1209	ex N736US	
☐ D-AKNS	Airbus A319-112	1277	ex N743UW	
☐ D-AKNT	Airbus A319-112	2607	ex D-AVXQ	
☐ D-AKNU	Airbus A319-112	2628	ex D-AVWB	
☐ D-AKNV	Airbus A319-112	2632	ex D-AVWE	
☐ D-AGWA	Airbus A319-132	2813	ex D-AVWM	
☐ D-AGWB	Airbus A319-132	2833	ex D-AVXI	
☐ D-AGWC	Airbus A319-132	2976	ex D-AVYX	
☐ D-AGWD	Airbus A319-132	3011	ex D-AVWB	
☐ D-AGWE	Airbus A319-132	3128	ex D-AVXB	
☐ D-AGWF	Airbus A319-132	3172	ex D-AVXG	
☐ D-AGWG	Airbus A319-132	3193	ex D-AVYS	
☐ D-AGWH	Airbus A319-132	3352	ex D-AVYX	
☐ D-AGWI	Airbus A319-132	3358	ex D-AVYZ	
☐ D-AGWJ	Airbus A319-132	3375	ex D-AVWB	
☐ D-AGWK	Airbus A319-132	3500	ex D-AVYW	
☐ D-AGWL	Airbus A319-132	3534	ex D-AVWB	
☐ D-AGWM	Airbus A319-132	3839	ex D-AVYQ	
☐ D-AGWN	Airbus A319-132	3841	ex D-AVYS	
☐ D-AGWO	Airbus A319-132	4166	ex D-AVWH	
☐ D-AGWP	Airbus A319-132	4227	ex D-AVYK	
☐ D-AGWQ	Airbus A319-132	4256	ex D-AVYP	
☐ D-AGWR	Airbus A319-132	4285	ex D-AVWS	
☐ D-AGWS	Airbus A319-132	4998	ex D-AVYG	
☐ D-AGWT	Airbus A319-132	5066	ex D-AVYL	
☐ D-AGWU	Airbus A319-132	5457	ex D-AVYL	
☐ D-AGWV	Airbus A319-132	5467	ex D-AVYM	
☐ D-AGWW	Airbus A319-132	5535	ex D-AVYN	
☐ D-AGWX	Airbus A319-132	5569	ex D-AVYO	
☐ D-AGWY	Airbus A319-132	5941	ex D-AVWD	
☐ D-AGWZ	Airbus A319-132	5978	ex D-AVWG	
☐ D-AIPL	Airbus A320-211	0094	ex 7T-VKO	♦
☐ D-AIPS	Airbus A320-211	0116	ex F-WWIK	♦
☐ D-AIPT	Airbus A320-211	0117	ex F-WWIL	♦
☐ D-AIPU	Airbus A320-211	0135	ex F-WWDB	♦
☐ D-AIPW	Airbus A320-211	0137	ex F-WWDD	♦
☐ D-AIPY	Airbus A320-211	0161	ex F-WWIA	♦
☐ D-AIPZ	Airbus A320-211	0162	ex F-WWDS	♦
☐ D-AIQA	Airbus A320-211	0172	ex F-WWIK	♦
☐ D-AIQB	Airbus A320-211	0200	ex F-WWDJ	
☐ D-AIQC	Airbus A320-211	0201	ex F-WWDL	♦
☐ D-AIQD	Airbus A320-211	0202	ex F-WWDM	♦
☐ D-AIQE	Airbus A320-211	0209	ex F-WWDY	♦
☐ D-AIQF	Airbus A320-211	0216	ex F-WWDR	♦
☐ D-AIQH	Airbus A320-211	0217	ex F-WWDS	
☐ D-AIQK	Airbus A320-211	0218	ex F-WWDX	
☐ D-AIQL	Airbus A320-211	0267	ex F-WWDY	♦
☐ D-AIQM	Airbus A320-211	0268	ex F-WWIB	♦
☐ D-AIQN	Airbus A320-211	0269	ex F-WWIC	♦
☐ D-AIQP	Airbus A320-211	0346	ex F-WWDX	♦
☐ D-AIQR	Airbus A320-211	0382	ex F-WWIZ	
☐ D-AIQS	Airbus A320-211	0401	ex F-WWBD	
☐ D-ACNF	Canadair CRJ-900NG	15243	ex C-GIAU	<EWG
☐ D-ACNH	Canadair CRJ-900NG	15247	ex C-GZQK	<EWG♦
☐ D-ACNI	Canadair CRJ-900NG	15248	ex C-GHZV	<EWG♦
☐ D-ACNK	Canadair CRJ-900NG	15251	ex C-GIBL	<EWG♦
☐ D-ACNL	Canadair CRJ-900NG	15252	ex C-GZQA	<EWG
☐ D-ACNN	Canadair CRJ-900NG	15254	ex C-GIAH	<EWG
☐ D-ACNP	Canadair CRJ-900NG	15259	ex C-GZQV	<EWG
☐ D-ACNV	Canadair CRJ-900NG	15268	ex C-GIAR	<EWG

HAHN AIR	Rooster (HR/HHN)			Hahn (HHN)

☐ D-CHRA	Cessna 525C Citationjet CJ4	0058	ex N5185V	
☐ D-CHRB	Cessna 525C Citationjet CJ4	0144	ex N5262W	♦
☐ D-CHRC	Cessna 525C Citationjet CJ4	0153	ex N5197M	♦

LGW - LUFTFAHRTGESELLSCHAFT WALTER Walter (HE/LGW)					Dortmund (DTM)
☐ D-ABQA	de Havilland DHC-8-402Q	4223	ex C-FTID		opf BER
☐ D-ABQB	de Havilland DHC-8-402Q	4226	ex C-FTUM		opf BER
☐ D-ABQC	de Havilland DHC-8-402Q	4231	ex C-FUCI		opf BER
☐ D-ABQD	de Havilland DHC-8-402Q	4234	ex C-FUCS		opf BER
☐ D-ABQE	de Havilland DHC-8-402Q	4239	ex C-FURQ		opf BER
☐ D-ABQF	de Havilland DHC-8-402Q	4245	ex C-FVGV		opf BER
☐ D-ABQG	de Havilland DHC-8-402Q	4250	ex C-FVUN		opf BER
☐ D-ABQH	de Havilland DHC-8-402Q	4256	ex C-FWGO		opf BER
☐ D-ABQI	de Havilland DHC-8-402Q	4264	ex C-FXIW		opf BER
☐ D-ABQJ	de Havilland DHC-8-402Q	4274	ex C-FYGN		opf BER
☐ D-ABQK	de Havilland DHC-8-402Q	4265	ex HB-JIK		opf BER
☐ D-ABQL	de Havilland DHC-8-402Q	4184	ex HB-JIJ		opf BER
☐ D-ABQM	de Havilland DHC-8-402Q	4119	ex N419KA		opf BER♦
☐ D-ABQN	de Havilland DHC-8-402Q	4124	ex C-FEUF		opf BER♦
☐ D-ABQO	de Havilland DHC-8-402Q	4129	ex N129KA		opf BER♦
☐ D-ABQP	de Havilland DHC-8-402Q	4137	ex C-FDLO		opf BER♦
☐ D-ABQQ	de Havilland DHC-8-402Q	4198	ex HB-JGA		opf BER♦

LUFTHANSA		Lufthansa (LH/DLH)			Frankfurt (FRA)

Member of Star Alliance

☐ D-AIBA	Airbus A319-112	4141	ex D-AVWG		
☐ D-AIBB	Airbus A319-112	4182	ex D-AVWK	Aalen	
☐ D-AIBC	Airbus A319-112	4332	ex D-AVXF	Siegburg	
☐ D-AIBD	Airbus A319-112	4455	ex D-AVYC	Pirmasens	
☐ D-AIBE	Airbus A319-112	4511	ex D-AVYH	Schönefeld	
☐ D-AIBF	Airbus A319-112	4796	ex D-AVYZ	Sinsheim	
☐ D-AIBG	Airbus A319-112	4841	ex D-AVWF	Kirchheim unter Teck	
☐ D-AIBH	Airbus A319-112	5239	ex D-AVYA	Herborn	
☐ D-AIBI	Airbus A319-112	5284	ex D-AVYY	Frankenthal	
☐ D-AIBJ	Airbus A319-112	5293	ex D-AVWA	Lorsch	
☐ D-AILA	Airbus A319-114	0609	ex D-AVYF	Frankfurt an der Oder	
☐ D-AILB	Airbus A319-114	0610	ex D-AVYG	Lutherstadt Wittenberg	
☐ D-AILC	Airbus A319-114	0616	ex D-AVYI	Rüsselsheim	
☐ D-AILD	Airbus A319-114	0623	ex D-AVYL	Dinkelsbühl	
☐ D-AILE	Airbus A319-114	0627	ex D-AVYO	Kelsterbach	
☐ D-AILF	Airbus A319-114	0636	ex D-AVYS	Trier	Star Alliance c/s
☐ D-AILH	Airbus A319-114	0641	ex D-AVYV	Norderstedt	
☐ D-AILI	Airbus A319-114	0651	ex D-AVYY	Ingolstadt	
☐ D-AILK	Airbus A319-114	0679	ex D-AVYG	Aschaffenburg	
☐ D-AILL	Airbus A319-114	0689	ex D-AVYL	Marburg	
☐ D-AILM	Airbus A319-114	0694	ex D-AVYR	Friedrichshafen	
☐ D-AILN	Airbus A319-114	0700	ex D-AVYU	Idar-Oberstein	
☐ D-AILP	Airbus A319-114	0717	ex D-AVYA	Tübingen	
☐ D-AILR	Airbus A319-114	0723	ex D-AVYD	Tegernsee	
☐ D-AILS	Airbus A319-114	0729	ex D-AVYF	Heide	
☐ D-AILT	Airbus A319-114	0738	ex D-AVYN	Straubing	
☐ D-AILU	Airbus A319-114	0744	ex D-AVYI	Verden	
☐ D-AILW	Airbus A319-114	0853	ex D-AVYO	Donaueschingen	
☐ D-AILX	Airbus A319-114	0860	ex D-AVYS	Fellbach	
☐ D-AILY	Airbus A319-114	0875	ex D-AVYC	Schweinfurt	
☐ D-AKNH	Airbus A319-112	0794	ex D-AVYD		
☐ D-AIPA	Airbus A320-211	0069	ex F-WWII	Buxtehude	
☐ D-AIPB	Airbus A320-211	0070	ex F-WWIJ	Heidelberg	
☐ D-AIPC	Airbus A320-211	0071	ex F-WWIO	Braunschweig	Star Alliance c/s
☐ D-AIPD	Airbus A320-211	0072	ex F-WWIP	Freiburg	Star Alliance c/s
☐ D-AIPE	Airbus A320-211	0078	ex F-WWIU	Kassel	
☐ D-AIPF	Airbus A320-211	0083	ex F-WWDE	Deggendorf	
☐ D-AIPH	Airbus A320-211	0086	ex F-WWDJ	Münster	
☐ D-AIPK	Airbus A320-211	0093	ex F-WWDQ	Wiesbaden	
☐ D-AIPM	Airbus A320-211	0104	ex F-WWIG	Troisdorf	
☐ D-AIPP	Airbus A320-211	0110	ex F-WWID	Starnberg	
☐ D-AIPR	Airbus A320-211	0111	ex F-WWIE	Kaufbeuren	
☐ D-AIQT	Airbus A320-211	1337	ex F-WWDO	Gotha	
☐ D-AIQU	Airbus A320-211	1365	ex F-WWIG	Backnang	
☐ D-AIQW	Airbus A320-211	1367	ex F-WWIH	Kleve	
☐ D-AIUA	Airbus A320-214/S	5935	ex D-AUBI		
☐ D-AIUB	Airbus A320-214/S	5972	ex D-AUBN		
☐ D-AIUC	Airbus A320-214/S	6006	ex D-AUBV		
☐ D-AIUD	Airbus A320-214/S	6033	ex D-AXAC		
☐ D-AIUE	Airbus A320-214/S	6092	ex D-AXAO		
☐ D-AIUF	Airbus A320-214/S	6141	ex D-AXAZ		
☐ D-AIUG	Airbus A320-214/S	6202	ex D-AVVH		
☐ D-AIUH	Airbus A320-214/S	6225	ex D-AVVM		
☐ D-AIUI	Airbus A320-214/S	6265	ex D-AVVS		
☐ D-AIUJ	Airbus A320-214/S	6301	ex D-AXAK		♦
☐ D-AIUK	Airbus A320-214/S	6423	ex D-AXAQ		♦

☐ D-AIUL	Airbus A320-214/S	6521	ex D-AXAZ		♦
☐ D-AIUM	Airbus A320-214/S	6577	ex D-AVVM		♦
☐ D-AIUN	Airbus A320-214/S	6549	ex D-AVVH		♦
☐ D-AIUO	Airbus A320-214/S	6636	ex D-AVVV		o/o♦
☐ D-AIUP	Airbus A320-214/S	6807	ex		o/o♦
☐ D-AIZA	Airbus A320-214	4097	ex D-AVVF		
☐ D-AIZB	Airbus A320-214	4120	ex D-AVVV		
☐ D-AIZC	Airbus A320-214	4153	ex D-AVVL	Budingen	
☐ D-AIZD	Airbus A320-214	4191	ex D-AVVD	Schwäbisch-Gmünd	
☐ D-AIZE	Airbus A320-214	4261	ex D-AXAC	Eisenach	
☐ D-AIZF	Airbus A320-214	4289	ex D-AXAF	Fulda	
☐ D-AIZG	Airbus A320-214	4324	ex D-AXAO	Sindelfingen	
☐ D-AIZH	Airbus A320-214	4363	ex D-AXAW	Hanau	
☐ D-AIZI	Airbus A320-214	4398	ex D-AVVL	Böblingen	
☐ D-AIZJ	Airbus A320-214	4449	ex D-AVVM	Herford	
☐ D-AIZK	Airbus A320-214	5122	ex D-AVVA		
☐ D-AIZL	Airbus A320-214	5181	ex D-AXAT	Esslingen	
☐ D-AIZM	Airbus A320-214	5203	ex D-AVVR		
☐ D-AIZN	Airbus A320-214	5425	ex D-AVVJ		
☐ D-AIZO	Airbus A320-214	5441	ex D-AVVP		
☐ D-AIZP	Airbus A320-214/S	5487	ex D-AXAA	Plauen	
☐ D-AIZV	Airbus A320-214/S	5658	ex D-AUBY		
☐ D-AIZW	Airbus A320-214/S	5694	ex D-AVVH	Wesel	
☐ D-AIZX	Airbus A320-214/S	5741	ex D-AVVT		
☐ D-AIZY	Airbus A320-214/S	5769	ex D-AVVX		
☐ D-AIZZ	Airbus A320-214/S	5831	ex D-AXAQ		
☐ D-	Airbus A320-214/S	6831	ex		o/o♦
☐ D-	Airbus A320-214/S	6892	ex		o/o♦
☐ D-	Airbus A320-214/S	6938	ex		o/o♦
☐ D-	Airbus A320-214/S	6953	ex		o/o♦
☐ D-	Airbus A320-214/S	6974	ex		o/o♦
☐ D-AIRA	Airbus A321-131	0458	ex F-WWIQ	Finkenwerder	
☐ D-AIRB	Airbus A321-131	0468	ex F-WWIS	Baden-Baden	
☐ D-AIRC	Airbus A321-131	0473	ex D-AVZC	Erlangen	
☐ D-AIRD	Airbus A321-131	0474	ex D-AVZD	Coburg	
☐ D-AIRE	Airbus A321-131	0484	ex D-AVZF	Osnabrück	
☐ D-AIRF	Airbus A321-131	0493	ex D-AVZH	Kempten	
☐ D-AIRH	Airbus A321-131	0412	ex D-AVZA	Garmisch-Partenkirchen	
☐ D-AIRK	Airbus A321-131	0502	ex D-AVZL	Freudenstadt/Schwarzwald	
☐ D-AIRL	Airbus A321-131	0505	ex D-AVZM	Kulmbach	
☐ D-AIRM	Airbus A321-131	0518	ex D-AVZT	Darmstadt	
☐ D-AIRN	Airbus A321-131	0560	ex D-AVZK	Kaiserslautern	
☐ D-AIRO	Airbus A321-131	0563	ex D-AVZN	Konstanz	
☐ D-AIRP	Airbus A321-131	0564	ex D-AVZL	Lunenburg	
☐ D-AIRR	Airbus A321-131	0567	ex D-AVZM	Wismar	
☐ D-AIRS	Airbus A321-131	0595	ex D-AVZX	Husum	
☐ D-AIRT	Airbus A321-131	0652	ex D-AVZI	Regensburg	
☐ D-AIRU	Airbus A321-131	0692	ex D-AVZT	Würzburg	
☐ D-AIRW	Airbus A321-131	0699	ex D-AVZY	Heilbronn	Star Alliance c/s
☐ D-AIRX	Airbus A321-131	0887	ex D-AVZI	Weimar	
☐ D-AIRY	Airbus A321-131	0901	ex D-AVZK	Flensburg	
☐ D-AIDA	Airbus A321-231	4360	ex D-AVZM	Pforzheim	
☐ D-AIDB	Airbus A321-231	4545	ex D-AVZZ	Bayreuth	
☐ D-AIDC	Airbus A321-231	4560	ex D-AZAB		
☐ D-AIDD	Airbus A321-231	4585	ex D-AVZC	Wilhelmshaven	
☐ D-AIDE	Airbus A321-231	4607	ex D-AZAK		
☐ D-AIDF	Airbus A321-231	4626	ex D-AZAO		
☐ D-AIDG	Airbus A321-231	4672	ex D-AZAF	Göttingen	
☐ D-AIDH	Airbus A321-231	4710	ex D-AVZD	Hildesheim	
☐ D-AIDI	Airbus A321-231	4753	ex D-AVZI	Salzgitter	
☐ D-AIDJ	Airbus A321-231	4792	ex D-AVZO	Remscheid	
☐ D-AIDK	Airbus A321-231	4819	ex D-AVZQ		
☐ D-AIDL	Airbus A321-231	4881	ex D-AVZC	Reutlingen	
☐ D-AIDM	Airbus A321-231	4916	ex D-AVZH	Recklinghausen	
☐ D-AIDN	Airbus A321-231	4976	ex D-AZAI	Neuss	
☐ D-AIDO	Airbus A321-231	4994	ex D-AZAJ		
☐ D-AIDP	Airbus A321-231	5049	ex D-AZAQ	Paderborn	
☐ D-AIDQ	Airbus A321-231	5028	ex D-AZAM		
☐ D-AIDT	Airbus A321-231	5087	ex D-AZAU		
☐ D-AIDU	Airbus A321-231	5186	ex D-AVZL		
☐ D-AIDV	Airbus A321-231	5413	ex D-AVZM		retro c/s
☐ D-AIDW	Airbus A321-231	6415	ex D-AZAO		♦
☐ D-AIDX	Airbus A321-231	6451	ex D-AVZD		♦
☐ D-AISB	Airbus A321-231	1080	ex D-AVZP	Hameln	
☐ D-AISC	Airbus A321-231	1161	ex D-AVZG	Speyer	
☐ D-AISD	Airbus A321-231	1188	ex F-WWDD	Chemnitz	
☐ D-AISE	Airbus A321-231	1214	ex D-AVZS	Neudstadt an der Weinstrasse	
☐ D-AISF	Airbus A321-231	1260	ex D-AVZI	Lippstadt	
☐ D-AISG	Airbus A321-231	1273	ex D-AVZU	Dormagen	
☐ D-AISH	Airbus A321-231	3265	ex D-AVZL	Wetzlar	
☐ D-AISI	Airbus A321-231	3339	ex D-AVZD	Bergheim	

☐	D-AISJ	Airbus A321-231	3360	ex D-AVZF	Gutersloh		
☐	D-AISK	Airbus A321-231	3387	ex D-AVZO	Emden		
☐	D-AISL	Airbus A321-231	3434	ex D-AVZD	Arnsberg		
☐	D-AISN	Airbus A321-231	3592	ex D-AZAA	Goppingen		
☐	D-AISO	Airbus A321-231	3625	ex D-AVZH	Bocholt		
☐	D-AISP	Airbus A321-231	3864	ex D-AVZK	Rosenheim		
☐	D-AISQ	Airbus A321-231	3936	ex D-AZAF	Lindau		
☐	D-AISR	Airbus A321-231	3987	ex D-AZAN	Donauworth		
☐	D-AIST	Airbus A321-231	4005	ex D-AVZD	Erbach		
☐	D-AISU	Airbus A321-231	4016	ex D-AVZF	Nordlingen		
☐	D-AISV	Airbus A321-231	4047	ex D-AZAG	Bingen		
☐	D-AISW	Airbus A321-231	4054	ex D-AZAR	Stade		
☐	D-AISX	Airbus A321-231	4073	ex D-AVZR			
☐	D-AISZ	Airbus A321-231	4085	ex D-AVZW			
☐	D-AIKA	Airbus A330-343X	570	ex F-WWYV	Minden		
☐	D-AIKB	Airbus A330-343X	576	ex F-WWKN	Cuxhaven		
☐	D-AIKC	Airbus A330-343X	579	ex F-WWKG	Hamm		
☐	D-AIKD	Airbus A330-343X	629	ex F-WWYF	Siegen		
☐	D-AIKE	Airbus A330-343X	636	ex F-WWYL	Landshut		
☐	D-AIKF	Airbus A330-343X	642	ex F-WWKV	Witten		
☐	D-AIKG	Airbus A330-343X	645	ex F-WWKE	Ludwigsburg		
☐	D-AIKH	Airbus A330-343X	648	ex F-WWKG			
☐	D-AIKI	Airbus A330-343X	687	ex F-WWYI			
☐	D-AIKJ	Airbus A330-343X	701	ex F-WWKD	Bottrop		
☐	D-AIKK	Airbus A330-343X	896	ex F-WWYX	Furth		
☐	D-AIKL	Airbus A330-343X	905	ex F-WWYC	Ingolstadt		
☐	D-AIKM	Airbus A330-343X	913	ex F-WWYJ			
☐	D-AIKN	Airbus A330-343X	922	ex F-WWYY			
☐	D-AIKO	Airbus A330-343X	989	ex F-WWKJ			
☐	D-AIKP	Airbus A330-343X	1292	ex F-WWYQ			
☐	D-AIKQ	Airbus A330-343X	1305	ex F-WWYV			
☐	D-AIKR	Airbus A330-343X	1314	ex F-WWKD			
☐	D-AIKS	Airbus A330-343E	1497	ex F-WWTQ			
☐	D-AIFA	Airbus A340-313X	352	ex F-WWJU	Dorsten		
☐	D-AIFC	Airbus A340-313X	379	ex F-WWJJ	Gander & Halifax		
☐	D-AIFD	Airbus A340-313X	390	ex F-WWJE	Giessen		
☐	D-AIFE	Airbus A340-313X	434	ex F-WWJT	Passau		
☐	D-AIFF	Airbus A340-313X	447	ex F-WWJB	Delmenhorst		
☐	D-AIGL	Airbus A340-313X	135	ex F-WWJS	Herne		
☐	D-AIGM	Airbus A340-313X	158	ex F-WWJN	Görlitz		
☐	D-AIGN	Airbus A340-313X	213	ex F-WWJM	Solingen	Star Alliance c/s	
☐	D-AIGO	Airbus A340-313X	233	ex F-WWJJ	Offenbach		
☐	D-AIGP	Airbus A340-313X	252	ex F-WWJM	Paderborn		
☐	D-AIGS	Airbus A340-313X	297	ex F-WWJK	Bergisch-Gladbach		
☐	D-AIGT	Airbus A340-313X	304	ex F-WWJY	Viersen		
☐	D-AIGU	Airbus A340-313X	321	ex F-WWJM	Castrop-Rauxel		
☐	D-AIGV	Airbus A340-313X	325	ex F-WWJN	Dinslaken		
☐	D-AIGW	Airbus A340-313X	327	ex F-WWJO	Gladbeck		
☐	D-AIGX	Airbus A340-313X	354	ex F-WWJV	Düren		
☐	D-AIGY	Airbus A340-313X	335	ex F-WWJS	Lünen		
☐	D-AIHA	Airbus A340-642	482	ex F-WWCS	Nürnberg	Star Alliance c/s	
☐	D-AIHB	Airbus A340-642	517	ex F-WWCR	Bremerhaven		
☐	D-AIHC	Airbus A340-642	523	ex F-WWCV	Essen		
☐	D-AIHD	Airbus A340-642	537	ex F-WWCZ	Stuttgart		
☐	D-AIHE	Airbus A340-642	540	ex F-WWCF	Leverkusen		
☐	D-AIHF	Airbus A340-642	543	ex F-WWCE	Lübeck		
☐	D-AIHH	Airbus A340-642	566	ex F-WWCJ	Wiesbaden		
☐	D-AIHI	Airbus A340-642	569	ex F-WWCB	Monchengladbach		
☐	D-AIHK	Airbus A340-642	580	ex F-WWCN	Mainz		
☐	D-AIHL	Airbus A340-642	583	ex F-WWCQ			
☐	D-AIHM	Airbus A340-642	762	ex F-WWCI	Wuppertal		
☐	D-AIHN	Airbus A340-642	763	ex F-WWCJ	Gummersback	Fanhansa c/s	
☐	D-AIHO	Airbus A340-642	767	ex F-WWCN			
☐	D-AIHP	Airbus A340-642	771	ex F-WWCQ			
☐	D-AIHQ	Airbus A340-642	790	ex F-WWCE		Fanhansa c/s	
☐	D-AIHR	Airbus A340-642	794	ex F-WWCF			
☐	D-AIHS	Airbus A340-642	812	ex F-WWCX			
☐	D-AIHT	Airbus A340-642	846	ex F-WWCH			
☐	D-AIHU	Airbus A340-642	848	ex F-WWCI			
☐	D-AIHV	Airbus A340-642	897	ex F-WWTI			
☐	D-AIHW	Airbus A340-642	972	ex F-WWCL			
☐	D-AIHX	Airbus A340-642	981	ex F-WWCN			
☐	D-AIHY	Airbus A340-642	987	ex F-WWCQ			
☐	D-AIHZ	Airbus A340-642	1005	ex F-WWCR			
☐	D-AIMA	Airbus A380-841	038	ex F-WWSH	Frankfurt am Main		
☐	D-AIMB	Airbus A380-841	041	ex F-WWAF	Munchen		
☐	D-AIMC	Airbus A380-841	044	ex F-WWAJ	Peking		
☐	D-AIMD	Airbus A380-841	048	ex F-WWAK	Tokio		
☐	D-AIME	Airbus A380-841	061	ex F-WWAV	Johannesburg		

☐ D-AIMF	Airbus A380-841	066	ex F-WWSN	Zürich	
☐ D-AIMG	Airbus A380-841	069	ex F-WWSO	Wien	
☐ D-AIMH	Airbus A380-841	070	ex F-WWSG	New York	
☐ D-AIMI	Airbus A380-841	072	ex F-WWSR	Berlin	
☐ D-AIMJ	Airbus A380-841	073	ex F-WWSP	Brüssel	
☐ D-AIMK	Airbus A380-841	146	ex F-WWAO	Düsseldorf	
☐ D-AIML	Airbus A380-841	149	ex F-WWSX	Hamburg	
☐ D-AIMM	Airbus A380-841	175	ex F-WWSP	Delhi	♦
☐ D-AIMN	Airbus A380-841	177	ex F-WWSR	San Francisco	♦
☐ D-ABEB	Boeing 737-330	25148/2077		Xanten	
☐ D-ABEC	Boeing 737-330	25149/2081		Karlsruhe	
☐ D-ABED	Boeing 737-330	25215/2082		Hagen	
☐ D-ABEE	Boeing 737-330	25216/2084		Ulm	
☐ D-ABEF	Boeing 737-330	25217/2094		Weiden i.d.Opf	
☐ D-ABEH	Boeing 737-330	25242/2102		Bad Kissingen	
☐ D-ABEI	Boeing 737-330	25359/2158	ex (D-ABJK)	Bamberg	
☐ D-ABEK	Boeing 737-330	25414/2164	ex (D-ABJL)		
☐ D-ABEN	Boeing 737-330	26428/2196	ex (D-ABJP)	Neubrandenburg	
☐ D-ABIF	Boeing 737-530	24820/1985		Landau	
☐ D-ABIN	Boeing 737-530	24938/2023		Langenhagen	
☐ D-ABIP	Boeing 737-530	24940/2034		Oberhausen	
☐ D-ABIR	Boeing 737-530	24941/2042		Anklam	
☐ D-ABIS	Boeing 737-530	24942/2048		Rendsburg	
☐ D-ABIT	Boeing 737-530	24943/2049		Neumünster	
☐ D-ABIU	Boeing 737-530	24944/2051		Limburg	
☐ D-ABIW	Boeing 737-530	24945/2063		Bad Nauheim	
☐ D-ABIX	Boeing 737-530	24946/2070		Iserlohn	
☐ D-ABIY	Boeing 737-530	25243/2086		Lingen	
☐ D-ABJB	Boeing 737-530	25271/2117		Rheine	
☐ D-ABTK	Boeing 747-430	29871/1293	ex (D-ABVI)	Kiel	
☐ D-ABTL	Boeing 747-430	29872/1299	ex (D-ABVG)	Dresden	
☐ D-ABVH	Boeing 747-430	25045/845	ex N6018N	Düsseldorf	
☐ D-ABVK	Boeing 747-430	25046/847	ex N6009F		
☐ D-ABVL	Boeing 747-430	26425/898	ex N60659	München	
☐ D-ABVM	Boeing 747-430	29101/1143	ex (V8-AC2)	Hessen	
☐ D-ABVN	Boeing 747-430	26427/915		Dortmund	
☐ D-ABVO	Boeing 747-430	28086/1080		Mülheim an der Ruhr	
☐ D-ABVP	Boeing 747-430	28284/1103		Bremen	
☐ D-ABVR	Boeing 747-430	28285/1106		Köln	
☐ D-ABVS	Boeing 747-430	28286/1109		Saarland	
☐ D-ABVT	Boeing 747-430	28287/1110			
☐ D-ABVU	Boeing 747-430	29492/1191		Bayern	
☐ D-ABVW	Boeing 747-430	29493/1205		Wolfsburg	
☐ D-ABVX	Boeing 747-430	29868/1237		Schleswig-Holstein	
☐ D-ABVY	Boeing 747-430	29869/1261		Nordrhein-Westfalen	
☐ D-ABVZ	Boeing 747-430	29870/1264		Niedersachsen	
☐ D-ABYA	Boeing 747-830	37827/1443	ex N5016R	Brandenburg	
☐ D-ABYC	Boeing 747-830	37828/1451		Sachsen	
☐ D-ABYD	Boeing 747-830	37829/1453		Mecklenburg-Vorpommern	
☐ D-ABYF	Boeing 747-830	37830/1456		Sachsen-Anhalt	
☐ D-ABYG	Boeing 747-830	37831/1470	ex N5022E	Baden-Württemberg	
☐ D-ABYH	Boeing 747-830	37832/1472		Thüringen	
☐ D-ABYI	Boeing 747-830	37833/1475		Potsdam	Fanhansa c/s
☐ D-ABYJ	Boeing 747-830	37834/1477		Hannover	
☐ D-ABYK	Boeing 747-830	37835/1480		Rheinland-Pfalz	
☐ D-ABYL	Boeing 747-830	37836/1492		Hessen	
☐ D-ABYM	Boeing 747-830	37837/1494		Bayern	
☐ D-ABYN	Boeing 747-830	37838/1497		Niedersachsen	
☐ D-ABYO	Boeing 747-830	37841/1498			
☐ D-ABYP	Boeing 747-830	37839/1500		Nordrhein-Westfalen	
☐ D-ABYQ	Boeing 747-830	37840/1503	ex N50281	Schleswig-Holstein	
☐ D-ABYR	Boeing 747-830	37842/1511		Bremen	
☐ D-ABYS	Boeing 747-830	37843/1512		Dresden	
☐ D-ABYT	Boeing 747-830	37844/1513		Köln	retro c/s
☐ D-ABYU	Boeing 747-830	37845/1514			
☐ D-ABYV	Boeing 747-830	37846/			o/o
☐ D-CDLH	Junkers Ju52/3m g8e	130714	ex N52JU	Tempelhof	painted as D-AQUI
☐ D-	Airbus A320-217Neo	6801	ex		o/o♦

LUFTHANSA CARGO		**Lufthansa Cargo (LH/GEC)**			**Frankfurt (FRA)**
☐ D-ALFA	Boeing 777-FBT	41674/1144		Good Day, USA	
☐ D-ALFB	Boeing 777-FBT	41675/1156		Jambo, Kenya	
☐ D-ALFC	Boeing 777-FBT	41676/1178		Ni Hao, China	
☐ D-ALFD	Boeing 777-FBT	41677/1208		Olá, Brazil	
☐ D-ALFE	Boeing 777-FBT	41678/1274		Hallo, Germany	
☐ D-ALCA	McDonnell-Douglas MD-11F	48781/625	ex N9020Q	Wilhelm Althen	

☐ D-ALCB	McDonnell-Douglas MD-11F	48782/626	ex N9166N		
☐ D-ALCC	McDonnell-Douglas MD-11F	48783/627		Karl-Ulrich Garnadt	
☐ D-ALCD	McDonnell-Douglas MD-11F	48784/628		100th Anniversary c/s	
☐ D-ALCE	McDonnell-Douglas MD-11F	48785/629		Marhaba Turkey	
☐ D-ALCF	McDonnell-Douglas MD-11F	48798/637			
☐ D-ALCG	McDonnell-Douglas MD-11F	48799/639		Konnichiwa Japan	
☐ D-ALCH	McDonnell-Douglas MD-11F	48801/640			
☐ D-ALCI	McDonnell-Douglas MD-11F	48800/641			
☐ D-ALCJ	McDonnell-Douglas MD-11F	48802/642		Namaste India	
☐ D-ALCK	McDonnell-Douglas MD-11F	48803/643	ex N9166N		
☐ D-ALCL	McDonnell-Douglas MD-11F	48804/644			
☐ D-ALCM	McDonnell-Douglas MD-11F	48805/645	ex N6069R		
☐ D-ALCN	McDonnell-Douglas MD-11F	48806/646			
☐ D-ALCR	McDonnell-Douglas MD-11F	48581/565	ex N581LT		[VCV]
☐ D-ALCS	McDonnell-Douglas MD-11F	48630/567	ex N630LT		[VCV]

LUFTHANSA CITYLINE — Hansaline (CL/CLH) — Frankfurt/Cologne (FRA/CGN)

☐ D-ACPM	Canadair CRJ-701ER	10080	ex C-GIAO	Heidenheim an der Brenz	wfs
☐ D-ACPN	Canadair CRJ-701ER	10083	ex C-GIAU	Quedlinburg	
☐ D-ACPO	Canadair CRJ-701ER	10085	ex C-FZYS	Spaichingen	
☐ D-ACPQ	Canadair CRJ-701ER	10091	ex C-GZJA	Lubbecke	Star Alliance c/s [CGN]
☐ D-ACPR	Canadair CRJ-701ER	10098		Weinheim an der Bergstrasse	[TUS]
☐ D-ACPS	Canadair CRJ-701ER	10100		Berchtesgaden	Star Alliance c/s wfs
☐ D-ACPT	Canadair CRJ-701ER	10103	ex C-GJLZ	Altötting	Star Alliance c/s [CGN]
☐ D-ACKA	Canadair CRJ-900LR	15072		Pfaffenhofen a.d.Ilm	
☐ D-ACKB	Canadair CRJ-900LR	15073	ex C-FJVT	Schliersee	
☐ D-ACKC	Canadair CRJ-900LR	15078		Mettman	
☐ D-ACKD	Canadair CRJ-900LR	15080		Wittlich	
☐ D-ACKE	Canadair CRJ-900LR	15081		Wernigerode	
☐ D-ACKF	Canadair CRJ-900LR	15083	ex C-FJVR	Prenzlau	
☐ D-ACKG	Canadair CRJ-900LR	15084	ex C-GIAO	Glücksburg	
☐ D-ACKH	Canadair CRJ-900LR	15085	ex C-GICL	Radebeul	
☐ D-ACKI	Canadair CRJ-900LR	15088	ex C-GIAP	Tuttlingen	
☐ D-ACKJ	Canadair CRJ-900LR	15089		Ilmenau	
☐ D-ACKK	Canadair CRJ-900LR	15094		Fürstenwalde	
☐ D-ACKL	Canadair CRJ-900LR	15095		Bad Bergzabern	
☐ D-ACNA	Canadair CRJ-900NG	15229	ex C-GZQA	Amberg	♦
☐ D-ACNB	Canadair CRJ-900NG	15230	ex C-GZQM	Wermelskirchen	♦
☐ D-ACNC	Canadair CRJ-900NG	15236	ex C-GIBO	Weil am Rhein	♦
☐ D-ACND	Canadair CRJ-900NG	15238	ex C-GIBT	Meersburg	♦
☐ D-ACNE	Canadair CRJ-900NG	15241	ex C-GICL	Heimstedt	♦
☐ D-AECA	Embraer ERJ-190LR	19000327	ex PT-TXP		
☐ D-AECB	Embraer ERJ-190LR	19000332	ex PT-TXS	Meißen	
☐ D-AECC	Embraer ERJ-190LR	19000333	ex PT-TXT		
☐ D-AECD	Embraer ERJ-190LR	19000337	ex PT-TXW		
☐ D-AECE	Embraer ERJ-190LR	19000341	ex PT-XQI		
☐ D-AECF	Embraer ERJ-190LR	19000359	ex PT-XNA	Kronberg/Taunus	
☐ D-AECG	Embraer ERJ-190LR	19000368	ex PT-XNG	Heppenheim/Bergstraße	
☐ D-AECH	Embraer ERJ-190LR	19000376	ex PT-XNM	Alzey	
☐ D-AECI	Embraer ERJ-190LR	19000381	ex PT-XNQ		
☐ D-AEBA	Embraer ERJ-195LR	19000314	ex PT-TXC		
☐ D-AEBB	Embraer ERJ-195LR	19000316	ex PT-TXE	Ingelheim a Rhein	
☐ D-AEBC	Embraer ERJ-195LR	19000320	ex PT-TXI		
☐ D-AEBD	Embraer ERJ-195LR	19000324	ex PT-TXM		
☐ D-AEBE	Embraer ERJ-195LR	19000350	ex PT-XQQ		
☐ D-AEBF	Embraer ERJ-195LR	19000411	ex PT-TBJ		
☐ D-AEBG	Embraer ERJ-195LR	19000423	ex PT-TBZ		
☐ D-AEBH	Embraer ERJ-195LR	19000447	ex PT-TBJ	Freising	
☐ D-AEBI	Embraer ERJ-195LR	19000464	ex PT-TOH	Erding	
☐ D-AEBJ	Embraer ERJ-195LR	19000486	ex PT-TPK		
☐ D-AEBK	Embraer ERJ-195LR	19000500	ex PT-TRF		
☐ D-AEBL	Embraer ERJ-195LR	19000507	ex PT-TSD		
☐ D-AEBM	Embraer ERJ-195LR	19000523	ex PT-TUK		
☐ D-AEBN	Embraer ERJ-195LR	19000532	ex PT-TUV		
☐ D-AEBO	Embraer ERJ-195LR	19000542	ex PT-TAU		
☐ D-AEBP	Embraer ERJ-195LR	19000553	ex PT-TBZ		
☐ D-AEBQ	Embraer ERJ-195LR	19000555	ex PT-TDJ		
☐ D-AEBR	Embraer ERJ-195LR	19000558	ex PT-TDN		
☐ D-AEBS	Embraer ERJ-195LR	19000565	ex PT-TDU	Hallbergmoos	
☐ D-AEMA	Embraer ERJ-195LR	19000290	ex PT-TZE		
☐ D-AEMB	Embraer ERJ-195LR	19000297	ex PT-TZL		
☐ D-AEMC	Embraer ERJ-195LR	19000300	ex PT-TZO		
☐ D-AEMD	Embraer ERJ-195LR	19000305	ex PT-TZT		
☐ D-AEME	Embraer ERJ-195LR	19000308	ex PT-TXH		

LUFTVERKEHR FRIESLAND HARLE — Harle

☐ D-IADE	Cessna 340A	340A0607	ex OE-FSK	

☐ D-IEST	Britten-Norman BN-2B-26 Islander	2253	ex I-DEPE	
☐ D-ILFA	Britten-Norman BN-2B-26 Islander	2243	ex G-BSWO	
☐ D-ILFD	Britten-Norman BN-2B-26 Islander	2296	ex JA02TY	
☐ D-ILFH	Britten-Norman BN-2B-26 Islander	2212	ex G-BPXS	

MHS AVIATION — Snowcap (M2/MHV) — Saarbrücken (SCN)

☐ D-BABY	Dornier 328-310 (328JET)	3186	ex I-AIRJ	>SUS♦
☐ D-BMAD	Dornier 328-300 (328JET)	3142	ex I-AIRX	British Airways c/s	>SUS
☐ D-CIRI	Dornier 328-110	3005	ex TF-CSC	British Airways c/s	>SUS
☐ D-CIRJ	Dornier 328-120	3035	ex N335LS		>M2
☐ D-CIRP	Dornier 328-120	3006	ex TF-CSD	British Airways c/s	>SUS
☐ D-CMHA	Dornier 328-110	3023	ex G-BWIR		♦
☐ D-CMHB	Dornier 328-110	3110	ex OE-LKA		♦

NIGHTEXPRESS — Executive (EXT) — Frankfurt (FRA)

☐ D-CCAS	Short SD.3-60	SH3737	ex G-OLBA	
☐ D-CRAS	Short SD.3-60	SH3744	ex N825BE	

PRIVATAIR — PrivatJet (PTG) — Düsseldorf (DUS)

☐ D-APBC	Boeing 737-8BK/W	33016/1588	ex N807SY	VIP
☐ D-APTA	Airbus A319-112	1263	ex LY-VEU	
☐ D-	Boeing 787-8	37306/315		o/o♦

PRIVATE WINGS — Private Wings (8W/PWF) — Ingolstadt-Manching

☐ D-BIRD	Dornier 328-310 (328JET)	3180	ex N422FJ	
☐ D-BJET	Dornier 328-310 (328JET)	3207	ex N328FG	
☐ D-CATZ	Dornier 328-110	3090	ex N404SS	
☐ D-CAWA	Dornier 328-110	3119	ex OE-LKC	♦
☐ D-CDAX	Dornier 328-110	3087	ex N463PS	
☐ D-CITO	Dornier 320-110	3063	ex CC-ACG	♦
☐ D-COSY	Dornier 328-110	3072	ex CC-AEY	♦
☐ D-CPWF	Dornier 328-110	3112	ex D-CFWF	
☐ D-CREW	Dornier 328-110	3113	ex D-CGAO	
☐ D-CSUE	Dornier 328-110	3019	ex N328DC	
☐ D-COCA	Beech 1900D	UE-224	ex N224YV	

PTL LUFTFAHRTUNTERNEHMEN — King Star (KST) — Landshut (QLG)

☐ D-IBAD	Beech B200 Super King Air	BB-1229	

REGIO-AIR — German Link (RAG) — Trollenhagen

☐ D-IBIJ	Cessna 402B	402B0327	ex YU-BIJ	<Goller
☐ D-IESS	Swearingen SA226TC Metro II	TC-338	ex N90141	

RHEIN-NECKAR AIR — (M2) — Mannheim (MHG)

☐ D-CIRJ	Dornier 328-120	3035	ex N335LS	<MHV

SUNEXPRESS DEUTSCHLAND — Sunrise (SXD) — Frankfurt (FRA)

☐ D-ASXA	Boeing 737-8Z9/W	28178/222	ex OE-LNK	
☐ D-ASXB	Boeing 737-8Z9/W	30420/1100	ex OE-LNP	
☐ D-ASXD	Boeing 737-8AS/W	33562/1466	ex EI-DCD	>CFG
☐ D-ASXE	Boeing 737-8CX/W	32365/1209	ex TC-SUG	<SXS
☐ D-ASXF	Boeing 737-8AS/W	33558/1441	ex EI-DAY	
☐ D-ASXG	Boeing 737-8CX/W	32366/1235	ex TC-SUH	<SXS
☐ D-ASXH	Boeing 737-8CX/W	32368/1289	ex TC-SUJ	<SXS
☐ D-ASXK	Boeing 737-86J/W	28070/106	ex D-ABAP	
☐ D-ASXL	Boeing 737-8EH/W	35835/3430	ex PR-GUC	<GLO
☐ D-ASXM	Boeing 737-8EH/W	35836/3466	ex PR-GUD	<GLO
☐ D-ASXN	Boeing 737-8EH/W	35838/3508	ex PR-GUF	<GLO
☐ D-ASXO	Boeing 737-8HX/W	29649/2515	ex TC-SUZ	♦
☐ D-ASXP	Boeing 737-8HX/W	29684/2539	ex TC-SNE	♦
☐ D-ASXS	Boeing 737-8AS/W	33563/1473	ex EI-DCE	
☐ D-ASXT	Boeing 737-8EH/W	35837/3473	ex PR-GUE	<GLO♦

TUIFLY — TuiJet (X3/TUI) — Hanover (HAJ)

☐ D-AHXC	Boeing 737-7K5/W	34693/2260		
☐ D-AHXE	Boeing 737-7K5/W	35135/2451		
☐ D-AHXF	Boeing 737-7K5/W	35136/2465		
☐ D-AHXG	Boeing 737-7K5/W	35140/2575		
☐ D-AHXJ	Boeing 737-7K5/W	35277/2609		
☐ D-ABKI	Boeing 737-86J/W	37748/3157	ex C-GBKI	♦

☐ D-AHFT	Boeing 737-8K5/W	30413/636	ex N1015B		
☐ D-AHFV	Boeing 737-8K5/W	30415/719	ex N1786B		
☐ D-AHFW	Boeing 737-8K5/W	30882/760	ex N1786B		
☐ D-AHFZ	Boeing 737-8K5/W	30883/783	ex N1786B	Mein Cewe Fotobuch c/s	
☐ D-AHLK	Boeing 737-8K5/W	35143/2763	ex C-FTLK	HF Kreuzfahrten c/s	
☐ D-ASUN	Boeing 737-8BK/W	33023/1682	ex TC-SNM		♦
☐ D-ATUA	Boeing 737-8K5/W	37245/3486			
☐ D-ATUB	Boeing 737-8K5/W	37247/3497	ex N1786B		
☐ D-ATUC	Boeing 737-8K5/W	34684/1870	ex N1786B	Dreamliner c/s	
☐ D-ATUD	Boeing 737-8K5/W	34685/1901		Haribo-Goldenbaren c/s	
☐ D-ATUE	Boeing 737-8K5/W	34686/1903		Dreamliner c/s	
☐ D-ATUF	Boeing 737-8K5/W	34687/1907	ex N1786B	Retro c/s	
☐ D-ATUG	Boeing 737-8K5/W	34688/1909			
☐ D-ATUH	Boeing 737-8K5/W	34689/1935	ex C-FYUH		
☐ D-ATUI	Boeing 737-8K5/W	37252/3554		Ice c/s	
☐ D-ATUJ	Boeing 737-8K5/W	39923/4001	ex N1787B	Paradiesvogel	Haribo Tropifrutti c/s
☐ D-ATUK	Boeing 737-8K5/W	39094/3641	ex C-GDGZ		
☐ D-ATUL	Boeing 737-8K5/W	38820/3653	ex C-GTUL		
☐ D-ATUM	Boeing 737-8K5/W	37240/4786			
☐ D-ATUN	Boeing 737-8K5/W	41660/5252			♦
☐ D-ATUO	Boeing 737-8K5/W	41661/5292			♦
☐ D-ATUP	Boeing 737-8K5/W	41662/5340			♦
☐ D-ATUQ	Boeing 737-8K5/W	41663/5369			♦
☐ D-ATUR	Boeing 737-8K5/W	41664/5380			♦
☐ D-ATUZ	Boeing 737-8K5/W	34691/2246	ex OO-JPT		o/o♦

WDL AVIATION   WDL (WDL)   Cologne (CGN)

☐ D-ALIN	British Aerospace 146 Srs.300	E3142	ex EI-DEW		[CGN]
☐ D-AMAX	British Aerospace 146 Srs.300	E3157	ex EI-DEX		[CGN]
☐ D-AMGL	British Aerospace 146 Srs.200	E2055	ex G-CBFL		♦
☐ D-AWBA	British Aerospace 146 Srs.300A	E3134	ex ZK-NZF		
☐ D-AWUE	British Aerospace 146 Srs.200	E2050	ex PK-PJP		

DQ-   FIJI (Republic of Fiji)

AIR KAIBU

☐ DQ-KVV	de Havilland DHC-6 Twin Otter 300	838	ex C-GIGZ	

AIR WAKAYA   Suva-Nausori (SUV)

☐ DQ-DHG	Cessna 208B Caravan I	208B1120	ex N127AX	dam 17Dec12
☐ DQ-FHG	Britten-Norman BN-2B-26 Islander	2230	ex G-BSAC	
☐ DQ-WPG	Cessna 208BEX Caravan I	208B5007	ex N2013Z	

FIJI AIRWAYS   Pac Sun (FJ/FJI)   Nadi (NAN)

☐ DQ-FJF	Boeing 737-7X2/W	28878/96	ex N1786B	Island of Koro	
☐ DQ-FJG	Boeing 737-8X2/W	29968/275	ex N1786B	Island of Kadavu	
☐ DQ-FJH	Boeing 737-8X2/W	29969/339	ex N1786B	Island of Gau	
☐ DQ-FJM	Boeing 737-86J/W	37754/3306	ex D-ABKL	Mamamanuca Islands	
☐ DQ-	Boeing 737-808/W	34969/2293	ex D-ABBX		o/o♦
☐ DQ-FJT	Airbus A330-243	1394	ex F-WWKD	Island of Taveuni	
☐ DQ-FJU	Airbus A330-243	1416	ex F-WWTK	Island of Namuka-i-Lau	
☐ DQ-FJV	Airbus A330-243	1465	ex F-WWCZ	Island of Yasawa-i-Rara	
☐ DQ-	Airbus A330-343E	1692	ex F-WW		o/o♦

FIJI LINK   Sunflower (PI/SUF)   Nadi (NAN)

☐ DQ-FDW	Britten-Norman BN-2A-26 Islander	602	ex 9M-MDC	Adi Makutu	
☐ DQ-FIE	de Havilland DHC-6 Twin Otter 300	660	ex N933CL	Spirit of Nadi	
☐ DQ-FJX	ATR 72-600	1221	ex F-WWET		♦
☐ DQ-FJY	ATR 42-600	1014	ex F-WWLW		♦
☐ DQ-FJZ	ATR 72-600	1146	ex F-WWEP		♦
☐ DQ-PSD	de Havilland DHC-6 Twin Otter 310	414	ex N38535		
☐ DQ-PSE	de Havilland DHC-6 Twin Otter 300	410	ex N974SW		

HIBISCUS AIR   Suva-Nausori (SUV)

☐ DQ-	Cessna U206F Stationair	U20602273	ex ZK-TFW	

ISLAND HOPPERS   Nadi (NAN)

☐ DQ-IBT	Aérespatiale AS350B Ecureuil 1	1572	ex ZK-IBT	
☐ DQ-KBD	Pacific Aerospace 750XL	169	ex ZK-KBD	
☐ DQ-KBP	Pacific Aerospace 750XL	178	ex ZK-KBP	

NORTHERN AIR SERVICES CHARTER				Suva-Nausori (SUV)
☐ DQ-FIC	Britten-Norman BN-2A-21 Islander	511	ex ZK-KHB	wfs
☐ DQ-JJS	Britten-Norman BN-2A-26 Islander	856	ex VH-IFA	
☐ DQ-SSS	Britten-Norman BN-2A-21 Islander	511	ex DQ-FIC	

PACIFIC ISLAND AIR				Nadi (NAN)
☐ DQ-GEE	de Havilland DHC-2 Beaver	1358	ex C-GSKY	FP
☐ DQ-HFJ	Aérospatiale AS355F1 Ecureuil 2	5158	ex VH-YUP	♦
☐ DQ-PIA	de Havilland DHC-3T Turbo Otter	115		FP♦
☐ DQ-SLM	Britten-Norman BN-2A-26 Islander	605	ex VH-XFI	
☐ DQ-YIR	Britten-Norman BN-2A-26 Islander	845	ex VH-FCO	

TURTLE AIRWAYS		Turtle (TLT)		Nadi-Newtown Beach
☐ DQ-TAL	de Havilland DHC-2 Beaver	1255	ex C-GLED	FP
☐ DQ-TAN	Cessna U206G Stationair 6 II	U20605574	ex VH-HBX	FP

D2- ANGOLA (Republic of Angola)				

AEROJET ANGOLA		Mabeco (MBC)		Luanda (LAD)
☐ D2-EBP	Embraer ERJ-145LR	145003	ex N850HK	
☐ D2-EDE	Embraer EMB.120ER Brasilia	120039	ex N188SW	
☐ D2-ENG	British Aerospace Jetstream 4121	41095	ex ZS-NYK	
☐ D2-FDK	Embraer EMB.120ER Brasilia	120281	ex N215SW	
☐ D2-FDQ	Antonov An-32A	2110	ex ER-AEV	
☐ D2-FDT	Embraer EMB.120RT Brasilia	120081	ex N103SK	
☐ D2-FER	Yakovlev Yak-40	9541844	ex RA-87994	wfs
☐ D2-FET	Embraer EMB.120ER Brasilia	120175	ex OM-SKY	
☐ D2-FHF	British Aerospace Jetstream 4101	41049	ex N149KM	

AIR 26		Ducard (DCD)		Luanda (LAD)
☐ D2-EYN	Embraer EMB.120ER Brasilia	120165	ex N264AS Nova Erce	
☐ D2-EYO	Embraer EMB.120RT Brasilia	120210	ex N269AS	
☐ D2-EYP	Embraer EMB.120RT Brasilia	120146	ex N262AS	
☐ D2-EYV	Embraer EMB.120ER Brasilia	120145	ex N284UE	[HLA]
☐ D2-EYQ	Embraer EMB.120ER Brasilia	120062	ex F-GFEO	
☐ D2-EZC	Embraer EMB.120ER Brasilia	120199	ex N652CT	wfs
☐ D2-EZZ	Embraer EMB.120FC Brasilia	120102	ex N126AM	Frtr
☐ D2-SRB	Embraer ERJ-135LR	145696	ex N834RP	<SEAA
☐ D2-SRC	Embraer ERJ-135LR	145724	ex N839RP	<SEAA

AIR J MICHEL				
☐ D2-FDR	LET L-410UVP	831039	ex UR-67411	

ALADA		Air Alada (RAD)		Luanda (LAD)
☐ D2-FAX	Antonov An-32A	1510	ex RA-48115 Kimoka	
☐ D2-FFR	Ilyushin Il-18D	0393607150	ex UR-75896	converted Il-22; wfs

ANGOLA AIR SERVICES				Luanda (LAD)
☐ D-BDTB	Dornier 328-310 (328JET)	3147	ex TF-MIK	wfs VIP
☐ D-BDTC	Dornier 328-310 (328JET)	3149	ex TF-MIL	wfs VIP
☐ D-BDTD	Dornier 328-310 (328JET)	3181	ex TF-MIO	wfs VIP
☐ D2-EBN	Learjet 45	45-069	ex SU-MSG	
☐ D2-ERU	Boeing 727-2S7	22020/1592	ex N681CA	
☐ D2-FHE	British Aerospace Jetstream 4101	41046	ex N146KM	wfs
☐ D2-FHK	Dornier 328-310 (328JET)	3161	ex D-BDTA	VIP
☐ ZS-PCA	Beech 1900C-1	UC-138	ex N138GA	

DIEXIM EXPRESS				Luanda (LAD)
☐ D2-FFE	Embraer EMB.120ER Brasilia	120242	ex N8078V	
☐ D2-FFO	Beech 350 Super King Air	FL-10	ex N350FH	
☐ D2-FFP	Embraer EMB.120RT Brasilia	120235	ex F-GJTF	
☐ D2-FFU	Embraer EMB.120ER Brasilia	120244	ex F-GTBH	[HLA]
☐ D2-FFW	Embraer ERJ-145MP	145360	ex F-OIJE Il Aladia	
☐ D2-FFY	Embraer EMB.120RT Brasilia	120171	ex N221CR	[HLA]
☐ D2-FXX	Learjet 45	45-066	ex N94CK	

FLY540 ANGOLA		(F5)		
☐ D2-FLB	ATR 72-202	470	ex M-ABEF	[LPA]

| ☐ D2-FLC | ATR 72-202 | 483 | ex M-ABEG | |
| ☐ D2-FLY | ATR 72-212A | 826 | ex F-WKVD | |

GIRA GLOBO		**Gira Globo (GGL)**		**Luanda (LAD)**
☐ D2-EBF	Beech 200 Super King Air	BB-836	ex S9-NAQ	
☐ D2-FCN	Ilyushin Il-76TD	0053462872	ex UR-76651	opf Angolan AF as T-900
☐ D2-FDG	Antonov An-32B	2201	ex RA-48116 Mulanda	
☐ D2-FEM	Ilyushin Il-76TD	0063469062	ex UR-76688 Rei-Ekuikui	opf Angolan AF as T-908
☐ D2-FEW	Ilyushin Il-76TD	0073475239	ex UR-76721	opf Angolan AF as T-904

GUICANGO		**(NCL)**		**Luanda (LAD)**
☐ D2-FDO	Embraer EMB.120RT Brasilia	120082	ex N102SK	♦
☐ D2-FFV	Antonov An-32	2510	ex HK-4369X	

HM AIRWAYS (HELI-MALONGO)				**Luanda (LAD)**
☐ D2-EYA	Bell 427	56037	ex N51804	
☐ D2-EYB	Bell 427	56046	ex N427MM	
☐ D2-EYC	Bell 427	56048	ex N804RM	
☐ D2-EYD	Bell 427	56049	ex N88PQ	
☐ D2-EYE	Bell 427	56050	ex N918RB	
☐ D2-FYF	Bell 427	56051	ex N96EA	
☐ D2-EYG	Bell 427	56052	ex N97EA	
☐ D2-EYH	Bell 427	56053	ex N97TZ	
☐ D2-EUO	de Havilland DHC-8-402Q	4312	ex C-GDCQ	
☐ D2-EUP	de Havilland DHC-8-402Q	4315	ex C-GDFF	
☐ D2-EUQ	de Havilland DHC-8-402Q	4322	ex C-GEVB	
☐ D2-EUR	de Havilland DHC-8-402Q	4325	ex C-GEZN	
☐ D2-EYI	Bell 430	49102	ex N41786	
☐ D2-EYJ	Bell 430	49108	ex N767MM	
☐ D2-EYK	Bell 430	49109	ex N825GB	
☐ D2-EYW	Bell 412EP			
☐ D2-EYX	Bell 412EP			
☐ D2-EYY	Bell 412EP			

SAL - SOCIEDADE DE AVIACAO LIGEIRA				**Luanda (LAD)**
☐ D2-ECN	Cessna F406 Caravan II	F406-0002	ex PH-MNS	
☐ D2-ECO	Cessna F406 Caravan II	F406-0011	ex D-IDAA	
☐ D2-ECP	Cessna F406 Caravan II	F406-0016	ex PH-LAS	
☐ D2-ECQ	Cessna F406 Caravan II	F406-0019	ex G-CVAN	
☐ D2-ECW	Beech 350 King Air	FL-102	ex S9-TAP	
☐ D2-ECX	Beech B200 Super King Air	BB-1362	ex N1565F	
☐ D2-EDA	Cessna 208B Caravan I	208B0568	ex N1215K	
☐ D2-EDB	Cessna 208B Caravan I	208B0665	ex N1256G	
☐ D2-EOD	Short SC.7 Skyvan 3	SH1938	ex CR-LOD	[LAD]

SEAA				**Luanda (LAD)**
☐ D2-SRA	Embraer ERJ-145EP	145155	ex EI-DKH	
☐ D2-SRB	Embraer ERJ-135LR	145696	ex N834RP	>DCD
☐ D2-SRC	Embraer ERJ-135LR	145724	ex N839RP	>DCD

SERVIS AIR				**Luanda (LAD)**
☐ D2-FGI	McDonnell-Douglas MD-82	53059/1942	ex I-DACY	
☐ D2-FGJ	McDonnell-Douglas MD-82	53220/2073	ex I-DATU	

SJL AERONÁUTICA				**Luanda (LAD)**
☐ D2-ESN	Fokker F.27 Friendship 500F	10610	ex PH-FTY	♦

SONAIR		**Sonair (SOR)**		**Luanda (LAD)**
☐ D2-EQD	Aérospatiale SA365N2 Dauphin 2	6521	ex F-GJIA	
☐ D2-EQE	Aérospatiale SA365N2 Dauphin 2	6531	ex F-WQSR	
☐ D2-EUO	Aérospatiale SA365N Dauphin 2	9000		
☐ D2-EVE	Aérospatiale SA365N2 Dauphin 2	6418	ex F-WQSR	
☐ D2-EVF	Aérospatiale SA365N2 Dauphin 2	6410	ex F-GHRX	
☐ D2-EXX	Aérospatiale SA365N2 Dauphin 2	6439	ex F-WQSR	
☐ D2-ERQ	Beech 1900D	UE-274	ex N11015	
☐ D2-EVJ	Beech 1900D	UE-111	ex N3119U	
☐ D2-EVK	Beech 1900D	UE-121	ex N3221A	
☐ D2-EVN	Beech 1900D	UE-370	ex (F-OHGD)	
☐ D2-EVR	Beech 1900D	UE-280	ex N11284	
☐ D2-EVX	Beech 1900D	UE-340	ex (F-GSVC)	
☐ D2-EVY	Beech 1900D	UE-249	ex N249GL	

☐ D2-EWR	Beech 1900D	UE-193	ex N69548	
☐ D2-EWW	Beech 1900D	UE-399	ex N854CA	
☐ D2-EWX	Beech 1900D	UE-405	ex N856CA	
☐ D2-EWY	Beech 1900D	UE-401	ex N840CA	
☐ D2-FFJ	Beech 1900D	UE-412	ex N44828	
☐ D2-FFN	Beech 1900D	UE-329	ex N23183	
☐ D2-EVA	de Havilland DHC-6 Twin Otter 310	728	ex V2-LDD	
☐ D2-EVB	de Havilland DHC-6 Twin Otter 310	810	ex V2-LDH	
☐ D2-EVC	de Havilland DHC-6 Twin Otter 310	809	ex V2-LDG	
☐ D2-EVH	de Havilland DHC-6 Twin Otter 300	511	ex HB-LOM	
☐ D2-FVM	de Havilland DHC-6 Twin Otter 310	794	ex HB-LRF	
☐ D2-FVN	de Havilland DHC-6 Twin Otter 310	817	ex N817L	
☐ D2-FVO	de Havilland DHC-6 Twin Otter 310	821	ex N821L	
☐ D2-FVP	de Havilland DHC-6 Twin Otter 310	743	ex 5Y-TMF	
☐ D2-FVQ	de Havilland DHC-6 Twin Otter 310	704	ex 5N-ASP	
☐ D2-EQH	Eurocopter EC225LP	2743		
☐ D2-EQI	Eurocopter EC225LP	2746		
☐ D2-EQL	Eurocopter EC225LP	2783	ex F-WWOX	
☐ D2-EQM	Eurocopter EC225LP	2784		
☐ D2-EVT	Eurocopter EC225LP		ex F-WQDI	
☐ D2-EWZ	Eurocopter EC225LP	2815	ex F-HUPM	
☐ D2-EZM	Eurocopter EC225LP	2900	ex G-CIDM	◆
☐ D2-EZN	Eurocopter EC225LP	2876	ex G-CIDK	◆
☐ D2-EZO	Eurocopter EC225LP	2913	ex F-WJXP	◆
☐ D2-EVS	Sikorsky S-76C	760603	ex C-GHRI	<CHC Helicopters Intl
☐ D2-EXG	Sikorsky S-76A	760042	ex ZS-RKE	<Heli-Union
☐ D2-EXH	Sikorsky S-76A	760268	ex ZS-RBE	<CHC Helicopter (Africa)
☐ D2-EXK	Sikorsky S-76C	760525	ex N9017U	
☐ D2-EXL	Sikorsky S-76C	760526	ex N9007U	
☐ D2-EXP	Sikorsky S-76C	760544	ex N2048K	
☐ D2-EXR	Sikorsky S-76C++	760758	ex N758N	◆
☐ D2-EZF	Sikorsky S-76C++	760811	ex N811H	
☐ D2-EZG	Sikorsky S-76C++	760812	ex N812N	
☐ D2-EZH	Sikorsky S-76C++	760813	ex N813E	◆
☐ D2-EZI	Sikorsky S-76C++	760797	ex N797Y	◆
☐ D2-EZJ	Sikorsky S-76C++	760809	ex N809D	◆
☐ D2-ESN	Fokker F.27 Friendship 500	10610	ex PH-FTY	
☐ D2-ESW	Fokker 50	20241	ex PH-RRM	[WOE]
☐ D2-ESZ	Aérospatiale AS332L2 II	2503	ex F-WQPA	
☐ D2-EVW	Boeing 737-7HB/W	35954/2310		
☐ D2-EWK	Beech 350 King Air	FL-294	ex S9-CAN	
☐ D2-EWS	Boeing 737-7HB/W	35956/2536		
☐ D2-EXN	Aérospatiale AS332L2 II	2590		
☐ N263SG	Boeing 747-481	29263/1204	ex B-LFC	<GTI
☐ N322SG	Boeing 747-481	30322/1250	ex B-LFD	<GTI

TAAG ANGOLA AIRLINES		***DTA (DT/DTA)***		***Luanda (LAD)***
☐ D2-TBF	Boeing 737-7M2/W	34559/2013	ex N6067U	
☐ D2-TBG	Boeing 737-7M2/W	34560/2036		
☐ D2-TBH	Boeing 737-7M2/W	34561/2043		
☐ D2-TBJ	Boeing 737-7M2/W	34562/2149		
☐ D2-TBK	Boeing 737-7HBC/W	35955/2531	ex D2-EVZ	
☐ D2-TED	Boeing 777-2M2ER	34565/581		
☐ D2-TEE	Boeing 777-2M2ER	34566/587		Kuitu Kuanavale
☐ D2-TEF	Boeing 777-2M2ER	34567/687		
☐ D2-TEG	Boeing 777-3M2ER	40805/935		Sagrada Esperanca
☐ D2-TEH	Boeing 777-3M2ER	40806/944		Welwitschia Marabilis
☐ D2-TEI	Boeing 777-3M2ER	43252/1198		Ebo
☐ D2-TBC	Boeing 737-2M2C	21173/447	ex D2-TAB	
☐ D2-TBO	Boeing 737-2M2	22776/891	ex N1782B	
☐ D2-TBX	Boeing 737-2M2	23351/1117		

TRANSAFRIK INTERNATIONAL		***(TFK)***		***Luanda/São Tomé (LAD/TMS)***
☐ 5X-TUA	Lockheed L-382G-11C Hercules	4301	ex S9-CAV	
☐ 5X-TUB	Lockheed L-382G-13C Hercules	4300	ex S9-CAW	opf UN
☐ 5X-TUD	Lockheed L-382G Hercules	4299	ex S9-DBF	opf UN
☐ 5X-TUE	Lockheed L-382E-25C Hercules	4385	ex S9-NAL	
☐ 5X-TUF	Lockheed L-328G Hercules	4383	ex S9-DBE	
☐ S9-BAE	Boeing 727-31F	18903/147	ex N210NE	
☐ S9-PAC	Boeing 727-44C (FedEx 3)	20475/854	ex C-GVFA	wfs

TROPICANA					Luanda (LAD)
☐ D2-EBF	Beech B200 Super King Air	BB-836	ex S9-NAQ		
☐ D2-FFM	Beech 1900D	UE-108	ex N118SK	Mavinga	

D4-   CAPE VERDE ISLANDS (Republic of Cape Verde)

CABO VERDE EXPRESS		Kabex (CVE)			Sal (SID)
☐ D4-CBL	LET L-410UVP-E10	902511	ex 9Q-CUM		
☐ D4-CBR	LET L-410UVP-E20	912533	ex D-CLED		
☐ D4-JCA	LET L-410UVP-E20	912604	ex OY-PEY		

TACV - TRANSPORTES AEREOS DE CABO VERDE/CAPE VERDE AIRLINES					
		Caboverde (VR/TCV)			Praia (RAI)
☐ D4-CBP	Boeing 757-2Q8	30045/957	ex N301AM	Emigranti	
☐ D4-CBT	ATR 72-212A	747	ex F-WWEH	Jorge Barbosa	
☐ D4-CBU	ATR 72-212A	755	ex F-WWEP	Baltizar Lopes	
☐ D4-CBV	ATR 42-500	669	ex F-WWLC		
☐ D4-CBX	Boeing 737-8Q8/W	30039/701	ex N734MA	Mindelo	
☐ OM-GTC	Boeing 737-430	27001/2316	ex G-CIEO		<RLX♦

D6-   COMOROS (Federal Islamic Republic of the Comores)

AB AVIATION		(AYD)		Moroni Prince Said Ibrahim (HAH)	
☐ ZS-OTD	Embraer EMB.120RT Brasilia	120230	ex N249CA	<Sahara African Avn♦	

COMORES AVIATION		Comores (O5/KMZ)			Moroni (YVA)
☐ D6-CAL	LET L-410UVP	800526	ex HA-LAB		
☐ D6-CAM	LET L-410UVP	851336	ex D6-GDH		
☐ D6-CAN	LET L-410UVP	841331	ex 9L-LCZ		

COMOROS ISLANDS AIRWAYS		Comores Airline (CIK)			Moroni (YVA)
☐ D6-CAS	Airbus A320-214	3040	ex EC-KAX		[KRT]

EC-   SPAIN (Kingdom of Spain)

AERONOVA		Aeronova (OVA)			Valencia (VLC)
☐ EC-GUS	Swearingen SA227AC Metro III	AC-648	ex N2685L		
☐ EC-GVE	Swearingen SA227AC Metro III	AC-669B	ex N2702Z		
☐ EC-HCH	Swearingen SA227AC Metro III	AC-658B	ex N2692P		
☐ EC-IXL	Swearingen SA227AC Metro III	AC-689B	ex D-COLC		
☐ EC-JCU	Swearingen SA227AC Metro III	AC-679B	ex N6UB		
☐ EC-IDG	ATR 42-320	003	ex F-OICG		

AIR EUROPA		Europa (UX/AEA)			Palma de Mallorca (PMI)
Member of SkyTeam					
☐ EC-JPF	Airbus A330-202	733	ex F-WWKU		
☐ EC-JQG	Airbus A330-202	745	ex F-WWYG	Estepona-Costa del Sol	
☐ EC-JQQ	Airbus A330-202	749	ex F-WWYJ		
☐ EC-JZL	Airbus A330-202	814	ex F-WWYJ	David Bisbal	
☐ EC-KOM	Airbus A330-202	931	ex F-WWKU		
☐ EC-KTG	Airbus A330-202	950	ex F-WWKQ		
☐ EC-LMN	Airbus A330-243	597	ex EI-EOL		
☐ EC-LNH	Airbus A330-243	551	ex EI-EON		
☐ EC-LQO	Airbus A330-243	505	ex 5B-DBS		
☐ EC-LQP	Airbus A330-243	526	ex 5B-DBT		
☐ EC-LVL	Airbus A330-243	461	ex EC-LKE		
☐ EC-LXA	Airbus A330-343E	670	ex OE-ICB	Los del Rio	
☐ EC-LXR	Airbus A330-343E	1097	ex EI-FBE		
☐ EC-MAJ	Airbus A330-243	992	ex A9C-KJ	Vicente del Bosque	
☐ EC-KUL	ATR 72-212A	809	ex F-WWET		<SWT♦
☐ EC-KVI	ATR 72-212A	824	ex F-WWEM		<SWT♦
☐ EC-LST	ATR 72-201F	234	ex SP-OLL		<SWT
☐ EC-LYB	ATR 72-212A	550	ex N550LL		<SWT♦

☐ EC-MAF	ATR 72-212A	568	ex OY-CIN		<SWT♦
☐ EC-IDA	Boeing 737-86Q/W	32773/1051	ex N73792		
☐ EC-IDT	Boeing 737-86Q/W	30281/1076	ex N73793		
☐ EC-III	Boeing 737-86Q/W	30284/1233			
☐ EC-ISN	Boeing 737-86Q/W	30291/1435			
☐ EC-JAP	Boeing 737-85P/W	33971/1580			
☐ EC-JBJ	Boeing 737-85P/W	33972/1598		Salamanca	
☐ EC-JBK	Boeing 737-85P/W	33973/1606			
☐ EC-JBL	Boeing 737-85P/W	33974/1610			
☐ EC-JHK	Boeing 737-85P/W	33975/1716	ex N1787B		SkyTeam c/s
☐ EC-JHL	Boeing 737-85P/W	33976/1740			
☐ EC-JNF	Boeing 737-85P/W	33977/1878		Lorenzo's Land	
☐ EC-KCG	Boeing 737-85P/W	33981/2269			
☐ EC-LPQ	Boeing 737-85P/W	35496/4015			
☐ EC-LPR	Boeing 737-85P/W	36588/3989			
☐ EC-LQX	Boeing 737-85P/W	36589/4116			
☐ EC-LTM	Boeing 737-85P/W	36591/4305			
☐ EC-LUT	Boeing 737-85P/W	36592/4434			
☐ EC-LVR	Boeing 737-85P/W	36593/4538			
☐ EC-LXV	Boeing 737-85P/W	36594/4666			
☐ EC-LYR	Boeing 737-85P/W	36595/4735	ex N1786B		
☐ EC-KRJ	Embraer ERJ-195LR	19000196	ex PT-SGE		
☐ EC-KXD	Embraer ERJ-195LR	19000244	ex PT-SIP		
☐ EC-KYO	Embraer ERJ-195LR	19000276	ex PT-TLQ		
☐ EC-KYP	Embraer ERJ-195LR	19000281	ex PT-TLV		
☐ EC-LCQ	Embraer ERJ-195LR	19000303	ex PT-TZR		
☐ EC-LEK	Embraer ERJ-195LR	19000344	ex PT-XQG		
☐ EC-LFZ	Embraer ERJ-195LR	19000357	ex PT-XQV		
☐ EC-LIN	Embraer ERJ-195LR	19000401	ex PT-XUG		
☐ EC-LKM	Embraer ERJ-195LR	19000425	ex PT-TBV		
☐ EC-LKX	Embraer ERJ-195LR	19000437	ex PT-TCX		
☐ EC-LLR	Embraer ERJ-195LR	19000452	ex PT-YCW		
☐ EC-KSS	Embraer ERJ-145MP	145230	ex D-ACIR	Trives	<PVG
☐ EC-	Boeing 787-8	36412/397			o/o♦
☐ SP-LRF	Boeing 787-8	35942/161		Franek	<LOT♦

AIR HORIZONT
Zaragosa (ZAZ)

☐ 9H-ZAZ	Boeing 737-436	25349/2156	ex G-DOCD	Corona de Aragon	wfs♦

AIR NOSTRUM
Nostru Air (YW/ANE)   **Valencia (VLC)**

☐ EC-LQV	ATR 72-600	995	ex F-WWLT		
☐ EC-LRH	ATR 72-600	999	ex F-WWLX		
☐ EC-LRR	ATR 72-600	1023	ex F-WWLQ		
☐ EC-LRU	ATR 72-600	1032	ex F-WWEQ		
☐ EC-LSQ	ATR 72-600	1041	ex F-WWED		
☐ EC-GYI	Canadair CRJ-200ER	7249	ex C-GDDM	Pinazo	
☐ EC-GZA	Canadair CRJ-200ER	7252	ex C-GDDO	Beniliure	wfs
☐ EC-HEK	Canadair CRJ-200ER	7320	ex C-GFCN	Cecilio Pla	
☐ EC-HHI	Canadair CRJ-200ER	7343	ex C-GFKQ	Virgen de Valvanera	[VCL]
☐ EC-HPR	Canadair CRJ-200ER	7430	ex C-GHDM	Mompo	[VLC]
☐ EC-HSH	Canadair CRJ-200ER	7466	ex C-GHWD	J Michavilla	
☐ EC-HYG	Canadair CRJ-200ER	7529	ex C-GIXG	E Sales Frances	[VLC]
☐ EC-ITU	Canadair CRJ-200ER	7866	ex C-GZSQ	Pons Arnau	
☐ EC-IVH	Canadair CRJ-200ER	7915	ex C-FADU	José Mongrell	
☐ EC-JCG	Canadair CRJ-200LR	7973	ex C-FCEU	José Vergara	
☐ EC-JCL	Canadair CRJ-200LR	7975	ex C-FCID	Rio Tormes	
☐ EC-JCM	Canadair CRJ-200LR	7981	ex C-FCNN	Beato de Liebana	all white
☐ EC-JCO	Canadair CRJ-200LR	7984	ex C-FCRX		
☐ EC-JEN	Canadair CRJ-200LR	7958	ex C-FBQO		wfs
☐ EC-JNX	Canadair CRJ-200LR	8058	ex C-FGEP	Catedral de Leon	all white
☐ EC-JOD	Canadair CRJ-200LR	8061	ex C-FGYE		all white
☐ EC-JOY	Canadair CRJ-200LR	8064	ex C-FHCW	Catedral de Leon	all white
☐ EC-JNB	Canadair CRJ-900ER	15057			
☐ EC-JTS	Canadair CRJ-900ER	15071	ex C-FJTF		
☐ EC-JTT	Canadair CRJ-900ER	15074	ex C-FJTJ		
☐ EC-JTU	Canadair CRJ-900ER	15079	ex C-FJTE		
☐ EC-JXZ	Canadair CRJ-900ER	15087	ex C-FLGI		
☐ EC-JYA	Canadair CRJ-900ER	15090	ex C-FLIX		
☐ EC-JYV	Canadair CRJ-900ER	15106	ex C-FLMJ		
☐ EC-JZS	Canadair CRJ-900ER	15111	ex C-FLMK		
☐ EC-JZT	Canadair CRJ-900ER	15113	ex C-FLMN		
☐ EC-JZU	Canadair CRJ-900ER	15115	ex C-FLMQ		
☐ EC-JZV	Canadair CRJ-900ER	15117	ex C-FLMS		>IBB
☐ EC-MEN	Canadair CRJ-900ER	15063	ex C-FIAP		♦
☐ EC-MFC	Canadair CRJ-900ER	15065	ex C-GLPP		♦

☐ EC-LJR	Canadair CRJ-1000ER	19002	ex C-GCBN	
☐ EC-LJS	Canadair CRJ-1000ER	19003	ex C-GIZJ	
☐ EC-LJT	Canadair CRJ-1000ER	19005	ex C-GIBJ	
☐ EC-LJX	Canadair CRJ-1000ER	19008		
☐ EC-LKF	Canadair CRJ-1000ER	19011	ex C-GHZZ	
☐ EC-LOJ	Canadair CRJ-1000ER	19018	ex C-GIAO	
☐ EC-LOV	Canadair CRJ-1000ER	19019	ex C-GIBT	
☐ EC-LOX	Canadair CRJ-1000ER	19020	ex C-GZQV	
☐ EC-LPG	Canadair CRJ-1000ER	19021	ex C-GZQW	
☐ EC-LPN	Canadair CRJ-1000ER	19022	ex C-GICB	

AIR PLUS ULTRA (PUE) Madrid-Barajas (MAD)

☐ EC-MFA	Airbus A340-313X	212	ex A9C-LG	wfs♦
☐ EC-MFB	Airbus A340-313X	215	ex A9C-LH	wfs♦

AIR SPA

☐ EC-JLC	Air Tractor AT-802A Fire Boss	802A-0214	

AIR TRACTOR EUROPE Valencia (VLC)

☐ EC-LMV	Air Tractor AT-802	802-0406	ex N8520L
☐ FC-LNT	Air Tractor AT-802	802-0411	ex N8522M
☐ EC-LRP	Air Tractor AI-802	802-0427	ex N85152
☐ EC-LRQ	Air Tractor AT-802	802-0431	ex N23579
☐ EC-LSB	Air Tractor AT-802	802-0438	ex N8516X
☐ EC-LSC	Air Tractor AT-802	802-0442	ex N8517Q
☐ EC-LSJ	Air Tractor AT-802	802-0432	ex N2358P
☐ EC-LSR	Air Tractor AT-802A	802A-0459	ex N2084F
☐ EC-LTN	Air Tractor AT-802A	802A-0461	ex N2358G
☐ EC-LXX	Air Tractor AT-802	802-0451	ex N8520K
☐ EC-LXY	Air Tractor AT-802	802-0454	ex N8518U
☐ EC-MDD	Air Tractor AT-802A	802A-0561	♦
☐ EC-MDN	Air Tractor AT-802A	802A-0562	♦

AIRNOR - AERONAVES DEL NORESTE Ponteareas

☐ EC-DXN	Eurocopter AS350B Ecureuil	1387	ex HB-XLU
☐ EC-IXH	Eurocopter AS355F1 Ecureuil	5009	ex D-HFAI
☐ EC-JJC	Eurocopter EC130B4 Ecureuil	3539	ex F-GSDF
☐ EC-JXC	Cessna 500 Citation	500-0278	ex OY-PCW

ALBASTAR (JQ/LAV) Palma de Mallorca (PMI)

☐ EC-LAV	Boeing 737-408	24352/1705	ex EC-KTM	Pino d'Urso	
☐ EC-LNC	Boeing 737-4K5	24130/1827	ex N721VX		
☐ EC-LTG	Boeing 737-4K5	24129/1783	ex N720VX		
☐ EC-MFS	Boeing 737-4Y0	25178/2199	ex OM-AEX		<AXE♦

ANGEL MARTINEZ RIDAO (AMO) Sevilla-Utrera

☐ EC-GGQ	Air Tractor AT-802	802-0028	ex N60660
☐ EC-GVN	Air Tractor AT-802	802-0065	ex N5059X
☐ EC-HMD	Air Tractor AT-802	802-0088	ex N9049K
☐ EC-HMZ	Air Tractor AT-802	802-0095	ex N9087Y
☐ EC-HXG	Air Tractor AT-802	802-0113	ex N91442
☐ EC-INH	Air Tractor AT-802	802-0139	ex N8507V
☐ EC-IXG	Air Tractor AT-802A Fire Boss	802A-0169	
☐ EC-JDJ	Air Tractor AT-802A Fire Boss	802A-0190	ex N85230
☐ EC-JIC	Air Tractor AT-802A	802-0192	ex N85178
☐ EC-JLB	Air Tractor AT-802A Fire Boss	802A-0206	ex N41744
☐ EC-JRM	Air Tractor AT-802A	802-0224	ex N85253
☐ EC-JTZ	Air Tractor AT-802A Fire Boss	802A-0230	ex N8516V
☐ EC-LLT	Air Tractor AT-802	802-0392	ex N8519F
☐ EC-LON	Air Tractor AT-802	802-0419	ex N8521E
☐ EC-FKV	Air Tractor AT-502	502-0162	ex N1529N
☐ EC-GDZ	Cessna 337G	33701687	ex N53532
☐ EC-IGT	Cessna T337G	P3370157	ex CC-CEA
☐ EC-GHI	Air Tractor AT-502B	502B-0360	ex N6095Z
☐ EC-IYL	Air Tractor AT-401	401-0739	ex N89KC
☐ EC-IYM	Air Tractor AT-401	401-0836	ex N1518V
☐ EC-JAY	Air Tractor AT-401	401-1150	
☐ EC-JBM	Air Tractor AT-502B	502B-0687	ex N8520K

AVIALSA – AVIACIÓN AGRICOLA DEL LEVANTE Valencia (VLC)

☐ EC-HOR	Air Tractor AT-802	802-0098	ex N9107X
☐ EC-JUB	Air Tractor AT-802A Fire Boss	802A-0236	ex N8520K
☐ EC-LBH	Air Tractor AT-802A Fire Boss	802A-0318	

□ EC-LBP	Air Tractor AT-802A Fire Boss	802A-0322	
□ EC-LGN	Air Tractor AT-802A	802A-0344	ex N5001N
□ EC-LGT	Air Tractor AT-802A	802A-0342	ex N8519F
□ EC-LGY	Air Tractor AT-802A	802A-0359	ex N85253
□ EC-LHI	Air Tractor AT-802	802-0361	ex N8520L
□ EC-LHR	Air Tractor AT-802A	802A-0368	ex N8523C
□ EC-LNG	Air Tractor AT-802	802-0407	ex N8520K
□ EC-LSS	Air Tractor AT-802	802-0466	ex N8521D
□ EC-MBH	Air Tractor AT-802	802-0458	♦

□ EC-EPP	Cessna T337H Super Skymaster	33701837	N1345L
□ EC-ETU	Cessna 337G Super Skymaster	33701573	ex N6AX
□ EC-HCA	Piper PA-34-200 Seneca	34-7650191	ex 9A-BPW

BINTER GROUP (NT/IBB) Las Palmas-Gran Canaria (LPA)

□ EC-GQF	ATR 72-202	489	ex F-WWLJ	
□ EC-GRU	ATR 72-202	493	ex F-WWLN	
□ EC-IYC	ATR 72-212A	709	ex F-WWEI	Los Gofiones
□ EC-IZO	ATR 72-212A	711	ex F-WWEK	Gofio
□ EC-JBI	ATR 72-212A	713	ex F-WWEM	Maspalomas Costa Canaria
□ EC-JEH	ATR 72-212A	716	ex F-WWEP	Perenquen
□ EC-JEV	ATR 72-212A	717	ex F-WWER	Los Sabandeños
□ EC-JQL	ATR 72-212A	726	ex F-WWEG	Teide
□ EC-KGI	ATR 72-212A	752	ex F-WWEM	Bentayga
□ EC-KGJ	ATR 72-212A	753	ex F-WWEN	Madeira
□ EC-KRY	ATR 72-212A	795	ex F-WWEV	Azero
□ EC-KSG	ATR 72-212A	796	ex F-WWEW	Malvasía Volcánica
□ EC-KYI	ATR 72-212A	850	ex F-WWET	Guarapo
□ EC-LAD	ATR 72-212A	864	ex F-WWEM	Baifo
□ EC-LFA	ATR 72-212A	902	ex F-WWER	Rapadura
□ EC-LGF	ATR 72-212A	907	ex F-WWEX	Pejeverde

□ EC-JZV	Canadair CRJ-900ER	15117	ex C-FLMS	<ANE

Binter Group comprises Binter Canarias, Canair and NAYSA, all flying interchangeably for those ops in Binter c/s

CANARYFLY/CANARIAS AERONÁUTICA Canary (PM/CNF) Las Palmas-Gran Canaria (LPA)

□ EC-GRP	ATR 72-202	488	ex F-WWLI		♦
□ EC-IRS	Swearingen SA227BC Metro III	BC-786B	ex N61AJ		
□ EC-JQC	Swearingen SA226AC Merlin IVA	AT-066	ex N5FY		
□ EC-LMX	ATR 42-320	115	ex EI-SLI	Villa Cisneros	<ABR wfs
□ EC-LYZ	ATR 42-300	226	ex F-GKNB	white c/s	
□ EC-LZR	ATR 72-202	441	ex OY-EDN		
□ OE-LIC	de Havilland DHC-8-314Q	503	ex D-BHAS	Steinmark c/s	<ISK♦

CAT HELICOPTERS Barcelona-Port

□ EC-KAF	Eurocopter AS355F2 Ecureuil II	5079	ex F-GJFU
□ EC-LHD	Eurocopter AS355F2 Ecureuil II	5381	ex F-HDLS

COMUNIDAD AUTÓNOMA DE EUSKADI - ERZAINTZA Vitoria (VIT)

□ EC-ERZ	Eurocopter AS350B2 Ecureuil	2261		opb Inaer
□ EC-EGV	Eurocopter AS365C3 Dauphin	5032	ex F-GBTB	wfs

CYGNUS AIR Gestair (XG/RGN) Madrid-Barajas (MAD)

□ EC-FTR	Boeing 757-256PCF	26239/553	ex EC-420
□ EC-KLD	Boeing 757-256PCF	24121/183	ex N28AT

COYOT AIR Madrid-Cuatro Vientos (MCV)

□ EC-IBV	Eurocopter AS350B3 Ecureuil	3489	ex F-WQPQ	
□ EC-KFO	Eurocopter AS350B3 Ecureuil	4247	ex F-WWPY	
□ EC-KGQ	Eurocopter AS350B3 Ecureuil	4253	ex F-WWPT	
□ EC-KGY	Eurocopter AS350B3 Ecureuil	4234	ex F-WWPG	
□ EC-KIS	Eurocopter AS350B3 Ecureuil	4264	ex F-WWPR	
□ EC-KSK	Eurocopter AS350B3 Ecureuil	4365	ex F-WQRA	<Inaer♦
□ EC-KSL	Eurocopter AS350B3 Ecureuil	4359	ex EC-067	
□ EC-KTY	Eurocopter AS350B3 Ecureuil	4517	ex F-WAHD	
□ EC-MBJ	Eurocopter AS350B3 Ecureuil	7573	ex F-HMFR	>Helitrans♦
□ EC-MCC	Eurocopter AS350B3 Ecureuil	3439	ex OB-1880-P	♦
□ EC-MCD	Eurocopter AS350B3 Ecureuil	3340	ex OB-1820-P	♦
□ EC-MCG	Eurocopter AS350B3 Ecureuil	3612	ex OB-1870-P	♦
□ EC-MCJ	Eurocopter AS350B1 Ecureuil	2558	ex OB-1855-P	♦

□ EC-FUH	Eurocopter AS355N Twin Ecureuil	5554	ex F-WYMB	
□ EC-HJF	Eurocopter AS355N Twin Ecureuil	5660		
□ EC-IDM	Eurocopter AS355N Twin Ecureuil	5698	ex F-WQPS	
□ EC-IKB	Eurocopter EC135T2	250	ex D-HTSF	♦

| ☐ EC-IZE | Eurocopter EC135T2 | 309 | | ♦ |
| ☐ EC-KNZ | Eurocopter EC135T2i | 606 | ex EC-032 | ♦ |

DGP CUERPO NACIONAL DE POLICIA — Madrid-Cuatro Vientos (MCV)

☐ EC-IKX	Eurocopter EC135P2	0222	ex G-79-07	21
☐ EC-KAP	Eurocopter EC135P2	0462	ex EC-068	22
☐ EC-KAQ	Eurocopter EC135P2+	0505	ex EC-069	23
☐ EC-KOA	Eurocopter EC135P2+	0536	ex EC-030	24
☐ EC-KOB	Eurocopter EC135P2+	0596	ex EC-035	25
☐ EC-KVY	Eurocopter EC135P2+	0650	ex EC-034	26
☐ EC-KXE	Eurocopter EC135P2+	0721	ex EC-032	27
☐ EC-LJZ	Eurocopter EC135P2+	0846	ex EC-094	28
☐ EC-LKA	Eurocopter EC135P2+	0851	ex EC-035	29
☐ EC-LOR	Eurocopter EC135P2+	0934	ex EC-031	30
☐ EC-LOS	Eurocopter EC135P2+	0935	ex EC-036	31
☐ EC-LTT	Eurocopter EC135P2+	0981	ex EC-030	32
☐ EC-LTU	Eurocopter EC135P2+	1044	ex EC-038	33

☐ EC-DUP	MBB Bo105CB	S-614	ex D-HDSJ	05	
☐ EC-DUY	MBB Bo105C	S-628	ex D-HDSX	06	wfs
☐ EC-DUZ	MBB Bo105CB	S-629	ex D-HDSY	07	
☐ EC-DXC	MBB Bo105CB	S-690	ex D-HDVD	08	
☐ EC-DXD	MBR Bo105CB	S-697	ex D-HDVK	09	
☐ EC-DXH	MBB Bo105CB	S-698	ex D-HDVL	10	
☐ EC-DXI	MBB Bo105CB	S-699	ex D-HDVM	11	
☐ EC-DYN	MBB Bo105CB	S-707	ex D-HDVU	13	
☐ EC-ECI	MBB Bo105C	S-720	ex D-HDRH	14	
☐ EC-EQY	MBB Bo105CBS	S-810	ex D-HDZT	15	
☐ EC-FNN	MBB Bo105CBS	S-870	ex EC-981	18	
☐ EC-FNO	MBB Bo105CBS	S-869	ex EC-982	17	

☐ EC-GBB	Beech 200 Super King Air	BB-182	ex EC-727	
☐ EC-IAX	Cessna 550 Citation I	550-0156	ex N205SC	43
☐ EC-ILJ	Cessna 421C	421C0272	ex LZ-CCA	♦
☐ EC-LEN	Eurocopter EC-225 LP	2759	ex EC-091	40

DGT - DIRECCION GENERAL DE TRAFICO — Madrid-Cuatro Vientos (MCV)

☐ EC-IKS	Eurocopter AS355N Twin Ecureuil	5710	
☐ EC-ISB	Eurocopter AS355N Twin Ecureuil	5715	
☐ EC-ISZ	Eurocopter AS355N Twin Ecureuil	5723	ex F-WWPF
☐ EC-IXI	Eurocopter AS355N Twin Ecureuil	5725	
☐ EC-JMK	Eurocopter AS355N Ecureuil II	5741	ex F-WWPP
☐ EC-KXU	Eurocopter AS355NP Ecureuil II	5768	
☐ EC-LAR	Eurocopter AS355NP Ecureuil II	5772	ex F-WEVS
☐ EC-LGC	Eurocopter AS355NP Ecureuil II	5775	ex EC-091
☐ EC-LGD	Eurocopter AS355NP Ecureuil II	5776	ex EC-091
☐ EC-MDO	Eurocopter AS355NP Ecureuil	5807	ex EC-005	♦

| ☐ EC-LBD | Eurocopter EC135T2+ | 711 | ex EC-001 |
| ☐ EC-LDF | Eurocopter EC135T2+ | 744 | ex EC-038 |

EVELOP AIRLINE (E9/EVE) — Palma de Mallorca (PMI)

☐ CS-TRH	Airbus A330-343	833	ex EC-KCP	<OBS
☐ EC-LZD	Airbus A320-214/S	5642	ex CS-TRM	
☐ EC-	Airbus A330-343E	1691	ex F-WW	o/o♦

FAASA – FUMIGACIÓN AÉREA ANDALUZA — Córdoba-Sebastián Almagro

☐ EC-KQX	AgustaWestland AW119Ke	14702	ex N52ME	
☐ EC-KQY	AgustaWestland AW119Ke	14703	ex N60ME	
☐ EC-KZT	AgustaWestland AW119Ke	14727	ex N106YS	
☐ EC-KZU	AgustaWestland AW119Ke	14728	ex N107YS	
☐ EC-KZV	AgustaWestland AW119Ke	14729	ex N108YS	
☐ EC-KZX	AgustaWestland AW119Ke	14730	ex N109YS	
☐ EC-LFK	AgustaWestland AW119Ke	14752	ex N202YS	
☐ EC-LFL	AgustaWestland AW119Ke	14753	ex N203YS	
☐ EC-LPK	AgustaWestland AW119Ke	14716	ex N626JP	
☐ EC-LRC	AgustaWestland AW119KeII	14783	ex N308YS	
☐ EC-LZH	AgustaWestland AW119KeII	14533	ex N149JM	

☐ EC-IXU	Bell 412	33037		♦
☐ EC-IXV	Bell 412	33068	ex N422EH	♦
☐ EC-MAP	Bell 412	33041	ex C-GWEU	
☐ EC-MAQ	Bell 412	33032	ex C-GUNX	
☐ EC-MAR	Bell 412	33031	ex N417EH	
☐ EC-MEI	Bell 412	33089	ex N167EH	♦
☐ EC-MEJ	Bell 412	33064	ex N169EH	♦

| ☐ EC-EHV | Bell 204 | 953 | | ♦ |

☐ EC-GKY	Bell 205	13274	ex HE.10B-37 (EC)	♦
☐ EC-GKZ	Bell 205	13275	ex HE.10B-38 (EC)	♦
☐ EC-HXL	Bell 222U	47540	ex TC-HLS	♦
☐ EC-IFB	Bell 222U	47572	ex TC-HKL	♦
☐ EC-JKI	Air Tractor AT-802A Fire Boss	802A-0205	ex N4141Z	
☐ EC-JTD	Agusta Bell 412HP	25801	ex SE-JIX	
☐ EC-JTF	Air Tractor AT-802A	802A-0219	ex N8519F	
☐ EC-KED	Agusta A119	14015	ex N119LF	
☐ EC-KFZ	Kamov Ka32A11BC	9804		
☐ EC-KGA	Kamov Ka32A11BC	9805		
☐ EC-KII	Agusta A119	14525	ex N630WB	
☐ EC-KSC	Agusta A119	14034	ex N873MB	
☐ EC-KSH	Kamov Ka32A11BC	9814		
☐ EC-LQB	Agusta A119	14519	ex N65TG	

FLIGHTLINE — Flight-Avia (FTL) — Barcelona (BCN)

☐ EC-FZB	Swearingen SA226TC Metro II	TC-221	ex EC-666
☐ EC-GFK	Swearingen SA226AT Merlin IVA	AT-062	ex EC-125
☐ EC-GXJ	Swearingen SA226TC Metro II	TC-374	ex OY-AUO
☐ EC-HCU	Swearingen SA226TC Metro II	TC-390	ex N19WP

GRUPO INAER AVIONES ANFIBIOS — Albecete/Alicante/Salamanca/Seville

☐ EC-HET	Canadair CL-215-1A10	1034	ex I-SISB	
☐ EC-HEU	Canadair CL-215-1A10	1038	ex I-SISC	
☐ EC-IQC	Air Tractor AT-802A Fire Boss	802A-0155	ex N8512Q	
☐ EC-IUJ	Air Tractor AT-802A Fire Boss	802A-0154	ex C-GYZB	
☐ EC-JJY	Air Tractor AT-802A Fire Boss	802A-0204	ex N41470	
☐ EC-MCQ	Canadair CL-215-6B11	2090	ex UD.14-04 (EC)	♦

HELIBRAVO AVIACIÓN — Salamanca

| ☐ EC-LSF | Eurocopter AS350B3 Ecureuil | 7416 |
| ☐ EC-LXO | Eurocopter AS350B3 Ecureuil | 7625 |

HELIMAR - HELICOPTERS DEL MARE NOSTRUM — Madrid-Cuatro Vientos

☐ EC-EVS	Bell 204 (UH-1B)	893	ex EC-463	wfs
☐ EC-EXO	Bell 204 (UH-1B)	202	ex EC-436	wfs
☐ EC-GIZ	Bell 205 (UH-1H)	5631	ex EC-297	
☐ EC-GJA	Bell 205 (UH-1H)	5387	ex EC-298	wfs
☐ EC-GJB	Bell 205 (UH-1H)	9262	ex EC-299	wfs
☐ EC-GSO	Bell 205 (UH-1H)	5466	ex N1217A	wfs
☐ EC-GLV	Bell 212	30587	ex N605LH	
☐ EC-IGP	Bell 212	30915	ex N5009N	
☐ EC-IGQ	Bell 212	30936	ex N5010F	
☐ EC-IGR	Bell 212	30989	ex N1074C	
☐ EC-KCN	Bell 212	30681	ex 5N-BEN	
☐ EC-DYK	Eurocopter AS350B Ecureuil	1863		
☐ EC-FME	Eurocopter AS350B2 Ecureuil	2448	ex EC-947	
☐ EC-GIY	Eurocopter AS350B1 Ecureuil	2175	ex EC-267	

HELICÓPTEROS INSULARES — Santa Cruz de Tenerife

☐ EC-JMP	Eurocopter AS350B Ecureuil	1761	ex OE-KXH
☐ EC-KFP	Eurocopter AS350B3 Ecureuil	3818	ex F-GYRE
☐ EC-LHH	Eurocopter AS350B3 Ecureuil	4931	

HELIDUERO — Córdoba-Palma del Rió

☐ EC-HXV	Bell 212	30647	ex PK-HMA
☐ EC-IXX	Bell 412	33043	ex N419EH
☐ EC-JIM	Bell 412EP	36191	ex N7015K
☐ EC-KDQ	Agusta A119 Koala	14031	ex I-CLMF
☐ EC-KEB	Bell 212	30972	ex LX-HEP
☐ EC-KEG	Agusta A119 Koala	14048	ex N325BC
☐ EC-KQD	Agusta A119 Koala	14012	ex VH-RPW
☐ EC-KQE	Agusta A119 Koala	14042	ex VH-RPS

HELIPISTAS — Ullastrell

| ☐ EC-HIL | Eurocopter EC120B Colibri | 1075 |

HELISWISS IBERICA — Iberswiss (HSW) — Barcelona-Sabadell

☐ EC-DXZ	Bell 206B Jetranger II	1051	ex HB-XFH
☐ EC-GUE	MBB Bo105 CBS-4	S-188	ex EC-234
☐ EC-HXI	Eurocopter EC120 B Colibri	1193	ex F-WQDD

HELITRANS PYRINEES   La Seu D'Urgell (LEU)

☐ EC-GDL	Eurocopter AS350B2 Ecureuil	2879	ex EC-890	
☐ EC-JTX	Eurocopter AS350B3 Ecureuil	3600	ex SE-JHC	
☐ EC-KLJ	Eurocopter AS350B3 Ecureuil	3804	ex EC-KFF	
☐ EC-LYC	Eurocopter AS350B3 Ecureuil	7599	ex F-WWXP	

IBERIA EXPRESS   (I2/IBS)   Madrid-Barajas (MAD)

☐ EC-FCB	Airbus A320-211	0158	ex EC-579	[MAD]
☐ EC-FDA	Airbus A320-211	0176	ex EC-581	[MAD]
☐ EC-FDB	Airbus A320-211	0173	ex EC-580	[MAD]
☐ EC-FGR	Airbus A320-211	0224	ex EC-586	[MAD]
☐ EC-FGV	Airbus A320-211	0207	ex EC-584	[MAD]
☐ EC-FLP	Airbus A320-211	0266	ex EC-881	[MAD]
☐ EC-FNR	Airbus A320-211	0323	ex EC-885	[MAD]
☐ EC-FQY	Airbus A320-211	0356	ex EC-886	[MAD]
☐ EC-JFG	Airbus A320-214	2143	ex F-WWBV	
☐ EC-JFH	Airbus A320-214	2104	ex F-WWBE	
☐ EC-JSK	Airbus A320-214	2807	ex F-WWIN	
☐ EC-KOH	Airbus A320-214	2248	ex XA-UDU	Fontibre
☐ FC-LEA	Airbus A320-214	1099	ex EC-HDO	Formentera
☐ EC-LKG	Airbus A320-214	1047	ex EC-HAF	♦
☐ EC-LKH	Airbus A320-214	1101	ex EC-HDP	
☐ EC-LLE	Airbus A320-214	1119	ex EC-HDT	
☐ EC-LRG	Airbus A320-214	1516	ex EC-HTA	
☐ EC-LUC	Airbus A320-214	1059	ex EC-HAG	
☐ EC-LUD	Airbus A320-214	1067	ex EC-HDK	
☐ EC-LUS	Airbus A320-216/S	5501	ex D-AXAG	
☐ EC-LVQ	Airbus A320-216	5590	ex D-AUBG	
☐ EC-LYE	Airbus A320-216/S	5729	ex F-WWIZ	
☐ EC-LYM	Airbus A320-216	5815	ex F-WWBM	
☐ EC-MBU	Airbus A320-214	1198	ex EI-EZR	♦
☐ EC-MCB	Airbus A320-214	1125	ex I-EEZK	♦
☐ EC-MEG	Airbus A320-214	1439	ex EI-CWU	♦
☐ EC-MEH	Airbus A320-214	1450	ex EI-CWV	♦

IBERIA LINEAS AEREAS DE ESPANA   Iberia (IB/IBE)   Madrid-Barajas (MAD)

Member of oneWorld

☐ EC-HGR	Airbus A319-111	1154	ex D-AVYY	Ribeira Sacra	
☐ EC-HKO	Airbus A319-111	1362	ex D-AVWJ	Gorbea	
☐ EC-JAZ	Airbus A319-111	2264	ex D-AVWQ	Las Medulas	
☐ EC-JDL	Airbus A319-111	2365	ex D-AVYN	Los Llanos de Aridane	
☐ EC-JEI	Airbus A319-111	2311	ex D-AVYG	Xativa	
☐ EC-JXJ	Airbus A319-111	2889	ex D-AVYH	Ciudad de Baeza	>VLG
☐ EC-KBX	Airbus A319-111	3078	ex D-AVYH	Oso Pardo	
☐ EC-KHM	Airbus A319-111	3209	ex D-AVWL	Búho Real	
☐ EC-KKS	Airbus A319-111	3320	ex D-AVYF	Halcõn Peregrino	retro c/s
☐ EC-KMD	Airbus A319-111	3380	ex D-AVWE	Petirrojo	
☐ EC-KOY	Airbus A319-111	3443	ex D-AVYN	Vencejo	
☐ EC-KUB	Airbus A319-111	3651	ex D-AVYR	Flamenco	
☐ EC-LEI	Airbus A319-111	3744	ex D-AVWZ	Vison Europeo	
☐ EC-MFO	Airbus A319-111	0938	ex F-GRHA		
☐ EC-MFP	Airbus A319-111	0998	ex F-GRHC		♦
☐ EC-IEF	Airbus A320-214	1655	ex F-WWDY	Castillo de Loarre	
☐ EC-IEG	Airbus A320-214	1674	ex F-WWIL	Costa Brava	
☐ EC-IEI	Airbus A320-214	1694	ex F-WWBT	Monasterio de Valldigna	[MAD]♦
☐ EC-ILR	Airbus A320-214	1793	ex F-WWIM	San Juan de la Pena	
☐ EC-ILS	Airbus A320-214	1809	ex F-WWBC	Sierra de Cameros	
☐ EC-IZH	Airbus A320-214	2225	ex F-WWID	San Pere de Roda	
☐ EC-IZR	Airbus A320-214	2242	ex F-WWDA	Urkiola	
☐ EC-JFN	Airbus A320-214	2391	ex F-WWDB	Sierra de las Nieves	
☐ EC-LUL	Airbus A320-216	5486	ex F-WWDE	Cangas de Onis	
☐ EC-LVD	Airbus A320-216	5570	ex F-WWIT	Valle de Mena	
☐ EC-LXQ	Airbus A320-216	5692	ex D-AVVG	Peñón de Ifach	
☐ EC-MCS	Airbus A320-214	6244	ex D-AVVP	Playa de los Lances	♦
☐ EC-MDK	Airbus A320-214/S	6328	ex D-AVVZ	PN Picos de Europa	♦
☐ EC-HUH	Airbus A321-211	1021	ex EC-HAC	Benidorm	
☐ EC-HUI	Airbus A321-211	1027	ex EC-HAE	Comunidad Autonoma de la Rioja	
☐ EC-IGK	Airbus A321-211	1572	ex EC-HTF	Costa Calida	
☐ EC-IJN	Airbus A321-211	1836	ex D-AVZN	Merida	
☐ EC-ILO	Airbus A321-211	1681	ex D-AVZW	Cueva de Nerja	
☐ EC-ILP	Airbus A321-211	1716	ex D-AVZT	Peniscola	
☐ EC-ITN	Airbus A321-211	2115	ex D-AVXG	Empuries	
☐ EC-IXD	Airbus A321-211	2220	ex D-AVZR	Valle de Aran	
☐ EC-JDM	Airbus A321-211	2357	ex D-AVZV	Cantabria	
☐ EC-JDR	Airbus A321-211	2488	ex D-AVXD	Sierra Cebollera	

☐ EC-JEJ	Airbus A321-211	2381	ex D-AVZI	Riofrio	
☐ EC-JGS	Airbus A321-211	2472	ex D-AVXA	Guadalupe	
☐ EC-JLI	Airbus A321-211	2563	ex D-AVZB	Delta Del Llobregat	
☐ EC-JNI	Airbus A321-211	2270	ex D-AVZA	Palmeral de Elche	
☐ EC-JQZ	Airbus A321-211	2736	ex D-AVZJ	Generalife	
☐ EC-JRE	Airbus A321-211	2756	ex D-AVZA	Villa de Uncastillo	
☐ EC-JZM	Airbus A321-211	2996	ex D-AVZP	Aquila Imperial	
☐ EC-LUB	Airbus A330-302	1377	ex F-WWYG	Tikal	
☐ EC-LUK	Airbus A330-302	1385	ex F-WWYQ	Costa Rica	
☐ EC-LUX	Airbus A330-302	1405	ex F-WWTO	Panamá	
☐ EC-LXK	Airbus A330-302	1426	ex F-WWCG	El Salvador	
☐ EC-LYF	Airbus A330-302	1437	ex F-WWKA	Juan Carlos I	
☐ EC-LZJ	Airbus A330-302	1490	ex F-WWTJ	Miami	
☐ EC-LZX	Airbus A330-302	1507	ex F-WWKG	Madrid	
☐ EC-MAA	Airbus A330-302	1515	ex F-WWKR	Rio de Janeiro	
☐ EC-	Airbus A330-302	1694	ex F-WW		o/o♦
☐ EC-GGS	Airbus A340-313	125	ex EC-154	Concha Espina	
☐ EC-GHX	Airbus A340-313	134	ex EC-155	Rosalia de Castro	
☐ EC-GJT	Airbus A340-313	145	ex EC-156	Rosa Chacel	wfs
☐ EC-GLE	Airbus A340-313	146	ex EC-157	Concepcion Arenal	
☐ EC-GUP	Airbus A340-313X	217	ex F-WWJG	Agustina de Aragon	
☐ EC-GUQ	Airbus A340-313X	221	ex F-WWJA	Beatriz Galindo	
☐ EC-HGV	Airbus A340-313X	329	ex F-WWJP	Maria Guerrero	
☐ EC-IIH	Airbus A340-313X	483	ex F-WWJI	Maria Barbara de Braganza	[MAD]
☐ EC-INO	Airbus A340-642	431	ex F-WWCI	Gaudi	
☐ EC-IOB	Airbus A340-642	440	ex F-WWCL	Julio Romero de Torres	
☐ EC-IQR	Airbus A340-642	460	ex F-WWCO	Salvador Dali	
☐ EC-IZX	Airbus A340-642	601	ex F-WWCS	Mariano Benlliure	
☐ EC-IZY	Airbus A340-642	604	ex F-WWCH	Ignacio de Zuloaga	
☐ EC-JBA	Airbus A340-642	606	ex F-WWCV	Joaquin Rodrigo	
☐ EC-JCY	Airbus A340-642	617	ex F-WWCL	Andres Segovia	
☐ EC-JCZ	Airbus A340-642	619	ex F-WWCP	Vincente Aleixandre	
☐ EC-JFX	Airbus A340-642	672	ex F-WWCB	Jacinto Benavente	
☐ EC-JLE	Airbus A340-642	702	ex F-WWCM	Santiago Ramon y Cajal	
☐ EC-JNQ	Airbus A340-642	727	ex F-WWCV	Antonio Machado	
☐ EC-JPU	Airbus A340-642	744	ex F-WWCF	Pio Baroja	
☐ EC-KZI	Airbus A340-642	1017	ex F-WWCS	Miguel Hernandez	
☐ EC-LCZ	Airbus A340-642	993	ex F-WWCK	Miguel Servet	
☐ EC-LEU	Airbus A340-642	960	ex F-WWCG	Rio Amazonas	
☐ EC-LEV	Airbus A340-642	1079	ex F-WWCE	Isaac Albeniz	
☐ EC-LFS	Airbus A340-642	1122	ex F-WWCF	Ciudad de Mexico	

INAER HELICOPTERS   Alicante-Mutxamel

☐ EC-KHV	AgustaWestland AW139	31089		
☐ EC-KLC	AgustaWestland AW139	31107		
☐ EC-LBM	AgustaWestland AW139	31226		
☐ EC-MBO	AgustaWestland AW139	41357	ex N611SM	♦
☐ EC-MBP	AgustaWestland AW139	41359	ex N467SH	♦
☐ EC-EEQ	Bell 212	30612	ex D-HOBB	
☐ EC-GID	Bell 212	31150	ex EC-367	
☐ EC-GXA	Bell 212	30812	ex LN-OQJ	
☐ EC-HTJ	Bell 212	30648	ex PK-HMC	
☐ EC-INN	Bell 212	31146	ex SE-JLP	
☐ EC-IYO	Bell 212	30946	ex C-GZMZ	
☐ EC-IYP	Bell 212	30533	ex C-FZPX	
☐ EC-MDM	Bell 212	30558	ex OB-2075-P	♦
☐ EC-MDU	Bell 212	30639	ex OB-1972-P	♦
☐ EC-MDV	Bell 212	30759	ex OB-1973-P	♦
☐ EC-IMZ	Bell 407	53547	ex C-GLZA	
☐ EC-JAR	Bell 407	53370	ex N54LM	
☐ EC-JBU	Bell 407	53241	ex I-FREC	
☐ EC-JBV	Bell 407	53613	ex C-FBXL	
☐ EC-JSD	Bell 407	53687	ex C-FHYS	
☐ EC-KCQ	Bell 407	53741	ex C-FLPB	
☐ EC-KZJ	Bell 407	53063	ex N407LH	
☐ EC-KZK	Bell 407	53132	ex N407DL	
☐ EC-LBS	Bell 407	53864	ex CC-CIO	
☐ EC-LXJ	Bell 407	53795	ex CC-CRA	
☐ EC-LYY	Bell 407	53727	ex CC-CIU	
☐ EC-GOP	Bell 412HP	36031	ex N4603T	
☐ EC-GPA	Bell 412HP	36071	ex N7238Y	
☐ EC-GSK	Bell 412	33092	ex SE-HVL	
☐ EC-HXX	Bell 412	33062	ex N4014U	
☐ EC-HXZ	Bell 412	33106	ex PK-HMT	
☐ EC-HZD	Bell 412	33056	ex N4031F	
☐ EC-IPM	Bell 412	33050	ex C-GJKT	

☐ EC-JFQ	Bell 412	33126	ex C-FAKF	
☐ EC-JJE	Bell 412	33004	ex N164EH	
☐ EC-JJQ	Bell 412EP	36376	ex N46372	
☐ EC-JXQ	Bell 412EP	36091	ex N5087V	
☐ EC-KBB	Bell 412EP	36426	ex N94479	
☐ EC-KBT	Bell 412EP	36423	ex C-FLOX	
☐ EC-KSJ	Bell 412EP	36467	ex C-FSVZ	
☐ EC-KTR	Bell 412EP	36472	ex C-FUMO	
☐ EC-KVC	Bell 412EP	36469	ex C-FSZW	
☐ EC-MAZ	Bell 412EP	36183	ex N52247	◆
☐ EC-JTO	Eurocopter AS350B3 Ecureuil	3091	ex LN-OPK	
☐ EC-JTP	Eurocopter AS350B3 Ecureuil	3445	ex SE-JHK	
☐ EC-KDO	Eurocopter AS350B3 Ecureuil	3677	ex LN-OMA	
☐ EC-KIE	Eurocopter AS350B3 Ecureuil	4286	ex F-WQDX	
☐ EC-KSK	Eurocopter AS350B3 Ecureuil	4365	ex F-WQRA	
☐ EC-KZL	Eurocopter AS350B3 Ecureuil	4688	ex F-WWPS	
☐ EC-LBU	Eurocopter AS350B3 Ecureuil	4780	ex F-WBGK	
☐ EC-LBV	Eurocopter AS350B3 Ecureuil	4781	ex F-WBGL	
☐ EC-MBQ	Eurocopter AS350B3 Ecureuil	4934	ex CC-ACX	◆
☐ EC-MCN	Eurocopter AS350B3 Ecureuil	3727	ex OB-1969-P	◆
☐ EC-INY	Eurocopter EC135T2	275	ex D-HECV	opf Junta Castilla y León-Sacyl
☐ FC-ITJ	Eurocopter EC135T2	306		opf Axencia Galega de Emerxencias
☐ EC-IUN	Eurocopter EC135T2	317		opf Axencia Galega de Emerxencias
☐ EC-JDG	Eurocopter EC135T2	354		opf Junta Castilla y León-Sacyl
☐ EC-JHT	Eurocopter EC135T2	396		opf C.Autónoma de Euskadi-Osakidetza
☐ EC-JUE	Eurocopter EC135T2	345	ex EC-067	opf Junta Castilla y León-Sacyl
☐ EC-KIJ	Eurocopter EC135T2+	579		opf Com Castilla La Mancha-SESCAM
☐ EC-KQT	Eurocopter EC135T2+	652	ex EC-003	opf Emerg Sanitarias de Extremadura
☐ EC-KUQ	Eurocopter EC135T2+	705	ex D-HECP	opf Emerg Sanitarias de Extremadura
☐ EC-LAX	Eurocopter EC135T2+	743		
☐ EC-JAK	Kamov Ka-32A11BC	9624	ex RA-31604	
☐ EC-JAL	Kamov Ka-32A11BC	9625	ex RA-31605	
☐ EC-JGV	Kamov Ka-32A11BC	9708/23		
☐ EC-JGX	Kamov Ka-32A11BC	9709/24		
☐ EC-JSP	Kamov Ka-32A11BC	9710		
☐ EC-JSQ	Kamov Ka-32A11BC	9712		
☐ EC-JUZ	Kamov Ka-32A11BC	9713		
☐ EC-JVA	Kamov Ka-32A11BC	9714		
☐ EC-JXG	Kamov Ka-32A11BC	9715		
☐ EC-KRI	Kamov Ka-32A11BC	9815		

☐ EC-DYQ	Bell 206B JetRanger	8677	ex HB-XML		
☐ EC-ERY	Sikorsky S-76 1S	760037	ex EC-364		opf Diputación Regional de Cantabria
☐ EC-EUT	Bell 206 L-3 LongRanger III	51337	ex N8212U		
☐ EC-FCO	Bell 206 L-3 LongRanger III	51179	ex N52CH		
☐ EC-FEL	Bell 412SP	25576	ex EC-607		
☐ EC-FTB	Sikorsky S61N	61741	ex EC-429	209	opf SASEMAR
☐ EC-FVO	Sikorsky S61N	61756	ex EC-575	210	opf SASEMAR
☐ EC-FZJ	Sikorsky S61N	61758	ex EC-717	758	opf SASEMAR
☐ EC-HEE	Eurocopter AS355N Ecureuil II	5645	ex F-OHVD		opf Comunidad de Madrid-Bomberos
☐ EC-ILE	Beech B200 Super King Air	BB-1792	ex N5092K	Mutxamel	
☐ EC-IUX	Beech B200 Super King Air	BB-1840	ex N816LD	Cartuja	
☐ EC-JES	Sikorsky S76C+	760576	ex N576ML	opf Serv Gardacostas da Xunta de Galicia	
☐ EC-JET	Sikorsky S76C+	760578	ex N578ML	opf Serv Gardacostas da Xunta de Galicia	
☐ EC-JKG	Bell 206 L-4 LongRanger IV	52068	ex OK-YIP		
☐ EC-KKO	Cessna 550 Citation Bravo	550-0992	ex N777EG		
☐ EC-KRU	Agusta Bell 412SP	25542	ex I-AGSF		
☐ EC-KUV	Agusta Bell 412SP	25602	ex I-MAGM		
☐ EC-KVH	Eurocopter EC145	9152	ex D-HMBN	opf Com Castilla La Manchas-SESCAM	
☐ EC-LBL	Agusta Bell 412SP	25600	ex ICGCL		
☐ EC-LIH	Beech B200GT Super King Air	BY-102	ex N6402G		◆
☐ EC-LKN	Eurocopter EC145	9300	ex D-HADF		
☐ EC-LYU	Eurocopter AS365N1 Dauphin II	6234	ex CC-AHR		
☐ EC-LZT	Eurocopter AS365N1 Dauphin II	6346	ex CC-AEF		◆
☐ EC-MAE	Agusta A109E	11619	ex F-HCHM		◆
☐ EC-MBN	Eurocopter AS355N Twin Ecureuil	5598	ex CC-ACW		◆
☐ EC-MEE	Eurocopter AS365N1 Dauphin II	6264	ex CC-AHS		◆

INTERCOPTERS   *Madrid-Cuatro Vientos*

☐ EC-KCM	Eurocopter EC-135 P2	0452	
☐ EC-KQA	Eurocopter EC-120 B Colibri	1532	ex F-WQAA
☐ EC-LQG	Agusta A109A-2	7388	ex I-SEIA

MAGRAMA – MINISTERIO DE AGRICULTURA, ALIMENTACION Y MEDIO AMBIENTE

☐ EC-GBP	Canadair CL215-1A10	1031	ex EC-983	op by Inaer
☐ EC-GBQ	Canadair CL215-1A10	1033	ex EC-956	op by Inaer
☐ EC-GBR	Canadair CL215-1A10	1051	ex EC-957	op by Inaer

☐ EC-GBS	Canadair CL215-1A10	1052	ex EC-985		op by Inaer
☐ EC-GBT	Canadair CL215-1A10	1054	ex EC-958		op by Inaer
☐ EC-HAP	CASA C212-400MP Aviocar	465	ex EC-011	Roche	op by Inaer
☐ EC-HTU	CASA C212-400MP Aviocar	470		Sancti Petri	op by Inaer
☐ EC-INX	CASA C212-400MP Aviocar	472		Doñana	op by Inaer
☐ EC-FUY	Agusta A109 C Max	7670	ex EC-453	Alcotán II	op by Inaer
☐ EC-GCQ	Agusta A109 C Max	7665	ex EC-895	Alcotán III	op by Inaer
☐ EC-JVG	Eurocopter AS365N3 Dauphin II	6718	ex F-WWOQ		op by Inaer
☐ EC-JXY	Eurocopter AS365N3 Dauphin II	6719	ex F-WWOI		op by Inaer
☐ EC-KTL	Eurocopter AS365N3 Dauphin II	6799	ex F-WQDN		op by Inaer
☐ EC-KTS	Eurocopter AS365N3 Dauphin II	6811			op by Inaer

MINISTERIO DE HACIENCA SERVICIO DE VIGILANCIA ADUANERA

☐ EC-LJB	CASA C212-200 Aviocar	323	ex TR.12D-79		op by Inaer
☐ EC-LJH	CASA C212-200 Aviocar	261	ex TR.12D-77		op by Inaer
☐ EC-LKJ	CASA C212-200 Aviocar	247	ex TR.12D-81		op by Inaer
☐ EC-LLN	CASA C212-300 Aviocar	359	ex TR.12D-76		op by Inaer
☐ EC-LSK	CASA C212-200 Aviocar	178	ex TR.12D-80		op by Inaer
☐ EC-LSL	CASA C212-200 Aviocar	311	ex TR.12D-7 8		op by Inaer
☐ EC-DVK	MBB Bo105CB4	S-630	ex D-HDSZ	Argos I	op by Inaer
☐ EC-DVL	MBB Bo105CB4	S-631	ex D-DHTA	Argos II	op by Inaer
☐ EC-FFV	MBB Bo105CBS5	S-852	ex D-HFHJ	Argos VI	op by Inaer
☐ EC-ESX	Eurocopter BK117A3	7176	ex EC-378		op by Inaer
☐ EC-IGM	Eurocopter AS365N1 Dauphin II	6616	ex F-WQDA		op by Inaer
☐ EC-JDQ	Eurocopter AS365N3 Dauphin II	6679	ex EC-IZQ		op by Inaer
☐ EC-KUH	Eurocopter AS365N3 Dauphin II	6803	ex F-WWOQ		op by Inaer

PAN AIR　　　　　Skyjet (PV/PNR)　　　　　Madrid-Barajas (MAD)

☐ EC-ELT	British Aerospace 146 Srs.200QT	E2102	ex EC-198	<TAY
☐ EC-FVY	British Aerospace 146 Srs.200QT	E2117	ex EC-615	<TAY
☐ EC-FZE	British Aerospace 146 Srs.200QT	E2105	ex EC-719	<TAY
☐ EC-GQO	British Aerospace 146 Srs.200QT	E2086	ex D-ADEI	<TAY
☐ EC-LMR	British Aerospace 146 Srs.300QT	E3151	ex OO-TAA	<TAY
☐ EC-LOF	British Aerospace 146 Srs.300QT	E3150	ex OO-TAK	<TAY
☐ EC-MCK	British Aerospace 146 Srs.300QT	E3153	ex OO-TAJ	<TAY♦
☐ EC-MCL	British Aerospace 146 Srs.300QT	E3154	ex OO-TAS	<TAY wfs♦
☐ EC-MEO	British Aerospace 146 Srs.300QT	E3186	ex OO-TAF	<TAF♦
☐ EC-MFT	British Aerospace 146 Srs.300QT	E3182	ex OO-TAE	<TAY♦

PRIVILEGE STYLE　　　　　Privilege (P6/PVG)　　　　　Palma de Mallorca (PMI)

☐ EC-HDS	Boeing 757-256	26252/900		Milagros Diaz	
☐ EC-ISY	Boeing 757-256	26241/572	ex N26ND	Cte Jesús Guil	
☐ EC-KSS	Embraer ERJ-145MP	145230	ex D-ACIR	Trives	>AEA
☐ EC-LZO	Boeing 767-35DER	27902/577	ex EI-FDI	Eduardo Barreiros	>FIN

ROTORSUN　　　　　Murcia

☐ EC-FHX	Bell 206B JetRanger III	3786	ex EC-698
☐ EC-HCC	Bell 206B JetRanger II	4505	ex C-GBUQ
☐ EC-JFP	Agusta AB206B JetRanger III	8647	ex EC-FYA

SAP – SOCIEDAD AERONÁUTICA PENINSULAR　　　　　Sevilla-San Pablos

☐ EC-BVL	Reims Cessna F.337E	F3370007	
☐ EC-CXC	Reims Cessna F.337F	F3370042	ex CS-AHH
☐ EC-EDB	Reims Cessna F.337G	F3370067	ex OO-EDU
☐ EC-GPF	Reims Cessna F.337G	F3370059	ex D-IOMS
☐ EC-GVX	Reims Cessna FTB.337G	FTB3370004	ex F-GCTO
☐ EC-GXC	Reims Cessna FTB.337G	FTB3370013	ex CS-AUX
☐ EC-HOG	Reims Cessna FTB.337G	FTB3370028	ex CS-DBV
☐ EC-DKD	Cessna 337G	33701797	ex N53706
☐ EC-FQA	Cessna 337G	33701713	ex N53575
☐ EC-GPQ	Cessna 337G	33701815	ex N617L	♦

SASEMAR – SOCIEDAD DE SALVAMENTO Y SEGURIDAD MARITIMA

☐ EC-JOU	AgustaWestland AW139	31034	ex I-RAII		op by Inaer
☐ EC-KJT	AgustaWestland AW139	31104	ex I-EASK		op by Inaer
☐ EC-KLM	AgustaWestland AW139	31201	ex I-EASB	201	op by Inaer
☐ EC-KLN	AgustaWestland AW139	31202		202	op by Inaer
☐ EC-KLV	AgustaWestland AW139	31205		203	op by Inaer
☐ EC-KXA	AgustaWestland AW139	31219	ex I-EASC	206	op by Inaer
☐ EC-LCH	AgustaWestland AW139	31257	ex I-RAIQ	204	op by Inaer
☐ EC-LEE	AgustaWestland AW139	31241		213	op by Inaer
☐ EC-LFP	AgustaWestland AW139	31296		207	op by Inaer

☐ EC-LFQ	AgustaWestland AW139	31298		211	op by Inaer
☐ EC-LIS	AgustaWestland AW139	31268		215	op by Inaer
☐ EC-LJA	AgustaWestland AW139	31318		205	op by Inaer
☐ EC-CDF	Beech 95-B55 Baron	TC-1555	ex E.20-9 (EC)		
☐ EC-COF	Beech 95-B55 Baron	TC-1844			
☐ EC-COG	Beech 95-B55 Baron	TC-1850			
☐ EC-COH	Beech 95-B55 Baron	TC-1856			
☐ EC-KEK	CASA CN-235-300	C166		101	op by Inaer
☐ EC-KEL	CASA CN-235-300	C169		102	op by Inaer
☐ EC-KEM	CASA CN-235-300	C171			
☐ EC-MCR	Eurocopter EC225LP	2892	ex EC-004	401	♦
☐ EC-MCP	Eurocopter EC225LP	2892	ex EC-004		♦

SERAIR TRANSWORLD PRESS		Cargopress (SEV)		Las Palmas-Gran Canaria (LPA)

☐ EC-GTM	Beech 1900C	UB-30	ex N7210R
☐ EC-GUD	Beech 1900C-1	UC-156	ex N156YV
☐ EC-GZG	Beech 1900C-1	UC-161	ex N55635
☐ EC-JDY	Beech 1900C-1	UC-91	ex N91YV

SKY HELICOPTEROS			Palma de Mallorca-Son Bonet

☐ EC-JFT	Cessna 560 Citation V Ultra	560-0506	ex G-OGRG
☐ EC-JIU	Cessna 525 Citation Jet I	525-0486	ex N334BD
☐ EC-KPQ	Eurocopter AS355N Ecureuil II	9612	ex F-WQAH
☐ EC-LBN	Eurocopter AS350B3 Ecureuil	4743	ex F-WEVS
☐ EC-LCD	Eurocopter AS355NP Ecureuil II	5758	ex F-WWPA
☐ EC-LHE	Eurocopter AS355NP Ecureuil II	5780	ex F-WETV
☐ EC-LMK	Eurocopter AS350B3 Ecureuil	7118	
☐ EC-LXH	Eurocopter AS350B3 Ecureuil	7575	
☐ EC-LXS	Eurocopter AS350B3 Ecureuil	7633	

SWIFTAIR		Swift (7J/SWT)		Madrid-Barajas (MAD)

☐ EC-ISX	ATR 42-320F	242	ex N242AT		no titles
☐ EC-IVP	ATR 42-300F	231	ex F-GKND		
☐ EC-JAD	ATR 42-300	321	ex F-GHPY		
☐ EC-JBN	ATR 42-300QC	218	ex F-GHPK	all-white	
☐ EC-JBX	ATR 42-300F	254	ex N255AE		
☐ EC-KAI	ATR 42-300F	141	ex EI-FXF		<ABR
☐ EC-INV	ATR 72-212F	274	ex N274AT		
☐ EC-IYH	ATR 72-202F	330	ex F-WQUI		
☐ EC-JQF	ATR 72-211F	147	ex SE-LVK		
☐ EC-JRP	ATR 72-212	446	ex D-AEWK		opf UN
☐ EC-JXF	ATR 72-211F	150	ex OY-CIV		
☐ EC-KAD	ATR 72-202	171	ex F-GKPC		>ABV
☐ EC-KIZ	ATR 72-202QC	204	ex F-GPOA		<FPO
☐ EC-KJA	ATR 72-202F	207	ex F-GPOB		<FPO
☐ EC-KKQ	ATR 72-212A	763	ex F-WWEB		
☐ EC-KUL	ATR 72-212A	809	ex F-WWET		>AEA
☐ EC-KVI	ATR 72-212A	824	ex F-WWEM		>AEA
☐ EC-LHV	ATR 72-202	416	ex F-WNUH		
☐ EC-LSN	ATR 72-202	192	ex PR-AZZ		>AEA
☐ EC-LST	ATR 72-201F	234	ex SP-OLL	all-white	>AEA
☐ EC-LYB	ATR 72-212A	550	ex N550LL		>AEA
☐ EC-LYJ	ATR 72-212A	468	ex OY-CIM		>ABV
☐ EC-MAF	ATR 72-212A	568	ex OY-CIN		>AEA
☐ EC-MEC	ATR 72-212A	595	ex OY-CIO		o/o♦
☐ EC-KLR	Boeing 737-3Q8SF	23766/1375	ex N237CP		
☐ EC-KTZ	Boeing 737-375F	23708/1395	ex N111KH		
☐ EC-KVD	Boeing 737-306F	23538/1288	ex N102KH		
☐ EC-LAC	Boeing 737-3M8F	24022/1662	ex N107KH		
☐ EC-LJI	Boeing 737-301SF	23512/1291	ex OO-TNI		
☐ EC-MAD	Boeing 737-4Y0SF	25261/2258	ex EI-STE		<ABR
☐ EC-MEY	Boeing 737-476SF	24438/2171	ex N248SY		♦
☐ EC-MFE	Boeing 737-476SF	24445/2539	ex N245SY		♦
☐ EC-MCI	Boeing 737-4Q8SF	26298/2564	ex N156GA		♦
☐ EC-	Boeing 737-476SF	24438/2171	ex N248SY		o/o♦
☐ EC-GQA	Embraer EMB-120RT Brasilia	120027	ex EC-GMT		Frtr
☐ EC-HAK	Embraer EMB-120RT Brasilia	120008	ex N212AS		Frtr
☐ EC-HCF	Embraer EMB-120RT Brasilia	120007	ex N211AS		Frtr
☐ EC-HFK	Embraer EMB-120RT Brasilia	120063	ex N7215U		Frtr
☐ EC-HMY	Embraer EMB-120RT Brasilia	120009	ex N214AS	all-white	Frtr
☐ EC-HTS	Embraer EMB-120RT Brasilia	120168	ex N168CA		Frtr
☐ EC-IMX	Embraer EMB-120RT Brasilia	120158	ex N312FV		Frtr
☐ EC-JBD	Embraer EMB.120RT Brasilia	120012	ex D-CAOB		Frtr
☐ EC-JBE	Embraer EMB.120RT Brasilia	120013	ex D-CAOA		Frtr

☐ EC-JKH	Embraer EMB.120RT Brasilia	120092	ex OM-SPY	
☐ EC-JUF	McDonnell-Douglas MD-83	53168/2061	ex N802NK	[MAD]
☐ EC-JUG	McDonnell-Douglas MD-83	49847/1585	ex N834NK	[MAD]
☐ EC-KCX	McDonnell-Douglas MD-83	49619/1483	ex N814NK	wfs
☐ EC-LEY	McDonnell-Douglas MD-83	53182/2068	ex I-SMED	wfs

TAF HELICOPTERS   Barcelona-Sabadell

☐ EC-IFU	Eurocopter EC135P2	0223	ex D-HECX	
☐ EC-IQZ	Eurocopter EC135P2	0293		
☐ EC-JVS	Eurocopter EC135P2	0436		
☐ EC-KDA	Eurocopter EC135P2+	0538	ex EC-030	
☐ EC-KPA	Eurocopter EC135P2+	0634	ex EC-034	
☐ EC-LAL	Eurocopter EC135P2+	0761	ex EC-036	
☐ EC-LCN	Eurocopter EC135P2+	0824	ex D-DECL	
☐ EC-FOQ	Eurocopter AS350B Ecureuil	2639	ex EC-906	
☐ EC-IOI	Eurocopter AS350B2 Ecureuil	3640	ex F-WQDH	
☐ EC-JEA	Eurocopter AS350B3 Ecureuil	3819	ex SE-JHX	
☐ EC-KFU	Eurocopter AS350B3 Ecureuil	4251	ex SE-JJO	
☐ EC-KNG	Eurocopter AS350B3 Ecureuil	4088	ex EC-KJF	
☐ EC-KRQ	Eurocopter AS350B3 Ecureuil	4370		
☐ EC-KTU	Eurocopter AS350B3 Ecureuil	4520		
☐ EC-DSU	MBB Bo105CBS	S-623	ex D-HDSS	
☐ EC-EMF	Agusta Bell 206B JetRanger II	8715		
☐ EC-FKK	Cessna 401	4010279	ex EC-907	
☐ EC-GUZ	Eurocopter AS355F-2 Twin Ecureuil	5454	ex N26ET	
☐ EC-KYJ	Eurocopter AS355NP Ecureuil II	5767		

TRABAJOS AÉREOS ESPEJO   Córdoba

☐ EC-EIO	Air Tractor AT-502	502-0019	ex EC-004	
☐ EC-ENM	Air Tractor AT-502A	503-0001	ex N7309X	cvtd from AT-503
☐ EC-FKU	Air Tractor AT-502	502-0125	ex N4548Y	
☐ EC-GMX	Air Tractor AT-802A	802A-0039	ex N5001X	
☐ EC-HKT	Air Tractor AT-802	802-0080	ex N90115	
☐ EC-IHJ	Air Tractor AT-802	802-0138	ex N8505Z	
☐ EC-JAC	Air Tractor AT-802A	802A-0177	ex N8525Z	
☐ EC-JMG	Air Tractor AT-802	802-0066	ex N98ZL	
☐ EC-LIX	Air Tractor AT-802	802-0046	ex CS-DIW	
☐ EC-BJJ	Reims Cessna F172H Skyhawk	F172-0338		
☐ EC-ETG	Hiller UH12J3	5067	ex N4027K	wfs
☐ EC-GJS	Beech F33A Bonanza	CE-576	ex EC-CON	
☐ EC-IMF	Cessna 550 Citation II	550-0443	ex D-CGAS	
☐ EC-IXP	Piper PA-31 Navajo	31-7812095	ex SE-IAC	
☐ EC-JDF	Bell 206B JetRanger III	2800	ex CS-HEP	
☐ EC-JJF	Reims Cessna FTB337G Milirole	FTB33700003	ex F-GGTN	Spirit of Corpal
☐ EC-LKR	Cessna U206F Stationair	U20603521	ex N63SJ	

URGEMER CANARIAS   Urgemer (UGC)   Las Palmas (LPA)

☐ EC-GHZ	Beech B200 Super King Air	BB-555	ex EC-795	
☐ EC-JJP	Beech B200 Super King Air	BB-845	ex OY-GRB	
☐ EC-KND	Beech B200 Super King Air	BB-1564	ex EC-KHR	

VOLOTEA AIRLINES   Volotea (V7/VOE)   Palma de Mallorca (PMI)

☐ EC-LPM	Boeing 717-2BL	55185/5145	ex N923ME	
☐ EI-EWI	Boeing 717-2BL	55170/5120	ex N906ME	
☐ EI-EWJ	Boeing 717-2BL	55171/5121	ex N907ME	
☐ EI-EXA	Boeing 717-2BL	55172/5122	ex N908ME	
☐ EI-EXB	Boeing 717-2BL	55173/5123	ex N909ME	
☐ EI-EXI	Boeing 717-2BL	55174/5124	ex N910ME	
☐ EI-EXJ	Boeing 717-2BL	55176/5126	ex N913ME	
☐ EI-FBJ	Boeing 717-2BL	55177/5127	ex N409BC	
☐ EI-FBK	Boeing 717-2BL	55182/5138	ex N920ME	
☐ EI-FBL	Boeing 717-2BL	55183/5140	ex N921ME	
☐ EI-FBM	Boeing 717-2BL	55192/5152	ex N926ME	
☐ EI-FCB	Boeing 717-2BL	55191/5151	ex N925ME	
☐ EI-FCU	Boeing 717-2BL	55190/5149	ex N799BC	
☐ EI-FGH	Boeing 717-2BL	55169/5119	ex EC-LQS	♦
☐ EI-FGI	Boeing 717-2BL	55167/5117	ex EC-LQI	♦
☐ EC-MEZ	Boeing 717-2CM	55059/5023	ex OH-BLG	♦
☐ EC-MFJ	Boeing 717-2CM	55060/5026	ex OH-BLH	♦
☐ EC-	Boeing 717-2CM	55061/5029	ex OH-BLI	o/o♦

VUELING AIRLINES   Vueling (VY/VLG)   Barcelona (BCN)

☐ EC-JVE	Airbus A319-112	2843	ex D-AVYT	

☐ EC-JXV	Airbus A319-112	2897	ex D-AVWH			
☐ EC-JXJ	Airbus A319-111	2889	ex D-AVYH	Ciudad de Baeza		<IBE♦
☐ EC-LRS	Airbus A319-112	3704	ex D-ABGR			<BER
☐ EC-LRZ	Airbus A319-112	3700	ex D-ABGQ			<BER
☐ EC-HGZ	Airbus A320-214	1208	ex F-WWIM			
☐ EC-HHA	Airbus A320-214	1221	ex F-WWBF			
☐ EC-HQI	Airbus A320-214	1396	ex F-WWIX	Mercé Suñé		
☐ EC-HQJ	Airbus A320-214	1430	ex F-WWBR			
☐ EC-HQL	Airbus A320-214	1461	ex F-WWDD	Click on Vueling		
☐ EC-HTD	Airbus A320-214	1550	ex F-WWDC	Unos vuelan, otras Vueling		
☐ EC-ILQ	Airbus A320-214	1736	ex F-WWDJ	La Padrera		
☐ EC-IZD	Airbus A320-214	2207	ex F-WWDS	Barceloning		
☐ EC-JFF	Airbus A320-214	2388	ex F-WWIH	Vueling the world		
☐ EC-JGM	Airbus A320-214	2407	ex F-WWDC	The joy of Vueling		
☐ EC-JSY	Airbus A320-214	2785	ex F-WWBU	Connie Baraja		
☐ EC-JTQ	Airbus A320-214	2794	ex F-WWBN	Vueling, que es gerundio		
☐ EC-JTR	Airbus A320-214	2798	ex F-WWIF	no Vueling, no party		
☐ EC-JYX	Airbus A320-214	2962	ex F-WWDJ	Elisenda Masana		
☐ EC-JZI	Airbus A320-214	2988	ex F-WWII	Vueling in love		
☐ EC-JZQ	Airbus A320-214	0992	ex TC-JLE	I Want to Vueling		
☐ EC-KCU	Airbus A320-216	3109	ex F-WWIR	My name is Ling. Vue Ling		
☐ EC-KDG	Airbus A320-214	3095	ex F-WWIY	Absolute Vueling		
☐ EC-KDH	Airbus A320-214	3083	ex F-WWIX	Ain't no Vueling high enough		
☐ EC-KDT	Airbus A320-216	3145	ex F-WWBM	Ready, steady, Vueling		
☐ EC-KDX	Airbus A320-216	3151	ex F-WWBU	Francisco José Ruiz Cortizo		
☐ EC-KFI	Airbus A320-216	3174	ex F-WWIP			
☐ EC-KHN	Airbus A320-216	3203	ex F-WWIG			
☐ EC-KJD	Airbus A320-216	3237	ex F-WWBJ			
☐ EC-KKT	Airbus A320-214	3293	ex F-WWDU	Vueling Together		
☐ EC-KLB	Airbus A320-214	3321	ex F-WWBY	Vuela y punto		
☐ EC-KLT	Airbus A320-216	3376	ex F-WWDI			
☐ EC-KMI	Airbus A320-216	3400	ex F-WWBT	How are you? I'm Vueling!		
☐ EC-KRH	Airbus A320-214	3529	ex D-AVVD	Vueling me softly		
☐ EC-LAA	Airbus A320-214	2678	ex A6-ABZ	Vueldone		
☐ EC-LAB	Airbus A320-214	2761	ex OE-LEV	Vueling voy, vueling vengo		
☐ EC-LLJ	Airbus A320-216	4661	ex F-WWII	Luke SkyVueling		
☐ EC-LLM	Airbus A320-214	4681	ex F-WWDX	Be happy, be Vueling		
☐ EC-LML	Airbus A320-214	4742	ex F-WWIR			
☐ EC-LOB	Airbus A320-214	4849	ex D-AUBJ	Vueling Europe		
☐ EC-LOC	Airbus A320-214	4855	ex F-WWBF	Vueling on heaven's door		
☐ EC-LOP	Airbus A320-214	4937	ex D-AXAG	All you need is Vueling		
☐ EC-LRN	Airbus A320-214	3995	ex D-ABDX			<BER
☐ EC-LSA	Airbus A320-214	4128	ex D-ABFB			<BER
☐ EC-LVA	Airbus A320-214	1171	ex EI-EZE			
☐ EC-LVB	Airbus A320-214	1210	ex EI-EZF			
☐ EC-LVC	Airbus A320-214	1372	ex OE-IBQ			
☐ EC-LVO	Airbus A320-214/S	5533	ex D-AXAS			
☐ EC-LVP	Airbus A320-214/S	5587	ex F-WWBY	Linking Europe c/s		
☐ EC-LVU	Airbus A320-214/S	5616	ex F-WWIU	Keep smiling, fly Vueling		o/o
☐ EC-LVX	Airbus A320-214/S	5673	ex D-AVVB	Vuelingsgefühle		
☐ EC-LZN	Airbus A320-214/S	5925	ex D-AUBE			
☐ EC-LZZ	Airbus A320-214	2620	ex OE-ICT			
☐ EC-MAH	Airbus A320-214/S	6039	ex F-WWIM			
☐ EC-MAI	Airbus A320-214/S	6045	ex F-WWIN			
☐ EC-MAN	Airbus A320-214/S	6079	ex F-WWIV	Vueling fa volare Roma		
☐ EC-MAO	Airbus A320-214/S	6081	ex F-WWBJ	Feel Home...fly Vueling		♦
☐ EC-MAX	Airbus A320-214	4478	ex F-HDGK			♦
☐ EC-MBE	Airbus A320-214	3476	ex A6-ABL			o/o♦
☐ EC-MBD	Airbus A320-214	3444	ex EI-FDT			o/o♦
☐ EC-MBF	Airbus A320-211	3492	ex EI-LIS			♦
☐ EC-MBK	Airbus A320-214	2658	ex OE-ICU			♦
☐ EC-MBL	Airbus A320-214	3833	ex CN-NMB			♦
☐ EC-MBM	Airbus A320-214	4463	ex F-HDMF			♦
☐ EC-MBY	Airbus A320-214	4674	ex D-ABFT			♦
☐ EC-MCU	Airbus A320-214	3907	ex EI-ERX			♦
☐ EC-	Airbus A320-214	6655	ex			o/o♦
☐ EC-LQJ	Airbus A320-232	1979	ex EI-EUK			
☐ EC-LQK	Airbus A320-232	2589	ex EI-EUP			
☐ EC-LQL	Airbus A320-232	1749	ex EI-EUF			
☐ EC-LQM	Airbus A320-232	2223	ex EI-EUN			
☐ EC-LQN	Airbus A320-232	2168	ex EI-EUM			
☐ EC-LQZ	Airbus A320-232	1933	ex EI-EUI			
☐ EC-LRA	Airbus A320-232	2479	ex EI-EUO			
☐ EC-LRE	Airbus A320-232	1914	ex EI-EUH			
☐ EC-LRM	Airbus A320-232	1349	ex EI-EUC			
☐ EC-LRY	Airbus A320-232	1862	ex EI-EUG			
☐ EC-LUN	Airbus A320-232	5479	ex F-WWBS			
☐ EC-LUO	Airbus A320-232/S	5530	ex F-WWDG			
☐ EC-LVS	Airbus A320-232/S	5599	ex D-AUBK			
☐ EC-LVT	Airbus A320-232/S	5612	ex D-AUBO			
☐ EC-LVV	Airbus A320-232/S	5620	ex F-WWII	Vueling for a dream		

☐ EC-LZE	Airbus A320-232/S	5885	ex F-WWIK		
☐ EC-LZF	Airbus A320-232/S	5940	ex F-WWDF		
☐ EC-LZM	Airbus A320-232/S	5877	ex (JA19JJ)		
☐ EC-MBS	Airbus A320-232/S	6123	ex F-WWDU	Be Premium	♦
☐ EC-MBT	Airbus A320-232/S	6128	ex D-AXAX	Vueling 10 Years	♦
☐ EC-MDZ	Airbus A320-232/S	6377	ex F-WWDK	Air Force Juan	o♦
☐ EC-MEA	Airbus A320-232/S	6400	ex F-WWIL		♦
☐ EC-MEL	Airbus A320-232/S	6450	ex D-AXAT	You're the Vueling that I want	♦
☐ EC-MEQ	Airbus A320-232/S	6483	ex F-WWDI	Keep Calm and Vueling	♦
☐ EC-MER	Airbus A320-232/S	6510	ex F-WWBD	Vueling my best dream	♦
☐ EC-MES	Airbus A320-232/S	6518	ex F-WWBU		♦
☐ EC-MFK	Airbus A320-232/S	6535	ex F-WWBY	Vueling Topic	♦
☐ EC-MFL	Airbus A320-232/S	6557	ex F-WWIK		♦
☐ EC-MFM	Airbus A320-232/S	6571	ex F-WWIR	Are you Vueling to me?	♦
☐ EC-MFN	Airbus A320-232/S	6594	ex F-WWDR		o/o♦
☐ EC-MGE	Airbus A320-232/S	6607	ex D-AVVS	#BuenVueling	♦
☐ EC-	Airbus A320-232/S	6841	ex		o/o♦
☐ EC-	Airbus A320-232/S	6851	ex		o/o♦
☐ EC-	Airbus A320-232/S	6883	ex		o/o♦
☐ EC-	Airbus A320-232/S	6949	ex		o/o♦
☐ EC-	Airbus A320-232/S	6966	ex		o/o♦
☐ LY-VEJ	Airbus A320-232	2275	ex M-ABIN		<NVD♦
☐ LY-VEM	Airbus A320-233	0747	ex EI-FBB		<NVD♦
☐ LY-VEO	Airbus A320-233	0558	ex F-ORAD		<NVD♦
☐ EC-	Airbus A321-231/S	6638	ex D-AVXX		o/o♦
☐ EC-	Airbus A321-231/S	6660	ex		o/o♦
☐ EC-	Airbus A321-231/S	6684	ex		o/o♦
☐ EC-	Airbus A321-231/S	6691	ex		o/o♦
☐ EC	Airbus A321-231/S	6740	ex		o/o♦

WAMOS AIR · Pullmantur (EB/PLM) · Madrid-Barajas (MAD)

☐ EC-KQC >SVA	Boeing 747-412	26549/1030	ex 9V-SMZ	
☐ EC-KSM	Boeing 747-412	27178/1015	ex 9V-SMW	
☐ EC-KXN	Boeing 747-4H6	25703/1025	ex N703AC	>SVA
☐ EC-LNA	Boeing 747-446	26346/897	ex N346AS	
☐ EC-MDS	Boeing 747-419	26910/1180	ex N342AS	>SVA♦

ZOREX · Zorex (ORZ) · Zaragoza (ZAZ)

☐ EC-HJC	Swearingen SA226TC Metro II	TC-318	ex OY-JEO
☐ EC-JYC	Swearingen SA226TC Metro II	TC-303	ex N117AR

EI- IRELAND (Eire)

AER ARANN ISLANDS · Galway (GWY)

☐ EI-AYN	Britten-Norman BN-2A-8 Islander	704	ex G-BBFJ	Inis-Mor
☐ EI-BCE	Britten-Norman BN-2A-26 Islander	519	ex G-BDUV	Inis-Meain
☐ EI-CUW	Pilatus BN-2B-20 Islander	2293	ex G-BWYW	

AER LINGUS · Shamrock (EI/EIN) · Dublin (DUB)

☐ EI-CVA	Airbus A320-214	1242	ex F-WWIT	St Schira/Scire	
☐ EI-CVB	Airbus A320-214	1394	ex F-WWIV	St Mobhi/Mobhi	
☐ EI-CVC	Airbus A320-214	1443	ex F-WWBS	St Kealin/Caolfhionn	
☐ EI-DEA	Airbus A320-214	2191	ex F-WWBX	St Fidelma/Fiedeilme	
☐ EI-DEB	Airbus A320-214	2206	ex F-WWBP	St Nathy/Naithi	
☐ EI-DEC	Airbus A320-214	2217	ex F-WWBH	St Fergal/Fearghal	
☐ EI-DEE	Airbus A320-214	2250	ex F-WWBE	St Ultan/Ultan	
☐ EI-DEF	Airbus A320-214	2256	ex F-WWBK	St Declan/Deaglan	
☐ EI-DEG	Airbus A320-214	2272	ex F-WWIB	St Fachtna/Fachtna	
☐ EI-DEH	Airbus A320-214	2294	ex F-WWBX	St Conleth/Connlaodh	
☐ EI-DEI	Airbus A320-214	2374	ex F-WWDU	St Oliver Plunkett/Oilibh Plunceid	opf VIR
☐ EI-DEJ	Airbus A320-214	2364	ex F-WWDI	St Kilian/Cillian	
☐ EI-DEK	Airbus A320-214	2399	ex F-WWIZ	St Eunan/Eunan	
☐ EI-DEL	Airbus A320-214	2409	ex F-WWDE	St Canice/Cainneach	
☐ EI-DEM	Airbus A320-214	2411	ex F-WWDG	St Ibar/Ibhar	
☐ EI-DEN	Airbus A320-214	2432	ex F-WWBK	St Kieran/Ciaran	
☐ EI-DEO	Airbus A320-214	2486	ex F-WWIV	St Senan/Seanan	Irish Rugby Team c/s
☐ EI-DEP	Airbus A320-214	2542	ex F-WWIU	St Eugene/Eoghan	
☐ EI-DER	Airbus A320-214	2583	ex F-WWDE	St Mel/Mel	
☐ EI-DES	Airbus A320-214	2635	ex F-WWDZ	St Pappin/Paipan	
☐ EI-DVE	Airbus A320-214	3129	ex F-WWBJ	St Aideen/Etaoin	
☐ EI-DVG	Airbus A320-214	3318	ex F-WWIV	St Flannan/Flannan	
☐ EI-DVH	Airbus A320-214	3345	ex F-WWBP		
☐ EI-DVI	Airbus A320-214	3501	ex F-WWBQ	St Emer/Eimaer	
☐ EI-DVJ	Airbus A320-214	3857	ex F-WWDL	St Macarthan/Macarthain	
☐ EI-DVK	Airbus A320-214	4572	ex D-AUBY	St Brigid/Birghid	

☐ EI-DVL	Airbus A320-214	4678	ex F-WWDR	St Moling/Molling	
☐ EI-DVM	Airbus A320-214	4634	ex F-WWDV		
☐ EI-DVN	Airbus A320-214	4715	ex D-AUBH		
☐ EI-EDP	Airbus A320-214	3781	ex F-WWIR		
☐ EI-EDS	Airbus A320-214	3755	ex F-WWBU	St Malachy/Maolmhaodhog	
☐ EI-EZW	Airbus A320-214	1983	ex I-EEZF	Rosie Lee	opf VIR
☐ EI-EZV	Airbus A320-214	2001	ex I-EEZG	Tartan Lassie	opf VIR
☐ EI-DAA	Airbus A330-202	397	ex F-WWKK	St Keeva/Caoimhe	
☐ EI-DUO	Airbus A330-202	841	ex F-WWYT	St Columba/Colum	
☐ EI-DUZ	Airbus A330-302	847	ex F-WWKM	St Aoife/Aoife	
☐ EI-EAV	Airbus A330-302	985	ex F-WWKF	Ronan	
☐ EI-EDY	Airbus A330-302	1025	ex F-WWYU	Maincin	
☐ EI-ELA	Airbus A330-302X	1106	ex F-WWYH	St Patrick/Padraig	
☐ EI-EWR	Airbus A330-202	330	ex 9M-XAD		♦
☐ EI-LAX	Airbus A330-202	269	ex F-WWKV	St Mella/Mella	
☐ EI-CPE	Airbus A321-211	0926	ex D-AVZQ	St Enda/Eanna	
☐ EI-CPG	Airbus A321-211	1023	ex D-AVZR	St Aidan/Aodhan	
☐ EI-CPH	Airbus A321-211	1094	ex F-WWDD	St Dervilla/Dearbhile	
☐ EI-EPR	Airbus A319-111	3169	ex EC-KEV	St Davnet/Damhnat	
☐ EI-EPS	Airbus A319-111	3377	ex EC-KME	St Fergus/Feargus	
☐ EI-EPT	Airbus A319-111	3054	ex EC-KBJ	St Rowan/Ruadhan	
☐ EI-EPU	Airbus A319-111	3102	ex EC-KDI	St Conleth/Conlaed	
☐ EI-LBR	Boeing 757-2Q8/W	28167/775	ex OH-LBR	St Columbanus/Columban	<ABR
☐ EI-LBS	Boeing 757-2Q8/W	27623/792	ex OH-LBS	St Otteran/Odhrán	<ABR
☐ EI-LBT	Boeing 757-2Q8/W	28170/801	ex OH-LBT	St Brendan/Breandan	<ABR

AIR CONTRACTORS   Contract (AG/ABR)   Dublin (DUB)

☐ EI-FXA	ATR 42-320F	282	ex N282AT		Lsd fr/opf FDX
☐ EI-FXB	ATR 42-320F	243	ex (N924FX)		Lsd fr/opf FDX
☐ EI-FXC	ATR 42-320F	310	ex (N925FX)		Lsd fr/opf FDX
☐ EI-FXD	ATR 42-300F	273	ex (N927FX)		Lsd fr/opf FDX
☐ EI-FXE	ATR 42-320F	327	ex (N926FX)		Lsd fr/opf FDX
☐ EI-FXF	ATR 42-300F	141	ex N928FX		>SWT
☐ EI-SLA	ATR 42-300F	149	ex SE-LST		
☐ EI-SLI	ATR 42-320	115	ex 5Y-BVD		>CNF
☐ EI-SLO	ATR 42-320F	121	ex HB-AFD		♦
☐ EI-FXG	ATR 72-202F	224	ex (N814FX)		
☐ EI-FXH	ATR 72-202F	229	ex N815FX		
☐ EI-FXI	ATR 72-202F	294	ex N818FX		
☐ EI-FXJ	ATR 72-202F	292	ex N813FX		
☐ EI-FXK	ATR 72-202F	256	ex N817FX		Lsd fr/opf FDX
☐ EI-REJ	ATR 72-202F	126	ex ES-KRA		
☐ EI-SLF	ATR 72-202F	210	ex OY-RUA		
☐ EI-SLG	ATR 72-202F	183	ex F-WQNI		
☐ EI-SLH	ATR 72-202F	157	ex OY-RTG		
☐ EI-SLJ	ATR 72-201	324	ex LY-PTK		
☐ EI-SLK	ATR 72-212	395	ex N642AS		
☐ EI-STB	Boeing 737-476SF	24440/2324	ex N116BT		
☐ EI-STC	Boeing 737-476SF	24446/2569	ex N119BT		
☐ EI-STE	Boeing 737-4Y0SF	25261/2258	ex N286AL		>SWT
☐ EI-STH	Boeing 737-429SF	25729/2217	ex N42XA		♦
☐ EI-EYK	Airbus A300B4-622RF	743	ex (JU-8128)		♦
☐ EI-EXR	Airbus A300B4-622RF	677	ex TC-ACM		♦
☐ EI-LBR	Boeing 757-2Q8/W	28167/775	ex OH-LBR	St Columbanus/Columban	>EIN
☐ EI-LBS	Boeing 757-2Q8/W	27623/792	ex OH-LBS	St Otteran/Odhrán	>EIN
☐ EI-LBT	Boeing 757-2Q8/W	28170/801	ex OH-LBT	St Brendan/Brreandan	>EIN
☐ EI-OZJ	Airbus A300B4-622RF	770	ex B-LDN		>AHK
☐ EI-STA	Boeing 737-31S	29057/2942	ex G-THOG		♦
☐ TF-BBD	Boeing 737-3Y0SF	24463/1701	ex OY-SEE		>BBD♦

CHC IRELAND   Dublin (DUB)

☐ EI-ICA	Sikorsky S-92A	920045	ex G-SARB		op by Irish Coastguard
☐ EI-ICD	Sikorsky S-92A	920052	ex G-SARC		op by Irish Coastguard
☐ EI-ICG	Sikorsky S-92A	920150	ex N150AL		op by Irish Coastguard
☐ EI-ICR	Sikorsky S-92A	920051	ex G-CGOC	Banrion n Speire	op by Irish Coastguard
☐ EI-ICU	Sikorsky S-92A	920034	ex G-CGMU		op by Irish Coastguard

CITYJET   City-Ireland (WX/BCY)   Dublin (DUB)

☐ EI-RJC	Avro 146-RJ85	E2333	ex G-CEHA	Achill Island	all white
☐ EI-RJD	Avro 146-RJ85	E2334	ex G-CEFL	Valentia Island	
☐ EI-RJE	Avro 146-RJ85	E2335	ex G-CEBU	St MacDara's Island	
☐ EI-RJF	Avro 146-RJ85	E2337	ex G-CEFN	Great Blasket Island	
☐ EI-RJG	Avro 146-RJ85	E2344	ex G-CEHB	Sherkin Island	
☐ EI-RJH	Avro 146-RJ85	E2345	ex G-CEIC	Inishturko/o	

☐ EI-RJI	Avro 146-RJ85	E2346	ex (G-CDZP)	Skellig Michael	all white
☐ EI-RJN	Avro 146-RJ85	E2351	ex N526XJ	Lake Isle of Inisheer	all white
☐ EI-RJO	Avro 146-RJ85	E2352	ex N527XJ	Inis Mor	
☐ EI-RJR	Avro 146-RJ85	E2364	ex N530XJ	Tory Island	
☐ EI-RJT	Avro 146-RJ85	E2366	ex N532XJ	Inishbofin	
☐ EI-RJU	Avro 146-RJ85	E2367	ex N533XJ	Cape Clear	
☐ EI-RJW	Avro 146-RJ85	E2371	ex N535XJ	Garinish Island	
☐ EI-RJX	Avro 146-RJ85	E2372	ex N536XJ	Scattery Island	
☐ EI-RJY	Avro 146-RJ85	E2307	ex N502XJ	Inishcealtra	
☐ EI-RJZ	Avro 146-RJ85	E2326	ex N512XJ		
☐ EI-WXA	Avro 146-RJ85	E2310	ex N503XJ		
☐ EI-REI	ATR 72-202	267	ex OY-RTB	Warrieor/Ainle	white c/s <STK♦
☐ OO-VLJ	Fokker 50	20105	ex PH-ARE	Owain Glyndwr	<VLM♦
☐ OO-VLP	Fokker 50	20209	ex PH-DMS		<VLM♦

NORWEGIAN AIR INTERNATIONAL   (NAI)   Dublin (DUB)

☐ EI-FHA	Boeing 737-8JP/W	39012/3982	ex LN-DYY	Vilhelm Bjerknes	♦
☐ EI-FHB	Boeing 737-8Q8/W	35283/2742	ex LN-NOE	Henrik Wergeland	♦
☐ EI-FHC	Boeing 737-8Q8/W	37159/2868	ex LN-NOL		6000th 737 c/s♦
☐ EI-FHD	Boeing 737-8JP/W	39011/3946	ex LN-DYX		♦
☐ EI-FHE	Boeing 737-8Q8/W	35280/2629	ex LN-NOD	Sonja Henie	♦
☐ EI-FHF	Boeing 737-8FZ/W	34954/2483	ex LN-NOB	Edvard Grieg	♦
☐ EI-FHG	Boeing 737-86N/W	37884/3223	ex LN-NOJ	Tycho Brahe	♦
☐ EI-FHH	Boeing 737-8FZ/W	31713/3215	ex LN-NOV	Evert Taube	♦
☐ EI-FHI	Boeing 737-8JP/W	39024/4610	ex LN-NGM	Carl Nielson	♦
☐ EI-LNA	Boeing 787-8	35304/102	ex (LN-BKA)	Sonia Henie	

RYANAIR   Ryanair (FR/RYR)   Dublin (DUB)

☐ EI-DAC	Boeing 737-8AS/W	29938/1240	
☐ EI-DAD	Boeing 737-8AS/W	33544/1249	
☐ EI-DAE	Boeing 737-8AS/W	33545/1252	
☐ EI-DAF	Boeing 737-8AS/W	29939/1262	
☐ EI-DAG	Boeing 737-8AS/W	29940/1265	
☐ EI-DAH	Boeing 737-8AS/W	33546/1269	
☐ EI-DAI	Boeing 737-8AS/W	33547/1271	
☐ EI-DAJ	Boeing 737-8AS/W	33548/1274	
☐ EI-DAK	Boeing 737-8AS/W	33717/1310	
☐ EI-DAL	Boeing 737-8AS/W	33718/1311	
☐ EI-DAM	Boeing 737-8AS/W	33719/1312	
☐ EI-DAN	Boeing 737-8AS/W	33549/1361	
☐ EI-DAO	Boeing 737-8AS/W	33550/1366	ex N1800B
☐ EI-DAP	Boeing 737-8AS/W	33551/1368	ex N6066U
☐ EI-DAR	Boeing 737-8AS/W	33552/1371	ex EI-DAQ
☐ EI-DAS	Boeing 737-8AS/W	33553/1372	ex EI-DAR
☐ EI-DCF	Boeing 737-8AS/W	33804/1529	
☐ EI-DCG	Boeing 737-8AS/W	33805/1530	
☐ EI-DCH	Boeing 737-8AS/W	33566/1546	
☐ EI-DCI	Boeing 737-8AS/W	33567/1547	
☐ EI-DCJ	Boeing 737-8AS/W	33564/1562	
☐ EI-DCK	Boeing 737-8AS/W	33565/1563	
☐ EI-DCL	Boeing 737-8AS/W	33806/1576	ex N1786B
☐ EI-DCM	Boeing 737-8AS/W	33807/1578	
☐ EI-DCN	Boeing 737-8AS/W	33808/1590	ex N60436
☐ EI-DCO	Boeing 737-8AS/W	33809/1592	
☐ EI-DCP	Boeing 737-8AS/W	33810/1595	
☐ EI-DCR	Boeing 737-8AS/W	33811/1613	
☐ EI-DCW	Boeing 737-8AS/W	33568/1631	
☐ EI-DCX	Boeing 737-8AS/W	33569/1635	
☐ EI-DCY	Boeing 737-8AS/W	33570/1637	
☐ EI-DCZ	Boeing 737-8AS/W	33815/1638	
☐ EI-DHA	Boeing 737-8AS/W	33571/1642	
☐ EI-DHB	Boeing 737-8AS/W	33572/1652	
☐ EI-DHC	Boeing 737-8AS/W	33573/1655	
☐ EI-DHD	Boeing 737-8AS/W	33816/1657	ex N1784B
☐ EI-DHE	Boeing 737-8AS/W	33574/1658	ex N1786B
☐ EI-DHF	Boeing 737-8AS/W	33575/1660	ex N1782B
☐ EI-DHG	Boeing 737-8AS/W	33576/1670	ex N1787B
☐ EI-DHH	Boeing 737-8AS/W	33817/1677	
☐ EI-DHN	Boeing 737-8AS/W	33577/1782	
☐ EI-DHO	Boeing 737-8AS/W	33578/1792	ex N1786B
☐ EI-DHP	Boeing 737-8AS/W	33579/1794	
☐ EI-DHR	Boeing 737-8AS/W	33822/1798	
☐ EI-DHS	Boeing 737-8AS/W	33580/1807	
☐ EI-DHT	Boeing 737-8AS/W	33581/1809	
☐ EI-DHV	Boeing 737-8AS/W	33582/1811	
☐ EI-DHW	Boeing 737-8AS/W	33823/1819	ex N1786B
☐ EI-DHX	Boeing 737-8AS/W	33585/1824	ex N60436
☐ EI-DHY	Boeing 737-8AS/W	33824/1826	ex N1781B

☐ EI-DHZ	Boeing 737-8AS/W	33583/1834		
☐ EI-DLB	Boeing 737-8AS/W	33584/1836	ex N5573L	
☐ EI-DLC	Boeing 737-8AS/W	33586/1844	ex N1786B	
☐ EI-DLD	Boeing 737-8AS/W	33825/1847		
☐ EI-DLE	Boeing 737-8AS/W	33587/1864		
☐ EI-DLF	Boeing 737-8AS/W	33588/1867		
☐ EI-DLG	Boeing 737-8AS/W	33589/1869	ex N1786B	
☐ EI-DLH	Boeing 737-8AS/W	33590/1886		
☐ EI-DLI	Boeing 737-8AS/W	33591/1894	ex N1786B	
☐ EI-DLJ	Boeing 737-8AS/W	34177/1899		National Express Coach c/s
☐ EI-DLK	Boeing 737-8AS/W	33592/1904	ex N1786B	
☐ EI-DLN	Boeing 737-8AS/W	33595/1926		
☐ EI-DLO	Boeing 737-8AS/W	34178/1929		
☐ EI-DLR	Boeing 737-8AS/W	33596/2057		
☐ EI-DLV	Boeing 737-8AS/W	33598/2063		
☐ EI-DLW	Boeing 737-8AS/W	33599/2078		
☐ EI-DLX	Boeing 737-8AS/W	33600/2082		
☐ EI-DLY	Boeing 737-8AS/W	33601/2088		
☐ EI-DPB	Boeing 737-8AS/W	33603/2112	ex N1787B	
☐ EI-DPC	Boeing 737-8AS/W	33604/2120	ex N1786B	
☐ EI-DPD	Boeing 737-8AS/W	33623/2123	ex N1786B	
☐ EI-DPF	Boeing 737-8AS/W	33606/2158		
☐ EI-DPG	Boeing 737-8AS/W	33607/2163		
☐ EI-DPH	Boeing 737-8AS/W	33624/2168		
☐ EI-DPI	Boeing 737-8AS/W	33608/2173		
☐ EI-DPJ	Boeing 737-8AS/W	33609/21/9	ex N1781B	
☐ EI-DPK	Boeing 737-8AS/W	33610/2183		
☐ EI-DPL	Boeing 737-8AS/W	33611/2189		
☐ EI-DPM	Boeing 737-8AS/W	33640/2198		
☐ EI-DPN	Boeing 737-8AS/W	35549/2200	ex N1787B	
☐ EI-DPO	Boeing 737-8AS/W	33612/2207	ex N1786B	
☐ EI-DPP	Boeing 737-8AS/W	33613/2213		
☐ EI-DPR	Boeing 737-8AS/W	33614/2219	ex N1786B	
☐ EI-DPT	Boeing 737-8AS/W	35550/2227	ex N1787B	
☐ EI-DPV	Boeing 737-8AS/W	35551/2236	ex N1779B	
☐ EI-DPW	Boeing 737-8AS/W	35552/2263		
☐ EI-DPX	Boeing 737-8AS/W	35553/2279		
☐ EI-DPY	Boeing 737-8AS/W	33615/2375	ex N1781B	
☐ EI-DPZ	Boeing 737-8AS/W	33616/2376		
☐ EI-DWA	Boeing 737-8AS/W	33617/2377		
☐ EI-DWB	Boeing 737-8AS/W	36075/2382		
☐ EI-DWC	Boeing 737-8AS/W	36076/2384		
☐ EI-DWD	Boeing 737-8AS/W	33642/2389	ex N1787B	
☐ EI-DWE	Boeing 737-8AS/W	36074/2391		
☐ EI-DWF	Boeing 737-8AS/W	33619/2396		
☐ EI-DWG	Boeing 737-8AS/W	33620/2397		
☐ EI-DWH	Boeing 737-8AS/W	33637/2408	ex N1787B	
☐ EI-DWI	Boeing 737-8AS/W	33643/2410		
☐ EI-DWJ	Boeing 737-8AS/W	36077/2411		
☐ EI-DWK	Boeing 737-8AS/W	36078/2415	ex N1786B	
☐ EI-DWL	Boeing 737-8AS/W	33618/2416	ex N1787B	
☐ EI-DWM	Boeing 737-8AS/W	36080/2430		
☐ EI-DWO	Boeing 737-8AS/W	36079/2440		
☐ EI-DWP	Boeing 737-8AS/W	36082/2443		
☐ EI-DWR	Boeing 737-8AS/W	36081/2448	ex N1786B	
☐ EI-DWS	Boeing 737-8AS/W	33625/2472	ex N1786B	
☐ EI-DWT	Boeing 737-8AS/W	33626/2489		
☐ EI-DWV	Boeing 737-8AS/W	33627/2492		
☐ EI-DWW	Boeing 737-8AS/W	33629/2507	ex N1781B	
☐ EI-DWX	Boeing 737-8AS/W	33630/2508		
☐ EI-DWY	Boeing 737-8AS/W	33638/2518	ex N1786B	
☐ EI-DWZ	Boeing 737-8AS/W	33628/2520	ex N1796B	
☐ EI-DYA	Boeing 737-8AS/W	33631/2529	ex N1786B	
☐ EI-DYB	Boeing 737-8AS/W	33633/2542		
☐ EI-DYC	Boeing 737-8AS/W	36567/2543	ex N1787B	
☐ EI-DYD	Boeing 737-8AS/W	33632/2544	ex N1786B	
☐ EI-DYE	Boeing 737-8AS/W	36568/2548		
☐ EI-DYF	Boeing 737-8AS/W	36569/2549	ex N1786B	
☐ EI-DYH	Boeing 737-8AS/W	36570/2573		
☐ EI-DYI	Boeing 737-8AS/W	36571/2574		
☐ EI-DYJ	Boeing 737-8AS/W	36572/2580		
☐ EI-DYK	Boeing 737-8AS/W	36573/2581		
☐ EI-DYL	Boeing 737-8AS/W	36574/2635	ex N1786B	
☐ EI-DYM	Boeing 737-8AS/W	36575/2636	ex N1787B	
☐ EI-DYN	Boeing 737-8AS/W	36576/2367	ex N1796B	
☐ EI-DYO	Boeing 737-8AS/W	33636/2728		
☐ EI-DYP	Boeing 737-8AS/W	37515/2729	ex N1786B	
☐ EI-DYR	Boeing 737-8AS/W	37513/2734		
☐ EI-DYS	Boeing 737-8AS/W	37514/2735		
☐ EI-DYT	Boeing 737-8AS/W	33634/2745		
☐ EI-DYV	Boeing 737-8AS/W	37512/2746		
☐ EI-DYW	Boeing 737-8AS/W	33635/2747		
☐ EI-DYX	Boeing 737-8AS/W	37517/2754		

☐ EI-DYY	Boeing 737-8AS/W	37521/2755	ex N1787B
☐ EI-DYZ	Boeing 737-8AS/W	37518/2760	
☐ EI-EBA	Boeing 737-8AS/W	37516/2761	
☐ EI-EBB	Boeing 737-8AS/W	37519/2779	ex N1787B
☐ EI-EBC	Boeing 737-8AS/W	37520/2780	ex N1795B
☐ EI-EBD	Boeing 737-8AS/W	37522/2781	ex N1796B
☐ EI-EBE	Boeing 737-8AS/W	37523/2788	
☐ EI-EBF	Boeing 737-8AS/W	37524/2791	ex N60697
☐ EI-EBG	Boeing 737-8AS/W	37525/2792	
☐ EI-EBH	Boeing 737-8AS/W	37526/2797	
☐ EI-EBI	Boeing 737-8AS/W	37527/2798	
☐ EI-EBK	Boeing 737-8AS/W	37528/2807	
☐ EI-EBL	Boeing 737-8AS/W	37529/2808	ex N1796B
☐ EI-EBM	Boeing 737-8AS/W	35002/2839	ex N1787B
☐ EI-EBN	Boeing 737-8AS/W	35003/2840	
☐ EI-EBO	Boeing 737-8AS/W	35004/2843	ex N1796B
☐ EI-EBP	Boeing 737-8AS/W	37531/2844	
☐ EI-EBR	Boeing 737-8AS/W	37530/2856	ex N1779B
☐ EI-EBS	Boeing 737-8AS/W	35001/2857	ex N1786B
☐ EI-EBT	Boeing 737-8AS/W	35000/2858	
☐ EI-EBV	Boeing 737-8AS/W	35009/2872	
☐ EI-EBW	Boeing 737-8AS/W	35010/2873	
☐ EI-EBX	Boeing 737-8AS/W	35007/2882	
☐ EI-EBY	Boeing 737-8AS/W	35006/2886	
☐ EI-EBZ	Boeing 737-8AS/W	35008/2887	
☐ EI-EFA	Boeing 737-8AS/W	35005/2892	ex N1786B
☐ EI-EFB	Boeing 737-8AS/W	37532/2893	
☐ EI-EFC	Boeing 737-8AS/W	35015/2901	
☐ EI-EFD	Boeing 737-8AS/W	35011/2903	ex N1787B
☐ EI-EFE	Boeing 737-8AS/W	37533/2905	
☐ EI-EFF	Boeing 737-8AS/W	35016/2917	ex N1786B
☐ EI-EFG	Boeing 737-8AS/W	35014/2921	ex N1786B
☐ EI-EFH	Boeing 737-8AS/W	35012/2923	ex N1787B
☐ EI-EFI	Boeing 737-8AS/W	35013/2924	ex N1786B
☐ EI-EFJ	Boeing 737-8AS/W	37536/2936	ex N1786B
☐ EI-EFK	Boeing 737-8AS/W	37537/2948	ex N1786B
☐ EI-EFL	Boeing 737-8AS/W	37534/2958	
☐ EI-EFM	Boeing 737-8AS/W	37535/2960	ex N1787B
☐ EI-EFN	Boeing 737-8AS/W	37538/2967	ex N1787B
☐ EI-EFO	Boeing 737-8AS/W	37539/2978	
☐ EI-EFP	Boeing 737-8AS/W	37540/2979	
☐ EI-EFR	Boeing 737-8AS/W	37541/3012	ex N1786B
☐ EI-EFS	Boeing 737-8AS/W	37542/3021	
☐ EI-EFT	Boeing 737-8AS/W	37543/3023	ex N1787B
☐ EI-EFV	Boeing 737-8AS/W	35017/3052	ex N60659
☐ EI-EFW	Boeing 737-8AS/W	35018/3078	ex N1786B
☐ EI-EFX	Boeing 737-8AS/W	35019/3079	ex N1787B
☐ EI-EFY	Boeing 737-8AS/W	35020/3084	ex N1786B
☐ EI-EFZ	Boeing 737-8AS/W	38489/3089	ex N1787B
☐ EI-EGA	Boeing 737-8AS/W	38490/3096	ex N1787B
☐ EI-EGB	Boeing 737-8AS/W	38491/3097	ex N1787B
☐ EI-EGC	Boeing 737-8AS/W	38492/3099	ex N1786B
☐ EI-EGD	Boeing 737-8AS/W	34981/3420	
☐ EI-EKA	Boeing 737-8AS/W	35022/3139	ex N1786B
☐ EI-EKB	Boeing 737-8AS/W	38494/3141	ex N1786B
☐ EI-EKC	Boeing 737-8AS/W	38495/3143	ex N1786B
☐ EI-EKD	Boeing 737-8AS/W	35024/3146	ex N1786B
☐ EI-EKE	Boeing 737-8AS/W	35023/3148	ex N1787B
☐ EI-EKF	Boeing 737-8AS/W	35025/3152	ex N1786B
☐ EI-EKG	Boeing 737-8AS/W	35021/3161	
☐ EI-EKH	Boeing 737-8AS/W	38493/3162	ex N1787B
☐ EI-EKI	Boeing 737-8AS/W	38496/3168	ex N1786B
☐ EI-EKJ	Boeing 737-8AS/W	38497/3173	ex N1796B
☐ EI-EKK	Boeing 737-8AS/W	38500/3174	ex N1787B
☐ EI-EKL	Boeing 737-8AS/W	38498/3179	ex N1796B
☐ EI-EKM	Boeing 737-8AS/W	38499/3181	ex N1786B
☐ EI-EKN	Boeing 737-8AS/W	35026/3187	ex N1787B
☐ EI-EKO	Boeing 737-8AS/W	35027/3198	ex N1795B
☐ EI-EKP	Boeing 737-8AS/W	35028/3199	ex N1786B
☐ EI-EKR	Boeing 737-8AS/W	38503/3202	ex N1786B
☐ EI-EKS	Boeing 737-8AS/W	38504/3203	ex N1786B
☐ EI-EKT	Boeing 737-8AS/W	38505/3206	ex N1786B
☐ EI-EKV	Boeing 737-8AS/W	38507/3211	
☐ EI-EKW	Boeing 737-8AS/W	38506/3221	ex N1786B
☐ EI-EKX	Boeing 737-8AS/W	35030/3222	ex N1787B
☐ EI-EKY	Boeing 737-8AS/W	35031/3230	
☐ EI-EKZ	Boeing 737-8AS/W	38508/3234	
☐ EI-EMA	Boeing 737-8AS/W	35032/3240	
☐ EI-EMB	Boeing 737-8AS/W	38511/3241	ex N1796B
☐ EI-EMC	Boeing 737-8AS/W	38510/3246	
☐ EI-EMD	Boeing 737-8AS/W	38509/3248	ex N1786B
☐ EI-EME	Boeing 737-8AS/W	35029/3254	
☐ EI-EMF	Boeing 737-8AS/W	34978/3256	ex N1786B

□ EI-EMH	Boeing 737-8AS/W	34974/3262		
□ EI-EMI	Boeing 737-8AS/W	34979/3263		National Express-UK Airport Transfers c/s
□ EI-EMJ	Boeing 737-8AS/W	34975/3271	ex N1786B	
□ EI-EMK	Boeing 737-8AS/W	38512/3272	ex N1786B	National Express Coach c/s
□ EI-EML	Boeing 737-8AS/W	38513/3283	ex N1786B	
□ EI-EMM	Boeing 737-8AS/W	38514/3284	ex N1786B	
□ EI-EMN	Boeing 737-8AS/W	38515/3286		
□ EI-EMO	Boeing 737-8AS/W	40283/3318		
□ EI-EMP	Boeing 737-8AS/W	40285/3322	ex N1787B	
□ EI-EMR	Boeing 737-8AS/W	40284/3323		
□ EI-ENA	Boeing 737-8AS/W	34983/3416	ex N1796B	
□ EI-ENB	Boeing 737-8AS/W	40289/3418		
□ EI-ENC	Boeing 737-8AS/W	34980/3419		
□ EI-ENE	Boeing 737-8AS/W	34976/3428		
□ EI-ENF	Boeing 737-8AS/W	35034/3451		
□ EI-ENG	Boeing 737-8AS/W	34977/3453	ex N1787B	
□ EI-ENH	Boeing 737-8AS/W	35033/3454	ex N1796B	
□ EI-ENI	Boeing 737-8AS/W	40300/3514	ex N1796B	
□ EI-ENJ	Boeing 737-8AS/W	40301/3514	ex N1796B	
□ EI-ENK	Boeing 737-8AS/W	40303/3524		
□ EI-ENL	Boeing 737-8AS/W	35037/3527	ex N1786B	
□ EI-ENM	Boeing 737-8AS/W	35038/3528	ex N1786B	
□ EI-ENN	Boeing 737-8AS/W	35036/3533		
□ EI-ENO	Boeing 737-8AS/W	40302/3534		
□ EI-ENP	Boeing 737 8AS/W	40304/3535		
□ EI-ENR	Boeing 737-8AS/W	35041/3538	ex N1786B	
□ EI-ENS	Boeing 737-8AS/W	40307/3541		
□ EI-ENT	Boeing 737-8AS/W	35040/3544	ex N1786B	
□ EI-ENV	Boeing 737-8AS/W	35039/3546	ex N1786B	
□ EI-ENW	Boeing 737-8AS/W	40306/3551	ex N1786B	
□ EI-ENX	Boeing 737-8AS/W	40305/3556		
□ EI-ENY	Boeing 737-8AS/W	35042/3559		
□ EI-ENZ	Boeing 737-8AS/W	40308/3561	ex N1786B	
□ EI-EPA	Boeing 737-8AS/W	34987/3568		
□ EI-EPB	Boeing 737-8AS/W	34986/3570	ex N1787B	
□ EI-EPC	Boeing 737-8AS/W	40312/3574		
□ EI-EPD	Boeing 737-8AS/W	40310/3578		
□ EI-EPE	Boeing 737-8AS/W	34984/3587		
□ EI-EPF	Boeing 737-8AS/W	40309/3593		
□ EI-EPG	Boeing 737-8AS/W	34985/3597	ex N1786B	
□ EI-EPH	Boeing 737-8AS/W	40311/3599		
□ EI-ESL	Boeing 737-8AS/W	34988/3767	ex N7235C	
□ EI-ESM	Boeing 737-8AS/W	34992/3772	ex N441BA	
□ EI-ESN	Boeing 737-8AS/W	34991/3780	ex N742BA	
□ EI-ESO	Boeing 737-8AS/W	34989/3787	ex N734BA	
□ EI-ESP	Boeing 737-8AS/W	34990/3789	ex N751BA	
□ EI-ESR	Boeing 737-8AS/W	34995/3795	ex N759BA	
□ EI-ESS	Boeing 737-8AS/W	35043/3800	ex N760BA	
□ EI-EST	Boeing 737-8AS/W	34994/3804	ex N761BA	
□ EI-ESV	Boeing 737-8AS/W	34993/3814	ex N762BA	
□ EI-ESW	Boeing 737-8AS/W	34997/3821		
□ EI-ESX	Boeing 737-8AS/W	34998/3822		
□ EI-ESY	Boeing 737-8AS/W	34999/3829		
□ EI-ESZ	Boeing 737-8AS/W	34996/3842		
□ EI-EVA	Boeing 737-8AS/W	40288/3884		
□ EI-EVB	Boeing 737-8AS/W	34982/3886		
□ EI-EVC	Boeing 737-8AS/W	40286/3905		
□ EI-EVD	Boeing 737-8AS/W	40287/3908		
□ EI-EVE	Boeing 737-8AS/W	35035/3920		
□ EI-EVF	Boeing 737-8AS/W	40291/3926		
□ EI-EVG	Boeing 737-8AS/W	40292/3928		
□ EI-EVH	Boeing 737-8AS/W	40290/3938		
□ EI-EVI	Boeing 737-8AS/W	38502/3945		
□ EI-EVJ	Boeing 737-8AS/W	38501/3953		
□ EI-EVK	Boeing 737-8AS/W	40298/3958		
□ EI-EVL	Boeing 737-8AS/W	40299/3974		
□ EI-EVM	Boeing 737-8AS/W	40296/3983		
□ EI-EVN	Boeing 737-8AS/W	40294/3992		
□ EI-EVO	Boeing 737-8AS/W	40297/4011	ex N1786B	
□ EI-EVP	Boeing 737-8AS/W	40293/4017	ex N1787B	
□ EI-EVR	Boeing 737-8AS/W	40295/4166		
□ EI-EVS	Boeing 737-8AS/W	40313/4169		
□ EI-EVT	Boeing 737-8AS/W	40315/4174		
□ EI-EVV	Boeing 737-8AS/W	40314/4190		
□ EI-EVW	Boeing 737-8AS/W	40318/4204		
□ EI-EVX	Boeing 737-8AS/W	40317/4211		
□ EI-EVY	Boeing 737-8AS.W	40319/4220	ex N1796B	
□ EI-EVZ	Boeing 737-8AS/W	40316/4227		
□ EI-EXD	Boeing 737-8AS/W	40320/4240		
□ EI-EXE	Boeing 737-8AS/W	40321/4249		
□ EI-EXF	Boeing 737-8AS/W	40322/4261		
□ EI-FEE	Boeing 737-8MD/W	44686/5072	ex N1786B	♦
□ EI-FEF	Boeing 737-8MD/W	44687/5099		♦

☐ EI-FEG	Boeing 737-8MD/W	44688/5111	ex N1786B	♦
☐ EI-FEH	Boeing 737-8MD/W	44689/5124		♦
☐ EI-FEI	Boeing 737-8MD/W	44690/5147		♦
☐ EI-FIA	Boeing 737-8AS/W	44691/5238		♦
☐ EI-FIB	Boeing 737-8AS/W	44692/5257		♦
☐ EI-FIC	Boeing 737-8AS/W	44693/5289		♦
☐ EI-FID	Boeing 737-8AS/W	44694/5301		♦
☐ EI-FIE	Boeing 737-8AS/W	44695/5316		♦
☐ EI-FIF	Boeing 737-8AS/W	44696/5344		♦
☐ EI-FIG	Boeing 737-8AS/W	44698/5352		♦
☐ EI-FIH	Boeing 737-8AS/W	44697/5374	ex N1796B	♦
☐ EI-FIJ	Boeing 737-8AS/W	44699/5393		♦
☐ EI-FIK	Boeing 737-8AS/W	44700/5402		♦
☐ EI-FIL	Boeing 737-8AS/W	44702/5429		o/o♦
☐ EI-	Boeing 737-8AS/W	44701/		o/o♦
☐ EI-	Boeing 737-8AS/W	44703/		o/o♦
☐ EI-	Boeing 737-8AS/W	44704/		o/o♦
☐ EI-	Boeing 737-8AS/W	61576/		o/o♦
☐ EI-	Boeing 737-8AS/W	61577/		o/o♦
☐ EI-	Boeing 737-8AS/W	61578/		o/o♦
☐ EI-	Boeing 737-8AS/W	61579/		o/o♦
☐ OM-CEX	Boeing 737-436	25839/2188	ex OK-WGY	<AXE♦
☐ OM-EEX	Boeing 737-4Q8	26302/2620	ex EI-FBR	<AXE♦
☐ OM-FEX	Boeing 737-8Q8	28213/50	ex N679AC	<AXE♦
☐ OM-HEX	Boeing 737-81Q/W	30785/1007	ex LN-NOC	<AXE♦
☐ YL-LCM	Airbus A320-211	0244	ex F-GJVF	<ART♦
☐ YL-LCN	Airbus A320-211	0662	ex N662WF	<ART♦

STOBART AIR		*Stobart Air (RE/STK)*		*Dublin (DUB)*

☐ EI-FAS	ATR 72-600	1083	ex F-WWET	St Connell/Conall	
☐ EI-FAT	ATR 72-600	1097	ex F-WWEJ	St Fursey/Fursa	
☐ EI-FAU	ATR 72-600	1098	ex F-WWEK	St Darragh/Dáire	
☐ EI-FAV	ATR 72-600	1105	ex F-WWER	St Eithne/Ethna	
☐ EI-FAW	ATR 72-600	1122	ex F-WWEK	St Cronan/Cronán	
☐ EI-FAX	ATR 72-600	1129	ex F-WWER	St Finnian/Finnian	
☐ EI-FCY	ATR 72-600	1139	ex F-WWED	Sir Oliver Plunkett/Oilibhéar Pluincéid	
☐ EI-FCZ	ATR 72-600	1159	ex F-WWEX	St Senan/Seanàn	Aer Lingus c/s♦
☐ EI-	ATR 72-600	1239	ex F-WW		o/o♦
☐ EI-CBK	ATR 42-310	199	ex F-WWEM	St Fintan/Fionntain	
☐ EI-EHH	ATR 42-300	196	ex G-SSEA	Fair Lady/Bebhinn	white c/s
☐ EI-REH	ATR 72-202	260	ex OY-RTA	Vision/Aisling	white c/s
☐ EI-REI	ATR 72-202	267	ex OY-RTB	Warrieor/Ainle	white c/s >BCS
☐ EI-REL	ATR 72-212A	748	ex F-WWEI	Flybe c/s	opf BEE
☐ EI-REM	ATR 72-212A	760	ex F-WWEW	St Gall/Gall	opf BEE

EK   ARMENIA (Republic of Armenia)

AIR ARMENIA		*(QN/ARR)*		*Yerevan-Zvartnots (EVN)*

☐ EK-RA01	Airbus A319-132CJ	0913	ex HZ-NAS	opf Govt
☐ EK73797	Boeing 737-505	26297/2578	ex VP-BEW	

AIR ARMENIA CARGO				

☐ EK11001	Antonov An-12BK	8346107	ex CCCP-11244	
☐ EK11810	Antonov An-12BP	5342908	ex UR-11810	
☐ EK12104	Antonov An-12BK	8346104	ex EX-334	
☐ EK32500	Antonov An-32B	2009	ex 9L-LFP	
☐ EK72928	Antonov An-72	36572060640	ex UR-CFI	♦
☐ EK76450	Ilyushin Il-76TD	1023414450	ex EK-76442	
☐ EY-415	Antonov An-12BK	8346104	ex EK12104	♦

ARARAT INTERNATIONAL AIRLINES		*(RRN)*		*Yerevan-Zvartnots (EVN)*

☐ EK82221	McDonnell-Douglas MD-82	53221/2079	ex LZ-LDE	>IRK
☐ EK82226	McDonnell-Douglas MD-82	53226/2087	ex I-DATH	>IRK
☐ EK82229	McDonnell-Douglas MD-82	53229/2105	ex LZ-LDL	>IRK

ATLANTIS EUROPEAN AIRWAYS		*(TD/LUR)*		*Yerevan-Zvartnots (EVN)*

☐ EK32008	Airbus A320-211	0229	ex N229AN	♦

AYK AVIA		*(AYK)*		*Yerevan-Zvartnots (EVN)*

☐ EK32120	Antonov An-32	1604	ex EK-32604	
☐ EK32803	Antonov An-32B	2803	ex S9-PSE	
☐ EK32805	Antonov An-32B	2805	ex ST-GSM	

170

☐ EK76992 Ilyushin Il-76TD 0073410292 ex EK-76707

RUS AVIATION		Reliable (R4/RLB)			Sharjah (SHJ)
☐ A6-JIL	Airbus A300B4-605RF	626	ex N77080	Sami	opb Unique Air
☐ A6-JIM	Airbus A300B4-605RF	643	ex N7082A	Darina	opb Unique Air
☐ EK76155	Ilyushin Il-76TD	0093421637	ex EK-76754		

SKIVA AIR		(KIR)		Sharjah (SHJ)
☐ EK2809	WSK-PZL Antonov An-28	1AJ009-09	ex ST-TRC	♦
☐ EK32109	Antonov An-32B	2109	ex ST-NSP	♦
☐ EK74036	Antonov An-74-200	36547098965	ex RA-74036	♦
☐ EK74052	Antonov An-72-200	36547098944	ex RA-74052	♦
☐ EK74923	Antonov An-74-200	36547096923	ex EK74043	♦

SKY NET AIRLINE		Skynet Air (SKJ)	
☐ EK-32968	British Aerospace Jetstream 32EP	968	ex ZK-ECR

SOUTH AIRLINES		(STH)		Sharjah (SHJ)
☐ EK26407	Antonov An-26	6407	ex 4L-BKA	
☐ EK26818	Antonov An-26B-100	57314101	ex 3X-GFD	
☐ EK26819	Antonov An-26	4507	ex 3X-GFG	
☐ EK26878	Antonov An-26	8303	ex 3X-GFH	
☐ EK32703	Antonov An-32A	1703	ex 3X-GHC	♦
☐ EK32709	Antonov An-32A	1709	ex 3X-GGS	♦
☐ EK72101	Antonov An-72-100	36572040548	ex 4L-VAS	
☐ EK72903	Antonov An-72	36572020385	ex D2-MBP	
☐ EK74045	Antonov An-74-200	36547098966	ex RA-74060	
☐ EK76778	Ilyushin Il-76TD	0083483502	Ex EY-627	♦

VETERAN AVIA		Veteran (VB/VBF)		Yerevan-Zvartnots (EVN)
☐ EK74799	Boeing 747-281BF	24399/750	ex N281RF	>ICL
☐ EK76783	Ilyushin Il-76MD	9903498974	ex RA-76783	
☐ UR-CMC	Ilyushin Il-76TD	1013407230	ex ER-IAL	

EP- IRAN (Islamic Republic of Iran)

ATA AIRLINES		Atalar Air (I3/TBZ)		
☐ EP-TAM	McDonnell-Douglas MD-83	53465/2093	ex UR-CHM	
☐ EP-TAN	McDonnell-Douglas MD-83	53520/2137	ex UR-CDN	
☐ EP-TAP	McDonnell-Douglas MD-83	53466/2101	ex UR-CHP	Shahriar
☐ EP-TAQ	McDonnell-Douglas MD-83	53488/2134	ex UR-CHQ	Alborz
☐ EP-TAR	McDonnell-Douglas MD-83	53198/1847	ex UR-CIK	
☐ EP-TAS	McDonnell-Douglas MD-83	49986/1842	ex UR-CJC	
☐ EP-TAB	Airbus A320-231	0362	ex UR-CJD	[TBZ]
☐ EP-TAC	Airbus A320-231	0405	ex UR-CJF	Sabalan
☐ EP-TAD	Airbus A320-231	0361	ex UR-CFW	

ATRAK AIR		(AK/ATR)		Tehrean-Mehrabad (THR)
☐ EP-TTA	Airbus A320-231	0393	ex UR-MUS	
☐ EP-TTB	Airbus A320-231	0314	ex 5U-AND	

CASPIAN AIRLINES		Caspian (IV/CPN)		Rasht (RAS)
☐ T7-AWA	Boeing 737-4H6	26467/2378	ex YR-AWA	[THR]♦
☐ T7-AWB	Boeing 737-4H6	26466/2372	ex YR-AWG	[THR]♦
☐ T7-AWC	Boeing 737-4H6	26451/2496	ex 9M-MMW	[THR]♦
☐ T7-AWD	Boeing 737-4H6	26464/2340	ex 9M-MMD	[THR]♦
☐ T9-AWE	Boeing 737-4H6	26443/2272	ex 9M-MMA	[THR]♦
☐ EP-CPD	McDonnell-Douglas MD-83	53188/2119	exUR-CLY	♦
☐ EP-CPU	McDonnell-Douglas MD-82	53223/2081	ex 4L-YAA	
☐ EP-CPV	McDonnell-Douglas MD-83	49938/1785	ex UR-CHN	
☐ EP-CPX	McDonnell-Douglas MD-83	53463/2089	ex UR-CJX	♦
☐ EP-CPZ	McDonnell-Douglas MD-83	53464/2091	ex UR-CJY	
☐ EP-CQA	Boeing 747-2J9F	21507/340	ex EP-SHA	

HELICOPTER SERVICES			Tehran
☐ EP-HEB	Aérospatiale AS350B2 Ecureuil	3050	ex F-WQDA
☐ EP-HEC	Aérospatiale AS350B3 Ecureuil	3621	ex F-WQDD
☐ EP-HED	Aérospatiale AS350B3 Ecureuil	3629	ex F-WQDJ

☐ EP-HEE	Aérospatiale AS350B3 Ecureuil	3644	ex F-WQDK		
☐ EP-HEF	Aérospatiale AS350B3 Ecureuil	3655			
☐ EP-HEG	Aérospatiale AS350B3 Ecureuil	3658			
☐ EP-HEH	Aérospatiale AS350B3 Ecureuil	3668			
☐ EP-HBJ	Bell 212	30504	ex N8112J		
☐ EP-HDV	Aérospatiale AS365N2 Dauphin 2	6467	ex F-GLMZ		
☐ EP-HTN	Bell 212	30885	ex N5009K		
☐ EP-HTO	Bell 205A-1	30163	ex N64743		
☐ EP-HTQ	Bell 205A-1	30189	ex N90039		
☐ EP-HUA	Bell 212	31176	ex HB-XPO		

IRAN AIR   Iranair (IR/IRA)   Tehran-Mehrabad (THR)

☐ EP-IBA	Airbus A300B4-605R	723	ex F-WWAL		
☐ EP-IBB	Airbus A300B4-605R	727	ex F-WWAZ		
☐ EP-IBC	Airbus A300B4-605R	632	ex SX-BEK		
☐ EP-IBD	Airbus A300B4-605R	696	ex SX-BEL		
☐ EP-IBG	Airbus A300B4-203F	299	ex EP-MDA		
☐ EP-IBH	Airbus A300B4-203F	302	ex EP-MDB		[THR]
☐ EP-IBI	Airbus A300B4-2C	151	ex TC-FLK		
☐ EP-IBJ	Airbus A300B4-2C	256	ex TC-FLL		
☐ EP-IBS	Airbus A300B2-203	080	ex F-WZEO		[THR]
☐ EP-IBT	Airbus A300B2-203	185	ex F-WZMB		[THR]
☐ EP-IBV	Airbus A300B2-203	187	ex F-WZMD		[IKA]
☐ EP-IBZ	Airbus A300B2-203	226	ex F-WZME		[THR]
☐ EP-ICE	Airbus A300B4-203F	139	ex TC-KZT		
☐ EP-ICF	Airbus A300B4-203F	173	ex TC-KZU		
☐ EP-IEB	Airbus A320-232	0575	ex EP-MHN		
☐ EP-IEC	Airbus A320-232	0857	ex EP-MHJ		
☐ EP-IED	Airbus A320-212	0345	ex VP-CBZ		[THR]
☐ EP-IEE	Airbus A320-211	0303	ex EK-32303		
☐ EP-IEF	Airbus A320-211	0312	ex EK-32312		
☐ EP-IEG	Airbus A320-211	2054	ex EK-32054		
☐ EP-IAA	Boeing 747SP-86	20998/275	ex N1785B		[THR]
☐ EP-IAB	Boeing 747SP-86	20999/278		Khorasan	[THR]
☐ EP-IAC	Boeing 747SP-86	21093/307		Fars	[THR]
☐ EP-IAD	Boeing 747SP-86	21758/371	ex N1800B	Khorasan	[THR]
☐ EP-IAG	Boeing 747-286M	21217/291		Azarabadegan	[IKA]
☐ EP-IAH	Boeing 747-286M	21218/300		Khuzestan	[THR]
☐ EP-IAI	Boeing 747-230M	22670/550	ex EP-AUA		
☐ EP-ICD	Boeing 747-21AC	24134/712	ex TC-AKZ		
☐ EP-CFD	Fokker 100	11442	ex PT-MRI		
☐ EP-CFE	Fokker 100	11422	ex F-GRMV		[THR]
☐ EP-CFH	Fokker 100	11443	ex F-GSTG		
☐ EP-CFI	Fokker 100	11511	ex PT-MRU		[THR]
☐ EP-CFJ	Fokker 100	11516	ex PT-MRV		[THR]
☐ EP-CFK	Fokker 100	11518	ex PT-MRW		[THR]
☐ EP-CFL	Fokker 100	11343	ex PT-MRY		[THR]
☐ EP-CFM	Fokker 100	11394	ex PT-MQL		
☐ EP-CFO	Fokker 100	11389	ex PT-MQE		
☐ EP-CFP	Fokker 100	11409	ex PT-MQN		
☐ EP-CFQ	Fokker 100	11429	ex PT-MQT		
☐ EP-CFR	Fokker 100	11383	ex PT-MQD		
☐ EP-IDA	Fokker 100	11292	ex PH-LMG		[THR]
☐ EP-IDD	Fokker 100	11294	ex PH-LMM		
☐ EP-IDF	Fokker 100	11298	ex PH-LMN		
☐ EP-IDG	Fokker 100	11302	ex PH-LMW		
☐ EP-IBK	Airbus A310-304	671	ex SU-MWB		
☐ EP-IBL	Airbus A310-304	436	ex A6-EKB		
☐ EP-IBP	Airbus A310-203	370	ex TC-JCR		[THR]
☐ EP-IBQ	Airbus A310-203	389	ex TC-JCS		[THR]
☐ EP-IRR	Boeing 727-286	20946/1052			[THR]
☐ EP-IRS	Boeing 727-286	20947/1070			[THR]
☐ EP-IRT	Boeing 727-286	21078/1114			[THR]
☐ UR-BXI	McDonnell-Douglas MD-82	53170/2065	ex G-CEPJ		<BKV♦
☐ UR-CHW	McDonnell-Douglas MD-82	49510/1514	ex S5-ACY		<BKV♦
☐ UR-CHX	McDonnell-Douglas MD-82	53162/2010	ex S5-ACZ		<BKV♦
☐ UR-CJZ	McDonnell-Douglas MD-82	49506/1400	ex G-CEPE		<BKV

IRAN AIRTOURS   (B9/IRB)   Tehran-Mehrabad/Mashad (THR/MHD)

☐ EP-MDC	McDonnell-Douglas MD-82	49524/1746	ex EP-ARA		
☐ EP-MDD	McDonnell-Douglas MD-82	49852/1959	ex EP-ARB		
☐ EP-MDE	McDonnell-Douglas MD-82	49523/1724	ex 4L-YAB		
☐ EP-MDF	McDonnell-Douglas MD-83	53184/2088	ex UR-BHJ		♦
☐ EP-MDG	McDonnell-Douglas MD-82	53232/2108	ex UR-CJR		♦
☐ UR-BXL	McDonnell-Douglas MD-82	49512/1548	ex G-CEPG		<BKV

☐ UR-BXM	McDonnell-Douglas MD-82	49505/1381	ex G-CEPD	<BKV
☐ UR-CGS	McDonnell-Douglas MD-82	49425/1240	ex G-CEPA	<BKV [THR for spares]
☐ UR-CGT	McDonnell-Douglas MD-82	49428/1241	ex G-CEPB	<BKV [THR for spares]
☐ UR-CHY	McDonnell-Douglas MD-82	53171/2067	ex G-CEPK	<UKM [MHD]
☐ UR-CHZ	McDonnell-Douglas MD-82	53169/2063	ex G-CEPI	<BKV [MHD]
☐ UR-CJQ	McDonnell-Douglas MD-82	49502/1300	ex G-CEPC	<BKV [MHD]

IRAN ASEMAN AIRLINES　　Aseman (EP/IRC)　　Tehran-Mehrabad (THR)

☐ EP-ATA	ATR 72-212	334	ex F-WWLQ	[SYZ]
☐ EP-ATH	ATR 72-212	339	ex F-WWLU	wfs
☐ EP-ATS	ATR 72-212	391	ex F-WWED	[SYZ]
☐ EP-ATU	ATR 72-212A	697	ex F-OIRA	
☐ EP-ATX	ATR 72-212A	573	ex F-OIRB	
☐ EP-ATZ	ATR 72-212	398	ex F-WWEK	
☐ EP-ASA	Boeing 727-228	22081/1594	ex LX-IRA	
☐ EP-ASB	Boeing 727-228	22082/1603	ex LX-IRB	
☐ EP-ASC	Boeing 727-228	22084/1638	ex LX-IRC	[THR]
☐ EP-ASD	Boeing 727-228	22085/1665	ex LX-IRD	
☐ EP-ATQ	Boeing 727-222F (FedEx 3)	21917/1616	ex A6-RCB	[THR]
☐ EP-ATT	Boeing 727-222F (FedEx 3)	21920/1634	ex A6-RCA	[THR]
☐ 3X-GFV	Boeing 727-230F	20905/1091	ex 4L-ABE	opf DHL♦
☐ EP-ASG	Fokker 100	11438	ex HL7210	
☐ EP-ASI	Fokker 100	11519	ex HL7215	
☐ EP-ASJ	Fokker 100	11378	ex HL7206	wfs
☐ EP-ASK	Fokker 100	11388	ex HL7208	wfs
☐ EP-ASM	Fokker 100	11433	ex F-GIOI	
☐ EP-ASO	Fokker 100	11454	ex F-GIOJ	wfs
☐ EP-ASP	Fokker 100	11504	ex HL7213	wfs
☐ EP-ASQ	Fokker 100	11513	ex HL7214	wfs
☐ EP-ASR	Fokker 100	11522	ex HL7216	wfs
☐ EP-AST	Fokker 100	11523	ex HL7217	wfs
☐ EP-ASU	Fokker 100	11430	ex PT-MQP	
☐ EP-ASX	Fokker 100	11431	ex PT-MQS	wfs
☐ EP-ASZ	Fokker 100	11421	ex PT-MQR	dam 10May14
☐ EP-ATB	Fokker 100	11401	ex PT-MQF	wfs
☐ EP-ATC	Fokker 100	11296	ex F-GPXM	wfs
☐ EP-ATD	Fokker 100	11387	ex F-GPXG	wfs
☐ EP-ATE	Fokker 100	11323	ex F-GPXJ	
☐ EP-ATF	Fokker 100	11476	ex F-GPXH	wfs
☐ EP-ATG	Fokker 100	11329	ex F-GPXK	wfs
☐ EP-AGY	Dassault Falcon 20E	286	ex F-WRQU	
☐ EP-APA	Airbus A340-311	002	ex M-YRGU	
☐ EP-APE	Airbus A320-231	0414	ex EP-MMK	♦
☐ EP-APF	Airbus A320-231	0354	ex EP-MML	♦
☐ EP-FIF	Dassault Falcon 20E	251	ex YI-AHG	

KISH AIR　　Kishair (Y9/KIS)　　Tehran-Mehrabad (THR)

☐ EP-LCI	McDonnell-Douglas MD-83	49844/1579	ex UR-CHR	
☐ EP-LCJ	McDonnell-Douglas MD-82	53221/2079	ex EK-82221	♦
☐ EP-LCK	McDonnell-Douglas MD-82	53224/2084	ex EK-82224	
☐ EP-LCL	McDonnell-Douglas MD-82	53229/2105	ex EK-82229	
☐ EP-LCM	McDonnell-Douglas MD-82	53226/2087	ex EK-82226	
☐ EP-LCN	McDonnell-Douglas MD-83	49569/1405	ex UR-BXN	
☐ EP-LCO	McDonnell-Douglas MD-83	53150/1831	ex UR-BXO	
☐ EP-LCP	Fokker 100	11495	ex (4L-)	
☐ EP-LCQ	Fokker 100	11492	ex (4L-)	
☐ EP-LCR	Fokker 100	11330	ex (4L-)	

MAHAN AIR　　Mahan Air (W5/IRM)　　Kerman (KER)

☐ EP-MHA	Airbus A300B2K-3C	160	ex EK-30060	wfs
☐ EP-MHF	Airbus A300B4-103	055	ex S7-AAZ	[IKA]
☐ EP-MHG	Airbus A300B4-203	204	ex AP-BFL	[IKA]
☐ EP-MHL	Airbus A300B4-203	175	ex SU-BMM	
☐ EP-MHM	Airbus A300B2K-3C	090	ex TC-SGA	
☐ EP-MHP	Airbus A300B2K-3C	244	ex EK-30044	
☐ EP-MMO	Airbus A300B4-622R	838	ex EX-35011	
☐ EP-MNG	Airbus A300B4-603	401	ex D-AIAK	
☐ EP-MNH	Airbus A300B4-603	405	ex D-AIAL	
☐ EP-MNI	Airbus A300B4-603	408	ex D-AIAM	
☐ EP-MNJ	Airbus A300B4-603	380	ex D-AIAH	
☐ EP-MNK	Airbus A300B4-603	618	ex D-AIAT	
☐ EP-MNL	Airbus A300B4-603	623	ex D-AIAU	
☐ EP-MNM	Airbus A300B4-605R	773	ex D-AIAX	
☐ EP-MNN	Airbus A300B4-605R	701	ex D-AIAZ	
☐ EP-MNQ	Airbus A300B4-603	553	ex EX-35010	

☐ EP-MNR	Airbus A300B4-603	411	ex EX-35009	
☐ EP-MNS	Airbus A300B4-603	414	ex EX-35008	
☐ EP-MNT	Airbus A300B4-603	546	ex EX-35007	
☐ EP-MNU	Airbus A300B4-605R	608	ex EX-35006	
☐ EP-MHO	Airbus A310-304	488	ex EK-31088	\<Blue Sky
☐ EP-MMJ	Airbus A310-304	526	ex JU-1010	[IKA]♦
☐ EP-MMN	Airbus A310-304	524	ex EX-301	
☐ EP-MMP	Airbus A310-304ER	586	ex F-OJHH	♦
☐ EP-MMX	Airbus A310-304	499	ex EP-VIP	VIP
☐ EP-MNF	Airbus A310-304	547	ex EK31047	
☐ EP-MNO	Airbus A310-304	595	ex EK-31095	
☐ EP-MNP	Airbus A310-308	620	ex EX-35004	
☐ EP-MNV	Airbus A310-304	567	ex EX-35003	
☐ EP-MOH	Airbus A310-304ER	537	ex F-OJHI	[IKA]
☐ EP-	Airbus A340-642	164	ex G-VAIR	[MHD]♦
☐ EP-	Airbus A340-642	371	ex YI-ASL	[MHD]♦
☐ EP-	Airbus A340-642	376	ex YI-ASM	[THR]♦
☐ EP-	Airbus A340-642	383	ex YI-ASN	[THR]♦
☐ EP-	Airbus A340-642	416	ex YI-NAD	[IKA]♦
☐ EP-	Airbus A340-642	449	ex YI-NAE	[IKA]♦
☐ EP-	Airbus A340-642	615	ex G-VSSH	[IKA]♦
☐ EP-MOH	Avro 146-RJ100	E3341	ex UR-CKF	
☐ EP-MOI	Avro 146-RJ100	E3362	ex UR-CKG	
☐ EP-MOP	Avro 146-RJ85	E2257	ex UR-CLU	
☐ EP-MOQ	Avro 146-RJ85	E2261	ex UR-CLV	VIP
☐ UR-CJW	Avro 146-RJ100	E3358	ex SX-DMC	\<UKM
☐ UR-CKJ	Avro 146-RJ100	E3343	ex SX-DMB	\<UKM
☐ EP-MNA	Boeing 747-422	24383/811	ex EK-74783	
☐ EP-MNB	Boeing 747-422	24363/740	ex EK-74763	
☐ EP-MNC	Boeing 747-422	26879/973	ex EK-74779	
☐ EP-MND	Boeing 747-3B3 (SCD)	23413/632	ex EK-74713	
☐ EP-MNE	Boeing 747-3B3 (SCD)	23480/641	ex EK-74780	
☐ EP-MMV	British Aerospace 146 Srs.200	E2079	ex EK27004	VIP
☐ EP-MOB	British Aerospace 146 Srs.300	E3212	ex EX-27001	
☐ EP-MOC	British Aerospace 146 Srs.300	E3158	ex G-UKRC	
☐ EP-MOD	British Aerospace 146 Srs.300	E3162	ex UR-	
☐ EP-MOE	British Aerospace 146 Srs.300	E3129	ex UR-CJM	
☐ EP-MOF	British Aerospace 146 Srs,300	E3149	ex UR-CIL	
☐ EP-MOK	British Aerospace 146 Srs.300	E3146	ex UR-CKY	♦
☐ EP-MOL	British Aerospace 146 Srs.300	E3159	ex UR-CKZ	♦
☐ EP-MOM	British Aerospace 146 Srs.300	E3165	ex UR-CJJ	>IRM
☐ UR-CKX	British Aerospace 146 Srs.300	E3131	ex LZ-HBE	\<UKM
☐ UR-CKY	British Aerospace 146 Srs.300	E3146	ex LZ-HBG	\<UKM
☐ EP-MMA	Airbus A340-311	020	ex EX-34001	
☐ EP-MMB	Airbus A340-311	056	ex EX-34002	
☐ EP-MMC	Airbus A340-313X	282	ex M-ABGQ	♦
☐ EP-	Airbus A321-131	0550	ex 2-WGLP	[IKA]♦

MERAJ AIR — Meraj (JI/MRJ) — Tehran-Mehrabad (THR)

☐ EP-AGA	Boeing 737-286	21317/483		VIP♦
☐ EP-AGB	Airbus A321-231	1202	ex F-WQSS	VIP♦
☐ EP-AJC	Airbus A320-232	0530	ex EP-IEA	
☐ EP-AJH	Airbus A320-233	1353	ex SU-PBG	♦
☐ EP-AJI	Airbus A320-233	1300	ex SU-PBH	♦
☐ EP-SIF	Airbus A300B4-622R	762	ex ZS-TSA	
☐ EP-SIG	Airbus A300B4-622R	750	ex B-2327	

NAFT AIR LINES/IRANIAN AIR TRANSPORT — Naft (IRG) — Ahwaz (AWZ)

☐ EP-EAH	Fokker 50	20234	ex D-AFKO	♦
☐ EP-GAS	Fokker 50	20224	ex PH-JXA	
☐ EP-NFK	Fokker 50	20235	ex EP-EAF	♦
☐ EP-NFT	Fokker 50	20220	ex PH-RRF	
☐ EP-OIL	Fokker 50	20222	ex PH-LNZ	
☐ EP-PET	Fokker 50	20283	ex PH-MXF	
☐ EP-AWZ	Fokker 100	11497	ex PH-AFO	
☐ EP-IOD	de Havilland DHC-6 Twin Otter 300	460		opf NIOC
☐ EP-IOE	de Havilland DHC-6 Twin Otter 300	425		opf NIOC
☐ EP-MIS	Fokker 100	11503	ex F-GPXI	
☐ EP-OPI	Fokker 100	11509	ex F-GLIR	
☐ EP-SUS	Fokker 100	11487	ex F-GPXA	

PAYAM	**Payamair (2F/IRP)**			**Karaj-Payam (QKC)**
☐ EP-TPH	Embraer EMB.110P1A Bandeirante	110453	ex EP-TPM	Tehran
☐ EP-TPI	Embraer EMB.110P1A Bandeirante	110438	ex EP-TPA	Kerrian
☐ EP-TPJ	Embraer EMB.110P1A Bandeirante	110442	ex EP-TPT	Kashan
☐ EP-TPK	Embraer EMB.110P1 Bandeirante	110386	ex EP-TPG	Esfahan
☐ EP-TPL	Embraer EMB.110P1 Bandeirante	110423	ex EP-TPS	Semnan
☐ EP-TPC	Bell 212	30516	ex 6-9202	
☐ EP-TPN	Bell 212	30517	ex 6-9203	

POUYA AIRLINES	**(PYA)**			
☐ EP-PUA	Antonov An-74TK-200			♦
☐ EP-PUB	Antonov An-74TK-200			♦
☐ EP-PUL	Ilyushin Il-76TD	0033448393	ex 15-2284	
☐ EP-PUM	Antonov An-74TK-200			♦
☐ EP-PUO	Ilyushin Il-76	1013409297	ex EP-GOL	
☐ EP-PUS	Ilyushin Il-76TD	1023409321	ex EP-GOM	

QESHM AIR	**Qeshm Air (QB/IRQ)**			**Tehran-Mehrabad (THR)**
☐ EP-FQK	Airbus A300B4-605R	584	ex TC-OAH	
☐ EP-FQL	Airbus A300B4-605R	744	ex TC-OAA	[IKA]
☐ EP-FQM	Airbus A300B4-605R	603	ex TC-OAZ	FS Persepolis c/s
☐ EP-FQN	Airbus A300B4-605R	749	ex TC-OAB	
☐ EP-FQO	Airbus A300B4-605R	764	ex TC-OAO	
☐ EP-FQX	Avro 146-RJ100	E3356	ex ey-570	♦
☐ EY-571	Avro 146-RJ85	E2363	ex EI-RJP	<TXP♦
☐ EY-572	Avro 146-RJ100	E3374	ex SX-DVE	<TXP wfs
☐ EY-573	Avro 146-RJ100	E3320	ex G-BZAT	<TXP wfs
☐ EY-574	Avro 146-RJ100	E3375	ex SX-DVF	<TXP wfs
☐ EP-FQA	Fokker 50	20274	ex EP-LCB	>SBT
☐ EP-FQB	Fokker 50	20263	ex EP-LCF	>SBT
☐ EP-FQC	Fokker 50	20275	ex EP-LCC	>SBT
☐ EP-FQD	Fokker 50	20265	ex EP-LCE	>SBT
☐ EP-FQF	Fokker 100	11462	ex UR-CKU	
☐ EP-FQG	Fokker 100	11444	ex UR-CKT	
☐ EP-FQI	Fokker 100	11475	ex UR-CKV	
☐ EP-FQJ	Fokker 100	11477	ex UR-CKW	
☐ EP-FQP	Airbus A320-214	0617	ex EY-632	♦
☐ EP-FQQ	Airbus A320-214	0611	ex EY-333	[THR]♦
☐ EP-FQR	Airbus A320-214	0607	ex EY-333	♦
☐ EY-631	Airbus A320-214	0607	ex VN-A306	<TXP wfs

SAHAND AIRLINES	**Sahand Air (IRS)**			**Shiraz (SYZ)**
☐ UR-CHO	McDonnell-Douglas MD-82	53231/2107	ex N597BC	<KHO

SEPAHAN AIRLINES	**Sepahan (H8/SON)**			**Isfahan (IFH)**
☐ EP-GPB	Ir.An-140-100	9006	ex HESA 90-06	
☐ EP-GPC	Ir.An-140-100	9007		
☐ EP-GPD	Ir.An-140-100	9008		
☐ EP-GPE	Ir.An-140-100	9009	ex HESA 90-09	
☐ EP-GPF	Ir.An-140-100	9010		
☐ H-228	Dornier 228-212	8210	ex EP-TAA	

SEPEHRAN AIRLINES				**Shiraz (SYZ)**
☐ EP-	Boeing 737-5L9	25066/2038	ex PK-TXG	wfs♦

TABAN AIRLINES	**Taban (HH/TBN)**			**Mashad (MHD)**
☐ EP-TBB	McDonnell-Douglas MD-88	53549/2185	ex UR-CIZ	
☐ EP-TBC	McDonnell-Douglas MD-88	53550/2187	ex UR-CJL	
☐ EP-TBD	McDonnell-Douglas MD-88	53547/2176	ex UR-CIY	
☐ EP-TBE	McDonnell-Douglas MD-88	53548/2180	ex UR-CJK	
☐ EP-TBF	McDonnell-Douglas MD-88	53546/2167	ex UR-CIX	
☐ EP-TBG	Avro 146-RJ85	E2289	ex UR-CKH	♦
☐ EP-TBH	Airbus A310-304	565	ex CS-TEX	♦
☐ YA-CAQ	Airbus A310-304	496	ex TC-JDA	Kabul	<AFG♦
☐ YA-CAV	Airbus A310-304ER	497	ex TC-JDB	Kandahar	<AFG [IKA]♦

TAFTAN AIRLINES	**(SBT)**			
☐ EP-FQA	Fokker 50	20274	ex EP-LCB	<IRQ♦

☐ EP-FQB	Fokker 50	20263	ex EP-LCF	<IRQ♦
☐ EP-FQC	Fokker 50	20275	ex EP-LCC	<IRQ♦
☐ EP-FQD	Fokker 50	20265	ex EP-LCE	<IRQ♦
☐ EP-TFN	Fokker 50	20302	ex PH-JCE	♦
☐ EP-TFT	Fokker 50	20298	ex PH-MXR	♦

ZAGROS AIRLINES   Zagros (ZV/IZG)   Abadan (ABD)

☐ EP-ZAI	Airbus A320-231	0376	ex UR-CKS	
☐ EP-ZAJ	Airbus A320-212	0407	ex UR-CKR	
☐ EP-ZAL	Airbus A320-212	0400	ex UR-CNA	♦
☐ UR-CNJ	Airbus A320-211	0311	ex YR-LCE	<DAT♦
☐ UR-CNK	Airbus A320-212	0426	ex YL-LCH	<DAT♦
☐ UR-CNO	Airbus A320-212	0395	ex ZS-DJD	<DAT♦

☐ EP-ZAA	McDonnell-Douglas MD-82	49634/1419	ex UR-CEW	
☐ EP-ZAB	McDonnell-Douglas MD-83	49930/1720	ex UR-CJB	
☐ EP-ZAC	McDonnell-Douglas MD-83	49949/1906	ex UR-CDR	
☐ EP-ZAD	McDonnell-Douglas MD-82	49279/1230	ex UR-CDI	
☐ EP-ZAE	McDonnell-Douglas MD-82	53066/1938	ex UR-CHJ	
☐ EP-ZAF	McDonnell-Douglas MD-82	53119/1956	ex UR-CDM	
☐ EP-ZAG	McDonnell-Douglas MD-82	49372/1252	ex UR-CDQ	
☐ EP-ZAK	McDonnell-Douglas MD-83	49627/1580	ex SX-BTM	
☐ EP-ZAM	McDonnell-Douglas MD-82	49483/1314	ex UR-CBO	
☐ EP-ZAQ	McDonnell-Douglas MD-83	49769/1559	ex UR-CDP	

ER-   MOLDOVA (Republic of Moldova)

AEROPORTUL INTERNATIONAL MARCULESTI/AIM AIR   (AMM)

☐ ER-MGJ	Mil Mi-8PS	10734	ex Romania 08	
☐ ER-MGY	Mil Mi-8PS	10731	ex YR-MLA	
☐ ER-MHD	Mil Mi-8MTV-1	95864	ex Moldova 02	
☐ ER-MHE	Mil Mi-8MTV-1	95865	ex LZ-...	
☐ ER-MHF	Mil Mi-8MTV-1	95862	ex LZ-...	
☐ ER-MHK	Mil Mi-8MTV-1	95863	ex UR-CIN	
☐ ER-MHQ	Mil Mi-8MTV-1	103M10	ex Bulgaria 510	

☐ ER-AFZ	Antonov An-72	36572070698	ex Moldova 72933	
☐ ER-AVK	Antonov An-26	13808	ex Romania 808	
☐ ER-AVL	Antonov An-26	13809	ex Romania 809	
☐ ER-AWF	Antonov An-72	36572070696	ex ER-72932	
☐ ER-MHC	Mil Mi-17P	150P04	ex Bulgaria 434	
☐ ER-MHS	Mil Mi-17	103M11	ex Bulgaria 410	
☐ ER-MHV	Mil Mi-17	103M13	ex Bulgaria 412	

AEROTRANS CARGO   Moldcargo (ATG)   Kishinev-Chisinau (KIV)

☐ ER-IAF	Ilyushin Il-76T	0003423699	ex 4L-SKL	
☐ ER-IAH	Ilyushin Il-76TD	1023414450	ex EK76540	operator not confirmed
☐ ER-IAP	Ilyushin Il-76TD	0063470088	ex EY-701	
☐ ER-IAV	Ilyushin Il-76TD	0063471150	ex UR-76704	
☐ ER-IAW	Ilyushin Il-76TD	0073479367	ex EY-702	
☐ ER-IBZ	Ilyushin Il-76T	083414432	ex EK76603	

☐ ER-BAM	Boeing 747-409BDSF	24312/954	ex D-ACGB	o/o♦
☐ I-MLDT	Fokker 50	20197	ex PH-KVD	Frtr	<MNL

AIR MOLDOVA   Air Moldova (9U/MLD)   Kishinev-Chisinau (KIV)

☐ ER-AXP	Airbus A320-233	0741	ex N452TA		>AZI
☐ ER-AXV	Airbus A320-211	0622	ex F-WQSG		
☐ ER-ECB	Embraer ERJ-190LR	19000325	ex PT-TXN		
☐ ER-ECC	Embraer ERJ-190LR	19000130	ex F-OSUD		
☐ ER-EMA	Embraer EMB.120RT Brasilia	120223	ex N246CA		wfs
☐ SX-BHS	Airbus A321-111	0642	ex F-GYAO		<HRM♦
☐ SX-BHT	Airbus A321-211	0666	ex EI-ESI		<HRM♦
☐ YR-OTN	McDonnell-Douglas MD-82	49119/1070	ex YR-MDM	Fly Romania c/s	<OTJ♦

CONTINENTAL   (CNW)   Kishinev-Chisinau (KIV)

☐ ER-BBS	Boeing 747-281F	23139/608	ex EK74739	♦

GRIXONA

☐ ER-IAK	Ilyushin Il-76TD	1023412399	ex EK76401	
☐ ER-ICS	Ilyushin Il-18D	187009303	ex UR-CEO	

MEGAVIATION (ARM)

☐ ER-MGV	Mil Mi-8MTV-1	93284	ex 9Q-CXC
☐ ER-MGX	Mil Mi-8MTV-1	93292	ex 9Q-CXG
☐ ER-MHX	Mil Mi-8	98628099	ex 3X-GFL
☐ ER-MYA	Mil Mi-8MTV-1	95637	ex ER-MHW	♦
☐ ER-MYB	Mil Mi-8MTV-1	93309	ex ER-MGW	♦
☐ ER-MYJ	Mil Mi-8MTV-1	96067	ex RF-92538	♦
☐ ER-YCG	Yakovlev Yak-42D	4520424811442 ex UR-CKO	
☐ ER-YCH	Yakovlev Yak-42D	4520423606235 ex UR-CFH	

PECOTOX-AIR Pecotox (PXA)

☐ ER-AZB	Antonov An-24RV	27307507	ex RA-47690	[TMS]
☐ ER-AZP	Antonov An-24RV	17307002	ex RA-47810	
☐ ER-AZX	Antonov An-24RV	47309804	ex RA-46687	
☐ ER-KGA	Kamov Ka32T	2991101	ex HA-HSB	
☐ ER-KGB	Kamov Ka32T	1788613	ex HA-HSD	
☐ ER-KGE	Kamov Ka32A	8708	ex RA-31586	
☐ ER-KGF	Kamov Ka32T	1583602	ex UR-AAC	
☐ ER-MGR	Mil Mi-8T	98308422	ex UR-AAD	
☐ ER-MGZ	Mil Mi-8PS	98417101	ex UR-22895	
☐ ER-MHB	Mil Mi-17P	415M01	ex LZ-MOE	
☐ ER-MHN	Mil Mi-8PS	8562	ex UR AAV	
☐ ER-MHP	Mil Mi-8MTV-1	95872	ex 4K-27038	

SKY PRIM AIR (KPM)

☐ ER-ICS	Ilyushin Il-18D	187009303	ex UR-CEO	♦
☐ ER-IAH	Ilyushin Il-76TD	1023414450	ex EK76540	♦
☐ ER-IAI	Ilyushin Il-76TD	1033418596	ex EK76381	♦
☐ ER-IAK	Ilyushin Il-76TD	1023412399	ex EK76401	♦
☐ ER-IAM	Ilyushin Il-76TD	1013409303	ex UP-I7626	♦
☐ ER-BAM	Boeing 747-409	24312	ex D-ACGB	♦

VALAN INTERNATIONAL CARGO Valan (VLN)

☐ ER-AVA	Antonov An-26B-100	11409	ex UR-26072	opf Skylink Arabia
☐ ER-AVB	Antonov An-26-100	3204	ex RA-26556	opf Skylink Arabia
☐ ER-AZO	Antonov An-26B	10606	ex EX-26001	♦
☐ ER-MGL	Mil Mi-17-IV	498M01		
☐ ER-MGM	Mil Mi-17-IV	96621		
☐ ER-MGQ	Mil Mi-8MTV-1	95603	ex EX-08012	♦
☐ ER-MHR	Mil Mi-8MTV-1	95952	ex RA-27125	
☐ ER-MHT	Mil Mi-17-IV	840M01		
☐ ER-MHY	Mil Mi-8MTV-1	95533	ex EX-08005	
☐ ER-MHZ	Mil Mi-8MTV-1	96078	ex RA-22503	
☐ ZS-PEL	Antonov An-32B	3004	ex ER-AFG	

ES- ESTONIA (Republic of Estonia)

AIREST Airest Cargo (AEG) Tallinn-Ylemiste (TLL)

☐ ES-LSA	SAAB SF.340AF	340A-055	ex LY-NSA	
☐ ES-LSB	SAAB SF.340AF	340A-045	ex LY-NSB	
☐ ES-LSC	SAAB SF.340AF	340A-037	ex LY-NSC	
☐ ES-LSD	SAAB SF.340AF	340A-080	ex SE-ISY	♦
☐ ES-LSE	SAAB SF.340AF	340A-132	ex ES-ASM	♦

AVIES Avies (U3/AIA) Tallinn-Ylemiste (TLL)

☐ ES-PJA	British Aerospace Jetstream 31	749	ex G-NOSS	
☐ ES-PJB	British Aerospace Jetstream 31	622	ex G-LOVB	
☐ ES-PJD	British Aerospace Jetstream 31	773	ex G-EIGG	
☐ ES-PJE	British Aerospace Jetstream 3201EP	841	ex SE-LHI	♦
☐ ES-PJF	British Aerospace Jetstream 3201EP	854	ex SE-LHE	♦
☐ ES-PJG	British Aerospace Jetstream 31	701	ex ES-LJD Tooru	
☐ ES-PJH	British Aerospace Jetstream 3201EP	855	ex SE-LHF	♦
☐ ES-PJR	British Aerospace Jetstream 32EP	949	ex SE-LNU	
☐ SE-FVP	British Aerospace Jetstream 31	719	ex G-BTXG	
☐ ES-PVC	Learjet 60	60-051	ex D-CHER	

ESTONIAN AIR Estonian (OV/ELL) Tallinn-Ylemiste (TLL)

☐ ES-ABJ	Boeing 737-33R	28873/2975	ex ZK-NGA	[TLL]
☐ ES-ACB	Canadair CRJ-900	15261	ex C-GIBH	
☐ ES-ACC	Canadair CRJ-900	15262	ex C-GIBQ	
☐ ES-ACD	Canadair CRJ-900	15276	ex C-GZQK	

☐ ES-AEA	Embraer ERJ-170STD	17000093	ex OH-LEE	<FIN
☐ ES-AEB	Embraer ERJ-170STD	17000106	ex OH-LEF	
☐ ES-AEC	Embraer ERJ-170STD	17000107	ex OH-LEG	<FIN
☐ ES-AED	Embraer ERJ-170STD	17000112	ex OH-LEH	<FIN

JP AIR CARGO   Tallinn-Ylemiste (TLL)

☐ ES-JFA	Swearingen SA227AC Metro III	AC-657	ex SX-BBX	Jussi	[BMA]

SMARTLYNX ESTONIA   Tallinn Cat (MYX)   Tallinn-Ylemiste (TLL)

☐ ES-SAK	Airbus A320-214	0888	ex EI-EZA	>CND♦
☐ ES-SAL	Airbus A320-214	566	ex EI-ERV	>CAI
☐ ES-SAM	Airbus A320-232	1896	ex EI-EZT	>CAI♦

ET-   ETHIOPIA (Federal Democratic Republic of Ethiopia)

ABYSSINIAN FLIGHT SERVICES   Addis Ababa (ADD)

☐ ET-AMI	Cessna 208B Caravan I	208B1260	ex N10966
☐ ET-AMV	Cessna 208B Caravan I	208B2001	ex N208GH
☐ ET-AOF	Cessna 208B Caravan I	208B2172	ex N62173

AQUARIUS AVIATION   Addis Ababa (ADD)

☐ ET-AQI	Rockwell Commander 690C	11693		
☐ ET-AQT	Rockwell Commander 690A	11252	ex N690PT	
☐ ET-	Dornier 228-200	8002	ex D-ILSW	wfs

ETHIOPIAN AIRLINES   Ethiopian (ET/ETH)   Addis Ababa (ADD)

Member of Star Alliance

☐ ET-ALK	Boeing 737-760/W	33764/1408			
☐ ET-ALM	Boeing 737-760/W	33765/1539			
☐ ET-ALN	Boeing 737-760/W	33766/1757	ex N1786B		
☐ ET-ALQ	Boeing 737-76N/W	33420/1459			
☐ ET-ANG	Boeing 737-7K9/W	34401/2216	ex OY-MRP		>SKK
☐ ET-ANH	Boeing 737-7K9/W	34402/2270	ex OY-MRR		>SKK
☐ ET-AOK	Boeing 737-790/W	33012/1306	ex M-ABDH		>SKK
☐ ET-ARB	Boeing 737-7Q8/W	30687/2252	ex N981LF		
☐ ET-ARD	Boeing 737-7Q8/W	30710/2188	ex N991LF		
☐ ET-ANZ	Boeing 737-8HO/W	37933/3437			
☐ ET-AOA	Boeing 737-8HO/W	37936/3459	ex N1786B		
☐ ET-AOB	Boeing 737-8HO/W	37937/3467	ex N1796B		
☐ ET-APF	Boeing 737-860/W	40961/3827			
☐ ET-APK	Boeing 737-860/W	40964/3991	ex N1786B		
☐ ET-APL	Boeing 737-860/W	40965/4075		>Malawian AL	
☐ ET-APM	Boeing 737-860/W	40962/4250			
☐ ET-APO	Boeing 737-860/W	40963/4231	ex N1787B		
☐ ET-AQM	Boeing 737-860/W	40966/4471			
☐ ET-AQN	Boeing 737-860/W	40967/4971			♦
☐ ET-AQO	Boeing 737-860/W	40968/5399			♦
☐ ET-AQP	Boeing 737-860/W	40969/			o/o♦
☐ ET-AQQ	Boeing 737-860/W	40970/			o/o♦
☐ ET-ASJ	Boeing 737-860/W	39442/5141			♦
☐ ET-AJS	Boeing 757-260PF	24845/300	ex N3519L		
☐ ET-AJX	Boeing 757-260PCF	25014/348			
☐ ET-AKC	Boeing 757-260	25353/408			
☐ ET-AKF	Boeing 757-260ER	26058/496			
☐ ET-ALZ	Boeing 757-231	30319/883	ex N720TW		
☐ ET-AMK	Boeing 757-23N	32449/974	ex C-GMYE		
☐ ET-AMT	Boeing 757-23N	27976/814	ex N520AT		
☐ ET-AMU	Boeing 757-23N	27975/779	ex N519AT		
☐ ET-ALH	Boeing 767-3BGER	30565/802	ex HB-IHW		
☐ ET-ALJ	Boeing 767-360ER/W	33767/918	ex N5020K	Avolon	
☐ ET-ALO	Boeing 767-360ER/W	33768/922			
☐ ET-ALP	Boeing 767-360ER	33769/933			
☐ ET-AMF	Boeing 767-3BGER	30563/786	ex B-2561		
☐ ET-AMG	Boeing 767-3BGER	30566/817	ex B-2562		
☐ ET-ANU	Boeing 767-3Q8ER	27993/619	ex N27993		
☐ ET-AQG	Boeing 767-306ER	28884/738	ex S7-FCS		
☐ ET-ANN	Boeing 777-260LR	40770/900		The Blue Nile	
☐ ET-ANO	Boeing 777-260LR	40771/908			
☐ ET-ANP	Boeing 777-260LR	40772/914			
☐ ET-ANQ	Boeing 777-260LR	40773/930		The Mount Kilimanjaro	
☐ ET-ANR	Boeing 777-260LR	40774/948		The Sahara	

☐ ET-AQL	Boeing 777-260LR	43814/1115			
☐ ET-APS	Boeing 777-F6N	41846/1043		The Renaissance Dam	
☐ ET-APU	Boeing 777-F6N	41817/1054			
☐ ET-ARH	Boeing 777-F60	42031/1242			♦
☐ ET-ARI	Boeing 777-F60	42032/1252	ex N5044K		♦
☐ ET-ARJ	Boeing 777-F60	42033/1334			o/o♦
☐ ET-AOO	Boeing 787-8	34743/39		Lake Tana	
☐ ET-AOP	Boeing 787-8	34744/44		Queen of Sheba	
☐ ET-AOQ	Boeing 787-8	34745/49	ex N1020K	Africa First	
☐ ET-AOR	Boeing 787-8	34746/71		Addis Ababa	
☐ ET-AOS	Boeing 787-8	34747/75		Lucy	
☐ ET-AOT	Boeing 787-8	34748/167			
☐ ET-AOU	Boeing 787-8	34749/164			
☐ ET-AOV	Boeing 787-8	34750/168		Taj Mahal	♦
☐ ET-ARE	Boeing 787-8	34751/196		Great Wall of China	♦
☐ ET-ARF	Boeing 787-8	34752/216			♦
☐ ET-ASG	Boeing 787-8	36111/258	ex N1005S	Mount Nyala	♦
☐ ET-ASH	Boeing 787-8	38754/283			♦
☐ ET-ASI	Boeing 787-8	38758/298			o/o♦
☐ ET-ANI	de Havilland DHC-8-402Q	4299	ex C-GBKC		
☐ ET-ANJ	de Havilland DHC-8-402Q	4303	ex C-GCLU		
☐ ET-ANK	de Havilland DHC-0-402Q	4304	ex C-GCPF		
☐ ET-ANL	de Havilland DHC-8-402Q	4307	ex C-GCPY		
☐ ET-ANV	de Havilland DHC-8-402Q	4317	ex C-GEHI		
☐ ET-ANW	de Havilland DHC-8-402Q	4320	ex C-GEUN		>SKK
☐ ET-ANX	de Havilland DHC-8-402Q	4330	ex C-GSNH		>SKK
☐ ET-ANY	de Havilland DHC-8-402Q	4334	ex C-GGFU		
☐ ET-AQB	de Havilland DHC-8-402Q	4419	ex C-GNKT		>Malawian AL
☐ ET-AQC	de Havilland DHC-8-402Q	4421	ex C-GPIZ		
☐ ET-AQD	de Havilland DHC-8-402Q	4427	ex C-GRTN		>SKK
☐ ET-AQE	de Havilland DHC-8-402Q	4428	ex C-GRUC		>SKK
☐ ET-AQF	de Havilland DHC-8-402Q	4429	ex C-GSMU		>SKK
☐ ET-ARL	de Havilland DHC-8-402Q	4469	ex C-GYOL		♦
☐ ET-ARM	de Havilland DHC-8-402Q	4472	ex C-GZED		♦
☐ ET-ARN	de Havilland DHC-8-402Q	4475	ex C-GZGX		♦
☐ ET-ASA	de Havilland DHC-8-402Q	4476	ex C-GZSD		♦
☐ ET-AIT	de Havilland DHC-6 Twin Otter 310	820	ex C-GDNG		
☐ ET-AIU	de Havilland DHC-6 Twin Otter 300	822	ex C-GDCZ		
☐ ET-AIX	de Havilland DHC-6 Twin Otter 300	835	ex C-GDFT		
☐ ET-AKG	Lockheed L-382G Hercules	5306			
☐ ET-AKU	Fokker 50	20333	ex PH-EXD		>KUH♦
☐ ET-AML	McDonnell-Douglas MD-11ERF	48758/615	ex N742BC		
☐ ET-AND	McDonnell-Douglas MD-11BCF	48780/624	ex N588BC		
☐ ET-APX	Boeing 777-36NER	42101/1150			
☐ ET-APY	Boeing 777-36NER	42102/1169			
☐ ET-ASK	Boeing 777-360ER	44550/1297			♦
☐ ET-ASL	Boeing 777-360ER	44551/1312			o/o♦
☐ ET-	Airbus A350-941	040	ex F-WW		o/o
☐ ET-	Airbus A350-941	043	ex F-WW		o/o

TEDDY AIR

☐ ET-ANF	Cessna 208B Caravan I	208B0367	ex 5Y-BMZ	

TRANS NATION AIRWAYS — Trans Nation (TNW) — Addis Ababa/Jeddah (ADD/JED)

☐ ET-AKZ	de Havilland DHC-8-202	469	ex C-GLOT	>BBZ
☐ ET-ALX	de Havilland DHC-8-202	475	ex ZK-ECR	
☐ ET-AMR	Bell 222UT	47554	ex N111DS	

EW- BELARUS (Republic of Belarus)

BELAVIA — Belavia (B2/BRU) — Minsk 1 (MHP)

☐ EW-254PA	Boeing 737-3Q8	26294/2550	ex N201LF	
☐ EW-282PA	Boeing 737-3Q8	26321/2764	ex B-5024	
☐ EW-283PA	Boeing 737-3Q8	26333/2786	ex B-2604	
☐ EW-308PA	Boeing 737-3K2	24328/1856	ex LN-KKH	
☐ EW-336PA	Boeing 737-3Q8	26312/2693	ex VQ-BHD	
☐ EW-366PA	Boeing 737-31S	29058/2946	ex YR-ADB	
☐ EW-386PA	Boeing 737-3K2	24327/1712	ex LY-FLJ	
☐ EW-404PA	Boeing 737-3L9	27061/2347	ex LY-FLE	♦
☐ EW-407PA	Boeing 737-36M	28332/2809	ex YR-BBA	♦
☐ EW-250PA	Boeing 737-524	26319/2748	ex N427LF	
☐ EW-251PA	Boeing 737-5Q8	27634/2889	ex PT-SSC	
☐ EW-252PA	Boeing 737-524	26340/2777	ex LY-AGZ	

179

☐ EW-253PA	Boeing 737-524	26339/2771	ex LY-AGQ	
☐ EW-290PA	Boeing 737-5Q8	27629/2834	ex N381LF	
☐ EW-294PA	Boeing 737-505	26338/2822	ex B-2975	

☐ EW-001PA	Boeing 737-8EV/W	33079/1075	ex N375BC	opf Govt, BBJ2
☐ EW-001PB	Boeing 767-32KER	33968/926	ex EZ-A700	opf Govt
☐ EW-100PJ	Canadair CRJ-200LR	7309	ex N400MJ	
☐ EW-276PJ	Canadair CRJ-200ER	7799	ex N698BR	
☐ EW-277PJ	Canadair CRJ-200ER	7852	ex N710BR	
☐ EW-301PJ	Canadair Challenger 850	8057	ex C-GWWW	
☐ EW-303PJ	Canadair CRJ-200ER	7436	ex OY-MBI	
☐ EW-340PO	Embraer ERJ-175LR	17000350	ex PT-TFE	
☐ EW-341PO	Embraer ERJ-175LR	17000352	ex PT-TGL	
☐ EW-399PO	Embraer ERJ-195LR	19000667	ex PR-EFO	♦
☐ EW-400PO	Embraer ERJ-195LR	19000668	ex PR-EFQ	♦
☐ EW-437PA	Boeing 737-8K5/W	27988/508	ex D-AHFP	♦
☐ EW-438PA	Boeing 737-86Q/W	30286/1280	ex D-ABBJ	♦
☐ EW-85703	Tupolev Tu-154M	91A878	ex CCCP-85703	
☐ EW-85741	Tupolev Tu-154M	91A896	ex ES-LTC	
☐ EW-85748	Tupolev Tu-154M	92A924		
☐ EW-85815	Tupolev Tu-154M	95A1010		opf Govt

GENEX — Aerogenex (GNX)

☐ EW-246TG	Antonov An-26B	14403	ex UR-26214 status uncertain	
☐ EW-259TG	Antonov An-26B	12706	ex UR-26094	
☐ EW-278TG	Antonov An-26B	13306	ex HA-TCZ	opf Vulkan Air
☐ EW-328TG	Antonov An-26B	12806	ex RA-26135	

GRODNO AIR

☐ EW-281CN	Antonov An-30	1402	ex RA-30001	
☐ EW-364TG	Antonov An-26B	4206	ex 3X-GEN Yurly Matviychuk	opf Vulkan Air
☐ EW-378TG	Antonov An-26B	14004	ex YL-RAE	opf Vulkan Air♦
☐ EW-427TI	Antonov An-12A	2340806	ex UP-AN213	♦

RUBY STAR — Rubystar (RSB) — Minsk-Machulishchy

☐ EW-355TH	Ilyushin Il-76TD	093495883	ex EW-78819	
☐ EW-356TH	Ilyushin Il-76TD	1013405159	ex EW-78848	
☐ EW-383TH	Ilyushin Il-76TD	1013405177	ex EY-608	
☐ EW-412TH	Ilyushin Il-76TD	0023437090	ex EK-76464	♦
☐ EW-430TH	Ilyushin Il-76TD	0043451528	ex RA-76476	♦

| ☐ EW-275TI | Antonov An-12BK | 00347210 | ex RA--13392 | |
| ☐ EW-338TI | Antonov An-12BP | 1340106 | ex UR-DWI | |

TRANSAVIA EXPORT — Transexport (TXC) — Minsk-Machulishchy

☐ EW-76734	Ilyushin Il-76TD	0073476312	ex CCCP-76734	>DVA
☐ EW-76735	Ilyushin Il-76TD	0073476314	ex CCCP-76735	[MSQ]
☐ EW-78769	Ilyushin Il-76MD	0083487607	ex CCCP-78769	[MSQ]
☐ EW-78779	Ilyushin Il-76TD	0083489662	ex CCCP-78779	[MSQ]
☐ EW-78787	Ilyushin Il-76MD	0083490698	ex CCCP-78787	[MSQ]
☐ EW-78799	Ilyushin Il-76TD	0093491754	ex CCCP-78799 Igor Vashkevich	[MSQ]
☐ EW-78801	Ilyushin Il-76TD	0093492763	ex CCCP-78801	[MSQ]
☐ EW-78808	Ilyushin Il-76TD	0093493794	ex CCCP-78808	[MSQ]
☐ EW-78819	Ilyushin Il-76TD	0093495883	ex CCCP-78819	
☐ EW-78827	Ilyushin Il-76TD	1003499997	ex CCCP-78827	[MSQ]
☐ EW-78839	Ilyushin Il-76TD	1003402047	ex CCCP-78839	[MSQ]
☐ EW-78843	Ilyushin Il-76TD	1003403082	ex CCCP-78543	

EX-   KYRGYZSTAN (Republic of Kyrgyzstan)

AIR BISHKEK — Eastok (KR/EAA) — Bishkek-Manas (FRU)

☐ EX-32002	Airbus A320-231	0386	ex EY-621	
☐ EX-37001	Boeing 737-301	23937/1587	ex E7-BBA	
☐ EX-37002	Boeing 737-3Z0	27521/2738	ex B-2957	>JUB
☐ UR-CME	Airbus A320-212	0671	ex N503NU	>ANR♦

AIR KYRGYZSTAN — Altyn Avia (QH/LYN) — Bishkek-Manas (FRU)

☐ EX-00001	Tupolev Tu-154M	92A945	ex EX-85762	
☐ EX-37301	Boeing 737-382	25162/2241	ex LY-SKW	
☐ EX-37401	Boeing 737-484	25361/2130	ex N761AS	
☐ EX-37501	Boeing 737-59D/W	26419/2186	ex G-GFFD	

AIR MANAS		Air Manas (ZM/MBB)			Bishkek-Manas (FRU)	
☐ EX-37402	Boeing 737-42R	29107/2997	ex TC-APD	Aichurok Pegasus Asia titles	<PGT
☐ EX-37801	Boeing 737-82R/W	35701/2496	ex TC-AAH	Hanim Pegasus Asia titles	<PGT♦

AVIA TRAFFIC COMPANY		Atomic (YK/AVJ)		Bishkek-Manas (FRU)
☐ EX-27007	British Aerospace 146 Srs.200	E2180	ex OO-DJG	
☐ EX-37005	Boeing 737-3Y0	24681/1929	ex N554MS	
☐ EX-37008	Boeing 737-330	23834/1454	ex LZ-BOW	
☐ EX-37010	Boeing 737-3L9	25125/2059	ex 4L-AJS	
☐ EX-37012	Boeing 737-33A	27463/2831	ex N218AW	

CENTRAL ASIAN			
☐ EX-08006	Mil Mi-8AMT	5948607093	ex RA-27118
☐ EX-08010	Mil Mi-8MTV-1	95986	ex ?
☐ EX-08014	Mil Mi-8MTV-1	95726	ex 4K-2511
☐ EX-08022	Mil Mi-8T	98308688	ex EX-40017
☐ EX-40016	Mil Mi-8T	7884	ex RA-22591

CLICK AIRWAYS			
☐ EX-76001	Ilyushin Il-76TD	1013408257	ex 4L-FFG
☐ EX-76002	Ilyushin Il-76TD	0093496903	ex EX-54001

HELI SKY			
☐ EX-08009	Mil Mi-171V	93878	ex ?
☐ EX-08015	Mil Mi-171V	103M04	ex EK17104
☐ EX-08016	Mil Mi-171V	103M07	ex EK17107
☐ EX-08023	Mil Mi-8MTV-1	95644	ex J2-
☐ EX-40007	Mil Mi-8MTV-1	95632	ex ST-BDU

MAXAVIA		(MAI)		Bishkek-Manas (FRU)
☐ UR-WRB	McDonnell-Douglas MD-82	49364/1276	ex N937AS	>BAY

S GROUP INTERNATIONAL		(IND)		Bishkek-Manas (FRU)
☐ EX-18007	Ilyushin Il-18E	185008601	ex EX-601	♦
☐ EX-18008	Ilyushin Il-18GrM	187010403	ex EX-75466	♦
☐ EX-32004	Airbus A320-231	0357	ex N567BB	

SKY BISHKEK		Juma Air (GY/BIS)	
☐ EX-34001	SAAB SF.340A	340A-146	ex N146PJ

SKY KG AIRLINES			
☐ EX-18006	Ilyushin Il-18D	187009904	ex EX-18005	reported op by Central AL

SKY WAY AIR			
☐ EX-126	Antonov An-26B	11508	ex UN-26075

SUPREME AVIATION			
☐ EX-40011	Mil Mi-8MTV-1	95483	ex ST-BDI

TEZJET		(TEZ)		Bishkek-Manas (FRU)
☐ EX-27002	British Aerospace 146 Srs.200	E2172	ex OO-DJH	♦

EY-   TAJIKISTAN (Republic of Tajikistan)

ASIA AIRWAYS			
☐ EY-401	Antonov An-12BP	8345607	ex EX-029	
☐ EY-402	Antonov An-12B	8346006	ex EX-031	wfs
☐ EY-403	Antonov An-12BK	00347107	ex EX-042	
☐ EY-406	Antonov An-12B	01347704	ex EK12704	♦
☐ EY-407	Antonov An-12			♦
☐ EY-408	Antonov An-12B	4020408	ex EK12408	♦
☐ EY-412	Antonov An-12			♦
☐ EY-512	Antonov An-72	36572060645	ex "02" red	♦
☐ EY-703	Ilyushin Il-76TD	0083488643	ex EY-690	

ASIAN EXPRESS AIRLINES		(KV/TXP)		Dushanbe (DYU)
☐ EY-571	Avro 146-RJ85	E2363	ex EI-RJP	>QSM
☐ EY-572	Avro 146-RJ100	E3374	ex SX-DVE	>QSM
☐ EY-573	Avro 146-RJ100	E3320	ex G-BZAT	>QSM
☐ EY-574	Avro 146-RJ100	E3375	ex SX-DVF	>QSM

KHATLON AIR		Khatlon (KHT)		
☐ EY-219	Mil Mi-8T	9754637	ex ST-MRF	♦
☐ EY-221	Mil Mi-8T	9754525	ex ST-DRW	♦
☐ EY-617	Ilyushin Il-76TD	0063467021	ex EK-76921	

SOMON AIR		Somon Air (4J/SMR)		Dushanbe (DYU)
☐ EY-545	Boeing 737-3K2	24326/1683	ex N412BC	
☐ EY-555	Boeing 737-3Y5	25613/2446	ex LN-KKV	
☐ EY-777	Boeing 737-8GJ/W	34960/2765	ex N960BB	Sadriddin Ayni
☐ EY-787	Boeing 737-8GJ/W	34955/2512	ex N349FD	Ismoil Somoni
☐ P4-SOM	Boeing 737-93YER	40889/3837	ex N1786B	Bobojon Ghafurov
☐ P4-TAJ	Boeing 737-93YER/W	40888/3771		Shirinsho Shotemur

TAJIK AIR		Tajikair (7J/TJK)		Dushanbe/Khudzhand (DYU/LBD)
☐ EY-87214	Yakovlev Yak-40K	9640851	ex HA-LJB	wfs
☐ EY-87434	Yakovlev Yak-40	9431035	ex EP-TUF	wfs
☐ EY-87963	Yakovlev Yak-40K	9831058	ex EP-EAK	wfs
☐ EY-87967	Yakovlev Yak-40K	9831158	ex EP-CPI	wfs
☐ EY-88267	Yakovlev Yak-40K	9720553	ex CCCP-88267	wfs
☐ EY-201	AVIC MA-60	0701		>EHN
☐ EY-444	Boeing 737-3L9	26441/2250	ex XA-UNG	
☐ EY-751	Boeing 757-2Q8	24964/424	ex N926JS	
☐ EY-752	Boeing 757-2Q8	27599/696	ex EI-EYZ	
☐ EY-753	Boeing 737-448	25736/2269	ex N151LF	
☐ EY-754	Boeing 737-4Q8	28202/3009	ex OO-VET	
☐ EY-25149	Mil Mi-8MTV-1	95190	ex CCCP-25149	
☐ EY-25167	Mil Mi-8MTV-1	95378	ex CCCP-25167	
☐ EY-25438	Mil Mi-8MTV-1	95579	ex CCCP-25438	
☐ EY-26205	Antonov An-26B	14107	ex CCCP-26205	
☐ EY-26658	Antonov An-26	7904	ex 26658	
☐ EY-28736	WSK-PZL/Antonov An-28	1AJ007-24	ex CCCP-28736	
☐ EY-28921	WSK-PZL/Antonov An-28	1AJ008-07	ex CCCP-28921	
☐ EY-46365	Antonov An-24B	07305906	ex CCCP-46365	wfs
☐ EY-46595	Antonov An-24B	97305105	ex UR-45595	
☐ EY-47693	Antonov An-24RV	27307510	ex CCCP-47693	>DAO
☐ EY-47802	Antonov An-24RV	17306901	ex UN-47802	
☐ EY-85692	Tupolev Tu-154M	90A865	ex EP-TUE	
☐ EY-85717	Tupolev Tu-154M	91A897	ex EP-EAA	
☐ LY-AWF	Boeing 737-522	26707/2512	ex C-FDCZ	<LLC
☐ LY-AWG	Boeing 737-522	26700/2490	ex C-FDCH	<LLC

EZ- TURKMENISTAN (Republic of Turkmenistan)

TURKMENISTAN AIRLINES		Turkmenistan (T5/TUA)		Askhabad (ASB)
☐ EZ-A101	Boeing 717-22K	55153/5072	ex N6202S	
☐ EZ-A102	Boeing 717-22K	55154/5078		
☐ EZ-A104	Boeing 717-22K	55195/5130		
☐ EZ-A105	Boeing 717-22K	55196/5133		
☐ EZ-A106	Boeing 717-22K	55186/5146		
☐ EZ-A107	Boeing 717-22K	55187/5147		
☐ EZ-A004	Boeing 737-82K/W	36088/2181	ex N1795B	
☐ EZ-A005	Boeing 737-82K/W	36089/2233		
☐ EZ-A015	Boeing 737-82K/W	39774/4440		
☐ EZ-A016	Boeing 737-82K/W	39775/4480	ex N5573B	
☐ EZ-A017	Boeing 737-82K/W	43863/4731		
☐ EZ-F422	Ilyushin Il-76TD	1023410348		[ASB]
☐ EZ-F423	Ilyushin Il-76TD	1033418608		[ASB]
☐ EZ-F424	Ilyushin Il-76TD	1033418592		[ASB]
☐ EZ-F425	Ilyushin Il-76TD	1023410336		[ASB]
☐ EZ-F426	Ilyushin Il-76TD	1033418609		
☐ EZ-F427	Ilyushin Il-76TD	1033418620		
☐ EZ-F428	Ilyushin Il-76TD	1043418624		
☐ EZ-S701	Sikorsky S-76C+	760463		opf Govt
☐ EZ-S702	Sikorsky S-76C+	760461		
☐ EZ-S703	Sikorsky S-76A+	760294	ex VH-XHL	

□ EZ-S70.	Sikorsky S-76A++	760032	ex G-BHBF	
□ EZ-	Sikorsky S-76C++	760708	ex G-CFJC	
□ EZ-A001	Boeing 737-341	26855/2305	ex EK-A001	
□ EZ-A002	Boeing 737-332	25994/2439	ex N301DE	
□ EZ-A003	Boeing 737-332	25995/2455	ex N302DE	
□ EZ-A006	Boeing 737-7GL/W	37236/2986	ex N1786B	
□ EZ-A007	Boeing 737-7GL/W	37234/2682		VIP
□ EZ-A008	Boeing 737-7GL/W	37237/2988	ex N1779B	
□ EZ-A009	Boeing 737-7GL/W	37235/2993	ex N3134C	
□ EZ-A010	Boeing 757-23A	25345/412	ex N58AW	
□ EZ-A011	Boeing 757-22K	28336/725		
□ EZ-A012	Boeing 757-22K	28337/726		
□ EZ-A014	Boeing 757-22K	30863/952		
□ EZ-A777	Boeing 777-22KLR	39548/889		opf Govt
□ EZ-A778	Boeing 777-22KLR	42296/1181		
□ EZ-A779	Boeing 777-22KLR	42297/1194		
□ EZ-B024	Canadair Challenger 870	10332	ex C-GZQQ	VIP
□ EZ-P710	Aérospatiale AS332L2	2577	ex F-WQDJ	opf Govt
□ EZ-P711	Aérospatiale AS332L2	2578	ex F-WWOU	opf Govt
□ EZ-S720	Sikorsky S-92	920017	ex N7118Z	opf Govt
□ EZ-S721	Sikorsky S-92	920026	ex N8103U	opf Govt

E3- ERITREA (State of Eritrea)

ERITREAN AIRLINES		**Eritrean (B8/ERT)**		**Asmara (ASM)**
□ E3-AAQ	Boeing 767-238ER	23309/129	ex N771WD	
□ UR-CME	Airbus A320-212	0671	ex N503NU	<ANR♦

MASSAWA AIRWAYS				**Massawa**
□ E3-AAV	AVIC MA-60			
□ E3-	Beech 1900D	UE-12	ex N45AR	
□ E3-	Beech 1900D	UE-27	ex N46AR	

RED SEA AIR			
□ E3-AAI	Harbin Y-12 II	0059	

E5- COOK ISLANDS

AIR RAROTONGA		**(GZ)**		**Rarotonga (RAR)**
□ E5-EFS	SAAB SF.340A	340A-049	ex ZK-EFS	
□ E5-TAI	Embraer EMB 110P1A Bandeirante	110447	ex VH-MWF	[RAR]
□ E5-FTS	Embraer EMB.110P1 Bandeirante	110239	ex ZK-FTS	
□ E5-TAK	Embraer EMB.110P1A Bandeirante	110448	ex ZK-TAK	
□ E5-TAL	Embraer EMB.110P2 Bandeirante	110245	ex VH-UQA	

E7- BOSNIA-HERZEGOVINA (Republic of Bosnia-Herzegovina)

BH AIR		**Air Bosna (JA/BON)**		**Banja Luka**
□ E7-AAD	ATR 72-212	464	ex T9-AAD	Sarajevo
□ E7-AAE	ATR 72-212	465	ex T9-AAE	Mostar
□ E7-ABA	CASA C.212-200	A48-1-302	ex T9-ABA	

ICAR AIR		**Tuzla Air (RAC)**	
□ E7-AAK	LET L-410UVP-E13	892321	ex T9-AAK

F- FRANCE (French Republic)

AERO SOTRAVIA			**Nangis les Loges**
□ F-GCPO	Piper PA-34-200T Seneca II	34-8070358	ex N8266V
□ F-GDHD	Britten-Norman BN-2A-9 Islander	591	ex F-WDHD
□ F-GMLJ	Cessna 414	414-0635	ex I-CCEE

AIGLE AZUR		**Aigle Azur (ZI/AAF)**	**Paris-Orly/Charles de Gaulle (ORY/CDG)**
□ F-HBAO	Airbus A320-214	4589	ex F-WWIQ
□ F-HBAP	Airbus A320-214	4675	ex F-WWDE
□ F-HBIB	Airbus A320-214	3289	ex D-ABDS
□ F-HBIO	Airbus A320-214	3242	ex D-ABDR
□ F-HBIS	Airbus A320-214	3136	ex EI-DVF

☐ F-HBIX	Airbus A320-214/S	6012	ex F-WWBU	
☐ F-HBAL	Airbus A319-111	2870	ex EC-JXA	
☐ F-HBMI	Airbus A319-114	0639	ex N573SX	
☐ F-HCZI	Airbus A319-112	4268	ex D-AVWP	

AIR CORSICA   Corsica (XK/CCM)   Ajaccio (AJA)

☐ F-GHQE	Airbus A320-211	0115		
☐ F-HBEV	Airbus A320-216	3952	ex F-WWBI	E Calanche de Piana
☐ F-HBSA	Airbus A320-216	3882	ex F-WWIP	A Scala di Santa Regina
☐ F-HZFM	Airbus A320-216	5887	ex D-AVVY	I Sanguinan
☐ F-HZPG	Airbus A320-216	5906	ex D-AVVR	U Capi Corsu
☐ F-GRPJ	ATR 72-212A	724	ex F-WWEI	L'Agriati
☐ F-GRPX	ATR 72-212A	734	ex F-WWEO	U Lioni di Roccapina
☐ F-GRPY	ATR 72-212A	742	ex F-WWEC	U Monte Cintu
☐ F-GRPZ	ATR 72-212A	745	ex F-WWEF	A Paglia Orba

AIR FRANCE   Airfrans (AF/AFR)   Paris Charles de Gaulle/Orly (CDG/ORY)

Member of SkyTeam

☐ F-GUGA	Airbus A318-111	2035	ex D-AUAD	
☐ F-GUGB	Airbus A318-111	2059	ex D-AUAF	
☐ F-GUGC	Airbus A318-111	2071	ex D-AUAG	
☐ F-GUGD	Airbus A318-111	2081	ex D-AUAH	
☐ F-GUGE	Airbus A318-111	2100	ex D-AUAI	
☐ F-GUGF	Airbus A318-111	2109	ex D-AUAJ	
☐ F-GUGG	Airbus A318-111	2317	ex D-AUAA	
☐ F-GUGH	Airbus A318-111	2344	ex D-AUAF	
☐ F-GUGI	Airbus A318-111	2350	ex D-AUAG	
☐ F-GUGJ	Airbus A318-111	2582	ex D-AUAE	
☐ F-GUGK	Airbus A318-111	2601	ex D-AUAF	
☐ F-GUGL	Airbus A318-111	2686	ex D-AUAA	
☐ F-GUGM	Airbus A318-111	2750	ex D-AUAB	
☐ F-GUGN	Airbus A318-111	2918	ex D-AUAB	
☐ F-GUGO	Airbus A318-111	2951	ex D-AUAD	
☐ F-GUGP	Airbus A318-111	2967	ex D-AUAF	
☐ F-GUGQ	Airbus A318-111	2972	ex D-AUAG	
☐ F-GUGR	Airbus A318-111	3009	ex D-AUAJ	
☐ F-GPMA	Airbus A319-113	0598	ex D-AVYD	
☐ F-GPMB	Airbus A319-113	0600	ex D-AVYC	
☐ F-GPMC	Airbus A319-113	0608	ex D-AVYE	
☐ F-GPMD	Airbus A319-113	0618	ex D-AVYJ	
☐ F-GPME	Airbus A319-113	0625	ex D-AVYQ	
☐ F-GPMF	Airbus A319-113	0637	ex D-AVYT	
☐ F-GRHB	Airbus A319-111	0985	ex D-AVYO	
☐ F-GRHE	Airbus A319-111	1020	ex D-AVYX	
☐ F-GRHF	Airbus A319-111	1025	ex D-AVYE	[TLS]
☐ F-GRHG	Airbus A319-111	1036	ex D-AVYS	
☐ F-GRHH	Airbus A319-111	1151	ex D-AVWK	
☐ F-GRHI	Airbus A319-111	1169	ex D-AVYX	
☐ F-GRHJ	Airbus A319-111	1176	ex D-AVWN	
☐ F-GRHK	Airbus A319-111	1190	ex D-AVYQ	
☐ F-GRHL	Airbus A319-111	1201	ex D-AVWT	
☐ F-GRHM	Airbus A319-111	1216	ex D-AVYF	
☐ F-GRHN	Airbus A319-111	1267	ex D-AVWB	
☐ F-GRHO	Airbus A319-111	1271	ex D-AVWC	
☐ F-GRHP	Airbus A319-111	1344	ex D-AVYQ	
☐ F-GRHQ	Airbus A319-111	1404	ex D-AVYB	
☐ F-GRHR	Airbus A319-111	1415	ex D-AVYF	
☐ F-GRHS	Airbus A319-111	1444	ex D-AVWA	
☐ F-GRHT	Airbus A319-111	1449	ex D-AVWD	
☐ F-GRHU	Airbus A319-111	1471	ex D-AVYR	
☐ F-GRHV	Airbus A319-111	1505	ex D-AVYF	
☐ F-GRHX	Airbus A319-111	1524	ex D-AVWC	
☐ F-GRHY	Airbus A319-111	1616	ex D-AVWG	
☐ F-GRHZ	Airbus A319-111	1622	ex D-AVYO	
☐ F-GRXA	Airbus A319-111	1640	ex D-AVYJ	
☐ F-GRXB	Airbus A319-111	1645	ex D-AVYC	
☐ F-GRXC	Airbus A319-111	1677	ex D-AVWF	
☐ F-GRXD	Airbus A319-111	1699	ex D-AVYG	
☐ F-GRXE	Airbus A319-111	1733	ex D-AVWT	
☐ F-GRXF	Airbus A319-111	1938	ex D-AVWG	
☐ F-GRXJ	Airbus A319-115LR	2456	ex D-AVYX	Dedicate
☐ F-GRXK	Airbus A319-115LR	2716	ex D-AVYX	Dedicate
☐ F-GRXL	Airbus A319-111	2938	ex D-AVWV	
☐ F-GRXM	Airbus A319-111	2961	ex D-AVYI	
☐ F-GFKY	Airbus A320-211	0285		Ville de Toulouse

☐ F-GHQJ	Airbus A320-211	0214		
☐ F-GHQL	Airbus A320-211	0239		
☐ F-GHQM	Airbus A320-211	0237		
☐ F-GKXA	Airbus A320-211	0287		Ville de Nantes
☐ F-GKXC	Airbus A320-214	1502	ex F-WWIG	
☐ F-GKXE	Airbus A320-214	1879	ex F-WWDX	
☐ F-GKXG	Airbus A320-214	1894	ex F-WWDV	
☐ F-GKXH	Airbus A320-214	1924		
☐ F-GKXI	Airbus A320-214	1949		
☐ F-GKXJ	Airbus A320-214	1900		
☐ F-GKXK	Airbus A320-214	2140	ex F-WWBR	
☐ F-GKXL	Airbus A320-214	2705		
☐ F-GKXM	Airbus A320-214	2721	ex F-WWXM	
☐ F-GKXN	Airbus A320-214	3008	ex F-WWBH	
☐ F-GKXO	Airbus A320-214	3420	ex F-WWIP	
☐ F-GKXP	Airbus A320-214	3470	ex F-WWBP	
☐ F-GKXQ	Airbus A320-214	3777	ex D-AVVH	
☐ F-GKXR	Airbus A320-214	3795	ex F-WWBM	
☐ F-GKXS	Airbus A320-214	3825	ex F-WWIV	SkyTeam c/s
☐ F-GKXT	Airbus A320-214	3859	ex F-WWDM	
☐ F-GKXU	Airbus A320-214	4063	ex F-WWBF	
☐ F-GKXV	Airbus A320-214	4084	ex D-AVVA	
☐ F-GKXY	Airbus A320-214	4105	ex D-AVVR	
☐ F-GKXZ	Airbus A320-214	4137	ex F-WWIZ	
☐ F-HBNA	Airbus A320-214	4335	ex F-WWIU	
☐ F-HBNB	Airbus A320-214	4402	ex F-WWBS	
☐ F-HBNC	Airbus A320-214	4601	ex F-WWID	
☐ F-HBND	Airbus A320-214	4604	ex F-WWIE	
☐ F-HBNE	Airbus A320-214	4664	ex F-WWIC	
☐ F-HBNF	Airbus A320-214	4714	ex F-WWBS	
☐ F-HBNG	Airbus A320-214	4747	ex F-WWIT	
☐ F-HBNH	Airbus A320-214	4800	ex F-WWIK	
☐ F-HBNI	Airbus A320-214	4820	ex F-WWIC	
☐ F-HBNJ	Airbus A320-214	4908	ex F-WWDK	
☐ F-HBNK	Airbus A320-214	5084	ex F-WWII	
☐ F-HBNL	Airbus A320-214	5129	ex F-WWBB	
☐ F-HEPA	Airbus A320-214	4139	ex F-WWIX	
☐ F-HEPB	Airbus A320-214	4241	ex F-WWDK	
☐ F-HEPC	Airbus A320-214	4267	ex F-WWBM	
☐ F-HEPD	Airbus A320-214	4295	ex F-WWIZ	
☐ F-HEPE	Airbus A320-214	4298	ex F-WWIC	
☐ F-HEPF	Airbus A320-214/S	5719	ex F-WWDX	
☐ F-HEPG	Airbus A320-214/S	5802	ex F-WWIX	
☐ F-HEPH	Airbus A320-214/S	5869	ex F-WWDK	
☐ F-GMZA	Airbus A321-111	0498	ex D-AVZK	
☐ F-GMZB	Airbus A321-111	0509	ex D-AVZN	
☐ F-GMZC	Airbus A321-111	0521	ex D-AVZW	
☐ F-GMZD	Airbus A321-111	0529	ex D-AVZA	
☐ F-GMZE	Airbus A321-111	0544	ex D-AVZF	
☐ F-GTAD	Airbus A321-212	0777	ex D-AVZI	
☐ F-GTAE	Airbus A321-212	0796	ex D-AVZN	SkyTeam c/s
☐ F-GTAH	Airbus A321-212	1133	ex D-AVZD	
☐ F-GTAJ	Airbus A321-212	1476	ex D-AVZF	
☐ F-GTAK	Airbus A321-212	1658	ex D-AVZP	
☐ F-GTAL	Airbus A321-212	1691	ex D-AVZY	
☐ F-GTAM	Airbus A321-212	1859	ex D-AVZY	
☐ F-GTAO	Airbus A321-212	3098	ex D-AVZQ	
☐ F-GTAP	Airbus A321-212	3372	ex D-AVZK	
☐ F-GTAQ	Airbus A321-212	3399	ex D-AVZQ	
☐ F-GTAR	Airbus A321-212	3401	ex D-AVZR	
☐ F-GTAS	Airbus A321-212	3419	ex D-AVZE	
☐ F-GTAT	Airbus A321-212	3441	ex D-AVZH	
☐ F-GTAU	Airbus A321-212	3814	ex D-AVZE	
☐ F-GTAX	Airbus A321-212	3930	ex D-AZAD	
☐ F-GTAY	Airbus A321-212	4251	ex D-AZAG	
☐ F-GTAZ	Airbus A321-212	4901	ex D-AVZG	
☐ F-GZCA	Airbus A330-203	422		
☐ F-GZCB	Airbus A330-203	443		
☐ F-GZCC	Airbus A330-203	448		
☐ F-GZCD	Airbus A330-203	458	ex (F-WWJH)	
☐ F-GZCE	Airbus A330-203	465	ex F-WWKM	
☐ F-GZCF	Airbus A330-203	481		
☐ F-GZCG	Airbus A330-203	498	ex F-WWKI	
☐ F-GZCH	Airbus A330-203	500		
☐ F-GZCI	Airbus A330-203	502	ex F-WWKJ	
☐ F-GZCJ	Airbus A330-203	503		
☐ F-GZCK	Airbus A330-203	516		
☐ F-GZCL	Airbus A330-203	519		
☐ F-GZCM	Airbus A330-203	567	ex (F-WWYT)	

☐ F-GZCN	Airbus A330-203	584		
☐ F-GZCO	Airbus A330-203	657		
☐ F-GLZC	Airbus A340-311	029		
☐ F-GLZH	Airbus A340-311	078		
☐ F-GLZI	Airbus A340-311	084		
☐ F-GLZJ	Airbus A340-313X	186		
☐ F-GLZK	Airbus A340-313X	207		
☐ F-GLZL	Airbus A340-313X	210		>ABD
☐ F-GLZM	Airbus A340-313X	237		
☐ F-GLZN	Airbus A340-313X	245		
☐ F-GLZO	Airbus A340-313X	246		
☐ F-GLZP	Airbus A340-313X	260		
☐ F-GLZR	Airbus A340-313X	307		
☐ F-GLZS	Airbus A340-313X	310		
☐ F-GLZU	Airbus A340-313X	377		
☐ F-GNIG	Airbus A340-313X	174		
☐ F-GNII	Airbus A340-313X	399		
☐ F-HPJA	Airbus A380-861	033	ex F-WWSB	
☐ F-HPJB	Airbus A380-861	040	ex F-WWSE	
☐ F-HPJC	Airbus A380-861	043	ex F-WWAB	
☐ F-HPJD	Airbus A380-861	049	ex F-WWAL	
☐ F-HPJE	Airbus A380-861	052	ex F-WWAN	
☐ F-HPJF	Airbus A380-861	064	ex F-WWAU	
☐ F-HPJG	Airbus A380-861	067	ex F-WWSQ	
☐ F-HPJH	Airbus A380-861	099	ex F-WWAF	
☐ F-HPJI	Airbus A380-861	115	ex F-WWSL	
☐ F-HPJJ	Airbus A380-861	117	ex F-WWSV	♦
☐ F-GITD	Boeing 747-428	25600/901		
☐ F-GITE	Boeing 747-428	25601/906		
☐ F-GITH	Boeing 747-428	32868/1325		
☐ F-GITI	Boeing 747-428	32869/1327		
☐ F-GITJ	Boeing 747-428	32871/1343		
☐ F-GSPA	Boeing 777-228ER	29002/129		
☐ F-GSPB	Boeing 777-228ER	29003/133		
☐ F-GSPC	Boeing 777-228ER	29004/138		
☐ F-GSPD	Boeing 777-228ER	29005/187		
☐ F-GSPE	Boeing 777-228ER	29006/189		
☐ F-GSPF	Boeing 777-228ER	29007/201		
☐ F-GSPG	Boeing 777-228ER	27609/195		
☐ F-GSPH	Boeing 777-228ER	28675/210		
☐ F-GSPI	Boeing 777-228ER	29008/258		
☐ F-GSPJ	Boeing 777-228ER	29009/263		
☐ F-GSPK	Boeing 777-228ER	29010/267		
☐ F-GSPL	Boeing 777-228ER	30457/284	ex N50281	
☐ F-GSPM	Boeing 777-228ER	30456/307		
☐ F-GSPN	Boeing 777-228ER	29011/314		
☐ F-GSPO	Boeing 777-228ER	30614/320		
☐ F-GSPP	Boeing 777-228ER	30615/327		
☐ F-GSPQ	Boeing 777-228ER	28682/331		
☐ F-GSPR	Boeing 777-228ER	28683/367		
☐ F-GSPS	Boeing 777-228ER	32306/370		
☐ F-GSPT	Boeing 777-228ER	32308/382		
☐ F-GSPU	Boeing 777-228ER	32309/383		
☐ F-GSPV	Boeing 777-228ER	28684/385		
☐ F-GSPX	Boeing 777-228ER	32698/392		
☐ F-GSPY	Boeing 777-228ER	32305/395		
☐ F-GSPZ	Boeing 777-228ER	32310/401		
☐ F-GSQA	Boeing 777-328ER	32723/466	ex N5017Q	
☐ F-GSQB	Boeing 777-328ER	32724/478		
☐ F-GSQC	Boeing 777-328ER	32727/480		
☐ F-GSQD	Boeing 777-328ER	32726/490		
☐ F-GSQE	Boeing 777-328ER	32851/492		
☐ F-GSQF	Boeing 777-328ER	32849/494	ex N50217	
☐ F-GSQG	Boeing 777-328ER	32850/500	ex N5028Y	
☐ F-GSQH	Boeing 777-328ER	32711/501		
☐ F-GSQI	Boeing 777-328ER	32725/502	ex N60697	
☐ F-GSQJ	Boeing 777-328ER	32852/510		
☐ F-GSQK	Boeing 777-328ER	32845/530	ex N5017Q	
☐ F-GSQL	Boeing 777-328ER	32853/545		
☐ F-GSQM	Boeing 777-328ER	32848/558		
☐ F-GSQN	Boeing 777-328ER	32960/565		
☐ F-GSQO	Boeing 777-328ER	32961/570		
☐ F-GSQP	Boeing 777-328ER	35676/573		
☐ F-GSQR	Boeing 777-328ER	35677/579		
☐ F-GSQS	Boeing 777-328ER	32962/608		
☐ F-GSQT	Boeing 777-328ER	32846/616		
☐ F-GSQU	Boeing 777-328ER	32847/624	ex N5022E	
☐ F-GSQV	Boeing 777-328ER	32854/636		

☐ F-GSQX	Boeing 777-328ER	32963/645	ex N5014K	
☐ F-GSQY	Boeing 777-328ER	35678/647		
☐ F-GZNA	Boeing 777-328ER	35297/671	ex N50217	
☐ F-GZNB	Boeing 777-328ER	32964/715		
☐ F-GZNC	Boeing 777-328ER	35542/723		Gille Dehove
☐ F-GZND	Boeing 777-328ER	35543/777	ex N1785B	
☐ F-GZNE	Boeing 777-328ER	37432/790		SkyTeam c/s
☐ F-GZNF	Boeing 777-328ER	37433/792	ex N50281	
☐ F-GZNG	Boeing 777-328ER	32968/795		
☐ F-GZNH	Boeing 777-328ER	35544/905	ex N5017V	
☐ F-GZNI	Boeing 777-328ER	39973/924		
☐ F-GZNJ	Boeing 777-328ER	38706/928		
☐ F-GZNK	Boeing 777-328ER	39971/931		
☐ F-GZNL	Boeing 777-328ER	40063/1001		
☐ F-GZNN	Boeing 777-328ER	40376/1013		SkyTeam c/s
☐ F-GZNO	Boeing 777-328ER	38665/1007	ex N5014K	
☐ F-GZNP	Boeing 777-328ER	37435/1290		♦
☐ F-GZNQ	Boeing 777-328ER	40064/1298		♦
☐ F-GZNR	Boeing 777-328ER	44553/1343		o/o♦
☐ F-GIUA	Boeing 747-428ERF	32866/1315	ex N5017Q	wfs
☐ F-GUOB	Boeing 777-F28	32965/732	ex N5023Q	
☐ F-GUOC	Boeing 777-F28	32966/752		

AIR FRANCE REGIONAL   Various

The majority of services are operated in full Air France colours with titles 'Air France by' the appropriate airline, Airlinair, Brit'Air, CCM Airlines, Regional and Cityjet.

AIR MEDITERRANÉE   Mediterranée (ML/BIE)   Tarbes (LDE)

☐ F-GYAN	Airbus A321-111	0535	ex F-WQQU	>HRM
☐ F-GYAO	Airbus A321-111	0642	ex F-WQQV	>HRM
☐ F-GYAP	Airbus A321-111	0517	ex HB-IOA	
☐ F-GYAQ	Airbus A321-211	0827	ex HB-IOI	
☐ F-GYAR	Airbus A321-211	0891	ex HB-IOJ	
☐ F-GYAZ	Airbus A321-111	0519	ex D-ANJA	
☐ SX-BHT	Airbus A321-211	0666	ex EI-ESI	>HRM
☐ F-HCOA	Boeing 737-5L9	28084/2788	ex OY-APB	
☐ F-HCOB	Boeing 737-59D	26422/2412	ex G-BVZE	
☐ SX-BHR	Boeing 737-5L9	29234/3068	ex TC-AAG	>HRM

AIRBUS TRANSPORT INTERNATIONAL   Super Transport (4Y/BGA)   Toulouse-Blagnac (TLS)

☐ F-GSTA	Airbus A300B4-608ST Beluga	655/001	ex F-WAST	Super Transporter 1
☐ F-GSTB	Airbus A300B4-608ST Beluga	751/002	ex F-WSTB	Super Transporter 2
☐ F-GSTC	Airbus A300B4-608ST Beluga	765/003	ex F-WSTC	Super Transporter 3
☐ F-GSTD	Airbus A300B4-608ST Beluga	776/004	ex F-WSTD	Super Transporter 4
☐ F-GSTF	Airbus A300B4-608ST Beluga	796/005	ex F-WSTF	Super Transporter 5

AIRLEC AIR ESPACE   Airlec (ARL)   Bordeaux (BOD)

☐ F-GGVG	Swearingen SA226T Merlin IIIB	T-293	ex D-IBBB
☐ F-GLPT	Swearingen SA226T Merlin IIIB	T-298	ex VH-AWU
☐ F-GRNT	Swearingen SA226T Merlin IIIB	T-312	ex N84GA
☐ F-HCRT	Cessna 550 Citation II	550-0257	ex N53RG

ALSAIR   Alsair (LSR)   Colmar (CMR)

☐ F-GEOU	Beech 65-C90 King Air	LJ-941	ex N3804C

ATLANTIQUE AIR ASSISTANCE   Triple A (TLB)   Nantes (NTE)

☐ F-GPYY	Beech 1900C-1	UC-115	ex N115YV

CHALAIR AVIATION/CATOVAIR   Chalair (CE/CLG)   Caen-Carpiquet (CFR)

☐ F-GOOB	Beech 1900C-1	UC-153	ex N153YV
☐ F-HBCA	Beech 1900D	UE-188	ex SE-KXV
☐ F-HBCB	Beech 1900D	UE-390	ex 3B-VTL
☐ F-HBCC	Beech 1900D	UE-350	ex 3B-VIP
☐ F-HBCE	Beech 1900D	UE-323	ex OY-CHU
☐ F-HBCG	Beech 1900D	UE-70	ex PH-RNG
☐ F-HETS	Beech 1900D	UE-360	ex PK-TVL
☐ F-BXPY	Beech 65-C90 King Air	LJ-684	
☐ F-GHVV	Beech 200 Super King Air	BB-676	ex N970AA
☐ F-GIJB	Beech 200 Super King Air	BB-13	ex N83MA

CORSAIR — Corsair (SS/CRL) — Ajaccio (AJA)

☐ F-GTUI	Boeing 747-422	26875/931	ex N186UA
☐ F-HBIL	Airbus A330-243	320	
☐ F-HCAT	Airbus A330-243	285	ex F-WWKB
☐ F-HSEA	Boeing 747-422	26877/944	ex F-WSEA
☐ F-HSKY	Airbus A330-343E	1359	ex F-WWCZ
☐ F-HSUN	Boeing 747-422	26880/984	ex F-WSUN
☐ F-HZEN	Airbus A330-343E	1376	ex F-WWYE

EUROPE AIRPOST — French Post (5O/FPO) — Paris-Charles de Gaulle (CDG)

☐ F-GFUF	Boeing 737-3B3QC	24388/1725			
☐ F-GIXB	Boeing 737-33AF	24789/1953	ex F-OGSD		
☐ F-GIXC	Boeing 737-38BQC	25124/2047	ex F-OGSS	Saint-Louis	wfs
☐ F-GIXE	Boeing 737-3B3QC	26850/2235	ex N854WT		
☐ F-GIXS	Boeing 737-3H6SF	27347/2615	ex 9M-MZB		
☐ F-GIXT	Boeing 737-39MQC	28898/2906	ex F-ODZZ		
☐ F-GZTA	Boeing 737-33VQC	29333/3084	ex HA-LKV		
☐ F-GZTB	Boeing 737-33VF	29336/3102	ex HA-LKU		
☐ F-GZTM	Boeing 737-3B3QC	24387/1693	ex ZS-ASL		♦
☐ F-GIXN	Boeing 737-4Y0SF	25181/2203	ex EI-STF		
☐ F-GPOA	ATR 72-202QC	204	ex F-ORAC	>SWT	
☐ F-GPOB	ATR 72-202QC	207	ex F-ORAN	>SWT	
☐ F-GZTC	Boeing 737-73V/W	32414/1214	ex G-EZJS		
☐ F-GZTD	Boeing 737-73V/W	32418/1300	ex G-EZJW		
☐ F-GZTE	Boeing 737-73S/W	29080/211	ex C-GTQI		
☐ F-GZTF	Boeing 737-73S/W	29081/215	ex C-GTQP		♦
☐ F-GZTI	Boeing 737-408SF	25063/2032	ex N563AC		
☐ F-GZTJ	Boeing 737-4S3SF	25595/2233	ex N595AG		

FINIST'AIR — Finistair (FTR) — Brest (BES)

☐ F-GHGZ	Cessna 208A Caravan I	208A00188	ex (N9769F)
☐ F-GJFI	Cessna 208B Caravan I	208B0230	ex N208GC
☐ F-HFTR	Cessna 208B Caravan I	208B2041	ex OY-PBU

FLEET MANAGEMENT AIRWAYS

☐ F-GUME	Beech 1900D	UE-371	ex CS-DOC

HELI-UNION — Heli Union (HLU) — Paris-Heliport/Toussus-le-Noble (JDP/TNF)

☐ F-GJPZ	Aérospatiale SA365N Dauphin 2	6115	ex LN-OLN	
☐ F-GKCU	Aérospatiale SA365N Dauphin 2	6011	ex PH-SEC	based Gabon
☐ F-GMAY	Aérospatiale SA365N Dauphin 2	6137		
☐ F-GNVT	Aérospatiale AS365N3 Dauphin 2	6772		based Gabon♦
☐ F-GRCF	Aérospatiale AS365N3 Dauphin 2	9000	ex (F-OHOD)	
☐ F-GTCH	Aérospatiela AS365N3 Dauphin 2	6710		based Gabon♦
☐ F-GVGV	Aérospatiale AS365N3 Dauphin 2	6724	ex F-WWOL	
☐ F-HUAJ	Aérospatiale AS365N3 Dauphin 3	6879	ex G-REDE	
☐ F-HUDT	Aérospatiale SA365N3 Dauphin 2	6745	ex D2-EWD	
☐ F-HURX	Aérospatiale AS365N3 Dauphin 2	9001	ex 5N-BNY	♦
☐ TJ-SAH	Aérospatiale SA365N Dauphin 2	6037	ex F-GMHI	
☐ F-GHOY	Aérospatiale AS332L1	9005	ex F-WQEB	
☐ F-GJTU	Aérospatiale AS350B3 Ecureuil	3449	ex EP-HEU	based Cayenne
☐ F-GYSH	Aérospatiale AS332L1	9006	ex F-WQEE	
☐ F-GYVL	Sikorsky S-76C+	760805	ex N805M	
☐ F-GZKP	Sikorsky S-76C+	760806	ex N806K	
☐ F-HUBH	AgustaWestland AW139	41387	ex N245MM	♦
☐ F-HUGF	AgustaWestland AW139	41388	ex N251MM	♦

HEX'AIR — Hex Airline (UD/HER) — Le Puy (LPY)

☐ F-GUPE	Beech 1900D	UE-248	ex N10882	>PEA

HOP! AIRLINAIR — Airlinair (A5/RLA) — Paris-Orly (ORY)

☐ F-GPYA	ATR 42-500	457	ex F-WWET	
☐ F-GPYB	ATR 42-500	480	ex F-WWLZ	
☐ F-GPYC	ATR 42-500	484	ex F-WWEB	
☐ F-GPYD	ATR 42-500	490	ex F-WWLJ	
☐ F-GPYF	ATR 42-500	495	ex F-WWLM	opf AFR
☐ F-GPYK	ATR 42-500	537	ex F-WWLC	opf AFR
☐ F-GPYL	ATR 42-500	542	ex F-WWLH	opf AFR
☐ F-GPYM	ATR 42-500	520	ex F-WWLR	opf AFR
☐ F-GPYN	ATR 42-500	539	ex F-WWLO	opf AFR
☐ F-GPYO	ATR 42-500	544	ex F-WWLH	
☐ F-GVZB	ATR 42-500	524	ex F-OHQL	

☐ F-GVZC	ATR 42-500	516	ex F-WNUA		
☐ F-GVZD	ATR 42-500	530	ex F-WNUJ		
☐ F-GKPD	ATR 72-202	177	ex F-WWE	all-white	
☐ F-GRPI	ATR 72-212A	722	ex F-WWEC		opf AFR
☐ F-GVZL	ATR 72-212A	553	ex F-OHJO		
☐ F-GVZM	ATR 72-212A	590	ex F-OHJT		
☐ F-GVZN	ATR 72-212A	563	ex F-OHJU		
☐ F-GVZP	ATR 72-212A	494	ex N494AE		
☐ F-GVZR	ATR 72-212A	498	ex N498AE		
☐ F-GVZS	ATR 72-212A	761	ex OY-CLU		
☐ F-GVZU	ATR 72-212A	500	ex N499AT		♦
☐ F-GVZV	ATR 72-212A	686	ex I-ADLJ		♦
☐ F-HAPL	ATR 72-212A	654	ex F-OIJG		
☐ F-HOPY	ATR 72-600	1237	ex F-WWEL		♦
☐ F-	ATR 72-600	1257	ex F-WWEI		o/o♦
☐ F-	ATR 72-600	1265	ex F-WW		o/o♦

HOP! BRIT'AIR *(DB/BZH)* *Morlaix (MXN)*

☐ F-GRJG	Canadair CRJ-100ER	7143	ex C-FMMQ		
☐ F-GRJI	Canadair CRJ-100ER	7147	ex C-FZAL		
☐ F-GRJJ	Canadair CRJ-100ER	7190	ex C-GBFF		
☐ F-GRJK	Canadair CRJ-100ER	7219	ex C-FMMQ		
☐ F-GRJL	Canadair CRJ-100FR	7221	ex C-FMNX		
☐ F-GRJM	Canadair CRJ-100ER	7222	ex C-FMMY		
☐ F-GRJN	Canadair CRJ-100ER	7262	ex C-FMLT		wfs
☐ F-GRJO	Canadair CRJ-100ER	7296	ex C-FMNW		
☐ F-GRJP	Canadair CRJ-100ER	7301	ex C-FVAZ		
☐ F-GRJQ	Canadair CRJ-100ER	7321	ex C-FMLS		
☐ F-GRJT	Canadair CRJ-100ER	7389	ex C-FMOS		
☐ F-GRZC	Canadair CRJ-701	10008	ex C-GHCO		
☐ F-GRZD	Canadair CRJ-701	10016	ex C-GJEZ		
☐ F-GRZE	Canadair CRJ-701	10032	ex C-GIBL		
☐ F-GRZF	Canadair CRJ-701	10036	ex C-GIBQ		
☐ F-GRZG	Canadair CRJ-701	10037	ex C-GIBT		
☐ F-GRZH	Canadair CRJ-701	10089	ex C-GIBI		
☐ F-GRZI	Canadair CRJ-701	10093			
☐ F-GRZJ	Canadair CRJ-701	10096			
☐ F-GRZK	Canadair CRJ-701	10198			
☐ F-GRZL	Canadair CRJ-701	10245			
☐ F-GRZM	Canadair CRJ-701	10263			
☐ F-GRZN	Canadair CRJ-701	10264			
☐ F-GRZO	Canadair CRJ-701	10265			
☐ F-HMLA	Canadair CRJ-1000	19004	ex C-GZQJ		
☐ F-HMLC	Canadair CRJ-1000	19006	ex C-GHKA		
☐ F-HMLD	Canadair CRJ-1000	19007	ex C-GIBR		
☐ F-HMLE	Canadair CRJ-1000	19009	ex C-GZQJ		
☐ F-HMLF	Canadair CRJ-1000	19010	ex C-GZQX		
☐ F-HMLG	Canadair CRJ-1000	19012	ex C-GZQW		
☐ F-HMLH	Canadair CRJ-1000	19013	ex C-GIAH		
☐ F-HMLI	Canadair CRJ-1000	19014	ex C-GIBJ		
☐ F-HMLJ	Canadair CRJ-1000	19015	ex C-GIAV		
☐ F-HMLK	Canadair CRJ-1000	19016	ex C-GZQA		
☐ F-HMLL	Canadair CRJ-1000	19017	ex C-GZQJ		
☐ F-HMLM	Canadair CRJ-1000	19023	ex C-GICL		
☐ F-HMLN	Canadair CRJ-1000	19024	ex C-GICP		
☐ F-HMLO	Canadair CRJ-1000	19041	ex C-GZYJ		♦

HOP! RÉGIONAL *Régional Europe (YS/RAE)* *Nantes (NTE)*

☐ F-GRGC	Embraer ERJ-145EP	145012	ex PT-SYI	
☐ F-GRGD	Embraer ERJ-145EP	145043	ex PT-SZI	
☐ F-GRGE	Embraer ERJ-145EP	145047	ex PT-SZM	
☐ F-GRGF	Embraer ERJ-145EP	145050	ex PT-SZP	
☐ F-GRGG	Embraer ERJ-145EP	145118	ex PT-SCT	
☐ F-GRGH	Embraer ERJ-145EP	145120	ex PT-SCW	
☐ F-GRGI	Embraer ERJ-145EP	145152	ex PT-SED	
☐ F-GRGJ	Embraer ERJ-145EP	145297	ex PT-SKO	
☐ F-GRGK	Embraer ERJ-145EP	145324	ex PT-SMQ	
☐ F-GRGL	Embraer ERJ-145EP	145375	ex PT-SOZ	
☐ F-GUBC	Embraer ERJ-145MP	145556	ex PT-SZR	
☐ F-GUBE	Embraer ERJ-145MP	145668	ex PT-SFC	
☐ F-GUBF	Embraer ERJ-145MP	145669	ex PT-SFD	
☐ F-GUBG	Embraer ERJ-145MP	14500890	ex PT-SYD	
☐ F-GUEA	Embraer ERJ-145MP	145342	ex PT-SNI	
☐ F-GUFD	Embraer ERJ-145MP	145197	ex PT-SGN	
☐ F-GVHD	Embraer ERJ-145MP	145178	ex PT-SEZ	
☐ F-HBXA	Embraer ERJ-170STD	17000237	ex PT-SFN	

☐ F-HBXB	Embraer ERJ-170STD	17000250	ex PT-SJB
☐ F-HBXC	Embraer ERJ-170STD	17000263	ex PT-SJR
☐ F-HBXD	Embraer ERJ-170STD	17000281	ex PT-TQH
☐ F-HBXE	Embraer ERJ-170STD	17000286	ex PT-TQM
☐ F-HBXF	Embraer ERJ-170STD	17000292	ex PT-TQS
☐ F-HBXG	Embraer ERJ-170STD	17000301	ex PT-XQA
☐ F-HBXH	Embraer ERJ-170STD	17000307	ex PT-XQH
☐ F-HBXI	Embraer ERJ-170STD	17000310	ex PT-XQX
☐ F-HBXJ	Embraer ERJ-170STD	17000312	ex PT-XQZ
☐ F-HBXK	Embraer ERJ-170LR	17000008	ex EI-DFG
☐ F-HBXL	Embraer ERJ-170LR	17000009	ex EI-DFH
☐ F-HBXM	Embraer ERJ-170LR	17000010	ex EI-DFI
☐ F-HBXN	Embraer ERJ-170LR	17000011	ex EI-DFJ
☐ F-HBXO	Embraer ERJ-170LR	17000032	ex EI-DFK
☐ F-HBXP	Embraer ERJ-170LR	17000036	ex EI-DFL
☐ F-HBLA	Embraer ERJ-190LR	19000051	ex PT-SIA
☐ F-HBLB	Embraer ERJ-190LR	19000060	ex PT-SIN
☐ F-HBLC	Embraer ERJ-190LR	19000080	ex PT-SJW
☐ F-HBLD	Embraer ERJ-190LR	19000113	ex PT-SQH
☐ F-HBLE	Embraer ERJ-190LR	19000123	ex PT-SQS
☐ F-HBLF	Embraer ERJ-190LR	19000158	ex PT-SAO
☐ F-HBLG	Embraer ERJ-190STD	19000254	ex PT-SIZ
☐ F-HBLH	Embraer ERJ-190STD	19000266	ex PT-TLG
☐ F-HBLI	Embraer ERJ-190STD	19000298	ex PT-TZM
☐ F-HBLJ	Embraer ERJ-190STD	19000311	ex PT-TZZ

INAER HELICOPTÈRES — Le Luc-Le Cannet

☐ F-HBOI	Eurocopter EC135T2+ Ecureuil	1011	ex 4K-AZ91	♦
☐ F-HCHL	Aérospatiale EC135P2 Ecureuil	0691	ex YR-RYC	♦
☐ F-HGOA	Eurocopter EC135T2+ Ecureuil	0668	ex G-PNTA	
☐ F-HMGI	Eurocopter EC135T2+ Ecureuil	0347	ex TC-HJF	♦
☐ F-HNCE	Eurocopter EC135T2+ Ecureuil	0762	ex G-PNTB	♦
☐ F-HOMG	Eurocopter EC135P2 Ecureuil	0441	ex OH-HMV	
☐ F-HORG	Eurocopter EC135P2 Ecureuil	0438	ex OH-HMI	
☐ F-HORL	Eurocopter EC135P2+ Ecureuil	0165	ex (D-HAAW)	♦
☐ F-HTLN	Eurocopter EC135T2+ Ecureuil	0810	ex G-PNTC	♦
☐ F-HTRS	Eurocopter EC135P2+ Ecureuil	0125	ex (D-HAAV)	♦

LA COMPAGNIE (B0/DJT) — Paris-Charles de Gaulle (CDG)

☐ F-HCIE	Boeing 757-204	27208/606	ex G-BYAT	♦
☐ F-HTAG	Boeing 757-256/W	29307/924	ex G-POWJ	♦

OPENSKIES (BOS) — Paris-Orly (ORY)

☐ F-GPEK	Boeing 757-236/W	25808/665	ex G-BPEK	Lauren
☐ F-HAVI	Boeing 757-26D/W	24473/301	ex N473AP	Violetta
☐ F-HAVN	Boeing 757-230/W	25140/382	ex D-ABNF	Gloria

OYONNAIR

☐ F-HEAL	Beech B200 Super King Air	BB-1928	ex N964RT
☐ F-HKIL	Cessba 510 Citation Mustang	510-0346	ex C-FBKD

PAN EUROPÉENNE AIR SERVICE (PEA) — Chambéry (CMF)

☐ F-GOPE	Beech 1900D	UE-103	ex (F-GMSA)	<HER
☐ F-GUPE	Beech 1900D	UE-248	ex N10882	<HER
☐ F-GYPE	Embraer ERJ-135LR	145492	ex PT-SXL	
☐ F-GZPE	Piaggio P.180 Avanti	1064		
☐ F-HAPE	Beech 1900D	UE-367	ex N30515	
☐ F-HBPE	Embraer ERJ-145LR	145106	ex PH-RXC	
☐ F-HCPE	Piaggio P.180 Avanti	1144		
☐ F-HIPE	Embraer EMB-505 Phenom 300	50500016	ex PT-PVD	

REGOURD AVIATION — Paris-Le Bourget (LBG)

☐ F-GIPH	Dassault Falcon 100	194	ex N61FC	
☐ F-GMOT	Dassault Falcon 50	111	ex N50AH	
☐ F-GVZJ	ATR 42-300	0093	ex F-WQNO	>AEH
☐ TR-LIW	ATR 42-300	148	ex F-HAEK	>EKA
☐ 5Y-EKA	Dornier 228-201	8108	ex LN-AAO	>Kasas

SECURITÉ CIVILE — Marseille (MRS)

☐ F-ZBEG	Canadair CL415	2015	ex C-FXBH	39
☐ F-ZBEU	Canadair CL415	2024	ex C-FZDE	42
☐ F-ZBFN	Canadair CL415	2006	ex C-FVUK	33
☐ F-ZBFP	Canadair CL415	2002	ex C-FBET	31

☐ F-ZBFS	Canadair CL415	2001	ex C-GSCT	32
☐ F-ZBFV	Canadair CL415	2013	ex C-FWPE	37
☐ F-ZBFW	Canadair CL415	2014	ex C-FWZH	38
☐ F-ZBFX	Canadair CL415	2007	ex C-FVUJ	34
☐ F-ZBFY	Canadair CL415	2010	ex C-FVDY	35
☐ F-ZBME	Canadair CL415	2057	ex C-GILN	44
☐ F-ZBMF	Canadair CL415	2063	ex C-FGZT	45
☐ F-ZBMG	Canadair CL415	2065	ex C-FLFW	48
☐ F-ZBAA	Conair Turbo Firecat	456/027	ex F-WEOL	22
☐ F-ZBAP	Conair Turbo Firecat	567/026	ex F-ZBDA	12
☐ F-ZBAZ	Conair Turbo Firecat	DHC-57/008	ex F-WEOL	01
☐ F-ZBCZ	Conair Turbo Firecat	DHC-94/036	ex F-ZBCA	23
☐ F-ZBEH	Conair Turbo Firecat	410/035	ex F-WEOJ	20
☐ F-ZBET	Conair Turbo Firecat	703/028	ex F-WEOJ	15
☐ F-ZBEW	Conair Turbo Firecat	621/025	ex F-WEOL	11
☐ F-ZBEY	Conair Turbo Firecat	400/017	ex F-WEOK	07
☐ F-ZBMA	Conair Turbo Firecat	461/021	ex C-GFZG	24
☐ F-ZBFJ	Beech B200 Super King Air	BB-1102	ex D-IWAN	98
☐ F-ZBFK	Beech B200 Super King Air	BB-876	ex F-GHSC	96
☐ F-ZBMB	Beech B200 Super King Air	BB-1379	ex F-GJFD	97
☐ F-ZBGO	Beech B300 King Air 350	FL-800	ex N8150M	
☐ F-ZBGP	Beech B300 King Air 350	FL-802	ex N8049T	
☐ F-ZBMC	de Havilland DHC-8-402QMRT	4040	ex C-FBAM	73
☐ F-ZBMD	de Havilland DHC-8-402QMRT	4043	ex C-FBSG	74
☐ F-ZBQJ	MBB BK.117C-2	9323	ex D-HMBG	
☐ F-ZBQK	MBB BK.117C-2	9372	ex D-HADC	
☐ F-ZBQL	MBB BK.117C-2	9452	ex D-HADK	

TRANSAVIA FRANCE	*France Soleil (TO/TVF)*			*Paris-Orly (ORY)*
☐ F-GZHA	Boeing 737-8GJ/W	34901/2267	ex (VT-SPN)	
☐ F-GZHB	Boeing 737-8GJ/W	34902/2309	ex (VT-SPO)	
☐ F-GZHC	Boeing 737-8K2/W	29651/2534		
☐ F-GZHD	Boeing 737-8K2/W	29650/2583		
☐ F-GZHE	Boeing 737-8K2/W	29678/2615	ex N1787B	
☐ F-GZHF	Boeing 737-8HX/W	29677/2946	ex PH-ZOM	
☐ F-GZHG	Boeing 737-8K2/W	30650/1158	ex PH-HZV	
☐ F-GZHI	Boeing 737-8K5/W	36120/4358		
☐ F-GZHJ	Boeing 737-86J/W	37778/4424		
☐ F-GZHK	Boeing 737-8K2/W	37790/4824	ex N1796B	
☐ F-GZHL	Boeing 737-8K2/W	37791/4858	ex N5573L	
☐ F-GZHM	Boeing 737-8K2/W	37792/4911		♦
☐ F-GZHN	Boeing 737-85H/W	29445/186	ex OY-SEI	
☐ F-GZHO	Boeing 737-8K2/W	43880/5270		♦
☐ F-GZHP	Boeing 737-8K2/W	44566/5345		♦
☐ F-GZHQ	Boeing 737-8K2/W	44567/5396		♦
☐ F-GZHR	Boeing 737-8K2/W	43913/		o/o♦
☐ F-GZHT	Boeing 737-8K2/W	41332/5390		♦
☐ F-GZHV	Boeing 737-85H/W	29444/178	ex OY-SEH	

TWIN JET	*Twinjet (T7/TJT)*			*Marseille (MRS)*
☐ F-GLND	Beech 1900D	UE-196	ex N3234G	
☐ F-GLNE	Beech 1900D	UE-197	ex N3234U	
☐ F-GLNF	Beech 1900D	UE-69	ex YR-RLA	
☐ F-GLNH	Beech 1900D	UE-73	ex YR-RLB	
☐ F-GLNK	Beech 1900D	UE-269	ex N11017	
☐ F-GRYL	Beech 1900D	UE-301	ex N22161	
☐ F-GTKJ	Beech 1900D	UE-348	ex N23406	
☐ F-GTVC	Beech 1900D	UE-349	ex N23430	opf Ministère de l'Interieur

XL AIRWAYS FRANCE	*Starway (SE/XLF)*			*Paris-Orly (ORY)*
☐ F-GRSQ	Airbus A330-243	501	ex F-WWKG	
☐ F-GSEU	Airbus A330-243	635	ex F-WWYO	
☐ F-HAXL	Boeing 737-8Q8/W	35279/2626	ex G-XLFR	
☐ F-HJUL	Boeing 737-8Q8/W	38819/3519		>LGL
☐ F-HXLF	Airbus A330-303	1360	ex F-WWKA	

F-O   PACIFIC TERRITORIES (French Polynesia and New Caledonia)

AIR ARCHIPELS	*Archipels (RHL)*			*Papeete (PPT)*
☐ F-OIQK	Beech B200C Super King Air	BL-149	ex N36949	
☐ F-OIQL	Beech B200C Super King Air	BL-148	ex N36948	
☐ F-OIQM	Beech B200 Super King Air	BB-1934	ex N37134	

AIR CALÉDONIE INTERNATIONAL	AirCal (TY/TPC)			Nouméa (NOU)
☐ F-OIPI	ATR 42-500	647	ex F-WWLE	
☐ F-OIPN	ATR 72-212A	735	ex F-WWEP	
☐ F-OIPS	ATR 72-212A	764	ex F-WWEC	
☐ F-ONCL	ATR 72-212A	759	ex F-WNCL	

AIR LOYAUTÉ	lazur (VZR)			Nouméa (NOU)
☐ F-GRSO	Beech B200C Super King Air	BL-11	ex (F-GYMD)	
☐ F-OIAY	de Havilland DHC-6 Twin Otter 300	507	ex P2-KSR	
☐ F-OIJI	de Havilland DHC-6 Twin Otter 300	277	ex (ZS-OVL)	
☐ F-ONCA	de Havilland DHC-6 Twin Otter 300	840	ex C-FZYG	
☐ F-ONOA	de Havilland DHC-6 Twin Otter 400	855	ex C-GNOA	

AIR MOOREA		Air Moorea (TAH)		Papeete (PPT)
☐ F-OIQF	de Havilland DHC-6 Twin Otter 300	815	ex N45KH	
☐ F-OIQP	de Havilland DHC-6 Twin Otter 300	715	ex 5Y-SKL	

AIR TAHITI		Air Tahiti (VT/VTA)		Papeete (PPT)
☐ F-OIQN	ATR 72-212A	719	ex F-WWET	
☐ F-OIQO	ATR 72-212A	731	ex F-WWEL	
☐ F-OIQR	ATR 72-212A	862	ex F-WWEJ	
☐ F-OIQT	ATR 72-212A	829	ex F-WWEW	
☐ F-OIQU	ATR 72-212A	751	ex F-WWEL	
☐ F-OIQV	ATR 72-212A	806	ex F-WWER	
☐ F-ORVB	ATR 42-600	1007	ex F-WWLP	
☐ F-ORVC	ATR 42-600	1013	ex F-WWLV	
☐ F-ORVN	ATR 72-600	1255	ex F-WWEG	o/o♦
☐ F-ORVS	ATR 72-600	1192	ex F-WWEI	♦

AIR TAHITI NUI		Tahiti Airlines (TN/THT)			Papeete (PPT)
☐ F-OJGF	Airbus A340-313X	385	ex F-WWJC	Mangareva	
☐ F-OJTN	Airbus A340-313X	395	ex C-GZIA	Bora Bora	
☐ F-OLOV	Airbus A340-313E	668	ex F-WWJD	Nuku Hiva	
☐ F-OSEA	Airbus A340-313X	438	ex F-WWJV	Rangiroa	
☐ F-OSUN	Airbus A340-313X	446	ex F-WWJA	Moorea	

AIR TETI'AROA				Papeete-Faaa
☐ F-OKAB	Britten-Norman BN-2T Islander	2310	ex G-CEUE	♦

AIRCALIN		Air Calin (SB/ACI)		Nouméa (NOU)
☐ F-OCQZ	de Havilland DHC-6 Twin Otter 300	412		
☐ F-OHSD	Airbus A330-202	507	ex F-WWYS	
☐ F-OIAQ	de Havilland DHC-6 Twin Otter 300	381	ex VH-RPZ	
☐ F-OJSB	Airbus A320-232	2152		
☐ F-OJSE	Airbus A330-202	510	ex F-WWYT	
☐ F-OZNC	Airbus A320-232	3547	ex VH-VQD	♦

F-O ATLANTIC / INDIAN OCEAN TERRITORIES (St Pierre & Miquelon and Réunion)

AIR AUSTRAL		Réunion (UU/REU)			St Denis-Gilot (RUN)
☐ F-OHSF	ATR 72-212A	650	ex F-WWEC		
☐ F-OLRA	Boeing 777-29MLR	40955/952		Antoine de Bertin	
☐ F-OMRU	ATR 72-212A	855	ex F-WWEI		
☐ F-ONGA	Boeing 737-89M/W	40910/3484			
☐ F-ONGB	Boeing 737-89M/W	40911/3504	ex N1786B		
☐ F-ONOU	Boeing 777-3Q8ER	35783/786	ex N5573S	Leon Dierx	Waterfalls c/s
☐ F-OREU	Boeing 777-39MER	37434/912			Waves c/s
☐ F-OSYD	Boeing 777-3Q8ER	35782/778	ex N5014K	C Leconte de Lisle	Volcano c/s
☐ F-OZSE	ATR 72-212A	813	ex F-WWEC	Eugène Dayot	>EWR
☐ F-O	Boeing 787-8	34510/			o/o♦
☐ F-O	Boeing 787-8	34491/			o/o♦

EWA AIR		(ZD/EWR)			Mayotte
☐ F-OZSE	ATR 72-212A	813	ex F-WWEC	Eugène Dayot	<REU

AIR ST-PIERRE		(PJ/SPM)		St-Pierre et Miquelon (FSP)
☐ F-OFSP	ATR 42-500	801	ex F-WWLT	
☐ F-OSPJ	Reims Cessna F406 Caravan II	F406-0091		

F-O   FRENCH CARIBBEAN (Guadeloupe & Saint-Barthélemy, Martinique and French Guyana)

AIR ANTILLES EXPRESS		(3S)		Pointe-à-Pitre (PTP)
☐ F-OHJG	de Havilland DHC-6 Twin Otter 300	603	ex Fr AF 603	<GUY
☐ F-OIXD	ATR 42-500	695	ex F-WWLQ	<GUY♦
☐ F-OIXE	ATR 42-500	807	ex F-WWLX	<GUY
☐ F-OIXH	ATR 42-500	831	ex F-WWLD	<GUY
☐ F-OIXO	ATR 72-600	1010	ex F-WWLS	<GUY

AIR CARAIBES	French West (TX/FWI)		
	Pointe-à-Pitre/Fort-de-France/ St Barthélemy/St Martin (PTP/FDF/SBH/SFG)		
☐ F-OIJH	ATR 72-212A	682	ex F-WWEE
☐ F-OIJK	ATR 72-212A	736	ex F-WWEQ
☐ F-OIXL	ATR 72-212A	888	ex F-WWES

AIR CARAIBES ATLANTIQUE	Car Line (CAJ)		Pointe-à-Pitre (PTP)
☐ F-GOTO	Airbus A330-323E	1021	ex F-WWYN
☐ F-HPTP	Airbus A330-323X	1268	ex F-WWKZ
☐ F-OFDF	Airbus A330-223	253	ex HB-IQD
☐ F-OONE	Airbus A330-323E	965	ex F-WWYL Region Guyane
☐ F-ORLY	Airbus A330-323X	758	ex F-WWYR

AIR GUYANE EXPRESS	Green Bird (3S/GUY)		Cayenne (CAY)
☐ F-OHJG	de Havilland DHC-6 Twin Otter 300	603	ex Fr AF 603	>3S
☐ F-OIJL	de Havilland DHC-6 Twin Otter 300	281	ex HB-LSV	
☐ F-OIJY	de Havilland DHC-6 Twin Otter 300	797	ex D-IFLY	
☐ F-OIXD	ATR 42-500	695	ex F-WWLQ	>3S
☐ F-OIXE	ATR 42-500	807	ex F-WWLX	>3S
☐ F-OIXF	LET L-410UVP-E20	092635	ex OK-2635	
☐ F-OIXG	LET L-410UVP-E20	2734	ex OK-AIS	
☐ F-OIXH	ATR 42-500	831	ex F-WWLD	>3S
☐ F-OIXI	LET L-410UVP-E20	2807	ex OK-ODR	
☐ F-OIXO	ATR 72-600	1010	ex F-WWLS	>3S
☐ F-OIXT	LET L-410UVP-E20	2903	ex OK-JDB	

AIRAWAK			Fort-de-France (FDF)
☐ F-OGXA	Britten-Norman BN-2A-26 Islander	788	ex D-IHUG
☐ F-OIXB	Cessna 402B II	402B1220	ex V2-LEW

INTER REGIONAL EXPRESS			Le Raizet
☐ F-OIXJ	Cessna 208B Caravan I	208B2325	

ST BARTH COMMUTER	Black Fin (SBU)		St Barthélemy (SBH)
☐ F-OHQY	Britten-Norman BN-2B-20 Islander	2251	ex V2-LFE
☐ F-OSBC	Cessna 208B Caravan I	208B2188	ex N1029J
☐ F-OSBH	Cessna 208B Caravan I	208B2117	ex N6137Y
☐ F-OSBM	Cessna 208B Caravan I	208B2391	ex N2025M

WANAIR			
☐ F-OHRX	Beech 1900D	UE-282	ex N11296

G-   UNITED KINGDOM (United Kingdom of Great Britain and Northern Ireland)

AIR CHARTER SCOTLAND	(EDC)		Perth Scone (PSL)
☐ G-SUGR	Embraer Legacy 650	14501199	ex PR-LBQ	♦
☐ G-WIRG	Embraer Legacy 650	14501184	ex PR-LBY	♦

ATLANTIC AIRLINES/WEST ATLANTIC	Neptune (NPT)		Coventry (CVT)
☐ G-BTPA	British Aerospace ATP (LFD)	2007	ex EC-HGC	
☐ G-BTPC	British Aerospace ATP (LFD)	2010	ex SE-MAI	
☐ G-BTPE	British Aerospace ATP (LFD)	2012	ex EC-HGE West Atlantic c/s	
☐ G-BTPF	British Aerospace ATP (LFD)	2013	ex EC-HCY	
☐ G-BTPG	British Aerospace ATP (LFD)	2014	ex (G-JEMF) West Atlantic c/s	
☐ G-BTPH	British Aerospace ATP (LFD)	2015	ex (G-JEMF)	
☐ G-BTTO	British Aerospace ATP (LFD)	2033	ex EC-HNA West Atlantic c/s	

☐ G-BUUP	British Aerospace ATP (LFD)	2008	ex G-MANU		
☐ G-BUUR	British Aerospace ATP (LFD)	2024	ex EC-GUX		
☐ G-MANH	British Aerospace ATP (LFD)	2017	ex G-LOGC		
☐ G-MANM	British Aerospace ATP (LFD)	2005	ex LZ-BPS		
☐ G-MANO	British Aerospace ATP (LFD)	2006	ex SE-MAN		
☐ G-JMCL	Boeing 737-322F	23951/1532	ex D-AGEA		
☐ G-JMCM	Boeing 737-3Y0F	24679/1897	ex EC-KRA		
☐ G-JMCO	Boeing 737-3T0SF	23569/1258	ex OO-TNA		
☐ G-JMCP	Boeing 737-3T0SF	23578/1358	ex OO-TNB		>AWC
☐ G-JMCR	Boeing 737-4Q8SF	25372/2280	ex N452KA		♦
☐ G-JMCT	Boeing 737-3Y0SF	24546/1811	ex G-ZAPV		
☐ G-JMCU	Boeing 737-301SF	23513/1327	ex OO-TNC		♦

AURIGNY AIR SERVICES · Ayline (GR/AUR) · Guernsey (GCI)

☐ G-BDTO	Britten-Norman BN-2A Mk.III-2 Trislander	1027	ex G-RBSI		
☐ G-BEVT	Britten-Norman BN-2A Mk.III-2 Trislander	1057			
☐ G-JOEY	Britten-Norman BN-2A Mk.III-2 Trislander	1016	ex G-BDGG	Joey	
☐ G-RBCI	Britten-Norman BN-2A Mk.III-2 Trislander	1035	ex G-BDWV		
☐ G-RLON	Britten-Norman BN-2A Mk.III-2 Trislander	1008	ex G-ITEX	Royal London Asset Mgt c/s	
☐ CS-TGG	Dornier 228-202K	8160	ex D-CORA		<RVP♦
☐ G-BWDB	ATR 72-202	449	ex F-WQNI		
☐ G-COBO	ATR 72-212A	852	ex F-WWEV		
☐ G-HUET	ATR 42-500	584	ex OY-YAS		♦
☐ G-NSEY	Embraer ERJ-195LR	19000671	ex PR-EGE		♦
☐ G-SAYE	Dornier 228-202K	8046	ex D-IFLM		♦
☐ G-VZON	ATR 72-212A	853	ex F-WWEW		
☐ OO-VLZ	Fokker 50	20264	ex TF-JMU	Deauville Normandie	<VLM♦

AV CARGO AIRLINES · London-Gatwick (LGW)

☐ N495DC	McDonnell-Douglas DC-10-30F	47818/305	ex Z-ALT		[LGG]
☐ Z-BAM	McDonnell-Douglas MD-11ERF	48746/597	ex N278WA	Lady Liege	>GAA
☐ Z-BPL	McDonnell-Douglas MD-11F	48756/623	ex N279WA	Hannah Mai	>GAA
☐ Z-BVT	McDonnell-Douglas MD-11BCF	48410/495	ex N575SH		[ZRH]

BA CITYFLYER · (CJ/CFE) · London City (LCY)

☐ G-LCYD	Embraer ERJ-170STD	17000294	ex PT-TQU	
☐ G-LCYE	Embraer ERJ-170STD	17000296	ex PT-TQW	
☐ G-LCYF	Embraer ERJ-170STD	17000298	ex PT-TQR	
☐ G-LCYG	Embraer ERJ-170STD	17000300	ex PT-TQZ	
☐ G-LCYH	Embraer ERJ-170STD	17000302	ex PT-XQB	
☐ G-LCYI	Embraer ERJ-170STD	17000305	ex PT-XQE	
☐ G-LCYJ	Embraer ERJ-190SR	19000339	ex PT-TXY	
☐ G-LCYK	Embraer ERJ-190SR	19000343	ex PT-XQK	
☐ G-LCYL	Embraer ERJ-190SR	19000346	ex PT-XQM	
☐ G-LCYM	Embraer ERJ-190SR	19000351	ex PT-XQR	
☐ G-LCYN	Embraer ERJ-190SR	19000392	ex PT-XNY	
☐ G-LCYO	Embraer ERJ-190SR	19000430	ex PT-TCQ	
☐ G-LCYP	Embraer ERJ-190SR	19000443	ex PT-TJD	
☐ G-LCYR	Embraer ERJ-190SR	19000563	ex PT-TDS	
☐ G-LCYS	Embraer ERJ-190SR	19000663	ex PR-EEX	
☐ G-LCYT	Embraer ERJ-190SR	19000670	ex PR-EGC	
☐ G-LCYU	Embraer ERJ-190SR	19000674	ex PR-EHF	
☐ G-CERZ	SAAB 2000	2000-042	ex SE-LSA	<EZE

BLUE ISLANDS · Blue Island (SI/BCI) · Jersey (JER)

☐ G-ISLF	ATR 42-500	546	ex D-BMMM	
☐ G-ISLG	ATR 42-320	019	ex F-HAAV	
☐ G-ISLH	ATR 42-300	0173	ex F-HEKF	
☐ G-ISLI	ATR 72-212A	0529	ex OY-CLM	
☐ G-ZEBS	ATR 42-320	066	ex F-HBSO	

BMI REGIONAL · Midland (BM/BMR) · Aberdeen/East Midlands-Nottingham (ABZ/EMA)

☐ G-EMBI	Embraer ERJ-145EP	145126	ex PT-SDG	
☐ G-EMBJ	Embraer ERJ-145MP	145134	ex PT-SDL	
☐ G-EMBN	Embraer ERJ-145EP	145201	ex PT-SGQ	
☐ G-RJXA	Embraer ERJ-145EP	145136	ex PT-SDP	
☐ G-RJXB	Embraer ERJ-145EP	145142	ex PT-SDS	
☐ G-RJXC	Embraer ERJ-145EP	145153	ex PT-SEE	

☐ G-RJXD	Embraer ERJ-145EP	145207	ex PT-SGX	
☐ G-RJXE	Embraer ERJ-145EP	145245	ex PT-SIJ	
☐ G-RJXF	Embraer ERJ-145EP	145280	ex PT-SJW	
☐ G-RJXG	Embraer ERJ-145EP	145390	ex PT-SQO	
☐ G-RJXH	Embraer ERJ-145EP	145442	ex PT-SUN	
☐ G-RJXI	Embraer ERJ-145EP	145454	ex PT-SUZ	>BEL
☐ G-RJXM	Embraer ERJ-145MP	145216	ex PH-RXA	
☐ G-RJXR	Embraer ERJ-145EP	145070	ex G-CCYH	
☐ G-RJXJ	Embraer ERJ-135ER	145473	ex PT-SVS	
☐ G-RJXK	Embraer ERJ-135ER	145494	ex PT-SXN	
☐ G-RJXL	Embraer ERJ-135ER	145376	ex PT-SQA	
☐ G-RJXP	Embraer ERJ-135ER	145431	ex G-CDFS	

BOND AIR SERVICES   Red Head (RHD)   Gloucestershire (GLO)

☐ G-BZRS	Eurocopter EC135T2+	0166	ex D-HECL	Polis Scotland
☐ G-CGPI	Eurocopter EC135T2+	0341	ex G-TAGG	Northern Lighthouse
☐ G-CGZD	Eurocopter EC135P2	0460	ex D-HHDL	East Anglian Air Ambulance
☐ G-CIDJ	Eurocopter EC135T2+	1010	ex 4X-AZ90	Scottish Air Ambulance♦
☐ G-DORS	Eurocopter EC135T2+	0517		Devon & Somerset Air Ambulance♦
☐ G-EMAA	Eurocopter EC135T2	0448		Midlands Air Ambulance
☐ G-GOWF	Eurocopter EC135T2+	0785		
☐ G-GWAA	Eurocopter EC135T2	0174	ex G-WMAS	Great Western Air Ambulance♦
☐ G-HBOB	Eurocopter EC135T2 ı	0664		Thames Valley & Chiltern Air Ambulance
☐ G-HEMC	Airbus Helicopters EC145T2	20012	ex D-HADM	East Anglian Air Ambulance♦
☐ G-HEMN	Eurocopter EC135T2+	1070		East Anglian Air Ambulance
☐ G-HWAA	Eurocopter EC135T2	0375		Midlands Air Ambulance
☐ G-KRNW	Eurocopter EC135T2	0175		Cornwall Air Ambulance
☐ G-NWAA	Eurocopter EC135T2	0427		North West Air Ambulance
☐ G-NWAE	Eurocopter EC135T2	0312	ex G-DAAT	North West Air Ambulance
☐ G-NWEM	Eurocopter EC135T2	0270	ex G-SSXX	North West Air Ambulance
☐ G-OMAA	Eurocopter EC135T2+	1144		owned by Midlands Air Ambulance
☐ G-SASA	Eurocopter EC135T2+	0147		Scottish Air Ambulance Service
☐ G-SASB	Eurocopter EC135T2+	0151		Scottish Air Ambulance Service
☐ G-SPHU	Eurocopter EC135T2+	0245	ex D-HKBA	Police Scotland
☐ G-WASC	Eurocopter EC135T2+	1074	ex D-HCBA	Wales Air Ambulance
☐ G-WASN	Eurocopter EC135T2+	0746		Wales Air Ambulance
☐ G-WASS	Eurocopter EC135T2+	0745		Wales Air Ambulance
☐ G-WONN	Eurocopter EC135T2+	0597		South & East Wales Police
☐ G-	Eurocopter EC135T2+	0274	ex OY-HPU	♦
☐ G-BUXS	MBB Bo.105DBS-4	S-41/913	ex G-PASA	
☐ G-CDBS	MBB Bo.105DBS-4	S-738	ex D-HDRZ	
☐ G-NDAA	MBB Bo.105DBS-4	S-135/914	ex G-WMAA	Great Western Air Ambulance
☐ G-NHAA	Aérospatiale AS365N2 Dauphin 2	6431	ex G-MLTY	Great North Air Ambulance♦
☐ G-NHAB	Aérospatiale AS365N2 Dauphin 2	6407	ex G-DAUF	Great North Air Ambulance♦
☐ G-NHAC	Aérospatiale AS365N2 Dauphin 2	6497	ex VP-BEO	Great North Air Ambulance♦
☐ G-SASS	MBB BK.117D2	20022	ex D-HCBT	Scottish Air Ambulance♦
☐ G-WAAS	MBB Bo.105DBS-4	S-138/911	ex G-ESAM	

BOND HELICOPTERS   Bond (BND)   Gloucestershire/Aberdeen (GLO/ABZ)

☐ G-REDJ	Aérospatiale AS332L2 II	2608	ex F-WWOJ	
☐ G-REDK	Aérospatiale AS332L2 II	2610	ex F-WWOM	
☐ G-REDM	Aérospatiale AS332L2 II	2614	ex F-WWOF	
☐ G-REDN	Aérospatiale AS332L2 II	2616	ex F-WQDH	
☐ G-REDO	Aérospatiale AS332L2 II	2622	ex F-WWOH	
☐ G-REDP	Aérospatiale AS332L2 II	2634	ex F-WWOB	
☐ G-REDR	Eurocopter EC225LP	2699		
☐ G-REDT	Eurocopter EC225LP	2701		
☐ G-REDV	Eurocopter EC225LP	2732		
☐ G-VINM	Eurocopter EC225LP	2942		
☐ G-PERA	AgustaWestland AW139	31322	ex N819JA	
☐ G-PERB	AgustaWestland AW139	41261	ex N389SH	
☐ G-PERD	AgustaWestland AW139	41270	ex LN-OEA	
☐ G-VINB	AgustaWestland AW139	31398		
☐ G-VINC	AgustaWestland AW139	31478		
☐ G-VINJ	AgustaWestland AW139	41355	ex N605SM	
☐ G-VIND	Sikorsky S-92A	920006	ex N192PH	♦
☐ G-VINF	Sikorsky S-92A	920008	ex N292PH	♦
☐ G-VING	Sikorsky S-92A	920207	ex N207RJ	♦
☐ G-VINK	Sikorsky S-92A	920223	ex N223P	♦
☐ G-VINL	Sikorsky S-92A	920226	ex N226Z	♦
☐ G-REDF	Eurocopter AS365N3 Dauphin 2	6884		
☐ G-REDG	Aérospatiale AS365N3 Dauphin 2	6907		
☐ G-REDH	Aérospatiale AS365N3 Dauphin 2	6911		

BRISTOW HELICOPTERS		Bristow (BHL)		Redhill/Aberdeen (KRH/ABZ)
☐ G-BLZJ	Aérospatiale AS332L	2123	ex LN-OMI	[ABZ]
☐ G-BMCX	Aérospatiale AS332L	2164	Lossiemouth	
☐ G-BRXU	Aérospatiale AS332L	2092	ex 5N-BGO	[NWI]
☐ G-BWMG	Aérospatiale AS332L	2046	ex 5N-BGP	wfs♦
☐ G-CGTJ	Aérospatiale AS332L	2488	ex 5N-BNU	wfs♦
☐ G-CGUB	Eurocopter EC225LP	2790	ex 9M-STH	
☐ G-TIGC	Aérospatiale AS332L	2024	ex (G-BJYH) Royal Burgh of Montrose	[ABZ]
☐ G-TIGE	Aérospatiale AS332L	2028	ex (G-BJYJ) City of Dundee	[NWI]
☐ G-TIGJ	Aérospatiale AS332L	2042	ex OB-2069-P	♦
☐ G-TIGS	Aérospatiale AS332L	2086	Findochty	[ABZ]
☐ G-ZZSA	Eurocopter EC225LP	2603	ex F-WWOJ	
☐ G-ZZSB	Eurocopter EC225LP	2615	ex F-WWOG	
☐ G-ZZSC	Eurocopter EC225LP	2654	ex F-WWOG	
☐ G-ZZSD	Eurocopter EC225LP	2658	ex F-WWOQ	
☐ G-ZZSE	Eurocopter EC225LP	2660	ex F-WWOJ	
☐ G-ZZSF	Eurocopter EC225LP	2662	ex F-WWOR	
☐ G-ZZSG	Eurocopter EC225LP	2714		
☐ G-ZZSI	Eurocopter EC225LP	2736	ex G-CGES	
☐ G-ZZSJ	Eurocopter EC225LP	2842		
☐ G-ZZSK	Eurocopter EC225LP	2849		
☐ G-ZZSL	Eurocopter EC225LP	2928		♦
☐ G-ZZSM	Eurocopter EC225LP	2937		♦
☐ G-CHNS	AgustaWestland AW139	31465		
☐ G-CHBY	AgustaWestland AW139	31310	ex OY-HLB	
☐ G-CIJW	AgustaWestland AW139	31571	ex I-EASS	♦
☐ G-CIJX	AgustaWestland AW139	31579		♦
☐ G-CIKO	AgustaWestland AW139	41378	ex N603SM	♦
☐ G-CIMU	AgustaWestland AW139	31583	ex N603SM	♦
☐ G-OENA	AgustaWestland AW189	47007	ex I-RAID	♦
☐ G-OENB	AgustaWestland AW189	49008		♦
☐ G-MCGM	AgustaWestland AW189	89001	ex I-EASN	opb Coastguard♦
☐ G-MCGN	AgustaWestland AW189	92001		opb Coastguard♦
☐ G-MCGO	AgustaWestland AW189			o/o♦
☐ G-MCGP	AgustaWestland AW189			o/o♦
☐ G-MCGR	AgustaWestland AW189			o/o♦
☐ G-MCGS	AgustaWestland AW189			o/o♦
☐ G-MCGT	AgustaWestland AW189			o/o♦
☐ G-MCGU	AgustaWestland AW189			o/o♦
☐ G-MCGV	AgustaWestland AW189			o/o♦
☐ G-MCGW	AgustaWestland AW189			o/o♦
☐ G-MCGX	AgustaWestland AW189			o/o♦
☐ G-MCGY	AgustaWestland AW189			o/o♦
☐ G-CFDV	Sikorsky S-76C++	760666	ex N45140	
☐ G-CGIW	Sikorsky S-76C+	760773	ex N773L	
☐ G-CGOU	Sikorsky S-76C+	760780	ex N20868	
☐ G-KAZA	Sikorsky S-76C+	760615	ex N81085	
☐ G-KAZB	Sikorsky S-76C+	760614	ex N8094S	
☐ G-CGYW	Sikorsky S-92A	920157	ex N157Q	
☐ G-CHHF	Sikorsky S-92A	920158	ex N158G	
☐ G-CHKI	Sikorsky S-92A	920175	ex N975F	
☐ G-CHMJ	Sikorsky S-92A	920178	ex N176U	
☐ G-CHYG	Sikorsky S-92A	920196	ex N196Q	
☐ G-CHYI	Sikorsky S-92A	920197	ex N197Y	♦
☐ G-CICH	Sikorsky S-92A	920209	ex N209X	
☐ C-CIGZ	Sikorsky S-92A	920224	ex N224XK	based Falklands♦
☐ G-CIHP	Sikorsky S-92A	920124	ex C-GKKN	based Falklands♦
☐ G-CIJC	Sikorsky S-92A	920240	ex N240E	♦
☐ G-GALC	Sikorsky S-92A	920200	ex N200BV	
☐ G-IACA	Sikorsky S-92A	920050	ex N81254	
☐ G-IACB	Sikorsky S-92A	920062	ex N4516G	
☐ G-IACC	Sikorsky S-92A	920063	ex N45158	
☐ G-IACD	Sikorsky S-92A	920065	ex N4515G Richard Enoch	
☐ G-IACE	Sikorsky S-92A	920066	ex N45148	
☐ G-IACF	Sikorsky S-92A	920068	ex N4509G	
☐ G-IACG	Sikorsky S-92A	920228	ex N228V	based Falklands♦
☐ G-IACG	Sikorsky S-92A	920228	ex N228V	♦
☐ G-MCGA	Sikorsky S-92A	920166	ex N166J	opb Coastguard
☐ G-MCGB	Sikorsky S-92A	920167	ex N167G	opb Coastguard
☐ G-MCGC	Sikorsky S-92A	920169	ex N169F Oscar Charlie	
☐ G-MCGD	Sikorsky S-92A	920171	ex N971E	
☐ G-MCGE	Sikorsky S-92A	920214	ex N214HM	opb Coastguard♦
☐ G-MCGF	Sikorsky S-92A	920222	ex N222XC	opb Coastguard♦
☐ G-MCGG	Sikorsky S-92A	920225	ex N225WK	opb Coastguard♦
☐ G-MCGH	Sikorsky S-92A	920234	ex N234TR	opb Coastguard♦
☐ G-MCGI	Sikorsky S-92A	920235	ex N235U	opb Coastguard♦
☐ G-MCGJ	Sikorsky S-92A	920248	ex N248N	o/o♦

☐ G-MCGK	Sikorsky S-92A	920251	ex N251Z		o/o♦
☐ G-XCII	Sikorsky S-92A	920174	ex N174X		
☐ G-BIMU	Sikorsky S-61N II	61752	ex N8511Z	Stac Pollaidh	SAR [NWI]
☐ G-BPWB	Sikorsky S-61N II	61822	ex EI-BHO	Portland Castle	SAR [NWI]
☐ G-ISSV	Eurocopter EC155 B1	6757			

BRITISH AIRWAYS   Speedbird (BA/BAW)   London-Heathrow/Gatwick & Manchester (LHR/LGW/MAN)

Member of oneWorld

☐ G-DBCA	Airbus A319-131	2098	ex D-AVYV	
☐ G-DBCB	Airbus A319-131	2188	ex D-AVYA	
☐ G-DBCC	Airbus A319-131	2194	ex D-AVYT	
☐ G-DBCD	Airbus A319-131	2389	ex D-AVYJ	
☐ G-DBCE	Airbus A319-131	2429	ex D-AVWG	
☐ G-DBCF	Airbus A319-131	2466	ex D-AVYA	
☐ G-DBCG	Airbus A319-131	2694	ex D-AVXD	
☐ G-DBCH	Airbus A319-131	2697	ex D-AVXE	
☐ G-DBCI	Airbus A319-131	2720	ex D-AVWC	
☐ G-DBCJ	Airbus A319-131	2981	ex D-AVXG	
☐ G-DBCK	Airbus A319-131	3049	ex D-AVYG	
☐ G-EUOA	Airbus A319-131	1513	ex D-AVYE	
☐ G-EUOB	Airbus A319-131	1529	ex D-AVWH	
☐ G-EUOC	Airbus A319-131	1537	ex D-AVYP	
☐ G-EUOD	Airbus A319-131	1558	ex D-AVYJ	
☐ G-EUOE	Airbus A319-131	1574	ex D-AVWF	
☐ G-EUOF	Airbus A319-131	1590	ex D-AVYW	
☐ G-EUOG	Airbus A319-131	1594	ex D-AVWU	
☐ G-EUOH	Airbus A319-131	1604	ex D-AVYM	
☐ G-EUOI	Airbus A319-131	1606	ex D-AVYN	
☐ G-EUPA	Airbus A319-131	1082	ex D-AVYK	
☐ G-EUPB	Airbus A319-131	1115	ex D-AVYT	
☐ G-EUPC	Airbus A319-131	1118	ex D-AVYU	The Firefly
☐ G-EUPD	Airbus A319-131	1142	ex D-AVWG	
☐ G-EUPE	Airbus A319-131	1193	ex D-AVYT	
☐ G-EUPF	Airbus A319-131	1197	ex D-AVWS	
☐ G-EUPG	Airbus A319-131	1222	ex D-AVYG	
☐ G-EUPH	Airbus A319-131	1225	ex D-AVYK	
☐ G-EUPJ	Airbus A319-131	1232	ex D-AVYJ	
☐ G-EUPK	Airbus A319-131	1236	ex D-AVYO	
☐ G-EUPL	Airbus A319-131	1239	ex D-AVYP	
☐ G-EUPM	Airbus A319-131	1258	ex D-AVYR	
☐ G-EUPN	Airbus A319-131	1261	ex D-AVWA	
☐ G-EUPO	Airbus A319-131	1279	ex D-AVYU	
☐ G-EUPP	Airbus A319-131	1295	ex D-AVWU	
☐ G-EUPR	Airbus A319-131	1329	ex D-AVYH	
☐ G-EUPS	Airbus A319-131	1338	ex D-AVYM	
☐ G-EUPT	Airbus A319-131	1380	ex D-AVWH	
☐ G-EUPU	Airbus A319-131	1384	ex D-AVWP	
☐ G-EUPV	Airbus A319-131	1423	ex D-AVYE	
☐ G-EUPW	Airbus A319-131	1440	ex D-AVYP	
☐ G-EUPX	Airbus A319-131	1445	ex D-AVWB	
☐ G-EUPY	Airbus A319-131	1466	ex D-AVYU	
☐ G-EUPZ	Airbus A319-131	1510	ex D-AVYY	
☐ G-EUUA	Airbus A320-232	1661	ex F-WWIH	
☐ G-EUUB	Airbus A320-232	1689	ex F-WWBE	
☐ G-EUUC	Airbus A320-232	1696	ex F-WWIO	
☐ G-EUUD	Airbus A320-232	1760	ex F-WWBN	
☐ G-EUUE	Airbus A320-232	1782	ex F-WWDO	
☐ G-EUUF	Airbus A320-232	1814	ex F-WWIY	
☐ G-EUUG	Airbus A320-232	1829	ex F-WWIU	
☐ G-EUUH	Airbus A320-232	1665	ex F-WWIG	
☐ G-EUUI	Airbus A320-232	1871	ex F-WWBI	
☐ G-EUUJ	Airbus A320-232	1883	ex F-WWBQ	
☐ G-EUUK	Airbus A320-232	1899	ex F-WWDO	
☐ G-EUUL	Airbus A320-232	1708	ex F-WWIV	
☐ G-EUUM	Airbus A320-232	1907	ex F-WWDN	
☐ G-EUUN	Airbus A320-232	1910	ex F-WWDP	
☐ G-EUUO	Airbus A320-232	1958	ex F-WWIT	
☐ G-EUUP	Airbus A320-232	2038	ex F-WWDB	
☐ G-EUUR	Airbus A320-232	2040	ex F-WWID	
☐ G-EUUS	Airbus A320-232	3301	ex F-WWIF	
☐ G-EUUT	Airbus A320-232	3314	ex F-WWIT	
☐ G-EUUU	Airbus A320-232	3351	ex F-WWID	
☐ G-EUUV	Airbus A320-232	3468	ex F-WWBO	
☐ G-EUUW	Airbus A320-232	3499	ex F-WWIN	
☐ G-EUUX	Airbus A320-232	3550	ex F-WWDM	
☐ G-EUUY	Airbus A320-232	3607	ex F-WWIC	
☐ G-EUUZ	Airbus A320-232	3649	ex F-WWDO	
☐ G-EUYA	Airbus A320-232	3697	ex F-WWBM	
☐ G-EUYB	Airbus A320-232	3703	ex F-WWBV	

☐ G-EUYC	Airbus A320-232	3721	ex F-WWBY	
☐ G-EUYD	Airbus A320-232	3726	ex F-WWDH	
☐ G-EUYE	Airbus A320-232	3912	ex F-WWBB	
☐ G-EUYF	Airbus A320-232	4185	ex F-WWIC	
☐ G-EUYG	Airbus A320-232	4238	ex F-WWDH	
☐ G-EUYH	Airbus A320-232	4265	ex F-WWBK	
☐ G-EUYI	Airbus A320-232	4306	ex F-WWIC	
☐ G-EUYJ	Airbus A320-232	4464	ex F-WWBQ	
☐ G-EUYK	Airbus A320-232	4551	ex F-WWBE	
☐ G-EUYL	Airbus A320-232	4725	ex F-WWDY	
☐ G-EUYM	Airbus A320-232	4791	ex F-WWIB	
☐ G-EUYN	Airbus A320-232	4975	ex F-WWDT	
☐ G-EUYO	Airbus A320-232/S	5634	ex F-WWDG	
☐ G-EUYP	Airbus A320-232/S	5784	ex F-WWIC	
☐ G-EUYR	Airbus A320-232/S	5856	ex F-WWBY	
☐ G-EUYS	Airbus A320-232/S	5948	ex F-WWDY	
☐ G-EUYT	Airbus A320-232/S	5985	ex F-WWIX	
☐ G-EUYU	Airbus A320-232/S	6028	ex F-WWDG	
☐ G-EUYV	Airbus A320-232/S	6091	ex F-WWDR	
☐ G-EUYW	Airbus A320-232/S	6129	ex F-WWDZ	
☐ G-EUYX	Airbus A320-232/S	6155	ex F-WWBM	
☐ G-EUYY	Airbus A320-232/S	6290	ex F-WWBB	
☐ G-GATH	Airbus A320-232	1482	ex OE-ICN	
☐ G-GATJ	Airbus A320-232	1509	ex OE-ICO	
☐ G-GATK	Airbus A320-232	1902	ex HA-LPD	
☐ G-GATL	Airbus A320-232	1834	ex HA-LPF	
☐ G-GATM	Airbus A320-232	1892	ex HA-LPE	
☐ G-GATN	Airbus A320-232	1613	ex OE-IDS	o/o
☐ G-GATO	Airbus A320-232	1663	ex OE-IDT	o/o
☐ G-GATP	Airbus A320-232	1804	ex OE-IDU	o/o
☐ G-GATS	Airbus A320-232	1672	ex OE-IDW	o/o
☐ G-GATR	Airbus A320-232	1771	ex PR-MAD	o/o
☐ G-MEDK	Airbus A320-232	2441	ex F-WWBQ	
☐ G-MIDO	Airbus A320-232	1987	ex F-WWIR	
☐ G-MIDS	Airbus A320-232	1424	ex F-WWBO	
☐ G-MIDT	Airbus A320-232	1418	ex F-WWBI	
☐ G-MIDX	Airbus A320-232	1177	ex F-WWDP	
☐ G-MIDY	Airbus A320-232	1014	ex F-WWDQ	
☐ G-TTOB	Airbus A320-232	1687	ex F-WWIM	
☐ G-TTOE	Airbus A320-232	1754	ex F-WWDH	
☐ G-EUXC	Airbus A321-231	2305	ex D-AVZE	
☐ G-EUXD	Airbus A321-231	2320	ex D-AVZO	
☐ G-EUXE	Airbus A321-231	2323	ex D-AVZP	
☐ G-EUXF	Airbus A321-231	2324	ex D-AVZQ	
☐ G-EUXG	Airbus A321-231	2351	ex D-AVZU	
☐ G-EUXH	Airbus A321-231	2363	ex D-AVZW	
☐ G-EUXI	Airbus A321-231	2536	ex D-AVZE	
☐ G-EUXJ	Airbus A321-231	3081	ex D-AVZL	
☐ G-EUXK	Airbus A321-231	3235	ex D-AVZI	
☐ G-EUXL	Airbus A321-231	3254	ex D-AVZV	
☐ G-EUXM	Airbus A321-231	3290	ex D-AVZC	
☐ G-MEDF	Airbus A321-231	1690	ex D-AVZX	
☐ G-MEDG	Airbus A321-231	1711	ex D-AVZK	
☐ G-MEDJ	Airbus A321-231	2190	ex D-AVZD	
☐ G-MEDL	Airbus A321-231	2653	ex D-AVZC	
☐ G-MEDM	Airbus A321-231	2799	ex D-AVZP	
☐ G-MEDN	Airbus A321-231	3512	ex D-AVZK	
☐ G-MEDU	Airbus A321-231	3926	ex D-AZAB	
☐ G-XLEA	Airbus A380-841	095	ex F-WWSK	
☐ G-XLEB	Airbus A380-841	121	ex F-WWAY	
☐ G-XLEC	Airbus A380-841	124	ex F-WWSC	
☐ G-XLED	Airbus A380-841	144	ex F-WWAK	
☐ G-XLEE	Airbus A380-841	148	ex F-WWAS	
☐ G-XLEF	Airbus A380-841	151	ex F-WWSI	
☐ G-XLEG	Airbus A380-841	161	ex F-WWSK	
☐ G-XLEH	Airbus A380-841	163	ex F-WWSM	
☐ G-XLEI	Airbus A380-841	173	ex F-WWSB	
☐ G-XLEJ	Airbus A380-841	192	ex F-WW	o/o♦
☐ G-XLEK	Airbus A380-841	194	ex F-WW	o/o♦
☐ G-XLEL	Airbus A380-841	215	ex F-WW	o/o♦
☐ G-DOCF	Boeing 737-436	25407/2178		
☐ G-DOCO	Boeing 737-436	25849/2381		
☐ G-DOCW	Boeing 737-436	25856/2422		
☐ G-DOCX	Boeing 737-436	25857/2451		
☐ G-GBTB	Boeing 737-436	25860/2545	ex OO-LTS	
☐ G-BNLF	Boeing 747-436	24048/773		
☐ G-BNLH	Boeing 747-436	24050/779	ex VH-NLH	[VCV]
☐ G-BNLJ	Boeing 747-436	24052/789	ex N60668	
☐ G-BNLK	Boeing 747-436	24053/790	ex N6009F	

☐ G-BNLN	Boeing 747-436	24056/802		
☐ G-BNLO	Boeing 747-436	24057/817		
☐ G-BNLP	Boeing 747-436	24058/828		
☐ G-BNLV	Boeing 747-436	25427/900		
☐ G-BNLW	Boeing 747-436	25432/903		
☐ G-BNLX	Boeing 747-436	25435/908		
☐ G-BNLY	Boeing 747-436	27090/959	ex N60659	
☐ G-BYGA	Boeing 747-436	28855/1190		
☐ G-BYGB	Boeing 747-436	28856/1194		
☐ G-BYGC	Boeing 747-436	25823/1195		
☐ G-BYGD	Boeing 747-436	28857/1196		
☐ G-BYGE	Boeing 747-436	28858/1198		
☐ G-BYGF	Boeing 747-436	25824/1200		
☐ G-BYGG	Boeing 747-436	28859/1212		
☐ G-CIVA	Boeing 747-436	27092/967		
☐ G-CIVB	Boeing 747-436	25811/1018		
☐ G-CIVC	Boeing 747-436	25812/1022		
☐ G-CIVD	Boeing 747-436	27349/1048	oneWorld c/s	
☐ G-CIVE	Boeing 747-436	27350/1050		
☐ G-CIVF	Boeing 747-436	25434/1058	ex (G-BNLY)	wfs
☐ G-CIVG	Boeing 747-436	25813/1059	ex N6009F	
☐ G-CIVH	Boeing 747-436	25809/1078		
☐ G-CIVI	Boeing 747-436	25814/1079		
☐ G-CIVJ	Boeing 747-436	25817/1102		
☐ G-CIVK	Boeing 747-436	25818/1104		
☐ G-CIVL	Boeing 747-436	27478/1108		
☐ G-CIVM	Boeing 747-436	28700/1116	oneWorld c/s	
☐ G-CIVN	Boeing 747-436	28848/1129		
☐ G-CIVO	Boeing 747-436	28849/1135	ex N6046P	
☐ G-CIVP	Boeing 747-436	28850/1144		
☐ G-CIVR	Boeing 747-436	25820/1146		
☐ G-CIVS	Boeing 747-436	28851/1148		
☐ G-CIVT	Boeing 747-436	25821/1149		
☐ G-CIVU	Boeing 747-436	25810/1154		
☐ G-CIVV	Boeing 747-436	25819/1156	ex N6009F	
☐ G-CIVW	Boeing 747-436	25822/1157		
☐ G-CIVX	Boeing 747-436	28852/1172		
☐ G-CIVY	Boeing 747-436	28853/1178		
☐ G-CIVZ	Boeing 747-436	28854/1183		
☐ G-BNWA	Boeing 767-336ER	24333/265	ex N6009F	
☐ G-BNWB	Boeing 767-336ER	24334/281	ex N6046P	
☐ G-BNWI	Boeing 767-336ER	24341/342		
☐ G-BNWM	Boeing 767-336ER	25204/376		
☐ G-BNWS	Boeing 767-336ER	25826/473	ex N6018N	
☐ G-BNWT	Boeing 767-336ER	25828/476		
☐ G-BNWV	Boeing 767-336ER	27140/490		
☐ G-BNWW	Boeing 767-336ER	25831/526		[LHR]
☐ G-BNWX	Boeing 767-336ER	25832/529		
☐ G-BNWY	Boeing 767-336ER	25834/608	ex N5005C	
☐ G-BNWZ	Boeing 767-336ER	25733/648		
☐ G-BZHA	Boeing 767-336ER	29230/702		
☐ G-BZHB	Boeing 767-336ER	29231/704		
☐ G-BZHC	Boeing 767-336ER	29232/708		
☐ G-RAES	Boeing 777-236ER	27491/76	ex (G-ZZZP)	
☐ G-VIIA	Boeing 777-236ER	27483/41	ex N5022E	
☐ G-VIIB	Boeing 777-236ER	27484/49	ex (G-ZZZG)	
☐ G-VIIC	Boeing 777-236ER	27485/53	ex (G-ZZZH)	
☐ G-VIID	Boeing 777-236ER	27486/56	ex (G-ZZZI)	
☐ G-VIIE	Boeing 777-236ER	27487/58	ex (G-ZZZJ)	
☐ G-VIIF	Boeing 777-236ER	27488/61	ex (G-ZZZK)	
☐ G-VIIG	Boeing 777-236ER	27489/65	ex (G-ZZZL)	
☐ G-VIIH	Boeing 777-236ER	27490/70	ex (G-ZZZM)	
☐ G-VIIJ	Boeing 777-236ER	27492/111	ex (G-ZZZN)	
☐ G-VIIK	Boeing 777-236ER	28840/117		
☐ G-VIIL	Boeing 777-236ER	27493/127		
☐ G-VIIM	Boeing 777-236ER	28841/130		
☐ G-VIIN	Boeing 777-236ER	29319/157		
☐ G-VIIO	Boeing 777-236ER	29320/182		
☐ G-VIIP	Boeing 777-236ER	29321/193		
☐ G-VIIR	Boeing 777-236ER	29322/203		
☐ G-VIIS	Boeing 777-236ER	29323/206		
☐ G-VIIT	Boeing 777-236ER	29962/217		
☐ G-VIIU	Boeing 777-236ER	29963/221		
☐ G-VIIV	Boeing 777-236ER	29964/228		
☐ G-VIIW	Boeing 777-236ER	29965/233		
☐ G-VIIX	Boeing 777-236ER	29966/236		
☐ G-VIIY	Boeing 777-236ER	29967/251		
☐ G-YMMA	Boeing 777-236ER	30302/242	ex N5017Q	
☐ G-YMMB	Boeing 777-236ER	30303/265		
☐ G-YMMC	Boeing 777-236ER	30304/268		
☐ G-YMMD	Boeing 777-236ER	30305/269		

☐ G-YMME	Boeing 777-236ER	30306/275		
☐ G-YMMF	Boeing 777-236ER	30307/281		
☐ G-YMMG	Boeing 777-236ER	30308/301		
☐ G-YMMH	Boeing 777-236ER	30309/303		
☐ G-YMMI	Boeing 777-236ER	30310/308		
☐ G-YMMJ	Boeing 777-236ER	30311/311		
☐ G-YMMK	Boeing 777-236ER	30312/312		
☐ G-YMML	Boeing 777-236ER	30313/334		
☐ G-YMMN	Boeing 777-236ER	30316/346		
☐ G-YMMO	Boeing 777-236ER	30317/361		
☐ G-YMMP	Boeing 777-236ER	30315/369		
☐ G-YMMR	Boeing 777-236ER	36516/771	ex N5014K	
☐ G-YMMS	Boeing 777-236ER	36517/784		
☐ G-YMMT	Boeing 777-236ER	36518/791		
☐ G-YMMU	Boeing 777-236ER	36519/796	ex N6009F	
☐ G-ZZZA	Boeing 777-236	27105/6	ex N77779	
☐ G-ZZZB	Boeing 777-236	27106/10	ex N77771	
☐ G-ZZZC	Boeing 777-236	27107/15	ex N5014K	
☐ G-STBA	Boeing 777-336ER	40542/879		
☐ G-STBB	Boeing 777-36NER	39286/887		
☐ G-STBC	Boeing 777-36NER	39287/901	ex N6018N	
☐ G-STBD	Boeing 777-36NER	38695/968		
☐ G-STBE	Boeing 777-36NER	38696/980		
☐ G-STBF	Boeing 777-336ER	40543/995		
☐ G-STBG	Boeing 777-336ER	38430/1135		
☐ G-STBH	Boeing 777-336ER	38431/1143		
☐ G-STBI	Boeing 777-336ER	43702/1171		
☐ G-STBJ	Boeing 777-336ER	43703/1182		
☐ G-STBK	Boeing 777-336ER	42121/1204		
☐ G-STBL	Boeing 777-336ER	42124/1221		
☐ G-ZBJA	Boeing 787-8	38609/108		
☐ G-ZBJB	Boeing 787-8	38610/111		
☐ G-ZBJC	Boeing 787-8	38611/114		
☐ G-ZBJD	Boeing 787-8	38619/121		
☐ G-ZBJE	Boeing 787-8	38612/173		
☐ G-ZBJF	Boeing 787-8	38613/177		
☐ G-ZBJG	Boeing 787-8	38614/187		
☐ G-ZBJH	Boeing 787-8	38615/197		
☐ G-ZBKA	Boeing 787-9	38616/346		o/o♦
☐ G-ZBKB	Boeing 787-9	38617/357		o/o♦
☐ G-ZBKC	Boeing 787-9	38621/360		o/o♦
☐ G-ZBKD	Boeing 787-9	38618/361		o/o♦
☐ G-ZBKE	Boeing 787-9	38620/374		o/o♦
☐ G-ZBKF	Boeing 787-9	38622/392		o/o♦
☐ G-ZBKG	Boeing 787-9	38623/396		o/o♦
☐ G-ZBKH	Boeing 787-9	38624/404		o/o♦
☐ G-ZBKI	Boeing 787-9	38625/406		o/o♦
☐ G-	Boeing 787-9	38626/		o/o
☐ G-	Boeing 787-9	38627/		o/o
☐ G-	Boeing 787-9	38628/		o/o
☐ G-	Boeing 787-9	38629/		o/o
☐ G-	Boeing 787-9	38630/		o/o
☐ G-	Boeing 787-9	38631/		o/o
☐ G-	Boeing 787-9	38632/		o/o
☐ G-EUNA	Airbus A318-112	4007	ex D-AUAC	
☐ G-EUNB	Airbus A318-112	4039	ex D-AUAF	

BRITISH INTERNATIONAL		**Brintel (BS/BIH)**		**Newquay (NQY)**
☐ G-ATBJ	Sikorsky S-61N	61269	ex N10043	based Falklands
☐ G-ATFM	Sikorsky S-61N	61270	ex CF-OKY	
☐ G-BFRI	Sikorsky S-61N II	61809		
☐ G-BTKL	MBB Bo105DB-4	S-422	ex D-HDMU	♦

CHC SCOTIA HELICOPTERS				**Aberdeen (ABZ)**
☐ G-BKZE	Aérospatiale AS332L	2102	ex F-WKQE	based Rzeszow
☐ G-CHCF	Aérospatiale AS332L2	2567		
☐ G-CHCG	Aérospatiale AS332L2	2592		
☐ G-CHCH	Aérospatiale AS332L2	2601		
☐ G-CHCI	Aérospatiale AS322L	2395	ex LN-OHD	based Rzeszow
☐ G-CHCJ	Eurocopter EC225LP	2745		
☐ G-CHCL	Eurocopter EC225LP	2674	ex F-WWOS	
☐ G-CHCM	Eurocopter EC225LP	2675	ex F-WWOV	
☐ G-CHCU	Aérospatiale AS332L2	2617	ex LN-OHL	based Rzeszow
☐ G-JENZ	Eurocopter EC225LP	2902		
☐ G-OAGA	Aérospatiale AS332LP	2878		

☐ G-OAGC	Aérospatiale AS332LP	2890			
☐ G-OAGD	Eurocopter EC225LP	2902	ex G-JENZ		♦
☐ G-OAGE	Eurocopter EC225LP	2949			♦
☐ G-PUMB	Aérospatiale AS332L1	2075	ex VH-LYS		
☐ G-PUMM	Aérospatiale AS332L2	2477	ex LN-OHM		
☐ G-PUMN	Aérospatiale AS332L2	2484	ex LN-OHF	<HKS based Rzeszow	
☐ G-PUMO	Aérospatiale AS332L2	2467			
☐ G-WNSN	Aérospatiale AS332LP	2688	ex VH-WEQ		
☐ G-WNSO	Eurocopter EC225LP	2681	ex PR-CHV		
☐ G-WNSP	Aérospatiale AS332LP	2707	ex 9M-AIT		
☐ G-CGIJ	AgustaWestland AW139	31203		opf Coastguard	
☐ G-CGWB	AgustaWestland AW139	31209		opf Coastguard	
☐ G-CHCV	AgustaWestland AW139	41005	ex UP-AW907		
☐ G-JEZA	AgustaWestland AW139	31255			
☐ G-SARD	AgustaWestland AW139	31208		opf Coastguard	
☐ G-SNSA	AgustaWestland AW139	31308	ex I-RAIQ		
☐ G-SNSB	AgustaWestland AW139	31295	ex PH-EUD		
☐ G-SNSE	AgustaWestland AW139	31561			♦
☐ G-CHCK	Sikorsky S-92A	920030	ex N8001N		
☐ G-CHCS	Sikorsky S-92A	920125	ex N2133X		
☐ G-WNSD	Sikorsky S-92A	920231	ex N231Y		♦
☐ G-WNSE	Sikorsky S-92A	920190	ex N190V		
☐ G-WNSG	Sikorsky S-92A	920058	ex OY-HKB		
☐ G-WNSI	Sikorsky S-92A	920024	ex 9M-AII I		♦
☐ G-WNSJ	Sikorsky S-92A	920185	ex N985X		
☐ G-WNSL	Sikorsky S-92A	920241			♦
☐ G-WNSM	Sikorsky S-92A	920237	ex N237MW		♦
☐ G-BTEU	Aérospatiale SA365N2 Dauphin 2	6392		Great North Air Ambulance	
☐ G-BTNC	Aérospatiale SA365N2 Dauphin 2	6409			
☐ G-CHCP	Agusta Bell AB139	31046	ex PH-IEH		
☐ G-CHCT	Agusta Bell AB139	31042	ex PH-TRH		

CITYWING   (V2)   Ronaldsway (IOM)

☐ OK-ASA	LET L-410UVP-E	902439	ex SP-KPY	Lsd fr/op by Van Air	
☐ OK-LAZ	LET L-410 UVP-E	902504	ex HA-LAZ	Lsd fr/opb Van Air♦	
☐ OK-RDA	LET L-410UVP-E	861813	ex HA-YFG	Lsd fr/opb Van Air	
☐ OK-TCA	LET L-410UVP-E	902431	ex SP-KPZ	Lsd fr/opb Van Air	
☐ OK-UBA	LET L-410UVP-E	892319	ex SP-TXA	Lsd fr/opb Van Air♦	
☐ G-GAVA	British Aerospace Jetstream 3102	785	ex G-CCPW	>LNQ dam 15Aug14♦	

DHL AIR   World Express (D0/DHK)   East Midlands-Nottingham/Brussels (EMA/BRU)

☐ G-BIKC	Boeing 757-236SF	22174/11			
☐ G-BIKF	Boeing 757-236SF	22177/16			
☐ G-BIKG	Boeing 757-236SF	22178/23			
☐ G-BIKI	Boeing 757-236SF	22180/25	ex OO-DLO		
☐ G-BIKJ	Boeing 757-236SF	22181/29			
☐ G-BIKK	Boeing 757-236SF	22182/30			
☐ G-BIKM	Boeing 757-236SF	22184/33	ex N8293V		
☐ G-BIKO	Boeing 757-236SF	22187/52			
☐ G-BIKP	Boeing 757-236SF	22188/54			
☐ G-BIKU	Boeing 757-236SF	23399/78			
☐ G-BIKV	Boeing 757-236SF	23400/81			
☐ G-BIKZ	Boeing 757-236SF	23532/98			
☐ G-BMRA	Boeing 757-236SF	23710/123			
☐ G-BMRB	Boeing 757-236SF	23975/145			
☐ G-BMRC	Boeing 757-236SF	24072/160			
☐ G-BMRD	Boeing 757-236SF	24073/166			
☐ G-BMRE	Boeing 757-236SF	24074/168			
☐ G-BMRF	Boeing 757-236SF	24101/175			
☐ G-BMRG	Boeing 757-236SF	24102/179	ex A9C-DHF		♦
☐ G-BMRH	Boeing 757-236SF	24266/210			
☐ G-BMRI	Boeing 757-236SF	24267/211	ex VT-BDK	<BDA♦	
☐ G-BMRJ	Boeing 757-236SF	24268/214			
☐ G-FCLD	Boeing 757-25PCF	28718/752	ex C-GJZX	>BDA♦	
☐ G-DHLE	Boeing 767-3JHF/W	37805/980			
☐ G-DHLF	Boeing 767-3JHF/W	37806/981			
☐ G-DHLG	Boeing 767-3JHF/W	37807/982			
☐ G-DHLH	Boeing 767-3JHF/W	37808/1036			
☐ G-DHLJ	Boeing 767-3JHF/W	37809/1039		>GTI	
☐ G-DHLK	Boeing 767-3JHF/W	37810/1041		>GTI	

DIRECT FLIGHT   (DCT)   Cranfield/Exeter (-/EXT)

☐ G-LUXE	British Aerospace 146 Srs.301	E3001	ex G-5-300	Atmospheric Research, opf FAAM	
☐ G-MAFA	Reims Cessna F406 Caravan II	F406-0036	ex G-DFLT	opf DEFRA	

☐ G-MAFB	Reims Cessna F406 Caravan II	F406-0080	ex F-WWSR	opf DEFRA
☐ G-SICA	Britten-Norman BN-2B-20 Islander	2304	ex G-SLAP	opf Shetland Islands Council
☐ G-SICB	Britten-Norman BN-2B-20 Islander	2260	ex G-NESU	opf Shetland Islands Council

EASTERN AIRWAYS — Eastflight (T3/EZE) — Humberside (HUY)

☐ G-MAJA	British Aerospace Jetstream 41	41032	ex G-4-032	
☐ G-MAJB	British Aerospace Jetstream 41	41018	ex G-BVKT	
☐ G-MAJC	British Aerospace Jetstream 41	41005	ex G-LOGJ	
☐ G-MAJD	British Aerospace Jetstream 41	41006	ex G-WAWR	
☐ G-MAJE	British Aerospace Jetstream 41	41007	ex G-LOGK	
☐ G-MAJF	British Aerospace Jetstream 41	41008	ex G-WAWL	
☐ G-MAJG	British Aerospace Jetstream 41	41009	ex G-LOGL	
☐ G-MAJH	British Aerospace Jetstream 41	41010	ex G-WAYR	
☐ G-MAJI	British Aerospace Jetstream 41	41011	ex G-WAND	
☐ G-MAJJ	British Aerospace Jetstream 41	41024	ex G-WAFT	
☐ G-MAJK	British Aerospace Jetstream 41	41070	ex SX-SEB	
☐ G-MAJL	British Aerospace Jetstream 41	41087	ex G-4-087	
☐ G-MAJT	British Aerospace Jetstream 41	41040	ex SX-SEC	
☐ G-MAJU	British Aerospace Jetstream 41	41071	ex N558HK	
☐ G-MAJW	British Aerospace Jetstream 41	41015	ex N303UE	
☐ G-MAJY	British Aerospace Jetstream 41	41099	ex N331UE	
☐ G-MAJZ	British Aerospace Jetstream 41	41100	ex N332UE	
☐ G-CDEA	SAAB 2000	2000-009	ex SE-009	
☐ G-CDEB	SAAB 2000	2000-036	ex SE-036	
☐ G-CDKA	SAAB 2000	2000-006	ex SE-006	BAW c/s
☐ G-CDKB	SAAB 2000	2000-032	ex SE-032	
☐ G-CERY	SAAB 2000	2000-008	ex D-AOLA	
☐ G-CERZ	SAAB 2000	2000-042	ex SE-LSA	>CFE
☐ G-CFLU	SAAB 2000	2000-055	ex SE-LSG	
☐ G-CFLV	SAAB 2000	2000-023	ex SE-023	
☐ G-CIEC	SAAB 2000	2000-037	ex HB-IZU	
☐ G-CGMB	Embraer ERJ-135ER	145189	ex F-GOHA	
☐ G-CGMC	Embraer ERJ-135ER	145198	ex F-GOHB	
☐ G-CGWV	Embraer ERJ-145MP	145362	ex F-GIJG	
☐ G-CHMR	Embraer ERJ-145MP	145405	ex OE-IAM	

EASYJET — Easy (U2/EZY) — London-Luton (LTN)

☐ G-EJAR	Airbus A319-111	2412	ex D-AVWH	Change for Good
☐ G-EZAA	Airbus A319-111	2677	ex D-AVYU	
☐ G-EZAB	Airbus A319-111	2681	ex D-AVYY	
☐ G-EZAC	Airbus A319-111	2691	ex D-AVXB	
☐ G-EZAD	Airbus A319-111	2702	ex D-AVXI	
☐ G-EZAF	Airbus A319-111	2715	ex D-AVYT	
☐ G-EZAG	Airbus A319-111	2727	ex D-AVXG	
☐ G-EZAI	Airbus A319-111	2735	ex D-AVXM	
☐ G-EZAJ	Airbus A319-111	2742	ex D-AVXP	
☐ G-EZAK	Airbus A319-111	2744	ex D-AVXQ	
☐ G-EZAL	Airbus A319-111	2754	ex D-AVWG	
☐ G-EZAM	Airbus A319-111	2037	ex HB-JZA	
☐ G-EZAN	Airbus A319-111	2765	ex D-AVWL	
☐ G-EZAO	Airbus A319-111	2769	ex D-AVWO	
☐ G-EZAP	Airbus A319-111	2777	ex D-AVYG	
☐ G-EZAS	Airbus A319-111	2779	ex D-AVYH	
☐ G-EZAT	Airbus A319-111	2782	ex D-AVYO	
☐ G-EZAU	Airbus A319-111	2795	ex D-AVWQ	
☐ G-EZAV	Airbus A319-111	2803	ex D-AVWV	
☐ G-EZAW	Airbus A319-111	2812	ex D-AVYU	
☐ G-EZAX	Airbus A319-111	2818	ex D-AVXA	
☐ G-EZAY	Airbus A319-111	2827	ex D-AVXE	
☐ G-EZAZ	Airbus A319-111	2829	ex D-AVXF	
☐ G-EZBA	Airbus A319-111	2860	ex D-AVWB	
☐ G-EZBB	Airbus A319-111	2854	ex D-AVXM	
☐ G-EZBC	Airbus A319-111	2866	ex D-AVWD	
☐ G-EZBD	Airbus A319-111	2873	ex D-AVWK	
☐ G-EZBE	Airbus A319-111	2884	ex D-AVXO	
☐ G-EZBF	Airbus A319-111	2923	ex D-AVYK	Inverness
☐ G-EZBG	Airbus A319-111	2946	ex D-AVXA	
☐ G-EZBH	Airbus A319-111	2959	ex D-AVXH	
☐ G-EZBI	Airbus A319-111	3003	ex D-AVYB	Romeo Alpha Juliet
☐ G-EZBJ	Airbus A319-111	3036	ex D-AVWJ	
☐ G-EZBK	Airbus A319-111	3041	ex D-AVWK	
☐ G-EZBL	Airbus A319-111	3053	ex D-AVYJ	
☐ G-EZBM	Airbus A319-111	3059	ex D-AVWE	Edinburgh
☐ G-EZBN	Airbus A319-111	3061	ex D-AVWH	
☐ G-EZBO	Airbus A319-111	3082	ex D-AVYK	
☐ G-EZBR	Airbus A319-111	3088	ex D-AVYY	
☐ G-EZBT	Airbus A319-111	3090	ex D-AVWM	
☐ G-EZBU	Airbus A319-111	3118	ex D-AVWW	

□	G-EZBV	Airbus A319-111	3122	ex D-AVWX	
□	G-EZBW	Airbus A319-111	3134	ex D-AVXE	
□	G-EZBX	Airbus A319-111	3137	ex D-AVXH	
□	G-EZBY	Airbus A319-111	3176	ex D-AVXJ	
□	G-EZBZ	Airbus A319-111	3184	ex D-AVYF	
□	G-EZDA	Airbus A319-111	3413	ex D-AVYH	
□	G-EZDB	Airbus A319-111	3411	ex D-AVYF	
□	G-EZDC	Airbus A319-111	2043	ex HB-JZB	
□	G-EZDD	Airbus A319-111	3442	ex D-AVYL	
□	G-EZDE	Airbus A319-111	3426	ex D-AVYP	
□	G-EZDF	Airbus A319-111	3432	ex D-AVYG	Spirit of easyJet 2014 James Baron
□	G-EZDH	Airbus A319-111	3466	ex D-AVWM	
□	G-EZDI	Airbus A319-111	3537	ex D-AVWC	
□	G-EZDJ	Airbus A319-111	3544	ex D-AVWJ	
□	G-EZDK	Airbus A319-111	3555	ex D-AVWP	
□	G-EZDL	Airbus A319-111	3569	ex D-AVWT	
□	G-EZDM	Airbus A319-111	3571	ex D-AVWU	Porto
□	G-EZDN	Airbus A319-111	3608	ex D-AVYJ	Amsterdam
□	G-EZDO	Airbus A319-111	3634	ex D-AVYP	
□	G-EZDP	Airbus A319-111	3675	ex D-AVYX	
□	G-EZDR	Airbus A319-111	3683	ex D-AVYZ	Keri Emerton
□	G-EZDS	Airbus A319-111	3702	ex D-AVWP	Christian Casella
□	G-EZDT	Airbus A319-111	3720	ex D-AVWR	
□	G-EZDU	Airbus A319-111	3735	ex D-AVWX	
□	G-EZDV	Airbus A319-111	3742	ex D-AVWY	
□	G-EZDW	Airbus A319-111	3746	ex D-AVXA	
□	G-EZDX	Airbus A319-111	3754	ex D-AVXB	
□	G-EZDY	Airbus A319-111	3763	ex D-AVXF	
□	G-EZDZ	Airbus A319-111	3774	ex D-AVXI	
□	G-EZEB	Airbus A319-111	2120	ex D-AVYK	
□	G-EZED	Airbus A319-111	2170	ex D-AVWT	
□	G-EZEG	Airbus A319-111	2181	ex D-AVWF	
□	G-EZEN	Airbus A319-111	2245	ex HB-JZI	♦
□	G-EZEV	Airbus A319-111	2289	ex D-AVYV	
□	G-EZEW	Airbus A319-111	2300	ex D-AVWH	
□	G-EZEZ	Airbus A319-111	2360	ex D-AVWP	
□	G-EZFA	Airbus A319-111	3788	ex D-AVXK	
□	G-EZFB	Airbus A319-111	3799	ex D-AVXN	
□	G-EZFC	Airbus A319-111	3808	ex D-AVYC	
□	G-EZFD	Airbus A319-111	3810	ex D-AVYF	
□	G-EZFE	Airbus A319-111	3824	ex D-AVYI	
□	G-EZFF	Airbus A319-111	3844	ex D-AVYT	
□	G-EZFG	Airbus A319-111	3845	ex D-AVYU	
□	G-EZFH	Airbus A319-111	3854	ex D-AVWA	
□	G-EZFI	Airbus A319-111	3888	ex D-AVWH	
□	G-EZFJ	Airbus A319-111	4040	ex D-AVYM	
□	G-EZFK	Airbus A319-111	4048	ex D-AVYP	
□	G-EZFL	Airbus A319-111	4056	ex D-AVYS	
□	G-EZFM	Airbus A319-111	4069	ex D-AVYT	
□	G-EZFN	Airbus A319-111	4076	ex D-AVYV	
□	G-EZFO	Airbus A319-111	4080	ex D-AVYW	Mandy Efthimiadis
□	G-EZFP	Airbus A319-111	4087	ex D-AVYX	
□	G-EZFR	Airbus A319-111	4125	ex D-AVWC	
□	G-EZFS	Airbus A319-111	4129	ex D-AVWE	
□	G-EZFT	Airbus A319-111	4132	ex D-AVWF	Sir George White
□	G-EZFU	Airbus A319-111	4313	ex D-AVXC	
□	G-EZFV	Airbus A319-111	4327	ex D-AVXE	
□	G-EZFW	Airbus A319-111	4380	ex D-AVYQ	
□	G-EZFX	Airbus A319-111	4385	ex D-AVYS	
□	G-EZFY	Airbus A319-111	4418	ex D-AVXJ	
□	G-EZFZ	Airbus A319-111	4425	ex D-AVXL	
□	G-EZGA	Airbus A319-111	4427	ex D-AVXM	
□	G-EZGB	Airbus A319-111	4437	ex D-AVXO	
□	G-EZGC	Airbus A319-111	4444	ex D-AVXP	
□	G-EZGD	Airbus A319-111	4451	ex D-AVYA	
□	G-EZGE	Airbus A319-111	4624	ex D-AVWK	
□	G-EZGF	Airbus A319-111	4635	ex D-AVWO	
□	G-EZGG	Airbus A319-111	4640	ex D-AVWP	
□	G-EZGH	Airbus A319-111	4667	ex D-AVYM	
□	G-EZGI	Airbus A319-111	4693	ex D-AVYP	
□	G-EZGJ	Airbus A319-111	4705	ex D-AVYR	
□	G-EZGK	Airbus A319-111	4717	ex D-AVYT	
□	G-EZGL	Airbus A319-111	4744	ex D-AVYB	
□	G-EZIB	Airbus A319-111	2427	ex HB-JZP	♦
□	G-EZIH	Airbus A319-111	2463	ex D-AVWV	
□	G-EZII	Airbus A319-111	2471	ex D-AVYK	
□	G-EZIJ	Airbus A319-111	2477	ex D-AVYU	
□	G-EZIK	Airbus A319-111	2481	ex D-AVYV	
□	G-EZIL	Airbus A319-111	2492	ex D-AVWM	Spirit of easyJet
□	G-EZIM	Airbus A319-111	2495	ex D-AVYO	
□	G-EZIN	Airbus A319-111	2503	ex D-AVYZ	
□	G-EZIO	Airbus A319-111	2512	ex D-AVWP	
□	G-EZIP	Airbus A319-111	2514	ex D-AVWQ	

☐ G-EZIR	Airbus A319-111	2527	ex D-AVWK	
☐ G-EZIS	Airbus A319-111	2528	ex D-AVWJ	
☐ G-EZIT	Airbus A319-111	2538	ex D-AVYN	
☐ G-EZIV	Airbus A319-111	2565	ex D-AVYY	
☐ G-EZIW	Airbus A319-111	2578	ex D-AVXE	Linate-Fiumicino Per Tutti c/s
☐ G-EZIX	Airbus A319-111	2605	ex D-AVXP	
☐ G-EZIY	Airbus A319-111	2636	ex D-AVWH	Discover Scotland
☐ G-EZIZ	Airbus A319-111	2646	ex D-AVWQ	
☐ G-EZMH	Airbus A319-111	2053	ex HB-JZD	
☐ G-EZNC	Airbus A319-111	2050	ex HB-JZC	
☐ G-EZPG	Airbus A319-111	2385	ex D-AVYD	
☐ G-EZSM	Airbus A319-111	2062	ex HB-JZE	
☐ G-EZOA	Airbus A320-214/S	6412	ex D-AXAM	♦
☐ G-EZOB	Airbus A320-214/S	6416	ex D-AXAO	♦
☐ G-EZOC	Airbus A320-214/S	6485	ex D-AXAW	♦
☐ G-EZOD	Airbus A320-214/S	6502	ex	♦
☐ G-EZOE	Airbus A320-214/S	6509	ex D-AXAY	♦
☐ G-EZOF	Airbus A320-214/S	6525	ex D-AVVC	♦
☐ G-EZTA	Airbus A320-214	3805	ex D-AVVD	
☐ G-EZTB	Airbus A320-214	3843	ex F-WWBO	
☐ G-EZTC	Airbus A320-214	3871	ex F-WWIG	
☐ G-EZTD	Airbus A320-214	3909	ex D-AVVB	
☐ G-EZTE	Airbus A320-214	3913	ex D-AVVF	
☐ G-EZTF	Airbus A320-214	3922	ex D-AVVG	
☐ G-EZTG	Airbus A320-214	3946	ex D-AVVJ	
☐ G-EZTH	Airbus A320-214	3953	ex D-AVVM	
☐ G-EZTI	Airbus A320-214	3975	ex D-AVVN	
☐ G-EZTJ	Airbus A320-214	3979	ex D-AVVO	
☐ G-EZTK	Airbus A320-214	3991	ex D-AVVP	
☐ G-EZTL	Airbus A320-214	4012	ex D-AVVC	
☐ G-EZTM	Airbus A320-214	4014	ex D-AVVD	
☐ G-EZTR	Airbus A320-214	4179	ex D-AVVX	
☐ G-EZTT	Airbus A320-214	4219	ex D-AVVM	
☐ G-EZTV	Airbus A320-214	4234	ex F-WWBZ	
☐ G-EZTX	Airbus A320-214	4286	ex F-WWIR	
☐ G-EZTY	Airbus A320-214	4543	ex D-AUBS	
☐ G-EZTZ	Airbus A320-214	4556	ex D-AUBW	
☐ G-EZUA	Airbus A320-214	4588	ex D-AVVE	
☐ G-EZUC	Airbus A320-214	4591	ex D-AVVF	
☐ G-EZUD	Airbus A320-214	4636	ex D-AXAZ	
☐ G-EZUF	Airbus A320-214	4676	ex D-AXAG	
☐ G-EZUG	Airbus A320-214	4680	ex D-AXAH	
☐ G-EZUH	Airbus A320-214	4708	ex D-AUBG	
☐ G-EZUI	Airbus A320-214	4721	ex D-AUBI	
☐ G-EZUJ	Airbus A320-214	4740	ex D-AVVI	
☐ G-EZUK	Airbus A320-214	4749	ex D-AVVL	
☐ G-EZUL	Airbus A320-214	5019	ex D-AXAH	
☐ G-EZUM	Airbus A320-214	5020	ex D-AXAI	
☐ G-EZUN	Airbus A320-214	5046	ex D-AXAN	
☐ G-EZUO	Airbus A320-214	5052	ex D-AUBA	
☐ G-EZUP	Airbus A320-214	5056	ex D-AUBB	
☐ G-EZUR	Airbus A320-214	5064	ex D-AUBD	
☐ G-EZUS	Airbus A320-214	5104	ex D-AUBS	
☐ G-EZUT	Airbus A320-214	5113	ex D-AUBW	
☐ G-EZUW	Airbus A320-214	5116	ex D-AUBY	
☐ G-EZUZ	Airbus A320-214	5187	ex D-AXAV	
☐ G-EZWA	Airbus A320-214	5201	ex D-AVVQ	
☐ G-EZWB	Airbus A320-214	5224	ex D-AXAZ	
☐ G-EZWC	Airbus A320-214	5236	ex D-AVVX	
☐ G-EZWD	Airbus A320-214	5249	ex D-AXAH	
☐ G-EZWE	Airbus A320-214	5289	ex D-AXAL	
☐ G-EZWF	Airbus A320-214	5319	ex D-AUBE	
☐ G-EZWG	Airbus A320-214/S	5318	ex F-WWBI	
☐ G-EZWH	Airbus A320-214/S	5542	ex D-AXAV	
☐ G-EZWI	Airbus A320-214/S	5592	ex D-AUBH	
☐ G-EZWJ	Airbus A320-214'S	5638	ex D-AUBS	
☐ G-EZWK	Airbus A320-214/S	5688	ex D-AVVF	
☐ G-EZWL	Airbus A320-214/S	5702	ex D-AVVI	
☐ G-EZWM	Airbus A320-214/S	5739	ex D-AVVS	
☐ G-EZWN	Airbus A320-214/S	5757	ex D-AVVV	
☐ G-EZWO	Airbus A320-214/S	5785	ex D-AXAF	
☐ G-EZWP	Airbus A320-214/S	5927	ex D-AUBF	
☐ G-EZWR	Airbus A320-214/S	5981	ex D-AUBO	
☐ G-EZWS	Airbus A320-214/S	6011	ex D-AUBW	
☐ G-EZWT	Airbus A320-214/S	6047	ex D-AXAF	
☐ G-EZWU	Airbus A320-214/S	6095	ex D-AXAP	
☐ G-EZWV	Airbus A320-214/S	6177	ex D-AVVD	
☐ G-EZWW	Airbus A320-214/S	6188	ex D-AVVF	♦
☐ G-EZWX	Airbus A320-214/S	6192	ex D-AVVG	♦
☐ G-EZWY	Airbus A320-214/S	6267	ex D-AVVT	♦
☐ G-EZWZ	Airbus A320-214/S	6353	ex F-WWIR	♦
☐ G-EZOF	Airbus A320-214/S	6525	ex D-AVVC	♦

☐ G-EZOG	Airbus A320-214/S	6541	ex D-AVVF			♦
☐ G-EZOH	Airbus A320-214/S	6546	ex D-AVVG			♦
☐ G-EZOI	Airbus A320-214/S	6562	ex D-AVVJ			♦
☐ G-EZOJ	Airbus A320-214/S	6565	ex D-AVVK			♦
☐ G-EZOK	Airbus A320-214/S	6568	ex F-WWIN			♦
☐ G-EZOL	Airbus A320-214/S	6572	ex D-AVVL	250th Airbus c/s		♦
☐ G-EZOM	Airbus A320-214/S	6587	ex D-AVVO			♦
☐ G-EZON	Airbus A320-214/S	6605	ex D-AVVR			♦
☐ G-EZOO	Airbus A320-214/S	6606	ex F-WWBB			o/o♦
☐ G-EZOP	Airbus A320-214/S	6633	ex D-AVVU			o/o♦
☐ G-EZOR	Airbus A320-214/S	6675	ex			o/o♦
☐ G-EZOT	Airbus A320-214/S	6680	ex			o/o♦
☐ G-EZOU	Airbus A320-214/S	6754	ex			o/o♦
☐ G-EZOV	Airbus A320-214/S	6788	ex			o/o♦
☐ G-EZOW	Airbus A320-214/S	6834	ex			o/o♦
☐ G-EZOX	Airbus A320-214/S	6837	ex			o/o♦
☐ G-EZOY	Airbus A320-214/S	6885	ex			o/o♦
☐ G-EZOZ	Airbus A320-214/S	6918	ex			o/o♦
☐ G-EZPA	Airbus A320-214/S	6947	ex			o/o♦
☐ G-EZPB	Airbus A320-214/S	6977	ex			o/o♦

FLYBE *Jersey (BE/BEE)* *Jersey/Exeter (JER/EXT)*

☐ G-ECOA	de Havilland DHC-8-402Q	4180	ex C-FMUE		
☐ G-ECOB	de Havilland DHC-8-402Q	4185	ex LN-WDT		
☐ G-ECOC	de Havilland DHC-8-402Q	4197	ex LN-WDU		
☐ G-ECOD	de Havilland DHC-8-402Q	4206	ex C-FPEX		
☐ G-ECOE	de Havilland DHC-8-402Q	4212	ex LN-WDV		
☐ G-ECOF	de Havilland DHC-8-402Q	4216	ex LN-WDW		
☐ G-ECOG	de Havilland DHC-8-402Q	4220	ex C-FSRQ		
☐ G-ECOH	de Havilland DHC-8-402Q	4221	ex C-FSRW		
☐ G-ECOI	de Havilland DHC-8-402Q	4224	ex C-FTIE		>BEL
☐ G-ECOJ	de Havilland DHC-8-402Q	4229	ex C-FTUS		
☐ G-ECOK	de Havilland DHC-8-402Q	4230	ex C-FTUT		>BEL
☐ G-ECOM	de Havilland DHC-8-402Q	4233	ex C-FUCR		
☐ G-ECOO	de Havilland DHC-8-402Q	4237	ex C-FUOH		
☐ G-ECOP	de Havilland DHC-8-402Q	4242	ex C-FUTG		
☐ G-ECOR	de Havilland DHC-8-402Q	4248	ex C-FVUJ		
☐ G-ECOT	de Havilland DHC-8-402Q	4251	ex C-FVUV		
☐ G-FLBA	de Havilland DHC-8-402Q	4253	ex C-FVVB		
☐ G-FLBB	de Havilland DHC-8-402Q	4255	ex C-FWGE		
☐ G-FLBC	de Havilland DHC-8-402Q	4257	ex C-FWGY		
☐ G-FLBD	de Havilland DHC-8-402Q	4259	ex C-FWZN	Spirit of Inverness	
☐ G-FLBE	de Havilland DHC-8-402Q	4261	ex C-FXAB	Spirit of Exeter	
☐ G-JECE	de Havilland DHC-8-402Q	4094	ex C-FDHU	The Wembley Grecians	
☐ G-JECF	de Havilland DHC-8-402Q	4095	ex C-FDHV		
☐ G-JECG	de Havilland DHC-8-402Q	4098	ex C-FAQH		
☐ G-JECH	de Havilland DHC-8-402Q	4103	ex C-FCQC		
☐ G-JECI	de Havilland DHC-8-402Q	4105	ex C-FCQK		
☐ G-JECJ	de Havilland DHC-8-402Q	4110	ex C-FCVN		
☐ G-JECK	de Havilland DHC-8-402Q	4113	ex C-FDRL		
☐ G-JECL	de Havilland DHC-8-402Q	4114	ex C-FDRN	The George Best	
☐ G-JECM	de Havilland DHC-8-402Q	4118	ex C-FFCE		
☐ G-JECN	de Havilland DHC-8-402Q	4120	ex C-FFCL		
☐ G-JECO	de Havilland DHC-8-402Q	4126	ex C-FFPT		
☐ G-JECP	de Havilland DHC-8-402Q	4136	ex C-FHEL		
☐ G-JECR	de Havilland DHC-8-402Q	4139	ex C-FHQM		
☐ G-JECX	de Havilland DHC-8-402Q	4155	ex C-FLKO		
☐ G-JECY	de Havilland DHC-8-402Q	4157	ex C-FLKV	Spirit of Liberum	
☐ G-JECZ	de Havilland DHC-8-402Q	4179	ex C-FMTY		
☐ G-JEDM	de Havilland DHC-8-402Q	4077	ex C-FGNP		
☐ G-JEDP	de Havilland DHC-8-402Q	4085	ex C-FDHO	Spirit of Belfast	
☐ G-JEDR	de Havilland DHC-8-402Q	4087	ex C-FDHI	Spirit of Dublin	
☐ G-JEDT	de Havilland DHC-8-402Q	4088	ex C-FDHP	Spirit of Edinburgh	
☐ G-JEDU	de Havilland DHC-8-402Q	4089	ex C-GEMU	Spirit of the Regions	
☐ G-JEDV	de Havilland DHC-8-402Q	4090	ex C-FDHX		
☐ G-JEDW	de Havilland DHC-8-402Q	4093	ex C-GFBW		
☐ G-KKEV	de Havilland DHC-8-402Q	4201	ex C-FOUU	Kevin Keegan	
☐ G-PRPA	de Havilland DHC-8-402Q	4187	ex N187WQ		o/o♦
☐ G-PRPB	de Havilland DHC-8-402Q	4333	ex N333NG		o/o♦
☐ G-PRPC	de Havilland DHC-8-402Q	4338	ex N338NG		o/o♦
☐ G-PRPD	de Havilland DHC-8-402Q	4332	ex N380NG		o/o♦
☐ G-PRPL	de Havilland DHC-8-402Q	4380	ex N380NG		♦

☐ G-FBJA	Embraer ERJ-175LR	17000326	ex PT-TIB		
☐ G-FBJB	Embraer ERJ-175LR	17000327	ex PT-TOB		
☐ G-FBJC	Embraer ERJ-175LR	17000328	ex PT-TOO		
☐ G-FBJD	Embraer ERJ-175LR	17000329	ex PT-TOZ		
☐ G-FBJE	Embraer ERJ-175LR	17000336	ex PT-TUS		
☐ G-FBJF	Embraer ERJ-175LR	17000341	ex PT-TBM		
☐ G-FBJG	Embraer ERJ-175LR	17000344	ex PT-TCY		
☐ G-FBJH	Embraer ERJ-175ST	17000351	ex PT-TFA		
☐ G-FBJI	Embraer ERJ-175ST	17000355	ex PT-THC		

☐ G-FBJJ	Embraer ERJ-175ST	17000358	ex PT-TJN		
☐ G-FBJK	Embraer ERJ 175ST	17000359	ex PT-TJQ		
☐ G-FBEE	Embraer ERJ-195LR	19000093	ex PT-SNN		[EXT]
☐ G-FBEF	Embraer ERJ-195LR	19000104	ex PT-SNY		
☐ G-FBEG	Embraer ERJ-195LR	19000120	ex PT-SQO		
☐ G-FBEH	Embraer ERJ-195LR	19000128	ex PT-SQX		
☐ G-FBEI	Embraer ERJ-195LR	19000143	ex PT-SYV		
☐ G-FBEJ	Embraer ERJ-195LR	19000155	ex PT-SAK		
☐ G-FBEK	Embraer ERJ-195LR	19000168	ex PT-SDC		[NQY]
☐ G-FBEL	Embraer ERJ-195LR	19000184	ex PT-SDS		[NQY]
☐ G-FBEM	Embraer ERJ-195LR	19000204	ex PT-SGN		[EXT]
☐ G-FBEN	Embraer ERJ-195LR	19000213	ex PT-SGW		[EXT]
☐ EI-REL	ATR 72-212A	748	ex F-WWEI	Flybe c/s	opb STK♦
☐ EI-REM	ATR 72-212A	760	ex F-WWEW	St Gall/Gall	opb STK♦
☐ G-CCGS	Dornier 328-110	3101	ex D-CPRX	Spirit of Norwich	opb LOG♦
☐ G-LENM	Avro 146-RJ85	E2273	ex G-CYGR		<Cello Avn♦
☐ G-LGNO	SAAB 2000	2000-013	ex SE-LOT	Spirit of Aberdeen	opb LOG♦
☐ G-LGNP	SAAB 2000	2000-018	ex OY-SFC		opb LOG♦
☐ G-LGNR	SAAB 2000	2000-004	ex OY-SFD		opb LOG♦

FLY WALES — Haverfordwest

| ☐ G-FLYW | Beech 200 Super King Air | BB-209 | ex G-LIVY |
| ☐ G-FSEU | Beech 200 Super King Air | BB-331 | ex N87LP |

FR AVIATION

☐ G-FFRA	AMD Falcon 20DC	132	ex N902FR	
☐ G-FRAD	AMD Falcon 20E	304	ex 9M-BDK	
☐ G-FRAF	AMD Falcon 20E	295	ex N911FR	
☐ G-FRAH	AMD Falcon 20DC	223	ex G-60-01	
☐ G-FRAI	AMD Falcon 20DC	270	ex N901FR	
☐ G-FRAJ	AMD Falcon 20DC	20	ex N903FR	
☐ G-FRAK	AMD Falcon 20DC	213	ex N905FR	
☐ G-FRAL	AMD Falcon 20DC	151	ex N904FR	
☐ G-FRAO	AMD Falcon 20DC	214	ex N906FR	
☐ G-FRAP	AMD Falcon 20DC	207	ex N908FR	
☐ G-FRAR	AMD Falcon 20DC	209	ex N909FR	
☐ G-FRAS	AMD Falcon 20C	82	ex RCAF117501	
☐ G-FRAT	AMD Falcon 20C	87	ex RCAF117502	
☐ G-FRAU	AMD Falcon 20C	97	ex RCAF117504	
☐ G-FRAW	AMD Falcon 20C	114	ex RCAF117507	
☐ G-MAFF	Britten-Norman BN-2T Turbine Islander	2119	ex G-BJED	
☐ G-MAFI	Dornier 228-202K	8115	ex D-CAAE	opf Oil Spill Response
☐ G-OMAF	Dornier 228-202K	8112	ex D-CAAD	opf Fisheries Patrol

HEBRIDEAN AIR SERVICES — Hebridean (HBR) — Cumbernauld

| ☐ G-HEBO | Britten-Norman BN-2B-26 Islander | 2268 | ex G-BUBK |
| ☐ G-HEBS | Britten-Norman BN-2B-26 Islander | 2267 | ex G-BUBJ |

INSTONE AIR SERVICES — (8G) — Coventry (CVT)

| ☐ G-APSA | Douglas DC-6A | 45497/995 | ex 4W-ABQ | [CVT] |

ISLES OF SCILLY SKYBUS — Scillonia (IOS) — Lands End-St Just (LEQ)

☐ G-BIHO	de Havilland DHC-6 Twin Otter 310	738	ex A6-ADB	
☐ G-BUBN	Britten-Norman BN-2B-26 Islander	2270		
☐ G-CBML	de Havilland DHC-6 Twin Otter 310	695	ex C-FZSP	
☐ G-CEWM	de Havilland DHC-6 Twin Otter 300	656	ex N70551	
☐ G-ISSG	de Havilland DHC-6 Twin Otter 310	572	ex C-GOYX	25th Anniversay c/s
☐ G-SBUS	Britten-Norman BN-2A-26 Islander	3013	ex G-BMMH	
☐ G-SSKY	Britten-Norman BN-2B-26 Islander	2247	ex G-BSWT	

JET2 — Channex (LS/EXS) — Leeds-Bradford /Manchester (LBA/MAN)

☐ G-CELA	Boeing 737-377F	23663/1323	ex VH-CZK	Jet2 Newcastle	
☐ G-CELB	Boeing 737-377	23664/1326	ex VH-CZL	Jet2 Yorkshire	
☐ G-CELC	Boeing 737-33A	23831/1471	ex N190FH	Jet2 Tunisia	wfs
☐ G-CELD	Boeing 737-33A	23832/1473	ex N191FH	Jet2 Espana	
☐ G-CELE	Boeing 737-33A	24029/1601	ex VH-CZX	Jet2 Belfast	
☐ G-CELF	Boeing 737-377	24302/1618	ex S7-ABB	Jet2 Sardinia	
☐ G-CELG	Boeing 737-377	24303/1620	ex S7-ABD	Helen Normington	
☐ G-CELH	Boeing 737-330QC	23525/1278	ex D-ABXD	Jet2 Faro	
☐ G-CELI	Boeing 737-330	23526/1282	ex D-ABXE	Jet2 Manchester	
☐ G-CELJ	Boeing 737-330	23529/1293	ex LZ-BOG	Jet2 Italia	
☐ G-CELK	Boeing 737-330	23530/1297	ex LZ-BOH	Jet2 Edinburgh	

☐ G-CELO	Boeing 737-33AQC	24028/1599	ex TF-ELO	Jet2 Faro		
☐ G-CELP	Boeing 737-330QC	23522/1246	ex TF-ELP	Jet2 Private Charter		
☐ G-CELR	Boeing 737-330QC	23523/1271	ex TF-ELR	Jet2 Corfu		
☐ G-CELS	Boeing 737-377	23660/1294	ex VH-CZH	Jet2 Leeds-Bradford		
☐ G-CELV	Boeing 737-377/W	23661/1314	ex VH-CZI	Jet2 Amsterdam		
☐ G-CELW	Boeing 737-377F	23659/1292	ex N659DG			
☐ G-CELX	Boeing 737-377F	23654/1273	ex VH-CZB	Jet2 Malaga		
☐ G-CELY	Boeing 737-377F	23662/1316	ex N622DG	Jet2 Ireland		
☐ G-CELZ	Boeing 737-377F	23658/1281	ex VH-CZF	Jet2 Paris		
☐ G-GDFB	Boeing 737-33A/W	25743/2206	ex SX-BBU			
☐ G-GDFE	Boeing 737-3Q8QC	24131/1541	ex OO-TNF			
☐ G-GDFG	Boeing 737-36Q/W	28658/2865	ex LN-KKQ	Music Hall Tavern		
☐ G-GDFH	Boeing 737-3Y5/W	25615/2478	ex LN-KKC	Jet2 Majorca		
☐ G-GDFK	Boeing 737-36N/W	28572/3031	ex N4620F			
☐ G-GDFL	Boeing 737-36N/W	28568/2987	ex OO-VEG			
☐ G-GDFM	Boeing 737-36N/W	28586/3090	ex OO-VEN	Jet2 Budapest		
☐ G-GDFN	Boeing 737-33V/W	29332/3072	ex YL-BBK			
☐ G-GDFO	Boeing 737-3U3/W	28740/3003	ex G-THOP			
☐ G-GDFT	Boeing 737-36Q/W	29141/3035	ex G-TOYM	Jet2 Murcia		
☐ G-GDFC	Boeing 737-8K2/W	28375/85	ex PH-HZC			
☐ G-GDFD	Boeing 737-8K5/W	27982/8	ex D-AHFB			
☐ G-GDFF	Boeing 737-85P	28385/421	ex EC-HGP			
☐ G-GDFP	Boeing 737-8Z9/W	28177/69	ex EI-EZB	Jet2 Paris		
☐ G-GDFR	Boeing 737-8Z9/W	30421/1345	ex EI-EZH	Jet2 Rome		
☐ G-GDFS	Boeing 737-86N/W	32243/869	ex OM-TVA	Jet2 Tunisia		
☐ G-GDFU	Boeing 737-8K5/W	30416/778	ex D-AHFX			♦
☐ G-GDFV	Boeing 737-85F/W	28821/151	ex F-WTDE	Jet2 Fuerteventura		
☐ G-GDFW	Boeing 737-8K5/W	27986/474	ex D-AHFM			
☐ G-GDFX	Boeing 737-8K5/W	27987/499	ex D-AHFO	Jet2 Vienna		
☐ G-GDFY	Boeing 737-86Q/W	30278/963	ex HA-LKE	Jet2 Kefalonia		
☐ G-GDFZ	Boeing 737-86Q/W	30276/920	ex EI-FDZ			
☐ G-JZHA	Boeing 737-8K5/W	30417/781	ex D-AHFY			
☐ G-JZHB	Boeing 737-8K5/W	28623/556	ex D-AHFS	Jet2 Malta		♦
☐ G-JZHC	Boeing 737-8K5/W	30593/528	ex D-AHFR	Jet2 Crete		♦
☐ G-JZHD	Boeing 737-808	34706/2014	ex EI-RUP			♦
☐ G-LSAA	Boeing 757-236	24122/187	ex N241CV	Jet2 Tenerife		
☐ G-LSAB	Boeing 757-27B/W	24136/169	ex N136CV	Jet2 Menorca		
☐ G-LSAC	Boeing 757-23A/W	25488/471	ex N254DG	Jet2 Lanzarote		
☐ G-LSAD	Boeing 757-236	24397/221	ex SX-BLW			
☐ G-LSAE	Boeing 757-27B/W	24135/165	ex OM-SNA	Jet2 Murcia		
☐ G-LSAG	Boeing 757-21B	24014/144	ex B-2801			
☐ G-LSAH	Boeing 757-21B	24015/148	ex B-2802			
☐ G-LSAI	Boeing 757-21B	24016/150	ex B-2803			
☐ G-LSAJ	Boeing 757-236	24793/292	ex G-CDUP	Jet2 New York	Jet2 Holidays c/s	
☐ G-LSAK	Boeing 757-23N	27973/735	ex N517AT			
☐ G-LSAN	Boeing 757-2K2/W	26635/608	ex HC-CIY			
☐ G-POWM	Airbus A320-232	2564	ex 4R-ABJ		<AWC♦	

LINKS AIR (LNQ) Humberside (HUY)

☐ G-GAVA	British Aerospace Jetstream 3102	785	ex G-CCPW	dam 15Aug14 >BPS	
☐ G-JIBO	British Aerospace Jetstream 3102	711	ex G-OJSA		
☐ G-LNKS	British Aerospace Jetstream 3102	772	ex G-JURA		

LITTLE RED

☐ EI-DEI	Airbus A320-214	2374	ex F-WWDU	Maggie May	opb EIN
☐ EI-EZW	Airbus A320-214	1983	ex I-EEZF	Rosie Lee	opb EIN
☐ EI-EZV	Airbus A320-214	2001	ex I-EEZG	Tartan Lassie	opb EIN
To cease ops 2015					

LOCH LOMOND SEAPLANES Luss

☐ G-DLAK	Cessna 208 Caravan I	20800340	ex A6-TDA	♦
☐ G-MDJE	Cessna 208 Caravan I	20800336	ex N208FM	FP

LOGANAIR Logan (LOG) Glasgow (GLA)

☐ G-BWWT	Dornier 328-110	3022	ex D-CDXO		
☐ G-BYHG	Dornier 328-110	3098	ex D-CDAE		
☐ G-BYMK	Dornier 328-110	3062	ex LN-ASK		
☐ G-BZOG	Dornier 328-110	3088	ex D-CDXN		
☐ G-CCGS	Dornier 328-110	3101	ex D-CPRX	Spirit of Norwich	opf BEE
☐ G-GNTB	SAAB SF.340AQC	340A-082	ex HB-AHL		
☐ G-GNTF	SAAB SF.340AQC	340A-113	ex SE-F13	all-white	
☐ G-LGNA	SAAB SF.340B	340B-199	ex N592MA	Flybe c/s	
☐ G-LGNB	SAAB SF.340B	340B-216	ex N595MA	Flybe c/s	
☐ G-LGNC	SAAB SF.340B	340B-318	ex SE-KXC	Flybe c/s	

□ G-LGND	SAAB SF.340B	340B-169	ex G-GNTH	Flybe c/s	
□ G-LGNE	SAAB SF.340B	340B-172	ex G-GNTI	Flybe c/s	
□ G-LGNF	SAAB SF.340B	340B-192	ex N192JE	Flybe c/s	
□ G-LGNG	SAAB SF.340B	340B-327	ex SE-C27	Flybe c/s	
□ G-LGNH	SAAB SF.340B	340B-333	ex SE-C33	Flybe c/s	
□ G-LGNI	SAAB SF.340B	340B-160	ex SE-F60	Flybe c/s	
□ G-LGNJ	SAAB SF.340B	340B-173	ex SE-F73	Flybe c/s	
□ G-LGNK	SAAB SF.340B	340B-185	ex SE-F85	Flybe c/s	
□ G-LGNL	SAAB SF.340B	340B-246	ex SE-G46	Flybe c/s	dam 02Jan15
□ G-LGNM	SAAB SF.340B	340B-187	ex SE-F47	Flybe c/s	
□ G-LGNN	SAAB SF.340B	340B-197	ex SE-F97	Flybe c/s	
□ G-BLDV	Britten-Norman BN-2B-26 Islander	2179	ex D-INEY		
□ G-BPCA	Britten-Norman BN-2B-26 Islander	2198	ex G-BLNX	Capt David Barclay MBE	
□ G-BVVK	de Havilland DHC-6 Twin Otter 310	666	ex LN-BEZ	Flybe c/s	
□ G-HIAL	de Havilland DHC-6 Twin Otter 400	917	ex C-GLVA		♦
□ G-LGNO	SAAB 2000	2000-013	ex SE-LOT	Spirit of Aberdeen	opf BEE
□ G-LGNP	SAAB 2000	2000-018	ex OY-SFC		opf BEE♦
□ G-LGNR	SAAB 2000	2000-004	ex OY-SFD		opf BEE♦
□ G-LGNS	SAAB 2000	2000-041	ex HB-IZX		♦
□ G-SGTS	de Havilland DHC-6 Twin Otter 400	918	ex C-FVIK		♦

MONARCH AIRLINES   Monarch (ZB/MON)   London-Luton (LTN)

□ G-MRJK	Airbus A320-214	1081	ex PH-BMC	
□ G-OZBW	Airbus A320-214	1571	ex G-OOPP	
□ G-OZBX	Airbus A320-214	1637	ex G-OOPU	
□ G-OZBY	Airbus A320-214	1320	ex G-OOAR	
□ G-ZBAH	Airbus A320-214	1413	ex EC-KBU	
□ G-ZBAP	Airbus A320-214	1605	ex M-RAFF	
□ G-ZBAR	Airbus A320-214	2142	ex 9H-AEF	<AMC
□ G-ZBAS	Airbus A320-214/S	6550	ex F-WWDS	♦
□ G-MARA	Airbus A321-231	0983	ex D-AVZB	[EMA]
□ G-OJEG	Airbus A321-231	1015	ex D-AVZN	
□ G-OZBE	Airbus A321-231	1707	ex D-AVZH	
□ G-OZBF	Airbus A321-231	1763	ex D-AVZB	
□ G-OZBG	Airbus A321-231	1941	ex D-AVXC	
□ G-OZBH	Airbus A321-231	2105	ex D-AVXB	
□ G-OZBI	Airbus A321-231	2234	ex D-AVZV	wfs
□ G-OZBL	Airbus A321-231	0864	ex G-MIDE	
□ G-OZBM	Airbus A321-231	1045	ex G-MIDJ	
□ G-OZBN	Airbus A321-231	1153	ex G-MIDK	
□ G-OZBO	Airbus A321-231	1207	ex G-MIDM	
□ G-OZBR	Airbus A321-231	1794	ex N586NK	
□ G-OZBS	Airbus A321-231	1428	ex G-TTIA	
□ G-OZBT	Airbus A321-231	3546	ex G-TTIH	
□ G-OZBU	Airbus A321-231	3575	ex G-TTII	
□ G-OZBZ	Airbus A321-231	1421	ex TC-OAN	
□ G-ZBAD	Airbus A321-231/S	5582	ex D-AVZH	
□ G-ZBAE	Airbus A321-231/S	5606	ex D-AVZO	
□ G-ZBAF	Airbus A321-231	2730	ex 5B-DCO	
□ G-ZBAG	Airbus A321-231	2793	ex 5B-DCP	
□ G-ZBAI	Airbus A321-231	2553	ex N566TA	
□ G-ZBAJ	Airbus A321-231	2610	ex N567TA	
□ G-ZBAK	Airbus A321-231	3458	ex JY-AYJ	
□ G-ZBAL	Airbus A321-231	3522	ex JY-AYK	
□ G-ZBAM	Airbus A321-231/S	6059	ex D-AVZT	
□ G-ZBAO	Airbus A321-231/S	6126	ex D-AVXH	
□ G-EOMA	Airbus A330-243	265	ex F-WWKU	[BHX]
□ G-SMAN	Airbus A330-243	261	ex F-WWKR	wfs
□ OY-JTY	Boeing 737-7Q8/W	30727/1005	ex VT-SJE	<JTG♦

OIL SPILL RESPONSE/T2 AVIATION   Robin Hood Doncaster Sheffield

□ G-MAFI	Dornier 228-202K	8115	ex D-CAAE	opb FR Avn♦
□ G-OSRA	Boeing 727-2S2F	22938/1832	ex N217FE	♦
□ G-OSRB	Boeing 727-2S2F	22929/1823	ex N480EC	♦
□ G-	Boeing 727-227F	21463/1353	ex N727EL	o/o♦

POLICE AVIATION SERVICE   Special (PLC)   Gloucester (GLO)

□ G-CPAO	Eurocopter EC135P2+	0843		Cheshire Police
□ G-CPAS	Eurocopter EC135P2+	0920		Cleveland Police
□ G-CPSH	Eurocopter EC135T2	0209	ex D-HECT	West Yorkshire Police
□ G-EMID	Eurocopter EC135P2+	0524		East Midlands Police
□ G-ESEX	Eurocopter EC135T2	0267	ex D-HECP	Central Counties Police
□ G-HEOI	Eurocopter EC135P2+	0825		West Mercia & Staffordshire Police
□ G-LASU	Eurocopter EC135T2	0228	ex D-HTSH	Lancashire Police
□ G-NMID	Eurocopter EC135T2+	0300		North Midlands Police
□ G-NWOI	Eurocopter EC135P2+	0887		National Police

☐ G-POLA	Eurocopter EC135P2+	0877		West Midlands Police
☐ G-PNSI	Eurocopter EC135T2	0337		Northern Ireland Police♦
☐ G-SUFK	Eurocopter EC135P2+	0730		Suffolk Police
☐ G-SURY	Eurocopter EC135T2	0283		South East Police
☐ G-TVHB	Eurocopter EC135P2+	0874		Chiltern Police
☐ G-WCAO	Eurocopter EC135T2+	0204	ex D-HECU	Western Counties Police
☐ G-DCPA	MBB BK.117C-1	7511	ex D-HECU	Devon & Cornwall Police♦
☐ G-DCPB	MBB BK.117C-2	9265	ex D-HMBZ	Devon & Cornwall Police
☐ G-MPSA	MBB BK.117C-2	9065		Metropolitan Police♦
☐ G-MPSB	MBB BK.117C-2	9068		Metropolitan Police♦
☐ G-MPSC	MBB BK.117C-2	9075		Metropolitan Police♦
☐ G-PSNR	MBB BK.117C-2	9488	ex G-LFRS	Northern Ireland Police
☐ G-PSNO	MBB BK.117C-2	9296	ex D-HADC	Northern Ireland Police♦
☐ G-PSNR	MBB BK.117C-2	9488	ex G-LFRS	Northern Ireland Police♦
☐ G-RESC	MBB BK.117C-1	7504	ex D-HELW	♦
☐ G-BXZK	MD Helicopters MD902 Explorer	900-00057	ex N9238T	Dorset Police
☐ G-CEMS	MD Helicopters MD902 Explorer	900-00089	ex PK-OCR	Yorkshire Air Ambulance
☐ G-CMBS	MD Helicopters MS902 Explorer	900-00111	ex N70124	West Yorkshire Police
☐ G-CNWL	MD Helicopters MD902 Explorer	900-0124	ex G-CIGX	Cornwall Air Ambulance♦
☐ G-COTH	MD Helicopters MD902 Explorer	900-00035	ex N3ND	Hertfordshire Air Ambulance
☐ G-EHAA	MD Helicopters MD902 Explorer	900-00079	ex G-GNAA	Essex Air Ambulance
☐ G-GMPX	MD Helicopters MD902 Explorer	900-00122	ex N9114R	Greater Manchester Police
☐ G-HAAT	MD Helicopters MD902 Explorer	900-00081	ex G-GMPS	
☐ G-HMDX	MD Helicopters MD902 Explorer	900-00121	ex N902RN	Maypas Helimedia
☐ G-KAAT	MD Helicopters MD902 Explorer	900-00056	ex G-PASS	Kent Air Ambulance
☐ G-KSSA	MD Helicopters MD902 Explorer	900-00123	ex N902CS	Surrey, Kent & Sussex Air Ambulance
☐ G-LNAA	MD Helicopters MD902 Explorer	900-00074	ex G-76-074	Cornwall Air Ambulance
☐ G-LNCT	MD Helicopters MD902 Explorer	900-00134	ex N40483	Lincs & Notts Air Ambulance
☐ G-SASH	MD Helicopters MD902 Explorer	900-00080	ex PH-SHF	Yorkshire Air Ambulance
☐ G-SASO	MD Helicopters MD902 Explorer	900-0013	ex N5646	Cornwall Air Ambulance
☐ G-SUSX	MD Helicopters MD902 Explorer	900-00065	ex N3065W	Sussex Air Ambulance
☐ G-WPAS	MD Helicopters MD902 Explorer	900-00053	ex N92237	Wiltshire Police & Air Ambulance
☐ G-YPOL	MD Helicopters MD902 Explorer	900-00078	ex N7038S	West Yorkshire Police
☐ G-CGTC	Britten-Norman BN-2T-4S Defender	4019		Northern Ireland Police
☐ G-DPPF	Agusta A109E Power	11216		Dyfed & Powys Police
☐ G-NETR	Aérospatiale AS355F1 Ecureuil 2	5164	ex G-JARV	British Transport Police
☐ G-NIAA	Beech 200 Super King Air	BB-		Northern Ireland Air Ambulance♦
☐ G-NTWK	Aérospatiale AS355F2 Ecureuil 2	5347	ex G-FTWO	British Transport Police
☐ G-WYPA	MBB Bo.105DBS-4	S-815	ex D-HDZY	

PREMIAIR AVIATION SERVICES　　　Premiere (PGL)　　　Denham

☐ G-URSA	Sikorsky S-76C++	760699	ex G-URSS	
☐ VP-BIR	Sikorsky S-76B	760430	ex N9HM	

RECONNAISSANCE VENTURES　　　(RVL)　　　Coventry (CVT)

☐ G-BCEN	Britten-Norman BN-2A-26 Islander	403	ex 4X-AYG	Maritime & Coastguard Agency
☐ G-BODY	Cessna 310R II	310R1503	ex N4897A	
☐ G-BWLF	Cessna 404 Titan	404-0414	ex G-BNXS	
☐ G-EGLT	Cessna 310R II	310R1874	ex G-BHTV	
☐ G-EXEX	Cessna 404 Titan	404-0037	ex SE-GZF	Maritime & Coastguard Agency
☐ G-FIND	Reims Cessna F406 Caravan II	0045	ex OY-PEU	
☐ G-LEAF	Reims Cessna F406 Caravan II	0018	ex EI-CKY	
☐ G-MAPP	Cessna 402B	402B-0583	ex D-INRH	
☐ G-MIND	Cessna 404 Titan	404-0004	ex G-SKKC	opf Enviroment Agency
☐ G-NOSE	Cessna 402B	402B0823	ex N98AR	Pollution control
☐ G-SOUL	Cessna 310R II	310R0140	ex N5020J	opf OSRL
☐ G-TASK	Cessna 404 Titan	404-0829	ex PH-MPC	Maritime & Coastguard Agency
☐ G-TURF	Reims Cessna F406 Caravan II	F406-0020	ex PH-FWF	Maritime & Coastguard Agency

SKYSOUTH　　　Skydrift (SDL)　　　Norwich / Shoreham (NWI/-)

☐ G-OETV	Piper PA-31-350 Chieftain	31-7852073	ex N27597	
☐ G-STHA	Piper PA-31-350 Chieftain	31-8052077	ex G-GLUG	

SOUTH WESTERN HELICOPTERS　　　Bristol (BRS)

☐ G-WPDA	Eurocopter EC135P1	0109	ex D-HIPT	opf Western Power Distribution
☐ G-WPDB	Eurocopter EC135P1	0112	ex D-HAIT	opf Western Power Distribution
☐ G-WPDC	Eurocopter EC135P1	0090	ex D-HKUG	opf Western Power Distribution
☐ G-WPDD	Eurocopter EC135P1	0071	ex D-HSOS	opf Western Power Distribution

THOMAS COOK AIRLINES　　　Kestrel (MT/TCX)　　　Manchester (MAN)

☐ LY-VEK	Airbus A320-232	2108	ex M-ABIK	<NVD♦
☐ LY-VEN	Airbus A320-233	1626	ex CC-COM	<NVD♦
☐ YL-LCK	Airbus A320-214	0936	ex OE-IBU	<ART♦
☐ YL-LCL	Airbus A320-214	0533	ex EI-DDL	Arisitides Sousa Mendes	<ART♦

☐ YL-LCO	Airbus A320-214	1873	ex N191AT		<ART♦
☐ G-DHJH	Airbus A321-211	1238	ex D-AVZL		
☐ G-NIKO	Airbus A321-211	1250	ex D-AVZF		
☐ G-TCDA	Airbus A321-211	2060	ex TC-JMG		
☐ G-TCDB	Airbus A321-211/S	5603	ex D-AIAB	Voyager Android	
☐ G-TCDC	Airbus A321-211	5872	ex D-AVZT		
☐ G-TCDD	Airbus A321-211/S	6038	ex D-AVZO		
☐ G-TCDE	Airbus A321-211/S	6056	ex D-AVZS		
☐ G-TCDF	Airbus A321-211/S	6114	ex D-AVXD		
☐ G-TCDG	Airbus A321-211/S	6122	ex D-AVXG		
☐ G-TCDV	Airbus A321-211	1972	ex OY-VKT		♦
☐ G-TCDW	Airbus A321-211	1921	ex OY-VKB		♦
☐ G-TCDX	Airbus A321-211	1887	ex OY-VKE		♦
☐ G-TCDY	Airbus A321-211	1881	ex OY-VKA		♦
☐ G-TCDZ	Airbus A321-211	1006	ex F-HBAF		
☐ G-TCDH	Airbus A321-211/S	6515	ex D-AVZZ		♦
☐ G-TCDJ	Airbus A321-211/S	6526	ex D-AZAF		♦
☐ G-TCDK	Airbus A321-211/S	6548	ex D-AZAJ		
☐ G-CHTZ	Airbus A330-243	398	ex F-WWBM		
☐ G-MDBD	Airbus A330-243	266	ex F-WWKG		
☐ G-MLJL	Airbus A330-243	254	ex F-WWKT		
☐ G-OJMB	Airbus A330-243	427	ex F-WWYH		
☐ G-OMYT	Airbus A330-243	301	ex G-MOJO		
☐ G-TCXB	Airbus A330-243	948	ex G-CINS		o/o♦
☐ G-VYGK	Airbus A330-243	1498	ex EC-330		♦
☐ OY-VKF	Airbus A330-243	309	ex G-CSJS		<VKG♦
☐ G-FCLI	Boeing 757-28A	26275/672	ex N161LF		
☐ G-JMAA	Boeing 757-3CQ	32241/960	ex N5002K		
☐ G-JMAB	Boeing 757-3CQ	32242/963	ex N1795B		
☐ G-JMCD	Boeing 757-25F	30757/928	ex C-GJZK		[SEN]
☐ G-JMCE	Boeing 757-25F	30758/932	ex C-GJZH		[SEN]
☐ G-TCBB	Boeing 757-236	29945/873	ex N945BB		
☐ G-TCBC	Boeing 757-236	29946/877	ex N946BB		
☐ G-WJAN	Boeing 757-21K	28674/746	ex C-GJZS		
☐ G-DAJC	Boeing 767-31KER/W	27206/533	ex C-GJJC		
☐ G-TCCA	Boeing 767-31KER/W	27205/528	ex G-SJMC		
☐ G-TCCB	Boeing 767-31KER/W	28865/657	ex G-DIMB		

THOMSON		**Thomson (BY/TOM)**		**London-Luton (LTN)**

☐ G-FDZA	Boeing 737-8K5/W	35134/2152	ex C-FPZA		
☐ G-FDZB	Boeing 737-8K5/W	35131/2242	ex C-FPZB		
☐ G-FDZD	Boeing 737-8K5/W	35132/2276	ex C-FTZD		
☐ G-FDZE	Boeing 737-8K5/W	35137/2482	ex C-GDZE		
☐ G-FDZF	Boeing 737-8K5/W	35138/2499	ex C-FEZF		
☐ G-FDZG	Boeing 737-8K5/W	35139/2538	ex C-FRZG		
☐ G-FDZJ	Boeing 737-8K5/W	34690/2184	ex C-FRZJ		
☐ G-FDZR	Boeing 737-8K5/W	35145/2849	ex C-FLZR		♦
☐ G-FDZS	Boeing 737-8K5/W	35147/2866	ex N1786B		
☐ G-FDZT	Boeing 737-8K5/W	37248/3532			
☐ G-FDZU	Boeing 737-8K5/W	37253/3562			
☐ G-FDZW	Boeing 737-8K5/W	37254/3586			
☐ G-FDZX	Boeing 737-8K5/W	37258/3655			
☐ G-FDZY	Boeing 737-8K5/W	37261/3844			
☐ G-FDZZ	Boeing 737-8K5/W	37262/3876			
☐ G-TAWA	Boeing 737-8K5/W	37264/3907			
☐ G-TAWB	Boeing 737-8K5/W	37242/3917			
☐ G-TAWC	Boeing 737-8K5/W	39922/3925			
☐ G-TAWD	Boeing 737-8K5/W	37265/3939			
☐ G-TAWF	Boeing 737-8K5/W	37244/3955			
☐ G-TAWG	Boeing 737-8K5/W	37266/3967			
☐ G-TAWH	Boeing 737-8K5/W	38107/3997			
☐ G-TAWI	Boeing 737-8K5/W	37267/4006	ex C-GEWI		
☐ G-TAWJ	Boeing 737-8K5/W	38108/4024	ex C-GVOJ		
☐ G-TAWK	Boeing 737-8K5/W	37239/4253	ex C-FQWK		
☐ G-TAWL	Boeing 737-8K5/W	37243/4299			
☐ G-TAWM	Boeing 737-8K5/W	37249/4360	ex N5515R		
☐ G-TAWN	Boeing 737-8K5/W	37251/4369	ex N5573K		
☐ G-TAWO	Boeing 737-8K5/W	37255/4384			
☐ G-TAWP	Boeing 737-8K5/W	37257/4412			
☐ G-TAWR	Boeing 737-8K5/W	37256/4416			
☐ G-TAWS	Boeing 737-8K5/W	37241/4842			
☐ G-TAWU	Boeing 737-8K5/W	37263/4875	ex N1787B		
☐ G-BYAW	Boeing 757-204/W	27234/663		Philip Stanley	
☐ G-BYAY	Boeing 757-204/W	28836/861	ex N1786B		
☐ G-CPEU	Boeing 757-236/W	29941/864	ex C-FLEU		
☐ G-CPEV	Boeing 757-236/W	29943/871	ex C-GOEV		
☐ G-OOBA	Boeing 757-28A/W	32446/950	ex C-GUBA		

☐ G-OOBB	Boeing 757-28A/W	32447/951	ex C-GTBB		
☐ G-OOBC	Boeing 757-28A/W	33098/1026			
☐ G-OOBD	Boeing 757-28A/W	33099/1028			
☐ G-OOBE	Boeing 757-28A/W	33100/1029			
☐ G-OOBF	Boeing 757-28A/W	33101/1041		TCS Expeditions titles	
☐ G-OOBG	Boeing 757-236/W	29942/867	ex C-FUBG		
☐ G-OOBH	Boeing 757-236/W	29944/872	ex C-FOBH	Dreamliner c/s	
☐ G-OOBN	Boeing 757-2G5ER	29379/919	ex HB-IHR		
☐ G-OOBP	Boeing 757-2G5ER	30394/922	ex HB-IHS		
☐ G-OBYE	Boeing 767-304ER/W	28979/691	ex ph-oye		
☐ G-OBYF	Boeing 767-304ER/W	28208/705	ex D-AGYF		
☐ G-OBYG	Boeing 767-304ER/W	29137/733			
☐ G-OBYH	Boeing 767-304ER/W	28883/737	ex SE-DZO		
☐ G-OOBM	Boeing 767-324ER/W	27568/593	ex VN-A765		[MAN]
☐ G-TUIA	Boeing 787-8	34422/92		Living the Dream	
☐ G-TUIB	Boeing 787-8	34423/94		Alfie	
☐ G-TUIC	Boeing 787-8	34424/96		Dream Maker	
☐ G-TUID	Boeing 787-8	36424/106		Angel of the Sky	
☐ G-TUIE	Boeing 787-8	37227/191	ex N1026G	Miles of Smiles	♦
☐ G-TUIF	Boeing 787-8	36428/198		#787pics	♦
☐ G-TUIG	Boeing 787-8	36426/260			♦
☐ G-TUIH	Boeing 787-8	37229/291			♦
☐ G-TUII	Boeing 787-8	37230/300			♦

TITAN AIRWAYS — Zap (ZT/AWC) — London-Stansted (STN)

☐ G-JMCP	Boeing 737-3T0SF	23578/1358	ex OO-TNB	<NPT
☐ G-POWC	Boeing 737-33AQC	25402/2159	ex SE-DPB	
☐ G-POWD	Boeing 767-36NER	30847/902	ex N308TL	
☐ G-POWG	Cessna 525A Citationjet CJ2	525A-0485		
☐ G-POWH	Boeing 757-256	29308/935	ex TC-OGT	
☐ G-POWI	Airbus A320-233	2791	ex EI-TAG	
☐ G-POWK	Airbus A320-233	4701	ex 9V-SLN	♦
☐ G-POWM	Airbus A320-232	2564	ex 4R-ABJ	>EXS♦
☐ G-ZAPW	Boeing 737-3L9QC	24219/1600	ex G-IGOX	
☐ G-ZAPX	Boeing 757-256	29309/936	ex EC-HIS	
☐ G-ZAPZ	Boeing 737-33AQC	25401/2067	ex SE-DPA	

VIRGIN ATLANTIC AIRWAYS — Virgin (VS/VIR) — London-Gatwick/Heathrow (LGW/LHR)

☐ G-VGBR	Airbus A330-343E	1329	ex F-WWTP	Golden Girl	
☐ G-VGEM	Airbus A330-343E	1215	ex B-18392	Diamond Girl	
☐ G-VINE	Airbus A330-343E	1231	ex N771RD	Champagne Belle	
☐ G-VKSS	Airbus A330-343E	1201	ex F-WWKU	Mademoiselle Rouge	
☐ G-VLUV	Airbus A330-343E	1206	ex B-18391	Lady Love	
☐ G-VNYC	Airbus A330-343E	1315	ex F-WWKE	Uptown Girl	
☐ G-VRAY	Airbus A330-343E	1296	ex F-WWKF	Miss Sunshine	
☐ G-VSXY	Airbus A330-343E	1195	ex F-WWKY	Beauty Queen	
☐ G-VUFO	Airbus A330-343E	1352	ex F-WWCR	Lady Stardust	
☐ G-VWAG	Airbus A330-343E	1341	ex F-WWCG	Miss England	
☐ G-VBLU	Airbus A340-642	723	ex F-WWCS	Soul Sister	
☐ G-VBUG	Airbus A340-642	804	ex F-WWCV	Lady Bird	
☐ G-VEIL	Airbus A340-642	575	ex F-WWCK	Queen of the Skies	
☐ G-VFIT	Airbus A340-642	753	ex F-WWCG	Dancing Queen	
☐ G-VFIZ	Airbus A340-642	764	ex F-WWCB	Bubbles	
☐ G-VGAS	Airbus A340-642	639	ex F-WWCI	Varga Girl	
☐ G-VGOA	Airbus A340-642	371	ex F-WWCK	Indian Princess	[LDE]
☐ G-VRED	Airbus A340-642	768	ex F-WWCH	Scarlet Lady	
☐ G-VWEB	Airbus A340-642	787	ex F-WWCZ	Surfer Girl	
☐ G-VWIN	Airbus A340-642	736	ex F-WWCL	Lady Luck	
☐ G-VWKD	Airbus A340-642	706	ex F-WWCQ	Miss Behavin'	
☐ G-VYOU	Airbus A340-642	765	ex F-WWCK	Emmeline Heansy	
☐ G-VAST	Boeing 747-41R	28757/1117		Ladybird	
☐ G-VBIG	Boeing 747-4Q8	26255/1081		Tinker Belle	
☐ G-VFAB	Boeing 747-4Q8	24958/1028		Lady Penelope	
☐ G-VGAL	Boeing 747-443	32337/1272	ex (EI-CVH)	Jersey Girl	
☐ G-VHOT	Boeing 747-4Q8	26326/1043		Tubular Belle	
☐ G-VLIP	Boeing 747-443	32338/1274	ex (EI-CVI)	Hot Lips	
☐ G-VROC	Boeing 747-41R	32746/1336		Mustang Sally	
☐ G-VROM	Boeing 747-443	32339/1275	ex CP-2603		
☐ G-VROS	Boeing 747-443	30885/1268	ex (EI-CVG)	English Rose	
☐ G-VROY	Boeing 747-443	32340/1277	ex (EI-CVK)	Pretty Woman	
☐ G-VWOW	Boeing 747-41R	32745/1287		Cosmic Girl	
☐ G-VXLG	Boeing 747-41R	29406/1177		Ruby Tuesday	
☐ G-VAHH	Boeing 787-9	37967/246		Dream Girl	♦
☐ G-VBEL	Boeing 787-9	37980/		Show Girl	o/o♦
☐ G-VBOW	Boeing 787-9	37979/		Pearly Queen	o/o♦

☐ G-VBZZ	Boeing 787-9	37976/408		Queen Bee	o/o♦
☐ G-VCRU	Boeing 787-9	37972/338		Olivia Rae	o/o♦
☐ G-VDIA	Boeing 787-9	37975/377		Lucy in the Sky	o/o♦
☐ G-VERY	Boeing 787-9			Miss Molly	o/o♦
☐ G-VFAN	Boeing 787-9	37978/		Pin-up Girl	o/o♦
☐ G-VMAP	Boeing 787-9	37977/		West End Girl	o/o♦
☐ G-VNEW	Boeing 787-9	40956/218		Birthday Girl	♦
☐ G-VOOH	Boeing 787-9	37968/256		Miss Chief	♦
☐ G-VOWS	Boeing 787-9	37974/373		Maid Marian	o/o♦
☐ G-VSPY	Boeing 787-9	37973/370		Miss Moneypenny	o/o♦
☐ G-VWHO	Boeing 787-9	37971/313		Mystery Girl	o/o♦
☐ G-VWOO	Boeing 787-9			Leading Lady	o/o♦
☐ G-VYNL	Boeing 787-9	37981/		Penny Lane	o/o♦
☐ G-VYUM	Boeing 787-9	37970/296		Ruby Murray	♦
☐ G-VZIG	Boeing 787-9	37969/267		Dream Jeannie	♦
☐ G-VELD	Airbus A340-313X	214	ex F-WWJY	African Queen	[LDE]
☐ G-VSUN	Airbus A340-313	114	ex F-WWJI	Rainbow Lady	[LDE]

WOODGATE EXECUTIVE AIR SERVICES   Belfast-Aldergrove (BFS)

☐ G-JAJK	Piper PA-31-350 Chieftain	31-8152014	ex G-OLDB		
☐ G-NIAA	Beech B200 Super King Air		ex D-IEFB	opf Northern Ireland Ambulance♦	

HA- HUNGARY (Hungarian Republic)

ABC AIR HUNGARY   ABC Hungary (AHU)   Budapest (BUD)

☐ HA-TAE	SAAB SF.340AF	340A-007	ex S5-BAT
☐ HA-TAF	SAAB SF.340AF	340A-011	ex LZ-SAC

BUDAPEST AIR SERVICE   Base (BPS)   Budapest (BUD)

☐ HA-FAI	Embraer EMB.120ER Brasilia	120123	ex F-GTSI	
☐ HA-FAL	Embraer EMB.120RT Brasilia	120176	ex F-GTSJ	opf ISK
☐ HA-FAN	Embraer EMB.120ER Brasilia	120104	ex F-GTSH	
☐ HA-YFD	LET L-410UVP-E17	892324		opf Hungarian Air Ambulance

CITYLINE HUNGARY   Cityhun (ZM/CNB)   Budapest (BUD)

☐ HA-TCN	Antonov An-26	7705	ex UR-26244	
☐ HA-TCO	Antonov An-26	2208	ex UR-CEP	<Hegedus

FARNAIR HUNGARY   Blue Strip (FAH)   Budapest (BUD)

☐ HA-FAM	Beech 1900D	UE-16	ex N16UE	
☐ HA-FAO	Swearingen SA227AC Metro III	AC-451B	ex SE-LEF	
☐ HA-FAT	Boeing 737-43QSF	28492/2837	ex N284CH	>KMI
☐ HA-FAU	Boeing 737-43QSF	28494/2839	ex N462PR	♦
☐ HA-FAV	Boeing 737-46QF	29000/3033	ex N690AC	♦
☐ HA-LAD	LET L-410UVP-E8A	902516		

FLEET AIR INTERNATIONAL   Budapest (BUD)

☐ HA-TAB	SAAB SF.340AF	340A-083	ex EC-IUP	
☐ HA-TAD	SAAB SF.340AF	340A-126	ex SE-LSP	
☐ HA-TAG	SAAB SF.340AF	340A-078	ex SE-LSR	
☐ HA-TVG	SAAB SF.340AQC	340A-066	ex SE-KCS	♦

TRAVEL SERVICE HUNGARY   Travelair (TVL)   Budapest (BUD)

☐ HA-LKG	Boeing 737-8CX/W	32362/1125	ex OK-TVB

WIZZ AIR   Wizz Air (W6/WZZ)   Budapest (BUD)

☐ HA-LPJ	Airbus A320-232	3127	ex F-WWBH
☐ HA-LPK	Airbus A320-232	3143	ex F-WWBI
☐ HA-LPL	Airbus A320-232	3166	ex F-WWIL
☐ HA-LPM	Airbus A320-232	3177	ex F-WWDG
☐ HA-LPN	Airbus A320-232	3354	ex F-WWIG
☐ HA-LPO	Airbus A320-232	3384	ex F-WWDO
☐ HA-LPQ	Airbus A320-232	3409	ex F-WWIC
☐ HA-LPR	Airbus A320-232	3430	ex F-WWBC
☐ HA-LPS	Airbus A320-232	3771	ex F-WWDS
☐ HA-LPT	Airbus A320-232	3807	ex F-WWDR
☐ HA-LPU	Airbus A320-232	3877	ex F-WWIJ
☐ HA-LPV	Airbus A320-232	3927	ex F-WWBR
☐ HA-LPW	Airbus A320-232	3947	ex F-WWBD
☐ HA-LPX	Airbus A320-232	3968	ex F-WWIN
☐ HA-LPY	Airbus A320-232	4109	ex D-AVVS

☐ HA-LPZ	Airbus A320-232	4174	ex F-WWDU	
☐ HA-LWA	Airbus A320-232	4223	ex F-WWBI	
☐ HA-LWB	Airbus A320-232	4246	ex F-WWDR	
☐ HA-LWC	Airbus A320-232	4323	ex F-WWDT	
☐ HA-LWD	Airbus A320-232	4351	ex F-WWBZ	
☐ HA-LWE	Airbus A320-232	4372	ex F-WWBM	
☐ HA-LWF	Airbus A320-232	3562	ex LZ-WZB	
☐ HA-LWG	Airbus A320-232	4308	ex LZ-WZC	
☐ HA-LWH	Airbus A320-232	4621	ex F-WWBV	
☐ HA-LWI	Airbus A320-232	4628	ex F-WWDH	
☐ HA-LWJ	Airbus A320-232	4683	ex F-WWIF	
☐ HA-LWK	Airbus A320-232	4716	ex F-WWBT	
☐ HA-LWL	Airbus A320-232	4736	ex F-WWIO	
☐ HA-LWM	Airbus A320-232	5021	ex F-WWIY	
☐ HA-LWN	Airbus A320-232	5075	ex F-WWIB	
☐ HA-LWO	Airbus A320-232	5123	ex F-WWBP	
☐ HA-LWP	Airbus A320-232	5139	ex F-WWIH	
☐ HA-LWQ	Airbus A320-232	5196	ex F-WWIP	
☐ HA-LWR	Airbus A320-232/S	5604	ex F-WWDZ	
☐ HA-LWS	Airbus A320-232/S	5608	ex F-WWIA	
☐ HA-LWT	Airbus A320-232/S	5615	ex F-WWIR	
☐ HA-LWU	Airbus A320-232/S	5617	ex F-WWIV	
☐ HA-LWV	Airbus A320-232/S	5660	ex UR-WUD	
☐ HA-LWX	Airbus A320-232/S	6001	ex F-WWBP	
☐ HA-LWY	Airbus A320-232/S	6058	ex F-WWDK	
☐ HA-LWZ	Airbus A320-232/S	6086	ex F-WWDN	
☐ HA-LYA	Airbus A320-232/S	6077	ex F-WWIK	
☐ HA-LYB	Airbus A320-232/S	6093	ex F-WWDV	
☐ HA-LYC	Airbus A320-232/S	6098	ex F-WWID	
☐ HA-LYD	Airbus A320-232/S	6115	ex F-WWBC	
☐ HA-LYE	Airbus A320-232/S	6131	ex F-WWIC	♦
☐ HA-LYF	Airbus A320-232/S	6195	ex F-WWDE	♦
☐ HA-LYG	Airbus A320-232/S	5539	ex UR-WUC	♦
☐ HA-LYH	Airbus A320-232/S	6235	ex F-WWIL	♦
☐ HA-LYI	Airbus A320-232/S	6352	ex F-WWDE	♦
☐ HA-LYJ	Airbus A320-232/S	6360	ex F-WWDC	♦
☐ HA-LYK	Airbus A320-232/S	6394	ex F-WWBQ	♦
☐ HA-LYL	Airbus A320-232/S	6489	ex F-WWDY	♦
☐ HA-LYM	Airbus A320-232/S	6544	ex F-WWDO	♦
☐ HA-LYN	Airbus A320-232/S	6559	ex F-WWIL	♦
☐ HA-LYO	Airbus A320-232/S	6576	ex F-WWBE	♦
☐ HA-LYP	Airbus A320-232/S	6589	ex F-WWDX	♦
☐ HA-LYQ	Airbus A320-232/S	6614	ex F-WWIA	o/o♦
☐ HA-LYR	Airbus A320-232/S	6631	ex	o/o♦
☐ HA-LYS	Airbus A320-232/S	6662	ex	o/o♦
☐ HA-LYT	Airbus A320-232/S	6683	ex	o/o♦
☐ HA-LYU	Airbus A320-232/S	5539	ex UR-WUC	♦
☐ HA-LYV	Airbus A320-232	3741	ex UR-WUB	♦
☐ HA-	Airbus A320-232/S	6951	ex	o/o♦

HB-   SWITZERLAND & LIECHSTENSTEIN (Swiss Confederation)

AIR GLACIERS   Air Glaciers (AGV)   Sion (SIR)

☐ HB-XQJ	Aérospatiale AS350B3 Ecureuil	3093	
☐ HB-XVB	Aérospatiale AS350B2 Ecureuil	2340	ex F-WYMK
☐ HB-ZCZ	Aérospatiale AS350B3 Ecureuil	3434	ex F-WQDG
☐ HB-ZHY	Aérospatiale AS350B3 Ecureuil	4220	
☐ HB-ZIS	Aérospatiale AS350B3 Ecureuil	4493	
☐ HB-ZNA	Aérospatiale AS350B3 Ecureuil	4082	ex EC-JSG
☐ HB-ZUT	Aérospatiale AS350B3 Ecureuil	4612	
☐ HB-CGW	Cessna U206G Stationair 6	U20604822	ex D-ELML
☐ HB-FDU	Pilatus PC-6/B1-H2 Turbo Porter	663	
☐ HB-GIL	Beech 200 Super King Air	BB-194	ex N502EB
☐ HB-GJI	Beech 200 Super King Air	BB-451	ex D-IBOW
☐ HB-GJM	Beech 200 Super King Air	BB-255	ex N32KD
☐ HB-ZEP	Eurocopter EC120B Colibri	1336	ex F-WWPO
☐ HB-ZIR	Eurocopter EC135T1	0105	ex OE-XAH
☐ HB-ZRK	Eurocopter EC135T1	0027	ex OE-XXR

(♦ at right of HB-ZRK row)

AIR ZERMATT   Air Zermatt (AZF)   Zermatt Heliport

☐ HB-ZCX	Aérospatiale AS350B2 Ecureuil	3105	ex I-AOLA
☐ HB-ZIA	Aérospatiale AS350B3 Ecureuil	4163	ex F-WQDB
☐ HB-ZKF	Aérospatiale AS350B3 Ecureuil	4541	ex (SE-JKU)
☐ HB-ZPB	Aérospatiale AS350B3 Ecureuil	7309	ex F-WWPU
☐ HB-ZVS	Aérospatiale AS350B3 Ecureuil	7569	
☐ HB-ZEF	Eurocopter EC135T2	0259	ex D-HECA
☐ HB-ZSU	Bell 429	57067	ex N425SR

BELAIR AIRLINES		Belair (4T/BHP)		Zurich (ZRH)	
☐ HB-IOP	Airbus A320-214	4187	ex D-AVVY		
☐ HB-IOQ	Airbus A320-214	3422	ex D-ABDT		
☐ HB-IOR	Airbus A320-214	4033	ex D-ABDZ		
☐ HB-IOS	Airbus A320-214	2968	ex D-ABDK		
☐ HB-IOZ	Airbus A320-214	4294	ex D-ABFH		
☐ HB-JOZ	Airbus A320-214	4631	ex (D-ABFR)		
☐ HB-IOX	Airbus A319-112	3604	ex D-ABGM		
☐ HB-JOY	Airbus A319-112	3245	ex D-ABGH		
All wear airberlin c/s					

EASYJET SWITZERLAND		Topswiss (DS/EZS)		Geneva (GVA)	
☐ HB-JYB	Airbus A319-111	4837	ex G-EZGR		
☐ HB-JYC	Airbus A319-111	4785	ex G-EZGO		
☐ HB-JYF	Airbus A319-111	4778	ex G-EZGM		♦
☐ HB-JYG	Airbus A319-111	4781	ex G-EZGN		♦
☐ HB-JYH	Airbus A319-111	4787	ex G-EZGP		♦
☐ HB-JZF	Airbus A319-111	2184	ex G-EZEH		
☐ HB-JZL	Airbus A319-111	2353	ex G-EZEY		
☐ HB-JZM	Airbus A319-111	2370	ex G-EZMK		
☐ HB-JZS	Airbus A319-111	3084	ex G-EZBP		
☐ HB-JZU	Airbus A319-111	2402	ex G-EZNM		
☐ HB-JZV	Airbus A319-111	2709	ex G-EZAE		
☐ HB-JZW	Airbus A319-111	2729	ex G-EZAH		
☐ HB-	Airbus A319-111	4744	ex G-EZGL		o/o♦
☐ HB-JXA	Airbus A320-214	5138	ex G-EZUX		
☐ HB-JXB	Airbus A320-214	5111	ex G-EZUV		♦
☐ HB-JXC	Airbus A320-214	5146	ex G-EZUY		♦
☐ HB-JXD	Airbus A320-214	5150	ex G-EZUU		♦
☐ HB-JYA	Airbus A320-214	4250	ex G-EZTW		
☐ HB-JYD	Airbus A320-214	4646	ex G-EZUE		
☐ HB-JYE	Airbus A320-214	4006	ex G-EZTN		
☐ HB-JZR	Airbus A320-214	4034	ex G-EZTO		
☐ HB-JZX	Airbus A320-214	4157	ex G-EZTP		
☐ HB-JZY	Airbus A320-214	4196	ex G-EZTS		
☐ HB-JZZ	Airbus A320-214	4233	ex G-EZTU		

EDELWEISS AIR		Edelweiss (WK/EDW)			Zurich (ZRH)
☐ HB-IHX	Airbus A320-214	0942	ex F-WWIU	Calvaro	
☐ HB-IHY	Airbus A320-214	0947	ex F-WWIY	Upali	
☐ HB-IHZ	Airbus A320-214	1026	ex F-WWDD	Viktoria	
☐ HB-IJV	Airbus A320-214	2024	ex F-WWDK	Macun	
☐ HB-IJW	Airbus A320-214	2134	ex F-WWBO	Shayan	
☐ HB-IQI	Airbus A330-223	291	ex F-WWKS		
☐ HB-JHQ	Airbus A330-343E	1193	ex F-WWKQ		<SWR
☐ HB-	Airbus A330-343E	1722	ex F-WW		o/o♦

ETIHAD REGIONAL		Darwin (F7/DWT)			Lugano (LUG)
☐ HB-IYD	SAAB 2000	2000-059	ex VP-BPP		
☐ HB-IYI	SAAB 2000	2000-016	ex D-AOLC		
☐ HB-IZH	SAAB 2000	2000-011	ex SE-011	Ticino	
☐ HB-IZJ	SAAB 2000	2000-015	ex (F-GOZJ)	Verbano	
☐ HB-IZP	SAAB 2000	2000-031	ex N168GC		
☐ HB-IZW	SAAB 2000	2000-039	ex YR-SBC		
☐ HB-IZZ	SAAB 2000	2000-048	ex SE-048	Ceresio	
☐ HB-ACA	ATR 72-212A	660	ex I-ADCB		
☐ HB-ACB	ATR 72-212A	662	ex OY-CKO		
☐ HB-ACC	ATR 72-212A	664	ex I-ADCD		♦
☐ HB-ACD	ATR 72-212A	664	ex I-ADCE		♦

FARNAIR SWITZERLAND		Farner (FT/FAT)			Basle (BSL)
☐ HB-AFG	ATR 72-201F	108	ex F-WQNA		
☐ HB-AFH	ATR 72-202F	313	ex F-GJKP	DHC c/s	
☐ HB-AFJ	ATR 72-202F	154	ex OY-RTE		
☐ HB-AFK	ATR 72-202F	232	ex F-GKOB		
☐ HB-AFL	ATR 72-202F	222	ex F-GKPF		
☐ HB-AFM	ATR 72-202F	364	ex B-22712		
☐ HB-AFN	ATR 72-202F	389	ex B-22716		
☐ HB-AFP	ATR 72-201F	381	ex B-22715		
☐ HB-AFR	ATR 72-201F	195	ex F-WKVC	DHL c/s	
☐ HB-AFS	ATR 72-201F	198	ex F-WKVJ		>ANG
☐ HB-AFV	ATR 72-202F	341	ex F-WKVJ		

☐ HB-AFW	ATR 72-202F	419	ex F-WNUD
☐ HB-AFX	ATR 72-202F	265	ex SP-LFB
☐ HB-AFF	ATR 42-320	264	ex F-GOBK

HOLIDAYJET		(GSW)		Zurich (ZRH)
☐ HB-JOG	Airbus A319-112	3818	ex D-AHIM	♦
☐ HB-JOH	Airbus A319-112	3589	ex D-AHIL	♦

HELVETIC AIRWAYS		Arabella (2L/OAW)		Zurich (ZRH)
☐ HB-JVL	Embraer ERJ-190LR	19000354	ex OE-IHD	♦
☐ HB-JVM	Embraer ERJ-190LR	19000349	ex OE-IXC	♦
☐ HB-JVN	Embraer ERJ-190LR	19000285	ex OE-IHA	♦
☐ HB-JVO	Embraer ERJ-190LR	19000294	ex OE-IHB	♦
☐ HB-JVP	Embraer ERJ-190LR	19000387	ex OE-IHE	♦
☐ HB-JVQ	Embraer ERJ-190LR	19000420	ex OE-IZF	♦
☐ HB-JVR	Embraer ERJ-190LR	19000435	ex OE-IXG	o/o♦
☐ HB-JVC	Fokker 100	11501	ex N1468A	
☐ HB-JVE	Fokker 100	11459	ex N1450A	
☐ HB-JVF	Fokker 100	11466	ex N1454D	
☐ HB-JVG	Fokker 100	11478	ex N1458H	
☐ HB-JVH	Fokker 100	11324	ex F-GPNK	
☐ HB-JVI	Fokker 100	11325	ex F-GPNL	[NWI]
☐ HB-JVK	Airbus A319-112	1886	ex VP-CAN	

PRIVATAIR		PrivatAir (PTI)		Geneva (GVA)
☐ HB-IGY	Dassault Falcon 900EX	95	ex F-WWFO	
☐ HB-IIQ	Boeing 737-7CN/W (BBJ)	30752/451	ex N1026G	Gulf Air c/s VIP
☐ HB-JJA	Boeing 737-7AK/W (BBJ)	34303/1758	ex VQ-BBS	>SAS♦
☐ HB-JJB	Boeing 737-306	27421/2438	ex PH-BTE	opf LC
☐ HB-JJC	Boeing 737-306	27420/2406	ex PH-BTD	opf LC
☐ HB-JJD	Boeing 757-236/W	25807/610	ex F-GPEJ	opf LC
☐ HB-JJE	Boeing 757-204/W	27219/596	ex G-OOBR	opf LC
☐ HB-JJF	Boeing 767-316ER/W	27613/652	ex CC-CBJ	opf LC♦
☐ HB-JJH	Boeing 737-752/W	33791/1557	ex N853AM Rivière Niari	opf LC♦
☐ HB-JJI	Boeing 737-752/W	33793/1597	ex N857AM	o/o♦

PRIVATE AIRWAYS				Sion (SIR)
☐ HB-FWV	Pilatus PC-12/47E	1416	ex HB-FSP	

SKYWORK AIRLINES		Skyfox (SX/SRK)		Bern (BRP)
☐ HB-AEO	Dornier 328-110	3061	ex OY-NCK	
☐ HB-AER	Dornier 328-110	3066	ex D-CPRP	
☐ HB-AES	Dornier 328-110	3021	ex D-CHIC	
☐ HB-AEV	Dornier 320-110	3056	ex I-IRTI Sonnenbär	
☐ HB-AEY	Dornier 328-130	3100	ex D-CCIR	

SWISS		Swiss (LX/SWR)		Zurich (ZRH)

Member of Star Alliance

☐ HB-IPT	Airbus A319-112	0727	ex D-AVYC	Rotsandnollen	
☐ HB-IPU	Airbus A319-112	0713	ex D-AVYB	Schrattenflue	
☐ HB-IPV	Airbus A319-112	0578	ex D-AVYA	Castelegns	
☐ HB-IPX	Airbus A319-112	0612	ex D-AVYH	Mont Racine	
☐ HB-IPY	Airbus A319-112	0621	ex D-AVYK	Les Ordons	
☐ HB-IJB	Airbus A320-214	0545	ex TC-JLA		
☐ HB-IJD	Airbus A320-214	0553	ex TC-JLH		
☐ HB-IJE	Airbus A320-214	0559	ex TC-JLI	Arosa	
☐ HB-IJF	Airbus A320-214	0562	ex TC-JLB	Regensdorf	
☐ HB-IJH	Airbus A320-214	0574	ex TC-JLD	Dübendorf	
☐ HB-IJI	Airbus A320-214	0577	ex F-WWDT	Saint-Prex	
☐ HB-IJJ	Airbus A320-214	0585	ex F-WWIV	Les Diablerets	
☐ HB-IJK	Airbus A320-214	0596	ex F-WWBH	Wissigstock	
☐ HB-IJL	Airbus A320-214	0603	ex F-WWBK	Nyon	
☐ HB-IJM	Airbus A320-214	0635	ex F-WWDD	Schilthorn	Star Alliance c/s
☐ HB-IJN	Airbus A320-214	0643	ex F-WWDI	Crans-Montana	Star Alliance c/s
☐ HB-IJO	Airbus A320-214	0673	ex F-WWBF	Verbier	Star Alliance c/s
☐ HB-IJP	Airbus A320-214	0681	ex F-WWBH	Nollen	
☐ HB-IJQ	Airbus A320-214	0701	ex F-WWDL	Locarno	
☐ HB-IJR	Airbus A320-214	0703	ex F-WWDS	Dammastock	
☐ HB-IJS	Airbus A320-214	0782	ex F-WWDS	Creux du Van	
☐ HB-IJU	Airbus A320-214	1951	ex F-WWIQ	Opfikon	
☐ HB-IJX	Airbus A320-214	1762	ex D-ALTG	Davos	

☐	HB-JLP	Airbus A320-214	4618	ex F-WWBP	
☐	HB-JLQ	Airbus A320-214	4673	ex F-WWBM	
☐	HB-JLR	Airbus A320-214	5037	ex F-WWDF	Bassersdorf
☐	HB-JLS	Airbus A320-214	5069	ex F-WWDC	Niederhasli
☐	HB-JLT	Airbus A320-214/S	5518	ex D-AXAM	Grenchen
☐	HB-IOC	Airbus A321-111	0520	ex D-AVZV	Eiger
☐	HB-IOD	Airbus A321-111	0522	ex TC-JMA	
☐	HB-IOF	Airbus A321-111	0541	ex TC-JMB	
☐	HB-IOH	Airbus A321-111	0664	ex D-AVZL	Pitz Palu
☐	HB-IOK	Airbus A321-111	0987	ex D-AVZC	Biefertenstock
☐	HB-IOL	Airbus A321-111	1144	ex D-AVZE	Kaiseregg
☐	HB-IOM	Airbus A321-212	4534	ex D-AVZL	Biel/Bienne
☐	HB-ION	Airbus A321-212	5567	ex D-AVZG	Lugano
☐	HB-IQA	Airbus A330-223	229	ex F-WWKS	Lauteraarhorn >BEL
☐	HB-IQC	Airbus A330-223	249	ex F-WWKI	Breithorn >BEL
☐	HB-JHA	Airbus A330-343E	1000	ex F-WWYX	Schwyz
☐	HB-JHB	Airbus A330-343E	1018	ex F-WWYJ	Sion
☐	HB-JHC	Airbus A330-343E	1029	ex F-WWYY	Bellinzona
☐	HB-JHD	Airbus A330-343E	1026	ex F-WWKE	St. Gallen
☐	HB-JHE	Airbus A330-343E	1084	ex F-WWKE	Fribourg
☐	HB-JHF	Airbus A330-343E	1089	ex F-WWKI	Bern
☐	HB-JHG	Airbus A330-343E	1101	ex F-WWYI	Glarus
☐	HB-JHH	Airbus A330-343E	1145	ex F-WWYD	Neuchatel
☐	HB-JHI	Airbus A330-343E	1181	ex F-WWKM	
☐	HB-JHJ	Airbus A330-343E	1188	ex F-WWYQ	Appenzell
☐	HB-JHK	Airbus A330-343E	1276	ex F-WWYI	Herisau
☐	HB-JHL	Airbus A330-343E	1290	ex F-WWKU	Sarnen
☐	HB-JHM	Airbus A330-343E	1355	ex F-WWCU	
☐	HB-JHN	Airbus A330-343E	1403	ex F-WWYI	
☐	HB-JHQ	Airbus A330-343E	1193	ex F-WWKQ	Chamsin >EDW
☐	HB-	Airbus A330-343E	1722	ex F-WW	o/o♦
☐	HB-JMA	Airbus A340-313X	538	ex F-WWJJ	Matterhorn
☐	HB-JMB	Airbus A340-313X	545	ex F-WWJL	Zurich
☐	HB-JMC	Airbus A340-313X	546	ex F-WWJM	Basel
☐	HB-JMD	Airbus A340-313X	556	ex F-WWJN	Liestal
☐	HB-JME	Airbus A340-313X	559	ex F-WWJP	Dom
☐	HB-JMF	Airbus A340-313X	561	ex F-WWJQ	Liskamm
☐	HB-JMG	Airbus A340-313X	562	ex F-WWJR	Luzern
☐	HB-JMH	Airbus A340-313E	585	ex F-WWJV	Chur
☐	HB-JMI	Airbus A340-313E	598	ex F-WWJX	Schaffhausen
☐	HB-JMJ	Airbus A340-313X	150	ex C-FYKX	Zug
☐	HB-JMK	Airbus A340-313X	169	ex OE-LAK	
☐	HB-JML	Airbus A340-313X	263	ex OE-LAL	Stans
☐	HB-JMM	Airbus A340-313X	154	ex C-FYKZ	Solothum
☐	HB-JMN	Airbus A340-313X	175	ex C-FYLG	Altdorf
☐	HB-JMO	Airbus A340-313X	179	ex C-FYLU	
☐	HB-JNA	Boeing 777-3DEER	44582/1363		o/o♦
☐	OE-LGO	de Havilland DHC-8-402Q	4281	ex C-GDLR	Innsbruck Star Alliance c/s <AUA♦
☐	OE-LGQ	de Havilland DHC-8-402Q	4003	ex C-GCGP	Wilder Kaiser Star Alliance c/s <AUA♦

SWISS GLOBAL AIR LINES   Euroswiss (SWU)   Basle/Lugano/Geneva/Zurich (BSL/LUG/GVA/ZRH)

☐	HB-IXO	Avro 146-RJ100	E3284	ex G-6-284	Brisen
☐	HB-IXP	Avro 146-RJ100	E3283	ex G-6-283	Chestenberg
☐	HB-IXQ	Avro 146-RJ100	E3282	ex G-6-282	Corno Gries
☐	HB-IXS	Avro 146-RJ100	E3280	ex G-6-280	Mont Velan
☐	HB-IXT	Avro 146-RJ100	E3259	ex G-BVYS	Ottenberg
☐	HB-IXU	Avro 146-RJ100	E3276	ex G-6-276	Pfannenstiel
☐	HB-IXV	Avro 146-RJ100	E3274	ex G-6-274	Saxer First
☐	HB-IXW	Avro 146-RJ100	E3272	ex G-6-272	Schafarnisch
☐	HB-IXX	Avro 146-RJ100	E3262	ex G-6-262	Siberen
☐	HB-IYQ	Avro 146-RJ100	E3384	ex G-CFAH	Piz Bruin
☐	HB-IYR	Avro 146-RJ100	E3382	ex G-CFAF	Vrenelisgärtli
☐	HB-IYS	Avro 146-RJ100	E3381	ex G-CFAE	Churfirsten
☐	HB-IYT	Avro 146-RJ100	E3380	ex G-CFAD	Bluemlisalp
☐	HB-IYU	Avro 146-RJ100	E3379	ex G-CFAC	Rot Turm Star Alliance c/s
☐	HB-IYV	Avro 146-RJ100	E3377	ex G-CFAB	Blümlisalp 3,663m Star Alliance c/s
☐	HB-IYW	Avro 146-RJ100	E3359	ex G-6-359	Spitzmeilen
☐	HB-IYY	Avro 146-RJ100	E3339	ex G-6-339	Titlis
☐	HB-IYZ	Avro 146-RJ100	E3338	ex G-6-338	Tour d'Ai

ZIMEX AVIATION   Zimex (C4/IMX)   Zurich (ZRH)

☐	HB-LOK	de Havilland DHC-6 Twin Otter 300	658	ex D-IASL	
☐	HB-LQV	de Havilland DHC-6 Twin Otter 300	643	ex 5A-LQV	
☐	HB-LRB	de Havilland DHC-6 Twin Otter 300	705	ex 5A-DHN	
☐	HB-LRN	de Havilland DHC-6 Twin Otter 300	636	ex ST-LRN	
☐	HB-LRO	de Havilland DHC-6 Twin Otter 300	523	ex F-GKTO	

☐ HB-LRR	de Havilland DHC-6 Twin Otter 300	505	ex 5Y-KZT		
☐ HB-LTG	de Havilland DHC-6 Twin Otter 300	628	ex D-IFLY		
☐ HB-LUC	de Havilland DHC-6 Twin Otter 300	351	ex PK-BAE		♦
☐ HB-LUE	de Havilland DHC-6 Twin Otter 300	233	ex PK-LTX		
☐ HB-LUM	de Havilland DHC-6 Twin Otter 300	420	ex PK-TWG		
☐ HB-LUX	de Havilland DHC-6 Twin Otter 400	845	ex C-FMJO		
☐ HB-FHZ	Pilatus PC-6/B2-H4	840	ex ZS-MTP		
☐ HB-FKR	Pilatus PC-6/B2-H4	872			
☐ HB-FLA	Pilatus PC-6/B2-H4	905			
☐ HB-FLB	Pilatus PC-6/B2-H4	906	ex 5A-FLE		
☐ HB-FLH	Pilatus PC-6/B2-H4	918			
☐ HB-AEM	Beech 1900D	UE-379	ex F-HALS		

HC- ECUADOR (Republic of Ecuador)

AEROMASTER AIRWAYS · Quito (UIO)

☐ HC-CBH	Bell 206L-1 LongRanger III	45354	ex N213HC	
☐ HC-CBT	Bell 427	56028	ex N40560	
☐ HC-CHG	Sikorsky S-64F Skycrane	64075	ex N722HT	

AEROPACSA · Aeropacsa (RPC) · Guayaquil (GYE)

☐ HC-BDV	Cessna TU206F Turbo Stationair II	U20603439		
☐ HC-CBD	Dornier 28D-2 Skyservant	4182	ex HK-4004	
☐ HC-CDI	Dornier 28D-2 Skyservant	4152	ex 58+77	

AERORELEASE · Guayaquil (GYE)

☐ HC-CQR	Mil Mi-171	S9489617098	ex HK-4900	♦

AEROVIC

☐ HC-CJH	Cessna 208B Caravan I	208B0962	ex N602RL	

AVIANCA ECUADOR · Aerogal (2K/GLG) · Shell-Mera/Quito (-/UIO)

☐ HC-CKL	Airbus A319-112	1866	ex N866MX		
☐ HC-CKM	Airbus A319-112	1872	ex N872MX		
☐ HC-CKN	Airbus A319-112	1882	ex N882MX		
☐ HC-CKO	Airbus A319-112	1925	ex N925MX		
☐ HC-CKP	Airbus A319-112	2126	ex EI-ERK		
☐ HC-CLF	Airbus A319-112	2078	ex N778CT		
☐ HC-CJM	Airbus A320-214	4379	ex F-WWIF		
☐ HC-CJV	Airbus A320-214	4547	ex D-AUBP		
☐ HC-CJW	Airbus A320-214	4487	ex N448AV	Star Alliance c/s	<AVA♦

EMETEBE TAXI AEREO · Emetebe (EMT) · Puerto Baquerizo Moreno

☐ HC-BNE	Piper PA-23-250 Aztec D	27-3959	ex N6742Y	
☐ HC-BZF	Britten-Norman BN-2A-27 Islander	200	ex F-BTGO	

LAC – LINEA AÉREA CUENCANA · (L5) · Cuenca (CUE)

☐ HC-CMY	Canadair CRJ-701	10004	ex N1RL	

LAN ECUADOR · Aerolane (XL/LNE) · Quito (UIO)

☐ HC-CPJ	Airbus A319-132	3671	ex CC-CYF	
☐ HC-CPQ	Airbus A319-132	4563	ex CC-BCA	♦
☐ HC-CPR	Airbus A319-132	3663	ex CC-CYE	
☐ HC-CPY	Airbus A319-132	4605	ex CC-BCC	
☐ HC-CPZ	Airbus A319-132	4598	ex CC-BCB	
☐ HC-CQU	Airbus A319-132	3770	ex CC-CYI	♦

SAEREO · Saereo (MZ/SRO) · Quito (UIO)

☐ HC-BUD	Gulfstream Commander 690C	11669	ex N844MA	
☐ HC-BVN	Beech 1900C	UB-53	ex N814BE	
☐ HC-BYH	Cessna T207A Stationair 8 II	20700749	ex N9905M	
☐ HC-BZO	Bell 407	53302	ex N8226A	
☐ HC-CBC	Beech 1900D	UE-17	ex N17YV	
☐ HC-CDM	Embraer EMB.120ER Brasilia	120088	ex N193SW	[UIO]
☐ HC-CEM	Embraer EMB.120ER Brasilia	120227	ex N198SW	[GUA]
☐ HC-CMR	Bell 429	57056	ex N4535X	
☐ N90215	Cessna 208B Caravan I	208B2332		

SERVICIO AEREO REGIONAL

☐ HC-BHC	Britten-Norman BN-2A-20 Islander	59	
☐ HC-CLI	Cessna 421C	1106	ex N6869G

SERVICIOS AEREOS AEROCONEXOS   Ciudadela

☐ HC-CMQ	Britten-Norman BN-2A-3 Islander	270	ex 9J-SKY	♦

SUDAMERICANA   Guayaquil (GYE)

☐ HC-COP	Boeing 737-5Y0	25176/2155	ex N461UF

TAME   Tame (EQ/TAE)   Quito (UIO)

☐ HC-CGJ	Airbus A320-214	0657	ex F-GRSE		[TUS]
☐ HC-CGW	Airbus A320-233	2084	ex N487TA	Ciudad de Quito	
☐ HC-CID	Airbus A320-232	0934	ex N934BV		
☐ HC-COC	Airbus A320-232	1368	ex N863AG		
☐ HC-COE	Airbus A320-233	1339	ex PR-MBM		
☐ HC-CPB	Airbus A320-233	1500	ex OE-ICR		
☐ HC-CGT	Airbus A319-132	2659	ex N511NK		
☐ HC-CGF	Embraer ERJ-190LR	19000137	ex PT-SYQ	Ciudad de Loja	
☐ HC-CGG	Embraer ERJ-190LR	19000141	ex PT-SYT	Ciudad de Manta	
☐ HC-CMO	Airbus A319-112	0946	ex F-WTBM		
☐ HC-CMP	Airbus A319-132	1934	ex N476TA		
☐ HC-COF	Airbus A319-112	949	ex OE-ISR		
☐ HC-COH	Airbus A330-243	348	ex F-WJKF		
☐ HC-COX	Embraer ERJ-190AR	19000372	ex PH-DNA		<DNM
☐ HC-COY	Embraer ERJ-190AR	19000373	ex PH-DNB		<DNM

TAME AMAZONIA

☐ HC-CPE	Quest Kodiak 100	100-0090	ex N90QK	♦
☐ HC-CPG	Quest Kodiak 1000	100-0106	ex N106QK	♦

TAMEXPRESS

☐ HC-CLT	ATR 42-500	844	ex F-WWLG
☐ HC-CMB	ATR 42-500	849	ex F-WWLH
☐ HC-CMH	ATR 42-500	854	ex F-WWLI

TRANS AM AERO EXPRESS   Aero Transam (7T/RTM)   Guayaquil (GYE)

☐ HC-CDX	ATR 42-300F	081	ex YV-914C	opf DHL

VIP-VUELOS INTERNOS PRIVADOS   Vipec (VUR)   Quito (UIO)

☐ HC-CFC	Dornier 328-110	3018	ex N422JS	[MYR]

HH-   HAITI (Republic of Haiti)

CARIBINTAIR/CARIBAIR   Caribintair (CRT)   Port-au-Prince (PAP)

☐ HH-CRT	LET L-410UVP-E	861721	ex LY-AZF	wfs
☐ HH-DMX	British Aerospace Jetstream 31	753	ex N842JS	

HANAIR

☐ HH-JEC	Britten-Norman BN-2A-26 Islander	150	ex 4X-CAH	

NATION AIR

☐ HH-NAT	LET L-410UVP	851439	ex HI-693CT

SUNRISE AIRWAYS   (KSZ)   Port-au-Prince (PAP)

☐ HH-SUN	British Aerospace Jetstream 32	922	ex HI888
☐ HH-YET	British Aerospace Jetstream 32	914	ex N914AE

TORTUG'AIR   Port-au-Prince (PAP)

☐ HH-CRB	LET L-410UVP	800413	ex HI-671CT	wfs
☐ HH-JET	British Aerospace Jetstream 32	883	ex N883CH	
☐ HH-LET	LET L-410UVP-E3	871927	ex PT-XCP	
☐ HH-TOR	LET L-410UVP-E3	871930	ex S9-BAO	
☐ HH-VOL	British Aerospace Jetstream 31	826	ex N250JT	
☐ N359AD	Embraer ERJ-145EP	145169	ex N978RP	<DYN♦

☐ YV315T	British Aerospace Jetstream 3102	697	ex TG-TAW	<SACSA

TROPICAL AIRWAYS

☐ HH-PRN	LET L-410UVP-E3	871906	ex HR-IBA

VISION AIR

☐ HH-RPL	Britten-Norman BN-2A Mk.III-2 Trislander	1040	ex XA-TYU

HI- DOMINICAN REPUBLIC (Republica Dominicana)

ACSA — Centuryflight (CEY) — Santo Domingo-Herrara (HEX)

☐ HI-744CT	Cessna 401B	401B0214	ex N7995Q
☐ HI772	British Aerospace Jetstream 3101	660	ex HI-772CT
☐ HI840	British Aerospace Jetstream 32EP	819	ex HI-840
☐ HI860	British Aerospace Jetstream 32EP	944	ex N944AE

AERODOMCA — Santo Domingo-Herrara (HEX)

☐ HI761	LET L-410UVP-E	871938	ex HI-761CT

AEROLINEAS MAS (N3/MAF) — Santo Domingo-La Isabela (JBQ)

☐ HI859	British Aerospace Jetstream 32	805	ex N493UE
☐ HI874	British Aerospace Jetstream 32	810	ex N494UE
☐ N170PC	British Aerospace Jetstream 31	717	

AIR INTER ISLAND — Santo Domingo-Herrara (HEX)

☐ HI-787	Britten-Norman BN-2A-8 Islander	542	ex HI-787SP	>Sky High

AIR SANTO DOMINGO — Aero Domingo (EX/SDO) — Santo Domingo-Herrara (HEX)

☐ HI-657CT	Short SD.3-60	SH3672	ex 8P-SCD	
☐ HI-679CT	LET L-410UVP-E	882023	ex HI-679CA	wfs
☐ HI-688CT	LET L-410UVP-E	861616	ex HI-688CA	wfs
☐ HI-760CT	Cessna 208B Caravan I	208B0802	ex N1326D	

CARIBAIR — Caribair (CBC) — Santo Domingo-Herrara (HEX)

☐ HI-569CT	Piper PA-31 Turbo Navajo B	31-700	ex HI-569CA		
☐ HI-585CA	Piper PA-31 Turbo Navajo B	31-850	ex N333GT		
☐ HI-666CT	LET L-410UVP	851517	ex TG-TJV		
☐ HI-697CT	LET L-410UVP-E9A	882040	ex S9-TAV		
☐ HI-698CT	LET L-410UVP-E9A	882039	ex S9-TAU		
☐ HI-713CT	LET L-410UVP	851340	ex HI-713CA		
☐ HI746CT	British Aerospace Jetstream 3101	692	ex HI-746CA	no titles	wfs
☐ HI-830	British Aerospace Jetstream 3101	780	ex HI-830CT		

DOMINICAN WINGS (DWI) — Santo Domingo-Herrara (HEX)

☐ HI-968	Airbus A320-233	0561	ex LY-VEP	♦

PAWA DOMINICANA — Pawa (7Q/PWD) — Santo Domingo-Herrara (HEX)

☐ HI-869	Douglas DC-9-32	47566/691	ex N949N	♦
☐ HI-876	Douglas DC-9-32	47046/168	ex N602NW	♦
☐ HI-965	Douglas DC-9-32	47235/436	ex YV371T	wfs♦
☐ HI-	Douglas DC-9-31	48139/1024	ex YV1879	[SDQ]♦
☐ HI-	McDonnell-Douglas MD-87	49727/1621	ex N599SH	[OPF]♦
☐ HI-	McDonnell-Douglas MD-87	49780/1674	ex N572SH	[OPF]♦
☐ HI-	McDonnell-Douglas MD083	49845/1573	ex N989PG	[HEX]♦

SAPAIR/SERVICIOS AEREOS PROFESIONALES

Proservicios (5S/PSV) — Santo Domingo-Herrara (HEX)

☐ HI819	British Aerospace Jetstream 31	811	ex HI-819
☐ HI851	British Aerospace Jetstream 32EP	940	ex HI-851
☐ HI856	British Aerospace Jetstream 32EP	919	ex HI-856
☐ HI858	British Aerospace Jetstream 32EP	938	ex HI-858
☐ HI875	British Aerospace Jetstream 3101	642	ex N642JX
☐ HI918	British Aerospace Jetstream 3102	641	ex LN-SVZ

☐ HI644	de Havilland DHC-6 Twin Otter 200	46	ex HI-644CT
☐ HI657	Short SD.3-60	SH3672	ex HI-657CT
☐ HI-720CT	Embraer EMB.120RT Brasilia	120038	ex N332JS

219

☐ N719JP	Beech 1900D	UE-84	ex ZS-PUC	

SKY HIGH AVIATION				Punta Cana
☐ HI-653	Britten-Norman BN-2A-26 Islander	8	ex HI-653CA	♦
☐ HI-787	Britten-Norman BN-2A-8 Islander	542	ex HI-787SP	<Air Inter Island♦

VOL AIR				Santo Domingo-Herrara (HEX)
☐ HI-785CT	Piper PA-31-350 Navajo Chieftain	31-7305066	ex N74923	
☐ HI-789CA	Britten-Norman BN-2A-21 Islander	849	ex HI-640CA	
☐ HI-845	Britten-Norman BN-2A-26 Islander	2005	ex HI-593CA	♦

HK- COLOMBIA (Republic of Colombia)

ADA – AEROLINEAS DE ANTIOQUIA		Antioquia (ANQ)		Medellin-Olaya Herrera (MDE)
☐ HK-4364	British Aerospace Jetstream 32EP	897	ex N482UE	
☐ HK-4381	British Aerospace Jetstream 32EP	898	ex N483UE	
☐ HK-4398	British Aerospace Jetstream 32EP	828	ex N473UE	
☐ HK-4515	British Aerospace Jetstream 32EP	900	ex N496UE	
☐ HK-4548	British Aerospace Jetstream 32EP	893	ex N479UE	
☐ HK-4792	British Aerospace Jetstream 32EP	865	ex N865CY	
☐ HK-4820	British Aerospace Jetstream 3201	895	ex N481UE	
☐ HK-	British Aerospace Jetstream 32	894	ex N894KA	wfs
☐ HK-2548	de Havilland DHC-6 Twin Otter 300	718	ex HK-2548X	
☐ HK-2603	de Havilland DHC-6 Twin Otter 300	749		
☐ HK-2669	de Havilland DHC-6 Twin Otter 300	760	ex HK-2669X Arcangel Rafael	
☐ HK-3972	Dornier 28D-2 Skyservant	4156	ex YS-400P	
☐ HK-4000	Dornier 28D-2 Skyservant	4177	ex YS-404P	
☐ HK-4042	Cessna T303 Crusader	T30300155	ex N6421C	
☐ HK-4073	Dornier 28D-2 Skyservant	4114	ex N952	
☐ HK-4849	Dornier 328-120	3084	ex HC-CFI	
☐ HK-4917	Dornier 328-110	3039	ex HC-CFS	
☐ HK-5053	Dornier 328-100			♦

AER CARIBE		(ACL)		
☐ HK-4052	Antonov An-32A	1805	ex YN-CBU	
☐ HK-4257	Antonov An-32B	3203	ex OB-1699	
☐ HK-4427	Antonov An-32A	1809	ex HK-4427X Marianita	
☐ HK-4832X	Antonov An-32B	3006	ex AMT-210	♦
☐ HK-4833X	Antonov An-32B	3404	ex AMT-211	♦
☐ HK-4728	Antonov An-26B	8205	ex EK-26205	
☐ HK-4729	Antonov An-26B	12602	ex EK-26093	
☐ HK-4730	Antonov An-26B	07309510	ex EK-26510	dam 07Aug14
☐ HK-4969	Beech 200C Super King Air	BL-14	ex N3697F	

AEROEXPRESSO DE LA FRONTERA				
☐ HK-3804P	Cessna 208B Caravan I	208B0315	ex HK-3804	
☐ HK-3539	Cessna 208 Caravan I	20800165	ex N9741F	
☐ HK-3916	Cessna 208B Caravan I	208B0372	ex YV1622	

AEROLINEAS ALAS DE COLOMBIA				
☐ HK-4825	Cessna 414	414-0838	ex N777NM	
☐ HK-5072	Cessna T207 Stationair	20700264	ex N469AM	♦

AEROLINEAS DE LA PAZ				Villavicencio (VVC)
☐ HK-1663	Cessna U206F Stationair	U20601962	ex N50961	
☐ HK-3035	Cessna T303 Crusader	T30300191		
☐ HK-4189	Douglas DC-3	4319	ex HK-3994	
☐ HK-4292X	Douglas DC-3	17061/34328	ex OB-1756	status?

AEROLINEAS DEL OCCIDENTE				
☐ HK-4920	Beech B300 King Air	FL-584	ex N33984	

AEROSUCRE		Aerosucre (KRE)		Barranquilla (BAQ)
☐ HK-4216	Boeing 737-230C	20253/223	ex HP-1134CMP	
☐ HK-4465	Boeing 727-222F (FedEx 3)	19915/681	ex N7642U	
☐ HK-4504	Boeing 727-2J0F (FedEx 3)	21108/1174	ex N284KH	
☐ HK-4544	Boeing 727-2J0F (FedEx 3)	21105/1158	ex N281KH	
☐ HK-4253X	Boeing 737-2H6C (Nordam 3)	21109/436	ex HP-1311CMP	
☐ HK-5026	Boeing 737-230	22120/715	ex CC-CDB	wfs♦

220

220

AERUPIA/AEROTAXI DEL UPIA — Villavicencio (VVC)

☐ HK-2713	Piper PA-34-220T Seneca III	34-8133241	
☐ HK-2822	Britten-Norman BN-2B-27 Islander	2109	ex N2643X
☐ HK-5014	Piper PA-31-325 Navajo	31-8312003	ex N41127

AIR CARIBE INTERNATIONAL

☐ HK-	Beech B200C Super King Air	BL-14	ex N3697F

AIR COLOMBIA — Villavicencio (VVC)

☐ HK-1175	Douglas DC-3	20432	
☐ HK-3292	Douglas DC-3	19661	ex N9101S
☐ HK-3293X	Douglas DC-3	9186	ex N46877

ALAS DE COLUMBIA

☐ HK-4924	Piper PA-34-200T Seneca	34-7770024	ex N995EA
☐ HK-4983	Cessna 421C	421C0346	ex N344ND

ALIANSA/AEROLINEAS ANDINAS — Villavicencio (VVC)

☐ HK-122	Douglas DC-3	4414	ex C-122	Frtr [VCV]
☐ HK-1315	Douglas DC-3	4307	ex PP-ANG	
☐ HK-2006	Douglas DC-3	43086	ex N43A	
☐ HK-2820	Douglas DC-3	20171	ex N151D	
☐ HK-3215	Douglas DC-3	26111/14666		
☐ HK-5016	AMC Turbo DC-3TP	14101/25546	ex ZS-OJM	

ANTES

☐ HK-4991	Cessna 208B Caravan I	208B0100	ex XA-UOH

AVIANCA — Avianca (AV/AVA) — Bogota-Eldorado (BOG)

Member of Star Alliance

☐ N589AV	Airbus A318-111	2575	ex N599EL	
☐ N590EL	Airbus A318-111	2328	ex XA-UBQ	
☐ N591EL	Airbus A318-111	2333	ex XA-UBR	
☐ N592EL	Airbus A318-111	2358	ex XA-UBS	
☐ N593EL	Airbus A318-111	2367	ex XA-UBT	
☐ N594EL	Airbus A318-111	2377	ex XA-UBU	
☐ N595EL	Airbus A318-111	2394	ex XA-UBV	
☐ N596EL	Airbus A318-111	2523	ex XA-UBW	
☐ N597EL	Airbus A318-111	2544	ex XA-UBX	
☐ N598EL	Airbus A318-111	2552	ex XA-UBY	
☐ N599EL	Airbus A318-111	2575	ex XA-UBZ	
☐ HK-4552	Airbus A319-112	3518	ex D-AVYZ	
☐ HK-4553	Airbus A319-112	3467	ex D-AVWN	
☐ N266CT	Airbus A319-112	2662	ex XA-UER	
☐ N422AV	Airbus A319-115	4200	ex D-AVYC	
☐ N519AV	Airbus A319-115	5119	ex D-AVYR	Star Alliance c/s
☐ N557AV	Airbus A319-115	5057	ex D-AVYM	
☐ N612MX	Airbus A319-112	1612	ex EI-CXA	
☐ N634MX	Airbus A319-112	1634	ex D-AVYH	
☐ N647AV	Airbus A319-115	3647	ex D-AVYQ	
☐ N690AV	Airbus A319-132/S	5944	ex D-AVWE	
☐ N691AV	Airbus A319-115	3691	ex D-AVWG	
☐ N694AV	Airbus A319-132/S	6068	ex D-AVWI	
☐ N695AV	Airbus A319-132/S	6099	ex D-AVWK	♦
☐ N723AV	Airbus A319-115/S	6167	ex D-AVWO	o/o♦
☐ N726AV	Airbus A319-115/S	6174	ex D-AVWP	♦
☐ N730AV	Airbus A312-132/S	6132	ex D-AVWL	o/o♦
☐ N741AV	Airbus A319-115/S	6617	ex D-AVYG	o/o♦
☐ N992TA	Airbus A319-112	2066	ex N602CT	<TAI
☐ HK-4549	Airbus A320-214	3408	ex F-WWBZ	
☐ HK-4659	Airbus A320-214	4100	ex F-WWDK	
☐ N195AV	Airbus A320-214	5195	ex D-AVVK	
☐ N281AV	Airbus A320-214	4281	ex F-WWIH	
☐ N284AV	Airbus A320-214	4284	ex F-WWIP	
☐ N345AV	Airbus A320-214	4345	ex F-WWBI	
☐ N398AV	Airbus A320-214	3988	ex F-WWBO	
☐ N401AV	Airbus A320-214	4001	ex F-WWDL	
☐ N411AV	Airbus A320-214	4011	ex F-WWIC	
☐ N416AV	Airbus A320-214	4167	ex F-WWBY	
☐ N417AV	Airbus A320-214	4175	ex D-AVVT	
☐ N426AV	Airbus A320-214	4026	ex F-WWDU	

☐ N446AV	Airbus A320-214	4046	ex D-AVVI		
☐ N448AV	Airbus A320-214	4487	ex HC-CJW	Star Alliance c/s	>GLG
☐ N451AV	Airbus A320-214	4051	ex F-WWIP		
☐ N454AV	Airbus A320-214	5454	ex D-AVVU	Star Alliance c/s	
☐ N477AV	Airbus A320-214/S	5477	ex F-WWBM	Star Alliance c/s	
☐ N481AV	Airbus A320-214	4381	ex F-WWBB		
☐ N536AV	Airbus A320-214	5360	ex D-AUBR	Star Alliance c/s	
☐ N538AV	Airbus A320-214	5398	ex F-WWBN		
☐ N562AV	Airbus A320-214/S	5622	ex F-WWBM		
☐ N567AV	Airbus A320-214	4567	ex F-WWBG		
☐ N599AV	Airbus A320-214	4599	ex F-WWBQ		
☐ N632AV	Airbus A320-214/S	5632	ex F-WWBE		
☐ N664AV	Airbus A320-214	3664	ex F-WWDX		
☐ N688TA	Airbus A320-214	5243	ex D-AVVZ	Star Alliance c/s	<TAI
☐ N724AV	Airbus A320-214/S	6153	ex F-WWBK		♦
☐ N728AV	Airbus A320-214/S	6209	ex F-WWDK		♦
☐ N740AV	Airbus A320-214/S	6411	ex F-WWDM		♦
☐ N763AV	Airbus A320-214	4763	ex F-WWBU		
☐ N789AV	Airbus A320-214	4789	ex F-WWDV		
☐ N821AV	Airbus A320-214	4821	ex F-WWIF		
☐ N862AV	Airbus A320-214	4862	ex F-WWBR		
☐ N961AV	Airbus A320-214	3961	ex F-WWDV		
☐ N980AV	Airbus A320-214	3980	ex F-WWIZ		
☐ N939AV	Airbus A320-214	4939	ex F-WWBN		
☐ N992AV	Airbus A320-214	3992	ex F-WWDE		
☐	Airbus A320-214	6692	ex		o/o♦
☐	Airbus A320-214	6739	ex		o/o♦
☐	Airbus A320-214	6746	ex		o/o♦
☐ N692AV	Airbus A321-231/S	5936	ex D-AZAV		
☐ N693AV	Airbus A321-231/S	6002	ex D-AVZC		
☐ N696AV	Airbus A321-231/S	6138	ex D-AVXK		♦
☐ N697AV	Airbus A321-231/S	6190	ex D-AZAE		♦
☐ N725AV	Airbus A321-231/S	6219	ex D-AZAW		♦
☐ N729AV	Airbus A321-231/S	6399	ex D-AZAE		♦
☐ N746AV	Airbus A321-211/S	6511	ex D-AVZY		o/o♦
☐ N	Airbus A321-231/S	6781	ex		o/o♦
☐ N279AV	Airbus A330-243	1279	ex F-WWYN		>TPU
☐ N280AV	Airbus A330-243	1400	ex F-WWKV	Star Alliance c/s	
☐ N342AV	Airbus A330-243	1342	ex F-WWCK	Star Alliance c/s	
☐ N508AV	Airbus A330-243	1508	ex F-WWKI		
☐ N941AV	Airbus A330-243	1492	ex F-WWTL		♦
☐ N968AV	Airbus A330-243	1009	ex F-WWYE		
☐ N969AV	Airbus A330-243	1016	ex F-WWYI		
☐ N973AV	Airbus A330-243	1073	ex F-WWKZ		
☐ N974AV	Airbus A330-243	1208	ex F-WWYM		
☐ N975AV	Airbus A330-243	1224	ex F-WWKJ		
☐ N	Airbus A330-243	1540	ex F-WW		o/o
☐ HK-4954	ATR 72-600	1092	ex F-WWEE		
☐ HK-4955	ATR 72-600	1114	ex F-WWEC		
☐ HK-4956	ATR 72-600	1116	ex F-WWEE		
☐ HK-4999	ATR 72-600	1126	ex F-WWEO		
☐ HK-5039	ATR 72-600	1124	ex F-WWEM		
☐ HK-5000	ATR 72-600	1142	ex F-WWEG		
☐ HK-5040	ATR 72-600	1151	ex F-WWEP		♦
☐ HK-5041	ATR 72-600	1160	ex F-WWEZ		♦
☐ HK-5109	ATR 72-600	1231	ex F-WWEF		♦
☐ N780AV	Boeing 787-8	37502/217		780	♦
☐ N781AV	Boeing 787-8	37503/228		781	♦
☐ N782AV	Boeing 787-8	37504/239		782	♦
☐ N783AV	Boeing 787-8	37505/242		783	♦
☐ N784AV	Boeing 787-8	37506/294		784	o/o♦
☐ N785AV	Boeing 787-8	37507/347		785	o/o♦
☐ N	Boeing 787-8	37508/367			o/o♦
☐ HK-4467	Fokker 50	20301	ex PH-MXZ		wfs
☐ HK-4469X	Fokker 50	20285	ex PH-AVJ		wfs
☐ HK-4470	Fokker 50	20297	ex PH-AVO		wfs
☐ HK-4487X	Fokker 50	20266	ex PH-LXW		wfs
☐ HK-4580	Fokker 50	20281	ex PR-OAW		wfs
☐ HK-4581	Fokker 50	20296	ex PR-OAX		wfs
☐ N330QT	Airbus A330-243F	1368	ex F-WWKQ		

AVIANCA CARGO	**Tampa (QT/TPA)**		**Medellin-Olaya Herrara (MDE)**

☐ N330QT	Airbus A330-243F	1368	ex F-WWKQ
☐ N331QT	Airbus A330-243F	1380	ex F-WWYK
☐ N332QT	Airbus A330-243F	1428	ex F-WWCI
☐ N334QT	Airbus A330-243F	1448	ex F-WWKU

☐ N335QT	Airbus A330-243F	1534	ex F-WWCJ	♦
☐ N771QT	Boeing 767-381F	33404/885	ex JA601F	

AVIHECO COLOMBIA   Bogota-Eldorado/Ibague (BOG/IBE)

☐ HK-3039	Bell 206L-2 LongRanger III	51052		
☐ HK-4267	Bell 206L-2 LongRanger III	51252	ex N37CA	
☐ HK-4306	Bell 206L-2 LongRanger III	51606	ex HC-BXA	
☐ HK-4334	Convair 580F	176	ex N631MB	Used by CIA/DAC
☐ HK-4736	Bell 212	30665	ex N665L	
☐ HK-4918	Bell 412EP	36252	ex N412TT	

CHARTER DEL CARIBE

☐ HK-4837	Cessna 421B	421B0464	ex N420GC

CHARTER EXPRESS

☐ HK-4858	Cessna P206	P206-0046	ex N2546X

CONVEYOR EXPRESS/LASER AEREO

☐ HK-4957	Piper PA-31-350 Navajo Chieftain	31-7305033	ex N58CR	♦
☐ HK-4958	Piper PA-31-325 Navajo	31-7612104	ex N83DW	♦

COPA AIRLINES COLOMBIA   (P5/RPB)   Bogota-Eldorado (BOG)

☐ HK-4505X	Embraer ERJ-190LR	19000114	ex PT-SQI	
☐ HK-4506X	Embraer ERJ-190LR	19000110	ex PT-SQE	
☐ HK-4507X	Embraer ERJ-190LR	19000122	ex PT-SQQ	
☐ HK-4508X	Embraer ERJ-190LR	19000138	ex PT-SYR	
☐ HK-4453X	Embraer ERJ-190LR	19000063	ex PT-SJB	
☐ HK-4454X	Embraer ERJ-190LR	19000061	ex PT-SIO	
☐ HK-4456X	Embraer ERJ-190LR	19000074	ex PT-SJN	
☐ HK-4559X	Embraer ERJ-190LR	19000200	ex PT-SGI	
☐ HK-4560X	Embraer ERJ-190LR	19000208	ex PT-SGR	
☐ HK-4599	Embraer ERJ-190LR	19000269	ex PT-TLJ	
☐ HK-4601	Embraer ERJ-190LR	19000251	ex PT-SIW	
☐ HP-1562CMP	Embraer ERJ-190AR	19000095	ex PT-SNP	<CMP
☐ HP-1563CMP	Embraer ERJ-190AR	19000098	ex PT-SNS	<CMP
☐ HP-1566CMP	Embraer ERJ-190AR	19000165	ex PT-SAX	<CMP
☐ HP-1371CMP	Boeing 737-7V3/W	30049/388		<CMP
☐ HP-1372CMP	Boeing 737-7V3/W	28607/399		<CMP
☐ HP-1373CMP	Boeing 737-7V3/W	30458/459	673	<CMP

EASYFLY   (EFY)   Bogota-Eldorado (BOG)

☐ HK-4502	British Aerospace Jetstream 4101	41091	ex N572HK	
☐ HK-4503	British Aerospace Jetstream 4101	41093	ex N574HK	
☐ HK-4521	British Aerospace Jetstream 4101	41092	ex N573HK	
☐ HK-4522	British Aerospace Jetstream 4101	41086	ex N568HK	
☐ HK-4551	British Aerospace Jetstream 4101	41089	ex N570HK	
☐ HK-4568	British Aerospace Jetstream 4101	41057	ex N552HK	
☐ HK-4585	British Aerospace Jetstream 4101	41067	ex N554HK	
☐ HK-4765	British Aerospace Jetstream 4101	41074	ex G-MAJV	
☐ HK-4775	British Aerospace Jetstream 4101	41039	ex G-MAJP	
☐ HK-4786	British Aerospace Jetstream 41	41098	ex G-MAJX	
☐ HK-4867	British Aerospace Jetstream 4101	41101		
☐ HK-4868	British Aerospace Jetstream 4101	41030	ex CX-CAF	
☐ N569HK	British Aerospace Jetstream 4101	41088		[MQY]
☐ HK-5070X	ATR 42-500	655	ex OH-ATD	♦
☐ HK-5071X	ATR 42-500	651	ex OH-ATC	♦
☐ HK-5117X	ATR 42-500	581	ex N581NC	♦

HELICOL   Helicol (HEL)   Bogota-Eldorado (BOG)

☐ HK-3303X	Bell 212	30654	ex N59608	
☐ HK-3336X	Bell 212	31207	ex N2180J	
☐ HK-3578G	Bell 412	33203		
☐ HK-3633X	Bell 206L-1 LongRanger II	45510	ex N57497	
☐ HK-4031X	Bell 212	31203	ex HK-3184X	
☐ HK-4213G	Bell 407	53405	ex (N2382Z)	
☐ HK-4731	Bell 412EP	36325		
☐ HK-4744	Bell 412	33009	ex N412HL	
☐ HK-4767	Bell 412	33065	ex N968FM	
☐ HK-4959	Beech 1900D	UE-168	ex N82539	
☐ HK-	Beech 1900D	UE-199	ex N81538	

HELIFLY

☐ HK-4928	Bell 206L LongRanger	45233	

HELIGOLFO

☐ HK-4840	Cessna 402B	402B0526	ex N354HC

HELISTAR COLOMBIA

☐ HK-4722	MBB BK.117C-2	9324	
☐ HK-4778	MBB BK.117C-2	9406	ex D-HMBE
☐ HK-4841	MBB BK.117C-2	9512	ex D-HADM
☐ HK-4847	MBB BK.117C-2	9520	ex D-HADN
☐ HK-4934	MBB BK.117C-2	9572	
☐ HK-4997	MBB BK.117C-2	9606	ex D-HADL
☐ HK-4779	Bell 412EP	36560	
☐ HK-4842	Bell 412EP	36594	ex N463XB

INTERANDES

☐ HK-3226	Cessna 208 Caravan I	20800002	ex N9182F

LAN AIRLINES COLOMBIA · LAN Colombia (4C/ARE) · Bogota-Eldorado (BOG)

Member of oneWorld

☐ HK-4473	de Havilland DHC-8Q-201	479	ex N985HA	
☐ HK-4480	de Havilland DHC-8Q-201	509	ex N998HA	
☐ HK-4491	de Havilland DHC-8Q-201	478	ex N983HA	
☐ HK-4495	de Havilland DHC-8Q-201	497	ex N996HA	
☐ HK-4509	de Havilland DHC-8Q-201	507	ex N997HA	
☐ HK-4513X	de Havilland DHC-8Q-201	468	ex N969HA	
☐ HK-4554X	de Havilland DHC-8Q-201	450	ex N965HA	
☐ CC-BAO	Airbus A320-214	4767	ex F-WWBZ	oneWorld c/s ♦
☐ CC-BAV	Airbus A320-214	4972	ex D-AVVC	

LATINA DE AVIACION · Villavicencio (VVC)

☐ HK-4173X	Beech 1900C-1	UC-14	ex N38015
☐ HK-2006	Douglas DC-3C	43086	ex N43A

LINEAS AEREAS CARGUERA DE COLOMBIA (L7/LAE) · Bogota-Eldorado (BOG)

☐ N418LA	Boeing 767-316F/W	34246/936	<LCO

LINEAS AÉREAS SURAMERICANAS · Suramericano (LAU) · Bogota-Eldorado (BOG)

☐ HK-1271	Boeing 727-24C (Raisbeck 3)	19524/428	ex N1781B	
☐ HK-4154	Boeing 727-51F (Raisbeck 3)	18804/162	ex N5607	Orion
☐ HK-4261	Boeing 727-251F (FedEx 3)	21156/1170	ex N296AJ	
☐ HK-4262	Boeing 727-2F9F/W (Duganair 3)	21427/1291	ex N299AJ	
☐ HK-4401	Boeing 727-2X3F (FedEx 3)	22609/1731	ex N797AJ	[BOG]
☐ HK-4636	Boeing 727-2S2F (FedEx 3)	22927/1821	ex N129FB	
☐ HK-4637	Boeing 727-2S2F (FedEx 3)	22928/1822	ex N131FB	

NACIONAL DE AVIACION COLOMBIA

☐ HK-4151X	LET L-410UVP-E	861610	ex N16100

PETROLEUM AIR SERVICE

☐ HK-4557	Beech 1900D	UE-50	ex HK-4557X
☐ HK-4564	Beech 1900D	UE-402	ex N842CA
☐ HK-4732	Beech 1900D	UE-160	ex N877NA
☐ HK-4959	Beech 1900D	UE-168	ex N82539
☐ HK-4963	Beech 1900D	UE-199	ex N81538
☐ HK-5003	Beech 1900D	UE-221	ex C-GHFB
☐ HK-4847	MBB BK.117C-2	9520	ex D-HADN
☐ HK-4934	MBB BK.117C-2	9572	
☐ HK-4997	MBB BK.117C-2	9606	ex D-HADL

SADELCA · Sadelca (SDK) · Neiva (NVA)

☐ HK-1149	Douglas DC-3	26593	ex HK-1149G	
☐ HK-2494	Douglas DC-3	16357/33105	ex N87611	
☐ HK-2664	Douglas DC-3	19433	ex HK-2665	Angela Sofia

☐ HK-5003	Beech 1900D	UE-221	ex C-GHFB	
☐ HK-3286	Douglas DC-3	6144	ex HP-86	dam 04Apr13
☐ HK-4296	Antonov An-32A	1704	ex ER-AXF	
☐ HK-4356	Antonov An-26B-100	5109	ex YN-CGC	

SARPA – RENT AIR/SERVICIOS AEREOS PANAMERICANOS   Medellin-Olaya Herrara (MDE)

☐ HK-4350	British Aerospace Jetstream 32EP	836	ex G-OEST	
☐ HK-4362	British Aerospace Jetstream 32EP	840	ex G-BYMA	
☐ HK-4394E	British Aerospace Jetstream 32EP	905	ex N486UE	EMS
☐ HK-4405	British Aerospace Jetstream 32EP	849	exHK-4405E EMS	
☐ HK-4411	British Aerospace Jetstream 32	870	ex N870CY	
☐ HK-4540X	British Aerospace Jetstream 32EP	933	ex N933CX	
☐ HK-4541	British Aerospace Jetstream 32EP	937	ex N937AE	
☐ HK-4772	British Aerospace Jetstream 32EP	950	ex N341TE	
☐ HK-4791	British Aerospace Jetstream 32EP	917	ex N917AE	
☐ HK-4803	British Aerospace Jetstream 3201	924	ex N924AE	
☐ HK-4854	British Aerospace Jetstream 32EP	921	ex N921AE	

☐ HK-4099	Agusta-Bell 212	5630		
☐ HK-4100	Agusta-Bell 212	5631		
☐ HK-4124	Bell 212	30844	ex N405RA	
☐ HK-4232	Bell 212	30993	ex XA-SRZ	
☐ HK-4233	Bell 212	31164	ex XA-LAM	
☐ HK-4826	Learjet 35A	35A-364		
☐ HK-4973	Embraer EMB.120ER Brasilia	120161	ex PT-SLE	
☐ HK-5013	Embraer EMB.120ER Brasilia	120147	ex PT-SLD	

SATENA   Satena (9R/NSE)   Bogota-Eldorado (BOG)

☐ HK-4747	ATR 42-512	526	ex FAC-1182	
☐ HK-4748	ATR 42-512	522	ex FAC-1183	
☐ HK-4806	ATR 42-512	513	ex N513NA	
☐ HK-4827	ATR 42-512	532	ex HK-4827X	
☐ HK-4862	ATR 42-512	571	ex VQ-VPE	
☐ HK-4949	ATR 42-512	621	ex F-OIQB	
☐ HK-4979	ATR 42-512	603	ex OY-CHI	dual reg FAC-1191
☐ HK-5104X	ATR 42-500	631	ex F-OIQD	♦
☐ HK-	ATR 42-600	1019	ex F-WWLF	dual reg FAC-1192	o/o♦

☐ FAC-1103	LET L-410UVP-E	902420	ex HK-4224	Lsd fr/opb SRC
☐ HK-4524X	Dornier 328-120	3082	ex FAC-1162 Bahia Solano	
☐ HK-4525	Embraer ERJ-145LR	145774	ex PT-SME Milenium I	
☐ HK-4528	Embraer ERJ-170LR	17000151	ex FAC-1180	
☐ HK-4828	ATR 72-212A	521	ex HK-4828X	
☐ HK-4532X	Dornier 328-120	3081	ex FAC-1163 El Antioqueño	
☐ HK-4533X	Dornier 328-120	3092	ex FAC-1164 El Casanereno	
☐ HK-4534X	Dornier 328-120	3103	ex FAC-1165 El Guambiano	
☐ HK-4535	Embraer ERJ-145LR	145776	ex PT-SMG Milenium II	
☐ HK-4863	ATR 72-212A	552	ex HK-4563X	
☐ HK-5036-X	Harbin Y-12E	017		♦
☐ HK-5037-X	Harbin Y-12E	018	also wears FAC-1107	♦

SEARCA   Searca (SRC)   Medellin-Olaya Herrara (MDE)

☐ HK-4266	Beech 1900C-1	UC-64	ex HK-4266X	
☐ HK-4282	Beech 1900C-1	UC-60	ex HK-4282X	
☐ HK-4476	Beech 1900D	UE-123	ex N123YV	
☐ HK-4499	Beech 1900D	UE-110	ex N110YV	
☐ HK-4512	Beech 1900D	UE-105	ex N105YV	
☐ HK-4537	Beech 1900D	UE-95	ex N95YV	
☐ HK-4558	Beech 1900D	UE-156	ex N156E	
☐ HK-4563	Beech 1900D	UE-113	ex N113YV	
☐ HK-4598	Beech 1900D	UE-183	ex N48544	
☐ HK-4600	Beech 1900D	UE-99	ex N99YV	
☐ HK-4630	Beech 1900D	UE-93	ex N93ZV	
☐ HK-4673	Beech 1900D	UE-104	ex N104YV	
☐ HK-4681	Beech 1900D	UE-213	ex N3199Q	
☐ HK-4709	Beech 1900D	UE-140	ex N140ZV	
☐ HK-5059	Beech 1900D	UE-181	ex N49543	♦

☐ HK-4038	LET L-410UVP-E	841323	ex HK-4038X	
☐ HK-4048	LET L-410UVP-E	912626	ex OM-111	
☐ HK-4105	LET L-410UVP-E	861613	ex HK-4105X	
☐ HK-4161	LET L-410UVP-E	861612	ex FAC 1105	
☐ HK-4367	LET L-410UVP-E20B	851334	ex CP-2252	
☐ FAC-1103	LET L-410UVP-E	902420	ex HK-4224	Lsd to/opf NSE

☐ HK-4794	Beechjet 400A	RK-21	ex N2920	
☐ HK-4801	Beechjet 400A	RK-173	ex N2273Z	
☐ HK-4989	Beech 200 Super King Air	BB-356	ex N79RR	

SELVA COLOMBIA		*Selva (SDV)*		*Villavicencio (VVC)*
☐ HK-4295	Antonov An-26	4702	ex LZ-NHA	Maribel
☐ HK-4388	Antonov An-26B-100	12402	ex LZ-NHE	
☐ HK-4607	Boeing 727-259F (FedEx 3)	22476/1747	ex N901LF	
☐ HK-4706	Antonov An-26B-100	12203	ex 3X-GFB	

SERVICARIBE EXPRESS			
☐ HK-4888X	Antonov An-26B	10406	ex UK-26003

TAS - TRANSPORTE AEREO DE SANTANDER			*Bucaramanga (BGA)*
☐ HK-4102	Dornier 28D-2 Skyservant	4187	ex D-IDES
☐ HK-4104	Dornier 28D-2 Skyservant	4193	ex D-IDRV
☐ HK-4139	Dornier 28D-2 Skyservant	4153	ex D-IDRF
☐ HK-4290X	Cessna 402C	402C0427	ex N717A

TAXI AÉREA DE CALDAS			
☐ HK-4610	Beech 1900D	UE-82	ex HK-4610X
☐ HK-4634	Beech 1900D	UE-54	ex N54YV

TAXI AÉREO CARIBENO			
☐ HK-4898	Piper PA-34-220T Seneca	34-8233010	ex N8456E
☐ HK-5021	Cessna TU206G Stationair	U20604645	ex N9998M ◆

TAXI AÉREO CUSIANA			*Bogota-Eldorado (BOG)*
☐ HK-2522	Cessna 402C II	402C0322	ex N2522P
☐ HK-4225	LET L-410UVP-E3	871929	ex HK-4225X
☐ HK-4260	LET L-410UVP-E3	871933	ex HK-4260X

TAXI AÉREO DE IBAGUE			
☐ HK-3743P	Cessna 208 Caravan I	20800216	ex HK-3743

TAXI AÉREO DE LA COSTA - TAXCO			
☐ HK-4978	Piper PA-31-325 Navajo	31-7612004	ex N727WN

TRANS ORIENTE			*Villavicencio (VVC)*
☐ HK-3981	Dornier 28D-2 Skyservant	4162	ex D-IDND
☐ HK-3982	Dornier 28D-2 Skyservant	4169	ex D-IDNC
☐ HK-3991X	Dornier 28D-2 Skyservant	4148	ex D-IDNF
☐ HK-3992X	Dornier 28D-2 Skyservant	4161	ex D-IDNE
☐ HK-4053X	Dornier 28D-1 Skyservant	4105	ex D-IDNH

TRANSPORTE AEREO DE COLOMBIA		*(TCB)*	
☐ HK-4147	LET L-410UVP-E	892341	ex HK-4147X
☐ HK-4196	LET L-410UVP-E	861617	ex HK-4196X

VERTICAL DE AVIACION – AIRFREIGHT AVIATION			*Bogota-Guaymaral*
☐ HK-3730X	Mil Mi-8TV-1	95728	ex CCCP-25112
☐ HK-3731X	Mil Mi-8TV-1	95586	ex CCCP-25447
☐ HK-3732X	Mil Mi-8TV-1	95729	ex CCCP-25113
☐ HK-3758X	Mil Mi-8TV-1	95908	ex HC-BSG
☐ HK-3779X	Mil Mi-8TV-1	95645	ex CCCP-25500
☐ HK-3780X	Mil Mi-8TV-1	95909	ex RA-27068
☐ HK-3862	Mil Mi-8TV-1	95923	ex CCCP-27087
☐ HK-3863	Mil Mi-8TV-1	95894	ex CCCP-27060
☐ HK-3864	Mil Mi-8TV-1	95893	ex CCCP-27059
☐ HK-3865	Mil Mi-8TV-1	95892	ex CCCP-27058
☐ HK-3882X	Mil Mi-8TV-1	96018	
☐ HK-3888X	Mil Mi-8TV-1	95838	
☐ HK-3908X	Mil Mi-8TV-1	95823	
☐ HK-3910X	Mil Mi-8TV-1	96008	ex RA-27185
☐ HK-3911X	Mil Mi-8TV-1	96124	ex RA-25768
☐ HK-4857	Mil Mi-8MTV-1	108M40	ex ZS-HJK
☐ HK-4878	Mil Mi-8MTV-1	108M11	ex Czech 0811
☐ HK-4883	Mil Mi-8MTV-1	108M33	ex ZS-HKC
☐ HK-4887	Mil Mi-8MTV-1	94235	ex YA-KMK
☐ HK-4916	Mil Mi-8MTV-1	108M03	ex ZS-HJO
☐ HK-3250	Bell 212	31219	ex HC-BSI
☐ HK-3723	Bell 212	32122	ex N1080V

☐ HK-4796	Mil Mi-171	59489617778	
☐ HK-4797	Mil Mi-171P	171P00784073403	
☐ HK-4838	British Aerospace Jetstream 32	926	ex N926AE
☐ HK-4844	British Aerospace Jetstream 32	888	ex N888CY
☐ HK-4852	Mil Mi-171	171C00784073402 ex YA-KMJ	
☐ HK-4899	Mil Mi-171	59489617122	ex B-7860

VIARCO   Villavicencio (VVC)

☐ HK-1315	Douglas DC-3	4307	ex PP-ANG
☐ HK-1842	Cessna U206F Stationair II	U20603487	ex (N8734Q)
☐ HK-3349X	Douglas DC-3	11825	ex FAE 92066/HC-AVC

VIAS AEREAS NACIONALES

☐ HK-3734	Cessna 208B Caravan I	208B0297	ex N5444B

VIVA COLOMBIA   Viva Colombia (VVC)   Medellin (MDE)

☐ HK-4811X	Airbus A320-214	1564	ex N260AV	
☐ HK-4817	Airbus A320-214	1725	ex N262AV	Helena
☐ HK-4818X	Airbus A320-214	1306	ex N136AG	Dani
☐ HK-4861X	Airbus A320-214	1867	ex N264AV	Tec Mario
☐ HK-4905	Airbus A320-214	1454	ex HK-4905X	
☐ HK-5051	Airbus A320-214	1757	ex EI-DJI	♦
☐ HK-5125X	Airbus A320-214	1370	ex EI-FGM	♦
☐ HK-	Airbus A320-214	1686	ex B-6320	o/o♦

WEST CARIBBEAN AIRWAYS

☐ HK-4125	LET L-410UVP-E	912605	ex OK-WDZ
☐ HK-4187X	LET L-410UVP-E	902432	ex HA-LAT

HL-   SOUTH KOREA (Republic of Korea)

AIR BUSAN   Air Busan (BX/ABL)   Busan-Gimhae (PVS)

☐ HL7711	Airbus A321-231	1636	ex D-AVZG
☐ HL7712	Airbus A321-231	1670	ex D-ABDM	♦
☐ HL7713	Airbus A321-231	1734	ex D-AVXD	♦
☐ HL7723	Airbus A321-231	2045	ex D-AVZC
☐ HL7761	Airbus A321-231	1227	ex N127AG
☐ HL8213	Airbus A321-231	1970	ex EI-LVB

☐ HL7250	Boeing 737-58E	25769/2737	
☐ HL7508	Boeing 737-48E	25772/2791	
☐ HL7510	Boeing 737-48E	25771/2816	
☐ HL7513	Boeing 737-48E	25776/2860	
☐ HL7517	Boeing 737-48E	25774/2909	

☐ HL7744	Airbus A320-232	2808	ex F-WWIO	♦
☐ HL7745	Airbus A320-232	2840	ex F-WWIE	♦
☐ HL7753	Airbus A320-232	2943	ex F-WWIM

AIR INCHEON   Air Incheon (KJ/AIH)   Seoul-Incheon (ICN)

☐ HL8271	Boeing 737-4Y0SF	24912/2064	ex N310MS
☐ HL8291	Boeing 737-4Y0SF	25190/2256	ex N519AG

AIR KOREA   (AKA)

☐ HL5107	Cessna 208 Caravan I	20800238	ex N9824F
☐ HL5111	Cessna 208 Caravan I	20800328	ex N36964
☐ HL5115	Cessna 208B Caravan I	208B2011	ex N22430

ASIANA AIRLINES   Asiana (OZ/AAR)   Seoul-Incheon/Kimpo (ICN/SEL)

Member of Star Alliance

☐ HL7737	Airbus A320-232	2397	ex F-WWIU
☐ HL7738	Airbus A320-232	2459	ex F-WWDM
☐ HL7762	Airbus A320-232	3244	ex F-WWBQ	dam 14Apr15
☐ HL7769	Airbus A320-232	3437	ex F-WWDX
☐ HL7772	Airbus A320-232	3483	ex F-WWDN
☐ HL7773	Airbus A320-232	3496	ex F-WWIL
☐ HL7776	Airbus A320-232	3641	ex F-WWBS
☐ HL7788	Airbus A320-232	3873	ex F-WWIH

☐ HL7594	Airbus A321-231	1356	ex D-AVZA
☐ HL7703	Airbus A321-231	1511	ex D-AVZA

☐ HL7722	Airbus A321-231	2041	ex D-AVZA		
☐ HL7729	Airbus A321-231	2110	ex D-AVXF		
☐ HL7730	Airbus A321-231	2226	ex D-AVZU		
☐ HL7731	Airbus A321-231	2247	ex D-AVZG		
☐ HL7735	Airbus A321-231	2290	ex D-AVZB		
☐ HL7763	Airbus A321-231	3297	ex D-AVZR		
☐ HL7767	Airbus A321-231	0802	ex N802BV		
☐ HL7789	Airbus A321-231	4112	ex D-AZAE		
☐ HL7790	Airbus A321-231	4142	ex D-AVZM		
☐ HL8004	Airbus A321-231	6299	ex D-AVZU		♦
☐ HL8018	Airbus A321-231	6395	ex D-AVXY		♦
☐ HL8236	Airbus A321-231	1174	ex N174AG		
☐ HL8255	Airbus A321-231	5035	ex D-AZAN		
☐ HL8256	Airbus A321-231	5169	ex D-AVZH		
☐ HL8257	Airbus A321-231	5173	ex D-AVZI		
☐ HL8265	Airbus A321-231	5287	ex D-AZAI		
☐ HL8266	Airbus A321-231	5350	ex D-AVZC		
☐ HL8267	Airbus A321-231	5382	ex D-AVZN		
☐ HL8277	Airbus A321-231	5462	ex D-AZAB		
☐ HL8278	Airbus A321-231	5500	ex D-AZAM		
☐ HL8279	Airbus A321-231	5636	ex D-AVZQ		
☐ HL8280	Airbus A321-231	5767	ex D-AZAR		
☐ HL8281	Airbus A321-231	5774	ex D-AZAW		
☐ HL	Airbus A321-231	6768	ex		o/o♦
☐ HL	Airbus A321-231	6796	ex		o/o♦
☐ HL7736	Airbus A330-323X	640	ex F-WWYR		
☐ HL7740	Airbus A330-323X	676	ex F-WWYA		
☐ HL7741	Airbus A330-323X	708	ex F-WWKL		
☐ HL7746	Airbus A330-323X	772	ex F-WWKE		
☐ HL7747	Airbus A330-323X	803	ex F-WWYE		
☐ HL7754	Airbus A330-323X	845	ex F-WWYZ		
☐ HL7792	Airbus A330-323X	1001	ex F-WWKL		
☐ HL7793	Airbus A330-323X	1055	ex F-WWYD		
☐ HL7794	Airbus A330-323X	1151	ex F-WWYS		
☐ HL7795	Airbus A330-323X	1211	ex F-WWYV		
☐ HL8258	Airbus A330-323E	1326	ex F-WWTM		
☐ HL8259	Airbus A330-323E	1340	ex F-WWCE		
☐ HL8282	Airbus A330-323E	1435	ex F-WWCU		
☐ HL8286	Airbus A330-323E	1464	ex F-WWCY		
☐ HL8293	Airbus A330-323E	1518	ex F-WWYD		
☐ HL7413	Boeing 747-48EMSF	25405/880			
☐ HL7414	Boeing 747-48EMSF	25452/892			
☐ HL7415	Boeing 747-48EMSF	25777/946			
☐ HL7417	Boeing 747-48EM	25779/1006			
☐ HL7418	Boeing 747-48E	25780/1035	ex N6018N		
☐ HL7419	Boeing 747-48EF	25781/1044			
☐ HL7420	Boeing 747-48EF	25783/1064			
☐ HL7421	Boeing 747-48EM	25784/1086			
☐ HL7423	Boeing 747-48EM	25782/1115			
☐ HL7428	Boeing 747-48E	28552/1160	ex N6018N		
☐ HL7436	Boeing 747-48EF	29170/1305	ex N1785B		
☐ HL7616	Boeing 747-446F	33748/1351	ex N401AL		
☐ HL7618	Boeing 747-446BDSF	26343/918	ex N364AS		
☐ HL7620	Boeing 747-419BDSF	29375/1228	ex N410SA		
☐ HL7247	Boeing 767-38E	25757/523			
☐ HL7248	Boeing 767-38E	25758/582			
☐ HL7506	Boeing 767-38E	25760/639			
☐ HL7507	Boeing 767-38EF	25761/616	ex N6005C		
☐ HL7514	Boeing 767-38E	25763/656		Tea Changum c/s	
☐ HL7515	Boeing 767-38E	25762/658	ex N6055X		
☐ HL7516	Boeing 767-38E	25759/668		Star Alliance c/s	
☐ HL7528	Boeing 767-38E	29129/693	ex N6005C		
☐ HL7500	Boeing 777-28EER	28685/400			
☐ HL7596	Boeing 777-28EER	28681/322			
☐ HL7597	Boeing 777-28EER	28686/359			
☐ HL7700	Boeing 777-28EER	30859/403	ex N5014K		
☐ HL7732	Boeing 777-28EER	29174/481			
☐ HL7739	Boeing 777-28EER	29175/526			
☐ HL7755	Boeing 777-28EER	30861/646			
☐ HL7756	Boeing 777-28EER	30860/659			
☐ HL7775	Boeing 777-28EER	30862/738			
☐ HL7791	Boeing 777-28EER	35525/853			
☐ HL8254	Boeing 777-28EER	40198/1027			
☐ HL8284	Boeing 777-28EER	40199/1117			
☐ HL7625	Airbus A380-841	152	ex F-WWAP		
☐ HL7626	Airbus A380-841	155	ex F-WWAQ		
☐ HL7634	Airbus A380-841	179	ex F-WWAF		♦
☐ HL7635	Airbus A380-841	183	ex F-WWSQ		o/o♦

☐ HL	Boeing 747-83QF	60117/1501	ex N823BA	o/o♦
☐ HL	Boeing 747-83QF	60118/1502	ex N826BA	o/o♦

EASTAR JET		**Eastarjet (ZE/ESR)**		**Seoul-Gimpo (GMP)**
☐ HL8023	Boeing 737-86N	28574/67	ex N846TM	♦
☐ HL8028	Boeing 737-8BK/W	30625/1248	ex N471JD	♦
☐ HL8029	Boeing 737-86N/W	28576/103	ex N859TM	o/o♦
☐ HL8264	Boeing 737-86J/W	28068/36	ex N862AG	
☐ HL8269	Boeing 737-8Q8/W	30684/1689	ex F-WTAD	
☐ HL8289	Boeing 737-883	30194/666	ex N394SA	
☐ HL8292	Boeing 737-883	28323/625	ex N233SA	
☐ HL8022	Boeing 737-73V	32426/1474	ex VT-JLG	♦
☐ HL8205	Boeing 737-73V	32412/1151	ex G-EZJP	
☐ HL8207	Boeing 737-73V	32413/1202	ex G-EZJR	

JEJU AIR		**(7C/JJA)**		**Cheju International (CJU)**
☐ HL7779	Boeing 737-85F	28824/180	ex VT-SPC	
☐ HL7780	Boeing 737-85F	28827/467	ex VT-SPD	
☐ HL8019	Boeing 737-86N/W	32694/1960	ex N839TM	♦
☐ HL8020	Boeing 737-86N/W	32683/2136	ex N854TM	♦
☐ HL8031	Boeing 737-8GJ/W	37361/3508	ex N374DC	♦
☐ HL8034	Boeing 737-8HX/W	38101/3803	ex N381AG	♦
☐ HL8206	Boeing 737-86J/W	30877/782	ex D-ABAE	
☐ HL8214	Boeing 737-86N/W	28608/410	ex D-ABBQ	
☐ HL8233	Boeing 737-85P/W	28383/266	ex EC-HBN	
☐ HL8234	Boeing 737-86Q/W	30285/1237	ex OO-VAS	
☐ HL8239	Boeing 737-82R	29344/849	ex TC-APU	
☐ HL8260	Boeing 737-8BK/W	30622/1108	ex VH-VOB	
☐ HL8261	Boeing 737-8BK/W	30624/1193	ex VH-VOD	
☐ HL8263	Boeing 737-82R/W	30658/1325	ex VH-VOV	
☐ HL8287	Boeing 737-8Q8/W	30665/1436	ex VH-VOU	
☐ HL8295	Boeing 737-8Q8/W	30694/1863	ex VT-SJG	
☐ HL8296	Boeing 737-8Q8/W	30695/1891	ex VT-SJH	
☐ HL8297	Boeing 737-83N/W	30673/1500	ex B-2863	♦
☐ HL8302	Boeing 737-8GJ/W	36367/3218	ex N460DC	♦

JIN AIR		**Jin Air (LJ/JNA)**		**Seoul-Incheon/Kimpo (ICN/SEL)**
☐ HL7555	Boeing 737-86N	30230/460	ex N1786B	
☐ HL7556	Boeing 737-86N	28615/482	ex N1787B	
☐ HL7557	Boeing 737-86N	28622/562	ex N1786B	
☐ HL7558	Boeing 737-86N	28625/590	ex N1786B	
☐ HL7559	Boeing 737-86N	28626/611	ex N1786B	
☐ HL7561	Boeing 737-8B5/W	29982/663		
☐ HL7562	Boeing 737-8B5	29983/678	ex N1768B	♦
☐ HL7563	Boeing 737-86N	28636/756		
☐ HL7564	Boeing 737-86N	28638/765		
☐ HL7565	Boeing 737-8B5/W	29984/848		♦
☐ HL7567	Boeing 737-86N	28647/878	ex N1768B	
☐ HL7798	Boeing 737-809/W	28236/739	ex B-16802	
☐ HL7743	Boeing 777-2B5ER	34208/584		♦

KOREA EXPRESS AIR		**Korea Express (XE/KEA)**		
☐ HL9495	Eurocopter EC135P2+	0897	ex N147AE	
☐ HL9496	Eurocopter EC135P2+	0942	ex N149AE	
☐ HL9497	Eurocopter EC135P2+	0946	ex N154AE	

KOREAN AIR		**Koreanair (KE/KAL)**		**Seoul-Incheon/Kimpo (ICN/SEL)**

Member of SkyTeam

☐ HL7538	Airbus A330-223	222	ex F-WWKP	
☐ HL7539	Airbus A330-223	226	ex F-WWKR	
☐ HL7552	Airbus A330-223	258	ex F-WWKQ	
☐ HL8211	Airbus A330-223	1133	ex F-WWKA	
☐ HL8212	Airbus A330-223	1155	ex F-WWKI	
☐ HL8227	Airbus A330-223	1200	ex F-WWKI	
☐ HL8228	Airbus A330-223	1203	ex F-WWYE	
☐ HL8276	Airbus A330-223	1393	ex F-WWYZ	
☐ HL7524	Airbus A330-322	206	ex HL7552	
☐ HL7525	Airbus A330-322	219	ex F-WWKO	
☐ HL7540	Airbus A330-322	241	ex F-WWKF	
☐ HL7550	Airbus A330-322	162	ex F-WWKK	
☐ HL7551	Airbus A330-322	172	ex F-WWKI	
☐ HL7553	Airbus A330-323X	267	ex F-WWKZ	
☐ HL7554	Airbus A330-323X	256	ex F-WWKN	

☐ HL7584	Airbus A330-323X	338	ex F-WWKP	
☐ HL7585	Airbus A330-323X	350	ex F-WWYF	
☐ HL7586	Airbus A330-323X	351	ex F-WWYH	
☐ HL7587	Airbus A330-323X	368	ex F-WWKF	
☐ HL7701	Airbus A330-323	425	ex F-WWYE	>CSA
☐ HL7702	Airbus A330-323	428	ex F-WWYF	
☐ HL7709	Airbus A330-323	484	ex F-WWKD	
☐ HL7710	Airbus A330-323	490	ex F-WWKF	
☐ HL7720	Airbus A330-323	550	ex F-WWKP	
☐ HL8001	Airbus A330-323E	1556	ex F-WWYK	♦
☐ HL8002	Airbus A330-323E	1576	ex F-WWYD	♦
☐ HL8003	Airbus A330-323E	1590	ex F-WWCL	♦
☐ HL8025	Airbus A330-323E	1611	ex F-WWCY	♦
☐ HL8026	Airbus A330-323E	1638	ex F-WWYZ	o/o♦
☐ HL8027	Airbus A330-343E	1647	ex F-WWKO	o/o♦
☐ HL7611	Airbus A380-861	035	ex (HL8226)	
☐ HL7612	Airbus A380-861	039	ex (HL-8226)	
☐ HL7613	Airbus A380-861	059	ex F-WWAY	
☐ HL7614	Airbus A380-861	068	ex F-WWSJ	
☐ HL7615	Airbus A380-861	075	ex F-WWSS	
☐ HL7619	Airbus A380-861	096	ex F-WWAP	
☐ HL7621	Airbus A380-861	126	ex F-WWSZ	
☐ HL7622	Airbus A380-861	128	ex F-WWAB	
☐ HL7627	Airbus A380-861	130	ex F-WWSD	
☐ HL7628	Airbus A380-861	156	ex F-WWAT	
☐ HL7560	Boeing 737-8B5/W	29981/622		
☐ HL7566	Boeing 737-8B5/W	29985/852		
☐ HL7568	Boeing 737-8B5/W	29986/891	SkyTeam c/s	
☐ HL7757	Boeing 737-8GQ/W	35790/2119		
☐ HL7758	Boeing 737-8GQ/W	35791/2150		
☐ HL7785	Boeing 737-8Q8/W	37162/2906	ex N1795B	
☐ HL7786	Boeing 737-8Q8/W	37163/2955	ex N1786B	
☐ HL8224	Boeing 737-8Q8/W	38822/3704		
☐ HL8225	Boeing 737-8Q8/W	38823/3818		
☐ HL8240	Boeing 737-8BK/W	39447/3794		
☐ HL8241	Boeing 737-8BK/W	38129/3852		
☐ HL8242	Boeing 737-8Q8/W	38824/3895		
☐ HL8243	Boeing 737-8Q8/W	38825/3927		
☐ HL8244	Boeing 737-8Q8/W	38826/3943		
☐ HL8245	Boeing 737-8Q8/W	38827/3980		
☐ HL8246	Boeing 737-8LH/W	41299/4057		
☐ HL8247	Boeing 737-8LH/W	41300/4214		
☐ HL7569	Boeing 737-9B5	29987/999	ex B-5110	
☐ HL7599	Boeing 737-9B5	29988/1026	ex N1795B	
☐ HL7704	Boeing 737-9B5	29989/1082	ex N1786B	
☐ HL7705	Boeing 737-9B5	29990/1162		
☐ HL7706	Boeing 737-9B5	29991/1188		
☐ HL7707	Boeing 737-9B5	29992/1190		
☐ HL7708	Boeing 737-9B5	29993/1208	ex N60659	
☐ HL7716	Boeing 737-9B5	29994/1320		
☐ HL7717	Boeing 737-9B5	29995/1332		
☐ HL7718	Boeing 737-9B5	29996/1338		
☐ HL7719	Boeing 737-9B5	29997/1416		
☐ HL7724	Boeing 737-9B5	29998/1494		
☐ HL7725	Boeing 737-9B5	29999/1512		
☐ HL7726	Boeing 737-9B5	30001/1729	ex N1786B	
☐ HL7727	Boeing 737-9B5	30000/1536	ex N6066U	
☐ HL7728	Boeing 737-9B5	30002/1620		
☐ HL8221	Boeing 737-9B5ER	37633/3645	ex N1786B	
☐ HL8223	Boeing 737-9B5ER	37634/3681		
☐ HL8248	Boeing 737-9B5ER	37635/4038		
☐ HL8249	Boeing 737-9B5ER	37636/4080	ex N1786B	
☐ HL8272	Boeing 737-9B5ER	42173/4468		
☐ HL8273	Boeing 737-9B5ER	42174/4479		
☐ HL7402	Boeing 747-4B5	26407/1155	ex N6038E	
☐ HL7404	Boeing 747-4B5	26409/1170	ex N6009F	
☐ HL7460	Boeing 747-4B5	26404/1107		
☐ HL7461	Boeing 747-4B5	26405/1118		
☐ HL7465	Boeing 747-4B5	26412/1284		opf Govt
☐ HL7472	Boeing 747-4B5	26403/1095		
☐ HL7473	Boeing 747-4B5	28335/1098		
☐ HL7490	Boeing 747-4B5	27177/1019		
☐ HL7491	Boeing 747-4B5	27341/1037		
☐ HL7492	Boeing 747-4B5	26397/1055		
☐ HL7493	Boeing 747-4B5	26398/1057		
☐ HL7494	Boeing 747-4B5	27662/1067		
☐ HL7495	Boeing 747-4B5	28096/1073		
☐ HL7498	Boeing 747-4B5	26402/1092		

☐ HL7400	Boeing 747-4B5F	26414/1295		
☐ HL7403	Boeing 747-4B5F	26408/1163	ex N60659	
☐ HL7434	Boeing 747-4B5F	32809/1316		
☐ HL7437	Boeing 747-4B5F	32808/1323		
☐ HL7438	Boeing 747-4B5ERF	33515/1329	ex N6005X	
☐ HL7439	Boeing 747-4B5ERF	33516/1338		
☐ HL7448	Boeing 747-4B5F	26416/1246		
☐ HL7449	Boeing 747-4B5F	26411/1248		
☐ HL7462	Boeing 747-4B5F	26406/1123		
☐ HL7466	Boeing 747-4B5F	26413/1286		
☐ HL7467	Boeing 747-4B5F	27073/1291		
☐ HL7499	Boeing 747-4B5ERF	33517/1340		
☐ HL7600	Boeing 747-4B5ERF	33945/1347		
☐ HL7601	Boeing 747-4B5ERF	33946/1350		
☐ HL7602	Boeing 747-4B5ERF	34301/1365		
☐ HL7603	Boeing 747-4B5ERF	34302/1368		
☐ HL7605	Boeing 747-4B5ERF	35526/1375		
☐ HL7609	Boeing 747-8HTF	37132/1425		
☐ HL7610	Boeing 747-8HTF	37133/1426		
☐ HL7617	Boeing 747-8B5F	37654/1474		
☐ HL7823	Boeing 747-8B5F	37655/1481	ex N774BA	
☐ HL7624	Boeing 747-8B5F	37656/1488	ex N957BA	
☐ HL	Boeing 747-8B5F	37657/1516		o/o♦
☐ HL7526	Boeing 777-2B5ER	27947/148	ex N50217	
☐ HL7530	Boeing 777-2B5ER	27945/59		
☐ HL7531	Boeing 777-2B5ER	27946/62		
☐ HL7574	Boeing 777-2B5ER	28444/305		
☐ HL7575	Boeing 777-2B5ER	28445/309		
☐ HL7598	Boeing 777-2B5ER	27949/356		
☐ HL7714	Boeing 777-2B5ER	27951/411		
☐ HL7715	Boeing 777-2B5ER	28372/416		
☐ HL7721	Boeing 777-2B5ER	33727/452		
☐ HL7733	Boeing 777-2B5ER	34206/520	ex N5023Q	
☐ HL7734	Boeing 777-2B5ER	34207/528		
☐ HL7750	Boeing 777-2B5ER	34209/633		
☐ HL7751	Boeing 777-2B5ER	34210/657	ex N6018N	
☐ HL7752	Boeing 777-2B5ER	34211/682		
☐ HL7764	Boeing 777-2B5ER	34214/684	ex N50281	
☐ HL7765	Boeing 777-2B5ER	34212/711		
☐ HL7766	Boeing 777-2B5ER	34213/730		
☐ HL7532	Boeing 777-3B5	28371/162		
☐ HL7533	Boeing 777-3B5	27948/178		
☐ HL7534	Boeing 777-3B5	27950/120	ex N5020K	
☐ HL7573	Boeing 777-3B5	27952/288		
☐ HL7782	Boeing 777-3B5ER	37643/785		
☐ HL7783	Boeing 777-3B5ER	37644/806	ex N5020K	SkyTeam c/s
☐ HL7784	Boeing 777-3B5ER	37136/823		
☐ HL8006	Boeing 777-3B5ER	37652/1315		o/o♦
☐ HL8007	Boeing 777-3B5ER	43815/1323		o/o♦
☐ HL8008	Boeing 777-3B5ER	43816/1339		o/o♦
☐ HL8010	Boeing 777-3B5ER	42120/1286		♦
☐ HL8011	Boeing 777-3B5ER	42123/1303		o/o♦
☐ HL8208	Boeing 777-3B5ER	37645/867		
☐ HL8209	Boeing 777-3B5ER	37646/875		
☐ HL8210	Boeing 777-3B5ER	40377/882	ex N5016R	
☐ HL8216	Boeing 777-3B5ER	37647/933		
☐ HL8217	Boeing 777-3B5ER	37648/938		
☐ HL8218	Boeing 777-3B5ER	37649/976		
☐ HL8250	Boeing 777-3B5ER	37650/1023		
☐ HL8274	Boeing 777-3B5ER	41998/1081		
☐ HL8275	Boeing 777-3B5ER	37651/1109		
☐ HL8005	Boeing 777-FB5	37642/1278		♦
☐ HL8226	Boeing 777-FB5	37640/1074		
☐ HL8251	Boeing 777-FB5	37639/989		
☐ HL8252	Boeing 777-FB5	37638/1026		
☐ HL8285	Boeing 777-FB5	37641/1172		
☐ HL8222	Boeing 737-7B5/W (BBJ1)	37660/2997	ex N719V	VIP
☐ HL	Boeing 747-8B5	40905/1506		o/o♦
☐ HL	Boeing 747-8B5	40906/1509		o/o♦
☐ HL	Boeing 747-8B5	40907/1524		o/o♦
☐ HL	Boeing 747-8B5	40908/1525		o/o♦
☐ HL	Boeing 787-8 (BBJ)	41987/11	ex N507BJ	♦

KOREAN AIR EXPRESS

☐ HL5231	Beech 1900D	UE-317	ex N713UE	
☐ HL5238	Beech 1900D	UE-222	ex N789BL	

KOREAN BUSINESS AIR SERVICE/KBAS

☐ HL2036   Canadair CL-215   1096

T'WAY AIR		Teeway (TW/TWB)		Cheong Ju (CJJ)
☐ HL8000	Boeing 737-86N/W	34249/1857	ex N106NG	
☐ HL8021	Boeing 737-8GJ/W	34899/2128	ex VT-SPL	♦
☐ HL8024	Boeing 737-8HX/W	36848/3394	ex N648AG	♦
☐ HL8030	Boeing 737-8Q8/W	41804/5305		♦
☐ HL8232	Boeing 737-8K5/W	27979/44	ex D-AHFE	
☐ HL8235	Boeing 737-8KG/W	39448/3362	ex N5002K	
☐ HL8237	Boeing 737-8Q8/W	30654/1295	ex N651LF	
☐ HL8253	Boeing 737-86J/W	28069/42	ex N962AG	
☐ HL8268	Boeing 737-83N/W	30660/1330	ex VT-SPH	
☐ HL8294	Boeing 737-8Q8/W	32798/1470	ex VH-VOW	

UB AIR

☐ HL9197   Bell 407   53082

HP-   PANAMA (Republic of Panama)

AIR PANAMA		Turismo Regional (79/PST)		Panama City-Albrook (BLB)
☐ HP-1763PST	Fokker 100	11315	ex PH-DIM	
☐ HP-1764PST	Fokker 100	11364	ex F-GIOG	
☐ HP-1894PST	Fokker 100	11390	ex PH-JXW	♦
☐ HP-1895PST	Fokker 100	11400	ex PH-KXJ	♦
☐ HP-1896PST	Fokker 100	11320	ex PH-LND	♦
☐ HP-639PS	Britten-Norman BN-2A-8 Islander	60	ex HP-639KN	
☐ HP-1153PS	Britten-Norman BN-2A-26 Islander	672	ex HP-1153XI	
☐ HP-1345PS	Cessna 208B Caravan I	208B0380	ex HP-1354AR	
☐ HP-1494PS	Britten-Norman BN-2A-3 Islander	673	ex CN-TCC	
☐ HP-1507PS	de Havilland DHC-6 Twin Otter 300	532	ex C-GQKZ	
☐ HP-1509PS	de Havilland DHC-6 Twin Otter 300	360	ex HP-1509APP	
☐ HP-1543PST	Fokker F.27 Friendship 400F	10268	ex HP-1543	
☐ HP-1542PST	Fokker F.27 Friendship 500F	10560	ex HP-1542PS	[BLB]
☐ HP-1604PST	Fokker F.27 Friendship 500F	10471	ex N716FE	
☐ HP-1605PST	Fokker 50	20178	ex LN-RND	
☐ HP-1606PST	Fokker 50	20179	ex LN-RNE	
☐ HP-1611PS	Cessna 208B Caravan I	208B1201	ex HP-1611	♦
☐ HP-1631PST	Fokker F.27 Friendship 500	10658	ex N725FE	
☐ HP-1670PS	SAAB SF.340B	340B-299	ex HP-1670PST	
☐ HP-1671PST	SAAB SF.340B	340B-294	ex N294CJ	
☐ HP-1759PST	Britten-Norman BN-2A-8 Islander	626	ex N9149D	
☐ HP-1793PST	Fokker 50	20162	ex YL-BAS	
☐ HP-1794PST	Fokker 50	20163	ex YL-BAT	
☐ HP-1796PST	Boeing 737-3B3QC	26851/2267	ex F-GIXF	

COPA AIRLINES		Copa (CM/CMP)		Panama City-Tucumen Intl (PTY)	

Member of Star Alliance

☐ HP-1370CMP	Boeing 737-71Q/W	29048/288	ex N82521	670	
☐ HP-1371CMP	Boeing 737-7V3/W	30049/388	ex N1787B	671	>RPB
☐ HP-1372CMP	Boeing 737-7V3/W	28607/399		672	>RPB
☐ HP-1373CMP	Boeing 737-7V3/W	30458/459		673	>RPB
☐ HP-1374CMP	Boeing 737-7V3/W	30459/494	ex N1787B	674	
☐ HP-1375CMP	Boeing 737-7V3/W	30460/558	ex N1787B	675	
☐ HP-1376CMP	Boeing 737-7V3/W	30497/574		676	
☐ HP-1377CMP	Boeing 737-7V3/W	30462/1161		677	
☐ HP-1378CMP	Boeing 737-7V3/W	30461/1173		678	
☐ HP-1379CMP	Boeing 737-7V3/W	30463/1221		679	
☐ HP-1380CMP	Boeing 737-7V3/W	30464/1241		680	
☐ HP-1520CMP	Boeing 737-7V3/W	33707/1376		681	
☐ HP-1521CMP	Boeing 737-7V3/W	33708/1379		682	
☐ HP-1524CMP	Boeing 737-7V3/W	33705/1505		683	
☐ HP-1525CMP	Boeing 737-7V3/W	33706/1518		684	
☐ HP-1530CMP	Boeing 737-7V3/W	34535/1962		687	
☐ HP-1531CMP	Boeing 737-7V3/W	34536/1995		688	
☐ HP-1522CMP	Boeing 737-8V3/W	33709/1387		480	
☐ HP-1523CMP	Boeing 737-8V3/W	33710/1397		481	
☐ HP-1526CMP	Boeing 737-8V3/W	34006/1585	ex N1782B	482	
☐ HP-1532CMP	Boeing 737-8V3/W	35068/2343		484	
☐ HP-1533CMP	Boeing 737-8V3/W	35067/2423		485	
☐ HP-1534CMP	Boeing 737-8V3/W	35125/2624		486	
☐ HP-1535CMP	Boeing 737-8V3/W	35126/2805	ex N1786B	487	

☐ HP-1536CMP	Boeing 737-8V3/W	35127/2963		488	
☐ HP-1537CMP	Boeing 737-8V3/W	36550/3114		489	
☐ HP-1538CMP	Boeing 737-8V3/W	36554/3130		490	
☐ HP-1539CMP	Boeing 737-8V3/W	29667/3151	ex N1787B	491	
☐ HP-1711CMP	Boeing 737-8V3/W	40663/3265		492	
☐ HP-1712CMP	Boeing 737-8V3/W	40664/3267	ex N1796B	493	
☐ HP-1713CMP	Boeing 737-8V3/W	40890/3455		494	
☐ HP-1714CMP	Boeing 737-8V3/W	40891/3476		495	
☐ HP-1715CMP	Boeing 737-8V3/W	40361/3500		496	
☐ HP-1716CMP	Boeing 737-8V3/W	40666/3567		497	
☐ HP-1717CMP	Boeing 737-8V3/W	40665/3595		498	
☐ HP-1718CMP	Boeing 737-8V3/W	38139/3611		499	
☐ HP-1719CMP	Boeing 737-8V3/W	37957/3695		550	
☐ HP-1720CMP	Boeing 737-8V3/W	37958/3739		551	
☐ HP-1721CMP	Boeing 737-8V3/W	40362/3751		552	
☐ HP-1722CMP	Boeing 737-8V3/W	38100/3761		533	
☐ HP-1723CMP	Boeing 737-8V3/W	37959/3781		554	
☐ HP-1724CMP	Boeing 737-8V3/W	38140/3810		555	
☐ HP-1725CMP	Boeing 737-8V3/W	38102/3839	ex N1787B	556	
☐ HP-1726CMP	Boeing 737-86N/W	38024/3919		557	
☐ HP-1727CMP	Boeing 737-8V3/W	40778/3956		558	
☐ HP-1728CMP	Boeing 737-86N/W	39396/3971		559	
☐ HP-1729CMP	Boeing 737-8V3/W	41088/3977		560	
☐ HP-1730CMP	Boeing 737-8V3/W	38141/3988		561	
☐ HP-1821CMP	Boeing 737-8V3/W	41089/4005		562	
☐ HP-1822CMP	Boeing 737-8V3/W	40779/4033		563	
☐ HP-1823CMP	Boeing 737-86N/W	39398/4051		564	Star Alliance c/s
☐ HP-1824CMP	Boeing 737-86N/W	39399/4083		565	
☐ HP-1825CMP	Boeing 737-8V3/W	40780/4179		566	
☐ HP-1826CMP	Boeing 737-86N/W	38031/4189	ex (HP-1836CMP)	567	
☐ HP-1827CMP	Boeing 737-8V3/W	38142/4221		568	
☐ HP-1828CMP	Boeing 737-8V3/W	38879/4233		569	
☐ HP-1829CMP	Boeing 737-8V3/W	38882/4361		570	
☐ HP-1830CMP	Boeing 737-8V3/W	40781/4396		571	Star Alliance c/s
☐ HP-1831CMP	Boeing 737-8V31/W	40788/4398		572	
☐ HP-1832CMP	Boeing 737-8V3/W	40789/4552		573	
☐ HP-1833CMP	Boeing 737-8V3/W	39884/4562		574	
☐ HP-1834CMP	Boeing 737-8V3/W	39885/4588		575	
☐ HP-1835CMP	Boeing 737-8V3/W	40790/4626		576	
☐ HP-1836CMP	Boeing 737-8V3/W	40782/4846		577	
☐ HP-1837CMP	Boeing 737-8V3/W	40783/4857		578	
☐ HP-1838CMP	Boeing 737-8V3/W	41445/4956		579	♦
☐ HP-1839CMP	Boeing 737-8V3/W	41446/4975		580	♦
☐ HP-1840CMP	Boeing 737-8V3/W	44155/5014	ex N1787B	581	♦
☐ HP-1841CMP	Boeing 737-8V3/W	44156/5059		582	♦
☐ HP-1842CMP	Boeing 737-8V3/W	40784/5100	ex N6067E	583	♦
☐ HP-1843CMP	Boeing 737-8V3/W	40785/5144		584	♦
☐ HP-1844CMP	Boeing 737-8V3/W	40786/5342		585	♦
☐ HP-1845CMP	Boeing 737-8V3/W	40787/5357			♦
☐ HP-1846CMP	Boeing 737-8V3/W	41447/			o/o♦
☐ HP-	Boeing 737-8V3/W	41448/			o/o♦
☐ HP-1540CMP	Embraer ERJ-190AR	19000012	ex PT-STL		
☐ HP-1556CMP	Embraer ERJ-190AR	19000016	ex PT-STQ		
☐ HP-1557CMP	Embraer ERJ-190AR	19000034	ex PT-SGI		
☐ HP-1558CMP	Embraer ERJ-190AR	19000038	ex PT-SGN		
☐ HP-1559CMP	Embraer ERJ-190AR	19000053	ex PT-SIC		
☐ HP-1560CMP	Embraer ERJ-190AR	19000056	ex PT-SIF		
☐ HP-1561CMP	Embraer ERJ-190AR	19000089	ex PT-SNI		
☐ HP-1562CMP	Embraer ERJ-190AR	19000095	ex PT-SNP		>RPB
☐ HP-1563CMP	Embraer ERJ-190AR	19000098	ex PT-SNS		>RPB
☐ HP-1564CMP	Embraer ERJ-190AR	19000100	ex PT-SNU		
☐ HP-1565CMP	Embraer ERJ-190AR	19000126	ex PT-SQV		
☐ HP-1566CMP	Embraer ERJ-190AR	19000165	ex PT-SAX		>RPB
☐ HP-1567CMP	Embraer ERJ-190AR	19000174	ex PT-SDJ		
☐ HP-1568CMP	Embraer ERJ-190AR	19000212	ex PT-SGV		
☐ HP-1569CMP	Embraer ERJ-190AR	19000222	ex PT-SHG		

DHL AERO EXPRESO (D5/DAE) Panama City-Tocumen Intl (PTY)

☐ HP-1810DAE	Boeing 757-27APCF	29611/910	ex N646AL	Ciudad de Panama
☐ HP-1910DAE	Boeing 757-27APCF	29607/832	ex N644AL	Ciudad de Colon
☐ HP-2010DAE	Boeing 757-27APCF	29610/904	ex N645AL	Ciudad de David

PANAIR CARGO/CARGO THREE Third Cargo (CTW) Panama City-Tocumen Intl (PTY)

☐ HP-1653CTW	Boeing 727-277F (FedEx 3)	21695/1481	ex N982JM	[PTY]
☐ HP-1754CTW	Boeing 727-225F	21857/1539	ex N755DH	

PARSA

☐ HP-512PS	Cessna U206E Stationair	U20601504	ex HP-512MF	

☐ HP-1507PS	de Havilland DHC-6 Twin Otter 300	532	
☐ HP-1509PS	de Havilland DHC-6 Twin Otter 300	360	
☐ HP-1688PS	Piper PA-34-2T Seneca II	34-7970141	ex HP-1688BL

HR- HONDURAS (Republic of Honduras)

AEROCARIBE DE HONDURAS

☐ HR-ASE	LET L-410UVP-E	861611	ex YS-IOC
☐ HR-AWA	LET L-410UVP-E3	882025	ex HI-681CT

AEROLINEAS SOSA — Sosa (NSO) — La Ceiba (LCE)

☐ HR-AIH	Britten-Norman BN-2A-21 Islander	513	ex C-GVZY	
☐ HR-ARE	LET L-410UVP	841312	ex S9-TBL	
☐ HR-ARJ	Nord 262A-14	15	ex N417SA	[LCE]
☐ HR-ARP	Nord 262A-27	33	ex N274A	wfs
☐ HR-ARU	Nord 262A-21	21	ex TG-ANP	[LCE]
☐ HR-ASI	LET L-410UVP-E3	871925	ex N888LT	
☐ HR-ATO	British Aerospace Jetstream 31	757	ex HR-ATE	
☐ HR-AUE	LET L-410UVP-E3	882029	ex TG-TAY	
☐ HR-AWW	Canadair CRJ-100ER	7037	ex N931CA	
☐ HR-AXJ	British Aerospace Jetstream 32	896	ex C-GQJV	
☐ HR-AXT	SAAB SF.340B	340B-267	ex N366PX	
☐ HR-AYT	Piper PA-31 Chieftain	31-8112060	ex HR-AVJ	♦

AEROVIAS CENTROAMERICAS - AVIAC

☐ HR-AJY	Douglas C-47	6068	ex HP-665	[TGU]
☐ HR-ALU	Douglas C-47-DL	4583	ex N28BA	
☐ HR-ATH	Douglas C-47	6102	ex HR-SAH	

CM AIRLINES — Tegucigalpa (TGU)

☐ HR-AVI	LET L-410UVP-E	952623	ex TG-TJL	
☐ HR-AXC	LET L-410UVP-E	902418	ex TG-TJH	
☐ HR-JMM	LET L-410UVP-E	902419	ex TG-TJG	
☐ TG-BJO	SAAB SF.340A	340A-142	ex N142XJ	<TGU
☐ TG-TAW	SAAB SF.340A	340A-117	ex YR-DAC	<TGU

EASYSKY — (EKY) — San Pedro Sula Ramon (SAP)

☐ HR-AVR	Boeing 737-232	23104/1062	ex N332DL	
☐ HR-AWG	British Aerospace Jetstream 31	764	ex C-FSEW	[SAP]
☐ HR-AWH	British Aerospace Jetstream 31	766	ex C-GPDC	
☐ HR-EMH	Boeing 737-5Y0	24900/2095	ex HC-CPC	♦
☐ HR-	Boeing 737-201	21816/592	ex XA-UHZ	♦

ISLENA AIRLINES — (WC/ISV) — La Ceiba (LCE)

☐ HR-AUX	ATR 42-320QC	394	ex 9A-CTU	
☐ HR-AVA	ATR 42-320	388	ex F-WQNC	
☐ HR-AXN	ATR 42-320	378	ex N378NA	
☐ HR-AYJ	ATR 72-600	1172	ex F-WWEM Avianca c/s	♦
☐ HR-AYM	ATR 72-600	1185	ex F-WWEB	♦
☐ HR-IAP	Short SD.3-60	SH3616	ex N345MV	
☐ HR-IAW	Short SD.3-60	SH3669	ex N361PA	
☐ HR-IBD	Cessna 208B Caravan I	208B....		
☐ HR-IBE	de Havilland DHC-6 Twin Otter			
☐ HR-IBH	Cessna 208B Caravan I			

LANHSA — LASA (LNH) — La Ceiba (LCE)

☐ HR-AWS	Cessna 402C	402C0069	ex N390TM	
☐ HR-AXG	British Aerospace Jetstream 3112	791	ex C-GNRG	
☐ HR-AXR	British Aerospace Jetstream 31	666	ex HH-	wfs
☐ HR-AYE	British Aerospace Jetstream 3112	747	ex C-GEMQ	♦

SETCO — Tegucigalpa (TGU)

☐ HR-AFB	Rockwell 500S Shrike Commander	3268	ex HR-315	[TGU]
☐ HR-AFC	Rockwell 500S Shrike Commander	3271	ex HR-317	[TGU]
☐ HR-AJY	Douglas DC-3	6068	ex HP-685	[TGU]
☐ HR-AKM	Rockwell 500S Shrike Commander	3098	ex HR-CNA	

HS- THAILAND (Kingdom of Thailand)

AIR INTER TRANSPORT

☐ HS-BIT   Piper PA-31-350 Navajo Chieftain   31-7752160   ex C-FJAL   ◆

ASIA ATLANTIC AIRWAYS		(HB/AAQ)		Bangkok-Suvarnabhumi (BKK)

☐ HS-AAB	Boeing 767-383ER	24846/309	ex N846TT
☐ HS-AAC	Boeing 767-322	25287/449	ex N781JM

ASIAN AIR		(DM/DEX)		Bangkok-Don Mueang (DMK)

☐ HS-DCM   Boeing 767-2J6ER   23307/126   ex N712AJ

BANGKOK AIRWAYS		Bangkok Air (PG/BKP)		Bangkok-Suvarnabhumi (BKK)

☐ HS-PGN	Airbus A319-132	3759	ex D-AVXD	Luang Prabang	
☐ HS-PGT	Airbus A319-132	3421	ex D-AVYM	Sukhothai	
☐ HS-PGX	Airbus A319-132	3424	ex D-AVYO	Hirsoshima	
☐ HS-PGY	Airbus A319-132	3454	ex D-AVWH	Angkor Wat	
☐ HS-PGZ	Airbus A319-132	3694	ex D-AVWH	Phnom Penh	
☐ HS PPA	Airbus A319-132	3911	ex D-AVYN	Si Satchanali	
☐ HS-PPB	Airbus A319-132	2648	ox N648BV	Rangkok	
☐ HS-PPC	Airbus A319-132	2660	ex N660BV	Chiang Mai	
☐ HS-PPF	Airbus A319-131	2634	ex EI-EXZ		
☐ HS-PPG	Airbus A319-132	2664	ex M-BOCA		
☐ HS-PPM	Airbus A319-132	2273	ex N874AC		◆
☐ HS-PGU	Airbus A320-232	2254	ex F-WWDC	Guilin	
☐ HS-PGV	Airbus A320-232	2310	ex F-WWDS	Krabi	
☐ HS-PGW	Airbus A320-232	2509	ex F-WWIQ	Samui	
☐ HS-PPD	Airbus A320-232	2531	ex D-ATAA		
☐ HS-PPE	Airbus A320-232	2417	ex PR-MAW	Mahamongkol	
☐ HS-PPH	Airbus A320-232	2783	ex PR-MBC		
☐ HS-PPJ	Airbus A320-232	2366	ex EI-FCR		
☐ HS-PPK	Airbus A320-232	2600	ex EI-FEN		◆
☐ HS-PGA	ATR 72-212A	710	ex F-WWEJ	Kut	dam 12Feb15
☐ HS-PGB	ATR 72-212A	708	ex F-WWEH	Phuket	
☐ HS-PGC	ATR 72-212A	715	ex F-WWEO	Nangyuan	
☐ HS-PGD	ATR 72-212A	833	ex F-WWEZ	Siem Reap	
☐ HS-PGF	ATR 72-212A	700	ex F-WWEW	Hua Hin	
☐ HS-PGG	ATR 72-212A	692	ex F-WWEO	Chang	
☐ HS-PGK	ATR 72-212A	680	ex F-WWEV	Apsara	
☐ HS-PGM	ATR 72-212A	704	ex F-WWEC	Tao	
☐ HS-PZA	ATR 72-600	1194	ex F-WWEK		◆
☐ HS-PZB	ATR 72-600	1230	ex F-WWEE		◆
☐ HS-	ATR 72-600	1269	ex F-WW		o/o◆

BUSINESS AIR		(8B/BCC)		Bangkok-Suvarnabhumi (BKK)

☐ HS-BIB   Boeing 767-341ER   24753/291   ex N753SJ
AOC suspended Jan15

CITY AIRWAYS		City Airways (E8/GTA)		Bangkok-Don Mueang (DMK)

☐ HS-GTE   Boeing 737-4H6   27087/2441   ex N114JF

HAPPY AIR		Happy Travel (HPY)		Bangkok-Suvamabhumi (BKK)

☐ HS-HPA   SAAB SF.340B   340A-255   ex N255AJ

JET ASIA AIRWAYS		Jet Asia (JF/JAA)		Bangkok-Suvamabhumi (BKK)

☐ HS-JAB	Boeing 767-222ER	21868/10	ex HS-BIA
☐ HS-JAE	Boeing 767-233ER	24324/252	ex N773JM
☐ HS-JAF	Boeing 767-233ER	24325/254	ex N780JM
☐ HS-JAK	Boeing 767-2J6ER	24007/204	ex N984JM
☐ HS-JAS	Boeing 767-336ER	25203/365	ex N797JM

KAN AIR/KANNITHI AVIATION		Kannithi Air (K8/KND)		Chiang Mai (CNX)

☐ HS-KAB	Cessna 208B Caravan I	208B2222	ex N6034P	
☐ HS-KAC	Beech 390 Premier 1	RB-48	ex D-IATT	
☐ HS-KAD	ATR 72-212A	777	ex M-IBAG	◆
☐ HS-KAF	ATR 72-212A	782	ex OY-CRV	◆

K-MILE AIR		(8K/KMI)			**Bangkok-Suvarnabhumi (BKK)**
☐ HS-KMA	Boeing 737-43QSF	28492/2837	ex HA-FAT		<FAH♦
☐ HS-SCK	Boeing 727-2J4F (FedEx 3)	22080/1598	ex VH-DHE		wfs

LEGACY AIR		(LGC)			**Utapao (UTP)**
☐ HS-LAA	SAAB SF.340A	340A-115	ex HS-SAC	Sensation	

NEWGEN AIRLINES		(E3/VGO)			**Bangkok-Don Mueang (DMK)**
☐ HS-NGA	Boeing 737-401	23991/1746	ex N424US	Al Roda	
☐ HS-NGB	Boeing 737-4H6	27673/2852	ex N104KR	Nittaya	♦
☐ HS-NGC	Boeing 737-4Q3	26603/2618	ex HS-GTE	Sunjutha	
☐ HS-NGD	Boeing 737-4Q3	26604/2684	ex N264LM	Amneh	♦

NOK AIR		Nok Air (DD/NOK)			**Bangkok-Don Mueang (DMK)**
☐ HS-DBA	Boeing 737-8AS/W	33813/1617	ex N840AC	Nok Yim Wan	
☐ HS-DBB	Boeing 737-8AS/W	33814/1618	ex N845AC	Nok Rak Yim	
☐ HS-DBC	Boeing 737-85P	28386/426	ex EC-HGQ	Nok Om Yim	
☐ HS-DBD	Boeing 737-8AS/W	33821/1698	ex N338CR	Nok Naanfa	
☐ HS-DBE	Boeing 737-83N/W	32577/973	ex VT-JGH	Nok Flamingo	
☐ HS-DBF	Boeing 737-8V3/W	29670/1711	ex HP-1529CMP	Nok Sod Sai	
☐ HS-DBG	Boeing 737-8FH/W	35094/2195	ex TC-AAK	Nok Baitoey	
☐ HS-DBH	Boeing 737-83N/W	32614/1201	ex VT-JGM	Nok Cartoon	
☐ HS-DBJ	Boeing 737-83N/W	32616/1212	ex VT-JGN	Nok Ra Rueng	
☐ HS-DBK	Boeing 737-86J/W	37774/4328	ex D-ABMM	Nok Sabai	
☐ HS-DBL	Boeing 737-8AS/W	33593/1914	ex EI-CLL	Nok Sanook	
☐ HS-DBM	Boeing 737-8AS/W	33594/1923	ex EI-DLM	Nok Sook Jai	
☐ HS-DBN	Boeing 737-8AS/W	33597/2060	ex EI-DLT	Nok Jai Dee	
☐ HS-DBO	Boeing 737-8AS/W	33621/2058	ex EI-DLS	Nok Dee Dee	
☐ HS-DBP	Boeing 737-8FZ/W	39336/4821		Nok Petchnaamngern	
☐ HS-DBQ	Boeing 737-86J/W	37794/4991		Nok Bussarakam 10th Anniversary c/s♦	
☐ HS-DBR	Boeing 737-86N/W	43420/5031		Nok Yoknapha	♦
☐ HS-DBS	Boeing 737-86N/W	43421/5137		Nok Tongchomphoo	♦
☐ HS-DQA	de Havilland DHC-8-402Q	4455	ex C-GWKW	Nok Anna	♦
☐ HS-DQB	de Havilland DHC-8-402Q	4458	ex C-GWRE	Nok Kao Neaw	♦
☐ HS-DQC	de Havilland DHC-8-402Q	4479	ex C-FDFZ	Nok Kao Pun	♦
☐ HS-DQD	ATR 72-600	4480	ex C-FCZD	Nok Kao Poon	♦
☐ HS-DRC	ATR 72-212A	740	ex M-IBAB	Nok Rom Ruen	♦
☐ HS-DRD	ATR 72-212A	754	ex M-IBAA	Nok Sailom	♦

NOKSCOOT		(XW/NCT)			**Bangkok-Don Mueang (DMK)**
☐ HS-XBA	Boeing 777-212ER	28521/330	ex 9V-SRF	Proud	♦
☐ HS-XBC	Boeing 777-212ER	30866/343	ex 9V-SRH	Plai Fah	♦

ORIENT THAI AIRLINES		Orient Thai (OX/OEA)		**Bangkok-Suvarnabhumi/Don Mueang (BKK/DMK)**
☐ HS-BRA	Boeing 737-324/W	23374/1204	ex N10323	[DMK]
☐ HS-BRB	Boeing 737-3T0/W	23375/1207	ex N14324	wfs
☐ HS-BRI	Boeing 737-3Z0	27138/2436	ex B-2533	
☐ HS-BRJ	Boeing 737-3Z0	27176/2495	ex B-2597	
☐ HS-BRK	Boeing 737-3Z0	25896/2558	ex B-2599	wfs
☐ HS-BRL	Boeing 737-3J6	25080/2254	ex B-2580	
☐ HS-BRQ	Boeing 737-3Z0	25892/2396	ex B-2587	wfs
☐ HS-STA	Boeing 747-422	26876/939	ex N187UA	
☐ HS-STB	Boeing 747-441	24956/917	ex PK-GSI	
☐ HS-STC	Boeing 747-412	26548/923	ex N584MD	
☐ HS-STI	Boeing 747-4Q8	28194/1100	ex G-VTOP	[BKK]
☐ HS-UTV	Boeing 747-346	23151/607	ex JA8166	[UTP]
☐ HS-UTW	Boeing 747-346	23067/588	ex JA812J	[DMK]
☐ HS-BKA	Boeing 767-3W0ER	28148/620	ex B-2568	
☐ HS-BKB	Boeing 767-346	23961/192	ex JA8265	[DMK]
☐ HS-BKD	Boeing 767-346	23962/193	ex JA8267	
☐ HS-BKE	Boeing 767-3W0ER	28264/644	ex JU-1012	>SVA dam 05Jan14
☐ HS-BKH	Boeing 767-346	23966/191	ex JA8266	
☐ HS-BKI	Boeing 767-346	23965/186	ex JA8264	♦
☐ HS-BKJ	Boeing 767-346	23963/224	ex JA8268	♦
☐ HS-BRD	Boeing 737-429	25247/2106	ex JA8931	
☐ HS-BRE	Boeing 737-429	25248/2120	ex JA8932	

R AIRLINES		(RK/RCT)		**Bangkok-Don Mueang (DMK)**
☐ HS-RCB	Airbus A320-212	0466	ex LY-VES	<NVD♦
☐ HS-RCC	Airbus A321-211	1017	ex M-ABFY	

RABBIT WINGS AIRWAYS

☐ HS-FGB	Piper PA-31-350 Navajo Chieftain	31-7652156	ex N64SS	♦

SIAM AIR TRANSPORT (O8/SQM) Bangkok-Don Mueang (DMK)

☐ HS-BRU	Boeing 737-3J6	25893/2489	ex B-2588	♦
☐ HS-BRV	Boeing 737-3L9	26440/2234	ex N338TH	♦

THAI AIRASIA Thai Asia (FD/AIQ) Bangkok-Don Mueang (DMK)

☐ HS-ABA	Airbus A320-216	3277	ex F-WWDH		
☐ HS-ABB	Airbus A320-216	3299	ex F-WWDZ		
☐ HS-ABC	Airbus A320-216	3338	ex F-WWBM		
☐ HS-ABD	Airbus A320-216	3394	ex F-WWBQ		
☐ HS-ABE	Airbus A320-216	3489	ex F-WWIR	Truly ASEAN c/s	
☐ HS-ABF	Airbus A320-216	3505	ex F-WWBS		
☐ HS-ABG	Airbus A320-216	3576	ex F-WWBN		
☐ HS-ABH	Airbus A320-216	3679	ex F-WWBD		
☐ HS-ABI	Airbus A320-216	3729	ex F-WWDK		
☐ HS-ABJ	Airbus A320-216	4019	ex F-WWDF		
☐ HS-ABK	Airbus A320-216	4088	ex F-WWBV	Thai Fight c/s	
☐ HS-ABL	Airbus A320-216	4126	ex F-WWIO		
☐ HS-ABM	Airbus A320-216	4278	ex F-WWID		
☐ HS-ABN	Airbus A320-216	4302	ex F-WWDM		
☐ HS-ABO	Airbus A320-216	4333	ex F-WWIM		
☐ HS-ABP	Airbus A320-216	4367	ex F-WWDR		
☐ HS-ABQ	Airbus A320-216	4386	ex F-WWDE		
☐ HS-ABR	Airbus A320-216	4390	ex F-WWDK		
☐ HS-ABS	Airbus A320-216	4426	ex F-WWBP		
☐ HS-ABT	Airbus A320-216	4557	ex F-WWDT		
☐ HS-ABU	Airbus A320-216	4807	ex 9M-AQL		♦
☐ HS-ABV	Airbus A320-216	4979	ex D-AVVM		
☐ HS-ABW	Airbus A320-216	4980	ex F-WWIZ		
☐ HS-ABX	Airbus A320-214	4917	ex 9M-AQJ		
☐ HS-ABY	Airbus A320-214	4964	ex 9M-AQK		
☐ HS-ABZ	Airbus A320-216	5283	ex F-WWIH		
☐ HS-BBA	Airbus A320-216	5344	ex F-WWDL		
☐ HS-BBB	Airbus A320-216	5353	ex F-WWIU		
☐ HS-BBC	Airbus A320-216/S	5468	ex F-WWBH		
☐ HS-BBD	Airbus A320-216/S	5593	ex F-WWDN		
☐ HS-BBE	Airbus A320-216/S	5703	ex F-WWBI		
☐ HS-BBF	Airbus A320-216/S	5762	ex F-WWIY		
☐ HS-BBG	Airbus A320-214/S	5812	ex F-WWBE		
☐ HS-BBH	Airbus A320-216/S	5839	ex F-WWIL		
☐ HS-BBI	Airbus A320-216/S	5851	ex F-WWBT		
☐ HS-BBJ	Airbus A320-216/S	5866	ex F-WWDJ		
☐ HS-BBK	Airbus A320-216/S	5918	ex F-WWDV		
☐ HS-BBL	Airbus A320-216/S	5959	ex F-WWIP		o/o
☐ HS-BBM	Airbus A320-216/S	6170	ex F-WWBR		♦
☐ HS-BBN	Airbus A320-216/S	6178	ex F-WWBU		♦
☐ HS-BBO	Airbus A320-216/S	6240	ex F-WWIN		♦
☐ HS-BBP	Airbus A320-216/S	6405	ex F-WWDT		♦
☐ HS-BBQ	Airbus A320-216/S	6428	ex F-WWID		♦
☐ HS-BBR	Airbus A320-216/S	6676	ex (JA01DJ)		o/o♦

THAI AIRASIA X (XJ/TAX) Bangkok-Don Mueang (DMK)

☐ HS-XTA	Airbus A330-343E	662	ex 9M-XXL	
☐ HS-XTB	Airbus A330-343	786	ex 9M-XXN	
☐ HS-XTC	Airbus A330-343	692	ex 9M-XXO	♦

THAI AIRWAYS INTERNATIONAL Thai (TG/THA) Bangkok-Suvarnabhumi (BKK)

Member of Star Alliance

☐ HS-TAR	Airbus A300B4-622R	681	ex F-WWAB	Yasothon	[DMK]
☐ HS-TAS	Airbus A300B4-622R	705	ex F-WWAT	Yala	[DMK]
☐ HS-TAT	Airbus A300B4-622R	782	ex F-WWAY	Srimuang	[BKK]
☐ HS-TAW	Airbus A300B4-622R	784	ex F-WWAL	Suranaree	[BKK]
☐ HS-TAX	Airbus A300B4-622R	785	ex F-WWAO	Thepsatri	[BKK]
☐ HS-TAY	Airbus A300B4-622R	786	ex F-WWAQ	Srisoonthorn	[BKK]
☐ HS-TAZ	Airbus A300B4-622R	787	ex F-WWAB	Srisubhan	[BKK]
☐ HS-TXA	Airbus A320-232	5198	ex D-AVVM	Ubon Ratchathani	♦
☐ HS-TXB	Airbus A320-232	5248	ex F-WWDC	Nakhon Phanom	♦
☐ HS-TXC	Airbus A320-232	5258	ex F-WWDQ	Nong Bua Lam Phu	♦
☐ HS-TXD	Airbus A320-232	5301	ex D-AXAU	Sing Buri	♦
☐ HS-TXE	Airbus A320-232	5436	ex F-WWIJ	Nakhon Si Thammarat	
☐ HS-TEA	Airbus A330-321	050	ex F-WWKI	Manorom	[TUP]

☐	HS-TEB	Airbus A330-321	060	ex F-WWKQ	Sri Sakhon	
☐	HS-TEC	Airbus A330-321	062	ex F-WWKR	Bang Rachan	[DMK]
☐	HS-TED	Airbus A330-321	064	ex F-WWKS	Donchedi	[BKK]
☐	HS-TEE	Airbus A330-321	065	ex F-WWKT	Kusuman	[BKK]
☐	HS-TEF	Airbus A330-321	066	ex F-WWKJ	Song Dao	[BKK]
☐	HS-TEG	Airbus A330-321	112	ex F-WWKM	Lam Plai Mat	[BKK]
☐	HS-TEH	Airbus A330-321	122	ex F-WWKG	Sai Buri	[BKK]
☐	HS-TEJ	Airbus A330-322	209	ex F-WWKN	Sudawadi	
☐	HS-TEK	Airbus A330-322	224	ex F-WWKD	Srichulalak	Royal Barge c/s
☐	HS-TEL	Airbus A330-322	231	ex F-WWKU	Thepamart	Star Alliance c/s
☐	HS-TEM	Airbus A330-323X	346	ex F-WWYE	Jiraprabha	[UTP]
☐	HS-TBA	Airbus A330-343E	1263	ex F-WWYC	Amnat Charoen	
☐	HS-TBB	Airbus A330-343E	1269	ex F-WWKV	Phrae	
☐	HS-TBC	Airbus A330-343E	1289	ex F-WWKP	Kanchanaburi	
☐	HS-TBD	Airbus A330-343E	1338	ex F-WWCB	Phayao	
☐	HS-TBE	Airbus A330-343E	1348	ex F-WWCN	Sakon Nakhon	
☐	HS-TBF	Airbus A330-343E	1374	ex F-WWYC	Sa Kaeo	
☐	HS-TBG	Airbus A330-343E	1408	ex F-WWTI	Samut Prakan	
☐	HS-TEN	Airbus A330-343E	990	ex F-WWKK	Suchada	
☐	HS-TEO	Airbus A330-343E	1003	ex F-WWKR	Chutamas	
☐	HS-TEP	Airbus A330-343E	1035	ex F-WWKS	Srianocha	
☐	HS-TEQ	Airbus A330-343E	1037	ex F-WWYA	Si Ayutthaya	
☐	HS-TER	Airbus A330-343E	1060	ex F-WWYQ	U Thong	
☐	HS-TES	Airbus A330-343E	1074	ex F-WWKJ	Sukhothai	
☐	HS-TET	Airbus A330-343E	1086	ex F-WWYV	Kirimas	
☐	HS-TEU	Airbus A330-343E	1090	ex F-WWYB	Chalburi	
☐	HS-TLA	Airbus A340-541	624	ex F-WWTN	Chiang Kham	[DMK]
☐	HS-TLB	Airbus A340-541	628	ex F-WWTO	Uttaradit	[DMK]
☐	HS-TLC	Airbus A340-541	698	ex F-WWTR	Phitsanulok	[DMK]
☐	HS-TLD	Airbus A340-541	775	ex F-WWTX	Kamphaeng Phet	[DMK]
☐	HS-TNA	Airbus A340-642	677	ex F-WWCJ	Watthana Nakhon	[UTP]
☐	HS-TNB	Airbus A340-642	681	ex F-WWCK	Saraburi	[UTP]
☐	HS-TNC	Airbus A340-642	689	ex F-WWCN	Chon Buri	[UTP]
☐	HS-TND	Airbus A340-642	710	ex F-WWCX	Phetchaburi	[UTP]
☐	HS-TNE	Airbus A340-642	719	ex F-WWCH	Nonthaburi	[UTP]
☐	HS-TNF	Airbus A340-642	953	ex F-WWCM	Mae Hong Son	[UTP]
☐	HS-TUA	Airbus A380-841	087	ex F-WWAO	Si Rattana	
☐	HS-TUB	Airbus A380-841	093	ex F-WWAN	Mancha Khiri	
☐	HS-TUC	Airbus A380-841	100	ex F-WWAT	Chaiya	
☐	HS-TUD	Airbus A380-841	122	ex F-WWSE	Phayuha Khiri	
☐	HS-TUE	Airbus A380-841	125	ex F-WWSQ	Si Racha	
☐	HS-TUF	Airbus A380-841	131	ex F-WWSU	Kamalasai	
☐	HS-TDA	Boeing 737-4D7	24830/1899		Songkhla	[DMK]
☐	HS-TDB	Boeing 737-4D7	24831/1922		Phuket	[DMK]
☐	HS-TDD	Boeing 737-4D7	26611/2318		Chumphon	
☐	HS-TDE	Boeing 737-4D7	26612/2330		Surin	[DMK]
☐	HS-TDF	Boeing 737-4D7	26613/2338		Si Sa Ket	[DMK]
☐	HS-TDG	Boeing 737-4D7	26614/2481		Kalasin	[DMK]
☐	HS-TDK	Boeing 737-4D7	28701/2977		Sri Surat	[DMK]
☐	HS-TGA	Boeing 747-4D7	32369/1273		Srisuriyothai	
☐	HS-TGB	Boeing 747-4D7	32370/1278		Si Satchanalai	
☐	HS-TGF	Boeing 747-4D7	33770/1335		Sri Ubon	
☐	HS-TGG	Boeing 747-4D7	33771/1337		Pathoomawadi	
☐	HS-TGH	Boeing 747-4D7BCF	24458/769		Chaiprakarn	[VCV]
☐	HS-TGJ	Boeing 747-4D7BCF	24459/777		Hariphunchai	wfs
☐	HS-TGO	Boeing 747-4D7	26609/1001		Bowonrangsi	
☐	HS-TGP	Boeing 747-4D7	26610/1047		Thepprasit	
☐	HS-TGR	Boeing 747-4D7	27723/1071		Siriwatthna	
☐	HS-TGT	Boeing 747-4D7	26616/1097		Watthanothai	
☐	HS-TGW	Boeing 747-4D7	27724/1111		Visuthakasatriya	
☐	HS-TGX	Boeing 747-4D7	27725/1134		Sirisobhakya	
☐	HS-TGY	Boeing 747-4D7	28705/1164	ex N60697	Dararasmi	
☐	HS-TGZ	Boeing 747-4D7	28706/1214		Phimara	
☐	HS-TJA	Boeing 777-2D7	27726/25		Lamphun	
☐	HS-TJB	Boeing 777-2D7	27727/32		U Thaithani	
☐	HS-TJC	Boeing 777-2D7	27728/44		Nakhon Nayok	
☐	HS-TJD	Boeing 777-2D7	27729/51		Mukdahan	
☐	HS-TJE	Boeing 777-2D7	27730/89		Chaiyaphum	
☐	HS-TJF	Boeing 777-2D7	27731/95		Phanom Sarakham	
☐	HS-TJG	Boeing 777-2D7	27732/100		Pattani	
☐	HS-TJH	Boeing 777-2D7	27733/113		Suphan Buri	
☐	HS-TJR	Boeing 777-2D7ER	34586/588		Nakhon Sawan	
☐	HS-TJS	Boeing 777-2D7ER	34587/595		Phra Nakhon	
☐	HS-TJT	Boeing 777-2D7ER	34588/596		Pathum Wan	
☐	HS-TJU	Boeing 777-2D7ER	34589/663		Phichit	
☐	HS-TJV	Boeing 777-2D7ER	34590/665		Nakhon Pathom	
☐	HS-TJW	Boeing 777-2D7ER	34591/672		Phetchabun	

☐ HS-TKA	Boeing 777-3D7	29150/156	ex N5028Y	Sriwanna	
☐ HS-TKB	Boeing 777-3D7	29151/170		Chainarai	
☐ HS-TKC	Boeing 777-3D7	29211/250		Kwanmuang	
☐ HS-TKD	Boeing 777-3D7	29212/260		Thepalai	
☐ HS-TKE	Boeing 777-3D7	29213/304		Sukhirin	
☐ HS-TKF	Boeing 777-3D7	29214/310		Chutamai	
☐ HS-TKK	Boeing 777-3ALER	41520/1030		Philavan	
☐ HS-TKL	Boeing 777-3ALER	41521/1049	ex N5022E	Sunanda	
☐ HS-TKM	Boeing 777-3ALER	41522/1082		Prabhasri	
☐ HS-TKN	Boeing 777-3ALER	41523/1091		Mendininat	
☐ HS-TKO	Boeing 777-3ALER	41524/1107		Vimolmassiri	
☐ HS-TKP	Boeing 777-3ALER	41525/1119		Sri Amphorn	
☐ HS-TKQ	Boeing 777-3ALER	41526/1129		Khemarat	
☐ HS-TKR	Boeing 777-3ALER	41527/1145		Hat Yai	
☐ HS-TKU	Boeing 777-3D7ER	42110/1166		Acharasobhit	
☐ HS-TKV	Boeing 777-3D7ER	42111/1215		Suchitra	◆
☐ HS-TKW	Boeing 777-3D7ER	42112/1228		Mukdasayam	◆
☐ HS-TKX	Boeing 777-3D7ER	42113/1267		Sudharma	◆
☐ HS-TKY	Boeing 777-3D7ER	42114/1310		Yubhaphaka	o/o◆
☐ HS-TKZ	Boeing 777-3D7ER	42115/1338		Sulalivan	o/o◆
☐ HS-TQA	Boeing 787-8	35315/190	ex N1008S	Ongkharak	◆
☐ HS-TQB	Boeing 787-8	35316/209		Chaturaphak Phiman	◆
☐ HS-TQC	Boeing 787-8	36110/226		Pran Buri	◆
☐ HS-TQD	Boeing 787-8	35320/244		Wapi Pathum	◆
☐ HS-TQE	Boeing 787-8	38757/287		Kosum Phisai	◆
☐ HS-TQF	Boeing 787-8	38759/331		Kong Krailat	o/o◆
☐ HS-TRA	ATR 72-201	164	ex F-WWEO	Lampang	[DMK]
☐ HS-TRB	ATR 72-201	167	ex F-WWEU	Chai Nat	[DMK]

THAI AVIATION SERVICES	**(TSL)**		**Nakhon si Thammarat**

☐ HS-HTE	Sikorsky S-76A++	760706	ex N2584R	
☐ HS-HTJ	Sikorsky S-76A++	760720	ex N720G	
☐ HS-HTL	Sikorsky S-76C++	760693	ex 9M-AIP	
☐ HS-HTN	Sikorsky S-76C++	760731	ex C-FZSZ	
☐ HS-HTP	Sikorsky S-76A++	760697	ex N25811	
☐ HS-HTT	Sikorsky S-76C++	760691	ex C-FRSA	
☐ HS-HTW	Sikorsky S-76C++	760724	ex C-FUWP	
☐ HS-HTZ	Sikorsky S-76C+	760561	ex C-GHRZ	
☐ HS-HTF	Sikorsky S-92A	920143	ex G-CHCZ	
☐ HS-HTH	Sikorsky S-92A	920146	ex N146UK	
A division of CHC Helicopters				

THAI EXPRESS AIR	**(TXZ)**		**Bangkok-Suvarnabhumi (BKK)**

☐ HS-EXA	Boeing 737-348QC	23809/1458	ex N809QC	[UTP]◆

THAI LION AIR	**(SL/TLM)**		**Bangkok-Don Mueang (DMK)**

☐ HS-LTH	Boeing 737-9GPER/W	38739/4657	ex N1786B	
☐ HS-LTI	Boeing 737-9GPER/W	38738/4643	ex N5515R	
☐ HS-LTJ	Boeing 737-9GPER/W	39823/5070		◆
☐ HS-LTK	Boeing 737-9GPER/W	38304/5162	ex (PK-LPJ)	◆
☐ HS-LTL	Boeing 737-9GPER/W	38748/4822	ex N5573B	
☐ HS-LTM	Boeing 737-9GPER/W	38749/4843	ex N1796B	
☐ HS-LTO	Boeing 737-9GPER/W	39824/5088		
☐ HS-LTP	Boeing 737-9GPER/W	38301/5176	ex (PK-LPK)	◆
☐ HS-LTQ	Boeing 737-9GPER/W	39832/5242		◆
☐ HS-LTR	Boeing 737-9GPER/W	39837/5347		◆
☐ HS-LTS	Boeing 737-9GPER/W	39839/5404		o/o◆
☐ HS-LTT	Boeing 737-9GPER/W	39860/5423		o/o◆

THAI FLYING SERVICE	**Thai Flying (TF/TFT)**		**Bangkok-Don Mueang (DMK)**

☐ HS-ITD	Beech King Air B300	FL-151	ex N10871	
☐ HS-SPL	Cessna 208B Caravan	208B1000	ex HS-SMI	

THAI SMILE AIRWAYS	**(WE/THD)**		**Bangkok-Suvamabhumi (BKK)**

☐ HS-TXF	Airbus A320-232	5553	ex F-WWID	Samul Songkhram	
☐ HS-TXG	Airbus A320-232/S	5806	ex F-WWBC	Prachin Buri	
☐ HS-TXH	Airbus A320-232/S	5828	ex F-WWBU	Satun	
☐ HS-TXJ	Airbus A320-232/S	5857	ex F-WWBZ	Ang Thong	
☐ HS-TXK	Airbus A320-232/S	5892	ex D-AVVL	Ranong	
☐ HS-TXL	Airbus A320-232/S	5951	ex F-WWDZ	Nong Khai	
☐ HS-TXM	Airbus A320-232/S	5979	ex F-WWIH	Krung Thep Nakhon	
☐ HS-TXN	Airbus A320-232/S	6113	ex D-AXAU	Udon Thani	
☐ HS-TXO	Airbus A320-232/S	6140	ex F-WWIX	Nakhon Ratchasima	◆
☐ HS-TXP	Airbus A320-232/S	6254	ex F-WWDP	Surat Thani	◆

☐ HS-TXQ	Airbus A320-232/S	6297	ex F-WWBJ	Phra Nakhon Si Autthaya	♦
☐ HS-TXR	Airbus A320-232/S	6374	ex D-AXAH	Trat	♦
☐ HS-TXS	Airbus A320-232/S	6417	ex F-WWDP	Roi Et	♦
☐ HS-	Airbus A320-232/S	6784	ex		o/o♦
☐ HS-	Airbus A320-232/S	6811	ex		o/o♦

THAI VIETJET AIR		**(TVJ)**		**Bangkok-Suvamabhumi (BKK)**

☐ HS-VKA	Airbus A320-214	2745	ex VN-A679	♦

UNITED OFFSHORE HELICOPTERS				**Songkhla**

☐ A7-GHD	AgustaWestland AW139	31233		
☐ A7-GHE	AgustaWestland AW139	31235		
☐ A7-GHF	AgustaWestland AW139	31242		
☐ HS-UOD	AgustaWestland AW139	41367	ex N620SM	♦
☐ HS-UOH	AgustaWestland AW139	31543	ex I-EASI	♦
☐ HS-UOJ	AgustaWestland AW139	31550	ex I-EASS	♦

HZ- SAUDI ARABIA (Kingdom of Saudi Arabia)

AVIATION HORIZONS				**Jeddah (JED)**

☐ HZ-FM1	Boeing 737-528/W	27425/2730	ex N463AC	♦
☐ HZ-HAA	Boeing 737-529/W	25419/2165	ex N419CT	♦

AL MAHA AIRWAYS				**Riyadh (RUH)**

☐ A7-LAA	Airbus A320-214/S	6347	ex (HZ-ALA)	♦
☐ A7-LAB	Airbus A320-214/S	6467	ex F-WWIO	♦
☐ A7-LAC	Airbus A320-214/S	6494	ex F-WWIH	♦
☐ A7-LAD	Airbus A320-214/S	6529	ex F-WWBI	♦
☐ A7-LAE	Airbus A320-214/S	6662	ex F-WWBZ	o/o♦
☐ HZ-	Airbus A320-214/S	6646	ex	o/o♦

ALPHA STAR AVIATION SERVICES		**(STT)**		**Riyadh (RUH)**

☐ HZ-A2	Airbus A320CJ-214	3164	ex HZ-AJ2	VIP
☐ HZ-A3	Airbus A320-214	0764	ex HZ-AJ3	VIP
☐ HZ-A4	Airbus A319-112	1494	ex HZ-AJW	VIP
☐ HZ-A5	Airbus A318CJ-112	2910	ex 9H-AFM	VIP
☐ HZ-A10	ATR 42-600	859	ex F-WWLJ	
☐ HZ-A11	ATR 72-600	1184	ex F-WKVH	♦
☐ HZ-A15	Airbus A320-216	3261	ex 9M-AHC	♦
☐ HZ-A	Airbus A319-112	6727	ex	o/o♦
☐ HZ-A	Airbus A330CJ-243	1676	ex F-WW	o/o♦

FLYNAS		**(XY/KNE)**		**Jeddah (JED)**

☐ VP-CXC	Airbus A320-214	2171	ex B-6028	
☐ VP-CXD	Airbus A320-214	2182	ex B-6029	
☐ VP-CXE	Airbus A320-214	2199	ex B-6030	♦
☐ VP-CXF	Airbus A320-214	1942	ex G-DHRG	
☐ VP-CXG	Airbus A320-214	1965	ex G-DHJZ	
☐ VP-CXH	Airbus A320-214	3256	ex VT-WAE	
☐ VP-CXI	Airbus A320-214	3218	ex A6-ABJ	
☐ VP-CXJ	Airbus A320-214/S	5716	ex D-AVVM	
☐ VP-CXK	Airbus A320-214	4055	ex M-ABGC	
☐ VP-CXL	Airbus A320-214	4735	ex CS-TRK	
☐ VP-CXM	Airbus A320-214	2776	ex EC-JSB	
☐ VP-CXN	Airbus A320-214	2569	ex 9K-CAA	
☐ VP-CXO	Airbus A320-214	3868	ex OE-IBV	
☐ VP-CXP	Airbus A320-214	3889	ex OE-IBX	
☐ VP-CXQ	Airbus A320-214	3933	ex OE-IBY	
☐ VP-CXR	Airbus A320-214	3894	ex F-WWDF	
☐ VP-CXS	Airbus A320-214	3787	ex F-WWBB	
☐ VP-CXT	Airbus A320-214	3817	ex F-WWIN	
☐ VP-CXU	Airbus A320-214	2123	ex SU-KBC	
☐ VP-CXV	Airbus A320-214	3809	ex CN-NMA	♦
☐ VP-CXW	Airbus A320-214	3475	ex F-WWDF	
☐ VP-CXX	Airbus A320-214	3425	ex F-WWIZ	
☐ VP-CXY	Airbus A320-214	3396	ex F-WWBR	
☐ VP-CXZ	Airbus A320-214	3361	ex F-WWIK	
☐ VP-CQT	Embraer ERJ-190LR	19000403	ex PT-TYW	[RUH]
☐ VP-CQW	Embraer ERJ-190LR	19000232	ex PT-SID	[EXT]
☐ VP-CQX	Embraer ERJ-190LR	19000233	ex PT-SIE	[AMM]
☐ 9M-XXK	Airbus A330-343E	1443	ex F-WWCS	Xklusive

SAUDI MEDEVAC

☐ HZ-MS54	AgustaWestland AW139	31539	ex I-RAIN	♦
☐ HZ-MS55	AgustaWestland AW139	31548	ex I-EASL	♦
☐ HZ-MS56	AgustaWestland AW139	31553	ex I-RAIK	♦

SAUDIA   Saudia (SV/SVA)   Jeddah (JED)

Member of SkyTeam

☐ HZ-ASA	Airbus A320-214	4081	ex F-WWBR		
☐ HZ-ASB	Airbus A320-214	4090	ex F-WWBZ		
☐ HZ-ASC	Airbus A320-214	4337	ex F-WWIV		
☐ HZ-ASD	Airbus A320-214	4364	ex F-WWDI		
☐ HZ-ASE	Airbus A320-214	4408	ex F-WWIE		
☐ HZ-ASF	Airbus A320-214	4955	ex D-AXAW		
☐ HZ-ASG	Airbus A320-214	5223	ex F-WWBM		
☐ HZ-AS11	Airbus A320-214	4015	ex F-WWBS		
☐ HZ-AS12	Airbus A320-214	4057	ex F-WWBC		
☐ HZ-AS13	Airbus A320-214	4104	ex F-WWDQ		
☐ HZ-AS14	Airbus A320-214	4115	ex F-WWDX		
☐ HZ-AS15	Airbus A320-214	4122	ex F-WWIF		
☐ HZ-AS16	Airbus A320-214	4135	ex F-WWIU		
☐ HZ-AS17	Airbus A320-214	4349	ex F-WWBV		
☐ HZ-AS18	Airbus A320-214	4357	ex F WWDH		
☐ HZ-AS19	Airbus A320-214	4376	ex F-WWIN		
☐ HZ-AS20	Airbus A320-214	4392	ex F-WWDO		
☐ HZ-AS21	Airbus A320-214	4414	ex D-AVVI		
☐ HZ-AS22	Airbus A320-214	4484	ex F-WWDN		
☐ HZ-AS23	Airbus A320-214	4519	ex F-WWDE		
☐ HZ-AS31	Airbus A320-214	4092	ex F-WWDE		
☐ HZ-AS32	Airbus A320-214	4273	ex F-WWBY		
☐ HZ-AS33	Airbus A320-214	4314	ex F-WWBP		
☐ HZ-AS34	Airbus A320-214	4397	ex F-WWIL		
☐ HZ-AS35	Airbus A320-214	4391	ex D-AVVG		
☐ HZ-AS36	Airbus A320-214	4393	ex D-AVVJ		
☐ HZ-AS37	Airbus A320-214	4394	ex F-WWDX		
☐ HZ-AS38	Airbus A320-214	4432	ex D-AVVP		
☐ HZ-AS39	Airbus A320-214	4442	ex F-WWIA		
☐ HZ-AS40	Airbus A320-214	4419	ex F-WWDU		
☐ HZ-AS41	Airbus A320-214	4454	ex F-WWBE		
☐ HZ-AS42	Airbus A320-214	4501	ex F-WWIM		
☐ HZ-AS43	Airbus A320-214	4517	ex F-WWBO		
☐ HZ-AS44	Airbus A320-214	4564	ex F-WWBD		
☐ HZ-AS45	Airbus A320-214	4823	ex F-WWII		
☐ HZ-ASH	Airbus A321-211	4467	ex D-AVZD		
☐ HZ-ASI	Airbus A321-211	4542	ex D-AVZR		
☐ HZ-ASJ	Airbus A321-211	4577	ex D-AZAG		
☐ HZ-ASK	Airbus A321-211	4590	ex D-AZAJ		
☐ HZ-ASL	Airbus A321-211	4838	ex D-AVZV		
☐ HZ-ASM	Airbus A321-211	4811	ex D-AVZP		
☐ HZ-ASN	Airbus A321-211	4925	ex D-AVZJ		
☐ HZ-ASO	Airbus A321-211	4962	ex D-AZAG		
☐ HZ-ASP	Airbus A321-211	5009	ex D-AZAK		
☐ HZ-ASQ	Airbus A321-211	5065	ex D-AVZM		
☐ HZ-ASR	Airbus A321-211	5285	ex D-AZAH		
☐ HZ-AST	Airbus A321-211	5314	ex D-AZAQ		
☐ HZ-ASU	Airbus A321-211	5447	ex D-AVZV		
☐ HZ-ASV	Airbus A321-211	5509	ex D-AZAO		
☐ HZ-ASW	Airbus A321-211	5549	ex D-AVZD		
☐ TC-OBR	Airbus A321-231	1008	ex N108DE		<OHY♦
☐ TC-OBV	Airbus A321-231	0806	ex TC-JMC		<OHY♦
☐ HZ-AQA	Airbus A330-343X	1108	ex F-WWKZ		
☐ HZ-AQB	Airbus A330-343X	1127	ex F-WWYP		
☐ HZ-AQC	Airbus A330-343X	1137	ex F-WWKM		
☐ HZ-AQD	Airbus A330-343X	1141	ex F-WWKL		
☐ HZ-AQE	Airbus A330-343X	1147	ex F-WWYB		
☐ HZ-AQF	Airbus A330-343X	1153	ex F-WWYT		
☐ HZ-AQG	Airbus A330-343X	1192	ex F-WWKO		
☐ HZ-AQH	Airbus A330-343X	1189	ex F-WWKA		
☐ HZ-AQI	Airbus A330-343X	1454	ex F-WWYG		
☐ HZ-AQJ	Airbus A330-343X	1473	ex F-WWYL		
☐ HZ-AQK	Airbus A330-343X	1462	ex F-WWCR		
☐ HZ-AQL	Airbus A330-343X	1513	ex F-WWKP	SkyTeam c/s	
☐ TC-OCA	Airbus A330-322	072	ex EC-IJH		<OHY
☐ TC-OCB	Airbus A330-342	098	ex B-HYA		<OHY
☐ TC-OCC	Airbus A330-322	143	ex 9M-MKS		<OHY
☐ TF-EAA	Airbus A330-223	343	ex N772RD		<ABD
☐ HZ-AIF	Boeing 747SP-68	22503/529			[JED]

☐ HZ-AIK	Boeing 747-368	23262/616	ex N6005C	[JED]
☐ HZ-AIL	Boeing 747-368	23263/619	ex N6009F	[JED]
☐ HZ-AIM	Boeing 747-368	23264/620	ex N6046P	[JED]
☐ HZ-AIN	Boeing 747-368	23265/622	ex N6046P	[JED]
☐ HZ-AIP	Boeing 747-368	23267/630	ex N6055X	[JED]
☐ HZ-AIQ	Boeing 747-368	23268/631	ex N6005C	[JED]
☐ HZ-AIR	Boeing 747-368	23269/643	ex N6038E	[JED]
☐ HZ-AIT	Boeing 747-368	23271/652	ex N6038N	[JED]
☐ HZ-AIU	Boeing 747-268F	24359/724	ex N6018N	[JED]
☐ EC-KXN	Boeing 747-4H6	25703/1025	ex N703AC	<PLM
☐ EC-KQC	Boeing 747-412	26549/1030	ex 9V-SMZ	<PLM♦
☐ EC-MDS	Boeing 747-419	26910/1180	ex N342AS	<PLM♦
☐ HZ-AIV	Boeing 747-468	28339/1122	ex N6005C	
☐ HZ-AIW	Boeing 747-468	28340/1138		
☐ HZ-AIX	Boeing 747-468	28341/1182		
☐ HZ-AIY	Boeing 747-468	28342/1216	ex N6009F	
☐ TC-ACF	Boeing 747-481SF	25645/979	ex N596MS	<RUN
☐ TC-ACG	Boeing 747-481SF	25641/928	ex N597MS	<RUN
☐ TC-ACJ	Boeing 747-433BCF	25075/868	ex B-2478	<RUN
☐ TC-ACM	Boeing 747-428ERF	32867/1318	ex F-GIUC	<RUN♦
☐ TF-AAC	Boeing 747-481	29262/1199	ex N262SG	<ABD
☐ TF-AAD	Boeing 747-4H6	28426/1130	ex HZ-AWA2	<ABD
☐ TF-AAE	Boeing 747-4H6	27672/1091	ex 9M-MPI	<ABD
☐ TF-AAG	Boeing 747-4H6	27043/1017	ex N774AS	<ABD
☐ TF-AAH	Boeing 747-4H6	29901/1301	ex 9M-MPQ	<ABD♦
☐ TF-AMF	Boeing 747-412BCF	24226/809	ex PH-MPR	<ABD
☐ TF-AMI	Boeing 747-412SF	27066/940	ex N706RB	<ABD
☐ TF-AML	Boeing 747-4H6SF	27044/1041	ex N401SA	<ABD
☐ TF-AMM	Boeing 747-4H6BDSF	25700/974	ex N740WA	<ABD
☐ TF-AMN	Boeing 747-4F6BDSF	27602/1161	ex N469AC	<ABD♦
☐ TF-AMP	Boeing 747-481SF	24801/805	ex LX-ZCV	<ABD
☐ TF-AMQ	Boeing 747-412F	26553/1069	ex N328SC	<ABD♦
☐ TF-AMS	Boeing 747-481	24920/832	ex JA8096	<ABD♦
☐ TF-AMU	Boeing 747-48EF	27603/1210	ex HL7426	<ABD
☐ TF-AMV	Boeing 747-412	28022/1082	ex 9V-SPI	<ABD
☐ 9M-MPD	Boeing 747-4H6	25701/997		<EZX
☐ 9M-MPK	Boeing 747-4H6	28427/1147		<EZX
☐ 9M-MPM	Boeing 747-4H6	28435/1152		<EZX♦
☐ HZ-AKA	Boeing 777-268ER	28344/98	ex N50217	
☐ HZ-AKB	Boeing 777-268ER	28345/99	ex N5023Q	
☐ HZ-AKC	Boeing 777-268ER	28346/101		
☐ HZ-AKD	Boeing 777-268ER	28347/103		
☐ HZ-AKE	Boeing 777-268ER	28348/109		
☐ HZ-AKF	Boeing 777-268ER	28349/114		
☐ HZ-AKG	Boeing 777-268ER	28350/119		
☐ HZ-AKH	Boeing 777-268ER	28351/124		
☐ HZ-AKI	Boeing 777-268ER	28352/143		
☐ HZ-AKJ	Boeing 777-268ER	28353/147		
☐ HZ-AKK	Boeing 777-268ER	28354/154		
☐ HZ-AKL	Boeing 777-268ER	28355/166		
☐ HZ-AKM	Boeing 777-268ER	28356/175		
☐ HZ-AKN	Boeing 777-268ER	28357/181		
☐ HZ-AKO	Boeing 777-268ER	28358/186		
☐ HZ-AKP	Boeing 777-268ER	28359/194		
☐ HZ-AKQ	Boeing 777-268ER	28360/219	ex N5016R	
☐ HZ-AKR	Boeing 777-268ER	28361/230	ex N5017V	
☐ HZ-AKS	Boeing 777-268ER	28362/255		
☐ HZ-AKT	Boeing 777-268ER	28363/298		
☐ HZ-AKU	Boeing 777-268ER	28364/306		
☐ HZ-AKV	Boeing 777-268ER	28365/323		
☐ HZ-AKW	Boeing 777-268ER	28366/351		
☐ HZ-AK11	Boeing 777-368ER	41048/982		
☐ HZ-AK12	Boeing 777-368ER	41050/986		
☐ HZ-AK13	Boeing 777-368ER	41049/992		
☐ HZ-AK14	Boeing 777-368ER	41051/999		
☐ HZ-AK15	Boeing 777-368ER	41052/1025		
☐ HZ-AK16	Boeing 777-368ER	41053/1061		
☐ HZ-AK17	Boeing 777-368ER	41054/1092		
☐ HZ-AK18	Boeing 777-368ER	41055/1131		
☐ HK-AK19	Boeing 777-368ER	41056/1142		
☐ HZ-AK20	Boeing 777-368ER	41058/1151		
☐ HZ-AK21	Boeing 777-368ER	41057/1157		
☐ HZ-AK22	Boeing 777-368ER	41059/1162		
☐ HZ-AK23	Boeing 777-368ER	42261/1251		♦
☐ HZ-AK24	Boeing 777-368ER	42262/1262		♦
☐ HZ-AK25	Boeing 777-368ER	42263/1269		♦
☐ HZ-AZ26	Boeing 777-368ER	42264/1288		♦
☐ HZ-AK27	Boeing 777-368ER	42265/1311		o/o♦
☐ HZ-AK28	Boeing 777-368ER	42266/1322		o/o♦

☐ HZ-AEA	Embraer ERJ-170LR	17000108	ex PT-SAQ	
☐ HZ-AEB	Embraer ERJ-170LR	17000114	ex PT-SAZ	
☐ HZ-AEC	Embraer ERJ-170LR	17000118	ex PT-SDF	
☐ HZ-AED	Embraer ERJ-170LR	17000119	ex PT-SDG	
☐ HZ-AEE	Embraer ERJ-170LR	17000121	ex PT-SDJ	
☐ HZ-AEF	Embraer ERJ-170LR	17000123	ex PT-SDM	
☐ HZ-AEG	Embraer ERJ-170LR	17000124	ex PT-SDN	
☐ HZ-AEH	Embraer ERJ-170LR	17000135	ex PT-SDY	
☐ HZ-AEI	Embraer ERJ-170LR	17000142	ex PT-SEG	
☐ HZ-AEJ	Embraer ERJ-170LR	17000145	ex PT-SEJ	
☐ HZ-AEK	Embraer ERJ-170LR	17000149	ex PT-SEN	
☐ HZ-AEL	Embraer ERJ-170LR	17000152	ex PT-SEQ	
☐ HZ-AEM	Embraer ERJ-170LR	17000155	ex PT-SES	
☐ HZ-AEN	Embraer ERJ-170LR	17000158	ex PT-SEW	
☐ HZ-AEO	Embraer ERJ-170LR	17000161	ex PT-SMB	
☐ HS-BKE	Boeing 767-3W0ER	28264/644	ex JU-1012	<OEA dam 05Jan14
☐ HZ-AI3	Boeing 747-87UF	37562/1429	ex N5023Q	
☐ HZ-AI4	Boeing 747-87UF	37563/1432	ex N958BA	
☐ HZ-AK71	Boeing 777-FFG	60337/1264		♦
☐ HZ-AK72	Boeing 777-FFG	60338/1328		o/o♦
☐ HZ-AK73	Boeing 777-FFG	60339/1342		o/o♦
☐ HZ-ANA	McDonnell-Douglas MD-11F	48773/609	ex N90187	[JED]
☐ HZ-ANB	McDonnell-Douglas MD-11F	48775/616	ex N91566	[JED]
☐ IIZ-ANC	McDonnell-Douglas MD-11F	48776/617	ex N91078	[JED]
☐ HZ-AND	McDonnell-Douglas MD-11F	48777/618	ex N9166N	[JED]
☐ HZ-APM	McDonnell-Douglas MD-90-30	53503/2229		[JED]
☐ HZ-APU	McDonnell-Douglas MD-90-30	53511/2255		[JED]
☐ HZ-	Boeing 787-9	41544/376		o/o♦
☐ HZ-	Boeing 787-9	41545/379		o/o♦
☐ HZ-	Boeing 787-9	41546/383		o/o♦

SAUDI GULF AIRLINES				*Dammam Intl (DMM)*

☐ HZ-SGA	Airbus A320-232/S	6455	ex F-WWBH	Riyadh	o/o♦
☐ HZ-SGB	Airbus A320-232/S	6474	ex F-WWBC	Dammam	o/o♦
☐ HZ-SGC	Airbus A320-232/S	6583	ex D-AVVN		o/o♦
☐ HZ-	Airbus A320-232/S	6735	ex		o/o♦

SNAS AVIATION		*Red Sea (RSE)*		*Riyadh/Bahrain (RUH/BAH)*

☐ HZ-SNA	Boeing 727-264F (FedEx 3)	20896/1051	ex A9C-SNA	all-white
☐ HZ-SNB	Boeing 727-223F (FedEx 3)	21084/1199	ex EC-HAH	all-white

Ops in association with DHL Worldwide (Bahrain)

H4- SOLOMON ISLANDS

PACIFIC AIR EXPRESS	*Solpac (PAQ)*	*Honiara/Brisbane, QLD (HIR/BNE)*

Ops cargo flights using aircraft leased from HeavyLift Cargo as required

SOLOMON AIRLINES		*Solomon (IE/SOL)*		*Honiara (HIR)*

☐ H4-AAI	Britten-Norman BN-2A-9 Islander	355	ex N355BN	
☐ H4-AAJ	Britten-Norman BN-2A-26 Islander	2154	ex T3-VIN	
☐ H4-BUS	Airbus A320-211	0302	ex N957PG	
☐ H4-NNP	de Havilland DHC-6 Twin Otter 300	491	ex YJ-RV1	
☐ H4-SID	de Havilland DHC-6 Twin Otter 300	442	ex VH-XFE	
☐ H4-SOL	de Havilland DHC-8-102	289	ex SX-BIW	Megapode

I - ITALY (Italian Republic)

AIR DOLOMITI		*Dolomiti (EN/DLA)*		*Trieste (TRS)*

☐ I-ADJK	Embraer ERJ-195LR	19000245	ex PT-SIQ	
☐ I-ADJL	Embraer ERJ-195LR	19000256	ex PT-STE	
☐ I-ADJM	Embraer ERJ-195LR	19000258	ex PT-STG	
☐ I-ADJN	Embraer ERJ-195LR	19000270	ex PT-TLK	
☐ I-ADJO	Embraer ERJ-195LR	19000280	ex PT-TLU	
☐ I-ADJP	Embraer ERJ-195LR	19000578	ex PT-TGI	I Puritani /incenzo Bellini
☐ I-ADJQ	Embraer ERJ-195LR	19000587	ex PT-THL	Ernani/Giuseppe Verdi
☐ I-ADJR	Embraer ERJ-195LR	19000595	ex PT-TIA	NormaVicenzo Bellini
☐ I-ADJS	Embraer ERJ-195LR	19000597	ex PT-TID	Gugllielmo Tell /Gioacchino Rossini
☐ I-ADJT	Embraer ERJ-195LR	19000606	ex PT-TJK	Tosca/Giacomo Puccini

AIR ITALY		*Air Italy (I9/AEY)*		*Milan-Malpensa (MXP)*

☐ EI-IGR	Boeing 737-36N/W	28561/2896	ex N561SM	
☐ EI-IGS	Boeing 737-36N/W	28562/2908	ex N562SM	>ISS

☐ EI-IGT	Boeing 737-73V/W	32421/1357	ex G-EZJZ	>ISS
☐ EI-IGU	Boeing 737-73V/W	32422/1363	ex G-EZKA	
☐ I-AIGH	Boeing 767-23BER	23973/208	ex N252MY	>ISS
☐ I-AIGJ	Boeing 767-304ER	28039/610	ex N769NA	>ISS

AIR ONE (ADH)

A number of Alitalia A320s fly in Air One c/s and with ADH flight numbers

AIR VALLÉE		Air Vallée (VK/RVL)		Aosta (AOT)
☐ SE-LEZ	Fokker 50	20128	ex PH-PRA	♦

ALIDAUNIA		Alida (D4/LID)		Foggia (FOG)
☐ I-AGSE	Agusta A109A II	7354		
☐ I-AGSH	Agusta A109A II	7384		
☐ I-LIDC	MBB BK.117C-1	7529	ex D-HMB.	
☐ I-LIDD	Agusta A109E Power	11107		
☐ I-LIDE	AgustaWestland AW139	31227	ex I-EASS	
☐ I-LIDF	Agusta A109S Grand	22077		
☐ I-LIDG	AgustaWestland AW109SP GranNew	.		♦
☐ I-LIDZ	Agusta A109E Power	11021		

ALISARDA		Merair (IG/ISS)			Olbia (OLB)
☐ EI-FDS	Boeing 737-86N/W	28595/285	ex OK-TVD		
☐ EI-FFK	Boeing 737-81Q/W	29051/479	ex C-FXGG		♦
☐ EI-FFM	Boeing 737-73S	29082/229	ex D-AHIA		♦
☐ EI-FFW	Boeing 737-85F/W	30477/976	ex N477MQ		♦
☐ EI-IGN	Boeing 737-84P/W	35074/2217	ex SP-IGN		
☐ EI-IGT	Boeing 737-73V/W	32421/1357	ex G-EZJZ		<AEY
☐ I-SMEB	McDonnell-Douglas MD-82	53064/1908	ex B-28001	Parco di Baia	
☐ I-SMEL	McDonnell-Douglas MD-82	49247/1151	ex HB-IKK	Parco Gaiola	
☐ I-SMEM	McDonnell-Douglas MD-82	49248/1152	ex HB-IKL	Penisola del sinis	
☐ I-SMEN	McDonnell-Douglas MD-83	53013/1738	ex EI-CRJ	Isole Egadi	
☐ I-SMEP	McDonnell-Douglas MD-82	49740/1618		Punta Campanella	
☐ I-SMER	McDonnell-Douglas MD-82	49901/1766	ex N6202S	Cinque Terre	
☐ I-SMES	McDonnell-Douglas MD-82	49902/1948		Isole Pelagie	
☐ I-SMET	McDonnell-Douglas MD-82	49531/1362		Miramare nel Golfo di Trieste	
☐ I-SMEV	McDonnell-Douglas MD-82	49669/1493		Isole di Ventotene e Santo Stefano	
☐ I-SMEZ	McDonnell-Douglas MD-82	49903/1949	ex PH-SEZ	Secche di Tor Patemo	
☐ EI-IGS	Boeing 737-36N/W	28562/2908	ex N562SM		<AEY
☐ I-AIGG	Boeing 767-304ER	28041/614	ex G-OBYC		♦
☐ I-AIGH	Boeing 767-23BER	23973/208	ex N252MY		<AEY
☐ I-AIGJ	Boeing 767-304ER	28039/610	ex N769NA		<AEY

ALITALIA		Alitalia (AZ/AZA)		Rome-Fiumicino (FCO)

Member of SkyTeam

☐ EI-IMB	Airbus A319-112	2033	ex I-BIMB	Isola del Giglio	
☐ EI-IMC	Airbus A319-112	2057	ex I-BIMC	Isola di Lipari	
☐ EI-IMD	Airbus A319-112	2074	ex I-BIMD	Isola di Capri	
☐ EI-IME	Airbus A319-112	1740	ex I-BIME	Isola di Panarea	
☐ EI-IMF	Airbus A319-112	2083	ex I-BIMF	Isola Tremiti	
☐ EI-IMG	Airbus A319-112	2086	ex I-BIMG	Isola di Pantelleria	
☐ EI-IMH	Airbus A319-112	2101	ex I-BIMH	Isola di Ventotene	
☐ EI-IMI	Airbus A319-112	1745	ex I-BIMI	Isola di Ponza	Fruili Venezia Guilia c/s
☐ EI-IMJ	Airbus A319-112	1779	ex I-BIMJ	Isola di Caprera	
☐ EI-IML	Airbus A319-112	2127	ex I-BIML	Isola La Maddalena	
☐ EI-IMM	Airbus A319-111	4759	ex D-AYVE	Vittorio Alfieri	
☐ EI-IMN	Airbus A319-111	4764	ex D-AVYG	Carlo Collodi	
☐ EI-IMO	Airbus A319-112	1770	ex I-BIMO	Isola d'Ischia	
☐ EI-IMP	Airbus A319-111	4859	ex D-AVWR	Italo Svevo	
☐ EI-IMR	Airbus A319-111	4875	ex D-AVYB	Italo Calvino	
☐ EI-IMS	Airbus A319-111	4910	ex D-AVYC	Guiseppe Parini	
☐ EI-IMT	Airbus A319-111	5018	ex F-WXAJ	Silvio Pellico	
☐ EI-IMU	Airbus A319-111	5130	ex D-AVYA	Pietro Verri	
☐ EI-IMV	Airbus A319-111	5294	ex D-AVWB	Filippo Tommaso Marinetti	
☐ EI-IMW	Airbus A319-111	5383	ex D-AVWJ		
☐ EI-IMX	Airbus A319-111	5424	ex D-AVWN		
☐ I-BIMA	Airbus A319-112	1722	ex D-AVWP	Isola d'Elba	
☐ EI-IKB	Airbus A320-214	1226	ex I-BIKB	Wolfgang Amadeus Mozart	
☐ EI-IKF	Airbus A320-214	1473	ex I-BIKF	Grecale	
☐ EI-IKG	Airbus A320-214	1480	ex I-BIKG	Scirocco	
☐ EI-IKL	Airbus A320-214	1489	ex I-BIKL	Libeccio	
☐ EI-IKU	Airbus A320-214	1217	ex I-BIKU	Fryderyk Chopin	
☐ I-BIKA	Airbus A320-214	0951	ex F-WWBT	Johann Sebastian Bach	

☐ I-BIKC	Airbus A320-214	1448	ex F-WWBV	Zefiro	
☐ I-BIKD	Airbus A320-214	1457	ex F-WWDE	Maestrale	
☐ I-BIKI	Airbus A320-214	1138	ex F-WWDJ	Girolamo Frescobaldi	
☐ I-BIKO	Airbus A320-214	1168	ex F-WWDL	George Bizet	
☐ I-WEBA	Airbus A320-214	3138	ex F-WWDI		
☐ I-WEBB	Airbus A320-214	3161	ex F-WWIC		
☐ EI-DSA	Airbus A320-216	2869	ex F-WWBE		Muoviamo chi muove l'Italia c/s
☐ EI-DSB	Airbus A320-216	2932	ex F-WWBX	Tomasi di Lampedusa	
☐ EI-DSC	Airbus A320-216	2995	ex F-WWIY	Lorenzo de'Medici	
☐ EI-DSD	Airbus A320-216	3076	ex F-WWIP	Edmondo de Amicis	
☐ EI-DSE	Airbus A320-216	3079	ex F-WWIL	Antonio Fogazzaro	
☐ EI-DSF	Airbus A320-216	3080	ex F-WWIV	Emilio Salgari	
☐ EI-DSG	Airbus A320-216	3115	ex F-WWIZ	Elio Vittorini	
☐ EI-DSI	Airbus A320-216	3213	ex F-WWIU	Carlo Emilio Gadda	
☐ EI-DSJ	Airbus A320-216	3295	ex F-WWDV	Ignazio Silone	
☐ EI-DSL	Airbus A320-216	3343	ex F-WWBO		
☐ EI-DSM	Airbus A320-216	3362	ex F-WWIR	Cesare Beccaria	Calabria c/s
☐ EI-DSN	Airbus A320-216	3412	ex F-WWIL		
☐ EI-DSP	Airbus A320-216	3482	ex F-WWDM	Ippolito Nievo	
☐ EI-DSU	Airbus A320-216	3563	ex F-WWBI	Beppe Fenoglio	
☐ EI-DSV	Airbus A320-216	3598	ex F-WWDJ		
☐ EI-DSW	Airbus A320-216	3609	ex F-WWIE	Vasco Pratolini	Jeep Renegade c/s
☐ EI-DSX	Airbus A320-216	3643	ex F-WWBT		
☐ EI DSY	Airbus A320-216	3666	ex F-WWDY		
☐ EI-DSZ	Airbus A320-216	3695	ex F WWBI		
☐ EI-DTA	Airbus A320-216	3732	ex F-WWDM	Ada Negri	
☐ EI-DTB	Airbus A320-216	3815	ex F-WWIF	Giacomo Leopardi	
☐ EI-DTC	Airbus A320-216	3831	ex F-WWBD	Dante Alighieri	
☐ EI-DTD	Airbus A320-216	3846	ex F-WWBY		
☐ EI-DTE	Airbus A320-216	3885	ex F-WWIY	Francesco Petrarca	
☐ EI-DTF	Airbus A320-216	3906	ex F-WWIM	Giovanni Boccaccio	
☐ EI-DTG	Airbus A320-216	3921	ex F-WWBK	Ludovico Ariosto	
☐ EI-DTH	Airbus A320-216	3956	ex F-WWBZ	Torquato Tasso	
☐ EI-DTI	Airbus A320-216	3976	ex F-WWIV	Niccolo Machiavelli	
☐ EI-DTJ	Airbus A320-216	3978	ex F-WWIX	Giovanni Pascoli	
☐ EI-DTK	Airbus A320-216	4075	ex F-WWBN	Giovanni Verga	
☐ EI-DTL	Airbus A320-216	4108	ex F-WWDS		
☐ EI-DTM	Airbus A320-216	4119	ex F-WWIE		
☐ EI-DTN	Airbus A320-216	4143	ex F-WWBB		
☐ EI-DTO	Airbus A320-216	4152	ex F-WWBJ		
☐ EI-EIA	Airbus A320-216	4195	ex F-WWIL	Elsa Morante	
☐ EI-EIB	Airbus A320-216	4249	ex F-WWDX		
☐ EI-EIC	Airbus A320-216	4520	ex D-AXAI		
☐ EI-EID	Airbus A320-216	4523	ex D-AUBU	Umberto Saba	
☐ EI-EIE	Airbus A320-216	4536	ex D-AXAL		
☐ EI-IXC	Airbus A321-112	0526	ex I-BIXC	Piazza del Campo Siena	
☐ EI-IXH	Airbus A321-112	0940	ex I-BIXH	Piazza della Signoria-Gubbio	
☐ EI-IXJ	Airbus A321-112	0959	ex I-BIXJ	Piazza del Municipio-Noto	
☐ EI-IXV	Airbus A321-112	0819	ex I-BIXV	Piazza del Rinascimento-Urbino	
☐ EI-IXZ	Airbus A321-112	0848	ex I-BIXZ	Piazza del Duomo Orvieto	
☐ I-BIXA	Airbus A321-112	0477	ex D-AVZE	Piazza del Duomo-Milano	
☐ I-BIXE	Airbus A321-112	0488	ex D-AVZG	Piazza di Spagna-Roma	[NWI]
☐ I-BIXK	Airbus A321-112	1220	ex D-AVZC	Piazza Ducale Vigevano	
☐ I-BIXL	Airbus A321-112	0513	ex D-AVZO	Piazza del Duomo-Lecce	
☐ I-BIXM	Airbus A321-112	0514	ex D-AVZP	Piazza di San Francesco-Assisi	
☐ I-BIXN	Airbus A321-112	0576	ex D-AVZR	Piazza del Duomo-Catania	
☐ I-BIXP	Airbus A321-112	0583	ex D-AVZT	Carlo Morelli	
☐ I-BIXQ	Airbus A321-112	0586	ex D-AVZU	Domenico Colapietro	
☐ I-BIXR	Airbus A321-112	0593	ex D-AVZW	Piazza del Campidoglio-Roma	
☐ I-BIXS	Airbus A321-112	0599	ex D-AVZZ	Piazza San Martino-Lucca	
☐ EI-DIP	Airbus A330-202	339	ex A6-EYW	Gian Lorenzo Bernini	
☐ EI-DIR	Airbus A330-202	272	ex A6-EYV	Filippo Brunelleschi	SkyTeam c/s
☐ EI-EJG	Airbus A330-202	1123	ex F-WWKY	Raffaello Sanzio	Calabria c/s
☐ EI-EJH	Airbus A330-202	1135	ex F-WWYU	Sandro Botticelli	
☐ EI-EJI	Airbus A330-202	1218	ex F-WWYT		
☐ EI-EJJ	Airbus A330-202	1225	ex F-WWKV		
☐ EI-EJK	Airbus A330-202	1252	ex F-WWKP		
☐ EI-EJL	Airbus A330-202	1283	ex F-WWKA	Piero della Francesca	
☐ EI-EJM	Airbus A330-202	1308	ex F-WWKH	Giovanni Battista Tiepolo	Expo 2015 c/s
☐ EI-EJN	Airbus A330-202	1313	ex F-WWYM	Il Tintoretto	
☐ EI-EJO	Airbus A330-202	1327	ex F-WWTN	Tiziano	
☐ EI-EJP	Airbus A330-202	1354	ex F-WWCT	Michelangelo Buonarroti	
☐ EI-DBK	Boeing 777-243ER	32783/455		Ostuni	
☐ EI-DBL	Boeing 777-243ER	32781/459		Sestriere	
☐ EI-DBM	Boeing 777-243ER	32782/463		Argentario	
☐ EI-DDH	Boeing 777-243ER	32784/477		Tropea	
☐ EI-ISA	Boeing 777-243ER	32855/413	ex I-DISA	Taormina	
☐ EI-ISE	Boeing 777-243ER	32856/421	ex I-DISE	Portofino	
☐ EI-ISB	Boeing 777-243ER	32859/426	ex I-DISB	Porto Rotondo	

☐ EI-ISD	Boeing 777-243ER	32860/439	ex I-DISD	Cortina d'Ampezzo
☐ EI-ISO	Boeing 777-243ER	32857/424	exI-DISO	Positano
☐ I-DISU	Boeing 777-243ER	32858/425		Madonna de Campiglio

ALITALIA CITYLINER — Cityliner (CT/CYL)

☐ EI-RDA	Embraer ERJ-175LR	17000330	ex PT-TPD	Parco Nazionale del Gran Paradiso
☐ EI-RDB	Embraer ERJ-175LR	17000331	ex PT-TPR	Parco Nazionale dello Stelvio
☐ EI-RDC	Embraer ERJ-175LR	17000333	ex PT-TSA	Parco Nazionale della Cinque Terre
☐ EI-RDD	Embraer ERJ-175LR	17000334	ex PT-TSP	Parco Nazionale d'Abruzzo
☐ EI-RDE	Embraer ERJ-175LR	17000335	ex PT-TUH	Parco dell'Etna
☐ EI-RDF	Embraer ERJ-175LR	17000337	ex PT-TUW	Parco Naturale Dolomiti Friulane
☐ EI-RDG	Embraer ERJ-175LR	17000338	ex PT-TVD	Parco Nazionale dell'Asinara
☐ EI-RDH	Embraer ERJ-175LR	17000339	ex PT-TZV	Parco Delta del Po
☐ EI-RDI	Embraer ERJ-175LR	17000340	ex PT-TAY	Parco Storico Monte Sole
☐ EI-RDJ	Embraer ERJ-175LR	17000342	ex PT-TBT	Parco Nazionale del Circeo
☐ EI-RDK	Embraer ERJ-175LR	17000343	ex PT-TBY	Parco Nazionale del Gargano
☐ EI-RDL	Embraer ERJ-175LR	17000345	ex PT-TDO	Parco Nazionale Val Grande
☐ EI-RDM	Embraer ERJ-175LR	17000346	ex PT-TDW	Parco Nazionale della Majella
☐ EI-RDN	Embraer ERJ-175LR	17000347	ex PT-TGA	Parco Nazionale dell'Alta Murgia
☐ EI-RDO	Embraer ERJ-175LR	17000348	ex PT-THB	Parco Nazionale della Maremma
☐ EI-RNA	Embraer ERJ-190LR	19000470	ex PT-TOQ	
☐ EI-RNB	Embraer ERJ-190LR	19000479	ex PT-TPC	Parco Nazionale del Pollino
☐ EI-RNC	Embraer ERJ-190LR	19000503	ex PT-TRL	Parco Nazionale Arcipelago Toscano
☐ EI-RND	Embraer ERJ-190LR	19000512	ex PT-TSQ	Parco Nazionale Dolomiti Bellunesi SkyTeam c/s
☐ EI-RNE	Embraer ERJ-190LR	19000520	ex PT-TUI	Parco Nazionale della Sila

BLU-EXPRESS — (BV/BPA) — Rome-Fiumicino (FCO)

☐ I-BPAC	Boeing 737-4K5	27074/2281	ex EI-CUN		♦
☐ I-BPAG	Boeing 737-31S	29059/2967	ex EI-DVY		
☐ I-BPAI	Boeing 737-31S	29060/2979	ex EI-DXB	Citta di Roma	

BLUE PANORAMA AIRLINES — Blue Panorama (BV/BPA) — Rome-Fiumicino (FCO)

☐ D-ANFE	ATR 72-202	272	ex SP-LFC		<ATV♦
☐ EI-CMD	Boeing 767-324ER/W	27392/568	ex N838TM	Città di Milano	>VCV♦
☐ EI-DBP	Boeing 767-35HER	26389/459	ex C-GGBJ		
☐ EI-FCV	Boeing 767-3X2ER	26260/552	ex N531CL		
☐ I-BPAL	Boeing 737-5K5	24927/1968	ex EI-EYV		
☐ I-BPAM	Boeing 737-3Y0	24909/2021	ex N265LM	Città di Firenze	
☐ OM-DEX	Boeing 737-46J	28867/2879	ex OO-JAM		<AXE♦

CARGOLUX ITALIA — Cargo Med (C8/ICV) — Milan-Malpensa (MXP)

☐ LX-RCV	Boeing 747-4R7F	30400/1235		Monviso	<CLX♦
☐ LX-TCV	Boeing 747-4R7F	30401/1311	ex N6046P	Monte Cervino	♦
☐ LX-YCV	Boeing 747-4R7F	35805/1407		City of Contern	<CLX

CITYFLY — City Fly (CII) — Rome-Urbe (ROM)

| ☐ I-LACO | Britten-Norman BN-2A-6 Islander | 17 | ex G-AWBY | | |

CORPO FORESTALE DELLO STATO — Rome-Ciampino (CIA)

☐ I-CFAG	Erickson/Sikorsky S-64E Skycrane	64088	ex N213AC	CFS-100	op by European Air-Crane
☐ I-CFAH	Erickson/Sikorsky S-64E Skycrane	64080	ex N174AC	CFS-101	op by European Air-Crane
☐ I-CFAI	Erickson/Sikorsky S-64E Skycrane	64067	ex N197AC	CFS-102	op by European Air-Crane
☐ I-CFAJ	Erickson/Sikorsky S-64E Skycrane	64078	ex N227AC	CFS-103	op by European Air-Crane

ELBAFLY — Elba-Island de Campo (EBA)

| ☐ E7-WDT | LET L-410UVP-E | 912615 | ex OK-WDT | | ♦ |

ELIDOLOMITI — Elidolomiti (EDO) — Belluno (BLX)

A subsidiary of Inaer Aviation Italia (qv)

ELIFRIULIA — Elifriulia (EFG) — Trieste (TRS)

☐ I-ASAP	Aérospatiale AS350B3 Ecureuil	7110		
☐ I-DYLL	Aérospatiale AS350B3 Ecureuil	4744		
☐ I-ENKY	Aérospatiale AS350B3 Ecureuil	4910		
☐ I-HSUN	Aérospatiale AS350B3 Ecureuil	4745		
☐ I-NEED	Aérospatiale AS350B3 Ecureuil			
☐ I-RISH	Aérospatiale AS350B3 Ecureuil	7374		
☐ I-ULYA	Aérospatiale AS350B3 Ecureuil	7354	ex F-WTBH	
☐ I-HELP	Eurocopter EC135T2	0469	ex D-HDOL	

☐ I-HFVG	Eurocopter EC135T2	1025	
☐ I-HUNK	Eurocopter EC135T2	0498	
☐ I-ORAO	Aérospatiale AS355N Ecureuil 2	5583	
☐ I-WIND	Eurocopter EC135T2i	0740	ex D-HAAT

ELILARIO ITALIA　　　　　　　　Lario (ELH)　　　Colico/Bergamo-Orio al Serio(-/BGY)

A subsidiary of Inaer Aviation Italia (qv)

ELILOMBARDA　　　　　　　　　　(EOA)　　　　　　　Calcinate del Pesce

☐ I-BSPL	Agusta A109S Grand	22075		
☐ I-CEPA	AgustaWestland AW139	31050		
☐ I-CESR	Agusta A109S Grand	22033		
☐ I-HELO	Agusta A109E Power	11605		
☐ I-MALF	Agusta-Bell 412EP	25975		EMS
☐ I-MECE	Agusta-Bell 412EP	25976		EMS
☐ I-MYRA	Agusta AW109SP	22245	ex M-ABFN	
☐ I-RAMM	Agusta A109S Grand	22157	ex (I-SCMA)	
☐ I-RYMA	Agusta AW109SP	22249	ex M-ABFO	
☐ I-VEGB	AgustaWestland AW139	41375	ex N622SM	♦
☐ I-VEGC	AgustaWestland AW139	41379	ex N621SM	♦

ELITALIANA

☐ I-PNTE	Agusta AW109S Grand	22173	ex I-PTFP
☐ I-PNTF	Agusta A109S Grand	22180	
☐ I-PNTH	Agusta A109S Grand	22181	

EUROPEAN AIR CRANE　　　　　　　　　　　　　　　　　　Florence (FLR)

European Air Crane is a subsidiary of Erikson Air Crane and ops Erickson/Sikorsky S-64E Skycranes for Corpo Forestale (I-)

HELI-ITALIA　　　　　　　　　　　　　　　　　　　　　　　Florence (FLR)

A subsidiary of Inaer Aviation Italia (qv)

INAER AVIATION ITALIA　　　　　　　　　　　　　　　　　　　　Colico

☐ I-CALI	Agusta A109S Grand	22128		
☐ I-CLOE	Agusta A109S Grand	22144	ex I-PTFP	
☐ I-CYMA	Agusta A109S Grand	22097		(EL)
☐ I-EITC	Agusta A109S Grand	22007		(EL)
☐ I-KERA	Agusta A109S Grand	22164		
☐ I-KORE	Agusta A109S Grand	22130	ex I-RAIS	
☐ I-LCCO	Agusta AW109SP GrandNew	22248		
☐ I-NAER	Agusta A109S Grand	22005	ex EC-JPP	
☐ I-NAES	Agusta A109S Grand	22169		(EL)
☐ I-RAKE	Agusta A109S Grand	22138		
☐ I-RELO	Agusta A109S Grand	22179		
☐ I-SNDR	Agusta AW109SP GrandNew	22244		
☐ I-AVCS	AgustaWestland AW139	31476		
☐ I-COLK	AgustaWestland AW139	31119		(EL)
☐ I-EITD	AgustaWestland AW139	31054	ex I-RAIC	(EL)
☐ I-PAAA	AgustaWestland AW139	31428		
☐ I-REDY	AgustaWestland AW139	31077		(ED)
☐ I-SRNT	AgustaWestland AW139	31588		♦
☐ I-AICO	MBB BK.117C-1	7542	ex D-HZBV	(EL)
☐ I-BBCK	MBB BK.117C-2	9678	ex D-HMBE	♦
☐ I-BLGN	MBB BK.117C-2	9438		dam 31Jly12
☐ I-CABO	MBB BK.117C-2	9205	ex EC-KYU	♦
☐ I-DENI	MBB BK.117C-1	7539		(EL)
☐ I-EITF	MBB BK.117C-2	9082	ex D-HMBI	(EL)
☐ I-EITG	MBB BK.117C-2	9086	ex D-HMBN	(EL)
☐ I-EITH	MBB BK.117C-2	9093	ex D-HMBB	(EL) EMS
☐ I-FNCS	MBB BK.117C-2	9187	ex D-HMBG	(EL)
☐ I-HDBX	MBB BK.117C-1	7546	ex D-HDBX	(HE) EMS
☐ I-HDBZ	MBB BK.117C-1	7547	ex D-HDBZ	(HE) EMS
☐ I-JUNO	MBB BK.117C-2	9271		
☐ I-LEDI	MBB BK.117C-2	9673		♦
☐ I-NAVY	MBB BK.117C-2	9189	ex D-HMBS	(EL)
☐ I-RAHB	MBB BK.117C-2	9335	ex D-HADF	
☐ I-STLV	MBB BK.117C-2	9229	ex D-HMBR	
☐ I-EFCN	Aérospatiale AS350B Ecureuil	1445		(ED)
☐ I-EITB	Agusta-Bell 412SP	25972		(EL)
☐ I-FLAQ	Agusta A109E Power	11076	ex F-GPVJ	
☐ I-PEBX	Airbus Helicopters EC145T2	20003	ex D-HADV	♦
☐ I-PEBZ	Airbus Helicopters EC145T2	20009	ex D-HADR	♦
☐ I-NUBJ	Agusta-Bell 412EP	25913		(EL)

☐ I-RCPM	Agusta A109E Power Elite	11172		(EL)
☐ I-RMTI	Agusta-Bell 412EP	25923		(EL)
☐ I-RNBR	Agusta-Bell 412EP	25921		dam 20Aug13 (EL)
☐ I-ZANL	Airbus Helicopters EC145T2	20023	ex D-HCBU	♦

The parent company of Elidolomiti (ED), Elilario (EL) and Helitalia (HE); also ops under its own name. The fleet given above gives an indication of the current operating company where known

MISTRAL AIR		Mistral (7M/MSA)		Rome-Ciampino (CIA)
☐ I-ADLK	ATR 72-212A	706	ex F-WWEF	Poste Italiane c/s♦
☐ I-ADLW	ATR 72-212A	707	ex F-WWEG	♦
☐ OY-CNJ	ATR 72-212F	414	ex N414WF	
☐ OY-YAB	ATR 72-212A	588	ex TC-YAB	Poste Italiane c/s♦
☐ OY-YAE	ATR 72-212A	705	ex TC-YAE	Poste Italiane c/s♦
☐ OY-YAI	ATR 72-212A	879	ex F-ORAA	wfs♦
☐ EI-CFQ	Boeing 737-3Y0QC	24255/1625	ex OY-JTH	Poste Italiane c/s♦
☐ EI-DVA	Boeing 737-36EQC	25159/2068	ex F-GIXM	
☐ EI-DVC	Boeing 737-33AQC	25426/2172	ex SE-DPC Libeccio	
☐ EI-ELZ	Boeing 737-4Q8	26308/2665	ex SX-BGV	
☐ EI-FGX	Boeing 737-3Q8	28054/3016	ex N54AU	Poste Italiane c/s♦
☐ OM-GTB	Boeing 737-49R	28882/2845	ex M-ABGN	<RLX♦
☐ I-MLRT	Fokker F.27 Friendship 500	10377	ex F-BPUE	<MNL♦
☐ LZ-LDP	McDonnell-Douglas MD-82	49973/1762	ex I-DACP	<BUC♦

NEOS		Moonflower (NO/NOS)		Milan-Malpensa (MXP)
☐ I-NEOS	Boeing 737-86N/W	32733/1078	Citta di Milano	
☐ I-NEOT	Boeing 737-86N/W	33004/1144	Citta di Torino	
☐ I-NEOU	Boeing 737-86N/W	29887/1263	Citta di Verona	
☐ I-NEOW	Boeing 737-86N/W	32685/2186	ex G-XLAN Lago Maggiore	
☐ I-NEOX	Boeing 737-86N/W	33677/1486	Citta di Bologna	
☐ I-NEOZ	Boeing 737-86N/W	34257/2024	ex EI-EOY	
☐ I-NDDL	Boeing 767-324ER/W	27568/593	ex G-OOBM	o/o♦
☐ I-NDMJ	Boeing 767-306ER/W	27958/589	ex EI-DMJ	
☐ I-NDOF	Boeing 767-306ER/W	27610/605	ex EI-DOF	

SW ITALIA		(CSW)		Milan-Malpensa (MXP)
☐ I-SWIA	Boeing 747-4R7F	29729/1189	ex 4K-SW800	♦

SKYBRIDGE AIROPS		Sky Airops (KYB)		Rome-Ciampano (CIA)
☐ I-SKYB	Embraer EMB.120RT Brasilia	120087	ex F-GTSG	wfs

SOREM/PROTEZIONE CIVILE			Rome-Ciampano/Urbe (CIA/ROM)	
☐ I-DPCC	Canadair CL415	2066	ex C-FNLH	27
☐ I-DPCD	Canadair CL415	2003	ex C-FTUA	7
☐ I-DPCE	Canadair CL415	2004	ex C-FTUS	8
☐ I-DPCF	Canadair CL415	2059	ex C-GIWU	23
☐ I-DPCG	Canadair CL415	2060	ex C-GJHU	24
☐ I-DPCH	Canadair CL415	2062	ex C-GJLB	25
☐ I-DPCI	Canadair CL415	2058	ex C-GISM	26
☐ I-DPCN	Canadair CL415	2070	ex C-FUEP	28
☐ I-DPCO	Canadair CL415	2009	ex C-FVRA	10
☐ I-DPCP	Canadair CL415	2020	ex C-FYCY	11
☐ I-DPCQ	Canadair CL415	2021	ex C-FYDA	12
☐ I-DPCR	Canadair CL415	2074	ex C-FZTY	31
☐ I-DPCS	Canadair CL415	2073	ex C-FZEG	29
☐ I-DPCT	Canadair CL415	2029	ex C-FZYS	18
☐ I-DPCU	Canadair CL415	2030	ex C-GALV	14
☐ I-DPCV	Canadair CL415	2035	ex C-GCXG	15	dam 09Apr14
☐ I-DPCW	Canadair CL415	2036	ex C-GDHW	16
☐ I-DPCY	Canadair CL415	2047	ex C-GFUS	20
☐ I-DPCZ	Canadair CL415	2048	ex C-GGCW	21
☐ I-SPEB	Air Tractor AT-802A	AT-802A-0217	ex EC-JQM	
☐ I-SPEF	Air Tractor AT-802A	AT-802A-0239	ex EC-JVD	
☐ I-SPEL	Air Tractor AT-802A	AT-802A-0325	ex EC-LGX	

JA   JAPAN

AIRASIA JAPAN		(JW/WAJ)		Nagoya Intl (NGO)
☐ JA02DJ	Airbus A320-216/W		ex	o/o♦

AIR DO | Air Do (HD/ADO) | Sapporo-Chitose (CTS)

☐ JA01AN	Boeing 737-781/W	33916/1781	ex N6066U	
☐ JA07AN	Boeing 737-781/W	33900/2071		
☐ JA08AN	Boeing 737-781/W	33877/2086		<ANA
☐ JA09AN	Boeing 737-781/W	33878/2145		<ANA
☐ JA12AN	Boeing 737-781/W	33881/2301		<ANA♦
☐ JA15AN	Boeing 737-781/W	33888/2394		
☐ JA01HD	Boeing 767-33AER	28159/689	ex OO-CTQ	
☐ JA98AD	Boeing 767-33AER	27476/687	ex N767AN	
☐ JA300K	Boeing 737-54K	27434/2872		
☐ JA301K	Boeing 737-54K	27435/2875		<ANA♦
☐ JA601A	Boeing 767-381	27943/669		
☐ JA8359	Boeing 767-381	25617/439		<ANA
☐ JA8595	Boeing 737-54K	28461/2850		

AIR DOLPHIN | | Okinawa-Naha (OKA)

☐ JA3428	Cessna P206C Super Skylane	P206-0517	ex N1610C
☐ JA5320	Britten-Norman BN-2B-20 Islander	2269	ex G-BUBM

AIR JAPAN | Air Japan (NQ/AJX) | Osaka-Itami/Kansi (ITM/KIX)

☐ JA55DZ	Cessna 208B Caravan I	208B0530	ex N164SA

AMAKUSA AIRLINES | Amakusa Air (AHX) | Kumamoto (KMJ)

☐ JA81AM	de Havilland DHC-8Q-103	537	ex C-FCSG	blue Dolphin c/s

ANA - ALL NIPPON AIRWAYS | All Nippon (NH/ANA) | Tokyo-Haneda (HND)

Member of Star Alliance

☐ JA8300	Airbus A320-211	0549	ex F-WWIT	
☐ JA8304	Airbus A320-211	0531	ex F-WWDY	
☐ JA8313	Airbus A320-211	0534	ex F-WWBC	
☐ JA8387	Airbus A320-211	0196	ex F-WWDE	
☐ JA8394	Airbus A320-211	0383	ex F-WWBF	
☐ JA8395	Airbus A320-211	0413	ex F-WWIM	
☐ JA8396	Airbus A320-211	0482	ex F-WWIO	
☐ JA8400	Airbus A320-211	0554	ex F-WWIG	
☐ JA8609	Airbus A320-211	0501	ex F-WWIN	
☐ JA8654	Airbus A320-211	0507	ex F-WWBT	
☐ JA8946	Airbus A320-211	0669	ex F-WWBD	
☐ JA8947	Airbus A320-211	0685	ex F-WWDR	
☐ JA8997	Airbus A320-211	0658	ex F-WWIU	
☐ JA301K	Boeing 737-54K	27435/2875		>ADO
☐ JA303K	Boeing 737-54K	28991/3017		
☐ JA305K	Boeing 737-54K	28993/3075	ex N1781B	
☐ JA8196	Boeing 737-54K	27966/2824		>AKX
☐ JA8404	Boeing 737-54K	27381/2708	ex N35108	
☐ JA8419	Boeing 737-54K	27430/2723		
☐ JA8596	Boeing 737-54K	28462/2853		>AKX
☐ JA02AN	Boeing 737-781/W	33872/1850		
☐ JA03AN	Boeing 737-781/W	33873/1871	ex N1787B	
☐ JA04AN	Boeing 737-781/W	33874/1890	ex N1781B	
☐ JA05AN	Boeing 737-781/W	33875/1971		
☐ JA06AN	Boeing 737-781/W	33876/1992		
☐ JA08AN	Boeing 737-781/W	33877/2086		>ADO
☐ JA09AN	Boeing 737-781/W	33878/2145		>ADO
☐ JA10AN	Boeing 737-781ER/W	33879/2157	ex N716BA	
☐ JA11AN	Boeing 737-781/W	33882/2268		
☐ JA12AN	Boeing 737-781/W	33881/2301		>ADO
☐ JA13AN	Boeing 737-781ER/W	33880/2232	ex N717BA	
☐ JA14AN	Boeing 737-781/W	33883/2370		
☐ JA16AN	Boeing 737-781/W	33889/2488		
☐ JA17AN	Boeing 737-781/W	33884/2513		
☐ JA18AN	Boeing 737-781/W	33885/2582		
☐ JA51AN	Boeing 737-881/W	33886/2607	ex N1786B	
☐ JA52AN	Boeing 737-881/W	33887/2643		
☐ JA53AN	Boeing 737-881/W	33891/2739		
☐ JA54AN	Boeing 737-881/W	33890/2833		
☐ JA55AN	Boeing 737-881/W	33892/2889		
☐ JA56AN	Boeing 737-881/W	33893/2926		
☐ JA57AN	Boeing 737-881/W	33894/2975	ex N1787B	
☐ JA58AN	Boeing 737-881/W	33895/3029	ex N1796B	
☐ JA59AN	Boeing 737-881/W	33886/3073		

☐ JA60AN	Boeing 737-881/W	33897/3126			
☐ JA61AN	Boeing 737-881/W	33898/3379			
☐ JA62AN	Boeing 737-881/W	33899/3414			
☐ JA63AN	Boeing 737-881/W	33901/3449	ex N1787B		
☐ JA64AN	Boeing 737-881/W	33902/3478	ex N1787B		
☐ JA65AN	Boeing 737-881/W	33903/3502	ex N1786B		
☐ JA66AN	Boeing 737-881/W	33909/3598			
☐ JA67AN	Boeing 737-881/W	33911/3682			
☐ JA68AN	Boeing 737-881/W	33910/4151			
☐ JA69AN	Boeing 737-881/W	33912/4228			
☐ JA70AN	Boeing 737-881/W	33913/4282			
☐ JA71AN	Boeing 737-881/W	33914/4334			
☐ JA72AN	Boeing 737-881/W	33915/4426			
☐ JA73AN	Boeing 737-881/W	33904/4561			
☐ JA74AN	Boeing 737-881/W	33905/4634			
☐ JA75AN	Boeing 737-881/W	33906/4851			
☐ JA76AN	Boeing 737-881/W	33907/4922			
☐ JA77AN	Boeing 737-881/W	44556/4985			♦
☐ JA78AN	Boeing 737-881/W	33908/5025			♦
☐ JA79AN	Boeing 737-881/W	44557/5101			
☐ JA80AN	Boeing 737-881/W	44558/5216			
☐ JA81AN	Boeing 737-881/W	44559/5330			
☐ JA602A	Boeing 767-381	27944/684			
☐ JA602F	Boeing 767-381F	33509/937			
☐ JA604A	Boeing 767-381ER	32973/881			
☐ JA604F	Boeing 767-381F	35709/947			
☐ JA605A	Boeing 767-381ER	32974/882			
☐ JA605F	Boeing 767-316F/W	30842/860	ex N316LA		
☐ JA606A	Boeing 767-381ER	32975/883		Fly Panda c/s	
☐ JA607A	Boeing 767-381ER	32976/884			
☐ JA608A	Boeing 767-381ER	32977/886			
☐ JA609A	Boeing 767-381ER	32978/888			
☐ JA610A	Boeing 767-381ER	32979/895			
☐ JA611A	Boeing 767-381ER	32980/914		Star Cluster c/s	
☐ JA612A	Boeing 767-381ER	33506/920			
☐ JA613A	Boeing 767-381ER	33507/924			
☐ JA614A	Boeing 767-381ER	33508/931		Star Alliance c/s	
☐ JA615A	Boeing 767-381ER	35877/951			
☐ JA616A	Boeing 767-381ER	35876/953			
☐ JA617A	Boeing 767-381ER	37719/971			
☐ JA618A	Boeing 767-381ER	37720/976			
☐ JA619A	Boeing 767-381ER/W	40564/993			
☐ JA620A	Boeing 767-381ER/W	40565/996			
☐ JA621A	Boeing 767-381ER/W	40566/998			
☐ JA622A	Boeing 767-381ER/W	40567/1000			
☐ JA623A	Boeing 767-381ER/W	40894/1001			
☐ JA624A	Boeing 767-381ER/W	40895/1010			
☐ JA625A	Boeing 767-381ER/W	40896/1012			
☐ JA626A	Boeing 767-381ER/W	40897/1018			
☐ JA627A	Boeing 767-381ER/W	40898/1023			
☐ JA8258	Boeing 767-381	23758/179	ex N6055X		
☐ JA8286	Boeing 767-381ERBCF	24400/269			
☐ JA8322	Boeing 767-381	25618/458			
☐ JA8323	Boeing 767-381ERBCF	25654/463			
☐ JA8324	Boeing 767-381	25655/465			
☐ JA8342	Boeing 767-381	27445/573			
☐ JA8356	Boeing 767-381ERBCF	25136/379			
☐ JA8357	Boeing 767-381	25293/401			
☐ JA8358	Boeing 767-381ERBCF	25616/432			
☐ JA8359	Boeing 767-381	25617/439			>ADO
☐ JA8360	Boeing 767-381	25055/352			
☐ JA8362	Boeing 767-381ERBCF	24632/285			
☐ JA8368	Boeing 767-381	24880/336			
☐ JA8567	Boeing 767-381	25656/510			
☐ JA8568	Boeing 767-381	25657/515			
☐ JA8569	Boeing 767-381	27050/516			
☐ JA8578	Boeing 767-381	25658/519			
☐ JA8579	Boeing 767-381	25659/520			
☐ JA8664	Boeing 767-381ER	27339/556			
☐ JA8669	Boeing 767-381	27444/567			
☐ JA8670	Boeing 767-381	25660/539			
☐ JA8674	Boeing 767-381	25661/543		Yume Jet You & Me c/s	
☐ JA8677	Boeing 767-381	25662/551			
☐ JA8970	Boeing 767-381ER	25619/645			
☐ JA8971	Boeing 767-381ER	27942/651			
☐ JA701A	Boeing 777-281	27938/77			
☐ JA702A	Boeing 777-281	27033/75			
☐ JA703A	Boeing 777-281	27034/81	ex N50217		
☐ JA704A	Boeing 777-281	27035/131			
☐ JA705A	Boeing 777-281	29029/137			
☐ JA706A	Boeing 777-281	27036/141			

☐	JA707A	Boeing 777-281ER	27037/247		
☐	JA708A	Boeing 777-281ER	28277/278		
☐	JA709A	Boeing 777-281ER	28278/286		
☐	JA710A	Boeing 777-281ER	28279/302		
☐	JA711A	Boeing 777-281	33406/482		Star Alliance c/s
☐	JA712A	Boeing 777-281	33407/495		Star Alliance c/s
☐	JA713A	Boeing 777-281	32647/509		
☐	JA714A	Boeing 777-281	28276/523		
☐	JA715A	Boeing 777-281ER	32646/563		
☐	JA716A	Boeing 777-281ER	33414/574		
☐	JA717A	Boeing 777-281ER	33415/580		
☐	JA741A	Boeing 777-281ER	40900/1005		
☐	JA742A	Boeing 777-281ER	40901/1016		
☐	JA743A	Boeing 777-281ER	40902/1090		
☐	JA744A	Boeing 777-281ER	40903/1102		
☐	JA745A	Boeing 777-281ER	40904/1112		
☐	JA8197	Boeing 777-281	27027/16	ex N5016R	
☐	JA8198	Boeing 777-281	27028/21		
☐	JA8199	Boeing 777-281	27029/29		
☐	JA8967	Boeing 777-281	27030/37		
☐	JA8968	Boeing 777-281	27031/38		
☐	JA8969	Boeing 777-281	27032/50		
☐	JA731A	Boeing 777-381ER	28281/488	ex N240BA	Star Alliance c/s
☐	JA732A	Boeing 777-381ER	27038/511		
☐	JA733A	Boeing 777-381ER	32648/529	ex N5014K	
☐	JA734A	Boeing 777-381ER	32649/557		
☐	JA735A	Boeing 777-381ER	34892/571		
☐	JA736A	Boeing 777-381ER	34893/589		
☐	JA751A	Boeing 777-381	28272/142	ex N5017Q	
☐	JA752A	Boeing 777-381	28274/160		
☐	JA753A	Boeing 777-381	28273/132		Sky Blue c/s
☐	JA754A	Boeing 777-381	27939/172		
☐	JA755A	Boeing 777-381	28275/104	ex N5017Q	
☐	JA756A	Boeing 777-381	27039/440		
☐	JA757A	Boeing 777-381	27040/442		
☐	JA777A	Boeing 777-381ER	32650/593		
☐	JA778A	Boeing 777-381ER	32651/606		
☐	JA779A	Boeing 777-381ER	34894/631		
☐	JA780A	Boeing 777-381ER	34895/639		
☐	JA781A	Boeing 777-381ER	27041/667		
☐	JA782A	Boeing 777-381ER	33416/691		
☐	JA783A	Boeing 777-381ER	27940/737		
☐	JA784A	Boeing 777-381ER	37950/833		
☐	JA785A	Boeing 777-381ER	37951/855		
☐	JA786A	Boeing 777-381ER	37948/866		
☐	JA787A	Boeing 777-381ER	37949/870		
☐	JA788A	Boeing 777-381ER	40686/873		
☐	JA789A	Boeing 777-381ER	40687/878		
☐	JA790A	Boeing 777-381ER	60136/1283		
☐	JA791A	Boeing 777-381ER	60137/1293		
☐	JA792A	Boeing 777-381ER	60138/1300		o/o
☐	JA801A	Boeing 787-8	34488/8	ex N1008S	
☐	JA802A	Boeing 787-8	34497/24	ex N1014X	
☐	JA803A	Boeing 787-8	34485/7		
☐	JA804A	Boeing 787-8	34486/9	ex N1006F	
☐	JA805A	Boeing 787-8	34514/31		
☐	JA806A	Boeing 787-8	34515/40		
☐	JA807A	Boeing 787-8	34508/41		
☐	JA808A	Boeing 787-8	34490/42		
☐	JA809A	Boeing 787-8	34494/47	ex N1015X	
☐	JA810A	Boeing 787-8	34506/48	ex N1008S	
☐	JA811A	Boeing 787-8	34502/51		
☐	JA812A	Boeing 787-8	40748/56		
☐	JA813A	Boeing 787-8	34521/67		
☐	JA814A	Boeing 787-8	34493/69		
☐	JA815A	Boeing 787-8	40899/66		
☐	JA816A	Boeing 787-8	34507/63		
☐	JA817A	Boeing 787-8	40749/59		
☐	JA818A	Boeing 787-8	42243/83	ex N1009N	
☐	JA819A	Boeing 787-8	42244/97		
☐	JA820A	Boeing 787-8	34511/101		
☐	JA821A	Boeing 787-8	42245/107		
☐	JA822A	Boeing 787-8	34512/110		♦
☐	JA823A	Boeing 787-8	42246/120		
☐	JA824A	Boeing 787-8	42247/132		
☐	JA825A	Boeing 787-8	34516/148		
☐	JA827A	Boeing 787-8	34509/147		
☐	JA828A	Boeing 787-8	42248/140		
☐	JA829A	Boeing 787-8	34520/179		♦
☐	JA831A	Boeing 787-8	34496/199		♦
☐	JA832A	Boeing 787-8	42249/203		♦

□ JA833A	Boeing 787-8	34524/202			♦
□ JA834A	Boeing 787-8	40750/206			♦
□ JA835A	Boeing 787-8	34525/243			♦
□ JA838A	Boeing 787-8	34528/299			o/o♦
□ JA872A	Boeing 787-8	34518/322			o/o♦
□ JA	Boeing 787-8	34489/			o/o
□ JA	Boeing 787-8	34499/			o/o
□ JA	Boeing 787-8	34500/			o/o
□ JA	Boeing 787-8	34501/			o/o
□ JA830A	Boeing 787-9	34522/146	ex N1792B		♦
□ JA833A	Boeing 787-9	34524/202			o/o♦
□ JA836A	Boeing 787-9	34527/280			♦
□ JA837A	Boeing 787-9	34526/295			o/o♦
□ JA839A	Boeing 787-9	34529/310			o/o♦
□ JA840A	Boeing 787-9	34534/319			o/o♦
□ JA873A	Boeing 787-9	34504/329		R2D2–Star Wars c/s	o/o♦
□ JA874A	Boeing 787-9	34520/345			o/o♦
□ JA875A	Boeing 787-9	34503/358			o/o♦
□ JA876A	Boeing 787-9	34531/369			o/o♦
□ JA877A	Boeing 787-9	43871/401			o/o♦
□ JA878A	Boeing 787-9	34532/414			o/o♦
□ JA392K	Boeing 737-46M	28550/2847	ex N8550F		>SNJ
□ JA	Airbus A330-343E	1483	ex N113NT		o/o♦
□ JA	Airbus A330-343E	1491	ex N115NT		o/o♦
□ JA	Airbus A330-343E	1542	ex N117NT		o/o♦
□ JA	Airbus A330-343E	1554	ex N116NT		o/o♦

ANA WINGS — Alfa Wing (EH/AKX) — Sapporo-Chitose (CTS)

□ JA302K	Boeing 737-54K	28990/3002	ex N1787B	
□ JA304K	Boeing 737-54K	28992/3030		
□ JA306K	Boeing 737-54K	29794/3109	ex N1786B	
□ JA307K	Boeing 737-54K	29795/3116	ex N60436	
□ JA352K	Boeing 737-5Y0	26097/2534	ex N97NK	
□ JA356K	Boeing 737-5L9	28083/2784	ex N8083N	
□ JA357K	Boeing 737-5L9	28131/2828	ex N88131	
□ JA358K	Boeing 737-5L9	28130/2825	ex N8130J	
□ JA359K	Boeing 737-5L9	28128/2817	ex N8128R	
□ JA8195	Boeing 737-54K	27433/2815		
□ JA8196	Boeing 737-54K	27966/2824		<ANA
□ JA8404	Boeing 737-54K	27381/2708	ex N35108	
□ JA8500	Boeing 737-54K	27431/2751		
□ JA8504	Boeing 737-54K	27432/2783		♦
□ JA8596	Boeing 737-54K	28462/2853		<ANA
□ JA460A	de Havilland DHC-8-402Q	4416	ex C-GOBK	
□ JA461A	de Havilland DHC-8-402Q	4430	ex C-GSNE	
□ JA462A	de Havilland DHC-8-402Q	4445	ex C-GUPG	
□ JA841A	de Havilland DHC-8-402Q	4080	ex C-GDLK	
□ JA842A	de Havilland DHC-8-402Q	4082	ex C-GFOD	
□ JA843A	de Havilland DHC-8-402Q	4084	ex C-GFQL	
□ JA844A	de Havilland DHC-8-402Q	4091	ex C-GHRI	
□ JA845A	de Havilland DHC-8-402Q	4096	ex C-FAQB	
□ JA846A	de Havilland DHC-8-402Q	4097	ex C-FAQD	
□ JA847A	de Havilland DHC-8-402Q	4099	ex C-FAQK	
□ JA848A	de Havilland DHC-8-402Q	4102	ex C-FCQA	
□ JA850A	de Havilland DHC-8-402Q	4108	ex C-FCVJ	
□ JA851A	de Havilland DHC-8-402Q	4109	ex C-FCVK	
□ JA852A	de Havilland DHC-8-402Q	4131	ex C-FGKC	
□ JA853A	de Havilland DHC-8-402Q	4135	ex C-FGKN	
□ JA854A	de Havilland DHC-8-402Q	4151	ex C-FJLH	
□ JA855A	de Havilland DHC-8-402Q	4292	ex C-GAUB	
□ JA856A	de Havilland DHC-8-402Q	4335	ex C-GGHS	
□ JA857A	de Havilland DHC-8-402Q	4362	ex C-GISU	
□ JA858A	de Havilland DHC-8-402Q	4385	ex C-GKVD	
□ JA859A	de Havilland DHC-8-402Q	4401	ex C-GLKE	

FIRST FLYING CO — Okinawa (OKA)

□ JA201D	de Havilland DHC-6 Twin Otter 400	915	ex C-GVEP	♦
□ JA202D	de Havilland DHC-6 Twin Otter 400	916	ex C-GVVA	♦

FUJI DREAM AIRLINES — (JH/FDA) — Shizuoka Mount Fuji (FSZ)

□ JA01FJ	Embraer ERJ-170STD	17000271	ex PT-SNB
□ JA02FJ	Embraer ERJ-170STD	17000289	ex PT-TQP
□ JA03FJ	Embraer ERJ-175STD	17000304	ex PT-XQD
□ JA04FJ	Embraer ERJ-170LR	17000129	ex N866RW
□ JA05FJ	Embraer ERJ-175STD	17000317	ex PT-XUL
□ JA06FJ	Embraer ERJ-175STD	17000332	ex PT-TPV

☐ JA07FJ	Embraer ERJ-175STD	17000361	ex PT-TKT	
☐ JA08FJ	Embraer ERJ-175STD	17000391	ex PR-EEP	
☐ JA09FJ	Embraer ERJ-175STD	17000464	ex PR-EKO	◆

HANKYU AIRLINES

| ☐ JA8229 | Cessna 208 Caravan I | 20800137 | ex N1570C |
| ☐ JA8890 | Cessna 208 Caravan I | 20800195 | ex N9776F |

HOKKAIDO AIR SYSTEM — North Air (NTH) — Sapporo-Chitose (CTS)

☐ JA01HC	SAAB SF.340B	340B-432	ex SE-B32
☐ JA02HC	SAAB SF.340B	340B-440	ex SE-B40
☐ JA03HC	SAAB SF.340B	340B-458	ex SE-B58

IBEX AIRLINES — Ibex (FW/IBX) — Sendai (SDJ)

☐ JA02RJ	Canadair CRJ-100ER	7033	ex OE-LRB	
☐ JA03RJ	Canadair CRJ-200ER	7624	ex C-GJZF	
☐ JA04RJ	Canadair CRJ-200ER	7798	ex C-FMLF	
☐ JA05RJ	Canadair CRJ-702ER	10279	ex C-FYDI	
☐ JA06RJ	Canadair CRJ-702ER	10303	ex C-GFFK	
☐ JA07RJ	Canadair CRJ-702ER	10327	ex C-GIBG	
☐ JA08RJ	Canadair CRJ-702ER	10333	ex C-GIAR	
☐ JA09RJ	Canadair CRJ-702ER	10334	cx C-GZQC	
☐ JA10RJ	Canadair CRJ-702ER	10340	ex C-GWGT	◆

J-AIR — (JL) — Nagoya-Komaki (NKM)

☐ JA201J	Canadair CRJ-200ER	7452	ex C-FMND	
☐ JA202J	Canadair CRJ-200ER	7484	ex C-FMLU	
☐ JA203J	Canadair CRJ-200ER	7626	ex C-FMNW	<JAL
☐ JA204J	Canadair CRJ-200ER	7643	ex C-FMNB	
☐ JA205J	Canadair CRJ-200ER	7767	ex C-FMLB	
☐ JA206J	Canadair CRJ-200ER	7834	ex C-FMMT	
☐ JA207J	Canadair CRJ-200ER	8050	ex C-FFVJ	
☐ JA208J	Canadair CRJ-200ER	8059	ex C-FMOW	
☐ JA209J	Canadair CRJ-200ER	8062	ex C-FMNQ	

☐ JA211J	Embraer ERJ-170STD	17000251	ex PT-SJC
☐ JA212J	Embraer ERJ-170STD	17000268	ex PT-SJW
☐ JA213J	Embraer ERJ-170STD	17000285	ex PT-TQL
☐ JA214J	Embraer ERJ-170STD	17000295	ex PT-TQV
☐ JA215J	Embraer ERJ-170STD	17000297	ex PT-TQX
☐ JA216J	Embraer ERJ-170STD	17000299	ex PT-TQY
☐ JA217J	Embraer ERJ-170STD	17000308	ex PT-XQW
☐ JA218J	Embraer ERJ-170STD	17000314	ex PT-XUI
☐ JA219J	Embraer ERJ-170STD	17000315	ex PT-XUJ
☐ JA220J	Embraer ERJ-170STD	17000322	ex PT-TBS
☐ JA221J	Embraer ERJ-170STD	17000353	ex PT-TGN
☐ JA222J	Embraer ERJ-170STD	17000356	ex PT-TIN
☐ JA223J	Embraer ERJ-170STD	17000362	ex PR-EAC
☐ JA224J	Embraer ERJ-170STD	17000379	ex PR-EDE
☐ JA225J	Embraer ERJ-170STD	17000389	ex PR-EEN

JAPAN AIR COMMUTER — Commuter (JC/JAC) — Amami (ASJ)

☐ JA841C	de Havilland DHC-8-402Q	4072	ex C-GEWI
☐ JA842C	de Havilland DHC-8-402Q	4073	ex C-GFCA
☐ JA843C	de Havilland DHC-8-402Q	4076	ex C-FDHZ
☐ JA844C	de Havilland DHC-8-402Q	4092	ex C-GFEN
☐ JA845C	de Havilland DHC-8-402Q	4101	ex C-FCPZ
☐ JA846C	de Havilland DHC-8-402Q	4107	ex C-FCVI
☐ JA847C	de Havilland DHC-8-402Q	4111	ex C-FCVS
☐ JA848C	de Havilland DHC-8-402Q	4121	ex C-FFCO
☐ JA849C	de Havilland DHC-8-402Q	4133	ex C-FGKJ
☐ JA850C	de Havilland DHC-8-402Q	4158	ex C-FLKW
☐ JA851C	de Havilland DHC-8-402Q	4177	ex C-FMTK

☐ JA001C	SAAB SF.340B	340B-419	ex SE-B19
☐ JA002C	SAAB SF.340B	340B-459	ex SE-B59
☐ JA8594	SAAB SF.340B	340B-399	ex SE-C99
☐ JA8642	SAAB SF.340B	340B-365	ex SE-C65
☐ JA8649	SAAB SF.340B	340B-368	ex SE-C68
☐ JA8703	SAAB SF.340B	340B-355	ex SE-C55
☐ JA8704	SAAB SF.340B	340B-361	ex SE-C61
☐ JA8886	SAAB SF.340B	340B-281	ex SE-G81
☐ JA8888	SAAB SF.340B	340B-331	ex SE-C31
☐ JA8900	SAAB SF.340B	340B-378	ex SE-C78

JAPAN AIRLINES INTERNATIONAL   *Japanair (JL/JAL)*   **Tokyo-Haneda (HND)**

Member of oneWorld

☐ JA301J	Boeing 737-846/W	35330/2095		♦
☐ JA302J	Boeing 737-846/W	35331/2162		
☐ JA303J	Boeing 737-846/W	35332/2225	ex N6066U	
☐ JA304J	Boeing 737-846/W	35333/2253		
☐ JA305J	Boeing 737-846/W	35334/2289		
☐ JA306J	Boeing 737-846/W	35335/2395	ex N6065Y	♦
☐ JA307J	Boeing 737-846/W	35336/2450		♦
☐ JA308J	Boeing 737-846/W	35337/2479	ex N1786B	
☐ JA309J	Boeing 737-846/W	35338/2522		
☐ JA310J	Boeing 737-846/W	35339/2510		
☐ JA311J	Boeing 737-846/W	35340/2571		
☐ JA312J	Boeing 737-846/W	35341/2584	ex N1786B	
☐ JA313J	Boeing 737-846/W	35342/2633	ex N1787B	
☐ JA314J	Boeing 737-846/W	35343/2701		♦
☐ JA315J	Boeing 737-846/W	35344/2731		♦
☐ JA316J	Boeing 737-846/W	35345/2762	ex N1787B	
☐ JA317J	Boeing 737-846/W	35346/2824		
☐ JA318J	Boeing 737-846/W	35347/2830	ex N1784B	
☐ JA319J	Boeing 737-846/W	35348/2867	ex N1795B	
☐ JA320J	Boeing 737-846/W	35349/2953	ex N1786B	♦
☐ JA321J	Boeing 737-846/W	35350/2977		
☐ JA322J	Boeing 737-846/W	35351/3002		
☐ JA323J	Boeing 737-846/W	35352/3057	ex N1787B	
☐ JA324J	Boeing 737-846/W	35353/3105	ex N1786B	
☐ JA325J	Boeing 737-846/W	35354/3117	ex N1787B	
☐ JA326J	Boeing 737-846/W	35355/3159	ex N1787B	♦
☐ JA327J	Boeing 737-846/W	35356/3201	ex N1796B	♦
☐ JA328J	Boeing 737-846/W	35357/3279	ex N1786B	♦
☐ JA329J	Boeing 737-846/W	35358/3315	ex N1796B	♦
☐ JA330J	Boeing 737-846/W	35359/3341		♦
☐ JA331J	Boeing 737-846/W	40346/3366	ex N1795B	♦
☐ JA332J	Boeing 737-846/W	40347/3385		♦
☐ JA333J	Boeing 737-846/W	40348/3465	ex N1799B	♦
☐ JA334J	Boeing 737-846/W	40349/3489	ex N1786B	♦
☐ JA335J	Boeing 737-846/W	40350/3525	ex N1787B	♦
☐ JA336J	Boeing 737-846/W	40351/3543	ex N1786B	♦
☐ JA337J	Boeing 737-846/W	40352/3604	ex N1786B	♦
☐ JA338J	Boeing 737-846/W	40355/3609		♦
☐ JA339J	Boeing 737-846/W	40354/3687		
☐ JA340J	Boeing 737-846/W	39190/3882		♦
☐ JA341J	Boeing 737-846/W	40356/3906		
☐ JA342J	Boeing 737-846/W	39191/4002		
☐ JA343J	Boeing 737-846/W	39192/4048		♦
☐ JA344J	Boeing 737-846/W	39193/4074		
☐ JA345J	Boeing 737-846/W	40947/4062		
☐ JA346J	Boeing 737-846/W	40948/4091		♦
☐ JA347J	Boeing 737-846/W	39194/4104		
☐ JA348J	Boeing 737-846/W	40353/4122		
☐ JA349J	Boeing 737-846/W	40950/4152		
☐ JA350J	Boeing 737-846/W	40954/4621		
☐ JA601J	Boeing 767-346ER	32886/875	ex N60697	
☐ JA602J	Boeing 767-346ER	32887/879		
☐ JA603J	Boeing 767-346ER	32888/880	ex N1794B	
☐ JA604J	Boeing 767-346ER	33493/905	oneWorld c/s	
☐ JA605J	Boeing 767-346ER	33494/911		
☐ JA606J	Boeing 767-346ER/W	33495/915		
☐ JA607J	Boeing 767-346ER/W	33496/917		
☐ JA608J	Boeing 767-346ER/W	33497/919		
☐ JA609J	Boeing 767-346ER	33845/921		
☐ JA610J	Boeing 767-346ER	33846/925		
☐ JA611J	Boeing 767-346ER	33847/927		
☐ JA612J	Boeing 767-346ER	33848/929		
☐ JA613J	Boeing 767-346ER	33849/935		
☐ JA614J	Boeing 767-346ER	33851/938		
☐ JA615J	Boeing 767-346ER	33850/942	ex N50217	
☐ JA616J	Boeing 767-346ER/W	35813/954		
☐ JA617J	Boeing 767-346ER/W	35814/957	ex N5023Q	Sky Sweet 767 c/s
☐ JA618J	Boeing 767-346ER/W	35815/964		
☐ JA619J	Boeing 767-346ER/W	37550/969		
☐ JA620J	Boeing 767-346ER/W	37547/974		
☐ JA621J	Boeing 767-346ER/W	37548/975		
☐ JA622J	Boeing 767-346ER	37549/977		
☐ JA623J	Boeing 767-346ER	36131/978	ex N1794B	
☐ JA651J	Boeing 767-346ER	40363/994		
☐ JA652J	Boeing 767-346ER	40364/995		
☐ JA653J	Boeing 767-346ER	40365/997		
☐ JA654J	Boeing 767-346ER	40366/999		

☐ JA655J	Boeing 767-346ER	40367/1007		
☐ JA656J	Boeing 767-346ER	40368/1009		Doraemon Jet c/s
☐ JA657J	Boeing 767-346ER	40369/1013		
☐ JA658J	Boeing 767-346ER	40370/1015		
☐ JA659J	Boeing 767-346ER	40371/1017		
☐ JA8269	Boeing 767-346	23964/225	ex N6046P	
☐ JA8299	Boeing 767-346	24498/277	ex N6055X	
☐ JA8364	Boeing 767-346	24782/327		
☐ JA8365	Boeing 767-346	24783/329		
☐ JA8397	Boeing 767-346	27311/547		
☐ JA8398	Boeing 767-346	27312/548		
☐ JA8399	Boeing 767-346	27313/554		
☐ JA8975	Boeing 767-346	27658/581		
☐ JA8976	Boeing 767-346	27659/667		
☐ JA8980	Boeing 767-346	28837/673		oneWorld c/s
☐ JA8986	Boeing 767-346	28838/680		
☐ JA8987	Boeing 767-346	28553/688		
☐ JA8988	Boeing 767-346	29863/772		
☐ JA007D	Boeing 777-289	27639/134		
☐ JA008D	Boeing 777-289	27640/146		
☐ JA009D	Boeing 777-289	27641/159	ex N5017V	
☐ JA010D	Boeing 777-289	27642/213		
☐ JA701J	Boeing 777-246ER	32889/410	ex (JA8989)	
☐ JA702J	Boeing 777-246ER	32890/417	ex (JA8990)	
☐ JA703J	Boeing 777-246ER	32891/427	ex N5023Q	
☐ JA704J	Boeing 777-246ER	32892/435	ex N50281	oneWorld c/s
☐ JA705J	Boeing 777-246ER	32893/446		
☐ JA706J	Boeing 777-246ER	33394/464		
☐ JA707J	Boeing 777-246ER	32894/475		
☐ JA708J	Boeing 777-246ER	32895/483		
☐ JA709J	Boeing 777-246ER	32896/489		
☐ JA710J	Boeing 777-246ER	33395/525		
☐ JA711J	Boeing 777-246ER	33396/533		
☐ JA712J	Boeing 777-246ER	37879		o/o
☐ JA713J	Boeing 777-246ER	37880		o/o
☐ JA714J	Boeing 777-246ER	37881		o/o
☐ JA715J	Boeing 777-246ER	37882		o/o
☐ JA716J	Boeing 777-246ER	37883		o/o
☐ JA771J	Boeing 777-246	27656/437	ex (JA711J)	oneWorld c/s
☐ JA772J	Boeing 777-246	27657/507		
☐ JA773J	Boeing 777-246	27653/635		
☐ JA8977	Boeing 777-289	27636/45		
☐ JA8978	Boeing 777-289	27637/79		
☐ JA8979	Boeing 777-289	27638/107		
☐ JA8983	Boeing 777-246	27366/39		
☐ JA8984	Boeing 777-246	27651/68		
☐ JA8985	Boeing 777-246	27652/72		
☐ JA731J	Boeing 777-346ER	32431/429	ex N5016R	
☐ JA732J	Boeing 777-346ER	32430/423	ex N5017V	oneWorld c/s
☐ JA733J	Boeing 777-346ER	32432/521		
☐ JA734J	Boeing 777-346ER	32433/527		Eco Jet c/s
☐ JA735J	Boeing 777-346ER	32434/577		
☐ JA736J	Boeing 777-346ER	32435/583		
☐ JA737J	Boeing 777-346ER	36126/668		
☐ JA738J	Boeing 777-346ER	32436/724		
☐ JA739J	Boeing 777-346ER	32437/736		
☐ JA740J	Boeing 777-346ER	36127/744		
☐ JA741J	Boeing 777-346ER	36128/812	ex N50281	
☐ JA742J	Boeing 777-346ER	36129/816	ex N1788B	
☐ JA743J	Boeing 777-346ER	36130/821	ex N6009F	
☐ JA751J	Boeing 777-346	27654/458		
☐ JA752J	Boeing 777-346	27655/460		oneWorld c/s
☐ JA8941	Boeing 777-346	28393/152		
☐ JA8943	Boeing 777-346	28395/196		
☐ JA8944	Boeing 777-346	28396/212		
☐ JA8945	Boeing 777-346	28397/238		
☐ JA821J	Boeing 787-8	34831/20		
☐ JA822J	Boeing 787-8	34832/23	ex N1003W	
☐ JA823J	Boeing 787-8	34833/21		
☐ JA824J	Boeing 787-8	34834/27		
☐ JA825J	Boeing 787-8	34835/33	ex N1006F	
☐ JA826J	Boeing 787-8	34836/37		
☐ JA827J	Boeing 787-8	34837/38	ex N787BK	
☐ JA828J	Boeing 787-8	34838/70		
☐ JA829J	Boeing 787-8	34839/84		
☐ JA830J	Boeing 787-8	34840/89		
☐ JA831J	Boeing 787-8	34847/152		
☐ JA832J	Boeing 787-8	34844/105		
☐ JA833J	Boeing 787-8	34846/125		
☐ JA834J	Boeing 787-8	34842/98		

☐ JA835J	Boeing 787-8	34850/159		
☐ JA836J	Boeing 787-8	38135/237		♦
☐ JA837J	Boeing 787-8	34860/222		♦
☐ JA838J	Boeing 787-8	34849/231		♦
☐ JA839J	Boeing 787-8	34853/252		♦
☐ JA840J	Boeing 787-8	34856/271	ex N1006K	♦
☐ JA864J	Boeing 787-8	34848/		o/o
☐ JA865J	Boeing 787-8	34851/		o/o
☐ JA866J	Boeing 787-8	34852/		o/o
☐ JA867J	Boeing 787-8	34858/		o/o
☐ JA	Boeing 787-8	34854/301		o/o
☐ JA	Boeing 787-8	34855/312		o/o
☐ JA	Boeing 787-8	34857/		o/o
☐ JA	Boeing 787-8	34859/385		o/o
☐ JA	Boeing 787-8	38134/		o/o
☐ JA203J	Canadair CRJ-200ER	7626	ex C-FMNW	>JLG
☐ JA861J	Boeing 787-9	34843/139	ex N789ZB	o/o
☐ JA862J	Boeing 787-9	34841/362		o/o♦
☐ JA863J	Boeing 787-9	38137/391		o/o♦
☐ JA8999	Boeing 737-446	29864/3111	ex N1786B	

JAPAN TRANSOCEAN AIR — JAI Ocean (NU/JTA) — Okinawa-Naha (OKA)

☐ JA8525	Boeing 737-4Q3	26605/2752		
☐ JA8597	Boeing 737-4Q3	27660/3043		
☐ JA8938	Boeing 737-4Q3	29485/3085		
☐ JA8939	Boeing 737-4Q3	29486/3088	ex N1800B	Jinbei Jet c/s
☐ JA8991	Boeing 737-446	27916/2718		
☐ JA8992	Boeing 737-446	27917/2729	ex N1792B	Jinbei Sakura Jimbei c/s
☐ JA8993	Boeing 737-446	28087/2812		
☐ JA8994	Boeing 737-446	28097/2907	ex N1786B	
☐ JA8995	Boeing 737-446	28831/2911		♦
☐ JA8996	Boeing 737-446	28832/2953	ex N1786B	
☐ JA8998	Boeing 737-446	28994/3044		

JETSTAR JAPAN — Orange Liner (GK/JJP) — Tokyo-Narita (TYO)

☐ JA01JJ	Airbus A320-232	5093	ex F-WWIN	
☐ JA02JJ	Airbus A320-232	5145	ex F-WWIL	
☐ JA03JJ	Airbus A320-232	5161	ex F-WWDL	
☐ JA04JJ	Airbus A320-232	5245	ex F-WWBY	
☐ JA05JJ	Airbus A320-232	5274	ex F-WWIJ	
☐ JA06JJ	Airbus A320-232/S	5281	ex F-WWDE	
☐ JA07JJ	Airbus A320-232/S	5355	ex F-WWBZ	
☐ JA08JJ	Airbus A320-232/S	5492	ex F-WWDH	
☐ JA09JJ	Airbus A320-232	5499	ex F-WWBP	
☐ JA10JJ	Airbus A320-232	5520	ex F-WWIN	
☐ JA11JJ	Airbus A320-232/S	5598	ex F-WWDR	
☐ JA12JJ	Airbus A320-232/S	5618	ex F-WWIX	
☐ JA13JJ	Airbus A320-232/S	5649	ex F-WWIL	
☐ JA14JJ	Airbus A320-232/S	5695	ex F-WWBJ	
☐ JA15JJ	Airbus A320-232/S	5701	ex F-WWBQ	
☐ JA16JJ	Airbus A320-232/S	5717	ex F-WWDV	
☐ JA17JJ	Airbus A320-232/S	5732	ex F-WWIE	
☐ JA18JJ	Airbus A320-232/S	5796	ex F-WWIO	
☐ JA19JJ	Airbus A320-232/S	6296	ex F-WWBF	♦
☐ JA20JJ	Airbus A320-232/S	6381	ex F-WWBI	♦

LINK AIRS — Fukuoka (FUK)

☐ JA01LK	ATR 72-600	1120	ex F-WKVH	o/o

NEW CENTRAL AIR SERVICE/SHIN CHUO KOKU — Tokyo-Chofu

☐ JA31CA	Dornier 228-212	8242	ex D-CBDO	
☐ JA32CA	Dornier 228-212	8243	ex D-CBDP	
☐ JA33CA	Dornier 228-212	8245	ex D-CDRS	
☐ JA34CA	Dornier 228-212NG	8300	ex D-CRAQ	
☐ JA35CA	Dornier 228-212NG	8304	ex D-CJAP	
☐ JA3453	Cessna TU206C Super Skywagon	U206-1218	ex N1775C	
☐ JA3669	Cessna TU206F Turbo Stationair	U20601964	ex N1704C	

NEW JAPAN AVIATION — Shin Nihon (NJA)

☐ JA80CT	Britten-Norman BN-2B-20 Islander	2234	ex G-CHEZ	
☐ JA127D	Britten-Norman BN-2B-20 Islander	2284		

NIPPON CARGO AIRLINES — Nippon Cargo (KZ/NCA) — Tokyo-Narita (NRT)

☐ JA04KZ	Boeing 747-4KZF	34283/1384		NCA Pegasus

☐ JA05KZ	Boeing 747-4KZF	36132/1394		NCA Apollo	
☐ JA06KZ	Boeing 747-4KZF	36133/1397		NCA Antares	
☐ JA07KZ	Boeing 747-4KZF	36134/1405		NCA Andromeda	
☐ JA08KZ	Boeing 747-4KZF	36135/1408		NCA Aries	
☐ JA11KZ	Boeing 747-8KZF	36136/1421	ex N5017Q		
☐ JA12KZ	Boeing 747-8KZF	36137/1422	ex N50217		
☐ JA13KZ	Boeing 747-8KZF	36138/1431	ex N6009F		
☐ JA14KZ	Boeing 747-8KZF	37394/1469	ex N772BA		
☐ JA15KZ	Boeing 747-8KZF	36139/1479	ex N942BA		
☐ JA16KZ	Boeing 747-8KZF	37393/1485	ex N808BA		
☐ JA17KZ	Boeing 747-8KZF	36140/1487	ex N815BA		
☐ JA18KZ	Boeing 747-8KZF	36141/1489	ex N783BA		
☐ JA19KZ	Boeing 747-8KZF	36142/			o/o
☐ JA20KZ	Boeing 747-8KZF	36143/			o/o
☐ JA21KZ	Boeing 747-8KZF	37395/			o/o
☐ JA22KZ	Boeing 747-8KZF	37396/			o/o
☐ JA24KZ	Boeing 747-8KZF	37397/			o/o
☐ JA25KZ	Boeing 747-8KZF	37398/			o/o

ORIENTAL AIR BRIDGE — Oriental Bridge (OC/ORC) — Nagasaki (NGS)

| ☐ JA801B | de Havilland DHC-8Q-201 | 566 | ex C-GDNG | |
| ☐ JA802B | de Havilland DHC-8Q-201 | 579 | ex C-FDHO | |

PEACH — Air Peach (MM/APJ) — Osaka-Kansai (KIX)

☐ JA801P	Airbus A320-214	4887	ex F-WWIQ	Peach Dream	
☐ JA802P	Airbus A320-214	4936	ex F-WWBU		
☐ JA803P	Airbus A320-214	5015	ex F-WWIG		
☐ JA804P	Airbus A320-214	5166	ex F-WWDJ		Violetta Rune c/s
☐ JA805P	Airbus A320-214	5304	ex F-WWDF	Mariko Jet	
☐ JA806P	Airbus A320-214	5384	ex F-WWIP		
☐ JA807P	Airbus A320-214	5440	ex F-WWII		
☐ JA808P	Airbus A320-214	5540	ex D-AXAU		
☐ JA809P	Airbus A320-214	5640	ex F-WWIK		
☐ JA810P	Airbus A320-214	5724	ex D-AVVP	Wing of Tohoku	
☐ JA811P	Airbus A320-214	5874	ex F-WWDO		
☐ JA812P	Airbus A320-214	6004	ex F-WWBR		
☐ JA813P	Airbus A320-214	6107	ex F-WWIT		♦
☐ JA814P	Airbus A320-214	6335	ex F-WWBM	Violetta Rune c/s	♦
☐ JA	Airbus A320-214	6640	ex		o/o♦
☐ JA	Airbus A320-214	6674	ex		o/o♦
☐ JA	Airbus A320-232	6835	ex		o/o♦

RAC - RYUKYU AIR COMMUTER — Okinawa-Naha (OKA)

☐ JA8935	de Havilland DHC-8Q-103B	593	ex C-GSAH	
☐ JA8936	de Havilland DHC-8Q-314	635	ex C-FIOX	
☐ JA8972	de Havilland DHC-8Q-103	472	ex C-GDKL	
☐ JA8973	de Havilland DHC-8Q-103	501	ex C-GDLD	
☐ JA8974	de Havilland DHC-8Q-103B	540	ex C-FDHP	
☐ JA5324	Britten-Norman BN-2B-20 Islander	2297	ex G-BWNG	
☐ JA5325	Britten-Norman BN-2B-20 Islander	2298	ex G-BWYX	

SKYMARK AIRLINES — Skymark (BC/SKY) — Osaka-Itami (ITM)

☐ JA73NA	Boeing 737-8HX/W	36849/3372	
☐ JA73NC	Boeing 737-8FZ/W	31743/3450	ex N1787B
☐ JA73ND	Boeing 737-8FZ/W	33440/3474	
☐ JA73NE	Boeing 737-82Y/W	40713/3501	ex N1787B
☐ JA73NF	Boeing 737-86N/W	38019/3642	
☐ JA73NG	Boeing 737-86N/W	36821/3738	ex N1786B
☐ JA73NJ	Boeing 737-86N/W	39405/3845	
☐ JA73NK	Boeing 737-86N/W	38023/3883	
☐ JA73NL	Boeing 737-8HX/W	38104/3933	
☐ JA73NM	Boeing 737-81D/W	39421/3940	
☐ JA73NN	Boeing 737-81D/W	39422/3975	
☐ JA73NP	Boeing 737-8HX/W	38109/4034	
☐ JA73NQ	Boeing 737-81D/W	39432/4310	
☐ JA73NR	Boeing 737-81D/W	39927/4340	
☐ JA73NT	Boeing 737-86N/W	41264/4460	
☐ JA73NU	Boeing 737-86N/W	38046/4511	
☐ JA73NX	Boeing 737-86N/W	38045/4606	
☐ JA73NY	Boeing 737-86N/W	41263/4633	
☐ JA737N	Boeing 737-8HX	36845/2339	
☐ JA737P	Boeing 737-8HX	29681/2493	ex N1795B
☐ JA737Q	Boeing 737-86N/W	35228/2630	
☐ JA737R	Boeing 737-86N/W	35630/2666	
☐ JA737T	Boeing 737-8Q8/W	35290/2818	
☐ JA737U	Boeing 737-8FZ/W	29680/2888	

☐ JA737X	Boeing 737-8AL/W	36692/3088	ex N1786B	
☐ JA737Y	Boeing 737-8FZ/W	29663/3113	ex N1786B	
☐ JA737Z	Boeing 737-82Y/W	40712/3308	ex N1786B	
Filed for brankruptcy protection Jan15; ops continue				

SOLASEED AIR — Newsky (6J/SNJ) — Miyazaki (KMI)

☐ JA801X	Boeing 737-81D/W	39415/3666		
☐ JA802X	Boeing 737-81D/W	39418/3816		Kumamon Go c/s
☐ JA803X	Boeing 737-86N/W	39395/3915		Paradise City Miyazaki c/s
☐ JA804X	Boeing 737-86N/W	38026/4016		North Miyazaki Republic of Himuka c/s
☐ JA805X	Boeing 737-86N/W	38035/4327		
☐ JA806X	Boeing 737-86N/W	38036/4339	ex N1786B	Amakusa Dream Year 2016 c/s
☐ JA807X	Boeing 737-81D/W	39431/4526		
☐ JA808X	Boeing 737-81D/W	39433/4611		Okinawa Yanbaru Flower Tour c/s
☐ JA809X	Boeing 737-86N/W	41247/4826		Takaharu c/s
☐ JA810X	Boeing 737-86N/W	41271/4920		♦
☐ JA811X	Boeing 737-86N/W	43406/5062		♦
☐ JA812X	Boeing 737-86N/W	43402/5319		♦
☐ JA392K	Boeing 737-46M	28550/2847	ex N8550F	<ANA

SPRING AIRLINES JAPAN — (9C/SJO) — Tokyo-Narita (NRT)

☐ JA01GR	Boeing 737-81D/W	39429/4413	ex N272LM	
☐ JA02GR	Boeing 737-86N/W	41256/4712		
☐ JA03GR	Boeing 737-86N/W	41272/4819		

STAR FLYER — (7G/SFJ) — Kitakyushu (KKJ)

☐ JA05MC	Airbus A320-214	4555	ex F-WWDG	
☐ JA06MC	Airbus A320-214	4720	ex F-WWDF	
☐ JA07MC	Airbus A320-214	5102	ex F-WWIS	
☐ JA08MC	Airbus A320-214	5393	ex F-WWBF	
☐ JA09MC	Airbus A320-214	5512	ex D-AXAK	City of Kitakyushu
☐ JA20MC	Airbus A320-214/S	5652	ex F-WWBO	
☐ JA21MC	Airbus A320-214/S	5773	ex D-AVVZ	
☐ JA22MC	Airbus A320-214/S	5862	ex D-AVVC	
☐ JA23MC	Airbus A320-214/S	5931	ex F-WWIG	

VANILLA AIR — (JW/VNL) — Tokyo-Narita (NRT)

☐ JA01VA	Airbus A320-216/S	5844	ex F-WWIN	
☐ JA02VA	Airbus A320-216/S	5901	ex F-WWDC	
☐ JA03VA	Airbus A320-216/S	5926	ex F-WWID	
☐ JA04VA	Airbus A320-216/S	6257	ex F-WWDR	
☐ JA05VA	Airbus A320-216/S	6282	ex F-WWII	♦
☐ JA06VA	Airbus A320-214/S	6320	ex F-WWIP	♦
☐ JA07VA	Airbus A320-214/S	6422	ex F-WWDR	♦
☐ JA08VA	Airbus A320-214/S	6447	ex F-WWII	♦

JU - MONGOLIA (State of Mongolia)

AERO MONGOLIA — Aero Mongolia (M0/MNG) — Ulan Bator (ULN)

☐ JU-8250	Fokker 50	20210	ex SE-MEI	
☐ JU-8251	Fokker 50	20251	ex PH-WXH	
☐ JU-8258	Fokker 50	20258	ex PH-KXU	

BLUE SKY AVIATION — Ulan Bator (ULN)

☐ JU-2114	Cessna 208B Caravan I	208B0782	ex N208BS	

CENTRAL MONGOLIAN AIRWAYS — Central Mongolia (CEM) — Ulan Bator (ULN)

☐ JU-5444	Mil Mi-8T	20409	ex JU-1024	
☐ JU-5445	Mil Mi-8T	98103227	ex JU-1025	
☐ JU-5446	Mil Mi-8T	20411	ex JU-1026	

HUNNU AIR — Trans Mongolia (MR/MML) — Ulan Bator (ULN)

☐ JU-8881	Fokker 50	20183	ex LN-RNF	Hunnu
☐ JU-8882	Fokker 50	20184	ex LN-RNG	Kidan
☐ JU-8883	Fokker 50	20181	ex OO-VLY	

MIAT MONGOLIAN AIRLINES — Mongol Air (OM/MGL) — Ulan Bator (ULN)

☐ EI-CSG	Boeing 737-8AS/W	29922/571	Ogedei Khaan	>TVS
☐ EI-CXV	Boeing 737-8CX/W	32364/1166	Khubelai Khaan	

☐ JU-1011	Boeing 767-3W0ER	28149/627	ex B-2569		
☐ JU-1015	Boeing 737-8SH/W	41318/4902		Guyug Khaan	◆
☐ JU-1021	Boeing 767-34GER	41519/1050		Chinggis Khaan	
☐ JU-1046	Antonov An-2	IG227-47	ex MONGOL-747		

SKY HORSE AVIATION/TENGERIN ELCH — Sky Horse (TNL) — Ulan Bator (ULN)

☐ JU-2030	LET L-410UVP-E1	861801	ex OK-RDE
☐ JU-2032	LET L-410UVP	810602	ex UR-67001

THOMAS AIR — Taimen (TME) — Ulan Bator (ULN)

☐ JU-1911	Pilatus PC-6/B2-B4 Porter	972	ex HB-FNR

JY- JORDAN (Hashemite Kingdom of Jordan)

AIR ARABIA JORDAN — (9P/PTR) — Amman-Marka (ADJ)

☐ JY-PTB	Airbus A320-212	0537	ex A9C-EC	
☐ JY-PTC	Airbus A320-214	3246	ex A6-ABM	◆

ARAB WINGS — Arab Wings (AWS) — Amman (AMM)

☐ JY-AWB	Beech B200 Super King Air	BB-1701	ex JY-AWZ	
☐ JY-AWD	Hawker 800XP	258520	ex JY-WJA	
☐ JY-AWE	Hawker 800XP	258539	ex JY-AW5	
☐ JY-AWG	Hawker 800XP	258504	ex TC-AHS	
☐ JY-AWH	Citation 680 Sovereign	680-0285	ex N61855	
☐ JY-CMC	Embraer Legacy 650	14501126	ex PT-TKX	
☐ JY-KME	Embraer Legacy 600	14501055	ex D-ADCN	
☐ JY-	Hawker 900XP	HA-177	ex UP-CSD	◆
☐ VP-CCC	Embraer Lineage 1000	19000278	ex JY-AAG	◆

BARQ AVIATION — Amman (AMM)

☐ OB-2049-P	Lockheed L-1011-100 Tristar	193B-1230	ex N194AT
☐ OB-2060-P	Lockheed L-1011-500 Tristar	193B-1238	ex N164AT
☐ OB-2061-P	Lockheed L-1011-500 Tristar	193B-1220	ex N1621T

JORDAN AVIATION — Jordan Aviation (R5/JAV) — Amman-Marka (ADJ)

☐ JY-JAB	Boeing 737-33A	23630/1312	ex N169AW	Noor	[AMM]
☐ JY-JAD	Boeing 737-322	24662/1862	ex N387UA		[AMM]
☐ JY-JAN	Boeing 737-322	23956/1564	ex N324UA	Amman	[AMM]
☐ JY-JAP	Boeing 737-46B	24124/1679	ex SX-BGX		
☐ JY-JAQ	Boeing 737-46J	27826/2694	ex D-ABRE		>LMU
☐ JY-JAX	Boeing 737-322	23955/1550	ex N323UA		[AMM]
☐ JY-JAC	Airbus A320-211	0029	ex N290SE		
☐ JY-JAG	Boeing 767-204ER	24757/299	ex G-SLVR		>SAI
☐ JY-JAI	Boeing 767-204ER	24736/296	ex G-SILC		[AMM]
☐ JY-JAL	Boeing 767-204ER	24239/243	ex G-BOPB		[AMM]
☐ JY-JAT	Airbus A320-211	2061	ex N261FG		
☐ JY-JAV	Airbus A310-222	357	ex 3B-STK	Zuhair	[AMM]

JORDAN INTERNATIONAL AIR CARGO — Amman-Marka (ADJ)

☐ JY-JID	Ilyushin Il-76MF	2013423808	ops as 360 (mil serial) and JID (without prefix)

ROYAL FALCON — (RL/RFJ) — Amman-Marka (ADJ)

☐ JY-JRD	Boeing 767-3P6ER	26237/544	ex N90GZ	>IAW
☐ JY-JRG	Airbus A320-212	814	ex EI-DJH	
☐ JY-RFF	Boeing 737-4K5	27831/2677	ex OO-TUB	>SNR

ROYAL JORDANIAN — Jordanian (RJ/RJA) — Amman (AMM)

Member of oneWorld

☐ JY-AYQ	Airbus A320-232	4670	ex F-WWBK		
☐ JY-AYR	Airbus A320-232	4817	ex F-WWIA		
☐ JY-AYS	Airbus A320-232	4853	ex F-WWBE		
☐ JY-AYU	Airbus A320-232	5128	ex D-AVVE	Sait	
☐ JY-AYW	Airbus A320-232	5367	ex F-WWDU	Irbid	
☐ JY-AYX	Airbus A320-231	2953	ex F-OHGX	Madaba	
☐ JY-BAA	Boeing 787-8	37983/194		Prince Hussein bin Abdullah	◆
☐ JY-BAB	Boeing 787-8	35319/214		Princess Iman Bint Abdullah	◆
☐ JY-BAC	Boeing 787-8	37164/219		Princess Salma Bint Abdullah	◆
☐ JY-BAE	Boeing 787-8	37166/221		Prince Hashem bin Adullah	◆

☐ JY-BAF	Boeing 787-8	36112/233		Amman	♦

☐ JY-AGQ	Airbus A310-304F	445	ex F-ODVF	Princess Raiyah
☐ JY-AGR	Airbus A310-304F	490	ex F-ODVG	Prince Faisal
☐ JY-AIE	Airbus A330-223	970	ex EI-EJY	Jordan River
☐ JY-AIF	Airbus A330-223	979	ex EI-EJZ	Prince Ali Ibn Al Hussain
☐ JY-AIG	Airbus A330-223	1002	ex EI-ESA	Prince Feisal Ibn Al-Hussein
☐ JY-AYL	Airbus A319-132	3428	ex D-AVYQ	Mafraq
☐ JY-AYM	Airbus A319-132	3685	ex D-AVWC	Ma'an
☐ JY-AYN	Airbus A319-132	3803	ex D-AVYB	Shobak
☐ JY-AYP	Airbus A319-132	3832	ex D-AVYL	Ajloun
☐ JY-AYT	Airbus A321-231	5099	ex D-AZAV	Karak
☐ JY-AYV	Airbus A321-231	5177	ex D-AVZJ	Madaba
☐ JY-EMA	Embraer ERJ-195LR	19000107	ex PT-SQB	
☐ JY-EMB	Embraer ERJ-195LR	19000131	ex PT-SYJ	
☐ JY-EMC	Embraer ERJ-175LR	17000223	ex PT-SCZ	Zay
☐ JY-EMD	Embraer ERJ-175LR	17000232	ex PT-SFI	Dana
☐ JY-EMG	Embraer ERJ-195LR	19000088	ex PT-SNG	
☐ JY-EMH	Embraer ERJ-175LR	17000316	ex PT-XUK	Azraq

ROYAL JORDANIAN XPRESS — Amman (AMM)

Wholly owned subsidiary of Royal Jordanian; leases aircraft from the parent as required.

ROYAL WINGS — Royal Wings (RY/RYW) — Amman (AMM)

☐ JY-AYI	Airbus A320-212	0569	ex F-OGYC	
☐ JY-AYW	Airbus A320-232	5367	ex F-WWDU	o/o♦

SOLITAIRE AIR — (STR) — Amman (AMM)

☐ JY-SOA	Boeing 737-33V	29338/3114	ex F-WTDK	FlyJordan c/s	♦

TEEBAH AIRLINES — Amman (AMM)

☐ YI-APW	Boeing 737-2B7	22885/966	ex 9L-LEG	>IAW

J2- DJIBOUTI (Republic of Djibouti)

DAALLO AIRLINES — Dalo Airlines (D3/DAO) — Djibouti/Dubai (JIB/DAB)

☐ EY-47693	Antonov An-24RV	27307510	ex CCCP-47693	<TJK
☐ EY-539	Boeing 737-3B7	23700/1461	ex AP-BIW	<ETJ♦
☐ UP-I1802	Ilyushin Il-18E	185008603	ex UN-75002	<MGK

J6- ST. LUCIA

INTER CARIBBEAN EXPRESS — Castries

☐ J6-UVF	Britten-Norman BN-2A-26 Islander	2165	ex J8-VAM	>SVD

J8- ST. VINCENT & GRENADINES (State of St. Vincent & Grenadines)

HARLEQUIN AIR — Vigie

☐ J8-HAA	Piper PA-31-350 Chieftain	31-8052107	ex N170PA
☐ J8-HAB	Piper PA-31-350 Navajo Chieftain	31-7652110	ex G-LYDC

MUSTIQUE AIRWAYS — Mustique (MAW) — Mustique (MQS)

☐ J8-CIW	Britten-Norman BN-2B-26 Islander	2018	ex J8-VAH
☐ J8-KIM	Rockwell 500S Shrike Commander	3253	ex J8-VBE
☐ J8-MQS	Aero Commander 500B	1400-144	ex J8-SJK
☐ J8-PIE	Britten-Norman BN-2A Islander	532	ex N619NA
☐ J8-PUG	Aero Commander 500U	1670-18	ex J8-VBD
☐ J6-SLU	Aero Commander 500B	1146-80	ex N6275X

ST LUCIA HELICOPTERS — Vigie

☐ J8-AAM	Aérospatiale AS350BA Ecureuil	1294	
☐ J8-AAQ	Aérospatiale AS3500B2 Ecureuil	4656	ex N535AE
☐ J8-AAR	Aérospatiale AS350BA Ecureuil	3869	ex N190AE

SVG AIR/GRENADINE AIRWAYS — Grenadines (SVD) — Kingston, St Vincent (SVD)

☐ J8-GAA	de Havilland DHC-6 Twin Otter 300	239	ex N239Z
☐ J8-GAL	de Havilland DHC-6 Twin Otter 300	510	ex V2-LFL

☐ J8-SUN	de Havilland DHC-6 Twin Otter 300	477	ex 8P-MLK	all-white	
☐ J8-VBQ	de Havilland DHC-6 Twin Otter 300	604	ex 8P-BGC	all-white	
☐ J8-VBS	de Havilland DHC-6 Twin Otter 300	249	ex V2-LGF	Trans Island 2000 c/s	
☐ J8-UVF	Britten-Norman BN-2B-26 Islander	2165	ex J6-UVF		<Inter Caribbean Express
☐ J8-VAQ	Cessna 402B II STOL	402B1038	ex N400XY		
☐ J8-VBI	Britten-Norman BN-2B-26 Islander	2025	ex J3-GAF		
☐ J8-VBJ	Britten-Norman BN-2A Islander	163	ex J3-GAG		
☐ J8-VBK	Britten-Norman BN-2A-26 Islander	570	ex J3-GAH		
☐ J8-VBL	Cessna 402C II	402C0640	ex N404MN		

LN-   NORWAY (Kingdom of Norway)

AIRWING   Norwing (NWG)   Oslo-Gardermoen (OSL)

☐ LN-AWA	Beech A100 King Air	B-213	ex SE-LDL	
☐ LN-FIX	Beech B200 Super King Air	BB-1898	ex N199GA	
☐ LN-ULV	Beech 200 Super King Air	BB-309	ex OY-PEB	

BERGEN AIR TRANSPORT   Bergen Air (BGT)   Bergen (BGO)

☐ LN-BAA	Beech B200 Super King Air	BB-1327	ex N67SD	
☐ LN-TWL	Beech B200 Super King Air	BB-1144	ex N120AJ	

BLUEWAY OFFSHORE NORGE   Stavanger (SVG)

☐ LN-OYW	Eurocopter EC225LP	2935		♦
☐ LN-OYX	Eurocopter EC225LP	2862	ex (OY-HOR)	

BRISTOW NORWAY

☐ LN-ONF	Eurocopter EC225LP 2	2750		♦
☐ LN-ONG	Eurocopter EC225LP 2	2755		♦
☐ LN-ONJ	Eurocopter EC225LR	2918		♦
☐ LN-ONK	Eurocopter EC255LR	2922		♦
☐ LN-ONL	Eurocopter EC225LR	2924		♦
☐ LN-ONA	Sikorsky S-92A	920144	ex N1016R	♦
☐ LN-ONB	Sikorsky S-92A	920145	ex N145MH	♦
☐ LN-ONC	Sikorsky S-92A	920148	ex N148FF	♦
☐ LN-OND	Sikorsky S-92A	920088	ex G-CGUX	♦
☐ LN-ONE	Sikorsky S-92A	920213	ex N213BS	♦
☐ LN-ONN	Sikorsky S-92A	920011	ex N7107S	Mona Lisa	♦
☐ LN-ONO	Sikorsky S-92A	920012	ex N7108Z	Madonna	♦
☐ LN-ONP	Sikorsky S-92A	920025	ex N8011N	♦
☐ LN-ONQ	Sikorsky S-92A	920032	ex N8036Q	♦
☐ LN-ONR	Sikorsky S-92A	920033	ex N8021R	♦
☐ LN-ONS	Sikorsky S-92A	920043	ex N8061E	♦
☐ LN-ONT	Sikorsky S-92A	920070	ex N4510G	♦
☐ LN-ONU	Sikorsky S-92A	920091	ex N2000Q	♦
☐ LN-ONV	Sikorsky S-92A	920092	ex N2010H	♦
☐ LN-ONW	Sikorsky S-92A	920090	ex N921AL	♦
☐ LN-ONX	Sikorsky S-92A	920137	ex N1133W	♦

CHC HELIKOPTER SERVICE   Helibus (HKS)   Stavanger/Bergen (SVG/BGO)

☐ LN-OAW	Aérospatiale AS332L	2053	ex VH-URY	
☐ LN-OHA	Aérospatiale AS332L	2396	ex F-WYMS	
☐ LN-OHE	Aérospatiale AS332L2 2	2474		
☐ LN-OHG	Aérospatiale AS332L2 2	2493		
☐ LN-OHJ	Aérospatiale AS332L2 2	2594		
☐ LN-OHK	Aérospatiale AS332L2 2	2613		
☐ LN-OHW	Eurocopter EC225LP 2	2715	ex F-WJXV	
☐ LN-OHY	Eurocopter EC225LP 2	2708	ex F-WWON	
☐ LN-OHZ	Eurocopter EC225LP	2691	ex (LN-OJN)	
☐ LN-OJA	Eurocopter EC225LP 2	2692		
☐ LN-OJB	Eurocopter EC225LP 2	2725		
☐ LN-OJC	Eurocopter EC225LP 2	2739		
☐ LN-OJD	Eurocopter EC225LP 2	2744	ex F-WWOY	
☐ LN-OJE	Eurocopter EC225LP 2	2716		
☐ LN-OJF	Eurocopter EC225LP 2	2721	ex F-WJXT	
☐ LN-OJG	Eurocopter EC225LP 2	2747		
☐ LN-OJK	Eurocopter EC225LP	2907		
☐ LN-OJL	Eurocopter EC225LP	2930		
☐ LN-OJN	Eurocopter EC225LP	2911		♦
☐ LN-OJO	Eurocopter EC225LP	2914		♦
☐ LN-OLD	Aérospatiale AS332L	2103	ex OY-HMI	
☐ LN-OMF	Aérospatiale AS332L	2067	ex G-PUMK	
☐ LN-OMH	Aérospatiale AS332L	2113	ex HZ-RH4	
☐ LN-OMX	Aérospatiale AS332L	2351	ex G-BTNZ	
☐ LN-OPH	Aérospatiale AS332L1	2347		

☐ LN-OPX	Aérospatiale AS332L1	9009				
☐ LN-OXX	Aérospatiale AS332L	2015	ex PR-CHZ			
☐ LN-OQA	Sikorsky S-92A	920013	ex (LN-ONO)			
☐ LN-OQB	Sikorsky S-92A	920014	ex (LN-OQA)			
☐ LN-OQC	Sikorsky S-92A	920018	ex (LN-OQB)			
☐ LN-OQE	Sikorsky S-92A	920047	ex N80071			
☐ LN-OQF	Sikorsky S-92A	920056	ex N4502R			
☐ LN-OQG	Sikorsky S-92A	920095	ex N20168			
☐ LN-OQH	Sikorsky S-92A	920097	ex N2021Y			
☐ LN-OQI	Sikorsky S-92A	920098	ex N2055A			
☐ LN-OQJ	Sikorsky S-92A	920110	ex N2126Z			
☐ LN-OQK	Sikorsky S-92A	920117	ex N21285			
☐ LN-OQL	Sikorsky S-92A	920132	ex N132GN			
☐ LN-OQM	Sikorsky S-92A	920186	ex N186U			
☐ LN-OQN	Sikorsky S-92A	920057	ex VH-LYJ			
☐ LN-OQO	Sikorsky S-92A	920060	ex G-WNSH			

CYBRAIR — Nesøya

☐ LN-NCC	de Havilland DHC-2 Beaver I	1167	ex N5CC		FP

FONNAFLY — Fonna (NOF) — Rosendal/Bergen/Oslo-Gardermoen/Voss (-/BGN/OSL/-)

☐ LN-OBD	Aérospatiale AS350B2 Ecureuil	3650	ex SE-JHI		
☐ LN-OVA	Aérospatiale AS350B3 Ecureuil	7149	ex SE-JLH		
☐ LN-OVE	Aérospatiale AS350B3 Ecureuil	7605	ex SE-JOP		
☐ LN-OVV	Aérospatiale AS350B3e Ecureuil	7382			
☐ LN-OYH	Aérospatiale AS350B3 Ecureuil	4461	ex EC-KTB		
☐ LN-FFF	Cessna U206G Stationair 6 II	U20604497	ex SE-GXB	Fonna 19	FP
☐ LN-HAI	Cessna U206F Stationair 6 II	U20603058	ex N4696Q		FP
☐ LN-HOO	Cessna TU206F Turbo Stationair 6 II	U20605490	ex (N649EU)	Fonna 10	FP
☐ LN-IKA	Cessna TU206F Turbo Stationair 6 II	U20606251	ex (N6356Z)	Fonna 11	FP
☐ LN-OEN	Eurocopter EC120B Colibri	1146	ex (LN-ONE)		

HELITRANS — Scanbird (9I/HDR) — Trondheim (TRD)

☐ LN-OAK	Aérospatiale AS350B3 Ecureuil	3212			
☐ LN-OFB	Aérospatiale AS350B3 Ecureuil	4691			
☐ LN-OFC	Aérospatiale AS350B3 Ecureuil	4763			
☐ LN-OFD	Aérospatiale AS350B3e Ecureuil	7796			♦
☐ LN-OGG	Aérospatiale AS350B1 Ecureuil	2021	ex SE-JLL		
☐ LN-OGL	Aérospatiale AS350B3 Ecureuil	3792	ex F-WQDD		
☐ LN-OGO	Aérospatiale AS350B3+ Ecureuil	7145			
☐ LN-OMD	Aérospatiale AS350B3 Ecureuil	3303	ex HB-ZCL		
☐ LN-OMV	Aérospatiale AS350B3 Ecureuil	3461	ex N785EB		
☐ LN-OPA	Aérospatiale AS350B3 Ecureuil	3589			
☐ LN-OTR	Aérospatiale AS350B3 Ecureuil	4751	ex F-WMXU		
☐ LN-OXE	Aérospatiale AS350B3 Ecureuil	4106	ex SE-JIO		
☐ LN-ABO	Cessna 185A Skywagon	185-0439	ex SE-EEM		
☐ LN-OPO	Bell 214B	28053	ex N214KR		
☐ LN-ORM	Bell 214B-1	28054	ex SE-HLE		

LUFTTRANSPORT — Luft Transport (LTR) — Bardufoss (BDU)

☐ LN-OLF	AgustaWestland AW139	31148			
☐ LN-OLO	AgustaWestland AW139	31139			
☐ LN-OLS	AgustaWestland AW139	31136			
☐ LN-OLU	AgustaWestland AW139	31135			
☐ LN-OLV	AgustaWestland AW139	31023	ex I-RAIB	Vaeroy	
☐ LN-LTA	Beech B200 Super King Air	BB-1868	ex N954RM		
☐ LN-LTB	Beech B200 Super King Air	BB-2001	ex N3501D		
☐ LN-LTC	Beech B200 Super King Air	BB-2002	ex N60102		
☐ LN-LTD	Beech B200 Super King Air	BB-2006	ex N61806		
☐ LN-LTE	Beech B200 Super King Air	BB-2007	ex N63007		
☐ LN-LTF	Beech B200 Super King Air	BB-2008	ex N63578		♦
☐ LN-LTG	Beech B200 Super King Air	BB-2009	ex N62509		
☐ LN-LTI	Beech B200 Super King Air	BB-2010	ex N6010T		
☐ LN-LTJ	Beech B200 Super King Air	BB-2011	ex N6011V		
☐ LN-LTK	Beech B200 Super King Air	BB-2004	ex N63924		
☐ LN-LTL	Beech B200 Super King Air	BB-2005	ex N6005S		
☐ LN-LTS	Dornier 228-212NG	8301	ex D-CNEW	Svalbard	
☐ LN-LYR	Dornier 228-202K	8166	ex D-CTCA	Kings Bay	
☐ LN-OLE	Aérospatiale SA365N2 Dauphin 2	6405	ex VT-CKR		
☐ LN-OLI	Agusta A109E Power	11204			
☐ LN-OLM	Aérospatiale AS365N3 Dauphin 2	6725	ex F-WWOT		
☐ LN-OLN	Aérospatiale AS365N3 Dauphin 2	6721	ex F-WWOF		
☐ LN-OLT	Aérospatiale AS365N3 Dauphin 3	6964	ex VF-WWOD		

NORD HELIKOPTER				**Alesund**
☐ LN-OWE	Aérospatiale AS350B3 Ecureuil	7578		
☐ LN-OWF	Aérospatiale AS350B3 Ecureuil	7587		
☐ LN-OWG	Aérospatiale AS350B3 Ecureiul	7858		♦

NORDLANDSFLY				**Mosjoen**
☐ LN-OSB	Aérospatiale AS350B3 Ecureuil	4752	ex I-IBLA	

NORSK HELIKOPTER		**Norske (NOR)**		**Stavanger (SVG)**
☐ LN-OEC	Sikorsky S-92A	920181	ex N181L	
☐ LN-OED	Sikorsky S-92A	920182	ex N982P	
☐ LN-OEE	Sikorsky S092A	920220	ex G-VINI	♦

NORSK LUFTAMBULANSE		**Helidoc (DOC)**		**Oslo/Drøbak (OSL/-)**
☐ LN-OOC	Eurocopter EC135P2+	0350	ex D-HECH	EMS
☐ LN-OOD	Eurocopter EC135P2+	0356	ex D-HECL	EMS
☐ LN-OOE	Eurocopter EC135P2+	0357	ex D-HECA	EMS
☐ LN-OOF	Eurocopter EC135P2+	0390	ex D-HECH	EMS
☐ LN-OOG	Eurocopter EC135P2+	0393	ex D-HECM	EMS
☐ LN-OOH	Eurocopter EC135P2+	0399	ex D-HECG	EMS
☐ LN-OOJ	Eurocopter EC135P2+	0588		EMS
☐ LN-OON	Eurocopter EC135P2+	1033		EMS
☐ LN-OOV	Eurocopter EC135P2+	1168		EMS♦
☐ LN-OOW	Eurocopter EC135P2+	1169		EMS♦
☐ LN-OOZ	Eurocopter EC135P2+	1170		EMS♦
☐ OE-XER	Eurocopter EC135	0221		
☐ LN-OOB	MBB BK.117D-2	20021	ex D-HCBS	♦
☐ LN-OOM	MBB BK.117C-2	9074	ex D-HMBB	

NORWEGIAN		**Nor Shuttle (DY/NAX)**		**Oslo-Gardermoen (OSL)**
☐ LN-KHA	Boeing 737-31S/W	29100/2984	ex SX-BGY	
☐ LN-KHB	Boeing 737-31S/W	29264/3070	ex SX-BGW	
☐ LN-KHC	Boeing 737-31S/W	29265/3073	ex SX-BGX	[QLA]
☐ LN-KKB	Boeing 737-33A	27457/2756	ex N457AN	
☐ LN-KKW	Boeing 737-3K9	24213/1794	ex CS-TLL	all white [QLA]
☐ LN-KKX	Boeing 737-33S/W	29072/3012	ex ZK-NGN	
☐ LN-DYA	Boeing 737-8JP/W	39162/2994	ex N1786B	
☐ LN-DYB	Boeing 737-8JP/W	39163/3054		
☐ LN-DYC	Boeing 737-8JP/W	39164/3196	ex N1787B	
☐ LN-DYD	Boeing 737-8JP/W	39002/3231	ex N1787B	
☐ LN-DYE	Boeing 737-8JP/W	39003/3401	ex N1787B	Ludvig Holberg
☐ LN-DYF	Boeing 737-8JP/W	39004/3482	ex N1787B	
☐ LN-DYG	Boeing 737-8JP/W	39165/3507	ex N1786B	
☐ LN-DYH	Boeing 737-8JP/W	40865/3410		Soren Kierkegaard
☐ LN-DYI	Boeing 737-8JP/W	40866/3432	ex N1787B	Aasmund Olavson Vinje
☐ LN-DYJ	Boeing 737-8JP/W	39045/3530		
☐ LN-DYK	Boeing 737-8JP/W	39046/3557		
☐ LN-DYL	Boeing 737-8JP/W	40867/3565		
☐ LN-DYM	Boeing 737-8JP/W	39005/3572		
☐ LN-DYN	Boeing 737-8JP/W	39006/3583		
☐ LN-DYO	Boeing 737-8JP/W	40868/3591		
☐ LN-DYP	Boeing 737-8JP/W	39047/3630		
☐ LN-DYQ	Boeing 737-8JP/W	40869/3651		
☐ LN-DYR	Boeing 737-8JP/W	40870/3660		
☐ LN-DYS	Boeing 737-8JP/W	390073665		
☐ LN-DYT	Boeing 737-8JP/W	39048/3686		
☐ LN-DYU	Boeing 737-8JP/W	39008/3725		
☐ LN-DYV	Boeing 737-8JP/W	39009/3790		
☐ LN-DYW	Boeing 737-8JP/W	39010/3871		
☐ LN-DYZ	Boeing 737-8JP/W	39013/4037		Aril Edwardsen
☐ LN-NGA	Boeing 737-8JP/W	39014/4067		Ludvig Walentin Karlsen
☐ LN-NGB	Boeing 737-8JP/W	39015/4090		Geirr Tveitt
☐ LN-NGC	Boeing 737-8JP/W	39016/4157		Jens Glad Balchen
☐ LN-NGD	Boeing 737-8JP/W	39049/4161		Ivo Caprino
☐ LN-NGE	Boeing 737-8JP/W	39050/4196		
☐ LN-NGF	Boeing 737-8JP/W	39017/4234		HC Ørstedt
☐ LN-NGG	Boeing 737-8JP/W	39018/4289		Gunnar Sønsteby
☐ LN-NGH	Boeing 737-8JP/W	39019/4295		Anders Zorn
☐ LN-NGI	Boeing 737-8JP/W	39020/4343		Wenche Foss
☐ LN-NGJ	Boeing 737-8JP/W	39021/4371		John Bauer
☐ LN-NGK	Boeing 737-8JP/W	39022/4528		Johan Falkberget
☐ LN-NGL	Boeing 737-8JP/W	39023/4572		Johan Frederik "Frits" Thaulow
☐ LN-NGN	Boeing 737-8JP/W	39025/4652		Georg Sverdrup
☐ LN-NGO	Boeing 737-8JP/W	39026/4676		Victor Borge

263

☐ LN-NGP	Boeing 737-8JP/W	39028/4701		Ivar Aasen
☐ LN-NGQ	Boeing 737-8JP/W	39027/4729		
☐ LN-NGR	Boeing 737-8JP/W	41121/4739		
☐ LN-NGS	Boeing 737-8JP/W	39029/4767	ex N17968	Regine Normann
☐ LN-NGT	Boeing 737-8JP/W	41125/4774	ex N5573B	Anton KH Jakobsen
☐ LN-NGU	Boeing 737-8JP/W	39030/4785		Harry S Pettersen
☐ LN-NGV	Boeing 737-8JP/W	39031/4841	ex N5573B	
☐ LN-NGW	Boeing 737-8JP/W	39032/4889	ex N1795B	Theodor Kittelsen
☐ LN-NGX	Boeing 737-8JP/W	39033/4927		
☐ LN-NGY	Boeing 737-8JP/W	41126/4972		Sigrid Undset ♦
☐ LN-NGZ	Boeing 737-8JP/W	41127/5013		o/o♦
☐ LN-NHA	Boeing 737-8JP/W	41129/5069		♦
☐ LN-NHB	Boeing 737-8JP/W	41134/5102		♦
☐ LN-NHC	Boeing 737-8JP/W	41128/5235		♦
☐ LN-NHD	Boeing 737-8JP/W	41131/5317	ex N1796B	♦
☐ LN-NHE	Boeing 737-8JP/W	41136/5415		♦
☐ LN-NHF	Boeing 737-8JP/W	42075/		o/o♦
☐ LN-NHH	Boeing 737-8JP/W	42069/		o/o♦
☐ LN-NHJ	Boeing 737-8JP/W	42078/		o/o♦
☐ LN-NHK	Boeing 737-8JP/W	42070/		o/o♦
☐ LN-NIA	Boeing 737-8JP/W	39444/3965		Johan Ludvig Runeberg
☐ LN-NIB	Boeing 737-86J/W	36879/3805	ex D-ABMA	
☐ LN-NIC	Boeing 737-8JP/W	38881/4316	ex N5515X	Fredrikke Marie Qvam
☐ LN-NID	Boeing 737-8JP/W	40544/4474		Christina Nilsson
☐ LN-NIE	Boeing 737-8JP/W	39435/4330		Asta Nielsen
☐ LN-NIF	Boeing 737-8JP/W	39434/4337		Minna Canth
☐ LN-NIG	Boeing 737-8JP/W	43878/5123		♦
☐ LN-NIH	Boeing 737-8JP/W	43879/5177		♦
☐ LN-NII	Boeing 737-8JP/W	43877/5204		♦
☐ LN-NOF	Boeing 737-86N/W	36809/2647		
☐ LN-NOG	Boeing 737-86N/W	35647/2927	ex N1786B	
☐ LN-NOH	Boeing 737-86N/W	36814/3015	ex N1779B	Selma Lagerlof
☐ LN-NOI	Boeing 737-86N/W	36820/3131		
☐ LN-NOM	Boeing 737-86N/W	28642/813	ex SE-RHA	
☐ LN-NON	Boeing 737-86N/W	28620/542	ex SE-RHB	
☐ LN-NOO	Boeing 737-86Q/W	30289/1399	ex N289CG	
☐ LN-NOR	Boeing 737-81D/W	39412/3553		
☐ LN-NOT	Boeing 737-8JP/W	37816/3194	ex N1796B	
☐ LN-NOU	Boeing 737-8FZ/W	29674/3140	ex N1787B	
☐ LN-NOW	Boeing 737-8JP/W	37817/3364	ex N1796B	Oda Krohg
☐ LN-NOX	Boeing 737-8JP/W	37818/3384		
☐ LN-NOY	Boeing 737-8JP/W	39419/3878		Knud Rasmussen
☐ LN-NOZ	Boeing 737-8JP/W	39420/3891		Gidsken Jakobsen
☐ OY-LHA	ATR 72-202	508	ex OY-RTC	<DTR

NORWEGIAN LONG HAUL		Norstar (DY/NLH)		Oslo-Gardermoen (OSL)
☐ EI-LNA	Boeing 787-8	35304/102	ex (LN-BKA)	Sonia Henie
☐ EI-LNB	Boeing 787-8	35305/112	ex (LN-BKB)	Thor Heyerdahl
☐ EI-LNC	Boeing 787-8	34795/136		
☐ EI-LND	Boeing 787-8	35310/153		Grete Waitz
☐ EI-LNE	Boeing 787-8	34796/165		Roald Amundsen
☐ EI-LNF	Boeing 787-8	35313/178		♦
☐ EI-LNG	Boeing 787-8	35314/183		Edvard Munch ♦
☐ EI-LNH	Boeing 787-8	36526/279		HC Andersen ♦
☐ EI-	Boeing 787-9	37307/400		o/o♦

SCANDINAVIAN AIRLINE SYSTEM	Scandinavian (SK/SAS)	Copenhagen-Kastrup (CPH)

For details see under Sweden (SE-)

SUNDT AIR		Midnight (MDT)		Oslo-Gardermoen (OSL)
☐ LN-ANP	Beech B200 Super King Air	BB-1971	ex N779BZ	
☐ LN-KYV	Beech 350ER King Air	FL-745	ex N80245	opf Kystverket
☐ LN-NOA	Beech B200 Super King Air	BB-829	ex N829AJ	
☐ LN-SOV	Cessna 680 Sovereign	680-0183		

WIDERØE'S FLYVESELSKAP		Widerøe (WF/WIF)		Bodo (BOO)
☐ LN-ILS	de Havilland DHC-8-103	396	ex C-GHRI	
☐ LN-WIA	de Havilland DHC-8-103B	359	ex C-GHRI	Nordland
☐ LN-WIB	de Havilland DHC-8-103B	360	ex C-GFBW	Finnmark
☐ LN-WIC	de Havilland DHC-8-103B	367	ex C-GDNG	Sogn og Fjordane
☐ LN-WID	de Havilland DHC-8-103B	369	ex C-FDHD	More og Romsdal
☐ LN-WIE	de Havilland DHC-8-103B	371	ex C-GFYI	Hordaland
☐ LN-WIF	de Havilland DHC-8-103B	372	ex C-GFOD	Nord-Tröndelag
☐ LN-WIG	de Havilland DHC-8-103B	382	ex C-GLOT	Troms
☐ LN-WIH	de Havilland DHC-8-103B	383	ex C-GFYI	Oslo
☐ LN-WII	de Havilland DHC-8-103B	384	ex C-GFOD	Nordkapp

□ LN-WIJ	de Havilland DHC-8-103B	386	ex C-GFQL	Hammerfest
□ LN-WIL	de Havilland DHC-8-103B	398	ex C-GFCF	Narvik
□ LN-WIM	de Havilland DHC-8-103B	403	ex C-GDIU	Vesterälen
□ LN-WIN	de Havilland DHC-8-103B	409	ex C-GDNG	Alstadhaug/Lofoten
□ LN-WIO	de Havilland DHC-8-103B	417	ex C-GFQL	Rost/Akershus
□ LN-WIP	de Havilland DHC-8-103A	239	ex C-FXNE	Alstahaug
□ LN-WIR	de Havilland DHC-8-103A	273	ex C-FZNU	Nordkyn
□ LN-WIT	de Havilland DHC-8-103	310	ex D-BIER	
□ LN-WIU	de Havilland DHC-8-103	378	ex C-FZKQ	
□ LN-WIV	de Havilland DHC-8-103	343	ex C-GJMQ	
□ LN-WFC	de Havilland DHC-8-311A	236	ex D-BEYT	
□ LN-WFH	de Havilland DHC-8-311A	238	ex C-FZOH	
□ LN-WFO	de Havilland DHC-8-311Q	493	ex C-GERC	
□ LN-WFP	de Havilland DHC-8-311Q	495	ex C-GFUM	
□ LN-WFS	de Havilland DHC-8-311Q	535	ex C-GEWI	Telemark
□ LN-WFT	de Havilland DHC-8-311Q	532	ex C-FATN	
□ LN-WFU	de Havilland DHC-8-314Q	592	ex OY-CJY	
□ LN-RDV	de Havilland DHC-8-402Q	4054	ex HA-LQA	
□ LN-RDY	de Havilland DHC-8-402Q	4062	ex HA-LQC	
□ LN-RDZ	de Havilland DHC-8-402Q	4063	ex HA-LQD	
□ LN-WDE	de Havilland DHC-8-402Q	4183	ex C-FNEC	
□ LN-WDF	de Havilland DHC-8-402Q	4244	ex C-FUTZ	
□ LN-WDG	de Havilland DHC 8-402Q	4266	ex C-FXJF	
□ LN-WDH	de Havilland DHC-8-402Q	4273	ex C-FYGI	
□ LN-WDI	de Havilland DHC-8-402Q	4286	ex C-FZFX	
□ LN-WDJ	de Havilland DHC-8-402Q	4290	ex C-GARX	
□ LN-WDK	de Havilland DHC-8-402Q	4337	ex C-GGIR	
□ LN-WDL	de Havilland DHC-8-402Q	4392	ex C-GLKA	Vestfold
□ LN-WSA	de Havilland DHC-8-202	435	ex C-GLUD	
□ LN-WSB	de Havilland DHC-8-202	440	ex C-GLUF	
□ LN-WSC	de Havilland DHC-8-202	441	ex C-GLUG	

LV- ARGENTINA (Republic of Argentina)

AEROLINEAS ARGENTINAS   *Argentina (AR/ARG)*   **Buenos Aires-Ezeiza (EZE)**

Member of SkyTeam

□ LV-FNI	Airbus A330-223	290	ex P4-TWM		
□ LV-FNJ	Airbus A330-223	300	ex P4-DLK		
□ LV-FNK	Airbus A330-223	358	ex EI-CXF		
□ LV-FNL	Airbus A330-243	364	ex EI-CXG		
□ LV-FVH	Airbus A330-202	1605	ex F-WWCQ		♦
□ LV-FVI	Airbus A330-202	1623	ex F-WWYQ		♦
□ LV-CEK	Airbus A340-312	094	ex EI-EHZ		
□ LV-CSD	Airbus A340-313X	123	ex B-HXM		
□ LV-CSE	Airbus A340-313X	126	ex B-HXN		
□ LV-CSF	Airbus A340-313X	128	ex B-HXO		
□ LV-CSX	Airbus A340-313X	373	ex F-GNIH		
□ LV-FPV	Airbus A340-313X	193	ex EC-GPB	SkyTeam c/s	
□ LV-FPU	Airbus A340-313X	170	ex G-CHSJ		
□ LV-ZPJ	Airbus A340-211	074	ex F-OHPG		[VCV]
□ LV-ZPX	Airbus A340-211	080	ex F-OHPH		[VCV]
□ LV-ZRA	Airbus A340-211	085	ex F-OHPI		[EZE]
□ LV-BYY	Boeing 737-7BD	33938/2863	ex N357AT		
□ LV-BZA	Boeing 737-76N/W	32674/1952	ex OK-GCA		
□ LV-BZO	Boeing 737-76N/W	32676/1974	ex OK-GCB		
□ LV-CAD	Boeing 737-76N/W	32680/2089	ex OK-GCC		
□ LV-CAM	Boeing 737-73V/W	30243/919	ex N243CL		
□ LV-CAP	Boeing 737-76N/W	32695/1919	ex OK-GCD		
□ LV-CBF	Boeing 737-76N/W	32696/1922	ex OK-GCE		
□ LV-CBG	Boeing 737-73V/W	30235/672	ex N384DF		
□ LV-CBS	Boeing 737-73V/W	30236/715	ex N385DF		
□ LV-CBT	Boeing 737-76N/W	34756/2208	ex OK-GCF		
□ LV-CCR	Boeing 737-73V/W	30237/730	ex N386DF		
□ LV-CMK	Boeing 737-7Q8/W	28240/832	ex N721LF		
□ LV-CPH	Boeing 737-7Q8/W	28238/817	ex N711LF		
□ LV-CSC	Boeing 737-7Q8/W	30630/1032	ex N351LF		
□ LV-CSI	Boeing 737-7Q8/W	30707975	ex N331LF		
□ LV-CVX	Boeing 737-7Q8/W	30641/1080	ex N151LF		
□ LV-CWL	Boeing 737-7Q8/W	30644/1107	ex N161LF		
□ LV-CXN	Boeing 737-7Q8/W	30638/858	ex N272LF		
□ LV-CYJ	Boeing 737-7Q8/W	30647/1159	ex N225LF		
□ LV-CYN	Boeing 737-7Q8/W	30648/1171	ex N301LF		
□ LV-CYO	Boeing 737-7Q8/W	30633/1220	ex N381LF		
□ LV-GOO	Boeing 737-7BD	35962/2932	ex N358AT		

☐ LV-CTB	Boeing 737-85F/W	30478/997	ex N478MQ		
☐ LV-CTC	Boeing 737-86J/W	30570/879	ex N570MQ		
☐ LV-CXS	Boeing 737-81D/W	39425/4167			
☐ LV-CXT	Boeing 737-81D/W	39426/4186			
☐ LV-FQB	Boeing 737-86J/W	36886/3777	ex D-ABKY		
☐ LV-FQC	Boeing 737-86J/W	37744/3694	ex D-ABKU		
☐ LV-FQY	Boeing 737-81D/W	39436/4764			
☐ LV-FQZ	Boeing 737-81D/W	41563/5086	ex N1796B		
☐ LV-FRK	Boeing 737-8BK/W	41560/4759			
☐ LV-FRQ	Boeing 737-8BK/W	41561/4860	ex N5573P		
☐ LV-FSK	Boeing 737-81D/W	41562/4960			
☐ LV-FUA	Boeing 737-8HX/W	40548/4995			
☐ LV-FUB	Boeing 737-81D/W	39893/5056			
☐ LV-FUC	Boeing 737-8SH/W	41347/5169			♦
☐ LV-FVM	Boeing 737-8SH/W	41329/5313			♦
☐ LV-FVN	Boeing 737-8SH/W	41331/5373			♦
☐ LV-BNM	Boeing 737-5K5	24926/1966	ex D-AHLD		[SFM]
☐ LV-VBX	McDonnell-Douglas MD-88	53047/2016		Parque Nacional Lanin	[UAQ]

AEROLINEAS FEDERAL ARGENTINA

☐ LV-ZPZ	British Aerospace Jetstream 32EP	931	ex N931AE

AMERICAN JET | Buenos Aires-Aeroparque (AEP)

☐ LV-BYJ	Swearingen SA227DC Metro 23	DC-889B	ex N889AJ
☐ LV-BYM	Swearingen SA227DC Metro 23	DC-856B	ex N3027B
☐ LV-BYN	Swearingen SA227DC Metro 23	DC-888B	ex N332AJ
☐ LV-CZJ	ATR 42-320	257	ex LV-CZJ
☐ LV-WTV	Dornier 228-201	8093	ex N228BM

ANDES LINEAS AEREAS | Aeroandes (OY/ANS) | Salta International (SLA)

☐ LV-AYD	McDonnell-Douglas MD-83	53015/1818	ex N824NK
☐ LV-BGV	McDonnell-Douglas MD-83	49904/1680	ex N960PG
☐ LV-CCJ	McDonnell-Douglas MD-83	49621/1495	ex EC-FTS
☐ LV-WGM	McDonnell-Douglas MD-83	49784/1627	ex N509MD

ARJET AIRLINES | Buenos Aires-Aeroparque (AEP)

☐ LV-ZYY	Boeing 737-236	21799/660	ex N914PG

AUSTRAL LINEAS AEREAS | Austral (AU/AUT) | Buenos Aires-Aeroparque (AEP)

☐ LV-CDY	Embraer ERJ-190AR	19000365	ex PT-XNE	
☐ LV-CDZ	Embraer ERJ-190AR	19000377	ex PT-XXN	
☐ LV-CET	Embraer ERJ-190AR	19000383	ex PT-XNR	
☐ LV-CEU	Embraer ERJ-190AR	19000389	ex PT-XNW	
☐ LV-CEV	Embraer ERJ-190AR	19000390	ex PT-XNX	
☐ LV-CHO	Embraer ERJ-190AR	19000395	ex PT-XUB	
☐ LV-CHQ	Embraer ERJ-190AR	19000397	ex PT-XUC	
☐ LV-CHR	Embraer ERJ-190AR	19000400	ex PT-TYF	
☐ LV-CHS	Embraer ERJ-190AR	19000402	ex PT-TYV	
☐ LV-CID	Embraer ERJ-190AR	19000409	ex PT-TBH	
☐ LV-CIE	Embraer ERJ-190AR	19000414	ex PT-TBL	
☐ LV-CIF	Embraer ERJ-190AR	19000421	ex PT-TBX	
☐ LV-CIG	Embraer ERJ-190AR	19000427	ex PT-TCL	
☐ LV-CIH	Embraer ERJ-190AR	19000428	ex PT-TCO	
☐ LV-CKZ	Embraer ERJ-190AR	19000439	ex PT-TCY	
☐ LV-CMA	Embraer ERJ-190AR	19000445	ex PT-TJF	
☐ LV-CMB	Embraer ERJ-190AR	19000448	ex PT-TJH	
☐ LV-CPI	Embraer ERJ-190AR	19000457	ex PT-TNY	
☐ LV-CPJ	Embraer ERJ-190AR	19000463	ex PT-TOG	
☐ LV-CPK	Embraer ERJ-190AR	19000474	ex PT-TOV	
☐ LV-FPS	Embraer ERJ-190AR	19000639	ex PR-ECH	SkyTeam c/s
☐ LV-FPT	Embraer ERJ-190AR	19000640	ex PR-ECI	SkyTeam c/s

BAIRES FLY | Buenos Aires-Aeroparque (AEP)

☐ LV-VDJ	Swearingen SA227AC Metro III	AC-729	ex N27283
☐ LV-WHG	Swearingen SA226TC Metro II	TC-344	ex N44CS
☐ LV-WJT	Swearingen SA227AC Metro III	AC-776B	ex N776NE
☐ LV-WTE	Swearingen SA227AC Metro III	AC-584	ex LV-PMF
☐ LV-ZMG	Swearingen SA227AC Metro III	AC-425	ex N721MA
☐ LV-CZX	Learjet 60	60-167	ex M-WISO
☐ LV-FUF	Learjet 60	60-165	ex N929GV

FLYING AMERICA				Buenos Aires-Aeroparque (AEP)	
☐ LV-BGH	Swearingen SA227AC Metro III	AC-467	ex TF-JMK		
☐ LV-YIC	Swearingen SA227AC Metro III	AC-448	ex LV-PNF		

HANGAR UNO				Buenos Aires-Don Torcuato	
☐ LV-WFR	Britten-Norman BN-2B-26 Islander	2263	ex G-BUBF	Puerto Carmelo titles	

HAWK AIR		Air Hawk (HKR)		Buenos Aires-Aeroparque (AEP)	
☐ LV-WHX	Piper PA-31 Turbo Navajo	31-353	ex N716DR		
☐ LV-WIR	Swearingen SA226T Merlin III	T-232	ex N56TA		Frtr
☐ LV-WNC	Swearingen SA226AT Merlin IVA	AT-036	ex N642TS		Frtr

LADE - LINEAS AEREAS DEL ESTADO		Lade (5U/LDE)		Comodoro Rivadavia (CRD)	
☐ T-81	de Havilland DHC-6 Twin Otter 200	165			
☐ T-82	de Havilland DHC-6 Twin Otter 200	167			
☐ T-85	de Havilland DHC-6 Twin Otter 200	173			
☐ T-86	de Havilland DHC-6 Twin Otter 200	225		Antarctic red c/s	
☐ T-87	de Havilland DHC-6 Twin Otter 200	158	ex LV-JMP		
☐ T-89	de Havilland DHC-6 Twin Otter 200	185	ex LV-JPX		
☐ T-90	de Havilland DI IC-6 Twin Otter 200	178	ex LV-JMR		
☐ T-31	SAAB SF.340B	340B-270	ex N284DC		
☐ T-32	SAAB SF.340B	340B-226	ex N285DC		
☐ T-33	SAAB SF.340B	340B-288	ex N288JJ		
☐ T-34	SAAB SF.340B	340B-217	ex N217JJ		

LAN ARGENTINA		Aero Dosmil (4M/DSM)		Buenos Aires-Aeroparque (AEP)	
☐ LV-BET	Airbus A320-233	1854	ex CC-COO		
☐ LV-BFO	Airbus A320-233	1877	ex CC-COQ		
☐ LV-BFY	Airbus A320-233	1858	ex CC-COP		
☐ LV-BGI	Airbus A320-233	1903	ex CC-COT		
☐ LV-BHU	Airbus A320-233	1512	ex CC-COH		
☐ LV-BOI	Airbus A320-233	1491	ex CC-COG		
☐ LV-BRA	Airbus A320-233	1304	ex CC-COC		
☐ LV-BRY	Airbus A320-233	1351	ex CC-COE		
☐ LV-BSJ	Airbus A320-233	1332	ex CC-COD		
☐ LV-BTM	Airbus A320-233	1548	ex CC-COK		
☐ LV-CQS	Airbus A320-233	1526	ex CC-COI		
☐ LV-FUX	Airbus A320-233	4543	ex CC-BAI		♦
☐ LV-CDQ	Boeing 767-316ER/W	35229/949	ex CC-CWN		
☐ LV-CFV	Boeing 767-316ER/W	34629/944	ex CC-CWG		

MACAIR JET		Jetmac (MCJ)		Buenos Aires-Aeroparque (AEP)	
☐ LV-ZOW	British Aerospace Jetstream 32EP	869	ex N869AE		
☐ LV-ZPW	British Aerospace Jetstream 32EP	861	ex N861AE		
☐ LV-ZRL	British Aerospace Jetstream 32EP	928	ex N928AE		
☐ LV-ZSB	British Aerospace Jetstream 32EP	942	ex N942AE		
☐ LV-ZST	British Aerospace Jetstream 32EP	941	ex N941AE		wfs

SERVICIOS AEREOS PATAGONICOS					
☐ LV-RBP	Swearingen SA227AC Metro III	AC-415	ex N173MA		
☐ LV-RBR	Swearingen SA227AC Metro III	AC-416	ex N177MA		
☐ LV-ZXA	Swearingen SA227DC Metro 23	DC-901B	ex LV-PIR	no titles	

SOL LINEAS AEREAS		Flight Sol (8R/OLS)		Rosario-Fisherton (ROS)	
☐ LV-BEW	SAAB SF.340A	340A-150	ex N150CN		
☐ LV-CEI	SAAB SF.340A	340A-012	ex N108PX		
☐ LV-CSK	SAAB SF.340B	340B-168	ex SE-LJR		
☐ LV-CYC	SAAB SF.340B	340B-310	ex N470LH		

TAPSA		Tapsa (V8/TPS)		Buenos Aires-Aeroparque (AEP)	
☐ LV-LSI	de Havilland DHC-6 Twin Otter 300	456	ex LV-PTW		

TRANSPORTES BRAGADO				Buenos Aires-Aeroparque (AEP)	
☐ LV-ZNU	Cessna 208B Caravan I	208B0718	ex LV-POC		

UNION AIR					
☐ LV-BGR	Swearingen SA227AC Metro III	AC-461B	ex EC-HXY		

LX-   LUXEMBOURG (Grand Duchy of Luxembourg)

CARGOLUX INTERNATIONAL AIRLINES   Cargolux (CV/CLX)   Luxembourg (LUX)

☐	LX-ACV	Boeing 747-4B5F	24200/748	ex D-ALAA	
☐	LX-DCV	Boeing 747-4B5BCF	24619/793	ex N790BA	
☐	LX-ECV	Boeing 747-4HQERF	37303/1416	ex N797BA	♦
☐	LX-JCV	Boeing 747-4EVERF	35171/1380	ex N558CL	o/o♦
☐	LX-OCV	Boeing 747-4R7F	29731/1222	Differdange	
☐	LX-RCV	Boeing 747-4R7F	30400/1235	Monviso	>ICV
☐	LX-SCV	Boeing 747-4R7F	29733/1281	Niederanven	
☐	LX-UCV	Boeing 747-4R7F	33827/1345	Bertrange	
☐	LX-VCV	Boeing 747-4R7F	34235/1366	City of Anchorage	
☐	LX-WCV	Boeing 747-4R7F	35804/1390	ex N5022E	Pétange	
☐	LX-YCV	Boeing 747-4R7F	35805/1407	City of Contern	>ICV
☐	LX-VCA	Boeing 747-8R7F	35808/1420	ex N5020K	City of Vianden	
☐	LX-VCB	Boeing 747-8R7F	35806/1423	ex N5014K	City of Esch-sur-Aizette	
☐	LX-VCC	Boeing 747-8R7F	35807/1424	ex N5573S	City of Ettelbruck	
☐	LX-VCD	Boeing 747-8R7F	35809/1436	City of Luxembourg	
☐	LX-VCE	Boeing 747-8R7F	35810/1454	City of Echternach	
☐	LX-VCF	Boeing 747-8R7F	35811/1461	City ofZhengzhou	
☐	LX-VCG	Boeing 747-8R7F	35812/1465	City of Diekirch	
☐	LX-VCH	Boeing 747-8R7F	35821/1473	ex N765BA	City of Troisvierges	
☐	LX-VCI	Boeing 747-8R7F	35822/1478	ex N775BA	City of Zhengzhou	
☐	LX-VCJ	Boeing 747-8R7F	38077/1490	ex N803BA	City of Zhengzhou	
☐	LX-VCK	Boeing 747-8R7F	38078/1491	ex N975BA	City of Contern	
☐	LX-VCL	Boeing 747-8R7F	35823/1504	ex N820BA	Joe Sutter-Father of the Boeing 747	♦
☐	LX-VCM	Boeing 747-8R7F	61169/1522	o/o♦

LUXAIR   Luxair (LG/LGL)   Luxembourg (LUX)

☐	LX-LGE	de Havilland DHC-8-402Q	4284	ex C-FXYV
☐	LX-LGF	de Havilland DHC-8-402Q	4349	ex C-GHDB
☐	LX-LGG	de Havilland DHC-8-402Q	4418	ex C-GOEA
☐	LX-LGH	de Havilland DHC-8-402Q	4420	ex C-GPID
☐	LX-LGM	de Havilland DHC-8-402Q	4425	ex C-GRSE
☐	LX-LGN	de Havilland DHC-8-402Q	4426	ex C-GRSO
☐	LX-LQA	de Havilland DHC-8-402Q	4468	ex C-GYPO
☐	LX-LGI	Embraer ERJ-145LU	145369	ex PT-SOU
☐	LX-LGJ	Embraer ERJ-145LU	145395	ex PT-SQS
☐	LX-LGW	Embraer ERJ-145LU	145135	ex PT-SDM
☐	LX-LGX	Embraer ERJ-145LU	145147	ex PT-SDX
☐	LX-LGY	Embraer ERJ-145LU	145242	ex PT-SIH
☐	LX-LGZ	Embraer ERJ-145LU	145258	ex PT-SIR
☐	F-HJUL	Boeing 737-8Q8/W	38819/3519	<XLF♦
☐	LX-LBA	Boeing 737-8C9/W	43537/5293	♦
☐	LX-LGQ	Boeing 737-7C9/W	33802/1442	Chateau de Berg
☐	LX-LGS	Boeing 737-7C9/W	33956/1634	Chateau de Senningen
☐	LX-LGU	Boeing 737-8C9/W	41047/4272	
☐	LX-LGV	Boeing 737-8C9/W	41190/4755	

SMART CARGO   West Lux (WLX)   Luxembourg (LUX)

☐	LX-WAE	British Aerospace ATP (LFD)	2037	ex SE-MAP

LY-   LITHUANIA (Republic of Lithuania)

AIR LITUANICA   (LT/LTU)   Vilnius (VNO)

☐	LY-LTF	Embraer ERJ-175LR	17000017	ex PP-PJD

AVIAVILSA   Aviavilsa (LVS)   Vilnius (VNO)

☐	LY-ETM	ATR 42-300F	067	ex (SE-MAS)	<DNU

AVION EXPRESS   Nordvind (X9/NVD)   Vilnius (VNO)

☐	LY-COM	Airbus A320-212	0528	ex VP-BRB	>CUB
☐	LY-VEJ	Airbus A320-232	2275	ex M-ABIN	>VLG♦
☐	LY-VEK	Airbus A320-232	2108	ex M-ABIK	>TCX♦
☐	LY-VEL	Airbus A320-232	1998	ex EI-EUB	>CFG♦
☐	LY-VEM	Airbus A320-233	0747	ex EI-FBB	>VLG♦
☐	LY-VEN	Airbus A320-233	1626	ex CC-COM	>TCX♦
☐	LY-VEO	Airbus A320-233	0558	ex F-ORAD	>VLG♦
☐	LY-VEQ	Airbus A320-214	0709	ex B-2459	>CUB
☐	LY-VES	Airbus A320-212	0466	ex N466AG	>RCT

☐ LY-VEV	Airbus A320-211	0211	ex G-YRGW	>CUB
☐ LY-VEW	Airbus A320-214	1005	ex N115MT	>CUB♦
☐ LY-VEZ	Airbus A320-212	0299	ex PH-AAZ	[YMX]
☐ LY-VET	Airbus A319-112	1778	ex N718CT	

DOT - DANU ORO TRANSPORTAS   Danu (R6/DNU)   Vilnius (VNO)

☐ LY-ARI	ATR 42-300	012A	ex F-WQBT	>SEH
☐ LY-DAT	ATR 42-500	445	ex F-WKVF	
☐ LY-ETM	ATR 42-300F	067	ex (SE-MAS)	>LVR
☐ LY-OOV	ATR 42-300F	005	ex EI-SLD	
☐ LY-RUM	ATR 42-300F	010	ex OY-RUM	
☐ LY-MCA	ATR 72-212A	212	ex SE-MCA	
☐ LY-RUN	SAAB SF.340A	340A-086	ex G-RUNG	<DTR
☐ LY-RUS	SAAB SF.340A	340A-074	ex SE-LTO	

GRAND CRU AIRLINES   (GCA)   Vilnius (VNO)

☐ LY-GCG	Boeing 737-4Y0	23870/1647	ex N870AG	♦
☐ LY-GGC	Boeing 737-3Q8	24492/1808	ex N225LF	
☐ LY-LGC	Boeing 737-382	24365/1695	ex OM-BEX	♦

SMALL PLANET AIRLINES   Small Planet (S5/LLC)   Vilnius (VNO)

☐ LY-SPA	Airbus A320-232	1715	ex EI-EZN	
☐ LY-SPB	Airbus A320-232	2987	ex P4-UAS	
☐ LY-SPC	Airbus A320-231	0415	ex EI-ETM	>LLP
☐ LY-SPD	Airbus A320-232	0990	ex VN-A195	
☐ LY-ONJ	Airbus A320-214	4203	ex 5A-ONJ	o/o♦
☐ LY-ONL	Airbus A320-214	4489	ex 5A-ONL	o/o♦
☐ LY-AQX	Boeing 737-322	24664/1877	ex SP-HAA	wfs
☐ LY-AWD	Boeing 737-522	26739/2494	ex C-FDCU	>VSV
☐ LY-AWE	Boeing 737-522	26684/2388	ex C-FCFR	>VSV
☐ LY-AWF	Boeing 737-522	26707/2512	ex C-FDCZ	>TJK
☐ LY-AWG	Boeing 737-522	26700/2490	ex C-FDCH	>TJK
☐ LY-AWH	Boeing 737-3Y0	23924/1542	ex N924RM	>VSV
☐ LY-FLB	Boeing 737-322/W	24667/1893	ex ES-LBA	
☐ LY-FLH	Boeing 737-382	25161/2226	ex N161AN	
☐ LY-SPE	Boeing 737-31S	29055/2923	ex LY-FLC	
☐ LY-AZV	Boeing 737-76N/W	37233/2578	ex EI-IGP	>VSV♦
☐ LY-FLG	Boeing 757-204	27237/602	ex G-BYAR	>VSV

TRANSAVIABALTIKA   Transbaltika (KTB)   Kaunus-Karmelava (KUN)

☐ LY-AVA	LET L-410UVP-E3	882036	ex Soviet AF 2036	
☐ LY-AVT	LET L-410UVP-E3	882033	ex Soviet AF 2033	
☐ LY-AVZ	LET L-410UVP-E	892336	ex RA-67610	

LZ-   BULGARIA (Republic of Bulgaria)

AIR BRIGHT   (RBI)   Plovdiv (PDV)

| ☐ LZ-ABR | Antonov An-26B | 13905 | ex YL-RAJ | |

AIR MAX   Aeromax (RMX)   Plovdiv (PDV)

☐ LZ-MNG	LET L-410UVP	841326	ex HA-LAY	[SOF]
☐ LZ-RMK	LET L-410UVP	851406	ex UR-67502	wfs
☐ LZ-RMV	LET L-410UVP-E	892215	ex HA-LAV	
☐ LZ-RMW	LET L-410UVP-E8A	902517	ex HA-LAE	

AIR SCORPIO   Scorpio Univers (SCU)   Sofia (SOF)

| ☐ LZ-CCB | Cessna 402B | 402B0581 | ex EC-HDF | |
| ☐ LZ-SAB | SAAB SF.340AF | 340A-020 | ex S5-BAM | |

AVIOSTART   (VSR)   Sofia (SOF)

| ☐ LZ-DAL | British Aerospace 146 Srs.200 | E2074 | ex ZS-PUZ | [SOF] |

BALKAN HOLIDAYS

| ☐ LZ-KBH | Kamov Ka-32A11BC | 8807 | ex LZ-MRA | |

BH AIR   Balkan Holidays (8H/BGH)   Sofia (SOF)

☐ LZ-BHB	Airbus A320-212	0294	ex OY-CNP	[MZJ]
☐ LZ-BHE	Airbus A320-211	0305	ex EI-DNK	
☐ LZ-BHF	Airbus A320-214	1087	ex EC-HDN	>VJC
☐ LZ-BHG	Airbus A320-232	2844	ex VT-INA	
☐ LZ-BHH	Airbus A320-232	2863	ex VT-INB	>AGY
☐ LZ-AOA	Airbus A319-112	3139	ex D-ABGE	
☐ LZ-AWA	Airbus A330-223	255	ex JY-JAJ	♦

BRIGHT FLIGHT   Sofia (SOF)

☐ LZ-FLA	Antonov An-26B	12010	ex HA-LCU	♦
☐ LZ-FLL	Antonov An-26B	12210	ex HA-LCV	♦

BULGARIA AIR   Flying Bulgaria (FB/LZB)   Sofia (SOF)

☐ LZ-ATS	ATR 42-300	130	ex F-WQNO	wfs
☐ LZ-BOT	Boeing 737-322	24665/1889	ex YU-AOU	♦
☐ LZ-BUR	Embraer ERJ-190AR	19000551	ex PT-TBV	
☐ LZ-FBA	Airbus A319-112	3564	ex D-AVWS	
☐ LZ-FBB	Airbus A319-112	3309	ex EI-DZW	
☐ LZ-FBC	Airbus A320-214	2540	ex EC-JMB	>OHY
☐ LZ-FBD	Airbus A320-214	2596	ex EC-JNA	>OHY
☐ LZ-FBE	Airbus A320-214	3780	ex D-AVVI	
☐ LZ-FBF	Airbus A319-111	3028	ex N950FR	
☐ LZ-HBB	British Aerospace 146 Srs.200	E2073	ex VH-NJU	[SOF]
☐ LZ-HBC	British Aerospace 146 Srs.200	E2093	ex VH-JJS	[SOF]
☐ LZ-HBZ	British Aerospace 146 Srs.200	E2103	ex G-JEAK	
☐ LZ-PLO	Embraer ERJ-190AR	19000584	ex PT-TGW	
☐ LZ-SOF	Embraer ERJ-190AR	19000492	ex PT-TPQ	
☐ LZ-TIM	Avro 146-RJ70	E1258	ex EI-CPJ	opf Bulgarian Govt
☐ LZ-VAR	Embraer ERJ-190AR	19000496	ex PT-TPT	

BULGARIAN AIR CHARTER   Bulgarian Charter (H6/BUC)   Sofia (SOF)

☐ LZ-LDC	McDonnell-Douglas MD-82	49217/1268	ex I-DAVC	[SOF]
☐ LZ-LDF	McDonnell-Douglas MD-82	49219/1310	ex I-DAVF	[SOF]
☐ LZ-LDG	McDonnell-Douglas MD-83	53149/1817	ex TC-FLN	
☐ LZ-LDJ	McDonnell-Douglas MD-82	53230/2106	ex I-DATM	[FCO]
☐ LZ-LDK	McDonnell-Douglas MD-82	49432/1378	ex I-DAVK	
☐ LZ-LDM	McDonnell-Douglas MD-82	53228/2104	ex EK-82228	
☐ LZ-LDN	McDonnell-Douglas MD-82	53216/2048	ex I-DATA	wfs
☐ LZ-LDP	McDonnell-Douglas MD-82	49973/1762	ex I-DACP	>MSA
☐ LZ-LDU	McDonnell-Douglas MD-82	53204/2009	ex I-DANU	
☐ LZ-LDS	McDonnell-Douglas MD-82	53218/2060	ex I-DATI	
☐ LZ-LDT	McDonnell-Douglas MD-82	53058/1927	ex I-DACZ	
☐ LZ-LDW	McDonnell-Douglas MD-82	49795/1639	ex I-DAVV	
☐ LZ-LDY	McDonnell-Douglas MD-82	49213/1243	ex I-DAWY	

CARGO AIR   (CGF)   Sofia (SOF)

☐ LZ-CGO	Boeing 737-301F	23237/1222	ex N503UW	
☐ LZ-CGP	Boeing 737-35BF	23970/1467	ex N221DL	
☐ LZ-CGQ	Boeing 737-3Y5F	25614/2467	ex N413BC	
☐ LZ-CGR	Boeing 737-448SF	24474/1742	ex N474EA	
☐ LZ-CGS	Boeing 737-4Q8SF	26306/2653	ex N831AV	

HELI AIR SERVICES   Heli Bulgaria (HLR)   Sofia (SOF)

☐ LZ-CCP	LET L-410UVP-E8C	912540	ex OK-WDA		opf UN
☐ LZ-CCQ	LET L-410UVP-E20	072621	ex OK-KIN		opf UN
☐ LZ-CCR	LET L-410UVP-E10	892301	ex SP-FTX		opf UN
☐ LZ-CCS	LET L-410UVP-E	902425	ex 3D-EER		opf UN
☐ LZ-CCT	LET L-410UVP-E20	912528	ex ST-DND		opf UN
☐ LZ-CCV	LET L-410UVP-E20	2720	ex OK-SLT		opf UN
☐ LZ-CCW	LET L-410UVP-E	912609	ex ES-LLC		opf UN
☐ LZ-LSB	LET L-410UVP-E2	861802		no titles	opf UN
☐ LZ-CEA	Agusta A109K2	10002	ex HB-XWB		

VIA - AIR VIA   Via Airways (VL/VIM)   Varna (VAR)

☐ LZ-MDA	Airbus A320-232	2732	ex F-WWBE	
☐ LZ-MDC	Airbus A320-232	4270	ex F-WWBS	>WOW
☐ LZ-MDD	Airbus A320-232	4305	ex F-WWDZ	>WOW
☐ LZ-MDR	Airbus A320-232	5158	ex D-AXAC	
☐ LZ-WOW	Airbus A320-232	2457	ex EI-EZG	>WOW

N   UNITED STATES OF AMERICA

ABX AIR		Abex (GB/ABX)		Wilmington-Airborne Airpark, OH (ILN)
☐ N226CY	Boeing 767-383ER BDSF	26544/412	ex EC-LKI	♦
☐ N315AA	Boeing 767-223SF	22317/109		
☐ N739AX	Boeing 767-232SCD	22216/26	ex N104DA	
☐ N740AX	Boeing 767-232SCD	22213/6	ex N101DA	
☐ N744AX	Boeing 767-232SCD	22221/53	ex N109DL	
☐ N745AX	Boeing 767-232SCD	22222/56	ex N110DL	
☐ N750AX	Boeing 767-232SCD	22227/83	ex N115DA	
☐ N752AX	Boeing 767-281F	23434/171	ex JA8255	
☐ N767AX	Boeing 767-281F	22785/51	ex JA8479	
☐ N768AX	Boeing 767-281F	22786/54	ex JA8480	
☐ N769AX	Boeing 767-281F	22787/58	ex JA8481	
☐ N773AX	Boeing 767-281F	22788/61	ex JA8482	
☐ N774AX	Boeing 767-281F	22789/67	ex JA8483	
☐ N775AX	Boeing 767-281F	22790/69	ex JA8484	
☐ N783AX	Boeing 767-281F	23016/80	ex JA8485	
☐ N787AX	Boeing 767-281F	23020/96	ex JA8489	
☐ N788AX	Boeing 767-281F	23021/103	ex JA8490	
☐ N792AX	Boeing 767-281SCD	23142/110	ex JA8240	
☐ N793AX	Boeing 767-281F	23143/114	ex JA8241	
☐ N794AX	Boeing 767-281F	23144/115	ex JA8242	
☐ N795AX	Boeing 767-281F	23145/116	ex JA8243	
☐ N796AX	Boeing 767-281BDSF	23146/121	ex PR-IOH	wfs♦
☐ N797AX	Boeing 767-281F	23147/123	ex JA8245	
☐ N798AX	Boeing 767-281SCD	23431/143	ex JA8251 DHL c/s	
☐ N219CY	Boeing 767-383ER BDSF	24358/263	ex G-VKNI	
☐ N220CY	Boeing 767-383ER BDSF	24729/358	ex EC-LKV DHL c/s	
☐ N317CM	Boeing 767-338ERF	24317/246	ex VH-OGC	
☐ N362CM	Boeing 767-338ERF	24316/242	ex VH-OGB	
☐ N363CM	Boeing 767-338ER BDSF	24853/319	ex VH-OGF	
☐ N364CM	Boeing 767-338ER BDSF	24531/278	ex VH-OGE	

ADI CHARTER		(Y7/DYN)		Pontiac-Oakland, MI (PTK)
☐ N359AD	Embraer ERJ-145EP	145169	ex N978RP	>Tortug'Air♦
☐ N459AD	Embraer ERJ-145EP	145185	ex N977RP	♦
☐ N974RP	Embraer ERJ-145MP	145203	ex XA-GLI	<CHQ♦
☐ N975RP	Embraer ERJ-145MP	145337	ex XA-HLI	<CHQ♦
☐ N976RP	Embraer ERJ-145MP	145322	ex XA-KAC	<CHQ♦

AERO AIR				Hillsboro, OR
☐ N401US	Douglas DC-7	45145/767	ex N6331C	Tanker
☐ N756Z	Douglas DC-7BF	45400/864	ex N347AA	engine testbed
☐ N838D	Douglas DC-7B	45347/936		Tanker
☐ N6353C	Douglas DC-7	45486/964		Tanker

AERO-FLITE				Spokane-Intl, WA (GEG)
☐ N354AC	Avro 146-RJ85	E2256	ex G-CHIU	161	waterbomber
☐ N355AC	Avro 146-RJ85	E2293	ex G-CHDG	162	waterbomber
☐ N366AC	Avro 146-RJ85	E2288	ex G-CGZB		for conversion to waterbomber♦
☐ N374AC	Avro 146-RJ85	E2266	ex G-CGZO		for conversion to waterbomber♦
☐ N379AC	Avro 146-RJ85	E2246	ex G-CGYS		for spares♦
☐ N839AC	Avro 146-RJ85	E2270	ex G-CLHX	160	waterbomber
☐ N262NR	Canadair CL215	1081	ex C-GDRS	262	opf Minnesota DNR
☐ N263NR	Canadair CL215	1082	ex C-GENU	263	Lsd fr/opf Minnesota DNR
☐ N264V	Canadair CL215	1090	ex C-GOFM	264	
☐ N266NR	Canadair CL215	1102	ex C-GOFO	266	Lsd fr/opf Minnesota DNR
☐ N267V	Canadair CL215	1103	ex C-GOFP	267	
☐ N907AS	British Aerospace 146 Srs.200	E2156	ex OB-1948-P		wfs♦

AIR AMERICA				San Juan-Luis Munoz Marin Intl, PR (SJU)
☐ N21WW	Piper PA-23-250 Aztec E	27-7554066	ex N54754	
☐ N30PT	Cessna 421C Golden Eagle	421C0157	ex N5284J	
☐ N707TL	Beech 65-E90 King Air	LW-173	ex N1573L	
☐ N2395Z	Piper PA-23-250 Aztec F	27-7954107	ex (AN-LAS)	
☐ N7049T	Britten-Norman BN-2A-21 Islander	643	ex C-GPAB	
☐ N62749	Piper PA-23-250 Aztec F	27-7654198		

AIR ARCTIC — Fairbanks-Intl, AK (FAI)

☐ N42WP	Piper PA-31-350 Chieftain	31-8252038	ex N41063	
☐ N234CE	Piper PA-31-350 Chieftain	31-8052203	ex N4504B	<Northern Alaska
☐ N820FS	Piper PA-31-350 Chieftain	31-7952185	ex TF-VLA	
☐ N4434D	Piper PA-31-350 Chieftain	31-7552020	ex PH-ASC	
☐ N7164D	Piper PA-31-350 Chieftain	31-8052013	ex C-GBGI	
☐ N3582P	Piper PA-31-350 Chieftain	31-8052103		
☐ N3589B	Piper PA-31-350 Chieftain	31-8052134		
☐ N27755	Piper PA-31-350 Chieftain	31-7852148		
☐ N59826	Piper PA-31-350 Navajo Chieftain	31-7652077		

AIR CARGO CARRIERS — Night Cargo (2Q/SNC) — Milwaukee-General Mitchell Intl, WI (MKE)

☐ N106SW	Short SD.3-30	SH3072		♦
☐ N167RC	Short SD.3-30	SH3038	ex N690RA	
☐ N264AC	Short SD.3-30	SH3103	ex N264AG	
☐ N334AC	Short SD.3-30	SH3029	ex VH-LSI	
☐ N336MV	Short SD.3-30	SH3018	ex PJ-DDB	
☐ N390GA	Short SD.3-30	SH3077	ex 4X-CSP	
☐ N936MA	Short SD.3-30	SH3036	ex G-BGNI	
☐ N2629P	Short SD.3-30	SH3079	ex G-BJLL	
☐ N124CA	Short SD.3-60	SH3652	ex G-BLJS	
☐ N151CA	Short SD.3-60	SH3653	ex G-BLJT	
☐ N360AB	Short SD.3-60	SH3756	ex G-BPKZ	
☐ N360RW	Short SD.3-60	SH3613	ex C-FCRB	
☐ N360SA	Short SD.3-60	SH3601	ex G-WIDE	
☐ N367AC	Short SD.3-60	SH3626	ex VH-MVW	
☐ N368AC	Short SD.3-60	SH3651	ex VH-BWO	
☐ N376AC	Short SD.3-60	SH3736	ex G-VBAC	
☐ N386MQ	Short SD.3-60	SH3709		♦
☐ N601CA	Short SD.3-60	SH3623	ex G-BKWM	
☐ N618AN	Short SD.3-60	SH3691	ex N881BC	
☐ N642AN	Short SD.3-60	SH3661	ex C-GPCE	
☐ N688AN	Short SD.3-60	SH3633	ex C-GPCJ	
☐ N701A	Short SD.3-60	SH3627	ex G-BKZP	
☐ N733CH	Short SD.3-60	SH3733	ex N569FU	
☐ N972AA	Short SD.3-60	SH3754	ex N263GA	
☐ N973AA	Short SD.3-60	SH3749	ex N749JT	
☐ N974AA	Short SD.3-60	SH3742	ex N742CC	
☐ N3732X	Short SD.3-60	SH3732	ex PK-DSN	
☐ N4498Y	Short SD.3-60	SH3625	ex G-BKZN	
☐ N409MN	Cessna 208B Caravan I	208B0846	ex N51666	♦
☐ N750CK	Cessna 650 Citation	650-7015		♦
☐ N907DB	Beech 300 King Air	FA-85		♦
☐ N960AA	AMD Falcon 20C	144	ex N385AC	
☐ N961AA	AMD Falcon 20D	205	ex N585AC	
☐ N1131G	Cessna 208B Caravan I	208B0661		♦
☐ N1241X	Cessna 208B Caravan I	208b0657	ex N52601	♦

AIR DIRECT — Rhinelander-Oneida County, WI (RHI)

☐ N800L	Piper PA-31 Turbo Navajo	31-426	ex C-GSGA
☐ N87395	Cessna 310R	310R0543	

AIR EAST — Latrobe, PA

Assoc with Vee Neal Aviation (qv)

AIR FLAMENCO/AIR CHARTER — (F4) — San Juan-Fernando Luis Ribas Dominici, PR (SIG)

☐ N203PR	Britten-Norman BN-2B-26 Islander	2248	ex G-BSWU	
☐ N821RR	Britten-Norman BN-2A-9 Islander	338	ex N146A	
☐ N901GD	Britten-Norman BN-2A-26 Islander	855	ex XA-JEK	The Spirit of Culebra
☐ N903GD	Britten-Norman BN-2A-8 Islander	625	ex HI636CT	
☐ N904GD	Britten-Norman BN-2B-26 Islander	2128	ex N902VL	
☐ N905GD	Britten-Norman BN-2A-9 Islander	339	ex C-FTAM	
☐ N906GD	Britten-Norman BN-2A-26 Islander	3008	ex VP-AAB	
☐ N907GD	Britten-Norman BN-2A-9 Islander	340	ex N161A	
☐ N908GD	Britten-Norman BN-2A-26 Islander	2040	ex C6-BUS	
☐ N913GD	Britten-Norman BN-2A-6 Islander	198	ex N7079N	
☐ N917GD	Britten-Norman BN-2A-27 Islander	789	ex N4915U	
☐ N915GD	Short SD.3-60	SH3755	ex N377AR	
☐ N916GD	Short SD.3-60	SH3751	ex N948RR	♦
☐ N918GD	Short SH.3-60	SH3741	ex N875GD	♦

AIR KEY WEST | Key West, FL

☐ N683KW	Partenavia P68C	305		♦
☐ N684KW	Partenavia P68C	387		♦
☐ N685KW	Britten-Norman BN-2T Islander	2120	ex G-BJEE	♦

AIR SUNSHINE | Air Sunshine (YI/RSI) | San Juan Intl, PR (SJU)

☐ N347AB	Cessna 402C	402C0347	ex N26548	
☐ N402RS	Cessna 402C	402C0402	ex N2663N	
☐ N603AB	Cessna 402C	402C0603	ex N84PB	
☐ N792BA	SAAB SF.340A	340A-092	ex N742BA	[FXE]
☐ N900MX	Beech 1900C	UB-55	ex N155GA	
Also trades as Tropical Transport Services				

AIR WISCONSIN | Air Wisconsin (ZW/WSN) | Appleton-Outagamie Co, WI (ATW)

Ops Canadair CRJ-200LRs for US Airways Express (qv)

AIRBORNE SUPPORT | Houma-Terrebonne, LA (HUM)

☐ N38WA	Rockwell 690A Turbo Commander	11169	ex XB-FLF	
☐ N932H	Basler Turbo 67 (DC-3TP)	3436/17101	ex N93HA	
☐ N14183	Piper PA-23 Aztec 250	27-4747	ex C-GQKP	
☐ N64766	Douglas C-47	27218	ex CAF12910	Sprayer
☐ N64767	Douglas C-47A	13303	ex CAF12941	Sprayer ♦
☐ N67024	Douglas DC-54D	10550	ex Bu50871	Sprayer
Assoc with Environmental Aviation Services				

AIRNET SYSTEMS | Columbus-Port Columbus Intl, OH/Dallas-Love Field, TX (CMH/DAL)

☐ N95BB	Beech 58 Baron	TH-333	ex N95BD
☐ N456WW	Beech 58 Baron	TH-444	ex N444TE
☐ N858LG	Beech 58 Baron	TH-518	ex N555GP
☐ N1814W	Beech 58 Baron	TH-287	
☐ N3695V	Beech 58 Baron	TH-1183	
☐ N9044V	Beech 58 Baron	TH-216	
☐ N17708	Beech 58 Baron	TH-813	
☐ N3RY	Cessna 208B Caravan I	208B0436	ex C-GSKR
☐ N102AN	Cessna 208B Caravan I	208B0906	ex N51666
☐ N103AN	Cessna 208B Caravan I	208B0928	
☐ N105AN	Cessna 208B Caravan I	208B0956	
☐ N106AN	Cessna 208B Caravan I	208B0917	ex N5207V
☐ N107AN	Cessna 208B Caravan I	208B0993	
☐ N1026V	Cessna 208B Caravan I	208B0319	
☐ N9539F	Cessna 208 Caravan I	20800092	
☐ N9642F	Cessna 208 Caravan I	20800110	
☐ N15WH	Learjet 35A	35A-085	
☐ N27BL	Learjet 35A	35A-163	ex YV-173CP
☐ N31WR	Learjet 35A	35A-313	ex TR-LZI
☐ N64CP	Learjet 35A	35A-264	ex VR-CDI
☐ N81FR	Learjet 35A	35A-081	ex N118DA
☐ N959SA	Learjet 35A	35A-076	
☐ N3547C	Piper PA-31-350 Chieftain	31-8052018	
☐ N3587P	Piper PA-31-350 Chieftain	31-8052120	
☐ N3590D	Piper PA-31-350 Chieftain	31-8052144	
☐ N40919	Piper PA-31-350 Chieftain	31-8152162	
All are freighters			

AIRPAC AIRLINES | Airpac (APC) | Seattle-Boeing Field, WA (BFI)

☐ N36PB	Piper PA-31-350 Navajo Chieftain	31-7405128	
☐ N627HA	Piper PA-31-350 Chieftain	31-7952241	
☐ N777KT	Piper PA-31-350 Navajo Chieftain	31-7552053	ex N1TW
☐ N3582X	Piper PA-31-350 Chieftain	31-8052105	
☐ N4490F	Piper PA-34-200T Seneca II	34-7670339	
☐ N8107D	Piper PA-34-200T Seneca II	34-8070010	
☐ N36319	Piper PA-34-200T Seneca II	34-7870318	

ALASKA AIR FUEL | Palmer, AK

☐ N3054V	Douglas C-54Q	10547	ex N76AU	Tanker
☐ N96358	Douglas C-54E	27284	ex Bu90398	Tanker

ALASKA AIRLINES | Alaska (AS/ASA) | Seattle-Tacoma Intl, WA (SEA)

☐ N703AS	Boeing 737-490	28893/3039	ex (N747AS)
☐ N705AS	Boeing 737-490	29318/3042	ex (N748AS)

☐ N706AS	Boeing 737-490	28894/3050	ex (N749AS)	Disneyworld titles	
☐ N708AS	Boeing 737-490	28895/3098			
☐ N713AS	Boeing 737-490	30161/3110	ex N1787B		
☐ N756AS	Boeing 737-4Q8	25097/2299			
☐ N760AS	Boeing 737-4Q8	25098/2320			
☐ N767AS	Boeing 737-490	27081/2354			
☐ N769AS	Boeing 737-4Q8	25103/2452			
☐ N778AS	Boeing 737-4Q8	25110/2586			
☐ N779AS	Boeing 737-4Q8	25111/2605			
☐ N786AS	Boeing 737-4S3	24795/1870	ex TF-FIE		
☐ N788AS	Boeing 737-490	28885/2891			
☐ N791AS	Boeing 737-490	28886/2902			
☐ N792AS	Boeing 737-490	28887/2903		Salmon Thirty Seven	
☐ N793AS	Boeing 737-490	28888/2990			
☐ N794AS	Boeing 737-490	28889/3000			
☐ N795AS	Boeing 737-490	28890/3006			
☐ N796AS	Boeing 737-490	28891/3027			
☐ N797AS	Boeing 737-490	28892/3036			
☐ N799AS	Boeing 737-490	29270/3038			
☐ N709AS	Boeing 737-490SF	28896/3099	ex N1787B		
☐ N762AS	Boeing 737-4Q8F	25099/2334			
☐ N763AS	Boeing 737-4Q8F	25100/2346			
☐ N764AS	Boeing 737-4Q8F	25101/2348			
☐ N765AS	Boeing 737-4Q8F	25102/2350			
☐ N768AS	Boeing 737-490F	27082/2356			
☐ N607AS	Boeing 737-790/W	29751/313			
☐ N609AS	Boeing 737-790/W	29752/350			
☐ N611AS	Boeing 737-790/W	29753/385			
☐ N612AS	Boeing 737-790/W	30162/406	ex N1787B		
☐ N613AS	Boeing 737-790/W	30163/430			
☐ N614AS	Boeing 737-790/W	30343/439			
☐ N615AS	Boeing 737-790/W	30344/472	ex N1787B		
☐ N618AS	Boeing 737-790/W	30543/536	ex N1787B		
☐ N619AS	Boeing 737-790/W	30164/597			
☐ N622AS	Boeing 737-790/W	30165/661			
☐ N625AS	Boeing 737-790/W	30792/754	ex N1795B		
☐ N626AS	Boeing 737-790/W	30793/763			
☐ N627AS	Boeing 737-790/W	30794/796	ex N1787B		
☐ N644AS	Boeing 737-790/W	30795/1277			
☐ N506AS	Boeing 737-890/W	35690/2627			
☐ N508AS	Boeing 737-890/W	35691/2662	ex N1786B		
☐ N512AS	Boeing 737-890/W	39043/2711			
☐ N513AS	Boeing 737-890/W	35192/2721	ex N1786B		
☐ N514AS	Boeing 737-890/W	35193/2727	ex N1786B		
☐ N516AS	Boeing 737-890/W	39044/2751			
☐ N517AS	Boeing 737-890/W	35197/2770			
☐ N518AS	Boeing 737-890/W	35693/2785			
☐ N519AS	Boeing 737-890/W	36482/2800	ex N1795B		
☐ N520AS	Boeing 737-890/W	36481/2812	ex N1786B		
☐ N523AS	Boeing 737-890/W	35194/2816			
☐ N524AS	Boeing 737-890/W	35195/2850	ex N1796B		
☐ N525AS	Boeing 737-890/W	35692/2859	ex N1786B		
☐ N526AS	Boeing 737-890/W	35196/2862	ex N1796B		
☐ N527AS	Boeing 737-890/W	35694/2913	ex N1796B		
☐ N528AS	Boeing 737-890/W	35695/2930			
☐ N529AS	Boeing 737-890/W	35198/3229	ex N1796B		
☐ N530AS	Boeing 737-890/W	36578/3257	ex N1786B		
☐ N531AS	Boeing 737-890/W	35199/3287	ex N1787B		
☐ N532AS	Boeing 737-890/W	36346/3317			
☐ N533AS	Boeing 737-890/W	35201/3511	ex N1786B		
☐ N534AS	Boeing 737-890/W	35202/3523			
☐ N535AS	Boeing 737-890/W	35200/3558			
☐ N536AS	Boeing 737-890/W	35203/3893			
☐ N537AS	Boeing 737-890/W	35204/3913			
☐ N538AS	Boeing 737-890/W	41188/4045			
☐ N546AS	Boeing 737-890/W	30022/1640			
☐ N548AS	Boeing 737-890/W	30020/1738			
☐ N549AS	Boeing 737-8FH/W	30824/1664			
☐ N551AS	Boeing 737-890/W	34593/1860			
☐ N552AS	Boeing 737-890/W	34595/1882	ex N1795B		
☐ N553AS	Boeing 737-890/W	34594/1906			
☐ N556AS	Boeing 737-890/W	35175/1980			
☐ N557AS	Boeing 737-890/W	35176/2010			
☐ N558AS	Boeing 737-890/W	35177/2031			
☐ N559AS	Boeing 737-890/W	35178/2026	ex N6067E	Salon Thirty Salmon II	ETOPS test a/c
☐ N560AS	Boeing 737-890/W	35179/2072		Spirit of the Islands c/s	
☐ N562AS	Boeing 737-890/W	35091/2084			
☐ N563AS	Boeing 737-890/W	35180/2090			
☐ N564AS	Boeing 737-890/W	35103/2099			
☐ N565AS	Boeing 737-890/W	35181/2134			

☐ N566AS	Boeing 737-890/W	35182/2164		
☐ N568AS	Boeing 737-890/W	35183/2166		
☐ N569AS	Boeing 737-890/W	35184/2192		75th anniversary c/s
☐ N570AS	Boeing 737-890/W	35185/2212		
☐ N577AS	Boeing 737-890/W	35186/2221	ex N1787B	
☐ N579AS	Boeing 737-890/W	35187/2226		
☐ N581AS	Boeing 737-890/W	35188/2259		
☐ N583AS	Boeing 737-890/W	35681/2333		
☐ N584AS	Boeing 737-890/W	35682/2365		
☐ N585AS	Boeing 737-890/W	35683/2385		
☐ N586AS	Boeing 737-890/W	35189/2393		
☐ N587AS	Boeing 737-890/W	35684/2422	ex N1786B	
☐ N588AS	Boeing 737-890/W	35685/2454	ex N1786B	
☐ N589AS	Boeing 737-890/W	35686/2458	ex N1786B	
☐ N590AS	Boeing 737-890/W	35687/2478		
☐ N592AS	Boeing 737-890/W	35190/2511	ex N1786B	
☐ N593AS	Boeing 737-890/W	35107/2545	ex N1786B	
☐ N594AS	Boeing 737-890/W	35191/2560	ex N1786B	
☐ N596AS	Boeing 737-890/W	35688/2587		
☐ N597AS	Boeing 737-890/W	35689/2601		
☐ N302AS	Boeing 737-990	30017/596	ex N737X	
☐ N303AS	Boeing 737-990	30016/683	ex N672AS	
☐ N305AS	Boeing 737-990	30013/774	ex (N673AS)	
☐ N306AS	Boeing 737-990/W	30014/802	ex (N674AS)	
☐ N307AS	Boeing 737-990/W	30015/838	ex N1788B	
☐ N309AS	Boeing 737-990/W	30857/902	ex N1786B	
☐ N315AS	Boeing 737-990/W	30019/1218		
☐ N317AS	Boeing 737-990/W	30856/1296	ex N1786B	
☐ N318AS	Boeing 737-990/W	30018/1326		
☐ N319AS	Boeing 737-990/W	33679/1344		
☐ N320AS	Boeing 737-990/W	33680/1380		
☐ N323AS	Boeing 737-990/W	30021/1454		
☐ N402AS	Boeing 737-990ER/W	41189/4212	ex N1786B	901
☐ N403AS	Boeing 737-990ER/W	41730/4242		902
☐ N407AS	Boeing 737-990ER/W	41731/4278	ex N1796B	903
☐ N408AS	Boeing 737-990ER/W	41732/4296		904
☐ N409AS	Boeing 737-990ER/W	41733/4338		905
☐ N413AS	Boeing 737-990ER/W	35205/4386		
☐ N419AS	Boeing 737-990ER/W	41734/4403		419
☐ N423AS	Boeing 737-990ER/W	35206/4425		423
☐ N431AS	Boeing 737-990ER/W	43255/4636		
☐ N433AS	Boeing 737-990ER/W	41704/4646		
☐ N435AS	Boeing 737-990ER/W	43292/4668		
☐ N440AS	Boeing 737-990ER/W	41705/4675		
☐ N442AS	Boeing 737-990ER/W	43293/4700		442
☐ N453AS	Boeing 737-990ER/W	36354/4747		453
☐ N457AS	Boeing 737-990ER/W	36355/4784		457
☐ N459AS	Boeing 737-990ER/W	36352/4832		
☐ N461AS	Boeing 737-990ER/W	36363/4850		
☐ N462AS	Boeing 737-990ER/W	36361/4887		
☐ N464AS	Boeing 737-990ER/W	40714/4903		
☐ N467AS	Boeing 737-990ER/W	36362/4925		
☐ N468AS	Boeing 737-990ER/W	41735/5012		
☐ N469AS	Boeing 737-990ER/W	41702/5043		♦
☐ N471AS	Boeing 737-990ER/W	41703/5110		♦
☐ N472AS	Boeing 737-990ER/W	60580/5358		♦
☐ N474AS	Boeing 737-990ER/W	40715/		o/o♦
☐ N477AS	Boeing 737-990ER/W	40716/		o/o♦
☐ N478AS	Boeing 737-990ER/W	44105/		o/o♦
☐ N479AS	Boeing 737-990ER/W	60576/		o/o♦
☐ N481AS	Boeing 737-990ER/W	44106/		o/o♦

ALASKA AIR TAXI

☐ N9620M	Cessna 207A Stationair 8	20700711
☐ N27987	Piper PA-31 Navajo	31-7912054
☐ N73100	Cessna 207A Stationair 8	20700559

ALASKA CENTRAL EXPRESS/ACE AIR CARGO   Ace Air (KO/AER)   Anchorage-Intl, AK (ANC)

☐ N110AX	Beech 1900C-1	UC-93	ex N575U	♦
☐ N111AX	Beech 1900C-1	UC-81	ex N5632C	
☐ N113AX	Beech 1900C-1	UC-41	ex N41UE	
☐ N114AX	Beech 1900C-1	UC-36	ex N1566C	
☐ N115AX	Beech 1900C-1	UC-2	ex N19NG	
☐ N116AX	Beech 1900C-1	UC-17	ex N17ZV	
☐ N117AX	Beech 1900C-1	UC-79	ex N79TR	
☐ N118AX	Beech 1900C-1	UC-116	ex N491QL	
☐ N119AX	Beech 1900C-1	UC-43	ex YV149T	

ALASKA SEAPLANE SERVICE	(J5)			Juneau-Intl, AK (JNU)
☐ N70SB	Cessna U206G Stationair	U20605554		♦
☐ N750KP	Cessna 208B Caravan I	208B0628	ex N750PA	FP
☐ N765KP	Piper PA-31-350 Chieftain	31-8253012		♦
☐ N777DH	de Havilland DHC-2 Beaver	47	ex CF-FHN	FP
☐ N1265U	Cessna 208 Caravan I	20800375		♦
☐ N4794C	de Havilland DHC-2 Beaver	342	ex 51-16545	FP
☐ N7687K	Cessna 180J Skywagon	18052703		FP
☐ N8200M	Piper PA-32-301 Saratoga	32-8006048		
☐ N8216T	Piper PA-32-301 Saratoga	32-8206037		
☐ N60077	de Havilland DHC-2 Beaver	1419	ex LV-GLJ	FP

ALASKA WEST AIR				Kenai Island Lake, AK (ENA)
☐ N49AW	de Havilland DHC-3 Turbo Otter	310	ex N21PG	FP
☐ N87AW	de Havilland DHC-3 Turbo Otter	52	ex C-FMPO	FP
☐ N222RL	de Havilland DHC-2 Turbo Beaver	1570/TB5	ex C-FOEB	FP
☐ N1018B	de Havilland DHC-3 Otter	392	ex C-FQOR	FP
☐ N1432Z	de Havilland DHC-2 Beaver	797	ex 54-1668	FP

ALLEGIANT AIR		Allegiant (G4/AAY)		Las Vegas-McCarran Intl, NV (LAS)
☐ N301NV	Airbus A319-111	2319	ex HB-JZK	301	
☐ N302NV	Airbus A319-112	2387	ex HB-JZN	302	
☐ N303NV	Airbus A319-112	2271	ex G-EZET	303	♦
☐ N304NV	Airbus A319-112	2265	ex HB-JZJ	304	♦
☐ N305NV	Airbus A319-111	2398	ex HB-JZO	305	♦
☐ N306NV	Airbus A319-111	2420	ex HB-JZT		♦
☐ N307NV	Airbus A319-111	2427	ex G-EZIB		o/o♦
☐ N308NV	Airbus A319-111	2450	ex G-EZIF		♦
☐ N310NV	Airbus A319-112	2224	ex VQ-BLY		
☐ N215NV	Airbus A320-214	1292	ex EC-HUJ		
☐ N216NV	Airbus A320-214	1318	ex EC-HUK		
☐ N217NV	Airbus A320-214	1347	ex EC-HUL		
☐ N218NV	Airbus A320-214	1229	ex EI-FCC	Make a Wish c/s	
☐ N219NV	Airbus A320-214	1255	ex EC-HSF		
☐ N220NV	Airbus A320-214	1262	ex EC-HYC		
☐ N221NV	Airbus A320-214	1288	ex EC-HYD		
☐ N222NV	Airbus A320-214	1530	ex EC-HTB	222	♦
☐ N223NV	Airbus A320-214	1540	ex EC-HTC	223	♦
☐ N224NV	Airbus A320-214	1694	ex EC-IEI		o/o♦
☐ N225NV	Airbus A320-214	0706	ex RP-C3221		o/o♦
☐ N226NV	Airbus A320-214	0745	ex RP-C3223		o/o♦
☐ N227NV	Airbus A320-214	0714	ex D-AHHH	227	♦
☐ N228NV	Airbus A320-214	0716	ex D-AHHD	228	♦
☐ N229NV	Airbus A320-214	0730	ex D-AHHG	229	♦
☐ N901NV	Boeing 757-204/W	26963/450	ex OH-AFL		
☐ N902NV	Boeing 757-204/W	26964/452	ex N964BV		
☐ N903NV	Boeing 757-204/W	26966/520	ex G-LSAM		
☐ N904NV	Boeing 757-204/W	26967/522	ex G-LSAL		
☐ N905NV	Boeing 757-204/W	27235/598	ex G-BYAO		
☐ N906NV	Boeing 757-204/W	27236/600	ex G-BYAP		
☐ N405NV	McDonnell-Douglas MD-83	49623/1499	ex SE-RFA		
☐ N406NV	McDonnell-Douglas MD-83	49900/1765	ex SE-RFC		
☐ N407NV	McDonnell-Douglas MD-83	53244/1901	ex SE-RFD		
☐ N408NV	McDonnell-Douglas MD-83	53246/1918	ex SE-RFB		
☐ N409NV	McDonnell-Douglas MD-83	49574/1413	ex SE-RDV		
☐ N410NV	McDonnell-Douglas MD-83	49965/2044	ex SE-DLV		
☐ N411NV	McDonnell-Douglas MD-83	53245/1978	ex HK-4413		
☐ N415NV	McDonnell-Douglas MD-83	49909/1625	ex SE-DII		
☐ N416NV	McDonnell-Douglas MD-83	49555/1402	ex SE-DIO		
☐ N417NV	McDonnell-Douglas MD-83	53347/1979	ex SE-DMD		
☐ N418NV	McDonnell-Douglas MD-83	49615/1543	ex SE-DID		
☐ N419NV	McDonnell-Douglas MD-83	53366/1999	ex SE-DME		
☐ N420NV	McDonnell-Douglas MD-83	49424/1284	ex SE-DFX		
☐ N421NV	McDonnell-Douglas MD-83	53275/1896	ex OY-KHR		
☐ N422NV	McDonnell-Douglas MD-83	49381/1231	ex OY-KGZ		
☐ N423NV	McDonnell-Douglas MD-83	53008/1895	ex SE-DIY		
☐ N424NV	McDonnell-Douglas MD-83	49421/1263	ex SE-DFU		
☐ N425NV	McDonnell-Douglas MD-83	49438/1353	ex SE-DFY		
☐ N426NV	McDonnell-Douglas MD-83	49437/1345	ex SE-DMI		
☐ N427NV	McDonnell-Douglas MD-83	49436/1303	ex OY-KHC		
☐ N429NV	McDonnell-Douglas MD-83	49385/1244	ex SE-DFT		
☐ N861GA	McDonnell-Douglas MD-83	49557/1436	ex SE-DPI	[TUS]
☐ N862GA	McDonnell-Douglas MD-83	49556/1415	ex LN-RMF	[TUS]
☐ N863GA	McDonnell-Douglas MD-83	49911/1653	ex OY-KHL	
☐ N864GA	McDonnell-Douglas MD-83	49912/1659	ex LN-RMJ	[IWA]
☐ N865GA	McDonnell-Douglas MD-83	49998/1800	ex SE-DIX	

☐ N866GA	McDonnell-Douglas MD-83	49910/1638	ex OY-KHK		
☐ N868GA	McDonnell-Douglas MD-83	49554/1379	ex LN-RMA		
☐ N869GA	McDonnell-Douglas MD-83	53294/1917	ex SE-DIZ		
☐ N871GA	McDonnell-Douglas MD-83	53296/1937	ex OY-KHT		
☐ N872GA	McDonnell-Douglas MD-83	53295/1922	ex LN-RMN		
☐ N873GA	McDonnell-Douglas MD-83	49658/1461	ex N946AS		
☐ N874GA	McDonnell-Douglas MD-83	49643/1423	ex N945AS		
☐ N875GA	McDonnell-Douglas MD-83	53468/2130	ex C-GKLN		
☐ N876GA	McDonnell-Douglas MD-83	53469/2116	ex C-GKLR		
☐ N877GA	McDonnell-Douglas MD-83	53467/2102	ex C-GKLJ		
☐ N878GA	McDonnell-Douglas MD-83	53487/2132	ex C-GKLQ		
☐ N879GA	McDonnell-Douglas MD-83	53486/2130	ex C-GKLN		
☐ N880GA	McDonnell-Douglas MD-83	49625/1503	ex OH-LMG		
☐ N881GA	McDonnell-Douglas MD-83	49708/1561	ex SE-RGO		
☐ N883GA	McDonnell-Douglas MD-83	49710/1547	ex SE-RGP		
☐ N884GA	McDonnell-Douglas MD-83	49401/1357	ex SE-RDS		
☐ N886GA	McDonnell-Douglas MD-83	49931/1754	ex N829NK		
☐ N887GA	McDonnell-Douglas MD-83	49932/1756	ex N830NK		
☐ N891GA	McDonnell-Douglas MD-83	49423/1283	ex LN-RLG		
☐ N892GA	McDonnell-Douglas MD-83	49826/1578	ex N861LF		[IWA]
☐ N893GA	McDonnell-Douglas MD-83	53051/1718	ex N881LF		
☐ N401NV	McDonnell-Douglas MD-88	49761/1623	ex N158PL		
☐ N402NV	McDonnell-Douglas MD-88	49763/1626	ex N160PL		
☐ N403NV	McDonnell-Douglas MD-88	49764/1632	ex N161PL		
☐ N404NV	McDonnell-Douglas MD-88	49765/1645	ex N162PL		
☐ N412NV	McDonnell-Douglas MD-88	49759/1606	ex N822ME		
☐ N414NV	McDonnell-Douglas MD-88	49766/1657	ex N823ME		

ALOHA AIR CARGO — Aloha (AAH) — Honolulu-Intl, HI (HNL)

☐ N301KH	Boeing 737-330F	27904/2691	ex N904JW		♦
☐ N302KH	Boeing 737-330SF	27905/2705	ex N905AU		♦
☐ N840AL	Boeing 737-2X6C	23124/1046	ex N747AS		
☐ N842AL	Boeing 737-290QC	23136/1032	ex N742AS	Manu Makamae	
☐ N843KH	SAAB SF.340AF	340A-046	ex XA-STX	Ke Kela	
☐ N844KH	SAAB SF.340AF	340A-108	ex OK-CCE	Hoku Ao	
☐ N845KH	SAAB SF.340AF	340A-111	ex SE-KXE		

ALPINE AIR EXPRESS — Alpine Air (5A/AIP) — Provo-Municipal, UT (PVU)

☐ N14MV	Beech 99	U-59	ex C-FGJT	
☐ N24BH	Beech 99	U-67	ex C-GVNQ	
☐ N95WA	Beech 99	U-6	ex N19RA	
☐ N99GH	Beech 99A	U-112	ex N86569	
☐ N216CS	Beech C99	U-216	ex C-GGPP	based HNL
☐ N236AL	Beech C99	U-236	ex RP-C2317	based HNL
☐ N237SL	Beech C99	U-237	ex RP-C2370	based HNL
☐ N238AL	Beech C99	U-238	ex RP-C2380	based HNL
☐ N239AL	Beech C99	U-239	ex RP-C2390	based HNL
☐ N326CA	Beech B99	U-135	ex N10RA	
☐ N899CA	Beech 99A	U-104	ex N1922T	
☐ N950AA	Beech B99	U-159	ex C-FCBU	
☐ N114AX	Beech 1900C	UB-36	ex N19RA	
☐ N125BA	Beech 1900C	UB-6	ex N125GP	
☐ N127BA	Beech 1900C	UB-7	ex N126GP	
☐ N133BA	Beech 1900C	UB-54	ex OB-1677-P	
☐ N153GA	Beech 1900C	UB-34	ex N734GL	based HNL
☐ N154GA	Beech 1900C	UB-25	ex N315BH	
☐ N172GA	Beech 1900C	UB-11	ex N11ZR	
☐ N190GA	Beech 1900C	UB-1	ex N1YW	
☐ N192GA	Beech 1900C	UB-17	ex N17ZR	based HNL
☐ N194GA	Beech 1900C	UB-8	ex CC-CAF	
☐ N197GA	Beech 1900C	UB-16	ex N16ZR	
☐ N198GA	Beech 1900C	UB-5	ex CC-CAS	
☐ N219VP	Beech 1900C	UB-14	ex N188GA	
☐ N60MJ	Beech 1900D	UE-60	ex N85445	

AMBLER AIR SERVICE — Ambler, AK

| ☐ N6230J | Piper PA-32R-300 Lance | 32R-7680337 | |

AMERICAN AIR FREIGHT — Laredo, TX

| ☐ N690WT | Rockwell 690B | 11455 | | ♦ |

AMERICAN AIRLINES — American (AA/AAL) — Dallas-Fort Worth, TX (DFW)

Member of oneWorld

| ☐ N700UW | Airbus A319-112 | 0885 | ex D-AVYF | 700 |

☐	N701UW	Airbus A319-112	0890	ex D-AVYG	701	Star Alliance c/s
☐	N702UW	Airbus A319-112	0896	ex D-AVYH	702	
☐	N703UW	Airbus A319-112	0904	ex D-AVYI	703	
☐	N704US	Airbus A319-112	0922	ex D-AVYQ	704	
☐	N705UW	Airbus A319-112	0929	ex D-AVYA	705	
☐	N708UW	Airbus A319-112	0972	ex D-AVYT	708	
☐	N709UW	Airbus A319-112	0997	ex D-AVYV	709	
☐	N710UW	Airbus A319-112	1019	ex D-AVYR	710	
☐	N711UW	Airbus A319-112	1033	ex D-AVYG	711	
☐	N712US	Airbus A319-112	1038	ex D-AVYW	712	
☐	N713UW	Airbus A319-112	1040	ex D-AVYH	713	
☐	N714US	Airbus A319-112	1046	ex D-AVYZ	714	
☐	N715UW	Airbus A319-112	1051	ex D-AVYV	715	
☐	N716UW	Airbus A319-112	1055	ex D-AVYM	716	
☐	N717UW	Airbus A319-112	1069	ex D-AVWC	717	Carolina Panthers c/s
☐	N721UW	Airbus A319-112	1095	ex D-AVYQ	721	
☐	N722US	Airbus A319-112	1097	ex D-AVYS	722	
☐	N723UW	Airbus A319-112	1109	ex D-AVWP	723	
☐	N724UW	Airbus A319-112	1122	ex D-AVYA	724	
☐	N725UW	Airbus A319-112	1135	ex D-AVWC	725	
☐	N730US	Airbus A319-112	1182	ex D-AVYD	730	
☐	N732UW	Airbus A319-112	1203	ex D-AVYA	732	
☐	N733UW	Airbus A319-112	1205	ex D-AVYB	733	Pittsburgh Steelers c/s
☐	N737US	Airbus A319-112	1245	ex D-AVYN	737	
☐	N738US	Airbus A319-112	1254	ex D-AVYQ	738	
☐	N740UW	Airbus A319-112	1265	ex D-AVWO	740	
☐	N741UW	Airbus A319-112	1269	ex D-AVWP	741	
☐	N742PS	Airbus A319-112	1275	ex N742US	742	retro PSA c/s
☐	N744P	Airbus A319-112	1287	ex N744US	744	Piedmont c/s
☐	N745VJ	Airbus A319-112	1289	ex N745UW	745	Allegheny c/s 'Vistajet'
☐	N746UW	Airbus A319-112	1297	ex D-AVWV	746	
☐	N747UW	Airbus A319-112	1301	ex D-AVWM	747	
☐	N748UW	Airbus A319-112	1311	ex D-AVYA	748	
☐	N749US	Airbus A319-112	1313	ex D-AVWG	749	
☐	N750UW	Airbus A319-112	1315	ex D-AVWH	750	
☐	N751UW	Airbus A319-112	1317	ex D-AVWK	751	
☐	N752US	Airbus A319-112	1319	ex D-AVWS	752	
☐	N753US	Airbus A319-112	1326	ex D-AVYG	753	
☐	N754UW	Airbus A319-112	1328	ex D-AVYJ	754	
☐	N755US	Airbus A319-112	1331	ex D-AVYN	755	
☐	N756US	Airbus A319-112	1340	ex D-AVYO	756	
☐	N757UW	Airbus A319-112	1342	ex D-AVYP	757	
☐	N758US	Airbus A319-112	1348	ex D-AVYS	758	
☐	N760US	Airbus A319-112	1354	ex D-AVWI	760	
☐	N762US	Airbus A319-112	1358	ex D-AVWD	762	
☐	N763US	Airbus A319-112	1360	ex D-AVWF	763	
☐	N764US	Airbus A319-112	1369	ex D-AVWM	764	
☐	N765US	Airbus A319-112	1371	ex D-AVWO	765	
☐	N766US	Airbus A319-112	1378	ex D-AVWG	766	
☐	N767UW	Airbus A319-112	1382	ex D-AVWN	767	
☐	N768US	Airbus A319-112	1389	ex D-AVYI	768	
☐	N769US	Airbus A319-112	1391	ex D-AVYJ	769	
☐	N770UW	Airbus A319-112	1393	ex D-AVYU	770	
☐	N3014R	Airbus A319-115/S	5842	ex D-AVXN	014	
☐	N4005X	Airbus A319-115/S	5753	ex D-AVXB	005	
☐	N5007E	Airbus A319-115/S	5781	ex D-AVXF	007	
☐	N6028Z	Airbus A319-115/S	6456	ex D-AVWZ		♦
☐	N8001N	Airbus A319-115/S	5678	ex D-AVYQ	001	
☐	N8009T	Airbus A319-115/S	5788	ex D-AVXH	009	
☐	N8027D	Airbus A319-115/S	6437	ex D-AVWY	027	♦
☐	N8030F	Airbus A319-115/S	6552	ex D-AVYD	030	♦
☐	N8031M	Airbus A319-115/S	6595	ex D-AVYF	031	♦
☐	N9002U	Airbus A319-115/S	5698	ex D-AVYR	002	
☐	N9004F	Airbus A319-115/S	5745	ex D-AVXA	004	
☐	N9006	Airbus A319-115/S	5761	ex D-AVXC	006	
☐	N9008U	Airbus A319-115/S	5786	ex D-AVXG	008	
☐	N9010R	Airbus A319-115/S	5789	ex D-AVXI	010	
☐	N9011P	Airbus A319-115/S	5798	ex D-AVXK	011	
☐	N9012	Airbus A319-115/S	5810	ex D-AVXL	012	
☐	N9013A	Airbus A319-115/S	5827	ex D-AVXM	013	
☐	N9015D	Airbus A319-115/S	5327	ex D-AVWC	015	
☐	N9016	Airbus A319-115/S	6040	ex D-AVWH	016	
☐	N9017P	Airbus A319-115/S	6085	ex D-AVWJ	017	♦
☐	N9018E	Airbus A319-115/S	6150	ex D-AVWM	018	♦
☐	N9019F	Airbus A319-115/S	6154	ex D-AVWN	019	♦
☐	N9021H	Airbus A319-115/S	6277	ex D-AVWR	021	♦
☐	N9022G	Airbus A319-115/S	6310	ex D-AVWS	022	♦
☐	N9023N	Airbus A319-115/S	6349	ex D-AVWT	023	♦
☐	N9025B	Airbus A319-115/S	6393	ex D-AVWV	025	♦
☐	N9026C	Airbus A319-115/S	6429	ex D-AVWX	026	♦
☐	N9029F	Airbus A319-115/S	6491	ex D-AVYA	029	♦
☐	N70020	Airbus A319-115/S	6263	ex D-AVWQ	020	♦

☐	N90024	Airbus A319-115/S	6384	ex D-AVWU	024	♦
☐	N93003	Airbus A319-115/S	5704	ex D-AVYS	003	
☐	N	Airbus A319-115/S	6644	ex		o/o♦
☐	N801AW	Airbus A319-132	0889	ex D-AVYM	801	
☐	N802AW	Airbus A319-132	0924	ex D-AVYR	802	
☐	N803AW	Airbus A319-132	0931	ex D-AVYK	803	
☐	N804AW	Airbus A319-132	1043	ex D-AVYY	804	
☐	N805AW	Airbus A319-132	1049	ex D-AVYU	805	
☐	N806AW	Airbus A319-132	1056	ex D-AVYO	806	
☐	N807AW	Airbus A319-132	1064	ex D-AVWB	807	
☐	N808AW	Airbus A319-132	1088	ex D-AVWM	808	
☐	N809AW	Airbus A319-132	1111	ex D-AVWT	809	
☐	N810AW	Airbus A319-132	1116	ex D-AVWV	810	
☐	N812AW	Airbus A319-132	1178	ex D-AVWP	812	
☐	N813AW	Airbus A319-132	1223	ex D-AVYH	813	
☐	N814AW	Airbus A319-132	1281	ex D-AVYC	814	
☐	N815AW	Airbus A319-132	1323	ex D-AVWW	815	
☐	N816AW	Airbus A319-132	1350	ex D-AVYV	816	
☐	N817AW	Airbus A319-132	1373	ex D-AVWA	817	
☐	N818AW	Airbus A319-132	1375	ex D-AVWB	818	
☐	N819AW	Airbus A319-132	1395	ex D-AVYX	819	
☐	N820AW	Airbus A319-132	1397	ex D-AVWQ	820	
☐	N821AW	Airbus A319-132	1406	ex D-AVYC	821	
☐	N822AW	Airbus A319-132	1410	ex D-AVYD	822	
☐	N823AW	Airbus A319-132	1463	ex D-AVYJ	823	
☐	N824AW	Airbus A319-132	1490	ex D-AVYA	824	
☐	N825AW	Airbus A319-132	1527	ex D-AVWG	825	
☐	N826AW	Airbus A319-132	1534	ex D-AVYO	826	Arizona flag c/s
☐	N827AW	Airbus A319-132	1547	ex D-AVWL	827	
☐	N828AW	Airbus A319-132	1552	ex D-AVWO	828	America West Heritage c/s
☐	N829AW	Airbus A319-132	1563	ex D-AVYS	829	
☐	N830AW	Airbus A319-132	1565	ex D-AVYT	830	
☐	N831AW	Airbus A319-132	1576	ex D-AVWQ	831	
☐	N832AW	Airbus A319-132	1643	ex D-AVYA	832	
☐	N833AW	Airbus A319-132	1844	ex D-AVWV	833	
☐	N834AW	Airbus A319-132	2302	ex D-AVWM	834	
☐	N835AW	Airbus A319-132	2458	ex D-AVYN	835	
☐	N836AW	Airbus A319-132	2570	ex D-AVXB	836	
☐	N837AW	Airbus A319-132	2595	ex D-AVXM	837	Arizona Cardinals c/s
☐	N838AW	Airbus A319-132	2615	ex D-AVXT	383	America West Heritage c/s
☐	N839AW	Airbus A319-132	2669	ex D-AVYH	839	
☐	N840AW	Airbus A319-132	2690	ex D-AVXA	840	
☐	N102UW	Airbus A320-214	0844	ex F-WWBG	102	
☐	N103US	Airbus A320-214	0861	ex F-WWBP	103	
☐	N104UW	Airbus A320-214	0863	ex F-WWBQ	104	
☐	N105UW	Airbus A320-214	0868	ex F-WWBU	105	
☐	N107US	Airbus A320-214	1052	ex F-WWIM	107	
☐	N108UW	Airbus A320-214	1061	ex F-WWBB	108	
☐	N109UW	Airbus A320-214	1065	ex F-WWBD	109	
☐	N110UW	Airbus A320-214	1112	ex F-WWBJ	110	
☐	N111US	Airbus A320-214	1114	ex F-WWBK	111	
☐	N112US	Airbus A320-214	1134	ex F-WWIV	112	
☐	N114UW	Airbus A320-214	1148	ex F-WWBQ	114	
☐	N117UW	Airbus A320-214	1224	ex F-WWBH	117	
☐	N118US	Airbus A320-214	1264	ex F-WWDE	118	
☐	N119US	Airbus A320-214	1268	ex F-WWDH	119	
☐	N121UW	Airbus A320-214	1294	ex F-WWBC	121	
☐	N122US	Airbus A320-214	1298	ex F-WWBM	122	
☐	N123UW	Airbus A320-214	1310	ex F-WWBX	123	
☐	N124US	Airbus A320-214	1314	ex F-WWDJ	124	
☐	N125UW	Airbus A320-214	4086	ex F-WWBU	125	
☐	N126UW	Airbus A320-214	4149	ex D-AVVJ	126	
☐	N127UW	Airbus A320-214	4202	ex D-AVVH	127	
☐	N128UW	Airbus A320-214	4242	ex F-WWDL	128	
☐	N601AW	Airbus A320-232	1935	ex D-ALAU	601	
☐	N602AW	Airbus A320-232	0565	ex D-ALAA	602	
☐	N604AW	Airbus A320-232	1196	ex F-WWDZ	604	[GYR]
☐	N620AW	Airbus A320-231	0052	ex N901BN	620	[GYR]
☐	N621AW	Airbus A320-231	0053	ex N902BN	621	[TUS]
☐	N624AW	Airbus A320-231	0055	ex N904BN	624	
☐	N625AW	Airbus A320-231	0064	ex N905BN	625	[TUS]
☐	N626AW	Airbus A320-231	0065	ex N906BN	626	[GYR]
☐	N631AW	Airbus A320-231	0077	ex N911GP	631	[GYR]
☐	N640AW	Airbus A320-232	0448	ex N931LF	640	
☐	N642AW	Airbus A320-232	0584	ex F-WWDZ	642	[GYR]
☐	N647AW	Airbus A320-232	0762	ex F-WWDE	647	[SAL]
☐	N649AW	Airbus A320-232	0803	ex F-WWDZ	649	
☐	N650AW	Airbus A320-232	0856	ex F-WWBM	650	
☐	N651AW	Airbus A320-232	0866	ex F-WWBS	651	
☐	N652AW	Airbus A320-232	0953	ex F-WWDR	652	

☐ N653AW	Airbus A320-232	1003	ex F-WWDK	653
☐ N654AW	Airbus A320-232	1050	ex F-WWIL	
☐ N655AW	Airbus A320-232	1075	ex F-WWIG	655	American Airlines c/s
☐ N656AW	Airbus A320-232	1079	ex F-WWIQ	656
☐ N657AW	Airbus A320-232	1083	ex F-WWIU	657
☐ N658AW	Airbus A320-232	1110	ex F-WWDI	658
☐ N659AW	Airbus A320-232	1166	ex F-WWDG	659	American Airlines c/s
☐ N660AW	Airbus A320-232	1234	ex F-WWIO	660
☐ N661AW	Airbus A320-232	1284	ex F-WWBK	661
☐ N662AW	Airbus A320-232	1274	ex F-WWDR	662
☐ N663AW	Airbus A320-232	1419	ex F-WWBJ	663
☐ N664AW	Airbus A320-232	1621	ex F-WWDK	664
☐ N665AW	Airbus A320-232	1644	ex F-WWDN	665
☐ N667AW	Airbus A320-232	1710	ex F-WWIX	667
☐ N668AW	Airbus A320-232	1764	ex F-WWBZ	668
☐ N669AW	Airbus A320-232	1792	ex F-WWDX	669
☐ N672AW	Airbus A320-232	2193	ex F-WWDZ	672
☐ N673AW	Airbus A320-232	2312	ex F-WWDJ	673
☐ N675AW	Airbus A320-232	2405	ex F-WWDA	675
☐ N676AW	Airbus A320-232	2422	ex F-WWBB	676
☐ N677AW	Airbus A320-232	2430	ex F-WWBJ	677
☐ N678AW	Airbus A320-232	2482	ex F-WWIN	678
☐ N679AW	Airbus A320-232	2613	ex F-WWIX	679
☐ N680AW	Airbus A320-232	2630	ex F-WWDX	680
☐ N150UW	Airbus A321-211	5504	ex D-AZAN	150
☐ N151UW	Airbus A321-211	5513	ex D-AZAP	151
☐ N152UW	Airbus A321-211	5588	ex D-AVZK	152
☐ N153UW	Airbus A321-211	5594	ex D-AVZL	153
☐ N154UW	Airbus A321-211	5644	ex D-AVZS	154
☐ N155UW	Airbus A321-211	5659	ex D-AVZV	155
☐ N156UW	Airbus A321-211	5684	ex D-AZAB	156
☐ N157UW	Airbus A321-211	5696	ex D-AZAG	157
☐ N161UW	Airbus A321-211	1403	ex D-AVZD	161
☐ N162UW	Airbus A321-211	1412	ex D-AVZF	162
☐ N163US	Airbus A321-211	1417	ex D-AVZG	163
☐ N165US	Airbus A321-211	1431	ex D-AVZB	165
☐ N167US	Airbus A321-211	1442	ex D-AVXA	167
☐ N169UW	Airbus A321-211	1455	ex D-AVXD	169
☐ N170US	Airbus A321-211	1462	ex D-AVZM	170
☐ N171US	Airbus A321-211	1465	ex D-AVZN	171
☐ N172US	Airbus A321-211	1472	ex D-AVZO	172
☐ N173US	Airbus A321-211	1481	ex D-AVZI	173
☐ N174US	Airbus A321-211	1492	ex D-AVZR	174
☐ N176UW	Airbus A321-211	1499	ex D-AVZT	176
☐ N177US	Airbus A321-211	1517	ex D-AVZF	177
☐ N178US	Airbus A321-211	1519	ex D-AVZH	178
☐ N179UW	Airbus A321-211	1521	ex D-AVZJ	179
☐ N180US	Airbus A321-211	1525	ex D-AVZV	180
☐ N181UW	Airbus A321-211	1531	ex D-AVZW	181
☐ N182UW	Airbus A321-211	1536	ex D-AVZB	182
☐ N183UW	Airbus A321-211	1539	ex D-AVZC	183
☐ N184US	Airbus A321-211	1651	ex D-AVZQ	184
☐ N185UW	Airbus A321-211	1666	ex D-AVZI	185
☐ N186US	Airbus A321-211	1701	ex D-AVZD	186
☐ N187US	Airbus A321-211	1704	ex D-AVZE	187
☐ N188US	Airbus A321-211	1724	ex D-AVXB	188
☐ N189UW	Airbus A321-211	1425	ex N164UW	189
☐ N190UW	Airbus A321-211	1436	ex N166US	190
☐ N191UW	Airbus A321-211	1447	ex N168US	191
☐ N192UW	Airbus A321-211	1496	ex N175US	192
☐ N193UW	Airbus A321-211	3584	ex D-AVZL	193
☐ N194UW	Airbus A321-211	3629	ex D-AVZI	194
☐ N195UW	Airbus A321-211	3633	ex D-AVZJ	195
☐ N196UW	Airbus A321-211	3879	ex D-AVZR	196
☐ N197UW	Airbus A321-211	3928	ex D-AZAC	197
☐ N198UW	Airbus A321-211	5444	ex D-AVZU	198
☐ N199UW	Airbus A321-211	5475	ex D-AZAG	188
☐ N101NN	Airbus A321-231/S	5834	ex D-AVZK	783
☐ N102NN	Airbus A321-231/S	5860	ex D-AVZQ	784
☐ N103NN	Airbus A321-231/S	5884	ex D-AVZW	785
☐ N104NN	Airbus A321-231/S	5895	ex D-AVZY	786
☐ N105NN	Airbus A321-231/S	5904	ex D-AZZA	787
☐ N106NN	Airbus A321-231/S	5932	ex D-AZAS	
☐ N107NN	Airbus A321-231/S	5938	ex D-AZAW	
☐ N108NN	Airbus A321-231/S	5946	ex D-AVZB	
☐ N109NN	Airbus A321-231/S	5955	ex D-AZAE	
☐ N110AN	Airbus A321-231/S	5975	ex D-AZAO	
☐ N111ZM	Airbus A321-231/S	5983	ex D-AZAQ	
☐ N112AN	Airbus A321-231/S	5991	ex D-AVZT	
☐ N113AN	Airbus A321-231/S	6020	ex D-AVZH	
☐ N114NN	Airbus A321-231/S	6046	ex D-AVZK	

☐ N115NN	Airbus A321-231/S	6063	ex D-AVZU		
☐ N116AN	Airbus A321-231/S	6070	ex D-AVZW		
☐ N117NN	Airbus A321-231/S	6094	ex D-AZAB		
☐ N118NN	Airbus A321-231/S	6162	ex D-AVXR		♦
☐ N119NN	Airbus A321-231/S	6222	ex D-AVZB		♦
☐ N120EE	Airbus A321-231/S	6227	ex D-AVZJ	852	♦
☐ N121AN	Airbus A321-231/S	6238	ex D-AVZA	853	♦
☐ N122NN	Airbus A321-231/S	6252	ex D-AVZF	854	♦
☐ N123NN	Airbus A321-231/S	6256	ex D-AVZI	855	♦
☐ N124AA	Airbus A321-231/S	6271	ex D-AVZO	856	♦
☐ N125AA	Airbus A321-231/S	6272	ex D-AVZP	857	♦
☐ N126AN	Airbus A321-231/S	6313	ex D-AZAB	858	♦
☐ N127AA	Airbus A321-231/S	6334	ex D-AVXF	859	♦
☐ N128AN	Airbus A321-231/S	6346	ex D-AVXJ	860	♦
☐ N129AA	Airbus A321-231/S	6401	ex D-AZAH	861	♦
☐ N130AN	Airbus A321-231/S	6407	ex D-AZAL	862	♦
☐ N131NN	Airbus A321-231/S	6472	ex D-AVZJ	863	♦
☐ N132AN	Airbus A321-231/S	6473	ex D-AVZI	864	♦
☐ N133AN	Airbus A321-231/S	6482	ex D-AVZO	865	♦
☐ N134AN	Airbus A321-231/S	6495	ex D-AVZT	866	♦
☐ N135NN	Airbus A321-231/S	6520	ex D-AZAB	867	♦
☐ N136AN	Airbus A321-231/S	6532	ex D-AZAI	868	♦
☐ N507AY	Airbus A321-231	3712	ex D-AVZP	507	
☐ N508AY	Airbus A321-231	3740	ex D-AZAL	508	
☐ N509AY	Airbus A321-231	3796	ex D-AZAS	509	
☐ N510UW	Airbus A321-231	3858	ex D-AVZI	510	
☐ N519UW	Airbus A321-231	3881	ex D-AVZT	519	
☐ N520UW	Airbus A321-231	3924	ex D-AZAA	520	
☐ N521UW	Airbus A321-231	3944	ex D-AZAJ	521	
☐ N523UW	Airbus A321-231	3960	ex D-AZAV	523	
☐ N524UW	Airbus A321-231	3977	ex F-WWIX	524	
☐ N534UW	Airbus A321-231	3989	ex D-AZAO	534	
☐ N535UW	Airbus A321-231	3993	ex D-AZAP	535	
☐ N536UW	Airbus A321-231	4025	ex D-AVZH	536	
☐ N537UW	Airbus A321-231	4041	ex D-AVZJ	537	
☐ N538UW	Airbus A321-231	4050	ex D-AZAK	538	
☐ N539UW	Airbus A321-231	4082	ex D-AVZV	539	
☐ N540UW	Airbus A321-231	4107	ex D-AZAD	540	
☐ N541UW	Airbus A321-231	4123	ex D-AZAI	541	
☐ N542UW	Airbus A321-231	4134	ex D-AZAL	542	
☐ N543UW	Airbus A321-231	4843	ex D-AVZW	543	
☐ N544UW	Airbus A321-231	4847	ex D-AVZX	544	
☐ N545UW	Airbus A321-231	4850	ex D-AVZY	545	
☐ N546UW	Airbus A321-231	4885	ex D-AVZD	546	
☐ N547UW	Airbus A321-231	4893	ex D-AVZE	547	
☐ N548UW	Airbus A321-231	4898	ex D-AVZF	548	
☐ N549UW	Airbus A321-231	4932	ex D-AVZK	549	
☐ N550UW	Airbus A321-231	4935	ex D-AVZL	550	
☐ N551UW	Airbus A321-231	4940	ex D-AZAB	551	
☐ N552UW	Airbus A321-231	4957	ex D-AZAE	552	
☐ N553UW	Airbus A321-231	4960	ex D-AZAF	553	
☐ N554UW	Airbus A321-231	4966	ex D-AVZB	554	
☐ N555AY	Airbus A321-231	5235	ex D-AVZM	555	
☐ N556UW	Airbus A321-231	5244	ex D-AVZW	556	
☐ N557UW	Airbus A321-231	5269	ex D-AZAC	557	
☐ N558UW	Airbus A321-231	5282	ex D-AZAG	558	
☐ N559UW	Airbus A321-231	5292	ex D-AZAJ	559	
☐ N560UW	Airbus A321-231	5300	ex D-AZAM	560	
☐ N561UW	Airbus A321-231	5317	ex D-AZAR	561	
☐ N562UW	Airbus A321-231	5332	ex D-AZAU	562	
☐ N563UW	Airbus A321-231	5368	ex D-AVZF	563	
☐ N564UW	Airbus A321-231	5374	ex D-AVZG	564	
☐ N565UW	Airbus A321-231	5409	ex D-AVZL	565	
☐ N566UW	Airbus A321-231	5422	ex D-AVZQ	566	
☐ N567UW	Airbus A321-231	5728	ex D-AZAV	567	
☐ N568UW	Airbus A321-231	5751	ex D-AZAM	568	
☐ N569UW	Airbus A321-231	5763	ex D-AZAP	569	
☐ N570UW	Airbus A321-231	5795	ex D-AVZD	570	
☐ N571UW	Airbus A321-231	5800	ex D-AVZE	571	
☐ N572UW	Airbus A321-231	5899	ex D-AVZZ	572	
☐ N573UW	Airbus A321-231	5939	ex D-AZAX	573	
☐ N575UW	Airbus A321-231	5980	ex D-AZAP	575	
☐ N576UW	Airbus A321-231	6027	ex D-AVZL	576	
☐ N578UW	Airbus A321-231	6035	ex D-AVZN	578	
☐ N579UW	Airbus A321-231	6100	ex D-AZAF	579	
☐ N580UW	Airbus A321-231	6133	ex D-AVXJ	580	
☐ N581UW	Airbus A321-231	6152	ex D-AVXO	581	
☐ N582UW	Airbus A321-231	6175	ex D-AVXW	582	
☐ N583UW	Airbus A321-231	6181	ex D-AVXY	583	
☐ N584UW	Airbus A321-231	6194	ex D-AZAH	584	♦
☐ N585UW	Airbus A321-231	6214	ex D-AZAV	585	♦
☐ N586UW	Airbus A321-231	6230	ex D-AZAO	586	♦
☐ N587UW	Airbus A321-231	6236	ex D-AZAU	587	♦

☐	N912UY	Airbus A321-231	6264	ex D-AVZL	912	♦
☐	N913US	Airbus A321-231	6255	ex D-AVZH	913	♦
☐	N914UY	Airbus A321-231	6337	ex D-AVXG	914	♦
☐	N915US	Airbus A321-231	6387	ex D-AVXV	915	♦
☐	N916US	Airbus A321-231	6420	ex D-AZAP	916	♦
☐	N917UY	Airbus A321-231	6427	ex D-AZAT	917	♦
☐	N918US	Airbus A321-231	6443	ex D-AVZB	918	♦
☐	N919US	Airbus A321-231	6479	ex D-AVZM	919	♦
☐	N920US	Airbus A321-231	6490	ex D-AVZR	920	♦
☐	N921US	Airbus A321-231	6523	ex D-AZAC	921	♦
☐	N922US	Airbus A321-231	6537	ex D-AVZN	922	♦
☐	N923US	Airbus A321-231	6543	ex D-AZAE	923	♦
☐	N924US	Airbus A321-231	6569	ex D-AZAR	924	♦
☐	N925UY	Airbus A321-231	6613	ex D-AVXO		o/o♦
☐	N927UW	Airbus A321-231	6625	ex D-AVXS	927	o/o♦
☐	N971UY	Airbus A321-231	6249	ex N911UY	971	♦
☐	N	Airbus A321-231	6618	ex		o/o♦
☐	N	Airbus A321-231/S	6647	ex		o/o♦
☐	N	Airbus A321-231/S	6650	ex		o/o♦
☐	N	Airbus A321-231/S	6656	ex		o/o♦
☐	N	Airbus A321-231/S	6667	ex		o/o♦
☐	N	Airbus A321-231/S	6687	ex		o/o♦
☐	N	Airbus A321-231/S	6711	ex		o/o♦
☐	N	Airbus A321-231/S	6723	ex		o/o♦
☐	N	Airbus A321-231/S	6745	ex		o/o♦
☐	N	Airbus A321-231/S	6761	ex		o/o♦
☐	N	Airbus A321-231/S	6802	ex		o/o♦
☐	N	Airbus A321-231/S	6812	ex		o/o♦
☐	N	Airbus A321-231/S	6822	ex		o/o♦
☐	N	Airbus A321-231/S	6840	ex		o/o♦
☐	N	Airbus A321-231/S	6844	ex		o/o♦
☐	N	Airbus A321-231/S	6866	ex		o/o♦
☐	N	Airbus A321-231/S	6899	ex		o/o♦
☐	N	Airbus A321-231/S	6928	ex		o/o♦
☐	N	Airbus A321-231/S	6935	ex		o/o♦
☐	N	Airbus A321-231/S	6940	ex		o/o♦
☐	N279AY	Airbus A330-243	1011	ex F-WWYG	279	
☐	N280AY	Airbus A330-243	1022	ex F-WWYP	280	
☐	N281AY	Airbus A330-243	1041	ex F-WWYT	281	
☐	N282AY	Airbus A330-243	1069	ex F-WWYG	282	
☐	N283AY	Airbus A330-243	1076	ex F-WWKP	283	
☐	N284AY	Airbus A330-243	1095	ex F-WWYS	284	
☐	N285AY	Airbus A330-243	1100	ex F-WWYF	285	
☐	N286AY	Airbus A330-243	1415	ex F-WWTM	286	
☐	N287AY	Airbus A330-243	1417	ex F-WWCE	287	
☐	N288AY	Airbus A330-243	1441	ex F-WWKI	288	
☐	N289AY	Airbus A330-243	1455	ex F-WWYH	289	
☐	N290AY	Airbus A330-243	1480	ex F-WWYV	290	
☐	N291AY	Airbus A330-243	1502	ex F-WWTX	291	
☐	N292AY	Airbus A330-243	1512	ex F-WWKO	292	
☐	N293AY	Airbus A330-243	1526	ex F-WWYH	293	
☐	N270AY	Airbus A330-323X	315	ex N670UW	270	
☐	N271AY	Airbus A330-323X	323	ex N671UW	271	
☐	N272AY	Airbus A330-323X	333	ex N672UW	272	
☐	N273AY	Airbus A330-323X	337	ex N673UW	273	
☐	N274AY	Airbus A330-323X	342	ex N674UW	274	
☐	N275AY	Airbus A330-323X	370	ex N675US	275	
☐	N276AY	Airbus A330-323X	375	ex N676UW	276	
☐	N277AY	Airbus A330-323X	380	ex N677UW	277	
☐	N278AY	Airbus A330-323X	388	ex N678US	278	
☐	N800NN	Boeing 737-823/W	29564/2964		3DY	
☐	N801NN	Boeing 737-823/W	29565/2972		3EA	
☐	N802NN	Boeing 737-823/W	31073/2982		3EB	
☐	N803NN	Boeing 737-823/W	29566/2995		3EC	
☐	N804NN	Boeing 737-823/W	29567/3004		3ED	
☐	N805NN	Boeing 737-823/W	31075/3013		3EE	
☐	N806NN	Boeing 737-823/W	29561/3028		3EF	
☐	N807NN	Boeing 737-823/W	31077/3035		3EF	
☐	N808NN	Boeing 737-823/W	33206/3042		3EH	
☐	N809NN	Boeing 737-823/W	33519/3050		3EJ	
☐	N810NN	Boeing 737-823/W	33207/3056		3EK	
☐	N811NN	Boeing 737-823/W	31079/3063		3EL	
☐	N812NN	Boeing 737-823/W	33520/3070		3EM	
☐	N813NN	Boeing 737-823/W	30918/3077		3EN	
☐	N814NN	Boeing 737-823/W	29562/3085		3EP	
☐	N815NN	Boeing 737-823/W	33208/3094		3ER	
☐	N816NN	Boeing 737-823/W	31081/3102		3ES	
☐	N817NN	Boeing 737-823/W	29558/3107		3ET	
☐	N818NN	Boeing 737-823/W	30910/3112		3EU	
☐	N819NN	Boeing 737-823/W	31083/3118		3EV	

☐	N820NN	Boeing 737-823/W	29559/3125		3EW
☐	N821NN	Boeing 737-823/W	30912/3137		3EX
☐	N822NN	Boeing 737-823/W	31085/3149		3EY
☐	N823NN	Boeing 737-823/W	29560/3156		3FA
☐	N824NN	Boeing 737-823/W	30916/3170		3FB
☐	N825NN	Boeing 737-823/W	31087/3178		3FC
☐	N826NN	Boeing 737-823/W	31089/3185		3FD
☐	N827NN	Boeing 737-823/W	33209/3193	ex N1786B	3FE
☐	N829NN	Boeing 737-823/W	33210/3200	ex N1787B	3FF
☐	N830NN	Boeing 737-823/W	31091/3209	ex N1786B	3FG
☐	N831NN	Boeing 737-823/W	33211/3217	ex N1796B	3FH
☐	N832NN	Boeing 737-823/W	33521/3228	ex N1786B	3FJ
☐	N833NN	Boeing 737-823/W	31093/3236	ex N1786B	3FK
☐	N834NN	Boeing 737-823/W	29576/3244	ex N1787B	3FL
☐	N835NN	Boeing 737-823/W	29577/3252	ex N1796B	3FM
☐	N836NN	Boeing 737-823/W	31095/3260	ex N1786B	3FN
☐	N837NN	Boeing 737-823/W	30908/3268	ex N1786B	3FP oneWorld c/s
☐	N838NN	Boeing 737-823/W	31097/3276		3FR oneWorld c/s
☐	N839NN	Boeing 737-823/W	29557/3282	ex N1786B	3FS
☐	N840NN	Boeing 737-823/W	33518/3291	ex N1786B	3FT
☐	N841NN	Boeing 737-823/W	30914/3298		3FU
☐	N842NN	Boeing 737-823/W	31099/3307	ex N1786B	3FV
☐	N843NN	Boeing 737-823/W	30906/3328	ex N1787B	3FW
☐	N844NN	Boeing 737-823/W	33212/3334		3FX
☐	N845NN	Boeing 737-823/W	40579/3340	ex N1786B	3FY
☐	N846NN	Boeing 737-823/W	31101/3347		3GA
☐	N847NN	Boeing 737-823/W	29575/3361		3GB
☐	N848NN	Boeing 737-823/W	31103/3367		3GC
☐	N849NN	Boeing 737-823/W	33213/3373		3GD
☐	N850NN	Boeing 737-823/W	40580/3380		3GE
☐	N851NN	Boeing 737-823/W	29556/3390		3GF
☐	N852NN	Boeing 737-823/W	40581/3396		3GG
☐	N853NN	Boeing 737-823/W	31105/3404		3GH
☐	N854NN	Boeing 737-823/W	33214/3412		3GJ
☐	N855NN	Boeing 737-823/W	40852/3422		3GK
☐	N856NN	Boeing 737-823/W	31107/3427		3GL
☐	N857NN	Boeing 737-823/W	30907/3434		3GM
☐	N858NN	Boeing 737-823/W	30904/3440		3GN
☐	N859NN	Boeing 737-823/W	29555/3456		3GP
☐	N860NN	Boeing 737-823/W	40583/3462		3GR
☐	N861NN	Boeing 737-823/W	31109/3468		3GS
☐	N862NN	Boeing 737-823/W	30905/3475		3GT
☐	N863NN	Boeing 737-823/W	30903/3481		3GU
☐	N864NN	Boeing 737-823/W	31111/3487		3GV
☐	N865NN	Boeing 737-823/W	29554/3493	ex N1787B	3GW
☐	N866NN	Boeing 737-823/W	40584/3499		3GX
☐	N867NN	Boeing 737-823/W	40762/3634		3GY
☐	N868NN	Boeing 737-823/W	40763/3668		3HA
☐	N869NN	Boeing 737-823/W	40764/3689		3HB
☐	N870NN	Boeing 737-823/W	40765/3748		3HE
☐	N871NN	Boeing 737-823/W	31127/3731		3HC
☐	N872NN	Boeing 737-823/W	33219/3740		3HD
☐	N873NN	Boeing 737-823/W	40766/3775		3HG
☐	N874NN	Boeing 737-823/W	31129/3764		3HF
☐	N875NN	Boeing 737-823/W	33220/3782		3HH
☐	N876NN	Boeing 737-823/W	40767/3793		3HJ
☐	N877NN	Boeing 737-823/W	31131/3808		3HF
☐	N878NN	Boeing 737-823/W	40768/3820		3HL
☐	N879NN	Boeing 737-823/W	31133/3833		3HM
☐	N880NN	Boeing 737-823/W	40769/3854		3HN
☐	N881NN	Boeing 737-823/W	31135/3862		3HP
☐	N882NN	Boeing 737-823/W	33221/3880		3HR
☐	N883NN	Boeing 737-823/W	31137/3892		
☐	N884NN	Boeing 737-823/W	33222/3914		
☐	N885NN	Boeing 737-823/W	31139/3935		
☐	N886NN	Boeing 737-823/W	33223/3950		
☐	N887NN	Boeing 737-823/W	31141/3964		
☐	N889NN	Boeing 737-823/W	33314/3981		
☐	N890NN	Boeing 737-823/W	31143/3999		
☐	N891NN	Boeing 737-823/W	33315/4022		
☐	N892NN	Boeing 737-823/W	31145/4040		
☐	N893NN	Boeing 737-823/W	33316/4053		
☐	N894NN	Boeing 737-823/W	31147/4066		
☐	N895NN	Boeing 737-823/W	31149/4079		
☐	N896NN	Boeing 737-823/W	33224/4093		
☐	N897NN	Boeing 737-823/W	33318/4106		
☐	N898NN	Boeing 737-823/W	33225/4129		
☐	N899NN	Boeing 737-823/W	31151/4142		
☐	N901AN	Boeing 737-823/W	29503/184		3AA
☐	N901NN	Boeing 737-823/W	33226/4155		
☐	N902AN	Boeing 737-823/W	29504/190		3AB
☐	N902NN	Boeing 737-323/W	31154/4168		
☐	N903AN	Boeing 737-823/W	29505/196		3AC

☐ N903NN	Boeing 737-823/W	31153/4183		
☐ N904AN	Boeing 737-823/W	29506/207		3AD
☐ N904NN	Boeing 737-823/W	33317/4197		
☐ N905AN	Boeing 737-823/W	29507/231		3AE
☐ N905NN	Boeing 737-823/W	31156/4210		3JP
☐ N906AN	Boeing 737-823/W	29508/240		3AF
☐ N906NN	Boeing 737-823/W	31155/4223		3JR
☐ N907AN	Boeing 737-823/W	29509/254		3AG
☐ N907NN	Boeing 737-823/W	31158/4235		3JS
☐ N908AN	Boeing 737-823/W	29510/263		3AH
☐ N908NN	Boeing 737-823/W	31157/4247		3JT
☐ N909AN	Boeing 737-823/W	29511/267	ex (N909AM)	3AJ
☐ N909NN	Boeing 737-823/W	31159/4259		3JU
☐ N910AN	Boeing 737-823/W	29512/271		3AK
☐ N910NN	Boeing 737-823/W	31160/4273		3JV
☐ N912AN	Boeing 737-823/W	29513/289		3AL
☐ N912NN	Boeing 737-823/W	33319/4286		3JW
☐ N913AN	Boeing 737-823/W	29514/293		3AM
☐ N913NN	Boeing 737-823/W	29571/4309		3JX
☐ N914AN	Boeing 737-823/W	29515/316		3AN
☐ N914NN	Boeing 737-823/W	31161/4315		3JY
☐ N915AN	Boeing 737-823/W	29516/322		3AP
☐ N915NN	Boeing 737-823/W	33227/4322		3KA
☐ N916AN	Boeing 737-823/W	29517/332		3AR
☐ N916NN	Boeing 737-823/W	31163/4333		3KB
☐ N917AN	Boeing 737-823/W	29518/344		3AS
☐ N917NN	Boeing 737-823/W	29572/4341		3KC
☐ N918AN	Boeing 737-823/W	29519/353		3AT
☐ N918NN	Boeing 737-823/W	33228/4352		3KD
☐ N919AN	Boeing 737-823/W	29520/363		3AU
☐ N919NN	Boeing 737-823/W	29573/4363		3KE
☐ N920AN	Boeing 737-823/W	29521/378		3AV
☐ N920NN	Boeing 737-823/W	31165/4373		3KF
☐ N921AN	Boeing 737-823/W	29522/383		3AW
☐ N921NN	Boeing 737-823/W	33229/4390		3KG
☐ N922AN	Boeing 737-823/W	29523/398		3AX
☐ N922NN	Boeing 737-823/W	29574/4401		3KH
☐ N923AN	Boeing 737-823/W	29524/405		3AY
☐ N923NN	Boeing 737-823/W	31167/4410		3KJ
☐ N924AN	Boeing 737-823/W	29525/434		3BA
☐ N924NN	Boeing 737-823/W	33486/4438		3KK
☐ N925AN	Boeing 737-823/W	29526/440		3BB
☐ N925NN	Boeing 737-823/W	31169/4444		3KL
☐ N926AN	Boeing 737-823/W	29527/453		3BC
☐ N926NN	Boeing 737-823/W	33321/4451		3KM
☐ N927AN	Boeing 737-823/W	30077/462		3BD
☐ N927NN	Boeing 737-823/W	31171/4459		3KN
☐ N928AN	Boeing 737-823/W	29528/473		3BE
☐ N928NN	Boeing 737-823/W	31172/4478		3KP
☐ N929AN	Boeing 737-823/W	30078/488		3BF
☐ N929NN	Boeing 737-823/W	33322/4489		3KR
☐ N930AN	Boeing 737-823/W	29529/503		3BG
☐ N930NN	Boeing 737-823/W	33487/4507		3KS
☐ N931AN	Boeing 737-823/W	30079/509		3BH
☐ N931NN	Boeing 737-823/W	33230/4523		3KT
☐ N932AN	Boeing 737-823/W	29530/527		3BJ
☐ N932NN	Boeing 737-823/W	33488/4530		3KU
☐ N933AN	Boeing 737-823/W	30080/531		3BK
☐ N933NN	Boeing 737-823/W	31173/4540		3KV
☐ N934AN	Boeing 737-823/W	29531/553		3BL
☐ N934NN	Boeing 737-823/W	33489/4558		3KW
☐ N935AN	Boeing 737-823/W	30081/559		3BM
☐ N935NN	Boeing 737-823/W	33231/4563		3KX
☐ N936AN	Boeing 737-823/W	29532/575		3BN
☐ N936NN	Boeing 737-823/W	31176/4580		3KY
☐ N937AN	Boeing 737-823/W	30082/579		3BP
☐ N937NN	Boeing 737-823/W	31178/4594		3LA
☐ N938AN	Boeing 737-823/W	29533/608		3BR
☐ N938NN	Boeing 737-823/W	33490/4605		3LB
☐ N939AN	Boeing 737-823/W	30083/612		3BS
☐ N939NN	Boeing 737-823/W	33491/4629		3LC
☐ N940AN	Boeing 737-823/W	30598/616		3BT
☐ N940NN	Boeing 737-823/W	33323/4655		3LD
☐ N941AN	Boeing 737-823/W	29534/624		3BU
☐ N941NN	Boeing 737-823/W	33232/4683		3LE
☐ N942AN	Boeing 737-823/W	30084/629		3BV
☐ N942NN	Boeing 737-823/W	33492/4691		3LF
☐ N943AN	Boeing 737-823/W	30599/635		3BW
☐ N943NN	Boeing 737-823/W	31177/4724		3LG
☐ N944AN	Boeing 737-823/W	29535/645		3BX
☐ N944NN	Boeing 737-823/W	31185/4742		3LH
☐ N945AN	Boeing 737-823/W	30085/649		3BY
☐ N945NN	Boeing 737-823/W	33233/4763		3LJ

☐	N946AN	Boeing 737-823/W	30600/655		3CA
☐	N946NN	Boeing 737-823/W	33234/4776		3LK
☐	N947AN	Boeing 737-823/W	29536/671	ex (N2292Z)	3CB
☐	N947NN	Boeing 737-823/W	31190/4811		3LL
☐	N948AN	Boeing 737-823/W	30086/679	ex (N2294B)	3CC
☐	N948NN	Boeing 737-823/W	31189/4835		3LM
☐	N949AN	Boeing 737-823/W	29537/699		3CD
☐	N949NN	Boeing 737-823/W	31192/4871		3LN
☐	N950AN	Boeing 737-823/W	30087/704		3CE
☐	N950NN	Boeing 737-823/W	31194/4891		3LP
☐	N951AA	Boeing 737-823/W	29538/720		3CF Astrojet c/s
☐	N951NN	Boeing 737-823/W	33327/4923		3LR
☐	N952AA	Boeing 737-823/W	30088/726		3CG
☐	N952NN	Boeing 737-823/W	31196/4951		3LS
☐	N953AN	Boeing 737-823/W	29539/741		3CH
☐	N953NN	Boeing 737-823/W	33328/4929		3LT
☐	N954AN	Boeing 737-823/W	30089/745		3CJ
☐	N954NN	Boeing 737-823/W	31197/4983		3LU
☐	N955AN	Boeing 737-823/W	29540/762		3CK
☐	N955NN	Boeing 737-823/W	31199/5033		3LV
☐	N956AN	Boeing 737-823/W	30090/764		3CL
☐	N956NN	Boeing 737-823/W	31200/5024		3LW
☐	N957AN	Boeing 737-823/W	29541/788		3CM
☐	N957NN	Boeing 737-823/W	31202/5071	ex N1787B	3LX
☐	N958AN	Boeing 737-823/W	30091/797		3CN
☐	N958NN	Boeing 737-823/W	31203/5113		3LY ♦
☐	N959AN	Boeing 737-823/W	30828/801		3CP
☐	N959NN	Boeing 737-823/W	33329/5142		3MA ♦
☐	N960AN	Boeing 737-823/W	29542/818		3CR
☐	N960NN	Boeing 737-823/W	33330/5156		3MB ♦
☐	N961AN	Boeing 737-823/W	30092/822		3CS
☐	N961NN	Boeing 737-823/W	31205/5171		3MC ♦
☐	N962AN	Boeing 737-823/W	30858/825		3CT
☐	N962NN	Boeing 737-823/W	33331/5191		3MD ♦
☐	N963AN	Boeing 737-823/W	29543/834		3CU
☐	N963NN	Boeing 737-823/W	31208/5207		3ME ♦
☐	N964AN	Boeing 737-823/W	30093/837		3CV
☐	N964NN	Boeing 737-823/W	31210/5226		3MF ♦
☐	N965AN	Boeing 737-823/W	29544/860		3CW
☐	N965NN	Boeing 737-823/W	33239/5251		3MG ♦
☐	N966AN	Boeing 737-823/W	30094/863		3CX
☐	N966NN	Boeing 737-823/W	33240/5288		3MH ♦
☐	N967AN	Boeing 737-823/W	29545/883		3CY
☐	N967NN	Boeing 737-823/W	31214/5304		3MJ ♦
☐	N968AN	Boeing 737-823/W	30095/886		3DA
☐	N968NN	Boeing 737-823/W	33241/5348		3MK ♦
☐	N969AN	Boeing 737-823/W	29546/910		3DB
☐	N969NN	Boeing 737-823/W	31215/5360	ex N1787B	3ML ♦
☐	N970AN	Boeing 737-823/W	30096/915		3DC
☐	N970NN	Boeing 737-823/W	31218/5394		♦
☐	N971AN	Boeing 737-823/W	29547/937		3DD
☐	N971NN	Boeing 737-823/W	31217/5413		♦
☐	N972AN	Boeing 737-823/W	30097/941		3DE
☐	N972NN	Boeing 737-823/W	33334/		o/o♦
☐	N973AN	Boeing 737-823/W	29548/971		3DF
☐	N973NN	Boeing 737-823/W	31219/		o/o♦
☐	N974AN	Boeing 737-823/W	30098/977		3DG
☐	N975AN	Boeing 737-823/W	29549/992		3DH
☐	N976AN	Boeing 737-823/W	30099/1001		3DJ
☐	N976NN	Boeing 737-823/W	33243/		o/o♦
☐	N977NN	Boeing 737-823/W	31225/		o/o♦
☐	N978AN	Boeing 737-823/W	30100/1022		3DL
☐	N978NN	Bieung 737-823/W	31226/		o/o♦
☐	N979AN	Boeing 737-823/W	29568/2838		3DM
☐	N980AN	Boeing 737-823/W	33203/2846		3DN
☐	N981AN	Boeing 737-823/W	29569/2870		3DP
☐	N982AN	Boeing 737-823/W	31067/2876		3DR
☐	N983AN	Boeing 737-823/W	29570/2899		3DS
☐	N987AN	Boeing 737-823/W	31069/2907		3DT
☐	N989AN	Boeing 737-823/W	33205/2915		3DU
☐	N990AN	Boeing 737-823/W	29563/2935		3DV
☐	N991AN	Boeing 737-823/W	30920/2945		3DW
☐	N992AN	Boeing 737-823/W	31071/2954		3DX
☐	N172AJ	Boeing 757-223/W	32400/1012		5FT
☐	N173AN	Boeing 757-223/W	32399/1005		5FS
☐	N174AA	Boeing 757-223/W	31308/998		5FR
☐	N175AN	Boeing 757-223/W	32394/992		5FK
☐	N176AA	Boeing 757-223/W	32395/994		5FL
☐	N177AN	Boeing 757-223/W	32396/996		5FM
☐	N178AA	Boeing 757-223/W	32398/1002	ex (N20171)	5FN
☐	N179AA	Boeing 757-223/W	32397/1000	ex (N20140)	5FP
☐	N181AN	Boeing 757-223/W	29591/852	ex N5573L	5EN

☐	N182AN	Boeing 757-223/W	29592/853		5EP	
☐	N183AN	Boeing 757-223ER/W	29593/862		5ER	
☐	N184AN	Boeing 757-223ER/W	29594/866	ex N1787B	5ES	
☐	N185AN	Boeing 757-223/W	32379/962		5ET	[ROW]
☐	N186AN	Boeing 757-223/W	32380/964		5EU	
☐	N187AN	Boeing 757-223/W	32381/965		5EV	
☐	N188AN	Boeing 757-223/W	32382/969		5EW	
☐	N189AN	Boeing 757-223/W	32383/970		5EX	
☐	N190AA	Boeing 757-223/W	32384/973		5EY	
☐	N191AN	Boeing 757-223/W	32385/977		5FA	
☐	N192AN	Boeing 757-223/W	32386/979		5FB	
☐	N193AN	Boeing 757-223/W	32387/981		5FC	
☐	N194AA	Boeing 757-223/W	32388/983		5FD	
☐	N195AN	Boeing 757-223/W	32389/984		5FE	
☐	N196AA	Boeing 757-223/W	32390/986		5FF	
☐	N197AN	Boeing 757-223/W	32391/988		5FG	
☐	N198AA	Boeing 757-223/W	32392/989		5FH	
☐	N199AN	Boeing 757-223/W	32393/991		5FJ	
☐	N200UU	Boeing 757-2B7/W	27809/673	ex N631AU	200	
☐	N201UU	Boeing 757-2B7/W	27810/678	ex N632AU	201	
☐	N202UW	Boeing 757-2B7/W	27811/681	ex N633AU	202	
☐	N203UW	Boeing 757-23N/W	30548/930	ex N642UW	203	
☐	N204UW	Boeing 757-23N/W	30886/945	ex N643UW	204	
☐	N205UW	Boeing 757-23N/W	30887/946	ex N644UW	205	
☐	N206UW	Boeing 757-2B7/W	27808/666	ex N630AU	206	
☐	N207UW	Boeing 757-28A	32448/967	ex N756NA	207	
☐	N601AN	Boeing 757-223/W	27052/661		5DU	[ROW]
☐	N602AN	Boeing 757-223/W	27053/664		5DV	
☐	N603AA	Boeing 757-223/W	27054/670		5DW	[ROW]
☐	N604AA	Boeing 757-223/W	27055/677		5DX	[ROW]
☐	N605AA	Boeing 757-223/W	27056/680		5DY	[ROW]
☐	N606AA	Boeing 757-223/W	27057/707		5EA	
☐	N607AM	Boeing 757-223/W	27058/712		5EB	
☐	N608AA	Boeing 757-223ER/W	27446/720		5EC	
☐	N609AA	Boeing 757-223ER/W	27447/722		5ED	
☐	N612AA	Boeing 757-223/W	24488/240		612	[ROW]
☐	N613AA	Boeing 757-223/W	24489/242		613	[ROW]
☐	N621AM	Boeing 757-223/W	24579/283		621	[ROW]
☐	N622AA	Boeing 757-223/W	24580/289		622	[ROW]
☐	N623AA	Boeing 757-223/W	24581/296		623	[ROW]
☐	N624AA	Boeing 757-223/W	24582/297		624	[ROW]
☐	N625AA	Boeing 757-223/W	24583/303		625	[ROW]
☐	N626AA	Boeing 757-223/W	24584/304		626	[ROW]
☐	N628AA	Boeing 757-223/W	24586/309		628	[ROW]
☐	N630AA	Boeing 757-223/W	24588/316		630	[ROW]
☐	N631AA	Boeing 757-223/W	24589/317		631	[ROW]
☐	N633AA	Boeing 757-223/W	24591/324		633	
☐	N634AA	Boeing 757-223/W	24592/327		634	
☐	N635AA	Boeing 757-223/W	24593/328		635	
☐	N639AA	Boeing 757-223/W	24597/345		639	[ROW]
☐	N640A	Boeing 757-223/W	24598/350		640	
☐	N645AA	Boeing 757-223/W	24603/370		5BR	[ROW]
☐	N646AA	Boeing 757-223/W	24604/375		5BS	
☐	N647AM	Boeing 757-223/W	24605/378		5BT	
☐	N649AA	Boeing 757-223/W	24607/383		5BV	
☐	N652AA	Boeing 757-223/W	24610/391		5BY	
☐	N653A	Boeing 757-223/W	24611/397		5CA	
☐	N654A	Boeing 757-223/W	24612/398		5CB	[ROW]
☐	N655AA	Boeing 757-223/W	24613/402		5CC	
☐	N656AA	Boeing 757-223/W	24614/404		5CD	
☐	N657AM	Boeing 757-223/W	24615/409		5CE	
☐	N658AA	Boeing 757-223/W	24616/410		5CF	
☐	N659AA	Boeing 757-223/W	24617/417		5CG Pride of American	
☐	N660AM	Boeing 757-223/W	25294/418		5CH	
☐	N662AA	Boeing 757-223/W	25296/425		5CK	
☐	N663AM	Boeing 757-223/W	25297/432		5CL	[ROW]
☐	N665AA	Boeing 757-223/W	25299/436		5CN	
☐	N666A	Boeing 757-223/W	25300/451		5CP	
☐	N668AA	Boeing 757-223/W	25333/460		5CS	[ROW]
☐	N669AA	Boeing 757-223/W	25334/463		5CT	wfs
☐	N670AA	Boeing 757-223/W	25335/468		5CU	
☐	N671AA	Boeing 757-223/W	25336/473		5CV	[ROW]
☐	N672AA	Boeing 757-223/W	25337/474		5CW	[ROW]
☐	N673AN	Boeing 757-223/W	29423/812		5EE	[ROW]
☐	N674AN	Boeing 757-223/W	29424/816		5EF	[ROW]
☐	N675AN	Boeing 757-223/W	29425/817		5EG	
☐	N676AN	Boeing 757-223/W	29426/827	ex N1798B	5EH	
☐	N677AN	Boeing 757-223/W	29427/828		5EJ	
☐	N678AN	Boeing 757-223/W	29428/837	ex N1787B	5EK	
☐	N679AN	Boeing 757-223/W	29589/842	ex N1800B	5EL Astrojet c/s	
☐	N680AN	Boeing 757-223/W	29590/847		5EM	[ROW]
☐	N681AA	Boeing 757-223/W	25338/483		5CX	[ROW]
☐	N682AA	Boeing 757-223/W	25339/484		5CY	[ROW]

☐ N683A	Boeing 757-223/W	25340/491		5DA	[ROW]
☐ N684AA	Boeing 757-223/W	25341/504		5DB	[ROW]
☐ N685AA	Boeing 757-223/W	25342/507		5DC	[ROW]
☐ N686AA	Boeing 757-223/W	25343/509		5DD	[ROW]
☐ N687AA	Boeing 757-223ER/W	25695/536		5DE	
☐ N688AA	Boeing 757-223ER/W	25730/548		5DF	
☐ N689AA	Boeing 757-223ER/W	25731/562		5DG	
☐ N690AA	Boeing 757-223ER/W	25696/566		5DH	
☐ N691AA	Boeing 757-223ER/W	25697/568		5DJ	
☐ N692AA	Boeing 757-223/W	26972/578		5DK	
☐ N693AA	Boeing 757-223/W	26973/580		5DL	[ROW]
☐ N694AN	Boeing 757-223/W	26974/582		5DM	[ROW]
☐ N695AN	Boeing 757-223/W	26975/621		5DN	[ROW]
☐ N696AN	Boeing 757-223/W	26976/627		5DP	[ROW]
☐ N697AN	Boeing 757-223/W	26977/633		5DR	[ROW]
☐ N698AN	Boeing 757-223/W	26980/635		5DS	[ROW]
☐ N699AN	Boeing 757-223/W	27051/660		5DT	[ROW]
☐ N901AW	Boeing 757-2S7	23321/76	ex N601RC	901	
☐ N902AW	Boeing 757-2S7	23322/79	ex N602RC	902	
☐ N904AW	Boeing 757-2S7	23566/96	ex N604RC	904	
☐ N905AW	Boeing 757-2S7	23567/97	ex N605RC	905	
☐ N906AW	Boeing 757-2S7	23568/99	ex N606RC	906	
☐ N908AW	Boeing 757-2G7/W	24233/244		908	
☐ N909AW	Boeing 757-2G7/W	24522/252		909	
☐ N910AW	Boeing 757-2G7/W	24523/256		910	wfs
☐ N935UW	Boeing 757-2B7/W	27201/605	ex N622AU	935	
☐ N936UW	Boeing 757-2B7/W	27244/607	ex N623AU	936	
☐ N937UW	Boeing 757-2B7/W	27245/630	ex N624AU	937	
☐ N938UW	Boeing 757-2B7/W	27246/643	ex N625VJ	938	
☐ N939UW	Boeing 757-2B7/W	27303/647	ex N626AU	939	
☐ N940UW	Boeing 757-2B7/W	27805/655	ex N627AU	940	
☐ N941UW	Boeing 757-2B7/W	27806/657	ex N628AU	941	
☐ N942UW	Boeing 757-2B7/W	27807/662	ex N629AU	942	
☐ N7667A	Boeing 757-223/W	25301/459		5CR	[ROW]
☐ N251AY	Boeing 767-2B7ER	24764/306	ex N651US	251	[CLT]
☐ N256AY	Boeing 767-2B7ER	26847/486	ex N656US	256	[CLT]
☐ N335AA	Boeing 767-223ER	22333/194		335	[ROW]
☐ N338AA	Boeing 767-223ER	22335/196		338	[MCI]
☐ N339AA	Boeing 767-223ER	22336/198		339	[MCI]
☐ N342AN	Boeing 767-323ER/W	33081/896		342	
☐ N343AN	Boeing 767-323ER/W	33082/899		343	member of OneWorld titles
☐ N344AN	Boeing 767-323ER/W	33083/900		344	
☐ N345AN	Boeing 767-323ER/W	33084/906		345	
☐ N346AN	Boeing 767-323ER/W	33085/907		346	
☐ N347AN	Boeing 767-323ER	33086/908		347	
☐ N348AN	Boeing 767-323ER/W	33087/910		348	
☐ N349AN	Boeing 767-323ER/W	33088/913		349	
☐ N350AN	Boeing 767-323ER/W	33089/916		350	
☐ N351AA	Boeing 767-323ER/W	24032/202		351	
☐ N352AA	Boeing 767-323ER/W	24033/205		352	
☐ N353AA	Boeing 767-323ER/W	24034/206		353	
☐ N354AA	Boeing 767-323ER/W	24035/211		354	
☐ N355AA	Boeing 767-323ER	24036/221		355	
☐ N357AA	Boeing 767-323ER/W	24038/227		357	
☐ N358AA	Boeing 767-323ER	24039/228		358	
☐ N359AA	Boeing 767-323ER/W	24040/230		359	
☐ N360AA	Boeing 767-323ER/W	24041/232		360	
☐ N361AA	Boeing 767-323ER/W	24042/235		361	
☐ N362AA	Boeing 767-323ER/W	24043/237		362	
☐ N363AA	Boeing 767-323ER/W	24044/238		363	
☐ N366AA	Boeing 767-323ER	25193/388		366	
☐ N368AA	Boeing 767-323ER	25195/404		368	
☐ N369AA	Boeing 767-323ER	25196/422		369	
☐ N371AA	Boeing 767-323ER	25198/431		371	
☐ N372AA	Boeing 767-323ER/W	25199/433		372	
☐ N373AA	Boeing 767-323ER/W	25200/435		373	
☐ N374AA	Boeing 767-323ER	25201/437		374	
☐ N376AN	Boeing 767-323ER	25445/447		376	
☐ N377AN	Boeing 767-323ER/W	25446/453		377	
☐ N378AN	Boeing 767-323ER/W	25447/469		378	
☐ N379AA	Boeing 767-323ER/W	25448/481		379	
☐ N380AN	Boeing 767-323ER/W	25449/489		380	
☐ N381AN	Boeing 767-323ER/W	25450/495		381	
☐ N382AN	Boeing 767-323ER/W	25451/498		382	
☐ N383AN	Boeing 767-323ER/W	26995/500		383	
☐ N384AA	Boeing 767-323ER/W	26996/512		384	
☐ N385AM	Boeing 767-323ER/W	27059/536		385	
☐ N386AA	Boeing 767-323ER/W	27060/540		386	
☐ N387AM	Boeing 767-323ER/W	27184/541		387	
☐ N388AA	Boeing 767-323ER/W	27448/563		388	
☐ N389AA	Boeing 767-323ER/W	27449/564		389	

☐	N390AA	Boeing 767-323ER/W	27450/565		390
☐	N391AA	Boeing 767-323ER/W	27451/566		391
☐	N392AN	Boeing 767-323ER/W	29429/700		392
☐	N393AN	Boeing 767-323ER/W	29430/701		393
☐	N394AN	Boeing 767-323ER/W	29431/703		394
☐	N395AN	Boeing 767-323ER/W	29432/709		395
☐	N396AN	Boeing 767-323ER/W	29603/739		396
☐	N397AN	Boeing 767-323ER/W	29604/744		397
☐	N398AN	Boeing 767-323ER/W	29605/748		398
☐	N399AN	Boeing 767-323ER/W	29606/752		399
☐	N7375A	Boeing 767-323ER	25202/441		375
☐	N39356	Boeing 767-323ER/W	24037/226		356
☐	N39364	Boeing 767-323ER/W	24045/240		364
☐	N39365	Boeing 767-323ER/W	24046/241		365
☐	N39367	Boeing 767-323ER	25194/394		367
☐	N750AN	Boeing 777-223ER	30259/332	ex (N798AN)	7BJ
☐	N751AN	Boeing 777-223ER	30798/333		7BK
☐	N752AN	Boeing 777-223ER	30260/339	ex (N799AN)	7BL
☐	N753AN	Boeing 777-223ER	30261/341	ex (N750AN)	7BM
☐	N754AN	Boeing 777-223ER	30262/345		7BN
☐	N755AN	Boeing 777-223ER	30263/354		7BP
☐	N756AM	Boeing 777-223ER	30264/358		7BR
☐	N757AN	Boeing 777-223ER	32636/363		7BS
☐	N758AN	Boeing 777-223ER	32637/371		7BT
☐	N759AN	Boeing 777-223ER	32638/376		7BU Pink Ribbon c/s
☐	N760AN	Boeing 777-223ER	31477/379		7BV
☐	N761AJ	Boeing 777-223ER	31478/393		7BW
☐	N762AN	Boeing 777-223ER	31479/399		7BX
☐	N765AN	Boeing 777-223ER	32879/433		7BY
☐	N766AN	Boeing 777-223ER	32880/445		7CA
☐	N767AJ	Boeing 777-223ER	33539/555		7CB
☐	N768AA	Boeing 777-223ER	33540/566		7CC
☐	N770AN	Boeing 777-223ER	29578/185		7AA
☐	N771AN	Boeing 777-223ER	29579/190		7AB
☐	N772AN	Boeing 777-223ER	29580/198		7AC
☐	N773AN	Boeing 777-223ER	29583/199		7AD
☐	N774AN	Boeing 777-223ER	29581/208		7AE
☐	N775AN	Boeing 777-223ER	29584/209		7AF
☐	N776AN	Boeing 777-223ER	29582/215		7AG
☐	N777AN	Boeing 777-223ER	29585/218		7AH
☐	N778AN	Boeing 777-223ER	29587/223		7AJ
☐	N779AN	Boeing 777-223ER	29955/225		7AK
☐	N780AN	Boeing 777-223ER	29956/241	ex N6055X	7AL
☐	N781AN	Boeing 777-223ER	29586/266		7AM
☐	N782AN	Boeing 777-223ER	30003/270		7AN
☐	N783AN	Boeing 777-223ER	30004/271		7AP
☐	N784AN	Boeing 777-223ER	29588/272		7AR
☐	N785AN	Boeing 777-223ER	30005/274		7AS
☐	N786AN	Boeing 777-223ER	30250/276		7AT
☐	N787AL	Boeing 777-223ER	30010/277		7AU
☐	N788AN	Boeing 777-223ER	30011/283		7AV
☐	N789AN	Boeing 777-223ER	30252/285		7AW
☐	N790AN	Boeing 777-223ER	30251/287		7AX
☐	N791AN	Boeing 777-223ER	30254/289		7AY
☐	N792AN	Boeing 777-223ER	30253/292		7BA
☐	N793AN	Boeing 777-223ER	30255/299		7BB
☐	N794AN	Boeing 777-223ER	30256/313		7BC
☐	N795AN	Boeing 777-223ER	30257/315		7BD
☐	N796AN	Boeing 777-223ER	30796/316		7BE
☐	N797AN	Boeing 777-223ER	30012/321	ex (N796AN)	7BF American Spirit
☐	N798AN	Boeing 777-223ER	30797/324		7BG
☐	N799AN	Boeing 777-223ER	30258/328	ex (N797AN)	7BH
☐	N717AN	Boeing 777-323ER	31543/1053		7LA
☐	N718AN	Boeing 777-323ER	41665/1062		7LB
☐	N719AN	Boeing 777-323ER	41668/1070		7LC
☐	N720AN	Boeing 777-323ER	33522/1075		7LD
☐	N721AN	Boeing 777-323ER	31546/1083		7LE
☐	N722AN	Boeing 777-323ER	31547/1095		7LF
☐	N723AN	Boeing 777-323ER	33125/1103		7LG
☐	N724AN	Boeing 777-323ER	31548/1113		7LH
☐	N725AN	Boeing 777-323ER	41666/1122		7LJ o/o
☐	N726AN	Boeing 777-323ER	31550/1160		7LK
☐	N727AN	Boeing 777-323ER	33541/1176		7LL
☐	N728AN	Boeing 777-323ER	31553/1191		7LM
☐	N729AN	Boeing 777-323ER	33127/1200		7LN
☐	N730AN	Boeing 777-323ER	31554/1217		7LP
☐	N731AN	Boeing 777-323ER	33523/1241		7LR
☐	N732AN	Boeing 777-323ER	31549/1257		7LS
☐	N733AR	Boeing 777-323ER	33524/1270		7LT ♦
☐	N734AR	Boeing 777-323ER	31480/1344		7LU o/o♦
☐	N735AT	Boeing 777-323ER	32439/		7LV o/o♦

□ N736AT	Boeing 777-323ER	33538/		7LW		o/o♦
□ N	Boeing 777-323ER	32439/				o/o
□ N	Boeing 777-323ER	41669/				o/o
□ N800AN	Boeing 787-8	40618/241		8AA		♦
□ N801AC	Boeing 787-8	40619/249		8AB		♦
□ N802AN	Boeing 787-8	40620/255		8AC		♦
□ N803AL	Boeing 787-8	40621/268		8AD		♦
□ N804AN	Boeing 787-8	40622/288		8AE		♦
□ N805AN	Boeing 787-8	40623/290		8AF		♦
□ N806AA	Boeing 787-8	40624/306		8AG		o/o♦
□ N807AA	Boeing 787-8	40625/320		8AH		o/o♦
□ N808AN	Boeing 787-8	40626/326		8AI		o/o♦
□ N809AN	Boeing 787-8	40627/336				o/o♦
□ N810AN	Boeing 787-8	40628/339				o/o♦
□ N811AB	Boeing 787-8	40629/378				o/o♦
□ N812AA	Boeing 787-8	40630/387				o/o♦
□ N813AN	Boeing 787-8	40631/389				o/o♦
□ N944UW	Embraer ERJ-190AR	19000058	ex PT-SIL	944		Republic
□ N945UW	Embraer ERJ-190AR	19000062	ex PT-SJA	945		Republic
□ N946UW	Embraer ERJ-190AR	19000072	ex PT-SJL	946		Republic
□ N947UW	Embraer ERJ-190AR	19000078	ex PT-SJU	947		Republic
□ N948UW	Embraer ERJ-190AR	19000081	ex PT-SJX	948		Republic
□ N949UW	Embraer ERJ-190AR	19000102	ex PT-SNW	949		Republic
□ N950UW	Embraer ERJ-190AR	19000106	ex PT-SQA	950		Republic
□ N951UW	Embraer ERJ-190AR	19000112	ex PT-SQG	951		Republic
□ N952UW	Embraer ERJ-190AR	19000119	ex PT-SQN	952		Republic
□ N953UW	Embraer ERJ-190AR	19000133	ex PT-SYL	953		Republic dam 09Feb15
□ N954UW	Embraer ERJ-190AR	19000139	ex PT-SYS	954		Republic
□ N955UW	Embraer ERJ-190AR	19000152	ex PT-SAH	955		Republic
□ N956UW	Embraer ERJ-190AR	19000156	ex PT-SAM	956		Republic
□ N957UW	Embraer ERJ-190AR	19000161	ex PT-SAQ	957		Republic
□ N958UW	Embraer ERJ-190AR	19000164	ex PT-SAT	958		Republic
□ N959UW	Embraer ERJ-190AR	19000166	ex N166HQ	959		
□ N961UW	Embraer ERJ-190AR	19000183	ex N168HQ	961		
□ N963UW	Embraer ERJ-190AR	19000191	ex N170HQ	963		
□ N965UW	Embraer ERJ-190AR	19000198	ex N172HQ	965		
□ N967UW	Embraer ERJ-190AR	19000211	ex N174HQ	967		
□ N298AA	McDonnell-Douglas MD-82	49310/1247		298		[ROW]
□ N403A	McDonnell-Douglas MD-82	49314/1256		403		
□ N424AA	McDonnell-Douglas MD-82	49336/1321		424		
□ N426AA	McDonnell-Douglas MD-82	49338/1327		426		
□ N454AA	McDonnell-Douglas MD-82	49559/1460		454		
□ N455AA	McDonnell-Douglas MD-82	49560/1462		455		
□ N456AA	McDonnell-Douglas MD-82	49561/1474		456		
□ N457AA	McDonnell-Douglas MD-82	49562/1475		457		[ROW]
□ N466AA	McDonnell-Douglas MD-82	49596/1510		466		
□ N467AA	McDonnell-Douglas MD-82	49597/1511		467		
□ N468AA	McDonnell-Douglas MD-82	49598/1513		468		
□ N469AA	McDonnell-Douglas MD-82	49599/1515		469		
□ N470AA	McDonnell-Douglas MD-82	49600/1516		470		
□ N471AA	McDonnell-Douglas MD-82	49601/1518		471		
□ N472AA	McDonnell-Douglas MD-82	49647/1520		472		
□ N473AA	McDonnell-Douglas MD-82	49648/1521		473		
□ N474	McDonnell-Douglas MD-82	49649/1526		474		
□ N475AA	McDonnell-Douglas MD-82	49650/1527		475		
□ N476AA	McDonnell-Douglas MD-82	49651/1528		476		[ROW]
□ N477AA	McDonnell-Douglas MD-82	49652/1529		477		
□ N478AA	McDonnell-Douglas MD-82	49653/1534		478		[ROW]
□ N479AA	McDonnell-Douglas MD-82	49654/1535		479		
□ N480AA	McDonnell-Douglas MD-82	49655/1536		480		
□ N481AA	McDonnell-Douglas MD-82	49656/1545		481		
□ N482AA	McDonnell-Douglas MD-82	49675/1546		482		
□ N483A	McDonnell-Douglas MD-82	49676/1550		483		
□ N484AA	McDonnell-Douglas MD-82	49677/1551		484		
□ N485AA	McDonnell-Douglas MD-82	49678/1555		485		
□ N486AA	McDonnell-Douglas MD-82	49679/1557		486		
□ N487AA	McDonnell-Douglas MD-82	49680/1558		487		
□ N488AA	McDonnell-Douglas MD-82	49681/1560		488		
□ N489AA	McDonnell-Douglas MD-82	49682/1562		489		
□ N490AA	McDonnell-Douglas MD-82	49683/1563		490		[ROW]
□ N491AA	McDonnell-Douglas MD-82	49684/1564		491		
□ N492AA	McDonnell-Douglas MD-82	49730/1565		492		[ROW]
□ N493AA	McDonnell-Douglas MD-82	49731/1566		493		
□ N494AA	McDonnell-Douglas MD-82	49732/1567		494		
□ N496AA	McDonnell-Douglas MD-82	49734/1619		496		
□ N499AA	McDonnell-Douglas MD-82	49737/1641		499		
□ N501AA	McDonnell-Douglas MD-82	49738/1648		501		
□ N505AA	McDonnell-Douglas MD-82	49799/1652		505		
□ N513AA	McDonnell-Douglas MD-82	49890/1686		513		
□ N552AA	McDonnell-Douglas MD-82	53034/1826		552		[ROW]

☐ N553AA	McDonnell-Douglas MD-82	53083/1828		553	[ROW]
☐ N554AA	McDonnell-Douglas MD-82	53084/1830		554	[ROW]
☐ N555AN	McDonnell-Douglas MD-82	53085/1839		555	
☐ N556AA	McDonnell-Douglas MD-82	53086/1840		556	[ROW]
☐ N557AN	McDonnell-Douglas MD-82	53087/1841		557	[ROW]
☐ N558AA	McDonnell-Douglas MD-82	53088/1852		558	[ROW]
☐ N559AA	McDonnell-Douglas MD-82	53089/1853		559	[ROW]
☐ N560AA	McDonnell-Douglas MD-82	53090/1858		560	[ROW]
☐ N561AA	McDonnell-Douglas MD-82	53091/1863		561	[ROW]
☐ N573AA	McDonnell-Douglas MD-82	53092/1864		573	[ROW]
☐ N574AA	McDonnell-Douglas MD-82	53151/1866		574	
☐ N575AM	McDonnell-Douglas MD-82	53152/1875		575	
☐ N576AA	McDonnell-Douglas MD-82	53153/1876		576	
☐ N578AA	McDonnell-Douglas MD-82	53155/1883		578	[ROW]
☐ N581AA	McDonnell-Douglas MD-82	53158/1891		581	
☐ N582AA	McDonnell-Douglas MD-82	53159/1892		582	
☐ N583AA	McDonnell-Douglas MD-82	53160/1893		583	
☐ N585AA	McDonnell-Douglas MD-82	53248/1903		585	
☐ N586AA	McDonnell-Douglas MD-82	53249/1904		586	
☐ N587AA	McDonnell-Douglas MD-82	53250/1907		587	[ROW]
☐ N954U	McDonnell-Douglas MD-82	49426/1399	ex N786JA	4UB	
☐ N955U	McDonnell-Douglas MD-82	49427/1401	ex N787JA	4UC	
☐ N3507A	McDonnell-Douglas MD-82	49801/1661		507	[ROW]
☐ N7506	McDonnell-Douglas MD-82	49800/1660		506	[ROW]
☐ N7508	McDonnell-Douglas MD-82	49802/1662		508	wfs
☐ N7509	McDonnell-Douglas MD-82	49803/1663		509	[ROW]
☐ N7512A	McDonnell-Douglas MD-82	49806/1673		512	[ROW]
☐ N7514A	McDonnell-Douglas MD-82	49891/1694		514	
☐ N7518A	McDonnell-Douglas MD-82	49895/1698		518	[ROW]
☐ N7520A	McDonnell-Douglas MD-82	49897/1708		520	
☐ N7521A	McDonnell-Douglas MD-82	49898/1709		521	[ROW]
☐ N7522A	McDonnell-Douglas MD-82	49899/1722		522	[ROW]
☐ N7525A	McDonnell-Douglas MD-82	49917/1735		525	[ROW]
☐ N7526A	McDonnell-Douglas MD-82	49918/1743		526	[ROW]
☐ N7528A	McDonnell-Douglas MD-82	49920/1750		528	
☐ N7537A	McDonnell-Douglas MD-82	49991/1780		537	[ROW]
☐ N7540A	McDonnell-Douglas MD-82	49994/1790		540	[ROW]
☐ N7541A	McDonnell-Douglas MD-82	49995/1791		541	
☐ N7542A	McDonnell-Douglas MD-82	49996/1792		542	[ROW]
☐ N7543A	McDonnell-Douglas MD-82	53025/1802		543	[ROW]
☐ N7546A	McDonnell-Douglas MD-82	53028/1813		546	[ROW]
☐ N7547A	McDonnell-Douglas MD-82	53029/1814		547	
☐ N7548A	McDonnell-Douglas MD-82	53030/1816		548	
☐ N7549A	McDonnell-Douglas MD-82	53031/1819		549	[ROW]
☐ N7550	McDonnell-Douglas MD-82	53032/1820		550	
☐ N14551	McDonnell-Douglas MD-82	53033/1822		551	[ROW]
☐ N16545	McDonnell-Douglas MD-82	53027/1805		545	[ROW]
☐ N33502	McDonnell-Douglas MD-82	49739/1649		502	
☐ N44503	McDonnell-Douglas MD-82	49797/1650		503	
☐ N70425	McDonnell-Douglas MD-82	49337/1325		425	
☐ N70504	McDonnell-Douglas MD-82	49798/1651		504	
☐ N70524	McDonnell-Douglas MD-82	49916/1729		524	[ROW]
☐ N433AA	McDonnell-Douglas MD-83	49451/1388		433	[ROW]
☐ N434AA	McDonnell-Douglas MD-83	49452/1389		434	
☐ N435AA	McDonnell-Douglas MD-83	49453/1390		435	[ROW]
☐ N436AA	McDonnell-Douglas MD-83	49454/1391		436	
☐ N437AA	McDonnell-Douglas MD-83	49455/1392		437	
☐ N438AA	McDonnell-Douglas MD-83	49456/1393		438	
☐ N439AA	McDonnell-Douglas MD-83	49457/1398		439	
☐ N564AA	McDonnell-Douglas MD-83	49346/1372		564	
☐ N565AA	McDonnell-Douglas MD-83	49347/1373		565	
☐ N566AA	McDonnell-Douglas MD-83	49348/1374		566	
☐ N567AM	McDonnell-Douglas MD-83	53293/2021		567	
☐ N568AA	McDonnell-Douglas MD-83	49349/1375		568	
☐ N569AA	McDonnell-Douglas MD-83	49351/1385		569	
☐ N570AA	McDonnell-Douglas MD-83	49352/1386		570	
☐ N571AA	McDonnell-Douglas MD-83	49353/1387		571	
☐ N590AA	McDonnell-Douglas MD-83	53253/1919		590	[ROW]
☐ N592AA	McDonnell-Douglas MD-83	53255/1932		592	[ROW]
☐ N593AA	McDonnell-Douglas MD-83	53256/1933		593	[ROW]
☐ N595AA	McDonnell-Douglas MD-83	53285/1989		595	[ROW]
☐ N596AA	McDonnell-Douglas MD-83	53286/2000		596	[ROW]
☐ N597AA	McDonnell-Douglas MD-83	53287/2006		597	
☐ N598AA	McDonnell-Douglas MD-83	53288/2011		598	
☐ N599AA	McDonnell-Douglas MD-83	53289/2012		599	
☐ N941AS	McDonnell-Douglas MD-83	49925/1616		4UK	[ROW]
☐ N961TW	McDonnell-Douglas MD-83	53611/2264		4XT	
☐ N962TW	McDonnell-Douglas MD-83	53612/2265		4XU	
☐ N963TW	McDonnell-Douglas MD-83	53613/2266		4XV	
☐ N964TW	McDonnell-Douglas MD-83	53614/2267		4XW	
☐ N965TW	McDonnell-Douglas MD-83	53615/2268		4XX	
☐ N966TW	McDonnell-Douglas MD-83	53616/2269		4XY	

☐ N967TW	McDonnell-Douglas MD-83	53617/2270		4YA	
☐ N968TW	McDonnell-Douglas MD-83	53618/2271		4YB	
☐ N969TW	McDonnell-Douglas MD-83	53619/2272		4YC	
☐ N970TW	McDonnell-Douglas MD-83	53620/2273		4YD	[TUL]
☐ N971TW	McDonnell-Douglas MD-83	53621/2274		4YE	[TUL]
☐ N972TW	McDonnell-Douglas MD-83	53622/2275		4YF	
☐ N975TW	McDonnell-Douglas MD-83	53625/2278		4YJ	
☐ N976TW	McDonnell-Douglas MD-83	53626/2279		4YK	[ROW]
☐ N978TW	McDonnell-Douglas MD-83	53628/2281		4YM	[ROW]
☐ N979TW	McDonnell-Douglas MD-83	53629/2282		4YN	
☐ N980TW	McDonnell-Douglas MD-83	53630/2283		4YP	
☐ N982TW	McDonnell-Douglas MD-83	53632/2285		4YR	
☐ N983TW	McDonnell-Douglas MD-83	53633/2286		4YS	
☐ N984TW	McDonnell-Douglas MD-83	53634/2287		4YT	
☐ N9401W	McDonnell-Douglas MD-83	53137/1872	ex N9001L	4WJ	
☐ N9402W	McDonnell-Douglas MD-83	53138/1886	ex N9001D	4WK	
☐ N9403W	McDonnell-Douglas MD-83	53139/1899	ex N9035C	4WL	
☐ N9404V	McDonnell-Douglas MD-83	53140/1923	ex N9075H	4WM	
☐ N9405T	McDonnell-Douglas MD-83	53141/1935		4WN	
☐ N9406W	McDonnell-Douglas MD-83	53126/2026	ex N6203U	4WP	
☐ N9407R	McDonnell-Douglas MD-83	49400/1356	ex EI-CKB	4WR	[ROW]
☐ N9409F	McDonnell-Douglas MD-83	53121/1971	ex N532MD	4WT	
☐ N9615W	McDonnell-Douglas MD-83	53562/2192		4XB	
☐ N9616G	McDonnell-Douglas MD-83	53563/2196		4XC	
☐ N9617R	McDonnell-Douglas MD-83	53564/2199		4XD	
☐ N9618A	McDonnell-Douglas MD-83	53565/2201		4XE	
☐ N9619V	McDonnell-Douglas MD-83	53566/2206		4XF	
☐ N9620D	McDonnell-Douglas MD-83	53591/2208		4XG	
☐ N9621A	McDonnell-Douglas MD-83	53592/2234		4XH	
☐ N9622A	McDonnell-Douglas MD-83	53593/2239		4XJ	
☐ N9624T	McDonnell-Douglas MD-83	53594/2241		4XK	
☐ N9625W	McDonnell-Douglas MD-83	53595/2244		4XL	
☐ N9626F	McDonnell-Douglas MD-83	53596//2247		4XM	
☐ N9627R	McDonnell-Douglas MD-83	53597/2249		4XN	[ROW]
☐ N9628W	McDonnell-Douglas MD-83	53598/2252		4XP	
☐ N9629H	McDonnell-Douglas MD-83	53599/2254		4XR	
☐ N9630A	McDonnell-Douglas MD-83	53561/2174	ex N90126	4XS	
☐ N9677W	McDonnell-Douglas MD-83	53627/2280		4YL	
☐ N9681B	McDonnell-Douglas MD-83	53631/2284	ex (N981TW)	4XT	
☐ N76200	McDonnell-Douglas MD-83	53290/2013		200	
☐ N76201	McDonnell-Douglas MD-83	53291/2019		201	
☐ N76202	McDonnell-Douglas MD-83	53292/2020		202	
☐ N430US	Boeing 737-4B7	24552/1797			[TUS]
☐ N450UW	Boeing 737-4B7	24933/1954	ex N775AU	450	[TUS]
☐ N453UW	Boeing 737-4B7	24980/1982	ex N778AU		[TUS]
☐ N454UW	Boeing 737-4B7	24996/1986	ex N779AU		[TUS]

AMERIFLIGHT   Amflight (A8/AMF)   Burbank Glendale-Pasadena, CA (BUR)

☐ N20FW	Beech 99A	U-111		
☐ N21FW	Beech 99A	U-117		
☐ N34AK	Beech 99A	U-105	ex N4099A	
☐ N51RP	Beech C99	U-212		
☐ N52RP	Beech C99	U-210	ex N66305	
☐ N53RP	Beech C99	U-195	ex N64997	[ELM]
☐ N55RP	Beech C99	U-198	ex N64002	
☐ N68TA	Beech C99	U-177	ex N177EE	
☐ N96AV	Beech C99	U-201		
☐ N102GP	Beech C99	U-208	ex (N114GE)	
☐ N104BE	Beech C99	U-221	ex N7203L	
☐ N106SX	Beech C99	U-166		
☐ N107SX	Beech C99	U-176		
☐ N108SX	Beech C99	U-184	ex N6787P	
☐ N130GP	Beech C99	U-222	ex N818FL	
☐ N131GP	Beech C99	U-225	ex J6-AAF	
☐ N134PM	Beech 99	U-34	ex N852SA	
☐ N164HA	Beech 99	U-60	ex N72TC	
☐ N174AV	Beech C99	U-174	ex N99CJ	
☐ N191AV	Beech C99	U-191	ex VR-CIB	
☐ N193SU	Beech C99	U-193	ex C-GFAT	
☐ N199AF	Beech B99	U-161	ex N12AK	
☐ N204AF	Beech C99	U-204	ex N575W	
☐ N206AV	Beech C99	U-206	ex N216EE	
☐ N213AV	Beech C99	U-213	ex N6656N	
☐ N221BH	Beech C99	U-168	ex N18AK	
☐ N223BH	Beech C99	U-173	ex N6460D	
☐ N225BH	Beech C99	U-181	ex N62936	
☐ N226BH	Beech C99	U-182	ex N6263D	
☐ N227AV	Beech C99	U-227	ex N2225H	
☐ N228BH	Beech C99	U-229	ex N3067L	
☐ N230BH	Beech C99	U-233	ex N72355	
☐ N234AV	Beech C99	U-234	ex N234BH	

☐ N235AV	Beech C99	U-235	ex N235BH
☐ N261SW	Beech C99	U-202	
☐ N330AV	Beech C99	U-230	ex N3063W
☐ N388AV	Beech C99	U-188	ex N799GL
☐ N802BA	Beech 99	U-29	ex N800BE
☐ N805BA	Beech 99A	U-147	ex N803BE
☐ N949K	Beech 99	U-36	
☐ N990AF	Beech C99	U-211	ex N113GP
☐ N991AF	Beech C99	U-214	ex N112GP
☐ N992AF	Beech C99	U-203	ex N541JC
☐ N997SB	Beech C99	U-192	ex N6534A
☐ N1924T	Beech 99A	U-115	ex N24AT
☐ N4199C	Beech C99	U-50	ex N7940
☐ N4299A	Beech B99	U-146	
☐ N6199D	Beech C99	U-169	
☐ N6724D	Beech C99	U-215	
☐ N7200Z	Beech C99	U-219	
☐ N7209W	Beech C99	U-224	
☐ N7862R	Beech 99A	U-85	
☐ N8226Z	Beech C99	U-190	ex 6Y-JVB
☐ N8227P	Beech C99	U-194	ex 6Y-JVA
☐ N62989	Beech C99	U-183	
☐ N63978	Beech C99	U-171	
☐ N81820	Beech C99	U-232	ex J6-AAG
☐ N19RZ	Beech 1900C-1	UC-75	ex JA190C
☐ N21RZ	Beech 1900C-1	UC-106	ex JA190B
☐ N26RZ	Beech 1900C-1	UC-134	ex JA190D
☐ N34RZ	Beech 1900C-1	UC-151	ex JA190A
☐ N49UC	Beech 1900C-1	UC-49	ex C-GCMJ
☐ N111YV	Beech 1900C-1	UC-111	ex F-GPYX
☐ N112YV	Beech 1900C-1	UC-112	ex VH-AFR
☐ N330AF	Beech 1900C	UB-38	ex N805BE
☐ N331AF	Beech 1900C	UB-44	ex N807BE
☐ N338AF	Beech 1900C-1	UC-57	ex A6-FCA
☐ N346AF	Beech 1900C-1	UC-71	ex A6-FCD
☐ N347AF	Beech 1900C-1	UC-66	ex A6-FCB
☐ N575G	Beech 1900C-1	UC-155	ex N155YV
☐ N718AF	Beech 1900C-1	UC-162	ex N575Y
☐ N1568G	Beech 1900C-1	UC-58	ex F-GNAD
☐ N2049K	Beech 1900C-1	UC-164	ex J6-AAJ
☐ N3052K	Beech 1900C	UB-70	
☐ N3071A	Beech 1900C	UB-46	ex N10RA
☐ N3229A	Beech 1900C	UB-51	
☐ N7203C	Beech 1900C	UB-28	
☐ N31701	Beech 1900C	UB-2	ex N121CZ
☐ N31702	Beech 1900C	UB-3	ex N122CZ
☐ N31703	Beech 1900C	UB-10	ex N123CZ
☐ N31704	Beech 1900C	UB-12	ex N124CZ
☐ N31705	Beech 1900C	UB-60	
☐ N179CA	Embraer EMB.120ER Brasilia	120179	ex PT-SQR
☐ N189CA	Embraer EMB.120ER Brasilia	120189	ex PT-SRC
☐ N201YW	Embraer EMB.120RT Brasilia	120201	ex N142EB
☐ N246AS	Embraer EMB.120ER Brasilia	120100	ex PP-SMS
☐ N247CA	Embraer EMB.120ER Brasilia	120225	ex PT-SSU
☐ N257AS	Embraer EMB.120ER Brasilia	120126	ex PT-SNS
☐ N258AS	Embraer EMB.120ER Brasilia	120131	ex PT-SNX
☐ N3BT	Piper PA-31-350 Navajo Chieftain	31-7752172	ex N27422
☐ N29UM	Piper PA-31-350 Navajo Chieftain	31-7652127	ex N29JM
☐ N555RG	Piper PA-31-350 Navajo Chieftain	31-7305103	ex N555RC
☐ N600TS	Piper PA-31-350 Navajo Chieftain	31-7305047	ex N537N
☐ N777MP	Piper PA-31-350 Navajo Chieftain	31-7552072	ex N59983
☐ N961CA	Piper PA-31-350 Navajo Chieftain	31-7652014	ex N961PS
☐ N3527D	Piper PA-31-350 Chieftain	31-7952137	
☐ N3540N	Piper PA-31-350 Chieftain	31-7952214	
☐ N3548B	Piper PA-31-350 Chieftain	31-8052025	
☐ N3553F	Piper PA-31-350 Chieftain	31-8052044	
☐ N4044P	Piper PA-31-350 Chieftain	31-8152004	
☐ N4087J	Piper PA-31-350 Chieftain	31-8152128	
☐ N4098A	Piper PA-31-350 Chieftain	31-8152200	
☐ N4502Y	Piper PA-31-350 Chieftain	31-8052189	
☐ N27426	Piper PA-31-350 Navajo Chieftain	31-7752175	
☐ N27677	Piper PA-31-350 Chieftain	31-7852101	
☐ N35336	Piper PA-31-350 Chieftain	31-7952189	
☐ N35805	Piper PA-31-350 Chieftain	31-8052090	
☐ N42076	Piper PA-31-350 Navajo Chieftain	31-7405209	ex G-OSPT
☐ N42079	Piper PA-31-350 Navajo Chieftain	31-7405488	ex G-BCOD
☐ N45004	Piper PA-31-350 Chieftain	31-8052163	
☐ N45014	Piper PA-31-350 Chieftain	31-8052171	
☐ N59820	Piper PA-31-350 Navajo Chieftain	31-7652073	
☐ N59973	Piper PA-31-350 Navajo Chieftain	31-7552079	

| ☐ N62858 | Piper PA-31-350 Navajo Chieftain | 31-7652115 | | |
| ☐ N66859 | Piper PA-31-350 Navajo Chieftain | 31-7405168 | | |

☐ N152AF	Swearingen SA227AC Metro III	AC-520	ex TG-4DHL	
☐ N155AF	Swearingen SA227AC Metro III	AC-455	ex N356AE	
☐ N191AF	Swearingen SA227AC Metro III	AC-491	ex N209CA	
☐ N360AE	Swearingen SA227AC Metro III	AC-675		[IGM]
☐ N362AE	Swearingen SA227AC Metro III	AC-677B		
☐ N377PH	Swearingen SA227AC Metro III	AC-574	ex (D-CABG)	
☐ N421MA	Swearingen SA227AC Metro III	AC-634	ex N3119Q	
☐ N422MA	Swearingen SA227AC Metro III	AC-635	ex N3119T	
☐ N423MA	Swearingen SA227AC Metro III	AC-636	ex N26823	
☐ N424MA	Swearingen SA227AC Metro III	AC-639		
☐ N426MA	Swearingen SA227AC Metro III	AC-645		
☐ N428MA	Swearingen SA227AC Metro III	AC-646		
☐ N443AF	Swearingen SA227AC Metro III	AC-443	ex N443NE	
☐ N473AF	Swearingen SA227AC Metro III	AC-473	ex N473NE	
☐ N475AF	Swearingen SA227AC Metro III	AC-475	ex N475NE	
☐ N476AF	Swearingen SA227AC Metro III	AC-476	ex N476NE	
☐ N488AF	Swearingen SA227AC Metro III	AC-488	ex N488NE	
☐ N529AF	Swearingen SA227AC Metro III	AC-752	ex XA-TML	
☐ N578AF	Swearingen SA227AC Metro III	AC-578	ex C-FJLE	
☐ N671AV	Swearingen SA227AC Metro III	AC-671		
☐ N672AV	Swearingen SA227AC Metro III	AC-672		
☐ N673AV	Swearingen SA227AC Metro III	AC-673		
☐ N698AF	Swearingen SA227AC Metro III	AC-698	ex N2711R	
☐ N709TR	Swearingen SA227AC Metro III	AC-709B		♦
☐ N801AF	Swearingen SA227AC Metro III	AC-701	ex C-GWXZ	
☐ N838AF	Swearingen SA227AC Metro III	AC-738	ex C-GWXX	

☐ N240DH	Swearingen SA227AT Expediter	AT-602B	ex N3117P	
☐ N241DH	Swearingen SA227AT Expediter	AT-607B	ex N3118A	
☐ N242DH	Swearingen SA227AT Expediter	AT-608B	ex N3118G	
☐ N243DH	Swearingen SA227AT Expediter	AT-609B	ex N3118H	
☐ N244DH	Swearingen SA227AT Expediter	AT-618B		
☐ N245DH	Swearingen SA227AT Expediter	AT-624B		
☐ N246DH	Swearingen SA227AT Expediter	AT-625B		
☐ N247DH	Swearingen SA227AT Expediter	AT-626B		
☐ N248DH	Swearingen SA227AT Expediter	AT-630B		
☐ N249DH	Swearingen SA227AT Expediter	AT-631B		
☐ N544UP	Swearingen SA227AT Expediter	AT-544	ex N68TA	
☐ N548UP	Swearingen SA227AT Expediter	AT-548	ex N548SA	
☐ N556UP	Swearingen SA227AT Expediter	AT-556	ex N3113B	
☐ N560UP	Swearingen SA227AT Expediter	AT-560	ex N3113A	
☐ N561UP	Swearingen SA227AT Expediter	AT-561	ex N3113F	
☐ N566UP	Swearingen SA227AT Expediter	AT-566	ex N3113N	
☐ N569UP	Swearingen SA227AT Expediter	AT-569	ex N31134	

☐ N94AF	Learjet 35A	35A-094	ex (N35PF)	
☐ N101WJ	Embraer EMB.110P1 Bandeirante	110203	ex N1102W	wfs♦
☐ N128CA	Learjet 35A	35A-248	ex C-GBFA	
☐ N237AF	Learjet 35A	35A-262	ex N237GA	
☐ N573G	Swearingen SA227AT Merlin IVC	AT-446B	ex N3008L	
☐ N807M	Swearingen SA227AT Merlin IVC	AT-454B	ex N3013T	

AMERIJET INTERNATIONAL — Amerijet (M6/AJT) — Fort Lauderdale-Hollywood Intl, FL (FLL)

☐ N199AJ	Boeing 727-2F9F	21426/1285	ex N83428	wfs
☐ N395AJ	Boeing 727-233F/W (Duganair 3)	21100/1148	ex N727SN	wfs
☐ N495AJ	Boeing 727-233F/W (Duganair 3)	20937/1103	ex C-GAAD	
☐ N598AJ	Boeing 727-212F/W (Duganair 3)	21947/1506	ex N86430	wfs
☐ N905AJ	Boeing 727-231F/W (Duganair 3)	21989/1590	ex N84357	[FLL]

☐ N316CM	Boeing 767-338ER BDSF	24146/231	ex VH-OGA	♦
☐ N319CM	Boeing 767-338ERSF	24407/247	ex VH-OGD	♦
☐ N741AX	Boeing 767-232SF	22215/17	ex N103DA	
☐ N743AX	Boeing 767-232SF	22218/31	ex N106DA	

AMERISTAR JET CHARTER — Ameristar (AJI) — Dallas-Addison, TX (ADS)

☐ N148TW	AMD Falcon 20C	148	ex N148WC	165
☐ N158TW	AMD Falcon 20C	158	ex N450MA	
☐ N204TW	AMD Falcon 20DC	204	ex EC-EGM	
☐ N221TW	AMD Falcon 20DC	221	ex EC-EIV	
☐ N223TW	AMD Falcon 20C	123	ex N45MR	
☐ N232TW	AMD Falcon 20C	32	ex F-GIVT	
☐ N236TW	AMD Falcon 20D	236	ex N936NW	
☐ N240TW	AMD Falcon 20C	40	ex C-GSKQ	
☐ N285TW	AMD Falcon 20EC	285	ex N285AP	
☐ N295TW	AMD Falcon 20C	5	ex F-GJPR	[ADS]
☐ N314TW	AMD Falcon 20EC	314	ex F-GDLU	
☐ N699TW	AMD Falcon 20DC	50	ex EC-EDO	

☐ N977TW	AMD Falcon 20DC	13	ex F-BTCY	[ADS]
☐ N85TW	Learjet 25D	25D-251	ex TG-VOC	
☐ N147TW	Learjet 25B	25B-023	ex N767SC	
☐ N237TW	Learjet 24D	24D-237	ex N825DM	
☐ N266TW	Learjet 24D	24D-266	ex N266BS	[ADS]
☐ N277TW	Learjet 24D	24D-277	ex N57BC	
☐ N330TW	Learjet 24F	24F-330	ex N511AT	
☐ N525TW	Learjet 25	25-011	ex N108GA	
☐ N888TW	Learjet 24D	24D-292	ex N800PC	[ADS]
☐ N176TW	Beech 65-E90 King Air	LW-76	ex ZS-LJF	
☐ N465TW	Boeing 737-205	23465/1226	ex N7368P	wfs
☐ N782TW	Douglas DC-9-15RC	45826/79	ex N229DE	[OSC]♦
☐ N783TW	Douglas DC-9-15F (ABS 3)	47010/97	ex N916R	
☐ N784TW	Douglas DC-9-15F (ABS 3)	47014/141	ex N923R	
☐ N785TW	Douglas DC-9-15F (ABS 3)	47015/156	ex N5373G	
☐ N786TW	McDonnell-Douglas MD-83	53123/1987	ex HK-4589	
☐ N787TW	McDonnell-Douglas MD-83	49945/1889	ex HK-4588X	

ANDREW AIRWAYS — Kodiak-Municipal, AK (KDK)

☐ N1544	de Havilland DHC-2 Beaver	1230	ex N67686	FP/WS
☐ N1545	de Havilland DHC-2 Beaver	1493	ex N123UA	FP/WS
☐ N5303X	Cessna U206G Stationair 6 II	U20605622		FP/WS
☐ N8429N	Piper PA-32-301 Saratoga	32-8106089		
☐ N47059	de Havilland DHC-2 Beaver	184	ex 9J-RGA	

APPALACHIAN AIR — Pikeville, KY

☐ N657BA	British Aerospace Jetstream 31	657	ex N412MX	♦

ARCTIC CIRCLE AIR — Saipan, N Marianas

☐ N675AC	Britten-Norman BN-2T Islander	2183	ex G-LEAP	

ARCTIC CIRCLE AIR SERVICE — Air Arctic (5F/CIR)
Aniak/Bethel/Dillingham-Municipal/Fairbanks-Intl, AK (ANI/BET/DLG/FAI)

☐ N168LM	Short SD.3-30	SH3104	ex N174Z	Frtr
☐ N261AG	Short SD.3-30	SH3117	ex 84-0470	Frtr

ASIA PACIFIC AIRLINES — Magellan (P9/MGE) — Guam (GUM)

☐ N319NE	Boeing 727-212F/W (Duganair 3)	21349/1289	ex N591DB	
☐ N705AA	Boeing 727-223F/W (Super 27)	22462/1751		
☐ N757MQ	Boeing 757-230	25436/419	ex RA-73008	wfs♦
☐ N727QM	Boeing 757-29J/W	27203/588	ex VQ-BKM	♦
☐ N86425	Boeing 727-212F/W (Duganair 3)	21459/1329	ex N296AS	

ASPEN HELICOPTERS — Aspen (AHF) — Oxnard, CA (OXR)

☐ N68VA	Partenavia P68C	440/C		♦
☐ N88N	Partenavia P68C	352-37	ex N9717N	
☐ N212AH	Bell 212	30959	ex C-FYMJ	
☐ N383SH	Bell 206L-3 LongRanger III	51073	ex N333SH	
☐ N617AC	Bell 407	53570	ex C-GZKD	
☐ N1085T	Bell 206L-1 LongRanger III	45376		
☐ N5012F	Bell 206B JetRanger III	2559		
☐ N8131	Piper PA-31-350 Chieftain	31-8152032	ex LN-REM	
☐ N39049	Bell 206B JetRanger III	3101		

ATI - AIR TRANSPORT INTERNATIONAL — Air Transport (8C/ATN) — Little Rock-Adams Field, AR (LIT)

☐ N286SC	Boeing 727-2A1F (FedEx 3)	21601/1694	ex N328AS	Beth	[MCO]
☐ N287SC	Boeing 727-2A1F (FedEx 3)	21345/1673	ex N327AS	Florence	[ILM]
☐ N357KP	Boeing 727-230F (FedEx 3)	20675/924	ex G-BPNY	Princess Kendall	[ILM]
☐ N801EA	Boeing 727-225F (FedEx 3)	22432/1658		Miss Ashley	[ILM]
☐ N815EA	Boeing 727-225F (FedEx 3)	22552/1773		Gudrund	[ILM]
☐ N531UA	Boeing 757-222F	25042/361			
☐ N557CM	Boeing 757-2B6PCF/W	23687/106	ex CN-RMZ	DHL c/s	
☐ N605DL	Boeing 757-232F	22812/46			
☐ N620DL	Boeing 757-232F	22910/111			
☐ N751CX	Boeing 757-2Q8PCF	26273/597	ex N556CM		[ILM]
☐ N752CX	Boeing 757-2G5C	24451/227	ex N151GX		
☐ N753CX	Boeing 757-2Y0C	26152/478	ex N259CA		
☐ N754CX	Boeing 757-2Y0C	26154/486	ex N763CA		
☐ N761CX	Boeing 767-223SCD	22318/111	ex N316AA		

☐ N762CX	Boeing 767-232SCD	22225/77	ex N748AX	
☐ N763CX	Boeing 767-232SCD	22223/74	ex N746AX	
☐ N791AX	Boeing 767-281BDSF	23141/108	ex PR-IOE	

ATLANTIC AIR CARGO
Miami-Intl, FL (MIA)

☐ N437GB	Douglas DC-3C	19999	ex HR-LAD	Frtr
☐ N705GB	Douglas DC-3C	13854	ex TG-SAA	Frtr

ATLANTIC SOUTHEAST AIRLINES
Acey (EV/ASQ)

Atlanta-Hartsfield Intl, GA/Orlando-Intl, FL (ATL/MCO)

Wholly owned subsidiary of SkyWest Airlines, merged with ExpressJet and ExpressJet Airlines and ops as Delta Connection; to be renamed Surejet

ATLAS AIR
Giant (5Y/GTI)
New York-JFK Intl, NY (JFK)

☐ N249BA	Boeing 747-409LCF	24309/766	ex B-18271		opf Boeing
☐ N263SG	Boeing 747-481	29263/1204	ex B-LFC		>SOR
☐ N322SG	Boeing 747-481	30322/1250	ex B-LFD		>SOR
☐ N408MC	Boeing 747-47UF	29261/1192	ex (N495MC)		>ACP
☐ N409MC	Boeing 747-47UF	30558/1242			
☐ N412MC	Boeing 747-47UF	30559/1244			
☐ N415MC	Boeing 747-47UF	32837/1304			>UAE
☐ N416MC	Boeing 747-47UF	32838/1307			>PAC
☐ N418MC	Boeing 747-47UF	32840/1319			
☐ N419MC	Boeing 747-48EF	28367/1096	ex TF-AMO		
☐ N429MC	Boeing 747-481BCF	24833/812	ex JA8095		[MZJ]
☐ N458MC	Boeing 747-446BCF	26356/1026	ex N356NA		
☐ N464MC	Boeing 747-446	26341/902	ex N349AS		
☐ N465MC	Boeing 747-446	24784/798	ex N287AS		
☐ N475MC	Boeing 747-47UF	29252/1165	ex G-GSSB		
☐ N476MC	Boeing 747-47UF	29256/1213	ex G-GSSA		>ETD
☐ N477MC	Boeing 747-47UF	29255/1184	ex G-GSSC		
☐ N492MC	Boeing 747-47UF	29253/1169			
☐ N493MC	Boeing 747-47UF	29254/1179			
☐ N496MC	Boeing 747-47UF	29257/1217			
☐ N497MC	Boeing 747-47UF	29258/1220			
☐ N498MC	Boeing 747-47UF	29259/1227			>PAC
☐ N499MC	Boeing 747-47UF	29260/1240			
☐ N718BA	Boeing 747-4H6LCF	27042/932	ex 9M-MPA		opf Boeing
☐ N747BC	Boeing 747-4J6LCF	25879/904	ex B-2464		opf Boeing
☐ N780BA	Boeing 747-409LCF	24310/778	ex B-18272		opf Boeing
☐ N850GT	Boeing 747-87UF	37570/1455		Spirit of Panalpina	
☐ N851GT	Boeing 747-87UF	37565/1458		Passion for Solutions	>PAC
☐ N852GT	Boeing 747-87UF	37571/1462			>PAC
☐ N853GT	Boeing 747-87UF	37572/1467			>PAC
☐ N854GT	Boeing 747-87UF	37566/1471			
☐ N855GT	Boeing 747-87UF	37567/1476			>ETD
☐ N856GT	Boeing 747-87UF	37561/1442	ex G-GSSD		
☐ N857GT	Boeing 747-87UF	37568/1444	ex G-GSSE		>PAC
☐ N858GT	Boeing 747-87UF	37569/1445	ex G-GSSF		>PAC
☐ N650GT	Boeing 767-231BDSF	22566/29	ex N702AX		
☐ N651GT	Boeing 767-231BDSF	22570/63	ex N707AX		
☐ N652GT	Boeing 767-231BDSF	22571/64	ex N708AX		
☐ N653GT	Boeing 767-231BDSF	22572/65	ex N709AX	DHL c/s	
☐ N655GT	Boeing 767-205ERF	23058/101	ex N713AX		
☐ N656GT	Boeing 767-281F	23017/82	ex N784AX	DHL c/s	◆
☐ N657GT	Boeing 767-281F	23018/84	ex N785AX		◆
☐ N658GT	Boeing 767-281F	23019/85	ex N786AX	DHL c/s	◆
☐ N659GT	Boeing 767-281F	23140/106	ex N790AX		◆
☐ N767MW	Boeing 767-277	22694/32	ex N767AT		opf MLW Avn
☐ N640GT	Boeing 767-3S1ER	25221/384	ex N585MS		
☐ N641GT	Boeing 767-38EER	25132/417	ex PR-VAF		
☐ N642GT	Boeing 767-3Y0ER	26207/503	ex C-GHPH		
☐ N643GT	Boeing 767-3JHF/W	37809/1039	ex G-DHLJ		<DHK>PAC
☐ N644GT	Boeing 767-3JHF/W	37810/1041	ex G-DHLK	DHL c/s	<DHK>PAC
☐ N355MC	Boeing 747-341SF	23395/629	ex PP-VNI		[MHV]
☐ N526MC	Boeing 747-2D7BSF	22337/479	ex HS-TGF	all-white	[ROW]
☐ N537MC	Boeing 747-271C	22403/524	ex LX-BCV	all-white	[ROW]
☐ N588GT	Boeing 757-26DPCF	24471/231	ex B-2808		wfs◆

BALD MOUNTAIN AIR SERVICE
Horner, AK (HOM)

☐ N74GS	Beech B200 Super King Air	BB-1135	ex ZS-LIZ	
☐ N104BM	de Havilland DHC-3 Turbo Otter	118	ex C-FBEP	

☐ N413JP	de Havilland DHC-3 Turbo Otter	314	ex C-GCDX	
☐ N716JP	de Havilland DHC-6 Twin Otter 300	527	ex TI-AZV	

BALTIA AIR LINES	*Baltia Flight (BTL)*	*Detroit-Willow Run, MI (YIP)*

☐ N706BL	Boeing 747-251B	21705/374	ex N623US	Spirit of Kathleen	[OSC]

BARON AVIATION SERVICES	*Show-Me (BVN)*	*Rolla-Vichy-National, MO (VIH)*

Ops Cessna 208/208B Caravans on behalf of Federal Express

BAY AIR	*Dillingham, AK*

☐ N364RA	de Havilland DHC-2 Beaver	364

BEMIDJI AIRLINES	*Bemidji (CH/BMJ)*	*Bemidji, MN (BJI)*

☐ N55SA	Beech 65-A80 Queen Air	LD-243	ex N794A	Queenaire 8800 conversion
☐ N95LL	Beech 65-A80 Queen Air	LD-235	ex N33TX	Queenaire 8800 conversion
☐ N103BA	Beech 65-B80 Queen Air	LD-435	ex N103EE	Queenaire 8800 conversion
☐ N104BA	Beech 65-B80 Queen Air	LD-411	ex N4258S	
☐ N106BA	Beech 65-B80 Queen Air	LD-409	ex N1338T	Queenaire 8800 conversion
☐ N110BA	Beech 65-B80 Queen Air	LD-279	ex N102KK	Queenaire 8800 conversion
☐ N111AR	Beech 65-80 Queen Air	LF-68	ex 62-3780	
☐ N131BA	Beech 65-B80 Queen Air	LD-297	ex N1555M	Queenaire 8800 conversion
☐ N132BA	Beech 65-B80 Queen Air	LD-331	ex C-GRID	Queenaire 8800 conversion
☐ N134BA	Beech 65-A80 Queen Air	LD-202	ex N848S	Queenaire 8800 conversion
☐ N135BA	Beech 65-80 Queen Air	LD-68	ex N29RG	Queenaire 8800 conversion
☐ N441MC	Beech 65-80 Queen Air	LF-45	ex 62-3847	
☐ N5078E	Beech 65-80 Queen Air	LF-76	ex 63-13637	
☐ N5078N	Beech 65-80 Queen Air	LF-16	ex 60-3467	
☐ N5078U	Beech 65-80 Queen Air	LF-32	ex 62-3834	
☐ N5079E	Beech 65-80 Queen Air	LF-52	ex 62-3854	
☐ N5080L	Beech 65-80 Queen Air	LF-59	ex 62-3861	
☐ N70NP	Beech 99	U-14	ex N914Y	
☐ N108BA	Beech 99	U-40	ex C-GQFD	
☐ N130BA	Beech 99A	U-80	ex N51PA	Frtr
☐ N137BA	Beech 99A	U-137	ex C-GAWW	
☐ N172EE	Beech C99	U-172	ex N993SB	
☐ N175EE	Beech C99	U-175	ex N994SB	
☐ N223CA	Beech C99	U-200	ex SE-IZX	
☐ N6645K	Beech C99	U-209		
☐ N7207E	Beech C99	U-223		
☐ N7212P	Beech C99	U-220		
☐ N60BA	Beech 65-E90 King Air	LW-79	ex N12AK	
☐ N227LC	Swearingen SA.227AC Metro III	AC-707B	ex N84GM	
☐ N611BA	Swearingen SA.227AC Metro III	AC-611B	ex VH-EEX	
☐ N619BA	Swearingen SA.227AC Metro III	AC-619B	ex VH-EEU	
☐ N6334S	Beech 58 Baron	TH-702		

BERING AIR	*Bering Air (8E/BRG)*	*Nome, AK (OME)*

☐ N204BA	Cessna 208B Caravan I	208B0752		
☐ N205BA	Cessna 208B Caravan I	208B0890		
☐ N806BA	Cessna 208B Caravan I	208B0943		
☐ N907BA	Cessna 208B Caravan I	208B1022		
☐ N1128L	Cessna 208B Caravan I	208B0536		
☐ N988BA	Cessna 208B Caravan I	208B2089		
☐ N141ME	Piper PA-31-350 Chieftain	31-8152117	ex N4086L	
☐ N4112D	Piper PA-31-350 T-1020	31-8353004		
☐ N4112E	Piper PA-31-350 T-1020	31-8353005		
☐ N4118G	Piper PA-31-350 T-1020	31-8453001		
☐ N41189	Piper PA-31-350 T-1020	31-8553002		
☐ N45052	Piper PA-31-350 Chieftain	31-8152063		
☐ N15GA	Beech 1900D	UE-37	ex F-HCHA	
☐ N79CF	Beech 200 Super King Air	BB-441		CatPass 250 conversion
☐ N148SK	Beech 1900D	UE-148		
☐ N326KW	Beech B200 Super King Air	BB-1360	ex HK-3703X	CatPass 250 conversion
☐ N349TA	CASA C.212-200	CC60-9-349	ex N316CA	Frtr
☐ N422CA	CASA C.212	CC40-5-238		
☐ N949BW	Beech B200 Super King Air	BB-1763		♦

BERRY AVIATION	*Berry (BYA)*	*San Marcos-Municipal, TX (HYI)*

☐ N92FE	de Havilland DHC-6 Twin Otter 300	242	ex TR-LGU	
☐ N165BA	Swearingen SA226TC Metro II	TC-215	ex N911HF	wfs
☐ N229SW	Embraer EMB.120ER Brasilia	120305	ex PT-SVX	♦
☐ N233SW	Embraer EMB.120ER Brasilia	120307	ex PT-SVZ	♦

☐ N235SW	Embraer EMB.120ER Brasilia	120310	ex PT-SXC	♦
☐ N339PH	Dornier 328-120	3015	ex D-CARR	
☐ N473PS	Dornier 328-120	3010	ex N332PH	
☐ N437YV	de Havilland DHC-8-202B	437	ex C-FDHD	
☐ N449YV	de Havilland DHC-8-202Q	449	ex C-GFHZ	
☐ N541AV	de Havilland DHC-8-201Q	541	ex C-FSQT	
☐ N651CT	Embraer EMB.120RT Brasilia	120197	ex N58733	
☐ N675BA	de Havilland DHC-6 Twin Otter 300	675	ex C-FUMY	
☐ N707TG	Embraer EMB.120RT Brasilia	120182	ex N17728	
☐ N789C	Swearingen SA227AC Metro III	AC-540	ex N389PH	
☐ N969AC	de Havilland DHC-6 Twin Otter 300	286	ex VH-FNU	
☐ N27442	Swearingen SA227AC Metro III	AC-750B		

BIG ISLAND AIR — Big Isle (BIG) — Kailua-Keahole Kona Intl, HI (KOA)

☐ N281A	Cessna 208 Caravan I	20800271	ex LV-WYX	
☐ N2150	Cessna 208BEX Caravan I	208B5054		♦

BIGHORN AIRWAYS — Bighorn (BHR) — Sheridan-County, WY/Casper-Natrona Co, WY (SHR/CPR)

☐ N107BH	CASA C.212-200	CC20-4-165	ex N212TH	
☐ N109BH	CASA C.212-200	CC35-1-192	ex N192PL	
☐ N110BH	Air Tractor AT-402A	402A-1135	ex C-GQKD	♦
☐ N112BH	CASA C.212-200	CC50-11-292	ex N311ST	
☐ N113BH	Cessna 180H Skywagon	18051844	ex N7944V	
☐ N115BH	Cessna 340A	340A1531	ex N2688Q	
☐ N117BH	CASA C.212-200	CC23-1-171	ex N349CA	
☐ N118BH	Cessna 340A	340A0003	ex N5168J	
☐ N213BH	Air Tractor AT-402B	402B-1279		♦
☐ N257MC	Dornier 228-202	8102	ex YV-648C	
☐ N263MC	Dornier 228-202	8141	ex N116DN	
☐ N266MC	Dornier 228-202	8150	ex D-CBDL	
☐ N441WJ	Cessna 441	441-0194	ex N26RF	
☐ N543CC	Bell 206B JetRanger III	3593	ex N2295W	
☐ N700WJ	Cessna 425 Conquest I	425-0036	ex F-GCQN	
☐ N4350S	Air Tractor AT-301	301-0030		
☐ N4351S	Air Tractor AT-301	301-0031		
☐ N6266C	Cessna T210N Turbo Centurion II	21063849		

BIZCHARTERS — Chicago-DuPage, IL (DPA)

☐ N234BZ	Embraer ERJ-135LR	145388	ex N736DT	♦
☐ N356BZ	Embraer ERJ-135LR	145288	ex N723AE	♦
☐ N735TS	Embraer ERJ-135LR	145386	ex PT-SQK	♦

BRISTOW US — Bristow Group L9/BTZ) — New Iberia-Air Logistics Heliport, LA

☐ N69AL	Bell 206L-4 LongRanger IV	52139	ex PT-YBH
☐ N76AL	Bell 206L-4 LongRanger IV	52165	ex N15EW
☐ N176AL	Bell 206L-4 LongRanger IV	52146	ex C-FOFE
☐ N177AL	Bell 206L-4 LongRanger IV	52157	ex C-GLZU
☐ N188AL	Bell 206L-4 LongRanger IV	52082	ex N84TV
☐ N192AL	Bell 206L-4 LongRanger IV	52342	
☐ N193AL	Bell 206L-4 LongRanger IV	52344	
☐ N196AL	Bell 206L-4 LongRanger IV	52380	ex N218K
☐ N206DB	Bell 206L-4 LongRanger IV	52127	
☐ N265AL	Bell 206L-4 LongRanger IV	52280	ex C-GFNY
☐ N266AL	Bell 206L-4 LongRanger IV	52281	ex C-GFNY
☐ N267AL	Bell 206L-4 LongRanger IV	52282	ex C-GAXE
☐ N268AL	Bell 206L-4 LongRanger IV	52283	
☐ N269AL	Bell 206L-4 LongRanger IV	52284	
☐ N271AL	Bell 206L-4 LongRanger IV	52287	
☐ N272AL	Bell 206L-4 LongRanger IV	52288	
☐ N275AL	Bell 206L-4 LongRanger IV	52285	
☐ N276AL	Bell 206L-4 LongRanger IV	52312	
☐ N278AL	Bell 206L-4 LongRanger IV	52313	
☐ N279AL	Bell 206L-4 LongRanger IV	52314	ex C-GAEP
☐ N280AL	Bell 206L-4 LongRanger IV	52315	
☐ N281AL	Bell 206L-4 LongRanger IV	52319	
☐ N403AL	Bell 407	53478	ex N4041F
☐ N405AL	Bell 407	53480	ex N40414
☐ N407AL	Bell 407	53044	
☐ N407TZ	Bell 407	53204	ex N487AL
☐ N408AL	Bell 407	53491	ex N6148U
☐ N409AL	Bell 407	53494	ex N9182V
☐ N410AL	Bell 407	53482	ex N388RT
☐ N431AL	Bell 407	53923	ex C-FYPN
☐ N447AL	Bell 407	53126	ex PT-YNM
☐ N477AL	Bell 407	53203	
☐ N487AL	Bell 407	53150	ex N847AL ♦

☐ N497AL	Bell 407	53172		
☐ N527AL	Bell 407	53211		
☐ N557AL	Bell 407	53243		
☐ N577AL	Bell 407	53247		
☐ N587AL	Bell 407	53248		
☐ N597AL	Bell 407	53091	ex N427AL	
☐ N607AL	Bell 407	53264		
☐ N617AL	Bell 407	53265		
☐ N627AL	Bell 407	53284		
☐ N637AL	Bell 407	53293	ex PT-YUW	based Alaska
☐ N647AL	Bell 407	53357	ex N60321	
☐ N667AL	Bell 407	53624	ex XA-SKY	
☐ N687AL	Bell 407	53366	ex N6302B	
☐ N697AL	Bell 407	53374	ex N6112Q	
☐ N727AL	Bell 407	53227	ex N298RS	
☐ N796RV	Bell 407	53037	ex RP-C2468	
☐ N937AL	Bell 407	53383	ex N63894	
☐ N520AL	Sikorsky S-76A++	760109	ex 5N-BCT	
☐ N720BG	Sikorsky S-76D	761013	ex N7613J	
☐ N722BG	Sikorsky S-76D	761016	ex N7616T	♦
☐ N723BG	Sikorsky S-76D	761019	ex N7619L	
☐ N860AL	Sikorsky S-76C	760527	ex N9042W	♦
☐ N861AL	Sikorsky S-76C	760529	ex N2032N	♦
☐ N862AL	Sikorsky S-76C	760531	ex N2021W	♦
☐ N863AL	Sikorsky S-76C	760536	ex N5009K	♦
☐ N864AL	Sikorsky S-76C	760557	ex N50093	♦
☐ N865AL	Sikorsky S-76C	760564	ex N70089	♦
☐ N866AL	Sikorsky S-76C	760562	ex N50085	♦
☐ N867AL	Sikorsky S-76C	760579	ex N7104Q	♦
☐ N868AL	Sikorsky S-76C	760580		♦
☐ N870AL	Sikorsky S-76C	760606	ex N8119N	
☐ N871AL	Sikorsky S-76C+	760627	ex N80907	
☐ N881AL	Sikorsky S-76C+	760673	ex N4512G	
☐ N883AL	Sikorsky S-76C	760677	ex N4514G	
☐ N884AL	Sikorsky S-76C	760721	ex N2975Q	
☐ N890BG	Sikorsky S-76C	760645	ex 9M-SPT	
☐ N891BG	Sikorsky S-76C	760679		♦
☐ N7644E	Sikorsky S-76D	761044		
☐ N7645T	Sikorsky S-76D	761045		
☐ N7646L	Sikorsky S-76D	761046		
☐ N7650G	Sikorsky S-76D	761050		♦
☐ N7653H	Sikorsky S-76D	761053		♦
☐ N7654Z	Sikorsky S-76D	761054		♦
☐ N227K	Sikorsky S-92A	920227		
☐ N254J	Sikorsky S-92A	920254		♦
☐ N257Z	Sikorsky S-92A	920257		♦
☐ N259CV	Sikorsky S-92A	920259		♦
☐ N262U	Sikorsky S-92A	920262		♦
☐ N292BG	Sikorsky S-92A	920194	ex N194H	♦
☐ N492BG	Sikorsky S-92A	920227	ex N227K	♦
☐ N592BG	Sikorsky S-92A	920243	ex N243Q	♦
☐ N692BG	Sikorsky S-92A	920093	ex PR-JAF	♦
☐ N892BG	Sikorsky S-92A	920211	ex N211MT	♦
☐ N932BG	Sikorsky S-92A	920021	ex N92UT	♦
☐ N933BG	Sikorsky S-92A	920155	ex N155N	♦
☐ N139TZ	AgustaWestland AW139	41202		♦
☐ N206XS	Bell 206B	3040		♦
☐ N439BG	AgustaWestland AW139	31312	ex G-CGSN	
☐ N523QK	Bell 412EP	36396	ex 9Y-BRS	♦
☐ N539BG	AgustaWestland AW139	41329	ex N512SM	
☐ N7007Q	Bell 412EP	36315	ex XA-TYA	♦

BROOKS AVIATION — Douglas-Municipal, GA (DQH)

☐ N99FS	Douglas DC-3	12425	ex (N89BF)

BUSINESS AVIATION COURIER — Dakota (DKT) — Sioux Falls-Joe Foss Field, SD (FSD)

☐ N76MD	Cessna 402B II	402B1055	ex N987PF
☐ N624CA	Cessna 402B	402B0876	ex D-IJOS
☐ N780MB	Cessna 402B	402B0249	ex N402RT
☐ N3796C	Cessna 402B	402B0803	
☐ N3813	Cessna 402B	402B0807	ex PK-VCE
☐ N80BS	Cessna 404 Titan II	404-0048	ex G-ZAPB
☐ N103RC	Cessna 404 Titan II	404-0108	ex C-FKQM
☐ N366AE	Swearingen SA.227AC Metro III	AC-681B	
☐ N685BA	Swearingen SA.227AC Metro III	AC-685	ex N685AV
☐ N797CF	Beech 65-C90 King Air	LJ-797	ex N61GA

☐ N3108B	Swearingen SA.227AC Metro III	AC-509	ex XA-TAK	
☐ N3116N	Swearingen SA.227AC Metro III	AC-596		

CAPE AIR (HYANNIS AIR SERVICE)   Cair (9K/KAP)

Hyannis-Barnstable Municipal, MA/Naples-Municipal, FL (HYA/APF)

☐ N18VV	Cessna 402C	402C0619	ex N180PB		
☐ N57PB	Cessna 402C II	402C0300	ex N3628M		♦
☐ N69SC	Cessna 402C II	402C0041	ex N5778C		
☐ N83PB	Cessna 402C II	402C0350	ex N26627		
☐ N106CA	Cessna 402C III	402C1020	ex TJ-AHQ		
☐ N120PC	Cessna 402C II	402C0079	ex N2612L		
☐ N121PB	Cessna 402C II	402C0507	ex N6874X		
☐ N160PB	Cessna 402C II	402C0493	ex N6841M		
☐ N161TA	Cessna 402C II	402C0070	ex N2611A		
☐ N223PB	Cessna 402C II	402C0105	ex N261PB		
☐ N247GS	Cessna 402C II	402C0637	ex N404BK		
☐ N256CA	Cessna 402C	402C0606	ex N402SX		♦
☐ N290CA	Cessna 402C II	402C0297	ex N401BK		
☐ N300SN	Cessna 402C II	402C0060	ex N5871C		
☐ N305AT	Cessna 402C	402C0030			♦
☐ N385CA	Cessna 402C II	402C0111	ex N26150		
☐ N401SX	Cessna 402C	402C0447	ex 9A-BPV		
☐ N401TJ	Cessna 402C II	402C0109	ex TJ-AFV		
☐ N402MQ	Cessna 402C	402C0095	ex N81PB		♦
☐ N402VN	Cessna 402C II	402C0488	ex (N6840D)		
☐ N404SX	Cessna 402C	402C0280			
☐ N406GA	Cessna 402C II	402C0329	ex N2642D		
☐ N466CA	Cessna 402C	402C0428	ex N6786R		♦
☐ N494BC	Cessna 402C II	402C0308	ex N67PB		
☐ N499CA	Cessna 402C II	402C1006	ex N410BK		
☐ N514NC	Cessna 402C II	402C0514	ex N125PB		
☐ N524CA	Cessna 402C II	402C0522	ex C-GSKG		
☐ N525RH	Cessna 402C II	402C0525	ex N68761		
☐ N548GA	Cessna 402C II	402C0653	ex N6773T		
☐ N618CA	Cessna 402C II	402C0620	ex VH-RGK		
☐ N660CA	Cessna 402C II	402C0406	ex C-GHMI		
☐ N663AA	Cessna 402C II	402C0123			
☐ N678JG	Cessna 402C II	402C0266	ex C-FAFB		
☐ N740CA	Cessna 402C	402C0277	ex N402NS		
☐ N747WS	Cessna 402C II	402C0080	ex C-GHYZ		
☐ N751CA	Cessna 402C II	402C0217	ex N402AT		
☐ N762EA	Cessna 402C II	402C0061	ex N5872C		
☐ N763EA	Cessna 402C II	402C0497	ex N763AN		
☐ N764EA	Cessna 402C II	402C0237	ex N2719T		
☐ N769EA	Cessna 402C II	402C0303	ex N3283M		
☐ N771EA	Cessna 402C II	402C0046	ex N5809C		
☐ N781EA	Cessna 402C II	402C0310	ex N822AN		
☐ N810BW	Cessna 402C II	402C0279	ex N810AN		
☐ N812AN	Cessna 402C II	402C0229	ex N2718P		
☐ N818AN	Cessna 402C II	402C0501	ex N6842Q		
☐ N890CA	Cessna 402C II	402C0006	ex N4643N		♦
☐ N1055	Cessna 402C II	402C0249			
☐ N1361G	Cessna 402C II	402C0270			
☐ N1376G	Cessna 402C II	402C0271	ex N156PB	special landscape c/s	
☐ N2611X	Cessna 402C II	402C0072			
☐ N2615G	Cessna 402C II	402C0101	ex C-GHGM		
☐ N2651S	Cessna 402C	402C0342			
☐ N2649Z	Cessna 402C II	402C0333			
☐ N2714B	Cessna 402C II	402C0210			
☐ N2714M	Cessna 402C II	402C0211			
☐ N3249M	Cessna 402C II	402C0296			
☐ N3292M	Cessna 402C II	402C0304			
☐ N4630N	Cessna 402C II	402C0001			
☐ N4652N	Cessna 402C II	402C0011			
☐ N5826C	Cessna 402C	402C0050			
☐ N6765T	Cessna 402C II	402C0629			
☐ N6786R	Cessna 402C	402C0428	ex N6788R		
☐ N6813J	Cessna 402C II	402C0641			
☐ N6875D	Cessna 402C II	402C0511		special Flagship Whalers c/s	
☐ N7037E	Cessna 402C II	402C0471	ex C-GGXH		
☐ N2711X	Cessna 402C	402C0116			♦
☐ N2713X	Cessna 402C	402C0207			♦
☐ N5820C	Cessna 402C	402C0047			♦
☐ N26156	Cessna 402C II	402C0112			
☐ N26514	Cessna 402C II	402C0344			
☐ N26632	Cessna 402C II	402C0404			
☐ N36911	Cessna 402C II	402C0314			
☐ N67786	Cessna 402C II	402C0631		special Key West Express c/s	
☐ N67886	Cessna 402C II	402C0435			
☐ N68391	Cessna 402C II	402C0483			

| ☐ N68752 | Cessna 402C II | 402C0518 | |
| ☐ N88833 | Cessna 402C II | 402C0265 | special flowers c/s |

☐ N510BN	Britten-Norman BN-2B-20 Islander	2239	ex G-BSPS	
☐ N520BN	Britten-Norman BN-2B-20 Islander	2240	ex G-HEBI	
☐ N530BN	Britten-Norman BN-2B-20 Islander	2209	ex G-BPLR	
☐ N540BN	Britten-Norman BN-2B-20	2207	ex G-BPLO	♦
☐ N6672C	Cessna 414A	414A-0053		
☐ N14834	ATR 42-320	193	ex F-WWEG	
☐ N42836	ATR 42-320	200	ex F-WWEN 836	

CARIBE RICO · Orlando, FL

| ☐ N274FS | Swearingen SA.226TC Metro II | TC-274 | ex C-FTJC |
| ☐ N1840M | Cessna 337F Skymaster | 33701440 | |

CARSON HELICOPTERS · Perkasie-Heliport, PA/Jackonsville Heliport, OR

☐ N349FC	Sikorsky S-61 (SH-3H)	61239	ex Bu151535	wfs
☐ N349RH	Sikorsky S-61 (UH-3H)	61117	ex Bu149702	
☐ N352DH	Sikorsky S-61 (SH-3H)	61161	ex N1048Y	
☐ N448JS	Sikorsky S-61N	61428	ex C-GJDR	
☐ N493RC	Sikorsky S-61N	61776	ex C-GSVO	
☐ N754WN	Sikorsky S-61N	61754	ex N617HM	
☐ N4263A	Sikorsky S-61R	61551	ex 65-5700	
☐ N4263F	Sikorsky S-61R	61533	ex 64-14230	
☐ N8167B	Sikorsky S-61A	61137	ex Bu149720	
☐ N42626	Sikorsky S-61R	61522	ex 63-9690	

CASTLE AVIATION · Castle (CSJ) · Akron-Canton Regional, OH (CAK)

☐ N31MG	Cessna 208B Caravan I	208B0776	ex N703PA	Frtr♦
☐ N24MG	Cessna 208B Caravan I	208B0850	ex N5261R	Frtr
☐ N27MG	Cessna 208B Caravan I	208B0650		Frtr
☐ N29MG	Cessna 208B Caravan I	208B0812	ex N52229	Frtr
☐ N1029Y	Cessna 208B Caravan I	208B0325		Frtr

| ☐ N49MG | Piper PA-60 Aerostar 600 | 60-0634-7961201 | ex N8232J | |
| ☐ N52MG | Ted Smith Aerostar 600A | 60-0530-172 | ex N8047J | |

CATALINA AIR TRANSPORT · Catalina Air (CBT) · Long Beach-Daugherty Field, CA (LGB)

☐ N403JB	Douglas DC-3	16943/34202	ex N17778
☐ N2298C	Douglas DC-3	16453/33201	ex (N352SA)
☐ N9680B	Cessna 208B Caravan I	208B0150	

CENTURION AIR CARGO · Challenge Cargo (WE/CWC) · Miami-Intl, FL (MIA)

☐ N901AR	Boeing 747-4R7F	25868/1125	ex LX-KCV	>KYE
☐ N902AR	Boeing 747-428ERF	32870/1344	ex F-GIUD	
☐ N903AR	Boeing 747-428ERF	33096/1317	ex F-GIUG	
☐ N904AR	Boeing 747-428ERF	33097/1361	ex VQ-BGY	o/o♦
☐ N984AR	McDonnell-Douglas MD-11BCF	48429/500	ex N429AN	[MZJ]
☐ N986AR	McDonnell-Douglas MD-11F	48426/468	ex EI-UPA	
☐ N987AR	McDonnell-Douglas MD-11F	48427/471	ex EI-UPE	[TUS]

CHAMPION AIR · Statesville, NC (SVH)

☐ N3DE	Embraer ERJ-145LR	145626	ex N856JJ
☐ N138DE	Embraer ERJ-145LR	145129	ex LX-LGV
☐ N500DE	Embraer ERJ-145EP	145084	ex LX-LGU

CHARTER AIR TRANSPORT · Stingray (VC/SRY) · Cleveland, OH (CLE)

☐ N650CT	Embraer EMB.120RT Brasilia	120198	ex N267AS	
☐ N652CT	Embraer EMB.120RT Brasilia	120289	ex N289YV	
☐ N653CT	Embraer EMB.120RT Brasilia	120243	ex N204SW	Via Air c/s
☐ N654CT	Embraer EMB.120ER Brasilia	120251	ex N251YV	Via Air c/s

COASTAL AIR TRANSPORT · Coastal (CXT) · St Croix-Alexander Hamilton, VI (STX)

| ☐ N676MF | Cessna 402B | 402B0106 | ex N7856Q | Cruzan Queen |
| ☐ N677MF | Cessna 404 Titan | 404-0421 | ex N96889 | |

COLUMBIA HELICOPTERS · Columbia Heli (WCO)
Aurora-State, OR/Lake Charles-Regional, LA (UAO/LCH)

| ☐ C-GHFF | Boeing Vertol 107 II | 406 | ex N195CH | >Helifor |

☐ N184CH	Kawasaki KV107-II	4001	ex Thai 4001	
☐ N185CH	Kawasaki KV107-II	4003	ex Thai 4003	
☐ N187CH	Kawasaki KV107-II	4012	ex HC-BZP	
☐ N188CH	Boeing Vertol 107 II	107	ex C-FHFW	
☐ N190CH	Boeing Vertol 107 II	2002	ex C-GHFY	◆
☐ N191CH	Boeing Vertol 107 II	2003	ex P2-CHD	
☐ N192CH	Kawasaki KV107-II	4011	ex JA9505	
☐ N196CH	Boeing Vertol 107 II	407		
☐ N6672D	Boeing Vertol 107 II	2	ex C-FHFV	
☐ N6674D	Boeing Vertol 107 II	4	ex C-FHFV	
☐ N6675D	Boeing Vertol 107 II	5	ex ZK-HCW	
☐ N6676D	Boeing Vertol 107 II	6		
☐ N6682D	Boeing Vertol 107 II	101	ex C-GHCD	
☐ N235CH	Boeing Vertol 234UT Chinook	MJ-002	ex G-BISO	
☐ N238CH	Boeing Vertol 234UT Chinook	MJ-005	ex C-FHFB	>Helifor
☐ N242CH	Boeing Vertol 234UT Chinook	MJ-023	ex HC-BYF	
☐ N246CH	Boeing Vertol 234LR Chinook	MJ-017	ex LN-OMK	
☐ N411CH	Boeing CH-47D Chinook		ex 87-0079	◆
☐ N412CH	Boeing CH-47D Chinook		ex 88-0109	◆
☐ N471CH	Boeing CH-47D Chinook	M3350	ex 90-0198	◆
☐ N472CH	Boeing CH-47D Chinook		ex 89-0138	◆
☐ N473CH	Boeing CH-47D Chinook		ex 92-0283	◆
☐ N474CH	Boeing CH-47D Chinook		ex 92-0300	◆
☐ N475CH	Boeing CH-47D Chinook		ex 88-0079	◆
☐ N476CH	Boeing CH-47D Chinook		ex 88-0097	◆
☐ P2-CHI	Boeing Vertol 234UT Chinook	MJ-003	ex N237CH	
☐ N111NS	Beech 200C Super King Air	BL-36		

COMMUTAIR   Commutair (C5/UCA)   Plattsburgh-Clinton County, NY (PLB)

Ops as United Express in full colours and using UA flight numbers. Commutair is a trading name of Champlain Enterprises. Leases 16 de Havilland DHC-8-200Qs from Horizon Airlines for service from Cleveland.

COMPASS AIRLINES   Compass Rose (CPZ)   Washington-Dulles-Intl, DC (IAD)

Ops as AA Express (Envoy) and Delta Connection

CORPORATE AIR   Air Spur (CPT)   Billings-Logan Intl, MT (BIL)

☐ N101UE	Beech 1900C-1	UC-101	ex N919GL	
☐ N330SB	Short SD.3-30	SH3013	ex (N277CC)	Frtr
☐ N331SB	Short SD.3-30	SH3015	ex N331CA	Frtr [HNL]

CORPORATE FLIGHT MANAGEMENT   Volunteer (VTE)   Smyrna, TN (MQY)

☐ N319UE	British Aerospace Jetstream 4101	41042	ex G-4-042	[MQY]
☐ N320UE	British Aerospace Jetstream 4101	41043	ex G-4-043	
☐ N325UE	British Aerospace Jetstream 4101	41063	ex G-4-063	
☐ N569ST	British Aerospace Jetstream 32EP	952	ex N952AE	
☐ N913AE	British Aerospace Jetstream 32	913	ex G-31-013	

CROMAN CORP   White City, OR

☐ N614CK	Sikorsky S-61N	61715	ex LN-OSJ	
☐ N615CK	Sikorsky S-61N	61814	ex C-GBFZ	
☐ N617CK	Sikorsky S-61N	61164		◆
☐ N618CK	Sikorsky S-61NM	61454	ex G-BCEB	
☐ N619CK	Sikorsky S-61N	61808	ex PR-AEL	
☐ N692CC	Sikorsky S-61A	61439		◆
☐ N693CC	Sikorsky S-61A	61215		◆
☐ N694CC	Sikorsky S-61A	61088		◆
☐ N611CK	Sikorsky SH-3H	61038	exN104BS	
☐ N612CK	Sikorsky SH-3H	61130	exN105BS	
☐ N613CK	Sikorsky SH-3H	613-2	exN105BS	

CSA AIR   Iron Air (IRO)   Iron Mountain-Ford, MI (IMT)

Ops Cessna Caravans leased from and on behalf of Federal Express

DELTA AIR LINES   Delta (DL/DAL)   Atlanta-Hartsfield Intl, GA (ATL)

Member of SkyTeam

☐ N301NB	Airbus A319-114	1058	ex D-AVYP	3101 City of Duluth
☐ N302NB	Airbus A319-114	1062	ex D-AVWA	3102
☐ N314NB	Airbus A319-114	1191	ex D-AVWO	3114
☐ N315NB	Airbus A319-114	1230	ex D-AVYM	3115
☐ N316NB	Airbus A319-114	1249	ex D-AVYW	3116

☐	N317NB	Airbus A319-114	1324	ex D-AVWT	3117
☐	N318NB	Airbus A319-114	1325	ex D-AVYF	3118
☐	N319NB	Airbus A319-114	1346	ex D-AVYR	3119
☐	N320NB	Airbus A319-114	1392	ex D-AVYT	3120
☐	N321NB	Airbus A319-114	1414	ex D-AVYL	3121
☐	N322NB	Airbus A319-114	1434	ex D-AVYO	3122
☐	N323NB	Airbus A319-114	1453	ex D-AVWE	3123
☐	N324NB	Airbus A319-114	1456	ex D-AVWF	3124
☐	N325NB	Airbus A319-114	1483	ex D-AVYU	3125
☐	N326NB	Airbus A319-114	1498	ex D-AVYC	3126
☐	N327NB	Airbus A319-114	1501	ex D-AVYD	3127
☐	N328NB	Airbus A319-114	1520	ex D-AVYN	3128
☐	N329NB	Airbus A319-114	1543	ex D-AVWJ	3129
☐	N330NB	Airbus A319-114	1549	ex D-AVWM	3130
☐	N331NB	Airbus A319-114	1567	ex D-AVYU	3131
☐	N332NB	Airbus A319-114	1570	ex D-AVWD	3132
☐	N333NB	Airbus A319-114	1582	ex D-AVYA	3133
☐	N334NB	Airbus A319-114	1659	ex D-AVYU	3134
☐	N335NB	Airbus A319-114	1662	ex D-AVYW	3135
☐	N336NB	Airbus A319-114	1683	ex D-AVWJ	3136
☐	N337NB	Airbus A319-114	1685	ex D-AVWL	3137
☐	N338NB	Airbus A319-114	1693	ex D-AVYD	3138
☐	N339NB	Airbus A319-114	1709	ex D-AVWG	3139
☐	N340NB	Airbus A319-114	1714	ex D-AVWN	3140
☐	N341NB	Airbus A319-114	1738	ex D-AVWV	3141
☐	N342NB	Airbus A319-114	1746	ex D-AVYA	3142
☐	N343NB	Airbus A319-114	1752	ex D-AVYH	3143
☐	N344NB	Airbus A319-114	1766	ex D-AVYU	3144
☐	N345NB	Airbus A319-114	1774	ex D-AVYD	3145
☐	N346NB	Airbus A319-114	1796	ex D-AVYX	3146
☐	N347NB	Airbus A319-114	1800	ex D-AVYZ	3147
☐	N348NB	Airbus A319-114	1810	ex D-AVWH	3148
☐	N349NB	Airbus A319-114	1815	ex D-AVWI	3149
☐	N351NB	Airbus A319-114	1820	ex D-AVWL	3151
☐	N352NB	Airbus A319-114	1824	ex D-AVWM	3152
☐	N353NB	Airbus A319-114	1828	ex D-AVWO	3153
☐	N354NB	Airbus A319-114	1833	ex D-AVWS	3154
☐	N355NB	Airbus A319-114	1839	ex D-AVWA	3155
☐	N357NB	Airbus A319-114	1875	ex D-AVYH	3157
☐	N358NB	Airbus A319-114	1897	ex D-AVYK	3158
☐	N359NB	Airbus A319-114	1923	ex D-AVWC	3159
☐	N360NB	Airbus A319-114	1959	ex D-AVWL	3160
☐	N361NB	Airbus A319-114	1976	ex D-AVYB	3161
☐	N362NB	Airbus A319-114	1982	ex D-AVYF	3162
☐	N363NB	Airbus A319-114	1990	ex D-AVYL	3163
☐	N364NB	Airbus A319-114	2002	ex D-AVWA	3164
☐	N365NB	Airbus A319-114	2013	ex D-AVWS	3165
☐	N366NB	Airbus A319-114	2026	ex D-AVWX	3166
☐	N368NB	Airbus A319-114	2039	ex D-AVYT	3168
☐	N369NB	Airbus A319-114	2047	ex D-AVWC	3169
☐	N370NB	Airbus A319-114	2087	ex D-AVWI	3170
☐	N371NB	Airbus A319-114	2095	ex D-AVYI	3171
☐	N309US	Airbus A320-211	0118	ex F-WWIM	3209
☐	N310NW	Airbus A320-211	0121	ex F-WWIO	3210
☐	N311US	Airbus A320-211	0125	ex F-WWIT	3211
☐	N312US	Airbus A320-211	0152	ex F-WWDT	3212
☐	N313US	Airbus A320-211	0153	ex F-WWDX	3213
☐	N314US	Airbus A320-211	0160	ex F-WWDZ	3214
☐	N315US	Airbus A320-211	0171	ex F-WWIJ	3215
☐	N316US	Airbus A320-211	0192	ex F-WWIY	3216
☐	N317US	Airbus A320-211	0197	ex F-WWDF	3217
☐	N318US	Airbus A320-211	0206	ex F-WWDK	3218
☐	N319US	Airbus A320-211	0208	ex F-WWDT	3219
☐	N320US	Airbus A320-211	0213	ex F-WWIB	3220
☐	N321US	Airbus A320-211	0262	ex F-WWID	3221
☐	N322US	Airbus A320-211	0263	ex F-WWDQ	3222
☐	N323US	Airbus A320-211	0272	ex F-WWBP	3223
☐	N324US	Airbus A320-211	0273	ex F-WWDS	3224
☐	N325US	Airbus A320-211	0281	ex F-WWBS	3225
☐	N326US	Airbus A320-211	0282	ex F-WWIA	3226
☐	N327NW	Airbus A320-211	0297	ex F-WWIO	3227
☐	N328NW	Airbus A320-211	0298	ex F-WWIP	3228
☐	N329NW	Airbus A320-211	0306	ex F-WWDG	3229
☐	N330NW	Airbus A320-211	0307	ex F-WWDJ	3230
☐	N331NW	Airbus A320-211	0318	ex F-WWBF	3231
☐	N332NW	Airbus A320-211	0319	ex F-WWBG	3232
☐	N333NW	Airbus A320-211	0329	ex F-WWDY	3233
☐	N334NW	Airbus A320-212	0339	ex F-WWBP	3234
☐	N335NW	Airbus A320-212	0340	ex F-WWBQ	3235
☐	N336NW	Airbus A320-212	0355	ex F-WWIE	3236
☐	N337NW	Airbus A320-212	0358	ex F-WWIO	3237
☐	N338NW	Airbus A320-212	0360	ex F-WWBY	3238

☐ N339NW	Airbus A320-212	0367	ex F-WWDG	3239	
☐ N340NW	Airbus A320-212	0372	ex F-WWIX	3240	
☐ N341NW	Airbus A320-212	0380	ex F-WWIS	3241	
☐ N342NW	Airbus A320-212	0381	ex F-WWIJ	3242	
☐ N343NW	Airbus A320-212	0387	ex F-WWBV	3243	
☐ N344NW	Airbus A320-212	0388	ex F-WWDC	3244	
☐ N345NW	Airbus A320-212	0399	ex F-WWIG	3245	
☐ N347NW	Airbus A320-212	0408	ex F-WWDN	3247	
☐ N348NW	Airbus A320-212	0410	ex F-WWDV	3248	
☐ N349NW	Airbus A320-212	0417	ex F-WWBR	3249	
☐ N350NA	Airbus A320-212	0418	ex F-WWDG	3250	
☐ N351NW	Airbus A320-212	0766	ex F-WWDG	3251	
☐ N352NW	Airbus A320-212	0778	ex F-WWDO	3252	
☐ N353NW	Airbus A320-212	0786	ex F-WWDP	3253	
☐ N354NW	Airbus A320-212	0801	ex F-WWDY	3254	
☐ N355NW	Airbus A320-212	0807	ex F-WWIC	3255	
☐ N356NW	Airbus A320-212	0818	ex F-WWBD	3256	
☐ N357NW	Airbus A320-212	0830	ex F-WWIN	3257	
☐ N358NW	Airbus A320-212	0832	ex F-WWIO	3258	
☐ N359NW	Airbus A320-212	0846	ex F-WWBH	3259	
☐ N360NW	Airbus A320-212	0903	ex F-WWDO	3260	
☐ N361NW	Airbus A320-212	0907	ex F-WWDQ	3261	
☐ N362NW	Airbus A320-212	0911	ex F-WWDT	3262	
☐ N363NW	Airbus A320-212	0923	ex F-WWDZ	3263	
☐ N364NW	Airbus A320-212	0962	ex F-WWBF	3264	
☐ N365NW	Airbus A320-212	0964	ex F-WWBJ	3265	
☐ N366NW	Airbus A320-212	0981	ex F-WWDE	3266	
☐ N367NW	Airbus A320-212	0988	ex F-WWIH	3267	
☐ N368NW	Airbus A320-212	0996	ex F-WWBV	3268	
☐ N369NW	Airbus A320-212	1011	ex F-WWDO	3269	
☐ N370NW	Airbus A320-212	1037	ex F-WWDY	3270	
☐ N371NW	Airbus A320-212	1535	ex F-WWIS	3271	
☐ N372NW	Airbus A320-212	1633	ex F-WWDO	3272	
☐ N373NW	Airbus A320-212	1641	ex F-WWIR	3273	
☐ N374NW	Airbus A320-212	1646	ex F-WWDS	3274	
☐ N375NC	Airbus A320-212	1789	ex F-WWDU	3275	
☐ N376NW	Airbus A320-212	1812	ex F-WWBB	3276	
☐ N377NW	Airbus A320-212	2082	ex F-WWIU	3277	
☐ N378NW	Airbus A320-212	2092	ex F-WWBP	3278	
☐ N851NW	Airbus A330-223	609	ex F-WWYZ	3351	
☐ N852NW	Airbus A330-223	614	ex F-WWKU	3352	
☐ N853NW	Airbus A330-223	618	ex F-WWKN	3353	
☐ N854NW	Airbus A330-223	620	ex F-WWYA	3354	
☐ N855NW	Airbus A330-223	621	ex F-WWYB	3355	
☐ N856NW	Airbus A330-223	631	ex F-WWYG	3356	
☐ N857NW	Airbus A330-223	633	ex F-WWYI	3357	
☐ N858NW	Airbus A330-223	718	ex F-WWYY	3358	
☐ N859NW	Airbus A330-223	722	ex F-WWKM	3359	
☐ N860NW	Airbus A330-223	778	ex F-WWKL	3360	
☐ N861NW	Airbus A330-223	796	ex F-WWKT	3361	
☐ N801NW	Airbus A330-323E	524	ex F-WWYZ	3301	
☐ N802NW	Airbus A330-323E	533	ex F-WWYD	3302	
☐ N803NW	Airbus A330-323E	542	ex F-WWYH	3303	
☐ N804NW	Airbus A330-323E	549	ex F-WWYJ	3304	
☐ N805NW	Airbus A330-323E	552	ex F-WWKQ	3305	
☐ N806NW	Airbus A330-323E	578	ex F-WWKD	3306	
☐ N807NW	Airbus A330-323E	588	ex F-WWKM	3307	
☐ N808NW	Airbus A330-323E	591	ex F-WWKO	3308	
☐ N809NW	Airbus A330-323E	663	ex F-WWKM	3309	
☐ N810NW	Airbus A330-323E	674	ex F-WWKT	3310	
☐ N811NW	Airbus A330-323E	690	ex F-WWKV	3311	
☐ N812NW	Airbus A330-323E	784	ex F-WWYX	3312	
☐ N813NW	Airbus A330-323E	799	ex F-WWKV	3313	
☐ N814NW	Airbus A330-323E	806	ex F-WWYN	3314	
☐ N815NW	Airbus A330-323E	817	ex F-WWYP	3315	
☐ N816NW	Airbus A330-323E	827	ex F-WWKG	3316	
☐ N817NW	Airbus A330-323E	843	ex F-WWYX	3317	
☐ N818NW	Airbus A330-323E	857	ex F-WWYD	3318	
☐ N819NW	Airbus A330-323E	858	ex F-WWYE	3319	
☐ N820NW	Airbus A330-323E	859	ex F-WWYF	3320	
☐ N821NW	Airbus A330-323E	865	ex F-WWYJ	3321	
☐ N822NW	Airbus A330-302	1627	ex F-WWYX	3322	o/o♦
☐ N823NW	Airbus A330-302	1628	ex F-WW		o/o♦
☐ N824NW	Airbus A330-302	1637	ex F-WW		o/o♦
☐ N	Airbus A330-302	1641	ex F-WW		o/o♦
☐ N	Airbus A330-302	1679	ex F-WW		o/o♦
☐ N603AT	Boeing 717-22A	55127/5074	ex N482HA		♦
☐ N607AT	Boeing 717-231	55074/5030	ex N599BC		♦
☐ N608AT	Boeing 717-231	55081/5045	ex N766BC		♦
☐ N717JL	Boeing 717-2BD	55042/5115	ex N983AT		♦

☐ N891AT	Boeing 717-2BD	55043/5131	ex (N984AT)		
☐ N892AT	Boeing 717-2BD	55044/5134	ex N7071U		
☐ N893AT	Boeing 717-2BD	55045/5136			
☐ N894AT	Boeing 717-2BD	55046/5137			
☐ N895AT	Boeing 717-2BD	55047/5139			
☐ N896AT	Boeing 717-2BD	55048/5141			
☐ N899AT	Boeing 717-2BD	55049/5143			
☐ N906AT	Boeing 717-231	55087/5060	ex N420TW		♦
☐ N910AT	Boeing 717-231	55086/5056	ex N2419C		♦
☐ N915AT	Boeing 717-231	55085/5055	ex N418TW		♦
☐ N919AT	Boeing 717-231	55084/5052	ex N2417F		♦
☐ N920AT	Boeing 717-231	55083/5049	ex N416TW		♦
☐ N921AT	Boeing 717-231	55082/5046	ex N415TW		♦
☐ N922AT	Boeing 717-2BD	55050/5144		9558	♦
☐ N923AT	Boeing 717-2BD	55051/5148			♦
☐ N924AT	Boeing 717-231	55080/5043	ex N413TW		♦
☐ N925AT	Boeing 717-231	55079/5042	ex N412TW		
☐ N926AT	Boeing 717-231	55078/5039	ex N411TW		♦
☐ N927AT	Boeing 717-231	55077/5038	ex N2410W		
☐ N928AT	Boeing 717-231	55076/5035	ex N409TW	9571	♦
☐ N929AT	Boeing 717-231	55075/5032	ex N408TW		
☐ N930AT	Boeing 717-231	55072/5025	ex N405TW		♦
☐ N933AT	Boeing 717-231	55071/5024	ex N2404A		
☐ N934AT	Boeing 717-231	55070/5022	ex N403TW		
☐ N935AT	Boeing 717-231	55069/5019	ex N402TW	9564	
☐ N937AT	Boeing 717-231	55091/5075	ex N424TW	9586	
☐ N938AT	Boeing 717-2BD	55098/5155		9561	♦
☐ N939AT	Boeing 717-2BD	55099/5156			♦
☐ N948AT	Boeing 717-2BD	55011/5012			♦
☐ N949AT	Boeing 717-2BD	55003/5004	ex N717XD		♦
☐ N951AT	Boeing 717-2BD	55013/5021			♦
☐ N953AT	Boeing 717-2BD	55015/5033			
☐ N954AT	Boeing 717-2BD	55016/5036			
☐ N955AT	Boeing 717-2BD	55017/5040			
☐ N956AT	Boeing 717-2BD	55018/5044			
☐ N957AT	Boeing 717-2BD	55019/5047			♦
☐ N958AT	Boeing 717-2BD	55020/5051			♦
☐ N959AT	Boeing 717-2BD	55021/5057			♦
☐ N960AT	Boeing 717-2BD	55022/5058			♦
☐ N961AT	Boeing 717-2BD	55023/5062			♦
☐ N963AT	Boeing 717-2BD	55024/5066			♦
☐ N964AT	Boeing 717-2BD	55025/5071			♦
☐ N965AT	Boeing 717-2BD	55026/5076			♦
☐ N966AT	Boeing 717-2BD	55027/5081			♦
☐ N967AT	Boeing 717-2BD	55028/5082			♦
☐ N968AT	Boeing 717-2BD	55029/5091			♦
☐ N969AT	Boeing 717-2BD	55030/5094		9531	♦
☐ N970AT	Boeing 717-2BD	55031/5096			♦
☐ N971AT	Boeing 717-2BD	55032/5097		9533	♦
☐ N972AT	Boeing 717-2BD	55033/5099		9534	♦
☐ N974AT	Boeing 717-2BD	55034/5101		9536	♦
☐ N975AT	Boeing 717-2BD	55035/5102			
☐ N977AT	Boeing 717-2BD	55036/5106			
☐ N978AT	Boeing 717-2BD	55037/5108			
☐ N979AT	Boeing 717-2BD	55038/5109			
☐ N981AT	Boeing 717-2BD	55040/5113			
☐ N982AT	Boeing 717-2BD	55041/5114			
☐ N983AT	Boeing 717-2BD	55052/5150		9560	♦
☐ N985AT	Boeing 717-231	55090/5068	ex N423TW		♦
☐ N986AT	Boeing 717-231	55089/5067	ex N422TW	9584	♦
☐ N987AT	Boeing 717-231	55088/5063	ex N2421A		♦
☐ N988AT	Boeing 717-23S	55068/5065	ex (EI-CWJ)		♦
☐ N989AT	Boeing 717-23S	55152/5085	ex (EI-CWK)		
☐ N990AT	Boeing 717-23S	55134/5088	ex (EI-CWM)		
☐ N993AT	Boeing 717-2BD	55137/5103		9538	♦
☐ N994AT	Boeing 717-2BD	55138/5104	ex N6206F		
☐ N995AT	Boeing 717-2BD	55139/5105			
☐ N996AT	Boeing 717-2BD	55140/5107			♦
☐ N997AT	Boeing 717-2BD	55141/5110			♦
☐ N998AT	Boeing 717-2BD	55142/5112			
☐ N301DQ	Boeing 737-732/W	29687/2667	ex N1795B	3601	
☐ N302DQ	Boeing 737-732/W	29648/2683		3602	
☐ N303DQ	Boeing 737-732/W	29688/2720	ex N1786B	3603	
☐ N304DQ	Boeing 737-732/W	29683/2724	ex N1787B	3604	
☐ N305DQ	Boeing 737-732/W	29645/2743		3605	
☐ N306DQ	Boeing 737-732/W	29633/2758		3606	
☐ N307DQ	Boeing 737-732/W	29679/2767		3607	
☐ N308DE	Boeing 737-732/W	29656/3022	ex N1786B	3608	
☐ N309DE	Boeing 737-732/W	29634/3031	ex N1796B	3609	
☐ N310DE	Boeing 737-732/W	29665/3058	ex N1786B	3610	
☐ N371DA	Boeing 737-832/W	29619/115	ex N1787B	3701	

☐	N372DA	Boeing 737-832/W	29620/118	ex N1782B	3702
☐	N373DA	Boeing 737-832/W	29621/123	ex N1800B	3703
☐	N374DA	Boeing 737-832/W	29622/128	ex N1787B	3704
☐	N375DA	Boeing 737-832/W	29623/145		3705
☐	N376DA	Boeing 737-832/W	29624/176		3706
☐	N377DA	Boeing 737-832/W	29625/264		3707
☐	N378DA	Boeing 737-832/W	30265/340		3708
☐	N379DA	Boeing 737-832/W	30349/351		3709
☐	N380DA	Boeing 737-832/W	30266/361		3710
☐	N381DN	Boeing 737-832/W	30350/365	ex (N381DA)	3711 SkyTeam c/s
☐	N382DA	Boeing 737-832/W	30345/389		3712
☐	N383DN	Boeing 737-832/W	30346/393	ex (N383DA)	3713
☐	N384DA	Boeing 737-832/W	30347/412		3714
☐	N385DN	Boeing 737-832/W	30348/418		3715
☐	N386DA	Boeing 737-832/W	30373/446	ex N1780B	3716
☐	N387DA	Boeing 737-832/W	30374/457	ex N1795B	3717
☐	N388DA	Boeing 737-832/W	30375/469		3718
☐	N389DA	Boeing 737-832/W	30376/513	ex N1787B	3719
☐	N390DA	Boeing 737-832/W	30536/518	ex N6063S	3720
☐	N391DA	Boeing 737-832/W	30560/535	ex N1787B	3721
☐	N392DA	Boeing 737-832/W	30561/564		3722
☐	N393DA	Boeing 737-832/W	30377/584	ex N1782B	3723
☐	N394DA	Boeing 737-832/W	30562/589		3724
☐	N395DN	Boeing 737-832/W	30773/604		3725
☐	N396DA	Boeing 737-832/W	30378/632	ex N1795B	3726
☐	N397DA	Boeing 737-832/W	30537/638		3727
☐	N398DA	Boeing 737-832/W	30774/641		3728
☐	N399DA	Boeing 737-832/W	30379/657		3729
☐	N3730B	Boeing 737-832/W	30538/662		3730
☐	N3731T	Boeing 737-832/W	30775/665		3731
☐	N3732J	Boeing 737-832/W	30380/674		3732
☐	N3733Z	Boeing 737-832/W	30539/685		3733
☐	N3734B	Boeing 737-832/W	30776/689		3734
☐	N3735D	Boeing 737-832/W	30381/694	ex (N3735J)	3735
☐	N3736C	Boeing 737-832/W	30540/709		3736
☐	N3737C	Boeing 737-832/W	30799/712		3737
☐	N3738B	Boeing 737-832/W	30382/723		3738
☐	N3739P	Boeing 737-832/W	30541/729		3739
☐	N3740C	Boeing 737-832/W	30800/732		3740
☐	N3741S	Boeing 737-832/W	30487/750		3741
☐	N3742C	Boeing 737-832/W	30835/755	ex N1781B	3742
☐	N3743H	Boeing 737-832/W	30836/770	ex N1795B	3743
☐	N3744F	Boeing 737-832/W	30837/805		3744
☐	N3745B	Boeing 737-832/W	32373/831		3745
☐	N3746H	Boeing 737-832/W	30488/842		3746
☐	N3747D	Boeing 737-832/W	32374/846	ex N1787B	3747
☐	N3748Y	Boeing 737-832/W	30489/865		3748
☐	N3749D	Boeing 737-832/W	30490/867		3749
☐	N3750D	Boeing 737-832/W	32375/870	ex N1787B	3750
☐	N3751B	Boeing 737-832/W	30491/892		3751
☐	N3752	Boeing 737-832/W	30492/894		3752
☐	N3753	Boeing 737-832/W	32626/899		3753
☐	N3754A	Boeing 737-832/W	29626/907		3754
☐	N3755D	Boeing 737-832/W	29627/914		3755 Skyteam c/s
☐	N3756	Boeing 737-832/W	30493/917	ex N1799B	3756
☐	N3757D	Boeing 737-832/W	30813/921		3757
☐	N3758Y	Boeing 737-832/W	30814/923		3758 SkyTeam c/s
☐	N3759	Boeing 737-832/W	30815/949		3759
☐	N3760C	Boeing 737-832/W	30816/952	ex N1787B	3760
☐	N3761R	Boeing 737-832/W	29628/964	ex N1784B	3761
☐	N3762Y	Boeing 737-832/W	30817/968		3762
☐	N3763D	Boeing 737-832/W	29629/1003	ex N1787B	3763
☐	N3764D	Boeing 737-832/W	30818/1006		3764
☐	N3765	Boeing 737-832/W	30819/1008	ex N1795B	3765
☐	N3766	Boeing 737-832/W	30820/1029		3766
☐	N3767	Boeing 737-832/W	30821/1031		3767
☐	N3768	Boeing 737-832/W	29630/1053		3768
☐	N3769L	Boeing 737-832/W	30822/1057		3769
☐	N3771K	Boeing 737-832/W	29632/1103		3771
☐	N3772H	Boeing 737-832/W	30823/3274		3772
☐	N3773D	Boeing 737-832/W	30825/3338	ex N1796B	3773
☐	N37700	Boeing 737-832/W	29631/1074		3770
☐	N801DZ	Boeing 737-932ER/W	31912/4603		3801
☐	N802DN	Boeing 737-932ER/W	31917/4628		3802
☐	N803DN	Boeing 737-932ER/W	31919/4639		3803
☐	N804DN	Boeing 737-932ER/W	31918/4650		3804
☐	N805DN	Boeing 737-932ER/W	31913/4664		3805
☐	N806DN	Boeing 737-932ER/W	31914/4672		3806
☐	N807DN	Boeing 737-932ER/W	31921/4682		3807
☐	N808DN	Boeing 737-932ER/W	31920/4693		3808
☐	N809DN	Boeing 737-932ER/W	31915/4704		3809 Spirit of Seattle
☐	N810DN	Boeing 737-932ER/W	31922/4708		3810

☐ N811DZ	Boeing 737-932ER/W	31916/4715		3811	
☐ N812DN	Boeing 737-932ER/W	31923/4722		3812	
☐ N813DN	Boeing 737-932ER/W	31925/4744		3813	
☐ N814DN	Boeing 737-932ER/W	31924/4751		3814	
☐ N815DN	Boeing 737-932ER/W	31926/4780		3815	
☐ N816DN	Boeing 737-932ER/W	31927/4791		3816	
☐ N817DN	Boeing 737-932ER/W	31929/4818		3817	
☐ N818DN	Boeing 737-932ER/W	31928/4829		3818	
☐ N819DN	Boeing 737-932ER/W	31930/4861		3819	♦
☐ N820DN	Boeing 737-932ER/W	31931/4883		3820	
☐ N821DN	Boeing 737-932ER/W	31932/4899		3821	
☐ N822DN	Boeing 737-932ER/W	31933/4947		3822	
☐ N823DN	Boeing 737-932ER/W	31934/4987		3823	
☐ N824DN	Boeing 737-932ER/W	31935/4998		3824	
☐ N825DN	Boeing 737-932ER/W	31936/5021		3825	
☐ N826DN	Boeing 737-932ER/W	31937/5036		3826	
☐ N827DN	Boeing 737-932ER/W	31938/5067		3827 C E Woolman	
☐ N828DN	Boeing 737-932ER/W	31939/5114		3828	♦
☐ N829DN	Boeing 737-932ER/W	31941/5143		3829	♦
☐ N830DN	Boeing 737-932ER/W	31940/5172		3830	♦
☐ N831DN	Boeing 737-932ER/W	31942/5210		3831	♦
☐ N832DN	Boeing 737-932ER/W	31943/5231		3832	♦
☐ N833DN	Boeing 737-932ER/W	31944/5250		3833	♦
☐ N834DN	Boeing 737-932ER/W	31946/5290		3834	♦
☐ N835DN	Boeing 737-932ER/W	31945/5299		3835	♦
☐ N836DN	Boeing 737-932ER/W	31947/5324		3836	♦
☐ N837DN	Boeing 737-932ER/W	31948/5332		3837	♦
☐ N838DN	Boeing 737-932ER/W	31949/5362	ex N1796B	3838	♦
☐ N839DN	Boeing 737-932ER/W	31950/5371		3839	♦
☐ N840DN	Boeing 737-932ER/W	31951/5391		3840	♦
☐ N841DN	Boeing 737-932ER/W	31952/		3841	o/o♦
☐ N842DN	Boeing 737-932ER/W	31953/		3842	o/o♦
☐ N843DN	Boeing 737-932ER/W	31954/		3843	o/o♦
☐ N844DN	Boeing 737-932ER/W	31955/		3844	o/o♦
☐ N845DN	Boeing 737-932ER/W	31956/		3845	o/o♦
☐ N846DN	Boeing 737-932ER/W	31957/		3846	o/o♦
☐ N847DN	Boeing 737-932ER/W	31958/		3847	o/o♦
☐ N848DN	Boeing 737-932ER/W	31959/		3848	o/o♦
☐ N849DN	Boeing 737-932ER/W	31960/		3849	o/o♦
☐ N314SQ	Boeing 747-412BCF	26554/1070	ex 9V-SCB		for spares [VCV]♦
☐ N661US	Boeing 747-451	23719/696	ex N401PW	6301	
☐ N662US	Boeing 747-451	23720/708	ex (N302US)	6302	
☐ N663US	Boeing 747-451	23818/715	ex (N303US)	6303	
☐ N664US	Boeing 747-451	23819/721	ex (N304US)	6304	
☐ N665US	Boeing 747-451	23820/726	ex (N305US)	6305	
☐ N666US	Boeing 747-451	23821/742	ex (N306US)	6306	
☐ N667US	Boeing 747-451	24222/799	ex (N307US)	6307	
☐ N668US	Boeing 747-451	24223/800	ex (N308US)	6308	
☐ N669US	Boeing 747-451	24224/803	ex (N309US)	6309	
☐ N670US	Boeing 747-451	24225/804	ex (N311US)	6310	
☐ N671US	Boeing 747-451	26477/1206		6311	[MZJ]
☐ N672US	Boeing 747-451	30267/1223		6312	[MZJ]
☐ N673US	Boeing 747-451	30268/1226		6313	
☐ N674US	Boeing 747-451	30269/1232		6314	
☐ N675NW	Boeing 747-451	33001/1297		6315	
☐ N676NW	Boeing 747-451	33002/1303		6316	[MZJ]
☐ N501US	Boeing 757-251	23190/53		5501 St Paul	[MZJ]
☐ N502US	Boeing 757-251	23191/55		5502 Minneapolis	[MZJ]
☐ N503US	Boeing 757-251	23192/59		5503 Detroit	[MZJ]
☐ N516US	Boeing 757-251	23204/104		5516 San Diego	[MZJ]
☐ N517US	Boeing 757-251	23205/105		5517 Portland	[MZJ]
☐ N519US	Boeing 757-251	23207/108		5519 Cleveland	
☐ N520US	Boeing 757-251	23208/109		5520 Philadelphia	[MZJ]
☐ N521US	Boeing 757-251	23209/110		5521 Denver	[MZJ]
☐ N522US	Boeing 757-251	23616/119		5522	
☐ N523US	Boeing 757-251	23617/121		5523 Dallas	
☐ N525US	Boeing 757-251	23619/124		5525 Miami	
☐ N526US	Boeing 757-251	23620/131		5526 Memphis	[MZJ]
☐ N527US	Boeing 757-251	23842/136		5527	[MZJ]
☐ N528US	Boeing 757-251	23843/137		5528	[MZJ]
☐ N529US	Boeing 757-251	23844/140		5529 New Orleans	
☐ N530US	Boeing 757-251	23845/188		5530 Omaha	
☐ N531US	Boeing 757-251	23846/190		5531 Newark	[MZJ]
☐ N532US	Boeing 757-251	24263/192		5532 Fort Myers	
☐ N533US	Boeing 757-251	24264/194		5533 Orange County	
☐ N534US	Boeing 757-251	24265/196		5534 Winnipeg	
☐ N535US	Boeing 757-251/W	26482/693		5635	
☐ N536US	Boeing 757-251/W	26483/695		5636	
☐ N537US	Boeing 757-251/W	26484/697		5637	
☐ N538US	Boeing 757-251/W	26485/699		5638	
☐ N539US	Boeing 757-251/W	26486/700		5639	

☐ N540US	Boeing 757-251/W	26487/701		5640	
☐ N541US	Boeing 757-251/W	26488/703		5641	
☐ N542US	Boeing 757-251/W	26489/705		5642	
☐ N543US	Boeing 757-251/W	26490/709		5643	
☐ N544US	Boeing 757-251/W	26491/710		5644	
☐ N545US	Boeing 757-251/W	26492/711		5645	
☐ N546US	Boeing 757-251/W	26493/713		5646	
☐ N547US	Boeing 757-251/W	26494/714		5647	
☐ N548US	Boeing 757-251/W	26495/715		5648	
☐ N549US	Boeing 757-251/W	26496/716		5649	
☐ N550NW	Boeing 757-251	26497/968		5650	
☐ N551NW	Boeing 757-251/W	26498/971		5651	
☐ N552NW	Boeing 757-251/W	26499/975		5652	
☐ N553NW	Boeing 757-251/W	26500/982		5653	
☐ N554NW	Boeing 757-251/W	26501/987		5654	
☐ N555NW	Boeing 757-251/W	33391/1011		5655	
☐ N556NW	Boeing 757-251/W	33392/1013		5656	
☐ N557NW	Boeing 757-251/W	33393/1016		5657	

Names prefixed 'City of'

☐ N393BC	Boeing 757-26D	33960/1045	ex B-2858		o/o♦
☐ N602DL	Boeing 757-232	22809/39		602	[MZJ]
☐ N603DL	Boeing 757-232	22810/41		603	[MZJ]
☐ N604DL	Boeing 757-232	22811/43		604	[MZJ]
☐ N609DL	Boeing 757-232/W	22816/65		609	[MZJ]
☐ N610DL	Boeing 757-232	22817/66		610 pink c/s	[MZJ]
☐ N612DL	Boeing 757-232	22819/73		612	
☐ N616DL	Boeing 757-232	22823/91		616	
☐ N617DL	Boeing 757-232	22907/92		617	
☐ N618DL	Boeing 757-232	22908/95		618	
☐ N623DL	Boeing 757-232	22913/118		623	
☐ N624AG	Boeing 757-2Q8/W	25624/541	ex F-GTIP	6818	[ATL]
☐ N624DL	Boeing 757-232/W	22914/120		624	[MZJ]
☐ N625DL	Boeing 757-232	22915/126		625	[MZJ]
☐ N626DL	Boeing 757-232	22916/128		626	[MZJ]
☐ N627DL	Boeing 757-232	22917/129		627	[MZJ]
☐ N628DL	Boeing 757-232	22918/133		628	[MZJ]
☐ N629DL	Boeing 757-232	22919/134		629	[MZJ]
☐ N630DL	Boeing 757-232	22920/135		630	[MZJ]
☐ N631DL	Boeing 757-232	23612/138		631	[MZJ]
☐ N633DL	Boeing 757-232	23614/157		633	
☐ N634DL	Boeing 757-232	23615/158		634	[MZJ]
☐ N635DL	Boeing 757-232	23762/159	ex 'N635DA'	635	
☐ N639DL	Boeing 757-232	23993/198		639	[BYH]
☐ N640DL	Boeing 757-232/W	23994/201		640	[BYH]
☐ N641DL	Boeing 757-232/W	23995/202		641	[BYH]
☐ N643DL	Boeing 757-232	23997/206		643	[BYH]
☐ N645DL	Boeing 757-232	24216/216		645	[BYH]
☐ N646DL	Boeing 757-232	24217/217		646	[MZJ]
☐ N647DL	Boeing 757-232	24218/222		647	[BYH]
☐ N648DL	Boeing 757-232/W	24372/223		648	[MZJ]
☐ N649DL	Boeing 757-232/W	24389/229		649	[MZJ]
☐ N650DL	Boeing 757-232/W	24390/230		650	[MZJ]
☐ N651DL	Boeing 757-232	24391/238		651	[MZJ]
☐ N652DL	Boeing 757-232	24392/239		652	[MZJ]
☐ N653DL	Boeing 757-232	24393/261		653	[MZJ]
☐ N654DL	Boeing 757-232	24394/264		654	
☐ N655DL	Boeing 757-232	24395/265		655	[MZJ]
☐ N656DL	Boeing 757-232	24396/266		656	
☐ N657DL	Boeing 757-232	24419/286		657	[MZJ]
☐ N658DL	Boeing 757-232/W	24420/287		658	
☐ N659DL	Boeing 757-232/W	24421/293		659	
☐ N660DL	Boeing 757-232/W	24422/294		660	
☐ N661DN	Boeing 757-232/W	24972/335		661	
☐ N662DN	Boeing 757-232/W	24991/342		662	
☐ N663DN	Boeing 757-232/W	24992/343		663	
☐ N664DN	Boeing 757-232/W	25012/347		664	
☐ N665DN	Boeing 757-232/W	25013/349		665	
☐ N666DN	Boeing 757-232/W	25034/354		666	
☐ N667DN	Boeing 757-232/W	25035/355		667	
☐ N668DN	Boeing 757-232	25141/376		668	
☐ N669DN	Boeing 757-232/W	25142/377		669	
☐ N670DN	Boeing 757-232	25331/415		670	
☐ N671DN	Boeing 757-232	25332/416		671	[GSO]
☐ N672DL	Boeing 757-232/W	25977/429		672	
☐ N673DL	Boeing 757-232	25978/430		673	[MZJ]
☐ N674DL	Boeing 757-232	25979/439		674	
☐ N675DL	Boeing 757-232	25980/448		675	
☐ N676DL	Boeing 757-232	25981/455		676	
☐ N677DL	Boeing 757-232	25982/456		677	[MZJ]
☐ N678DL	Boeing 757-232	25983/465		678	
☐ N679DA	Boeing 757-232	26955/500		679	
☐ N680DA	Boeing 757-232	26956/502		680	

☐	N681DA	Boeing 757-232	26957/516		681	[SAT]
☐	N682DA	Boeing 757-232	26958/518		682	
☐	N683DA	Boeing 757-232	27103/533		683	
☐	N684DA	Boeing 757-232	27104/535		684	
☐	N685DA	Boeing 757-232	27588/667		685	
☐	N686DA	Boeing 757-232/W	27589/689		686	
☐	N687DL	Boeing 757-232/W	27586/800		687	
☐	N688DL	Boeing 757-232/W	27587/803		688	
☐	N689DL	Boeing 757-232/W	27172/807		689	
☐	N690DL	Boeing 757-232/W	27585/808		690	
☐	N692DL	Boeing 757-232/W	29724/820	ex N1799B	692	
☐	N693DL	Boeing 757-232/W	29725/826	ex N1799B	693	
☐	N694DL	Boeing 757-232	29726/831		694 The Spirit of Freedom	
☐	N695DL	Boeing 757-232/W	29727/838	ex N1795B	695	
☐	N696DL	Boeing 757-232	29728/845	ex N1795B	696	
☐	N697DL	Boeing 757-232	30318/880	ex N1795B	697	
☐	N698DL	Boeing 757-232	29911/885		698	
☐	N699DL	Boeing 757-232/W	29970/887	ex N1795B	699	
☐	N702TW	Boeing 757-2Q8/W	28162/732		6801	
☐	N703TW	Boeing 757-2Q8ER/W	27620/736		6802	
☐	N704X	Boeing 757-2Q8/W	28163/741		6803	
☐	N705TW	Boeing 757-231/W	28479/742		6811	
☐	N706TW	Boeing 757-2Q8/W	28165/743		6804	
☐	N707TW	Boeing 757-2Q8ER/W	27625/744		6805	
☐	N709TW	Boeing 757-2Q8/W	28168/754		6806	
☐	N710TW	Boeing 757-2Q8/W	28169/757		6807	
☐	N711ZX	Boeing 757-231/W	28481/758		6814	
☐	N712TW	Boeing 757-2Q8ER/W	27624/760		6808	
☐	N713TW	Boeing 757-2Q8/W	28173/764		6809	
☐	N717TW	Boeing 757-231/W	28485/854		6812	
☐	N718TW	Boeing 757-231/W	28486/869		6815	
☐	N721TW	Boeing 757-231/W	29954/874		6810	
☐	N722TW	Boeing 757-231/W	29385/893	ex N1795B	6816	
☐	N723TW	Boeing 757-231/W	29378/907		6817	
☐	N727TW	Boeing 757-231/W	30340/901		6813	
☐	N750AT	Boeing 757-212ER	23126/45	ex 9V-SGL	6902	
☐	N751AT	Boeing 757-212ER	23125/44	ex 9V-SGK	6901	
☐	N752AT	Boeing 757-212ER	23128/48	ex 9V-SGN	6904	
☐	N757AT	Boeing 757-212ER	23127/47	ex 9V-SGM	6903	
☐	N819DX	Boeing 757-26D	33959/1044	ex N346BC		wfs♦
☐	N823DX	Boeing 757-26D	33967/1050	ex N338BC		last 757 built wfs♦
☐	N900PC	Boeing 757-26D/W	28446/740		691	
☐	N6700	Boeing 757-232/W	30337/890		6700	
☐	N6701	Boeing 757-232	30187/892		6701	
☐	N6702	Boeing 757-232/W	30188/898		6702	
☐	N6703D	Boeing 757-232	30234/908	ex N1795B	6703	
☐	N6704Z	Boeing 757-232	30396/914	ex N1795B	6704	
☐	N6705Y	Boeing 757-232	30397/917		6705	
☐	N6706Q	Boeing 757-232	30422/921		6706	
☐	N6707A	Boeing 757-232	30395/927		6707	
☐	N6708D	Boeing 757-232	30480/934		6708	
☐	N6709	Boeing 757-232	30481/937		6709	
☐	N6710E	Boeing 757-232	30482/939		6710	
☐	N6711M	Boeing 757-232	30483/941		6711	
☐	N6712B	Boeing 757-232	30484/942		6712	
☐	N6713Y	Boeing 757-232/W	30777/944		6713	
☐	N6714Q	Boeing 757-232/W	30485/949		6714	
☐	N6715C	Boeing 757-232/W	30486/953		6715	
☐	N6716C	Boeing 757-232	30838/955		6716	
☐	N67171	Boeing 757-232/W	30839/959		6717	
☐	N	Boeing 757-26D	33966/1049	ex B-2875		o/o♦
☐	N	Boeing 757-26D	33961/1046	ex B-2880		o/o♦
☐	N581NW	Boeing 757-351/W	32982/1001	ex N753JM	5801	
☐	N582NW	Boeing 757-351/W	32981/1014		5802 The Bernie Epple	
☐	N583NW	Boeing 757-351/W	32983/1019		5803	
☐	N584NW	Boeing 757-351/W	32984/1020		5804	
☐	N585NW	Boeing 757-351/W	32985/1021		5805	
☐	N586NW	Boeing 757-351/W	32987/1022		5806	
☐	N587NW	Boeing 757-351/W	32986/1023		5807	
☐	N588NW	Boeing 757-351/W	32988/1024		5808	
☐	N589NW	Boeing 757-351/W	32989/1025		5809	
☐	N590NW	Boeing 757-351/W	32990/1027	ex N1795B	5810	
☐	N591NW	Boeing 757-351/W	32991/1030		5811	
☐	N592NW	Boeing 757-351/W	32992/1033		5812	
☐	N593NW	Boeing 757-351/W	32993/1034	ex N1795B	5813	
☐	N594NW	Boeing 757-351	32994/1035		5814	
☐	N595NW	Boeing 757-351/W	32995/1036	ex N1795B	5815	
☐	N596NW	Boeing 757-351	32996/1037		5816	
☐	N121DE	Boeing 767-332	23435/162		121	
☐	N124DE	Boeing 767-332	23438/189		124	
☐	N125DL	Boeing 767-332	24075/200		125	

☐	N126DL	Boeing 767-332	24076/201		126	
☐	N127DL	Boeing 767-332	24077/203		127	
☐	N128DL	Boeing 767-332	24078/207		128	
☐	N129DL	Boeing 767-332	24079/209		129	
☐	N130DL	Boeing 767-332	24080/216		130	
☐	N131DN	Boeing 767-332	24852/320		131	[MZJ]
☐	N132DN	Boeing 767-332	24981/345		132	[VCV]
☐	N133DN	Boeing 767-332	24982/348		133	[VCV]
☐	N134DL	Boeing 767-332	25123/353		134	[VCV]
☐	N135DL	Boeing 767-332	25145/356		135	[MZJ]
☐	N136DL	Boeing 767-332	25146/374		136	
☐	N137DL	Boeing 767-332	25306/392		137	
☐	N138DL	Boeing 767-332	25409/410		138	
☐	N139DL	Boeing 767-332	25984/427		139	
☐	N140LL	Boeing 767-332	25988/499		1401	
☐	N143DA	Boeing 767-332	25991/721		1403	
☐	N144DA	Boeing 767-332	27584/751		1404	
☐	N152DL	Boeing 767-3P6ER/W	24984/339	ex A4O-GM	1502	
☐	N153DL	Boeing 767-3P6ER/W	24985/340	ex A4O-GN	1503	
☐	N154DL	Boeing 767-3P6ER	25241/389	ex A4O-GO	1504	
☐	N155DL	Boeing 767-3P6ER/W	25269/390	ex A4O-GP	1505	
☐	N156DL	Boeing 767-3P6ER/W	25354/406	ex A4O-GR	1506	
☐	N169DZ	Boeing 767-332ER/W	29689/706		1601	
☐	N171DN	Boeing 767-332ER/W	24759/304		171	
☐	N171DZ	Boeing 767-332ER/W	29690/717		1701	
☐	N172DN	Boeing 767-332ER/W	24775/312		172	
☐	N172DZ	Boeing 767-332ER/w	29691/719		1702	
☐	N173DN	Boeing 767-332ER	24800/313		173	[VCV]
☐	N173DZ	Boeing 767-332ER/W	29692/723		1703	
☐	N174DN	Boeing 767-332ER/W	24802/317		174	
☐	N174DZ	Boeing 767-332ER/W	29693/725		1704	
☐	N175DN	Boeing 767-332ER/W	24803/318		175	
☐	N175DZ	Boeing 767-332ER/W	29696/740		1705	SkyTeam c/s
☐	N176DN	Boeing 767-332ER/W	25061/341		176	
☐	N176DZ	Boeing 767-332ER	29697/745		1706	Skyteam c/s
☐	N177DN	Boeing 767-332ER	25122/346		177	
☐	N177DZ	Boeing 767-332ER/W	29698/750		1707	
☐	N178DN	Boeing 767-332ER/W	25143/349		178	
☐	N178DZ	Boeing 767-332ER	30596/795		1708	
☐	N179DN	Boeing 767-332ER/W	25144/350		179	
☐	N180DN	Boeing 767-332ER/W	25985/428		180	
☐	N181DN	Boeing 767-332ER/W	25986/446		181	
☐	N182DN	Boeing 767-332ER/W	25987/461		182	
☐	N183DN	Boeing 767-332ER/W	27110/492		183	
☐	N184DN	Boeing 767-332ER	27111/496		184	
☐	N185DN	Boeing 767-332ER/W	27961/576		185	
☐	N186DN	Boeing 767-332ER/W	27962/585		186	
☐	N187DN	Boeing 767-332ER/W	27582/617		187	
☐	N188DN	Boeing 767-332ER	27583/631		188	
☐	N189DN	Boeing 767-332ER/W	25990/646		189	
☐	N190DN	Boeing 767-332ER	28447/653		190	
☐	N191DN	Boeing 767-332ER/W	28448/654		191	
☐	N192DN	Boeing 767-332ER/W	28449/664		192	
☐	N193DN	Boeing 767-332ER/W	28450/671		193	
☐	N194DN	Boeing 767-332ER/W	28451/675		194	
☐	N195DN	Boeing 767-332ER/W	28452/676		195	
☐	N196DN	Boeing 767-332ER/W	28453/679		196	
☐	N197DN	Boeing 767-332ER/W	28454/683		197	
☐	N198DN	Boeing 767-332ER/W	28455/685		198	
☐	N199DN	Boeing 767-332ER/W	28456/690		199	
☐	N394DL	Boeing 767-324ER/W	27394/572	ex HL7505	1521	
☐	N764RD	Boeing 767-3Y0ER	26204/464	ex PR-VAD		[MZJ]
☐	N1200K	Boeing 767-332ER/W	28457/696		1200	
☐	N1201P	Boeing 767-332ER/W	28458/697		1201	
☐	N1402A	Boeing 767-332	25989/506		1402	
☐	N1501P	Boeing 767-3P6ER/W	24983/334	ex A4O-GL	1501	
☐	N1602	Boeing 767-332ER/W	29694/735		1602	
☐	N1603	Boeing 767-332ER/W	29695/736		1603	
☐	N1604R	Boeing 767-332ER/W	30180/749		1604	
☐	N1605	Boeing 767-332ER/W	30198/753		1605	
☐	N1607B	Boeing 767-332ER/W	30388/787		1607	
☐	N1608	Boeing 767-332ER/W	30573/788		1608	
☐	N1609	Boeing 767-332ER/W	30574/789		1609	
☐	N1610D	Boeing 767-332ER/W	30594/790		1610	
☐	N1611B	Boeing 767-332ER/W	30595/794		1611	
☐	N1612T	Boeing 767-332ER/W	30575/838		1612	
☐	N1613B	Boeing 767-332ER/W	32776/847		1613	
☐	N16065	Boeing 767-332ER/W	30199/755		1606	
☐	N825MH	Boeing 767-432ER	29703/758	ex N6067U	1801	
☐	N826MH	Boeing 767-432ER	29713/769		1802	
☐	N827MH	Boeing 767-432ER	29705/773	ex N76400	1803	
☐	N828MH	Boeing 767-432ER	29699/791		1804	

☐ N829MH	Boeing 767-432ER	29700/801		1805	
☐ N830MH	Boeing 767-432ER	29701/803		1806	
☐ N831MH	Boeing 767-432ER	29702/804		1807	
☐ N832MH	Boeing 767-432ER	29704/807		1808	
☐ N833MH	Boeing 767-432ER	29706/810		1809	
☐ N834MH	Boeing 767-432ER	29707/813		1810	
☐ N835MH	Boeing 767-432ER	29708/814		1811	
☐ N836MH	Boeing 767-432ER	29709/818		1812	
☐ N837MH	Boeing 767-432ER	29710/820		1813	
☐ N838MH	Boeing 767-432ER	29711/821		1814	
☐ N839MH	Boeing 767-432ER	29712/824		1815	
☐ N840MH	Boeing 767-432ER	29718/830		1816	
☐ N841MH	Boeing 767-432ER	29714/855		1817	
☐ N842MH	Boeing 767-432ER	29715/856		1818	
☐ N843MH	Boeing 767-432ER	29716/865		1819	
☐ N844MH	Boeing 767-432ER	29717/871		1820	
☐ N845MH	Boeing 767-432ER	29719/874		1821	
☐ N701DN	Boeing 777-232LR	29740/697	ex N5016R	7101	
☐ N702DN	Boeing 777-232LR	29741/704		7102	
☐ N703DN	Boeing 777-232LR	32222/767		7103	
☐ N704DK	Boeing 777-232LR	29739/772	ex N5016R	7104	
☐ N705DN	Boeing 777-232LR	29742/773		7105	
☐ N706DN	Boeing 777-232LR	30440/776	ex N5023Q	7106	
☐ N707DN	Boeing 777-232LR	39091/781		7107	
☐ N708DN	Boeing 777-232LR	39254/789		7108	
☐ N709DN	Boeing 777-232LR	40559/854		7109	
☐ N710DN	Boeing 777-232LR	40560/857		7110	
☐ N860DA	Boeing 777-232ER	29951/202		7001	
☐ N861DA	Boeing 777-232ER	29952/207		7002	
☐ N862DA	Boeing 777-232ER	29734/235	ex N5022E	7003	
☐ N863DA	Boeing 777-232ER	29735/245	ex N5014K	7004	
☐ N864DA	Boeing 777-232ER	29736/249	ex N50217	7005	
☐ N865DA	Boeing 777-232ER	29737/257		7006	
☐ N866DA	Boeing 777-232ER	29738/261		7007	
☐ N867DA	Boeing 777-232ER	29743/387		7008	
☐ N401EA	Douglas DC-9-51	47682/788	ex N920VJ	9885	[MZJ]
☐ N600TR	Douglas DC-9-51	47783/899	ex YV-40C	9886	[MZJ]
☐ N670MC	Douglas DC-9-51	47659/807	ex HB-ISP	9882	[MZJ]
☐ N676MC	Douglas DC-9-51	47652/798	ex OE-LDL	9881	[MZJ]
☐ N677MC	Douglas DC-9-51	47756/873	ex OE-LDO	9884	[MZJ]
☐ N760NC	Douglas DC-9-51	47708/813		9851	[MZJ]
☐ N761NC	Douglas DC-9-51	47709/814		9852	[MZJ]
☐ N762NC	Douglas DC-9-51	47710/818		9853	[MZJ]
☐ N765NC	Douglas DC-9-51	47718/834		9856	[MZJ]
☐ N769NC	Douglas DC-9-51	47757/877		9860	[MZJ]
☐ N772NC	Douglas DC-9-51	47774/884		9863	[MZJ]
☐ N774NC	Douglas DC-9-51	47776/889		9865	[MZJ]
☐ N776NC	Douglas DC-9-51	47786/905		9867	[MZJ]
☐ N777NC	Douglas DC-9-51	47787/912		9868	[MZJ]
☐ N778NC	Douglas DC-9-51	48100/927		9869	[MZJ]
☐ N781NC	Douglas DC-9-51	48121/935		9872	[MZJ]
☐ N783NC	Douglas DC-9-51	48108/937		9874	wfs
☐ N478DN	McDonnell-Douglas MD-82	53004/1846	ex SE-DIR		for spares [BYH]♦
☐ N482DN	McDonnell-Douglas MD-82	53314/1946	ex SE-DMB		for spares [BYH]
☐ N490DN	McDonnell-Douglas MD-82	49384/1237	ex LN-ROP		[BYH]
☐ N491DN	McDonnell-Douglas MD-82	49422/1264	ex LN-ROT		[BYH]
☐ N492DN	McDonnell-Douglas MD-82	49728/1553	ex SE-DIK		for spares [BYH]♦
☐ N493DN	McDonnell-Douglas MD-82	49604/1456	ex OY-KHE		for spares [BYH]♦
☐ N494DN	McDonnell-Douglas MD-82	53368/2003	ex LN-RMS		for spares [BYH]♦
☐ N495DN	McDonnell-Douglas MD-82	53365/1998	ex LN-RMR		for spares [BYH]
☐ N497DN	McDonnell-Douglas MD-82	49613/1519	ex OY-KHG		for spares [BYH]♦
☐ N900DE	McDonnell-Douglas MD-88	53372/1970		9000	
☐ N901DE	McDonnell-Douglas MD-88	53378/1980		9001	
☐ N902DE	McDonnell-Douglas MD-88	53379/1983		9002	
☐ N903DE	McDonnell-Douglas MD-88	53380/1986		9003	
☐ N904DE	McDonnell-Douglas MD-88	53409/1990		9004	
☐ N904DL	McDonnell-Douglas MD-88	49535/1347		904	
☐ N905DE	McDonnell-Douglas MD-88	53410/1992		9005	
☐ N905DL	McDonnell-Douglas MD-88	49536/1348		905	
☐ N906DE	McDonnell-Douglas MD-88	53415/2027		9006	
☐ N906DL	McDonnell-Douglas MD-88	49537/1355		906	
☐ N907DE	McDonnell-Douglas MD-88	53416/2029		9007	
☐ N907DL	McDonnell-Douglas MD-88	49538/1365		907	
☐ N908DE	McDonnell-Douglas MD-88	53417/2032		9008	
☐ N908DL	McDonnell-Douglas MD-88	49539/1366		908	
☐ N909DE	McDonnell-Douglas MD-88	53418/2033		9009	
☐ N909DL	McDonnell-Douglas MD-88	49540/1395		909	dam 05Mar15
☐ N910DE	McDonnell-Douglas MD-88	53419/2036		9010	
☐ N910DL	McDonnell-Douglas MD-88	49541/1416		910	

☐ N911DE	McDonnell-Douglas MD-88	49967/2037	9011	
☐ N911DL	McDonnell-Douglas MD-88	49542/1433	911	
☐ N912DE	McDonnell-Douglas MD-88	49997/2038	9012	
☐ N912DL	McDonnell-Douglas MD-88	49543/1434	912	
☐ N913DE	McDonnell-Douglas MD-88	49956/2039	9013	
☐ N913DL	McDonnell-Douglas MD-88	49544/1443	913	
☐ N914DE	McDonnell-Douglas MD-88	49957/2049	9014	
☐ N914DL	McDonnell-Douglas MD-88	49545/1444	914	
☐ N915DE	McDonnell-Douglas MD-88	53420/2050	9015	
☐ N915DL	McDonnell-Douglas MD-88	49546/1447	915	
☐ N916DE	McDonnell-Douglas MD-88	53421/2051	9016	
☐ N916DL	McDonnell-Douglas MD-88	49591/1448	916	
☐ N917DE	McDonnell-Douglas MD-88	49958/2054	9017	
☐ N917DL	McDonnell-Douglas MD-88	49573/1469	917	
☐ N918DE	McDonnell-Douglas MD-88	49959/2055	9018	
☐ N918DL	McDonnell-Douglas MD-88	49583/1470	918	[VCV]
☐ N919DE	McDonnell-Douglas MD-88	53422/2058	9019	
☐ N919DL	McDonnell-Douglas MD-88	49584/1471	919	
☐ N920DE	McDonnell-Douglas MD-88	53423/2059	9020	
☐ N920DL	McDonnell-Douglas MD-88	49644/1473	920	
☐ N921DL	McDonnell-Douglas MD-88	49645/1480	921	
☐ N922DL	McDonnell-Douglas MD-88	49646/1481	922	
☐ N923DL	McDonnell-Douglas MD-88	49705/1491	923	
☐ N024DL	McDonnell-Douglas MD-88	49711/1492	924	[VCV]
☐ N925DL	McDonnell-Douglas MD-88	49712/1500	925	
☐ N926DL	McDonnell-Douglas MD-88	49713/1523	926	
☐ N927DA	McDonnell-Douglas MD-88	49714/1524	927	
☐ N928DL	McDonnell-Douglas MD-88	49715/1530	928	
☐ N929DL	McDonnell-Douglas MD-88	49716/1531	929	
☐ N930DL	McDonnell-Douglas MD-88	49717/1532	930	
☐ N931DL	McDonnell-Douglas MD-88	49718/1533	931	
☐ N932DL	McDonnell-Douglas MD-88	49719/1570	932	
☐ N933DL	McDonnell-Douglas MD-88	49720/1571	933	
☐ N934DL	McDonnell-Douglas MD-88	49721/1574	934	
☐ N935DL	McDonnell-Douglas MD-88	49722/1575	935	
☐ N936DL	McDonnell-Douglas MD-88	49723/1576	936	
☐ N937DL	McDonnell-Douglas MD-88	49810/1588	937	
☐ N938DL	McDonnell-Douglas MD-88	49811/1590	938	
☐ N939DL	McDonnell-Douglas MD-88	49812/1593	939	
☐ N940DL	McDonnell-Douglas MD-88	49813/1599	940	
☐ N941DL	McDonnell-Douglas MD-88	49814/1602	941	
☐ N942DL	McDonnell-Douglas MD-88	49815/1605	942	
☐ N943DL	McDonnell-Douglas MD-88	49816/1608	943	
☐ N944DL	McDonnell-Douglas MD-88	49817/1612	944	
☐ N945DL	McDonnell-Douglas MD-88	49818/1613	945	
☐ N946DL	McDonnell-Douglas MD-88	49819/1629	946	
☐ N947DL	McDonnell-Douglas MD-88	49878/1664	947	
☐ N948DL	McDonnell-Douglas MD-88	49879/1666	948	
☐ N949DL	McDonnell-Douglas MD-88	49880/1676	949	
☐ N950DL	McDonnell-Douglas MD-88	49881/1677	950	
☐ N951DL	McDonnell-Douglas MD-88	49882/1679	951	
☐ N952DL	McDonnell-Douglas MD-88	49883/1683	952	
☐ N953DL	McDonnell-Douglas MD-88	49884/1685	953	
☐ N954DL	McDonnell-Douglas MD-88	49885/1689	954	
☐ N955DL	McDonnell-Douglas MD-88	49886/1691	955	
☐ N956DL	McDonnell-Douglas MD-88	49887/1699	956	
☐ N957DL	McDonnell-Douglas MD-88	49976/1700	957	
☐ N958DL	McDonnell-Douglas MD-88	49977/1701	958	
☐ N959DL	McDonnell-Douglas MD-88	49978/1710	959	
☐ N960DL	McDonnell-Douglas MD-88	49979/1711	960	
☐ N961DL	McDonnell-Douglas MD-88	49980/1712	961	
☐ N962DL	McDonnell-Douglas MD-88	49981/1725	962	
☐ N963DL	McDonnell-Douglas MD-88	49982/1726	963	
☐ N964DL	McDonnell-Douglas MD-88	49983/1747	964	
☐ N965DL	McDonnell-Douglas MD-88	49984/1748	965	
☐ N966DL	McDonnell-Douglas MD-88	53115/1795	966	
☐ N967DL	McDonnell-Douglas MD-88	53116/1796	967	
☐ N968DL	McDonnell-Douglas MD-88	53161/1808	968	
☐ N969DL	McDonnell-Douglas MD-88	53172/1810	969	
☐ N970DL	McDonnell-Douglas MD-88	53173/1811	970	
☐ N971DL	McDonnell-Douglas MD-88	53214/1823	971	
☐ N972DL	McDonnell-Douglas MD-88	53215/1824	972	
☐ N973DL	McDonnell-Douglas MD-88	53241/1832	973	
☐ N974DL	McDonnell-Douglas MD-88	53242/1833	974	
☐ N975DL	McDonnell-Douglas MD-88	53243/1834	975	
☐ N976DL	McDonnell-Douglas MD-88	53257/1845	976	
☐ N977DL	McDonnell-Douglas MD-88	53258/1848	977	
☐ N978DL	McDonnell-Douglas MD-88	53259/1849	978	
☐ N979DL	McDonnell-Douglas MD-88	53266/1859	979	
☐ N980DL	McDonnell-Douglas MD-88	53267/1860	980	
☐ N981DL	McDonnell-Douglas MD-88	53268/1861	981	
☐ N982DL	McDonnell-Douglas MD-88	53273/1870	982	
☐ N983DL	McDonnell-Douglas MD-88	53274/1873	983	

☐	N984DL	McDonnell-Douglas MD-88	53311/1912		984
☐	N985DL	McDonnell-Douglas MD-88	53312/1914		985
☐	N986DL	McDonnell-Douglas MD-88	53313/1924		986
☐	N987DL	McDonnell-Douglas MD-88	53338/1926		987
☐	N988DL	McDonnell-Douglas MD-88	53339/1928		988
☐	N989DL	McDonnell-Douglas MD-88	53341/1936		989
☐	N990DL	McDonnell-Douglas MD-88	53342/1939		990
☐	N991DL	McDonnell-Douglas MD-88	53343/1941		991
☐	N992DL	McDonnell-Douglas MD-88	53344/1943		992
☐	N993DL	McDonnell-Douglas MD-88	53345/1950		993
☐	N994DL	McDonnell-Douglas MD-88	53346/1952		994
☐	N995DL	McDonnell-Douglas MD-88	53362/1955		995
☐	N996DL	McDonnell-Douglas MD-88	53363/1958		996
☐	N997DL	McDonnell-Douglas MD-88	53364/1961		997
☐	N998DL	McDonnell-Douglas MD-88	53370/1963		998
☐	N999DN	McDonnell-Douglas MD-88	53371/1965		999
☐	N301EV	McDonnell-Douglas MD-90-30	53535/2158	ex B-17911	for spares [BYH]♦
☐	N302EV	McDonnell-Douglas MD-90-30ER	53534/2153	ex B-17923	for spares {BYH}♦
☐	N303EV	McDonnell-Douglas MD-90-30	53554/2166	ex B-17921	for spares [BYH]♦
☐	N901DA	McDonnell-Douglas MD-90-30	53381/2100	ex N902DC	9201
☐	N902DA	McDonnell-Douglas MD-90-30	53382/2094		9202
☐	N903DA	McDonnell-Douglas MD-90-30	53383/2095		9203
☐	N904DA	McDonnell-Douglas MD-90-30	53384/2096		9204
☐	N905DA	McDonnell-Douglas MD-90-30	53385/2097		9205
☐	N906DA	McDonnell-Douglas MD-90-30	53386/2099		9206
☐	N907DA	McDonnell-Douglas MD-90-30	53387/2115		9207
☐	N908DA	McDonnell-Douglas MD-90-30	53388/2117		9208
☐	N909DA	McDonnell-Douglas MD-90-30	53389/2122		9209
☐	N910DN	McDonnell-Douglas MD-90-30	53390/2123		9210
☐	N911DA	McDonnell-Douglas MD-90-30	53391/2126		9211
☐	N912DN	McDonnell-Douglas MD-90-30	53392/2136		9212
☐	N913DN	McDonnell-Douglas MD-90-30	53393/2154		9213
☐	N914DN	McDonnell-Douglas MD-90-30	53394/2156		9214
☐	N915DN	McDonnell-Douglas MD-90-30	53395/2159		9215
☐	N916DN	McDonnell-Douglas MD-90-30	53396/2161		9216
☐	N917DN	McDonnell-Douglas MD-90-30	53552/2163	ex N593BC	9217
☐	N918DH	McDonnell-Douglas MD-90-30	53553/2165	ex N648NW	9218
☐	N919DN	McDonnell-Douglas MD-90-30ER	53576/2195	ex N647NW	9219
☐	N920DN	McDonnell-Douglas MD-90-30	53582/2198	ex B-2256	9220
☐	N921DN	McDonnell-Douglas MD-90-30	53583/2200	ex B-2257	9221
☐	N922DX	McDonnell-Douglas MD-90-30	53584/2203	ex B-2258	9222
☐	N923DN	McDonnell-Douglas MD-90-30	53585/2224	ex B-2262	9223
☐	N924DN	McDonnell-Douglas MD-90-30	53586/2233	ex B-2263	9224
☐	N925DN	McDonnell-Douglas MD-90-30	53587/2240	ex B-2265	9225
☐	N926DH	McDonnell-Douglas MD-90-30	53588/2248	ex B-2268	9226
☐	N927DN	McDonnell-Douglas MD-90-30	53589/2259	ex B-2269	9227
☐	N928DN	McDonnell-Douglas MD-90-30	53590/2261	ex B-2270	9228
☐	N929DN	McDonnell-Douglas MD-90-30	53459/2141	ex OH-BLC	9229
☐	N930DN	McDonnell-Douglas MD-90-30	53458/2140	ex OH-BLU	9230
☐	N931DN	McDonnell-Douglas MD-90-30	53544/2197	ex OH-BLD	9231
☐	N932DN	McDonnell-Douglas MD-90-30	53457/2138	ex OH-BLE	9232
☐	N933DN	McDonnell-Douglas MD-90-30	53543/2194	ex OH-BLF	9233
☐	N934DN	McDonnell-Douglas MD-90-30	53462/2149	ex HB-JIF	9234
☐	N935DN	McDonnell-Douglas MD-90-30	53460/2142	ex HB-JID	9235
☐	N936DN	McDonnell-Douglas MD-90-30	53461/2147	ex HB-JIE	9236
☐	N937DN	McDonnell-Douglas MD-90-30	53352/2098	ex JA8062	
☐	N938DN	McDonnell-Douglas MD-90-30	53353/2120	ex JA8063	
☐	N939DN	McDonnell-Douglas MD-90-30	53356/2157	ex JA8066	
☐	N940DN	McDonnell-Douglas MD-90-30	53359/2164	ex JA8004	
☐	N941DN	McDonnell-Douglas MD-90-30	53555/2207	ex JA001D	
☐	N942DN	McDonnell-Douglas MD-90-30	53556/2210	ex JA002D	
☐	N943DN	McDonnell-Douglas MD-90-30	53557/2211	ex JA003D	
☐	N944DN	McDonnell-Douglas MD-90-30	53558/2212	ex JA004D	
☐	N945DN	McDonnell-Douglas MD-90-30	53559/2236	ex JA005D	
☐	N946DN	McDonnell-Douglas MD-90-30	53354/2125	ex JA8064	
☐	N947DN	McDonnell-Douglas MD-90-30	53355/2131	ex JA8065	
☐	N948DN	McDonnell-Douglas MD-90-30	53357/2164	ex JA8069	
☐	N949DN	McDonnell-Douglas MD-90-30	53358/2179	ex JA8070	
☐	N950DN	McDonnell-Douglas MD-90-30	53360/2190	ex JA8020	
☐	N951DN	McDonnell-Douglas MD-90-30	53361/2202	ex JA8029	
☐	N952DN	McDonnell-Douglas MD-90-30	53560/2245	ex JA006D	
☐	N953DN	McDonnell-Douglas MD-90-30	53523/2143	ex B-2250	9253
☐	N954DN	McDonnell-Douglas MD-90-30	53524/2146	ex B-2251	9254
☐	N955DN	McDonnell-Douglas MD-90-30	53525/2150	ex B-2252	9255
☐	N956DN	McDonnell-Douglas MD-90-30	53526/2170	ex B-2253	9256
☐	N957DN	McDonnell-Douglas MD-90-30	53527/2175	ex B-2254	9257
☐	N958DN	McDonnell-Douglas MD-90-30	53528/2177	ex B-2255	9258
☐	N959DN	McDonnell-Douglas MD-90-30	53529/2220	ex B-2259	9259
☐	N960DN	McDonnell-Douglas MD-90-30	53530/2222	ex B-2260	9260
☐	N961DN	McDonnell-Douglas MD-90-30	53531/2228	ex B-2261	9261
☐	N962DN	McDonnell-Douglas MD-90-30	53532/2253	ex B-2266	9262
☐	N963DN	McDonnell-Douglas MD-90-30	53533/2258	ex B-2267	9263

[MZJ

□ N964DN	McDonnell-Douglas MD-90-30	60001/4001	ex B-2100	9264 AVIC II assembled	
□ N965DN	McDonnell-Douglas MD-90-30	60002/4002	ex B-2103	9265 AVIC II assembled	

□ N447CA	Canadair CRJ-200ER	7552	ex C-GJLL		wfs
□ N682BR	Canadair CRJ-200ER	7691	ex C-FVAZ		[IGM]♦
□ N684BR	Canadair CRJ-200ER	7708	ex C-FMLF		[IGM]
□ N754NW	Douglas DC-9-41	47178/323	ex OY-KGB	9754	[MZJ]
□ N756NW	Douglas DC-9-41	47180/354	ex SE-DBU	9756	[MZJ]
□ N758NW	Douglas DC-9-41	47286/359	ex OY-KGC	9758	[MZJ]
□ N931TW	McDonnell-Douglas MD-83	49527/1382			[BYH]♦
□ N971EV	Canadair CRJ-200ER	7528	ex N664BR		wfs♦
□ N8986E	Douglas DC-9-31	47402/482	ex 5N-INZ	9993	[MZJ]
□ N	Airbus A321-200	6923	ex		o/o♦
□ N	Airbus A321-200	6926	ex		o/o♦

DELTA CONNECTION (DL/DAL)
Cincinnati-Northern Kentucky Intl, OH/Atlanta-Hartsfield Intl, GA/Orlando-Intl, FL (CVG/ATL/MCO)

□ N716CA	Canadair CRJ-100ER	7250	ex C-FMMW	7250	Comair [IGM]
□ N721CA	Canadair CRJ-100ER	7259	ex C-FMLI	7259	Comair [IGM]
□ N739CA	Canadair CRJ-100ER	7273	ex C-FMNQ	7273	Comair [IGM]
□ N784CA	Canadair CRJ-100ER	7319	ex C-FMLI	7319	Comair [IGM]
□ N786CA	Canadair CRJ-100ER	7333	ex C-FMNQ	7333	Comair [IGM]
□ N797CA	Canadair CRJ-100ER	7344	ex C-FMKV	7344	Comair [IGM]
□ N594SW	Canadair CRJ-100ER	7285	ex N767CA	7285	SkyWest
□ N779CA	Canadair CRJ-100ER	7306	ex C-FMMB	7306	SkyWest
□ N781CA	Canadair CRJ-100ER	7312	ex C-FMMY	7312	SkyWest
□ N783CA	Canadair CRJ-100ER	7315	ex C-FMKW	7315	SkyWest<COM
□ N809CA	Canadair CRJ-100ER	7366	ex C-FMMB	7366	SkyWest<COM
□ N420CA	Canadair CRJ-200ER	7451	ex C-FVAZ	7451	Comair [IGM]
□ N810CA	Canadair CRJ-200ER	7370	ex C-FMMW	7370	Comair [IGM]
□ N811CA	Canadair CRJ-200ER	7380	ex C-FMLQ	7380	Comair [IGM]
□ N812CA	Canadair CRJ-200ER	7381	ex C-FMLS	7381	Comair [IGM]
□ N814CA	Canadair CRJ-200ER	7387	ex C-GFVM	7387	Comair [IGM]
□ N815CA	Canadair CRJ-200ER	7397	ex C-FMML	7397	Comair [IGM]
□ N805AY	Canadair CRJ-200LR	8005	ex C-FDQP	8005	Endeavor [IGM]
□ N812AY	Canadair CRJ-200LR	8012	ex C-	8012	Endeavor [IGM]
□ N813AY	Canadair CRJ-200LR	8013	ex C-	8013	Endeavor [IGM]
□ N819AY	Canadair CRJ-200LR	8019	ex C-FMLQ	8019	Endeavor
□ N820AY	Canadair CRJ-200LR	8020	ex C-FMLS	8020	Endeavor
□ N821AY	Canadair CRJ-200LR	8021	ex C-FMLT	8021	Endeavor [IGM]
□ N823AY	Canadair CRJ-200LR	8023	ex C-FMMT	8023	Endeavor [IGM]
□ N824AY	Canadair CRJ-200LR	8024	ex C-FMNH	8024	Endeavor [IGM]
□ N825AY	Canadair CRJ-200LR	8025	ex C-FMNW	8025	Endeavor [IGM]
□ N826AY	Canadair CRJ-200LR	8026	ex C-FMNX	8026	Endeavor [IGM]
□ N827AY	Canadair CRJ-200LR	8027	ex C-FMNY	8027	Endeavor [IGM]
□ N829AY	Canadair CRJ-200LR	8029	ex C-FMOW	8029	Endeavor [IGM]
□ N831AY	Canadair CRJ-200LR	8031	ex C-FETZ	8031	Endeavor wfs
□ N832AY	Canadair CRJ-200LR	8032	ex C-FMNQ	8032	Endeavor
□ N833AY	Canadair CRJ-200LR	8033	ex C-FMLU	8033	Endeavor
□ N834AY	Canadair CRJ-200LR	8034	ex C-FEXV	8034	Endeavor
□ N835AY	Canadair CRJ-200LR	8035	ex C-FMMB	8035	Endeavor
□ N836AY	Canadair CRJ-200LR	8036	ex C-FMML	8036	Endeavor
□ N840AY	Canadair CRJ-200LR	8040	ex C-FEZX	8040	Endeavor
□ N8390A	Canadair CRJ-200LR	7390	ex C-FMOW	8390 Spirit of Memphis Belle	Endeavor wfs
□ N8409N	Canadair CRJ-200LR	7409	ex C-FMLI	8409	Endeavor
□ N8412F	Canadair CRJ-200LR	7412	ex C-FMLT	8412	Endeavor wfs
□ N8416B	Canadair CRJ-200LR	7416	ex C-FMNW	8416	Endeavor [IGM]
□ N8423C	Canadair CRJ-200LR	7423	ex C-FMNQ	8423	Endeavor [IGM]
□ N8432A	Canadair CRJ-200LR	7432	ex C-GHRR	8432	Endeavor
□ N8444F	Canadair CRJ-200LR	7444	ex C-FMMT	8444	Endeavor [IGM]
□ N8458A	Canadair CRJ-200LR	7458	ex C-FMMN	8458	Endeavor
□ N8475B	Canadair CRJ-200LR	7475	ex C-FMNH	8475	Endeavor [IGM]
□ N8477R	Canadair CRJ-200LR	7477	ex C-FMNX	8477	Endeavor
□ N8488D	Canadair CRJ-200LR	7488	ex C-FMMN	8488	Endeavor [IGM]
□ N8492C	Canadair CRJ-200LR	7492	ex C-FMMY	8492	Endeavor [IGM]
□ N8495B	Canadair CRJ-200LR	7495	ex C-FMKW	8495	Endeavor [IGM]
□ N8501F	Canadair CRJ-200LR	7501	ex C-FMLS	8501	Endeavor [IGM]
□ N8505Q	Canadair CRJ-200LR	7505	ex C-FMNH	8505	Endeavor [IGM]
□ N8506C	Canadair CRJ-200LR	7506	ex C-FMNW	8506	Endeavor [IGM]
□ N8515F	Canadair CRJ-200LR	7515	ex C-FMOI	8515	Endeavor [IGM]
□ N8516C	Canadair CRJ-200LR	7516	ex C-FMMB	8516	Endeavor [IGM]
□ N8525B	Canadair CRJ-200LR	7525	ex C-FMKW	8525	Endeavor [IGM]
□ N8532G	Canadair CRJ-200LR	7532	ex C-FMLT	8532	Endeavor [IGM]
□ N8533D	Canadair CRJ-200LR	7533	ex C-FMLV	8533	Endeavor [IGM]
□ N8541D	Canadair CRJ-200LR	7541	ex C-FVAZ	8541	Endeavor [IGM]
□ N8543F	Canadair CRJ-200LR	7543	ex C-FMNQ	8543	Endeavor [IGM]
□ N8554A	Canadair CRJ-200LR	7554	ex C-FMKV	8554	Endeavor [IGM]
□ N8560F	Canadair CRJ-200LR	7560	ex C-FMLQ	8560	Endeavor [IGM]

☐ N8577D	Canadair CRJ-200LR	7577	ex C-FMML	8577		Endeavor [IGM]
☐ N8580A	Canadair CRJ-200LR	7580	ex C-FMMW	8580		Endeavor [IGM]
☐ N8587E	Canadair CRJ-200LR	7587	ex C-FMLB	8587		Endeavor [IGM]
☐ N8665A	Canadair CRJ-200LR	7665	ex C-FMOI	8665		Endeavor
☐ N8673D	Canadair CRJ-200LR	7673	ex C-FMNB	8673		Endeavor [IGM]
☐ N8674A	Canadair CRJ-200LR	7674	ex C-FMKV	8674		Endeavor [IGM]
☐ N8894A	Canadair CRJ-200LR	7894	ex C-FMMT	8894		Endeavor wfs
☐ N8896A	Canadair CRJ-200LR	7896	ex C-FMNW	8896		Endeavor [IGM]
☐ N8907A	Canadair CRJ-200LR	7907	ex C-FMML	8907		Endeavor wfs
☐ N8908D	Canadair CRJ-200LR	7908	ex C-FMMN	8908		Endeavor [IGM]
☐ N8914A	Canadair CRJ-200LR	7914	ex C-FMKV	8914		Endeavor [IGM]
☐ N8918B	Canadair CRJ-200LR	7918	ex C-FMLF	8918		Endeavor [IGM]
☐ N8936A	Canadair CRJ-200LR	7936	ex C-FMMB	8936		Endeavor
☐ N8943A	Canadair CRJ-200LR	7943	ex C-FMNB	8943		Endeavor
☐ N8944B	Canadair CRJ-200LR	7944	ex C-FMKV	8944 Spirit of Beale St		Endeavor
☐ N8946A	Canadair CRJ-200LR	7946	ex C-FMKZ	8946		Endeavor
☐ N8948B	Canadair CRJ-200LR	7948	ex C-FMLF	8948		Endeavor [IGM]
☐ N8970D	Canadair CRJ-200LR	7970	ex C-FMMW	8970		Endeavor
☐ N8971A	Canadair CRJ-200LR	7971	ex C-FMMX	8971		Endeavor [IGM]
☐ N8974C	Canadair CRJ-200LR	7974	ex C-FMKV	8974		Endeavor
☐ N8976E	Canadair CRJ-200LR	7976	ex C-FMKZ	8976		Endeavor
☐ N451CA	Canadair CRJ-200ER	7562	ex C-GJVH	7562		ExpressJet wfs
☐ N528CA	Canadair CRJ-200ER	7841	ex C-FVAZ	7841		ExpressJet
☐ N680BR	Canadair CRJ-200ER	7679	ex C-FMLI			ExpressJet wfs
☐ N681BR	Canadair CRJ-200ER	7680	ex C-FMLQ			ExpressJet wfs
☐ N683BR	Canadair CRJ-200ER	7692	ex C-FMND			ExpressJet [IGM]
☐ N686BR	Canadair CRJ-200ER	7715	ex C-FMNH			ExpressJet
☐ N820AS	Canadair CRJ-200ER	7188	ex C-FMMQ	820		ExpressJet
☐ N825AS	Canadair CRJ-200ER	7207	ex C-FMNX	825		ExpressJet [VCV]
☐ N833AS	Canadair CRJ-200ER	7246	ex C-FMMB	833		ExpressJet
☐ N835AS	Canadair CRJ-200ER	7258	ex C-FMLF	835		ExpressJet
☐ N837AS	Canadair CRJ-200ER	7271	ex C-FVAZ	837		ExpressJet
☐ N838AS	Canadair CRJ-200ER	7276	ex C-FMMB	838		ExpressJet
☐ N839AS	Canadair CRJ-200ER	7284	ex C-FMKV	839		ExpressJet
☐ N840AS	Canadair CRJ-200ER	7290	ex C-FMLQ	840		ExpressJet
☐ N841AS	Canadair CRJ-200ER	7300	ex C-FMOW	841		ExpressJet
☐ N842AS	Canadair CRJ-200ER	7304	ex C-FMLU	842		ExpressJet
☐ N843AS	Canadair CRJ-200ER	7310	ex C-FMMW	843		ExpressJet
☐ N844AS	Canadair CRJ-200ER	7317	ex C-FMLB	844		ExpressJet
☐ N845AS	Canadair CRJ-200ER	7324	ex C-FMMT	845		ExpressJet
☐ N846AS	Canadair CRJ-200ER	7328	ex C-FMNY	846		ExpressJet
☐ N847AS	Canadair CRJ-200ER	7335	ex C-FMOI	847		ExpressJet
☐ N848AS	Canadair CRJ-200ER	7339	ex C-FMMQ	848		ExpressJet
☐ N849AS	Canadair CRJ-200ER	7347	ex C-FMLB	849		ExpressJet
☐ N850AS	Canadair CRJ-200ER	7355	ex C-FMNH	850		ExpressJet
☐ N851AS	Canadair CRJ-200ER	7360	ex C-FMOW	851		ExpressJet
☐ N852AS	Canadair CRJ-200ER	7369	ex C-FMMQ	852		ExpressJet
☐ N853AS	Canadair CRJ-200ER	7374	ex C-FMKV	853		ExpressJet
☐ N854AS	Canadair CRJ-200ER	7382	ex C-FMLT	854		ExpressJet
☐ N855AS	Canadair CRJ-200ER	7395	ex C-GGKY	855		ExpressJet
☐ N856AS	Canadair CRJ-200ER	7404	ex C-FMKV	856		ExpressJet
☐ N857AS	Canadair CRJ-200ER	7411	ex C-FMLS	857		ExpressJet
☐ N858AS	Canadair CRJ-200ER	7417	ex C-FMNX	858		ExpressJet
☐ N859AS	Canadair CRJ-200ER	7421	ex C-FVAZ	859		ExpressJet
☐ N860AS	Canadair CRJ-200ER	7433	ex C-FMNB	860		ExpressJet
☐ N861AS	Canadair CRJ-200ER	7445	ex C-FMNH	861		ExpressJet
☐ N867AS	Canadair CRJ-200ER	7463	ex C-FMNB	867		ExpressJet
☐ N868AS	Canadair CRJ-200ER	7474	ex C-FMMT	868		ExpressJet
☐ N870AS	Canadair CRJ-200ER	7530	ex C-FMLQ	870		ExpressJet
☐ N871AS	Canadair CRJ-200ER	7537	ex C-FMNX	871		ExpressJet
☐ N872AS	Canadair CRJ-200ER	7542	ex C-FMND	872		ExpressJet
☐ N873AS	Canadair CRJ-200ER	7549	ex C-GJLI	873		ExpressJet
☐ N874AS	Canadair CRJ-200ER	7551	ex C-GJLK	874		ExpressJet>SKW
☐ N875AS	Canadair CRJ-200ER	7559	ex C-GJLQ	875		ExpressJet>SKW
☐ N876AS	Canadair CRJ-200ER	7576	ex C-FMMB	876		ExpressJet
☐ N877AS	Canadair CRJ-200ER	7579	ex C-FMMQ	877		ExpressJet
☐ N878AS	Canadair CRJ-200ER	7590	ex C-FMLQ	878		ExpressJet
☐ N879AS	Canadair CRJ-200ER	7600	ex C-FMOW	879		ExpressJet
☐ N880AS	Canadair CRJ-200ER	7606	ex C-FMMB	880		ExpressJet
☐ N881AS	Canadair CRJ-200ER	7496	ex C-GIXF	881		ExpressJet
☐ N882AS	Canadair CRJ-200ER	7503	ex C-GJAO	882		ExpressJet
☐ N883AS	Canadair CRJ-200ER	7504	ex C-GIZD	883		ExpressJet
☐ N884AS	Canadair CRJ-200ER	7513	ex C-GIZF	884		ExpressJet
☐ N885AS	Canadair CRJ-200ER	7521	ex C-GJDX	885		ExpressJet>SKW
☐ N886AS	Canadair CRJ-200ER	7531	ex C-GJJC	886		ExpressJet>SKW
☐ N889AS	Canadair CRJ-200ER	7538	ex C-GJJG	889		ExpressJet>SKW
☐ N900EV	Canadair CRJ-200ER	7608	ex C-FMMN	900		ExpressJet
☐ N901EV	Canadair CRJ-200ER	7616	ex C-FMKZ	901		ExpressJet
☐ N902EV	Canadair CRJ-200ER	7620	ex C-FMLQ	902		ExpressJet
☐ N903EV	Canadair CRJ-200ER	7621	ex C-FMLS	903		ExpressJet
☐ N904EV	Canadair CRJ-200ER	7628	ex C-FMNY	904		ExpressJet
☐ N905EV	Canadair CRJ-200ER	7632	ex C-FMND	905		ExpressJet

☐	N906EV	Canadair CRJ-200ER	7642	ex C-FMMY	906	ExpressJet
☐	N907EV	Canadair CRJ-200ER	7648	ex C-FMLF	907	ExpressJet
☐	N908EV	Canadair CRJ-200ER	7654	ex C-FMMT	908	ExpressJet
☐	N909EV	Canadair CRJ-200ER	7658	ex C-FMNY	909	ExpressJet
☐	N910EV	Canadair CRJ-200ER	7727	ex C-FMML	7727	ExpressJet>SKW
☐	N914EV	Canadair CRJ-200ER	7752	ex C-FMND	914	ExpressJet
☐	N915EV	Canadair CRJ-200ER	7754	ex C-FMLU	7754	ExpressJet>SKW
☐	N916EV	Canadair CRJ-200ER	7757	ex C-FMML	916	ExpressJet
☐	N917EV	Canadair CRJ-200ER	7769	ex C-FMLI	917	ExpressJet
☐	N919EV	Canadair CRJ-200ER	7780	ex C-FMOW	919	ExpressJet
☐	N920EV	Canadair CRJ-200ER	7810	ex C-FMOW	920	ExpressJet
☐	N921EV	Canadair CRJ-200ER	7819	ex C-FMMQ	921	ExpressJet
☐	N922EV	Canadair CRJ-200ER	7822	ex C-FMMY	922	ExpressJet
☐	N923EV	Canadair CRJ-200ER	7826	ex C-FMKZ	923	ExpressJet
☐	N924EV	Canadair CRJ-200ER	7830	ex C-FMLQ	924	ExpressJet
☐	N925EV	Canadair CRJ-200ER	7831	ex C-FMLS	925	ExpressJet
☐	N926EV	Canadair CRJ-200ER	7843	ex C-FMNQ	926	ExpressJet
☐	N927EV	Canadair CRJ-200ER	7844	ex C-FMLU	927	ExpressJet
☐	N931EV	Canadair CRJ-200ER	8015	ex C-FMKZ	931	ExpressJet
☐	N933EV	Canadair CRJ-200ER	8022	ex C-FEHV	933	ExpressJet
☐	N936EV	Canadair CRJ-200ER	8038	ex C-FEZT	936	ExpressJet
☐	N937EV	Canadair CRJ-200ER	8042	ex C-FFAB	937	ExpressJet
☐	N970EV	Canadair CRJ-200ER	7527	ex N663BR	970	ExpressJet [IGM]
☐	N972EV	Canadair CRJ-200ER	7534	ex N665BR	972	ExpressJet [IGM]
☐	N973EV	Canadair CRJ-200ER	7575	ex N708BR	973	ExpressJet [IGM]
☐	N974EV	Canadair CRJ-200ER	7594	ex N672BR	974	ExpressJet
☐	N975EV	Canadair CRJ-200ER	7599	ex N673BR	975	ExpressJet [IGM]
☐	N976EV	Canadair CRJ-200ER	7601	ex N674BR	976	ExpressJet
☐	N977EV	Canadair CRJ-200ER	7720	ex N687BR	977	ExpressJet [IGM]
☐	N978EV	Canadair CRJ-200ER	7723	ex N688BR	978	ExpressJet [IGM]
☐	N979EV	Canadair CRJ-200ER	7737	ex N689BR	979	ExpressJet
☐	N980EV	Canadair CRJ-200ER	7759	ex N692BR	980	ExpressJet
☐	N981EV	Canadair CRJ-200ER	7768	ex N694BR	981	ExpressJet
☐	N473CA	Canadair CRJ-200ER	7668	ex C-FMMN	472	Shuttle America♦
☐	N653BR	Canadair CRJ-200ER	7438	ex C-FMLF	460	Shuttle America♦
☐	N667BR	Canadair CRJ-200ER	7535	ex C-FMNH	461	Shuttle America♦
☐	N702BR	Canadair CRJ-200ER	7462	ex N851FJ	459	Shuttle America♦
☐	N406SW	Canadair CRJ-200ER	7030	ex C-FMNH	7030	SkyWest
☐	N409SW	Canadair CRJ-200ER	7056	ex C-FMMX	7056	SkyWest [TUS]
☐	N410SW	Canadair CRJ-200ER	7066	ex C-FMOL	7066	SkyWest [TUS]
☐	N411SW	Canadair CRJ-200ER	7067	ex C-FMOS	7067	SkyWest wfs
☐	N416SW	Canadair CRJ-200ER	7089	ex N60SR	7089	SkyWest
☐	N418SW	Canadair CRJ-200ER	7446	ex C-FMNW	7446	SkyWest
☐	N426SW	Canadair CRJ-200ER	7468	ex C-FMLF	7468	SkyWest
☐	N427SW	Canadair CRJ-200ER	7497	ex C-FMLB	7497	SkyWest
☐	N429SW	Canadair CRJ-200ER	7518	ex C-FMMN	7518	SkyWest
☐	N430SW	Canadair CRJ-200ER	7523	ex C-FMNB	7523	SkyWest
☐	N431SW	Canadair CRJ-200ER	7536	ex C-FMNW	7536	SkyWest
☐	N432SW	Canadair CRJ-200ER	7548	ex C-GJFG	7548	SkyWest
☐	N433SW	Canadair CRJ-200ER	7550	ex C-GJFH	7550	SkyWest
☐	N437SW	Canadair CRJ-200ER	7564	ex C-GJIA	7564	SkyWest
☐	N438SW	Canadair CRJ-200ER	7574	ex C-FMLU	7574	SkyWest
☐	N439SW	Canadair CRJ-200ER	7578	ex C-FMMN	7578	SkyWest
☐	N440SW	Canadair CRJ-200ER	7589	ex C-FMLI	7589	SkyWest
☐	N441SW	Canadair CRJ-200ER	7602	ex C-FMND	7602	SkyWest
☐	N442SW	Canadair CRJ-200ER	7609	ex C-FMMQ	7609	SkyWest
☐	N443SW	Canadair CRJ-200ER	7638	ex C-FMMN	7638	SkyWest
☐	N445SW	Canadair CRJ-200ER	7651	ex C-FMLS	7651	SkyWest
☐	N446SW	Canadair CRJ-200ER	7666	ex C-FMMB	7666	SkyWest
☐	N447SW	Canadair CRJ-200ER	7677	ex C-FMLB	7677	SkyWest
☐	N448SW	Canadair CRJ-200ER	7678	ex C-FMLF	7678	SkyWest
☐	N449SW	Canadair CRJ-200ER	7699	ex C-FMMQ	7699	SkyWest
☐	N452SW	Canadair CRJ-200ER	7716	ex C-FMNW	7716	SkyWest
☐	N453SW	Canadair CRJ-200ER	7743	ex C-FMLV	7743	SkyWest
☐	N454SW	Canadair CRJ-200ER	7749	ex C-FMOS	7749	SkyWest
☐	N455CA	Canadair CRJ-200ER	7592	ex C-FMLT	7592	SkyWest
☐	N455SW	Canadair CRJ-200ER	7760	ex C-FMMW	7760	SkyWest
☐	N457SW	Canadair CRJ-200ER	7773	ex C-FMLV	7773	SkyWest
☐	N459SW	Canadair CRJ-200ER	7782	ex C-FMND	7782	SkyWest
☐	N460SW	Canadair CRJ-200ER	7803	ex C-FMLV	7803	SkyWest
☐	N461SW	Canadair CRJ-200ER	7811	ex C-FVAZ	7811	SkyWest
☐	N463SW	Canadair CRJ-200ER	7820	ex C-FMMW	7820	SkyWest
☐	N465SW	Canadair CRJ-200ER	7845	ex C-FMOI	7845	SkyWest
☐	N466SW	Canadair CRJ-200ER	7856	ex C-FMKZ	7856	SkyWest
☐	N477CA	Canadair CRJ-200ER	7670	ex C-FMMW	7670	SkyWest
☐	N487CA	Canadair CRJ-200ER	7729	ex C-FMMQ	7729	SkyWest
☐	N601XJ	Canadair CRJ-200LR	8044	ex C-FFHW		SkyWest♦
☐	N602XJ	Canadair CRJ-200LR	8045	ex C-FMKZ		SkyWest♦
☐	N629BR	Canadair CRJ-200ER	7251	ex (N533CA)	7251	SkyWest
☐	N659BR	Canadair CRJ-200ER	7509	ex C-FMOS	7509	SkyWest
☐	N675BR	Canadair CRJ-200ER	7635	ex (N536CA)	7635	SkyWest

☐	N685BR	Canadair CRJ-200ER	7712	ex (N532CA)	7712	SkyWest
☐	N823AS	Canadair CRJ-200ER	7196	ex C-FMKZ	823	SkyWest♦
☐	N824AS	Canadair CRJ-200ER	7203	ex C-FMLB	824	SkyWest♦
☐	N862AS	Canadair CRJ-200ER	7476	ex C-FMNW	7476	SkyWest<ASQ
☐	N863AS	Canadair CRJ-200ER	7487	ex C-FMML	7487	SkyWest<ASQ
☐	N864AS	Canadair CRJ-200ER	7502	ex C-FMLT	864	SkyWest<ASQ
☐	N866AS	Canadair CRJ-200ER	7517	ex C-FMML	7517	SkyWest<ASQ
☐	N869AS	Canadair CRJ-200ER	7479	ex C-FMOS	869	SkyWest<ASQ
☐	N875AS	Canadair CRJ-200ER	7559	ex C-GJLQ	875	SkyWest<ASQ
☐	N889AS	Canadair CRJ-200ER	7538	ex C-GJJG	889	SkyWest<ASQ
☐	N910EV	Canadair CRJ-200ER	7727	ex C-FMML	7727	SkyWest<ASQ
☐	N913EV	Canadair CRJ-200ER	7731	ex C-FMMX	7731	SkyWest
☐	N912EV	Canadair CRJ-200ER	7728	ex C-FMMN	7728	SkyWest
☐	N915EV	Canadair CRJ-200ER	7754	ex C-FMLU	7754	SkyWest<ASQ
☐	N928EV	Canadair CRJ-200ER	8006	ex C-FMMB	928	SkyWest♦
☐	N929EV	Canadair CRJ-200ER	8007	ex C-FMMN		SkyWest
☐	N930EV	Canadair CRJ-200ER	8014	ex C-FMKW	930	SkyWest♦
☐	N932EV	Canadair CRJ-200ER	8016	ex C-FMLB		SkyWest
☐	N8884E	Canadair CRJ-200LR	7884	ex C-FMKV		SkyWest♦
☐	N8903A	Canadair CRJ-200LR	7903	ex C-FMNQ		SkyWest♦
☐	N8923A	Canadair CRJ-200LR	7923	ex C-FMLV		SkyWest♦
☐	N8932C	Canadair CRJ-440LR	7932	ex C-FMND		SkyWest♦
☐	N8933B	Canadair CRJ-200LR	7933	ex C-FMNQ		SkyWest♦
☐	N8965E	Canadair CRJ-200LR	7965	ex C-FMOI		SkyWest♦
☐	N8968E	Canadair CRJ-200LR	7968	ex C-FMMN		SkyWest♦
☐	N8982A	Canadair CRJ-200LR	7982	ex C-FMLT		SkyWest♦
☐	N800AY	Canadair CRJ-440LR	8000	ex C-FMMW	8000	Endeavor
☐	N801AY	Canadair CRJ-440LR	8001	ex C-FMMX	8001	Endeavor
☐	N830AY	Canadair CRJ-440LR	8030	ex C-FVAZ	8030	Endeavor [IGM]
☐	N839AY	Canadair CRJ-440LR	8039	ex C-FMMW	8039	Endeavor wfs
☐	N841AY	Canadair CRJ-440LR	8041	ex C-FMMY	8041	Endeavor wfs
☐	N8588D	Canadair CRJ-440LR	7588	ex C-GJSZ	8588	Endeavor [IGM]
☐	N8598B	Canadair CRJ-440LR	7598	ex C-FMNY	8598	Endeavor [IGM]
☐	N8604C	Canadair CRJ-440LR	7604	ex C-FMLU	8604	Endeavor [IGM]
☐	N8611A	Canadair CRJ-440LR	7611	ex C-FMMX	8611	Endeavor
☐	N8623A	Canadair CRJ-440LR	7623	ex C-FMLV	8623	Endeavor [IGM]
☐	N8631E	Canadair CRJ-440LR	7631	ex C-FVAZ	8631	Endeavor [IGM]
☐	N8646A	Canadair CRJ-440LR	7646	ex C-FMKZ	8646	Endeavor [IGM]
☐	N8659B	Canadair CRJ-440LR	7659	ex C-FMOS	8659	Endeavor [IGM]
☐	N8672A	Canadair CRJ-440LR	7672	ex C-FMMY	8672	Endeavor [IGM]
☐	N8683B	Canadair CRJ-440LR	7683	ex C-FMLV	8683	Endeavor [IGM]
☐	N8688C	Canadair CRJ-440LR	7688	ex C-FMNY	6888	Endeavor [IGM]
☐	N8694A	Canadair CRJ-440LR	7694	ex C-FMLU	8694	Endeavor [IGM]
☐	N8696C	Canadair CRJ-440LR	7696	ex C-FMMB	8696	Endeavor
☐	N8698A	Canadair CRJ-440LR	7698	ex C-FMMN	8698	Endeavor [IGM]
☐	N8709A	Canadair CRJ-440LR	7709	ex C-FMLI	8709	Endeavor [IGM]
☐	N8710A	Canadair CRJ-440LR	7710	ex C-FMLQ	8710	Endeavor [IGM]
☐	N8718E	Canadair CRJ-440LR	7718	ex C-FMNY	8718	Endeavor [IGM]
☐	N8721B	Canadair CRJ-440LR	7721	ex C-FVAZ	8721	Endeavor
☐	N8733G	Canadair CRJ-440LR	7733	ex C-FMNB	8733	Endeavor [IGM]
☐	N8736A	Canadair CRJ-440LR	7736	ex C-FMKZ	8736	Endeavor [IGM]
☐	N8745B	Canadair CRJ-440LR	7745	ex C-FMNH	8745	Endeavor [IGM]
☐	N8747B	Canadair CRJ-440LR	7747	ex C-FMNX	8747	Endeavor [IGM]
☐	N8751D	Canadair CRJ-440LR	7751	ex C-FVAZ	8751	Endeavor [IGM]
☐	N8758D	Canadair CRJ-440LR	7758	ex C-FMMN	8758	Endeavor [IGM]
☐	N8771A	Canadair CRJ-440LR	7771	ex C-FMLS	8771	Endeavor [IGM]
☐	N8775A	Canadair CRJ-440LR	7775	ex C-FMNH	8775	Endeavor [IGM]
☐	N8783E	Canadair CRJ-440LR	7783	ex C-FMNQ	8783	Endeavor [IGM]
☐	N8790A	Canadair CRJ-440LR	7790	ex C-FMMW	8790	Endeavor [IGM]
☐	N8794B	Canadair CRJ-440LR	7794	ex C-FMKV	8794	Endeavor [IGM]
☐	N8797A	Canadair CRJ-440LR	7797	ex C-FMLB	8797	Endeavor [IGM]
☐	N8800G	Canadair CRJ-440LR	7800	ex C-FMLQ	8800	Endeavor
☐	N8808H	Canadair CRJ-440LR	7808	ex C-FMNY	8808	Endeavor [IGM]
☐	N8836A	Canadair CRJ-440LR	7836	ex C-FMNW	8836	Endeavor [IGM]
☐	N8837B	Canadair CRJ-440LR	7837	ex C-FMNX	8837	Endeavor [IGM]
☐	N8839E	Canadair CRJ-440LR	7839	ex C-FMOS	8839	Endeavor
☐	N8847A	Canadair CRJ-440LR	7847	ex C-FMML	8847	Endeavor
☐	N8855A	Canadair CRJ-440LR	7855	ex C-FMKW	8855	Endeavor [IGM]
☐	N8869B	Canadair CRJ-440LR	7869	ex C-FMOS	8869	Endeavor
☐	N8877A	Canadair CRJ-440LR	7877	ex C-FMML	8877	Endeavor
☐	N8883E	Canadair CRJ-440LR	7883	ex C-FMNB	8883	Endeavor
☐	N8886A	Canadair CRJ-440LR	7886	ex C-FMKZ	8886	Endeavor wfs
☐	N8888D	Canadair CRJ-440LR	7888	ex C-FMLF	8888	Endeavor [IGM]
☐	N8891A	Canadair CRJ-440LR	7891	ex C-FMLS	8891	Endeavor
☐	N8913A	Canadair CRJ-440LR	7913	ex C-FMNB	8913	Endeavor
☐	N8921B	Canadair CRJ-440LR	7921	ex C-FMLS	8921	Endeavor
☐	N8924B	Canadair CRJ-440LR	7924	ex C-FMMT	8924	Endeavor
☐	N8928A	Canadair CRJ-440LR	7928	ex C-FMNY	8928	Endeavor [IGM]
☐	N8930E	Canadair CRJ-440LR	7930	ex C-FMOW	8930	Endeavor
☐	N8938A	Canadair CRJ-440LR	7938	ex C-FMMN	8938	Endeavor
☐	N8940E	Canadair CRJ-440LR	7940	ex C-FMMW	8940	Endeavor
☐	N8960A	Canadair CRJ-440LR	7960	ex C-FMOW	8960	Endeavor

☐ N8964E	Canadair CRJ-440LR	7964	ex C-FMLU	8964		Endeavor
☐ N8969A	Canadair CRJ-440LR	7969	ex C-FMMQ	8969		Endeavor
☐ N8972E	Canadair CRJ-440LR	7972	ex C-FMMY	8972		Endeavor
☐ N8977A	Canadair CRJ-440LR	7977	ex C-FMLB	8977		Endeavor
☐ N8980A	Canadair CRJ-440LR	7980	ex C-FMLQ	8980		Endeavor
☐ N8986B	Canadair CRJ-440LR	7986	ex C-FMNW	8986		Endeavor
☐ N8828D	Canadair CRJ-440LR	7828	ex C-FMLF			SkyWest♦
☐ N8942A	Canadair CRJ-440LR	7942	ex C-FMMY			SkyWest♦
☐ N378CA	Canadair CRJ-701ER	10097	ex C-GIAJ	10097		Comair>GJS
☐ N371CA	Canadair CRJ-701ER	10082	ex C-GIAR	10082		ExpressJet
☐ N376CA	Canadair CRJ-701ER	10092		10092		ExpressJet
☐ N390CA	Canadair CRJ-701ER	10106		10106		ExpressJet
☐ N391CA	Canadair CRJ-701ER	10108		10108		ExpressJet
☐ N398CA	Canadair CRJ-701ER	10112		10112		ExpressJet
☐ N609SK	Canadair CRJ-701ER	10020	ex N701EV	10020		ExpressJet
☐ N611SK	Canadair CRJ-701ER	10035	ex N702EV	10035		ExpressJet>SKW
☐ N613SK	Canadair CRJ-701ER	10038	ex N703EV	10038		ExpressJet>SKW
☐ N614SK	Canadair CRJ-701ER	10051	ex N705EV	10051		ExpressJet>SKW
☐ N750EV	Canadair CRJ-701ER	10161				ExpressJet
☐ N707EV	Canadair CRJ-701ER	10057	ex C-GIAZ			ExpressJet
☐ N708EV	Canadair CRJ-701ER	10060	ex C-GIBI			ExpressJet
☐ N709EV	Canadair CRJ-701ER	10068	ex C-GICB			ExpressJet
☐ N710EV	Canadair CRJ-701ER	10071	ex C-GICP			ExpressJet
☐ N712EV	Canadair CRJ-701ER	10074	ex C-GHZZ			ExpressJet
☐ N713EV	Canadair CRJ-701ER	10081	ex C-GIAP			ExpressJet
☐ N716EV	Canadair CRJ-701ER	10084	ex C-GIAV			ExpressJet
☐ N717EV	Canadair CRJ-701ER	10088	ex C-GIBH			ExpressJet
☐ N718EV	Canadair CRJ-701ER	10095				ExpressJet
☐ N719EV	Canadair CRJ-701ER	10099	ex C-GICL			ExpressJet
☐ N720EV	Canadair CRJ-701ER	10115	ex C-GIAW			ExpressJet
☐ N722EV	Canadair CRJ-701ER	10127				ExpressJet
☐ N723EV	Canadair CRJ-701ER	10132				ExpressJet
☐ N724EV	Canadair CRJ-701ER	10138	ex C-GIBT			ExpressJet
☐ N730EV	Canadair CRJ-701ER	10141	ex C-GIAP			ExpressJet
☐ N738EV	Canadair CRJ-701ER	10146				ExpressJet
☐ N740EV	Canadair CRJ-701ER	10151				ExpressJet
☐ N744EV	Canadair CRJ-701ER	10157				ExpressJet
☐ N748EV	Canadair CRJ-701ER	10158				ExpressJet
☐ N751EV	Canadair CRJ-701ER	10163				ExpressJet
☐ N752EV	Canadair CRJ-701ER	10166				ExpressJet
☐ N753EV	Canadair CRJ-701ER	10169				ExpressJet
☐ N754EV	Canadair CRJ-701ER	10173	ex C-FCRJ			ExpressJet
☐ N755EV	Canadair CRJ-701ER	10185				ExpressJet
☐ N758EV	Canadair CRJ-701ER	10210				ExpressJet
☐ N759EV	Canadair CRJ-701ER	10211				ExpressJet
☐ N760EV	Canadair CRJ-701ER	10212				ExpressJet
☐ N761ND	Canadair CRJ-701ER	10213				ExpressJet
☐ N317CA	Canadair CRJ-701ER	10055	ex C-GZXI			GoJet
☐ N340CA	Canadair CRJ-701ER	10062	ex C-GIBL			GoJet
☐ N355CA	Canadair CRJ-701ER	10067	ex C-GIBT			GoJet
☐ N368CA	Canadair CRJ-701ER	10075	ex C-GIAD			GoJet
☐ N369CA	Canadair CRJ-701ER	10079	ex C-GZUD	10079		GoJet
☐ N374CA	Canadair CRJ-701ER	10090		10090		GoJet
☐ N378CA	Canadair CRJ-701ER	10097	ex C-GIAJ	10097		GoJet<COM
☐ N642CA	Canadair CRJ-701ER	10125		10125		GoJet
☐ N653CA	Canadair CRJ-701ER	10129	ex C-GZUC	10129		GoJet
☐ N655CA	Canadair CRJ-701ER	10134		10134		GoJet
☐ N656CA	Canadair CRJ-701ER	10143	ex C-GIAU	10143		GoJet
☐ N658CA	Canadair CRJ-701ER	10148	ex C-GIAU	10148		GoJet
☐ N669CA	Canadair CRJ-701ER	10176		10176		GoJet
☐ N668CA	Canadair CRJ-701ER	10162				GoJet
☐ N690CA	Canadair CRJ-701ER	10182		10182		GoJet
☐ N741EV	Canadair CRJ-701ER	10155	ex C-FBQS			GoJet
☐ N215AG	Canadair CRJ-701ER	10009	ex N601QX			SkyWest
☐ N216AG	Canadair CRJ-701ER	10023	ex N606QX			SkyWest
☐ N218AG	Canadair CRJ-701ER	10205	ex N618QX			SkyWest
☐ N227AG	Canadair CRJ-701ER	10015	ex D-ACPD			SkyWest
☐ N331CA	Canadair CRJ-701ER	10061	ex C-GIBJ	10061		SkyWest
☐ N603SK	Canadair CRJ-702ER	10248	ex C-FHUC	10248		SkyWest
☐ N603QX	Canadair CRJ-701ER	10011	ex C-GHCZ			SkyWest<QXE
☐ N604SK	Canadair CRJ-702ER	10249		10239		SkyWest
☐ N606SK	Canadair CRJ-702ER	10250		10250		SkyWest
☐ N607SK	Canadair CRJ-702ER	10251	ex C-FIBQ	10251		SkyWest
☐ N608SK	Canadair CRJ-702ER	10252		10252		SkyWest
☐ N611SK	Canadair CRJ-701ER	10035	ex N702EV	10035		SkyWest<ASQ
☐ N613SK	Canadair CRJ-701ER	10038	ex N703EV	10038		SkyWest<ASQ
☐ N614SK	Canadair CRJ-701ER	10051	ex N705EV	10051		SkyWest<ASQ
☐ N630SK	Canadair CRJ-701ER	10328	ex C-GIBQ			SkyWest

☐ N632SK	Canadair CRJ-702ER	10330	ex C-GZQF		SkyWest
☐ N633SK	Canadair CRJ-702ER	10331	ex C-GHZZ		SkyWest
☐ N625CA	Canadair CRJ-701ER	10113		10113	SkyWest
☐ N641CA	Canadair CRJ-701ER	10122		10122	SkyWest
☐ N161PQ	Canadair CRJ-900ER	15161			Endeavor
☐ N176PQ	Canadair CRJ-900ER	15176			Endeavor>ASQ
☐ N181PQ	Canadair CRJ-900ER	15181			Endeavor>ASQ
☐ N272PQ	Canadair CRJ-900ER	15272	ex C-GZQG		Endeavor
☐ N279PQ	Canadair CRJ-900ER	15279	ex C-GIBN		Endeavor
☐ N292PQ	Canadair CRJ-900LR	15292	ex C-GZQJ		Endeavor
☐ N293PQ	Canadair CRJ-900LR	15293	ex C-GHZZ		Endeavor
☐ N294PQ	Canadair CJR-900LR	15294	ex C-GIBL		Endeavor
☐ N295PQ	Canadair CRJ-900LR	15295			Endeavor
☐ N296PQ	Canadair CRJ-900LR	15296			Endeavor
☐ N297PQ	Canadair CRJ-900LR	15297			Endeavor
☐ B298PQ	Canadair CRJ-900LR	15298			Endeavor
☐ N299PQ	Canadair CRJ-900LR	15299			Endeavor
☐ N300PQ	Canadair CRJ-900LR	15300	ex C-GIBQ		Endeavor
☐ N301PQ	Canadair CRJ-900LR	15301			Endeavor
☐ N302PQ	Canadair CRJ-900LR	15302			Endeavor
☐ N303PQ	Canadair CRJ-900ER	15303			Endeavor
☐ N304PQ	Canadair CRJ-900ER	15304			Endeavor
☐ N305PQ	Canadair CRJ-900ER	15305			Endeavor
☐ N306PQ	Canadair CRJ-900ER	15306			Endeavor
☐ N307PQ	Canadair CRJ-900LR	15307			Endeavor
☐ N308PQ	Canadair CRJ-900LR	15308			Endeavor
☐ N309PQ	Canadair CRJ-900LR	15309			Endeavor
☐ N310PQ	Canadair CRJ-900LR	15310			Endeavor
☐ N311PQ	Canadair CRJ-900LR	15311			Endeavor
☐ N313PQ	Canadair CRJ-900LR	15313	ex C-GWFQ		Endeavor♦
☐ N314PQ	Canadair CRJ-900LR	15314	ex C-GWFV		Endeavor♦
☐ N315PQ	Canadair CRJ-900LR	15315	ex C-GWFX		Endeavor♦
☐ N316PQ	Canadair CRJ-900LR	15316	ex C-GWFY		Endeavor♦
☐ N319PQ	Canadair CRJ-900LR	15319	ex C-GIBJ		Endeavor♦
☐ N320PQ	Canadair CRJ-900LR	15320	ex C-GIBL		Endeavor♦
☐ N324PQ	Canadair CRJ-900LR	15324	ex C-GZQE		Endeavor♦
☐ N325PQ	Canadair CRJ-900LR	15325	ex C-GZQJ		Endeavor♦
☐ N326PQ	Canadair CRJ-900LR	15326	ex C-GIAO		Endeavor♦
☐ N329PQ	Canadair CRJ-900LR	15329			Endeavor♦
☐ N330PQ	Canadair CRJ-900LR	15330			Endeavor♦
☐ N331PQ	Canadair CRJ-900LR	15331			Endeavor♦
☐ N335PQ	Canadair CJR-900LR	15335	ex C-GWFI		Endeavor♦
☐ N336PQ	Canadair CRJ-900LR	15336	ex C-GWFK		Endeavor♦
☐ N337PQ	Canadair CRJ-900LR	15337			Endeavor♦
☐ N341PQ	Canadair CRJ-900LR	15341	ex C-GWFY		Endeavor♦
☐ N348PQ	Canadair CRJ-900LR	15348	ex C-GZUJ		Endeavor♦
☐ N349PQ	Canadair CRJ-900LR	15349	ex C-GZUQ		Endeavor♦
☐ N600LR	Canadair CRJ-900ER	15142			Endeavor
☐ N601LR	Canadair CRJ-900ER	15145			Endeavor
☐ N602LR	Canadair CRJ-900ER	15151			Endeavor
☐ N604LR	Canadair CRJ-900ER	15152			Endeavor
☐ N605LR	Canadair CRJ-900LR	15160			Endeavor
☐ N901XJ	Canadair CRJ-900LR	15130			Endeavor
☐ N902XJ	Canadair CRJ-900LR	15131	ex C-FNWB		Endeavor
☐ N903XJ	Canadair CRJ-900LR	15134	ex C-FOFO		Endeavor
☐ N904XJ	Canadair CRJ-900LR	15135			Endeavor
☐ N905XJ	Canadair CRJ-900LR	15137			Endeavor
☐ N906XJ	Canadair CRJ-900LR	15138			Endeavor
☐ N907XJ	Canadair CRJ-900LR	15139	ex C-FOVM		Endeavor
☐ N908XJ	Canadair CRJ-900LR	15140	ex C-FOWF		Endeavor
☐ N909XJ	Canadair CRJ-900LR	15141			Endeavor
☐ N910XJ	Canadair CRJ-900LR	15143			Endeavor
☐ N912XJ	Canadair CRJ-900LR	15144			Endeavor
☐ N913XJ	Canadair CRJ-900LR	15148	ex C-FQYX		Endeavor
☐ N914XJ	Canadair CRJ-900LR	15149			Endeavor
☐ N915XJ	Canadair CRJ-900LR	15150			Endeavor
☐ N916XJ	Canadair CRJ-900LR	15154			Endeavor
☐ N917XJ	Canadair CRJ-900LR	15155			Endeavor
☐ N918XJ	Canadair CRJ-900LR	15156			Endeavor
☐ N919XJ	Canadair CRJ-900LR	15163	ex C-FSQZ		Endeavor
☐ N920XJ	Canadair CRJ-900LR	15167			Endeavor
☐ N921XJ	Canadair CRJ-900LR	15172			Endeavor
☐ N922XJ	Canadair CRJ-900LR	15174	ex C-FTTY		Endeavor
☐ N923XJ	Canadair CRJ-900LR	15177			Endeavor
☐ N924XJ	Canadair CRJ-900LR	15179			Endeavor
☐ N925XJ	Canadair CRJ-900LR	15183			Endeavor
☐ N926XJ	Canadair CRJ-900LR	15184		928	Endeavor
☐ N927XJ	Canadair CRJ-900LR	15188			Endeavor
☐ N928XJ	Canadair CRJ-900LR	15190			Endeavor
☐ N929XJ	Canadair CRJ-900LR	15191			Endeavor
☐ N930XJ	Canadair CRJ-900LR	15192			Endeavor
☐ N931XJ	Canadair CRJ-900LR	15193			Endeavor

☐ N932XJ	Canadair CRJ-900LR	15194			Endeavor
☐ N933XJ	Canadair CRJ-900LR	15196	ex C-GIBN		Endeavor
☐ N934XJ	Canadair CRJ-900LR	15198			Endeavor
☐ N935XJ	Canadair CRJ-900LR	15199			Endeavor
☐ N936XJ	Canadair CRJ-900LR	15201			Endeavor
☐ N937XJ	Canadair CRJ-900LR	15210			Endeavor
☐ N131EV	Canadair CRJ-900ER	15217			ExpressJet
☐ N132EV	Canadair CRJ-900ER	15219			ExpressJet
☐ N133EV	Canadair CRJ-900ER	15222			ExpressJet
☐ N134EV	Canadair CRJ-900ER	15223			ExpressJet
☐ N135EV	Canadair CRJ-900ER	15225	ex C-GIBI		ExpressJet
☐ N136EV	Canadair CRJ-900ER	15226			ExpressJet
☐ N137EV	Canadair CRJ-900ER	15227			ExpressJet
☐ N138EV	Canadair CRJ-900ER	15235	ex C-GZQW		ExpressJet
☐ N146PQ	Canadair CRJ-900ER	15146			ExpressJet
☐ N147PQ	Canadair CRJ-900ER	15147			ExpressJet
☐ N153PQ	Canadair CRJ-900ER	15153			ExpressJet
☐ N166PQ	Canadair CRJ-900ER	15166			ExpressJet
☐ N176PQ	Canadair CRJ-900ER	15176			ExpressJet<FLG
☐ N181PQ	Canadair CRJ-900ER	15181			ExpressJet<FLG
☐ N186PQ	Canadair CRJ-900ER	15186			ExpressJet
☐ N195PQ	Canadair CRJ-900ER	15195	ex C-FVWD		ExpressJet
☐ N197PQ	Canadair CRJ-900ER	15197	ex C-GZQV		ExpressJet
☐ N200PQ	Canadair CRJ-900FR	15200	ex C-GWVU		ExpressJet
☐ N228PQ	Canadair CRJ-900ER	15228			ExpressJet
☐ N232PQ	Canadair CRJ-900ER	15232	ex C-GZQR		ExpressJet
☐ N538CA	Canadair CRJ-900ER	15157			ExpressJet
☐ N582CA	Canadair CRJ-900ER	15171	ex C-		ExpressJet
☐ N606LR	Canadair CRJ-900LR	15173			ExpressJet
☐ N607LR	Canadair CRJ-900LR	15178			ExpressJet
☐ N676CA	Canadair CRJ-900ER	15127			ExpressJet
☐ N678CA	Canadair CRJ-900ER	15125	ex C-		ExpressJet
☐ N691CA	Canadair CRJ-900ER	15136			ExpressJet
☐ N695CA	Canadair CRJ-900ER	15097	ex C-	30th Anniversary c/s	ExpressJet
☐ N181GJ	Canadair CRJ-900	15204	ex C-GSKK		GoJet♦
☐ N162PQ	Canadair CRJ-900ER	15162	ex C-FSQJ		SkyWest
☐ N170PQ	Canadair CRJ-900ER	15170			SkyWest
☐ N187PQ	Canadair CRJ-900ER	15187			SkyWest
☐ N548CA	Canadair CRJ-900ER	15159			SkyWest
☐ N549CA	Canadair CRJ-900ER	15164	ex C-		SkyWest
☐ N554CA	Canadair CRJ-900ER	15168	ex C-		SkyWest
☐ N679CA	Canadair CRJ-900ER	15132	ex C-		SkyWest
☐ N689CA	Canadair CRJ-900ER	15133			SkyWest
☐ N692CA	Canadair CRJ-900ER	15092	ex C-		SkyWest
☐ N693CA	Canadair CRJ-900ER	15096	ex C-		SkyWest
☐ N800SK	Canadair CRJ-900ER	15060			SkyWest
☐ N802SK	Canadair CRJ-900ER	15061			SkyWest
☐ N803SK	Canadair CRJ-900ER	15062	ex C-FJTQ		SkyWest
☐ N804SK	Canadair CRJ-900ER	15067	ex C-		SkyWest
☐ N805SK	Canadair CRJ-900ER	15069	ex C-GZQT		SkyWest
☐ N806SK	Canadair CRJ-900ER	15070	ex C-GZQV		SkyWest
☐ N807SK	Canadair CRJ-900ER	15082	ex C-		SkyWest
☐ N809SK	Canadair CRJ-900ER	15086	ex C-FLCX		SkyWest
☐ N810SK	Canadair CRJ-900ER	15093	ex C-		SkyWest
☐ N812SK	Canadair CRJ-900ER	15098	ex C-		SkyWest
☐ N813SK	Canadair CRJ-900ER	15099	ex C-		SkyWest
☐ N814SK	Canadair CRJ-900ER	15100	ex C-		SkyWest
☐ N815SK	Canadair CRJ-900ER	15101	ex C-		SkyWest
☐ N816SK	Canadair CRJ-900ER	15105	ex C-		SkyWest
☐ N817SK	Canadair CRJ-900ER	15107	ex C-		SkyWest
☐ N820SK	Canadair CRJ-900ER	15108	ex C-		SkyWest
☐ N821SK	Canadair CRJ-900ER	15109	ex C-	35th anniversary c/s	SkyWest
☐ N822SK	Canadair CRJ-900ER	15203	ex C-		SkyWest
☐ N823SK	Canadair CRJ-900ER	15205	ex C-		SkyWest
☐ N824SK	Canadair CRJ-900ER	15208	ex C-		SkyWest
☐ N825SK	Canadair CRJ-900ER	15212	ex C-		SkyWest
☐ N897SK	Canadair CRJ-900ER	15103	ex VN-A802		SkyWest
☐ N898SK	Canadair CRJ-900ER	15110	ex VN-A803		SkyWest
☐ N899SK	Canadair CRJ-900ER	15112	ex VN-A804		SkyWest
☐ N295SK	Embraer ERJ-140LR	145513	ex PT-SYF		Shuttle America wfs♦
☐ N297SK	Embraer ERJ-140LR	145522	ex PT-SYN		Shuttle America wfs♦
☐ N299SK	Embraer ERJ-140LR	145532	ex PT-STW		Shuttle America [IGM]♦
☐ N371SK	Embraer ERJ-140LR	145535	ex PT-STZ		Shuttle America wfs♦
☐ N372SK	Embraer ERJ-140LR	145538	ex PT-SZC		Shuttle America wfs♦
☐ N373SK	Embraer ERJ-140LR	145543	ex PT-SZG		Shuttle America wfs♦
☐ N374SK	Embraer ERJ-140LR	145544	ex PT-SZH		Shuttle America [IGM]♦
☐ N375SK	Embraer ERJ-140LR	145569	ex PT-SBF		Shuttle America [IGM]♦
☐ N376SK	Embraer ERJ-140LR	145578	ex PT-SBO		Shuttle America [IGM]♦
☐ N377SK	Embraer ERJ-140LR	145579	ex PT-SBP		Shuttle America wfs♦

☐	N378SK	Embraer ERJ-140LR	145593	ex PT-SCC		Shuttle America wfs♦
☐	N379SK	Embraer ERJ-140LR	145606	ex PT-SCP		Shuttle America [IGM]♦
☐	N380SK	Embraer ERJ-140LR	145613	ex PT-SCX		Shuttle America [IGM]♦
☐	N381SK	Embraer ERJ-140LR	145619	ex PT-SDH		Shuttle America wfs♦
☐	N382SK	Embraer ERJ-140LR	145624	ex PT-SDM		Shuttle America [IGM]♦
☐	N10575	Embraer ERJ-145LR	145640	ex PT-SEC		ExpressJet
☐	N11137	Embraer ERJ-145XR	145721	ex PT-SGX		ExpressJet
☐	N11544	Embraer ERJ-145LR	145557	ex PT-SZS		ExpressJet
☐	N11551	Embraer ERJ-145LR	145411	ex PT-STI		ExpressJet
☐	N11193	Embraer ERJ-145XR	14500938	ex PT-SCJ		ExpressJet
☐	N11165	Embraer ERJ-145XR	14500819	ex PT-SNT		ExpressJet
☐	N11176	Embraer ERJ-145XR	14500881	ex PT-SXV		ExpressJet
☐	N11181	Embraer ERJ-145XR	14500904	ex PT-SYN		ExpressJet
☐	N11184	Embraer ERJ-145XR	14500917	ex PT-SVX		ExpressJet
☐	N11189	Embraer ERJ-145XR	14500931	ex PT-SCA		ExpressJet
☐	N11192	Embraer ERJ-145XR	14500936	ex PT-SCI		ExpressJet
☐	N11199	Embraer ERJ-145XR	14500953	ex PT-SFA		ExpressJet
☐	N12163	Embraer ERJ-145XR	14500811	ex PT-SNN		ExpressJet
☐	N12167	Embraer ERJ-145XR	14500834	ex PT-SQG		ExpressJet
☐	N12175	Embraer ERJ-145XR	14500878	ex PT-SXT		ExpressJet
☐	N12201	Embraer ERJ-145XR	14500959	ex PT-SFG		ExpressJet
☐	N12569	Embraer ERJ-145LR	145630	ex PT-SDS		ExpressJet
☐	N14162	Embraer ERJ-145XR	14500808	ex PT-SNK		ExpressJet
☐	N14168	Embraer ERJ-145XR	14500840	ex PT-SQL		ExpressJet
☐	N14171	Embraer ERJ-145XR	14500859	ex PT-SQZ		ExpressJet
☐	N14173	Embraer ERJ-145XR	14500872	ex PT-SXK		ExpressJet
☐	N14174	Embraer ERJ-145XR	14500876	ex PT-SXR		ExpressJet
☐	N14179	Embraer ERJ-145XR	14500896	ex PT-SYI		ExpressJet
☐	N14188	Embraer ERJ-145XR	14500929	ex PT-SOY		ExpressJet
☐	N14198	Embraer ERJ-145XR	14500951	ex PT-SCZ		ExpressJet
☐	N14570	Embraer ERJ-145LR	145632	ex PT-SDU		ExpressJet
☐	N14907	Embraer ERJ-145LR	145468	ex PT-SVN		ExpressJet
☐	N16170	Embraer ERJ-145XR	14500850	ex PT-SQT		ExpressJet
☐	N16178	Embraer ERJ-145XR	14500889	ex PT-SYC		ExpressJet
☐	N16183	Embraer ERJ-145XR	14500914	ex PT-SYV		ExpressJet
☐	N18557	Embraer ERJ-145LR	145596	ex PT-SCF		ExpressJet
☐	N19554	Embraer ERJ-145LR	145587	ex PT-SBX		ExpressJet
☐	N22909	Embraer ERJ-145LR	145459	ex PT-SVE		ExpressJet
☐	N33182	Embraer ERJ-145XR	14500909	ex PT-SYS		ExpressJet
☐	N825MJ	Embraer ERJ-145LR	145179	ex PT-SGB		Freedom [BNA]
☐	N826MJ	Embraer ERJ-145LR	145214	ex PT-SHB		Freedom [BNA]
☐	N827MJ	Embraer ERJ-145LR	145217	ex PT-SHD		Freedom [BNA]
☐	N828MJ	Embraer ERJ-145LR	145218	ex PT-SHE		Freedom [BNA]
☐	N831MJ	Embraer ERJ-145LR	145273	ex PT-SJP		Freedom [BNA]
☐	N836MJ	Embraer ERJ-145LR	145359	ex PT-SNY		Freedom
☐	N838MJ	Embraer ERJ-145LR	145384	ex PT-SQI		Freedom
☐	N856MJ	Embraer ERJ-145LR	145626	ex PT-SDO		Freedom
☐	N257JQ	Embraer ERJ-145LR	14500812	ex PT-SNO	257	Shuttle America♦
☐	N258JQ	Embraer ERJ-145LR	145768	ex PT-SJZ	258	Shuttle America♦
☐	N259JQ	Embraer ERJ-145LR	145763	ex PT-SJU	259	Shuttle America♦
☐	N263SK	Embraer ERJ-145LR	145199	ex PT-SGP		Shuttle America>SLI
☐	N265SK	Embraer ERJ-145LR	145226	ex PT-SHL	265	Shuttle America♦
☐	N266SK	Embraer ERJ-145LR	145241	ex PT-SIG	266	Shuttle America♦
☐	N267SK	Embraer ERJ-145LR	145268	ex PT-SJK	437	Shuttle America [IGM]♦
☐	N268SK	Embraer ERJ-145LR	145270	ex PT-SJM		Shuttle America [IGM]♦
☐	N269SK	Embraer ERJ-145LR	145293	ex PT-SYG	269	Shuttle America♦
☐	N270SK	Embraer ERJ-145LR	145304	ex PT-SKV	270	Shuttle America♦
☐	N271SK	Embraer ERJ-145LR	145305	ex PT-SKW	8271	Shuttle America♦
☐	N272SK	Embraer ERJ-145LR	145306	ex PT-SKX	8272	Shuttle America
☐	N273SK	Embraer ERJ-145LR	145331	ex PT-SMX	8273	Shuttle America
☐	N274SK	Embraer ERJ-145LR	145344	ex PT-SNK	8274	Shuttle America
☐	N275SK	Embraer ERJ-145LR	145345	ex PT-SNL	439	Shuttle America wfs♦
☐	N276SK	Embraer ERJ-145LR	145348	ex PT-SNO	8276	Shuttle America♦
☐	N277SK	Embraer ERJ-145LR	145355	ex PT-SNU	440	Shuttle America wfs♦
☐	N278SK	Embraer ERJ-145LR	145370	ex PT-SOV	8278	Shuttle America♦
☐	N279SK	Embraer ERJ-145LR	145379	ex PT-SQD		Shuttle America wfs♦
☐	N280SK	Embraer ERJ-145LR	145381	ex PT-SQF	280	Shuttle America♦
☐	N281SK	Embraer ERJ-145LR	145391	ex PT-SQP	281	Shuttle America♦
☐	N282SL	Embraer ERJ-145LR	145409	ex PT-STG	282	Shuttle America {IGM}♦
☐	N283SK	Embraer ERJ-145LR	145424	ex PT-STV	442	Shuttle America [IGM]♦
☐	N284SK	Embraer ERJ-145LR	145427	ex PT-STY		Shuttle America [IGM]♦
☐	N285SK	Embraer ERJ-145LR	145435	ex PT-SUG	444	Shuttle America wfs♦
☐	N286SK	Embraer ERJ-145LR	145443	ex PT-SUO	817	Shuttle America ♦
☐	N287SK	Embraer ERJ-145LR	145460	ex PT-SVF	818	Shuttle America ♦
☐	N288SK	Embraer ERJ-145LR	145461	ex PT-SVG	288	Shuttle America ♦
☐	N289SK	Embraer ERJ-145LR	145463	ex PT-SVI		Shuttle America [IGM]♦
☐	N290SK	Embraer ERJ-145LR	145474	ex PT-SVT	290	Shuttle America♦
☐	N291SK	Embraer ERJ-145LR	145486	ex PT-SXF	JRX	Shuttle America wfs♦
☐	N292SK	Embraer ERJ-145LR	145488	ex PT-SXH		Shuttle America wfs♦
☐	N293SK	Embraer ERJ-145LR	145500	ex PT-SXT	293	Shuttle America♦

☐ N294SK	Embraer ERJ-145LR	145497	ex PT-SXQ	294	Shuttle America♦
☐ N296SK	Embraer ERJ-145LR	145514	ex PT-SYG	296	Shuttle America♦
☐ N298SK	Embraer ERJ-145LR	145508	ex PT-SYA	298	Shuttle America♦
☐ N370SK	Embraer ERJ-145LR	145515	ex PT-SYH	370	Shuttle America♦
☐ N561RP	Embraer ERJ-145LR	145447	ex PT-SUS	8561	Shuttle America
☐ N562RP	Embraer ERJ-145LR	145451	ex PT-SUW	8562	Shuttle America
☐ N563RP	Embraer ERJ-145LR	145509	ex PT-SYB	8563	Shuttle America
☐ N564RP	Embraer ERJ-145LR	145524	ex PT-SYP	8564	Shuttle America
☐ N565RP	Embraer ERJ-145LR	145679	ex PT-SFL	8565	Shuttle America
☐ N566RP	Embraer ERJ-145LR	145691	ex PT-SFX	8566	Shuttle America
☐ N567RP	Embraer ERJ-145LR	145698	ex PT-SGD	8567	Shuttle America
☐ N568RP	Embraer ERJ-145LR	145800	ex PT-SNE	8568	Shuttle America
☐ N569RP	Embraer ERJ-145LR	14500816	ex PT-SNR	8569	Shuttle America
☐ N570RP	Embraer ERJ-145LR	14500821	ex PT-SNV	8570	Shuttle America
☐ N571RP	Embraer ERJ-145LR	14500827	ex PT-SNZ	8571	Shuttle America
☐ N572RP	Embraer ERJ-145LR	14500828	ex PT-SQB	8572	Shuttle America
☐ N573RP	Embraer ERJ-145LR	14500837	ex PT-SQJ	8573	Shuttle America
☐ N574RP	Embraer ERJ-145LR	14500845	ex PT-SQP	8574	Shuttle America
☐ N575RP	Embraer ERJ-145LR	14500847	ex PT-SQR	8575	Shuttle America
☐ N576RP	Embraer ERJ-145LR	14500856	ex PT-SQX	8576	Shuttle America
☐ N577RP	Embraer ERJ-145LR	14500862	ex PT-SXC	8577	Shuttle America
☐ N578RP	Embraer ERJ-145LR	14500865	ex PT-SXE	8578	Shuttle America
☐ N579RP	Embraer ERJ-145LR	14500871	ex PT-SXI	8579	Shuttle America
☐ N973RP	Embraer ERJ-145LR	145444	ex XA-FLI		Shuttle America♦
☐ N974RP	Embraer ERJ-145MP	145203	ex XA-GLI		Shuttle America<TYR>DYN♦
☐ N975RP	Embraer ERJ-145MP	145337	ox XA-HLI		Shuttle America<TYR>DYN♦
☐ N976RP	Embraer ERJ-145MP	145322	ex XA-KAC		Shuttle America<I YR>DYN♦
☐ N746CZ	Embraer ERJ-170LR	17000180	ex VH-ZHA		Compass
☐ N747CZ	Embraer ERJ-170LR	17000187	ex VH-ZHB		Compass
☐ N748CZ	Embraer ERJ-170LR	17000191	ex VH-ZHC		Compass
☐ N749CZ	Embraer ERJ-170LR	17000227	ex VH-ZHD		Compass
☐ N751CZ	Embraer ERJ-170LR	17000247	ex VH-ZHE		Compass
☐ N752CZ	Embraer ERJ-170LR	17000255	ex VH-ZHF		Compass [BNA]
☐ N818MD	Embraer ERJ-170SU	17000039	ex PT-SUI	818	Republic♦
☐ N823MD	Embraer ERJ-170SU	17000044	ex PT-SUO		Shuttle America
☐ N824MD	Embraer ERJ-170SU	17000045	ex PT-SUO		Shuttle America
☐ N855RW	Embraer ERJ-170SE	17000077	ex PT-SZC		Shuttle America
☐ N859RW	Embraer ERJ-170SE	17000082	ex PT-SZH		Shuttle America
☐ N860RW	Embraer ERJ-170SE	17000084	ex PT-SZJ		Shuttle America
☐ N862RW	Embraer ERJ-170SE	17000098	ex PT-SZY		Shuttle America
☐ N867RW	Embraer ERJ-170SU	17000130	ex PT-SDT		Shuttle America
☐ N868RW	Embraer ERJ-170SU	17000131	ex PT-SDU		Shuttle America
☐ N869RW	Embraer ERJ-170SE	17000133	ex PT-SDW		Shuttle America
☐ N870RW	Embraer ERJ-170SE	17000138	ex PT-SEC		Shuttle America
☐ N602CZ	Embraer ERJ-175LR	17000171	ex PT-SMN		Compass
☐ N603CZ	Embraer ERJ-175LR	17000176	ex PT-SMT		Compass
☐ N604CZ	Embraer ERJ-175LR	17000181	ex PT-SMY		Compass
☐ N605CZ	Embraer ERJ-175LR	17000186	ex PT-SUD		Compass
☐ N606CZ	Embraer ERJ-175LR	17000188	ex PT-SUH		Compass
☐ N607CZ	Embraer ERJ-175LR	17000192	ex PT-SUT		Compass
☐ N608CZ	Embraer ERJ-175LR	17000195	ex PT-SXA		Compass
☐ N609CZ	Embraer ERJ-175LR	17000197	ex PT-SXJ		Compass
☐ N610CZ	Embraer ERJ-175LR	17000198	ex PT-SXK		Compass
☐ N612CZ	Embraer ERJ-175LR	17000201	ex PT-SXQ		Compass
☐ N613CZ	Embraer ERJ-175AR	17000203	ex PT-SXS		Compass
☐ N614CZ	Embraer ERJ-175AR	17000205	ex PT-SCA		Compass
☐ N615CZ	Embraer ERJ-175LR	17000207	ex PT-SCC		Compass
☐ N616CZ	Embraer ERJ-175LR	17000209	ex PT-SCG		Compass
☐ N617CZ	Embraer ERJ-175LR	17000210	ex PT-SCH		Compass
☐ N619CZ	Embraer ERJ-175LR	17000213	ex PT-SCK		Compass
☐ N620CZ	Embraer ERJ-175LR	17000214	ex PT-SCL		Compass
☐ N621CZ	Embraer ERJ-175LR	17000218	ex PT-SCP		Compass
☐ N622CZ	Embraer ERJ-175LR	17000219	ex PT-SCQ		Compass
☐ N623CZ	Embraer ERJ-175LR	17000221	ex PT-SCT		Compass
☐ N624CZ	Embraer ERJ-175LR	17000222	ex PT-SCX		Compass
☐ N625CZ	Embraer ERJ-175AR	17000225	ex PT-SFB		Compass
☐ N626CZ	Embraer ERJ-175AR	17000226	ex PT-SFC		Compass
☐ N627CZ	Embraer ERJ-175AR	17000229	ex PT-SFF		Compass
☐ N628CZ	Embraer ERJ-175AR	17000233	ex PT-SFJ		Compass
☐ N629CZ	Embraer ERJ-175AR	17000236	ex PT-SFM		Compass
☐ N630CZ	Embraer ERJ-175AR	17000238	ex PT-SFO		Compass
☐ N631CZ	Embraer ERJ-175AR	17000239	ex PT-SFP		Compass
☐ N632CZ	Embraer ERJ-175AR	17000244	ex PT-SFV		Compass
☐ N633CZ	Embraer ERJ-175AR	17000245	ex PT-SFW		Compass
☐ N634CZ	Embraer ERJ-175AR	17000246	ex PT-SFX		Compass
☐ N635CZ	Embraer ERJ-175AR	17000252	ex PT-SJD		Compass
☐ N636CZ	Embraer ERJ-175AR	17000253	ex PT-SJE		Compass
☐ N637CZ	Embraer ERJ-175AR	17000256	ex PT-SJI		Compass
☐ N638CZ	Embraer ERJ-175AR	17000259	ex PT-SJL		Compass

☐ N639CZ	Embraer ERJ-175AR	17000262	ex PT-SJP		Compass
☐ N201JQ	Embraer ERJ-175LR	17000235	ex PT-SFL		Shuttle America
☐ N202JQ	Embraer ERJ-175LR	17000240	ex PT-SFQ		Shuttle America
☐ N203JQ	Embraer ERJ-175LR	17000242	ex PT-SFT		Shuttle America
☐ N204JQ	Embraer ERJ-175LR	17000243	ex PT-SFU		Shuttle America
☐ N206JQ	Embraer ERJ-175LR	17000249	ex PT-SJA		Shuttle America
☐ N207JQ	Embraer ERJ-175LR	17000254	ex PT-SJG		Shuttle America
☐ N208JQ	Embraer ERJ-175LR	17000257	ex PT-SJJ		Shuttle America
☐ N209JQ	Embraer ERJ-175LR	17000258	ex PT-SJK		Shuttle America
☐ N210JQ	Embraer ERJ-175LR	17000260	ex PT-SJN		Shuttle America
☐ N211JQ	Embraer ERJ-175LR	17000261	ex PT-SJO		Shuttle America
☐ N212JQ	Embraer ERJ-175LR	17000264	ex PT-SJS		Shuttle America
☐ N213JQ	Embraer ERJ-175LR	17000265	ex PT-SJT		Shuttle America
☐ N214JQ	Embraer ERJ-175LR	17000267	ex PT-SJV		Shuttle America
☐ N215JQ	Embraer ERJ-175LR	17000270	ex PT-SNA		Shuttle America
☐ N216JQ	Embraer ERJ-175LR	17000273	ex PT-SNH		Shuttle America
☐ N958WH	Embraer ERJ-175LR	17000248	ex PT-SFZ	8205	Shuttle America
☐ N412XJ	SAAB SF.340B	340B-412	ex SE-B12		Mesaba
☐ N413XJ	SAAB SF.340B	340B-413	ex SE-B13		Mesaba
☐ N449XJ	SAAB SF.340B	340B-449	ex SE-B49		Mesaba
☐ N184CJ	SAAB SF.340B	340B-184	ex N300CE		Endeavor [BGR]
☐ N191MJ	SAAB SF.340B	340B-191	ex N301AE		Endeavor [BGR]
☐ N193CJ	SAAB SF.340B	340B-193	ex N302CE		Endeavor [BGR]
☐ N194CJ	SAAB SF.340B	340B-194	ex N303CE		Endeavor [AUW]
☐ N198CJ	SAAB SF.340B	340B-198	ex N304CE		Endeavor [BGR]
☐ N202SR	SAAB SF.340B	340B-202	ex N305CE		Endeavor [AUW]
☐ N203CJ	SAAB SF.340B	340B-203	ex N306CE		Endeavor [AUW]
☐ N204CJ	SAAB SF.340B	340B-204	ex N307CE		Endeavor [AUW]
☐ N210CJ	SAAB SF.340B	340B-210	ex N308CE		Endeavor [AUW]
☐ N277MJ	SAAB SF.340B	340B-277	ex N357BE		Endeavor [BGR]
☐ N362PX	SAAB SF.340B	340B-258	ex SE-G58		Endeavor [BGR]
☐ N334CJ	SAAB SF.340B	340B-334	ex N312CE		Endeavor [AUW]
☐ N341CJ	SAAB SF.340B	340B-341	ex N341SB		Endeavor [BGR]
☐ N344CJ	SAAB SF.340B	340B-344	ex N344SB		Endeavor [BGR]
☐ N346CJ	SAAB SF.340B	340B-346	ex N346SB		Endeavor [BGR]
☐ N350CJ	SAAB SF.340B	340B-350	ex N350CF		Endeavor [SGF]
☐ N352CJ	SAAB SF.340B	340B-352	ex N317CE		Endeavor [BGR]

DESERT AIR TRANSPORT — Anchorage, AK (ANC)

☐ N153PA	Convair 240-27	304	ex 51-7892	
☐ N272R	Douglas DC-3	13678	ex NC88824	
☐ N44587	Douglas DC-3	12857	ex N353SA	[ANC]

DOLPHIN AIRLINES

☐ N251SA	de Havilland DHC-6 Twin Otter 300	524	ex YV-529C
☐ N288SA	de Havilland DHC-6 Twin Otter 300	389	ex V2-LEY

DYNAMIC AIRWAYS/AVIATION — Dynamic Air (DYA) — Greensboro, NC (GSO)

☐ N253MY	Boeing 767-23BER	23974/214	ex I-AIGI	♦
☐ N254MY	Boeing 767-336ER	25443/419	ex VH-ZXG	♦
☐ N767DA	Boeing 767-246	23213/118	ex JA8232	
☐ N768DA	Boeing 767-246	23214/122	ex HS-JAD	wfs
☐ N881YV	Boeing 767-241ERF	23803/161	exN768QT	>21 Air♦
☐ N770JM	Boeing 767-233ER	24145/236	ex C-GDSY	
☐ N999YV	Boeing 767-241ERF	23801/1700	ex N769QT	>21 Air♦
☐ N897JM	Douglas DC-9-32	47592/712	ex C-FTMY	[MHV]
☐ N8100L	de Havilland DHC-8-103	146	ex N829EX	♦
☐ N8300S	de Havilland DHC-8-315Q	577	ex OY-CLI	[YYR]
☐ N8300T	de Havilland DHC-8-314	358	ex ZS-NMA	

EAGLE AIR TRANSPORT

☐ N10EA	de Havilland DHC-6 Twin Otter 200	199	ex C-FRXU
☐ N30EA	de Havilland DHC-6 Twin Otter 200	191	ex SE-KOK
☐ N40EA	Cessna 208A Caravan I	208A00065	ex N799FE
☐ N70EA	de Havilland DHC-6 Twin Otter 200	139	ex N719AS
☐ N220EA	Cessna 208B Caravan I	208B0151	ex N9697B

EASTERN AIRLINES — (EA/EAL) — Miami-Intl, FL (MIA)

☐ N266EA	Boeing 737-8AL/W	35070/2115	ex 5Y-KYB	Spirit of Captain Eddie Rickenbacker[MIA]♦

EG & G				Las Vegas-McCarran, NV (LAS)
☐ N273RH	Boeing 737-66N	29890/1276	ex N824SR	
☐ N288DP	Boeing 737-66N	29892/1305	ex N892SR	
☐ N319BD	Boeing 737-66N	28649/887	ex N649MT	
☐ N365SR	Boeing 737-66N	29891/1294	ex N891RD	
☐ N859WP	Boeing 737-66N	28652/938	ex N645DM	
☐ N869HH	Boeing 737-66N	28650/932	ex N628SR	
☐ N20RA	Beech 1900C	UB-42	ex (N272HK)	
☐ N623RA	Beech 1900C-1	UC-163	ex N3043L	
☐ N654BA	Beech B200C Super King Air	BL-54	ex N6563C	
☐ N661BA	Beech B200C Super King Air	BL-61	ex N6564C	
☐ N662BA	Beech B200C Super King Air	BL-62	ex N6566C	

ELITE AIRWAYS		Mainer (MNU)		Portland Intl, ME (PWM)
☐ N91EA	Canadair CRJ-200ER	7705	ex PH-ACJ	
☐ N92EA	Canadair CRJ-200ER	7732	ex EC-IKZ	
☐ N93EA	Canadair CRJ-200ER	7563	ex EC-IAA	
☐ N96EA	Canadair CRJ-200ER	7700	ex PH-ABY	
☐ N97EA	Canadair CRJ-100ER	7027	ex C-GRGQ	
☐ N	Canadair CRJ-701ER	10086	ex D-ACPP	♦

EMERALD COAST AIR				Mobile, AL
☐ N71EC	de Havilland DHC-6 Twin Otter 100	37	ex C-FDTJ	

EMPIRE AIRLINES	Empire Air (EM/EMO)	Coeur d'Alene, ID/Spokane-Intl, WA (COE/GEG)

Ops Cessna 208 Caravans and ATR 42/72s plus Fokker F.27 Friendship 500s leased from, and operated on behalf of, FedEx

ENDEAVOR AIR	Flagship (9E/FLG)	Memphis-Intl, TN/Minneapolis-St Paul Intl, MN (MEM/MSP)

Ops for Delta Connection; filed Chapter 11 01Apr12

ENVOY		Eagle Flight (MQ/ENY)		Dallas-Fort Worth, TX (DFW)
☐ N868CA	Canadair CRJ-100LR	7427	ex C-FMML	7427	SkyWest
☐ N417SW	Canadair CRJ-200ER	7400	ex C-FMMW	7400	SkyWest
☐ N423SW	Canadair CRJ-200ER	7456	ex C-FMMB	7456	SkyWest
☐ N435SW	Canadair CRJ-200ER	7555	ex C-GJHK	7555	SkyWest
☐ N464SW	Canadair CRJ-200ER	7827	ex C-FMLB	7827	SkyWest
☐ N862AS	Canadair CRJ-200ER	7476	ex C-FMNW	7476	ExpressJet>SKW
☐ N863AS	Canadair CRJ-200ER	7487	ex C-FMML	7487	ExpressJet>SKW
☐ N864AS	Canadair CRJ-200ER	7502	ex C-FMLT	864	ExpressJet>SKW
☐ N866AS	Canadair CRJ-200ER	7517	ex C-FMML	7517	ExpressJet>SKW
☐ N869AS	Canadair CRJ-200ER	7479	ex C-FMOS	869	ExpressJet>SKW
☐ N955SW	Canadair CRJ-200ER	7817	ex C-FMML	7817	SkyWest♦
☐ N500AE	Canadair CRJ-701ER	10025	ex C-GJEX		
☐ N501BG	Canadair CRJ-701ER	10017	ex C-GIAH		
☐ N502AE	Canadair CRJ-701ER	10018	ex C-GJUI		
☐ N503AE	Canadair CRJ-701ER	10021	ex C-GIAP		
☐ N504AE	Canadair CRJ-701ER	10044	ex C-GHZZ		
☐ N505AE	Canadair CRJ-701ER	10053	ex C-GIAU		
☐ N506AE	Canadair CRJ-701ER	10056	ex C-GIAX		
☐ N507AE	Canadair CRJ-701ER	10059	ex C-GIBH		
☐ N508AE	Canadair CRJ-701ER	10072	ex C-GHZV		
☐ N509AE	Canadair CRJ-701ER	10078	ex C-GZUC		
☐ N510AE	Canadair CRJ-701ER	10105			
☐ N511AE	Canadair CRJ-701ER	10107			
☐ N512AE	Canadair CRJ-701ER	10110			
☐ N513AE	Canadair CRJ-701ER	10114			
☐ N514AE	Canadair CRJ-701ER	10119			
☐ N515AE	Canadair CRJ-701ER	10121			
☐ N516AE	Canadair CRJ-701ER	10123			
☐ N517AE	Canadair CRJ-701ER	10124			
☐ N518AE	Canadair CRJ-701ER	10126			
☐ N519AE	Canadair CRJ-701ER	10131			
☐ N520DC	Canadair CRJ-701ER	10140			
☐ N521AE	Canadair CRJ-701ER	10142			
☐ N522AE	Canadair CRJ-701ER	10147			
☐ N523AE	Canadair CRJ-701ER	10152			
☐ N524AE	Canadair CRJ-701ER	10154			
☐ N525AE	Canadair CRJ-702ER	10302	ex C-GIAX		
☐ N526EA	Canadair CRJ-702ER	10304	ex C-GICL		
☐ N527EA	Canadair CRJ-702ER	10305	ex C-GIAP		
☐ N528EG	Canadair CRJ-702ER	10306			
☐ N529EA	Canadair CRJ-702ER	10307			

☐ N530EA	Canadair CRJ-702ER	10308				
☐ N531EG	Canadair CRJ-702ER	10309	ex C-GIAO			
☐ N532EA	Canadair CRJ-702ER	10310	ex C-GIBJ			
☐ N533AE	Canadair CRJ-702ER	10311	ex C-GIBR			
☐ N534AE	Canadair CRJ-702ER	10312	ex C-GZQA			
☐ N535EA	Canadair CRJ-702ER	10313	ex C-GZQX			
☐ N536EA	Canadair CRJ-702ER	10315	ex C-GIAH			
☐ N537EA	Canadair CRJ-702ER	10316	ex C-GIAP			
☐ N538EG	Canadair CRJ-702ER	10317				
☐ N539EA	Canadair CRJ-702ER	10318				
☐ N540EG	Canadair CRJ-702ER	10319	ex C-GIAV			
☐ N541EA	Canadair CRJ-702ER	10320	ex C-GZQF			
☐ N542EA	Canadair CRJ-702ER	10321	ex C-GZQI			
☐ N543EA	Canadair CRJ-702ER	10323	ex C-GZQV			
☐ N544EA	Canadair CRJ-702ER	10324	ex C-GICL			
☐ N545PB	Canadair CRJ-702ER	10325	ex C-GZQO			
☐ N546FF	Canadair CRJ-702ER	10326	ex C-GZQP			
☐ N241LR	Canadair CRJ-900ER	15066	ex EI-DOT	CYA		Mesa♦
☐ N942LR	Canadair CRJ-900ER	15076	ex EI-DRI			Mesa♦
☐ N943LR	Canadair CRJ-900ER	15068	ex EI-DOU			Mesa♦
☐ N946LR	Canadair CRJ-900ER	15104	ex EI-DUK			Mesa♦
☐ N547NN	Canadair CRJ-900	15317	ex C-GWGQ			PSA♦
☐ N548NN	Canadair CRJ-900	15318				PSA♦
☐ N549NN	Canadair CRJ-900	15322	ex C-GICL			PSA♦
☐ N550NN	Canadair CRJ-900	15323	ex C-GIAH			PSA♦
☐ N551NN	Canadair CRJ-900	15327	ex C-GICP			PSA♦
☐ N552NN	Canadair CRJ-900	15328				PSA♦
☐ N553NN	Canadair CRJ-900	15333				PSA♦
☐ N554NN	Canadair CRJ-900	15334				PSA♦
☐ N555NN	Canadair CRJ-900	15338		555		PSA♦
☐ N556NN	Canadair CRJ-900	15339	ex C-GWFV	556		PSA♦
☐ N557NN	Canadair CRJ-900	15340		557		PSA♦
☐ N558NN	Canadair CRJ-900	15342		558		PSA♦
☐ N559NN	Canadair CRJ-900	15343		559		PSA♦
☐ N560NN	Canadair CRJ-900	15345		560		PSA♦
☐ N561NN	Canadair CRJ-900	15346		561		PSA♦
☐ N562NN	Canadair CRJ-900	15347	ex C-GZUH	562		PSA♦
☐ N563NN	Canadair CRJ-900	15350	ex C-GZUR	563		PSA♦
☐ N564NN	Canadair CRJ-900	15351	ex C-GZUY	564		PSA♦
☐ N565NN	Canadair CRJ-900	15352	ex C-GZVR	565		PSA♦
☐ N566NN	Canadair CRJ-900	15353	ex C-GZVU	566		PSA♦
☐ N567NN	Canadair CRJ-900	15354	ex C-GZWO	567		PSA♦
☐ N568NN	Canadair CRJ-900	15355	ex C-GZWV	568		PSA♦
☐ N569NN	Canadair CRJ-900	15356	ex C-GZXH	569		PSA♦
☐ N570NN	Canadair CRJ-900	15357	ex C-GZXU	570		PSA♦
☐ N571NN	Canadair CRJ-900	15360		571		PSA♦
☐ N572NN	Canadair CRJ-900	15361	ex C-GIBN	572		PSA♦
☐ N573NN	Canadair CRJ-900	15362	ex C-GIBT	573		PSA♦
☐ N574NN	Canadair CRJ-900	15365		574		PSA♦
☐ N575NN	Canadair CRJ-900	15366		575		PSA♦
☐ N576NN	Canadair CRJ-900	15367		576		PSA♦
☐ N329EN	de Havilland DHC-8-311	290	ex SU-UAD	HDG		Piedmont♦
☐ N337EN	de Havilland DHC-8-311A	284	ex SU-UAE	HDH		Piedmont♦
☐ N800AE	Embraer ERJ-140LR	145425	ex PT-XGF			wfs
☐ N801AE	Embraer ERJ-140LR	145469	ex PT-SVO			wfs
☐ N802AE	Embraer ERJ-140LR	145471	ex PT-SVQ			wfs
☐ N803AE	Embraer ERJ-140LR	145483	ex PT-SXC	100th ERJ	Spirit of Eagle titles	wfs
☐ N804AE	Embraer ERJ-140LR	145487	ex PT-SXG			
☐ N805AE	Embraer ERJ-140LR	145489	ex PT-SXI			wfs
☐ N806AE	Embraer ERJ-140LR	145503	ex PT-SXW			
☐ N807AE	Embraer ERJ-140LR	145506	ex PT-SXZ		Make A Wish c/s	wfs
☐ N808AE	Embraer ERJ-140LR	145519	ex PT-SYK			
☐ N809AE	Embraer ERJ-140LR	145521	ex PT-SYM			
☐ N810AE	Embraer ERJ-140LR	145525	ex PT-SYQ			wfs
☐ N811AE	Embraer ERJ-140LR	145529	ex PT-STT			wfs
☐ N812AE	Embraer ERJ-140LR	145531	ex PT-STV			wfs
☐ N813AE	Embraer ERJ-140LR	145539	ex PT-SZD			
☐ N814AE	Embraer ERJ-140LR	145541	ex PT-SZF			wfs
☐ N815AE	Embraer ERJ-140LR	145545	ex PT-SZI			
☐ N816AE	Embraer ERJ-140LR	145552	ex PT-SZO			wfs
☐ N817AE	Embraer ERJ-140LR	145554	ex PT-SZQ			
☐ N818AE	Embraer ERJ-140LR	145561	ex PT-SZW			
☐ N819AE	Embraer ERJ-140LR	145566	ex PT-SBC			
☐ N820AE	Embraer ERJ-140LR	145576	ex PT-SBM			
☐ N821AE	Embraer ERJ-140LR	145577	ex PT-SBN			
☐ N822AE	Embraer ERJ-140LR	145581	ex PT-SBS			
☐ N823AE	Embraer ERJ-140LR	145582	ex PT-SBT			
☐ N824AE	Embraer ERJ-140LR	145584	ex PT-SBV			
☐ N825AE	Embraer ERJ-140LR	145589	ex PT-SBZ			

☐ N826AE	Embraer ERJ-140LR	145592	ex PT-SCA		
☐ N827AE	Embraer ERJ-140LR	145602	ex PT-SCL		
☐ N828AE	Embraer ERJ-140LR	145604	ex PT-SCN		
☐ N829AE	Embraer ERJ-140LR	145609	ex PT-SCS		
☐ N830AE	Embraer ERJ-140LR	145615	ex PT-SDD		
☐ N831AE	Embraer ERJ-140LR	145616	ex PT-SDE		
☐ N832AE	Embraer ERJ-140LR	145627	ex PT-SDP	wfs	
☐ N833AE	Embraer ERJ-140LR	145629	ex PT-SDR		
☐ N834AE	Embraer ERJ-140LR	145631	ex PT-SDT	wfs	
☐ N835AE	Embraer ERJ-140LR	145634	ex PT-SDW	wfs	
☐ N836AE	Embraer ERJ-140LR	145635	ex PT-SDX		
☐ N837AE	Embraer ERJ-140LR	145647	ex PT-SEH	wfs	
☐ N838AE	Embraer ERJ-140LR	145651	ex PT-SEL		
☐ N839AE	Embraer ERJ-140LR	145653	ex PT-SEN		
☐ N840AE	Embraer ERJ-140LR	145656	ex PT-SEQ	[SJT]	
☐ N841AE	Embraer ERJ-140LR	145667	ex PT-SFB		
☐ N842AE	Embraer ERJ-140LR	145673	ex PT-SFG		
☐ N843AE	Embraer ERJ-140LR	145680	ex PT-SFM		
☐ N844AE	Embraer ERJ-140LR	145682	ex PT-SFO		
☐ N845AE	Embraer ERJ-140LR	145685	ex PT-SFR		
☐ N846AE	Embraer ERJ-140LR	145692	ex PT-SFY		
☐ N847AE	Embraer ERJ-140LR	145707	ex PT-SGK		
☐ N848AE	Embraer ERJ-140LR	145710	ex PT-SGO		
☐ N849AE	Embraer ERJ-140LR	145716	ex PT-SGT	wfs	
☐ N850AE	Embraer ERJ-140LR	145722	ex PT-SGY		
☐ N851AE	Embraer ERJ-140LR	145734	ex PT-SHK		
☐ N852AE	Embraer ERJ-140LR	145736	ex PT-SHM		
☐ N853AE	Embraer ERJ-140LR	145742	ex PT-SJB		
☐ N854AE	Embraer ERJ-140LR	145743	ex PT-SJC		
☐ N855AE	Embraer ERJ-140LR	145747	ex PT-SJG		
☐ N856AE	Embraer ERJ-140LR	145748	ex PT-SJH		
☐ N857AE	Embraer ERJ-140LR	145752	ex PT-SJL		
☐ N858AE	Embraer ERJ-140LR	145754	ex PT-SJN	[SJT]	
☐ N600BP	Embraer ERJ-145LR	145044	ex N813HK		
☐ N601DW	Embraer ERJ-145LR	145046	ex N814HK		
☐ N602AE	Embraer ERJ-145LR	145048	ex N815HK		
☐ N603KC	Embraer ERJ-145LR	145055	ex N816HK		
☐ N604AE	Embraer ERJ-145LR	145058	ex N604DG		
☐ N605KS	Embraer ERJ-145LR	145059	ex N818HK		
☐ N607AE	Embraer ERJ-145LR	145064	ex N820HK		
☐ N608LM	Embraer ERJ-145LR	145068	ex N821HK		
☐ N609DP	Embraer ERJ-145LR	145069	ex N822HK		
☐ N610AE	Embraer ERJ-145LR	145073	ex PT-SAR		
☐ N611AE	Embraer ERJ-145LR	145074	ex PT-SAS		
☐ N612AE	Embraer ERJ-145LR	145079	ex PT-SAX		
☐ N613AE	Embraer ERJ-145LR	145081	ex (N826HK)		
☐ N614AE	Embraer ERJ-145LR	145086			
☐ N615AE	Embraer ERJ-145LR	145087			
☐ N616AE	Embraer ERJ-145LR	145092			
☐ N617AE	Embraer ERJ-145LR	145093	ex PT-SBP		
☐ N618AE	Embraer ERJ-145LR	145097	ex PT-SBT		
☐ N619AE	Embraer ERJ-145LR	145101			
☐ N620AE	Embraer ERJ-145LR	145102			
☐ N621AE	Embraer ERJ-145LR	145105			
☐ N622AE	Embraer ERJ-145LR	145108			
☐ N623AE	Embraer ERJ-145LR	145109			
☐ N624AE	Embraer ERJ-145LR	145111			
☐ N625AE	Embraer ERJ-145LR	145115	ex PT-SCR		
☐ N626AE	Embraer ERJ-145LR	145117	ex PT-SCT		
☐ N627AE	Embraer ERJ-145LR	145121	ex PT-SCX		
☐ N628AE	Embraer ERJ-145LR	145124	ex PT-SDA		
☐ N629AE	Embraer ERJ-145LR	145130	ex PT-SDH		
☐ N630AE	Embraer ERJ-145LR	145132	ex PT-SDJ		
☐ N631AE	Embraer ERJ-145LR	145139	ex PT-SDQ		
☐ N632AE	Embraer ERJ-145LR	145143	ex PT-SDT		
☐ N633AE	Embraer ERJ-145LR	145148	ex PT-SDY		
☐ N634AE	Embraer ERJ-145LR	145150	ex PT-SEB		
☐ N635AE	Embraer ERJ-145LR	145158			
☐ N636AE	Embraer ERJ-145LR	145160			
☐ N637AE	Embraer ERJ-145LR	145170			
☐ N638AE	Embraer ERJ-145LR	145172			
☐ N639AE	Embraer ERJ-145LR	145182	ex PT-SGE		
☐ N640AE	Embraer ERJ-145LR	145183	ex PT-SGF		
☐ N641AE	Embraer ERJ-145LR	145191	ex PT-SGJ		
☐ N642AE	Embraer ERJ-145LR	145193	ex PT-SGK		
☐ N643AE	Embraer ERJ-145LR	145200		200th titles	
☐ N644AE	Embraer ERJ-145LR	145204	ex PT-SGW		
☐ N645AE	Embraer ERJ-145LR	145212	ex PT-SGZ		
☐ N646AE	Embraer ERJ-145LR	145213	ex PT-SHA		
☐ N647AE	Embraer ERJ-145LR	145222	ex PT-SHH		
☐ N648AE	Embraer ERJ-145LR	145225	ex PT-SHJ		
☐ N649PP	Embraer ERJ-145LR	145234	ex PT-SIB		

☐ N650AE	Embraer ERJ-145LR	145417	ex PT-STO		
☐ N651AE	Embraer ERJ-145LR	145422	ex PT-STT		
☐ N652RS	Embraer ERJ-145LR	145432	ex PT-SUD		
☐ N653AE	Embraer ERJ-145LR	145433	ex PT-SUE		
☐ N654AE	Embraer ERJ-145LR	145437	ex PT-SUI		
☐ N655AE	Embraer ERJ-145LR	145452	ex PT-SUX		
☐ N656AE	Embraer ERJ-145LR	145740	ex PT-SHV		
☐ N657AE	Embraer ERJ-145LR	145744	ex PT-SJD		
☐ N658AE	Embraer ERJ-145LR	145760	ex PT-SJO		
☐ N659AE	Embraer ERJ-145LR	145762	ex PT-SJT		
☐ N660CL	Embraer ERJ-145LR	145764	ex PT-SJV		
☐ N661JA	Embraer ERJ-145LR	145766	ex PT-SJX		
☐ N662EH	Embraer ERJ-145LR	145777	ex PT-SMG		
☐ N663AR	Embraer ERJ-145LR	145778	ex PT-SMH		
☐ N664MS	Embraer ERJ-145LR	145779	ex PT-SMI		
☐ N665BC	Embraer ERJ-145LR	145783	ex PT-SMK		
☐ N668HH	Embraer ERJ-145LR	145785	ex PT-SMM		
☐ N669MB	Embraer ERJ-145LR	145788	ex PT-SMQ		
☐ N670AE	Embraer ERJ-145LR	145790	ex PT-SMR		
☐ N672AE	Embraer ERJ-145LR	145794	ex PT-SMV		
☐ N674RJ	Embraer ERJ-145LR	14500801	ex PT-SNF		
☐ N678AE	Embraer ERJ-145LR	14500813	ex PT-SNP		
☐ N679AE	Embraer ERJ-145LR	14500814	ex PT-SNQ		
☐ N681AE	Embraer ERJ-145LR	14500824	ex PT-SNX		
☐ N682AE	Embraer ERJ-145LR	14500826	ex PT-SNY		
☐ N683AE	Embraer ERJ-145LR	14500833	ex PT-SQF		
☐ N686AE	Embraer ERJ-145LR	14500843	ex PT-SQN		
☐ N688AE	Embraer ERJ-145LR	14500849	ex PT-SQS		
☐ N689EC	Embraer ERJ-145LR	14500853	ex PT-SQV		
☐ N690AE	Embraer ERJ-145LR	14500858	ex PT-SXM		
☐ N691AE	Embraer ERJ-145LR	14500860	ex PT-SXA		
☐ N692AE	Embraer ERJ-145LR	14500866	ex PT-SXF		
☐ N693AE	Embraer ERJ-145LR	14500868	ex PT-SXG		
☐ N694AE	Embraer ERJ-145LR	14500869	ex PT-SXN		
☐ N695AE	Embraer ERJ-145LR	14500870	ex PT-SXH		
☐ N696AE	Embraer ERJ-145LR	14500874	ex PT-SXO		
☐ N697AB	Embraer ERJ-145LR	14500875	ex PT-SXQ		
☐ N698CB	Embraer ERJ-145LR	14500877	ex PT-SXS		
☐ N699AE	Embraer ERJ-145LR	14500883	ex PT-SXW		
☐ N900AE	Embraer ERJ-145LR	14500885	ex PT-SXX		
☐ N902BC	Embraer ERJ-145LR	14500887	ex PT-SXZ		
☐ N905JH	Embraer ERJ-145LR	14500892	ex PT-SYE		
☐ N906AE	Embraer ERJ-145LR	14500894	ex PT-SYG		
☐ N907AE	Embraer ERJ-145LR	14500895	ex PT-SYH		
☐ N908AE	Embraer ERJ-145LR	14500897	ex PT-SYJ		
☐ N909AE	Embraer ERJ-145LR	14500899	ex PT-SYK		
☐ N918AE	Embraer ERJ-145LR	14500902	ex PT-SYM		
☐ N922AE	Embraer ERJ-145LR	14500906	ex PT-SYO		
☐ N923AE	Embraer ERJ-145LR	14500907	ex PT-SYQ		
☐ N925AE	Embraer ERJ-145LR	14500908	ex PT-SYR		
☐ N928AE	Embraer ERJ-145LR	14500911	ex PT-SYT		
☐ N931AE	Embraer ERJ-145LR	14500912	ex PT-SYU		
☐ N932AE	Embraer ERJ-145LR	14500915	ex PT-SYW		
☐ N933JN	Embraer ERJ-145LR	14500918	ex PT-SYY		
☐ N935AE	Embraer ERJ-145LR	14500920	ex PT-SYZ		
☐ N939AE	Embraer ERJ-145LR	14500923	ex PT-SOU		
☐ N941LT	Embraer ERJ-145LR	14500926	ex PT-SOW		
☐ N942LL	Embraer ERJ-145LR	14500930	ex PT-SOZ		
☐ N667GB	Embraer ERJ-145LR	145784	ex PT-SML		ExpressJet♦
☐ N671AE	Embraer ERJ-145LR	145793	ex PT-SMU		ExpressJet♦
☐ N673AE	Embraer ERJ-145LR	145797	ex PT-SMX		ExpressJet♦
☐ N675AE	Embraer ERJ-145LR	14500806	ex PT-SNI		ExpressJet♦
☐ N676AE	Embraer ERJ-145LR	14500807	ex PT-SNJ		ExpressJet♦
☐ N677AE	Embraer ERJ-145LR	14500810	ex PT-SNL		ExpressJet♦
☐ N680AE	Embraer ERJ-145LR	14500820	ex PT-SNU		ExpressJet♦
☐ N684JW	Embraer ERJ-145LR	14500835	ex PT-SQH		ExpressJet♦
☐ N685AE	Embraer ERJ-145LR	14500836	ex PT-SQI		ExpressJet♦
☐ N687JS	Embraer ERJ-145LR	14500846	ex PT-SQQ		ExpressJet♦
☐ N606AE	Embraer ERJ-145LR	145062	ex N819HK		TransStates♦
☐ N200NN	Embraer ERJ-175LR	17000456	ex PR-EKE	0	Compass♦
☐ N201NN	Embraer ERJ-175LR	17000461	ex PR-EKK	1	Compass♦
☐ N202NN	Embraer ERJ-175LR	17000467	ex PR-EKS	2	Compass♦
☐ N203NN	Embraer ERJ-175LR	17000473	ex PR-EKY	3	Compass♦
☐ N204NN	Embraer ERJ-175LR	17000477	ex PR-	4	Compass o/o♦
☐ N401YX	Embraer ERJ-175LR	17000363	ex PR-EAH	A01	Republic
☐ N402YX	Embraer ERJ-175LR	17000364	ex PR-EAI	A02	Republic
☐ N403YX	Embraer ERJ-175LR	17000365	ex PR-EAK	A03	Republic
☐ N404YX	Embraer ERJ-175LR	17000367	ex PR-EAY	A04	Republic
☐ N405YX	Embraer ERJ-175LR	17000368	ex PR-EBO	A05	Republic

☐ N406YX	Embraer ERJ-175LR	17000369	ex PR-EBP	A06		Republic
☐ N407YX	Embraer ERJ-175LR	17000370	ex PR-EBU	A07		Republic
☐ N408YX	Embraer ERJ-175LR	17000371	ex PR-EBX	A08		Republic
☐ N409YX	Embraer ERJ-175LR	17000372	ex PR-EBY	A09		Republic
☐ N410YX	Embraer ERJ-175LR	17000373	ex PR-ECL	A10		Republic
☐ N411YX	Embraer ERJ-175LR	17000374	ex PR-ECQ	A11		Republic
☐ N412YX	Embraer ERJ-175LR	17000375	ex PR-ECS	A12		Republic
☐ N413YX	Embraer ERJ-175LR	17000376	ex PR-ECX	A13		Republic
☐ N414YX	Embraer ERJ-175LR	17000377	ex PR-ECY	A14		Republic
☐ N415YX	Embraer ERJ-175LR	17000378	ex PR-EDB	A15		Republic
☐ N416YX	Embraer ERJ-175LR	17000381	ex PR-EDO	A16		Republic
☐ N417YX	Embraer ERJ-175LR	17000382	ex PR-EDQ	A17		Republic
☐ N418YX	Embraer ERJ-175LR	17000383	ex PR-EDT	A18		Republic
☐ N419YX	Embraer ERJ-175LR	17000384	ex PR-EEA	A19		Republic
☐ N420YX	Embraer ERJ-175LR	17000385	ex PR-EEC	A20		Republic
☐ N421YX	Embraer ERJ-175LR	17000386	ex PR-EEG	A21		Republic
☐ N422YX	Embraer ERJ-175LR	17000387	ex PR-EEH	A22		Republic
☐ N423YX	Embraer ERJ-175LR	17000392	ex PR-EEV	A23		Republic
☐ N424YX	Embraer ERJ-175LR	17000393	ex PR-EEW	A24		Republic
☐ N425YX	Embraer ERJ-175LR	17000396	ex PR-EFG	A25		Republic
☐ N426YX	Embraer ERJ-175LR	17000397	ex PR-EFI	A26		Republic♦
☐ N427YX	Embraer ERJ-175LR	17000402	ex PR-EFV	A27		Republic♦
☐ N428YX	Embraer ERJ-175LR	17000403	ex PR-EFW	A28		Republic♦
☐ N429YX	Embraer ERJ-175LR	17000408	ex PR-EGN	A29		Republic♦
☐ N430YX	Embraer ERJ-175LR	17000409	ex PR-EGQ	A30		Republic♦
☐ N431YX	Embraer ERJ-175LR	17000413	ex PR-EGX	A31		Republic♦
☐ N432YX	Embraer ERJ-175LR	17000415	ex PR-EGZ	A32		Republic♦
☐ N433YX	Embraer ERJ-175LR	17000416	ex PR-EHC	A33		Republic♦
☐ N434YX	Embraer ERJ-175LR	19000418	ex PR-EHD	A34		Republic♦
☐ N435YX	Embraer ERJ-175LR	17000423	ex PR-EHN	A35		Republic♦
☐ N436YX	Embraer ERJ-175LR	17000424	ex PR-EHO	A36		Republic♦
☐ N437YX	Embraer ERJ-175LR	17000366	ex PR-EAU	A37		Republic♦
☐ N438YX	Embraer ERJ-175LR	17000428	ex PR-EHT	A38		Republic♦
☐ N439YX	Embraer ERJ-175LR	17000434	ex PR-EHZ	A39		Republic♦
☐ N440YX	Embraer ERJ-175LR	17000435	ex PR-EIA	A40		Republic♦
☐ N441YX	Embraer ERJ-175LR	17000444	ex PR-EIR	A41		Republic♦
☐ N442YX	Embraer ERJ-175LR	17000446	ex PR-EIT	A42		Republic♦
☐ N443YX	Embraer ERJ-175LR	17000447	ex PR-EIU	A43		Republic♦
☐ N444YX	Embraer ERJ-175LR	17000453	ex PR-EKB	A44		Republic♦
☐ N445YX	Embraer ERJ-175LR	17000455	ex PR-EKD	A45		Republic♦
☐ N446YX	Embraer ERJ-175LR	17000457	ex PR-EKF	A46		Republic♦
☐ N447YX	Embraer ERJ-175LR	17000463	ex PR-EKM	A47		Republic♦

EP AVIATION/AAR AIRLIFT

☐ N602AR	CASA C212-200	161	ex 9H-AAR	
☐ N603AR	CASA C212-200	162	ex 9H-AAS	
☐ N604AR	CASA C212-200	289	ex N966BW	
☐ N605AR	CASA C212-200	290	exN962BW	
☐ N606AR	CASA C212-200	304	ex N967BW	
☐ N607AR	CASA C212-200	309	ex N2357G	
☐ N620AR	CASA C212-200	379	ex N6369C	♦
☐ N621AR	CASA C212-200	393	ex N4399T	♦
☐ N961BW	CASA C212-200	248	ex N202FN	
☐ N963BW	CASA C212-200	320	ex N204FN	
☐ N969BW	CASA C212-200	262	ex N262MA	
☐ N511AV	de Havilland DHC-8-103	051	ex C-GAAN	
☐ N634AR	de Havilland DHC-8-103	003	ex N810LR	
☐ N635AR	de Havilland DHC-8-103	047	ex N801LR	
☐ N636AR	de Havilland DHC-8-102	086	ex N150RN	
☐ N637AR	de Havilland DHC-8-102	265	ex N308RD	
☐ N638AR	de Havilland DHC-8-103	389	ex N826EX	
☐ N979HA	de Havilland DHC-8-103	373	ex C-GFQL	
☐ N990AV	de Havilland DHC-8-102	099	ex C-GZTC	
☐ N654AR	Swearingen SA226DC Metro 23	DC-868B	ex C-FAFI	
☐ N850AR	Sikorsky S-92A	920140	ex N140SR	
☐ N851AR	Sikorsky S-92A	920142	ex N142KT	
☐ N955BW	Swearingen SA226DC Metro 23	DC-821B	ex N821JB	
☐ N956BW	Swearingen SA227DC Metro 23	DC-864B	ex C-GKAF	
☐ N1269J	CASA CN235-10	C012	ex N983BW	
☐ N2696S	CASA CN235-10	C007	ex N981BW	

ERA HELICOPTERS   Anchorage-Intl South, AK/Lake Charles-Regional, LA (ANC/LCH)

☐ N108TA	Aérospatiale AS350BA AStar	3080
☐ N109TA	Aérospatiale AS350B2 AStar	3103
☐ N118TA	Aérospatiale AS350B2 AStar	3110
☐ N159JK	Aérospatiale AS350B2 AStar	3253
☐ N161EH	Aérospatiale AS350B2 AStar	2144
☐ N166EH	Aérospatiale AS350B2 AStar	2194

☐ N178EH	Aérospatiale AS350B2 AStar	2264	
☐ N181EH	Aérospatiale AS350B2 AStar	2680	
☐ N182EH	Aérospatiale AS350B2 AStar	2681	
☐ N183EH	Aérospatiale AS350B2 AStar	2752	
☐ N185EH	Aérospatiale AS350B2 AStar	2823	
☐ N186EH	Aérospatiale AS350B2 AStar	2844	
☐ N187EH	Aérospatiale AS350B2 AStar	2839	
☐ N188EH	Aérospatiale AS350B2 AStar	2954	
☐ N190EH	Aérospatiale AS350B2 AStar	2974	
☐ N191EH	Aérospatiale AS350B2 AStar	2505	
☐ N192EH	Aérospatiale AS350B2 AStar	2582	
☐ N193EH	Aérospatiale AS350B2 AStar	2599	
☐ N194EH	Aérospatiale AS350B2 AStar	2608	
☐ N195EH	Aérospatiale AS350B2 AStar	2615	
☐ N196EH	Aérospatiale AS350B2 AStar	2976	
☐ N212EH	Aérospatiale AS350B2 AStar	3151	
☐ N214EH	Aérospatiale AS350B2 AStar	3163	
☐ N215EH	Aérospatiale AS350B2 AStar	3172	
☐ N216EH	Aérospatiale AS350B2 AStar	3184	
☐ N217EH	Aérospatiale AS350B2 AStar	3197	
☐ N217FD	Aérospatiale AS350B2 AStar	4221	ex N646PT
☐ N323AH	Aérospatiale AS350B2 Astar	4649	
☐ N328BF	Aérospatiale AS350B2 AStar	4284	
☐ N420JA	Aérospatiale AS350B2 AStar	4212	
☐ N603WB	Aérospatiale AS350B2 Astar	4225	
☐ N725SG	Aérospatiale AS350B2 AStar	2856	ex N43MH
☐ N747WB	Aérospatiale AS350B2 AStar	2768	
☐ N4061G	Aérospatiale AS350BA Ecureuil	3051	ex F-OHVB
☐ N40584	Aérospatiale AS350B2 Ecureiul	2924	ex F-OHNT
☐ N18EA	Agusta A109E Power	11210	ex N261CF
☐ N334JT	Agusta A109E Power	11738	
☐ N512LD	Agusta A109E Power	11683	
☐ N530KS	Agusta A109E Power	11694	
☐ N820FT	Agusta A109E Power	11701	
☐ N903RW	Agusta A109E Power	11601	ex N3ZJ
☐ N910LB	Agusta A109E Power	11682	
☐ N108AG	Agusta A119 Koala	14053	ex N911AM
☐ N126RD	Agusta A119 Koala	14504	ex N6QY
☐ N203JP	Agusta A119 Koala	14535	
☐ N330JN	Agusta A119 Koala	14510	
☐ N514RE	Agusta A119 Koala II	14701	
☐ N602FB	Agusta A119 Koala	14528	
☐ N628RL	Agusta A119 Koala II	14713	
☐ N709CG	Agusta A119 Koala	14052	ex N18YC
☐ N715RT	Agusta A119 Koala	14516	
☐ N802SM	Agusta A119 Koala II	14711	
☐ N822MM	Agusta A119 Koala	14055	ex N6QX
☐ N915BE	Agusta A119 Koala	14519	
☐ N920JD	Agusta A119 Koala II	14754	ex N920LD
☐ N109DR	AgustaWestland AW139	31311	
☐ N113CV	AgustaWestland AW139	31390	
☐ N119MW	AgustaWestland AW139	41307	
☐ N159RB	AgustaWestland AW139	41281	♦
☐ N328SH	AgustaWestland AW139	41309	
☐ N403CB	AgustaWestland AW139	41206	ex N116YS
☐ N404JG	AgustaWestland AW139	41351	
☐ N415JH	AgustaWestland AW139	41224	
☐ N482LA	AgustaWestland AW139	41272	
☐ N524JD	AgustaWestland AW139	41301	
☐ N540DJ	AgustaWestland AW139	41002	
☐ N553RD	AgustaWestland AW139	41369	♦
☐ N561RV	AgustaWestland AW139	41263	♦
☐ N603PW	AgustaWestland AW139	31309	
☐ N604DP	AgustaWestland AW139	44352	
☐ N726MD	AgustaWestland AW139	41320	
☐ N730VM	AgustaWestland AW139	41362	♦
☐ N804CB	AgustaWestland AW139	41277	
☐ N808FG	AgustaWestland AW139	31383	
☐ N811TA	AgustaWestland AW139	41269	
☐ N829SN	AgustaWestland AW139	41244	ex N471SM
☐ N971TG	AgustaWestland AW139	41333	
☐ N357EH	Bell 212	31209	
☐ N358EH	Bell 212	31211	
☐ N359EH	Bell 212	31212	ex C-GRVN
☐ N361EH	Bell 212	30554	ex XA-TRY
☐ N362EH	Bell 212	30853	ex XA-TRX
☐ N399EH	Bell 212	30810	ex XA-AAM
☐ N500EH	Bell 212	30945	
☐ N508EH	Bell 212	30908	

☐ N523EH	Bell 212	31214	ex C-GRWX

☐ N89EM	Eurocopter EC135T1	0049	ex N94387
☐ N127JL	Eurocopter EC135P2+	0976	
☐ N133JG	Eurocopter EC135P2+	0915	ex N203AE
☐ N228BJ	Eurocopter EC135P2+	0982	
☐ N302NM	Eurocopter EC135P2+	0987	
☐ N320TV	Eurocopter EC135P2	0467	ex N220AE
☐ N324XM	Eurocopter EC135P2+	0991	
☐ N325DB	Eurocopter EC135P2+	0985	
☐ N357TC	Eurocopter EC135P2+	0626	
☐ N430TM	Eurocopter EC135P2	0457	ex N220AE
☐ N517JF	Eurocopter EC135P2+	0777	ex D-HCBJ
☐ N551BA	Eurocopter EC135P2	0188	
☐ N602SH	Eurocopter EC135P2+	0937	
☐ N605SS	Eurocopter EC135P2	0461	
☐ N611LS	Eurocopter EC135P2	0472	
☐ N812DR	Eurocopter EC135P2+	0752	

☐ N328PK	Sikorsky S-76C	760604		♦
☐ N531BH	Sikorsky S-76C++	760725	ex N2579T	
☐ N547WM	Sikorsky S-76C++	760722	ex N2579P	
☐ N573EH	Sikorsky S-76A++	760373	ex B-	
☐ N575EH	Sikorsky S-76A++	760366	ex N621LH	
☐ N577EH	Sikorsky S-76A++	760222	ex N15459	
☐ N578EH	Sikorsky S-76A++	760099	ex N223BF	
☐ N905RD	Sikorsky S-76C+	760610	ex N8109K	
☐ N911LV	Sikorsky S-76A++	760281		
☐ N927MS	Sikorsky S-76C	760605		♦

☐ N109RR	Eurocopter EC225LP	2777		
☐ N168EH	Bell 412	33058	ex VH-NSI	
☐ N186LA	MBB BK-117C-2	9185	ex XA-UPM	
☐ N225EW	Eurocopter EC225LP	2809		
☐ N271X	Sikorsky S-92A	920271		♦
☐ N412SG	Eurocopter EC225LP	2825	ex OY-HNA	
☐ N421EH	Bell 412	33067	ex N57413	
☐ N602JS	Eurocopter EC225LP	2821	ex F-HUMB	
☐ N702LM	MBB BK-117C-2	9197	ex N803PH	
☐ N968KC	MBB BK-117C-2	9226		

ERICKSON AERO TANKER

☐ N291EA	McDonnell-Douglas MD-87	53039/1881	ex N826TH	101	air tanker♦
☐ N292EA	McDonnell-Douglas MD-87	53208/1865	ex SE-DMM	102	wfs♦
☐ N293EA	McDonnell-Douglas MD-87	53209/1867	ex SE-DMN	103	air tanker♦
☐ N294EA	McDonnell-Douglas MD-87	53210/1871	ex EC-FFI	104	wfs♦
☐ N295EA	McDonnell-Douglas MD-87	53211/1874	ex SE-DMP	105	air tanker♦
☐ N296EA	McDonnell-Douglas MD-87	53212/1877	ex EC-LUJ	106	wfs♦
☐ N297EA	McDonnell-Douglas MD-87	53213/1879	ex EC-FHK	107	wfs♦

ERICKSON AIR CRANE   Central Point, OR

☐ N154AC	Erickson/Sikorsky S-64E Skycrane	64037	ex 68-18435	733 Georgia Peach	
☐ N159AC	Erickson/Sikorsky S-64F Skycrane	64084	ex 68-18476	741	
☐ N164AC	Erickson/Sikorsky S-64E Skycrane	64034	ex C-FCRN	730 The Incredible Hulk	
☐ N171AC	Erickson/Sikorsky S-64F Skycrane	64090	ex 69-18482		[Central Point]
☐ N172AC	Erickson/Sikorsky S-64F Skycrane	64061	ex C-FCRN		
☐ N173AC	Erickson/Sikorsky S-64E Skycrane	64015	ex PR-HRB		
☐ N176AC	Erickson/Sikorsky S-64E Skycrane	64003	ex C-GZJK		
☐ N194AC	Erickson/Sikorsky S-64E Skycrane	64017	ex C-GFLH	746	
☐ N217AC	Erickson/Sikorsky S-64E Skycrane	64064	ex N542SB	732 Malcolm	
☐ N218AC	Erickson/Sikorsky S-64E Skycrane	64033	ex N545SB	749 Elsie	
☐ N229AC	Erickson/Sikorsky S-64E Skycrane	64018	ex N4099Y		
☐ N236AC	Erickson/Sikorsky S-64E Skycrane	64089			
☐ N237AC	Erickson/Sikorsky S-64E Skycrane	64095	ex 70-18487		
☐ N238AC	Erickson/Sikorsky S-64F Skycrane	64016	ex N543CH		[Central Point]
☐ N243AC	Erickson/Sikorsky S-64E Skycrane	64022	ex N544CH		[Central Point]
☐ N247AC	Erickson/Sikorsky S-64E Skycrane	64052	ex C-GJRY		
☐ N253AC	Erickson/Sikorsky S-64F Skycrane	64042	ex N7073C		[Central Point]
☐ N957AC	Erickson/Sikorsky S-64E Skycrane	64065	ex C-GESG	745	
☐ N4099M	Erickson/Sikorsky S-64E Skycrane	64028	ex 67-18426		
☐ N6962R	Erickson/Sikorsky S-64E Skycrane	64058	ex HC-CAT	741 Olga	

EVERGREEN HELICOPTERS   (7E)

McMinnville, OR/Anchorage-Merrill, AK/ Galveston, TX (RNC/MRI/GLS)

☐ N33AZ	Bell 206L-3 LongRanger III	51110	
☐ N60EV	Sikorsky S-61 (H-3E)	61643	ex 69-5799

☐ N61EV	Sikorsky S-61R (CH-3E)	61566	ex 65-12791	
☐ N70DB	Bell 206B JetRanger	1730		
☐ N105EV	Beech 1900D	UE-64	ex N1900R	
☐ N139EV	AgustaWestland AW139	31006	ex UAE 4003	[AUH]
☐ N140EV	AgustaWestland AW139	31025	ex UAE 4004	[AUH]
☐ N171CJ	Beech 1900D	UE-71	ex N85704	
☐ N202EV	Lockheed P2V-5 Neptune	726-5387	ex Bu131502 141	Tanker
☐ N212EV	Bell 212	30881	ex HK-4064X	
☐ N330JF	Aérospatiale SA.330J Puma	1514	ex 9M-SSD	
☐ N350EV	Aérospatiale AS350B2 AStar	2961	ex N142LG	
☐ N353EV	Aérospatiale AS350B2 AStar	2444	ex C-GJVG	
☐ N359EV	Aérospatiale AS350B3 AStar	3797	ex I-BALO	
☐ N405PC	Learjet 35A	35A-651	ex HB-VJK	
☐ N405R	Aérospatiale SA.330J Puma	1475	ex PP-MGB	
☐ N423CA	CASA C.212-200	CC40-6-240		>US Air Force
☐ N437CA	CACA C.212-200	CC29-1-180	ex ZS-PRL	
☐ N502FS	CASA C.212-200	CD58-1-294	ex N31BR	
☐ N730TS	MBB Bo.105S	S-895	ex N204PC	
☐ N822H	Bell 214ST	28139	ex N6957Y	
☐ N823H	Bell 214ST	28141	ex N59805	
☐ N3195S	Bell 206L-3 LongRanger III	51136		
☐ N5007F	Bell 206L-1 LongRanger III	45186		
☐ N16974	Bell 212	30886	ex 9Y-DPB	

EVERTS AIR ALASKA Everts (VTS) Fairbanks-Intl, AK (FAI)

☐ N108NS	Piper PA-32R-300 Lance	32R-7680288	ex N108TA	
☐ N148RF	Piper PA-32R-300 Lance	32R-7680076	ex N844JH	
☐ N575JD	Cessna 208B Caravan I	208B0595	ex N5268V	dam 22Jan15
☐ N6969J	Piper PA-32R-300 Lance	32R-7680398		

Tatonduk Outfitters is an associated partner

EVERTS AIR CARGO Everts (VTS) Fairbanks-Intl, AK (FAI)

☐ N100CE	Douglas C-118A	44662/629	ex N51599	
☐ N151	Douglas DC-6B	45496/992	ex C-GICD	
☐ N351CE	Douglas C-118A	44599/505	ex 53-3228	
☐ N400UA	Douglas DC-6A	44258/467	ex YV-296C	
☐ N501XP	Douglas DC-6B	45177	ex C-GKUG	
☐ N501YP	Douglas DC-6A	45531	ex C-GIBS	
☐ N551CE	Douglas DC-6B	45179/865	ex N60759	
☐ N555SQ	Douglas DC-6B	45137/830	ex N37585	
☐ N6174C	Douglas DC-6A	44075/451	ex C-GBYN	Good Grief
☐ N747CE	Douglas C-118A	44661/628	ex N233HP	
☐ N851CE	Douglas DC-6A	45531	ex N501YP	♦
☐ N9056R	Douglas DC-6A/B	45498/1005	ex C-FCZZ	
☐ N904CE	Douglas DC-9-32CF	47040/172	ex N904AX	[FAI]
☐ N930CE	Douglas DC-9-33F	47363/445	ex N930AX	
☐ N932CE	Douglas DC-9-33CF (ABS 3)	47465/584	ex N932AX	
☐ N935CE	Douglas DC-9-33RC (ABS 3)	47413/521	ex N935AX	
☐ N952AX	Douglas DC-9-41F (ABS 3)	47615/751	ex JA8432	[FAI]
☐ N7CE	Cessna 206H Stationair	20608030		♦
☐ N744DA	Pilatus PC-12/47	744	ex HB-FSB	
☐ N964AS	McDonnell-Douglas MD-83	53078/1996		[TUS]
☐ N965AS	McDonnell-Douglas MD-83	53079/2004		♦
☐ N5180	Cessna 180E Skywagon	18051077		
☐ N1105G	Embraer EMB.120FC Brasilia	120105	ex PT-SMX	
☐ N1110J	Embraer EMB.120FC Brasilia	120110	ex PT-SNC	
☐ N7848B	Curtiss C-46R Commando	273	ex HP-238	Dumbo
☐ N54514	Curtiss C-46D Commando	33285	ex 51-1122	Maid in Japan
☐ N73444	McDonnell-Douglas MD-83SF	49470/1417		

Tatonduk Outfitters is an associated partner

EVERTS AIR FUEL Fairbanks-Intl, AK (FAI)

☐ N23AC	Curtiss c-46F Commando	22451		♦
☐ N1651M	Curtiss C-46F Commando	22399	ex 44-70586	
☐ N1822M	Curtiss C-46F Commando	22521	ex 44-18698	Salmon Ella
☐ N1837M	Curtiss C-46F Commando	22388	ex CF-FNC	Hot Stuff dam 08Jly13
☐ N54584	Curtiss C-46 Commando	22388	ex 44-78495	♦
☐ N251CE	Douglas C-118A	44612/532	ex Bu153693 532	
☐ N444CE	Douglas DC-6B	45478/962	ex C-GHLZ	Spirit of America
☐ N451CE	Douglas C-118B	43712/358	ex N840CS	
☐ N517EE	Douglas C-118B	43693		♦
☐ N751CE	Douglas C-118		ex 131571	♦
☐ N951CE	Douglas C-118A	43696	ex 131593	
☐ N5307S	Douglas C-118B	43704	ex N651CE	♦
☐ N6586C	Douglas DC-6B/F	45222/849		

☐ N7780B	Douglas DC-6A	45372/875		The Aviator
☐ N7919C	Douglas DC-6B	43554	ex PH-DFM	

EXPRESSJET AIRLINES — Jet Link (EV/ASQ)
Cleveland, OH/Houston-Intercontinental, TX/Newark, NJ (CLE/IAH/EWR)

Ops schedule flights as Delta Connection, Envoy and United Express

FALCON AIR EXPRESS — Panther (6F/FAO)

☐ N120MN	McDonnell-Douglas MD-83	53120/1964	ex EI-CFZ		
☐ N125MN	McDonnell-Douglas MD-83	53125/1993	ex EI-CER		
☐ N305FA	McDonnell-Douglas MD-83	49398/1332	ex N566MS		wfs
☐ N306FA	McDonnell-Douglas MD-83	49344/1370	ex N562AA		
☐ N307FA	McDonnell-Douglas MD-83	53199/1968	ex N307MS		[MZJ]

FALCON AIR SERVICE

☐ N128ST	Cessna 208B Caravan I	208B1133	
☐ N213LA	Cessna 208B Caravan I	208B1096	ex N777VW
☐ N350JW	Beech B300 King Air	FL-208	ex C-FJOL
☐ N688FA	Cessna 208B Caravan I	208B1103	ex N688RP
☐ N891DF	Cessna 208B Caravan I	208B1148	

FEDEX EXPRESS — FedEx (FX/FDX) — Memphis-Intl, TN (MEM)

☐ N650FE	Airbus A300F4-605R	726	ex F-WWAP	Molly Mickler
☐ N651FE	Airbus A300F4-605R	728	ex F-WWAJ	Diane Kathleen
☐ N652FE	Airbus A300F4-605R	735	ex F-WWAN	Rachel Patricia
☐ N653FE	Airbus A300F4-605R	736	ex F-WWAD	Samantha Massey
☐ N654FE	Airbus A300F4-605R	738	ex F-WWAX	Richard
☐ N655FE	Airbus A300F4-605R	742	ex F-WWAJ	Dion
☐ N656FE	Airbus A300F4-605R	745	ex F-WWAP	Devin
☐ N657FE	Airbus A300F4-605R	748	ex F-WWAM	Lizzie
☐ N658FE	Airbus A300F4-605R	752	ex F-WWAE	Tristian
☐ N659FE	Airbus A300F4-605R	757	ex F-WWAF	Jayden
☐ N660FE	Airbus A300F4-605R	759	ex F-WWAG	Zack
☐ N661FE	Airbus A300F4-605R	760	ex F-WWAL	Caleb
☐ N662FE	Airbus A300F4-605R	761	ex F-WWAK	Tessa
☐ N663FE	Airbus A300F4-605R	766	ex F-WWAO	Domenick
☐ N664FE	Airbus A300F4-605R	768	ex F-WWAA	Amanda
☐ N665FE	Airbus A300F4-605R	769	ex F-WWAM	Ethan
☐ N667FE	Airbus A300F4-605R	771	ex F-WWAF	Sean
☐ N668FE	Airbus A300F4-605R	772	ex F-WWAP	Tianna
☐ N669FE	Airbus A300F4-605R	774	ex F-WWAE	Kaitlyn
☐ N670FE	Airbus A300F4-605R	777	ex F-WWAQ	Amrit
☐ N671FE	Airbus A300F4-605R	778	ex F-WWAV	Drew
☐ N672FE	Airbus A300F4-605R	779	ex F-WWAZ	Young Joe
☐ N673FE	Airbus A300F4-605R	780	ex F-WWAU	Mark
☐ N674FE	Airbus A300F4-605R	781	ex F-WWAN	Thea
☐ N675FE	Airbus A300F4-605R	789	ex F-WWAZ	Byron
☐ N676FE	Airbus A300F4-605R	790	ex F-WWAV	Jade
☐ N677FE	Airbus A300F4-605R	791	ex F-WWAD	Clifford
☐ N678FE	Airbus A300F4-605R	792	ex F-WWAF	Allison
☐ N679FE	Airbus A300F4-605R	793	ex F-WWAG	Ty
☐ N680FE	Airbus A300F4-605R	794	ex F-WWAH	Tierney
☐ N681FE	Airbus A300F4-605R	799	ex F-WWAJ	Kaci
☐ N682FE	Airbus A300F4-605R	800	ex F-WWAK	Gabrial
☐ N683FE	Airbus A300F4-605R	801	ex F-WWAL	Xenophon
☐ N684FE	Airbus A300F4-605R	802	ex F-WWAM	Daniel
☐ N685FE	Airbus A300F4-605R	803	ex F-WWAB	Landon Ostlie
☐ N686FE	Airbus A300F4-605R	804	ex F-WWAO	Alex
☐ N687FE	Airbus A300F4-605R	873	ex F-WWAO	Aika
☐ N688FE	Airbus A300F4-605R	874	ex F-WWAP	
☐ N689FE	Airbus A300F4-605R	875	ex F-WWAQ	
☐ N690FE	Airbus A300F4-605R	876	ex F-WWAR	
☐ N691FE	Airbus A300F4-605R	877	ex F-WWAS	
☐ N692FE	Airbus A300F4-605R	878	ex F-WWAT	Gabriel
☐ N716FD	Airbus A300B4-622F	358	ex HL7287	Halle	[VCV]
☐ N717FD	Airbus A300B4-622F	361	ex HL7280	Roben	
☐ N718FD	Airbus A300B4-622F	365	ex HL7281	Anna	[VCV]
☐ N719FD	Airbus A300B4-622F	388	ex HL7290	Cale	
☐ N720FD	Airbus A300B4-622F	417	ex HL7291	Kristin Marie	[VCV]
☐ N721FD	Airbus A300B4-622RF	477	ex D-ASAE	Kathryn	
☐ N722FD	Airbus A300B4-622RF	479	ex HL7535	Selina	
☐ N723FD	Airbus A300B4-622RF	543	ex HL7536	Cody	
☐ N724FD	Airbus A300B4-622RF	530	ex F-OIHA	Anacarina	
☐ N725FD	Airbus A300B4-622RF	572	ex SU-GAT	Zebradedra	
☐ N726FD	Airbus A300B4-622RF	575	ex SU-GAU		
☐ N727FD	Airbus A300B4-622RF	579	ex SU-GAV	Mira	
☐ N728FD	Airbus A300B4-622RF	581	ex SU-GAW	Cassie	
☐ N729FD	Airbus A300B4-622RF	657	ex TF-ELU	Kaylee	

☐ N730FD	Airbus A300B4-622RF	659	ex TF-ELB	Kailey	
☐ N731FD	Airbus A300B4-605RF	709	ex B-2320	Bryan	
☐ N732FD	Airbus A300B4-605RF	713	ex B-2321	Safaa	
☐ N733FD	Airbus A300B4-605RF	715	ex B-2322	Lily	
☐ N740FD	Airbus A300B4-622RF	559	ex F-WQTD		
☐ N741FD	Airbus A300B4-622RF	611	ex A7-AFC	Serena	
☐ N742FD	Airbus A300B4-622RF	613	ex A7-AFD	Britton	
☐ N743FD	Airbus A300B4-622RF	630	ex A7-AFA		
☐ N744FD	Airbus A300B4-622RF	664	ex A7-ABN	Grace	
☐ N745FD	Airbus A300B4-622RF	668	ex A7-ABO	Vale	
☐ N746FD	Airbus A300B4-622RF	688	ex A7-ABW	Lucy	
☐ N748FD	Airbus A300B4-622RF	633	ex N633AN		
☐ N749FD	Airbus A300B4-622RF	536	ex TF-ELD	Andrea	
☐ N750FD	Airbus A300B4-622RF	555	ex F-HEEE	Saki	
☐ N751FD	Airbus A300B4-622RF	625	ex F-HDDD	Tey	
☐ N401FE	Airbus A310-203F	191	ex D-AICA	David	[VCV]
☐ N402FE	Airbus A310-203F	201	ex D-AICB	Carlye	[VCV]
☐ N405FE	Airbus A310-203F	237	ex D-AICF	Mariah	[VCV]
☐ N409FE	Airbus A310-203F	273	ex D-AICL	Jake	[VCV]
☐ N410FE	Airbus A310-203F	356	ex D-AICM	Carolyn	
☐ N411FE	Airbus A310-203F	359	ex D-AICN	Barbra	[VCV]
☐ N414FE	Airbus A310-203F	400	ex D-AICS	Tanner	[VCV]
☐ N416FE	Airbus A310-222F	288	ex F-WGYR	Patrick	[VCV]
☐ N417FE	Airbus A310-222F	333	ex N802PA	Kyle	[VCV]
☐ N418FE	Airbus A310-222F	343	ex N803PA	Rachel	[VCV]
☐ N419FE	Airbus A310-222F	345	ex N804PA	Krystle	[VCV]
☐ N421FE	Airbus A310-222F	342	ex N806PA	Caitlin	[VCV]
☐ N423FE	Airbus A310-203F	281	ex PH-MCA	Trey	
☐ N425FE	Airbus A310-203F	264	ex PH-AGD	Jerome	[VCV]
☐ N426FE	Airbus A310-203F	245	ex PH-AGB	Shana	
☐ N427FE	Airbus A310-203F	362	ex PH-AGH	Zackary	
☐ N428FE	Airbus A310-203F	248	ex PH-AGC	Kristina	[VCV]
☐ N429FE	Airbus A310-203F	364	ex PH-AGI	Conner	
☐ N430FE	Airbus A310-203F	394	ex PH-AGK	Kelleen	
☐ N431FE	Airbus A310-203F	316	ex F-WWAD	Asumi	[VCV]
☐ N435FE	Airbus A310-203F	369	ex F-GEME	Ceara	[VCV]
☐ N436FE	Airbus A310-203F	454	ex F-GEMG	Gillian	[VCV]
☐ N443FE	Airbus A310-203F	283	ex PH-AGE	Katelin	
☐ N445FE	Airbus A310-203F	297	ex PH-AGF	Nicholas	[VCV]
☐ N447FE	Airbus A310-222F	251	ex HB-IPB	Shaunna	[VCV]
☐ N450FE	Airbus A310-222F	162	ex F-GPDJ	Selna	
☐ N453FE	Airbus A310-222F	267	ex D-ASAL	Rush	
☐ N454FE	Airbus A310-222F	278	ex D-ASAK	Marissa	
☐ N455FE	Airbus A310-222F	331	ex F-WWAH	Sara	
☐ N456FE	Airbus A310-222F	318	ex F-OHPQ	Simon	[VCV]
☐ N801FD	Airbus A310-324F	539	ex D-ASAD	Amos	
☐ N802FD	Airbus A310-324F	542	ex D-ASAD	Saeed	[VCV]
☐ N803FD	Airbus A310-324F	378	ex N853CH	Rylan	
☐ N804FD	Airbus A310-324F	549	ex N101MP	Paige	
☐ N805FD	Airbus A310-324F	456	ex F-OGYR	Fernando	
☐ N806FD	Airbus A310-324F	458	ex F-OGYN	Addisyn	[VCV]
☐ N807FD	Airbus A310-324F	492	ex F-WQTA	Joshua	
☐ N808FD	Airbus A310-324F	439	ex F-OHPU	Berkeley	
☐ N809FD	Airbus A310-324F	449	ex F-OHPV	Gavin	
☐ N810FD	Airbus A310-324F	452	ex F-OHPY	Sebastian	
☐ N811FD	Airbus A310-324F	457	ex F-OGYM		
☐ N812FD	Airbus A310-324F	467	ex F-OGYS	Agyei	[VCV]
☐ N813FD	Airbus A310-324F	500	ex N501RR		[VCV]
☐ N814FD	Airbus A310-324F	534	ex N534RR		[VCV]
☐ N815FD	Airbus A310-324F	638	ex F-OJAF	Tommy	[VCV]
☐ N816FD	Airbus A310-304F	593	ex F-OGQR	Phoenix	[VCV]
☐ N817FD	Airbus A310-304F	552	ex TF-ELS		
☐ N900FX	ATR 42-320F	170	ex N14825		opb CFS
☐ N901FX	ATR 42-320F	172	ex N26826		opb CFS
☐ N903FX	ATR 42-320F	179	ex N14828		opb CFS
☐ N906FX	ATR 42-320F	280	ex N97841		opb MTN
☐ N907FX	ATR 42-320F	286	ex N86842		opb MTN
☐ N908FX	ATR 42-300F	023	ex N972NA		opb CFS
☐ N909FX	ATR 42-300F	275	ex N275BC		opb MTN
☐ N910FX	ATR 42-300F	277	ex N277AT		opb MTN
☐ N911FX	ATR 42-300F	045	ex N424MQ		opb CFS
☐ N912FX	ATR 42-300F	047	ex N47AE		opb CFS
☐ N913FX	ATR 42-320F	250	ex N251AE		opb CFS
☐ N914FX	ATR 42-300F	293	ex N293AT		opb MTN
☐ N915FX	ATR 42-320F	269	ex N269AT		opb MTN
☐ N916FX	ATR 42-300F	314	ex N314AM		opb MTN
☐ N917FX	ATR 42-320F	354	ex N351AT		opb CFS
☐ N918FX	ATR 42-300F	262	ex N262AT		opb MTN
☐ N919FX	ATR 42-320F	266	ex N265AE		opb CFS
☐ N920FX	ATR 42-320F	325	ex N325AT		opb MTN
☐ N921FX	ATR 42-300F	319	ex N319AM		opb MTN

☐ N923FX	ATR 42-310F	135	ex C-GATK	
☐ EI-FXK	ATR 72-202F	256	ex N817FX	opb ABR
☐ N426AT	ATR 72-212	426	ex F-WWED	wfs
☐ N800FX	ATR 72-212	336	ex N630AS	opb MTN
☐ N801FX	ATR 72-212	338	ex N632AS	opb CFS
☐ N802FX	ATR 72-212	344	ex N633AS	opb MTN
☐ N803FX	ATR 72-212	362	ex N631AS	opb CFS
☐ N804FX	ATR 72-212	370	ex N634AS	opb MTN
☐ N805FX	ATR 72-212F	372	ex N635AS	opb CFS
☐ N806FX	ATR 72-212	375	ex N636AS	opb MTN
☐ N807FX	ATR 72-212	383	ex N637AS	opb CFS
☐ N810FX	ATR 72-202F	220	ex N722TE	opb MTN
☐ N811FX	ATR 72-202F	283	ex N723TE	opb MTN
☐ N812FX	ATR 72-212F	404	ex D-AEWI	opb MTN
☐ N816FX	ATR 72-212F	347	ex D-AEWG	opb CFS
☐ N819FX	ATR 72-212F	359	ex D-AEWH	opb CFS
☐ N820FX	ATR 72-212F	248	ex N248AT	opb MTN
☐ N821FX	ATR 72-212F	253	ex N252AM	opb CFS
☐ N771FD	Boeing 757-222	24799/291	ex N511UA	[VCV]
☐ N770FD	Boeing 757-222	24743/270	ex N507UA 770	[VCV]
☐ N772FD	Boeing 757-222	24840/306	ex N515UA 772	[VCV]♦
☐ N773FD	Boeing 757-222	24872/312	ex N519UA	
☐ N774FD	Boeing 757-222	26709/563	ex N585UA	[VCV]♦
☐ N775FD	Boeing 757-222	25043/353	cx N530UA 775	[VCV]♦
☐ N776FD	Boeing 757-222	25129/372	cx N534UA 776	[VCV]♦
☐ N777FD	Boeing 757-222	25222/385	ex N538UA 777	[VCV]♦
☐ N778FD	Boeing 757-222	25223/386	ex N539UA 778	[VCV]♦
☐ N779FD	Boeing 757-222	25252/393	ex N540UA 787	[VCV]♦
☐ N780FD	Boeing 757-222SF	25253/394	ex N541UA	
☐ N781FD	Boeing 757-222	26673/497	ex N567UA 781	[VCV]♦
☐ N782FD	Boeing 757-222	26677/499	ex N569UA	[VCV]♦
☐ N783FD	Boeing 757-222	26678/501	ex N570UA	[VCV]
☐ N784FD	Boeing 757-222SF	26681/506	ex N571UA 784 Neave	
☐ N785FD	Boeing 757-222SF	26682/508	ex N572UA	
☐ N786FD	Boeing 757-222SF	24995/341	ex N527UA	
☐ N787FD	Boeing 757-222	26685/512	ex N573UA	[VCV]♦
☐ N788FD	Boeing 757-222	26686/513	ex N574UA 788	[VCV]♦
☐ N789FD	Boeing 757-222	26689/515	ex N575UA	[VCV]♦
☐ N790FD	Boeing 757-222	26693/527	ex N577UA	[VCV]♦
☐ N791FD	Boeing 757-222	26694/531	ex N578UA 791	[VCV]♦
☐ N792FD	Boeing 757-222	26697/539	ex N579UA	[VCV]♦
☐ N793FD	Boeing 757-222	26698/542	ex N580UA	[VCV]♦
☐ N794FD	Boeing 757-222SF	26701/543	ex N581UA Rubyrose	
☐ N795FD	Boeing 757-222SF	26706/559	ex N584UA Shane	
☐ N796FD	Boeing 757-222SF	26710/567	ex N586UA 796	
☐ N797FD	Boeing 757-222SF	28143/719	ex N592UA	
☐ N798FD	Boeing 757-222SF	28144/724	ex N593UA	
☐ N799FD	Boeing 757-222	28145/727	ex N594UA	[VCV]♦
☐ N901FD	Boeing 757-2B7F	27122/525	ex N610AU	
☐ N902FD	Boeing 757-2B7SF	27123/534	ex N927UW	>MAL
☐ N903FD	Boeing 757-2B7SF	27124/540	ex N928UW Makayia	
☐ N905FD	Boeing 757-2B7SF	27145/546	ex N930UW	
☐ N906FD	Boeing 757-2B7SF	27148/564	ex N931UW Laura	
☐ N909FD	Boeing 757-2B7SF	27200/589	ex N934UW	>MAL
☐ N910FD	Boeing 757-236SF	25054/362	ex G-OOOK Jiatian	
☐ N912FD	Boeing 757-28ASF	24260/204	ex N517NA	
☐ N913FD	Boeing 757-28ASF	24017/162	ex C-FTDV Brayden	
☐ N914FD	Boeing 757-28ASF	24367/208	ex G-FCLG Bella	
☐ N915FD	Boeing 757-236SF	24120/174	ex 4X-EBO	
☐ N916FD	Boeing 757-27BSF	24137/178	ex 4X-EBY Mallory	
☐ N917FD	Boeing 757-23AF	24291/215	ex CX-PUD Kirby	
☐ N918FD	Boeing 757-23AERF	24290/212	ex N290AN Dexter	
☐ N919FD	Boeing 757-23ASF	24636/259	ex G-FJEA Evan	
☐ N920FD	Boeing 757-23AERF	24289/209	ex G-OAVB Sophia	
☐ N921FD	Boeing 757-23ASF	24924/333	ex N924AW	
☐ N922FD	Boeing 757-23ASF	24293/220	ex N293AW	
☐ N923FD	Boeing 757-28ASF	26266/514	ex G-BYAF	
☐ N924FD	Boeing 757-28ASF	26267/538	ex G-BYAK	
☐ N925FD	Boeing 757-204SF	27238/604	ex G-BYAS	
☐ N926FD	Boeing 757-2S7SF	23323/80	ex N903AW Clare	
☐ N927FD	Boeing 757-204SF	27220/618	ex G-BYAU	
☐ N928FD	Boeing 757-28ASF	24369/226	ex G-JMCF Annsley	
☐ N930FD	Boeing 757-2Y0SF	25240/388	ex N240MQ	
☐ N933FD	Boeing 757-21BSF	24330/200	ex B-2804 Fabian	
☐ N934FD	Boeing 757-21BSF	24331/203	ex B-2805 Shae	
☐ N935FD	Boeing 757-2T7ERSF	22780/15	ex G-MONB Desirée	
☐ N936FD	Boeing 757-2T7ERSF	23293/56	ex G-MONE Piper	
☐ N937FD	Boeing 757-2T7SF	23895/132	ex N513NA Aley	
☐ N938FD	Boeing 757-23AERSF	24292/219	ex G-OJIB	
☐ N939FD	Boeing 757-23ASF	24528/250	ex N549AX	
☐ N940FD	Boeing 757-236SF	24772/271	ex N247SS	

☐ N941FD	Boeing 757-225SF	22691/155	ex TF-LLY	Erika	
☐ N942FD	Boeing 757-225SF	22612/114	ex N226LC		
☐ N943FD	Boeing 757-2G5SF	23929/153	ex N929RD		
☐ N944FD	Boeing 757-2G5SF	24497/228	ex N497EA	Reagan	
☐ N946FD	Boeing 757-236SF	24398/224	ex G-CPEL		
☐ N947FD	Boeing 757-236SF	24882/323	ex G-BPEC	Giovanna	
☐ N948FD	Boeing 757-236SF	25059/363	ex G-BPED	Anissa	
☐ N949FD	Boeing 757-236SF	25060/364	ex G-BPEE		
☐ N950FD	Boeing 757-236SF	25806/601	ex G-BPEI	Mia	
☐ N951FD	Boeing 757-236SF	28665/747	ex G-CPEM		
☐ N952FD	Boeing 757-236SF	28666/751	ex G-CPEN		
☐ N953FD	Boeing 757-236SF	28667/762	ex G-CPEO		
☐ N954FD	Boeing 757-236SF	29113/784	ex G-CPER	Mika	
☐ N955FD	Boeing 757-236SF	29114/793	ex G-CPES	Elke	
☐ N956FD	Boeing 757-236SF	29115/798	ex G-CPET		
☐ N957FD	Boeing 757-21BSF	24774/288	ex N802PG		
☐ N958FD	Boeing 757-236	24371/225	ex N579SH		[VCV]
☐ N959FD	Boeing 757-236SF	25133/374	ex N522NA	Kylie	
☐ N960FD	Boeing 757-236SF	25593/466	ex G-OOOZ		
☐ N961FD	Boeing 757-2Y0SF	25268/400	ex G-CPEP	Byanca	
☐ N962FD	Boeing 757-2G5SF	24176/173	ex CS-TLX	Nina	
☐ N963FD	Boeing 757-28ASF	24368/213	ex N639AX		
☐ N964FD	Boeing 757-258SF	24884/325	ex 4X-EBS	Brooke	
☐ N965FD	Boeing 757-258SF	27622/745	ex G-STRZ		
☐ N966FD	Boeing 757-28ASF	25626/549	ex G-BYAL		
☐ N967FD	Boeing 757-28ASF	26269/612	ex OH-AFJ	Jessi	
☐ N968FD	Boeing 757-28ASF	26274/676	ex G-FCLH		
☐ N969FD	Boeing 757-28ASF	28164/749	ex G-FCLB		
☐ N970FD	Boeing 757-28ASF	28166/756	ex G-FCLC	Jordyn	
☐ N971FD	Boeing 757-28ASF	26277/658	ex N750NA	Darcy	
☐ N972FD	Boeing 757-28ASF	28203/802	ex G-TCBA		
☐ N973FD	Boeing 757-2Y0SF	26151/472	ex TF-FIK	Abigaile	
☐ N974FD	Boeing 757-2Y0SF	26158/526	ex G-OOOX	Eva	
☐ N975FD	Boeing 757-2B7SF	27146/551	ex G-OOBI	Meriel	
☐ N976FD	Boeing 757-2B7SF	27147/552	ex G-OOBJ		
☐ N977FD	Boeing 757-236SF	24118/163	ex N630SH		
☐ N978FD	Boeing 757-236SF	24119/167	ex YV2242	Mackenzie Ann	
☐ N979FD	Boeing 757-236SF	25592/453	ex N169CA		
☐ N985FD	Boeing 757-230SF	24737/267	ex N741PA		
☐ N986FD	Boeing 757-231SF	28482/770	ex N595SH	Tanner	
☐ N987FD	Boeing 757-231SF	28483/777	ex N596SH	James	
☐ N988FD	Boeing 757-222SF	26705/556	ex N583UA		
☐ N989FD	Boeing 757-231SF	28480/750	ex N592SH		
☐ N990FD	Boeing 757-232SF	22909/101	ex N619DL		
☐ N991FD	Boeing 757-232SF	22911/112	ex N621DL		
☐ N992FD	Boeing 757-232SF	22912/113	ex N622DL		
☐ N993FD	Boeing 757-2Q8SF	24965/438	ex SU-BPY	Jasmine	
☐ N994FD	Boeing 757-23ASF	25490/510	ex N490AN	Lindora	
☐ N995FD	Boeing 757-2Q8SF	25131/458	ex N594BC	Risa	
☐ N996FD	Boeing 757-2Q8SF	26270/558	ex N595BC		
☐ N997FD	Boeing 757-230SF	24738/274	ex N473AC	Analise	
☐ N998FD	Boeing 757-230SF	24747/275	ex EI-IGC		
☐ N999FD	Boeing 757-230SF	24748/285	ex N493AC	Meredith	
☐ N68085	Boeing 757-222	26702/550	ex N582UA		[VCV]♦
☐ N68087	Boeing 757-222	24891/319	ex (N774FD)		[VCV]♦
☐ N101FE	Boeing 767-3S2ERF	42706/1058	ex N60659	101 Hannah	
☐ N102FE	Boeing 767-32SERF	42707/1061		102 Kara	
☐ N103FE	Boeing 767-32SERF	43544/1063		103 Selah	
☐ N104FE	Boeing 767-32SERF	42708/1064		104 Birdie	
☐ N106FE	Boeing 767-32SERF	42709/1070		106 Evelyn	♦
☐ N107FE	Boeing 767-3S2ERF	44377/1071		107 Grayson	♦
☐ N108FE	Boeing 767-3S2ERF	44378/1072		108 Luci	♦
☐ N109FE	Boeing 767-32SERF	42710/1073		109 Stephanie	♦
☐ N110FE	Boeing 767-32SERF	43542/1074		110 Margo	♦
☐ N112FE	Boeing 767-3S2ERF	43543/1075		112 Jordan	♦
☐ N113FE	Boeing 767-3S2ERF	42711/1076		113 Brandon	♦
☐ N114FE	Boeing 767-3S2ERF	42712/1077		114 Jade	♦
☐ N115FE	Boeing 767-3S2ERF	42713/1078		115 Rosabella	♦
☐ N117FE	Boeing 767-3S2ERF	44379/1079		117 Rylee	♦
☐ N118FE	Boeing 767-3S2ERF	42714/1080		118	♦
☐ N120FE	Boeing 767-3S2ERF	44380/1081		120 Brianna	♦
☐ N121FE	Boeing 767-3S2ERF	43545/			o/o♦
☐ N122FE	Boeing 767-3S2ERF	42715/		122	o/o♦
☐ N123FE	Boeing 767-3S2ERF	42716/		123	o/o♦
☐ N124FE	Boeing 767-3S2ERF	43546/			o/o♦
☐ N125FE	Boeing 767-3S2ERF	42717/		125	o/o♦
☐ N126FE	Boeing 767-3S2ERF	42718/		126	o/o♦
☐ N128FE	Boeing 767-3S2ERF	42719/		128 Jaxon	o/o♦
☐ N130FE	Boeing 767-3S2ERF	42720/		130	o/o♦
☐ N132FE	Boeing 767-3S2ERF	42721/		132	o/o♦
☐ N135FE	Boeing 767-3S2ERF	42722/		135	o/o♦
☐ N138FE	Boeing 767-3S2ERF	42723/		138	o/o♦

☐ N297FE	Boeing 767-32LERF/W	41068/1027	ex 4K-SW808	wfs♦
☐ N298FE	Boeing 767-32LERF	41069/1032	ex 4K-SW880	wfs♦
☐ N68077	Boeing 767-316ERF/W	30780/806	ex PR-ACG	<TUS♦
☐ N68078	Boeing 767-316ERF/W	32572/846	ex N312LA	<LCO♦
☐ N68079	Boeing 767-316ERF/W	32573/848	ex PR-ADY	<TUS♦
☐ N	Boeing 767-3S2ERF	42724/		o/o♦
☐ N	Boeing 767-3S2ERF	42725/		o/o♦
☐ N	Boeing 767-3S2ERF	42726/		o/o♦
☐ N	Boeing 767-3S2ERF	42727/		o/o♦
☐ N	Boeing 767-3S2ERF	42728/		o/o♦
☐ N	Boeing 767-3S2ERF	42729/		o/o♦
☐ N	Boeing 767-3S2ERF	42730/		o/o♦
☐ N	Boeing 767-3S2ERF	42731/		o/o♦
☐ N	Boeing 767-3S2ERF	42732/		o/o♦
☐ N850FD	Boeing 777-FS2	37721/813	Saad	
☐ N851FD	Boeing 777-FS2	37722/834		
☐ N852FD	Boeing 777-FS2	37723/848		
☐ N853FD	Boeing 777-FS2	37724/829	Talon	
☐ N854FD	Boeing 777-FS2	37725/890	Faith	
☐ N855FD	Boeing 777-FS2	37726/892	Ariana	
☐ N856FD	Boeing 777-FS2	37727/884	Zoe	
☐ N857FD	Boeing 777-FS2	37728/886	Braydon	
☐ N858FD	Boeing 777-FS2	37729/936		
☐ N859FD	Boeing 777-FS2	37730/1134	859 Charli	
☐ N860FD	Boeing 777-FS2	37731/	860	o/o
☐ N861FD	Boeing 777-FS2	37732/973	861	
☐ N862FD	Boeing 777-FS2	37733/975	862 Erica	
☐ N863FD	Boeing 777-FS2	37734/998	863 Madeline	
☐ N864FD	Boeing 777-FS2	37735/1015	864 Leah	
☐ N865FD	Boeing 777-FS2	40671/	865	o/o
☐ N866FD	Boeing 777-FS2	40672/	866	o/o
☐ N867FD	Boeing 777-FS2	40673/	867	o/o
☐ N868FD	Boeing 777-FS2	40674/1320	868	o/o
☐ N869FD	Boeing 777-FS2	40675/1336	869	o/o
☐ N870FD	Boeing 777-FS2	40676/	870	o/o
☐ N873FD	Boeing 777-FS2	40679/	873	o/o
☐ N876FD	Boeing 777-FS2	40682/	876	o/o
☐ N877FD	Boeing 777-FS2	40683/	877	o/o
☐ N878FD	Boeing 777-FS2	40684/	878	o/o
☐ N879FD	Boeing 777-FS2	40685/	879	o/o
☐ N880FD	Boeing 777-F28	32967/718	ex F-GUOA	880	
☐ N882FD	Boeing 777-F28	32969/827	ex N449BA	882 LeeAnna	
☐ N883FD	Boeing 777-FHT	39285/897	ex N5022E	883 Abbi	
☐ N884FD	Boeing 777-FS2	37137/917	884	
☐ N885FD	Boeing 777-FS2	41064/967	885	
☐ N886FD	Boeing 777-FS2	41065/1041	886 Amara	
☐ N887FD	Boeing 777-FS2	41066/1048	887 Juliana	
☐ N888FD	Boeing 777-FS2	42704/	888	o/o
☐ N889FD	Boeing 777-FS2	41067/1057	889 Sydney	
☐ N890FD	Boeing 777-FS2	41439/1033	890 Alexis	
☐ N891FD	Boeing 777-FS2	41440/	891	o/o
☐ N892FD	Boeing 777-FS2	38707/960	892	
☐ N893FD	Boeing 777-FS2	41736/	893	o/o
☐ N894FD	Boeing 777-FS2	41737/	894	o/o
☐ N895FD	Boeing 777-FS2	41749/1152	895 Kimberley	
☐ N896FD	Boeing 777-FS2	41750/	896	o/o
☐ N897FD	Boeing 777-FS2	42705/	897	o/o
☐ C-FEXB	Cessna 208B Caravan I	208B0539	ex N758FX	>MAL
☐ C-FEXF	Cessna 208B Caravan I	208B0508	ex N749FX	>MAL
☐ C-FEXV	Cessna 208B Caravan I	208B0482	ex N738FX	>MAL
☐ C-FEXY	Cessna 208B Caravan I	208B0226	ex N896FE	>MAL
☐ N700FX	Cessna 208B Caravan I	208B0419		opb CFS
☐ N701FX	Cessna 208B Caravan I	208B0420		opb WIG
☐ N702FX	Cessna 208B Caravan I	208B0422		opb BVN
☐ N703FX	Cessna 208B Caravan I	208B0423		opb IRO
☐ N705FX	Cessna 208B Caravan I	208B0425		opb CFS
☐ N706FX	Cessna 208B Caravan I	208B0426		opb IRO
☐ N707FX	Cessna 208B Caravan I	208B0427		opb PCM
☐ N709FX	Cessna 208B Caravan I	208B0430		opb CFS
☐ N710FX	Cessna 208B Caravan I	208B0431		opb CPT
☐ N711FX	Cessna 208B Caravan I	208B0433		opb CFS
☐ N712FX	Cessna 208B Caravan I	208B0435		opb IRO
☐ N713FX	Cessna 208B Caravan I	208B0438		opb PCM
☐ N715FX	Cessna 208B Caravan I	208B0440		opb MTN
☐ N716FX	Cessna 208B Caravan I	208B0442		opb CPT
☐ N717FX	Cessna 208B Caravan I	208B0445		opb IRO
☐ N718FX	Cessna 208B Caravan I	208B0448		opb BVN
☐ N719FX	Cessna 208B Caravan I	208B0450		opb BVN
☐ N720FX	Cessna 208B Caravan I	208B0452		opb CFS dam 31Jan15
☐ N721FX	Cessna 208B Caravan I	208B0453	ex N5132T	opb MTN
☐ N722FX	Cessna 208B Caravan I	208B0454	ex N5133E	opb PCM
			ex N51342	

☐ N723FX	Cessna 208B Caravan I	208B0456		opb BVN
☐ N724FX	Cessna 208B Caravan I	208B0458		opb CPT
☐ N725FX	Cessna 208B Caravan I	208B0460		opb WIG
☐ N726FX	Cessna 208B Caravan I	208B0465	ex N5267K	opb PCM
☐ N727FX	Cessna 208B Caravan I	208B0468	ex N5121N	opb IRO
☐ N728FX	Cessna 208B Caravan I	208B0471	ex N5061W	opb CFS
☐ N729FX	Cessna 208B Caravan I	208B0474	ex N2617Z	opb MTN
☐ N730FX	Cessna 208B Caravan I	208B0477	ex N5066U	opb CPT
☐ N731FX	Cessna 208B Caravan I	208B0480		opb WIG
☐ N740FX	Cessna 208B Caravan I	208B0484		opb MTN
☐ N741FX	Cessna 208B Caravan I	208B0486	ex N5145P	opb BVN
☐ N742FX	Cessna 208B Caravan I	208B0489		opb MTN
☐ N744FX	Cessna 208B Caravan I	208B0492	ex N5148B	opb PCM
☐ N745FX	Cessna 208B Caravan I	208B0495	ex N5162W	opb BVN
☐ N746FX	Cessna 208B Caravan I	208B0498	ex N51743	opb CFS
☐ N747FE	Cessna 208B Caravan I	208B0238		opb MTN
☐ N747FX	Cessna 208B Caravan I	208B0501	ex N51017	opb MTN
☐ N748FE	Cessna 208B Caravan I	208B0241		opb WIG
☐ N748FX	Cessna 208B Caravan I	208B0503	ex N52609	opb PCM
☐ N749FE	Cessna 208B Caravan I	208B0242		opb BVN
☐ N750FX	Cessna 208B Caravan I	208B0511	ex N5211Q	opb PCM
☐ N751FE	Cessna 208B Caravan I	208B0245		opb CPT
☐ N751FX	Cessna 208B Caravan I	208B0514	ex N5262W	opb BVN
☐ N752FE	Cessna 208B Caravan I	208B0247		opb IRO
☐ N752FX	Cessna 208B Caravan I	208B0517	ex N5214J	opb CFS
☐ N753FX	Cessna 208B Caravan I	208B0520	ex N51942	opb BVN
☐ N754FX	Cessna 208B Caravan I	208B0526	ex N5201M	opb PCM
☐ N755FX	Cessna 208B Caravan I	208B0529	ex N5264E	opb WIG
☐ N756FE	Cessna 208B Caravan I	208B0251		opb BVN
☐ N756FX	Cessna 208B Caravan I	208B0532		opb CFS
☐ N760FE	Cessna 208B Caravan I	208B0252		opb CPT
☐ N761FE	Cessna 208B Caravan I	208B0254		opb IRO
☐ N762FE	Cessna 208B Caravan I	208B0255		opb PCM
☐ N763FE	Cessna 208B Caravan I	208B0256		opb PCM
☐ N764FE	Cessna 208B Caravan I	208B0258		opb MTN
☐ N765FE	Cessna 208B Caravan I	208B0259		opb BVN
☐ N766FE	Cessna 208B Caravan I	208B0260		opb CPT
☐ N767FE	Cessna 208B Caravan I	208B0262		opb IRO
☐ N768FE	Cessna 208B Caravan I	208B0263		opb PCM
☐ N770FE	Cessna 208B Caravan I	208B0265		opb BVN
☐ N771FE	Cessna 208B Caravan I	208B0267		opb PCM
☐ N772FE	Cessna 208B Caravan I	208B0268		opb PCM
☐ N773FE	Cessna 208B Caravan I	208B0269		opb BVN
☐ N774FE	Cessna 208B Caravan I	208B0271		opb BVN
☐ N775FE	Cessna 208B Caravan I	208B0272		opb CFS
☐ N778FE	Cessna 208B Caravan I	208B0275		opb CFS
☐ N779FE	Cessna 208B Caravan I	208B0276		opb CFS
☐ N780FE	Cessna 208B Caravan I	208B0277		opb WIG
☐ N781FE	Cessna 208B Caravan I	208B0278		opb PCM
☐ N782FE	Cessna 208B Caravan I	208B0280		opb PCM
☐ N783FE	Cessna 208B Caravan I	208B0281		opb WIG
☐ N784FE	Cessna 208B Caravan I	208B0282		opb IRO
☐ N785FE	Cessna 208B Caravan I	208B0283		opb PCM
☐ N786FE	Cessna 208B Caravan I	208B0284		opb BVN
☐ N787FE	Cessna 208B Caravan I	208B0285		opb MTN
☐ N788FE	Cessna 208B Caravan I	208B0286		opb CFS
☐ N789FE	Cessna 208B Caravan I	208B0287		opb WIG
☐ N790FE	Cessna 208B Caravan I	208B0288		opb PCM
☐ N792FE	Cessna 208B Caravan I	208B0290		opb MTN
☐ N794FE	Cessna 208B Caravan I	208B0292		opb CPT
☐ N795FE	Cessna 208B Caravan I	208B0293		opb IRO
☐ N796FE	Cessna 208B Caravan I	208B0212	ex C-FEXY	opb CPT
☐ N797FE	Cessna 208B Caravan I	208B0042	ex C-FEXH	opb CPT
☐ N798FE	Cessna 208B Caravan I	208B0174	ex C-FEDY	opb CPT
☐ N804FE	Cessna 208B Caravan I	208B0039	ex F-GETN	opb WIG
☐ N807FE	Cessna 208B Caravan I	208B0041	ex F-GETO	opb WIG
☐ N820FE	Cessna 208B Caravan I	208B0111	ex F-GHHC	opb MTN
☐ N828FE	Cessna 208B Caravan I	208B0122	ex F-GHHD	opb IRO
☐ N831FE	Cessna 208B Caravan I	208B0225	ex F-GHHE	opb MTN
☐ N841FE	Cessna 208B Caravan I	208B0144		opb BVN
☐ N843FE	Cessna 208B Caravan I	208B0147		opb IRO
☐ N844FE	Cessna 208B Caravan I	208B0149		opb PCM
☐ N845FE	Cessna 208B Caravan I	208B0152		opb BVN
☐ N846FE	Cessna 208B Caravan I	208B0154		opb CPT
☐ N847FE	Cessna 208B Caravan I	208B0156		opb MTN
☐ N848FE	Cessna 208B Caravan I	208B0158		opb MTN
☐ N849FE	Cessna 208B Caravan I	208B0162		opb MTN
☐ N850FE	Cessna 208B Caravan I	208B0164		opb CFS
☐ N851FE	Cessna 208B Caravan I	208B0166		opb CPT
☐ N852FE	Cessna 208B Caravan I	208B0168		opb MTN
☐ N853FE	Cessna 208B Caravan I	208B0170		opb MTN
☐ N855FE	Cessna 208B Caravan I	208B0203		opb MTN
☐ N856FE	Cessna 208B Caravan I	208B0176		opb CFS

☐ N857FE	Cessna 208B Caravan I	208B0177		opb PCM
☐ N858FE	Cessna 208B Caravan I	208B0178		opb IRO
☐ N859FE	Cessna 208B Caravan I	208B0181		opb CFS
☐ N860FE	Cessna 208B Caravan I	208B0182		opb CPT
☐ N861FE	Cessna 208B Caravan I	208B0183		opb BVN
☐ N862FE	Cessna 208B Caravan I	208B0184		opb MTN
☐ N863FE	Cessna 208B Caravan I	208B0186		opb CPT
☐ N864FE	Cessna 208B Caravan I	208B0187		opb CPT
☐ N865FE	Cessna 208B Caravan I	208B0188		opb WIG
☐ N866FE	Cessna 208B Caravan I	208B0189	ex HK-3924X	opb BVN
☐ N867FE	Cessna 208B Caravan I	208B0191		opb CPT
☐ N869FE	Cessna 208B Caravan I	208B0195		opb MTN
☐ N870FE	Cessna 208B Caravan I	208B0196		opb WIG
☐ N871FE	Cessna 208B Caravan I	208B0198		opb IRO
☐ N872FE	Cessna 208B Caravan I	208B0200		opb PCM
☐ N873FE	Cessna 208B Caravan I	208B0202		opb CFS
☐ N874FE	Cessna 208B Caravan I	208B0205		opb MTN
☐ N875FE	Cessna 208B Caravan I	208B0206		opb CFS
☐ N876FE	Cessna 208B Caravan I	208B0207		opb CFS
☐ N877FE	Cessna 208B Caravan I	208B0232		opb CPT
☐ N878FE	Cessna 208B Caravan I	208B0211		opb MTN
☐ N879FE	Cessna 208B Caravan I	208B0213		opb PCM
☐ N880FE	Cessna 208B Caravan I	208B0215		opb CFS
☐ N881FE	Cessna 208B Caravan I	208B0204		opb MTN
☐ N882FE	Cessna 208B Caravan I	208B0208		opb CFS
☐ N884FE	Cessna 208B Caravan I	208B0233		opb IRO
☐ N885FE	Cessna 208B Caravan I	208B0185		opb CPT
☐ N886FE	Cessna 208B Caravan I	208B0190		opb PCM
☐ N887FE	Cessna 208B Caravan I	208B0216		opb MTN
☐ N888FE	Cessna 208B Caravan I	208B0217		opb WIG
☐ N889FE	Cessna 208B Caravan I	208B0218		opb BVN
☐ N890FE	Cessna 208B Caravan I	208B0219		opb CPT
☐ N891FE	Cessna 208B Caravan I	208B0221		opb PCM
☐ N894FE	Cessna 208B Caravan I	208B0224		opb BVN
☐ N895FE	Cessna 208B Caravan I	208B0015	ex C-FEXG	opb CFS
☐ N897FE	Cessna 208B Caravan I	208B0227		opb CFS
☐ N898FE	Cessna 208B Caravan I	208B0228		opb WIG
☐ N899FE	Cessna 208B Caravan I	208B0235		opb CFS
☐ N900FE	Cessna 208B Caravan I	208B0054	ex (F-GJHL)	opb BVN
☐ N902FE	Cessna 208B Caravan I	208B0002		opb BVN
☐ N903FE	Cessna 208B Caravan I	208B0003		opb CPT
☐ N904FE	Cessna 208B Caravan I	208B0004		opb CPT
☐ N905FE	Cessna 208B Caravan I	208B0005		opb MTN
☐ N906FE	Cessna 208B Caravan I	208B0006		opb IRO
☐ N907FE	Cessna 208B Caravan I	208B0007		opb IRO
☐ N908FE	Cessna 208B Caravan I	208B0008		opb PCM
☐ N909FE	Cessna 208B Caravan I	208B0009		opb WIG
☐ N910FE	Cessna 208B Caravan I	208B0010		opb CPT
☐ N911FE	Cessna 208B Caravan I	208B0011		opb WIG
☐ N912FE	Cessna 208B Caravan I	208B0012		opb BVN
☐ N914FE	Cessna 208B Caravan I	208B0014		opb IRO
☐ N916FE	Cessna 208B Caravan I	208B0016		opb CPT
☐ N918FE	Cessna 208B Caravan I	208B0018		opb CFS
☐ N919FE	Cessna 208B Caravan I	208B0019		opb WIG
☐ N920FE	Cessna 208B Caravan I	208B0020		opb PCM
☐ N921FE	Cessna 208B Caravan I	208B0021		opb MTN
☐ N922FE	Cessna 208B Caravan I	208B0022		opb BVN
☐ N923FE	Cessna 208B Caravan I	208B0023		opb IRO
☐ N924FE	Cessna 208B Caravan I	208B0024		opb CPT
☐ N925FE	Cessna 208B Caravan I	208B0025		opb IRO
☐ N926FE	Cessna 208B Caravan I	208B0026		opb CPT
☐ N927FE	Cessna 208B Caravan I	208B0027		opb IRO
☐ N928FE	Cessna 208B Caravan I	208B0028		opb BVN
☐ N929FE	Cessna 208B Caravan I	208B0029		opb BVN
☐ N930FE	Cessna 208B Caravan I	208B0030		opb PCM
☐ N931FE	Cessna 208B Caravan I	208B0031		opb WIG
☐ N933FE	Cessna 208B Caravan I	208B0033		opb CPT
☐ N934FE	Cessna 208B Caravan I	208B0034		opb BVN
☐ N935FE	Cessna 208B Caravan I	208B0035		opb WIG
☐ N936FE	Cessna 208B Caravan I	208B0036		opb CPT
☐ N937FE	Cessna 208B Caravan I	208B0037		opb WIG
☐ N938FE	Cessna 208B Caravan I	208B0038		opb MTN
☐ N939FE	Cessna 208B Caravan I	208B0180		opb BVN
☐ N940FE	Cessna 208B Caravan I	208B0040		opb CFS
☐ N943FE	Cessna 208B Caravan I	208B0043		opb MTN
☐ N946FE	Cessna 208B Caravan I	208B0048	ex (N948FE)	opb IRO
☐ N947FE	Cessna 208B Caravan I	208B0050	ex (N950FE)	opb WIG
☐ N950FE	Cessna 208B Caravan I	208B0056	ex (N956FE)	dam 30Dec14
☐ N952FE	Cessna 208B Caravan I	208B0060	ex (N960FE)	opb CPT
☐ N953FE	Cessna 208B Caravan I	208B0062	ex (N962FE)	opb CFS
☐ N954FE	Cessna 208B Caravan I	208B0064	ex (N964FE)	opb IRO
☐ N955FE	Cessna 208B Caravan I	208B0066	ex (N966FE)	opb MTN
☐ N956FE	Cessna 208B Caravan I	208B0068	ex (N968FE)	opb CFS

☐ N957FE	Cessna 208B Caravan I	208B0070	ex (N970FE)			opb BVN
☐ N958FE	Cessna 208B Caravan I	208B0071				opb WIG
☐ N959FE	Cessna 208B Caravan I	208B0073				opb WIG
☐ N960FE	Cessna 208B Caravan I	208B0075				opb CFS
☐ N961FE	Cessna 208B Caravan I	208B0077				opb BVN
☐ N962FE	Cessna 208B Caravan I	208B0078				opb MTN
☐ N963FE	Cessna 208B Caravan I	208B0080				opb WIG
☐ N964FE	Cessna 208B Caravan I	208B0083				opb CPT
☐ N965FE	Cessna 208B Caravan I	208B0084				opb CFS
☐ N966FE	Cessna 208B Caravan I	208B0086				opb WIG
☐ N967FE	Cessna 208B Caravan I	208B0088				opb MTN
☐ N968FE	Cessna 208B Caravan I	208B0090				opb PCM
☐ N969FE	Cessna 208B Caravan I	208B0092				opb PCM
☐ N970FE	Cessna 208B Caravan I	208B0093				opb BVN
☐ N971FE	Cessna 208B Caravan I	208B0094				opb CPT
☐ N972FE	Cessna 208B Caravan I	208B0096				opb CPT
☐ N975FE	Cessna 208B Caravan I	208B0101				opb MTN
☐ N976FE	Cessna 208B Caravan I	208B0103				opb CFS
☐ N977FE	Cessna 208B Caravan I	208B0104				opb CPT
☐ N980FE	Cessna 208B Caravan I	208B0108				opb CPT
☐ N981FE	Cessna 208B Caravan I	208B0110				opb WIG
☐ N983FE	Cessna 208B Caravan I	208B0113				opb CFS
☐ N984FE	Cessna 208B Caravan I	208B0115				opb PCM
☐ N985FE	Cessna 208B Caravan I	208B0117				opb PCM
☐ N985FX	Cessna 208B Caravan I	208B2369				
☐ N986FE	Cessna 208B Caravan I	208B0194				opb IRO
☐ N986FX	Cessna 208B Caravan I	208B2377				
☐ N987FE	Cessna 208B Caravan I	208B0201				opb PCM
☐ N987FX	Cessna 208B Caravan I	208B2390				
☐ N988FX	Cessna 208B Caravan I	208B2400				
☐ N989FE	Cessna 208B Caravan I	208B0124				opb WIG
☐ N989FX	Cessna 208B Caravan I	208B2403				
☐ N990FE	Cessna 208B Caravan I	208B0125				opb CPT
☐ N990FX	Cessna 208B Caravan I	208B2276				
☐ N991FE	Cessna 208B Caravan I	208B0127				opb CPT
☐ N991FX	Cessna 208B Caravan I	208B2279				
☐ N992FE	Cessna 208B Caravan I	208B0128				opb CFS
☐ N992FX	Cessna 208B Caravan I	208B2288				
☐ N993FE	Cessna 208B Caravan I	208B0130				opb IRO
☐ N993FX	Cessna 208B Caravan i	208B2289				
☐ N994FE	Cessna 208B Caravan I	208B0132				opb BVN
☐ N994FX	Cessna 208B Caravan I	208B2315				
☐ N995FE	Cessna 208B Caravan I	208B0133				opb PCM
☐ N996FE	Cessna 208B Caravan I	208B0135				opb WIG
☐ N997FE	Cessna 208B Caravan I	208B0197				opb CPT
☐ N998FE	Cessna 208B Caravan I	208B0139				opb WIG
☐ N999FE	Cessna 208B Caravan I	208B0231				opb MTN
☐ N357FE	McDonnell-Douglas MD-10-10F	46939/203	ex N1849U	Channelle		
☐ N358FE	McDonnell-Douglas MD-10-10F	46633/297	ex N1839U	Kurt		
☐ N359FE	McDonnell-Douglas MD-10-10F	46635/307	ex N1842U	Michaela		
☐ N360FE	McDonnell-Douglas MD-10-10F	46636/309	ex N1843U	Phillip		[SIN]
☐ N361FE	McDonnell-Douglas MD-10-10F	48260/344	ex N1844U	Sion		
☐ N362FE	McDonnell-Douglas MD-10-10F	48261/347	ex N1845U	Cole		
☐ N363FE	McDonnell-Douglas MD-10-10F	48263/353	ex N1847U	Carter		
☐ N365FE	McDonnell-Douglas MD-10-10F	46601/6	ex N1802U	Joey		
☐ N366FE	McDonnell-Douglas MD-10-10F	46602/8	ex N1803U	Gretchen		
☐ N367FE	McDonnell-Douglas MD-10-10F	46605/15	ex N1806U	Lathan		[VCV]
☐ N368FE	McDonnell-Douglas MD-10-10F	46606/17	ex N1807U	Cindy		
☐ N369FE	McDonnell-Douglas MD-10-10F	46607/25	ex N1808U	Jessie		[VCV]
☐ N370FE	McDonnell-Douglas MD-10-10F	46608/26	ex N1809U	Jay		
☐ N371FE	McDonnell-Douglas MD-10-10F	46609/27	ex N1810U	Vincent		[VCV]
☐ N372FE	McDonnell-Douglas MD-10-10F	46610/32	ex N1811U	Gus		
☐ N373FE	McDonnell-Douglas MD-10-10F	46611/35	ex N1812U			
☐ N374FE	McDonnell-Douglas MD-10-10F	46612/39	ex N1813U	Brittnie		[VCV]
☐ N375FE	McDonnell-Douglas MD-10-10F	46613/42	ex N1814U			
☐ N377FE	McDonnell-Douglas MD-10-10F	47965/59	ex N1833U	Shelby		[VCV]
☐ N381FE	McDonnell-Douglas MD-10-10F	46615/76	ex N1816U	Duval		
☐ N383FE	McDonnell-Douglas MD-10-10F	46616/86	ex N1817U	Cody		
☐ N385FE	McDonnell-Douglas MD-10-10F	46619/119	ex N1820U	Lindsay		
☐ N386FE	McDonnell-Douglas MD-10-10F	46620/138	ex N1821U	TJ	first MD-10 conversion	[VCV]
☐ N387FE	McDonnell-Douglas MD-10-10F	46621/140	ex N1822U	Joel		[VCV]
☐ N389FE	McDonnell-Douglas MD-10-10F	46623/154	ex N1824U	Tayvon		[VCV]
☐ N390FE	McDonnell-Douglas MD-10-10F	46624/155	ex N1825U	Rasik		
☐ N392FE	McDonnell-Douglas MD-10-10F	46626/198	ex N1827U	Axton		[VCV]
☐ N394FE	McDonnell-Douglas MD-10-10F	46628/207	ex N1829U	Parker		
☐ N395FE	McDonnell-Douglas MD-10-10F	46629/208	ex N1830U	Audreon		[VCV]
☐ N396FE	McDonnell-Douglas MD-10-10F	46630/209	ex N1831U	Adrienne		
☐ N397FE	McDonnell-Douglas MD-10-10F	46631/210	ex N1832U	Stefani		[VCV]
☐ N398FE	McDonnell-Douglas MD-10-10F	46634/298	ex N1841U	Kacie		[VCV]
☐ N399FE	McDonnell-Douglas MD-10-10F	48262/351	ex N1846U	Tariq		[VCV]
☐ N550FE	McDonnell-Douglas MD-10-10F	46521/55	ex N121AA	Adam		
☐ N554FE	McDonnell-Douglas MD-10-10F	46708/62	ex N153AA			

☐ N556FE	McDonnell-Douglas MD-10-10F	46710/70	ex N160AA	Kirsten	[VCV]
☐ N559FE	McDonnell-Douglas MD-10-10F	46930/112	ex N167AA	Francesca	
☐ N560FE	McDonnell-Douglas MD-10-10F	46938/153	ex N168AA	Deonna	
☐ N562FE	McDonnell-Douglas MD-10-10F	46947/247	ex N126AA	Janai	
☐ N564FE	McDonnell-Douglas MD-10-10F	46984/250	ex N128AA	Ava	
☐ N566FE	McDonnell-Douglas MD-10-10F	46989/271	ex N130AA	Ben	
☐ N567FE	McDonnell-Douglas MD-10-10F	46994/273	ex N131AA	Meagan	
☐ N569FE	McDonnell-Douglas MD-10-10F	47828/319	ex N133AA	Stas	[VCV]
☐ N570FE	McDonnell-Douglas MD-10-10F	47829/321	ex N134AA	Joelle	
☐ N571FE	McDonnell-Douglas MD-10-10F	47830/323	ex N135AA	Ella	
☐ N10060	McDonnell-Douglas MD-10-10F	46970/269	ex N581LF	Haylee	
☐ N40061	McDonnell-Douglas MD-10-10F	46973/272	ex N591LF	Garrett	
☐ N68049	McDonnell-Douglas MD-10-10CF	47803/139		Dusty	
☐ N68050	McDonnell-Douglas MD-10-10CF	47804/142		Merideth Allison	[VCV]
☐ N68051	McDonnell-Douglas MD-10-10CF	47805/145		Todd	
☐ N68052	McDonnell-Douglas MD-10-10CF	47806/148		Brock	[VCV]
☐ N68053	McDonnell-Douglas MD-10-10CF	47807/173		Chayne	
☐ N68054	McDonnell-Douglas MD-10-10CF	47808/177		Eren	[VCV]
☐ N68057	McDonnell-Douglas MD-10-10CF	48264/379	ex N1848U	Nelson	[VCV]
☐ N302FE	McDonnell-Douglas MD-10-30CF	46801/103	ex N102TV	Cori	[VCV]
☐ N303FE	McDonnell-Douglas MD-10-30CF	46802/110	ex N103TV	Macy	
☐ N304FE	McDonnell-Douglas MD-10-30CF	46992/257	ex EC-DSF	Claire	
☐ N306FE	McDonnell-Douglas MD-10-30F	48287/409		John	
☐ N307FE	McDonnell-Douglas MD-10 30F	48291/412		Erin Lee	
☐ N308FE	McDonnell-Douglas MD-10-30F	48297/416		Ann	
☐ N311FE	McDonnell-Douglas MD-10-30CF	46871/219	ex LN-RKB	Sherrese	
☐ N312FE	McDonnell-Douglas MD-10-30CF	48300/433		Genevieve	[VCV]
☐ N313FE	McDonnell-Douglas MD-10-30F	48311/440		Bilal	
☐ N315FE	McDonnell-Douglas MD-10-30F	48313/443		Roxanna	
☐ N316FE	McDonnell-Douglas MD-10-30F	48314/444		Sarah	
☐ N317FE	McDonnell-Douglas MD-10-30CF	46835/277	ex N106WA	Madison	[VCV]
☐ N318FE	McDonnell-Douglas MD-10-30CF	46837/282	ex N108WA	Mason	
☐ N319FE	McDonnell-Douglas MD-10-30CF	47820/317	ex N112WA	Seth	
☐ N320FE	McDonnell-Douglas MD-10-30F	47835/326	ex OO-SLD	Maura	
☐ N321FE	McDonnell-Douglas MD-10-30F	47836/330	ex OO-SLE	Athena	
☐ N521FE	McDonnell-Douglas MD-11F	48478/514	ex N807DE	Janie	
☐ N522FE	McDonnell-Douglas MD-11F	48476/510	ex N805DE	Katelyn	
☐ N523FE	McDonnell-Douglas MD-11F	48479/536	ex N808DE	David	
☐ N524FE	McDonnell-Douglas MD-11F	48480/538	ex N809DE		[VCV]
☐ N525FE	McDonnell-Douglas MD-11F	48565/542	ex N810DE	McKinnon	
☐ N527FE	McDonnell-Douglas MD-11F	48601/562	ex N812DE		[VCV]
☐ N528FE	McDonnell-Douglas MD-11F	48623/605	ex N814DE	Trinity	
☐ N529FE	McDonnell-Douglas MD-11F	48624/622	ex N815DE		
☐ N572FE	McDonnell-Douglas MD-11ER	48755/613	ex N730BC	Masaki	
☐ N573FE	McDonnell-Douglas MD-11BCF	48769/603	ex N746BC	Tom	
☐ N574FE	McDonnell-Douglas MD-11F	48499/486	ex N499HE		
☐ N575FE	McDonnell-Douglas MD-11F	48500/493	ex N485LS	Sonni	
☐ N576FE	McDonnell-Douglas MD-11F	48501/513	ex N501FR	Keeley	
☐ N577FE	McDonnell-Douglas MD-11F	48469/519	ex B-18172	Tobias	[VCV]
☐ N578FE	McDonnell-Douglas MD-11F	48458/449	ex N489GX	Stephen	
☐ N579FE	McDonnell-Douglas MD-11F	48470/546	ex B-18151	Nash	[VCV]
☐ N580FE	McDonnell-Douglas MD-11F	48471/558	ex B-18152	Ashton	
☐ N582FE	McDonnell-Douglas MD-11F	48420/451	ex N1751A	Jamie	
☐ N583FE	McDonnell-Douglas MD-11F	48421/452	ex N1752K	Nancy	
☐ N584FE	McDonnell-Douglas MD-11F	48436/483	ex N1768D	Jeffrey Wellington	
☐ N585FE	McDonnell-Douglas MD-11F	48481/482	ex N1759	Katherine	Panda Express c/s
☐ N586FE	McDonnell-Douglas MD-11F	48487/469	ex N1753	Dylan	
☐ N587FE	McDonnell-Douglas MD-11F	48489/492	ex N1754	Trina	
☐ N588FE	McDonnell-Douglas MD-11F	48490/499	ex N1755	Kendra	
☐ N589FE	McDonnell-Douglas MD-11F	48491/503	ex N1756	Shaun	
☐ N590FE	McDonnell-Douglas MD-11F	48505/462	ex N1757A	Stan	
☐ N591FE	McDonnell-Douglas MD-11F	48527/504	ex N1758B	Mandy	
☐ N592FE	McDonnell-Douglas MD-11F	48550/526	ex N1760A	Joshua	
☐ N593FE	McDonnell-Douglas MD-11F	48551/527	ex N1761R	Harrison	
☐ N594FE	McDonnell-Douglas MD-11F	48552/530	ex N1762B	Derek	
☐ N595FE	McDonnell-Douglas MD-11F	48553/531	ex N1763	Avery	
☐ N596FE	McDonnell-Douglas MD-11F	48554/535	ex N1764B	Peyton	
☐ N597FE	McDonnell-Douglas MD-11F	48596/537	ex N1765B	Corbin	
☐ N598FE	McDonnell-Douglas MD-11F	48597/540	ex N1766A	Kate	
☐ N599FE	McDonnell-Douglas MD-11F	48598/550	ex N1767A	Mariana	
☐ N601FE	McDonnell-Douglas MD-11F	48401/447	ex N111MD	Jim Riedmeyer	
☐ N602FE	McDonnell-Douglas MD-11F	48402/448	ex N211MD	Malcolm Baldrige 1990	
☐ N603FE	McDonnell-Douglas MD-11F	48459/470		Elizabeth	
☐ N604FE	McDonnell-Douglas MD-11F	48460/497		Hollis	
☐ N605FE	McDonnell-Douglas MD-11F	48514/515		April Star	
☐ N606FE	McDonnell-Douglas MD-11F	48602/549		Charles & Teresa	
☐ N607FE	McDonnell-Douglas MD-11F	48547/517		Christina	
☐ N608FE	McDonnell-Douglas MD-11F	48548/521		Colton	
☐ N609FE	McDonnell-Douglas MD-11F	48549/545		Scott	
☐ N610FE	McDonnell-Douglas MD-11F	48603/551		Marisa	
☐ N612FE	McDonnell-Douglas MD-11F	48605/555		Alyssa	

☐ N613FE	McDonnell-Douglas MD-11F	48749/598		Krista	
☐ N614FE	McDonnell-Douglas MD-11F	48528/507		Cristy	
☐ N615FE	McDonnell-Douglas MD-11F	48767/602		Youhei	
☐ N616FE	McDonnell-Douglas MD-11F	48747/594		Shanita	
☐ N617FE	McDonnell-Douglas MD-11F	48748/595		Travis	
☐ N618FE	McDonnell-Douglas MD-11F	48754/604		Justin	
☐ N619FE	McDonnell-Douglas MD-11F	48770/607		Lyndon	
☐ N620FE	McDonnell-Douglas MD-11F	48791/635		Grady	
☐ N621FE	McDonnell-Douglas MD-11F	48792/636		Connor	
☐ N623FE	McDonnell-Douglas MD-11F	48794/638		Meghan	
☐ N624FE	McDonnell-Douglas MD-11F	48443/458	ex HB-IWA	Corinne	
☐ N625FE	McDonnell-Douglas MD-11BCF	48753/608	ex N785BC	Robyn	
☐ N628FE	McDonnell-Douglas MD-11F	48447/464	ex HB-IWE	Noah	
☐ N631FE	McDonnell-Douglas MD-11F	48454/477	ex HB-IWI		
☐ N642FE	McDonnell-Douglas MD-11F	48485/502	ex 9M-TGR	Elise	
☐ N643FE	McDonnell-Douglas MD-11F	48486/509	ex 9M-TGS	Haley	
☐ N644FE	McDonnell-Douglas MD-11F	48444/459	ex 9M-TGP	Adriana	[VCV]
☐ N645FE	McDonnell-Douglas MD-11F	48446/463	ex 9M-TGQ	Carmen	[VCV]
☐ N68092	McDonnell-Douglas MD-11CF	48632/582	ex N276WA		[VCV]
☐ N274FE	Boeing 727-233F (FedEx 3)	22039/1614	ex C-GYNA	Jessica	[VCV]

FLIGHT ALASKA　　　　　　　Tundra (TUD)　　　　　Dillingham-Memorial, AK (DLG)

☐ N207JP	Cessna 207 Skywagon	20700255		♦
☐ N755AB	Cessna 207A Stationair 8 II	20700622	ex HP-916	
☐ N916AC	Cessna 207 Skywagon	20700061	ex ZK-JFJ	
☐ N1653U	Cessna 207 Skywagon	20700253		
☐ N1704U	Cessna 207 Skywagon	20700304		
☐ N6470H	Cessna 207A Stationair 7 II	20700534		
☐ N7318U	Cessna 207A Skywagon	20700396		
☐ N7380U	Cessna 207A Skywagon	20700428		
☐ N7394U	Cessna 207A Skywagon	20700437		
☐ N9935M	Cessna 207A Skywagon	20700751		
☐ N70076	Cessna 207A Skywagon	20700547		
☐ N91060	Cessna T207 Turbo Skywagon	20700047		

FLORIDA AIR TRANSPORT　　　Florida Transport (FBN)　　　Fort Lauderdale-Executive, FL (FXE)

☐ N70BF	Douglas DC-6A	43720/373	ex XA-SCZ
☐ N460WA	Douglas C-54E	27359	ex 44-9133

40 MILE AIR　　　　　　　Mile-Air (Q5/MLA)　　　　　Tok-Junction, AK (TKJ)

☐ N87TS	Piper PA-31 Turbo Navajo B	31-7300969	ex N4426Y
☐ N207DG	Cessna T207 Turbo Skywagon	20700070	ex N91902
☐ N734GW	Cessna U206G Stationair 6	U20604832	
☐ N1541F	Cessna 185D Skywagon	185-0896	
☐ N4978C	Cessna U206G Stationair	U20603870	
☐ N5200X	Cessna U206G Stationair 6	U20605591	

FREEDOM AIR　　　　　　　Freedom (FP/FRE)　　　　　Agana, GU (GUM)

☐ N44FA	Cessna 207A Stationair 8	20700659	ex N75975
☐ N74NF	Short SD.3-60	SH3721	ex N121PC
☐ N76NF	Short SD.3-30	SH3044	ex N3445B
☐ N131FA	Piper PA-23-250 Aztec D	27-4097	ex N234SP
☐ N330FA	Short SD.3-30	SH3112	ex N188LM
☐ N4168R	Piper PA-32-300 Cherokee Six C	32-40484	
☐ N4171R	Piper PA-32-300 Cherokee Six C	32-40504	
☐ N7576Z	Cessna U206G Stationair	U20606375	
☐ N8628N	Piper PA-32-300 Cherokee Six	32-7140021	

FREIGHT RUNNERS EXPRESS　　　Freight Runners (FRG)　　　Milwaukee-General Mitchell Intl, WI (MKE)

☐ N109CZ	Beech 99	U-109	ex N2880A	Frtr
☐ N199CZ	Beech 99	U-30	ex N3RP	Frtr
☐ N299CZ	Beech 99	U-74	ex C-FCVJ	Frtr
☐ N399CZ	Beech 99	U-91	ex N195WA	Frtr
☐ N499CZ	Beech 99A	U-81	ex N36AK	Frtr
☐ N599CZ	Beech 99A	U-89	ex 5Y-BJW	Frtr
☐ N699CZ	Beech 99	U-10	ex (N84SD)	Frtr
☐ N799CZ	Beech 99	U-68	ex N196WA	Frtr
☐ N899CZ	Beech 99A	U-96	ex N199CA	Frtr
☐ N999CZ	Beech 99A	U-116	ex C-GZAM	
☐ N75GB	Cessna 402B	402B0912		
☐ N191CZ	Beech 1900C	UB-59	ex D-CARA	
☐ N192CZ	Beech 1900C-1	UC-118	ex N439QA	
☐ N193CZ	Beech 1900C-1	UC-73	ex ZS-OZZ	
☐ N402CZ	Cessna 402B	402B0213	ex C-GKFK	
☐ N1517U	Cessna 207 Skywagon	20700117		Frtr

☐ N1518U	Cessna 207 Skywagon	20700118		Frtr
☐ N7886Q	Cessna 402B	402B0214		

FRONTIER AIRLINES   Frontier Flight (F9/FFT)   Denver-International, CO (DEN)

☐ N902FR	Airbus A319-111	1515	ex D-AVYM		
☐ N904FR	Airbus A319-111	1579	ex D-AVWS	Trumpeter Swan	[GYR]
☐ N905FR	Airbus A319-111	1583	ex D-AVYC	Seal	
☐ N906FR	Airbus A319-111	1684	ex D-AVWK	Pronghorn Antelope	
☐ N908FR	Airbus A319-111	1759	ex D-AVYL	Blue Heron	
☐ N910FR	Airbus A319-112	1781	ex D-AVYK	Cougar	
☐ N912FR	Airbus A319-111	1803	ex D-AVWE	Red Fox Pup	
☐ N918FR	Airbus A319-111	1943	ex D-AVWH	Whitetail Deer	
☐ N919FR	Airbus A319-111	1980	ex D-AVYD	Ocelot	
☐ N920FR	Airbus A319-111	1997	ex D-AVYO	Coyote	
☐ N921FR	Airbus A319-111	2010	ex D-AVWO	Mountain Goat	
☐ N922FR	Airbus A319-111	2012	ex D-AVWR	Red Fox	
☐ N923FR	Airbus A319-111	2019	ex D-AVWV	Racoon	
☐ N924FR	Airbus A319-111	2030	ex D-AVYG	Polar Bear Cubs	
☐ N925FR	Airbus A319-111	2103	ex D-AVWH	Dall's Sheep	
☐ N926FR	Airbus A319-111	2198	ex D-AVYD	Black-tailed Deer Fawn	
☐ N927FR	Airbus A319-111	2209	ex D-AVYL	Bottle-nosed Dolphin	
☐ N928FR	Airbus A319-111	2236	ex D-AVWK	Bobcat	
☐ N929FR	Airbus A319-111	2240	ex D-AVWP	Lynx	
☐ N931FR	Airbus A319-111	2253	ex D-AVYR	Bear cub	
☐ N932FR	Airbus A319-111	2258	ex D-AVYK	Bald Eagle	
☐ N933FR	Airbus A319-111	2260	ex D-AVYX	Hawk	
☐ N934FR	Airbus A319-111	2287	ex D-AVYU	Lynx pup	
☐ N935FR	Airbus A319-111	2318	ex D-AVYJ	Sea Otter	
☐ N938FR	Airbus A319-111	2406	ex D-AVWA	Arctic Fox	
☐ N939FR	Airbus A319-111	2448	ex D-AVWL	Emperor Penguins	
☐ N941FR	Airbus A319-112	2483	ex D-AVYY	Gray Wolf	
☐ N943FR	Airbus A319-112	2518	ex D-AVWT	Fawn	
☐ N947FR	Airbus A319-111	2806	ex D-AVYK	Leopard	
☐ N948FR	Airbus A319-112	2836	ex D-AVXR	Pelican	
☐ N949FR	Airbus A319-112	2857	ex D-AVYL	White Ermine	
☐ N951FR	Airbus A319-112	4127	ex N412MX		
☐ N952FR	Airbus A319-112	4204	ex N204MX		
☐ N953FR	Airbus A319-112	4254	ex N254MX		
☐ N954FR	Airbus A319-112	1786	ex N786CT		
☐ N201FR	Airbus A320-214	3389	ex F-WWDQ	Elk	
☐ N202FR	Airbus A320-214	3431	ex F-WWDT	Colorado	
☐ N203FR	Airbus A320-214	1806	ex D-ALTI		
☐ N204FR	Airbus A320-214	2325	ex N270AV		
☐ N205FR	Airbus A320-214	4253	ex D-AXAB	Killer Whale	
☐ N206FR	Airbus A320-214	4272	ex F-WWBX	Polar Bear	
☐ N207FR	Airbus A320-214	4307	ex D-AXAK		
☐ N208FR	Airbus A320-214	4562	ex D-AUBX		
☐ N209FR	Airbus A320-214	4641	ex D-AVVO		
☐ N210FR	Airbus A320-214	4668	ex F-WWBJ		
☐ N211FR	Airbus A320-214	4688	ex F-WWIU		
☐ N213FR	Airbus A320-214	4704	ex F-WWDQ		
☐ N214FR	Airbus A320-214	4727	ex F-WWDZ		
☐ N216FR	Airbus A320-214	4745	ex F-WWIS		
☐ N218FR	Airbus A320-214	1615	ex N261AV		
☐ N219FR	Airbus A320-214	1860	ex N263AV		
☐ N220FR	Airbus A320-214/S	5661	ex D-AUBZ		
☐ N221FR	Airbus A320-214	3205	ex RP-C8607		
☐ N223FR	Airbus A320-214	2695	ex D-AAAN		
☐ N227FR	Airbus A320-214/S	6184	ex F-WWBY	Grizzly Bear-Grizwald	♦
☐ N228FR	Airbus A320-214/S	5526	ex G-ZBAA	Orville the Red Cardinal	♦
☐ N229FR	Airbus A320-214/S	5581	ex G-ZBAB	229	♦

FRONTIER FLYING SERVICES   Frontier-Air (2F/FTA)   Fairbanks, AK (FAI)

☐ N404GV	Beech 1900C-1	UC-154	ex N154YV	
☐ N575A	Beech 1900C-1	UC-83	ex N80334	
☐ N575Q	Beech 1900C-1	UC-160	ex N160AM	
☐ N575Z	Beech 1900C-1	UC-136	ex N21483	
☐ N815GV	Beech 1900C-1	UC-78	ex N121WV	
☐ N1553C	Beech 1900C	UC-24	ex N31226	
☐ N15503	Beech 1900C-1	UC-72		
☐ N17GN	Cessna 207A Stationair 8 II	20700693	ex C-GDFK	
☐ N23CF	Cessna 207 Skywagon	20700276		
☐ N104K	Cessna 207 Skywagon	20700122	ex C-GUHZ	
☐ N327CT	Cessna 207A Stationair 7 II	20700535	ex N6475H	
☐ N747SQ	Cessna 207A Skywagon	20700387	ex N1787U	
☐ N1668U	Cessna 207 Skywagon	20700268		
☐ N1754U	Cessna T207 Stationair	20700354		
☐ N5277J	Cessna 207A Stationair 8 II	20700772	ex N9975M	

☐ N6207H	Cessna 207A Stationair 7 II	20700551	ex C-FSEE	
☐ N7320U	Cessna 207A Skywagon	20700397		
☐ N7340U	Cessna 207A Skywagon	20700407		
☐ N7373U	Cessna 207A Skywagon	20700423		
☐ N7384U	Cessna 207A Stationair 7 II	20700431		
☐ N7389U	Cessna 207A Stationair 7 II	20700432		
☐ N9399M	Cessna 207A Stationair 8 II	20700652	ex VH-UAA	
☐ N9794M	Cessna 207A Stationair 8 II	20700730		>Fly BVI
☐ N9869M	Cessna 207A Stationair 8 II	20700744		
☐ N9946M	Cessna 207A Stationair 7 II	20700588		
☐ N9948M	Cessna 207A Stationair 8 II	20700759		
☐ N9996M	Cessna 207A Stationair 8 II	20700779		
☐ N73067	Cessna 207A Stationair 7 II	20700558		
☐ N91002	Cessna 207 Stationair	20700003		
☐ N28AN	Cessna 208B Caravan I	208B0751		
☐ N92JJ	Cessna 208B Caravan I	208B1074	ex N208FD	
☐ N126AR	Cessna 208B Caravan I	208B1004		♦
☐ N208SD	Cessna 208B Caravan I	208B0491	ex (N610DK)	
☐ N215MC	Cessna 208B Caravan I	208B0730	ex N12328	
☐ N233PC	Cessna 208B Caravan I	208B1179		♦
☐ N303GV	Cessna 208B Caravan I	208B0581		
☐ N405GV	Cessna 208B Caravan I	208B0892	ex C-GWCA	
☐ N407GV	Cessna 208B Caravan I	208B0616	ex N5262X	
☐ N409GV	Cessna 208B Caravan i	208B1110	ex N208BR	
☐ N410GV	Cessna 208B Caravan I	208B0632	ex N5264U	
☐ N411GV	Cessna 208B Caravan I	208B0672		
☐ N715HE	Cessna 208B Caravan I	208B0603	ex N715HL	
☐ N717PA	Cessna 208B Caravan I	208B0804	ex N12890	
☐ N814GV	Cessna 208B Caravan I	208B0958	ex XA-TVS	
☐ N838GV	Cessna 208B Caravan I	208B0838	ex N838FB	
☐ N1232Y	Cessna 208B Caravan I	208B0566	ex N5246Z	
☐ N1242Y	Cessna 208B Caravan I	208B0939	ex N124LA	
☐ N1275N	Cessna 208B Caravan I	208B0756		
☐ N1296Y	Cessna 208B Caravan I	208B1079	ex N52JJ	
☐ N3252Y	Cessna 208B Caravan I	208B1008		♦
☐ N12373	Cessna 208B Caravan I	208B0697		♦
☐ N44AC	Piper PA-31-350 Chieftain	31-8052147	ex N3590M	
☐ N137CS	Piper PA-31-350 Chieftain	31-8152137	ex C-GVPP	
☐ N200AK	Piper PA-31-350 Chieftain	31-8052180		♦
☐ N3516A	Piper PA-31-350 Chieftain	31-7952106		
☐ N3536B	Piper PA-31-350 Chieftain	31-7952205		
☐ N4112K	Piper PA-31-350 T-1020	31-8353006		
☐ N4301C	Piper PA-31-350 T-1020	31-8353001	ex C-FKGX	
☐ N4501B	Piper PA-31-350 Chieftain	31-8052168		
☐ N35497	Piper PA-31-350 Chieftain	31-8052039		
☐ N168LM	Short SD.3-30	SH3104		♦
☐ N261AG	Short SD.3-30	SH3117		♦
☐ N406GV	Reims Cessna F406 Caravan II	F406-0049	ex 9M-PMS	
☐ N861FT	Reims Cessna F406 Caravan II	F406-0034	ex OO-LMO	
☐ N6590Y	Reims Cessna F406 Caravan II	F406-0052	ex F-WZDU	
☐ N6591R	Reims Cessna F406 Caravan II	F406-0054	ex F-WZDX	
☐ N91361	Cessna 180H Skywagon	18052045		

FUGA AIR CHARTER — Scottsdale, AZ (SCF)

| ☐ N735TS | Embraer ERJ-135LR | 145386 | ex PT-SQK | ♦ |

GALLUP FLYING SERVICE — Gallup-Municipal, NM (GUP)

☐ N425RM	Cessna 425	425-0180	ex N68731	
☐ N986GM	Cessna 414A Chancellor	414A0089	ex N612CB	
☐ N6640C	Cessna 414A Chancellor	414A0044		
☐ N7909Q	Cessna T310Q	310Q0620		
☐ N8840K	Cessna 414A Chancellor	414A0236		
☐ N29359	Cessna 210L Centurion II	21059858		
☐ N68149	Cessna 414A Chancellor	414A0642		

GATEWAY CANYONS AIR TOURS — Grand Junction, CO

| ☐ N301GC | Aérospatiale AS350B3 Astar | 7068 | ex N949AE | |

GB AIRLINK — Island Tiger (GBX)   Fort Lauderdale-Hollywood Intl, FL (FLL)

☐ N30GB	Beech H-18	BA-688		Frtr
☐ N80GB	Short SC.7 Skyvan 3	SH1888	ex LX-ABC	Frtr
☐ N231SK	Volpar Turboliner	AF-856	ex N346V	Frtr♦
☐ N320GB	Beech G-18S	BA-509		Frtr♦
☐ N911E	Beech E-18S	BA-10	ex N501J	Frtr

GO! EXPRESS   Honolulu-Intl, HI (HNL)

Opb Mokulele Airlines

GOJET AIRLINES   Lindbergh (G7/GJS)   St Louis-Lambert Intl, MO (STL)

GoJet Airlines is a wholly owned subsidiary of Trans States Airlines and ops feeder services for United Express.

GRAND CANYON AIRLINES   Canyon View (CVU)

Grand Canyon-National Park, AZ/Valle-J Robidoux, AZ (GCN/VLE)

☐ N74GC	de Havilland DHC-6 Twin Otter 300	559	ex J6-AAK		
☐ N171GC	de Havilland DHC-6 Twin Otter 300	406	ex J8-VBR	>LCB	
☐ N173GC	de Havilland DHC-6 Twin Otter 300	295	ex C-GLAZ		
☐ N177GC	de Havilland DHC-6 Twin Otter 300	263	ex N102AC		
☐ N189GC	de Havilland DHC-6 Twin Otter 300	722	ex TI-BFO	♦	
☐ N190GC	de Havilland DHC-6 Twin Otter 300	285	ex TI-BDM		
☐ N227SA	de Havilland DHC-6 Twin Otter 300	517	ex N43SP		
☐ N297SA	de Havilland DHC-6 Twin Otter 300	297		♦	
☐ N192GC	Cessna 208B Caravan I	208B2026	ex N708RL		

GRANT AVIATION   (GV/GUN)   Emmonak, AK (EMK)

☐ N8NZ	Cessna 207A Stationair 7 II	20700421	ex VH-XXL
☐ N48CF	Cessna T207A Turbo Skywagon	20700366	
☐ N207EX	Cessna 207 Stationair	20700100	ex N91167
☐ N9651M	Cessna 207A Stationair 8 II	20700715	
☐ N9728M	Cessna 207A Stationair 8 II	20700721	
☐ N28KE	Piper PA-31-350 Chieftain	31-8152049	ex C-GVSX
☐ N77HV	Piper PA-31-350 Chieftain	31-8152193	ex C-GLCN
☐ N78GA	Piper PA-31-350 Chieftain	31-8352030	ex XA-DAM
☐ N417PM	Piper PA-31-350 Chieftain	31-8052051	ex N357CT
☐ N4105D	Piper PA-31-350 Chieftain	31-8252027	
☐ N25JA	Cessna 208B Caravan I	208B1212	

GREAT LAKES AIRLINES   Lakes Air (ZK/GLA)   Cheyenne, WY (CYS)

☐ N100UX	Beech 1900D	UE-100		Fly Telluride
☐ N122UX	Beech 1900D	UE-122	ex N122YV	
☐ N153GL	Beech 1900D	UE-153	ex N153ZV	
☐ N154GL	Beech 1900D	UE-154	ex N154ZV	Sierra Vista
☐ N169GL	Beech 1900D	UE-169		dam 01Sep13
☐ N170GL	Beech 1900D	UE-170	ex N170YV	Garden City, NE
☐ N184UX	Beech 1900D	UE-184	ex N184YV	
☐ N192GL	Beech 1900D	UE-192	ex N192YV	Telluride, CO
☐ N195GL	Beech 1900D	UE-195	ex N195YV	Miles City, MT
☐ N201GL	Beech 1900D	UE-201	ex N201YQ	Pierre, SD
☐ N202UX	Beech 1900D	UE-202	ex N202ZK	
☐ N208GL	Beech 1900D	UE-208	ex N208YV	Fly Telluride
☐ N210GL	Beech 1900D	UE-210	ex N210UX	
☐ N211GL	Beech 1900D	UE-211	ex N211UX	Laramie, WY
☐ N219GL	Beech 1900D	UE-219	ex N219YV	
☐ N220GL	Beech 1900D	UE-220	ex N220UX	Hays, KS
☐ N231YV	Beech 1900D	UE-231		
☐ N240GL	Beech 1900D	UE-240	ex N240YV	Devil's Tower, WY
☐ N245GL	Beech 1900D	UE-245	ex N245YV	
☐ N247GL	Beech 1900D	UE-247	ex N247YV	
☐ N251GL	Beech 1900D	UE-251	ex N251ZV	Grand Tetons
☐ N253GL	Beech 1900D	UE-253	ex N253YV	
☐ N254GL	Beech 1900D	UE-254	ex N10840	Grand Island, NE
☐ N255GL	Beech 1900D	UE-255	ex N10860	>SCE
☐ N257GL	Beech 1900D	UE-257	ex N257YV	
☐ N261GL	Beech 1900D	UE-261	ex N261YV	Scotts Bluff, NE
☐ N71GL	Embraer EMB.120ER Brasilia	120071	ex N267UE	
☐ N96ZK	Embraer EMB.120ER Brasilia	120096	ex N452UE	
☐ N108UX	Embraer EMB.120ER Brasilia	120108	ex N451UE	
☐ N293UX	Embraer EMB.120ER Brasilia	120293	ex PT-SVN	
☐ N297UX	Embraer EMB.120ER Brasilia	120297	ex PT-SVQ	
☐ N299UX	Embraer EMB.120ER Brasilia	120299	ex PT-SVT	

GREAT SOUTHERN AIRWAYS

☐ N341GS	Convair C-131F	281	ex Bu140998
☐ N342GS	Convair C-131F	299	ex Bu141016
☐ N343GS	Convair C-131F	305	ex Bu141022

| ☐ N344GS | Convair C-131F | 311 | ex Bu141028 | |
| ☐ N8149H | Convair C-131F | | ex Bu141008 | ♦ |

GRIFFINGS ISLAND AIRLINES — Sandusky-Griffing, OH (SKY)

☐ N428S	Piper PA-32-301 Saratoga	32-8106021	
☐ N442S	Britten-Norman BN-2A-20 Islander	770	ex N6863G
☐ N450S	Beech B200 Super King Air	BB-1035	ex N7GA

GULF & CARIBBEAN AIR — Trans Auto (TSU) — Fort Lauderdale-Hollywood Intl, FL (FLL)

☐ N431FL	AMD Falcon 20	249	ex N451DP		
☐ N461FL	AMD Falcon 20	94	ex N566YT		
☐ N471FL	AMD Falcon 20C	163	ex N258PE		
☐ N481FL	AMD Falcon 20-5	27	ex N326VW		
☐ N511FL	AMD Falcon 20-5	122	ex N302TT		
☐ N521FL	AMD Falcon 20-5	68	ex N458SW		
☐ N531FL	AMD Falcon 20-5	113	ex N22WJ		
☐ N541FL	AMD Falcon 20-5	48	ex N23ND		
☐ N581FL	AMD Falcon 20F	440	ex N205JC		♦
☐ N131FL	Convair 580	155	ex N5804	13	Frtr
☐ N141FL	Convair 580F	111	ex N302K	14	Frtr
☐ N151FL	Convair 580	51	ex N5810	15	Frtr
☐ N171FL	Convair 580	318	ex N300K		Frtr
☐ N181FL	Convair 580	387	ex N301K	18	Frtr
☐ N191FL	Convair 580	326	ex N923DR	19	Frtr
☐ N351FL	Convair 5800	279	ex C-FKFS		Frtr
☐ N361FL	Convair 5800	343	ex C-FKFS		
☐ N371FL	Convair 5800	309	ex C-FMKF		Frtr
☐ N381FL	Convair 5800	276	ex C-FKFS		Frtr
☐ N391FL	Convair 5800	278	ex C-GKFD		Frtr
☐ N991FL	Convair 580	508	ex C-GTTG		Frtr
☐ N7813B	Convair 340-70	265	ex 53-7813		wfs
☐ N8149P	Convair C-131F	292	ex Bu141009		wfs
☐ N51211	Convair 580	489	ex N5121		wfs
☐ N51255	Convair 580	383	ex N45LC		wfs
☐ N215WE	Boeing 727-2S2F	22936/1830	ex N215FE		
☐ N216WE	Boeing 727-2S2F	22937/1831	ex N216FE		
☐ N251FL	Boeing 727-277F/W (Duganair 3)	20551/1054	ex C-GYKF	717	
☐ N281FL	Boeing 727-281F (Raisbeck 3)	21455/1316	ex C-GKFJ		♦

GULF ATLANTIC AIRWAYS

☐ N750DR	Cessna 310R	310R0064	ex 3A-MDP	
☐ N860CR	Cessna 560 Citation V	560-0500		♦
☐ N891CA	Cessna 500 Citation I	500-0168	ex N135MA	
☐ N939TW	Cessna 560 Citation V	560-0185	ex N989TW	
☐ N83223	Piper PA-44-180T Seminole	44-8107036		♦

HAVANA AIR — Miami, FL (MIA)

| ☐ N745VA | Boeing 737-405 | 24271/1738 | ex N427BV | opb RBY♦ |
| ☐ P4-MDD | McDonnell-Douglas MD-82 | 49972/1757 | ex PJ-MDD | <INA♦ |

HAWAIIAN AIRLINES — Hawaiian (HA/HAL) — Honolulu-Intl, HI (HNL)

☐ N370HA	Airbus A330-243	1511	ex F-WWKN	Kuamo'o	
☐ N373HA	Airbus A330-243	1530	ex F-WWCE	Kūkalani'ehu	
☐ N374HA	Airbus A330-243	1565	ex F-WWYY	Melemele	
☐ N375HA	Airbus A330-243	1606	ex F-WWCR		♦
☐ N378HA	Airbus A330-243	1615	ex F-WWYN		♦
☐ N380HA	Airbus A330-243	1104	ex F-WWYX		
☐ N381HA	Airbus A330-243	1114	ex F-WWYN		
☐ N382HA	Airbus A330-243	1171	ex F-WWYA	Iwakeli'i	
☐ N383HA	Airbus A330-243	1217	ex F-WWKR		
☐ N384HA	Airbus A330-243	1259	ex F-WWYV	Hokupa'a	
☐ N385HA	Airbus A330-243	1295	ex F-WWYD	Manalakalani	
☐ N386HA	Airbus A330-243	1302	ex F-WWKO	Heiheionakeiki	
☐ N388HA	Airbus A330-243	1310	ex F-WWKN	Nahiku	
☐ N389HA	Airbus A330-243	1316	ex F-WWKJ	Keali'iokonaikalewa	
☐ N390HA	Airbus A330-243	1389	ex F-WWYU	Nāmāhoe	
☐ N391HA	Airbus A330-243	1399	ex F-WWYI	Hokulei	
☐ N392HA	Airbus A330-243	1404	ex F-WWYM	Hikianalia	
☐ N393HA	Airbus A330-243	1422	ex F-WWTX	Lehuakona	
☐ N395HA	Airbus A330-243	1469	ex F-WWKZ	A'a	
☐ N396HA	Airbus A330-243	1488	ex F-WWYZ	Keoe	
☐ N399HA	Airbus A330-243	1496	ex F-WWTP	Kūmsu	
☐ N	Airbus A330-243	1672	ex F-WW		o/o♦
☐ N475HA	Boeing 717-22A	55121/5050		I'Iwi	

☐ N476HA	Boeing 717-22A	55118/5053		Elepaio	
☐ N477HA	Boeing 717-22A	55122/5061		Apapane	
☐ N478HA	Boeing 717-22A	55123/5064		Amakihi	
☐ N479HA	Boeing 717-22A	55124/5069		Akepa	
☐ N480HA	Boeing 717-22A	55125/5070		Pueo	
☐ N481HA	Boeing 717-22A	55126/5073		Alauahio	
☐ N483HA	Boeing 717-22A	55128/5079	ex N604AT		
☐ N484HA	Boeing 717-22A	55129/5080		Oma'o	
☐ N485HA	Boeing 717-22A	55130/5089		Palila	
☐ N486HA	Boeing 717-22A	55131/5092		Akiki	
☐ N487HA	Boeing 717-22A	55132/5098		Lo	
☐ N488HA	Boeing 717-23S	55001/5002	ex VH-NXF		
☐ N489HA	Boeing 717-23S	55002/5003	ex VH-NXB		
☐ N490HA	Boeing 717-23S	55151/5041	ex VH-NXC		
☐ N491HA	Boeing 717-2BL	55175/5125	ex N912ME		[HNL]
☐ N492HA	Boeing 717-2BL	55181/5135	ex N919ME	Ewa Ewa	
☐ N493HA	Boeing 717-2BL	55184/5142	ex N922ME	Ua'u	
☐ N580HA	Boeing 767-33AER/W	28140/850		Kolea	
☐ N581HA	Boeing 767-33AER/W	28141/853		Manu o Ku	
☐ N582HA	Boeing 767-33AER/W	28139/857		Ake Ake	
☐ N583HA	Boeing 767-33AER	25531/423	ex D-AMUP	A	
☐ N587HA	Boeing 767-33AER/W	33421/887		Pakalakala	
☐ N588HA	Boeing 767-3CBER/W	33466/890		Iwa	
☐ N590HA	Boeing 767-3CBER/W	33467/894		Koa'e Ula	
☐ N592HA	Boeing 767-3CBER/W	33468/898		Hunakai	
☐ N594HA	Boeing 767-332	23275/136	ex N116DL		

HORIZON AIR		*Horizon Air (QX/QXE)*		*Seattle-Tacoma Intl, WA (SEA)*	
☐ N600QX	Canadair CRJ-701ER	10005	ex C-GCRA	600	>ASQ
☐ N603QX	Canadair CRJ-701ER	10011	ex C-GHCZ	603	>SKW
☐ N604QX	Canadair CRJ-701ER	10019	ex C-GIAJ	604	>ASQ
☐ N605QX	Canadair CRJ-701ER	10022	ex C-GIAR	605	>ASQ
☐ N608QX	Canadair CRJ-701ER	10026	ex C-GIAX	608	>ASQ
☐ N611QX	Canadair CRJ-701ER	10041	ex C-GICP	611	>ASQ
☐ N612QX	Canadair CRJ-701ER	10042	ex C-GHZV	612	>ASQ
☐ N613QX	Canadair CRJ-701ER	10045	ex C-GIAD	613	>SKW
☐ N614QX	Canadair CRJ-701ER	10049	ex C-GIAJ	614	>ASQ
☐ N615QX	Canadair CRJ-701ER	10065	ex C-GIBQ	615	>ASQ
☐ N616QX	Canadair CRJ-701ER	10128	ex C-	616	>SKW
☐ N617QX	Canadair CRJ-701ER	10130	ex C-	617	>SKW
☐ N619QX	Canadair CRJ-701ER	10246	ex C-	619	>SKW
☐ N358PH	de Havilland DHC-8-202Q	506	ex C-FWBB		>UCA
☐ N359PH	de Havilland DHC-8-202Q	514	ex C-GEOA	City of Kelowna	>UCA
☐ N360PH	de Havilland DHC-8-202Q	515	ex C-GEWI	City of Medford	>UCA
☐ N361PH	de Havilland DHC-8-202Q	516	ex C-GFOD	City of Sun Valley	>UCA
☐ N362PH	de Havilland DHC-8-202Q	518	ex C-FDHI		>UCA
☐ N363PH	de Havilland DHC-8-202Q	520	ex C-FDHP	City of Boise	>UCA
☐ N364PH	de Havilland DHC-8-202Q	524	ex C-FDHX	Cities of Seattle/Tacoma	>UCA
☐ N365PH	de Havilland DHC-8-202Q	526	ex C-FDHZ	City of Pocatello	>UCA
☐ N366PH	de Havilland DHC-8-202Q	510	ex C-GELN	City of Redding	>UCA
☐ N367PH	de Havilland DHC-8-202Q	511	ex C-GDLD		>UCA
☐ N368PH	de Havilland DHC-8-202Q	512	ex C-GDFT	City of Idaho Falls	>UCA
☐ N369PH	de Havilland DHC-8-202Q	513	ex C-FWBB		>UCA
☐ N374PH	de Havilland DHC-8-202Q	528	ex C-GDIU		>UCA
☐ N375PH	de Havilland DHC-8-202Q	529	ex C-GDKL		>UCA
☐ N379PH	de Havilland DHC-8-202Q	530	ex C-GDLK		>UCA
☐ N400QX	de Havilland DHC-8-402Q	4030	ex C-GFCF		
☐ N401QX	de Havilland DHC-8-402Q	4031	ex C-GFCW		
☐ N402QX	de Havilland DHC-8-402Q	4032	ex C-GFOD		
☐ N403QX	de Havilland DHC-8-402Q	4037	ex C-FDHP		
☐ N404QX	de Havilland DHC-8-402Q	4046	ex C-GDKL		
☐ N405QX	de Havilland DHC-8-402Q	4047	ex C-GDLD		
☐ N406QX	de Havilland DHC-8-402Q	4048	ex C-GDLK		
☐ N407QX	de Havilland DHC-8-402Q	4049	ex C-GDNK		
☐ N408QX	de Havilland DHC-8-402Q	4050	ex C-GFCA		
☐ N409QX	de Havilland DHC-8-402Q	4051	ex C-GFCW		
☐ N410QX	de Havilland DHC-8-402Q	4053	ex C-GFQL		
☐ N411QX	de Havilland DHC-8-402Q	4055	ex C-GFUM		
☐ N412QX	de Havilland DHC-8-402Q	4059	ex C-FGNP		
☐ N413QX	de Havilland DHC-8-402Q	4060	ex C-FNGB		
☐ N414QX	de Havilland DHC-8-402Q	4061	ex C-GDFT		
☐ N415QX	de Havilland DHC-8-402Q	4081	ex C-GELN		
☐ N416QX	de Havilland DHC-8-402Q	4083	ex C-GDNK		
☐ N417QX	de Havilland DHC-8-402Q	4086	ex C-FCSG		
☐ N418QX	de Havilland DHC-8-402Q	4143	ex C-FHQX		
☐ N419QX	de Havilland DHC-8-402Q	4145	ex C-FHRD		
☐ N420QX	de Havilland DHC-8-402Q	4147	ex C-FJLA		
☐ N421QX	de Havilland DHC-8-402Q	4149	ex C-FJLF		
☐ N422QX	de Havilland DHC-8-402Q	4150	ex C-FJLG		

☐ N423QX	de Havilland DHC-8-402Q	4153	ex C-FJLO		
☐ N426QX	de Havilland DHC-8-402Q	4154	ex C-FJLX		
☐ N427QX	de Havilland DHC-8-402Q	4156	ex C-FLKU		
☐ N428QX	de Havilland DHC-8-402Q	4160	ex C-FLTL		
☐ N429QX	de Havilland DHC-8-402Q	4161	ex C-FLTT		
☐ N430QX	de Havilland DHC-8-402Q	4163	ex C-FMES		
☐ N431QX	de Havilland DHC-8-402Q	4164	ex C-FMEU		
☐ N432QX	de Havilland DHC-8-402Q	4166	ex C-FMFH		
☐ N433QX	de Havilland DHC-8-402Q	4210	ex C-FPQB		
☐ N434MK	de Havilland DHC-8-402Q	4227	ex C-FTUQ	Milton G Koult II	
☐ N435QX	de Havilland DHC-8-402Q	4232	ex C-FUCO		
☐ N436QX	de Havilland DHC-8-402Q	4236	ex C-FUOF		
☐ N437QX	de Havilland DHC-8-402Q	4240	ex C-FUSM		
☐ N438QX	de Havilland DHC-8-402Q	4243	ex C-FUTP		
☐ N439QX	de Havilland DHC-8-402Q	4246	ex C-FVGY		
☐ N440QX	de Havilland DHC-8-402Q	4347	ex C-GHCV		
☐ N441QX	de Havilland DHC-8-402Q	4348	ex C-GHCY		
☐ N442QX	de Havilland DHC-8-402Q	4352	ex C-GHWA		
☐ N443QX	de Havilland DHC-8-402Q	4353	ex C-GILG		
☐ N444QX	de Havilland DHC-8-402Q	4355	ex C-GHYE		
☐ N445QX	de Havilland DHC-8-402Q	4358	ex C-GILN		
☐ N446QX	de Havilland DHC-8-402Q	4363	ex C-GISZ		
☐ N447QX	de Havilland DHC-8-402Q	4364	ex C-GITK		
☐ N448QX	de Havilland DHC-8-402Q	4409	ex C-GMYH		
☐ N449QX	de Havilland DHC-8-402Q	4410	ex C-GNGZ		
☐ N450QX	de Havilland DHC-8-402Q	4452	ex C-GVYA	450	
☐ N451QX	de Havilland DHC-8-402Q	4457	ex C-GWLB		
☐ N452QX	de Havilland DHC-8-402Q	4459	ex C-GWTH		
☐ N453QX	de Havilland DHC-8-402Q	4489	ex C-FFVS		♦

IBC AIRWAYS   Chasqui (II/CSQ)   Miami-Intl, FL (MIA)

☐ N367PX	SAAB SF.340B	340B-271	ex SE-G71	
☐ N431BC	SAAB SF.340B	340B-260	ex N363PX	
☐ N481BC	SAAB SF.340B	340B-274	ex N368PX	
☐ N611BC	SAAB SF.340A	340A-060	ex N403BH	Frtr
☐ N631BC	SAAB SF.340A	340A-061	ex N404BH	Frtr
☐ N641BC	SAAB SF.340A	340A-069	ex N340SL	Frtr
☐ N651BC	SAAB SF.340A	340A-076	ex N76XJ	Frtr
☐ N661BC	SAAB SF.340A	340A-125	ex N125CH	Frtr
☐ N671BC	SAAB SF.340A	340A-084	ex N163PW	Frtr
☐ N691BC	SAAB SF.340A	340A-041	ex XA-BML	Frtr
☐ N901BC	SAAB SF.340A	340A-088	ex XA-MDG	Frtr
☐ N241BC	Embraer ERJ-145EPF	145077	ex N803HK	[MIA]
☐ N261BC	Embraer ERJ-145EPF	145082	ex N804HK	[FTL]
☐ N841BC	Swearingen SA227TC Metro II	TC-282	ex N248AM	
☐ N851BC	Swearingen SA227AT Merlin IVC	AT-495B	ex N9UA	

ILIAMNA AIR TAXI   Iliamna Air (V8/IAR)   Iliamna, AK (ILI)

☐ N715HL	Pilatus PC-12/45	292	ex N292PB	
☐ N715TL	Pilatus PC-12/45	548	ex HB-FST	
☐ N3682Z	Beech 58 Baron	TH-1159		
☐ N1748U	Cessna 207 Skywagon	20700348		
☐ N7379U	Cessna 207A Stationair 7 II	20700427		
☐ N9720M	Cessna 207A Stationair 8 II	20700720		
☐ N62230	de Havilland DHC-2 Beaver	707	ex 53-7899	FP
☐ N68088	de Havilland DHC-2 Beaver	1197	ex 56-4447	FP

INTER-ARCHIPELAGO AIRWAYS

☐ N77X	Cessna 208B Caravan I	208B0904	
☐ N119RW	Agusta A119	14508	♦

INTER COASTAL AIR   Bayamon, PR

☐ N402AJ	Cessna 402B	402B0884	ex N884RC

INTERNATIONAL AIR RESPONSE   Coolidge-Municipal, AZ(CHD)

☐ N117TG	Lockheed C-130A-1A Hercules	3018	ex 54-1631	31 Iron Butterfly	
☐ N118TG	Lockheed C-130A-1A Hercules	3219	ex 57-0512	32	
☐ N119TG	Lockheed C-130A Hercules	3227	ex N138FF	88	[CHD]
☐ N120TG	Lockheed C-130A Hercules	3035	ex N130SA		
☐ N121TG	Lockheed C-130A Hercules	3119	ex N132FF	83	based St Athan
☐ N133HP	Lockheed C-130A-1A Hercules	3189	ex N8026J		
☐ N4887C	Douglas DC-7B	45351/903		33	

ISLAND AIR — Moku (MKU) — Honolulu-Intl, HI (HNL)

☐ N342AT	ATR 72-212	345	ex N345AT	Ho'opa'a
☐ N941WP	ATR 72-212	349	ex N348AE	Manawanui
☐ N942WP	ATR 72-212	425	ex N425AT	Pa'ahana
☐ N943WP	ATR 72-212	420	ex N420AT	Ho'olauna
☐ N945WP	ATR 72-212	434	ex N434AT	Hilina'i ◆
☐ N360WP	de Havilland DHC-8-402Q	4481	ex C-FENO	◆
☐ N361WP	de Havilland DHC-8-402Q	4482	ex C-FEGY	◆

ISLAND AIR CHARTERS — Barracuda (ISC) — Fort Lauderdale-Hollywood Intl, FL (FLL)

☐ N138LW	Britten-Norman BN-2A-27 Islander	138	ex YR-BNF
☐ N779KS	Britten-Norman BN-2A-27 Islander	779	ex YR-BNE

ISLAND AIR SERVICE — Kodiak-Municipal, AK (ADQ)

☐ N27MR	Britten-Norman BN-2A-26 Islander	884	ex XC-DUN	
☐ N91AK	de Havilland DHC-2 Beaver	737		FP◆
☐ N1162W	Beech 65-B80 Queen Air	LD-350	ex C-FXKZ	
☐ N5891V	Britten-Norman BN-2A-26 Islander	3011	ex J8-VAN	

ISLAND AIR TRANSPORT

☐ N9015Q	Douglas C-54D	22178	ex 43-17228	◆

ISLAND AIRLINES — Nantucket-Memorial, MA (ACK)

☐ N402BK	Cessna 402C II	402C689	ex N550CQ
☐ N404NS	Cessna 402C II	402C0421	ex N79FC
☐ N406BK	Cessna 402C III	402C0807	ex N1235A
☐ N407BK	Cessna 402C II	402C0238	ex N279CB
☐ N409BK	Cessna 402C II	402C0651	ex N67220

ISLAND AIRWAYS — Charlevoix-Municipal, MI (CVX)

☐ N19WA	Britten-Norman BN-2A-8 Islander	524	ex N307SK
☐ N80KM	Britten-Norman BN-2A Islander	80	ex G-BNXA
☐ N95BN	Britten-Norman BN-2A-8 Islander	95	ex G-AXKB
☐ N137MW	Britten-Norman BN-2A Islander	137	ex G-AXWH
☐ N866JA	Britten-Norman BN-2A-6 islander	185	ex G-31-185

ISLAND SEAPLANE SERVICE — Honolulu-Keehi Lagoon SPB, HI

☐ N110AW	de Havilland DHC-2 Beaver	690	ex N11015	Fantasy Islands c/s	FP

ISLAND WINGS AIR SERVICE — Ketchikan-Waterfront SPB, AK (WFB)

☐ N1117F	de Havilland DHC-2 Beaver	1369	ex N6783L	FP

JETBLUE AIRWAYS — JetBlue (B6/JBU) — New York-JFK Intl, NY (JFK)

☐ N503JB	Airbus A320-232	1123	ex F-WWBR	Blue Bird
☐ N504JB	Airbus A320-232	1156	ex F-WWBV	Shades Of Blue
☐ N505JB	Airbus A320-232	1173	ex F-WWDN	Blue Skies
☐ N506JB	Airbus A320-232	1235	ex F-WWIN	Wild Blue Yonder
☐ N507JT	Airbus A320-232	1240	ex D-ANNB	Blue Crew
☐ N508JL	Airbus A320-232	1257	ex D-ANNC	May the Force be with Blue
☐ N509JB	Airbus A320-232	1270	ex F-WWDF	True Blue
☐ N510JB	Airbus A320-232	1280	ex F-WWBA	Out Of The Blue
☐ N516JB	Airbus A320-232	1302	ex F-WWBQ	Royal Blue
☐ N517JB	Airbus A320-232	1327	ex F-WWDU	Blue Moon
☐ N519JB	Airbus A320-232	1398	ex F-WWIY	It Had To Be Blue
☐ N520JB	Airbus A320-232	1446	ex F-WWBT	Blue Velvet
☐ N521JB	Airbus A320-232	1452	ex F-WWBY	Baby Blue
☐ N523JB	Airbus A320-232	1506	ex F-WWII	Born To Be Blue
☐ N524JB	Airbus A320-232	1528	ex F-WWIN	Blue Belle
☐ N526JL	Airbus A320-232	1546	ex D-ANND	Blues Just Want To Have Fun
☐ N527JL	Airbus A320-232	1557	ex D-ANNE	Blue Bayou
☐ N529JB	Airbus A320-232	1610	ex F-WWDE	Ole Blue Eyes
☐ N531JL	Airbus A320-232	1650	ex D-ANNF	All Blue Can Jet
☐ N534JB	Airbus A320-232	1705	ex F-WWIU	Bada Bing, Bada Blue
☐ N535JB	Airbus A320-232	1739	ex F-WWBQ	Estrella Azul
☐ N536JB	Airbus A320-232	1784	ex F-WWDS	Canyon Blue
☐ N537JT	Airbus A320-232	1785	ex D-ANNI	Red White and Blue
☐ N547JB	Airbus A320-232	1849	ex F-WWDF	Forever Blue
☐ N552JB	Airbus A320-232	1861	ex F-WWDM	Blue Jay
☐ N554JB	Airbus A320-232	1898	ex F-WWBK	Sacre' Bleu!
☐ N556JB	Airbus A320-232	1904	ex F-WWDD	Betty Blue
☐ N558JB	Airbus A320-232	1915	ex F-WWIF	Song Sung Blue

☐ N559JB	Airbus A320-232	1917	ex F-WWIR	Here's Looking At Blue, Kid
☐ N561JB	Airbus A320-232	1927	ex F-WWIC	La Vie En Blue
☐ N562JB	Airbus A320-232	1948	ex F-WWDF	The Name Is Blue, jetBlue
☐ N563JB	Airbus A320-232	2006	ex F-WWBY	Blue Chip
☐ N564JB	Airbus A320-232	2020	ex F-WWBZ	Absolute Blue
☐ N565JB	Airbus A320-232	2031	ex F-WWDT	Bippity Boppity Blue
☐ N566JB	Airbus A320-232	2042	ex F-WWDU	Blue Suede Shoes
☐ N568JB	Airbus A320-232	2063	ex F-WWDE	Blue Sapphire
☐ N569JB	Airbus A320-232	2075	ex F-WWDF	Blues Brothers
☐ N570JB	Airbus A320-232	2099	ex F-WWBD	Devil With A Blue Dress On
☐ N571JB	Airbus A320-232	2125	ex F-WWIX	Blue Monday
☐ N579JB	Airbus A320-232	2132	ex F-WWDB	Can't Stop Lovin' Blue
☐ N580JB	Airbus A320-232	2136	ex F-WWBB	Mo Better Blue
☐ N583JB	Airbus A320-232	2150	ex F-WWII	Bluesville
☐ N584JB	Airbus A320-232	2149	ex F-WWID	Blue Fox
☐ N585JB	Airbus A320-232	2159	ex F-WWIC	I Got Blue Babe
☐ N586JB	Airbus A320-232	2160	ex F-WWIN	Blue Flight Special
☐ N587JB	Airbus A320-232	2177	ex F-WWIT	Blue Kid In Town
☐ N588JB	Airbus A320-232	2201	ex F-WWIT	Hopelessly Devoted To Blue
☐ N589JB	Airbus A320-232	2215	ex F-WWBJ	Blue Skies Ahead
☐ N590JB	Airbus A320-232	2231	ex F-WWIH	Liberty Blue
☐ N591JB	Airbus A320-232	2246	ex F-WWIS	Tale Of Blue Cities
☐ N592JB	Airbus A320-232	2259	ex F-WWBI	American Blue
☐ N593JB	Airbus A320-232	2280	ex F-WWDT	I Only Have Eyes For Blue
☐ N594JB	Airbus A320-232	2284	ex F-WWBQ	Whole Lotta Blue
☐ N595JB	Airbus A320-232	2286	ex F-WWBR	Rhythm & Blues
☐ N597JB	Airbus A320-232	2307	ex F-WWIC	For The Love Of Blue
☐ N598JB	Airbus A320-232	2314	ex F-WWDK	Me & You & A Plane Named Blue
☐ N599JB	Airbus A320-232	2336	ex F-WWIN	If The Blue Fits
☐ N603JB	Airbus A320-232	2352	ex F-WWIL	Viva La Blue
☐ N605JB	Airbus A320-232	2368	ex F-WWDO	Blue Yorker
☐ N606JB	Airbus A320-232	2384	ex F-WWIE	Idlewild Blue
☐ N607JB	Airbus A320-232	2386	ex F-WWIG	Beantown Blue
☐ N608JB	Airbus A320-232	2415	ex F-WWDP	..And Along Came Blue
☐ N612JB	Airbus A320-232	2447	ex F-WWBU	Blue Look Maaahvelous
☐ N613JB	Airbus A320-232	2449	ex F-WWBX	Bahama Blue
☐ N615JB	Airbus A320-232	2461	ex F-WWDR	Blue Bravest City of NY Fire Dept c/s
☐ N618JB	Airbus A320-232	2489	ex F-WWDX	Can't Get Enough Of Blue
☐ N621JB	Airbus A320-232	2491	ex F-WWDY	Do-be-do-be Blue
☐ N623JB	Airbus A320-232	2504	ex F-WWBM	All We Need Is Blue
☐ N624JB	Airbus A320-232	2520	ex F-WWBN	Blue-T-Ful
☐ N625JB	Airbus A320-232	2535	ex F-WWII	CompanyBlue
☐ N627JB	Airbus A320-232	2577	ex F-WWDB	A Friend Like Blue
☐ N629JB	Airbus A320-232	2580	ex F-WWBH	Bright Lights, Blue City
☐ N630JB	Airbus A320-232	2640	ex F-WWBY	Honk If You love Blue
☐ N632JB	Airbus A320-232	2647	ex F-WWIF	Clear Blue Sky
☐ N633JB	Airbus A320-232	2671	ex F-WWDF	Major Blue
☐ N634JB	Airbus A320-232	2710	ex F-WWIZ	B*L*U*E
☐ N635JB	Airbus A320-232	2725	ex F-WWDQ	All Because of Blue
☐ N636JB	Airbus A320-232	2755	ex F-WWDL	All Wrapped Up In Blue
☐ N637JB	Airbus A320-232	2781	ex F-WWDY	Big Blue Bus
☐ N638JB	Airbus A320-232	2802	ex F-WWIL	Blue begins with you
☐ N639JB	Airbus A320-232	2814	ex F-WWIV	A Little Blue Will Do
☐ N640JB	Airbus A320-232	2832	ex F-WWBD	Blue Better Believe It
☐ N641JB	Airbus A320-232	2848	ex F-WWIK	Blue Come Back Now Ya Hear
☐ N643JB	Airbus A320-232	2871	ex F-WWBF	Blue Jersey
☐ N644JB	Airbus A320-232	2880	ex F-WWBO	Blue Loves Ya, Baby
☐ N645JB	Airbus A320-232	2900	ex F-WWDE	Blues Have More Fun
☐ N646JB	Airbus A320-232	2945	ex F-WWIP	Bravo Lima Uniform Echo
☐ N648JB	Airbus A320-232	2970	ex F-WWDI	That's What I Like About Blue
☐ N649JB	Airbus A320-232	2977	ex F-WWBD	Fancy Meeting Blue Here
☐ N651JB	Airbus A320-232	2992	ex F-WWIS	I'm Having a Blue Moment
☐ N652JB	Airbus A320-232	3029	ex F-WWBT	Out With The Old, In With The Blue
☐ N653JB	Airbus A320-232	3039	ex F-WWDH	Breath of Fresh Blue
☐ N655JB	Airbus A320-232	3072	ex F-WWIN	special colours, Blue 100
☐ N656JB	Airbus A320-232	3091	ex F-WWIQ	California Blue
☐ N657JB	Airbus A320-232	3119	ex F-WWBC	Denim Blue
☐ N658JB	Airbus A320-232	3150	ex F-WWBT	Woo-Hoo JetBlue
☐ N659JB	Airbus A320-232	3190	ex F-WWIQ	Simply Blue
☐ N661JB	Airbus A320-232	3228	ex F-WWBD	Let the Blue Times Roll
☐ N662JB	Airbus A320-232	3263	ex F-WWDO	Glad to be Blue
☐ N663JB	Airbus A320-232	3287	ex F-WWDG	Paint the town blue
☐ N665JB	Airbus A320-232	3348	ex F-WWBV	Something about blue
☐ N703JB	Airbus A320-232	3381	ex F-WWDM	It's up to blue, New York, New York
☐ N705JB	Airbus A320-232	3416	ex F-WWIN	Big Blue People Seater
☐ N706JB	Airbus A320-232	3451	ex F-WWBE	As blue as it gets
☐ N708JB	Airbus A320-232	3479	ex F-WWDJ	All that and a bag of blue chips
☐ N709JB	Airbus A320-232	3488	ex F-WWIK	Brand Spanking Blue
☐ N712JB	Airbus A320-232	3517	ex F-WWDQ	Enough about me..Let's talk about Blue
☐ N715JB	Airbus A320-232	3554	ex F-WWBD	How's My Flying? Call 1-800-JetBlue
☐ N729JB	Airbus A320-232	3572	ex F-WWBJ	If You Can Read This, Your Blue Close
☐ N746JB	Airbus A320-232	3622	ex F-WWIL	Some Like It Blue
☐ N760JB	Airbus A320-232	3659	ex F-WWDU	The Blues Were Made For Flying

☐ N763JB	Airbus A320-232	3707	ex F-WWIQ	Unforgetably blue	
☐ N766JB	Airbus A320-232	3724	ex F-WWDG	Etjay Luebay	
☐ N768JB	Airbus A320-232	3760	ex F-WWDC	Blue Crew	
☐ N775JB	Airbus A320-232	3800	ex F-WWBT	Canard Bleu	
☐ N779JB	Airbus A320-232	3811	ex F-WWID	Blue Ribbon	
☐ N784JB	Airbus A320-232	4578	ex F-WWDZ	Blue Infinity and Beyond	
☐ N789JB	Airbus A320-232	4612	ex F-WWDC	What's Blue and White and Flies All Over	
☐ N793JB	Airbus A320-232	4647	ex F-WWDN	My Other Ride is a JetBlue E190	
☐ N794JB	Airbus A320-232	4904	ex F-WWBX	Pretty Fly for a Blue Guy	
☐ N796JB	Airbus A320-232	5060	ex F-WWBQ	100% Blue	
☐ N804JB	Airbus A320-232	5142	ex F-WWBE	Got Blue ?	
☐ N805JB	Airbus A320-232/S	5148	ex D-AVVP	You Had Me at Blue	
☐ N806JB	Airbus A320-232/S	5302	ex F-WWBE	Objects in Mirror are Bluer than they Appear	
☐ N807JB	Airbus A320-232/S	5312	ex D-AUBC	1 Fly JetBlue 2 Repeat step 1	
☐ N809JB	Airbus A320-232/S	5349	ex F-WWBV	Blue by Popular Demand	
☐ N821JB	Airbus A320-232/S	5417	ex F-WWDQ	Blue Yorker	
☐ N827JB	Airbus A320-232/S	5677	ex F-WWDE	It Takes Blue to Tango	
☐ N828JB	Airbus A320-232/S	5723	ex F-WWID	Simon Says, "Fly JetBlue"	
☐ N834JB	Airbus A320-232/S	5782	ex F-WWDP	Keep Blue and Carry On	
☐ N903JB	Airbus A321-231/S	5783	ex D-AVZA	Bigger, Brighter, Bluer	
☐ N905JB	Airbus A321-231/S	5854	ex D-AVZP	Blue Swayed	
☐ N907JB	Airbus A321-231/S	5865	ex D-AVZS	Blue Really Got Me Goin'	
☐ N913JB	Airbus A321-231/S	5909	ex D-AZAB	Blue Kid on the Block	
☐ N923JB	Airbus A321-231/S	5960	ex D-AZAJ	It's Mint to Be	
☐ N929JB	Airbus A321-231/S	6031	ex D-AVZM	One Giant Leap for Mint Kind	
☐ N934JB	Airbus A321-231/S	6130	ex D-AVXI	Fly in Mint Condition	♦
☐ N935JB	Airbus A321-231/S	6185	ex D-AVXZ		♦
☐ N937JB	Airbus A321-231/S	6245	ex D-AVZD	Never a Dull MoMint	♦
☐ N942JB	Airbus A321-231/S	6279	ex D-AVZS	Menta Fresca	♦
☐ N943JT	Airbus A321-231/S	6326	ex D-AVXD	Blue-Carpet TreatMint	♦
☐ N944JT	Airbus A321-231/S	6359	ex D-AVXM	I was Mint for Lovin' Blue	♦
☐ N945JT	Airbus A321-231/S	6390	ex D-AVXX	A Blue Mintality	♦
☐ N946JT	Airbus A321-231/S	6425	ex D-AZAS		♦
☐ N947JB	Airbus A321-231/S	6448	ex D-AVZC	Una Nueva Menta-lidad	♦
☐ N948JB	Airbus A321-231/S	6560	ex D-AZAO		♦
☐ N949JT	Airbus A321-231/S	6575	ex D-AVXF		♦
☐ N950JT	Airbus A321-231/S	6609	ex D-AVXN		o/o♦
☐ N	Airbus A321-231/S	6621	ex		o/o♦
☐ N	Airbus A321-231/S	6649	ex		o/o♦
☐ N	Airbus A321-231/S	6663	ex		o/o♦
☐ N	Airbus A321-231/S	6725	ex		o/o♦
☐ N	Airbus A321-231/S	6729	ex		o/o♦
☐ N	Airbus A321-231/S	6767	ex		o/o♦
☐ N	Airbus A320-231/S	6793	ex		o/o♦
☐ N	Airbus A321-231/S	6809	ex		o/o♦
☐ N	Airbus A321-231/S	6842	ex		o/o♦
☐ N	Airbus A321-231/S	6859	ex		o/o♦
☐ N	Airbus A321-231/S	6887	ex		o/o♦
☐ N	Airbus A321-231/S	6894	ex		o/o♦
☐ N	Airbus A321-231/S	6903	ex		o/o♦
☐ N	Airbus A321-231/S	6930	ex		o/o♦
☐ N	Airbus A321-231/S	6968	ex		o/o♦
☐ N178JB	Embraer ERJ-190AR	19000004	ex PT-STD	It's A Blue Thing	
☐ N179JB	Embraer ERJ-190AR	19000006	ex PT-STF	Come Fly With Blue	
☐ N183JB	Embraer ERJ-190AR	19000007	ex PT-STG	Azul Brasileiro	
☐ N184JB	Embraer ERJ-190AR	19000008	ex PT-STH	Outta the Blue	
☐ N187JB	Embraer ERJ-190AR	19000009	ex PT-STI	Dream Come Blue	
☐ N190JB	Embraer ERJ-190AR	19000011	ex PT-STK	Luiz F Kahl	
☐ N192JB	Embraer ERJ-190AR	19000014	ex PT-STO	Yes, I'm a Natural Blue	
☐ N193JB	Embraer ERJ-190AR	19000017	ex PT-STR	Peek-a-Blue	
☐ N197JB	Embraer ERJ-190AR	19000020	ex PT-STU	Color Me Blue	
☐ N198JB	Embraer ERJ-190AR	19000021	ex PT-STV	Big Apple Blue	
☐ N203JB	Embraer ERJ-190AR	19000023	ex PT-STX	Look at Blue now	
☐ N206JB	Embraer ERJ-190AR	19000025	ex PT-STZ	Blue-It's the New Black	
☐ N216JB	Embraer ERJ-190AR	19000026	ex PT-SGA	Blue Getaway	
☐ N228JB	Embraer ERJ-190AR	19000030	ex PT-SGE	Blue 4 You	
☐ N229JB	Embraer ERJ-190AR	19000032	ex PT-SGG	Blue Amigo	
☐ N231JB	Embraer ERJ-190AR	19000033	ex PT-SGH	Blue Bonnet	
☐ N236JB	Embraer ERJ-190AR	19000035	ex PT-SGJ	Blue by Design	
☐ N238JB	Embraer ERJ-190AR	19000039	ex PT-SGO	Blue Clipper	
☐ N239JB	Embraer ERJ-190AR	19000040	ex PT-SGP	Blissfully Blue	
☐ N247JB	Embraer ERJ-190AR	19000042	ex PT-SGR	Blue is so You	
☐ N249JB	Embraer ERJ-190AR	19000045	ex PT-SGU	Blueprint	
☐ N258JB	Embraer ERJ-190AR	19000047	ex PT-SGW	Blue Send Me	
☐ N265JB	Embraer ERJ-190AR	19000049	ex PT-SGY	Blue Streak	
☐ N266JB	Embraer ERJ-190AR	19000054	ex PT-SID	Blue Sweet Blue	
☐ N267JB	Embraer ERJ-190AR	19000065	ex PT-SJD	Bluesmobile	
☐ N273JB	Embraer ERJ-190AR	19000073	ex PT-SJM	Carribean Blue	
☐ N274JB	Embraer ERJ-190AR	19000082	ex PT-SJY	Good, Better, Blue	
☐ N279JB	Embraer ERJ-190AR	19000090	ex PT-SNJ	Indigo Blue	

☐ N281JB	Embraer ERJ-190AR	19000103	ex PT-SNX	Lady in Blue
☐ N283JB	Embraer ERJ-190AR	19000125	ex PT-SQU	Pretty in Blue
☐ N284JB	Embraer ERJ-190AR	19000144	ex PT-SVY	Sincerely Blue
☐ N292JB	Embraer ERJ-190AR	19000179	ex PT-SDN	Parlez-Blue?
☐ N294JB	Embraer ERJ-190AR	19000185	ex PT-SDT	Room with a blue
☐ N296JB	Embraer ERJ-190AR	19000219	ex PT-SHC	Blue's your daddy
☐ N298JB	Embraer ERJ-190AR	19000249	ex PT-SIT	Cool Blue
☐ N304JB	Embraer ERJ-190AR	19000257	ex PT-STF	Midnight Blue
☐ N306JB	Embraer ERJ-190AR	19000272	ex PT-TLM	Blue Orleans
☐ N307JB	Embraer ERJ-190AR	19000286	ex PT-TZA	Mi Corazon Azul
☐ N309JB	Embraer ERJ-190AR	19000289	ex PT-TZD	Rhapsody in Blue
☐ N316JB	Embraer ERJ-190AR	19000292	ex PT-TZG	Usto Schulz
☐ N317JB	Embraer ERJ-190AR	19000363	ex PT-XNC	Deja Blue
☐ N318JB	Embraer ERJ-190AR	19000364	ex PT-XND	Blue Jean Baby
☐ N323JB	Embraer ERJ-190AR	19000384	ex PT-XNS	Only Blue
☐ N324JB	Embraer ERJ-190AR	19000388	ex PT-XNV	Blue Traveller
☐ N328JB	Embraer ERJ-190AR	19000422	ex PT-TGY	Blue Warrior
☐ N329JB	Embraer ERJ-190AR	19000433	ex PT-TCT	My Other Ride is a JetBlue A320
☐ N334JB	Embraer ERJ-190AR	19000446	ex PT-TJG	#Follow @JetBlue
☐ N337JB	Embraer ERJ-190AR	19000473	ex PT-TOU	I'm with Blue
☐ N339JB	Embraer ERJ-190AR	19000490	ex PT-TPP	BYO Blue
☐ N346JB	Embraer ERJ-190AR	19000504	ex PT-TRO	Blueberry
☐ N348JB	Embraer ERJ-190AR	19000511	ex PT-TSH	Mystic Blue
☐ N351JB	Embraer ERJ-190AR	19000549	ex PT-TBP	JBlu
☐ N353JB	Embraer ERJ-190AR	19000576	ex PT-TGC	Blue La La
☐ N354JB	Embraer ERJ-190AR	19000601	ex PT-TIX	Bluetopia
☐ N355JB	Embraer ERJ-190AR	19000617	ex PT-TJV	Rendezblue
☐ N358JB	Embraer ERJ-190AR	19000618	ex PT-TKC	Blue's on First
☐ N368JB	Embraer ERJ-190AR	19000623	ex PT-TKK	Powered by Blue
☐ N373JB	Embraer ERJ-190AR	19000624	ex PT-TKM	Best in Blue
☐ N374JB	Embraer ERJ-190AR	19000629	ex PT-TKS	I'm a Blue Believer
☐ N375JB	Embraer ERJ-190AR	19000637	ex PR-ECA	Blue State of Mind

JIM HANKINS AIR SERVICE   Hankins (HKN)   Jackson-Hawkins Field, MS (HKS)

☐ N22BR	Beech H-18	BA-729	ex N402AP	Frtr
☐ N368HC	Beech H-18	BA-630	ex N8217	Frtr
☐ N495DM	Beech C-45H	AF-225	ex N6630R	Frtr
☐ N4209V	Volpar Turboliner	AF-884	ex HB-GFX	Frtr
☐ N92756	Beech H-18	BA-728	ex JA5133	Frtr
☐ N3BA	Douglas DC-3	12172	ex N94530	Frtr
☐ N40XL	Beech 58 Baron	TH-400	ex N80LM	
☐ N366MQ	Short SD.3-60	SH3639	ex G-BLEH	
☐ N899DD	Beech 58 Baron	TH-899	ex VH-BWJ	
☐ N958JH	Beech 65-C90A King Air	LJ-1108	ex N438SP	
☐ N3106W	Beech 58 Baron	TH-408		
☐ N6652A	Beech 58 Baron	TH-1045		
☐ N8061A	Douglas DC-3	6085	ex (N351SA)	Frtr

KALITTA AIR   Connie (K4/CKS)   Detroit-Willow Run, MI (YIP)

☐ N624US	Boeing 747-251B	21706/377		[OSC]
☐ N629US	Boeing 747-251F	22388/444		[OSC]
☐ N701CK	Boeing 747-259B (SCD)	21730/372	ex N924FT	[OSC]
☐ N703CK	Boeing 747-212BSF	21939/449	ex N319FV	[OSC]
☐ N704CK	Boeing 747-246F	23391/654	ex JA8171	
☐ N708CK	Boeing 747-212BSF	21937/419	ex N526UP	[OSC]
☐ N712CK	Boeing 747-122 (SCD)	19754/60	ex N854FT	[OSC]
☐ N746CK	Boeing 747-246F	22989/571	ex JA811J	
☐ N747CK	Boeing 747-221F	21743/384	ex JA8165	[OSC]
☐ N748CK	Boeing 747-221F	21744/392	ex JA8160	[OSC]
☐ N790CK	Boeing 747-251BSF	23112/595	ex N632NW	[OSC]
☐ N791CK	Boeing 747-251F	23888/682	ex N640US	[OSC]
☐ N792CK	Boeing 747-212F	24177/710	ex N644NW	[OSC]
☐ N793CK	Boeing 747-222BSF	23736/673	ex N645NW	
☐ N794CK	Boeing 747-222BSF	23737/675	exN646NW	
☐ N795CK	Boeing 747-251BSF	23111/594	ex N631NW	
☐ N402KZ	Boeing 747-481F	34017/1363	ex JA02KZ	◆
☐ N403KZ	Boeing 747-481f	34018/1378	ex JA03KZ	◆
☐ N740CK	Boeing 747-4H6FCF	24405/745	ex N73714	
☐ N741CK	Boeing 747-4H6FCF	24315/738	ex N73713	
☐ N742CK	Boeing 747-446BCF	24424/760	ex JA8072	
☐ N743CK	Boeing 747-446BCF	26350/961	ex JA8906	
☐ N744CK	Boeing 747-446BCF	26353/980	ex JA8909	
☐ N745CK	Boeing 747-446BCF	26361/1188	ex JA8915	
☐ N769CK	Boeing 747-430M	24966/846	ex D-ABTE	[OSC]◆
☐ N782CK	Boeing 747-4HQERF	37304/1419	ex N798BA	

KALITTA CHARTERS   Kalitta (K9/KFS)   Detroit-Willow Run, MI (YIP)

☐ N65FS	Beech 58 Baron	TH-1084	ex N6681Y	♦
☐ N400RP	Beech 58 Baron	TH-319	ex N1036W	♦
☐ N1847F	Beech 58 Baron	TH-1291		♦
☐ N1859K	Beech 58 Baron	TH-1299		♦
☐ N2027V	Beech 58 Baron	TH-965		♦
☐ N3703Q	Beech 58 Baron	TH-1189		♦
☐ N720CK	Boeing 727-2B6F (Raisbeck 3)	21298/1246	ex N721SK	
☐ N722CK	Boeing 727-2H3F (Raisbeck 3)	20948/1084	ex N722SK	
☐ N723CK	Boeing 727-2H3F (Raisbeck 3)	20545/877	ex N723SK	[OSC]
☐ N724CK	Boeing 727-225F (Raisbeck 3)	20383/831	ex N8840E	
☐ N725CK	Boeing 727-224F/W (Raisbeck 3)	22252/1697	ex N746DH	
☐ N726CK	Boeing 727-2M7 (FedEx 3)	21951/1680	ex N750DH	
☐ N728CK	Boeing 727-221	22541/1797	ex N727M	[OSC]
☐ N729CK	Boeing 727-264F/W	22982/1802	ex N751DH	
☐ N752DH	Boeing 727-223F	22466/1763	ex N709AA	[OSC]
☐ N88BG	Learjet 35A	35A-090	ex I-FIMI	♦
☐ N122JW	Learjet 35A	35A-217	ex N111RF	♦
☐ N400JE	Learjet 35A	35A-120		♦
☐ N474AN	Learjet 35A	35A-295	ex N94AA	♦
☐ N730CK	Boeing 737-4C9	26437/2249	ex UR-GAV	[OSC]♦
☐ N915CK	Douglas DC-9-15RC	47086/219	ex N915R	
☐ N916CK	Douglas DC-9-33RC	47291/343	ex N933AX	
☐ N917CK	Douglas DC-9-15RC	47152/170	ex N166DE	

KALITTA FLYING SERVICES   Kalitta (KFS)
Detroit-Willow Run, MI/Morristown, TN/El Paso, TX (YIP/MRX/ESP)

☐ N70CK	AMD Falcon 20C	128	ex N228CK	
☐ N192CK	AMD Falcon 20DC	192	ex N192R	
☐ N226CK	AMD Falcon 20DC	226	ex N226R	
☐ N227CK	AMD Falcon 20DC	227	ex N227R	
☐ N229CK	AMD Falcon 20DC	229	ex N229R	
☐ N240CK	AMD Falcon 20-5	24	ex N240TJ	
☐ N808CK	AMD Falcon 20F-5	108	ex N108R	
☐ N820CK	AMD Falcon 20-5	120	ex N647JP	♦
☐ N995CK	AMD Falcon 20DC	95	ex N950RA	
☐ N998CK	AMD Falcon 20DC	98	ex N980R	
☐ N39CK	Learjet 25	25-005	ex XA-SDQ	
☐ N71CK	Learjet 36A	36A-035	ex VH-BIB	
☐ N72CK	Learjet 35A	35A-165	ex N16BJ	
☐ N73CK	Learjet 35A	35A-092	ex N39WA	
☐ N76CK	Learjet 25	25-020	ex N500JS	
☐ N88BG	Learjet 35A	35A-090		♦
☐ N150CK	Learjet 25D	25D-150	ex N251JA	
☐ N237CK	Learjet 35A	35A-237	ex N11UF	
☐ N298CK	Learjet 35A	35A-298	ex N298NW	
☐ N431CK	Learjet 35A	35A-431	ex N355PC	♦
☐ N474AN	Learjet 35A	35A-295		♦
☐ N818CK	Learjet 25B	25B-118	ex N118MB	
☐ N870CK	Learjet 35A	35A-170	ex N88NJ	♦
☐ N905CK	Learjet 36	36-005	ex N9108Z	
☐ N913CK	Learjet 35	35-013	ex N535TA	

All freighters; sister company of Kalitta Charters

KAMAKA AIR   Honolulu-Intl, HI (HNL)

☐ N145KA	Cessna 208B Caravan I	208B2019		
☐ N231H	Beech E-18S	BA-281	ex N23Y	
☐ N248KA	Cessna 208B Caravan I	208B2408		
☐ N933T	Beech Super H-18	BA-665		
☐ N9796N	Douglas C-117D	43375	ex C-FLED	

KAISERAIR   (KAI)   Oakland, CA (OAK)

☐ N732KA	Boeing 737-59D/W	25065/2028	ex N565EL	♦
☐ N737KA	Boeing 737-7BX	30740/776	ex VH-VBT Lani	

KATMAI AIR   (KT)   King Salmon, AK/Anchorage-Lake Hood SPB, AK (AKN/LHD)

☐ N45GB	de Havilland DHC-2 Turbo Beaver	1623/TB14	ex C-FNPW	FP
☐ N490K	de Havilland DHC-2 Beaver	1268	ex N513F	FP
☐ N491K	de Havilland DHC-3 Turbo Otter	434	ex N49KA	FP
☐ N492K	Piper PA-31-350 Chieftain	31-8052176	ex C-GAWL	
☐ N493K	de Havilland DHC-2 Beaver		ex 56-0408	FP♦
☐ N495K	Cessna U206F Stationair II	U20602549	ex N1274V	FP

☐ N496K	Cessna U206G Stationair	U20603953	ex N756BE	FP
☐ N498K	Cessna T207A Stationair 8	20700624	ex N73762	FP
☐ N499K	Cessna T207A Stationair 8	20700632	ex N73835	FP; dam 21Jly13
☐ N3125N	de Havilland DHC-3 Otter	394	ex C-FAXD	
☐ N9644G	Cessna U206F Stationair	U20601844		FP

KENAI RIVER XPRESS — Soldotna, AK

| ☐ N150BA | de Havilland DHC-3 Turbo Otter | 15 | ex C-FODL | |

KENMORE AIR — Kenmore (M5/KEN) — Kenmore SPB, WA (KEH)

☐ N77MV	de Havilland DHC-2 Beaver	1273	ex 57-6168		FP
☐ N384N	de Havilland DHC-2 Beaver	562	ex N73527		FP♦
☐ N900KA	de Havilland DHC-2 Beaver	1676	ex LN-BFH	Maggie Evening Magazine	FP
☐ N1018F	de Havilland DHC-2 Beaver	710	ex N62SJ		FP
☐ N1433Z	de Havilland DHC-2 Beaver	595	ex 53-2802		FP
☐ N1455T	de Havilland DHC-2 Turbo Beaver III	1647/TB26	ex C-FOEI		FP
☐ N5484	de Havilland DHC-2 Beaver	1600			FP♦
☐ N6781L	de Havilland DHC-2 Beaver	788	ex N10LU		FP
☐ N9744T	de Havilland DHC-2 Turbo Beaver III	1692/TB60	ex N1944		FP
☐ N9766Z	de Havilland DHC-2 Beaver	504	ex N13454		FP
☐ N17598	de Havilland DHC-2 Beaver	1129	ex VP-FAH		FP
☐ N64389	de Havilland DHC-2 Beaver	1637	ex N616W		FP
☐ N72355	de Havilland DHC-2 Beaver	1164	ex N62355		FP
☐ N50KA	de Havilland DHC-3 Turbo Otter	221	ex C-GLMT	K5 Evening c/s	FP
☐ N58JH	de Havilland DHC-3 Turbo Otter	131	ex N8510Q		FP
☐ N87KA	de Havilland DHC-3 Turbo Otter	11	ex N8262V		FP
☐ N606KA	de Havilland DHC-3 Turbo Otter	37	ex N8260L		FP
☐ N707KA	de Havilland DHC-3 Turbo Otter	106	ex N888KA		FP
☐ N765KA	de Havilland DHC-3 Turbo Otter	26	ex N26DE		FP
☐ N2634Y	de Havilland DHC-3 Turbo Otter	59	ex C-GIWQ		FP
☐ N3125S	de Havilland DHC-3 Turbo Otter	407	ex RCAF 9424	Seattle Hospital c/s	FP
☐ N90422	de Havilland DHC-3 Turbo Otter	152	ex 55-3296	Expedia.com titles	FP
☐ N2803K	Cessna 180K Skywagon	18053074			FP
☐ N2849K	Cessna 180K Skywagon	18053096			FP

KENMORE AIR EXPRESS

☐ N72KA	Cessna 208B Caravan I	208B0326	ex N1030N	FP
☐ N426KM	Cessna 208 Caravan I	20800306	ex N12656	FP
☐ N4107Q	Piper PA-31-350 Chieftain	31-8253008		
☐ N40796	Piper PA-31-350 Chieftain	31-8152084		

KEY LIME AIR — Key Lime (LYM) — Denver-International, CO (DEN)

☐ N259DS	Dornier 328-310 (328JET)	3197	ex N901SJ	♦
☐ N356SK	Dornier 328-310 (328JET)	3163	ex D-BDXH	♦
☐ N358SK	Dornier 328-310 (328JET)	3188		♦
☐ N394DC	Dornier 328-310 (328JET)	3174	ex N38VP	
☐ N395DC	Dornier 328-310 (328JET)	3178	ex N905HB	
☐ N398DC	Dornier 328-300 (328JET)	3206	ex OE-HRJ	
☐ N62Z	Swearingen SA226TC Metro II	TC-237	ex N5437M	
☐ N276CA	Swearingen SA226TC Metro II	TC-276	ex N103GS	
☐ N326BA	Swearingen SA226TC Metro II	TC-269	ex C-GYXC	
☐ N509SS	Swearingen SA226TC Metro II	TC-206	ex N261S	
☐ N770S	Swearingen SA226TC Metro II	TC-248		
☐ N81418	Swearingen SA226TC Metro II	TC-223	ex EC-GNM	
☐ N184SW	Swearingen SA227AC Metro III	AC-647	ex CX-TAA	
☐ N508FA	Swearingen SA227AC Metro III	AC-508	ex ZK-NSW	
☐ N542FA	Swearingen SA227AC Metro III	AC-542	ex ZK-NSX	
☐ (N640KL)	Swearingen SA227AC Metro III	AC-640	ex N425MA	
☐ (N655KL)	Swearingen SA227AC Metro III	AC-655B	ex N2691W	
☐ (N731KY)	Swearingen SA227AC Metro III	AC-731	ex N2728G	
☐ N765FA	Swearingen SA227AC Metro III	AC-765	ex ZK-NSI	
☐ N769KL	Swearingen SA227AC Metro III	AC-769B	ex HZ-SN10	
☐ N779BC	Swearingen SA227BC Metro III	BC-779B	ex XA-RXW	
☐ N787C	Swearingen SA227AC Metro III	AC-550	ex N31110	
☐ N787KL	Swearingen SA227BC Metro III	BC-787B	ex XA-SAQ	
☐ N788KL	Swearingen SA227AC Metro III	AC-788B	ex A9C-DHA	
☐ N366DC	Embraer EMB.120ER Brasilia	120288	ex N220SW	
☐ N820DC	Swearingen SA227DC Metro 23	DC-820B	ex XA-SHD	
☐ N882DC	Swearingen SA227DC Metro 23	DC-882B	ex C-GAFQ	

KING AIR — Naknek, AK

| ☐ N4602F | Piper PA-32-300 Cherokee Six | 32-7640118 | | |

☐ N5371G	de Havilland DHC-2 Beaver	1075	ex 56-0362	FP
☐ N7942V	Cessna 180H Skywagon	18051842		FP
☐ N8421A	Piper PA-32-301 Cherokee Six	32-8106085		
☐ N44851	Piper PA-32-300 Cherokee Six	32-7740107		

KIRLAND AVIATION   Boca Raton, FL (BCT)

☐ N301UE	British Aerospace Jetstream 41	41012	ex G-4-012	wfs
☐ N328UE	British Aerospace Jetstream 41	41083	ex G-4-083	wfs
☐ N423KA	British Aerospace Jetstream 41	41023	ex N41023	[LYH]♦

KOLOB CANYONS AIR SERVICES   Kolob (KCR)   Cedar City, UT (CDC)

☐ N2BZ	Aero Commander 500S Shrike	3227	ex N57150	
☐ N57RS	Rockwell 690A Turbo Commander	11149	ex N5KW	
☐ N66GW	Rockwell 690A Turbo Commander	11174	ex N6B	
☐ N90AT	Rockwell 690A Turbo Commander	11272	ex N888PB	
☐ N98PJ	Rockwell 690A Turbo Commander	11320	ex N220HC	
☐ N690TR	Rockwell 690A Turbo Commander	11034	ex EC-EFS	
☐ N900DT	Aero Commander 500S Shrike	3056	ex N9008N	
☐ N8536	Aero Commander 500S Shrike	3267	ex N57117	
☐ N9096N	Aero Commander 500S Shrike	3076		♦
☐ N123KC	Piper PA-32R-300 Lance	32R-7680431		
☐ N457KA	Pilatus PC-12/45	157	ex HB-FOI	
☐ N474KA	Learjet 35A	35A-174	ex N773DL	♦
☐ N649KA	Swearingen SA227AC Metro III	AC-649	ex C6-REX	
☐ N652KA	Swearingen SA227AC Metro III	AC-652B	ex C6-FPO	
☐ N746KA	Swearingen SA227AC Metro III	AC-746B		♦
☐ N6851J	Piper PA-32R-300 Lance	32r-7680370		

L-3 FLIGHT INTERNATIONAL AVIATION   Invader Jack (IVJ)   Newport News-Williamsburg Intl, VA (PHF)

☐ N10FN	Learjet 36	36-015	ex N14CF	
☐ N12FN	Learjet 36	36-016	ex N616DJ	
☐ N16FN	Learjet 36A	36A-027	ex N27MJ	
☐ N26FN	Learjet 36	36-011	ex N26MJ	
☐ N39FN	Learjet 35	35-006	ex N39DM	
☐ N50FN	Learjet 35A	35A-070	ex N543PA	
☐ N51FN	Learjet 35A	35A-069	ex N48GP	
☐ N52FN	Learjet 35A	35A-424	ex N508GP	
☐ N54FN	Learjet 25C	25C-083	ex N200MH	
☐ N55FN	Learjet 35A	35A-202	ex D-CGPD	
☐ N83FN	Learjet 36	36-007	ex N83DM	
☐ N84FN	Learjet 36	36-002	ex N84DM	
☐ N118FN	Learjet 35A	35A-118	ex N88JA	
☐ N710GS	Learjet 35	35-032	ex N711MA	
☐ N208SA	Cessna 208B Caravan I	208B0831		♦
☐ N404E	de Havilland DHC-8-402	4067	ex C-GEOZ	♦
☐ N925WP	Beech 300 King Air	FL-711		♦
☐ N5055J	Beech 300 King Air	FL-855		♦

LAB FLYING SERVICE   (JF/LAB)   Juneau-Intl, AK/Haines-Municipal, AK (JNU/HNS)

☐ N54KA	Piper PA-32-300 Cherokee Six	32-7840197		
☐ N666EB	Piper PA-32-300 Cherokee Six	32-7940115	ex N2116G	
☐ N2897X	Piper PA-32-300 Cherokee Six	32-7940187		
☐ N2930Q	Piper PA-32R-300 Lance	32R-7780269		
☐ N4485X	Piper PA-32-300 Cherokee Six	32-7640026		
☐ N5686V	Piper PA-32R-300 Lance	32R-7780361		
☐ N6968J	Piper PA-32R-300 Lance	32R-7680397		
☐ N7718C	Piper PA-32-300 Cherokee Six	32-7640049		
☐ N8127Q	Piper PA-32-300 Cherokee Six	32-7940269		
☐ N8493C	Piper PA-32R-300 Lance	32R-7680118		
☐ N39636	Piper PA-32-300 Cherokee Six	32-7840172		
☐ N3523Y	Piper PA-31-350 Chieftain	31-7952115		
☐ N6314V	Helio H-295 Courier II	2534		
☐ N7333L	Piper PA-34-200T Seneca II	34-7670099		
☐ N54732	Piper PA-31-350 Navajo Chieftain	31-7405254		

LAKE & PENINSULA AIRLINES   Port Alsworth, AK (PTA)

☐ N454SF	Cessna 208B Caravan I	208B0797	ex N5180C	
☐ N756BW	Cessna U206G Stationair	U20603969		FP/WS
☐ N9602F	Cessna 208 Caravan I	20800103		

LAKE CLARK AIR   Port Alsworth, AK (PTA)

☐ N31TN	Beech B99	U-49	ex N98RZ	♦
☐ N991AK	Beech 99	U-28	ex N33TN	[ANC]

☐ N992AK	Beech C99	U-167	ex C-FNMF	◆
☐ N993AK	Piper PA-31-350 Navajo Chieftain	31-7305015	ex N7146T	
☐ N995AK	Piper PA-31-350 Navajo Chieftain	31-7752089	ex N75RA	
☐ N996AK	Cessna U206E Stationair	U20601519	ex N9119M	
☐ N997AK	Cessna 207 Skywagon	20700019	ex N91028	
☐ N8300Q	Cessna U206F Stationair II	U20603161		FP
☐ N73123	Cessna 207A Skywagon	20700561	ex V3-HFK	

LEIS AIR — Honolulu, HI

☐ N865MA	Cessna 208B Caravan I	208B0996	ex N747CG	◆
☐ N866MA	Cessna 208B Caravan I	208B0934	ex N108JA	◆

LOGISTIC AIR — Reno, NV (RNO)

☐ N617US	Boeing 747-251F	21121/261		[MZJ]
☐ N618US	Boeing 747-251F	21122/269		[MZJ]
☐ N722LA	Boeing 727-2F2F	22992/1804	ex TC-JCA	wfs
☐ N908AX	Douglas DC-9-31	47008/98	ex VH-TJK	[MZJ]
☐ N941AX	Douglas DC-9-31	47419/602	ex VH-TJQ	[MZJ]
☐ N982AX	Douglas DC-9-32	47317/385	ex N1261L	[MZJ]
☐ S2-AFA	Boeing 747-121SCD	19650/24	ex N617FF	◆
☐ 5U-ACF	Boeing 747-146B	23150/601	ex CP-2480	◆

LYNDEN AIR CARGO — Lynden (L2/LYC) — Anchorage-Intl, AK (ANC)

☐ N401LC	Lockheed L-382G-31C Hercules	4606	ex ZS-RSJ	
☐ N403LC	Lockheed L-382G-31C Hercules	4590	ex N903SJ	
☐ N404LC	Lockheed L-382G-38C Hercules	4763	ex N909SJ	[IGM]
☐ N405LC	Lockheed L-382G-69C Hercules	5025	ex ZS-OLG	
☐ P4-LAE	Lockheed L-382G Hercules	5225	ex P2-LAE	◆

M & N AVIATION — Jonah (MJ/JNH) — San Juan-Munoz Marin Intl, PR (SJU)

☐ N405MN	Pilatus PC-12/45	405		◆
☐ N787RA	Cessna 208B Caravan I	208B1019	ex N52144	

MARIANAS AIR TRANSFER — N Mariana Island, MP

☐ N8639N	Piper PA-32-300 Cherokee Six	32-7140032	
☐ N32728	Piper PA-32-300 Cherokee Six	32-7540061	

MARTINAIRE — Martex (MRA) — Dallas-Addison, TX (ADS)

☐ N78SA	Cessna 208B Caravan I	208B0467	ex N5058J
☐ N162SA	Cessna 208B Caravan I	208B0548	ex N1219N
☐ N1031P	Cessna 208B Caravan I	208B0404	
☐ N1037N	Cessna 208B Caravan I	208B0334	ex (C-GWFN)
☐ N1116W	Cessna 208B Caravan I	208B0411	
☐ N1119V	Cessna 208B Caravan I	208B0383	
☐ N1120W	Cessna 208B Caravan I	208B0388	
☐ N4591B	Cessna 208B Caravan I	208B0137	ex (N997FE)
☐ N4602B	Cessna 208B Caravan I	208B0140	ex (N999FE)
☐ N4625B	Cessna 208B Caravan I	208B0159	
☐ N4655B	Cessna 208B Caravan I	208B0160	
☐ N4662B	Cessna 208B Caravan I	208B0161	
☐ N4674B	Cessna 208B Caravan I	208B0165	
☐ N4687B	Cessna 208B Caravan I	208B0167	
☐ N9331B	Cessna 208B Caravan I	208B0055	ex (N955FE)
☐ N9469B	Cessna 208B Caravan I	208B0079	
☐ N9471B	Cessna 208B Caravan I	208B0081	
☐ N9505B	Cessna 208B Caravan I	208B0085	
☐ N9546B	Cessna 208B Caravan I	208B0126	
☐ N9714B	Cessna 208B Caravan I	208B0153	
☐ N9760B	Cessna 208B Caravan I	208B0102	
☐ N9761B	Cessna 208B Caravan I	208B0107	
☐ N9762B	Cessna 208B Caravan I	208B0109	
☐ N9766B	Cessna 208B Caravan I	208B0112	
☐ N9956B	Cessna 208B Caravan I	208B0119	
☐ N12155	Cessna 208B Caravan I	208B0562	ex (C-FKAX)

MAVERICK HELICOPTERS — Las Vegas-McCarran Intl/Grand Canyon-National Park (LAS/GCN)

☐ N805MH	Eurocopter EC130B4	3799
☐ N806MH	Eurocopter EC130B4	3833
☐ N807MH	Eurocopter EC130B4	3912
☐ N808MH	Eurocopter EC130B4	3914
☐ N809MH	Eurocopter EC130B4	3927
☐ N810MH	Eurocopter EC130B4	3949
☐ N812MH	Eurocopter EC130B4	3956
☐ N813MH	Eurocopter EC130B4	3967

☐ N814MH	Eurocopter EC130B4	4020		
☐ N815MH	Eurocopter EC130B4	4022		
☐ N816MH	Eurocopter EC130B4	4038		
☐ N817MH	Eurocopter EC130B4	4125		
☐ N818MH	Eurocopter EC130B4	4131		
☐ N821MH	Eurocopter EC130B4	4134		
☐ N822MH	Eurocopter EC130B4	4142		
☐ N823MH	Eurocopter EC130B4	4158		
☐ N824MH	Eurocopter EC130B4	4173		
☐ N846MH	Eurocopter EC130B4	4248		
☐ N847MH	Eurocopter EC130B4	4266		
☐ N848MH	Eurocopter EC130B4	4290		
☐ N849MH	Eurocopter EC130B4	4313		
☐ N850MH	Eurocopter EC130B4	4327		
☐ N851MH	Eurocopter EC130B4	4340		
☐ N852MH	Eurocopter EC130B4	4356		
☐ N853MH	Eurocopter EC130B4	4417		
☐ N854MH	Eurocopter EC130B4	4433		
☐ N856MH	Eurocopter EC130B4	4437		
☐ N857MH	Eurocopter EC130B4	4457		
☐ N858MH	Eurocopter EC130B4	4503		
☐ N862MH	Eurocopter EC130B4	4545		
☐ N863MH	Eurocopter EC130B4	4570		
☐ N864MH	Eurocopter EC130B4	4616		
☐ N867MH	Eurocopter EC130B4	4770		
☐ N868MH	Eurocopter EC130B4	4797		

McNEELY CHARTER SERVICE — Mid-South (MDS)
West Memphis-Municipal, AR/Malden, MO (AWM/MAW)

☐ N106GA	Beech Baron 58	TH-437	ex N4379W	
☐ N262AG	Short SD.3-30	SH3120	ex 84-0473	
☐ N320MC	Swearingen SA227AC Metro III	AC-688	ex EC-GEN	
☐ N866D	Mitsubishi MU-2B-36 (MU-2L)	656	ex N666D	
☐ N2699Y	Swearingen SA227AC Metro III	AC-666		wfs

MENARD — Eau Claire, WI

☐ N534M	Beech 1900D	UE-333	ex N23235	
☐ N536M	Beech 1900D	UE-334		
☐ N548M	Embraer ERJ-135SE	145364	ex PT-SOP	
☐ N549M	Embraer ERJ-135SE	145450	ex N948AL	
☐ N563M	Cessna 560 Citation	560-0550		♦
☐ N564M	Cessna 560 Citation	560-0569		♦

MERLIN AIRWAYS — Avalon (MEI)

☐ N575EG	Swearingen SA227AC Metro III	AC-575		♦
☐ N708EG	Swearingen SA227AC Metro III	AC-708B	ex N27188	

MESA AIRLINES — Air Shuttle (YV/ASH) — Phoenix-Sky Harbor Intl, AZ/Albuquerque-Intl, NM (PHX/ABQ)

Ops for American, Delta and United

MIAMI AIR INTERNATIONAL — Biscayne (LL/BSK) — Miami-Intl, FL (MIA)

☐ N732MA	Boeing 737-81Q/W	30618/830	ex D-AXLI	
☐ N733MA	Boeing 737-81Q/W	30619/856	ex D-AXLJ	
☐ N738MA	Boeing 737-8Q8/W	32799/1467		Diane
☐ N739MA	Boeing 737-8Q8/W	30670/1481		Ely
☐ N752MA	Boeing 737-48E	28198/2806	ex HL7509	
☐ N753MA	Boeing 737-48E	28053/2954	ex HL7518	

MIAMI AIR LEASE — Miami Air (MG/MGD) — Miami-Opa Locka, FL (OPF)

☐ N41527	Convair 440-72	346	ex C-FPUM

MIDWEST CONNECT — Skyway-Ex (AL/SYX) — Milwaukee-General Mitchell Intl, WI (MKE)

☐ N407SW	Canadair CRJ-200ER	7034	ex C-FMNY	Mesa
☐ N471CA	Canadair CRJ-200ER	7655	ex C-FMNH	SkyWest
☐ N472CA	Canadair CRJ-200ER	7667	ex C-FMML	SkyWest
☐ N479CA	Canadair CRJ-200ER	7675	ex C-FMKW	SkyWest
☐ N494CA	Canadair CRJ-200ER	7765	ex C-FMKW	SkyWest
☐ N495CA	Canadair CRJ-200ER	7774	ex C-FMMT	SkyWest
☐ N498CA	Canadair CRJ-200ER	7792	ex C-FMMY	SkyWest
☐ N507CA	Canadair CRJ-200ER	7796	ex C-GZFC	SkyWest
☐ N699BR	Canadair CRJ-200ER	7801	ex C-FMLS	SkyWest
☐ N709BR	Canadair CRJ-200ER	7850	ex C-FMMW	SkyWest
☐ N983CA	Canadair CRJ-100ER	7169	ex C-FMNX	SkyWest

☐ N984CA	Canadair CRJ-100ER	7171	ex C-FMML		SkyWest
☐ N986CA	Canadair CRJ-100ER	7174	ex C-FMNX		SkyWest
☐ N988CA	Canadair CRJ-100ER	7204	ex C-FMMT		SkyWest [TUS]

Ops flights for Republic Airlines

MINDEN AIR — Minden, NV (MEV)

☐ N446MA	British Aerospace 146 Srs.200	E2111	ex C-FBAO	46 Fireliner	Waterbomber
☐ N556MA	British Aerospace 146 Srs.200	E2106	ex C-GRNZ		for tanker conversion [MEV]
☐ N1247M	Cessna 337E Super Skymaster	33701247			

MISSISSIPPI AIR EXPRESS — Madison, MS

☐ N999RK	Cessna 414	0610			♦

MISTY FJORDS AIR — Ketchikan, AK (WFB)

☐ N6868B	de Havilland DHC-3 Turbo Otter	274	ex C-GKPB	
☐ N7336	de Havilland DHC-2 Beaver	1229		
☐ N9204H	Cessna A185F Skywagon	18503421		♦

MOKULELE AIRLINES/GO! EXPRESS   Speedbuggy (MW/MUL)   Kailua/Kona-Keahole-Kona Intl, HI (KOA)

☐ N825MA	Cessna 208BEX Caravan I	208B5065		
☐ N835MA	Cessna 208B Caravan I	208B2335	ex N6059K	
☐ M839MA	Cessna 208B Caravan I	208B2392	ex N81118	
☐ N840MA	Cessna 208B Caravan I	208B2423	ex N6062Q	
☐ N841MA	Cessna 208B Caravan I	208B1084		♦
☐ N847MA	Cessna 208BEX Caravan I	208B5075		
☐ N852MA	Cessna 208BEX Caravan I	208B5081		
☐ N856MA	Cessna 208BEX Caravan I	208B5084		
☐ N857MA	Cessna 208B Caravan I	208B2422	ex N8117N	
☐ N859MA	Cessna 208B Caravan I	208B2424	ex N8117T	
☐ N861MA	Cessna 208B Caravan I	208B0825	ex N98RR	dam 22Oct13
☐ N862MA	Cessna 208B Caravan I	208B1138	ex N115KW	
☐ N863MA	Cessna 208B Caravan I	208B1049	ex N208LR	
☐ N879MA	Cessna 208BEX Caravan I	208B5019	ex N9521Z	♦
☐ N887MA	Cessna 208BEX Caravan I	208B5178		♦

MOUNTAIN AIR CARGO   Mountain (MTN)   Kinston-Regional Jetport, NC (ISO)

☐ N2679U	Short SD.3-30	SH3071	ex N330AE	
☐ N26288	Short SD.3-30	SH3074	ex G-BIYF	

NATIONAL AIRLINES   National Cargo (N8/MUA)   Detroit-Willow Run, MI (YIP)

☐ N135CA	Boeing 757-2Y0	26160/555	ex G-FCLJ	♦
☐ N15ECA	Boeing 757-2Y0	26161/557	ex G-FCLK	♦
☐ N168CA	Boeing 757-2Z0C	27259/609	ex B-2837	[ROW]
☐ N176CA	Boeing 757-28A	24543/268	ex G-STRW	
☐ N567CA	Boeing 757-223	24608/384	ex N650AA	
☐ N155CA	Douglas DC-8-73CF	46073/485	ex N803UP	[ROW]
☐ N919CA	Boeing 747-428BCF	25302/884	ex TF-ALF	
☐ N952CA	Boeing 747-428MBCF	25238/872	ex TF-NAC	wfs

Entered Chapter 11 Oct14; ops continue

NATIVE AMERICAN AIR SERVICE — Phoenix-Williams Gateway, AZ (CHD)

☐ N317NA	Pilatus PC-12/45	223	ex N223PD	Air Ambulance
☐ N562NA	Pilatus PC-12/45	174	ex N174PC	Air Ambulance
☐ N613NA	Pilatus PC-12/45	197	ex N197PC	Air Ambulance
☐ N970NA	Pilatus PC-12/45	226	ex N308NA	Air Ambulance

NEPTUNE AVIATION SERVICES — Missoula-Intl, MT (MSO)

☐ N443NA	Lockheed P2V-7 Neptune	726-7168	ex N139HP	
☐ N445NA	Lockheed P2V-7 Neptune	726-7102	ex N140HP	
☐ N807NA	Lockheed P2V-5 Neptune	426-5305	ex N1386K	07
☐ N1386C	Lockheed P2V-5 Neptune	426-5268	ex Bu128422	44
☐ N4235N	Lockheed P2V-5 Neptune	726-7158	ex Bu144681	10
☐ N9855F	Lockheed P2V-7 Neptune	426-5326	ex Bu131445	06
☐ N96264	Lockheed P2V-5 Neptune	426-5192	ex Bu128346	12
☐ N96278	Lockheed P2V-5 Neptune	426-5340	ex Bu131459	05
☐ N146FF	British Aerospace 146 Srs.200	E2049	ex N608AW	Tanker 40
☐ N192DD	British Aerospace 146 Srs.200	E2192	ex OO-MJE	[MSO]♦
☐ N193DD	British Aerospace 146 Srs.200	E2196	ex OO-DJJ	♦
☐ N471NA	British Aerospace 146 Srs.200	E2136	ex N145FF	Tanker 41

☐ N472NA	British Aerospace 146 Srs.200	E2138	ex N18FF	Tanker 10
☐ N473NA	British Aerospace 146 Srs.200	E2045	ex OY-RCA	Tanker 01
☐ N474NA	British Aerospace 146 Srs.200	E2084	ex N291UE	Tanker 02
☐ N301TS	Beech B100 King Air	BE-76		♦
☐ N485AS	Dassault Falcon 100	219		♦

NEW ENGLAND AIRLINES New England (EJ/NEA) Westerly-State, RI (WST)

☐ N401WB	Britten-Norman BN-2A Islander	66	ex N598JA
☐ N403WB	Britten-Norman BN-2A-26 Islander	46	ex N123NE
☐ N404WB	Britten-Norman BN-2A-26 Islander	564	ex N304SK
☐ N405WB	Piper PA-32-300 Cherokee Six	32-7640043	ex N345CS
☐ N406WB	Piper PA-32-300 Cherokee Six	32-7640058	ex N8303C
☐ N408WB	Piper PA-32-300 Cherokee Six	32-7240092	ex N4885T

NORD AVIATION Santa Teresa-Dona Ana County, NM (EPZ)

☐ N16LJ	Learjet 55	126	ex N7260J	
☐ N321L	Douglas C-117D	43345	ex N307SF	Frtr
☐ N738WB	Beech D50C Twin Bonanza	DH-286	ex N344WG	Frtr
☐ N9375Y	Beech H18	BA-564		
☐ N57626	Douglas DC-3	4564	ex NC57626	Frtr

NORTH STAR AIR CARGO Sky Box (SBX) Milwaukee-General Mitchell Intl, WI (MKE)

☐ N50DA	Short SC.7 Skyvan	SH1852	ex G-AWVM	Frtr
☐ N51NS	Short SC.7 Skyvan	SH1843	ex N20DA	Frtr
☐ N549WB	Short SC.7 Skyvan	SH1911	ex XA-SRD	Frtr
☐ N731E	Short SC.7 Skyvan	SH1853	ex N80JJ	

NORTHERN AIR CARGO Yukon (NC/NAC) Anchorage-Intl, AK (ANC)

☐ N320DL	Boeing 737-232F	23092/1023	
☐ N321DL	Boeing 737-232F	23093/1024	
☐ N322DL	Boeing 737-232F	23094/1026	
☐ N360WA	Boeing 737-301SF	23553/1406	ex A6-HMK
☐ N361NC	Boeing 737-301SF	23260/1146	ex TF-BBI

OHANA

☐ N801HC	ATR 42-500	629	ex OK-JFL	Kaiahulu
☐ N804HC	ATR 42-500	623	ex OK-JFJ	Holo Kaomi
☐ N805HC	ATR 42-500	625	ex OK-JFL	Hikipua

OMEGA AERIAL REFUELLING

☐ N707MQ	Boeing 707-368C	21368/925	ex HZ-HM3
☐ N974VV	McDonnell-Douglas DC-10-40		
	(KDC-10)	46974/274	ex JA8538

OMEGA AIR San Antonio, TX (SAT)

☐ N623RH	Boeing 707-338C	19623/671	ex A20-623	wfs♦
☐ N624RH	Boeing 707-338C	19624/689	ex A20-624	wfs♦
☐ N629RH	Boeing 707-338C	19629/737	ex A20-629	wfs♦
☐ N707GF	Boeing 707-3K1C	20804/883	ex YR-ABB	wfs♦

OMNI AIR INTERNATIONAL Omni (OY/OAE) Tulsa-Intl, OK (TUL)

☐ N225AX	Boeing 767-224ER	30434/825	ex N68155	
☐ N234AX	Boeing 767-224ER	30436/833	ex N67157	
☐ N342AX	Boeing 767-328ER	27136/497	ex N225LF	
☐ N351AX	Boeing 767-33AER	27908/578	ex I-DEIF	
☐ N378AX	Boeing 767-33AER	28147/622	ex I-DEIL	
☐ N387AX	Boeing 767-319ER	24875/371	ex N875AW	
☐ N396AX	Boeing 767-319ER	26264/555	ex N411LF	
☐ N423AX	Boeing 767-324ER	27569/601	ex N767NA	♦
☐ N441AX	Boeing 767-36NER	29898/754	ex N768NA	♦
☐ N531AX	McDonnell-Douglas DC-10-30ERF	48316/437	ex N244NW	[GYR]
☐ N621AX	McDonnell-Douglas DC-10-30ER	48319/438	ex N240NW	[GYR]
☐ N918AX	Boeing 777-222ER	26935/88	ex N789UA	
☐ N927AX	Boeing 777-222ER	26943/92	ex N790UA	

ORANGE AIR Orlando-Sanford Intl, FL (SFB)

☐ N918AV	McDonnell-Douglas MD-82	49104/1085	ex ZA-ARD	♦
☐ N926AV	McDonnell-Douglas MD-83	49630/1591	ex LV-BEG	♦

OSPREY EXPRESS — Portland, ME

☐ N887ME	Cessna 208 Caravan I	20800402	ex N719MZ	FP

PACIFIC AIRWAYS — (3F) — Ketchikan-Harbor SPB, AK (WFB)

☐ N12UA	de Havilland DHC-2 Beaver	700	ex C-GSIN	FP
☐ N96DG	de Havilland DHC-2 Beaver	702	ex N99132	FP
☐ N264P	de Havilland DHC-2 Beaver	464	ex N23RF	FP
☐ N5595M	de Havilland DHC-2 Beaver	1571	ex 105	FP
☐ N9294Z	de Havilland DHC-2 Beaver	1379	ex 58-2047	FP

PACIFIC HELICOPTOR TOURS — Kahului, HI (OGG)

☐ N27FU	Bell UH-1H	4113	ex 63-08821
☐ N1076C	Bell 204	5436	ex Bu157841
☐ N5743H	Bell 206B JetRanger	3042	
☐ N6131P	Bell UH-1H	5787	ex 66-16093
☐ N6651H	Bell 206L-1 LongRanger	45211	
☐ N8079E	Bell UH-1H	4762	ex 65-09718
☐ N80780	Bell UH-1H	4527	ex 64-13820

PACIFIC WINGS — Tsunami (LW/NMI) — Kahului-Intl, HI (OGG)

☐ N301PW	Cessna 208B Caravan I	208B0983	
☐ N302PW	Cessna 208B Caravan I	208B0984	
☐ N306PW	Cessna 208B Caravan I	208B1240	ex N208TD
☐ N307PW	Cessna 208B Caravan I	208B1254	ex N12959
☐ N308PW	Cessna 208B Caravan I	208B1273	ex N5166T

PAPILLON GRAND CANYON AIRWAYS — (HI) — Grand Canyon-National Park, AZ, (GCN)

☐ N425EH	Aérospatiale AS350B2 AStar	4197	35	
☐ N763AE	Aérospatiale AS350B3 AStar	7789		♦
☐ N830PA	Aérospatiale AS350B3 AStar	7246		
☐ N832PA	Aérospatiale AS350B3 AStar	7307		
☐ N833PA	Aérospatiale AS350B3 AStar	7403	ex N6871A	
☐ N834PA	Aérospatiale AS350B3 AStar	7415		
☐ N835PA	Aérospatiale AS350B3 AStar	7501		
☐ N836PA	Aérospatiale AS350B3 AStar	7508		
☐ N839PA	Aérospatiale AS350B3 AStar	7675		
☐ N840PA	Aérospatiale AS350B3 AStar	7718		
☐ N841PA	Aérospatiale AS350B3 AStar	7748		♦
☐ N890PA	Aérospatiale AS350B2 AStar	4554	37	
☐ N891PA	Aérospatiale AS350B2 AStar	4557	ex N895PA	33	
☐ N892PA	Aérospatiale AS350B2 AStar	4581		
☐ N942AE	Aérospatiale AS350B3 AStar	7865		♦
☐ N178PA	Bell 206L-1 LongRanger III	45319	ex F-ODUB	8
☐ N333ER	Bell 206L-1 LongRanger III	45203	ex B7VG	12
☐ N2072M	Bell 206L-1 LongRanger II	45720		2
☐ N3893U	Bell 206L-3 LongRanger III	51020		9
☐ N3895D	Bell 206L-1 LongRanger II	45590		1
☐ N4227E	Bell 206L-1 LongRanger III	45702	ex N725RE	18
☐ N5745Y	Bell 206L-1 LongRanger III	45531		11
☐ N20316	Bell 206L-1 LongRanger II	45687		21
☐ N22425	Bell 206L-1 LongRanger II	45743		29
☐ N27694	Bell 206L-1 LongRanger II	45282		4
☐ N38885	Bell 206L-1 LongRanger II	45726		20
☐ N50046	Bell 206L-1 LongRanger II	45173		28
☐ N57491	Bell 206L-1 LongRanger II	45505		15
☐ N130GC	Eurocopter EC130B4	3562	41	
☐ N130PH	Eurocopter EC130B4	3670	38	dam Jun13
☐ N132GC	Eurocopter EC130B4	3756	43	
☐ N133PH	Eurocopter EC130B4	3939	ex N202AE	49
☐ N135PH	Eurocopter EC130B4	3695	39	
☐ N136PH	Eurocopter EC130B4	3896	46	
☐ N137PH	Eurocopter EC130B4	3775	40	
☐ N138PH	Eurocopter EC130B4	3790	ex F-WWXB	44
☐ N151GC	Eurocopter EC130B4	4402	51	
☐ N152GC	Eurocopter EC130B4	4448	52	
☐ N153GC	Eurocopter EC130B4	7074		
☐ N154GC	Eurocopter EC130B4	7077		
☐ N155GC	Eurocopter EC130B4	7091		♦
☐ N156GC	Eurocopter EC130B4	7296		
☐ N779PA	Eurocopter EC130B4	4318		
☐ N830GC	Eurocopter EC130T2	7507		♦
☐ N831GC	Eurocopter EC130T2	7582		
☐ N832GC	Eurocopter EC130T2	7667		
☐ N833GC	Eurocopter EC130T2	7747		

☐ N834GC	Eurocopter EC130T2	7829		♦
☐ N835GC	Eurocopter EC130B4	7833		♦
☐ N836GC	Eurocopter EC130T2	8012		♦
☐ N368PA	MD Helicopters MD900 Explorer	900-00012	ex N901CF	
☐ N407PA	Bell 407	53567	ex N16FR	

PARADIGM AIR CARRIERS   Gazelle (PMM)

☐ N698SS	Boeing 727-223	21369/1275	ex N864AA

PENAIR/PENINSULA AIRWAYS   Peninsula (KS/PEN)   Anchorage-Intl, AK (ANC)

☐ N340AQ	SAAB SF.340AF	340A-019	ex C-GYQM		
☐ N364PX	SAAB SF.340B	340B-262	ex SE-G62		
☐ N365PX	SAAB SF.340B	340B-265	ex SE-G65		
☐ N369PX	SAAB SF.340B	340B-295	ex SE-G95		
☐ N403XJ	SAAB SF.340B	340B-403	ex SE-B03		
☐ N404XJ	SAAB SF.340B	340B-404	ex SE-B04		
☐ N406XJ	SAAB SF.340B	340B-406	ex SE-B06		
☐ N410XJ	SAAB SF.340B	340B-410	ex SE-B10		
☐ N424XJ	SAAB SF.340B	340B-424	ex SE-B24		
☐ N662PA	SAAB SF.340AF	340A-109	ex N109XJ		
☐ N665PA	SAAB SF.340B	340B-181	ex N590MA		
☐ N675PA	SAAB SF.340B	340B-206	ex N593MA	Spirit of Bristol Bay	
☐ N677PA	SAAB SF.340B	340B-328	ex VH-XDZ		
☐ N679PA	SAAB SF.340B	340B-345	ex N345CV		
☐ N685PA	SAAB SF.340B	340B-212	ex N594MA	Spirit of the Aleutians	
☐ N508RH	SAAB 2000	2000-027	ex N5124		o/o♦
☐ N4327P	Piper PA-32-301 Saratoga	32-8406002			
☐ N9304F	Cessna 208 Caravan I	20800008			
☐ N9481F	Cessna 208 Caravan I	20800070			

PHI - PETROLEUM HELICOPTERS   Petroleum (PHM)   Lafayette-Regional, LA (LFT)

☐ N151AE	Aérospatiale AS350B3 AStar	3814		
☐ N153AE	Aérospatiale AS350B3 AStar	3829		
☐ N350LG	Aérospatiale AS350B3 AStar	3690	ex N499AE	
☐ N351LG	Aérospatiale AS350B3 AStar	3722	ex N580AE	
☐ N352LG	Aérospatiale AS350B3 AStar	3777	ex N142AE	
☐ N386P	Aérospatiale AS350B3 AStar	7638	ex N547AE	
☐ N389P	Aérospatiale AS350B3 AStar	7627	ex N553AE	
☐ N392P	Aérospatiale AS350B3 AStar	7662		
☐ N393P	Aérospatiale AS350B3 AStar	7669		
☐ N394P	Aérospatiale AS350B3 AStar	7694		
☐ N395P	Aérospatiale AS350B3 AStar	7698		
☐ N397P	Aérospatiale AS350B3 AStar	7795		♦
☐ N498AE	Aérospatiale AS350B3 AStar	3687		
☐ N585AE	Aérospatiale AS350B3 AStar	3736		
☐ N587AE	Aérospatiale AS350B3 AStar	3730		
☐ N590AE	Aérospatiale AS350B3 AStar	3733		
☐ N970AE	Aérospatiale AS350B2 AStar	3235		
☐ N972AE	Aérospatiale AS350B3 AStar	3234		EMS
☐ N973AE	Aérospatiale AS350B3 AStar	3229	ex C-GFIH	EMS
☐ N4031L	Aérospatiale AS350B2 AStar	2907		based Antarctica
☐ N4036H	Aérospatiale AS350B2 AStar	2919		based Antarctica
☐ N139PH	AgustaWestland AW139	41253		
☐ N140PH	AgustaWestland AW139	41254	ex N380SH	
☐ N141PH	AgustaWestland AW139	41266		
☐ N145PH	AgustaWestland AW139	41271		
☐ N146PH	AgustaWestland AW139	41280		
☐ N148PH	AgustaWestland AW139	41300		
☐ N149PH	AgustaWestland AW139	41303		
☐ N151PH	AgustaWestland AW139	41312		
☐ N152PH	AgustaWestland AW139	41316		
☐ N153PH	AgustaWestland AW139	41317		
☐ N241PH	Beech B200 Super King Air	BB-1182	ex N416CS	
☐ N246PH	Beech B200 Super King Air	BB-1373		
☐ N248PH	Beech B200 Super King Air	BB-1618	ex N827HT	
☐ N332P	Beech B200GT Super King Air	BY-178	ex N5078Z	
☐ N911CM	Beech B200 Super King Air	BB-1551	ex N247PH	
☐ N203PH	Bell 206L-3 LongRanger III	51520	ex N31077	
☐ N204PH	Bell 206L-3 LongRanger III	51465	ex N41791	
☐ N207PH	Bell 206L-3 LongRanger III	51495	ex N8591X	
☐ N209PH	Bell 206L-3 LongRanger III	51531	ex N8594X	
☐ N214PH	Bell 206L-3 LongRanger III	51131	ex N4835	
☐ N215PH	Bell 206L-3 LongRanger III	51575	ex N53119	
☐ N219PH	Bell 206L-3 LongRanger III	51509	ex N8593X	

☐	N221PH	Bell 206L-3 LongRanger III	51494	ex N8590X
☐	N225PH	Bell 206L-3 LongRanger III	51556	ex N6251Y
☐	N228PH	Bell 206L-4 LongRanger IV	52033	ex N7074W
☐	N229PH	Bell 206L-3 LongRanger III	51184	ex N54641
☐	N230PH	Bell 206L-3 LongRanger III	51506	ex N206FS
☐	N231PH	Bell 206L-3 LongRanger III	51540	
☐	N233PH	Bell 206L-3 LongRanger III	51529	
☐	N236PH	Bell 206L-3 LongRangerIII	51345	
☐	N668PH	Bell 206L-3 LongRanger III	51487	ex N8589X
☐	N3107N	Bell 206L-3 LongRanger III	51512	
☐	N3108E	Bell 206L-3 LongRanger III	51498	
☐	N6160Z	Bell 206L-3 LongRanger III	51610	
☐	N7077F	Bell 206L-4 LongRanger IV	52038	
☐	N8588X	Bell 206L-3 LongRanger III	51486	
☐	N32041	Bell 206L-3 LongRanger III	51539	ex C-FLXL
☐	N62127	Bell 206L-4 LongRanger IV	52023	
☐	N401PH	Bell 407	53615	ex N407MD
☐	N402PH	Bell 407	53159	
☐	N403PH	Bell 407	53267	ex N8595X
☐	N404PH	Bell 407	53188	
☐	N406PH	Bell 407	53198	
☐	N407H	Bell 407	53464	ex N407XM
☐	N407PH	Bell 407	53003	ex C-FWRD
☐	N408PH	Bell 407	53228	
☐	N409PH	Bell 407	53626	ex N45655
☐	N410PH	Bell 407	53636	ex C-FDXK
☐	N411PH	Bell 407	53637	
☐	N412P	Bell 407	54135	♦
☐	N412PH	Bell 407	53862	
☐	N415PH	Bell 407	53390	ex N492PH
☐	N416PH	Bell 407	53276	
☐	N417PH	Bell 407	53038	
☐	N418PH	Bell 407	53640	ex N418PH
☐	N419P	Bell 407	54133	
☐	N420PH	Bell 407	53747	ex C-FLZR
☐	N421PH	Bell 407	53749	ex C-FLZP
☐	N422PH	Bell 407	53675	
☐	N424PH	Bell 407	53682	
☐	N425PH	Bell 407	53684	
☐	N426PH	Bell 407	53751	
☐	N427PH	Bell 407	53863	
☐	N428PH	Bell 407	53754	
☐	N429PH	Bell 407	53772	
☐	N430PH	Bell 407	53870	
☐	N431P	Bell 407	53857	
☐	N432PH	Bell 407	53681	
☐	N433P	Bell 407	53861	
☐	N434PH	Bell 407	53773	
☐	N439PH	Bell 407	53999	ex N424QA
☐	N440PH	Bell 407	53327	ex N724PH
☐	N441PH	Bell 407	54081	
☐	N442PH	Bell 407	54089	
☐	N443PH	Bell 407	54090	
☐	N445PH	Bell 407	54096	
☐	N447PH	Bell 407	53114	
☐	N448PH	Bell 407	54111	ex N470ZB
☐	N449PH	Bell 407	54117	
☐	N450PH	Bell 407	54125	
☐	N451PH	Bell 407	54127	
☐	N452P	Bell 407	53568	
☐	N452PH	Bell 407	53457	
☐	N453P	Bell 407	53572	
☐	N457PH	Bell 407	53121	♦
☐	N467PH	Bell 407	53142	
☐	N490PH	Bell 407	53378	ex N6387C
☐	N491PH	Bell 407	53386	ex N6390Y
☐	N493PH	Bell 407	53393	
☐	N494PH	Bell 407	53396	
☐	N495PH	Bell 407	53397	
☐	N496PH	Bell 407	53398	
☐	N498PH	Bell 407	53399	
☐	N501PH	Bell 407	53401	
☐	N510PH	Bell 407	53209	
☐	N612PH	Bell 407	53199	
☐	N719PH	Bell 407	53266	
☐	N720PH	Bell 407	53277	
☐	N721PH	Bell 407	53278	
☐	N722PH	Bell 407	53288	
☐	N723PH	Bell 407	53283	
☐	N740PH	Bell 407	53435	ex N6077V
☐	N742PH	Bell 407	53461	
☐	N4999	Bell 407	53323	

☐ N412SM	Bell 412EP	36213	ex N426DR	EMS
☐ N480PH	Bell 412EP	36589	ex N461QZ	
☐ N481PH	Bell 412EP	36596	ex N466QH	
☐ N482PH	Bell 412EP	36597	ex N467AB	
☐ N483PH	Bell 412EP	36598	ex N4663B	
☐ N484PH	Bell 412EP	36599	ex N467BB	
☐ N485PH	Bell 412EP	36600	ex N467FB	
☐ N486PH	Bell 412EP	36601	ex N467EB	
☐ N487PH	Bell 412EP	36668		♦
☐ N488PH	Bell 412EP	36669		♦
☐ 4X-BDT	Bell 412SP	33150	ex N142PH	♦
☐ N301PH	Eurocopter EC135P2	0355		
☐ N302PH	Eurocopter EC135P2	0364		EMS
☐ N303PH	Eurocopter EC135P2	0372		
☐ N304PH	Eurocopter EC135P2	0386		
☐ N305PH	Eurocopter EC135P2	0395		
☐ N307PH	Eurocopter EC135P2	0398		
☐ N308PH	Eurocopter EC135P2	0401		
☐ N309PH	Eurocopter EC135P2	0403		
☐ N311PH	Eurocopter EC135P2	0413		
☐ N312PH	Eurocopter EC135P2	0404		PHi Air Medical
☐ N314PH	Eurocopter EC135P2	0409		
☐ N317PH	Eurocopter EC135P2	0423		
☐ N320PH	Eurocopter EC135P2+	0430		
☐ N323PH	Eurocopter EC135P2+	0434		
☐ N324PH	Eurocopter EC135P2+	0571		
☐ N325PH	Eurocopter EC135P2+	0576		
☐ N326PH	Eurocopter EC135P2+	0435		
☐ N327PH	Eurocopter EC135P2+	0445	ex D-HECB	
☐ N328PH	Eurocopter EC135P2+	0450	ex D-HECG	
☐ N329PH	Eurocopter EC135P2+	0489		
☐ N330PH	Eurocopter EC135P2+	0514		
☐ N332PH	Eurocopter EC135P2+	0519		
☐ N343PH	Eurocopter EC135P2+	0456		
☐ N344PH	Eurocopter EC135P2+	0459		
☐ N370PH	Eurocopter EC135P2+	0464		
☐ N376PH	Eurocopter EC135P2+	0523		
☐ N380PH	Eurocopter EC135P2+	0593		
☐ N381PH	Eurocopter EC135P2+	0611		
☐ N382PH	Eurocopter EC135P2+	0618		
☐ N383PH	Eurocopter EC135P2+	0622		
☐ N384PH	Eurocopter EC135P2+	0653		
☐ N385PH	Eurocopter EC135P2+	0670		
☐ N388PH	Eurocopter EC135P2+	0701		
☐ N389PH	Eurocopter EC135P2+	0710		
☐ N390PH	Eurocopter EC135P2+	0733		
☐ N391PH	Eurocopter EC135P2+	0748		
☐ N709P	Sikorsky S-76C-2	760716		
☐ N714P	Sikorsky S-76C+	760719	ex N2576T	
☐ N718P	Sikorsky S-76C-2	760686		
☐ N725P	Sikorsky S-76C-2	760688		
☐ N738P	Sikorsky S-76C-2	760668		
☐ N742P	Sikorsky S-76C	760607		
☐ N745P	Sikorsky S-76C	760619		
☐ N746P	Sikorsky S-76C	760623		
☐ N753P	Sikorsky S-76C	760726		
☐ N759P	Sikorsky S-76C-2	760690		
☐ N760PH	Sikorsky S-76A	760078	ex VH-BJR	
☐ N761PH	Sikorsky S-76A	760224	ex VH-BJS	
☐ N762P	Sikorsky S-76A	760060	ex N76NY	
☐ N763P	Sikorsky S-76A	760166	ex C-GHJT	
☐ N764P	Sikorsky S-76A	760276	ex N913UK	
☐ N769P	Sikorsky S-76C	760671		
☐ N770PH	Sikorsky S-76A	760231	ex N911MJ	
☐ N772P	Sikorsky S-76C	760730		
☐ N776P	Sikorsky S-76A	760275	ex N911UK	
☐ N778P	Sikorsky S-76A	760035	ex N4253S	
☐ N779P	Sikorsky S-76C+	760655	ex N4501G	
☐ N781P	Sikorsky S-76C+	760630		
☐ N784P	Sikorsky S-76C	760634		
☐ N785P	Sikorsky S-76C	760635		
☐ N786P	Sikorsky S-76C	760643		
☐ N787P	Sikorsky S-76C-2	760692		
☐ N790P	Sikorsky S-76C	760675	ex N45138	
☐ N794P	Sikorsky S-76C	760737		
☐ N796P	Sikorsky S-76C-2	760681		
☐ N797P	Sikorsky S-76C	760742		
☐ N798P	Sikorsky S-76C-2	760685		
☐ N1545K	Sikorsky S-76A	760047		
☐ N1545X	Sikorsky S-76A	760050		
☐ N1546G	Sikorsky S-76A	760076		

☐ N1546K	Sikorsky S-76A	760082		
☐ N5435V	Sikorsky S-76A	760158		
☐ PP-MCS	Sikorsky S-76A	760077	ex N1547D	
☐ PR-CHG	Sikorsky S-76C+	760658	ex N658A	based Brazil
☐ PR-CHI	Sikorsky S-76C+	760670	ex N4514K	based Brazil
☐ N274Z	Sikorsky S-92A	920274		♦
☐ N392PH	Sikorsky S-92A	920015		
☐ N492PH	Sikorsky S-92A	920016	ex N592PH	
☐ N592PH	Sikorsky S-92A	920027		
☐ N692PH	Sikorsky S-92A	920028		
☐ N792PH	Sikorsky S-92A	920037		
☐ N892PH	Sikorsky S-92A	920038	ex N8092S	
☐ N921PH	Sikorsky S-92A	920073		
☐ N922PH	Sikorsky S-92A	920096		
☐ N923PH	Sikorsky S-92A	920104		
☐ N924PH	Sikorsky S-92A	920116		
☐ N925PH	Sikorsky S-92A	920118		
☐ N926PH	Sikorsky S-92A	920121		
☐ N927PH	Sikorsky S-92A	920122	ex N2148A	
☐ N928PH	Sikorsky S-92A	920149	ex N2148A	
☐ N929PH	Sikorsky S-92A	920151	ex N2199M	
☐ N930PH	Sikorsky S-92A	920160	ex N1604	
☐ N931PH	Sikorsky S-92A	920161	ex N161U	
☐ N932PH	Sikorsky S-92A	920164	ex N164V	
☐ N933PH	Sikorsky S-92A	920165	ex N165U	
☐ N935PH	Sikorsky S-92A	920178	ex N178F	
☐ N936PH	Sikorsky S-92A	920180	ex N980A	
☐ N937PH	Sikorsky S-92A	920201	ex N201WK	
☐ N939PH	Sikorsky S-92A	920202	ex N202Y	
☐ N940PH	Sikorsky S-92A	920206	ex N206YL	
☐ N941PH	Sikorsky S-92A	920210	ex N210FD	
☐ N942PH	Sikorsky S-92A	920217	ex N217Y	
☐ N943PH	Sikorsky S-92A	920218	ex N218PY	
☐ N944PH	Sikorsky S-92A	920238		♦
☐ N945PH	Sikorsky S-92A	920246		♦
☐ N946PH	Sikorsky S-92A	920252		♦
☐ N947PH	Sikorsky S-92A	920256		♦
☐ N948PH	Sikorsky S-92A	920260		♦
☐ N949PH	Sikorsky S-92A	920264		♦
☐ N992PH	Sikorsky S-92A	920055	ex N4502G	
☐ N32HH	Learjet 31A	31A-201		
☐ N132PH	Learjet 31A	31A-242		
☐ N217AE	MBB BK-117B-2	7152	ex N217UC	
☐ N226PH	Bell 212	31106	ex N27805	
☐ N227PH	Bell 212	30953	ex N3131S	
☐ N232PH	Learjet 45	45-2044		♦
☐ N911TL	MBB BK-117B-1	7198	ex N911AF	
☐ N3208H	Bell 212	31304		
☐ N5736J	Bell 212	31140		

PHOENIX AIR		**Gray Bird (PH/PHA)**		**Cartersville, GA (VPC)**
☐ N164PA	Grumman G-159 Gulfstream I	54	ex N26AJ	
☐ N171PA	Grumman G-159 Gulfstream I	192	ex YV-76CP	
☐ N185PA	Grumman G-159 Gulfstream I	26	ex YV-82CP	
☐ N190PA	Grumman G-159 Gulfstream I (LFD)	195	ex N1900W	Frtr
☐ N192PA	Grumman G-159 Gulfstream I	149	ex N684FM	[VPC]
☐ N193PA	Grumman G-159 Gulfstream I (LFD)	125	ex N5NA	Frtr
☐ N195PA	Grumman G-159C Gulfstream IC	88	ex C-GPTN	
☐ N196PA	Grumman G-159 Gulfstream I	139	ex C-FRTU	
☐ N198PA	Grumman G-159C Gulfstream IC	27	ex N415CA	
☐ N810CB	Grumman G-159C Gulfstream 1	23	ex N186PA	
☐ N163PA	Grumman G-1159A Gulfstream III-SMA	249	ex F-249	
☐ N165PA	Grumman G-1159 Gulfstream IIB	775	ex N692EB	
☐ N173PA	Grumman G-1159A Gulfstream III-SMA	313	ex F-313	
☐ N183PA	Grumman G-1159A Gulfstream III	385	ex N883PA	
☐ N184PA	Grumman G-1159A Gulfstream III	318	ex N17NC	
☐ N186PA	Grumman G-1159A Gulfstream III-SMA	317	ex N90EP	
☐ N197PA	Grumman G-1159A Gulfstream III-SM	329	ex N152PA	
☐ N32PA	Learjet 36A	36A-025	ex N800BL	
☐ N54PA	Learjet 36	36-004	ex N180GC	
☐ N56PA	Learjet 36A	36A-023	ex N6YY	
☐ N62PG	Learjet 36A	36A-031	ex N20UG	
☐ N71PG	Learjet 36	36-013	ex D-CBRD	
☐ N80PG	Learjet 35	35-063	ex N663CA	

362

□ N524PA	Learjet 35	35-033	ex N31FN	
□ N527PA	Learjet 36A	36A-019	ex N540PA	coded VA27
□ N541PA	Learjet 35	35-053	ex N53FN	coded OR41
□ N542PA	Learjet 35	35-030	ex C-GKPE	coded GA42
□ N544PA	Learjet 35A	35A-247	ex N523PA	coded NY
□ N545PA	Learjet 36A	36A-028	ex N75TD	coded GA45
□ N547PA	Learjet 36	36-012	ex N712JE	coded AK47
□ N549PA	Learjet 35A	35A-119	ex (N64DH)	coded GA49
□ N568PA	Learjet 35A	35A-205	ex N59FN	
□ N751AC	Learjet 35A	35A-101		♦

PIEDMONT AIRLINES — Piedmont (PT/PDT) — Salisbury-Wicomico Regional, MD (SBY)

A wholly owned subsidiary of American Airlines

PLANEMASTERS — Planemaster (PMS) — Chicago-Du Page, IL (DPA)

□ N274PM	Cessna 208B Caravan I	208B0705	ex N9183L	Frtr
□ N279PM	Cessna 208B Caravan I	208B0623	ex N104VE	Frtr
□ N281PM	Cessna 208B Caravan I	208B0902		Frtr
□ N282PM	Cessna 208B Caravan I	208B0981		Frtr
□ N286PM	Cessna 208B Caravan I	208B0631		Frtr
□ N1256P	Cessna 208B Caravan I	208B0564	ex N5162W	Frtr

| ⊔ N41AU | IAI 1125 Astra | 041 | |

POLAR AIR CARGO — Polar (PO/PAC) — New York-JFK Intl, NY (JFK)

□ N416MC	Boeing 747-47UF	32838/1307		<GTI
□ N450PA	Boeing 747-46NF	30808/1257	The Spirit of Long Beach	
□ N451PA	Boeing 747-46NF	30809/1259	Wings of Change	
□ N452PA	Boeing 747-46NF	30810/1260	Polar Spirit	
□ N453PA	Boeing 747-46NF	30811/1283		
□ N454PA	Boeing 747-46NF	30812/1310		
□ N498MC	Boeing 747-47UF	29259/1227		<GTI
□ N643GT	Boeing 767-3JHF/W	37809/1039	ex G-DHLJ	<GTI
□ N644GT	Boeing 767-3JHF/W	37810/1041	ex G-DHLK	DHL c/s	<GTI
□ N851GT	Boeing 747-87UF	37565/1458	Passion for Solutions	DHL c/s <GTI♦
□ N852GT	Boeing 747-87UF	37571/1462		<GTI
□ N853GT	Boeing 747-87UF	37572/1467		<GTI
□ N857GT	Boeing 747-87UF	37568/1444	ex G-GSSE	<GTI♦
□ N858GT	Boeing 747-87UF	37569/1445	ex G-GSSF	<GTI♦

PRIORITY AIR — New Orleans-Lakefront, LA (NEW)

| □ N46SA | Swearingen SA226T Merlin III | T-231 | ex N20QN | EMS |

PRIORITY AIR CHARTER — Priority Air (PRY) — Kidron-Stolzfus Airfield, OH

□ N179SA	Cessna 208B Caravan I	208B0594	ex N5268M	
□ N208TF	Cessna 208B Caravan I	208B0592	ex N208CR	
□ N228PA	Cessna 208B Caravan I	208B0930	ex N2418W	
□ N716BT	Cessna 208B Caravan I	208B0843	ex N5260Y	
□ N866MA	Cessna 208B Caravan I	208B0934	ex N108JA	♦
□ N885SP	Cessna 208B Caravan I	208B0463	ex 5Y-PAP	
□ N268PA	Pilatus Porter PC-12/45	268	ex C-GFIL	♦
□ N467KS	Douglas DC-3/65TP	20175	ex N145RD	
□ N467PA	Douglas DC-3	14994/26439	ex YV2119	♦
□ N812PA	Pilatus Porter PC-12	106	ex N82HR	
□ N813PA	Pilatus Porter PC-12	104		
□ N814PA	Pilatus Porter PC-12	110	ex N108U	

PRO AIRE CARGO — Osh Kosh, WI (OSH)

□ N196TC	Cessna 310R II	310R1801		♦
□ N314U	Cessna 310R II	310R1852	ex N2888A	
□ N500FS	Cessna 310R II	310R0630	ex N98881	
□ N1203W	Cessna 310R II	310R2106	ex G-BIBC	
□ N1533T	Cessna 310R II	310R0111		
□ N3286M	Cessna 310R II	310R1894		
□ N3482G	Cessna 310R II	310R0850		
□ N3640G	Cessna 310R II	310R0880		♦
□ N3845G	Cessna 310R II	310R0929		
□ N5215C	Cessna 310R II	310R1515		♦
□ N6122C	Cessna 310R II	310R1290		
□ N6832Y	Cessna 310R II	310R2112		♦
□ N98904	Cessna 310R II	310R1240		
□ N401VA	Piper PA-31T Cheyenne	31T-8275001		♦
□ N6384X	Cessna 402B	402B1347		♦

☐ N37127   Cessna 404   404-0114   ◆

PROMECH AIR   (Z3)   Ketchikan-Harbor SPB, AK (WFB)

☐ N92AK	de Havilland DHC-2 Beaver	1031		FP♦
☐ N1108Q	de Havilland DHC-2 Beaver	416	ex 5-1G851	FP♦
☐ N4787C	de Havilland DHC-2 Beaver	1330	ex C-FGMK	FP♦
☐ N64393	de Havilland DHC-2 Beaver	845	ex 54-1701	FP♦
☐ N64397	de Havilland DHC-2 Beaver	760	ex 53-7943	FP♦
☐ N379PM	de Havilland DHC-3 Turbo Otter	379		FP♦
☐ N435B	de Havilland DHC-3 Turbo Otter	183	ex C-GIGZ	opf Key West Seaplanes FP
☐ N3952B	de Havilland DHC-3 Turbo Otter	225	ex C-GGON	FP

PSA AIRLINES   Blue Streak (JIA)   Dayton-Cox Intl, OH (DAY)

A wholly owned subsidiary of American Airlines, ops services as an Envoy commuter using AA flight numbers

PTARMIGAN AIR   Bethel, AK

☐ N102SY	de Havilland DHC-2 Beaver	1367	ex 58-2035
☐ N734Q	de Havilland DHC-2 Beaver	1395	ex N217GB

RAM AIR SERVICES   Atlanta-Peachtree, GA (PDK)

☐ N702RS	SAAB SF.340B	340B-233	ex N233CJ
☐ N703RS	SAAB SF.340B	340B-252	ex N252CJ

RAVN ALASKA   Erah (7H/ERR)   Anchorage-Intl South, AK (ANC)

☐ N880EA	de Havilland DHC-8-106	392	ex VH-QQJ
☐ N883EA	de Havilland DHC-8-106	260	ex C-GGEW
☐ N884EA	de Havilland DHC-8-106	387	ex N824EX
☐ N885EA	de Havilland DHC-8-106	341	ex N842EX
☐ N886EA	de Havilland DHC-8-103	215	ex N215AL
☐ N887EA	de Havilland DHC-8-106	351	ex SX-BVE
☐ N889EA	de Havilland DHC-8-106	322	ex N803LR
☐ N891EA	de Havilland DHC-8-106	335	ex OY-RUI

REDDING AERO ENTERPRISES   Boxer (BXR)   Redding-Municipal, CA (RDD)

☐ N681RC	Cessna 402C II	402C0002	ex N4633N	
☐ N2610G	Cessna 402C II	402C0064		
☐ N2613B	Cessna 402C II	402C0083		
☐ N2712F	Cessna 402C II	402C0121		
☐ N5849C	Cessna 402C II	402C0052		
☐ N36908	Cessna 402C II	402C0313		
☐ N68379	Cessna 402C	402C0469	ex N350RC	
☐ N121HA	Cessna 208B Caravan I	208B0068	ex N6540Q	
☐ N915CD	Beech 65-C90 King Air	LJ-748		◆
☐ N932C	Cessna 208B Caravan I	208B0032	ex N932FE	
☐ N9623B	Cessna 208B Caravan I	208B0138		◆
☐ N37223	Cessna 310R	310R0963		

REEVE AIR ALASKA   Anchorage, AK (ANC)

☐ N16SC	Piper PA-31 Navajo	31-639	ex N16NA

REPUBLIC AIRWAYS   Brickyard (RPA)   Chicago-O'Hare, IL/Washington-Dulles, DC (ORD/DUL)

☐ N34NG	de Havilland DHC-8-402Q	4340	ex C-GGSI	
☐ N187WQ	de Havilland DHC-8-402Q	4187	ex C-FNQG	
☐ N188WQ	de Havilland DHC-8-402Q	4188	ex C-FNQH	
☐ N196WQ	de Havilland DHC-8-402Q	4196	ex C-FOJT	
☐ N202WQ	de Havilland DHC-8-402Q	4202	ex C-FOUY	
☐ N203WQ	de Havilland DHC-8-402Q	4203	ex C-FPDY	
☐ N204WQ	de Havilland DHC-8-402Q	4204	ex C-FPEF	
☐ N208WQ	de Havilland DHC-8-402Q	4208	ex C-FPPW	
☐ N209WQ	de Havilland DHC-8-402Q	4209	ex C-FPQA	
☐ N213WQ	de Havilland DHC-8-402Q	4213	ex C-FQXO	
☐ N214WQ	de Havilland DHC-8-402Q	4214	ex C-FQXP	
☐ N328NG	de Havilland DHC-8-402Q	4328	ex C-GPNN	
☐ N323NG	de Havilland DHC-8-402Q	4323	ex C-GEVP	
☐ N332NG	de Havilland DHC-8-402Q	4332	ex C-GFKK	
☐ N336NG	de Havilland DHC-8-402Q	4336	ex C-GGIF	
☐ N333NG	de Havilland DHC-8-402Q	4333	ex C-GGFI	wfs
☐ N338NG	de Havilland DHC-8-402Q	4338	ex C-GGQY	
☐ N339NG	de Havilland DHC-8-402Q	4339	ex C-GGRI	
☐ N341NG	de Havilland DHC-8-402Q	4341	ex C-GGSV	<FLG
☐ N345NG	de Havilland DHC-8-402Q	4345	ex C-GHCF	

364

☐ N346NG	de Havilland DHC-8-402Q	4346	ex C-GHCO	
☐ N356NG	de Havilland DHC-8-402Q	4356	ex C-GILK	
☐ N342NG	de Havilland DHC-8-402Q	4342	ex C-GGUB	
☐ N502LX	de Havilland DHC-8-402Q	4168	ex C-FMIU	
☐ N507LX	de Havilland DHC-8-402Q	4181	ex C-FMUF	
☐ N508LX	de Havilland DHC-8-402Q	4182	ex C-FMUH	
☐ N510LX	de Havilland DHC-8-402Q	4186	ex C-FNER	
☐ N810MD	Embraer ERJ-170SU	17000026	ex PT-SKT	
☐ N813MA	Embraer ERJ-170SU	17000031	ex PT-SKZ	
☐ N815MD	Embraer ERJ-170SU	17000034	ex PT-SUD	
☐ N818MD	Embraer ERJ-170SU	17000039	ex PT-SUI	
☐ N821MD	Embraer ERJ-170SU	17000042	ex PT-SUL	>SLI
☐ N826MD	Embraer ERJ-170SU	17000046	ex PT-SUP	>SLI
☐ N871RW	Embraer ERJ-170SU	17000140	ex PT-SEE	
☐ N872RW	Embraer ERJ-170SU	17000143	ex PT-SEH	
☐ N873RW	Embraer ERJ-170SU	17000144	ex PT-SEI	
☐ N874RW	Embraer ERJ-170SU	17000148	ex PT-SEM	
☐ N163HQ	Embraer ERJ-190AR	19000255	ex PT-STD	
☐ N164HQ	Embraer ERJ-190AR	19000275	ex PT-TLP	
☐ N165HQ	Embraer ERJ-190AR	19000291	ex PT-TZF	
☐ N167HQ	Embraer ERJ-190AR	19000173	ex N960UW	>SLI
☐ N169HQ	Embraer ERJ-190AR	19000188	ex N962UW	>SLI
☐ N175HQ	Embraer ERJ-190AR	19000216	ex N968UW	>.SLI
☐ N176HQ	Embraer ERJ-190AR	19000461	cx PT-TOC	
☐ N177HQ	Embraer ERJ-190AR	19000481	ex PT-TPG	

ROYAL AIR FREIGHT — Air Royal (RAX) — Pontiac-Oakland, MI (PTK)

☐ N4TB	AMD Falcon 20F-5B	432	ex N355DG	
☐ N20WK	AMD Falcon 20-5	310	ex N724JC	
☐ N120RA	AMD Falcon 20DC	211	ex N764LA	
☐ N123RA	AMD Falcon 20DC	30	ex N514SA	
☐ N166RA	AMD Falcon 20F	449	ex N73MR	
☐ N220WE	AMD Falcon 20F	349	ex N287SA	
☐ N211FJ	AMD Falcon 20	347		♦
☐ N224WE	AMD Falcon 20F	272	ex N770RR	
☐ N239CD	AMD Falcon 20F-5	339	ex N38TJ	
☐ N247PL	AMD Falcon 20F	247		♦
☐ N733JB	AMD Falcon 20F	256		♦
☐ N766RA	AMD Falcon 20F	360	ex N349MR	
☐ N900RA	AMD Falcon 20C	59	ex N159MV	
☐ N34A	Embraer EMB.110P1 Bandeirante	110350	ex N4361Q	
☐ N49RA	Embraer EMB.110P1A Bandeirante	110424	ex C-GPRV	
☐ N64DA	Embraer EMB.110P1 Bandeirante	110385	ex PT-SFC	
☐ N72RA	Embraer EMB.110P1 Bandeirante	110377	ex C-GHOV	[PTK]
☐ N73RA	Embraer EMB.110P1 Bandeirante	110413	ex C-GPNW	
☐ N25MD	Learjet 25	25-054	ex N509G	
☐ N604AS	Learjet 25D	25D-292	ex N711VK	
☐ N688GS	Learjet 25B	25B-123	ex N906SU	
☐ N876MC	Learjet 24B	24B-217	ex C-FZHT	
☐ N2094L	Learjet 25B	25B-095	ex C-GRCO	
☐ N10UF	Learjet 35A	35A-166	ex N719JB	
☐ N41RA	Learjet 35A	35A-215	ex N35ED	
☐ N62RA	Learjet 35A	35A-312	ex N369BA	
☐ N76RA	Learjet 35A	35A-140	ex N40BD	
☐ N81RA	Learjet 35A	35A-472	ex N612SQ	
☐ N198GJ	Learjet 35A	35A-198	ex I-ALPT	
☐ N235EA	Learjet 35A	35A-061	ex N238RC	
☐ N351AS	Learjet 35A	35A-146	ex N55AS	
☐ N399BA	Learjet 35A	35A-371	ex LV-ALF	
☐ N731RA	Learjet 35A	35A-328	ex N408MG	
☐ N800GJ	Learjet 35A	35A-352	ex N35CZ	
☐ N841TF	Learjet 35A	35A-416	ex N841TT	
☐ N945W	Learjet 35A	35A-301	ex N98AC	
☐ N220RA	Beech B200 Super King Air	BB-1130	ex N418DN	♦
☐ N551RA	Learjet 55	55-076	ex C-GKTM	♦
☐ N728FR	Cessna 310R	310R1248	ex N98993	
☐ N1768E	Cessna 310R	1566		♦
☐ N2643D	Cessna 310R	310R1686		
☐ N5279J	Cessna 402B	402B1202	ex N6841M	
☐ N5373J	Cessna 402B	402B0367	ex C-GCXI	
☐ N87341	Cessna 310R	310R0520		

RUST'S FLYING SERVICE/RUSTAIR — Anchorage-Lake Hood SPB, AK (LHD)

| ☐ N121KT | de Havilland DHC-2 Beaver | 1407 | ex N692F | FP/WS |

□ N122KT	Piper PA-32-300 Cherokee Six	32-7940190	ex N2898W	
□ N125KT	Cessna A185F Skywagon	18503494		FP♦
□ N320KT	de Havilland DHC-3 Otter	73	exC-GRNI	FP
□ N424KT	de Havilland DHC-3 Turbo Otter	338	ex N338D	FP/WS
□ N626KT	Cessna U206G Stationair 6 II	U20604426	ex N756WY	FP
□ N675HP	Cessna 208 Caravan I	20800289	ex N850HP	FP
□ N727KI	de Havilland DHC-3 Turbo Otter	419	ex N427PM	FP/WS
□ N828KT	Piper PA-32-350 Chieftain	31-8052098	ex SE-KDB	
□ N929KT	de Havilland DHC-3 Turbo Otter	461	ex N271PA	FP/WS
□ N1292F	Cessna A185F Skywagon	18502668		FP♦
□ N2740X	de Havilland DHC-2 Beaver	579	ex C-GIJO	FP/WS
□ N2899J	de Havilland DHC-3 Turbo Otter	425	ex C-GLCR	FP/WS
□ N4444Z	de Havilland DHC-2 Beaver	1307	ex N123PG	FP/WS
□ N4596U	Cessna U206G Stationair 6 II	U20604990		FP
□ N4661Z	Cessna U206G Stationair 6 II	U20605998		FP
□ N4891Z	Cessna U206G Stationair 6 II	U20606044		FP
□ N68083	de Havilland DHC-2 Beaver	1254	ex 57-2580	FP/WS

RVR AVIATION — Arlington, TX

| □ N403RW | Embraer ERJ-135LR | 145262 | ex PT-SIV | |

RYAN AIR/ARCTIC TRANSPORTATION SERVICES
Ryan Air (7S/RYA) — Unalakleet-Municipal, AK (UNK)

□ N26TA	Cessna 207A Stationair 8	20700725	ex N9759M	
□ N624DR	Cessna 207A Stationair 7 II	20700517	ex N917AC	
□ N624ER	Cessna 207A Stationair 8 II	20700752	ex N9936M	
□ N7305U	Cessna 207AT207A Stationair 7	20700392		
□ N7605U	Cessna 207A Stationair 7	20700443		
□ N9475M	Cessna 207A Stationair 8	20700695		
□ N9736M	Cessna 207A Stationair 8	20700722		
□ N9829M	Cessna 207A Stationair 8	20700741		
□ N9956M	Cessna 207A Stationair 8	20700763		
□ N73217	Cessna 207A Stationair 8	20700572		
□ N73467	Cessna T207A Stationair 8 II	20700594		
□ N73503	Cessna 207A Stationair 8	20700599		
□ N73789	Cessna T207A Stationair 8	20700629		
□ N352CA	CASA C212-200	CC40-1-190		
□ N424CA	CASA C212-200	CC40-7-242		
□ N439RA	CASA C212-200	CC50-9-287	ex N287MA	
□ N440RA	CASA C212-200	CC20-6-174	ex N687MA	dam 2009
□ N707RA	Cessna 208BEX Caravan I	208B5120		♦

SANDBAR AIR

| □ N524DB | Cessna 208 Caravan I | 20800389 | ex N5244W | |

SAN JUAN AIRLINES — Mariner (2G/MRR) — Seattle-Lake Union, WA/Seattle-Renton (LKS/RNT)

□ N90YC	de Havilland DHC-2 Beaver	1338	ex N127WA	FP
□ N67681	de Havilland DHC-2 Beaver	1158	ex N215LU	FP
□ N67684	de Havilland DHC-2 Beaver	1208	ex N67894	FP
□ N67685	de Havilland DHC-2 Beaver	1250	ex N128WA	FP
□ N67689	de Havilland DHC-2 Beaver	1242	ex N67675	FP

Aslo trades as Northwest Seaplanes

SCENIC AIRLINES — Scenic (YR/SCE) — Las Vegas-North, NV/Page, AZ (VGT/PGA)

□ N97AR	de Havilland DHC-6 Twin Otter 300	365	ex PJ-TSE	
□ N142SA	de Havilland DHC-6 Twin Otter 300	241	ex N385EX	
□ N146SA	de Havilland DHC-6 Twin Otter 300	514	ex N27RA	
□ N148SA	de Havilland DHC-6 Twin Otter 300	409	ex N548N	
□ N228SA	de Havilland DHC-6 Twin Otter 300	253	ex N103AC	
□ N297SA	de Havilland DHC-6 Twin Otter 300	297	ex N852TB	
□ N359AR	de Havilland DHC-6 Twin Otter 300	359	ex N149SA	
□ N692AR	de Havilland DHC-6 Twin Otter 300	692	ex N230SA	

SCOTT AIR — Klawock, AK

□ N1229C	Cessna 208B Caravan I	208B0589		♦
□ N1229X	Cessna 208 Caravan I	20800212		♦
□ N32009	Cessna 208 Caravan I	20800022		♦

SEABORNE AIRLINES — Seaborne (BB/SBS) — San Juan-Munoz Marin Intl, PR (SJU)

| □ N283AE | SAAB SF.340B | 340B-283 | ex VH-UYI | |
| □ N327SA | SAAB SF.340B | 340B-166 | ex C-GTJY | |

☐ N334CJ	SAAB SF.340B	340B-334	ex N312CE
☐ N336SA	SAAB SF.340B	340B-336	ex C-FTLW
☐ N341CJ	SAAB SF.340B	340B-341	ex N341SB
☐ N343CJ	SAAB SF.340B	340B-343	ex N315CE
☐ N350CJ	SAAB SF.340B	340B-350	ex N350CF
☐ N353SA	SAAB SF.340B	340B-351	ex C-FSPB
☐ N562CP	de Havilland DHC-6 Twin Otter 300	562	ex TI-BAL

SEAPORT AIRLINES　　　　Sasquatch (K5/SQH)　　　　　　　Portland, OR

☐ N29MG	Cessna 208B Caravan I	208B0512	
☐ N803TH	Cessna 208B Caravan I	208B0321	ex N1027G
☐ N950PA	Cessna 208B Caravan I	208B1063	ex N208ED
See also Wings of Alaska			

SERVANT AIR　　　　　　　　　　　　　　　　　　　　　　　Kodiak, AK

☐ N208GE	Cessna 208 Caravan I	20800062	ex HH-CAT	
☐ N770SF	Beech B200 Super King Air	BB-916		◆
☐ N4181W	Piper PA-32-300 Cherokee Six	32-40263		◆

SEVEN STARS AIR CARGO　　　　　　　　　　　　　　　　　Caroline, PR

☐ N749T	Beech E-18S	BA-55	ex N4641A	Frtr
☐ N8711H	Beech E-18S	BA-87		◆

SHUTTLE AMERICA　　　　　　　Mercury (S5/TCF)
Wilmington-Newcastle, DE/Windsor Locks-Bradley Intl, CT (ILG/BDL)

Ops aircraft for Delta Connection in full colours; wholly owned by Republic Airlines

SIERRA PACIFIC AIRLINES　　　Sierra Pacific (SI/SPA)　　　Tucson-Intl, AZ (TUS)

☐ N541AS	Boeing 737-528	27424/2720	ex G-GFFE	◆
☐ N703S	Boeing 737-2T4 (AvAero 3)	22529/750	ex N703ML	
☐ N712S	Boeing 737-2Y5 (AvAero 3)	23038/949	ex ZK-NAF	

SIERRA WEST AIRLINES　　　　Platinum West (P8/PKW)　　　Oakdale, CA (SCK)

☐ N63NE	Swearingen SA227AC Metro III	AC-763B		Frtr
☐ N563TR	Swearingen SA227AT Expediter	AT-563	ex VH-EER	Frtr
☐ N564TR	Swearingen SA227AT Expediter	AT-564	ex VH-EEO	Frtr
☐ N567TR	Swearingen SA227AT Expediter	AT-567	ex VH-EEP	Frtr
☐ N681TR	Swearingen SA227AC Metro III	AC-682	ex N921BC	Frtr
☐ N31TK	Learjet 31A	31A-059		Frtr◆
☐ N209TR	Boeing 727-223F	20994/1190	ex HZ-SND	[ELP]◆
☐ N221TR	Learjet 35A	35A-221	ex VH-FSY	Frtr
☐ N242DR	Learjet 35A	35A-242	ex VH-FSZ	Frtr
☐ N283SA	AMD Falcon 20DC	83	ex (N82SR)	Frtr
☐ N425JF	AMD Falcon 20	64	ex N513AG	Frtr
☐ N589DC	AMD Falcon 20	45		Frtr◆
☐ N655TR	Learjet 55	55-006		Frtr◆
☐ N844L	Learjet 35	35-014		◆

SILLER HELICOPTERS

☐ N45917	Sikorsky S-61V-1	61271	◆

SILVER AIRWAYS　　　　　　　　(3M/SIL)　　　Fort Lauderdale-Hollwood, FL (FLL)

☐ N301AG	SAAB SF.340B	340B-420	ex N420XJ		
☐ N303AG	SAAB SF.340B	340B-414	ex N414XJ		
☐ N304AG	SAAB SF.340B	340B-418	ex N418XJ	Prop Me Up	
☐ N317AG	SAAB SF.340B	340B-417	ex N417XJ		
☐ N325AG	SAAB SF.340B	340B-425	ex JU-9907		[BGR]
☐ N327AG	SAAB SF.340B	340B-427	ex N427XJ		
☐ N328AG	SAAB SF.340B	340B-428	ex N428XJ		
☐ N331AG	SAAB SF.340B	340B-430	ex N430XJ		
☐ N334AG	SAAB SF.340B	340B-434	ex N434XJ		
☐ N336AG	SAAB SF.340B	340B-436	ex N436XJ		
☐ N341AG	SAAB SF.340B	340B-437	ex N437XJ		
☐ N343AG	SAAB SF.340B	340B-443	ex N443XJ	One by One	
☐ N344AG	SAAB SF.340B	340B-444	ex N444XJ	Ellie's Dream	
☐ N346AG	SAAB SF/340B	340B-446	ex N446XJ	Team Victory	
☐ N347AG	SAAB SF.340B	340B-447	ex N447XJ		
☐ N348AG	SAAB SF.340B	340B-448	ex N448XJ		
☐ N350AG	SAAB SF.340B	340B-450	ex N450XJ	Smooth Landing	
☐ N351AG	SAAB SF.340B	340B-445	ex N445XJ		
☐ N352AG	SAAB SF.340B	340B-442	ex N442XJ		

☐ N356AG	SAAB SF.340B	340B-411	ex N411XJ	Establish Yourself
☐ N359AG	SAAB SF.340B	340B-415	ex N415XJ	Transformation
☐ N361AG	SAAB SF.340B	340B-451	ex N451XJ	
☐ N362AG	SAAB SF.340B	340B-438	ex N438XJ	
☐ N412XJ	SAAB SF.340B	340B-412		♦
☐ N413XJ	SAAB SF.340B	340B-413		♦
☐ N38537	Beech 1900D	UE-158		
☐ N81533	Beech 1900D	UE-137		
☐ N81535	Beech 1900D	UE-147		
☐ N81536	Beech 1900D	UE-152		

SKAGWAY AIR SERVICE — Skagway, AK (SGY)

☐ N1132Q	Piper PA-32-300 Cherokee Six	32-7740046
☐ N2884M	Piper PA-32-300 Cherokee Six	32-7840058
☐ N8200M	Piper PA-32-301 Saratoga	32-8006048
☐ N8216T	Piper PA-32-301 Saratoga	32-8206037
☐ N9540K	Piper PA-34-200T Seneca II	34-7670208
☐ N31589	Piper PA-32-300 Cherokee Six	32-7840135
☐ N40698	Piper PA-32-300 Cherokee Six	32-7440056

SKYBUS JET CARGO — Las Vegas, NV (LAS)

| ☐ N721CX | McDonnell-Douglas DC-8-72CF | 46013/427 | ex F-RAFG | [ROW]♦ |
| ☐ N807DH | McDonnell-Douglas DC-8-73CF | 45990/375 | exOB-2059-P | wfs |

SKY KING — Songbird (5K/SGB) — Lakeland Linder, FL (LAL)

| ☐ N417XA | Boeing 737-484 | 25417/2160 | ex N741AS | ♦ |

SKY LEASE CARGO — (GG/KYE) — Greensboro-Piedmont Triad Intl, NC (GSO)

☐ N950AR	McDonnell-Douglas MD-11F	48461/475	ex B-2170	
☐ N951AR	McDonnell-Douglas MD-11F	48495/461	ex B-2171	[MIA]
☐ N952AR	McDonnell-Douglas MD-11F	48497/512	ex B-2173	
☐ N953AR	McDonnell-Douglas MD-11F	48520/541	ex B-2175	
☐ N954AR	McDonnell-Douglas MD-11F	48498/522	ex B-2174	[MIA]
☐ N955AR	McDonnell-Douglas MD-11F	48496/496	ex B-2172	
☐ N956AR	McDonnell-Douglas MD-11CF	48629/586	ex PH-MCT	[MIA]
☐ N504TA	Airbus A300B4-203F	216	ex N861PA	wfs
☐ N821SC	Airbus A300B4-203F	211	extC-ALU	[CCS]
☐ N901AR	Boeing 747-4R7F	25868/1125	ex LX-KCV	<CWC

SKYWAY ENTERPRISES — Skyway Inc (SKZ) — Orlando-Kissimmee, FL/Detroit-Willow Run, IL (ISM/YIP)

☐ N367MQ	Short SD.3-60	SH3640	ex G-BLGA	
☐ N377MQ	Short SD.3-60	SH3699	ex G-BMUY	
☐ N378MQ	Short SD.3-60	SH3700	ex G-BMXP	
☐ N381MQ	Short SD.3-60	SH3703	ex G-BMXT	
☐ N382MQ	Short SD.3-60	SH3704	ex G-BMXU	[ISM]
☐ N383MQ	Short SD.3-60	SH3706	ex G-BNBB	
☐ N385MQ	Short SD.3-60	SH3707	ex G-BNBC	
☐ N112PS	Douglas DC-9-15F (ABS 3)	47013/129	ex N557AS	
☐ N306JA	Learjet 24D	24D-306		♦

SKYWEST AIRLINES — SkyWest (OO/SKW) — Salt Lake City-Intl, UT/Los Angeles-Intl, CA (SLC/LAX)

☐ N217SW	Embraer EMB.120ER Brasilia	120286	ex PT-SVG
☐ N224SW	Embraer EMB.120ER Brasilia	120294	ex PT-SVO
☐ N237SW	Embraer EMB.120ER Brasilia	120314	ex N659CT
☐ N296SW	Embraer EMB.120ER Brasilia	120325	ex PT-SXR
☐ N298SW	Embraer EMB.120ER Brasilia	120328	ex N658CT
☐ N291SW	Embraer EMB.120ER Brasilia	120318	ex N660CT
☐ N299SW	Embraer EMB.120ER Brasilia	120329	ex PT-SXV
☐ N576SW	Embraer EMB.120ER Brasilia	120345	ex PT-SBZ
All believed wfs			
☐ N947SW	Canadair CRJ-200ER	7786	ex C-FMMB	7786

SMOKEY BAY AIR — (2E) — Homer, AK (HOM)

☐ N36GB	Cessna U206F Stationair	U20601854	ex N9654G	FP
☐ N710MH	Cessna U206F Stationair	U20602383		FP
☐ N756ZV	Cessna U206G Stationair	U20604495		FP

SOUTH AERO   Albuquerque-Intl, NM (ABQ)

☐ N54ZP	Cessna 404 Titan II	404-0694	ex N6764X	
☐ N165SA	Cessna 404 Titan II	404-0622	ex N5244J	
☐ N809RQ	Cessna 404 Titan II	404-0809	ex N809RC	
☐ N920RC	Cessna 404 Titan	404-0092	ex PT-WQT	
☐ N5388J	Cessna 404 Titan II	404-0666		

☐ N29AN	Cessna 208B Caravan I	208B0753		
☐ N42MG	Cessna 402C II	402C0320	ex N36992	
☐ N108AN	Cessna 208B Caravan I	208B0975		
☐ N2688X	Cessna 414A	414A0336		
☐ N6420N	Cessna A185F Skywagon	18504307		♦
☐ N6479N	Cessna T210N Turbo Centurion II	21063053		♦
☐ N7213N	Cessna T210N Turbo Centurion II	21063207		

SOUTHERN AIR   Southern Air (9S/SOO)   Columbus-Rickenbacker, OH (LCK)

☐ N748SA	Boeing 747-206M (EUD/(SF))	21110/271	ex PH-BUH	[MHV]
☐ N758SA	Boeing 747-281F	23138/604	ex JA8167	[MHV]
☐ N760SA	Boeing 747-230M	21221/299	ex N509MC	[MHV]
☐ N761SA	Boeing 747-2F6SF	21832/421	ex N534MC	[MHV]
☐ N765SA	Boeing 747-2F6B (SCD)	21833/423	ex N535FC	[MHV]
☐ N815SA	Boeing 747-2L5BSF	22107/469	ex B-HMF	[MHV]
☐ N820SA	Boeing 747-243M	23476/647	ex TF-AMD	[MHV]

☐ N494SA	Boeing 737-4H6SF	27674/2877	ex 9M-MQO	
☐ N495SA	Boeing 737-45DSF	27157/2502	ex SP-LLC	
☐ N496SA	Boeing 747-4H6SF	26455/2507	ex 9M-MMY	
☐ N498SA	Boeing 737-4Q8SF	26334/2782	ex N991LF	DHL c/s	♦
☐ N499SA	Boeing 737-4K5SF	26316/2711	ex N281LF	o/o♦
☐ N558CL	Boeing 747-4EVERF	35171/1380	ex B-2440	
☐ N714SA	Boeing 777-FZB	37988/1002		
☐ N774SA	Boeing 777-FZB	37986/844	ex N5023Q	
☐ N775SA	Boeing 777-FZB	37987/852		
☐ N777SA	Boeing 777-FZB	37989/1011		

SOUTHERN SEAPLANE   Southern Skies (SSC)   Belle Chase-Southern Seaplane SPB, LA (BCS)

☐ N522SS	Cessna A185F Skywagon	18504388	ex N96PA	FP
☐ N732EJ	Cessna 210L Centurion	21061454		FP
☐ N1574P	Cessna 210L Centurion	21061258		FP♦
☐ N2272X	Cessna U206E Skywagon	U20601556	ex VQ-LAP	FP
☐ N2429E	Cessna A185E Skywagon	185-1172	ex N8H	FP
☐ N21058	de Havilland DHC-2 Beaver	630	ex CF-HOE	FP
☐ N61301	Cessna A185F Skywagon	18504144		FP
☐ N70822	Cessna U206F Stationair	U20602099		FP

SOUTHWEST AIRLINES   Southwest (WN/SWA)   Dallas-Love Field, TX (DAL)

☐ N892AT	Boeing 717-2BD	55044/5134	ex N7071U	742	
☐ N932AT	Boeing 717-231	55073/5028	ex N406TW	783	
☐ N936AT	Boeing 717-231	55058/5017	ex N401TW	778	[GYR]
☐ N940AT	Boeing 717-2BD	55004/5005	ex N717XE	702	[GYR]
☐ N942AT	Boeing 717-2BD	55005/5006		703	
☐ N943AT	Boeing 717-2BD	55006/5007		704	[GYR]
☐ N944AT	Boeing 717-2BD	55007/5008		705	
☐ N945AT	Boeing 717-2BD	55008/5009		706	[GYR]
☐ N946AT	Boeing 717-2BD	55009/5010		707	[GYR]
☐ N947AT	Boeing 717-2BD	55010/5011		708	[GYR]
☐ N950AT	Boeing 717-2BD	55012/5018		710	[GYR]
☐ N952AT	Boeing 717-2BD	55014/5027		712	[GYR]
☐ N980AT	Boeing 717-2BD	55039/5111		737	[GYR]
☐ N991AT	Boeing 717-23S	55135/5090	ex N6202S	763	
☐ N992AT	Boeing 717-2BD	55136/5100	ex N6202D	764	[GYR]

☐ N317WN	Boeing 737-3Q8	24068/1506	ex G-EZYE	
☐ N340LV	Boeing 737-3K2	23738/1360	ex PH-HVJ	
☐ N342SW	Boeing 737-3H4	24133/1682		
☐ N345SA	Boeing 737-3K2	23786/1386	ex PH-HVK	
☐ N346SW	Boeing 737-3H4	24153/1690		
☐ N349SW	Boeing 737-3H4	24408/1734		
☐ N352SW	Boeing 737-3H4/W	24888/1942		Lone Star One
☐ N353SW	Boeing 737-3H4/W	24889/1947		
☐ N354SW	Boeing 737-3H4/W	25219/2092		
☐ N355SW	Boeing 737-3H4/W	25250/2103		
☐ N356SW	Boeing 737-3H4/W	25251/2105		
☐ N357SW	Boeing 737-3H4/W	26594/2294		
☐ N358SW	Boeing 737-3H4/W	26595/2295		
☐ N359SW	Boeing 737-3H4/W	26596/2297		
☐ N360SW	Boeing 737-3H4/W	26571/2307		
☐ N361SW	Boeing 737-3H4/W	26572/2309		

☐ N362SW	Boeing 737-3H4/W	26573/2322	
☐ N363SW	Boeing 737-3H4/W	26574/2429	Heroes of the Heart
☐ N364SW	Boeing 737-3H4/W	26575/2430	
☐ N365SW	Boeing 737-3H4/W	26576/2433	
☐ N366SW	Boeing 737-3H4/W	26577/2469	
☐ N367SW	Boeing 737-3H4/W	26578/2470	
☐ N368SW	Boeing 737-3H4/W	26579/2473	
☐ N369SW	Boeing 737-3H4/W	26580/2477	
☐ N370SW	Boeing 737-3H4/W	26597/2497	
☐ N371SW	Boeing 737-3H4/W	26598/2500	
☐ N372SW	Boeing 737-3H4/W	26599/2504	
☐ N373SW	Boeing 737-3H4/W	26581/2509	
☐ N374SW	Boeing 737-3H4/W	26582/2515	
☐ N375SW	Boeing 737-3H4/W	26583/2520	
☐ N376SW	Boeing 737-3H4/W	26584/2570	
☐ N378SW	Boeing 737-3H4/W	26585/2579	
☐ N379SW	Boeing 737-3H4/W	26586/2580	
☐ N380SW	Boeing 737-3H4/W	26587/2610	
☐ N382SW	Boeing 737-3H4/W	26588/2611	
☐ N383SW	Boeing 737-3H4/W	26589/2612	Arizona One
☐ N384SW	Boeing 737-3H4/W	26590/2613	
☐ N385SW	Boeing 737-3H4/W	26600/2617	
☐ N386SW	Boeing 737-3H4/W	26601/2626	
☐ N387SW	Boeing 737-3H4/W	26602/2627	
☐ N388SW	Boeing 737-3H4/W	26591/2628	
☐ N389SW	Boeing 737-3H4/W	26592/2629	
☐ N390SW	Boeing 737-3H4/W	26593/2642	
☐ N391SW	Boeing 737-3H4/W	27378/2643	
☐ N392SW	Boeing 737-3H4/W	27379/2644	
☐ N394SW	Boeing 737-3H4/W	27380/2645	
☐ N395SW	Boeing 737-3H4/W	27689/2667	
☐ N396SW	Boeing 737-3H4/W	27690/2668	
☐ N397SW	Boeing 737-3H4/W	27691/2695	
☐ N398SW	Boeing 737-3H4/W	27692/2696	
☐ N399WN	Boeing 737-3H4/W	27693/2697	
☐ N600WN	Boeing 737-3H4/W	27694/2699	
☐ N601WN	Boeing 737-3H4/W	27695/2702	Jack Vidal
☐ N602SW	Boeing 737-3H4/W	27953/2713	
☐ N603SW	Boeing 737-3H4/W	27954/2714	
☐ N604SW	Boeing 737-3H4/W	27955/2715	
☐ N605SW	Boeing 737-3H4/W	27956/2716	
☐ N606SW	Boeing 737-3H4/W	27926/2740	
☐ N607SW	Boeing 737-3H4/W	27927/2741	June M Morris
☐ N608SW	Boeing 737-3H4/W	27928/2742	
☐ N609SW	Boeing 737-3H4/W	27929/2744	California One
☐ N610WN	Boeing 737-3H4/W	27696/2745	
☐ N611SW	Boeing 737-3H4/W	27697/2750	
☐ N612SW	Boeing 737-3H4/W	27930/2753	
☐ N613SW	Boeing 737-3H4/W	27931/2754	
☐ N614SW	Boeing 737-3H4/W	28033/2755	
☐ N615SW	Boeing 737-3H4/W	27698/2757	
☐ N616SW	Boeing 737-3H4/W	27699/2758	
☐ N617SW	Boeing 737-3H4/W	27700/2759	ex N1786B
☐ N618WN	Boeing 737-3H4/W	28034/2761	
☐ N619SW	Boeing 737-3H4/W	28035/2762	
☐ N620SW	Boeing 737-3H4/W	28036/2766	
☐ N621SW	Boeing 737-3H4/W	28037/2767	
☐ N622SW	Boeing 737-3H4/W	27932/2779	
☐ N623SW	Boeing 737-3H4/W	27933/2780	
☐ N624SW	Boeing 737-3H4/W	27934/2781	
☐ N625SW	Boeing 737-3H4/W	27701/2787	
☐ N626SW	Boeing 737-3H4/W	27702/2789	
☐ N627SW	Boeing 737-3H4/W	27935/2790	
☐ N628SW	Boeing 737-3H4/W	27703/2795	
☐ N629SW	Boeing 737-3H4/W	27704/2796	25 Silver One
☐ N630WN	Boeing 737-3H4/W	27705/2797	
☐ N631SW	Boeing 737-3H4/W	27706/2798	
☐ N632SW	Boeing 737-3H4/W	27707/2799	
☐ N633SW	Boeing 737-3H4/W	27936/2807	
☐ N634SW	Boeing 737-3H4/W	27937/2808	
☐ N635SW	Boeing 737-3H4/W	27708/2813	
☐ N636WN	Boeing 737-3H4/W	27709/2814	
☐ N637SW	Boeing 737-3H4/W	27710/2819	
☐ N638SW	Boeing 737-3H4/W	27711/2820	
☐ N639SW	Boeing 737-3H4/W	27712/2821	
☐ N640SW	Boeing 737-3H4/W	27713/2840	
☐ N641SW	Boeing 737-3H4/W	27714/2841	
☐ N642WN	Boeing 737-3H4/W	27715/2842	
☐ N643SW	Boeing 737-3H4/W	27716/2843	
☐ N644SW	Boeing 737-3H4/W	28329/2869	
☐ N645SW	Boeing 737-3H4/W	28330/2870	
☐ N646SW	Boeing 737-3H4/W	28331/2871	
☐ N647SW	Boeing 737-3H4/W	27717/2892	

☐ N648SW	Boeing 737-3H4/W	27718/2893			
☐ N649SW	Boeing 737-3H4/W	27719/2894			
☐ N650SW	Boeing 737-3H4/W	27720/2901			
☐ N651SW	Boeing 737-3H4/W	27721/2915			
☐ N652SW	Boeing 737-3H4/W	27722/2916			
☐ N653SW	Boeing 737-3H4/W	28398/2917			
☐ N654SW	Boeing 737-3H4/W	28399/2918			
☐ N655WN	Boeing 737-3H4/W	28400/2931			
☐ N656SW	Boeing 737-3H4/W	28401/2932			
☐ N657SW	Boeing 737-3L9	23331/1111	ex N960WP		
☐ N658SW	Boeing 737-3L9	23332/1118	ex N961WP		
☐ N659SW	Boeing 737-301	23229/1112	ex N950WP		
☐ N660SW	Boeing 737-301	23230/1115	ex N949WP		
☐ N663SW	Boeing 737-3Q8	23256/1128	ex N329US		
☐ N665WN	Boeing 737-3Y0	23497/1227	ex G-MONF		
☐ N669SW	Boeing 737-3A4	23752/1484	ex N758MA		
☐ N670SW	Boeing 737-3G7	23784/1533	ex N779MA		
☐ N684WN	Boeing 737-3T0	23941/1520	ex EC-EID		
☐ N685SW	Boeing 737-3Q8	23401/1209	ex G-BOWR		
☐ N686SW	Boeing 737-317	23175/1110	ex EI-CHU		
☐ N687SW	Boeing 737-3Q8	23388/1187	ex N103GU		
☐ N691WN	Boeing 737-3G7	23781/1494	ex N784MA		
☐ N694SW	Boeing 737-3T5	23061/1080	ex N744MA		
☐ N697SW	Boeing 737-3T0	23838/1505	ex N764MA		
☐ N508SW	Boeing 737-5H4	24185/1932			
☐ N511SW	Boeing 737-5H4	24188/2029			
☐ N514SW	Boeing 737-5H4	25153/2078			
☐ N515SW	Boeing 737-5H4	25154/2080			
☐ N520SW	Boeing 737-5H4	25319/2134			
☐ N521SW	Boeing 737-5H4	25320/2136			
☐ N522SW	Boeing 737-5H4	26564/2202			
☐ N523SW	Boeing 737-5H4	26565/2204			
☐ N524SW	Boeing 737-5H4	26566/2224			
☐ N525SW	Boeing 737-5H4	26567/2283			
☐ N526SW	Boeing 737-5H4	26568/2285			
☐ N527SW	Boeing 737-5H4	26569/2287			
☐ N528SW	Boeing 737-5H4	26570/2292			
☐ N200WN	Boeing 737-7H4/W	32482/1638	ex N1795B		
☐ N201LV	Boeing 737-7H4/W	29854/1650		Fred J Jones	
☐ N202WN	Boeing 737-7H4/W	33999/1653			
☐ N203WN	Boeing 737-7H4/W	32483/1656			
☐ N204WN	Boeing 737-7H4/W	29855/1663			
☐ N205WN	Boeing 737-7H4/W	34010/1668	ex N1784B		
☐ N206WN	Boeing 737-7H4/W	34011/1675			
☐ N207WN	Boeing 737-7H4/W	34012/1678			
☐ N208WN	Boeing 737-7H4/W	29856/1679			
☐ N209WN	Boeing 737-7H4/W	32484/1683	ex N1787B		
☐ N210WN	Boeing 737-7H4/W	34162/1690			
☐ N211WN	Boeing 737-7H4/W	34163/1699			
☐ N212WN	Boeing 737-7H4/W	32485/1708			
☐ N213WN	Boeing 737-7H4/W	34217/1717			
☐ N214WN	Boeing 737-7H4/W	32486/1721		Maryland One	
☐ N215WN	Boeing 737-7H4/W	32487/1723		Ron Chapman	
☐ N216WR	Boeing 737-7H4/W	32488/1735	ex N1784B		
☐ N217JC	Boeing 737-7H4/W	34232/1737	ex (N217WN)		
☐ N218WN	Boeing 737-7H4/W	32489/1741			
☐ N219WN	Boeing 737-7H4/W	32490/1744	ex N1786B		
☐ N220WN	Boeing 737-7H4/W	32491/1756			
☐ N221WN	Boeing 737-7H4/W	34259/1776	ex N1786B		
☐ N222WN	Boeing 737-7H4/W	34290/1780			
☐ N223WN	Boeing 737-7H4/W	32492/1799	ex N1795B		
☐ N224WN	Boeing 737-7H4/W	32493/1801	ex N1786B	Slam Dunk One	
☐ N225WN	Boeing 737-7H4/W	34333/1820			
☐ N226WN	Boeing 737-7H4/W	32494/1822	ex N1786B		
☐ N227WN	Boeing 737-7H4/W	34450/1831	ex N1786B		
☐ N228WN	Boeing 737-7H4/W	32496/1835	ex N1780B		
☐ N229WN	Boeing 737-7H4/W	32498/1858			
☐ N230WN	Boeing 737-7H4/W	34592/1868		Colorado One	5000th 737 built
☐ N231WN	Boeing 737-7H4/W	32499/1881	ex N1787B		
☐ N232WN	Boeing 737-7H4/W	32500/1888			
☐ N233LV	Boeing 737-7H4/W	32501/1893			
☐ N234WN	Boeing 737-7H4/W	32502/1905			
☐ N235WN	Boeing 737-7H4/W	34630/1916	ex N1787B		
☐ N236WN	Boeing 737-7H4/W	34631/1928	ex N1786B		
☐ N237WN	Boeing 737-7H4/W	34632/1930			
☐ N238WN	Boeing 737-7H4/W	34713/1950			
☐ N239WN	Boeing 737-7H4/W	34714/1954	ex N1786B		
☐ N240WN	Boeing 737-7H4/W	32503/1959	ex N1786B		
☐ N241WN	Boeing 737-7H4/W	32504/1965			
☐ N242WN	Boeing 737-7H4/W	32505/1969			
☐ N243WN	Boeing 737-7H4/W	34863/1973			

☐	N244WN	Boeing 737-7H4/W	34864/1977		
☐	N245WN	Boeing 737-7H4/W	32506/1982		
☐	N246LV	Boeing 737-7H4/W	32507/1984	ex N1786B	
☐	N247WN	Boeing 737-7H4/W	32508/1989		
☐	N248WN	Boeing 737-7H4/W	32509/2000		
☐	N249WN	Boeing 737-7H4/W	34951/2005		
☐	N250WN	Boeing 737-7H4/W	34972/2019		
☐	N251WN	Boeing 737-7H4/W	32510/2025		
☐	N252WN	Boeing 737-7H4/W	34973/2027		
☐	N253WN	Boeing 737-7H4/W	32511/2038		
☐	N254WN	Boeing 737-7H4/W	32512/2040		
☐	N255WN	Boeing 737-7H4/W	32513/2049		
☐	N256WN	Boeing 737-7H4/W	32514/2059		
☐	N257WN	Boeing 737-7H4/W	32515/2062		
☐	N258WN	Boeing 737-7H4/W	32516/2076		
☐	N259WN	Boeing 737-7H4/W	35554/2092		
☐	N260WN	Boeing 737-7H4/W	32518/2114	ex N1786B	
☐	N261WN	Boeing 737-7H4/W	32517/2133	ex N1787B	
☐	N262WN	Boeing 737-7H4/W	32519/2139	ex N1786B	
☐	N263WN	Boeing 737-7H4/W	32520/2153		
☐	N264LV	Boeing 737-7H4/W	32521/2161		
☐	N265WN	Boeing 737-7H4/W	32522/2174		
☐	N266WN	Boeing 737-7H4/W	32523/2182	ex N1787B	Colleen Barrett
☐	N267WN	Boeing 737-7H4/W	32525/2193		
☐	N268WN	Boeing 737-7H4/W	32524/2199		
☐	N269WN	Boeing 737-7H4/W	32526/2204		
☐	N270WN	Boeing 737-705/W	29089/83	ex VP-BBT	
☐	N271LV	Boeing 737-705/W	29090/109	ex VP-BBU	
☐	N272WN	Boeing 737-7H4/W	32527/2224	ex N1786B	
☐	N273WN	Boeing 737-7H4/W	32528/2238		
☐	N274WN	Boeing 737-7H4/W	32529/2244		
☐	N275WN	Boeing 737-7H4/W	36153/2256		
☐	N276WN	Boeing 737-7H4/W	32530/2262		
☐	N277WN	Boeing 737-7H4/W	32531/2274		
☐	N278WN	Boeing 737-7H4/W	36441/2281	ex N1787B	
☐	N279WN	Boeing 737-7H4/W	32532/2284	ex N1786B	
☐	N280WN	Boeing 737-7H4/W	32533/2294		Missouri One c/s
☐	N281WN	Boeing 737-7H4/W	36528/2307		Southwest's 500th Boeing 737
☐	N282WN	Boeing 737-7H4/W	32534/2318		
☐	N283WN	Boeing 737-7H4/W	36610/2322		
☐	N284WN	Boeing 737-7H4/W	32535/2328	ex N1786B	
☐	N285WN	Boeing 737-7H4/W	32536/2337		
☐	N286WN	Boeing 737-7H4/W	32471/1535	ex N471WN	
☐	N287WN	Boeing 737-7H4/W	32537/2344	ex N1786B	
☐	N288WN	Boeing 737-7H4/W	36611/2350	ex N1786B	
☐	N289CT	Boeing 737-7H4/W	36633/2354	ex N1786B	
☐	N290WN	Boeing 737-7H4/W	36632/2363		
☐	N291WN	Boeing 737-7H4/W	32539/2378		
☐	N292WN	Boeing 737-7H4/W	32538/2383		
☐	N293WN	Boeing 737-7H4/W	36612/2387		
☐	N294WN	Boeing 737-7H4/W	32540/2390	ex N1786B	
☐	N295WN	Boeing 737-7H4/W	32541/2409		
☐	N296WN	Boeing 737-7H4/W	36613/2413		
☐	N297WN	Boeing 737-7H4/W	32542/2417		
☐	N298WN	Boeing 737-7H4/W	32543/2438		
☐	N299WN	Boeing 737-7H4/W	36614/2442		
☐	N400WN	Boeing 737-7H4/W	27891/806		
☐	N401WN	Boeing 737-7H4/W	29813/810		
☐	N402WN	Boeing 737-7H4/W	29814/811	ex N1786B	
☐	N403WN	Boeing 737-7H4/W	29815/821	ex N1786B	
☐	N404WN	Boeing 737-7H4/W	27892/880	ex N1787B	
☐	N405WN	Boeing 737-7H4/W	27893/881	ex N1786B	
☐	N406WN	Boeing 737-7H4/W	27894/885	ex N1786B	
☐	N407WN	Boeing 737-7H4/W	29817/903	ex N1786B	
☐	N408WN	Boeing 737-7H4/W	27895/934	ex N1786B	
☐	N409WN	Boeing 737-7H4/W	27896/945	ex N1787B	
☐	N410WN	Boeing 737-7H4/W	27897/946	ex N1786B	
☐	N411WN	Boeing 737-7H4/W	29821/950	ex N1786B	
☐	N412WN	Boeing 737-7H4/W	29818/956	ex N1795B	
☐	N413WN	Boeing 737-7H4/W	29819/960		
☐	N414WN	Boeing 737-7H4/W	29820/967	ex N1795B	
☐	N415WN	Boeing 737-7H4/W	29836/980	ex N1787B	
☐	N416WN	Boeing 737-7H4/W	32453/990	ex N1786B	
☐	N417WN	Boeing 737-7H4/W	29822/993	ex N1786B	The Rollin W King
☐	N418WN	Boeing 737-7H4/W	29823/1000		The Winning Spirit
☐	N419WN	Boeing 737-7H4/W	29824/1017	ex N1786B	
☐	N420WN	Boeing 737-7H4/W	29825/1039		
☐	N421LV	Boeing 737-7H4/W	32452/1040		
☐	N422WN	Boeing 737-7H4/W	29826/1093		
☐	N423WN	Boeing 737-7H4/W	29827/1101		
☐	N424WN	Boeing 737-7H4/W	29828/1105		
☐	N425LV	Boeing 737-7H4/W	29829/1109		
☐	N426WN	Boeing 737-7H4/W	29830/1114		

☐ N427WN	Boeing 737-7H4/W	29831/1119			
☐ N428WN	Boeing 737-7H4/W	29844/1243			
☐ N429WN	Boeing 737-7H4/W	33658/1256			
☐ N430WN	Boeing 737-7H4/W	33659/1257			
☐ N431WN	Boeing 737-7H4/W	29845/1259			
☐ N432WN	Boeing 737-7H4/W	33715/1297	ex N1786B		
☐ N433LV	Boeing 737-7H4/W	33716/1301			
☐ N434WN	Boeing 737-7H4/W	32454/1313			
☐ N435WN	Boeing 737-7H4/W	32455/1328			
☐ N436WN	Boeing 737-7H4/W	32456/1342			
☐ N437WN	Boeing 737-7H4/W	29832/1349			
☐ N438WN	Boeing 737-7H4/W	29833/1353			
☐ N439WN	Boeing 737-7H4/W	29834/1356		The Donald G Ogden	
☐ N440LV	Boeing 737-7H4/W	29835/1358			
☐ N441WN	Boeing 737-7H4/W	29837/1360			
☐ N442WN	Boeing 737-7H4/W	32459/1365	ex (N442LV)		
☐ N443WN	Boeing 737-7H4/W	29838/1369		The Spirit of Hope	
☐ N444WN	Boeing 737-7H4/W	29839/1374	ex N1786B		
☐ N445WN	Boeing 737-7H4/W	29841/1388			
☐ N446WN	Boeing 737-7H4/W	29842/1401	ex N1787B		
☐ N447WN	Boeing 737-7H4/W	33720/1405			
☐ N448WN	Boeing 737-7H4/W	33721/1409		The Spirit of Kitty Hawk	
☐ N449WN	Boeing 737-7H4/W	32469/1427			
☐ N450WN	Boeing 737-7H4/W	32470/1429	ex N60668		
☐ N451WN	Boeing 737-7H4/W	32495/1458			
☐ N452WN	Boeing 737-7H4/W	29846/1461			
☐ N453WN	Boeing 737-7H4/W	29847/1476			
☐ N454WN	Boeing 737-7H4/W	29851/1477			
☐ N455WN	Boeing 737-7H4/W	32462/1480			
☐ N456WN	Boeing 737-7H4/W	32463/1484			
☐ N457WN	Boeing 737-7H4/W	33856/1485			
☐ N458WN	Boeing 737-7H4/W	33857/1490			
☐ N459WN	Boeing 737-7H4/W	32497/1492			
☐ N460WN	Boeing 737-7H4/W	32464/1499			
☐ N461WN	Boeing 737-7H4/W	32465/1510			
☐ N462WN	Boeing 737-7H4/W	32466/1513			
☐ N463WN	Boeing 737-7H4/W	32467/1515			
☐ N464WN	Boeing 737-7H4/W	32468/1517			
☐ N465WN	Boeing 737-7H4/W	33829/1519			
☐ N466WN	Boeing 737-7H4/W	30677/1520			
☐ N467WN	Boeing 737-7H4/W	33830/1521			
☐ N468WN	Boeing 737-7H4/W	33858/1523			
☐ N469WN	Boeing 737-7H4/W	33859/1525			
☐ N470WN	Boeing 737-7H4/W	33860/1528			
☐ N472WN	Boeing 737-7H4/W	33831/1537			
☐ N473WN	Boeing 737-7H4/W	33832/1541			
☐ N474WN	Boeing 737-7H4/W	33861/1543	ex N1786B		
☐ N475WN	Boeing 737-7H4/W	32474/1545			
☐ N476WN	Boeing 737-7H4/W	32475/1549			
☐ N477WN	Boeing 737-7H4/W	33988/1552			
☐ N478WN	Boeing 737-7H4/W	33989/1555			
☐ N479WN	Boeing 737-7H4/W	33990/1558			
☐ N480WN	Boeing 737-7H4/W	33998/1561			
☐ N481WN	Boeing 737-7H4/W	29853/1564			
☐ N482WN	Boeing 737-7H4/W	29852/1568			
☐ N483WN	Boeing 737-7H4/W	32472/1570			
☐ N484WN	Boeing 737-7H4/W	33841/1575	ex N1786B		
☐ N485WN	Boeing 737-7H4/W	32473/1577	ex N1786B		
☐ N486WN	Boeing 737-7H4/W	33852/1579			
☐ N487WN	Boeing 737-7H4/W	33854/1583			
☐ N488WN	Boeing 737-7H4/W	33853/1587			
☐ N489WN	Boeing 737-7H4/W	33855/1589	ex N1780B		
☐ N490WN	Boeing 737-7H4/W	32476/1591		100 H-E-B titles	
☐ N491WN	Boeing 737-7H4/W	33867/1598			
☐ N492WN	Boeing 737-7H4/W	33866/1605			
☐ N493WN	Boeing 737-7H4/W	32477/1616			
☐ N494WN	Boeing 737-7H4/W	33868/1621			
☐ N495WN	Boeing 737-7H4/W	33869/1625			
☐ N496WN	Boeing 737-7H4/W	32478/1626			
☐ N497WN	Boeing 737-7H4/W	32479/1628			
☐ N498WN	Boeing 737-7H4/W	32480/1633			
☐ N499WN	Boeing 737-7H4/W	32481/1636			
☐ N550WN	Boeing 737-76Q/W	30279/1010	ex VT-SIR		
☐ N551WN	Boeing 737-76Q/W	30280/1025	ex VT-SIS		
☐ N552WN	Boeing 737-7BX/W	30744/989	ex VH-VBQ		
☐ N553WN	Boeing 737-7BX/W	30745/1027	ex VH-VBR		
☐ N554WN	Boeing 737-7BX/W	30746/1085	ex VH-VBS		
☐ N555LV	Boeing 737-7BD/W	36726/3585			
☐ N556WN	Boeing 737-7BD/W	33936/3613			
☐ N557WN	Boeing 737-790/W	30166/700	ex N623AS		◆
☐ N558WN	Boeing 737-73V/W	30248/1118	ex HL8204		[PAE]
☐ N559WN	Boeing 737-73V/W	30249/1128	ex C-GZEJ		[PAE]
☐ N560WN	Boeing 737-790/W	30542/532	ex N617AS	560	◆

☐	N561WN	Boeing 737-73V	32417/1285	ex HL8216		[PAE]♦
☐	N562WN	Boeing 737-790/W	30778/724	ex N624AS	562	♦
☐	N563WN	Boeing 737-752/W	34296/1783	ex HK-4660X	563	wfs♦
☐	N564WN	Boeing 737-73V/W	30244/1148	ex C-FENJ	564	wfs♦
☐	N565WN	Boeing 737-76Q	30282/1143	ex B-2680	565	[PAE]♦
☐	N566WN	Boeing 737-7CT/W	32753/1222	ex C-FWAD	566	wfs♦
☐	N567WN	Boeing 737-7CT/W	32747/1239	ex C-FWAF	567	wfs♦
☐	N568WN	Boeing 737-76N	32583/994	ex N847TM		wfs♦
☐	N569WN	Boeing 737-7CT/W	33656/1246	ex C-FWAI	569	wfs♦
☐	N570WN	Boeing 737-7CT/W	33657/1254	ex C-FWAO	570	wfs♦
☐	N700GS	Boeing 737-7H4/W	27835/4			
☐	N701GS	Boeing 737-7H4/W	27836/6	ex N35108		
☐	N703SW	Boeing 737-7H4/W	27837/12	ex N1792B		
☐	N704SW	Boeing 737-7H4/W	27838/15			
☐	N705SW	Boeing 737-7H4/W	27839/20			
☐	N706SW	Boeing 737-7H4/W	27840/24			
☐	N707SA	Boeing 737-7H4/W	27841/1	ex N737X		
☐	N708SW	Boeing 737-7H4/W	27842/2			
☐	N709SW	Boeing 737-7H4/W	27843/3			
☐	N710SW	Boeing 737-7H4/W	27844/34	ex N1787B		
☐	N711HK	Boeing 737-7H4/W	27845/38		The Herbert D Kelleher	
☐	N712SW	Boeing 737-7H4/W	27846/53			
☐	N713SW	Boeing 737-7H4/W	27847/54		Shamu c/s	
☐	N714CB	Boeing 737-7H4/W	27848/61		Southwest Classic colours	
☐	N715SW	Boeing 737-7H4/W	27849/62		Shamu c/s	
☐	N716SW	Boeing 737-7H4/W	27850/64			
☐	N717SA	Boeing 737-7H4/W	27851/70	ex N1799B		
☐	N718SW	Boeing 737-7H4/W	27852/71	ex N3134C		
☐	N719SW	Boeing 737-7H4/W	27853/82			
☐	N720WN	Boeing 737-7H4/W	27854/121	ex N1787B		
☐	N723SW	Boeing 737-7H4/W	27855/199	ex N1787B		
☐	N724SW	Boeing 737-7H4/W	27856/201	ex N1787B		
☐	N725SW	Boeing 737-7H4/W	27857/208	ex N1786B		
☐	N726SW	Boeing 737-7H4/W	27858/213			
☐	N727SW	Boeing 737-7H4/W	27859/274	ex N1786B	Nevada One c/s	
☐	N728SW	Boeing 737-7H4/W	27860/276	ex N1787B		
☐	N729SW	Boeing 737-7H4/W	27861/278	ex N1786B		
☐	N730SW	Boeing 737-7H4/W	27862/284	ex N1795B		
☐	N731SA	Boeing 737-7H4/W	27863/318	ex N1786B		
☐	N732SW	Boeing 737-7H4/W	27864/319	ex N1787B		
☐	N733SA	Boeing 737-7H4/W	27865/320	ex N1787B		
☐	N734SA	Boeing 737-7H4/W	27866/324	ex N1795B		
☐	N735SA	Boeing 737-7H4/W	27867/354	ex N1786B		
☐	N736SA	Boeing 737-7H4/W	27868/357	ex N1786B		
☐	N737JW	Boeing 737-7H4/W	27869/358			
☐	N738CB	Boeing 737-7H4/W	27870/360	ex N1786B		
☐	N739GB	Boeing 737-7H4/W	29275/144	ex N1786B		
☐	N740SW	Boeing 737-7H4/W	29276/155			
☐	N741SA	Boeing 737-7H4/W	29277/157			
☐	N742SW	Boeing 737-7H4/W	29278/172		Nolan Ryan Express	
☐	N743SW	Boeing 737-7H4/W	29279/175	ex N60436		
☐	N744SW	Boeing 737-7H4/W	29490/232	ex N1781B		
☐	N745SW	Boeing 737-7H4/W	29491/237	ex "N728SW"		
☐	N746SW	Boeing 737-7H4/W	29798/299	ex N1786B		
☐	N747SA	Boeing 737-7H4/W	29799/306			
☐	N748SW	Boeing 737-7H4/W	29800/331	ex N1786B		
☐	N749SW	Boeing 737-7H4/W	29801/343	ex N1786B		
☐	N750SA	Boeing 737-7H4/W	29802/366			
☐	N751SW	Boeing 737-7H4/W	29803/373	ex N1786B		
☐	N752SW	Boeing 737-7H4/W	29804/387			
☐	N754SW	Boeing 737-7H4/W	29849/416	ex N1787B		
☐	N755SA	Boeing 737-7H4/W	27871/419	ex N1787B		
☐	N756SA	Boeing 737-7H4/W	27872/422	ex N1786B		
☐	N757LV	Boeing 737-7H4/W	29850/425	ex N1786B		
☐	N758SW	Boeing 737-7H4/W	27873/437	ex N1786B		
☐	N759GS	Boeing 737-7H4/W	30544/448	ex N1786B		
☐	N760SW	Boeing 737-7H4/W	27874/468	ex N1786B		
☐	N761RR	Boeing 737-7H4/W	27875/495			
☐	N762SW	Boeing 737-7H4/W	27876/512	ex N1786B		
☐	N763SW	Boeing 737-7H4/W	27877/520	ex N1786B		
☐	N764SW	Boeing 737-7H4/W	27878/521	ex N1787B		
☐	N765SW	Boeing 737-7H4/W	29805/525	ex N1786B		
☐	N766SW	Boeing 737-7H4/W	29806/537	ex N1786B		
☐	N767SW	Boeing 737-7H4/W	29807/541	ex N1787B		
☐	N768SW	Boeing 737-7H4/W	30587/580	ex N1002R		
☐	N769SW	Boeing 737-7H4/W	30588/592			
☐	N770SA	Boeing 737-7H4/W	30589/595			
☐	N771SA	Boeing 737-7H4/W	27879/599			
☐	N772SW	Boeing 737-7H4/W	27880/601			
☐	N773SA	Boeing 737-7H4/W	27881/603	ex N1786B		
☐	N774SW	Boeing 737-7H4/W	27882/609	ex N1786B		
☐	N775SW	Boeing 737-7H4/W	30590/617	ex N1786B		
☐	N776WN	Boeing 737-7H4/W	30591/620	ex N1786B		

☐ N777QC	Boeing 737-7H4/W	30592/621	ex N1786B	
☐ N778SW	Boeing 737-7H4/W	27883/626	ex N1786B	
☐ N779SW	Boeing 737-7H4/W	27884/628	ex N1786B	
☐ N780SW	Boeing 737-7H4/W	27885/643	ex N1786B	
☐ N781WN	Boeing 737-7H4/W	30601/646		New Mexico One
☐ N782SA	Boeing 737-7H4/W	29808/670	ex N1787B	
☐ N783SW	Boeing 737-7H4/W	29809/675	ex N1785B	
☐ N784SW	Boeing 737-7H4/W	29810/677	ex N1786B	
☐ N785SW	Boeing 737-7H4/W	30602/693	ex N1786B	
☐ N786SW	Boeing 737-7H4/W	29811/698	ex N1787B	
☐ N787SA	Boeing 737-7H4/W	29812/705	ex N1786B	
☐ N788SA	Boeing 737-7H4/W	30603/707	ex N1786B	
☐ N789SW	Boeing 737-7H4/W	29816/718	ex N1786B	
☐ N790SW	Boeing 737-7H4/W	30604/721	ex N1786B	
☐ N791SW	Boeing 737-7H4/W	27886/736	ex N1786B	
☐ N792SW	Boeing 737-7H4/W	27887/737		
☐ N793SA	Boeing 737-7H4/W	27888/744	ex N1786B	Spirit One
☐ N794SW	Boeing 737-7H4/W	30605/748	ex N1781B	
☐ N795SW	Boeing 737-7H4/W	30606/780	ex N1786B	
☐ N796SW	Boeing 737-7H4/W	27889/784	ex N1786B	
☐ N797MX	Boeing 737-7H4/W	27890/803		
☐ N798SW	Boeing 737-7AD/W	28436/41	ex N700EW	
☐ N799SW	Boeing 737-7Q8/W	28209/14	ex 9Y-TJI	
☐ N900WN	Boeing 737-7H4/W	32544/2460		
⊓ N901WN	Boeing 737-7H4/W	32545/2462		
☐ N902WN	Boeing 737-7H4/W	36615/2469		
☐ N903WN	Boeing 737-7H4/W	32457/2473		
☐ N904WN	Boeing 737-7H4/W	36616/2480	ex N1780B	
☐ N905WN	Boeing 737-7H4/W	36617/2491	ex N1786B	
☐ N906WN	Boeing 737-7H4/W	36887/2494		
☐ N907WN	Boeing 737-7H4/W	36619/2500		
☐ N908WN	Boeing 737-7H4/W	36620/2509	ex N1786B	
☐ N909WN	Boeing 737-7H4/W	32458/2517		Beats Music c/s
☐ N910WN	Boeing 737-7H4/W	36618/2521	ex N1786B	
☐ N912WN	Boeing 737-7H4/W	36621/2532	ex N1786B	
☐ N913WN	Boeing 737-7H4/W	29840/2536	ex N1787B	
☐ N914WN	Boeing 737-7H4/W	36622/2540	ex N1787B	
☐ N915WN	Boeing 737-7H4/W	36888/2546		
☐ N916WN	Boeing 737-7H4/W	36623/2558		
☐ N917WN	Boeing 737-7H4/W	36624/2562	ex N1787B	
☐ N918WN	Boeing 737-7H4/W	29843/2572		
☐ N919WN	Boeing 737-7H4/W	36625/2591		
☐ N920WN	Boeing 737-7H4/W	32460/2597	ex N1796B	
☐ N921WN	Boeing 737-7H4/W	36626/2600		
☐ N922WN	Boeing 737-7H4/W	32461/2620		
☐ N923WN	Boeing 737-7H4/W	36627/2634		
☐ N924WN	Boeing 737-7H4/W	36628/2640		
☐ N925WN	Boeing 737-7H4/W	36630/2656	ex N1786B	
☐ N926WN	Boeing 737-7H4/W	36629/2663	ex N1786B	
☐ N927WN	Boeing 737-7H4/W	36889/2679		
☐ N928WN	Boeing 737-7H4/W	36890/2687		
☐ N929WN	Boeing 737-7H4/W	36631/2689		
☐ N930WN	Boeing 737-7H4/W	36636/2784	ex N6067E	
☐ N931WN	Boeing 737-7H4/W	36637/2799	ex N1799B	
☐ N932WN	Boeing 737-7H4/W	36639/2837	ex N1786B	
☐ N933WN	Boeing 737-7H4/W	36640/2847		
☐ N934WN	Boeing 737-7H4/W	36642/2878		
☐ N935WN	Boeing 737-7H4/W	36641/2894		
☐ N936WN	Boeing 737-7H4/W	36643/2909	ex N1787B	
☐ N937WN	Boeing 737-7H4/W	36644/2925	ex N1787B	
☐ N938WN	Boeing 737-7H4/W	36645/2929	ex N1786B	Heroes of the Heart Meteorology
☐ N939WN	Boeing 737-7H4/W	36646/2933	ex N1787B	
☐ N940WN	Boeing 737-7H4/W	36900/2943	ex N1786B	
☐ N941WN	Boeing 737-7H4/W	36647/2961	ex N1796B	
☐ N942WN	Boeing 737-7H4/W	36648/2985	ex N1787B	
☐ N943WN	Boeing 737-7H4/W	36913/3195	ex N1786B	
☐ N944WN	Boeing 737-7H4/W	36659/3220		
☐ N945WN	Boeing 737-7H4/W	36660/3226	ex N1787B	
☐ N946WN	Boeing 737-7H4/W	36918/3251	ex N1786B	
☐ N947WN	Boeing 737-7H4/W	36924/3290	ex N1787B	
☐ N948WN	Boeing 737-7H4/W	36662/3296		
☐ N949WN	Boeing 737-7H4/W	36663/3358	ex N1786B	
☐ N950WN	Boeing 737-7H4/W	36664/3365	ex N1799B	
☐ N951WN	Boeing 737-7H4/W	36665/3388		
☐ N952WN	Boeing 737-7H4/W	36667/3477		
☐ N953WN	Boeing 737-7H4/W	36668/3510	ex N1786B	
☐ N954WN	Boeing 737-7H4/W	36669/2547		
☐ N955WN	Boeing 737-7H4/W	36671/3603		
☐ N956WN	Boeing 737-7H4/W	36672/3629		
☐ N957WN	Boeing 737-7H4/W	41528/3657		
☐ N958WN	Boeing 737-7H4/W	36673/3661		
☐ N959WN	Boeing 737-7H4/W	36674/3696		
☐ N960WN	Boeing 737-7H4/W	36675/3715		

☐	N961WN	Boeing 737-7H4/W	36962/3719			
☐	N962WN	Boeing 737-7H4/W	36963/3724			
☐	N963WN	Boeing 737-7H4/W	36676/3726			
☐	N964WN	Boeing 737-7H4/W	36965/3759			
☐	N965WN	Boeing 737-7H4/W	36677/3774			
☐	N966WN	Boeing 737-7H4/W	36066/3788			
☐	N967WN	Boelng 737-7H4/W	36967/3791			
☐	N968WN	Boeing 737-7H4/W	36679/3872			
☐	N969WN	Boeing 737-7H4/W	41777/3874			
☐	N7701B	Boeing 737-76N/W	32681/1526	ex N149AT	301	
☐	N7702A	Boeing 737-7BD/W	33917/1550	ex N166AT	302	
☐	N7703A	Boeing 737-76N/W	32653/1566	ex N168AT	303	
☐	N7704B	Boeing 737-7BD/W	33918/1572	ex N167AT	304	
☐	N7705A	Boeing 737-76N/W	32744/1584	ex N169AT	305	
☐	N7706A	Boeing 737-76N/W	32661/1593	ex N173AT	306	
☐	N7707C	Boeing 737-76N/W	32667/1623	ex N174AT	307	
☐	N7708E	Boeing 737-76N/W	32652/1627	ex N175AT	308	
☐	N7709A	Boeing 737-76N/W	32654/1641	ex N176AT	309	
☐	N7710A	Boeing 737-76N/W	32656/1671	ex N184AT	310	
☐	N7711N	Boeing 737-76N/W	32657/1687	ex N240AT	311	
☐	N7712G	Boeing 737-76N/W	32660/1710	ex N261AT	312	
☐	N7713A	Boeing 737-7BD/W	33919/1730	ex N267AT	7713	
☐	N7714B	Boeing 737-76N/W	32679/1514	ex N126AT	300	
☐	N7715E	Boeing 737-7BD/W	33921/1778	ex N272AT	315	
☐	N7716A	Boeing 737-76N/W	32662/1788	ex N273AT	316	
☐	N7717D	Boeing 737-76N/W	32664/1804	ex N276AT	317	
☐	N7718B	Boeing 737-76N/W	32665/1827	ex N278AT	318	
☐	N7719A	Boeing 737-76N/W	32666/1833	ex N279AT	319	
☐	N7720F	Boeing 737-7BD/W	33922/1845	ex N281AT	7720	
☐	N7721E	Boeing 737-7BD/W	34479/1874	ex N283AT	7721	
☐	N7722B	Boeing 737-76N/W	32668/1876	ex N284AT	322	
☐	N7723E	Boeing 737-76N/W	32670/1898	ex N285AT	323	
☐	N7724A	Boeing 737-7BD/W	36725/2815	ex N354AT	324	
☐	N7725A	Boeing 737-76N/W	32671/1925	ex N287AT	325	
☐	N7726A	Boeing 737-7BD/W	33924/1940	ex N288AT	326	
☐	N7727A	Boeing 737-76N/W	32673/1943	ex N289AT	327	
☐	N7728D	Boeing 737-7BD/W	33925/1967	ex N290AT	7728	
☐	N7729A	Boeing 737-76N/W	32675/1970	ex N291AT	329	
☐	N7730A	Boeing 737-76N/W	33926/1997	ex N292AT	330	
☐	N7731A	Boeing 737-76N/W	32677/2002	ex N295AT	331	
☐	N7732A	Boeing 737-7BD/W	34861/2041	ex N296AT	332	
☐	N7733B	Boeing 737-76N/W	32678/2055	ex N299AT	333	
☐	N7734H	Boeing 737-7BD/W	33923/2083	ex N300AT	334	
☐	N7735A	Boeing 737-7BD/W	34862/2094	ex N307AT	7735	
☐	N7736A	Boeing 737-7BD/W	35109/2126	ex N308AT	336	
☐	N7737E	Boeing 737-7BD/W	33929/2129	ex N309AT	337	
☐	N7738A	Boeing 737-7BD/W	33930/2143	ex N311AT	338	
☐	N7739A	Boeing 737-7BD/W	35110/2147	ex N312AT	339	
☐	N7740A	Boeing 737-7BD/W	33927/2169	ex N313AT	340	
☐	N7741C	Boeing 737-7BD/W	35788/2178	ex N315AT	341	
☐	N7742B	Boeing 737-7BD/W	33928/2190	ex N316AT	7742	
☐	N7743B	Boeing 737-7BD/W	36718/2568	ex N344AT	7743	
☐	N7744A	Boeing 737-7BD/W	33931/2214	ex N318AT	7744	
☐	N7745A	Boeing 737-7BD/W	33933/2278	ex N326AT	345	
☐	N7746C	Boeing 737-7BD/W	33934/2296	ex N328AT	346	
☐	N7747C	Boeing 737-7BD/W	36091/2304	ex N329AT	347	
☐	N7748A	Boeing 737-7BD/W	36399/2312	ex N330AT	348	
☐	N7749B	Boeing 737-7BD/W	36724/2813	ex N353AT	356	
☐	N7750A	Boeing 737-7BD/W	36716/2505	ex N336AT	350	
☐	N7751A	Boeing 737-7BD/W	36717/2526	ex N337AT	351	
☐	N7752B	Boeing 737-7BD/W	33943/2552	ex N338AT	352	
☐	N7811F	Boeing 737-76N/W	28654/986	ex D-ABBS		
☐	N7812G	Boeing 737-79N/W	32582/1013	ex D-ABBT		
☐	N7813P	Boeing 737-7K9/W	30041/909	ex N341TR		
☐	N7814B	Boeing 737-7K9/W	30042/931	ex N342TR		
☐	N7815L	Boeing 737-7BK/W	30288/1322	ex N488AC	7815	♦
☐	N7816B	Boeing 737-7L9/W	28009/221	ex VP-BSP	7816	wfs♦
☐	N7817J	Boeing 737-7L9/W	28013/682	ex D-AGEY	7817	wfs♦
☐	N7818L	Boeing 737-76N/W	28609/417	ex OO-JAN	7818	wfs♦
☐	N7819A	Boeing 737-7Q8	30649/1048	ex A4O-BS	7819	wfs♦
☐	N7820L	Boeing 737-79P	28253/1247	ex B-2683	7820	wfs♦
☐	N7821L	Boeing 737-7CT/W	32748/1266	ex C-FWAQ	7821	[PAE]♦
☐	N7822A	Boeing 737-76N	32596/1028	ex N848TM	7822	[PAE]♦
☐	N7823A	Boeing 737-7CT/W	32749/1281	ex C-FWBG	7823	[PAE]♦
☐	N7825A	Boeing 737-7CT/W	32750/1286	ex C-FWBL	7825	[PAE]♦
☐	N7826B	Boeing 737-79P	30035/1288	ex B-5032	7826	[PAE]♦
☐	N7827A	Boeing 737-79P	28255/1284	ex 2-TBXA	7827	[PAE]♦
☐	N7828A	Boeing 737-7CT/W	33697/1303	ex C-FWBW	7828	[PAE]♦
☐	N7830A	Boeing 737-7L9/W	28008/203	ex OY-JTW	7830	[PAE]♦
☐	N7831B	Boeing 737-7CT/W	32752/1339	ex C-FWCC	7831	[PAE]♦
☐	N7834A	Boeing 737-752/W	33789/1524	ex XA-HAM	7834	[PAE]♦
☐	N7844A	Boeing 737-752/W	35118/2151	ex XA-GMV	7844	[PAE]♦

☐ N500WR	Boeing 737-8H4/W	36898/4967	ex (N8636E)	8636	♦
☐ N8301J	Boeing 737-8H4/W	36980/3952		Warrior One	
☐ N8302F	Boeing 737-8H4/W	36680/3979			
☐ N8303R	Boeing 737-8H4/W	36681/3993			
☐ N8305E	Boeing 737-8H4/W	36683/4009			
☐ N8306H	Boeing 737-8H4/W	36983/4019			
☐ N8307K	Boeing 737-8H4/W	36987/4027			
☐ N8308K	Boeing 737-8H4/W	36682/4039			
☐ N8309C	Boeing 737-8H4/W	36985/4043			
☐ N8310C	Boeing 737-8H4/W	38807/4058			
☐ N8311Q	Boeing 737-8H4/W	38808/4073			
☐ N8312C	Boeing 737-8H4/W	38809/4084			
☐ N8313F	Boeing 737-8H4/W	38810/4088			
☐ N8314L	Boeing 737-8H4/W	36990/4100			
☐ N8315C	Boeing 737-8H4/W	38811/4108			
☐ N8316H	Boeing 737-8H4/W	36684/4113			
☐ N8317M	Boeing 737-8H4/W	36992/4126			
☐ N8318F	Boeing 737-8H4/W	36685/4143			
☐ N8319F	Boeing 737-8H4/W	36994/4162			
☐ N8320J	Boeing 737-8H4/W	36686/4163			
☐ N8321D	Boeing 737-8H4/W	36687/4195			
☐ N8322X	Boeing 737-8H4/W	36997/4200		8322	
☐ N8323C	Boeing 737-8H4/W	37005/4232	ex N1786B	8323	
☐ N8324A	Boeing 737-8H4/W	35966/4239		8324	
☐ N8325D	Boeing 737-8H4/W	37003/4255		8325	
☐ N8326F	Boeing 737-8H4/W	35969/4263		8326	
☐ N8327A	Boeing 737-8H4/W	37009/4269		8327	
☐ N8328A	Boeing 737-8H4/W	38818/4285		8328	
☐ N8329B	Boeing 737-8H4/W	37006/4292		8329	
☐ N8600F	Boeing 737-8H4/W	39882/4007			
☐ N8601C	Boeing 737-8H4/W	38874/4050			
☐ N8602F	Boeing 737-8H4/W	38110/4059			
☐ N8603F	Boeing 737-8H4/W	38875/4069			
☐ N8604K	Boeing 737-8H4/W	39883/4078			
☐ N8605E	Boeing 737-8H4/W	36891/4297		8605	
☐ N8606C	Boeing 737-8H4/W	35964/4312	ex (N8331A)	8606	
☐ N8607M	Boeing 737-8H4/W	36634/4318	ex (N8332K)	8607	
☐ N8608N	Boeing 737-8H4/W	36638/4323	ex (N8333J)	8608	
☐ N8609A	Boeing 737-8H4/W	36893/4335		8609	
☐ N8610A	Boeing 737-8H4/W	36635/4362		8610	
☐ N8611F	Boeing 737-8H4/W	36892/4367		8611	
☐ N8612K	Boeing 737-8H4/W	36973/4389		8612	
☐ N8613K	Boeing 737-8H4/W	36998/4397		8613	
☐ N8614M	Boeing 737-8H4/W	36908/4420		8614	
☐ N8615E	Boeing 737-8H4/W	36933/4613		8615	
☐ N8616C	Boeing 737-8H4/W	36914/4627		8616	
☐ N8617E	Boeing 737-8H4/W	36912/4631		8617	
☐ N8618N	Boeing 737-8H4/W	36915/4667		8618	
☐ N8619F	Boeing 737-8H4/W	33939/4670		8619	
☐ N8620H	Boeing 737-8H4/W	42526/4674		8620	
☐ N8621A	Boeing 737-8H4/W	36917/4706		8621	
☐ N8622A	Boeing 737-8H4/W	36919/4717	ex N1786B	8622	
☐ N8623F	Boeing 737-8H4/W	36731/4734		8623	
☐ N8624J	Boeing 737-8H4/W	37004/4845		8624	
☐ N8625A	Boeing 737-8H4/W	36896/4849		8625	
☐ N8626B	Boeing 737-8H4/W	36894/4854		8626	
☐ N8627B	Boeing 737-8H4/W	36895/4874		8627	
☐ N8628A	Boeing 737-8H4/W	42384/4888		8628	
☐ N8629A	Boeing 737-8H4/W	36897/4896		8629	
☐ N8630B	Boeing 737-8H4/W	42521/4914		8630	
☐ N8631A	Boeing 737-8H4/W	42385/4928		8631	
☐ N8632A	Boeing 737-8H4/W	60082/4935	ex N1786B	8632	
☐ N8633A	Boeing 737-8H4/W	36905/4942		8633	
☐ N8634A	Boeing 737-8H4/W	42522/4955		8634	
☐ N8635F	Boeing 737-8H4/W	60083/4962		8635	
☐ N8637A	Boeing 737-8H4/W	42523/4974		8637	
☐ N8638A	Boeing 737-8H4/W	36911/4977		8638	
☐ N8639B	Boeing 737-8H4/W	60086/4999		8639	
☐ N8640D	Boeing 737-8H4/W	60084/5001		8640	
☐ N8641B	Boeing 737-8H4/W	60085/5011	ex N8639B	8641	
☐ N8642E	Boeing 737-8H4/W	42525/5022		8642 Heart One	
☐ N8643A	Boeing 737-8H4/W	42524/5030		8643	
☐ N8644C	Boeing 737-8H4/W	35973/5032		8644	
☐ N8645A	Boeing 737-8H4/W	36907/5038		8645 Heart Two	
☐ N8646B	Boeing 737-8H4/W	36935/5042		8646	
☐ N8647A	Boeing 737-8H4/W	42528/5044		8647	
☐ N8648A	Boeing 737-8H4/W	42531/5064		8648	
☐ N8649A	Boeing 737-8H4/W	42527/5084		8649	
☐ N8650F	Boeing 737-8H4/W	36909/5105		8650	
☐ N8651A	Boeing 737-8H4/W	36920/5125	ex N1795D	8651	
☐ N8652B	Boeing 737-8H4/W	36971/5151		8652	
☐ N8653A	Boeing 737-8H4/W	37037/5192		8653	♦
☐ N8654B	Boeing 737-8H4/W	37045/5198		8654	♦

☐ N8655D	Boeing 737-8H4/W	42529/5200		8655	♦
☐ N8656B	Boeing 737-8H4/W	42530/5221		8656	♦
☐ N8657B	Boeing 737-8H4/W	42535/5227		8657	♦
☐ N8658A	Boeing 737-8H4/W	36899/5229	8658	8658	♦
☐ N8659D	Boeing 737-8H4/W	36901/5269		8659	♦
☐ N8660A	Boeing 737-8H4/W	36654/5273		8660	♦
☐ N8661A	Boeing 737-8H4/W	36906/5283		8661	♦
☐ N8662F	Boeing 737-8H4/W	36936/5309	ex N1786B	8662	♦
☐ N8663A	Boeing 737-8H4/W	36902/5329		8663	♦
☐ N8664J	Boeing 737-8H4/W	36649/5350		8664	♦
☐ N8665D	Boeing 737-8H4/W	36652/5370		8665	♦
☐ N8667D	Boeing 737-8H4/W	36657/5392		8667	♦
☐ N8668A	Boeing 737-8H4/W	36903/5411		8668	o/o♦
☐ N8669B	Boeing 737-8H4/W	36655/		8669	o/o♦
☐ N8670A	Boeing 737-8H4/W	36656/		8670	o/o♦
☐ N8671D	Boeing 737-8H4/W	36937/		8671	o/o♦
☐ N8672F	Boeing 737-8H4/W	36715/		8672	o/o♦
☐ N8673F	Boeing 737-8H4/W	36940/		8673	o/o♦
☐ N8674B	Boeing 737-8H4/W	36941/		8674	o/o♦
☐ N8675A	Boeing 737-8H4/W	36734/		8675	o/o♦
☐ N8676A	Boeing 737-8H4/W	35976/		8676	o/o♦
☐ N	Boeing 737-8H4/W	37043/			o/o
☐ N	Boeing 737-8H4/W	38806/			o/o

SPECTRUM AIR SERVICES (XSA) Atlanta-Kalb, GA (PDK)

☐ N70X	Canadair CL-600-2B16 Challenger	5073	♦
☐ N70XF	Canadair CL-600-2B16 Challenger	1032	♦
☐ N675MS	Cessna 208 Caravan I	20800370	

SPEEDSTAR EXPRESS Lake Elsinore, CA

☐ N192AV	Cessna 208 Caravan I	20800215	ex N192RA
☐ N923MA	de Havilland DHC-6 Twin Otter 200	168	ex N923HM
☐ N926MA	de Havilland DHC-6 Twin Otter 200	133	ex N953SM
☐ N9641F	Cessna 208 Caravan I	20800122	

SPERNAK AIRWAYS Anchorage-Merrill, AK (MRI)

☐ N29CF	Cessna 207 Skywagon	20700353		FP
☐ N6492H	Cessna 207A Stationair 7 II	20700544		FP
☐ N7392U	Cessna 207A Stationair 7 II	20700435		FP
☐ N73047	Cessna 207A Stationair 7 II	20700556	ex XB-EXR	FP
☐ N91038	Cessna 207 Skywagon	20700027		FP

SPIRIT AIR Salmon-Lemhi County, ID (SMN)

☐ N80GV	Piper PA-31-350 Navajo Chieftain	31-7552003	ex N61487
☐ N376ME	Cessna T206H Turbo Stationair	T20608225	
☐ N838SA	Quest Kodiak 100	100-0002	
☐ N4438	Britten-Norman BN-2A-20 Islander	766	ex N443S
☐ N6561B	Britten-Norman BN-2A-20 Islander	520	ex YV-1073P
☐ N7067Z	Cessna T210M Turbo Centurion	21062572	ex C-GPTX
☐ N8514C	Piper PA-34-200T Seneca II	34-7670147	
☐ N31932	Piper PA-31-350 Navajo Chieftain	31-7405144	ex N888TV

SPIRIT AIRLINES Spirit Wings (NK/NKS) Fort Lauderdale-Hollywood Intl, FL (FLL)

☐ N502NK	Airbus A319-132	2433	ex D-AVWX	
☐ N503NK	Airbus A319-132	2470	ex D-AVYJ	
☐ N504NK	Airbus A319-132	2473	ex D-AVYP	
☐ N505NK	Airbus A319-132	2485	ex D-AVYI	
☐ N506NK	Airbus A319-132	2490	ex D-AVWH	
☐ N507NK	Airbus A319-132	2560	ex D-AVYV	
☐ N508NK	Airbus A319-132	2567	ex D-AVWM	
☐ N509NK	Airbus A319-132	2603	ex D-AVXO	
☐ N510NK	Airbus A319-132	2622	ex D-AVYT	
☐ N512NK	Airbus A319-132	2673	ex D-AVYO	
☐ N514NK	Airbus A319-132	2679	ex D-AVYV	
☐ N515NK	Airbus A319-131	2698	ex EI-ECX	
☐ N519NK	Airbus A319-132	2723	ex EI-ECY	
☐ N516NK	Airbus A319-132	2704	ex D-AVXJ	
☐ N517NK	Airbus A319-132	2711	ex D-AVYM	
☐ N519NK	Airbus A319-132	2723	ex EI-ECY	o/o
☐ N521NK	Airbus A319-132	2797	ex EI-ESG	
☐ N522NK	Airbus A319-132	2893	ex D-AVYY	
☐ N523NK	Airbus A319-132	2898	ex D-AVWN	
☐ N524NK	Airbus A319-132	2929	ex D-AVYU	
☐ N525NK	Airbus A319-132	2942	ex D-AVWX	
☐ N526NK	Airbus A319-132	2963	ex D-AVYM	
☐ N527NK	Airbus A319-132	2978	ex D-AVXD	
☐ N528NK	Airbus A319-132	2983	ex D-AVXI	

☐ N529NK	Airbus A319-132	3007	ex D-AVYL		
☐ N530NK	Airbus A319-132	3017	ex D-AVXL		
☐ N531NK	Airbus A319-132	3026	ex D-AVWC		
☐ N532NK	Airbus A319-132	3165	ex D-AVYX		
☐ N533NK	Airbus A319-132	3393	ex D-AVWJ		
☐ N534NK	Airbus A319-132	3395	ex D-AVWK		
☐ N601NK	Airbus A320-232	4206	ex D-AVVI		
☐ N602NK	Airbus A320-232	4264	ex D-AXAD		
☐ N603NK	Airbus A320-232	4321	ex D-AXAM		
☐ N604NK	Airbus A320-232	4431	ex D-AVVO		
☐ N605NK	Airbus A320-232	4548	ex F-WWIV		
☐ N606NK	Airbus A320-232	4592	ex F-WWIR		
☐ N607NK	Airbus A320-232	4595	ex F-WWIZ		
☐ N608NK	Airbus A320-232	4902	ex F-WWBT		
☐ N609NK	Airbus A320-232	4951	ex F-WWDI		
☐ N611NK	Airbus A320-232	4996	ex F-WWBJ		
☐ N612NK	Airbus A320-232	5029	ex F-WWBN		
☐ N613NK	Airbus A320-232	5042	ex F-WWDO		
☐ N614NK	Airbus A320-232	5132	ex F-WWDS		
☐ N615NK	Airbus A320-232	5159	ex F-WWDF		
☐ N616NK	Airbus A320-232	5370	ex F-WWDV		
☐ N617NK	Airbus A320-232	5387	ex F-WWIY		
☐ N618NK	Airbus A320-232/S	5458	ex F-WWBB		
☐ N619NK	Airbus A320-232/S	5517	ex F-WWDL		
☐ N620NK	Airbus A320-232/S	5624	ex F-WWBC		
☐ N621NK	Airbus A320-232/S	5672	ex F-WWBX		
☐ N622NK	Airbus A320-232/S	5804	ex F-WWBB		
☐ N623NK	Airbus A320-232/S	5861	ex F-WWDF		
☐ N624NK	Airbus A320-232/S	5880	ex F-WWII		
☐ N625NK	Airbus A320-232/S	5954	ex F-WWIC		
☐ N626NK	Airbus A320-232/S	5999	ex F-WWBO		
☐ N627NK	Airbus A320-232/S	6082	ex F-WWBQ		
☐ N628NK	Airbus A320-232/S	6193	ex F-WWDC		♦
☐ N629NK	Airbus A320-232/S	6300	ex F-WWBZ		♦
☐ N630NK	Airbus A320-232/S	6304	ex F-WWBH		♦
☐ N631NK	Airbus A320-232/S	6327	ex F-WWIZ		♦
☐ N632NK	Airbus A320-232/S	6331	ex F-WWBD		♦
☐ N633NK	Airbus A320-232/S	6345	ex F-WWBU		♦
☐ N634NK	Airbus A320-232/S	6370	ex F-WWIY		♦
☐ N635NK	Airbus A320-232/S	6383	ex F-WWDS		♦
☐ N636NK	Airbus A320-232/S	6424	ex F-WWDV		♦
☐ N637NK	Airbus A320-232/S	6436	ex F-WWBE		♦
☐ N638NK	Airbus A320-232/S	6463	ex F-WWIE		♦
☐ N639NK	Airbus A320-232/S	6487	ex F-WWDL		♦
☐ N640NK	Airbus A320-232/S	6507	ex F-WWIZ		♦
☐ N641NK	Airbus A320-232/S	6566	ex F-WWIM		♦
☐ N642NK	Airbus A320-232/S	6586	ex F-WWDV		o/o♦
☐ N643NK	Airbus A320-232/S	6616	ex F-WWBO		o/o♦
☐ N587NK	Airbus A321-231	2476	ex D-AVXB	Spirit of Jamaica	
☐ N588NK	Airbus A321-231	2590	ex D-AVZK		
☐ N	Airbus A321-231	6672	ex		o/o♦
☐ N	Airbus A321-231	6736	ex		o/o♦
☐ N	Airbus A321-231	6770	ex		o/o♦
☐ N	Airbus A321-231	6804	ex		o/o♦
☐ N	Airbus A321-231/S	6867	ex		o/o♦
☐ N	Airbus A321-231/S	6884	ex		o/o♦
☐ N	Airbus A320-271Neo	6799	ex		o/o♦
☐ N	Airbus A320-271Neo	6833	ex		o/o♦
☐ N	Airbus A320-271Neo	6920	ex		o/o♦

SUBURBAN AIR FREIGHT   Sub Air (SUB)   Omaha-Eppley Airfield, NE (OMA)

☐ N114MN	Aero Commander 680FL	1553-107	ex (N2611L)	
☐ N290MP	Aero Commander 680FL	1535-104		
☐ N309VS	Aero Commander 680FL	1659-128	ex N6626V	
☐ N2828S	Aero Commander 680FL	1329-14		
☐ N5035E	Aero Commander 680FL	1764-147		
☐ N9011N	Aero Commander 680FL	1836-153		
☐ N103SX	Beech 1900C	UC-103	ex N205CA	♦
☐ N124GP	Beech 1900C	UB-23	ex N23VK	
☐ N130UE	Beech 1900C	UC-130	ex VH-EEY	
☐ N149SF	Beech 1900C-1	UC-149	ex N575X	
☐ N253SF	Beech 1900C-1	UC-53	ex N31764	♦
☐ N420CM	Beech 1900C-1	UC-131		
☐ N719GL	Beech 1900C	UB-19	ex N314BH	♦
☐ N208QC	Cessna 208B Caravan I	208B0774	ex N5261R	
☐ N864SF	Cessna 208B Caravan I	208B0864		

SUN AIR EXPRESS   Fort Lauderdale, FL (FXX)

☐ N27196	Piper PA-31-350 Navajo Chieftain	31-7752095	♦
☐ N45038	Piper PA-31-350 Navajo Chieftain	31-8052292	♦

SUN COUNTRY AIRLINES   Sun Country (SY/SCX)   Minneapolis/St Paul Intl, MN (MSP)

☐ N710SY	Boeing 737-73V	30241/1034	ex N241CL		
☐ N711SY	Boeing 737-73V	30245/1058	ex G-EZJJ		
☐ N712SY	Boeing 737-7Q8	28219/183	ex PR-GOU		
☐ N713SY	Boeing 737-7Q8	30635/713	ex PR-GIL		
☐ N714SY	Boeing 737-752/W	33786/1403	ex N850AM		
☐ N715SY	Boeing 737-752/W	33787/1421	ex N852AM		
☐ N716SY	Boeing 737-7Q8/W	30629/1011	ex D-ABBV		
☐ N801SY	Boeing 737-8Q8/W	30332/777	ex N1787B	The Phoenix	
☐ N804SY	Boeing 737-8Q8/W	30689/908		Laughlin Luck	
☐ N805SY	Boeing 737-8Q8/W	30032/985	ex N1781B	The Spirit of Minnesota	
☐ N808SY	Boeing 737-8BK/W	33021/1667	ex D-APBD		♦
☐ N809SY	Boeing 737-8Q8/W	30683/1669			
☐ N813SY	Boeing 737-8Q8	28237/769	ex OY-SED		
☐ N814SY	Boeing 737-8BK/W	30620/991	ex VH-VOA		
☐ N815SY	Boeing 737-8BK/W	30623/1136	ex VH-VOC		
☐ N816SY	Boeing 737-8Q8/W	30637/800	ex N281LF		
☐ N817SY	Boeing 737-8K2/W	30392/833	ex PH-HZM		
☐ N818SY	Boeing 737-8BK/W	29646/2282	ex ET-AMZ		
☐ N819SY	Boeing 737-86N/W	34254/1897	ex B-5148		♦
☐ N820SY	Boeing 737-8FH/W	39951/5166	ex N1796B		♦
☐ N821SY	Boeing 737-8FH/W	39952/5217	ex N1786B		♦

SUNDANCE HELICOPTERS   Las Vegas, NV

☐ N53SH	Aérospatiale AS350B2 AStar	2009	♦
☐ N201AE	Aérospatiale AS350B2 AStar	3895	♦
☐ N230SH	Aérospatiale AS350B2 AStar	2337	♦
☐ N250SH	Aérospatiale AS350B2 AStar	3874	♦
☐ N313LV	Aérospatiale AS350B2 AStar	3296	♦
☐ N340SH	Aérospatiale AS350B2 AStar	4190	♦
☐ N345SH	Aérospatiale AS350B2 AStar	3345	♦
☐ N351WM	Aérospatiale AS350B2 AStar	2167	♦
☐ N507SH	Aérospatiale AS350B2 AStar	4747	♦
☐ N612SH	Aérospatiale AS350B2 AStar	4757	♦
☐ N708SH	Aérospatiale AS350B2 AStar	7098	♦
☐ N712SH	Aérospatiale AS350B2 AStar	7102	♦
☐ N735SH	Aérospatiale AS350B2 AStar	7315	♦
☐ N745SH	Aérospatiale AS350B2 AStar	7455	♦
☐ N749SH	Aérospatiale AS350B2 AStar	7449	♦
☐ N751H	Aérospatiale AS350B2 AStar	3403	♦
☐ N808HD	Aérospatiale AS350BA AStar	2347	♦
☐ N884SH	Aérospatiale AS350B2 AStar	2884	♦
☐ N966SH	Aérospatiale AS350B2 AStar	3787	♦
☐ N3819	Aérospatiale AS350B2 AStar	3877	♦
☐ N208SH	Eurocopter EC130T2	7644	♦
☐ N213SH	Eurocopter EC130T2	7651	♦
☐ N216SH	Eurocopter EC130T2	7674	♦
☐ N220SH	Eurocopter EC130T2	7710	♦
☐ N222SH	Eurocopter EC130T2	7943	♦
☐ N223SH	Eurocopter EC130T2	7953	♦
☐ N231SH	Eurocopter EC130T2	7993	♦
☐ N237SH	Eurocopter EC130T2	8005	♦
☐ N98AL	Bell 206B JetRanger	2985	♦
☐ N145SH	Cessna 208BEX Caravan I	208B5099	♦
☐ N388JC	Bell 206L-1 LongRanger	45568	♦
☐ N392SH	Eurocopter EC130B4	3922	♦
☐ N399SH	Eurocopter EC130B4	3992	♦
☐ N452SH	Eurocopter EC130B4	4528	♦
☐ N663SH	Eurocopter EC130B4	4663	♦

SUNSHINE HELICOPTERS   Kahului Heliport, HI

☐ N131WS	Eurocopter EC130B4	3521	ex C-FAAT
☐ N132WS	Eurocopter EC130B4	3527	ex N478DV
☐ N801MH	Eurocopter EC130B4	3654	
☐ N802MH	Eurocopter EC130B4	3707	
☐ N803MH	Eurocopter EC130B4	3735	
☐ N804MH	Eurocopter EC130B4	3750	
☐ N288WS	Aérospatiale AS350BA AStar	2087	ex N288BA
☐ N4075S	Aérospatiale AS350BA AStar	3043	
☐ N6094H	Aérospatiale AS350BA AStar	2694	

☐ N6094S   Aérospatiale AS350BA AStar   2722

SURF AIRLINES   Santa Monica, CA

☐ N805SA	Pilatus Porter PC-12/45	569	ex N569AF	
☐ N806SA	Pilatus Porter PC-12/45	558	ex N558AF	
☐ N807SA	Pilatus Porter PC-12/45	547	ex N547AF	
☐ N809SA	Pilatus Porter PC-12/47E	1490		◆
☐ N816SA	Pilatus Porter PC-12/47E	1499		◆
☐ N817SA	Pilatus Porter PC-12/47E	1504		◆
☐ N819SA	Pilatus Porter PC-12/47E	1512		◆
☐ N821SA	Pilatus Porter PC-12/47E	1516		◆

SWIFT AIR   Swiftflight (Q7/SWQ)   Phoenix, AZ (PHX)

☐ N418US	Boeing 737-401	23985/1676		◆
☐ N420US	Boeing 737-401	23987/1698		◆
☐ N421US	Boeing 737-401	23988/1714		
☐ N440US	Boeing 737-4B7	24811/1890		◆
☐ N458UW	Boeing 737-4B7	25022/2010	ex N783AU	◆
☐ N801TJ	Boeing 737-4B7	24892/1944	ex N448US	
☐ N802TJ	Boeing 737-4B7	24874/1936	ex N447US	wfs
☐ N803TJ	Boeing 737-45D	27156/2492	ex SP-LLB	
☐ N727NY	Boeing 727-232	20646/967	ex N59792	VIP [MQY]

TAILWIND INTERNATIONAL   Cherry (CCY)   Dallas-Addison, TX (ADS)

☐ N207CA	AMD Falcon 20	153	ex N70MD
☐ N209CA	AMD Falcon 20C	71	ex N195AS
☐ N218CA	AMD Falcon 20DC	218	ex EC-EEU
☐ N234CA	AMD Falcon 20C	17	ex N55TH

TALKEETNA AIR TAXI   Talkeetna, AK (TKA)

☐ N2YV	de Havilland DHC-3 Otter	207		◆
☐ N60WT	de Havilland DHC-2 Beaver	491	ex N4081F	FP/WS
☐ N100BW	de Havilland DHC-3 Otter	58	ex C-GOFD	FP/WS
☐ N144Q	de Havilland DHC-2 Beaver	1465		FP/WS
☐ N185FK	Cessna A185F Skywagon	18502513	ex N1796R	FP/WS
☐ N510PR	de Havilland DHC-3 Turbo Otter	250	ex VH-OTV	FP/WS
☐ N561TA	de Havilland DHC-2 Beaver	581	ex CF-HGV	FP/WS
☐ N565TA	de Havilland DHC-3 Turbo Otter	46	ex C-FQOQ	FP/WS
☐ N1694M	Cessna A185E Skywagon	18501879		FP/WS
☐ N8190Y	de Havilland DHC-2 Beaver	824	ex C-GPUP	FP/WS

TALON AIR SERVICE   Talon Flight (TFF)   Soldotna, AK

| ☐ N252TA | de Havilland DHC-3 Turbo Otter | 252 | ex C-FTKA |
| ☐ N253TA | Cessna 208 Caravan I | 20800222 | ex N788TW |

TANANA AIR SERVICE   Tan Air (4E/TNR)   Ruby, AK (RBY)

☐ N97CR	Piper PA-32R-300 Lance	32R-7780078	ex JA3776
☐ N866CS	Cessna A185F Skywagon	18502866	ex N866ST
☐ N1587U	Cessna 207 Stationair	20700187	
☐ N4352F	Piper PA-32R-300 Lance	32R-7680441	
☐ N4803S	Piper PA-32-260 Cherokee Six B	32-1188	
☐ N31606	Piper PA-32-300 Cherokee Six	32-7840137	
☐ N75387	Piper PA-32R-300 Lance	32R-7680298	

TAQUAN AIR SERVICE   Taquan (K3)   Metlakatla/Ketchikan-Waterfront SPB, AK (MTM/WFB)

☐ N1018A	de Havilland DHC-2 Beaver	178	ex N52409	FP
☐ N5160G	de Havilland DHC-2 Beaver	236	ex 51-16483	FP
☐ N37756	de Havilland DHC-2 Beaver	1456	ex G-203	FP
☐ N67673	de Havilland DHC-2 Beaver	1284	ex 57-2586	FP
☐ N68010	de Havilland DHC-2 Beaver	1243	ex 57-6150	FP

TBM   Tulare-Mefford Field, CA/Visalia-Municipal, CA (TLR/VIS)

☐ N466TM	Lockheed C-130A-1A Hercules	3173	ex 57-0466	64	Tanker
☐ N473TM	Lockheed C-130A-1A Hercules	3081	ex 56-0473	63	Tanker
☐ N531BA	Lockheed C-130A-1A Hercules	3139	ex 56-0531	67	[VIS]

TEMSCO HELICOPTERS   Temsco (TMS)   Ketchikan-Temsco Heliport, AK

☐ N94TH	Aérospatiale AS350B AStar	2548	ex (N6951T)
☐ N141TH	Aérospatiale AS350B2 AStar	1167	ex N98MB
☐ N142AE	Aérospatiale AS350B3 AStar	7035	
☐ N143TH	Aérospatiale AS350B2 AStar	9043	

☐ N145TH	Aérospatiale AS350B2 AStar	9060			
☐ N146TH	Aérospatiale AS350B2 AStar	9065			
☐ N147TH	Aérospatiale AS350B2 AStar	9070			
☐ N148TH	Aérospatiale AS350B2 AStar	4623			
☐ N149TH	Aérospatiale AS350B2 AStar	9071			
☐ N288CH	Aérospatiale AS350B2 AStar	2383			♦
☐ N403AE	Aérospatiale AS350B3 AStar	3281			
☐ N405AE	Aérospatiale AS350B3 AStar	3286			
☐ N570AE	Aérospatiale AS350B2 AStar	7489			
☐ N802TH	Aérospatiale AS350B2 AStar	9023			
☐ N911CV	Aérospatiale AS350B3 AStar	3142	ex N40729		
☐ N970TH	Aérospatiale AS350BA AStar	9011			
☐ N4022D	Aérospatiale AS350B2 AStar	2891			
☐ N6015S	Aérospatiale AS350BA AStar	1884			
☐ N6080R	Aérospatiale AS350BA AStar	2685			
☐ N6094E	Aérospatiale AS350BA AStar	2750			
☐ N6094U	Aérospatiale AS350BA AStar	2751			
☐ N6302Y	Aérospatiale AS350B2 AStar	9007			
☐ N57954	Aérospatiale AS350B AStar	1127	ex N35977		
☐ N57958	Aérospatiale AS350B AStar	1512			
☐ N214TH	Bell 214B-1	28031	ex N4374D		
☐ N502TH	Bell 205A-1	30030	ex C-FKHQ		
☐ N16920	Bell 212	30865			
☐ N83230	Bell 212	30560			

10 TANKER AIR CARRIER

☐ N450AX	McDonnell-Douglas DC-10-10	46942/162	ex N161AA	910	waterbomber [OSC]♦
☐ N522AX	McDonnell-Douglas DC-10-30	48315/436	ex N243NW		waterbomber♦
☐ N612AX	McDonnell-Douglas DC-10-30ER	48290/435	ex N239NW	910	waterbomber♦
☐ N17805	McDonnell-Douglas DC-10-30	47957/201	ex F-GPVB	911	waterbomber♦

TRADEWIND AVIATION   Oxford, CT

☐ N87T	Douglas DC-3	6148	ex N31MC	Frtr
☐ N131FS	Douglas DC-3	16172/32920	ex N67PA	Frtr
☐ N133FS	Douglas DC-3	15757/27202	ex N53NA	Frtr
☐ N135FS	Douglas DC-3	20063	ex NC63107	Frtr
☐ N138FS	Douglas DC-3	9967	ex N303SF	Frtr
☐ N783T	Douglas DC-3	4219	ex N783V	Frtr

TRANS STATES AIRLINES   Waterski (AX/LOF)   St Louis-Lambert Intl, MO (STL)

Ops commuter services for American Airlines as American Connection and United Air Lines as United Express from St Louis, MO, Baltimore-Washington, MD, Newark, NJ, Chicago, IL and Pittsburgh, PA. Go Jet Airlines is a wholly owned subsidiary based in St Louis, MO operating CRJ-700s for United Express.

TRANSAIR/TRANS EXECUTIVE AIRLINES OF HAWAII
Maui (P6/MUI)   Honolulu-Intl, HI (HNL)

☐ N221LM	Short SD.3-60	SH3722	ex N722PC	Frtr
☐ N351TA	Short SD.3-60	SH3759	ex N159CC	Frtr
☐ N729PC	Short SD.3-60	SH3729	ex 6Y-JMX	Frtr
☐ N808KR	Short SD.3-60	SH3734	ex D-CFAO	Frtr
☐ N808TR	Short SD.3-60	SH3718	ex VQ-TSK	Frtr
☐ N827BE	Short SD.3-60	SH3746	ex N746SA	Frtr
☐ N4476F	Short SD.3-60	SH3731	ex 5N-BFT	
☐ N306AL	Boeing 737-2T4C	23066/992	ex XA-RCB	
☐ N587CA	Convair 640	463	ex C-FPWO	
☐ N737CS	Boeing 737-2T4F	23272/1093	ex VT-BOI	
☐ N413JG	Boeing 737-28Q	23148/1059	ex C-FLWJ	♦
☐ N809TA	Boeing 737-209F	23796/1420	ex 9M-PMZ	♦
☐ N810TA	Boeing 737-275C	21116/427	ex 9M-PML	

TRANSNORTHERN AVIATION   Anchorage, AK (ANC)

☐ N27TN	Douglas C-117D	43332	ex N99857	
☐ N782C	Swearingen SA.227AC Metro III	AC-525	ex N31078	
☐ N3114G	Swearingen SA227AC Metro III	AC-583	ex (N505TN)	

TROPIC AIR CHARTERS   Fort Lauderdale Executive, FL (FXE)

☐ N131JL	Britten-Norman BN-2A-6 Islander	225	ex G-51-225	
☐ N200MU	Britten-Norman BN-2A-27 Islander	78	ex 6Y-JSX	
☐ N296TA	Britten-Norman BN-2A-8 Islander	384	ex J8-VBN	
☐ N297TA	Britten-Norman BN-2A-26 Islander	741	ex N196TA	

TROPICAL TRANSPORT SERVICES — San Juan-Munoz Marin Intl, PR (SJU)

☐ N351AB	Cessna 402C	402C0351	
☐ N347AB	Cessna 402C	402C0347	
☐ N402AS	Cessna 402C	402C0402	
☐ N603AB	Cessna 402C	402C0603	
☐ N744BA	SAAB SF.340A	340A-105	ex SE-F05
☐ N792BA	SAAB SF.340A	340A-092	ex SE-E92
☐ N900MX	Beech 1900C	UB-55	

TURBO FLITE AVIATION — Missoula, MT

☐ N383EC	CASA CN-235-300	C177	ex N528LD	
☐ N385RS	CASA CN-235-300	C042		
☐ N825CE	CASA CN-235-200	C130		♦
☐ N835CE	CASA CN-235-300	C176	ex N248MD	
☐ N5025	CASA CN-235-200	C030	ex N235TF	
☐ N504WJ	de Havilland DHC-6 Twin Otter 300	503		♦
☐ N562CP	de Havilland DHC-6 Twin Otter 300	562		♦

21 AIR — Greensboro, NC (GSO)

☐ N881YV	Boeing 767-241ERF	23803/161	ex N768QT	<DYA♦
☐ N999YV	Boeing 767-241ERF	23801/1700	ex N769QT	<DYA♦

UFLY AIRWAYS (6F/FAO) — Miami, FL (MIA)

☐ N836NK	McDonnell-Douglas MD-83	53045/1777	ex N833RA
☐ N836RA	McDonnell-Douglas MD-83	53046/1794	ex YV-44C

ULTIMATE JETCHARTERS dba Ultimate Air Shuttle (UJC) — Cincinnati-Lunken Field (LUK)

☐ N328WW	Dornier 328-310 (328JET)	3116	ex D-BGAD	♦
☐ N359SK	Dornier 328-310 (328JET)	3202	ex D-BDXU	♦
☐ N406FJ	Dornier 328-310 (328JET)	3156	ex D-BDXK	♦
☐ N407FJ	Dornier 328-310 (328JET)	3157	ex D-BDXL	♦
☐ N411FJ	Dornier 328-310 (328JET)	3166	ex D-BDXW	♦
☐ N419FJ	Dornier 328-310 (328JET)	3173	ex D-BDXH	♦
☐ N425FJ	Dornier 328-310 (328JET)	3189	ex D-BDXI	♦
☐ N429FJ	Dornier 328-310 (328JET)	3194	ex D-BDXJ	♦

UNITED AIR LINES   United (UA/UAL)   Chicago-O'Hare Intl, IL/San Francisco-Intl, CA (ORD/SFO)

Member of Star Alliance. Ex Continental aircraft are listed by last 3 digits within types.

☐ N801UA	Airbus A319-131	0686	ex D-AVYI	4001
☐ N802UA	Airbus A319-131	0690	ex D-AVYO	4002
☐ N803UA	Airbus A319-131	0748	ex D-AVYL	4003
☐ N804UA	Airbus A319-131	0759	ex D-AVYR	4004
☐ N805UA	Airbus A319-131	0783	ex D-AVYY	4005
☐ N806UA	Airbus A319-131	0788	ex D-AVYW	4006
☐ N807UA	Airbus A319-131	0798	ex D-AVYX	4007
☐ N808UA	Airbus A319-131	0804	ex D-AVYF	4008
☐ N809UA	Airbus A319-131	0825	ex D-AVYZ	4009
☐ N810UA	Airbus A319-131	0843	ex D-AVYR	4010
☐ N811UA	Airbus A319-131	0847	ex D-AVYB	4011
☐ N812UA	Airbus A319-131	0850	ex D-AVYK	4012
☐ N813UA	Airbus A319-131	0858	ex D-AVYP	4013
☐ N814UA	Airbus A319-131	0862	ex D-AVYT	4014
☐ N815UA	Airbus A319-131	0867	ex D-AVYU	4015
☐ N816UA	Airbus A319-131	0871	ex D-AVYY	4016
☐ N817UA	Airbus A319-131	0873	ex D-AVYX	4017
☐ N818UA	Airbus A319-131	0882	ex D-AVYE	4018
☐ N819UA	Airbus A319-131	0893	ex D-AVYV	4019
☐ N820UA	Airbus A319-131	0898	ex D-AVYZ	4020
☐ N821UA	Airbus A319-131	0944	ex D-AVYC	4021
☐ N822UA	Airbus A319-131	0948	ex D-AVYE	4022
☐ N823UA	Airbus A319-131	0952	ex D-AVYF	4023
☐ N824UA	Airbus A319-131	0965	ex D-AVYH	4024
☐ N825UA	Airbus A319-131	0980	ex D-AVYN	4025
☐ N826UA	Airbus A319-131	0989	ex D-AVYU	4026
☐ N827UA	Airbus A319-131	1022	ex D-AVYD	4027
☐ N828UA	Airbus A319-131	1031	ex D-AVYF	4028
☐ N829UA	Airbus A319-131	1211	ex D-AVYC	4029
☐ N830UA	Airbus A319-131	1243	ex D-AVWI	4030
☐ N831UA	Airbus A319-131	1291	ex D-AVWF	4031
☐ N832UA	Airbus A319-131	1321	ex D-AVWQ	4032
☐ N833UA	Airbus A319-131	1401	ex D-AVYA	4033
☐ N834UA	Airbus A319-131	1420	ex D-AVYM	4034

☐ N835UA	Airbus A319-131	1426	ex D-AVYN	4035
☐ N836UA	Airbus A319-131	1460	ex D-AVYI	4036
☐ N837UA	Airbus A319-131	1474	ex D-AVYS	4037
☐ N838UA	Airbus A319-131	1477	ex D-AVYG	4038
☐ N839UA	Airbus A319-131	1507	ex D-AVYX	4039
☐ N840UA	Airbus A319-131	1522	ex D-AVYZ	4040
☐ N841UA	Airbus A319-131	1545	ex D-AVWK	4041
☐ N842UA	Airbus A319-131	1569	ex D-AVWA	4042
☐ N843UA	Airbus A319-131	1573	ex D-AVWE	4043
☐ N844UA	Airbus A319-131	1581	ex D-AVWT	4044
☐ N845UA	Airbus A319-131	1585	ex D-AVYD	4045
☐ N846UA	Airbus A319-131	1600	ex D-AVWW	4046
☐ N847UA	Airbus A319-131	1627	ex D-AVYB	4047
☐ N848UA	Airbus A319-131	1647	ex D-AVYK	4048
☐ N849UA	Airbus A319-131	1649	ex D-AVYP	4049
☐ N850UA	Airbus A319-131	1653	ex D-AVYR	4050
☐ N851UA	Airbus A319-131	1664	ex D-AVYX	4051
☐ N852UA	Airbus A319-131	1671	ex D-AVWD	4052
☐ N853UA	Airbus A319-131	1688	ex D-AVWM	4053
☐ N854UA	Airbus A319-131	1731	ex D-AVWS	4054
☐ N855UA	Airbus A319-131	1737	ex D-AVWU	4055
☐ N401UA	Airbus A320-232	0435	ex F-WWDD	4501
☐ N402UA	Airbus A320-232	0439	ex F-WWIJ	4502
☐ N403UA	Airbus A320-232	0442	ex F-WWIY	4703
☐ N404UA	Airbus A320-232	0450	ex F-WWII	4704
☐ N405UA	Airbus A320-232	0452	ex F-WWBF	4705
☐ N406UA	Airbus A320-232	0454	ex F-WWBJ	4506
☐ N407UA	Airbus A320-232	0456	ex F-WWDB	4507
☐ N408UA	Airbus A320-232	0457	ex F-WWDG	4508
☐ N409UA	Airbus A320-232	0462	ex F-WWDQ	4709
☐ N410UA	Airbus A320-232	0463	ex F-WWDV	4910
☐ N411UA	Airbus A320-232	0464	ex F-WWDX	4711
☐ N412UA	Airbus A320-232	0465	ex F-WWIM	4712
☐ N413UA	Airbus A320-232	0470	ex F-WWBM	4713
☐ N414UA	Airbus A320-232	0472	ex F-WWIU	4814
☐ N415UA	Airbus A320-232	0475	ex F-WWBP	4615
☐ N416UA	Airbus A320-232	0479	ex F-WWDH	4616
☐ N417UA	Airbus A320-232	0483	ex F-WWIT	4617
☐ N418UA	Airbus A320-232	0485	ex F-WWIZ	4618
☐ N419UA	Airbus A320-232	0487	ex F-WWDJ	4619
☐ N420UA	Airbus A320-232	0489	ex F-WWDM	4620
☐ N421UA	Airbus A320-232	0500	ex F-WWDZ	4621
☐ N422UA	Airbus A320-232	0503	ex F-WWIV	4622
☐ N423UA	Airbus A320-232	0504	ex F-WWBO	4623
☐ N424UA	Airbus A320-232	0506	ex F-WWBQ	4624
☐ N425UA	Airbus A320-232	0508	ex F-WWBY	4625
☐ N426UA	Airbus A320-232	0510	ex F-WWBZ	4626
☐ N427UA	Airbus A320-232	0512	ex F-WWDD	4627
☐ N428UA	Airbus A320-232	0523	ex F-WWDE	4628
☐ N429UA	Airbus A320-232	0539	ex F-WWIX	4629
☐ N430UA	Airbus A320-232	0568	ex F-WWDC	4630
☐ N431UA	Airbus A320-232	0571	ex F-WWDH	4631
☐ N432UA	Airbus A320-232	0587	ex F-WWBB	4632
☐ N433UA	Airbus A320-232	0589	ex F-WWBD	4633
☐ N434UA	Airbus A320-232	0592	ex F-WWBF	4634
☐ N435UA	Airbus A320-232	0613	ex F-WWBQ	4635
☐ N436UA	Airbus A320-232	0638	ex F-WWDE	4636
☐ N437UA	Airbus A320-232	0655	ex F-WWIK	4637
☐ N438UA	Airbus A320-232	0678	ex F-WWBJ	4838
☐ N439UA	Airbus A320-232	0683	ex F-WWDQ	4839
☐ N440UA	Airbus A320-232	0702	ex F-WWDP	4840
☐ N441UA	Airbus A320-232	0751	ex F-WWIU	4841
☐ N442UA	Airbus A320-232	0780	ex F-WWDQ	4842
☐ N443UA	Airbus A320-232	0820	ex F-WWBT	4643
☐ N444UA	Airbus A320-232	0824	ex F-WWBZ	4844
☐ N445UA	Airbus A320-232	0826	ex F-WWIL	4845
☐ N446UA	Airbus A320-232	0834	ex F-WWIP	4846
☐ N447UA	Airbus A320-232	0836	ex F-WWIR	4847
☐ N448UA	Airbus A320-232	0842	ex F-WWBF	4848
☐ N449UA	Airbus A320-232	0851	ex F-WWBJ	4849
☐ N451UA	Airbus A320-232	0865	ex F-WWBR	4851
☐ N452UA	Airbus A320-232	0955	ex F-WWBD	4852
☐ N453UA	Airbus A320-232	1001	ex F-WWBH	4853
☐ N454UA	Airbus A320-232	1104	ex F-WWDC	4654
☐ N455UA	Airbus A320-232	1105	ex F-WWDE	4655
☐ N456UA	Airbus A320-232	1128	ex F-WWIJ	4656
☐ N457UA	Airbus A320-232	1146	ex F-WWBM	4857
☐ N458UA	Airbus A320-232	1163	ex F-WWDK	4858
☐ N459UA	Airbus A320-232	1192	ex F-WWDX	4859
☐ N460UA	Airbus A320-232	1248	ex F-WWIS	4860
☐ N461UA	Airbus A320-232	1266	ex F-WWDC	4661
☐ N462UA	Airbus A320-232	1272	ex F-WWDI	4962

☐ N463UA	Airbus A320-232	1282	ex F-WWBJ	4663	Jim Briggs
☐ N464UA	Airbus A320-232	1290	ex F-WWBR	4664	
☐ N465UA	Airbus A320-232	1341	ex F-WWDP	4865	
☐ N466UA	Airbus A320-232	1343	ex F-WWDQ	4666	
☐ N467UA	Airbus A320-232	1359	ex F-WWBH	4867	
☐ N468UA	Airbus A320-232	1363	ex F-WWIE	4668	
☐ N469UA	Airbus A320-232	1409	ex F-WWDF	4869	
☐ N470UA	Airbus A320-232	1427	ex F-WWBN	4870	
☐ N471UA	Airbus A320-232	1432	ex F-WWBA	4871	
☐ N472UA	Airbus A320-232	1435	ex F-WWBC	4872	
☐ N473UA	Airbus A320-232	1469	ex F-WWDL	4873	
☐ N474UA	Airbus A320-232	1475	ex F-WWDQ	4874	
☐ N475UA	Airbus A320-232	1495	ex F-WWIC	4875	
☐ N476UA	Airbus A320-232	1508	ex F-WWBB	4876	
☐ N477UA	Airbus A320-232	1514	ex F-WWBF	4877	
☐ N478UA	Airbus A320-232	1533	ex F-WWIQ	4878	
☐ N479UA	Airbus A320-232	1538	ex F-WWIT	4879	
☐ N480UA	Airbus A320-232	1555	ex F-WWBP	4880	
☐ N481UA	Airbus A320-232	1559	ex F-WWDH	4881	
☐ N482UA	Airbus A320-232	1584	ex F-WWBN	4882	
☐ N483UA	Airbus A320-232	1586	ex F-WWBR	4883	
☐ N484UA	Airbus A320-232	1609	ex F-WWBZ	4884	
☐ N485UA	Airbus A320-232	1617	ex F-WWDD	4885	
☐ N486UA	Airbus A320-232	1620	ex F-WWDG	4886	
☐ N487UA	Airbus A320-232	1669	ex F-WWIJ	4887	
☐ N488UA	Airbus A320-232	1680	ex F-WWBF	4888	
☐ N489UA	Airbus A320-232	1702	ex F-WWIT	4889	
☐ N490UA	Airbus A320-232	1728	ex F-WWBI	4890	
☐ N491UA	Airbus A320-232	1741	ex F-WWBU	4891	
☐ N492UA	Airbus A320-232	1755	ex F-WWDZ	4892	
☐ N493UA	Airbus A320-232	1821	ex F-WWIO	4893	
☐ N494UA	Airbus A320-232	1840	ex F-WWDC	4894	
☐ N495UA	Airbus A320-232	1842	ex F-WWBP	4895	
☐ N496UA	Airbus A320-232	1845	ex F-WWDR	4896	
☐ N497UA	Airbus A320-232	1847	ex F-WWDE	4897	
☐ N498UA	Airbus A320-232	1865	ex F-WWIK	4898	
☐ N16701	Boeing 737-724/W	28762/29	ex N1786B	0701	
☐ N24702	Boeing 737-724/W	28763/32		0702	
☐ N16703	Boeing 737-724/W	28764/37		0703	
☐ N14704	Boeing 737-724/W	28765/43		0704	
☐ N25705	Boeing 737-724/W	28766/46		0705	
☐ N24706	Boeing 737-724/W	28767/47		0706	
☐ N23707	Boeing 737-724/W	28768/48	ex N1787B	0707	
☐ N23708	Boeing 737-724/W	28769/52		0708	
☐ N16709	Boeing 737-724/W	28779/93		0709	
☐ N15710	Boeing 737-724/W	28780/94		0710	
☐ N54711	Boeing 737-724/W	28782/97	ex N1786B	0711	
☐ N15712	Boeing 737-724/W	28783/105	ex N1786B	0712	
☐ N16713	Boeing 737-724/W	28784/107	ex N1786B	0713	
☐ N33714	Boeing 737-724/W	28785/119	ex N1786B	0714	
☐ N24715	Boeing 737-724/W	28786/125	ex N1795B	0715	
☐ N13716	Boeing 737-724/W	28787/156	ex N1782B	0716	
☐ N29717	Boeing 737-724/W	28936/182	ex N1786B	0717	
☐ N13718	Boeing 737-724/W	28937/185	ex N1786B	0718	
☐ N17719	Boeing 737-724/W	28938/195	ex N1786B	0719	
☐ N13720	Boeing 737-724/W	28939/214	ex N1786B	0720	
☐ N23721	Boeing 737-724/W	28940/219		0721	
☐ N27722	Boeing 737-724/W	28789/247	ex N1786B	0722	
☐ N21723	Boeing 737-724/W	28790/253	ex N1787B	0723	
☐ N27724	Boeing 737-724/W	28791/283	ex N1787B	0724	
☐ N39726	Boeing 737-724/W	28796/315	ex N1787B	0726	
☐ N38727	Boeing 737-724/W	28797/317	ex N1786B	0727	
☐ N39728	Boeing 737-724/W	28944/321	ex N1786B	0728	
☐ N24729	Boeing 737-724/W	28945/325	ex N1784B	0729	
☐ N17730	Boeing 737-724/W	28798/338	ex N1786B	0730	
☐ N14731	Boeing 737-724/W	28799/346	ex N1786B	0731	
☐ N16732	Boeing 737-724/W	28948/352	ex N60436	0732	
☐ N27733	Boeing 737-724/W	28800/364	ex N1786B	0733	Sir Samuel J LeFrak
☐ N27734	Boeing 737-724/W	28949/371	ex N1786B	0734	
☐ N14735	Boeing 737-724/W	28950/376	ex N1786B	0735	
☐ N24736	Boeing 737-724/W	28803/380	ex N1786B	0736	
☐ N13750	Boeing 737-724/W	28941/286		0750	
☐ N15751	Boeing 737-71Q/W	29047/235	ex HP-1369CMP	0751	wfs♦
☐ N17752	Boeing 737-71Q/W	29048/288	ex HP-1370CMP		o/o♦
☐ N25201	Boeing 737-824/W	28958/443	ex N1786B	0201	
☐ N24202	Boeing 737-824/W	30429/581	ex N1786B	0202	
☐ N33203	Boeing 737-824/W	30613/591	ex N1786B	0203	
☐ N35204	Boeing 737-824/W	30576/606	ex N1795B	0204	
☐ N27205	Boeing 737-824/W	30577/615	ex N1786B	0205	
☐ N11206	Boeing 737-824/W	30578/618	ex N1786B	0206	
☐ N36207	Boeing 737-824/W	30579/627	ex N1786B	0207	

☐ N26208	Boeing 737-824/W	30580/644	ex N1786B	0208
☐ N33209	Boeing 737-824/W	30581/647	ex N1786B	0209
☐ N26210	Boeing 737-824/W	28770/56		0210
☐ N24211	Boeing 737-824/W	28771/58		0211
☐ N24212	Boeing 737-824/W	28772/63		0212
☐ N27213	Boeing 737-824/W	28773/65		0213
☐ N14214	Boeing 737-824/W	28774/74		0214
☐ N26215	Boeing 737-824/W	28775/76		0215
☐ N12216	Boeing 737-824/W	28776/79		0216
☐ N16217	Boeing 737-824/W	28777/81		0217
☐ N12218	Boeing 737-824/W	28778/84		0218
☐ N14219	Boeing 737-824/W	28781/88		0219
☐ N18220	Boeing 737-824/W	28929/134	ex N60436	0220
☐ N12221	Boeing 737-824/W	28930/153	ex N1796B	0221
☐ N34222	Boeing 737-824/W	28931/159		0222
☐ N18223	Boeing 737-824/W	28932/162	ex N1786B	0223
☐ N24224	Boeing 737-824/W	28933/165	ex N1782B	0224
☐ N12225	Boeing 737-824/W	28934/168	ex N1782B	0225
☐ N26226	Boeing 737-824/W	28935/171	ex N1787B	0226
☐ N13227	Boeing 737-824/W	28788/262	ex N1787B	0227
☐ N14228	Boeing 737-824/W	28792/281	ex N1787B	0228
☐ N17229	Boeing 737-824/W	28793/287	ex N1786B	0229
☐ N14230	Boeing 737-824/W	28794/296	ex N1787B	0230
☐ N14231	Boeing 737-824/W	28795/300	ex N1787B	0231
☐ N26232	Boeing 737-824/W	28942/304		0232
☐ N17233	Boeing 737-824/W	28943/328	ex N1787B	0233
☐ N16234	Boeing 737-824/W	28946/334	ex N1787B	0234
☐ N14235	Boeing 737-824/W	28947/342		0235
☐ N35236	Boeing 737-824/W	28801/367	ex N1786B	0236
☐ N14237	Boeing 737-824/W	28802/374		0237
☐ N12238	Boeing 737-824/W	28804/386	ex N1786B	0238
☐ N27239	Boeing 737-824/W	28951/391	ex N1787B	0239
☐ N14240	Boeing 737-824/W	28952/394	ex N1786B	0240
☐ N54241	Boeing 737-824/W	28953/395	ex N1787B	0241
☐ N14242	Boeing 737-824/W	28805/402	ex N1786B	0242
☐ N18243	Boeing 737-824/W	28806/403	ex N1786B	0243
☐ N17244	Boeing 737-824/W	28954/409	ex N1787B	0244
☐ N17245	Boeing 737-824/W	28955/411	ex N1786B	0245
☐ N27246	Boeing 737-824/W	28956/413	ex N1786B	0246
☐ N36247	Boeing 737-824/W	28807/431	ex N1786B	0247
☐ N13248	Boeing 737-824/W	28808/435	ex N1786B	0248
☐ N14249	Boeing 737-824/W	28809/438	ex N1786B	0249
☐ N14250	Boeing 737-824/W	28957/441	ex N1786B	0250
☐ N73251	Boeing 737-824/W	30582/650	ex N1786B	0251
☐ N37252	Boeing 737-824/W	30583/656	ex N1787B	0252
☐ N37253	Boeing 737-824/W	30584/660		0253
☐ N76254	Boeing 737-824/W	30779/667	ex N1786B	0254
☐ N37255	Boeing 737-824/W	30610/686	ex N1787B	0255
☐ N73256	Boeing 737-824/W	30611/692	ex N1787B	0256
☐ N38257	Boeing 737-824/W	30612/706	ex N1786B	0257
☐ N77258	Boeing 737-824/W	30802/708	ex N1786B	0258
☐ N73259	Boeing 737-824/W	30803/854	ex N1786B	0259
☐ N35260	Boeing 737-824/W	30855/862	ex N1786B	0260
☐ N77261	Boeing 737-824/W	31582/897	ex N1786B	0261
☐ N33262	Boeing 737-824/W	32402/901	ex N1786B	0262
☐ N37263	Boeing 737-824/W	31583/906	ex N1786B	0263
☐ N33264	Boeing 737-824/W	31584/916	ex N1786B	0264
☐ N76265	Boeing 737-824/W	31585/928	ex N1786B	0265
☐ N33266	Boeing 737-824/W	32403/930		0266
☐ N37267	Boeing 737-824/W	31586/939	ex N1786B	0267
☐ N38268	Boeing 737-824/W	31587/957	ex N1786B	0268
☐ N76269	Boeing 737-824/W	31588/966	ex N1786B	0269
☐ N73270	Boeing 737-824/W	31632/970	ex N1787B	0270
☐ N35271	Boeing 737-824/W	31589/982	ex N1786B	0271
☐ N36272	Boeing 737-824/W	31590/987	ex N1795B	0272
☐ N37273	Boeing 737-824/W	31591/1012	ex N1787B	0273
☐ N37274	Boeing 737-824/W	31592/1062		0274
☐ N73275	Boeing 737-824/W	31593/1077		0275
☐ N73276	Boeing 737-824/W	31594/1079		0276
☐ N37277	Boeing 737-824/W	31595/1099		0277
☐ N73278	Boeing 737-824/W	31596/1390		0278
☐ N79279	Boeing 737-824/W	31597/1411	ex N1787B	0279
☐ N36280	Boeing 737-824/W	31598/1423		0280
☐ N37281	Boeing 737-824/W	31599/1425		0281
☐ N34282	Boeing 737-824/W	31634/1440		0282
☐ N73283	Boeing 737-824/W	31606/1456		0283
☐ N33284	Boeing 737-824/W	31635/1475		0284
☐ N78285	Boeing 737-824/W	33452/1540		0285
☐ N33286	Boeing 737-824/W	31600/1506		0286
☐ N37287	Boeing 737-824/W	31636/1509		0287
☐ N76288	Boeing 737-824/W	33451/1516		0288
☐ N33289	Boeing 737-824/W	31607/1542	ex N1786B	0289
☐ N37290	Boeing 737-824/W	31601/1567		0290

☐ N73291	Boeing 737-824/W	33454/1611		0291	
☐ N33292	Boeing 737-824/W	33455/1622		0292	
☐ N37293	Boeing 737-824/W	33453/1743		0293	
☐ N33294	Boeing 737-824/W	34000/1762		0294	
☐ N77295	Boeing 737-824/W	34001/1779		0295	
☐ N77296	Boeing 737-824/W	34002/1787		0296	
☐ N39297	Boeing 737-824/W	34003/1791		0297	
☐ N37298	Boeing 737-824/W	34004/1813		0298	
☐ N73299	Boeing 737-824/W	34005/1821	ex N1786B	0299	
☐ N78501	Boeing 737-824/W	31602/1994	ex N1786B	0501	
☐ N76502	Boeing 737-824/W	31603/2017		0502	
☐ N76503	Boeing 737-824/W	33461/2023		0503	
☐ N76504	Boeing 737-824/W	31604/2035		0504	
☐ N76505	Boeing 737-824/W	32834/2048	ex N1786B	0505	
☐ N78506	Boeing 737-824/W	32832/2065		0506	
☐ N87507	Boeing 737-824/W	31637/2487	ex N1786B	0507	
☐ N76508	Boeing 737-824/W	31639/2514		0508	
☐ N78509	Boeing 737-824/W	31638/2523	ex N1787B	0509	
☐ N77510	Boeing 737-824/W	32828/2579		0510	
☐ N78511	Boeing 737-824/W	33459/2598		0511	
☐ N87512	Boeing 737-824/W	33458/2602		0512	
☐ N87513	Boeing 737-824/W	31621/2655		0513	
☐ N76514	Boeing 737-824/W	31626/2680		0514	
☐ N76515	Boeing 737-824/W	31623/2713		0515	
☐ N76516	Boeing 737-824/W	37096/2718		0516	Star Alliance c/s
☐ N76517	Boeing 737-824/W	31628/2723		0517	
☐ N77518	Boeing 737-824/W	31605/2768		0518	Capt Marlon Green
☐ N76519	Boeing 737-824/W	30132/3138	ex N1796B	0519	
☐ N77520	Boeing 737-824/W	31658/3158	ex N1786B	0520	
☐ N79521	Boeing 737-824/W	31662/3169	ex N1796B	0521	
☐ N76522	Boeing 737-824/W	31660/3175	ex N1786B	0522	
☐ N76523	Boeing 737-824/W	37101/3216	ex N1786B	0523	
☐ N78524	Boeing 737-824/W	31642/3224		0524	
☐ N77525	Boeing 737-824/W	31659/3253	ex N1787B	0525	
☐ N76526	Boeing 737-824/W	38700/3289		0526	
☐ N87527	Boeing 737-824/W	38701/3305		0527	
☐ N76528	Boeing 737-824/W	31663/3464		0528	
☐ N76529	Boeing 737-824/W	31652/3490		0529	
☐ N77530	Boeing 737-824/W	39998/3521		0530	
☐ N87531	Boeing 737-824/W	39999/3549		0531	
☐ N30401	Boeing 737-924/W	30118/820		0401	
☐ N79402	Boeing 737-924/W	30119/857		0402	
☐ N38403	Boeing 737-924/W	30120/884	ex N1786B	0403	
☐ N32404	Boeing 737-924/W	30121/893	ex N1787B	0404	
☐ N72405	Boeing 737-924/W	30122/911	ex N1786B	0405	
☐ N73406	Boeing 737-924/W	30123/943	ex N1786B	0406	
☐ N35407	Boeing 737-924/W	30124/951	ex N1786B	0407	
☐ N37408	Boeing 737-924/W	30125/962	ex N1787B	0408	
☐ N37409	Boeing 737-924/W	30126/1004	ex N1787B	0409	
☐ N75410	Boeing 737-924/W	30127/1021	ex N1786B	0410	
☐ N71411	Boeing 737-924/W	30128/1052		0411	
☐ N31412	Boeing 737-924/W	30129/1112		0412	
☐ N37413	Boeing 737-924ER/W	31664/2474		0413	
☐ N47414	Boeing 737-924ER/W	32827/2490	ex N1787B	0414	
☐ N39415	Boeing 737-924ER/W	32826/2516		0415	
☐ N39416	Boeing 737-924ER/W	37093/2528		0416	
☐ N38417	Boeing 737-924ER/W	31665/2541		0417	
☐ N39418	Boeing 737-924ER/W	33456/2547		0418	
☐ N37419	Boeing 737-924ER/W	31666/2553		0419	
☐ N37420	Boeing 737-924ER/W	33457/2565		0420	
☐ N27421	Boeing 737-924ER/W	37094/2577		0421	
☐ N37422	Boeing 737-924ER/W	31620/2614		0422	
☐ N39423	Boeing 737-924ER/W	32829/2645		0423	
☐ N38424	Boeing 737-924ER/W	37095/2651		0424	
☐ N75425	Boeing 737-924ER/W	33460/2657		0425	
☐ N75426	Boeing 737-924ER/W	31622/2676		0426	
☐ N37427	Boeing 737-924ER/W	37097/2707		0427	
☐ N75428	Boeing 737-924ER/W	31633/2737		0428	
☐ N75429	Boeing 737-924ER/W	30130/2750		0429	
☐ N77430	Boeing 737-924ER/W	37098/2774	ex N1786B	0430	
☐ N77431	Boeing 737-924ER/W	32833/2787		0431	
☐ N75432	Boeing 737-924ER/W	32835/2817		0432	
☐ N75433	Boeing 737-924ER/W	33527/2842		0433	
☐ N37434	Boeing 737-924ER/W	33528/2891		0434	
☐ N75435	Boeing 737-924ER/W	33529/2916		0435	
☐ N75436	Boeing 737-924ER/W	33531/2947		0436	
☐ N37437	Boeing 737-924ER/W	33532/2959		0437	
☐ N78438	Boeing 737-924ER/W	33533/2971		0438	
☐ N57439	Boeing 737-924ER/W	33534/2990	ex N1786B	0439	
☐ N45440	Boeing 737-924ER/W	33535/2996		0440	
☐ N53441	Boeing 737-924ER/W	30131/3014	ex N1787B	0441	
☐ N53442	Boeing 737-924ER/W	33536/3027		0442	

☐ N38443	Boeing 737-924ER/W	31655/3393	ex N1786B	0443	
☐ N36444	Boeing 737-924ER/W	31643/3417	ex N1786B	0444	
☐ N73445	Boeing 737-924ER/W	40000/3615		0445	
☐ N38446	Boeing 737-924ER/W	31661/3894		0446	
☐ N36447	Boeing 737-924ER/W	31650/3924		0447	
☐ N78448	Boeing 737-924FR/W	40003/3942		0448	
☐ N81449	Boeing 737-924ER/W	31651/3978		0449	
☐ N39450	Boeing 737-924ER/W	40004/3984		0450	
☐ N38451	Boeing 737-924ER/W	31646/3990		0451	
☐ N68452	Boeing 737-924ER/W	40005/4032		0452	
☐ N68453	Boeing 737-924ER/W	41742/4052		0453	
☐ N38454	Boeing 737-924ER/W	31640/4068		0454	
☐ N34455	Boeing 737-924ER/W	41743/4086		0455	
☐ N37456	Boeing 737-924ER/W	37205/4164		0456	
☐ N28457	Boeing 737-924ER/W	41744/4182		0457	
☐ N38458	Boeing 737-924ER/W	37199/4188		0458	
☐ N38459	Boeing 737-924ER/W	37206/4218		0459	
☐ N34460	Boeing 737-924ER/W	37200/4224		0460	
☐ N39461	Boeing 737-924ER/W	37201/4230		0461	
☐ N37462	Boeing 737-924ER/W	37207/4254		0462	
☐ N39463	Boeing 737-924ER/W	37208/4260		0463	
☐ N37464	Boeing 737-924ER/W	41745/4290		0464	
☐ N37465	Boeing 737-924ER/W	36599/4302		0465	
☐ N37466	Boeing 737-924ER/W	31644/4326		0466	
☐ N38467	Boeing 737-924ER/W	33537/4344		0467	
☐ N37468	Boeing 737-924ER/W	32836/4356		0468	
☐ N36469	Boeing 737-924ER/W	36600/4374		0469	
☐ N37470	Boeing 737-924ER/W	37099/4392		0470	
☐ N37471	Boeing 737-924ER/W	37102/4408		0471	
☐ N36472	Boeing 737-924ER/W	31653/4436		0472	
☐ N38473	Boeing 737-924ER/W	38702/4452		0473	
☐ N37474	Boeing 737-924ER/W	31648/4457		0474	
☐ N37475	Boeing 737-924ER/W	37100/4473		0475	
☐ N39476	Boeing 737-924ER/W	38703/4506		0476	o/o
☐ N27477	Boeing 737-924ER/W	31647/4531		0477	
☐ N28478	Boeing 737-924ER/W	31649/4546		0478	
☐ N68801	Boeing 737-924ER/W	42740/4549		801	
☐ N68802	Boeing 737-924ER/W	42739/4567		802	
☐ N66803	Boeing 737-924ER/W	42817/4589		803	
☐ N69804	Boeing 737-924ER/W	42816/4614		804	
☐ N68805	Boeing 737-924ER/W	42818/4625		805	
☐ N69806	Boeing 737-924ER/W	42742/4661		806	
☐ N68807	Boeing 737-924ER/W	42819/4686		807	
☐ N68808	Boeing 737-924ER/W	42820/4690		808	
☐ N64809	Boeing 737-924ER/W	42821/4718		809	
☐ N69810	Boeing 737-924ER/W	42744/4733		810	
☐ N68811	Boeing 737-924ER/W	42175/4737		811	
☐ N67812	Boeing 737-924ER/W	43530/4758		812	
☐ N69813	Boeing 737-924ER/W	43531/4773		813	
☐ N66814	Boeing 737-924ER/W	42745/4787		814	
☐ N67815	Boeing 737-924ER/W	43532/4795		815	
☐ N69816	Boeing 737-924ER/W	42176/4802		816	
☐ N68817	Boeing 737-924ER/W	42747/4809		817	
☐ N69818	Boeing 737-924ER/W	42177/4825		818	
☐ N69819	Boeing 737-924ER/W	43533/4836		819	
☐ N63820	Boeing 737-924ER/W	43534/4847		820	
☐ N68821	Boeing 737-924ER/W	43535/4868		821	8000th 737 built
☐ N68822	Boeing 737-924ER/W	42178/4876		822	
☐ N68823	Boeing 737-924ER/W	42746/4894		823	
☐ N69824	Boeing 737-924ER/W	42179/4907		824	
☐ N66825	Boeing 737-924ER/W	42748/4918		825	
☐ N69826	Boeing 737-924ER/W	42180/4939		826	
☐ N67827	Boeing 737-924ER/W	44581/4950		827	♦
☐ N66828	Boeing 737-924ER/W	44580/4958		828	♦
☐ N69829	Boeing 737-924ER/W	44561/4965			♦
☐ N69830	Boeing 737-924ER/W	44560/4976			♦
☐ N66831	Boeing 737-924ER/W	44562/5029	ex N5200K	831	♦
☐ N65832	Boeing 737-924ER/W	44563/5047		832	♦
☐ N69833	Boeing 737-924ER/W	44565/5074		833	♦
☐ N68834	Boeing 737-924ER/W	44564/5092		834	♦
☐ N69835	Boeing 737-924ER/W	60087/5107		835	♦
☐ N68836	Boeing 737-924ER/W	60088/5118		836	♦
☐ N66837	Boeing 737-924ER/W	60122/5168		837	♦
☐ N69838	Boeing 737-924ER/W	60121/5183		838	♦
☐ N69839	Boeing 737-924ER/W	60316/5214		839	♦
☐ N66840	Boeing 737-924ER/W	42181/5246		841	♦
☐ N68841	Boeing 737-924ER/W	42182/5254		842	♦
☐ N68842	Boeing 737-924ER/W	42183/5258		843	♦
☐ N68843	Boeing 737-924ER/W	60317/5271		840	♦
☐ N64844	Boeing 737-924ER/W	42184/5282		844	♦
☐ N67845	Boeing 737-924ER/W	42185/5286		855	♦
☐ N67846	Boeing 737-924ER/W	42186/5294		846	♦
☐ N69847	Boeing 737-924ER/W	42187/5328		847	♦

☐ N66848	Boeing 737-924ER/W	42188/5339		848	♦
☐ N62849	Boeing 737-924ER/W	42204/5366		849	♦
☐ N68880	Boeing 737-924ER/W	42199/5383		0880	♦
☐ N61881	Boeing 737-924ER/W	42200/5408		0881	♦
☐ N61882	Boeing 737-924ER/W	42201/5416		0882	o/o♦
☐ N62883	Boeing 737-924ER/W	42202/		0883	o/o♦
☐ N62884	Boeing 737-924ER/W	42203/		0884	o/o♦
☐ N69885	Boeing 737-924ER/W	42189/		0885	o/o♦
☐ N61886	Boeing 737-924ER/W	42190/		0886	o/o♦
☐ N61887	Boeing 737-924ER/W	42192/		0887	o/o♦
☐ N69888	Boeing 737-924ER/W	42191/		0888	o/o♦
☐ N62889	Boeing 737-924ER/W	42193/		0899	o/o♦
☐ N63890	Boeing 737-924ER/W	42194/		0890	o/o♦
☐ N68891	Boeing 737-924ER/W	42196/		0891	o/o♦
☐ N62892	Boeing 737-924ER/W	42195/		0892	o/o♦
☐ N104UA	Boeing 747-422	26902/1141		8104	
☐ N105UA	Boeing 747-451	26473/985	ex N60659	8105	
☐ N107UA	Boeing 747-422	26900/1168		8107	
☐ N116UA	Boeing 747-422	26908/1193		8116	
☐ N117UA	Boeing 747-422	28810/1197		8117	
☐ N118UA	Boeing 747-422	28811/1201		8118	
☐ N119UA	Boeing 747-422	28812/1207		8419	
☐ N120UA	Boeing 747-422	29166/1209		8120	
☐ N121UA	Boeing 747-422	29167/1211		8121	
☐ N122UA	Boeing 747-422	29168/1218		8122	
☐ N127UA	Boeing 747-422	28813/1221		8127	
☐ N128UA	Boeing 747-422	30023/1245		8128	
☐ N171UA	Boeing 747-422	24322/733		8171	
☐ N174UA	Boeing 747-422	24381/762		8174	
☐ N175UA	Boeing 747-422	24382/806		8175	
☐ N177UA	Boeing 747-422	24384/819		8177	
☐ N178UA	Boeing 747-422	24385/820		8178	
☐ N179UA	Boeing 747-422	25158/866		8179	
☐ N180UA	Boeing 747-422	25224/867		8180	
☐ N181UA	Boeing 747-422	25278/881	ex N6005C	8181	
☐ N182UA	Boeing 747-422	25279/882		8182	
☐ N194UA	Boeing 747-422	26892/1088		8494	
☐ N195UA	Boeing 747-422	26899/1113		8195	[TUP]
☐ N197UA	Boeing 747-422	26901/1121		8197	
☐ N199UA	Boeing 747-422	28717/1126		8199	
☐ N502UA	Boeing 757-222/W	24623/246		5702	
☐ N505UA	Boeing 757-222/W	24626/254		5705	
☐ N509UA	Boeing 757-222	24763/284		5409	
☐ N510UA	Boeing 757-222/W	24780/290		5710	
☐ N512UA	Boeing 757-222/W	24809/298		5712	
☐ N513UA	Boeing 757-222	24810/299		5413	[GYR]
☐ N514UA	Boeing 757-222	24839/305		5414	
☐ N516UA	Boeing 757-222	24860/307		5416	
☐ N518UA	Boeing 757-222/W	24871/311		5718	
☐ N520UA	Boeing 757-222	24890/313		5420	[GYR]
☐ N522UA	Boeing 757-222	24931/320		5422	
☐ N523UA	Boeing 757-222	24932/329		5423	[GYR]
☐ N526UA	Boeing 757-222	24994/339		5426	
☐ N528UA	Boeing 757-222	25018/346		5428	
☐ N529UA	Boeing 757-222	25019/352		5429	
☐ N533UA	Boeing 757-222	25073/367		5433	[TUS]
☐ N535UA	Boeing 757-222	25130/373		5435	
☐ N536UA	Boeing 757-222	25156/380		5436	[VCV]
☐ N537UA	Boeing 757-222	25157/381		5437	
☐ N543UA	Boeing 757-222ER	25698/401		5543	
☐ N544UA	Boeing 757-222ER/W	25322/405		5544	
☐ N545UA	Boeing 757-222ER	25323/406		5545	
☐ N546UA	Boeing 757-222ER/W	25367/413		5546	
☐ N547UA	Boeing 757-222ER	25368/414		5547	
☐ N548UA	Boeing 757-222ER	25396/420		5548	
☐ N549UA	Boeing 757-222/W	25397/421		5949	[GSO]
☐ N550UA	Boeing 757-222ER	25398/426		5550	
☐ N551UA	Boeing 757-222ER	25399/427		5551	[GYR]
☐ N552UA	Boeing 757-222ER	26641/431		5552	[GYR]
☐ N553UA	Boeing 757-222	25277/434		5453	[GYR]
☐ N554UA	Boeing 757-222/W	26644/435		5754	[GYR]
☐ N555UA	Boeing 757-222/W	26647/442		5755	[GYR]
☐ N556UA	Boeing 757-222	26650/447		5456	[GYR]
☐ N557UA	Boeing 757-222	26653/454		5757	[GYR]
☐ N558UA	Boeing 757-222	26654/462		5458	[GYR]
☐ N559UA	Boeing 757-222	26657/467		5459	[GYR]
☐ N560UA	Boeing 757-222	26660/469		5760	[GYR]
☐ N561UA	Boeing 757-222	26661/479		5461	[GYR]
☐ N562UA	Boeing 757-222	26664/487		5462	[GYR]
☐ N563UA	Boeing 757-222	26665/488		5463	[GYR]
☐ N564UA	Boeing 757-222	26666/490		5464	[GYR]

☐ N565UA	Boeing 757-222	26669/492		5465	[GYR]
☐ N566UA	Boeing 757-222	26670/494		5466	[GYR]
☐ N568UA	Boeing 757-222/W	26674/498		5468
☐ N587UA	Boeing 757-222/W	26713/570		5687
☐ N588UA	Boeing 757-222/W	26717/571		5688
☐ N589UA	Boeing 757-222ER/W	20707/773	ex N3509J	5589
☐ N590UA	Boeing 757-222ER/W	28708/785		5590
☐ N595UA	Boeing 757-222ER/W	28748/789		5595
☐ N596UA	Boeing 757-222ER/W	28749/794		5596
☐ N597UA	Boeing 757-222/W	28750/841		5597
☐ N598UA	Boeing 757-222/W	28751/844	ex N1787B	5598
☐ N58101	Boeing 757-224/W	27291/614		0101
☐ N14102	Boeing 757-224/W	27292/619		0102
☐ N33103	Boeing 757-224/W	27293/623		0103
☐ N17104	Boeing 757-224/W	27294/629		104
☐ N17105	Boeing 757-224/W	27295/632		0105
☐ N14106	Boeing 757-224/W	27296/637		0106 Sam E Ashmore
☐ N14107	Boeing 757-224/W	27297/641		107
☐ N21108	Boeing 757-224/W	27298/645		0108
☐ N12109	Boeing 757-224/W	27299/648		0109
☐ N13110	Boeing 757-224/W	27300/650		110
☐ N57111	Boeing 757-224/W	27301/652		0111
☐ N18112	Boeing 757-224/W	27302/653		0112
☐ N13113	Boeing 757-224/W	27555/668		0113
☐ N12114	Boeing 757-224/W	27556/682		0114
☐ N14115	Boeing 757-224/W	27557/686		0115
☐ N12116	Boeing 757-224/W	27558/702		0116
☐ N19117	Boeing 757-224/W	27559/706		0117
☐ N14118	Boeing 757-224/W	27560/748	ex (N19118)	0118
☐ N18119	Boeing 757-224/W	27561/753		0119
☐ N14120	Boeing 757-224/W	27562/761		0120
☐ N14121	Boeing 757-224/W	27563/766		121
☐ N17122	Boeing 757-224/W	27564/768		0122
☐ N26123	Boeing 757-224/W	28966/781		123
☐ N29124	Boeing 757-224/W	27565/786		0124
☐ N12125	Boeing 757-224/W	28967/788	ex N1787B	0125
☐ N17126	Boeing 757-224/W	27566/790		126
☐ N48127	Boeing 757-224/W	28968/791		0127
☐ N17128	Boeing 757-224/W	27567/795		128
☐ N29129	Boeing 757-224/W	28969/796		129
☐ N19130	Boeing 757-224/W	28970/799		0130
☐ N34131	Boeing 757-224/W	28971/806		131
☐ N33132	Boeing 757-224/W	29281/809		132
☐ N17133	Boeing 757-224/W	29282/840		133
☐ N67134	Boeing 757-224/W	29283/848	ex N1800B	134
☐ N41135	Boeing 757-224/W	29284/851		0135
☐ N19136	Boeing 757-224/W	29285/856		0136
☐ N34137	Boeing 757-224/W	30229/899		0137
☐ N13138	Boeing 757-224/W	30351/903	ex N1795B	0138
☐ N17139	Boeing 757-224/W	30352/911		0139
☐ N41140	Boeing 757-224/W	30353/913		0140
☐ N19141	Boeing 757-224/W	30354/933		0141
☐ N75851	Boeing 757-324/W	32810/990		0851
☐ N57852	Boeing 757-324/W	32811/995		852
☐ N75853	Boeing 757-324/W	32812/997		853
☐ N75854	Boeing 757-324/W	32813/999		854
☐ N57855	Boeing 757-324/W	32814/1038		855
☐ N74856	Boeing 757-324/W	32815/1039		0856
☐ N57857	Boeing 757-324/W	32816/1040		0857
☐ N75858	Boeing 757-324/W	32817/1042		0858
☐ N56859	Boeing 757-324/W	32818/1043		859 last 757-300 built
☐ N73860	Boeing 757-33N/W	32584/972	ex N550TZ	860
☐ N75861	Boeing 757-33N/W	32585/976	ex N551TZ	861
☐ N57862	Boeing 757-33N/W	32586/978	ex N552TZ	863
☐ N57863	Boeing 757-33N/W	32587/980	ex N553TZ	863
☐ N57864	Boeing 757-33N/W	32588/985	ex N554TZ	864
☐ N77865	Boeing 757-33N/W	32589/1003	ex N555TZ	865
☐ N78866	Boeing 757-33N/W	32591/1007	ex N557TZ	866
☐ N77867	Boeing 757-33N/W	32592/1008	ex N558TZ	867
☐ N57868	Boeing 757-33N/W	32590/1017	ex N556TZ	868
☐ N57869	Boeing 757-33N/W	32593/1018	ex N559TZ	869
☐ N57870	Boeing 757-33N/W	33525/1031	ex N560TZ	0870
☐ N77871	Boeing 757-33N/W	33526/1032	ex N561TZ	871
☐ N68159	Boeing 767-224ER	30438/845		159	[GYR]
☐ N641UA	Boeing 767-322ER	25091/360		6341
☐ N642UA	Boeing 767-322ER	25092/367		6342
☐ N643UA	Boeing 767-322ER	25093/368		6343
☐ N644UA	Boeing 767-322ER	25094/369		6344
☐ N646UA	Boeing 767-322ER	25283/420		6346
☐ N647UA	Boeing 767-322ER	25284/424		6347
☐ N648UA	Boeing 767-322ER	25285/443		6348

☐ N649UA	Boeing 767-322ER	25286/444		6349
☐ N651UA	Boeing 767-322ER	25389/452		6351
☐ N652UA	Boeing 767-322ER	25390/457		6352
☐ N653UA	Boeing 767-322ER	25391/460		6353 Star Alliance c/s
☐ N654UA	Boeing 767-322ER	25392/462		6354
☐ N655UA	Boeing 767-322ER	25393/468		6355
☐ N656UA	Boeing 767-322ER	25394/472		6356
☐ N657UA	Boeing 767-322ER	27112/479		6357
☐ N658UA	Boeing 767-322ER	27113/480		6358
☐ N659UA	Boeing 767-322ER	27114/485		6359
☐ N660UA	Boeing 767-322ER	27115/494		6360
☐ N661UA	Boeing 767-322ER	27158/507		6361
☐ N662UA	Boeing 767-322ER	27159/513		6362
☐ N663UA	Boeing 767-322ER	27160/514		6363
☐ N664UA	Boeing 767-322ER/W	29236/707		6664
☐ N665UA	Boeing 767-322ER/W	29237/711		6665
☐ N666UA	Boeing 767-322ER/W	29238/715		6666
☐ N667UA	Boeing 767-322ER/W	29239/716		6667
☐ N668UA	Boeing 767-322ER/W	30024/742		6668
☐ N669UA	Boeing 767-322ER/W	30025/757		6669
☐ N670UA	Boeing 767-322ER/W	29240/763		6670
☐ N671UA	Boeing 767-322ER/W	30026/766		6671
☐ N672UA	Boeing 767-322ER/W	30027/773		6672
☐ N673UA	Boeing 767-322ER/W	29241/779		6673
☐ N674UA	Boeing 767-322ER/W	29242/782		6674
☐ N675UA	Boeing 767-322ER/W	29243/800		6675
☐ N676UA	Boeing 767-322ER/W	30028/834		6676
☐ N677UA	Boeing 767-322ER/W	30029/852		6677
☐ N66051	Boeing 767-424ER	29446/799	ex (N76401)	051
☐ N67052	Boeing 767-424ER	29447/805	ex (N87402)	052
☐ N59053	Boeing 767-424ER	29448/809	ex (N47403)	053
☐ N76054	Boeing 767-424ER	29449/816	ex (N87404)	054
☐ N76055	Boeing 767-424ER	29450/826		0055
☐ N66056	Boeing 767-424ER	29451/842		056
☐ N66057	Boeing 767-424ER	29452/859		057
☐ N67058	Boeing 767-424ER	29453/862		058
☐ N69059	Boeing 767-424ER	29454/864		0059
☐ N78060	Boeing 767-424ER	29455/866		060
☐ N68061	Boeing 767-424ER	29456/868		061
☐ N76062	Boeing 767-424ER	29457/869		0062
☐ N69063	Boeing 767-424ER	29458/872		063
☐ N76064	Boeing 767-424ER	29459/873		064
☐ N76065	Boeing 767-424ER	29460/876		065
☐ N77066	Boeing 767-424ER	29461/878		066
☐ N204UA	Boeing 777-222ER	28713/191		2904
☐ N206UA	Boeing 777-222ER	30212/216		2906
☐ N209UA	Boeing 777-222ER	30215/259		2609
☐ N210UA	Boeing 777-222	30216/264		2510
☐ N211UA	Boeing 777-222	30217/282		2511
☐ N212UA	Boeing 777-222	30218/293		2512
☐ N213UA	Boeing 777-222	30219/295		2513
☐ N214UA	Boeing 777-222	30220/296		2514
☐ N215UA	Boeing 777-222	30221/297		2515
☐ N216UA	Boeing 777-222ER	30549/291		2616
☐ N217UA	Boeing 777-222ER	30550/294		2617
☐ N218UA	Boeing 777-222ER	30222/317		2618 10 Years Star Alliance c/s
☐ N219UA	Boeing 777-222ER	30551/318		2619
☐ N220UA	Boeing 777-222ER	30223/340		2620
☐ N221UA	Boeing 777-222ER	30552/347		2621
☐ N222UA	Boeing 777-222ER	30553/352		2622
☐ N223UA	Boeing 777-222ER	30224/357		2623
☐ N224UA	Boeing 777-222ER	30225/375		2624
☐ N225UA	Boeing 777-222ER	30554/377		2625 Spirit of United
☐ N226UA	Boeing 777-222ER	30226/380		2626
☐ N227UA	Boeing 777-222ER	30555/381		2627
☐ N228UA	Boeing 777-222ER	30556/384		2628
☐ N229UA	Boeing 777-222ER	30557/388		2629
☐ N768UA	Boeing 777-222	26919/11		2368
☐ N769UA	Boeing 777-222	26921/12		2369
☐ N771UA	Boeing 777-222	26932/3	ex N7773	2371
☐ N772UA	Boeing 777-222	26930/5	ex (N77775)	2372
☐ N773UA	Boeing 777-222	26929/4	ex N7774	2473 Richard H Leung, Customer
☐ N774UA	Boeing 777-222	26936/2	ex N7772	2374
☐ N775UA	Boeing 777-222	26947/22		2475
☐ N776UA	Boeing 777-222	26937/27		2376
☐ N777UA	Boeing 777-222	26916/7		2377
☐ N778UA	Boeing 777-222	26940/34		2478
☐ N779UA	Boeing 777-222	26941/35		2379
☐ N780UA	Boeing 777-222	26944/36		2380
☐ N781UA	Boeing 777-222	26945/40		2481
☐ N782UA	Boeing 777-222ER	26948/57		2982

☐ N783UA	Boeing 777-222ER	26950/60		2983	
☐ N784UA	Boeing 777-222ER	26951/69		2984	
☐ N785UA	Boeing 777-222ER	26954/73		2985	
☐ N786UA	Boeing 777-222ER	26938/52		2986	
☐ N787UA	Boeing 777-222ER	26939/43		2987	
☐ N788UA	Boeing 777-222ER	26942/82		2988	
☐ N791UA	Boeing 777-222ER	26933/93		2991	
☐ N792UA	Boeing 777-222ER	26934/96		2992	
☐ N793UA	Boeing 777-222ER	26946/97		2993	
☐ N794UA	Boeing 777-222ER	26953/105		2994	Star Alliance c/s
☐ N795UA	Boeing 777-222ER	26927/108		2995	
☐ N796UA	Boeing 777-222ER	26931/112		2996	
☐ N797UA	Boeing 777-222ER	26924/116		2997	
☐ N798UA	Boeing 777-222ER	26928/123		2998	
☐ N799UA	Boeing 777-222ER	26926/139		2999	
☐ N78001	Boeing 777-224ER	27577/161		0001 Gordon M Bethune	
☐ N78002	Boeing 777-224ER	27578/165		002	
☐ N78003	Boeing 777-224ER	27579/167		003	
☐ N78004	Boeing 777-224ER	27580/169		004	
☐ N78005	Boeing 777-224ER	27581/177		005	
☐ N77006	Boeing 777-224ER	29476/183		006 Robert F Six	
☐ N74007	Boeing 777-224ER	29477/197		0007	
☐ N78008	Boeing 777-224ER	29478/200		0008	
☐ N78009	Boeing 777-224ER	29479/211		0009	
☐ N76010	Boeing 777-224ER	29480/220		010	
☐ N79011	Boeing 777-224ER	29859/227		0011	
☐ N77012	Boeing 777-224ER	29860/234		0012	
☐ N78013	Boeing 777-224ER	29861/243		013	
☐ N77014	Boeing 777-224ER	29862/253		014	
☐ N27015	Boeing 777-224ER	28678/273		015	
☐ N57016	Boeing 777-224ER	28679/279		016	
☐ N78017	Boeing 777-224ER	31679/391		017	
☐ N37018	Boeing 777-224ER	31680/397		018	
☐ N77019	Boeing 777-224ER	35547/617		019	
☐ N69020	Boeing 777-224ER	31687/625		020	
☐ N76021	Boeing 777-224ER	39776/858		021	
☐ N77022	Boeing 777-224ER	39777/868		022	
☐ N27901	Boeing 787-8	34821/45		0901	
☐ N26902	Boeing 787-8	34822/50		0902	
☐ N27903	Boeing 787-8	34823/52		0903	
☐ N20904	Boeing 787-8	34824/53		0904	
☐ N45905	Boeing 787-8	34825/55		0905	
☐ N26906	Boeing 787-8	34829/77		0906	
☐ N29907	Boeing 787-8	34830/117		0907	
☐ N27908	Boeing 787-8	36400/124		0908	
☐ N26909	Boeing 787-8	34827/135		0909	
☐ N26910	Boeing 787-8	34826/145		0910	
☐ N28912	Boeing 787-8	34828/186		0912	♦
☐ N30913	Boeing 787-8	35879/238		0913	♦
☐ N38950	Boeing 787-9	36401/181		0950	♦
☐ N19951	Boeing 787-9	36402/223		0951	♦
☐ N26952	Boeing 787-9	36403/263		0952	♦
☐ N35953	Boeing 787-9	36404/269	ex N8571C	0953	♦
☐ N13954	Boeing 787-9	36405/275		0954	♦
☐ N38955	Boeing 787-9	37814/297		0955	o/o♦
☐ N45956	Boeing 787-9	40918/324		0956	o/o♦
☐ N27957	Boeing 787-9	36409/334		0957	o/o♦
☐ N27958	Boeing 787-9	36406/342		0958	o/o♦
☐ N27959	Boeing 787-9	36407/348		0959	o/o♦
☐ N26960	Boeing 787-9	36408/355		0960	o/o♦
☐ N29961	Boeing 787-9	37811/363		0961	o/o♦
☐ N36962	Boeing 787-9	35880/365		0962	o/o♦
☐ N17963	Boeing 787-9	37812/390		0963	o/o♦
☐ N27964	Boeing 787-9	37813/398		0964	o/o♦
☐ N27965	Boeing 787-9	37815/402		0965	o/o♦
☐ N16944	Embraer ERJ-145EP	145045	ex PT-SZK	944	[IGM]♦
☐ N14945	Embraer ERJ-145EP	145049	ex PT-SZO	945	[IGM]♦
☐ N12946	Embraer ERJ-145EP	145052	ex PT-SZR	946	[IGM]♦
☐ N14947	Embraer ERJ-145EP	145054	ex PT-SZT	947	[IGM]♦
☐ N13949	Embraer ERJ-145LR	145057	ex PT-SZW	949	[IGM]♦

UNITED EXPRESS   United (UA)
Chicago-O'Hare Intl, IL/San Francisco-Intl, CA/Denver, CO (ORD/SFO/DEN)

☐ N81535	Beech 1900D	UE-147	Silver
☐ N81536	Beech 1900D	UE-152	Silver
☐ N53545	Beech 1900D	UE-185	Silver
☐ N81546	Beech 1900D	UE-187	Silver

☐ N69549	Beech 1900D	UE-194			Silver
☐ N81556	Beech 1900D	UE-239			Silver
☐ N87557	Beech 1900D	UE-246			Silver
☐ N830AS	Canadair CRJ-200ER	7236	ex C-FMNW		ExpressJet
☐ N832AS	Canadair CRJ-200ER	7243	ex C-FMNQ		ExpressJet
☐ N834AS	Canadair CRJ-200ER	7254	ex C-FMKV		ExpressJet
☐ N836AS	Canadair CRJ-200ER	7263	ex C-FMLU		ExpressJet
☐ N652BR	Canadair CRJ-200ER	7429	ex C-FMMQ	458	SkyWest♦
☐ N903SW	Canadair CRJ-200ER	7425	ex C-FMOI	7425	SkyWest
☐ N905SW	Canadair CRJ-200ER	7437	ex C-FMLB	7437	SkyWest
☐ N908SW	Canadair CRJ-200ER	7540	ex C-FMOW	7540	SkyWest
☐ N909SW	Canadair CRJ-200ER	7558	ex C-GJHL	7558	SkyWest
☐ N910SW	Canadair CRJ-200ER	7566	ex C-GJHY	7566	SkyWest
☐ N912SW	Canadair CRJ-200ER	7595	ex C-FMNH	7595	SkyWest
☐ N913SW	Canadair CRJ-200ER	7597	ex C-FMNX	7597	SkyWest
☐ N915SW	Canadair CRJ-200ER	7615	ex C-GKJQ	7615	SkyWest
☐ N916SW	Canadair CRJ-200ER	7634	ex C-FMLU	7634	SkyWest
☐ N917SW	Canadair CRJ-200ER	7641	ex C-FMMX	7641	SkyWest
☐ N918SW	Canadair CRJ-200ER	7645	ex C-FMKW	7645	SkyWest
☐ N919SW	Canadair CRJ-200ER	7657	ex C-FMNX	7657	SkyWest
☐ N920SW	Canadair CRJ-200ER	7660	ex C-FMOW	7660	SkyWest
☐ N923SW	Canadair CRJ-200ER	7664	ex C-FMLU	7664	SkyWest
☐ N924SW	Canadair CRJ-200ER	7681	ex C-FMLS	7681	SkyWest
☐ N925SW	Canadair CRJ-200ER	7682	ex C-FMLI	7682	SkyWest
☐ N926SW	Canadair CRJ-200ER	7687	ex C-FMNX	7687	SkyWest
☐ N927SW	Canadair CRJ-200ER	7693	ex C-FMNQ	7693	SkyWest
☐ N928SW	Canadair CRJ-200ER	7701	ex C-FMMX	7701	SkyWest
☐ N929SW	Canadair CRJ-200ER	7703	ex C-FMNB	7703	SkyWest
☐ N930SW	Canadair CRJ-200ER	7713	ex C-FMLV	7713	SkyWest
☐ N932SW	Canadair CRJ-200ER	7714	ex C-FMMT	7714	SkyWest
☐ N934SW	Canadair CRJ-200ER	7722	ex C-FMND	7722	SkyWest
☐ N935SW	Canadair CRJ-200ER	7725	ex C-FMOI	7725	SkyWest
☐ N936SW	Canadair CRJ-200ER	7726	ex C-FMMB	7726	SkyWest
☐ N937SW	Canadair CRJ-200ER	7735	ex C-FMKW	7735	SkyWest
☐ N938SW	Canadair CRJ-200ER	7741	ex C-FMLS	7741	SkyWest
☐ N939SW	Canadair CRJ-200ER	7742	ex C-FMLT	7742	SkyWest
☐ N941SW	Canadair CRJ-200ER	7750	ex C-FMOW	7750	SkyWest
☐ N943SW	Canadair CRJ-200ER	7762	ex C-FMMY	7762	SkyWest
☐ N945SW	Canadair CRJ-200ER	7770	ex C-FMLQ	7770	SkyWest
☐ N946SW	Canadair CRJ-200ER	7776	ex C-FMNW	7776	SkyWest
☐ N948SW	Canadair CRJ-200ER	7789	ex C-GXTU	7789	SkyWest
☐ N951SW	Canadair CRJ-200ER	7795	ex C-FMKW	7795 30th anniversary c/s	SkyWest
☐ N952SW	Canadair CRJ-200ER	7805	ex C-FMNH	7805	SkyWest
☐ N953SW	Canadair CRJ-200ER	7813	ex C-GZGP	7813	SkyWest
☐ N954SW	Canadair CRJ-200ER	7815	ex C-FMOI	7815	SkyWest
☐ N956SW	Canadair CRJ-200ER	7825	ex C-FMKW	7825	SkyWest
☐ N957SW	Canadair CRJ-200ER	7829	ex C-FMLI	7829	SkyWest
☐ N958SW	Canadair CRJ-200ER	7833	ex C-FMLV	7833	SkyWest
☐ N959SW	Canadair CRJ-200ER	7840	ex C-FMOW	7840	SkyWest
☐ N960SW	Canadair CRJ-200ER	7853	ex C-FMNB	7853	SkyWest
☐ N961SW	Canadair CRJ-200ER	7857	ex C-FMLB	7857	SkyWest
☐ N962SW	Canadair CRJ-200ER	7859	ex C-FMLI	7859	SkyWest
☐ N963SW	Canadair CRJ-200ER	7865	ex C-FMNH	7865	SkyWest
☐ N964SW	Canadair CRJ-200ER	7868	ex C-GZTD	7867	SkyWest
☐ N965SW	Canadair CRJ-200ER	7871	ex C-FVAZ	7871	SkyWest
☐ N967SW	Canadair CRJ-200ER	7872	ex C-FMND	7872	SkyWest
☐ N969SW	Canadair CRJ-200ER	7876	ex C-FMMB	7876	SkyWest
☐ N970SW	Canadair CRJ-200ER	7881	ex C-GZUJ	7881	SkyWest
☐ N971SW	Canadair CRJ-200ER	7947	ex C-FMLB	7947	SkyWest
☐ N973SW	Canadair CRJ-200ER	7949	ex C-FMLI	7949	SkyWest
☐ N975SW	Canadair CRJ-200ER	7951	ex C-FMLS	7951	SkyWest
☐ N976SW	Canadair CRJ-200ER	7952	ex C-FMLT	7952	SkyWest
☐ N978SW	Canadair CRJ-200ER	7953	ex C-FMLV	7953	SkyWest
☐ N979SW	Canadair CRJ-200ER	7954	ex C-FMMT	7954	SkyWest
☐ N980SW	Canadair CRJ-200ER	7955	ex C-FMNH	7955	SkyWest
☐ N982SW	Canadair CRJ-200ER	7956	ex C-FMNW	7956	SkyWest
☐ N983SW	Canadair CRJ-200ER	7961	ex C-FVAZ	7961	SkyWest
☐ N986SW	Canadair CRJ-200ER	7967	ex C-FMML	7967	SkyWest
☐ N715SF	Canadair CRJ-440LR	7115	ex LV-WPF		Mesa
☐ N17175	Canadair CRJ-440LR	7175	ex LV-WXB		Mesa [TUS]
☐ N151GJ	Canadair CRJ-702ER	10216			GoJet
☐ N152GJ	Canadair CRJ-702ER	10218			GoJet
☐ N153GJ	Canadair CRJ-702ER	10219			GoJet
☐ N154GJ	Canadair CRJ-702ER	10224			GoJet
☐ N155GJ	Canadair CRJ-702ER	10225			GoJet
☐ N156GJ	Canadair CRJ-702ER	10227			GoJet
☐ N157GJ	Canadair CRJ-702ER	10230			GoJet
☐ N158GJ	Canadair CRJ-702ER	10237			GoJet
☐ N159GJ	Canadair CRJ-702ER	10238			GoJet

☐	N160GJ	Canadair CRJ-702ER	10239			GoJet
☐	N161GJ	Canadair CRJ-702ER	10253			GoJet
☐	N162GJ	Canadair CRJ-702ER	10254			GoJet
☐	N163GJ	Canadair CRJ-702ER	10255			GoJet
☐	N164GJ	Canadair CRJ-702ER	10256			GoJet
☐	N165GJ	Canadair CRJ-702ER	10257			GoJet
☐	N166GJ	Canadair CRJ-702ER	10266			GoJet
☐	N167GJ	Canadair CRJ-702ER	10269			GoJet
☐	N168GJ	Canadair CRJ-702ER	10272	ex C-GHZZ		GoJet
☐	N169GJ	Canadair CRJ-702ER	10273			GoJet
☐	N170GJ	Canadair CRJ-702ER	10280	ex C-GICN		GoJet
☐	N171GJ	Canadair CRJ-702ER	10282	ex C-GIAR		GoJet
☐	N172GJ	Canadair CRJ-702ER	10283			GoJet
☐	N173GJ	Canadair CRJ-702ER	10287			GoJet
☐	N174GJ	Canadair CRJ-702ER	10296			GoJet
☐	N175GJ	Canadair CRJ-702ER	10297			GoJet
☐	N354CA	Canadair CRJ-701ER	10064	ex C-GIBO		GoJet
☐	N367CA	Canadair CRJ-701ER	10069	ex C-GICL	10069	GoJet
☐	N379CA	Canadair CRJ-701ER	10102		10102	GoJet
☐	N659CA	Canadair CRJ-701ER	10153		10153	GoJet
☐	N501MJ	Canadair CRJ-701ER	10047	ex C-FZVM		Mesa
☐	N502MJ	Canadair CRJ-701ER	10050	ex C-GIAI		Mesa
☐	N503MJ	Canadair CRJ-701ER	10058	ex C-GIBG		Mesa
☐	N504MJ	Canadair CRJ-701ER	10066	ex C-GIBR		Mesa
☐	N505MJ	Canadair CRJ-701ER	10070	ex C-GICN		Mesa
☐	N506MJ	Canadair CRJ-701ER	10073	ex C-GHZY		Mesa
☐	N507MJ	Canadair CRJ-701ER	10077	ex C-GIAH		Mesa
☐	N508MJ	Canadair CRJ-701ER	10087	ex C-FZZE		Mesa
☐	N509MJ	Canadair CRJ-701ER	10094			Mesa
☐	N510MJ	Canadair CRJ-701ER	10101			Mesa
☐	N511MJ	Canadair CRJ-701ER	10104			Mesa
☐	N512MJ	Canadair CRJ-701ER	10109			Mesa
☐	N513MJ	Canadair CRJ-701ER	10111			Mesa
☐	N514MJ	Canadair CRJ-701ER	10116			Mesa
☐	N515MJ	Canadair CRJ-701ER	10117			Mesa
☐	N516LR	Canadair CRJ-701ER	10258			Mesa
☐	N518LR	Canadair CRJ-701ER	10259			Mesa
☐	N519LR	Canadair CRJ-701ER	10260	ex C-FLGD		Mesa
☐	N521LR	Canadair CRJ-701ER	10261	ex C-FMHJ		Mesa
☐	N522LR	Canadair CRJ-701ER	10262			Mesa
☐	N217AG	Canadair CRJ-701ER	10031	ex N609QX		SkyWest
☐	N219AG	Canadair CRJ-701ER	10246	ex N619QX		SkyWest
☐	N223AG	Canadair CRJ-701ER	10010	ex ZS-NLV		SkyWest
☐	N224AG	Canadair CRJ-701ER	10024	ex ZS-NLT		SkyWest
☐	N225AG	Canadair CRJ-701ER	10033	ex ZS-NBD		Skywest
☐	N613QX	Canadair CRJ-701ER	10045	ex C-GIAD		SkyWest<QXE
☐	N631SK	Canadair CRJ-702ER	10329	ex C-GIBR		SkyWest
☐	N701SK	Canadair CRJ-701ER	10133		10133	SkyWest
☐	N702SK	Canadair CRJ-701ER	10136		10136	SkyWest
☐	N703SK	Canadair CRJ-701ER	10139		10139	SkyWest
☐	N705SK	Canadair CRJ-701ER	10145		10145	SkyWest
☐	N706SK	Canadair CRJ-701ER	10149		10149	SkyWest
☐	N707SK	Canadair CRJ-701ER	10003	ex C-FBKA	10003	SkyWest
☐	N708SK	Canadair CRJ-701ER	10156		10156	SkyWest
☐	N709SK	Canadair CRJ-701ER	10159		10159	SkyWest
☐	N710SK	Canadair CRJ-701ER	10170		10170	SkyWest
☐	N712SK	Canadair CRJ-701ER	10172	ex C-GIAR	10172	SkyWest
☐	N713SK	Canadair CRJ-701ER	10174		10174	SkyWest
☐	N715SK	Canadair CRJ-701ER	10179		10179	SkyWest
☐	N716SK	Canadair CRJ-701ER	10180		10180	SkyWest
☐	N718SK	Canadair CRJ-701ER	10184		10184	SkyWest
☐	N719SK	Canadair CRJ-701ER	10188		10188	SkyWest
☐	N724SK	Canadair CRJ-701ER	10189		10189	SkyWest
☐	N726SK	Canadair CRJ-701ER	10190		10190	SkyWest
☐	N727SK	Canadair CRJ-701ER	10191		10191	SkyWest
☐	N728SK	Canadair CRJ-701ER	10192		10192	SkyWest
☐	N730SK	Canadair CRJ-701ER	10193		10193	SkyWest
☐	N732SK	Canadair CRJ-701ER	10194		10194	SkyWest
☐	N738SK	Canadair CRJ-701ER	10195		10195	SkyWest
☐	N740SK	Canadair CRJ-701ER	10196		10196	SkyWest
☐	N742SK	Canadair CRJ-701ER	10197		10197	SkyWest
☐	N743SK	Canadair CRJ-701ER	10199		10199	SkyWest
☐	N744SK	Canadair CRJ-701ER	10200		10200	SkyWest
☐	N745SK	Canadair CRJ-701ER	10201		10201	SkyWest
☐	N746SK	Canadair CRJ-701ER	10202	ex C-FEUP	10202	SkyWest
☐	N748SK	Canadair CRJ-701ER	10203		10203	SkyWest
☐	N750SK	Canadair CRJ-701ER	10207		10207	SkyWest
☐	N751SK	Canadair CRJ-701ER	10208		10208	SkyWest
☐	N752SK	Canadair CRJ-701ER	10209		10209	SkyWest
☐	N753SK	Canadair CRJ-701ER	10214	ex C-FEVZ	10214	SkyWest
☐	N754SK	Canadair CRJ-701ER	10215		10215	SkyWest

☐ N755SK	Canadair CRJ-701ER	10220	ex C-FFVX	10220		SkyWest
☐ N756SK	Canadair CRJ-701ER	10221		10221		SkyWest
☐ N758SK	Canadair CRJ-701ER	10222		10222		SkyWest
☐ N760SK	Canadair CRJ-701ER	10223		10223		SkyWest
☐ N762SK	Canadair CRJ-702ER	10226		10226		SkyWest
☐ N763SK	Canadair CRJ-702ER	10228		10228		SkyWest
☐ N764SK	Canadair CRJ-702ER	10229	ex C-FGRE	10229		SkyWest
☐ N765SK	Canadair CRJ-702ER	10231		10231		SkyWest
☐ N766SK	Canadair CRJ-702ER	10232		10232		SkyWest
☐ N767SK	Canadair CRJ-702ER	10233		10233		SkyWest
☐ N768SK	Canadair CRJ-702ER	10234		10234		SkyWest
☐ N770SK	Canadair CRJ-702ER	10243		10243		SkyWest
☐ N771SK	Canadair CRJ-702ER	10244		10244		SkyWest
☐ N772SK	Canadair CRJ-702ER	10235		10235		SkyWest
☐ N773SK	Canadair CRJ-702ER	10236		10236		SkyWest
☐ N774SK	Canadair CRJ-702ER	10240		10240		SkyWest
☐ N776SK	Canadair CRJ-702ER	10241		10241		SkyWest
☐ N778SK	Canadair CRJ-702ER	10242		10242		SkyWest
☐ N779SK	Canadair CRJ-702ER	10276		10276		SkyWest
☐ N780SK	Canadair CRJ-702ER	10277		10277		SkyWest
☐ N782SK	Canadair CRJ-702ER	10278		10278		SkyWest
☐ N783SK	Canadair CRJ-702ER	10281	ex C-GICP	10281		SkyWest
☐ N784SK	Canadair CRJ-702ER	10284	ex C-GZQB	10284		SkyWest
☐ N785SK	Canadair CRJ-702ER	10285		10285		SkyWest
☐ N786SK	Canadair CRJ-702ER	10286		10286		SkyWest
☐ N787SK	Canadair CRJ-702ER	10288		10288		SkyWest
☐ N788SK	Canadair CRJ-702ER	10290		10290		SkyWest
☐ N789SK	Canadair CRJ-702ER	10291		10291		SkyWest
☐ N790SK	Canadair CRJ-702ER	10292		10292		SkyWest
☐ N791SK	Canadair CRJ-702ER	10293		10293		SkyWest
☐ N792SK	Canadair CRJ-702ER	10294		10294		SkyWest
☐ N793SK	Canadair CRJ-702ER	10295		10295		SkyWest
☐ N794SK	Canadair CRJ-702ER	10298		10298		SkyWest
☐ N795SK	Canadair CRJ-702ER	10299		10299		SkyWest
☐ N796SK	Canadair CRJ-702ER	10300		10300		SkyWest
☐ N797SK	Canadair CRJ-702ER	10301		10301		SkyWest
☐ N248LR	Canadair CRJ-900	15274	ex C-GUHY			Mesa [PHX]
☐ N249LR	Canadair CRJ-900	15275	ex C-GUID			Mesa [PHX]
☐ N326MS	Canadair CRJ-900	15124	ex A6-HLM			Mesa
☐ N329MS	Canadair CRJ-900	15126	ex A6-HLS			Mesa
☐ N944LR	Canadair CRJ-900ER	15075	ex EI-DRK			Mesa♦
☐ N945LR	Canadair CRJ-900ER	15077	ex EI-DRJ			Mesa♦
☐ N947LR	Canadair CRJ-900ER	15116	ex EI-DVP			Mesa♦
☐ N948LR	Canadair CRJ-900ER	15118	ex EI-DVR			Mesa♦
☐ N950LR	Canadair CRJ-900ER	15119	ex EI-DVS			Mesa♦
☐ N951LR	Canadair CRJ-900ER	15123	ex EI-DVT			Mesa♦
☐ N351PH	de Havilland DHC-8-202Q	490	ex C-GFUM	763		Commutair<QXE
☐ N358PH	de Havilland DHC-8-202Q	506	ex C-FWBB	775		Commutair<QXE
☐ N359PH	de Havilland DHC-8-202Q	514	ex C-GEOA	764		Commutair<QXE
☐ N360PH	de Havilland DHC-8-202Q	515	ex C-GEWI	762		Commutair<QXE
☐ N361PH	de Havilland DHC-8-202Q	516	ex C-GFOD	767		Commutair<QXE
☐ N362PH	de Havilland DHC-8-202Q	518	ex C-FDHI	766		Commutair<QXE
☐ N363PH	de Havilland DHC-8-202Q	520	ex C-FDHP	760		Commutair<QXE
☐ N364PH	de Havilland DHC-8-202Q	524	ex C-FDHX	765		Commutair<QXE
☐ N365PH	de Havilland DHC-8-202Q	526		773		Commutair<QXE
☐ N366PH	de Havilland DHC-8-202Q	510	ex C-GELN	769		Commutair<QXE
☐ N367PH	de Havilland DHC-8-202Q	511	ex C-GDLD	774		Commutair<QXE
☐ N368PH	de Havilland DHC-8-202Q	512	ex C-GDFT	768		Commutair<QXE
☐ N369PH	de Havilland DHC-8-202Q	513	ex C-FWBB	770		Commutair<QXE
☐ N374PH	de Havilland DHC-8-202Q	528	ex C-GDIU	771		Commutair<QXE
☐ N375PH	de Havilland DHC-8-202Q	529	ex C-GDKL	761		Commutair<QXE
☐ N379PH	de Havilland DHC-8-202Q	530	ex C-GDLK	772		Commutair<QXE
☐ N192PF	de Havilland DHC-8-301	192	ex N3554T			Commutair♦
☐ N837CA	de Havilland DHC-8-311Q	554	ex OE-LTN	355		Commutair
☐ N838CA	de Havilland DHC-8-311Q	527	ex OE-LTM	356		Commutair
☐ N839CA	de Havilland DHC-8-311Q	553	ex OE-LTO	357		Commutair
☐ N857CA	de Havilland DHC-8-311Q	531	ex OE-LTN	359		Commutair
☐ N876CA	de Havilland DHC-8-311Q	438	ex OE-LTG	358		Commutair
☐ N351NG	de Havilland DHC-8-402Q	4351	ex C-GHVS			[YYZ]
☐ N354NG	de Havilland DHC-8-402Q	4354				[YYZ]
☐ N341NG	de Havilland DHC-8-402Q	4341	ex C-GGSV			Pinnacle>RPA
☐ N221SW	Embraer EMB.120ER Brasilia	120290	ex PT-SVK			SkyWest
☐ N223SW	Embraer EMB.120ER Brasilia	120291	ex PT-SVL			SkyWest
☐ N234SW	Embraer EMB.120ER Brasilia	120308	ex PT-SXA			SkyWest
☐ N236SW	Embraer EMB.120ER Brasilia	120312	ex PT-SXE			SkyWest
☐ N237SW	Embraer EMB.120ER Brasilia	120314	ex PT-SXG			SkyWest
☐ N270YV	Embraer EMB.120ER Brasilia	120270	ex PT-SUR			SkyWest

☐	N290SW	Embraer EMB.120ER Brasilia	120317	ex PT-SXJ		SkyWest
☐	N292SW	Embraer EMB.120ER Brasilia	120319	ex PT-SXL		SkyWest
☐	N294SW	Embraer EMB.120ER Brasilia	120321	ex PT-SXN		SkyWest
☐	N295SW	Embraer EMB.120ER Brasilia	120322	ex PT-SXO		SkyWest
☐	N297SW	Embraer EMB.120ER Brasilia	120327	ex PT-SXT		SkyWest
☐	N308SW	Embraer EMB.120ER Brasilia	120326	ex PT-SXS		SkyWest
☐	N560SW	Embraer EMB.120ER Brasilia	120334	ex PT-SXX		SkyWest
☐	N561SW	Embraer EMB.120ER Brasilia	120335	ex PT-SXY		SkyWest
☐	N562SW	Embraer EMB.120ER Brasilia	120336	ex PT-SXZ		SkyWest
☐	N563SW	Embraer EMB.120ER Brasilia	120338			SkyWest
☐	N564SW	Embraer EMB.120ER Brasilia	120339	ex PT-SAC		SkyWest
☐	N565SW	Embraer EMB.120ER Brasilia	120340	ex PT-SAI		SkyWest
☐	N566SW	Embraer EMB.120ER Brasilia	120341	ex PT-SAF		SkyWest
☐	N567SW	Embraer EMB.120ER Brasilia	120342	ex PT-SAL		SkyWest
☐	N568SW	Embraer EMB.120ER Brasilia	120343	ex PT-SAZ		SkyWest
☐	N569SW	Embraer EMB.120ER Brasilia	120344	ex PT-SBY		SkyWest
☐	N578SW	Embraer EMB.120ER Brasilia	120346	ex PT-SCA		SkyWest
☐	N579SW	Embraer EMB.120ER Brasilia	120347	ex PT-SCB		SkyWest
☐	N580SW	Embraer EMB.120ER Brasilia	120348	ex PT-SCC		SkyWest
☐	N581SW	Embraer EMB.120ER Brasilia	120349	ex PT-SCZ		SkyWest
☐	N582SW	Embraer EMB.120ER Brasilia	120350	ex PT-SDC		SkyWest
☐	N583SW	Embraer EMB.120ER Brasilia	120351	ex PT-SEF		SkyWest
☐	N584SW	Embraer EMB.120ER Brasilia	120352	ex PT-SEG		SkyWest
☐	N585SW	Embraer EMB.120ER Brasilia	120353	ex PT-SEH		SkyWest
☐	N586SW	Embraer EMB.120ER Brasilia	120354	ex PT-SEJ		SkyWest
☐	N16501	Embraer ERJ-135ER	145145	ex PT-SDV	501	[IGM]
☐	N16502	Embraer ERJ-135ER	145166	ex PT-SFF	502	[IGM]
☐	N19503	Embraer ERJ-135ER	145176	ex PT-SFI	503	[IGM]
☐	N25504	Embraer ERJ-135ER	145186	ex PT-SFK	504	[CLE]
☐	N14505	Embraer ERJ-135ER	145192	ex PT-SFN	505	[IGM]
☐	N27506	Embraer ERJ-135ER	145206	ex PT-SFT	506	[IGM]
☐	N17507	Embraer ERJ-135ER	145215	ex PT-SFW	507	[IGM]
☐	N14508	Embraer ERJ-135ER	145220	ex PT-SFY	508	[IGM]
☐	N15509	Embraer ERJ-135ER	145238	ex PT-SID	509	[IGM]
☐	N16510	Embraer ERJ-135ER	145251	ex PT-SJI	510	[IGM]
☐	N16511	Embraer ERJ-135ER	145267	ex PT-SIZ	511	[IGM]
☐	N27512	Embraer ERJ-135ER	145274	ex PT-SJQ	512	[IGM]
☐	N17513	Embraer ERJ-135LR	145292	ex PT-SKJ	513	[IGM]
☐	N14514	Embraer ERJ-135LR	145303	ex PT-SKU	514	wfs
☐	N29515	Embraer ERJ-135LR	145309	ex PT-SMA	515	wfs
☐	N14516	Embraer ERJ-135LR	145323	ex PT-SMP	516	[IGM]
☐	N24517	Embraer ERJ-135LR	145332	ex PT-SMY	517	[IGM]
☐	N28518	Embraer ERJ-135LR	145334	ex PT-SNA	518	[IGM]
☐	N12519	Embraer ERJ-135LR	145366	ex PT-SOQ	519	[IGM]
☐	N16520	Embraer ERJ-135LR	145372	ex PT-SOX	520	[IGM]
☐	N17521	Embraer ERJ-135LR	145378	ex PT-SQC	521	[IGM]
☐	N14522	Embraer ERJ-135LR	145383	ex PT-SQH	522	[IGM]
☐	N27523	Embraer ERJ-135LR	145389	ex PT-SQN	523	[IGM]
☐	N17524	Embraer ERJ-135LR	145399	ex PT-SQW	524	ExpressJet
☐	N16525	Embraer ERJ-135LR	145403	ex PT-STA	525	ExpressJet
☐	N11526	Embraer ERJ-135LR	145410	ex PT-STH	526	ExpressJet
☐	N15527	Embraer ERJ-135LR	145413	ex PT-STJ	527	ExpressJet
☐	N12528	Embraer ERJ-135LR	145504	ex PT-SXX	528	ExpressJet
☐	N28529	Embraer ERJ-135LR	145512	ex PT-SYE	529	ExpressJet
☐	N12530	Embraer ERJ-135LR	145533	ex PT-STX	530	ExpressJet
☐	N11535	Embraer ERJ-145LR	145518	ex PT-SYJ	535	ExpressJet
☐	N11536	Embraer ERJ-145LR	145520	ex PT-SYL	536	ExpressJet
☐	N21537	Embraer ERJ-145LR	145523	ex PT-SYO	537	ExpressJet
☐	N13538	Embraer ERJ-145LR	145527	ex PT-STS	538	ExpressJet
☐	N11539	Embraer ERJ-145LR	145536	ex PT-SZA	539	ExpressJet
☐	N12540	Embraer ERJ-145LR	145537	ex PT-SZB	540	ExpressJet
☐	N16541	Embraer ERJ-145LR	145542	ex PT-SZF	541	ExpressJet
☐	N14542	Embraer ERJ-145LR	145547	ex PT-SZK	542	ExpressJet
☐	N14543	Embraer ERJ-145LR	145553	ex PT-SZP	543	ExpressJet
☐	N26545	Embraer ERJ-145LR	145558	ex PT-SZT	545	ExpressJet
☐	N16546	Embraer ERJ-145LR	145562	ex PT-SZX	546	ExpressJet
☐	N11547	Embraer ERJ-145LR	145563	ex PT-SZY	547	ExpressJet
☐	N11548	Embraer ERJ-145LR	145565	ex PT-SBB	548	ExpressJet
☐	N26549	Embraer ERJ-145LR	145571	ex PT-SBH	549	ExpressJet
☐	N13550	Embraer ERJ-145LR	145575	ex PT-SBL	550	ExpressJet
☐	N12552	Embraer ERJ-145LR	145583	ex PT-SBU	552	ExpressJet
☐	N13553	Embraer ERJ-145LR	145585	ex PT-SBW	553	ExpressJet
☐	N15555	Embraer ERJ-145LR	145594	ex PT- (SCD)	555	ExpressJet
☐	N18556	Embraer ERJ-145LR	145595	ex PT-SCE	556	ExpressJet
☐	N14558	Embraer ERJ-145LR	145598	ex PT-SCG	558	ExpressJet
☐	N16559	Embraer ERJ-145LR	145603	ex PT-SCM	559	ExpressJet
☐	N17560	Embraer ERJ-145LR	145605	ex PT-SCO	560	ExpressJet
☐	N16561	Embraer ERJ-145LR	145610	ex PT-SCT	561	ExpressJet
☐	N14562	Embraer ERJ-145LR	145611	ex PT-SCV	562	ExpressJet
☐	N12563	Embraer ERJ-145LR	145612	ex PT-SCW	563	ExpressJet

☐ N12564	Embraer ERJ-145LR	145618	ex PT-SDG	564	ExpressJet
☐ N11565	Embraer ERJ-145LR	145621	ex PT-SDJ	565	ExpressJet
☐ N13566	Embraer ERJ-145LR	145622	ex PT-SDK	566	ExpressJet
☐ N12567	Embraer ERJ-145LR	145623	ex PT-SDL	567	ExpressJet
☐ N14568	Embraer ERJ-145LR	145628	ex PT-SDQ	568	ExpressJet
☐ N16571	Embraer ERJ-145LR	145633	ex PT-SDV	571	ExpressJet
☐ N15572	Embraer ERJ-145LR	145636	ex PT-SDY	572	ExpressJet
☐ N14573	Embraer ERJ-145LR	145638	ex PT-SDZ	573	ExpressJet
☐ N15574	Embraer ERJ-145LR	145639	ex PT-SEB	574	ExpressJet
☐ N12900	Embraer ERJ-145LR	145511	ex PT-SYD	900	ExpressJet
☐ N48901	Embraer ERJ-145LR	145501	ex PT-SXU	901	ExpressJet
☐ N14902	Embraer ERJ-145LR	145496	ex PT-SXO	902	ExpressJet
☐ N13903	Embraer ERJ-145LR	145479	ex PT-SVY	903	ExpressJet
☐ N14904	Embraer ERJ-145LR	145477	ex PT-SVW	904	ExpressJet
☐ N14905	Embraer ERJ-145LR	145476	ex PT-SVV	905	ExpressJet
☐ N29906	Embraer ERJ-145LR	145472	ex PT-SVR	906	ExpressJet
☐ N13908	Embraer ERJ-145LR	145465	ex PT-SVK	908	ExpressJet
☐ N15910	Embraer ERJ-145LR	145455	ex PT-SVA	910	ExpressJet
☐ N16911	Embraer ERJ-145LR	145446	ex PT-SUR	911	ExpressJet
☐ N15912	Embraer ERJ-145LR	145439	ex PT-SUK	912	ExpressJet
☐ N13913	Embraer ERJ-145LR	145438	ex PT-SUJ	913	ExpressJet
☐ N13914	Embraer ERJ-145LR	145430	ex PT-SUB	914	ExpressJet
☐ N36915	Embraer ERJ-145LR	145421	ex PT-STS	915	ExpressJet
☐ N14916	Embraer ERJ-145LR	145415	ex PT-STL	916	ExpressJet
☐ N29917	Embraer ERJ-145LR	145414	ex PT-STK	917	ExpressJet
☐ N16918	Embraer ERJ-145LR	145397	ex PT-SQU	918	ExpressJet
☐ N16919	Embraer ERJ-145LR	145393	ex PT-SQQ	919	ExpressJet
☐ N14920	Embraer ERJ-145LR	145380	ex PT-SQE	920	ExpressJet
☐ N12921	Embraer ERJ-145LR	145354	ex PT-SNT	921	ExpressJet
☐ N12922	Embraer ERJ-145LR	145338	ex PT-SNE	922	ExpressJet
☐ N14923	Embraer ERJ-145LR	145318	ex PT-SMJ	923	ExpressJet
☐ N12924	Embraer ERJ-145LR	145311	ex PT-SMC	924	ExpressJet
☐ N14925	Embraer ERJ-145EP	145004	ex PT-SYA	925	ExpressJet [RFD]
☐ N15926	Embraer ERJ-145EP	145005	ex PT-SYB	926	ExpressJet [RFD]
☐ N16927	Embraer ERJ-145EP	145006	ex PT-SYC	927	ExpressJet [RFD]
☐ N17928	Embraer ERJ-145EP	145007	ex PT-SYD	928	ExpressJet [IGM]
☐ N13929	Embraer ERJ-145EP	145009	ex PT-SYF	929	ExpressJet [IGM]
☐ N14930	Embraer ERJ-145EP	145011	ex PT-SYH	930	ExpressJet [IGM]
☐ N15932	Embraer ERJ-145EP	145015	ex PT-SYL	932	ExpressJet [IGM]
☐ N14933	Embraer ERJ-145EP	145018	ex PT-SYO	933	ExpressJet [RFD]
☐ N12934	Embraer ERJ-145EP	145019	ex PT-SYP	934	ExpressJet [IGM]
☐ N13935	Embraer ERJ-145EP	145022	ex PT-SYS	935	ExpressJet [IGM]
☐ N13936	Embraer ERJ-145EP	145025	ex PT-SYV	936	ExpressJet [IGM]
☐ N14937	Embraer ERJ-145EP	145026	ex PT-SYW	937	ExpressJet [IGM]
☐ N14938	Embraer ERJ-145EP	145029	ex PT-SYX	938	ExpressJet [IGM]
☐ N14939	Embraer ERJ-145EP	145030	ex PT-SYY	939	ExpressJet [IGM]
☐ N14940	Embraer ERJ-145EP	145033	ex PT-SZA	940	ExpressJet [IGM]
☐ N15941	Embraer ERJ-145EP	145035	ex PT-SZB	941	ExpressJet
☐ N14942	Embraer ERJ-145EP	145037	ex PT-SZD	942	ExpressJet wfs
☐ N15948	Embraer ERJ-145EP	145056	ex PT-SZV	948	ExpressJet [IGM]
☐ N14950	Embraer ERJ-145LR	145061	ex PT-SAE	950	ExpressJet
☐ N16951	Embraer ERJ-145LR	145063	ex PT-SAG	951	ExpressJet [IGM]
☐ N14952	Embraer ERJ-145LR	145067	ex PT-SAL	952	ExpressJet [IGM]
☐ N14953	Embraer ERJ-145LR	145071	ex PT-SAP	953	ExpressJet [IGM]
☐ N16954	Embraer ERJ-145LR	145072	ex PT-SAQ	954	ExpressJet [IGM]
☐ N13955	Embraer ERJ-145LR	145075	ex PT-SAT	955	ExpressJet [IGM]
☐ N13956	Embraer ERJ-145LR	145078	ex PT-SBB	956	ExpressJet wfs
☐ N12957	Embraer ERJ-145LR	145080	ex PT-SBD	957	ExpressJet wfs
☐ N13958	Embraer ERJ-145LR	145085	ex PT-SBH	958	ExpressJet wfs
☐ N14959	Embraer ERJ-145LR	145091	ex PT-SBM	959	ExpressJet [IGM]
☐ N14960	Embraer ERJ-145LR	145100	ex PT-SBW	960 100th c/s	ExpressJet wfs
☐ N16961	Embraer ERJ-145LR	145103	ex PT-S	961	ExpressJet
☐ N27962	Embraer ERJ-145LR	145110	ex PT-S	962	ExpressJet
☐ N16963	Embraer ERJ-145LR	145116	ex PT-SCS	963	ExpressJet
☐ N13964	Embraer ERJ-145LR	145123	ex PT-SCZ	964	ExpressJet
☐ N13965	Embraer ERJ-145LR	145125	ex PT-SDC	965	ExpressJet
☐ N19966	Embraer ERJ-145LR	145131	ex PT-SDI	966	ExpressJet
☐ N13968	Embraer ERJ-145LR	145138	ex PT-SDP	968	ExpressJet
☐ N13969	Embraer ERJ-145LR	145141	ex PT-SDR	969	ExpressJet
☐ N13970	Embraer ERJ-145LR	145146	ex PT-SDW	970	ExpressJet
☐ N22971	Embraer ERJ-145LR	145149	ex PT-SDZ	971	ExpressJet
☐ N14972	Embraer ERJ-145LR	145151	ex PT-SEC	972	ExpressJet
☐ N15973	Embraer ERJ-145LR	145159	ex PT-SEM	973	ExpressJet
☐ N14974	Embraer ERJ-145LR	145161	ex PT-SEO	974	ExpressJet
☐ N13975	Embraer ERJ-145LR	145163	ex PT-SEP	975	ExpressJet
☐ N16976	Embraer ERJ-145LR	145171	ex PT-SEV	976	ExpressJet
☐ N14977	Embraer ERJ-145LR	145175	ex PT-SEX	977	ExpressJet
☐ N13978	Embraer ERJ-145LR	145180	ex PT-SGC	978	ExpressJet
☐ N13979	Embraer ERJ-145LR	145181	ex PT-SGD	979	ExpressJet
☐ N15980	Embraer ERJ-145LR	145202	ex PT-SGT	980	ExpressJet
☐ N16981	Embraer ERJ-145LR	145208	ex PT-SGY	981	ExpressJet
☐ N15983	Embraer ERJ-145LR	145239	ex PT-SIE	983	ExpressJet
☐ N17984	Embraer ERJ-145LR	145246	ex PT-SIK	984	ExpressJet

☐ N15985	Embraer ERJ-145LR	145248	ex PT-SIL	985	ExpressJet
☐ N15986	Embraer ERJ-145LR	145254	ex PT-SIO	986	ExpressJet
☐ N16987	Embraer ERJ-145LR	145261	ex PT-SIU	987	ExpressJet
☐ N13988	Embraer ERJ-145LR	145265	ex PT-SIX	988	ExpressJet
☐ N13989	Embraer ERJ-145LR	145271	ex PT-SJN	989	ExpressJet
☐ N14991	Embraer ERJ-145LR	145278	ex PT-SJU	991	ExpressJet
☐ N13992	Embraer ERJ-145LR	145284	ex PT-SKB	992	ExpressJet
☐ N14993	Embraer ERJ-145LR	145289	ex PT-SKG	993	ExpressJet
☐ N13994	Embraer ERJ-145LR	145291	ex PT-SKI	994	ExpressJet
☐ N13995	Embraer ERJ-145LR	145295	ex PT-SKM	995	ExpressJet
☐ N12996	Embraer ERJ-145LR	145296	ex PT-SKN	996	ExpressJet
☐ N13997	Embraer ERJ-145LR	145298	ex PT-SKP	997	ExpressJet
☐ N14998	Embraer ERJ-145LR	145302	ex PT-SKT	998	ExpressJet
☐ N16999	Embraer ERJ-145LR	145307	ex PT-SKY	999	ExpressJet
☐ N18102	Embraer ERJ-145XR	145643	ex PT-SEE	102	ExpressJet
☐ N24103	Embraer ERJ-145XR	145645	ex PT-SEF	103	ExpressJet
☐ N41104	Embraer ERJ-145XR	145646	ex PT-SEG	104	ExpressJet
☐ N14105	Embraer ERJ-145XR	145649	ex PT-SEJ	105	ExpressJet
☐ N11107	Embraer ERJ-145XR	145654	ex PT-SEO	107	ExpressJet
☐ N17108	Embraer ERJ-145XR	145655	ex PT-SEP	108	ExpressJet
☐ N11109	Embraer ERJ-145XR	145657	ex PT-SER	109	ExpressJet
☐ N34110	Embraer ERJ-145XR	145658	ex PT-SES	110	ExpressJet
☐ N34111	Embraer ERJ-145XR	145659	ex PT-SET	111	ExpressJet
☐ N16112	Embraer ERJ-145XR	145660	ex PT-SEU	112	ExpressJet
☐ N18114	Embraer ERJ-145XR	145664	ex PT-SEY	114	ExpressJet
☐ N17115	Embraer ERJ-145XR	145666	ex PT-SFA	115	ExpressJet
☐ N14116	Embraer ERJ-145XR	145672	ex PT-SFF	116	ExpressJet
☐ N14117	Embraer ERJ-145XR	145674	ex PT-SFH	117	ExpressJet
☐ N13118	Embraer ERJ-145XR	145675	ex PT-SFI	118	ExpressJet
☐ N11119	Embraer ERJ-145XR	145677	ex PT-SFK	119	ExpressJet
☐ N18120	Embraer ERJ-145XR	145681	ex PT-SFN	120	ExpressJet
☐ N11121	Embraer ERJ-145XR	145683	ex PT-SFP	121	ExpressJet
☐ N12122	Embraer ERJ-145XR	145684	ex PT-SFQ	122	ExpressJet
☐ N13123	Embraer ERJ-145XR	145688	ex PT-SFU	123	ExpressJet
☐ N13124	Embraer ERJ-145XR	145689	ex PT-SFV	124	ExpressJet
☐ N14125	Embraer ERJ-145XR	145690	ex PT-SFW	125	ExpressJet
☐ N12126	Embraer ERJ-145XR	145693	ex PT-SFZ	126	ExpressJet
☐ N11127	Embraer ERJ-145XR	145697	ex PT-SGC	127	ExpressJet
☐ N24128	Embraer ERJ-145XR	145700	ex PT-SGE	128	ExpressJet
☐ N21129	Embraer ERJ-145XR	145703	ex PT-SGH	129	ExpressJet
☐ N21130	Embraer ERJ-145XR	145704	ex PT-SGI	130	ExpressJet
☐ N31131	Embraer ERJ-145XR	145705	ex PT-SGJ	131	ExpressJet
☐ N13132	Embraer ERJ-145XR	145708	ex PT-SGL	132	ExpressJet
☐ N13133	Embraer ERJ-145XR	145712	ex PT-SGP	133	ExpressJet
☐ N25134	Embraer ERJ-145XR	145714	ex PT-SGR	134	ExpressJet
☐ N12135	Embraer ERJ-145XR	145718	ex PT-SGU	135	ExpressJet
☐ N12136	Embraer ERJ-145XR	145719	ex PT-SGV	136	ExpressJet
☐ N17138	Embraer ERJ-145XR	145727	ex PT-SHD	138	ExpressJet
☐ N23139	Embraer ERJ-145XR	145731	ex PT-SHH	139	ExpressJet
☐ N11140	Embraer ERJ-145XR	145732	ex PT-SHI	140	ExpressJet
☐ N26141	Embraer ERJ-145XR	145733	ex PT-SHJ	141	ExpressJet
☐ N12142	Embraer ERJ-145XR	145735	ex PT-SHL	142	ExpressJet
☐ N14143	Embraer ERJ-145XR	145739	ex PT-SHT	143	ExpressJet
☐ N21144	Embraer ERJ-145XR	145741	ex PT-SJA	144	ExpressJet
☐ N12145	Embraer ERJ-145XR	145745	ex PT-SJE	145	ExpressJet
☐ N17146	Embraer ERJ-145XR	145746	ex PT-SJF	146	ExpressJet
☐ N16147	Embraer ERJ-145XR	145749	ex PT-SJI	147	ExpressJet
☐ N14148	Embraer ERJ-145XR	145751	ex PT-SJK	148	ExpressJet
☐ N16149	Embraer ERJ-145XR	145753	ex PT-SJM	149	ExpressJet
☐ N11150	Embraer ERJ-145XR	145756	ex PT-SJP	150	ExpressJet
☐ N27152	Embraer ERJ-145XR	145759	ex PT-SJR	152	ExpressJet
☐ N21154	Embraer ERJ-145XR	145772	ex PT-SMC	154	ExpressJet
☐ N12157	Embraer ERJ-145XR	145787	ex PT-SMP	157	ExpressJet
☐ N14158	Embraer ERJ-145XR	145791	ex PT-SMS	158	ExpressJet
☐ N17159	Embraer ERJ-145XR	145792	ex PT-SMT	159	ExpressJet
☐ N12160	Embraer ERJ-145XR	145799	ex PT-SMZ	160	ExpressJet
☐ N13161	Embraer ERJ-145XR	14500805	ex PT-SNH	161	ExpressJet
☐ N11164	Embraer ERJ-145XR	14500817	ex PT-SNS	164	ExpressJet
☐ N12166	Embraer ERJ-145XR	14500831	ex PT-SQE	166	ExpressJet
☐ N17169	Embraer ERJ-145XR	14500844	ex PT-SQO	169	ExpressJet
☐ N12172	Embraer ERJ-145XR	14500864	ex PT-SXD	172	ExpressJet
☐ N14177	Embraer ERJ-145XR	14500888	ex PT-SYA	177	ExpressJet
☐ N14180	Embraer ERJ-145XR	14500900	ex PT-SYL	180	ExpressJet
☐ N17185	Embraer ERJ-145XR	14500922	ex PT-SOT	185	ExpressJet
☐ N14186	Embraer ERJ-145XR	14500924	ex PT-SOV	186	ExpressJet
☐ N11187	Embraer ERJ-145XR	14500927	ex PT-SOX	187	ExpressJet
☐ N27190	Embraer ERJ-145XR	14500934	ex PT-SCC	190	ExpressJet
☐ N11191	Embraer ERJ-145XR	14500935	ex PT-SCH	191	ExpressJet
☐ N11194	Embraer ERJ-145XR	14500940	ex PT-SCL		ExpressJet
☐ N12195	Embraer ERJ-145XR	14500943	ex PT-SCO	195	ExpressJet
☐ N17196	Embraer ERJ-145XR	14500945	ex PT-SCQ	196	ExpressJet
☐ N21197	Embraer ERJ-145XR	14500947	ex PT-SCS	197	ExpressJet

☐ N27200	Embraer ERJ-145XR	14500956	ex PT-SFE	200		ExpressJet
☐ N13202	Embraer ERJ-145XR	14500962	ex PT-SFJ	202		ExpressJet
☐ N14203	Embraer ERJ-145XR	14500964	ex PT-SFL	203		ExpressJet
☐ N14204	Embraer ERJ-145XR	14500968	ex PT-SFT	204		ExpressJet
☐ N806HK	Embraer ERJ-145ER	145112	ex PT-SCO			Trans States
☐ N807HK	Embraer ERJ-145ER	145119	ex PT-SCV			Trans States
☐ N810HK	Embraer ERJ-145LR	145231	ex PT-SHV			Trans States
☐ N811HK	Embraer ERJ-145ER	145256	ex PT-SIQ			Trans States
☐ N825HK	Embraer ERJ-145LR	145510	ex XA-QAC			Trans States wfs♦
☐ N829HK	Embraer ERJ-145LR	145281	ex PR-PSM			Trans States
☐ N832HK	Embraer ERJ-145LR	145771	ex PT-SMB			Trans States
☐ N833HK	Embraer ERJ-145LR	145240	ex HB-JAB			Trans States
☐ N834HK	Embraer ERJ-145LR	145269	ex PR-PSL			Trans States
☐ N835HK	Embraer ERJ-145LR	145670	ex PT-SFE			Trans Stares
☐ N836HK	Embraer ERJ-145LR	145695	ex PT-SGA			Trans States
☐ N838HK	Embraer ERJ-145LR	145321	ex HB-JAG			Trans States
☐ N839HK	Embraer ERJ-145LR	14500829	ex PT-SQC			Trans States
☐ N841HK	Embraer ERJ-145LR	145382	ex HB-JAJ			Trans States
☐ N842HK	Embraer ERJ-145LR	14500830	ex PT-SQD			Trans States
☐ N843HK	Embraer ERJ-145LR	14500822	ex PT-SNW			Trans States
☐ N844HK	Embraer ERJ-145LR	14500838	ex PT-SQK			Trans States
☐ N845HK	Embraer ERJ-145LR	14500842	ex PT-SQM			Trans States
☐ N846HK	Embraer ERJ-145LR	14500855	ex PT-SQW			Trans States
☐ N847HK	Embraer ERJ-145LR	14500857	ex PT-SQY			Trans States
☐ N853HK	Embraer ERJ-145MP	145407	ex PR-PSN			Trans States
☐ N854HK	Embraer ERJ-145MP	145408	ex PR-PSO			Trans States
☐ N855HK	Embraer ERJ-145LR	145387	ex PR-PSK			Trans States
☐ N856HK	Embraer ERJ-145MP	145441	ex PR-PSP			Trans States
☐ N857HK	Embraer ERJ-145EU	145418	ex F-GRGM			Trans States
☐ N10156	Embraer ERJ-145XR	145786	ex PT-SMN			Trans States♦
☐ N11106	Embraer ERJ-145XR	145650	ex PT-SEK			Trans States♦
☐ N11113	Embraer ERJ-145XR	145662	ex PT-SEW			Trans States♦
☐ N11155	Embraer ERJ-145XR	145782	ex PT-SMJ			Trans States♦
☐ N14153	Embraer ERJ-145XR	145761	ex PT-SJS			Trans States♦
☐ N16151	Embraer ERJ-145XR	145758	ex PT-SJQ			Trans States♦
☐ N18101	Embraer ERJ-145XR	145590	ex PT-SDC			Trans States♦
☐ N631RW	Embraer ERJ-170SE	17000007	ex PT-SKX			Shuttle America
☐ N632RW	Embraer ERJ-170SE	17000050	ex PT-SUU			Shuttle America
☐ N633RW	Embraer ERJ-170SE	17000054	ex PT-SUZ			Shuttle America
☐ N634RW	Embraer ERJ-170SE	17000055	ex PT-SVE			Shuttle America
☐ N635RW	Embraer ERJ-170SE	17000056	ex PT-SVF			Shuttle America
☐ N636RW	Embraer ERJ-170SE	17000052	ex PT-SVK			Shuttle America
☐ N637RW	Embraer ERJ-170SE	17000051	ex PT-SUV			Shuttle America
☐ N638RW	Embraer ERJ-170SE	17000053	ex PT-SUY			Shuttle America
☐ N639RW	Embraer ERJ-170SE	17000057	ex PT-SVG			Shuttle America
☐ N640RW	Embraer ERJ-170SE	17000058	ex PT-SVH			Shuttle America
☐ N641RW	Embraer ERJ-170SE	17000062	ex PT-SVN			Shuttle America
☐ N642RW	Embraer ERJ-170SE	17000063	ex PT-SVO			Shuttle America
☐ N643RW	Embraer ERJ-170SE	17000060	ex PT-SVL			Shuttle America
☐ N644RW	Embraer ERJ-170SE	17000061	ex PT-SVM			Shuttle America
☐ N645RW	Embraer ERJ-170SE	17000064	ex PT-SVP			Shuttle America
☐ N646RW	Embraer ERJ-170SE	17000066	ex PT-SVR			Shuttle America
☐ N647RW	Embraer ERJ-170SE	17000067	ex PT-SVS			Shuttle America
☐ N648RW	Embraer ERJ-170SE	17000068	ex PT-SVT			Shuttle America
☐ N649RW	Embraer ERJ-170SE	17000070	ex PT-SVV			Shuttle America
☐ N650RW	Embraer ERJ-170SE	17000071	ex PT-SVW			Shuttle America
☐ N651RW	Embraer ERJ-170SE	17000072	ex PT-SVX			Shuttle America
☐ N652RW	Embraer ERJ-170SE	17000075	ex PT-SZA			Shuttle America
☐ N653RW	Embraer ERJ-170SE	17000076	ex PT-SZB			Shuttle America
☐ N654RW	Embraer ERJ-170SE	17000104	ex PT-SAK			Shuttle America
☐ N655RW	Embraer ERJ-170SE	17000105	ex PT-SAM			Shuttle America
☐ N656RW	Embraer ERJ-170SE	17000113	ex PT-SAY			Shuttle America
☐ N657RW	Embraer ERJ-170SE	17000115	ex PT-SDC			Shuttle America
☐ N856RW	Embraer ERJ-170SE	17000078	ex PT-SZD			Shuttle America
☐ N857RW	Embraer ERJ-170SE	17000079	ex PT-SZE			Shuttle America
☐ N858RW	Embraer ERJ-170SE	17000080	ex PT-SZF			Shuttle America
☐ N861RW	Embraer ERJ-170SE	17000094	ex PT-SZU			Shuttle America
☐ N863RW	Embraer ERJ-170SE	17000100	ex PT-SAB			Shuttle America
☐ N864RW	Embraer ERJ-170SE	17000117	ex PT-SDE			Shuttle America
☐ N865RW	Embraer ERJ-170SE	17000122	ex PT-SDK			Shuttle America
☐ N88301	Embraer ERJ-175LR	17000388	ex PR-EEM	301		Mesa
☐ N87302	Embraer ERJ-175LR	17000394	ex PR-EFC	302		Mesa
☐ N87303	Embraer ERJ-175LR	17000398	ex PR-EFK	303		Mesa
☐ N89304	Embraer ERJ-175LR	17000406	ex PR-EGI	304		Mesa♦
☐ N93305	Embraer ERJ-175LR	17000412	ex PR-EGW	305		Mesa♦
☐ N87306	Embraer ERJ-175LR	17000414	ex PR-EGY	306		Mesa♦
☐ N84307	Embraer ERJ-175LR	17000419	ex PR-EHG	307		Mesa♦
☐ N89308	Embraer ERJ-175LR	17000422	ex PR-EHM	308		Mesa♦
☐ N86309	Embraer ERJ-175LR	17000426	ex PR-EHQ	309		Mesa♦
☐ N88310	Embraer ERJ-175LR	17000427	ex PR-EHS	310		Mesa o/o♦

☐ N86311	Embraer ERJ-175LR	17000429	ex PR-EHU	311	Mesa o/o♦
☐ N89312	Embraer ERJ-175LR	17000432	ex PR-EHX	312	Mesa♦
☐ N82313	Embraer ERJ-175LR	17000433	ex PR-EHY	313	Mesa♦
☐ N89314	Embraer ERJ-175LR	17000436	ex PR-EIF	314	Mesa ♦
☐ N86315	Embraer ERJ-175LR	17000437	ex PR-EIG	315	Mesa♦
☐ N89316	Embraer ERJ-175LR	17000438	ex PR-EIH	316	Mesa♦
☐ N89317	Embraer ERJ-175LR	17000442	ex PR-EIN	317	Mesa♦
☐ N87318	Embraer ERJ-175LR	17000443	ex PR-EIP	318	Mesa♦
☐ N87319	Embraer ERJ-175LR	17000448	ex PR-EIV	319	Mesa♦
☐ N85320	Embraer ERJ-175LR	17000454	ex PR-EKC	320Mesa	♦☐
N89321	Embraer ERJ-175LR	17000459	ex PR-EKH	321	Mesa♦
☐ N86322	Embraer ERJ-175LR	17000465	ex PR-EKT	322	Mesa♦
☐ N85323	Embraer ERJ-175LR	17000469	ex PR-EKU	323	Mesa♦
☐ N86324	Embraer ERJ-175LR	17000471	ex PR-EKW	324	Mesa♦
☐ N88325	Embraer ERJ-175LR	17000474	ex PR-ELD	325	Mesa♦
☐ N88326	Embraer ERJ-175LR	17000478	ex PR-	326	Mesa o/o♦
☐ N103SY	Embraer ERJ-175LR	17000390	ex PR-EEO		SkyWest
☐ N105SY	Embraer ERJ-175LR	17000395	ex PR-EFD		SkyWest
☐ N106SY	Embraer EJR-175LR	17000399	ex PR-EFP		SkyWest♦
☐ N107SY	Embraer ERJ-175LR	17000400	ex PR-EFR		SkyWest♦
☐ N108SY	Embraer ERJ-175LR	17000401	ex PR-EFU		SkyWest♦
☐ N109SY	Embraer ERJ-175LR	17000404	ex PR-EFU		SkyWest♦
☐ N110SY	Embraer ERJ-175LR	17000405	ex PR-EGG		SkyWest♦
☐ N113SY	Embraer ERJ-175LR	17000407	ex PR-EGK		SkyWest♦
☐ N114SY	Embraer ERJ-175LR	17000410	ex PR-EGR		SkyWest♦
☐ N116SY	Embraer ERJ-175LR	17000411	ex PR-EGU		SkyWest♦
☐ N117SY	Embraer ERJ-175LR	17000416	ex PR-EHB		SkyWest♦
☐ N118SY	Embraer ERJ-175LR	17000420	ex PR-EHH		SkyWest♦
☐ N119SY	Embraer ERJ-175LR	17000421	ex PR-EHL		SkyWest♦
☐ N120SY	Embraer ERJ-175LR	17000425	ex PR-EHP		SkyWest♦
☐ N121SY	Embraer ERJ-175LR	17000430	ex PR-EHV		SkyWest♦
☐ N122SY	Embraer ERJ-175LR	17000431	ex PR-EHW		SkyWest♦
☐ N124SY	Embraer ERJ-175LR	17000439	ex PR-EII		SkyWest♦
☐ N125SY	Embraer ERJ-175LR	17000440	ex PR-EIL		SkyWest♦
☐ N127SY	Embraer ERJ-175LR	17000441	ex PR-EIM		SkyWest♦
☐ N128SY	Embraer ERJ-175LR	17000445	ex PR-EIQ		SkyWest♦
☐ N130SY	Embraer ERJ-175LR	17000449	ex PR-EIW		SkyWest♦
☐ N131SY	Embraer ERJ-175LR	17000450	ex PR-EIX		SkyWest♦
☐ N132SY	Embraer ERJ-175LR	17000451	ex PR-EIZ		SkyWest♦
☐ N133SY	Embraer ERJ-175LR	17000452	ex PR-EKA		SkyWest♦
☐ N134SY	Embraer ERJ-175LR	17000458	ex PR-EKG		SkyWest♦
☐ N135SY	Embraer ERJ-175LR	17000460	ex PR-EKI		SkyWest♦
☐ N136SY	Embraer ERJ-175LR	17000462	ex PR-EKL		SkyWest♦
☐ N138SY	Embraer ERJ-175LR	17000466	ex PR-EKQ		SkyWest♦
☐ N139SY	Embraer ERJ-175LR	17000468	ex PR-EKP		SkyWest♦
☐ N140SY	Embraer ERJ-175LR	17000470	ex PR-EKV		SkyWest♦
☐ N141SY	Embraer ERJ-175LR	17000472	ex PR-EKX		SkyWest♦
☐ N142SY	Embraer ERJ-175LR	17000475	ex PR-ELK		SkyWest♦
☐ N143SY	Embraer ERJ-175LR	17000476	ex PR-ELQ		SkyWest o/o♦
☐ N	Embraer ERJ-175LR	17000483	ex OR-		SkyWest o/o♦
☐ N356CJ	SAAB SF.340B	340B-356	ex N356SB		[MNZ]

UNIVERSAL AIRLINES		**Pacific Northern (PNA)**		**Victoria-Regional, TX (VCT)**
☐ N170UA	Douglas DC-6A	45518/998	ex N870TA	
☐ N500UA	Douglas DC-6A	44597/501	ex N766WC	
☐ N905GA	Convair 580	121	ex C-FMGC	

UPS AIRLINES		**UPS (5X/UPS)**		**Louisville-Intl, KY (SDF)**
☐ N120UP	Airbus A300F4-622R	805	ex F-WWAR	
☐ N121UP	Airbus A300F4-622R	806	ex F-WWAP	
☐ N122UP	Airbus A300F4-622R	807	ex F-WWAX	
☐ N124UP	Airbus A300F4-622R	808	ex F-WWAT	
☐ N125UP	Airbus A300F4-622R	809	ex F-WWAU	
☐ N126UP	Airbus A300F4-622R	810	ex F-WWAB	
☐ N127UP	Airbus A300F4-622R	811	ex F-WWAD	
☐ N128UP	Airbus A300F4-622R	812	ex F-WWAE	
☐ N129UP	Airbus A300F4-622R	813	ex F-WWAF	
☐ N130UP	Airbus A300F4-622R	814	ex F-WWAG	
☐ N131UP	Airbus A300F4-622R	815	ex F-WWAH	
☐ N133UP	Airbus A300F4-622R	816	ex F-WWAJ	
☐ N134UP	Airbus A300F4-622R	817	ex F-WWAL	
☐ N135UP	Airbus A300F4-622R	818	ex F-WWAM	
☐ N136UP	Airbus A300F4-622R	819	ex F-WWAN	
☐ N137UP	Airbus A300F4-622R	820	ex F-WWAO	
☐ N138UP	Airbus A300F4-622R	821	ex F-WWAQ	
☐ N139UP	Airbus A300F4-622R	822	ex F-WWAS	
☐ N140UP	Airbus A300F4-622R	823	ex F-WWAV	
☐ N141UP	Airbus A300F4-622R	824	ex F-WWAY	

☐ N142UP	Airbus A300F4-622R	825	ex F-WWAA
☐ N143UP	Airbus A300F4-622R	826	ex F-WWAB
☐ N144UP	Airbus A300F4-622R	827	ex F-WWAD
☐ N145UP	Airbus A300F4-622R	828	ex F-WWAE
☐ N146UP	Airbus A300F4-622R	829	ex F-WWAG
☐ N147UP	Airbus A300F4-622R	830	ex F-WWAJ
☐ N148UP	Airbus A300F4-622R	831	ex F-WWAM
☐ N149UP	Airbus A300F4-622R	832	ex F-WWAN
☐ N150UP	Airbus A300F4-622R	833	ex F-WWAO
☐ N151UP	Airbus A300F4-622R	834	ex F-WWAP
☐ N152UP	Airbus A300F4-622R	835	ex F-WWAQ
☐ N153UP	Airbus A300F4-622R	839	ex F-WWAR
☐ N154UP	Airbus A300F4-622R	840	ex F-WWAS
☐ N156UP	Airbus A300F4-622R	845	ex F-WWAU
☐ N157UP	Airbus A300F4-622R	846	ex F-WWAV
☐ N158UP	Airbus A300F4-622R	847	ex F-WWAX
☐ N159UP	Airbus A300F4-622R	848	ex F-WWAZ
☐ N160UP	Airbus A300F4-622R	849	ex F-WWAF
☐ N161UP	Airbus A300F4-622R	850	ex F-WWAG
☐ N162UP	Airbus A300F4-622R	851	ex F-WWAJ
☐ N163UP	Airbus A300F4-622R	852	ex F-WWAK
☐ N164UP	Airbus A300F4-622R	853	ex F-WWAL
☐ N165UP	Airbus A300F4-622R	854	ex F-WWAM
☐ N166UP	Airbus A300F4-622R	861	ex F-WWAU
☐ N167UP	Airbus A300F4-622R	862	ex F-WWAH
☐ N168UP	Airbus A300F4-622R	863	ex F-WWAV
☐ N169UP	Airbus A300F4-622R	864	ex F-WWAX
☐ N170UP	Airbus A300F4-622R	865	ex F-WWAZ
☐ N171UP	Airbus A300F4-622R	866	ex F-WWAE
☐ N172UP	Airbus A300F4-622R	867	ex F-WWAF
☐ N173UP	Airbus A300F4-622R	868	ex F-WWAG
☐ N174UP	Airbus A300F4-622R	869	ex F-WWAN
☐ N570UP	Boeing 747-44AF	35667/1388	
☐ N572UP	Boeing 747-44AF	35669/1396	
☐ N573UP	Boeing 747-44AF	35662/1401	
☐ N574UP	Boeing 747-44AF	35663/1403	
☐ N575UP	Boeing 747-44AF	35664/1406	
☐ N576UP	Boeing 747-44AF	35665/1410	
☐ N577UP	Boeing 747-44AF	35666/1412	
☐ N578UP	Boeing 747-45EBCF	27154/994	ex B-16461
☐ N579UP	Boeing 747-45EBCF	26062/1016	ex B-16465
☐ N580UP	Boeing 747-428F	25632/968	ex LX-ICV
☐ N581UP	Boeing 747-4R7F	25866/1002	ex LX-FCV
☐ N582UP	Boeing 747-4R7F	29053/1139	ex LX-LCV
☐ N583UP	Boeing 747-4R7F	25867/1008	ex LX-GCV
☐ N401UP	Boeing 757-24APF	23723/139	
☐ N402UP	Boeing 757-24APF	23724/141	
☐ N403UP	Boeing 757-24APF	23725/143	
☐ N404UP	Boeing 757-24APF	23726/147	
☐ N405UP	Boeing 757-24APF	23727/149	
☐ N406UP	Boeing 757-24APF	23728/176	
☐ N407UP	Boeing 757-24APF	23729/181	
☐ N408UP	Boeing 757-24APF	23730/184	
☐ N409UP	Boeing 757-24APF	23731/186	
☐ N410UP	Boeing 757-24APF	23732/189	
☐ N411UP	Boeing 757-24APF	23851/191	
☐ N412UP	Boeing 757-24APF	23852/193	
☐ N413UP	Boeing 757-24APF	23853/195	
☐ N414UP	Boeing 757-24APF	23854/197	
☐ N415UP	Boeing 757-24APF	23855/199	
☐ N416UP	Boeing 757-24APF	23903/318	
☐ N417UP	Boeing 757-24APF	23904/322	
☐ N418UP	Boeing 757-24APF	23905/326	
☐ N419UP	Boeing 757-24APF	23906/330	
☐ N420UP	Boeing 757-24APF	23907/334	
☐ N421UP	Boeing 757-24APF	25281/395	
☐ N422UP	Boeing 757-24APF	25324/399	
☐ N423UP	Boeing 757-24APF	25325/403	
☐ N424UP	Boeing 757-24APF	25369/407	
☐ N425UP	Boeing 757-24APF	25370/411	
☐ N426UP	Boeing 757-24APF	25457/477	
☐ N427UP	Boeing 757-24APF	25458/481	
☐ N428UP	Boeing 757-24APF	25459/485	
☐ N429UP	Boeing 757-24APF	25460/489	
☐ N430UP	Boeing 757-24APF	25461/493	
☐ N431UP	Boeing 757-24APF	25462/569	ex OY-USA
☐ N432UP	Boeing 757-24APF	25463/573	ex OY-USB
☐ N433UP	Boeing 757-24APF	25464/577	ex OY-USC
☐ N434UP	Boeing 757-24APF	25465/579	ex OY-USD
☐ N435UP	Boeing 757-24APF	25466/581	
☐ N436UP	Boeing 757-24APF	25467/625	

☐ N437UP	Boeing 757-24APF	25468/628	
☐ N438UP	Boeing 757-24APF	25469/631	
☐ N439UP	Boeing 757-24APF	25470/634	
☐ N440UP	Boeing 757-24APF	25471/636	
☐ N441UP	Boeing 757-24APF	27386/638	
☐ N442UP	Boeing 757-24APF	27387/640	
☐ N443UP	Boeing 757-24APF	27388/642	
☐ N444UP	Boeing 757-24APF	27389/644	
☐ N445UP	Boeing 757-24APF	27390/646	
☐ N446UP	Boeing 757-24APF	27735/649	
☐ N447UP	Boeing 757-24APF	27736/651	
☐ N448UP	Boeing 757-24APF	27737/654	
☐ N449UP	Boeing 757-24APF	27738/656	
☐ N450UP	Boeing 757-24APF	25472/659	
☐ N451UP	Boeing 757-24APF	27739/675	
☐ N452UP	Boeing 757-24APF	25473/679	
☐ N453UP	Boeing 757-24APF	25474/683	
☐ N454UP	Boeing 757-24APF	25475/687	
☐ N455UP	Boeing 757-24APF	25476/691	
☐ N456UP	Boeing 757-24APF	25477/728	
☐ N457UP	Boeing 757-24APF	25478/729	
☐ N458UP	Boeing 757-24APF	25479/730	
☐ N459UP	Boeing 757-24APF	25480/733	
☐ N460UP	Boeing 757-24APF	25481/734	
☐ N461UP	Boeing 757-24APF	28265/755	
☐ N462UP	Boeing 757-24APF	28266/759	
☐ N463UP	Boeing 757-24APF	28267/763	
☐ N464UP	Boeing 757-24APF	28268/765	
☐ N465UP	Boeing 757-24APF	28269/767	
☐ N466UP	Boeing 757-24APF	25482/769	
☐ N467UP	Boeing 757-24APF	25483/771	
☐ N468UP	Boeing 757-24APF	25484/774	
☐ N469UP	Boeing 757-24APF	25485/776	
☐ N470UP	Boeing 757-24APF	25486/778	
☐ N471UP	Boeing 757-24APF	28842/813	
☐ N472UP	Boeing 757-24APF	28843/815	
☐ N473UP	Boeing 757-24APF	28846/823	ex N5573L
☐ N474UP	Boeing 757-24APF	28844/879	
☐ N475UP	Boeing 757-24APF	28845/882	
☐ N301UP	Boeing 767-34AERF/W	27239/580	
☐ N302UP	Boeing 767-34AERF/W	27240/590	
☐ N303UP	Boeing 767-34AERF/W	27241/594	
☐ N304UP	Boeing 767-34AERF/W	27242/598	
☐ N305UP	Boeing 767-34AERF/W	27243/600	
☐ N306UP	Boeing 767-34AERF/W	27759/622	
☐ N307UP	Boeing 767-34AERF/W	27760/624	
☐ N308UP	Boeing 767-34AERF/W	27761/626	
☐ N309UP	Boeing 767-34AERF/W	27740/628	
☐ N310UP	Boeing 767-34AERF/W	27762/630	
☐ N311UP	Boeing 767-34AERF/W	27741/632	
☐ N312UP	Boeing 767-34AERF/W	27763/634	
☐ N313UP	Boeing 767-34AERF/W	27764/636	
☐ N314UP	Boeing 767-34AERF/W	27742/638	
☐ N315UP	Boeing 767-34AERF/W	27743/640	
☐ N316UP	Boeing 767-34AERF/W	27744/660	
☐ N317UP	Boeing 767-34AERF/W	27745/666	
☐ N318UP	Boeing 767-34AERF/W	27746/670	
☐ N319UP	Boeing 767-34AERF/W	27758/672	
☐ N320UP	Boeing 767-34AERF/W	27747/674	
☐ N321UP	Boeing 767-34AERF/W	27748/678	
☐ N322UP	Boeing 767-34AERF/W	27749/682	
☐ N323UP	Boeing 767-34AERF/W	27750/724	
☐ N324UP	Boeing 767-34AERF/W	27751/726	
☐ N325UP	Boeing 767-34AERF/W	27752/728	
☐ N326UP	Boeing 767-34AERF/W	27753/730	
☐ N327UP	Boeing 767-34AERF/W	27754/732	
☐ N328UP	Boeing 767-34AERF/W	27755/756	
☐ N329UP	Boeing 767-34AERF/W	27756/760	
☐ N330UP	Boeing 767-34AERF/W	27757/764	
☐ N331UP	Boeing 767-34AERF/W	32843/854	
☐ N332UP	Boeing 767-34AERF/W	32844/858	
☐ N334UP	Boeing 767-34AERF/W	37856/979	ex N5023Q
☐ N335UP	Boeing 767-34AERF/W	37857/983	336
☐ N336UP	Boeing 767-34AERF/W	37858/986	337
☐ N337UP	Boeing 767-34AERF/W	37944/988	338
☐ N338UP	Boeing 767-34AERF/W	37859/989	339
☐ N339UP	Boeing 767-34AERF/W	37860/991	340
☐ N340UP	Boeing 767-34AERF/W	37861/992	341
☐ N341UP	Boeing 767-34AERF/W	37865/1002	342
☐ N342UP	Boeing 767-34AERF/W	37945/1003	343
☐ N343UP	Boeing 767-34AERF/W	37866/1005	344
☐ N344UP	Boeing 767-34AERF/W	37867/1006	345
☐ N345UP	Boeing 767-34AERF/W		

☐ N346UP	Boeing 767-34AERF/W	37868/1008		346
☐ N347UP	Boeing 767-34AERF/W	37871/1020		347
☐ N348UP	Boeing 767-34AERF/W	37872/1022		348
☐ N349UP	Boeing 767-34AERF/W	37947/1024		349
☐ N350UP	Boeing 767-34AERF/W	37873/1025		350
☐ N351UP	Boeing 767-34AERF/W	37874/1026		351
☐ N352UP	Boeing 767-34AERF/W	37875/1028		352
☐ N353UP	Boeing 767-34AERF/W	37877/1035		353
☐ N354UP	Boeing 767-34AERF/W	37862/1044		354
☐ N355UP	Boeing 767-34AERF/W	37863/1046		355
☐ N356UP	Boeing 767-34AERF/W	37869/1048		356
☐ N357UP	Boeing 767-34AERF/W	37876/1051		357
☐ N358UP	Boeing 767-34AERF/W	37864/1053		358
☐ N359UP	Boeing 767-34AERF/W	37870/1056		359
☐ N360UP	Boeing 767-34AERF/W	37946/1057		360
☐ N361UP	Boeing 767-34AERF/W	37878/1059		361
☐ N250UP	McDonnell-Douglas MD-11F	48745/596	ex N798BA	
☐ N251UP	McDonnell-Douglas MD-11F	48744/592	ex N797BA	
☐ N252UP	McDonnell-Douglas MD-11F	48768/601	ex PP-SFA	
☐ N253UP	McDonnell-Douglas MD-11F	48439/554	ex PP-VPM	
☐ N254UP	McDonnell-Douglas MD-11F	48406/547	ex PP-VPL	
☐ N255UP	McDonnell-Douglas MD-11F	48404/523	ex PP-VPJ	
☐ N256UP	McDonnell-Douglas MD-11F	48405/524	ex PP-VPK	
☐ N257UP	McDonnell-Douglas MD-11F	48451/505	ex HS-TMG	
☐ N258UP	McDonnell-Douglas MD-11F	48416/466	ex HS-TMD	
☐ N259UP	McDonnell-Douglas MD-11F	48417/467	ex HS-TME	
☐ N260UP	McDonnell-Douglas MD-11F	48418/501	ex HS-TMF	
☐ N270UP	McDonnell-Douglas MD-11F	48576/574	ex JA8585	
☐ N271UP	McDonnell-Douglas MD-11F	48572/556	ex JA8581	
☐ N272UP	McDonnell-Douglas MD-11F	48571/552	ex JA8580	
☐ N273UP	McDonnell-Douglas MD-11F	48574/566	ex JA8583	
☐ N274UP	McDonnell-Douglas MD-11F	48575/568	ex JA8584	
☐ N275UP	McDonnell-Douglas MD-11F	48774/610	ex JA8589	
☐ N276UP	McDonnell-Douglas MD-11F	48579/599	ex JA8588	
☐ N277UP	McDonnell-Douglas MD-11F	48578/588	ex JA8587	
☐ N278UP	McDonnell-Douglas MD-11F	48577/583	ex JA8586	
☐ N279UP	McDonnell-Douglas MD-11F	48573/559	ex JA8582	
☐ N280UP	McDonnell-Douglas MD-11F	48634/614	ex N38WF	
☐ N281UP	McDonnell-Douglas MD-11F	48538/533	ex N48WF	
☐ N282UP	McDonnell-Douglas MD-11F	48452/472	ex N74WF	
☐ N283UP	McDonnell-Douglas MD-11F	48484/484	ex V5-NMC	
☐ N284UP	McDonnell-Douglas MD-11F	48541/621	ex PP-VTU	
☐ N285UP	McDonnell-Douglas MD-11F	48457/498	ex PP-VTH	
☐ N286UP	McDonnell-Douglas MD-11F	48453/473	ex V5-NMD	
☐ N287UP	McDonnell-Douglas MD-11F	48539/571	ex PP-VTP	
☐ N288UP	McDonnell-Douglas MD-11F	48540/611	ex PP-VTK	
☐ N289UP	McDonnell-Douglas MD-11F	48455/487	ex PP-VTJ	
☐ N290UP	McDonnell-Douglas MD-11F	48456/494	ex PP-VTI	
☐ N291UP	McDonnell-Douglas MD-11F	48477/511	ex N806DE	
☐ N292UP	McDonnell-Douglas MD-11F	48566/543	ex N811DE	
☐ N293UP	McDonnell-Douglas MD-11F	48473/481	ex N802DE	
☐ N294UP	McDonnell-Douglas MD-11F	48472/480	ex N801DE	
☐ N295UP	McDonnell-Douglas MD-11F	48475/489	ex N804DE	
☐ N296UP	McDonnell-Douglas MD-11F	48474/485	ex N803DE	

US AIRWAYS	**US Air (US/USA)**
	Pittsburgh-Greater Pittsburgh Intl, PA/Phoenix-Sky Harbor Intl, AZ (PIT/PHX)

Ops merged with Americal Airlines 08Apr15

US AIRWAYS EXPRESS	**Air Express (USX)**
	Charlotte, NC/Philadelphia, PA/Pittsburgh, PA (CLT/PHL/PIT)

☐ N401AW	Canadair CRJ-200LR	7280	ex C-FMLQ	401	Air Wisconsin
☐ N403AW	Canadair CRJ-200LR	7288	ex C-FMLF	403	Air Wisconsin
☐ N404AW	Canadair CRJ-200LR	7294	ex C-FMMT	404	Air Wisconsin
☐ N405AW	Canadair CRJ-200LR	7362	ex C-FMND	405	Air Wisconsin
☐ N406AW	Canadair CRJ-200LR	7402	ex C-FMMY	406	Air Wisconsin
☐ N407AW	Canadair CRJ-200LR	7424	ex C-FMLU	407	Air Wisconsin
☐ N408AW	Canadair CRJ-200LR	7568	ex C-FMNY	408	Air Wisconsin
☐ N409AW	Canadair CRJ-200LR	7447	ex C-FMNX	409	Air Wisconsin
☐ N410AW	Canadair CRJ-200LR	7490	ex C-FMMW	410	Air Wisconsin
☐ N411ZW	Canadair CRJ-200LR	7569	ex C-FMNZ	411	Air Wisconsin
☐ N412AW	Canadair CRJ-200LR	7582	ex C-FMMY	412	Air Wisconsin
☐ N413AW	Canadair CRJ-200LR	7585	ex C-FMKW	413	Air Wisconsin
☐ N414ZW	Canadair CRJ-200LR	7586	ex C-FMKZ	414	Air Wisconsin
☐ N415AW	Canadair CRJ-200LR	7593	ex C-FMLV	415	Air Wisconsin
☐ N416AW	Canadair CRJ-200LR	7603	ex C-FMNQ	416	Air Wisconsin
☐ N417AW	Canadair CRJ-200LR	7610	ex C-FMMW	417	Air Wisconsin
☐ N418AW	Canadair CRJ-200LR	7618	ex C-FMLF	418	Air Wisconsin
☐ N419AW	Canadair CRJ-200LR	7633	ex C-FMNQ	419	Air Wisconsin

☐ N420AW	Canadair CRJ-200LR	7640	ex C-FMMW	420		Air Wisconsin
☐ N421ZW	Canadair CRJ-200LR	7346	ex N587ML	421		Air Wisconsin
☐ N422AW	Canadair CRJ-200LR	7341	ex N586ML	422		Air Wisconsin
☐ N423AW	Canadair CRJ-200LR	7636	ex C-FMMB	423		Air Wisconsin
☐ N424AW	Canadair CRJ-200LR	7656	ex C-FMNW	424		Air Wisconsin
☐ N425AW	Canadair CRJ-200LR	7663	ex C-FMNQ	425		Air Wisconsin
☐ N426AW	Canadair CRJ-200LR	7669	ex C-FMMQ	426		Air Wisconsin
☐ N427ZW	Canadair CRJ-200LR	7685	ex C-FMNH	427		Air Wisconsin
☐ N428AW	Canadair CRJ-200LR	7695	ex C-FMOI	428		Air Wisconsin
☐ N429AW	Canadair CRJ-200LR	7711	ex CFMLS	429		Air Wisconsin
☐ N430AW	Canadair CRJ-200LR	7719	ex C-FMOS	430		Air Wisconsin
☐ N431AW	Canadair CRJ-200LR	7256	ex N575ML	431		Air Wisconsin
☐ N432AW	Canadair CRJ-200LR	7257	ex N576ML	432		Air Wisconsin
☐ N433AW	Canadair CRJ-200LR	7289	ex N580ML	433		Air Wisconsin
☐ N434AW	Canadair CRJ-200LR	7322	ex N582ML	434		Air Wisconsin
☐ N435AW	Canadair CRJ-200LR	7724	ex C-FMLU	435		Air Wisconsin
☐ N436AW	Canadair CRJ-200LR	7734	ex C-FMKV	436		Air Wisconsin
☐ N437AW	Canadair CRJ-200LR	7744	ex C-FMMT	437		Air Wisconsin
☐ N438AW	Canadair CRJ-200LR	7748	ex C-GFAX	438		Air Wisconsin
☐ N439AW	Canadair CRJ-200LR	7753	ex C-FZZO	439		Air Wisconsin
☐ N440AW	Canadair CRJ-200LR	7766	ex C-FMKZ	440		Air Wisconsin
☐ N441ZW	Canadair CRJ-200LR	7777	ex C-FMNX	441		Air Wisconsin
☐ N442AW	Canadair CRJ-200LR	7778	ex C-FMNY	442		Air Wisconsin
☐ N443AW	Canadair CRJ-200LR	7781	ex C-FVAZ	443		Air Wisconsin
☐ N444ZW	Canadair CRJ-200LR	7788	ex C-FMMN	444		Air Wisconsin
☐ N445AW	Canadair CRJ-200LR	7804	ex C-FMMT	445		Air Wisconsin
☐ N446AW	Canadair CRJ-200LR	7806	ex C-FMNW	446		Air Wisconsin
☐ N447AW	Canadair CRJ-200LR	7812	ex C-FMND	447		Air Wisconsin
☐ N448AW	Canadair CRJ-200LR	7814	ex C-FMLU	448		Air Wisconsin
☐ N449AW	Canadair CRJ-200LR	7818	ex C-FMMN	449		Air Wisconsin
☐ N450AW	Canadair CRJ-200LR	7823	ex C-FMNB	450		Air Wisconsin
☐ N451AW	Canadair CRJ-200LR	7832	ex C-FMLT	451		Air Wisconsin
☐ N452AW	Canadair CRJ-200LR	7835	ex C-FMNH	452		Air Wisconsin
☐ N453AW	Canadair CRJ-200LR	7838	ex C-FMNY	453		Air Wisconsin
☐ N454AW	Canadair CRJ-200LR	7842	ex C-FMND	454		Air Wisconsin
☐ N455AW	Canadair CRJ-200LR	7848	ex C-FMMN	455		Air Wisconsin
☐ N456ZW	Canadair CRJ-200LR	7849	ex C-FMMQ	456		Air Wisconsin
☐ N457AW	Canadair CRJ-200LR	7854	ex C-FMKV	457		Air Wisconsin
☐ N458AW	Canadair CRJ-200LR	7861	ex C-FMLS	458		Air Wisconsin
☐ N459AW	Canadair CRJ-200LR	7863	ex C-FMLV	459		Air Wisconsin
☐ N460AW	Canadair CRJ-200LR	7867	ex C-GZTD	460		Air Wisconsin
☐ N461AW	Canadair CRJ-200LR	7870	ex C-FMOW	461		Air Wisconsin
☐ N462AW	Canadair CRJ-200LR	7875	ex C-FMOI	462		Air Wisconsin
☐ N463AW	Canadair CRJ-200LR	7878	ex C-FMMN	463		Air Wisconsin
☐ N464AW	Canadair CRJ-200LR	7890	ex C-FMLQ	464		Air Wisconsin
☐ N465AW	Canadair CRJ-200LR	7893	ex C-FMLV	465		Air Wisconsin
☐ N466AW	Canadair CRJ-200LR	7899	ex C-FMOS	466		Air Wisconsin
☐ N467AW	Canadair CRJ-200LR	7900	ex C-FMOW	467		Air Wisconsin
☐ N468AW	Canadair CRJ-200LR	7916	ex C-FMKZ	468		Air Wisconsin
☐ N469AW	Canadair CRJ-200LR	7917	ex C-FMLB	469		Air Wisconsin
☐ N470ZW	Canadair CRJ-200LR	7927	ex C-FMNX	470		Air Wisconsin
☐ N471ZW	Canadair CRJ-200ER	7457	ex N655BR			Air Wisconsin
☐ N17231	Canadair CRJ-200ER	7231	ex C-FMLS			Mesa
☐ N37178	Canadair CRJ-200ER	7178	ex C-GAVO			Mesa
☐ N77286	Canadair CRJ-200ER	7286	ex C-FMKZ			Mesa [TUS]
☐ N202PS	Canadair CRJ-200ER	7858	ex C-FMLF	202		PSA
☐ N206PS	Canadair CRJ-200ER	7860	ex C-FMLQ	206		PSA
☐ N207PS	Canadair CRJ-200ER	7873	ex C-FMNQ	207		PSA
☐ N209PS	Canadair CRJ-200ER	7874	ex C-FMLU	209		PSA
☐ N213PS	Canadair CRJ-200ER	7879	ex C-FMMQ	213		PSA
☐ N215PS	Canadair CRJ-200ER	7880	ex C-FMMW	215		PSA
☐ N216PS	Canadair CRJ-200ER	7882	ex C-FMMY	216		PSA
☐ N218PS	Canadair CRJ-200ER	7885	ex C-FMKW	218		PSA
☐ N220PS	Canadair CRJ-200ER	7887	ex C-FMLB	220		PSA
☐ N221PS	Canadair CRJ-200ER	7889	ex C-FMLI	221		PSA
☐ N223JS	Canadair CRJ-200ER	7892	ex C-FMLT	223		PSA
☐ N226JS	Canadair CRJ-200ER	7895	ex C-FMNH	226		PSA
☐ N228PS	Canadair CRJ-200ER	7897	ex C-FMNX	228		PSA
☐ N229PS	Canadair CRJ-200ER	7898	ex C-FMNY	229		PSA
☐ N230PS	Canadair CRJ-200ER	7904	ex C-FMLU	230		PSA
☐ N237PS	Canadair CRJ-200ER	7906	ex C-FMMB	237		PSA
☐ N241PS	Canadair CRJ-200ER	7909	ex C-FMMQ	241		PSA
☐ N242JS	Canadair CRJ-200ER	7911	ex C-FMMX	242		PSA
☐ N244PS	Canadair CRJ-200ER	7912	ex C-FMMY	244		PSA
☐ N245PS	Canadair CRJ-200ER	7919	ex C-FMLI	245		PSA
☐ N246PS	Canadair CRJ-200ER	7920	ex C-FMLQ	246		PSA
☐ N247JS	Canadair CRJ-200ER	7922	ex C-FMLT	247		PSA
☐ N248PS	Canadair CRJ-200ER	7925	ex C-FMNH	248		PSA
☐ N249PS	Canadair CRJ-200ER	7926	ex C-FMNW	249		PSA
☐ N250PS	Canadair CRJ-200ER	7929	ex C-FMOS	250		PSA
☐ N251PS	Canadair CRJ-200ER	7931	ex C-FVAZ	251		PSA

☐ N253PS	Canadair CRJ-200ER	7934	ex C-FMLU	253		PSA
☐ N254PS	Canadair CRJ-200ER	7935	ex C-FMOI	254		PSA
☐ N256PS	Canadair CRJ-200ER	7937	ex C-FMML	256		PSA
☐ N257PS	Canadair CRJ-200ER	7939	ex C-FMMQ	257		PSA
☐ N258PS	Canadair CRJ-200ER	7941	ex C-FMMX	258		PSA
☐ N259PS	Canadair CRJ-200ER	7945	ex C-FMKW	259		PSA
☐ N260JS	Canadair CRJ-200ER	7957	ex C-FMNX	260		PSA
☐ N261PS	Canadair CRJ-200ER	7959	ex C-FMOS	261		PSA
☐ N262PS	Canadair CRJ-200ER	7962	ex C-FMND	262		PSA
☐ N468CA	Canadair CRJ-200ER	7649	ex C-FMLI	7649		SkyWest
☐ N492SW	Canadair CRJ-100ER	7168	ex N982CA	7168		SkyWest♦
☐ N496CA	Canadair CRJ-200ER	7791	ex C-FMMX	791		SkyWest
☐ N506CA	Canadair CRJ-200ER	7793	ex C-FMNB	793		SkyWest
☐ N821AS	Canadair CRJ-200ER	7194	ex C-FMKV	821		SkyWest♦
☐ N874AS	Canadair CRJ-200ER	7551	ex C-GJLK	874		SkyWest<BTA
☐ N885AS	Canadair CRJ-200ER	7521	ex C-GJDX	885		SkyWest<BTA
☐ N886AS	Canadair CRJ-200ER	7531	ex C-GJJC	886		SkyWest<ASQ
☐ N906SW	Canadair CRJ-200ER	7510	ex C-FMOW	7510		SkyWest
☐ N907SW	Canadair CRJ-200ER	7511	ex C-FVAZ	7511		SkyWest
☐ N944SW	Canadair CRJ-200ER	7764	ex C-FMKV	7764		SkyWest
☐ N702PS	Canadair CRJ-701ER	10135	ex C-	702		PSA
☐ N703PS	Canadair CRJ-701ER	10137	ex C-	703		PSA
☐ N705PS	Canadair CRJ-701ER	10144	ex C-	705		PSA
☐ N706PS	Canadair CRJ-701ER	10150	ex C-FBLQ	706		PSA
☐ N708PS	Canadair CRJ-701ER	10160	ex C-	708	Star Alliance c/s	PSA
☐ N709PS	Canadair CRJ-701ER	10165	ex N165MD	709		PSA
☐ N710PS	Canadair CRJ-701ER	10167	ex N167MD	710		PSA
☐ N712PS	Canadair CRJ-701ER	10168	ex N168MD	712		PSA
☐ N716PS	Canadair CRJ-701ER	10171	ex N171MD	716		PSA
☐ N718PS	Canadair CRJ-701ER	10175	ex C-FCQX	718		PSA
☐ N719PS	Canadair CRJ-701ER	10177	ex N177MD	719		PSA
☐ N720PS	Canadair CRJ-701ER	10178	ex N175MD	720		PSA
☐ N723PS	Canadair CRJ-701ER	10181	ex C-FCRE	723		PSA
☐ N725PS	Canadair CRJ-701ER	10186	ex C-	725		PSA
☐ N243LR	Canadair CRJ-900	15064	ex C-GLPN	#CYC		Mesa
☐ N244LR	Canadair CRJ-900	15233	ex C-GUHF	#CYD		Mesa
☐ N245LR	Canadair CRJ-900	15234	ex C-GUHH	#CYE		Mesa
☐ N246LR	Canadair CRJ-900	15239	ex C-GUHT	#CYF		Mesa
☐ N247LR	Canadair CRJ-900	15273	ex C-GUHU			Mesa [PHX]
☐ N902FJ	Canadair CRJ-900ER	15002	ex C-GDNH			Mesa
☐ N903FJ	Canadair CRJ-900ER	15003	ex C-GZQA			Mesa
☐ N904FJ	Canadair CRJ-900ER	15004	ex C-GZQB			Mesa
☐ N905J	Canadair CRJ-900ER	15005	ex C-GZQC			Mesa
☐ N906FJ	Canadair CRJ-900ER	15006	ex C-GZQE			Mesa
☐ N907FJ	Canadair CRJ-900ER	15007	ex C-GZQF			Mesa
☐ N908FJ	Canadair CRJ-900ER	15008	ex C-GZQG			Mesa
☐ N909FJ	Canadair CRJ-900ER	15009	ex C-GZQI			Mesa
☐ N910FJ	Canadair CRJ-900ER	15010	ex C-GZQJ			Mesa
☐ N911FJ	Canadair CRJ-900ER	15011	ex C-GZQK			Mesa
☐ N912FJ	Canadair CRJ-900ER	15012	ex C-GZQL			Mesa
☐ N913FJ	Canadair CRJ-900ER	15013	ex C-GZQM			Mesa
☐ N914FJ	Canadair CRJ-900ER	15014	ex C-GZQO			Mesa
☐ N915FJ	Canadair CRJ-900ER	15015	ex C-GZQP			Mesa
☐ N916FJ	Canadair CRJ-900ER	15016	ex C-GZQQ			Mesa
☐ N917FJ	Canadair CRJ-900ER	15017	ex C-GZQR			Mesa
☐ N918FJ	Canadair CRJ-900ER	15018	ex C-			Mesa
☐ N919FJ	Canadair CRJ-900ER	15019	ex C-			Mesa
☐ N920FJ	Canadair CRJ-900ER	15020	ex C-			Mesa
☐ N921FJ	Canadair CRJ-900ER	15021	ex C-			Mesa
☐ N922FJ	Canadair CRJ-900ER	15022	ex C-			Mesa
☐ N923FJ	Canadair CRJ-900ER	15023	ex C-			Mesa
☐ N924FJ	Canadair CRJ-900ER	15024	ex C-			Mesa
☐ N925FJ	Canadair CRJ-900ER	15025	ex C-			Mesa
☐ N926LR	Canadair CRJ-900ER	15026	ex C-			Mesa
☐ N927LR	Canadair CRJ-900ER	15027	ex C-			Mesa
☐ N928LR	Canadair CRJ-900ER	15028	ex C-			Mesa
☐ N929LR	Canadair CRJ-900ER	15029	ex C-			Mesa
☐ N930LR	Canadair CRJ-900ER	15030	ex C-			Mesa
☐ N931LR	Canadair CRJ-900ER	15031	ex C-			Mesa
☐ N932LR	Canadair CRJ-900ER	15032	ex C-			Mesa
☐ N933LR	Canadair CRJ-900ER	15033	ex C-			Mesa
☐ N934FJ	Canadair CRJ-900ER	15034	ex C-			Mesa
☐ N935LR	Canadair CRJ-900ER	15035	ex C-			Mesa
☐ N938LR	Canadair CRJ-900ER	15038	ex C-			Mesa
☐ N939LR	Canadair CRJ-900ER	15039	ex C-			Mesa
☐ N942LR	Canadair CRJ-900ER	15042	ex C-			Mesa
☐ N956LR	Canadair CRJ-900ER	15056	ex C-			Mesa
☐ N804EX	de Havilland DHC-8-102A	227	ex C-GFYI	ESA		Piedmont
☐ N805EX	de Havilland DHC-8-102A	228	ex C-GLOT	ESB		Piedmont

☐ N806EX	de Havilland DHC-8-102A	263	ex C-GEVP	ESC	Piedmont
☐ N807EX	de Havilland DHC-8-102A	292	ex C-GFQL	ESD	Piedmont
☐ N808EX	de Havilland DHC-8-102A	299	ex C-GDKL	ESE	Piedmont
☐ N809EX	de Havilland DHC-8-102A	302	ex PT-MFI	ESF	Piedmont
☐ N810EX	de Havilland DHC-8-102A	308	ex C-GDKL	ESG	Piedmont
☐ N812EX	de Havilland DHC-8-102A	312	ex C-GDNG	ESH	Piedmont
☐ N814EX	de Havilland DHC-8-102A	318	ex C-GDNG	ESI	Piedmont
☐ N815EX	de Havilland DHC-8-102A	321	ex C-GDFT	ESJ	Piedmont
☐ N816EX	de Havilland DHC-8-102A	329	ex C-GEVP	ESK	Piedmont
☐ N837EX	de Havilland DHC-8-102A	217	ex N976HA	ERH	Piedmont
☐ N838EX	de Havilland DHC-8-102A	220	ex N977HA	ERK	Piedmont
☐ N839EX	de Havilland DHC-8-102	226	ex N803EX	ERL	Piedmont
☐ N906HA	de Havilland DHC-8-102	009	ex C-GHRI	HAS	Piedmont
☐ N907HA	de Havilland DHC-8-102	011	ex C-GESR	HSB	Piedmont
☐ N908HA	de Havilland DHC-8-102	015	ex C-GIBQ	HSC	Piedmont
☐ N911HA	de Havilland DHC-8-102	034	ex C-GEOA	HSF	Piedmont
☐ N912HA	de Havilland DHC-8-102	040	ex C-GEOA	HSG	Piedmont
☐ N914HA	de Havilland DHC-8-102	053	ex C-GETI	HSH	Piedmont
☐ N930HA	de Havilland DHC-8-102	126	ex C-GFQL	HSW	Piedmont
☐ N931HA	de Havilland DHC-8-102	132	ex C-GFOD	HSZ	Piedmont
☐ N933HA	de Havilland DHC-8-102	134	ex C-GFUM	HBA	Piedmont
☐ N935HA	de Havilland DHC-8-102	142	ex C-GLOT	HBC	Piedmont
☐ N936HA	de Havilland DHC-8-102	145	ex C-GFQL	HRA	Piedmont
☐ N937HA	de Havilland DHC-8-102	148	ex C-GLOT	HRB	Piedmont
☐ N938HA	de Havilland DHC-8-102	152	ex C-GFUM	HRC	Piedmont
☐ N940HA	de Havilland DHC-8-102	156	ex C-GLOT	HRE	Piedmont
☐ N941HA	de Havilland DHC-8-102	161	ex C-GETI	HRF	Piedmont
☐ N942HA	de Havilland DHC-8-102	163	ex C-GFUM	HRG	Piedmont
☐ N943HA	de Havilland DHC-8-102	167	ex C-GFOD	HRH	Piedmont
☐ N975HA	de Havilland DHC-8-102	176		HRI	Piedmont
☐ N326EN	de Havilland DHC-8-311	234	ex N386DC	HDF	Piedmont
☐ N327EN	de Havilland DHC-8-311A	261	ex N379DC	HDD	Piedmont
☐ N328EN	de Havilland DHC-8-311A	281	ex N380DC	HDC	Piedmont
☐ N330EN	de Havilland DHC-8-311A	274	ex N805SA	HDI	Piedmont
☐ N331EN	de Havilland DHC-8-311A	279	ex N806SA	HDJ	Piedmont
☐ N333EN	de Havilland DHC-8-311	221	ex N803SA	HDK	Piedmont
☐ N335EN	de Havilland DHC-8-311	375	ex N804SA	HDN	Piedmont
☐ N336EN	de Havilland DHC-8-311A	336	ex N284BC	HAD	Piedmont
☐ N343EN	de Havilland DHC-8-311A	340	ex OE-LLZ	HDE	Piedmont
☐ N801HK	Embraer ERJ-145ER	145053	ex PT-SZS	TRK	Trans States
☐ N808HK	Embraer ERJ-145ER	145157	ex PT-SEK	TRD	Trans States
☐ N809HK	Embraer ERJ-145ER	145187	ex PT-SGH	TRE	Trans States
☐ N812HK	Embraer ERJ-145ER	145373	ex PT-SOY	TRG	Trans States
☐ N801MA	Embraer ERJ-170SU	17000012	ex PT-SKE	801	Republic
☐ N802MD	Embraer ERJ-170SU	17000013	ex PT-SKF	802	Republic
☐ N803MD	Embraer ERJ-170SU	17000015	ex PT-SKI	803	Republic
☐ N805MD	Embraer ERJ-170SU	17000018	ex PT-SKL	805	Republic
☐ N806MD	Embraer ERJ-170SU	17000019	ex PT-SKM	806	Republic>SLI
☐ N807MD	Embraer ERJ-170SU	17000020	ex PT-SKN	807	Republic
☐ N808MD	Embraer ERJ-170SU	17000021	ex PT-SKO	808	Republic
☐ N809MD	Embraer ERJ-170SU	17000022	ex PT-SKP	809	Republic
☐ N811MD	Embraer ERJ-170SU	17000028	ex PT-SKV	811	Republic
☐ N812MD	Embraer ERJ-170SU	17000030	ex PT-SKY	812	Republic
☐ N813MA	Embraer ERJ-170SU	17000031	ex PT-SKZ	813	Republic
☐ N814MD	Embraer ERJ-170SU	17000033	ex PT-SUB	814	Republic
☐ N816MA	Embraer ERJ-170SU	17000037	ex PT-SUG	816	Republic
☐ N817MD	Embraer ERJ-170SU	17000038	ex PT-SUH	817	Republic
☐ N819MD	Embraer ERJ-170SU	17000040	ex PT-SUJ	819	Republic
☐ N820MD	Embraer ERJ-170SU	17000041	ex PT-SUK	820	Republic
☐ N821MD	Embraer ERJ-170SU	17000042	ex PT-SUL	821	Republic>SLI
☐ N822MD	Embraer ERJ-170SU	17000043	ex PT-SUM	822	Republic
☐ N826MD	Embraer ERJ-170SU	17000046	ex PT-SUP	826	Republic>SLI
☐ N827MD	Embraer ERJ-170SU	17000047	ex PT-SUQ	827	Republic
☐ N828MD	Embraer ERJ-170SU	17000048	ex PT-SUR	828	Republic
☐ N829MD	Embraer ERJ-170SU	17000049	ex PT-SUT	829	Republic
☐ N873RW	Embraer ERJ-170SU	17000144	ex PT-	703	Republic
☐ N874RW	Embraer ERJ-170SU	17000148	ex PT-	704	Republic
☐ N101HQ	Embraer ERJ-175LR	17000156	ex PT-SEU		Republic
☐ N102HQ	Embraer ERJ-175LR	17000157	ex PT-SEV		Republic
☐ N103HQ	Embraer ERJ-175LR	17000159	ex PT-SEX		Republic
☐ N104HQ	Embraer ERJ-175LR	17000160	ex PT-SMA		Republic
☐ N105HQ	Embraer ERJ-175LR	17000163	ex PT-SMF		Republic
☐ N106HQ	Embraer ERJ-175LR	17000164	ex PT-SMG		Republic
☐ N107HQ	Embraer ERJ-175LR	17000165	ex PT-SMH		Republic
☐ N108HQ	Embraer ERJ-175LR	17000166	ex PT-SMI		Republic
☐ N109HQ	Embraer ERJ-175LR	17000168	ex PT-SMK		Republic
☐ N110HQ	Embraer ERJ-175LR	17000172	ex PT-SMP		Republic
☐ N111HQ	Embraer ERJ-175LR	17000173	ex PT-SMQ		Republic
☐ N112HQ	Embraer ERJ-175LR	17000174	ex PT-SMR		Republic

☐ N113HQ	Embraer ERJ-175LR	17000177	ex PT-SMU		Republic
☐ N114HQ	Embraer ERJ-175LR	17000179	ex PT-SMW		Republic
☐ N115HQ	Embraer ERJ-175LR	17000182	ex PT-SMZ		Republic
☐ N116HQ	Embraer ERJ-175LR	17000183	ex PT-SUA		Republic
☐ N117HQ	Embraer ERJ-175LR	17000184	ex PT-SUB		Republic
☐ N118HQ	Embraer ERJ-175LR	17000189	ex PT-SUI		Republic
☐ N119HQ	Embraer ERJ-175LR	17000190	ex PT-SUQ		Republic
☐ N120HQ	Embraer ERJ-175LR	17000193	ex PT-SUV		Republic
☐ N121HQ	Embraer ERJ-175LR	17000194	ex PT-SUY		Republic
☐ N122HQ	Embraer ERJ-175LR	17000196	ex PT-SXF		Republic
☐ N123HQ	Embraer ERJ-175LR	17000199	ex PT-SXM		Republic
☐ N124HQ	Embraer ERJ-175LR	17000200	ex PT-SXO		Republic
☐ N125HQ	Embraer ERJ-175LR	17000202	ex PT-SXR		Republic
☐ N126HQ	Embraer ERJ-175LR	17000204	ex PT-SXU		Republic
☐ N127HQ	Embraer ERJ-175LR	17000206	ex PT-SCB		Republic
☐ N128HQ	Embraer ERJ-175LR	17000208	ex PT-SCF		Republic
☐ N129HQ	Embraer ERJ-175LR	17000211	ex PT-SCI		Republic
☐ N130HQ	Embraer ERJ-175LR	17000212	ex PT-SCJ		Republic
☐ N131HQ	Embraer ERJ-175LR	17000215	ex PT-SCM		Republic
☐ N132HQ	Embraer ERJ-175LR	17000216	ex PT-SCN		Republic
☐ N133HQ	Embraer ERJ-175LR	17000217	ex PT-SCO		Republic
☐ N134HQ	Embraer ERJ-175LR	17000220	ex PT-SCS		Republic
☐ N135HQ	Embraer ERJ-175LR	17000224	ex PT-SFA		Republic
☐ N136HQ	Embraer ERJ-170LR	17000228	ex PT-SFE		Republic
☐ N137HQ	Embraer ER.I-170LR	17000231	ex PT-SFH		Republic
☐ N138HQ	Embraer ERJ-170LR	17000234	cx PT-SFK		Republic
☐ N339CJ	SAAB SF.340B	340B-339	ex N339SB	LNA	[MNZ]
☐ N144ZV	Beech 1900D	UE-144			Mesa wfs

USDA FOREST SERVICE   Boise, ID (BOI)

☐ N105NJ	Bell UH-1H	9265	ex 66-17071		
☐ N106NJ	Bell UH-1H	5724	ex 66-16030		
☐ N107NJ	Bell UH-1H	13682	ex 74-22358		
☐ N107Z	Bell UH-1	22342	ex 83-24194		
☐ N109Z	Bell UH-1	20854	ex 69-16422		
☐ N120FC	Bell UH-1H	12565	ex 70-16260		
☐ N121FC	Bell UH-1H	4404	ex N4396H		
☐ N122FC	Bell UH-1H	4749	ex 65-09705		
☐ N124FC	Bell UH-1H	4457	ex 64-13750		
☐ N128FC	Bell UH-1H	12136	ex 69-15848		
☐ N205BH	Bell EH-1H	11373	ex 69-15085		
☐ N205FD	Bell UH-1H	5305	ex 66-0822		
☐ N205KS	Bell UH-1H	9526	ex N3132B		
☐ N242KC	Bell UH-1H	10040	ex 67-17842		
☐ N338WN	Bell UH-1H	4138	ex N81735		
☐ N339WN	Bell UH-1H	4175	ex 63-12979		
☐ N340WN	Bell UH-1H	5125	ex 65-10081		
☐ N341WN	Bell UH-1H	5174	ex 65-10130		
☐ N343WN	Bell UH-1H		ex 73-21764		♦
☐ N344WN	Bell UH-1H	13153	ex 71-20329		
☐ N345WN	Bell UH-1F	13328	ex 72-21629		
☐ N346WN	Bell UH-1F	12318	ex 70-15708		
☐ N347WN	Bell UH-1E	13549	ex 73-22066		
☐ N387M	Bell UH-1H	11769	ex 69-15481		
☐ N388M	Bell UH-1H	13368	ex 73-21680		
☐ N394M	Bell UH-1H	4392	ex 64-13685		
☐ N395M	Bell UH-1H	4706	ex 65-09662		
☐ N398M	Bell UH-1H	5028	ex 65-09984		
☐ N407KC	Bell UH-1H	8595	ex N240KC		♦
☐ N408KC	Bell UH-1H	9923	ex N141KC		
☐ N441FA	Bell UH-1H	5610	ex N4212Y		
☐ N481DF	Bell UH-1H	13318	ex 72-21019		♦
☐ N488DF	Bell UH-1H	11527	ex N305SB		♦
☐ N489DF	Bell EH-1X	12224	ex 69-15936	standby♦	
☐ N490DF	Bell UH-1H	12375	ex 70-15765		♦
☐ N491DF	Bell EH-1H	12146	ex 69-15858		♦
☐ N492DF	Bell EH-1H	11433	ex 69-15145	standby♦	
☐ N493DF	Bell EH-1H	12001	ex 69-15713	standby♦	
☐ N494DF	Bell EH-1X	11303	ex 69-15015		♦
☐ N495DF	Bell EH-1H	12218	ex 69-15930		♦
☐ N496DF	Bell EH-1H	11964	ex 69-15676		♦
☐ N497DF	Bell EH-1H	11553	ex 69-15265		♦
☐ N498DF	Bell UH-1H	12153	ex 69-15865		♦
☐ N499DF	Bell UH-1H	12846	ex 71-20022		♦
☐ N541FA	Bell UH-1H	8529	ex N4212C		
☐ N777SF	Bell UH-1H	12220			♦
☐ N915MF	Bell UH-1H		ex 65-9750		♦
☐ N925MF	Bell UH-1H		ex 65-9871		♦
☐ N935MF	Bell UH-1H		ex 65-9836		♦
☐ N945MF	Bell UH-1H		ex 66-16634		♦
☐ N955MF	Bell UH-1H		ex 69-15213		♦

☐	N965MF	Bell UH-1H		ex 66-16070	◆
☐	N987SF	Bell UH-1H		ex 66-16639	◆
☐	N6132N	Bell UH-1H		ex 66-16040	◆
☐	N60124	Bell UH-1H	10419		◆
☐	N29FC	Cessna U206C Stationair	U206-1191	ex N29246	
☐	N111Z	Cessna TU206F Turbo Stationair	U20602919	ex N1761Q	
☐	N126Z	Cessna TU206F Turbo Stationair	U20602367	ex N2399U	
☐	N146FC	Cessna P206A Stationair	P206-0247	ex N163SF	
☐	N166Z	Cessna TU206G Turbo Stationair 6	U20606923	ex N136Z	
☐	N527NR	Cessna U206 Stationair	U206-0278	ex N5278U	
☐	N764	Cessna U206F Stationair	U20602672		◆
☐	N106FS	de Havilland DHC-2 Beaver	477	ex N31521	
☐	N191Z	de Havilland DHC-2 Beaver	1006		
☐	N192Z	de Havilland DHC-2 Beaver	1347	ex N1927	
☐	N193Z	de Havilland DHC-2 Beaver	1162	ex N197Z	
☐	N904AK	de Havilland DHC-2 Beaver	1266	ex N9262Z	
☐	N4932	de Havilland DHC-2 Beaver	471	ex 52-6099	
☐	N422DF	Marsh S-2T Turbo Tracker	286C	ex N518DF	◆
☐	N424DF	Marsh S-2T Turbo Tracker	289C	ex N519DF	◆
☐	N425DF	Marsh S-2T Turbo Tracker	294C	ex N522DF	◆
☐	N426DF	Marsh S-2T Turbo Tracker	293C	ex N520DF	◆
☐	N427DF	Marsh S-2T Turbo Tracker	326C	ex N524DF	◆
☐	N428DF	Marsh S-2T Turbo Tracker	137C	ex N511DF	◆
☐	N431DF	Marsh S-2T Turbo Tracker	109C	ex N504DF	◆
☐	N432DF	Marsh S-2T Turbo Tracker	112C	ex N505DF	◆
☐	N433DF	Marsh S-2T Turbo Tracker	130C	ex N510DF	◆
☐	N434DF	Marsh S-2T Turbo Tracker	335C	ex N527DF	◆
☐	N435DF	Marsh S-2T Turbo Tracker	329C	ex N526DF	◆
☐	N436DF	Marsh S-2T Turbo Tracker	224C	ex Bu152337	◆
☐	N437DF	Marsh S-2T Turbo Tracker	123C	ex N507DF	dam 04Oct13 ◆
☐	N438DF	Marsh S-2T Turbo Tracker	173C	ex N513DF	◆
☐	N439DF	Marsh S-2T Turbo Tracker	129C	ex N509DF	◆
☐	N440DF	Marsh S-2T Turbo Tracker	148C	ex N512DF	◆
☐	N441DF	Marsh S-2T Turbo Tracker	277C	ex N517DF	◆
☐	N442DF	Marsh S-2T Turbo Tracker	295C	ex Bu152826	◆
☐	N444DF	Marsh S-2T Turbo Tracker	187C	ex N515DF	◆
☐	N445DF	Marsh S-2T Turbo Tracker	232C	ex N516DF	◆
☐	N448DF	Marsh S-2T Turbo Tracker	234C	ex Bu152347	◆
☐	N449DF	Marsh S-2T Turbo Tracker	307C	ex N523DF	◆
☐	N450DF	Marsh S-2T Turbo Tracker	228C	ex Bu152341	◆
☐	N400DF	Rockwell OV-10A Bronco	305-122M-65	ex Bu155454	◆
☐	N401DF	Rockwell OV-10A Bronco	305-128M-68	ex Bu155457	standby ◆
☐	N402DF	Rockwell OV-10A Bronco	305-132M-70	ex Bu155459	◆
☐	N403DF	Rockwell OV-10A Bronco	305-148M-78	ex Bu155467	standby ◆
☐	N407DF	Rockwell OV-10A Bronco	305-164M-86	ex Bu155475	◆
☐	N408DF	Rockwell OV-10A Bronco	305-178M-90	ex Bu155480	◆
☐	N409DF	Rockwell OV-10A Bronco	305-18M-12	ex Bu155401	◆
☐	N410DF	Rockwell OV-10A Bronco	305-158M-82	ex Bu155471	◆
☐	N413DF	Rockwell OV-10A Bronco	305-20M-13	ex Bu155402	◆
☐	N414DF	Rockwell OV-10A Bronco	305-26M-16	ex Bu155415	◆
☐	N415DF	Rockwell OV-10A Bronco	305-68M-38	ex Bu155427	◆
☐	N418DF	Rockwell OV-10A Bronco	305-70M-39	ex Bu155428	◆
☐	N421DF	Rockwell OV-10A Bronco	305-206M-107	ex Bu155496	◆
☐	N429DF	Rockwell OV-10A Bronco	305A-17M-11	ex Bu155400	◆
☐	N469DF	Rockwell OV-10A Bronco		ex Bu155395	◆
☐	N470DF	Rockwell OV-10A Bronco		ex Bu155502	◆
☐	N473DF	Rockwell OV-10A Bronco		ex Bu155406	◆
☐	N114Z	Short SD.3-60	SH3048		◆
☐	N142Z	Short SD.3-60	SH3421		◆
☐	N145Z	Short SD.3-60	SH3425		◆
☐	N148Z	Short SD.3-60	SH3428		◆
☐	N151Z	Short SD.3-60	SH3407		◆
☐	N161Z	Short SD.3-60	SH3412		◆
☐	N162Z	Short SD.3-60	SH3401		◆
☐	N163Z	Short SD.3-60	SH3414		◆
☐	N106Z	Bell 206A JetRanger	508	ex N950NS	
☐	N102NJ	Bell 206B JetRanger	1671	ex N33PX	
☐	N103NJ	Bell 206A JetRanger	361	ex N619DE	
☐	N109FC	Piper PA-31-350 Chieftain	31-8012073	ex N61850	
☐	N115Z	Basler BT-67	16819/33567	ex N146Z	
☐	N141Z	de Havilland DHC-6 Twin Otter 300	803	ex C-GDNG	
☐	N143Z	de Havilland DHC-6 Twin Otter 300	437	ex N300LJ	
☐	N144Z	Cessna 550 Citation Bravo	550-0926	ex N100Z	
☐	N147Z	Aero Commander 500B	1432-152		
☐	N149Z	Beech B200C Super King Air	BL-124	ex N107Z	
☐	N162NR	Cessna 180A	32805		◆
☐	N173Z	Short SD.3-30	SH3116	ex 84-0469	

☐ N175Z	Short SD.3-30	SH3115	ex 84-0468	
☐ N178Z	Short SD.3-30	SH3119	ex 84-0472	
☐ N179Z	Short SD.3-30	SH3109	ex 84-0462	
☐ N182Z	Beech 200 Super King Air	BB-402	ex N318W	
☐ N185FC	Cessna 185E	185-0982		♦
☐ N194Z	Aero Commander 500B	1510-182		
☐ N214GB	Beech B200 Super King Air	BB-1668		♦
☐ N391M	Cessna 185C	185-0684		♦
☐ N392M	Bell 206A JetRanger	362	ex N3750U	
☐ N457DF	Beech 58 Baron	TH-1354		♦
☐ N2728X	Cessna 180H Skywagon	18051528		♦
☐ N4704A	Cessna A185E Skywagon	18502426		♦

US HELICOPTERS   Wingate-US Heliport, NC

☐ N36TV	Aérospatiale AS350B AStar	1858	ex N69TL	
☐ N117HD	Aérospatiale AS350B2 AStar	7464		♦
☐ N117TV	Aérospatiale AS350B AStar	1857		♦
☐ N119TV	Aérospatiale AS350B AStar	2122	ex N477HD	
☐ N125HD	Aérospatiale AS350B2 AStar	7899		♦
☐ N129TV	Aérospatiale AS350BA AStar	2897	ex N10BC	
☐ N132TV	Aérospatiale AS350B AStar	1636		♦
☐ N355TV	Aérospatiale AS350B AStar	2647	ex TG-JBG	
☐ N357TV	Aérospatiale AS350B AStar	2376	ex N795WC	
☐ N606HD	Aérospatiale AS350B2 AStar	7601		
☐ N888TV	Aérospatiale AS350B AStar	2007		
☐ N915HD	Aérospatiale AS350B2 AStar	3583	ex N311SJ	♦
☐ N933HD	Aérospatiale AS350B2 AStar	7799	ex N801H	
☐ N955HD	Aérospatiale AS350B AStar	1596		
☐ N977V	Aérospatiale AS350B AStar	3462		
☐ N104TV	Bell 206B JetRanger	2379		♦
☐ N109US	Bell 206B JetRanger	2164		♦
☐ N155TV	Bell 206L-3 LongRanger	51339		♦
☐ N316TV	Bell 206B JetRanger III	2704	ex N188TV	♦
☐ N515TV	Bell 206B JetRanger	2130		♦
☐ N977V	Bell 206L-3 JetRanger	3462		♦

USA JET AIRLINES   Jet USA (UJ/JUS)   Detroit-Willow Run, MI (YIP)

☐ N191US	Douglas DC-9-15	45718/17	ex N300ME	VIP
☐ N192US	Douglas DC-9-15RC	47156/228	ex N9357	VIP
☐ N194US	Douglas DC-9-15RC (ABS 3)	47016/173	ex N9349	[YIP]
☐ N195US	Douglas DC-9-15RC (ABS 3)	47017/186	ex N9352	VIP
☐ N196US	Douglas DC-9-15RC	47155/216	ex N9355	
☐ N205US	Douglas DC-9-32CF	47690/843	ex N724HB	
☐ N208US	Douglas DC-9-32F (ABS 3)	47220/296	ex N935F	
☐ N215US	Douglas DC-9-32 (ABS 3)	47480/607	ex N986US	wfs
☐ N231US	Douglas DC-9-32 (ABS 3)	48114/919	ex XA-TXG	[YIP]
☐ N327US	Douglas DC-9-33F (ABS 3)	47414/536	ex N940F	
☐ N727US	Boeing 727-223F (FedEx 3)	22470/1771	ex N715AA	
☐ N822AA	AMD Falcon 20DC	195	ex N195MP	
☐ N826AA	AMD Falcon 20DC	67	ex N821AA	
☐ N827AA	AMD Falcon 20EC	298	ex OE-GNN	
☐ N829AA	Learjet 25B	25B-100	ex N25TK	
☐ N831US	McDonnell-Douglas MD-83f	49791/1644	ex N791MD	
☐ N948AS	McDonnell-Douglas MD-83	53021/1801		[YIP]
☐ N949NS	McDonnell-Douglas MD-83	53022/1809	ex N949AS	[VCV]

US DEPARTMENT OF ENERGY   Energy (NRG)

☐ N617DE	Bell 407	53867	ex N342AB	
☐ N618DE	Bell 407	53798		♦
☐ N619DE	Bell 407	53410	ex N617DE	
☐ N793BP	Bell 407	53934	ex N934BP	
☐ N794BP	Bell 407	53942	ex N942BP	
☐ N116SR	MBB BK117A-3	7012	ex N39189	
☐ N117SR	MBB BK117A-3	7084	ex N426MB	
☐ N185XP	Beech B200 Super King Air	BB-952	ex N1852B	
☐ N229DE	Douglas DC-9-15RC	45826/79	ex N29AF	♦
☐ N411DE	Bell 412	36030		♦
☐ N412DE	Bell 412	36033		♦
☐ N6451D	Beech B200 Super King Air	BB-1009		♦
☐ N792BP	Beech B200GT Super King Air	BY-10		
☐ N7232R	Beech B200C Super King Air	BL-69	ex N2811B	♦
☐ N2065S	Bell 204L-4 LongRanger	52002		

VEE NEAL AVIATION				Latrobe, PA
☐ N646VN	British Aerospace Jetstream 31	646	ex N646SA	
☐ N858CY	British Aerospace Jetstream 3201	858	ex N423AM	

VENT AIRLINES		Valkyrie (VKY)		
☐ N575EG	Swearingen SA227AC Metro III	AC-575	ex N378PH	

VIEQUES AIR LINK	Vieques (V4/VES)			Vieques, PR (VQS)
☐ N663VL	Britten-Norman BN-2B-26 Islander	2110	ex N663J	
☐ N861VL	Britten-Norman BN-2B-26 Islander	2155	ex N861JA	
☐ N902VL	Britten-Norman BN-2A-20 Islander	685	ex N148ES	
☐ N903VL	Britten-Norman BN-2A-26 Islander	2019	ex N2159X	
☐ N904VL	Britten-Norman BN-2A-26 Islander	3014	ex HK-3813	no titles
☐ N907VL	Britten-Norman BN-2A-9 Islander	343	ex N723JM	
☐ N908VL	Britten-Norman BN-2B-26 Islander	2187	ex N728JM	
☐ N12NX	Cessna 402C	402C0290	ex N768EA	
☐ N335VL	Cessna 208B Caravan I	208B0964	ex N5260Y	
☐ N905VL	Britten-Norman BN-2A Mk.III-2			
	Trislander	1048	ex N905GD	
☐ N906VL	Britten-Norman BN-2A Mk.III-2			
	Trislander	1060	ex N906GD	
☐ N6880A	Cessna 402C	402C0616		

VIRGIN AMERICA	Redwood (VX/VRD)			San Francisco, CA (SFO)
☐ N521VA	Airbus A319-115	2773	ex D-AVWZ	let there be flight
☐ N522VA	Airbus A319-112	2811	ex D-AVYP	
☐ N523VA	Airbus A319-112	3181	ex D-AVYB	
☐ N524VA	Airbus A319-112	3204	ex D-AVWK	dark horse
☐ N525VA	Airbus A319-112	3324	ex D-AVYG	
☐ N526VA	Airbus A319-112	3347	ex D-AVYW	
☐ N527VA	Airbus A319-112	3417	ex D-AVYK	tubular belle
☐ N528VA	Airbus A319-112	3445	ex D-AVYR	fog cutter
☐ N529VA	Airbus A319-112	3684	ex D-AVWB	moodlights, camera, action
☐ N530VA	Airbus A319-112	3686	ex D-AVWD	gogo dancer
☐ N361VA	Airbus A320-214/S	5515	ex D-AXAL	jersey girl
☐ N621VA	Airbus A320-214	2616	ex F-WWDJ	air colbert
☐ N622VA	Airbus A320-214	2674	ex F-WWID	California Dreaming
☐ N623VA	Airbus A320-214	2740	ex PR-MHH	three if by air
☐ N624VA	Airbus A320-214	2778	ex F-WWDX	red, white & blue
☐ N625VA	Airbus A320-214	2800	ex F-WWIJ	Jefferson Airplane
☐ N626VA	Airbus A320-214	2830	ex F-WWDO	unicorn chaser
☐ N627VA	Airbus A320-214	2851	ex F-WWIQ	
☐ N628VA	Airbus A320-214	2993	ex F-WWIT	
☐ N629VA	Airbus A320-214	3037	ex PR-MHL	Midnight Ride
☐ N630VA	Airbus A320-214	3101	ex F-WWIG	superfly
☐ N631VA	Airbus A320-214	3135	ex F-WWDL	chic mobile
☐ N632VA	Airbus A320-214	3155	ex F-WWDH	youtube air
☐ N633VA	Airbus A320-214	3230	ex F-WWBE	the tim clark express
☐ N634VA	Airbus A320-214	3359	ex F-WWII	mach daddy
☐ N635VA	Airbus A320-214	3398	ex F-WWBS	my other ride's a spaceship
☐ N636VA	Airbus A320-214	3460	ex F-WWBJ	
☐ N637VA	Airbus A320-214	3465	ex F-WWBN	an airplane named desire
☐ N638VA	Airbus A320-214	3503	ex D-AVVB	san francisco pride
☐ N639VA	Airbus A320-214	3016	ex 9K-CAE	
☐ N640VA	Airbus A320-214	3349	ex 9K-CAF	
☐ N641VA	Airbus A320-214	3656	ex 9K-CAG	
☐ N642VA	Airbus A320-214	3670	ex 9K-CAH	breanna jewel
☐ N835VA	Airbus A320-214	4448	ex D-AVVZ	
☐ N836VA	Airbus A320-214	4480	ex D-AUBD	
☐ N837VA	Airbus A320-214	4558	ex D-AUBT	
☐ N838VA	Airbus A320-214	4559	ex F-WWDY	
☐ N839VA	Airbus A320-214	4610	ex F-WWIY	
☐ N840VA	Airbus A320-214	4616	ex F-WWBI	bytheway
☐ N841VA	Airbus A320-214	4655	ex F-WWDS	#nerdbird
☐ N842VA	Airbus A320-214	4805	ex F-WWBK	Real Steel
☐ N843VA	Airbus A320-214	4814	ex F-WWDR	¡VAmanos!
☐ N844VA	Airbus A320-214	4851	ex F-WWBB	sol plane
☐ N845VA	Airbus A320-214	4867	ex F-WWDM	stay hungry, stay foolish
☐ N846VA	Airbus A320-214	4894	ex F-WWIU	glitter girl
☐ N847VA	Airbus A320-214	4948	ex F-WWDH	scarlettoO'air
☐ N848VA	Airbus A320-214	4959	ex F-WWDJ	bellapierre
☐ N849VA	Airbus A320-214	4991	ex F-WWBB	fly bye baby
☐ N851VA	Airbus A320-214	4999	ex F-WWBR	Friends of Arjay Miller
☐ N852VA	Airbus A320-214	5004	ex F-WWDL	safady voyager
☐ N853VA	Airbus A320-214	5034	ex F-WWIP	mt hoodie
☐ N854VA	Airbus A320-214	5058	ex F-WWBG	stand up flyer

☐ N855VA	Airbus A320-214	5179	ex F-WWDU screw it, let's do it	
☐ N	Airbus A320-214	6669	ex	o/o♦
☐ N	Airbus A320-214	6706	ex	o/o♦
☐ N	Airbus A320-214	6795	ex	o/o♦
☐ N	Airbus A320-214	6823	ex	o/o♦
☐ N	Airbus A320-214	6876	ex	o/o♦
☐ N	Airbus A320-214	6972	ex	o/o♦

VISION AIR   Ruby (V2/RBY)   Las Vegas North, NV (VGT)

☐ N402VA	Dornier 228-202K	8085	ex G-BWEX	
☐ N403VA	Dornier 228-202K	8171	ex 9M-BAS	
☐ N404VA	Dornier 228-202	8120	ex N279MC	
☐ N405VA	Dornier 228-202	8144	ex N264MC	
☐ N409VA	Dornier 228-202	8097	ex N228ME	
☐ N329MX	Dornier 328-120	3049	ex D-CAOS	
☐ N661CS	Boeing 767-375ER	25864/426	ex CC-CRH all white	♦
☐ N732VA	Boeing 737-3T0	23366/1174	ex N34315	
☐ N742VA	Boeing 737-448	24773/1850	ex TC-MNH	
☐ N745VA	Boeing 737-405	24271/1738	ex N427BV	opf Havana Air
☐ N767VA	Boeing 767-222ER	21870/13	ex N609UA	[MEX]
☐ N768VA	Boeing 767-222ER	21869/11	ex N608UA	wfs
☐ N769VA	Boeing 767-222ER	21866/7	ex N605UA	

WARBELOWS AIR   Warbelow (4W/WAV)   Fairbanks-Intl, AK (FAI)

☐ N3527U	Piper PA-31-350 Chieftain	31-7952141		
☐ N4082T	Piper PA-31-350 Chieftain	31-8152089		
☐ N27663	Piper PA-31-350 Chieftain	31-7852094		♦
☐ N27917	Piper PA-31-350 Chieftain	31-7852007		♦
☐ N59764	Piper PA-31-350 Navajo Chieftain	31-7652037		
☐ N59829	Piper PA-31-350 Navajo Chieftain	31-7652081		
☐ N8763Q	Cessna U206F Stationair	U20603516		

WARD AIR   Juneau-Intl, AK (JNU)

☐ N767RR	Cessna T310Q	310Q0455	ex N7676Q	
☐ N62353	de Havilland DHC-2 Beaver	1363	ex 58-2031	FP
☐ N62355	de Havilland DHC-2 Beaver	1045	ex N67897	FP
☐ N62357	de Havilland DHC-2 Beaver	1145	ex N64391	FP
☐ N62358	de Havilland DHC-2 Beaver	627	ex N67693	FP
☐ N63354	de Havilland DHC-3 Turbo Otter	30	ex C-FWAF	FP
☐ N93023	Cessna U206G Stationair II	U20603526	ex N8773Q	FP
☐ N93024	Cessna U206G Stationair II	U20604392	ex N756VN	FP
☐ N93025	Cessna A185F Skywagon	18503163		FP
☐ N93356	de Havilland DHC-3 Turbo Otter	144	ex N62KA	FP

WATERMAKERS AIR   Fort Lauderdale, FL

☐ N146WM	Cessna 208B Caravan I	208B0818	ex N811FL	
☐ N208JH	Cessna 208B Caravan I	208B1144	ex N1273E	

WEST AIRPAC   Valley (PCM)   Fresno-Air Terminal, CA / Chico-Municipal, CA (FAT/CIC)

Ops Cessna Caravans leased from, and operated on behalf of, FedEx

WESTERN AIR EXPRESS   Western Express (WAE)   Boise, ID (BOI)

☐ N158WA	Swearingen SA226TC Metro II	TC-411	ex N5974V	
☐ N160WA	Swearingen SA226TC Metro IIA	TC-399	ex N56EA	
☐ N162WA	Swearingen SA226TC Metro IIA	TC-418	ex C-GRET	
☐ N167WA	Cessna 402B II	402B1044	ex N98680	
☐ N7947Q	Cessna 402B	402B0397		

WESTERN AIRWAYS   Houston-Sugar Land, TX (SGR)

☐ N42WA	Canadair CRJ-100LR	7024	ex C-GRWO	

WESTERN GLOBAL AIRLINES   (WGN)   Sarasot, FL (SRQ)

☐ N382WA	McDonnell-Douglas MD-11F	48411/453	ex N703GC	[MZJ]♦
☐ N383WA	McDonnell-Douglas MD-11F	48412/454	ex N705GC	[SBD]♦
☐ N415JN	McDonnell-Douglas MD-11F	48415/576	ex N304MS	♦
☐ N435KD	McDonnell-Douglas MD-11F	48435/478	ex N384WA	
☐ N542KD	McDonnell-Douglas MD-11F	48542/570	ex OH-NGA	♦
☐ N543JN	McDonnell-Douglas MD-11F	48543/572	ex B-2178	
☐ N545JN	McDonnell-Douglas MD-11F	48545/587	ex B-2179	[OSC]♦

WESTWIND AIR — Molalla, OR

☐ N2AV	Cessna 208 Caravan I	20800057	ex N208NN
☐ N2WF	Cessna U206F Stationair	U20602849	♦

WESTWIND AVIATION — Phoenix-Deer Valley, AZ (DVT)

☐ N122JB	Cessna 208B Caravan I	208B1025	ex N5090V
☐ N208WW	Cessna 208B Caravan I	208B0721	
☐ N785WW	Cessna 208B Caravan I	208B0792	ex N5267T
☐ N786WW	Cessna 208B Caravan I	208B1099	ex N12744
☐ N9317M	Cessna T207A Stationair 8 II	20700680	
☐ N9482M	Cessna T207A Stationair 8 II	20700698	

WIGGINS AIRWAYS (PIPER EAST) — Wiggins (WIG) — Norwood-Memorial, MA (OWD)

☐ N189WA	Beech 99	U-76	ex N139BA
☐ N190WA	Beech C99	U-207	ex N207CS
☐ N191WA	Beech 99A	U-136	ex C-GPCF
☐ N192WA	Beech B99	U-152	ex C-GEOI
☐ N193WA	Beech 99	U-17	ex N10MV
☐ N194WA	Beech 99	U-64	ex C-FAWX
☐ N195WA	Beech 99	U-38	ex N202BH
☐ N196WA	Beech C99	U-179	ex N995SB
☐ N197WA	Beech 99A	U-130	ex C-FOZU
☐ N198WA	Beech 99A	U-142	ex N133BA
☐ N24AN	Embraer EMB.110P2 Bandeirante	110318	ex F-GBRM
☐ N115WA	Embraer EMB.110P1A Bandeirante	110451	ex N36AN
☐ N116WA	Embraer EMB.110P1 Bandeirante	110399	ex N64CZ
☐ N117WA	Embraer EMB.110P1 Bandeirante	110388	ex N62CZ
☐ N118WA	Embraer EMB.110P1 Bandeirante	110250	ex N710NH
☐ N119WA	Embraer EMB.110P2 Bandeirante	110372	ex N31AN ♦
☐ N120WA	Embraer EMB.110P1 Bandeirante	110404	ex N51BA ♦
☐ N830AC	Embraer EMB.110P1 Bandeirante	110205	♦
☐ N91RK	Beech A100 King Air	B-226	ex N9126S

WINGS OF ALASKA — Wings Alaska (K5/WAK) — Juneau-Intl, AK (JNU)

☐ N336AK	de Havilland DHC-3 Turbo Otter	333	ex N567KA	FP
☐ N337AK	de Havilland DHC-3 Turbo Otter	418	ex N2783J	FP
☐ N338AK	de Havilland DHC-3 Turbo Otter	262	ex N62355	FP
☐ N339AK	de Havilland DHC-3 Turbo Otter	454	ex N28TH	FP
☐ N753AK	de Havilland DHC-3 Turbo Otter	7	ex N342AK	FP
☐ N39AK	Cessna 207A Stationair 8 II	20700597	ex N73482	FP/WS
☐ N62AK	Cessna 207A Stationair 8 II	20700780	ex N9997M	FP/WS
☐ N96AK	Cessna 207A Stationair 8 II	20700782	ex N1347Q	FP/WS
☐ N331AK	Cessna 208B Caravan I	208B0739	ex N5264S	
☐ N332AK	Cessna 208B Caravan I	208B0779	ex N5264S	FP/WS

WORLD ATLANTIC AIRLINES — (K8/WAL) — Miami, FL (MIA)

☐ N802WA	McDonnell-Douglas MD-83	53052/1731	ex N751LF	The Pride of Miami Tech
☐ N803WA	McDonnell-Douglas MD-82	49507/1425	ex N705MT	Amos
☐ N804WA	McDonnell-Douglas MD-83	49345/1371	ex N563AA	Zahira
☐ N805WA	McDonnell-Douglas MD-83	53470/2134	ex N951TW	
☐ N806WA	McDonnell-Douglas MD-83	53251/1909	ex N588AA	♦

WRIGHT AIR SERVICE — Wright Flyer (WRF) — Fairbanks-Intl, AK (FAI)

☐ N32WA	Cessna 208B Caravan I	208B0234	ex C-FKEL	wfs
☐ N143WA	Cessna 208BEX Caravan I	208B5002		
☐ N540ME	Cessna 208B Caravan I	208B0540	ex N1329G	
☐ N900WA	Cessna 208B Caravan I	208B0659	ex N52613	
☐ N976E	Cessna 208B Caravan I	208B0976	ex N5263D	
☐ N999WV	Cessna 208B Caravan I	208B2082	ex N5236L	
☐ N1323R	Cessna 208B Caravan I	208B0745		
☐ N4365U	Cessna 208B Caravan I	208B0253	ex N208CC	
☐ N9FW	Piper PA-31-350 Navajo Chieftain	31-7405468	ex N61441	
☐ N54WA	Piper PA-31-350 Navajo Chieftain	31-7652067	ex N942LU	
☐ N7426L	Piper PA-31 Turbo Navajo B	31-812		
☐ N8795Q	Cessna U206G Stationair	U20603547		

XTRAAIRWAYS — Ruby Mountain (XP/CXP) — Elko-JC Harris Field, NV (EKO)

☐ N43XA	Boeing 737-4S3	24796/1887	ex TF-ELV	
☐ N134AS	Boeing 737-484	25314/2124	ex YR-BAL	♦
☐ N148AS	Boeing 737-484	27149/2471	ex VQ-BNX	♦
☐ N279AD	Boeing 737-4Q8	26279/2221	ex SX-BGS	BHS♦

☐ N843TM	Boeing 737-4Y0	24691/1904	ex VP-BGP	♦

YUKON AVIATION — Bethel, AK (BET)

☐ N150HH	Bell 206B JetRanger III	701	
☐ N1322F	Cessna A185F Skywagon	18502825	
☐ N1653U	Cessna 207 Super Skywagon	20700253	
☐ N4237V	Bell 204 (UH-1B)	261	ex 60-0315
☐ N29970	Cessna A185F Skywagon II	18504292	ex (C-GMTU)
☐ N91060	Cessna T207 Turbo Skywagon	20700047	

OB- PERU (Republic of Peru)

AERONAVES VIVE PERU — Trujillo

☐ OB-2091-P	Beech B200 Super King Air	BB-1359	ex N90GA	♦
☐ OB-2029-P	Beech B200 Super King Air	BB-1666	ex N401CG	♦

AEROMASTER DEL PERU

☐ OB-1995-P	Bell 214ST	28196	ex N726HT

AERO TRANSPORTE - ATSA — ATSA (AMP) — Lima-Jorge Chavez Intl (LIM)

☐ OB-1629	Piper PA-42 Cheyenne III	42-8001067	ex N183CC	
☐ OB-1633-P	Piper PA-42 Cheyenne III	42-7801003	ex N134KM	
☐ OB-1687-P	Piper PA-42 Cheyenne III	42-8001016	ex N69PC	
☐ OB-1714	Piper PA-42 Cheyenne III	42-8001013	ex N275AB	
☐ OB-1803-P	Piper PA-42 Cheyenne III	42-7800002	ex N911VJ	
☐ OB-1703	IAI-1125 Astra	004	ex N425TS	
☐ OB-1770-P	Fokker 50	20280	exOB-1770	
☐ OB-1778-P	Antonov An-26B-100	14205	ex OB-1777-T	
☐ OB-1868-P	Antonov An-32B	2802	ex OB-1462	<Transaer
☐ OB-1875	Beech 1900D	UE-68	ex N168AZ	
☐ OB-1881-P	Beech B300 Super King Air	FL-470	ex N350MS	
☐ OB-1907-P	Antonov An-32B	3107	ex OB-1907-T	<Transaer
☐ OB-1924-P	Antonov An-32B	3109	ex OB-1924-T	<Transaer
☐ OB-1962-P	Antonov An-32A	2602	ex OB-1962-T	
☐ OB-1983-P	Beech B200 Super King Air	BB-1549	ex N549SC	
☐ OB-1985	Beech 1900D	UE-138	ex N239SC	
☐ OB-2023	IAI Gulfstream G200	034	ex N108SC	
☐ OB-2043-P	Fokker 50	20115	ex PH-EDJ	
☐ OB-2088	Beech B200 Super King Air	BB-1526	ex N527SC	♦

AERODIANA

☐ OB-1870-P	Cessna 208B Caravan I	208B1278	ex OB-1870-T
☐ OB-1882-P	Cessna 208B Caravan I	208B1306	ex OB-1882-T
☐ OB-1963-P	Cessna 208B Caravan I	208B2252	ex OB-1963T
☐ OB-2001-P	Cessna 208B Caravan II	208B2313	ex OB-2001-T
☐ OB-2021-P	Cessna 208B Caravan II	208B2387	ex OB-2021-T

AIR MAJORO — Air Majoro (MJP) — Lima-Jorge Chavez Intl (LIM)

☐ OB-1920-P	Cessna 402C II	402C0442	ex N6790B
☐ OB-1919-P	Cessna 207A Skywagon 7	20700761	ex N9951M
☐ OB-1921-P	Cessna 402C II	402C0419	ex N419RC
☐ OB-1929-P	Cessna 207A Skywagon 7	20700717	ex N61CQ
☐ OB-1936-P	Cessna 207A Skywagon 7	20700767	ex N9965M
☐ OB-2077-P	Beech 200C	BL-5	ex N469SP

AIR PERU EXPRESS

☐ N377AR	Short SD.3-60	SH3755	ex SE-LHY	<ROX
☐ N948RR	Short SD.3-60	SH3751	ex G-BVMX	<ROX
☐ OB-2087-P	Short SD.3-60	SH3764	ex N764JR	♦

AMAZON SKY — (AMT) — Lima-Jorge Chavez Intl (LIM)

☐ OB-1859-P	Antonov An-26B-100	6209	ex UR-VYV	
☐ OB-2015-P	Antonov An-26-100	4002	ex OB-2015-T	
☐ OB-2085-P	Antonov An-32	3302	ex UR-CLZ	♦

COYOTAIR PERU

☐ OB-1973-P	Bell 212	30757	ex EC-GXG	>Inaer

HELICOPTEROS DEL PACIFICO

☐ OB-2078-P	Mil Mi-8MSB	MSB8330003	♦

HELISUR/HELICOPTEROS DEL SUR — Iquitos (IQT)

☐ OB-1639-P	Mil Mi-8AMT	59489607212	ex OB-1639-T
☐ OB-1663	Mil Mi-8AMT	94704	ex RA-27126
☐ OB-1826	Mil Mi-8MTV-1	93281	
☐ OB-1934-P	Mil Mi-8MTV-1	96264	ex RA-25809
☐ OB-2071-P	Mil Mi-8AMT	59489611137	ex RA-22977
☐ OB-1584	Mil Mi-17 (Mi-8MTV-1)	95432	ex RA-70879
☐ OB-1585	Mil Mi-17 (Mi-8MTV-1)	223M103	ex RA-70951
☐ OB-1691	Mil Mi-17 (Mi-8MTV-1)	96153	ex RA-27193
☐ OB-1760	Mil Mi-17 (Mi-8MTV-1)	93823	
☐ OB-1761	Mil Mi-17 (Mi-8MTV-1)	93477	
☐ OB-1878-P	Mil Mi-171	59489614258	ex HK-4312
☐ OB-1935-P	Mil Mi-171C	171C00643083909U	ex RA-22471
☐ OB-1987P	Mil Mi-171C	171C00643083806U	ex RA-22438
☐ OB-1988P	Mil Mi-171C	171C00643083807U	ex RA-22437
☐ OB-1989P	Mil Mi-171C	171C00643083808U	ex RA-22435
☐ OB-1990P	Mil Mi-171C	171C00643083809U	ex RA-22433
☐ OB-2018-P	Mil Mi-171C	171C00643116101U	
☐ OB-2019-P	Mil Mi-171C	171C00643116102U	
☐ OB-2020-P	Mil Mi-171C	171C00643116103U	
☐ OB-2074-P	Mil Mi-171C	171C00643116104U	♦

INAER HELICOPTER PERU

☐ OB-1973-P	Bell 212	30757	ex EC-GXG	<Coyotair
☐ OB-2027-P	Bell 412EP	36254	ex C-GMVX	

LAN PERU — (LP/LPE) — Lima-Jorge Chavez Intl (LIM)

☐ CC-COU	Airbus A319-132	2089	ex D-AVWL
☐ CC-COX	Airbus A319-132	2096	ex D-AVYN
☐ CC-CPE	Airbus A319-132	2321	ex D-AVYO
☐ CC-CPF	Airbus A319-132	2572	ex D-AVXC
☐ CC-CPI	Airbus A319-132	2585	ex D-AVXH
☐ CC-CPM	Airbus A319-132	2864	ex D-AVWC
☐ CC-CPO	Airbus A319-132	2872	ex D-AVWJ
☐ CC-CPQ	Airbus A319-132	2886	ex D-AVXP
☐ CC-CQK	Airbus A319-132	2892	ex D-AVYV
☐ CC-CQL	Airbus A319-132	2894	ex D-AVWE
☐ CC-CYJ	Airbus A319-132	3772	ex D-AVXH

LC BUSRE — Busre (W4/LCB) — Lima-Jorge Chavez Intl (LIM)

☐ N436YV	de Havilland DHC-8Q-202	436	ex C-GDNG
☐ N444YV	de Havilland DHC-8Q-202	444	ex C-GFRP
☐ N447YV	de Havilland DHC-8Q-202	447	ex C-GFYI
☐ N448YV	de Havilland DHC-8Q-202	448	ex C-GLOT
☐ N454YV	de Havilland DHC-8Q-202	454	ex C-GEOA
☐ N987HA	de Havilland DHC-8Q-202	425	ex C-GFHZ

MOVIL AIR TOURS

☐ OB-2029-P	Cessna 208B Caravan I	208B2379	ex OB-2029-T	
☐ OB-2030-P	Cessna 208B Caravan I	208B2343	ex OB-2030-T	
☐ OB-2072-P	Cessna 208B Caravan I	108B5061	ex OB-2072-T	♦

PERUVIAN AIRLINES — Peruvian (P9/PVN) — Lima-Jorge Chavez Intl (LIM)

☐ OB-1823-P	Boeing 737-2T2 (Nordam 3)	22793/892	ex OB-1823	[LIM]
☐ OB-1839-P	Boeing 737-204	22640/867	ex N640AD	wfs
☐ OB-1841-P	Boeing 737-204	22058/629	ex N58AD	
☐ OB-1851-P	Boeing 737-230 (Nordam 3)	22133/772	ex N133AD	
☐ OB-1954-P	Boeing 737-247 (Nordam 3)	23188/1071	ex HC-CGA	
☐ OB-2036-P	Boeing 737-3M8	25071/2039	ex N250AG	
☐ OB-2037-P	Boeing 737-3Q8	26296/2581	ex N296AG	
☐ OB-2040-P	Boeing 737-3K2	24329/1858	ex N923AG	♦
☐ OB-2041-P	Boeing 737-53C	24825/1894	ex N248AG	♦
☐ OB-2079-P	Boeing 737-48E	27630/2848	ex N763AG	
☐ OB-2089-P	Boeing 737-3Y0QC	23685/1357	ex N835AC	[LIM]♦
☐ OB-2090-P	Boeing 737-3Q8QC	24132/1555	ex N846AC	[LIM]♦

SERVICIOS AEREOS DE LOS ANDES (AND) Miraflores, Lima

☐ OB-1813-P	Bell 212	30811	ex OB-1762-T	
☐ OB-1906-P	Bell 212	30544	ex C-FLBF	
☐ OB-1910-P	Bell 212	30798	ex C-GSLL	
☐ OB-1965-P	Bell 212	30615	ex C-GAZX	
☐ OB-2026-P	Bell 212	31123	ex CC-ACL	
☐ OB-1846-P	Aérospatiale AS350B3 Ecureuil	3698	ex I-EWAY	é
☐ OB-1864-P	de Havilland DHC-6 Twin Otter 300	282	ex CC-PCI	
☐ OB-1897	de Havilland DHC-6 Twin Otter 300	521	ex OB-1897-P	
☐ OB-1904-P	Aérospatiale AS350B3 Ecureuil	4572		
☐ OB-1913-P	de Havilland DHC-6 Twin Otter 300	391	ex C-GHVV	
☐ OB-1937-P	Aérospatiale AS350B3 Ecureuil	4800		
☐ OB-1939-P	Bell 205A-1	30136	ex C-GCZG	
☐ OB-1958-P	Bell 412HP	36065	ex C-FDDI	
☐ OB-2027-P	Bell 414EP	36254		♦
☐ OB-2047-P	Bell 412EP	36255	ex C-GMVY	
☐ OB-2076-P	de Havilland DHC-8Q-202	4010	ex N404AV	

STAR PERU Star Up (2I/SRU) Lima-Jorge Chavez Intl (LIM)

☐ OB-1877-P	British Aerospace 146 Srs.100	E1199	ex A5-RGE	
☐ OD-1879 P	British Aerospace 146 Srs.100	E1095	ex A5-RGD	
☐ OB-1885-P	British Aerospace 146 Srs.200	E2087	cx N292UE	
☐ OB-1914-P	British Aerospace 146 Srs.300	E3181	ex G-JEBA	
☐ OB-1923-P	British Aerospace 146 Srs.300	E3185	ex G-JEBB	
☐ OB-1930-P	British Aerospace 146 Srs.200	E2201	ex D-AJET	
☐ OB-1943-P	British Aerospace 146 Srs.200	E2133	ex OB-1943-T	
☐ OB-1978-P	British Aerospace 146 Srs.200QT	E2114	ex OB-1978-T	
☐ OB-2014T	British Aerospace 146 Srs.200	E2058	ex ZS-PYM	[LIM]
☐ OB-1769	Antonov An-24RV	57310110	ex ER-AWX Leonid	wfs
☐ OB-1772	Antonov An-26B-100	10704	ex OB-1772-P	wfs

TACA PERU Trans Peru (T0/TPU) Lima-Jorge Chavez Intl (LIM)

☐ N279AV	Airbus A330-243	1279	ex F-WWYN	<AVA
☐ N491TA	Airbus A320-233	2301	ex F-WWDF	
☐ N521TA	Airbus A319-132	3276	ex D-AVYK	
☐ N988TA	Embraer ERJ-190LR	19000399	ex PT-XUE	
Aircraft frequently rotated with Avianca Central America (qv)				

TRANSAER

☐ OB-1868-P	Antonov An-32B	2802	ex OB-1462	>AMP
☐ OB-1907-P	Antonov An-32B	3107	ex OB-1907-T	>AMP
☐ OB-1924-P	Antonov An-32B	3109	ex OB-1924-T	>AMP

TRANSPORTES AEREOS CIELOS ANDINOS Lima-Jorge Chavez Intl (LIM)

☐ OB-1828	Antonov An-26	7409	ex OB-1828-P	wfs
☐ OB-1876-P	Antonov An-26B-100	11506	ex OB-1876-T	
☐ OB-1893-P	Antonov An-26-100	8401	ex OB-1893-T	

OD- LEBANON (Republic of Lebanon)

MED AIRWAYS (MED) Beirut (BEY)

☐ OD-AMR	Canadair CRJ-200ER	7255	ex N630BR	

MIDDLE EAST AIRLINES Cedar Jet (ME/MEA) Beirut (BEY)

Member of SkyTeam

☐ OD-MRL	Airbus A320-232	5000	ex D-AVVV	
☐ OD-MRM	Airbus A320-232	4632	ex D-AXAY	
☐ OD-MRN	Airbus A320-232	4339	ex F-OMRN	
☐ OD-MRO	Airbus A320-232	4296	ex F-OMRO	
☐ OD-MRR	Airbus A320-232	3837	ex F-WWBJ	
☐ OD-MRS	Airbus A320-232	3804	ex F-WWDJ	
☐ OD-MRT	Airbus A320-232	3736	ex F-ORMK	
☐ T7-MRA	Airbus A320-214	5162	ex F-OMRA	
☐ T7-MRB	Airbus A320-214	5152	ex F-OMRB	
☐ T7-MRC	Airbus A320-214	5253	ex F-OMRC	
☐ T7-MRD	Airbus A320-214/S	5746	ex F-OMRD SkyTeam c/s	♦
☐ OD-MEA	Airbus A330-243	984	ex F-WWKE	
☐ OD-MEB	Airbus A330-243	998	ex F-WWYT	
☐ OD-MEC	Airbus A330-243	995	ex F-WWKQ	

☐ OD-MED	Airbus A330-243	926	ex F-ORMA	
☐ OD-RMI	Airbus A321-231	1977	ex F-ORMI	retro c/s
☐ OD-RMJ	Airbus A321-231	2055	ex F-ORMJ	

WINGS OF LEBANON AVIATION	**Wings Lebanon (WLB)**	**Beirut (BEY)**

☐ OD-HAJ	Boeing 737-3Q8	26313/2704	ex G-THOE	>TSC

OE- AUSTRIA (Republic of Austria)

AUSTRIAN	**Austrian (OS/AUA)**	**Vienna-Schwechat (VIE)**

Member of Star Alliance

☐ OE-LDA	Airbus A319-112	2131	ex D-AVWS	Sofia	
☐ OE-LDB	Airbus A319-112	2174	ex D-AVYP	Bucharest	
☐ OE-LDC	Airbus A319-112	2262	ex D-AVWE	Kiev	
☐ OE-LDD	Airbus A319-112	2416	ex D-AVWN	Moscow	
☐ OE-LDE	Airbus A319-112	2494	ex D-AVYL	Baku	
☐ OE-LDF	Airbus A319-112	2547	ex D-AVYA	Sarajevo	
☐ OE-LDG	Airbus A319-112	2652	ex D-AVYF	Tbilisi	
☐ OE-LBJ	Airbus A320-214	1553	ex D-ALTF	Hohe Tauern	
☐ OE-LBL	Airbus A320-214	2009	ex D-ALTL	Ausseerland	
☐ OE-LBM	Airbus A320-214	1504	ex D-ALTE	Arlberg	
☐ OE-LBN	Airbus A320-214	0768	ex F-WWDH	Osttirol	
☐ OE-LBO	Airbus A320-214	0776	ex F-WWDM	Pyhrn-Eisenwürzen	
☐ OE-LBP	Airbus A320-214	0797	ex F-WWDV	Neusiedlersee	retro c/s
☐ OE-LBQ	Airbus A320-214	1137	ex F-WWDF	Ray Charles	
☐ OE-LBR	Airbus A320-214	1150	ex F-WWBP	Frida Kahlo	
☐ OE-LBS	Airbus A320-214	1189	ex F-WWDV	Waldviertel	
☐ OE-LBT	Airbus A320-214	1387	ex F-WWIS	Wörthersee	
☐ OE-LBU	Airbus A320-214	1478	ex F-WWDS	Mühlviertel	
☐ OE-LBV	Airbus A320-214	1385	ex D-ALTB	Wienviertel	
☐ OE-LBW	Airbus A320-214	1678	ex OH-LXE	Innviertel	
☐ OE-LBX	Airbus A320-214	1735	ex OH-LXG	Mostviertel	Star Alliance c/s
☐ OE-LBA	Airbus A321-111	0552	ex D-AVZH	Salzkammergut	
☐ OE-LBB	Airbus A321-111	0570	ex D-AVZQ	Pinzgau	
☐ OE-LBC	Airbus A321-111	0581	ex D-AVZS	Südtirol	
☐ OE-LBD	Airbus A321-211	0920	ex D-AVZN	Steirisches Weinland	
☐ OE-LBE	Airbus A321-211	0935	ex D-AVZR	Wachau	
☐ OE-LBF	Airbus A321-211	1458	ex D-AVXE	Wien	
☐ OE-LAE	Boeing 767-3Z9ER/W	30383/812		Wiener Sangerknaben	
☐ OE-LAT	Boeing 767-31AER	25273/393	ex PH-MCK	Thailand	
☐ OE-LAW	Boeing 767-3Z9ER	26417/448		China	
☐ OE-LAX	Boeing 767-3Z9ER/W	27095/467		Salzburger Festspiele	
☐ OE-LAY	Boeing 767-3Z9ER/W	29867/731	ex D-ABUV	Japan	
☐ OE-LAZ	Boeing 767-3Z9ER/W	30331/759	ex D-ABUW	India	
☐ OE-LPA	Boeing 777-2Z9ER	28698/87	ex N5022E	Melbourne	
☐ OE-LPB	Boeing 777-2Z9ER	28699/163		Sydney	
☐ OE-LPC	Boeing 777-2Z9ER	29313/386		Don Bradman	
☐ OE-LPD	Boeing 777-2Z9ER	35960/607		America	
☐ OE-LPE	Boeing 777-2Q8ER	27607/135	ex VN-A147	Blue Danube	
☐ OE-LGA	de Havilland DHC-8-402Q	4014	ex C-GDNG	Kärnten	
☐ OE-LGB	de Havilland DHC-8-402Q	4015	ex C-GDOE	Tirol	
☐ OE-LGC	de Havilland DHC-8-402Q	4026	ex C-GEVP	Salzburg	
☐ OE-LGD	de Havilland DHC-8-402Q	4027	ex C-GEWI	Land Steiermark	
☐ OE-LGE	de Havilland DHC-8-402Q	4042	ex C-FNGB	Land Oberösterreich	
☐ OE-LGF	de Havilland DHC-8-402Q	4068	ex C-GERC	Land Niederösterreich	
☐ OE-LGG	de Havilland DHC-8-402Q	4074	ex C-GFCF	Stadt Budapest	
☐ OE-LGH	de Havilland DHC-8-402Q	4075	ex C-GFCW	Vorarlberg	
☐ OE-LGI	de Havilland DHC-8-402Q	4100	ex C-FAQR	Eisenstadt	
☐ OE-LGJ	de Havilland DHC-8-402Q	4104	ex C-FCQH	Baden	
☐ OE-LGK	de Havilland DHC-8-402Q	4280	ex C-FYMK	Burgenland	
☐ OE-LGL	de Havilland DHC-8-402Q	4310	ex C-GCQB	Altenrhein	
☐ OE-LGM	de Havilland DHC-8-402Q	4319	ex C-GEII	Villach	
☐ OE-LGN	de Havilland DHC-8-402Q	4326	ex C-GEZY	Gmunden	
☐ OE-LGO	de Havilland DHC-8-402Q	4281	ex C-GDLR	Innsbruck	Star Alliance c/s♦
☐ OE-LGP	de Havilland DHC-8-402Q	4016	ex PH-DHQ	Spirit of Alpbach	Star Alliance c/s♦
☐ OE-LGQ	de Havilland DHC-8-402Q	4003	ex C-GCGP	Wilder Kaiser	Star Alliance c/s >SWR♦
☐ OE-LGR	de Havilland DHC-8-402Q	4045	ex C-GPDJ	Tyrolean Spirit	Star Alliance c/s♦
☐ OE-LFH	Fokker 70	11554	ex PH-EZN	Stadt Salzburg	
☐ OE-LFI	Fokker 70	11529	ex PH-WXF	Stadt Klagenfurt	
☐ OE-LFJ	Fokker 70	11532	ex PH-WXG	Stadt Graz	
☐ OE-LFP	Fokker 70	11560	ex PH-EZW	Wels	
☐ OE-LFQ	Fokker 70	11568	ex PH-EZC	Dornbirn	

☐ OE-LFR	Fokker 70	11572	ex PH-EZD	Steyr	
☐ OE-LVA	Fokker 100	11490	ex PH-ZFB	Riga	
☐ OE-LVB	Fokker 100	11502	ex PH-ZFE	Vilnius	
☐ OE-LVC	Fokker 100	11446	ex PH-ZFF	Tirana	
☐ OE-LVD	Fokker 100	11515	ex PH-ZFG	Skopje	
☐ OE-LVE	Fokker 100	11499	ex PH-ZFH	Zagreb	
☐ OE-LVF	Fokker 100	11483	ex PH-ZFI	Yerevan	
☐ OE-LVG	Fokker 100	11520	ex PH-ZFJ	Krakow	Star Alliance c/s
☐ OE-LVH	Fokker 100	11456	ex PH-ZFK	Minsk	
☐ OE-LVI	Fokker 100	11468	ex PH-ZFL	Prague	
☐ OE-LVJ	Fokker 100	11359	ex PH-ZFM	Bratislava	
☐ OE-LVK	Fokker 100	11397	ex PH-ZFQ	Burgenland	
☐ OE-LVL	Fokker 100	11404	ex PH-ZFR	Odessa	
☐ OE-LVM	Fokker 100	11361	ex PH-ZFN	Krasnodar	
☐ OE-LVN	Fokker 100	11367	ex PH-ZFO	Dniepropetrovsk	
☐ OE-LVO	Fokker 100	11460	ex PH-ZFS	Chisinau	
☐ OE-LSM	Embraer ERJ-145MP	145322	ex PT-SMN		>CHQ♦
☐ OE-LSP	Embraer ERJ-145MP	145337	ex PT-SND		>CHQ
☐ OE-LSR	Embraer ERJ-145MP	145203	ex PT-SGU		>CHQ

FLYING BULLS   Salzburg (SZG)

☐ N996DM	Douglas DC-6B	45563/1034	ex V5-NCF	Red Bull
☐ N6123C	North American B-25J Mitchell	108-47647	ex 44-86893A	
☐ OE-EDM	Cessna 208 Caravan I	20800257	ex N666CS	FP
☐ OE-LDM	Douglas DC-6B	45563/1034	ex N996DM	

Ops some pleasure flights as well as airshow appearances

INTERSKY   Intersky 3L/ISK)   Freidrichschafen-Lowental (FDH)

☐ HA-FAL	Embraer EMB.120RT Brasilia	120176	ex F-GTSJ		opb BPS
☐ OE-LIA	de Havilland DHC-8Q-314	505	ex D-BHAT		
☐ OE-LIB	ATR 72-600	1038	ex F-WWEZ		
☐ OE-LIC	de Havilland DHC-8Q-314	503	ex D-BHAS	Steinmark c/s	>CNF
☐ OE-LID	ATR 72-600	1042	ex F-WWEE		
☐ OE-LSB	de Havilland DHC-8Q-314	525	ex C-FDHY	Espace Mittelland	

NIKI   FlyNiki (HG/NLY)   Vienna-Schwecat (VIE)

☐ OE-LNA	Airbus A319-112	3661	ex D-ABGN		♦
☐ OE-LNB	Airbus A319-112	3447	ex D-ABGK		♦
☐ OE-LNC	Airbus A319-112	3728	ex D-ABGP		♦
☐ OE-LND	Airbus A319-112	3689	ex D-ABGO		♦
☐ OE-LNE	Airbus A319-112	3415	ex D-ABGJ		♦
☐ OE-LEA	Airbus A320-214	2529	ex F-WWID	Rock'n Roll	
☐ OE-LEB	Airbus A320-214	4231	ex D-AXAA	Polka	
☐ OE-LEC	Airbus A320-214	4316	ex D-AXAL		
☐ OE-LEE	Airbus A320-214	2749	ex F-WWDB		
☐ OE-LEF	Airbus A320-214	4368	ex D-AXAY		
☐ OE-LEG	Airbus A320-214	4581	ex D-AXAP		
☐ OE-LEH	Airbus A320-214	4594	ex D-AVVG		
☐ OE-LEL	Airbus A320-214	2668	ex SP-IAG	Soul	
☐ OE-LEN	Airbus A320-214	3093	ex D-ABDP		♦
☐ OE-LEQ	Airbus A320-214	5464	ex D-AVVW		>IAW
☐ OE-LEU	Airbus A320-214	2902	ex F-WWDH		
☐ OE-LEV	Airbus A320-214	5246	ex D-ABNB		♦
☐ OE-LEX	Airbus A320-214	2867	ex F-WWBC	Jazz	
☐ OE-LEY	Airbus A320-214/S	5648	ex D-AUBV		
☐ OE-IXG	Embraer ERJ-190LR	19000435	ex D-ARJG		
☐ OE-LES	Airbus A321-211	3504	ex D-AVZI	Boogie Woogie	
☐ OE-LET	Airbus A321-211	3830	ex D-AVZG	Heavy Metal	
☐ OE-LEW	Airbus A321-211	4611	ex D-AZAL	Cancan	
☐ OE-LEZ	Airbus A321-211	4648	ex D-AZAV		

PEOPLE'S VIENNALINE   (PE/PEV)   St Gallen-Altenrhein (ACH)

☐ OE-LMK	Embraer ERJ-170STD	17000150	ex OH-LEO

PINK AVIATION

☐ OE-FDE	Short SC.7 Skyvan Mk.3	SH1886	♦
☐ OE-FDI	Short SC.7 Skyvan Mk.3	SH1932	♦
☐ OE-FDN	Short SC.7 Skyvan Mk.3	SH1964	♦
☐ OE-FDP	Short SC.7 Skyvan Mk.3	SH1924	♦

TYROLEAN JET SERVICE   Tyroljet (TJS)   Innsbruck (INN)

☐ OE-FSG	Cessna 525A Citation Jet CJ2	525A-0203	ex N736LB

☐ OE-GLS	Cessna 650 Citation VII	650-7110	ex N657JW	
☐ OE-GMG	Cessna 650 Citation VII	650-7102	ex D-CNCJ	
☐ OE-HGE	Gulfstream G200	240	ex N440GA	
☐ OE-HMS	Dornier 328JET Envoy3	3121	ex D-BDXI	VIP wfs
☐ OE-IEL	Bombardier BD-700 Global Express	9099	ex C-GZKL	
☐ OE-IZI	Gulfstream G550	5302	ex D-ASAF	
☐ OE-LIP	Airbus A319CJ-115	3632	ex D-AHAD	
☐ OE-LOV	Airbus A319CJ-115	3513	ex D-ALEY	VIP
☐ OE-LUX	Airbus A318CJ-112	4169	ex 9H-AFT	VIP

WELCOME AIR		Welcomeair (2W/WLC)		Innsbruck (INN)

☐ OE-LIR	Dornier 328-110	3115	ex D-CDXG	Phönix

OH- FINLAND (Republic of Finland)

ALANDIA AIR				Mariehamn (MHQ)

☐ SE-ISR	SAAB SF.340A	340A-017	ex 9G-CTS	[ARN]
☐ SE-KCH	SAAB SF.340B	340B-171	ex 5Y-FLB	>NTJ
☐ SE-KXD	SAAB SF.340B	340B-248	ex N248DP	>NTJ♦
☐ SE-LJM	SAAB SF.340A	340A-112	ex LY-RIK	>NTJ
☐ SE-LJN	SAAB SF.340A	340A-114	ex LY-DIG	>NTJ
☐ SE-	SAAB SF.340B	340B-249	ex N249CJ	[BGR]

BLUE1		Bluefinn (KF/BLF)		Helsinki-Vantaa (HEL)

Member of Star Alliance

☐ OH-BLI	Boeing 717-2CM	55061/5029	ex SE-REP	Sky Trickle	
☐ OH-BLJ	Boeing 717-23S	55065/5048	ex SE-REL	Pearl Mist	
☐ OH-BLM	Boeing 717-23S	55066/5054	ex SE-REM	Spring Rain	wfs
☐ OH-BLN	Boeing 717-2K9	55053/5016	ex EC-KHX		Star Alliance c/s
☐ OH-BLO	Boeing 717-2K9	55056/5015	ex EC-KFR	Forest Pond	
☐ OH-BLP	Boeing 717-23S	55064/5037	ex EC-KNE	Star Twinkle	
☐ OH-BLQ	Boeing 717-23S	55067/5059	ex EC-KRO	Play of Waves	

FINNAIR		Finnair (AY/FIN)		Helsinki-Vantaa (HEL)

Member of oneWorld

☐ OH-LVA	Airbus A319-112	1073	ex F-WWID	
☐ OH-LVB	Airbus A319-112	1107	ex D-AVWS	
☐ OH-LVC	Airbus A319-112	1309	ex D-AVWY	
☐ OH-LVD	Airbus A319-112	1352	ex D-AVYW	oneWorld c/s
☐ OH-LVG	Airbus A319-112	1916	ex D-AVYG	
☐ OH-LVH	Airbus A319-112	1184	ex EI-CZE	
☐ OH-LVI	Airbus A319-112	1364	ex F-WQQZ	
☐ OH-LVK	Airbus A319-112	2124	ex D-AVWB	
☐ OH-LVL	Airbus A319-112	2266	ex D-AVWS	

☐ OH-LXA	Airbus A320-214	1405	ex F-WWDH	
☐ OH-LXB	Airbus A320-214	1470	ex F-WWDO	
☐ OH-LXC	Airbus A320-214	1544	ex F-WWIX	
☐ OH-LXD	Airbus A320-214	1588	ex F-WWBQ	
☐ OH-LXF	Airbus A320-214	1712	ex F-WWIY	
☐ OH-LXH	Airbus A320-214	1913	ex F-WWIZ	
☐ OH-LXI	Airbus A320-214	1989	ex F-WWDN	
☐ OH-LXK	Airbus A320-214	2065	ex F-WWIQ	
☐ OH-LXL	Airbus A320-214	2146	ex F-WWDN	
☐ OH-LXM	Airbus A320-214	2154	ex F-WWDP	

☐ OH-LZA	Airbus A321-211	0941	ex D-AVZT	
☐ OH-LZB	Airbus A321-211	0961	ex D-AVZU	
☐ OH-LZC	Airbus A321-211	1185	ex D-AVZI	
☐ OH-LZD	Airbus A321-211	1241	ex D-AVZG	
☐ OH-LZE	Airbus A321-211	1978	ex D-AVZV	
☐ OH-LZF	Airbus A321-211	2208	ex D-AVZI	
☐ OH-LZG	Airbus A321-231/S	5758	ex D-AZAO	
☐ OH-LZH	Airbus A321-231/S	5803	ex D-AVZF	
☐ OH-LZI	Airbus A321-231/S	5922	ex D-AZAI	
☐ OH-LZK	Airbus A321-231/S	5961	ex D-AZAL	
☐ OH-LZL	Airbus A321-231/S	6083	ex D-AVZY	

☐ OH-LTM	Airbus A330-302E	994	ex F-WWKO	Marimekko Metsänväki c/s
☐ OH-LTN	Airbus A330-302E	1007	ex F-WWYC	
☐ OH-LTO	Airbus A330-302E	1013	ex F-WWKD	Marimekko Unikko c/s
☐ OH-LTP	Airbus A330-302E	1023	ex F-WWYQ	
☐ OH-LTR	Airbus A330-302E	1067	ex F-WWKY	
☐ OH-LTS	Airbus A330-302E	1078	ex F-WWYU	

☐ OH-LTT	Airbus A330-302E	1088	ex F-WWKH		
☐ OH-LTU	Airbus A330-302E	1173	ex F-WWYN		
☐ OH-LQA	Airbus A340-311	058	ex G-VFLY		
☐ OH-LQB	Airbus A340-313X	835	ex F-WWJG		
☐ OH-LQC	Airbus A340-313X	844	ex F-WWJI		
☐ OH-LQD	Airbus A340-313X	921	ex F-WWJK		
☐ OH-LQE	Airbus A340-313X	938	ex F-WWJL		
☐ OH-LQF	Airbus A340-313X	168	ex F-GNIF		
☐ OH-LQG	Airbus A340-313X	174	ex F-GNIG		
☐ OH-LKE	Embraer ERJ-190LR	19000059	ex PT-SEW		>FCM
☐ OH-LKF	Embraer ERJ-190LR	19000066	ex PT-SJE		>FCM
☐ OH-LKG	Embraer ERJ-190LR	19000079	ex PT-SJV		>FCM
☐ OH-LKH	Embraer ERJ-190LR	19000086	ex PT-SNE		>FCM
☐ OH-LKI	Embraer ERJ-190LR	19000117	ex PT-SQL		>FCM
☐ OH-LKK	Embraer ERJ-190LR	19000127	ex PT-SQW		>FCM
☐ OH-LKL	Embraer ERJ-190LR	19000153	ex PT-SAI		>FCM
☐ OH-LKM	Embraer ERJ-190LR	19000160	ex PT-SAP		>FCM
☐ OH-LKN	Embraer ERJ-190LR	19000252	ex PT-SIX	oneWorld c/s	>FCM
☐ OH-LKO	Embraer ERJ-190LR	19000267	ex PT-TLH		>FCM
☐ OH-LKP	Embraer ERJ-190LR	19000416	ex PT-TBN		>FCM
☐ OH-LKR	Embraer ERJ-190LR	19000436	ex PT-TCV		>FCM

ERJ-190 fleet also opb Flybe Nordic

☐ EC-LZO	Boeing 767-35DER	27902/577	ex EI-FDI	Eduardo Barreiros	<PVG♦
☐ OH-LEE	Embraer ERJ-170STD	17000093	ex PT-SZT		>ELL
☐ OH-LEG	Embraer ERJ-170STD	17000107	ex PT-SAP		>ELL
☐ OH-LEH	Embraer ERJ-170STD	17000112	ex PT-SAX		>ELL
☐ OH-LWA	Airbus A350-941	018	ex F-WZFM		o/o♦
☐ OH-LWB	Airbus A350-941	019	ex F-WZFN		o/o♦
☐ OH-LWC	Airbus A350-941	020	ex F-WZFO		o/o♦
☐ OH-	Airbus A350-941	022	ex F-WZ		o/o♦
☐ SP-LRC	Boeing 787-8	35940/86	ex N1791B		<LOT♦

FLYBE NORDIC		*Finncom (FC/FCM)*			*Helsinki-Vantaa (HEL)*
☐ OH-ATE	ATR 72-212A	741	ex F-WWEB		
☐ OH-ATF	ATR 72-212A	744	ex F-WWEE		
☐ OH-ATG	ATR 72-212A	757	ex F-WWER		
☐ OH-ATH	ATR 72-212A	769	ex F-WWEH		
☐ OH-ATI	ATR 72-212A	783	ex F-WWEB		
☐ OH-ATJ	ATR 72-212A	792	ex F-WWEM		
☐ OH-ATK	ATR 72-212A	848	ex F-WWEN		
☐ OH-ATL	ATR 72-212A	851	ex F-WWEU		
☐ OH-ATM	ATR 72-212A	916	ex F-WWEN		
☐ OH-ATN	ATR 72-212A	959	ex F-WWEL		
☐ OH-ATO	ATR 72-212A	977	ex F-WWEV		
☐ OH-ATP	ATR 72-212A	1050	ex F-WWEV		
☐ OH-LKE	Embraer ERJ-190LR	19000059	ex PT-SEW		<FIN
☐ OH-LKF	Embraer ERJ-190LR	19000066	ex PT-SJE		<FIN
☐ OH-LKG	Embraer ERJ-190LR	19000079	ex PT-SJV		<FIN
☐ OH-LKH	Embraer ERJ-190LR	19000086	ex PT-SNE		<FIN
☐ OH-LKI	Embraer ERJ-190LR	19000117	ex PT-SQL		<FIN
☐ OH-LKK	Embraer ERJ-190LR	19000127	ex PT-SQW		<FIN
☐ OH-LKL	Embraer ERJ-190LR	19000153	ex PT-SAI		<FIN
☐ OH-LKM	Embraer ERJ-190LR	19000160	ex PT-SAP		<FIN
☐ OH-LKN	Embraer ERJ-190LR	19000252	ex PT-SIX		<FIN
☐ OH-LKO	Embraer ERJ-190LR	19000267	ex PT-TLH		<FIN
☐ OH-LKP	Embraer ERJ-190LR	19000416	ex PT-TBN		<FIN
☐ OH-LKR	Embraer ERJ-190LR	19000436	ex PT-TCV		<FIN
☐ OH-LEI	Embraer ERJ-170STD	17000120	ex PT-SDI	Finnair c/s	
☐ OH-LEK	Embraer ERJ-170STD	17000127	ex PT-SDQ	Finnair c/s	

Finnair ERJ-190 fleet also operated; to be renamed Nordic Regional Airlines May15

JETTIME FINLAND		*Jet Time (JTF)*			*Helsinki-Vantaa (HEL)*
☐ OH-JTV	Boeing 737-7L9/W	28015/785	ex OY-JTV		
☐ OH-JTZ	Boeing 737-73S	29083/392	ex OY-JTZ		♦

NORDIC GLOBAL AIRLINES		*Nordic Global (NJ/NGB)*			*Helsinki-Vantaa (HEL)*
☐ OH-LGC	McDonnell-Douglas MD-11F	48512/529	ex N512SU		
☐ OH-LGD	McDonnell-Douglas MD-11BCF	48513/564	ex N518AY		
☐ OH-NGB	McDonnell-Douglas MD-11F	48546/589	ex B-16107		

To cease ops 31May15

SCANWINGS		*Skywings (ABF)*			*Helsinki-Vantaa (HEL)*
☐ OH-BAX	Beech 65-C90 King Air	LJ-984	ex LN-FOD		

☐ OH-BCX	Beech 65-C90 King Air	LJ-770	ex (YV-2301P)
☐ OH-BEX	Beech 65-C90 King Air	LJ-978	ex N725KR
☐ OH-SWI	Cessna 525A CitationJet CJ2	525A-0408	ex G-MNRM

UTIN LENTO

| ☐ OH-SIS | Cessna 208 Caravan I | 20800105 | ex LN-PBD |

OK- CZECH REPUBLIC

AIR BOHEMIA

| ☐ OK-OKV | Piper PA-42 Cheyenne III | 42-8001011 | ex D-IABA | ♦ |

AIR PRAGUE

☐ OK-GIO	Beech 65-C90GTX King Air	LJ-2009	ex N8109K
☐ OK-TOS	Beech B200 Super King Air	BB-825	ex I-MTOP
☐ OK-UNO	Beech B200 Super King Air	BB-1905	ex I-REEF

CENTRAL CONNECT AIRLINES — Jobair (3B/JBR) — Ostrava (OSR)

| ☐ OK-CCC | SAAB SF.340B | 340B-208 | ex YR-VGM | |
| ☐ OK-CCG | SAAB SF.340A | 340A-104 | ex N104CQ | Frtr [OSR] |

CSA CZECH AIRLINES — CSA Lines (OK/CSA) — Prague-Ruzyne (PRG)

Member of SkyTeam

☐ OK-MEK	Airbus A319-112	3043	ex D-AVWL		
☐ OK-MEL	Airbus A319-112	3094	ex D-AVWN		
☐ OK-NEM	Airbus A319-112	3406	ex D-AVYB		
☐ OK-NEN	Airbus A319-112	3436	ex D-AVYJ		
☐ OK-NEO	Airbus A319-112	3452	ex D-AVYY		
☐ OK-NEP	Airbus A319-112	3660	ex D-AVYT		City of Prague c/s
☐ OK-OER	Airbus A319-112	3892	ex D-AVWK		
☐ OK-PET	Airbus A319-112	4258	ex D-AVWM		
☐ OK-REQ	Airbus A319-112	4713	ex D-AVYS		
☐ OK-GFQ	ATR 72-212A	674	ex VT-JCF		
☐ OK-GFR	ATR 72-212A	681	ex VT-JCH		
☐ OK-GFS	ATR 72-212A	679	ex VT-JCG		
☐ OK-KFN	ATR 42-500	637	ex F-WWLR	Prerov	
☐ OK-KFO	ATR 42-500	633	ex F-WWLN	Sokolov	
☐ OK-KFP	ATR 42-500	639	ex F-WWLT	Svitavy	
☐ OK-MEH	Airbus A320-214	3031	ex F-WWBU	Beskydy	wfs♦
☐ OK-MEI	Airbus A320-214	3060	ex F-WWDY		wfs
☐ OK-MEJ	Airbus A320-214	3097	ex F-WWID		
☐ OK-XGD	Boeing 737-55S	26542/2337	ex (OO-SYO)	Poprad	all white [PRG]
☐ OK-XGE	Boeing 737-55S	26543/2339	ex (OO-SYP)	Kosice	SkyTeam c/s [PRG]
☐ OK-YBA	Airbus A330-323	425	ex HL7701		<KAL
☐ OK-YFT	ATR 72-212	387	ex EI-SLL		SkyTeam c/s

HOLIDAYS CZECH AIRLINES — Czech Holidays (HCC) — Prague-Ruzyne (PRG)

| ☐ OK-HCA/ | Airbus A320-214 | 4699 | ex F-WWDO | Prague loves You titles | >TVQ |
| ☐ OK-HCB | Airbus A320-214 | 2180 | ex G-OOPX | | >TVS |

LR AIRLINES — Lady Racine (LRB) — Ostrava (OSR)

| ☐ OK-LRA | LET L-410UVP-E | 892216 | ex CCCP-67605 | Lady Racine |

SILESIA AIR — (SUA)

☐ OK-SLA	Cessna 525 Citationjet	525-0310	ex D-IIJS	
☐ OK-SLS	Cessna 560 Citation V	560-0088	ex D-CMCM	
☐ OK-SLX	Cessna 560XL Citation Excel	560-5243	ex N243CH	
☐ OK-XLS	Cessna Citation XLS+	560-6060	ex N51160	

SILVER AIR — Solid (SLD) — Prague-Ruzyne (PRG)

| ☐ OK-SLD | LET L-410UVP-E20 | 902503 | ex LZ-CCG | Ceska Posta titles |
| ☐ OK-WDC | LET L-410UVP-E8D | 912531 | | |

SKY AIR

| ☐ OK-PRG | Beech 65-C90A King Air | LJ-1340 | ex N24TF |

SMARTWINGS		(QS/TVS)		Prague-Ruzyne (PRG)
☐ OK-SWT	Boeing 737-7Q8	29346/1264	ex EI-EUV	
☐ OK-SWW	Boeing 737-7Q8	28254/1283	ex EI-EUU	
☐ OK-TSA	Boeing 737-8S3/W	29250/792	ex TC-APH	<TVS>SEJ
☐ OK-TSF	Boeing 737-8GJ/W	37360/2783	ex YR-BGS	♦
☐ OK-TSH	Boeing 737-804/W	28231/538	ex VP-BFA	♦
☐ OK-TVP	Boeing 737-8K5/W	32907/1117	ex D-AHLR	>SWG
☐ OK-TVW	Boeing 737-86Q/W	30295/1600	ex HB-IIR	
☐ OK-TVY	Boeing 737-8Q8/W	30724/2286	ex C-GTVY	

TRAVEL SERVICE		Skytravel (QS/TVS)		Prague-Ruzyne (PRG)
☐ EI-CSG	Boeing 737-8AS/W	29922/571		Ogedei Khaan	<MGL♦
☐ OK-TSA	Boeing 737-8S3/W	29250/792	ex TC-APH		>QS
☐ OK-TSC	Boeing 737-8FH/W	35093/2176	ex C-GTQX		
☐ OK-TSD	Boeing 737-8Q8/W	41795/4895			
☐ OK-TSE	Boeing 737-81D/W	39437/4775	ex N5573K		
☐ OK-TSJ	Boeing 737-8AS/W	29921/560	ex C-FTCX		<CJA♦
☐ OK-TSL	Boeing 737-8AS/W	29923/576	ex C-FTCZ		<CJA♦
☐ OK-TVE	Boeing 737-86Q/W	30294/1469	ex C-GRKB		>SWG♦
☐ OK-TVF	Boeing 737-8FH/W	29669/1692	ex C-GTVF		
☐ OK-TVG	Boeing 737-8Q8/W	30719/2257	ex C-GTVG		>SWG
☐ OK-TVH	Boeing 737-8Q8/W	35275/2604	ex C-GVVH		>SWG
☐ OK-TVJ	Boeing 737-8Q8/W	29351/1471	ex C-FTAH		<SWG♦
☐ OK-TVK	Boeing 737-86N/W	32740/1444	ex C-FGVK		>SWG
☐ OK-TVL	Boeing 737-8FN/W	37076/3147			
☐ OK-TVM	Boeing 737-8FN/W	37077/3163	ex N1796B		
☐ OK-TVO	Boeing 737-8CX/W	32360/1084	ex PR-GOK		>SEJ
☐ OK-TVR	Boeing 737-86N/W	38018/3618	ex OM-TVR		
☐ OK-TVS	Boeing 737-86N/W	39404/3633			
☐ OK-TVT	Boeing 737-86N/W	39394/3899			
☐ OK-TVU	Boeing 737-86N/W	38025/3968			
☐ OK-TVV	Boeing 737-86N/W	38027/4030			
☐ OK-TVX	Boeing 737-8Z9/W	33833/1680	ex OE-LNR	Airport Prague c/s	>SEJ
☐ OK-HCB	Airbus A320-214	2180	ex G-OOPX		<HCC
☐ OK-TSI	Boeing 737-9GJER/W	37363/3843	ex M-ABIJ		
☐ YL-LCA	Airbus A320-211	0333	ex 4X-ABC		<ART♦
☐ YL-LCD	Airbus A320-211	0359	ex C-FMSV		<ART♦

VAN AIR		Eurovan (V9/VAA)		Brno-Turany
☐ OK-ASA	LET L-410UVP-E	902439	ex SP-KPY	
☐ OK-RDA	LET L-410UVP-E	861813	ex HA-YFG	opf Citywing
☐ OK-TCA	LET L-410UVP-E	902431	ex SP-KPZ	opf Citywing
☐ OK-UBA	LET L-410UVP-E19	892319	ex SP-TXA	opf Citywing

OM- SLOVAKIA (Slovak Republic)

AIR CARGO GLOBAL		(UB/CCC)		Bratislava-MR Stefanik (BTS)
☐ OM-ACA	Boeing 747-481F	34016/1360	ex N401KZ	♦
☐ OM-ACG	Boeing 747-409BDSF	24311/869	ex D-ACGA	

AIREXPLORE		Galileo (ED/AXE)		Bratislava-MR Stefanik (BTS)
☐ OM-AEX	Boeing 737-4Y0	25178/2199	ex D-AEFL	>LAV
☐ OM-CEX	Boeing 737-436	25839/2188	ex OK-WGY	>RYR
☐ OM-DEX	Boeing 737-46J	28867/2879	ex OO-JAM	>BPA
☐ OM-EEX	Boeing 737-4Q8	26302/2620	ex EI-FBR	>RYR♦
☐ OM-FEX	Boeing 737-8Q8	28213/50	ex N679AC	>RYR♦
☐ OM-GEX	Boeing 737-8AS/W	29919/341	ex N637AC	>PAU♦
☐ OM-HEX	Boeing 737-81Q/W	30785/1007	ex LN-NOC	>RYR♦

AIR TEC			
☐ OM-PRH	LET L-410UVP-E	831138	

AIR TRANSPORT EUROPE			Poprad
☐ OM-ATO	Agusta A109K2	10037	ex D-HPRK	
☐ OM-ATR	Bell 429	57143	ex OK-BHY	♦

DUBNICA AIR			Slavnica
☐ OM-DAC	LET L-410UVP	810712	ex OM-PGB	
☐ OM-ODQ	LET L-410UVP	841320	ex OK-ODQ	
☐ OM-SAB	LET L-410MA	750405	ex 0405 Slovak AF	

GO2SKY		(RLX)		Bratislava-MR Stefanik (BTS)
☐ OM-GTA	Boeing 737-4Q8	24332/1866	ex N332TR	
☐ OM-GTB	Boeing 737-49R	28882/2845	ex M-ABGN	>MSA
☐ OM-GTC	Boeing 737-430	27001/2316	ex G-CIEO	>TCV♦

SLOVAK GOVERNMENT FLYING SERVICE	Slovak Government (SSG)			Bratislava-MR Stefanik (BTS)
☐ OM-BYE	Yakovlev Yak-40	9440338	ex OK-BYE	VIP
☐ OM-BYL	Yakovlev Yak-40	9940560	ex OK-BYL	VIP
☐ OM-BYO	Tupolev Tu-154M	89A803	ex OK-BYO	
☐ OM-BYR	Tupolev Tu-154M	98A1012		VIP

TRAVEL SERVICE SLOVAKIA				Slovak Travel (TVQ)
☐ OM-HCA	Airbus A320-214	4699	ex OK-HCA	Prague loves You titles	<HCC
☐ OM-TSG	Boeing 737-82R/W	30666/1460	ex OK-TSG		♦

UTAIR EUROPE				
☐ OM-AVA	Mil Mi-8MTV-1	95901	ex RA-27065	♦

OO- BELGIUM (Kingdom of Belgium)

AIR SERVICE LIEGE		(BNJ)		Liege (LGG)
☐ N194ER	Cessna 510 Citation Mustang	510-0432		
☐ OO-AMR	Cessna 525A Citationjet CJ2+	525A-0495	ex N5218T	
☐ OO-ASL	Beech B200C Super King Air	BL-49	ex OK-LFB	
☐ OO-EDV	Cessna 525B Citationjet CJ3	525B-0200	ex N5073G	
☐ OO-PRM	Cessna 510 Citation Mustang	510-0125	ex N4073S	

BRUSSELS AIRLINES		Beeline (SN/BEL)		Brussels-National (BRU)

Member of Star Alliance

☐ OO-SSA	Airbus A319-111	2392	ex N936FR	
☐ OO-SSB	Airbus A319-111	2400	ex N937FR	
☐ OO-SSC	Airbus A319-112	1086	ex F-OHJX	
☐ OO-SSD	Airbus A319-112	1102	ex EI-DEY	
☐ OO-SSE	Airbus A319-111	2700	ex M-ABGB	
☐ OO-SSF	Airbus A319-111	2763	ex M-ABGA	
☐ OO-SSG	Airbus A319-112	1160	ex EI-CZF	
☐ OO-SSH	Airbus A319-112	2925	ex OE-IDQ	♦
☐ OO-SSI	Airbus A319-111	3895	ex SX-OAF	♦
☐ OO-SSK	Airbus A319-112	1336	ex F-WQRU	
☐ OO-SSM	Airbus A319-112	1388	ex F-WQRV	
☐ OO-SSN	Airbus A319-112	1963	ex N259AD	
☐ OO-SSP	Airbus A319-111	0644	ex F-GPMG	
☐ OO-SSQ	Airbus A319-112	3790	ex N790MX	
☐ OO-SSR	Airbus A319-112	4275	ex N275MX	
☐ OO-SSU	Airbus A319-111	2230	ex G-EZEM	
☐ OO-SSV	Airbus A319-111	2196	ex G-EZEI	
☐ OO-SSW	Airbus A319-111	3255	ex EI-ETG	
☐ OO-SNA	Airbus A320-214	1441	ex D-ALTC	
☐ OO-SNB	Airbus A320-214	1493	ex D-ALTD	Rackham	Tintin comic c/s
☐ OO-SNC	Airbus A320-214	1797	ex D-ALTH	
☐ OO-SND	Airbus A320-214	1838	ex D-ALTJ	
☐ OO-SNF	Airbus A320-214	2810	ex EI-DET	
☐ OO-SNG	Airbus A320-214	1885	ex F-GKXF	
☐ OO-TCQ	Airbus A320-214	2114	ex G-TCAD	♦
☐ OO-SFM	Airbus A330-301	030	ex F-GMDA	
☐ OO-SFN	Airbus A330-301	037	ex F-GMDB	
☐ OO-SFO	Airbus A330-301	045	ex F-GMDC	
☐ OO-SFU	Airbus A330-223	324	ex M-ABFL	
☐ OO-SFV	Airbus A330-322	095	ex 9M-MKR	
☐ OO-SFW	Airbus A330-322	082	ex EI-DVB	
☐ OO-SFY	Airbus A330-223	229	ex HB-IQA	<SWR
☐ OO-SFZ	Airbus A330-223	249	ex HB-IQC	<SWR
☐ OO-DWA	Avro 146-RJ100	E3308	ex G-BXEU	
☐ OO-DWB	Avro 146-RJ100	E3315	ex G-6-315	
☐ OO-DWC	Avro 146-RJ100	E3322	ex G-6-322	
☐ OO-DWD	Avro 146-RJ100	E3324	ex G-6-324	
☐ OO-DWE	Avro 146-RJ100	E3327	ex G-6-327	
☐ OO-DWF	Avro 146-RJ100	E3332	ex G-6-332	
☐ OO-DWG	Avro 146-RJ100	E3336	ex G-6-336	

422

☐ OO-DWH	Avro 146-RJ100	E3340	ex G-6-340	
☐ OO-DWI	Avro 146-RJ100	E3342	ex G-6-342	
☐ OO-DWJ	Avro 146-RJ100	E3355	ex G-6-355	
☐ OO-DWK	Avro 146-RJ100	E3360	ex G-6-360	
☐ OO-DWL	Avro 146-RJ100	E3361	ex G-6-361	
☐ G-ECOI	de Havilland DHC-8-402Q	4224	ex C-FTIE	<BEE
☐ G-ECOK	de Havilland DHC-8-402Q	4230	ex C-FTUT	<BEE
☐ G-RJXI	Embraer ERJ-145EP	145454	ex PT-SUZ Star Alliance c/s	<BMR♦

JETAIRFLY — Beauty (TB/JAF) — Brussels-National (BRU)

☐ OO-CAN	Boeing 737-8AS/W	29933/1038	ex C-FYQN		<CJT♦
☐ OO-JAA	Boeing 737-8BK/W	29660/2355	ex C-FUAA	Victory	
☐ OO-JAD	Boeing 737-8K5/W	39093/3601			
☐ OO-JAF	Boeing 737-8K5/W	35133/2313	ex N1780B	Smile	
☐ OO-JAH	Boeing 737-8K5/W	37260/3688		Perspective	
☐ OO-JAQ	Boeing 737-8K5/W	35148/2790	ex C-FOAQ	Vision	
☐ OO-JAU	Boeing 737-8K5/W	37250/4345	ex C-FJAU	Excellence	
☐ OO-JAV	Boeing 737-8K5/W	40943/4407	ex N5573L	Happiness	
☐ OO-JAX	Boeing 737-8K5/W	37238/3452	ex N1787B	Brightness	
☐ OO-JAY	Boeing 737-8K5/W	40944/4431		Elegance	
☐ OO-JBG	Boeing 737-8K5/W	35142/2660	ex C-GLBG	Gerard Brackx	>SWG
☐ OO-JEF	Boeing 737-8K5/W	44271/4805		Affection	
☐ OO-JLO	Boeing 737 8K5/W	34692/2249	ex CN-RPG	Grace	
☐ OO-JPT	Boeing 737-8K5/W	34691/2246	ex CN-RPF	Sky	
☐ OO-JAO	Boeing 737-7K5/W	35141/2603	ex D-AHXI	Playing to Win	
☐ OO-JAR	Boeing 737-7K5/W	35150/2825		Enjoy	
☐ OO-JAS	Boeing 737-7K5/W	35144/2652	ex D-AHXK		
☐ OO-JDL	Boeing 787-8	34425/137		Diamond	
☐ OO-JEB	Embraer ERJ100-100STD	19000607	ex PT-TJM	Navigator	
☐ OO-JEM	Embraer ERJ190-100STD	19000603	ex PT-TJC	Explorer	
☐ OO-JNL	Boeing 767-304ER/W	29384/784	ex PH-OYJ		♦
☐ OO-JOS	Boeing 737-7K5/W	35282/2585	ex D-AHXH	Aurora	♦
☐ OO-JVA	Embraer ERJ190-100STD	19000689	ex PR-EKZ	Jewel	♦

NOORDZEE HELIKOPTERS VLAANDEREN (NHV)
Den Helder/Ostend/Antwerp-Deurne/Kortrijk-Wevelgem (-/OST/ANR/KJK)

☐ CS-HHR	Aérospatiale AS365N3 Dauphin 2	6841	ex F-OJTU		<HPL
☐ OO-NAT	Eurocopter EC155B1 Dauphin	6735	ex PH-SHN		
☐ OO-NHD	Aérospatiale AS365NE Dauphin 2	6831			
☐ OO-NHE	Aérospatiale AS365N3 Dauphin 2	6843			
☐ OO-NHJ	Eurocopter EC155B1 Dauphin	6842	ex (OO-NHI)		based Caithness
☐ OO-NHK	Aérospatiale AS365N3 Dauphin 2	6876			based Ivory Coast
☐ OO-NHM	Aérospatiale AS365N3 Dauphin 2	6740	ex C-FYRC		
☐ OO-NHN	Aérospatiale AS365N3 Dauphin 2	6783	ex D2-EWF		based Liberia
☐ OO-NHO	Aérospatiale AS365N3 Dauphin 2	6809	ex D2-EWH		based Liberia
☐ OO-NHP	Eurocopter EC155B1 Dauphin	6762	ex G-ISSU		
☐ OO-NHQ	Eurocopter EC155B1 Dauphin	6778	ex G-ISST		based Humberside
☐ OO-NHU	Aérospatiale AS365SR Dauphin	6665	ex F-WWOS	Flipper 2	
☐ OO-NHV	Aérospatiale AS365N3 Dauphin 2	6510	ex F-GVHN	Flipper 1	
☐ OO-NHX	Aérospatiale AS365N3 Dauphin 2	6706	ex OY-HMO		
☐ OO-NHY	Aérospatiale AS365N3 Dauphin 2	6754			
☐ OO-NHZ	Aérospatiale AS365N2 Dauphin 2	6450	ex N4H	Samu 59	EMS
☐ OO-NSH	Eurocopter EC155B1 Dauphin	6681	ex D-HAZA		based Humberside
☐ OO-NSZ	Aérospatiale AS365N2 Dauphin 2	6420	ex LN-OCO		♦
☐ 9G-NHG	Aérospatiale AS365N3 Dauphin 2	6881			
☐ 9G-NHH	Aérospatiale AS365N3 Dauphin 2	6891	ex OO-NHH		
☐ OO-ECB	Eurocopter EC120B Colibri	1096	ex F-WQDK		
☐ OO-NHB	Eurocopter EC145B	9083	ex D-HMBG		EMS
☐ OO-NHF	MD Helicopters MD900 Explorer	900-00015	ex N9015P		EMS
☐ OO-NHI	MD Helicopters MD900 Explorer	900-0137	ex N40789		♦
☐ PH-NHR	Aérospatiale AS332L2	2572	ex G-CHLF		
☐ PH-NHS	Aérospatiale AS332L2	2599	ex G-CHLJ		
☐ PH-NHU	Eurocopter EC175B	5004			
☐ PH-NHV	Eurocopter EC175B	5002	ex F-WJXA		♦

THOMAS COOK AIRLINE BELGIUM — Thomas Cook (HQ/TCW) — Brussels-National (BRU)

☐ OO-TCH	Airbus A320-214	1929	ex D-AICM		
☐ OO-TCS	Airbus A319-132	2362	ex M-ABEL	Sunshine	
☐ OO-TCT	Airbus A320-212	1402	ex D-AICJ		♦
☐ OO-TCV	Airbus A320-214	1968	ex D-AICN		♦
☐ OO-TCW	Airbus A320-214	1954	ex OY-VKS		♦

TNT AIRWAYS — Quality (3V/TAY) — Liege (LGG)

☐ OE-IAE	Boeing 737-4Q8SF	25105/2505	ex N772AS	♦

☐ OE-IAF	Boeing 737-4Y0SF	25184/2227	ex F-GIXU	♦
☐ OE-IAG	Boeing 737-4Q8F	25168/2210	ex N515AC	[DTH]♦
☐ OE-IAP	Boeing 737-4M0SF	29206/3058	ex PK-GZK	
☐ OE-IAQ	Boeing 737-4M0SF	29207/3078	ex PK-GZL	
☐ OE-IAR	Boeing 737-4M0SF	29208/3081	ex PK-GZM	
☐ OE-IAS	Boeing 737-4M0SF	29209/3087	ex PK-GZN	
☐ OE-IAT	Boeing 737-4M0SF	29210/3091	ex PK-GZO	
☐ OE-IBW	Boeing 737-4Q8SF	25109/2561	ex N416BC	♦
☐ OO-TNN	Boeing 737-45DF	27131/2458	ex EI-EMW	
☐ OO-TNO	Boeing 737-49RSF	28881/2833	ex EI-DOS	
☐ OO-TNP	Boeing 737-45DF	27256/2589	ex EI-EOD	
☐ OO-TNQ	Boeing 737-4M0SF	29205/3056	ex OE-IAO	
☐ EC-ELT	British Aerospace 146 Srs.200QT	E2102	ex EC-198	>PNR
☐ EC-FVY	British Aerospace 146 Srs.200QT	E2117	ex EC-615	>PNR
☐ EC-FZE	British Aerospace 146 Srs.200QT	E2105	ex EC-719	>PNR
☐ EC-GQO	British Aerospace 146 Srs.200QT	E2086	ex D-ADEI	>PNR♦
☐ OO-TAQ	British Aerospace 146 Srs.200QT	E2078	ex G-BNPJ	[EXT]
☐ EC-LMR	British Aerospace 146 Srs.300QT	E3151	ex OO-TAA	>PNR
☐ EC-LOF	British Aerospace 146 Srs.300QT	E3150	ex OO-TAK	>PNR
☐ EC-MCK	British Aerospace 146 Srs.300QT	E3153	ex OO-TAJ	>PNR♦
☐ EC-MCL	British Aerospace 146 Srs.300QT	E3154	ex OO-TAS	>PNR♦
☐ OO-TAD	British Aerospace 146 Srs.300QT	E3166	ex G-TNTM	
☐ OO-TAE	British Aerospace 146 Srs.300QT	E3182	ex G-TNTG	>PNR
☐ OO-TAF	British Aerospace 146 Srs.300QT	E3186	ex G-TNTK	>PNR
☐ OO-TAH	British Aerospace 146 Srs.300QT	E3168	ex G-TNTL	
☐ OO-TAJ	British Aerospace 146 Srs.300QT	E3153	ex G-TNTE	>PNR
☐ OO-TAS	British Aerospace 146 Srs.300QT	E3154	ex EC-FFY	>PNR
☐ OE-IBZ	Boeing 737-34S BDSF	29108/2983	ex TF-TNM	
☐ OE-LFB	Boeing 757-23APF	24868/314	ex VQ-BOX	♦
☐ OO-TFA	Boeing 757-28AF	25622/530	ex OH-AFK	opf NATO
☐ OO-THA	Boeing 747-4HAERF	35232/1381	Peter Abeles 1924-1999	
☐ OO-THB	Boeing 747-4HAERF	35234/1386	Ken Thomas 1913-1997	
☐ OO-THC	Boeing 747-4HAERF	35235/1389	ex N50217	opf UAE
☐ OO-THD	Boeing 747-4HAERF	35236/1399		opf UAE
☐ OO-TNL	Boeing 737-34SSF	29109/3001	ex N132MN	
☐ OO-TSA	Boeing 777-FHT	38969/947		
☐ OO-TSB	Boeing 777-FHT	39286/963	ex N778SA	
☐ OO-TSC	Boeing 777-FHT	37138/977		
☐ SE-RLA	Boeing 767-232SCD	22224/76	ex N747AX	<SWN♦

VLM AIRLINES		Rubens (VG/VLM)		Antwerp-Deurne (ANR)
☐ OO-VLF	Fokker 50	20208	ex PH-DMT	Panamarenko	
☐ OO-VLI	Fokker 50	20226	ex PH-JXC		
☐ OO-VLJ	Fokker 50	20105	ex PH-ARE	Owain Glyndwr	>BCY
☐ OO-VLL	Fokker 50	20144	ex TF-JMG	City of Groningen	
☐ OO-VLM	Fokker 50	20135	ex PH-VLM		
☐ OO-VLN	Fokker 50	20145	ex PH-VLN	Spirit of Reenstar	
☐ OO-VLO	Fokker 50	20127	ex ES-AFL	Angela Dirkin	>Vizion Air
☐ OO-VLP	Fokker 50	20209	ex PH-DMS		>BCY
☐ OO-VLQ	Fokker 50	20159	ex EC-GBH	City of Manchester	
☐ OO-VLR	Fokker 50	20121	ex PH-ARF	City of Luxembourg	
☐ OO-VLS	Fokker 50	20109	ex EC-GBG	City of Antwerp	
☐ OO-VLZ	Fokker 50	20264	ex TF-JMU	Deauville Normandie	>AUR

OY-   DENMARK (Kingdom of Denmark)

AIR GREENLAND		Greenland (GL/GRL)		Nuuk Godthaab (GOH)
☐ OY-HGA	Aérospatiale AS350B2 Ecureuil	2600		
☐ OY-HGK	Aérospatiale AS350B2 Ecureuil	2570	ex C-FNJW	
☐ OY-HGO	Aérospatiale AS350B3 Ecureuil	3919		
☐ OY-HGP	Aérospatiale AS350B3 Ecureuil	4062		
☐ OY-HGS	Aérospatiale AS350B3 Ecureuil	4226		
☐ OY-HGT	Aérospatiale AS350B3 Ecureuil	4279		
☐ OY-HGU	Aérospatiale AS350B3 Ecureuil	4466	ex F-WWXM	
☐ OY-HGV	Aérospatiale AS350B3 Ecureuil	4469		♦
☐ OY-HUD	Aérospatiale AS350B3 Ecureuil	7152		
☐ OY-HUE	Aérospatiale AS350B3 Ecureuil	7172		
☐ OY-GRG	de Havilland DHC-8-202Q	504	ex C-FXBO	
☐ OY-GRH	de Havilland DHC-8-202Q	488	ex C-GCTX	
☐ OY-GRJ	de Havilland DHC-8-202Q	496	ex C-GLVB	
☐ OY-GRK	de Havilland DHC-8-202Q	498	ex C-GLUZ	
☐ OY-GRM	de Havilland DHC-8-202Q	434	ex C-FRIQ	
☐ OY-GRO	de Havilland DHC-8-202Q	482	ex C-FEBU	♦
☐ OY-CBU	de Havilland DHC-7-103	020		Nipiki

☐ OY-GRN	Airbus A330-223	230	ex F-WIHL	Norsaq
☐ OY-HAF	Sikorsky S-61N	61267	ex N10045	Nattoralik
☐ OY-HAG	Sikorsky S-61N	61268	ex N10046	Kussak
☐ OY-HCY	Bell 212	31166		Piseeq 2
☐ OY-HDM	Bell 212	31142	ex N57545	
☐ OY-HDN	Bell 212	31136	ex N5752K	Miteq
☐ OY-HMD	Bell 212	31125	ex (LN-ORI)	
☐ OY-PCL	Beech B200 Super King Air	BB-1675	ex N2355Z	

ALSIE EXPRESS   Mermaid (6I/MMD)   Sønderborg (SGD)

| ☐ OY-CLY | ATR 72-212A | 799 | ex 4K-AZ66 |
| ☐ OY-CLZ | ATR 72-212A | 818 | ex 4K-AZ67 |

ATLANTIC AIRWAYS   Faroeline (RC/FLI)   Vagar (FAE)

☐ OY-HIM	AgustaWestland AW139	31492	ex G-OAGB	◆
☐ OY-HMB	Bell 212	30686	ex LN-OSR	
☐ OY-HSJ	Bell 412	36069	ex N412SX	
☐ OY-HSR	Bell 412EP	36133	ex N62734	
☐ OY-RCC	Avro 146-RJ100	E3357	ex HB-IYX	>SCW
☐ OY-RCE	Avro 146-RJ85	E2233	ex HB-IXH	>DAP
☐ OY-RCG	Airbus A319-115	5079	ex D-AVYN	
☐ OY-RCH	Airbus A319-112	2186	ex 9H-AEJ	<AMC
☐ OY-RCI	Airbus A319-112	3905	ex SX-OAJ	

BENAIR AIR SERVICE   Birdie (BDI)   Stauning (STA)

☐ OY-ARJ	Cessna 414	414-0614	ex D-IAWM	
☐ OY-BJP	Swearingen SA227AC Metro III	AC-499	ex F-GHVG	
☐ OY-HDD	Bell 206B JetRanger III	3649	ex N130S	
☐ OY-MUG	Short SD.3-60	SH3716	ex G-BNDM	all-white
☐ OY-PBH	LET L-410UVP-E20	972736	ex OK-EDA	
☐ OY-PBI	LET L-410UVP-E20	871936	ex OK-SDM	
☐ OY-PBV	Short SD.3-60	SH3747	ex G-GPBV	
☐ OY-PBW	Short SD.3-60	SH3760	ex VH-SEG	

BLUE WEST HELICOPTERS GREENLAND   Tassiilaq

| ☐ OY-HIT | Aérospatiale AS350B Ecureuil | 9087 | ex TF-BWH |

CIMBER   Cimber (QA/CIM)   Sonderborg (SGD)

☐ OY-RJB	Canadair CRJ-200LR	7419	ex D-ACIN	wfs
☐ OY-RJG	Canadair CRJ-200LR	7104	ex D-ACLU	wfs◆
☐ OY-RJH	Canadair CRJ-200LR	7090	ex D-ACLS	wfs◆
☐ OY-RJI	Canadair CRJ-200LR	7093	ex D-ACLT	wfs◆
☐ OY-RJJ	Canadair CRJ-200ER	7784	ex HA-LNC	wfs
☐ OY-RJK	Canadair CRJ-200ER	7622	ex EC-IDC	wfs
☐ OY-RJL	Canadair CRJ-200ER	7661	ex EC-IGO	wfs
☐ OY-RJM	Canadair CRJ-200ER	7591	ex EC-IBM	wfs

Acquired by SAS Dec14

COPENHAGEN AIRTAXI   Aircat (CAT)   Copenhagen-Roskilde (RKE)

☐ OY-CAC	Partenavia P.68B	179	
☐ OY-CAT	Britten-Norman BN-2B-26 Islander	2224	ex EC-FFZ
☐ OY-CDC	Partenavia P.68C	211	ex D-GEMD

DANCOPTER   Dancopter (DOP)   Holsted Heliport & Esbjerg (-/EBJ)

☐ OY-HJA	Eurocopter EC155B1 Dauphin 2	6828		
☐ OY-HJB	Eurocopter EC155B1 Dauphin 2	6871		◆
☐ OY-HJJ	Eurocopter EC155B1 Dauphin 2	6662	ex 5H-EXO	
☐ OY-HJP	Eurocopter EC155B1 Dauphin 2	6655	ex F-WWOI	
☐ OY-HSK	Eurocopter EC155B1 Dauphin 2	6660	ex N155EW	
☐ OY-HSL	Eurocopter EC155B1 Dauphin 2	6658		
☐ OY-HOK	Eurocopter EC225LP	2839	ex F-WWOI	
☐ OY-HOM	Eurocopter EC225LP	2838		
☐ OY-HOS	Eurocopter EC225LP	2841		

DANISH AIR TRANSPORT   Danish (DX/DTR)   Kolding-Vamdrup

☐ OY-LHA	ATR 72-202	508	ex OY-RTC	>NAX
☐ OY-LHB	ATR 72-202	496	ex OY-RTF	
☐ OY-LHC	ATR 72-212	405	ex EI-SLN	◆
☐ OY-RUB	ATR 72-202	301	ex F-WQNS	
☐ OY-RUD	ATR 72-201	162	ex LY-ATR	
☐ OY-RUG	ATR 72-202	0509	ex OY-RTD	

☐ OY-JRJ	ATR 42-320	036	ex F-WQIS		based BSG
☐ OY-JRK	Airbus A320-231	0444	ex S5-AAS		>ADR♦
☐ OY-JRU	McDonnell-Douglas MD-87	49403/1404	ex SE-RBA		
☐ OY-JRY	ATR 42-300	063	ex F-WQOC		>SEH
☐ OY-JRZ	Airbus A320-233	2102	ex EI-FGO		♦
☐ OY-LHD	Airbus A320-231	0113	ex XY-AGI		♦
☐ OY-RUE	McDonnell-Douglas MD-83	49936/1778	ex YR-HBZ	Coca Cola/FIFA c/s	
☐ OY-RUF	ATR 42-500	515	ex F-GVIJ		
☐ OY-RUO	ATR 42-500	514	ex OY-CIL		
☐ OY-RUP	Airbus A320-231	0406	ex N406PR		♦

GREENLANDCOPTER

☐ OY-HHI	Aérospatiale AS350B3 Ecureuil	7440	

JET TIME — Jettime (JO/JTG) — Copenhagen-Kastrup (CPH)

☐ OY-JZU	ATR 72-212A	723	ex (XY-AJU)	Gyrid Viking	>SAS♦
☐ OY-JZV	ATR 72-212A	789	ex F-GVZT	Gudlög Viking	>SAS♦
☐ OY-JZW	ATR 72-212A	773	ex PP-PTL		♦
☐ OY-JZY	ATR 72-212A	500	ex N540AM		>SAS
☐ OY-JZZ	ATR 72-212A	548	ex N548AT		>SAS
☐ OY-YAF	ATR 72-212A	982	ex TC-YAF		[BLL]♦
☐ OY-JZA	ATR 72-600	1110	ex F-WWEW	Rorik Viking	>SAS
☐ OY-JZB	ATR 72-600	1121	ex F-WWEJ	Palnetoke Viking	>SAS
☐ OY-JZC	ATR 72-600	1120	ex F-WKVI	Torver Viking	>SAS
☐ OY-JZD	ATR 72-600	1131	ex F-WWET	Fjølnur Viking	>SAS
☐ OY-JZE	ATR 72-600	1164	ex F-WWEE	Skagul Viking	>SAS♦
☐ OY-JZF	ATR 72-600	1165	ex F-WWEF	Skjalm Viking	>SAS♦
☐ OY-JZG	ATR 72-600	1171	ex F-WWEL	Njal Viking	>SAS♦
☐ OY-JZH	ATR 72-600	1177	ex F-WWER	Nord Viking	>SAS♦
☐ OY-	ATR 72-600	1177	ex F-WW		o/o♦
☐ OY-JTA	Boeing 737-33A	23631/1337	ex N371FA		
☐ OY-JTB	Boeing 737-3Y0	24464/1753	ex RP-C4010		
☐ OY-JTC	Boeing 737-3L9/W	23718/1402	ex 9M-AAB		
☐ OY-JTD	Boeing 737-3Y0/W	24678/1853	ex 9M-AAY		
☐ OY-JTE	Boeing 737-3L9/W	27834/2692	ex G-OGBE		
☐ OY-JTF	Boeing 737-382QC	24364/1657	ex OK-GCG		
☐ OY-JTJ	Boeing 737-301SF	23741/1498	ex EC-JUV		
☐ OY-JTI	Boeing 737-448SF	25052/2036	ex N448KA		
☐ OY-JTK	Boeing 737-4Y0SF	24903/1978	ex N451KA		
☐ OY-JTL	Boeing 737-42CSF	24231/1871	ex N455KA		♦
☐ OY-JTS	Boeing 737-7K2/W	33465/1316	ex PH-XRW		
☐ OY-JTT	Boeing 737-73S/W	29079/194	ex OY-MRU		
☐ OY-JTU	Boeing 737-7L9/W	28010/396	ex OY-MRG		
☐ OY-JTY	Boeing 737-7Q8/W	30727/1005	ex VT-SJE		>MON

NORTH FLYING — North Flying (M3/NFA) — Aalborg (AAL)

☐ OY-CCJ	Learjet 35A	35A-468	ex N468LM		
☐ OY-CYV	Cessna 550 Citation II	550-0440	ex N120TC		
☐ OY-DLY	Piper PA-31 Turbo Navajo	31-229	ex G-AWOW		
☐ OY-NLA	Cessna 650 Citation III	650-0070	ex N38ED		
☐ OY-NPD	Swearingen SA227DC Metro 23	DC-865B	ex 9M-BCH		
☐ OY-NPE	Swearingen SA227DC Metro 23	DC-867B	ex N23VJ		
☐ OY-NPF	Swearingen SA227DC Metro 23	DC-880B	ex TF-JME		
☐ OY-NPG	Swearingen SA227DC Metro 23	DC-896B	ex VH-TWL		♦

PRIMERA AIR SCANDINAVIA — Primera (PF/PRI) — Billund (BLL)

☐ OY-PSA	Boeing 737-8Q8/W	30688/2280	ex TF-JXD	
☐ OY-PSC	Boeing 737-86N/W	33419/1251	ex TF-JXF	
☐ OY-PSE	Boeing 737-809/W	30664/743	ex TF-JXI	
☐ OY-PSF	Boeing 737-7Q8/W	28210/22	ex TF-JXG	
☐ OY-PSG	Boeing 737-7BX/W	30743/922	ex VH-VBP	

SCANDINAVIAN AIRLINE SYSTEM — Scandinavian (SK/SAS) — Copenhagen-Kastrup (CPH)

For details see under Sweden (SE-)

STAR AIR — Whitestar (S6/SRR) — Copenhagen-Kastrup (CPH)

☐ OY-SRF	Boeing 767-219ERSF	23327/134	ex N327MR	
☐ OY-SRG	Boeing 767-219ERSF	23328/149	ex N328MT	
☐ OY-SRH	Boeing 767-204ERSF	24457/256	ex N457GE	
☐ OY-SRI	Boeing 767-25ESF	27193/527	ex N622EV	
☐ OY-SRJ	Boeing 767-25ESF	27195/535	ex N625EV	
☐ OY-SRK	Boeing 767-204ERSF	23072/107	ex N307MT	
☐ OY-SRL	Boeing 767-232SF	22219/37	ex N107DL	

☐ OY-SRM	Boeing 767-25ESF	27192/524	ex N621EV		
☐ OY-SRN	Boeing 767-219ERSF	23326/124	ex N326MR		
☐ OY-SRO	Boeing 767-25ESF	27194/532	ex N623EV		
☐ OY-SRP	Boeing 767-232SF	22220/38	ex N108DL		
☐ OY-SRT	Boeing 767-232SCD	22226/78	ex N749AX		♦

SUN AIR OF SCANDINAVIA		*Sunscan (EZ/SUS)*			*Billund (BLL)*
☐ D-BMAD	Dornier 328-300 (328JET)	3142	ex I-AIRX	British Airways c/s	<MHV♦
☐ D-CIRI	Dornier 328-110	3005	ex TF-CSC	British Airways c/s	<MHV
☐ D-CIRP	Dornier 328-120	3006	ex TF-CSD	British Airways c/s	<MHV
☐ OY-JJB	Dornier 328-300 (328JET)	3199	ex HB-AEU	JoinJet c/s	
☐ OY-NCJ	Dornier 328-310 (328JET)	3186	ex D-BABY	JoinJet c/s	<MHV♦
☐ OY-NCL	Dornier 328-310 (328JET)	3192	ex N427FJ		
☐ OY-NCM	Dornier 328-310 (328JET)	3190	ex N426FJ		
☐ OY-NCN	Dornier 328-310 (328JET)	3193	ex N428FJ		
☐ OY-NCO	Dornier 328-310 (328JET)	3210	ex OE-HAB		
☐ OY-NCP	Dornier 328-300 (328JET)	3132	ex N328AC		
☐ OY-NCT	Dornier 328-310 (328JET)	3213	ex OE-LJR		
☐ OY-NCU	Dornier 328-300 (328JET)	3122	ex N353SK	British Airways c/s	
☐ OY-NCW	Dornier 328-300 (328JET)	3131	ex D-BGAL	British Airways c/s	
☐ OY-JJA	British Aerospace 125 Srs.800XPR	258496	ex (OY-JJC)		
☐ OY-JJD	Beech 400A	RK-133	ex I-TOPB		
⊔ OY-JJE	Beech 400	RK-29	ex I-IPIZ		
☐ OY-SVB	British Aerospace Jetstream 31	985	ex JA8591		
☐ OY-SVF	British Aerospace Jetstream 31	686	ex G-BSFG	Skien	
☐ D-BABY	Dornier 328-310 (328JET)	3186	ex I-AIRJ	JoinJet c/s	<MHV♦
☐ OY-	British Aerospace 125 Srs.800sp	258637	ex N637XP		♦

THOMAS COOK AIRLINES SCANDINAVIA		*Viking (DK/VKG)*		*Copenhagen-Kastrup (CPH)*
☐ OY-TCD	Airbus A321-211/S	6314	ex D-AZAC	♦
☐ OY-TCE	Airbus A321-211/S	6342	ex D-AVXH	♦
☐ OY-TCF	Airbus A321-211/S	6351	ex D-AVXK	♦
☐ OY-TCG	Airbus A321-211/S	6389	ex D-AVXW	♦
☐ OY-TCH	Airbus A321-211/S	6438	ex D-AZAX	♦
☐ OY-TCI	Airbus A321-211/S	6468	ex D-AVZH	o/o♦
☐ OY-VKC	Airbus A321-211	1932	ex D-AVXB	
☐ OY-VKD	Airbus A321-211	1960	ex G-EFPA	
☐ OY-	Airbus A321-211/S	6376	ex	o/o♦
☐ OY-	Airbus A321-211/S	6960	ex	o/o♦
☐ OY-VKF	Airbus A330-243	309	ex G-CSJS	>TCX
☐ OY-VKG	Airbus A330-343X	349	ex F-WWYG	
☐ OY-VKH	Airbus A330-343X	356	ex F-WWYJ	
☐ OY-VKI	Airbus A330-343X	357	ex C-GVKI	

P-   KOREA (Democratic People's Republic of Korea)

AIR KORYO		*Air Koryo (JS/KOR)*		*Pyongyang (FNJ)*
☐ P-532	Antonov An-24RV	47309707		
☐ P-533	Antonov An-24RV	47309708		
☐ P-537	Antonov An-24B	67302408		
☐ P-551	Tupolev Tu-154B	75A129	ex 551	
☐ P-552	Tupolev Tu-154B	76A143	ex 552	
☐ P-561	Tupolev Tu-154B-2	83A573		
☐ P-632	Tupolev Tu-204-300	1450742364012	ex RA-64012	
☐ P-633	Tupolev Tu-204-100	1450741964048	ex RA-64048	
☐ P-671	Antonov An-148-100	03-08		
☐ P-672	Antonov An-148-100B	04-02		o/o♦
☐ P-813	Tupolev Tu-134B-3	66215		
☐ P-814	Tupolev Tu-134B-3	66368		
☐ P-835	Ilyushin Il-18D	188011205	ex 835	
☐ P-836	Ilyushin Il-18V	185008204	ex 836	wfs
☐ P-881	Ilyushin Il-62M	3647853		
☐ P-882	Ilyushin Il-62M	2850236	no titles	opf Govt
☐ P-885	Ilyushin Il-62M	3933913	ex 885	
☐ P-912	Ilyushin Il-76MD	1003403104		
☐ P-913	Ilyushin Il-76MD	1003404126		
☐ P-914	Ilyushin Il-76MD	1003404146		

PH-   NETHERLANDS (Kingdom of the Netherlands)

AIR CHARTERS EUROPE			*Groningen-Eelde*
☐ PH-ACF	Beech 1900D	UE-383	ex N800CA

AIS AIRLINES   Spinner (IS/PNX)   Amsterdam-Schiphol (AMS)

☐ PH-CCI	British Aerospace Jetstream 32	860	ex 4X-CII
☐ PH-DCI	British Aerospace Jetstream 32	916	ex 4X-CIJ
☐ PH-HCI	British Aerospace Jetstream 32	864	ex LN-FAN(2)
☐ PH-LCI	British Aerospace Jetstream 31	718	ex G-OAKI
☐ PH-NCI	British Aerospace Jetstream 32EP	844	ex SE-LHB
☐ PH-OCI	British Aerospace Jetstream 32EP	846	ex SE-LHC
☐ PH-RCI	British Aerospace Jetstream 32EP	848	ex SE-LHH
☐ PH-	British Aerospace Jetstream 32EP	953	ex LN-FAQ

ARKEFLY/TUI NETHERLANDS   Arkefly (OR/TFL)   Amsterdam-Schiphol (AMS)

☐ PH-TFA	Boeing 737-8FH/W	35100/2424	ex N1786B	Ferdinand Fransen	
☐ PH-TFB	Boeing 737-8K5/W	35149/2820	ex N1781B		
☐ PH-TFC	Boeing 737-8K5/W	35146/2875	ex N1787B		
☐ PH-TFD	Boeing 737-86N/W	38014/3588			
☐ PH-TFF	Boeing 737-86N/W	35220/2406	ex EI-EPO		
☐ PH-TFK	Boeing 787-8	36427/182	#dreamcatcher		♦
☐ PH-TFL	Boeing 787-8	37228/245			♦
☐ PH-TFM	Boeing 787-8	36429/281	#Driemliner		♦

CHC AIRWAYS   Schreiner (SCH)   Rotterdam (RTM)

☐ 5A-DLX	de Havilland DHC-8-311A	254	ex PH-SDK	>PEO

CHC HELICOPTERS NETHERLANDS   (HNL)   den Helder (DHR)

☐ PH-EUE	AgustaWestland AW139	31387		
☐ PH-EUF	AgustaWestland AW139	31406		
☐ PH-EUG	AgustaWestland AW139	31407		
☐ PH-EUJ	AgustaWestland AW139	31511		
☐ PH-SHK	AgustaWestland AW139	31030	ex I-RAIA	
☐ PH-SHL	AgustaWestland AW139	31041		
☐ PH-SHP	AgustaWestland AW139	31099		
☐ PH-EUI	Sikorsky S-92A	920046	ex G-WNSF	
☐ PH-SHN	Eurocopter EC155B1 Dauphin 2	6755		♦
☐ PH-SHO	Eurocopter EC155B1 Dauphin 2	6739	ex F-WWOV	

CORENDON DUTCH AIRLINES   (CND)   Amsterdam-Schiphol (AMS)

☐ CS-TQU	Boeing 737-8K2/W	30646/1122	ex PH-HZY	<MMZ♦
☐ ES-SAK	Airbus A320-214	0888	ex EI-EZA	<MYX♦
☐ PH-CDE	Boeing 737-8KN/W	35795/2829	ex A6-FDB	
☐ PH-CDF	Boeing 737-804/W	28227/452	ex G-CDZH	

DENIM AIR ACMI   (J7/DNM)   Amsterdam-Schiphol (AMS)

☐ OY-CHT	ATR 42-300	080	ex PJ-DAJ	♦
☐ PH-DNA	Embraer ERJ-190AR	19000372	ex A9C-MC	>TAE
☐ PH-DNB	Embraer ERJ-190AR	19000373	ex A9C-MD	>TAE
☐ PH-DND	Embraer ERJ-145MP	145406	ex EI-FFL	♦
☐ PH-JXN	Fokker 50	20239	ex EC-GFP	opf UN
☐ PH-MJP	Fokker 100	11505	ex D-AFKE	♦

HELI HOLLAND   Emmer-Compascuum

☐ PH-EQR	Eurocopter EC155B Dauphin 2	4557	ex D-HLEW
☐ PH-EQU	Eurocopter EC155B1 Dauphin 2	6708	ex 3A-MAG
☐ PH-HHO	Eurocopter EC155B1 Dauphin 2	6683	ex 4K-AZ45

KLM CITYHOPPER   City (WA/KLC)   Amsterdam-Schiphol (AMS)

☐ PH-EZA	Embraer ERJ-190LR	19000224	ex PT-SHI
☐ PH-EZB	Embraer ERJ-190LR	19000235	ex PT-SIG
☐ PH-EZC	Embraer ERJ-190LR	19000250	ex PT-SIU
☐ PH-EZD	Embraer ERJ-190LR	19000279	ex PT-TLT
☐ PH-EZE	Embraer ERJ-190LR	19000288	ex PT-TZC
☐ PH-EZF	Embraer ERJ-190LR	19000304	ex PT-TZS
☐ PH-EZG	Embraer ERJ-190LR	19000315	ex PT-TXD
☐ PH-EZH	Embraer ERJ-190LR	19000319	ex PT-TXH
☐ PH-EZI	Embraer ERJ-190LR	19000322	ex PT-TXK
☐ PH-EZK	Embraer ERJ-190LR	19000326	ex PT-TXO
☐ PH-EZL	Embraer ERJ-190LR	19000334	ex PT-TXU
☐ PH-EZM	Embraer ERJ-190LR	19000338	ex PT-TXX
☐ PH-EZN	Embraer ERJ-190LR	19000342	ex PT-XQJ
☐ PH-EZO	Embraer ERJ-190LR	19000345	ex PT-XQL
☐ PH-EZP	Embraer ERJ-190LR	19000347	ex PT-XQN

☐ PH-EZR	Embraer ERJ-190LR	19000375	ex PT-XNL		
☐ PH-EZS	Embraer ERJ-190LR	19000380	ex PT-XNP		
☐ PH-EZT	Embraer ERJ-190LR	19000519	ex PT-TUG		
☐ PH-EZU	Embraer ERJ-190LR	19000522	ex PT-TUI		
☐ PH-EZV	Embraer ERJ-190LR	19000528	ex PT-TUQ		
☐ PH-EZW	Embraer ERJ-190LR	19000533	ex PT-TUX		
☐ PH-EZX	Embraer ERJ-190LR	19000545	ex PT-TBI	SkyTeam c/s	
☐ PH-EZY	Embraer ERJ-190LR	19000649	ex PR-EDD		
☐ PH-EZZ	Embraer ERJ-190LR	19000654	ex PR-EDX		
☐ PH-EXA	Embraer ERJ-190LR	19000655	ex PR-EDY		
☐ PH-EXB	Embraer ERJ-190LR	19000658	ex PR-EEF		
☐ PH-EXC	Embraer ERJ-190LR	19000659	ex PR-EEI		
☐ PH-EXD	Embraer ERJ-190LR	19000661	ex PR-EEQ		
☐ PH-KBX	Fokker 70	11547		VIP; opf Royal Flight	
☐ PH-KZA	Fokker 70	11567			
☐ PH-KZB	Fokker 70	11562			
☐ PH-KZC	Fokker 70	11566			
☐ PH-KZD	Fokker 70	11582			
☐ PH-KZE	Fokker 70	11576			
☐ PH-KZF	Fokker 70	11577	ex (G-BVTH)		
☐ PH-KZI	Fokker 70	11579	ex (I-REJC)		
☐ PH-KZK	Fokker 70	11581	ex (I-REJD)		
☐ PH-KZL	Fokker 70	11536	ex 9V-SLK		
☐ PH-KZM	Fokker 70	11561	ex 9V-SLL		
☐ PH-KZN	Fokker 70	11553	ex PK-PFE		
☐ PH-KZO	Fokker 70	11538	ex G-BVTE		
☐ PH-KZP	Fokker 70	11539	ex G-BVTF		
☐ PH-KZR	Fokker 70	11551	ex G-BVTG		
☐ PH-KZS	Fokker 70	11540	ex F-GLIS		
☐ PH-KZT	Fokker 70	11541	ex F-GLIT		
☐ PH-KZU	Fokker 70	11543	ex F-GLIU		
☐ PH-KZW	Fokker 70	11558	ex F-GLIX		wfs
☐ PH-WXC	Fokker 70	11574	ex I-REJI		
☐ PH-WXD	Fokker 70	11563	ex HA-LMD		

KLM ROYAL DUTCH AIRLINES   KLM (KL/KLM)   Amsterdam-Schiphol (AMS)

Member of SkyTeam

☐ PH-AOA	Airbus A330-203	682	ex F-WWYE	dam-Amsterdam
☐ PH-AOB	Airbus A330-203	686	ex F-WWYH	Potsdamer Platz-Berlin
☐ PH-AOC	Airbus A330-203	703	ex F-WWKE	Place de la Concorde-Paris
☐ PH-AOD	Airbus A330-203	738	ex F-WWYC	Piazza del Duomo-Milano
☐ PH-AOE	Airbus A330-203	770	ex F-WWKD	Parliament Square-Edinburgh
☐ PH-AOF	Airbus A330-203	801	ex F-WWYC	Federation Square-Melbourne
☐ PH-AOH	Airbus A330-203	811	ex F-WWYH	Senaatintori/Senate Square-Helsinki
☐ PH-AOI	Airbus A330-203	819	ex F-WWYR	Plaza de la Independencia-Madrid
☐ PH-AOK	Airbus A330-203	834	ex F-WWKZ	Radhuspladsen-Kobenhavn
☐ PH-AOL	Airbus A330-203	900	ex F-WWKP	Piccadilly Circus-London
☐ PH-AOM	Airbus A330-203	1161	ex F-WWKP	Piazza San Marco-Venezia
☐ PH-AON	Airbus A330-203	925	ex F-WWKB	Museumplein-Amsterdam
☐ PH-AKA	Airbus A330-303	1287	ex F-WWYP	Times Square-New York
☐ PH-AKB	Airbus A330-303	1294	ex F-WWKK	Piazza Navonna-Roma
☐ PH-AKD	Airbus A330-303	1300	ex F-WWYC	Plaza de la Catedral-La Habana
☐ PH-AKE	Airbus A330-303	1381	ex F-WWYL	Praça do Rosio-Lisboa
☐ PH-AKF	Airbus A330-303	1580	ex F-WWCD	Hofplein-Rotterdam ♦
☐ PH-BGD	Boeing 737-7K2/W	30366/2675		Goudhaantje/Goldcrest
☐ PH-BGE	Boeing 737-7K2/W	30371/2705		Ortolaan/Ortolan Bunting
☐ PH-BGF	Boeing 737-7K2/W	30365/2714		Grote Zilverreiger/Great White Heron
☐ PH-BGG	Boeing 737-7K2/W	30367/2835		Koeningseider/King Eider
☐ PH-BGH	Boeing 737-7K2/W	38053/3119		Grutto/Godwit
☐ PH-BGI	Boeing 737-7K2/W	30364/3172	ex N1786B	Vink/Finch
☐ PH-BGK	Boeing 737-7K2/W	38054/3292	ex N1786B	Noordse Stormvogel/Fulmar
☐ PH-BGL	Boeing 737-7K2/W	30369/3407		Tjiftjaf/Warbler
☐ PH-BGM	Boeing 737-7K2/W	39255/3569		Cormorant
☐ PH-BGN	Boeing 737-7K2/W	38125/3584		Jan van Gent/Gannet
☐ PH-BGO	Boeing 737-7K2/W	38126/3590		Bird of Paradise
☐ PH-BGP	Boeing 737-7K2/W	38127/3632		Pelikaan/Pelican
☐ PH-BGQ	Boeing 737-7K2/W	39256/3675	ex N1796B	Golden Oriole
☐ PH-BGR	Boeing 737-7K2/W	39446/3728		Zwarte Wouw/Black Kite
☐ PH-BGT	Boeing 737-7K2/W	38634/3762		Hen Harrier
☐ PH-BGU	Boeing 737-7K2/W	39257/3779		Koekoek/Cuckoo
☐ PH-BGW	Boeing 737-7K2/W	38128/3797		Kingfisher
☐ PH-BGX	Boeing 737-7K2/W	38635/3811		Scholekster/Oystercatcher
☐ PH-BCA	Boeing 737-8K2/W	37820/3480		Flamingo
☐ PH-BCB	Boeing 737-8K2/W	39443/3648		Great Shearwater
☐ PH-BCD	Boeing 737-8K2/W	42149/4458		Koperwiek/Redwing
☐ PH-BCE	Boeing 737-8K2/W	42151/4852		Bluethroat/Blauborst ♦
☐ PH-BGA	Boeing 737-8K2/W	37593/2569	ex N1786B	Redshank

	Reg	Type	MSN	Ex	Name	Notes
☐	PH-BGB	Boeing 737-8K2/W	37594/2594		Whimbiel/Regenwulp	
☐	PH-BGC	Boeing 737-8K2/W	30361/2619		Pintail/Pijlstaart	
☐	PH-BXA	Boeing 737-8K2/W	29131/198	ex N1786B	Zwann/Swan	retro c/s
☐	PH-BXB	Boeing 737-8K2/W	29132/261	ex N1786B	Valk/Falcon	
☐	PH-BXC	Boeing 737-8K2/W	29133/305		Karhoen/Grouse	
☐	PH-BXD	Boeing 737-8K2/W	29134/355	ex N1784B	Arend/Eagle	
☐	PH-BXE	Boeing 737-8K2/W	29595/552	ex N1787B	Havik/Hawk	
☐	PH-BXF	Boeing 737-8K2/W	29596/583	ex N1787B	Zwalluw/Swallow	
☐	PH-BXG	Boeing 737-8K2/W	30357/605	ex N1787B	Kraanvogel/Crane	
☐	PH-BXH	Boeing 737-8K2/W	29597/630	ex N1786B	Gans/Goose	
☐	PH-BXI	Boeing 737-8K2/W	30358/633	ex N1787B	Zilvermeeuw/Herring Gull	
☐	PH-BXK	Boeing 737-8K2/W	29598/639	ex N1015G	Gierzwalluw/Swift	>TRA
☐	PH-BXL	Boeing 737-8K2/W	30359/659		Sperwer/Sparrow Hawk	
☐	PH-BXM	Boeing 737-8K2/W	30355/714	ex N1786B	Kluut/Avocet	
☐	PH-BXN	Boeing 737-8K2/W	30356/728	ex N1787B	Merel/Blackbird	
☐	PH-BXU	Boeing 737-8BK/W	33028/1936		Albatross	
☐	PH-BXV	Boeing 737-8K2/W	30370/2205	ex N1786B	Roodborstje/Robin	
☐	PH-BXW	Boeing 737-8K2/W	30360/2467	ex N1784B	Partridge	
☐	PH-BXY	Boeing 737-8K2/W	30372/2503		Fuut/Grebe	
☐	PH-BXZ	Boeing 737-8K2/W	30368/2533	ex N1786B	Uil/Owl	
☐	PH-BXO	Boeing 737-9K2/W	29599/866	ex N1786B	Plevier/Plover	SkyTeam c/s
☐	PH-BXP	Boeing 737-9K2/W	29600/924	ex N1786B	Merkroet/Crested Coot	
☐	PH-BXR	Boeing 737-9K2/W	29601/959	ex N1786B	Nachtegaal/Nightingale	
☐	PH-BXS	Boeing 737-9K2/W	29602/981	ex N1786B	Buizard/Buzzard	
☐	PH-BXT	Boeing 737-9K2/W	32944/1498		Zeestern/Sea Tern	
☐	PH-BFA	Boeing 747-406	23999/725	ex N6018N	City of Atlanta	
☐	PH-BFB	Boeing 747-406	24000/732		City of Bangkok	
☐	PH-BFC	Boeing 747-406M	23982/735	ex N6038E	City of Calgary	KLM Asia titles
☐	PH-BFD	Boeing 747-406M	24001/737		City of Dubai/Doebai	KLM Asia titles
☐	PH-BFE	Boeing 747-406M	24201/763	ex N6046P	City of Melbourne	
☐	PH-BFF	Boeing 747-406M	24202/770	ex N6046P	City of Freetown	
☐	PH-BFG	Boeing 747-406	24517/782		City of Guayaquil	
☐	PH-BFH	Boeing 747-406M	24518/783	ex N60668	City of Hong Kong	KLM Asia titles
☐	PH-BFI	Boeing 747-406M	25086/850		City of Jakarta	
☐	PH-BFK	Boeing 747-406M	25087/854		City of Karachi	
☐	PH-BFL	Boeing 747-406	25356/888		City of Lima	
☐	PH-BFM	Boeing 747-406M	26373/896		City of Mexico	KLM Asia titles
☐	PH-BFN	Boeing 747-406	26372/969		City of Nairobi	
☐	PH-BFO	Boeing 747-406M	25413/938		City of Orlando	
☐	PH-BFP	Boeing 747-406M	26374/992		City of Paramaribo	KLM Asia titles
☐	PH-BFR	Boeing 747-406M	27202/1014		City of Rio de Janeiro	
☐	PH-BFS	Boeing 747-406M	28195/1090		City of Seoul	
☐	PH-BFT	Boeing 747-406M	28459/1112		City of Tokyo	
☐	PH-BFU	Boeing 747-406M	28196/1127		City of Beijing	
☐	PH-BFV	Boeing 747-406M	28460/1225		City of Vancouver	
☐	PH-BFW	Boeing 747-406M	30454/1258		City of Shanghai	
☐	PH-BFY	Boeing 747-406M	30455/1302		City of Johannesburg	KLM Asia titles
☐	PH-BQA	Boeing 777-206ER	33711/454	ex N5014K	Albert Plesman	
☐	PH-BQB	Boeing 777-206ER	33712/457		Borobudur	
☐	PH-BQC	Boeing 777-206ER	29397/461		Chichen-Itza	
☐	PH-BQD	Boeing 777-206ER	33713/465		Daarjeeling Railway	
☐	PH-BQE	Boeing 777-206ER	28691/468		Epidaurus	
☐	PH-BQF	Boeing 777-206ER	29398/474		Ferrara City	KLM Asia titles
☐	PH-BQG	Boeing 777-206ER	32704/476		Galapagos Islands	
☐	PH-BQH	Boeing 777-206ER	32705/493	ex N5016R	Hadrian's Wall	
☐	PH-BQI	Boeing 777-206ER	33714/497		Iguazu Falls	KLM Asia titles
☐	PH-BQK	Boeing 777-206ER	29399/499		Mount Kilimanjaro	KLM Asia titles
☐	PH-BQL	Boeing 777-206ER	34711/552		Litomyšl Castle	KLM Asia titles
☐	PH-BQM	Boeing 777-206ER	34712/559		Machu Picchu	
☐	PH-BQN	Boeing 777-206ER	32720/561		Nahanni National Park	
☐	PH-BQO	Boeing 777-206ER	35295/609		Old Rauma	
☐	PH-BQP	Boeing 777-206ER	32721/630		Pont du Gard	
☐	PH-BVA	Boeing 777-306ER	35671/694	(ex PH-BQR)	De Hoge Veluwe National Park	
☐	PH-BVB	Boeing 777-306ER	36145/706		Nationaal Park Fulufjället	
☐	PH-BVC	Boeing 777-306ER	37582/787		Nationaal Park Sian Ka'an	KLM Asia titles
☐	PH-BVD	Boeing 777-306ER	35979/807		National Park Amboseli	SkyTeam c/s
☐	PH-BVF	Boeing 777-306ER	39972/915			
☐	PH-BVG	Boeing 777-306ER	38867/1020		Nationaal Park Wolong	
☐	PH-BVI	Boeing 777-306ER	35947/1029		Nationaal Park Vuurland	
☐	PH-BVK	Boeing 777-306ER	42172/1106		Nationaal Park Yellowstone	
☐	PH-BVN	Boeing 777-306ER	44549/1280		Nationaal Park Tijuca	♦
☐	PH-BVO	Boeing 777-306ER	35946/1292		Nationaal Park Kaziranga	♦
☐	PH-BVP	Boeing 777-306ER	44555/			o/o♦
☐	PH-BVR	Boeing 777-306ER	61603/			o/o♦
☐	PH-BVS	Boeing 777-306ER	61604/			o/o♦
☐	PH-BVU	Boeing 777-306ER	61702/			o/o♦
☐	PH-BHA	Boeing 787-9	36113/356			o/o♦
☐	PH-BHC	Boeing 787-9	38760/368			o/o♦

☐ PH-BHD	Boeing 787-9	38763/381			o/o♦
☐ PH-BHE	Boeing 787-9	42485/			o/o♦
☐ PH-BHF	Boeing 787-9	38765/412			o/o♦
☐ PH-BHG	Boeing 787-9	42486/422			o/o♦
☐ PH-BHH	Boeing 787-9	38766/			o/o♦
☐ PH-BHI	Boeing 787-9	38767/			o/o♦
☐ PH-BHL	Boeing 787-9	38755/			o/o♦
☐ PH-BHM	Boeing 787-9	38769/			o/o♦
☐ PH-BHP	Boeing 787-9	38775/			o/o♦
☐ PH-BHQ	Boeing 787-9	38766/			o/o♦

MARTINAIR HOLLAND — Martinair (MP/MPH) — Amsterdam-Schiphol (AMS)

☐ PH-MPQ	Boeing 747-412BCF	24975/838	ex D-ACGC		wfs
☐ PH-CKA	Boeing 747-406ERF	33694/1326			
☐ PH-CKB	Boeing 747-406ERF	33695/1328			
☐ PH-CKC	Boeing 747-406ERF	33696/1341			
☐ PH-MPP	Boeing 747-412BCF	24061/717	ex D-ACGD		wfs
☐ PH-MPS	Boeing 747-412BCF	24066/791	ex N728BA		
☐ PH-MCP	McDonnell-Douglas MD-11CF	48616/577	ex N90187		
☐ PH-MCR	McDonnell-Douglas MD-11CF	48617/581			[AMS]
☐ PH-MCS	McDonnell-Douglas MD-11CF	48618/584			wfs
☐ PH-MCU	McDonnell-Douglas MD-11F	48757/606		Prinses Maxima	
☐ PH-MCW	McDonnell-Douglas MD-11CF	48788/632			
☐ PH-MCY	McDonnell-Douglas MD-11F	48445/460	ex N626FE		[AMS]

TESSEL AIR

☐ PH-LBR	Cessna 208 Caravan I	20800101	ex N99U		FP

TRANSAVIA — Transavia (HV/TRA) — Amsterdam-Schiphol (AMS)

☐ PH-XRA	Boeing 737-7K2/W	30784/873	ex N1786B	Leontien van Moorsel	
☐ PH-XRB	Boeing 737-7K2/W	28256/1298			
☐ PH-XRC	Boeing 737-7K2/W	29347/1318	ex OY-TDZ		
☐ PH-XRD	Boeing 737-7K2/W	30659/1329			
☐ PH-XRE	Boeing 737-7K2/W	30668/1482			
☐ PH-XRV	Boeing 737-7K2/W	34170/1701		Rotterdam The Hague Airport	
☐ PH-XRX	Boeing 737-7K2/W	33464/1299		Stadprins Akkedeer	
☐ PH-XRY	Boeing 737-7K2/W	33463/1292			
☐ PH-XRZ	Boeing 737-7K2/W	33462/1278			
☐ PH-BXK	Boeing 737-8K2/W	29598/639	ex N1015G	Gierzwalluw/Swift	<KLM
☐ PH-GGX	Boeing 737-8EH/W	36596/3180	ex PR-GGX		<GLO
☐ PH-GUA	Boeing 737-8EH/W	37601/3301	ex PR-GUA		<GLO
☐ PH-GUB	Boeing 737-8EH/W	35832/3309	ex PR-GUB		<GLO♦
☐ PH-HSA	Boeing 737-8K2/W	34171/2950	ex9Y-TJS		
☐ PH-HSB	Boeing 737-8K2/W	34172/3242	ex N1786B		
☐ PH-HSC	Boeing 737-8K2/W	34173/3266			
☐ PH-HSD	Boeing 737-8K2/W	39260/3581	ex N1787B		
☐ PH-HSE	Boeing 737-8K2/W	39259/3635			
☐ PH-HSF	Boeing 737-8K2/W	39261/3998	ex N1786B		
☐ PH-HSG	Boeing 737-8K2/W	39262/4021			
☐ PH-HSI	Boeing 737-8K2/W	42148/4404	ex N5573B		
☐ PH-HSJ	Boeing 737-8K2/W	42150/4810	ex (PH-BCE)		
☐ PH-HSK	Boeing 737-8K2/W	41330/5354			♦
☐ PH-HSM	Boeing 737-8K2/W	42067/5389			♦
☐ PH-HSN	Boeing 737-8K2/W	41340/			o/o♦
☐ PH-HSO	Boeing 737-8K2/W	41342/			o/o♦
☐ PH-HSQ	Boeing 737-8K2/W	41355/			o/o♦
☐ PH-HSW	Boeing 737-8K2/W	37160/2880	ex 9Y-TJR		
☐ PH-HZD	Boeing 737-8K2/W	28376/252	ex N1786B		
☐ PH-HZE	Boeing 737-8K2/W	28377/277	ex N1786B	City of Rhodos	
☐ PH-HZF	Boeing 737-8K2/W	28378/291	ex N1796B		
☐ PH-HZG	Boeing 737-8K2/W	28379/498	ex N1786B	Sunweb c/s	
☐ PH-HZI	Boeing 737-8K2/W	28380/524			
☐ PH-HZJ	Boeing 737-8K2/W	30389/549	ex N1796B		
☐ PH-HZK	Boeing 737-8K2/W	30390/555	ex N1786B		
☐ PH-HZL	Boeing 737-8K2/W	30391/814	ex N1786B		
☐ PH-HZN	Boeing 737-8K2/W	32943/1478			
☐ PH-HZO	Boeing 737-8K2/W	34169/2243			
☐ PH-HZW	Boeing 737-8K2/W	29345/1132	ex VT-SPZ		
☐ PH-HZX	Boeing 737-8K2/W	28248/1126			

VIZION AIR — Maastricht

☐ OO-VLO	Fokker 50	20127	ex ES-AFL	Angela Dirkin	<VLM♦

PJ-   NETHERLANDS ANTILLES

DIVI DIVI AIR | Divi Air (DVR) | Curacao (CUR)

☐ PJ-BMV	Cessna 402B	402B0865	ex C-GCKB	
☐ PJ-SEA	Britten-Norman BN-2A-26 Islander	311	ex C-FFXS	FlyDivi.com titles
☐ PJ-SKY	Britten-Norman BN-2A-26 Islander	885	ex C-FDYT	

INSEL AIR | Inselair (7I/INC) | Curacao (CUR)

☐ PJ-KVG	Fokker 50	20211	ex PH-KVG	
☐ PJ-KVI	Fokker 50	20218	ex PH-KVI	
☐ PJ-KVK	Fokker 50	20219	ex PH-KVK	
☐ PJ-KVL	Fokker 50	20278	ex P4-KVL	♦
☐ PJ-KVM	Fokker 50	20288	ex P4-KVM	♦
☐ PJ-MDA	McDonnell-Douglas MD-83	49449/1354	ex 9A-CBJ	
☐ PJ-MDB	McDonnell-Douglas MD-82	48021/1078	ex N812NK	
☐ PJ-MDC	McDonnell-Douglas MD-82	49434/1446	ex N434AG	
☐ PJ-MDE	McDonnell-Douglas MD-82	49971/1755	ex N971AG	
☐ PJ-MDF	McDonnell-Douglas MD-83	53014/1740	ex N534WP	
☐ PJ-VIA	Embraer EMB.110P1 Bandeirante	110387	ex E5-TAI	[CUR]
☐ PJ-VIC	Embraer EMB.110P1 Bandeirante	110261	ex VH-BWC	[CUR]
☐ PJ-VIP	Embraer EMB.110P1 Bandeirante	110382	ex YV-249C Curacao	

WINAIR/WINDWARD ISLANDS AIRWAYS Windward (WM/WIA) | St Maarten (SXM)

☐ PJ-WII	de Havilland DHC-6 Twin Otter 300	682	ex C-GKGQ	
☐ PJ-WIJ	de Havilland DHC-6 Twin Otter 300	533	ex C-FAKB	
☐ PJ-WIL	de Havilland DHC-6 Twin Otter 300	358	ex C-FCSY	
☐ PJ-WIT	de Havilland DHC-6 Twin Otter 300	588	ex C-FBBW	
☐ PJ-WJR	de Havilland DHC-6 Twin Otter 300	476	ex N476R	
☐ PJ-AIW	Britten-Norman BN-2A-26 Islander	2038	ex C-GZKG	
☐ PJ-CIW	Britten-Norman BN-2B-26 Islander	876	ex C-GZTP	

WINDWARD EXPRESS AIRWAYS | St Maarten (SXM)

☐ PJ-WEA	Britten-Norman BN-2A-27 Islander	659	ex N659CM	
☐ PJ-WEB	Britten-Norman BN-2A-26 Islander	2208	ex 8P-TAG	
☐ PJ-WED	Britten-Norman BN-2A-20 Islander	2153	ex PZ-TBL	

PK-   INDONESIA (Republic of Indonesia)

AIR BORN

☐ PK-BAA	de Havilland DHC-6 Twin Otter 310	611	ex C-FBKB	FP
☐ PK-BAC	de Havilland DHC-6 Twin Otter 300	576	ex N54LM	
☐ PK-BAF	de Havilland DHC-6 Twin Otter 300	518	ex C-GSOZ	
☐ PK-BAG	MBB Bo105CBS-5	S-908	ex PK-TWP	
☐ PK-BAH	MBB Bo105CBS-5	S-920	ex PK-TWQ	

AIR MALEO | Jakarta-Halim (HLP)

| ☐ PK-ZMM | Fokker F.27 Friendship 600 | 10349 | ex N19QQ | |
| ☐ PK-ZMV | Fokker F.27 Friendship 600 | 10385 | ex N19NN | |

AIRFAST INDONESIA | Airfast (AFE) | Balikpapan/Jayapura (BPN/DJJ)

☐ PK-OCF	de Havilland DHC-6 Twin Otter 400	866	ex C-FGAL	
☐ PK-OCG	de Havilland DHC-6 Twin Otter 400	868	ex C-FAFI	
☐ PK-OCJ	de Havilland DHC-6 Twin Otter 300	522	ex A6-MBM	
☐ PK-OCK	de Havilland DHC-6 Twin Otter 310	616	ex 9Q-CLE	all-white
☐ PK-OCL	de Havilland DHC-6 Twin Otter 300	689	ex N689WJ	Santigi
☐ PK-	de Havilland DHC-6 Twin Otter 400	914	ex C-FMJO	♦
☐ PK-OAW	Beech 65-B80 Queen Air	LD-308	ex PK-JBF	
☐ PK-OCA	IPTN/Bell 412	34009/NB09	ex PK-XFJ	
☐ PK-OCB	IPTN/Bell 412	34007/NB07	ex PK-XFH	
☐ PK-OCC	CASA-Nurtanio C.212-200	50N/CC4-2-210	ex PK-NZJ	
☐ PK-OCE	Bell 212	30981	ex PK-VBZ	
☐ PK-OCP	Boeing 737-27A	23794/1424	ex B-2625	
☐ PK-OCS	McDonnell-Douglas MD-83	53124/1991	ex N786BC	
☐ PK-OCT	McDonnell-Douglas MD-82	49889/1761	ex N823RA	
☐ PK-OCU	McDonnell-Douglas MD-82	53017/1797	ex N824RA	
☐ PK-ODB	Aérospatiale AS350B3 Ecureuil	4595	ex PK-FLZ	
☐ PK-ODC	Aérospatiale AS350B3 Ecureuil	7346	ex ZK-IFK	

☐ PK-ODD	Bell 412EP	36464	ex N419EV	
☐ PK-OKE	Embraer ERJ-135LR	145726	ex N135SV	♦
☐ PK-OIA	Bell 407	53850	ex N332RB	
☐ PK-OIB	Bell 407	53796	ex N53796	
☐ PK-OME	Embraer Legacy 600	145516	ex PT-SAG	VIP
☐ PK-OMI	Mil Mi-171	171C0036010530U		
☐ PK-OMS	Mil Mi-171			♦
☐ PK-OSP	British Aerospace 146 Srs.100	E1124	ex G-CBXY	opf Metro TV; VIP

ALFA TRANS DIRGANTARA

☐ PK-ASA	Cessna 208B Caravan I	208B2183	ex N1014A
☐ PK-ASC	Cessna 208 Caravan I	20800539	ex N2033Y

ASIALINK CARGO EXPRESS (KP/AKC) Jakarta-Soekarno Hatta (CGK)

☐ PK-KRA	Fokker F.27 Friendship 500	10632	ex N19XF	Lara	
☐ PK-KRJ	Fokker F.27 Friendship 500	10660	ex TC-MBB		[BXM]
☐ PK-KRL	Fokker F.27 Friendship 500	10654	ex TC-MBA		
☐ PK-KRP	Fokker 50F	20119	ex PH-LMB		

ASIAN ONE AIR

☐ PK-LTF	Cessna 208B Caravan I	208B0922	ex N786DM

AVIASTAR MANDIRI Aviastar (MV/VIT) Banjarmasin (BDJ)

☐ PK-BRP	de Havilland DHC-6 Twin Otter 300	356	ex N972SW	
☐ PK-BRQ	de Havilland DHC-6 Twin Otter 300	702	ex N702PV	
☐ PK-BRS	de Havilland DHC-6 Twin Otter 300	299	ex C-FPNZ	
☐ PK-BRT	de Havilland DHC-6 Twin Otter 300	380	ex (F-GUTR)	
☐ PK-BRZ	de Havilland DHC-6 Twin Otter 300	357	ex C-FCSX	
☐ PK-BRE	British Aerospace 146 Srs.200	E2139	ex C-GRNU	
☐ PK-BRF	British Aerospace 146 Srs.200	E2210	ex PK-LNJ	
☐ PK-BRI	British Aerospace 146 Srs.200	E2227	ex G-BVMS	wfs
☐ PK-KRA	Fokker F.27 Friendship 500	10632	ex N19XF	

BATIK AIR (ID/BTK) Jakarta-Soekarno Hatta (CGK)

☐ PK-LAF	Airbus A320-214/S	6164	ex F-WWBO	♦
☐ PK-LAG	Airbus A320-214/S	6280	ex F-WWIE	♦
☐ PK-LAH	Airbus A320-214/S	6309	ex F-WWDY	♦
☐ PK-LAI	Airbus A320-214/S	6356	ex D-AXAD	♦
☐ PK-LAJ	Airbus A320-214/S	6361	ex D-AXAE	♦
☐ PK-LAK	Airbus A320-214/S	6372	ex F-WWIK	♦
☐ PK-LAL	Airbus A320-214/S	6505	ex F-WWIX	♦
☐ PK-	Airbus A320-214/S	6628	ex	o/o♦
☐ PK-	Airbus A320-214/S	6695	ex	o/o♦
☐ PK-	Airbus A320-214/S	6700	ex	o/o♦
☐ PK-	Airbus A320-214/S	6786	ex	o/o♦
☐ PK-	Airbus A320-214/S	6806	ex	o/o♦
☐ PK-	Airbus A320-214/S	6846	ex	o/o♦
☐ PK-	Airbus A320-214/S	6962	ex	o/o♦
☐ PK-	Airbus A320-214/S	6963	ex	o/o♦
☐ PK-	Airbus A320-214/S	6969	ex	o/o♦
☐ PK-LBK	Boeing 737-8GP/W	39822/5048		♦
☐ PK-LBL	Boeing 737-8GP/W	39821/5026		♦
☐ PK-LBQ	Boeing 737-8GP/W	39825/5127	ex N1787B	♦
☐ PK-LBR	Boeing 737-8GP/W	40061/5130		♦
☐ PK-LBS	Boeing 737-8GP/W	39827/5157		♦
☐ PK-LBT	Boeing 737-8GP/W	39828/5179		♦
☐ PK-LBU	Boeing 737-8GP/W	38308/5225	ex N1795B	♦
☐ PK-LBV	Boeing 737-8GP/W	39831/5255		♦
☐ PK-LBW	Boeing 737-8GP/W	39834/5267	ex N1787B	♦
☐ PK-LBY	Boeing 737-8GP/W	39833/5278	ex N6063S	♦
☐ PK-LBZ	Boeing 737-8GP/W	39835/5307		♦
☐ PK-LDE	Boeing 737-8GP/W	39836/5315		♦
☐ PK-LDF	Boeing 737-8GP/W	38309/5375		♦
☐ PK-LBG	Boeing 737-9GPER/W	38688/4414	ex (PK-LKW)	
☐ PK-LBH	Boeing 737-9GPER/W	38730/4430	ex (PK-LKV)	
☐ PK-LBI	Boeing 737-9GPER/W	38743/4711	ex (PK-LLP)	
☐ PK-LBJ	Boeing 737-9GPER/W	38742/4726	ex (PK-LLO)	
☐ PK-LBM	Boeing 737-9GPER/W	38689/4441	ex (PK-LKZ)	
☐ PK-LBO	Boeing 737-9GPER/W	38731/4463	ex (PK-LKY)	

CARDIG AIR (8F/CAD) Jakarta-Soekarno Hatta (CGK)

☐ PK-BBB	Boeing 737-347SF	23598/1289	ex N312WA	Creativity
☐ PK-BBS	Boeing 737-301SF	23258/1126	ex OE-IAU	

☐ PK-BBY	Boeing 737-3Q8F	23535/1301	ex EI-ETW	

CITILINK		*Superlink (QG/CTV)*		*Jakarta-Halim (HLP)*
☐ PK-GLG	Airbus A320-214	3861	ex A9C-BAV	
☐ PK-GLH	Airbus A320-214	3147	ex JA206A	
☐ PK-GLI	Airbus A320-214	3148	ex JA207A	
☐ PK-GLK	Airbus A320-214	5351	ex D-AUBM	
☐ PK-GLL	Airbus A320-214	5379	ex F-WWIX	
☐ PK-GLM	Airbus A320-214	5394	ex D-AUBX	
☐ PK-GLN	Airbus A320-214	5399	ex D-AVVA	
☐ PK-GLO	Airbus A320-214	5415	ex D-AVVG	
☐ PK-GLP	Airbus A320-214	5511	ex F-WWDJ	
☐ PK-GLQ	Airbus A320-214	5541	ex F-WWDT	
☐ PK-GLR	Airbus A320-214	5551	ex F-WWDU	
☐ PK-GLS	Airbus A320-214	5556	ex F-WWDX	
☐ PK-GLT	Airbus A320-214	5560	ex D-AUBA	
☐ PK-GLU	Airbus A320-214	5571	ex D-AUBB	
☐ PK-GLV	Airbus A320-214	5574	ex D-AUBC	
☐ PK-GLW	Airbus A320-214	5597	ex D-AUBJ	
☐ PK-GLX	Airbus A320-214/S	5777	ex D-AXAC	
☐ PK-GLY	Airbus A320-214/S	5830	ex F-WWBV	
☐ PK-GLZ	Airbus A320-214/S	6118	ex F-WWBE	♦
☐ PK-GQA	Airbus A320-214/S	6207	ex F-WWDJ	♦
☐ PK-GQC	Airbus A320-214/S	6224	ex D-AVVL	♦
☐ PK-GQD	Airbus A320-214/S	6243	ex D-AVVO	♦
☐ PK-GQE	Airbus A320-214/S	6270	ex D-AVVU	♦
☐ PK-GQF	Airbus A320-214/S	6322	ex F-WWIT	♦
☐ PK-GQG	Airbus A320-214/S	6333	ex F-WWBK	♦
☐ PK-GQH	Airbus A320-214/S	6408	ex D-AXAL	♦
☐ PK-GQI	Airbus A320-214/S	6434	ex F-WWIA	♦
☐ PK-GQJ	Airbus A320-214/S	6503	ex F-WWIT	♦
☐ PK-GQK	Airbus A320-214/S	6596	ex D-AVVP	♦
☐ PK-	Airbus A320-214/S	6898	ex	o/o♦
☐ PK-	Airbus A320-214/S	6919	ex	o/o♦
☐ PK-	Airbus A320-214/S	6932	ex	o/o♦
☐ PK-GLA	Airbus A320-233	1635	ex HA-LPB	
☐ PK-GLC	Airbus A320-233	0892	ex HA-LPC	
☐ PK-GLD	Airbus A320-233	0839	ex HA-LPA	
☐ PK-GLE	Airbus A320-232	2598	ex N598AG	
☐ PK-GLF	Airbus A320-232	2692	ex N692AG	
☐ PK-GLJ	Airbus A320-232	4961	ex (VT-KRA)	
☐ PK-GGN	Boeing 737-3U3	28735/3029	ex N5573K	
☐ PK-GGO	Boeing 737-3U3	28736/3032	ex N3134C	[CGK]
☐ PK-GGP	Boeing 737-3U3	28737/3037	ex N1020L	[CGK]
☐ PK-GGQ	Boeing 737-3U3	28739/3064	ex N1024A	[CGK]
☐ PK-GGR	Boeing 737-3U3	28741/3079	ex N1026G	[CGK]

DERAYA AIR TAXI		*Deraya (DRY)*		*Jakarta-Halim (HLP)*
☐ PK-DCC	Cessna 402C II	402C0250	ex N444DS	
☐ PK-DCJ	Cessna 402B	402B0615	ex N3759C	
☐ PK-DCZ	Cessna 402B	402B0890	ex N5203J	
☐ PK-DGA	British Aerospace ATP(LFD	2026	ex G-JEMD	
☐ PK-DGC	British Aerospace ATPF	2052	ex G-BUKJ	♦
☐ PK-DSB	Short SD.3-30	SH3056	ex DQ-SUN	
☐ PK-DSH	Short SD.3-60	SH3757	ex N350TA	
☐ PK-DSR	Short SD.3-30	SH3060	ex DQ-FIJ	
☐ PK-DSS	Short SD.3-60	SH3743	ex N743RW	
☐ PK-LPN	Cessna U206F Stationair II	U20602789	ex PK-UFO	

DIMONIM AIR				*Jakarta-Soekarno Hatta (CGK)*
☐ PK-HVA	Cessna 208B Caravan I	208B	ex	♦
☐ PK-HVC	Cessna 208B Caravan I	208B	ex	♦
☐ PK-HVH	ATR 72-202	373	ex OM-VRA	♦
☐ PK-HVT	Cessna 208B Caravan I	208B	ex	♦

DIRGANTARA AIR SERVICE	*Dirgantara (DIR)*		*Jakarta-Halim/Bandarmasin/Pontianak (HLP/BDJ/PNK)*	
☐ PK-VIM	Britten-Norman BN-2A-3 Islander	634	ex 9V-BEB	
☐ PK-VIS	Britten-Norman BN-2A-21 Islander	485	ex G-BEGB	
☐ PK-VIU	Britten-Norman BN-2A-21 Islander	781	ex PK-KNH	
☐ PK-VIX	Britten-Norman BN-2A-21 Islander	2027	ex G-BIUF	
☐ PK-VIY	Britten-Norman BN-2A-21 Islander	2133	ex G-BJOR	
☐ PK-VMB	Gippsland GA-8 Airvan	GA8-03-031	ex VH-BOI	
☐ PK-VMC	Gippsland GA-8 Airvan	GA8-03-033	ex VH-BNL	
☐ PK-VMD	Gippsland GA-8 Airvan	GA8-03-041	ex VH-FDR	
☐ PK-VME	Gippsland GA-8 Airvan	GA8-03-042	ex VH-JYN	

434

| □ PK-VSN | CASA-Nurtanio C.212-100 | 22N/A4-19-136 | ex PK-XCU |
| □ PK-XNE | CASA-Nurtanio CN235-110 | N056 | |

EASTINDO (ESD) Jakarta-Halim (HLP)

□ PK-RGA	Beech 1900D	UE-376	ex N31425
□ PK-RGD	Beech 1900D	UE-400	ex N835CA
□ PK-RGG	Aérospatiale AS350b3 Ecureuil	7286	
□ PK-RGP	Britten-Norman BN-2B-20 Islander	2249	ex PK-HNG
□ PK-RGQ	Britten-Norman BN-2T Turbo Islander	2303	ex N2536Y

ENGGANG AIR SERVICE

□ PK-RSA	Agusta A1095P	22226		
□ PK-RSC	Cessna 208B Caravan I	208B2330	ex N9025C	dam 09Sep14
□ PK-RSE	Cessna 208B Caravan I	208B2283	ex N6019C	
□ PK-RSO	Cessna 650 Citation VII	650-7073	ex PK-RJB	
□ PK-RSS	Embraer Legacy 600	14501020	ex PT-RJO	
□ PK-RSP	Cessna 208B Caravan I	208B2254	ex N60336	

EXPRESSAIR/TRAVEL EXPRESS (XAR) Ujung Pandang

□ PK-TXI	Boeing 737-322	24671/1913	ex N396UA	
□ PK-TXJ	Boeing 737-3M8	24413/1884	ex N16EA	
□ PK-TXZ	Boeing 737-36N	28558/2876	ex N282CS	
□ PK-TZA	Boeing 737-33V	29340/3121	ex N281CS	
□ PK-TZC	Boeing 737-33V	29337/3113	ex N279CS	♦
□ PK-	Boeing 737-3L9	27833/2688	ex N4973S	o/o

□ PK-TXL	Dornier 328-110	3037	ex N425JS	
□ PK-TXM	Dornier 328-110	3032	ex N423JS	
□ PK-TXN	Dornier 328-110	3030	ex N328JS	
□ PK-TXO	Dornier 328-110	3045	ex N432JS	
□ PK-TXP	Dornier 328-110	3038	ex N426JS	
□ PK-TXQ	Dornier 328-110	3043	ex N429JS	
□ PK-TXR	Dornier 328-120	3008	ex N472PS	
□ PK-TXT	Dornier 328-310 (328JET)	3165	ex N365SK	
□ PK-TXW	Dornier 328-110	3044	ex N430JS	[CGK]

□ PK-TXD	Boeing 737-284	22400/766	ex SX-BCK	Grace	wfs
□ PK-TXH	Boeing 737-529	25218/2111	ex N22YH	
□ PK-TXK	Boeing 737-2B7 (Nordam 3)	22880/927	ex PK-CJJ	
□ PK-TXY	Boeing 737-204	22057/621	ex PK-CJD	

GARUDA INDONESIA Indonesia (GA/GIA) Jakarta-Soekarno Hatta (CGK)

Member of SkyTeam

□ PK-GPH	Airbus A330-243	1020	ex F-WWYL	
□ PK-GPI	Airbus A330-243	1052	ex F-WWKQ	
□ PK-GPJ	Airbus A330-243	988	ex F-WWKI	
□ PK-GPK	Airbus A330-243	1028	ex F-WWYZ	
□ PK-GPL	Airbus A330-243	1184	ex F-WWKT	
□ PK-GPM	Airbus A330-243	1214	ex F-WWKH	
□ PK-GPN	Airbus A330-243	1261	ex F-WWKF	
□ PK-GPO	Airbus A330-243	1288	ex F-WWKL	
□ PK-GPP	Airbus A330-243	1364	ex F-WWKK	
□ PK-GPQ	Airbus A330-243	1410	ex F-WWTZ	
□ PK-GPS	Airbus A330-243	1474	ex F-WWYM	

□ PK-GPA	Airbus A330-341	138	ex F-WWKH	
□ PK-GPC	Airbus A330-341	140	ex F-WWKU	
□ PK-GPD	Airbus A330-341	144	ex F-WWKG	
□ PK-GPE	Airbus A330-341	148	ex F-WWKD	
□ PK-GPF	Airbus A330-341	153	ex F-WWKY	SkyTeam c/s
□ PK-GPG	Airbus A330-341	165	ex F-WWKL	
□ PK-GPR	Airbus A330-343	1446	ex F-WWKQ	
□ PK-GPT	Airbus A330-343	1548	ex F-WWCZ	♦
□ PK-GPU	Airbus A330-343	1560	ex F-WWYR	♦
□ PK-GPV	Airbus A330-343	1577	ex F-WWYN	♦
□ PK-GPW	Airbus A330-343	1585	ex F-WWKU	♦
□ PK-	Airbus A330-343	1654	ex F-WW	o/o♦
□ PK-	Airbus A330-343	1671	ex F-WW	o/o♦
□ PK-	Airbus A330-343	1698	ex F-WW	o/o♦
□ PK-	Airbus A330-343	1703	ex F-WW	o/o♦

□ PK-GAA	ATR 72-600	1119	ex F-WWEH	
□ PK-GAC	ATR 72-600	1132	ex F-WWEU	
□ PK-GAD	ATR 72-600	1140	ex F-WWEE	
□ PK-GAE	ATR 72-600	1149	ex F-WWEN	♦
□ PK-GAF	ATR 72-600	1152	ex F-WWEQ	♦
□ PK-GAG	ATR 72-600	1157	ex F-WWEV	dam 03Feb15♦

☐ PK-GAH	ATR 72-600	1181	ex F-WWEV		♦
☐ PK-GAI	ATR 72-600	1191	ex F-WWEH		♦
☐ PK-GAJ	ATR 72-600	1243	ex F-WWES		♦
☐ PK-	ATR 72-600	1251	ex F-WWEF		o/o♦
☐ PK-GEG	Boeing 737-83N/W	30033/1149	ex N323TZ		
☐ PK-GEH	Boeing 737-83N/W	30643/1106	ex N319TZ		
☐ PK-GEI	Boeing 737-86N/W	29883/1083	ex N29883		
☐ PK-GEJ	Boeing 737-86N/W	33003/1121	ex G-XLAG		
☐ PK-GEK	Boeing 737-85F/W	30568/793	ex N568MQ		
☐ PK-GEL	Boeing 737-8AS/W	29927/727	ex EI-CSN		
☐ PK-GEM	Boeing 737-8AS/W	29928/735	ex EI-CSO		
☐ PK-GEN	Boeing 737-8AS/W	29929/753	ex EI-CSP		
☐ PK-GEO	Boeing 737-8AS/W	29930/757	ex EI-CSQ		
☐ PK-GEP	Boeing 737-8AS/W	29931/1020	ex EI-CSR		
☐ PK-GEQ	Boeing 737-86N/W	32659/1709	ex EC-JEX		
☐ PK-GER	Boeing 737-86J/W	30876/759	ex D-ABAD		
☐ PK-GFA	Boeing 737-86N/W	36549/3331			
☐ PK-GFC	Boeing 737-86N/W	39390/3348			
☐ PK-GFD	Boeing 737-8U3/W	40807/3337			
☐ PK-GFE	Boeing 737-86N/W	36804/3374			
☐ PK-GFF	Boeing 737-8U3/W	36436/3370			
☐ PK-GFG	Boeing 737-8BK/W	37819/3402	ex N1786B		
☐ PK-GFH	Boeing 737-8U3/W	36850/3389			
☐ PK-GFI	Boeing 737-86N/W	36805/3438			
☐ PK-GFJ	Boeing 737-86N/W	37885/3445	ex N1796B		
☐ PK-GFK	Boeing 737-86N/W	37887/3463			
☐ PK-GFL	Boeing 737-86N/W	36808/3505	ex N1787B		
☐ PK-GFM	Boeing 737-8U3/W	39920/3518			
☐ PK-GFN	Boeing 737-86N/W	38033/3607			
☐ PK-GFO	Boeing 737-86N/W	39403/3674	ex N1795B		
☐ PK-GFP	Boeing 737-8U3/W	38821/3684			
☐ PK-GFQ	Boeing 737-81D/W	39416/3766			
☐ PK-GFR	Boeing 737-81D/W	39417/3802			
☐ PK-GFS	Boeing 737-86N/W	36830/3860			
☐ PK-GFT	Boeing 737-86N/W	38032/3869			
☐ PK-GFU	Boeing 737-86N/W	38040/4482			
☐ PK-GFV	Boeing 737-8U3/W	38885/4490			
☐ PK-GFW	Boeing 737-8U3/W	39929/4520	ex N6065Y		
☐ PK-GFX	Boeing 737-8U3/W	39928/4453			
☐ PK-GFY	Boeing 737-85N/W	38043/4619			
☐ PK-GFZ	Boeing 737-86N/W	38044/4635			
☐ PK-GMA	Boeing 737-8U3/W	30151/2942	ex N1784B		
☐ PK-GMC	Boeing 737-8U3/W	30155/3081	ex N1786B		
☐ PK-GMD	Boeing 737-8U3/W	30156/3100			
☐ PK-GME	Boeing 737-8U3/W	30157/3123			
☐ PK-GMF	Boeing 737-8U3/W	30140/3129			
☐ PK-GMG	Boeing 737-8U3/W	30141/3166	ex N1796B		
☐ PK-GMH	Boeing 737-8U3/W	30142/3213	ex N1786B	SkyTeam c/s	
☐ PK-GMI	Boeing 737-8U3/W	30143/3243	ex N1786B		
☐ PK-GMJ	Boeing 737-8U3/W	30144/3249	ex N1787B		
☐ PK-GMK	Boeing 737-8U3/W	29666/3171	ex N1787B		
☐ PK-GML	Boeing 737-8U3/W	31763/3177	ex N1787B		
☐ PK-GMM	Boeing 737-8U3/W	30145/3285			
☐ PK-GMN	Boeing 737-8U3/W	30146/3303			
☐ PK-GMO	Boeing 737-8U3/W	30147/3327	ex N1786B		
☐ PK-GMP	Boeing 737-8U3/W	30148/3353	ex N1787B		
☐ PK-GMQ	Boeing 737-8U3/W	30149/3405	ex N1787B		
☐ PK-GMR	Boeing 737-8U3/W	30150/3429			
☐ PK-GMS	Boeing 737-8U3/W	38071/3855			
☐ PK-GMU	Boeing 737-8U3/W	38073/3930			
☐ PK-GMV	Boeing 737-8U3/W	38074/3960			
☐ PK-GMW	Boeing 737-8U3/W	38069/4026			
☐ PK-GMX	Boeing 737-8U3/W	38070/3996			
☐ PK-GMY	Boeing 737-8U3/W	38884/4446	ex N5573P		
☐ PK-GMZ	Boeing 737-8U3/W	38072/4582			
☐ PK-GNA	Boeing 737-8U3/W	41310/4692			
☐ PK-GNC	Boeing 737-8U3/W	41312/4720			
☐ PK-GND	Boeing 737-8U3/W	41794/4761			
☐ PK-GNE	Boeing 737-8U3/W	39936/4800			
☐ PK-GNF	Boeing 737-8U3/W	39939/4866	ex N5573L		
☐ PK-GNG	Boeing 737-8U3/W	39891/4901			
☐ PK-GNH	Boeing 737-8U3/W	40547/4961			
☐ PK-GNI	Boeing 737-86N/W	41267/4957			♦
☐ PK-GNJ	Boeing 737-8U3/W	41796/4969			♦
☐ PK-GNK	Boeing 737-8U3/W	41798/5049			♦
☐ PK-GNL	Boeing 737-86N/W	41253/5078			♦
☐ PK-GNM	Boeing 737-8U3/W	41322/5057	ex N1796B		♦
☐ PK-GNN	Boeing 737-86N/W	41270/5116			♦
☐ PK-GNO	Boeing 737-8U3/W	41800/5109			♦
☐ PK-GNP	Boeing 737-8U3/W	41605/5245			♦
☐ PK-GNQ	Boeing 737-8U3/W	39954/5284			♦
☐ PK-GNR	Boeing 737-8U3/W	39955/5335			♦

☐ PK-GNS	Boeing 737-8U3/W	41607/5385	♦
☐ PK-GIA	Boeing 777-3U3ER	40074/1104	
☐ PK-GIC	Boeing 777-3U3ER	40075/1121	
☐ PK-GID	Boeing 777-3U3ER	29146/1141	
☐ PK-GIE	Boeing 777-3U3ER	29147/1148	
☐ PK-GIF	Boeing 777-3U3ER	29148/1203	♦
☐ PK-GIG	Boeing 777-3U3ER	29143/1234	♦
☐ PK-GIH	Boeing 777-3U3ER	29144/1305	o/o♦
☐ PK-GIJ	Boeing 777-3U3ER	40072/1332	o/o♦
☐ PK-GRA	Canadair CRJ-1000ER	19025	ex C-GZQO SkyTeam c/s
☐ PK-GRC	Canadair CRJ-1000ER	19026	ex C-GIAU
☐ PK-GRE	Canadair CRJ-1000ER	19027	ex C-GIAV
☐ PK-GRF	Canadair CRJ-1000ER	19028	ex C-GIBJ
☐ PK-GRG	Canadair CRJ-1000ER	19029	ex C-GIBQ
☐ PK-GRH	Canadair CRJ-1000ER	19030	ex C-GZQA
☐ PK-GRI	Canadair CRJ-1000ER	19031	ex C-GZQL
☐ PK-GRJ	Canadair CRJ-1000ER	19032	ex C-GIAH
☐ PK-GRK	Canadair CRJ-1000ER	19033	ex C-GIAO
☐ PK-GRL	Canadair CRJ-1000ER	19034	ex C-GICB
☐ PK-GRM	Canadair CRJ-1000ER	19035	ex C-GZQF
☐ PK-GRN	Canadair CRJ-1000ER	19036	ex C-GZQK
☐ PK-GRO	Canadair CRJ-1000ER	19038	ex C-GIAU
☐ PK-GRP	Canadair CRJ-1000ER	19039	ex C-GIAV
☐ PK-GRQ	Canadair CRJ-1000ER	19040	♦
☐ PK-GGC	Boeing 737-5U3	28727/2937	ex N1786B wfs
☐ PK-GGD	Boeing 737-5U3	28728/2938	ex N1786B
☐ PK-GGE	Boeing 737-5U3	28729/2950	ex N60436
☐ PK-GGF	Boeing 737-5U3	28730/2952	
☐ PK-GGG	Boeing 737-3U3	28731/2949	wfs
☐ PK-GSG	Boeing 747-4U3	25704/1011	
☐ PK-GSH	Boeing 747-4U3	25705/1029	ex N6038E

GATARI AIR SERVICE — Gatari (GHS) — Jakarta-Halim (HLP)

☐ PK-HMB	Bell 212	30502	ex PK-DBY
☐ PK-HMM	Bell 212	30958	ex PK-PGF
☐ PK-HNS	ATR 42-500	601	ex PK-TSQ
☐ PK-HNT	ATR 42-500	614	ex OY-EDE
☐ PK-HNY	Kawasaki/MBB BK-117B-1	1052	ex JA6614

GT AIR — Jakarta-Halim (HLP)

☐ PK-LTT	Dornier 28D-1 Skyservant	4031	ex PK-VRB
☐ PK-LTU	Dornier 28D-1 Skyservant	4026	ex PK-VRA

HEVILIFT AVIATION INDONESIA

☐ PK-FUF	de Havilland DHC-6 Twin Otter 300	578	ex P2-KSS
☐ PK-IRN	de Havilland DHC-6 Twin Otter 400	859	ex C-GVAQ

INDONESIA AIR TRANSPORT — Intra (I8/IDA) — Jakarta-Halim (HLP)

☐ PK-TRD	Aérospatiale SA365C Dauphin 2	5058	ex N3606Q
☐ PK-TRE	Aérospatiale SA365C Dauphin 2	5004	ex N3604G
☐ PK-TSH	Aérospatiale SA365N Dauphin 2	6008	ex N801BA
☐ PK-TSI	Aérospatiale SA365N Dauphin 2	6026	ex N87SV
☐ PK-TSW	Aérospatiale AS365N2 Dauphin 2	6470	ex HL9204
☐ PK-TSX	Aérospatiale AS365N2 Dauphin 2	6472	ex HL9206
☐ PK-THS	ATR 42-500	0559	ex SP-EDF
☐ PK-THT	ATR 42-500	611	ex I-ADLZ
☐ PK-TRW	Beech 1900D	UE-177	ex N3237H
☐ PK-TRX	Beech 1900D	UE-186	ex N3233J
☐ PK-TSF	Bell 212	30974	ex N27664
☐ PK-TSG	Bell 212	30753	ex N81FC
☐ PK-TSJ	Fokker F.27 Friendship 500RFC	10525	ex N702A wfs
☐ PK-TSO	Fokker 50	20186	ex PH-ZDB
☐ PK-TSP	Fokker 50	20316	ex PK-TWJ
☐ PK-TSY	ATR 42-300	118	ex LY-ARY
☐ PK-TSZ	ATR 42-300	059	ex LY-ARJ

INDONESIA AIRASIA — (QZ/AWQ) — Jakarta-Soekarno Hatta (CGK)

☐ PK-AXA	Airbus A320-216	3610	ex F-WWIG
☐ PK-AXD	Airbus A320-216	3182	ex 9M-AFX
☐ PK-AXE	Airbus A320-216	3715	ex F-WWIZ
☐ PK-AXF	Airbus A320-216	3765	ex F-WWDO
☐ PK-AXG	Airbus A320-216	3813	ex F-WWIE
☐ PK-AXH	Airbus A320-216	3875	ex F-WWII

☐ PK-AXI	Airbus A320-216	3963	ex F-WWID	
☐ PK-AXJ	Airbus A320-216	4035	ex F-WWIJ	
☐ PK-AXK	Airbus A320-216	4147	ex F-WWBC	
☐ PK-AXL	Airbus A320-216	4346	ex F-WWBT	
☐ PK-AXM	Airbus A320-216	4462	ex F-WWBI	
☐ PK-AXR	Airbus A320-216	2881	ex 9M-AFJ	
☐ PK-AXS	Airbus A320-216	2885	ex 9M-AFK	
☐ PK-AXT	Airbus A320-216	3486	ex 9M-AHK	
☐ PK-AXU	Airbus A320-216	3549	ex 9M-AHN	
☐ PK-AXV	Airbus A320-216	4889	ex RP-C8190	
☐ PK-AXW	Airbus A320-216	5137	ex F-WWDV	
☐ PK-AXX	Airbus A320-216	5215	ex F-WWBC	
☐ PK-AXY	Airbus A320-216	5359	ex F-WWDM	
☐ PK-AXZ	Airbus A320-216	5420	ex F-WWDR	
☐ PK-AZA	Airbus A320-216	5165	ex B-508L	
☐ PK-AZC	Airbus A320-214	2425	ex CS-TKL	
☐ PK-AZD	Airbus A320-216/S	5627	ex F-WWBI	
☐ PK-AZE	Airbus A320-214/S	5098	ex F-WWIQ	
☐ PK-AZF	Airbus A320-216/S	5706	ex F-WWDC	
☐ PK-AZG	Airbus A320-216/S	5657	ex JA05AJ	
☐ PK-AZH	Airbus A320-216	5325	ex JA03AJ	
☐ PK-AZI	Airbus A320-216	5200	ex JA02AJ	
☐ PK-AZJ	Airbus A320-216	5153	ex JA01AJ	
☐ PK-	Airbus A320-216/S	6178	ex	o/o
☐ PK-AWO	Boeing 737-322	24659/1836	ex 9M-AEA	
☐ PK-AWX	Boeing 737-3Y0	24547/1813	ex 9M-AEC	wfs

INDONESIA AIRASIA X (XT/IDX) Jakarta-Soekarno Hatta (CGK)

☐ PK-XRA	Airbus A330-343E	716	ex 9M-XXQ	♦
☐ PK-XRC	Airbus A330-343E	654	ex 9M-XXR	♦

JAYAWIJAYA DIRGANTARA (JWD) Jakarta-Halim (HLP)

☐ PK-JRU	Fokker F27-500 Friendship	10629	ex PK-VKT

JHONLIN AIR TRANSPORT (JLB)

☐ PK-JBA	ATR 42-600	1004	ex F-WWLZ
☐ PK-JBB	Hawker 900XP	HA-0188	ex N188XP
☐ PK-JBC	Cessna 208B Caravan I	208B2002	ex N224SK
☐ PK-JBE	Bell 429	57040	ex N449QB
☐ PK-JBH	Hawker 900XP	HA-0071	
☐ PK-JBK	Beech 350 King Air	RL-619	ex N60819
☐ PK-JBL	Bell 407	53987	ex N416AB
☐ PK-JBN	Piper PA-31 Navajo C	31-8012055	ex PK-IKJ
☐ PK-JBS	Cessna 208B Caravan I	208B2255	ex N6034H

KALSTAR AVIATION Kalstar (KD/KLS) Berau Kalimaru (BEJ)

☐ PK-KSD	ATR 42-212A	585	ex 2-ASIA	♦
☐ PK-KSE	ATR 42-320	415	ex N415AN	
☐ PK-KSI	ATR 42-320	348	ex N38AN	
☐ PK-KSO	ATR 42-320	202	ex N21837	
☐ PK-	ATR 42-500	518	ex 8Q-VAR	o/o♦
☐ PK-KDA	Embraer ERJ-195LR	19000029	ex G-FBEA	♦
☐ PK-KDC	Embraer ERJ-195LR	19000057	ex G-FBEB	♦
☐ PK-KSA	ATR 72-600	1080	ex F-WWEQ	
☐ PK-KSC	ATR 72-212A	638	ex 2-CSLA	♦
☐ PK-KSM	Boeing 737-529	26537/2265	ex PK-RAW	
☐ PK-KSP	Boeing 737-59D	26421/2279	ex N457US	
☐ PK-KST	Boeing 737-3MB	25040/2017	ex PK-ECK	
☐ PK-KSU	ATR 72-600	1108	ex F-WWEU	

KURA-KURA AVIATION

☐ PK-WLU	Gippsland GA-8 Airvan	03-031	
☐ PK-WLV	Gippsland GA-8 Airvan	03-033	

LION AIRLINES Lion Inter (JT/LNI) Jakarta-Soekarno Hatta (CGK)

☐ 9M-LMF	ATR 72-600	1081	ex F-WWER	>MXD
☐ 9M-LMG	ATR 72-600	1089	ex (PK-WGL)	>MXD
☐ 9M-LMH	ATR 72-600	1095	ex F-WWEH	>MXD
☐ 9M-LMJ	ATR 72-600	1123	ex F-WWEL	>MXD
☐ 9M-LMK	ATR 72-600	1130	ex F-WWES	>MXD
☐ 9M-LML	ATR 72-600	1135	ex F-WWEX	>MXD
☐ 9M-LMM	ATR 72-600	1147	ex F-WWEL	>MXD
☐ 9M-LMO	ATR 72-600	1154	ex F-WWES	>MXD♦
☐ 9M-LMP	ATR 72-600	1161	ex F-WWEB	>MXD♦

☐ 9M-LMQ	ATR 72-600	1179	ex F-WWET	>MXD♦
☐ 9M-LMR	ATR 72-600	1186	ex F-WWEC	>MXD♦
☐ PK-LIF	Boeing 737-4Y0	24467/1733	ex PK-MBL	[CGK]
☐ PK-LIG	Boeing 737-4Y0	24513/1779	ex PK-MBM	[CGK]
☐ PK-LIH	Boeing 737-4Y0	24520/1803	ex HL7260	wfs
☐ PK-LII	Boeing 737-46B	24123/1663	ex EC-GRX	
☐ PK-LIR	Boeing 737-4Y0	24692/1963	ex EC-IRA	[SUB]
☐ PK-LIS	Boeing 737-4Y0	24693/1972	ex OK-WGG	
☐ PK-LIT	Boeing 737-4Y0	24512/1777	ex PK-GWV	[CGK]
☐ PK-LIW	Boeing 737-4Y0	24684/1841	ex EI-CVN	
☐ PK-LJQ	Boeing 737-8GP/W	38317/3985		
☐ PK-LJR	Boeing 737-8GP/W	37292/4008		
☐ PK-LJS	Boeing 737-8GP/W	37293/4046		
☐ PK-LJU	Boeing 737-8GP/W	37294/4071	ex N1786B	
☐ PK-LJV	Boeing 737-8GP/W	38721/4077		
☐ PK-LJW	Boeing 737-8GP/W	37295/4092		
☐ PK-LJY	Boeing 737-8GP/W	38722/4125		
☐ PK-LKG	Boeing 737-8GP/W	38681/4180		
☐ PK-LKH	Boeing 737-8GP/W	37297/4193		
☐ PK-LKI	Boeing 737-8GP/W	38724/4206		
☐ PK-LKJ	Boeing 737-8GP/W	38682/4226		
☐ PK-LKK	Boeing 737-8GP/W	38725/4238		
☐ PK-LKP	Boeing 737-8GP/W	38685/4314		
☐ PK-LKQ	Boeing 737-8GP/W	38727/4320		
☐ PK-LKR	Boeing 737-8GP/W	38686/4332		
☐ PK-LKT	Boeing 737-8GP/W	38733/4517	ex (PK-LLI)	
☐ PK-LKU	Boeing 737-8GP/W	38691/4514	ex (PK-LLH)	
☐ PK-LKV	Boeing 737-8GP/W	38735/4583	ex N5573B	
☐ PK-LKW	Boeing 737-8GP/W	38734/4578	ex (PK-LLK)	
☐ PK-LKZ	Boeing 737-8GP/W	38740/4687		
☐ PK-LOG	Boeing 737-8GP/W	38745/4740	ex N5573L	
☐ PK-LOH	Boeing 737-8GP/W	38744/4762		
☐ PK-LOI	Boeing 737-8GP/W	38746/4777	ex N5573L	
☐ PK-LOJ	Boeing 737-8GP/W	38747/4783		
☐ PK-LOM	Boeing 737-8GP/W	38750/4867		
☐ PK-LOO	Boeing 737-8GP/W	39814/4879		♦
☐ PK-LOP	Boeing 737-8GP/W	39815/4890		♦
☐ PK-LOQ	Boeing 737-8GP/W	39816/4924	ex N1795B	♦
☐ PK-LOR	Boeing 737-8GP/W	39818/4936		♦
☐ PK-LOV	Boeing 737-8GP/W	39817/4954		♦
☐ PK-LFF	Boeing 737-9GPER/W	35679/2093	ex N6055X	
☐ PK-LFG	Boeing 737-9GPER/W	35680/1981	ex N900ER	
☐ PK-LFH	Boeing 737-9GPER/W	35710/2285	ex N1786B	
☐ PK-LFI	Boeing 737-9GPER/W	35711/2319	ex N1780B	
☐ PK-LFJ	Boeing 737-9GPER/W	35712/2349	ex (PK-LAJ)	
☐ PK-LFK	Boeing 737-9GPER/W	35713/2437	ex N1781B	
☐ PK-LFL	Boeing 737-9GPER/W	35714/2461	ex (PK-LAL)	
☐ PK-LFM	Boeing 737-9GPER/W	35715/2485	ex N1786B	
☐ PK-LFO	Boeing 737-9GPER/W	35716/2504	ex N1786B	
☐ PK-LFP	Boeing 737-9GPER/W	35717/2455		
☐ PK-LFQ	Boeing 737-9GPER/W	35718/2670		
☐ PK-LFR	Boeing 737-9GPER/W	35719/2694		
☐ PK-LFS	Boeing 737-9GPER/W	35720/2756		
☐ PK-LFT	Boeing 737-9GPER/W	35721/2793		
☐ PK-LFU	Boeing 737-9GPER/W	35722/2836	ex N1784B	
☐ PK-LFV	Boeing 737-9GPER/W	35723/2848	ex N1787B	
☐ PK-LFW	Boeing 737-9GPER/W	35724/2879		
☐ PK-LFY	Boeing 737-9GPER/W	35725/2897	ex N1786B	
☐ PK-LFZ	Boeing 737-9GPER/W	35726/2904		
☐ PK-LGJ	Boeing 737-9GPER/W	35727/2934	ex N1796B	
☐ PK-LGK	Boeing 737-9GPER/W	35728/2984	ex N1786B	
☐ PK-LGL	Boeing 737-9GPER/W	35729/3008		
☐ PK-LGM	Boeing 737-9GPER/W	35730/3075		
☐ PK-LGO	Boeing 737-9GPER/W	35731/3093		
☐ PK-LGP	Boeing 737-9GPER/W	35732/3111		
☐ PK-LGQ	Boeing 737-9GPER/W	35733/3135		
☐ PK-LGR	Boeing 737-9GPER/W	35734/3153		
☐ PK-LGS	Boeing 737-9GPER/W	35735/3183		
☐ PK-LGT	Boeing 737-9GPER/W	35736/3207	ex N1787B	
☐ PK-LGU	Boeing 737-9GPER/W	35737/3225	ex N1787B	
☐ PK-LGV	Boeing 737-9GPER/W	37268/3297		
☐ PK-LGW	Boeing 737-9GPER/W	37269/3321		
☐ PK-LGY	Boeing 737-9GPER/W	37270/3333		
☐ PK-LGZ	Boeing 737-9GPER/W	37271/3345	ex N1786B	
☐ PK-LHH	Boeing 737-9GPER/W	37279/3375		
☐ PK-LHI	Boeing 737-9GPER/W	37276/3381		
☐ PK-LHJ	Boeing 737-9GPER/W	37272/3411		
☐ PK-LHK	Boeing 737-9GPER/W	37273/3423	ex N1787B	
☐ PK-LHL	Boeing 737-9GPER/W	37274/3441		
☐ PK-LHM	Boeing 737-9GPER/W	37277/3513		

☐ PK-LHO	Boeing 737-9GPER/W	37278/3555		
☐ PK-LHP	Boeing 737-9GPER/W	37279/3573		
☐ PK-LHQ	Boeing 737-9GPER/W	37280/3537		
☐ PK-LHR	Boeing 737-9GPER/W	37281/3627		
☐ PK-LHS	Boeing 737-9GPER/W	37282/3663		
☐ PK-LHT	Boeing 737-9GPER/W	37283/3699		
☐ PK-LHU	Boeing 737-9GPER/W	38300/3717		
☐ PK-LHV	Boeing 737-9GPER/W	37284/3735		
☐ PK-LHW	Boeing 737-9GPER/W	38302/3753		
☐ PK-LHY	Boeing 737-9GPER/W	37285/3765		
☐ PK-LHZ	Boeing 737-9GPER/W	38305/3807		
☐ PK-LJF	Boeing 737-9GPER/W	37286/3813		
☐ PK-LJG	Boeing 737-9GPER/W	37287/3831		
☐ PK-LJH	Boeing 737-9PGER/W	37288/3849		
☐ PK-LJI	Boeing 737-9GPER/W	38310/3867		
☐ PK-LJJ	Boeing 737-9GPER/W	37289/3888		
☐ PK-LJK	Boeing 737-9GPER/W	38311/3900		
☐ PK-LJL	Boeing 737-9GPER/W	37290/3918		
☐ PK-LJM	Boeing 737-9GPER/W	38313/3936		
☐ PK-LJO	Boeing 737-9GPER/W	38315/3954		
☐ PK-LJP	Boeing 737-9GPER/W	37291/3966		
☐ PK-LJT	Boeing 737-9GPER/W	38720/4056		
☐ PK-LJW	Boeing 737-9GPER/W	37295/4092		
☐ PK-LJZ	Boeing 737-9GPER/W	37296/4128		
☐ PK-LKF	Boeing 737-9GPER/W	38723/4140		
☐ PK-LKL	Boeing 737-9GPER/W	38683/4236		
☐ PK-LKM	Boeing 737-9GPER/W	38726/4284	ex N1787B	
☐ PK-LKO	Boeing 737-9GPER/W	38684/4266		
☐ PK-LLF	Boeing 737-9GPER/W	38732/4484		>MXD
☐ PK-LOF	Boeing 737-9GPER/W	38741/4679		
☐ PK-LPF	Boeing 737-9GPER/W	39880/5081		♦
☐ PK-LPH	Boeing 737-9GPER/W	39878/5096		♦
☐ PK-LPI	Boeing 737-9GPER/W	38299/5134		♦
☐ 9M-LNF	Boeing 737-9GPER/W	38687/4368		>MXD
☐ 9M-LNG	Boeing 737-9GPER/W	38729/4380		>MXD
☐ 9M-LNJ	Boeing 737-9GPER/W	38690/4495	ex (PK-LLG)	>MXD
☐ PK-LHF	Boeing 747-412	24063/736	ex N240BA	
☐ PK-LHG	Boeing 747-412	24065/761	ex N465BB	
☐ PK-LIO	McDonnell-Douglas MD-90-30	53490/2133	ex N902RA	[CGK]
☐ PK-LIP	McDonnell-Douglas MD-90-30	53551/2144	ex N903RA	[CGK]
☐ PK-LIU	Boeing 737-3G7	23218/1076	ex N380WL	
☐ PK-LIV	Boeing 737-3G7	23219/1090	ex N390WL	
☐ PK-	Airbus A330-343E	1675	ex F-WW	o/o♦
☐ PK-	Airbus A330-343E	1683	ex F-WW	o/o♦
☐ PK-	Airbus A330-343E	1680	ex F-WW	o/o♦
☐ PK-	Airbus A330-343E	1693	ex F-WW	o/o♦

MANUNGGAL AIR SERVICE (MNS) Jakarta-Halim (HLP)

☐ PK-VTN	British Aerospace 146 Srs.100	E1104	ex PK-VKD	[HLP]
☐ PK-VTP	Aérospatiale/MBB Transall C-160P	234	ex PK-PTP	
☐ PK-VTR	Aérospatiale/MBB Transall C-160P	233	ex PK-PTO	[HLP]
☐ PK-VTS	Aérospatiale/MBB Transall C-160P	207	ex PK-PTY	[HLP]
☐ PK-VTZ	Aérospatiale/MBB Transall C-160P	208	ex PK-PTZ	

MIMIKA AIR

☐ PK-LTV	de Havilland DHC-6 Twin Otter 300	634	ex N933DR	

MY INDO AIRLINES (MYU) Jakarta-Halim (HLP)

☐ PK-MYI	Boeing 737-3Z0F	23448/1168	ex 9M-NEJ	♦

NAM AIR (NM/NAM) Jakarta-Soekarno-Hatta (CGK)

☐ PK-NAM	Boeing 737-524/W	27900/2736	ex N16632	Bersinar
☐ PK-NAN	Boeing 737-524/W	27901/2743	ex N24633	Kehidupan

NATIONAL UTILITY HELICOPTERS

☐ PK-URL	Bell 412EP	36313	ex ZK-HVM	
☐ PK-URZ	Bell 206LT LongRanger	52067	ex PK-YRQ	
☐ PK-USA	Bell 212	30753	ex PK-BRU	
☐ PK-USS	Bell 212	30974	ex PK-BRV	

NYAMAN AIR

☐ PK-FUD	Sikorsky S-76C++	760412	ex VH-FLE	
☐ PK-FUE	Sikorsky S-76C++	760682	ex VH-FLF	
☐ PK-FUF	de Havilland DHC-6 Twin Otter 300	578	ex P2-KSS	
☐ PK-FUH	Aérospatiale AS350B3 Ecureuil	3242	ex P2-HCZ	

☐ PK-FUI	Aérospatiale AS350B3 Ecureuil	3634	ex P2-HCY		
☐ PK-FUJ	Bell 412HP	36046	ex VT-UHA		

NUSANTARA AIR CHARTER (SJK) Jakarta-Halim (HLP)

☐ PK-JKG	ATR 42-500	667	ex OY-CLO		
☐ PK-JKH	ATR 72-212A	538	ex D-ANAC		
☐ PK-JKM	Canadair Challenger 601-3A	5120	ex N408TB		
☐ PK-JKP	Avro 146-RJ100	E3243	ex VH-NBU	Anugrah	opf PT Anugrah
☐ PK-JKW	British Aerospace 146 Srs.200	E2204	ex PK-LNI	Athirah	

NUSANTARA BUANA AIR

☐ PK-DCP	CASA-Nurtanio C212-A4	14N/A4-11-101	ex PK-XCM	
☐ PK-DYR	Piper PA-31T Cheyenne II	31T-7820054	ex VH-MWT	
☐ PK-TLE	CASA-Nurtanio C212-200	87N/CC4-38-282	ex PK-VSA	
☐ PK-TLG	CASA-Nurtanio C212-200	93N/4-413	ex PK-VSF	
☐ PK-TLH	CASA-Nurtanio C212-200	90N/410	ex PK-BRN	
☐ PK-TLI	CASA-Nurtanio C212-200	91N/411	ex PK-BRM	
☐ PK-TMC	Piper PA-31T Cheyenne II	31T-7920084	ex PK-PCI	

PEGASUS AIR SERVICES

☐ PK-ICG	Aérospatiale EC135P2	0437	ex PK-JTI	
☐ PK-ICT	Cessna 208B Caravan I	208B2319	ex N60208	
☐ PK-ICY	Cessna 208B Caravan I	208B2354	ex PK-LTY	

PELITA AIR Pelita (6D/PAS) Jakarta-Halim/Pondok Cabe (HLP/PCB)

☐ PK-PCN	CASA-Nurtanio C212-A4	56N/CC4-8-216	ex PK-XDE	[PCB]
☐ PK-PCO	CASA-Nurtanio C.212-A4	55N/CC4-7-215	ex PK-XDD	
☐ PK-PCP	CASA-Nurtanio C212-A4	48N/AB4-20-208	ex PK-XAV	
☐ PK-PCQ	CASA-Nurtanio C212-A4	47N/AB4-19-207	ex PK-XAU	[PCB]
☐ PK-PCR	CASA-Nurtanio C212-A4	46N/AB4-18-206	ex PK-XAT	
☐ PK-PCS	CASA-Nurtanio C212-A4	45N/AB4-17-205	ex PK-XAS	
☐ PK-PCT	CASA-Nurtanio C212-A4	44N/AB4-16-204	ex PK-XAR	
☐ PK-PCU	CASA-Nurtanio C212-A4	43N/AB4-15-203	ex PK-XAQ	
☐ PK-PCV	CASA-Nurtanio C212-100	21N/A4-18-132	ex PK-XCT	
☐ PK-PCY	CASA-Nurtanio C212-100	2N/C4-2-39	ex PK-PCL	
☐ PK-PGQ	Nurtanio/MBB Bo.105CB	N60/S-458		
☐ PK-PGR	Nurtanio/MBB Bo.105CB	N62/S-460		
☐ PK-PGU	Nurtanio/MBB Bo.105C	N12/S-218	ex PK-XZJ	
☐ PK-PGZ	Nurtanio/MBB Bo.105CB	N65/S-553		
☐ PK-PIH	Nurtanio/MBB Bo.105CB	N68/S-556		
☐ PK-PIJ	Nurtanio/MBB Bo.105CB	N70/S-558	ex PK-XYN	
☐ PK-PIM	Nurtanio/MBB Bo.105CB	N72/S-560	ex PK-XYP	
☐ PK-PUA	Sikorsky S-76A	76-0179	ex N5446U	>TVV
☐ PK-PUD	Sikorsky S-76A	76-0195	ex N3121A	>TVV
☐ PK-PUE	Sikorsky S-76A	76-0200		>TVV
☐ PK-PUW	Sikorsky S-76C++	760816	ex N816H	
☐ PK-PUX	Sikorsky S-76C++	760821	ex N821A	
☐ PK-PUY	Sikorsky S-76C++	760816	ex N816H	
☐ PK-PUZ	Sikorsky S-76C++	760820	ex N820G	
☐ PK-PAV	ATR 72-212A	908	ex OY-YAJ	♦
☐ PK-PAW	ATR 72-212A	746	ex M-YWAB	
☐ PK-PAX	ATR 42-500	627	ex F-OIQC	Bontang ♦
☐ PK-PCI	Piper PA-31T Cheyenne II	31T-7920084	ex N189GH	
☐ PK-PEI	Aérospatiale SA330J Puma	1299		
☐ PK-PEK	Aérospatiale SA330G Puma	1283		
☐ PK-PEO	Aérospatiale SA330J Puma	1261		
☐ PK-PFZ	Fokker 100	11486	ex PH-ZFA	
☐ PK-PJJ	Avro 146-RJ85	E2239	ex G-6-239	VIP
☐ PK-PJN	Fokker 100	11288	ex PH-LMU	Minas
☐ PK-PJY	Fokker F.28 Fellowship 4000	11146	ex PH-EXN	Aceh
☐ PK-PSV	de Havilland DHC-7-103	105	ex C-GFOD	
☐ PK-PSW	de Havilland DHC-7-103	100	ex C-GFCF	
☐ PK-PSX	de Havilland DHC-7-103	094	ex C-GFYI	
☐ PK-PUG	IPTN/Aérospatiale AS332C	NSP2/2020	ex PK-XSB	
☐ PK-PUH	IPTN/Aérospatiale AS332C	NSP3/2021	ex PK-XSC	
☐ PK-PUJ	Bell 412EP	36282	ex N2012Y	
☐ PK-PUK	Bell 412EP	36288	ex N2028L	
☐ PK-PUL	Bell 430	49088	ex N3005J	

PREMIAIR Jakarta-Halim (HLP)

☐ N227GV	Embraer Lineage 1000	19000159	ex PP-XTF	
☐ N377CJ	Boeing 737-73Q/W (BBJ1)	30789/602	ex N349BA	
☐ PK-DHK	Embraer Legacy 600	14501046	ex PT-SED	
☐ PK-RJA	Embraer Legacy 600	14501134	ex D-ADCQ	

☐ PK-RJP	Embraer Legacy 650	14501172	ex PT-TJY	
☐ PK-RNI	Embraer Legacy 600	14501045	ex G-CFJA	

RPX REPUBLIC EXPRESS		**Public Express (RH/RPH)**		**Jakarta-Soekarno Hatta (CGK)**

☐ PK-RPH	Boeing 737-2K2C (AvAero 3)	20943/405	ex F-GGVP	[PCB]
☐ PK-RPI	Boeing 737-2K2C (AvAero 3)	20944/408	ex F-GGVQ	

SABANG MERAUKE RAYA AIR CHARTER		**Samer (SMC)**		**Medan (MES)**

☐ PK-NCZ	CASA-Nurtanio C212-A4	79N/274		
☐ PK-ZAB	CASA-Nurtanio C212-A4	23N/A4-20-140	ex PK-XCV	
☐ PK-ZAN	CASA-Nurtanio C212-A4	4N/A4-1-60	ex A-2102	
☐ PK-ZAO	CASA-Nurtanio C212-A4	6N/A4-3-64	ex A-2101	
☐ PK-ZAQ	CASA-Nurtanio C212-A4	82N/CC4-33-277	ex PK-JSR	
☐ PK-ZAV	CASA-Nurtanio C212-A4	81N/CC4-32-276	ex PK-JSS	
☐ PK-ZAE	Britten-Norman BN-2A-21 Islander	565	ex G-BEGH	[MES]
☐ PK-ZAK	Piper PA-31 Turbo Navajo	31-407	ex PK-FJA	

SKY AVIATION		**(SYA)**		

☐ PK-ECD	Fokker 50	20271	ex PH-LXK	wfs
☐ PK-ECE	Fokker 50	20277	ex PH-LXR	wfs
☐ PK-ECF	Fokker 50	20279	ex PH-LXT	wfs
☐ PK-ECG	Fokker 50	20254	ex PH-KXN	wfs
☐ PK-ECH	Fokker 50	20255	ex PH-KXS	wfs
☐ PK-ECC	Cessna 208B Caravan I	208B0643	ex HS-GAA	wfs
☐ PK-ECL	Sukhoi SSJ 100-95B	95022		wfs
☐ PK-ECM	Sukhoi SSJ 100-95B	95027		wfs
☐ PK-ECN	Sukhoi SSJ 100-95B	95031		wfs
☐ PK-RJI	Fokker 100	11328	ex G-BWXF	wfs
Ceased ops Mar14; may restart				

SRIWIJAYA AIR		**Sriwijaya (SJ/SJY)**		**Jakarta-Soekarno Hatta (CGK)**

☐ PK-CJA	Boeing 737-284	22301/683	ex PK-IJS	Brenda	
☐ PK-CJE	Boeing 737-2T4	23446/1165	ex ET-ALE	Citra	
☐ PK-CJF	Boeing 737-284	22343/695	ex SX-BCI		
☐ PK-CJH	Boeing 737-2B7 (Nordam 3)	22883/935	ex N271AU		[CGK]
☐ PK-CJI	Boeing 737-2B7 (Nordam 3)	23135/1054	ex PK-ALV	Membalong	[CGK]
☐ PK-CJK	Boeing 737-236	22032/742	ex PK-ALK		[CGK]
☐ PK-CJL	Boeing 737-284	21301/474	ex PK-TXE		
☐ PK-CJM	Boeing 737-2B7 (Nordam 3)	22884/956	ex PK-TXC		[CGK]
☐ PK-CJO	Boeing 737-284	22300/674	ex PK-IJR	Lomasasta	
☐ PK-CJP	Boeing 737-2B7 (Nordam 3)	23132/1044	ex PK-ALN	Lenggang	[CGK]
☐ PK-CJC	Boeing 737-33A	24025/1556	ex SE-RCP		
☐ PK-CJS	Boeing 737-3L9	27925/2763	ex N104VR		
☐ PK-CJT	Boeing 737-33A	24791/1984	ex N791AW		
☐ PK-CJY	Boeing 737-3Q8	24698/1846	ex PK-GHS		
☐ PK-CKE	Boeing 737-3Q8	24987/2268	ex N596BC		
☐ PK-CKF	Boeing 737-3Y0	25179/2205	ex N381DF		
☐ PK-CKH	Boeing 737-3Y0	24907/2013	ex N383DF		
☐ PK-CKI	Boeing 737-3Y0	25187/2248	ex N382DF		
☐ PK-CKJ	Boeing 737-3L9	27337/2594	ex N581MS	Kemurahan	
☐ PK-CKK	Boeing 737-3L9	27336/2587	ex N308MS	Kejujura	
☐ PK-CKL	Boeing 737-3Q8	26293/2541	ex PK-GGV	Keikhlasan	
☐ PK-CKP	Boeing 737-36N	28559/2882	ex B-2601	Perlindungan	
☐ PK-CJW	Boeing 737-4Y0	24690/1885	ex N690MD		
☐ PK-CKA	Boeing 737-4Q8	25169/2237	ex N483JC		
☐ PK-CKC	Boeing 737-4Q8	26285/2416	ex N587BC		
☐ PK-CKD	Boeing 737-4Y0	25180/2201	ex N251MD	Bersebah	
☐ PK-CKN	Boeing 737-4Q8	26281/2380	ex D-ABRF	Sukacita	
☐ PK-CLC	Boeing 737-524/W	27323/2616	ex N27610	Citra	
☐ PK-CLD	Boeing 737-524/W	27333/2660	ex N17620	Kedahsyatan	
☐ PK-CLE	Boeing 737-524/W	27326/2633	ex N14613	Kemuliaan	
☐ PK-CLF	Boeing 737-524/W	27327/2634	ex N17614		
☐ PK-CLH	Boeing 737-524/W	27330/2648	ex N16617		
☐ PK-CLI	Boeing 737-524/W	27332/2659	ex N17619		
☐ PK-CLJ	Boeing 737-524/W	27527/2672	ex N19623		
☐ PK-CLK	Boeing 737-524/W	27317/2576	ex N14604	Melayani	
☐ PK-CLL	Boeing 737-524/W	27528/2675	ex N13642	Mengabdi	
☐ PK-CLM	Boeing 737-524/W	27526/2669	ex N18622		
☐ PK-CLN	Boeing 737-524/W	27529/2683	ex N46625	Berbagi	
☐ PK-CLO	Boeing 737-524/W	27334/2661	ex N19621		
☐ PK-CMA	Boeing 737-524/W	27531/2700	ex N17627	Ketaatan	
☐ PK-CMC	Boeing 737-524/W	27534/2726	ex N59630	Megah	
☐ PK-CMD	Boeing 737-524/W	27535/2728	ex N62631	Lomasasta	

☐ PK-CLA	Boeing 737-86N/W	28591/233	ex SU-MWD	Brenda	
☐ PK-CLQ	Boeing 737-81Q/W	29050/444	ex N905AG	Kebahagiaan	
☐ PK-CLS	Boeing 737-8K5/W	27985/470	ex D-AHFL	Kepercayaan	
☐ PK-CLT	Boeing 737-8K5/W	27991/248	ex D-AHFK	Emilio	
☐ PK-CME	Boeing 737-8Q8/W	30702/1953	ex 2-MFFB	Kebersamaan	♦
☐ PK-CMF	Boeing 737-86Q/W	32885/1147	ex B-2675	Kemumian	♦
☐ PK-CMI	Boeing 737-8Q8/W	28214/78	ex HL8262	Kebenaran	♦

SUSI AIR/ASI PUDJIASTUTI AVIATION   Sky Queen (SQS)   Medan (MES)

☐ PK-BVA	Cessna 208B Caravan I	208B2126	ex N61905
☐ PK-BVB	Cessna 208B Caravan I	208B2163	ex N208CC
☐ PK-BVD	Cessna 208B Caravan I	208B2141	ex N61932
☐ PK-BVE	Cessna 208B Caravan I	208B2142	ex N6194X
☐ PK-BVF	Cessna 208B Caravan I	208B2143	ex N61983
☐ PK-BVG	Cessna 208B Caravan I	208B2146	ex N6203C
☐ PK-BVH	Cessna 208B Caravan I	208B2151	ex N6204C
☐ PK-BVI	Cessna 208B Caravan I	208B2177	ex N1015J
☐ PK-BVJ	Cessna 208B Caravan I	208B2194	ex N1016M
☐ PK-BVK	Cessna 208B Caravan I	208B2198	ex N10200
☐ PK-BVL	Cessna 208B Caravan I	208B2206	ex N1021S
☐ PK-BVN	Cessna 208B Caravan I	208B2214	exN60059
☐ PK-BVO	Cessna 208B Caravan I	208B2217	ex N1022G
☐ PK-BVP	Cessna 208B Caravan I	208B2218	ex N1022Z
☐ PK-BVQ	Cessna 208B Caravan I	208B2225	ex N10225
☐ PK-BVR	Cessna 208B Caravan I	208B2229	ex N1023Q
☐ PK-BVS	Cessna 208B Caravan I	208B2293	ex N9012S
☐ PK-BVU	Cessna 208B Caravan I	208B2257	ex N6033H
☐ PK-BVW	Cessna 208B Caravan I	208B2258	ex N258CC
☐ PK-BVZ	Cessna 208B Caravan I	208b2273	ex N3042C
☐ PK-VVA	Cessna 208B Caravan I	208B1066	ex N12690
☐ PK-VVB	Cessna 208B Caravan I	208B1285	ex N4117B
☐ PK-VVD	Cessna 208B Caravan I	208B1303	ex N20722
☐ PK-VVF	Cessna 208B Caravan I	208B1177	ex N1307K
☐ PK-VVH	Cessna 208B Caravan I	208B1078	ex N278ST
☐ PK-VVI	Cessna 208B Caravan I	208B1205	ex RP-C2929
☐ PK-VVJ	Cessna 208B Caravan I	208B2086	ex N2232Y
☐ PK-VVM	Cessna 208B Caravan I	208B2093	ex N2154L
☐ PK-VVO	Cessna 208B Caravan I	208B2111	ex N61611
☐ PK-VVR	Cessna 208B Caravan I	208B1085	ex N12722
☐ PK-VVS	Cessna 208B Caravan I	208B1117	ex N12775
☐ PK-VVT	Cessna 208B Caravan I	208B2068	ex N61413
☐ PK-	Cessna 208B Caravan i	208B2273	ex N3042C
☐ PK-	Cessna 208B Caravan I	208B2293	ex N9012S

☐ PK-BVC	Pilatus PC-6/B2-H4 Turbo Porter	983	ex HB-FJC
☐ PK-BVM	Pilatus PC-6/B2-H4 Turbo Porter	975	ex HB-FNU
☐ PK-BVT	Pilatus PC-6/B2-H4 Turbo Porter	968	ex HB-FNM
☐ PK-BVY	Pilatus PC-6/B2-H4 Turbo Porter	973	ex HB-FNS
☐ PK-VVK	Pilatus PC-6/B2-H4 Turbo Porter	958	
☐ PK-VVP	Pilatus PC-6/B2-H4 Turbo Porter	957	
☐ PK-VVU	Pilatus PC-6/B2-H4 Turbo Porter	967	ex HB-FNK
☐ PK-VVW	Pilatus PC-6/B2-H4 Turbo Porter	982	ex HB-FJB

☐ PK-BVV	Piaggio P.180 Avanti	1209	ex N128PA
☐ PK-BVX	Piaggio P.180 Avanti	1204	ex N134PA
☐ PK-VVC	Agusta AW119 Mk II	14751	ex N409SM
☐ PK-VVV	Agusta A109S	22089	
☐ PK-VVX	Piaggio P.180 Avanti	1192	ex N146PA

TRANSNUSA AVIATION MANDIRI   (M8/TNU)   Denpasar (DPS)

☐ PK-TNA	Fokker 50	20261	ex PK-BRX	
☐ PK-TNB	Fokker 50	20282	ex PK-BRY	
☐ PK-TNC	Fokker 50	20240	ex D2-ESR	
☐ PK-TND	Fokker 50	20260	ex OB-1829-P	
☐ PK-TNS	Fokker 50	20307	ex PK-BRW	
☐ PK-TNJ	ATR 42-600	1015	ex F-WWLX	♦
☐ PK-TNR	Fokker 70	11585	ex VN-A504	♦

TRANSWISATA AIR   (TWT)   Jakarta-Halim (HLP)

☐ PK-TWM	Fokker F.28 Fellowship 4000	11183	ex ZS-JAV	wfs
☐ PK-TWN	Fokker 100	11335	ex PH-SXI	
☐ PK-TWU	Aérospatiale/Nurtanio AS332C	NSP09/2109	ex PK-XSI	
☐ PK-TWV	Boll 412EP	36153	ex HL9251	
☐ PK-TWW	CASA-Nurtanio C.212-200	102N/422	ex PK-XCX	

TRAVIRA AIR   Paramita (TVV)   Denpasar (DPS)

☐ PK-PUA	Sikorsky S-76A	760179	ex N5446U	<PAS

☐ PK-PUD	Sikorsky S-76A	760195	ex N3121A	<PAS
☐ PK-PUE	Sikorsky S-76A	760200		<PAS
☐ PK-TVA	Sikorsky S-76C++	760662	ex 9M-SPQ	
☐ PK-TVF	Sikorsky S-76A	760154	ex VH-CPH	
☐ PK-TVP	Sikorsky S-76C	760421	ex N899KK	
☐ PK-TVQ	Sikorsky S-76A	760286	ex N30DJ	
☐ PK-TVP	Sikorsky S-76C	760436	ex N476X	
☐ PK-TVU	Sikorsky S-76C	760298	ex N520AL	
☐ PK-NZU	IPTN/MBB Bo.105CB	N121/S-719	ex PK-IWJ	
☐ PK-TUA	Aérospatiale AS350B2 Ecureuil	7061	ex F-OKFR	
☐ PK-TUB	de Havilland DHC-8Q-315	590	ex C-GJTR	
☐ PK-TUC	Bell 412EP	36544	ex N3537H	
☐ PK-TUD	de Havilland DHC-8Q-315	582	ex C-GLWO	wfs
☐ PK-TVB	IPTN/MBB Bo.105CB	N6/S-177	ex PK-PGV	
☐ PK-TVH	Beech 1900D	UE-364	ex N30469	
☐ PK-TVI	Cessna 208 Caravan I	20800313	ex C-FAMB	FP
☐ PK-TVK	Beech 1900D	UE-375	ex N31424	air ambulance
☐ PK-TVN	Cessna 208 Caravan I	20800358	ex N1229N	FP
☐ PK-TVO	Hawker 800XP	258579	ex N50309	
☐ PK-TVW	Cessna 208 Caravan I	20800418	ex N20869	FP
☐ PK-TVX	Cessna 208 Caravan I	20800421	ex N2098U	FP
☐ PK-TVZ	Boeing 737-5L9	28996/2998	ex N737RH	VIP
☐ PK-	ATR 42-600	1017	ex F-WWLB	o/o♦

TRIGANA AIR SERVICE — Trigana (TGN) — Jakarta-Halim (HLP)

☐ PK-YRE	ATR 42-300	027	ex F-GPZB	
☐ PK-YRH	ATR 42-300	097	ex F-ODGN	
☐ PK-YRK	ATR 42-300	106	ex N422TE	
☐ PK-YRN	ATR 42-300	102	ex N421TE	
☐ PK-YRR	ATR 42-310	214	ex F-GHPI	
☐ PK-YRV	ATR 42-300	190	ex G-BYHA	wfs
☐ PK-YSF	Boeing 737-4Y0	23869/1639	ex PK-YTZ	
☐ PK-YSY	Boeing 737-347SF	23597/1287	ex PK-BBA	
☐ PK-YSZ	Boeing 737-3Z0F	23451/1240	ex N23451	
☐ PK-	Boeing 737-301SF	23930/1539	ex EC-LTO	o/o♦
☐ ZS-SMG	Boeing 737-3Y0F	23499/1242	ex VP-BCJ	<SFR
☐ PK-TVG	Bell 412EP	36559	ex N437HB	
☐ PK-YPX	de Havilland DHC-6 Twin Otter 300	684	ex HB-LTF	
☐ PK-YRC	Cessna TU206D Skywagon	U206-1269	ex PK-MCA	
☐ PK-YRF	de Havilland DHC-6 Twin Otter 300	462	ex D-ISKY	♦
☐ PK-YRI	ATR 72-202	326	ex F-WQUF	
☐ PK-YRJ	de Havilland DHC-4A Caribou	27	ex N666NC	
☐ PK-YRQ	Bell 206L-4 LongRanger IV	52069	ex F-GPGC	
☐ PK-YRU	de Havilland DHC-6 Twin Otter 300	685	ex VH-VHP	dam 11Jan15
☐ PK-YRX	ATR 72-202	342	ex F-WQRY	
☐ PK-YRY	ATR 72-202	201	ex F-WQAL	
☐ PK-YSA	Boeing 737-228 (Nordam 3)	23007/948	ex PK-MBZ	
☐ PK-YSC	Boeing 737-228 (Nordam 3)	23004/941	ex PK-MBY	
☐ PK-YSD	Boeing 737-217 (AvAero 3)	22260/784	ex PK-MBQ	[CGK]

TRI-MG INTRA-ASIA AIRLINES — Trilines (GM/TMG) — Jakarta-Halim (HLP)

☐ PK-YGG	Boeing 737-301SF	23743/1510	ex N433RC		
☐ PK-YGH	Boeing 737-36MSF	28567/2971	ex N558MS		wfs♦
☐ PK-YGJ	Cessna T206H Turbo Stationair	T20608220	ex N206F		
☐ PK-YGP	Boeing 737-210C (Nordam 3)	21822/605	ex 9M-NEA	Galactico	
☐ PK-YGR	Boeing 727-223F (FedEx 3)	20993/1189	ex N117JB	Zenith	
☐ PK-YGZ	Boeing 727-31F (FedEx 3)	20112/700	ex OO-DHO	Noble Witness	

UNINDO AIRCHARTER

☐ PK-UAD	Bell 206L-4 LongRanger IV	52076	ex N8AY	

WINGS ABADI AIR — Wings Abadi (IW/WON) — Jakarta-Soekarno Hatta (CGK)

☐ PK-WFF	ATR 72-212A	869	ex F-WWET	
☐ PK-WFG	ATR 72-212A	882	ex F-WWEL	
☐ PK-WFH	ATR 72-212A	883	ex F-WWEM	
☐ PK-WFI	ATR 72-212A	871	ex F-WWEV	
☐ PK-WFJ	ATR 72-212A	898	ex F-WWEI	
☐ PK-WFK	ATR 72-212A	905	ex F-WWEV	
☐ PK-WFL	ATR 72-212A	915	ex F-WWEM	
☐ PK-WFM	ATR 72-212A	922	ex F-WWEV	
☐ PK-WFO	ATR 72-212A	936	ex F-WWEL	
☐ PK-WFP	ATR 72-212A	937	ex F-WWEM	
☐ PK-WFQ	ATR 72-212A	943	ex F-WWES	
☐ PK-WFR	ATR 72-212A	946	ex F-WWEW	

☐ PK-WFS	ATR 72-212A	957	ex F-WWEJ	
☐ PK-WFT	ATR 72-212A	961	ex F-WWEN	
☐ PK-WFU	ATR 72-212A	964	ex F-WWEQ	
☐ PK-WFV	ATR 72-212A	985	ex F-WWEF	
☐ PK-WFW	ATR 72-212A	1024	ex F-WWEK	
☐ PK-WFY	ATR 72-212A	1048	ex F-WWEU	
☐ PK-WFZ	ATR 72-212A	1055	ex F-WWEX	
☐ PK-WGF	ATR 72-212A	1062	ex F-WWEM	
☐ PK-WGG	ATR 72-600	1063	ex F-WWEX	
☐ PK-WGH	ATR 72-600	1067	ex F-WWED	
☐ PK-WGI	ATR 72-600	1074	ex F-WWEK	
☐ PK-WGJ	ATR 72-600	1079	ex F-WWEP	
☐ PK-WGK	ATR 72-600	1106	ex F-WWES	
☐ PK-WGL	ATR 72-600	1118	ex F-WWEG	
☐ PK-WGM	ATR 72-600	1168	ex F-WWEI	◆
☐ PK-WGO	ATR 72-600	1104	ex F-WWEQ Lion Wings titles	
☐ PK-WGP	ATR 72-600	1176	ex F-WWEQ	◆
☐ PK-WGQ	ATR 72-600	1188	ex F-WWEE	◆
☐ PK-WGR	ATR 72-600	1193	ex F-WWEJ	◆
☐ PK-WGS	ATR 72-600	1134	ex HS-LFH	◆
☐ PK-WGT	ATR 72-600	1220	ex F-WWES	◆
☐ PK-WGU	ATR 72-600	1225	ex F-WWEX	◆
☐ PK-WGV	ATR 72-600	1227	ex F-WWEB	◆
☐ PK-WCW	ATR 72-600	1234	ex F-WWEI	◆
☐ PK-WGY	ATR 72-600	1238	ex F-WWEM	◆
☐ PK-WGZ	ATR 72-600	1244	ex F-WWET	◆
☐ PK-WHF	ATR 72-600	1247	ex F-WWEW	◆
☐ PK-WHG	ATR 72-600	1250	ex F-WWEB	o/o◆
☐ PK-WHH	ATR 72-600	1256	ex F-WWEH	o/o◆
☐ PK-	ATR 72-600	1263	ex F-WW	o/o◆
☐ PK-WIF	McDonnell-Douglas MD-82	49481/1308	ex N72821	[CGK]
☐ PK-WIH	McDonnell-Douglas MD-82	49582/1411	ex N57837	wfs
☐ PK-WII	McDonnell-Douglas MD-82	49263/1163	ex PK-LMI	[SUB]
☐ PK-WIO	McDonnell-Douglas MD-82	49102/1076	ex PK-LMQ	[CGK]
☐ PK-WIY	McDonnell-Douglas MD-82	49250/1186	ex PK-LMY	wfs
☐ PK-WID	de Havilland DHC-8-301	116	ex N116TY	
☐ PK-WIE	de Havilland DHC-8-301	108	ex N108TY	

PP-, PR-, PT- BRAZIL (Federative Republic of Brazil)

ABAETE LINHAS AEREAS/ATA (ABJ) Salvador, BA (SSA)

☐ PT-OGK	Cessna 208A Caravan I	20800078	ex N65575
☐ PT-OGR	Cessna 208A Caravan I	20800100	ex N838FE
☐ PT-OGS	Cessna 208A Caravan I	20800034	ex N811FE
☐ PT-OGT	Cessna 208A Caravan I	20800038	ex N815FE
☐ PT-OGU	Cessna 208A Caravan I	20800066	ex N826FE
☐ PP-ATT	Cessna 402B	402B0631	ex N3786C
☐ PT-GKO	Embraer EMB.110E Bandeirante	110119	
☐ PT-JBD	Cessna 402B	402B0404	
☐ PT-JTZ	Cessna 402B	402B0532	
☐ PT-LKZ	Cessna 402B	402B1074	ex N1554G
☐ PT-MCA	Embraer EMB.121A1 Xingu	121058	
☐ PT-MFO	Embraer EMB.110C Bandeirante	110058	ex FAB2158
☐ PT-MFQ	Embraer EMB.110C Bandeirante	110121	ex FAB2188
☐ PT-MFS	Embraer EMB.110C Bandeirante	110054	ex FAB2160
☐ PT-RGV	Embraer EMB.821 Caraja	820136	ex PT-ZNA
☐ PT-VCH	Embraer EMB.821 Caraja	821012	
☐ PT-VKD	Embraer EMB.821 Caraja	820159	

AERO RIO TAXI AEREO Rio de Janeiro, RJ

☐ PR-GJR	Bell 429	57189	ex C-GZES	◆
☐ PR-RJZ	Cessna 208B Caravan I	208B2131	ex (VH-NQB)	
☐ PR-ROZ	Dassault Falcon 900EX EASy	235	ex N235FJ	
☐ PR-WZR	Cessna 208BEX Caravan I	208B5135		◆

AEROLEO TAXI AERO Rio de Janeiro-Santos Dumont, RJ/Macae & Sao Tome, RJ (SDU/MEA)

☐ PR-EDA	Sikorsky S-76A	760279	ex N710AL	<ALG
☐ PR-GPC	Sikorsky S-76A	760266	ex N703AL	<ALG
☐ PR-LBA	Sikorsky S-76C+	760705	ex N2584Q	<ALG
☐ PR-LCT	Sikorsky S-76C+	760723	ex N723Y	<ALG
☐ PR-LCV	Sikorsky S-76C+	760672	ex N4508N	<ALG
☐ PR-LCX	Sikorsky S-76C+	760704	ex N231Y	<ALG
☐ PR-LCZ	Sikorsky S-76C+	760707	ex N415Y	<ALG
☐ PR-LDA	Sikorsky S-76C+	760756	ex N756N	<ALG

☐ PR-LDB	Sikorsky S-76C+	760759	ex N759L	<ALG
☐ PR-LDC	Sikorsky S-76C+	760783		
☐ PR-LDE	Sikorsky S-76C+	760784		
☐ PR-LDG	Sikorsky S-76C+	760785		
☐ PR-LDH	Sikorsky S-76C+	760777	ex N777LQ	
☐ PR-LDJ	Sikorsky S-76C	760530	ex N22CP	
☐ PR-LDK	Sikorsky S-76C	760608	ex N176PG	
☐ PR-LDN	Sikorsky S-76C++	760654	ex G-CEOR	
☐ PR-LDP	Sikorsky S-76C	760534	ex N115PD	
☐ PR-LDQ	Sikorsky S-76C++	760718	ex VH-TZK	
☐ PR-LDT	Sikorsky S-76C+	760553	ex N767LL	
☐ PR-LDV	Sikorsky S-76C++	760768	ex G-CGRK	
☐ PR-LDW	Sikorsky S-76C++	760744	ex G-CFFZ	
☐ PR-LDX	Sikorsky S-76C++	760818	ex N818V	
☐ PR-LDZ	Sikorsky S-76C++	760803	ex G-CGVW	
☐ PR-LEA	Sikorsky S-76C-2	760804	ex 9Y-HWO	♦
☐ PR-LEC	Sikorsky S-76C	760505	ex N932FF	
☐ PR-NLF	Sikorsky S-76A	760085	ex N1547K	<ALG
☐ PT-HOR	Sikorsky S-76A	760003	ex N476AL	<ALG
☐ PT-YAY	Sikorsky S-76A	760277	ex N708AL	<ALG
☐ PT-YAZ	Sikorsky S-76A	760227	ex N422AL	♦
☐ PR-JAA	Sikorsky S-92A	920099	ex N2059J	
☐ PR-JAW	Sikorsky S-92A	920163	ex N163L	
☐ PR-JAR	Sikorsky S092A	920154	ex N2198J	♦
☐ PR-JBE	Sikorsky S-92A	920170	ex N970P	♦
☐ PR-JBH	Sikorsky S-92A	920159	ex N159Y	
☐ PR-JBI	Sikorsky S-92A	920179	ex N179P	
☐ PR-JBK	Sikorsky S-92A	920191	ex N191Q	♦
☐ PR-JBO	Sikorsky S-92A	920192	ex N192K	
☐ PR-JBP	Sikorsky S-92A	920236	ex N236Z	♦
☐ PR-JBQ	Sikorsky S-92A	920239	ex N239Q	♦

ALGAR AVIATION TAXI AEREO — Uberlandia

☐ PP-ECC	Daher Scotata TAM-700N	1040	ex N900BX	♦
☐ PR-ATA	Cessna 208B Caravan I	208B0880		♦
☐ PT-TIC	Piaggio P.180 Avanti	1217		

ALP AEREO TAXI

☐ PR-VCI	Cessna 208B Caravan I	208B2034	♦

AMERICA DO SUL TAXI AEREO – ASTA — Astair (SUL)

☐ PP-OSP	Cessna 208B Caravan I	208B2236	ex N5296X

AMAZONAVES TAXI AEREO — Tefe/Manaus, AM (-/MAO)

☐ PP-AMV	Cessna 208B Caravan I	208B2179	ex N5036Q	
☐ PP-AMX	Cessna 208B Caravan I	208B2267	ex N50549	
☐ PP-ITZ	Cessna 208B Caravan I	208B0499	ex N5188N	
☐ PT-FLW	Cessna 208B Caravan I	208B0451	ex N1213Z	
☐ PT-MET	Cessna 208B Caravan I	208B0509	ex N5073G	
☐ PT-EUS	Embraer EMB.810C Seneca	810230		opb Tio Taxi Aereo
☐ PT-OLJ	Embraer EMB.810C Seneca	810330		
☐ PT-SHU	Embraer EMB.110P1A Bandeirante	110466		

APUI TAXI AEREO — Manaus-Ponta Pelada, AM (PLL)

☐ PT-GKX	Embraer EMB.110P Bandeirante	110129	
☐ PT-ODY	Embraer EMB.110 Bandeirante	110039	ex FAB 2147

ATLAS AIR

☐ PR-BRU	Mil Mi-171A1	171A0100761053..U	opf Petrobras
☐ PR-RUS	Mil Mi-171A1	171A010076105304U	opf Petrobras

AVIANCA BRAZIL — Oceanair (O6/ONE) — Rio de Janeiro-Santos Dumont, RJ (SDU)

☐ PR-AVH	Airbus A318-121	3001	ex CC-CVA
☐ PR-AVJ	Airbus A318-121	3030	ex CC-CVB
☐ PR-AVK	Airbus A318-121	3062	ex CC-CVF
☐ PR-AVL	Airbus A318-121	3214	ex CC-CVH
☐ PR-AVO	Airbus A318-121	3216	ex CC-CVN
☐ PR-ONC	Airbus A318-121	3371	ex CC-CVP
☐ PR-OND	Airbus A318-121	3390	ex CC-CVR
☐ PR-ONG	Airbus A318-121	3438	ex CC-CVS
☐ PR-ONH	Airbus A318-121	3469	ex CC-CVU
☐ PR-ONI	Airbus A318-121	3509	ex CC-CVV

☐ PR-ONM	Airbus A318-121	3585	ex CC-CZJ		
☐ PR-ONO	Airbus A318-121	3602	ex CC-CZN		
☐ PR-ONP	Airbus A318-121	3606	ex CC-CZQ		
☐ PR-ONQ	Airbus A318-121	3635	ex CC-CZR		
☐ PR-ONR	Airbus A318-121	3642	ex CC-CZS		
☐ PR-AVP	Airbus A320-214	4891	ex F-WWIS		
☐ PR-AVQ	Airbus A320-214	4913	ex F-WWDA		
☐ PR-AVR	Airbus A320-214	4941	ex D-AXAP		
☐ PR-AVU	Airbus A320-214	4942	ex F-WWBV		
☐ PR-OCA	Airbus A320-214/S	6125	ex F-WWDY		♦
☐ PR-OCB	Airbus A320-214/S	6139	ex F-WWIS		♦
☐ PR-OCD	Airbus A320-214/S	6173	ex F-WWBS		♦
☐ PR-OCH	Airbus A320-214/S	6528	ex D-AVVD		♦
☐ PR-OCI	Airbus A320-214/S	6536	ex D-AVVE		♦
☐ PR-OCM	Airbus A320-214/S	6561	ex F-WWBT		♦
☐ PR-OCN	Airbus A320-214/S	6598	ex D-AVVQ		o/o♦
☐ PR-ONK	Airbus A320-214	5278	ex F-WWBB		
☐ PR-ONL	Airbus A320-214	5299	ex D-AXAR		
☐ PR-ONS	Airbus A320-214	5754	ex F-WWIB		
☐ PR-ONT	Airbus A320-214	5841	ex F-WWIM		
☐ PR-ONW	Airbus A320-214/S	6050	ex D-AXAG		
☐ PR-ONX	Airbus A320-214/S	6057	ex D-AXAI		
☐ PR-ONY	Airbus A320-214/S	6103	ex F-WWIE		♦
☐ PR-ONZ	Airbus A320-214/S	6110	ex F-WWIU		♦
☐ PR-	Airbus A320-214/S	6634	ex		o/o♦
☐ PR-	Airbus A320-214/S	6651	ex		o/o♦
☐ PR-	Airbus A320-214/S	6689	ex		o/o♦
☐ PR-	Airbus A320-214/S	6856	ex		o/o♦
☐ PR-	Airbus A320-214/S	6871	ex		o/o♦
☐ PR-OCF	Airbus A330-243	1586	ex F-WWKZ		wfs♦
☐ PR-OCL	Airbus A330-243	1540	ex F-WXAJ		wfs♦
☐ PR-ONV	Airbus A330-243F	1506	ex F-WWKF		
☐ PR-	Airbus A330-243	1608	ex F-WWCU		o/o
☐ PR-	Airbus A330-243	1657	ex F-WW		o/o♦
☐ PR-OAD	Fokker 100	11370	ex N1412A		
☐ PR-OAE	Fokker 100	11426	ex N1436A		
☐ PR-OAF	Fokker 100	11415	ex N1430D		dam 28Mar14
☐ PR-OAG	Fokker 100	11412	ex N1427A		
☐ PR-OAI	Fokker 100	11417	ex N1432A		
☐ PR-OAJ	Fokker 100	11418	ex N1433B		
☐ PR-OAK	Fokker 100	11425	ex N1435D		
☐ PR-OAL	Fokker 100	11435	ex N1440A		
☐ PR-OAM	Fokker 100	11436	ex N1441A		
☐ PR-OAQ	Fokker 100	11467	ex N1455K		
☐ PR-OAR	Fokker 100	11481	ex N1461C		
☐ PR-OAS	Fokker 100	11405	ex N1422J		[CGH]
☐ PR-OAT	Fokker 100	11411	ex N1426A		
☐ PR-OAU	Fokker 100	11427	ex N1437B		
☐ PR-AVB	Airbus A319-115	4222	ex D-AVYJ		
☐ PR-AVC	Airbus A319-115	4287	ex D-AVWT		
☐ PR-AVD	Airbus A319-115	4336	ex D-AVXG		
☐ PR-OAN	Embraer EMB.120RT Brasilia	120051	ex N237AS		wfs
☐ PR-ONJ	Airbus A319-115	5193	ex D-AVYT		

AZUL   Azul (AD/AZU)   Sao Paulo-Viracopos, SP (VCP)

☐ PR-AIV	Airbus A330-243	532	ex A9C-KI	Nação Azul	Brazilian Flag c/s♦
☐ PR-AIW	Airbus A330-243	462	ex 2-LYSE	Welcome to Azul	♦
☐ PR-AIX	Airbus A330-243	372	ex VH-XFB	I ♥ Azul	♦
☐ PR-AIY	Airbus A330-243	494	ex EI-EYO	Don't Worry, Be Azul	♦
☐ PR-AIZ	Airbus A330-243	527	ex EI-FEL	América Azul	♦
☐ PR-	Airbus A330-243	529	ex TC-JNV		o/o♦
☐ PP-PTV	ATR 42-500	503	ex F-WNUA		♦
☐ PP-PTW	ATR 42-500	510	ex F-WNUB		♦
☐ PR-TKC	ATR 42-500	609	ex I-ADLU		♦
☐ PR-TKD	ATR 42-500	604	ex I-ADLP		♦
☐ PR-TKE	ATR 42-500	556	ex F-WKVC		♦
☐ PR-TKF	ATR 42-500	579	ex F-OIJB		♦
☐ PR-TTK	ATR 42-500	504	ex F-WQNK		♦
☐ PP-PTM	ATR 72-212A	798	ex F-WWEO		wfs♦
☐ PP-PTN	ATR 72-212A	832	ex F-WWEI		♦
☐ PP-PTO	ATR 72-212A	837	ex Г-WWEO		♦
☐ PP-PTR	ATR 72-212A	785	ex F-WWED		♦
☐ PP-PTT	ATR 72-212A	846	ex F-WWEL		♦
☐ PP-PTU	ATR 72-212A	891	ex F-WWEW	Tudo Azul	♦
☐ PP-PTX	ATR 72-212A	666	ex F-WKVE		♦
☐ PP-PTY	ATR 72-212A	911	ex F-WWEE		♦

☐	PP-PTZ	ATR 72-212A	918	ex F-WWEP		♦
☐	PR-TKA	ATR 72-212A	926	ex F-WWEB		♦
☐	PR-TKN	ATR 72-212A	580	ex EC-HCG		♦
☐	PR-AKA	ATR 72-600	1245	ex F-WWEU	É Azul uai	♦
☐	PR-AKB	ATR 72-600	1253	ex F-WWEE		o/o♦
☐	PR-AQA	ATR 72-600	1052	ex F-WWEK	Para sempre Azul	
☐	PR-AQB	ATR 72-600	1054	ex F-WWEP	Azul blanc et rouge	
☐	PR-AQC	ATR 72-600	1057	ex F-WWER	Azzurro	
☐	PR-AQD	ATR 72-600	1060	ex F-WWEU	Azulissimo	
☐	PR-AQE	ATR 72-600	1066	ex F-WWEC	100% Azul	
☐	PR-AQF	ATR 72-600	1072	ex F-WWEI	Bonito e Azul	
☐	PR-AQG	ATR 72-600	1076	ex F-WWEM	Falcão Azul	
☐	PR-AQH	ATR 72-600	1082	ex F-WWES	Infinito Azul	
☐	PR-AQI	ATR 72-600	1088	ex F-WWEZ	É Azul, É Azul	
☐	PR-AQJ	ATR 72-600	1094	ex F-WWEG	Alma Azul	
☐	PR-AQK	ATR 72-600	1100	ex F-WWEM	Azul Fever	
☐	PR-AQL	ATR 72-600	1102	ex F-WWEO	Dia Lindo, Dia Azul	
☐	PR-AQM	ATR 72-600	1113	ex F-WWEB	Pantanal Azul	
☐	PR-AQN	ATR 72-600	1115	ex F-WWED	Azulmania	
☐	PR-AQO	ATR 72-600	1138	ex F-WWEI	Vamos de Azul	
☐	PR-AQP	ATR 72-600	1144	ex F-WWEI	Guerreiro Azul	
☐	PR-AQQ	ATR 72-600	1166	ex F-WWEG	Eu Sempre Sonhei Azul	♦
☐	PR-AQR	ATR 72-600	1173	ex F-WWEN	Se você fosse uma cor, seria o Azul	♦
☐	PR-AQS	ATR 72-600	1180	ex F-WWEU	Lindo voo Azul	♦
☐	PR-AQT	ATR 72-600	1190	ex F-WWEG	Lua Azul	♦
☐	PR-AQV	ATR 72-600	1195	ex F-WWEL	Gralha Azul	♦
☐	PR-AQW	ATR 72-600	1232	ex F-WWEG	Com você tudo fica Azul	♦
☐	PR-AQX	ATR 72-600	1233	ex F-WWEH	Je suis Azul	♦
☐	PR-AQZ	ATR 72-600	1241	ex F-WWEQ	Azul, asas do Brasil	♦
☐	PR-AQY	ATR 72-600	1236	ex F-WWEK	Orgulho de ser Azul	♦
☐	PR-ATB	ATR 72-600	969	ex F-WWLT	La Ville Rose	
☐	PR-ATE	ATR 72-600	972	ex F-WWLW	Alfa Zulu Uniform Lima	
☐	PR-ATG	ATR 72-600	988	ex F-WWLO	Planeta Azul	
☐	PR-ATH	ATR 72-600	991	ex F-WWLQ	Meu Coração é Azul	
☐	PR-ATJ	ATR 72-600	996	ex F-WWLU	Viva Azul !	
☐	PR-ATK	ATR 72-600	1020	ex F-WWLN	Azul Viagens	
☐	PR-ATP	ATR 72-600	1026	ex F-WWLS	Uma vez Azul, sempre Azul	
☐	PR-ATQ	ATR 72-600	1027	ex F-WWLT	O Nordeste é Azul	
☐	PR-ATR	ATR 72-600	966	ex F-WWLQ	Azul Tango Romeo	
☐	PR-ATU	ATR 72-600	1033	ex F-WWER	Azul Anil	
☐	PR-ATV	ATR 72-600	1043	ex F-WWEF	Magia Azul	
☐	PR-ATW	ATR 72-600	1046	ex F-WWEI	Horizonte Azul	
☐	PR-ATZ	ATR 72-600	1047	ex F-WWEL	Imensidão Azul	
☐	PR-TKI	ATR 72-600	967	ex F-WKVB		♦
☐	PR-TKJ	ATR 72-600	971	ex F-WWLV		♦
☐	PR-TKK	ATR 72-600	987	ex F-WWLN		♦
☐	PR-TKL	ATR 72-600	992	ex F-WWLR		♦
☐	PR-TKM	ATR 72-600	998	ex F-WWLW		♦
☐	PR-	ATR 72-600	1270	ex F-WW		o/o♦
☐	PP-PJA	Embraer ERJ-175LR	17000272	ex PT-SNF	Azul dos Pampas	[POA]♦
☐	PP-PJB	Embraer ERJ-175LR	17000277	ex PT-TQD		[POA]♦
☐	PP-PJC	Embraer ERJ-175LR	17000287	ex PT-TQN		[POA]♦
☐	PP-PJE	Embraer ERJ-175LR	17000291			[POA]♦
☐	PP-PJF	Embraer ERJ-175LR	17000309			[POA]♦
☐	PP-PJJ	Embraer ERJ-190LR	19000163	ex HB-JQE		♦
☐	PP-PJK	Embraer ERJ-190LR	19000178	ex HB-JQF		♦
☐	PP-PJL	Embraer ERJ-190LR	19000189	ex HB-JQG		♦
☐	PP-PJM	Embraer ERJ-190LR	19000432		Seu' Antonio	♦
☐	PP-PJN	Embraer ERJ-190LR	19000441		Madiba Azul	♦
☐	PP-PJO	Embraer ERJ-190LR	19000450			♦
☐	PP-PJP	Embraer ERJ-190LR	19000460			♦
☐	PP-PJQ	Embraer ERJ-190LR	19000493		Brasileirissimo Luciano do Valle	♦
☐	PP-PJR	Embraer ERJ-190LR	19000495			♦
☐	PP-PJT	Embraer ERJ-190LR	19000506			♦
☐	PP-PJU	Embraer ERJ-190LR	19000541			♦
☐	PP-PJV	Embraer ERJ-190LR	19000550		Daniela Mercury é Azul	♦
☐	PR-AZA	Embraer ERJ-190AR	19000150	ex N290JB	Azulville	
☐	PR-AZB	Embraer ERJ-190AR	19000241	ex N840JE	Azul Paulista	
☐	PR-AZC	Embraer ERJ-190AR	19000242	ex N841JS	Ceu Azul	
☐	PR-AZD	Embraer ERJ-190AR	19000271	ex PT-TLL	Passaro Azul	
☐	PR-AZE	Embraer ERJ-190AR	19000282	ex PT-TLW	Verda, Amarelo e Azul	
☐	PR-AZF	Embraer ERJ-190AR	19000295		Voce que e Feito de Azul	
☐	PR-AZG	Embraer ERJ-190AR	19000329		A Terra e Azul	
☐	PR-AZH	Embraer ERJ-190AR	19000330		Azulcenter	
☐	PR-AZI	Embraer ERJ-190AR	19000336		Adorinha Azul	
☐	PR-AZL	Embraer ERJ-190AR	19000147	ex N288JB	O Rio de Janeiro continua Azul	
☐	PR-AUA	Embraer ERJ-195AR	19000652		Canarinho Azul	
☐	PR-AUB	Embraer ERJ-195AR	19000660		Anjo Azul	
☐	PR-AUC	Embraer ERJ-195AR	19000662		Fernando de Noronha é Azul	

☐ PR-AUD	Embraer ERJ-195AR	19000669		Azulzinho	
☐ PR-AUE	Embraer ERJ-195AR	19000677		Azultec	♦
☐ PR-AUF	Embraer ERJ-195AR	19000678		Incrivelmente Azul	♦
☐ PR-AUH	Embraer ERJ-195AR	19000685		Ozires Silva	♦
☐ PR-AUI	Embraer ERJ-195AR	19000686		Ada Rogato Pioneria Zaul	♦
☐ PR-AUJ	Embraer ERJ-195AR	19000688		Cmte Omar Fontana-Pioneiro da Aviação	♦
☐ PR-AXA	Embraer ERJ-195AR	19000491		Azul Safira	
☐ PR-AXB	Embraer ERJ-195AR	19000498		Céu Azul de Brasilia	
☐ PR-AXC	Embraer ERJ-195AR	19000510		Azul Tropical	
☐ PR-AXD	Embraer ERJ-195AR	19000514		Azulão	
☐ PR-AXE	Embraer ERJ-195AR	19000521		Axé Azul	
☐ PR-AXF	Embraer ERJ-195AR	19000530		Azul acima de Tude	
☐ PR-AXG	Embraer ERJ-195AR	19000540		Trovão Azul	
☐ PR-AXH	Embraer ERJ-195AR	19000569		Verão Azul	50 Cities c/s
☐ PR-AXN	Embraer ERJ-195AR	19000590		Dias Azuis	
☐ PR-AXI	Embraer ERJ-195AR	19000575		Piloto Azul	
☐ PR-AXJ	Embraer ERJ-195AR	19000580		O Sol é Azul	
☐ PR-AXK	Embraer ERJ-195AR	19000585		Águia Branca	
☐ PR-AXL	Embraer ERJ-195AR	19000588		Flecha Azul	
☐ PR-AXO	Embraer ERJ-195AR	19000592		Simplesmente Azul	
☐ PR-AXP	Embraer ERJ-195AR	19000600		Coração Azul	
☐ PR-AXQ	Embraer ERJ-195AR	19000609		João Bosco é Azul	
☐ PR-AXR	Embraer ERJ-195AR	19000615		Agente de Aeroporto Azul	
☐ PR-AXS	Embraer ERJ-195AR	19000620		Espirito Azul	
☐ PR-AXT	Embraer ERJ-195AR	19000621		Sangue Azul	
☐ PR-AXU	Embraer ERJ-195AR	19000626		Azul Bossa Nova	
☐ PR-AXV	Embraer ERJ-195AR	19000628		Espirito de União	
☐ PR-AXW	Embraer ERJ-195AR	19000638		Nas Asas Azuis de Milton Nascimento	
☐ PR-AXX	Embraer ERJ-195AR	19000647		Estrela Azul	
☐ PR-AXY	Embraer ERJ-195AR	19000648		Azul de Norte a Sul	
☐ PR-AXZ	Embraer ERJ-195AR	19000650		Céu Azul de Brigadeiro	
☐ PR-AYA	Embraer ERJ-195AR	19000237	ex PT-SIK	Azul e Brasil	
☐ PR-AYB	Embraer ERJ-195AR	19000239		Tudo Azul	
☐ PR-AYC	Embraer ERJ-195AR	19000240		A Liberdade e Azul	
☐ PR-AYD	Embraer ERJ-195AR	19000247		Azalou	
☐ PR-AYE	Embraer ERJ-195AR	19000260	ex PT-STI	Azul do Cor da Mar	
☐ PR-AYF	Embraer ERJ-195AR	19000353		Tripulante Azul	
☐ PR-AYG	Embraer ERJ-195AR	19000356		Tudo Novo, Tudo Azul	
☐ PR-AYH	Embraer ERJ-195AR	19000361		Céu, Sol, Sul, Azul	
☐ PR-AYI	Embraer ERJ-195AR	19000366		Azul Celeste	
☐ PR-AYJ	Embraer ERJ-195AR	19000370		Azul Real	
☐ PR-AYK	Embraer ERJ-195AR	19000374		Diamante Azul	
☐ PR-AYL	Embraer ERJ-195AR	19000378		Amazonia Azul	
☐ PR-AYM	Embraer ERJ-195AR	19000382		Cada Vez mais Azul	
☐ PR-AYN	Embraer ERJ-195AR	19000386		Blue Angels	
☐ PR-AYO	Embraer ERJ-195AR	19000391		Rosa e Azul	
☐ PR-AYP	Embraer ERJ-195AR	19000396		Arara Azul	
☐ PR-AYQ	Embraer ERJ-195AR	19000407			
☐ PR-AYR	Embraer ERJ-195AR	19000413			
☐ PR-AYS	Embraer ERJ-195AR	19000419			
☐ PR-AYT	Embraer ERJ-195AR	19000429			
☐ PR-AYU	Embraer ERJ-195AR	19000434		#sennasempre	
☐ PR-AYV	Embraer ERJ-195AR	19000449			
☐ PR-AYW	Embraer ERJ-195AR	19000458		Vento Azul	
☐ PR-AYX	Embraer ERJ-195AR	19000471		Azul e Verde	
☐ PR-AYY	Embraer ERJ-195AR	19000475		Sorriso Azul	
☐ PR-AYZ	Embraer ERJ-195AR	19000484		Azul de A a Z	
☐ PP-PTF	ATR 42-300	072	ex LV-ZNV		wfs
☐ PP-PTI	ATR 42-320	374	ex F-WQNP		
☐ PR-TTF	ATR 42-300	021	ex F-WQNS		<TTL

BHS - BRAZILIAN HELICOPTER SERVICES
Sao Paulo-Marte, SP, Farol de Sao Tome, SP, Macae & Sao Tome, RJ

☐ PR-BGA	Eurocopter EC225LP	2773	ex G-LCAS	
☐ PR-BGH	Eurocopter EC225LP	2798	ex C-GLIS	
☐ PR-BGK	Eurocopter EC225LP	2801	ex C-GMJI	
☐ PR-BGL	Eurocopter EC225LP	2822	ex G-JSKN	
☐ PR-BGR	Eurocopter EC225LP	2899	ex G-HALI	♦
☐ PR-CHW	Eurocopter EC225LP	2740	ex G-DRIT	
☐ PR-CHX	Eurocopter EC225LP	2729	ex G-CLAR	
☐ PR-CHY	Eurocopter EC225LP	2722	ex G-LJAM	
☐ PR-PLL	Eurocopter EC225LP	2680	ex N225EH	
☐ PR-VLL	Eurocopter EC225LP	2685	ex N247CF	
☐ PR-YCL	Eurocopter EC225LP2	2708	ex LN-OHY	
☐ PP-MEM	Sikorsky S-76A+	760092	ex N176PA	
☐ PP-MET	Sikorsky S-76A	760229	ex N31217	
☐ PP-MPM	Sikorsky S-76C	760375	ex N775AB	
☐ PR-BGC	Sikorsky S-76-2	760601	ex C-GGIU	
☐ PR-BGD	Sikorsky S-76C+	760568	ex C-GHRY	

☐ PR-BGE	Sikorsky S-76C+	760546	ex C-FCHC	
☐ PR-BGG	Sikorsky S-76C+	760602	ex C-FGDO	
☐ PR-BGI	Sikorsky S-76C+	760537	ex C-GEJL	
☐ PR-BGJ	Sikorsky S-76C+	760570	ex C-GHRW	
☐ PR-BGO	Sikorsky S-76C+	760603	ex C-GHRI	
☐ PR-BGP	Sikorsky S-76C+	760596	ex C-GARC	
☐ PR-BGQ	Sikorsky S-76C	760598	ex C-GOLH	<CHC Helicopters Intl
☐ PR-CHA	Sikorsky S-76C++	760625	ex C-GBQE	
☐ PR-CHB	Sikorsky S-76A++	760004	ex C-GIME	
☐ PR-CHC	Sikorsky S-76C++	760632	ex C-GBQF	
☐ PR-CHD	Sikorsky S-76C++	760636	ex C-GBQG	
☐ PR-CHE	Sikorsky S-76C++	760642	ex C-GBQH	
☐ PR-CHG	Sikorsky S-76C++	760658		♦
☐ PR-CHI	Sikorsky S-76CH	760670	ex N4514K	♦
☐ PR-CHJ	Sikorsky S-76CH	760674	ex N4513G	♦
☐ PR-CHL	Sikorsky S-76A++	760160	ex D2-EXF	♦
☐ PR-CHM	Sikorsky S-76C-2	760711	ex C-FWOX	♦
☐ PR-CHO	Sikorsky S-76C++	760657	ex PR-CHF	♦
☐ PR-CHP	Sikorsky S-76C++	760743	ex C-FYDD	
☐ PR-CHQ	Sikorsky S-76C++	760734	ex C-FXFK	
☐ PT-YGM	Sikorsky S-76A	760067	ex ZS-RJK	<CHC Helicopters Africa
☐ PT-YIM	Sikorsky S-76A	760144	ex XA-SRS	
☐ PT-YQM	Sikorsky S-76A	760051	ex ZS-RGZ	<CHC Helicopters Africa
☐ PR-BGB	Sikorsky S-92A	920141	ex C-GJMY	
☐ PR-BGM	Sikorsky S-92A	920153	ex C-GNUA	
☐ PR-BGN	Sikorsky S-92A	920152	ex G-WNSA	
☐ PR-BGT	Sikorsky S-92A	920183	ex C-GUQI	
☐ PR-CHR	Sikorsky S-92A	920112	ex C-FRWL	
☐ PR-CHS	Sikorsky S-92A	920113	ex C-FPKW	
☐ PR-CHT	Sikorsky S-92A	920119	ex C-GDHU	
☐ PR-CHU	Sikorsky S-92A	920127	ex C-GFHO	
☐ PR-BGF	Eurocopter EC120B Colibri	1181		♦
☐ PR-BGS	Agusta A109E Power	11621		♦
☐ PR-BGX	AgustaWestland AW139	31492	ex OY-HIM	♦
☐ PR-BGY	AgustaWestland AW139	31551		♦
☐ PR-BGZ	AgustaWestland AW139	31552	ex G-SNSD	♦
☐ PR-MEK	Aérospatiale SA365N Dauphin 2	6030	ex PH-SSX	

COLT TRANSPORTES AEREO		(XCA)		Sao Paulo-Congonhas, SP (CGH)
☐ PR-IOX	Boeing 737-4B6SF	26529/2584	ex N529TP	
☐ PR-IOY	Boeing 737-4B6SF	26526/2219	ex N526TP	

CTA – CLEITON TAXI AEREO				
☐ PR-ETA	Mitsubishi MU-2B-60 Marquise	1507SA	ex N308TC	
☐ PR-SLD	Cessna 208B Caravan I	208B1154		♦
☐ PR-VDB	Cessna 208BEX Caravan I	208B5146		♦
☐ PT-CQT	Cessna 208B Caravan I	208B0314	ex N1018X	♦

FLYWAYS LINHAS AÉREAS				Rio de Janeiro-Galeao, RJ (GIG)
☐ PR-TKN	ATR 72-212A	580	ex EC-HCG	o/o♦

FRETAX TAXI AEREO				
☐ PR-JOH	Cessna 208B Caravan I	208B0323	ex N465BA	
☐ PR-MSH	Cessna 208B Caravan I	208B0700	ex N700RH	

GOL TRANSPORTES AEREOS	Gol Transporte (G3/GLO)			Sao Paulo-Congonhas, SP (CGH)
☐ PR-GEA	Boeing 737-7EH/W	37595/3026		
☐ PR-GEC	Boeing 737-7EH/W	37608/3678		
☐ PR-GED	Boeing 737-7EH/W	37609/3799		
☐ PR-GEE	Boeing 737-73V/W	32415/1260	ex N243AW	
☐ PR-GEI	Boeing 737-76N/W	34758/2266	ex TC-JKI	o/o♦
☐ PR-GIF	Boeing 737-73S	29076/98	ex OY-MLY	
☐ PR-GIG	Boeing 737-73S	29077/104	ex OY-MLZ	
☐ PR-GIH	Boeing 737-76N/W	32743/1503	ex N750AL	
☐ PR-GII	Boeing 737-7L9	28011/1203	ex OY-MRL	
☐ PR-GIJ	Boeing 737-7L9	28012/1092	ex OY-MRK	
☐ PR-GIM	Boeing 737-73V	30238/913	ex G-EZJE	
☐ PR-GIN	Boeing 737-73V	30242/690	ex G-EZJD	
☐ PR-GOG	Boeing 737-76Q	30275/900	ex N795BA	
☐ PR-GOH	Boeing 737-76N	32440/954	ex N1786B	
☐ PR-GOI	Boeing 737-76N	32574/983	ex N1786B	
☐ PR-GOM	Boeing 737-76N	28613/463	ex N312ML	
☐ PR-GON	Boeing 737-76N	30051/436	ex N311ML	
☐ PR-GOR	Boeing 737-76N	33380/1231		
☐ PR-GOV	Boeing 737-76N	28580/135	ex N580HE	

□ PR-GOW	Boeing 737-76N	28584/170	ex N584SR			
□ PR-GOX	Boeing 737-7K9	28088/19	ex N100UN			
□ PR-GOY	Boeing 737-7K9	28089/25	ex N101UN			
□ PR-VBH	Boeing 737-73V	30239/944	ex N239CG			
□ PR-VBI	Boeing 737-73V	30246/1064	ex N346CL			
□ PR-VBO	Boeing 737-73V	30247/1066	ex G-EZJL			
□ PR-VBP	Boeing 737-7EA	32407/904	ex N160CK			♦
□ PR-VBU	Boeing 737-76N/W	29905/372	ex N746AL			♦
□ PR-VBV	Boeing 737-76N/W	30050/429	ex N748AL			♦
□ PR-VBW	Boeing 737-7BX	30739/758	ex 6V-AHO			
□ PR-VBX	Boeing 737-7BX	30738/716	ex 6V-AHN			
□ PR-GGA	Boeing 737-8EH/W	35063/2476	ex N1787B			
□ PR-GGB	Boeing 737-8EH/W	35064/2498				
□ PR-GGD	Boeing 737-8EH/W	34275/2588				
□ PR-GGE	Boeing 737-8EH/W	35824/2665	ex N1786B			
□ PR-GGF	Boeing 737-8EH/W	35826/2749				
□ PR-GGG	Boeing 737-8EH/W	36566/2809				
□ PR-GGH	Boeing 737-8EH/W	36147/2864	ex N1787B			
□ PR-GGJ	Boeing 737-8EH/W	35825/2786	ex N1796B			
□ PR-GGK	Boeing 737-8EH/W	35065/2561				
□ PR-GGL	Boeing 737-8EH/W	36148/2890				
□ PR-GGM	Boeing 737-8EH/W	36149/2920	ex N1786B			
□ PR-GGN	Boeing 737-8EH/W	35827/2991	ex N1781B			
□ PR-GGO	Boeing 737-8EH/W	35828/3025				
□ PR-GGP	Boeing 737-8EH/W	35829/3076	ex N1787B			
□ PR-GGQ	Boeing 737-8EH/W	37596/3103	ex N1786B			
□ PR-GGR	Boeing 737-8EH/W	36150/3106	ex N1787B			
□ PR-GGT	Boeing 737-8EH/W	35830/3115				
□ PR-GGU	Boeing 737-8EH/W	37597/3133				
□ PR-GGV	Boeing 737-8EH/W	37598/3136				
□ PR-GGW	Boeing 737-8EH/W	35831/3165	ex PH-GGW			
□ PR-GGX	Boeing 737-8EH/W	36596/3180	ex PH-GGX		>TRA	
□ PR-GGY	Boeing 737-8EH/W	37599/3191				
□ PR-GGZ	Boeing 737-8EH/W	37600/3205	ex PH-GGZ			
□ PR-GIT	Boeing 737-809	28403/117	ex TC-APM			♦
□ PR-GIU	Boeing 737-809	29103/129	ex TC-APZ			
□ PR-GIV	Boeing 737-86N/W	28578/89	ex VT-JNA			
□ PR-GIW	Boeing 737-86N/W	28575/91	ex VT-JNB			
□ PR-GOP	Boeing 737-8BK	30621/1194	ex N461LF	Victoria		
□ PR-GTA	Boeing 737-8EH/W	34474/1843	ex N6067U			
□ PR-GTB	Boeing 737-8EH/W	34475/2020				
□ PR-GTC	Boeing 737-8EH/W	34277/2028	ex N1786B			
□ PR-GTE	Boeing 737-8EH/W	34278/2052				
□ PR-GTF	Boeing 737-8EH/W	34279/2061				
□ PR-GTG	Boeing 737-8EH/W	34654/2075				
□ PR-GTH	Boeing 737-8EH/W	34655/2091				
□ PR-GTI	Boeing 737-8EH/W	34280/2100				
□ PR-GTJ	Boeing 737-8EH/W	34656/2110				
□ PR-GTK	Boeing 737-8EH/W	34281/2116				
□ PR-GTL	Boeing 737-8EH/W	34962/2215	ex N1786B			
□ PR-GTM	Boeing 737-8EH/W	34963/2240				
□ PR-GTN	Boeing 737-8EH/W	34267/2311				
□ PR-GTO	Boeing 737-8EH/W	34964/2332				
□ PR-GTP	Boeing 737-8EH/W	34965/2341				
□ PR-GTQ	Boeing 737-8EH/W	36146/2358				
□ PR-GTR	Boeing 737-8EH/W	34966/2367				
□ PR-GTT	Boeing 737-8EH/W	34268/2407				
□ PR-GTU	Boeing 737-8EH/W	34269/2412	ex N1786B			
□ PR-GTV	Boeing 737-8EH/W	34270/2420				
□ PR-GTY	Boeing 737-8EH/W	34273/2464				
□ PR-GTZ	Boeing 737-8EH/W	34274/2468	ex N1795B			
□ PR-GUA	Boeing 737-8EH/W	37601/3301	ex PH-GUA		>TRA	
□ PR-GUB	Boeing 737-8EH/W	35832/3309	ex PH-GUB		>TRA	
□ PR-GUC	Boeing 737-8EH/W	35835/3430	ex D-ASXL		>SXD	
□ PR-GUD	Boeing 737-8EH/W	35836/3466	ex D-ASXM		>SXD	
□ PR-GUE	Boeing 737-8EH/W	35837/3473			>SXD	
□ PR-GUF	Boeing 737-8EH/W	35838/3508	ex D-ASXN		>SXD	
□ PR-GUG	Boeing 737-8EH/W	35842/3639				
□ PR-GUH	Boeing 737-8EH/W	35843/3667	ex N17868			
□ PR-GUI	Boeing 737-8EH/W	35844/3722				
□ PR-GUJ	Boeing 737-8EH/W	35851/3745				
□ PR-GUK	Boeing 737-8EH/W	35852/3760				
□ PR-GUL	Boeing 737-8EH/W	35845/3785				
□ PR-GUM	Boeing 737-8EH/W	35846/3823				
□ PR-GUN	Boeing 737-8EH/W	37610/3912				
□ PR-GUO	Boeing 737-8EH/W	35850/4124				
□ PR-GUP	Boeing 737-8HX/W	38876/4114				
□ PR-GUQ	Boeing 737-8HX/W	39604/4160				
□ PR-GUR	Boeing 737-8HX/W	38877/4144				
□ PR-GUT	Boeing 737-8HX/W	38878/4203				
□ PR-GUU	Boeing 737-8EH/W	39607/4248				
□ PR-GUV	Boeing 737-8EH/W	39609/4283				

☐ PR-GUW	Boeing 737-8EH/W	39608/4291		
☐ PR-GUX	Boeing 737-8EH/W	39611/4319		
☐ PR-GUY	Boeing 737-8EH/W	39612/4329		
☐ PR-GUZ	Boeing 737-8EH/W	39613/4353		
☐ PR-GXA	Boeing 737-8EH/W	39614/4387		
☐ PR-GXB	Boeing 737-8EH/W	39615/4382	ex N1787B	
☐ PR-GXC	Boeing 737-8EH/W	39616/4432		
☐ PR-GXD	Boeing 737-8EH/W	39617/4435	ex N5515R	
☐ PR-GXE	Boeing 737-8EH/W	39618/4501		
☐ PR-GXF	Boeing 737-8EH/W	39619/4509		
☐ PR-GXG	Boeing 737-8EH/W	39620/4529		
☐ PR-GXH	Boeing 737-8EH/W	39621/4544		
☐ PR-GXI	Boeing 737-8EH/W	39622/4551		
☐ PR-GXJ	Boeing 737-8EH/W	39623/4553		
☐ PR-GXK	Boeing 737-8EH/W	39624/4623		
☐ PR-GXL	Boeing 737-8EH/W	39625/4591		
☐ PR-GXM	Boeing 737-8EH/W	39629/4713	ex N5515R	
☐ PR-GXN	Boeing 737-8EH/W	39631/4741		
☐ PR-GXO	Boeing 737-8EH/W	39632/4757		
☐ PR-GXP	Boeing 737-8EH/W	41163/4771		
☐ PR-GXQ	Boeing 737-8EH/W	39633/4779	ex N1786B	
☐ PR-GXR	Boeing 737-8EH/W	39634/4801	ex N5573K	
☐ PR-GXT	Boeing 737-8EH/W	39636/4844	ex N5573K	
☐ PR-GXU	Boeing 737-8EH/W	39637/4856		
☐ PR-GXV	Boeing 737-8EH/W	39639/4931		
☐ PR-GXW	Boeing 737-8EH/W	39640/4933		♦
☐ PR-GXX	Boeing 737-8EH/W	41166/5224		♦
☐ PR-GXY	Boeing 737-8EH/W	40738/5386		♦
☐ PR-VBJ	Boeing 737-86N/W	36434/2706		♦
☐ PR-VBL	Boeing 737-8EH/W	34272/2449	ex PR-GTW	♦
☐ PR-WJC	Boeing 737-341	25051/2127	ex PR-BRF	[OPF]
☐ PR-WJG	Boeing 737-322	24452/1728	ex N359UA	wfs
☐ PR-WJJ	Boeing 737-341	24935/1935	ex PP-VON	wfs
☐ PR-WJK	Boeing 737-33A	23830/1462	ex N238MQ	wfs

HELISUL TAXI AEREO   Foz do Iguaçu, PR

☐ PR-HEM	Aérospatiale AS350B2 Ecureuil	2828	ex N110LN	♦
☐ PR-HES	Agusta A109K2	10028	ex N912VR	♦
☐ PR-HTA	Helibras HS.350B2 Esquilo	AS3523		
☐ PR-KEB	Beech 200 Super King Air	BB-835	ex N84PN	
☐ PT-HGB	Bell 206B JetRanger III	4298	ex C-FRIN	
☐ PT-HMI	Helibras HS.350B Esquilo	1639/HB1046		
☐ PT-HML	Helibras HS.350B Esquilo	1642/HB1049		
☐ PT-HOY	Bell 206B JetRanger III	4171	ex N4171J	
☐ PT-HTC	Bell 206B JetRanger III	3449	ex N2113Z	
☐ PT-YAP	Bell 206B JetRanger III	3481	ex N215RG	
☐ PT-YEL	Bell 206L-4 LongRanger IV	52198	ex N6593X	

LATIN AIR CARGO   Rio de Janeiro-Galeao, RJ (GIG)

☐ PP-YOU	McDonnell-Douglas DC-10-30F	46978/256	ex (PR-LSA	o/o♦

LIDER TAXI AEREO/AIR BRASIL   (LID)   Belo Horizonte, MG/Rio de Janeiro-Galeao, RJ (-/GIG)

☐ PR-LCA	Sikorsky S-76C+	760554	ex N2039K	♦
☐ PR-LCC	Sikorsky S-76C+	760555	ex N2039S	♦
☐ PR-LCD	Sikorsky S-76C	760549		♦
☐ PR-LCE	Sikorsky S-76C+	760556	ex N2040F	♦
☐ PR-LCF	Sikorsky S-76C+	760558	ex N20380	♦
☐ PR-LCG	Sikorsky S-76C+	760559	ex N20374	♦
☐ PR-LCH	Sikorsky S-76C+	760560	ex (5N-BGF)	♦
☐ PR-LCI	Sikorsky S-76C+	760563	ex N7008G	♦
☐ PR-LCJ	Sikorsky S-76C+	760571	ex N7094T	♦
☐ PR-LCK	Sikorsky S-76C+	760573	ex N7096T	♦
☐ PR-LCM	Sikorsky S-76C+	760624	ex N80736	♦
☐ PR-LCN	Sikorsky S-76C+	760626	ex N80876	♦
☐ PR-LCO	Sikorsky S-76C	760628	ex N80601	♦
☐ PR-LCP	Sikorsky S-76C	760631	ex N80259	♦
☐ PR-LCR	Sikorsky S-76C	760617	ex N81189	♦
☐ PP-MMF	Dassault Falcon 2000LX	202	ex F-WWMA	♦
☐ PR-EAS	Beech 65-C90GTx	LJ-2030	ex N8130J	
☐ PR-MGP	Beech 65-C90GTx	LJ-2050	ex N5050B	
☐ PR-PRA	Raytheon Premier 1A	RB-169	ex N837JM	♦
☐ PR-PRE	Raytheon Premier 1A	RB-1394	ex N239RF	♦
☐ PT-HOX	Bell 212	31175	ex N212CE	♦
☐ PT-HTP	Bell 212	32132	ex N5748Z	♦
☐ PT-JAA	British Aerospace 125 Srs 800B	258190	ex PT-OHB	♦
☐ PT-WHC	Beechcraft 400XP	RK-58	ex N56356	♦
☐ PT-WHD	Beeccraft 400XP	RK-77	ex N8277Y	♦

□ PT-WHE	Beechcraft 400A	RK-81	ex N8167G	◆

LYNX AVIACAO TAXI AEREO

□ PP-WTH	Embraer ERJ-135LR	145402	ex N739AE	◆
□ PR-WTH	Embraer ERJ-135LR	145715	ex N837RP	◆

MANAUS AEROTAXI   *Manaus-Eduardo Gomes, AM (MAO)*

□ PR-MPD	Rockwell 690B Turbo Commander	11513	ex N690BA	
□ PR-MPE	Cessna 208 Caravan I	20800510	ex N6144K	FP
□ PR-MPF	Cessna 650 Citation III	650-0087	ex PP-AIO	
□ PT-LIK	Mitsubishi MU-2B-60 Marquise	1546SA	ex N472MA	
□ PT-WDB	Embraer EMB.110C Bandeirante	110051	ex FAB2150	◆

MAP LINHAS AEREAS   *Mas Air (PAM)*   *Manaus-Ponta Pelada, AM (PLL)*

□ PR-MPN	ATR 42-320	020	ex PR-TTG	
□ PR-MPO	ATR 42-320	091	ex PP-PTD	
□ PR-MPY	ATR 72-202	519	ex F-WNUC	
□ PR-MPZ	ATR 72-202	523	ex F-WNUD	
□ PR-STY	ATR 72-202	367	ex OM-VRB	◆
□ PT-SOF	Embraer EMB.110P1A Bandeirante	110486		
□ PT-WDB	Embraer EMB.110C Bandeirante	110051	ex 2159 Brazil	

MODERN LOGISTICS   *(MWM)*   *Sao Paulo-Guarulhos, SP (GRU)*

□ PP-YBA	Boeing 737-4Y0F	24683/1901	ex N837TM	o/o◆

OMNI TAXI AEREO   *Jacarepagua*

□ PR-OHA	AgustaWestland AW139	41302	ex N491SM	
□ PR-OHB	AgustaWestland AW139	41304	ex N492SM	
□ PR-OHC	AgustaWestland AW139	41305	ex N496SM	
□ PR-OHD	AgustaWestland AW139	41306	ex N493SM	
□ PR-OHJ	AgustaWestland AW139	41335	ex N515SM	
□ PR-OHL	AgustaWestland AW139	41337	ex N516SM	
□ PR-OHN	AgustaWestland AW139	41331	ex N518SM	
□ PR-OHQ	AgustaWestland AW139	41380	ex N625SM	
□ PR-OMF	AgustaWestland AW139	31053	ex A6-AWB	
□ PR-OMM	AgustaWestland AW139	41006	ex A6-AWG	
□ PR-OMN	AgustaWestland AW139	41205		◆
□ PR-OMP	AgustaWestland AW139	31095	ex A6-AWD	
□ PR-OHR	AgustaWestland AW139	41382		◆
□ PR-OHE	Sikorsky S-92A	920172	ex N972S	
□ PR-OHF	Sikorsky S-92A	920177	ex N977Y	
□ PR-OHG	Sikorsky S-92A	920187	ex N187N	
□ PR-OHI	Sikorsky S-92A	920184	ex N184W	
□ PR-OHO	Sikorsky S-92A	920208	ex N208Y	
□ PR-HGB	Sikorsky S-76C	760498	ex N431MB	
□ PR-HGC	Sikorsky S-76C+	760472	ex N162AD	
□ PR-HGD	Sikorsky S-76C+	760470	ex N241KK	◆
□ PR-OHH	Eurocopter EC225LP	2818		◆
□ PR-OHM	Agusta A109E Power	11794		◆
□ PR-OMW	Eurocopter EC225LP	2835		◆

ORTIZ TAXI AEREO   *Rio Branco, AC*

□ PR-OTZ	Cessna 208B Caravan I	208B2333		

PANTANAL   *Pantanal (GP/PTN)*   *Sao Paulo-Congonhas, SP (CGH)*

□ PT-MFT	ATR 42-320	306	ex G-BXEH	wfs

☐ PT-MFU	ATR 42-310	070	ex F-GHJE	wfs
☐ PT-MFV	ATR 42-300	043	ex F-GGLR	wfs
☐ PT-MZD	Airbus A319-132	1096	ex D-AVYR	
☐ PT-MZJ	Airbus A320-232	1251	ex F-WWIV	<TAM

PASSAREDO TRANSPORTES AEREOS   Passaredo (2Z/PTB)   Ribeirao Preto, SP (RAO)

☐ PP-PTP	ATR 72-212A	865	ex F-WWEO	Tuiuiu	♦
☐ PP-PTQ	ATR 72-212A	874	ex F-WWEZ	Quero-Quero	♦
☐ PR-PDD	ATR 72-212A	562	ex F-WKVE	Beija-flor	
☐ PR-PDE	ATR 72-212A	565	ex F-WNUE	Joao de Barro	
☐ PR-PDH	ATR 72-212A	572	ex EI-FAN	Tucano	
☐ PR-PDJ	ATR 72-212A	575	ex EI-EYY	Andorinha	
☐ PR-PDK	ATR 72-212A	593	ex EI-EZK	Arara	
☐ PR-PDA	ATR 72-600	1022	ex F-WWEW	Bem-te-vi	
☐ PR-PDB	ATR 72-600	1028	ex F-WWLU	Canario	
☐ PR-PDC	ATR 72-600	1040	ex F-WWEC	Sabia	
☐ PR-PDI	ATR 72-600	1059	ex F-WWET	Pica-pau	
☐ PT-PSS	Embraer ERJ-145MP	145336	ex EI-EHW		

PEC TAXI AEREO

| ☐ PT-PTA | Cessna 208B Caravan I | 208B0763 | ex N5165P | ♦ |

PIQUIATUBA TAXI AEREO   Piquiatuba, PA

☐ PP-AMZ	Cessna 208B Caravan I	208B2073	ex N2210K	♦
☐ PR-MDP	Embraer EMB.120RT Brasilia	120250	ex N250YV	♦
☐ PT-MES	Cessna 208B Caravan I	208B0507		♦

PUMA AIR   Puma Brasil (Z4/PLY)   Belem, PA (BEL)

| ☐ N191AQ | Boeing 737-322 | 24247/1634 | ex PR-GLQ | [LIM] |
| ☐ PR-PUA | Boeing 737-322 | 24668/1905 | ex PR-GLK | wfs |

RICO LINHAS AEREAS/TAXI AEREO   Rico (C7/RLE)   Manaus-Eduardo Gomez, AM (MAO)

☐ PP-MDB	Cessna 560 Citation XLS	560-5552	ex N5231S	
☐ PT-GJC	Embraer EMB.110C Bandeirante	110055		
☐ PT-WJA	Embraer EMB.110P1 Bandeirante	110265	ex PT-OHF	
☐ PT-WJG	Embraer EMB.120ER Brasilia	120064	ex PT-PCA	wfs
☐ PT-WRU	Cessna 208 Caravan I	20800284		FP

RIO BRANCO AEROTAXI   Rio Branco, AC

| ☐ PR-SBR | Cessna 208B Caravan I | 208B2253 | ex N5163C | |

RIO LINHAS AEREAS   (R3/RIO)   Curitiba (CWB)

☐ PR-IOA	Boeing 727-214F	21512/1343	ex N750US	
☐ PR-IOC	Boeing 727-264F (FedEx 3)	22984/1813	ex N764AT	
☐ PR-IOD	Boeing 727-264F (FedEx 3)	23014/1816	ex N765AT	
☐ PR-IOF	Boeing 727-214F	21692/1479	ex N786AT	
☐ PR-IOG	Boeing 727-214F	21691/1480	ex N785AT	
☐ PR-RLJ	Boeing 727-214F	21513/1365	ex N751US	[CWB]
☐ PP-WSA	Boeing 737-4Q8SF	25375/2598	ex N339LF	

RIO MADEIRA AEROTAXI - RIMA

| ☐ PT-MEC | Cessna 208B Caravan I | 208B0342 | ex N1045C | ♦ |

RURAIMA TAXI AEREO

| ☐ PT-WIO | Cessna 208B Caravan I | 208B0521 | ex N5058J | ♦ |

SETE LINHAS AEREAS   Sete   Goiania, GO (GYN)

☐ PT-MEG	Cessna 208B Caravan I	208B0352	ex N1114N	
☐ PT-MEH	Cessna 208B Caravan I	208B0354	ex N1114W	
☐ PT-MEI	Cessna 208B Caravan I	208B0358	ex N1115P	
☐ PT-MEK	Cessna 208B Caravan I	208B0360	ex N1115W	
☐ PT-MEL	Cessna 208B Caravan I	208B0361	ex N1116G	
☐ PR-STD	Mitsubishi MU-2B-60 Marquise	1536SA		
☐ PR-STE	Embraer EMB.120ER Brasilia	120295	ex N295UX	
☐ PR-STI	Embraer EMB.120RT Brasilia	120276	ex PR-TUH	
☐ PR-STZ	Embraer EMB.120ER	120285	ex N216SW	
☐ PT-LHH	Mitsubishi MU-2B-60 Marquise	1508SA	ex N618RT	♦
☐ PT-LHT	Learjet 35A	35A-479	ex N30SA	

☐ PT-WST	Mitsubishi MU-2B-36A	711SA	ex N171CA	
☐ PT-WYT	Mitsubishi MU-2B-36A	722SA	ex N722MU	

SIDERAL AIR CARGO — Sideral (SID) — Curitiba, PR (CWB)

☐ PR-SDJ	Boeing 737-4Y0SF	24906/2009	ex N309MS	
☐ PR-SDL	Boeing 737-3S3F	24060/1519	ex N312AW	
☐ PR-SDU	Boeing 747-4B6SF	24808/1888	ex N248JT	
☐ PR-SDV	Boeing 737-4Q8SF	25377/2717	ex N347AT	♦
☐ PT-MFE	ATR 42-300	295	ex F-WWLU	wfs♦

SIGA TAXI AEREO

☐ PR-GRB	Pilatus PC-12	147856	♦

SOL LINHAS AEREAS

☐ PR-VLA	LET L-410UVP-E20	882101	ex OK-TDA

TAM CARGO — Absa Cargo (M3/TUS) — Sao Paulo-Viracopos, SP (VCP)

☐ PR-ABB	Boeing 767-316F/W	29881/778	ex CC-CZX		<LAN
☐ PR-ABD	Boeing 767-316F/W	34245/934			<LCO
☐ PR-ACG	Boeing 767-316F/W	30780/806	ex CC-CZY		<LAN>FDX
☐ PR-ACO	Boeing 767-316F	35817/959	ex N526LA		♦
☐ PR-ACQ	Boeing 767-346F/W	35818/960	ex N422LA		♦
☐ PR-ADY	Boeing 767-316ERF/W	32573/848	ex N314LA	TAM Cargo c/s	<LCO>FDX

TAM LINHAS AEREAS — TAM (JJ/TAM) — Sao Paulo-Congonhas, SP (GGH)

Member of oneWorld

☐ PR-MAL	Airbus A319-132	1801	ex D-AVWD		
☐ PR-MAM	Airbus A319-132	1826	ex D-AVWN		
☐ PR-MAN	Airbus A319-132	1831	ex D-AVWR		
☐ PR-MAO	Airbus A319-132	1837	ex D-AVYQ		
☐ PR-MAQ	Airbus A319-132	1855	ex D-AVYA		
☐ PR-MBN	Airbus A319-132	3032	ex D-AVWG		
☐ PR-MBU	Airbus A319-132	3588	ex D-AVYG		
☐ PR-MBV	Airbus A319-132	3595	ex D-AVYC		
☐ PR-MBW	Airbus A319-132	3710	ex D-AVWQ		
☐ PR-MYB	Airbus A319-112	3727	ex D-AVWT		
☐ PR-MYC	Airbus A319-112	3733	ex D-AVWW		
☐ PR-MYL	Airbus A319-112	4734	ex D-AVYA		
☐ PR-MYM	Airbus A319-112	4756	ex D-AVYD		
☐ PT-MZC	Airbus A319-132	1092	ex D-AVYD		
☐ PT-MZE	Airbus A319-132	1103	ex D-AVWD		
☐ PT-MZF	Airbus A319-132	1139	ex D-AVYO		
☐ PT-TMA	Airbus A319-132	4000	ex D-AVYA		
☐ PT-TMB	Airbus A319-132	4163	ex D-AVYF		
☐ PT-TMC	Airbus A319-132	4171	ex D-AVWJ		
☐ PT-TMD	Airbus A319-132	4192	ex D-AVYA	Rio 450 años c/s	
☐ PT-TME	Airbus A319-132	4389	ex D-AVXH		
☐ PT-TMF	Airbus A319-132	2467	ex D-ABGB		
☐ PT-TMG	Airbus A319-132	4773	ex D-AVYI		
☐ PT-TMH	Airbus A319-132	2784	ex N601LF		
☐ PT-TMI	Airbus A319-132	5345	ex D-AVWF		
☐ PT-TML	Airbus A319-132	2887	ex CC-CPX		♦
☐ PR-MHA	Airbus A320-214	2924	ex F-WWDV		
☐ PR-MHB	Airbus A320-214	1692	ex F-GRSN		
☐ PR-MHE	Airbus A320-214	3111	ex F-WWIS		
☐ PR-MHF	Airbus A320-214	3180	ex F-WWDT		
☐ PR-MHG	Airbus A320-214	3002	ex F-WWBB		
☐ PR-MHI	Airbus A320-214	3035	ex F-WWDE		
☐ PR-MHJ	Airbus A320-214	3047	ex F-WWDQ		
☐ PR-MHK	Airbus A320-214	3058	ex F-WWDX		
☐ PR-MHM	Airbus A320-214	3211	ex F-WWIR		
☐ PR-MHO	Airbus A320-214	3278	ex F-WWDK		
☐ PR-MHP	Airbus A320-214	3266	ex F-WWBS		
☐ PR-MHQ	Airbus A320-214	3284	ex F-WWDQ		
☐ PR-MHR	Airbus A320-214	3313	ex F-WWIQ		
☐ PR-MHS	Airbus A320-214	3325	ex F-WWBF		
☐ PR-MHU	Airbus A320-214	3391	ex F-WWDR		
☐ PR-MHV	Airbus A320-214	3540	ex F-WWIO		
☐ PR-MHW	Airbus A320-214	3630	ex F-WWBQ		
☐ PR-MHX	Airbus A320-214	3565	cx F WWBM		
☐ PR-MHY	Airbus A320-214	3594	ex F-WWDG		
☐ PR-MHZ	Airbus A320-214	3658	ex F-WWDT		
☐ PR-MYA	Airbus A320-214	3662	ex F-WWDV		
☐ PR-MYD	Airbus A320-214	3750	ex F-WWBR		
☐ PR-MYE	Airbus A320-214	3908	ex F-WWIR		

☐	PR-MYF	Airbus A320-214	3972	ex F-WWIQ		
☐	PR-MYG	Airbus A320-214	4320	ex F-WWDJ		
☐	PR-MYH	Airbus A320-214	4441	ex F-WWDY		
☐	PR-MYI	Airbus A320-214	4446	ex D-AVVY		
☐	PR-MYJ	Airbus A320-214	4465	ex D-AVVL		
☐	PR-MYK	Airbus A320-214	4544	ex D-AXAN		
☐	PR-MYN	Airbus A320-214	4953	ex D-AXAU		
☐	PR-MYO	Airbus A320-214	4974	ex D-AVVK		
☐	PR-MYP	Airbus A320-214	5066	ex D-AUBE		
☐	PR-MYQ	Airbus A320-214	5101	ex D-AUBQ		
☐	PR-MYR	Airbus A320-214	5107	ex D-AUBT		
☐	PR-MYS	Airbus A320-214	5109	ex D-AUBU		
☐	PR-MYT	Airbus A320-214	5184	ex D-AXAU		
☐	PR-MYU	Airbus A320-214	5209	ex F-WWBJ		
☐	PR-MYV	Airbus A320-214	5222	ex D-AXAX		
☐	PR-MYW	Airbus A320-214	5240	ex F-WWBT		
☐	PR-MYX	Airbus A320-214	5342	ex D-AUBK		
☐	PR-MYY	Airbus A320-214/S	5591	ex F-WWDC		
☐	PR-MYZ	Airbus A320-214/S	5621	ex F-WWBB		
☐	PR-TYA	Airbus A320-214/S	5643	ex F-WWIO		
☐	PR-TYD	Airbus A320-214/S	5749	ex D-AVVU		
☐	PR-TYF	Airbus A320-214/S	5752	ex F-WWIA		
☐	PR-TYG	Airbus A320-214/S	5845	ex D-AXAT		
☐	PR-TYH	Airbus A320-214/S	5883	ex D-AVVI	10,000 faces c/s	
☐	PR-	Airbus A320-214/S	6157	ex		o/o
☐	PR-MAA	Airbus A320-232	1595	ex F-WWBU		
☐	PR-MAG	Airbus A320-232	1832	ex F-WWBD	Sao Paulo 450 Anos	
☐	PR-MAK	Airbus A320-232	1825	ex F-WWIX		
☐	PR-MAP	Airbus A320-232	1857	ex F-WWBZ		
☐	PR-MAR	Airbus A320-232	1888	ex F-WWBS		
☐	PR-MAS	Airbus A320-232	2372	ex F-WWDQ		
☐	PR-MAV	Airbus A320-232	2393	ex F-WWIR		
☐	PR-MAY	Airbus A320-232	2661	ex F-WWIV		
☐	PR-MAZ	Airbus A320-232	2513	ex F-WWIY		
☐	PR-MBA	Airbus A320-232	2734	ex F-WWBF		
☐	PR-MBB	Airbus A320-232	2737	ex F-WWBH		
☐	PR-MBD	Airbus A320-232	2838	ex F-WWID		
☐	PR-MBE	Airbus A320-232	2859	ex F-WWIU		
☐	PR-MBF	Airbus A320-232	2896	ex F-WWBZ		
☐	PR-MBG	Airbus A320-232	1459	ex OE-LOR		
☐	PR-MBH	Airbus A320-232	2904	ex F-WWDP		
☐	PR-MBL	Airbus A320-233	2044	ex HC-CDZ		
☐	PR-MBO	Airbus A320-232	3156	ex F-WWDK		
☐	PR-MBP	Airbus A320-232	1215	ex G-TTOA		
☐	PR-MBQ	Airbus A320-232	1652	ex N533JB		
☐	PR-MBR	Airbus A320-232	1802	ex N542JB		
☐	PR-MBS	Airbus A320-232	1835	ex N544JB		
☐	PR-MBT	Airbus A320-233	2014	ex HC-CDY		
☐	PR-MBX	Airbus A320-232	1591	ex N528JB		
☐	PR-MBY	Airbus A320-232	1891	ex N550JB		
☐	PR-MBZ	Airbus A320-232	1827	ex N546JB		
☐	PT-MZG	Airbus A320-232	1143	ex F-WWBG		
☐	PT-MZH	Airbus A320-232	1158	ex F-WWBY		
☐	PT-MZI	Airbus A320-232	1246	ex F-WWIR		
☐	PT-MZJ	Airbus A320-232	1251	ex F-WWIV		>PTN
☐	PT-MZL	Airbus A320-232	1376	ex F-WWIN		
☐	PT-MZT	Airbus A320-232	1486	ex F-WWDV		
☐	PT-MZU	Airbus A320-232	1518	ex F-WWIJ		
☐	PT-MZW	Airbus A320-232	1580	ex F-WWBK		
☐	PT-MZY	Airbus A320-232	1628	ex F-WWDO		
☐	PT-MZZ	Airbus A320-232	1593	ex F-WWBT		
☐	PT-MXA	Airbus A321-231	3222	ex D-AVZF		
☐	PT-MXB	Airbus A321-231	3229	ex D-AVZG		
☐	PT-MXC	Airbus A321-231	3294	ex D-AVZE		
☐	PT-MXD	Airbus A321-231	3761	ex D-AZAP		
☐	PT-MXE	Airbus A321-231	3816	ex D-AVZB		
☐	PT-MXF	Airbus A321-231	4352	ex D-AVZC		
☐	PT-MXG	Airbus A321-231	4358	ex D-AVZK		
☐	PT-MXH	Airbus A321-231	4570	ex D-AZAX		
☐	PT-MXI	Airbus A321-231	4662	ex D-AZAD		
☐	PT-MXJ	Airbus A321-231	5528	ex D-AZAW		
☐	PT-MXL	Airbus A321-231/S	5947	ex D-AVZJ		
☐	PT-MXM	Airbus A321-231/S	5987	ex D-AZAR		
☐	PT-MXN	Airbus A321-231/S	6097	ex D-AZAC		
☐	PT-MXO	Airbus A321-231/S	6121	ex D-AVXF		
☐	PT-MXP	Airbus A321-231/S	6163	ex D-AVXS		♦
☐	PT-MXQ	Airbus A321-231/S	6165	ex D-AVXT		♦
☐	PT-XPA	Airbus A321-211/S	6409	ex D-AZAM		♦
☐	PT-XPB	Airbus A321-211/S	6414	ex D-AZAN		♦
☐	PT-XPC	Airbus A321-211/S	6592	ex D-AVXK		♦
☐	PT-XPD	Airbus A321-211/S	6632	ex D-AVXW		o/o♦

☐ PT-	Airbus A321-211/S	6670	ex	o/o♦
☐ PT-	Airbus A321-211/S	6685	ex	o/o♦
☐ PT-MVA	Airbus A330-223	232	ex A6-EYX	[MIA]
☐ PT-MVB	Airbus A330-223	238	ex A6-EYY	♦
☐ PT-MVC	Airbus A330-223	247	ex F-WWKH	
☐ PT-MVD	Airbus A330-223	259	ex A6-EYB	
☐ PT-MVE	Airbus A330-223	361	ex A6-EYA	[QSC]
☐ PT-MVF	Airbus A330-203	466	ex F-WWKP	
☐ PT-MVG	Airbus A330-203	472	ex F-WWKQ	
☐ PT-MVL	Airbus A330-203	700	ex F-WWKB	
☐ PT-MVQ	Airbus A330-223	968	ex F-WWYN	
☐ PT-MVS	Airbus A330-223	1112	ex F-WWYJ	
☐ PT-MVT	Airbus A330-223	1118	ex F-WWKS	
☐ PT-MOA	Boeing 767-316ER/W	41995/1049	ex CC-BDN	♦
☐ PT-MOB	Boeing 767-316ER/W	40592/1031	ex CC-BDE	♦
☐ PT-MOC	Boeing 767-316ER/W	41746/1033	ex CC-BDF	♦
☐ PT-MOE	Boeing 767-316ER/W	41996/1052	ex CC-BDO	♦
☐ PT-MOF	Boeing 767-316ER/W	41997/1055	ex CC-BDP	♦
☐ PT-MOG	Boeing 767-316ER/W	29227/698	ex CC-CZW	♦
☐ PT-MSO	Boeing 767-316ER/W	41747/1034	ex CC-BDG	
☐ PT-MSS	Boeing 767-316ER/W	41748/1037	ex CC-BDH	
☐ PT-MSV	Boeing 767-316ER/W	40593/1038	ex CC-BDI	
☐ PT-MSW	Boeing 767-316ER/W	42213/1040	ex CC-BDJ	
☐ PT-MSX	Boeing 767-316ER/W	41993/1042	ex CC-BDK	
☐ PT-MSY	Boeing 767-316ERW	42214/1043	ex CC-BDL	
☐ PT-MSZ	Boeing 767-316ER/W	41994/1045	ex CC-BDM	♦
☐ PT-MUA	Boeing 777-32WER	37664/727	ex N5573S	
☐ PT-MUB	Boeing 777-32WER	37665/733	ex N6009F	
☐ PT-MUC	Boeing 777-32WER	37666/740		
☐ PT-MUD	Boeing 777-32WER	37667/751		
☐ PT-MUE	Boeing 777-32WER	38886/1036		
☐ PT-MUF	Boeing 777-32WER	38887/1042		
☐ PT-MUG	Boeing 777-32WER	38888/1052		
☐ PT-MUH	Boeing 777-32WER	38889/1059		
☐ PT-MUI	Boeing 777-32WER	40589/1118		
☐ PT-MUJ	Boeing 777-32WER	40588/1128		
☐ PT-MSN	Airbus A340-541	445	ex C-GKOL	<ACA [GRU]

TAXI AEREO RIBEIRO				Curitiba, PR (CWB)
☐ PT-SFS	Embraer EMB.110P1 Bandeirante	110401		

TOTAL LINHAS AEREAS		(TTL)		Pampula Intl, MG (PLU)
☐ PR-TTB	Boeing 727-223 (FedEx 3)	22007/1643	ex N891AA	
☐ PR-TTO	Boeing 727-2M7F (FedEx 3)	21200/1206	ex N721RW	
☐ PR-TTP	Boeing 727-2M7F (FedEx 3)	21502/1339	ex N998PG	[GRU]
☐ PT-MTQ	Boeing 727-243F	22053/1620	ex N198PC	[GIG]
☐ PT-MTT	Boeing 727-243F	22167/1752	ex N270PC	
☐ PR-TKB	ATR 42-500	610	ex I-ADLV	dam 30May14♦
☐ PR-TTF	ATR 42-300	021	ex F-WQNS	>TIB
☐ PR-TTH	ATR 42-500	506	ex F-WQNL	
☐ PR-TTM	ATR 42-500	551	ex D-BNNN	

TWO TAXI AEREO		Brasil Cargo (OWT)		Belem, PA (BEL)
☐ PP-ITY	Cessna 208B Caravan I	208B0560		♦
☐ PR-BAT	Cessna 208B Caravan I	208B2169	ex N5180K	
☐ PR-CRF	Cessna 208B Caravan I	208B2227	ex N5260M	
☐ PR-IHP	Cessna 208B Caravan I	208B2110	ex N5264E	
☐ PR-MAU	Cessna 208B Caravan I	208B0621	ex ZP-CAD	♦
☐ PR-OGP	Cessna 208A Caravan I	20800050	ex N817FE	♦
☐ PR-OZA	Cessna 208B Caravan I	208B0157	ex N4615B	♦
☐ PR-WOT	Cessna 208B Caravan I	208B2240	ex N5166T	♦
☐ PT-MEA	Cessna 208B Caravan I	208B0333	ex N1037L	♦
☐ PT-MEB	Cessna 208B Caravan I	208B0335	ex N1038G	♦
☐ PT-MED	Cessna 208B Caravan I	208B0343	ex N1052C	♦
☐ PT-MEJ	Cessna 208B Caravan I	208B0359	ex N1115V	♦
☐ PT-MEM	Cessna 208B Caravan I	208B0405		♦
☐ PT-MEN	Cessna 208B Caravan I	208B0408		♦
☐ PT-MEO	Cessna 208B Caravan I	208B0412		♦
☐ PT-MEY	Cessna 208B Caravon I	208B0518		♦
☐ PT-MHC	Cessna 208B Caravan I	208B0543		♦
☐ PT-WZN	Cessna 208B Caravan I	208B0698		♦

VARIG Varig (RG/VRN) Rio de Janeiro-Galeao, RJ/Porto Alegre-Canoas, RS (GIG/POA)

☐ PR-GOQ	Boeing 737-76N	33417/1215	
☐ PR-VBM	Boeing 737-7EA	32406/859	ex N815PG
☐ PR-VBQ	Boeing 737-76N	30135/1068	ex PR-GOO
☐ PR-VBY	Boeing 737-73A/W	28499/390	ex N738AL
☐ PR-VBZ	Boeing 737-73A/W	28500/414	ex N739AL
☐ PR-VBF	Boeing 737-8EH/W	34276/2716	
☐ PR-VBG	Boeing 737-8EH/W	35066/2700	
☐ PR-VBK	Boeing 737-8EH/W	34271/2445	ex PR-GTX

VERA CRUZ TAXI AEREO Vera Cruz, SP

☐ PR-CFJ	Cessna 208B Caravan I	208B1217	ex N52136
☐ PR-VCB	Cessna 208B Caravan I	208B1236	ex N208GH
☐ PR-VCE	Cessna 208B Caravan I	208B1286	ex N5147B
☐ PT-MEV	Cessna 208B Caravan I	208B0512	ex N5076K

XP TAXI AEREO

☐ PR-VXP	Cessna 208B Caravan I	208B1281	ex N5249W

PZ- SURINAME (Republic of Suriname)

BLUE WING AIRLINES Blue Tail (BWI) Paramaribo-Zorg en Hoop (ORG)

☐ PZ-TGQ	Cessna U206G Stationair 6	U20605917	ex PZ-TAO		
☐ PZ-TLV	Cessna U206G Stationair 6	U20606951			
☐ PZ-TSA	WSK/PZL Antonov An-28	1AJ007-21	ex PZ-TGW		
☐ PZ-TSB	Cessna 208 Caravan I	20800098	ex N207RM		
☐ PZ-TSD	de Havilland DHC-6 Twin Otter 200	117	ex VH-JEA		
☐ PZ-TSF	Reims Cessna F406 Caravan II	F406-0033	ex VH-JVN		
☐ PZ-TSH	de Havilland DHC-6 Twin Otter 200	145	ex VH-TZR		
☐ PZ-TSK	Cessna 208B Caravan I	208B0488	ex N1301K	Supervan 300 conversion	
☐ PZ-TSN	WSK/PZL Antonov An-28	1AJ007-20	ex YV-528C		wfs
☐ PZ-	de Havilland DHC-6 Twin Otter 300	90	ex VH-BVS		♦

CARIBBEAN COMMUTER AIRWAYS

☐ PZ-TYD	Britten-Norman BN-2A Islander	3009	ex F-OHQX	Island of Dominica
☐ PZ-TYL	Britten-Norman BN-2A Islander	2211	ex N887MA	Island of St Lucia

FLY ALLWAYS (EDR) Paramaribo-Zanderij Intl (PBM)

☐ PZ-TFA	Fokker 70	11556	ex PH-KZV	o/o♦
☐ PZ-TFB	Fokker 70	11570	ex PH-WXA	♦

GUM AIR Gum Air (GUM) Paramaribo-Zorg en Hoop (ORG)

☐ PZ-TBB	Cessna 208B Caravan I	208B5020	ex N8135F		
☐ PZ-TBH	Cessna 208B Caravan I	208B0923	ex N1132W	Spirit of Pike	
☐ PZ-TBK	Cessna 208B Caravan I	208B2464	ex N208AE		♦
☐ PZ-TBS	Cessna 208B Caravan I	208B1284	ex N4114A		
☐ PZ-TBT	Cessna 208B Caravan I	208B1111	ex N412BZ		
☐ PZ-PBD	Cessna U206G Stationair	U20603786	ex PZ-TBD		♦
☐ PZ-TBA	GAF Nomad N22B	N22B-66			
☐ PZ-TBG	Cessna U206B Super Skywagon	U206-0832	ex N3832G		
☐ PZ-TBY	de Havilland DHC-6 Twin Otter 300	646	ex N7015A		
☐ PZ-TVC	Cessna 404 Titan	404-0243	ex YV-236CP		
☐ PZ-TVU	Cessna TU206G Stationair 6	U20604783	ex PZ-PVU		

SURINAM AIRWAYS Surinam (PY/SLM) Paramaribo-Zanderij Intl/Zorg en Hoop (PBM/ORG)

☐ PZ-TCN	Boeing 737-36N	28668/2890	ex N668AN
☐ PZ-TCO	Boeing 737-36N	28669/2897	ex N669AN
☐ PZ-TCP	Airbus A340-311	049	ex F-GLZG
☐ PZ-TCQ	Boeing 737-3Q8	26295/2557	ex N295AN

SURINAM AIRWAYS COMMUTER

☐ PZ-TYD	Britten-Norman BN-2A-26 Islander	3009	Village of Djoemoe

P2- PAPUA NEW GUINEA (Independent State of Papua New Guinea)

AIR NIUGINI   Niugini (PX/ANG)   Port Moresby (POM)

☐ P2-PXP	de Havilland DHC-8-402Q	4022	ex C-GKZV		
☐ P2-PXQ	de Havilland DHC-8-402Q	4033	ex C-GLPE		
☐ P2-PXR	de Havilland DHC-8-402Q	4038	ex C-GLGV		
☐ P2-PXS	de Havilland DHC-8-402Q	4262	ex C-FXAW		
☐ P2-PXT	de Havilland DHC-8-402Q	4329	ex C-GNIU		
☐ P2-PXU	de Havilland DHC-8-402Q	4316	ex C-GEHE		
☐ P2-ANC	Fokker 100	11471	ex PH-MXW		
☐ P2-AND	Fokker 100	11473	ex PT-MRQ		
☐ P2-ANE	Fokker 100	11264	ex PH-THY		
☐ P2-ANF	Fokker 100	11351	ex PH-FDI		
☐ P2-ANH	Fokker 100	11301	ex C-GPNL		
☐ P2-ANJ	Fokker 100	11472	ex PH-EZU	City of Lae	
☐ P2-ANQ	Fokker 100	11451	ex PH-ZDJ		
☐ P2-ANR	Fokker 70	11578	ex PH-KZG		♦
☐ P2-PXC	Boeing 737-86Q/W	30290/1406	ex EC-ISE		<ICE
☐ P2-PXD	Boeing 737-7L9/W	28007/136	ex D-ALAD		
☐ P2-PXE	Boeing 737-8BK/W	33024/1688	ex M-ABGK		
☐ P2-PXV	Boeing 767-341ER	30341/768	ex A6-JBD		<ICE
☐ P2-PXW	Boeing 767-383ER	25365/395	ex TF-FIB		<ICE
☐ P2-PXZ	ATR 72-201F	198	ex HB-AFS		<FAT

AIR SANGA   Port Moresby (POM)

☐ P2-ASZ	Pacific Aerospace 750XL	179	ex ZK-KBQ	
☐ P2-MDC	Cessna U206F Stationair	U20602738	ex N1753C	

AIRLINES OF PAPUA NEW GUINEA   Balus (CG/TOK)   Port Moresby (POM)

☐ P2-MCG	de Havilland DHC-8-102	006	ex C-GJCB		
☐ P2-MCH	de Havilland DHC-8-102	012	ex C-GPYD		
☐ P2-MCI	de Havilland DHC-8-102	197	ex ZK-NET		
☐ P2-MCK	de Havilland DHC-8-102	041	ex VH-QQD		
☐ P2-MCL	de Havilland DHC-8-102	027	ex VH-WZJ		
☐ P2-MCM	de Havilland DHC-8-102	211	ex C-FNCG		
☐ P2-MCN	de Havilland DHC-8-102	380	ex VH-QQH		
☐ P2-MCO	de Havilland DHC-8-103	366	ex S2-AER		♦
☐ P2-MCP	de Havilland DHC-8-102	033	ex VH-TNX		
☐ P2-MCQ	de Havilland DHC-8-102	243	ex VH-TNW		
☐ P2-MCT	de Havilland DHC-8-102	135	ex VH-QQH		
☐ P2-MCU	de Havilland DHC-8-102	208	ex VH-QQJ		
☐ P2-MCW	de Havilland DHC-8-102	067	ex VH-QQI		
☐ P2-MCY	de Havilland DHC-8-102A	237	ex C-FNCG		
☐ P2-EMO	de Havilland DHC-6 Twin Otter 300	726	ex N726JM		
☐ P2-MCR	de Havilland DHC-6 Twin Otter 300	219	ex P2-MFY		
☐ P2-MCZ	de Havilland DHC-6 Twin Otter 300	330	ex N901WW		wfs

ASIA PACIFIC AIRLINES   (A6/MLP)   Tabubil (TBG)

☐ P2-NAT	de Havilland DHC-8-103	170	ex VH-JSJ	
☐ P2-NAX	de Havilland DHC-8-103	229	ex VH-JSI	opf OK Tedi Mining
☐ P2-NAZ	de Havilland DHC-8-102	316	ex C-GFUM	Spirit of Tabubil

CENTRAL AVIATION SERVICES   Mount Hagen (HGU)

☐ P2-BWC	Pacific Aerospace 750XL	136	ex ZK-JQQ	
☐ P2-BWE	Pacific Aerospace 750XL	161	ex ZK-KAU	
☐ P2-BWF	Pacific Aerospace 750XL	159	ex ZK-KAX	
☐ P2-CAC	Kawasaki BK117B2	1012	ex VH-NGH	
☐ P2-OMA	Pacific Aerospace 750XL	175	ex ZK-KBM	
☐ P2-OMH	Piper PA-31T Cheyenne	31T-7520037	ex P2-KDA	

COLUMBIA HELICOPTERS

☐ P2-CHE	Boeing-Vertol BV-107-100	108	ex N109CH	
☐ P2-CHI	Boeing-Vertol BV-234UT	MJ-003	ex N237CH	
☐ P2-CHJ	Boeing-Vertol BV-234UT	MJ-022	ex N245CH	
☐ P2-CHK	Boeing-Vertol BV-234UT	MJ-006	ex N239CH	

HELIFIX OPERATIONS   Port Moresby (POM)

☐ P2-HFA	Cessna 208B Caravan I	208B0954	ex N1242A	♦
☐ P2-HFB	Cessna 208B Caravan I	208B1016	ex N1242L	♦
☐ P2-HFD	Cessna 208B Caravan I	208B0727	ex ZS-NAP	♦

☐ P2-HFN	Bell 407	53500	ex D-HJSP	♦
☐ P2-HFQ	Bell 407	53559	ex VH-CUX	♦
☐ P2-HFR	Bell 212	53221	ex VH-NPN	♦
☐ P2-HFS	Bell 407	53158	ex D-HUTA	♦
☐ P2-HFT	Bell 212	32125	ex A6-BBY	
☐ P2-HFU	Bell 212	31227	ex A6-BAB	
☐ P2-HFX	Bell 206L-3 LongRanger 3	51480	ex D-HWPP	♦
☐ P2-HFY	Bell 206L-3 LongRanger 3	51324	ex VH-NDI	♦
☐ P2-HFY	Bell 206L-3 LongRanger 3	52106	ex VH-RHC	♦
☐ P2-POL	Bell 407	53338		♦

HELI NIUGINI   Madang (MAG)

☐ P2-HBI	Bell 407	53097	ex N692RH	♦
☐ P2-HBT	Bell 407	53186	ex VH-CJN	♦
☐ P2-HBU	Bell 407	53809	ex N404BH	♦
☐ P2-HBV	Bell 407	53845	ex N345PB	♦
☐ P2-HBW	Bell 407	53946	ex N365PB	♦
☐ P2-HBK	Kawasaki BK117B-2	1046	ex ZK-HBK	♦
☐ P2-HBL	Kawasaki BK117B-2	1021	ex ZK-HLU	♦
☐ P2-HBN	Kawasaki BK117B-2	1073	ex VH-KHO	♦
☐ P2-HBO	Kawasaki BK117A-3	1002	ex ZK-HAW	♦
☐ P2-HBQ	Kawasaki BK117B-2	1075	ex ZK-HLI	♦
☐ P2-HBR	Kawasaki BK117B-2	1035	ex ZK-HHL	♦
☐ P2-HNA	Kawasaki BK117B-2	1041	ex ZK-HOU	♦
☐ P2-HNB	Kawasaki BK117B-2	1024	ex ZK-HNB	♦
☐ P2-HNC	Eurocopter BK117B-2	7177	ex ZK-IQL	♦
☐ P2-HBA	Mil Mi-8AMT	59849605182	ex RA-27101	♦
☐ P2-HBB	Mil Mi-8AMT	59489607904	ex RA-27106	♦
☐ P2-HBE	Mil Mi-8MTV-1	95651	ex RA-25503	♦
☐ P2-HBH	Bell 206L-3 LongRanger III	51012	ex SE-HOR	♦
☐ P2-HBS	Bell 206L-1 LongRanger II	45645	ex P2-JND	♦
☐ P2-HBX	Bell 205A-1	30109	ex VH-AWU	♦
☐ P2-HBY	Bell 205A-1	30131	ex VH-NNN	♦

HEVI-LIFT   (IU/GCW)   Mount Hagen/Cairns (HGU/CNS)

☐ P2-AVV	ATR 42-320	304	ex VH-AVV	
☐ P2-KSJ	ATR 42-320	096	ex (P2-HLB)	
☐ P2-KSL	ATR 42-500	497	ex OY-RUJ	♦
☐ P2-KSR	ATR 42-320	194	ex VH-FLE	
☐ P2-KSV	ATR 42-500	501	ex OY-RUL	
☐ P2-HCC	Bell 206L-1 LongRanger III	45427	ex N5019T	
☐ P2-HCD	Bell 206L-1 LongRanger III	45528	ex C-GGHZ	
☐ P2-HCG	Bell 206L-1 LongRanger III	51256	ex N919AC	
☐ P2-HCM	Bell 206L-1 LongRanger III	45608	ex P2-NHE	
☐ P2-HCO	Bell 206L-3 LongRanger III	51178	ex N3204K	
☐ P2-HCU	Bell 206L-3 LongRanger III	51416	ex N254EV	♦
☐ P2-DFA	Bell 212	30807	ex D-HGPP	
☐ P2-DFB	Bell 212	30799	ex P2-HCJ	♦
☐ P2-HCK	Bell 212	30583	ex N212SX	
☐ P2-HCQ	Bell 212	30860	ex JA9528	
☐ P2-HCW	Bell 212	30520	ex PK-EBO	
☐ P2-HCX	Bell 212	30584	ex D-HAGT	
☐ P2-HLV	Bell 212	30508	ex VH-SYV	
☐ P2-HCF	Bell 412HP	36032	ex N30YM	
☐ P2-HCP	Bell 412EP	36381	ex C-GUHZ	
☐ P2-HCS	Bell 412HP	33160	ex VH-HQQ	
☐ P2-HCV	Bell 412EP	36424	ex N416EV	
☐ P2-	Bell 412EP	30381	ex N413EV	
☐ P2-IRM	de Havilland DHC-6 Twin Otter 400	853	ex C-FVAT	
☐ P2-IRN	de Havilland DHC-6 Twin Otter 400	859	ex C-GVAQ	
☐ P2-KSG	de Havilland DHC-6 Twin Otter 300	509	ex VH-WPT	
☐ P2-KSI	de Havilland DHC-6 Twin Otter 300	706	ex VH-HPY	
☐ P2-KSO	de Havilland DHC-6 Twin Otter 300			
☐ P2-KST	de Havilland DHC-6 Twin Otter 300	520	ex YJ-RV5	
☐ P2-KSU	de Havilland DHC-6 Twin Otter 300			
☐ P2-KSW	de Havilland DHC-6 Twin Otter 300	703	ex P2-MCX	
☐ P2-KSY	de Havilland DHC-6 Twin Otter 400	875	ex C-FVAT	♦
☐ P2-HCA	Bell 407	53054	ex N417AL	
☐ P2-HCB	Bell 407	53141	ex N437AL	
☐ P2-HCL	Bell 407	53823	ex C-GRUS	
☐ P2-HCR	Bell 407	53294	ex N53EE	
☐ P2-KSN	Beech 200C Super King Air	BL-22	ex P2-HCN	
☐ P2-MHL	Mil Mi-8MTV-1	95721	ex ER-MHL	♦

| ☐ P2-MHM | Mil Mi-8MTV-2 | 95881 | ex ER-MHM | |

ISLAND NATIONAIR   Port Moresby (POM)

| ☐ P2-IHL | Bell 407 | 53000 | ex VH-CJT | ♦ |
| ☐ P2-SJC | MBB BK117B-1 | 1027 | ex VH-CSG | |

LINK PNG   (PX/ANG)   Port Moresby (POM)

☐ P2-ANK	de Havilland DHC-8Q-202	461	ex C-GFBW	♦
☐ P2-ANM	de Havilland DHC-8Q-314	523	ex D-BPAD	♦
☐ P2-ANN	de Havilland DHC-8-315	401	ex JY-RWB	♦
☐ P2-ANO	de Havilland DHC-8-311A	252	ex D-BOBU	♦
☐ P2-ANX	de Havilland DHC-8Q-202	463	ex D-BHAL	♦
☐ P2-PXI	de Havilland DHC-8Q-201	460	ex C-GHQO	♦
☐ P2-PXL	de Havilland DHC-8-314	385	ex C-FEZD	♦

McDERMOTT AVIATION   Port Moresby (POM)

☐ P2-LNJ	Beech 200C Super King Air	BL-41	ex VH-OYK	♦
☐ P2-MBH	Bell 214B-1	28063	ex N214BH	♦
☐ P2-MLJ	Bell 214B-1	28066	ex N214JL	♦
☐ P2-MSA	Bell 214B-1	28065	ex N28065	♦
☐ P2-ZMY	Beech 200 Super King Air	BB-1449	ex VH-ZMY	♦

MISSIONARY AVIATION FELLOWSHIP   Mount Hagen (HGU)

☐ P2-MEW	GippsAero GA-8-TC320 Airvan	GA8-TC320-10-157	ex VH-CQJ	♦
☐ P2-MFG	GippsAero GA-8-TC320 Airvan	GA8-TC320-09-152	ex VH-WOQ	♦
☐ P2-MFK	GippsAero GA-8-TC320 Airvan	GA8-TC320-08-130	ex VH-MTF	♦
☐ P2-MFL	GippsAero GA-8-TC320 Airvan	GA8-TC320-09-146	ex VH-BQY	♦
☐ P2-MFM	GippsAero GA-8-TC320 Airvan	GA8-TC320-09-149	ex VH-BQE	♦
☐ P2-MKK	GippsAero GA-8-TC320 Airvan	GA8-TC320-11-164	ex VH-BYQ	♦
☐ P2-MAF	Cessna 208 Caravan I	20800198	ex PK-MPN	♦
☐ P2-MAG	Cessna 208 Caravan I	20800397	ex N534TC	♦
☐ P2-MAI	Cessna U206G Stationair	U206G05734	ex P2-DMH	♦
☐ P2-MFB	de Havilland DHC-6 Twin Otter 300	289	ex N910HD	♦
☐ P2-MFD	Cessna TU206G Stationair	TU206G06347	ex P2-SIM	♦
☐ P2-MFN	Cessna TU206G Stationair	TU206G05541	ex N4788X	♦
☐ P2-MFO	Cessna TU206G Stationair	TU206G05456	ex P2-SDB	♦
☐ P2-MFT	de Havilland DHC-6 Twin Otter 300	565	ex N565DH	♦
☐ P2-MFU	de Havilland DHC-6 Twin Otter 300	182	ex TJ-AHV	♦

NATIONAL AVIATION SERVICES   Port Moresby (POM)

☐ P2-NAJ	Britten-Norman BN-2A-26 Islander	100	ex P2-ALE	
☐ P2-NAM	Britten-Norman BN-2A-26 Islander	76	ex P2-ALD	
☐ P2-NAV	Britten-Norman BN-2A-26 Islander	81	ex VH-CSU	

NORTH COAST AVIATION   Lae (LAE)   Madang (MAG)

☐ P2-ARB	Pacific Aerospace 750XL	181	ex ZK-KBS	
☐ P2-BJD	Pacific Aerospace 750XL	124	ex P2-SDB	
☐ P2-ISM	Britten-Norman BN-2A-20 Islander	227	ex VH-EDI	
☐ P2-NCA	Pacific Aerospace 750XL	134	ex ZK-JQO	
☐ P2-TLF	Pacific Aerospace 750XL	166	ex P2-SDE	♦

PACIFIC HELICOPTERS   Goroka (GKA)

☐ P2-PAN	Bell 212	30663	ex N212XL	♦
☐ P2-PAR	Bell 212	30978	ex XC-DES	♦
☐ P2-PAU	Bell 212	30973	ex A6-BBG	♦
☐ P2-PAY	Bell 212	30630	ex C-GBPH	♦
☐ P2-PAZ	Bell 212	30673	ex D-HAFQ	♦
☐ P2-FXA	Eurocopter AS350BA AStar	1745	ex VH-BXQ	♦
☐ P2-FXB	Eurocopter AS350FX II AStar	2040	ex JA9496	♦
☐ P2-FXC	Eurocopter AS350BA AStar	1608	ex P2-PHH	♦
☐ P2-FXD	Eurocopter AS350BA AStar	1448	ex P2-PHQ	♦
☐ P2-FXE	Eurocopter AS350FX II AStar	2504	ex C-GFQR	♦
☐ P2-FXF	Eurocopter AS350FX II AStar	2164	ex DQ-FIH	♦
☐ P2-PHK	Eurocopter AS350B2 AStar	3299	ex I-DLER	♦
☐ P2-PHV	Eurocopter AS350BA AStar	1087	ex ZK-HDK	♦
☐ P2-PHX	Eurocopter AS350BA AStar	1817		♦
☐ P2-PHY	Eurocopter AS350R2 AStar	1907	ex N5616Q	♦
☐ P2-PHY	Eurocopter AS350BA AStar	1873	ex ZK-HSN	♦
☐ P2-BKA	Kawasaki BK117B-2	1064	ex ZK-IME	♦
☐ P2-BKB	Eurocopter BK117B-2	7069	ex ZK-HQO	♦
☐ P2-BKC	Kawasaki BK117B-2	1058	ex ZK-IZY	♦

□ P2-BKD	Kawasaki BK117B-2	1045	ex 9N-AEL	♦
□ P2-PBA	Bell 206L-1 LongRanger II	45642	ex VH-SCV	♦
□ P2-PBB	Bell 206L-3 LongRanger III	51400	ex N86EC	♦
□ P2-PBC	Bell 206L-1 LongRanger II	45349	ex N1077N	♦
□ P2-PBG	Bell 206L-4 LongRanger IV	52043	ex 5B-CKA	♦
□ P2-PHP	Eurocopter SA315B	2472	ex N1217N	♦

SIL AVIATION — Aiyura (AYU)

□ P2-SIB	Quest Kodiak 100	100-0008	ex N498KQ
□ P2-SID	Quest Kodiak 100	100-0048	ex N499KQ
□ P2-SIH	Bell 206L-3 LongRanger III	51156	ex N3198Z
□ P2-SIR	Quest Kodiak 100	100-0038	ex N497KQ
□ P2-SIT	Quest Kodiak 100	100-0077	ex N77KQ

SOUTHWEST AIR — Mendi (MDU)

□ P2-SHA	Bell 206L-3 LongRanger III	51533	ex VH-IRE	
□ P2-SHG	Bell 407	53260	ex VH-ICL	
□ P2-SWE	de Havilland DHC-6 Twin Otter 300	480	ex P2-RDL	
□ P2-SWF	Embraer EMB.110P1 Bandeirante	110237	ex N691RA	[BNE]
□ P2-SWZ	Beech B200 Super King Air	BB-1412	ex N38VV	

SUNBIRD AVIATION — Port Moresby (POM)

| □ P2-SBB | Britten-Norman BN-2T Islander | 880 | ex N121MT |
| □ P2-SBC | Britten-Norman BN-2T Islander | 3010 | ex RP-C788 |

TRANSNIUGINI AIRWAYS — Port Moresby (POM)

| □ P2-BOB | Beech 95-B55 Baron | TC-1682 | ex VH-MHM |
| □ P2-TNT | Pacific Aerospace 750XL | 143 | ex ZK-JNG |

TRAVEL AIR — (4P) — Madang (MAG)

□ P2-TAE	Fokker 50	20202	ex PH-FZG
□ P2-TAF	Fokker 50	20192	ex PH-LMT
□ P2-TAG	Fokker 50	20177	ex PH-TAG
□ P2-TAH	Fokker 50	20122	ex PH-FZF

TROPIC AIR COMMUTER — Port Moresby (POM)

□ P2-AMH	Cessna 208B Caravan I	208B0785	ex N785SC	
□ P2-BEN	Cessna 208B Caravan I	208B0424	ex VH-LSA	
□ P2-DRS	Beech B200 Super King Air	BB-1695	exP2-MAX	
□ P2-JAU	Beech 200C Super King Air	BL-39	ex P2-SIA	
□ P2-JON	Beech 200 Super King Air	BA-1418	ex VH-MWU	
□ P2-JWM	Cessna 208B Caravan I	208B0945	ex N830CE	
□ P2-MAX	Beech 200 Super King Air	BB-1695	ex N909DD	♦
□ P2-MEH	Cessna 525B CitationJet	525B0027	ex VH-ARZ	♦

UNAPU FREIGHT SERVICES — Port Moresby (POM)

| □ P2-ENB | Britten-Norman BN-2B-26 Islander | 2197 | ex VH-KQM |

P4- ARUBA

ARUBA AIRLINES — (AG/ARU) — Aruba (AUA)

| □ P4-AAA | Airbus A320-232 | 0582 | ex B-6026 |
| □ P4-AAC | Airbus A320-232 | 0573 | ex N181LF |

INSEL AIR ARUBA — Insel Aruba (8I/NLU) — Aruba (AUA)

□ P4-FKA	Fokker 70	11528	ex PJ-JCH	♦
□ P4-FKB	Fokker 70	11537	ex PJ-JCT	♦
□ P4-FKC	Fokker 70	11583	ex PJ-FKC	♦
□ P4-MDD	McDonnell-Douglas MD-82	49972/1757	ex PJ-MDD	>Havana Air
□ P4-MDG	McDonnell-Douglas MD-83	49935/1773	ex PJ-MDG	♦
□ P4-MDH	McDonnell-Douglas MD-83	53624/2277	ex N974TW	♦

LAMIA — (LMD) — Aruba (AUA)

□ CP-2933	Avro 146-RJ85	E2348	ex YV2768	[CBB]♦
□ P4-GIU	Avro 146-RJ85	E2349	ex EI-RJL	[NWI]
□ P4-TIZ	Avro 146-RJ85	E2350	ex EI-RJM	[VLV]
□ YV3035	Avro 146-RJ85	E2370	ex P4-ARI	[VLV]♦

LYNDEN AIR CARGO

☐ P2-LAC	Lockheed L-382G Hercules	4676	ex N406LC		♦
☐ P4-LAD	Lockheed L-382G Hercules	4698	ex N402LC		♦
☐ P4-LAE	Lockheed L-382G Hercules	5225	ex N407LC		♦

TIARA AIR		Tiara (3P/TNM)		Aruba (AUA)
☐ P4-TIA	Short SD.3-60	SH3619	ex C-GPCG	
☐ P4-TIB	Short SD.3-60	SH3621	ex C-GPCN	
☐ P4-TIC	Short SD.3-60	SH3614	ex HP-1315APP	[AUA]
☐ P4-TID	Learjet 35A	35A-200	ex N200LJ	

RA- RUSSIA (Russian Federation)

AEROBRATSK		Aerobra (BRP)		Bratsk (BTK)
☐ RA-22856	Mil Mi-8T	98415350	ex CCCP-22856	
☐ RA-24261	Mil Mi-8T	98734147	ex CCCP-24261	
☐ RA-88205	Yakovlev Yak-40	9630749	ex CCCP-88205	
☐ RA-88215	Yakovlev Yak-40K	9630150	ex CCCP-88215	

AEROFLOT RUSSIAN AIRLINES		Aeroflot (SU/AFL)		Moscow-Sheremetyevo (SVO)

Member of SkyTeam

☐ VP-BDM	Airbus A319-111	2069	ex D-AVYJ	A Borodin	
☐ VP-BDN	Airbus A319-111	2072	ex D-AVYL	A Dargomyzhsky	
☐ VP-BDO	Airbus A319-111	2091	ex D-AVWU	I Stravinsky	
☐ VP-BWA	Airbus A319-111	2052	ex D-AVYA	S Prokofiev	
☐ VQ-BBA	Airbus A319-111	3794	ex D-AVXM	S Cheliuskin	
☐ VQ-BCO	Airbus A319-111	3942	ex D-AVWR	A Hachaturian	
☐ VQ-BCP	Airbus A319-111	3998	ex D-AVYZ	D Mendeleev	
☐ VP-BDK	Airbus A320-214	2106	ex F-WWDR		SkyTeam c/s
☐ VP-BID	Airbus A320-214	5421	ex D-AVVI	I Tamm	
☐ VP-BJA	Airbus A320-214	5536	ex F-WWDM	I Mechnikov	
☐ VP-BKC	Airbus A320-214	3545	ex F-WWIT	I Kruzenshtern	
☐ VP-BKX	Airbus A320-214	3410	ex F-WWIJ	G Sedov	
☐ VP-BKY	Airbus A320-214	3511	ex F-WWBZ	M Rostropovich	
☐ VP-BLH	Airbus A320-214	5565	ex F-WWIE	P Cherenkov	
☐ VP-BLL	Airbus A320-214	5572	ex F-WWBJ	N Basov	
☐ VP-BLP	Airbus A320-214	5578	ex F-WWBN	A Popov	
☐ VP-BLR	Airbus A320-214	5585	ex F-WWBQ	P Yablochkov	
☐ VP-BNT	Airbus A320-214	5614	ex F-WWIF	Dobrolet	retro c/s
☐ VP-BME	Airbus A320-214	3699	ex F-WWBO	N Mikluho-Maklay	
☐ VP-BMF	Airbus A320-214	3711	ex F-WWIV	G Shelihov	
☐ VP-BNL	Airbus A320-214	5580	ex D-AUBE	A Suvorov	
☐ VP-BQP	Airbus A320-214	2875	ex F-WWBJ	A Rublev	
☐ VP-BQU	Airbus A320-214	3373	ex F-WWDG	A Nikitin	
☐ VP-BQV	Airbus A320-214	2920	ex F-WWDY	V Vasnetsov	
☐ VP-BQW	Airbus A320-214	2947	ex F-WWBV	V Vereschchagin	
☐ VP-BRX	Airbus A320-214	3063	ex F-WWDZ	V Surikov	
☐ VP-BRY	Airbus A320-214	3052	ex F-WWDT	K Brulloff	
☐ VP-BRZ	Airbus A320-214	3157	ex F-WWDM	V Serov	
☐ VP-BTI	Airbus A320-214	5873	ex D-AVVF	V Meyerhold	
☐ VP-BWD	Airbus A320-214	2116	ex F-WWDY	A Aliabiev	
☐ VP-BWE	Airbus A320-214	2133	ex F-WWDX	N Rimsky-Korsakov	
☐ VP-BWF	Airbus A320-214	2144	ex F-WWBY	D Shostakovich	
☐ VP-BWM	Airbus A320-214	2233	ex F-WWII	S Rackhmaninov	
☐ VP-BZO	Airbus A320-214	3574	ex F-WWBK	V Bering	
☐ VP-BZP	Airbus A320-214	3631	ex D-AVYG	E Haborov	
☐ VP-BZQ	Airbus A320-214	3627	ex F-WWIS	Yu. Lisiansky	
☐ VP-BZR	Airbus A320-214	3640	ex F-WWBR	F Bellinghausen	
☐ VP-BZS	Airbus A320-214	3644	ex F-WWBU	M Lazarev	
☐ VQ-BAX	Airbus A320-214	3778	ex F-WWIM	G Nevelskoy	
☐ VQ-BAY	Airbus A320-214	3786	ex D-AVVL	S Krasheninnikov	
☐ VQ-BAZ	Airbus A320-214	3789	ex F-WWBC	V Obruchev	
☐ VQ-BBB	Airbus A320-214	3823	ex F-WWIT	Yu Gagarin	
☐ VQ-BBC	Airbus A320-214	3835	ex F-WWBI	N Przhevalsky	
☐ VQ-BCM	Airbus A320-214	3923	ex F-WWBN	G Titov	
☐ VQ-BCN	Airbus A320-214	3954	ex F-WWBV	V Chelomey	
☐ VQ-BEH	Airbus A320-214	4133	ex F-WWIS	I Pavlov	
☐ VQ-BEJ	Airbus A320-214	4160	ex D-AVVO	I Kurchatov	
☐ VQ-BHL	Airbus A320-214	4453	ex F-WWIX	S Vavilov	
☐ VQ-BHN	Airbus A320-214	4498	ex D-AUBL	N Lobachevsky	
☐ VQ-BIR	Airbus A320-214	4625	ex F-WWBZ	S Kovalevskaya	
☐ VQ-BIT	Airbus A320-214	4656	ex D-AXAB	L Landau	
☐ VQ-BIU	Airbus A320-214	4684	ex D-AUBA	K Timiriazev	
☐ VQ-BIV	Airbus A320-214	4649	ex F-WWDP	A Kolmogorov	

☐	VQ-BIW	Airbus A320-214	4579	ex D-AUBZ	V Glushko
☐	VQ-BKS	Airbus A320-214	4692	ex F-WWDI	A Chizhevsky
☐	VQ-BKT	Airbus A320-214	4712	ex F-WWBR	V Vernadsky
☐	VQ-BKU	Airbus A320-214	4835	ex D-AXAN	A Nikolaev
☐	VQ-BPU	Airbus A320-214	5921	ex F-WWDX	D Likhachev
☐	VQ-BPV	Airbus A320-214/S	5970	ex F-WWBC	A Stoletov
☐	VQ-BPW	Airbus A320-214/S	5982	ex F-WWBF	A Vishnevsky
☐	VQ-BRV	Airbus A320-214/S	5967	ex F-WWIS	A Butlerov
☐	VQ-BRW	Airbus A320-214/S	5974	ex F-WWBE	S Botkin
☐	VQ-BSE	Airbus A320-214/S	5989	ex D-AUBQ	B Petrovsky
☐	VQ-BSG	Airbus A320-214/S	6017	ex D-AUBY	Yu Senkevich
☐	VQ-BSH	Airbus A320-214/S	6022	ex D-AUBZ	P Beliaev
☐	VQ-BSI	Airbus A320-214/S	6043	ex F-WWDC	V Komarov
☐	VQ-BSJ	Airbus A320-214/S	6044	ex D-AXAE	B Egorov
☐	VQ-BSL	Airbus A320-214/S	6060	ex F-WWDM	K Feoktistov
☐	VQ-BST	Airbus A320-214/S	6071	ex D-AXAL	P Popovich
☐	VQ-BSU	Airbus A320-214/S	6090	ex D-AXAN	G Zhukov
☐		Airbus A320-214/S	6939	ex	o/o♦
☐	VP-BDC	Airbus A321-211	5271	ex D-AZAD	V Alekseev
☐	VP-BOC	Airbus A321-211	5720	ex D-AZAT	S Mikhalkov
☐	VP-BOE	Airbus A321-211	5755	ex D-AZAN	G Vishnevskaya
☐	VP-BQR	Airbus A321-211	2903	ex D-AVZD	I Repin
☐	VP-BQS	Airbus A321-211	2912	ex D-AVZL	I Kramskoi
☐	VP-BQT	Airbus A321-211	2965	ex D-AVZE	I Shishkin
☐	VP-BQX	Airbus A321-211	2957	ex D-AVZU	I Ayvazovsky
☐	VP-BRW	Airbus A321-211	3191	ex D-AVZW	N Rerih
☐	VP-BTG	Airbus A321-211	5790	ex D-AVZC	K Stanislavsky
☐	VP-BTL	Airbus A321-211	5881	ex D-AVZV	Y Vakhtangov	Manchester United c/s
☐	VP-BTR	Airbus A321-211	5913	ex D-AZAC	S Diaghilev
☐	VP-BUM	Airbus A321-211	3267	ex D-AVZQ	A Deineka
☐	VP-BUP	Airbus A321-211	3334	ex D-AVZY	M Shagal
☐	VP-BWN	Airbus A321-211	2330	ex D-AVZR	A Skriabin
☐	VP-BWO	Airbus A321-211	2337	ex D-AVZS	P Chaikovsky
☐	VP-BWP	Airbus A321-211	2342	ex D-AVZT	M Musorgsky
☐	VQ-BEA	Airbus A321-211	4058	ex D-AZAS	I Michurin
☐	VQ-BED	Airbus A321-211	4074	ex D-AVZT	N Pirogov
☐	VQ-BEE	Airbus A321-211	4099	ex D-AZAA	I Sechenov
☐	VQ-BEF	Airbus A321-211	4103	ex D-AZAC	N Zhukovsky
☐	VQ-BEG	Airbus A321-211	4116	ex D-AZAF	K Tsiolkovsky
☐	VQ-BEI	Airbus A321-211	4148	ex D-AVZS	S Korelov
☐	VQ-BHK	Airbus A321-211	4461	ex D-AVZB	M Keldysh
☐	VQ-BHM	Airbus A321-211	4500	ex D-AVZG	N Vavilov
☐	VQ-BOH	Airbus A321-211	5044	ex D-AZAP	A Prokorov
☐	VQ-BOI	Airbus A321-211	5059	ex D-AZAS	N Semenov
☐	V	Airbus A321-211	6924	ex	o/o♦
☐	VP-BLX	Airbus A330-243	963	ex F-WWYJ	E Sveetlanov
☐	VP-BLY	Airbus A330-243	973	ex F-WWKA	V Vysctsky
☐	VQ-BBE	Airbus A330-243	1014	ex F-WWKU	I Brodsky
☐	VQ-BBF	Airbus A330-243	1045	ex F-WWYB	A Griboedov
☐	VQ-BBG	Airbus A330-243	1047	ex F-WWKD	N Gogol
☐	VP-BDD	Airbus A330-343E	1356	ex F-WWCV	A Modzhaysky
☐	VP-BDE	Airbus A330-343E	1371	ex F-WWKY	L Kantorovich
☐	VQ-BCQ	Airbus A330-343E	1058	ex F-WWYX	SkyTeam c/s
☐	VQ-BCU	Airbus A330-343E	1065	ex F-WWYJ	V Mayakovsky
☐	VQ-BCV	Airbus A330-343E	1072	ex F-WWYK	B Pasternak
☐	VQ-BEK	Airbus A330-343E	1077	ex F-WWKN	A Tvardovskiy
☐	VQ-BEL	Airbus A330-343E	1103	ex F-WWYR	F Tyutchev
☐	VQ-BMV	Airbus A330-343E	1284	ex F-WWYA	P Kapitsa
☐	VQ-BMX	Airbus A330-343E	1299	ex F-WWKQ	A Sakharov
☐	VQ-BMY	Airbus A330-343E	1301	ex F-WWYL	I Frank
☐	VQ-BNS	Airbus A330-343E	1264	ex F-WWYT	A Bakulev
☐	VQ-BPI	Airbus A330-343E	1323	ex F-WWTJ	L Yashin
☐	VQ-BPJ	Airbus A330-343E	1328	ex F-WWTO	V Brumei
☐	VQ-BPK	Airbus A330-343E	1345	ex F-WWCI	I Kulibin
☐	VQ-BQX	Airbus A330-343E	1232	ex F-WWYI	O Mandelshtam
☐	VQ-BQY	Airbus A330-343E	1247	ex F-WWYQ	M Sholokhov
☐	VQ-BQZ	Airbus A330-343E	1270	ex F-WWYG	N Burdenko
☐	VP-BON	Boeing 737-8LJ/W	41200/5063		N Berdyaev	♦
☐	VP-BRF	Boeing 737-8LJ/W	41195/4590		S Obraztsov
☐	VP-BRH	Boeing 737-8LJ/W	41196/4665		B Kustodiev
☐	VP-BRR	Boeing 737-8LJ/W	41197/4710		A Solzhenitsyn
☐	VP-BZA	Boeing 737-8LJ/W	41198/4753		Ch Aytmatov
☐	VP-BZB	Boeing 737-8LJ/W	41199/4897		K Simonov
☐	VQ-BVO	Boeing 737-8LJ/W	41203/5253		V Belinsky	♦
☐	VQ-BVP	Boeing 737-8LJ/W	41204/5291		L Gumilev	♦
☐	VQ-BWA	Boeing 737-8LJ/W	41207/5377			♦
☐	VP-BGC	Boeing 777-3M0ER	41680/1079		P Bagration
☐	VP-BGD	Boeing 777-3M0ER	41681/1084	ex N5016R	M Barclay-de-Tolly

☐ VP-BGE	Boeing 777-3M0ER	41679/1068	ex N5016R	M Kutuzov		
☐ VP-BGF	Boeing 777-3M0ER	41686/1097		D Davydov		
☐ VQ-BQB	Boeing 777-3M0ER	41687/1161		AA Kuprin		
☐ VQ-BQC	Boeing 777-3M0ER	41688/1175		I Bunin		
☐ VQ-BQD	Boeing 777-3M0ER	41682/1185		A Chekhov		
☐ VQ-BQE	Boeing 777-3M0ER	41683/1190		M Lermontov		
☐ VQ-BQF	Boeing 777-3M0ER	41684/1199		A Blok		
☐ VQ-BQG	Boeing 777-3M0ER	41689/1205			SkyTeam c/s♦	
☐ VQ-BUA	Boeing 777-3M0ER	41685/1281		S Esenin	♦	
☐ VQ-BUB	Boeing 777-3M0ER	41690/1294		M Bulgakov	♦	
☐ VQ-BUC	Boeing 777-3M0ER	41691/1299			o/o♦	
☐ RA-96005	Ilyushin Il-96-300	74393201002	ex CCCP-96005	V Chkalov		
☐ RA-96007	Ilyushin Il-96-300	74393201004		A Mayorov		
☐ RA-96008	Ilyushin Il-96-300	74393201005		IA Moiseyev		
☐ RA-96010	Ilyushin Il-96-300	74393201007		Nikolaj Karpajev	dbf 03Jun14	
☐ RA-96011	Ilyushin Il-96-300	74393201008		K Kokkinaki		
☐ RA-96015	Ilyushin Il-96-300	74393201012		M Gromov		
☐ RA-89014	Sukhoi SSJ 100-95B	95025		V Sysovskiy		
☐ RA-89015	Sukhoi SSJ 100-95B	95029			SkyTeam c/s	
☐ RA-89017	Sukhoi SSJ 100-95B	95035		P Khmelnitsky		
☐ RA-89022	Sukhoi SSJ 100-95B	95039		I Orlovets		
☐ RA-89023	Sukhoi SSJ 100-95B	95041		P Mikhaylov		
☐ RA-89024	Sukhoi SSJ 100-95B	95044		D Barilov		
☐ RA-89025	Sukhoi SSJ 100-95B	95047		Kh Tskhovrebov		
☐ RA-89026	Sukhoi SSJ 100-95B	95051		G Benkunsky	♦	
☐ RA-89027	Sukhoi SSJ 100-95B	95053		V Borisov	♦	
☐ RA-89028	Sukhoi SSJ 100-95B	95059		B Bugaev	♦	
☐ RA-89032	Sukhoi SSJ 100-95B	95043	ex 97002	D Ezersky	wfs	
☐ RA-89041	Sukhoi SSJ 100-95B	95063		M Vodopyanov	♦	
☐ RA-89042	Sukhoi SSJ 100-95B	95068		E Barabash	♦	
☐ RA-89043	Sukhoi SSJ 100-95B	95074		B Velling	♦	
☐ RA-89044	Sukhoi SSJ 100-95B	95076		A Vitkovsky	♦	
☐ RA-89045	Sukhoi SSJ 100-95B	95079		I Voedilo	♦	
☐ RA-89046	Sukhoi SSJ 100-95B	95082		D Glinka	♦	
☐ RA-89047	Sukhoi SSJ 100-95B	95084		A Gruzdin	♦	
☐ RA-89052	Sukhoi SSJ 100-95B	95088		M Efimov	♦	
☐ RA-	Sukhoi SSJ 100-95B	95089			o/o♦	
☐ RA-	Sukhoi SSJ 100-95B	95090			o/o♦	
☐ RA-	Sukhoi SSJ 100-95B	95091			o/o♦	
☐ RA-	Sukhoi SSJ 100-95B	95094			o/o♦	

AEROKUZBASS — Novokuznetsk (NKZ) — Novokuznetsk (NOZ)

☐ RA-22725	Mil Mi-8T	98308700	ex CCCP-22725	
☐ RA-24430	Mil Mi-8T	98625661	ex CCCP-24430	dam 05Dec13

AEROLIMOUSINE — (LIN) — Moscow-Vnukovo (VKO)

☐ RA-02810	BAe 125-700A	257012	ex N449EB	
☐ RA-87908	Yakovlev Yak-40	9721354	ex CCCP-87908	

AIRBRIDGE CARGO — AirBridge Cargo (RU/ABW) — Moscow Sheremetyevo(SVO)

☐ VP-BIG	Boeing 747-46NERF	35420/1395	ex N5022E	
☐ VP-BIK	Boeing 747-46NERF	35421/1400		
☐ VP-BIM	Boeing 747-4HAERF	35237/1402		
☐ VQ-BHE	Boeing 747-4KZF	36784/1411	ex N384NC	
☐ VQ-BIA	Boeing 747-4KZF	36785/1418	ex N385NY	
☐ VQ-BJB	Boeing 747-446F	33749/1352	ex N402AL	
☐ VQ-BUU	Boeing 747-4EVERF	35170/1376	ex N368DF	♦
☐ VQ-BWW	Boeing 747-406ERF	35233/1382	ex PH-CKD	♦
☐ VQ-BGZ	Boeing 747-8HVF	37580/1430		
☐ VQ-BLQ	Boeing 747-8HVF	37581/1448		
☐ VQ-BLR	Boeing 747-8HVF	37668/1452	ex N1788B	
☐ VQ-BRH	Boeing 747-8HVF	37669/1463	ex N769BA	
☐ VQ-BRJ	Boeing 747-8HVF	37670/1482	ex N959BA	
☐ VQ-BVR	Boeing 747-867F	60687/1505		♦
☐ VQ-BVF	Boeing 737-46QF	29001/3040	ex N691AC	♦

AK BARS AERO — Bugavia (2B/BGM) — Bugulma (UUA)

☐ VQ-BHF	Canadair CRJ-200LR	7802	ex N510CA	
☐ VQ-BHG	Canadair CRJ-200LR	7816	ex N518CA	
☐ VQ-BHH	Canadair CRJ-200LR	7824	ex N526CA	
☐ VQ-BHI	Canadair CRJ-200LR	7809	ex N514CA	
☐ VQ-BHJ	Canadair CRJ-200LR	7821	ex N523CA	
☐ VQ-BJZ	Canadair CRJ-200ER	7500	ex N130MN	
☐ VQ-BLZ	Canadair CRJ-200LR	7520	ex N129MN	

☐ VQ-BOJ	Canadair CRJ-200ER	7740	ex N128MN
☐ VQ-BOL	Canadair CRJ-200ER	7739	ex N677SA
☐ VQ-BOM	Canadair CRJ-200ER	7707	ex N486CA
☐ VQ-BOP	Canadair CRJ-200ER	7689	ex N483CA
☐ VQ-BOQ	Canadair CRJ-200ER	7613	ex N458CA
☐ VQ-BOR	Canadair CRJ-200ER	7313	ex N639BR
☐ VQ-BOT	Canadair CRJ-200ER	7414	ex N649BR
☐ VQ-BOU	Canadair CRJ-200ER	7535	ex N667BR
☐ RA-85799	Tupolev Tu-154M	94A983	
☐ RA-85833	Tupolev Tu-154M	01A1020	
☐ RA-87209	Yakovlev Yak-40K	9810657	ex CCCP-87209 all-white
☐ RA-87447	Yakovlev Yak-40	9430436	ex CCCP-87447 AK Bars Bank titles
☐ RA-87494	Yakovlev Yak-40	9541745	ex CCCP-87494
☐ RA-87938	Yakovlev Yak-40K	9710153	ex CCCP-87938

Scheduled services suspended Jan15

ALROSA AVIATION — Mirny (6R/DRU) — Mirny (MJZ)

☐ RA-22394	Mil Mi-8T	7296	ex CCCP-22394
☐ RA-22570	Mil Mi-8T	7816	ex CCCP-22570
☐ RA-22571	Mil Mi-8T	7817	ex CCCP-22571
☐ RA-22731	Mil Mi-8T	98308847	ex CCCP-22731
☐ RA-22744	Mil Mi-8T	98311127	ex CCCP-22744
☐ RA-22879	Mil Mi-8T	98415832	ex CCCP-22879
☐ RA-22899	Mil Mi-8T	98417179	ex CCCP-22899
☐ RA-22902	Mil Mi-8T	98420099	ex CCCP-22902
☐ RA-24256	Mil Mi-8T	98734114	ex CCCP-24256
☐ RA-24257	Mil Mi-8T	98734121	ex CCCP-24257
☐ RA-24435	Mil Mi-8T	98625845	ex CCCP-24435
☐ RA-24451	Mil Mi-8T	98628263	ex CCCP-24451
☐ RA-24506	Mil Mi-8T	98520843	ex CCCP-24506
☐ RA-24536	Mil Mi-8T	98522588	ex CCCP-24536
☐ RA-24741	Mil Mi-8T	98417837	ex CCCP-24741
☐ RA-25228	Mil Mi-8T	7763	ex CCCP-25228
☐ RA-25313	Mil Mi-8T	98203720	ex CCCP-25313
☐ RA-25333	Mil Mi-8T	98206010	ex CCCP-25333
☐ RA-25376	Mil Mi-8T	98209062	ex CCCP-25376
☐ RA-25606	Mil Mi-8T	99150564	ex CCCP-25606
☐ RA-85654	Tupolev Tu-154M	89A796	ex CCCP-86654
☐ RA-85675	Tupolev Tu-154M	90A835	ex CCCP-85675 Vladimir Kuzakov
☐ RA-85684	Tupolev Tu-154M	90A851	ex CCCP-85684
☐ RA-85728	Tupolev Tu-154M	92A910	ex CCCP-85728
☐ RA-85757	Tupolev Tu-154M	92A939	ex EP-MHX
☐ RA-85770	Tupolev Tu-154M	93A952	[NOZ]
☐ RA-85782	Tupolev Tu-154M	93A966	ex UN-85782
☐ EI-ECL	Boeing 737-86N/W	32655/1662	ex LN-NOP ♦
☐ EI-ECM	Boeing 737-86N/W	32658/1695	ex LN-NOQ ♦
☐ EI-FCH	Boeing 737-83N/W	32576/875	ex M-ABFV
☐ RA-06036	Mil Mi-26	34001212426	ex CCCP-06036
☐ RA-06081	Mil Mi-26	34001212471	ex CCCP-06081
☐ RA-26552	Antonov An-26	3107	ex CCCP-26552 [YKS]
☐ RA-26628	Antonov An-26	5309	ex CCCP-26628 wfs
☐ RA-26668	Antonov An-26B-100	8201	ex CCCP-26668
☐ RA-46488	Antonov An-24RV	27308106	ex CCCP-46488
☐ RA-46621	Antonov An-24RV	37308708	ex CCCP-46621
☐ RA-47272	Antonov An-24B	07306402	ex CCCP-47272
☐ RA-47694	Antonov An-24B	27307601	ex CCCP-47694
☐ RA-65146	Tupolev Tu-134B-3	61000	ex YL-LBA
☐ RA-65653	Tupolev Tu-134A	0351009	ex CCCP-65653 [MHP]
☐ RA-65751	Tupolev Tu-134B-3	63536	ex 4L-AAC
☐ RA-76360	Ilyushin Il-76TD	1033414492	
☐ RA-76420	Ilyushin Il-76TD	1023413446	jt ops with TIS

AMUR ARTEL STARATELEI AVIAKOMPANIA — Khabarovsk-Novy (KHV)

☐ RA-26001	Antonov An-26	9705	ex CCCP-26001
☐ RA-26048	Antonov An-26B	10901	ex CCCP-26048
☐ RA-46612	Antonov An-24RV	37308609	ex CCCP-46612

ANGARA AIRLINES — Sarma (2G/AGU) — Irkutsk-One (IKT)

☐ RA-46625	Antonov An-24RV	37308804	ex CCCP-46625
☐ RA-46662	Antonov An-24RV	47309410	ex CCCP-46662
☐ RA-46697	Antonov An-24RV	47309908	ex CCCP-46697
☐ RA-46712	Antonov An-24RV	57310408	ex EX-24408
☐ RA-47366	Antonov An-24RV	77310804	ex CCCP-47366
☐ RA-47818	Antonov An-24RV	17307107	ex CCCP-47818
☐ RA-47848	Antonov An-24B	17307410	ex CCCP-47848

☐ RA-61709	Antonov An-148-100	27015040009		♦
☐ RA-61710	Antonov An-148-100	27015040010		♦
☐ RA-61711	Antonov An-148-100	41-07		
☐ RA-61713	Antonov An-148-100	41-10		
☐ RA-61714	Antonov An-148-100	42-01		
☐ RA-26511	Antonov An-26-100	6808	ex CCCP-26511	
☐ RA-26543	Antonov An-26	2709	ex CCCP-26543	
☐ RA-26655	Antonov An-26-100	7802	ex CCCP-26655	wfs

ARKHANGELSK 2ND AVIATION ENTERPRISE — Arkhangelsk-Vaslearo

☐ RA-67553	LET L-410UVP-E	851430	ex CCCP-67553
☐ RA-67564	LET L-410UVP-E	851604	ex CCCP-67564
☐ RA-67567	LET L-410UVP-E	861607	ex CCCP-67567
☐ RA-67602	LET L-410UVP-E	892229	ex CCCP-67602
☐ RA-67603	LET L-410UVP-E	892214	ex CCCP-67603
☐ RA-67606	LET L-410UVP-E	892322	ex CCCP-67606
☐ RA-06039	Mil Mi-26T	34001212429	ex CCCP-06039
☐ RA-06042	Mil Mi-26T	34001212432	ex CCCP-06042
☐ RA-06044	Mil Mi-26T	34001212434	ex CCCP-06044
☐ RA-22341	Mil Mi-8T	7166	ex CCCP-22341
☐ RA-22762	Mil Mi-8T	98311485	ex CCCP-22762
☐ RA-24012	Mil Mi-8MTV-1	95713	ex CCCP-24012

ATRAN - AVIATRANS CARGO AIRLINES — Atran (V8/VAS) — Moscow-Domodedovo (DME)

☐ RA-11868	Antonov An-12BK	9346310	ex CCCP-11868
☐ RA-12990	Antonov An-12B	00347304	ex CCCP-12990
☐ VP-BCK	Boeing 737-46QSF	28758/2939	ex N782AG
☐ VP-BCJ	Boeing 737-46QSF	28663/2922	ex N682AG

AURORA AIRLINES — Satair (HZ/SHU) — Ulyanovsk-Tsentralny (ULY)

☐ VP-BUK	Airbus A319-111	3281	ex D-AVYP		
☐ VP-BUN	Airbus A319-111	3298	ex D-AVYI		
☐ VP-BUO	Airbus A319-111	3336	ex D-AVYS		
☐ VP-BWK	Airbus A319-111	2222	ex D-AVYI		
☐ VP-BWL	Airbus A319-111	2243	ex D-AVWV		
☐ VQ-BBD	Airbus A319-111	3838	ex D-AVYP		♦
☐ VQ-BWV	Airbus A319-112	3108	ex RP-C8603		♦
☐ RA-67251	de Havilland DHC-8-311	533	ex C-FWFH		
☐ RA-67253	de Havilland DHC-8-311	451	ex C-GAPW		
☐ RA-67255	de Havilland DHC-8-315	581	ex C-GLKW		
☐ RA-67257	de Havilland DHC-8-201	457	ex C-GYDI		
☐ RA-67261	de Havilland DHC-8-315Q	556	ex C-GOJE		
☐ RA-67263	de Havilland DHC-8-201	428	ex C-GOSW		
☐ RA-11364	Antonov An-12BK	00347601	ex CCCP-11364		
☐ RA-46530	Antonov An-24B	57310009	ex CCCP-46530		
☐ RA-48984	Antonov An-12B	402913	ex UR-48984		
☐ RA-64026	Tupolev Tu-204-300	1450743364026			[VVO]
☐ RA-64038	Tupolev Tu-204-300	1450744464038		small Sberbank Rossii titles	[VVO]
☐ RA-64039	Tupolev Tu-204-300	1450741564039		small Sberbank Rossii titles	[VVO]
☐ RA-64040	Tupolev Tu-204-300	1450744565040			[VVO]
☐ RA-67283	de Havilland DHC-6 Twin Otter 400	881	ex C-GVEP		♦
☐ RA-73002	Boeing 737-5L9	28997/3008	ex LY-AYS		
☐ RA-73003	Boeing 737-2J8 (Nordam 3)	22859/890	ex N235WA		wfs
☐ RA-73005	Boeing 737-232 (Nordam 3)	23100/1038	ex N328DL		wfs
☐ RA-73006	Boeing 737-548	25737/2232	ex LY-AYW		♦
☐ RA-73013	Boeing 737-5L9	28721/2856	ex OY-APH		
☐ RA-	de Havilland DHC-6 Twin Otter 400	889	ex C-GVZQ		♦

AVIAKOMPANIYA PANH — Chita

☐ RA-67038(2)	LET L-410UVP-E20	2912	ex OK-SLW(2)	♦
☐ RA-67039(2)	LET L-410UVP-E20	2914	ex OK-JDP(2)	♦

AVIACON ZITOTRANS — Zitotrans (ZR/AZS) — Ekaterinburg-Koltsovo (SVX)

☐ RA-76352	Ilyushin Il-76TD	1023411378	ex EP-SFB	opf UN WFP
☐ RA-76370	Ilyushin Il-76TD	1023414458		
☐ RA-76386	Ilyushin Il-76TD	1033418600	ex UK 76386	
☐ RA-76502	Ilyushin Il-76TD	1003401004	ex EW-78828	
☐ RA-76807	Ilyushin Il-76TD	1013405176	ex CCCP-76807	opf UN WFP
☐ RA-76842	Ilyushin Il-76TD	1033418616		
☐ RA-76846	Ilyushin Il-76TD	0093497936	ex EP-TPU	

467

AVIALIFT

☐ RA-87273	Yakovlev Yak-40	9310297	ex CCCP-87273	♦

AVIASTAR – TUPOLEV Tupolevair (4B/TUP) Moscow-Zhukovsky/Domodedovo (-/DME)

☐ RA-64021	Tupolev Tu-204-100C	1450742964021		
☐ RA-64024	Tupolev Tu-204-100C	1450741364024	ex LY-AGT	DHL c/s
☐ RA-64032	Tupolev Tu-204-100C	1450742264032		

BARKOL AVIAKOMPANIA Moscow-Bykovo/Volgograd-Gurmak (BKA/VOG)

☐ RA-87227	Yakovlev Yak-40K	9841559	ex CCCP-87227	♦
☐ RA-87280	Yakovlev Yak-40	9322025	ex CCCP-87280	VIP
☐ RA-88228	Yakovlev Yak-40	9641750		VIP

BURYAT AIRLINES Bural (BUN) Ulan Ude-Mukhino (UUD)

☐ RA-46506	Antonov An-24RV	37308402	ex CCCP-46506	
☐ RA-46614	Antonov An-24RV	37308701	ex CCCP-46614	
☐ RA-46661	Antonov An-24RV	47309305	ex UR-CDY	
☐ RA-47361	Antonov An-24RV	67310705	ex CCCP-47361	wfs
☐ RA-47799	Antonov An-24RV	17306808	ex CCCP-47799	

CENTER-SOUTH AIRLINES Center-South (DF/CTS) Belgorod (EGO)

☐ RA-65096	Tupolev Tu-134A-3	60257	ex CCCP-65096	
☐ RA-65097	Tupolev Tu-134A-3	60540	ex CCCP-65097	
☐ RA-65102	Tupolev Tu-134A-3	60267	ex CCCP-65102	
☐ RA-65108	Tupolev Tu-134A-3	60332	ex CCCP-65108	[PEE]
☐ RA-65559	Tupolev Tu-134A-3	7349909	ex CCCP-65559	
☐ RA-65574	Tupolev Tu-134B-3	03564753	ex 17 red	
☐ RA-65576	Tupolev Tu-134B-3	63285	ex CCCP-65576 Alexsandr Fedorchenko	
☐ RA-65700	Tupolev Tu-134B-3M	64783	ex 46 red	
☐ RA-65727	Tupolev Tu-134B-3	03564820	ex CCCP-65727	
☐ RA-65747	Tupolev Tu-134B-3	03564715		♦
☐ RA-65784	Tupolev Tu-134A-3	62715	ex CCCP-65784	
☐ RA-65805	Tupolev Tu-134B-3	64775	ex CCCP-64775	
☐ RA-65906	Tupolev Tu-134AK	66175	ex CCCP-65906	
☐ RA-65944	Tupolev Tu-134A-3	12096	ex CCCP-65944	♦
☐ RA-89004	Sukhoi SSJ 100-95B	95012	ex 95012	Oleg Kuprikov
☐ RA-89007	Sukhoi SSJ 100-95B	95015	ex 95015	Sergey Melnikov
☐ RA-89053	Sukhoi SSJ 100-95LR	95009	ex 97009	♦

CHUKOTAVIA (ADZ) Anadyr (DYR)

☐ RA-22728	Mil Mi-8T	98308799	ex CCCP-22728	
☐ RA-24199	Mil Mi-8T	98943825	ex CCCP-24199	
☐ RA-24497	Mil Mi-8T	98734707	ex CCCP-24497	
☐ RA-24498	Mil Mi-8T	98734729	ex CCCP-24498	
☐ RA-24503	Mil Mi-8T	96520730	ex CCCP-24503	
☐ RA-24531	Mil Mi-8T	98522401	ex CCCP-24531	
☐ RA-24719	Mil Mi-8T	98417340	ex CCCP-24719	
☐ RA-24738	Mil Mi-8T	98417759	ex CCCP-24738	
☐ RA-25158	Mil Mi-8T	99047875	ex CCCP-25158	
☐ RA-25189	Mil Mi-8T	98943829	ex CCCP-25189	
☐ RA-25470	Mil Mi-8MTV-1	95614	ex CCCP-25470	
☐ RA-25988	Mil Mi-8T	7520	ex CCCP-25988	
☐ RA-26099	Antonov An-26B-100	11905	ex CCCP-26099	
☐ RA-26128	Antonov An-26B	12702	ex CCCP-26128	
☐ RA-26590	Antonov An-26B	13910	ex CCCP-26590	
☐ RA-46616	Antonov An-24RV	37308703	ex CCCP-46616	
☐ RA-47159	Antonov An-24B	89901701	ex CCCP-47159	
☐ RA-67281	de Havilland DHC-6 Twin Otter 400	860	ex C-GFVT	
☐ RA-67282	de Havilland DHC-6 Twin Otter 400	861	ex C-GNVA	dam 05Feb14
☐ RA-67826	de Havilland DHC-6 Twin Otter 400	919	ex C-GFVT	♦
☐ RA-	de Havilland DHC-6 Twin Otter 400	922	ex C-FGAL	o/o♦

DEXTER AIR TAXI

☐ RA-01500	Pilatus PC-12/47	803	ex OY-PLB
☐ RA-01501	Pilatus PC-12/47	841	ex HB-FSP
☐ RA-01502	Pilatus PC-12/47	862	ex HB-FSU
☐ RA-01503	Pilatus PC-12/47	882	ex HB-FQN
☐ RA-01504	Pilatus PC-12NG	1026	ex HB-FQQ
☐ RA-01505	Pilatus PC-12NG	1029	ex HB-FQH
☐ RA-01506	Pilatus PC-12NG	1061	ex HB-FRO

☐ RA-01507	Pilatus PC-12NG	1064	ex HB-FRS
☐ RA-01509	Pilatus PC-12/47	745	ex HB-FSC
☐ RA-01510	Pilatus PC-12/47	723	ex HB-FRJ
☐ RA-01511	Pilatus PC-12NG	1324	ex OK-PCB
☐ RA-01514	Pilatus PC-12/45	607	ex N607ST
☐ RA-01515	Pilatus PC-12		
☐ RA-01508	Pilatus PC-12/45	471	ex ZS-AGI

DONAVIA — Donavia (D9/DNV) — Rostov-on-Don (ROV)

☐ VP-BBT	Airbus A319-112	1805	ex C-GKNW	
☐ VP-BBU	Airbus A319-112	1630	ex C-FBLJ	
☐ VP-BIS	Airbus A319-112	1808	ex OH-LVF	
☐ VP-BIV	Airbus A319-115LR	3065	ex F-GRXN	
☐ VP-BNB	Airbus A319-112	2751	ex N945FR	
☐ VP-BNJ	Airbus A319-111	2241	ex N930FR	
☐ VP-BNN	Airbus A319-111	1841	ex N914FR	
☐ VP-BQK	Airbus A319-111	3179	ex EC-KFT	
☐ VP-BWG	Airbus A319-111	2093	ex D-AVYE	
☐ VP-BWJ	Airbus A319-111	2179	ex D-AVYU	♦
☐ RA-89034	Sukhoi SSJ 100-95LR	95062		o/o♦
☐ RA-89035	Sukhoi SSJ 100-95LR	95067		o/o♦
☐ RA-89036	Sukhoi SSJ 100-95LR	95070		o/o♦
☐ RA-89037	Sukhoi SSJ 100-95LR	95077		o/o♦
☐ RA-89038	Sukhoi SSJ 100-95LR	95083		o/o♦
☐ VP-BWY	Boeing 737-528	27305/2574	ex F-GJNO	[MME]
☐ VP-BWZ	Boeing 737-528	27304/2572	ex F-GJNN	[MME]
☐ VQ-BAN	Boeing 737-4Q8	25113/2656	ex N782AS	[MPL]
☐ VQ-BAO	Boeing 737-4Q8	25114/2666	ex N783AS	[RIX]

FLIGHT INSPECTIONS & SYSTEMS — Specair (LTS) — Moscow-Bykovo/Khabarovsk-Novy (BKA/KHV)

☐ RA-26088	Antonov An-26ASLK	11209	ex CCCP-26088	Calibrator/Flying laboratory
☐ RA-26571	Antonov An-26ASLK	3909	ex CCCP-26571	Calibrator/Flying laboratory
☐ RA-26625	Antonov An-26ASLK	5203	ex CCCP-26625	Calibrator/Flying laboratory
☐ RA-26631	Antonov An-26ASLK	5503	ex CCCP-26631	Calibrator/Flying laboratory
☐ RA-26673	Antonov An-26ASLK	8408	ex CCCP-26673	Calibrator/Flying laboratory
☐ RA-46395	Antonov An-24KPA	07036209	ex CCCP-46395	Calibrator/Flying laboratory

GAZPROMAVIA — Gazprom (4G/GZP) — Moscow-Ostafyevo/Moscow-Vnukovo (-/VKO)

☐ RA-04086	Eurocopter EC135T2+	0924	
☐ RA-04087	Eurocopter EC135T2+	0927	
☐ RA-04088	Eurocopter EC135T2+	0952	
☐ RA-04089	Eurocopter EC135T2+	0955	
☐ RA-04090	Eurocopter EC135T2+	0863	
☐ RA-04091	Eurocopter EC135T2+	0899	
☐ RA-04092	Eurocopter EC135T2+	0904	
☐ RA-04093	Eurocopter EC135T2+	0906	
☐ RA-24143	Mil Mi-8T	98841441	ex UN-24143
☐ RA-06104	Mil Mi-8T	99047812	ex 4K-25157
☐ RA-06105	Mil Mi-8T	98943859	ex CCCP-26564(2)
☐ RA-06162	Mil Mi-8T	98943931	ex CCCP-06162
☐ RA-22233	Mil M-8AMT	8AMT00643104803U	
☐ RA-22443	Mil Mi-8AMT	8AMT00643073109U	
☐ RA-22508	Mil Mi-8T	99357517	
☐ RA-22962	Mil Mi-8PK	99357695	
☐ RA-22963	Mil Mi-8T	99457734	
☐ RA-22964	Mil Mi-8TM	99357706	
☐ RA-22967	Mil Mi-8AMT	59489614234	
☐ RA-24015	Mil Mi-8T	99150857	ex CCCP-25015
☐ RA-24158	Mil Mi-8T	98941827	ex CCCP-24158
☐ RA-24167	Mil Mi-8T	98941977	ex CCCP-24167
☐ RA-24179	Mil Mi-8T	98943215	ex CCCP-24179
☐ RA-25155	Mil Mi-8PS	99047812	ex CCCP-25155
☐ RA-25410	Mil Mi-8MTV-1	96126	
☐ RA-25411	Mil Mi-8MTV-1	96127	
☐ RA-25412	Mil Mi-8MTV-1	96148	
☐ RA-25614	Mil Mi-8T	99150825	ex LY-HBD
☐ RA-25616	Mil Mi-8T	99150834	ex CCCP-25616
☐ RA-25776	Mil Mi-8MTV-1	96103	
☐ RA-25794	Mil Mi-8MTV-1	96203	
☐ RA-25798	Mil Mi-8MTV-1	96009	
☐ RA-25799	Mil Mi-8MTV-1	96010	
☐ RA-25800	Mil Mi-8MTV-1	96012	
☐ RA-27077	Mil Mi-8MTV-1	95915	
☐ RA-27078	Mil Mi-8MTV-1	95916	
☐ RA-27140	Mil Mi-8MTV-1	96202	

☐ RA-27145	Mil Mi-8T	99257347		
☐ RA-27159	Mil Mi-8T	99257231	ex CCCP-27159	
☐ RA-27197	Mil M-8MTV-1	96011		
☐ RA-27199	Mil Mi-8MTV-1	96014		
☐ RA-22453	Mil Mi-171C	171C00066433202U		
☐ RA-22454	Mil Mi-171C	171C00066433203U		
☐ RA-22455	Mil Mi-171C	171C00066433110U		
☐ RA-22456	Mil Mi-171C	171C00066433201U		
☐ RA-22459	Mil Mi-171C	171C00066433204U		
☐ RA-22460	Mil Mi-171C	171C00066433205U		
☐ RA-22461	Mil Mi-171C	171C00066433206U		
☐ RA-22462	Mil Mi-171C	171C00066433207U		
☐ RA-22463	Mil Mi-171C	171C00066433208U		
☐ RA-22464	Mil Mi-171C	171C00066433209U		
☐ RA-22465	Mil Mi-171C	171C00066433210U		
☐ RA-22466	Mil Mi-171C	171C00066343301U		
☐ RA-22468	Mil Mi-171C	171C00066433302U		
☐ RA-22469	Mil Mi-171C	171C00066343303U		
☐ RA-89018	Sukhoi SSJ 100-95LR	95033		
☐ RA-89019	Sukhoi SSJ 100-95LR	95056	ex 89019	
☐ RA-89020	Sukhoi SSJ 100-95LR	95055	ex 89020	
☐ RA-89029	Sukhoi SSJ 100-95LR	95057	ex 89029	
☐ RA-89030	Sukhoi SSJ 100-95LR	95030		♦
☐ RA-89031	Sukhoi SSJ 110-95LR	95064		♦
☐ RA-89048	Sukhoi SSJ 100-95LR	95073		♦
☐ RA-89049	Sukhoi SSJ 100-95LR	95078		♦
☐ RA-	Sukhoi SSJ 100-95LR	95080		o/o♦
☐ RA-	Sukhoi SSJ 100-95LR	95092		o/o♦
☐ RA-42436	Yakovlev Yak-42D	4520421605018		
☐ RA-42437	Yakovlev Yak-42D	4520423606018		
☐ RA-42438	Yakovlev Yak-42D	4520423609018		VIP
☐ RA-42439	Yakovlev Yak-42D	4520423904019		
☐ RA-42442	Yakovlev Yak-42D	4520421402019		VIP
☐ RA-42451	Yakovlev Yak-42D	4520422708018		VIP
☐ RA-42452	Yakovlev Yak-42D	4520423409016	ex RA-42431	
☐ RA-21505	Yakovlev Yak-40K	9830159	ex CCCP-21505	
☐ RA-73000	Boeing 737-76N	28630/664	ex VT-JNP	
☐ RA-73004	Boeing 737-76N	28635/734	ex VT-JNQ	
☐ RA-74008	Antonov An-74TK-100	36547095900	ex UR-74008	
☐ RA-85625	Tupolev Tu-154M	87A752	ex CCCP-85625	
☐ RA-85751	Tupolev Tu-154M	92A933		
☐ RA-85774	Tupolev Tu-154M	93A956		[ULY]
☐ RA-88186	Yakovlev Yak-40K	9620648	ex CCCP-88186	
☐ RA-88300	Yakovlev Yak-40K	9641451	ex OK-GEO	
☐ VP-BNZ	Boeing 737-7HD/W (BBJ1)	35959/2029		VIP

GLOBUS — Globus (GH/GLP)

☐ VP-BDF	Boeing 737-8Q8/W	30672/1497	ex EI-EWK	
☐ VP-BDG	Boeing 737-8Q8/W	30669/1479	ex EI-EWL	
☐ VP-BDH	Boeing 737-8Q8/W	30667/1448	ex EI-EWN	
☐ VP-BND	Boeing 737-83N/W	28245/1054	ex N315TZ	
☐ VP-BNG	Boeing 737-83N/W	30640/1035	ex N314TZ	
☐ VP-BQD	Boeing 737-83N/W	28239/847	ex N301TZ	
☐ VP-BQF	Boeing 737-83N/W	28243/984	ex N310TZ	
☐ VP-BUG	Boeing 737-86J/W	37741/2686	ex N741SM	
☐ VQ-BKV	Boeing 737-8ZS/W	37084/3605		
☐ VQ-BKW	Boeing 737-8ZS/W	37085/3654		
☐ VQ-BVK	Boeing 737-8GJ/W	41401/5165		<SBI♦
☐ VQ-BVL	Boeing 737-8GJ/W	41399/5055	ex (VT-SZL)	<SBI♦
☐ VQ-BVM	Boeing 737-8GJ/W	41400/5094	ex (VT-SZM)	<SBI♦
☐ VP-BAN	Boeing 737-4Y0	26071/2361	ex N314PW	

GROZNY-AVIA — (GZ/GOZ) — Grozny (GRV)

☐ RA-42353	Yakovlev Yak-42D	4520424711396	ex LY-AAT	
☐ RA-42365	Yakovlev Yak-42D	4520424811447	ex CCCP-42365	♦
☐ RA-42379	Yakovlev Yak-42D	4520421014543	ex EP-YAE	
☐ RA-42385	Yakovlev Yak-42D	4520423016309	ex ER-YCC	small NK Air titles
☐ RA-42418	Yakovlev Yak-42D	4520423219118	ex CCCP-42418	

I FLY — Russian Sky (H5/RSY)

☐ EI-DUA	Boeing 757-256	26247/860	ex N241LF	
☐ EI-DUD	Boeing 757-256	26249/881	ex N271LF	
☐ EI-ETI	Airbus A330-322	171	ex D-AERS	
☐ EI-EWT	Boeing 757-28A	29381/958	ex N754NA	

470

| ☐ EI-FBU | Airbus A330-322 | 120 | ex D-AERK | | |

IKAR — Krasjet (IK/KAR) — Magadan-Sokol (GDX)

☐ VP-BDI	Boeing 767-38AER	29618/792	ex N618SH		<NWS♦
☐ VP-BMC	Boeing 767-3Q8ER	30301/762	ex N431LF	Pegas c/s	<NWS
☐ VP-BOY	Boeing 767-3G5ER	29435/720	ex EI-CZH	Pegas c/s	<NWS
☐ VP-BOZ	Boeing 767-3G5ER	28111/612	ex EI-CXO	Pegas c/s	<NWS
☐ VQ-BTQ	Boeing 767-3Q8ER	28207/695	ex B-5018		♦

| ☐ RA-28723 | WSK-PZL/Antonov An-28 | 1AJ007-08 | ex CCCP-28723 | | wfs |
| ☐ RA-28726 | WSK-PZL/Antonov An-28 | 1AJ007-11 | ex CCCP-28726 | | wfs |

ILIN AVIAKOMPANIA — Yakutsk-Magan

| ☐ RA-67664 | LET L-410UVP-E | 902526 | ex CCCP-67664 Anatoli Kryuchkov | |

IRAERO — IrAero (IO/IAE) — Irkutsk-One (IKT)

☐ RA-08824	Antonov An-24RV	97310810V	ex CCCP-08824	
☐ RA-46408	Antonov An-24B	87304003	ex CCCP-46408	♦
☐ RA-46505	Antonov An-24RV	37308309	ex CCCP-46505	
☐ RA-46640	Antonov An-24RV	37308908	ex CCCP-46640	
☐ RA-46846	Antonov An-24RV	27307504	ex ER-AWC	
☐ RA-47804	Antonov An-24RV	17306903	ex CCCP-47804	
☐ RA-47805	Antonov An-24RV	17306907	ex ER-AWD	
☐ RA-48096	Antonov An-24RV	57310406	ex CCCP-48096	
☐ RA-93934	Antonov An-24B	09902310	ex CCCP-93934	

☐ RA-26051	Antonov An-26B	10906	ex CCCP-26051	
☐ RA-26131	Antonov An-26B	12707	ex CCCP-26131	
☐ RA-26138	Antonov An-26B	12810	ex CCCP-26138	
☐ RA-26515	Antonov An-26	6910	ex CCCP-26515	
☐ RA-26665	Antonov An-26	8108	ex CCCP-26665	
☐ RA-26692	Antonov An-26B-100	9409	ex CCCP-26692	

☐ VP-BAO	Canadair CRJ-100ER	7177	ex F-GPTB	<RLU
☐ VQ-BIX	Canadair CRJ-200ER	7546	ex N446CA	<RLU
☐ VQ-BIY	Canadair CRJ-200ER	7539	ex N443CA	
☐ VQ-BMK	Canadair CRJ-200ER	7668	ex N473CA	<RLU
☐ VQ-BML	Canadair CRJ-200ER	7650	ex N469SM	

IZHAVIA — Izhavia (I8/IZA) — Izhevsk (IJK)

☐ RA-42343	Yakovlev Yak-42D	4520421708285	ex UR-42343	
☐ RA-42368	Yakovlev Yak-42D	4520422914166	ex EP-TAV	
☐ RA-42380	Yakovlev Yak-42D	4520422014549	ex CU-T1242	
☐ RA-42421	Yakovlev Yak-42D	4520422303017		
☐ RA-42450	Yakovlev Yak-42D	4520424601019		♦
☐ RA-42455	Yakovlev Yak-42D	4520424404018	ex YL-LBT	
☐ RA-42549	Yakovlev Yak-42D	11040105	ex ER-YCD	

☐ RA-46620	Antonov An-24RV	37308707	ex CCCP-46620	
☐ RA-46637	Antonov An-24RV	37308903	ex CCCP-46637	
☐ RA-47315	Antonov An-24RV	67310502	ex CCCP-47315	

JET-2000 — Moscow Jet (JTT)

| ☐ RA-74015 | Antonov An-74D | 36547098969 | | |

JET AIR GROUP — Sistema (JSI) — Moscow-Sheremetyevo (SME)

| ☐ RA-65723 | Tupolev Tu-134A-3M | 66440 | ex CCCP-65723 | VIP |
| ☐ RA-65930 | Tupolev Tu-134A-3M | 66500 | ex CCCP-65930 | VIP |

KATEKAVIA — Katekavia (ZF/KTK) — Sharypovo/Krasnoyarsk-Yernelyanovo (-/KJA)

☐ RA-46494	Antonov An-24RV	27308207	ex CCCP-46494	
☐ RA-46603	Antonov An-24RV	37308510	ex CCCP-46603	♦
☐ RA-46674	Antonov An-24RV	47309606	ex CCCP-46674	
☐ RA-46693	Antonov An-24RV	47309904	ex CCCP-46693	
☐ RA-47820	Antonov An-24RV	17307201	ex CCCP-47820	

☐ VP-BAS	Boeing 757-28A	28161/723	ex EI-ETS		♦
☐ VP-BLT	Boeing 757-28A	28174/865	ex N752NA		♦
☐ VP-BLV	Boeing 757-28A	30043/925	ex N755NA	Azur Air c/s	♦
☐ VP-BPB	Boeing 757-231/W	28484/825	ex N926LG	Azur Air c/s	♦
☐ VQ-BEY	Boeing 757-2Q8/W	29382/1010	ex OH-LBX	Azur Air c/s	♦
☐ VQ-BEZ	Boeing 757-2Q8/W	29377/857	ex OH-LBU	Azur Air c/s	♦
☐ VQ-BKB	Boeing 757-2Q8/W	26271/592	ex TC-SNB	Azur Air c/s	♦

☐ VQ-BKF	Boeing 757-2Q8/W	26268/590	ex TC-SND	♦
☐ VQ-BQA	Boeing 757-2Q8	30044/954	ex TC-ETE	♦
☐ VP-BXW	Boeing 767-3Q8ER	27618/727	ex XA-APB	♦
☐ VQ-BUO	Boeing 767-33AER	27909/591	ex (LZ-AWB) Azur Air c/s	o/o♦
☐ VQ-BUP	Boeing 767-33AER	28043/734	ex (CS-TKR)	o/o♦

KAZAN AIR ENTERPRISES — Kazan Osnovnoi/Khanty Mansisk (KZN/-)

☐ RA-06171	Mil Mi-8T	98420128	ex CCCP-06171	
☐ RA-06175	Mil Mi-8T	8621	ex CCCP-06175	
☐ RA-22674	Mil Mi-8T	8127	ex CCCP-22674	
☐ RA-22679	Mil Mi-8T	8133	ex CCCP-22679	
☐ RA-22734	Mil Mi-8T	98308901	ex CCCP-22734	
☐ RA-22871	Mil Mi-8T	98415671	ex CCCP-22871	
☐ RA-22873	Mil Mi-8T	98415711	ex CCCP-22873	
☐ RA-25408	Mil Mi-8T	98233135	ex CCCP-25408	
☐ RA-25519	Mil Mi-8T	9775214	ex CCCP-25519	
☐ RA-25599	Mil Mi-8T	99150362	ex CCCP-25599	
☐ RA-27023	Mil Mi-8T	9754622	ex CCCP-27023	
☐ RA-27100	Mil Mi-8PS-11	8705		
☐ RA-27176	Mil Mi-8PS	8710	ex TC-HSA	
☐ RA-67667	LET L-410UVP-E3	902408	ex Soviet AF 2408	
☐ RA-67672	LET L-410UVP-E	872013	ex Soviet AF 2013	no titles
☐ RA-67675	LET L-410UVP-E	882027	ex Soviet AF 2027	[Kazan]

KHABAROVSK AIRLINES — Nikolaevsk-na-Amure

☐ RA-46529	Antonov An-24RV	57310008	ex CCCP-4652	♦
☐ RA-46714	Antonov An-24RV	57310105	ex EX-051	♦
☐ RA-47321	Antonov An-24RV	67310507	ex TC-TOR	♦
☐ RA-47359	Antonov An-24RV	67310608	ex UR-47359	♦
☐ RA-47367	Antonov An-24RV	77310806		♦
☐ RA-49624	Antonov An-24RT	0911504	ex CCCP-49264	♦
☐ RA-25196	Mil Mi-8T	99047381	ex CCCP-25196	
☐ RA-26105	Antonov An-26B-100	12003	ex CCCP-26105	
☐ RA-26174	Antonov An-26B-100	97308304	ex CCCP-26174	
☐ RA-46528	Antonov An-24RV	47310007	ex CCCP-46528	
☐ RA-67035	LET L-410UVP-E20	132907	ex OK-JDF	
☐ RA-67036	LET L-410UVP-E20	132908	ex OK-JDG	
☐ RA-67040	LET L-410UVP-E20	2913	ex OK-JDO	♦
☐ RA-88251	Yakovlev Yak-40K	9710552	ex CCCP-88251	

KNAAPO — Komsomolsk na Amur (KXK)

☐ RA-11371	Antonov An-12BP	00347406	ex 22 red	
☐ 11789	Antonov An-12BP	6343905	ex LZ-BFB	
☐ 48978	Antonov An-12BK	9346410	ex CCCP-48978	wfs

KOLAVIA — Kogalym (7K/KGL) — Kogalym (KGP)

☐ RA-22501	Mil Mi-8T	99357415		
☐ RA-22641	Mil Mi-8T	8026	ex CCCP-22641	
☐ RA-22980	Mil Mi-8AMT	59489607603	ex RA-22509	opf UN as UNO-756
☐ RA-24588	Mil Mi-8T	98839385	ex CCCP-24588	
☐ RA-25328	Mil Mi-8T	98203998	ex CCCP-25328	
☐ RA-25342	Mil Mi-8T	98206652	ex CCCP-25342	
☐ RA-25761	Mil Mi-8MTV-1	96073		
☐ RA-27066	Mil Mi-8MTV-1	95902	ex CCCP-27066	
☐ EI-ETH	Airbus A321-231	0668	ex TC-OAF MetroJet c/s	
☐ EI-ETJ	Airbus A321-231	0663	ex TC-OAE	
☐ EI-ETK	Airbus A321-231	0787	ex TC-OAI	
☐ EI-ETL	Airbus A321-231	0954	ex TC-OAK	wfs
☐ EI-FBF	Airbus A321-231	1060	ex B-6285	
☐ EI-FBH	Airbus A321-231	1293	ex B-6300	
☐ EI-FBV	Airbus A321-211	0852	ex G-OOPE	wfs
☐ EI-FSB	Airbus A321-211	1554	ex F-WXAK Metrojet c/s	♦
☐ EI-FDL	Airbus A320-232	2029	ex TC-KLA MetroJet c/s	wfs
☐ EI-FDM	Airbus A320-232	2077	ex TC-KLB Metrojet c/s	♦
☐ RA-67218	Canadair Challenger 850	8074	ex C-FOMN	VIP
☐ RA-67220	Canadair Challenger 850	8091	ex C-FTSF	VIP
☐ RA-85761	Tupolev Tu-154M	93A944		[DME]
☐ RA-85784	Tupolev Tu-154M	93A968		[SGC]

Also ops as MetroJet

KOMAVIA TRANS — (KMA) — Syktyvkar (SCW)

☐ RA-	Embraer ERJ-145LI	145701	ex B-3060	o/o♦

☐ RA-	Embraer ERJ-145LI	145755	ex B-3061	o/o♦
☐ RA-	Embraer ERJ-145LI	14500815	ex B-3065	o/o♦
☐ RA-	Embraer ERJ-145LI	14500823	ex B-3066	o/o♦
☐ VQ-BWL	Embraer ERJ-145LI	14500804	ex M-EMBB	♦
☐ VQ-BWM	Embraer ERJ-145LI	14500823	ex 2-DOPW	♦
☐ VQ-BWO	Embraer ERJ-145LI	14500815	ex M-EMBC	♦
☐ VQ-BWP	Embraer ERJ-145LI	145781	ex M-EMBA	♦
☐ RA-67021	LET L-410UVP-E20	2810	ex OK-SBA	
☐ RA-67022	LET L-410UVP-E20	2811	ex OK-SLW	
☐ RA-67023	LET L-410UVP-E20	2816	ex OK-VDD	
☐ RA-67024	LET L-410UVP-E20	2909	ex OK-JDH	

KOSMOS — Kosmos (KSM) — Moscow-Vnukovo (VKO)

☐ RA-11025	Antonov An-12B	6344103	ex CCCP-11025	
☐ RA-11363	Antonov An-12BK	00347505	ex CCCP-11363	
☐ RA-12988	Antonov An-12B	00347206	ex CCCP-12988	
☐ RA-65719	Tupolev Tu-134AK	63637	ex CCCP-65719	VIP
☐ RA-65726	Tupolev Tu-134AK	63720	ex CCCP-65726	VIP
☐ RA-65956	Tupolev Tu-134A-3	2351709	ex CCCP-65956	
☐ RA-85700	Tupolev Tu-154M	91A875	ex LZ-HMY	
☐ RA-85773	Tupolev Tu-154M	93A955	ex EP-TUB	♦
☐ RA-85777	Tupolev Tu-154M	93A959	ex EP-TUA	♦
☐ RA-85849	Tupolev Tu 154M	89A815		
☐ RA-93913	Antonov An-12BP	4342609	ex CCCP-93913	♦

KOSTROMA AIR ENTERPRISE — Kostroma (KMW)

☐ RA-26081	Antonov An-26B-100	11703	ex UR-BXU
☐ RA-26595	Antonov An-26	13401	ex CCCP-26595 Yuri Smimov
☐ RA-27210	Antonov An-26-100	5410	ex CCCP-27210 Marshal Novikov

KRASAVIA — Siberian Sky (SSJ) — Krasnoyarsk (KJA)

☐ RA-46466	Antonov An-24RV	27307904	ex CCCP-46466	
☐ RA-46642	Antonov An-24RV	37308910	ex CCCP-46642	
☐ RA-46682	Antonov An-24RV	47309704	ex CCCP-46682	
☐ RA-47306	Antonov An-24RV	57310306	ex CCCP-47306	
☐ RA-49287	Antonov An-24RV	27307607	ex YR-AME	
☐ RA-26005	Antonov An-26	9809	ex CCCP-26005	
☐ RA-26008	Antonov An-26B-100	9902	ex CCCP-26008	
☐ RA-26056	Antonov An-26B	11005	ex CCCP-26056	
☐ RA-26118	Antonov An-26B-100	12207	ex CCCP-26118	
☐ RA-26121	Antonov An-26B	12305	ex UR-BXT	
☐ RA-42340	Yakovlev Yak-42D	4520424606270	ex CCCP-42340	♦
☐ RA-42359	Yakovlev Yak-42D	4520423811417	ex LY-AAW	♦
☐ RA-42370	Yakovlev Yak-42D	4520422914203	ex CCCP-42370	
☐ RA-67017	Let 410UVP-E20	2812	ex OK-SLZ	
☐ RA-67018	Let 410UVP-E20	2813	ex OK-ODJ	
☐ RA-67020	Let 410UVP-E20	2814	ex OK-ODS	
☐ RA-69354	Antonov An-32A	1606	ex CCCP-69354	
☐ RA-69355	Antonov An-32A	1607	ex CCCP-69355	
☐ RA-87900	Yakovlev Yak-40K	9720254	ex CCCP-87900	

LUKIAVIATRANS — (LKV) — Velikie Luki/Pskov-Kresty (VLU/PKV)

☐ RA-30007	Antonov An-30D	1408	ex CCCP-30007	
☐ RA-30039	Antonov An-30	0710	ex CCCP-30039	
☐ RA-30075	Antonov An-30	1306	ex CCCP-30075 Mikhail Razzhivak	♦

LUKOIL AVIA — (LUK)

☐ RA-42424	Yakovlev Yak-42D	4520421302016	ex UN-42424
☐ RA-88297	Yakovlev Yak-40	9530142	ex «01» red
☐ VP-CLR	Boeing 737-7EM/W (BBJ1)	34865/1865	

MCHS ROSSII — Sumes (SUM) — Moscow-Zhukovsky

☐ RF-31121	Beriev Be-200ChS	76820003001	ex 301 black Pyotr Streletski
☐ RF-31130	Beriev Be-200ChS	76820003102	ex RF-31361 Ivan Shamanov
☐ RF-31360	Beriev Be-200ChS	76820001402	ex RF-32766 Ivan Sukhomlin
☐ RF-32765	Beriev Be-200ChS	76820001301	ex RA-32515 Ivan Borzov
☐ RF-32767	Beriev Be-200ChS	76820002501	ex RF-31120 Vasili Rakov
☐ RF-32768	Beriev Be-200ChS	76820002602	Yevgeni Preobrazhenski
☐ RA-76362	Ilyushin Il-76TD	1033416533	Anatoliy Lyapidevskiy
☐ RA-76363	Ilyushin Il-76TD	1033417540	Vasiliy Molokov
☐ RA-76429	Ilyushin Il-76TD	1043419639	Sigizmund Levanevski
☐ RA-76840	Ilyushin Il-76TD	1033417553	Nikolay Kamanin

☐ RA-76841	Ilyushin Il-76TD	1033418601		Mavrikiy Slepnyov	
☐ RA-76845	Ilyushin Il-76TD	1043420696		Mikhail Vodop'yanov	
☐ RF-31122	Antonov An-74P	47136012	ex 210	Alexander Belyakov	
☐ RF-31124	Mil Mi-26T	34001212522	ex RA-06279		
☐ RF-31215	Mil Mi-26T				
☐ RF-31350	Antonov An-74P	36547097940	ex RF-31112	Georgi Baidukov	
☐ RF-31353	Mil Mi-8MTV-2	96223	ex RF-31110		
☐ RA-32821	Mil Mi-26T	34001212603	ex RF-31005		
☐ RA-42441	Yakovlev Yak-42D	4520421402018	ex EP-LAN	Velerij Chkalov	VIP
☐ RA-42446	Yakovlev Yak-42D	4520423308017	ex UN-42446	Vladimir Kokkinaki	
☐ RA-61715	Antonov An-148-100EM	27015042015	ex RF-32815	Aleksander Pokryshkin	
☐ RA-61717	Antonov An-148-100EM	27015042017		Ivan Kozhedub	
☐ RA-86570	Ilyushin Il-62M	1356344		Mikhail Gromov	
☐ RA-	Sukhoi SSJ 100-95LR	95061			o/o♦
☐ RA-	Sukhoi SSJ 100-95LR	95069			o/o♦

MERIDIAN AIR

| ☐ RA-65724 | Tupolev Tu-134A-3m | 66445 | ex CCCP-65724 | wfs |
| ☐ RA-65737 | Tupolev Tu-134B-3 | 64195 | | |

NK AIR

☐ RA-42342	Yakovlev Yak-42D	4520421706302	ex EK-42342	small Grozny Avia titles	♦
☐ RA-42373	Yakovlev Yak-42D	4520423914323	ex UR-CER	small Grozny Avia titles	♦
☐ RA-42408	Yakovlev Yak-42D	4520424116698	ex EP-YAC	small Grozny Avia titles	♦

NORDAVIA REGIONAL AIRLINES — Dvina (5N/AUL) — Arkhangelsk-Talegi (ARH)

☐ VP-BKU	Boeing 737-505	25789/2229	ex G-GFFB	
☐ VP-BKV	Boeing 737-505	27155/2449	ex N215BV	
☐ VP-BOI	Boeing 737-505	24650/1792	ex G-GFFG	[BOH]
☐ VP-BQI	Boeing 737-5Y0	25186/2236	ex OM-SEA	
☐ VP-BQL	Boeing 737-5Y0	25185/2220	ex OM-SEF	
☐ VP-BRG	Boeing 737-53C	24826/2041	ex OM-SED	
☐ VP-BRI	Boeing 737-5Y0	25289/2288	ex OM-SEG	
☐ VP-BRK	Boeing 737-5Y0	25288/2286	ex OM-SEC	
☐ VP-BRN	Boeing 737-5Y0	25191/2260	ex OM-SEB	
☐ VP-BRP	Boeing 737-505	24651/1842	ex LN-BRD	
☐ RA-47199	Antonov An-24RV	27307703	ex CCCP-47199	[ARH]
☐ RA-47305	Antonov An-24RV	57310305	ex CCCP-47305	

NORDSTAR — Taimyr (Y7/TYA)

☐ VQ-BKN	ATR 42-500	827	ex F-WNUC
☐ VQ-BKO	ATR 42-500	823	ex F-WNUB
☐ VQ-BKP	ATR 42-500	835	ex F-WWLE
☐ VQ-BKQ	ATR 42-500	839	ex F-WWLF
☐ VQ-BPE	ATR 42-500	641	ex OH-ATA
☐ VQ-BDN	Boeing 737-8K5/W	32905/1046	ex D-AHLP
☐ VQ-BDO	Boeing 737-8K5/W	32906/1087	ex D-AHLQ
☐ VQ-BDP	Boeing 737-8Q8/W	28221/226	ex N282AG
☐ VQ-BDW	Boeing 737-8K5/W	27977/9	ex D-AHFC
☐ VQ-BDZ	Boeing 737-8K5/W	27978/40	ex D-AHFD
☐ VQ-BKR	Boeing 737-8AS/W	33559/1443	ex N592MS
☐ VQ-BNG	Boeing 737-86J/W	37747/3120	ex D-ABKH
☐ VQ-BPM	Boeing 737-8AS/W	33812/1615	ex EI-DCS
☐ VQ-BQT	Boeing 737-8AS/W	33561/1463	ex N591MS
☐ VP-BKT	Boeing 737-33R	28871/2900	ex PP-VPY

NORDWIND — (N4/NWS) — Moscow-Sheremetyevo (SVO)

☐ VP-BGH	Airbus A321-232	3034	ex EI-EWP	
☐ VP-BRD	Airbus A321-232	3120	ex EI-EYB	
☐ VQ-BOD	Airbus A321-211	1233	ex M-ABEE	
☐ VQ-BOE	Airbus A321-211	1219	ex M-ABED	
☐ VQ-BRM	Airbus A321-231	1276	ex EI-EUT	
☐ VQ-BRN	Airbus A321-231	1843	ex D-ALAB	
☐ VQ-BRO	Airbus A321-232	2927	ex N927AG	
☐ VQ-BRU	Airbus A321-232	2933	ex N933AG	
☐ VP-BOW	Boeing 737-8Q8/W	30040/1693	ex UR-CLR	♦
☐ VP-BPI	Boeing 737-83N/W	28244/958	ex N308TZ	
☐ VP-BPY	Boeing 737-83N/W	28247/1091	ex N318TZ	
☐ VQ-BPZ	Boeing 737-8BK/W	33027/1918	ex N756DB	♦
☐ VQ-BUV	Boeing 737-86N/W	32691/2033	ex B-5143	♦
☐ VQ-BVY	Boeing 737-8Q8/W	32841/1705	ex UR-CLS	♦

☐ VP-BDI	Boeing 767-38AER	29618/792	ex N618SH	>KAR♦
☐ VP-BMC	Boeing 767-3Q8ER	30301/762	ex N431LF	>KAR
☐ VP-BOQ	Boeing 767-304ER/W	28042/649	ex G-OBYD	
☐ VP-BOY	Boeing 767-3G5ER	29435/720	ex EI-CZH	>KAR
☐ VP-BOZ	Boeing 767-3G5ER	28111/612	ex EI-CXO	>KAR
☐ VP-BRL	Boeing 767-3D7ER	26328/637	ex EI-EXL	
☐ VQ-BMQ	Boeing 767-306ER	28098/607	ex N765NA	
☐ VQ-BOG	Boeing 767-341ER	30342/774	ex VP-BWQ	
☐ VQ-BPT	Boeing 767-306ER	27957/587	ex N281LF	
☐ VQ-BVD	Boeing 767-319ER	30586/808	ex 5Y-KYW	o/o♦
☐ VP-BJB	Boeing 777-21BER	27606/121	ex B-2062	
☐ VP-BJF	Boeing 777-21BER	32703/472	ex B-2070	
☐ VQ-BUD	Boeing 777-2Q8ER	27608/164	ex VN-A151	♦

ORENAIR Orenburg (R2/ORB) Orenburg-Tsentralny (REN)

☐ VP-BPG	Boeing 737-8AS/W	29924/578	ex EI-CSI	
☐ VP-BVU	Boeing 737-8LJ/W	41202/5206	ex N1781B	♦
☐ VQ-BCJ	Boeing 737-8AS/W	29932/1030	ex EI-CSS	
☐ VQ-BFY	Boeing 737-86N/W	29884/1094	ex N117MN	
☐ VQ-BFZ	Boeing 737-86N/W	28644/839	ex N116MN	
☐ VQ-BIZ	Boeing 737-86N/W	28645/840	ex N548MS	
☐ VQ-BJC	Boeing 737-8K5/W	27992/523	ex D-AHFQ	
☐ VQ-BJX	Boeing 737-86N/W	32735/1104	ex TC-APJ	
☐ VQ-BNK	Boeing 737-8K5/W	30414/703	ex D-AHFU	
☐ VQ-BPX	Boeing 737-8Q8/W	35278/2625	ex D-APBB	[BUD]♦
☐ VQ-BSR	Boeing 737-8AS/W	33622/2101	ex EI-DLZ	
☐ VQ-BSS	Boeing 737-8AS/W	33602/2109	ex EI-DPA	
☐ VQ-BUE	Boeing 737-8GJ/W	34900/2167	ex VT-SPM	♦
☐ VQ-BUF	Boeing 737-8GJ/W	34897/2069	ex VT-SPJ	♦
☐ VQ-BVV	Boeing 737-8LJ/W	41201/5153	ex N1795B	♦
☐ VP-BHB	Boeing 777-2Q8ER	29402/517	ex F-OMAY	
☐ VP-BLA	Boeing 777-2Q8ER	28676/246	ex F-ORUN	
☐ VQ-BNU	Boeing 777-2Q8ER	29908/229	ex F-OPAR	

ORENBURZHYE

☐ RA-67043	LET L410UVP-E20	2918	ex OK-JDS	♦
☐ RA-67044	LET L410UVP-E20	3002	ex OK-JDW	♦

PETROPAVLOVSK-KAMCHATSKY AIR ENTERPRISE
Petrokam (PTK) Petropavlovsk Kamchatsky-Yelizovo (PKC)

☐ RA-67007	LET L-410UVP-E20	2723	ex OK-SLV	
☐ RA-67008	LET L-410UVP-E20	2724	ex OK-SDT	
☐ RA-67009	LET L-410UVP-E20	2725	ex OK-SDU	
☐ RA-67645	LET L-410UVP-E	902438	ex CCCP-67645	
☐ RA-67662	LET L-410UVP-E	902520	ex CCCP-67662	
☐ RA-26085	Antonov An-26B-100	12310	ex UR-BXP	
☐ RA-26122	Antonov An-26B	12401	ex CCCP-26122	
☐ RA-26251	Antonov An-26-100	9109		
☐ RA-28714	PZL-Antonov An-28	1AJ-006-24	ex CCCP-28714	♦
☐ RA-87385	Yakovlev Yak-40K	9411632	ex CCCP-87385	
☐ RA-87947	Yakovlev Yak-40K	9621145	ex CCCP-87947	
☐ RA-87949	Yakovlev Yak-40K	9621345	ex CCCP-87949	
☐ RA-87988	Yakovlev Yak-40	9541244	ex CCCP-87988	

POBEDA (DP/PBD) Moscow-Vnukovo (VKO)

☐ VQ-BAW	Boeing 737-8MA/W	43666/5386		♦
☐ VQ-BTC	Boeing 737-8MA/W	43662/5119		♦
☐ VQ-BTD	Boeing 737-8MA/W	43664/5185		♦
☐ VQ-BTE	Boeing 737-81D/W	39441/5077	ex N1786B	♦
☐ VQ-BTG	Boeing 737-8FZ/W	41992/4908		♦
☐ VQ-BTH	Boeing 737-8LJ/W	39947/5051	ex N447DC	♦
☐ VQ-BTI	Boeing 737-8LJ/W	39948/5023	ex N448DC	♦
☐ VQ-BTJ	Boeing 737-8LJ/W	39950/5133		♦
☐ VQ-BTS	Boeing 737-8FZ/W	41991/4870		♦
☐ VQ-BWG	Boeing 737-8LJ/W	41205/5302		♦
☐ VQ-BWH	Boeing 737-8LJ/W	41206/5318		♦

POLAR AIRLINES Air Sakha (PI/RKA) Batagai

☐ RA-46333	Antonov An-24B	97305510	ex CCCP-46333	[YKS]
☐ RA-46510	Antonov An-24RV	37308406	ex CCCP-46510	
☐ RA-46646	Antonov An-24RV	37309105	ex CCCP-46646	
☐ RA-46665	Antonov An-24RV	47309506	ex CCCP-46665	
☐ RA-46834	Antonov An-24RV	17306801	ex CCCP-46834	

☐ RA-47260	Antonov An-24B	27307802	ex CCCP-47260	
☐ RA-47352	Antonov An-24RV	67310601	ex CCCP-47352	
☐ RA-47353	Antonov An-24RV	67310602	ex CCCP-47353	♦
☐ RA-47357	Antonov An-24RV	67310606	ex CCCP-47357	
☐ RA-47360	Antonov An-24RV	67310704	ex CCCP-47360	
☐ RA-47363	Antonov An-24RV	77310707	ex CCCP-47363	
☐ RA-47786	Antonov An-24B	89901601	ex CCCP-47786	
☐ RA-67623	LET L-410UVP-E	902405	ex CCCP-67623	
☐ RA-67670	LET L-410UVP-E3	902416	ex ES-LLA	
☐ RA-67676	LET L-410UVP-E	872007	ex 2007	
☐ RA-67693	LET L-410UVP-E	952624	ex OK-ADT	
☐ RA-67694	LET L-410UVP-E	952625	ex OK-ADU	
☐ RA-26030	Antonov An-26B-100	10501	ex CCCP-26030	
☐ RA-26538	Antonov An-26-100	2102	ex CCCP-26538	
☐ RA-26604	Antonov An-26	4506	ex UR-26604	

PSKOVAVIA	*Pskovavia (PSW)*		*Pskov-Kresty (PKV)*

☐ RA-26041	Antonov An-26B	10707	ex CCCP-26041	
☐ RA-26086	Antonov An-26B	12302	ex CCCP-26086	
☐ RA-26134	Antonov An-26B	12805	ex CCCP-26134	
☐ RA-26142	Antonov An-26B	12904	ex OB-1442	
☐ RA-46473	Antonov An-24RV	27308101	ex EW-46483	
☐ RA-46651	Antonov An-24RV	47309202	ex CCCP-46651	
☐ RA-46667	Antonov An-24RV	47309508	ex CCCP-46667	
☐ RA-47362	Antonov An-24RV	67310706	ex UR-47362	
☐ RA-47697	Antonov An-24RV	27306704	ex EW-47697	♦
☐ RA-47800	Antonov An-24RV	17306809	ex CCCP-47800	♦

RED WINGS AIRLINES	*Remont Air (WZ/RWZ)*		*Moscow-Vnukovo (VKO)*

☐ RA-64017	Tupolev Tu-204-100	1450742564017	
☐ RA-64018	Tupolev Tu-204-100	1450741964018	
☐ RA-64019	Tupolev Tu-204-100	1450741064019	
☐ RA-64020	Tupolev Tu-204-100	1450743164020	
☐ RA-64043	Tupolev Tu-204-100	1450743764043	
☐ RA-64046	Tupolev Tu-204-100	1450743864046	
☐ RA-64049	Tupolev Tu-204-100	1450744864049	
☐ RA-64050	Tupolev Tu-204-100	1450741964050	
☐ RA-89001	Sukhoi SSJ 100-95B	95008	♦
☐ RA-89002	Sukhoi SSJ 100-95B	95010	♦
☐ RA-89021	Sukhoi SSJ 100-95B	95021	♦

ROSSIYA AIRLINES	*Russia (FV/SDM)*		*Moscow-Vnukovo/St Petersburg-Pulkovo (VKO/LED)*

☐ EI-ETN	Airbus A319-111	1654	ex B-2225	
☐ EI-ETO	Airbus A319-111	1679	ex B-2223	
☐ EI-ETP	Airbus A319-111	1753	ex B-2339	
☐ EI-EYL	Airbus A319-111	2465	ex N940FR	
☐ EI-EYM	Airbus A319-111	2497	ex N942FR	
☐ EI-EZC	Airbus A319-112	2879	ex B-6232	
☐ EI-EZD	Airbus A319-112	2913	ex B-6233	
☐ RA-73025	Airbus A319CJ-115	4024	ex F-WHUF	VIP
☐ RA-73026	Airbus A31CJ9-115	4679	ex F-WHUJ	VIP
☐ VP-BIQ	Airbus A319-111	1890	ex N917FR	
☐ VP-BIT	Airbus A319-111	1761	ex N909FR	
☐ VP-BIU	Airbus A319-114	0649	ex N574SX	
☐ VQ-BAQ	Airbus A319-111	1560	ex N903FR	
☐ VQ-BAR	Airbus A319-111	1488	ex N901FR	
☐ VQ-BAS	Airbus A319-111	1863	ex N913FR	FK Zenith St Petersburg c/s
☐ VQ-BAT	Airbus A319-112	1876	ex N916FR	
☐ VQ-BAU	Airbus A319-111	1851	ex N915FR	
☐ VQ-BAV	Airbus A319-111	1743	ex N907FR	
☐ EI-EYR	Airbus A320-214	2930	ex A6-ABG	
☐ EI-EYS	Airbus A320-214	2964	ex A6-ABH	
☐ EI-FAJ	Airbus A320-214	3044	ex A6-ABI	
☐ VP-BWH	Airbus A320-214	2151	ex F-WWIR	
☐ VP-BWI	Airbus A320-214	2163	ex F-WWBD	♦
☐ VQ-BBM	Airbus A320-214	1578	ex EC-HZU	
☐ VQ-BDQ	Airbus A320-214	1767	ex EC-KDD	
☐ VQ-BDR	Airbus A320-214	1130	ex EC-IMU	
☐ VQ-BDY	Airbus A320-214	1657	ex EC-KBQ	
☐ VQ-BFM	Airbus A320-214	1379	ex EC-HQG	♦
☐ VQ-BCG	Airbus A320-214	1200	ex EC-HGY	♦
☐ RA-61701	Antonov An-148-100B	2701504001		
☐ RA-61702	Antonov An-148-100B	2701504002		
☐ RA-61703	Antonov An-148-100B	2701504003		

☐ RA-61704	Antonov An-148-100B	2701504004		
☐ RA-61705	Antonov An-148-100B	2701504005		
☐ RA-61706	Antonov An-148-100B	2701504006		
☐ EI-DZH	Boeing 767-3Q8ER	29390/870	ex N101LF	
☐ EI-EAR	Boeing 767-3Q8ER	27616/714	ex N364LF	
☐ EI-ECB	Boeing 767-3Q8ER	27617/722	ex N151LF	
☐ RA-64504	Tupolev Tu-214	41202004		
☐ RA-64505	Tupolev Tu-214	42204005		
☐ RA-64506	Tupolev Tu-214	44204006		

ROYAL FLIGHT (ABG) Moscow-Vnukovo (VKO)

☐ VP-BOO	Boeing 757-204/W	28834/850	ex G-BYAX	♦
☐ VQ-BTB	Boeing 757-28A/W	28835/858	ex G-FCLF	
☐ VQ-BTM	Boeing 757-256/W	26253/902	ex YL-BDC	
☐ VQ-BTN	Boeing 757-256/W	26251/897	ex YL-BDB	
☐ VQ-BTR	Boeing 757-28A/W	28171/805	ex G-FCLE	
☐ RA-76457	Ilyushin Il-76T	093421621	ex CCCP-76457	opb UN as UNO-823♦
☐ RA-76780	Ilyushin Il-76T	0013430901	ex CCCP-76780 all-white	opb UN as UNO-824♦
☐ RA-76799	Ilyushin Il-76TD	1003403075	ex CCCP-76799	<ESL♦

RUSLINE Rusline Air (7R/RLU) Moscow-Sheremetyevo (SVO)

☐ VP-BAO	Canadair CRJ-100ER	7177	ex F-GPTB	>IAE
☐ VP-BVB	Canadair CRJ-100ER	7245	ex N713CA	
☐ VP-BVC	Canadair CRJ-100LR	7441	ex N409CA	
☐ VP-BVD	Canadair CRJ-100LR	7440	ex N408CA	
☐ VP-BVK	Canadair CRJ-100ER	7408	ex N818CA	
☐ VQ-BNA	Canadair CRJ-100LR	7473	ex N435CA	
☐ VQ-BNB	Canadair CRJ-100LR	7364	ex N807CA	
☐ VQ-BND	Canadair CRJ-100LR	7483	ex N442CA	
☐ VQ-BNE	Canadair CRJ-100LR	7482	ex N436CA	
☐ VQ-BNL	Canadair CRJ-100ER	7106	ex F-GRJE	
☐ VQ-BNY	Canadair CRJ-100ER	7108	ex F-GRJF	
☐ VP-BMN	Canadair CRJ-200ER	7179	ex N620BR	
☐ VP-BMR	Canadair CRJ-200ER	7192	ex N623BR	[DME]
☐ VP-BVK	Canadair CRJ-200ER	7408	ex N818CA	
☐ VQ-BBW	Canadair CRJ-200ER	7426	ex N651BR	
☐ VQ-BEV	Canadair CRJ-200ER	7467	ex N703BR	
☐ VQ-BFA	Canadair CRJ-200ER	7627	ex N466CA	
☐ VQ-BFB	Canadair CRJ-200ER	7637	ex N467CA	
☐ VQ-BFF	Canadair CRJ-200ER	7470	ex N705BR	
☐ VQ-BFI	Canadair CRJ-200ER	7671	ex N478CA	
☐ VQ-BIX	Canadair CRJ-200ER	7539	ex N443CA	>IAE
☐ VQ-BMK	Canadair CRJ-200ER	7668	ex N473CA	>IAE
☐ VQ-BBX	Embraer EMB.120ER Brasilia	120205	ex N205CA	
☐ VQ-BCB	Embraer EMB.120ER Brasilia	120231	ex N280AS	
☐ VQ-BCL	Embraer EMB.120ER Brasilia	120304	ex N227SW	

RUSSIAN STATE TRANSPORT

☐ RA-65719	Tupolev Tu-134AK	63637	ex CCCP-65719	VIP
☐ RA-65726	Tupolev Tu-134AK	63720	ex CCCP-65726	VIP
☐ RA-65904	Tupolev Tu-134A-3	63953	ex CCCP-65904	
☐ RA-65905	Tupolev Tu-134A-3	63965	ex CCCP-65905	
☐ RA-65911	Tupolev Tu-134A-3	63972	ex CCCP-65911	
☐ RA-65956	Tupolev Tu-134A-3	2351709	ex CCCP-65956	
☐ RA-96012	Ilyushin Il-96-300	74393201009		Presidential a/c
☐ RA-96014	Ilyushin Il-96-300	74393202014		o/o
☐ RA-96016	Ilyushin Il-96-300PU	74393202010	ex (RA-96013)	Presidential a/c
☐ RA-96017	Ilyushin Il-96-300S	74393202011		
☐ RA-96018	Ilyushin Il-96-300PU	74393202018		VIP
☐ RA-96019	Ilyushin Il-96-300	74393202019		
☐ RA-96020	Ilyushin Il-96-300PU	74393202020		
☐ RA-96021	Ilyushin Il-96-300	74393203021		o/o
☐ RA-64515	Tupolev Tu-214SR	44507015		
☐ RA-64516	Tupolev Tu-214SR	42709016		
☐ RA-64517	Tupolev Tu-214SR	41709017		
☐ RA-64520	Tupolev Tu-214PU	44709020		
☐ RA-64521	Tupolev Tu-214	43911021		
☐ RA-64522	Tupolev Tu-214SUS	43911022		
☐ RA-64524	Tupolev Tu-214SUS	43003024		
☐ RA-64057	Tupolev Tu-204-300A	1450744164057		
☐ RA-64058	Tupolev Tu-204-300A	1450744164058		
☐ RA-87968	Yakovlev Yak-40	9841258	ex CCCP-87968	

☐ RA-87971	Yakovlev Yak-40D	9831558	ex CCCP-87971		VIP
☐ RA-87972	Yakovlev Yak-40	9921658	ex CCCP-87972		

S7 AIRLINES	**Siberian Airlines (S7/SBI)**	**Novosibirsk-Tolmachevo (OVB)**

Member of oneWorld

☐ VP-BHF	Airbus A319-114	1819	ex N350NB		
☐ VP-BHG	Airbus A319-114	1870	ex N356NB		
☐ VP-BHI	Airbus A319-114	2028	ex N367NB		
☐ VP-BHJ	Airbus A319-114	2369	ex N372NB		
☐ VP-BHK	Airbus A319-114	2373	ex N373NB		
☐ VP-BHL	Airbus A319-114	2464	ex N374NB		
☐ VP-BHP	Airbus A319-114	2618	ex N376NB		
☐ VP-BHQ	Airbus A319-114	2641	ex N377NB		
☐ VP-BHV	Airbus A319-114	2474	ex N375NB		
☐ VP-BTN	Airbus A319-114	1126	ex N307NB		
☐ VP-BTO	Airbus A319-114	1129	ex N308NB		
☐ VP-BTP	Airbus A319-114	1131	ex N309NB		
☐ VP-BTQ	Airbus A319-114	1149	ex N310NB		
☐ VP-BTS	Airbus A319-114	1164	ex N311NB		
☐ VP-BTT	Airbus A319-114	1167	ex N312NB		
☐ VP-BTU	Airbus A319-114	1071	ex N303NB		
☐ VP-BTV	Airbus A319-114	1078	ex N304NB		
☐ VP-BTW	Airbus A319-114	1090	ex N305NB		
☐ VP-BTX	Airbus A319-114	1091	ex N306NB		
☐ VQ-BQW	Airbus A319-115LR	2279	ex F-GRXI		
☐ VP-BCP	Airbus A320-214	3473	ex F-WWBY		
☐ VP-BCS	Airbus A320-214	3490	ex F-WWIS		
☐ VP-BCZ	Airbus A320-214	3446	ex F-WWIT		
☐ VP-BDT	Airbus A320-214	3494	ex F-WWIC		
☐ VP-BOG	Airbus A320-214	5559	ex F-WWIG		
☐ VP-BOJ	Airbus A320-214	5607	ex D-AUBN		
☐ VP-BOL	Airbus A320-214/S	6066	ex F-WWDS		
☐ VP-BOM	Airbus A320-214/S	6171	ex D-AVVC		♦
☐ VQ-BCI	Airbus A320-214	2623	ex EC-JNT		
☐ VQ-BDE	Airbus A320-214	3866	ex F-WWDZ		
☐ VQ-BDF	Airbus A320-214	3880	ex F-WWIL		
☐ VQ-BES	Airbus A320-214	4032	ex F-WWIH		
☐ VQ-BET	Airbus A320-214	4150	ex F-WWBG		
☐ VQ-BOA	Airbus A320-214	5001	ex F-WWBM		
☐ VQ-BPL	Airbus A320-214	5026	ex F-WWBK		
☐ VQ-BPN	Airbus A320-214	5167	ex F-WWBV		
☐ VQ-BRC	Airbus A320-214	5106	ex F-WWIU		
☐ VQ-BRD	Airbus A320-214	5031	ex F-WWBE		
☐ VQ-BRG	Airbus A320-214	5134	ex F-WWDA		
☐ VP-BVH	Boeing 767-33AER	28495/643	ex N495AN		
☐ VQ-BBI	Boeing 767-328ER	27428/586	ex EC-JJJ		
☐ VQ-BQH	Airbus A321-211	3070	ex CN-ROM		
☐ VQ-BQI	Airbus A321-211	2726	ex CN-ROF		
☐ VQ-BQJ	Airbus A321-211	2076	ex CN-RNY		
☐ VQ-BQK	Airbus A321-211	2064	ex CN-RNX		
☐ VQ-BVK	Boeing 737-8GJ/W	41401/5165			>GLP♦
☐ VQ-BVL	Boeing 737-8GJ/W	41399/5055	ex (VT-SZL)		>GLP♦
☐ VQ-BVM	Boeing 737-8GJ/W	41400/5094	ex (VT-SZM)		>GLP♦

SARATOV AIRLINES	**Saratov Air (6W/SOV)**	**Saratov-Tsentralny (RTW)**

☐ RA-42316	Yakovlev Yak-42D	4520422202030	ex CCCP-42316		
☐ RA-42326	Yakovlev Yak-42D	4520424402154	ex CCCP-42326		
☐ RA-42328	Yakovlev Yak-42D	4520421505058	ex CCCP-42328		
☐ RA-42361	Yakovlev Yak-42D	4520423811427	ex CCCP-42361		
☐ RA-42378	Yakovlev Yak-42D	4520421014494	ex TC-FAR		
☐ RA-42389	Yakovlev Yak-42D	4520424016542	ex CCCP-42389		
☐ RA-42432	Yakovlev Yak-42D	4520424410016	ex TC-ALY		no titles
☐ RA-42550	Yakovlev Yak-42D	11140205	ex CCCP-42550		
☐ RA-42557	Yakovlev Yak-42D	4520423302017	ex UP-Y4201		
☐ VQ-BRX	Embraer ERJ-195AR	19000169	ex VP-CQR		
☐ VQ-BRY	Embraer ERJ-195AR	19000157	ex VP-CQS		
☐ VQ-BUQ	Embraer ERJ-195LR	19000069	ex G-FBEC		o/o♦
☐ VQ-BUR	Embraer ERJ-195LR	19000084	ex G-FBED		o/o♦

SEVERSTAL	**Severstal (D2/SSF)**	**Cherepovets (CEE)**

☐ RA-67229	Canadair CRJ-200LR	7403	ex D-ACHD		
☐ RA-67230	Canadair CRJ-200LR	7407	ex D-ACHE		
☐ RA-67231	Canadair CRJ-200LR	7464	ex D-ACHI		
☐ RA-67234	Canadair CRJ-200ER	7514	ex EC-HXM		
☐ RA-67239	Canadair CRJ-200LR	7989	ex EC-JEE		♦

| ☐ RA-67240 | Canadair CRJ-200LR | 8008 | ex EC-JEF | ♦ |

☐ RA-87224	Yakovlev Yak-40K	9841259	ex CCCP-87224	VIP opf Yava Group
☐ RA-88188	Yakovlev Yak-40	9620848	ex CCCP-88188	
☐ RA-88296	Yakovlev Yak-40	9421634	ex VN-A445	VIP

SHAR INK — Sharink (UGP) — Moscow-Ostafyevo

☐ RA-25770	Mil Mi-8PS-11	8709	ex CCCP-25770	VIP
☐ RA-74001	Antonov An-74TK-100	36547070655	ex ST-BDS	<Sakha Avn School♦
☐ RA-74020	Antonov An-74TK-100	36547195014		
☐ RA-74047	Antonov An-74-200	36547097941	ex ST-PRC	
☐ RA-76403	Ilyushin Il-76TD	1023412414	ex UP-I7620	

SIBERIAN LIGHT AVIATION

| ☐ RA-28719 | WSK/PZL Antonov An-28 | 1AJ007-04 | ex CCCP-28719 | ♦ |
| ☐ RA-28728 | WSK/PZL Antonov An-28 | 1AJ007-13 | ex CCCP-28728 | ♦ |

SIBNIA

☐ 11767	Antonov An-12BP	401909	ex RA-11767
☐ 65721	Tupolev Tu-134A	66130	ex 65721
☐ 87251	Yakovlev Yak-40	9310826	ex CCCP-87251
☐ 87460	Yakovlev Yak-40	9431936	ex RA-87460
☐ 87829	Yakovlev Yak-40	9240125	ex RA-87829
☐ 88164	Yakovlev Yak-40	9611846	ex RA-88164

SIRIUS AERO — Sirius Aero (CIG) — Moscow-Vnukovo (VKO)

| ☐ RA-65926 | Tupolev Tu-134AK | 66101 | ex CCP-65926 | ♦ |
| ☐ RA-65978 | Tupolev Tu-134A-3 | 63357 | ex CCCP-65978 Svetlana | VIP |

SKOL — (CDV) — Surgut (SGC)

☐ RA-06033	Mil Mi-26T	34001212423	ex CCCP-06033
☐ RA-06035	Mil Mi-26T	23001212425	ex CCCP-06035
☐ RA-06086	Mil Mi-26T	23001212479	ex CCCP-06086
☐ RA-06260	Mil Mi-26T	34001212120	
☐ RA-06277	Mil Mi-26T	34001212410	
☐ RA-06294	Mil Mi-26T	34001212123	
☐ RA-06298	Mil Mi-26T	34001212094	

☐ RA-87340	Yakovlev Yak-40	9510939	ex CCCP-87340
☐ RA-87940	Yakovlev Yak-40	9540444	ex CCCP-87940
☐ RA-88226	Yakovlev Yak-40	9641350	ex CCCP-88226
☐ RA-88306	Yakovlev Yak-40KD	9640651	ex OK-GEL

STATE AIRLINE 224 FLIGHT UNIT

☐ RA-76686	Ilyushin Il-76MD	0063468045	ex CCCP-76686	
☐ RA-78762	Ilyushin Il-76MD	0083486574	ex CCCP-78762	
☐ RA-78796	Ilyushin Il-76MD	0093491735	ex CCCP-78796	
☐ RA-78816	Ilyushin Il-76MD	0093495486	ex CCCP-78816	
☐ RA-78817	Ilyushin Il-76MD	0093495851	ex CCCP-78817	
☐ RA-78831	Ilyushin Il-76MD	1003401017	ex CCCP-78831	
☐ RA-78838	Ilyushin Il-76MD	1003402044	ex CCCP-78838	
☐ RA-78842	Ilyushin Il-76MD	1003403069	ex CCCP-78842	
☐ RA-78854	Ilyushin Il-76MD-90	1013407220	ex CCCP-78854	

☐ RA-82014	Antonov An-124-100	9773954732039	ex CCCP-82014	
☐ RA-82030	Antonov An-124-100	9773054732045	ex CCCP-82030	
☐ RA-82032	Antonov An-124-100	9773053832057	ex CCCP-82032 Vladimir Gladilin	
☐ RA-82038	Antonov An-124-100	9773054955077	ex "09" black	♦
☐ RA-82039	Antonov An-124-100	9773052055082	ex CCCP-82039	
☐ RA-82040	Antonov An-124-100	9773053355086	ex CCCP-82040	
☐ RF-82041	Antonov An-124-100	9773054055089	ex RA-82041	♦

SVERDLOVSK 2ND AIR ENTERPRISE — Pyshma (UKU) — Yekaterinburg-Koltsovo (SVX)

☐ RA-74006	Antonov An-74	36547095896	ex CCCP-74006	
☐ RA-74048	Antonov An-74D	36547098943		all-white,no titles VIP
☐ RA-87503	Yakovlev Yak-40	9520240	ex CCCP-87503	VIP. opf Kolsto Ural [SVX]

TATARSTAN AIR

☐ RA-67171	Cessna 208B Caravan I	208B2412	ex M95406
☐ RA-67173	Cessna 208B Caravan I	208B2428	ex N8129L
☐ RA-67174	Cessna 208B Caravan I	208B2430	ex N8130K
☐ RA-67175	Cessna 208B Caravan I	208B2420	ex N9540J
☐ RA-67176	Cessna 208B Caravan I	208B2426	ex N81287

☐ RA-67178	Cessna 208B Caravan I	208B2429	ex N81301	
☐ RA-67179	Cessna 208BEX Caravan I	208B5036	ex N8148N	♦
☐ RA-67181	Cessna 208BEX Caravan I	208B5038	ex N8148V	♦
☐ RA-67182	Cessna 208BEX Caravan I	208B5043	ex N81491	♦
☐ RA-67183	Cessna 208BEX Caravan I	208B5044	ex N8149Q	
☐ RA-67184	Cessna 208BEX Caravan I	208B5045	ex N8149Y	♦
☐ RA-67185	Cessna 208BEX Caravan I	208B5046	ex N81594	♦
☐ RA-67187	Cessna 208BEX Caravan I	208B5048	ex N8150S	♦

TOMSKAVIA		Tomsk Avia (TSK)		Tomsk (TOF)
☐ RA-46627	Antonov An-24RV	37308806	ex CCCP-46627	
☐ RA-46679	Antonov An-24RV	47309701	ex CCCP-46679	
☐ RA-47254	Antonov An-24RV	27307706	ex CCCP-47254	
☐ RA-47255	Antonov An-24RV	27307707		
☐ RA-47355	Antonov An-24RV	67310604	ex CCCP-47355	
☐ RA-26039	Antonov An-26B-100	10702	ex CCCP-26039	[TOF]
☐ RA-26209	Antonov An-26B-100	14302	ex CCCP-26209	
☐ RA-26518	Antonov An-26-100	7009	ex UN-26518	
☐ RA-26688	Antonov An-26-100	9004	ex CCCP-26688	[TOF]
☐ RA-67413	Cessna 208B Caravan I	208B2393	ex N2015A	
☐ RA-67438	Cessna 208B Caravan I	208B2386	ex N2010H	
☐ RA-67443	Cessna 208B Caravan I	208B2394	ex N2017J	
AOC suspended Apr15				

TRANSAERO AIRLINES		Transoviet (UN/TSO)		Moscow-Domodedovo (DME)
☐ EI-CXK	Boeing 737-4S3	25596/2255	ex G-OGBA	
☐ EI-CZK	Boeing 737-4Y0	24519/1781	ex N519AP	
☐ EI-DDK	Boeing 737-4S3	24165/1720	ex N758BC	
☐ EI-DDY	Boeing 737-4Y0	24904/1988	ex HA-LEV	
☐ EI-DNM	Boeing 737-4S3	24166/1722	ex EC-JHX	
☐ EI-DTV	Boeing 737-5Y0	25183/2218	ex B-2549	
☐ EI-DTW	Boeing 737-5Y0	25188/2238	ex B-2550	
☐ EI-DTX	Boeing 737-5Q8	28052/2965	ex LY-AZX	
☐ EI-UNG	Boeing 737-524	28915/2993	ex N14654	
☐ EI-UNH	Boeing 737-524	28916/2994	ex N14655	Imperial c/s
☐ VP-BPA	Boeing 737-5K5	25037/2022	ex D-AHLI	
☐ VP-BPD	Boeing 737-5K5	25062/2044	ex D-AHLN	
☐ VP-BYI	Boeing 737-524	28921/3052	ex N14660	
☐ VP-BYJ	Boeing 737-524	28923/3060	ex N14662	
☐ VP-BYN	Boeing 737-524	28924/3063	ex N17663	
☐ VP-BYO	Boeing 737-524	28922/3055	ex N23661	
☐ VP-BYP	Boeing 737-524	28927/3074	ex N14667	
☐ VP-BYQ	Boeing 737-524	28919/3045	ex N18658	
☐ VP-BYT	Boeing 737-524	28928/3077	ex N14668	
☐ EI-ETX	Boeing 737-7Q8	29359/1659	ex HA-LOS	
☐ EI-EUW	Boeing 737-7Q8	29350/1452	ex HA-LOI	
☐ EI-EUX	Boeing 737-7Q8	29352/1491	ex HA-LOL	
☐ EI-EUY	Boeing 737-7Q8	29354/1581	ex HA-LOP	
☐ EI-EUZ	Boeing 737-7Q8	29355/1609	ex HA-LOR	
☐ EI-RUL	Boeing 737-7K9	34320/1763	ex B-5107	
☐ EI-RUM	Boeing 737-7K9	34321/1802	ex B-5106	
☐ EI-EDZ	Boeing 737-8K5/W	27980/45	ex D-AHFF	
☐ EI-EEA	Boeing 737-8K5/W	27989/59	ex D-AHFG	
☐ EI-RUA	Boeing 737-86J/W	30498/450	ex D-ABAV	
☐ EI-RUB	Boeing 737-85P/W	33982/2338	ex EC-KEO	
☐ EI-RUC	Boeing 737-86R/W	30494/786	ex ET-ANA	
☐ EI-RUD	Boeing 737-86R/W	30495/876	ex B-2665	
☐ EI-RUE	Boeing 737-85P/W	28388/533	ex EC-HKQ	
☐ EI-RUF	Boeing 737-85P/W	28536/540	ex EC-HKR	
☐ EI-RUG	Boeing 737-86N	28610/449	ex VT-SJF	
☐ EI-RUH	Boeing 737-8K5/W	28228/484	ex LX-LGT	
☐ EI-RUI	Boeing 737-85P	28387/522	ex EC-HJQ	
☐ EI-RUJ	Boeing 737-81Q/W	29049/424	ex N982CQ	
☐ EI-RUK	Boeing 737-86N	28621/570	ex VT-SPE	
☐ EI-RUN	Boeing 737-808	34702/1917	ex B-5168	♦
☐ EI-RUO	Boeing 737-808	34703/1941	ex B-5169	♦
☐ EI-RUR	Boeing 737-8MC/W	44435/5351	ex N1782B	
☐ EI-RUS	Boeing 737-8MC/W	44437/5595		o/o♦
☐ EI-UNJ	Boeing 737-86J/W	36883/3709	ex D-ABKV	
☐ EI-UNK	Boeing 737-86J/W	36119/3750	ex D-ABKX	
☐ EI-XLB	Boeing 747-446	26359/1153	ex N913UN	
☐ EI-XLC	Boeing 747-446	27100/1236	ex N919UN	wfs
☐ EI-XLD	Boeing 747-446	26360/1166	ex N914UN	
☐ EI-XLE	Boeing 747-446	26362/1202	ex N916UN	
☐ EI-XLF	Boeing 747-446	27645/1282	ex N921MM	

☐ EI-XLG	Boeing 747-446	29899/1208	ex N917UN	
☐ EI-XLH	Boeing 747-446	27650/1234	ex N918UN	
☐ EI-XLI	Boeing 747-446	27648/1253	ex N920UN	
☐ EI-XLJ	Boeing 747-446	27646/1280	ex N922UN	
☐ EI-XLK	Boeing 747-412	29950/1241	ex N747NB	wfs
☐ EI-XLL	Boeing 747-412	28031/1266	ex N747NP	
☐ EI-XLM	Boeing 747-412	28028/1270	ex N747WV	
☐ EI-XLN	Boeing 747-412	28029/1276	ex N747JV	
☐ EI-XLO	Boeing 747-412	28025/1289	ex N747KD	
☐ EI-XLZ	Boeing 747-444	29119/1187	ex N747ZA	
☐ VP-BKJ	Boeing 747-444	26638/995	ex N7716Q	wfs
☐ VP-BKL	Boeing 747-444	28468/1162	ex N3508M	
☐ VP-BVR	Boeing 747-444	26637/943	ex (VP-BKG)	
☐ VQ-BHW	Boeing 747-4F6	28959/1158	ex ZS-SBK	wfs
☐ VQ-BHX	Boeing 747-4F6	28960/1167	ex ZS-SBS	wfs
☐ EI-CXZ	Boeing 767-216ER	24973/347	ex N502GX	
☐ EI-DBF	Boeing 767-3Q8ER	24745/355	ex F-GHGF	
☐ EI-DBG	Boeing 767-3Q8ER	24746/378	ex F-GHGG	
☐ EI-DBU	Boeing 767-37EER	25077/385	ex F-GHGH	
☐ EI-DBW	Boeing 767-201ER	23899/182	ex N647US	
☐ EI-DFS	Boeing 767-33AER	25346/403	ex ET-AKW	
☐ EI-RUU	Boeing 767-36NER	30110/775	ex VP-BAY	
☐ EI-RUV	Boeing 767-36NER	30111/776	ex VP-BAZ	
☐ EI-RUW	Boeing 767-36NFR	30107/761	ex VP-BAV	
☐ EI-RUX	Boeing 767-36NER	30109/767	ex VP-BAX	
☐ EI-RUY	Boeing 767-3Q8ER	29387/840	ex EC-HSV	
☐ EI-RUZ	Boeing 767-3Q8ER	30048/828	ex EC-HPU	
☐ EI-UNA	Boeing 767-3P6ER	26233/501	ex A4O-GU	
☐ EI-UNB	Boeing 767-3P6ER	26234/538	ex A4O-GY	
☐ EI-UNC	Boeing 767-319ER	29388/785	ex N381LF	
☐ EI-UND	Boeing 767-3P6ER	26236/436	ex A4O-GS	
☐ EI-UNE	Boeing 767-3Q8ER	29383/747	ex 5Y-KYY	
☐ EI-UNF	Boeing 767-3P6ER	26238/440	ex A4O-GT	
☐ EI-UNR	Boeing 777-212ER	28523/239	ex 9V-SRE	
☐ EI-UNS	Boeing 777-212ER	28514/153	ex 9V-SRD	
☐ EI-UNT	Boeing 777-212ER	28999/150	ex 9V-SRC	
☐ EI-UNU	Boeing 777-212ER	28998/149	ex 9V-SRB	
☐ EI-UNV	Boeing 777-222ER	28714/205	ex N205UA	
☐ EI-UNW	Boeing 777-222ER	30214/254	ex N208UA	
☐ EI-UNX	Boeing 777-222ER	30213/232	ex N207UA	
☐ EI-UNY	Boeing 777-222	26918/9	ex N767UA	
☐ EI-UNZ	Boeing 777-222	26925/13	ex N770UA	
☐ EI-UNL	Boeing 777-312	28515/180	ex 9V-SYA	
☐ EI-UNM	Boeing 777-312	28534/192	ex 9V-SYD	
☐ EI-UNN	Boeing 777-312	28517/188	ex 9V-SYC	
☐ EI-UNP	Boeing 777-312	28516/184	ex 9V-SYB	
☐ EI-XLP	Boeing 777-312	28531/244	ex 9V-SYE	
☐ EI-CXN	Boeing 737-329	23772/1432	ex OO-SDW	wfs
☐ EI-CXR	Boeing 737-329	24355/1709	ex OO-SYA	
☐ EI-DOH	Boeing 737-31S	29056/2928	ex VT-SAX	
☐ EI-ERP	Boeing 737-3S3	29245/3061	ex LN-KKY	
☐ RA-64051	Tupolev Tu-204-100S	1450742964051		
☐ RA-64052	Tupolev Tu-204-100S	1450742964052		
☐ RA-64509	Tupolev Tu-214	43406009		
☐ RA-64518	Tupolev Tu-214	44709018		
☐ RA-64549	Tupolev Tu-214	42507013	ex RA-64513	
☐ RA-64051	Tupolev Tu-204-120C	64051		♦
☐ RA-64052	Tupolev Tu-204-120C	64052		♦
☐ VP-BGU	Boeing 747-346	23482/640	ex N740UN	[DME]
☐ VP-BGW	Boeing 747-346	24019/695	ex N742UN	wfs
☐	Airbus A380-861	212	ex F-WW	o/o♦
☐	Airbus A321-211	6678	ex	o/o♦
☐	Airbus A321-211	6726	ex	o/o♦
☐	Airbus A321-211	6783	ex	o/o♦
☐	Airbus A321-211	6817	ex	o/o♦

TSSKB PROGRESS AVIAKOMPANIA		*Progress (PSS)*		*Samara-Bezymyanka (KUF)*
☐ RA-26130	Antonov An-26B-100	12704	ex CCCP-26130	
☐ RA-26180	Antonov An-26	9737810	ex CCCP-26180	
☐ RA-26191	Antonov An-24B	19902309	ex CCCP-26191	

TURUKHAN AVIAKOMPANIA		*(UT)*		*Turukhansk*
☐ RA-46468	Antonov An-24RV	27307906	ex CCCP-46468	♦
☐ RA-46491	Antonov An-24RV	27308204	ex 3X-GEB	♦
☐ RA-46493	Antonov An-24RV	27308206	ex CCCP-46493	♦
☐ RA-46497	Antonov An-24RV	27308210	ex CCCP-46497	♦

481

☐ RA-46520	Antonov An-24RV	37308506	ex CCCP-46520	◆
☐ RA-46532	Antonov An-24RV	57310101	ex CCCP-46532	◆
☐ RA-46604	Antonov An-24RV	37308601	ex CCCP-46604	◆
☐ RA-46609	Antonov An-24RV	37308606	ex CCCP-46609	◆
☐ RA-46619	Antonov An-24RV	37308706	ex CCCP-46619	◆
☐ RA-46650	Antonov An-24RV	47309201	ex CCCP-46650	◆
☐ RA-46689	Antonov An-24RV	47309806	ex CCCP-46689	◆
☐ RA-46692	Antonov An-24RV	47309903	ex CCCP-46692	◆
☐ RA-47264	Antonov An-24RV	27307806	ex CCCP-47264	◆
☐ RA-47295	Antonov An-24RV	07306608	ex CCCP-47295	◆
☐ RA-47351	Antonov An-24RV	67310510	ex YL-LCI	◆
☐ RA-47358	Antonov An-24RV	67310607	ex CCCP-47358	◆
☐ RA-49278	Antonov An-24RV	47309808	ex YR-AMJ	◆
☐ RA-49279	Antonov An-24RV	17306905	ex UN-49279	◆
☐ RA-22697	Mil Mi-8TB	8156		◆
☐ RA-22778	Mil Mi-8TB	98311800		◆
☐ RA-22825	Mil Mi-8TB	7625		◆
☐ RA-22861	Mil Mi-8TB	98415471		◆
☐ RA-22864	Mil Mi-8TB	98415527		◆
☐ RA-22900	Mil Mi-8TB	98420071		◆
☐ RA-24191	Mil Mi-8TB	98943692		◆
☐ RA-24286	Mil Mi-8TB	98734433		◆
☐ RA-24287	Mil Mi-8TB	98734449		◆
☐ RA-24441	Mil Mi-8TB	98625989		◆
☐ RA-24519	Mil Mi-8TB	98522095		◆
☐ RA-24689	Mil Mi-8TB	9815749		◆
☐ RA-24708	Mil Mi-8TB	98103562		◆
☐ RA-25361	Mil Mi-8TB	98206821		◆
☐ RA-25537	Mil Mi-8TB	99254376		◆
☐ RA-22494	Mil Mi-171	8AMT00643084107U		◆
☐ RA-25172	Mil Mi-17	95481		◆
☐ RA-26102	Antonov An-26B	11909	ex CCCP-26102	◆
☐ RA-26620	Antonov An-26B-100	5104	ex CCCP-26620	◆
☐ RA-26662	Antonov An-26-100	8101	ex CCCP-26662	◆
☐ RA-27068	Mil Mi-17	95904		◆
☐ RA-65052	Tupolev Tu-134A-3	49825	ex CCCP-65052	◆
☐ RA-65083	Tupolev Tu-134A-3	60090	ex UN-65083	◆
☐ RA-65560	Tupolev Tu-134A-3	60231		◆
☐ RA-65565	Tupolev Tu-143AK	63998		◆

URAL AIRLINES   Sverdlovsk Air (U6/SVR)   Yekaterinburg-Koltsovo (SVX)

☐ VP-BBQ	Airbus A320-214	2278	ex A6-ABC	
☐ VP-BFZ	Airbus A320-214	0735	ex G-BXKD	
☐ VP-BIE	Airbus A320-214	3099	ex JA205A	
☐ VP-BKB	Airbus A320-214	3189	ex JA208A	
☐ VP-BMT	Airbus A320-214	2349	ex A6-ABD	
☐ VP-BMW	Airbus A320-214	2166	ex CN-NME	
☐ VP-BQZ	Airbus A320-211	0157	ex TS-INH	[LDE]
☐ VP-BTZ	Airbus A320-214	3107	ex RP-C8605	
☐ VQ-BAG	Airbus A320-214	1063	ex EC-KLU	
☐ VQ-BCY	Airbus A320-214	1484	ex EC-HQM	
☐ VQ-BCZ	Airbus A320-214	1777	ex G-OOPW	
☐ VQ-BDJ	Airbus A320-214	2175	ex N268AV	
☐ VQ-BDM	Airbus A320-214	2187	ex N269AV	
☐ VQ-BFV	Airbus A320-214	1152	ex N266AV	
☐ VQ-BFW	Airbus A320-214	2327	ex N271AV	
☐ VQ-BLO	Airbus A320-214	1751	ex 6Y-JMJ	
☐ VQ-BNI	Airbus A320-214	3472	ex RP-C3246	◆
☐ VQ-BQN	Airbus A320-214	3433	ex RP-C3245	◆
☐ VQ-BRE	Airbus A320-214	2998	ex JA204A	
☐ VP-BVP	Airbus A321-211	2707	ex F-GYAJ	
☐ VQ-BCX	Airbus A321-211	1720	ex G-OOAV	
☐ VQ-BDA	Airbus A321-211	1012	ex TC-KTY	
☐ VQ-BKG	Airbus A321-211	0991	ex EI-CPF	
☐ VQ-BKH	Airbus A321-211	0841	ex EI-CPD	
☐ VQ-BKJ	Airbus A321-211	0815	ex EI-CPC	
☐ VQ-BOB	Airbus A321-211	1905	ex EI-ERT	
☐ VQ-BOC	Airbus A321-231	1199	ex EI-ERS	
☐ VQ-BOF	Airbus A321-211	0775	ex EI-EPM	
☐ VQ-BOZ	Airbus A321-211	2117	ex EI-ERU	
☐ VP-BJV	Airbus A319-112	1603	ex N681AC	◆
☐ VQ-BTP	Airbus A319-111	3834	ex EI-EWF	
☐ VQ-BTY	Airbus A319-112	3385	ex 2-ABIE	◆
☐ VQ-BTZ	Airbus A319-112	3388	ex 2-ABIF	◆

UTAIR AIRLINES		UTair (UT/UTA)		Tyumen-Roshchino (TJM)
☐ RA-01971	AgustaWestland AW139	31422	ex I-RAIU	
☐ RA-01972	AgustaWestland AW139	31429	ex I-RAIX	
☐ RA-01975	AgustaWestland AW139			
☐ RA-01976	AgustaWestland AW139			
☐ RA-01977	AgustaWestland AW139			
☐ RA-01992	AgustaWestland AW139			
☐ RA-	AgustaWestland AW139	31454	ex I-RAIR	
☐ VQ-BHZ	Boeing 737-46M	28549/2844	ex OK-CGT	
☐ VQ-BIC	Boeing 737-45S	28478/3132	ex OK-FGS	opf UN
☐ VQ-BID	Boeing 737-45S	28477/3131	ex OK-FGR	opf UN
☐ VQ-BIE	Boeing 737-45S	28476/3103	ex OK-EGP	
☐ VQ-BIF	Boeing 737-45S	28474/3028	ex OK-DGN	
☐ VQ-BIG	Boeing 737-45S	28473/3014	ex OK-DGM	
☐ VP-BFO	Boeing 737-524/W	27319/2590	ex N58606	
☐ VP-BFW	Boeing 737-524/W	27325/2630	ex N11612	
☐ VP-BVL	Boeing 737-524	28926/3069	ex N13665	
☐ VP-BVN	Boeing 737-524	27540/2776	ex N33637	
☐ VP-BVZ	Boeing 737-524/W	28925/3066	ex N14664	
☐ VP-BXO	Boeing 737-524/W	27314/2566	ex N14601	
☐ VP-BXQ	Boeing 737-524/W	27315/2571	ex N69602	
☐ VP-BXR	Boeing 737-524/W	27316/2573	ex N69603	
☐ VP-BXU	Boeing 737-524/W	27318/2582	ex N14605	
☐ VP-BXV	Boeing 737-524/W	27322/2607	ex N14609	wfs
☐ VP-BXY	Boeing 737-524/W	27328/2640	ex N37615	
☐ VP-BYK	Boeing 737-524	28918/3026	ex N23657	
☐ VP-BYL	Boeing 737-524	28920/3048	ex N15659	
☐ VP-BYM	Boeing 737-524	28917/3019	ex N11656	
☐ VQ-BAC	Boeing 737-524/W	27321/2597	ex N33608	
☐ VQ-BAD	Boeing 737-524/W	27331/2652	ex N16618	
☐ VQ-BAE	Boeing 737-524/W	27320/2596	ex N16607	
☐ VQ-BJL	Boeing 737-524/W	28913/2985	ex N14652	
☐ VQ-BJM	Boeing 737-524/W	28912/2980	ex N11651	
☐ VQ-BJN	Boeing 737-524/W	28911/2973	ex N16650	
☐ VQ-BJO	Boeing 737-524/W	28910/2972	ex N16649	
☐ VQ-BJP	Boeing 737-524/W	28905/2934	ex N17644	
☐ VQ-BJQ	Boeing 737-524/W	28902/2926	ex N11641	
☐ VQ-BJS	Boeing 737-524/W	28901/2924	ex N17640	
☐ VQ-BJT	Boeing 737-524/W	28900/2913	ex N14639	
☐ VQ-BJU	Boeing 737-524/W	28899/2912	ex N19638	
☐ VQ-BJV	Boeing 737-524/W	28914/2986	ex N14653	
☐ VQ-BPO	Boeing 737-524/W	28903/2927	ex N16642	
☐ VQ-BPP	Boeing 737-524/W	28906/2935	ex N14654	
☐ VQ-BPQ	Boeing 737-524/W	28907/2956	ex N16646	
☐ VQ-BPR	Boeing 737-524/W	28908/2958	ex N16647	
☐ VQ-BPS	Boeing 737-524/W	28909/2960	ex N16648	
☐ VP-BUL	Boeing 737-8LP/W	41707/4637		wfs
☐ VQ-BJF	Booeing 737-8AS/W	32778/1140	ex VQ-BBR	
☐ VQ-BJG	Boeing 737-8AS/W	32779/1167	ex VQ-BBS	
☐ VQ-BJH	Boeing 737-8AS/W	32780/1178	ex VQ-BCH	
☐ VQ-BJI	Boeing 737-8AS/W	29937/1238	ex VQ-BDV	
☐ VQ-BJJ	Boeing 737-8AS/W	29936/1236	ex VQ-BDU	
☐ VQ-BMG	Boeing 737-8LP/W	41841/5095		wfs♦
☐ VQ-BQP	Boeing 737-8GU/W	37553/3646		
☐ VQ-BQQ	Boeing 737-8GU/W	37552/3620		
☐ VQ-BQR	Boeing 737-8GU/W	36386/3710		
☐ VQ-BQS	Boeing 737-8GU/W	36387/3729		
☐ VQ-BRK	Boeing 737-8LP/W	41708/4839		wfs
☐ VQ-BRP	Boeing 737-8LP/W	41709/5002		wfs♦
☐ VQ-BRQ	Boeing 737-8LP/W	41710/5019		wfs♦
☐ VQ-BRR	Boeing 737-8LP/W	41836/4881	ex N5573P	wfs
☐ VP-BAB	Boeing 767-224ER	30430/811	ex N76151	[MCI]
☐ VP-BAG	Boeing 767-224ER	30435/827	ex N76156	
☐ VP-BAI	Boeing 767-224ER	30437/839	ex N67158	
☐ VP-BAL	Boeing 767-224ER	30439/851	ex N68160	wfs♦
☐ VP-BAQ	Boeing 767-224ER	30431/815	ex N73152	wfs
☐ VP-BAU	Boeing 767-224ER	30432/819	ex N76153	wfs♦
☐ VP-BAW	Boeing 767-224ER	30433/823	ex N69154	wfs
☐ VQ-BSX	Boeing 767-306ER	27612/647	ex P4-KCA	♦
☐ VQ-BSY	Boeing 767-306ER	27614/661	ex P4-KCB	♦
☐ VQ-BGH	Canadair CRJ-200LR	7114	ex C-GGDU	wfs
☐ VQ-BGL	Canadair CRJ-200LR	7128	ex C-GFNJ	wfs
☐ VQ-BGM	Canadair CRJ-200LR	7130	ex C-GGEV	wfs
☐ VQ-BGO	Canadair CRJ-200LR	7135	ex C-GEFJ	
☐ VQ-BGR	Canadair CRJ-200LR	7220	ex C-GFOA	opf UN
☐ VQ-BGT	Canadair CRJ-200LR	7266	ex C-GGDQ	wfs

☐ VQ-BGU	Canadair CRJ-200LR	7298	ex C-GEDO		wfs
☐ VQ-BGV	Canadair CRJ-200LR	7378	ex C-GFMQ		wfs
☐ VQ-BGX	Canadair CRJ-200LR	7394	ex C-GGDR		wfs
☐ RA-07229	Eurocopter AS350B3e Ecureuil				
☐ RA-07234	Aérospatiale AS350B3e Ecureuil				
☐ RA-07239	Aérospatiale AS350B3e Ecureuil				
☐ RA-07241	Aérospatiale AS355NP Twin Squirrel				
☐ RA-07235	Eurocopter AS355NP Twin Squirrel				
☐ RA-85016	Tupolev Tu-154M	90A844	ex LZ-MIH		
☐ RA-85018	Tupolev Tu-154M	90A852	ex LZ-MIR		
☐ RA-85681	Tupolev Tu-154M	90A848	ex LZ-LTE	Abakan	
☐ RA-85813	Tupolev Tu-154M	95A990		Vladimir Kuleshov	[TJM]
☐ RA-89034	Sukhoi SSJ 100-95LR	95061			o/o♦
☐ VP-BYW	ATR 72-201	174	ex ES-KRE		[TJM]
☐ VQ-BGK	Boeing 737-9LFER/W	41843/5190			o/o♦
☐ VQ-	Boeing 737-9LFER/W	41712/5336	ex N1798B		o/o♦

UTAIR CARGO

☐ RA-74009	Antonov An-74	36547095898	ex ER-AEN	[TJM]
☐ RA-74013	Antonov An-74-200	36547098960	ex ST-WTS	
☐ RA-74016	Antonov An-74TK-200	365470991034		opf UNO as UN-051P
☐ RA-74032	Antonov An-74TK-200	36547098962	ex UR-74032	opf UN as UN-
☐ RA-74035	Antonov An-74TK-200	36547098963		opf UNO as UNO-051P
☐ RA-26010	Antonov An-26B	9906	ex CCCP-28010	
☐ RA-26636	Antonov An-26-100	6306	ex EP-TQB	
☐ RA-88289	Antonov An-26B	11804	ex 88289	

UTAIR EXPRESS   UTAir-Express (UR/UTX)   Syktyvkar (SCW)

☐ RA-13344	Antonov An-24RV	37308310	ex CCCP-13344	
☐ RA-46519	Antonov An-24RV	37308505	ex CCCP-46519	
☐ RA-46610	Antonov An-24RV	37308607	ex CCCP-46610	
☐ RA-46848	Antonov An-24RV	27307506	ex CCCP-46848	[SGC]
☐ RA-47271	Antonov An-24RV	07306401	ex BNMAU-6401	
☐ RA-47273	Antonov An-24B	07306403	ex CCCP-47273	
☐ RA-47821	Antonov An-24RV	17307202	ex CCCP-47821	
☐ RA-47827	Antonov An-24B	17307208	ex CCCP-47827	
☐ VP-BCB	ATR 42-300	054	ex I-NOWT	
☐ VP-BLI	ATR 42-300	233	ex D-BCRQ	[TOF]
☐ VP-BLJ	ATR 42-300	255	ex D-BCRR	[MGL]
☐ VP-BLO	ATR 42-300	289	ex D-BCRT	
☐ VP-BPJ	ATR 42-300	165	ex N15823	[TOF]
☐ VP-BPK	ATR 42-300	166	ex N16824	
☐ VP-BYX	ATR 72-201	251	ex ES-KRK	wfs
☐ VQ-BLC	ATR 72-212A	942	ex F-WWER	
☐ VQ-BLD	ATR 72-212A	945	ex F-WWEV	
☐ VQ-BLE	ATR 72-212A	950	ex F-WWEC	
☐ VQ-BLF	ATR 72-212A	951	ex F-WWED	
☐ VQ-BLG	ATR 72-212A	952	ex F-WWEE	
☐ VQ-BLH	ATR 72-212A	953	ex F-WWEF	
☐ VQ-BLI	ATR 72-212A	963	ex F-WWEP	
☐ VQ-BLJ	ATR 72-212A	965	ex F-WWER	
☐ VQ-BLK	ATR 72-212A	975	ex F-WWET	
☐ VQ-BLL	ATR 72-212A	976	ex F-WWEU	
☐ VQ-BLM	ATR 72-212A	980	ex F-WWEZ	
☐ VQ-BLN	ATR 72-212A	981	ex F-WWEB	
☐ VQ-BMA	ATR 72-212A	983	ex F-WWED	
☐ VQ-BMB	ATR 72-212A	984	ex F-WWEE	
☐ VQ-BMD	ATR 72-212A	990	ex F-WWEH	
☐ RA-26636	Antonov An-26B-100	6306	ex EP-TQB	
☐ RA-26520	Antonov An-26B-100	7101	ex CCCP-26520	

UVAUGA   Pilot Air (UHS)   Ulyanovsk-Tsentralny (ULY)

☐ RA-26025	Antonov An-26B	10308	ex CCCP-26025	
☐ RA-26513	Antonov An-26	6810	ex CCCP-26513	
☐ RA-26544	Antonov An-26	2710	ex CCCP-26544	
☐ RA-85609	Tupolev Tu-154M	84A704	ex CCCP-85609	no titles [ULY]

VIM AIRLINES   MovAir (NN/MOV)   Moscow-Domodedovo (DME)

☐ RA-73009	Boeing 757-230	25437/422	ex D-ABNI	
☐ RA-73010	Boeing 757-230	25438/428	ex D-ABNK	wfs
☐ RA-73011	Boeing 757-230	25439/437	ex D-ABNL	
☐ RA-73012	Boeing 757-230	25440/443	ex D-ABNM	
☐ RA-73016	Boeing 757-230	26433/521	ex D-ABNP	

☐ RA-73017	Boeing 757-230	26434/532	ex D-ABNR	
☐ RA-73018	Boeing 757-230	26435/537	ex D-ABNS	
☐ VP-BDY	Airbus A319-111	2442	ex G-EZID	♦
☐ VP-BDZ	Airbus A319-111	2446	ex G-EZIE	♦
☐ VQ-BTK	Airbus A319-111	3403	ex AP-ECD	
☐ VQ-BTL	Airbus A319-111	3364	ex AP-EDB	
☐ VQ-	Boeing 767-31AER	27619/595	ex N195AT	wfs♦

VOLGA-DNEPR AIRLINES — Volga Dnepr (VI/VDA) — Ulyanovsk-Vostochniy East

☐ RA-82042	Antonov An-124-100	9773054055093	ex CCCP-82042
☐ RA-82043	Antonov An-124-100	9773054155101	ex CCCP-82043
☐ RA-82044	Antonov An-124-100	9773054155109	ex CCCP-82044
☐ RA-82045	Antonov An-124-100	9773052255113	ex CCCP-82045
☐ RA-82046	Antonov An-124-100	9773052255117	ex RA-82067
☐ RA-82047	Antonov An-124-100	9773053259121	
☐ RA-82074	Antonov An-124-100	9773051459142	
☐ RA-82078	Antonov An-124-100	9773054559153	
☐ RA-82079	Antonov An-124-100	9773052062157	
☐ RA-82081	Antonov An-124-100M	9773051462165	
☐ RA-76503	Ilyushin Il-76-90VD	2113422748	
☐ RA-76511	Ilyushin Il-76-90VD	2123422752	
☐ RA-76950	Ilyushin Il-76-90VD	2053420697	Vladimir Kokkinaki
☐ RA-76951	Ilyushin Il-76-90VD	2073421704	
☐ RA-76952	Ilyushin Il-76-90VD	2093422743	

VOLOGDA AIR ENTERPRISE — Vologda Air (VGV) — Vologda-Grishino (VGD)

☐ RA-87284	Yakovlev Yak-40	9311927	ex CCCP-87277	
☐ RA-87669	Yakovlev Yak-40	9021760	ex EW-87669	
☐ RA-87842	Yakovlev Yak-40	9331030	ex CCCP-87842	
☐ RA-87905	Yakovlev Yak-40K	9720754	ex CCCP-87905	
☐ RA-87966	Yakovlev Yak-40	9820958	ex CCCP-87966	♦
☐ RA-88231	Yakovlev Yak-40	9642050	ex CCCP-88231	
☐ RA-88247	Yakovlev Yak-40	9642051	ex EP-LBJ	

VOSTOK AIRLINES — Vostok (VTK) — Khabarovsk-Novy (KHV)

☐ RA-28920	WSK/PZL Antonov An-28	1AJ008-06	ex CCCP-28920
☐ RA-28929	WSK/PZL Antonov An-28	1AJ008-16	ex CCCP-28929
☐ RA-28933	WSK/PZL Antonov An-28	1AJ008-20	ex CCCP-28933
☐ RA-28941	WSK/PZL Antonov An-28	1AJ009-07	ex CCCP-28941
☐ RA-28942	WSK/PZL Antonov An-28	1AJ009-08	ex CCCP-28942
☐ RA-41901	Antonov An-38-100	4163847010001	Vera
☐ RA-41902	Antonov An-38-100	4163847010002	Nadezhda
☐ RA-41903	Antonov An-38-100	4163838010003	Lyubov

YAK-SERVIS

☐ RA-21506	Yakovlev Yak-40KD	9840259	ex CCCP-21506

YAKUTIA AIRLINES — Air Yakutia (R3/SYL) — Yakutsk (YKS)

☐ VP-BKD	de Havilland DHC-8Q-402	4162	ex LX-LGC	
☐ VP-BNU	de Havilland DHC-8Q-402	4171	ex LX-LGD	
☐ VP-BOS	de Havilland DHC-8Q-402	4159	ex LX-LGA	
☐ VQ-BNH	de Havilland DHC-8-311	402	ex C-FBXO	♦
☐ VQ-BVI	de Havilland DHC-8-311	381	ex C-GXXD	♦
☐ VQ-BVJ	de Havilland DHC-8-311	379	ex C-GXXE	♦
☐ RA-26660	Antonov An-26-100	97308008	ex CCCP-26660	
☐ RA-41250	Antonov An-140-100	05A001		[YKS]
☐ RA-41251	Antonov An-140-100	07A012		[YKS]
☐ RA-41252	Antonov An-140-100	09A014		
☐ RA-41253	Antonov An-140-100	36525305032	ex UR-14008	
☐ RA-46479	Antonov An-24RV	27308007	ex ER-AZM	
☐ RA-46496	Antonov An-24RV	27308209	ex CCCP-46496	
☐ RA-47304	Antonov An-24RV	57310304	ex CCCP-47304	
☐ RA-47353	Antonov An-24RV	67310602	ex CCCP-47353	
☐ RA-85707	Tupolev Tu-154M	91A882	ex UR-85707	
☐ RA-85812	Tupolev Tu-154M	94A1005	AirUnion c/s	[YKS]
☐ RA-89011	Sukhoi SSJ 100-95B	95019		wfs
☐ RA-89012	Sukhoi SSJ 100-95B	95020	Roman Dmitriev	wfs
☐ VP-BEP	Boeing 737-8Q8/W	32797/1287	ex EI-ETZ	
☐ VQ-BEO	Boeing 737-76Q/W	30293/1496	ex D-ABBN	
☐ VQ-BMP	Boeing 737-86N/W	28617/504	ex SE-RHS	
☐ VQ-BOY	Boeing 737-85F/W	28825/188	ex D-ABBR	
☐ VQ-BPY	Boeing 757-236PCF	25597/441	ex N597AG	♦

YAMAL AIRLINES	Yamal (YC/LLM)			Salekhard-Nepalkovo (SLY)
☐ VP-BBN	Airbus A320-232	1918	ex EI-ELD	
☐ VP-BCN	Airbus A320-232	1993	ex EI-ELN	
☐ VP-BCU	Airbus A320-232	1969	ex EI-ELE	
☐ VP-BHW	Airbus A320-232	2413	ex OE-IBF	
☐ VP-BHX	Airbus A320-214	2439	ex M-ABFH	
☐ VP-BHZ	Airbus A320-214	2419	ex M-ABFG	
☐ VQ-BNR	Airbus A320-214	1054	ex N105SR	
☐ VP-BBA	Canadair CRJ-200LR	7607	ex D-ACRE	
☐ VP-BBC	Canadair CRJ-200LR	7619	ex D-ACRF	
☐ VP-BBE	Canadair CRJ-200LR	7630	ex D-ACRG	
☐ VP-BBM	Canadair CRJ-200LR	7738	ex D-ACRH	
☐ VQ-BBV	Canadair CRJ-200ER	7454	ex N654BR	wfs
☐ VQ-BPA	Canadair CRJ-200LR	7583	ex D-ACRD	
☐ VQ-BPB	Canadair CRJ-200LR	7573	ex D-ACRC	
☐ VQ-BPC	Canadair CRJ-200LR	7570	ex D-ACRB	
☐ VQ-BPD	Canadair CRJ-200LR	7567	ex D-ACRA	
☐ VQ-BSA	Canadair CRJ-200LR	7910	ex LY-AZQ	♦
☐ RA-26113	Antonov An-26B	12110	ex UR-BXV	[SCW]
☐ RA-26133	Antonov An-26B-100	12709	ex CCCP-26133	
☐ RA-67015	LET L-410UVP-E20	2805	ex OK-ODM	
☐ RA-67016	LET L-410UVP-E20	2804	ex OK-ODO	
☐ RA-67219	Canadair Challenger 850	8090	ex C-FTSV	VIP
☐ VP-BKW	Boeing 737-4M0	29204/3051	ex N204BV	
☐ VQ-BII	Boeing 737-48E	25773/2905	ex N773SJ	
☐ VQ-BIK	Boeing 737-48E	25775/2925	ex N775SJ	
☐ VQ-BNM	Boeing 737-5Q8	28201/2999	ex N171LF	
☐ VQ-BSM	Airbus A321-231	1967	ex OD-RMH	
☐ VQ-BSQ	Airbus A321-231	1956	ex OD-RMG	

RDPL- LAOS (Lao People's Democratic Republic)

LAO AIRLINES	Lao (QV/LAO)			Vientiane (VTE)
☐ RDPL-34173	ATR 72-202	870	ex F-WNUD	
☐ RDPL-34174	ATR 72-202	878	ex F-WNUF	
☐ RDPL-34175	ATR 72-202	929	ex F-WKVF	
☐ RDPL-34176	ATR 72-202	938	ex F-WKVJ	
☐ RDPL-34222	ATR 72-600	1049	ex F-WKVC	
☐ RDPL-34225	ATR 72-600	1155	ex F-WWET	♦
☐ RDPL-34228	ATR 72-600	1189	ex F-WWEF	♦
☐ RDPL-34168	CAIC MA60	0402		wfs
☐ RDPL-34169	CAIC MA60	0403		wfs
☐ RDPL-34171	CAIC MA60	0507		wfs
☐ RDPL-34172	CAIC MA60	0508		wfs
☐ RDPL-34188	Airbus A320-214	4596	ex F-WWIX	
☐ RDPL-34199	Airbus A320-214	4639	ex F-WWBN	
☐ RDPL-34223	Airbus A320-214	5356	ex D-AUBN	
☐ RDPL-34224	Airbus A320-214	5396	ex D-AUBY	

LAO CENTRAL AIRLINES	Lao Central (LF/LCI)			Vientiane (VTE)
☐ RDPL-34158	LET 410UVP-E	902437	ex ER-LID	[VTE]
☐ RDPL-34183	Boeing 737-4K5	24127/1707	ex OO-TUA	[VTE]
☐ RDPL-34189	Boeing 737-4Y0	24314/1680	ex YR-BAI	[VTE]
☐ RDPL-34195	Sukhoi SSJ 100-95B	95026		[VTE]
Ops suspended May14; due to restart mid 2015				

LAO SKYWAYS	(LLL)			Vientiane (VTE)
☐ HS-SAB	Dornier 228-212	8007	ex D-ISIS	
☐ HS-SAE	Dornier 228-212	8124	ex 5Y-BWN	
☐ RDPL-34162	Aérospatiale AS350B2 Ecureuil	2262	ex ZK-HDM	
☐ RDPL-34181	Aérospatiale AS350B2 Ecureuil	1661	ex ZK-HND	
☐ RDPL-34182	Aérospatiale AS350B2 Ecureuil	2811	ex ZK-HVE	
☐ RDPL-34140	Mil Mi-17 (Mi-8MTV-1)	95984	ex CCCP-27121	
☐ RDPL-34149	Cessna 208B Caravan I	208B1159	ex N12879	
☐ RDPL-34160	Cessna 208B Caravan I	208B2006	ex N2251Z	
☐ RDPL-34178	Mil Mi-8T-17-1V			
☐ RDPL-34190	Mil Mi-8T			
☐ RDPL-34226	AVIC MA-60			
☐ RDPL-34262	AVIC MA-60			
☐ RDPL-34320	Mil Mi-8MTV-1			♦

RP- PHILIPPINES (Republic of the Philippines)

AIRASIA PHILIPPINES		Cool Red (PQ/APG)		Manila-Ninoy Aquino Intl (MNL)
☐ RP-C8189	Airbus A320-216	4797	ex F-WWIH	

AIRASIA ZEST		Zest Airways (Z2/EZD)		Manila-Sangley Point (SGL)
☐ RP-C8897	Airbus A320-232	2141	ex N581JB	wfs
☐ RP-C8970	Airbus A320-216	3064	ex 9M-AFR	
☐ RP-C8971	Airbus A320-216	2956	ex 9M-AFN	
☐ RP-C8972	Airbus A320-216	2826	ex 9M-AFH	
☐ RP-C8974	Airbus A320-216	3568	ex 9M-AHO Solair Resort c/s	♦
☐ RP-C8986	Airbus A320-216	3018	ex 9M-AFQ	
☐ RP-C8987	Airbus A320-214	1286	ex 9M-AQT	
☐ RP-C8988	Airbus A320-232	2147	ex RP-C8898	
☐ RP-C8991	Airbus A320-232	4533	ex D-AXAK	[KUL]
☐ RP-C8992	Airbus A320-232	2137	ex G-TTOI	
☐ RP-C8993	Airbus A320-232	0667	ex N403AC	
☐ RP-C8994	Airbus A320-233	0743	ex N416AC	
☐ RP-C8995	Airbus A320-232	0872	exB-6256	
☐ RP-C8996	Airbus A320-233	0874	ex N593SH	
☐ RP-C0997	Airbus A320-232	2576	ex EI-EWE	
☐ RP-C3889	LET L-410UVP	851511	ex RA-67544 Fleuris titles	
☐ RP-C5000	ITPN CASA CN-235	2/001N	ex PK-MNA	
☐ RP-C8892	CAIC MA60	0703	ex B-956L	
☐ RP-C8894	CAIC MA60	0710	ex B-956L	
☐ RP-C8895	CAIC MA60	0711	ex B-963L	
☐ RP-C8896	CAIC MA60	0712	ex B-964L	

AIR JUAN				Manila
☐ RP-C1718	Bell 407	54337		♦
☐ RP-C2303	Cessna 208B Caravan I	208B2338	ex N20320	♦

AIR LINK INTERNATIONAL AIRWAYS				Manila-Sangley Point (SGL)
☐ RP-C180	Cessna 414	414-0402	ex RP.180	
☐ RP-C1102	Beech 88 Queen Air	LP-44	ex RP-94	
☐ RP-C2252	NAMC YS-11A-212	2079	ex RP-C1931	

CANADIAN HELICOPTERS PHILIPPINES				Manila
☐ RP-C276	Sikorsky S-76A	760011	ex HS-HTY	♦

CARGOHOUSE				
☐ RP-C6021	Cessna 208B Caravan I	208B2263	ex N3042E	

CEBGO		Seair (DG/SGD)		
		Manila Ninoy Aquino Intl/Diosdado Macapagal Intl (MNL/CRK)		
☐ RP-C2128	LET L-410UVP-E3	882102	ex S9-BOX	
☐ RP-C2328	LET L-410UVP-E3	872004	ex S9-BOY	
☐ RP-C2428	LET L-410UVP-E3	871909	ex 3D-DAM	
☐ RP-C2728	LET L-410UVP-E	861708	ex RP-C5888 jungle c/s	
☐ RP-C3318	LET L-410UVP-E3	871934	ex 3C-QRH	
☐ RP-C3328	LET L-410UVP-E3	872003	ex RP-C528	
☐ RP-C3263	Airbus A320-214	4574	ex D-AVVJ	♦
☐ RP-C3267	Airbus A320-214	4927	ex F-WWBH	♦
☐ RP-C3269	Airbus A320-214	5250	ex F-WWDK	♦
☐ RP-C3270	Airbus A320-214	5320	ex F-WWDH	
☐ RP-C4328	Dornier 328-110	3042	ex D-CPRT	wfs
☐ RP-C4737	Boeing 737-2T4C	23065/989	ex JY-TWC	wfs
☐ RP-C5320	Airbus A319-132	3801	ex 9V-TRB	<TGW
☐ RP-C5328	Dornier 328-110	3046	ex D-CPRS	wfs
☐ RP-C6328	Dornier 328-120	3027	ex N653JC	wfs
☐ RP-C7328	Dornier 328-110	3069	ex G-BYML	wfs

CEBU PACIFIC AIR		Cebu Air (5J/CEB)		Manila-Sangley Point (SGL)
☐ RP-C3189	Airbus A319-111	2556	ex D-AVYG	
☐ RP-C3190	Airbus A319-111	2586	ex D-AVXI	
☐ RP-C3191	Airbus A319-111	2625	ex D-AVYZ	
☐ RP-C3192	Airbus A319-111	2638	ex D-AVWJ	
☐ RP-C3193	Airbus A319-111	2786	ex D-AVYV	
☐ RP-C3194	Airbus A319-111	2790	ex D-AVWN	
☐ RP-C3195	Airbus A319-111	2831	ex D-AVXH	

☐ RP-C3196	Airbus A319-111	2821	ex D-AVXC	
☐ RP-C3197	Airbus A319-111	2852	ex D-AVXL	
☐ RP-C3198	Airbus A319-111	2876	ex D-AVWL	
☐ RP-C3236	Airbus A320-214	5067	ex F-WWBX	
☐ RP-C3237	Airbus A320-214	5045	ex F-WWDZ	
☐ RP-C3238	Airbus A320-214	5067	ex F-WWBX	
☐ RP-C3242	Airbus A320-214	2994	ex F-WWIU	
☐ RP-C3243	Airbus A320-214	3048	ex F-WWDR	
☐ RP-C3244	Airbus A320-214	3272	ex F-WWBZ	
☐ RP-C3249	Airbus A320-214	3762	ex F-WWDI	
☐ RP-C3250	Airbus A320-214	3767	ex F-WWDP	
☐ RP-C3260	Airbus A320-214	4447	ex F-WWII	
☐ RP-C3261	Airbus A320-214	4508	ex F-WWBJ	
☐ RP-C3262	Airbus A320-214	4537	ex F-WWIF	
☐ RP-C3264	Airbus A320-214	4852	ex D-AUBM	
☐ RP-C3265	Airbus A320-214	4861	ex D-AUBO	
☐ RP-C3266	Airbus A320-214	4870	ex D-AUBR	
☐ RP-C3268	Airbus A320-214	4993	ex F-WWBF	
☐ RP-C3271	Airbus A320-214	5381	ex F-WWIG	
☐ RP-C3272	Airbus A320-214/S	5442	ex F-WWIK	
☐ RP-C3273	Airbus A320-214/S	5498	ex D-AXAF	
☐ RP-C3274	Airbus A320-214/S	5669	ex F-WWBU	
☐ RP-C3275	Airbus A320-214/S	5687	ex F-WWDJ	
☐ RP-C3276	Airbus A320-214/S	5917	ex D-AUBC	
☐ RP-C3277	Airbus A320-214/S	5934	ex F-WWIT	
☐ RP-C3278	Airbus A320-214/S	6021	ex F-WWBY	
☐ RP-C3279	Airbus A320-214/S	6051	ex F-WWDH	
☐ RP-C4100	Airbus A320-214/S	6317	ex F-WWIH	♦
☐ RP-C4101	Airbus A320-214/s	6325	ex F-WWIX	♦
☐ RP-C4102	Airbus A320-214/S	6418	ex D-AXAP	♦
☐ RP-C4103	Airbus A320-214/S	6441	ex F-WWBJ	♦
☐ RP-C	Airbus A320-214/S	6777	ex	o/o♦
☐ RP-C	Airbus A320-214/S	6782	ex	o/o♦
☐ RP-C	Airbus A320-214/S	6786	ex	o/o♦
☐ RP-C	Airbus A320-214/S	6927	ex	o/o♦
☐ RP-C	Airbus A320-214/S	6937	ex	o/o♦
☐ RP-C3341	Airbus A330-343E	1420	ex F-WWTR	
☐ RP-C3342	Airbus A330-343E	1445	ex F-WWKP	
☐ RP-C3343	Airbus A330-343E	1495	ex F-WWTO	
☐ RP-C3344	Airbus A330-343E	1527	ex F-WWYO	♦
☐ RP-C3345	Airbus A330-343E	1552	ex F-WWKV	♦
☐ RP-C3346	Airbus A330-343E	1602	ex F-WWCH	♦
☐ RP-C7250	ATR 72-212A	779	ex F-WWER	
☐ RP-C7251	ATR 72-212A	784	ex F-WWEC	
☐ RP-C7252	ATR 72-212A	820	ex F-WWEJ	
☐ RP-C7253	ATR 72-212A	828	ex F-WWEV	
☐ RP-C7255	ATR 72-212A	842	ex F-WWEH	
☐ RP-C7256	ATR 72-212A	847	ex F-WWEI	
☐ RP-C7257	ATR 72-212A	857	ex F-WWEB	
☐ RP-C7258	ATR 72-212A	944	ex F-WWET	

FIL-ASIAN AIRWAYS

| ☐ RP-C3591 | NAMC YS-11A-214 | 2147 | | |

### INTERISLAND AIRLINES		Tri-Bird (ISN)		Manila-Ninoy Aquino Intl (MNL)
☐ RP-C8101	British Aerospace 125 Srs.700A	257151	ex N825MS	
☐ RP-C8108	British Aerospace 125 Srs.700A	257008	ex N618KR	

### ISLAND TRANSVOYAGER		(ITI)		Manila-Sangley Point (SGL)
☐ RP-C1008	Dornier 228-212	8193	ex D-CARD	
☐ RP-C2289	Dornier 228-212	8177	ex B-11150	wfs
☐ RP-C4200	ATR 42-500	554	ex DQ-PSA	♦
☐ RP-C4201	ATR 42-500	689	ex OY-CLR	

### JET EAGLE INTERNATIONAL				Subic Bay
☐ RP-C2813	British Aerospace Jetstream 3201	853	ex VH-OAB	♦
☐ RP-C7573	Cessna 208B Caravan I	208B2266	ex N30197	
☐ RP-C7574	Cessna 208B Caravan I	208B2328	ex N90327	

### LLOYD HELICOPTER				Manila
☐ RP-C176	Sikorsky S-76A+	760112	ex VH-LAQ	♦

488

MAJESTIC AIR CARGO

☐ RP-C7110	Boeing 727-227F	21249/1219	ex N76753	wfs

NORTHSKY AIR | | | | Tuguegarao

☐ RP-C8825	Cessna 402B	402B-0628	ex N1048	♦

PACIFICAIR | Pacific West (GX/PFR) | | Manila-Sangley Point (SGL)

☐ RP-C1103	Beech H-18	BA-660	ex N638CZ
☐ RP-C1358	Beech H-18 Tri-Gear	BA-750	ex RP-C1986
☐ RP-C2132	Britten-Norman BN-2A-21 Islander	422	ex G-BCSG

PAL EXPRESS | Orient Pacific (2P/GAP) | | Manila-Ninoy Aquino Intl (MNL)

☐ RP-C3227	Airbus A320-214	2183	ex OY-VKP	
☐ RP-C3228	Airbus A320-214	2162	ex RP-C3226	
☐ RP-C8393	Airbus A320-214	4777	ex F-WWDN	
☐ RP-C8395	Airbus A320-214	4984	ex D-AVVR	
☐ RP-C8396	Airbus A320-214	5007	ex D-AVVY	
☐ RP-C8397	Airbus A320-214	5012	ex D-AVVZ	
☐ RP-C8398	Airbus A320-214	5103	ex D-AUBR	
☐ RP-C8399	Airbus A320-214	5310	ex D-AUBB	♦
☐ RP-C8604	Airbus A320-214	3087	ex F-WWBV	
☐ RP-C8606	Airbus A320-214	3187	ex F-WWDY	
☐ RP-C8615	Airbus A320-214	3731	ex F-WWDL	♦
☐ RP-C8616	Airbus A320-214	5081	ex D-AUBJ	
☐ RP-C8618	Airbus A320-214	5140	ex D-AVVI	
☐ RP-C3016	de Havilland DHC-8-314Q	653	ex C-FNEA	
☐ RP-C3017	de Havilland DHC-8-314Q	657	ex C-FOUN	
☐ RP-C3018	de Havilland DHC-8-314Q	658	ex C-FPDR	
☐ RP-C3020	de Havilland DHC-8-314Q	583	ex OY-EDM	
☐ RP-C3030	de Havilland DHC-8-402Q	4064	ex LN-WDD	
☐ RP-C3031	de Havilland DHC-8-402Q	4069	ex LN-WDA	
☐ RP-C3032	de Havilland DHC-8-402Q	4070	ex LN-WDB	
☐ RP-C3033	de Havilland DHC-8-402Q	4071	ex LN-WDC	
☐ RP-C3036	de Havilland DHC-8-402Q	4023	ex LN-RDH	
☐ RP-C8780	Airbus A330-343E	1456	ex F-WWYJ	Philippine Airlines c/s

PHILIPPINE AIRLINES | Philippine (PR/PAL) | | Manila-Ninoy Aquino Intl (MNL)

☐ RP-C3221	Airbus A320-214	0706	ex F-WWIM	
☐ RP-C3223	Airbus A320-214	0745	ex F-WWIR	
☐ RP-C8609	Airbus A320-214	3273	ex F-WWIC	
☐ RP-C8610	Airbus A320-214	3310	ex F-WWIO	
☐ RP-C8611	Airbus A320-214	3455	ex F-WWBH	
☐ RP-C8612	Airbus A320-214	3553	ex F-WWIZ	
☐ RP-C8613	Airbus A320-214	3579	ex F-WWBY	
☐ RP-C8614	Airbus A320-214	3652	ex F-WWDQ	
☐ RP-C8619	Airbus A320-214	5315	ex F-WWIL	
☐ RP-C8620	Airbus A320-214	5371	ex F-WWDX	
☐ RP-C9901	Airbus A321-231/S	5715	ex D-AZAS	
☐ RP-C9902	Airbus A321-231/S	5747	ex D-AZAL	
☐ RP-C9903	Airbus A321-231/S	5787	ex D-AVZB	
☐ RP-C9905	Airbus A321-231/S	5820	ex D-AVZH	
☐ RP-C9906	Airbus A321-231/S	5825	ex D-AVZI	
☐ RP-C9907	Airbus A321-231/S	5838	ex D-AVZR	
☐ RP-C9909	Airbus A321-231/S	6074	ex D-AVZX	
☐ RP-C9910	Airbus A321-231/S	6201	ex D-AZAM	♦
☐ RP-C9911	Airbus A321-231/S	6253	ex D-AVZG	♦
☐ RP-C9912	Airbus A321-231/S	6291	ex D-AVZT	♦
☐ RP-C9914	Airbus A321-231/S	6295	ex D-AVZX	♦
☐ RP-C9915	Airbus A321-231/S	6330	ex D-AVXE	♦
☐ RP-C9916	Airbus A321-231/S	6363	ex D-AVXN	♦
☐ RP-C9917	Airbus A321-231/S	6371	ex D-AVXR	♦
☐ RP-C9918	Airbus A321-231/S	6493	ex D-AVZS	♦
☐ RP-C9919	Airbus A321-231/S	6531	ex D-AZAG	♦
☐ RP-C9921	Airbus A321-231/S	6539	ex D-AZAD	♦
☐ RP-C9923	Airbus A321-231/S	6573	ex D-AVXD	♦
☐ RP-C9924	Airbus A321-231/S	6623	ex D-AVXR	o/o♦
☐ RP-C	Airbus A321-231/S	6658	ex	o/o♦
☐ RP-C	Airbus A321-231/S	6734	ex	o/o♦
☐ RP-C	Airbus A321-231/S	6828	ex	o/o♦
☐ RP-C	Airbus A321-231/S	6850	ex	o/o♦
☐ RP-C	Airbus A321-231/S	6869	ex	o/o♦
☐ RP-C	Airbus A321-231/S	6947	ex	o/o♦

☐ RP-C3330	Airbus A330-301	183	ex F-OHZM	[MNL]
☐ RP-C3336	Airbus A330-301	198	ex F-OHZR	
☐ RP-C3340	Airbus A330-301	203	ex F-OHZT	wfs
☐ RP-C8760	Airbus A330-343E	1510	ex F-WWKM	
☐ RP-C8762	Airbus A330-343E	1531	ex F-WWCG	♦
☐ RP-C8763	Airbus A330-343E	1546	ex F-WWCX	♦
☐ RP-C8764	Airbus A330-343E	1553	ex F-WWYA	♦
☐ RP-C8765	Airbus A330-343E	1559	ex F-WWYQ	♦
☐ RP-C8766	Airbus A330-343E	1566	ex F-WW	♦
☐ RP-C8771	Airbus A330-343E	1568	ex F-WWKJ	♦
☐ RP-C8781	Airbus A330-343E	1460	ex F-WWCP	
☐ RP-C8782	Airbus A330-343E	1449	ex F-WWKY	
☐ RP-C8783	Airbus A330-343E	1463	ex F-WWCX	
☐ RP-C8784	Airbus A330-343E	1467	ex F-WWKL	
☐ RP-C8785	Airbus A330-343E	1475	ex F-WWYQ	
☐ RP-C8786	Airbus A330-343E	1482	ex F-WWCM	
☐ RP-C8789	Airbus A330-343E	1504	ex F-WWTZ	
☐ RP-C3431	Airbus A340-313X	176	ex F-OHPK	wfs
☐ RP-C3435	Airbus A340-313X	302	ex (EC-LTB)	
☐ RP-C3436	Airbus A340-313X	318	ex F-WJKM	
☐ RP-C3437	Airbus A340-313X	332	ex F-WJKN	
☐ RP-C3438	Airbus A340-313X	387	ex EC-LHM	
☐ RP-C3439	Airbus A340-313X	459	ex EC-ICF	
☐ RP-C3441	Airbus A340-313X	474	ex EC-IDF	♦
☐ RP-C7772	Boeing 777-3F6ER	38719/1153		
☐ RP-C7773	Boeing 777-3F6ER	38718/1096		
☐ RP-C7774	Boeing 777-3F6ER	35556/1056		
☐ RP-C7775	Boeing 777-3F6ER	35555/1022		
☐ RP-C7776	Boeing 777-36NER	37712/841	ex N5020K	
☐ RP-C7777	Boeing 777-36NER	37709/826		
☐ RP-C5168	Gulfstream G150	259	ex N746GA	
☐ RP-C7471	Boeing 747-4F6	27261/1005	ex N751PR	[MZJ]
☐ RP-C7472	Boeing 747-4F6	27262/1012	ex N752PR	[MZJ]
☐ RP-C7473	Boeing 747-4F6	27828/1039	ex N753PR	[MZJ]
☐ RP-C7475	Boeing 747-469M	27663/1068	ex N754PR	[MZJ]

ROYAL STAR AVIATION — Manila-Sangley Point (SGL)

☐ RP-C1098	Agusta A109E Power	11041	ex CS-HEM	
☐ RP-C2812	British Aerospace Jetstream 3217	923	ex N93BA	
☐ RP-C8299	British Aerospace Jetstream 4101	41080	ex N327UE	
☐ RP-C8328	Dornier 328-300 (328JET)	3136	ex N360SK	
☐ RP-C8558	Cessna 208B Caravan I	208B2167	ex N169WD	♦
☐ RP-C8568	Cessna 560 Citation Excel	560-6050	ex N713DH	♦
☐ RP-C9555	Dornier 328-310 (328JET)	3160	ex N821MW	♦

SKYJET — (M8/MSJ) — Manila-Ninoy Aquino Intl (MNL)

☐ RP-C8538	British Aerospace 146 Srs.100	E1015	ex PK-VTA	
☐ RP-C	British Aerospace 146 Srs.100	E1104	ex PK-VTN	o/o♦

SORIANO AVIATION — Soriano (SOY) — Manila-Sangley Point (SGL)

☐ RP-C2282	Dornier 228-202K	8173	ex N23UA	
☐ RP-C2283	Dornier 228-202K	8077	ex F-ODZH	
☐ RP-C2287	Dornier 228-202K	8174	ex VH-YJD	

SE-   SWEDEN (Kingdom of Sweden)

ARCTIC AIR — Arjeplog

☐ SE-HKK	Agusta Bell206B JetRanger III	8603	ex Armén 06283	
☐ SE-JOA	Bell 206L1 LongRanger	45548	ex G-LILA	
☐ SE-JPB	Bell 206L1 LongRanger II	45783	ex G-KATG	

ARCTIC AIRLINK — Luleå (LLA)

☐ SP-MRC	SAAB SF.340A	340A-143	ex EC-IRR	<IGA♦

AMAPOLA FLYG — Amapola (HP/APF) — Stockholm-Arlanda/Malmö-Sturup (ARN/MMX)

☐ SE-KTC	Fokker 50	20124	ex OY-MMG	
☐ SE-KTD	Fokker 50	20125	ex OY-MMH	
☐ SE-LIO	Fokker 50	20146	ex PH-PRC	
☐ SE-LIP	Fokker 50F	20147	ex PH-PRD	
☐ SE-LIR	Fokker 50	20151	ex PH-PRE	
☐ SE-LIS	Fokker 50	20152	ex PH-PRF	

☐ SE-LJG	Fokker 50	20168	ex LX-LGC	
☐ SE-LJH	Fokker 50	20171	ex LX-LGD	
☐ SE-LJI	Fokker 50F	20180	ex LX-LGE	
☐ SE-LJV	Fokker 50F	20103	ex VT-CAA	
☐ SE-LJY	Fokker 50F	20259	ex OY-PAA	
☐ SE-MFB	Fokker 50F	20252	ex PH-KXM	
☐ SE-MFJ	Fokker 50F	20149	ex YL-BAR	♦

BRAATHENS REGIONAL   Braathens (DC/BRX)   Trollhättan (THN)

☐ SE-MDA	ATR 72-212A	778	ex EI-REN	Anders Källson
☐ SE-MDB	ATR 72-212A	822	ex EI-RER	Pigge
☐ SE-MDC	ATR 72-212A	894	ex F-WWED	
☐ SE-MDH	ATR 72-212A	917	ex F-WWEO	
☐ SE-MDI	ATR 72-212A	930	ex F-WWEF	
☐ SE-KXK	SAAB 2000	2000-012	ex F-GOZI	opf SAS
☐ SE-LOM	SAAB 2000	2000-035	ex LY-SBK	opf SAS
☐ SE-LSB	SAAB 2000	2000-043	ex OH-SAU	
☐ SE-LSE	SAAB 2000	2000-046	ex OH-SAW	Malmö Avn c/s
☐ SE-LTU	SAAB 2000	2000-062	ex HB-IYG	opf SAS
☐ SE-LTV	SAAB 2000	2000-063	ex HB-IYH	opf SAS
☐ SE-LTX	SAAB 2000	2000-024	ex HB-IZM	
☐ SE-LXH	SAAB 2000	2000-007	ex LY-SBQ	Love
☐ SE-LXK	SAAB 2000	2000-056	ex ER-SFA	
☐ SE-MFF	SAAB 2000	2000-038	ex YR-SBA	
☐ SE-MFK	SAAB 2000	2000-005	ex D-AOLB	
☐ SE-MFM	SAAB 2000	2000-022	ex OY-SFB	
☐ SE-ISG	SAAB SF.340B	340B-162	ex SE-F62	

FLY LOGIC/NORTH EXPRESS   Logic/NorthExpress (LOD/NOX)   Malmö-Sturup (MMX)

☐ SE-GIN	Piper PA-31 Navajo C	31-7512039	
☐ SE-IDR	Piper PA-31 Navajo C	31-7712085	ex LN-DAB
☐ SE-KCP	Swearingen SA226TC Metro II	TC-330	ex N7217N

MALMÖ AVIATION   Scanwings (TF/SCW)   Stockholm-Bromma/Malmö-Sturup (BMA/MMX)

☐ SE-DJN	Avro 146-RJ85	E2231	ex HB-IXG	
☐ SE-DJO	Avro 146-RJ85	E2226	ex HB-IXF	
☐ SE-DSO	Avro 146-RJ100	E3221	ex N504MM	
☐ SE-DSP	Avro 146-RJ100	E3242	ex N505MM	
☐ SE-DSR	Avro 146-RJ100	E3244	ex N506MM	
☐ SE-DSS	Avro 146-RJ100	E3245	ex N507MM	
☐ SE-DST	Avro 146-RJ100	E3247	ex N508MM	
☐ SE-DSU	Avro 146-RJ100	E3248	ex N509MM	
☐ SE-DSV	Avro 146-RJ100	E3250	ex N510MM	
☐ SE-DSX	Avro 146-RJ100	E3255	ex N511MM	
☐ SE-DSY	Avro 146-RJ100	E3263	ex N512MM	
☐ SE-RJI	Avro 146-RJ100	E3357	ex OY-RCC	<FLI♦
☐ SE-LSE	SAAB 2000	2000-046	ex OH-SAW	<BRX

NEXT JET   Nextjet (2N/NTJ)   Stockholm-Bromma (BMA)

☐ SE-LLO	British Aerospace ATP	2023	ex G-MANP	
☐ SE-MAK	British Aerospace ATP	2040	ex G-MANF	
☐ SE-MAL	British Aerospace ATP	2045	ex G-MANE	
☐ SE-MEE	British Aerospace ATP	2019	ex CS-TGL	
☐ SE-MEX	British Aerospace ATP	2018	ex CS-TFJ	
☐ SE-ISE	SAAB SF.340A	340A-156	ex YL-BAP	
☐ SE-KCH	SAAB SF.340B	340B-171	ex 5Y-FLB	<Alandia
☐ SE-KXD	SAAB SF.340B	340B-248	ex N248DP	<Alandia♦
☐ SE-KXI	SAAB SF.340B	340B-176	ex XA-AFR	
☐ SE-KXJ	SAAB SF.340B	340B-189	ex XA-TKT	
☐ SE-LEP	SAAB SF.340A	340A-127	ex B-12200	
☐ SE-LJM	SAAB SF.340A	340A-112	ex LY-RIK	<Alandia
☐ SE-LJN	SAAB SF.340A	340A-114	ex LY-DIG	<Alandia
☐ SE-LJS	SAAB SF.340B	340B-215	ex D-CDEO	
☐ SE-LJT	SAAB SF.340B	340B-221	ex D-CASD	
☐ SE-LMR	SAAB SF.340A	340A-141	ex OK-UFO	

NORDFLYG AIR LOGISTICS   Nyköping-Skavsta (NYO)

☐ SE-LSK	Cessna 208B Caravan I	208B1012	ex N5236L

NORRLANDSFLYG AMBULANS   Lifeguard Sweden (HMF)   Göteburg/Säve (GSE)

☐ SE-HAJ	Sikorsky S-76C	760510	ex OH-HCJ	SAR

☐ SE-HAV	Sikorsky S-76C	760377	ex N50KH	SAR
☐ SE-HEJ	Sikorsky S-76C+	760604	ex N71141	SAR
☐ SE-HOJ	Sikorsky S-76C+	760605	ex N8125H	SAR
☐ SE-JEZ	Sikorsky S-76A	760215	ex N72WW	EMS
☐ SE-JOB	Sikorsky S-76C++	760683	ex N4511A	SAR
☐ SE-JOJ	Sikorsky S-76C++	760678	ex N4510Q	SAR
☐ SE-JUC	Sikorsky S-76A	760219	ex N18KH	EMS
☐ SE-JUY	Sikorsky S-76C	760407	ex N154AE	SAR

NOVAIR — Navigator (N9/NVR) — Stockholm-Arlanda (ARN)

☐ SE-RDN	Airbus A321-231	2211	ex D-AVZK
☐ SE-RDO	Airbus A321-231	2216	ex D-AVZN
☐ SE-RDP	Airbus A321-231	2410	ex D-AVZK

SCANDINAVIAN AIRAMBULANCE — Luleå (LLA)

☐ SE-JIA	Aérospatiale AS365N3 Dauphin	6415	ex XA-RWZ	♦
☐ SE-JIB	Aérospatiale AS365N2 Dauphin	6404	ex LN-OLJ	♦
☐ SE-JIC	Aérospatiale AS365N2 Dauphin	6417	ex N915ME	♦
☐ SE-JID	Aérospatiale AS365N3 Dauphin	6788	ex N650LH	♦
☐ SE-JRB	Aérospatiale AS365N3 Dauphin	6782	ex A6-SBK	♦
☐ SE-IUX	Beech 200 Super King Air	BB-675	ex N26SD	
☐ SE-IXC	Beech B200 Super King Air	BB-1210	ex N7213J	
☐ SE-KFP	Beech B200C Super King Air	BL-132	ex N5962F	
☐ SE-LTL	Beech 200 Super King Air	BB-582	ex LN-MOA	
☐ SE-LVU	Beech B200 Super King Air	BB-1692	ex N772TP	
☐ SE-LVV	Beech B200 Super King Air	BB-1537	ex N3237M	
☐ SE-MAZ	Beech B200 Super King Air	BB-1522	ex ZS-OBB	
☐ SE-JJC	MBB BK117C2	9076	ex D-HMBN	♦
☐ SE-JRE	MBB BK117D2	20014		op in Finland♦
☐ SE-JRF	MBB BK117D2	20015		op in Finland♦
☐ SE-JRG	MBB BK117D2	20017	ex D-HADH	♦
☐ SE-JRO	MBB BK117C2	9202	ex LN-OOQ	♦
☐ SE-DZZ	Learjet 35A	35A-415	ex D-COSY	
☐ SE-JIE	Eurocopter EC135P2+	0715		♦
☐ SE-JFN	Eurocopter EC135T2	0214		♦
☐ SE-JRC	Bell 429	57154	ex C-GWEG	♦

SCANDINAVIAN AIRLINE SYSTEM — Scandinavian (SK/SAS)
Copenhagen-Kastrup/Oslo-Gardermoen/Stockholm-Arlanda (CPH/OSL/ARN)

Member of Star Alliance

☐ OY-KAL	Airbus A320-232	2883	ex OE-IBJ	Jon Viking
☐ OY-KAM	Airbus A320-232	2911	ex OE-IBL	Randver Viking
☐ OY-KAN	Airbus A320-232	2958	ex OE-IBM	Refil Viking
☐ OY-KAO	Airbus A320-232	2990	ex OE-IBO	Amled Viking
☐ OY-KAP	Airbus A320-232	3086	ex VT-INI	Viglek Viking
☐ OY-KAR	Airbus A320-232	3159	ex VT-INJ	Vermund Viking
☐ OY-KAS	Airbus A320-232	3335	ex VT-INO	Igulfast Viking
☐ OY-KAT	Airbus A320-232	3192	ex VT-INK	Hildegun Viking
☐ OY-KAU	Airbus A320-232	3227	ex VT-INL	Hjorvard Viking
☐ OY-KAW	Airbus A320-232	2817	ex M-ABFP	Tyke Viking
☐ OY-KAY	Airbus A320-232	2856	ex M-ABFN	Runar Viking
☐ SE-RJE	Airbus A320-232	1183	ex EC-KEC	Ottar Viking
☐ SE-RJF	Airbus A320-232	1383	ex EC-KOX	Adils Viking
☐ LN-RKI	Airbus A321-232	1817	ex D-AVZK	Gunnhild Viking
☐ LN-RKK	Airbus A321-232	1848	ex SE-REG	Svipdag Viking
☐ OY-KBB	Airbus A321-232	1642	ex D-AVZN	Hjörulf Viking
☐ OY-KBE	Airbus A321-232	1798	ex D-AVZG	Emma Viking
☐ OY-KBF	Airbus A321-232	1807	ex D-AVZH	Skapti Viking
☐ OY-KBH	Airbus A321-232	1675	ex D-AVZV	Sulke Viking
☐ OY-KBK	Airbus A321-232	1587	ex D-AVZK	Arne Viking
☐ OY-KBL	Airbus A321-232	1619	ex D-AVZB	Gunnbjörn Viking
☐ LN-RKH	Airbus A330-343X	497	ex F-WWYP	Emund Viking	
☐ LN-RKM	Airbus A330-343X	496	ex OY-KBN	Eystein Viking	
☐ LN-RKN	Airbus A330-343X	568	ex SE-REF	Erik Viking	
☐ LN-RKO	Airbus A330-343X	515	ex SE-REE	Sigrid Viking	
☐ LN-RKR	Airbus A330-343	1660	ex F-WW		o/o♦
☐	Airbus A330-343	1673	ex F-WW		o/o♦
☐ LN-RKF	Airbus A340-313X	413	ex SE-REA	Godfred Viking
☐ LN-RKG	Airbus A340-313X	424	ex SE-REB	Gudrod Viking
☐ LN-RKP	Airbus A340-313X	167	ex CC-CQG	Torfinn Viking
☐ OY-KBA	Airbus A340-313X	435	ex F-WWJU	Adalstein Viking
☐ OY-KBC	Airbus A340-313X	467	ex F-WWJE	Freydis Viking

☐ OY-KBD	Airbus A340-313X	470	ex F-WWJF	Toste Viking	
☐ OY-KBI	Airbus A340-313X	430	ex F-WWJR	Rurik Viking	
☐ OY-KBM	Airbus A340-313X	450	ex F-WWJD	Astrid Viking	Star Alliance c/s
☐ OY-JZA	ATR 72-600	1110	ex F-WWEW	Rorik Viking	<JTG
☐ OY-JZB	ATR 72-600	1121	ex F-WWEJ	Palnetoke Viking	<JTG
☐ OY-JZC	ATR 72-600	1120	ex F-WKVI	Torver Viking	<JTG
☐ OY-JZD	ATR 72-600	1131	ex F-WWET	Fjølnur Viking	<JTG
☐ OY-JZE	ATR 72-600	1164	ex F-WWEE	Skagul Viking	<JTG♦
☐ OY-JZF	ATR 72-600	1165	ex F-WWEF	Skjalm Viking	<JTG♦
☐ OY-JZG	ATR 72-600	1171	ex F-WWEL	Njal Viking	<JTG♦
☐ OY-JZH	ATR 72-600	1177	ex F-WWER	Nord Viking	<JTG♦
☐ OY-JZU	ATR 72-212A	723	ex (XY-AJU)	Gyrid Viking	<JTG♦
☐ OY-JZV	ATR 72-212A	789	ex F-GVZT	Gudlög Viking	<JTG♦
☐ OY-JZY	ATR 72-212A	500	ex N540AM		<JTG
☐ OY-JZZ	ATR 72-212A	548	ex N548AT		<JTG
☐ LN-RCT	Boeing 737-683	30189/303	ex OY-KKF	Fridlev Viking	
☐ LN-RCU	Boeing 737-683	30190/335	ex SE-DNZ	Sigfrid Viking	
☐ LN-RCW	Boeing 737-683	28308/333	ex SE-DNY	Yngvar Viking	
☐ LN-RGK	Boeing 737-683	28313/447	ex SE-DTH	Vile Viking	
☐ LN-RPA	Boeing 737-683	28290/100	ex N5002K	Amljot Viking	
☐ LN-RPB	Boeing 737-683	28294/137	ex N1787B	Bure Viking	
☐ LN-RPE	Boeing 737-683	28306/329	ex SE-DOT	Edla Viking	
☐ LN-RPF	Boeing 737-683	28307/330	ex N1784B	Frede Viking	
☐ LN-RPG	Boeing 737-683	28310/255	ex N1787B	Geirmund Viking	
☐ LN-RPH	Boeing 737-683	28605/375	ex N1786B	Hamdor Viking	[ARN]
☐ LN-RPS	Boeing 737-683	28298/191	ex OY-KKC	Gautrek Viking	
☐ LN-RPT	Boeing 737-683	28299/193	ex OY-KKD	Ellida Viking	
☐ LN-RPW	Boeing 737-683	28289/92	ex OY-KKA	Alvid Viking	
☐ LN-RPX	Boeing 737-683	28291/112	ex SE-DNN	Nanna Viking	
☐ LN-RPY	Boeing 737-683	28292/116	ex SE-DNO	Olof Viking	
☐ LN-RPZ	Boeing 737-683	28293/120	ex OY-KKB	Bera Viking	
☐ LN-RRC	Boeing 737-683	28300/209	ex OY-KKG	Sindre Viking	
☐ LN-RRD	Boeing 737-683	28301/227	ex OY-KKH	Embla Viking	
☐ LN-RRO	Boeing 737-683	28288/49	ex SE-DNM	Bernt Viking	
☐ LN-RRP	Boeing 737-683	28311/382	ex SE-DTU	Vilborg Viking	
☐ LN-RRR	Boeing 737-683	28309/368	ex SE-DTF	Torbjörn Viking	
☐ LN-RRX	Boeing 737-683	28296/21	ex SE-DNR	Ragnfast Viking	
☐ LN-RRY	Boeing 737-683	28297/30	ex SE-DNS	Signe Viking	
☐ LN-RRZ	Boeing 737-683	28295/149	ex SE-DNP	Gisla Viking	
☐ OY-KKS	Boeing 737-683	28322/614	ex LN-RPC	Ramveig Viking	
☐ SE-DNX	Boeing 737-683	28304/270	ex G-CDRA	Torvald Viking	
☐ SE-DOR	Boeing 737-683	28305/290	ex G-CDRB	Elisabeth Viking	
☐ HB-JJA	Boeing 737-7AK/W (BBJ)	34303/1758	ex VQ-BBS	Eivind Viking	<PTI♦
☐ LN-RNN	Boeing 737-783	28315/464	ex OY-KKI	Borgny Viking	
☐ LN-RNO	Boeing 737-783	28316/476	ex OY-KKR	Gjuke Viking	
☐ LN-RNU	Boeing 737-783/W	34548/3116	ex N1786B	Hans Viking	
☐ LN-RNW	Boeing 737-783/W	34549/3210		Granmar Viking	
☐ LN-RPJ	Boeing 737-783	30192/486	ex N1786B	Grimhild Viking	
☐ LN-RPK	Boeing 737-783	28317/500	ex N1786B	Heimer Viking	
☐ LN-RRA	Boeing 737-783/W	30471/2288	ex (SE-DYD)	Steinar Viking	
☐ LN-RRB	Boeing 737-783/W	32276/2331	ex (SE-DYC)	Dag Viking	
☐ LN-RRM	Boeing 737-783	28314/458	ex SE-DTI	Erland Viking	
☐ LN-RRN	Boeing 737-783	30191/404	ex SE-DTG	Solveig Viking	
☐ LN-TUD	Boeing 737-705	28217/142	ex N1786B	Magrete Skulesdatter	
☐ LN-TUF	Boeing 737-705	28222/245	ex N1786B	Tyra Haraldsdatter	
☐ LN-TUH	Boeing 737-705	29093/471	ex N1786B	Margrete Ingesdatter	
☐ LN-TUJ	Boeing 737-705/W	29095/773		Eirik Blodöks	
☐ LN-TUK	Boeing 737-705/W	29096/794		Inge Bärdsson	
☐ LN-TUL	Boeing 737-705/W	29097/1072	ex N1786B	Hakon IV Hakonsson	
☐ LN-TUM	Boeing 737-705/W	29098/1116		Øystein Magnusson	
☐ SE-RER	Boeing 737-7BX	30736/658	ex N341MS	Svein Viking	
☐ SE-RES	Boeing 737-7BX	30737/687	ex N343MS	Rut Viking	
☐ SE-RET	Boeing 737-76N/W	32734/1090	ex N588SC	Katarina Viking	
☐ SE-REU	Boeing 737-76N/W	33005/1134	ex N629SC	Folke Viking	
☐ SE-REX	Boeing 737-76N/W	33418/1226	ex N286CS	Lodin Viking	
☐ SE-REY	Boeing 737-76N/W	32737/1130	ex EI-CXE	Kristina Viking	
☐ SE-REZ	Boeing 737-76N/W	32738/1392	ex N280SC	Margareta Viking	
☐ SE-RJR	Boeing 737-76N/W	33420/1459	ex ET-ALQ	Styrbjörn Viking	♦
☐ SE-RJS	Boeing 737-76N/W	32684/1889	ex TC-SAC	Sigvalde Viking	♦
☐ SE-RJT	Boeing 737-76N/W	32741/1487	ex ET-ALU	Tora Viking	♦
☐ SE-RJU	Boeing 737-76N/W	29885/1120	ex EI-CXD	Ubbe Viking	
☐ SE-RJX	Boeing 737-76N/W	34754/2172	ex TC-SAD	Vagn Viking	♦
☐ LN-RCN	Boeing 737-883	28318/529	ex SE-DTK	Hedrun Viking	
☐ LN-RCX	Boeing 737-883	30196/733	ex SE-DYH	Sigfrid Viking	
☐ LN-RCY	Boeing 737-883	28324/767	ex SE-DTT	Eylime Viking	
☐ LN-RCZ	Boeing 737-883	30197/798	ex SE-DTS	Glitne Viking	
☐ LN-RGA	Boeing 737-86N/W	39397/4003	ex N1786B	Svarthöfde Viking	
☐ LN-RGB	Boeing 737-86N/W	38034/4280	ex N1786B	Benedicte Viking	
☐ LN-RGC	Boeing 737-86N/W	41257/4321		Cecilia Viking	

☐	LN-RGD	Boeing 737-86N/W	41258/4393		Dygve Viking	
☐	LN-RGE	Boeing 737-86N/W	38037/4376		Egil Viking	
☐	LN-RGF	Boeing 737-86N/W	38038/4429		Torolf Viking	
☐	LN-RGG	Boeing 737-86N/W	38039/4469		Asgerd Viking	
☐	LN-RGH	Boeing 737-86N/W	41266/4770		Odvar Viking	
☐	LN-RGI	Boeing 737-86N/W	35646/4788		Turid Viking	
☐	LN-RPL	Boeing 737-883	30469/673	ex (SE-DYC)	Svanevit Viking	
☐	LN-RPM	Boeing 737-883	30195/696	ex (SE-DYD)	Frigg Viking	
☐	LN-RPN	Boeing 737-883	30470/717	ex (SE-DYG)	Bergfora Viking	
☐	LN-RPO	Boeing 737-883	30467/634	ex VQ-BFU	Thorleif Viking	
☐	LN-RPR	Boeing 737-883	30468/668	ex VQ-BFR	Ore Viking	
☐	LN-RRE	Boeing 737-85P/W	35706/2586		Knut Viking	
☐	LN-RRF	Boeing 737-85P/W	35707/2610		Froydis Viking	
☐	LN-RRG	Boeing 737-85P/W	35708/2653		Einar Viking	
☐	LN-RRH	Boeing 737-883/W	34546/2898	ex N1786B	Freja Viking	
☐	LN-RRJ	Boeing 737-883/W	34547/2956	ex N5573L	Frida Viking	
☐	LN-RRK	Boeing 737-883	32278/1169	ex SE-DYG	Gerud Viking	
☐	LN-RRL	Boeing 737-883/W	28328/1424	ex SE-DYT	Jarlabanke Viking	Star Alliance c/s
☐	LN-RRS	Boeing 737-883	28325/1014	ex (SE-DYM)	Ymer Viking	
☐	LN-RRT	Boeing 737-883	28326/1036	ex (SE-DYN)	Lodyn Viking	
☐	LN-RRU	Boeing 737-883	28327/1070	ex (SE-DYP)	Vingolf Viking	
☐	LN-RRW	Boeing 737-883	32277/1554	ex SE-DTR	Saga Viking	Star Alliance c/s
☐	OY-KFA	Canadair CRJ-900	15206	ex C-GIAW	Johan Viking	
☐	OY-KFB	Canadair CRJ-900	15211		Alfhild Viking	
☐	OY-KFC	Canadair CRJ-900	15218		Bertil Viking	
☐	OY-KFD	Canadair CRJ-900	15221		Estrid Viking	
☐	OY-KFE	Canadair CRJ-900	15224	ex C-GIBH	Ingemar Viking	
☐	OY-KFF	Canadair CRJ-900	15231	ex C-GZQO	Karl Viking	
☐	OY-KFG	Canadair CRJ-900	15237		Maria Viking	
☐	OY-KFH	Canadair CRJ-900	15240	ex C-GZQU	Ella Viking	
☐	OY-KFI	Canadair CRJ-900	15242	ex C-GIAP	Rolf Viking	
☐	OY-KFK	Canadair CRJ-900	15244	ex C-GBSZ	Hardenknud Viking	
☐	OY-KFL	Canadair CRJ-900	15246		Regin Viking	
☐	OY-KFM	Canadair CRJ-900	15250	ex LN-RNL	Fafner Viking	♦
☐	OY-KBO	Airbus A319-132	2850	ex D-AVXK	Christian Valdemar Viking	retro c/s
☐	OY-KBP	Airbus A319-132	2888	ex D-AVYG	Viger Viking	
☐	OY-KBR	Airbus A319-131	3231	ex D-AVYV	Sten Viking	
☐	OY-KBT	Airbus A319-131	3292	ex D-AVYC	Ragnvald Viking	
☐	SE-KXK	SAAB 2000	2000-012	ex F-GOZI		opb BRX♦
☐	SE-LOM	SAAB 2000	2000-035	ex LY-SBK		opb BRX♦
☐	SE-LTU	SAAB 2000	2000-062	ex HB-IYG		opb BRX♦
☐	SE-LTV	SAAB 2000	2000-063	ex HB-IYH		opb BRX♦

SJÖFARTSVERKET/SWEDISH MARITIME ADMINISTRATION
Sweden Rescue
Göteburg/Säve (GSE)

☐	SE-JRH	AgustaWestland AW139	31499	ex (I-RAIE)	♦
☐	SE-JRI	AgustaWestland AW139	31507	ex (I-PTFG)	♦
☐	SE-JRJ	AgustaWestland AW139	31524		♦
☐	SE-JRK	AgustaWestland AW139	31542		SAR♦
☐	SE-JRL	AgustaWestland AW139	31558		♦
☐	SE-JRM	AgustaWestland AW139	31597		SAR♦
☐	SE-JRN	AgustaWestland AW139	31598		♦
☐	SE-HAJ	Sikorsky S-76C	760510	ex OH-HCJ	SAR
☐	SE-HAV	Sikorsky S-76C	760377	ex N50KH	SAR
☐	SE-JOB	Sikorsky S-76C++	760683	ex N4511A	SAR
☐	SE-JOJ	Sikorsky S-76C++	760678	ex N4510Q	SAR
☐	SE-JUY	Sikorsky S-76C	760407	ex N154AE	SAR

SMA HELICOPTER RESCUE
Lifeguard Sweden (HMF)
Göteburg/Säve (GSE)

| ☐ | SE-JEZ | Sikorsky S-76A | 760215 | ex N72WW | EMS |

TUIFLY NORDIC
Bluescan (6B/BLX)
Stockholm-Arlanda (ARN)

☐	SE-DZV	Boeing 737-804/W	32904/1302		
☐	SE-RFT	Boeing 737-8K5/W	38097/3548	ex N1787B	
☐	SE-RFU	Boeing 737-8K5/W	37259/3673	ex N1786B	
☐	SE-RFV	Boeing 737-86N/W	32669/1895	ex EI-EOX	
☐	SE-RFX	Boeing 737-8K5/W	37246/3994		
☐	SE-RFY	Boeing 737-8K5/W	44272/4827		
☐	SE-RFR	Boeing 767-38AER/W	29617/741	ex VP-BWT	
☐	SE-RFS	Boeing 767-304ER/W	28040/613	ex G-OBYB	

WEST AIR SWEDEN
Air Sweden (PT/SWN)
Lidköping (LDK)

| ☐ | SE-KXP | British Aerospace ATP LFD | 2056 | ex LX-WAF | |

☐ SE-LGU	British Aerospace ATPF	2022	ex N853AW	[MMX]
☐ SE-LGV	British Aerospace ATPF	2034	ex N857AW	[IOM]
☐ SE-LGX	British Aerospace ATPF	2036	ex N859AW	
☐ SE-LGY	British Aerospace ATPF	2035	ex (LX-WAZ)	
☐ SE-LGZ	British Aerospace ATP LFD	2021	ex LX-WAW	
☐ SE-LHX	British Aerospace ATPF	2020	ex LX-WAN	
☐ SE-LHZ	British Aerospace ATPF	2059	ex LX-WAL	
☐ SE-LNX	British Aerospace ATPF	2061	ex LX-WAK	
☐ SE-LNY	British Aerospace ATPF	2062	ex (LX-WAJ)	
☐ SE-LPR	British Aerospace ATPF	2057	ex LX-WAP	
☐ SE-LPS	British Aerospace ATP LFD	2043	ex LX-WAO	
☐ SE-LPT	British Aerospace ATPF	2058	ex LX-WAS	[MMX]
☐ SE-LPU	British Aerospace ATPF	2060	ex LX-WAM	
☐ SE-LPV	British Aerospace ATP LFD	2041	ex LX-WAV	
☐ SE-LPX	British Aerospace ATPF	2063	ex LX-WAX	
☐ SE-MAF	British Aerospace ATPF	2002	ex G-MAUD	
☐ SE-MAH	British Aerospace ATPF	2004	ex G-MANJ	
☐ SE-MAJ	British Aerospace ATP LFD	2038	ex LX-WAD	
☐ SE-MAO	British Aerospace ATP LFD	2011	ex LX-WAT	
☐ SE-MAR	British Aerospace ATPF	2053	ex G-OBWR	
☐ SE-MAY	British Aerospace ATPF	2044	ex G-BTPN	
☐ SE-MEG	British Aerospace ATP	2031	ex CS-TGN	[MMX]
☐ SE-DUX	Canadair CRJ-200F	7010	ex C-FJGI	opf Posten Norge
☐ SE-DUY	Canadair CRJ-200F	7023	ex C-FJGK	opf Posten Norge
☐ SE-MGI	ATR 72-202	241	ex SX-BIF	[SGD]
☐ SE-MGJ	ATR 72-202	290	ex SX-BIG	[SGD]
☐ SE-MGT	ATR 72-201	145	ex F-GVZF	
☐ SE-RIF	Canadair CRJ-200F	7142	ex OE-LCJ	opf Posten Norge
☐ SE-RLA	Boeing 767-232SCD	22224/76	ex N747AX	>TAY♦

SP-   POLAND (Republic of Poland)

ENTER AIR   Enter (E4/ENT)   Warsaw-Okecie (WAW)

☐ SP-ENA	Boeing 737-4Q8	26320/2563	ex HL7592	
☐ SP-ENB	Boeing 737-4Q8	26299/2602	ex HL7527	
☐ SP-ENC	Boeing 737-4Q8	25376/2689	ex EI-DXG	
☐ SP-ENE	Boeing 737-4Q8	25374/2562	ex TC-TJC	
☐ SP-ENF	Boeing 737-4C9	25429/2215	ex SE-RID	
☐ SP-ENH	Boeing 737-405	25795/2867	ex LN-BUF	
☐ SP-ENI	Boeing 737-43Q	28489/2827	ex OO-VEP	
☐ SP-ENK	Boeing 737-46J	28038/2794	ex 9M-MQP	
☐ SP-ENR	Boeing 737-8Q8/W	30652/1018	ex A4O-BN	♦
☐ SP-ENT	Boeing 737-8AS/W	29926/722	ex M-ABGY	♦
☐ SP-ENU	Boeing 737-83N/W	30675/898	ex D4-CBY	♦
☐ SP-ENV	Boeing 737-8BK/W	33014/1367	ex OO-VAC	
☐ SP-ENW	Boeing 737-86J/W	28073/200	ex D-ABAS	
☐ SP-ENX	Boeing 737-8Q8/W	30627/752	ex D-ABBU	
☐ SP-ENY	Boeing 737-86N/W	28592/258	ex SE-RHX	
☐ SP-ENZ	Boeing 737-85F/W	28823/174	ex D-ABBM	

EXIN   Exin (EXN)   Katowice-Muchoeiec (KTW)

☐ SP-EKA	Antonov An-26B	12008	ex RA-26107	wfs
☐ SP-EKB	Antonov An-26	1310	ex 1310 Polish AF	[KTW]
☐ SP-EKC	Antonov An-26	1407	ex 1407 Polish AF	
☐ SP-EKD	Antonov An-26	1402	ex 1402 Polish AF	[KTW]
☐ SP-EKE	Antonov An-26	1509	ex 1509 Polish AF	[KTW]
☐ SP-EKF	Antonov An-26	1604	ex 1604 Polish AF	[KTW]
☐ SP-FDR	Antonov An-26B	11305	ex RA-26067	wfs
☐ SP-FDS	Antonov An-26B	12205	ex RA-26116	wfs
☐ SP-FDT	Antonov An-26B	12102	ex RA-26110	wfs

LOT - POLISH AIRLINES   Pollat (LO/LOT)   Warsaw-Okecie (WAW)

Member of Star Alliance

☐ SP-LRA	Boeing 787-8	35938/61	ex N1026G	
☐ SP-LRB	Boeing 787-8	37894/78		
☐ SP-LRC	Boeing 787-8	35940/86	ex N1791B	>FIN
☐ SP-LRD	Boeing 787-8	35941/87		
☐ SP-LRE	Boeing 787-8	35939/88		
☐ SP-LRF	Boeing 787-8	35942/161	Franek	>AEA
☐ SP-EQB	de Havilland DHC-8-402Q	4407	ex C-GMXR	wfs♦
☐ SP-EQC	de Havilland DHC-8-402Q	4408	ex C-GMYD	♦
☐ SP-EQD	de Havilland DHC-8-402Q	4411	ex C-GHND	♦
☐ SP-EQE	de Havilland DHC-8-402Q	4417	ex C-GOCX	wfs♦
☐ SP-EQF	de Havilland DHC-8-402Q	4422	ex C-GPKS	wfs♦

☐ SP-EQG	de Havilland DHC-8-402Q	4423	ex C-GPYN	♦
☐ SP-EQH	de Havilland DHC-8-402Q	4424	ex C-GPZF	♦
☐ SP-EQI	de Havilland DHC-8-402Q	4442	ex C-GUIT	♦
☐ SP-EQK	de Havilland DHC-8-402Q	4443	ex C-GUIZ	♦
☐ SP-EQL	de Havilland DHC-8-402Q	4451	ex C-GVWZ	♦
☐ SP-LDB	Embraer ERJ-170STD	17000024	ex PT-SKR	
☐ SP-LDE	Embraer ERJ-170LR	17000029	ex PT-SKW	
☐ SP-LDF	Embraer ERJ-170LR	17000035	ex PT-SUE	
☐ SP-LDG	Embraer ERJ-170LR	17000065	ex PT-SVQ	
☐ SP-LDH	Embraer ERJ-170LR	17000069	ex PT-SVU	
☐ SP-LDI	Embraer ERJ-170LR	17000073	ex PT-SVY	
☐ SP-LDK	Embraer ERJ-170LR	17000074	ex PT-SVZ	Star Alliance c/s
☐ SP-LIA	Embraer ERJ-175LR	17000125	ex PT-SDO	Mamma Mia c/s
☐ SP-LIB	Embraer ERJ-175LR	17000132	ex PT-SDV	
☐ SP-LIC	Embraer ERJ-175LR	17000134	ex PT-SDX	
☐ SP-LID	Embraer ERJ-175LR	17000136	ex PT-SDZ	
☐ SP-LIE	Embraer ERJ-175LR	17000153	ex EI-DVW	retro c/s
☐ SP-LIF	Embraer ERJ-175LR	17000154	ex EI-DVV	
☐ SP-LIG	Embraer ERJ-175LR	17000283	ex PT-TQJ	VIP; opf Govt♦
☐ SP-LIH	Embraer ERJ-175LR	17000288	ex PT-TQO	VIP; opf Govt♦
☐ SP-LII	Embraer ERJ-175LR	17000290	ex PT-TQQ	600th EJet c/s
☐ SP-LIK	Embraer ERJ-175LR	17000303	ex PT-XQC	Welcome to Poland c/s
☐ SP-LIL	Embraer ERJ-175LR	17000306	ex PT-XQF	Welcome to Polanc c/s
☐ SP-LIM	Embraer ERJ-175LR	17000311	ex PT-XQY	
☐ SP-LIN	Embraer ERJ-175LR	17000313	ex PT-XUH	Black Energy/Mike Tyson c/s
☐ SP-LIO	Embraer ERJ-175LR	17000321	ex PT-XUP	Welcome to Poland c/s
☐ SP-LNA	Embraer ERJ-195LR	19000415	ex PT-TBM	
☐ SP-LNB	Embraer ERJ-195LR	19000444	ex PT-TJE	
☐ SP-LNC	Embraer ERJ-195LR	19000462	ex PT-TOD	
☐ SP-LND	Embraer ERJ-195LR	19000516	ex PT-TUD	
☐ SP-LNE	Embraer ERJ-195LR	19000583	ex PT-TGO	
☐ SP-LNF	Embraer ERJ-195LR	19000596	ex PT-TIB	
☐ SP-LGG	Embraer ERJ-145MP	145329	ex PT-SMK	[WAW]
☐ SP-LGH	Embraer ERJ-145MP	145329	ex PT-SMV	[WAW]
☐ SP-LGO	Embraer ERJ-145MP	145560	ex PT-SZV	Pomocy logo	[WAW]
☐ SP-LLE	Boeing 737-45D	27914/2804		♦
☐ SP-LLF	Boeing 737-45D	28752/2874		♦
☐ SP-LLG	Boeing 737-45D	28753/2895	ex SX-BGN	♦

SKYTAXI — Iguana (TE/IGA) — Wroclaw (WRO)

☐ SP-MRB	SAAB SF.340AQC	340A-100	ex OE-GIF	all white
☐ SP-MRC	SAAB SF.340A	340A-143	ex EC-IRR	>Arctic Airlink
☐ SP-MRE	SAAB SF.340A	340A-151	ex ES-ASN	

SMALL PLANET AIRLINES POLSKA — Skypol (P7/LLP) — Warsaw-Okecie (WAW)

☐ LY-SPC	Airbus A320-231	0415	ex EI-ETM	<LLC
☐ SP-HAB	Airbus A320-232	1411	ex G-TCAC	
☐ SP-HAC	Airbus A320-233	0739	ex N413AC	
☐ SP-HAD	Airbus A320-232	2016	ex P4-SAS	>SWM
☐ SP-HAE	Airbus A320-214	0883	ex XU-704	all white	wfs
☐ SP-HAF	Airbus A320-214	0914	ex XU-702	wfs
☐ SP-HAG	Airbus A320-232	1723	ex OE-IDN	♦
☐ SP-HAH	Airbus A320-233	2118	ex OE-IDP	♦
☐ SP-HAI	Airbus A320-233	1007	ex B-6027	♦

SPRINTAIR — Sprintair (SRN) — Warsaw-Okecie (WAW)

☐ SP-KPC	SAAB SF.340A	340A-070	ex SE-KCT	
☐ SP-KPE	SAAB SF.340AQC	340A-130	ex SE-ISL	
☐ SP-KPF	SAAB SF.340AQC	340A-135	ex SE-KCU	
☐ SP-KPG	SAAB SF.340AQC	340A-065	ex SE-KCR	
☐ SP-KPH	SAAB SF.340AQC	340A-015	ex SE-ISP	
☐ SP-KPK	SAAB SF.340AF	340A-026	ex VH-ZLY	
☐ SP-KPL	SAAB SF.340A	340A-038	ex VH-ZRX	
☐ SP-KPN	SAAB SF.340A	340A-118	ex SE-F18	
☐ SP-KPO	SAAB SF.340AQC	340A-010	ex SE-LTI	
☐ SP-KPR	SAAB SF.340AQC	340A-139	ex OH-FAE	
☐ SP-KPU	SAAB SF.340AF	340A-145	ex SE-ISD	
☐ SP-KPV	SAAB SF.340A	340A-071	ex SE-LGS	
☐ SP-KPZ	SAAB SF.340AF	340A-087	ex SE-KUT	
☐ SP-SPA	ATR 72-202	246	ex D-ANFD	♦
☐ SP-KTL	LET L-410UVP-E16A	902414	ex SP-TXB	

TRAVEL SERVICE POLAND		Jet Travel (3Z/TVP)		Warsaw-Okecie (WAW)
☐ SP-TVZ	Boeing 737-8BK/W	29643/2303	ex OK-TVN	

ST-   SUDAN (Republic of the Sudan)

AIR TAXI		(WAM)		Khartoum (KRT)
☐ ST-TKO	Antonov An-32B	3110	ex ER-AWL Deena	

ALFA AIRLINES		Alfa Sudan (AAJ)	
☐ ST-ARP	Antonov An-24RV	37308809	ex EK-46630
☐ ST-AQR	Ilyushin Il-76TD	0043453575	ex 9L-LCX
☐ ST-AWT	Antonov An-26	3508	ex RA-58646
☐ ST-EWD	Ilyushin Il-76TD	0063466989	ex UR-CAP

ALOK AIR			Alok Air (LOK)
☐ ST-AWZ	Antonov An-24RV	77310808	ex 4L-AVL Pay Pay
☐ S9-TLN	Antonov An-24RV		♦

AZZA TRANSPORT		Azza Transport (AZZ)		Khartoum (KRT)
☐ ST-ARV	Antonov An-12BP	7345310	ex EK-11028	
☐ ST-AZH	Antonov An-12BK	003470076	ex UR-CFD	
☐ ST-AZN	Antonov An-12	9346808	ex UR-CFC	opb Sudanese AF

BADR AIRLINES		Badr Air (J4/BDR)		Khartoum (KRT)
☐ C5-BDV	Boeing 737-5H6	27356/2654	ex 4L-AJV	♦
☐ ST-BDE	Ilyushin Il-76TD	1013408252	ex RA-76809	
☐ ST-BDN	Ilyushin Il-76TD	1023413443	ex UK 76448	
☐ ST-BDR	Mil Mi-8S	10733	ex LY-HBB	
☐ ST-SAL	Antonov An-26B	17311907	ex RA-26100	
☐ 4L-AJB	Boeing 737-5H6	27354/2637	ex N495MS	<AJD
☐ 4L-AJO	Boeing 737-36N	28673/2995	ex N641CS	<AJD♦

BENTIU AIR TRANSPORT		Bentiu Air (BNT)		Sharjah/Khartoum (SHJ/KRT)
☐ ST-NDC	Antonov An-26	10908	ex RA-26052	
☐ ST-SRA	Antonov An-26	11807	ex RA-08827	

BLUE BIRD AIRLINES		Bluebird Sudan (BLB)		Khartoum (KRT)
☐ ST-AFP	de Havilland DHC-6 Twin Otter 300	479	ex C-GDVN-X	opf UNICEF
☐ ST-ARH	Fokker 50	20131	ex LN-BBB	
☐ ZS-TIL	Beech 1900D	UE-21	ex 5Y-RAE	opf Red Cross

DELTA AIR COMPANY			
☐ ST-DAC	Ilyushin Il-76TD	1033416515	ex UR-CIG ♦

DOVE AIR		Doveair (DOV)	
☐ ST-HIS	Antonov An-26B-100	10310	ex UN-26026
☐ ST-MRS	Tupolev Tu-134B-3	63333	ex UN-65699 wfs

EL DINDER			
☐ ST-ISG	WSK-PZL Antonov An-28	1AJ005-01	ex EK-28501

EL MAGAL AVIATION			Khartoum (KRT)
☐ ST-APJ	Antonov An-12BP	2400701	ex RA-11308
☐ ST-BEN	Antonov An-26	6907	ex UR-26514

GREEN FLAG AVIATION			
☐ ST-BDT	Antonov An-74	36547097935	ex RA-74046 [IEV]
☐ ST-EWX	Ilyushin Il-76TD	1013409282	ex UN-76810
☐ ST-GFA	Mil Mi-17	202M27	ex RA-70958
☐ ST-GFC	Mil Mi-17	212M147	ex RA-70891
☐ ST-GFD	Antonov An-30A-100	0605	ex UR-30030
☐ ST-GFE	Mil Mi-17	212M148	ex RA-70892
☐ ST-GFF	Antonov An-74	36547097932	ex T9-ABE
☐ ST-GFK	Mil Mi-172		

KATA TRANSPORTATION		Katavia (KTV)		Khartoum (KRT)
☐ ST-AZM	Antonov An-12BK	00346907	ex 05 red	

MID AIRLINES		Nile (NYL)		Khartoum (KRT)
☐ ST-ARG	Fokker 50	20130	ex LN-BBA	
☐ ST-ARZ	Fokker 50	20134	ex LN-BBC	[KRT]

SUDAN AIRWAYS		Sudanair (SD/SUD)		Khartoum (KRT)
☐ JY-JAQ	Boeing 737-46J	27826/2694	ex D-ABRE	<JAV
☐ ST-ANH	Beech 65-C90 King Air	LJ-823		
☐ ST-ASF	Fokker 50	20155	ex PH-PRG	
☐ ST-ASI	Fokker 50	20247	ex G-UKTB	
☐ ST-ASO	Fokker 50	20256	ex G-UKTD	
☐ ST-AST	Airbus A310-322	437	ex SU-BOW	[KRT]
☐ ST-ATA	Airbus A300B4-622R	775	ex TF-ELC	Alqaswa	
☐ ST-ATB	Airbus A300B4-622R	666	ex TF-ELB	Elburag	
☐ ST-SFS	Beech 200 Super King Air	BB-539	ex N555SK	

SUN AIR		Sun Group (S6/SNR)		Khartoum (KRT)
☐ JY-RFF	Boeing 737-4K5	27831/2677	ex OO-TUB	<RFJ
☐ ST-SDA	Boeing 737-2T4	23274/1099	ex B-2508	[ALG]
☐ ST-SDB	Boeing 737-2T4	23273/1097	ex B-2507	[ALG]

TARCO AIR		(TRQ)		
☐ C5-AAL	Boeing 737-332	25996/2488	ex N259DG	
☐ C5-AAN	Boeing 737-522	26687/2402	ex 4L-AJE	<AAZ
☐ ST-AWR	Ilyushin Il-76TD	0033447365	ex RDPL-34138	
☐ ST-MRL	Yakovlev Yak-42D	4520424116690	ex UN-42703	
☐ ST-NSP	Antonov An-32B	2109	ex ER-AZW	
☐ ST-TAB	Yakovlev Yak-42D	4520421401018	ex UR-42449	
☐ ST-TAC	Yakovlev Yak-42D	4520423304016	ex UR-42426	
☐ ST-TAR	Yakovlev Yak-42D	4520423307017	ex UP-Y4211	
☐ ST-TOM	WSK-PZL Antonov An-28	1AJ006-03	ex 9Q-CFY	

SOUTH SUDAN

International radio call sign prefix Z8- was allocated to South Sudan in 2012 and, if adopted as nationality prefix, may therefore appear on aircraft in due course

GOLDEN WINGS AVIATION				Juba (JUB)
☐ ZS-SKA	Fokker 70	11559	ex PH-ZFT	opb SKA♦

INTERSTATE AIRWAYS				Juba (JUB)
☐ ZS-CMR	Canadair CRJ-100LR	7326	ex N785CA	opb KEM♦
☐ ZS-CRJ	Canadair CRJ-100LR	7338	ex N798CA	opb KEM♦

KUSH AIR		(KUH)		Juba (JUB)
☐ EK4104	LET L410UVP-E	861606	ex UP-L4104	
☐ ET-AKU	Fokker 50	20333	ex PH-EXD	Spirit of the South c/s	<ETH♦
☐ EY-324	Antonov An-32B	1709	ex EK32709	c/n unconfirmed♦
☐ ST-ALM	Antonov An-32			
☐ ST-APS	Ilyushin Il-76TD	102349316	ex RA-76837	
☐ ST-KNF	Antonov An-26	13006	ex Ukraine 14 blue	
☐ 5Y-BYE	Fokker 50	20204	ex 9M-MGJ	opb Skyward Intl; dam 06Sep14
☐ 5Y-BSM	LET L410UVP-E9	871939	ex 3D-SIG	
☐ 5Y-NIK	LET L-410UVPE-9	912619	ex OK-WDW	

NOVA AIRWAYS		Novanile (O9/NOV)		
☐ ST-NVB	Canadair CRJ-200ER	7807	ex HA-LND	
☐ ST-NVC	Canadair CRJ-200ER	7686	ex HA-LNB	
☐ ST-NVD	Canadair CRJ-200ER	7653	ex C-GTLG	
☐ ST-NVE	Canadair CRJ-200ER	7662	ex C-GUTX	♦
☐ ST-NVG	Boeing 737-58E	29122/2991	ex M-ABES	dam 19Dec13

SOUTHERN STAR AIRWAYS				Juba (JUB)
☐ 5Y-BZI	de Havilland DHC-8-102	105	ex 9Q-CWP	<ALW

498

SOUTH SUPREME AIRLINES		(JUA)			Juba (JUB)
☐ C5-JUA	Boeing 737-306	23541/1309	ex A6-JUD		♦
☐ C5-SMC	Canadair CRJ-100ER	7162	ex F-GRJU		
☐ C5-SMS	Boeing 737-3Y0	23927/1580	ex 3X-GGR		♦
☐ C5-SSA	Fokker 50	20138	ex ST-NEW		dam 07Jan14
☐ EK26310	Antonov An-26B	13310	ex UR-CFX		♦
☐ EK26710	Antonov An-26B-100	12710	ex ER-AZU		
☐ EK26804	Antonov An-26	8004	ex ER-AUW		
☐ ST-AQD	Antonov An-26B	11008	ex EX-28087		♦
☐ ST-	Canadair CRJ-100ER	7375	ex F-GRJR		[MXN]♦
☐ 4L-AJY	Boeing 737-33A	27452/2679	ex N270AE		<AJD
☐ 5Y-DAD	LET L410UVP-E	902436	ex ST-DMS		♦

SU-   EGYPT (Arab Republic of Egypt)

AIR ARABIA EGYPT		Arabia Egypt (E5/RBG)			Alexandria (ALY)
☐ SU-AAB	Airbus A320-214	3152	ex A6-ABN		

AIR CAIRO		(SM/MSC)			Cairo-Intl (CAI)
☐ SU-BPU	Airbus A320-214	2937	ex F-WWIJ		
☐ SU-BPV	Airbus A320-214	2966	ex F-WWDC		
☐ SU-BPW	Airbus A320-214	3282	ex F-WWDP		
☐ SU-BPX	Airbus A320-214	3323	ex F-WWBE		
☐ SU-BSM	Airbus A320-214	3626	ex A6-ABO		♦
☐ SU-BSN	Airbus A320-214	3840	ex A6-ABQ		♦
☐ SU-GCD	Airbus A320-232	2094	ex F-WWBX		<MSR♦

AIR GO EGYPT		(AGY)			Cairo-Intl (CAI)
☐ LZ-BHH	Airbus A320-232	2863	ex VT-INB		<BGH♦
☐ SU-GCL	Airbus A320-231	0322	ex SU-RAA	Reem	♦

AIR LEISURE		(ALD)			Cairo-Intl (CAI)
☐ SU-BME	McDonnell-Douglas MD-83	49628/1582	ex F-GRML		wfs♦
☐ SU-GBN	Airbus A340-212	159	ex F-WWJV	Cleo Express	<MSR♦
☐ SU-GBO	Airbus A340-212	178	ex F-WWJD	Hathor Express	<MSR♦

AIR SINAI		Air Sinai (4D/ASD)			Cairo-Intl (CAI)

A wholly owned subsidiary of Egyptair; ops services with aircraft leased from the parent

ALEXANDRIA AIRLINES		(XH/KHH)			Alexandria (ALY)
☐ SU-KHM	Boeing 737-5C9	26438/2413	ex JY-JA1		>DAV
☐ SU-KHO	Boeing 737-3S3	29244/3059	ex JY-JAY		

ALMASRIA UNIVERSAL AIRLINES		Almasria (UJ/LMU)			Cairo-Intl (CAI)
☐ JY-JAQ	Boeing 737-46J	27826/2694	ex D-ABRE		<JAV♦
☐ SU-TCD	Airbus A321-231	1366	ex EI-EUD		
☐ SU-TCE	Airbus A320-232	0977	ex 4R-MRB		
☐ SU-TCF	Airbus A320-232	1561	ex 9V-SLE		o/o♦

AMC AIRLINES		AMC Airlines (MZ/AMV)			Cairo-Intl (CAI)
☐ SU-BPZ	Boeing 737-86N/W	35213/2300			

AVIATOR		(AVV)			Cairo-Intl (CAI)
☐ SU-GBJ	Boeing 737-566	25352/2169		Philae	<MSR♦

CAIRO AVIATION		(CCE)			Cairo-Intl (CAI)
☐ SU-EAF	Tupolev Tu-204-120	1450743764027	ex RA-64027		[ULY]
☐ SU-EAG	Tupolev Tu-204-120S	1450743764028	ex RA-64028	TNT c/s	[CAI]
☐ SU-EAH	Tupolev Tu-204-120	1450743164023			[CAI]
☐ SU-EAI	Tupolev Tu-204-120	1450743164025			[CAI]
☐ SU-EAJ	Tupolev Tu-204-120S	1450742264029	ex RA-64029	TNT c/s	[CAI}

EGYPTAIR		Egyptair (MS/MSR)			Cairo-Intl (CAI)

Member of Star Alliance

| ☐ SU-GBA | Airbus A320-231 | 0165 | ex F-WWDV | Aswan | |
| ☐ SU-GBB | Airbus A320-231 | 0166 | ex F-WWID | Luxor | |

☐ SU-GBC	Airbus A320-231	0178	ex F-WWIQ	Hurghada	
☐ SU-GBD	Airbus A320-231	0194	ex F-WWIZ	Taba	
☐ SU-GBE	Airbus A320-231	0198	ex F-WWDG	El Alamein	
☐ SU-GBF	Airbus A320-231	0351	ex F-WWDM	Sharm El Sheikh	[CAI]
☐ SU-GBG	Airbus A320-231	0366	ex F-WWDD	Saint Catherine	
☐ SU-GBZ	Airbus A320-232	2070	ex F-WWDJ		
☐ SU-GCA	Airbus A320-232	2073	ex F-WWIO		
☐ SU-GCB	Airbus A320-232	2079	ex F-WWDV		
☐ SU-GCC	Airbus A320-232	2088	ex F-WWBH		
☐ SU-GCD	Airbus A320-232	2094	ex F-WWBX		>MSC
☐ SU-GCE	Airbus A330-243	600	ex F-WWYK		
☐ SU-GCF	Airbus A330-243	610	ex F-WWKS		
☐ SU-GCG	Airbus A330-243	666	ex F-WWKQ		
☐ SU-GCH	Airbus A330-243	683	ex F-WWYF		
☐ SU-GCI	Airbus A330-243	696	ex F-WWYR		
☐ SU-GCJ	Airbus A330-243	709	ex F-WWKK		
☐ SU-GCK	Airbus A330-243	726	ex F-WWKP		
☐ SU-GDS	Airbus A330-343X	1143	ex F-WWKQ		
☐ SU-GDT	Airbus A330-343X	1230	ex F-WWYR		
☐ SU-GDU	Airbus A330-343X	1238	ex F-WWKI		
☐ SU-GDV	Airbus A330-343X	1246	ex F-WWKY		
☐ SU-GCM	Boeing 737-866/W	35558/2054			
☐ SU-GCN	Boeing 737-866/W	35559/2113	ex N1795B		
☐ SU-GCO	Boeing 737-866/W	35561/2369	ex N1795B		
☐ SU-GCP	Boeing 737-866/W	35560/2434	ex N1786B		
☐ SU-GCR	Boeing 737-866/W	35562/2826	ex N1786B		
☐ SU-GCS	Boeing 737-866/W	35563/2695			
☐ SU-GCZ	Boeing 737-866/W	35568/2795			
☐ SU-GDA	Boeing 737-866/W	35565/2999	ex N1796B		
☐ SU-GDB	Boeing 737-866/W	35567/3017	ex N1786B		
☐ SU-GDC	Boeing 737-866/W	35564/3040	ex N1779B		
☐ SU-GDD	Boeing 737-866/W	35566/3061			
☐ SU-GDE	Boeing 737-866/W	35569/3043	ex N1786B		
☐ SU-GDX	Boeing 737-866/W	40757/3409	ex N1786B		
☐ SU-GDY	Boeing 737-866/W	40758/3442			
☐ SU-GDZ	Boeing 737-866/W	40759/3472			
☐ SU-GEA	Boeing 737-866/W	40760/3492	ex N1786B		
☐ SU-GEB	Boeing 737-866/W	40800/3677	ex N1786B		
☐ SU-GEC	Boeing 737-866/W	40801/3819			
☐ SU-GED	Boeing 737-866/W	40802/4095			
☐ SU-GEE	Boeing 737-866/W	40803/4136			
☐ SU-GBR	Boeing 777-266	28424/80		Nefertari	
☐ SU-GBS	Boeing 777-266	28425/85		Tiye	[CAI]
☐ SU-GBX	Boeing 777-266ER	32629/362		Neit	>BBC
☐ SU-GBY	Boeing 777-266ER	32630/368			>BBC
☐ SU-GDL	Boeing 777-36NER	38284850			
☐ SU-GDM	Boeing 777-36NER	38285/862			
☐ SU-GDN	Boeing 777-36NER	38288/896			
☐ SU-GDO	Boeing 777-36NER	38289/907	ex N5023Q		
☐ SU-GDP	Boeing 777-36NER	38290/918			
☐ SU-GDR	Boeing 777-36NER	38291/926			
☐ SU-GAC	Airbus A300B4-203F	255	ex F-WZMY	New Valley	
☐ SU-GAS	Airbus A300B4-622RF	561	ex F-WWAN	Cheops	
☐ SU-GAY	Airbus A300B4-622RF	607	ex F-WWAB	Seti 1	
☐ SU-GBH	Boeing 737-566	25084/2019			[CAI]
☐ SU-GBJ	Boeing 737-566	25352/2169		Philae	>Aviator
☐ SU-GBK	Boeing 737-566	26052/2276			
☐ SU-GBL	Boeing 737-566	26051/2282		Ramesseum	
☐ SU-GBM	Airbus A340-212	156	ex F-WWJK	Osiris Express	[CAI]
☐ SU-GBN	Airbus A340-212	159	ex F-WWJV	Cleo Express	>ALD
☐ SU-GBO	Airbus A340-212	178	ex F-WWJD	Hathor Express	>ALD
☐ SU-GBT	Airbus A321-231	0680	ex D-AVZB	Red Sea	
☐ SU-GBU	Airbus A321-231	0687	ex D-AVZR	Sinai	
☐ SU-GBV	Airbus A321-231	0715	ex D-AVZX	Mediterranean	
☐ SU-GBW	Airbus A321-231	0725	ex D-AVZA	The Nileno titles	

EGYPTAIR EXPRESS   Cairo-Intl (CAI)

☐ SU-GCT	Embraer ERJ-170LR	17000167	ex PT-SMJ	
☐ SU-GCU	Embraer ERJ-170LR	17000169	ex PT-SML	
☐ SU-GCV	Embraer ERJ-170LR	17000170	ex PT-SMM	
☐ SU-GCW	Embraer ERJ-170LR	17000175	ex PT-SMS	
☐ SU-GCX	Embraer ERJ-170LR	17000178	ex PT-SMV	
☐ SU-GCY	Embraer ERJ-170LR	17000185	ex PT-SUC	
☐ SU-GDF	Embraer ERJ-170LR	17000266	ex PT-SJU	
☐ SU-GDG	Embraer ERJ-170LR	17000269	ex PT-SJZ	
☐ SU-GDH	Embraer ERJ-170LR	17000274	ex PT-TQA	
☐ SU-GDI	Embraer ERJ-170LR	17000276	ex PT-TQC	
☐ SU-GDJ	Embraer ERJ-170LR	17000282	ex PT-TQI	

☐ SU-GDK   Embraer ERJ-170LR   17000284   ex PT-TQK

FLYEGYPT	(FEG)	Cairo-Intl (CAI)

☐ SU-TMG   Boeing 737-86J/W   32918/1255   ex D-ABBG   ♦

NESMA AIRLINES	(NE/NMA)	Cairo-Intl (CAI)

☐ SU-NMA	Airbus A320-232	1697	ex G-MIDR	Bertha
☐ SU-NMB	Airbus A320-232	1732	ex G-MIDP	Fatima
☐ SU-NMC	Airbus A320-232	2676	ex N676AG	Noura

NILE AIR	Nile Bird (NP/NIA)	Cairo-Intl (CAI)

☐ SU-BQB	Airbus A320-232	3183	ex N621SA	
☐ SU-BQC	Airbus A320-232	3219	ex N623SA	
☐ SU-BQJ	Airbus A320-232	2874	ex N874AC	♦

PETROLEUM AIR SERVICES	Pas Air (PER)	Al Arish/Hurghada (AAC/HRG)

☐ SU-CAC	Bell 206L-3 LongRanger III	51004	
☐ SU-CAE	Bell 206L-3 LongRanger III	51030	
☐ SU-CAF	Bell 206L-3 LongRanger III	51031	
☐ SU-CAG	Bell 206B JetRanger III	3574	
☐ SU-CAH	Bell 206B JetRanger III	3581	
☐ SU-CAI	Bell 206L-3 LongRanger III	51018	

☐ SU-CAB	Bell 212	31223	
☐ SU-CAJ	Bell 212	31247	
☐ SU-CAL	Bell 212	31215	ex N3889A
☐ SU-CAM	Bell 212	31249	
☐ SU-CAN	Bell 212	31250	
☐ SU-CAO	Bell 212	31260	
☐ SU-CAQ	Bell 212	31262	
☐ SU-CAR	Bell 212	31263	
☐ SU-CAS	Bell 212	31264	
☐ SU-CAU	Bell 212	35036	

☐ SU-CAV	Bell 412HP	36037	ex XA-TNO
☐ SU-CAX	Bell 412HP	36081	ex N2156S
☐ SU-CAY	Bell 412EP	36158	ex N6489P
☐ SU-CAZ	Bell 412EP	36184	ex N55248
☐ SU-CBI	Bell 412EP	36353	ex C-FCSC
☐ SU-CBL	Bell 412EP	36377	ex C-FENJ
☐ SU-CBM	Bell 412EP	36379	ex C-FEON
☐ SU-CBO	Bell 412EP	36410	ex C-FIRW
☐ SU-CBR	Bell 412EP	36432	ex C-FMQV
☐ SU-CBS	Bell 412EP	36468	ex C-FTCJ
☐ SU-CBT	Bell 412EP	36492	ex C-FVDY
☐ SU-CBX	Bell 412EP	36541	ex N3545

☐ SU-CBA	de Havilland DHC-7-102	093	ex C-GFYI
☐ SU-CBB	de Havilland DHC-7-102	096	ex C-GEWQ
☐ SU-CBC	de Havilland DHC-7-102	097	ex C-GFQL
☐ SU-CBD	de Havilland DHC-7-102	098	ex C-GEWQ
☐ SU-CBE	de Havilland DHC-7-102	099	ex C-GFBW

☐ SU-CBF	de Havilland DHC-8-315Q	584	ex C-FDHX
☐ SU-CBG	de Havilland DHC-8-315Q	585	ex C-FDHY
☐ SU-CBH	de Havilland DHC-8-315Q	594	ex C-FPJH
☐ SU-CBJ	de Havilland DHC-8-315Q	607	ex C-FBNT
☐ SU-CBN	de Havilland DHC-8-315Q	632	ex C-FIOY

☐ SU-CBP	Eurocopter EC135P2+	0604	ex D-HTSI
☐ SU-CBQ	Eurocopter EC135P2+	0607	ex D-HECP
☐ SU-CBV	AgustaWestland AW139	41209	ex N139DH
☐ SU-CBY	Canadair CRJ-900ER	15278	ex C-GIBL

SMART AVIATION	Smart Aviation (M4/SME)	Cairo-Intl (CAI)

☐ SU-SMA	Cessna 680 Sovereign	680-0118	ex (N2UJ)	
☐ SU-SMB	Cessna 680 Sovereign	680-0167	ex N5180C	
☐ SU-SMC	Cessna 680 Sovereign	680-0246	ex N5162W	
☐ SU-SMD	Cessna 680 Sovereign	680-0270	ex N41221	
☐ SU-SME	Cessna 680 Sovereign	680-0274	ex N41222	

☐ SU-SMG	Beech 350 King Air	FL-721	ex N6021C	
☐ SU-SMH	de Havilland DHC-8-402Q	4367	ex C-GJFG	>BBC
☐ SU-SMI	de Havilland DHC-8-402Q	4368	ex C-GJFP	>BBC

TRISTAR AIR	*Triple Star (TSY)*	*Cairo-Intl (CAI)*
☐ SU-BMZ Airbus A300B4-203F	129	ex N825SC

SU-Y PALESTINE

PALESTINIAN AIRLINES		*(PNW)*	
☐ SU-YAH	Fokker 50	20123	ex PH-FZJ	>NIN
☐ SU-YAI	Fokker 50	20143	ex PH-FZI	>NIN

SX-   GREECE (Hellenic Republic)

AEGEAN AIRLINES		*Aegean (A3/AEE)*	*Athens-Eleftherios Venizelos Intl (ATH)*

Member of Star Alliance

☐ SX-DGB	Airbus A320-232	4165	ex F-WWBX	
☐ SX-DGC	Airbus A320-232	4094	ex SX-OAS	
☐ SX-DGD	Airbus A320-232	4065	ex SX-OAP	
☐ SX-DGE	Airbus A320-232	3990	ex SX-OAM	
☐ SX-DGI	Airbus A320-232	3162	ex SX-OAI	
☐ SX-DGJ	Airbus A320-232	3316	ex SX-OAH	
☐ SX-DGK	Airbus A320-232	3748	ex SX-OAQ	
☐ SX-DGL	Airbus A320-232	3812	ex SX-OAR	
☐ SX-DGN	Airbus A320-232	2828	ex P4-TAS	
☐ SX-DGO	Airbus A320-232	3519	ex P4-XAS	♦
☐ SX-DGR	Airbus A320-232	3484	ex P4-WAS	♦
☐ SX-DGU	Airbus A320-232	2359	ex M-ABIM	♦
☐ SX-DGV	Airbus A320-232	1856	ex TC-JLJ	o/o♦
☐ SX-DGW	Airbus A320-232	1909	ex TC-JLK	♦
☐ SX-DGX	Airbus A320-232	1956	ex TC-JLL	o/o♦
☐ SX-DGY	Airbus A320-232/S	6611	ex F-WWDM	o/o♦
☐ SX-DGZ	Airbus A320-232/S	6643	ex	o/o♦
☐ SX-DNA	Airbus A320-232/S	6655	ex	o/o♦
☐ SX-DVG	Airbus A320-232	3033	ex F-WWBX Ethos	
☐ SX-DVH	Airbus A320-232	3066	ex F-WWIF Nostos	
☐ SX-DVI	Airbus A320-232	3074	ex F-WWIO Kinesis	
☐ SX-DVJ	Airbus A320-232	3365	ex F-WWIS Exelixis	
☐ SX-DVK	Airbus A320-232	3392	ex F-WWDS	
☐ SX-DVL	Airbus A320-232	3423	ex F-WWIV	
☐ SX-DVM	Airbus A320-232	3439	ex F-WWDY	
☐ SX-DVN	Airbus A320-232	3478	ex F-WWDI	
☐ SX-DVQ	Airbus A320-232	3526	ex F-WWDU	
☐ SX-DVR	Airbus A320-232	3714	ex D-AVVB	
☐ SX-DVS	Airbus A320-232	3709	ex F-WWIT	
☐ SX-DVT	Airbus A320-232	3745	ex F-WWIJ	
☐ SX-DVU	Airbus A320-232	3753	ex F-WWBS Pheidias	
☐ SX-DVV	Airbus A320-232	3773	ex F-WWDT Cleisthenes	
☐ SX-DVW	Airbus A320-232	3785	ex F-WWIU Nikos Kazantzakis	
☐ SX-DVX	Airbus A320-232	3829	ex F-WWIZ	
☐ SX-DVY	Airbus A320-232	3850	ex F-WWDG	
☐ SX-	Airbus A320-232	6862	ex	o/o♦
☐ SX-DGA	Airbus A321-231	3878	ex D-AVZP	
☐ SX-DGP	Airbus A321-232	3302	ex OE-ICK	
☐ SX-DGQ	Airbus A321-232	3322	ex OE-ICM	
☐ SX-DGS	Airbus A321-231	1428	ex G-OZBS	o/o♦
☐ SX-DGT	Airbus A321-231	1433	ex G-OZBP	♦
☐ SX-DVO	Airbus A321-231	3462	ex D-AVZU Philoxenia	
☐ SX-DVP	Airbus A321-231	3527	ex D-AVZZ	
☐ SX-DVZ	Airbus A321-231	3820	ex D-AVZF	
☐ SX-BNR	Learjet 60	60-231	ex D-CDNX	
☐ SX-DGF	Airbus A319-132	2468	ex D-ABGC	<BER

AEROLAND AIRWAYS			*Athens-Eleftherios Venizelos Intl (ATH)*
☐ SX-ARW	Cessna 208B Caravan I	208B1174	ex N13080 Isle of Chios
☐ SX-ARX	Cessna 208B Caravan I	208B1182	ex N1300G Isle of Lesvos
☐ SX-ARY	Cessna 208B Caravan I	208B1301	ex N2028N Isle of Paros

AIR INTERSALONIKA			*Thessaloniki (SKG)*
☐ SX-HKY	Agusta A109K2	10034	ex I-AGIK	♦
☐ SX-HMY	Agusta A109K2	10020	ex I-AGKL	♦

ASTRA AIRLINES — Greek Star (A2/AZI) — Thessaloniki (SKG)

☐ ER-AXP	Airbus A320-233	0741	ex N452TA		\<MLD♦
☐ SX-DIO	Airbus A320-232	0527	ex PH-AAY	Hara	
☐ SX-DIP	ATR 72-202	328	ex SP-LFE	Nicolaos	
☐ SX-DIX	British Aerospace 146 Srs.300	E3193	ex I-ADJF	Erriki	
☐ SX-DIZ	British Aerospace 146 Srs.300	E3206	ex G-JEBE	Maja	

AVIATOR AIRWAYS — Aviator (AVW) — Athens-Eleftherios Venizelos Intl (ATH)

☐ SX-APJ	Beech 200 Super King Air	BB-401	ex OY-JAO	

BLUE BIRD AIRWAYS — Cadia Bird (BZ/BBG) — Athens-Eleftherios Venizelos Intl (ATH)

☐ SX-TZE	Boeing 737-48E	27632/2857	ex EI-DOV	
☐ YR-HBD	McDonnell-Douglas MD-83	49808/1836	ex I-SMEC	\<OTJ♦

ELLINAIR — (EL/ELN) — Thessaloniki (SKG)

☐ SX-EMI	Avro 146-RJ85	E2305	ex G-CHPB	Thessaloniki	
☐ SX-EMS	Avro 146-RJ85	E2296	ex G-CHIN	Athens	♦

EPSILON AVIATION — Night Rider (GRV) — Athens-Eleftherios Venizelos Intl (ATH)

☐ SX-BMM	Swearingen SA227AC Metro III	BC-774B	ex N774MW	Mike
☐ SX-BNN	Swearingen SA227AC Metro III	BC-771B	ex N771MW	Nick

GAINJET — (GNJ) — Athens-Eleftherios Venizelos Intl (ATH)

☐ N577DA	Bombardier 604 Challenger	5398	ex N477DM		
☐ N597DA	Bombardier 604 Challenger	5359	ex N497DM		
☐ SX-ATF	Boeing 737-406	25423/2184	ex PH-BTB		
☐ SX-DGM	Embraer Legacy 600	145-01023	ex PT-SVY		
☐ SX-GAB	Gulfstream G-450	4172	ex N572GA		
☐ SX-GJJ	Gulfstream G-550	5350	ex N750GA		
☐ SX-GJN	Bombardier Global Express XRS	9260	ex N651GS		
☐ SX-RFA	Boeing 757-23N/W	30232/888	ex EI-LTO		VIP
☐ SX-VIP	Boeing 737-3Y0	24680/1927	ex N553MS		
☐ VP-CSH	Gulfstream G-450	4202	ex N202GA		

HERMES AIRLINES — (H3/HRM) — Athens-Eleftherios Venizelos Intl (ATH)

☐ F-GYAN	Airbus A321-111	0535	ex F-WQQU		\<BIE>JBW♦
☐ SX-BDS	Airbus A320-232	1422	ex 4L-AJF		♦
☐ SX-BDT	Airbus A320-214	0879	ex 4L-AJD		♦
☐ SX-BHR	Boeing 737-5L9	29234/3068	ex TC-AAG		\<BIE
☐ SX-BHS	Airbus A321-111	0642	ex F-GYAO		\<BIE>MLD
☐ SX-BHT	Airbus A321-211	0666	ex EI-ESI		\<BIE>MLD

MINOAN AIR — Minoan (MAV) — Heraklion (HER)

☐ SX-BRM	Fokker 50	20207	ex PH-KVF	Bella	[MST]
☐ SX-BRS	Fokker 50	20206	ex PH-KVE		>ALX
☐ SX-BRV	Fokker 50	20199	ex PH-ZDI	Victor	[MST]
☐ SX-MAR	Fokker 50	20189	ex YL-BAO	Stamitis	

OLYMPIC AIR — Olympic (OA/NOA) — Athens-Eleftherios Venizelos Intl (ATH)

☐ SX-BIT	de Havilland DHC-8-402Q	4148	ex G-JECV	
☐ SX-BIU	de Havilland DHC-8-402Q	4152	ex G-JECW	
☐ SX-OBA	de Havilland DHC-8-402Q	4267	ex G-PTHA	
☐ SX-OBB	de Havilland DHC-8-402Q	4268	ex G-PTHB	
☐ SX-OBC	de Havilland DHC-8-402Q	4276	ex G-PTHC	
☐ SX-OBD	de Havilland DHC-8-402Q	4311	ex G-PTHD	
☐ SX-OBE	de Havilland DHC-8-402Q	4314	ex G-PTHE	
☐ SX-OBF	de Havilland DHC-8-402Q	4318	ex G-PTHF	
☐ SX-OBG	de Havilland DHC-8-402Q	4321	ex G-PTHG	
☐ SX-OBH	de Havilland DHC-8-402Q	4327	ex G-PTHH	
☐ SX-BIO	de Havilland DHC-8-102	330	ex C-GZQZ	Katerina Thanou
☐ SX-BIP	de Havilland DHC-8-102	347	ex C-GZRA	Voula Patoulidou
☐ SX-BIQ	de Havilland DHC-8-102	361	ex C-GZRD	Kahi Kahiasvili
☐ SX-BIR	de Havilland DHC-8-102	364	ex C-GZRF	Kostas Kenteris

SKY EXPRESS — Air Crete (GQ/SEH) — Heraklion (HER)

☐ OY-JRY	ATR 42-300	063	ex F-WQOC	\<DTR♦
☐ SX-DIA	British Aerospace Jetstream 41	41075	ex G-CEYV	dam 02Feb15
☐ SX-GRY	ATR 42-300	012A	ex LY-ARI	\<DNU
☐ SX-ROD	British Aerospace Jetstream 41	41076	ex G-CEYW	
☐ SX-SEH	British Aerospace Jetstream 41	41014	ex G-ISAY	

SKYGREECE AIRLINES		(GW/SGR)		Athens (ATH)
☐ SX-BPN	Boeing 767-31AER	26470/416	ex N328MP	

SWIFTAIR HELLAS		Med-Freight (MDF)	Athens-Eleftherios Venizelos Intl (ATH)	
☐ SX-BGU	Swearingen SA227AC Metro III	AC-615B	ex EC-HJO	
☐ SX-BKZ	Swearingen SA227AC Metro III	AC-694B	ex SX-BKW	
☐ SX-BMT	Swearingen SA227AC Metro III	AC-699B	ex EC-GYB	

S2- BANGLADESH (People's Republic of Bangladesh)

BANGLA INTERNATIONAL AIRLINES			Dhaka (DAC)	
☐ S2-AFY	Bell 407	53648	ex N9133D	♦

BIMAN BANGLADESH AIRLINES		Bangladesh (BG/BBC)		Dhaka (DAC)
☐ S2-AFO	Boeing 777-3E9ER	40122/964	The Palki	
☐ S2-AFP	Boeing 777-3E9ER	40123/971	Arun Alo	
☐ S2-AHK	Boeing 777-266ER	32629/362	ex SU-GBX	<MSR♦
☐ S2-AHL	Boeing 777-266ER	32630/368	ex SU-GBY	<MSR
☐ S2-AHM	Boeing 777-3E9ER	40120/1170	Aakash Pradeep	
☐ S2-AHN	Boeing 777-3E9ER	40121/1186	Raanga Prsvat	
☐ SU-SMI	de Havilland DHC-8-402Q	4368	ex C-GJFP	<SME♦
☐ S2-ACO	Douglas DC-10-30	46993/263	ex 9V-SDB	City of Hazrat Shah Makhdoom (RA) wfs
☐ S2-ACP	Douglas DC-10-30	46995/275	ex 9V-SDD	[DAC]
☐ S2-ACR	Douglas DC-10-30	48317/445	The New Era	[DAC]
☐ S2-ACV	Fokker F.28 Fellowship 4000	11124	ex PK-YPV	[DAC]
☐ S2-ACW	Fokker F.28 Fellowship 4000	11148	ex PK-YPJ	[DAC]
☐ S2-ADF	Airbus A310-325	700	ex F-WWCB	City of Chittagong
☐ S2-ADK	Airbus A310-325	594	ex N594RC	
☐ S2-AFL	Boeing 737-83N/W	28648/888	ex PR-GOZ	
☐ S2-AFM	Boeing 737-83N/W	28653/948	ex PR-GIA	
☐ S2-AGQ	de Havilland DHC-8-400Q	4367	ex SU-SMH	<SME♦

BISMILLAH AIRLINES		Bismillah (5Z/BML)		Dhaka/Sharjah (DAC/SHJ)
☐ S2-ADW	Hawker Siddeley HS.748 Srs 2A/347	1766	ex G-BGMN	Frtr [DAC]
☐ S2-AEE	Hawker Siddeley HS.748 Srs 2A/242	1647	ex G-ORCP	Frtr

EASY FLY EXPRESS		Easy Express (8E/EFX)		Dhaka (DAC)
☐ S2-AAX	Hawker Siddeley HS.748 Srs.2A/242	1767	ex G-BGMO	

NOVOAIR		(VQ)		Dhaka (DAC)
☐ S2-AGJ	Embraer ERJ-145EU	145573	ex G-EMBX	♦
☐ S2-AGK	Embraer ERJ-145EU	145546	ex G-EMBW	♦
☐ S2-AGL	Embraer ERJ-145EU	145300	ex G-EMBP	♦

REGENT AIRWAYS		Regent (RX/RGE)		Chittagong (CGP)
☐ S2-AHA	de Havilland DHC-8-314Q	521	ex D-BLEJ	
☐ S2-AHB	de Havilland DHC-8-314Q	543	ex D-BEBA	
☐ S2-AHC	Boeing 737-7V3/W	29360/1644	ex N171LF	
☐ S2-AHD	Boeing 737-7K5/W	30714/2202	ex D-AHXA	
☐ S2-AHE	de Havilland DHC-6 Twin Otter 400	874	ex C-GLVA	opf Chevron

SKY AIR		(C3)		Dhaka (DAC)
☐ S2-AGN	Boeing 737-209F (AvAero 3)	24197/1581	ex 9M-PMW	♦

TAC AIRLINES			Dhaka (DAC)	
☐ S2-AEJ	McDonnell-Douglas MD-83	53189/2121	ex N9414W	opb UBD

TRUE AVIATION			Dhaka (DAC)	
☐ S2-AGA	Antonov An-26B	13504	ex UR-ELA	♦
☐ S2-AGZ	Antonov An-26B	13408	ex UR-ELP	to be confirmed♦

UNITED AIRWAYS		United Bangladesh (4H/UBD)		Dhaka (DAC)
☐ S2-AEH	McDonnell-Douglas MD-83	49937/1784	ex YR-HBA	
☐ S2-AEI	McDonnell-Douglas MD-83	53183/2071	ex N583AN	
☐ S2-AEJ	McDonnell-Douglas MD-83	53189/2121	ex N9414W	opf TAC AL

☐ S2-AEU	McDonnell-Douglas MD-83	49790/1643	ex G-FLTL	
☐ S2-AFV	McDonnell-Douglas MD-83	53377/2057	ex SX-BPP	[DAC]
☐ S2-AES	de Havilland DHC-8-103	363	ex N810WP	
☐ S2-AFE	ATR 72-212	385	ex N385FA	
☐ S2-AFF	Airbus A310-325	672	ex M-ABCX	
☐ S2-AFN	ATR 72-212	379	ex PK-MFA	dam 20Jly14
☐ S2-AFU	ATR 72-202	402	ex SP-LFF	
☐ S2-AFW	Airbus A310-325	674	ex F-HBOS	

US-BANGLA AIRLINES   Dhaka (DAC)

☐ S2-AGU	de Havilland DHC-8-402Q	4041	ex D-ADHR
☐ S2-AGV	de Havilland DHC-8-402Q	4044	ex D-ADHS

YOUNGONE

☐ S2-ACU	Cessna 208B Caravan I	208B0612	ex N1215A
☐ S2-AEK	Piaggio P.180 Avanti	1212	ex D-IMIA
☐ S2-AEQ	Pilatus PC-12/45	538	
☐ S2-AEV	Piaggio P.180 Avanti	1193	

S5-   SLOVENIA (Republic of Slovenia)

ADRIA AIRWAYS   Adria (JP/ADR)   Ljubljana (LJU)

Member of Star Alliance

☐ S5-AAK	Canadair CRJ-900ER	15128			
☐ S5-AAL	Canadair CRJ-900ER	15129			
☐ S5-AAN	Canadair CRJ-900ER	15207			
☐ S5-AAO	Canadair CRJ-900ER	15215			
☐ S5-AAU	Canadair CRJ-900ER	15283	ex C-GZQM		
☐ S5-AAV	Canadair CRJ-900ER	15284	ex C-GZQR	Vesna	
☐ OY-JRK	Airbus A320-231	0444	ex S5-AAS		DTR♦
☐ S5-AAD	Canadair CRJ-200LR	7166	ex C-FZWS		
☐ S5-AAE	Canadair CRJ-200LR	7170	ex C-GAIK		[LJU]
☐ S5-AAF	Canadair CRJ-200LR	7272	ex C-FMND		[LJU]
☐ S5-AAG	Canadair CRJ-200LR	7384	ex C-FMMT	Star Alliance c/s	
☐ S5-AAP	Airbus A319-132	4282	ex D-AVWR		
☐ S5-AAR	Airbus A319-132	4301	ex D-AVXB		
☐ S5-AAX	Airbus A319-111	1000	ex F-GRHD		♦
☐ S5-AAZ	Canadair CRJ-701ER	10014	ex D-ACPC	Łódź	♦

AERO4M   Aerocutter (H4/AEH)   Ljubljana (LJU)

☐ F-GRGP	Embraer ERJ-135ER	145188	ex PT-SFL		opf EKA♦
☐ F-GVZJ	ATR 42-300	0093	ex F-WQNO		<Regourd >RJM Avn♦
☐ F-HTOP	Embraer ERJ-135LR	14500886	ex LX-LGK		opf EKA♦
☐ S5-ACK	ATR 72-212	369	ex TR-LHI		♦

LINXAIR   Repidlinx (LIX)

☐ S5-BAR	Cessna 525A Citation CJ2+	525A-0423	ex N806CJ	
☐ S5-BAS	Cessna 525A Citation CJ2+	525A-0348	ex N5076J	♦
☐ S5-BAV	Cessna 560 Citation XLS	560-5660	ex N602MA	
☐ S5-BAZ	Cessna 560 Citation Excel	560-5236	ex N236LD	
☐ S5-BDG	Cessna 560 Citation Excel	560-5215	ex M-CEXL	

SOLINAIR   Solinair (SOP)   Portoroz (POW)

☐ S5-ABV	Boeing 737-4K5SF	24128/1715	ex TC-MNG	
☐ S5-ABZ	Boeing 737-4K5SF	24126/1697	ex TC-MCF	♦
☐ S5-BBS	SAAB SF.340A	340A-064	ex SE-E64	

S7-   SEYCHELLES (Republic of Seychelles)

AIR SEYCHELLES   Seychelles (HM/SEY)   Mahe (SEZ)

☐ S7-AAF	de Havilland DHC-6 Twin Otter 300	623	ex S7-AAO	Isle of Praslin	
☐ S7-AAJ	de Havilland DHC-6 Twin Otter 310	499	ex PH-STB	Isle of Desroches	
☐ S7-AAR	de Havilland DHC-6 Twin Otter 300	539	ex PH-STF	Isle of Farquhar	
☐ S7-BRD	de Havilland DHC-6 Twin Otter 400	899	ex C-GUVT	Isle of Bird	♦
☐ S7-CUR	de Havilland DHC-6 Twin Otter 400	846	ex C-GLVA	Spirit of Curieuse	
☐ S7-LDI	de Havilland DHC-6 Twin Otter 400	898	ex C-GFAP	Isle of La Digue	♦
☐ A6-EIA	Airbus A320-232	1944	ex PH-MPD	Amirantes	<ETD♦
☐ A6-EYY	Airbus A330-243	751	ex VT-EYY	Aldabra	opb ETD

☐ A6-EYZ	Airbus A330-243	807	ex VT-JWE	Vallée de Mai	opb ETD
☐ S7-AAA	Britten-Norman BN-2A-27 Islander	540	ex G-BDZP	Isle of Remire	wfs
☐ S7-PAL	Short SD.3-60	SH3758	ex G-KBAC	Isle de Palme	
☐ S7-PRI	Short SD.3-60	SH3724	ex G-BNMU	Isle of La Digue	

HELICOPTER SEYCHELLES — Mahe (SEZ)

| ☐ S7-NEL | Agusta A.109C | 7630 | |
| ☐ S7-NMK | Bell 206B JetRanger | 4633 | ex N707MK |

IDC AIRCRAFT — Mahe (SEZ)

☐ S7-AAI	Reims Cessna F406 Caravan II	F406-0051	ex N7148P	
☐ S7-AAU	Britten-Norman BN-2A-21 Islander	589	ex A2-01M	opf Coast Guard
☐ S7-IDC	Beech 1900D	UE-212	ex N3217U	opf Coast Guard
☐ S7-MAC	Dornier 228-201	8056	ex ZS-MJH	♦

ZIL AIR — Mahe (SEZ)

| ☐ S7-BOS | Beech B200GT Super King Air | BY-141 | ex N8141U | ♦ |

S9-   SAO TOME (Democratic Republic of São Tomé & Principe)

AFRICA'S CONNECTION   (ACH)

| ☐ S9-AUN | Dornier 228-201 | 8076 | ex 5N-AUN |
| ☐ S9-RAS | Dornier 228-201 | 8068 | ex TR-LHE |

TC-   TURKEY (Republic of Turkey)

ANADOLU JET   (AJA)   Ankara/Esenboga International (ESB)

☐ TC-SAF	Boeing 737-73V	32419/1321	ex TC-JKS		<SXS wfs
☐ TC-SAG	Boeing 737-73V	32420/1341	ex TC-JKT		<SXS [LDE]
☐ TC-SAO	Boeing 737-76N/W	34753/2165	ex TC-JKL	Anamur	<SXS
☐ TC-SAP	Boeing 737-76N/W	34755/2187	ex TC-JKM	Kalkan	<SXS
☐ TC-SAZ	Boeing 737-7GL/W	34759/2320	ex TC-JKP	Akçakoca	<SXS
☐ TC-SBB	Boeing 737-7GL/W	34760/2352	ex TC-JKR	Gelibolu	<SXS
☐ TC-SAH	Boeing 737-8FH/W	35092/2160	ex TC-JHI	Hendek	<SXS
☐ TC-SAU	Boeing 737-8GJ/W	34958/2688	ex TC-JHG	Pamukkale	<SXS
☐ TC-SAV	Boeing 737-8GJ/W	34959/2719	ex TC-JHH	Kemer	<SXS
☐ TC-SBE	Boeing 737-8BK/W	29644/2231	ex EI-EZM		<SXS
☐ TC-SBF	Boeing 737-86Q/W	30296/1647	ex TC-JHJ	Silifke	<SXS
☐ TC-SBG	Boeing 737-86J/W	28071/133	ex EI-FBP		<SXS
☐ TC-SBI	Boeing 737-8AS/W	29920/362	ex N641AC		<SXS
☐ TC-SBJ	Boeing 737-8AS/W	29916/210	ex N645AC		<SXS
☐ TC-SBM	Boeing 737-8AS/W	29918/307	ex N649AC		<SXS
☐ TC-SBN	Boeing 737-86N/W	32690/2250	ex 9M-FFC		<SXS♦
☐ TC-SBP	Boeing 737-86N/W	32672/1932	ex OE-IDK		<SXS♦
☐ TC-SBR	Boeing 737-86N/W	32693/1951	ex OE-IDL		<SXS♦
☐ TC-SBS	Boeing 737-8AS/W	29917/298	ex N636AC		<SXS♦
☐ TC-SBV	Boeing 737-86N/W	32736/1113	ex F-HJER		<SXS
☐ TC-SBZ	Boeing 737-86N/W	28628/573	ex HL7796		<SXS♦
☐ TC-SCD	Boeing 737-8Q8/W	41805/5325			o/o♦
☐ TC-SEE	Boeing 737-8CX/W	32363/1139	ex N363MQ		<SXS♦
☐ TC-SNI	Boeing 737-8FH/W	29671/1700	ex EI-DMZ		<SXS
☐ TC-SUO	Boeing 737-86Q/W	30272/824	ex VH-VOE		<SXS
☐ TC-YAL	Embraer ERJ-190LR	19000227	ex VP-CQY	Edremit	<BRJ♦
☐ TC-YAN	Embraer ERJ-190LR	19000367	ex VP-CQY	Istanbul	<BRJ♦
☐ TC-	Boeing 737-9GJER/W	34952/2426	ex N396DC		o/o♦
☐ TC-	Boeing 737-9GJER/W	34956/2608	ex N462DC		o/o♦

ATLASGLOBAL   Atlasjet (KK/KKK)   Antalya (AYT)

☐ TC-ATB	Airbus A321-211	1503	ex 6Y-JMH
☐ TC-ATE	Airbus A321-211	0675	ex F-WTAX
☐ TC-ATF	Airbus A321-211	0761	ex F-WTAV
☐ TC-ATH	Airbus A321-211	1953	ex F-ORMF
☐ TC-ATR	Airbus A321-211	1451	ex F-HCAI
☐ TC-ATY	Airbus A321-211	0808	ex F-GUAA
☐ TC-ATZ	Airbus A321-211	0823	ex F-HBAB
☐ TC-ETF	Airbus A321-231	1438	ex N585NK
☐ TC-ETH	Airbus A321-231	0968	ex TC-IEF
☐ TC-ETJ	Airbus A321-231	0974	ex TC-IEG
☐ TC-ETM	Airbus A321-131	0604	ex TC-TUB
☐ TC-ETN	Airbus A321-131	0614	ex TC-TUC
☐ TC-ETV	Airbus A321-231	1950	ex EI-LVA

☐ TC-ABL	Airbus A320-214	1390	ex OE-ICV	♦
☐ TC-ATD	Airbus A319-112	1124	ex EI-ELO	
☐ TC-ATK	Airbus A320-232	2747	ex OE-IBD	
☐ TC-ATM	Airbus A320-232	2753	ex OE-IBE	
☐ TC-ATT	Airbus A320-233	1624	ex EI-TAB	

BORA JET — Bora Jet (YB/BRJ) — Istanbul-Sabiha Gokcen Intl (SAW)

☐ TC-YAG	Embraer ERJ-190LR	19000263	ex EI-FCN	Siirt	♦
☐ TC-YAH	Embraer ERJ-190LR	19000264	ex EI-FCO		♦
☐ TC-YAI	Embraer ERJ-190LR	19000201	ex EI-FCL		♦
☐ TC-YAJ	Embraer ERJ-190LR	19000230	ex EI-FCM		♦
☐ TC-YAK	Embraer ERJ-190LR	19000310	ex D-AEMF		♦
☐ TC-YAL	Embraer ERJ-190LR	19000227	ex VP-CQY	Edremit	>AJA♦
☐ TC-YAM	Embraer ERJ-190LR	19000217	ex VP-CQZ		♦
☐ TC-YAN	Embraer ERJ-190LR	19000367	ex VP-CQV	Istanbul	>AJA♦
☐ TC-YAC	ATR 72-212A	701	ex OY-EDC		[BLL]

CORENDON AIRLINES — Corendon (XC/CAI) — Istanbul-Sabiha Gokcen Intl (SAW)

☐ TC-TJG	Boeing 737-86J/W	29120/202	ex D-ABAT	
☐ TC-TJH	Boeing 737-86J/W	29121/239	ex D-ABAU	
☐ TC-TJI	Boeing 737-8S3/W	29246/475	ex TC-SGK	
☐ TC-TJJ	Boeing 737-8S3/W	29247/493	ex TC-SGL	Detur c/s
☐ TC-TJL	Boeing 737-86J/W	32920/1293	ex D-AXLK	
☐ TC-TJM	Boeing 737-8Q8/W	28218/160	ex N282AG	
☐ TC-TJN	Boeing 737-85P/W	28535/480	ex EC-HJP	
☐ TC-TJO	Boeing 737-86N/W	34253/1866	ex B-5146	>♦
☐ TC-TJP	Boeing 737-8BK/W	33022/1672	ex EI-EOJ	♦
☐ TC-TJS	Boeing 737-81B/W	34252/1851	ex M-ABID	♦
☐ ES-SAL	Airbus A320-214	566	ex EI-ERV	<MYX♦
☐ ES-SAM	Airbus A320-232	1896	ex EI-EZT	<MYX♦
☐ TC-TJB	Boeing 737-3Q8	27633/2878	ex N304FL	Ayhan Saracoglu	Kids & Co c/s

FREEBIRD AIRLINES — Freebird (FH/FHY) — Istanbul-Ataturk (IST)

☐ TC-FBH	Airbus A320-214	4207	ex F-WWBP	
☐ TC-FBJ	Airbus A320-232	0580	ex N580CG	
☐ TC-FBO	Airbus A320-214	5096	ex F-WWIO	
☐ TC-FBR	Airbus A320-232	2524	ex VT-DKZ	
☐ TC-FBV	Airbus A320-214	4658	ex F-WWIM	
☐ TC-FHB	Airbus A320-214	3025	ex D-AAAP	♦
☐ TC-FHC	Airbus A320-214	3852	ex F-HBII	♦
☐ TC-FHE	Airbus A320-232	2804	ex F-WTDA	
☐ TC-FBG	Airbus A321-231	0771	ex HL7588	

GOZEN AIR SERVICE

| ☐ TC-KHC | de Havilland DHC-6 Twin Otter 400 | 857 | ex C-GVVA | |

MARIN AIR — Antalya/Bodrum-Marina/Marmaris-Marina (AYT/-/-)

| ☐ TC-KEU | Cessna 208 Caravan I | 20800317 | ex N52234 | FP |

MNG CARGO AIRLINES — Black Sea (MB/MNB) — Istanbul-Ataturk (IST)

☐ TC-MCA	Airbus A300C4-605RF	755	ex TF-ELW	
☐ TC-MCC	Airbus A300B4-622RF	734	ex N734JJ	
☐ TC-MCD	Airbus A300B4-605RF	521	ex B-2306	
☐ TC-MCE	Airbus A300B4-605RF	525	ex B-2307	
☐ TC-MCG	Airbus A300B4-622RF	739	ex N739AA	
☐ TC-MND	Airbus A300C4-203F	212	ex ZS-SDG	>CEL
☐ TC-MNV	Airbus A300C4-605RF	758	ex TF-ELG	
☐ TC-MCZ	Airbus A330-243F	1332	ex F-WWTS	Murathan
☐ TC-MDG	Canadair Challenger 601-3A	5110	ex N308BX	
☐ TC-MJA	Canadair Global 5000	9405	ex C-GFAP	
☐ TC-RZA	Canadair BD-100 Challnger 300	20284	ex N284JC	

MYCARGO AIRLINES — (9T/RUN) — Istanbul-Ataturk (IST)

☐ TC-ACF	Boeing 747-481SF	25645/979	ex N596MS	>SVA
☐ TC-ACG	Boeing 747-481SF	25641/928	ex N597MS	>SVA
☐ TC-ACH	Boeing 747-433BCF	24998/840	ex B-2477	
☐ TC-ACJ	Boeing 747-433BCF	25075/868	ex B-2478	>SVA
☐ TC-ACM	Boeing 747-428ERF	32867/1318	ex F-GIUC	>SVA♦

☐ TC-ACE	Airbus A300B4-203F	154	ex N320SC		
☐ TC-ACU	Airbus A300B4-203F	183	ex N512TA		wfs
☐ TC-ACY	Airbus A300B4-203F	107	ex N59107		[SAW]
☐ TC-ACZ	Airbus A300B4-203F	105	ex N317FV		wfs

ONUR AIR · Onur Air (8Q/OHY) · Istanbul-Ataturk (IST)

☐ LZ-FBC	Airbus A320-214	2540	ex EC-JMB		<LZB♦
☐ LZ-FBD	Airbus A320-214	2596	ex EC-JNA		<LZB♦
☐ TC-OBG	Airbus A320-233	0916	ex N590SH		
☐ TC-OBL	Airbus A320-232	0640	ex TC-OGI		
☐ TC-OBM	Airbus A320-232	0676	ex TC-OGJ		
☐ TC-OBN	Airbus A320-232	2571	ex LZ-WZA		
☐ TC-OBO	Airbus A320-232	2688	ex HA-LPH		
☐ TC-OBS	Airbus A320-232	0543	ex EI-EEL		
☐ TC-OBU	Airbus A320-232	0661	ex EI-EEI		
☐ TC-ODA	Airbus A320-233	0912	ex B-2348		
☐ TC-OBF	Airbus A321-231	0963	ex OE-IAA		
☐ TC-OBJ	Airbus A321-231	0835	ex N835AG		>GZQ
☐ TC-OBK	Airbus A321-231	0792	ex EI-LVD	Rana	
☐ TC-OBR	Airbus A321-231	1008	ex N108DE		>SVA
☐ TC-OBV	Airbus A321-231	0806	ex TC-JMC		>SVA
☐ TC-OBY	Airbus A321-231	0810	ex TC-JMD		
☐ TC-OBZ	Airbus A321-231	0811	ex TC-SKI		
☐ TC-ONJ	Airbus A321-131	0385	ex D-AVZG	Kaptan Koray Sahin	
☐ TC-ONS	Airbus A321-131	0364	ex D-AVZD	Funda	
☐ TC-OCA	Airbus A330-322	072	ex EC-IJH		>SVA
☐ TC-OCB	Airbus A330-342	098	ex B-HYA		>SVA
☐ TC-OCC	Airbus A330-322	143	ex 9M-MKS		>SVA
☐ TC-OCD	Airbus A330-322	087	ex VN-A368		

PEGASUS AIRLINES · Sunturk (PC/PGT) · Istanbul-Ataturk (IST)

☐ TC-DCA	Airbus A320-214/S	5879	ex D-AVVH	Pinar	
☐ TC-DCB	Airbus A320-214/S	5902	ex D-AVVP	Talya	
☐ TC-DCC	Airbus A320-214/S	5950	ex D-AUBJ	Melis	
☐ TC-DCD	Airbus A320-214/S	5995	ex D-AUBS	Deniz	
☐ TC-DCE	Airbus A320-214/S	6465	ex F-WWIG		♦
☐ TC-DCG	Airbus A320-216/S	6597	ex F-WWDF		o/o♦
☐ TC-DCH	Airbus A320-216/S	6619	ex F-WWBJ		o/o♦
☐ TC-DCI	Airbus A320-216/S	6666	ex		o/o♦
☐ TC-AAH	Boeing 737-82R/W	35701/2496		Hanim	>MBB
☐ TC-AAI	Boeing 737-82R/W	35699/2712		Gülce	
☐ TC-AAJ	Boeing 737-82R/W	35702/2810	ex N1787B	Ece	
☐ TC-AAL	Boeing 737-82R/W	35984/2937	ex N1786B	Selin	
☐ TC-AAN	Boeing 737-82R/W	38173/3011		Merve	
☐ TC-AAO	Boeing 737-86N/W	28619/534	ex EI-DJU		
☐ TC-AAR	Boeing 737-86N/W	28624/585	ex EI-DGZ		
☐ TC-AAS	Boeing 737-82R/W	40871/3212	ex N1787B	Dilara	
☐ TC-AAT	Boeing 737-82R/W	40872/3227	ex N1786B	Isik	
☐ TC-AAU	Boeing 737-82R/W	40873/3238		Duru	
☐ TC-AAV	Boeing 737-82R/W	40696/3295	ex N1787B	Sude Naz	
☐ TC-AAY	Boeing 737-82R/W	40874/3316		Damla	
☐ TC-AAZ	Boeing 737-82R/W	40875/3325		Mina	
☐ TC-ABP	Boeing 737-82R/W	40876/3326	ex N1786B	Nisa	
☐ TC-ACP	Boeing 737-82R/W	40697/3354		Derin	
☐ TC-ADP	Boeing 737-82R/W	40720/3526		Nisa Nur	
☐ TC-AEP	Boeing 737-82R/W	40724/3563		Irem Naz	
☐ TC-AGP	Boeing 737-82R/W	40728/3579		Sebnem	
☐ TC-AHP	Boeing 737-82R/W	40721/3600	ex N1787B	Iram Naz	
☐ TC-AIP	Boeing 737-82R/W	40877/3602	ex N1787B	Hande	
☐ TC-AIS	Boeing 737-82R/W	38174/3857		Sevde Nil D	
☐ TC-AJP	Boeing 737-82R/W	35983/3617	ex N1787B	Masal	
☐ TC-AMP	Boeing 737-82R/W	40723/3622		Nil	
☐ TC-ANP	Boeing 737-82R/W	40722/3637		Lidya	
☐ TC-ARP	Boeing 737-82R/W	40272/3652		Nehir	
☐ TC-ASP	Boeing 737-82R/W	40011/3662		Ipek	
☐ TC-AVP	Boeing 737-82R/W	38175/3877		Yagmur A	Pegasus Asia titles
☐ TC-AZP	Boeign 737-82R/W	38176/3896		Maya	Pegasus Asia titles
☐ TC-CCP	Boeing 737-86J/W	37746/3109	ex D-ABKG		
☐ TC-CPA	Boeing 737-82R/W	40725/3909		Sena	
☐ TC-CPB	Boeing 737-82R/W	38177/3947		Doğa	
☐ TC-CPC	Boeing 737-82R/W	40878/3972		Öykü	
☐ TC-CPD	Boeing 737-82R/W	40726/4013		Berra	Pegasus Asia c/s
☐ TC-CPE	Boeing 737-82R/W	38178/4023		Bade	Pegasus Asia c/s
☐ TC-CPF	Boeing 737-82R/W	40879/4267		Zeynep	
☐ TC-CPG	Boeing 737-82R/W	40880/4288		Ceren	
☐ TC-CPI	Boeing 737-82R/W	40014/4298	ex N5573K	Almira	
☐ TC-CPJ	Boeing 737-82R/W	40881/4513		Beren K	

☐ TC-CPK	Boeing 737-82R/W	40009/4736		Asli	
☐ TC-CPL	Boeing 737-82R/W	40010/4807	ex N5573B	Aslihan	
☐ TC-CPM	Boeing 737-82R/W	40012/5222		Jasmin Yalcin	♦
☐ TC-CPN	Boeing 737-82R/W	40013/5300		Ada E	♦
☐ TC-CPO	Boeing 737-8AS/W	33641/2222	ex EI-DPS	Hayal	
☐ TC-CPP	Boeing 737-804/W	32903/1127	ex SE-DZN		♦
☐ TC-CPR	Boeing 737-8GJ/W	34905/2392	ex EI-FGC	Firedevs	♦
☐ TC-CPS	Boeing 737-8GJ/W	37366/3628	ex VT-SGU	Peri	♦
☐ TC-CPU	Boeing 737-86N/W	35216/2321	ex D-AAAM	Sarya	♦
☐ TC-CPV	Boeing 737-86J/W	36884/3732	ex D-ABKW	Hira	♦
☐ TC-IZB	Boeing 737-86J/W	37743/2834	ex D-ABKE	Defne	
☐ TC-IZC	Boeing 737-86J/W	37745/3044	ex D-ABKF	Noa Nehir	
☐ TC-IZD	Boeing 737-83N/W	32348/933	ex M-ABFU	Buglem Sera	
☐ TC-IZE	Boeing 737-86J/W	37740/2638	ex D-ABKB	Elif	
☐ TC-IZG	Boeing 737-8AS/W	33605/2140	ex EI-DPE	Karya Damla	♦
☐ TC-IZI	Boeing 737-8GJ/W	34904/2347	ex VT-SPR	Ayse	♦
☐ TC-IZJ	Boeing 737-82R/W	35700/2435	ex TC-AAE	Hayirli	♦
☐ TC-	Boeing 737-82R/W	40729/			o/o
☐ TC-APD	Boeing 737-42R	29107/2997		Aichurok Pegasus Asia titles	>MBB

SEABIRD AIRLINES

☐ TC-SBU	de Havilland DHC-6 Twin Otter 300	321	ex C-GLKB		FP

SUNEXPRESS — Sunexpress (XQ/SXS) — Antalya (AYT)

☐ TC-SAF	Boeing 737-73V	32419/1321	ex TC-JKS		opf AJA<THY wfs
☐ TC-SAG	Boeing 737-73V	32420/1341	ex TC-JKT		opf AJA<THY [LDE]
☐ TC-SAO	Boeing 737-76N/W	34753/2165	ex TC-JKL	Anamur	>AJA
☐ TC-SAP	Boeing 737-76N/W	34755/2187	ex TC-JKM	Kalkan	>AJA
☐ TC-SAZ	Boeing 737-7GL/W	34759/2320	ex TC-JKP	Akçakoca	>AJA
☐ TC-SBB	Boeing 737-7GL/W	34760/2352	ex TC-JKR	Gelibolu	>AJA
☐ TC-SAH	Boeing 737-8FH/W	35092/2160	ex TC-JHI		>AJA
☐ TC-SAI	Boeing 737-8AS/W	33818/1685	ex EI-DHI		>AJA
☐ TC-SAJ	Boeing 737-8AS/W	33819/1691	ex EI-DHJ		>AJA
☐ TC-SAK	Boeing 737-8AS/W	33820/1696	ex EI-DHK		>AJA
☐ TC-SAU	Boeing 737-8GJ/W	34958/2688	ex TC-JHG		>AJA
☐ TC-SAV	Boeing 737-8GJ/W	34959/2719	ex TC-JHH		>AJA
☐ TC-SBE	Boeing 737-8BK/W	29644/2231	ex EI-EZM		>AJA
☐ TC-SBF	Boeing 737-86Q/W	30296/1647	ex TC-JHU	Silifke	>AJA
☐ TC-SBG	Boeing 737-86J/W	28071/133	ex EI-FBP		>AJA
☐ TC-SBI	Boeing 737-8AS/W	29920/362	ex N641AC		>AJA
☐ TC-SBJ	Boeing 737-8AS/W	29916/210	ex N645AC		>AJA
☐ TC-SBM	Boeing 737-8AS/W	29918/307	ex N649AC		>AJA
☐ TC-SBN	Boeing 737-86N/W	32690/2250	ex 9M-FFC		>AJA
☐ TC-SBP	Boeing 737-86N/W	32672/1932	ex OE-IDK		>AJA♦
☐ TC-SBR	Boeing 737-86N/W	32693/1951	ex OE-IDL		>AJA♦
☐ TC-SBS	Boeing 737-8AS/W	29917/298	ex N636AC		>AJA♦
☐ TC-SBV	Boeing 737-86N/W	32736/1113	ex F-HJER		>AJA
☐ TC-SBZ	Boeing 737-86N/W	28628/573	ex HL7796		>AJA♦
☐ TC-SCF	Boeing 737-8AL/W	40554/5410			o/o♦
☐ TC-SCL	Boeing 737-81D/W	39430/4442	ex EI-FGS		o/o♦
☐ TC-SED	Boeing 737-86N/W	32361/1098	ex N361MQ		♦
☐ TC-SEE	Boeing 737-8CX/W	32363/1139	ex N363MQ		>AJA♦
☐ TC-SNF	Boeing 737-8HC/W	36529/2566	ex N1787B		
☐ TC-SNG	Boeing 737-8HC/W	36530/2622	ex N1786B		
☐ TC-SNH	Boeing 737-8FH/W	30826/1732	ex EI-ECD		
☐ TC-SNI	Boeing 737-8FH/W	29671/1700	ex EI-DMZ		>AJA
☐ TC-SNJ	Boeing 737-86J/W	30827/1632	ex D-ABBO		
☐ TC-SNL	Boeing 737-86N/W	34251/1817	ex EC-JKZ		
☐ TC-SNN	Boeing 737-8HC/W	40775/3250			
☐ TC-SNO	Boeing 737-8HC/W	40776/3273	ex N1795B		
☐ TC-SNP	Boeing 737-8HC/W	40777/3320	ex N1786B		
☐ TC-SNR	Boeing 737-8HC/W	40754/3352	ex N1795B		
☐ TC-SNT	Boeing 737-8HC/W	40755/3400	ex N1786B		
☐ TC-SNU	Boeing 737-8HC/W	40756/3457	ex N1796B		
☐ TC-SNV	Boeing 737-86J/W	28072/147	ex D-ABAR		
☐ TC-SNY	Boeing 737-8K5/W	27981/7	ex D-AHFA		
☐ TC-SNZ	Boeing 737-86N/W	28616/483	ex N357MS		♦
☐ TC-SUG	Boeing 737-8CX/W	32365/1209			>SXD
☐ TC-SUH	Boeing 737-8CX/W	32366/1235			>SXD
☐ TC-SUI	Boeing 737-8CX/W	32367/1253			
☐ TC-SUJ	Boeing 737-8CX/W	32368/1289			>SXD
☐ TC-SUL	Boeing 737-85F/W	28822/166	ex SE-DVO		
☐ TC-SUM	Boeing 737-85F/W	28826/238	ex SE-DVR	25th Anniversary c/s	
☐ TC-SUO	Boeing 737-86Q/W	30272/824	ex VH-VOE		>AJA
☐ TC-SUU	Boeing 737-86Q/W	30274/845	ex VH-VOF		
☐ TC-SUV	Boeing 737-86N/W	30807/829	ex N50089	25th Anniversary c/s	
☐ TC-SUY	Boeing 737-86N/W	30806/790	ex G-OXLB		
☐ TC-	Boeing 737-8GJ/W	39428/4348	ex N119TN		o/o♦

| ☐ TC-SCA | Boeing 737-9GJER/W | 34952/2426 | ex N396DC | | o/o♦ |

TAILWIND AIRLINES — Tailwind (TI/TWI) — Istanbul-Ataturk (IST)

☐ TC-TLA	Boeing 737-4Q8	25107/2526	ex N774AS	M Demir Uz	
☐ TC-TLB	Boeing 737-4Q8	25108/2551	ex N775AS	M Safi Ergin	
☐ TC-TLC	Boeing 737-4Q8	25112/2638	ex N780AS	Capt Z Kllic	
☐ TC-TLD	Boeing 737-4Q8	28199/2826	ex N784AS	Capt M Akgün	
☐ TC-TLE	Boeing 737-4Q8	27628/2858	ex N785AS	A Güney	
☐ TC-TLG	Boeing 737-8K5/W	27983/218	ex D-AHFH	H Aydin	♦
☐ TC-TLH	Boeing 737-8K5/W	27984/220	ex D-AHFI		♦

THK - TURK HAVA KURUMU — Hur Kus (THK) — Ankara (ANK)

☐ TC-TKH	Canadair CL215	1104	ex C-GOFR	268
☐ TC-TKJ	Canadair CL215	1007		298
☐ TC-TKK	Canadair CL215	1030	ex C-FTUW	205
☐ TC-TKL	Canadair CL215	1011	ex C-FTUU	209
☐ TC-TKM	Canadair CL215	1097	ex I-SRMD	299
☐ TC-TKT	Canadair CL215	1097		5
☐ TC-TKV	Canadair CL215	1072	ex I-CFST	7
☐ TC-TKY	Canadair CL215	1108	ex I-CFSZ	9
☐ TC-TKZ	Canadair CL215	1076	ex I-SRMC	6
☐ TC-CAU	Cessna 208 Caravan I	20800248	ex N1123X	
☐ TC-CAV	Cessna 208 Caravan I	20800256	ex N1249T	
☐ TC-CAY	Cessna 402B Utiliner	402B1073	ex 10007 Turkey	
☐ TC-CAZ	Cessna 421C Golden Eagle II	421C0089	ex 10006 Turkey	
☐ TC-FAH	Piper PA-42-720 Cheyenne IIIA	42-5501033		
☐ TC-THK	Piper PA-42-720 Cheyenne IIIA	42-5501031	ex TC-FAG	
☐ TC-ZTP	Cessna 402B	402B0412	ex N69289	
☐ TC-ZVJ	Cessna 402B	402B1084	ex N1552G	

TURKISH AIRLINES — Turkish (TK/THY) — Istanbul-Ataturk (IST)

Member of Star Alliance

☐ TC-JLM	Airbus A319-132	2738	ex D-AVXN	Sinop
☐ TC-JLN	Airbus A319-132	2739	ex D-AVXO	Karabuk
☐ TC-JLO	Airbus A319-132	2631	ex TC-OGU	Ahlat
☐ TC-JLP	Airbus A319-132	2655	ex TC-OGV	Koycegiz
☐ TC-JLR	Airbus A319-132	3142	ex SX-OAV	Bakirköy
☐ TC-JLS	Airbus A319-132	4629	ex D-AVWM	Salihli
☐ TC-JLT	Airbus A319-132	4665	ex D-AVYL	Adilcevaz
☐ TC-JLU	Airbus A319-132	4695	ex D-AVYQ	Sultanahmet
☐ TC-JLV	Airbus A319-132	4755	ex D-AVYC	Sapanca
☐ TC-JLY	Airbus A319-132	4774	ex D-AVYK	Bergama
☐ TC-JLZ	Airbus A319-132	4790	ex D-AVYY	Edirnekapi
☐ TC-JUA	Airbus A319-132	2404	ex TC-IZM	Silivri
☐ TC-JUB	Airbus A319-132	2414	ex TC-IZR	Yeşilköy
☐ TC-JUD	Airbus A319-132	2452	ex TC-IZH	Bahçelievler
☐ TC-JAI	Airbus A320-232	3259	ex N569MS	Dumlupinar
☐ TC-JBI	Airbus A320-232	3308	ex N568MS	Uzungöl
☐ TC-JLJ	Airbus A320-232	1856	ex EI-DIV	Sirnak [IST]
☐ TC-JLL	Airbus A320-232	1956	ex EI-DIX	Duzce
☐ TC-JPA	Airbus A320-232	2609	ex F-WWBU	Mus
☐ TC-JPB	Airbus A320-232	2626	ex F-WWDS	Rize
☐ TC-JPC	Airbus A320-232	2928	ex F-WWDZ	Hasankeyf
☐ TC-JPD	Airbus A320-232	2934	ex F-WWIC	Isparta
☐ TC-JPE	Airbus A320-232	2941	ex F-WWIF	GumushaneStar Alliance c/s dam 25Apr15
☐ TC-JPF	Airbus A320-232	2984	ex F-WWIE	Yozgat — Star Alliance c/s
☐ TC-JPG	Airbus A320-232	3010	ex F-WWBJ	Osmaniye
☐ TC-JPH	Airbus A320-232	3185	ex F-WWDX	Kars
☐ TC-JPI	Airbus A320-232	3208	ex F-WWIS	Dogubevazit
☐ TC-JPJ	Airbus A320-232	3239	ex F-WWBK	Edremit
☐ TC-JPK	Airbus A320-232	3257	ex F-WWDI	Erdek
☐ TC-JPL	Airbus A320-232	3303	ex F-WWIJ	Göreme
☐ TC-JPM	Airbus A320-232	3341	ex F-WWBN	Harput
☐ TC-JPN	Airbus A320-232	3558	ex F-WWBE	Mardin
☐ TC-JPO	Airbus A320-232	3567	ex F-WWBP	Çankin
☐ TC-JPP	Airbus A320-232	3603	ex F-WWDL	Harran
☐ TC-JPR	Airbus A320-232	3654	ex F-WWDR	Kusadasi
☐ TC-JPS	Airbus A320-232	3718	ex F-WWBK	Burdur
☐ TC-JPT	Airbus A320-232	3719	ex D-AVVC	Ihlara
☐ TC-JPU	Airbus A320-214	3896	ex A9C-BAT	Aksaray
☐ TC-JPV	Airbus A320-214	3931	ex A9C-BAS	Sisli
☐ TC-JPY	Airbus A320-214	3949	ex A9C-BAP	Beykoz
☐ TC-JUE	Airbus A320-232	2156	ex 9V-VLE	Akhisar
☐ TC-JUF	Airbus A320-232	2164	ex 9V-VLF	Inegöl
☐ TC-JUG	Airbus A320-232	2395	ex 9V-JSC	Alanya

☐ TC-JUI	Airbus A320-232	2401	ex 9V-JSD	Kadirli	
☐ TC-JUJ	Airbus A320-232	2522	ex N532CL	Hatay	
☐ TC-JUK	Airbus A320-232	2602	ex PR-MAX	Palandöken	
☐ TC-JMH	Airbus A321-231	3637	ex D-AVZM	Didim	
☐ TC-JMI	Airbus A321-231	3673	ex D-AVZZ	Milas	
☐ TC-JMJ	Airbus A321-231	3688	ex D-AZAG	Tekirdag	
☐ TC-JMK	Airbus A321-231	3738	ex D-AZAK	Uskudar	
☐ TC-JML	Airbus A321-231	3382	ex G-TTIG	Eminonu	
☐ TC-JMM	Airbus A321-232	2916	ex OE-ICI	Erciyes	
☐ TC-JMN	Airbus A321-232	2919	ex OE-ICJ	Esenler	
☐ TC-JRA	Airbus A321-231	2823	ex D-AVZE	Kutahya	Star Alliance c/s
☐ TC-JRB	Airbus A321-231	2868	ex D-AVZI	Kirikkale	
☐ TC-JRC	Airbus A321-231	2999	ex D-AVZV	Sakarya	
☐ TC-JRD	Airbus A321-231	3015	ex D-AVZX	Balikesir	
☐ TC-JRE	Airbus A321-231	3126	ex D-AVZS	Beypazari	
☐ TC-JRF	Airbus A321-231	3207	ex D-AVZY	Fethiye	
☐ TC-JRG	Airbus A321-231	3283	ex D-AVZZ	Finike	
☐ TC-JRH	Airbus A321-231	3350	ex D-AVZI	Yalova	
☐ TC-JRI	Airbus A321-231	3405	ex D-AVZS	Adiyaman	
☐ TC-JRJ	Airbus A321-231	3429	ex D-AVZC	Corum	
☐ TC-JRK	Airbus A321-231	3525	ex D-AVZY	Batman	
☐ TC-JRL	Airbus A321-231	3539	ex D-AVZB	Tarsus	
☐ TC-JRM	Airbus A321-231	4643	ex D-AZAU	Afyonkarahisar	
☐ TC-JRN	Airbus A321-231	4654	ex D-AZAC	Sariyer	
☐ TC-JRO	Airbus A321-231	4682	ex D-AZAI	Uludag	
☐ TC-JRP	Airbus A321-231	4698	ex D-AZAP	Urgüp	
☐ TC-JRR	Airbus A321-231	4706	ex D-AZAR	Emirgan	
☐ TC-JRS	Airbus A321-231	4761	ex D-AVZJ	Datja	
☐ TC-JRT	Airbus A321-231	4779	ex D-AVZL	Alacati	
☐ TC-JRU	Airbus A321-231	4788	ex D-AVZN	Florya	
☐ TC-JRV	Airbus A321-231	5077	ex D-AVZO	Ümraniye	
☐ TC-JRY	Airbus A321-231	5083	ex D-AZAT	Beyoğlu	
☐ TC-JRZ	Airbus A321-231	5118	ex D-AZAW	Maltepe	
☐ TC-JSA	Airbus A321-231	5154	ex D-AVZE	Gaziosmanpaşa	
☐ TC-JSB	Airbus A321-231	5205	ex D-AVZS	Mut	
☐ TC-JSC	Airbus A321-231	5254	ex D-AVZZ	Arnavutköy	
☐ TC-JSD	Airbus A321-231	5388	ex D-AVZR	Kiz Kulesi	
☐ TC-JSE	Airbus A321-231/S	5450	ex D-AVZX	Kizilirmak	
☐ TC-JSF	Airbus A321-231/S	5465	ex D-AZAC	Niğde	
☐ TC-JSG	Airbus A321-231/S	5490	ex D-AZAJ	Ordu	
☐ TC-JSH	Airbus A321-231/S	5546	ex D-AVZC	Van	
☐ TC-JSI	Airbus A321-231/S	5584	ex D-AVZI	Tunceli	
☐ TC-JSJ	Airbus A321-231/S	5633	ex D-AVZP	Keçiören	
☐ TC-JSK	Airbus A321-231/S	5663	ex D-AVZW	Kula	
☐ TC-JSL	Airbus A321-231/S	5667	ex D-AVZX	Kulu	
☐ TC-JSM	Airbus A321-231/S	5689	ex D-AZAC	Ayder	
☐ TC-JSN	Airbus A321-231/S	6508	ex D-AVZX		♦
☐ TC-JSO	Airbus A321-231/S	6563	ex D-AZAP		♦
☐ TC-JSP	Airbus A321-231/S	6599	ex D-AVXL		♦
☐ TC-JSR	Airbus A321-231/S	6652	ex		o/o♦
☐ TC-JSS	Airbus A321-231/S	6657	ex		o/o♦
☐ TC-JST	Airbus A321-231/S	6682	ex		o/o♦
☐ TC-JSU	Airbus A321-231/S	6709	ex		o/o♦
☐ TC-JSV	Airbus A321-231/S	6751	ex		o/o♦
☐ TC-JSY	Airbus A321-231/S	6758	ex		o/o♦
☐ TC-JSZ	Airbus A321-231/S	6766	ex		o/o♦
☐ TC-	Airbus A321-231/S	6791	ex		o/o♦
☐ TC-	Airbus A321-231/S	6798	ex		o/o♦
☐ TC-	Airbus A321-231/S	6827	ex		o/o♦
☐ TC-	Airbus A321-231/S	6861	ex		o/o♦
☐ TC-	Airbus A321-231/S	6879	ex		o/o♦
☐ TC-	Airbus A321-231/S	6895	ex		o/o♦
☐ TC-	Airbus A321-231/S	6905	ex		o/o♦
☐ TC-	Airbus A321-231/S	6913	ex		o/o♦
☐ TC-	Airbus A321-231/S	6915	ex		o/o♦
☐ TC-	Airbus A321-231/S	6957	ex		o/o♦
☐ TC-JIL	Airbus A330-202	882	ex VT-JWH	Yedigöler	
☐ TC-JIM	Airbus A330-202	901	ex VT-JWL	Erenköy	
☐ TC-JIN	Airbus A330-202	932	ex VT-JWN	Tarabya	
☐ TC-JIO	Airbus A330-223	869	ex OE-ICX		♦
☐ TC-JIP	Airbus A330-223	876	ex OE-IDC		♦
☐ TC-JIR	Airbus A330-223	949	ex OE-ICY		♦
☐ TC-JIS	Airbus A330-223	961	ex OE-ICZ		♦
☐ TC-JIT	Airbus A330-223	977	ex OE-IDA		♦
☐ TC-JIV	Airbus A330-223	1213	ex PT-MVU		♦
☐ TC-JNA	Airbus A330-203	697	ex F-WWYS	Gaziantep	
☐ TC-JNB	Airbus A330-203	704	ex F-WWKF	Konya	
☐ TC-JNC	Airbus A330-203	742	ex F-WWYF	Bursa	
☐ TC-JND	Airbus A330-203	754	ex F-WWYL	Antalya	
☐ TC-JNE	Airbus A330-203	774	ex F-WWKG	Kayseri	
☐ TC-JNF	Airbus A330-202	463	ex A7-AFN	Canakkale	

☐ TC-JNG	Airbus A330-202	504	ex A7-AFO	Eskisehir	
☐ TC-JNV	Airbus A330-243	529	ex A9C-KH	Çatalhöyük	
☐ TC-JOM	Airbus A330-302	1535	ex F-WXAT		<AAW♦
☐ TC-JCI	Airbus A330-243F	1442	ex F-WWKK	Kervan	
☐ TC-JDO	Airbus A330-223F	1004	ex F-WWYE	Meric	
☐ TC-JDP	Airbus A330-223F	1092	ex F-WWKS	Firat	
☐ TC-JDR	Airbus A330-243F	1344	ex F-WWCJ	Gediz	
☐ TC-JDS	Airbus A330-243F	1418	ex F-WWCB	Trakya	
☐ TC-JOU	Airbus A330-243F	1550	ex F-WWKL		♦
☐ 9M-MUC	Airbus A330-223F	1164	ex F-WWKG		<MAS
☐ TC-JNH	Airbus A330-343E	1150	ex F-WWYM	Topkapi	
☐ TC-JNI	Airbus A330-343E	1160	ex F-WWKH	Konak	
☐ TC-JNJ	Airbus A330-343E	1170	ex F-WWKZ	Kapadokya	
☐ TC-JNK	Airbus A330-343E	1172	ex F-WWYK	Sanliurfa	
☐ TC-JNL	Airbus A330-343E	1204	ex F-WWYF		
☐ TC-JNM	Airbus A330-343E	1212	ex F-WWYY		
☐ TC-JNN	Airbus A330-343E	1228	ex F-WWKZ	Selcuklu	
☐ TC-JNO	Airbus A330-343E	1298	ex F-WWKG	Boğaziçi	
☐ TC-JNP	Airbus A330-343E	1307	ex F-WWYX	Gökçeada	
☐ TC-JNR	Airbus A330-343E	1311	ex F-WWKY	Haliç Golden Horn	
☐ TC-JNS	Airbus A330-303	1458	ex F-WWYP	Hattuşaş	
☐ TC-JNT	Airbus A330-303	1476	ex F-WWYR	Truva	
☐ TC-JNZ	Airbus A330-303	1487	ex F-WWYY	Kartaikaya	
☐ TC-JOA	Airbus A330-303	1501	ex F-WWTV	Pamukkale	
☐ TC-JOB	Airbus A330-303	1514	ex F-WWKQ	Bozcaada	
☐ TC-JOC	Airbus A330-303	1522	ex F-WWKU	Göbeklitepe	dam 04Mar15♦
☐ TC-JOD	Airbus A330-303	1529	ex F-WWCC	Malazgirt	♦
☐ TC-JOE	Airbus A330-303	1571	ex F-WWKO		dam 04Mar15♦
☐ TC-JOF	Airbus A330-303	1616	ex F-WWKT		♦
☐ TC-JOG	Airbus A330-303	1620	ex F-WWKK		♦
☐ TC-JOH	Airbus A330-303	1622	ex F-WWYF		♦
☐ TC-JOI	Airbus A330-303	1629	ex F-WWKH		o/o♦
☐ TC-JOJ	Airbus A330-303	1640	ex F-WWCM		o/o♦
☐ TC-JOK	Airbus A330-303	1642	ex F-WW		o/o♦
☐ TC-JOL	Airbus A330-303	1644	ex F-WW		o/o♦
☐ TC-	Airbus A330-303	1696	ex F-WW		o/o♦
☐ TC-JDK	Airbus A340-311	025	ex F-WWJP	Isparta	[IST]
☐ TC-JDL	Airbus A340-311	057	ex F-WWJF	Ankara	[SAW]
☐ TC-JDM	Airbus A340-311	115	ex F-WWJN	Izmir	
☐ TC-JDN	Airbus A340-313X	180	ex F-WWJU	Adana	
☐ TC-JIH	Airbus A340-313X	270	ex F-WWJP	Kocaeli	
☐ TC-JII	Airbus A340-313X	331	ex F-WWJQ	Mersin	
☐ TC-JKF	Boeing 737-76N/W	32684/1889	ex EI-EDT		>SXS
☐ TC-JKG	Boeing 737-76N/W	34754/2172	ex OM-NGH		>SXS
☐ TC-JKJ	Boeing 737-752/W	34297/1808	ex N297MD	Eyup	
☐ TC-JKK	Boeing 737-752/W	34298/1812	ex N298MD	Fatih	
☐ TC-JKO	Boeing 737-752/W	34300/1848	ex N343CT	Kadiköy	
☐ TC-JKS	Boeing 737-73V	32419/1321	ex G-EZJX		>SXS wfs
☐ TC-JKT	Boeing 737-73V	32420/1341	ex G-EZJY		>SXS [LDE]
☐ TC-JFC	Boeing 737-8F2/W	29765/80		Van	
☐ TC-JFD	Boeing 737-8F2/W	29766/87		Artvin	
☐ TC-JFE	Boeing 737-8F2/W	29767/95	ex N1786B	Hatay	
☐ TC-JFF	Boeing 737-8F2/W	29768/99	ex N1786B	Bingöl	
☐ TC-JFG	Boeing 737-8F2/W	29769/102	ex N1787B	Mardin	
☐ TC-JFH	Boeing 737-8F2/W	29770/114	ex N1787B	Igdir	
☐ TC-JFI	Boeing 737-8F2/W	29771/228	ex N1795B	Sivas	Star Alliance c/s
☐ TC-JFJ	Boeing 737-8F2/W	29772/242	ex N1786B	Agri	
☐ TC-JFK	Boeing 737-8F2/W	29773/259	ex N1786B	Zonguldak	
☐ TC-JFL	Boeing 737-8F2/W	29774/269	ex N1786B	Ordu	
☐ TC-JFM	Boeing 737-8F2/W	29775/279	ex N1786B	Nigde	
☐ TC-JFN	Boeing 737-8F2/W	29776/308		Bitlis	
☐ TC-JFO	Boeing 737-8F2/W	29777/309		Batman	
☐ TC-JFP	Boeing 737-8F2/W	29778/349	ex N1787B	Amasya	
☐ TC-JFR	Boeing 737-8F2/W	29779/370	ex N1786B	Giresun	
☐ TC-JFT	Boeing 737-8F2/W	29780/454	ex N1787B	Kastamonu	
☐ TC-JFU	Boeing 737-8F2/W	29781/461	ex N1795B	Elazig	
☐ TC-JFV	Boeing 737-8F2/W	29782/490	ex N1786B	Tunceli	
☐ TC-JFY	Boeing 737-8F2/W	29783/497	ex N1786B	Manisa	
☐ TC-JFZ	Boeing 737-8F2/W	29784/539		Bolu	
☐ TC-JGA	Boeing 737-8F2/W	29785/544	ex N1786B	Malatya	
☐ TC-JGB	Boeing 737-8F2/W	29786/566	ex N1786B	Foca	
☐ TC-JGC	Boeing 737-8F2/W	29787/771	ex N1786B	Abant	
☐ TC-JGD	Boeing 737-8F2/W	29788/791	ex N1787B	Nevsehir	
☐ TC-JGF	Boeing 737-8F2/W	29790/1088	ex N1786B	Ardahan	
☐ TC-JGG	Boeing 737-8F2/W	34405/1828		Erzincan	
☐ TC-JGH	Boeing 737-8F2/W	34406/1852		Tokat	
☐ TC-JGI	Boeing 737-8F2/W	34407/1873		Siirt	
☐ TC-JGJ	Boeing 737-8F2/W	34408/1880		Aydin	

☐ TC-JGK	Boeing 737-8F2/W	34409/1924	ex N1786B	Kirsehir
☐ TC-JGL	Boeing 737-8F2/W	34410/1927	ex N1787B	Karaman
☐ TC-JGM	Boeing 737-8F2/W	34411/1944		Hakkari
☐ TC-JGN	Boeing 737-8F2/W	34412/1949		Bilecik
☐ TC-JGO	Boeing 737-8F2/W	34413/1972	ex N1786B	Kilis
☐ TC-JGP	Boeing 737-8F2/W	34414/1978	ex N1786B	Bartin
☐ TC-JGR	Boeing 737-8F2/W	34415/1988	ex N1786B	Usak
☐ TC-JGS	Boeing 737-8F2/W	34416/1996		Kahramanmaras
☐ TC-JGT	Boeing 737-8F2/W	34417/2009		Avanos
☐ TC-JGU	Boeing 737-8F2/W	34418/2012		Bodrum
☐ TC-JGV	Boeing 737-8F2/W	34419/2021	ex N60668	Cesme
☐ TC-JGY	Boeing 737-8F2/W	35738/2592		Manavgat
☐ TC-JGZ	Boeing 737-8F2/W	35739/2654		Midyat
☐ TC-JHA	Boeing 737-8F2/W	35740/2673		Mudanya
☐ TC-JHB	Boeing 737-8F2/W	35741/2685		Safranbolu
☐ TC-JHC	Boeing 737-8F2/W	35742/2708		Iskenderun
☐ TC-JHD	Boeing 737-8F2/W	35743/2717		Serik
☐ TC-JHE	Boeing 737-8F2/W	357442733	ex N1786B	Burhanlye
☐ TC-JHF	Boeing 737-8F2/W	35745/2748		Ayvalik
☐ TC-JHK	Boeing 737-8F2/W	40975/3824	ex N3134C	Besiktas
☐ TC-JHL	Boeing 737-8F2/W	40976/3870		Unye
☐ TC-JHM	Boeing 737-8F2/W	40980/4041		Burgaz
☐ TC-JHN	Boeing 737-8F2/W	40981/4082		Yesilirmak
☐ TC-JHO	Boeing 737-8F2/W	40987/4324	ex N5515X	Köprübaşı
☐ TC-JHP	Boeing 737-8F2/W	42000/4336		Dicie
☐ TC-JHR	Boeing 737-8F2/W	40989/4394		Manisa
☐ TC-JHS	Boeing 737-8F2/W	40991/4411	ex N5515X	Amasya
☐ TC-JHT	Boeing 737-8F2/W	42001/4423		Bingöl
☐ TC-JHU	Boeing 737-8F2/W	42002/4437		Amasra
☐ TC-JHV	Boeing 737-8F2/W	40992/4778		
☐ TC-JHY	Boeing 737-8F2/W	42003/4798		
☐ TC-JHZ	Boeing 737-8F2/W	42004/4814	ex N5573K	Iznik
☐ TC-JVA	Boeing 737-8F2/W	40988/4833		
☐ TC-JVB	Boeing 737-8F2/W	40990/4865	ex N5573B	
☐ TC-JVC	Boeing 737-8F2/W	42005/4886		Sahinbey ♦
☐ TC-JVD	Boeing 737-8F2/W	42007/4900		♦
☐ TC-JVE	Boeing 737-8F2/W	42006/4915		♦
☐ TC-JVF	Boeing 737-8F2/W	42008/4934		♦
☐ TC-JVG	Boeing 737-8F2/W	42009/4963	ex N1796B	Artvin ♦
☐ TC-JYA	Boeing 737-9F2ER/W	40973/3669	ex N973TK	Selçuk
☐ TC-JYB	Boeing 737-9F2ER/W	40974/3693	ex N974TK	Denizli
☐ TC-JYC	Boeing 737-9F2ER/W	40977/3948	ex N977TK	Ereğli
☐ TC-JYD	Boeing 737-9F2ER/W	40978/4020	ex N978TK	Bayburt
☐ TC-JYE	Boeing 737-9F2ER/W	40979/4044	ex N981TK	Tuz Gölü
☐ TC-JYF	Boeing 737-9F2ER/W	40982/4098	ex N982TK	Çiragan
☐ TC-JYG	Boeing 737-9F2ER/W	40983/4110	ex N983TK	Ünye
☐ TC-JYH	Boeing 737-9F2ER/W	40984/4134	ex N984TK	Of
☐ TC-JYI	Boeing 737-9F2ER/W	40985/4176	ex N985TK	Mugla
☐ TC-JYJ	Boeing 737-9F2ER/W	40986/4308	ex N986TK	Ermirdağ
☐ TC-JYL	Boeing 737-9F2ER/W	42010/5263		♦
☐ TC-JYM	Boeing 737-9F2ER/W	42011/5303		♦
☐ TC-JYN	Boeing 737-9F2ER/W	42012/5387		♦
☐ TC-JYO	Boeing 737-9F2ER/W	42013/5400		♦
☐ TC-JYP	Boeing 737-9F2ER/W	42014/		o/o♦
☐ TC-JJE	Boeing 777-3F2ER	40707/895	ex N5020K	Dolmabahce
☐ TC-JJF	Boeing 777-3F2ER	40708/899	ex N6009F	Beylerbeyi
☐ TC-JJG	Boeing 777-3F2ER	40791/903	ex N50281	Yildiz
☐ TC-JJH	Boeing 777-3F2ER	40792/906	ex N5016R	Rumeli
☐ TC-JJI	Boeing 777-3F2ER	40709/909	ex N5020K	Ege
☐ TC-JJJ	Boeing 777-3F2ER	40710/913		Erzurum
☐ TC-JJK	Boeing 777-3F2ER	40711/916	ex N50812	Akdeniz
☐ TC-JJL	Boeing 777-3F2ER	40793/919		Karadeniz
☐ TC-JJM	Boeing 777-3F2ER	40794/923		Marmara
☐ TC-JJN	Boeing 777-3F2ER	40795/940		Anadolu
☐ TC-JJO	Boeing 777-3F2ER	40796/953		Istanbul
☐ TC-JJP	Boeing 777-3F2ER	40797/959	ex N1794B	Ankara
☐ TC-JJR	Boeing 777-3F2ER	44116/1214		Erciyes ♦
☐ TC-JJS	Boeing 777-3F2ER	44117/1222		Zigana ♦
☐ TC-JJT	Boeing 777-3F2ER	44118/1233		Çukurova ♦
☐ TC-JJU	Boeing 777-3F2ER	60401/1256		Büyükada ♦
☐ TC-JJV	Boeing 777-3F2ER	44119/1277		Heybeliada ♦
☐ TC-JJY	Boeing 777-3F2ER	44120/1287		Kinaliada ♦
☐ TC-JJZ	Boeing 777-3F2ER	44122/1291		♦
☐ TC-LJA	Boeing 777-3F2ER	44121/1296		♦
☐ TC-LJB	Boeing 777-3F2ER	44124/1331		o/o♦
☐ TC-LJC	Boeing 777-3F2ER	44123/1337		o/o♦
☐ TC-LJD	Boeing 777-3F2ER	44125/		o/o♦
☐ TC-DAP	Gulfstream G550	5212	ex N512GA	
☐ TC-JCZ	Airbus A310-304F	480	ex F-WWCZ	Ergene
☐ TC-LER	Airbus A310-304F	646	ex A6-EFA	<KZU♦

513

ULS CARGO		(GO/KZU)			Istanbul-Ataturk (IST)
☐ TC-ABK	Airbus A300B4-203	101	ex N59101	Adiyaman	
☐ TC-AGK	Airbus A300B4-203F	117	ex G-CEXH	Siirt 5	
☐ TC-KZV	Airbus A300B4-103F	041	ex PH-EAN	Siirt 4	wfs
☐ TC-LER	Airbus A310-304F	646	ex A6-EFA		>THY
☐ TC-SGM	Airbus A310-308F	592	ex A6-EFB		
☐ TC-VEL	Airbus A310-304F	622	ex A6-EFC		

UNSPED PAKET SERVISI/UPS		Unsped (UNS)			Istanbul-Ataturk (IST)
☐ TC-UPS	Swearingen SA226TC Merlin IVA	AT-044	ex TC-BPS	Beril	opf UPS

TF- ICELAND (Republic of Iceland)

AIR ATLANTA ICELANDIC		Atlanta (CC/ABD)		Keflavik (KEF)
☐ TF-AAC	Boeing 747-481	29262/1199	ex N262SG	>SVA
☐ TF-AAD	Boeing 747-4H6	28426/1130	ex HZ-AWA2	>SVA
☐ TF-AAE	Boeing 747-4H6	27672/1091	ex TF-AAE	>SVA
☐ TF-AAG	Boeing 747-4H6	27043/1017	ex N774AS	>SVA
☐ TF-AAH	Boeing 747-4H6	29901/1301	ex 9M-MPQ	>SVA
☐ TF-AMF	Boeing 747-412BCF	24226/809	ex PH-MPR	>SVA
☐ TF-AMI	Boeing 747-412BDSF	27066/940	ex N706RB	>SVA
☐ TF-AML	Boeing 747-4H6SF	27044/1041	ex N401SA	>SVA
☐ TF-AMM	Boeing 747-4H6BDSF	25700/974	ex N740WA	>SVA
☐ TF-AMN	Boeing 747-4F6BDSF	27602/1161	ex N469AC	>SVA♦
☐ TF-AMP	Boeing 747-481BCF	24801/805	ex LX-ZCV	.>SVA
☐ TF-AMQ	Boeing 747-412F	26553/1069	ex N328SC	>SVA♦
☐ TF-AMS	Boeing 747-481	24920/832	ex JA8096	>SVA
☐ TF-AMU	Boeing 747-48EF	27603/1210	ex HL7426	>SVA
☐ TF-AMV	Boeing 747-412	28022/1082	ex 9V-SPI	>SVA
☐ TF-	Boeing 747-428ERF	32867/1318	ex F-GUIC	o/o♦
☐ TF-AAA	Boeing 747-236B SCD	22442/526	ex N361FC	[FJR]
☐ TF-AAB	Boeing 747-236M	22304/502	ex N362FM	[FJR]
☐ TF-EAA	Airbus A330-223	343	ex N772RD	>SVA
☐ TF-EAB	Airbus A340-313X	210	ex F-GLZL	<AFR opf MDG

AIR ICELAND		Faxi (FXI)		Akureyri/Reykjavik (AEY/REK)
☐ TF-JMM	Fokker 50	20214	ex D-AFKM	
☐ TF-JMN	Fokker 50	20223	ex D-AFKN	
☐ TF-JMR	Fokker 50	20243	ex TF-FIR	Asdis
☐ TF-JMS	Fokker 50	20244	ex TF-FIS	Sigdis
☐ TF-JMT	Fokker 50	20250	ex TF-FIT	Freydis
☐ TF-JMG	de Havilland DHC-8-202Q	445	ex C-GLRT	
☐ TF-JMK	de Havilland DHC-8-202Q	446	ex C-GLSG	

BLUEBIRD CARGO		Blue Cargo (BF/BBD)		Keflavik (KEF)
☐ TF-BBD	Boeing 737-3Y0SF	24463/1701	ex OY-SEE	>ABR
☐ TF-BBE	Boeing 737-36ESF	25256/2123	ex N314FL	
☐ TF-BBF	Boeing 737-36ESF	25264/2194	ex N316FL	
☐ TF-BBG	Boeing 737-36ESF	25263/2187	ex N317FL	
☐ TF-BBH	Boeing 737-4Y0F	23865/1582	ex N865FC	
☐ TF-BBJ	Boeing 737-476F	24436/1998	ex N937NZ	♦

EAGLE AIR ICELAND		Artic Eagle (FEI)		Reykjavik (REK)
☐ TF-ORA	British Aerospace Jetstream 32	925	ex OY-SVR	
☐ TF-ORB	Cessna 207A Stationair 8 II	20700781	ex OY-SUC	
☐ TF-ORC	British Aerospace Jetstream 3212	981	ex OY-SVY	
☐ TF-ORD	British Aerospace Jetstream 3102	740	ex G-FARA	
☐ TF-ORF	Cessna 441 Conquest II	441-0057	ex N441AK	

ICELANDAIR		Iceair (FI/ICE)		Keflavik/Reykjavik (KEF/REK)
☐ TF-FIA	Boeing 757-256/W	29310/938	ex EC-HIT	Herdubreid
☐ TF-FIC	Boeing 757-23N	30735/931	ex M-ABDG	Magni
☐ TF-FIG	Boeing 757-23APF	24456/237	ex N571CA	
☐ TF-FIH	Boeing 757-208PCF	24739/273		
☐ TF-FII	Boeing 757-208/W	24760/281		Fanndis
☐ TF-FIJ	Boeing 757-208/W	25085/368	ex G-BTEJ	Surtsey
☐ TF-FIK	Boeing 757-256/W	26254/905	ex EI-ERF	Sóldis ♦
☐ TF-FIN	Boeing 757-208/W	28989/780	ex N1790B	Eldborg
☐ TF-FIO	Boeing 757-208/W	29436/859		Krafla
☐ TF-FIP	Boeing 757-208/W	30423/916	ex N1006K	Leifur Eriksson
☐ TF-FIR	Boeing 757-256/W	26242/593	ex EC-FYJ	Askja

☐ TF-FIS	Boeing 757-256/W	26245/617	ex VQ-BCK	Grimsvötn	
☐ TF-FIT	Boeing 757-256/W	26244/616	ex VP-BFG	Helgafell	
☐ TF-FIU	Boeing 757-256/W	26243/603	ex PH-ITA	Hekla Aurora	Northern Lights c/s
☐ TF-FIV	Boeing 757-208/W	30424/956		Katla	
☐ TF-FIW	Boeing 757-27B	24838/302	ex VP-BFI	Búrfell	all white
☐ TF-FIX	Boeing 757-308/W	29434/1004	ex N60659	Hengill	
☐ TF-FIY	Boeing 757-256/W	29312/943	ex P2-ANB	Grábrók	
☐ TF-FIZ	Boeing 757-256/W	30052/948	ex EC-HIX	Keilir	
☐ TF-ISD	Boeing 757-223/W	24596/344	ex N638AA	Snæfellsjökull	
☐ TF-ISF	Boeing 757-223	24595/337	ex N637AM	Laki	
☐ TF-ISL	Boeing 757-223/W	25295/423	ex N661AA	Öræfajökull	
☐ TF-ISK	Boeing 757-223/W	24606/379	ex N648AA	Eldfell	
☐ TF-ISY	Boeing 757-223/W	24594/336	ex N636AM		wfs♦
☐ TF-ISZ	Boeing 757-223/W	24600/357	ex N642AA	Eiriksjökull	♦
☐ TF-LLX	Boeing 757-256/W	29311/940	ex A6-RKA	Skjaldbreidur	
☐ TF-FIB	Boeing 767-383ER	25365/395	ex N365SR		>ANG
☐ P2-PXC	Boeing 737-86Q/W	30290/1406	ex EC-ISE		>ANG
☐ P2-PXV	Boeing 767-341ER	30341/768	ex A6-JBD		>ANG

LOFTLEIDIR ICELANDIC

Ops charter flights and ACMI leases using the AOC of its parent, Icelandair, from whom the aircraft are leased

MYFLUG   Myflug (MYA)   Myvatn (MVA)

☐ TF-MYA	Beech B200 Super King Air	BB-1646	ex N399CW
☐ TF-MYF	Cessna U206G Stationair 6 II	U20606614	ex TC-FAE
☐ TF-MYY	Cessna U206F Stationair	U20602831	ex N35960

NATURE AIR

☐ TF-BFN	de Havilland DHC-6 Twin Otter 300	772	ex N189GC	♦

NORLANDAIR   Akureyri (AEY)

☐ TF-NLB	Beech B200 Super King Air	BB-1689	ex N225TL
☐ TF-NLC	de Havilland DHC-6 Twin Otter 300	413	ex TF-JMC
☐ TF-NLD	de Havilland DHC-6 Twin Otter 300	475	ex TF-JMD

WESTMANN ISLANDS AIRLINES   Reykjavik (REK)

☐ TF-VEV	Piper PA-31-350 Chieftain	31-8152007	ex N4051Q
☐ TF-VEY	Partenavia P.68B	109	ex G-JVMR

WOW AIR   (WW/WOW)   Keflavik (KEF)

☐ LZ-MDC	Airbus A320-232	4270	ex F-WWBS	<VIM
☐ LZ-MDD	Airbus A320-232	4305	ex F-WWDZ	<VIM
☐ TF-DAD	Airbus A321-211/S	6232	ex VQ-BMI	♦
☐ TF-MOM	Airbus A321-211/S	6210	ex VQ-BTT	♦
☐ TF-WOW	Airbus A320-232	2457	ex LZ-WOW	<VIM

TG-   GUATEMALA (Republic of Guatemala)

AEREO RUTA MAYA/JUNGLE FLYING   Ruta Maya (MMG)   Guatemala City-La Aurora (GUA)

☐ TG-AGY	LET L-410UVP	851404	ex HR-IBC	
☐ TG-ARM	Cessna 208B Caravan I	208B0768	ex N5152X	
☐ TG-JCC	Embraer EMB.110P1 Bandeirante	110348	ex N57DA	
☐ TG-JCE	de Havilland DHC-6 Twin Otter 300	420	ex TI-AYQ	
☐ TG-JCO	Embraer EMB.110P2 Bandeirante	110354	ex N102EB	
☐ TG-JFT	Cessna 208B Caravan I	208B0622	ex N52601	
☐ TG-TJD	LET L-410UVP	851421		♦
☐ TG-TJL	LET L-410UVP	952623		♦

AERO CENTRO GUATEMALA

☐ N66KQ	Quest Kodiak 100	100-0066	

AVIATECA GUATEMALA   (GU/GUG)   Guatemala City-La Aurora (GUA)

☐ TG-TRA	ATR 42-300QC	312	ex 9A-CTS	
☐ TG-TRB	ATR 42-300QC	317	ex 9A-CTT	wfs
☐ TG-TRC	ATR 72-600	1167	ex F-WWEH	♦
☐ TG-TRD	ATR 72-600	1174	ex F-WWEB	♦
☐ TG-TRE	ATR 72-600	1196	ex F-WWEM	♦
☐ TG-TRF	ATR 72-600	1199	ex F-WWEQ	♦

AVCOM				Guatemala City-La Aurora (GUA)
☐ TG-JAD	Rockwell 500S Shrike Commander	3123	ex N500MT	
☐ TG-JAM	Aero Commander 500B	1594-205	ex TG-HIA	
☐ TG-JWC	Rockwell 500S Shrike Commander	3209		

DHL DE GUATEMELA		(L3/JOS)		Guatemala City-La Aurora (GUA)
☐ TG-DHP	ATR 42-300	052	ex YV-876C	DHL c/s

MESOAMERICA AIR SERVICES			
☐ TG-JCB	Cessna 404	0235	ex N88719

MILLENIUM AVIATION TRANSPORTES			
☐ TG-MMM	Cessna 208 Caravan I	20800014	ex YV-1122P

TRANSPORTES AEREOS GUATEMALTECOS		(5U/TGU)		Guatemala City-La Aurora (GUA)
☐ TG-TAG	Embraer EMB.110P1A Bandeirante	110441	ex VH-LNB	
☐ TG-TAK	Embraer EMB.110P1 Bandeirante	110405	ex C-FPCO	
☐ TG-TAM	Embraer EMB.110P1 Bandeirante	110220	ex N101RA	
☐ TG-TAN	Embraer EMB.110P1 Bandeirante	110342	ex C-GPCQ	
☐ TG-TAY	Embraer EMB.110P1 Bandeirante	110218	ex TG-JCU	
☐ TG-BJO	SAAB SF.340A	340A-142	ex N142XJ	>CM A/L
☐ TG-JLG	Beech 300 King Air	FA-179	ex N1548K	
☐ TG-TAA	Piper PA-34-200T Seneca			
☐ TG-TAB	Bell 206L LongRanger I	45315	ex N2775G	
☐ TG-TAQ	SAAB SF.340A	340A-140	ex C-GCPU	♦
☐ TG-TAR	SAAB SF.340A	340A-116	ex YR-DAA	[GUA]
☐ TG-TAW	SAAB SF.340A	340A-117	ex YR-DAC	>CM A/L
☐ YV315T	British Aerospace Jetstream 31	697	ex TG-TAW	

TI- COSTA RICA (Republic of Costa Rica)

AEROBELL AIR CHARTERS			San José-Tobias Bolanos (SYQ)
☐ TI-BAD	Bell 407	53403	ex N501TH
☐ TI-BAJ	Cessna 208B Caravan I	208B1180	ex N5058J
☐ TI-BAY	Cessna 208B Caravan I	208B1218	

AERODIVA			Pavas
☐ TI-BEC	Beech B200 Super King Air	BB-364	ex EC-KNT ♦

AVIONES TAXI AEREO			San José-Juan Santamaria (SJO)
☐ TI-ABA	Piper PA-23-250 Aztec D	27-4229	ex TI-1089C wfs
☐ TI-ACA	Piper PA-23-250 Aztec C	27-3515	ex TI-1058C
☐ TI-AST	Piper PA-23-250 Aztec E	27-7554074	ex N54763
☐ TI-ATZ	de Havilland DHC-6 Twin Otter 200	169	ex N931MA

NATUREAIR		(5C/NRR)		Pavas
☐ TI-AZC	de Havilland DHC-6 Twin Otter 300	433	ex N239SA	VistaLiner
☐ TI-AZD	de Havilland DHC-6 Twin Otter 300	697	ex N178GC	
☐ TI-BDZ	de Havilland DHC-6 Twin Otter 300	267	ex N140SA	
☐ TI-BFN	de Havilland DHC-6 Twin Otter 300	556	ex N241SA	
☐ TI-BFV	de Havilland DHC-6 Twin Otter 300	264	ex N72GC	♦
☐ TI-BBC	Cessna 208B Caravan I	208B1210	ex N183GC	
☐ TI-BCS	Dornier 228-212	8236	ex XA-AIR	
☐ TI-BEI	Cessna 208B Caravan I	208B0900	ex N181GC	

PARADISE AIR			San José-Tobias Bolanos (SYQ)
☐ N13AV	Gippsland GA-8 Airvan	GA8-03-028	ex VH-ARW

SANSA		(RZ/LRS)		San José-Juan Santamaria (SJO)
☐ TI-BCX	Cessna 208B Caravan I	208B2058	ex N5040E	
☐ TI-BDL	Cessna 208B Caravan I	208B2097	ex N208LD(1)	
☐ TI-BDW	Cessna 208B Caravan I	208B2176	ex N208LD(1)	
☐ TI-BDX	Cessna 208B Caravan I	208B2246	ex N5091J	
☐ TI-BDY	Cessna 208B Caravan I	208B2248		

TACA COSTA RICA	TACA CostaRica (TI/TAT)	San José-Juan Santamaria (SJO)

Ops aircraft of Avianca Central America (YS-)

TJ- CAMEROON (Republic of Cameroon)

AIR LEASING CAMEROON   Douala (DLA)

☐ TJ-ALD	Fokker F.28 Fellowship 4000	11173	ex TT-EAS	[HLA]
☐ TJ-ALF	Fokker F.28 Fellowship 4000	11226	ex N477AU	wfs
☐ TJ-ALG	Fokker F.28 Fellowship 4000	11227	ex N159AD	

CAMAIR   Camairco (QC/CRC)   Douala (DLA)

☐ TJ-CAC	Boeing 767-33AER	28138/822		Le Dja	
☐ TJ-QCA	Boeing 737-7BD/W	34480/1900	ex N480AC		
☐ TJ-QCB	Boeing 737-7BD/W	33920/1753	ex N339AG		
☐ TJX-SD	AVIC MA60			probable mis-paint	♦
☐ TJX-SE	AVIC MA60			probable mis-paint	♦

CHC CAMEROON   Douala (DLA)

| ☐ TJ-CQD | Aérospatiale SA365N Dauphin 2 | 6062 | ex 5N-ARM |

ELYSIAN AIRLINES   (E4/GIE)   Yaounde Nsimalen Intl (NSI)

| ☐ TJ-TAA | British Aerospace 146-200 | E2178 | ex YR-JFK | ♦ |

JETFLY.COM

| ☐ TJ-PHT | Dornier 228-202K | 8143 | ex F-OGOF |

NATIONAL AIRWAYS CAMEROON   (9O)   Yaounde (YAO)

| ☐ ZS-NTT | Beech 200 Super King Air | BB-350 | ex N125MS |

TL- CENTRAL AFRICAN REPUBLIC

KARINOU AIRLINES   (U5/KRN)   Bangui (BGF)

| ☐ TL-AEG | Boeing 737-2H4 (AvAero 3) | 23109/1016 | ex OD-AMB |
| ☐ TL-ASM | Boeing 737-36N | 28560/2888 | ex N11AQ |

MINAIR   Ormine (OMR)   Bangui (BGF)

| ☐ TL-AEE | LET L-410UVP | 902501 | ex HA-LAO |
| ☐ ZS-TAS | Cessna 208B Caravan I | 208B0378 | ex N208SA |

WESTWIND AVIATION

| ☐ TL-AEW | Hawker Siddeley HS.780 Andover Andover S.1 | Set 13 | ex XS606 |

TN- PEOPLE'S REPUBLIC OF CONGO

AERO FRET BUSINESS   Brazzaville/Pointe Noir (BZV/PNR)

☐ TN-AHH	Antonov An-24RV	47309705	ex 9XR-DB	[QRA]
☐ TN-AHU	Antonov An-12BK	7345403	ex EX-124	
☐ TN-AIW	Yakovlev Yak-40	9321028	ex UR-88299	

AEROSERVICE   Congoserv (RSR)   Brazzaville/Pointe Noire (BZV/PNR)

☐ TN-ACY	Cessna 402B	402B0810	ex TR-LTN
☐ TN-ADN	Britten-Norman BN-2A-9 Islander	647	ex TL-AAQ
☐ TN-ADY	Britten-Norman BN-2A-9 Islander	764	ex TR-LWL
☐ TN-AEK	Cessna 404 Titan II	404-0132	ex TR-LXI
☐ TN-AFC	CASA C.212-300	DF72-1-397	ex D4-CBA

AIR CONGO INTERNATIONAL/SOC NOUVELLE AIR CONGO   Brazzaville (BZV)

☐ TN-AHL	AVIC 1 MA-60	0405	ex B-762L
☐ TN-AHO	AVIC 1 MA-60	0408	ex B-800L
☐ TN-AJF	AVIC 1 MA-60	0905	

CANADIAN AIRWAYS CONGO				Brazzaville (BZV)
☐ TN-AIT	Boeing 737-2T5	22395/729	ex EK-73777	
☐ TN-AIX	Boeing 737-2T5	22632/847	ex 4L-NAM	wfs
☐ TN-AJL	McDonnell-Douglas MD-82	49278/1183	ex UR-WRE	<WRC

CONGO AIRWAYS				Brazzaville (BZV)
☐ TN-AIR	Douglas DC-9-32	47730/828	ex ZS-GAJ	<GBB

EC AIR		(LC)		Brazzaville (BZV)
☐ HB-JJB	Boeing 737-306	27421/2438	ex PH-BTE	opb PTI
☐ HB-JJC	Boeing 737-306	27420/2406	ex PH-BTD	opb PTI [OSR]
☐ HB-JJD	Boeing 757-236	25807/610	ex F-GPEJ	Fleuve Congo	opb PTI
☐ HB-JJE	Boeing 757-204/W	27219/596	ex G-OOBR Riviere Sangha	opb PTI
☐ HB-JJF	Boeing 767-316ER/W	27613/652	ex CC-CBJ	opb PTI♦
☐ HB-JJH	Boeing 737-752/W	33791/1557	ex N853AM Rivière Niari	opb PTI♦
☐ 9A-BTD	Fokker 100	11407	ex N1424M	<TDR♦

EQUAFLIGHT SERVICE		Equaflight (5E/EKA)		Brazzaville (BZV)
☐ F-GRGP	Embraer ERJ-135ER	145188	ex PT-SFL	opb AEH
☐ F-HTOP	Embraer ERJ-135LR	14500886	ex LX-LGK	opb AEH♦
☐ TN-AIJ	Embraer EMB.120ER Brasilia	120209	ex F-HBBB	[DNR]
☐ TR-LIW	ATR 42-300	148	ex F-HAEK	

MISTRAL AVIATION				
☐ TN-AJG	Douglas DC-9-32	47313/268	ex S9-DAB	♦
☐ TN-AJM	Douglas DC-9-32	47198/302	ex TR-LHG	[HLA]♦

TRANS AIR CONGO		Trans-Congo (Q8/TSG)	Brazzaville/Pointe Noire (BZV/PNR)
☐ OD-HAJ	Boeing 737-3Q8	26313/2704	ex G-THOE	<WLB
☐ TN-AHI	Boeing 737-247 (Nordam 3)	23609/1403	ex N328DL	
☐ TN-AHM	LET L-410UVP	820830	ex UR-MLD	
☐ TN-AIM	Boeing 737-232 (AvAero 3)	23083/1008	ex OD-WOL	
☐ TN-AIN	Boeing 737-236	23172/1091	ex N843AL	
☐ TN-AIZ	Boeing 737-33A	25138/2153	ex N552MS	
☐ TN-AJJ	Boeing 737-3Q8	24986/2192	ex N330LF	
☐ ZS-GAB	McDonnell-Douglas MD-82	49165/1117	ex 3D-GAA	<GBB♦

TR-   GABON (Gabonese Republic)

AFRIC AVIATION		(L8/EKG)		Port Gentil (POG)
☐ TR-LIT	Embraer EMB.120ER Brasilia	120213	ex EC-LHY	wfs
☐ TR-LIW	ATR 42-300	148	ex F-HAEK	
☐ ZS-BBM	Embraer ERJ-145LR	145597	ex PR-PSH	opb SET♦
☐ ZS-OLY	Beech 1900D	UE-39	ex N39ZV	<SLT♦
☐ ZS-XCB	ATR 72-212	460	ex F-WNUC	opb SET♦

AFRIJET BUSINESS SERVICE				Libreville (LBV)
☐ CS-DVF	ATR 72-202	350	ex SE-MGM	>LZF♦
☐ ZS-AFR	ATR 42-500	643	ex OH-ATB	opb SET for Shell Gabon♦

ALLEGIANCE AIRWAYS GABON		(ATG)		Libreville (LBV)
☐ ZS-BIL	Boeing 737-277	22650/1981	ex UP-B3702	opb GRF♦
☐ ZS-CFA	British Aerospace 125-1000A	259024	ex ZS-ABG	opb SLE♦
☐ ZS-SRW	Embraer EMB.120RT Brasilia	120018	ex N95644	opb NTN♦

AVIREX		Avirex-Gabon (G2/AVX)		Libreville (LBV)
☐ TR-LEB	Cessna 402B	402B1078	ex TN-AEZ	
☐ TR-LEI	Piper PA-31 Turbo Navajo B	31-7300904	ex N4330B	
☐ TR-LFG	Cessna 404 Titan II	404-0844	ex TJ-AHY	
☐ TR-LVR	Cessna 207 Skywagon	20700310	ex N1710U	

NOUVELLES AIR AFFAIRES GABON	Nouvelle Affaires (NVS)			Libreville (LBV)
☐ TR-AAG	Canadair Challenger 601-3A	5071	ex N500PC	
☐ TR-CLB	de Havilland DHC-8Q-314	545	ex D-BDTM	
☐ TR-LBV	Beech 1900D	UE-321	ex ZS-OCX	
☐ TR-LFO	Beech 1900D	UE-313	ex ZS-OCV	
☐ TR-LFX	Cessna 208B Caravan I	208B0796	ex N99FX	
☐ TR-LGQ	Fokker 100	11424	ex F-GIOH	[BTS]

SCD AVIATION/AFRICA CONNECTION

☐ D-CAAL	Dornier 228-202K	8152		<Advanced Avn
☐ TR-LRS	Embraer EMB.120 Brasilia	120239	ex F-GTBG	wfs

SKY GABON   *Sky Gabon (SKG)*

☐ C-FHNM	Convair 580F	454	ex N583P	<NRL
☐ I-MLUT	Fokker F.27 Friendship 500	10369	ex F-BPUA	<MNL

TS-   TUNISIA

NOUVELAIR   *Nouvelair (BJ/LBT)*   *Monastir (MIB)*

☐ TS-INA	Airbus A320-214	1121	ex F-WWBT	Dora	
☐ TS-INB	Airbus A320-214	1175	ex F-WWDO		
☐ TS-INC	Airbus A320-214	1744	ex F-WWBS	Youssef	
☐ TS-INF	Airbus A320-212	0937	ex SU-KBA		
☐ TS-INH	Airbus A320-214	4623	ex F-WWBY	Mohamed Aziz Milad	
☐ TS-INN	Airbus A320-212	0793	ex D-AICB		>LAA
☐ TS-INO	Airbus A320-214	3480	ex F-WWDK		
☐ TS-INP	Airbus A320-214	1597	ex SU-KBD		
☐ TS-INQ	Airbus A320-214	2158	ex EI-FDV		
☐ TS-INR	Airbus A320-214	3487	cx RP-C3247		♦
☐ TS-INS	Airbus A320-232	3089	ex EI-EYE		♦
☐ TS-INV	Canadair Challenger 604	5628	ex TS-IBT		

SYPHAX AIRLINES   *Syphax (FS/SYA)*   *Sfax Thyna (SFA)*

☐ TS-IEF	Airbus A319-112	3853	ex D-AHIN	Karama
☐ TS-IEG	Airbus A319-112	3872	ex D-AHIO	El Horria

TUNISAIR   *Tunair (TU/TAR)*   *Tunis-Carthage (TUN)*

☐ TS-IMC	Airbus A320-211	0124	ex F-WWIS		
☐ TS-IMD	Airbus A320-211	0205	ex F-WWDO	Khereddine	
☐ TS-IME	Airbus A320-211	0123	ex F-OGYC	Tabarka	
☐ TS-IMF	Airbus A320-211	0370	ex F-WWIP	Djerba	
☐ TS-IMG	Airbus A320-211	0390	ex F-WWDL	Abou el Kacem Chebbi	
☐ TS-IMH	Airbus A320-211	0402	ex F-WWBN	Ali Belhaouane	
☐ TS-IMI	Airbus A320-211	0511	ex F-WWDC	Jugurtha	
☐ TS-IML	Airbus A320-211	0958	ex F-WWBI	Gafsa El Ksar	
☐ TS-IMM	Airbus A320-211	0975	ex F-WWIR	Le Bardo	
☐ TS-IMN	Airbus A320-211	1187	ex F-WWDU	Ibn Khaldoun	
☐ TS-IMP	Airbus A320-211	1700	ex F-WWIS	La Galite	
☐ TS-IMR	Airbus A320-214	4344	ex D-AXAS	Habib Bourguiba	
☐ TS-IMS	Airbus A320-214	4689	ex D-AUBC	Dougga	
☐ TS-IMT	Airbus A320-214	5204	ex F-WWIZ	Aziza Othmana	
☐ TS-IMU	Airbus A320-214	5474	ex F-WWBI	Sousse	
☐ TS-IMV	Airbus A320-214	5610	ex F-WWIB	Ibn El Jazzar	
☐ TS-IMW	Airbus A320-214/S	6338	ex F-WWBN	Farhad Hachet	♦
☐ TS-	Airbus A320-214/S	6922	ex		o/o♦
☐ TS-IOK	Boeing 737-6H3	29496/268	ex N1786B	Kairouan	
☐ TS-IOL	Boeing 737-6H3	29497/282	ex N1786B	Tozeur Nefta	
☐ TS-IOM	Boeing 737-6H3	29498/310	ex N1786B	Carthage	
☐ TS-ION	Boeing 737-6H3	29499/510	ex N1786B	Utique	
☐ TS-IOP	Boeing 737-6H3	29500/543		El Jem	
☐ TS-IOQ	Boeing 737-6H3	29501/563	ex N1787B	Bizerte	
☐ TS-IOR	Boeing 737-6H3	29502/816	ex N1786B	Tahar Haddad	
☐ TS-IFM	Airbus A330-243	1631	ex F-WWKR		o/o♦
☐ TS-IFN	Airbus A330-243	1641	ex F-WWKA		o/o♦
☐ TS-IMJ	Airbus A319-114	0869	ex D-AVYW	El Kantaoui	
☐ TS-IMK	Airbus A319-114	0880	ex D-AVYD	Kerkenah	
☐ TS-IMO	Airbus A319-114	1479	ex D-AVYT	Hannibal	
☐ TS-IMQ	Airbus A319-112	3096	ex D-AVWZ	Alyssa	>AAW
☐ TS-IOG	Boeing 737-5H3	26639/2253		Sfax	wfs
☐ TS-IOH	Boeing 737-5H3	26640/2474		Hammamet	wfs
☐ TS-IOI	Boeing 737-5H3	27257/2583		Mahdia	wfs
☐ TS-IOJ	Boeing 737-5H3	27912/2701		Monastir	wfs
☐ TS-IPA	Airbus A300B4-605R	558		Sidi Bou Said	
☐ TS-IPB	Airbus A300B4-605R	563	ex A6-EKD	Tunis	
☐ TS-IPC	Airbus A300B4-605R	505	ex A6-EKE	Amilcar	
			ex F-OIHB		

TUNISAIR EXPRESS   *Tunexpress (UG/SEN)*   *Tunis-Carthage (TUN)*

☐ TS-ISA	Canadair CRJ-900	15091		Didon

☐ TS-LBA	ATR 42-300	245	ex G-BXBV	Alyssa
☐ TS-LBC	ATR 72-202	281	ex F-WWLK	Tahar Haddad
☐ TS-LBD	ATR 72-202	756	ex F-WWEQ	Hasdrubal
☐ TS-LBE	ATR 72-202	794	ex F-WWEU	
☐ ZS-PYU	Beech 1900D	UE-107	ex N107YV	

TUNISAVIA	*Tunisavia (TAJ)*	*Tunis-Carthage (TUN)*

☐ TS-HSD	Aérospatiale SA365N Dauphin 2	6117	ex F-WXFC
☐ TS-HSE	Aérospatiale SA365N Dauphin 2	6150	ex F-WYMN
☐ TS-LIB	de Havilland DHC-6 Twin Otter 300	716	ex TS-DIB
☐ TS-LSF	de Havilland DHC-6 Twin Otter 300	575	ex TS-DSF

TT- TCHAD (Republic of Chad)

AIR HORIZON	*Tchad-Horizon (TPK)*	*N'Djamena (NDJ)*

Ops cargo flights with Antonov An-12 frtrs leased from other operators as required

AVMAX TCHAD	*N'Djamena (NDJ)*

☐ TT-DAC	de Havilland DHC-8-311	216	ex C-GOFW	
☐ TT-DAV	de Havilland DHC-8-301	184	ex C-GRGF	♦

RJM AVIATION	*N'Djamena (NDJ)*

☐ F-GVZJ	ATR 42-300	093	ex F-WQNO	< AEH♦
☐ TT-DAG	Embraer EMB.120RT Brasilia	120253	ex F-GTVA	

TOUMAÏ AIR TCHAD	*(9D/THE)*	*N'Djamena (NDJ)*

☐ TT-EAS	Fokker F-28 Fellowship 4000	11204	ex TJ-ALC	[NDJ]
☐ TT-EAZ	Boeing 737-322	24673/1920	ex 4L-IMO	Bamina [ADD]

TU- IVORY COAST (Republic of the Ivory Coast)

AIR CÔTE d'IVOIRE	*Cote d'Ivoire (HF/VRE)*	*Abidjan (ABJ)*

☐ TU-TSA	Airbus A319-115LR	2213	ex F-GRXG	
☐ TU-TSB	Airbus A319-115LR	2228	ex F-GRXH	
☐ TU-TSK	de Havilland DHC-8-402Q	4474	ex C-GZDV	♦
☐ TU-TSL	de Havilland DHC-8-402Q	4484	ex C-FBUO	♦
☐ TU-TSN	Airbus A319-112	1429	ex N429AG	
☐ TU-	Airbus A319-111	6834	ex	o/o♦
☐ ZS-GAO	Airbus A320-231	067	ex N628AW	<GBB♦

AIR INTER IVOIRE	*Inter Ivoire (NTV)*	*Abidjan (ABJ)*

☐ TU-TDM	Grumman G.159 Gulfstream I	20	ex TJ-WIN	[MAD]
☐ TU-TGF	Piper PA-31-350 Navajo Chieftain	31-7305072	ex N74930	
☐ TU-TJF	Piper PA-23-250 Aztec F	27-7654072	ex N62594	
☐ TU-TJL	Piper PA-31T Cheyenne II	31T-7720033	ex N82152	
☐ TU-TJN	Beech 58 Baron	TH-776	ex HB-GGE	

IAS HELICOPTERS	

☐ TU-HAC	Aérospatiale AS365N3 Dauphin	6738	ex C-GSAB	♦
☐ TU-HAD	Aérospatiale AS365N3 Dauphin	6657	ex C-GGJV	♦
☐ TU-HAF	Aéspatiale AS365N3 Dauphin	6593	ex C-GGVW	♦
☐ TU-THO	Aérospatiale SA365C2 Dauphin	5071	ex F-GFEC	♦
☐ TU-THP	Aérospatiale SA365N Dauphin	6066	ex F-GERJ	♦
☐ TU-THQ	Aérospatiale SA365C2 Dauphin	5007	ex EC-DXM	♦
☐ TU-HAB	Aérospatiale AS350B Ecureuil	1792	ex F-GECM	♦

IVOIRIENNE DE TRANSPORTS AERIENS	*(IVN)*

☐ TU-PAD	Hawker Siddeley HS.748 Srs.2B/426	1799	ex 4R-SER	>EHN

MAXAIR	*Abidjan (ABJ)*

☐ TU-TSG	Beech 200 Super King Air	BB-616	ex F-GGMV	♦
☐ TU-TSH	Beech B200 Super King Air	BB-1058	ex CN-TLH	♦

SOPHIA AIRLINES/COTAIR	

☐ TU-TBB	LET L-410UVP	851423	ex 3D-GAM
☐ TU-TBS	LET L-410UVP	810724	ex 3D-BHK

☐ TU-TCV	LET L-410UVP	851507	ex UR-SEV	
☐ TU-TPI	Cessna U206G Stationair	U20603733	ex LN-MAQ	wfs♦

WESTAIR CARGO AIRLINES				Westcar (WSC)
☐ 3D-RED	Boeing 737-268C	20575/295	ex 3D-PHS	wfs

TY-   BENIN (Republic of Benin)

AIR TAXI BENIN				Cotonou (COO)
☐ TY-ATB	Piper PA-30-160B Twin Comanche	30-1379	ex F-BUVZ	

SOC BENINOISE DES HYDROCARBURES				Cotonou (COO)
☐ TY-ABC	AgustaWestland AW139	41347	ex N459SH	opb Benin AF♦

TRANS AIR BENIN				Cotonou (COO)

Ops services with aircraft leased from Trans Air Congo as required

WESTAIR BENIN			(WH/WSF)	
☐ YU-ANP	Boeing 737-2K3 (Nordam 3)	23912/1401	Zadar	<AGX

TZ-   MALI (Republic of Mali)

AIR MALI		(I5/CMM)		Bamako (BKO)
☐ TZ-RCA	Canadair CRJ-200ER	7392	ex N646BR	opf VBW
☐ TZ-RMA	McDonnell-Douglas MD-87	49832/1703	ex I-AFRB	[BKO]
☐ TZ-RMB	McDonnell-Douglas MD-87	49841/1751	ex EC-EYZ	[BKO]
☐ TZ-RMC	McDonnell-Douglas MD-87	49842/1763	ex EC-EZA	

AVION EXPRESS		Avion Express (VXP)		Bamako (BKO)
☐ 3X-GED	SAAB SF.340A	340A-051	ex ZS-PMN	wfs
☐ 3X-GEJ	SAAB SF.340A	340A-136	ex ZK-NLN	wfs

TOMBOUCTOU AVIATION		(TBT)		
☐ TZ-BSA	BAC One-Eleven 492GM (QTA 3)	260	ex YR-MIA	VIP [MJI]
☐ TZ-BSB	BAC One-Eleven 401AK	086	ex YR-CJL	VIP wfs

T3-   KIRIBATI (Republic of Kiribati)

AIR KIRIBATI		(4A/AKL)		Tarawa-Bonriki Intl (TRW)
☐ T3-ATC	CASA C.212-200	CC30-1-236		
☐ T3-ATI	Harbin Y-12 II	0077		
☐ T3-	de Havilland DHC-6 Twin Otter 300	647	ex N360CM	
☐ T3-	de Havilland DHC-6 Twin Otter 300	831	ex N831WJ	♦

T8A-   PALAU (Republic of Palau)

PALAU PACIFIC AIRWAYS		(P7/PAU)		Koror (ROR)
☐ OM-GEX	Boeing 737-8AS/W	29919/341	ex N637AC	<AXE♦

UK   UZBEKISTAN (Republic of Uzbekistan)

AVIALEASING	Twinarrow (V2/TWN)	Tashkent-Vostochny/Miami-Opa Locka, FL (TAS/OPF)		
☐ UK 11418	Antonov An-12B	402504	ex RA-11996	based OPF
☐ UK-12001	Antonov An-12BP	5343202	ex CCCP-11711	
☐ UK 12002	Antonov An-12B	402002	ex RA-11373	
UK 11418 ops cargo flights for Bahamasair and DHL				

SILK ROAD CARGO BUSINESS		(S9/URS)		
☐ VQ-BNW	Airbus A300-622RF	0733	ex N733MY	

UZBEKISTAN AIRWAYS		Uzbek (HY/UZB)	Tashkent-Vostochny/Samarkand (TAS/SKD)		
☐ UK 32011	Airbus A320-214	4371	ex D-AVVA		
☐ UK 32012	Airbus A320-214	4395	ex D-AVVK		
☐ UK 32014	Airbus A320-214	4417	ex F-WWDM		
☐ UK 32015	Airbus A320-214	4485	ex D-AUBF		
☐ UK 32016	Airbus A320-214	4492	ex D-AUBJ		
☐ UK 32017	Airbus A320-214	4651	ex D-AXAA		
☐ UK 32018	Airbus A320-214	4724	ex D-AUBK		
☐ UK 32019	Airbus A320-214	4770	ex F-WWDC		
☐ UK 32020	Airbus A320-214	4952	ex D-AXAT		
☐ UK 75700	Boeing 757-23P	28338/731			opf Govt
☐ UK 75701	Boeing 757-23P	30060/875	ex VP-BUB	Urgench	
☐ UK 75702	Boeing 757-23P	30061/886	ex VP-BUD	Shahrisabz	
☐ VP-BUH	Boeing 757-231	30339/896	ex N726TW		
☐ VP-BUI	Boeing 757-231	28487/878	ex N719TW		
☐ VP-BUJ	Boeing 757-231	28488/884	ex N724TW		
☐ UK 67000	Boeing 767-33PER	35796/958	ex N5014K		VIP; opf Govt
☐ UK 67001	Boeing 767-33PERF	28370/635	ex VP-BUA	Samarkand	
☐ UK 67002	Boeing 767-33PER	28392/650	ex VP-BUZ	Khiva	
☐ UK 67003	Boeing 767-33PER	40534/1019			
☐ UK 67004	Boeing 767-33PER	40536/1021			
☐ UK 67005	Boeing 767-33PER	40533/1047	ex N940BA		
☐ UK 67006	Boeing 767-33PER	40535/1054			
☐ VP-BUE	Boeing 767-3CBER	33469/904	ex N594HA		
☐ VP-BUF	Boeing 767-33PER	33078/928			
☐ UK 76351	Ilyushin Il-76TD	1013408240	ex RA-76351		[TAS]
☐ UK 76358	Ilyushin Il-76TD	1023410339			[TAS]
☐ UK 76359	Ilyushin Il-76TD	1033414483			[TAS]
☐ UK 76426	Ilyushin Il-76TD	1043419644			[TAS]
☐ UK 76428	Ilyushin Il-76TD	1043419648	ex 76428		
☐ UK 76449	Ilyushin Il-76TD	1023403058	ex 76449		[TAS]
☐ UK 76782	Ilyushin Il-76TD	0093498971	ex CCCP-76782		[TAS]
☐ UK 76793	Ilyushin Il-76TD	0093498951	ex CCCP-76793		[TAS]
☐ UK 76794	Ilyushin Il-76TD	0093498954	ex CCCP-76794		[TAS]
☐ UK 76805	Ilyushin Il-76TD	1003403109	ex CCCP-76805		
☐ UK 76824	Ilyushin Il-76TD	1023410327	ex CCCP-76824		[TAS]
☐ UK 91102	Ilyushin Il-114-100	1063800202			
☐ UK 91104	Ilyushin Il-114-100	2093800204			
☐ UK 91105	Ilyushin Il-114-100	2063800205	ex 91105		
☐ UK 91106	Ilyushin Il-114-100	2083800206	ex 91106		
☐ UK 91107	Ilyushin Il-114-100	2103800207			
☐ UK 91108	Ilyushin Il-114-100	10.3800208			
☐ UK 91109	Ilyushin Il-114-100	0.3800209			
☐ UK 31001	Airbus A310-324	574	ex F-OGQY	Tashkent	wfs
☐ UK 31002	Airbus A310-324	576	ex F-OGQZ	Fergana	wfs
☐ UK 31003	Airbus A310-324	706	ex F-WWCM	Bukhara	[TAS]
☐ UK 31004	Airbus A300B4-622RF	717	ex HL7299		
☐ UK 31005	Airbus A300B4-622RF	722	ex HL7244		
☐ UK 80001	Avro 146-RJ85	E2312	ex G-6-312		VIP opf Govt
☐ UK 80002	Avro 146-RJ85	E2309	ex G-6-309		
☐ UK 80003	Avro 146-RJ85	E2319	ex G-6-319		

UP- KAZAKHSTAN (Republic of Kazakhstan)

AIR ALMATY		(K7/LMY)		Almaty (ALA)
☐ UP-I7601	Ilyushin Il-76TD	1013409295	ex YL-LAJ	
☐ UP-I7618	Ilyushin Il-76TD	0013428831	ex UN-76022	

AIR ASTANA		Astanaline (KC/KZR)		Astana/Almaty (TSE/ALA)
☐ P4-KBA	Airbus A320-232	5401	ex F-WWBQ	Manshuk
☐ P4-KBB	Airbus A320-232/S	5613	ex F-WWIC	Roza
☐ P4-KBC	Airbus A320-232/S	5734	ex F-WWIG	Gaziza
☐ P4-KBD	Airbus A320-232/S	5870	ex D-AVVE	
☐ P4-KBE	Airbus A320-232/S	5968	ex D-AUBM	
☐ P4-KBF	Airbus A320-232/S	6037	ex F-WWIL	
☐ P4-KBG	Airbus A320-232/S	6029	ex D-AXAB	
☐ P4-VAS	Airbus A320-232	3141	ex F-WWDO	
☐ P4-EAS	Boeing 757-2G5/W	29488/830	ex D-AMUG	
☐ P4-FAS	Boeing 757-2G5/W	29489/834	ex D-AMUH	
☐ P4-GAS	Boeing 757-2G5/W	28112/708	ex D-AMUI	
☐ P4-KCU	Boeing 757-23N/W	27971/690	ex N558AX	
☐ P4-MAS	Boeing 757-28A/W	28833/782	ex B-2852	

☐ P4-KCC	Embraer ERJ-190LR	19000418	ex PT-TBP		
☐ P4-KCD	Embraer ERJ-190LR	19000431	ex PT-TCR		
☐ P4-KCE	Embraer ERJ-190LR	19000487	ex PT-TPL		
☐ P4-KCF	Embraer ERJ-190LR	19000537	ex PT-TVE		
☐ P4-KCG	Embraer ERJ-190LR	19000543	ex PT-TAX	Hiuaz	
☐ P4-KCH	Embraer ERJ-190LR	19000547	ex PT-TBN	DINA	
☐ P4-KCI	Embraer ERJ-190LR	19000604	ex PT-TJL	Amina	
☐ P4-KCJ	Embraer ERJ-190LR	19000653	ex PR-EDV		
☐ P4-KCK	Embraer ERJ-190LR	19000657	ex PR-EED		
☐ P4-KCA	Boeing 767-306ER	27612/647	ex PH-BZI		wfs
☐ P4-KDA	Airbus A321-231	5357	ex D-AVZE	Kulyash	
☐ P4-KDB	Airbus A321-231	5404	ex D-AVZK	Aliya	
☐ P4-KEA	Boeing 767-3KYER/W	42220/1060			
☐ P4-KEB	Boeing 767-3KYER/W	42221/1062			
☐ P4-KEC	Boeing 767-3KYER/W	42223/1068			♦
☐ P4-NAS	Airbus A321-131	1042	ex N104AQ		
☐ P4-OAS	Airbus A321-231	1204	ex N120ED		
☐ P4-YAS	Airbus A319-132	3614	ex D-AVYL		

AIR TRUST (RTR)

☐ UP-I6209	Ilyushin Il-62M	3357947	ex UN-86586	
☐ UP-I7626	Ilyushin Il-76M	1013409303	ex YU-AMJ	
☐ UP I7644	Ilyushin Il-76TD	0033448404	ex UP-I7623	

BEK AIR (Z9/BEK) Almaty (ALA)

☐ UP-F1004	Fokker 100	11445	ex PK-RGE	
☐ UP-F1005	Fokker 100	11500	ex D-AFKD	
☐ UP-F1007	Fokker 100	11496	ex D-AFKC	
☐ UP-F1009	Fokker 100	11470	ex D-AFKF	
☐ UP-F1010	Fokker 100	11527	ex D-AFKB	♦
☐ UP-F1011	Fokker 100	11517	ex D-AFKA	♦
☐ UP-F1014	Fokker 100	11322	ex 4L-GIA	
☐ UP-Y4021	Yakovlev Yak-40	9302229	ex UN-87306	wfs
☐ UP-Y4022	Yakovlev Yak-40	9411533	ex UP-Y4023(1)	wfs
☐ UP-Y4023	Yakovlev Yak-40	9621148	ex UN-88191	wfs
☐ UP-Y4024	Yakovlev Yak-40	9711552	ex UN-88260	wfs

BERKUT STATE AIR COMPANY (BEC) Almaty (ALA)

☐ UP-A2001	Airbus A320CJ-214	3199	ex UN-A2001	VIP opf Govt
☐ UP-B5701	Boeing 757-2M6ER	23454/102	ex UN-B5701	VIP opf Govt
☐ UP-I7605	Ilyushin Il-76TD	1033416520	ex UN-76374	
☐ UP-MI702	Mil Mi-172 (Mi-8MTV-3)	398C01	ex UN-17201	VIP
☐ UP-MI814	Mil Mi-8MTV-1	96275	ex UN-25401	VIP
☐ UN-85464	Tupolev Tu-154B-2	80A464	ex 85464	opf Govt

CASPIY (TLG) Aktau Shevchenko (SCO)

☐ UP-F1001	Fokker 100	11384	ex N110MN	
☐ UP-F1002	Fokker 100	11371	ex N371MX	
☐ UP-F1003	Fokker 100	11375	ex N375MX	
☐ UP-F1008	Fokker 100	11347	ex N347MX	
☐ UP-D3001	Dornier 328-300 (328JET)	3124	ex N355SK	
☐ UP-	Dornier 328-300 (328JET)	3108	ex N351SK	wfs♦

EURO-ASIA AIR INTERNATIONAL Kazeur (KZE) Almaty/Sharjah (ALA/SHJ)

☐ UP-AW609	AgustaWestland AW139	31379		
☐ UP-T3409	Tupolev Tu-134B-3	62820	ex UN-65720	VIP♦
☐ UP-Y4026	Yakovlev Yak-40	9510639	ex UN-87337 Aibike titles	VIP
☐ UP-Y4027	Yakovlev Yak-40K	9741856	ex UN-87935	VIP
☐ UP-Y4030?	Yakovlev Yak-40	9541444	ex UN-87990	

KAZAIRJET

☐ UP-AN721	Antonov An-72	36572030425	ex UN-72904	
☐ UP-Y4015	Yakovlev Yak-40	9530842	ex UN-87543	♦

KAZAVIASPAS Spakas (KZS)

☐ UP-AN301	Antonov An-30	0604	ex UN-30029	
☐ UP-I7604	Ilyushin Il-76TD	1033414485	ex UN-76371	
☐ UP-M1706	Mil Mi-171C	171C00073983304U		♦
☐ UP-M1707	Mil Mi-17V-5	398M23		♦
☐ UP-T3407	Tupolev Tu-134A	49912	ex UN-65070	
☐ UP-T5406	Tupolev Tu-154M	93A965	ex UN-85781	

SCAT		Vlasta (DV/VSV)		Shymkent (CIT)
☐ UP-AN404	Antonov An-24B	17307303	ex UN-26196	
☐ UP-AN405	Antonov An-24B	77303508	ex UN-46265	
☐ UP-AN407	Antonov An-24B	87305305	ex UN-46310	
☐ UP-AN408	Antonov An-24B	97305608	ex UN-46340	
☐ UP-AN410	Antonov An-24B	07306104	ex UN-46381	
☐ UP-AN411	Antonov An-24B	87304106	ex UN-46421	
☐ UP-AN412	Antonov An-24B	87304309	ex UN-46438	
☐ UP-AN413	Antonov An-24RV	27308305	ex UN-46500	
☐ UP-AN414	Antonov An-24RV	37308805	ex UN-46626	[CIT]
☐ UP-AN415	Antonov An-24RV	47309505	ex UN-46664	
☐ UP-AN416	Antonov An-24RV	47309604	ex UN-46672	
☐ UP-AN417	Antonov An-24RV	47309910	ex UN-46699	
☐ UP-AN418	Antonov An-24B	89901810	ex UN-47176	
☐ UP-AN419	Antonov An-24RV	27307609	ex UN-47258	
☐ UP-AN420	Antonov An-24B	07306308	ex UN-47270	
☐ UP-AN421	Antonov An-24B	07306407	ex UN-47277	
☐ UP-AN422	Antonov An-24B	07306504	ex UN-47284	
☐ UP-AN423	Antonov An-24RV	67310509	ex UN-47350	wfs
☐ UP-AN424	Antonov An-24RV	27307509	ex UN-47692	
☐ UP-AN425	Antonov An-24B	79901307	ex UN-47763	
☐ UP-AN426	Antonov An-24B	17307406	ex UN-47844	
☐ LY-AWD	Boeing 737-522	26739/2494	ex C-FDCU	<LLC
☐ LY-AWE	Boeing 737-522	26684/2388	ex C-FCFR	<LLC
☐ LY-AWH	Boeing 737-3Y0	23924/1542	ex N924RM	<LLC
☐ LY-AYZ	Boeing 737-548	25739/2271	ex EI-CDH	
☐ UP-B3710	Boeing 737-505	29116/3005	ex 4L-TGF	
☐ UP-B3712	Boeing 737-35B	25069/2053	ex LY-AQV	[VNO]
☐ UP-CJ004	Canadair CRJ-200LR	7901	ex LY-AYJ	
☐ UP-CJ005	Canadair CRJ-200LR	7902	ex LY-AYK	
☐ UP-CJ007	Canadair CRJ-200ER	7702	ex N585SC	
☐ UP-CJ008	Canadair CRJ-200LR	7365	ex OE-LCN	
☐ UP-CJ011	Canadair CRJ-200ER	7746	ex EC-ILF	
☐ UP-CJ012	Canadair CRJ-200ER	7785	ex EC-INF	
☐ UP-CJ	Canadair CRJ-200LR	8010	ex S5-AAJ	o/o
☐ LY-AZV	Boeing 737-76N/W	37233/2578	ex EI-IGP	<LLC♦
☐ LY-FLG	Boeing 757-204	27237/602	ex G-BYAR	opf Sunday AL <LLC
☐ UP-AN202	Antonov An-12BP	3341201	ex UN-11367	
☐ UP-AN601	Antonov An-26	0503	ex UN-26027	
☐ UP-B5702	Boeing 757-21B	25083/359	ex N508AG	opf Sunday AL
☐ UP-B5703	Boeing 757-21B	25259/392	ex B-2818	opf Sunday AL
☐ UP-Y4203	Yakovlev Yak-42D	4250421116567	ex UN-42401	
☐ UP-Y4210	Yakovlev Yak-42D	4520422306016	ex UN-42428	wfs

SEMEYAVIA		Ertis (SMK)		Semipalatinsk (PLX)
☐ UP-Y4016	Yakovlev Yak-40K	9810557	ex UN-87208	
☐ UP-Y4017	Yakovlev Yak-40K	9810157	ex UN-87204	

7TH SKY				Almaty (ALA)
☐ UP-CJ009	Canadair CRJ-100LR	7354	ex C-GLVF	
☐ UP-CJ010	Canadair CRJ-100LR	7359	ex C-GLVE	Sapsan c/s

SUNDAY AIRLINES				Shymkent (CIT)
☐ LY-FLG	Boeing 757-204	27237/602	ex G-BYAR	opb VSV <LLC♦
☐ UP-B5702	Boeing 757-21B	25083/359	ex N508AG	opb VSV♦
☐ UP-B5703	Boeing 757-21B	25259/392	ex B-2818	opb VSV♦
☐ UP-B5704	Boeing 757-21B	25884/461	ex B-2822	opf VSV
☐ UP-B6703	Boeing 767-332ER	30597/797	ex B-2499	♦

ZHEZ AIR		(KZH)		
☐ UP-L4102	LET L-410UVP-E	902512	ex UR-SVI	
☐ UP-L4108	LET L-410UVP-E20	2801	ex UN-87929	

UR- UKRAINE

EROJET		Jet Express (BJU)		
☐ UR-ALC	SAAB SF.340B	340B-163	ex UR-IMF	

AEROSTAR		Aerostar (UAR)		Kiev-Zhulyany/Kiev-Borispol (IEV/KBP)
☐ UR-DAV	Dornier 328-310 (328JET)	3169	ex N328DP	[BSL]

524

AEROVIS AIRLINES/AVFL LOGISTICS		**Aeroviz (VIZ)**		**Rivnu (RWN)**
☐ UR-CBF	Antonov An-12BP	2340507	ex LZ-SFW	
☐ UR-CBG	Antonov An-12BP	6343705	ex UR-11302	
☐ UR-CEZ	Antonov An-12B	6344304	ex RA-98118	
☐ UR-CFB	Antonov An-12BP	6343802	ex 02 red	

AIR SIRIN				
☐ TT-WAK	Ilyushin Il-18D	172011401	ex 3X-GGR	
☐ 4L-AFT	Antonov An-26B	10610	ex 3X-GHK	

AIR URGA		**Urga (3N/URG)**		**Kirovograd-Khmelyovoye (KGO)**
☐ UR-ELL	Antonov An-24RV	67310503	ex UR-47316	opf UN
☐ UR-ELM	Antonov An-24RV	67310506	ex UR-47319	
☐ UR-ELN	Antonov An-24B	89901607	ex UR-47155	opf UN
☐ UR-ELO	Antonov An-24RV	47309507	ex UR-46666	
☐ UR-ELT	Antonov An-24RV	27307809	ex XU-054	
☐ UR-46311	Antonov An-24B	97305307	ex LZ-MND	opf UN
☐ UR-ELB	Antonov An-26B	14005	ex UR-26201	opf UN
☐ UR-ELD	Antonov An-26B	14010	ex UR-26203	opf UN
☐ UR-FI E	Antonov An-26B	12108	ex UR-26111	opf UN
☐ UR-ELF	Antonov An-26B-100	12204	ex UR-26115	opf UN
☐ UR-ELG	Antonov An-26B	12902	ex UR-26140	opf UN
☐ UR-ELH	Antonov An-26B	12908	ex UR-26143	opf UN
☐ UR-ELI	Antonov An-26B	14009	ex HA-TCM	
☐ UR-APM	SAAB SF.340B	340B-230	ex SE-KTE	
☐ UR-ARO	SAAB SF.340B	340B-276	ex SE-KTK	wfs
☐ UR-ELJ	SAAB SF.340B	340B-259	ex JU-9901	
☐ UR-ELQ	SAAB SF.340B	340B-239	ex N239CJ	
☐ UR-ELS	SAAB SF.340B	340B-214	ex N311CE	♦
☐ UR-ELU	SAAB SF.340B	340B-360	ex N875PC	
☐ UR-ELV	SAAB SF.340B	340B-242	ex N242CJ	
☐ UR-ELZ	SAAB SF.340B	340B-359	ex JU-9905	
☐ UR-ESA	SAAB SF.340B	340B-449	ex N449XJ	♦
☐ UR-ESB	SAAB SF.340B	340B-426	ex N426XJ	♦
☐ UR-IMS	SAAB SF.340B	340B-228	ex YR-VGP	
☐ UR-IMX	SAAB SF.340B	340B-225	ex YR-VGR	

ANTONOV AIRLINES		**Antonov Bureau (ADB)**		**Kiev-Gostomel**
☐ UR-82007	Antonov An-124-100	19530501005	ex CCCP-82007	
☐ UR-82008	Antonov An-124-100M-150	19530501006	ex CCCP-82008	
☐ UR-82009	Antonov An-124-100	19530501007	ex CCCP-82009	
☐ UR-82027	Antonov An-124-100	19530502288	ex CCCP-82027	
☐ UR-82029	Antonov An-124-100	19530502630	ex CCCP-82029	
☐ UR-82072	Antonov An-124-100	9773053359136	ex RA-82072	
☐ UR-82073	Antonov An-124-100	9773054359139	ex RA-82073	
☐ UR-09307	Antonov An-22A	043481244	ex CCCP-09307	
☐ UR-74010	Antonov An-74T	36547030450	ex CCCP-74010	VIP
☐ UR-82060	Antonov An-225 Mriya	19530503763	ex CCCP-82060	

ATLASJET UKRAINE		**(UH/UJX)**		**Lvov (LWO)**
☐ UR-AJA	Airbus A320-214	1213	ex VQ-BHS	
☐ UR-AJB	Airbus A320-233	0733	ex EI-FBA	
☐ UR-AJC	Airbus A320-214	1390	ex TC-ABL	o/o♦

AVIA EXPRESS				
☐ UR-MAG	LET L-410	820924	ex D-COXB	♦

BRAVO AIRWAYS		**(BAY)**		**Kiev-Borispol (KBP)**
☐ TT-DBC	Douglas DC-8-73CF	45991/380	ex N602AL	[NBO]♦
☐ UR-WRB	McDonnell-Douglas MD-82	49364/1276	ex N937AS	<MaxAvia
☐ UR-CNE	Boeing 737-505	24828/1925	ex N828DG	>UKM♦

BUKOVYNA AIRLINES		**Bukovyna (BQ/BKV)**		**Chernovtsy (CWC)**
☐ UR-BXI	McDonnell-Douglas MD-82	53170/2065	ex G-CEPJ	>IRA
☐ UR-BXL	McDonnell-Douglas MD-82	49512/1548	ex G-CEPG	>IRB
☐ UR-BXM	McDonnell-Douglas MD-82	49505/1381	ex G-CEPD	>IRB [ARN]
☐ UR-CGS	McDonnell-Douglas MD-82	49425/1240	ex G-CEPA	>IRB
☐ UR-CGT	McDonnell-Douglas MD-82	49428/1241	ex G-CEPB	>IRB
☐ UR-CHW	McDonnell-Douglas MD-82	49510/1514	ex S5-ACY	>IRA

☐ UR-CHX	McDonnell-Douglas MD-82	53162/2010	ex S5-ACZ	>IRA
☐ UR-CHZ	McDonnell-Douglas MD-82	53169/2063	ex G-CEPI	>IRB
☐ UR-CJA	McDonnell-Douglas MD-82	49277/1181	ex LZ-LDR	wfs
☐ UR-CJQ	McDonnell-Douglas MD-82	49502/1300	ex G-CEPC	>IRB
☐ UR-CJZ	McDonnell-Douglas MD-82	49506/1400	ex G-CEPE	>IRA
☐ UR-BXN	McDonnell-Douglas MD-83	49569/1405	ex LZ-LDV	>IRK

CAVOK AIRLINES

☐ UR-CCP	Antonov An-12AP	2340505	ex LZ-CBM	♦
☐ UR-CJN	Antonov An-12B	01348007	ex EK-12006	
☐ UR-CKL	Antonov An-12BK	01348005	ex EX-169	
☐ UR-CKM	Antonov An-12BP	02348207	ex UP-AN211	
☐ UR-CNN	Antonov An-12B	7345004	ex EW-394TI	♦
☐ UR-CKC	Antonov An74TK-100	36547095905	ex ER-AUL	

CHALLENGE AERO

☐ UR-CLH	Yakovlev Yak-40	9530642	ex RA-87541	
☐ UR-RTS	Yakovlev Yak-40	9530541	ex 4L-EUN	

CONSTANTA AIRLINES Constanta (UZA) Zaporozhye (OZH)

☐ UR-ALM	Yakovlev Yak-40K	9741756	ex UR-CAR	VIP
☐ UR-FRU	Yakovlev Yak-40	9440737	ex RA-87211	VIP opf Sumy Frunze

DART AIRLINES (DAT) Kiev-Zhulyany (IEV)

☐ UR-CEL	McDonnell-Douglas MD-83	49390/1269	ex XU-ZAA	>SAW♦
☐ UR-CHL	McDonnell-Douglas MD-83	49395/1286	ex XU-U4E	♦
☐ UR-CNJ	Airbus A320-211	0311	ex YL-LCE	>IZG♦
☐ UR-CNK	Airbus A320-212	0426	ex YL-LCH	>IZG♦
☐ UR-CNO	Airbus A320-212	0395	ex ZS-DJD	>IZG♦
☐ UR-CNU	Airbus A320-212	0525	ex EI-DXY	>SAW♦

DNIPROAVIA Dniepro (Z6/UDN) Dnepropetrovsk-Kodaki (DNK)

☐ UR-DNA	Embraer ERJ-145EU	145088	ex G-EMBF	wfs
☐ UR-DNB	Embraer ERJ-145EU	145094	ex G-EMBG	[KBP]
☐ UR-DNE	Embraer ERJ-145EU	145357	ex G-EMBS	[CFE]
☐ UR-DNF	Embraer ERJ-145EU	145404	ex G-EMBT	
☐ UR-DNG	Embraer ERJ-145EP	145394	ex G-ERJG	
☐ UR-DNI	Embraer ERJ-145EP	145325	ex G-ERJF	[WAW]
☐ UR-DNL	Embraer ERJ-145EU	145042	ex G-EMBE	wfs
☐ UR-DNN	Embraer ERJ-145LR	145665	ex I-EXMH	[WAW]
☐ UR-DNO	Embraer ERJ-145EP	145237	ex G-ERJB	[WAW]
☐ UR-DNP	Embraer ERJ-145EP	145290	ex G-ERJD	
☐ UR-DNQ	Embraer ERJ-145EP	145315	ex G-ERJE	[WAW]
☐ UR-DNS	Embraer ERJ-145LR	145652	ex I-EXMG	wfs
☐ UR-DNT	Embraer ERJ-145LR	145709	ex SE-RAG	
☐ UR-DNU	Embraer ERJ-145LR	145738	ex I-EXMM	wfs
☐ UR-DNV	Embraer ERJ-145LR	145445	ex F-WKXF	wfs
☐ UR-DNW	Embraer ERJ-145LR	145316	ex I-EXMU	[WAW]
☐ UR-DNZ	Embraer ERJ-145LR	145436	ex F-WKXL	
☐ UR-DPA	Embraer ERJ-145LR	145330	ex F-WKXM	wfs
☐ UR-DPB	Embraer ERJ-145LR	145250	ex F-WKXI	
☐ UR-DNH	Boeing 737-5Y0	24696/1960	ex N246ST	wfs

EAST CLIPPER

☐ UR-AKP	Yakovlev Yak-40	9120817	ex Serbia 71502	

EUROPE AIR

☐ UR-EAA	Ilyushin Il-76TD	0033446350	ex UP-I7625	♦

KHARKIV AIRLINES Larisa (KW/KHK) Kharkov (HRK)

Ops temporarily suspended 31Mar15

KHORS AIR Aircompany Khors (KO/KHO) Kiev-Borispol (KBP)

☐ UR-CBN	McDonnell-Douglas MD-82	49490/1352	ex N72830	♦
☐ UR-CEL	McDonnell-Douglas MD-83	49390/1269	ex XU-ZAA	>KCA
☐ UR-CHL	McDonnell-Douglas MD-83	49395/1286	ex XU-U4E	>KCA
☐ UR-CHO	McDonnell-Douglas MD-82	53231/2107	ex N597BC	[THR]
☐ UR-CJE	McDonnell-Douglas MD-83	49857/1687	ex SX-BTF	[THR]

□ UR-NAC	Learjet 60		60-016	ex UR-CHH	

MERIDIAN/CARGO AIR CHARTERING		**(MEM)**			**Poltava (PLV)**
□ UR-BAB	Antonov An-26B-100		11603	ex UR-26077	
□ UR-CHT	Antonov An-26B		77305901	ex UR-VIV	
□ UR-MDA	Antonov An-26-100		87307108		

MOTOR SICH AIRLINES		**Motor Sich (M9/MSI)**			**Zaporozhye (OZH)**
□ UR-MSA	Mil Mi-2		547620042		
□ UR-MSC	Mil Mi-2		549509115		
□ UR-MSD	Mil Mi-2		547619042		
□ UR-MSE	Mil Mi-2		549437105		
□ UR-MSG	Mil Mi-2		514424095		
□ UR-MSH	Mil Mi-2		547746082	ex 12 yellow	♦
□ UR-MSS	Mil Mi-2		549434105		♦
□ UR-MST	Mil Mi-2		549132035	ex UR-BBF	♦
□ UR-MSV	Mil Mi-2		549716046		♦
□ UR-BXC	Antonov An-24RV		37308902	ex UR-46636	
□ UR-MSB	Mil Mi-8MSB		9732911		
□ UR-MSF	Mil Mi-8MSB		9744312		
□ UR-MSI	Antonov An-24RV		27307608	ex UR-47699	
□ UR-11316	Antonov An-12BK		9346810	ex RA-11316	
□ UR-11819	Antonov An-12BP		6344009	ex CCCP-11819	no titles
□ UR-14005	Antonov An-140		36525305021		
□ UR-14007	Antonov An-140-100		36525305029		
□ UR-42410	Yakovlev Yak-42D		4520421219029	ex UP-Y4205	[OZH]
□ UR-47297	Antonov An-24RV		07306610	ex CCCP-47297	
□ UR-74026	Antonov An-74TK-200		36547096919	ex HK-3810X	opf UN
□ UR-87215	Yakovlev Yak-40		9510540	ex OK-FEJ	
□ UR-88310	Yakovlev Yak-40		9940760	ex 5R-MUB	

MRK AIRLINES		**Aviamars (6V/MRW)**			**Kiev-Borispol (KBP)**
□ UR-CGQ	SAAB SF.340A		340A-097	ex N771DF	
□ UR-CGR	SAAB SF-340A		340A-124	ex N340JW	

SHOVKOVIY SHLYAH		**Way Aero (S8/SWW)**			**Kiev-Zhulyany (IEV)**
□ UR-CAF	Antonov An-12BP		3341209	ex 4K-AZ56	
□ UR-CGX	Antonov An-12BP		5343510	ex 4K-AZ60	

SOUTH AIRLINES		**Southline (YG/OTL)**			**Odessa-Tsentralny (ODS)**
□ EK-73755	Boeing 737-229C (Nordam 3)		21139/437	ex EX-050	
□ UR-47256	Antonov An-24RV		27307708	ex CCCP-47256	

STATE AVIATION ENTERPRISE UKRAINE					**Kiev-Borispol (KBP)**
□ UR-AWB	Antonov An-74TK-300		36547098984	ex UR-YVA	
□ UR-PAA	Mil Mi-8MTV-1		804M01		
□ UR-PAB	Mil Mi-8MTV-1		804M02		
□ UR-65556	Tupolev Tu-134A-3		66372	ex CCCP-65556	
□ UR-65718	Tupolev Tu-134A-3		63668	ex CCCP-65718	
□ UR-86527	Ilyushin Il-62M		4037758	ex CCCP-86527	
□ UR-86528	Ilyushin Il-62M		4038111	ex CCCP-86528	

UKRAINE AIRALLIANCE		**Ukraine Alliance (UKL)**			**Kiev-Borispol (KBP)**
□ UR-CAH	Antonov An-12BK		8345604	ex ER-AXX	
□ UR-CAJ	Antonov An-12BK		8346106	ex ER-AXZ	
□ UR-CAK	Antonov An-12BP		6343707	ex ER-ACI	
□ UR-CGV	Antonov An-12BP		6344610	ex EW-266TI	
□ UR-CGW	Antonov An-12B		402410	ex EW-265TI	

UKRAINE INTERNATIONAL AIRLINES		**Ukraine International (PS/AUI)**			**Kiev-Borispol (KBP)**
□ UR-GAK	Boeing 737-5Y0/W		26075/2374	ex PT-SLN	
□ UR-GAS	Boeing 737-528/W		25236/2443	ex S5-AAM	
□ UR-GAT	Boeing 737-528/W		25237/2464	ex F-GJNM	
□ UR-GAU	Boeing 737-5Y0/W		25182/2211	ex N182GE	
□ UR-GAW	Boeing 737-5Y0/W		24898/2079	ex N898ED	
□ UR-GBC	Boeing 737-5L9/W		28722/2868	ex UR-DND	
□ UR-GBE	Boeing 737-548/W		24968/1975	ex UR-AAK	
□ UR-GBF	Boeing 737-548/W		24919/1970	ex UR-AAM	
□ UR-PSA	Boeing 737-8HX/W		29658/2970	ex N1787B	
□ UR-PSB	Boeing 737-8HX/W		29654/3018		
□ UR-PSC	Boeing 737-8HX/W		29662/3182	ex N1787B	

☐ UR-PSD	Boeing 737-8HX/W	29686/3259		
☐ UR-PSE	Boeing 737-84R/W	38119/3962	ex UR-AAN	
☐ UR-PSF	Boeing 737-84R/W	38120/4018	ex UR-AAO	♦
☐ UR-PSG	Boeing 737-85R	29038/297	ex VT-JNJ	
☐ UR-PSH	Boeing 737-85R	29040/465	ex VT-JNM	
☐ UR-EMA	Embraer ERJ-190LR	19000494	ex UR-DSA	
☐ UR-EMB	Embraer ERJ-190LR	19000501	ex UR-DSB	
☐ UR-EMC	Embraer ERJ-190LR	19000589	ex PT-THT	
☐ UR-EMD	Embraer ERJ-190LR	19000602	ex PT-TIZ	
☐ UR-EME	Embraer ERJ-190LR	19000608	ex PT-TJW	
☐ UR-FAA	Boeing 737-3Y0SF	24462/1691	ex N105KH	
☐ UR-GAH	Boeing 737-32Q/W	29130/3105	ex N1779B	Mayrni
☐ UR-GAO	Boeing 737-4Z9	25147/2043	ex OE-LNH	
☐ UR-GBA	Boeing 737-36N/W	28670/2948	ex OO-VEX	
☐ UR-GBD	Boeing 737-36Q/W	28659/2680	ex UR-DNJ	
☐ UR-GEA	Boeing 767-322ER/W	25280/391	ex UR-DNM	
☐ UR-GEB	Boeing 767-33AER/W	25530/414	ex UR-AAI	wfs
☐ UR-GEC	Boeing 767-33AER/W	25533/454	ex UR-AAJ	[IEV]
☐ UR-GED	Boeing 767-33AER/W	25536/504	ex UR-VVV	[BUD]
☐ UR-PSI	Boeing 737-9KVER/W	41534/4524	ex N60697	
☐ UR-PSJ	Boeing 737-9KVER/W	41535/4654		
☐ UR-PSK	Boeing 737-94XER/W	36086/2910	ex TC-SKN	
☐ UR-PSL	Boeing 737-94XER/W	36087/2928	ex TC-SKP	

UM AIR   Mediterranee Ukraine (UF/UKM)   Kiev-Borispol (KBP)

☐ UR-CHY	McDonnell-Douglas MD-82	53171/2067	ex G-CEPK	>IRM
☐ UR-CJW	Avro 146-RJ100	E3358	ex SX-DMC	>IRM
☐ UR-CKJ	Avro 146-RJ100	E3343	ex SX-DMB	>IRM
☐ UR-CKN	McDonnell-Douglas MD-83	53186/2092	ex YR-HBB	♦
☐ UR-CKX	British Aerospace 146 Srs.300	E3131	ex LZ-HBE	>IRM
☐ UR-CNE	Boeing 737-505	24828/1925	ex N828DG	<BAY♦

UNIVERSAL AVIA   Kharkiv Universal (HBU)   Rivnu (RWN)

☐ UR-CWD	Mil Mi8MTV-1	95662	ex UR-25514	♦
☐ UR-CWE	Mil Mi-8T	98730521	ex UR-24225	♦
☐ UR-67439	LET L-410UVP	841204	ex YL-KAH	

UTAIR UKRAINE   (UTN)

☐ UR-UTE	ATR 42-300	057	ex VP-BCG	wfs
☐ UR-UTP	Boeing 737-8Q8	28226/77	ex EI-EZP	
☐ UR-UTQ	Boeing 737-83N/W	30679/1404	ex B-2865	
☐ UR-UTR	Boeing 737-8Q8/W	28215/75	ex N806SY	
☐ UR-UTX	Canadair CRJ-200LR	7119	ex VQ-BGI	wfs
☐ UR-UTY	Canadair CRJ-100LR	7122	ex VQ-BGK	[CGN]
☐ UR-UTZ	Canadair CRJ-100LR	7121	ex VQ-BGJ	[CGN]

WINDROSE AIR   Wind Rose (7W/WRC)   Kiev-Borispol (BPL)

☐ UR-DNR	Embraer ERJ-145LR	145641	ex F-WKXA	
☐ UR-WRE	McDonnell-Douglas MD-82	49278/1183	ex UR-CDA	>Canadian AW Congo
☐ UR-WRH	Airbus A321-231	2462	ex G-TTID	>ABQ
☐ UR-WRI	Airbus A321-231	2682	ex G-TTIE	
☐ UR-WRJ	Airbus A321-231	1869	ex UR-DAT	>ABQ
☐ UR-WRK	Airbus A320-212	0235	ex UR-DAE	
☐ UR-WRM	Airbus A320-212	0645	ex UR-DAI	
☐ UR-WRO	Airbus A321-211	0781	ex G-OOPH	>ABQ
☐ UR-WRQ	Airbus A330-223	296	ex OE-ICN	

YAN AIR   (YE/ANR)   Kiev-Zhulyany (IEV)

☐ UR-CJU	McDonnell-Douglas MD-83	49631/1596	ex XU-703	♦
☐ UR-CME	Airbus A320-212	0671	ex N503NU	<EAA>ERT♦
☐ UR-CMK	Airbus A320-212	0445	ex EX-32001	>KMF♦
☐ UR-CNF	Boeing 737-3Z0	27126/2370	ex N295AL	♦
☐ UR-VNP	Boeing 737-4Y0	23980/1667	ex EY-538	♦
☐ UR-YAB	SAAB SF.340A	340A-134	ex OE-GIR	
☐ UR-YAC	SAAB SF.340A	340A-153	ex OE-GOD	
☐ UR-YAD	Airbus A320-211	0726	ex N281LF	

YUZMASHAVIA   Dnepropetrovsk-Kodaki (DNK)

☐ UR-78785	Ilyushin Il-76TD	0083489691	ex RA-78785	
☐ UR-78786	Ilyushin Il-76TD	0083490693	ex CCCP-78786	
☐ UR-87951	Yakovlev Yak-40K	9810957	ex CCCP-87951	

ZETAVIA | Zetavia (ZK/ZAV)

☐ UR-CID	Ilyushin Il-76TD	0063465956	ex EK-76640
☐ UR-CIE	Ilyushin Il-76T	093420594	ex EK-76633(2)
☐ UR-CIF	Ilyushin Il-76TD	1023412395	ex EK-76677(2)
☐ UR-CIU	Ilyushin Il-76TD	0053458741	ex RA-76628
☐ UR-CIV	Ilyushin Il-76TD	0083471147	ex UP-I7642
☐ UR-CMB	Ilyushin Il-76TD	0033446325	ex ER-IAD

VH-   AUSTRALIA (Commonwealth of Australia)

AD-ASTRAL AVIATION SERVICES | Perth International, WA (PER)

☐ VH-FWA	Beech 1900C	UB-61	ex N818BE
☐ VH-KFN	Beech 1900C-1	UC-173	ex N412CM
☐ VH-NOA	Beech 1900D	UE-94	ex PK-OCW
☐ VH-VOA	Beech 1900C	UB-62	ex ZS-NAV

ADAGOLD AVIATION | Brisbane (BNE)

Uses Air Tahiti Nui A340s on Defence Force charters

ADVANCE AVIATION | Emerald, QLD (EMD)

☐ VH-BCQ	Piper PA-31-350 Chieftain	31-7952134	ex N35265
☐ VH-FLL	Cessna 208 Caravan I	20800359	ex N908KA
☐ VH-FLZ	Beech Baron 58	TH-274	ex VH-OTP
☐ VH-FWJ	Piper PA-31 Navajo C	31-7712092	ex ZK-PNX
☐ VH-LWW	Piper PA-31 Navajo C	31-8112034	ex VH-NMT
☐ VH-TQC	Cessna 210N Centurion	21063325	ex N44ZP

AEROLINK AIR SERVICES | Sydney-Bankstown, NSA (BWU)

☐ VH-OZF	Embraer EMB.110P2 Bandeirante	110201	ex G-EIIO	[MBH]
☐ VH-SIN	Piper PA-31 Navajo	31-785	ex N7418L	
☐ VH-WBR	Embraer EMB.110P2 Bandeirante	110292	ex DQ-WBI	
☐ VH-XMA	Cessna 310R	310R0628	ex N31HS	

AIR FRASER ISLAND | Harvey Bay, QLD (HVB)

☐ VH-ATP	Piper PA-31-350 Chieftain	31-7405447	ex N61404
☐ VH-BFS	GippsAero GA-8 Airvan	GA8-03-035	
☐ VH-BNX	GippsAero GA-8 Airvan	GA8-03-032	
☐ VH-RDZ	Cessna 402A	402A0125	ex ZK-CSX

AIR FRONTIER | Darwin, NT (DRW)

☐ VH-AKG	Beech Baron 58	TH-1011	ex N2070D	
☐ VH-CMH	Beech Baron 58	TH-108	ex VH-HWQ	
☐ VH-DMD	Beech Baron 58	TH-1294	ex N1839Y	
☐ VH-HMF	Beech Baron 58	TH-196	ex N9335Q	
☐ VH-PRH	Beech Baron 58	TH-380	ex N3013W	
☐ VH-XGF	Beech Baron 58	TH-379	ex N3078V	
☐ VH-BNZ	Cessna 210N Centurion	210N64837	ex N4911U	
☐ VH-DCX	Cessna 210N Centurion	210N62990	ex (N6414N)	
☐ VH-MCE	Cessna 210M Centurion	210M62633	ex N761YV	
☐ VH-MDU	Cessna 210M Centurion	210M61634	ex (N732NB)	♦
☐ VH-MOK	Cessna 210R Centurion	210R64933	ex N6306U	
☐ VH-RQD	Cessna 210M Centurion	210M61693	ex N1775C	
☐ VH-SGX	Cessna 210N Centurion	210N64684	ex N1307U	
☐ VH-UBK	Cessna 210L Centurion	210L59512	ex N4612Q	
☐ VH-VIG	Cessna 210N Centurion	210N63714	ex N5197C	♦
☐ VH-WRD	Cessna 210M Centurion	210M62942	ex (N4738Y)	
☐ VH-XRJ	Cessna 210M Centurion	210M62012	ex N7363M	
☐ VH-DMF	Piper PA-31/A1 Navajo	31-447	ex N6483L	
☐ VH-JMD	Piper PA-31-350 Chieftain	31-7401260	ex VH-SOW	
☐ VH-LHE	Piper PA-31-350 Chieftain	31-7305028	ex N2GG	
☐ VH-PDN	Piper PA-31 Navajo	31-177	ex N9131Y	
☐ VH-RNG	Piper PA-31-350 Chieftain	31-7852142	ex N27713	
☐ VH-VTR	Piper PA-31-350 Chieftain	31-7952165	ex VH-MYF	
☐ VH-WYY	Piper PA-31 Navajo	31-657	ex VH-WZN	
☐ VH-GWH	Grumman G-21A Goose	B-49	ex N121GL	
☐ VH-JBH	Beech 65-B80 Queen Air	LD-443	ex VH-AMQ	
☐ VH-MHL	Cessna 207	20700059	ex N91076	♦
☐ VH-MRH	Beech 65-B80 Queen Air	LD-456	ex VH-BQA	
☐ VH-SKJ	Cessna 404	0086	ex VH-BPO	
☐ VH-SKW	Cessna 404	0042	ex VH-PNY	

☐ VH-TFP	Cessna 310R	310R1844	ex N59EX	
☐ VH-SWP	Beech 65-B80 Queen Air	LD-472	ex VH-MWK	
☐ VH-UBW	Cessna 207	20700137	ex N1537U	♦

AIR LINK (ZL) Dubbo, NSW (DBO)

☐ VH-BWQ	Cessna 310R	310R1401	ex N4915A
☐ VH-DVR	Piper PA-31-350 Chieftain	31-7952052	ex N27936
☐ VH-DVW	Piper PA-31-350 Chieftain	31-7952011	ex VH-LHH
☐ VH-HSL	Cessna 310R	310R0946	ex N8643G
☐ VH-JMP	Cessna 310R	310R1270	ex N125SP
☐ VH-MZF	Piper PA-31-350 Chieftain	31-8252039	ex N41064
☐ VH-RUE	Beech 1900D	UE-53	ex ZK-JNG
☐ VH-TDL	Piper PA-39 Twin Comanche C/R	39-152	ex VH-NHC

AIR MELBOURNE Melbourne-Moorabbin (MBW)

| ☐ VH-NPY | Agusta A109E | 11501 | ex N42-501 | ♦ |
| ☐ VH-XUM | Agusta A109E | 11684 | ex VH-BRB | ♦ |

AIR SOUTH REGIONAL Adelaide, SA (ADL)

☐ VH-LOA	Beech B200 Super King Air	BB-1463	ex ZS-PLK	
☐ VH-YEG	Embraer EMB.120ER Brasilia	120152	ex VH-NHC	♦
☐ VH-YOA	Beech 1900D	UE-143	ex ZS-SSX	
☐ VH-ZOA	Beech 1900D	UE-85	ex VH-VNT	

AIR WHITSUNDAY SEAPLANES (RWS) Whitsunday, QLD

☐ VH-AQV	de Havilland DHC-2 Beaver	1257	ex N67685	FP wfs
☐ VH-AWD	de Havilland DHC-2 Beaver	1066	ex VH-AYS	FP
☐ VH-AWI	de Havilland DHC-2 Beaver	298	ex VH-HQE	FP
☐ VH-AWY	de Havilland DHC-2 Beaver	1444	ex VH-SSG	FP
☐ VH-PGB	Cessna 208 Caravan I	20800346	ex N209E	FP
☐ VH-PGT	Cessna 208 Caravan I	20800345	ex N208E	FP

AIRLINES OF TASMANIA Hobart, TAS (HBA)

☐ VH-AEU	Britten-Norman BN-2B-26 Islander	2130	ex G-BJON	
☐ VH-BTD	Piper PA-31 Navajo C	31-7912041	ex VH-ATG	
☐ VH-BTI	Piper PA-31 Navajo C	31-8212003	ex ZK-VNA	
☐ VH-CCN	Cessna 404 Titan II	404-0801	ex VH-WZK	
☐ VH-EXC	Rockwell Commander 500B	3251	ex N57162	
☐ VH-LCD	Cessna U206G Stationair 6	20604523	ex N673AA	
☐ VH-LTW	Piper PA-31-350 Stationair 6	31-8152025	ex N40725	
☐ VH-MYS	Cessna U206G Stationair 6	20605162	ex N4921U	
☐ VH-OBL	Britten-Norman BN-2A-20 Islander	2035	ex ZK-OBL	
☐ VH-RQW	Britten-Norman BN-2A-26 Islander	73	ex P2-ALI	
☐ VH-RTP	Britten-Norman BN-2A-6 Islander	79	ex G-AXIN	♦
☐ VH-TZY	Piper PA-31-350 Chieftain	31-7405166	ex N622WR	
☐ VH-WZM	Cessna 404 Titan II	404-0837	ex N68075	

AIRNORTH REGIONAL Topend (TL/ANO) Darwin, NT

☐ VH-ANK	Embraer EMB.120ER Brasilia	120155	ex VH-YDD		
☐ VH-ANN	Embraer EMB.120ER Brasilia	120203	ex VH-BRP		
☐ VH-ANQ	Embraer EMB.120RT Brasilia	120079	ex VH-tfx		♦
☐ VH-ANZ	Embraer EMB.120RT Brasilia	120135	ex VH-XFR		
☐ VH-DIL	Embraer EMB.120ER Brasilia	120153	ex N285UE		
☐ VH-ANA	Swearingen SA227DC Metro 23	DC-871B	ex VH-HCB		
☐ VH-ANO	Embraer ERJ-170LR	17000099	ex B-KXB	Savannah	
☐ VH-ANT	Embraer ERJ-170LR	17000357	ex PT-TJI	Currajong	
☐ VH-ANV	Embraer ERJ-170LR	17000280	ex PT-TQG	Makikit Timor	
☐ VH-ANW	Swearingen SA227DC Metro 23	DC-873B	ex N3031Q		
☐ VH-ANY	Swearingen SA227DC Metro 23	DC-840B	ex N3022L		
☐ VH-SWO	Embraer ERJ-170LR	17000081	ex B-KXA		

ALLIANCE AIRLINES Alli (QQ/UTY) Brisbane-International, QLD (BNE)

☐ VH-FKO	Fokker 50	20160	ex OO-VLV	
☐ VH-FKP	Fokker 50	20161	ex VH-AHX	[ADL]
☐ VH-FKV	Fokker 50	20303	ex B-12273	
☐ VH-FKW	Fokker 50	20306	ex B-12275	
☐ VH-FKX	Fokker 50	20312	ex B-12276	
☐ VH-FKY	Fokker 50	20284	ex B-12271	
☐ VH-FKZ	Fokker 50	20286	ex B-12272	
☐ VH-JFB	Fokker 70	11521	ex HP-1731PST	
☐ VH-JFE	Fokker 70	11545	ex HP-1732PST	
☐ VH-NKH	Fokker 70	11549	ex OE-LFG	used for spares♦

☐ VH-NKU	Fokker 70	11555	ex OE-LFK	♦
☐ VH-NKZ	Fokker 70	11573	ex OE-LFL	used for spares♦
☐ VH-QQR	Fokker 70	11564	ex YR-KMA	
☐ VH-QQV	Fokker 70	11565	ex YR-KMB	
☐ VH-QQW	Fokker 70	11569	ex YR-KMC	
☐ VH-QQX	Fokker 70	11571	ex 9H-AFS	
☐ VH-QQY	Fokker 70	11575	ex 9H-AFZ	
☐ VH-FKA	Fokker 100	11345	ex N885US	
☐ VH-FKC	Fokker 100	11349	ex P2-ANB	
☐ VH-FKD	Fokker 100	11357	ex N888AU	
☐ VH-FKF	Fokker 100	11365	ex N890US	
☐ VH-FKG	Fokker 100	11366	ex N891US	
☐ VH-FKJ	Fokker 100	11372	ex N892US	
☐ VH-FKK	Fokker 100	11379	ex N894US	
☐ VH-FKL	Fokker 100	11380	ex N895US	[BNE]
☐ VH-FWH	Fokker 100	11316	ex G-BXNF	all white	>VAU
☐ VH-FWI	Fokker 100	11318	ex G-FIOR	all white
☐ VH-XWM	Fokker 100	11276	ex D-AGPA	
☐ VH-XWN	Fokker 100	11278	ex D-AGPB	
☐ VH-XWO	Fokker 100	11280	ex D-AGPC	
☐ VH-XWP	Fokker 100	11281	ex D-AGPD	
☐ VH-XWQ	Fokker 100	11300	ex D-AGPE	[BTS]
☐ VH-XWR	Fokker 100	11306	ex D-AGPG	
☐ VH-XWS	Fokker 100	11314	ex D-AGPL	
☐ VH-XWT	Fokker 100	11338	ox D-AGPQ	

ARNHEM LAND COMMUNITY AIRLINES/LAYNHA AIR   *Cairns, QLD (CNS)*

☐ VH-BPL	GippsAero GA-8 Airvan	GA8-07-117		
☐ VH-LHC	GippsAero GA-8 Airvan	GA8-04-057	ex VH-LHH	
☐ VH-LHD	GippsAero GA-8 Airvan	GA8-04-051	ex VH-SFX	
☐ VH-LHV	GippsAero GA-8 Airvan	GA8-04-045	ex VH-UAF	
☐ VH-MFA	GippsAero GA-8 Airvan	GA8-08-129	ex VH-BCE	
☐ VH-MFF	GippsAero GA-8 Airvan	GA8-06-100	ex P2-MFJ	
☐ VH-MFI	GippsAero GA-8 Airvan	GA8-04-065	ex P2-MFI	
☐ VH-MFX	GippsAero GA-8 Airvan	GA8-04-053	ex VH-TMN	
☐ VH-MQI	GippsAero GA-8-TC320 Airvan	GA8-10-154	ex VH-WOP	
☐ VH-MQR	GippsAero GA-8-TC320 Airvan	GA8-10-155	ex VH-WOG	
☐ VH-MTR	GippsAero GA-8 Airvan	GA8-05-073	ex PK-MPK	opb MAF
☐ VH-KBN	Cessna U206G Stationair	06630	ex N9731Z	
☐ VH-LHL	Cessna 210N Centurion	63739	ex VH-UBO	
☐ VH-LHQ	Cessna U206G Stationair	03773	ex VH-LGN	
☐ VH-LHX	Cessna U206G Stationair	03555	ex VH-STK	
☐ VH-UBV	Cessna U206G Stationair	05671	ex VH-WKH	♦

AUSTRALIAN HELICOPTERS   *Brisbane (BNE)*

☐ VH-CQJ	Bell 412EP	36374		based MKY
				opf Queensland Ambulance Svces
☐ VH-EPR	Bell 412EP	36204	ex VH-CFE	♦
☐ VH-LSY	Bell 412	36015	ex N555BA	opf AAAC
☐ VH-PXY	Bell 412EP	36434	ex C-GUNQ	♦
☐ VH-RHJ	Bell 412EP	36236		based Cooktown
☐ VH-VAO	Bell 412EP	36507	ex N358AB	opf Victoria Ambulance Svces
☐ VH-VAS	Bell 412EP	36504	ex N357JB	opf Victoria Ambulance Svces
☐ VH-VAU	Bell 412EP	36203	ex EC-KZM	opf Victoria Ambulance Svces
☐ VH-CWP	Aerospatiale AS350B3	4176		
☐ VH-HHO	Aerospatiale AS350BA AStar	2181	ex JA9803	based ADL
☐ VH-HPO	Aerospatiale AS350BA AStar	2186	ex RP-C1900	
☐ VH-HQO	Aerospatiale AS350BA AStar	1607	ex VH-HCF	
☐ VH-LSA	Agusta Bell AB412	25571	ex I-RECE	based ADL
☐ VH-LSV	Agusta Bell AB412	36015	ex ZK-HIU	opf AAAC
☐ VH-NDY	Bell 206B JetRanger III	3810	ex VH-BHY	opf Channel 7 News; based ADL
☐ VH-NPC	Hughes MD369E	0117E	ex ZK-HRQ	based Newcastle
☐ VH-NPH	Hughes MD369E	0352E	ex VH-WHC	based Newcastle
☐ VH-OSA	Eurocopter EC130B4	3968		based ADL
☐ VH-VSA	MBB BK117B-2	7186	ex SE-JUL	bsd ADL
☐ VH-YXF	AgustaWestland AW139	31591		opf Victoria Ambulance Svces♦

AVIAIR   *Kununurra, WA (KNX)*

☐ VH-KSA	Cessna 208B Caravan I	208B0516	ex N6302B	
☐ VH-LNH	Cessna 208B Caravan I	208B0590	ex N590TA	
☐ VH-LNN	Cessna 208B Caravan I	208B0801	ex 9M-PMB	
☐ VH-LNO	Cessna 208B Caravan I	208B0925	ex N125AR	
☐ VH-LWA	Cessna 208B Caravan I	208B1173		
☐ VH-TOV	Cessna 208B Caravan I	208B0769	ex VH-UZB	♦
☐ VH-TUY	Cessna 208B Caravan I	208B1200	ex P2-TZZ	
☐ VH-TWZ	Cessna 208B Caravan I	208B0648	ex VH-UZF	♦

| ☐ VH-FGH | GippsAero GA-8 Airvan | GA8-02-012 | ex VH-WOG |
| ☐ VH-RKD | Piper PA-31-350 Chieftain | 31-8152048 | ex N4076Z |

AVTEX AVIATION   Sydney-Bankstown, NSW (BWU)

| ☐ VH-MKK | Piper PA-31-350 Navajo Chieftain | 31-7652068 | ex VH-OZQ |
| ☐ VH-PGW | Piper PA-31P-350 Mojave | 31P-8414036 | ex N855MH |

BOND HELICOPTERS AUSTRALIA   Darwin, NT (DRW)

☐ VH-NWC	Eurocopter EC225LP Super Puma	2826	ex	
☐ VH-NWG	Eurocopter EC225LP Super Puma	2879	ex	
☐ VH-NWJ	Eurocopter EC225LP Super Puma	2944		♦
☐ VH-NYV	Aerospatiale AS332L Super Puma	2048	ex C-GOSE	
☐ VH-NYW	Sikorsky S-92A	920232	ex N232F	♦
☐ VH-NYX	Aerospatiale AS332L Super Puma	2007	ex C-FYZD	
☐ VH-NYZ	Sikorsky S-92A	920233	ex N233Q	♦

BRISTOW HELICOPTERS (AUSTRALIA)
Perth-Jandakot/Karratha/Barrow Island, WA/Darwin, NT (-/KTA/BWB/DRW)

☐ VH-BHH	Aérospatiale AS332L	2059	ex G-TIGW	
☐ VH-BHK	Aérospatiale AS332L	2096	ex G-TIGU	
☐ VH-BHX	Aérospatiale AS332L	2079	ex G-BRWE City of Albany	
☐ VH-BHY	Aérospatiale AS332L	2129	ex B-HZY	[KTA]
☐ VH-BXZ	Aérospatiale AS332L	2078	ex G-TIGT	
☐ VH-BYT	Aérospatiale AS332L	2083	ex G-CEYJ	
☐ VH-BYV	Aerospatiale AS332L	2061	ex G-TIGO	
☐ VH-BZC	Aérospatiale AS332L	2036	ex 9M-BEM	
☐ VH-BZU	Aérospatiale AS332L	2045	ex G-TIGM	
☐ VH-ZFB	Eurocopter EC225LP	2695	ex 9M-STX	
☐ VH-ZFC	Eurocopter EC225LP	2709	ex G-ZZSP	
☐ VH-ZFD	Eurocopter EC225LP	2724	ex G-CFZE	
☐ VH-ZFE	Eurocopter EC225LP	2728	ex G-CFZY	
☐ VH-ZFH	Eurocopter EC225LP	2723	ex G-ZZSH	
☐ VH-ZFK	Eurocopter EC225LP	2792	ex 9M-STI	
☐ VH-ZFL	Eurocopter EC225LP	2898	ex F-WJXD	♦
☐ VH-ZFS	Eurocopter EC225LP	2785	ex G-CGUA	♦
☐ VH-BKE	Kawasaki/MBB BK117B-2	1042	ex ZK-HLI	
☐ VH-BKK	Kawasaki/MBB BK117B-1	1044	ex JA9993	
☐ VH-TZI	Sikorsky S-76C++	760774	ex G-CGLS	
☐ VH-TZL	Sikorsky S-76C+	760735	ex G-CFPY	
☐ VH-TZR	Sikorsky S-76C+	760775	ex G-CGLU	
☐ VH-ZFJ	Sikorsky S-76C+	760733	ex G-CFPV	
☐ VH-ZFM	AgustaWestland AW139	41233	ex N370SH	
☐ VH-ZFN	AgustaWestland AW139	41228	ex N368SH	
☐ VH-ZFO	AgustaWestland AW139	41339	ex N433SH	
☐ VH-ZFP	AgustaWestland AW139	41370	ex N490SH	♦
☐ VH-ZUO	Sikorsky S-92A	920203		
☐ VH-ZUQ	Sikorsky S-92A	920205		
☐ VH-ZUV	Sikorsky S-92A	920219	ex N219X	♦
☐ VH-ZUW	Sikorsky S-92A	920221	ex N221ER	♦

BROOME AIR SERVICES   Broome, WA (BME)

☐ VH-CRN	Cessna 208B Caravan I	208B0428	ex VH-URT	
☐ VH-CVN	Cessna 208B Caravan I	208B0676	ex N12372	♦
☐ VH-LZK	Cessna 208B Caravan I	208B0991	ex N12374	♦
☐ VH-NCK	Cessna 208B Caravan I	208B1129	ex N229CF	
☐ VH-NFT	Cessna 208B Caravan I	208B1057	ex N990AM	♦
☐ VH-NTC	Cessna 208B Caravan I	208B0418	ex VH-DEX	♦
☐ VH-TLH	Cessna 208B Caravan I	208B0800	ex 9M-PMA	
☐ VH-AOI	Cessna 210N Centurion II	21064609	ex N9821Y	
☐ VH-AMG	Cessna 210N Centurion II	21064075	ex C-GTSW	
☐ VH-EGB	Cessna 210M Centurion II	21062858	ex N6969B	
☐ VH-FOK	Cessna 210N Centurion II	21063041	ex N6559N	
☐ VH-TWD	Cessna 210L Centurion II	21064356	ex N6372Y	
☐ VH-DMN	Beech Baron 58	TH-1103	ex VH-HUG	
☐ VH-ENT	Cessna 404 Titan II	404-0818	ex ZK-ECP	
☐ VH-KEZ	Cessna 402C	402C0262	ex N40BH	
☐ VH-LBB	Cessna 402C	402C0283	ex N470A	
☐ VH-MSM	Beech B200 Super King Air	BB-1464	ex N133LC	♦
☐ VH-MWX	Beech B200 Super King Air	BB-1424	ex N8236K	
☐ VH-OZO	Cessna 404 Titan II	404-0653	ex P2-ALG	♦
☐ VH-SKC	Cessna 404 Titan II	404-0404	ex VH-TWZ	
☐ VH-TDQ	Cessna U206F Stationair	20602801		
☐ VH-WSF	Beech Baron 58	TH-549	ex VH-WZG	
☐ VH-ZOR	Beech 200 Super King Air	BB-762	ex N762KA	

532

☐ VH-ZXM	Beech 200 Super King Air	BB-1470	ex LN-MOI	♦

BROOME AVIATION   Broome, WA (BME)

☐ VH-DZH	Cessna 210L Centurion II	21061247	ex VH-SJQ	
☐ VH-KDM	Cessna 210N Centurion II	21063041	ex N6467N	
☐ VH-KJL	Cessna 210L Centurion II	21060776	ex N1765C	
☐ VH-PBV	Cessna 210M Centurion II	21062350	ex N761LW	♦
☐ VH-SJG	Cessna 210L Centurion II	21063529	ex N6450A	
☐ VH-SKQ	Cessna 210L Centurion II	21061243	ex N1629C	
☐ VH-TCI	Cessna 210L Centurion II	21060548	ex N94225	
☐ VH-WTX	Cessna 210L Centurion II	21060222	ex (N93025)	
☐ VH-BBU	Cessna U206G Stationair	20604109	ex N756HS	
☐ VH-DAW	Cessna 310R II	310R0148	ex N5028J	
☐ VH-DLF	Cessna 404	404-0683	ex N6763K	
☐ VH-JOR	Cessna 404	404-0642	ex D-IEEE	
☐ VH-MOV	Cessna 208 Caravan I	20800369	ex N5257C	Floatplane♦
☐ VH-NUX	Cessna 208 Caravan I	20800334	ex N76EA	♦
☐ VH-PGA	Cessna 208 Caravan I	20800312	ex N1127W	Floatplane♦
☐ VH-SHZ	Cessna U206G Stationair	U206G03726	ex (N9909N)	
☐ VH-TLD	Cessna 208B Caravan I	208B0339	ex P2-TSJ	

CAIRNS SEAPLANES   Cairns, QLD (CNS)

☐ VH-CXS	de Havilland DHC-2 Beaver	1360	ex N211AW	FP

CARE FLIGHT   (CFH)   Sydney/Darwin/Katherine/Gove (SYD/DRW/KTH/GOV)

☐ VH-ZCI	Beech B200 Super King Air	BB-1875	ex VH-WJY	
☐ VH-ZCJ	Beech B200 Super King Air	BB1853	ex N93RR	
☐ VH-ZCN	Beech B200 Super King Air	BB-1987	ex N987KA	
☐ VH-ZCO	Beech B200 Super King Air	BB-1955	ex N215ML	
☐ VH-ZCY	Beech B200 Super King Air	BB-1459	ex LN-MOD	
☐ VH-LWI	Bell 412EP	36573	ex C-GKSY	based SYD
☐ VH-XCF	Bell 412	33019		
☐ VH-XCI	Bell 412EP	36397	ex VT-AZN	
☐ VH-XCK	Bell 412EP	36398	ex C-FHWU	
☐ VH-XCN	Bell 412HP	36023	ex C-GBKI	
☐ VH-XCO	Bell 412HP	36022	ex VH-ESA	
☐ VH-XCY	Bell 412EP	36402	ex C-GLGP	
☐ VH-BIF	Kawasaki BK117B-2	1084	ex ZK-IFB	based SYD
☐ VH-BKV	Kawasaki BK117B-2	1109	ex JA01CJ	♦
☐ VH-CXJ	Learjet 45	152	ex N33013Q	
☐ VH-EHQ	MBB BK117C-1	7502	ex N911RR	♦
☐ VH-EIG	Beech 400XP	RK-406	ex N140QS	based DRW♦
☐ VH-IME	Kawasaki BK117B-2	1097	ex JA6684	based SYD
☐ VH-VVI	Learjet 45	262		
☐ VH-XCE	Aérospatiale AS350BA Ecureuil	2649	ex VH-CMS	
☐ VH-XCW	Bell 230	23019	ex VH-XCQ	
☐ VH-YHF	AgustaWestland AW139	31108	ex VH-ESJ	based DRW
☐ VH-ZCF	Agusta A109E	11122	ex VH-IAG	
Ops medical flights for NSW, NT and Queensland Governments				

CASAIR   Perth-International, WA (PER)

☐ VH-KGX	Swearingen SA226TC Metro II	TC-326	ex VH-UUK	
☐ VH-NGX	Swearingen SA226TC Metro II	TC-287	ex VH-WGV	
☐ VH-OGX	Swearingen SA226TC Metro II	TC-395	ex VH-TFQ	
☐ VH-WGX	Swearingen SA226TC Metro II	TC-312	ex N1015B	
☐ VH-ZGX	Swearingen SA227TT Merlin III	TT-534	ex N90GT	
☐ VH-SWT	Beech 58 Baron	TH-560	ex N9380S	

CATALINA AIRLINES   Perth-International, WA (PER)

☐ VH-NMO	Grumman G-111 Albatross	148329	ex N42MY	
☐ VH-OPH	Cessna 208 Caravan	20800157	ex N501P	

CHARTAIR   Alice Springs, NT (ASP)

☐ VH-JJN	Beech 58 Baron	TH-1276	ex N3837M	
☐ VH-KEW	Beech 58 Baron	TH-803	ex N23877	♦
☐ VH-MLB	Beech 58 Baron	TH-1675	ex N81215	♦
☐ VH-SMW	Beech 58 Baron	TH-694	ex N6076S	
☐ VH-WZT	Beech 58 Baron	TH-542	ex VH-TYR	
☐ VH-BYK	Cessna 210L Centurion	21060435	ex N2691W	
☐ VH-HZL	Cessna 210N Centurion	21063276	ex N9SA	
☐ VH-IDZ	Cessna 210M Centurion II	21062530	ex N761UN	
☐ VH-JLC	Cessna 210N Centurion II	21063490	ex VH-OKH	

☐ VH-KST	Cessna 210M Centurion II	21062521	ex ZK-KLG	
☐ VH-LPO	Cessna 210L Centurion	21060489	ex VH-YEH	♦
☐ VH-LTB	Cessna 210N Centurion II	21064679	ex N670A	
☐ VH-NQP	Cessna 210N Centurion II	21064572	ex N9678Y	
☐ VH-OKJ	Cessna 210M Centurion II	21061602	ex VH-FZO	
☐ VH-RDH	Cessna 210N Centurion II	21065374	ex N5427Y	
☐ VH-SYT	Cessna 210L Centurion	21061052	ex N2086S	
☐ VH-TFF	Cessna 210N Centurion	21064277	ex N6169Y	♦
☐ VH-TFL	Cessna 210M Centurion II	21063678	ex N671AA	
☐ VH-TWP	Cessna 210M Centurion II	21061841	ex N1636C	
☐ VH-WMP	Cessna 210M Centurion II	21062731	ex N6278B	
☐ VH-BPI	Cessna 310R	310R0936	ex N8556G	♦
☐ VH-COQ	Cessna 310R	310R1643	ex N2635Y	
☐ VH-JZW	Cessna 310R	310R0073	ex N8213Q	
☐ VH-LJF	Cessna 310R	310R0691	ex N41TV	
☐ VH-PBI	Cessna 310R	310R0831	ex N3423G	
☐ VH-XXT	Cessna 310R	310R1617	ex N2631B	
☐ VH-CAJ	Cessna 402C II	402C0026	ex N5717C	
☐ VH-CYT	Cessna 402C	402C0293	ex VH-OKZ	
☐ VH-HOR	Cessna 402C	402C0108	ex P2-KSR	
☐ VH-LAE	Cessna 402C	402C0097	ex N2614Z	
☐ VH-NGP	Cessna 402C	402C0644	ex N644MA	
☐ VH-NMQ	Cessna 402C	402C0451	ex VH-RMQ	
☐ VH-OVU	Cessna 402C	402C0802	ex V5-VAC	
☐ VH-TFM	Cessna 402C II	402C0067	ex N2610Y	
☐ VH-TZH	Cessna 402C II	402C0617	ex N6880Y	
☐ VH-UCD	Cessna 402C II	402C0049	ex N5825C	
☐ VH-FTW	Beech 95-B55 Baron	TC-2123	ex N24097	
☐ VH-JFO	Cessna 441	441-0126	ex N337C	♦
☐ VH-JFU	Cessna 441	4410-158	ex N3TK	
☐ VH-JLT	Cessna 441	4410138	ex VH-KUZ	
☐ VH-NGC	Cessna 208B Caravan I	208B0916	ex VH-SMH	
☐ VH-NGK	Cessna 208B Caravan I	208B1203	ex HB-CZE	
☐ VH-OCS	Cessna 441	441-0030	ex N441MM	
☐ VH-TPK	Cessna U206G Stationair	U206G04599	ex N9949M	
☐ VH-TYH	Cessna 208B Caravan I	208B2045	ex N308TC	
☐ VH-TYQ	Cessna 208B Caravan I	208B2050	ex N309TC	

CHC HELICOPTERS (AUSTRALIA)	Hems (HEM)			Adelaide-International, SA (ADL)
☐ VH-LAF	Aérospatiale AS332L1	2319	ex LN-OBT	<CHC Scotia
☐ VH-LHG	Aérospatiale AS332L1	2317	ex LN-OBR	
☐ VH-LHH	Aérospatiale AS332L1	2407	ex 9M-STU	<CHC Intl
☐ VH-LHJ	Aérospatiale AS332L	2063	ex G-BSOI	
☐ VH-LOF	Aérospatiale AS332L	2058	ex G-CDSV	<CHC Intl
☐ VH-LOJ	Aérospatiale AS332L	2312	ex C-FWPE	<CHC Intl
☐ VH-LYH	Aérospatiale AS332L	2468	ex C-GGKX	
☐ VH-LYI	Aérospatiale AS332L	2381	ex C-GGKY	
☐ VH-LYP	Aérospatiale AS332L	9008	ex C-GOSA	
☐ VH-SRU	Eurocopter EC225LP	2910		♦
☐ VH-TQP	Eurocopter EC225LP	2851	ex G-ITAV	
☐ VH-TQU	Eurocopter EC225LP	2827	ex G-YRKE	
☐ VH-TQV	Eurocopter EC225LP	2848		
☐ VH-WEV	Eurocopter EC225LP	2768	ex G-NNCY	
☐ VH-WEX	Eurocopter EC225LP	2775	ex G-CMJK	
☐ VH-WGV	Eurocopter EC225LP	2794		
☐ VH-WSO	Eurocopter EC225LP	2779		
☐ VH-PXE	AgustaWestland AW139	41311	ex N426SH	
☐ VH-PXF	AgustaWestland AW139	31444	ex G-SNSC	
☐ VH-SYJ	AgustaWestland AW139	31114		opf NSW Air Ambulance
☐ VH-SYV	AgustaWestland AW139	31126		opf NSW Air Ambulance
☐ VH-SYZ	AgustaWestland AW139	31155		opf NSW Air Ambulance
☐ VH-WEJ	AgustaWestland AW139	31319	ex G-CGRG	
☐ VH-WEK	AgustaWestland AW139	31320	ex G-CGRH	
☐ VH-EPH	Bell 412EP	36419	ex N3070R	opf NSW Air Ambulance
☐ VH-EPK	Bell 412EP	36100	ex N412HH	opf NSW Air Ambulance
☐ VH-EWA	Bell 412EP	36312	ex C-GUOP	
☐ VH-NSC	Bell 412	33029	ex VH-CRQ	EMS, based CBR
☐ VH-NSP	Bell 412	33091	ex N22976	EMS
☐ VH-VAA	Bell 412EP	36274	ex C-GLZM	opf Victoria Ambulance Sve
☐ VH-VAB	Bell 412EP	36275		opf Victoria Ambulance Sve
☐ VH-HRP	Sikorsky S-76A+	760122	ex N176CH	based East Sale opf RAAF
☐ VH-LAH	Sikorsky S-76A+	760089	ex RJAF 725	based NTL
☐ VH-LAI	Sikorsky S-76A+	760103	ex RJAF 727	
☐ VH-LHN	Sikorsky S-76A++	760300	ex B-HZE	
☐ VH-LHY	Sikorsky S-76A+	760105	ex RJAF 729	based Pearce
☐ VH-LHZ	Sikorsky S-76A+	760113	ex RJAF 732	RAAF rescue

☐ VH-LOH	Sikorsky S-92A	920036	ex N8068D	Alice	
☐ VH-LYX	Sikorsky S-92A	920198			
☐ VH-PVD	Aérosapatiale SA.365N3 Dauphin	6846	ex F-WWOK		based MEN
☐ VH-PVE	Eurocopter EC135T2	0834			based MEN
☐ VH-PVG	Aérospatiale SA.365N3 Dauphin 2	6539	ex (HB-XQS)		based MEN
☐ VH-PVH	Aérospatiale AS365N3 Dauphin 2	6604	ex F-WQDC		based MEN
☐ VH-SYB	Eurocopter EC145+	9203	ex D-HMBZ		
☐ VH-SYG	Eurocopter EC145+	9235	ex D-HMBJ		

COBHAM AVIATION SERVICES AUSTRALIA   National Jet (NC/NJS)   Adelaide-International, SA (ADL)

☐ VH-NJH	Avro 146-RJ100	E3301	ex G-BXAS		
☐ VH-NJI	Avro 146-RJ100	E3265	ex VH-NBK		
☐ VH-NJP	Avro 146-RJ100	E3354	ex G-BZAW		
☐ VH-NJQ	Avro 146-RJ100	E3328	ex G-BZAU		
☐ VH-NJU	Avro 146-RJ85	E2287	ex G-CIKF		o/o♦
☐ VH-NJW	Avro 146-RJ85	E2329	ex G-CDYK		♦
☐ VH-NJY	Avro 146-RJ100	E3331	ex G-BZAV		
☐ VH-NXD	Boeing 717-23S	55062/5031	ex VH-VQD		
☐ VH-NXE	Boeing 717-23S	55063/5034	ex VH-VQE		
☐ VH-NXG	Boeing 717-2K9	55057/5020	ex VH-LAX		
☐ VH-NXH	Boeing 717-2K9	55055/5014	ex VH-IMD		
☐ VH-NXI	Boeing 717-2K9	55054/5013	ex VH-IMP		
☐ VH-NXJ	Boeing 717-2BL	55166/5116	ex N902ME		
☐ VH-NXK	Boeing 717-231	55092/5077	ex VH-YQF		
☐ VH-NXL	Boeing 717-231	55093/5083	ex VH-YQG		
☐ VH-NXM	Boeing 717-231	55094/5084	ex VH-YQH		
☐ VH-NXN	Boeing 717-231	55095/5087	ex VH-YQI		
☐ VH-NXO	Boeing 717-231	55096/5093	ex VH-YQJ		
☐ VH-NXQ	Boeing 717-231	55097/5095	ex VH-YQK		
☐ VH-NXR	Boeing 717-2BL	55168/5116	ex N904ME		
☐ VH-YQS	Boeing 717-2BL	55178/5128	ex N406BC		
☐ VH-YQT	Boeing 717-2BL	55179/5129	ex N917ME		
☐ VH-YQU	Boeing 717-2BL	55180/5132	ex N795BC		
☐ VH-YQV	Boeing 717-2BL	55193/5153	ex N927ME		
☐ VH-YQW	Boeing 717-2BL	55194/5154	ex N928ME	The Tassie Devil	
☐ VH-NJC	British Aerospace 146 Srs.100	E1013	ex G-6-013		
☐ VH-NJF	British Aerospace 146 Srs.300QT	E3198	ex G-BTLD		
☐ VH-NJG	British Aerospace 146 Srs.200	E2170	ex G-BSOH		
☐ VH-NJL	British Aerospace 146 Srs.300QT	E3213	ex G-BVPE		
☐ VH-NJM	British Aerospace 146 Srs.300QT	E3194	ex G-BTHT		
☐ VH-NJN	British Aerospace 146 Srs.300	E3217	ex G-BUHW		
☐ VH-NJR	British Aerospace 146 Srs.100	E1152	ex G-BRLN		
☐ VH-NJV	British Aerospace 146 Srs.100QT	E1002	ex G-BSTA		
☐ VH-NJZ	British Aerospace 146 Srs.300QT	E3126	ex G-BPNT		
☐ VH-YAE	British Aerospace 146 Srs.200	E2107	ex N294UE		
☐ VH-LCL	de Havilland DHC-8-202Q	492	ex C-GEOA		opf RAN
☐ VH-ZZA	de Havilland DHC-8-202MPA	419	ex C-FWWU		opf Custom Coastwatch
☐ VH-ZZB	de Havilland DHC-8-202MPA	424	ex C-FXBC		opf Custom Coastwatch
☐ VH-ZZC	de Havilland DHC-8-202MPA	433	ex C-FXFK		opf Custom Coastwatch
☐ VH-ZZE	de Havilland DHC-8Q-315MPA	640	ex C-FHQG		opf Custom Coastwatch
☐ VH-ZZF	de Havilland DHC-8Q-315MPA	643	ex C-FJKS		opf Custom Coastwatch
☐ VH-ZZG	de Havilland DHC-8Q-315MPA	644	ex C-FJKU		opf Custom Coastwatch
☐ VH-ZZI	de Havilland DHC-8-202MPA	550	ex C-GDLD		opf Custom Coastwatch
☐ VH-ZZJ	de Havilland DHC-8-202MPA	551	ex C-FDHI		opf Custom Coastwatch
☐ VH-ZZN	de Havilland DHC-8-315	399	ex VH-JSQ		opf Custom Coastwatch
☐ VH-ZZP	de Havilland DHC-8-202	411	ex VH-JSH		
☐ VH-NJA	Embraer ERJ-190LR	19000404	ex D-AEMG		♦
☐ VH-YZE	Reims Cessna F406 Vigilant	F406-0076	ex VH-ZZE		opf Custom Coastwatch
☐ VH-YZF	Reims Cessna F406 Vigilant	F406-0078	ex VH-ZZF		opf Custom Coastwatch
☐ VH-YZG	Reims Cessna F406 Vigilant	F406-0079	ex VH-ZZG		opf Custom Coastwatch

CORPORATE AIR   Goulburn, NSW (GUL)

☐ VH-VED	Cessna 441 Conquest II	441-0272	ex N394G		
☐ VH-VEH	Cessna 441 Conquest II	441-0238	ex N3NC		
☐ VH-VEJ	Cessna 441 Conquest II	441-0249	ex N911ER		
☐ VH-VEW	Cessna 441 Conquest II	441-0264	ex C-FWCP		
☐ VH-VEY	Cessna 441 Conquest II	441-0295	ex N181MD		
☐ VH-VEZ	Cessna 441 Conquest II	441-0182	ex VH-AZB		
☐ VH-VEA	Cessna 404 Titan II	404-0219	ex VH-ARQ		
☐ VH-VEB	Beech Baron 58	TH-399	ex VH-CYT		
☐ VH-VEC	Cessna 404 Titan II	404-0217	ex VH-CSV		
☐ VH-VEF	SAAB SF.340B	340B-408	erx VH-VNX		♦
☐ VH-VEG	Beech Baron 58	TH-822	ex VH-WIM		
☐ VH-VEK	Swearingen SA227DC Metro 23	DC-845B	ex VH-KED		
☐ VH-VEM	SAAB SF.340B	340B-364	ex C-GMNM		

☐ VH-VEO	SAAB SF.340B	340B-366	ex C-FTJV
☐ VH-VEP	SAAB SF.340B	340B-377	ex C-FTJW
☐ VH-VER	Cessna 404	4040611	ex VH-BUY
☐ VH-VEU	Swearingen SA227TC Metro 23	DC-797B	ex VH-KDJ

DE BRUIN AIR · Mount Gambier, SA (MGB)

☐ VH-OAE	British Aerospace Jetstream 32EP	851	ex N851JX
☐ VH-OAM	British Aerospace Jetstream 32EP	859	ex N859AE
☐ VH-OAV	Vulcanair P.68C	460/C	
☐ VH-OTX	Piper PA-60 Aerostar 602P	62P-0879-8165015 ex N6891M

EASTERN AUSTRALIA AIRLINES · (EAQ) · Sydney-Kingsford Smith, NSW (SYD)

A wholly-owned subsidiary of Qantas and ops scheduled services in full colours as QantasLink

EXPRESS FREIGHTERS AUSTRALIA · (EFA) · Sydney-Kingsford Smith, NSW (SYD)

☐ VH-XMB	Boeing 737-376SF	23478/1251	ex ZK-JNG	opf QF Freight
☐ VH-XML	Boeing 737-376SF	23486/1286	ex ZK-JNF	opf QF Freight
☐ VH-XMO	Boeing 737-376SF	23488/1352	ex ZK-JNH	opf QF Freight
☐ VH-XMR	Boeing 737-376SF	23490/1390	ex ZK-JNA	opf QF Freight
☐ VH-EFR	Boeing 767-381F	33510/939	ex N324MY	opf QF Freight

GAM AIR SERVICES · Melbourne-Essendon, VIC (MEB)

☐ VH-DZC	Rockwell 500S Shrike Commander	3226	ex G-BDAL
☐ VH-KAK	Rockwell 500S Shrike Commander	3269	ex N57163
☐ VH-LTP	Rockwell 500S Shrike Commander	3323	ex N12RS
☐ VH-MEH	Rockwell 500S Shrike Commander	3258	ex N57213
☐ VH-UJI	Rockwell 500S Shrike Commander	3301	ex VH-TWS
☐ VH-UJL	Rockwell 500S Shrike Commander	3088	ex N9120N
☐ VH-UJM	Rockwell 500S Shrike Commander	3117	ex N5007H
☐ VH-UJN	Rockwell 500S Shrike Commander	3151	ex ZS-NRO
☐ VH-UJR	Rockwell 500S Shrike Commander	3311	ex VH-PAR
☐ VH-UJS	Rockwell 500S Shrike Commander	1797-12	ex VH-EXF
☐ VH-UJU	Rockwell 500S Shrike Commander	3055	ex VH-PWO
☐ VH-UJV	Rockwell 500S Shrike Commander	3161	ex N712PC
☐ VH-UJX	Aero Commander 500S Shrike	1839-31	ex VH-EXI
☐ VH-YJC	Rockwell 500S Shrike Commander	3176	ex VH-ACZ
☐ VH-YJJ	Rockwell 500S Shrike Commander	3178	ex VH-ACJ
☐ VH-YJL	Aero Commander 500S Shrike	1875-48	ex VH-ACL
☐ VH-YJM	Rockwell 500S Shrike Commander	3186	ex RP-C1268
☐ VH-YJO	Aero Commander 500B	1506-180	ex VH-WRU
☐ VH-YJR	Rockwell 500S Shrike Commander	3231	ex VH-PCO
☐ VH-YJS	Rockwell 500S Shrike Commander	3315	ex VH-FGS
☐ VH-YJU	Aero Commander 500U Shrike	1765-49	ex F-ODHD

☐ VH-AAG	Aero Commander 690A	11101	ex N57101
☐ VH-NBT	Rockwell Commander 681B	6047	ex VH-NYE
☐ VH-PCV	Rockwell 690ATurbo Commander	11283	ex N57228
☐ VH-UJA	Aero Commander 680FL	1521-100	ex PK-MAG
☐ VH-VJD	Dornier 228-202K	8157	ex D2-EBT
☐ VH-VJE	Dornier 228-202	8041	ex 5N-DOC
☐ VH-VJJ	Dornier 228-202	8025	ex 5N-DOA
☐ VH-VJN	Dornier 228-202	8040	ex V7-0811
☐ VH-YJA	Aero Commander 680FL	1734-140	ex RP-C699

GOLD COAST SEAPLANES · Coolangatta, QLD (OOL)

| ☐ VH-IDO | de Havilland DHC-2 Beaver | 1545 | | FP |

GOLDEN EAGLE AIRLINES · Port Hedland, WA (PHE)

☐ VH-FML	Piper PA-31 Navajo C	31-8112015	ex N40540
☐ VH-KTS	Piper PA-31 Navajo C	31-7912014	ex N27833
☐ VH-NMK	Piper PA-31-350 Chieftain	31-8152163	ex P2-RHA
☐ VH-NPA	Piper PA-31-350 Chieftain	31-8452016	ex N41171
☐ VH-PJY	Cessna U206G Stationair 6 II	U20605120	ex N4829U

GOLDFIELDS AIR SERVICES · (GOS) · Kalgoorlie, WA (KGI)

☐ VH-LNX	Cessna 402C	402C0295	ex ZS-LNX	
☐ VH-KFX	Beech B200 Super King Air	BB-1862	ex N225WC	♦
☐ VH-NTE	Beech 200 Super King Air	BB-529	ex VH-SWP	
☐ VH-NTG	Beech B200C Super King Air	BL-9	ex VH-KZL	
☐ VH-NTS	Beech B200C Super King Air	BL-30	ex VH-TNQ	
☐ VH-OOT	Cessna 310R	1635	ex VH-PEE	
☐ VH-TSI	Cessna 402C	402C0492	ex N6841L	♦
☐ VH-TUZ	Beech B60 Duke	P-578	ex N3834N	
☐ VH-UFD	Beech A60 Duke	P-237	ex N1869W	

GREAT WESTERN AVIATION   Brisbane, QLD (BNE)

☐ VH-DEH	Piper PA-31 Turbo Navajo C	31-7812123	ex N27792
☐ VH-FMO	Piper PA-31 Navajo	31-8012052	ex N35574
☐ VH-FMU	Piper PA-31 Navajo	31-8212015	ex N41033
☐ VH-KTU	Piper PA-31 Turbo Navajo C	31-7912079	ex N35301
☐ VH-NAD	Piper PA-31 Navajo	31-8212004	ex N4099T
☐ VH-OMM	Piper PA-31-350	31-8152153	ex N4091B
☐ VH-SGV	Beech 200 Super King Air	BB-718	ex N6728N
☐ VH-XGV	Beech 200 Super King Air	BB-1230	ex N224P

HARDY AVIATION   Darwin, NT (DRW)

☐ VH-ANM	Cessna 404 Titan II	404-0010	ex VH-BPM	
☐ VH-ANP	Cessna 404 Titan II	404-0064	ex N404MP	
☐ VH-HAZ	Cessna 404 Titan II	404-0046	ex G-BYLR	
☐ VH-HMA	Cessna 404 Titan II	404-0122	ex N37158	
☐ VH-HVR	Cessna 404 Titan II	404-0673	ex N404MT	
☐ VH-SZP	Cessna 404 Titan II	404-0637	ex ZS-OVU	
☐ VH-UOP	Cessna 404 Titan II	404-0636	ex N5280J	
☐ VH-AZW	Cessna 441 Conquest II	441-0028	ex VH-FWA	
☐ VH-JVB	Cessna 441 Conquest	441-0231	ex N441YA	
☐ VH-JVE	Cessna 441 Conquest	441-0068	ex N3WM	
☐ VH-JVN	Cessna 441 Conquest	441-0247	ex N5HG	
☐ VH-JVY	Cessna 441 Conquest	441-0074	ex N441RK	
☐ VH-ANS	Cessna 210M Centurion II	21062784	ex N784ED	
☐ VH-ARJ	Cessna 402B	402B0629	ex N3784C	[DRW]
☐ VH-ASN	Embraer EMB.120ER Brasilia	120056	ex N334JS	
☐ VH-BEM	Cessna 402B	404B0590	ex N402HA	
☐ VH-CNH	Swearingen SA227DC Metro 23	DC-899B	ex YV-256T	
☐ VH-HPA	Cessna U206G Stationair 6	U20605002	ex VH-WIW	
☐ VH-HVH	Swearingen SA227DC Metro 23	DC-886B	ex N3006M	
☐ VH-JZL	Cessna TU206G Stationair 6	U20604721	ex N732TS	
☐ VH-MJN	Cessna 210M Centurion	21061888	ex N732YU	
☐ VH-MKS	Swearingen SA226TC Metro II	TC-262	ex N49GW	
☐ VH-MMA	Douglas DC-3	9593	ex VH-MWQ	
☐ VH-MNH	Beech Baron 58	TH-1137	ex N67249	
☐ VH-NOK	Cessna 210M Centurion II	21062063	ex N9127M	
☐ VH-RAP	Cessna U206F Stationair	U20602989	ex VH-DXU	
☐ VH-RUY	Cessna 402C	402C0273	ex N1774G	
☐ VH-SGO	Beech 58 Baron	TH-1185	ex N3702D	
☐ VH-SQL	Cessna 402C II	402C0326	ex VH-OAS	
☐ VH-TFG	Swearingen SA227AC Metro III	AC-504	ex N31072	
☐ VH-TGD	Swearingen SA227AC Metro III	AC-667B	ex C-FAFS	
☐ VH-XSM	Beech E55 Baron	TE-804	ex P2-COE	

HELIWEST   Perth, WA (PER)

☐ VH-BHO	Bell 206L3 LongRanger	51354	ex JA9893	
☐ VH-BHT	Bell 206L1 LongRanger	45223	ex N4643E	
☐ VH-CYJ	Bell 206L3 LongRanger	51245	ex JA9767	
☐ VH-LHP	Bell 206L3 LongRanger	51002	ex G-CJCB	
☐ VH-ZHP	Bell 206L3 LongRanger	45308	ex N2774V	
☐ VH-ZWV	Bell 206L3 LongRanger	51040	ex N209RM	
☐ VH-XRA	MBB Bo.105LSA-3	2015	ex N31RX	
☐ VH-XRF	MBB Bo.105LSA-3	2032	ex N999SA	
☐ VH-XRG	MBB Bo.105LSA-3	2037	ex C-FRIQ	
☐ VH-XRI	MBB Bo.105LSA-3	2041	ex N404AB	
☐ VH-XRQ	MBB Bo.105LSA-3	2016	ex TC-HCR	
☐ VH-XRU	MBB Bo.105LSA-3	2043	ex HZ-SRC	
☐ VH-XRX	MBB Bo.105LSA-3	2033	ex N315LS	
☐ VH-XRU	MBB Bo.105LSA-3	2043	ex HZ-SRC	
☐ VH-BII	Aérospatiale AS350B2	2267	ex N13HF	
☐ VH-BIN	Bell 206B JetRanger III	2019	ex VH-UEE	
☐ VH-JVC	Aerospatiale AS350BA AStar	1516	ex P2-PHB	
☐ VH-LRW	Aérospatiale AS350B2	1819	ex N78KR	
☐ VH-NRW	Aérospatiale AS350B2	3232	ex N350JG	
☐ VH-RPK	Bell 206B JetRanger III	2626	ex VH-LAL	
☐ VH-VJG	Bell 206B JetRanger III	2169	ex 9M-AVM	
☐ VH-XSQ	Bell 427	56010	ex N378JC	
☐ VH-XWC	MBB BK.117B-2	7232	ex N911SX	♦
☐ VH-ZMN	Bell 206B JetRanger III	3591	ex VH-UPT	

HINTERLAND AVIATION   Hinterland (OI/HND)   Cairns, QLD (CNS)

☐ VH-ETF	Cessna 208B Caravan I	208B1175	ex G-GOTF

☐ VH-HJS	Beech B200 Super King Air	BB-1178	ex ZK-LRJ	♦
☐ VH-HLJ	Beech B200 Super King Air	BB-945	ex RP-C11577	
☐ VH-MRZ	Cessna 208B Caravan I	208B1048	ex N1266V	
☐ VH-TFK	Cessna 402C III	402C1011	ex VH-PVU	
☐ VH-TFO	Cessna 404 Titan II	404-0076	ex N32L	
☐ VH-TFQ	Cessna 208B Caravan I	208B1216	ex N84BP	
☐ VH-TFS	Cessna 208B Caravan I	208B1006	ex N1247N	
☐ VH-TFU	Cessna 404 Titan	404-0834	ex VH-SZO	
☐ VH-TFY	Cessna 310R	310R1213	ex VH-TQF	
☐ VH-TFZ	Cessna 402C II	402C0408	ex VH-RMI	
☐ VH-TSI	Cessna 402C	402C0492	ex N6841L	

HNZ AUSTRALIA   Karratha, WA (KTA)

☐ VH-NZQ	AgustaWestland AW109SP	22301		♦
☐ VH-NZU	AgustaWestland AW109SP	22281		♦
☐ VH-NZW	AgustaWestland AW109SP	22302		♦
☐ VH-WCD	Eurocopter AS350B3	3266	ex HB-ZBW	♦
☐ VH-WOE	Eurocopter AS350B2	2469	ex ZK-IBH	♦
☐ VH-WKA	Eurocopter EC145	9158	ex N315DD	♦
☐ VH-WKC	Eurocopter EC145	9209	ex N957AL	♦

JETGO AUSTRALIA   (JG/JGO)   Brisbane, QLD (BNE)

☐ VH-JGB	Embraer ERJ-135LR	145728	ex N135SZ	
☐ VH-JTG	Embraer ERJ-135LR	145687	ex XA-AMM	
☐ VH-JZG	Embraer ERJ-135LR	145713	ex N836RP	
☐ VH-ZJG	Embraer ERJ-140LR	145522	ex N297SK	o/o♦

JETSTAR AIRWAYS   Jetstar (JQ/JST)   Melbourne-Tullamarine, VIC (MEL)

☐ VH-JQG	Airbus A320-232	2169	ex F-WWDQ	
☐ VH-JQL	Airbus A320-232	2185	ex F-WWDB	
☐ VH-JQX	Airbus A320-232	2197	ex F-WWDH	
☐ VH-VFD	Airbus A320-232	4922	ex F-WWIK	
☐ VH-VFF	Airbus A320-232	5039	ex F-WWDG	
☐ VH-VFH	Airbus A320-232	5211	ex F-WWBN	
☐ VH-VFI	Airbus A320-232	5270	ex F-WWIF	
☐ VH-VFJ	Airbus A320-232	5311	ex F-WWBH	
☐ VH-VFK	Airbus A320-232	5334	ex D-AUBI	
☐ VH-VFL	Airbus A320-232/S	5489	ex F-WWDF	Little Athletics c/s
☐ VH-VFN	Airbus A320-232/S	5566	ex F-WWIP	Celebrating 100 aircraft c/s
☐ VH-VFO	Airbus A320-232/S	5631	ex D-AUBQ	
☐ VH-VFP	Airbus A320-232/S	5775	ex D-AXAA	
☐ VH-VFQ	Airbus A320-232/S	5780	ex D-AXAE	
☐ VH-VFT	Airbus A320-232/S	5532	ex (B-KJA)	
☐ VH-VFU	Airbus A320-232/S	5814	ex F-WWBK	
☐ VH-VFV	Airbus A320-232/S	5858	ex F-WWDE	
☐ VH-VFX	Airbus A320-232/S	5871	ex F-WWDM	
☐ VH-VFY	Airbus A320-232/S	6362	ex F-WWDG	♦
☐ VH-VGA	Airbus A320-232	4899	ex F-WWBS	
☐ VH-VGD	Airbus A320-232	4527	ex D-AXAJ	
☐ VH-VGF	Airbus A320-232	4497	ex F-WWIK	10th anniversary c/s
☐ VH-VGH	Airbus A320-232	4495	ex D-AUBK	
☐ VH-VGI	Airbus A320-232	4466	ex F-WWBU	
☐ VH-VGJ	Airbus A320-232	4460	ex F-WWBH	
☐ VH-VGN	Airbus A320-232	4434	ex D-AVVT	
☐ VH-VGO	Airbus A320-232	4356	ex D-AXAV	
☐ VH-VGP	Airbus A320-232	4343	ex F-WWBH	Powderfinger c/s
☐ VH-VGQ	Airbus A320-232	4303	ex F-WWDY	
☐ VH-VGR	Airbus A320-232	4257	ex F-WWIQ	
☐ VH-VGT	Airbus A320-232	4178	ex F-WWDZ	
☐ VH-VGU	Airbus A320-232	4245	ex F-WWDQ	
☐ VH-VGV	Airbus A320-232	4229	ex F-WWBU	
☐ VH-VGY	Airbus A320-232	4177	ex D-AVVW	
☐ VH-VGZ	Airbus A320-232	3917	ex F-WWBF	
☐ VH-VQA	Airbus A320-232	3783	ex F-WWIS	
☐ VH-VQC	Airbus A320-232	3668	ex F-WWID	
☐ VH-VQE	Airbus A320-232	3495	ex F-WWIJ	
☐ VH-VQF	Airbus A320-232	3474	ex F-WWDE	
☐ VH-VQG	Airbus A320-232	2787	ex F-WWBV	
☐ VH-VQH	Airbus A320-232	2766	ex F-WWDG	Go Roos c/s
☐ VH-VQJ	Airbus A320-232	2703	ex F-WWIS	
☐ VH-VQK	Airbus A320-232	2651	ex F-WWIM	
☐ VH-VQL	Airbus A320-232	2642	ex F-WWBZ	
☐ VH-VQM	Airbus A320-232	2608	ex F-WWBS	
☐ VH-VQP	Airbus A320-232	2573	ex F-WWBD	
☐ VH-VQQ	Airbus A320-232	2537	ex F-WWIJ	
☐ VH-VQR	Airbus A320-232	2526	ex F-WWDQ	
☐ VH-VQS	Airbus A320-232	2515	ex F-WWIE	
☐ VH-VQU	Airbus A320-232	2455	ex F-WWDJ	
☐ VH-VQW	Airbus A320-232	2329	ex F-WWDZ	

| ☐ VH-VQZ | Airbus A320-232 | 2292 | ex 9V-VQZ |
| ☐ VH-XSJ | Airbus A320-232/S | 5482 | ex 9V-JST |

☐ VH-VWT	Airbus A321-231	3717	ex D-AVZQ
☐ VH-VWU	Airbus A321-231	3948	ex D-AZAL
☐ VH-VWW	Airbus A321-231	3916	ex D-AVZX
☐ VH-VWX	Airbus A321-231	3899	ex D-AVZW
☐ VH-VWY	Airbus A321-231	1408	ex N584NK
☐ VH-VWZ	Airbus A321-231	1195	ex N583NK

☐ VH-VKA	Boeing 787-8	36227/123		
☐ VH-VKB	Boeing 787-8	36228/134	ex N1015X	
☐ VH-VKD	Boeing 787-8	36229/142		
☐ VH-VKE	Boeing 787-8	36230/162		
☐ VH-VKF	Boeing 787-8	36231/175		◆
☐ VH-VKG	Boeing 787-8	36232/189		◆
☐ VH-VKH	Boeing 787-8	36233/200		◆
☐ VH-VKI	Boeing 787-8	36235/257	ex N8571B	◆
☐ VH-VKJ	Boeing 787-8	36236/278		o/o◆
☐ VH-VKK	Boeing 787-8	36237/321		o/o◆
☐ VH-VKL	Boeing 787-8	36238/344		o/o◆

| ☐ VH-EBE | Airbus A330-202 | 842 | ex F-WWYV |
| ☐ VH-EBK | Airbus A330-202 | 945 | ex F-WWYV |

KAKADU AIR SERVICES   Jabiru, NT (JAB)

☐ VH-DZZ	Cessna 208 Caravan I	20800197	ex N708A	
☐ VH-KNA	GippsAero GA-8 Airvan	GA8-04-044	ex VH-IXN	
☐ VH-KNB	GippsAero GA-8 Airvan	GA8-07-109		
☐ VH-KNE	GippsAero GA-8 Airvan	GA8-08-133		
☐ VH-KNP	GippsAero GA-8 Airvan	GA8-04-063	ex VH-YAH	
☐ VH-KNQ	Cessna 208B Caravan I	208B2193	ex N2028N	
☐ VH-ZME	Cessna 402C	402C0422	ex N6787Z	
☐ VH-ZMG	Cessna 402C	402C0263	ex P2-SIB	◆

KARRATHA FLYING SERVICES   Karratha, WA (KTA)

☐ VH-KFE	Beech B200 Super King Air	BB-1172	ex VH-FDG
☐ VH-KFH	Beech B200 Super King Air	BB-1641	ex VH-HWO
☐ VH-KFX	Beech B200 Super King Air	BB-1862	ex N225WC
☐ VH-XFM	DHC-6 Twin Otter 200	164	ex P2-POM
☐ VH-ZKF	de Havilland DHC-6 Twin Otter 100	43	ex VH-TZL

KATHERINE AVIATION   Katherine, NT (KTR)

☐ VH-ECL	Beech Baron 58	TH-1078		
☐ VH-EDR	Beech Baron 58	TH-046	ex N4683A	◆
☐ VH-EYH	Beech Baron 58	TH-246	ex N1564W	◆
☐ VH-JCY	Beech Baron 58	TH-1295	ex N1851X	◆
☐ VH-OKB	Beech Baron 58	TH-602	ex VH-FER	◆
☐ VH-OKI	Beech Baron 58	TH-788	ex N4571S	◆
☐ VH-SDL	Beech Baron 58	TH-455	ex N4424W	◆

☐ VH-ARH	Cessna 210L Centurion	21060841	EX n5130v
☐ VH-DOB	Cessna 210L Centurion	21059658	ex N5158Q
☐ VH-FTM	Cesna 210L Centurion	21061159	ex N2198S
☐ VH-HGZ	Cessna T210L Centurion	21060430	ex N93843
☐ VH-HZN	Cessna 210N Centurion	21063975	ex N4667Y
☐ VH-MDZ	Cessna 210M Centurion	21061773	ex (N732TZ)
☐ VH-MLW	Cessna 210M Centurion	21062812	ex (N6667B)
☐ VH-NPL	Cessna 210N Centurion	21064037	ex N4903Y
☐ VH-TEV	Cessna 210L Centurion	21061374	ex N732AY
☐ VH-TLJ	Cessna 210N Centurion	21064151	ex N5284Y
☐ VH-UBL	Cessna 210N Centurion	21064712	ex N1638U
☐ VH-ZAC	Cessna T210N Centurion	21063688	ex N4954C

| ☐ VH-IGU | Cessna 402B | 4021070 | ex N1542G |
| ☐ VH-NQT | Beech 200 Super King Air | BB-305 | ex N11AB |

KIMBERLEY AIR   Kununurra, WA (KNS)

☐ VH-MBQ	Cessna 208 Caravan I	20800278	ex VH-NRP	
☐ VH-MGK	Cessna U206G Stationair	U206G03952	ex VH-SBA	◆
☐ VH-NLV	Cessna 210N Centurion	21063093	ex VH-APU	◆
☐ VH-SJW	Cessna 210M	21062219	ex N761FJ	
☐ VH-TFT	Cessna 210N	21063448	ex N5456A	
☐ VH-UBO	Gippsaero GA-8 Airvan	GA8-09-148		◆

KING ISLAND AIRLINES   Melbourne-Moorabbin, VIC (MBW)

| ☐ VH-KGQ | Embraer EMB.110P1 Bandeirante | 110221 | ex VH-XFD |

☐ VH-KIB	Piper PA-31-350 Navajo Chieftain	31-7305035	ex VH-TXD	
☐ VH-KIG	Piper PA-31-350 Chieftain	31-7852146	ex VH-HRL	
☐ VH-KIO	Piper PA-31-350 Navajo Chieftain	31-7405487	ex VH-DMV	
☐ VH-KIY	Piper PA-31-350 Chieftain	31-7952061	ex VH-KGN	

KJM AIR   Adelaide, SA (ADE)

| ☐ VH-KMS | Beech B200 Super King Air | BB-1667 | ex N968MB | |

MACHJET   Sunshine Coast (MCY)

☐ VH-JLU	Cessna S550 Citation II	S550-0076	ex N25DY	
☐ VH-MWZ	Beech B200 Super King Air	BB-1430	ex VH-MSM	
☐ VH-SIY	Cessna 525 CitationJet CJ-1	525-0002	ex N54BP	
☐ VH-WJK	Beech B200 Super King Air	BB-1083	ex VH-ZEK	

MAROOMBA AIRLINES   (KN)   Perth-International, WA (PER)

☐ VH-QQC	de Havilland DHC-8-102	008	ex VH-JSZ	<SKP
☐ VH-QQD	de Havilland DHC-8-102	245	ex S2-AAA	♦
☐ VH-QQG	de Havilland DHC-8-102	036	ex 5W-FAA	<SKP
☐ VH-QQK	de Havilland DHC-8-102	326	ex N846EX	♦
☐ VH-QQL	de Havilland DHC-8-102A	388	ex N825EX	♦
☐ VH-ITA	Beech B200 Super King Air	BB-1244	ex F-OINC	
☐ VH-MQZ	Beech B200 Super King Air	BB-1961	ex N74061	
☐ VH-RIO	Hawker 800XP*	258594	ex N323MP	opf RFDS
☐ VH-RIU	Hawker 800XP	258723	ex M-YCEF	♦

MILITARY SUPPORT SERVICES   Brisbane (BNE)

| ☐ VH-MQD | CASA C.212-200 | CC50-7-272 | ex N433CA | |
| ☐ VH-MQE | CASA C.212-200 | CD51-6-318 | ex N7241E | |

NETWORK AVIATION AUSTRALIA   Perth-International, WA (PER)

☐ VH-NHF	Fokker 100	11458	ex PH-AQD	
☐ VH-NHG	Fokker 100	11514	ex PH-ZFU	
☐ VH-NHI	Fokker 100	11479	ex PH-ZFZ	
☐ VH-NHJ	Fokker 100	11464	ex PH-ZFY	
☐ VH-NHK	Fokker 100	11465	ex PH-AQB	
☐ VH-NHM	Fokker 100	11449	ex PH-AQA	
☐ VH-NHN	Fokker 100	11469	ex PH-ZFX	
☐ VH-NHO	Fokker 100	11312	ex D-AGPJ	
☐ VH-NHP	Fokker 100	11399	ex D-AGPS	
☐ VH-NHQ	Fokker 100	11506	ex PH-ZFV	
☐ VH-NHV	Fokker 100	11482	ex PH-ZFW	
☐ VH-NQE	Fokker 100	11457	ex PH-AQC	
☐ VH-NHA	Embraer EMB.120ER Brasilia	120269	ex N209SW	wfs
☐ VH-NHY	Embraer EMB.120ER Brasilia	120054	ex VH-NIF	wfs

PEARL AVIATION   Perth-International, WA (PER)

☐ VH-FIX	Beech 350 King Air	FL-90	ex D-CKRA	Calibrator
☐ VH-FIY	Beech B300 King Air	FL-760	ex N8010C	
☐ VH-FIZ	Beech B350i King Air	FL-779	ex D-CAUB	
☐ VH-OYA	Beech 200 King Air	BB-365	ex P2-SML	
☐ VH-OYD	Beech B200 King Air	BB-1041	ex N200BK	
☐ VH-OYT	Beech 200T King Air	BT-6/BB-489	ex VH-PPJ	[BNE]
☐ VH-TLX	Beech 200 King Air	BB-550	ex P2-MBM	[DRW]
☐ VH-PPF	Dornier 328-110	3057	ex N439JS	
☐ VH-PPG	Dornier 328-110	3053	ex D-CIAB	
☐ VH-PPJ	Dornier 328-110	3059	ex D-CCAD	
☐ VH-PPQ	Dornier 328-110	3051	ex D-CEAD	
☐ VH-PPV	Dornier 328-110	3052	ex D-CDAD	

Rotate between DRW, MEB, BNE and PER

☐ VH-OYB	Swearingen SA227DC Metro 23	DC-848B	ex N452LA	
☐ VH-OYG	Swearingen SA227DC Metro 23	DC-875B	ex VH-SWM	
☐ VH-OYI	Swearingen SA227DC Metro 23	DC-839B	ex VH-DMI	
☐ VH-OYN	Swearingen SA227DC Metro 23	DC-870B	ex VH-DMO	

PEL-AIR   Pelflight (PFY)   Sydney Kingsford-Smith, NSW/Brisbane, QLD (SYD/BNE)

☐ VH-AJG	IAI 1124 Westwind	281	ex N1124F	
☐ VH-AJJ	IAI 1124 Westwind	248	ex N25RE	
☐ VH-AJP	IAI 1124 Westwind	238	ex 4X-CMJ	
☐ VH-AJV	IAI 1124 Westwind	282	ex N186G	
☐ VH-KNR	IAI 1124A Westwind II	340	ex N118MP	

☐ VH-KNS	IAI 1124 Westwind	323	ex N816H	
☐ VH-KNU	IAI 1124 Westwind	317	ex VH-UUZ	EMS
☐ VH-EKT	SAAB SF.340AF	340A-085	ex F-GGBJ	
☐ VH-KDB	SAAB SF.340AF	340A-008	ex PH-KJK	
☐ VH-KDK	SAAB SF.340AF	340A-016	ex SE-E16	
☐ VH-SLD	Learjet 35A	35A-145	ex (N166AG)	based Nowra; RAN fleet support
☐ VH-SLE	Learjet 35A	35A-428	ex N17LH	based Nowra; RAN fleet support
☐ VH-SLF	Learjet 36A	36A-049	ex N136ST	based Nowra; RAN fleet support
☐ VH-SLJ	Learjet 36	36-014	ex N200Y	based Nowra; RAN fleet support
☐ VH-VAD	Beech B200C Super King Air	BL-154	ex VH-ZKA	Victorian Ambulance Service
☐ VH-VAE	Beech B200C Super King Air	BL-155	ex VH-ZKB	Victorian Ambulance Service
☐ VH-VAH	Beech B200C Super King Air	BL-156	ex N6388B	Victorian Ambulance Service
☐ VH-VAI	Beech B200C Super King Air	BL-157	ex N6350V	Victorian Ambulance Service

PELICAN AIR — Sydney-Bankstown (BWU)

☐ VH-OTD	Britsh Aerospace Jetstream 32	978	ex G-BZYP	♦
☐ VH-OTE	British Aerospace Jetstream 32	980	ex G-CBEP	♦

POLAR AVIATION — Port Hedland, WA (PHE)

☐ VH-BIV	Cessna 210N Centurion II	21063398	ex N5373A	
☐ VH-BLW	Beech Baron 58	TH-490	ex N1349K	
☐ VH-CFL	Cessna 208B Caravan I	208B0434	ex N1203D	
☐ VH-ILD	Beech 95-E55 Baron	TE-788	ex N4055A	
☐ VH-NSM	Beech 58 Baron	TH-1798	ex N1098C	
☐ VH-NWT	Cessna 208B Caravan I	208B0733	ex N1269N	
☐ VH-YSS	Beech 58 Baron	TH-1583	ex N56569	

QANTAS AIRWAYS — Qantas (QF/QFA) — Sydney-Kingsford Smith, NSW (SYD)

Member of oneWorld

☐ VH-EBA	Airbus A330-202	508	ex F-WWKM	Cradle Mountain	♦
☐ VH-EBB	Airbus A330-202	522	ex F-WWYQ	Albany	♦
☐ VH-EBC	Airbus A330-202	506	ex F-WWYU	Surfers Paradise	♦
☐ VH-EBD	Airbus A330-202	513	ex F-WWYV	Traralgon	♦
☐ VH-EBF	Airbus A330-202	853	ex F-WWYU		♦
☐ VH-EBG	Airbus A330-203	887	ex F-WWKD	Barossa Valley	
☐ VH-EBH	Airbus A330-203	892	ex F-WWYT	Hunter Valley	
☐ VH-EBI	Airbus A330-203	898	ex F-WWKM	Yarra Valley	
☐ VH-EBJ	Airbus A330-202	940	ex F-WWKL	Margaret River	♦
☐ VH-EBL	Airbus A330-203	976	ex F-WWKU	Whitsundays	
☐ VH-EBM	Airbus A330-202	1061	ex F-WWKU	Tamar Valley	
☐ VH-EBN	Airbus A330-202	1094	ex F-WWKM	Clare Valley	
☐ VH-EBO	Airbus A330-202	1169	ex F-WWKJ	Kimberley	
☐ VH-EBP	Airbus A330-202	1174	ex F-WWKS	Ningaloo Reef	
☐ VH-EBQ	Airbus A330-202	1198	ex F-WWYZ	Wolgan Valley	
☐ VH-EBR	Airbus A330-202	1251	ex F-WWXK	Lockyer Valley	
☐ VH-EBS	Airbus A330-202	1258	ex F-WWYS	Swan Valley	
☐ VH-EBV	Airbus A330-202	1365	ex F-WWKN	Kangaroo Island	
☐ VH-QPA	Airbus A330-303	553	ex F-WWKS	Kununurra	
☐ VH-QPB	Airbus A330-303	558	ex F-WWYO	Freycinet Peninsula	
☐ VH-QPC	Airbus A330-303	564	ex F-WWYQ	Broken Hill	
☐ VH-QPD	Airbus A330-303	574	ex F-WWYU	Port Macquarie	
☐ VH-QPE	Airbus A330-303	593	ex F-WWKP	Port Lincoln	
☐ VH-QPF	Airbus A330-303	595	ex F-WWKR	Esperance	
☐ VH-QPG	Airbus A330-303	603	ex F-WWYN	Mount Gambier	
☐ VH-QPH	Airbus A330-303	695	ex F-WWYQ	Noosa	
☐ VH-QPI	Airbus A330-303	705	ex F-WWKG	Cairns	
☐ VH-QPJ	Airbus A330-303	712	ex F-WWYM	Port Stephens	
☐ VH-OQA	Airbus A380-842	014	ex F-WWSK	Nancy Bird Walton	
☐ VH-OQB	Airbus A380-842	015	ex F-WWSL	Hudson Fysh	
☐ VH-OQC	Airbus A380-842	022	ex F-WWSR	Paul McGinness	
☐ VH-OQD	Airbus A380-842	026	ex F-WWSX	Fergus McMaster	
☐ VH-OQE	Airbus A380-842	027	ex F-WWSY	Lawrence Hargrave	
☐ VH-OQF	Airbus A380-842	029	ex F-WWSA	Charles Kingsford Smith	
☐ VH-OQG	Airbus A380-842	047	ex F-WWAD	Charles Ulm	
☐ VH-OQH	Airbus A380-842	050	ex F-WWAE	Reginald Ansett	
☐ VH-OQI	Airbus A380-842	055	ex F-WWAP	David Warren	
☐ VH-OQJ	Airbus A380-842	062	ex F-WWAQ	Bert Hinkler	
☐ VH-OQK	Airbus A380-842	063	ex F-WWSK	John/Reginald Duigen	
☐ VH-OQL	Airbus A380-842	074	ex F-WWSL	Phyllis Arnott	
☐ VH-OQM	Airbus A380-842	091	ex F-WW		o/o
☐ VH-OQN	Airbus A380-842	1003	ex F-WW	Lester Brain	o/o♦
☐ VH-VXA	Boeing 737-838/W	29551/1042	ex (N979AN)	Broome	
☐ VH-VXB	Boeing 737-838/W	30101/1045	ex (N980AN)	Yananyi	
☐ VH-VXC	Boeing 737-838/W	30897/1049	ex (N981AN)	Gippsland	

☐ VH-VXD	Boeing 737-838/W	29552/1063	ex (N982AN)	Tenterfield	
☐ VH-VXE	Boeing 737-838/W	30899/1071	ex (N983AN)	Coffs Harbour	
☐ VH-VXF	Boeing 737-838/W	29553/1096	ex (N984AN)	Sunshine Coast	
☐ VH-VXG	Boeing 737-838/W	30901/1102	ex (N985AM)	Port Douglas	
☐ VH-VXH	Boeing 737-838/W	33478/1137	ex (N986AM)	Warrnambool	
☐ VH-VXI	Boeing 737-838/W	33479/1141	ex (N987AM)	Oonadatta	
☐ VH-VXJ	Boeing 737-838/W	33480/1157	ex (N988AM)	Coober Pedy	
☐ VH-VXK	Boeing 737-838/W	33481/1160	ex (N989AM)	Katherine	
☐ VH-VXL	Boeing 737-838/W	33482/1172		Charleville	
☐ VH-VXM	Boeing 737-838/W	33483/1177	ex N6055X	Mount Hotham	
☐ VH-VXN	Boeing 737-838/W	33484/1180		Freemantle	
☐ VH-VXO	Boeing 737-838/W	33485/1183		Kakadu	Prostate Cancer c/s
☐ VH-VXP	Boeing 737-838/W	33722/1324		Logan	
☐ VH-VXQ	Boeing 737-838/W	33723/1335		Redlands	
☐ VH-VXR	Boeing 737-838/W	33724/1340		Shepparton	
☐ VH-VXS	Boeing 737-838/W	33725/1352		St Helens	
☐ VH-VXT	Boeing 737-838/W	33760/1412	ex N1787B	Townsville	
☐ VH-VXU	Boeing 737-838/W	33761/1420		Wollongong	
☐ VH-VYA	Boeing 737-838/W	33762/1532		Narooma	
☐ VH-VYB	Boeing 737-838/W	33763/1534		Cape Otway	
☐ VH-VYC	Boeing 737-838/W	33991/1612		Arnhem Land	
☐ VH-VYD	Boeing 737-838/W	33992/1706		Eudunda	
☐ VH-VYE	Boeing 737-838/W	33993/1712	ex N1786B	Alice Springs	
☐ VH-VYF	Boeing 737-838/W	33994/1727	ex N1784B	Evandale	
☐ VH-VYG	Boeing 737-838/W	33995/1736	ex N6046P	Australind	
☐ VH-VYH	Boeing 737-838/W	34180/1815		Queanbeyan	
☐ VH-VYI	Boeing 737-838/W	34181/1840		Bathurst Island	
☐ VH-VYJ	Boeing 737-838/W	34182/1842	ex N1782B	Cann River	
☐ VH-VYK	Boeing 737-838/W	34183/1846	ex N1784B	Moree	
☐ VH-VYL	Boeing 737-838/W	34184/1854	ex N1786B	Wangaratta	
☐ VH-VZA	Boeing 737-838/W	34195/2502	ex N1779B	Port Augusta	
☐ VH-VZB	Boeing 737-838/W	34196/2623	ex N1786B	Lake Macquarie	
☐ VH-VZC	Boeing 737-838/W	34197/2649		Innisfail	
☐ VH-VZD	Boeing 737-838/W	34198/2659		Geelong	Optus c/s
☐ VH-VZE	Boeing 737-838/W	34199/2661	ex N1786B	Bunbury	
☐ VH-VZL	Boeing 737-838/W	34194/3621	ex N1787B	Newcastle	
☐ VH-VZM	Boeing 737-838/W	34192/3644		Bathurst	
☐ VH-VZO	Boeing 737-838/W	34191/3692	ex N1786B	Bendigo	
☐ VH-VZP	Boeing 737-383/W	39362/3714		Whyalla	
☐ VH-VZR	Boeing 737-838/W	34193/3754		Coral Bay	
☐ VH-VZS	Boeing 737-838/W	39358/3769		Tamworth	
☐ VH-VZT	Boeing 737-838/W	34186/3798		Kalgoorlie	
☐ VH-VZU	Boeing 737-838/W	34187/3826		Lorne	
☐ VH-VZV	Boeing 737-838/W	34189/3856		Palm Cove	
☐ VH-VZW	Boeing 737-838/W	39359/3881		Beaconfield	
☐ VH-VZY	Boeing 737-838/W	39363/3944		Temora	
☐ VH-VZX	Boeing 737-838/W	34188/3910		Daylesford	
☐ VH-VZZ	Boeing 737-838/W	39445/4010		Walpole	
☐ VH-XZA	Boeing 737-838/W	39367/4150		Leeton	
☐ VH-XZB	Boeing 737-838/W	39360/4192		Mudgee	
☐ VH-XZC	Boeing 737-838/W	39361/4199		Walwa	
☐ VH-XZD	Boeing 737-838/W	39368/4400		Moranbah	
☐ VH-XZE	Boeing 737-838/W	39369/4421		Pine Creek	
☐ VH-XZF	Boeing 737-838/W	39370/4450		Cygnet	
☐ VH-XZG	Boeing 737-838/W	39371/4477		Bungendore	
☐ VH-XZH	Boeing 737-838/W	39372/4521	ex N5573L	Mclaren Vale	
☐ VH-XZI	Boeing 737-838/W	39364/4630		Kalbarri	
☐ VH-XZJ	Boeing 737-838/W	39365/4669		Mendoowoorrji	Aboriginal c/s
☐ VH-XZK	Boeing 737-838/W	39366/4705		Cook	
☐ VH-XZL	Boeing 737-838/W	44573/5009		Flinders	
☐ VH-XZM	Boeing 737-838/W	44574/5018		Coonawarra	
☐ VH-XZN	Boeing 737-838/W	44575/5060		Wagga Wagga	
☐ VH-XZO	Boeing 737-838/W	44576/5108		Leichhardt	
☐ VH-XZP	Boeing 737-838/W	44577/5164		James Strong	retro c/s
☐ VH-OEB	Boeing 747-48E	25778/983	ex HL7416	Phillip Island	
☐ VH-OEE	Boeing 747-438ER	32909/1308	ex N747ER	Nullarbor	
☐ VH-OEF	Boeing 747-438ER	32910/1313	ex N60659	City of Sydney	
☐ VH-OEG	Boeing 747-438ER	32911/1320		Parkes	
☐ VH-OEH	Boeing 747-438ER	32912/1321	ex N5020K	Hervey Bay	
☐ VH-OEI	Boeing 747-438ER	32913/1330		Ceduna	
☐ VH-OEJ	Boeing 747-438ER	32914/1331	ex N60668	Wunala	
☐ VH-OJI	Boeing 747-438	24887/826	ex N6009F	Longreach	
☐ VH-OJM	Boeing 747-438	25245/875		Gosford	
☐ VH-OJS	Boeing 747-438	25564/1230		Hamilton Island	
☐ VH-OJT	Boeing 747-438	25565/1233		Fraser Island	
☐ VH-OJU	Boeing 747-438	25566/1239		Lord Howe Island	
☐ VH-OGG	Boeing 767-338ER	24929/343		City of Rockhampton	[VCV]
☐ VH-OGH	Boeing 767-338ER	24930/344		City of Parramatta	[VCV]
☐ VH-OGK	Boeing 767-338ER	25316/397	ex N6018N	Mackay	[VCV]
☐ VH-OGM	Boeing 767-338ER	25575/451		Bundaberg	[ASP]
☐ VH-OGO	Boeing 767-338ER	25577/550		Unity	[ASP]

☐ VH-OGP	Boeing 767-338ER	28153/615		Forbes	[VCV]
☐ VH-OGQ	Boeing 767-338ER	28154/623		Birdsville	[VCV]
☐ VH-OGR	Boeing 767-338ER	28724/662		Corowa	[ASP]
☐ VH-OGS	Boeing 767-338ER	28725/665		Roma	[ASP]
☐ VH-OGT	Boeing 767-338ER	29117/710		Maroochydore	[ASP]
☐ VH-OGU	Boeing 767-338ER	29118/713		Byron Bay	[ASP]
☐ VH-OGV	Boeing 767-338ER	30186/796			[VCV]

QANTAS FREIGHT (XM/XME) Brisbane (BNE)

☐ VH-EFR	Boeing 767-381F	33510	ex N324MY		opb EFA♦
☐ VH-NJF	British Aerospace146 Srs.300QT	E3198	ex G-BTLD		<NJS
☐ VH-NJM	British Aerospace146 Srs.300QT	E3194	ex G-BTHT		<NJS
☐ VH-NJV	British Aerospace146 Srs.100QC	E1002	ex G-BSTA		<NJS
☐ VH-XMB	Boeing 737-376F	23478	ex ZK-JNG		opb EFA
☐ VH-XML	Boeing 737-376F	23486	ex ZK-JNF	Qantas Freight c/s	opb EFA
☐ VH-XMO	Boeing 737-376F	23488	ex ZK-JNH		opb EFA
☐ VH-XMR	Boeing 737-376F	23490	ex ZK-JNA		opb EFA

QANTASLINK Q Link (QLK) various

☐ VH-TQG	de Havilland DHC-8-201	430	ex C-GDNG	Pixie Rourke	Eastern Australia
☐ VH-TQS	de Havilland DHC-8-202	418	ex 9M-EKB		Eastern Australia
☐ VH-TQX	de Havilland DHC-8-202	439	ex N439SD		Eastern Australia
☐ VH-SBB	de Havilland DHC-8-315Q	539	ex C-FDHO		Eastern Australia [TMW]
☐ VH-SBG	de Havilland DHC-8-315Q	575	ex C-GSAH		Eastern Australia
☐ VH-SBI	de Havilland DHC-8-315Q	605	ex C-FZKU		Eastern Australia
☐ VH-SBJ	de Havilland DHC-8-315Q	578	ex C-FDHI		Eastern Australia
☐ VH-SBT	de Havilland DHC-8-315Q	580	ex C-FDHP		Eastern Australia [TMW]
☐ VH-SBV	de Havilland DHC-8-315Q	595	ex C-GIHK		Eastern Australia
☐ VH-SBW	de Havilland DHC-8-315Q	599	ex C-GZPN		Eastern Australia
☐ VH-SCE	de Havilland DHC-8-315Q	602	ex C-GZPP		Eastern Australia
☐ VH-TQD	de Havilland DHC-8-315Q	598	ex C-GZDO		Eastern Australia
☐ VH-TQE	de Havilland DHC-8-315Q	596	ex C-GDOE		Eastern Australia
☐ VH-TQH	de Havilland DHC-8-315Q	597	ex C-GZDM		Eastern Australia
☐ VH-TQK	de Havilland DHC-8-315Q	600	ex C-GZPO		Eastern Australia
☐ VH-TQL	de Havilland DHC-8-315Q	603	ex C-GZPQ		Eastern Australia
☐ VH-TQM	de Havilland DHC-8-315Q	604	ex C-FZHW		Eastern Australia
☐ VH-TQY	de Havilland DHC-8-315Q	552	ex C-FDHP		Eastern Australia [TMW]
☐ VH-TQZ	de Havilland DHC-8-315Q	555	ex C-GDNK		Eastern Australia [TMW]
☐ VH-LQB	de Havilland DHC-8-402Q	4343	ex C-GGUK		Sunstate
☐ VH-LQD	de Havilland DHC-8-402Q	4371	ex C-GJFZ	City of Greater Geraldton	Sunstate
☐ VH-LQF	de Havilland DHC-8-402Q	4375	ex C-GJKV		Sunstate
☐ VH-LQG	de Havilland DHC-8-402Q	4376	ex C-GJLE	Town of Exmouth	Sunstate
☐ VH-LQH	de Havilland DHC-8-402Q	4431	ex C-GSZD		Sunstate
☐ VH-LQJ	de Havilland DHC-8-402Q	4414	ex C-GNZW		Sunstate
☐ VH-LQK	de Havilland DHC-8-402Q	4415	ex C-GOAO		Sunstate
☐ VH-LQL	de Havilland DHC-8-402Q	4449	ex C-GVRK		Sunstate
☐ VH-LQM	de Havilland DHC-8-402Q	4450	ex C-GVXE		Sunstate
☐ VH-LQQ	de Havilland DHC-8-402Q	4461	ex C-GWRF		Sunstate♦
☐ VH-QOA	de Havilland DHC-8-402Q	4112	ex C-FDHG	Gladstone:	Sunstate
☐ VH-QOB	de Havilland DHC-8-402Q	4116	ex C-FERF	Yeppoon	Sunstate
☐ VH-QOC	de Havilland DHC-8-402Q	4117	ex C-FFCD	Mackay	Sunstate
☐ VH-QOD	de Havilland DHC-8-402Q	4123	ex C-FFQL	Emerald	Sunstate
☐ VH-QOE	de Havilland DHC-8-402Q	4125	ex C-FFQE		Sunstate
☐ VH-QOF	de Havilland DHC-8-402Q	4128	ex C-FFQM		Sunstate
☐ VH-QOH	de Havilland DHC-8-402Q	4132	ex C-FGKH	Breast Cancer c/s	Sunstate
☐ VH-QOI	de Havilland DHC-8-402Q	4189	ex C-FNQL	Tamworth	Sunstate
☐ VH-QOJ	de Havilland DHC-8-402Q	4192	ex C-FNZU	Riverina	Sunstate
☐ VH-QOK	de Havilland DHC-8-402Q	4215	ex C-FQXU		Sunstate
☐ VH-QOM	de Havilland DHC-8-402Q	4217	ex C-FRLL		Sunstate
☐ VH-QON	de Havilland DHC-8-402Q	4218	ex C-FRLP		Sunstate
☐ VH-QOP	de Havilland DHC-8-402Q	4238	ex C-FUOI	Coffs Harbour	Sunstate
☐ VH-QOR	de Havilland DHC-8-402Q	4241	ex C-FUST	Eyre Peninsula	Sunstate
☐ VH-QOS	de Havilland DHC-8-402Q	4263	ex C-FXAZ	Mildura	Sunstate
☐ VH-QOT	de Havilland DHC-8-402Q	4269	ex C-FXYP		Sunstate
☐ VH-QOU	de Havilland DHC-8-402Q	4275	ex C-FYGQ		Sunstate
☐ VH-QOV	de Havilland DHC-8-402Q	4277	ex C-FYIC		Sunstate
☐ VH-QOW	de Havilland DHC-8-402Q	4285	ex C-FZFT	Taronga Zoo c/s	Sunstate
☐ VH-QOX	de Havilland DHC-8-402Q	4287	ex C-FZGC		Sunstate
☐ VH-QOY	de Havilland DHC-8-402Q	4288	ex C-FZGG		Sunstate

REX – REGIONAL EXPRESS (ZL/RXA) Orange, NSW/Wagga Wagga, NSW (OAG/WGA)

☐ VH-EKD	SAAB SF.340A	340A-155	ex SE-F55		[WGA]♦
☐ VH-EKH	SAAB SF.340B	340B-369	ex SE-C69		Sharkcage Diving c/s
☐ VH-EKX	SAAB SF.340B	340B-257	ex (F-GNVQ)		
☐ VH-KDQ	SAAB SF.340B	340B-325	ex SE-KVO		
☐ VH-KDV	SAAB SF.340B	340B-322	ex SE-KVN		
☐ VH-KRX	SAAB SF.340B	340B-290	ex N361BE		

☐	VH-NRX	SAAB SF.340B	340B-291	ex N362BE	
☐	VH-OLL	SAAB SF.340B	340B-175	ex N143NC	
☐	VH-OLM	SAAB SF.340B	340B-205	ex SE-G05	
☐	VH-ORX	SAAB SF.340B	340B-293	ex N363BE	
☐	VH-PRX	SAAB SF.340B	340B-303	ex N366BE	
☐	VH-REX	SAAB SF.340B	340B-384	ex N384AE	
☐	VH-RXE	SAAB SF.340B	340B-275	ex N275CJ	
☐	VH-RXN	SAAB SF.340B	340B-279	ex N358BE	
☐	VH-RXQ	SAAB SF.340B	340B-200	ex YR-VGN	
☐	VH-RXS	SAAB SF.340B	340B-285	ex N359BE	
☐	VH-RXX	SAAB SF.340B	340B-209	ex N355BE	
☐	VH-SBA	SAAB SF.340B	340B-311	ex SE-KXA	City of Wagga Wagga c/s
☐	VH-TRX	SAAB SF.340B	340B-287	ex N360BE	Kay Hull Plane
☐	VH-VNA	SAAF SF.340B	340B-301	ex ZK-VAA	♦
☐	VH-YRX	SAAB SF.340B	340B-178	ex N178CT	
☐	VH-ZJS	SAAB SF.340B	340B-186	ex HS-HPI	
☐	VH-ZLA	SAAB SF.340B	340B-371	ex N371AE	
☐	VH-ZLC	SAAB SF.340B	340B-373	ex N373AE	
☐	VH-ZLF	SAAB SF.340B	340B-374	ex N374AE	
☐	VH-ZLG	SAAB SF.340B	340B-375	ex N375AE	
☐	VH-ZLH	SAAB SF.340B	340B-376	ex N376AE	
☐	VH-ZLJ	SAAB SF.340B	340B-380	ex N380AE	
☐	VH-ZLK	SAAB SF.340B	340B-381	ex N381AE	
☐	VH-ZLO	SAAB SF.340B	340B-382	ex N382AE	
☐	VH-ZLQ	SAAB SF.340B	340B-370	ex N370AM	
☐	VH-ZLR	SAAB SF.340B	340B-229	ex SE-KSK	
☐	VH-ZLS	SAAB SF.340B	340B-383	ex N383AE	
☐	VH-ZLV	SAAB SF.340B	340B-386	ex N386AE	
☐	VH-ZLW	SAAB SF.340B	340B-387	ex N387AE	
☐	VH-ZLX	SAAB SF.340B	340B-182	ex ER-SGB	
☐	VH-ZRB	SAAB SF.340B	340B-389	ex N389AE	
☐	VH-ZRC	SAAB SF.340B	340B-390	ex N390AE	
☐	VH-ZRE	SAAB SF.340B	340B-391	ex N391AE	
☐	VH-ZRH	SAAB SF.340B	340B-392	ex N392AE	
☐	VH-ZRI	SAAB SF.340B	340B-394	ex N394AE	
☐	VH-ZRJ	SAAB SF.340B	340B-396	ex N396AE	
☐	VH-ZRK	SAAB SF.340B	340B-397	ex N397AE	
☐	VH-ZRL	SAAB SF.340B	340B-398	ex N398AE	
☐	VH-ZRM	SAAB SF.340B	340B-400	ex N400BR	
☐	VH-ZRN	SAAB SF.340B	340B-393	ex N393AE	
☐	VH-ZRY	SAAB SF.340B	340B-401	ex N901AE	
☐	VH-ZRZ	SAAB SF.340B	340B-388	ex N388AE	
☐	VH-ZXS	SAAB SF.340B	340B-179	ex HS-HPE	

ROSSAIR CHARTER (RFS) Adelaide, SA (ADL)

☐	VH-NAX	Cessna 441	4410106	ex VH-HXM	
☐	VH-TFB	Cessna 441	4410260	ex N68597	
☐	VH-XBC	Cessna 441	4410297	ex N441MT	
☐	VH-XMD	Cessna 441	4410025	ex N441HD	
☐	VH-XMJ	Cessna 441	4410113	ex N990AR	
☐	VH-LOA	Beech B200 Super King Air	BB-1463	ex ZS-PLK	♦

ROYAL FLYING DOCTOR SERVICE

☐	VH-AMQ	Beech B200 Super King Air	BL-166	ex N80666	South Eastern
☐	VH-AMR	Beech B200 Super King Air	BL-167	ex N80467	South Eastern
☐	VH-AMS	Beech B200C Super King Air	BL-168	ex N81458	South Eastern
☐	VH-FDA	Beech B200 Super King Air	BB-1986	ex N986KA	Queensland
☐	VH-FDB	Beech B200 Super King Air	BB-1977	ex N7317A	Queensland
☐	VH-FDC	Pilatus PC-12/45	426		Queensland
☐	VH-FDD	Beech B200 Super King Air	BB-1697	ex N40483	Queensland
☐	VH-FDE	Pilatus PC-12/45	332		Central Operations
☐	VH-FDF	Beech B200 Super King Air	BB-1696	ex N40481	Queensland
☐	VH-FDG	Beech B200 Super King Air	BB-2012	ex N60312	Queensland
☐	VH-FDI	Beech B200C Super King Air	BL-162	ex N80562	Queensland
☐	VH-FDJ	Pilatus PC-12/47	861	ex HB-FST	Central Operations
☐	VH-FDK	Pilatus PC-12/47	466		Central Operations
☐	VH-FDL	Beech B200 Super King Air	BB-2021	ex N5021C	Queensland♦
☐	VH-FDM	Beech B200C Super King Air	BL-161	ex N80761	Queensland
☐	VH-FDN	Beech B200C Super King Air	BL-58	ex N58FM	Queensland♦
☐	VH-FDO	Beech B200 Super King Air	BB-2020	ex N5020U	Queensland♦
☐	VH-FDP	Pilatus PC-12/45	434		Queensland
☐	VH-FDR	Beech B200 Super King Air	BB-1881	ex N36801	Queensland
☐	VH-FDS	Beech B200C Super King Air	BL-158		Queensland
☐	VH-FDT	Beech B200 Super King Air	BB-1990	ex N990KA	Queensland
☐	VH-FDW	Beech B200 Super King Air	BB-1880	ex N61800	Queensland
☐	VH-FDZ	Beech B200 Super King Air	BB-1882	ex N37082	Queensland
☐	VH-FFI	Beech B200 Super King Air	BB-1037	ex VH-FDI	Queensland
☐	VH-FGR	Pilatus PC-12/45	438	ex HB-FRW	Central Operations

☐ VH-FGS	Pilatus PC-12/45	440	ex HB-FRX	Central Operations
☐ VH-FGT	Pilatus PC-12/45	442	ex HB-FRY	Central Operations
☐ VH-FMP	Pilatus PC-12/45	122		Central Operations
☐ VH-FMW	Pilatus PC-12/45	123		Central Operations
☐ VH-FMZ	Pilatus PC-12/45	138		Central Operations
☐ VH-FVA	Pilatus PC-12/47E	1182		Central Operations
☐ VH-FVB	Pilatus PC-12/47E	1187	ex HB-FTI	Central Operations
☐ VH-FVD	Pilatus PC-12/47E	1206	ex HB-FTT	Central Operations
☐ VH-FVE	Pilatus PC-12/47E	1221	ex HB-FQQ	Central Operations
☐ VH-FVF	Pilatus PC-12/47E	1228	ex HB-FQY	Central Operations
☐ VH-LTQ	Beech B200 Super King Air	BL-170	ex N50600	South Eastern
☐ VH-MSH	Beech B200 Super King Air	BB-1787	ex N44857	South Eastern
☐ VH-MSZ	Beech 200 Super King Air	BB-866	ex ZK-PBG	South Eastern
☐ VH-MVJ	Beech B200 Super King Air	BB-1842	ex N50152	South Eastern
☐ VH-MVL	Beech B200 Super King Air	BB-1333	ex N1101W	South Eastern
☐ VH-MVP	Beech B200 Super King Air	BB-1812	ex VH-AMR	South Eastern
☐ VH-MVS	Beech B200 Super King Air	BB-1813	ex VH-AMQ	South Eastern
☐ VH-MVW	Beech B200 Super King Air	BB-1980	ex N980KA	South Eastern
☐ VH-MVX	Beech B200C Super King Air	BL-153	ex N3203R	South Eastern
☐ VH-MVY	Beech B200 Super King Air	BB-1324	ex N7087N	South Eastern
☐ VH-MWH	Beech B200 Super King Air	BB-2003	ex N32030	South Eastern
☐ VH-MWK	Beech B200C Super King Air	BL-152	ex N3202W	South Eastern
☐ VH-MWO	Pilatus PC-12/45	379		Western Operations
☐ VH-MWV	Beech B200 Super King Air	BB-1814	ex VH-AMS	South Eastern
☐ VH-NAJ	Beech B300C Super King Air	FM-47	ex N81307	South Eastern
☐ VH-NAO	Beech B300C Super King Air	FM-49	ex N81339	South Eastern
☐ VH-NQA	Beech B200C Super King Air	BL-68	ex VH-FDS	Queensland
☐ VH-NQB	Pilatus PC-12/45	428	ex VH-FDM	Queensland
☐ VH-NQC	Cessna 208B Grand Caravan	208B2138	ex N52645	Queensland
☐ VH-NQD	Cessna 208B Grand Caravan	208B2139	ex N50756	Queensland
☐ VH-NWO	Pilatus PC-12/45	396	ex HB-FQQ	Western Operations
☐ VH-OWA	Pilatus PC-12/47E	1115	ex HB-FQR	Western Operations
☐ VH-OWB	Pilatus PC-12/47E	1104	ex HB-FQD	Western Operations
☐ VH-OWD	Pilatus PC-12/47E	1140	ex HB-FRN	Western Operations
☐ VH-OWG	Pilatus PC-12/47E	1155	ex HB-FSV	Western Operations
☐ VH-OWI	Pilatus PC-12/47E	1232	ex HB-FRD	Western Operations
☐ VH-OWJ	Pilatus PC-12/47E	1411	ex HB-FSK	Western Operations
☐ VH-OWP	Pilatus PC-12/47E	1032	ex HB-FQL	Western Operations
☐ VH-OWQ	Pilatus PC-12/47E	1052	ex HB-FRF	Western Operations
☐ VH-OWR	Pilatus PC-12/47E	1082	ex HB-FSK	Western Operations
☐ VH-OWS	Pilatus PC-12/47E	1428	ex HB-FQB	Western Operations
☐ VH-OWU	Pilatus PC-12/47E	1433	ex HB-FQG	Western Operations
☐ VH-OWX	Pilatus PC-12/47E	1439	ex HB-FQM	Western Operations
☐ VH-SQR	Beech B300 Super King Air	FL-939	ex N5039E	South Eastern♦
☐ VH-VWO	Pilatus PC-12/45	400	ex HB-FQR	Western Operations
☐ VH-YWO	Pilatus PC-12/45	725		Western Operations
☐ VH-ZWO	Pilatus PC-12/45	467	ex HB-FQM	Western Operations

SEAIR PACIFIC GOLD COAST — Gold Coast, QLD (OOL)

☐ VH-LMD	Cessna 208 Caravan I	20800217	ex 9M-FBA	FP
☐ VH-LMZ	Cessna 208 Caravan I	20800173	ex LN-SEA	FP
☐ VH-LYT	Cessna 208B Caravan I	208B1208	ex N1320B	
☐ VH-OZH	Cessna 208B Caravan I	208B0464	ex N13313	
☐ VH-TLZ	Cessna 208B Caravan I	208B0789	ex TI-BAP	♦
☐ VH-VCW	Cessna 208B Caravan I	208B1102	ex N678HC	
☐ VH-MBF	Britten-Norman BN-2A-8 Islander	646	ex P2-MBF	
☐ VH-MBK	Britten-Norman BN-2A Islander	158	ex P2-MBD	[OOL]
☐ VH-MWQ	Beech 200 Super King Air	BB-1416	ex N8254H	
☐ VH-RUT	Britten-Norman BN-2A Islander	165	ex G-AXYT	♦
☐ VH-SDU	Cessna 210M Centurion	21062253	ex VH-OUR	

SEAWING AIRWAYS — Sydney Rose Bay, NSW (RSE)

☐ VH-SWB	de Havilland DHC-2 Beaver	1557	ex ZK-CKD	FP

SHARP AIRLINES — Hamilton, VIC (HML)

☐ VH-HWR	Swearingen SA227DC Metro 23	DC-851B	ex N3025T	
☐ VH-MYI	Swearingen SA227DC Metro 23	DC-869B	ex 9M-APB	
☐ VH-SEZ	Swearingen SA227AC Metro III	AC-637	ex ZK-RCA	
☐ VH-SWK	Swearingen SA227DC Metro 23	DC-826B	ex N52ML	
☐ VH-UUB	Swearingen SA227DC Metro 23	DC-894B	ex N3032F	
☐ VH-UUN	Swearingen SA227AC Metro III	AC-686	ex N686AV	
☐ VH-SMO	Cessna 441	441-0132	ex N441SS	
☐ VH-YHV	Cessna 441	441-0147	ex N504AC	

SHINE AVIATION SERVICES — Geraldtown, WA (GET)

☐ VH-ADE	Piper PA-31-325 Navajo	31-7712006	ex N62996	

☐ VH-AFY	Piper PA-31 Navajo	31-8012084	ex ZK-CJO
☐ VH-EKG	Beech 1900D	UE-135	ex ZS-SSY
☐ VH-HHX	Beech Baron 58	TH-270	ex VH-WGS
☐ VH-ITF	Piper PA-31 Navajo	31-7812014	ex N27435
☐ VH-PGO	Piper PA-31-350 Chieftain	31-7852109	ex VH-SFH
☐ VH-PNS	Partenavia P.68B	71	
☐ VH-SXS	Beech Baron 58	TH-81	ex ZK-EJJ
☐ VH-SZD	Cessna 404	4040050	ex 5Y-BGE
☐ VH-TBU	GippsAero GA-8 Airvan	GA8-02-011	ex VH-ARQ
☐ VH-VHT	Cessna 404	4040226	ex ZS-OJN
☐ VH-XSY	Beech Baron 58	TH-425	ex ZK-TWB

SHOAL AIR   Kunanurra, WA (KNS)

☐ VH-EDE	Cessna 210 Centurion	210L60517	ex (N94149)	
☐ VH-BKD	Cessna 210 Centurion	21063127	ex N6635N	
☐ VH-MNN	Cessna 210 Centurion	21060746	ex ZS-MNM	
☐ VH-OTB	Cessna 210 Centurion	21060067	ex ZK-FMG	
☐ VH-RLP	Cessna 210-5 Centurion	21050213	ex (N8213Z)	
☐ VH-SMP	Cessna 210 Centurion	210L61544	ex N732JG	
☐ VH-WNI	Cessna 210 Centurion	210M62462	ex N761RR	
☐ VH-ARN	Cessna 310R	310R0611	ex VH-ARS	
☐ VH-DVN	Cessna 310R	310R0329	ex N87269	
☐ VH-JVO	Cessna 310R	310R0539	ex N145FB	♦
☐ VH-SUE	Cessna 310P	310P0132	ex N5832M	
☐ VH-TWY	Cessna 310R	310R0090	ex N69336	♦
☐ VH-UJF	Cessna 310R	310R1342	ex N6215C	
☐ VH-BFL	GippsAero GA-8 Airvan	GA8-06-107		
☐ VH-HJR	Piper PA-31-350 Chieftain	31-8252016	ex VH-MZX	
☐ VH-KFF	Piper PA-31-350 Chieftain	31-7952125	ex VH-UOT	
☐ VH-KFW	Piper PA-31 Turbo Navajo	31-366	ex VH-WGU	
☐ VH-NLG	Cessna U206G Stationair	U206G03930	ex ZS-JGH	♦
☐ VH-WOU	Cessna 207 Skywagon	20700099	ex N91164	
☐ VH-WOX	Cessna 207 Skywagon	20700130	ex VH-DMS	
☐ VH-WOY	Cessna 207A Skywagon	20700707	ex N9529M	

SHORTSTOP AIR CHARTER   Melbourne-Essendon, VIC (MEB)

☐ VH-OVC	Swearingen SA226T Merlin II	T-318	ex OE-FOW	
☐ VH-OVM	Douglas DC-3	16354/33102	ex VH-JXD	Arthur Schutt MBE

SKIPPERS AVIATION   Perth-International, WA (PER)

☐ VH-XFP	de Havilland DHC-8-102A	346	ex VH-TQU	
☐ VH-XFQ	de Havilland DHC-8-106	306	ex VH-TQW	
☐ VH-XFT	de Havilland DHC-8-102	52	ex ZK-NEW	
☐ VH-XFU	de Havilland DHC-8-102	151	ex ZK-NEV	
☐ VH-XFV	de Havilland DHC-8-314A	350	ex D-BMUC	
☐ VH-XFW	de Havilland DHC-8-314A	356	ex D-BKIM	
☐ VH-XFX	de Havilland DHC-8-314A	313	ex D-BHAM	
☐ VH-XFZ	de Havilland DHC-8-314A	365	ex D-BACH	
☐ VH-XKI	de Havilland DHC-8-315Q	587	ex C-GKUX	
☐ VH-XKJ	de Havilland DHC-8-315Q	588	ex C-GLPG	
☐ VH-XUA	Embraer EMB.120ER Brasilia	120045	ex N272UE	
☐ VH-XUB	Embraer EMB.120ER Brasilia	120181	ex VH-XFW	
☐ VH-XUC	Embraer EMB.120ER Brasilia	120208	ex VH-XFV	Pelsaert Princess
☐ VH-XUD	Embraer EMB.120ER Brasilia	120140	ex VH-XFZ	Monket Mia Flyer
☐ VH-XUE	Embraer EMB.120ER Brasilia	120115	ex VH-XFQ	
☐ VH-XUF	Embraer EMB.120ER Brasilia	120207	ex N268UE	
☐ VH-WAI	Swearingen SA227DC Metro 23	DC-874B	ex N3032L	
☐ VH-WAJ	Swearingen SA227DC Metro 23	DC-876B	ex N3033U	
☐ VH-WAX	Swearingen SA227DC Metro 23	DC-877B	ex N30337	
☐ VH-WBA	Swearingen SA227DC Metro 23	DC-883B	ex N30042	
☐ VH-WBQ	Swearingen SA227DC Metro 23	DC-884B	ex N30046	Laverton
☐ VH-FMQ	Cessna 441 Conquest II	441-0109	ex N26226	
☐ VH-LBY	Cessna 441 Conquest II	441-0023	ex VH-TFW	
☐ VH-LBZ	Cessna 441 Conquest II	441-0038	ex VH-HWD	
☐ VH-SJQ	Cessna 441 Conquest II	441-0173	ex N2722Y	
☐ VH-XKM	Fokker 100	11410	ex PH-KXR	[PER]
☐ VH-XKN	Fokker 100	11420	ex PH-LXG	[PER]

SKYFORCE AVIATION   (SZF)   Sydney-Bankstown, NSW (BWU)

☐ VH-PDL	Convair 580F	137	ex ZK-PNR	[BWU]
☐ VH-PDW	Convair 580F	86	ex C-GKFQ	
☐ VH-PDX	Convair 580F	126	ex C-FIWN	

☐ VH-SIF	British Aerospace 146 Srs.200QC	E2119	ex G-ZAPN		
☐ VH-SJF	British Aerospace 146 Srs.200QC	E2148	ex G-ZAPK		
☐ VH-SUF	British Aerospace 146 Srs.200	E2130	ex ZK-ECO		♦

SKYTRADERS   Melbourne-Tullamarine, VIC (MEL)

☐ VH-VHA	CASA C.212 Srs.400	474		Ginger	Wheels or skis
☐ VH-VHB	CASA C.212 Srs.400	475		Gadget	Wheels or skis
☐ VH-VHD	Airbus A319-115LR	1999	ex F-GYAS		
☐ VH-VCJ	Airbus A319-132LR	1880	ex SX-DGH		

SKYTRANS REGIONAL   (Q6/SKP)   Cairns, QLD (CNS)

☐ VH-QQA	de Havilland DHC-8-102	005	ex P2-MCN
☐ VH-QQG	de Havilland DHC-8-102	036	ex 5W-FAA

SLINGAIR   Kununurra, WA (KNX)

☐ VH-HAM	Cessna 208 Caravan I	20800296	ex N208MM
☐ VH-KSA	Cessna 208B Caravan I	208B0516	ex N6302B
☐ VH-LNH	Cessna 208B Caravan I	208B0590	ex N590TA
☐ VH-LNN	Cessna 208B Caravan I	208B0801	ex 9M-PMB
☐ VH-LNO	Cessna 208B Caravan I	208B0925	ex N125AR
⊓ VH-LWA	Cessna 208B Caravan I	208B1173	
☐ VH-TUY	Cessna 208B Caravan I	208B1200	ex P2-TZZ
☐ VH-FGH	GippsAero GA-8 Airvan	GA8-02-012	ex VH-WOG
☐ VH-JVO	Cessna 310R	310R0539	ex N145FB
☐ VH-NLG	Cessna U206G Stationair	U20603930	ex ZS-JGH
☐ VH-NLV	Cessna 210N Centurion II	21063093	ex VH-APU
☐ VH-NLZ	Cessna 210N Centurion II	21063769	ex VH-RZZ
☐ VH-RKD	Piper PA-31-350 Chieftain	31-8152048	ex N4076Z
☐ VH-TWY	Cessna 310R	310R0090	ex N69336
☐ VH-URX	Cessna 210N Centurion II	21064449	ex N6595Y

SUNSTATE AIRLINES   Sunstate (SSQ)   Brisbane, QLD (BNE)

Wholly owned by Qantas and ops scheduled services in full colours as QantasLink (qv)

SYDNEY SEAPLANES   Sydney Rose Bay, NSW

☐ VH-AAM	de Havilland DHC-2 Beaver	1492	ex VH-IMR	Caledonia	FP
☐ VH-NOO	de Havilland DHC-2 Beaver	1535	ex VH-IDI	Cambria	FP
☐ VH-PXT	Cessna T206H Stationair	20608729	ex N353SC		FP♦
☐ VH-SXF	Cessna 208 Caravan I	20800405	ex N1122Y	Corsair	FP
☐ VH-ZWH	Cessna 208 Caravan I	20800399	ex N877AA		FP♦

TASFAST AIR FREIGHT   Hobart, TAS (HBT)

☐ VH-EDV	Piper PA-31-350 Navajo Chieftain	31-7305025	ex N86568		
☐ VH-IBI	Piper PA-31-350 Navajo Chieftain	31 7552035	ex ZK-NSO		
☐ VH-LCE	Piper PA-31-350 Navajo Chieftain	31-7305088	ex N305SP		
☐ VH-MYX	Piper PA-31-350 Navajo Chieftain	31-7552098	ex P2-SAS		
☐ VH-TBJ	Piper PA-31-350 Navajo Chieftain	31-8052038	ex G-PLAC		
☐ VH-POV	Cessna 208B Caravan I	208B1182	ex SX-ARX		♦

TASMAN CARGO AIRLINES   Freightexpress (HJ/TMN)   Hobart, TAS (HBT)

☐ VH-TCA	Boeing 757-236PCF	25620/449	ex G-CSVS	DHL c/s	<BCS

TIGERAIR AUSTRALIA   (TR/TGV)   Melbourne-Tullamarine, VIC (MEL)

☐ VH-VNB	Airbus A320-232	2906	ex 9V-TAG		
☐ VH-VNC	Airbus A320-232	3275	ex F-WWDE		
☐ VH-VND	Airbus A320-232	3296	ex F-WWDX		
☐ VH-VNF	Airbus A320-232	3332	ex F-WWBI		
☐ VH-VNG	Airbus A320-232	3674	ex 9V-TAJ		
☐ VH-VNH	Airbus A320-232	3734	ex F-WWDN		
☐ VH-VNJ	Airbus A320-232	2982	ex 9V-TAI		
☐ VH-VNK	Airbus A320-232	3986	ex 9V-TAK		
☐ VH-VNO	Airbus A320-232	4053	ex 9V-TAL		
☐ VH-VNP	Airbus A320-232	2952	ex 9V-TAH		
☐ VH-VNQ	Airbus A320-232	5218	ex F-WWBD	Sarah	
☐ VH-VNR	Airbus A320-232	5900	ex D-AVVO		
☐ VH-XUG	Airbus A320-232	6032	ex F-WWDQ		
☐ VH-	Airbus A320-232	6522	ex		o/o♦
☐ VH-	Airbus A320-232	6750	ex		o/o♦

TOLL AVIATION (TFX) Brisbane, QLD

☐ VH-UUO	Swearingen SA227AC Metro III	AC-530	ex ZK-NST	
☐ VH-UZG	Swearingen SA227AC Metro III	AC-553	ex N220CT	
☐ VH-UZP	Swearingen SA227AC Metro III	AC-498	ex OY-BPL	David Fell
☐ VH-UZS	Swearingen SA227AC Metro III	AC-517	ex VH-UUG	
☐ VH-UZW	Swearingen SA227AC Metro III	AC-526	ex OY-GAW	Toll c/s
☐ VH-HPB	Swearingen SA227DC Metro 23	DC-808B	ex N808SK	
☐ VH-HPE	Swearingen SA227DC Metro 23	DC-823B	ex N823MM	Toll c/s
☐ VH-TOQ	ATR 42-300F	079	ex EI-SLB	Toll c/s
☐ VH-TOX	ATR 42-300F	024	ex EI-SLE	Toll c/s
☐ VH-UZI	Swearingen SA227AT Expediter	AT-570	ex N570UP	
☐ VH-UZN	Swearingen SA227DC Metro 23	DC-881B	ex N6BN	The Australian c/s
☐ ZK-FXT	Boeing 737-3B7F	23862/1586	ex N527AU	opb AWK♦
☐ ZK-JTQ	Boeing 737-476F	24442/2371	ex VH-TJQ	opb AWK♦
☐ ZK-TLD	Boeing 737-3B7SF	23706/1499	ex N520AU	opb AWK
☐ ZK-TLE	Boeing 737-3S1SF	24834/1896	ex N919GF	opb AWK

VIRGIN AUSTRALIA Kanga (VA/VAU) Brisbane-International, QLD (BNE)

☐ VH-XFC	Airbus A330-243	1293	ex F-WWYU	Mooloolaba Beach	
☐ VH-XFD	Airbus A330-243	1306	ex F-WWYY	Bells Beach	
☐ VH-XFE	Airbus A330-243	1319	ex F-WWTE	Manly Beach	
☐ VH-XFG	Airbus A330-243	1407	ex F-WWTU	Terrigal Beach	
☐ VH-XFH	Airbus A330-243	1452	ex F-WWYD	Duranbah Beach	
☐ VH-XFJ	Airbus A330-243	1561	ex F-WWYS	Gnaraloo Bay	♦
☐ VH-BZG	Boeing 737-8FE/W	37822/3355	ex (VH-VUW)	Vivonne Bay	
☐ VH-VOK	Boeing 737-8FE/W	33758/1359		Johanna Beach	
☐ VH-VOL	Boeing 737-8FE/W	33759/1364		Newport Beach	
☐ VH-VOM	Boeing 737-8FE/W	33794/1373		Fairhaven Beach	
☐ VH-VON	Boeing 737-8FE/W	33795/1375		Greenmount Point	
☐ VH-VOO	Boeing 737-8FE/W	33796/1377	ex ZK-PBA	Peaceful Bay	
☐ VH-VOP	Boeing 737-8FE/W	33797/1389	ex ZK-PBB	Indian Head	♦
☐ VH-VOQ	Boeing 737-8FE/W	33798/1391		Margaret River	
☐ VH-VOR	Boeing 737-8FE/W	33799/1462	ex ZK-PBF	Rainbow Beach	♦
☐ VH-VOS	Boeing 737-8FE/W	33800/1483		Chiton Rocks	
☐ VH-VOT	Boeing 737-8FE/W	33801/1504		Scarborough Beach	
☐ VH-VOX	Boeing 737-8BK/W	33017/1446	ex ZK-PBC	Coolum Beach	
☐ VH-VOY	Boeing 737-8FE/W	33996/1551	ex ZK-PBD	Brighton Beach	♦
☐ VH-VUA	Boeing 737-8FE/W	33997/1559		Vestey's Beach	
☐ VH-VUB	Boeing 737-8FE/W	34013/1573	ex ZK-PBJ	Trigg Beach	♦
☐ VH-VUC	Boeing 737-8FE/W	34014/1582		Peregian Beach	
☐ VH-VUD	Boeing 737-8FE/W	34015/1594	ex ZK-PBG	Tallows Beach	♦
☐ VH-VUE	Boeing 737-8FE/W	34167/1676	ex N1786B	Curl Curl Beach	
☐ VH-VUF	Boeing 737-8FE/W	34168/1697		Hobart Honey	
☐ VH-VUG	Boeing 737-8FE/W	34438/1948		Jasmine Tasman	
☐ VH-VUH	Boeing 737-8FE/W	34440/2003	ex ZK-PBI	Lady Rebecca	♦
☐ VH-VUI	Boeing 737-8FE/W	34441/2015		Kewarra Beach	
☐ VH-VUJ	Boeing 737-8FE/W	34443/2056		Rosebud Beach	
☐ VH-VUK	Boeing 737-8FE/W	36602/2353		Seaford Beach Diva	
☐ VH-VUL	Boeing 737-8FE/W	36603/2356	ex N1782B	Ocean Grove Beach	
☐ VH-VUM	Boeing 737-8BK/W	29675/2414	ex N1786B	Holloways Beach	
☐ VH-VUN	Boeing 737-8BK/W	29676/2432		Carrickalinga Beach	
☐ VH-VUO	Boeing 737-8FE/W	36601/2525	ex ZK-PBM	Eighty Mile Beach	♦
☐ VH-VUP	Boeing 737-8FE/W	36604/2650	ex ZK-PBK	Lighthouse Beach	♦
☐ VH-VUQ	Boeing 737-8FE/W	36605/2710	ex ZK-PBL	Merewether Beach	♦
☐ VH-VUR	Boeing 737-8FE/W	36606/3059	ex N1786B	Star City	
☐ VH-VUS	Boeing 737-8FE/W	36607/3082		Seaspray Beach	
☐ VH-VUT	Boeing 737-8FE/W	36608/3132	ex N5573L	Alma Bay	
☐ VH-VUU	Boeing 737-8FE/W	36609/3232	ex N1782B	Kingscliff Beach	
☐ VH-VUV	Boeing 737-8FE/W	37821/3288	ex N1796B	Binalong Bay	
☐ VH-VUW	Boeing 737-8KG/W	39449/3398		Pebbly Beach	
☐ VH-VUX	Boeing 737-8FE/W	37823/3415	ex N1786B	Nightcliff Beach	
☐ VH-VUY	Boeing 737-8KG/W	39450/3494	ex N1796B	Snapper Rocks	
☐ VH-VUZ	Boeing 737-8FE/W	39921/3536	ex N1786B	Lennox Head	
☐ VH-YFC	Boeing 737-81D/W	39413/3592		Bondi Beach	
☐ VH-YFE	Boeing 737-81D/W	39414/3623		Sunshine Beach	
☐ VH-YFF	Boeing 737-8FE/W	40994/3664		Wineglass Bay	
☐ VH-YFG	Boeing 737-8FE/W	40999/3941		Hanson Bay	
☐ VH-YFH	Boeing 737-3FE/W	40996/3801		Mindil Beach	
☐ VH-YFI	Boeing 737-8FE/W	41000/3963		Porpoise Bay	
☐ VH-YFJ	Boeing 737-8FE/W	41001/4089		Surfers Paradise Beach	
☐ VH-YFK	Boeing 737-8FE/W	41004/3861		Long Beach	
☐ VH-YFL	Boeing 737-8FE/W	41002/4047		Sandy Bay	
☐ VH-YFN	Boeing 737-8FE/W	41009/4456		Ballina Beach	
☐ VH-YFP	Boeing 737-8FE/W	41011/4476		Nobby's Beach	
☐ VH-YFQ	Boeing 737-8FE/W	41010/4494		Whiting Beach	
☐ VH-YFR	Boeing 737-8FE/W	41012/4543		Scamander Beach	
☐ VH-YIA	Boeing 737-8FE/W	37824/3718	ex N1786B	Henley Beach	
☐ VH-YIB	Boeing 737-8FE/W	37825/3758		Trinity Beach	

☐ VH-YID	Boeing 737-8FE/W	38709/3851		Tapu'itea	
☐ VH-YIE	Boeing 737-8FE/W	38708/3875		Fingal Beach	
☐ VH-YIF	Boeing 737-8FE/W	38710/3904		Sorrento Beach	
☐ VH-YIG	Boeing 737-8FE/W	38711/3921		Kings Beach	
☐ VH-YIH	Boeing 737-8FE/W	38712/4070		Hastings Point	
☐ VH-YIJ	Boeing 737-8FE/W	39924/4109		Pennington Bay	
☐ VH-YIL	Boeing 737-8FE/W	38713/4123		Seventy Five Mile Beach	
☐ VH-YIM	Boeing 737-8FE/W	38716/4119		Bridgewater Bay	
☐ VH-YIO	Boeing 737-8FE/W	38714/4132		Lammeroo Beach	
☐ VH-YIQ	Boeing 737-8FE/W	38715/4156		Hyams Beach	
☐ VH-YIR	Boeing 737-8FE/W	39925/4172		Cactus Beach	
☐ VH-YIS	Boeing 737-8FE/W	39926/4201		Casuarina Beach	
☐ VH-YIT	Boeing 737-8FE/W	38717/4194		Lammermoor Beach	
☐ VH-YIU	Boeing 737-8FE/W	40699/4560		Middleton Beach	
☐ VH-YIV	Boeing 737-8FE/W	40698/4571		Stanwell Park	
☐ VH-YIW	Boeing 737-8FE/W	40700/5085	ex N6046P	Mona Vale Beach	♦
☐ VH-YIY	Boeing 737-8FE/W	40701/5280		Stanwell Park	♦
☐ VH-YIZ	Boeing 737-8FE/W	40702/5061		Black Rock	♦
☐ VH-YVA	Boeing 737-8FE/W	40995/3680		Eurong Beach	
☐ VH-YVC	Boeing 737-8FE/W	40997/3832		Jetty Beach	
☐ VH-YVD	Boeing 737-8FE/W	40998/3848	ex N1786D	Salmon Beach	
☐ VH-VOZ	Boeing 777-3ZGER	35302/745		Palm Beach	
☐ VH-VPD	Boeing 777-3ZGER	37938/756		Avalon Beach	
☐ VH-VPE	Boeing 777-3ZGER	37939/764		Noosa Heads Beach	
☐ VH-VPF	Boeing 777-3ZGER	37940/801		Caves Beach	
☐ VH-VPH	Boeing 777-3ZGER	37943/898		St Kilda Beach	
☐ VH-ZPA	Embraer ERJ-190AR	19000148	ex PT-SAB	Apollo Beach	
☐ VH-ZPB	Embraer ERJ-190AR	19000162	ex PT-SAR	Bicheno Beach	
☐ VH-ZPC	Embraer ERJ-190AR	19000170	ex PT-SDF	Cabarita Beach	
☐ VH-ZPD	Embraer ERJ-190AR	19000176	ex PT-SDL	Dudley Beach	
☐ VH-ZPE	Embraer ERJ-190AR	19000187	ex PT-SDV	Coogee Beach	
☐ VH-ZPF	Embraer ERJ-190AR	19000193	ex PT-SGB	Whitehaven Beach	
☐ VH-ZPG	Embraer ERJ-190AR	19000195	ex PT-SGD	Glenelg Beach	
☐ VH-ZPH	Embraer ERJ-190AR	19000199	ex PT-SGD	Honeymoon Cove	
☐ VH-ZPI	Embraer ERJ-190AR	19000202	ex PT-SGK	Seven Mile Beach	
☐ VH-ZPJ	Embraer ERJ-190AR	19000209	ex PT-SGS	Jervis Bay	
☐ VH-ZPK	Embraer ERJ-190AR	19000218	ex PT-SHB	Aussie Rob	
☐ VH-ZPL	Embraer ERJ-190AR	19000220	ex PT-SHD	Clifton Beach	
☐ VH-ZPM	Embraer ERJ-190AR	19000262	ex PT-TLC	Maroochydore Beach	
☐ VH-ZPN	Embraer ERJ-190AR	19000312	ex PT-TXA	Arrawarra Beach	
☐ VH-ZPO	Embraer ERJ-190AR	19000321	ex PT-TXJ	Boomerang Beach	
☐ VH-ZPQ	Embraer ERJ-190AR	19000412	ex PT-TBK	Main Beach	[BNA]
☐ VH-ZPR	Embraer ERJ-190AR	19000424	ex PT-TCG	Dundee Beach	
☐ VH-ZPT	Embraer ERJ-190AR	19000451	ex PT-TJX	Little Beach	
☐ VH-VBY	Boeing 737-7FE/W	34323/1751		Kingston Beach	
☐ VH-VBZ	Boeing 737-7FE/W	34322/1777		Cronulla Beach	

VIRGIN AUSTRALIA REGIONAL AIRLINES   *(VA/VAU)*   *Perth-International, WA (PER)*

☐ VH-FVH	ATR 72-500	954	ex F-WWEG	Four Mile Beach	
☐ VH-FVI	ATR 72-500	955	ex F-WWEH	Mission Beach	
☐ VH-FVL	ATR 72-500	974	ex F-WWES	Preston Beach	
☐ VH-FVM	ATR 72-500	979	ex F-WWEX	Woolamai Beach	
☐ VH-FVU	ATR 72-500	978	ex OY-CJU	Double Island Point	
☐ VH-FVX	ATR 72-500	986	ex OY-CJV	Kirra Beach	
☐ VH-FVN	ATR 72-600	1039	ex F-WWEB	Whitehaven Beach	
☐ VH-FVP	ATR 72-600	1025	ex F-WWLR	Wategos Beacch	
☐ VH-FVQ	ATR 72-600	1053	ex F-WWEO	Christies Beach	
☐ VH-FVR	ATR 72-600	1058	ex F-WWES	Yallingup Beach	
☐ VH-FVY	ATR 72-600	1073	ex F-WWEJ	Marcoola Beach	
☐ VH-FVZ	ATR 72-600	1087	ex F-WWEX	Angourie Beach	
☐ VH-VPI	ATR 72-600	1107	ex F-WWET	Bronte Beach	
☐ VH-VPJ	ATR 72-600	1169	ex F-WWEJ	Monkey Mia	♦
☐ VH-FNA	Fokker 50	20106	ex PH-EXG	Rockingham Beach	
☐ VH-FNB	Fokker 50	20107	ex PH-EXF	Shire of Esperance	
☐ VH-FND	Fokker 50	20129	ex PH-EXB		
☐ VH-FNE	Fokker 50	20212	ex PH-PRJ		
☐ VH-FNF	Fokker 50	20200	ex PH-PRH		
☐ VH-FNH	Fokker 50	20113	ex PH-EXY	Shire of Carnarvon	
☐ VH-FNI	Fokker 50	20114	ex PH-EXZ	City of Geraldton	
☐ VH-FSL	Fokker 50	20249	ex PH-KXH		
☐ VH-FNC	Fokker 100	11334	ex D-AGPO		
☐ VH-FNJ	Fokker 100	11489	ex G-BVJA	Talbot Bay	
☐ VH-FNN	Fokker 100	11326	ex PH-CFD		
☐ VH-FNR	Fokker 100	11488	ex G-BVJB	Lake Argyle	
☐ VH-FNT	Fokker 100	11461	ex B-12297		
☐ VH-FNU	Fokker 100	11373	ex OO-TUF	Roebuck Bay	

☐ VH-FNY	Fokker 100	11484	ex N108ML		
☐ VH-FSQ	Fokker 100	11450	ex N450DR	Bills Bay	
☐ VH-FSW	Fokker 100	11391	ex D-AGPR		
☐ VH-FWH	Fokker 100	11316	ex G-BXNF	all white	<UTY♦
☐ VH-FZH	Fokker 100	11303	ex PH-CXF		♦
☐ VH-FZI	Fokker 100	11333	ex PH-CXN		♦
☐ VH-FZO	Fokker 100	11305	ex PH-LMY		
☐ VH-FNP	Airbus A320-231	0429	ex G-BYTH	Honeymoon Cove	
☐ VH-YUD	Airbus A320-232	1922	ex G-MEDH	Port Beach	

WEST WING AVIATION — Mount Isa, QLD (ISA)

☐ VH-BAM	Cessna 208B Caravan	208B1220	ex N920RD		
☐ VH-NDC	Cessna 208B Caravan I	208B2215	ex N2056W		♦
☐ VH-NTQ	Cessna 208 Caravan	20800183	ex ZK-PMT		♦
☐ VH-TIY	Cessna 208B Caravan I	208B0649	ex P2-TWW		
☐ VH-TQB	Cessna 208B Caravan I	208B2128	ex 5X-AMK		♦
☐ VH-UZY	Cessna 208B Caravan I	208B0937	ex EC-IEX		
☐ VH-WZJ	Cessna 208B Caravan I	208B1108	ex N208JJ		
☐ VH-ABP	Beech Baron 58	TH-709	ex N6771S		
☐ VH-BWC	Beech Baron 58	TH-478	ex VH-BAM		
☐ VH-EMK	Beech 1900C-1	UC-159	ex N159GL		♦
☐ VH-EZN	Beech Baron 58	TH-1222	ex N3722P		
☐ VH-LSB	Beech Baron 58	TH-819	ex N206SB		
☐ VH-SBM	Beech B200 Super King Air	BB-964	ex VH-HTU		
☐ VH-SKZ	Cessna 404 Titan II	404-0080	ex VH-JOH		
☐ VH-TAN	Cessna 402C	402C1008	ex N1237D		
☐ VH-TIV	Cessna 402B	402B0623	ex N3774C		
☐ VH-VCB	Beech 200 Super King Air	BB-579	ex P2-MML		
☐ VH-WZD	Britten-Norman BN.2A-21 Islander	450	ex VH-USD		
☐ VH-WZF	Britten-Norman BN-2A-21 Islander	537	ex 5Y-RAJ		
☐ VH-WZY	Cessna 208B Caravan I	208B1035	ex VH-ZGS		
☐ VH-XDA	Cessna 404 Titan II	404-0408	ex VH-HOA		
☐ VH-XDP	Cessna 404 Titan II	404-0845	ex ZS-PNW		
☐ VH-XDV	Beech B200 Super King Air	BB-1100	ex N63971		
☐ VH-XDW	Beech B200 Super King Air	BB-1258	ex N2748X		
☐ VH-XDY	Beech 1900D	UE-396	ex N838CA		

WETTENHALL AIR SERVICES — Deniliquin, NSW (DNQ)

☐ VH-MAV	Rockwell 500S Shrike Commander	3280	ex N81512	
☐ VH-SSL	Swearingen SA226T Merlin	T-210	ex N173SP	

WHITSUNDAY AIR SERVICES — Hamilton Island, QLD (HTI)

☐ VH-WTY	Cessna 208 Caravan I	20800522	ex N1027V	
☐ VH-ZDA	DHC-2 Beaver I	803	ex N317DH	

VN- VIETNAM (Socialist Republic of Vietnam)

HAI AU AVIATION — Hanoi-Noi Bai, SPB

☐ VN-B446	Cessna 208BEX Caravan I	208B		FP♦
☐ VN-B468	Cessna 208BEX Caravan I	208B5121		FP♦
☐ VN-B469	Cessna 208BEX Caravan I	208B5122	ex N3051H	FP♦

JETSTAR PACIFIC AIRLINES — Pacific Express (BL/PIC) — Ho Chi Minh City (SGN)

☐ VN-A198	Airbus A320-232	4459	ex D-AXAB	
☐ VN-A555	Airbus A320-232	2331	ex 9V-TAC	
☐ VN-A556	Airbus A320-232	2340	ex 9V-TAD	
☐ VN-A557	Airbus A320-232	2670	ex EI-EWS	
☐ VN-A558	Airbus A320-232	2922	ex EI-EYC	
☐ VN-A559	Airbus A320-232	3012	ex EI-EYD	
☐ VN-A560	Airbus A320-232	3621	ex RP-C8989	
☐ VN-A561	Airbus A320-232/S	6136	ex F-WWIO	♦
☐ VN-A345	Airbus A321-231	2261	ex D-AVZJ	<HVN♦
☐ VN-A347	Airbus A321-231	2267	ex D-AVZL	<HVN♦

VASCO — Vasco Air (VFC) — Ho Chi Minh City (SGN)

☐ VN-B212	ATR 72-212A	685	ex F-WWEH	<HVN
☐ VN-B594	Beech B200 Super King Air	BB-1329	ex VH-SWC	

VIETJET — (VJ/VJC)

☐ LZ-BHF	Airbus A320-214	1087	ex EC-HDN	<BGH♦

☐ VN-A650	Airbus A320-214/S	6457	ex F-WWBO			♦
☐ VN-A655	Airbus A320-214/S	6498	ex F-WWIP			♦
☐ VN-A656	Airbus A320-214/S	6584	ex F-WWDT			♦
☐ VN-A658	Airbus A320-214/S	6341	ex F-WWBP			♦
☐ VN-A659	Airbus A320-214/S	6378	ex D-AXAI			♦
☐ VN-A666	Airbus A320-214	3739	ex 9K-EAA	Giá rẻ hơn, bay nhiều thêm		
☐ VN-A668	Airbus A320-214	3791	ex 9K-EAB			
☐ VN-A669	Airbus A320-214	4049	ex 9K-EAD			
☐ VN-A678	Airbus A320-214/S	6025	ex D-AXAA			
☐ VN-A680	Airbus A320-214	4475	ex RP-C8389			
☐ VN-A681	Airbus A320-214	4512	ex RP-C8391			
☐ VN-A682	Airbus A320-214	5742	ex F-WWDR			
☐ VN-A686	Airbus A320-214/S	5822	ex F-WWBR			
☐ VN-A688	Airbus A320-214	2712	ex SP-IAF			
☐ VN-A689	Airbus A320-232	4190	ex SX-OAT			
☐ VN-A690	Airbus A320-214	4415	ex RP-C8388			♦
☐ VN-A691	Airbus A320-214	4504	ex RP-C8390			♦
☐ VN-A692	Airbus A320-214	4907	ex RP-C8394			♦
☐ VN-A699	Airbus A320-232	4193	ex SX-OAU			
☐ VN-A695	Airbus A320-214	3646	ex RP-C3248			♦
☐ VN-A696	Airbus A320-214/S	6242	ex F-WWBI			♦
☐ VN-A	Airbus A320-214/S	6738	ex		o/o♦
☐ VN-A	Airbus A320-214/S	6778	ex		o/o♦
☐ VN-A	Airbus A320-214/S	6881	ex		o/o♦
☐ VN-A	Airbus A320-214/S	6929	ex		o/o♦
☐ VN-A	Airbus A320-214/S	6944	ex		o/o♦
☐ VN-A	Airbus A320-214/S	6955	ex		o/o♦
☐ VN-A651	Airbus A321-211/S	5295	ex D-AZAK	9000th Airbus Aircraft titles	♦
☐ VN-A	Airbus A321-211/S	6696	ex		o/o♦
☐ VN-A	Airbus A321-211/S	6848	ex		o/o♦
☐ VN-A	Airbus A321-211/S	6936	ex		o/o♦

VIETNAM AIRLINES — Vietnam Airlines (VN/HVN) — Hanoi-Noi Bal (HAN)

Member of SkyTeam

☐ VN-A322	Airbus A321-231	4311	ex D-AVZU		
☐ VN-A323	Airbus A321-231	4669	ex D-AZAE		
☐ VN-A324	Airbus A321-231	4703	ex D-AZAQ		
☐ VN-A325	Airbus A321-231	4737	ex D-AVZB		
☐ VN-A326	Airbus A321-231	4783	ex D-AVZM		
☐ VN-A327	Airbus A321-231	4826	ex D-AVXS	SkyTeam c/s	
☐ VN-A329	Airbus A321-231	4863	ex D-AZAA		
☐ VN-A331	Airbus A321-231	4945	ex D-AZAC		
☐ VN-A332	Airbus A321-231	4971	ex D-AZAH		
☐ VN-A334	Airbus A321-231	5164	ex D-AVZG		
☐ VN-A335	Airbus A321-231	5241	ex D-AVZV		
☐ VN-A336	Airbus A321-231	5247	ex D-AVZX		
☐ VN-A338	Airbus A321-231	5251	ex D-AVZY		
☐ VN-A339	Airbus A321-231	5275	ex D-AZAE		
☐ VN-A344	Airbus A321-231	2255	ex D-AVZH		
☐ VN-A345	Airbus A321-231	2261	ex D-AVZJ		>PIC
☐ VN-A347	Airbus A321-231	2267	ex D-AVZL		>PIC
☐ VN-A348	Airbus A321-231	2303	ex D-AVZC		>VAV
☐ VN-A349	Airbus A321-231	2480	ex D-AVXC		>VAV
☐ VN-A350	Airbus A321-231	2974	ex D-AVZN		
☐ VN-A351	Airbus A321-231	3005	ex D-AVZI		
☐ VN-A352	Airbus A321-231	3013	ex D-AVZW		
☐ VN-A353	Airbus A321-231	3022	ex D-AVZY		
☐ VN-A354	Airbus A321-231	3198	ex D-AVZX		
☐ VN-A356	Airbus A321-231	3315	ex D-AVZA		
☐ VN-A357	Airbus A321-231	3355	ex D-AVZB		
☐ VN-A358	Airbus A321-231	3600	ex D-AZAC		
☐ VN-A359	Airbus A321-231	3737	ex D-AZAJ		
☐ VN-A360	Airbus A321-231	3862	ex D-AVZJ		
☐ VN-A361	Airbus A321-231	3964	ex D-AZAW		
☐ VN-A362	Airbus A321-231	3966	ex D-AVZC		
☐ VN-A363	Airbus A321-231	4136	ex D-AZAT		
☐ VN-A365	Airbus A321-231	4213	ex D-AVZG		
☐ VN-A366	Airbus A321-231	4277	ex D-AZAO		
☐ VN-A367	Airbus A321-231	4315	ex D-AVZV		
☐ VN-A390	Airbus A321-231	5297	ex D-AZAL		
☐ VN-A392	Airbus A321-231	5306	ex D-AZAO		
☐ VN-A393	Airbus A321-231	5340	ex D-AZAW		
☐ VN-A394	Airbus A321-231	5343	ex D-AZAX		>VAV
☐ VN-A395	Airbus A321-231	5385	ex D-AVZP		
☐ VN-A396	Airbus A321-231	5392	ex D-AVZB		
☐ VN-A397	Airbus A321-231	5418	ex D-AVZO		
☐ VN-A398	Airbus A321-231	5427	ex D-AVZS		>VAV
☐ VN-A399	Airbus A321-231	5438	ex D-AVZZ		
☐ VN-A601	Airbus A321-231	5456	ex D-AVZY		
☐ VN-A602	Airbus A321-231	5469	ex D-AZAD		

☐ VN-A603	Airbus A321-231	5495	ex D-AZAL	
☐ VN-A604	Airbus A321-231	5555	ex D-AVZF	
☐ VN-A605	Airbus A321-231	5699	ex D-AZAH	
☐ VN-A606	Airbus A321-231	5709	ex D-AZAQ	
☐ VN-A608	Airbus A321-231	5916	ex D-AZAF	
☐ VN-A609	Airbus A321-231	5958	ex D-AZAH	
☐ VN-A610	Airbus A321-231	5994	ex D-AZAU	
☐ VN-A611	Airbus A321-231	6266	ex D-AVZM	♦
☐ VN-A612	Airbus A321-231	6344	ex D-AVXI	o/o♦
☐ VN-A	Airbus A321-231	6748	ex	o/o♦
☐ VN-A	Airbus A321-231	6756	ex	o/o♦
☐ VN-A	Airbus A321-231	6810	ex	o/o♦
☐ VN-A371	Airbus A330-223	275	ex HB-IQG	
☐ VN-A372	Airbus A330-223	294	ex HB-IQJ	
☐ VN-A374	Airbus A330-223	299	ex HB-IQK	
☐ VN-A375	Airbus A330-223	366	ex HB-IQP	
☐ VN-A376	Airbus A330-223	943	ex EI-ELI	
☐ VN-A377	Airbus A330-223	962	ex EI-ELJ	
☐ VN-A378	Airbus A330-223	1019	ex F-WJKM	
☐ VN-A379	Airbus A330-223	1256	ex F-WWYO	
☐ VN-A381	Airbus A330-223	1266	ex F-WWKR	
☐ VN-A383	Airbus A330-223	946	ex D-ANJB	
☐ VN-B210	ATR 72-212A	678	ex F-WWET	
☐ VN-B212	ATR 72-212A	685	ex F-WWEH	>VFC
☐ VN-B214	ATR 72-212A	688	ex F-WWEK	
☐ VN-B218	ATR 72-212A	877	ex F-WWEE	
☐ VN-B219	ATR 72-212A	886	ex F-WWEP	
☐ VN-B220	ATR 72-212A	890	ex F-WWEV	
☐ VN-B221	ATR 72-212A	892	ex F-WWEX	
☐ VN-B223	ATR 72-212A	896	ex F-WWEG	
☐ VN-B225	ATR 72-212A	897	ex F-WW	
☐ VN-B233	ATR 72-212A	912	ex F-WWEG	
☐ VN-B236	ATR 72-212A	914	ex F-WWEJ	
☐ VN-B237	ATR 72-212A	925	ex F-WWEZ	
☐ VN-B239	ATR 72-212A	927	ex F-WWEC	
☐ VN-B240	ATR 72-212A	939	ex F-WWEO	
☐ VN-A141	Boeing 777-2Q8ER	28688/436		
☐ VN-A142	Boeing 777-2Q8ER	32701/443		
☐ VN-A143	Boeing 777-26KER	33502/450		
☐ VN-A144	Boeing 777-26KER	33503/453		
☐ VN-A145	Boeing 777-26KER	33504/491		
☐ VN-A146	Boeing 777-26KER	33505/486		
☐ VN-A149	Boeing 777-2Q8ER	32716/518	ex (VN-A147)	
☐ VN-A150	Boeing 777-2Q8ER	32717/541		
☐ VN-A861	Boeing 787-9	35151/303		o/o♦
☐ VN-A862	Boeing 787-9	35152/318		o/o♦
☐ VN-A	Boeing 787-9	35153/333		o/o♦
☐ VN-A	Boeing 787-9	35154/353		o/o♦
☐ VN-A	Boeing 787-9	38761/380		o/o♦
☐ VN-A	Boeing 787-9	38762/388		o/o♦
☐ VN-A312	Airbus A320-232	2522	ex N532CL	o/o
☐ VN-A502	Fokker 70	11580	ex PH-EZL	
☐ VN-A886	Airbus A350-941	014	ex F-WZFI	o/o♦
☐ VN-A	Airbus A350-941	015	ex F-WZFJ	o/o♦
☐ VN-A	Airbus A350-941	016	ex F-WZFK	o/o♦
☐ VN-A	Airbus A350-941	017	ex F-WZ	o/o♦

VP-A ANGUILLA (British Overseas Territory)

ANGUILLA AIR SERVICES *(Q3/AXL)* **Anguilla-Wallbake (AXA)**

☐ VP-AAN	Cessna 402C	402C0029	
☐ VP-AAS	Britten-Norman BN-2A-26 Islander	206	ex G-ISLA

CARIBE AIR CHARTERS **Anguilla-Wallbake (AXA)**

☐ VP-AAJ	Britten-Norman BN-2A-26 Islander	2006	ex V4-AAC

TRANS ANGUILLA AIRLINES **Anguilla-Wallbake/St Thomas-Cyril E King, VI (AXA/STT)**

☐ VP-AAA	Britten-Norman BN-2A-21 Islander	382	ex N361RA

☐ VP-AAF   Britten-Norman BN-2B-21 Islander   2024   ex N21DA

VP-C CAYMAN ISLANDS (British Overseas Territory)

CAYMAN AIRWAYS   Cayman (KX/CAY)   Georgetown, Grand Cayman (GCM)

☐ VP-CAY	Boeing 737-3Q8	26286/2424	ex N241LF	Spirit of Recovery
☐ VP-CKW	Boeing 737-36E	26322/2769	ex EI-CRZ	
☐ VP-CKY	Boeing 737-3Q8	26282/2355	ex N262KS	The Cayman Islands
☐ VP-CKZ	Boeing 737-36E	27626/2792	ex EI-CSU	

CAYMAN AIRWAYS EXPRESS   Georgetown, Grand Cayman (GCM)

☐ VP-CXA	de Havilland DHC-6 Twin Otter 300	602	ex N602DH
☐ VP-CXB	de Havilland DHC-6 Twin Otter 300	563	ex N563DH

CHC HELICOPTERS

☐ VP-CHB	Aérespatiale AS.332L	2582	ex LN-OHI	op in Falklands
☐ VP-CHD	Sikorsky S-76C++	760764	ex C-FZUT	
☐ VP-CHF	AgustaWestland AW139	31474	ex G-LLOV	♦
☐ VP-CHJ	AgustaWestland AW139	31479	ex G-FTOM	♦

VP-F FALKLAND ISLANDS (British Overseas Territory)

BRITISH ANTARCTIC SURVEY   Penguin (BAN)   Rothera Base, Antarctica

☐ VP-FAZ	de Havilland DHC-6 Twin Otter 300	748	ex C-GEOA	Wheels or skis
☐ VP-FBB	de Havilland DHC-6 Twin Otter 310	783	ex C-GDKL	Wheels or skis
☐ VP-FBC	de Havilland DHC-6 Twin Otter 310	787	ex C-GDIU	Wheels or skis
☐ VP-FBL	de Havilland DHC-6 Twin Otter 300	839	ex C-GDCZ	Wheels or skis
☐ VP-FBQ	de Havilland DHC-7-110	111	ex G-BOAX	

FIGAS - FALKLAND ISLANDS GOVERNMENT AIR SERVICES   Port Stanley (PSY)

☐ VP-FBD	Britten-Norman BN-2B-26 Islander	2160	ex G-BKJK	
☐ VP-FBM	Britten-Norman BN-2B-26 Islander	2200	ex G-BLNZ	
☐ VP-FBN	Britten-Norman BN-2B-26 Islander	2216	ex G-BRFY	Fishery Patrol
☐ VP-FBO	Britten-Norman BN-2B-26 Islander	2218	ex G-BRGA	Fishery Patrol
☐ VP-FBR	Britten-Norman BN-2B-26 Islander	2252	ex G-BTLX	

VP-L BRITISH VIRGIN ISLANDS (British Overseas Territory)

BVI AIRWAYS

☐ N487UE	British Aerospace Jetstream 32	906	ex G-31-906

FLY BVI

☐ N208RL	Cessna 208B Caravan I	208B0865	ex N5206T	<FTA

VI AIR LINK

☐ VP-LNB	Beech A100 King Air	B-166	ex N79NB

VP-M MONTSERRAT (British Overseas Territory)

AIR MONTSERRAT   Plymouth (MNI)

☐ VP-MNI	Britten-Norman BN-2B-27 Islander	183	ex C-GLTX
☐ VP-MNT	Britten-Norman BN-2B-26 Islander	2186	

VQ-T TURKS & CAICOS ISLANDS (British Overseas Territory)

CAICOS EXPRESS AIRWAYS   Caicos (CXE)   Providenciales (PLS)

☐ VQ-TIN	Cessna 402C	402C0227	ex N68CT
☐ VQ-TRF	Cessna 402C	402C0021	ex N402RR

GLOBAL AIRWAYS   Providenciales (PLS)

☐ VQ-TBF	Piper PA-23 Aztec 250C	27-2615	ex N5517Y
☐ VQ-TGA	Cessna 401A	401A0114	ex N401DD
☐ VQ-TGS	Piper PA-23 Aztec 250E	27-7554008	ex C-GWVS

INTERCARIBBEAN AIRWAYS		Islandways (JY/IWY)		Providenciales (PLS)
☐ VQ-TBC	Embraer EMB.120ER Brasilia	120283	ex N639AS	
☐ VQ-TDG	Embraer EMB.120ER Brasilia	120275	ex N503AS	
☐ VQ-TEL	Embraer EMB.120ER Brasilia	120273	ex N501AS	♦
☐ VQ-TMJ	Embraer EMB.120ER Brasilia	120274	ex N502AS	
☐ VQ-TVG	Embraer EMB.120ER Brasilia	120268	ex N286AS	♦
☐ VQ-TCI	Beech B200C Super King Air	BL-125	ex VH-BRF	
☐ VQ-TDA	Britten-Norman BN-2A-27 Islander	504	ex HI-704CT	
☐ VQ-TRJ	Cessna 401A	401A0061	ex N60EM	

VT- INDIA (Republic of India)

AIRASIA INDIA		Ariya (I5/IAD)		Chennai (MAA)
☐ VT-ATB	Airbus A320-216/S	6034	ex 9M-AJF	♦
☐ VT-ATF	Airbus A320-216/S	6015	ex F-WWBV	
☐ VT-JRT	Airbus A320-216/S	6262	ex 9M-AJT The Pioneer c/s	♦
☐ VT-RED	Airbus A320-216/S	5824	ex 9M-AQW	♦
☐ VT-	Airbus A320-216	4070	ex 9M-AHU	♦
☐ VT-	Airbus A320-216/S	6096	ex	o/o

AIR COSTA		(LB/LEP)	
☐ VT-LBR	Embraer ERJ-190LR	19000593	ex EI-FCT
☐ VT-LNR	Embraer ERJ-170LR	17000293	ex G-CHJU
☐ VT-LSR	Embraer ERJ-170LR	17000278	ex G-CHJI
☐ VT-LVR	Embraer ERJ-190LR	19000608	ex EI-FDJ

AIR INDIA		Airindia (AI/AIC)	Mumbai-Chhatrapatti Shivaji Intl (BOM)

Member of Star Alliance

☐ VT-SCA	Airbus A319-112	2593	ex D-AVXL	
☐ VT-SCB	Airbus A319-112	2624	ex D-AVYX	
☐ VT-SCC	Airbus A319-112	2629	ex D-AVWC	
☐ VT-SCF	Airbus A319-112	2907	ex D-AVWT	
☐ VT-SCG	Airbus A319-112	3271	ex D-AVYH	
☐ VT-SCH	Airbus A319-112	3288	ex D-AVWM	
☐ VT-SCI	Airbus A319-112	3300	ex D-AVYN	
☐ VT-SCJ	Airbus A319-112	3305	ex D-AVYO	
☐ VT-SCK	Airbus A319-112	3344	ex D-AVYT	
☐ VT-SCL	Airbus A319-112	3551	ex D-AVWO	
☐ VT-SCM	Airbus A319-112	3620	ex D-AVYN	
☐ VT-SCN	Airbus A319-112	3687	ex D-AVWE	
☐ VT-SCO	Airbus A319-112	3822	ex D-AVYH	
☐ VT-SCP	Airbus A319-112	3874	ex D-AVWF	
☐ VT-SCQ	Airbus A319-112	3918	ex D-AVYY	
☐ VT-SCR	Airbus A319-112	3970	ex D-AVYB	
☐ VT-SCS	Airbus A319-112	4020	ex D-AVYH	
☐ VT-SCT	Airbus A319-112	4029	ex D-AVYJ	
☐ VT-SCU	Airbus A319-112	4052	ex D-AVYQ	
☐ VT-SCV	Airbus A319-112	4089	ex D-AVYY	
☐ VT-SCW	Airbus A319-112	4121	ex D-AVWB	
☐ VT-SCX	Airbus A319-112	4164	ex D-AVYZ	
☐ VT-EDC	Airbus A320-214	4201	ex F-WWBD	
☐ VT-EDD	Airbus A320-214	4212	ex F-WWDJ	
☐ VT-EDE	Airbus A320-214	4236	ex F-WWDE	
☐ VT-EDF	Airbus A320-214	4237	ex F-WWDG	
☐ VT-EXA	Airbus A320-214/S	6446	ex D-AXAS	♦
☐ VT-	Airbus A320-214/S	6690	ex	o/o♦
☐ VT-	Airbus A320-214/S	6771	ex	o/o♦
☐ VT-	Airbus A320-214/S	6803	ex	o/o♦
☐ VT-EPB	Airbus A320-231	0045	ex F-WWDY	
☐ VT-EPC	Airbus A320-231	0046	ex F-WWDG	
☐ VT-EPF	Airbus A320-231	0049	ex F-WWIA	
☐ VT-EPG	Airbus A320-231	0050	ex F-WWDR	
☐ VT-EPH	Airbus A320-231	0051	ex F-WWIB	
☐ VT-EPI	Airbus A320-231	0056	ex F-WWIC	
☐ VT-EPJ	Airbus A320-231	0057	ex F-WWIF 50 years titles	
☐ VT-EPS	Airbus A320-231	0096	ex F-WWDU	
☐ VT-ESA	Airbus A320-231	0396	ex F-WWBK	
☐ VT-ESB	Airbus A320-231	0398	ex F-WWDQ	
☐ VT-ESC	Airbus A320-231	0416	ex F-WWBP	
☐ VT-ESD	Airbus A320-231	0423	ex F-WWIT	
☐ VT-ESE	Airbus A320-231	0431	ex F-WWBQ	
☐ VT-ESF	Airbus A320-231	0432	ex F-WWBS Star Alliance c/s	

☐ VT-ESG	Airbus A320-231	0451	ex F-WWIN		
☐ VT-ESI	Airbus A320-231	0486	ex F-WWBH	50 years titles	
☐ VT-ESJ	Airbus A320-231	0490	ex F-WWDT	50 years titles	
☐ VT-ESK	Airbus A320-231	0492	ex F-WWBU	50 years titles	
☐ VT-ESL	Airbus A320-231	0499	ex F-WWDO		
☐ VT-PPA	Airbus A321-211	3130	ex D-AVZT		
☐ VT-PPB	Airbus A321-211	3146	ex D-AVZU		
☐ VT-PPD	Airbus A321-211	3212	ex D-AVZA		
☐ VT-PPE	Airbus A321-211	3326	ex D-AVZW		
☐ VT-PPF	Airbus A321-211	3340	ex D-AVZH		
☐ VT-PPG	Airbus A321-211	3367	ex D-AVZG		
☐ VT-PPH	Airbus A321-211	3498	ex D-AVZG		
☐ VT-PPI	Airbus A321-211	3557	ex D-AVZQ		
☐ VT-PPJ	Airbus A321-211	3573	ex D-AVZC		
☐ VT-PPK	Airbus A321-211	3619	ex D-AVZF		
☐ VT-PPL	Airbus A321-211	3752	ex D-AZAM		
☐ VT-PPM	Airbus A321-211	3792	ex D-AZAR		
☐ VT-PPN	Airbus A321-211	3955	ex D-AZAU		
☐ VT-PPO	Airbus A321-211	4002	ex D-AVZB		
☐ VT-PPQ	Airbus A321-211	4009	ex D-AVZE		
☐ VT-PPT	Airbus A321-211	4078	ex D-AVZU		
☐ VT-PPU	Airbus A321-211	4096	ex D-AVZY		
☐ VT-PPV	Airbus A321-211	4138	ex D-AZAU		
☐ VT-PPW	Airbus A321-211	4155	ex D-AVZZ		
☐ VT-PPX	Airbus A321-211	4280	ex D-AZAP		
☐ VT-EGF	Boeing 737-2A8F	22282/681	ex N8292V		[DEL]
☐ VT-EGG	Boeing 737-2A8F	22283/689	ex N8290V		[DEL]
☐ VT-EGI	Boeing 737-2A8F	22285/798			[DEL]
☐ VT-EGJ	Boeing 737-2A8F	22286/799			[DEL]
☐ VT-EHH	Boeing 737-2A8F	22863/907			[DEL]
☐ VT-ESN	Boeing 747-437	27164/1003		Tanjore	wfs
☐ VT-ESO	Boeing 747-437	27165/1009		Khajurao	
☐ VT-ESP	Boeing 747-437	27214/1034		Ajanta	
☐ VT-EVA	Boeing 747-437	28094/1089		Agra	
☐ VT-EVB	Boeing 747-437	28095/1093		Velha Goa	
☐ VT-ALJ	Boeing 777-337ER	36308/643		Bihar	
☐ VT-ALK	Boeing 777-337ER	36309/652		Chattisgarh	
☐ VT-ALL	Boeing 777-337ER	36310/656		Goa	
☐ VT-ALM	Boeing 777-337ER	36311/713		Himachal Pradesh	
☐ VT-ALN	Boeing 777-337ER	36312/719		Jammu and Kashmir	
☐ VT-ALO	Boeing 777-337ER	36313/798		Karnataka	
☐ VT-ALP	Boeing 777-337ER	36314/804		Madhya Pradesh	
☐ VT-ALQ	Boeing 777-337ER	36315/809		Manipur	
☐ VT-ALR	Boeing 777-337ER	36316/814		Meghalaya	
☐ VT-ALS	Boeing 777-337ER	36317/864		Mizoram	
☐ VT-ALT	Boeing 777-337ER	36318/871		Nagaland	
☐ VT-ALU	Boeing 777-337ER	36319/880		Orissa	
☐ VT-ALV	Boeing 777-337ER	36320/			o/o
☐ VT-ALW	Boeing 777-337ER	36321/			o/o
☐ VT-ALX	Boeing 777-337ER	36322/			o/o
☐ VT-ANA	Boeing 787-8	36273/25	ex N1020K		
☐ VT-ANB	Boeing 787-8	36279/26	ex N10230		
☐ VT-ANC	Boeing 787-8	36274/28			
☐ VT-AND	Boeing 787-8	36278/29	ex N10230		
☐ VT-ANE	Boeing 787-8	36280/30			
☐ VT-ANG	Boeing 787-8	36275/32			
☐ VT-ANH	Boeing 787-8	36276/35	ex N1020L		
☐ VT-ANI	Boeing 787-8	36277/46	ex N6067B		
☐ VT-ANJ	Boeing 787-8	36281/54			
☐ VT-ANK	Boeing 787-8	36282/60			
☐ VT-ANL	Boeing 787-8	36283/65			
☐ VT-ANM	Boeing 787-8	36284/72			
☐ VT-ANN	Boeing 787-8	36285/90	ex N1008S		
☐ VT-ANO	Boeing 787-8	36286/91	ex N8289V		
☐ VT-ANP	Boeing 787-8	36287/158			
☐ VT-ANQ	Boeing 787-8	36288/180			
☐ VT-ANR	Boeing 787-8	36289/208			
☐ VT-ANS	Boeing 787-8	36290/232			
☐ VT-ANT	Boeing 787-8	36291/250			
☐ VT-ANU	Boeing 787-8	36292/273		Star Alliance c/s	
☐ VT-ANV	Boeing 787-8	36293/311			o/o
☐ VT-ANW	Boeing 787-8	36294/			o/o
☐ VT-ANX	Boeing 787-8	36295/			o/o
☐ VT-ANY	Boeing 787-8	36296/			o/o
☐ VT-ANZ	Boeing 787-8	36297/			o/o
☐ VT-NAA	Boeing 787-8	36298/			o/o
☐ VT-NAC	Boeing 787-8	36299/			o/o
☐ VT-	Boeing 787-8	36280/			o/o

☐ VT-ALF	Boeing 777-237LR	36305/793	Jharkhand	
☐ VT-ALG	Boeing 777-237LR	36306/800	Kerala	wfs
☐ VT-ALH	Boeing 777-237LR	36307/805	Maharashtra	[used for spares BOM]

AIR INDIA EXPRESS — Express India (IX/AXB) — Mumbai-Chhatrapatti Shivaji Intl (BOM)

☐ VT-AXH	Boeing 737-8HG/W	36323/2108	
☐ VT-AXI	Boeing 737-8HG/W	36324/2132	
☐ VT-AXJ	Boeing 737-8HG/W	36325/2142	
☐ VT-AXM	Boeing 737-8HG/W	36326/2148	
☐ VT-AXN	Boeing 737-8HG/W	36327/2154	
☐ VT-AXP	Boeing 737-8HG/W	36328/2177	
☐ VT-AXQ	Boeing 737-8HG/W	36329/2258	
☐ VT-AXR	Boeing 737-8HG/W	36330/2317	
☐ VT-AXT	Boeing 737-8HG/W	36331/2324	
☐ VT-AXU	Boeing 737-8HG/W	36332/2381	
☐ VT-AXW	Boeing 737-8HG/W	36334/2612	
☐ VT-AXX	Boeing 737-8HG/W	36335/2672	
☐ VT-AXZ	Boeing 737-8HG/W	36336/2782	ex N1786B
☐ VT-AYA	Boeing 737-8HG/W	36337/2861	ex N6065Y
☐ VT-AYB	Boeing 737-8HG/W	36338/2962	
☐ VT-AYC	Boeing 737-8HG/W	36339/3039	ex N1786B
☐ VT-AYD	Boeing 737-8HG/W	36340/3122	ex N1786B

AIR INDIA REGIONAL — Allied (9I/LLR) — Delhi-Indira Gandhi Intl (DEL)

☐ VT-ABA	ATR 42-320	390	ex F-WQNK	
☐ VT-ABB	ATR 42-320	392	ex F-WQNL	
☐ VT-ABD	ATR 42-320	356	ex F-WQNF	
☐ VT-ABO	ATR 42-320	406	ex F-WQNE	
☐ VT-AII	ATR 72-600	1197	ex F-WNUB	♦
☐ VT-AIT	ATR 72-600	1226	ex F-WWEZ	♦
☐ VT-AIU	ATR 72-600	1246	ex F-WWEV	o/o♦
☐ VT-AIV	ATR 72-600	1252	ex F-WWED	o/o♦
☐ VT-RJB	Canadair CRJ-701LR	10217	ex D-ALTE	Air India Regional c/s
☐ VT-RJC	Canadair CRJ-701ER	10052	ex B-KBB	Air India Regional c/s
☐ VT-RJD	Canadair CRJ-701ER	10048	ex G-DUOD	Air India Regional c/s
☐ VT-RJE	Canadair CRJ-701ER	10029	ex N290RB	Air India Regional c/s

AIR PEGASUS — (PPL) — Bangalore (BLR)

☐ VT-APA	ATR 72-212A	699	ex M-ABFC	♦

BLUE DART AVIATION — Blue Dart (BZ/BDA) — Chennai (MAA)

☐ VT-BDK	Boeing 757-236SF	24267/211	ex OO-DPL		>DHK
☐ VT-BDM	Boeing 757-23NSF	27598/692	ex EI-LTA	Vision VIII	
☐ VT-BDN	Boeing 757-25CPCF	25898/475	ex N7273	Vision IX	
☐ VT-BDO	Boeing 757-204PCF	26962/440	ex N226EA	Vision X	
☐ VT-BDQ	Boeing 757-28APCF	26276/704	ex N391LF	Vision XI	
☐ G-FCLD	Boeing 757-25PCF	28718/752	ex C-GJZX		<DHK♦
☐ VT-BDH	Boeing 737-25C	24236/1585	ex B-2524	Vision IV	wfs

FUTURA TRAVELS

☐ VT-ASH	Beech 1900D	UE-361	ex C-GSKQ
☐ VT-FTL	Hawker 850XP	258980	ex N3188X

GO AIR — Goair (G8/GOW) — Mumbai-Chhatrapatti Shivaji Intl (BOM)

☐ VT-GOI	Airbus A320-214	5016	ex D-AXAF
☐ VT-GOJ	Airbus A320-214	5112	ex F-WWIK
☐ VT-GOK	Airbus A320-214	5232	ex F-WWBS
☐ VT-GOL	Airbus A320-214/S	5463	ex F-WWBE
☐ VT-GOM	Airbus A320-214/S	5552	ex D-AXAX
☐ VT-GON	Airbus A320-214/S	5675	ex F-WWBZ
☐ VT-GOO	Airbus A320-214/S	5811	ex D-AXAL
☐ VT-GOP	Airbus A320-214/S	5809	ex F-WWBD
☐ VT-GOQ	Airbus A320-214/S	5990	ex F-WWBH
☐ VT-GOR	Airbus A320-214/S	6062	ex F-WWII
☐ VT-WAF	Airbus A320-214	3306	ex F-WWIM
☐ VT-WAG	Airbus A320-214	3597	ex D-AVVE
☐ VT-WAH	Airbus A320-214	3616	ex F-WWII
☐ VT-WAI	Airbus A320-214	3798	ex F-WWBP
☐ VT-WAJ	Airbus A320-214	3827	ex F-WWIX
☐ VT-WAK	Airbus A320-214	3900	ex F-WWDU
☐ VT-WAL	Airbus A320-214	3915	ex F-WWBC
☐ VT-WAM	Airbus A320-214	4399	ex F-WWBC
☐ VT-WAN	Airbus A320-214	4438	ex F-WWDF

HELIGO CHARTERS				**Mumbai**
☐ VT-HLC	AgustaWestland AW139	31106	ex A6-AWE	
☐ VT-HLD	AgustaWestland AW139	31281		
☐ VT-HLG	Bell 412EP	36272	ex A6-BAU	♦
☐ VT-HLI	Aérospatiale AS365N3 Dauphin 2	6773	ex PR-MEL	♦
☐ VT-HLJ	Aérospatiale AS365N3 Dauphin 2	6776	ex PR-MEM	♦
☐ VT-HLK	Bell 412	36280	ex PK-URH	♦
☐ VT-HLP	AgustaWestland AW139	41268	ex N3885H	

INDIGO		**Ifly (6E/IGO)**		**Bangalore (BLR)**
☐ VT-IAL	Airbus A320-232/S	5992	ex D-AUBR	
☐ VT-IAN	Airbus A320-232/S	6010	ex F-WWBT	
☐ VT-IAO	Airbus A320-232/S	6036	ex D-AXAD	
☐ VT-IAP	Airbus A320-232/S	6208	ex D-AVVI	♦
☐ VT-IAQ	Airbus A320-232/S	6247	ex D-AVVQ	♦
☐ VT-IAR	Airbus A320-232/S	6275	ex D-AVVV	♦
☐ VT-IAS	Airbus A320-232/S	6289	ex D-AVVW	♦
☐ VT-IAX	Airbus A320-232/S	6287	ex F-WWIU	♦
☐ VT-IAY	Airbus A320-232/S	6336	ex D-AXAB	♦
☐ VT-IDA	Airbus A320-232	4918	ex 9V-TRC	♦
☐ VT-IDB	Airbus A320-232	4973	ex PK-RMO	♦
☐ VT-IDC	Airbus A320-232	5073	ex PK-RMP	♦
☐ VT-IDD	Airbus A320-232	5335	ex 9V-TRS	♦
☐ VT-IDE	Airbus A320-232	5375	ex 9V-TRT	♦
☐ VT-IDF	Airbus A320-232	5426	ex 9V-TRU	♦
☐ VT-IDH	Airbus A320-232	5194	ex 9V-TRP	o/o♦
☐ VT-IDI	Airbus A320-232	5188	ex 9V-TRO	♦
☐ VT-IDJ	Airbus A320-232	4812	ex 9V-TAX	♦
☐ VT-IDK	Airbus A320-232	5228	ex 9V-TRQ	♦
☐ VT-IDL	Airbus A320-232	5120	ex 9V-TRG	♦
☐ VT-IEA	Airbus A320-232	4603	ex D-AXAR	
☐ VT-IEB	Airbus A320-232	4609	ex D-AXAT	
☐ VT-IEC	Airbus A320-232	4614	ex F-WWBF	
☐ VT-IED	Airbus A320-232	4630	ex F-WWDJ	
☐ VT-IEE	Airbus A320-232	4637	ex F-WWIB	
☐ VT-IEF	Airbus A320-232	4752	ex F-WWBG	
☐ VT-IEG	Airbus A320-232	4762	ex F-WWBQ	
☐ VT-IEH	Airbus A320-232	4757	ex F-WWBI	
☐ VT-IEI	Airbus A320-232	4813	ex D-AXAI	
☐ VT-IEJ	Airbus A320-232	4818	ex D-AXAK	
☐ VT-IEK	Airbus A320-232	4868	ex D-AUBQ	
☐ VT-IEL	Airbus A320-232	4888	ex D-AVVE	
☐ VT-IEM	Airbus A320-232	4947	ex D-AXAR	
☐ VT-IEN	Airbus A320-232	4954	ex D-AXAV	
☐ VT-IEO	Airbus A320-232	4965	ex F-WWBC	
☐ VT-IEP	Airbus A320-232	5027	ex D-AXAJ	
☐ VT-IEQ	Airbus A320-232	5036	ex D-AXAM	
☐ VT-IER	Airbus A320-232	5076	ex F-WWBY	
☐ VT-IES	Airbus A320-232	5090	ex F-WWDN	
☐ VT-IET	Airbus A320-232	5094	ex D-AUBM	
☐ VT-IEU	Airbus A320-232	5092	ex D-AUBL	
☐ VT-IEV	Airbus A320-232	5080	ex F-WWIF	
☐ VT-IEW	Airbus A320-232	5155	ex D-AXAB	
☐ VT-IEX	Airbus A320-232	5190	ex F-WWID	
☐ VT-IEY	Airbus A320-232	5230	ex D-AUBP	
☐ VT-IEZ	Airbus A320-232	5231	ex D-AVVN	
☐ VT-IFA	Airbus A320-232	5259	ex D-AXAJ	
☐ VT-IFB	Airbus A320-232	5262	ex F-WWDZ	
☐ VT-IFC	Airbus A320-232	5291	ex D-AXAO	
☐ VT-IFD	Airbus A320-232	5298	ex D-AXAQ	
☐ VT-IFE	Airbus A320-232	5313	ex F-WWDG	
☐ VT-IFF	Airbus A320-232	5365	ex F-WWDT	
☐ VT-IFG	Airbus A320-232	5411	ex D-AVVF	
☐ VT-IFH	Airbus A320-232/S	5437	ex D-AVVO	
☐ VT-IFI	Airbus A320-232/S	5460	ex D-AVVV	
☐ VT-IFJ	Airbus A320-232/S	5473	ex D-AVVX	
☐ VT-IFK	Airbus A320-232/S	5476	ex D-AVVY	
☐ VT-IFL	Airbus A320-232/S	5507	ex D-AXAI	
☐ VT-IFM	Airbus A320-232/S	5537	ex D-AXAT	
☐ VT-IFN	Airbus A320-232/S	5577	ex D-AUBD	
☐ VT-IFO	Airbus A320-232/S	5641	ex F-WWIN	
☐ VT-IFP	Airbus A320-232/S	5676	ex D-AVVC	
☐ VT-IFQ	Airbus A320-232/S	5683	ex D-AVVD	
☐ VT-IFR	Airbus A320-232/S	5712	ex F-WWDL	
☐ VT-IFS	Airbus A320-232/S	5727	ex F-WWIT	
☐ VT-IFT	Airbus A320-232/S	5744	ex F-WWDU	
☐ VT-IFU	Airbus A320-232/S	5807	ex D-AXAK	
☐ VT-IFV	Airbus A320-232/S	5829	ex D-AXAP	
☐ VT-IFW	Airbus A320-232/S	5893	ex D-AVVM	
☐ VT-IFX	Airbus A320-232/S	5898	ex D-AVVN	

☐ VT-IFY	Airbus A320-232/S	5923	ex D-AUBD	
☐ VT-IFZ	Airbus A320-232/S	5952	ex D-AUBK	
☐ VT-IGH	Airbus A320-232	4008	ex F-WWDZ	
☐ VT-IGI	Airbus A320-232	4113	ex F-WWDV	
☐ VT-IGJ	Airbus A320-232	4156	ex F-WWBM	
☐ VT-IGK	Airbus A320-232	4216	ex F-WWBE	
☐ VT-IGL	Airbus A320-232	4312	ex F-WWBD	
☐ VT-IGS	Airbus A320-232	4328	ex F-WWIB	
☐ VT-IGT	Airbus A320-232	4384	ex F-WWBN	
☐ VT-IGU	Airbus A320-232	4488	ex D-AUBH	
☐ VT-IGV	Airbus A320-232	4481	ex F-WWDL	
☐ VT-IGW	Airbus A320-232	4506	ex D-AUBN	
☐ VT-IGX	Airbus A320-232	4518	ex D-AXAH	
☐ VT-IGY	Airbus A320-232	4535	ex F-WWDX	
☐ VT-IGZ	Airbus A320-232	4552	ex D-AUBR	
☐ VT-INP	Airbus A320-232	3357	ex F-WWIH	
☐ VT-INQ	Airbus A320-232	3414	ex F-WWIM	
☐ VT-INR	Airbus A320-232	3453	ex F-WWBF	
☐ VT-INS	Airbus A320-232	3457	ex F-WWBI	
☐ VT-INT	Airbus A320-232	3497	ex F-WWIM	
☐ VT-INU	Airbus A320-232	3541	ex F-WWIP	
☐ VT-INV	Airbus A320-232	3618	ex F-WWIJ	
☐ VT-INX	Airbus A320-232	3782	ex D-AVVK	
☐ VT-INY	Airbus A320-232	3863	ex F-WWDY	
☐ VT-INZ	Airbus A320-232	3943	ex F-WWDT	
☐ VT-	Airbus A320-232	5449	ex 9V-TRV	o/o♦
☐ VT-	Airbus A320-232/S	6023	ex 9V-TRO	o/o♦
☐ VT-	Airbus A320-271Neo	6720	ex	o/o♦
☐ VT-	Airbus A320-271Neo	6744	ex	o/o♦
☐ VT-	Airbus A320-271Neo	6819	ex	o/o♦
☐ VT-	Airbus A320-271Neo	6829	ex	o/o♦
☐ VT-	Airbus A320-271Neo	6860	ex	o/o♦
☐ VT-	Airbus A320-271Neo	6868	ex	o/o♦
☐ VT-	Airbus A320-271Neo	6952	ex	o/o♦

JAGSON AIRLINES   Delhi-Indira Gandhi Intl (DEL)

☐ VT-ESS	Dornier 228-201	8017	ex A5-RGC
☐ VT-EUM	Dornier 228-201	8096	ex D-CAAL
☐ VT-JJA	Mil Mi-172	365C157	
☐ VT-JJB	Mil Mi-172	365C158	

JET AIRWAYS   Jet Airways (9W/JAI)   Mumbai-Chhatrapatti Shivaji Intl (BOM)

☐ VT-JWJ	Airbus A330-202	885	ex F-WWKS	
☐ VT-JWK	Airbus A330-202	888	ex F-WWKL	
☐ VT-JWM	Airbus A330-202	923	ex F-WWYZ	
☐ VT-JWP	Airbus A330-202	947	ex F-WWKM	
☐ VT-JWQ	Airbus A330-202	956	ex F-WWYA	
☐ VT-JWR	Airbus A330-302	1351	ex F-WWCQ	
☐ VT-JWS	Airbus A330-302	1361	ex F-WWKF	
☐ VT-JWT	Airbus A330-302	1370	ex F-WWKU	
☐ VT-JWU	Airbus A330-302	1391	ex F-WWYX	
☐ VT-JWV	Airbus A330-202	923	ex A6-EYB	♦
☐ VT-JCA	ATR 72-212A	572	ex F-WQKD	
☐ VT-JCD	ATR 72-212A	636	ex F-WQMC	
☐ VT-JCJ	ATR 72-212A	771	ex F-WWEJ	
☐ VT-JCK	ATR 72-212A	775	ex F-WWEN	
☐ VT-JCL	ATR 72-212A	791	ex F-WWEK	
☐ VT-JCP	ATR 72-212A	841	ex F-WWES	
☐ VT-JCQ	ATR 72-212A	843	ex F-WWEJ	
☐ VT-JCR	ATR 72-212A	919	ex F-WWER	
☐ VT-JCS	ATR 72-212A	920	ex F-WWES	
☐ VT-JCT	ATR 72-212A	924	ex F-WWEX	
☐ VT-JCU	ATR 72-212A	928	ex F-WWED	
☐ VT-JCV	ATR 72-212A	932	ex F-WWEH	
☐ VT-JBB	Boeing 737-8HX/W	36846/2368	ex N846AG	
☐ VT-JBC	Boeing 737-8HX/W	36847/2388	ex N847AG	
☐ VT-JBD	Boeing 737-85R/W	35099/2439		
☐ VT-JBE	Boeing 737-85R/W	35106/2530	ex N1786B	
☐ VT-JBF	Boeing 737-85R/W	35082/2550	ex N1786B	
☐ VT-JBG	Boeing 737-85R/W	35083/2535	ex N1786B	
☐ VT-JBH	Boeing 737-85R/W	35289/2811	ex N1786B	
☐ VT-JBJ	Boeing 737-85R/W	36551/2974	ex N1786B	
☐ VT-JBK	Boeing 737-85R/W	36553/3074	ex N1786B	
☐ VT-JBM	Boeing 737-86N/W	36817/3055	ex N1786B	
☐ VT-JBN	Boeing 737-86N/W	36818/3087	ex N1786B	
☐ VT-JBP	Boeing 737-86N/W	36819/3101	ex N1779B	

☐ VT-JBQ	Boeing 737-85R/W	36694/3264	ex N1787B	
☐ VT-JBR	Boeing 737-85R/W	36695/3281		
☐ VT-JBS	Boeing 737-85R/W	36698/3433		
☐ VT-JBT	Boeing 737-8BK/W	33024/1688	ex VT-AXC	
☐ VT-JBU	Boeing 737-86N/W	36825/3763		
☐ VT-JBV	Boeing 737-86N/W	36827/3836		
☐ VT-JBW	Boeing 737-8AL/W	37960/3809		
☐ VT-JBX	Boeing 737-8AL/W	37961/3847		
☐ VT-JFA	Boeing 737-86N/W	38029/4111		
☐ VT-JFB	Boeing 737-86N/W	39401/4127		
☐ VT-JFC	Boeing 737-86N/W	38030/4139		
☐ VT-JFD	Boeing 737-8AL/W	39051/4205		
☐ VT-JFE	Boeing 737-8AL/W	39053/4270		
☐ VT-JFF	Boeing 737-8AL/W	39055/4342	ex N5573K	
☐ VT-JFP	Boeing 737-8AL/W	39068/4696		
☐ VT-JFQ	Boeing 737-8AL/W	39063/4727		
☐ VT-JFR	Boeing 737-8AL/W	39064/4793		
☐ VT-JFS	Boeing 737-8AL/W	39065/4884		
☐ VT-JFT	Boeing 737-8AL/W	39066/4932		♦
☐ VT-JFW	Boeing 737-85R/W	42799/4984		♦
☐ VT-JFX	Boeing 737-85R/W	42800/5054		♦
☐ VT-JFY	Boeing 737-85R/W	42804/5068		♦
☐ VT-JFZ	Boeing 737-8Rr/w	39069/5112		♦
☐ VT-JGA	Boeing 737-85R	30410/1228		dam 13Apr15
☐ VT-JGE	Boeing 737-83N/W	32663/1608	ex EI-DIL	
☐ VT-JGF	Boeing 737-8FH/W	29639/1643	ox EI-DIM	
☐ VT-JGG	Boeing 737-8FH/W	29668/1686	ex EI-DIN	
☐ VT-JGK	Boeing 737-83N/W	32579/1002	ex EI-DKR	
☐ VT-JGP	Boeing 737-85R/W	34798/1920		
☐ VT-JGQ	Boeing 737-85R/W	34797/2007		
☐ VT-JGR	Boeing 737-85R/W	34799/2044		
☐ VT-JGS	Boeing 737-85R/W	34800/2085		
☐ VT-JGT	Boeing 737-85R/W	34801/2125		
☐ VT-JGU	Boeing 737-85R/W	34802/2170		
☐ VT-JGV	Boeing 737-85R/W	34803/2209		
☐ VT-JGW	Boeing 737-85R/W	34804/2297		
☐ VT-JNL	Boeing 737-85R	29039/326	ex N1786B	
☐ VT-JNN	Boeing 737-85R	29041/489	ex N1786B	
☐ VT-JTA	Boeing 737-85R/W	42805/5184		♦
☐ VT-JTB	Boeing 737-85R/W	39070/5196		♦
☐ VT-JBZ	Boeing 737-96NER/W	36539/2596	ex M-ABER	
☐ VT-JEH	Boeing 777-35RER	35166/678	ex N5014K	
☐ VT-JEK	Boeing 777-35RER	35165/696		
☐ VT-JEM	Boeing 777-35RER	35162/666	ex TC-JJB	
☐ VT-JEQ	Boeing 777-35RER	35161/693	ex HS-TKJ	
☐ VT-JGC	Boeing 737-95R	30412/1314		
☐ VT-JGD	Boeing 737-95R	33740/1350		
☐ VT-JGL	Boeing 737-76N/W	32738/1392	ex EI-DMD	
☐ VT-JGX	Boeing 737-75R/W	34805/2360	ex N1781B	
☐ VT-JGY	Boeing 737-75R/W	34806/2404		
☐ VT-JGZ	Boeing 737-76N/W	35218/2342	ex N1781B	

JETKONNECT		**Sahara (S2/JLL)**		**Delhi-Indira Gandhi Intl (DEL)**
☐ VT-JCM	ATR 72-212A	793	ex F-WWEN	
☐ VT-JCN	ATR 72-212A	825	ex F-WWEN	
☐ VT-JCW	ATR 72-212A	933	ex F-WWEI	
☐ VT-JCX	ATR 72-600	1056	ex F-WWEQ	
☐ VT-JCY	ATR 72-600	1064	ex F-WTDH	
☐ VT-JCZ	ATR 72-600	1075	ex F-WWEL	
☐ VT-JDC	ATR 72-212A	772	ex M-IBAC	
☐ VT-JDD	ATR 72-212A	758	ex M-IBAD	
☐ VT-JBL	Boeing 737-85R/W	35651/3000		
☐ VT-JGJ	Boeing 737-83N/W	32578/998	ex EI-DKP	
☐ VT-JLE	Boeing 737-8AS/W	33555/1426	ex EI-DAV	
☐ VT-JLF	Boeing 737-8AS/W	33556/1428	ex EI-DAW	
☐ VT-SJI	Boeing 737-8K9/W	34399/2030		
☐ VT-SJJ	Boeing 737-8K9/W	34400/2053		
☐ VT-JBY	Boeing 737-96NER/W	35227/2621	ex M-ABEP	
☐ VT-JLB	Boeing 737-7Q8	28250/1142	ex A4O-BT	
☐ VT-JLH	Boeing 737-96NER/W	35223/2559	ex M-ABEN	
☐ VT-JLJ	Boeing 737-96NER/W	35225/2590	ex M-ABEO	
☐ VT-SIZ	Boeing 737-7BK	33025/1707	ex N325CT	
☐ VT-SJA	Boeing 737-7BK	33026/1715	ex N326CT	

MDLR AIRLINES				**Mumbai-Chhatrapatti Shivaji Intl (BOM)**
☐ VT-MDL	Avro 146-RJ70	E1229	ex G-BUFI	[DEL]
☐ VT-MDM	Avro 146-RJ70	E1230	ex G-CDNB	[DEL]

☐ VT-MDN	Avro 146-RJ70	E1252	ex G-CDNC	[BCM]

NORTHEAST SHUTTLE

☐ VT-EIO	Dornier 228-201	8037	ex D-IDBG	
☐ VT-NER	Dornier 228-212	8191	ex 9N-AIY	

PINNACLE AIR   Bangalore (BLR)

☐ VT-VTP	Cessna 208 Caravan I	2308	ex N6019U	

SPICEJET   SpiceJet (SG/SEJ)   Delhi-Indira Ghandi International (DEL)

☐ OK-TSA	Boeing 737-8S3/W	29250/792	ex TC-APH		<QS♦
☐ OK-TVO	Boeing 737-8CX/W	32360/1084	ex PR-GOK		<TVS♦
☐ OK-TVX	Boeing 737-8Z9/W	33833/1680	ex OE-LNR	Airport Prague c/s	<TVS♦
☐ VT-SGG	Boeing 737-8GJ/W	36368/3310		Chilli	
☐ VT-SGH	Boeing 737-8GJ/W	36369/3363		Turmeric	
☐ VT-SGJ	Boeing 737-86J/W	29641/1654	ex G-CGPP	Cumin	
☐ VT-SGQ	Boeing 737-8GJ/W	37365/3539	ex N1796B		
☐ VT-SGV	Boeing 737-8GJ/W	37362/3830	ex N1782B	Nigella	
☐ VT-SGX	Boeing 737-86J/W	37751/3932		Parsley	
☐ VT-SGY	Boeing 737-8GJ/W	37765/3986		Cayenne	
☐ VT-SGZ	Boeing 737-8GJ/W	39423/4025		Caraway	
☐ VT-SPF	Boeing 737-8GJ/W	34896/1861		Coriander	
☐ VT-SPK	Boeing 737-8GJ/W	34898/2104		Fennel	
☐ VT-SPL	Boeing 737-8GJ/W	34899/2128		Cardamom	
☐ VT-SPP	Boeing 737-86N/W	35217/2359		Rosemary	
☐ VT-SZA	Boeing 737-8GJ/W	39424/4054		Sage	
☐ VT-SZB	Boeing 737-8GJ/W	39427/4225	ex N1786B	Sumac	
☐ VT-SZI	Boeing 737-8GJ/W	37364/4638		Gambooge	
☐ VT-SZJ	Boeing 737-8GJ/W	41397/4769	ex N1786B	Saffron	
☐ VT-SZK	Boeing 737-8GJ/W	41398/4910		Red Chilli	♦
☐ VT-SUA	de Havilland DHC-8-402Q	4373	ex C-GJJU	Saunf	
☐ VT-SUB	de Havilland DHC-8-402Q	4374	ex C-GJKC	Heeng	
☐ VT-SUC	de Havilland DHC-8-402Q	4377	ex C-GKLF	Tulsi	
☐ VT-SUD	de Havilland DHC-8-402Q	4378	ex C-GKLZ	Tejpatta	
☐ VT-SUE	de Havilland DHC-8-402Q	4379	ex C-GKMS	Elaichi	
☐ VT-SUF	de Havilland DHC-8-402Q	4382	ex C-GKOI	Kesar	
☐ VT-SUG	de Havilland DHC-8-402Q	4387	ex C-GKVM	Jeera	
☐ VT-SUH	de Havilland DHC-8-402Q	4389	ex C-GKVP	Dhania	
☐ VT-SUI	de Havilland DHC-8-402Q	4395	ex C-GLEP	Haldi	
☐ VT-SUJ	de Havilland DHC-8-402Q	4396	ex C-GLFS	Daichini	
☐ VT-SUK	de Havilland DHC-8-402Q	4398	ex C-GLKU	Sarson	
☐ VT-SUL	de Havilland DHC-8-402Q	4400	ex C-GLUM	Javitri	
☐ VT-SUM	de Havilland DHC-8-402Q	4402	ex C-GLKV	Jaiphal	
☐ VT-SUO	de Havilland DHC-8-402Q	4404	ex C-GMOU	Laung	
☐ VT-SUP	de Havilland DHC-8-402Q	4412	ex C-GNHX	Imli	
☐ VT-SPU	Boeing 737-9GJER/W	34953/2466		Anise	

VENTURA AIRCONNECT

☐ VT-VAK	Cessna 208B Caravan I	208B2281	ex N90015	
☐ VT-VAM	Cessna 208B Caravan I	208B2269	ex N9000F	

VISTARA   (UK/VTI)   Delhi-Indira Ghandi Intl (DEL)

☐ VT-TTB	Airbus A320-232/S	6223	ex F-WWDT	♦
☐ VT-TTC	Airbus A320-232/S	6278	ex F-WWID	♦
☐ VT-TTD	Airbus A320-232/S	6311	ex F-WHUL	♦
☐ VT-TTE	Airbus A320-232/S	6343	ex F-WXAG	♦
☐ VT-TTF	Airbus A320-232/S	6388	ex F-WWDF	♦
☐ VT-TTG	Airbus A320-232/S	6513	ex F-WWBN	♦
☐ VT-	Airbus A320-232/S	6741	ex	o/o♦
☐ VT-	Airbus A320-232/S	6800	ex	o/o♦
☐ VT-	Airbus A320-232/S	6824	ex	o/o♦

V2- ANTIGUA (State of Antigua and Barbuda)

LIAT - THE CARIBBEAN AIRLINE   LIAT (LI/LIA)   Antigua-VC Bird Intl (ANU)

☐ V2-LID	ATR 42-600	1006	ex F-WWLO	
☐ V2-LIF	ATR 42-600	1008	ex F-WWLQ	
☐ V2-LIG	ATR 42-600	1009	ex F-WWLR	
☐ V2-LIK	ATR 42-600	1012	ex F-WWLU	♦
☐ V2-LIM	ATR 42-600	1018	ex F-WWLC	♦
☐ V2-LDQ	de Havilland DHC-8-102	113	ex EI-BWX	[ANU]

☐ V2-LDU	de Havilland DHC-8-103	270	ex EI-CBV		
☐ V2-LEF	de Havilland DHC-8-103	144	ex HS-SKH		
☐ V2-LEU	de Havilland DHC-8-311	408	ex C-FWBB	Sir Frank de Lisle	wfs
☐ V2-LFF	de Havilland DHC-8-314	410	ex N285BC		
☐ V2-LFV	de Havilland DHC-8-311A	283	ex PH-SDR		[ANU]
☐ V2-LGB	de Havilland DHC-8-311A	266	ex C-GZTB		
☐ V2-LGI	de Havilland DHC-8-311A	325	ex C-FHXB		
☐ V2-LGN	de Havilland DHC-8-311	230	ex PJ-DHL		
☐ V2-LIA	ATR 72-600	1077	ex (VT-JDA)		
☐ V2-LIB	ATR 72-600	1103	ex F-WWEP		
☐ V2-LIC	ATR 72-600	1091	ex F-WWED		
☐ V2-LIH	ATR 72-600	1112	ex F-WWEZ		

V3- BELIZE

MAYA ISLAND AIR	**Myland (MY/MYD)**		**Belize City-Municipal/San Pedro (TZA/SPR)**
☐ V3-HGF	Cessna 208B Caravan I	208B0927	ex N52627
☐ V3-HGJ	Cessna 208B Caravan I	208B0946	ex N52639
☐ V3-HGO	Cessna 208B Caravan I	208B0995	ex N1241G
☐ V3-HGP	Cessna 208B Caravan I	208B0998	exN12419
☐ V3-HGQ	Cessna 208B Caravan I	208B0973	ex N1248G
☐ V3-HGW	Cessna 208B Caravan I	208B1095	ex N1273Z
☐ V3-HHA	Cessna 208B Caravan I	208B1292	ex N4117D
☐ V3-HGE	Britten-Norman BN-2A-26 Islander	911	ex N103NE
☐ V3-HGI	Gippsland GA-8 Airvan	GA8-01-008	ex VH-AUV
☐ V3-HGK	Britten-Norman BN-2A-26 Islander	853	ex N271RS

TROPIC AIR	**Tropiser (9N/TOS)**		**San Pedro (SPR)**
☐ V3-HFV	Cessna 208B Caravan I	208B0647	ex N5268M
☐ V3-HGV	Cessna 208B Caravan I	208B1072	ex N5185V
☐ V3-HGX	Cessna 208B Caravan I	208B1162	ex N5108G
☐ V3-HHC	Cessna 208B Caravan I	208B2004	
☐ V3-HHE	Cessna 208B Caravan I	208B2062	exN52475
☐ V3-HHG	Cessna 208B Caravan I	208B2051	ex N5270K
☐ V3-HHI	Cessna 208B Caravan I	208B2149	ex N52234
☐ V3-HHK	Cessna 208B Caravan I	208B2249	ex N52038
☐ V3-HHL	Cessna 208B Caravan I	208B	
☐ V3-HHM	Cessna 208B Caravan I	208B	
☐ V3-HDT	Cessna 207A Stationair 8	20700716	ex (N9696M)
☐ V3-HSS	Beech A100 King Air	B-222	ex C-GVMI ♦

V4- ST KITTS & NEVIS (Federation of St Christopher and Nevis)

AIR ST KITTS & NEVIS			**Basseterre-Golden Rock (SKB)**
☐ N785PA	Cessna 208B Caravan I	208B0994	ex C6-NFS
☐ N920HL	Cessna 208B Caravan I	208B2232	opf DHL
☐ N930HL	Cessna 208B Caravan I	208B2238	opf DHL

V5- NAMIBIA (Republic of Namibia)

AIR NAMIBIA		**Namibia (SW/NMB)**	**Windhoek-Eros/Hosea Kutako Intl (ERS)**
☐ V5-ANF	Embraer ERJ-135ER	145243	ex F-GOHC	<RAE
☐ V5-ANG	Embraer ERJ-135ER	145335	ex F-GOHE	<RAE
☐ V5-ANH	Embraer ERJ-135ER	145347	ex F-GOHF	<RAE
☐ V5-ANI	Embraer ERJ-135ER	145252	ex F-GOHD	<RAE
☐ V5-ANK	Airbus A319-112	3586	ex D-ABGL	
☐ V5-ANL	Airbus A319-112	3346	ex D-ABGI	
☐ V5-ANM	Airbus A319-112	5366	ex D-AVWG	
☐ V5-ANN	Airbus A319-112	5400	ex D-AVWK	
☐ V5-ANO	Airbus A330-243	1451	ex F-WWYC	
☐ V5-ANP	Airbus A330-243	1466	ex F-WWCD	
☐ V5-NME	Airbus A340-311	051	ex D-AIMG	[LDE]
☐ V5-NMF	Airbus A340-311	047	ex D-AIMF	[LDE]
☐ V5-OUB	Beech 1900C	UB-20	ex V5-MMN	

BAY AIR AVIATION	**Nomad Air (NMD)**		**Walvis Bay (WVB)**
☐ V5-FUR	Cessna 310Q	310Q0456	ex ZS-FUR

CARAVAN AIR

☐ V5-GPX   Cessna 208 Caravan I   20800177   ex ZS-MVY

COMPION AVIATION		Compion (COX)		Windhoek-Eros (ERS)

☐ V5-NPR	Cessna 310Q	310Q0985	ex ZS-NPR	
☐ V5-SOS	Cessna 402C	402C0437	ex V5-AAS	EMS International SOS titles

DESERT AIR				Windhoek-Eros (ERS)

☐ V5-DAC	Rockwell 840 Turbo Commander	11732	ex N8VL	
☐ V5-DOL	Rockwell 690B Turbo Commander	11422	ex D2-EBX	♦
☐ V5-MAC	Rockwell 690B Turbo Commander	11557	ex N75WA	
☐ V5-MAX	Cessna 208B Caravan I	208B0706	ex N910HE	
☐ V5-MKR	Cessna T210N Turbo Centurion II	21063060	ex ZS-LAS	
☐ V5-MKS	Cessna T310R II	310R0583	ex N410AS	
☐ V5-SKY	Cessna T210L Turbo Centurion II	21059953	ex ZS-SKY	Sossus Air Taxi titles
☐ V5-TEM	Beech Baron 58	TH-812	ex V5-LZG	

NAMIBIA COMMERCIAL AIRWAYS		Med Rescue (MRE)		Windhoek-Eros (ERS)

☐ ZS-NAT	Britten-Norman BN-2T Turbine Islander	2158	ex 7Q-CAV	
☐ V5-NCG	Douglas DC-6B	45564/1040	ex GBM112	Batuleur

SEFOFANE AIR				Windhoek-Eros (ERS)

☐ V5-BAT	Cessna T210N Turbo Centurion II	21064543	ex ZS-MUG
☐ V5-BUZ	Cessna T210N Turbo Centurion II	21063539	ex ZS-OXI
☐ V5-KUD	Cessna 210N Centurion II	21063834	ex ZS-KUD
☐ V5-MTB	Cessna T210N Turbo Centurion II	21062933	ex ZS-MTB
☐ V5-RNO	Cessna 208B Caravan I	208B1304	ex N41138
☐ ZS-SUN	Cessna 208B Caravan I	208B0307	ex V5-SUN

WESTAIR AVIATION		Westair Wings (WAA)		Windhoek-Eros (ERS)

☐ V5-AAG	Cessna 210M Centurion II	21062077	ex N9646M	tail magnetometer
☐ V5-LWH	Cessna 310R	310R0571	ex ZS-LWH	
☐ V5-LXZ	Cessna 210M Centurion II	21063931	ex ZS-LXZ	
☐ V5-MDY	Cessna 402B	402B1353	ex D2-FFW	
☐ V5-ROB	Cessna 208B Caravan I	208B....		
☐ V5-SAC	Cessna 340A	340A0945	ex ZS-KUH	
☐ V5-WAA	Cessna 404 Titan II (RAM)	404-0210	ex N88668	Ghost Rider
☐ V5-WAB	Cessna 310Q	310Q0727	ex N4541Q	
☐ V5-WAC	Cessna 404 Titan II	404-0616	ex ZS-KRJ	
☐ V5-WAD	Cessna 310R	310R1340	ex ZS-KEE	
☐ V5-WAE	Cessna 402C	402C0430	ex ZS-NPA	
☐ V5-WAG	Cessna 310R	310R1668	ex V5-KRK	
☐ V5-WAK	Reims Cessna F406 Caravan II	F406-0048	ex G-FLYN	DHL titles

WILDERNESS AIR

☐ V5-ECO	Cessna 208B Caravan I	208B2037	ex N2193K
☐ V5-RNO	Cessna 208B Caravan I	208B1304	ex N41138

V6-   MICRONESIA (Federated States of Micronesia)

CAROLINE ISLAND AIR			Pohnpei (PNI)

☐ V6-01FM	Britten-Norman BN-2A-27 Islander	2014	ex V6-SFM
☐ V6-02FM	Beech 65-80 Queen Air	LC-84	ex N349N
☐ V6-03FM	Britten-Norman BN-2A-21 Islander	660	ex VH-AUN

V7-   MARSHALL ISLANDS (Republic of the Marshall Islands)

AIR MARSHALL ISLANDS		Air Marshalls (CMW)		Majuro Intl (MAJ)

☐ V7-0210	de Havilland DHC-8-102	218	ex ZK-NEU
☐ V7-9206	Dornier 228-212	8194	ex MI-9206
☐ V7-9207	Dornier 228-212	8201	ex MI-9207

V8-   BRUNEI (Negara Brunei Darussalam)

BRUNEI SHELL

☐ V8-GAS	Sikorsky S-92A	920042	ex N8068V
☐ V8-OIL	Sikorsky S-92A	920041	ex N8086L

| ☐ V8-SAR | Sikorsky S-92A | 920039 | ex V8-SHL | ♦ |

ROYAL BRUNEI AIRLINES — Brunei (BI/RBA) — Bandar Seri Begawan (BWN)

☐ V8-RBS	Airbus A320-232	2135	ex F-WWIV	
☐ V8-RBT	Airbus A320-232	2139	ex F-WWDO	
☐ V8-RBU	Airbus A320-232	2195	ex 9V-TAB	
☐ V8-RBV	Airbus A320-232	3071	ex A7-ADU	
☐ V8-	Airbus A320-232	6708	ex	o/o♦
☐ V8-	Airbus A320-232	6816	ex	o/o♦
☐ V8-DLA	Boeing 787-8	34785/128		
☐ V8-DLB	Boeing 787-8	34786/130		
☐ V8-DLC	Boeing 787-8	34789/156		
☐ V8-DLD	Boeing 787-8	34788/166		
☐ V8-RBP	Airbus A319-132	2023	ex D-AVWW	
☐ V8-RBR	Airbus A319-132	2032	ex D-AVYK	

XA- MEXICO (United Mexican States)

AEREO CALAFIA — Calafia (CFV) — Los Cabos (SJD)

☐ XA-AVT	Cessna 208B Caravan I	208B0301	ex XA-SFJ	
☐ XA-BTS	Cessna 208B Caravan I	208B1093	ex XA-UCT	
☐ XA-HVB	Cessna 208B Caravan I	208B1104	ex N4047W	dam 17Sep14
☐ XA-TWN	Cessna 208B Caravan I	208B0931	ex N5296M	dam 17Sep14
☐ XA-UGI	Cessna 208B Caravan I	208B1211	ex N5166U	
☐ XA-VVT	Cessna 208B Caravan I	208B1269		
☐ XA-JVT	Embraer EMB-120ER Brasilia	120330	ex N393SW	
☐ XA-OVB	Embraer ERJ-145ER	145083	ex N183EC	
☐ XA-TQW	Cessna 206H Stationair	20608072	ex N4002B	

AEREO OWEN — Los Mochis (LMM)

| ☐ XA-OWN | Embraer EMB-120 Brasilia | 120272 | ex N500DN | ♦ |

AERO BINIZA — Biniza (BZS) — Oaxaca (OAX)

| ☐ XA-GIL | Cessna 208B Caravan I | 208B1088 | ex N817SB | |
| ☐ XA-UAB | Cessna 208B Caravan I | 208B1017 | ex XA-TVS | |

AERO CUAHONTE — Cuahonte (CUO) — Uruapan (UPN)

☐ XA-GUU	Swearingen SA226TC Metro II	TC-389	ex XA-STV	
☐ XA-HUO	Swearingen SA226AC Metro II			
☐ XA-KOC	Cessna 402C	402C0301	ex N3271M	
☐ XA-SER	Swearingen SA226AT Metro II	TC-413	ex N139WW	
☐ XA-UNB	Dornier 228-202K	8139	ex F-OGOL	
☐ XA-UOR	Dornier 228-212	8237	ex F-OGVE	

AERO DAVINCI INTERNACIONAL — Aero Davinci (DVI) — Reynosa (REX)

| ☐ XA-AFL | Swearingen SA226TC Metro II | | | |
| ☐ XA-TGV | Swearingen SA226TC Metro II | TC-350 | ex N4254Y | |

AERO JBR — (AJB)

| ☐ XA-UFJ | NAMC YS-11A-607 | 2071 | ex XA-TTY | wfs |

AERO SUDPACIFICO — (SDP)

| ☐ XA-SJY | Swearingen SA226TC Metro II | TC-340 | ex N247AM | |
| ☐ XA- | Swearingen SA226TC Metro II | TC-386 | ex N32AG | |

AEROCEDROS — Ensenada (ESE)

☐ XA-RYV	Convair 440-0	474	ex XB-CSE	
☐ XA-STJ	Cessna 402B	402B0801	ex N3792C	
☐ XA-TFY	Convair 440-0	472	ex N411GA	
☐ XA-TFZ	Convair 440-94	439	ex N44829	

Ops Convair 440s for Soc Coop Prod Pesque Pescado

AERODAN — Aerodan (ROD) — Saltillo (SLW)

| ☐ XA-YYS | NAMC YS-11A-205 | 2077 | ex N917AX | |

AEROFUTURO — Mexico City-Toluca (TLC)

| ☐ XA-UGN | Swearingen SA226TC Metro II | TC-353 | ex XA-SFS | |

AEROLAMSA — Playa del Carmen (PCM)

☐ XA-TYL	El Gavilan 358	003	ex TG-TDA
☐ XA-UBD	Britten-Norman BN-2A Mk.III-2		
	Trislander	1044	ex YV-2523P

AEROLINEAS CENTAURO — Centauro (CTR) — Durango (DGO)

☐ XA-JAD	Cessna U206G Stationair 6 II	U20605279	
☐ XA-NAQ	Cessna U206G Stationair 6	U20603880	ex XB-CJQ
☐ XA-PIQ	Britten-Norman BN-2A-26 Islander	892	ex XC-DUJ
☐ XA-RNC	Cessna TU206G Stationair 6 II	U20605747	ex XB-CGX

AEROMAR — Trans-Aeromar (VW/TAO) — Mexico City-Toluca (TLC)

☐ XA-TAH	ATR 42-500	471	ex F-WWLS	
☐ XA-TAI	ATR 42-500	474	ex F-WWLF	
☐ XA-TKJ	ATR 42-500	561	ex F-WWLW	
☐ XA-TLN	ATR 42-500	564	ex F-WWEC	
☐ XA-TPR	ATR 42-500	586	ex F-WWEA	
☐ XA-TPS	ATR 42-500	594	ex F-WWEX	
☐ XA-TRI	ATR 42-500	607	ex F-WWEA	
☐ XA-TRJ	ATR 42-500	608	ex F-WWEB	
☐ XA-UAU	ATR 42-500	462	ex I-ADLF	Edo de Veracruz
☐ XA-UAV	ATR 42-500	476	ex I-ADLG	
☐ XA-UFA	ATR 42-500	412	ex F-WQNH	
☐ XA-MKH	ATR 72-600	1096	ex F-WWEI	AeroMexico Express c/s
☐ XA-NLP	ATR 72-600	1086	ex F-WWEW	AeroMexico Express c/s
☐ XA-SJJ	ATR 42-320	039	ex N71296	
☐ XA-SYH	ATR 42-320	062	ex XA-PEP	Presidente Aleman
☐ XA-TIC	ATR 42-320	058	ex F-OGNF	
☐ XA-UOZ	Canadair CRJ-200ER	7544	ex N119MN	
☐ XA-UPA	Canadair CRJ-200ER	7545	ex N122MN	
☐ XA-UTF	Canadair CRJ-200ER	7851	ex EC-IRI	

AEROMEXICO — AeroMexico (AM/AMX) — Mexico City-Benito Juarez Intl (MEX)

Member of SkyTeam

☐ EI-DRD	Boeing 737-752/W	35117/2122	ex N1786B	
☐ EI-DRE	Boeing 737-752/W	35787/2111		
☐ N126AM	Boeing 737-7BK/W	30617/812	ex EI-EOV	
☐ N423AM	Boeing 737-73V/W	32423/1433	ex G-EZKB	
☐ N784XE	Boeing 737-752/W	33784/1393	ex XA-BAM	
☐ N788XA	Boeing 737-752/W	33788/1439	ex XA-GAM	
☐ N842AM	Boeing 737-752/W	32842/1814		
☐ N851AM	Boeing 737-752/W	29363/1417	ex XA-EAM	
☐ N904AM	Boeing 737-752/W	28262/1565	ex N854AM	
☐ N906AM	Boeing 737-752/W	29356/1586		
☐ N908AM	Boeing 737-752/W	30038/1601		
☐ N997AM	Boeing 737-76Q/W	30283/1156	ex G-OSLH	
☐ XA-AAM	Boeing 737-752/W	33783/1381		
☐ XA-AGM	Boeing 737-752/W	35786/2098		
☐ XA-CAM	Boeing 737-752/W	33785/1398		
☐ XA-CTG	Boeing 737-752/W	35123/2374		
☐ XA-CYM	Boeing 737-752/W	35124/2456	ex N1779B	
☐ XA-GOL	Boeing 737-752/W	35785/2011		
☐ XA-MAH	Boeing 737-752/W	35122/2348		
☐ XA-NAM	Boeing 737-752/W	33790/1533	ex (XA-IAM)	
☐ XA-PAM	Boeing 737-752/W	34293/1747		
☐ XA-QAM	Boeing 737-752/W	34294/1761	ex N1786B	
☐ XA-VAM	Boeing 737-752/W	34295/1765		
☐ EI-DRA	Boeing 737-852/W	35114/2037	ex N1779B	
☐ EI-DRC	Boeing 737-852/W	35116/2081		
☐ N342AM	Boeing 737-8Z9/W	34262/1720	ex OE-LNS	
☐ N359AM	Boeing 737-8CX/W	32359/1041	ex PR-GOJ	
☐ N520AM	Boeing 737-81Q/W	29052/557	ex VP-BMI	
☐ N825AM	Boeing 737-852/W	36699/5091		
☐ N845AM	Boeing 737-852/W	36706/5219	ex N1787B	♦
☐ N858AM	Boeing 737-8Q8/W	30671/1307	ex C-GLBW	
☐ N859AM	Boeing 737-8Q8/W	32796/1272	ex N641LF	
☐ N860AM	Boeing 737-83N/W	28249/1123	ex N151LF	
☐ N861AM	Boeing 737-83N/W	30706/929	ex N161LF	
☐ N875AM	Boeing 737-852/W	36705/5149		♦
☐ N950AM	Boeing 737-852/W	35115/2070	ex EI-DRB	
☐ N957AM	Boeing 737-852/W	39957/5379		♦
☐ N958AM	Boeing 737-852/W	39958/5361		♦
☐ XA-AMA	Boeing 737-852/W	36700/4137		
☐ XA-AMB	Boeing 737-852/W	36703/4496		
☐ XA-AMC	Boeing 737-852/W	36704/4539		

☐ XA-AME	Boeing 737-852/W	36708/4559			
☐ XA-AMG	Boeing 737-81D/W	39439/4853			
☐ XA-AMJ	Boeing 737-852/W	36701/4185			
☐ XA-AMK	Boeing 737-852/W	36702/4222			
☐ XA-AML	Boeing 737-852/W	36707/5045			♦
☐ XA-AMM	Boeing 737-852/W	39944/4949			♦
☐ XA-AMN	Boeing 737-852/W	39945/4989			♦
☐ XA-AMO	Boeing 737-852/W	43665/5337			♦
☐ XA-AMS	Boeing 737-852/W	43661/5295			♦
☐ XA-JOY	Boeing 737-852/W	35121/2327	ex N1782B		
☐ XA-MIA	Boeing 737-852/W	35119/2273			
☐ XA-ZAM	Boeing 737-852/W	35120/2290	ex N1780B		
☐ N961AM	Boeing 787-8	35306/115			
☐ N964AM	Boeing 787-8	35307/122			
☐ N965AM	Boeing 787-8	35308/127			
☐ N966AM	Boeing 787-8	35311/155			
☐ N967AM	Boeing 787-8	35312/163			
☐ XA-AMR	Boeing 787-8	36844/264			♦
☐ XA-AMX	Boeing 787-8	36843/251			♦
☐	Boeing 787-8	37165/330			o/o♦
☐	Boeing 787-8	37167/359			o/o♦
☐ N745AM	Boeing 777-2Q8ER	32718/554			
☐ N746AM	Boeing 777-2Q8ER	32719/562			
☐ N774AM	Boeing 777-2Q8ER	28689/365	ex N301LF		
☐ N776AM	Boeing 777-2Q8ER	28692/373	ex N181LF		
☐ XA-FRJ	Boeing 767-283ER	24728/305	ex N728CG		
☐ XA-JBC	Boeing 767-284ER	24762/307	ex XA-RVY		
☐ XA-MAT	Boeing 767-3Y0ER	24947/351	ex N942AC		
☐ XA-TPM	McDonnell-Douglas MD-87	49671/1463	ex PZ-TCG	District of Para	[MEX]
☐ XA-TOJ	Boeing 767-283ER	24727/301	ex PT-TAI		[MAD]
☐ XA-	McDonnell-Douglas MD-83	49397/1331	ex N838AM		wfs

AEROMEXICO CONNECT *Costera (5D/SLI)* *Monterrey-Escobedo Intl/Vera Cruz (MTY/VER)*

☐ XA-ACB	Embraer ERJ-145LR	145221	ex N264SK		
☐ XA-ALI	Embraer ERJ-145LR	145795	ex PT-SMW		
☐ XA-BLI	Embraer ERJ-145LR	145798	ex PT-SMY		
☐ XA-CLI	Embraer ERJ-145LR	14500803	ex PT-SNG		
☐ XA-ELI	Embraer ERJ-145LR	14500861	ex PT-SXB		
☐ XA-ILI	Embraer ERJ-145LR	145564	ex D-ACIA		
☐ XA-JLI	Embraer ERJ-145LR	145426	ex N971RP		
☐ XA-KLI	Embraer ERJ-145LR	145440	ex N972RP		
☐ XA-QLI	Embraer ERJ-145LR	145588	ex HB-JAX		
☐ XA-RAC	Embraer ERJ-145LR	145313	ex N830HK		
☐ XA-RLI	Embraer ERJ-145LR	145559	ex HB-JAS		
☐ XA-SLI	Embraer ERJ-145LR	145580	ex HB-JAW		
☐ XA-TAC	Embraer ERJ-145LR	145475	ex N823HK		
☐ XA-TLI	Embraer ERJ-145LR	145601	ex HB-JAY		
☐ XA-ULI	Embraer ERJ-145LR	145570	ex HB-JAU		
☐ XA-VAC	Embraer ERJ-145LR	145232	ex N831HK		
☐ XA-VLI	Embraer ERJ-145LR	145574	ex HB-JAV		
☐ XA-WAC	Embraer ERJ-145LR	145255	ex N837HK		
☐ XA-WLI	Embraer ERJ-145LR	145434	ex HB-JAN		
☐ XA-XAC	Embraer ERJ-145LR	145128	ex N260SK		
☐ XA-XLI	Embraer ERJ-145LR	145456	ex HB-JAO		
☐ XA-YAC	Embraer ERJ-145LR	145168	ex N262SK		
☐ XA-YLI	Embraer ERJ-145LR	145400	ex HB-JAL		
☐ XA-ZAC	Embraer ERJ-145LR	145199	ex N263SK		<CHQ [QRO]
☐ XA-ZLI	Embraer ERJ-145LR	145420	ex HB-JAM		
☐ XA-ACP	Embraer ERJ-170SU	17000019	ex N806MD		<RPA
☐ XA-ACQ	Embraer ERJ-170SU	17000042	ex N821MD		<RPA
☐ XA-ACV	Embraer ERJ-170SU	17000046	ex N826MD	SkyTeam c/s	<RPA
☐ XA-GAM	Embraer ERJ-170ST	17000146	ex 5Y-KYL		♦
☐ XA-GAQ	Embraer ERJ-170ST	17000141	ex 5Y-KYG		♦
☐ XA-GAY	Embraer ERJ-170LR	17000087	ex HC-CEX		♦
☐ XA-GAZ	Embraer ERJ-170LR	17000092	ex HC-CEY		♦
☐ XA-SAC	Embraer ERJ-170ST	17000139	ex OH-LEL		
☐ XA-	Embraer ERJ-170STD	17000025	ex SP-LDC		♦
☐ XA-AAC	Embraer ERJ-190LR	19000121	ex PT-SQP		
☐ XA-ACC	Embraer ERJ-190LR	19000499	ex PT-TRE		
☐ XA-ACE	Embraer ERJ-190LR	19000518	ex PT-TUF		
☐ XA-ACI	Embraer ERJ-190LR	19000525	ex PT-TUN		
☐ XA-ACJ	Embraer ERJ-190LR	19000531	ex PT-TUT		
☐ XA-ACK	Embraer ERJ-100LR	19000538	ex PT-TYQ		
☐ XA-ACM	Embraer ERJ-190LR	19000546	ex PT-TXF		
☐ XA-ACN	Embraer ERJ-190LR	19000552	ex PT-TBX		
☐ XA-ACS	Embraer ERJ-190LR	19000554	ex PT-TCJ		
☐ XA-ACT	Embraer ERJ-190LR	19000557	ex PT-TDM		
☐ XA-BAC	Embraer ERJ-190LR	19000129	ex PT-SQP		

☐ XA-CAC	Embraer ERJ-190LR	19000135	ex PT-SYN	
☐ XA-DAC	Embraer ERJ-190LR	19000455	ex PT-TJZ	
☐ XA-EAC	Embraer ERJ-190LR	19000145	ex PT-SYX	
☐ XA-FAC	Embraer ERJ-190LR	19000234	ex PT-SIF	
☐ XA-GAD	Embraer ERJ-190LR	19000651	ex PR-EDK	
☐ XA-GAE	Embraer ERJ-190LR	19000664	ex PR-EEY	◆
☐ XA-GAF	Embraer ERJ-190LR	19000666	ex PR-EFL	
☐ XA-GAG	Embraer ERJ-190AR	19000188	ex N169HQ	<RPA◆
☐ XA-GAH	Embraer ERJ-190AR	19000216	ex N175HQ	◆
☐ XA-GAI	Embraer ERJ-190LR	19000672	ex PR-EGT	◆
☐ XA-GAK	Embraer ERJ-190LR	19000673	ex PR-EGV	◆
☐ XA-GAL	Embraer ERJ-190AR	19000173	ex N167HQ	◆
☐ XA-GAR	Embraer ERJ-190AR	19000197	ex N171HQ	◆
☐ XA-GAW	Embraer ERJ-190LR	19000679	ex PR-EIB	◆
☐ XA-HAC	Embraer ERJ-190LR	19000466	ex PT-TOJ	
☐ XA-IAC	Embraer ERJ-190LR	19000238	ex PT-SIL	
☐ XA-JAC	Embraer ERJ-190LR	19000248	ex PT-SIS	
☐ XA-MAC	Embraer ERJ-190LR	19000408	ex PT-TBG	
☐ XA-	Embraer ERJ-190AR	19000173	ex N167HQ	<RPA◆
☐ XA-	Embraer ERJ-190AR	19000206	ex N173HQ	wfs◆
☐ XA-ACF	Embraer ERJ-175LR	17000137	ex PP-PJG	
☐ XA-AXC	Embraer ERJ-175LR	17000126	ex PP-PJI	
☐ XA-GAB	Embraer ERJ-175LR	17000147	ex PP-PJH	

AERONAVES TSM (VTM) Saltilo (SLW)

☐ XA-DHL	Douglas DC-9-33F (ABS 3)	47193/311	ex N941F	
☐ XA-UOG	Douglas DC-9-33RC (ABS 3)	47194/324	ex N944F	
☐ XA-UPS	Douglas DC-9-33RC (ABS 3)	47462/564	ex N934AX	
☐ XA-UQT	Douglas DC-9-32CF	47147/208	ex N905AX	
☐ XA-URM	Douglas DC-9-32CF	47148/246	ex N909AX	
☐ XA-	Douglas DC-9-15F	47061/207	ex N915F	◆
☐ XA-ADQ	Swearingen SA226TC Metro II	TC-409	ex C-FLNG	
☐ XA-ADS	Swearingen SA226TC Metro II	TC-404	ex C-FGPW	
☐ XA-TSM	Swearingen SA226TC Metro IIA	TC-412	ex XA-SXB	
☐ XA-UFO	Swearingen SA226TC Metro II	TC-281	ex N396RY	
☐ XA-UKP	Swearingen SA226TC Metro II	TC-376	ex N637PJ	
☐ XA-AFT	Swearingen SA227AC Metro III	AC-581	ex C-FAFE	Frtr
☐ XA-DCX	Swearingen SA227AC Metro III	AC-497	ex XA-UKJ	
☐ XA-EEE	Swearingen SA227AC Metro III	AC-503	ex N102GS	
☐ XA-EGC	Swearingen SA227AC Metro III	AC-724	ex N106GS	
☐ XA-MIO	Swearingen SA227AC Metro III	AC-693B	ex N446MA	
☐ XA-PNG	Swearingen SA227AC Metro III	AC-687B	ex N445MA	
☐ XA-SLW	Swearingen SA227AC Metro III	AC-628B	ex N280EM	
☐ XA-SUS	Swearingen SA227AC Metro III	AC-430B	ex M430PF	
☐ XA-TYX	Swearingen SA227AC Metro III	AC-627B	ex N799BW	
☐ XA-UAJ	Swearingen SA227AC Metro III	AC-586	ex N911EJ	Frtr
☐ XA-UAL	Swearingen SA227AC Metro III	AC-704	ex N704C	
☐ XA-UKJ	Swearingen SA227AC Metro III	AC-532	ex N372PH	
☐ XA-UMW	Swearingen SA227AC Metro III	AC-717	ex N434MA	
☐ XA-UNQ	Swearingen SA227AC Metro III	AC-565	ex N163WA	
☐ XA-UOS	Swearingen SA227AC Metro III	AC-760B	ex N760TR	
☐ XA-	Swearingen SA227AC Metro III	AC-595	ex N446GL	
☐ XA-	Swearingen SA227AC Metro III	AC-617	ex N617BT	
☐ XA-	Swearingen SA227AC Metro III	AC-761B	ex N61NE	
☐ XA-ADJ	Learjet 24	24-060	ex N90J	
☐ XA-SAU	Hawker 125-700A	NA0220	ex N725CC	
☐ XA-TRQ	Learjet 24	24-112	ex N104GA	
☐ XA-TYF	Convair 600F	101	ex N94279	
☐ XA-UGH	Swearingen SA226AT Merlin IV	AT-009	ex N479VK	
☐ XA-UJI	Convair 640F	88	ex N73137	
☐ XA-UMI	Convair 640F	48	ex N3417	
☐ XA-UNH	Convair 640	332	ex N640R	
☐ XA-UTX	McDonnell-Douglas MD-83SF	49663/1437	ex N9307R	◆
☐ XA-	Convair 640F	104	ex N640CM	
☐ XA-	Swearingen SA227AT Merlin IVC	AT-434B	ex N434TR	
☐ XA-	McDonnell-Douglas MD-82SF	49342/1337	ex N430AA	
☐ XA-	McDonnell-Douglas MD-82SF	49558/1451	ex N453AA	o/o◆

AEROPACIFICO Transportes Pacifico (TFO) Los Mochis (LMM)

☐ XA-AFE	LET L-410UVP-E	902508	ex N19RZ	
☐ XA-UEP	British Aerospace Jetstream 31	794	ex N417UE	

AEROPOSTAL DE MEXICO Postal Cargo (PCG) Mexico City-Benito Juarez Intl (MEX)

☐ XA-RSH	Lockheed C-130A Hercules	3224	ex HP-1162TLN	[MEX]
☐ XA-RYZ	Lockheed C-130A Hercules	3225	ex N9691N	[MEX]

☐ XA-TXS	Douglas DC-8-63CF (BAC 3)	46054/453	ex N796AL		[QRO]

AEROTRON AIR ADVENTURE — Aerotron (TRN) — Puerto Vallarta (PVR)

☐ XA-ADZ	Cessna 402	402-0113	ex N772EA	
☐ XA-TNI	Cessna 208B Caravan I	208B0728		opf Air Adventure

AEROTUCAN — (RTU) — Oaxaca (OAX)

☐ XA-TDS	Cessna 208B Caravan I	208B0559	ex N51396

AEROUNION — AeroUnion (6R/TNO) — Mexico City-Benito Juarez Intl (MEX)

☐ XA-EFR	Boeing 767-241ERSF	23804/178	ex N767QT	
☐ XA-FPP	Airbus A300B4-203F	227	ex N227TN	
☐ XA-LRC	Boeing 767-241ERSF	23802/172	ex N770QT	
☐ XA-LRL	Airbus A300B4-203F	210	ex N2101R	
☐ XA-MRC	Airbus A300B4-203F	247	ex N247AX	
☐ XA-TWQ	Airbus A300B4-203F	045	ex G-HLAB	Tata

AIR TRIBE

☐ XA-TRB	Convair 580	52	ex N588X	[OPF]
☐ XA-UPL	Convair 580	24	ex N584E	

ALCON SERVICIOS AEREOS — Alcon (AOA)

☐ XA-TND	NAMC YS-11A-306	2073	ex N111PH

ALTERNATIVE AIR — (TIV) — Merida

☐ XA-UFT	British Aerospace Jetstream 32	862	ex N862JX

ASESA

☐ XA-BNA	Bell 412EP	36627	ex N489WH	♦
☐ XA-BNB	Bell 412EP	36628	ex N489TB	♦
☐ XA-BNC	Bell 412EP	36629	ex N489VB	♦
☐ XA-BND	Bell 412EP	36630	ex N491EA	♦
☐ XA-BNE	Bell 412EP	36633	ex N491CB	♦

COMERCIAL AEREA — (CRS)

☐ XA-ESV	Cessna 208B Caravan I	208B0807	ex N5261R
☐ XA-SNS	Cessna 425 Conquest I	425-0108	ex N70GM

DANAUS LINEAS AEREAS — (NAU) — Querétaro (QRO)

☐ XA-URT	Boeing 737-247	23184/1061	ex XA-UJB		
☐ XA-URU	Boeing 737-247	23186/1066	ex XA-UIU	Pena de Bernal	♦

ESTAFETA CARGA AEREA — (E7/ESF) — San Luis Potosi (SLP)

☐ XA-AJA	Boeing 737-3Y0SF	23747/1363	ex N331AW
☐ XA-ECA	Boeing 737-3M8SF	24024/1689	ex N784DC
☐ XA-EMX	Boeing 737-375F	23707/1388	ex N336AW
☐ XA-SPO	Canadair CRJ-100FR	(PF)7085	ex F-GRJD
☐ XA-GGB	Boeing 737-3M8SF	24023/1675	ex N783DC
☐ XA-ESA	Canadair CRJ-100LR (PF)	7088	ex F-GRJC

FLYMEX — Integrales (NTG) — Toluca (TLC)

☐ XA-AAS	Dornier 328-300 (328JET)	3127	ex N430Z	
☐ XA-ALA	Dornier 328-310 (328JET)	3167	ex N117LM	VIP
☐ XA-FAS	Dornier 328-300 (328JET)	3125	ex N410Z	
☐ XA-MAX	Embraer Legacy 600	145540	ex EC-IIR	♦
☐ XA-MHA	Embraer Legacy 600	14500965	ex N965LL	♦

GLOBAL AIR — Damojh (DMJ) — Mexico City-Benito Juarez Intl (MEX)

☐ XA-TWR	Boeing 737-2H4 (AvAero 3)	21812/611	ex XA-TPW	no titles	
☐ XA-UBB	Boeing 737-291	21750/574	ex N988UA		[MEX]
☐ XA-UHY	Boeing 737-2C3	21016/406	ex XA-MAB		[MEX]
☐ XA-UMQ	Boeing 737-2Q3	24103/1565	ex N243AG		

HELI CAMPECHE/HELISERVICIO — Helicampeche (HEC) — Campeche/Mexico City (CPE/-)

☐ XA-HCA	Bell 412EP	36581	ex N450XB
☐ XA-HCB	Bell 412EP	36583	ex N448UB
☐ XA-HCC	Bell 412EP	36338	ex XA-UCC

☐ XA-HCD	Bell 412EP	36331	ex XA-UBF	
☐ XA-HCF	Bell 412EP	36604	ex N470TB	
☐ XA-HCG	Bell 412EP	36605	ex N475DB	
☐ XA-HCH	Bell 412EP	36609	ex N475MB	
☐ XA-HCI	Bell 412EP	36610	ex N475CB	
☐ XA-HCJ	Bell 412EP	36611	ex N475BA	
☐ XA-HCK	Bell 412EP	36641	ex N496HB	♦
☐ XA-HCP	Bell 412EP	36645	ex N7832L	♦
☐ XA-HSA	Bell 412EP	36582	ex N446UB	
☐ XA-HSD	Bell 412EP	36446	ex N31011	
☐ XA-HSG	Bell 412EP	36473	ex N321FB	
☐ XA-HSH	Bell 412EP	36479	ex N142AW	
☐ XA-HSJ	Bell 412EP	36337	ex N45388	
☐ XA-HSK	Bell 412EP	36340	ex N45389	
☐ XA-HSL	Bell 412EP	36334	ex OB-2013-P	
☐ XA-HSM	Bell 412EP	36324	ex N8067M	♦
☐ XA-HSN	Bell 412EP	36488	ex N332TB	
☐ XA-HSO	Bell 412EP	36489	ex N331AB	
☐ XA-SMW	Bell 412HP	36038	ex SU-CAW	
☐ XA-TXR	Bell 412EP	36289	ex N2029N	
☐ XA-TXV	Bell 412EP	36317	ex N7020C	
☐ XA-TXZ	Bell 412EP	36314	ex N7030B	
☐ XA-ADL	Bell 407	53447	ex N61201	
☐ XA-HCM	Bell 429	57165	ex N498DT	♦
☐ XA-HCN	Bell 429	57166	ex N498EH	♦
☐ XA-JOL	Bell 206B JetRanger III	786	ex N31AL	<OLOG
☐ XA-LOC	Bell 206B JetRanger III	3284		<OLOG
☐ XA-SMX	Bell 206L-4 LongRanger IV	52005	ex N2064W	
☐ XA-TPC	Bell 407	53313	ex N60664	
☐ XA-	Eurocopter EC155R1	6765	ex G-ISSW	

INTERJET	**ABC Aerolineas (4O/AIJ)**		**Toluca (TLC)**

☐ XA-ABC	Airbus A320-214	3690	ex F-WWBE	
☐ XA-ACO	Airbus A320-214	1322	ex F-WQUX	
☐ XA-ALM	Airbus A320-214	1308	ex F-WQUU	
☐ XA-BAV	Airbus A320-214	5372	ex D-AUBU	
☐ XA-BIC	Airbus A320-214	3374	ex XA-MXL	
☐ XA-BIO	Airbus A320-214	4730	ex F-WWIL	
☐ XA-DOS	Airbus A320-214	4235	ex OE-IAX	
☐ XA-ECO	Airbus A320-214	4733	ex F-WWIN	
☐ XA-FOG	Airbus A320-214	2048	ex N141LF	
☐ XA-FUA	Airbus A320-214/S	5867	ex D-AVVD	
☐ XA-GAC	Airbus A320-214/S	5933	ex D-AUBH	
☐ XA-IJA	Airbus A320-214	1244	ex F-WQUT	
☐ XA-IJT	Airbus A320-214	1132	ex F-WQUR	
☐ XA-ILY	Airbus A320-214	3123	ex N213MX	
☐ XA-ING	Airbus A320-214	4304	ex OE-IAY	
☐ XA-INJ	Airbus A320-214	1162	ex F-WQUV	
☐ XA-IUA	Airbus A320-214/S	5653	ex D-AUBX	
☐ XA-JAV	Airbus A320-214	5221	ex D-AXAW	
☐ XA-JCV	Airbus A320-214	3514	ex F-WWDO	
☐ XA-JMA	Airbus A320-214/S	5665	ex D-AVVA	
☐ XA-KNO	Airbus A320-214	2539	ex D-ABDA	
☐ XA-LHG	Airbus A320-214/S	5878	ex D-AVVG	
☐ XA-MLR	Airbus A320-214	2227	ex EC-JAB	
☐ XA-MTO	Airbus A320-214	4924	ex D-AXAB	
☐ XA-MTY	Airbus A320-214	1179	ex XA-AIJ	
☐ XA-MXM	Airbus A320-214	3286	ex F-WWDR	
☐ XA-MYR	Airbus A320-214	3021	ex HB-IOV	
☐ XA-ROA	Airbus A320-214	0707	ex N707CG	wfs
☐ XA-SUN	Airbus A320-214	4411	ex EI-ERY	
☐ XA-TLC	Airbus A320-214	3312	ex F-WWIP	
☐ XA-UHE	Airbus A320-214	3149	ex F-WWBS	
☐ XA-VAI	Airbus A320-214	3160	ex F-WWDR	
☐ XA-VCT	Airbus A320-214	5163	ex F-WWDI	
☐ XA-VFI	Airbus A320-214	1780	ex N471LF	
☐ XA-VIP	Airbus A320-214	3304	ex XA-MXK	
☐ XA-VTA	Airbus A320-214	1259	ex XA-ITJ	
☐ XA-WAB	Airbus A320-214	5358	ex D-AUBQ	
☐ XA-XII	Airbus A320-214	3508	ex F-WWBU	
☐ XA-YES	Airbus A320-214	4933	ex D-AXAE	
☐ XA-ZIH	Airbus A320-214	3667	ex F-WWDZ	
☐ XA-ABM	Sukhoi SSJ 100-95B	95036	ex I-PDVZ	
☐ XA-ALJ	Sukhoi SSJ 100-95B	95046	ex I-PDVY	♦
☐ XA-BMO	Sukhoi SSJ 100-95B	95048	ex I-PDVW	♦
☐ XA-GCD	Sukhoi SSJ 100-95B	95052	ex I-PDVW	♦
☐ XA-IJR	Sukhoi SSJ 100-95B	95024	ex I-PDVX	
☐ XA-JLG	Sukhoi SSJ 100-95B	95023	ex I-PDVW	
☐ XA-JLP	Sukhoi SSJ 100-95B	95042	ex I-PDVZ	♦
☐ XA-JLV	Sukhoi SSJ 100-95B	95028	ex I-PDVY	

☐ XA-LLV	Sukhoi SSJ 100-95B	95049	ex I-PDVZ	♦
☐ XA-LME	Sukhoi SSJ 100-95B	95045	ex I-PDVX	♦
☐ XA-NSG	Sukhoi SSJ 100-95B	95034	ex I-PDVW	
☐ XA-OAA	Sukhoi SSJ 100-95B	95038	ex 97012	
☐ XA-OUI	Sukhoi SSJ 100-95B	95050	ex I-PDVW	♦
☐ XA-PBA	Sukhoi SSJ 100-95B	95040	ex I-PDVY	♦
☐ XA-PPY	Sukhoi SSJ 100-95B	95054	ex	♦
☐ XA-	Sukhoi SSJ 100-95B	95065	ex	o/o♦
☐ XA-	Sukhoi SSJ 100-95B	95066	ex	o/o♦
☐ XA-	Sukhoi SSJ 100-95B	95071	ex	o/o♦
☐ XA-	Sukhoi SSJ 199-95B	95081	ex	o/o♦

LINEAS AEREAS COMERCIALES (LCM)

☐ XB-MIC	Cessna 208B Caravan I	208B0496	ex N5165T

MAGNICHARTERS Grupomonterrey (GMT) Monterrey-Gen Mariano Ecobedo Intl (MTY)

☐ XA-MAA	Boeing 737-377	23655/1274	ex N812AR		
☐ XA-MAB	Boeing 737-301	23232/1169	ex N502UW		
☐ XA-MAI	Boeing 737-322	24537/1774	ex N368UA		
☐ XA-UNM	Boeing 737-322	24248/1636	ex N187AQ		
☐ XA-UNY	Boeing 737-322	24455/1752	ex N184AQ		
☐ XA-UQA	Boeing 737-322	23952/1534	ex N192AQ		
☐ XA-UQX	Boeing 737-33A/W	23827/1444	ex N195AQ		
☐ XA-UTE	Boeing 737-322	24670/1909	ex N300VJ		
☐ XA-UUI	Boeing 737-3K2	28085/2722	ex N280CL		♦
☐ XA-MAD	Boeing 737-277 (Nordam 3)	22652/831	ex N185AW	Magni titles	
☐ XA-MAE	Boeing 737-277 (Nordam 3)	22648/789	ex N181AW		
☐ XA-UTS	Boeing 737-55D	27130/2448	ex N188PP		

MASAIR Mas Carga (MY/MAA) Mexico City-Benito Juarez Intl (MEX)

☐ N420LA	Boeing 767-316ERF/W	34627/948		<LCO

MAYAIR (7M/MYI) Mexico City-Benito Juarez Intl (MEX)

☐ XA-AIR	Dornier 228-212	8236	ex F-OGVA	
☐ XA-UAF	Dornier 228-212	8238	ex F-OHQK	
☐ XA-UUU	Fokker 50	20194	ex SE-LIT	♦

MCS AEROCARGA Mexico City-Benito Juarez Intl (MEX)

☐ XA-	Canadair CRJ-100PF	7120	ex C-FWSC	♦

SERVICIOS AEREOS MTT

☐ XA-MTA	Pilatus PC-12/47	884	ex N884XY

TAR - TRANSPORTES AEREOS REGIONALES (LCT)

☐ XA-BPK	Embraer ERJ-145LR	145507	ex N846MJ	
☐ XA-MFH	Embraer ERJ-145LR	145568	ex N850MJ	
☐ XA-RHF	Embraer ERJ-145LR	145481	ex N844MJ	♦

TRANSPORTES AEREOS PEGASO

☐ XA-ERA	MBB BK117C-2			♦
☐ XA-THI	MBB BK117C-2			♦
☐ XA-UPU	MBB BK117C-2			♦
☐ XA-UQC	MBB BK117C-2			♦
☐ XA-UQV	MBB BK117C-2			♦
☐ XA-TVP	Eurocopter EC155B1			♦
☐ XA-TYM	Eurocopter EC155B1			♦
☐ XA-USY	Eurocopter EC155B1	6972		♦

TRANSPORTES AEREOS TERRESTRES

☐ XA-TAT	de Havilland DHC-6 Twin Otter 300	237	
☐ XA-	de Havilland DHC-6 Twin Otter 300	601	ex N471SC

VIGO JET Vigo Jet (VGJ) Mexico City-Benito Juarez Intl (MEX)

☐ XA-LMA	North American Sabreliner 40A	282-137	ex N881DM	
☐ XA-MJE	North American Sabreliner 40EL	282-65	ex XA-GGE	Frtr
☐ XA-TXX	Swearingen SA227AC Metro III	AC-484	ex N341AE	
☐ XA-UIS	Cessna 650 Citation III	650-0186	ex N386CW	

VIVA AEROBUS   (VIV)   Monterrey-Escobedo Intl (MTY)

☐ EI-ERH	Airbus A320-232	2157	ex G-TTOJ	
☐ EI-EUA	Airbus A320-232	2210	ex EC-IYG	
☐ XA-TAR	Airbus A320-232	2908	ex 4R-ABG	♦
☐ XA-VAA	Airbus A320-232/S	6574	ex F-WWIY	♦
☐ XA-VAE	Airbus A320-232/S	6602	ex F-WWBP	o/o♦
☐ XA-VAF	Airbus A320-232	2443	ex OE-ICG	
☐ XA-VAG	Airbus A320-232	2752	ex HA-LPI	
☐ XA-VAH	Airbus A320-232	3743	ex VH-VQB	♦
☐ XA-	Airbus A320-232/S	6755	ex	o/o♦
☐ XA-	Airbus A320-232/S	6813	ex	o/o♦
☐ XA-	Airbus A320-232/S	6820	ex	o/o♦
☐ XA-	Airbus A320-232/S	6901	ex	o/o♦
☐ XA-	Airbus A320-232/S	6958	ex	o/o♦
☐ EI-EOZ	Boeing 737-3Q8	24962/2139	ex SE-RHT	
☐ XA-TAR	Boeing 737-301	23259/1132	ex HS-AEF	[MTY]
☐ XA-VAB	Boeing 737-36N	28566/2964	ex N296CS	
☐ XA-VIA	Boeing 737-3B7	23856/1501	ex N521AU	
☐ XA-VIB	Boeing 737-3B7	23378/1339	ex HS-AAU	
☐ XA-VIF	Boeing 737-301	23552/1382	ex PK-AWV	[MTY]
☐ XA-VIH	Boeing 737-301	23554/1408	ex PK-AWW	[MTY]
☐ XA-VIJ	Boeing 737-3Y0	24677/1837	ex PK-AWC	[CEN]
☐ XA-VIK	Boeing 737-3L9	26442/2277	ex PK-AWN	
☐ XA-VIL	Boeing 737-33A	25010/2008	ex TS-IEC	
☐ XA-VIM	Boeing 737-33A	25032/2014	ex TS-IED	
☐ XA-VIQ	Boeing 737-33A	27267/2600	ex N267AN	
☐ XA-VIR	Boeing 737-33A	27285/2608	ex LN-KKE	
☐ XA-VIS	Boeing 737-33A	27457/2756	ex LN-KKB	
☐ XA-VIT	Boeing 737-3K2	27635/2721	ex ZK-SJE	
☐ XA-VIV	Boeing 737-301	23560/1463	ex N573US	wfs
☐ XA-VIW	Boeing 737-36Q	28660/2883	ex N660AG	
☐ XA-VIX	Boeing 737-3B7	23312/1162	ex N390US	
☐ XA-VAD	Boeing 737-3U3	28742/2992	ex N297CS	

VOLARIS   (V4/VOI)   Toluca (TLC)

☐ N501VL	Airbus A319-133	2979	ex D-AVXF	Angela	
☐ N502VL	Airbus A319-132	3463	ex D-AVWL	Armando	
☐ N503VL	Airbus A319-132	3491	ex D-AVYU	Daniel	
☐ N504VL	Airbus A319-132	3590	ex D-AVYK	Denisse	
☐ XA-VOA	Airbus A319-132	2771	ex D-AVWP	Alma	
☐ XA-VOB	Airbus A319-133	2780	ex D-AVYJ	Blanca	
☐ XA-VOC	Airbus A319-132	2997	ex D-AVXK	Carlos	
☐ XA-VOD	Airbus A319-133	3045	ex D-AVWO	Daniel	
☐ XA-VOE	Airbus A319-133	3069	ex D-AVWT	Esteban	Jose Cuervo Express c/s
☐ XA-VOF	Airbus A319-133	3077	ex D-AVWQ	Felipe	
☐ XA-VOG	Airbus A319-133	3175	ex D-AVXI	Gerardo	
☐ XA-VOH	Airbus A319-133	3253	ex D-AVWU	Humberto	
☐ XA-VOI	Airbus A319-132	2657	ex D-AVYN		
☐ XA-VOJ	Airbus A319-133	3279	ex D-AVYM		
☐ XA-VOK	Airbus A319-133	3450	ex D-AVYT	Kevin	
☐ XA-VOL	Airbus A319-132	2666	ex D-AVWX	Laura	
☐ XA-VOP	Airbus A319-133	4403	ex D-AVXI		
☐ XA-VOQ	Airbus A319-133	4422	ex D-AVXK	Sonia	
☐ N505VL	Airbus A320-233	4798	ex D-AVVT	Enrique	
☐ N506VL	Airbus A320-233	4828	ex F-WWIJ	Erick	
☐ N507VL	Airbus A320-233	4832	ex D-AXAM	Hugo	
☐ N508VL	Airbus A320-233	4950	ex D-AXAS	Humberto	
☐ N509VL	Airbus A320-233	5062	ex D-AUBC	Jessica	
☐ N510VL	Airbus A320-233	5207	ex D-AVVS	Juan	
☐ N511VL	Airbus A320-233	5212	ex D-AVVU	Juan	
☐ N512VL	Airbus A320-233	5308	ex D-AUBA	Judith	
☐ N513VL	Airbus A320-233	5322	ex D-AUBF	Liliana	
☐ N514VL	Airbus A320-233	5337	ex D-AUBJ	Luis	
☐ N515VL	Airbus A320-233	5391	ex D-AUBW	Luis	
☐ N516VL	Airbus A320-232	2204	ex XA-VOU	Paloma	
☐ N517VL	Airbus A320-233	4741	ex XA-VOX	Mijail	
☐ N518VL	Airbus A320-233	5488	ex D-AXAB	Raúl	
☐ N519VL	Airbus A320-233/S	5510	ex D-AXAJ	Ricardo	
☐ N520VL	Airbus A320-233/S	5595	ex D-AUBI	Ricardo	
☐ N521VL	Airbus A320-233/S	5651	ex D-AUBW	Roberto	
☐ N522VL	Airbus A320-233/S	5776	ex D-AXAB	Rocio	
☐ N523VL	Airbus A320-233/S	6014	ex D-AUBX	Rodrigo	
☐ N524VL	Airbus A320-233/S	6161	ex D-AVVB	Itzali	♦
☐ N525VL	Airbus A320-233/S	6332	ex D-AXAA	Mayra	♦
☐ N526VL	Airbus A320-233/S	6470	ex D-AXAU	Lorena	♦
☐ XA-VLB	Airbus A320-233/S	5988	ex F-WWBK	Stephany	
☐ XA-VLC	Airbus A320-233/S	5996	ex F-WWBN	Francisco	
☐ XA-VLD	Airbus A320-233/S	6109	ex D-AXAS	Patty	♦

☐ XA-VLE	Airbus A320-233/S	6288	ex F-WWIV	Eduardo	♦
☐ XA-VLF	Airbus A320-233/S	6321	ex D-AVVX	Sabrina	♦
☐ XA-VLJ	Airbus A321-233/S	6601	ex D-AVXM		o/o♦
☐ XA-VLK	Airbus A320-233/S	6610	ex D-AVVT		o/o♦
☐ XA-VOM	Airbus A320-233	3624	ex F-WWIM	Margarita	
☐ XA-VON	Airbus A320-233	3672	ex F-WWIN	Noemi	
☐ XA-VOV	Airbus A320-232	3524	ex EI-ERB	Valerie	
☐ XA-VOW	Airbus A320-232	3543	ex EI-ERC	Victor	
☐ XA-VOY	Airbus A320-233/S	5793	ex F-WWIR	Yessica	
☐ XA-VOZ	Airbus A320-233/S	5819	ex F-WWBO	Zahira	
☐	Airbus A320-233/S	6705	ex		o/o♦
☐	Airbus A320-233/S	6778	ex		o/o♦
☐	Airbus A320-233/S	6943	ex		o/o♦
☐	Airbus A320-233/S	6970	ex		o/o♦
☐ XA-VLH	Airbus A321-231/S	6558	ex D-AZAN		♦

WESTAIR DE MEXICO

☐ XA-TLA	Swearingen SA227AC Metro III	AC-723	ex N2725D	

XT-   BURKINA FASO (People's Democratic Republic of Burkina Faso)

AIR BURKINA | Burkina (2J/VBW) | Ouagadougou (OUA)

☐ TZ-RCA	Canadair CRJ-200ER	7392	ex N646BR	opb CMM♦
☐ XT-ABC	McDonnell-Douglas MD-87	49834/1714	ex I-AFRA	[OLB]
☐ XT-ABD	McDonnell-Douglas MD-87	49840/1745	ex EC-EYY	[OLB]
☐ XT-ABS	Embraer ERJ-170STD	17000027	ex SP-LDD	♦
☐ XT-ABT	Embraer ERJ-170STD	17000023	ex SP-LDA	♦

COLOMBE AIRLINES | (CBL) | Ouagadougou (OUA)

☐ CS-DVF	ATR 72-202	350	ex SE-MGM	<LZF♦
☐ N589BC	McDonnell-Douglas MD-83	49662/1429	ex SE-RDM	[OUA]♦

TRANSAFRICAINE AIR CARGO

☐ TN-AID	Fokker F.27-500F	10615	ex N19AY	

XU-   CAMBODIA (Kingdom of Cambodia)

BASSAKA AIR | (5B/BSX) | Phnom Penh-Pochentong (PNH)

☐ XU-112	Airbus A320-214	0648	ex VN-A309	♦
☐ XU-113	Airbus A320-214	0650	ex VN-A311	♦

CAMBODIA ANGKOR AIR | (K6/VAV) | Phnom Penh-Pochentong (PNH)

☐ XU-235	ATR 72-212A	899	ex VN-B227	
☐ XU-236	ATR 72-212A	906	ex VN-B231	
☐ XU-348	Airbus A321-231	5427	ex VN-A398	<HVN
☐ XU-349	Airbus A321-231	2480	ex VN-A349	<HVN
☐ XU-350	Airbus A321-231	5343	ex VN-A394	<HVN
☐ XU-351	Airbus A321-231	2303	ex VN-A348	<HVN♦

CAMBODIA BAYON AIRLINES | (BD/BAY) | Phnom Penh-Pochentong (PNH)

☐ XU-001	AVIC MA-60	1108		♦

HELISTAR CAMBODIA | | Siem Reap (REP)

☐ XU-188	Aérospatiale AS350B2 Ecureuil	4625	
☐ ZK-HJY	Aérospatiale AS350B2 Ecureuil	2005	

SKY ANGKOR AIRLINES | (ZA/SWM) | Phnom Penh-Pochentong (PNH)

☐ XU-ZAB	Airbus A320-231	0476	ex N476PB	[VTE]
☐ XU-ZAC	Airbus A320-231	0430	ex N286AT	
☐ XU-701	Airbus A320-212	0421	ex PK-TAA	♦
☐ XU-705	Airbus A320-232	2016	ex SP-HAD	<LLP♦

XY-   MYANMAR (Union of Myanmar)

AIR BAGAN | (W9/JAB) | Yangon (RGN)

☐ XY-AGE	Airbus A310-222	320	ex B-2302	[RGN]

☐ XY-AGF	Fokker 100	11282	ex N854US		[RGN]
☐ XY-AIC	ATR 42-320	159	ex N34820		[RGN]
☐ XY-AID	ATR 42-300	152	ex N34817		
☐ XY-AIH	ATR 72-212	469	ex F-OHFZ		
☐ XY-AIK	ATR 72-212	592	ex I-ATSL		

AIR KBZ		**Jade Air (K7/KBZ)**			**Yangon (RGN)**
☐ XY-AIY	ATR 72-212A	547	ex N547NA		
☐ XY-AJC	ATR 72-212A	541	ex N541AT		
☐ XY-AJD	ATR 72-212A	545	ex N545AT		
☐ XY-AJE	ATR 72-600	1068	ex F-WKVJ		
☐ XY-AJJ	ATR 72-600	1085	ex F-WWEV		
☐ XY-AJT	ATR 72-212A	658	ex OY-CJM		♦
☐ XY-AJW	ATR 72-600	1224	ex F-WTDS		♦
☐ XY-AIW	ATR 42-212A	582	ex EC-HEZ		
☐ XY-	ATR 42-500	602	ex OY-CGD		wfs♦

AIR MANDALAY		**(6T/AMY)**			**Mandalay/Yangon (MDL/RGN)**
☐ XY-AEY	ATR 72-212	393	ex F-OHFS	Hanna	[RGN]
☐ XY-AIJ	ATR 42-320	268	ex F-OHRN		wfs
☐ XY-AIR	ATR 72-212	467	ex EI-CMJ	Hezan	wfs
☐ XY-ALD	Embraer ERJ-145EP	145060	ex N160EC		♦
☐ XY-ALE	Embraer ERJ-145EP	145089	ex N189EC		♦

APEX AIRLINES					**Yangon (RGN)**
☐ XY-AJV	ATR 72-600	1229	ex F-WKVH		♦

ASIAN WINGS		**Asian Star (YJ/AWM)**			**Yangon (RGN)**
☐ XY-AGN	Airbus A321-112	0765	ex I-BIXT		
☐ XY-AIF	ATR 72-212A	765	ex F-WWED		
☐ XY-AIS	ATR 72-212A	626	ex I-ATPA		
☐ XY-AIU	ATR 72-212A	557	ex I-ADLN		
☐ XY-AJQ	ATR 72-212A	634	ex I-ADLS		♦

FMI AIR		**(ND/FMI)**			**Yangon (RGN)**
☐ XY-ALA	Canadair CRJ-200LR	7486	ex C-FBZA		♦
☐ XY-	Canadair CRJ-100SE	7136	ex C-GZCU		♦
☐ XY-	Canadair CRJ-200LR	7439	ex C-GSBX		♦

GOLDEN MYANMAR AIRLINES		**(Y5/YMR)**			**Yangon (RGN)**
☐ XY-AGS	Airbus A320-232	1407	ex EI-EUE		
☐ XY-AGT	Airbus A320-232	2128	ex P4-PAS		dam 14Apr14
☐ XY-AJM	ATR 72-600	1148	ex F-WKVG		
☐ XY-AJS	ATR 72-600	1156	ex F-WKVG		♦

MANN YADANARPON AIRLINES		**(7Y/MYP)**			**Mandalay (MDL)**
☐ XY-AJO	ATR 72-600	1127	ex F-WKVG		
☐ XY-AJP	ATR 72-600	1137	ex F-WKVJ		

MYANMAR NATIONAL AIRLINES		**Unionair (MM/UBA)**			**Yangon (RGN)**
☐ XY-AEZ	ATR 72-212	475	ex F-OGUO	all-white	
☐ XY-AIA	ATR 72-212	422	ex F-WQNQ		
☐ XY-AIG	ATR 72-212A	781	ex F-WWET		
☐ XY-AJN	ATR 72-212A	787	ex EI-REO		
☐ XY-	ATR 72-600	1267	ex F-WW		o/o♦
☐ XY-AGB	Fokker F.28 Fellowship 4000	11184	ex YU-AOH		
☐ XY-AGH	Fokker F.28 Fellowship 4000	11161	ex ZS-JAV		
☐ XY-AGP	Embraer ERJ-190AR	19000154	ex N161HL		
☐ XY-AGQ	Embraer ERJ-190AR	19000231	ex N162HL		
☐ XY-AIB	ATR 42-320	178	ex F-WQNM		
☐ XY-AIO	Xian MA60	0806			
☐ XY-AIP	Xian MA60	0807			♦
☐ XY-AIQ	Xian MA60	0808			♦
☐ XY-AJA	Beech 1900D	UE-325	ex ZS-OYM		
☐ XY-AJK	Cessna 208B Caravan I	208B5066	ex N81530		
☐ XY-AJL	Cessna 208B Caravan I	208B5067	ex N8153K		

MYANMAR AIRWAYS INTERNATIONAL		**Myanmar (8M/MMA)**			**Yangon (RGN)**
☐ XY-AGG	Airbus A320-231	0114	ex S5-AAC		[KUL]

☐ XY-AGL	Airbus A320-231	0316	ex M-ABCW	wfs
☐ XY-AGO	Airbus A320-214	0973	ex EI-EYH	
☐ XY-AGR	Airbus A319-112	1791	ex OH-LVE	
☐ XY-AGU	Airbus A319-111	1180	ex EI-FCP	
☐ XY-AGV	Airbus A319-111	1247	ex EI-FDB	

YANGON AIRWAYS — Air Yangon (YH/AYG) — Yangon (RGN)

☐ XY-AIM	ATR 72-212	479	ex F-OIYA
☐ XY-AIN	ATR 72-212	481	ex F-OIYB
☐ XY-AJI	ATR 72-212A	797	ex EI-REP

YA-   AFGHANISTAN (State of Afghanistan)

AFGHAN JET INTERNATIONAL — (HN/AJI) — Sharjah (SHJ)

☐ YA-AJH	Canadair CRJ-200LR	7431	ex EK20017
☐ YA-AJK	Canadair CRJ-200LR	7499	ex EK20018

ARIANA AFGHAN AIRLINES — Ariana (FG/AFG) — Kabul (KBL)

☐ C5-AAF	Airbus A320-231	0373	ex EY-624		<AAZ♦
☐ YA-CAQ	Airbus A310-304	496	ex TC-JDA	Kabul	>TBN
☐ YA-CAV	Airbus A310-304ER	497	ex TC-JDB	Kandahar	>TBN
☐ YA-FAM	Boeing 727-223 (Raisbeck 3)	21088/1255	ex N861AA		
☐ YA-FAN	Boeing 727-227F (FedEx 3)	21245/1202	ex 9L-LFD		[KBL]
☐ YA-FAS	Boeing 727-223 (Raisbeck 3)	21388/1345	ex N876AA		wfs
☐ YA-FAT	Boeing 727-221/W (Duganair 3)	22542/1799	ex 5N-BFY		
☐ YA-GAX	de Havilland DHC-6 Twin Otter 300	331			
☐ YA-PIE	Boeing 737-4Y0	26086/2475	ex TC-JEY		dam 07Nov14
☐ YA-PIR	Boeing 737-232 (Nordam 3)	23077/996	ex N305DL		

EAST HORIZON AIRLINES — (EE/EHN) — Kabul (KBL)

☐ EY-201	AVIC MA60	0701		<TJK♦
☐ TU-PAD	Hawker-Siddeley HS.748 Srs.2B/426	1799	ex 4R-SER	<IVN
☐ YA-EHC	Antonov An-24RV	57310203	ex UR-ELK	♦
☐ YA-EHD	Antonov An-24RV	57310109	ex UR-ELW	
☐ YA-EH01	CASA C.212-100	AA1-11-9G	ex T.12B-53	
☐ YA-EH02	CASA C.212-100	A1-12-22	ex T.12B-18	
☐ YA-EH03	CASA C.212-100	A11-12-31	ex T.12B-23	
☐ YA-EH04	CASA C.212-100	AA1-4-99	ex T.12B-48	

KAM AIR — Kamgar (RQ/KMF) — Kabul (KBL)

☐ YA-KMD	McDonnell-Douglas MD-83	49785/1628	ex EI-CIW	
☐ YA-KMF	McDonnell-Douglas MD-82	49704/1490	ex N959U	
☐ YA-KMG	McDonnell-Douglas MD-83	49567/1367	ex N9306T	
☐ YA-KMO	McDonnell-Douglas MD-87	53010/1921	ex N542PT	
☐ YA-KMZ	McDonnell-Douglas MD-87	53337/1962	ex N541PT	
☐ YA-KME	Mil Mi-8AMT	00804092692U	ex EX-40004	
☐ YA-KMH	Mil Mi-8AMT	00804092601U	ex EX-40003	
☐ YA-KML	Mil Mi-8MTV-1	95219	ex Soviet Army 14 blue	
☐ YA-KMS	Mil Mi-8T	9743808		
☐ YA-KMT	Mil Mi-8T	4285		
☐ YA-KMU	Mil Mi-8T	9733102		
☐ YA-KMV	Mil Mi-8T	4774		
☐ YA-KMW	Mil Mi-8T	98308444	ex ST-SHR	
☐ YA-KMX	Mil Mi-8T	4143		
☐ YA-WTA	Mil Mi-8AMT	00804092603U	ex EX-40005	
☐ YA-WTB	Mil Mi-8AMT	00804092604U	ex EX-40006	
☐ UR-CMK	Airbus A320-212	0445	ex EX-32001	<ANR♦
☐ YA-KAM	Boeing 767-222	21879/49	ex N619UA	
☐ YA-KMA	Airbus A320-231	0480	ex VT-EYL	City of Kabul	>SFW
☐ YA-KMC	Antonov An-24RV	37309008	ex Z3-AAI	
☐ YA-VIA	Cessna 421B	421B0912	ex N241DR	
☐ 4L-AJC	Boeing 737-33R	28873/2975	ex M-ABGT	<AJD♦
☐ 4L-TZS	Boeing 747-281F	24576/818	ex VP-BII	

SAFI AIRWAYS — (4Q/SFW) — Kabul (KBL)

☐ YA-AQS	Boeing 767-2J6ER	23745/156	ex B-2554	City of Kabul
☐ YA-AQT	Boeing 757-2K2/W	26330/717	ex EI-EXX	City of Mazar-E-Sharif
☐ YA-HSB	Boeing 737-3J6	23303/1237	ex B-2532	City of Mazar	[CAI]
☐ YA-KMA	Airbus A320-231	0480	ex VT-EYL	City of Kabul	<KMF
☐ YA-SFL	Boeing 737-3J6	23302/1224	ex B-2531	City of Herar	[CAI]
☐ YA-TTD	Airbus A320-214	0994	ex B-2416	City of Kandahar
☐ YA-TTE	Airbus A319-112	1018	ex EI-FBO	City of Herat

☐ YA-TTF   Airbus A319-112   0734   ex EI-FCG   City of Farah

YI-   IRAQ (Republic of Iraq)

AL-NASER AIRLINES   (6N/MHK)   Baghdad-Al Muthana (BGW)

Reg	Type	C/N	Ex	Notes	Remarks
☐ JY-SOP	Boeing 767-233	22526/92	ex JY-JRF		wfs
☐ YI-APZ	Boeing 737-201 (Nordam 3)	22354/736	ex JY-JRA		
☐ YI-AQS	Boeing 737-48E	25765/2335	ex N765TA	Naser	
☐ 9H-TEQ	Airbus A340-642	416	ex (9H-SUN)		<HFM♦

IRAQI AIRWAYS   Iraqi (IA/IAW)   Baghdad-Al Muthana/Intl (BGW/SDA)

Reg	Type	C/N	Ex	Notes
☐ YI-ASE	Boeing 737-81Z/W	40104/4515		
☐ YI-ASF	Boeing 737-81Z/W	40105/4719	ex N1786B	
☐ YI-ASG	Boeing 737-81Z/W	40089/4837		
☐ YI-ASH	Boeing 737-81Z/W	40076/4873		
☐ YI-ASI	Boeing 737-81Z/W	40077/4943	ex N1786B	♦
☐ YI-ASJ	Boeing 737-81Z/W	40090/4921	ex N1786B	♦
☐ YI-ASK	Boeing 737-81Z/W	40078/5145	ex N1787B	♦
☐ YI-ASQ	Boeing 737-81Z/W	40079/5249		♦
☐ YI-ASR	Boeing 737-81Z/W	40080/5287		♦
☐ YI-ASS	Boeing 737-81Z/W	40081/5322		o/o♦
☐ YI-AST	Boeing 737-81Z/W	40082/5388		♦
☐ YI-	Boeing 737-81Z/W	40087/		o/o♦
☐ YI-AQA	Canadair CRJ-900	15189	ex C-FULE	
☐ YI-AQB	Canadair CRJ-900	15202	ex C-FWPF	
☐ YI-AQC	Canadair CRJ-900	15213	ex C-FWZH	
☐ YI-AQD	Canadair CRJ-900	15220	ex C-FYED	
☐ YI-AQE	Canadair CRJ-900	15265	ex C-GZQU	
☐ YI-AQF	Canadair CRJ-900	15266	ex C-GICN	
☐ YI-AGR	Airbus A321-231	4067	ex D-ANJB	
☐ YI-AGS	Airbus A321-231	4044	ex D-ANJA	
☐ YI-APW	Boeing 737-2B7 (Nordam 3)	22885/966	ex 9L-LEG	wfs
☐ YI-APY	Boeing 737-201 (Nordam 3)	22274/682	ex J2-KCM	wfs
☐ YI-AQK	Boeing 737-7BD/W	33935/2315	ex N331AT	
☐ YI-AQL	Boeing 737-7BD/W	35789/2201	ex N317AT	
☐ YI-AQM	Boeing 767-33P6ER	26235/502	ex N90GV	
☐ YI-AQQ	Boeing 747-446	27099/1031	ex JY-	
☐ YI-AQW	Boeing 767-3P6ER	26237/544	ex JY-JRD	<RFJ
☐ YI-AQY	Airbus A330-202	1339	ex (9M-XXJ)	
☐ YI-AQZ	Boeing 777-29MLR	40993/1006	ex N736FE	
☐ YI-ARA	Airbus A320-214	5115	ex OE-LEM	
☐ YI-ARB	Airbus A320-214	5290	ex D-ABND	
☐ YI-ARD	Airbus A320-214	5464	ex OE-LEQ	<NLY
☐ YI-ASA	Boeing 747-4H6	28433/1290	ex 9M-MPO	
☐ 4L-MRK	Boeing 747-281F	25171/886	ex VP-BIJ	<TZS♦

ZAGROSJET   (Z4/GZQ)   Erbil (EBL)

Reg	Type	C/N	Ex	Remarks
☐ TC-OBJ	Airbus A321-231	0835	ex N835AG	<OHY♦
☐ YI-AQU	Airbus A321-231	1878	ex TC-ATO	

YJ-   VANUATU (Republic of Vanuatu)

AIR SAFARIS

Reg	Type	C/N	Ex
☐ YJ-CCM	Cessna A.185F Skywagon	18503403	ex N18TK

AIR TAXI   Port Vila (VLI)

Reg	Type	C/N	Ex	Remarks
☐ YJ-AL1	Britten-Norman BN-2A-25 Islander		ex VH-RGE	
☐ YJ-AL2	Britten-Norman BN-2A-27 Islander	609	ex VH-SKG	♦

AIR VANUATU   Air Van (NF/AVN)   Port Vila (VLI)

Reg	Type	C/N	Ex	Name	Remarks
☐ YJ-AV1	Boeing 737-8Q8/W	30734/2477	ex N1779B	Spirit of Vanuatu	
☐ YJ-AV3	Britten-Norman BN-2A-21 Islander	483	ex F-OCXP		
☐ YJ-AV4	Harbin Y-12 IV	028	ex B-958L		
☐ YJ-AV5	Harbin Y-12 IV	029	ex B-978L		
☐ YJ-AV6	Harbin Y-12 IV	032	ex B-979L		
☐ YJ-AV11	de Havilland DHC-6 Twin Otter 300	564	ex N564DH		♦
☐ YJ-AV71	ATR 72-212A	720	ex M-ABFJ	Betty Emma	♦
☐ YJ-AV72	ATR 72-212A	876	ex F-WNUG		
☐ YJ-RV10	de Havilland DHC-6 Twin Otter 300	679	ex OY-SLI	Melanesian Princess	
☐ YJ-RV16	Britten-Norman BN-2A-27 Islander	104	ex ZK-FLU		dam 01Apr13

UNITY AIRLINES — Port Vila (VLI)

☐ YJ-008	Britten-Norman BN-2B-20 Islander	2172	ex JA5290
☐ YJ-009	Britten-Norman BN-2A-26 Islander	65	ex V7-0009
☐ YJ-0019	Britten-Norman BN-2A Mk.III-2	1055	ex SX-CPG

YK- SYRIA (Syrian Arab Republic)

CHAM WINGS AIRLINES — (6Q/SAW) — Damascus (DAM)

☐ UR-CEL	McDonnell-Douglas MD-83	49390/1269	ex XU-ZAA	<DAT♦
☐ UR-CNU	Airbus A320-212	0525	ex EI-DXY	<DAT♦

SYRIAN ARAB AIRLINES — Syrianair (RB/SYR) — Damascus (DAM)

☐ YK-AKA	Airbus A320-232	0886	ex F-WWDH	Ugarit	
☐ YK-AKB	Airbus A320-232	0918	ex F-WWIJ	Ebla	
☐ YK-AKC	Airbus A320-232	1032	ex F-WWDV	Afamia	
☐ YK-AKD	Airbus A320-232	1076	ex F-WWIK	Mari	
☐ YK-AKE	Airbus A320-232	1085	ex F-WWIX	Bosra	
☐ YK-AKF	Airbus A320-232	1117	ex F-WWBN	Amrit	[DAM]
☐ YK-ANA	Antonov An-24B	87304203			
☐ YK-ANC	Antonov An-26	3007			Govt operated
☐ YK-ANE	Antonov An-26	3103			Govt operated
☐ YK-ANF	Antonov An-26	3104			Govt operated
☐ YK-ANG	Antonov An-26B	10907			Govt operated
☐ YK-ANH	Antonov An-26B	11406			Govt operated
☐ YK-AQA	Yakovlev Yak-40	9341932			Govt operated
☐ YK-AQB	Yakovlev Yak-40	9530443			Govt operated
☐ YK-AQD	Yakovlev Yak-40	9830158			VIP Govt operated
☐ YK-AQE	Yakovlev Yak-40K	9830258			Govt operated
☐ YK-AQF	Yakovlev Yak-40	9931859			Govt operated
☐ YK-SQG	Yakovlev Yak-40K	9941959	ex YK-AQG		♦
☐ YK-ATA	Ilyushin Il-76TD	093421613			Govt operated
☐ YK-ATB	Ilyushin Il-76T	093421619			Govt operated
☐ YK-ATD	Ilyushin Il-76T	0013431915			Govt operated
☐ YK-AYA	Tupolev Tu-134B-3	63992			
☐ YK-AYB	Tupolev Tu-134B-3	63994			
☐ YK-AYE	Tupolev Tu-134B-3	66187			
☐ YK-AYF	Tupolev Tu-134B-3	63190			[DAM]

YL- LATVIA (Republic of Latvia)

AIR BALTIC — AirBaltic (BT/BTI) — Riga-Spilve (RIX)

☐ YL-BBI	Boeing 737-33A/W	27454/2703	ex PT-SSQ	
☐ YL-BBJ	Boeing 737-36Q/W	30333/3117	ex D-ADIA	
☐ YL-BBL	Boeing 737-33V/W	29334/3089	ex HA-LKS	
☐ YL-BBO	Boeing 737-33V	29335/3094	ex G-THOO	
☐ YL-BBR	Boeing 737-31S	29266/3092	ex G-OTDA	
☐ YL-BBS	Boeing 737-31S	29267/3093	ex G-GSPN	
☐ YL-BBX	Boeing 737-36Q/W	30334/3120	ex D-ADIB	
☐ YL-BBY	Boeing 737-36Q/W	30335/3129	ex D-ADIC	
☐ YL-BBD	Boeing 737-53S	29075/3101	ex F-GJNU	
☐ YL-BBE	Boeing 737-53S	29073/3083	ex EI-DDT	
☐ YL-BBM	Boeing 737-522	26680/2366	ex N680MV	
☐ YL-BBN	Boeing 737-522	26683/2368	ex N683MV	
☐ YL-BBQ	Boeing 737-522	26691/2408	ex N691MV	
☐ YL-BAE	de Havilland DHC-8-402Q	4289	ex C-FZGL	
☐ YL-BAF	de Havilland DHC-8-402Q	4293	ex C-GAUI	
☐ YL-BAH	de Havilland DHC-8-402Q	4296	ex C-GBJA	
☐ YL-BAI	de Havilland DHC-8-402Q	4302	ex C-GCKV	
☐ YL-BAJ	de Havilland DHC-8-402Q	4309	ex C-GCQG	
☐ YL-BAQ	de Havilland DHC-8-402Q	4313	ex C-GDDU	
☐ YL-BAX	de Havilland DHC-8-402Q	4324	ex C-GLTI	
☐ YL-BAY	de Havilland DHC-8-402Q	4331	ex C-GKLC	
☐ YL-BBT	de Havilland DHC-8-402Q	4438	ex C-GTZH	
☐ YL-BBU	de Havilland DHC-8-402Q	4439	ex C-GTZU	
☐ YL-BBV	de Havilland DHC-8-402Q	4444	ex C-GUJL	
☐ YL-BBW	de Havilland DHC-8-402Q	4448	ex C-GUTD	
☐ YL-BAZ	Fokker 50	20153	ex LY-BAZ	[BGY]
☐ YL-BDC	Boeing 757-256/W	26253/902	ex XU-882	

PRIMERA AIR NORDIC | (6F) | Riga-Spilve (RIX)

☐ YL-PSB	Boeing 737-8Q8/W	30722/2261	ex OY-PSB	♦
☐ YL-PSD	Boeing 737-86N/W	28618/514	ex OY-PSD	♦
☐ YL-PSH	Boeing 737-86N/W	34247/1830	ex OY-PSH	♦

RAF-AVIA | Mitavia (MTL) | Riga-Spilve (RIX)

☐ YL-RAA	Antonov An-26B	11206	ex RA-26064	
☐ YL-RAB	Antonov An-26B	10508	ex RA-26032	
☐ YL-RAC	Antonov An-26	9903	ex CCCP-79169	
☐ YL-RAD	Antonov An-26B	13909	ex RA-26589	
☐ YL-RAI	Antonov An-26B	10103	ex UR-DWD	
☐ YL-RAG	SAAB SF.340A	340A-052	ex SE-E52	Frtr
☐ YL-RAH	SAAB SF.340A	340A-081	ex EC-IRD	Frtr

SMARTLYNX | (6Y/ART) | Riga-Spilve (RIX)

☐ YL-BBC	Airbus A320-211	0142	ex SX-BVD		
☐ YL-LCA	Airbus A320-211	0333	ex 4X-ABC		>TVS
☐ YL-LCD	Airbus A320-211	0359	ex C-FMSV		>TVS
☐ YL-LCK	Airbus A320-214	0936	ex OE-IBU		>TCX
☐ YL-LCL	Airbus A320-214	0533	ex EI-DDL	Arisitides Sousa Mendes	>TCX
☐ YL-LCM	Airbus A320-211	0244	ex F-GJVF		>RYR
☐ YL-LCN	Airbus A320-211	0662	ex N662WF		>RYR♦
☐ YL-LCO	Airbus A320-214	1873	ex N191AT		>TCX
☐ YL-LCP	Airbus A320-232	1823	ex EI-EZS		♦

YN-   NICARAGUA (Republic of Nicaragua)

LA COSTENA | Managua (MGA)

☐ YN-CGS	Cessna 208B Caravan I	208B0781	ex YV-184T	
☐ YN-CGU	Cessna 208B Caravan I	208B0607	ex HP-1400	
☐ YN-CHG	ATR 42-320	323	ex F-OHGL	
☐ YN-CIE	ATR 42-320	400	ex N400LC	♦

YR-   ROMANIA (Republic of Romania)

AIR BUCHAREST | (BUR) | Bucharest-Baneasa (BBU)

☐ YR-TIB	Boeing 737-3L9	27924/2760	ex OE-ITA

BLUE AIR | Blue Messenger (0B/BMS) | Bucharest-Otopeni (OTP)

☐ YR-BAE	Boeing 737-4Y0	28723/2886	ex EI-CXL	
☐ YR-BAJ	Boeing 737-430	27002/2323	ex EI-COI	
☐ YR-BAK	Boeing 737-430	27005/2359	ex EI-COJ	
☐ YR-BAO	Boeing 737-42C	24813/2062	ex F-WTBB	
☐ YR-BAQ	Boeing 737-4D7	28702/2978	ex VQ-BDB	♦
☐ YR-BAR	Boeing 737-4Q8	25371/2195	ex N707DB	
☐ YR-BAS	Boeing 737-430	27007/2367	ex HS-GTC	♦
☐ YR-BAU	Boeing 737-4Y0	26066/2301	ex N606AN	♦
☐ YR-BAZ	Boeing 737-405	24644/1938	ex LN-BRI	
☐ YR-BAC	Boeing 737-377	23653/1260	ex ZK-SLA	♦
☐ YR-BAF	Boeing 737-322F	24453/1730	ex N360UA	
☐ YR-BAG	Boeing 737-5L9	24778/1816	ex N494ST	
☐ YR-BMB	Boeing 737-85R/W	29037/177	ex VQ-BEN	♦

CARPATAIR | Carpatair (V3/KRP) | Timisoara-Giarmata (TSR)

☐ YR-FKA	Fokker 100	11340	ex C-GKZC	
☐ YR-FKB	Fokker 100	11369	ex C-GKZK	>VOE
☐ YR-FZA	Fokker 100	11395	ex ER-FZA	♦
☐ YR-FKB	Fokker 100	11369	ex C-GKZK	♦

TAROM | Tarom (RO/ROT) | Bucharest-Otopeni (OTP)

Member of SkyTeam

☐ YR-ATA	ATR 42-500	566	ex F-WWLF	Dunarea
☐ YR-ATB	ATR 42-500	569	ex F-WWLH	Bistrita
☐ YR-ATC	ATR 42-500	589	ex F-WWLR	Mures
☐ YR-ATD	ATR 42-500	591	ex F-WWLS	Cris
☐ YR-ATE	ATR 42-500	596	ex F-WWLY	Olt
☐ YR-ATF	ATR 42-500	599	ex F-WWEB	Arges
☐ YR-ATG	ATR 42-500	605	ex F-WWLG	Dambovita

☐ YR-ATH	ATR 72-212	861	ex F-WWEH	Somes	
☐ YR-ATI	ATR 72-212	867	ex F-WWER	Ialomita	
☐ YR-BGA	Boeing 737-38J	27179/2524	ex N5573K	Alba Iulia	
☐ YR-BGB	Boeing 737-38J	27180/2529		Bucuresti	
☐ YR-BGD	Boeing 737-38J	27182/2663		Deva	
☐ YR-BGE	Boeing 737-38J	27395/2671		Timisoara	
☐ YR-BGF	Boeing 737-78J/W	28440/795		Brâila	SkyTeam c/s
☐ YR-BGG	Boeing 737-78J/W	28442/827		Craiova	retro c/s
☐ YR-BGH	Boeing 737-78J/W	28438/1394		Hunedoara	
☐ YR-BGI	Boeing 737-78J/W	28439/1419		Iasi	
☐ YR-LCA	Airbus A310-325	636	ex F-WQAV	Transilvania	
☐ YR-LCB	Airbus A310-325	644	ex F-WQAX	Moldova	
☐ YR-ASA	Airbus A318-111	2931	ex D-AUAC	Aurel Vlaicu - Aviation Pioneer	
☐ YR-ASB	Airbus A318-111	2955	ex D-AUAE	Traian Vuia - Aviation Pioneer	
☐ YR-ASC	Airbus A318-111	3220	ex D-AUAF	Henri Coanda - Aviation Pioneer	
☐ YR-ASD	Airbus A318-111	3225	ex D-AUAG	Smaranda Brăescu	

TEN AIRWAYS		Tender Air (X5/OTJ)		Bucharest-Otopeni (OTP)

☐ YR-HBD	McDonnell-Douglas MD-83	49808/1836	ex I-SMEC		>BBG
☐ YR-OTH	McDonnell-Douglas MD-83	49620/1484	ex YR-HBH		
☐ YR-OTK	McDonnell-Douglas MD-82	49139/1091	ex YR-MDK		Stage 4 demonstrator
☐ YR-OTL	McDonnell-Douglas MD-83	48079/1016	ex YR-MDL	Trawelair c/s	♦
☐ YR-OTN	McDonnell-Douglas MD-82	49119/1070	ex YR-MDM	Fly Romania c/s	>MLD

Filed for insolvency protection Feb15

VEGA OFFSHORE			

| ☐ YR-GSP | Bell 429 | 57037 | ex C-GKKJ |

YS- EL SALVADOR (Republic of El Salvador)

AVIANCA CENTRAL AMERICA		Taca (TA/TAI)		San Salvador-Comalapa Intl (SAL)

Member of Star Alliance

☐ N471TA	Airbus A319-132	1066	ex D-AVWE		wfs
☐ N477TA	Airbus A319-132	1952	ex D-AVWK		
☐ N478TA	Airbus A319-132	2339	ex D-AVWG		
☐ N479TA	Airbus A319-132	2444	ex D-AVWS		
☐ N480TA	Airbus A319-132	3057	ex D-AVYV		
☐ N520TA	Airbus A319-132	3248	ex D-AVWH		
☐ N522TA	Airbus A319-132	5219	ex D-AVYV	Star Alliance c/s	
☐ N524TA	Airbus A319-132	5280	ex D-AVYX	Star Alliance c/s	
☐ N703AV	Airbus A319-132/S	5406	ex D-AVWL		
☐ N990TA	Airbus A319-112	1598	ex XA-UAQ		
☐ N490TA	Airbus A320-232	2282	ex F-WWBO		
☐ N492TA	Airbus A320-233	2434	ex F-WWDL		
☐ N493TA	Airbus A320-233	2917	ex F-WWDR		
☐ N494TA	Airbus A320-233	3042	ex F-WWDM		
☐ N495TA	Airbus A320-233	3103	ex F-WWIH		
☐ N496TA	Airbus A320-233	3113	ex F-WWIU		
☐ N497TA	Airbus A320-233	3378	ex F-WWDK		
☐ N498TA	Airbus A320-233	3418	ex F-WWIO		
☐ N499TA	Airbus A320-233	3510	ex F-WWBX		
☐ N603AV	Airbus A320-233/S	5840	ex D-AXAS		
☐ N680TA	Airbus A320-233	3538	ex F-WWIF		
☐ N682TA	Airbus A320-233	3581	ex F-WWDC		
☐ N683TA	Airbus A320-233	4906	ex F-WWDE		
☐ N684TA	Airbus A320-233	4944	ex F-WWBZ		
☐ N685TA	Airbus A320-233	5068	ex D-AUBF		
☐ N686TA	Airbus A320-214	5238	ex D-AVVY		
☐ N687TA	Airbus A320-233	1334	ex EI-TAD		
☐ N688TA	Airbus A320-214	5243	ex D-AVVZ	Star Alliance c/s	>AVA
☐ N689TA	Airbus A320-214	5333	ex F-WWBU	Star Alliance c/s	
☐ N	Airbus A320-232	6775	ex		o/o♦
☐ N935TA	Embraer ERJ-190AR	19000205	ex TI-BCF		
☐ N936TA	Embraer ERJ-190AR	19000215	ex TI-BCG		
☐ N937TA	Embraer ERJ-190AR	19000221	ex TI-BCH		
☐ N938TA	Embraer ERJ-190AR	19000228	ex TI-BCI		
☐ N982TA	Embraer ERJ-190AR	19000259	ex PT-STH		
☐ N983TA	Embraer ERJ-190AR	19000265	ex PT-TLF		
☐ N984TA	Embraer ERJ-190AR	19000273	ex PT-TLN		
☐ N985TA	Embraer ERJ-190AR	19000287	ex PT-TZB		
☐ N986TA	Embraer ERJ-190AR	19000360	ex PT-XNB		
☐ N987TA	Embraer ERJ-190AR	19000393	ex PT-XNZ		
☐ N989TA	Embraer ERJ-190AR	19000482	ex PT-TPH		
☐ N564TA	Airbus A321-231	2862	ex D-AVZB		

☐ N568TA	Airbus A321-231	2687	ex D-AVZE	
☐ N570TA	Airbus A321-231	3869	ex D-AVZO	

VUELA AIRLINES	**(VAR)**		**San Salvador-Comalapa Intl (SAL)**
☐ N1235V	Airbus A319-132	2718	ex 5B-DCF
☐ N1821V	Airbus A319-132	2383	ex 5B-DCN

YU- SERBIA (Republic of Serbia)

AIR SERBIA		**JAT (JU/ASL)**		**Belgrade (BEG)**
☐ YU-APA	Airbus A319-132	2277	ex F-ORAH	
☐ YU-APB	Airbus A319-132	2296	ex N229RG	♦
☐ YU-APC	Airbus A319-131	2621	ex EI-EYA	Novak Djokovic
☐ YU-APD	Airbus A319-132	2335	ex EI-LIR	♦
☐ YU-APE	Airbus A319-132	3252	ex XA-VOS	
☐ YU-APF	Airbus A319-132	3317	ex XA-VOT	
☐ YU-API	Airbus A319-132	1140	ex A6-SAA	♦
☐ YU-APJ	Airbus A319-132	1159	ex A6-SAB	♦
☐ YU-ALN	ATR 72-202	180	ex F-WWEP	
☐ YU-ALO	ATR 72-202	186	ex F-WWEW	
☐ YU-ALP	ATR 72-202	189	ex F-WWED	
☐ YU-ALT	ATR 72-500	555	ex OY-CJT	
☐ YU-ALU	ATR 72-500	536	ex OY-NAB	
☐ YU-ALV	ATR 72-212A	727	ex F-GRPK	♦
☐ YU-AND	Boeing 737-3H9	23329/1134		Aviolet c/s
☐ YU-ANF	Boeing 737-3H9	23330/1136		[BEG]
☐ YU-ANH	Boeing 737-3H9	23415/1171	ex TC-CYO	wfs
☐ YU-ANI	Boeing 737-3H9	23416/1175	ex Z3-AAA	Aviolet c/s
☐ YU-ANJ	Boeing 737-3H9	23714/1305	ex TC-MIO	
☐ YU-ANK	Boeing 737-3H9	23715/1310		Aviolet c/s
☐ YU-ANL	Boeing 737-3H9	23716/1321	ex Z3-ARF	[BEG]
☐ YU-ANV	Boeing 737-3H9	24140/1524		
☐ YU-ANW	Boeing 737-3H9	24141/1526	ex TS-IED	wfs
☐ YU-AOV	Boeing 737-341	26852/2273	ex LZ-BOO	wfs
☐ YU-APG	Airbus A320-232	2587	ex VH-VQO	
☐ YU-APH	Airbus A320-232	2645	ex SP-ACK	Vlade Divac

AVIOGENEX		**Genex (AGX)**		**Belgrade (BEG)**
☐ YU-ANP	Boeing 737-2K3 (Nordam 3)	23912/1401	Zadar	wfs
To be liquidated				

YV- VENEZUELA (Bolivarian Republic of Venezuela)

AEROANDINAS				
☐ YV3014	British Aerospace Jetstream 3202	871	ex G-ISLB	♦

AERO EJECUTIVOS		**Venejecutiv (VEJ)**		**Caracas-Simon Bolivar Intl (CCS)**
☐ YV1434	LET L-410UVP-E3	872014	ex YV-1026CP	
☐ YV1854	Douglas DC-3	6135	ex YV-500C	
☐ YV201T	Douglas DC-3	11775	ex YV-1179C	
☐ YV-426C	Douglas DC-3	4093	ex N10DC	
☐ YV-440C	Douglas DC-3	2201	ex N31PB	Caballo Viejo status?

AEROBOL - AEROVIAS BOLIVAR			**Ciudad Bolivar (CBL)**
☐ YV-315C	Cessna U206G Stationair 6	U20604323	ex YV-1465P
☐ YV-387C	Cessna U206G Stationair 6	U20605398	ex YV-1310P
☐ YV-389C	Cessna U206G Stationair 6		
☐ YV-408C	Cessna U206G Stationair 6		
☐ YV-615C	Cessna U206G Stationair 6	U20604759	ex YV-1704P
☐ YV-849C	Cessna U206G Stationair 6		
☐ YV-946C	Cessna U206G Stationair 6		
☐ YV-270C	Britten-Norman BN-2A-20 Islander	573	ex YV-142CP
☐ YV-288C	Cessna 207A Stationair 8	20700708	ex YV-2143P
☐ YV-380C	Cessna 207A Stationair 8		

AEROMED				
☐ YV1752	LET L-410UVP-E	861719	ex YV-1176C	

AEROPOSTAL — Alven (ALV) — Caracas-Simon Bolivar Intl (CCS)

☐ YV445T	McDonnell-Douglas MD-82	49969/1719	ex N969AG	El Valenciano	
☐ YV505T	McDonnell-Douglas MD-82	49794/1600	ex N794AG	El Barquisimetano	
☐ YV563T	McDonnell-Douglas MD-82	53225/2086	ex I-DATG		wfs
☐ YV2793	McDonnell-Douglas MD-82	49796/1713	ex YV444T	El Varguense	
☐ YV2957	McDonnell-Douglas MD-82	53233/2110	ex N261PH	El Bolivarense	
☐ YV2992	McDonnell-Douglas MD-82	53206/2034	ex N263PH	El Cumanes	
☐ YV137T	Douglas DC-9-51 (ABS 3)	47771/883	ex YV-15C	El Neoespartano	[CCS]
☐ YV139T	Douglas DC-9-51	47695/806	ex YV-43C	Pa'lante!	[CCS]

AEROSERVICIOS RANGER — Caracas-La Carlota/Lagunillas/Tumeremo (-/LGY/TMO)

☐ YV-429C	Bell 206B JetRanger III	1959	ex N9910K	
☐ YV-431C	Bell 206B JetRanger III	2588		
☐ YV-433C	Bell 206B JetRanger II	2106	ex YV-330CP	
☐ YV-455C	Bell 206B JetRanger	1481	ex N218AL	
☐ YV-457C	Bell 206B JetRanger III	2470	ex N50056	
☐ YV-571C	Bell 206B JetRanger	273	ex N59Q	
☐ YV-572C	Bell 206B JetRanger	644	ex N7906J	
☐ YV1204	Britten-Norman BN-2A-26 Islander	56	ex YV-920C	
☐ YV1241	Britten-Norman BN-2A-26 Islander	149	ex YV-921C	

AEROVIAS CARIBE EXPRESS

☐ YV158T	Cessna 208B Caravan I	208B0444	ex YV-1088CP

AIR VENEZUELA

☐ YV-687CP	Beech 1900C	UB-57	ex N816BE

ALBATROS AIRLINES — (G2/GAL) — Maracay (MYC)

☐ YV2484	Cessna 208B Caravan I	208B2125	ex N52691		
☐ YV2489	Cessna 208B Caravan I	208B2132	ex N5183U		
☐ YV2776	Embraer EMB-120RT Brasilia	120150	ex PR-GDC		
☐ YV2777	Embraer EMB-120RT Brasilia	120074	ex PT-WKI		
☐ YV2814	Embraer EMB-120RT Brasilia	120130	ex YV2775		
☐ YV3001	Boeing 737-5L9	28995/2947	ex N102ES	Esmeralda	♦

ASERCA AIRLINES — Arosca (R7/OCA) — Caracas-Simon Bolivar Intl (CCS)

☐ YV153T	McDonnell-Douglas MD-82	49486/1317	ex YV388T		
☐ YV348T	McDonnell-Douglas MD-82	49120/1071	ex N993PG		
☐ YV481T	McDonnell-Douglas MD-83	49846/1581	ex N953PG		
☐ YV485T	McDonnell-Douglas MD-83	49668/1467	ex N668SH		
☐ YV494T	McDonnell-Douglas MD-82	49521/1690	ex N574SH		
☐ YV539T	McDonnell-Douglas MD-83	49848/1592	ex N848SH		
☐ YV2754	McDonnell-Douglas MD-82	49259/1161	ex N248AA		
☐ YV2971	McDonnell-Douglas MD-83	53472/2178	ex N981AS		
☐ YV2990	McDonnell-Douglas MD-83	53473/2183	ex N982AS		♦
☐ YV3024	McDonnell-Douglas MD-83	53453/2112	ex N977AS		♦
☐ YV	McDonnell-Douglas MD-87	49727/1621	ex N599SH		o/o♦
☐ YV-120T	North American Sabreliner 40A	282-106	ex N854RB		
☐ YV2220	Douglas DC-9-31	48155/1050	ex YV297T	Nuestra Señora de Lourdes	[CCS]
☐ YV2259	Douglas DC-9-31	48120/949	ex YV243T	San Miguel Arcangel	wfs
☐ YV2431	Douglas DC-9-31	48119/943	ex YV242T	San Francisco de Asis	wfs

AVIOR AIRLINES/AVIOR EXPRESS — Avior (9V/ROI) — Barcelona (BLA)

☐ YV1364	Beech 1900D	UE-270	ex YV-401C		
☐ YV1365	Beech 1900D	UE-268	ex YV-402C		
☐ YV1368	Beech 1900D	UE-304	ex YV-406C		>ATK
☐ YV1369	Beech 1900D	UE-342	ex YV-438C		
☐ YV1370	Beech 1900D	UE-343	ex YV-466C		
☐ YV1372	Beech 1900D	UE-331	ex YV-660C		
☐ YV1373	Beech 1900D	UE-355	ex YV-663C		
☐ YV1374	Beech 1900D	UE-356	ex YV-664C		
☐ YV187T	Boeing 737-2H4 (AvAero 3)	22964/933	ex N92SW		wfs
☐ YV343T	Boeing 737-232 (Nordam 3)	23101/1041	ex N329DL		wfs
☐ YV491T	Boeing 737-2T5 (Nordam 3)	22979/950	ex HC-CFH		
☐ YV1576	Boeing 737-2H4 (AvAero 3)	22826/878	ex N85SW		
☐ YV2732	Boeing 737-2Y5 (Nordam 3)	23848/1418	ex YV488T		
☐ YV2794	Boeing 737-232 (Nordam 3)	23089/1019	ex YV341T		
☐ YV2823	Boeing 737-232 (Nordam 3)	23090/1020	ex YV342T		
☐ YV2937	Boeing 737-2Y5 (Nordam 3)	23847/1414	ex YV495T		

☐ YV2917	Fokker 50	20193	ex PH-ZDE		
☐ YV2936	Fokker 50	20195	ex PH-ZDG		♦
☐ YV2948	Fokker 50	20198	ex PH-ZDH		♦
☐ YV2976	Fokker 50	20188	ex PH-ZDD		♦
☐ YV2977	Fokker 50	20187	ex PH-ZDC		♦
☐ YV3010	Fokker 50	20237	ex PH-JXM		♦
☐ YV1766	Cessna 208B Caravan I	208B0793	ex YV-925C		
☐ YV2928	Boeing 737-401	23885/1512	ex N405CJ		
☐ YV2946	Boeing 737-401	23886/1487	ex YV534T		
☐ YV3011	Boeing 737-401	23989/1716	ex N422US		♦
☐ YV	Boeing 737-401	23990/1732	ex N423US		[BLA]♦

CARIBBEAN FLIGHTS		Carflights (CIF)		Valencia Intl (VLN)

☐ YV-912C	Douglas DC-3	14506/25951	ex CP-2255	Falcon

CHAPI AIR				Marquetia

☐ YV1416	Britten-Norman BN-2A Mk.III-2 Trislander	1034	ex YV-872C	
☐ YV1996	Britten-Norman BN-2A-7 Islander	242	ex YV178T	
☐ YV2238	Britten-Norman BN-2A-8 Islander	296	ex YV1115C	dam 16Jan15

COMERAVIA		(CVV)		Cuidad Bolivar (CBL)

☐ YV396T	Short SD.3-60	SH3713	ex G-XPSS	
☐ YV1232	LET L-410UVP	810640	ex UR-67064	
☐ YV1233	LET L-410UVP	851427	ex YV-1185C	
☐ YV1332	LET L-410UVP	831028	ex YV-906C	
☐ YV1333	LET L-410UVP-E	861709	ex YV-1108CP	

COSTA AIRLINES		(COT)		Maracaibo (MAR)

☐ YV550T	Canadair CRJ-200ER	7172	ex N27172	o/o

CONVIASA		Conviasa (V0/VCV)	Caracas-Simon Bolivar Intl (CCS)

☐ YV2969	Cessna 208BEX Caravan I	208B5062			♦
☐ YV2970	Cessna 208BEX Caravan I	208B5071			♦
☐ YV2993	Cessna 208BEX Caravan I	208B5082			♦
☐ YV2994	Cessna 208BEX Caravan I	208B5083	ex PP-PEX		♦
☐ YV2995	Cessna 208BEX Caravan I	208B			♦
☐ YV3032	Cessna 208BEX Caravan I	208B			♦
☐ YV3033	Cessna 208B Caravan I	208B5140			♦
☐ YV3034	Cessna 208B Caravan I	208B5142			♦
☐ YV2849	Embraer ERJ-190AR	19000509	ex (UR-DSD)		
☐ YV2850	Embraer ERJ-190AR	19000505	ex PT-TSB		
☐ YV2851	Embraer ERJ-190AR	19000515	ex (UR-DSE)		
☐ YV2911	Embraer ERJ-190AR	19000610	ex PT-TJP		
☐ YV2912	Embraer ERJ-190AR	19000612	ex PT-TJR		
☐ YV2913	Embraer ERJ-190AR	19000622	ex PT-TKL		
☐ YV2943	Embraer ERJ-190AR	19000634	ex PR-EBS		
☐ YV2944	Embraer ERJ-190AR	19000634	ex PR-EBT		
☐ YV2953	Embraer ERJ-190AR	19000643	ex PR-ECN		
☐ YV2954	Embraer ERJ-190AR	19000644	ex PR-ECP		
☐ YV2964	Embraer ERJ-190AR	19000646	ex PR-ECW		
☐ YV2965	Embraer ERJ-190AR	19000645	ex PR-ECV		
☐ YV2966	Embraer ERJ-190AR	19000485	ex PT-TPJ		
☐ YV3016	Embraer ERJ-190STD	19000177	ex PR-LET	opf Petróleos de Venezuela♦	
☐ YV3052	Embraer ERJ-190AR	19000675	ex PR-EHI	o/o♦	
☐ YV3071	Embraer ERJ-190AR	19000676	ex PR-EHK	o/o♦	
☐ YV	Embraer ERJ-190AR	19000687	ex PR-EIY	o/o♦	
☐ YV	Embraer ERJ-190AR	19000690	ex PR-	o/o♦	
☐ EI-CMD	Boeing 767-324ER/W	27392/568	ex N838TM	<BPA♦	
☐ YV475T	Boeing 737-230	22124/727	ex N214AG	wfs	
☐ YV476T	Boeing 737-230	22121/720	ex N212AG	wfs	
☐ YV1004	Airbus A340-211	031	ex F-WQTN	Simon Bolivan El Libertador	
☐ YV1005	ATR 42-320	491	ex F-WQNK	[CCS]	
☐ YV1007	Boeing 737-322	23949/1493	ex N317UA	[MIA]	
☐ YV1008	ATR 42-320	346	ex F-WQNB	[CCS]	
☐ YV1009	ATR 42-320	487	ex F-WQNL		
☐ YV1111	Canadair CRJ-701ER	10270	ex N627CP		
☐ YV1115	Canadair CRJ-701ER	10271	ex N628CP		
☐ YV1850	ATR 72-201	276	ex F-WQNE	[CCS]	
☐ YV2088	Canadair CRJ-701ER	10274	ex N259CP		
☐ YV2115	Canadair CRJ-701ER	10275	ex N230CP		
☐ YV2421	ATR 72-212	482	ex F-WQNB		
☐ YV2422	ATR 72-212	486	ex F-WQNA		

☐ YV2556	Boeing 737-3G7	24712/1869	ex N311AW		[MIA]
☐ YV2557	Boeing 737-3G7	24633/1809	ex N306AW		wfs
☐ YV2558	Boeing 737-232 (Nordam 3)	23096/1028	ex XA-UIZ		
☐ YV2559	Boeing 737-232 (Nordam 3)	23097/1029	ex XA-UIY		
☐ 9M-XXJ	Airbus A330-343E	1423	ex F-WWRY	Harmonious DiverXity	<XAX♦

ESTELAR LATINOAMERICA (ETR) Caracas-Simon Bolivar Intl (CCS)

☐ YV497T	Boeing 737-247	23603/1361	ex N632CC	The Spirit of the Warrior	
☐ YV498T	Boeing 737-2E3 (AvAero 3)	22703/811	ex HC-FCO		
☐ YV2722	Boeing 737-2Y5 (Nordam 3)	24031/1523	ex YV399T	The Air Warrior	
☐ YV2792	Boeing 737-2B7	22887/976	ex N240CD		wfs
☐ YV2918	Boeing 737-329	23773/1441	EX 773KR	The Legend of the Warrior	

HELITEC Maturin (MUN)

☐ YV147T	Swearingen SA227AC Metro III	AC-744B	ex YV-947CP
☐ YV171T	Swearingen SA227AC Metro III	AC-594	ex YV-1000C
☐ YV185T	Swearingen SA227DC Metro 23	DC-904B	ex N904NJ
☐ YV221T	Swearingen SA227DC Metro 23	DC-879B	ex N6ER
☐ YV393T	Swearingen SA227AC Metro III		
☐ YV1412	Swearingen SA227TT Merlin IIIC	TT-465	ex YV-696CP
☐ YV1574	Swearingen SA227TT Merlin 300	TT-435	ex YV-808CP

KAVOK AIRLINES Catatumbo (KVA)

| ☐ YV2472 | British Aerospace Jetstream 32EP | | |

LASER Laser (QL/LER) Caracas-Simon Bolivar Intl (CCS)

☐ YV469T	McDonnell-Douglas MD-81	53299/2075	ex N819AG	
☐ YV480T	McDonnell-Douglas MD-81	53043/1982	ex N820AG	
☐ YV492T	McDonnell-Douglas MD-81	53301/2082	ex N821AG	
☐ YV1240	McDonnell-Douglas MD-81	49907/1734	ex N228RF	
☐ YV1243	McDonnell-Douglas MD-81	49908/1749	ex N908RF	
☐ YV2923	McDonnell-Douglas MD-82	49563/1485	ex N458AA	
☐ YV2927	McDonnell-Douglas MD-82	49924/1759	ex N7532A	
☐ YV2945	McDonnell-Douglas MD-82	49564/1486	ex N495AA	
☐ YV3053	McDonnell-Douglas MD-82	49566/1497	ex N461AA	♦
☐ YV	McDonnell-Douglas MD-82	49565/1496	ex N460AA	
☐ YV167T	Douglas DC-9-32 (ABS 3)	47281/427	ex YV-1121C	[SFB]
☐ YV231T	Douglas DC-9-32	47133/230	ex HK-4310X	[CCS]
☐ YV331T	Douglas DC-9-31	48157/1054	ex N934LK	
☐ YV332T	Douglas DC-9-31	48158/1056	ex N935DS	[CCS]

LINEA TURISTICA AEREOTUY Aereotuy (L4/TUY) Caracas-Simon Bolivar Intl (CCS)

☐ YV-463T	Cessna 560 Citation V	560-0175	ex N43LD	
☐ YV1182	Cessna 208B Caravan I	208B0729	ex YV-659C	
☐ YV1184	de Havilland DHC-7-102	030	ex YV-639C	
☐ YV1185	de Havilland DHC-7-102	005	ex YV-638C	wfs
☐ YV1188	Cessna 208B Caravan I	208B0955	ex YV-863C	
☐ YV382T	ATR 42-320	110	ex LN-FAP	[CCS]

PERLA AIRLINES (PLV)

| ☐ YV335T | McDonnell-Douglas MD-83 | 49232/1178 | ex N931AS | wfs |
| ☐ YV529T | McDonnell-Douglas MD-83 | 53024/1825 | ex N958AS | |

PETROLEOS DE VENEZUELA/PDVSA

☐ YV0171	Aérospatiale AS355NP		
☐ YV0178	Aérospatiale AS355NP	5793	
☐ YV0188	Aérospatiale AS350B3C Ecureuil		
☐ YV0190	Aérospatiale AS355NP	5789	
☐ YV2762	Beech 1900D		
☐ YV2861	Beech 1900D	UE-308	ex N904CG	♦
☐ YV2869	Beech 1900D		

PROFLIGHT VENEZUELA

| ☐ YV215T | British Aerospace Jetstream 31 | 784 | ex N430UE |
| ☐ YV | British Aerospace Jetstream 32 | 934 | ex N934AE |

RUTACA Rutaca (5R/RUC) Ciudad Bolivar (CBL)

☐ YV169T	Boeing 737-2S3 (Nordam 3)	21776/577	ex YV-1155C	[CBL]
☐ YV369T	Boeing 737-230 (Nordam 3)	22113/649	ex OB-1837-P	
☐ YV379T	Boeing 737-230 (Nordam 3)	22115/694	ex N215AG	
☐ YV380T	Boeing 737-230 (Nordam 3)	22127/745	ex N227AG	

☐ YV390T	Boeing 737-230 (Nordam 3)	22128/752	ex N128AG	
☐ YV472T	Boeing 737-242	22074/619	ex N131MS	
☐ YV1381	Boeing 737-2S3 (Nordam 3)	21774/563	ex YV-216C	Vinotinto c/s
☐ YV	Boeing 737-244	22581/796	ex HC-CFR	[CBL]
☐ YV-229C	Cessna U206G Stationair	U20603541	ex YV-1153P	
☐ YV-785C	Cessna U206G Stationair	U20603889	ex YV-1314P	
☐ YV-786C	Cessna U206G Stationair 6	U20605125	ex YV-1719P	
☐ YV1943	Cessna U206G Stationair 6	U20605354	ex YV-210C	
☐ YV1946	Cessna U206G Stationair 6	U20604803	ex YV-793C	
☐ YV1947	Cessna U206F Stationair	U20603192	ex YV-789C	
☐ YV1948	Cessna U206G Stationair 6	U20604150	ex YV-379C	
☐ YV-209C	Cessna U206D Super Skywagon	U206-1338	ex N72247	
☐ YV1671	Cessna U206F	U20602386	ex YV-214C	
☐ YV1950	Cessna 208B Caravan I	208B0555	ex YV-791C	
☐ YV1951	Cessna 208B Caravan I	208B0527	ex YV-790C	
☐ YV3063	Boeing 737-3Q8	26311/2681	ex N221LF	◆

SASCA – SERVICIOS AEREOS SUCRE　　　(SSU)　　　　　　　　　　Porlamar

☐ YV183T	Cessna 208B Caravan I	208B0669	ex YV-1149C	
☐ YV315T	British Aerospace Jetstream 3102	697	ex TG-TAW	>Tortug'Air
☐ YV2211	British Aerospace Jetstream 31	645	ex YV263T	

SBA - SANTA BARBARA AIRLINES　　Santa Barbara (S3/BBR)　　　　Maracaibo (MAR)

☐ YV1421	ATR 42-320	300	ex YV-1017C	
☐ YV1422	ATR 42-320	340	ex YV-1018C	wfs
☐ YV1423	ATR 42-320	360	ex YV-1015C Virgen del Carmen	
☐ YV1424	ATR 42-320	368	ex YV-1014C Mi Chinita	
☐ YV2314	ATR 42-300	038	ex PR-TTD	
☐ YV288T	Boeing 757-21B	24402/233	ex N742PA	
☐ YV304T	Boeing 757-21B	24714/262	ex N816PG	
☐ YV450T	Boeing 757-236	24370/218	ex N580SH	
☐ YV528T	Boeing 767-3P6ER	24349/244	ex N960PG	
☐ YV545T	Boeing 767-3P6ER	23764/158	ex N964PG	
☐ YV-1038C	Cessna 208B Caravan I	208B0889	ex N52677	
☐ YV-1039C	Cessna 208B Caravan I	208B0901	ex N5267K	

SERAMI　　　　　　　　　　　　　　(SRE)　　　　　　　　Cuidad Bolivar (CBL)

☐ YV2355	Cessna 208B Caravan I	208B1242	ex N52178	
☐ YV2367	Cessna 210		ex YV-1156C	
☐ YV2368	Cessna 404	4040851	ex YV-160T	

SOLAR CARGO　　　　　　　Solarcargo (OLC)　　　　　　　　Valencia (VLN)

☐ YV524T	McDonnell-Douglas DC-10-30F	47840/337	ex N612GC	
☐ YV1402	Antonov An-26	7207	ex YV1110C	[VLN]
☐ YV1403	Antonov An-26	9810	ex YV-1134C	[VLN]

SUNDANCE AIR　　　　　　Danceair (SUV)

☐ YV537T	British Aerospace Jetstram 31	755	ex N743PE	
☐ YV547T	British Aerospace Jetstream 3102	721	ex N310SA	
☐ YV1544	LET L-410UVP	831032	ex YV-1114C	
☐ YV2063	LET L-410UVP	831010	ex YV-1025C	

TRANSAVEN – TRANSPORTE AEREO VENEZUELA　(VEN)　　　　Caracas-Simon Bolivar Intl (CCS)

☐ YV1417	LET L-410UVP	830939	ex YV-980C	[BON]
☐ YV1446	Cessna 402B	402B1079	ex YV-	
☐ YV2082	LET L-410UVP-E	902430	ex YV-1175C	
☐ YV2083	LET L-410UVP-E	892314	ex YV-1113C	
☐ YV2170	Britten-Norman BN-2A Mk.III-1			
	Trislander	1007	ex YV-1117C	

TRANSCARGA　　　　　　　Tiaca (T7/TIW)　　　　Caracas-Simon Bolivar Intl (CCS)

☐ N831JM	Airbus A300B4-203F	220	ex EI-SAF	[SFB]
☐ N832JM	Airbus A300B4-203F	152	ex EI-OZE	[SFB]
☐ N833JM	Airbus A300B4-203	234	ex EI-OZH	[SFB]◆
☐ N834JM	Airbus A300B4-203F	236	ex EI-OZD	[SFB]
☐ N835JM	Airbus A300B4-203F	259	ex EI-OZF	[LDE]◆
☐ YV560T	Airbus A300B4-203F	261	ex N251AX	[SFB]◆
☐ YV562T	Airbus A300B4-203F	274	ex N830JM	◆
☐ YV276T	Cessna 402B	402B1234	ex N4188G	
☐ YV277T	Cessna 402B	402B1024	ex N98635	

☐ YV1114	Cessna 402B	402B0814	ex N3826C	
☐ YV1149	Aero Commander 500B	500B-899	ex YV-941C	ex c/n 500A-899-B
☐ YV2546	Embraer EMB.120ER Brasilia	120017	ex N125AM	
☐ YV2694	Embraer EMB.120RT Brasilia	120021	ex N223AS	
☐ YV2789	Cessna 412B			
☐ YV2791	Cessna 402B			

TRANSMANDU		*(TMD)*		*Ciudad Bolivar (CBL)*
☐ YV1019	British Aerospace Jetstream 32	911	ex N491UE	
☐ YV2532	British Aerospace Jetstream 32EP	965	ex N965AE	
☐ YV2536	British Aerospace Jetstream 32	964	ex YV2272?	
☐ YV1258	Cessna U206F	U20602122	ex YV-193C	
☐ YV2456	British Aerospace Jetstream 32	884	ex N476UE	
☐ YV2536	British Aerospace Jetstream 32EP	966	ex N966AE	

VENEXCARGO		*(VNX)*		
☐ YV1442	Swearingen SA226TC Metro II	TC-213	ex YV-852CP	

VENEZOLANA		*Venezolana (VNE)*		*Caracas-Simon Bolivar Intl (CCS)*
☐ YV268T	Boeing 737-232 (AvAero 3)	23099/1035	ex N327DL	
☐ YV287T	Boeing 737-217 (AvAero 3)	22728/911	ex N168WP	
☐ YV296T	Boeing 737-2T5 (AvAero 3)	22024/641	ex N166WP	
☐ YV302T	Boeing 737-2T5 (AvAero 3)	23087/1013	ex N315DL	
☐ YV502T	Boeing 737-2A1	21598/512	ex N976UA	
☐ YV513T	Boeing 737-230	23158/1089	ex N89DL	
☐ YV535T	Boeing 737-230	23153/1075	ex N2DL	
☐ YV191T	McDonnell-Douglas MD-83	49392/1272	ex N392AP	
☐ YV179T	British Aerospace Jetstream 31	759	ex YV-1086C	
☐ YV180T	British Aerospace Jetstream 31	770	ex YV-1093C	
☐ YV290T	British Aerospace Jetstream 41	41020	ex N306UE	
☐ YV514T	McDonnell-Douglas MD-82	49511/1537	ex N511JZ	

VENSECAR INTERNACIONAL		*Vecar (V4/VEC)*		*Caracas-Simon Bolivar Intl (CCS)*
☐ YV567T	Boeing 737-4Q3SF	29487/3122	ex N493SA	DHL c/s
☐ YV573T	Boeing 737-4Q3SF	26606/2898	ex N230PA	DHL c/s♦
☐ YV2308	ATR 42-300F	061	ex YV157T 302	DHL c/s

WYNGS AVIATION				
☐ YV1106	Beech 1900D	UE-241	ex YV-1152CP	

Z-   ZIMBABWE (Republic of Zimbabwe)

AIR ZIMBABWE		*Air Zimbabwe (UM/AZW)*		*Harare-International (HRE)*
☐ Z-WPA	Boeing 737-2N0	23677/1313	ex C9-BAG	Mbuya Nehanda	
☐ Z-WPB	Boeing 737-2N0	23678/1405		Great Zimbabwe	
☐ Z-WPC	Boeing 737-2N0	23679/1415		Matojeni	[HRE]
☐ Z-WPE	Boeing 767-2N0ER	24713/287		Victoria Falls	
☐ Z-WPF	Boeing 767-2N0ER	24867/333		Chimanimani	
☐ Z-WPJ	CAIC MA60	0301	ex B-674L	Nyami-Nyami	
☐ Z-WPK	CAIC MA60	0302		A'sambeni	
☐ Z-WPL	CAIC MA60	0303			
☐ Z-WPM	Airbus A320-214	0630	ex M-YWAT		
☐ Z-WPN	Airbus A320-211	1973	ex M-YWAU		[JNB]

DHL AVIATION (ZIMBABWE)				*Harare-International (HRE)*
☐ Z-KPS	Cessna 208B Caravan I	208B0303	ex N31SE	

FLYAFRICA.COM		*(Z7/FZW)*		*Harare-International (HRE)*
☐ Z-FAA	Boeing 737-55S	26539/2300	ex T7-FAA	♦
☐ Z-FAB	Boeing 737-55S	26540/2317	ex T7-FAB	♦

GLOBAL AFRICA AVIATION		*(GAA)*		*Harare-International (HRE)*
☐ Z-GAB	McDonnell-Douglas MD-11ERF	48746/597	ex Z-BAM	Lady Liege	<AV Cargo♦
☐ Z-GAC	McDonnell-Douglas MD-11F	48756/623	ex Z-BPL	Hannah Mai	<AV Cargo♦

UNITED AIR CHARTERS		*Unitair (UAC)*		*Harare-Charles Prince*
☐ Z-BWK	Cessna U206G Stationair	U20603546	ex N8794Q	
☐ Z-UAC	Beech 58 Baron	TH-211	ex 9J-ADK	

☐ Z-UTD	Britten-Norman BN-2A Mk.III-2 Trislander	1055	ex A2-AGY	
☐ Z-WHG	Beech 95-D55 Baron	TE-761	ex VP-WHG	
☐ Z-WHH	Beech 65-80 Queen Air	LD-101	ex VP-WHH	
☐ Z-WHX	Britten-Norman BN-2A-7 Islander	192	ex VP-WHX	
☐ Z-WKL	Cessna U206F Stationair	U20601707	ex ZS-ILV	
☐ Z-WTA	Cessna U206F Stationair	U20602547	ex OO-SPX	
☐ Z-WTF	Cessna 414A Chancellor	414A0062	ex G-METR	
☐ Z-YHS	Cessna U206C Super Skywagon	U206-1029	ex VP-YHS	

ZK- NEW ZEALAND (Dominion of New Zealand)

AERIUS HELICOPTERS — Te Puke

☐ ZK-HZU	Aérospatiale AS350B Ecureuil	1471	ex JA9294

AIR CHATHAMS — Chatham (CV/CVA) — Chatham Island (CHT)

☐ ZK-AWP	Douglas DC-3C	16387/33135	ex A3-AWP	
☐ ZK-CIB	Convair 580	327A	ex C-FCIB	
☐ ZK-CIC	Swearingen SA227AC Metro III	AC-623B	ex N623AV	Frtr
☐ ZK-CIE	Convair 580	399	ex N565EA	
☐ ZK-CIF	Convair 580	381	ex N566EA	
☐ ZK-KAI	Cessna U206G Stationair	U20603711		
☐ ZK-LYP	Britten-Norman BN-2A-27 Islander	821	ex A3-LYP	

AIR FREIGHT NZ — Air Freight (AFN) — Auckland-Intl (AKL)

☐ ZK-FTA	Convair 580F	168	ex C-GKFP	opf Parceline
☐ ZK-KFH	Convair 580F	42	ex C-FKFL	
☐ ZK-KFJ	Convair 580F	114	ex C-GKFJ	
☐ ZK-KFL	Convair 580F	372	ex C-FKFL	opf Parceline
☐ ZK-KFS	Convair 5800	277	ex C-FKFS	Frtr
☐ ZK-JSH	British Aerospace Jetstream 31	838	ex G-IBLW	♦
☐	British Aerospace Jetstream 32	976	ex VH-OTR	opf Life Flight Trust♦

AFN code is for domestic use only; not registered with ICAO

AIR GISBORNE — Gisborne (GIS)

☐ ZK-DCP	Piper PA-34-200T Seneca	34-8070355	ex N8263M	
☐ ZK-SFC	Piper PA-34-200T Seneca	34-7770054	ex VH-PZG	
☐ ZK-SKL	Beech King Air C90A	LJ-1372	ex N454P	♦

AIR MANAWATU — Flight Med — Fielding

☐ ZK-LAL	Partenavia P.68B	70	ex VH-PNY

AIR MILFORD — Queenstown (ZQN)

☐ ZK-DWX	Cessna U206F	U20606241	ex N59268
☐ ZK-ENW	Cessna A185F	18503133	ex N80651
☐ ZK-SKA	Cessna 208 Caravan I	20800524	ex VH-SKH
☐ ZK-SKB	Cessna 208 Caravan I	20800244	ex VH-BSX

AIR NAPIER — Air Napier (NPR) — Napier-Hawkes Bay (NPR)

☐ ZK-ELK	Piper PA-32-260 Cherokee Six	32-7600009	ex N8768C
☐ ZK-MSL	Piper PA-34-200T Seneca	34-7770224	ex N5600V
☐ ZK-NPR	Piper PA-31 Navajo	31-777	ex ZK-DOM
☐ ZK-WUG	Piper PA-34-200T Seneca	34-7970329	ex N2891R

AIR NELSON — Link (RLK) — Nelson (NSN)

Wholly owned by Air New Zealand; ops as part of Air New Zealand Link (qv)

AIR NEW ZEALAND — NewZealand (NZ/ANZ) — Auckland-Intl (AKL)

Member of Star Alliance

☐ ZK-OAB	Airbus A320-232	4553	ex F-WWDF	All Blacks c/s
☐ ZK-OJA	Airbus A320-232	2085	ex F-WWIN	
☐ ZK-OJB	Airbus A320-232	2090	ex F-WWBM	
☐ ZK-OJC	Airbus A320-232	2112	ex F-WWDQ	
☐ ZK-OJD	Airbus A320-232	2130	ex F-WWDK	
☐ ZK-OJE	Airbus A320-232	2148	ex F-WWIH	
☐ ZK-OJF	Airbus A320-232	2153	ex F-WWIS	
☐ ZK-OJG	Airbus A320-232	2173	ex F-WWDJ	
☐ ZK-OJH	Airbus A320-232	2257	ex F-WWDE	Star Alliance c/s
☐ ZK-OJI	Airbus A320-232	2297	ex F-WWBU	
☐ ZK-OJK	Airbus A320-232	2445	ex EI-EWD	

☐ ZK-OJM	Airbus A320-232	2533	ex F-WWIB		
☐ ZK-OJN	Airbus A320-232	2594	ex F-WWBC		
☐ ZK-OJO	Airbus A320-232	2663	ex F-WWBM		
☐ ZK-OJQ	Airbus A320-232	4584	ex F-WWIO		
☐ ZK-OJR	Airbus A320-232	4884	ex F-WWIP		
☐ ZK-OJS	Airbus A320-232	4926	ex F-WWIT		
☐ ZK-OXA	Airbus A320-232/S	5629	ex F-WWBH		
☐ ZK-OXB	Airbus A320-232/S	5682	ex F-WWDH		
☐ ZK-OXC	Airbus A320-232/S	5847	ex D-AXAU		
☐ ZK-OXD	Airbus A320-232/S	5962	ex F-WWIY		
☐ ZK-OXE	Airbus A320-232/S	5993	ex F-WWBM		
☐ ZK-OXF	Airbus A320-232/S	6182	ex F-WWBV		◆
☐ ZK-OXG	Airbus A320-232/S	6460	ex F-WWDZ		◆
☐ ZK-OXH	Airbus A320-232/S	6471	ex F-WWIQ		◆
☐ ZK-OXI	Airbus A320-232/S	6533	ex F-WWBQ		◆
☐ ZK-OXJ	Airbus A320-232/S	6694	ex		o/o◆
☐ ZK-OXK	Airbus A320-232/S	6706	ex		o/o◆
☐ ZK-	Airbus A320-232/S	6789	ex		o/o◆
☐ ZK-NCG	Boeing 767-319ER/W	26912/509			
☐ ZK-NCI	Boeing 767-319ER/W	26913/558	ex N6009F		
☐ ZK-NCJ	Boeing 767-319ER/W	26915/574	ex N6018N		
☐ ZK-NCK	Boeing 767-319ER/W	26971/663			
☐ ZK-NCL	Boeing 767-319ER/W	28745/677			
☐ ZK-OKA	Boeing 777-219ER	29404/534			
☐ ZK-OKB	Boeing 777-219ER	34376/537			
☐ ZK-OKC	Boeing 777-219ER	34377/546		Fern leaf c/s	
☐ ZK-OKD	Boeing 777-219ER	29401/550			
☐ ZK-OKE	Boeing 777-219ER	32712/564			
☐ ZK-OKF	Boeing 777-219ER	34378/575			
☐ ZK-OKG	Boeing 777-219ER	29403/591			
☐ ZK-OKH	Boeing 777-219ER	34379/605			
☐ ZK-OKM	Boeing 777-319ER	38405/902			
☐ ZK-OKN	Boeing 777-319ER	38406/911			
☐ ZK-OKO	Boeing 777-319ER	38407/921		The Desolation of Smaug c/s	
☐ ZK-OKP	Boeing 777-319ER	39041/972		The Hobbit c/s	
☐ ZK-OKQ	Boeing 777-319ER	40689/984		All Blacks c/s	
☐ ZK-OKR	Boeing 777-319ER	44546/1206			
☐ ZK-OKS	Boeing 777-319ER	44547/1237			
☐ ZK-NZC	Boeing 787-9	41988/126	ex N789EX		o/o
☐ ZK-NZD	Boeing 787-9	41989/133	ex N789FT		o/o
☐ ZK-NZE	Boeing 787-9	34334/169	ex N1012N	Blacks c/s	
☐ ZK-NZF	Boeing 787-9	34335/213			
☐ ZK-NZG	Boeing 787-9	37963/236			
☐ ZK-NZH	Boeing 787-9	37964/351			o/o◆
☐ ZK-NZI	Boeing 787-9	37965/			o/o◆
☐ ZK-NZJ	Boeing 787-9	37966/			o/o◆
☐ ZK-NZK	Boeing 787-9	43217/			o/o◆
☐ ZK-NZL	Boeing 787-9	43218/			o/o◆
☐ ZK-NGG	Boeing 737-319	25606/3123	ex N1795B		
☐ ZK-NGI	Boeing 737-319	25608/3128	ex N1786B		
☐ ZK-NGJ	Boeing 737-319	25609/3130	ex N1786B		last 737-300 built

AIR NEW ZEALAND LINK — Christchurch-Intl/Nelson/Hamilton (CHC/NSN/HLZ)

☐ ZK-MCA	ATR 72-212A	597	ex F-WQKC		Mount Cook
☐ ZK-MCB	ATR 72-212A	598	ex F-WQKG		Mount Cook
☐ ZK-MCC	ATR 72-212A	714	ex F-WQMV		Mount Cook
☐ ZK-MCF	ATR 72-212A	600	ex F-WQKH		Mount Cook
☐ ZK-MCJ	ATR 72-212A	624	ex F-WQKI		Mount Cook
☐ ZK-MCO	ATR 72-212A	628	ex F-WQKJ		Mount Cook
☐ ZK-MCP	ATR 72-212A	630	ex F-WQKK		Mount Cook
☐ ZK-MCU	ATR 72-212A	632	ex F-WQKL		Mount Cook
☐ ZK-MCW	ATR 72-212A	646	ex F-WQMG		Mount Cook
☐ ZK-MCX	ATR 72-212A	687	ex F-WQMN		Mount Cook
☐ ZK-MCY	ATR 72-212A	703	ex F-WQMR		Mount Cook
☐ ZK-MVA	ATR 72-600	1051	ex F-WWEJ		Mount Cook
☐ ZK-MVB	ATR 72-600	1065	ex F-WKVB	All Blacks c/s	Mount Cook
☐ ZK-MVC	ATR 72-600	1084	ex F-WWEU		Mount Cook
☐ ZK-MVD	ATR 72-600	1117	ex F-WWEF		Mount Cook
☐ ZK-MVE	ATR 72-600	1182	ex F-WWEW		Mount Cook◆
☐ ZK-MVF	ATR 72-600	1228	ex F-WWEC		Mount Cook◆
☐ ZK-MVG	ATR 72-600	1264	ex F-WW		Mount Cook o/o◆
☐ ZK-MVH	ATR 72-600		ex F-WW		Mount Cook o/o◆
☐ ZK-MVI	ATR 72-600		ex F-WW		Mount Cook o/o◆
☐ ZK-EAB	Beech 1900D	UE-425	ex N2335Z		Eagle
☐ ZK-EAC	Beech 1900D	UE-426	ex N51226		Eagle
☐ ZK-EAD	Beech 1900D	UE-427	ex N50127		Eagle

☐ ZK-EAE	Beech 1900D	UE-428	ex N3188L		Eagle
☐ ZK-EAF	Beech 1900D	UE-429	ex N50069		Eagle
☐ ZK-EAG	Beech 1900D	UE-430	ex N50430	All Blacks c/s	Eagle
☐ ZK-EAH	Beech 1900D	UE-431	ex N51321		Eagle
☐ ZK-EAI	Beech 1900D	UE-432	ex N5032L		Eagle
☐ ZK-EAJ	Beech 1900D	UE-433	ex N4469Q		Eagle
☐ ZK-EAM	Beech 1900D	UE-436	ex N5016C		Eagle
☐ ZK-EAN	Beech 1900D	UE-437	ex N50307		Eagle
☐ ZK-EAO	Beech 1900D	UE-438	ex N4470D		Eagle
☐ ZK-EAP	Beech 1900D	UE-439	ex N50899		Eagle
☐ ZK-EAQ	Beech 1900D	UE-363	ex N846CA		Eagle
☐ ZK-EAR	Beech 1900D	UE-388	ex VH-EAS		Eagle
☐ ZK-NEA	de Havilland DHC-8-311Q	611	ex C-FCPO		Air Nelson
☐ ZK-NEB	de Havilland DHC-8-311Q	615	ex C-FDRG		Air Nelson
☐ ZK-NEC	de Havilland DHC-8-311Q	616	ex C-FEDG		Air Nelson
☐ ZK-NED	de Havilland DHC-8-311Q	617	ex C-FERB		Air Nelson
☐ ZK-NEE	de Havilland DHC-8-311Q	618	ex C-FFBY		Air Nelson
☐ ZK-NEF	de Havilland DHC-8-311Q	620	ex C-FFCC		Air Nelson
☐ ZK-NEG	de Havilland DHC-8-311Q	621	ex C-FFOZ		Air Nelson
☐ ZK-NEH	de Havilland DHC-8-311Q	623	ex C-FGAI		Air Nelson
☐ ZK-NEJ	de Havilland DHC-8-311Q	625	ex C-FFPA		Air Nelson
☐ ZK-NEK	de Havilland DHC-8-311Q	629	ex C-FHPZ		Air Nelson
☐ ZK-NEM	de Havilland DHC-8-311Q	630	ex C-FHQB		Air Nelson
☐ ZK-NEO	de Havilland DHC-8-311Q	633	ex C-FIOS		Air Nelson
☐ ZK-NEP	de Havilland DHC-8-311Q	634	ex C-FIOV		Air Nelson
☐ ZK-NEQ	de Havilland DHC-8-311Q	636	ex C-FJKL		Air Nelson
☐ ZK-NER	de Havilland DHC-8-311Q	639	ex C-FJKO		Air Nelson
☐ ZK-NES	de Havilland DHC-8-311Q	641	ex C-FJKP		Air Nelson
☐ ZK-NET	de Havilland DHC-8-311Q	642	ex C-FJKQ		Air Nelson
☐ ZK-NEU	de Havilland DHC-8-311Q	647	ex C-FLTZ		Air Nelson
☐ ZK-NEW	de Havilland DHC-8-311Q	648	ex C-FLUH		Air Nelson
☐ ZK-NEZ	de Havilland DHC-8-311Q	654	ex C-FNPY		Air Nelson
☐ ZK-NFA	de Havilland DHC-8-311Q	659	ex C-FPPN		Air Nelson
☐ ZK-NFB	de Havilland DHC-8-311Q	670	ex C-FVUF		Air Nelson
☐ ZK-NFI	de Havilland DHC-8-311Q	671	ex C-FWGQ		Air Nelson

AIR SAFARIS & SERVICES — Airsafari (SRI) — Lake Tekapo

☐ ZK-BZV	Cessna 180D	18050935	ex N6435X	
☐ ZK-NMD	GAF N24A Nomad	N24A-060	ex VH-DHU	
☐ ZK-NME	GAF N24A Nomad	N24A-122	ex 5W-FAT	
☐ ZK-SAE	Gippsland GA-8 Airvan	GA8-04-055	ex VH-VFF	
☐ ZK-SAF	Gippsland GA-8 Airvan	GA8-02-017	ex VH-AAP	
☐ ZK-SAU	Gippsland GA-8-TC-320 Airvan	GA8-TC320-09-144		
☐ ZK-SAZ	Gippsland GA-8 Airvan	GA8-05-078		
☐ ZK-SEY	Cessna T207A Stationair 8	20700661	ex N76012	
☐ ZK-SRI	Cessna 208B Caravan I	208B0636	ex N208PR	

AIRSCAPADE — Te Anau (TEU)

☐ ZK-AKY	de Havilland DH89B Dragon Rapide	6653	ex NZ525	opb Croydon Aircraft Trust
☐ ZK-JGB	Douglas R4D-1 Skytrain	4363	ex N451ZS	♦

AIR2THERE — Airtothere — Paraparaumu (PPQ)

☐ ZK-MYH	Cessna 208B Caravan I	208B0604	ex N64BP	
☐ ZK-MYM	Beech B200 Super King Air	BB-1466	ex VH-ZMQ	EMS, opf Manawatu Air Ambulance
☐ ZK-MYS	Piper PA-31-350 Navajo Chieftain	31-7652032	ex ZK-MCM	
☐ ZK-WHW	Piper PA-31 Navajo	31-437	ex N6476L	

AIR WANGANUI COMMUTER — Medicare — Wanganui (WAG)

☐ ZK-MKG	Beech C90B King Air	LJ-1367	ex N111MU	
☐ ZK-WTH	Piper PA-31P-350 Navajo Chieftain	31P-8414003	ex N9187Y	

AIR WEST COAST — Air West — Greymouth (GMN)

☐ ZK-COY	Cessna 210-5A	205-0570		♦
☐ ZK-VIR	Cessna P210N Centurion	P21000482	ex N731KK	

AIRWORK NEW ZEALAND — Airwork (AWK) — Auckland-Intl/Christchurch (AWK/CHC)

☐ ZK-FXT	Boeing 737-3B7SF	23862/1586	ex N527AU	opf TFX
☐ ZK-JTQ	Boeing 737-476F	24442/2371	ex VH-JTQ	opf TFX
☐ ZK-TLA	Boeing 737-3B7SF	23383/1425	ex N508AU	
☐ ZK-TLD	Boeing 737-3B7SF	23706/1499	ex N520AU	opf TFX
☐ ZK-TLE	Boeing 737-3S1SF	24834/1896	ex N919GF	opf TFX
☐ ZK-TLF	Boeing 737-4Q8SF	24709/2115	ex N709AG	[KUL]
☐ ZK-	Boeing 737-476SF	24435/1959	ex N938NZ	o/o♦
☐ ZK-	Boeing 737-476SF	24436/1998	ex N937NZ	o/o♦
☐ ZK-	Boeing 737-476SF	24437/2162	ex N939NZ	o/o♦

| ☐ ZK- | Boeing 737-476SF | 24444/2454 | exN944NZ | | o/o♦ |
| ☐ ZK- | Boeing 737-476SF | | ex N936NZ | | o/o♦ |

☐ ZK-LFT	Swearingen SA227AC Metro III	AC-582	ex ZK-PAA		EMS; opf Life Flight NZ
☐ ZK-NSS	Swearingen SA227AC Metro III	AC-692B	ex N2707D		EMS
☐ ZK-POB	Swearingen SA227AC Metro III	AC-606B	ex D-CABG		opf SkyLink
☐ ZK-POE	Swearingen SA227CC Metro 23	CC-843B	ex N30228		opf NZ Post
☐ ZK-POF	Swearingen SA227CC Metro 23	CC-844B	ex N30229		

☐ ZK-ECI	British Aerospace Jetstream 32EP	946	ex ZK-JSU		opf Inflite Charters
☐ ZK-ECJ	British Aerospace Jetstream 32EP	969	ex ZK-JSR		opf Inflite Charters
☐ ZK-FOP	Piper PA-31-350 Navajo Chieftain	31-7405227	ex N888SG		EMS
☐ ZK-HGU	MBB BK.117B-2	7229	ex N164AM		♦
☐ ZK-HQC	MBB BK.117A-3	7014	ex N135CP		
☐ ZK-INI	MBB BK.117B-2	7179	ex N5405G		♦
☐ ZK-PAX	Fokker F.27 Friendship 500	10596	ex HB-ILJ	all-white	
☐ ZK-POH	Fokker F.27 Friendship 500	10680	ex VT-NEH	all-white	

ALPINE HELICOPTERS · Wanaka (WKA)

☐ ZK-HAA	Aérospatiale AS350B2 Ecureuil	3700	ex ZK-IDV		♦
☐ ZK-HBN	Aérospatiale AS350B2 Ecureuil	2266	ex JA9852		
☐ ZK-HIH	Aérospatiale AS350BA AStar	1723	ex JA6018		
☐ ZK-HOT	Aérospatiale AS350B2 Ecureuil	2653	ex ZK-HTB		

ANDERSON HELICOPTERS · Hokitika (HKK)

| ☐ ZK-HKA | Aérospatiale AS350B2 Ecureuil | 2887 | ex RP-C1591 | |
| ☐ ZK-HSG | Bell 206B JetRanger | 1555 | ex C-GLDR | |

AORAKI MOUNT COOK SKIPLANES · Aoraki Mount Cook (MON)

☐ ZK-BKG	Cessna 180 Skywagon	30376	ex N1676C	WS
☐ ZK-CBS	Cessna A185 Skywagon	185-0398	ex N11B	WS
☐ ZK-MCN	Pilatus PC-6/B2-H4 Turbo Porter	824	ex HB-FCV	WS♦
☐ ZK-MCR	Cessna A185F Skywagon	18504429	ex N714XT	WS
☐ ZK-MCT	Pilatus PC-6/B2-H4 Turbo Porter	841	ex HB-FIO	WS
☐ ZK-MCV	Cessna A185F Skywagon	18504395	ex N714FV	WS

ARDMORE HELICOPTERS · Ardmore (AMZ)

| ☐ ZK-HYH | Bell 206B JetRanger | 3290 | ex ZK-HGS | |

ASHWORTH HELICOPTERS · Gisborne (GIS)

| ☐ ZK-HHC | Bell 206B JetRanger | 1715 | ex N101HS | |
| ☐ ZK-IWA | Bell 206L-3 LongRanger | 51543 | ex JA6114 | |

ASPIRING AIR/ASPIRING HELICOPTERS (OI) · Wanaka (WKA)

☐ ZK-EVT	Britten-Norman BN-2A-26 Islander	152	ex YJ-RV19	Lake Wanaka
☐ ZK-HAH	Aérospatiale AS350B2 Ecureuil	4734		
☐ ZK-HMM	Aérospatiale AS350B2 Ecureuil	2436	ex ZK-IWJ	♦

AUCKLAND REGIONAL HEALTH TRUST · Auckland-Mechanics Bay

| ☐ ZK-HKZ | Kawasaki BK117B-2 | 1089 | ex HL9210 | EMS |
| ☐ ZK-HLN | Kawasaki BK117B-2 | 1017 | ex JA9696 | EMS |

AUCKLAND SEAPLANES · Auckland Harbour

| ☐ ZK-AMA | de Havilland DHC-2 Beaver | 1477 | ex C-GBVR | FP |

AVIA AIR CHARTERS · Hamilton (HLZ)

| ☐ ZK-LTD | Piper PA-31 Navajo | 31-7300918 | ex VH-JKC | ♦ |

BECK HELICOPTERS · Eltham

☐ ZK-HDU	Bell 206B JetRanger	1337	ex N59524	
☐ ZK-HHB	Garlick-Bell UH-1B Iroquois	3114	ex N123MS	
☐ ZK-HHF	Tamarack-Bell UH-1P Iroquois	7009	ex N2412G	
☐ ZK-HHU	Tamarack-Bell UH-1P Iroquois	7016	ex N156UH	
☐ ZK-HKO	Bell 206B JetRanger II	2140		

CENTRAL SOUTH ISLAND HELICOPTERS · Herbert

☐ ZK-HDN	McDonnell MD-520N	LN080	ex N955SD	
☐ ZK-HDW	McDonnell MD-520N	LN072	ex N905SD	
☐ ZK-HGO	Aérospatiale AS350BA AStar	2182	ex JA9813	
☐ ZK-HTO	Bell 206B JetRanger	2265	ex N16892	

| ☐ ZK-HUE | Garlick-Bell UH-1L Iroquois | 6046 | ex N9770N | |
| ☐ ZK-IOJ | Aérospatiale AS350B3 Ecureuil | 7815 | | ♦ |

CHRISTIAN AVIATION — Christian — Ardmore (AMZ)

☐ ZK-CAL	Piper PA-31-350 Navajo Chieftain	31-7405241	ex ZK-EVD	
☐ ZK-CAM	Piper PA-31 Navajo	31-261	ex ZK-DCE	
☐ ZK-CAO	Piper PA-34-220T Seneca	34-7670251		♦
☐ ZK-MVY	Piper Aerostar 600	60-0649-7961206	ex VH-MVY	

EAGLE AIRWAYS — Eagle (EAG) — Hamilton (HLZ)

50% owned by Air New Zealand; ops as part of Air New Zealand Link (qv); EAG code is for domestic use only and is not registered with ICAO

FLIGHT 2000 — Ardmore (AMZ)

| ☐ ZK-DAK | Douglas DC-3 | 15035/26480 | ex VH-SBT | RNZAF colours |

FLIGHTCARE — Napier-Hawkes Bay (NPR)

| ☐ ZK-DRD | Cessna P206 Stationair | P206-0135 | ex F-OCFB | EMS |
| ☐ ZK-WLG | Cessna 421C Golden Eagle | 421C0492 | ex VH-BRN | EMS |

FLY MY SKY — Auckland-Intl/Ardmore (AKL/AMZ)

☐ ZK-DLA	Britten-Norman BN-2B-2 Islander	2131	ex VH-ISL	[AMZ]
☐ ZK-EVO	Britten-Norman BN-2A-26 Islander	785	ex 5W-FAQ	♦
☐ ZK-PIY	Britten-Norman BN-2A-20 Islander	344	ex JA5218	
☐ ZK-PIZ	Britten-Norman BN-2B-26 Islander	2012	ex N2132M	
☐ ZK-SFK	Britten-Norman BN-2A-6 Islander	236	ex VH-CPG	

FOX GLACIER HELICOPTERS — Fox Glacier (FGL)

☐ ZK-HGE	Aérospatiale AS350B Ecureuil	1145	ex F-WYMB	
☐ ZK-HHM	Aérospatiale AS350B2 Ecreuil	1076	ex JA9229	
☐ ZK-HKU	Aérospatiale AS350BA AStar	1132	ex N5774U	♦
☐ ZK-HSE	Aérospatiale AS350B Ecureuil	2051	ex JA9726	

GARDEN CITY HELICOPTERS — Christchurch-Intl (CHC)

☐ ZK-FDN	Beech C90AKing Air	LJ-1606	ex N699TT	
☐ ZK-FDR	Beech B200C Super King Air	BL-31	ex VH-KFN	
☐ ZK-HGH	Aérospatiale AS350BA AStar	1443	ex N144AE	EMS, opf Canterbury West Coast Air Rescue Trust
☐ ZK-HJC	Kawasaki BK.117B-2	1061	ex JA6626	EMS, opf Canterbury RHT
☐ ZK-HQT	Aérospatiale AS350BA AStar	1729	ex JA9359	EMS, opf Nelson/Marlborough RHT
☐ ZK-HUG	Aérospatiale AS350BA AStar	2038	ex JA9492	
☐ ZK-IHL	Aérospatiale AS350B3 Ecureuil	7219		
☐ ZK-IHM	Kawasaki BK117B-2	1018	ex VH-RLI	
☐ ZK-IQT	Eurocopter EC120B	1370	ex VH-ADC	
☐ ZK-IVB	MBB BK.117B-2	7061	ex N143AM	♦
☐ ZK-KBF	Cessna 421B	421B0943	ex VH-ADG	EMS, opf NZ Flying Doctor Service
☐ ZK-NFD	Cessna 441 Conquest II	4410141	ex VH-CFD	EMS, opf NZ Flying Doctor Service

GISBORNE HELICOPTERS — Airmed — Gisborne (GIS)

☐ ZK-HNY	Bell 407	53052	ex VH-RRR	
☐ ZK-HQP	McDonnell MD-520N	LN093	ex N911TC	
☐ ZK-IKO	Aérospatiale AS350B2 Ecureuil	3528	ex N468AE	♦

GLACIER SOUTHERN LAKE HELICOPTERS — Queenstown (ZQN)

☐ ZK-HQG	Aérospatiale AS350B2 Ecrueil	4641		
☐ ZK-IDM	Aérospatiale AS350B2 Ecureuil	9026	ex D-HRHR	
☐ ZK-IDT	Aérospatiale AS350B3 Ecureuil	7721		
☐ ZK-IQG	Aérospatiale AS350B2 Ecureuil	7524	ex C-GLFI	♦
☐ ZK-IVW	Aérospatiale AS350B2 Ecureuil	7335		
☐ ZK-IBL	Aérospatiale AS350BA AStar	2075	ex JA9741	

GLENORCHY AIR SERVICES — Milford Sound (MFN)

☐ ZK-JRR	Gippsland GA-8 Airvan	GA8-01-006	ex VH-FOV	
☐ ZK-LOR	Gippsland GA-8 Airvan	GA8-03-034	ex VH-BMX	
☐ ZK-MIF	Cessna U206G Stationair	U20603926	ex ZK-EJE	

GOLDEN BAY AIR — Golden Bay — Takaka (KTF)

| ☐ ZK-ZAG | Piper PA-34-220T Seneca | 34-8333002 | ex C-GOKO | |
| ☐ ZK-ZIG | Piper PA32R-301 Saratoga | 32-8013045 | ex N8161Q | |

GREAT BARRIER AIRLINES	**Great Barrier (GBA)**			**Auckland-North Shore**
☐ ZK-ENZ	Piper PA-32-260 Cherokee Six	32-1117	ex ZK-DBP	Tomtit
☐ ZK-FVD	Britten-Norman BN-2A-26 Islander	316	ex G-BJWN	Pigeon
☐ ZK-LGC	Britten-Norman BN-2A Mk.III-1			
	Trislander	1042	ex G-RHOP	wfs
☐ ZK-LGF	Britten-Norman BN-2A Mk.III-1			
	Trislander	1023	ex YJ-LGF	wfs
☐ ZK-LOU	Britten-Norman BN-2A Mk.III-1			
	Trislander	322	ex VH-MRJ	wfs
☐ ZK-NSN	Piper PA-31 Turbo Navajo	31-687	ex VH-CFP	Bellbird
☐ ZK-PLA	Partenavia P.68B	86	ex A6-ALO	Tui
☐ ZK-RDT	Embraer EMB.820C Navajo	820127	ex PT-RDT	
☐ ZK-REA	Britten-Norman BN-2A-26 Islander	43	ex ZK-FWH	Brown Teal

HELETRANZ				**Albany**
☐ ZK-HFS	Aérospatiale AS355F2 Ecureuil II	5388	ex OK-BIC	
☐ ZK-HST	Aérospatiale AS350B2 Ecureuil	4538		
☐ ZK-HTV	Eurocopter EC120B	1041	ex VH-AVM	
☐ ZK-IRP	Bell 427	56078	ex N450KB	

HELI A1				**Kiokio**
☐ ZK-IUU	Aérospatiale AS350B3 Ecureuil	3724	ex ZK-HUU	♦
☐ ZK-IZZ	Aérospatiale AS350BA AStar	1821	ex ZK-HZZ	

HELI HARVEST				**Ardmore (AMZ)**
☐ ZK-HHL	Aérospatiale AS332L1 .	2240	ex JA9679	

HELI 7				**Tauranga City (TRG)**
☐ ZK-IKK	MBB Bo105DBS-4	S-656	ex 9M-SAR	♦
☐ ZK-IMO	MBB Bo105CB-4	S-583	ex N918ET	♦

HELI SIKA				**Poronui Station**
☐ ZK-HIU	Aérospatiale AS350BA AStar	1088	ex JA9224	

HELI SOUTH				**Balclutha**
☐ ZK-HMS	Bell 206B JetRanger	3803	ex N3191L	
☐ ZK-HXP	Bell 206B JetRanger	3334	ex N2062D	
☐ ZK-IDG	Bell 206B JetRanger	3495	ex N20KK	
☐ ZK-ISM	Bell 206B JetRanger	3667	ex JA9746	
☐ ZK-ITK	Bell 206L-1 LongRanger	45628	ex C-GZFT	♦
☐ ZK-ITL	Bell 206L-4 LongRanger	52073	ex VT-PLS	

HELI TOURS				**Queenstown (ZQN)**
☐ ZK-HQN	Aérospatiale AS350BA AStar	1807	ex ZK-HGF	

HELICOPTER SERVICES (BAY OF PLENTY)	**Care Flight**			**Taupo (TUO)**
☐ ZK-FPZ	de Havilland DHC-2 Beaver	6474	ex N6474	
☐ ZK-HKC	Aérospatiale AS350B3 Ecureuil	3427	ex ZK-HEA	
☐ ZK-HZD	Aérospatiale AS350BA AStar	1265	ex ZK-HBV	
☐ ZK-HZO	Aérospatiale AS350BA AStar	1034	ex VH-SRA	
☐ ZK-IHF	Aérospatiale AS355F2 Ecureuil II	5140	ex JA9570	

HELICOPTERS HAWKES BAY				**Bridge Pa Aerodrome**
☐ ZK-HBJ	Bell 206B JetRanger	1211	ex ZK-HQN	
☐ ZK-IJG	Aérospatiale AS350BA AStar	1558	ex VH-INW	♦
☐ ZK-INR	McDonnell MD-520N	LN009	ex N809M	

HELICOPTERS OTAGO				**Taieri Aerodrome**
☐ ZK-HWI	Bell 206B JetRanger	3770	ex N3181B	
☐ ZK-HWK	Bell 206B JetRanger	1521	ex VH-FJE	
☐ ZK-HWN	Bell 206B JetRanger	1995	ex C-GIZK	
☐ ZK-HWQ	Bell 206B JetRanger	3185	ex N3893Y	
☐ ZK-IWM	Bell 206B JetRanger	4150	ex JA6064	
☐ ZK-HJK	Kawasaki BK.117B-2	1020	ex VH-HJQ	EMS
☐ ZK-HQI	MBB BK.117B-2	7139	ex P2-HBM	
☐ ZK-HUP	Kawasaki BK.117B-2	1031		EMS, opf Otago RHT
☐ ZK-IME	Kawasaki BK.117B-2	1074	ex VH-EMS	EMS
☐ ZK-IWY	Bell 206L LongRanger 4	52301	ex C-GFTE	

☐ ZK-IWZ	Bell 206L LongRanger 3	51123	ex N412TV	

HELICORP — Hamilton (HLZ)

☐ ZK-IGE	Eurocopter EC120	1555		◆
☐ ZK-IPV	Eurocopter EC130B4	4556		◆

HELILINK — Auckland-Mechanics Bay

☐ ZK-HDG	Aérospatiale AS355F1 Ecureuil II	5212	ex N5802T	opf Inflite Charters
☐ ZK-HKG	Aérospatiale AS355F1 Ecureuil II	5267	ex VH-NWA	
☐ ZK-HLF	Kawasaki BK.117B-2	1070	ex JA6642	EMS, opf Lifeflight
☐ ZK-HPA	Aérospatiale AS355F1 Ecureuil II	5010	ex N813CE	
☐ ZK-HVN	Bell 427	56017	ex N324FH	opf Inflite Charters
☐ ZK-HXE	Aérospatiale AS355F1 Ecureuil II	5219	ex JA9576	
☐ ZK-ITR	Agusta A109E	11127	ex I-PAXE	EMS, opf Taranaki RHT

HELITRIPS — Onehunga-Pike's Point

☐ ZK-IRL	Bell 206L-1 LongRanger	45549	ex C-GLEO	◆

HELIVIEW HELICOPTER FLIGHTS — Cromwell/Raetihi Aerodromes

☐ ZK-HTK	Bell 206L-1 LongRanger	45766	ex N60GK	◆
☐ ZK-IHI	McDonnell MD-600N	RN047	ex VT-SSH	

HELIWORKS QUEENSTOWN — Queenstown (ZQN)

☐ ZK-HJP	Aérospatiale AS350BA AStar	2322	ex JA9875	
☐ ZK-HYS	Aérospatiale AS350B2 Ecureuil	2447	ex PK-OCZ	opf Alpine Heliski NZ
☐ ZK-IDF	Aérospatiale AS350B3 Ecureuil	7421		

HIGH COUNTRY HELICOPTERS — Riversdale

☐ ZK-IMJ	Aérospatiale AS350B2 Ecureuil	9057	ex VH-DHQ	◆

HNZ/HELICOPTERS NEW ZEALAND — Nelson (NSN)

☐ ZK-HBU	Aérospatiale AS350B2 Ecureuil	2286	ex VH-WDH	
☐ ZK-HDB	Aérospatiale AS350B2 Ecureuil	2518	ex PK-UHN	
☐ ZK-HJV	Aérospatiale AS350B2 Ecureuil	2846	ex PK-TVX	
☐ ZK-HJY	Aérospatiale AS350B2 Ecureuil	2005	ex JA9463	
☐ ZK-HMQ	Aérospatiale AS350B2 Ecureuil	9045	ex ZK-HYM	
☐ ZK-HNR	Aérospatiale AS350B2 Ecureuil	2486	ex VH-WCW	
☐ ZK-HNW	Aérospatiale AS350B2 Ecureuil	3908	ex C-FMBC	
☐ ZK-HUK	Aérospatiale AS350B2 Ecureuil	2532	ex VH-WCO	
☐ ZK-HVU	Aérospatiale AS350B2 Ecureuil	2132	ex VH-WDQ	
☐ ZK-IHD	Aerospatiale AS350B3 Ecureuil	3190	ex VH-WCN	
☐ RP-C2013	AgustaWestland AW139	41268	ex VT-HLF	◆
☐ RP-C2139	AgustaWestland AW139	41322	ex N430SH	◆
☐ ZK-HNE	AgustaWestland AW139	31031	ex N139WH	
☐ ZK-HNO	AgustaWestland AW139	31156	ex VH-NZF	
☐ ZK-HNZ	AgustaWestland AW139	31103	ex I-EASS	
☐ ZK-IHP	AgustaWestland AW139	31146	ex VH-NZZ	◆
☐ ZK-HDY	Bell 412EP	36099	ex A6-AGS	
☐ ZK-HNX	Aérospatiale AS350BA AStar	1828	ex VH-WKZ	

INFINITY HELILINE — Wanaka (WKA)

☐ ZK-HBX	Aérospatiale AS350BA Ecureuil	1391	ex ZK-HYP	

ISLAND AIR CHARTERS — Tauranga (TRG)

☐ ZK-PAI	Cessna TU206A Stationair	U206-0511	ex ZK-SUN	
☐ ZK-WWH	Cessna U206G Stationair	U20603550	ex ZK-MCH	

JETCONNECT — Qantas Jetconnect (QF/QNZ) — Auckland-Intl (AKL)

☐ ZK-ZQA	Boeing 737-838/W	34200/2989	ex VH-VZF	Jean Batten
☐ ZK-ZQB	Boeing 737-838/W	34201/3006	ex VH-VZG	Sir William Hudson
☐ ZK-ZQC	Boeing 737-838/W	34202/3048	ex VH-VZH	Katherine Mansfield
☐ ZK-ZQD	Boeing 737-838/W	34203/3515		Sir Edmund Hilary
☐ ZK-ZQE	Boeing 737-838/W	34185/3542	ex N1786B	William Pickering
☐ ZK-ZQF	Boeing 737-838/W	34204/3562		Ernest Rutherford
☐ ZK-ZQG	Boeing 737-838/W	34190/3683		Ernest Rutherford
☐ ZK-ZQH	Boeing 737-838/W	39357/3743		Charles Upham

KAIKOURA HELICOPTERS   Kaikoura Whaleway

☐ ZK-HBO	Bell 206B JetRanger	570	ex N8190J	

KAPITI HELIWORKS   Paraparaumu-Kapiti Coast (PPQ)

☐ ZK-IBM	Bell 206B JetRanger	1290	ex ZK-HBM	♦

LAKELAND HELICOPTERS   Murupara

☐ ZK-HJX	RHH-Bell UH-1H Iroquois	13710	ex N2386	
☐ ZK-HSP	Hagglund-Bell UH-1H Iroquois	5352	ex N226MS	wfs
☐ ZK-HSX	RHH-Bell UH-1H Iroquois	10320	ex N375AV	
☐ ZK-HYG	Williams-Bell UH-1H Iroquois	4568	ex N205HA	
☐ ZK-HZX	Hagglund-Bell UH-1H Irqouois	11892	ex N3061A	
☐ ZK-HCH	Bell 206B JetRanger	2258	ex N16859	
☐ ZK-HIX	Bell 206B JetRanger	869	ex VH-YDA	
☐ ZK-HWO	Bell 206B JetRanger	838	ex N38AL	
☐ ZK-IBW	Aérospatiale AS350B3 Ecureuil	7020		♦

MAINLAND AIR SERVICES   Dunedin (DUD)

☐ ZK JAS	Piper PA-34-220T Seneca	34-48010	ex VH-YSB	♦
☐ ZK-LSP	Piper PA-34-220T Seneca	34-48022	ex VH-YSI	♦
☐ ZK-VIP	Piper PA-31-350 Navajo Chieftain	31-7405482	ex N33WH	♦

MARLBOROUGH HELICOPTERS   Omaka Aerodrome

☐ ZK-HJI	Bell 206B JetRanger	4083	ex JA9866
☐ ZK-HTA	Bell 206L LongRanger 3	51220	ex JA9710
☐ ZK-HZE	Bell 206B JetRanger	769	ex C-FTPG

MILFORD SOUND FLIGHTS   Queenstown (ZQN)

☐ ZK-DBV	Britten-Norman BN-2A-26 Islander	164	ex VH-EQX
☐ ZK-MCD	Britten-Norman BN-2A-26 Islander	719	ex G-BCAG
☐ ZK-MCE	Britten-Norman BN-2A-26 Islander	724	ex G-BCHB
☐ ZK-MCM	Gippsland GA-8 Airvan	GA8-07-119	
☐ ZK-MCZ	Gippsland GA-8 Airvan	GA8-07-116	
☐ ZK-ZQN	Gippsland GA-8 Airvan	GA-8-13-196	ex VH-ARZ

MILFORD SOUND HELICOPTERS   Te Anau

☐ ZK-HYM	Aérospatiale AS350B2 Ecureuil	3287	ex ZK-HBV
☐ ZK-ITY	Aérospatiale AS350B3 Ecureuil 2	4949	

MOUNT COOK AIRLINE   Mountcook (NM/NZM)   Christchurch-Intl (CHC)

77% owned by Air New Zealand; ops scheduled services as Air New Zealand Link in full colours using NZ flight numbers

MOUNT HUTT HELICOPTERS   Methven

☐ ZK-HBC	McDonnell MD-520N	LN018	ex G-NEEN	
☐ ZK-HDQ	Aérospatiale AS350BA AStar	1932	ex VH-BHX	
☐ ZK-IBC	Aérospatiale AS350BA AStar	2562	ex VH-WHW	♦

MOUNTAIN AIR   Taumarunui

☐ ZK-DOV	Cessna 206 Super Skywagon	206-0248	ex N5248U

MOUNTAIN HELICOPTERS   Fox Glacier

☐ ZK-HFJ	McDonnell MD-520N	LN027	ex N198RM

NOKOMAI HELICOPTERS   Lumsden

☐ ZK-HWG	Aérospatiale AS350B2 Ecureuil	2816	ex ZK-IHW

NORTH SHORE HELICOPTERS   North Shore

☐ ZK-HAX	MBB Bo105CBS-4	S.888	ex Dubai P-793
☐ ZK-HGB	Aérospatiale AS350BA AStar	2550	
☐ ZK-HGD	Bell 206B JetRanger	4143	ex N7KR
☐ ZK-IFC	Eurocopter EC130B4	3938	ex ZK-IMR
☐ ZK-IGL	Eurocopter EC135P2	0195	ex ZK-ITF
☐ ZK-IGM	Eurocopter EC130B4	3770	

NORTHLAND EMERGENY SERVICES TRUST	*Helimed*			*Whangarei*
☐ ZK-IAL	Sikorsky S-76A	760133	ex N76LP	EMS
☐ ZK-IKM	Sikorsky S-76A	760106	ex VH-XHA	EMS
☐ ZK-ISJ	Sikorsky S-76A	760012	ex VH-CFH	EMS

OVER THE TOP				*Queenstown (ZQN)*
☐ ZK-HEK	Eurocopter EC120B	1023	ex VH-CXX	◆
☐ ZK-ICU	Aérospatiale AS350B3 AStar	2485	ex JA6090	
☐ ZK-ICY	Aérospatiale AS350B3 Ecureuil	7745		
☐ ZK-IDN	Eurocopter EC130B4	4084	ex ZK-HKV	◆
☐ ZK-IFE	Eurocopter EC120B	1502		
☐ ZK-IKJ	Aérospatiale AS350B3 Ecureuil	4536	ex G-CFHE	◆
☐ ZK-IUP	Eurocopter EC130B4	4118		

PACIFIC HELICOPTERS				*Christchurch-IAP (CHC)*
☐ ZK-HUQ	Aérospatiale AS355F2 Ecureuil II	5512	ex ZK-HLI	

PHILIPS SEARCH & RESCUE SERVICES	*Philips*			*Taupo (TUO)*
☐ ZK-HIG	Bell 222U	47537	ex N226LL	◆
☐ ZK-HNP	Aérospatiale AS350B2 Ecureuil	1611		wfs
☐ ZK-HZJ	Aérospatiale AS350B2 Ecureuil	2460	ex ZK-HIF	EMS, opf Taupo RHT
☐ ZK-HZL	Aérospatiale AS350BA AStar	1218	ex N3610D	EMS, opf Rotorua RHT dam 19Apr14
☐ ZK-HZM	Aérospatiale AS350B2 Ecureuil	1985	ex JA9466	EMS, opf Tauranga RHT
☐ ZK-HZN	Aérospatiale AS350BA AStar	1815		EMS, opf Palmerston North RHT
☐ ZK-HZQ	Bell 222B	47147	ex N222EA	EMS, opf Waikato RHT
☐ ZK-IPT	Kawasaki BK.117B-2	1080	ex HL9466	EMS
☐ ZK-IRU	Kawasaki BK.117B-2	1101	ex VH-BKS	EMS
☐ ZK-KOH	Mitsubishi Mu-2B-30	521	ex VH-KOH	◆
☐ ZK-NSP	Piper PA-31-350 Navajo Chieftain	31-7552069	ex N59980	EMS

PICTON FLOAT PLANE				*Picton Harbour*
☐ ZK-MCG	Cessna U206G Stationair	U20603551		◆

PRECISION HELICOPTERS				*Urenui*
☐ ZK-HFE	Bell 206B JetRanger	3978	ex JA9752	
☐ ZK-IBF	Bell 206B JetRanger	919	ex 5W-HWR	
☐ ZK-IED	MBB BK.117A-3	7059	ex N236KH	◆
☐ ZK-ITM	Aérospatiale AS350B3 Ecureuil	4735	ex CC-CXX	◆

REID HELICOPTERS NELSON				*Wakefield*
☐ ZK-HEX	Aérospatiale AS350BA AStar	1654	ex TG-EVE	
☐ ZK-HNA	Aérospatiale AS350BA AStar	1606	ex VH-KWX	
☐ ZK-IOR	Aérospatiale AS350BA AStar	1646	ex ZK-HWF	◆

RIDGE AIR				*Blenheim-Marlborough (BHE)*
☐ ZK-BJM	Piper PA-34-220T Seneca	34-48048	ex N21GP	
☐ ZK-VAD	Cessna 402C	402C0076	ex VH-COH	

SALT AIR				*Kerikeri-Bay of Islands/Paihia (KKE/-)*
☐ ZK-IJH	Bell 206L-3 LongRanger	51335	ex N35CH	
☐ ZK-ILM	Bell 206L-3 LongRanger	51278	ex N992SH	
☐ ZK-MAB	Gippsland GA8 Airvan	GA8-08-139	ex VH-BQY	◆

SILVER FERN HELICOPTERS				*North Shore*
☐ ZK-HKV	Eurocopter EC130B4	4084	ex F-WWPJ	
☐ ZK-IND	Bell 206L-1 LongRanger	45776	ex N3186P	

SKYLINE AVIATION				*Napier-Hawkes Bay (NPR)*
☐ ZK-HFZ	Aérospatiale AS350BA AStar	1784	ex JA9373	EMS, opf Eastland RHT
☐ ZK-HYP	Aérospatiale AS350BA AStar	1393	ex N5744Y	EMS, opf Eastland RHT
☐ ZK-IBK	Kawasaki BK.117B-2	1053	ex ZK-HEN	EMS, opf Hawkes Bay RHT
☐ ZK-LWN	Piper PA-31 Navajo	31-8112056	ex N40938	
☐ ZK-MFT	Cessna 421C Golden Eagle	421-0886	ex N9501L	EMS, opf NZ Air Ambulance Service
☐ ZK-PLK	Beech B200C Super King Air	BL-64	ex N188TC	
☐ ZK-ZZA	Beech C90A King Air	LJ-1407	ex N90NZ	

SKYWORK HELICOPTERS　　　　　　　　　　　　　　　　　　　　　*Warkworth*

☐ VH-IUU	Kaman K-MAX	029	ex ZK-HEE	based Woollongong, NSW
☐ ZK-HEE	Aérospatiale AS350B3 Ecureuil	3780	ex VH-EQQ	♦
☐ ZK-HQQ	Aérospatiale AS350BA AStar	2240	ex JA9832	
☐ ZK-HQR	Bell 206B JetRanger	1644	ex RP-C1941	
☐ ZK-HSS	Aérospatiale AS350B3 Ecureuil	4923	ex PK-URD	♦
☐ ZK-HUU	Aérospatiale AS350B3 Ecureuil	3724		
☐ ZK-HWW	Aérospatiale AS350BA AStar	1299		
☐ ZK-HZZ	Aérospatiale AS355N Ecureuil II	5691	ex VP-CLF	

SOUNDSAIR TRAVEL & TOURISM　　　*Soundsair*　　　　　　*Wellington (WLG)*

☐ ZK-PDM	Cessna 208 Caravan I	20800240	ex N1289N	
☐ ZK-SAA	Cessna 208B Caravan I	208B0862	ex N208DG	
☐ ZK-SAN	Cessna 208 Caravan I	20800360	ex ZK-TZR	
☐ ZK-SAW	Cessna 208B Caravan I	208B2087	ex N771AL	♦
☐ ZK-SAY	Cessna 208B Caravan I	208B0861	ex ZK-MJL	
☐ ZK-PLS	Pilatus PC-12	363	ex VH-KWO	o/o♦

SOUTH EAST AIR　　　　　　　　　　*South East*　　　　　　*Invercargill (IVC)*

☐ ZK-FWZ	Britten-Norman BN-2A-26 Islander	52	ex T3-ATH	Stewart Island Flights titles
☐ ZK-FXE	Britten-Norman BN-2A-26 Islander	110	ex F-OCFR	Stewart Island Flights titles
☐ ZK-JEM	Cessna A185E Skywagon	18501780	ex VH-JBM	

SOUTHERN ALPS AIR　　　　　　　　　　　　　　　　　　　　　*Wanaka (WKA)*

☐ ZK-FMA	Cessna A185F Skywagon	18503513	ex N2177Q	
☐ ZK-FQY	Cessna 207	20700293		♦
☐ ZK-JMS	Cessna U206F Stationair	U20601838	ex ZK-PDZ	
☐ ZK-RLM	Cessna U206F Stationair	U20601752	ex ZK-EEE	

SOUTHERN LAKES HELICOPTERS　　　　　　　　　　　　　　　　　*Te Anau*

☐ ZK-HMD	Aérospatiale AS350B2 Ecureuil	2782	ex N350SL	
☐ ZK-IBR	Aérospatiale AS350B3 Ecureuil	4899	ex ZK-IDF	
☐ ZK-IDE	Aérospatiale AS350B3 Ecureuil	4544	ex ZK-IDF	opf Antarctic New Zealand
☐ ZK-IRM	Aérospatiale AS350B3 Ecureuil	4048		

SUNAIR AVIATION　　　　　　　　*Sunair (SAV)*　　　　*Tauranga City (TRG)*

☐ ZK-DGS	Piper PA-23-250 Aztec	27-7304959	ex N14370	
☐ ZK-DIR	Piper PA-23-250 Aztec	27-4242	ex VH-PRB	
☐ ZK-ECM	Piper PA-23-250 Aztec	27-8154001	ex VH-JEL	
☐ ZK-ERM	Piper PA-23-250 Aztec	27-7405435	ex N54129	
☐ ZK-EVP	Piper PA-23-250 Aztec	27-8054053	ex N2566Z	
☐ ZK-FVP	Piper PA-23-250 Aztec	27-7854096	ex VH-FVP	
☐ ZK-MTY	Piper PA-23-250 Aztec	27-7654137	ex VH-MTY	
☐ ZK-PIW	Piper PA-23-250 Aztec	27-7305089	ex VH-RCI	
☐ ZK-PIX	Piper PA-23-250 Aztec	27-4738	ex N14174	
☐ ZK-TDM	Piper PA-23-250 Aztec	27-7754045	ex VH-TDM	
☐ ZK-WDP	Piper PA-23-250 Aztec	27-8054025	ex T3-64Z	♦

TARANAKI AIR AMBULANCE　　　　　　　　　　　　　　　*New Plymouth (NPL)*

☐ ZK-MJF	Piper PA-31 Navajo	31-7912089	ex C-GVEV	EMS

TASMAN HELICOPTERS ABOVE & BEYOND　　　　　　　　　　*Motueka (MZP)*

☐ ZK-INN	Eurocopter EC120B	1570	

TAUPO'S FLOATPLANE　　　　　　　　　　　　　　　　　*Taupo Lakefront*

☐ ZK-EFI	Cessna U206G Stationair	U20603525	ex N8772Q	FP
☐ ZK-FPO	Cessna U206G Stationair	U20605772	ex C-GGMI	FP

THE HELICOPTER LINE　　*Queenstown/Franz Josef Glacier/Fox Glacier/Mount Cook (ZQN/WHO/FGL/MON)*

☐ ZK-HBR	Aérospatiale AS350BA AStar	1386	ex N5774U	
☐ ZK-HJE	Aérospatiale AS350BA AStar	1307	ex N4428V	
☐ ZK-HJQ	Aérospatiale AS350BA AStar	1295	ex C-FBXE	opf Glacier H/Cs
☐ ZK-HKR	Aérospatiale AS350BA AStar	1234	ex N3606X	♦
☐ ZK-HRQ	Aérospatiale AS350BA AStar	1311	ex VH-RLO	
☐ ZK-HAE	Aérospatiale AS350B2 Ecureuil	3625	ex I-EXPO	
☐ ZK-HAO	Aérospatiale AS350B2 Ecureuil	7622		
☐ ZK-HDL	Aérospatiale AS350B2 Ecureuil	2981	ex 9M-BBB	
☐ ZK-HFF	Aérospatiale AS350B2 Ecureuil	4967	ex N351BE	♦
☐ ZK-HFK	Aérospatiale AS350B2 Ecureuil	1397	ex VH-WCD	opf Glacier H/Cs

☐ ZK-HGV	Aérospatiale AS350B2 Ecureuil	3944	ex VH-FLL	
☐ ZK-HNQ	Aérospatiale AS350B2 Ecureuil	1972	ex JA9450	
☐ ZK-HRM	Aérospatiale AS350B2 Ecureuil	2721	ex C-FCFM	
☐ ZK-HRV	Aérospatiale AS350B2 Ecureuil	2777	ex N975AE	
☐ ZK-HSM	Aérospatiale AS350B2 Ecureuil	3529		
☐ ZK-HSO	Aérospatiale AS350B2 Ecureuil	3004	ex N945AE	♦
☐ ZK-HTD	Aérospatiale AS350B2 Ecureuil	3351	ex N946AE	
☐ ZK-HYY	Aérospatiale AS350B2 Ecureuil	3886	ex N354P	♦
☐ ZK-IBV	Aérospatiale AS350B2 Ecureuil	3761		
☐ ZK-ICD	Aérospatiale AS350B2 Ecureuil	2107		
☐ ZK-IDQ	Aérospatiale AS350B3 Ecureuil	3178	ex ZK-IPV	
☐ ZK-HKF	Aérospatiale AS355F1 Ecureuil 2	5200	ex VH-HJK	
☐ ZK-HKY	Aérospatiale AS355F1 Twin Star	5123	ex N909CH	
☐ ZK-HMB	Aérospatiale AS355F1 Twin Star	5016	ex N57812	
☐ ZK-HML	Aérospatiale AS355F1 Twin Star	5032	ex N5776A	
☐ ZK-HPI	Aérospatiale AS355F1 Twin Star	5211	ex N5802N	
☐ ZK-HPZ	Aérospatiale AS355F1 Twin Star	5107	ex N87906	
☐ ZK-IAV	Aérospatiale AS355F1 Twin Star	5041		

TWIN COAST HELICOPTERS — Whangarei (WRE)

☐ ZK-ICV	Bell 206L LongRanger	45017	ex N5084F

VIRGIN SAMOA (PBL)

☐ ZK-PBF	Boeing 737-8FE/W	33799/1462	ex VH-VOR	Tapu'itea

Ops trans-Tasman services alongside the other ZK- registered 737s

VOLCANIC AIR — Volcanic — Rotorua Lakefront

☐ ZK-FEO	Cessna U206G Stationair	U20603797	ex N9063G	FP
☐ ZK-IAB	Aérospatiale AS350BA AStar	1785	ex JA9389	
☐ ZK-IVA	Bell 206B JetRanger	2407	ex C-GQZL	♦
☐ ZK-VAS	de Havilland DHC-3 Otter	35	ex C-FXGA	FP

WAIRARAPA HELICOPTERS — Masterton-Hood (MRO)

☐ ZK-HPK	Bell 206B JetRanger	2280	ex ZK-HBD	
☐ ZK-IBQ	Aérospatiale AS350BA AStar	2050	ex XA-JCF	♦

WAY TO GO HELISERVICES — Rangiora

☐ ZK-HKW	Aérospatiale AS350BA AStar	1360	ex VH-HBK

WINGS & WATER — Lake Te Anau

☐ ZK-DRH	Cessna U206C Skywagon	U206-1179	ex N29227	FP

WINGS OVER WHALES — Kaikoura (KBZ)

☐ ZK-KBZ	Gippsland GA-8 Airvan	GA8-03-024	♦

ZP- PARAGUAY (Republic of Paraguay)

AEROLINEAS PARAGUAYAS — ARPA (PAY)

☐ ZP-TAZ	Cessna 208B Caravan I	208B0686

TAM MERCOSUR — Paraguaya (PZ/LAP) — Asuncion (ASU)

Ops services with Fokker 100 aircraft leased from parent (80% owner), TAM Brasil, as required

ZS- SOUTH AFRICA (Republic of South Africa)

AFRICA CHARTER AIRLINE — Africa Sky (FSK) — Lanseria (HLA)

☐ ZS-IAB	Boeing 737-210C	20917/344	ex N834AL	
☐ ZS-SID	Boeing 737-244F	22583/809		wfs♦
☐ ZS-SIF	Boeing 737-244F	22585/828		
☐ ZS-SIT	Boeing 737-236	21790/599	ex V5-AND	opf Exxaro Coal♦
☐ ZS-TFT	Boeing 737-3Q8	26301/2623	ex 5R-MFI	♦
☐ ZS-TRI	McDonnell-Douglas MD-83	49707/1487	ex N315FV	

AIR-TEC AFRICA/AIRCRAFT SYSTEMS SA — Bethlehem

☐ ZS-ATA	LET L-410UVP-E20	872017	ex 5Y-BRM	opf UN
☐ ZS-ATB	LET L-410UVP-E20	892340	ex ST-CAU	

☐ ZS-ATD	LET L-410UVP-E	902527	ex ST-CAT	
☐ ZS-ATE	LET L-410UVP-E20	932731	ex 5Y-EXV	opf UN
☐ ZS-ATF	LET L-410UVP-E3	902403	ex ST-DMR	
☐ ZS-ATG	LET L-410UVP	882103	ex 5N-BEB	opf UN
☐ ZS-ATH	LET L-410UVP-E20	912530	ex CP-2349	
☐ ZS-ATI	LET L-410UVP-E20	902409	ex F-OTKE	opf ICRC
☐ ZS-ATJ	LET L-410UVP-E20	062636	ex PR-NHA	
☐ ZS-ATK	LET L-410UVP-E20	062637	ex PR-NHB	♦
☐ ZS-ATN	LET L-410UVP-E20	072639	ex PR-NHC	♦
☐ ZS-EPB	LET L-410UVP-E20	902413	ex F-ORTE	opf UN
☐ ZS-MWM	LET L-410UVP-E20	912613	ex 7Q-YKV	opf ICRC
☐ ZS-OOF	LET L-410UVP-E20	871920	ex 5H-PAJ	
☐ ZS-PNI	LET L-410UVP-E20	871904	ex 5Y-BSV	opf ICRC
☐ ZS-OSE	LET L-420	922729A	ex N420Y	[UHE]
☐ ZS-OUE	LET L-420	012735A	ex OK-GDM	opf UN

AIRLINK — Link (4Z/LNK) — Johannesburg-OR Tambo (JNB)

☐ ZS-ASW	Avro 146-RJ85	E2313	ex N505XJ	
☐ ZS-ASX	Avro 146-RJ85	E2314	ex N506XJ	
☐ ZS-ASY	Avro 146-RJ85	E2316	ex N507XJ	
☐ ZS-ASZ	Avro 146-RJ85	E2318	ex N508XJ	
☐ ZS-SSH	Avro 146-RJ85	E2285	ex G-CGMT	
☐ ZS-SSI	Avro 146-RJ85	E2383	ex G-LCYB	
☐ ZS-SSJ	Avro 146-RJ85	E2385	ex G-LCYC	
☐ ZS-SSK	Avro 146-RJ85	E2251	ex G-CGSM	
☐ ZS-SYO	Avro 146-RJ85	E2394	ex OH-SAP	
☐ ZS-SYP	Avro 146-RJ85	E2393	ex OH-SAO	
☐ ZS-TCO	Avro 145-RJ85	E2388	ex G-CHRZ	♦
☐ ZS-TCP	Avro 145-RJ85	E2389	ex G-CHSF	♦
☐ ZS-NRE	British Aerospace Jetstream 41	41048	ex G-4-048	
☐ ZS-NRF	British Aerospace Jetstream 41	41050	ex G-4-050	
☐ ZS-NRG	British Aerospace Jetstream 41	41051	ex G-4-051	
☐ ZS-NRH	British Aerospace Jetstream 41	41054	ex G-4-054	
☐ ZS-NRI	British Aerospace Jetstream 41	41061	ex G-4-061	
☐ ZS-NRJ	British Aerospace Jetstream 41	41062	ex G-4-062	
☐ ZS-OEX	British Aerospace Jetstream 41	41103	ex G-4-103	
☐ ZS-OMZ	British Aerospace Jetstream 41F	41037	ex VH-CCW	
☐ ZS-OTM	Embraer ERJ-135LR	145485	ex PT-SXE	op as Swaziland Airlink
☐ ZS-OTN	Embraer ERJ-135LR	145491	ex PT-SXK	
☐ ZS-OUV	Embraer ERJ-135LR	145493	ex PT-SXM	op as Airlink Zimbabwe
☐ ZS-SJX	Embraer ERJ-135LR	145428	ex PT-STZ	
☐ ZS-SNV	Embraer ERJ-135LR	145551	ex N845RP	
☐ ZS-SNW	Embraer ERJ-135LR	145720	ex N838RP	
☐ ZS-SNX	Embraer ERJ-135LR	145620	ex N844RP	
☐ ZS-SNZ	Embraer ERJ-135LR	145725	ex N840RP	
☐ ZS-SUV	Embraer ERJ-135LR	145663	ex PT-TJA	
☐ ZS-SWN	Embraer ERJ-135ER	145453	ex SE-RAB	
☐ ZS-SWV	Embraer ERJ-135LR	145737	ex XA-ASF	
☐ ZS-SYT	Embraer ERJ-135LR	145358	ex N732DH	
☐ ZS-TCB	Embraer ERJ-135ER	145210	ex SE-RAA	
☐ ZS-TCE	Embraer ERJ-135LR	145356	ex N731BE	
☐ ZS-TFK	Embraer ERJ-135LR	145249	ex N713AE	♦
☐ ZS-TFL	Embraer ERJ-135LR	145368	ex N733KR	♦
☐ ZS-DFA	Embraer ERJ-145EP	145165	ex N165EC	♦
☐ ZS-SYB	Embraer ERJ-145MP	145308	ex G-CGYK	

AVEX AIR — (AVE)

☐ ZS-AAK	Dornier 328-300 (328JET)	3162	ex OY-NCR
☐ ZS-AAL	Beech 350 King Air	FL-438	ex N438GC
☐ ZS-AAT	Dornier 328-310 (328JET)	3146	ex OY-NCV
☐ ZS-SYU	Embraer EMB.505 Phenom 300	50500021	ex N521EC
☐ ZS-XXL	Cessna 208B Caravan I	208B1219	ex N9208

AWESOME FLIGHT SERVICES — Awesome (ASM) — Lanseria (HLA)

☐ VH-NOA	Beech 1900D	UE-96	ex PK-OCW	
☐ ZS-FAB	Beech 1900D	UE-227	ex N87554	♦
☐ ZS-FAN	Beech 1900D	UE-198	ex N47542	♦
☐ ZS-JAG	Beech 1900D	UE-115	ex VH-VAZ	♦
☐ ZS-OKN	Beech 1900D	UE-23	ex V5-OKN	
☐ ZS-PRG	Beech 1900D	UE-90	ex VH-VAU	
☐ ZS-SEM	Beech 1900D	UE-91	ex VH-VNT	♦
☐ ZS-ARA	Learjet 35A	35A-349	ex N252WJ	
☐ ZS-FOX	Dassault Falcon 10	72	ex N50TY	

BATELEUR AIR CHARTER (BEU)

☐ ZS-CCL	Beech 1900D	UE-89	ex N891SK
☐ ZS-PHX	Beech 1900D	UE-145	ex N145SK

CEMAIR (5Z/KEM) Johannesburg-OR Tambo (JNB)

☐ ZS-CMB	Canadair CRJ-100ER	7215	ex N989CA	>PRF♦
☐ ZS-CMD	Canadair CRJ-100ER	7141	ex N969CA	♦
☐ ZS-CMR	Canadair CRJ-100LR	7326	ex N785CA	opf Interstate
☐ ZS-CRJ	Canadair CRJ-100LR	7338	ex N798CA	opf Interstate
☐ ZS-KEM	Canadair CRJ-200ER	7297	ex N720SW	
☐ ZS-	Canadair CRJ-100ER	7292	ex N595SW	o/o♦
☐ ZS-	Canadair CRJ-100ER	7293	ex N597SW	wfs♦
☐ ZS-DHC	de Havilland DHC-8-102	030	ex N713M	♦

CHC HELICOPTERS (AFRICA) Cape Town-International (CPT)

☐ ZS-RFU	Sikorsky S-76C+	760417	ex G-SSSE	
☐ ZS-RKO	Sikorsky S-76A++	760135	ex VH-LAX	
☐ ZS-RKP	Sikorsky S-76A++	760198	ex VH-LAY	Marine 2
☐ ZS-RNG	Sikorsky S-76A++	760036	ex D2-EXJ	based BSG <CHC Scotia
☐ ZS-RPI	Sikorsky S-76A++	760049	ex G-BHGK	based BSG <CHC Scotia
☐ ZS-HVJ	Sikorsky S-61N	61493	ex N9119Z	wfs
☐ ZS-KEI	Convair 580	141	ex N5822	
☐ ZS-LYL	Convair 580	39	ex N511GA	
☐ ZS-RDI	Bell 206L-3 LongRanger III	51392	ex N521EV	
☐ ZS-RDV	Sikorsky S-61N	61716	ex G-BIHH	based SSG
☐ ZS-RGV	Bell 212	30952	ex C-FRUU	
☐ ZS-RLK	Sikorsky S-61N	61772	ex G-BEWM	
☐ ZS-RLL	Sikorsky S-61N	61778	ex G-BFFK	
☐ ZS-RNP	Bell 212	30893	ex C-FPKW	based Malabo
☐ ZS-RNR	Bell 212	30829	ex C-FRWL	based Malabo

A member of CHC Helicopter Corp; ops from bases in Equatorial Guinea, Namibia and Angola as well as South Africa

COMAIR Commercial (MN/CAW) Johannesburg-OR Tambo (JNB)

☐ ZS-OKG	Boeing 737-376	23483/1264	ex VH-TAI	BAW c/s	
☐ ZS-OKH	Boeing 737-376	23479/1259	ex VH-TAH	BAW c/s	
☐ ZS-OKI	Boeing 737-376	23489/1356	ex VH-TAX	BAW c/s	
☐ ZS-OKJ	Boeing 737-376	23487/1306	ex VH-TAV	BAW c/s	
☐ ZS-OKK	Boeing 737-376	23485/1277	ex VH-TAK	BAW c/s	
☐ ZS-OAA	Boeing 737-4L7	26960/2483	ex VH-RON	BAW c/s	
☐ ZS-OAF	Boeing 737-4S3	25116/2061	ex PP-VTL	Kulula c/s	
☐ ZS-OAG	Boeing 737-4H6	27168/2435	ex JA737D	BAW c/s	
☐ ZS-OAM	Boeing 737-4S3	24164/1702	ex EI-DFE	BAW c/s	
☐ ZS-OAO	Boeing 737-4S3	24163/1700	ex EI-DFD	Kulula c/s	
☐ ZS-OAP	Boeing 737-4S3	24167/1736	ex EI-DFF	BAW c/s	
☐ ZS-OAR	Boeing 737-476	28152/2829	ex VH-TJZ		♦
☐ ZS-OAV	Boeing 737-4H6	27086/2426	ex JA737C		
☐ ZS-OTF	Boeing 737-436	25305/2147	ex G-DOCC	BAW c/s	
☐ ZS-OTG	Boeing 737-436	25840/2197	ex G-DOCJ	BAW c/s	<SFR
☐ ZS-OTH	Boeing 737-436	25841/2222	ex G-DOCK	BAW c/s	
☐ ZS-ZWA	Boeing 737-8LD/W	40851/4094		Kulula c/s	
☐ ZS-ZWB	Boeing 737-8LD/W	40852/4229		Kulula c/s	
☐ ZS-ZWC	Boeing 737-8LD/W	40853/4252		Kulula c/s	
☐ ZS-ZWD	Boeing 737-8LD/W	40855/4279		Kulula c/s	
☐ ZS-ZWI	Boeing 737-85R/W	30403/749	ex N801VL	BAW c/s	
☐ ZS-ZWO	Boeing 737-8K2/W	28373/51	ex PH-HZA		
☐ ZS-ZWP	Boeing 737-86N/W	28612/455	ex OK-PIK	Kulula c/s	
☐ ZS-ZWQ	Boeing 737-8K2/W	28374/57	ex PH-HZB	Kulula c/s	
☐ ZS-ZWR	Boeing 737-85P/W	28382/256	ex EC-HBM	BAW c/s	
☐ ZS-ZWS	Boeing 737-86N/W	32732/1056	ex M-ABDO	Europcar c/s	
☐ ZS-ZWT	Boeing 737-8K5/W	27990/246	ex OO-JBV	Europcar c/s	

DHL AVIATION Worldstar (DHV) Lanseria (HLA)

Utilises Cessna 208B Caravans and ATR 42s opb Solenta Aviation in full DHL c/s

DODSON INTERNATIONAL CHARTER Pretoria-Wonderboom (PRY)

☐ ZS-OJJ	AMI Turbo DC-3TP	16213/32961	ex N8194Q	opf UN/Red Cross

EXECUTIVE TURBINE AIR CHARTER/AIRCRAFT CONTRACTS AFRICA Lanseria (HLA)

☐ ZS-JAZ	Beech 1900D	UE-6	ex VT-AVJ

☐ ZS-OUG	Beech 1900D	UE-14	ex (ZS-OPI)	all-white	
☐ ZS-OYG	Beech 1900D	UE-230	ex 5N-BCQ	all-white	
☐ ZS-PKB	Beech 1900D	UE-3	ex N3YV		>TravelMax
☐ ZS-PZE	Beech 1900D	UE-32	ex N83611		
☐ ZS-ETA	Embraer EMB.120ER Brasilia	120277	ex N213SW		
☐ ZS-LFM	Beech B200 Super King Air	BB-954	ex N1839S		
☐ ZS-PRC	Beech B200 Super King Air	BB-1341	ex OY-GEU		Beech 1300 conversion

FAIR AVIATION   (FAV)   Lanseria (HLA)

☐ ZS-PCC	Beech 1900C	UC-143	ex 9J-AWS	
☐ ZS-SBR	British Aerospace 146 Srs.300	E3120	ex N611NW	wfs
☐ ZS-SOP	British Aerospace 146 Srs.300	E3187	ex G-BSYT	[HLA]
☐ ZS-SOR	British Aerospace 146 Srs.300	E3155	ex G-BTNU	wfs
☐ ZS-	British Aerospace 146 Srs.200	E2067	ex N146QT	wfs

FEDERAL AIR   Fedair (FDR)   Durban-Virginia (VIR)

☐ ZS-DRC	Beech 1900C-1	UC-166	ex N166GL		♦
☐ ZS-OXN	Beech 1900D	UE-83	ex N831SK	all-white	
☐ ZS-PJY	Beech 1900D	UE-204	ex N204GL		opf UN
☐ ZS-PRH	Beech 1900D	UE-316	ex N21716	all-white	<SLE
☐ ZS-PWY	Beech 1900D	UE-87	ex N87SK	all-white	
☐ ZS-DAT	Pilatus PC-12/45	242	ex HB-FRM		
☐ ZS-FDR	Beech 200 Super King Air	BB-1234	ex N971LE		
☐ ZS-KNL	Cessna 402C II	402C0646	ex N6814D		
☐ ZS-LXO	Beech 58 Baron	TH-886	ex N23527		
☐ ZS-OJC	Cessna 208B Caravan I	208B0593	ex N1194F		
☐ ZS-THR	Cessna 208B Caravan I	208B0571	ex N282FV		
☐ 5H-FED	Cessna 208B Caravan I	208B0437	ex ZS-FED		

FREEDOM AIR

☐ 5Y-FAE	Embraer EMB.120RT Brasilia	120156	ex ZS-PPF

FLYSAFAIR   Cargo (FA/SFR)   Johannesburg-OR Tambo (JNB)

☐ ZS-JRC	Boeing 737-42JF	27143/2457	ex N143HF		
☐ ZS-JRD	Boeing 737-4Y0	24917/2017	exEI-JRD		
☐ ZS-JRE	Boeing 737-4Y0	26065/2284	exEI0JRE	FlySafair c/s	
☐ ZS-JRF	Boeing 737-4L7C	26961/2517	ex N117BT		
☐ ZS-JRI	Boeing 737-4Q8	25095/2265	ex N754AS		♦
☐ ZS-JRK	Boeing 737-4Q8	25096/2278	ex N755AS		♦
☐ ZS-OTG	Boeing 737-436	25840/2197	ex G-DOCJ		>CAW
☐ ZS-JIV	Lockheed L-382G-35C Hercules	4673	ex EI-JIV		♦
☐ ZS-JIZ	Lockheed L-382G-35C Hercules	4695	ex F-GNMM		>ABR
☐ ZS-ORB	Lockheed L-382G-14C Hercules	4248	ex PK-YRW		
☐ ZS-RSC	Lockheed L-382G-28C Hercules	4475	ex D2-		
☐ ZS-RSF	Lockheed L-382G-31C Hercules	4562	ex S9-CAI		opf UN
☐ ZS-RSG	Lockheed L-382G-31C Hercules	4565	ex S9-CAJ		
☐ ZS-SMG	Boeing 737-3Y0SF	23499/1242	ex 5Y-BXK		>TGN
☐ ZS-SMJ	Boeing 737-3Y0SF	23500/1243	ex 5Y-BXK		
☐ 5Y-BXL	Boeing 737-33A	23634/1423	ex N175AW		

FUGRO AIRBORNE SURVEYS   Lanseria (HLA)

☐ PR-FAS	Cessna 208B Caravan I	208B0462	ex C-GRCK	
☐ VH-FAY	Cessna 208B Caravan I	208B0884	ex C-GJQV	
☐ VH-FGQ	Cessna 208 Caravan I	20800251	ex C-GFAV	
☐ ZS-FSB	Cessna 208B Caravan I	208B0860	ex PR-SSB	
☐ ZS-MSJ	Cessna 208 Caravan I	20800030	ex A2-AHJ	
☐ VH-TEM	CASA C.212-200F	CC37-1-138	ex P2-CNP	
☐ ZS-AIU	Cessna 404 Titan II	404-0082	ex A2-AIU	
☐ ZS-FMG	Piper PA-31-350 Chieftain	79-52155	ex 9H-FMG	♦
☐ ZS-FTA	Cessna 210N Centurion II	21063562	ex VH-JBH	
☐ ZS-KRG	Cessna 404 Titan II	404-0676	ex N6761Y	
☐ ZS-SSY	Reims Cessna F406 Caravan II	F406-0037	ex PR-FAG	

GLOBAL AVIATION LEASING   (GBB)   Johannesburg-OR Tambo (JNB)

☐ ZS-GAG	Douglas DC-9-32	47190/240	ex 5X-GLO	
☐ ZS-GAJ	Douglas DC-9-32	47730/828	ex 3D-MRW	>Congo Airways
☐ ZS-GAR	Douglas DC-9-32	47132/229	ex 3D-MRO	[JNB]
☐ ZS-GAT	Douglas DC-9-32	47797/913	ex 3D-MRT	[JNB]
☐ ZS-GAU	Douglas DC-9-32	47798/914	ex 3D-MRU	
☐ S9-GAS	McDonnell-Douglas DC-10-10	47832/318	ex ZS-GAS	[TIP]

☐ ZS-GAB	McDonnell-Douglas MD-82	49165/1117	ex 3D-GAA	>TSG
☐ ZS-GAC	McDonnell-Douglas DC-10-30F	46978/256	ex N607GC	[MIA]
☐ ZS-GAO	Airbus A320-231	067	ex N628AW	>VRE
☐ ZS-GAP	McDonnell-Douglas DC10-10	46646/285	ex S9-GAP	[JNB]
☐ ZS-GAZ	Airbus A320-231	081	ex N632AW	♦
☐ ZS-TOG	McDonnell-Douglas MD-82	49905/1767	ex N905TA	[JNB]

GRYPHON AIRLINES   (6P/GRF)   Johannesburg-OR Tambo (JNB)

☐ ZS-BIL	Boeing 737-277	22650/1981	ex UP-B3702	opf ATG♦
☐ ZS-TRJ	McDonnell-Douglas MD-87	49829/1678	ex EC-GRM	[JNB]♦

INTERAIR   Inline (D6/ILN)   Johannesburg-OR Tambo (JNB)

☐ ZS-IJA	Boeing 737-201	22751/857	ex N245US	
☐ ZS-IJB	Boeing 767-266ERM	23180/99	ex N573JW	
☐ ZS-SIH	Boeing 737-244	22587/835		
☐ ZS-SIM	Boeing 737-244	22828/881		wfs

JET 4 NOW

☐ ZS-EVE	Boeing 737-230 (Nordam 3)	22123/726	ex UP-B3707	>ALX

KING AIR CHARTER   Lanseria (HLA)

☐ ZS-HFG	Bell 206B JetRanger	1864		
☐ ZS-JSC	Beech B200 Super King Air	BB-1985	ex N71850	
☐ ZS-LFW	Beech B200 Super King Air	BB-999	ex 9Q-CPV	
☐ ZS-LRS	Beech 200C Super King Air	BL-20	ex 5Y-LRS	
☐ ZS-MPC	Cessna 402C II	402C0426	ex C9-MEB	
☐ ZS-NHW	Grumman G-159 Gulfstream I	141	ex N800PA	
☐ ZS-OED	Beech B200 Super King Air	BB-1149	ex N200HF	
☐ ZS-RFS	Bell 206L-4 LongRanger IV	52116	ex N4252S	
☐ ZS-RXR	Bell 205A-1	30290	ex D-HAFW	
☐ ZS-SHH	Beech 1900D	UE-36	ex N136MJ	

KULULA.COM   Johannesburg-OR Tambo (JNB)

Wholly owned low cost, no frills subsidiary of Comair who op the aircraft

MANGO   Tulca (JE/MNO)   Johannesburg-OR Tambo (JNB)

☐ ZS-SJG	Boeing 737-8BG/W	32353/711	ex N1786B	
☐ ZS-SJH	Boeing 737-8BG/W	32354/725	ex PH-HZQ	
☐ ZS-SJK	Boeing 737-8BG/W	32355/807	ex PH-HZT	
☐ ZS-SJL	Boeing 737-8BG/W	32356/819	ex PH-HZZ	
☐ ZS-SJP	Boeing 737-8BG/W	32358/955	ex PH-HZU	
☐ ZS-SJR	Boeing 737-844/W	32631/1176	ex N6067U	
☐ ZS-SJT	Boeing 737-844/W	32633/1225		

MCC AVIATION   (MCC)   Lanseria (HLA)

☐ ZS-JSM	British Aerospace Jetstream 41	41052	ex ZK-JSM	
☐ ZS-NOM	British Aerospace Jetstream 41	41047	ex G-MAJO	

MGC AIRLINES   Maseru (MSU)

☐ ZS-NMJ	Canadair CRJ-200ER	7161	ex C-GAUG	
☐ ZS-NMK	Canadair CRJ-200ER	7198	ex C-GBMF	

NAC CHARTER   Slipstream (SLE)   Lanseria (HLA)

☐ ZS-MCE	Beech B200 Super King Air	BB-884	ex N49JG	
☐ ZS-NBJ	Beech B200 Super King Air	BB-1070	ex SE-KND	
☐ ZS-OCI	Beech 200 Super King Air	BB-121	ex TR-LDX	
☐ ZS-ODI	Beech 200 Super King Air	BB-1542	ex N202JT	
☐ ZS-OUI	Beech 200 Super King Air	BB-688	ex 5R-MGH	Catpass 250 conversion
☐ ZS-PLJ	Beech B200 Super King Air	BB-1401	ex VH-YDH	
☐ ZS-SMC	Beech B200 Super King Air	BB-1489	ex N1563M	
☐ ZS-CFA	British Aerospace 125-1000A	259024	ex ZS-ABG	opf ATG
☐ ZS-EPV	Pacific Aerospace 750XL	144		
☐ ZS-HKV	Aérospatiale AS350B Ecureuil	1528		
☐ ZS-MJW	Piper PA-46-350P Malibu	46-36519	ex N2441L	
☐ ZS-MKI	Beech 65-C90A King Air	LJ-1099	ex Z-MKI	
☐ ZS-PNN	Beech 95-B55 Baron	TC-1794	ex A2-EAH	
☐ ZS-RDR	Bell 206B JetRanger III	4183	ex Z-RDR	
☐ ZS-RJO	Bell 407	53206		
☐ ZS-RPC	Bell 407	53365	ex C-GAHJ	
☐ ZS-SHJ	Pacific Aerospace 750XL	148	ex ZK-JSU	
☐ ZS-SRR	Pilatus PC-12/45	319		

☐ ZS-SUW	Beech 390 Premier I	RB-66	ex G-VONJ
☐ ZS-TOW	Learjet 35A	35A-475	ex 3D-ADC
☐ ZS-TVT	Beech Baron 58	TH-1962	ex N584J

NATIONAL AIRWAYS CORP   Aeromed (NTN)   Lanseria (HLA)

☐ ZS-CHR	Beech 1900D	UE-4	ex V5-OWN	♦
☐ ZS-ONI	Beech 1900D	UE-312	ex D2-EVL	
☐ ZS-OOW	Beech 1900D	UE-57	ex N57ZV	
☐ ZS-OSF	Beech 1900D	UE-35	ex N35YV	
☐ ZS-OYD	Beech 1900D	UE-191	ex VH-IAR	<Air Express Algeria
☐ ZS-OYF	Beech 1900D	UE-214	ex VH-IMS	<Air Express Algeria
☐ ZS-OYL	Beech 1900D	UE-324	ex A6-YST	
☐ ZS-OZZ	Beech 1900C-1	UC-73	ex N1570B	
☐ ZS-PRH	Beech 1900D	UE-316	ex N21716	>FDR
☐ ZS-SET	Beech 1900D	UE-265	ex VT-AVR	
☐ ZS-SNJ	Beech 1900D	UE-131	ex N131YV	
☐ ZS-SNK	Beech 1900D	UE-132	ex N132YV	
☐ ZS-SRZ	Beech 1900D	UE-133	ex N133YV	
☐ ZS-SVI	Beech 1900D	UE-173	ex N173YV	

☐ ZS-ACS	Beech B200 Super King Air	BB-961	ex A2-AHA	
☐ ZS-KGW	Beech B200 Super King Air	BB-381	ex N4848M	
☐ ZS-OTS	Beech B200 Super King Air	BB-1113		
☐ ZS-PCH	Beech B200 Super King Air	BB-1856	ex N61596	
☐ ZS PLL	Beech B200 Super King Air	BB-1189	ex VH-KBH	based KBL
☐ ZS-SON	Beech B200C Super King Air	BL-136	ex N136BL	

☐ ZS-BCI	SOCATA TBM-850	397	ex F-OIKI	
☐ ZS-CCK	Beech 350 King Air	BB-1987		
☐ ZS-CFA	Hawker 1000A	259024	ex ZS-ABG	
☐ ZS-DED	Beech 58 Baron	TH-1941	ex A2-CAS	
☐ ZS-DFC	Embraer ERJ-145MP	145339	ex PR-PSR	>ZR
☐ ZS-DIX	Beech 65-C90 King Air	LJ-669		
☐ ZS-KMN	Beech 58 Baron	TH-153	ex F-ODMJ	
☐ ZS-LMF	Beechjet 400A	RK-146	ex N746TA	
☐ ZS-OXV	Cessna 208B Caravan I	208B0563	ex N330AK	
☐ ZS-RWN	Aérospatiale AS350BA Ecureuil	1866	ex F-GJAM	
☐ ZS-SGV	Hawker 900XP	HA-0067	ex N3217H	
☐ ZS-SHY	Beech 350 King Air	FL-543	ex N543KA	
☐ ZS-SME	Hawker 900XP	HA-0104	ex N6434R	
☐ ZS-SMV	Embraer EMB.120ER Brasilia	120162	ex F-GHIB	♦
☐ ZS-SRW	Embraer EMB.120RT Brasilia	120018	ex N95644	opf ATG♦

NATURELINKCHARTER   (NRK)

| ☐ ZS-PGY | Embraer EMB.120RT Brasilia | 120194 | ex N269UE |
| ☐ ZS-POE | Embraer EMB.120RT Brasilia | 120137 | ex N137H |

NELAIR CHARTER   Nelair (NLC)   Nelspruit (NLP)

☐ ZS-EDG	Cessna U206 Super Skywagon	U206-0382	ex N2182F
☐ ZS-EVB	Piper PA-30 Twin Comanche 160B	30-1218	ex N8134Y
☐ ZS-IKZ	Piper PA-32-300 Cherokee Six E	32-7240070	ex ZS-XAS
☐ ZS-JGW	Cessna 401B	401B0106	ex N7966Q
☐ ZS-JZX	Piper PA-34-200T Seneca II	34-7770269	ex N5911V
☐ ZS-LTL	Cessna 310Q	310Q0025	ex N8925Z
☐ ZS-LVR	Douglas DC-3	20475	ex N5000E
☐ ZS-MHE	Piper PA-31-350 Navajo Chieftain	31-7305096	ex N74950
☐ ZS-MSO	Piper PA-32-300 Cherokee Six	32-7540083	ex N33050
☐ ZS-NAO	Cessna T210L Centurion II	21060092	ex N59104
☐ ZS-NKG	Cessna 208 Caravan I	20800178	ex 5Y-NKG
☐ ZS-PHI	Grumman G-159 Gulfstream I	164	ex N290AS
☐ ZS-RAN	Cessna 402B	402B0439	ex ZS-XAV

PHOEBUS APOLLO AVIATION/FLYEXALL Phoebus (PE/PHB)   Johannesburg-Rand (QRA)

☐ ZS-DIW	Douglas DC-3	11991	ex SAAF 6871 Pegasus	
☐ ZS-PAI	Douglas C-54E	27319	ex N4989K Atlas	
☐ ZS-PAK	Douglas DC-9-32	47368/505	ex D6-CAW	
☐ ZS-PAL	Douglas DC-9-34CF	47704/819	ex 5N-BHC	[JNB]

QWILA AIR   Q-Charter   Lanseria (HLA)

☐ ZS-NUF	Beech 200C Super King Air	BL-4	ex V5-AAL	
☐ ZS-OKL	Beech 1900D	UE-48	ex 5Y-OKL	
☐ ZS-PRE	Beech 1900C	UB-15	ex N715GL	all-white
☐ ZS-SLG	Cessna 208B Caravan I	208B0772	ex N208LT	

ROSSAIR   Rossair Charter (RSS)

| ☐ ZS-OLP | Beech 1900C | UB-18 | ex Z-DHS |

☐ ZS-OLW	Beech 1900D	UE-33	ex N33YV		
☐ ZS-PIR	Beech 1900D	UE-29	ex PH-RAG		

ROVOS AIR   *Rovos (6P/VOS)*   **Pretoria-Wonderboom (PRY)**

☐ ZS-ARV	Convair 340-67	228	ex CP-2237		[PRY]
☐ ZS-AUA	Douglas DC-4	42934	ex PH-DDS	Flying Dutchman colours	
☐ ZS-BRV	Convair 340-67	215	ex CP-2236		[PRY]
☐ ZS-CRV	Douglas DC-3	13331	ex ZS-PTG	Delaney	

SA EXPRESS   *Expressways (XZ/EXY)*   **Johannesburg-OR Tambo (JNB)**

☐ ZS-NMC	Canadair CRJ-200ER	7225	ex N626BR	
☐ ZS-NMD	Canadair CRJ-200ER	7233	ex N627BR	
☐ ZS-NME	Canadair CRJ-200ER	7240	ex N628BR	
☐ ZS-NMF	Canadair CRJ-200ER	7287	ex N634BR	
☐ ZS-NMG	Canadair CRJ-200ER	7772	ex 5N-BJI	
☐ ZS-NMH	Canadair CRJ-200ER	7787	ex 5N-BJK	
☐ ZS-NMI	Canadair CRJ-200ER	7153	ex C-FZAN	
☐ ZS-NML	Canadair CRJ-200ER	7201	ex C-GBLX	
☐ ZS-NMM	Canadair CRJ-200ER	7234	ex C-FMMT	
☐ ZS-NMN	Canadair CRJ-200ER	7237	ex C-FMMX	
☐ ZS-NMO	de Havilland DHC-8-402Q	4122	ex C-FFCU	
☐ ZS-NMS	de Havilland DHC-8-402Q	4127	ex C-FFPH	
☐ ZS-YBP	de Havilland DHC-8-402Q	4142	ex G-JECS	
☐ ZS-YBR	de Havilland DHC-8-402Q	4144	ex G-JECT	
☐ ZS-YBT	de Havilland DHC-8-402Q	4146	ex G-JECU	
☐ ZS-YBU	de Havilland DHC-8-402Q	4344	ex G-FLBF	
☐ ZS-YBW	de Havilland DHC-8-402Q	4350	ex G-FLBG	
☐ ZS-YBX	de Havilland DHC-8-402Q	4366	ex G-FLBH	
☐ ZS-YBY	de Havilland DHC-8-402Q	4370	ex G-FLBJ	
☐ ZS-YBZ	de Havilland DHC-8-402Q	4175	ex HB-JQB	
☐ ZS-NBF	Canadair CRJ-701ER	10028	ex D-ACSB	
☐ ZS-NBG	Canadair CRJ-701ER	10039	ex D-ACSC	
☐ ZS-TBE	Canadair CRJ-701	10006	ex F-GRZA	
☐ ZS-TBH	Canadair CRJ-701	10007	ex F-GRZB	

SAHARA AFRICAN AVIATION   **Nelspruit (NLP)**

☐ ZS-AAF	Embraer EMB.120RT Brasilia	120262	ex N268CA	♦
☐ ZS-AAG	Embraer EMB.120ER Brasilia	120252	ex N259CA	opf MXE♦
☐ ZS-OTD	Embraer EMB.120RT Brasilia	120230	ex N249CA	>AYD♦
☐ ZS-PBT	Embraer EMB.120ER Brasilia	120260	ex N223BD	
☐ ZS-SOB	Embraer EMB.120ER Brasilia	120186	ex VH-TWF	♦
☐ ZS-SOC	Embraer EMB.120ER Brasilia	120266	ex VH-TWZ	♦
☐ ZS-TBR	Embraer EMB.120QC Brasilia	120264	ex N462CA	wfs
☐ ZS-TBJ	Embraer EMB.120ER Brasilia	120267	ex N463CA	

SKYHAUL   *Skyhaul (HAU)*   **Johannesburg-OR Tambo (JNB)**

☐ ZS-SKI	Convair 580	186	ex EC-GHN	>LAC SkyCongo
☐ ZS-SKK	Convair 580	135	ex EC-GKH	>LAC SkyCongo
☐ ZS-SKL	Convair 580F	458	ex EC-GBF	

SKYWISE   *(S8/SWZ)*   **Johannesburg-OR Tambo (JNB)**

☐ ZS-SPU	Boeing 737-3S3	24059/1517	ex N240AG	opb BRH♦
☐ ZS-VDB	Boeing 737-31L	27345/2625	ex N745TP	opb BRH♦

SOLENTA AVIATION   *(SL/SET)*   **Lanseria (HLA)**

☐ ZS-AFR	ATR 42-500	643	ex OH-ATB	opf Afrijet Business Service/Shell Gabon
☐ ZS-ATR	ATR 42-300F	060	ex PH-XLC	[HLA]
☐ ZS-LUC	ATR 42-320	032	ex PH-RAK	
☐ ZS-OVP	ATR 42-300F	088	ex F-WQNG	opf DHL
☐ ZS-OVR	ATR 42-300F	116	ex F-WQNB	opf DHL
☐ ZS-OVS	ATR 42-320F	075	ex F-WQNU	opf DHL
☐ ZS-XCC	ATR 42-500	528	ex F-WKVI	
☐ ZS-XCD	ATR 42-300F	228	ex N422WA	DHL c/s [MST]
☐ ZS-XCG	ATR 42-500	443	ex SP-EDE	opf Shell♦
☐ ZS-AEA	Beech 1900D	UE-385	ex HB-AEL	
☐ ZS-MKE	Beech 1900D	UE-44	ex PH-ACY	opf UN
☐ ZS-NAC	Beech 1900D	UE-28	ex N28YV	
☐ ZS-OCX	Beech 1900D	UE-321		♦
☐ ZS-OLW	Beech 1900D	UE-33		opf ICRC
☐ ZS-OLY	Beech 1900D	UE-39	ex N39ZV	opf UN
☐ ZS-OYC	Beech 1900D	UE-117	ex VH-NTL	
☐ ZS-OYE	Beech 1900D	UE-200	ex VH-IAV	opb Tullow Air

☐ ZS-OYJ	Beech 1900D	UE-273	ex 5Y-NAC		
☐ ZS-OYK	Beech 1900D	UE-318	ex VH-NBN	all-white	opb Tullow Air
☐ ZS-PJX	Beech 1900D	UE-102	ex P2-MBX		
☐ ZS-ZED	Beech 1900D	UE-260	ex N260GL		opf UN
☐ ZS-BBH	Embraer ERJ-145LR	145607	ex PR-PSI		
☐ ZS-BBI	Embraer ERJ-145LR	145223	ex N18982		
☐ ZS-BBJ	Embraer ERJ-145LR	145277	ex N13990		
☐ ZS-BBK	Embraer ERJ-135LR	145396	ex N737MW		♦
☐ ZS-BBM	Embraer ERJ-145LR	145597	ex PR-PSH		opf EKG
☐ ZS-NIZ	Cessna 208B Caravan I	208B0353	ex 5Y-NIZ		opf DHL
☐ ZS-OHE	Beech 1900C-1	UC-48	ex 9J-AFJ		
☐ ZS-OTV	Cessna 208B Caravan I	208B0545	ex 5Y-OTV		
☐ ZS-PEA	Beech 200C Super King Air	BL-29	ex N500PH	all-white	
☐ ZS-XCA	ATR 72-212A	463	ex PR-TTJ		
☐ ZS-XCB	ATR 72-212	460	ex F-WNUC		opf EKG
☐ ZS-XCE	ATR 72-202F	396	ex F-WKVD		
☐ ZS-XCF	ATR 72-201F	227	ex LX-WAB	DHL c/s	
☐ ZS-ZAA	LET L-410UVP-E20	2919	ex OK-JDT		♦
☐ ZS-ZAB	LET L-410UVP-E20	2920			♦
☐ ZS-ZAC	LET L-410UVP-E20	3001	ex OK-JDX		♦
☐ ZS-ZAD	LET L-410UVP-E20	3003	ex OK-JPA		♦
☐ 5Y-OBY	Cessna 208B Caravan I	208B0345	ex ZS-OBY		opf DHL

SOUTH AFRICAN AIRWAYS	**Springbok (SA/SAA)**	**Johannesburg-OR Tambo (JNB)**

Member of Star Alliance

☐ ZS-SFG	Airbus A319-131	2326	ex D-AVYT		
☐ ZS-SFH	Airbus A319-131	2355	ex D-AVWC		
☐ ZS-SFI	Airbus A319-131	2375	ex D-AVWR		
☐ ZS-SFJ	Airbus A319-131	2379	ex D-AVWU		
☐ ZS-SFK	Airbus A319-131	2418	ex D-AVYI		
☐ ZS-SFL	Airbus A319-131	2438	ex D-AVWP		
☐ ZS-SFM	Airbus A319-131	2469	ex D-AVYH		
☐ ZS-SFN	Airbus A319-131	2501	ex D-AVWD		
☐ ZS-SZA	Airbus A320-232	5637	ex F-WWIJ		
☐ ZS-SZB	Airbus A320-232	5680	ex F-WWDF		
☐ ZS-SZC	Airbus A320-232	5956	ex F-WWIO		
☐ ZS-SZD	Airbus A320-232	6007	ex F-WWBS		
☐ ZS-SZE	Airbus A320-232	6147	ex F-WWBD		♦
☐ ZS-SZF	Airbus A320-232	6189	ex F-WWBX		♦
☐ ZS-SZG	Airbus A320-232	6200	ex F-WWDG		♦
☐ ZS-SZH	Airbus A320-232	6306	ex F-WWDU		♦
☐ ZS-SZI	Airbus A320-232	6439	ex F-WWBF		♦
☐ ZS-SZJ	Airbus A320-232	6478	ex F-WWBM		
☐ ZS-SZY	Airbus A320-232	5011	ex F-WWIA		
☐ ZS-SZZ	Airbus A320-232	4990	ex D-AVVU		
☐ ZS-	Airbus A320-214	6694	ex		o/o♦
☐ ZS-	Airbus A320-214	6712	ex		o/o♦
☐ ZS-	Airbus A320-214	6730	ex		o/o♦
☐ ZS-	Airbus A320-214	6753	ex		o/o♦
☐ ZS-	Airbus A320-232	6948	ex		o/o♦
☐ ZS-SXU	Airbus A330-243	1271	ex F-WWYX		[JNB]
☐ ZS-SXV	Airbus A330-243	1249	ex F-WWYH		
☐ ZS-SXW	Airbus A330-243	1236	ex F-WWKA		
☐ ZS-SXX	Airbus A330-243	1223	ex F-WWYL		
☐ ZS-SXY	Airbus A330-243	1210	ex F-WWYS		
☐ ZS-SXZ	Airbus A330-243	1191	ex F-WWKL		
☐ ZS-SXA	Airbus A340-313E	544	ex F-WWJS		
☐ ZS-SXB	Airbus A340-313E	582	ex F-WWJT		
☐ ZS-SXC	Airbus A340-313E	590	ex F-WWJY		
☐ ZS-SXD	Airbus A340-313E	643	ex VT-JWA	Siyanqoba	special c/s
☐ ZS-SXE	Airbus A340-313E	646	ex VT-JWB		
☐ ZS-SXF	Airbus A340-313E	651	ex VT-JWC		
☐ ZS-SXG	Airbus A340-313X	378	ex F-WJKF		
☐ ZS-SXH	Airbus A340-313X	197	ex F-WJKP		
☐ ZS-SNA	Airbus A340-642	410	ex F-WWCE		
☐ ZS-SNB	Airbus A340-642	417	ex F-WWCG		
☐ ZS-SNC	Airbus A340-642	426	ex F-WWCH		Star Alliance c/s
☐ ZS-SND	Airbus A340-642	531	ex F-WWCX		
☐ ZS-SNE	Airbus A340-642	534	ex F-WWCY		
☐ ZS-SNF	Airbus A340-642	547	ex F-WWCI		
☐ ZS-SNG	Airbus A340-642	557	ex F-WWCG		
☐ ZS-SNH	Airbus A340-642	626	ex F-WWCF		
☐ ZS-SNI	Airbus A340-642	630	ex F-WWCG		
☐ ZS-SJA	Boeing 737-8S3/W	29248/561			

☐ ZS-SJB	Boeing 737-8S3/W	29249/653	ex N1786B	
☐ ZS-SJC	Boeing 737-85F/W	28828/565	ex N1786B	
☐ ZS-SJD	Boeing 737-85F/W	28829/582		
☐ ZS-SJE	Boeing 737-85F/W	28830/669	ex N1786B	
☐ ZS-SJF	Boeing 737-85F/W	30006/688	ex N1787B	
☐ ZS-SJM	Boeing 737-85F/W	30476/789	ex N788BA	
☐ ZS-SJN	Boeing 737-85F/W	30569/850	ex N1786B	
☐ ZS-SJO	Boeing 737-8BG/W	32357/918	ex PH-HZS	
☐ ZS-SJS	Boeing 737-844/W	32632/1205		
☐ ZS-SJU	Boeing 737-844/W	32634/1383		
☐ ZS-SJV	Boeing 737-844/W	32635/1407	ex N1787B	Star Alliance c/s
☐ ZS-SBA	Boeing 737-3Y0F	26070/2349	ex N700JZ	
☐ ZS-SBB	Boeing 737-3Y0F	26072/2369	ex N701JZ	

SPRINGBOK CLASSIC AIR — Spring Classic (SPB) — Johannesburg-Rand (QRA)

☐ ZS-CFC	Beech E-18S	BA-216		

STAR AIR CARGO — Brightstar (BRH) — Johannesburg-OR Tambo (JNB)

☐ ZS-PUI	Boeing 737-2B7 (Nordam 3)	22890/986	ex 5N-BFJ	
☐ ZS-SFX	Boeing 737-2B7 (Nordam 3)	22889/983	ex 5N-BFH	wfs
☐ ZS-SPU	Boeing 737-3S3	24059/1517	ex N240AG	opf SWZ
☐ ZS-SVT	Boeing 737-2K9	23405/1178	ex 7Q-YKX	
☐ ZS-SVV	Boeing 737-236	22030/693	ex CC-CZO	[JNB]
☐ ZS-VDB	Boeing 737-31L	27345/2625	ex N745TP	opf SWZ
☐ ZS-VDP	Boeing 737-31L	27346/2636	ex N346TP	>LAM

STARS AWAY AVIATION — (STX) — Cape Town-International (CPT)

☐ ZS-YDB	Douglas DC-8-62AF	46162/555	ex 9G-AED	

SWIFT FLITE

☐ ZS-NKE	Embraer EMB.120ER Brasilia	120296	ex N226SW	

TAB AIR CHARTER

☐ ZS-TAA	Embraer EMB.120ER Brasilia	120280	ex PR-UHT	
☐ ZS-TAE	Beech 200 Super King Air	BB-704	ex A2-AJK	

TRAMON AIR — Tramon (TMX) — Lanseria (HLA)

☐ ZS-ALX	Grumman G-159 Gulfstream I	086	ex N10TB	

UTAIR SOUTH AFRICA — Lanseria (HLA)

☐ ZS-HFI	Mil Mi-8MTV-1	95907	ex RA-27071	
☐ ZS-HFL	Mil Mi-8MTV-1	95958	ex RA-27131	
☐ ZS-HFM	Mil Mi-8MTV-1	94622	ex RA-25558	
☐ ZS-RUB	Mil Mi-8MTV-1	95960	ex RA-27133	
☐ ZS-SCF	Mil Mi-8MTV-1	93442	ex RA-25829	
☐ ZS-SCG	Mil Mi-8MTV-1	95955	ex RA-27128	
☐ ZS-SUF	Mil Mi-8MTV-1	93345	ex RA-22978	
☐ ZS-TUT	Mil Mi-8MTV-1	95151	ex RA-25413	

WESTAIR WINGS CHARTERS

☐ ZS-DHL	Reims Cessna F406 Caravan II	F406-0062	ex V5-DHL	♦

Z3-   MACEDONIA (Republic of Macedonia)

BUSINESS AIR — Cucer-Sandevo

☐ Z3-DAG	Piper PA-34-200T Seneca IV	34-47014	ex G-PFCI	

3A-   MONACO (Principality of Monaco)

HELI AIR MONACO — Heli Air (YO/MCM) — Monte Carlo Heliport (MCM)

☐ 3A-MAC	Aérospatiale AS350B Ecureuil	1673	ex HB-XBC	
☐ 3A-MAX	Aérospatiale AS350BA Ecureuil	1794	ex F-GMBN	
☐ 3A-MFC	Eurocopter EC130B4 Ecureuil	3768		
☐ 3A-MIL	Aérospatiale AS350BA Ecureuil	17090	ex F-GMBV	
☐ 3A-MPJ	Eurocopter EC130B4 Ecureuil	3662		
☐ 3A-MTA	Aérospatiale AS350B2 Ecureuil	2545	ex F-GHUT	
☐ 3A-MTT	Aérospatiale AS350B2 Ecureuil	1967	ex I-LUPJ	
☐ 3A-MWI	Aérospatiale AS350B3 Ecureuil	4484	ex F-HBRR	

☐ 3A-MCM	Aérospatiale SA365N Dauphin 2	6076	ex F-WQEE
☐ 3A-MXC	Aérospatiale AS355N Dauphin 2	5699	ex LX-HBP
☐ 3A-MXL	Aérospatiale AS355N Ecureuil 2	5713	

MONACAIR (MCR) Monte Carlo Heliport (MCM)

☐ 3A-MBD	Eurocopter EC155B1 Dauphin	6892	ex F-WJXU
☐ 3A-MDF	Agusta A109SP Grand	22215	
☐ 3A-MPG	Eurocopter EC155B1	6771	ex F-WQDN

3B- MAURITIUS (Republic of Mauritius)

AIR MAURITIUS — AirMauritius (MK/MAU) — Plaisance (MRU)

☐ 3B-NAU	Airbus A340-312	076	ex F-WWJG	Pink Pigeon
☐ 3B-NAY	Airbus A340-313X	152	ex F-WWJX	Cardinal
☐ 3B-NBD	Airbus A340-313X	194	ex F-WWJP	Parakeet
☐ 3B-NBE	Airbus A340-313X	268	ex F-WWJG	Paille en Queue
☐ 3B-NBI	Airbus A340-313E	793	ex F-WWJE	Le Flamboyant
☐ 3B-NBJ	Airbus A340-313E	800	ex F-WWJF	Le Chamarel
☐ 3B-NBF	Airbus A319-112	1592	ex D-AVYX	Mon Choisy
☐ 3R-NBG	ATR 72-212A	690	ex F-WWEM	Port Mathurin
☐ 3B-NBH	Airbus A319-112	1936	ex D-AVWF	Blue Bay
☐ 3B-NBL	Airbus A330-202	1057	ex F-WWYF	Nenuphar
☐ 3B-NBM	Airbus A330-202	883	ex F-WWKK	Trochetia
☐ 3B-NBN	ATR 72-212A	921	ex F-WWET	Ile Aux Aigrettes
☐ 3B-NZD	Bell 206B JetRanger III	4464		
☐ 3B-NZE	Bell 206B JetRanger III	4465		
☐ 3B-NZF	Bell 206B JetRanger III	4496	ex N8152H	

3C- EQUATORIAL GUINEA (Republic of Equatorial Guinea)

AIR ANNOBON — San Antonio de Palé (NBN)

| ☐ 3C-MAA | Avro 146-RJ85 | E2365 | ex EI-RJS | Mebana |

CEIBA INTERCONTINENTAL — Ceiba Line (C2/CEL) — Malabo (SSG)

☐ CS-FAF	Boeing 737-8FB/W	41159/4973		Mbasogo	opb WHT♦
☐ TC-MND	Airbus A300C4-203F	212	ex ZS-SDG		<MNB
☐ 3C-LLG	ATR 42-320	0335	ex F-ODYE		[LPA]
☐ 3C-LLH	ATR 42-500	671	ex F-WWYE		
☐ 3C-LLI	ATR 72-212A	790	ex F-WWEJ		
☐ 3C-LLM	ATR 72-212A	810	ex F-WWEX		
☐ 3C-LLS	Boeing 777-2FBLR	40668/937		Djibloho	opb WHT
☐ 3C-LLU	Boeing 767-306ER	30393/781	ex HB-JJG	Kie Ntem	VIP
☐ 3C-LLY	Boeing 737-8FB/W	41157/4782		Bioko	
☐ 3C-LLW	Boeing 737-8FB/W	41158/5180		Evinayong	♦
☐ 3C-MAB	Boeing 777-2FBLR	60116/1258			[BSL]♦

CRONOS AIRLINES — (C8/CRA) — Malabo (SSG)

☐ ZS-AKK	Embraer ERJ-135LR	145301	ex N724AE	o/o♦
☐ ZS-SMO	British Aerospace 146 Srs.300	E3169	ex G-BSNS	♦
☐ ZS-SOP	British Aerospace 146 Srs.300	E3187	ex G-BSYT	opb FAV
☐ 3C-AKK	British Aerospace 146 Srs.200	E2069	ex ZS-SOW	♦

GEASA — Geasa (GEA) — Malabo (SSG)

| ☐ 3C-LLU | Boeing 767-306ER | 30393/781 | ex HB-JJG | VIP; opf CEL |

GENERAL WORKS AVIACION — (GWK) — Malabo (SSG)

☐ 3C-GWA	Fokker F.28 Fellowship 4000	11240	ex HC-CDG	wfs
☐ 3C-GWC	Fokker F.28 Fellowship 4000	11238	ex TU-TIY	
☐ 3C-GWD	Fokker F.28 Fellowship 4000	11224	ex HC-CDW	

GUINEA EQUATORIAL AIRLINES — Malabo (SSG)

| ☐ 3C-LGE | Dassault Falcon 50 | 246 | ex F-GTJF | |
| ☐ 3C-LLP | LET L-410UVP-E20 | 092713 | ex OK-2713 | opf Govt |

NATIONALE GABON — Malabo (SSG)

| ☐ ZS-PMS | SAAB SF.340A | 340A-059 | ex N327PX | [HLA] |

PUNTO AZUL		(ZR)			Malabo (SSG)
☐ ZS-DFC	Embraer ERJ-145MP	145339	ex PR-PSR		<NTN♦
☐ 3C-MAC	Embraer ERJ-145MP	145244	ex ZS-DBF		♦

3DC- SWAZILAND (Kingdom of Swaziland)

EASTERN AIRWAYS				Manzini-Matsapha (MTS)
☐ 3D-PAT	LET L-410UVP-E	902507	ex OK-VAA	

4K- AZERBAIJAN (Republic of Azerbaijan)

AZERBAIJAN AIRLINES		Azal (J2/AHY)			Baku-Bina (BAK)
☐ 4K-AZ54	Airbus A320-212	0331	ex 9H-ADZ		
☐ 4K-AZ77	Airbus A320-214	2846	ex D-ABDH	Lerik	
☐ 4K-AZ78	Airbus A320-214	2853	ex D-ABDI	Naftalin	
☐ 4K-AZ79	Airbus A320-214	2865	ex D-ABDJ	Oghuz	
☐ 4K-AZ80	Airbus A320-214	2991	ex HB-IOT	Shirvan	
☐ 4K-AZ83	Airbus A320-214	2685	ex D-ABDD	Julfa	
☐ 4K-AZ84	Airbus A320-214	3006	ex HB-IOU	Kirdamir	
☐ 4K-AI07	Airbus A320-214CJ	6285	ex F-WWIQ	Baku-7	VIP♦
☐ VP-BBR	Boeing 787-8	37920/211	ex N1789B		♦
☐ VP-BBS	Boeing 787-8	37921/247	ex N8570Z	Ordubad	♦
☐ 4K-AI01	Boeing 767-32LER	40342/990	ex 4K-BAKU-1	Baku-1	opf Govt
☐ 4K-AI02	Airbus A319CJ-115	2487	ex 4K-AZ01	Baku-2	opf Govt
☐ 4K-AI08	Airbus A340-642	779	ex VP-CCC		VIP
☐ 4K-AZ03	Airbus A319-111	2516	ex D-AVWS	Ganja	
☐ 4K-AZ04	Airbus A319-111	2588	ex D-AVXJ	Guba	
☐ 4K-AZ05	Airbus A319-111	2788	ex D-AVYY	Gazakh	
☐ 4K-AZ10	Tupolev Tu-154M	98A1013			
☐ 4K-AZ11	Boeing 757-22L	29305/894	ex VP-BBR	Sumgayit	
☐ 4K-AZ12	Boeing 757-22L	30834/947	ex VP-BBS	Nakhchivan	
☐ 4K-AZ38	Boeing 757-256	26246/620	ex N262CT	Qobustan	
☐ 4K-AZ43	Boeing 757-2M6	23453/100	ex V8-RBB		
☐ 4K-AZ52	Embraer ERJ170-100LR	17000002	ex M-YRGO	Zagataia	
☐ 4K-AZ64	Embraer ERJ190-100AR	19000627	ex PT-TKP	Gabala	
☐ 4K-AZ65	Embraer ERJ190-100AR	19000630	ex PR-EAE	Gusar	
☐ 4K-AZ66	Embraer ERJ190-100AR	19000631	ex PR-EAF	Salyan	
☐ 4K-AZ67	Embraer ERJ190-100AR	19000636	ex PR-EBV	Khankandi	
☐ 4K-AZ81	Boeing 767-32LER	40343/1004	ex N5023Q	Babek	
☐ 4K-AZ82	Boeing 767-32LER	41063/1030		Koroglu	
☐ 4K-AZ85	Airbus A340-542	886	ex F-WWTG	Karabakh	
☐ 4K-AZ86	Airbus A340-542	894	ex F-WWTH	Nakhchivan	

SILK WAY AIRLINES		Silk Line (ZP/AZQ)		Baku-Bina (BAK)
☐ 4K-AZ19	Ilyushin Il-76TD	0053460820	ex UR-76408	
☐ 4K-AZ31	Ilyushin Il-76TD	1013405184	ex RA-76426	
☐ 4K-AZ40	Ilyushin Il-76TD	1043419632	ex RA-76366	
☐ 4K-AZ41	Ilyushin Il-76TD	1093420673		
☐ 4K-AZ60	Ilyushin Il-76MD	0093499982	ex RA-76822	
☐ 4K-AZ61	Ilyushin Il-76TD	1023412411	ex 4K-AZ16	
☐ 4K-AZ100	Ilyushin Il-76TD-90	2073421708		
☐ 4K-AZ101	Ilyushin Il-76TD-90	2083421716		
☐ 4K-AZ23	Antonov An-12BK	8345605	ex RA-11715	
☐ 4K-AZ63	Antonov An-12BP	9346308	ex UR-CBU	
☐ 4K-AZ93	Antonov An-12BK	7345203	ex UR-CGU	

SILK WAY HELICOPTERS				Baku-Zabrat
☐ 4K-AZ115	AgustaWestland AW139	31482	ex I-EASN	♦
☐ 4K-AZ117	AgustaWestland AW139	31491	ex I-EASH	♦
☐ 4K-AZ121	AgustaWestland AW139	31495		♦
☐ 4K-AZ125	AgustaWestland AW139	31506		♦
☐ 4K-AZ127	AgustaWestland AW139	31510	ex I-EASJ	♦
☐ 4K-88888	AgustaWestland AW139	31530	ex I-EASG	♦
☐ 4K-AZ02	Aérospatiale AS.332LI Super Puma	2627	ex F-WWOT	
☐ 4K-AZ11	Sikorsky S-92A	920108	ex N2096D	
☐ 4K-AZ24	Aérospatiale AS.332L1 Super Puma	2625	ex F-WWOM	
☐ 4K-AZ46	Eurocopter EC155B1 Dauphin	6685	ex F-WWOK	
☐ 4K-AZ47	Eurocopter EC155B1 Dauphin	6693	ex F-WWOI	
☐ 4K-AZ50	Sikorsky S-92A+	920135	ex N135NL	
☐ 4K-AZ51	Sikorsky S-92A+	920136	ex N136CL	
☐ 4K-AZ73	Mil Mi-171C	171C0031084210U		

SILK WAY WEST AIRLINES (7L/AZG) Baku-Bina (BAK)

☐ VQ-BVB	Boeing 747-83QF	44444/1493	ex (4K-SW881)	♦
☐ VQ-BVC	Boeing 747-83QF	44937/1496	ex (4K-SW882)	♦
☐ 4K-SW008	Boeing 747-4R7F	29732/1231	ex LX-PCV	♦
☐ 4K-SW888	Boeing 747-4R7F	29730/1203	ex LX-NCV	♦
☐ 4K-SW808	Boeing 767-32LERF/W	41068/1027		[JAX]♦
☐ 4K-SW880	Boeing 767-32LERF	41069/1032		[JAX]♦

SKY WIND Sky Wind Baku-Bina (BAK)

☐ 4K-78129	Ilyushin Il-76MD	0083489683	ex ER-IBC

SW BUSINESS AVIATION (ESW)

☐ 4K-AZ808	ATR 42-500	673	ex F-WWLG
☐ 4K-8888	Boeing 727-251	22543/1700	ex 4K-AZ9

4L- GEORGIA (Republic of Georgia)

AVIAEXPORT Tbilisi-Lochini (TBS)

☐ 4L-ABE	Boeing 727-230F (FedEx 3)	20905/1091	cx HZ SNC

AVIASERVICE

☐ 4L-AVB	Mil Mi-171	171E00196610		♦
☐ 4L-GGG	Aérospatiale AS332L1	2833		♦
☐ 4L-SSS	Aéspatiale AS332L1	2820	ex F-WWOS	♦

BRAVO AIR (BRZ)

☐ 4L-GSS	Antonov An-26	5106	ex EY-323	
☐ 4L-IKE	Antonov An-26	5407	ex EY-322	♦

FLY ADJARA

☐ 4L-BKL	Antonov An-26	3709	ex 23 red

FLYVISTA (GT) Tbilisi-Lochini (TBS)

☐ 4L-AJC	Boeing 737-33R	28873/2975	ex M-ABGT	<AJD>KMF♦
☐ 9H-AJW	Boeing 737-3U3	28733/2969	ex 4L-AJW	♦

GEORGIAN AIRWAYS Tamazi (A9/TGZ) Tbilisi-Lochini (TBS)

☐ 4L-GAA	Canadair CL-600-2B19 (Chal 850)	8046	ex 4L-GAF	opf Govt
☐ 4L-GAF	Gulfstream GIV-X	4106	ex A6-FLG	
☐ 4L-GAL	Canadair CRJ-200ER	7076	ex F-GRJB	
☐ 4L-GAM	Cessna T206 Stationair	T20608957	ex D-EXAL	
☐ 4L-TGB	Canadair CRJ-200LR	7442	ex OY-MBJ	
☐ 4L-TGG	Canadair CRJ-200LR	7386	ex OY-MAV	
☐ 4L-TGI	Boeing 737-505	26336/2805	ex B-2973	
☐ 4L-TGM	Boeing 737-76N/W	29904/347	ex EI-EZI	
☐ 4L-TGN	Boeing 737-7BK/W	33015/1384	ex VH-VBV	
☐ 4L-TGS	Canadair CRJ-200LR	7373	ex EK-20073	

GEORGIAN INTERNATIONAL AIRLINES (4L/GIL) Batumi (BUS)

☐ 4L-GIB	Fokker 100	11320	ex PH-LND	o/o♦

GEORGIAN STAR INTERNATIONAL/AG AIR (GST) Tbilisi-Lochini (TBS)

☐ 4L-ACE	Boeing 747-329SF	24837/810	ex VP-BIC	wfs
☐ 4L-ADA	Airbus A300F4-203	157	ex A6-MDA	
☐ 4L-IMA	Boeing 737-322	24717/1930	ex N208MG	[AMM]
☐ 4L-NAL	Boeing 737-2Q8	21960/642	ex E3-NAS	[ASM]

SKY GEORGIA Gremi (QB/GFG) Tbilisi-Lochini (TBS)

☐ 4L-GNN	Douglas DC-9-51	47657/787	ex UR-BYL	[TBS]

THE CARGO AIRLINES Toka (TZS) Tbilisi-Lochini (TBS)

☐ 4L-ABA	Airbus A300B4-203F	157	ex A6-MDA	♦
☐ 4L-ABI	Airbus A300F4-203	277	ex EY-647	♦
☐ 4L-AMS	Airbus A300B4-203F	126	ex S5-ABS	♦
☐ 4L-BIC	Airbus A300F4-203	292	ex 4L-ABS	♦

☐ 4L-MRK	Boeing 747-281F	25171/886	ex VP-BIJ	>IAW

TUSHETI (USB)

☐ 4L-AAA	Eurocopter EC155B	6630	ex F-WQDH
☐ 4L-TBS	Mil Mi-8MTV	103M12	ex BAF-111
☐ 4L-TIS	Mil Mi-8T	8231	ex TC-HAG
☐ 4L-TLS	Mil Mi-8MTV	95588	
☐ 4L-TLT	MBB Bo.105CB	S-249	ex 4L-QOR

VISTA GEORGIA (AJD) Tbilisi-Lochini (TBS)

☐ 4L-AJB	Boeing 737-5H6	27354/2637	ex N495MS	>BDR
☐ 4L-AJC	Boeing 737-33R	28873/2975	ex M-ABGT	>GT♦
☐ 4L-AJG	Boeing 737-37Q	28537/2904	ex G-ODSK	♦
☐ 4L-AJH	Boeing 737-505	25794/2803	ex EI-FDE	♦
☐ 4L-AJO	Boeing 737-36N	28673/2995	ex N641CS	>BDR
☐ 4L-AJW	Boeing 737-3U3	28733/2969	ex EI-FCW	>GT♦
☐ 4L-AJY	Boeing 737-33A	27452/2679	ex N270AE	>JUA

4O- MONTENEGRO (Republic of Montenegro)

AIRWAYS MONTENEGRO

☐ 4O-VIP	Eurocopter EC120B Colibri	1203	ex D-HOER	♦

MONTENEGRO AIRLINES Montair (YM/MGX) Podgorica/Tivat (TGD/TIV)

☐ 4O-AOK	Fokker 100	11272	ex YU-AOK	Sveti Petar Cetinjski	[TGD]
☐ 4O-AOL	Fokker 100	11268	ex ZA-ARC	Podgorica	wfs
☐ 4O-AOM	Fokker 100	11321	ex YU-AOM	Bar	
☐ 4O-AOP	Fokker 100	11332	ex YU-AOP	Boka	
☐ 4O-AOT	Fokker 100	11350	ex YU-AOT		wfs
☐ 4O-AOA	Embraer ERJ-195LR	19000180	ex PT-SDO		
☐ 4O-AOB	Embraer ERJ-195LR	19000283	ex PT-TLX		
☐ 4O-AOC	Embraer ERJ-195LR	19000358	ex PT-PVM		
☐ 4O-AOD	Embraer ERJ-190LR	19000665	ex PR-EEZ		♦

4R- SRI LANKA (Democratic Socialist Republic of Sri Lanka)

AERO LANKA Serendib (QL/RNL) Colombo-Bandaranayike Intl/Ratmalana (CMB/RML)

☐ 4R-SEA	Cessna 404	404-0833	ex N404AM

CINNAMON AIR

☐ 4R-CAE	Cessna 208 Caravan	20800364	ex N14RP

FITS AVIATION Expoavia (8D/EXV) Colombo-Bandaranayike Intl/Ratmalana (CMB/RML)

☐ 4R-EXD	Ilyushin Il-18GrM	187009802	ex YR-IMZ	<RMV
☐ 4R-EXJ	Douglas DC-8-63CF (BAC 3)	46049/479	ex N867BX	[NBO]
☐ 4R-EXK	Fokker F.27 Friendship 500RF	10631	ex 4R-MRA	
☐ 4R-EXH	Fokker F.27 Friendship 500RF	10642	ex A4O-FG	wfs
☐ 4R-EXL	Cessna 208B Caravan I	208B2298	ex N9012U	
☐ 4R-EXM	McDonnell-Douglas MD-82SF	53217/2053	ex N982FA	♦

HELITOURS Colombo-Ratmalana (RML)

☐ 4R-HTA	Bell 412	33096	ex SUH-4201	
☐ 4R-HTB	Bell 412	33095	ex SUH-4204	
☐ 4R-HTC	Mil Mi-171	171E0144116001U		♦
☐ 4R-HTD	Mil Mi-171	171E0144116002U		♦
☐ 4R-HTE	Mil Mi-171	171E0144116003U		♦
☐ 4R-HTF	Mil Mi-171	171E0144116004U		♦
☐ 4R-HTN	AVIC MA-60	0708		
☐ 4R-HTO	AVIC MA-60	0709		

LANKAN CARGO (RLN) Colombo-Bandaranayike Intl (CMB)

☐ TU-TAB	Boeing 727-223F	20190/738	ex N315NE

MIHIN LANKA (MJ/MLR) Colombo-Bandaranayike Intl (CMB)

☐ 4R-MRC	Airbus A321-231	3106	ex G-TTIF	
☐ 4R-MRD	Airbus A321-231	1946	ex EI-EUJ	
☐ 4R-MRE	Airbus A320-232	2731	ex EI-EWU	
☐ 4R-MRF	Airbus A319-112	1893	ex B-MAM	♦

SAFFRON AVIATION — Colombo-Ratmalana (RML)

☐ 4R-CAE	Cessna 208 Caravan I	20800364	ex N14RP	♦
☐ 4R-CAF	Cessna 208 Caravan I	20801337	ex N126JW	♦
☐ 4R-CAG	Cessna 208B Caravan I	208B0959	ex N623ZC	♦

SIMPLIFLY — Colombo-Bandaranayike Intl (CMB)

☐ 4R-HDA	Cessna T206H Skywagon	T20608646	ex N216WH	FP

SRILANKAN — Srilankan (UL/ALK) — Colombo-Bandaranayike Intl (CMB)

Member of oneWorld

☐ 4R-ABK	Airbus A320-214	2584	ex 9K-CAB		
☐ 4R-ABL	Airbus A320-232	2345	ex M-ABDD		
☐ 4R-ABM	Airbus A320-214	4694	ex F-WWDK	City of Anuradhapura	
☐ 4R-ABN	Airbus A320-214	4869	ex F-WWDO	City of Kalyanipura	
☐ 4R-ABO	Airbus A320-214	4915	ex F-WWDC	City of Yalpanam	
☐ 4R-ABP	Airbus A320-214	5086	ex F-WWIJ		
☐ 4R-ALA	Airbus A330-243	303	ex F-WWYH		
☐ 4R-ALB	Airbus A330-243	306	ex F-WWYL		
☐ 4R-ALC	Airbus A330-243	311	ex F-WWYN		
☐ 4R-ALD	Airbus A330-243	313	ex F-WWYP		
☐ 4R-ALG	Airbus A330-243	404	ex G-WWBB		
☐ 4R-ALH	Airbus A330-243	627	ex EI-EOK	oneWorld c/s	
☐ 4R-ALJ	Airbus A330-243	456	ex G-OJMC		
☐ 4R-ALL	Airbus A330-343	1564	ex F-WWYX	City of Sri Jayawardenepura	♦
☐ 4R-ALM	Airbus A330-343	1583	ex F-WWKF	The City of Sihagiri	♦
☐ 4R-ALN	Airbus A330-343	1604	ex F-WWCP	City of Kolomtota	♦
☐ 4R-ALO	Airbus A330-343	1650	ex F-WW		o/o♦
☐ 4R-	Airbus A330-343	1689	ex F-WW		o/o♦
☐ 4R-	Airbus A330-343	1669	ex F-WW		o/o♦
☐ 4R-ADA	Airbus A340-311	032	ex F-WWJT		
☐ 4R-ADB	Airbus A340-311	033	ex F-WWJU		
☐ 4R-ADC	Airbus A340-311	034	ex F-WWJY		
☐ 4R-ADE	Airbus A340-312	367	ex F-GTUA		
☐ 4R-ADF	Airbus A340-312	374	ex F-GTUB	City of Magam-Ruhunupura	
☐ 4R-ADG	Airbus A340-313X	381	ex B-HXL		
☐ 4R-ABQ	Airbus A321-231	3397	ex A7-ADX		
☐ 4R-ABR	Airbus A321-231	3636	ex A7-ADY		♦

SRILANKAN AIR TAXI

☐ 4R-	de Havilland DHC-6 Twin Otter 300	276	ex C-FBBA	

4X- ISRAEL (State of Israel)

ARKIA ISRAELI AIRLINES — Arkia (IZ/AIZ) — Tel Aviv-Ben Gurion/Sde Dov (TLV/SDV)

☐ 4X-AVT	ATR 72-212A	894	ex F-WWEN
☐ 4X-AVU	ATR 72-212A	587	ex F-WWES
☐ 4X-AVW	ATR 72-212A	583	ex F-WWER
☐ 4X-AVX	ATR 72-212A	656	ex F-WWEJ
☐ 4X-AVZ	ATR 72-212A	577	ex F-WWEN
☐ 4X-BAU	Boeing 757-3E7/W	30178/906	ex N1003M
☐ 4X-BAW	Boeing 757-3E7/W	30179/912	
☐ 4X-EMA	Embraer ERJ-195LR	19000172	ex EC-KOZ
☐ 4X-EMB	Embraer ERJ-190LR	19000616	ex G-CIDI

AYIT AVIATION — Ayit (AYT) — Beer-Sheba (BEV)

☐ 4X-AGP	Short SC.7 Skyvan 3-100	SH1893	ex VH-IBS	
☐ 4X-AHP	de Havilland DHC-6 Twin Otter 100	75	ex C-FCSF	
☐ 4X-AYS	Britten-Norman BN-2A-8 Islander	376	ex (G-BJWL)	wfs
☐ 4X-AYT	Britten-Norman BN-2A Islander	96		♦
☐ 4X-DZY	Beech B80A Queen Air	LD-487	ex IDFAF-108	

CARGO AIRLINES — CAL (5C/ICL) — Tel Aviv-Ben Gurion (TLV)

☐ EK74799	Boeing 747-281BF	24399/750	ex N281RF	<VPB♦
☐ 4X-ICA	Boeing 747-4EVFER	35172/1383	ex N369DF	♦
☐ 4X-ICB	Boeing 747-412F	26561/1042	ex N491EV	♦
☐ 4X-ICM	Boeing 747-271C	21965/438	ex N539MC	all-white

EL AL ISRAEL AIRLINES | EIAI (LY/ELY) | Tel Aviv-Ben Gurion (TLV)

☐ 4X-EKA	Boeing 737-858/W	29957/204	ex N1786B	801	
☐ 4X-EKB	Boeing 737-858/W	29958/249	ex N1786B	802 Ashkelon	
☐ 4X-EKC	Boeing 737-858/W	29959/314	ex N1795B	803 Beit Shean	
☐ 4X-EKF	Boeing 737-8HX/W	29638/2766		804 Kinneret	
☐ 4X-EKH	Boeing 737-85P/W	35485/2871		807 Hadera	
☐ 4X-EKI	Boeing 737-86N/W	28587/192	ex N802NA	812	
☐ 4X-EKJ	Boeing 737-85P/W	35486/2908	ex N1786B		
☐ 4X-EKL	Boeing 737-85P/W	35487/2941	ex N1796B		
☐ 4X-EKP	Boeing 737-8Q8/W	30639/935	ex 5W-SAO	Nahariya	
☐ 4X-EKR	Boeing 737-804/W	30466/505	ex G-CDZM	Givatayim	
☐ 4X-EKS	Boeing 737-8Q8/W	36433/2702	ex N1796B		
☐ 4X-ELA	Boeing 747-458	26055/1027		201 Tel Aviv-Jaffa	
☐ 4X-ELB	Boeing 747-458	26056/1032	ex N60697	202 Haifa	
☐ 4X-ELC	Boeing 747-458	27915/1062	ex N6009F	203 Beer Sheva	
☐ 4X-ELD	Boeing 747-458	29328/1215		204 Jerusalem	
☐ 4X-ELE	Boeing 747-412	26551/1045	ex 9V-SPB		
☐ 4X-ELF	Boeing 747-412F	26563/1036	ex 9V-SFA		
☐ 4X-ELH	Boeing 747-412	26555/1075	ex EC-LGL	Ashdod	
☐ 4X-EAF	Boeing 767-27EER	24854/326	ex F-GHGE	606 Dallat El Carmel	wfs
☐ 4X-EAJ	Boeing 767-330ER	25208/381	ex N208LS	635 Bat Yam	
☐ 4X-EAK	Boeing 767-3Q8ER	27600/655	ex N271LF	612 Rehovot	
☐ 4X-EAL	Boeing 767-33AER	27477/780	ex N477AN	613 Mishmar HaEmek	
☐ 4X-EAM	Boeing 767-3Q8ER	28132/692	ex UR-VVT	614 Daliat el Carmel	
☐ 4X-EAP	Boeing 767-3Y0ER	24953/405	ex TF-FIA	634 Herzliya	
☐ 4X-EAR	Boeing 767-352ER	26262/583	ex VN-A769	633 Kfar Saba	
☐ 4X-ECA	Boeing 777-258ER	30831/319		101 Galillee	
☐ 4X-ECB	Boeing 777-258ER	30832/325		102 Negev	
☐ 4X-ECC	Boeing 777-258ER	30833/335		103 Hasharon	
☐ 4X-ECD	Boeing 777-258ER	33169/405		104 Carmel	
☐ 4X-ECE	Boeing 777-258ER	36083/648	ex N5017Q	105 Sderot	
☐ 4X-ECF	Boeing 777-258ER	36084/655	ex N5022E	106	
☐ 4X-EHA	Boeing 737-958ER/W	41552/4632	ex N1786B		
☐ 4X-EHB	Boeing 737-958ER/W	41553/4697	ex N5573P		
☐ 4X-EHC	Boeing 737-958ER/W	41554/4990			♦
☐ 4X-EHD	Boeing 737-958ER/W	41555/5311	ex N1787B	834	♦
☐ 4X-EHE	Boeing 737-958ER/W	41556/4840	ex N1796B		
☐ 4X-EKD	Boeing 737-758	29960/327	ex N1786B	701 Eilat Red Sea	
☐ 4X-EKE	Boeing 737-758	29961/442	ex N1786B	702 Nazareth	

ISRAIR | Israir (6H/ISR) | Tel Aviv-Ben Gurion (TLV)

☐ 4X-ABF	Airbus A320-232	4354	ex F-WWDC
☐ 4X-ABG	Airbus A320-232	4413	ex F-WWIR
☐ 4X-ATH	ATR 72-212A	931	ex F-WWEG
☐ 4X-ATI	ATR 72-212A	962	ex F-WWEO

MOONAIR | (MOO) | Tel Aviv-Sde Dov (SDV)

☐ 4X-CBY	Piper PA-23-250 Aztec E	27-7304990	ex N405PB
☐ 4X-CCJ	Piper PA-31-350 Navajo Chieftain	31-7405140	ex G-FOEL

PHI HELICOPTERS | | Haifa

☐ 4X-BDW	MBB BK.117A-4	7092

UP

☐ 4X-EKM	Boeing 737-804/W	30465/502	ex G-CDZL	Ramla	
☐ 4X-EKO	Boeing 737-86Q/W	30287/1308	ex D-ATUI	Lod	
☐ 4X-EKT	Boeing 737-8BK/W	33030/1968	ex 5B-DBZ	Bet Shemesh	♦
☐ 4X-EKU	Boeing 737-8Z9/W	33834/1938	ex OE-LNT	Raanana	

5A- LIBYA (Socialist People's Libyan Arab Jamahiriya)

AFRIQIYAH AIRWAYS | Afriqiyah (8U/AAW) | Tripoli-Ben Gashir Intl (TIP)

☐ LY-ONJ	Airbus A320-214	4203	ex EI-ONJ	[VNO]♦
☐ LY-ONL	Airbus A320-214	4489	ex EI-ONL	[VNO]♦
☐ 5A-ONA	Airbus A320-214	3224	ex F-WWBY	
☐ 5A-ONB	Airbus A320-214	3236	ex F-WWBI	
☐ 5A-ONK	Airbus A320-214	4330	ex F-WWIJ	[TIP]
☐ 5A-ONM	Airbus A320-214	4521	ex F-WWDI	dam 14Jly14
☐ 5A-ONN	Airbus A320-214	5414	ex F-WWDN	dam 14Jly14
☐ 5A-ONO	Airbus A320-214	5448	ex D-AVVD	

☐ TS-IMQ	Airbus A319-112	3096	ex D-AVWZ	Alyssa	<TAR
☐ 5A-ONC	Airbus A319-111	3615	ex D-AVYM		dam 13Jly14
☐ 5A-OND	Airbus A319-111	3657	ex D-AVYS		
☐ 5A-ONE	Airbus A340-213	151	ex HZ-WBT4		VIP/opf Govt
☐ 5A-ONH	Airbus A330-202	1043	ex F-WWKM		dam 14Jly14
☐ 5A-ONI	Airbus A319-111	4004	ex D-AVYC		dam 14Jly14
☐ 5A-ONQ	Airbus A330-302	1499	ex F-WWTS		[TLS]
☐ 5A-ONR	Airbus A330-302	1535	ex F-WWCK		>THY
☐ 5A-	Airbus A330-202	1543	ex F-WW		o/o

AIR KURFA (7F/KAV)

☐ 5A-DGR	British Aerospace Jetstream 32	945	ex HL5214	wfs

AIR LIBYA Air Libya (7Q/TLR) Tripoli-Mitiga/Benghazi (MJI/BEN)

☐ 5A-DKV	Boeing 727-2D6	22374/1711	ex 7T-VEV	
☐ 5A-DKX	Boeing 727-2D6	22765/1801	ex 7T-VEX	[BEN]
☐ 5A-DKY	Boeing 737-2D6 (Nordam 3)	22766/853	ex 7T-VEY	wfs
☐ 5A-FLA	Avro RJ100	E3232	ex G-CEIH	
☐ 5A-FLC	British Aerospace 146 Srs.200	E2077	ex ZS-SOV	
☐ 5Y-BRU	LET L410UVP-E9	952539	ex 5X-UAY	<XAK

BURAQ AIR Buraqair (UZ/BRQ) Tripoli-Mitiga/Benghazi (MJI/BEN)

☐ 5A-DMG	Boeing 737-8GK/W	34948/2074	ex N1787B	Tripoli	
☐ 5A-DMH	Boeing 737-8GK/W	34949/2106		Benghazi	dam 14Jly14
☐ 5A-MAB	Boeing 737-406	24857/1902	ex PH-BDU		
☐ 5A-WAC	Boeing 737-4B6	26531/2453	ex N563MS		
☐ 5A-WAD	Boeing 737-55D	27419/2401	ex N587SC		

GHADAMES AIR TRANSPORT (OG/GHT) Tripoli-Ben Gashir Intl (TIP)

☐ C5-LIM	Douglas DC-9-31	48146/1044	ex C5-LPS	
☐ YR-CRY	Fokker 100	11493	ex 9Q-CHO	[MLA]♦
☐ 5A-WAT	Airbus A320-212	0438	ex F-WTDD	

GLOBAL AVIATION (GAK) Tripoli-Mitiga (MJI)

☐ 5A-DNO	Ilyushin Il-76T	0043451509		
☐ 5A-DQB	Ilyushin Il-86	51483208069	ex UN-86101	[FJR]

LIBYAN AIR CARGO Libac (LCR) Tripoli-Mitiga (MJI)

☐ 5A-DJQ	Lockheed L-382G-40C Hercules	4798	ex N501AK		
☐ 5A-DJR	Lockheed L-382E-15C Hercules	4302	ex RP-C99		
☐ 5A-DKL	Antonov An-124-100	19530502761			wfs
☐ 5A-DNY	Ilyushin Il-62M	3052657	ex TL-ABW	Ghadamis	
☐ 5A-DOA	Antonov An-26B	12306	ex LAAF 8207	Wadi Jaref	
☐ 5A-DOF	Antonov An-26B	13007	ex LAAF 8302	Ben Weleed	
☐ 5A-DOG	Antonov An-26-100	13008	ex LAAF 8303	Albayda	
☐ 5A-DOM	Lockheed L-382G-62C Hercules	4992	ex N4268M		
☐ 5A-DOO	Lockheed L-382G-64C Hercules	5000	ex 119 Libyan AF		wfs
☐ 5A-DRS	Ilyushin Il-76M	1033414474	ex RA-76367		

LIBYAN AIRLINES Libair (LN/LAA) Tripoli-Ben Gashir Intl (TIP)

☐ TS-INN	Airbus A320-212	0793	ex D-AICB	<LBT dam 14Jly14
☐ 5A-LAH	Airbus A320-214	4405	ex F-WWBX	dam 14Jly14
☐ 5A-LAJ	Airbus A320-214	4490	ex D-AUBI	dam 14Jly14
☐ 5A-LAK	Airbus A320-214	4526	ex F-WWDO	
☐ 5A-LAO	Airbus A320-214	5373	ex F-WWID	wfs
☐ 5A-LAP	Airbus A320-214	5405	ex F-WWBY	
☐ 5A-LAQ	Airbus A320-214	5494	ex F-WWBO	
☐ 5A-LAA	Canadair CRJ-900	15120	ex C-FPQO	
☐ 5A-LAC	Canadair CRJ-900	15122	ex C-FPUN	
☐ 5A-LAD	Canadair CRJ-900	15214		
☐ 5A-LAE	Canadair CRJ-900	15216		wfs
☐ 5A-LAM	Canadair CRJ-900	15257	ex C-GZQW	
☐ 5A-LAN	Canadair CRJ-900	15258	ex C-GIBO	
☐ 5A-DCT	de Havilland DHC-6 Twin Otter 300	627		
☐ 5A-DCV	de Havilland DHC-6 Twin Otter 300	637		
☐ 5A-DCX	de Havilland DHC-6 Twin Otter 300	641		
☐ 5A-DCZ	de Havilland DHC-6 Twin Otter 300	645		
☐ 5A-DDE	de Havilland DHC-6 Twin Otter 300	677		
☐ 5A-DHN	de Havilland DHC-6 Twin Otter 300	705		
☐ 5A-DHY	de Havilland DHC-6 Twin Otter 300	661	ex C-GELZ	
☐ 5A-DJG	de Havilland DHC-6 Twin Otter 300	744	ex C-GFHQ	

☐ 5A-DJH	de Havilland DHC-6 Twin Otter 300	747	ex C-GEOA	
☐ 5A-DJI	de Havilland DHC-6 Twin Otter 300	757	ex C-GERL	
☐ 5A-DJJ	de Havilland DHC-6 Twin Otter 300	769	ex C-GETI	
☐ 5A-DGC	Cessna 402C II	402C0045	ex N5800C	
☐ 5A-DHG	Cessna 402C II	402C0464	ex N8737Q	
☐ 5A-DHH	Cessna 402C II	402C0444	ex N6790F	
☐ 5A-DHZ	Swearingen SA226AT Merlin IIIB	T-345	ex OO-HSC	
☐ 5A-DJB	Swearingen SA226AT Merlin IIIB	T-388	ex OO-SXC	
☐ 5A-LAF	ATR 42-500	691	ex F-WWLM	
☐ 5A-LAG	ATR 42-500	802	ex F-WWLU	
☐ 5A-LAR	Airbus A330-202	1412	ex F-WWCK	
☐ 5A-LAS	Airbus A330-202	1424	ex F-WWTP	dam 20Jly14
☐ 5A-LAT	Airbus A330-202	1505	ex F-WWKE	♦
☐ 5A-LAU	Airbus A330-202	1543	ex F-WWCT	o/o♦

LIBYAN WINGS

Tripoli-Ben Gashir Intl (TIP)

☐ 5A-WLA	Airbus A319-112	2878	ex RP-C8600	wfs♦
☐ 5A-WLB	Airbus A319-112	2954	ex D-AAAN	wfs♦

PETRO AIR

(PEO)

Tripoli-Ben Gashir Intl (TIP

☐ 5A-AGR	de Havilland DHC-8Q-315	601	ex PH-AGR	
☐ 5A-DDC	de Havilland DHC-6 Twin Otter 300	662	ex TJ-CQE	
☐ 5A-DLX	de Havilland DHC-8-311	254	ex PH-SKD	<CHC A/W [MLA]
☐ 5A-DSO	Fokker F-28 Fellowship 2000	11110	ex HB-AAS	
☐ 5A-PAA	Embraer ERJ-170LR	17000275	ex PT-TQB	
☐ 5A-PAB	Embraer ERJ-170LR	17000279	ex PT-TQF	
☐ 5A-PAC	de Havilland DHC-6 Twin Otter 400	854	ex C-GUVA	
☐ 5A-SOC	Embraer ERJ-170LR	17000162		dam 06Dec13

TOBRUK AIR

Tobruk Air (7T/TBQ)

Tripoli-Ben Gashir Intl (TIP)

Ops cargo flights with Douglas DC-10-30F and Ilyushin Il-76 aircraft leased from other operators when required

5H-   TANZANIA (United Republic of Tanzania)

ADVENTURE SERVICES

☐ 5H-DEB	Cessna 208BEX Caravan I	208B5014	ex N8134H	>Northern Air

AIR EXCEL

Tinga-Tinga (XLL)

Arusha (ARK)

☐ 5H-FIA	Cessna 208B Caravan I	208B2284	ex N9005N	
☐ 5H-GEN	Cessna 208B Caravan I	208B5028	ex N81471	
☐ 5H-IKI	Cessna 208B Caravan I	208B2005	ex N421WF	
☐ 5H-MEK	Cessna 208B Caravan i	208B2017	ex N2293Y	
☐ 5H-SMK	Cessna 208B Caravan I	208B0654	ex VT-TAP	
☐ 5H-VAN	Cessna 208B Caravan I	208B1214	ex N13204	
☐ 5H-XLL	Cessna 208BEX Caravan I	208B1192	ex 5H-FAC	
☐ 5H-AES	LET L-410UVP-E20	871811	ex 5H-PAD	
☐ 5H-EMK	Cessna TU206G Turbo Stationair 8 II	U20604638	ex 5H-SDA	
☐ 5H-WOW	Reims Cessna F406 Caravan II	F406-0060	ex PH-GUG	

AIR TANZANIA

Tanzania (TC/ATC)

Dar-es-Salaam (DAR)

☐ 5H-MWF	de Havilland DHC-8-311	474	ex G-BRYW	
☐ 5Y-WWA	Canadair CRJ-200ER	7350	ex EC-HHV	<DAC East Africa

AS SALAAM AIR

Zanzibar (ZNZ)

☐ 5H-HAD	Cessna 208B Caravan I	208B1137	ex N486WC	
☐ 5H-KJS	Cessna 208B Caravan I	208B1149	ex N1275D	
☐ 5H-NPC	Cessna TU206F Stationair	U20602598	ex ET-ALF	

AURIC AIR SERVICES

Mwanza (MWZ)

☐ 5H-AAA	Cessna 208B Caravan I	208B2282	ex N3034D	
☐ 5H-AAB	Cessna 208B Caravan I	208B2395	ex N20294	
☐ 5H-AAC	Cessna 208B Caravan I	208B2371	ex N2021G	
☐ 5H-AAE	Cessna 208BEX Caravan I	208B5101	ex N8158X	♦
☐ 5H-AAF	Cessna 208BEX Caravan I	208B5102	ex N8160R	♦
☐ 5H-DTS	Cessna 208B Caravan I	208B2159	ex 5H-DTA	
☐ 5H-KKC	Cessna 208B Caravan I	208B2207	ex N60253	
☐ 5H-NCS	Cessna 208B Caravan I	208B1311	ex N2123S	
☐ 5H-TMS	Cessna 208B Caravan I	208B2055	ex N2208Y	
☐ 5H-TWO	Piper PA-34-200T Seneca	34-8170030	ex ZS-KTK	

COASTAL AVIATION — Dar-es-Salaam (DAR)

☐ 5H-BAD	Cessna 208B Caravan I	208B0586	ex N5QP	
☐ 5H-BAT	Cessna 208B Caravan I	208B1030	ex N12554	
☐ 5H-BEE	Cessna 208B Caravan I	208B2264	ex N3041Q	
☐ 5H-GUS	Cessna 208B Caravan I	208B1317	ex N21738	
☐ 5H-HOT	Cessna 208B Caravan I	208B0677	ex N1256N	
☐ 5H-JOE	Cessna 208B Caravan I	208B0570	ex N9EU	
☐ 5H-LUV	Cessna 208B Caravan I	208B2274	ex N30391	
☐ 5H-LXJ	Cessna 208B Caravan I	208B1230	ex N1084Y	
☐ 5H-MAD	Cessna 208B Caravan I	208B0872	ex N1294K	
☐ 5H-NEG	Cessna 208B Caravan I	208B2296	ex N9014K	
☐ 5H-POA	Cessna 208B Caravan I	208B0965	ex N1129Y	
☐ 5H-SUN	Cessna 208B Caravan I	208B0754	ex 5H-PAF	
☐ 5H-VIP	Cessna 208B Caravan I	208B0714	ex N208FK	
☐ 5H-ZEB	Cessna 208B Caravan I	208B0994	ex N785PA	♦
☐ 5H-CCT	Cessna TU206G Stationair 6	U20604597	ex ZS-MXV	
☐ 5H-FAB	Pilatus PC-12/45	202	ex C-PSRK	
☐ 5H-GUN	Cessna U206G Stationair 6	U20605223	ex 5H-TGT	
☐ 5H-MAG	Pilatus PC-12/45	857	ex 5H-SUZ	
☐ 5H-TOY	Cessna 404 Titan II	404-0668	ex 5Y-MCK	
☐ 5H-XII	Pilatus PC-12/45	121	ex HB-FOT	

EVERETT AVIATION — Dar-es-Salaam (DAR)

☐ 5H-EXT	AgustaWestland AW139	41344	ex N435SH	♦
☐ 5H-EXU	AgustaWestland AW139	41346	ex N438SH	♦
☐ 5H-EXV	AgustaWestland AW139	41350	ex N449SH	♦

FASTJET — Grey Bird (FTZ) — Dar-es-Salaam (DAR)

☐ 5H-FJA	Airbus A319-111	2176	ex G-EZEF	[DUB]
☐ 5H-FJC	Airbus A319-112	1145	ex F-GYJM	
☐ 5H-FJD	Airbus A319-131	2268	ex ZS-SFD	♦
☐ 5H-YAH	Canadair CRJ-100ER	7011	ex C-GKTX	

FLIGHTLINK AIR CHARTERS — Dar-es-Salaam (DAR)

☐ 5H-ETG	Cessna 560 Citation V	560-0070	ex N570VP	
☐ 5H-FHM	Embraer EMB120RT Brasilia	120196	ex ZS-PSB	♦
☐ 5H-FLF	Cessna 208 Caravan I	20800021	ex 5Y-HAA	
☐ 5H-FLI	Cessna T206H Stationair	T20608988	ex N9040U	
☐ 5H-FLL	Cessna 208 Caravan I	20800004	ex 5Y-MAK	>FDR
☐ 5H-FLS	Cessna 208B Caravan I	208B2302	ex N90151	

FLY SAFARI AIR LINK — Dar-es-Salaam (DAR)

☐ 5H-EWA	Cessna 208 Caravan I	20800109	ex 5H-TFC	
☐ 5H-FOX	Cessna 208B Caravan I	208B0074	ex 5Y-BTM	
☐ 5H-LOL	Cessna 208B Caravan I	208B5085	ex N8154D	
☐ 5H-LUX	Cessna 510 Citation Mustang	510-0342	ex N578CT	♦
☐ 5H-SAL	Cessna 206H Stationair	20608056	ex 5Y-PKS	

KILWA AIR

☐ 5H-KLA	Britten-Norman BN-2B-21 Islander	2002	ex 5X-MHB	
☐ 5H-MLB	Cessna T210N Centurion II	21064259	ex ZS-LVC	

LAKE VICTORIA FLYING SAFARIS — Arusha (ARK)

☐ 5H-DKG	Piper PA-32 Cherokee Six	32-40472	ex 5H-MTI	

NOMAD AVIATION/SOLENTA AVIATION

☐ 5H-EGG	Cessna 208B Caravan I	208B0476	ex 5Y-EGG	
☐ 5H-FED	Cessna 208B Caravan I	208B0437	ex ZS-FED	
☐ 5H-OJF	Cessna 208B Caravan I	208B0481	ex ZS-OJF	
☐ 5H-TIN	Cessna 208B Caravan I	208B0261	ex ZS-TIN	

NORTHERN AIR — Arusha (ARK)

☐ 5H-DEB	Cessna 208BEX Caravan I	208B5014	ex N8134H	<Adventure Svces
☐ 5H-SJF	Cessna 208B Caravan I	208B0950	ex N1130T	
☐ 5H-SUZ	Cessna 208B Caravan I	208B1247	ex 5H-TOM	

PELICAN AVIATION & TOURS — Dar-es-Salaam (DAR)

☐ 5H-AMH	Cessna 208BEX Caravan I	208B5108	ex N81608	♦

PRECISION AIR — Precisionair (PW/PRF) — Arusha (ARK)

☐ 5H-PAG	ATR 42-300	384	ex F-WQJO	
☐ 5H-PWH	ATR 42-600	1001	ex F-WWLK	Tanga
☐ 5H-PWE	ATR 42-500	815	ex F-WWLZ	Kigoma
☐ 5H-PWF	ATR 42-500	819	ex F-WWLA	Bukoba
☐ 5H-PWI	ATR 42-600	1003	ex F-WWLM	Mji wa iringa
☐ 5H-PWA	ATR 72-212A	780	ex F-WWES	
☐ 5H-PWB	ATR 72-212A	834	ex F-WWEB	
☐ 5H-PWC	ATR 72-212A	866	ex F-WWEP	
☐ 5H-PWD	ATR 72-212A	880	ex F-WWEI	
☐ 5H-PWG	ATR 72-212A	923	ex F-WWEW	Kilimanjaro
☐ 5H-PAY	Reims Cessna 406 Caravan II	F406-0035	ex ZS-OGY	

REGIONAL AIR SERVICES — Regional Services (8N/REG) — Arusha (ARK)

☐ 5H-BYO	Cessna 208B Caravan I	208B0443	ex 5Y-BYO
☐ 5H-MUA	Cessna 208B Caravan I	208B0487	ex 5Y-BLM
☐ 5H-NHB	Cessna 208B Caravan I	208B0328	ex 5Y-NHB
☐ 5H-RES	Cessna 208B Caravan I	208B1020	ex N110WY
☐ 5H-RIO	Cessna 208B Caravan I	208B2381	ex N381BB
☐ A6-MAR	de Havilland DHC-6 Twin Otter 300	841	ex N9045S
☐ 5H-KEG	de Havilland DHC-6 Twin Otter 310	799	ex 5Y-KEG

SAFARI EXPRESS AIRWAYS

☐ 5H-ABG	de Havilland DHC-8-315Q	574	ex C-FBLY
☐ 5H-SGH	Beech 1900D	UE-263	ex ZS-SGH
☐ 5H-SPB	Beech 1900D	UE-300	ex EC-IJO
☐ 5H-SPC	Beech 1900D	UE-319	ex ZS-SHA

SEAPLANES AFRICA — Zanzibar (ZNZ)

☐ 5H-QIK	Cessna U206B Stationair	U206-0705	ex N79MT	FP

SHINE AIR

☐ 5H-MIK	Cessna 208B Caravan I	208B1026	ex 5H-FEE	◆

SKY AVIATION TANZANIA — Dar-es-Salaam (DAR)

☐ 5H-MUK	British Aerospace 146 Srs.300	E3118	ex 5H-FTZ	◆
☐ 5H-NAC	Cessna 208B Caravan I	208B0757	ex N1307D	
☐ 5H-SKT	Piper PA-31-350 Chieftain	31-8152058	ex A2-AHP	
☐ 5H-SKX	Cessna 402B	402B-0829	ex 5Y-EAL	
☐ 5H-SKY	Piper PA-32-300 Cherokee Six	32-770061	ex N3258Q	

TANZANAIR - TANZANIAN AIR SERVICES — Dar-es-Salaam (DAR)

☐ 5H-DJS	Beech B300 King Air	FL-830	ex N830HB
☐ 5H-GHL	Cessna U206F Stationair II	U20602583	ex 5H-JBJ
☐ 5H-LDS	Cessna 310I	310I0029	ex 5Y-AJN
☐ 5H-TZE	Reims Cessna F406 Caravan II	F406-0046	ex OY-PED
☐ 5H-TZT	Cessna 208B Caravan I	208B0664	ex ZS-PSR
☐ 5H-TZU	Cessna 208B Caravan I	208B0639	ex ZS-PJJ
☐ 5H-TZX	Beech B200 Super King Air	BB-1196	ex Z-ZLT

TROPICAL AIR (ZANZIBAR) — Zanzibar (ZNZ)

☐ 5N-ALO	Cessna 208B Caravan I	208B0668	ex ZS-OFK	
☐ 5H-AMI	ATR 42-300	151	ex LZ-ATR	
☐ 5H-ATR	ATR 42-320	308	ex 5H-PAA	
☐ 5H-CRY	LET L-410UVP-E20	982631	ex 5H-ZAA	
☐ 5H-MXN	Aérospatiale AS350B2 Ecureuil	9074	ex ZS-RYY	◆
☐ 5H-NOW	Cessna 208B Caravan I	208B2209	ex N6026F	op in Gabon
☐ 5H-TAR	Piper PA-34-200T Seneca II	34-7970038	ex 5H-MNF	
☐ 5H-TZO	Partenavia P.68B	149	ex 5H-AZY	
☐ 5H-YES	Cessna 208B Caravan I	208B2092	ex N22562	op in Gabon

ZANAIR — Zanair (B4/TAN) — Zanzibar (ZNZ)

☐ 5H-ARD	Cessna 207A Stationair 8	20700700	ex ZS-OFX	◆
☐ 5H-CAR	Cessna 208B Caravan I	208B2035	ex N2327X	
☐ 5H-CAT	Cessna 208B Caravan I	208B2199	ex N1009U	
☐ 5H-LAU	Cessna 404 Titan II	404-0675	ex 5Y-SAB	◆
☐ 5H-LET	LET L-410UVP-E9	892226	ex 9L-LBK	
☐ 5H-WAI	Cessna F406 Caravan II	F406-0016	ex D2-ECP	
☐ 5H-ZAP	LET L-410UVPE-E9	871824	ex 9L-LBV	dam 29Jan14

☐ 5H-ZAR	Cessna 404 Titan II	404-0835	ex 5H-AEL	
☐ 5H-ZAY	Cessna 404 Titan II	404-0207	ex N798A	
☐ 5H-ZAZ	Cessna 402C	402C0029	ex 5Y-NNM	

ZANTAS AIR SERVICE   Dar-es-Salaam (DAR)

☐ 5H-FZA	Cessna 208BEX Caravan I	208B5012	ex N8133T	♦
☐ 5H-NBL	Cessna 208B Caravan I	208B1293	ex N4115R	
☐ 5H-NWA	Cessna 208B Caravan I	208B0891	ex 5H-TAK	
☐ 5H-TAQ	Cessna 208BEX Caravan I	208B5029	ex N8144D	
☐ 5H-TAZ	Cessna 208B Caravan I	208B1186	ex N12998	

5N-   NIGERIA (Federal Republic of Nigeria)

AERO CONTRACTORS   Aeroline (NG/NIG)   Lagos (LOS)

☐ 5N-AQK	Aérospatiale SA365N Dauphin 2	6108		opf NNPC
☐ 5N-AQL	Aérospatiale SA365N Dauphin 2	6109		opf NNPC
☐ 5N-BAF	Aérospatiale SA365N2 Dauphin 2	6430	ex F-WYMC	opf NNPC
☐ 5N-BDA	Aérospatiale SA365N Dauphin 2	6077	ex 8P-PHM	
☐ 5N-BET	Aérospatiale SA365N Dauphin 2	6087	ex TJ-DEM	
☐ 5N-BIX	Aérospatiale AS365N3 Dauphin 2	6657	ex PH-SHI	
☐ 5N-ESO	Aérospatiale SA365N Dauphin 2	6072	ex PH-SSP	
☐ 5N-STO	Aérospatiale SA365N Dauphin 2	6106	ex PH-SSV	
☐ 5N-BIZ	Boeing 737-4B7	24558/1845	ex N436US	
☐ 5N-BJA	Boeing 737-4B7	24873/1931	ex N446US	
☐ 5N-BOB	Boeing 737-42C	24232/2060	ex EI-CWE	
☐ 5N-BOC	Boeing 737-42C	24814/2270	ex EI-CWF	
☐ 5N-BOT	Boeing 737-4U3	25713/2531	ex PK-GWK	o/o
☐ 5N-BPQ	Boeing 737-4M0	29201/3018	ex N605SC	
☐ 5N-BPR	Boeing 737-4M0	29202/3025	ex N608SC	
☐ 5N-BQL	Boeing 737-4M0	29203/3049	ex N643CS	
☐ 5N-BKQ	Boeing 737-522	26695/2423	ex VP-BSW	
☐ 5N-BKR	Boeing 737-522	26699/2485	ex VP-BSX	
☐ 5N-BLC	Boeing 737-522	26692/2421	ex VP-BSV	
☐ 5N-BLD	Boeing 737-522	26675/2345	ex VP-BSU	
☐ 5N-BLE	Boeing 737-522	26672/2343	ex VP-BSQ	
☐ 5N-BLG	Boeing 737-522	25387/2179	ex VP-BTI	
☐ 5N-AOA	Aérospatiale AS355F Ecureuil 2	5277	ex F-WZFB	opf NNPC
☐ 5N-AOB	Aérospatiale AS355F Ecureuil 2	5278	ex F-WZFV	opf NNPC
☐ 5N-BKG	Eurocopter EC225LP	2681		
☐ 5N-BKH	Eurocopter EC225LP	2727		
☐ 5N-BJO	de Havilland DHC-8Q-311	534	ex C-FLGJ	
☐ 5N-BPT	de Havilland DHC-8-402Q	4078	ex G-JEDN	
☐ 5N-BPU	de Havilland DHC-8-402Q	4079	ex G-JEDO	
☐ 5N-RSN	AgustaWestland AW139	31060	ex 5N-BJB	opf River States Govt

AIR PEACE   (APK)   Lagos (LOS)

☐ 5N-BQQ	Boeing 737-524/W	27533/2725	ex N14629		♦
☐ 5N-BQR	Boeing 737-528/W	25235/2428	ex N254SC		♦
☐ 5N-BQS	Boeing 737-524/W	27530/2686	ex N32626		♦
☐ 5N-BQT	Dornier 328-310 (328JET)	3221	ex VP-CJD		VIP
☐ 5N-BQU	Dornier 328-310 (328JET)	3171	ex N328DA	Helen	wfs♦
☐ 5N-BQV	Dornier 328-310 (328JET)	3200	ex D-BDBJ	Ojochide	wfs
☐ 5N-BRN	Boeing 737-528/W	25234/2411	ex N261SC	Ugochukwu	♦

AIR TARABA

☐ 5N-BOZ	Embraer ERJ-145EU	145617	ex M-ABFA	
☐ 5N-	Embraer ERJ-145LR	145488	ex N292SK	

ALLIED AIR CARGO   Bambi (4W/AJK)   Lagos (LOS)

☐ 5N-JRT	Boeing 737-4Y0SF	26081/2442	ex N291CS	[VQQ]♦
☐ 5N-OTT	Boeing 737-406SF	24529/1770	ex N737WF	
☐ 5N-RKT	Boeing 737-4Q8SF	26300/2604	ex N263VT	wfs

ARIK AIR   Arik Air (W3/ARA)   Lagos (LOS)

☐ 5N-MJC	Boeing 737-7BD/W	33932/2234	ex N320AT	Martin
☐ 5N-MJD	Boeing 737-7BD/W	36073/2248	ex N323AT	Michael
☐ 5N-MJE	Boeing 737-7GL/W	34761/2401	ex N737AV	McTighe
☐ 5N-MJF	Boeing 737-7GL/W	34762/2427	ex N737BV	Queen of Angles
☐ 5N-MJG	Boeing 737-7BD/W	33944/2576	ex N346AT	Claudiana
☐ 5N-MJH	Boeing 737-7BD/W	36719/2589	ex N347AT	Margaret
☐ 5N-MJI	Boeing 737-76N/W	28640/799	ex N740AL	City of Freetown

☐ 5N-MJJ	Boeing 737-76N/W	28641/809	ex N741AL	City of Benin	
☐ 5N-MJK	Boeing 737-76N/W	30830/855	ex N742AL	Ville de Niamey	
☐ 5N-JEA	Canadair CRJ-900ER	15058	ex C-FHRH	Anthony	
☐ 5N-JEB	Canadair CRJ-900ER	15059	ex C-FHRK	Patrick	
☐ 5N-JEC	Canadair CRJ-900ER	15054	ex C-FGNB	John Paul II	
☐ 5N-JED	Canadair CRJ-900ER	15114	ex C-FMEP	Abraham	
☐ 5N-JEE	Canadair CRJ-1000	19037	ex C-GZQW		
☐ CS-TFW	Airbus A340-542	910	ex F-WJKH	Our Lady of Perpetual Help	>HFY
☐ CS-TFX	Airbus A340-542	912	ex F-WJKI	Captin Bob Hayes, OON	>HFY
☐ 5N-BKU	de Havilland DHC-8-402Q	4207	ex C-FPPU	Christopher	
☐ 5N-BKV	de Havilland DHC-8-402Q	4219	ex C-FSRN	Cyprian	
☐ 5N-BKW	de Havilland DHC-8-402Q	4465	ex C-GXRE	Nicholas	♦
☐ 5N-BKX	de Havilland DHC-8-402Q	4470	ex C-GYPY	Stephen	♦
☐ 5N-JIC	Airbus A330-223	891	ex EI-EWH	Joseph of the Holy Family	
☐ 5N-JID	Airbus A330-223	927	ex EI-EWG	Our Lady of Grace	
☐ 5N-JMA	Hawker 800XP	258658	ex N658XP		
☐ 5N-JMB	Hawker 800XP	258659	ex N659XP		
☐ 5N-MJA	Boeing 737-322	24360/1692	ex N354UA	Abubakar	[NWI]
☐ 5N-MJB	Boeing 737-322	24454/1750	ex N361UA	Ibrahim	[SEN]
☐ 5N-MJN	Boeing 737-86N/W	35638/2789	ex N1796B		
☐ 5N-MJO	Boeing 737-86N/W	35640/2819	ex N358MT	Augustine	
☐ 5N-MJP	Boeing 737-8JE/W	38970/3030	ex N1787B	Sultan of Sokoto	
☐ 5N-MJQ	Boeing 737-8JE/W	38971/3065		City of Calabar	
☐ 5N-	ATR 72-600	4465	ex C-GXRE		♦

ASSOCIATED AVIATION — Associated (SCD) — Lagos (LOS)

☐ 5N-BHV	Boeing 727-227F (FedEx 3)	21364/1261	ex N86426		[LOS]
☐ 5N-BIT	Embraer EMB.120RT Brasilia	120050	ex N190SW		
☐ 5N-BJM	Embraer ERJ-145LR	1450984	ex PT-SKE		
☐ 5N-BJX	Boeing 727-225F	20627/947	ex N361KP		wfs
☐ 5N-BNQ	Boeing 727-2B7F	22162/1717	ex N762AT		

ATLANTIC AVIATION

☐ 5N-BOK	Sikorsky S-76C+	760466	ex C-GLAY		♦
☐ 5N-BOL	Sikorsky S-76C+	760575	ex C-GHRE		♦

AZMAN AIR — (AZM) — Kano (KAN)

☐ 5N-YSM	Boeing 737-36N	28557/2862	ex G-TOYF	Alhaji Yunusa Sarina	
☐ 5N-HAI	Boeing 737-36N	28570/3010	ex G-TOYH	Hajiya Aisha Yunusa	

BRISTOW HELICOPTERS (NIGERIA) — Bristow Helicopters (BHN)
Lagos/Calabar/Eket/Port Harcourt/Warri (LOS/CBQ/-/PHC/-)

☐ 5N-BFE	Bell 206L-4 LongRanger IV	52272	ex N20796		
☐ 5N-BFF	Bell 206L-4 LongRanger IV	52273	ex N2080C		
☐ 5N-BFG	Bell 206L-4 LongRanger IV	52274	ex N2080W		
☐ 5N-BFH	Bell 206L-4 LongRanger IV	52275	ex N2081K		
☐ 5N-BFV	Bell 206L-4 LongRanger IV	52160	ex 5N-ESC		
☐ 5N-BHH	Bell 206L-4 LongRanger IV	52291	ex N274AL		
☐ 5N-BCZ	Bell 412SP	33179	ex B-55521		
☐ 5N-BDY	Bell 412EP	36267	ex N506AL		
☐ 5N-BDZ	Bell 412EP	36278	ex 9Y-ALI		
☐ 5N-BFU	Bell 412EP	36318	ex N7022F		
☐ 5N-BGS	Bell 412EP	33186	ex N464AC		
☐ 5N-BHB	Bell 412EP	36273	ex XA-TTF		
☐ 5N-BHD	Bell 412EP	36354	ex N4202A		
☐ 5N-BIM	Bell 412EP	36373	ex N31195		
☐ 5N-BIO	Bell 412EP	36378	ex N106AL		
☐ 5N-BIP	Bell 412EP	36383	ex N105AL		
☐ 5N-BIQ	Bell 412EP	36385	ex N115AL		
☐ 5N-BIR	Bell 412EP	36386	ex N107AL		
☐ 5N-BIS	Bell 412EP	36387	ex N132AL		
☐ 5N-BML	Bell 412EP	36433	ex G-OIBU		
☐ 5N-BDH	Eurocopter EC155B	6591	ex F-WQDQ		opf Shell Nigeria
☐ 5N-BDI	Eurocopter EC155B	6602			opf Shell Nigeria
☐ 5N-BDJ	Eurocopter EC155B	6607			opf Shell Nigeria
☐ 5N-BDK	Eurocopter EC155B	6608			opf Shell Nigeria
☐ 5N-BDL	Eurocopter EC155B	6610	ex F-WQDA		opf Shell Nigeria
☐ 5N-BDM	Eurocopter EC155B	6611	ex F-WQDH		opf Shell Nigeria
☐ 5N-BGC	Sikorsky S-76C+	760481	ex LN-ONY		
☐ 5N-BGD	Sikorsky S-76C+	760540	ex N864AL		
☐ 5N-BGE	Sikorsky S-76C+	760545	ex N20509		
☐ 5N-BIL	Sikorsky S-76C+	760591	ex N869AL		

☐ 5N-BJT	Sikorsky S-76C+	760638	ex N872AL		
☐ 5N-BJU	Sikorsky S-76C+	760640	ex N876AL		
☐ 5N-BKM	Sikorsky S-76C+	760660	ex N45083		
☐ 5N-BMD	Sikorsky S-76C+	760456	ex LN-ONZ		
☐ 5N-BMI	Sikorsky S-76C+	760732	ex G-CFPU		
☐ 5N-BMX	Sikorsky S-76C+	760754	ex G-CFRD		
☐ 5N-BNZ	Sikorsky S-76C++	760802	ex G-CGUJ		
☐ 5N-BQJ	Sikorsky S-76C+	760656	ex G-CGRU		
☐ 5N-BRJ	Sikorsky S-76C++	760778	ex G-CGOP		
☐ 5N-BRS	Sikorsky S-76C	760669	ex G-CEYZ		
☐ 5N-BSC	Sikorsky S-76C	760664	ex 9M-SPW		♦
☐ 5N-	Sikorsky S-76C	760618	ex N877AL		♦
☐ 5N-	Sikorsky S-76C	760639	ex N493KC		♦
☐ 5N-	Sikorsky S-76C+	760652	ex N879AL		
☐ 5N-BEM	Bell 407	53246	ex N567AL		
☐ 5N-BEO	Bell 407	53190	ex N467AL		
☐ 5N-BEP	Bell 407	53107	ex N427AL		
☐ 5N-BES	Bell 206B	3216	ex N139H		♦
☐ 5N-BFI	Bell 407	53550	ex N2531G		
☐ 5N-BES	Bell 206B JetRanger III	3216	ex N139H		
☐ 5N-BIW	Cessna 208 Caravan I	20800403	ex N1316N		FP
☐ 5N-BJE	Aérospatiale AS365N2 Dauphin 2	6446	ex EP-HCK		
☐ 5N-BJS	Cessna 560 Citation XLS	560-5703	ex N560MP		
☐ 5N-BKJ	Aérospatiale AS332L	2170	ex G-PUMI		
☐ 5N-BLX	Sikorsky S-92A	920082	ex G-CFCA		
☐ 5N-BMN	Sikorsky S-92A	920103	ex G-CGCI		
☐ 5N-BOA	Sikorsky S-92A	920075	ex N92TZ		c/n unconfirmed♦
☐ 5N-BPC	Sikorsky S-92A	920212	ex G-CICJ		

CAVERTON HELICOPTERS (CJR) Lagos (LOS)

☐ 5N-BOI	AgustaWestland AW139	31380			
☐ 5N-BOJ	AgustaWestland AW139	31385			
☐ 5N-BOX	AgustaWestland AW139	31386	ex I-EASH		
☐ 5N-CHX	AgustaWestland AW139	31394			
☐ 5N-CML	AgustaWestland AW139	31389	ex I-RAIL		
☐ 5N-CNL	AgustaWestland AW139	31388			
☐ 5N-BHK	Aérospatiale SA365N Dauphin 2	6128	ex CS-HFH		<HeliPortugal
☐ 5N-BHS	Aérospatiale AS350B2 Ecureuil	1871	ex CS-HDK		<HeliPortugal
☐ 5N-BHT	Aérospatiale AS350B2 Ecureuil	1222	ex CS-HEO		<HeliPortugal
☐ 5N-BIK	Aérospatiale AS365N Dauphin 2	6138	ex F-GNVS		<HeliPortugal
☐ 5N-BJV	de Havilland DHC-6 Twin Otter 300	816	ex HB-LUB		
☐ 5N-BNV	Sikorsky S-76C++	760752	ex F-HELB		
☐ 5N-BNW	Sikorsky S-76C2	760788	ex F-GTNB		
☐ 5N-BNX	Sikorsky S-76C2	760786	ex F-GZAT		
☐ 5N-LAG	Bell 412EP	36495	ex N362MH		
☐ 5N-LSG	Bell 412EP	36495	ex N362KB		
☐ 5N-SHE	de Havilland DHC-6 Twin Otter 400	864	ex C-GUVA		

CHANCHANGI AIRLINES (5B/NCH) Kaduna (KAD)

☐ 5N-BMB	Boeing 737-3J6	25079/2016	ex B-2536		
☐ 5N-BMC	Boeing 737-3Z0	25089/2027	ex B-2537		[BEG]
☐ 5N-IZB	Boeing 737-2X6C	23292/1113	ex ZS-IAD		♦

CHC NIGERIA

☐ 5N-BQA	AgustaWestland AW139	31458	ex C-GUFI		♦
☐ 5N-BQB	AgustaWestland AW139	31540			♦

DANA AIRLINES Dana Air (9J/DAN) Kaduna (KAD)

☐ 5N-BKI	McDonnell-Douglas MD-82	49482/1309	ex 5N-BII		♦
☐ 5N-DEV	McDonnell-Douglas MD-83	49947/1900	ex N934JM	Guru	
☐ 5N-JAI	McDonnell-Douglas MD-83	53016/1850	ex N968AS		
☐ 5N-JOY	McDonnell-Douglas MD-83	49944/1888	ex N935JM	Ananda	
☐ 5N-SAI	McDonnell-Douglas MD-83	53018/1779	ex N943AS		
☐ 5N-SRI	McDonnell-Douglas MD-83	53020/1789	ex N947AS		
☐ SU-KHM	Boeing 737-5C9	26438/2413	ex JY-JA1		<KHH
☐ 5N-AUN	Dornier 228-201	8076	ex D-CEPT		
☐ 5N-BCA	Piper PA-23 Aztec 250D	27-4220	ex G-AYZN		
☐ 5N-BRG	Beech 1900D	UE-7	ex ZS-OYA		♦
☐ 5N-BRH	Beech 1900D	UE-26	ex ZS-PJF		
☐ 5N-DOB	Dornier 228-202	8026	ex N232RP		
☐ 5N-DOL	Dornier 228-202	8145	ex N241RP		[ABV]
☐ 5N-DOW	Dornier 328-110	3070	ex D-CASI		
☐ 5N-DOX	Dornier 328-110	3073	ex OE-LKF		
☐ 5N-DOY	Dornier 328-110	3089	ex OE-LKG		

DISCOVERY AIR		(DO/DCV)			Lagos (LOS)
☐ 5N-BQO	Boeing 737-36N/W	28571/3022	ex N571TP		wfs
☐ 5N-BQP	Boeing 737-33R	28870/2899	ex G-TOYK		wfs
AOC suspended Jan15; to be reinstated					

EASY LINK		Flyme (FYE)			
☐ 5N-BCM	LET L-410UVP-E	902502	ex HI-692CT		

FIRST NATION AIRLINES		(FRN)			Lagos (LOS)
☐ 5N-FND	Airbus A319-113	0647	ex EI-DVD	Endurance	
☐ 5N-FNE	Airbus A319-113	0660	ex EI-DVU	Faith	

HAK AIR		(HKL)			Lagos (LOS)
☐ 5N-BOT	Boeing 737-4U3	25713/2531	ex PK-GWK		[CGK]
☐ 5N-BOU	Boeing 737-4U3	25715/2537	ex PK-GWM		
☐ 5N-BOV	Boeing 737-4U3	25716/2540	ex PK-GWN		[CGK]
☐ 5N-BOW	Boeing 737-4U3	25718/2548	ex PK-GWP		[CGK]

IRS AIRLINES		Silverbird (LVB)			Lagos (LOS)
☐ 5N-CEO	Fokker 100	11295	ex N860US	Hajiya Babba	
☐ 5N-HIR	Fokker 100	11498	ex G-CFBU	Khalifa	
☐ 5N-SAT	Fokker 100	11293	ex PH-MJO		wfs
☐ 5N-SIK	Fokker 100	11286	ex SE-DUU	Halima	dam 10May14
☐ 5N-SMR	Fokker 100	11291	ex PH-MJN		[LOS]
☐ 5N-NCZ	Fokker F.28 Fellowship 4000	11241	ex ZS-OPS		

JEDAIR					Lagos (LOS)
☐ 5N-BMS	Boeing 737-2R8C	21710/546	ex ZS-SMX		♦
☐ 5N-IHS	Beech 200 Super King Air	BB-663	ex 5N-AMT		

KABO AIR		Kabo (N9/QNK)			Kano (KAN)
☐ 5N-ASG	Boeing 767-332	23436/163	ex N122DL		wfs♦
☐ 5N-DKB	Boeing 747-251B	23548/644	ex N637US		
☐ 5N-JRM	Boeing 747-251B	23549/651	ex N638US		
☐ 5N-MAD	Boeing 747-251B	23547/642	ex N636US		
☐ 5N-MDK	Boeing 747-422	26878/966	ex N135KB		

MAXAIR		(NR/NGL)			Katsina (KAT)
☐ 5N-BMG	Boeing 747-346	23638/658	ex JA8177		
☐ 5N-DBM	Boeing 747-346	23968/693	ex JA8184		
☐ 5N-DDK	Boeing 747-346	23967/692	ex JA8183		
☐ 5N-HMB	Boeing 747-438	25067/857	ex VH-OJK		
☐ 5N-MBB	Boeing 747-346	24018/694	ex HS-UTS		[CGK]

MED-VIEW AIRLINES		(VL/MEV)			Kano (KAN)
☐ 5N-BPA	Boeing 737-484	25362/2142	ex N362AS		
☐ 5N-BPB	Boeing 737-484	25430/2174	ex N304AS		
☐ 5N-BQM	Boeing 737-5Q8	28055/3024	ex N361LF		
☐ 5N-MAA	Boeing 737-4D7	28703/2962	ex HS-TDH		♦
☐ 5N-MAB	Boeing 737-4D7	28704/2968	ex HS-TDJ		♦

NESTOIL					
☐ 5N-BRK	AgustaWestland AW139	41258	ex N12AR		♦
☐ 5N-BRL	AgustaWestland AW139	41259	ex N90AR		♦

OVERLAND AIRWAYS		Overland (OJ/OLA)			Lagos/Abuja (LOS/ABV)
☐ 5N-BCO	Beech 1900D	UE-225	ex N225GL		[HLA]
☐ 5N-BCP	Beech 1900D	UE-116	ex N116YV		
☐ 5N-BCR	ATR 42-320	031	ex F-WQNR		
☐ 5N-BCS	ATR 42-300	025	ex EC-IYE		
☐ 5N-BND	ATR 42-320	363	ex F-WKVD		
☐ 5N-BPE	ATR 72-202	316	ex F-WNUA		
☐ 5N-BPF	ATR 72-202	352	ex F-WNUF		
☐ 5N-BPG	ATR 72-202	365	ex F-WKVH		dam 29Nov14
☐ 5N-BRQ	ATR 42-320	351	ex F-WKVF		♦

PRIME AIR SERVICES

| ☐ M-BETY | Dornier 328-310 (328JET) | 3176 | ex UR-AER | VIP |

SKYBIRD AIR   (KYC)

☐ 5N-SPE	Dornier 328JET Envoy 3	3151	ex D-BDXT
☐ 5N-SPM	Dornier 328JET Envoy 3	3141	ex D-BDXY
☐ 5N-BMH	Dornier 328-300 (328JET)	3120	ex 5N-SPN

SKYPOWER EXPRESS AIRWAYS   Nigeria Express (EAN)   Lagos (LOS)

| ☐ 5N-AXR | Embraer EMB.110P1A Bandeirante | 110459 | ex PT-SHM |
| ☐ 5N-BMA | Boeing 737-3Q4SF | 24209/1492 | ex ZK-TLB | [AMM] |

TOPBRASS AVIATION   Brass Line (BRL)   Lagos (LOS)

☐ 5N-BIA	de Havilland DHC-8-315Q	608	ex C-FBOA
☐ 5N-TBB	de Havilland DHC-8-315Q	613	ex D2-EYL
☐ 5N-TBC	de Havilland DHC-8-315Q	614	ex D2-EYM

5R-   MADAGASCAR (Democratic Republic of Madagascar)

AEROMARINE   Antananarivo ((TNR)

☐ F-ODQI	Piper PA-31-350 Navajo Chieftain	31-7305065	ex F-BUOI
☐ 5R-MCJ	Piper PA-23-250 Aztec C	27-3644	ex N6449Y
☐ 5R-MCR	Piper PA-31 Turbo Navajo	31-162	ex N9122Y
☐ 5R-MIK	Piper PA-23-250 Aztec B	27-2191	ex TL-ABA
☐ 5R-MKG	Beech 99	U-21	ex F-GFPE
☐ 5R-MLI	Cessna 207A Stationair 7 II	20700496	ex 5R-MVR
☐ 5R-MLJ	Cessna 310R II	310R1372	ex F-GBGB
☐ 5R-MLK	Beech 95-C55 Baron	TE-101	ex F-BOJG
☐ 5R-MLT	Cessna 310R II	310R0328	ex F-BXLT

AIR MADAGASCAR   Air Madagascar (MD/MDG)   Antananarivo (TNR)

☐ TF-EAB	Airbus A340-313X	210	ex F-GLZL	opb ABD
☐ 5R-EAA	Airbus A340-313X	319	ex F-GLZT
☐ 5R-EJA	ATR 72-600	1239	ex F-WWEN	♦
☐ 5R-MFH	Boeing 737-3Q8	26305/2651
☐ 5R-MGC	de Havilland DHC-6 Twin Otter 300	328
☐ 5R-MGD	de Havilland DHC-6 Twin Otter 300	329
☐ 5R-MGF	de Havilland DHC-6 Twin Otter 300	482
☐ 5R-MJE	ATR 72-212A	694	ex F-WWEQ
☐ 5R-MJF	ATR 72-212A	698	ex F-WWEU
☐ 5R-MJG	ATR 42-500	649	ex F-WWLG
☐ 5R-MVT	ATR 42-320	044	ex F-WQAD
☐ 5R-MLA	Piper PA-31-350 Chieftain	31-7952076
☐ 5R-	ATR 72-600	1248	ex F-WWEX	o/o♦

MADAGASCAR TRANS AIR   Ivato

| ☐ 5R-MKK | Piper PA-34-200T Seneca | 34-7970480 | ex ZS-KIG |

MALAGASY AIRLINES   (MLG)   Antananarivo (TNR)

☐ 5R-MDB	Cessna 402B	402B0572	ex ZS-RES
☐ 5R-MHJ	Piper PA-23-250 Aztec	27-409	ex 5R-MVJ
☐ 5R-MKS	Cessna 402B	402B0014	ex 5R-MVC
☐ 5R-MLZ	Cessna TU206G Stationair 6	U20604526	ex F-BVQK

TIKO AIR   Antananarivo (TNR)

| ☐ 5R-MJT | ATR 42-320 | 221 | ex (5R-TIK) |

5T-   MAURITANIA (Islamic Republic of Mauritania)

MAURITANIA AIRLINES INTERNATIONAL   (L6/MAI)   Nouakchott (NKC)

☐ 5T-CLA	Boeing 737-55S	28469/2849	ex OK-CGH
☐ 5T-CLB	Boeing 737-55S	28470/2861	ex OK-CGJ
☐ 5T-CLC	Boeing 737-7EE/W	34263/1739	ex N426HZ
☐ 5T-CLD	Embraer ERJ-145LR	14500852	ex N852EC	♦

5U- NIGER (Republic of Niger)

NIGER AIRLINES (6N/NIN) Niamey (NIM)

☐ SU-YAH	Fokker 50	20123	ex PH-FZJ	<PNW♦
☐ SU-YAI	Fokker 50	20143	ex PH-FZI	<PNW♦

5V- TOGO (Togolese Republic)

ASKY (KP/SKK) Lome (LFW)

☐ ET-ANW	de Havilland DHC-8-402Q	4320	ex C-GEUN	<ETH
☐ ET-ANX	de Havilland DHC-8-402Q	4330	ex C-GSNH	<ETH
☐ ET-AQD	de Havilland DHC-8-402Q	4427	ex C-GRTN	<ETH
☐ ET-AQE	de Havilland DHC-8-402Q	4428	ex C-GRUC	<ETH
☐ ET-AQF	de Havilland DHC-8-402Q	4429	ex C-GSMU	<ETH
☐ ET-ANG	Boeing 737-7K9/W	34401/2216	ex OY-MRP	<ETH
☐ ET-ANH	Boeing 737-7K9/W	34402/2270	ex OY-MRR	<ETH
☐ ET-AOK	Boeing 737-790/W	33012/1306	ex M-ABDH	<ETH

5W- SAMOA (Independent State of Western Samoa)

POLYNESIAN AIRLINES Polynesian (PH/PAO) Apia (APW)

☐ 5W-FAW	de Havilland DHC-6 Twin Otter 300	827	ex C-FTLQ	Gogo
☐ 5W-FAY	de Havilland DHC-6 Twin Otter 300	690	ex VH-UQW	Gillian

SAMOA AIR Apia (APW)

☐ 5W-CSJ	Britten-Norman BN-2A-9 Islander	833	ex DQ-FCX

5X- UGANDA (Republic of Uganda)

EAGLE AIR UGANDA African Eagle (H7/EGU) Entebbe (EBB)

☐ 5X-EBZ	Beech 1900C-1	UC-174	ex ZS-PIT
☐ 5X-EIV	LET L-410UVP-E9	962632	ex 5Y-BPX
☐ 5X-GNF	LET L-410UVP-E8	892320	ex OK-UDA

KAMPALA EXECUTIVE AVIATION Kampala

☐ 5X-KED	Pilatus PC-12/47	872	ex D-FSYB	♦

UGANDA AIR CARGO Uganda Cargo (UCC) Entebbe (EBB)

☐ 5X-UCF	Lockheed L-382G Hercules	4610	ex (PH-AID)
☐ 5X-UYX	Harbin Y-12-IV	026	ex Uganda AF
☐ 5X-UYZ	Harbin Y-12-IV	021	ex Uganda AF
☐ 5X-UXZ	Harbin Y-12-IV	027	ex Uganda AF
☐ 5X-	Lockheed L-382G Hercules	4388	ex ZS-ORC

5Y- KENYA

ABERDAIR AVIATION Aberdav (BDV) Nairobi-Wilson (WIL)

☐ 5Y-BTL	Rockwell 690A Turbo Commander	11103	ex N690CE	
☐ 5Y-FEW	Aérospatiale AS350B3 Ecureuil	7360	ex F-HMRR	♦
☐ 5Y-FWG	Embraer EMB.120RT Brasilia	120261	ex ZS-PVF	
☐ 5Y-FWH	Cessna 208 Caravan I	20800158	ex ET-A	♦
☐ 5Y-MNJ	Aérospatiale AS350B3e Ecureuil	7392	ex F-	♦
☐ 5Y-NKW	Aérospatiale AS350B3 Ecureuil	7194	ex F-GOLK	♦
☐ 5Y-SOP	Cessna 208B Caravan I	208B2367	ex N20166	♦
☐ 9G-FWC	Embraer EMB.110P1 Bandeirante	110381	ex S9-DAI	♦

AFRICAN EXPRESS AIRWAYS Express Jet (XU/AXK) Nairobi-Jomo Kenyatta Intl (NBO)

☐ 5Y-AXD	Douglas DC-9-32	47088/180	ex 9L-LDF	[NBO]
☐ 5Y-AXF	Douglas DC-9-32	47093/237	ex 9L-LDG	
☐ 5Y-AXJ	Embraer EMB.120ER Brasilia	120078	ex 5X-TEZ	
☐ 5Y-AXL	McDonnell-Douglas MD-82	49204/1179	ex I-DAWL	
☐ 5Y-AXN	McDonnell-Douglas MD-82	49207/1189	ex N461LF	

AIRKENYA EXPRESS (P2/XAK) Nairobi-Wilson (WIL)

☐ 5Y-BGH	de Havilland DHC-6 Twin Otter 300	574	ex N4226J	
☐ 5Y-BIO	de Havilland DHC-6 Twin Otter 300	579	ex 5H-MRB	
☐ 5H-BMP	de Havilland DHC-7-102	080	ex 5Y-BMP	
☐ 5Y-BRU	LET L-410UVP-E9	912539	ex 5X-UAY	>TLR
☐ 5Y-BTZ	de Havilland DHC-8-102	203	ex VH-TNU	
☐ 5Y-BXW	Cessna 208B Caravan I	208B2189	ex N1008P	
☐ 5Y-BZJ	Cessna 208B Caravan I	208B2310	ex N60200	
☐ 5Y-CCV	Cessna 208BEX Caravan I	208B5031	ex N81450	♦
☐ 5Y-CDK	de Havilland DHC-7-110	054	ex PK-PKT	♦
☐ 5Y-HNB	Aérospatiale AS350B Ecureuil	4108	ex TG-GAD	
☐ 5Y-PJH	de Havilland DHC-6 Twin Otter 300			
☐ 5Y-PJP	de Havilland DHC-6 Twin Otter 300	424	ex ZS-LGN	

AIRTRAFFIC Aircare (ATY) Nairobi-Wilson (WIL)

☐ 5Y-BUX	Dornier 228-201	8080	ex SX-BHI	
☐ 5Y-BYC	Dornier 228-202	8058	ex D-IMIK	
☐ 5Y-CBJ	Dornier 228-201	8066	ex D-IKBA	
☐ 5Y-CCD	Dornier 228-201	8002	ex D-ILWS	♦
☐ 5Y-CBV	Dornier 228-201	8035	ex D-ILWB	♦
☐ 5Y-BTF	Beech 1900C-1	UC-132	ex OY-GEG	
☐ 5Y-BZH	Beech 1900D	UE-294	ex N187RL	
☐ 5Y-CEI	Embraer EMB.120ER Brasilia	120121	ex N331CR	♦

AIRWORKS KENYA (SAVANNAH AIR SERVICES/FEDERAL AIR) Nairobi-Wilson (WIL)

☐ 5Y-NFY	Cessna 208B Caravan I	208B0294	ex ZS-NFY	
☐ 5Y-NKV	Cessna 208B Caravan I	208B0387	ex ZS-NKV	
☐ 5Y-NLM	Cessna 208B Caravan I	208B0375	ex ZS-NLM	opf UN
☐ 5Y-NUU	Cessna 208B Caravan I	208B0567	ex ZS-NUU	♦
☐ 5Y-NXZ	Cessna 208B Caravan I	208B0357	ex ZS-NXZ	
☐ 5Y-ODS	Cessna 208B Caravan I	208B0538	ex ZS-ODS	
☐ 5Y-SAV	Cessna 208B Caravan I	208B0312	ex N208PA	
☐ 5Y-NPT	Beech 1900C	UC-113	ex ZS-NPT	♦
☐ 5Y-ODG	Beech 1900C	UC-158	ex ZS-ODG	♦

ALS/COMPION AVIATION (K4/ALW) Nairobi-Wilson (WIL)

☐ 5Y-BVP	Beech 1900D	UE-136	ex ZS-PHM	opf ICRC
☐ 5Y-BVT	Beech 1900D	UE-226	ex 5H-SXY	
☐ 5Y-BVV	Beech 1900C	UB-29	ex ZS-OUC	
☐ 5Y-BVX	Beech 1900D	UE-101	ex ZS-PJG	
☐ 5Y-DHL	Beech 1900C-1	UC-100	ex N15305	opf ICRC
☐ 5Y-LKG	Beech 1900C	UB-63	ex C-FUCB	opf Kenya Airlink
☐ 5Y-SGL	Beech 1900C-1	UC-114	ex V5-SGL	opf UN Humanitarian Service
☐ 5Y-BVO	de Havilland DHC-8-102	007	ex C-GFQI	
☐ 5Y-BXH	de Havilland DHC-8-102	205	ex C-FLAD	
☐ 5Y-BXI	de Havilland DHC-8-102	376	ex C-GRGQ	
☐ 5Y-BXU	de Havilland DHC-8-106	344	ex C-GFKC	
☐ 5Y-BZI	de Havilland DHC-8-102	105	ex 9Q-CWP	>Southern Star
☐ 5Y-CAU	de Havilland DHC-8-102	010	ex 5H-KMC	
☐ 5Y-PRV	de Havilland DHC-8-102	185	ex C-FGQI	
☐ 5Y-STN	de Havilland DHC-8-102	179	ex C-FCON	
☐ 5Y-BLA	Beech 200C Super King Air	BL-10	ex C-FAMB	
☐ 5Y-BVY	Embraer ERJ-135LR	145599	ex N843RP	
☐ 5Y-BVZ	Embraer ERJ-135LR	145661	ex N842RP	
☐ 5Y-CAV	Embraer ERJ-135MP	145385	ex N538CL	opf UN
☐ 5Y-CBX	Beech B300 King Air	FA-39		♦

ASTRAL AVIATION Astral Cargo (8V/ACP) Nairobi-Jomo Kenyatta Intl (NBO)

☐ N408MC	Boeing 747-47UF	29261/1192	ex (N495MC)	<GTI
☐ 5Y-GMA	Boeing 727-22Q9F	21930/1508	ex N740DH	♦
☐ 5Y-JUU	Fokker F-27 Friendship 500	10448	ex A6-FCZ	
☐ 5Y-SAN	Douglas DC-9-34CF	47706/821	ex S9-PSR	
☐ 5Y-UAE	Douglas DC-9-34CF	47707/823	ex 9L-LFK	

AVRO EXPRESS Nairobi-Wilson (WIL)

☐ 5Y-BXT	Hawker Siddeley HS.748-2B/266	1701	ex 3X-GEW	Frtr
☐ 5Y-CBI	Hawker Siddeley HS.748-2B/378	1784	ex ZS-TPW	Frtr
☐ 5Y-	Hawker Siddeley HS.748-2A/270	1687	ex N687AP	Frtr♦
☐ 5Y-	Hawker Siddeley HS.748-2A/242	1689	ex N748D	Frtr♦
☐ 5Y-	Hawker Siddeley HS.748-2A/275	1697	ex G-OSOE	Frtr♦
☐ 5Y-	Hawker Siddeley HS.748-2A/287	1736	ex ZS-DBM	Frtr♦

BLUE BIRD AVIATION — Cobra (BBZ) — Nairobi -Wilson (WIL)

☐ ET-AKZ	de Havilland DHC-8-202	469	ex C-GLOT	<TNW
☐ 5Y-VVN	de Havilland DHC-8-102	062	ex VH-TQN	
☐ 5Y-VVP	de Havilland DHC-8-106	339	ex C-FLPP	
☐ 5Y-VVR	de Havilland DHC-8-102	204	ex VH-TQQ	[YYB]
☐ 5Y-VVS	de Havilland DHC-8-102	349	ex VH-TQT	wfs
☐ 5Y-VVT	de Havilland DHC-8-102	362	ex VH-TQV	
☐ 5Y-VVI	de Havilland DHC-8-402Q	4056	ex D-ADHD	opf UN
☐ 5Y-VVO	de Havilland DHC-8-402Q	4066	ex D-ADHE	
☐ 5Y-VVU	de Havilland DHC-8-402QPF	4008	ex SE-LSM	
☐ 5Y-VVW	de Havilland DHC-8-402QPF	4011	ex LN-RDL	
☐ 5Y-VVX	de Havilland DHC-8-402QPF	4018	ex LN-RDB	
☐ 5Y-VVY	de Havilland DHC-8-402QPF	4009	ex LN-RDD	
☐ 5Y-VVZ	de Havilland DHC-8-402QPF	4024	ex LN-RDI	
☐ 5Y-HHC	LET L-410A	720204	ex OK-DDU	wfs
☐ 5Y-HHE	Beech 200 Super King Air	BB-547	ex ZS-NIP	
☐ 5Y-VVC	LET L-410UVP-E20	922728	ex ZS-NIJ	wfs
☐ 5Y-VVE	LET L-410UVP-E20	922726	ex 5Y-TTT	wfs
☐ 5Y-VVG	Fokker 50	20137	ex N137NM	
☐ 5Y-VVH	Fokker 50	20203	ex N203NM	
☐ 5Y-VVL	LET L-410UVP-E7	872018	ex 5Y-HHL	wfs
☐ 5Y-VVM	Beech 1900D	UE-175	ex N61HA	

BLUE SKY AVIATION — Mawingu (SBK) — Nairobi-Wilson (WIL)

☐ 5Y-BOD	LET L-410UVP-E20	982727	ex OK-DDF
☐ 5Y-BSA	LET L-410UVP-E9	892323	ex OK-UDC
☐ 5Y-VVA	LET L-410UVP-E9	962633	ex OK-BDL

CAPITAL AIRLINES — Capital Delta (CPD) — Nairobi Wilson (WIL)

☐ 5Y-JAI	Beech 200 Super King Air	BB-557	ex OY-PAM	
☐ 5Y-NKI	Beech 200 Super King Air	BB-525	ex ZS-MFC	
☐ 5Y-SJB	Beech 200 Super King Air	BB-467	ex 5H-MUN	CatPass 250 conversion

CARGO2FLY — Nairobi Wilson (WIL)

☐ 5Y-CCE	Fokker F.27-500 Friendship	10370	ex N19GQ	♦

CEZANNE AIR EXPRESS — Nairobi-Wilson (WIL)

☐ 5Y-JON	Britten-Norman BN-2B-20 Islander	2203	ex 5H-JON

DAC EAST AFRICA/DAC AVIATION — Nairobi-Wilson (WIL)

☐ 5Y-BVS	Cessna 208B Caravan I	208B2007		
☐ 5Y-DAA	Cessna 208BEX Caravan I	208B5025	ex N8136S	♦
☐ 5Y-DAB	Cessna 208BEX Caravan I	208B5026	ex N8138F	♦
☐ 5Y-DAE	Cessna 208BEX Caravan I	208B5055	ex N8153M	♦
☐ 5Y-DEA	Cessna 208BEX Caravan I	208B5013		♦
☐ 5Y-BWG	de Havilland DHC-8-311Q	406	ex C-FTYU	opf UN
☐ 5Y-PTA	de Havilland DHC-8-315	397	ex N788BC	<Trident Avn opf UN
☐ 5Y-QHW	de Havilland DHC-8-402Q	4052	ex G-JEDI	♦
☐ 5Y-QOE	de Havilland DHC-8-402Q	4054	ex G-JEDK	>JamboJet♦
☐ 5Y-WJF	de Havilland DHC-8-202Q	456	ex N456YV	
☐ 5Y-BWR	Canadair CRJ-100LR	7004	ex C-FYFS	opf UN
☐ 5Y-WWA	Canadair CRJ-200ER	7350	ex EC-HHV	>ATC

EAST AFRICAN AIR CHARTER — Nairobi-Wilson (WIL)

☐ 5Y-ALY	Cessna U206F Stationair	U20602266	ex N15588U	
☐ 5Y-ART	Cessna 210L Centurion II	21059817		
☐ 5Y-BIX	Reims Cessna F406 Caravan II	F406-0055	ex N65912	
☐ 5Y-BLN	Cessna 208B Caravan I	208B0558	ex N50938	
☐ 5Y-BMH	Cessna 310R	310R0501	ex N87216	
☐ 5Y-EOC	Cessna 208B Caravan I	208B0737	ex N1266A	

EXECUTIVE TURBINE KENYA — Nairobi-Wilson (WIL)

☐ 5Y-BTG	Beech 1900C-1	UC-96	ex ZS-PBY	[WIL]

FALCON AIR CHARTERS

☐ 5Y-GSV	Cessna 208 Caravan I	20800024	ex N9358F

FLEX AIR CARGO — Nairobi-Wilson (WIL)

□ 5Y-BSI	Beech 1900C-1	UC-172	ex 5Y-BBI	
□ 5Y-BUC	Cessna 208B Caravan I	208B0400	ex ZS-NLO	
□ 5Y-LEX	Cessna 208B Caravan I	208B0738	ex ZS-CAT	

FLY540 — Swift Tango (5H/FFV) — Nairobi-Jomo Kenyatta Intl (NBO)

□ 5Y-BTT	Beech 1900C-1	UC-125	ex ZS-POU	
□ 5Y-BUN	ATR 42-320	205	ex ZS-OZX	[WIL]
□ 5Y-BUZ	de Havilland DHC-8-106	253	ex C-FOBU	
□ 5Y-BVG	Beech 1900D	UE-62	ex N62ZV	
□ 5Y-BXB	de Havilland DHC-8-102	213	ex N825PH	
□ 5Y-BXC	Canadair CRJ-100ER	7184	ex C-FOVP	
□ 5Y-BXD	Canadair CRJ-100ER	7042	ex C-GLGU	
□ 5Y-CAC	Cessna 208B Caravan I	208B0525	ex 5Y-YEP	
□ 5Y-NON	Cessna 208 Caravan I	20800036	ex ZS-NON	
□ 5Y-XXB	Douglas DC-9-14 (ABS 3)	45711/4	ex N500ME	
□ 5Y-	Douglas DC-9-15	45740/62	ex ZS-MNT	VIP >EXZ

FLY SAX — (B5/EXZ) — Nairobi-Jomo Kenyatta Intl (NBO)

□ 5Y-BSS	Beech 1900C-1	UC-88	ex ZS-PJA	
□ 5Y-EEE	Fokker F.28 Fellowship 4000	11229	ex 5Y-MNT	
□ 5Y-SAX	Douglas DC-9-15	45740/62	ex ZS-MNT	VIP <FFV
□ 5Y-XXA	Douglas DC-9-14 (ABS 3)	45725/19	ex N600ME	

FREEDOM AIRLINES EXPRESS — Nairobi-Wilson (WIL)

| □ 5Y-FAM | Embraer EMB.120RT Brasilia | 120247 | ex N258CA | |
| □ 5Y-UPL | Canadair CRJ-100ER | 7040 | ex C-GTLF | [WIL] |

JAMBOJET — Nairobi-Jomo Kenyatta Intl (NBO)

□ 5Y-KQA	Boeing 737-3U8	28746/2863		
□ 5Y-KQB	Boeing 737-3U8	28747/2884		
□ 5Y-KYM	Boeing 737-306	28719/2930	ex PH-BTH	
□ 5Y-QOE	de Havilland DHC-8-402Q	4054	ex G-JEDK	<DAC E Africa♦

JUBBA AIRWAYS — Jubba (6J/JBW) — Nairobi-Jomo Kenyatta Intl (NBO)

□ F-GYAN	Airbus A321-111	0535	ex F-WQQU	<BIE ♦
□ 5Y-BXG	Boeing 737-247 (Nordam 3)	23519/1299	ex YA-GAE	wfs
□ 5Y-BZL	Boeing 737-4B7	24550/1793	ex EY-537	
□ 5Y-BXZ	Boeing 737-247 (Nordam 3)	23516/1257	ex EX-25004	
□ 5Y-CCR	Boeing 737-3Z0	27521/2738	ex EX-37002	<EEA

KASAS/BLUEWAVE AVIATION — Nairobi-Wilson (WIL)

□ 5Y-BRX	Dornier 228-100	7004	ex SE-KKX	
□ 5Y-BTU	Dornier 228-201	8030	ex D-CCAL	
□ 5Y-BUV	Dornier 228-201	8050	ex A6-ZYE	
□ 5Y-CCS	Dornier 228-202K	8152	ex D-CAAL	♦
□ 5Y-EKA	Dornier 228-201	8108	ex LN-AAO	<Regourd
□ 5Y-CAX	Dassault Falcon 10	140		♦

KEN AIR

| □ 5Y- | Cessna 208B Caravan I | 208B2348 | ex N2025X | |

KENYA AIRWAYS — Kenya (KQ/KQA) — Nairobi-Jomo Kenyatta Intl (NBO)

Member of SkyTeam

□ 5Y-CYA	Boeing 737-8HX/W	40549/5115		o/o♦
□ 5Y-CYB	Boeing 737-8HX/W	40550/5170		♦
□ 5Y-CYC	Boeing 737-86N/W	43400/5237		♦
□ 5Y-CYD	Boeing 737-8HX/W	40553/5372		♦
□ 5Y-KYD	Boeing 737-86N/W	35632/2690		
□ 5Y-KYE	Boeing 737-8Q8/W	35286/2757	ex N1796B	
□ 5Y-KYF	Boeing 737-86N/W	35637/2803		
□ 5Y-KQS	Boeing 777-2U8ER	33683/522	Mount Elgon	
□ 5Y-KQT	Boeing 777-2U8ER	33682/514	Mount Kenya	
□ 5Y-KQU	Boeing 777-2U8ER	33681/479	Mount Kilimanjaro	
□ 5Y-KZY	Boeing 777-36NER	41819/1197	Victoria Falls	
□ 5Y-KZX	Boeing 777-3U8ER	42097/1211		♦
□ 5Y-KYZ	Boeing 777-2U8ER	36124/614	Mount Longonot	

☐ 5Y-KZZ	Boeing 777-36NER	41818/1140		Maasai Mara
☐ 5Y-KZA	Boeing 787-8	35510/157		The Great Rift Valley
☐ 5Y-KZB	Boeing 787-8	35511/184		The Zambezi River ◆
☐ 5Y-KZC	Boeing 787-8	36040/192		◆
☐ 5Y-KZD	Boeing 787-8	36041/204		Tsavo National Park ◆
☐ 5Y-KZE	Boeing 787-8	36042/212		Serengeti Plains ◆
☐ 5Y-KZF	Boeing 787-8	36043/223		◆
☐ 5Y-KZG	Boeing 787-8	36044/289		◆
☐ 5Y-KZH	Boeing 787-8	36045/307		o/o◆
☐ 5Y-KZI	Boeing 787-8	36046/317		o/o◆
☐ 5Y-FFA	Embraer ERJ-190AR	19000562	ex PT-TDR	
☐ 5Y-FFB	Embraer ERJ-190AR	19000572	ex PT-TEY	SkyTeam c/s
☐ 5Y-FFC	Embraer ERJ-190AR	19000577	ex PT-TGD	
☐ 5Y-FFD	Embraer ERJ-190AR	19000579	ex PT-TGM	
☐ 5Y-FFE	Embraer ERJ-190AR	19000586		
☐ 5Y-FFF	Embraer ERJ-190AR	19000594	ex PT-THY	
☐ 5Y-FFG	Embraer ERJ-190AR	19000599	ex PT-TIK	
☐ 5Y-FFH	Embraer ERJ-190AR	19000619	ex PT-TKD	
☐ 5Y-FFJ	Embraer ERJ-190AR	19000633	ex PR-EAQ	
☐ 5Y-FFK	Embraer ERJ-190AR	19000642	ex PR-ECM	
☐ 5Y-KYP	Embraer ERJ-190AR	19000398	ex PT-TYG	
☐ 5Y-KYQ	Embraer ERJ-190AR	19000440	ex PT-TDY	
☐ 5Y-KYR	Embraer ERJ-190AR	19000468	ex PT-TOK	
☐ 5Y-KYS	Embraer ERJ-190AR	19000478	ex PT-TPA	
☐ 5Y-KYT	Embraer ERJ-190AR	19000544	ex PT-TAZ	
☐ 5Y-KQC	Boeing 737-3U8SF	29088/3034		
☐ 5Y-KQD	Boeing 737-3U8SF	29750/3095	ex N5573L	
☐ 5Y-KQE	Boeing 737-76N/W	30133/877		
☐ 5Y-KQF	Boeing 737-76N/W	30136/1145		
☐ 5Y-KQG	Boeing 737-7U8/W	32371/1242	ex N715BA	
☐ 5Y-KQH	Boeing 737-7U8/W	32372/1327		
☐ 5Y-KQX	Boeing 767-36NER	30854/844		[SNN]
☐ 5Y-KQZ	Boeing 767-36NER	30853/837		[SNN]
☐ 5Y-KYH	Embraer ERJ-170LR	17000230	ex PT-SFG	
☐ 5Y-KYJ	Embraer ERJ-170LR	17000128	ex B-KXD	
☐ 5Y-KYK	Embraer ERJ-170LR	17000111	ex B-KXC	
☐ 5Y-KYN	Boeing 737-306	28720/2957	ex PH-BTI	
☐ 5Y-KYX	Boeing 767-3P6ER	24484/260	ex N244AV	[ADD]

KENYA FOREST SERVICE

☐ 5Y-FOR	Cessna 208B Caravan I	208B2384	ex N20288	
☐ 5Y-FSK	Aérospatiale AS350B3 Ecureuil	7664		◆

MOMBASA AIR SAFARI — Skyrover (RRV) — Mombasa (MBA)

☐ 5Y-CAJ	Cessna 208B Caravan I	208B0401	ex 5H-AXL	◆
☐ 5Y-CBB	Cessna 208B Caravan I	208B0725	ex N208LF	◆
☐ 5Y-CCA	Cessna 208B Caravan I	208B1248	ex 5H-DAN	◆
☐ 5Y-CCU	Cessna 208B Caravan I	208B0814	ex ZS-ORU	◆
☐ 5Y-VAN	Cessna 208B Caravan I	208B0346	ex ZS-OHC	
☐ 5Y-WOW	Douglas DC-3/65ARTP	14165/25610	ex ZS-OJK	

PAN AFRICAN AIRWAYS — Nairobi-Jomo Kenyatta Intl (NBO)

☐ 5Y-CDP	Douglas DC-9-31	48145/1042	ex C5-AEB	>Som-Air◆

PHOENIX AVIATION — Nairobi-Wilson (WIL)

☐ 5Y-FDK	Beech 200 Super King Air	BB-531	ex 5Y-FOK	
☐ 5Y-JJZ	Beech B200 Super King Air	BB-1127	ex G-BMNF	
☐ 5Y-NJS	Beech 200 Super King Air	BB-837	ex ZS-LBD	
☐ 5Y-RJA	Beech 200 Super King Air	BB-619		
☐ 5Y-SMB	Beech 200 Super King Air	BB-379	ex 5Y-DDE	
☐ 5Y-TPA	Beech 200 Super King Air	BB-650	ex ZS-PSP	
☐ 5Y-CDH	Cessna 208B Caravan I	208B0608	ex N608AG	◆
☐ 5Y-MJA	Cessna 208B Caravan I	208B2203	ex N2059S	
☐ 5Y-MNG	Cessna Citation 550 Bravo	550-0876	ex N876CA	
☐ 5Y-MSA	Cessna Citation 550 Bravo	550-0975	ex N175CM	
☐ 5Y-RIS	Beech 350 King Air	FL-149	ex N149KA	
☐ 5Y-SIR	Cessna 550 Citation Bravo	550-0995	ex N550PD	

QUEENSWAY AIR SERVICES — Nairobi-Wilson (WIL)

☐ 5Y-BKT	Beech 200 Super King Air	BB-256	ex ZS-NTM	

RIBWAY CARGO AIRLINES   Nairobi-Jomo Kenyatta Intl (NBO)

☐ 5Y-RCA	Douglas DC-8-73AF	46044/432	ex N606AL	[ILN]♦

ROSSAIR KENYA

☐ 5Y-RDS	Douglas/AMI Turbo DC-3	15640/27085	ex N146JR	

SAFARILINK AVIATION   (XLK)   Nairobi-Wilson (WIL)

☐ 5Y-BOP	Cessna 208B Caravan I	208B0642	ex N208GJ	
☐ 5Y-NUU	Cessna 208B Caravan I	208B0567	ex ZS-NUU	
☐ 5Y-SLA	Cessna 208B Caravan I	208B0574	ex F-OGXY	
☐ 5Y-SLB	Cessna 208B Caravan I	208B0394	ex 5Y-BNS	♦
☐ 5Y-SLE	Cessna 208B Caravan I	208B2091	ex (5Y-SLC)	
☐ 5Y-SLG	Cessna 208B Caravan I	208B2241	ex N60259	
☐ 5Y-SLH	Vessna 208B Caravan I	208B2360		♦
☐ 5Y-ZBI	Cessna 208B Caravan I	208B0324	ex N1029P	
☐ 5Y-SLD	de Havilland DHC-8-102	331	ex C-FLPQ	
☐ 5Y-SLF	de Havilland DHC-6 Twin Otter 300	513	ex ZS-SCJ	

SAFE AIR KENYA   (K3/SAQ)

☐ 5Y-TCO	Hawker Siddeley HS.748 Srs.2B/360LFD	1772	ex VH-IPA	

748 AIR SERVICES   Sefeas (SVT)   Nairobi-Wilson (WIL)

☐ 5Y-JGM	de Havilland DHC-8-102A	287	ex N828PH	opf UN
☐ 5Y-IHO	de Havilland DHC-8-106	268	ex C-FOEN	
☐ 5Y-MAJ	de Havilland DHC-8-102	153	ex C-GYDH	♦
☐ 5Y-RHM	de Havilland DHC-8-102	177	ex C-GYDL	♦
☐ 5Y-SMJ	de Havilland DHC-8-401Q	4013	ex LN-RDA	
☐ 5Y-BSX	Hawker Siddeley HS.780 Andover C.1	Set 20	ex 9Q-COE	wfs
☐ 5Y-EVG	Aérospatiale AS350B2 Ecureuil	4439	ex ZK-IHT	
☐ 5Y-FAJ	Cessna 208B Caravan I	208B2356	ex N20168	♦
☐ 5Y-ZBL	Cessna 208B Caravan I	208B0338	ex N1042Y	

SEVERIN AIR SAFARIS

☐ 5Y-SXC	Cessna 208B Caravan I	208B2372	ex N20194	♦
☐ 5Y-SXS	Cessna 208B Caravan I	208B2108	ex N6130K	

SKYTRAILS   Skytrail   Mombasa (MBA)

☐ 5Y-AFD	Cessna TU206B Skywagon	U206-0724	ex N3424L	
☐ 5Y-SKN	Fokker 50	20110	ex PH-GER	

SKYWARD INTERNATIONAL AVIATION   (SEW)   Nairobi-Wilson (WIL)

☐ 5Y-JXJ	Fokker 50	20232	ex PH-JXJ	♦
☐ 5Y-JXK	Fokker 50	20233	ex PH-JXK	♦
☐ 5Y-MIS	Fokker 50	20111	ex PH-AMP	>Haajara Airline
☐ 5Y-SED	Fokker 50	20108	ex PH-MUJ	♦
☐ 5Y-SIB	Fokker 50	20167	ex 9M-MGF	dam 04Jan15♦
☐ 5Y-SVN	Fokker 50	20116	ex PH-GHK	♦
☐ 5Y-JLH	Canadair CRJ-100LR	7113	ex C-FZGN	
☐ 5Y-SIA	Fokker 100	11307	ex PH-CMM	

SKYWAYS KENYA   Nairobi-Wilson (WIL)

☐ 5Y-BMB	Douglas DC-3	17108/34375	ex N2025A	wfs

SOLENTA AVIATION (KENYA)   Nairobi-Jomo Kenyatta Intl (NBO)

☐ 5Y-OBY	Cessna 208B Caravan I	208B0345	ex ZS-OBY	DHL c/s
☐ 5Y-TLC	Cessna 208B Caravan I	208B0472	ex ZS-TLC	DHL c/s

SUPERIOR AVIATION SERVICES   Skycargo (SUK)   Nairobi-Wilson (WIL)

☐ 5Y-ATH	Piper PA-23-250 Aztec E	27-7305138		
☐ 5Y-PEA	Beech 58 Baron	TH-1067	ex N60664	

TRACKMARK CARGO   Nairobi-Wilson (WIL)

☐ 5Y-BNH	Cessna 208B Caravan I	208B0385	ex ZS-NYS	
☐ 5Y-TVM	Cessna 208B Caravan I	208B0355	ex N9697C	

TRANSWORLD SAFARIS — Nairobi-Wilson (WIL)

☐ 5Y-ROH	Piper PA-31-350 Chieftain	31-8152038	ex N217JP	

TRIDENT AVIATION/ENTERPRISES — Nairobi-Wilson (WIL)

☐ 5Y-BTP	de Havilland DHC-8-102	104	ex 6Y-JMT	opf UN
☐ 5Y-DAC	de Havilland DHC-8-102	251	ex C-GZAN	opf UN
☐ 5Y-EMD	de Havilland DHC-8-102	110	ex 6Y-JMZ	opf UN
☐ 5Y-ENA	de Havilland DHC-8-102	297	ex N836EX	opf UN
☐ 5Y-GRS	de Havilland DHC-8-102	355	ex SX-BIS	opf UN
☐ 5Y-MOC	de Havilland DHC-8-315	374	ex C-FDYW	
☐ 5Y-PTA	de Havilland DHC-8-315	397	ex N788BC	
☐ 5Y-TAJ	de Havilland DHC-5E Buffalo	108	ex C-GDOB	opf UN-WFP
☐ 5Y-XNZ	de Havilland DHC-5D Buffalo	81	ex PK-XNZ	

TROPIC AIR — Nairobi-Wilson (WIL)

☐ 5Y-BRT	Cessna 208B Caravan I	208B0682	ex ZS-ELE	
☐ 5Y-BSY	Cessna 208B Caravan I	208B0907	ex N32211	
☐ 5Y-BWV	Aérospatiale AS350B3 Ecureuil	4482	ex ZS-RBS	
☐ 5Y-BYG	Aérospatiale AS350B3 Ecureuil	4296	ex ZS-RDU	
☐ 5Y-CCJ	Cessna 208 Caravan I	20800194	ex N388NT	♦
☐ 5Y-CCP	Aérospatiale AS350B3c Ecureuil	7448	ex ZS-HNO	♦

UNIWORLD AIR CARGO — Nairobi-Jomo Kanyatta Intl (NBO)

☐ HP-1813UCG	Douglas DC-9-33F (ABS 3)	47384/543	ex 5Y-DBH	♦

YELLOW WINGS AIR SERVICES/KENAIR

☐ 5Y-ELO	Cessna 208B Caravan I	208B2201	ex N1032L	
☐ 5Y-YWA	Cessna 208B Caravan I	208B2348	ex N2025X	♦

ZB AIR (Z BOSCOVIC AIR CHARTER) — Bosky (ZBA) — Nairobi-Wilson (WIL)

☐ 5Y-OPM	Cessna 208B Caravan I	208B0330	ex N1034S	
☐ 5Y-ZBD	Cessna 208B Caravan I	208B1109	ex N1275Z	
☐ 5Y-ZBE	Cessna 208B Caravan I	208B2072	ex N2212X	
☐ 5Y-ZBG	Cessna 208B Caravan I	208B2318	ex N60207	
☐ 5Y-ZBR	Cessna 208B Caravan I	208B0446	ex N12922	
☐ 5Y-ZBT	Cessna 208B Caravan I	208B1243	ex N1226X	
☐ 5Y-ZBW	Cessna 208B Caravan I	208B0409	ex N1115W	
☐ 5Y-ZBX	Cessna 208B Caravan I	208B1170	ex N1308N	
☐ 5Y-AIS	Beech 95-D55 Baron	TE-680		
☐ 5Y-AUN	Cessna U206F Stationair	U20602531	ex N1244V	
☐ 5Y-AYZ	Cessna 310R	310R0121	ex N4940J	
☐ 5Y-AZS	Cessna 310R	310R0524	ex N87350	
☐ 5Y-ZBK	Beech B200 Super King Air	BB-1714	ex N3214D	
☐ 5Y-ZBM	Cessna U206H Stationair 6	U20608114	ex N259ME	
☐ 5Y-ZBO	Cessna U206H Stationair	U20608131	ex N373ME	

6O-   SOMALIA (Democratic Republic of Somalia)

GALEYR AIRLINE — Mogadishu (MGQ)

☐ 5Y-BOD	LET L-410UVP	982727		♦

HAAJARA AIRLINE

☐ 5Y-MIS	Fokker 50	20111	ex PH-AMP	<SEW

SOM-AIR — Mogadishu (MGQ)

☐ 5Y-CDP	Douglas DC-9-31	48145/1042	ex C5-AEB	<Pan African AW♦

6V-   SENEGAL (Republic of Senegal)

AERO SERVICES — Servo (RSG) — Dakar (DKR)

☐ 6V-AHF	Cessna 208B Caravan I	208B0634	ex N12386	
☐ 6V-AHI	Cessna 402C	402C0120	ex F-OHCM	

ASECNA — (XKX) — Dakar (DKR)

☐ 6V-AFW	ATR 42-300	117	ex F-WWEN	Calibrator/Pax

SENEGALAIR

☐ 6V-AIE	British Aerospace Jetstream 32	899	ex N484UE	

SENEGAL AIRLINES   *(DN/SGG)*   *Dakar (DKR)*

☐ A6-FLA	de Havilland DHC-8Q-402	4454	ex C-GWLV	<FVS♦
☐ 6V-AJA	Airbus A320-231	076	ex ZS-GAS	♦

TRANSAIR   *Dakar (DKR)*

☐ 6V-AIP	Embraer EMB.120RT Brasilia	120103	ex EC-HHN	♦

6Y- JAMAICA

AIRWAYS INTERNATIONAL/JAMAICA AIR SHUTTLE (ARW)

☐ 6Y-JSA	Beech 99	U-58	ex V2-ANU	
☐ 6Y-JSI	Beech 99	U-98	ex V2-DOM	

FLY JAMAICA   *(OJ/FJM)*   *Kingston-Norman Manley Intl (KIN)*

☐ N767WA	Boeing 767-319ER	24876/413	ex N762NA	♦

INTERNATIONAL AIRLINK   *Kingston-Tinson Peninsula (KTP)*

☐ 6Y-JRD	Cessna U206G Stationair 6	U20604522	ex N9019M	

SKYLAN AIRWAYS   *(SKA)*

☐ 6Y-JIC	British Aerospace Jetstream 32EP	920	ex N920AE	

TIMAIR   *Montego Bay (MBJ)*

☐ 6Y-JLU	Britten-Norman BN-2B-26 Islander	2170	ex 6Y-JLG	
☐ 6Y-JNA	Cessna U206G Stationair	U20603837	ex N4515C	
☐ 6Y-JNJ	Cessna U206G Stationair 6	U20606359	ex N2447N	
☐ 6Y-JNL	Cessna U206G Stationair 6	U20605620	ex N712RS	

7O- YEMEN (Republic of Yemen)

BLUE BIRD AVIATION   *(BBY)*   *Sana'a (SAH)*

☐ 7O-ADS	de Havilland DHC-8-102	280	ex C-FMCZ	♦
☐ 7O-ADU	de Havilland DHC-8-102	327	ex C-FHLO	♦
☐ 7O-BBC	de Havilland DHC-8-202	432	ex C-GXIC	♦

FELIX AIRWAYS   *Felix (F0/FXX)*   *Sana'a (SAH)*

☐ 7O-FAB	Canadair CRJ-702NG	10268		
☐ 7O-FAI	Canadair CRJ-200LR	7307	ex N636BR	
☐ 7O-FAJ	Canadair CRJ-200LR	7308	ex N637BR	

YEMENIA/YEMEN AIRWAYS *Yemeni (IY/IYE)*   *Sana'a (SAH)*

☐ 7O-ADA	Boeing 727-2N8	21842/1512	ex 4W-ACJ		opf Govt
☐ 7O-ADD	Lockheed L-382C-86D Hercules	4827	ex 1160		jt ops with Air Force
☐ 7O-ADE	Lockheed L-382C-86D Hercules	4825	ex 1150		jt ops with Air Force
☐ 7O-ADF	Ilyushin Il-76TD	1033418578	ex RA-76380		jt ops with Air Force
☐ 7O-ADH	de Havilland DHC-6 Twin Otter 310	764	ex (VQ-TAN)		
☐ 7O-ADI	de Havilland DHC-6 Twin Otter 300	664	ex HB-LRT		<FAT
☐ 7O-ADP	Airbus A330-243	625	ex F-WWYD	Sana'a	
☐ 7O-ADR	Airbus A310-324ET	568	ex F-OGYO	Socotra	
☐ 7O-ADT	Airbus A330-243	632	ex F-WWYH	Aden	
☐ 7O-ADV	Airbus A310-325	702	ex F-OHPR	Seiyun	
☐ 7O-ADW	Airbus A310-325	704	ex F-OHPS	Marib	
☐ 7O-ADY	de Havilland DHC-8-103	333	ex C-FSID		
☐ 7O-AFA	Airbus A320-233	4653	ex F-WWIA	Mukalla	
☐ 7O-AFB	Airbus A320-233	4691	ex F-WWBO	Mareb	
☐ 7O-YMN	Boeing 747SP-27	21786/413	ex A7-AHM		opf Govt

7Q- MALAWI (Republic of Malawi)

MALAWIAN AIRLINES   *(3W/MWI)*   *Blantyre (BLZ)*

☐ ET-APL	Boeing 737-860/W	40965/4075		<ETH
☐ ET-AQB	de Havilland DHC-8-402Q	4419	ex C-GNKT	<ETH

7T-   ALGERIA (Democratic & Popular Republic of Algeria)

AIR ALGERIE   Air Algerie (AH/DAH)   Algiers (ALG)

	Reg	Type	c/n	ex	Name	
☐	7T-VJA	Airbus A330-202	1613	ex F-WWCZ		♦
☐	7T-VJB	Airbus A330-202	1630	ex F-WWKP		o/o♦
☐	7T-VJC	Airbus A330-202	1649	ex F-WW		o/o♦
☐	7T-VJV	Airbus A330-202	644	ex F-WWKD	Tinhinan	
☐	7T-VJW	Airbus A330-202	647	ex F-WWKF	Lalla Setti	
☐	7T-VJX	Airbus A330-202	650	ex F-WWKK	Mers el Kebir	
☐	7T-VJY	Airbus A330-202	653	ex F-WWYK	Monts des Beni Chougrane	
☐	7T-VJZ	Airbus A330-202	667	ex F-WWKR	Teddis	
☐	7T-VUI	ATR 72-212A	644	ex F-OHGM		
☐	7T-VUJ	ATR 72-212A	648	ex F-OHGN		
☐	7T-VUK	ATR 72-212A	652	ex F-OHGO		
☐	7T-VUL	ATR 72-212A	672	ex F-OHGP		
☐	7T-VUM	ATR 72-212A	677	ex F-OHGQ		
☐	7T-VUN	ATR 72-212A	684	ex F-OHGR		
☐	7T-VUO	ATR 72-212A	901	ex F-WWEP		
☐	7T-VUP	ATR 72-212A	903	ex F-WWES		
☐	7T-VUQ	ATR 72-212A	909	ex F-WWEB		
☐	7T-VUS	ATR 72-212A	913	ex F-WWEI		
☐	7T-VUT	ATR 72-600	1223	ex F-WWEV		♦
☐	7T-VUV	ATR 72-600	1258	ex F-WWEJ		o/o♦
☐	7T-VVQ	ATR 72-212A	676	ex F-WWEA		
☐	7T-VVR	ATR 72-212A	683	ex F-WWEF		
☐	7T-	ATR 72-600	1266	ex F-WW		o/o♦
☐	7T-	ATR 72-600	1266	ex F-WW		o/o♦
☐	7T-VJQ	Boeing 737-6D6	30209/1115		Kasbah d'Alger	
☐	7T-VJR	Boeing 737-6D6	30545/1131	ex N1786B		
☐	7T-VJS	Boeing 737-6D6	30210/1150	ex N60559		
☐	7T-VJT	Boeing 737-6D6	30546/1152			
☐	7T-VJU	Boeing 737-6D6	30211/1164			
☐	7T-VCC	Boeing 737-8ZQ/W	40886/3747		Ahaggar	<DTH
☐	7T-VJJ	Boeing 737-8D6/W	30202/610	ex N1786B	Jugurtha	
☐	7T-VJK	Boeing 737-8D6/W	30203/640	ex N1781B	Mansourah	
☐	7T-VJL	Boeing 737-8D6/W	30204/652	ex N1786B	Allizi	
☐	7T-VJM	Boeing 737-8D6/W	30205/691	ex N1786B	Ihrane	
☐	7T-VJN	Boeing 737-8D6/W	30206/751	ex n1786b	Oued Tafna	
☐	7T-VJO	Boeing 737-8D6/W	30207/868	ex N1787B	Tinerkouk	
☐	7T-VJP	Boeing 737-8D6/W	30208/896	ex N1787B	Mont Tahat	
☐	7T-VKA	Boeing 737-8D6/W	34164/1748		Monts Chaboro	
☐	7T-VKB	Boeing 737-8D6/W	34165/1768	ex N1784B	Mont de l'Assekhrem	
☐	7T-VKC	Boeing 737-8D6/W	34166/1773	ex N1786B		
☐	7T-VKD	Boeing 737-8D6/W	40858/3406	ex N1786B		
☐	7T-VKE	Boeing 737-8D6/W	40859/3446			
☐	7T-VKF	Boeing 737-8D6/W	40860/3471	ex N1787B		
☐	7T-VKG	Boeing 737-8D6/W	40861//3596	ex N1786B		
☐	7T-VKH	Boeing 737-8D6/W	40862/3625	ex N1786B		
☐	7T-VKI	Boeing 737-8D6/W	40863/3658			
☐	7T-VKJ	Boeing 737-8D6/W	40864/3691			
☐	7T-VCV	Beech A100 King Air	B-93	ex N9369Q		
☐	7T-VHL	Lockheed L-382-51D Hercules	4886	ex N4160M		
☐	7T-VJG	Boeing 767-3D6ER	24766/310			
☐	7T-VJH	Boeing 767-3D6ER	24767/323			
☐	7T-VJI	Boeing 767-3D6ER	24768/332	ex N6009F		
☐	7T-VRF	Beech A100 King Air	B-147	ex N1828W		

AIR EXPRESS ALGERIA   Algiers (ALG)

	Reg	Type	c/n	ex		
☐	ZS-OXR	LET L-410UVP-E20	972730	ex 5H-HSA		<Air-Tec Africa
☐	7T-VAE	LET L-410UVP-E20	872011	ex OK-SDT		
☐	7T-VAF	LET L-410UVP-E20	082629	ex CCCP-67698		
☐	7T-VAG	LET L-410UVP-E20	2915	ex OK-JDR		
☐	7T-	LET L-410UVP-E20	972730	ex ZS-OXR		
☐	ZS-ORV	Beech 1900D	UE-42	ex (ZS-OPK)	opf UN WFP >NAC	
☐	ZS-OUE	LET L-420	012735A	ex OK-GDM	<Air-Tec Africa	
☐	ZS-OYD	Beech 1900D	UE-191	ex VH-IAR	>NAC	

STAR AVIATION   Algiers (ALG)

	Reg	Type	c/n	ex	
☐	7T-VNA	Pilatus PC-6/B2-H4 Turbo Porter	817	ex HB-FFV	
☐	7T-VNB	Beech 1900D	UE-305	ex 7T-WRF	
☐	7T-VND	de Havilland DHC-6 Twin Otter 300	502	ex HB-LRS	
☐	7T-VNE	de Havilland DHC-6 Twin Otter 300	717	ex HB-LTD	
☐	7T-VNG	Beech 1900D	UE-296	ex HB-AEK	

☐ 7T-	Cessna 525A Citation CJ2+	525A-0246	ex N2051A

TASSILI AIRLINES — Tassili Air (SF/DTH) — Hassi Messaoud (HME)

☐ 7T-VCL	de Havilland DHC-8-402Q	4167	ex C-FMIT		
☐ 7T-VCM	de Havilland DHC-8-402Q	4169	ex C-FMIV		
☐ 7T-VCN	de Havilland DHC-8-402Q	4173	ex C-FMKF		
☐ 7T-VCO	de Havilland DHC-8-402Q	4178	ex C-FMTN		
☐ 7T-VCP	de Havilland DHC-8-202	661	ex C-FRIZ		
☐ 7T-VCQ	de Havilland DHC-8-202	664	ex C-FTGX		
☐ 7T-VCR	de Havilland DHC-8-202	665	ex C-FTUE		
☐ 7T-VCS	de Havilland DHC-8-202	666	ex C-FUCF		
☐ 7T-VCG	Pilatus PC-6/B2-H4 Turbo Porter	917	ex HB-FLJ		
☐ 7T-VCH	Pilatus PC-6/B2-H4 Turbo Porter	929	ex HB-FLX		
☐ 7T-VCI	Pilatus PC-6/B2-H4 Turbo Porter	933	ex HB-FLY		
☐ 7T-VCJ	Pilatus PC-6/B2-H4 Turbo Porter	934	ex HB-FLZ		
☐ 7T-VCK	Pilatus PC-6/B2-H4 Turbo Porter	930	ex HB-FMA		
☐ 7T-VCA	Boeing 737-8ZQ/W	40884/3575	ex N1786B	Tassili n'Ajjer	
☐ 7T-VCB	Boeing 737-8ZQ/W	40885/3606		La Tanezrouft	
☐ 7T-VCC	Boeing 737-8ZQ/W	40886/3747		Ahaggar	>DAH
☐ 7T-VCD	Boeing 737-8ZQ/W	40887/3786		Assekrem	
☐ 7T-VIG	Cessna 208B Caravan I	208B0391	ex N1122N		
☐ 7T-VII	Cessna 208B Caravan I	208B0393	ex N1123G		
☐ 7T-VIL	Cessna 208B Caravan I	208B0601	ex N1247H		
☐ 7T-VIM	Cessna 208B Caravan I	208B0602	ex N1247K		
☐ 7T-VIO	Beech 1900D	UE-366	ex N30511		
☐ 7T-VIP	Beech 1900D	UE-369	ex N30538		
☐ 7T-VIQ	Beech 1900D	UE-381	ex N31683		VIP

8P- BARBADOS

TRANS ISLAND AIR 2000 — Trans Island (TRD) — Bridgetown-Grantley Adams (BGI)

Services performed by Twin Otters operated by SVG Air (J8-)

8Q- MALDIVES (Republic of Maldives)

FLYME/VILLA AIR — (VP/VQI) — Male (MLE)

☐ 8Q-VAQ	ATR 42-500	606	ex I-ADLQ	
☐ 8Q-VAS	ATR 72-600	1069	ex F-WWEF	
☐ 8Q-VAT	ATR 72-600	1109	ex F-WWEV	
☐ 8Q-VAV	ATR 72-212A	701	ex OY-EDC	♦
☐ 8Q-VAW	ATR 72-212A	702	ex OY-EDD	♦
☐ 8Q-VAU	Cessna 208 Caravan I	20800550	ex N81523	♦

ISLAND AVIATION SERVICES — Male (MLE)

☐ 8Q-IAF	de Havilland DHC-6 Twin Otter 315	447	ex C-CKBQ	FP♦
☐ 8Q-IAJ	de Havilland DHC-6 Twin Otter 300	276	ex C-GKSQ	FP♦
☐ 8Q-IAK	de Havilland DHC-6 Twin Otter 315	557	ex C-GYDS	FP♦
☐ 8Q-IAL	de Havilland DHC-6 Twin Otter 300	358	ex C-GXWG	FP♦

MALDIVIAN — (DQA) — Male (MLE)

☐ 8Q-AMD	de Havilland DHC-8-202	429	ex C-GDKL	
☐ 8Q-IAK	de Havilland DHC-8-315Q	557	ex C-GYDS	♦
☐ 8Q-IAM	de Havilland DHC-8-311Q	499	ex C-GUZV	
☐ 8Q-IAO	de Havilland DHC-8-314Q	544	ex D-BHOQ	
☐ 8Q-IAP	de Havilland DHC-8-315Q	491	ex LN-WFE	
☐ 8Q-IAQ	de Havilland DHC-8-202	542	ex C-FIKT	
☐ 8Q-IAN	Airbus A320-214	2347	ex EC-KHJ	
☐ 8Q-IAI	Airbus A321-211	2599	ex EC-JMR	♦

MALDIVIAN AIR TAXI — Male (MLE)

☐ 8Q-MAD	de Havilland DHC-6 Twin Otter 300	273	ex C-FAKB	FP
☐ 8Q-MAF	de Havilland DHC-6 Twin Otter 300	449	ex C-FWKQ	FP
☐ 8Q-MAH	de Havilland DHC-6 Twin Otter 300	374	ex C-FMYV	FP
☐ 8Q-MAI	de Havilland DHC-6 Twin Otter 300	279	ex C-GKBM	FP
☐ 8Q-MAJ	de Havilland DHC-6 Twin Otter 300	837	ex C-GJDP	FP
☐ 8Q-MAN	de Havilland DHC-6 Twin Otter 300	435	ex C-FWKZ	FP
☐ 8Q-MAO	de Havilland DHC-6 Twin Otter 300	259	ex C-FKBI	FP
☐ 8Q-MAP	de Havilland DHC-6 Twin Otter 300	571	ex C-FKBX	FP
☐ 8Q-MAT	de Havilland DHC-6 Twin Otter 200	146	ex 8Q-NTA	FP
☐ 8Q-MAW	de Havilland DHC-6 Twin Otter 300	722	ex C-FWKO	FP

☐	8Q-MAX	de Havilland DHC-6 Twin Otter 300	755	ex C-FWKX		FP
☐	8Q-MAZ	de Havilland DHC-6 Twin Otter 300	774	ex C-FWKU		FP
☐	8Q-MBA	de Havilland DHC-6 Twin Otter 300	691	ex D-IHAI		FP
☐	8Q-MBB	de Havilland DHC-6 Twin Otter 300	659	ex HB-LUG		FP
☐	8Q-MBC	de Havilland DHC-6 Twin Otter 300	256	ex H4-SIB		
☐	8Q-MBD	de Havilland DHC-6 Twin Otter 300	283	ex D-IBVP		
☐	8Q-MBE	de Havilland DHC-6 Twin Otter 300	561	ex OY-ATY		FP
☐	8Q-MBF	de Havilland DHC-6 Twin Otter 300	375	ex C-GIZQ		FP
☐	8Q-MBG	de Havilland DHC-6 Twin Otter 300	288	ex N102SK		FP
☐	8Q-MBH	de Havilland DHC-6 Twin Otter 300	585	ex N226SA		FP
☐	8Q-OEQ	de Havilland DHC-6 Twin Otter 100	044	ex C-FOEQ		FP
☐	8Q-IAS	de Havilland DHC-8-315Q	546	ex OE-LIE		

MEGA GLOBAL MALDIVES — Sandbar (LV/MEG) — Male (MLE)

☐	8Q-MEE	Boeing 767-306ER	27959/609	ex VP-BWW		♦
☐	8Q-MEF	Boeing 767-306ER	27960/625	ex VP-BWX		♦
☐	8Q-MEG	Boeing 767-3P6ER	24496/270	ex N183AQ		
☐	8Q-MEH	Boeing 767-3Y0ER	26206/487	ex C-GHPF		
☐	8Q-MEI	Boeing 757-204	25623/528	ex EI-EXW		

TRANS MALDIVIAN AIRWAYS — Trans Maldivian (TMW) — Male (MLE)

☐	8Q-TAB	de Havilland DHC-6 Twin Otter 300	582	ex ZS-SAI		FP
☐	8Q-TAC	de Havilland DHC-6 Twin Otter 300	580	ex ZS-PZO		FP
☐	8Q-TAD	de Havilland DHC-6 Twin Otter 300	701	ex C-GYXF		FP♦
☐	8Q-TAE	de Havilland DHC-6 Twin Otter 300	372	ex C-FTWU		FP♦
☐	8Q-TMB	de Havilland DHC-6 Twin Otter 300	587	ex C-GASV		FP
☐	8Q-TME	de Havilland DHC-6 Twin Otter 300	798	ex 8Q-HIH		FP
☐	8Q-TMF	de Havilland DHC-6 Twin Otter 300	657	ex 8Q-HII		FP
☐	8Q-TMG	de Havilland DHC-6 Twin Otter 310	597	ex 8Q-HIJ	The Beach House c/s	FP
☐	8Q-TMH	de Havilland DHC-6 Twin Otter 300	668	ex HK-4194X		FP
☐	8Q-TMI	de Havilland DHC-6 Twin Otter 300	754	ex N107JM		FP
☐	8Q-TMJ	de Havilland DHC-6 Twin Otter 300	781	ex N781JM		FP
☐	8Q-TMK	de Havilland DHC-6 Twin Otter 300	751	ex N710PV		FP
☐	8Q-TML	de Havilland DHC-6 Twin Otter 300	640	ex N709PV		FP
☐	8Q-TMN	de Havilland DHC-6 Twin Otter 300	700	ex (PH-OHN)		FP
☐	8Q-TMO	de Havilland DHC-6 Twin Otter 300	234	ex C-FBZN		FP
☐	8Q-TMP	de Havilland DHC-6 Twin Otter 300	652	ex VH-KZN		FP
☐	8Q-TMQ	de Havilland DHC-6 Twin Otter 300	753	ex N162AY		FP
☐	8Q-TMR	de Havilland DHC-6 Twin Otter 320	270	ex N270CM		FP
☐	8Q-TMS	de Havilland DHC-6 Twin Otter 300	663	ex PK-TWH		FP
☐	8Q-TMU	de Havilland DHC-6 Twin Otter 300	467	ex C-FOIM		FP
☐	8Q-TMV	de Havilland DHC-6 Twin Otter 300	625	ex C-FNBL		FP
☐	8Q-TMW	de Havilland DHC-6 Twin Otter 300	768	ex C-GDQM		FP
☐	8Q-TMX	de Havilland DHC-6 Twin Otter 400	848	ex C-FPPL		FP
☐	8Q-TMY	de Havilland DHC-6 Twin Otter 400	849	ex C-GLCU		FP
☐	8Q-TMZ	de Havilland DHC-6 Twin Otter 400	850	ex C-GLTI		FP

8R- GUYANA (Co-operative Republic of Guyana)

AIR GUYANA — (WOL) — Georgetown-Ogle (OGL)

☐	N524AT	Boeing 757-23NEM	30233/895	ex M-ABDF		[KIN]
☐	8R-WAL	Cessna 208B Caravan I	208B0990	ex N208KT		
☐	8R-	LET L-410UVP-E20	2903	ex OK-JDB		

AIR SERVICES GUYANA — Georgetown-Ogle (OGL)

☐	8R-ASL	Cessna 208B Caravan I	208B0707	ex V3-HIK		
☐	8R-BHR	Cessna 208B Caravan I	208B0611	ex YN-CGB		
☐	8R-BKP	Cessna 208B Caravan I	208B0758	ex YN-CFO		
☐	8R-GCB	Cessna 208B Caravan I	208B0614	ex YN-CHA		
☐	8R-GFA	Cessna 208B Caravan I	208B0478	ex V3-HFP		
☐	8R-YAC	Cessna 208B Caravan I	208B0647	ex V3-HFV		
☐	8R-GAA	Piper PA-34-200T Seneca II	34-7870451	ex 8R-GGJ		
☐	8R-GER	Britten-Norman BN-2A-27 Islander	478	ex G-BDJX		
☐	8R-GFI	Britten-Norman BN-2A-9 Islander	677	ex G-AZGU		
☐	8R-GFM	Cessna U206F Stationair	U20601731	ex N9531G		
☐	8R-GHB	Cessna U206G Stationair 6	U20604889	ex 8R-GPF		
☐	8R-GTR	Bell 206L-4 LongRanger	52138	ex XC-PBC		
☐	8R-GYA	Cessna U206G Stationair	U20603654	ex 8R-GGF		R/STOL conv
☐	8R-GZR	Cessna 208B Caravan I	208B0407	ex V3-HSS		

RORAIMA AIRWAYS — Roraima (ROR) — Georgetown-Ogle (OGL)

☐	8R-GRA	Britten-Norman BN-2A-26 Islander	3006	ex N42540		
☐	8R-GRB	Britten-Norman BN-2B-26 Islander	431	ex N431V		

☐ 8R-GRC	Britten-Norman BN-2B-27 Islander	2114	ex SX-DKA	

TRANS GUYANA AIRWAYS — Trans Guyana (TGY) — Georgetown-Ogle (OGL)

☐ 8R-GAS	Cessna 208B Caravan I	208B1234	ex N1141H	
☐ 8R-GGA	Britten-Norman BN-2A Mk III Trislander	366	ex G-LCEC	
☐ 8R-GGB	Britten-Norman BN-2A Mk III Trislander	1039	ex G-BEDP	dam 21Sep14
☐ 8R-GGY	Britten-Norman BN-2A-26 Islander	470	ex N81567	dam 06Jly14
☐ 8R-GHM	Britten-Norman BN-2A-27 Islander	216	ex PT-IAS	
☐ 8R-GHR	Cessna 208B Caravan I	208B0519	ex PT-MEZ	
☐ 8R-GHT	Cessna 208B Caravan I	208B0572	ex TI-BBG	
☐ 8R-GTG	Cessna 208B Caravan I	208B0397	ex N397TA	

9A- CROATIA (Republic of Croatia)

CROATIA AIRLINES — Croatia (OU/CTN) — Zagreb (ZAG)

Member of Star Alliance

☐ 9A-CQA	de Havilland DHC-8-402Q	4205	ex C-FPEL	Slavonija	
☐ 9A-CQB	de Havilland DHC-8-402Q	4211	ex C-FPQD	Lika	
☐ 9A-CQC	de Havilland DHC-8-402Q	4258	ex C-FWIJ	Istra	
☐ 9A-CQD	de Havilland DHC-8-402Q	4260	ex C-FWZU	Dalmacija	
☐ 9A-CQE	de Havilland DHC-8-402Q	4300	ex C-GBKD	Zagorje	
☐ 9A-CQF	de Havilland DHC-8-402Q	4301	ex C-GCKE	Primorje	
☐ 9A-CTG	Airbus A319-112	0767	ex D-AVYA	Zadar	
☐ 9A-CTH	Airbus A319-112	0833	ex D-AVYJ	Zagreb	
☐ 9A-CTI	Airbus A319-112	1029	ex D-AVYC	Vukova	Star Alliance c/s
☐ 9A-CTJ	Airbus A320-214	1009	ex F-WWDN	Dubrovnik	
☐ 9A-CTK	Airbus A320-214	1237	ex F-WWIK	Split	
☐ 9A-CTL	Airbus A319-112	1252	ex D-AVYS	Pula	

LIMITLESS AIRWAYS — (LIM) — Zadar (RJK)

☐ 9A-SLA	Airbus A320-214	0828	ex 2-ERIK	[ZAG]♦

TRADE AIR — Tradeair (C3/TDR) — Zagreb (ZAG)

☐ 9A-BTD	Fokker 100	11407	ex N1424M	>3C
☐ 9A-BTE	Fokker 100	11416	ex N1431B	Sun Adria c/s

9G- GHANA (Republic of Ghana)

AFRICA WORLD AIRLINES/FLYAFRICA — Blackstar (AW/AFW) — Accra (ACC)

☐ 9G-AET	Embraer ERJ-145LI	14500992	ex B-3039	
☐ 9G-AEU	Embraer ERJ-145LI	14500996	ex B-3035	
☐ 9G-AFB	Embraer ERJ-145LI	14501059	ex B-3089	

AIR GHANA — (GHN) — Accra (ACC)

☐ ZS-OKM	Beech 1900D	UE-74	ex N74YV		
☐ 9G-AGL	Boeing 737-4Q8F	25163/2264	ex N350AT	DHL c/s	♦

AIRLIFT INTERNATIONAL — (ALE) — Accra (ACC)

☐ 9G-RAC	Douglas DC-8-63PF (BAC 3)	46093/496	ex N816AX	wfs

ANTRAK AIR — Antrak (O4/ABV) — Accra (ACC)

☐ EC-KAD	ATR 72-202	171	ex F-GKPC	<SWT♦
☐ EC-LYJ	ATR 72-212A	468	ex OY-CIM	<SWT

CITYLINK — CityLink (CTQ) — Accra (ACC)

☐ 9G-CTQ	SAAB SF.340A	340A-137	ex YR-DAB	wfs
☐ 9G-LET	LET L-410UVP-E20	871922	ex ZS-OOH	

GIANAIR

☐ 9G-ASG	British Aerospace Jetstream 32EP	795	ex LN-HTB	
☐ 9G-GAS	British Aerospace Jetstream 32	970	ex SE-LXE	

JOHNSONS AIR		(JON)			Accra (ACC)
☐ 9G-SIM	Douglas DC-8-63CF (BAC 3)	46061/480	ex N826AX		wfs♦
☐ 9G-TOP	Douglas DC-8-63CF	46151/540	ex 9G-MKN		wfs♦

PETROLEUM HELICOPTERS					
☐ 9G-AEQ	Sikorsky S-76A	760193	ex N792P		♦

MERIDIAN AIRWAYS		Merid Air (MAG)			Accra (ACC)
☐ 9G-AXA	Douglas DC-8-63F (BAC 3)	46113/521	ex N811AX		wfs

STARBOW		Easy Shuttle (S9/IKM)			Accra (ACC)
☐ A6-FLR	de Havilland DHC-8-402Q	4486	ex C-FFWY		<FVS♦
☐ 9G-FWD	Embraer EMB.110P1 Bandeirante	110347	ex VH-CEG		♦
☐ 9G-SBB	British Aerospace 146 Srs.300	E3123	ex G-UKHP		
☐ 9G-SBC	British Aerospace 146 Srs.300	E3183	ex G-BUHB		
☐ 9G-SBD	British Aerospace 146 Srs.200	E2059	ex ZS-PUM		dam 28Oct14

9H-   MALTA (Republic of Malta)

AIR MALTA		Air Malta (KM/AMC)			Luqa (MLA)
☐ 9H-AEF	Airbus A320-214	2142	ex F-WWBZ	Valletta	>MON
☐ 9H-AEI	Airbus A320-214	2189	ex XA-SOB		retro c/s
☐ 9H-AEK	Airbus A320-214	2291	ex F-WWBT	San Gijan	
☐ 9H-AEN	Airbus A320-214	2665	ex F-WWBN	Bormia	
☐ 9H-AEO	Airbus A320-214	2768	ex F-WWDK	Isla-Cita'Invicta	
				Valletta European Capital of Culture c/s	
☐ 9H-AEH	Airbus A319-112	2122	ex D-AVWA	Floriana	
☐ 9H-AEJ	Airbus A319-112	2186	ex D-AVWX	San Pawl il-Bahr	>FLI
☐ 9H-AEL	Airbus A319-112	2332	ex D-AVYZ	Marsaxlokk	
☐ 9H-AEM	Airbus A319-112	2382	ex D-AVWW	Birgu	
☐ 9H-AEP	Airbus A320-214	3056	ex F-WWDV	Nadur	
☐ 9H-AEQ	Airbus A320-214	3068	ex F-WWIJ	Tarxien	

AIR X CHARTER		(AXY)			Luqa (MLA)
☐ 9H-AHA	Boeing 737-505	24647/2143	ex N647EL		♦
☐ 9H-JPC	Embraer Legacy 600	14501010	ex D-ATWO		♦
☐ 9H-KAP	Embraer Legacy 600	14501089	ex 2-KAPP		♦
☐ 9H-OME	Boeing 737-505	24274/2035	ex (HA-SHC)		♦
☐ 9H-WFC	Embraer Legacy 600	14500988	ex D-AONE		

FUGRO MALTA					Luqa (MLA)
☐ 9H-FMF	Piper PA-31 Turbo Navajo	31-245	ex OY-BHF		
☐ 9H-FMH	Piper PA-31-350 Navajo Chieftain	31-7552075	ex PH-OTH		

HI FLY MALTA		Moonraker (5M/HFM)			Luqa (MLA)
☐ 9H-TEP	Airbus A340-642	391	ex G-VMEG		[THR]♦

MALETH-AERO		(MLT)			Luqa (MLA)
☐ 9H-BHA	Boeing 737-529	26538/2298	ex VP-BHA		[KTW]♦
☐ 9H-GGG	Boeing 737-7ZX (BBJ1)	40119/4620			[CHC]♦
☐ 9H-MTF	Boeing 737-329	23774/1443	ex SX-MTF		♦

MEDAVIA		Medavia (N5/MDM)			Luqa (MLA)
☐ 9H-AET	Dornier 328-110	3117	ex D-COMM		
☐ 9H-AEW	de Havilland DHC-8-102	222	ex PH-SDH		
☐ 9H-AEY	de Havilland DHC-8-315Q	508	ex G-BRYX		dam 14Jly14
☐ 9H-AFD	de Havilland DHC-8-315Q	458	ex G-BRYU		
☐ 9H-AFH	Beech 1900D	UE-372	ex PH-RAR		opf ICRC
☐ 9H-AFI	Beech 1900D	UE-31	ex PH-RAH		

9J-   ZAMBIA (Republic of Zambia)

AIRWAVES AIRLINK		Airlimited (WLA)			Lusaka (LUN)
☐ 9J-CGC	Cessna 208B Caravan I	208B0742	ex N878C		

PROFLIGHT COMMUTER SERVICES   Proflight-Zambia (P0/PFZ)   Lusaka (LUN)

☐ ZS-CMB	Canadair CRJ-100ER	7215	ex N989CA	<KEM♦
☐ 7Q-YMJ	Piper PA-23-250 Aztec D	27-4104	ex ZS-FTO	
☐ 9J-ABD	Cessna P206D Super Skylane	P206-0461	ex ZS-FDA	
☐ 9J-KKN	Piper PA-31-350 Chieftain	31-8052113	ex ZS-KKN	
☐ 9J-OMY	British Aerospace Jetstream 41F	41036	ex ZS-OMY	
☐ 9J-PCR	Cessna 208B Caravan I	208B1302	ex N2047V	
☐ 9J-PCS	British Aerospace Jetstream 32	824	ex N3108	
☐ 9J-PCT	British Aerospace Jetstream 32EP	903	ex VP-CEX	
☐ 9J-PCU	British Aerospace Jetstream 32EP	800	ex N290MA	
☐ 9J-PCW	British Aerospace Jetstream 41	41034	ex ZS-OMF	
☐ 9J-PCXf	British Aerospace Jetstream 41	41035	ex ZS-OMS	
☐ 9J-PLJ	Britten-Norman BN-2A-21 Islander	799	ex Botswana OA3	
☐ 9J-UAS	Britten-Norman BN-2A Islander	155	ex Z-UAS	
☐ 9J-WEX	Britten-Norman BN-2A Islander	619	ex Z-WEX	
☐ 9J-	British Aerospace Jetstream 31	691	ex ZS-JSL	

ROYAL AIR CHARTERS   Lusaka (LUN)

☐ 9J-CID	Cessna 208B Caravan I	208B1307	ex N20527
☐ 9J-PKP	Embraer EMB.120ER Brasilia	120316	ex N591M

ZAMBIA FLYING DOCTOR

☐ 9J-DOC	Beech B200 Super King Air	BB-1046	ex 9J MED

9K-   KUWAIT (State of Kuwait)

JAZEERA AIRWAYS   Jazeera (J9/JZR)   Kuwait City (KWI)

☐ 9K-CAD	Airbus A320-214	2822	ex F-WWDC	
☐ 9K-CAI	Airbus A320-214	3919	ex F-WWBH	
☐ 9K-CAJ	Airbus A320-214	3939	ex F-WWDR	
☐ 9K-CAK	Airbus A320-214	4162	ex F-WWBS	
☐ 9K-CAL	Airbus A320-214	5033	ex D-AXAL	
☐ 9K-CAM	Airbus A320-214	5625	ex F-WWBK	
☐ 9K-CAN	Airbus A320-214	5833	ex F-WWDG	
☐ 9K-CAO	Airbus A320-214	6124	ex D-AXAW	♦

KUWAIT AIRWAYS   Kuwaiti (KU/KAC)   Kuwait City (KWI)

☐ 9K-AHI	Airbus A300C4-620	344	ex PK-MAY	Al-Sabahiya	opf Govt {KWI]
☐ 9K-AMA	Airbus A300B4-605R	673	ex F-WWAQ	Failaka	
☐ 9K-AMB	Airbus A300B4-605R	694	ex F-WWAV	Burghan	
☐ 9K-AMC	Airbus A300B4-605R	699	ex F-WWAM	Wafra	
☐ 9K-AMD	Airbus A300B4-605R	719	ex F-WWAB	Wara	
☐ 9K-AME	Airbus A300B4-605R	721	ex F-WWAG	Al-Rawdhatain	
☐ 9K-AKA	Airbus A320-212	0181	ex F-WWIU	Bubbyan	
☐ 9K-AKB	Airbus A320-212	0182	ex F-WWIV	Kubber	
☐ 9K-AKC	Airbus A320-212	0195	ex F-WWDP	Qurtoba	
☐ 9K-AKD	Airbus A320-212	2046	ex F-WWBG	Al-Mubarakiya	opf Govt
☐ 9K-AKE	Airbus A320-214/S	6350	ex F-WWBY	Al Boom	♦
☐ 9K-AKF	Airbus A320-214/S	6375	ex F-WWDO	Sanbouk	♦
☐ 9K-AKG	Airbus A320-214/S	6458	ex F-WWDU	Bateel	♦
☐ 9K-AKH	Airbus A320-214/S	6476	ex F-WWBK	Jalboot	♦
☐ 9K-AKI	Airbus A320-214/S	6500	ex F-WWIS	Shuwi	♦
☐ 9K-AKJ	Airbus A320-214/S	6516	ex F-WWBP		♦
☐ 9K-AKK	Airbus A320-214/S	6538	ex F-WWIB	Tashalah	o/o♦
☐ 9K-APB	Airbus A330-243	1643	ex F-WWKF		o/o♦
☐ 9K-APA	Airbus A330-243	1626	ex F-WWYV		o/o♦
☐ 9K-	Airbus A330-243	1653	ex F-WW		o/o♦
☐ 9K-	Airbus A330-243	1678	ex F-WW		o/o♦
☐ 9K-	Airbus A330-243	1681	ex F-WW		o/o♦
☐ 9K-ADE	Boeing 747-469M	27338/1046		Al-Jabariya	opf Govt
☐ 9K-ALA	Airbus A310-308	647	ex F-WWCQ	Al-Jahra	
☐ 9K-ALB	Airbus A310-308	649	ex F-WWCV	Gharnada	
☐ 9K-ALC	Airbus A310-308	663	ex JY-AGT	Kazma	
☐ 9K-ALD	Airbus A310-308	648	ex F-WWCR	Al-Salmiya	opf Govt
☐ 9K-ANA	Airbus A340-313	089	ex F-WWJX	Warba	
☐ 9K-ANB	Airbus A340-313	090	ex F-WWJZ	Bayan	
☐ 9K-ANC	Airbus A340-313	101	ex F-WWJE	Meskan	
☐ 9K-AND	Airbus A340-313	104	ex F-WWJJ	Al-Riggah	
☐ 9K-AOA	Boeing 777-269ER	28743/125		Al-Gurain	
☐ 9K-AOB	Boeing 777-269ER	28744/145		Garouh	

9M- MALAYSIA (Federation of Malaysia)

AIRASIA		Asian express (AK/AXM)		Kuala Lumpur-Don Muang (DMK)
☐ 9M-AFA	Airbus A320-214	2612	ex F-WWBV	The Apprentice Asia c/s
☐ 9M-AFB	Airbus A320-214	2633	ex F-WWDY	
☐ 9M-AFC	Airbus A320-214	2656	ex F-WWIO	
☐ 9M-AFD	Airbus A320-214	2683	ex F-WWIT	
☐ 9M-AFE	Airbus A320-214	2699	ex F-WWDN	
☐ 9M-AFF	Airbus A320-214	2760	ex F-WWDT	
☐ 9M-AFG	Airbus A320-214	2816	ex F-WWIX	
☐ 9M-AFI	Airbus A320-216	2842	ex F-WWIG	
☐ 9M-AFL	Airbus A320-216	2926	ex F-WWDX	♦
☐ 9M-AFM	Airbus A320-216	2944	ex F-WWIN	
☐ 9M-AFO	Airbus A320-216	2989	ex F-WWIK	
☐ 9M-AFP	Airbus A320-216	3000	ex F-WWBL	1Malaysia c/s
☐ 9M-AFS	Airbus A320-216	3117	ex F-WWBB	
☐ 9M-AFT	Airbus A320-216	3140	ex F-WWDN	mface c/s
☐ 9M-AFU	Airbus A320-216	3154	ex F-WWDE	
☐ 9M-AFV	Airbus A320-216	3173	ex F-WWIO	
☐ 9M-AFW	Airbus A320-216	3404	ex F-WWBX	The AirAsia Mobile App c/s
☐ 9M-AFX	Airbus A320-216	3182	ex F-WWDU	
☐ 9M-AFY	Airbus A320-216	3194	ex F-WWIV	
☐ 9M-AFZ	Airbus A320-216	3201	ex F-WWID	
☐ 9M-AHA	Airbus A320-216	3223	ex F-WWBV	
☐ 9M-AHB	Airbus A320-216	3232	ex F-WWBF	
☐ 9M-AHD	Airbus A320-216	3291	ex F-WWDT	
☐ 9M-AHE	Airbus A320-216	3327	ex F-WWBH	Tune Talk c/s
☐ 9M-AHF	Airbus A320-216	3353	ex F-WWIE	
☐ 9M-AHG	Airbus A320-216	3370	ex F-WWDF	Ninetology c/s
☐ 9M-AHH	Airbus A320-216	3427	ex F-WWBB	
☐ 9M-AHJ	Airbus A320-216	3477	ex F-WWDH	
☐ 9M-AHL	Airbus A320-216	3521	ex F-WWDS	Prince Lubricants c/s
☐ 9M-AHM	Airbus A320-216	3536	ex F-WWID	
☐ 9M-AHP	Airbus A320-216	3582	ex F-WWDE	
☐ 9M-AHQ	Airbus A320-216	3628	ex F-WWIU	
☐ 9M-AHR	Airbus A320-216	3701	ex F-WWBP	green Lion c/s
☐ 9M-AHS	Airbus A320-216	3776	ex F-WWDX	
☐ 9M-AHT	Airbus A320-216	3997	ex F-WWDH	
☐ 9M-AHV	Airbus A320-216	4079	ex F-WWBP	
☐ 9M-AHW	Airbus A320-216	4098	ex F-WWDJ	
☐ 9M-AHX	Airbus A320-216	4263	ex F-WWBG	
☐ 9M-AHY	Airbus A320-216	4293	ex F-WWIY	
☐ 9M-AHZ	Airbus A320-216	4361	ex F-WWDP	
☐ 9M-AJA	Airbus A320-216/S	5897	ex F-WWBJ	
☐ 9M-AJB	Airbus A320-216/S	5905	ex F-WWDL	
☐ 9M-AJC	Airbus A320-216/S	5914	ex F-WWDT	
☐ 9M-AJD	Airbus A320-216/S	5863	ex (PK-AZK)	
☐ 9M-AJE	Airbus A320-216/S	5908	ex F-WWDN	
☐ 9M-AJG	Airbus A320-216/S	6048	ex F-WWDF	
☐ 9M-AJH	Airbus A320-216/S	6064	ex F-WWDO	
☐ 9M-AJI	Airbus A320-216/S	6075	ex F-WWIJ	
☐ 9M-AJJ	Airbus A320-216/S	6084	ex F-WWDL	
☐ 9M-AJK	Airbus A320-216/S	6088	ex F-WWDP	♦
☐ 9M-AJL	Airbus A320-216/S	6105	ex F-WWIH	♦
☐ 9M-AJM	Airbus A320-216/S	6096	ex F-WWDX	
☐ 9M-AJN	Airbus A320-216/S	6145	ex F-WWIZ	♦
☐ 9M-AJO	Airbus A320-216/S	6169	ex F-WWBH	♦
☐ 9M-AJP	Airbus A320-216/S	6158	ex F-WWBN	♦
☐ 9M-AJQ	Airbus A320-216/S	6204	ex F-WWDH	♦
☐ 9M-AJR	Airbus A320-216/S	6215	ex F-WWDO	♦
☐ 9M-AJS	Airbus A320-216	4989	ex RP-C8191	♦
☐ 9M-AJU	Airbus A320-216/S	6492	ex F-WWIK	♦
☐ 9M-AQA	Airbus A320-216	4404	ex F-WWBG	
☐ 9M-AQB	Airbus A320-216	4458	ex F-WWBF	
☐ 9M-AQC	Airbus A320-216	4793	ex F-WWID	
☐ 9M-AQD	Airbus A320-216	4882	ex F-WWIO	
☐ 9M-AQE	Airbus A320-216	4571	ex PK-AXP	
☐ 9M-AQF	Airbus A320-216	4582	ex PK-AXQ	
☐ 9M-AQG	Airbus A320-216	4477	ex PK-AXN	
☐ 9M-AQH	Airbus A320-216	4969	ex D-AVVB	
☐ 9M-AQI	Airbus A320-216	4486	ex PK-AXO	
☐ 9M-AQM	Airbus A320-216	5149	ex F-WWBU	
☐ 9M-AQN	Airbus A320-216	5272	ex F-WWII	
☐ 9M-AQO	Airbus A320-216	5347	ex F-WWIT	
☐ 9M-AQP	Airbus A320-216	5397	ex D-AUBZ	
☐ 9M-AQQ	Airbus A320-216/S	5428	ex F-WWIC	
☐ 9M-AQR	Airbus A320-216	5430	ex D-AVVM	
☐ 9M-AQS	Airbus A320-216	5431	ex F-WWIF	
☐ 9M-AQU	Airbus A320-216/S	5505	ex F-WWBU	
☐ 9M-AQV	Airbus A320-216/S	5619	ex F-WWIH	

☐ 9M-AQX	Airbus A320-216/S	5547	ex JA04AJ			
☐ 9M-AQY	Airbus A320-216/S	5846	ex F-WWBN			
☐ 9M-AQZ	Airbus A320-216/S	5888	ex F-WWIQ			
☐ 9M-	Airbus A320-216/S	6262	ex F-WWDX			o/o♦
☐ 9M-	Airbus A320-216/S	6676	ex			o/o♦
☐ 9M-	Airbus A320-216/S	6702	ex			o/o♦
☐ 9M-	Airbus A320-216/S	6961	ex			o/o♦

AIRASIA X (D7/XAX) Kuala Lumpur-Sultan Abdul Aziz Shah (KUL)

☐ 9M-XAA	Airbus A330-301	054	ex N54AN		
☐ 9M-XBA	Airbus A330-343E	1619	ex F-WWYI		o/o♦
☐ 9M-XXA	Airbus A330-343E	952	ex F-WWKR	Xuberance	
☐ 9M-XXB	Airbus A330-343E	974	ex F-WWKD	Xhilaration	
☐ 9M-XXC	Airbus A330-343E	1048	ex F-WWKI	Midnight Xcapade	
☐ 9M-XXD	Airbus A330-343E	1066	ex F-WWYI	Soaring Xpectations	
☐ 9M-XXE	Airbus A330-343E	1075	ex F-WWKS	Pioneering Xpedition	
☐ 9M-XXF	Airbus A330-343E	1126	ex F-WWYQ	Northern Xposure	
☐ 9M-XXG	Airbus A330-343E	1131	ex F-WWYY	Southern Xross	
☐ 9M-XXH	Airbus A330-343E	1165	ex F-WWYG	Xtraordinary 1000	
☐ 9M-XXI	Airbus A330-343E	1411	ex F-WWCM	Xakura Blossom	
☐ 9M-XXJ	Airbus A330-343E	1423	ex F-WWRY	Harmonious DiverXity	>VCV
☐ 9M-XXK	Airbus A330-343E	1433	ex F-WWCS	Xklusive	>KNE
☐ 9M-XXM	Airbus A330-343	741	ex B-HWJ		
☐ 9M-XXP	Airbus A330-343E	1481	ex F-WWYX	Xiao Long Bao	
☐ 9M-XXS	Airbus A330-343E	1533	ex F-WWCI	Xiaolin Spirit	♦
☐ 9M-XXT	Airbus A330-343E	1549	ex F-WWKD	Xcintillating PhoeniX c/s♦	
☐ 9M-XXU	Airbus A330-343E	1581	ex F-WWCM		♦
☐ 9M-XXV	Airbus A330-343E	1589	ex F-WWCI	Global Xpansion	♦
☐ 9M-XXY	Airbus A330-343E	1600	ex F-WWYC		♦
☐ 9M-XXW	Airbus A330-343E	1596	ex F-WWYO		♦
☐ 9M-XXZ	Airbus A330-343E	1612	ex F-WWKS		♦
☐ 9M-	Airbus A330-343E	1646	ex F-WWKM		o/o♦
☐ 9M-	Airbus A330-343E	1659	ex F-WW		o/o♦
☐ 9M-	Airbus A330-343E	1666	ex F-WW		o/o♦
☐ 9M-	Airbus A330-343E	1668	ex F-WW		o/o♦
☐ 9M-	Airbus A330-343E	1670	ex F-WW		o/o♦
☐ 9M-	Airbus A330-343E	1674	ex F-WW		o/o♦
☐ 9M-	Airbus A330-343E	1734	ex F-WW		o/o♦
☐ 9M-	Airbus A330-343E	1740	ex F-WW		o/o♦
☐ 9M-	Airbus A330-343E	1743	ex F-WW		o/o♦
☐ 9M-XAB	Airbus A340-313X	273	ex C-GDVW		
☐ 9M-XAC	Airbus A340-313X	278	ex C-GDVZ		

AWAN INSPIRASI Miri

☐ 9M-AIK	Sikorsky S-76C+	760622	ex C-GHRK	
☐ 9M-AIM	Eurocopter EC225LP	2769	ex F-WGYO	
☐ 9M-AIN	Eurocopter EC225LP	2804		
☐ 9M-AIO	Eurocopter EC225LP	2572	ex F-WWOA	
☐ 9M-AIP	AgustaWestland AW139	41319		♦
☐ 9M-AIR	AgustaWestland AW139	31485		♦
☐ 9M-AIW	AgustaWestland AW139	31498		♦

EAGLEXPRESS AIR (9A/EZX)

☐ 9M-ACM	Boeing 747-428C	25628/934	ex N697AC	
☐ 9M-MPD	Boeing 747-4H6	25701/997		>SVA
☐ 9M-MPK	Boeing 747-4H6	28427/1147		<MAS>SVA
☐ 9M-MPM	Boeing 747-4H6	28435/1152		>SVA♦

FIREFLY (FY/FFM) Penang (PEN)

☐ 9M-FYA	ATR 72-212A	812	ex F-WWEB	
☐ 9M-FYB	ATR 72-212A	814	ex F-WWED	
☐ 9M-FYC	ATR 72-212A	821	ex F-WWEK	
☐ 9M-FYD	ATR 72-212A	830	ex F-WWEE	
☐ 9M-FYE	ATR 72-212A	840	ex F-WWER	
☐ 9M-FYF	ATR 72-212A	860	ex F-WWEF	
☐ 9M-FYG	ATR 72-212A	868	ex F-WWES	
☐ 9M-FYH	ATR 72-212A	934	ex F-WWEJ	
☐ 9M-FYI	ATR 72-212A	935	ex F-WWEK	
☐ 9M-FYJ	ATR 72-212A	941	ex F-WWEQ	
☐ 9M-FYK	ATR 72-212A	947	ex F-WWEX	
☐ 9M-FYL	ATR 72-212A	948	ex F-WWEZ	
☐ 9M-FIA	ATR 72-600	1093	ex F-WWEF	Exim Bank c/s
☐ 9M-FIB	ATR 72-600	1128	ex F-WWEQ	
☐ 9M-FIC	ATR 72-600	1158	ex F-WWEW	♦
☐ 9M-FID	ATR 72-600	1178	ex F-WWES	♦
☐ 9M-FIE	ATR 72-600	1235	ex F-WWEJ	♦

| ☐ 9M-FIF | ATR 72-600 | 1259 | ex F-WWEK | o/o♦ |

GADING SARI AVIATION SERVICES (GSB) Kuala Lumpur-Sultan Abdul Aziz Shah (KUL)

| ☐ 9M-GSA | Boeing 737-4B7F | 24559/1847 | ex EC-LKB | |
| ☐ 9M-GSB | Boeing 737-46QSF | 28661/2910 | ex N661AG | |

HEVILIFT

☐ 9M-AVM	Eurocopter EC135P2+ Ecureuil	0789	ex D-HECM	♦
☐ 9M-HBS	Eurocopter EC155B1	6977		♦
☐ 9M-HLL	Sikorsky S-76C			♦
☐ 9M-HLM	Sikorsky S-76C++			♦
☐ 9M-HLN	Sikorsky S-76C			♦

HORNBILL SKYWAYS

| ☐ 9M-WSC | Beech B300 King Air | FL-826 | ex N826KA | |

LAYANG-LAYANG AEROSPACE Layang (LAY) Miri (MYY)

☐ 9M-LLB	GAF N22C Nomad	N22C-95	ex VH-SNL	
☐ 9M-LLH	Bell 206B JetRanger III	2919	ex VH-WNA	
☐ 9M-LLI	GAF N22C Nomad	N22B-69	ex VH-MSF	
☐ 9M-LLM	Bell 206B JetRanger			
☐ 9M-LLR	MBB Bo105CBS			
☐ 9M-LLT	Bell 206B JetRanger	969	ex G-TUCH	
☐ 9M-LLU	Bolkow 105C			

MALAYSIA AIRLINES Malaysian (MH/MAS) Kuala Lumpur-Sultan Abdul Aziz Shah (KUL)

Member of oneWorld

☐ 9M-MKA	Airbus A330-322	067	ex F-WWKK	[KUL]
☐ 9M-MTA	Airbus A330-323E	1209	ex F-WWYG	dam 14Mar15
☐ 9M-MTB	Airbus A330-323E	1219	ex F-WWYX	
☐ 9M-MTC	Airbus A330-323E	1229	ex F-WWYJ	
☐ 9M-MTD	Airbus A330-323E	1234	ex F-WWYN	
☐ 9M-MTE	Airbus A330-323E	1243	ex F-WWYP	oneWorld c/s
☐ 9M-MTF	Airbus A330-323E	1281	ex F-WWKO	
☐ 9M-MTG	Airbus A330-323E	1318	ex F-WWYI	
☐ 9M-MTH	Airbus A330-323E	1336	ex F-WWTY	
☐ 9M-MTI	Airbus A330-323E	1337	ex F-WWTZ	
☐ 9M-MTJ	Airbus A330-323E	1347	ex F-WWCM	
☐ 9M-MTK	Airbus A330-323E	1388	ex F-WWYT	
☐ 9M-MTL	Airbus A330-323E	1395	ex F-WWKH	
☐ 9M-MTM	Airbus A330-323E	1431	ex F-WWCN	
☐ 9M-MTN	Airbus A330-323E	1470	ex F-WWYF	
☐ 9M-MTO	Airbus A330-323E	1489	ex F-WWTI	oneWorld c/s
☐ 9M-	Airbus A330-343E	1665	ex F-WW	o/o♦
☐ 9M-MNA	Airbus A380-841	078	ex F-WWSU	
☐ 9M-MNB	Airbus A380-841	081	ex F-WWAJ	
☐ 9M-MNC	Airbus A380-841	084	ex F-WWAD	
☐ 9M-MND	Airbus A380-841	089	ex F-WWSO	oneWorld c/s
☐ 9M-MNE	Airbus A380-841	094	ex F-WWAV	
☐ 9M-MNF	Airbus A380-841	114	ex F-WWSG	100th A380 c/s
☐ 9M-MMB	Boeing 737-4H6	26444/2308		wfs
☐ 9M-MMC	Boeing 737-4H6	26453/2332		wfs
☐ 9M-MMH	Boeing 737-4H6	27084/2391		[KUL]
☐ 9M-MMJ	Boeing 737-4H6	27097/2399		wfs
☐ 9M-MMK	Boeing 737-4H6	27083/2403		wfs
☐ 9M-MML	Boeing 737-4H6	27085/2407		wfs
☐ 9M-MMR	Boeing 737-4H6	26468/2445		[KUL]
☐ 9M-MMT	Boeing 737-4H6	27170/2462		wfs
☐ 9M-MMU	Boeing 737-4H6	26447/2479	ex VT-JAV	wfs
☐ 9M-MMW	Boeing 737-4H6	26451/2496		wfs
☐ 9M-MMX	Boeing 737-4H6	26452/2501		wfs
☐ 9M-MMZ	Boeing 737-4H6	26457/2521		[KUL]
☐ 9M-MQA	Boeing 737-4H6	26458/2525		[KUL]
☐ 9M-MQB	Boeing 737-4H6	26459/2530		[KUL]
☐ 9M-MQE	Boeing 737-4H6	26462/2542		wfs
☐ 9M-MQF	Boeing 737-4H6	26463/2560		[KUL]
☐ 9M-MQI	Boeing 737-4H6	27353/2632	ex 9H-ADJ	wfs
☐ 9M-MQK	Boeing 737-4H6	27384/2673		wfs
☐ 9M-MQQ	Boeing 737-4Y0	24915/2055	ex SX-BKL	wfs
☐ 9M-FFD	Boeing 737-85F/W	30007/746	ex ZS-SJI	
☐ 9M-FFE	Boeing 737-85F/W	30567/761	ex ZS-SJJ	
☐ 9M-FFF	Boeing 737-8FZ/W	39320/3690		
☐ 9M-MLD	Boeing 737-8GQ/W	35793/2428	ex N793AW	

☐ 9M-MLE	Boeing 737-8FH/W	35105/2501	ex N126RB		
☐ 9M-MLF	Boeing 737-8FZ/W	29657/3335	ex N1786B		
☐ 9M-MLG	Boeing 737-8FZ/W	31779/3395	ex N1787B		
☐ 9M-MLH	Boeing 737-8FZ/W	31723/3435	ex N1788B		
☐ 9M-MLI	Boeing 737-8FZ/W	31793/3503			
☐ 9M-MLJ	Boeing 737-8FZ/W	39319/3564			
☐ 9M-MLK	Boeing 737-8FZ/W	39321/3778			
☐ 9M-MLL	Boeing 737-8FZ/W	39322/3834			
☐ 9M-MLM	Boeing 737-8H6/W	39323/3885			
☐ 9M-MLN	Boeing 737-8H6/W	39324/4042			
☐ 9M-MLO	Boeing 737-8H6/W	39325/4085			
☐ 9M-MLP	Boeing 737-8H6/W	39326/4208			
☐ 9M-MLQ	Boeing 737-8H6/W	39327/4237			
☐ 9M-MLR	Boeing 737-8H6/W	39328/4257	ex N1796B		
☐ 9M-MLS	Boeing 737-8H6/W	39333/4618			
☐ 9M-MLT	Boeing 737-8H6/W	39334/4656			
☐ 9M-MLU	Boeing 737-8H6/W	39940/4872	ex N1786B		
☐ 9M-MLV	Boeing 737-8H6/W	39941/4917			♦
☐ 9M-MSA	Boeing 737-8H6/W	40143/4346			
☐ 9M-MSB	Boeing 737-8H6/W	40144/4385			
☐ 9M-MSC	Boeing 737-8H6/W	40145/4405			
☐ 9M-MSD	Boeing 737-8H6/W	40146/4447			
☐ 9M-MSE	Boeing 737-8H6/W	40147/4502			
☐ 9M-MSF	Boeing 737-8H6/W	40148/4512			
☐ 9M-MSG	Boeing 737-8H6/W	40149/4574	ex N5573K		
☐ 9M-MSH	Boeing 737-8H6/W	40150/4616			
☐ 9M-MSI	Boeing 737-8H6/W	40151/4640			
☐ 9M-MSJ	Boeing 737-8H6/W	40152/4685			
☐ 9M-MXA	Boeing 737-8H6/W	40128/3421	ex N1786B	1972 MAS c/s	
☐ 9M-MXB	Boeing 737-8H6/W	40129/3458	ex N1795B		
☐ 9M-MXC	Boeing 737-8H6/W	40130/3495	ex N1786B	oneWorld c/s	
☐ 9M-MXD	Boeing 737-8H6/W	40131/3577	ex N1787B		
☐ 9M-MXE	Boeing 737-8H6/W	40132/3723			
☐ 9M-MXF	Boeing 737-8H6/W	40133/3806			
☐ 9M-MXG	Boeing 737-8H6/W	40134/3873			
☐ 9M-MXH	Boeing 737-8H6/W	40135/3911			
☐ 9M-MXI	Boeing 737-8H6/W	40136/4287			
☐ 9M-MXJ	Boeing 737-8H6/W	40137/4131			
☐ 9M-MXK	Boeing 737-8H6/W	40138/4217	ex N6046P		
☐ 9M-MXL	Boeing 737-8H6/W	40139/4246			
☐ 9M-MXM	Boeing 737-8H6/W	40140/4276			
☐ 9M-MXN	Boeing 737-8H6/W	40141/4287			
☐ 9M-MXO	Boeing 737-8H6/W	40142/4317	ex N5573K		
☐ 9M-MXP	Boeing 737-8H6/W	40153/4723			
☐ 9M-MXQ	Boeing 737-8H6/W	40154/4749			
☐ 9M-MXR	Boeing 737-8H6/W	40155/4772			
☐ 9M-MXS	Boeing 737-8H6/W	40156/4815	ex N1796B		
☐ 9M-MXT	Boeing 737-8H6/W	40157/4848			
☐ 9M-MXU	Boeing 737-8H6/W	40158/4930	ex N1786B		♦
☐ 9M-MXV	Boeing 737-8H6/W	40159/4964			♦
☐ 9M-MXW	Boeing 737-8H6/W	40160/5040			♦
☐ 9M-MXX	Boeing 737-8H6/W	40161/5052	ex N1787B		♦
☐ 9M-MXY	Boeing 737-8H6/W	40162/5208			♦
☐ 9M-MPK	Boeing 747-4H6	28427/1147		Johor Bahru	>EZX
☐ 9M-MPN	Boeing 747-4H6	28432/1247		Pangkor	[KUL]
☐ 9M-MPP	Boeing 747-4H6	29900/1296		Putrajaya	wfs
☐ 9M-MPR	Boeing 747-4H6F	28434/1371			
☐ 9M-MPS	Boeing 747-4H6F	29902/1374			
☐ 9M-MRA	Boeing 777-2H6ER	28408/64	ex N5017V		
☐ 9M-MRB	Boeing 777-2H6ER	28409/74	ex N50217		
☐ 9M-MRC	Boeing 777-2H6ER	28410/78			
☐ 9M-MRE	Boeing 777-2H6ER	28412/115			
☐ 9M-MRF	Boeing 777-2H6ER	28413/128			
☐ 9M-MRG	Boeing 777-2H6ER	28414/140			
☐ 9M-MRH	Boeing 777-2H6ER	28415/151			
☐ 9M-MRJ	Boeing 777-2H6ER	28417/222			
☐ 9M-MRL	Boeing 777-2H6ER	29065/329			
☐ 9M-MRM	Boeing 777-2H6ER	29066/336			
☐ 9M-MRN	Boeing 777-2H6ER	28419/394			[KUL]
☐ 9M-MRP	Boeing 777-2H6ER	28421/496	ex N5016R		
☐ 9M-MRQ	Boeing 777-2H6ER	28422/498			
☐ 9M-MUA	Airbus A330-223F	1136	ex F-WWYZ		
☐ 9M-MUB	Airbus A330-223F	1148	ex F-WWYL		
☐ 9M-MUC	Airbus A330-223F	1164	ex F-WWKG		>THY
☐ 9M-MUD	Airbus A330-223F	1180	ex F-WWYR		

MALINDO AIRWAYS		**(MXD)**	**Kuala Lumpur-Sultan Abdul Aziz Shah (KUL)**	
☐ 9M-LMF	ATR 72-600	1081	ex F-WWER	<LNI
☐ 9M-LMG	ATR 72-600	1089	ex (PK-WGL)	<LNI

☐ 9M-LMH	ATR 72-600	1095	ex F-WWEH	<LNI
☐ 9M-LMJ	ATR 72-600	1123	ex F-WWEL	<LNI
☐ 9M-LMK	ATR 72-600	1130	ex F-WWES	<LNI
☐ 9M-LML	ATR 72-600	1135	ex F-WWEX	<LNI
☐ 9M-LMM	ATR 72-600	1147	ex F-WWEL	<LNI
☐ 9M-LMO	ATR 72-600	1154	ex F-WWES	<LNI♦
☐ 9M-LMP	ATR 72-600	1161	ex F-WWEB	<LNI♦
☐ 9M-LMQ	ATR 72-600	1179	ex F-WWET	<LNI♦
☐ 9M-LMR	ATR 72-600	1186	ex F-WWEC	<LNI♦
☐ 9M-LNF	Boeing 737-9GPER/W	38687/4368		<LNI
☐ 9M-LNG	Boeing 737-9GPER/W	38729/4380	ex (PK-)	<LNI
☐ 9M-LNH	Boeing 737-9GPER/W	38732/4484	ex (PK-LLF)	<LNI
☐ 9M-LNJ	Boeing 737-9GPER/W	38690/4495	ex (PK-LLG)	<LNI
☐ 9M-LNK	Boeing 737-9GPER/W	38737/4600	ex (PK-LLL)	<LNI
☐ 9M-LNL	Boeing 737-9GPER/W	38736/4592	ex N1786B	
☐ 9M-LNM	Boeing 737-8GP/W	39826/5122	ex N1796B	♦
☐ 9M-LNP	Boeing 737-8GP/W	39830/5159		♦

MASWINGS   (MWG)   Kota Kinabalu Intl (BXI)

☐ 9M-MWA	ATR 72-212A	817	ex F-WWEG		
☐ 9M-MWB	ATR 72-212A	856	ex F-WWEX		
☐ 9M-MWC	ATR 72-212A	863	ex F-WWEL		
☐ 9M-MWD	ATR 72-212A	873	ex F-WWEX		
☐ 9M-MWE	ATR 72-212A	885	ex F-WWEO		
☐ 9M-MWF	ATR 72-212A	889	ex F-WWET		
☐ 9M-MWG	ATR 72-212A	895	ex F-WWEE		
☐ 9M-MWH	ATR 72-212A	900	ex F-WWEO		
☐ 9M-MWI	ATR 72-212A	904	ex F-WWET	Bario	
☐ 9M-MWJ	ATR 72-212A	910	ex F-WWEH		
☐ 9M-MYA	ATR 72-600	1099	ex F-WWEL		
☐ 9M-MYB	ATR 72-600	1153	ex F-WWER		♦
☐ 9M-MYC	ATR 72-600	1170	ex F-WWEK		♦
☐ 9M-MYD	ATR 72-600	1187	ex F-WWED		♦
☐ 9M-SSA	de Havilland DHC-6 Twin Otter 400	880	ex C-GVVA		
☐ 9M-SSB	de Havilland DHC-6 Twin Otter 400	883	ex C-GFAP		
☐ 9M-SSC	de Havilland DHC-6 Twin Otter 400	886	ex C-FVGY		
☐ 9M-SSD	de Havilland DHC-6 Twin Otter 400	893	ex C-GFVT		♦
☐ 9M-SSE	de Havilland DHC-6 Twin Otter 400	894	ex C-GNVA		♦
☐ 9M-SSF	de Havilland DHC-6 Twin Otter 400	909	ex C-GVOT		♦
☐ 9M-MGE	Fokker 50	20166			[SZB]

MHS AVIATION/MALAYSIAN HELICOPTER SERVICES   Kerteh/Miri (KTE/MYY)

☐ 9M-SPB	Aérospatiale AS332L2	2636	ex F-WWOO		
☐ 9M-SPC	Aérospatiale AS332L2	2639	ex F-WWOJ		
☐ 9M-SPD	Aérospatiale AS332L2	2646	ex F-WWOO		
☐ 9M-SPE	Eurocopter EC225LP	2782	ex F-WWOP		
☐ 9M-SPF	Eurocopter EC225LP	2803	ex F-WJXL		
☐ 9M-SPG	Eurocopter EC255LP	2852	ex F-WWOY		
☐ 9M-SPH	Eurcopter EC225LP	2870	ex F-WWON		♦
☐ 9M-SPI	Eurocopter EC225LP	2868	ex F-WTAO		
☐ 9M-STK	Eurocopter EC225LP		ex VN-		
☐ 9M-STV	Aérospatiale AS332L1	2408			
☐ 9M-STW	Aérospatiale AS332L1	2312	ex LN-OBQ	<CHC Helicopters Intl	
☐ 9M-AIM	Eurocopter EC225LP	2769			
☐ 9M-SPP	Sikorsky S-76C+	760661	ex N45067		
☐ 9M-SPR	Sikorsky S-76C	760663	ex N4508G		
☐ 9M-STB	Sikorsky S-76C	760384			
☐ 9M-STC	Sikorsky S-76C	760392			
☐ 9M-STD	Sikorsky S-76C	760397			
☐ 9M-STF	Sikorsky S-76C	760400			
☐ 9M-STG	Sikorsky S-76C	760385	ex ZS-RTC		
☐ 9M-	Sikorsky S-76C+	760533	ex N76AF		♦
☐ 9M-	Sikorsky S-76C++	760609	ex N928DZ		
☐ 9M-	Sikorsky S-76C+	760613	ex N760MP		♦
☐ 9M-	Sikorsky S-76C++	760739	ex N269PA		♦
☐ 9M-AVP	Sikorsky S-61N	61768	ex G-BEKJ		
☐ 9M-SNA	Aérospatiale AS365N2 Dauphin 2	6246	ex N634LH	based Dengkil	
☐ 9M-SSV	Aérospatiale AS355F2 Ecureuil 2	5476		based Dengkil	
☐ 9M-SSW	Aérospatiale AS355F2 Twin Star	5467	ex N467CL	based Dengkil	
☐ 9M-SSZ	Aérospatiale AS355F2 Ecureuil 2	5292	ex 3A-MVV	based Dengkil	
☐ 9M-STL	Beech 1900D	UE-373	ex N31110		
☐ 9M-STM	Beech 1900D	UE-374	ex N31419		

NEPTUNE AIR   Warisan (N7/NEP)

☐ 9M-NEF	Boeing 737-3S3F	23811/1445	ex N811AN	

| ☐ 9M-NEP | Boeing 727-277F (FedEx 3) | 22641/1753 | ex VH-VLI | |

PAN MALAYSIAN AIR TRANSPORT — Pan Malaysia (PMA)
Subang-Sultan Abdul Aziz Shah International (SZB)

| ☐ 9M-PIH | Short SC.7 Skyvan 3 | SH1962 | ex G-BFUM | |

RAYA AIRWAYS — Transmile (TH/RMY) — Subang-Sultan Abdul Aziz Shah Intl (SZB)

☐ 9M-TGB	Boeing 727-2F2F/W (Duganair 3)	22998/1810	ex VH-DHF	
☐ 9M-TGE	Boeing 727-247F (FedEx 3)	21697/1471	ex PK-TMA	
☐ 9M-TGF	Boeing 727-247F (FedEx 3)	21698/1474	ex N209UP	
☐ 9M-TGG	Boeing 727-247F (FedEx 3)	21699/1485	ex N207UP	
☐ 9M-TGH	Boeing 727-247F (FedEx 3)	21701/1493	ex N208UP	
☐ 9M-TGJ	Boeing 727-247F (FedEx 3)	21700/1489	ex HS-SCH	[SZB]
☐ 9M-TGK	Boeing 727-247F (FedEx 3)	21392/1305	ex HS-SCJ	[SZB]
☐ 9M-TGM	Boeing 727-225F (FedEx 3)	22549/1737	ex N902RF	[SZB]
☐ 9M-TGN	Boeing 727-225F (FedEx 3)	21856/1537	ex N8887Z	[SZB]

SABAH AIR — Sabah Air (SAX) — Kota Kinabalu-Intl (BKI)

☐ 9M-AUA	GAF N22B Nomad	N22B-7		
☐ 9M-AWC	Bell 206B JetRanger III	2336		
☐ 9M-AYN	Bell 206B JetRanger III	3022	ex N5738M	
☐ 9M-AZK	Bcll 206L-3 LongRanger III	51484	ex N4196G	
☐ 9M-BKK	Aérospatiale AS355NA Ecureuil			
☐ 9M-MOH	Aérospatiale AS355NP Ecureuil			
☐ 9M-SAC	Bell 206B JetRanger III	2510		

SAZMA AVIATION

| ☐ 9M-SBO | Sikorsky S-76C++ | 760739 | ex N269PA | ♦ |

9N-   NEPAL (Federal Democratic Republic of Nepal)

AIR KASTHAMANDAP — Kathmandu (KTM)

☐ 9N-AIZ	Pacific Aerospace 750XL	154	ex ZK-JJH	
☐ 9N-AJB	Pacific Aerospace 750XL	160	ex ZK-KAZ	
☐ 9N-AJF	Pacific Aerospace 750XL	162	ex ZK-KAO	

BUDDHA AIR — Buddha Air (U4/BHA) — Kathmandu (KTM)

☐ 9N-AEE	Beech 1900D	UE-286	ex N11194	
☐ 9N-AEW	Beech 1900D	UE-328	ex N23179	
☐ 9N-AGH	Beech 1900D	UE-409	ex N4192N	
☐ 9N-AIM	ATR 42-300	388	ex F-WQNF	
☐ 9N-AIN	ATR 42-320	403	ex F-WQNA	
☐ 9N-AIT	ATR 42-320	409	ex F-WKVF	
☐ 9N-AJO	ATR 72-212A	535	ex F-WNUF	
☐ 9N-AJS	ATR 72-212A	531	ex B-3023	
☐ 9N-AJX	ATR 72-212A	578	ex F-WNUB	

GOMA AIR — Kathmandu (KTM)

☐ 9N-AJT	Cessna 208B Caravan I	208B0694	ex N694MA	dam 02May11
☐ 9N-AJU	Cessna 208B Caravan I	208B0770	ex N74KA	dam 27May13
☐ 9N-AKY	LET L-410UVP-E20	2917	ex OK-JDL	♦

MAKALU AIR — Kathmandu (KTM)

| ☐ 9N-AJG | Cessna 208B Caravan I | 208B0746 | ex N998LA | |

HIMALAYA AIRWAYS — (H9) — Kathmandu (KTM)

| ☐ 9N- | Airbus A320-214/S | 6626 | ex | o/o♦ |
| ☐ 9N | Airbus A320-214/S | 6686 | ex | o/o♦ |

MOUNTAIN HELICOPTERS

| ☐ 9N-AJJ | Aérospatiale AS350B2 Ecureuil | 3568 | ex ZS-RXR | |
| ☐ 9N-AJP | Aérospatiale AS350B3 Ecureuil | 4681 | ex EC-KZY | |

NEPAL AIRLINES — Nepal (RA/RNA) — Kathmandu (KTM)

☐ 9N-ABM	de Havilland DHC-6 Twin Otter 300	455	ex N302EH	Munal	♦
☐ 9N-ABT	de Havilland DHC-6 Twin Otter 300	812	ex C-GHHI	Gauthali	
☐ 9N-ABU	de Havilland DHC-6 Twin Otter 300	814	ex C-GHHY	Jureli	
☐ 9N-ABX	de Havilland DHC-6 Twin Otter 300	830	ex C-GIQS	Malewa	

☐ 9N-ACA	Boeing 757-2F8	23850/142		Karnali	
☐ 9N-ACB	Boeing 757-2F8C	23863/182	ex N5573K	Gandaki	
☐ 9N-AKQ	AVIC MA60		ex B-831L	Rara	
☐ 9N-AKR	AVIC MA60				o/o♦
☐ 9N-AKS	Harbin Y12E		ex B-963L		♦
☐ 9N-AKT	Harbin Y12E				o/o♦
☐ 9N-AKU	Harbin Y12E				o/o♦
☐ 9N-AKV	Harbin Y12E				o/o♦
☐ 9N-AKW	Airbus A320-232/S	6445	ex D-AXAR	Sagarmatha	♦
☐ 9N-AKX	Airbus A320-233/W	6555	ex D-AVVI	Lumbini	♦

SAURYA AIRLINES — Kathmandu (KTM)

| ☐ 9N-ALE | Canadair CRJ-200ER | 7493 | ex EC-HTZ | ♦ |

SHREE AIRLINES — Pokhara/Surkhet (PKR/SKH)

☐ 9N-ADD	Mil Mi-17-1 (Mi-8ATM)	59489607385	ex RA-22160	
☐ 9N-ADL	Mil Mi-17-1 (Mi-8ATM)	59489605283	ex RA-27093	[KTM]
☐ 9N-ADM	Mil Mi-8AMTV-1	95640	ex CCCP-25495	opf UN as UN0754
☐ 9N-AJA	Mil Mi-17	95895	ex 9N-ADN	
☐ 9N-AKG	Aérospatiale AS350B3 Ecureuil			

SIMRIK AIRLINES (RMK) — Kathmandu (KTM)

☐ 9N-AFA	de Havilland DHC-6 Twin Otter 300	665	ex VT-ERV
☐ 9N-AGI	Beech 1900C-1	UC-97	ex N97YV
☐ 9N-AGL	Beech 1900C-1	UC-108	ex N15656
☐ 9N-AIE	Dornier 228-202K	8165	ex 9M-VAA
☐ 9N-AIO	British Aerospace Jetstream 4101	41055	ex N316UE
☐ 9N-AIP	British Aerospace Jetstream 4101	41058	ex N322UE
☐ 9N-AIQ	British Aerospace Jetstream 4101	41064	ex N326UE
☐ 9N-AJH	Dornier 228-212	8198	ex VH-ATZ

SITA AIRLINES — Kathmandu (KTM)

| ☐ 9N-AHR | Dornier 228-202 | 8154 | ex C-GSAU |

TARA AIR (TB) — Kathmandu (KTM)

☐ 9N-ABM	de Havilland DHC-6 Twin Otter 300	455	ex N302EH	<RNA
☐ 9N-ABQ	de Havilland DHC-6 Twin Otter 300	655		<RNA [DOP]
☐ 9N-AET	de Havilland DHC-6 Twin Otter 300	619	ex C-GBQA	
☐ 9N-AEV	de Havilland DHC-6 Twin Otter 300	729	ex C-FWQF	
☐ 9N-AHS	Dornier 228-212	8218	ex RP-C2101	
☐ 9N-AKE	Dornier 228-212	8244	ex 8Q-IAR	
☐ 9N-AKK	Dornier 228-212	8239	ex RP-C1198	

YETI AIRLINES (YT/NYT) — Kathmandu (KTM)

☐ 9N-AHU	British Aerospace Jetstream 41	41072	ex N555HK
☐ 9N-AHV	British Aerospace Jetstream 41	41077	ex N561HK
☐ 9N-AHW	British Aerospace Jetstream 41	41078	ex N562HK
☐ 9N-AHY	British Aerospace Jetstream 41	41066	ex N553HK
☐ 9N-AIB	British Aerospace Jetstream 41	41017	ex G-CDYH
☐ 9N-AIH	British Aerospace Jetstream 41	41085	ex N567HK
☐ 9N-AJC	British Aerospace Jetstream 41	41096	ex G-MAJM

9Q-   DEMOCRATIC REPUBLIC OF CONGO

AIR FAST CONGO — Lubumbashi-Luano (FBM)

| ☐ 9Q-CDP | LET L-410UVP-E | 902519 | ex 9L-LCL |

AIR KASAI — Kinshasa-Ndolo (NLO)

☐ 9Q-CFA	LET L-410UVP-E	871921	ex 5V-TTF	
☐ 9Q-CFH	WSK-PZL Antonov An-2	1G137-35	ex ES-CAK	
☐ 9Q-CFL	Antonov An-26B	14003	ex RA-26593	opb Services Air
☐ 9Q-CFM	Antonov An-26B	10405	ex RA-26235	
☐ 9Q-CFP	Antonov An-26	10605	ex RA-26237	
☐ 9Q-CFT	WSK-PZL Antonov An-2	1G223-14	ex EK-40390	
☐ 9Q-CFU	WSK-PZL Antonov An-2	1G137-49	ex ES-CAJ	
☐ 9Q-CGD	Boeing 737-3S3QC	23788/1393	ex OE-IBS	<Gomair dam Dec13

AIR KATANGA — Lubumbashi-Luano (FBM)

☐ 9Q-CYD	Beech 1900C	UB-40	ex N495KL	
☐ 9Q-CVF	Hawker Siddeley 125-731	25118	ex N118DA	wfs
☐ 9Q-CYJ	Aérospatiale AS350B2 Ecureuil	3032	ex G-REAL	

AIR TROPIQUES — Kinshasa-Ndolo (NLO)

☐ 9Q-CEJ	Beech 1900C	UB-74	ex ZS-ODR	
☐ 9Q-CEO	LET L-410UVP	820837	ex 5R-MGZ	
☐ 9Q-CLN	Fokker F.27 Friendship 100	10152	ex ZS-OEH	wfs

BLUE AIRLINES — (BUL) — Kinshasa-N'djili (FIH)

☐ 9Q-CZO	Antonov An-26	13402	ex UR-26596

BLUESKY AIRLINES — Kinshasa-N'djili (FIH)

☐ 9Q-CSZ	McDonnell-Douglas MD-83	53063/1851	ex N969AS	♦

BUSINESS AVIATION OF CONGO — Kinshasa-Ndolo (NLO)

☐ 9Q-CYM	LET L-410UVP-E3	902402	ex RA-67620	wfs

BUSY BEE CONGO

☐ 9Q-CTD	LET L-410AB	710002	ex 5Y-HHF
☐ 9Q-CSW	LET L-410A	730209	ex 5Y-HHB

CAA – COMPAGNIE AFRICAINE D'AVIATION — (BU/ALX) — Kinshasa-N'djili (FIH)

☐ SX-BRS	Fokker 50	20206	ex PH-KVE	<MAV♦
☐ ZS-EVE	Boeing 737-230 (Nordam 3)	22123/726	ex UP-B3701	<Jet 4 Now♦
☐ 9Q-CAB	Fokker 50	20276	ex PH-LXP	
☐ 9Q-CAT	Airbus A320-212	0189	ex F-GTHL	
☐ 9Q-CCI	Fokker 50	20176	ex LN-RNC	
☐ 9Q-CCO	Airbus A320-211	0342	ex N342DK	
☐ 9Q-CIB	McDonnell-Douglas MD-82	49394/1285	ex N94EV	wfs
☐ 9Q-CJB	Fokker 50	20205	ex TF-JMO	♦
☐ 9Q-CPB	Airbus A320-212	0279	ex ZS-EJI	♦

GOMAIR — Goma (GOM)

☐ 9Q-CBX	Boeing 737-291	22089/632	ex N2089	
☐ 9Q-CGB	Boeing 727-22	19195/406	ex 9T-TCL	
☐ 9Q-CGD	Boeing 737-3S3QC	23788/1393	ex OE-IBS	>Air Kasai
☐ 9Q-CGW	Boeing 737-210	19594/102	ex C-GJLN	

ITAB – INTERNATIONAL TRANS AIR BUSINESS — Lubumbashi-Luano (FBM)

☐ 9Q-CAP	Shorts SD3.60	SH.3612	ex YN-CGG	
☐ 9Q-CDJ	Boeing 737-2Q8C	21959/610	ex ZS-PVU	
☐ 9Q-CFJ	HS.125-600B	256051	ex N601JA	VIP
☐ 9Q-CIT	G159 Gulfstream	193	ex ZS-JIS	
☐ 9Q-CJC	Partenavia P.68	227-19-TC	ex 7Q-YFZ	
☐ 9Q-CJF	HS.125-600B	256031	ex 9Q-CGF	VIP
☐ 9Q-COE	G159 Gulfstream	156	ex N41LH	

KIN AVIA — Kinshasa-N'Djili (FIH)

☐ 9Q-CEG	LET L-410UVP-E	912607	ex 3D-WDR	
☐ 9Q-CEN	LET L-410UVP-E3	892325	ex 3D-DEN	
☐ 9Q-CKA	LET L-410UVP-E	861722	ex 3D-CCF	
☐ 9Q-CMA	LET L-410UVP-E	902515	ex 3D-FTN	wfs
☐ 9Q-CRJ	LET L-410UVP-E	872006	ex 3D-MSC	

KORONGO AIRLINES — (ZC/KGO) — Lubumbashi-Luano (FBM)

☐ OO-LTM	Boeing 737-3M8/W	25070/2037	ex F-GMTM

LIGNES AERIENNES CONGOLAISES — Congolaise (V4/LCG) — Kinshasa-Ndolo (NLO)

☐ 9Q-CLG	Boeing 737-2L9	22071/620	ex ZS-PIV	[PGF]

MALU AVIATION — Kinshasa-Ndolo (NLO)

☐ 9Q-CKN	Nord 262C-61	74	ex (F-OHRB)
☐ 9Q-CLD	Short SC.7 Skyvan 3	SH1870	ex SE-LDK
☐ 9Q-CTC	G159 Gulfstream	1	ex 3X-GER
☐ 9q-	Short SD.3-60	SH3752	ex N136LR

SERVICES AIR — Kinshasa-N'Djili (FIH)

☐ 9Q-CNJ	Boeing 727-2S2F	22934/1828	ex N3588W	
☐ 9Q-CVS	Boeing 727-2S2F	22931/1825	ex N252CY	
☐ 9Q-CVN	Boeing 727-2S2F	22933/1827	ex N211FE	[FIH]♦

☐ 9Q-CVV	Boeing 727-2S2F	22935/1829	ex N213FE	[FIH]♦
☐ 9Q-	Boeing 727-2S2F	22925/1819	ex N203FE	[FIH]♦
☐ 5X-HJI	Airbus A310-304F	413	ex VT-EJI	
☐ 9Q-CFL	Antonov An-26B	14003	ex RA-26593	

STELLAVIA

☐ 9Q-CLL	HS.748 Srs.2A	1561	ex 9L-LBF	Frtr

SWALA AIRLINES   Bukavu (BKY)

☐ 9Q-CSD	Short SC.7 Skyvan 3A-100	SH1831	ex ZS-ORN	
☐ 9Q-CSL	Dornier 228-202	8069	ex D-ILWD	
☐ 9Q-CST	Short SC.7 Skyvan	SH1860	ex 5S-TB. Austria	
☐ 9Q-CXF	Short SC.7 Skyvan 3M-100	SH1915	ex (5Y-)	

TRANS AIR CARGO SERVICES   Kinshasa-N'djili (FIH)

☐ 9Q-CJG	Douglas DC-8-62F	46110/487	ex ZS-POL	
☐ 9Q-CJL	Douglas DC-8-62F (BAC 3)	45909/307	ex N802BN	
☐ 9Q-CJO	McDonnell-Douglas DC-8-73CF	46133/534	ex 3X-GHH	
☐ 9Q-CMP	Boeing 727-22C	19892/640	ex 3D-KMJ	wfs
☐ 9Q-CYS	NAMC YS-11A-205	2051	ex 3D-CYS	wfs

WILL AIRLIFT   Kinshasa-N'djili (FIH)

☐ 9Q-CNR	Douglas DC-9-32	47090/190	ex ZS-NRC	wfs

WIMBI DIRA AIRWAYS   Wimbidiera (WDA)   Kinshasa-N'djili (FIH)

☐ 9Q-CWE	Douglas DC-9-32 (ABS 3)	47701/822	ex N212ME	

9U-   BURUNDI (Republic of Burundi)

AIR BURUNDI   Air Burundi (PBU)   Bujumbura (BJM)

☐ 9U-BHG	Beech 1900C-1	UC-147	ex TN-AFK	
☐ 9U-BHU	AVIC MA-60		ex B-1019L	[BJM]

9V-   SINGAPORE (Republic of Singapore)

AIRMARK SINGAPORE   Singapore-Seletar (XSP)

Leases aircraft from other operators as required

JETSTAR ASIA AIRWAYS   Jetstar Asia (3K/JSA)   Singapore-Changi (SIN)

☐ 9V-JSA	Airbus A320-232	2316	ex F-WWDR	Asia's Got Talent c/s
☐ 9V-JSB	Airbus A320-232	2356	ex F-WWIQ	
☐ 9V-JSE	Airbus A320-232	2423	ex VH-JQW	
☐ 9V-JSF	Airbus A320-232	2453	ex VH-JQH	
☐ 9V-JSH	Airbus A320-232	2604	ex VH-VQA	
☐ 9V-JSI	Airbus A320-232	4443	ex F-WWIC	
☐ 9V-JSJ	Airbus A320-232	4515	ex F-WWBN	
☐ 9V-JSK	Airbus A320-232	4772	ex F-WWDH	
☐ 9V-JSL	Airbus A320-232	4786	ex F-WWDU	
☐ 9V-JSM	Airbus A320-232	4872	ex F-WWDQ	
☐ 9V-JSN	Airbus A320-232	4914	ex D-AVVO	
☐ 9V-JSO	Airbus A320-232	5305	ex D-AXAY	
☐ 9V-JSP	Airbus A320-232	5323	ex F-WWIN	
☐ 9V-JSQ	Airbus A320-232	5390	ex F-WWIZ	
☐ 9V-JSR	Airbus A320-232	5433	ex F-WWIH	
☐ 9V-JSS	Airbus A320-232/S	5472	ex F-WWBK	
☐ 9V-JSU	Airbus A320-232/S	5708	ex F-WWDN	
☐ 9V-JSV	Airbus A320-232/S	5813	ex F-WWBH	

SCOOT   Scooter (TZ/SCO)   Singapore-Changi (SIN)

☐ 9V-OTB	Boeing 777-212ER	28508/83	ex 9V-SQB	Big Yella Fella	
☐ 9V-OTC	Boeing 777-212ER	28509/86	ex 9V-SQC	Goin' Scootin' [ROW]
☐ 9V-OTD	Boeing 777-212ER	28510/90	ex 9V-SQD	Maju lah
☐ 9V-OTE	Boeing 777-212ER	28519/237	ex 9V-SQH	Scootalicious
☐ 9V-OTF	Boeing 777-212ER	28522/337	ex 9V-SRG	Bo-Eng Boeing ♦
☐ 9V-OFA	Boeing 787-8	37117/314		o/o♦
☐ 9V-OFB	Boeing 787-8	37118/335		o/o♦
☐ 9V-OFC	Boeing 787-8	37120/349		o/o♦
☐ 9V-OFD	Boeing 787-8	37121/375		o/o♦

☐ 9V-OFE	Boeing 787-8	37122/415		o/o♦
☐ 9V-OJA	Boeing 787-9	37112/240	Dream Start	♦
☐ 9V-OJB	Boeing 787-9	37113/272	Barry	♦
☐ 9V-OJC	Boeing 787-9	37114/284	Inspiring Spirit	♦
☐ 9V-OJD	Boeing 787-9	37115/308		o/o♦
☐ 9V-OJE	Boeing 787-9	37116/316		o/o♦
☐ 9V-OJF	Boeing 787-9	37119/337		o/o♦

SILKAIR · *Silkair (MI/SLK)* · Singapore-Changi (SIN)

☐ 9V-SBD	Airbus A319-132	1698	ex D-AVYE	
☐ 9V-SBE	Airbus A319-132	2568	ex D-AVXA	
☐ 9V-SBF	Airbus A319-132	3104	ex D-AVYI	
☐ 9V-SBG	Airbus A319-133	4215	ex D-AVYH	
☐ 9V-SBH	Airbus A319-133	4259	ex D-AVWO	
☐ 9V-SLC	Airbus A320-232	0969	ex F-WWBO	wfs
☐ 9V-SLE	Airbus A320-232	1561	ex F-WWBC	wfs
☐ 9V-SLF	Airbus A320-232	2058	ex F-WWBK	
☐ 9V-SLG	Airbus A320-233	2252	ex F-WWBB	
☐ 9V-SLH	Airbus A320-233	2517	ex F-WWIG	
☐ 9V-SLI	Airbus A320-233	2775	ex F-WWDS	
☐ 9V-SLJ	Airbus A320-233	3570	ex F-WWBD	
☐ 9V-SLK	Airbus A320-233	3821	ex F-WWIQ	
☐ 9V-SLL	Airbus A320-233	4118	ex D-AVVU	
☐ 9V-SLM	Airbus A320-233	4457	ex D-AXAA	
☐ 9V-SLO	Airbus A320-233	5050	ex F-WWDY	
☐ 9V-SLP	Airbus A320-233	5089	ex F-WWIM	
☐ 9V-SLQ	Airbus A320-233	5296	ex D-AXAN	
☐ 9V-SLR	Airbus A320-233	5531	ex D-AXAR	
☐ 9V-SLS	Airbus A320-233	5794	ex D-AXAG	
☐ 9V-MGA	Boeing 737-8SA/W	44217/4765		
☐ 9V-MGB	Boeing 737-8SA/W	44218/4808		
☐ 9V-MGC	Boeing 737-8SA/W	44219/4882		
☐ 9V-MGD	Boeing 737-8SA/W	44220/4926	ex N1796B	
☐ 9V-MGE	Boeing 737-8SA/W	44221/5021		♦
☐ 9V-MGF	Boeing 737-8SA/W	44222/5089		♦
☐ 9V-MGG	Boeing 737-8SA/W	44223/5140		♦
☐ 9V-MGH	Boeing 737-8SA/W	44224/5148		♦
☐ 9V-MGI	Boeing 737-8SA/W	44225/5260		♦
☐ 9V-MGJ	Boeing 737-8SA/W	44226/5355		♦

SINGAPORE AIRLINES · *Singapore (SQ/SIA)* · Singapore-Changi (SIN)

Member of Star Alliance

☐ 9V-SSA	Airbus A330-343E	1485	ex F-WWKV	
☐ 9V-SSB	Airbus A330-343E	1517	ex F-WWYC	
☐ 9V-SSC	Airbus A330-343E	1544	ex F-WWCU	
☐ 9V-SSD	Airbus A330-343E	1562	ex F-WWYU	♦
☐ 9V-SSE	Airbus A330-343E	1597	ex F-WWYP	♦
☐ 9V-SSF	Airbus A330-343E	1609	ex F-WWCV	♦
☐ 9V-SSG	Airbus A330-343E	1633	ex F-WWYK	o/o♦
☐ 9V-SSH	Airbus A330-343E	1648	ex F-WWKU	o/o♦
☐ 9V-STA	Airbus A330-343E	978	ex F-WWKZ	
☐ 9V-STB	Airbus A330-343E	983	ex F-WWYZ	
☐ 9V-STC	Airbus A330-343E	986	ex F-WWKG	
☐ 9V-STD	Airbus A330-343E	997	ex F-WWYM	
☐ 9V-STE	Airbus A330-343E	1006	ex F-WWYB	
☐ 9V-STF	Airbus A330-343E	1010	ex F-WWYF	
☐ 9V-STG	Airbus A330-343E	1012	ex F-WWKA	
☐ 9V-STH	Airbus A330-343E	1015	ex F-WWKV	
☐ 9V-STI	Airbus A330-343E	1085	ex F-WWKA	
☐ 9V-STJ	Airbus A330-343E	1098	ex F-WWKQ	
☐ 9V-STK	Airbus A330-343E	1099	ex F-WWYD	
☐ 9V-STL	Airbus A330-343E	1105	ex F-WWKR	
☐ 9V-STM	Airbus A330-343E	1107	ex F-WWKP	
☐ 9V-STN	Airbus A330-343E	1124	ex F-WWYK	
☐ 9V-STO	Airbus A330-343E	1132	ex F-WWYL	
☐ 9V-STP	Airbus A330-343E	1146	ex F-WWYV	
☐ 9V-STQ	Airbus A330-343E	1149	ex F-WWYH	
☐ 9V-STR	Airbus A330-343E	1156	ex F-WWKK	
☐ 9V-STS	Airbus A330-343E	1157	ex F-WWYX	
☐ 9V-STT	Airbus A330-343E	1382	ex F-WWYN	
☐ 9V-STU	Airbus A330-343E	1401	ex F-WWKZ	
☐ 9V-STV	Airbus A330-343E	1427	ex F-WWCH	
☐ 9V-STW	Airbus A330-343E	1447	ex F-WWKS	
☐ 9V-STY	Airbus A330-343E	1453	ex F-WWYE	
☐ 9V-STZ	Airbus A330-343E	1477	ex F-WWYS	

☐	9V-SKA	Airbus A380-841	003	ex F-WWSA		
☐	9V-SKB	Airbus A380-841	005	ex F-WWSB		
☐	9V-SKC	Airbus A380-841	006	ex F-WWSC		
☐	9V-SKD	Airbus A380-841	008	ex F-WWSE		
☐	9V-SKE	Airbus A380-841	010	ex F-WWSG		
☐	9V-SKF	Airbus A380-841	012	ex F-WWSI		
☐	9V-SKG	Airbus A380-841	019	ex F-WWSP		
☐	9V-SKH	Airbus A380-841	021	ex F-WWSQ		
☐	9V-SKI	Airbus A380-841	034	ex F-WWSC		
☐	9V-SKJ	Airbus A380-841	045	ex F-WWSG		
☐	9V-SKK	Airbus A380-841	051	ex F-WWAH		
☐	9V-SKL	Airbus A380-841	058	ex F-WWSI		
☐	9V-SKM	Airbus A380-841	065	ex F-WWSM		
☐	9V-SKN	Airbus A380-841	071	ex F-WWSX		
☐	9V-SKP	Airbus A380-841	076	ex F-WWSC		
☐	9V-SKQ	Airbus A380-841	079	ex F-WWST		
☐	9V-SKR	Airbus A380-841	082	ex F-WWSH		
☐	9V-SKS	Airbus A380-841	085	ex F-WWAH		
☐	9V-SKT	Airbus A380-841	092	ex F-WWSA		
☐	9V-SQJ	Boeing 777-212ER	30875/406			
☐	9V-SQK	Boeing 777-212ER	33368/428			
☐	9V-SQL	Boeing 777-212ER	33370/451			
☐	9V-SQM	Boeing 777-212ER	33372/485			
☐	9V-SQN	Boeing 777-212ER	33373/487	ex N5023Q		
☐	9V-SRJ	Boeing 777-212ER	28527/372			
☐	9V-SRK	Boeing 777-212ER	28529/389	ex N5022E		wfs
☐	9V-SRL	Boeing 777-212ER	32334/409			
☐	9V-SRM	Boeing 777-212ER	32320/438			
☐	9V-SRN	Boeing 777-212ER	32318/441			wfs
☐	9V-SRO	Boeing 777-212ER	32321/447			
☐	9V-SRP	Boeing 777-212ER	33369/448			
☐	9V-SRQ	Boeing 777-212ER	33371/449			
☐	9V-SVA	Boeing 777-212ER	28524/350	ex V8-BLC		[SIN]
☐	9V-SVB	Boeing 777-212ER	28525/353	ex V8-BLD		
☐	9V-SVC	Boeing 777-212ER	28526/355	ex V8-BLE		
☐	9V-SVD	Boeing 777-212ER	30869/366	ex V8-BLF		[SIN]
☐	9V-SVE	Boeing 777-212ER	30870/374			
☐	9V-SVF	Boeing 777-212ER	30871/378	ex V8-BLA		
☐	9V-SVG	Boeing 777-212ER	30872/398	ex V8-BLB		
☐	9V-SVH	Boeing 777-212ER	28532/407	ex N5022E		
☐	9V-SVI	Boeing 777-212ER	32316/412			
☐	9V-SVJ	Boeing 777-212ER	32335/415			
☐	9V-SVL	Boeing 777-212ER	32336/422			
☐	9V-SVM	Boeing 777-212ER	30874/430			
☐	9V-SVN	Boeing 777-212ER	30873/431	ex N5028Y		
☐	9V-SVO	Boeing 777-212ER	28533/471			
☐	9V-SNA	Boeing 777-312ER	42240/1279			♦
☐	9V-SNB	Boeing 777-312ER	42241/1340			o/o♦
☐	9V-SWA	Boeing 777-312ER	34568/586	ex N6018N		
☐	9V-SWB	Boeing 777-312ER	33377/592			
☐	9V-SWD	Boeing 777-312ER	34569/600			
☐	9V-SWE	Boeing 777-312ER	34570/602			
☐	9V-SWF	Boeing 777-312ER	34571/603			
☐	9V-SWG	Boeing 777-312ER	34572/604			
☐	9V-SWH	Boeing 777-312ER	34573/615			
☐	9V-SWI	Boeing 777-312ER	34574/618			
☐	9V-SWJ	Boeing 777-312ER	34575/623			
☐	9V-SWK	Boeing 777-312ER	34576/644	ex N6009F		
☐	9V-SWL	Boeing 777-312ER	34577/673			
☐	9V-SWM	Boeing 777-312ER	34578/701			
☐	9V-SWN	Boeing 777-312ER	34579/703			
☐	9V-SWO	Boeing 777-312ER	34580/708			
☐	9V-SWP	Boeing 777-312ER	34581/710			
☐	9V-SWQ	Boeing 777-312ER	34582/716			
☐	9V-SWR	Boeing 777-312ER	34583/722			
☐	9V-SWS	Boeing 777-312ER	34584/729			
☐	9V-SWT	Boeing 777-312ER	34585/759			
☐	9V-SWU	Boeing 777-312ER	42235/1124			
☐	9V-SWV	Boeing 777-312ER	42236/1136	ex N50217		
☐	9V-SWW	Boeing 777-312ER	42237/1184			
☐	9V-SWY	Boeing 777-312ER	42238/1250			♦
☐	9V-SWZ	Boeing 777-312ER	42239/1266			♦
☐	9V-SYF	Boeing 777-312	30868/360			
☐	9V-SYG	Boeing 777-312	28528/364			
☐	9V-SYH	Boeing 777-312	32317/420	ex N5020K		
☐	9V-SYI	Boeing 777-312	32327/484	ex N5028Y		
☐	9V-SYJ	Boeing 777-312	33374/503	ex N50217		
☐	9V-SYK	Boeing 777-312	33375/505			
☐	9V-SYL	Boeing 777-312	33376/515			

SINGAPORE AIRLINES CARGO — SinCargo (SQ/SQC) — Singapore-Changi (SIN)

☐ 9V-SFC	Boeing 747-412F	26560/1052		>CAO
☐ 9V-SFF	Boeing 747-412F	28026/1105		
☐ 9V-SFG	Boeing 747-412F	26558/1173		
☐ 9V-SFJ	Boeing 747-412F	26559/1285		[VCV]
☐ 9V-SFK	Boeing 747-412F	28030/1298		
☐ 9V-SFL	Boeing 747-412F	32897/1322	ex N5022E	[VCV]
☐ 9V-SFM	Boeing 747-412F	32898/1333		
☐ 9V-SFN	Boeing 747-412F	32899/1342		
☐ 9V-SFO	Boeing 747-412F	32900/1349		
☐ 9V-SFP	Boeing 747-412F	32902/1364		
☐ 9V-SFQ	Boeing 747-412F	32901/1369		

SWIFT AIRCARGO — Singapore-Changi (SIN)

☐ N583AN	McDonnell-Douglas MD-83	53183/2071	ex HK-4184X	>UBD
☐ N991JM	McDonnell-Douglas MD-83	53122/1984	ex 4L-LAU	
☐ N992JM	McDonnell-Douglas MD-83	49948/1905	ex 4L-LUL	
☐ 9V-	McDonnell-Douglas MD-83	53189/2121	ex N9414W	>TAC Airlines

TIGERAIR — Stripe (TR/TGW) — Singapore-Changi (SIN)

☐ RP-C6320	Airbus A320-232	5194	ex F-WWIG	
☐ 9V-TAE	Airbus A320-232	2724	ex F-WWDO	
☐ 9V-TAF	Airbus A320-232	2728	ex F-WWDU	
☐ 9V-TAM	Airbus A320-232	4181	ex F-WWIA	
☐ 9V-TAN	Airbus A320-232	4210	ex F-WWBR	
☐ 9V-TAO	Airbus A320-232	4421	ex F-WWDZ	
☐ 9V-TAP	Airbus A320-232	4445	ex F-WWIH	
☐ 9V-TAQ	Airbus A320-232	4469	ex F-WWBV	
☐ 9V-TAR	Airbus A320-232	4491	ex F-WWIB	
☐ 9V-TAS	Airbus A320-232	4493	ex F-WWID	
☐ 9V-TAT	Airbus A320-232	4532	ex F-WWDR	
☐ 9V-TAU	Airbus A320-232	4561	ex F-WWBB	
☐ 9V-TAV	Airbus A320-232	4608	ex F-WWIK	
☐ 9V-TAY	Airbus A320-232	4874	ex F-WWDY	
☐ 9V-TAZ	Airbus A320-232	4879	ex F-WWIN	
☐ 9V-TJR	Airbus A320-232	4645	ex VH-FJR	
☐ 9V-TRD	Airbus A320-232	4931	ex D-AXAD	
☐ 9V-TRH	Airbus A320-232/S	5496	ex F-WWBT	
☐ 9V-TRI	Airbus A320-232/S	5596	ex F-WWDQ	
☐ 9V-TRK	Airbus A320-232/S	5697	ex F-WWBN	
☐ 9V-TRL	Airbus A320-232/S	5721	ex D-AVVO	
☐ 9V-TRM	Airbus A320-232/S	5805	ex D-AXAJ	
☐ 9V-TRO	Airbus A320-232/S	6023	ex RP-C6319	wfs♦
☐ 9V-TRN	Airbus A320-232/S	5915	ex D-AUBB	
☐ 9V-TRV	Airbus A320-232	5449	ex PK-RMT	♦
☐ 9V-TRW	Airbus A320-232/S	5605	ex PK-RMU	♦
☐ 9V-TRX	Airbus A320-232/S	5662	ex PK-RMV	♦
☐ 9V-TRA	Airbus A319-132	3757	ex D-AVXC	[KUL]
☐ 9V-TRB	Airbus A319-132	3801	ex RP-C5320	[KUL]

9XR- RWANDA (Rwanda Republic)

RWANDAIR — Rwandair (WB/RWD) — Kigali (KGL)

☐ ET-ALX	de Havilland DHC-8-202	475	ex ZK-ECR		<TNW
☐ 7Q-YKW	Boeing 737-522	25384/2149	ex N917UA	Sapitwa	wfs
☐ 9XR-WF	Boeing 737-84Y/W	40892/3737			
☐ 9XR-WG	Boeing 737-84Y/W	40893/3817			
☐ 9XR-WH	Canadair CRJ-900ER	15286	ex C-GHZY		
☐ 9XR-WI	Canadair CRJ-900ER	15287	ex C-GIAD		
☐ 9XR-WJ	Boeing 737-7K5/W	30717/2228	ex D-AHXB		
☐ 9XR-WK	Boeing 737-7K5/W	30726/2298	ex D-AHXD		
☐ 9XR-WL	de Havilland DHC-8-402Q	4464	ex C-GXKR		
☐ 9XR-WM	Boeing 787-8	35507/17	ex (CN-RGB)		o/o
☐ 9XR-WN	Boeing 787-8	35508/19	ex (CN-RGC)		o/o

SILVERBACK CARGO FREIGHTERS — Silverback (VRB) — Kigali (KGL)

☐ 9XR-SC	Douglas DC-8-62F	46068/463	ex N990CF	wfs
☐ 9XR-SD	Douglas DC-8-62F	45956/376	ex N994CF	wfs

9Y- TRINIDAD & TOBAGO (Republic of Trinidad & Tobago)

BRIKO AIR SERVICE (BKO)

☐ 9Y-BKO	British Aerospace Jetstream 31	939	ex N340TE	[MIA]
☐ 9Y-JET	British Aerospace Jetstream 31	932	ex N338TE	
☐ 9Y-TIY	Cessna 402C	402C0265	ex N3146M	

BRISTOW CARIBBEAN Port of Spain (POS)

☐ 9Y-BCO	Bell 412EP	36401	ex N8087N	
☐ 9Y-BOB	Bell 412SP	36256	ex N368AL	
☐ 9Y-EVS	Bell 412SP	33212	ex XA-SBJ	<OLOG
☐ 9Y-JAW	Bell 412EP	36588	ex N460WB	
☐ 9Y-ONE	Bell 412EP	36421	ex N387AL	
☐ 9Y-SKY	Bell 412EP	36420	ex XA-HSS	
☐ 9Y-TNT	Bell 412EP	36414	ex N386AL	
☐ 9Y-AG311	AgustaWestland AW139			
☐ 9Y-AG312	AgustaWestland AW139			
☐ 9Y-AG313	AgustaWestland AW139			
☐ 9Y-AG314	AgustaWestland AW139			
☐ 9Y-DEL	AgustaWestland AW139	41221	ex N239BG	
☐ 9Y-ELL	AgustaWestland AW139	41363	ex N485SH	♦
☐ 9Y-ENT	AgustaWestland AW139	41368	ex N487SH	
☐ 9Y-TAJ	AgustaWestland AW139	41234	ex N339BG	
☐ 9Y-	AgustaWestland AW139	41374	ex N492SH	♦
☐ 9Y-DDG	Sikorsky S-76D	761015	ex N721BG	♦
☐ 9Y-HWO	Sikorsky S-76C	760804	ex N804L	

CARIBBEAN AIRLINES/EXPRESS Caribbean Airlines (BW/BWA) Port of Spain (POS)

☐ 9Y-TTA	ATR 72-600	968	ex F-WWLS		
☐ 9Y-TTB	ATR 72-600	973	ex F-WWLX		
☐ 9Y-TTC	ATR 72-600	989	ex F-WWLP		
☐ 9Y-TTD	ATR 72-600	993	ex F-WWLS		
☐ 9Y-TTE	ATR 72-600	997	ex F-WWLV		
☐ 9Y-ANU	Boeing 737-8Q8/W	28235/697	ex (9Y-SLU)		
☐ 9Y-BGI	Boeing 737-8Q8/W	28232/547	ex N1786B		
☐ 9Y-GEO	Boeing 737-8Q8/W	28225/433	ex PH-HSX		
☐ 9Y-JMF	Boeing 737-8Q8/W	30730/2399	ex N351LF		
☐ 9Y-JMB	Boeing 737-8Q8/W	30661/1186	ex 7O-ADN	Air Jamaica c/s	♦
☐ 9Y-JMC	Boeing 737-8Q8/W	28252/1195	ex N341LF		♦
☐ 9Y-JMD	Boeing 737-8Q8/W	30720/2235	ex F-WTAC		♦
☐ 9Y-JME	Boeing 737-86J/W	32919/1279	ex D-ABBH		♦
☐ 9Y-KIN	Boeing 737-8Q8/W	28234/680	(ex 9Y-ANU)		
☐ 9Y-MBJ	Boeing 737-85P/W	33980/2245	ex EC-KBV		
☐ 9Y-POS	Boeing 737-8Q8/W	28230/506			
☐ 9Y-SLU	Boeing 737-83N/W	28246/1081	ex N317TZ		
☐ 9Y-SXM	Boeing 737-8HO/W	37935/3716			
☐ 9Y-TAB	Boeing 737-8Q8/W	28233/598			
☐ 9Y-LGW	Boeing 767-316ER/W	26327/621	ex CC-CEB		
☐ 9Y-LHR	Boeing 767-316ER/W	27597/602	ex CC-CDP	MADIBA Nelson Mandela 1918-2013	

NATIONAL HELICOPTER SERVICES

☐ 9Y-LAS	Sikorsky S-76C	760680	ex N760ST	♦

JET AND TURBOPROP AIRLINERS IN NON-AIRLINE SERVICE

☐ YI-ASB	Airbus A300B-B4-2C	239	Government of Iraq
☐ A7-AFE	Airbus A310-308	667	Qatar Amiri Flight
☐ EC-HLA	Airbus A310-324ET	489	EADS Military Transport Aircraft Division
☐ F-RADA	Airbus A310-304	421	French Air Force
☐ F-RADB	Airbus A310-304	422	French Air Force
☐ F-RADC	Airbus A310-304	418	French Air Force
☐ F-WNOV	Airbus A310-304	498	Novespace
☐ HS-TYQ	Airbus A310-324	591	Royal Thai Air Force (also 60202)
☐ HZ-NSA	Airbus A310-304	431	Al-Atheer Establishment
☐ N461VA	Airbus A310-222	367	Van Vliet International
☐ N461WA	Airbus A310-222	372	Van Vliet International
☐ 9K-ALD	Airbus A310-308	648	Government of Kuwait
☐ J-757	Airbus A310-304	473	Pakistan Air Force
☐ T.22-1	Airbus A310-304	550	Spanish Air Force
☐ T.22-2	Airbus A310-304	551	Spanish Air Force
☐ 10+22	Airbus A310-304	503	German Air Force
☐ 10+23	Airbus A310-304	503	German Air Force
☐ 10+24	Airbus A310-304	434	German Air Force
☐ 10+25	Airbus A310-304	484	German Air Force
☐ 10+26	Airbus A310-304	522	German Air Force
☐ 10+27	Airbus A310-304	523	German Air Force
☐ 15001	Airbus A310-304	446	Royal Canadian Air Force
☐ 15002	Airbus A310-304	482	Royal Canadian Air Force
☐ 15003	Airbus A310-304	425	Royal Canadian Air Force
☐ 15004	Airbus A310-304	444	Royal Canadian Air Force
☐ 15005	Airbus A310-304	441	Royal Canadian Air Force
☐ A6-AAM	Airbus A318 Elite	1599	Dana Executive Jets
☐ A6-AJC	Airbus A318 Elite	3985	AJA - Al Jaber Aviation
☐ B-6186	Airbus A318 Elite	3333	China Eastern Business Aviation Service
☐ B-6936	Airbus A318 Elite	4732	GCL Poly Energy Holding
☐ HZ-RCA	Airbus A318 Elite	3932	Mid East Jet
☐ LX-GJC	Airbus A318 Elite	3100	Global Jet Concept
☐ M-HHHH	Airbus A318 Elite	4650	Kutus
☐ N777UE	Airbus A318 Elite	5478	Universal Entertainment
☐ OE-ICE	Airbus A318 Elite	4503	Avcon Jet
☐ VP-BKG	Airbus A318 Elite	4878	China Sonangol International
☐ VP-CCH	Airbus A318 Elite	4211	Gama Aviation
☐ VP-CKH	Airbus A318 Elite	3530	National Air Services (NAS)
☐ VP-CKS	Airbus A318 Elite	3238	National Air Services (NAS)
☐ VP-CYB	Airbus A318 Elite	5545	BAA Jet Management
☐ VQ-BDD	Airbus A318 Elite	3751	Royal Flight of Jordan
☐ A4O-AJ	Airbus A319CJ	4992	Oman Royal Flight
☐ A6-AFH	Airbus A319CJ	4228	ExecuJet Middle East
☐ A6-ESH	Airbus A319CJ	0910	Sharjah Ruler's Flight
☐ A7-HHJ	Airbus A319CJ	1335	Qatar Amiri Flight
☐ A7-MED	Airbus A319-133LR	4114	Qatar Amiri Flight
☐ A7-MHH	Airbus A319CJ	3994	Qatar Amiri Flight
☐ B-4090	Airbus A319-115	5023	Government of PRC
☐ B-4091	Airbus A319-115	5088	Government of PRC
☐ B-6933	Airbus A319CJ	4583	Business Aviation Asia
☐ D-ACBN	Airbus A319CJ	3243	DC Aviation
☐ D-ADNA	Airbus A319CJ	1053	DC Aviation
☐ D-ALEX	Airbus A319CJ	5963	K5 Aviation
☐ D-ALXX	Airbus A319CJ	4470	K5 Aviation
☐ EK-RA01	Airbus A319CJ	0913	Government of Armenia
☐ G-NMAK	Airbus A319CJ	2550	Al Kharafi Aviation
☐ G-NOAH	Airbus A319CJ	3826	Acropolis Aviation
☐ HL8080	Airbus A319CJ	5768	SK Telecom
☐ HS-TYR	Airbus A319CJ	1908	Royal Thai Air Force (Also 60221)
☐ LX-GVV	Airbus A319CJ	3542	Global Jet Luxembourg
☐ LX-MCE	Airbus A319CJ	2592	Global Jet Luxembourg
☐ LZ-AOB	Airbus A319-112	3188	Government of Bulgaria
☐ M-KATE	Airbus A319CJ	4151	Global Jet Concept
☐ M-RBUS	Airbus A319CJ	3856	Global Jet Concept
☐ N3618F	Airbus A319CJ	2748	Pharmair
☐ OE-LGS	Airbus A319CJ	3046	K5 Aviation
☐ VP-CJG	Airbus A319CJ	4353	MJet
☐ P4-MGU	Airbus A319CJ	5445	Global Jet Concept
☐ P4-MIS	Airbus A319CJ	3133	Global Jet Concept
☐ P4-RLA	Airbus A319CJ	4319	System Capital Management
☐ P4-VNL	Airbus A319CJ	2921	Global Jet Concept
☐ TC-ANA	Airbus A319CJ	1002	Government of Turkey
☐ TU-VAS	Airbus A319CJ	2192	Government of Ivory Coast
☐ UP-A2101	Airbus A319CJ	5538	Comlux KZ
☐ UR-ABA	Airbus A319CJ	3260	Government of Ukraine
☐ VP-BED	Airbus A319CJ	3073	Planair

☐ VP-BEX	Airbus A319CJ	2706	Planair
☐ VP-CAD	Airbus A319CJ	5040	
☐ VP-CAN	Airbus A319-112	1886	National Air Services (NAS)
☐ VP-CCJ	Airbus A319CJ	2421	Al Salam 319
☐ VP-CIE	Airbus A319CJ	1589	Mid East Jet
☐ VP-CSN	Airbus A319CJ	3356	Maz Aviation
☐ VP-CVX	Airbus A319CJ	1212	VW Air Services
☐ VQ-BKK	Airbus A319CJ	1485	TAG Aviation Asia
☐ VQ-BVQ	Airbus A319CJ	4842	Rizon Jet
☐ VT-IAH	Airbus A319CJ	2837	Reliance Commercial Dealers
☐ 4K-A102	Airbus A319CJ	2487	Government of Azerbaijan
☐ 6V-ONE	Airbus A319CJ	1556	Government of Senegal
☐ 9H-AGC	Airbus A319CJ	4583	Hilly Sky Group
☐ 9H-AGF	Airbus A319CJ	5261	Comlux Aviation Malta
☐ 9H-AVK	Airbus A319CJ	4622	Comlux Aviation Malta
☐ 9K-GEA	Airbus A319CJ	3957	Government of Kuwait
☐ 9M-NAA	Airbus A319CJ	2949	Royal Malaysian Air Force
☐ 0001	Airbus A319CJ	1468	Venezuelan Air Force
☐ 2101	Airbus A319CJ	2263	Brazilian Air Force
☐ 2801	Airbus A319CJ	2801	Czech Air Force
☐ 3085	Airbus A319CJ	3085	Czech Air Force
☐ 15+01	Airbus A319CJ	3897	German Air Force
☐ 15+02	Airbus A319CJ	4060	German Air Force
☐ MM62174	Airbus A319CJ	1157	Italian Air Force
☐ MM62209	Airbus A319CJ	1795	Italian Air Force
☐ MM62243	Airbus A319CJ	2507	Italian Air Force
☐ A4O-AA	Airbus A320-232	2566	Oman Royal Flight
☐ A6-DLM	Airbus A320-232	2403	Abu Dhabi Amiri Flight
☐ A6-HMS	Airbus A320-232	3379	Fujairah Amiri Flight
☐ A7-AAG	Airbus A320-232	0927	Qatar Amiri Flight
☐ A7-HSJ	Airbus A320-232/S	5255	Qatar Amiri Flight
☐ A7-MBK	Airbus A320-232	4170	Qatar Amiri Flight
☐ CS-TFY	Airbus A320-232	1868	Masterjet
☐ D-ATRA	Airbus A320-232	0659	DLR Flugbetriebe
☐ F-WWBA	Airbus A320-111	0001	Airbus
☐ HS-TYT	Airbus A320-214CJ	6112	Royal Thai Air Force
☐ HZ-XY7	Airbus A320-214	2165	National Air Services (NAS)
☐ KOC001	Airbus A320-214	4507	Government of Cambodia
☐ UK32000	Airbus A320-214	4528	Government of Uzbekistan
☐ VP-CHA	Airbus A320-232/S	5182	Aviation Link
☐ VP-CSS	Airbus A320-232CJ	3402	SAAD Air
☐ 9K-AKD	Airbus A320-212	2046	Government of Kuwait
☐ 9M-NAB	Airbus A320-232CJ	4199	Royal Malaysian Air Force
☐ 554	Airbus A320-214CJ	3723	Royal Air Force of Oman
☐ 555	Airbus A320-214CJ	4117	Royal Air Force of Oman
☐ 556	Airbus A320-214CJ	4795	Royal Air Force of Oman
☐ A7-HHM	Airbus A330-202	605	Qatar Amiri Flight
☐ A7-HJJ	Airbus A330-202	487	Qatar Amiri Flight
☐ EC-330	Airbus A330-203MRTT	747	EADS Military Transport Aircraft Division
☐ EC-377	Airbus A330-243	1312	Royal Air Force
☐ EC-339	Airbus A330-243MRTT	1080	United Arab Emirates Air Force
☐ F-RARF	Airbus A330-223	240	French Air Force
☐ F-WWCB	Airbus A330-203MRTT	571	Airbus Military
☐ F-WWKB	Airbus A330-203	925	Airbus
☐ F-WWKR	Airbus A330-243	1053	Constellation Aviation
☐ TC-TUR	Airbus A330-243 Prestige	1240	Government of Turkey
☐ UP-A3001	Airbus A330-243 Prestige	863	Government of Kazakhstan
☐ D-ADNA	Airbus A330-243 Prestige	1053	DC Aviation
☐ VP-CAC	Airbus A330-243 Prestige	1053	Specialized Aviation
☐ VP-CBE	Airbus A330-202	1321	Hong Kong Jet
☐ ZZ330	Airbus A330-243MRTT	1046	Royal Air Force
☐ ZZ331	Airbus A330-243MRTT	1248	Royal Air Force
☐ ZZ332	Airbus A330-243MRTT	1275	Royal Air Force
☐ ZZ333	Airbus A330-243MRTT	1312	Royal Air Force
☐ ZZ334	Airbus A330-243MRTT	1033	Royal Air Force
☐ ZZ335	Airbus A330-243MRTT	1334	Royal Air Force
☐ ZZ336	Airbus A330-243MRTT	1363	Royal Air Force
☐ ZZ337	Airbus A330-243MRTT	1390	Royal Air Force
☐ ZZ338	Airbus A330-243MRTT	1419	Royal Air Force
☐ ZZ339	Airbus A330-243MRTT	1439	Royal Air Force
☐ 1301	Airbus A330-243MRTT	1186	United Arab Emirates Air Force
☐ 1302	Airbus A330-243MRTT	1250	United Arab Emirates Air Force
☐ 2401	Airbus A330-202MRTT	980	Royal Saudi Air Force
☐ 2402	Airbus A330-202MRTT	996	Royal Saudi Air Force
☐ 2403	Airbus A330-202MRTT	1235	Royal Saudi Air Force
☐ 2404	Airbus A330-202MRTT	1379	Royal Saudi Air Force
☐ 2405	Airbus A330-202MRTT	1478	Royal Saudi Air Force
☐ 2406	Airbus A330-202MRTT	1516	Royal Saudi Air Force
☐ A7-AAH	Airbus A340-313X	528	Qatar Amiri Flight
☐ A7-HHH	Airbus A340-541	495	Qatar Amiri Flight

☐ A7-HHK	Airbus A340-211	026	Qatar Amiri Flight
☐ D-AAAL	Airbus A340-541	464	Lufthansa Technik
☐ D-AAAU	Airbus A340-642	468	Lufthansa Technik
☐ D-AIGZ	Airbus A340-313X	347	German Air Force
☐ F-RAJA	Airbus A340-212	075	French Air Force
☐ F-RAJB	Airbus A340-212	081	French Air Force
☐ F-WJKH	Airbus A340-541	1091	Kuwait Airways
☐ F-WJKI	Airbus A340-541	1102	Kuwait Airways
☐ F-WWAI	Airbus A340-311	001	Airbus
☐ F-WWCA	Airbus A340-642	360	Airbus
☐ HZ-A1	Airbus A340-211	009	Alpha Star Aviation
☐ HZ-HMS2	Airbus A340-213X	204	Saudi Ministry of Defense and Aviation
☐ HZ-124	Airbus A340-213	004	Government of Saudi Arabia
☐ M-IABU	Airbus A340-313E	955	Global Jet Concept
☐ PK-GBB	Airbus A340-541	1102	Government of Kuwait
☐ SU-GGG	Airbus A340-212	061	Government of Egypt
☐ TS-KRT	Airbus A340-542	902	Government of Tunisia
☐ VP-BMS	Airbus A340-541	560	Las Vegas Sands
☐ VP-CCC	Airbus A340-642	779	AJ Walter Aviation
☐ VP-CDD	Airbus A340-642	924	Government of Jordan
☐ V8-001	Airbus A340-212	046	Brunei Sultan Flight
☐ 7T-VPP	Airbus A340-541	917	Government of Algeria
☐ 9K-GBA	Airbus A340-541	1091	Government of Kuwait
☐ 9K-GBB	Airbus A340-541		Government of Kuwait
☐ 16+01	Airbus A340-313X	274	German Air Force
☐ 16+02	Airbus A340-313X	355	German Air Force
☐ F-WWDD	Airbus A380-861	004	Airbus
☐ F-WWOW	Airbus A380-841	001	Airbus
☐ EX-001	Antonov An-12B	5343606	Government of DR Congo
☐ RF-11260	Antonov An-12BK	8346003	
☐ UP-AN205	Antonov An-12BK	02348304	Kazakhstan Emercom
☐ 11529	Antonov An-12B	6344109	RSK Mig
☐ EW-007DD	Antonov An-26AFS	4708	Government of Belarus
☐ EW-009DD	Antonov An-26SLK	6604	Government of Belarus
☐ RF-00714	Antonov An-26	8310	DOSAAF
☐ RF-26256	Antonov An-26	6301	FSB
☐ RF-26257	Antonov An-26	8907	FSB
☐ RF-26258	Antonov An-26	9009	FSB
☐ RF-26259	Antonov An-26	12007	FSB
☐ RF-26260	Antonov An-26	13101	FSB
☐ RF-26261	Antonov An-26	13701	FSB
☐ RF-26262	Antonov An-26	13804	FSB
☐ RF-26265	Antonov An-26	13004	FSB
☐ RF-26266	Antonov An-26	13610	FSB
☐ RF-26267	Antonov An-26	13803	FSB
☐ RF-26268	Antonov An-26	14008	FSB
☐ RF-26269	Antonov An-26	14006	FSB
☐ RF-26270	Antonov An-26	14309	FSB
☐ RF-26271	Antonov An-26	8910	FSB
☐ RF-26272	Antonov An-26	14210	FSB
☐ RF-26273	Antonov An-26	13005	FSB
☐ RF-26274	Antonov An-26	13506	FSB
☐ RF-26275	Antonov An-26	2609	FSB
☐ RF-26276	Antonov An-26	9701	FSB
☐ RF-26276P	Antonov An-26		FSB
☐ RF-26277	Antonov An-26	9703	FSB
☐ RF-26278	Antonov An-26	13010	FSB
☐ RF-26279	Antonov An-26	14109	FSB
☐ RF-26280	Antonov An-26	11208	FSB
☐ RF-26281	Antonov An-26	11002	FSB
☐ RF-26282	Antonov An-26	14110	FSB
☐ RF-26283	Antonov An-26	9808	FSB
☐ RF-47323	Antonov An-26	5708	Directorate for Nuclear Technical Support
☐ RF-47324	Antonov An-26	10002	Directorate for Nuclear Technical Support
☐ RF-47325	Antonov An-26	8306	Directorate for Nuclear Technical Support
☐ RF-56300	Antonov An-26	1004	Russian Ministry of the Interior
☐ RF-56301	Antonov An-26	3207	Russian Ministry of the Interior
☐ RF-56302	Antonov An-26	4701	Russian Minsitry of the Interior
☐ RF-56303	Antonov An-26	7601	Russian Ministry of the Interior
☐ RF-56304	Antonov An-26	8307	Russian Ministry of the Interior
☐ RF-56305	Antonov An-26	8705	Russian Ministry of the Interior
☐ RF-56306	Antonov An-26	0403	Russian Ministry of the Interior
☐ RF-56307	Antonov An-26	1501	Russian Minsitry of the Interior
☐ RF-56308	Antonov An-26	8008	Russian Ministry of the Interior
☐ RF-56309	Antonov An-26	0605	Russian Ministry of the Interior
☐ RF-56310	Antonov An-26	11504	Russian Ministry of the Interior
☐ TJ-26633	Antonov An-26	5910	Tajikistan Air Force
☐ 26092	Antonov An-26	12705	NIIIS
☐ 26588	Antonov An-26B	13908	Aerogeophysical Flight Test Centre
☐ 26639	Antonov An-26KPA	10609	LII im Gromova

☐ 26691	Antonov An-26B	9205	NIIIS Nizhny Novgorod
☐ 29113	Antonov An-26	1301	LII Zhukovski
☐ UR-NTE	Antonov An-28	1AJ004-02	WSK/PZL
☐ D2-MBO	Antonov An-30A-100	1401	Angolan Air Force
☐ RA-30063	Antonov An-30D	1202	Aerogeophysical Flight Test Centre
☐ RA-30073	Antonov An-30	1304	Aerogeophysical Flight Test Centre
☐ RF-30080	Antonov An-30	1505	UN
☐ 30031	Antonov An-30A-100	0606	Government of Kazakhstan
☐ 30508	Antonov An-30	0508	UN
☐ ST-PAW	Antonov An-32B	3209	Sudan Police Air Wing
☐ 3C-4GE	Antonov An-32B	3603	Government of Equatorial Guinea
☐ 48119	Antonov An-32A	2209	RSK Mig
☐ 41910	Antonov An-38-200	3802002	Novosibirsk Aircraft Production Association
☐ UR-EXA	Antonov An-70	770102	Antonov Design Bureau
☐ D2-FEP	Antonov An-72	36572070688	Angolan Air Force
☐ D2-FGE	Antonov An-72	36572070695	Angolan Air Force
☐ D2-FGF	Antonov An-72		Anglolan Air Force
☐ RA-72946	Antonov An-72	36572090801	Russian Ministry of the Interior; wfs CKL
☐ RA-74003	Antonov An-74	36574070690	Republikha Sakha
☐ RF-72010	Antonov An-72	36572040550	FSB
☐ RF-72011	Antonov An-72	36572092841	FSB
☐ RF-72012	Antonov An-72	36572093866	FSB
☐ RF-72014	Antonov An-72	36572030468	FSB
☐ RF-72015	Antonov An-72	36572060620	FSB
☐ RF-72016	Antonov An-72	36572061625	FSB
☐ RF-72017	Antonov An-72P	36576090808	FSB
☐ RF-72018	Antonov An-72P	36576094880	FSB
☐ RF-72019	Antonov An-72P	36576090810	FSB
☐ RF-72020	Antonov An-72P	36576091825	FSB
☐ RF-72021	Antonov An-72P	36576091827	FSB
☐ RF-72022	Antonov An-72P	36576091830	FSB
☐ RF-72023	Antonov An-72P	36576096913	FSB
☐ RF-72024	Antonov An-72P	36576091830	FSB
☐ RF-72025	Antonov An-72P	36576094885	FSB
☐ RF-72026	Antonov An-72P	36576095895	FSB
☐ RF-72027	Antonov An-72P	36576095899	FSB
☐ RF-72028	Antonov An-72P	36576093870	FSB
☐ RF-72907	Antonov An-72	36572020375	Russian Ministry of the Interior
☐ RF-72922	Antonov An-72	36572040560	Russian Ministry of the Interior
☐ RF-72923	Antonov An-72	36572060590	Russian Ministry of the Interior
☐ RF-72924	Antonov An-2	36572060600	Russian Ministry of the Interior
☐ RF-72979	Antonov An-72	36572095908	Russian Ministry of the Interior
☐ ST-PRK	Antonov An-72-100	36572060642	Government of Sudan
☐ ST-PRM	Antonov An-72-100D	36572096914	Sudan Police Air Wing
☐ UP-72850	Antonov An-72-100	36576092850	Government of Kazakhstan
☐ 3C-CMN	Antonov An-72	36572092858	Government of Equatorial Guinea
☐ RA-74005	Antonov An-74TK-100	36547094892	FMBA Rossii
☐ ST-PRB	Antonov An-74	36547096918	Sudan Government
☐ ST-PRD	Antonov An-74-200	36547096924	
☐ 5A-CAA	Antonov An-74TK-300	3654701211080	Libyan DCA
☐ RDPL-34177	Antonov An-74TK-100	365470991005	Government of Laos
☐ ST-PRK	Antonov An-74	36547098956	Government of Sudan
☐ 5A-CAA	Antonov An-74TK-300	3654701211080	Libyan DCA
☐ 74008	Antonov An-74TK-200	3654701221089	Kazakhstan Ministry of the Interior
☐ 74082	Antonov An-74T-200A		Government of Kazakhstan
☐ RA-61707	Antonov An-148-100E	27015040007	FSB
☐ RA-61712	Antonov An-148-100EA	27015040012	FSB
☐ RA-61719	Antonov An-148-100EA	27015042019	FSB
☐ UR-UKR	Antonov An-148-100	0110	Antonov Design Bureau
☐ UR-NTN	Antonov An-158	0102	Antonov
☐ F-WWLY	ATR 42-600	811	ATR
☐ N313CG	ATR 42-320	358	US Department of Justice
☐ N366FM	ATR 42-320	549	US Department of Justice
☐ PNC-0243	ATR 42-300	287	Policia Nacional Colombiana
☐ TR-KJD	ATR 42F-312	131	Government of Gabon
☐ TT-ABE	ATR 42-300	230	Government of Tchad
☐ AR-	ATR 72-212A	788	Pakistan Navy
☐ F-WWEY	ATR 72-600	098	ATR
☐ HS-GCA	ATR 72-500	872	Royal Thai Air Force (Also 60313)
☐ HS-GCC	ATR 72-500	887	Royal Thai Air Force (Also 60315)
☐ HS-GCD	ATR 72-500	893	Royal Thai Air Force (Also 60316)
☐ PR-AZT	ATR-72-202	450	Imetame

☐ 7T-VPE	ATR 72-600	1200	Government of Algeria
☐ N162W	BAC One-Eleven 401AK	087	Northrop Grumman Systems
☐ N164W	BAC One-Eleven 401AK	090	Northrop Grumman Systems
☐ N999BW	BAC One-Eleven 419EP	120	Business Jet Access
☐ YR-BRE	BAC One-Eleven 561RC	405	Romavia
☐ YR-BRI	BAC One-Eleven 561RC	409	Romavia
☐ A6-AAB	Avro RJ100	E3387	Abu Dhabi Amiri Flight
☐ A6-LIW	Avro RJ70	E1267	Abu Dhabi Amiri Flight
☐ A6-RJ1	Avro RJ85	E2323	Dubai Air Wing
☐ A6-RJ2	Avro RJ85	E2325	Dubai Air Wing
☐ A9C-AWL	Avro RJ100	E3386	Bahrain Amiri Air Force
☐ A9C-BDF	Avro RJ85	E2390	Bahrain Amiri Air Force
☐ A9C-HWR	Avro RJ85	E2306	Bahrain Amiri Flight
☐ CP-2634	BAe 146-200	E2096	Minero San Cristobal
☐ G-BVRJ	Avro RJ70	E1254	Qinetiq
☐ G-LENM	Avro RJ85	E2273	Cello Aviation
☐ G-LUXE	BAe 146-300	E3001	Natural Environment Research Countil
☐ G-OFOA	BAe 146-100	E1006	Formula 1 Management
☐ G-OFOM	BAe 146-100	E1144	Formula 1 Management
☐ G-RAJJ	BAe 146-200	E2108	Cello Aviation
☐ G-SMLA	BAe 146-200	E2047	Jota Aviation
☐ G-TYPH	BAe 146-200	E2200	BAE Systems Corporate Air Travel
☐ LZ-LIM	Avro RJ70	E1258	Government of Bulgaria
☐ N114M	BAe 146-100	E1068	Montex Drilling
☐ PK-OSP	BAe 140-100	E1124	Metro TV
☐ QQ101	Avro RJ100	E3368	QinetiQ
☐ TJ-TAA	Bae 146-200	E2178	
☐ UK-80001	Avro RJ85	E2312	Government of Uzbekistan
☐ ZE700	BAe 146-100	E1021	Royal Air Force
☐ ZE701	BAe 146-100	E1029	Royal Air Force
☐ ZE707	BAe 146-200QC	E2188	Royal Air Force
☐ ZE708	BAe 146-200QC	E2211	Royal Air Force
☐ XS646	BAe Andover C.1	Set 30	QinetiQ
☐ C-FBIJ	BAe Jetstream 31	817	Les N Little
☐ FAB 045	BAe Jetstream 32	907	Bolivian Air Force
☐ FAB 046	BAe Jetstream 32	947	Bolivian Air Force
☐ G-BWWW	BAe Jetstream 31	614	BAE Systems (Operations)
☐ G-NFLA	BAe Jetstream 31	637	Cranfield Institute of Technology
☐ G-PLAJ	BAe Jetstream 31	738	Skybird
☐ HP-	BAe Jetstream 31	635	RML Alquileres
☐ HS-DCA	BAe Jetstream 31 Super	960	Thai Department of Aviation
☐ N380JT	BAe Jetstream 31	743	Monarca Air Freight
☐ N404GJ	BAe Jetstream 31	754	Northeast Air & Sea Services
☐ N408PP	BAe Jetstream 31	605	Sky High Aircraft
☐ N618SC	BAe Jetstream 31	618	KSC Enterprises
☐ N695MA	Bae Jetstream 31	695	M2 Aircraft Management
☐ N752VN	BAe Jetstream 31	752	Pentagon Group
☐ N849JS	BAe Jetstream 31	812	Driscoll Health Care Services
☐ N904EH	BAe Jetstream 31	613	Jetstream VIP
☐ RP-C2813	BAe Jetstream 32EP	853	Balesin Island Club
☐ TC-RSA	BAe Jetstream 32	986	Redstar Aviation
☐ 9Q-CFI	BAe Jetstream 32	960	Gecamines
☐ B-HRS	BAe Jetstream 41MPA	41102	Hong Kong Government Flying Service
☐ B-HRT	BAe Jetstream 41MPA	41104	Hong Kong Government Flying Service
☐ N602JF	BAe Jetstream 41	41038	FABCO Equipment I
☐ N679AS	BAe Jetstream 41	41056	Northstar Aviation
☐ N767KM	BAe Jetstream 41	41021	Soar Aircorp
☐ RP-C8298	BAe Jetstream 41	41013	Hyperlink Water & Electricity
☐ ZS-NOM	BAe Jetstream 41	41047	MGC Aircraft Management
☐ 41060	BAe Jetstream 41	41060	Royal Thai Army
☐ 41094	BAe Jetstream 41	41094	Royal Thai Army
☐ F-GVLC	Beech 1900	UC-168	JDP
☐ N27NG	Beech 1900D	UE-382	Northrop Grumman Systems
☐ N124YV	Beech 1900D	UE-124	US Department of State
☐ N191CS	Beech 1900D	UE-392	Freeport-McMoran
☐ N258AW	Beech 1900D	UE-258	US Department of State
☐ N378AW	Beech 1900D	UE-378	US Department of State
☐ N408SN	Beech 1900D	UE-408	US Department of State
☐ N470MM	Beech 1900D	UE-394	Schwan's Shared Services
☐ N640MW	Beech 1900C-1	UC-1	Marvin Lumber & Cedar
☐ N655MW	Beech 1900D	UE-377	Marvin Lumber & Cedar
☐ N1883M	Beech 1900D	UE-354	Meijer Stores Limited Partnership
☐ N83413	Beech 1900D	UE-25	Hawker Beechcraft
☐ N85516	Beech 1900D	UE-61	US Department of State
☐ TT-ABB	Beech 1900D	UE-406	Government of Tchad
☐ TU-VAP	Beech 1900D		Republican Forces of Côte d'Ivoire
☐ VH-EMI	Beech 1900C-1	UC-109	Hawker Pacific
☐ YV1894	Beech 1900D	UE-157	Toyota of Venezuela

☐ 5N-MPA	Beech 1900D	UE-149	Mobil Producing Nigeria
☐ 5N-MPN	Beech 1900D	UE-77	Mobil Producing Nigeria
☐ 5Y-JIA	Beech 1900D	UE-267	Government of Somalia
☐ 1906	Beech 1900C-1	UC-6	Republic of China Air Force
☐ 1907	Beech 1900C-1	UC-7	Republic of China Air Force
☐ RA-21511	Beriev Be-200	7682000002	Beriev TANTK
☐ D2-MAN	Boeing 707-321B	20025	Government of Angola
☐ D2-TPR	Boeing 707-3J6B	20715	Government of Angola
☐ EP-AJE/1001	Boeing 707-386C	21396	Iranian Air Force
☐ EP-NHA	Boeing 707-3J9C	21123	Government of Iran
☐ N88ZL	Boeing 707-330B	18928	Lowa
☐ N404PA	Boeing 707-32B	18835	US Air Force
☐ N707JT	Boeing 707-138B	18740	John Travolta
☐ 9Q-CLK	Boeing 707-138B	17702	Government of DRC
☐ TC-91	Boeing 707-387B	21070	Argentine Air Force
☐ TK.17-1	Boeing 707-331B	20060	Spanish Air Force
☐ TK.17-2	Boeing 707-331C	18757	Spanish Air Force
☐ TK.17-3	Boeing 707-365C	21367	Spanish Air Force
☐ 264	Boeing 707-3J6B	20721	Israeli Air Force
☐ 290	Boeing 707-3W6C	21956	Israeli Air Force
☐ 295	Boeing 707-366C	20919	Israeli Air Force
☐ 1002	Boeing 707-3J9C	20832	Iranian Air Force
☐ 2002	Boeing 707-370C	20891	Iranian Air Force
☐ 5-8301	Boeing 707-3J9C	20830	Iranian Air Force
☐ 5-8306	Boeing 707-3J9C	20835	Iranian Air Force
☐ 5-8310	Boeing 707-3J9C	21126	Iranian Air Force
☐ A9C-BA	Boeing 727-2M7RE/W	21824	Bahrain Amiri Flight
☐ C5-GAE	Boeing 727-051	19124	Royal Air
☐ C5-GAF	Boeing 727-095	19252	Government of Gambia
☐ C5-GOG	Boeing 727-1H2RE/W	20533	Government of Gambia
☐ FAC-1203	Boeing 727-151C	19868	Colombian Air Force
☐ FAC-1204	Boeing 727-2X3F	22608	Colombian Air Force
☐ FAE-620	Boeing 727-230	21620	Ecuadorian Air Force
☐ FAE-691	Boeing 727-134	19691	Ecuadorian Air Force
☐ HZ-AB3	Boeing 727-2U5RE	22362	Al Anwa Establishment
☐ HZ-RKR	Boeing 727-021	19006	Shazin Trading
☐ HZ-SKI	Boeing 727-212RE	21460	Al Tameer
☐ J2-KBA	Boeing 727-191	19394	Government of Djibouti
☐ M-FAHD	Boeing 727-076RE	19254	Flightec International
☐ M-FTOH	Boeing 727-269	22359	Strong Aviation
☐ M-STAR	Boeing 727-2X8	22687	Starling Aviation
☐ N25AZ	Boeing 727-030	18370	Aviation Consultants
☐ N30MP	Boeing 727-021	18998	MP Aviation
☐ N289MT	Boeing 727-223	22467	Raytheon
☐ N311AG	Boeing 727-017RE	20512	Vallejo Investments
☐ N408EC	Boeing 727-2S2FRE	22929	TAG Aviation (Stansted)
☐ N422BN	Boeing 727-227	20735	Roush Air
☐ N606DH	Boeing 727-030	18365	Clementine Aviation
☐ N706JP	Boeing 727-035	19835	Dodson Services
☐ N724CL	Boeing 727-051	19121	Clay Lacy Aviation
☐ N724YS	Boeing 727-281	21474	Fry's Electronics
☐ N727AH	Boeing 727-021	19261	Classic Designs of Tampa Bay
☐ N727BM	Boeing 727-230F	21442	Link Air Charter
☐ N727NA	Boeing 727-30C/W	19011	Air Linkers
☐ N727NK	Boeing 727-212	21945	FBA Airplane
☐ N794AJ	Boeing 727-227F/W	21243	Zero Gravity
☐ N800AK	Boeing 727-023/W	20045	Westar Aviation Services
☐ N908JE	Boeing 727-031RE	20115	JEGE
☐ N17773	Boeing 727-227	21045	Elan Express
☐ P4-FLY	Boeing 727-022	19148	Aviation Connexions
☐ P4-JLD	Boeing 727-193	19620	Government of Tatarstan
☐ S9-SVE	Boeing 727-030	18366	JR Executive
☐ TJ-AAM	Boeing 727-2R1	21636	Government of Cameroon
☐ TU-VAO	Boeing 727-2Y4	22968	Government of Côte d'Ivoire
☐ TY-24A	Boeing 727-256	20819	Government of Benin
☐ TZ-001	Boeing 727-2K5	21853	Government of Mali
☐ VP-BAP	Boeing 727-021	19260	Malibu Consulting
☐ VP-BDJ	Boeing 727-023	20046	Westar Aviation Services
☐ VP-BPZ	Boeing 727-017RE	20327	Peter Nygard
☐ VP-CCA	Boeing 727-2L4	21010	Layale Enterprises
☐ VP-CJN	Boeing 727-076	20371	Starling Aviation
☐ VP-CMO	Boeing 727-212/W	21948	Transatlantic Aviation
☐ VP-CZY	Boeing 727-2P1RE	21595	Jet Aviation Business Jets
☐ XC-FAD/3501	Boeing 727-014	18912	Mexican Air Force
☐ XC-FPA	Boeing 727-264	22413	Mexican Federal Police
☐ XC-MPF	Boeing 727-264F/W	22664	Mexican Federal Police
☐ XC-NPF	Boeing 727-264	22663	Mexican Federal Police
☐ XC-OPF	Boeing 727-264/W	22676	Mexican Federal Police
☐ XT-BBE	Boeing 727-14	18990	Government of Burkina Faso
☐ XT-BFA	Boeing 727-282RE	22430	Government of Burkina Faso

☐ YA-FAY	Boeing 727-228	22289	Afghan Air Force
☐ ZS-PVX	Boeing 727-2N6RE	22825	Fortune Air
☐ 5Y-GMA	Boeing 727-2Q9F	21930	Aerospace Consortium
☐ 6V-AEF	Boeing 727-2M1RE	21091	Government of Senegal
☐ 7O-ADA	Boeing 727-2n8	21842	Government of Yemen
☐ 9Q-CBA	Boeing 727-223	21526	Government of DRC
☐ 9Q-CDC	Boeing 727-030/W	18934	Government of DRC
☐ 9Q-CDJ	Boeing 727-041	20424	Government of DRC
☐ 9T-TCK	Boeing 727-022C	19806	Congolese Air Force
☐ 9T-TCL	Boeing 727-022C	19195	Congolese Air Force
☐ 3504	Boeing 727-014F	18909	Mexican Air Force
☐ 3505	Boeing 727-264	22661	Mexican Air Force
☐ 3506	Boeing 727-264	22662	Mexican Air Force
☐ 3517	Boeing 727-264	22412	Mexican Air Force
☐ AI-7304	Boeing 737-2Q8	21518	Indonesian Air Force
☐ A9C-DAA	Boeing 737-268	22050	Delmun Aviation Services
☐ C-FFAL	Boeing 737-2R8C	21711	Xstrata Canada
☐ C-GXNR	Boeing 737-2S2C	21929	Xstrata Canada
☐ FAE630	Boeing 737-236	21798	Ecuadorian Air Force
☐ FAP-350	Boeing 737-244	19707	Peruvian Air Force
☐ FAP-352	Boeing 737-244	23042	Peruvian Air Force
☐ HZ-MIS	Boeing 737-2K5	22600	Arabasco
☐ K2412	Boeing 737-2A8	23036	Indian Air Force
☐ K2413	Boeing 737-2A8	23037	Indian Air Force
☐ K3186	Boeing 737-2A8	20484	Indian Air Force
☐ K-3187	Boeing 737-2A8	20483	Indian Air Force
☐ N73HK	Boeing 737-2S9	21957	Executive Jet Aviation (Cayman Islands)
☐ N370BC	Boeing 737-247	23468	Basic Capital Majestic
☐ N500VP	Boeing 737-2H4	22062	VIP Holdings
☐ N733TW	Boeing 737-2H4	22732	Commercial Jet Partners
☐ N902WG	Boeing 737-2H6	22620	Gary 737
☐ VP-CAQ	Boeing 737-2V6	22431	Jet Connections
☐ VP-CBA	Boeing 737-2W8	22628	Casbah
☐ 5N-BMS	Boeing 737-2R8C	21710	JedAir
☐ 0207	Boeing 737-2N1	21167	Venezuelan Air Force
☐ 3520	Boeing 737-2B7	23133	Mexican Air Force
☐ A-7305	Boeing 737-4U3	25714	Indonesian Air Force
☐ A-7306	Boeing 737-4U3	25719	Indonesian Air Force
☐ B-10001	Boeing 737-4JQ	28492	Government of Republic of China
☐ EZ-A001	Boeing 737-341	26855	Government of Turkmenistan
☐ FAC1208	Boeing 737-4S3SF	25594	Colombian Air Force
☐ FAC1209	Boeing 737-46BC	25262	Colombian Air Force
☐ FAP356	Boeing 737-528	27426	Peruvian Air Force (also OB-1860)
☐ G-CIBE	Boeing 737-4Q8	26298	International Student Recruitment UK
☐ G-RAJG	Boeing 737-476	24439	Cello Aviation
☐ G-THOC	Boeing 737-59D	24694	TAG Aviation
☐ HS-CMV	Boeing 737-4Z6	27906	Royal Thai Air Force (also 11-111)
☐ HS-HRH	Boeing 737-448	24866	Royal Thai Air Force
☐ M-AZIZ	Boeing 737-505	24649	Azizi
☐ NAF916	Boeing 737-505	25791	Nigerian Air Force
☐ N35LX	Boeing 737-330	23528	Lockheed Martin Corp
☐ N37NY	Boeing 737-4YO	23976	Piedmont Aviation Services
☐ N129AC	Boeing 737-4Q8	26280	Juliet Romeo Aviation
☐ N274EL	Boeing 737-505	24274	European Aviation
☐ N321GG	Boeing 737-5H6	26445	GoGo
☐ N334CS	Boeing 737-3M8QC	24021	US Marshals Service
☐ N444HE	Boeing 737-39A/W	23800	Alticor
☐ N640CS	Boeing 737-4Y0	26078	US Marshals Service
☐ N788LS	Boeing 737-3L9	24220	Las Vegas Sands
☐ N789LS	Boeing 737-35B	24269	Las Vegas Sands
☐ N999FJ	Boeing 737-33A	27456	
☐ PR-CID	Boeing 737-33A	25033	Club Nautico Agua Limpa
☐ T-04	Boeing 737-5H6	26456	Argentine Air Force
☐ T7-CVG	Boeing 737-505	24645	Edge Aerodynamix
☐ XC-LJG	Boeing 737-322	24361	Mexican Air Force (also TP-03)
☐ XC-UJB	Boeing 737-33A	24095	Mexican Air Force (also TP-02)
☐ 4X-AOO	Boeing 737-4A8	24707	ELTA Electronics
☐ 5R-MRM	Boeing 737-3Z9	24081	Government of Madagascar
☐ 9H-MTF	Boeing 737-329	23774	Multiflight
☐ 99-999	Boeing 737-53A	24866	Royal Thai Air Force
☐ 921	Boeing 737-58N	28866	Chilean Air Force
☐ 922	Boeing 737-330QC	23524	Chilean Air Force
☐ 85101	Boeing 737-3Z8	23152	Korean Air Force
☐ A30-006	Boeing 737-7ES	33987	Royal Australian Air Force
☐ B-4080	Boeing 737-85N/W	36774	Government of PRC
☐ B-4081	Boeing 737-86N/W	36775	Governtment of PRC
☐ B-4082	Boeing 737-89L/W	40018	Government of PRC
☐ B-4083	Boeing 737-89L/W	40037	Government of PRC
☐ D-AAAM	Boeing 737-76N/W	35218	Lufthansa Technik
☐ HS-TYS	Boeing 737-8Z6/W	35478	Royal Thai Air Force (also 55-555)

☐ N660CP	Boeing 737-78D/W	36721	ConocoPhillips Alaska
☐ N668CP	Boeing 737-76N/W	38028	ConocoPhillips Alaska
☐ N737A	Boeing 737-7AX	30181	Saudi Aramco Aviation
☐ N737AT	Boeing 737-7HJC	36756	US Dept of Defense
☐ N738A	Boeing 737-7AX	30182	Saudi Aramco Aviation
☐ N743A	Boeing 737-7AXC	30184	Saudi Aramco Aviation
☐ N744A	Boeing 737-7AXC/W	30185	Saudi Aramco Aviation
☐ N959BP	Boeing 737-7BD/W	36720	ConocoPhillips Alaska
☐ 3701	Boeing 737-8AR/W	30139	Republic of China Air Force
☐ 65-328	Boeing 737-7ES/W	35328	Republic of Korea Air Force
☐ A36-001	Boeing 737 BBJ1	30829	Royal Australian Air Force
☐ A36-002	Boeing 737 BBJ1	30790	Royal Australian Air Force
☐ A6-AIN	Boeing 737 BBJ1	29268	Abu Dhabi Amiri Flight
☐ A6-DAS	Boeing 737 BBJ1	29858	Abu Dhabi Amiri Flight
☐ A6-DFR	Boeing 737 BBJ1	30884	Abu Dhabi Amiri Flight
☐ A6-HRS	Boeing 737 BBJ1	29251	Dubai Air Wing
☐ A6-RJX	Boeing 737 BBJ1	29865	Royal Jet
☐ A6-RJY	Boeing 737 BBJ1	29857	Royal Jet
☐ A6-RJZ	Boeing 737 BBJ1	29269	Royal Jet
☐ A6-002	Boeing 737 BBJ1	33963	Turkish Air Force
☐ B-5273	Boeing 737 BBJ1	38633	Deer Jet
☐ B-5286	Boeing 737 BBJ1	41658	Nanshan Jet
☐ B-LEX	Boeing 737 BBJ1	34683	Metrojet
☐ FAC0001	Boeing 737 BBJ1	29272	Colombian Air Force
☐ HL7227	Boeing 737 BBJ1	35977	Hanwha Chemical Corp
☐ HL7759	Boeing 737 BBJ1	35990	Samsung Techwin Aviation
☐ HL7787	Boeing 737 BBJ1	36852	Hyundai
☐ HL8270	Boeing 737 BBJ1	40586	Samsung Techwin Aviation
☐ HL8290	Boeing 737 BBJ1	41375	Hyundai Motor Co
☐ HZ-MF1	Boeing 737 BBJ1	33405	Saudi Ministry of Finance & Economy
☐ HZ-MF2	Boeing 737 BBJ1	33499	Saudi Ministry of Finance & Economy
☐ HZ-101	Boeing 737 BBJ1	32805	Royal Saudi Air Force
☐ K-5012	Boeing 737 BBJ1	36106	Indian Air Force
☐ K-5013	Boeing 737 BBJ1	36107	Indian Air Force
☐ K-5014	Boeing 737 BBJ1	36108	Indian Air Force
☐ LY-TVG	Boeing 737 BBJ1	60406	Hansel Prime
☐ M53-01	Boeing 737 BBJ1	29274	Royal Malaysian Air Force
☐ M-GEAA	Boeing 737 BBJ1	38408	Wuleen Investment
☐ M-URUS	Boeing 737 BBJ1	34622	Global Jet Concept
☐ M-YBBJ	Boeing 737 BBJ1	36027	Global Jet Austria
☐ N1TS	Boeing 737 BBJ1	39109	First Visual Air
☐ N43PR	Boeing 737 BBJ1	28581	The Town & Country Food Markets
☐ N50TC	Boeing 737 BBJ1	29024	Tracinda
☐ N90R	Boeing 737 BBJ1	32775	Swiftlite Aircraft
☐ N92SR	Boeing 737 BBJ1	37111	Star Flight Express
☐ N108MS	Boeing 737 BBJ1	33102	Las Vegas Sands
☐ N111VM	Boeing 737 BBJ1	36090	
☐ N162WC	Boeing 737 BBJ1	30329	The Washington Companies
☐ N260DV	Boeing 737 BBJ1	29142	RDV Leasing
☐ N301SR	Boeing 737 BBJ1	38854	Essar Shipping & Logistics
☐ N315TS	Boeing 737 BBJ1	30772	Tudor-Saliba
☐ N367BJ	Boeing 737 BBJ1	33102	Turkish Air Force
☐ N380BJ	Boeing 737 BBJ1	37700	
☐ N500LS	Boeing 737 BBJ1	29054	Hayes Productions
☐ N720MM	Boeing 737 BBJ1	33010	MGM Resorts Aviation
☐ N721UF	Boeing 737 BBJ1	30327	F&L Aviaton III
☐ N737AG	Boeing 737 BBJ1	30496	Funair
☐ N737CC	Boeing 737 BBJ1	29135	Mid East Jet
☐ N737ER	Boeing 737 BBJ1	30754	Boetti Air
☐ N737L	Boeing 737 BBJ1	30751	Legatum Aviation
☐ N737LE	Boeing 737 BBJ1	28579	Universal Jet Aviation
☐ N742PB	Boeing 737 BBJ1	29200	Chartwell Partners
☐ N788DP	Boeing 737 BBJ1	29441	DP World
☐ N800KS	Boeing 737 BBJ1	30782	AEJ Services
☐ N834BA	Boeing 737 BBJ1	29102	Boeing
☐ N835BA	Boeing 737 BBJ1	30572	Boeing
☐ N836BA	Boeing 737 BBJ1	30756	Boeing
☐ N887LS	Boeing 737-BBJ1	29233	Las Vegas Sands
☐ N888TY	Boeing 737 BBJ1	29749	TY Air
☐ N2708E	Boeing 737 BBJ1	39095	Artjet Three
☐ N7600K	Boeing 737 BBJ1	32628	SAS Institute
☐ N8767	Boeing 737 BBJ1	32807	Avjet
☐ N79711	Boeing 737 BBJ1	30547	Dallah Albaraka
☐ OE-IRF	Boeing 737 BBJ1	38855	Art Aviation
☐ PR-BBS	Boeing 737 BBJ1	32575	Banco Safra
☐ P4-AFK	Boeing 737 BBJ1	36493	Premier Avia
☐ P4-ASL	Boeing 737 BBJ1	29791	Arabasco
☐ P4-BBJ	Boeing 737 BBJ1	30070	JetMagic
☐ P4-KAZ	Boeing 737 BBJ1	32774	Prime Aviation
☐ P4-LIG	Boeing 737 BBJ1	37592	Petroff Air
☐ P4-MAK	Boeing 737 BBJ1	40761	VIPJet
☐ P4-NGK	Boeing 737 BBJ1	37583	Itera Holdings

☐ TS-IOO	Boeing 737 BBJ1	29149	Government of Tunisia
☐ TT-ABD	Boeing 737 BBJ1	29136	Government of Tchad
☐ TZ-PRM	Boeing 737 BBJ1	30328	Government of Mali
☐ VP-BBJ	Boeing 737 BBJ1	29273	Unifund
☐ VP-BBW	Boeing 737 BBJ1	30076	GAMA Aviation
☐ VP-BEL	Boeing 737 BBJ1	29139	Orient Global
☐ VP-BFT	Boeing 737 BBJ1	36714	Jet Aviation Business Jets
☐ VP-BIZ	Boeing 737 BBJ1	34477	ACM Aviation
☐ VP-BJJ	Boeing 737 BBJ1	30330	Avenir Worldwide
☐ VP-BOP	Boeing 737 BBJ1	40117	Longtail Aviation
☐ VP-BRT	Boeing 737 BBJ1	32970	Global Jet Concept
☐ VP-BWR	Boeing 737 BBJ1	29317	Usal
☐ VP-BYA	Boeing 737 BBJ1	29972	Saudi Oger
☐ VP-CAE	Boeing 737 BBJ1	38608	Pacific Sky Air Charter Services
☐ VP-CPA	Boeing 737 BBJ1	30031	Mid East Jet
☐ VQ-BTA	Boeing 737 BBJ1	29188	Gulf Wings
☐ ZS-RSA	Boeing 737 BBJ1	32627	South African Air Force
☐ 3C-EGE	Boeing 737 BBJ1	33367	Government of Equatorial Guinea
☐ 5N-FGT	Boeing 737 BBJ1	34260	Government of Nigeria
☐ 5U-GRN	Boeing 737 BBJ1	28976	Government of Niger
☐ 9H-BBJ	Boeing 737 BBJ1	30791	Privajet
☐ 01-0015	Boeing 737 BBJ1	32916	US Air Force
☐ 01-0040	Boeing 737 BBJ1	29971	US Air Force
☐ 01-0041	Boeing 737 BBJ1	33080	US Air Force
☐ 02-0042	Boeing 737 BBJ1	33500	US Air Force
☐ 02-0201	Boeing 737 BBJ1	30755	US Air Force
☐ 02-0202	Boeing 737 BBJ1	30753	US Air Force
☐ 02-0203	Boeing 737 BBJ1	33434	US Air Force
☐ 05-0730	Boeing 737 BBJ1	34807	US Air Force
☐ 05-0932	Boeing 737 BBJ1	34808	US Air Force
☐ 05-4613	Boeing 737 BBJ1	34809	US Air Force
☐ 06-003	Boeing 737 BBJ1	33964	Turkish Air Force
☐ A-001	Boeing 737 BBJ2	41706	Government of Indonesia
☐ A6-AUH	Boeing 737 BBJ2	33473	Abu Dhabi Presidential Flight
☐ A6-HEH	Boeing 737 BBJ2	32825	Dubai Air Wing
☐ A6-MRM	Boeing 737 BBJ2	32450	Dubai Air Wing
☐ A6-MRS	Boeing 737 BBJ2	35238	Dubai Air Wing
☐ CN-MVI	Boeing 737 BBJ2	37545	Government of Morocco
☐ D-AACM	Boeing 737 BBJ2	37663	ACM Air Charter
☐ EW-001PA	Boeing 737 BBJ2	33079	Government of Belarus
☐ HS-TYS	Boeing 737 BBJ2	35478	Royal Thai Air Force
☐ HZ-HR5	Boeing 737 BBJ2	32438	Saudi Oger
☐ HZ-102	Boeing 737 BBJ2	32451	Royal Saudi Air Force
☐ N371BC	Boeing 737 BBJ2	32791	Mid East Jet
☐ N713JM	Boeing 737 BBJ2	42510	Geermu
☐ N737GG	Boeing 737 BBJ2	40118	737 Two Aviation
☐ N737M	Boeing 737 BBJ2	33361	EIE Eagle
☐ OE-ILX	Boeing 737 BBJ2	32777	Global Jet Austria
☐ VP-BBZ	Boeing 737 BBJ2	39899	GAMA Aviation
☐ VP-BZL	Boeing 737 BBJ2	32915	Lowa
☐ VP-CBB	Boeing 737 BBJ2	32806	A S Bugshan & Bros
☐ VP-CSK	Boeing 737 BBJ2	34620	Nofa Aviation
☐ VQ-BOS	Boeing 737 BBJ2	35792	Bayham Holdings
☐ HZ-ATR	Boeing 737 BBJ3	39317	Saudi Ministry of Finance
☐ HZ-MF6	Boeing 737 BBJ3	39317	Saudi Ministry of Finance
☐ VP-BDB	Boeing 737 BBJ3	38890	Dallah Group
☐ VP-CEC	Boeing 737 BBJ3	37546	Peridot Associated
☐ VP-CKK	Boeing 737 BBJ3	37560	National Air Services
☐ 9K-GCC	Boeing 737 BBJ3	37632	Government of Kuwait
☐ A4O-SO	Boeing 747-SP27	21785	Oman Amiri Flight
☐ A9C-HAK	Boeing 747-SPZ5	23610	Bahrain Amiri Flight
☐ C-GTFF	Boeing 747-SPB5	22484	Pratt & Whitney Canada
☐ HZ-HM1A	Boeing 747-3G1	23070	Government of Saudi Arabia
☐ HZ-HM1B	Boeing 747-SP68	21652	Government of Saudi Arabia
☐ HZ-HM1C	Boeing 747-SP68	22750	Government of Saudi Arabia
☐ N905NA	Boeing 747-123	20107	NASA
☐ N747A	Boeing 747-SP27	21992	Fry's Electronics
☐ N747GE	Boeing 747-121F	19651	General Electric
☐ N787RR	Boeing 747-267B	21966	Rolls-Royce North America
☐ P4-FSH	Boeing 747-SP31	21963	Ernest Angley Ministries
☐ VP-BAT	Boeing 747-SP21	21648	Qatar Amiri Flight
☐ VP-BLK	Boeing 747-SP31	21961	Las Vegas Sands
☐ VQ-BMS	Boeing 747-SP21	21649	Las Vegas Sands
☐ 7O-YMN	Boeing 747-SP27	21786	Government of Yemen
☐ 5-8101	Boeing 747-131F	19668	Iranian Air Force
☐ 5-8102	Boeing 747-131F	19678	Iranian Air Force
☐ 5-8108	Boeing 747-270C	21180	Iranian Air Force
☐ 5-8107	Boeing 747-131F	20082	Iranian Air Force
☐ 5-8115	Boeing 747-2J9F	21507	Iranian Air Force
☐ 82-8000	Boeing 747 VC-25A	23824	US Air Force

☐ 92-9000	Boeing 747 VC-25A	23825	US Air Force
☐ A4O-OMN	Boeing 747-430	32445	Oman Amiri Flight
☐ A6-COM	Boeing 747-433	25074	Dubai Air Wing
☐ A6-GGP	Boeing 747-412F	28032	Dubai Air Wing
☐ A6-HRM	Boeing 747-422	26903	Dubai Air Wing
☐ A6-MMM	Boeing 747-422	26906	Dubai Air Wing
☐ A6-UAE	Boeing 747-48E	28551	Abu Dhabi Amiri Flight
☐ A6-YAS	Boeing 747-4F6	28961	Abu Dhabi Amiri Flight
☐ A9C-HMK	Boeing 747-4P8	33684	Bahrain Amiri Flight
☐ HZ-HM1	Boeing 747-468	28343	Government of Saudi Arabia
☐ HZ-WBT7	Boeing 747-4J6	25880	Kingdom Holding
☐ V8-ALI	Boeing 747-430	26426	Government of Brunei
☐ 9K-ADE	Boeing 747-469SCD	27338	Government of Kuwait
☐ 20-1101	Boeing 747-47C	24730	Japan Air Self Defence Force
☐ 20-1102	Boeing 747-47C	24731	Japan Air Self Defence Force
☐ A4O-HMS	Boeing 747-8H0	39749	Oman Amiri Flight
☐ A6-PFA	Boeing 747-8Z5	37500	Abu Dhabi Amiri Flight
☐ A7-HHE	Boeing 747-8KB	37544	Qatar Amiri Flight
☐ A7-HJA	Boeing 747-8KB	37075	Qatar Amiri Flight
☐ N458BJ	Boeing 747-8JA	40065	Government of Saudi Arabia
☐ N5017Q	Boeing 747-8KZF	36136	Boeing
☐ VQ-BSK	Boeing 747-8ZJ	42096	Worldwide Aircraft Holding
☐ 9K-GAA	Boeing 747-8JK	38636	Government of Kuwait
☐ EZ-A010	Boeing 757-23A	25345	Government of Turkmenistan
☐ G-TCSX	Boeing 757-2K2/W	26330	TAG Aviation
☐ HZ-HMED	Boeing 757-23A	25495	Government of Saudi Arabia
☐ M-RISE	Boeing 757-23N/W	27972	Talos Aviation
☐ N119NA	Boeing 757-223/W	24487	US Dept of Justice
☐ N610G	Boeing 757-22L	29304	Comco
☐ N757A	Boeing 757-200	22212	Boeing
☐ N757AG	Boeing 757-256/W	29306	Funair
☐ N757HW	Boeing 757-225	22194	Honeywell Aviation Services
☐ N757MA	Boeing 757-24Q	28463	Mid East Jet
☐ N757SS	Boeing 757-236	22176	Juliet Romeo Aviation
☐ N770BB	Boeing 757-2J4/W	25220	The Yucaipa Companies
☐ N801DM	Boeing 757-256	26240	MLW Aviation
☐ N805AM	Boeing 757-2Q8	26272	US Air Force
☐ N874TW	Boeing 757-223/W	24524	US Dept of Justice
☐ N903TB	Boeing 757-2Q8/W	28172	L-3 Communications
☐ NZ7571	Boeing 757-2K2	26633	Royal New Zealand Air Force
☐ NZ7572	Boeing 757-2K2	26634	Royal New Zealand Air Force
☐ T-01	Boeing 757-23A	25487	Argentine Air Force
☐ UK-75700	Boeing 757-23P	28338	Government of Uzbekistan
☐ UP-B5701	Boeing 757-2M6	23454	Government of Kazakhstan
☐ VQ-BTF	Boeing 757-23A/W	24923	Aquis
☐ XC-UJM	Boeing 757-225/W	22690	Mexican Air Force (also TP-01)
☐ 9H-AVM	Boeing 757-23A/W	24527	JetMagic
☐ 09-0015	Boeing 757-C32A	25044	US Air Force
☐ 09-0016	Boeing 757- C32A	28160	US Air Force
☐ 98-0001	Boeing 757- C32A	29025	US Air Force
☐ 98-0002	Boeing 757- C32A	29026	US Air Force
☐ 99-0003	Boeing 757- C32A	29027	US Air Force
☐ 99-0004	Boeing 757- C32A	29028	US Air Force
☐ A9C-HMH	Boeing 767-4F2ER	34205	Bahrain Amiri Flight
☐ EW-001PB	Boeing 767-32KER	33968	Government of Belarus
☐ N673BF	Boeing 767-238ER	23402	Polaris Aviation Solutions
☐ N767A	Boeing 767-2AXER	33685	Saudi Aramco Aviation
☐ N767KS	Boeing 767-24QER	28270	Mid East Jet
☐ N804MS	Boeing 767-3P6ER	27255	Las Vegas Sands
☐ N2767	Boeing 767-238ER	23896	Elan Express
☐ P4-MES	Boeing 767-33AER	33425	Global Jet Concept
☐ UK67000	Boeing 767-33PER	35796	Government of Uzbekistan
☐ V8-MHB	Boeing 767-27GER	25537	Brunei Sultan's Flight
☐ VP-BKS	Boeing 767-3P6ER	27254	Kalair
☐ VP-CME	Boeing 767-231	22567	Mid East Jet
☐ ZS-DJI	Boeing 767-216ER	23624	Aeronexus
☐ 4K-A101	Boeing 767-32LER	40341	Government of Azerbaijan
☐ 4X-AGM	Boeing 767-328ER	27135	Israeli Aircraft Industries
☐ 985	Boeing 767-3Y0ER	26205	Chilean Air Force
☐ A6-ALN	Boeing 777-2ANER	29953	Abu Dhabi Amiri Flight
☐ A6-SIL	Boeing 777-35RER	36563	Abu Dhabi Amiri Flight
☐ N777AS	Boeing 777-24Q	29271	Mid East Jet
☐ TR-KPR	Boeing 777-236	27108	Government of Gabon
☐ VP-CAL	Boeing 777-2KQLR	40753	Aviation Link
☐ A6-PFC	Boeing 787-8	35303	Abu Dhabi Amiri Flight
☐ HZ-MF8	Boeing 787-8	40059	Saudi Ministry of Finance
☐ N787BA	Boeing 787-8	40690	Boeing

☐ N787EX	Boeing 787-8	40691	Boeing
☐ N787FT	Boeing 787-8	40694	Boeing
☐ N7874	Boeing 787-8	40693	Boeing
☐ VP-BDA	Boeing 787-9	37109	Kalair
☐ XC-MEX/TP-01	Boeing 787-8	40695	Mexican Air Force
☐ B-970L	CAIC ARJ21-700	101	China Aviation Industry Corp
☐ B-991L	CAIC ARJ21-700	102	China Aviation Industry Corp
☐ B-992L	CAIC ARJ21-700	103	China Aviation Industry Corp
☐ B-1110L	CAIC ARJ21-700	104	China Aviation Industry Corp
☐ B-3570	Canadair Challenger 850	8102	Yalian Jet
☐ B-4005	Canadair Challenger 800	7138	Government of PRC
☐ B-4006	Canadair Challenger 800	7149	Government of PRC
☐ B-4007	Canadair Challenger 800	7180	Government of PRC
☐ B-4010	Canadair Challenger 800	7189	Government of PRC
☐ B-4011	Canadair Challenger 800	7193	Government of PRC
☐ B-4701	Canadair CRJ-200SE	7639	China Ocean Aviation
☐ B-4702	Canadair CRJ-200SE	7455	China Ocean Aviation
☐ B-7695	Canadair CRJ-200ER	7268	ZYB Lily Jet
☐ B-7697	Canadair Challenger 850	8089	ZYB Lily Jet
☐ B-7767	Canadair Challenger 850	8106	ZYB Lily Jet
☐ B-7795	Canadair Challegner 850	8098	ZYB Lily Jet
☐ B-7797	Canadair Challenger 850	8096	Business Aviation Asia
☐ C-FBZA	Canadair CRJ-200LR	7486	Avionco
☐ C-FIPΓ	Conodair Challenger 850	8107	ACASS Canada
☐ C-GDTD	Canadair Challenger 850	8067	Flightexec
☐ C-GSLL	Canadair Challenger 850	8103	Image Air Charter
☐ C-GSUW	Canadair Challenger 850	8047	Suncor Energy
☐ D-AAIJ	Canadair Challenger 850	8065	Imperial Jet
☐ EI-EEZ	Canadair Challenger 850	8085	Private Sky
☐ G-IGWT	Canadair Challenger 850	8078	Skywings
☐ G-SHAL	Canadair Challenger 850	8066	TAG Aviation
☐ LY-LTY	Canadair Challenger 850	8055	Charter Jets
☐ LY-VTA	Canadair CRJ-200LR	7617	Charter Jets
☐ LY-ZAB	Canadair CRJ-200LR	7248	KlasJet
☐ M-ABGH	Canadair CRJ-100SE	7351	Carolina Turbine Sales
☐ M-ANTA	Canadair Challenger 850	8094	Miklos Services
☐ M-FZMH	Canadair Challenger 850	8068	Arabian Jets
☐ M-HLAN	Canadair Challenger 850	8104	Wonder Air International
☐ M-LILJ	Canadair Challenger 850	8060	Raise In Development
☐ M-LILY	Canadair Challenger 850	8108	TAG Aviation Asia
☐ M-TAKE	Canadair Challenger 850	8079	Jet Airlines
☐ N96AP	Canadair CRJ-200LR	7730	Two Creeks Partners
☐ N141SH	Canadair CRJ-200ER	7206	Stewart-Haas Racing
☐ N155MW	Canadair CRJ-200LR	7021	MWR Racing
☐ N169CA	Canadair Challenger 850	8088	Carnegie Institution of Washington
☐ N296TX	Canadair Challenger 850	8053	Skyward Dragon
☐ N480SJ	Canadair CRJ-200ER	7755	Set Jet
☐ N500PR	Canadair Challenger 800	7846	Penske Racing
☐ N501LS	Canadair Challenger 800	7584	Boston Enterprises
☐ N529DB	Canadair Challenger 800	7152	Hardwicke Properties
☐ N601LS	Canadair Challenger 800	7008	Directional Visions
☐ N678RS	Canadair Challenger 850	7176	Cyberjet
☐ N702SJ	Canadair CRJ-200ER	7489	Set Jet
☐ N711WM	Canadair Challenger 800	7140	Gaughan Flying
☐ N719AV	Canadair CRJ-100ER	7159	Three Amp
☐ N888AU	Canadair CRJ-200 Phoenix	7211	Jet Asia
☐ N888GY	Canadair CRJ-200 ExecLiner	7471	Airod
☐ N888WU	Canadair CRJ-200ER	7481	888WU
☐ N890RL	Canadair CRJ-200SE	7717	IFG Properties
☐ N895CL	Canadair Challenger 850	8095	Averitt Air
☐ N999YG	Canadair Challenger 800	7075	Burrell Aviation
☐ OD-TAL	Canadair CRJ-100LR	7086	Emerald Jets
☐ OE-ILI	Canadair Challenger 850	8048	VistaJet
☐ OE-ILV	Canadair Challenger 850	8082	VistaJet
☐ OE-ILY	Canadair Challenger 850	8076	VistaJet
☐ OE-ILZ	Canadair Challenger 850	8086	VistaJet
☐ OE-ISA	Canadair Challenger 850	8043	Avcon Jet
☐ OE-ISF	Canadair Challenger 850	8056	International Jet Management
☐ OY-VEG	Canadair Challenger 850	8075	ExecuJet Scandinavia
☐ OY-VGA	Canadair Challenger 850	8077	ExecuJet Scandinavia
☐ P4-VIP	Canadair CRJ-100ER	7158	Premier Avia
☐ RP-C8638	Canadair CRJ-200ER	7756	
☐ TC-EJA	Canadair CRJ-200ER	7763	MNG Jets
☐ T7-OAM	Canadair Challenger 850	8084	Aviraventures
☐ UP-C8502	Canadair Challenger 850	8049	Comlux KZ
☐ UP-C8503	Canadair Challenger 850	8093	Comlux KZ
☐ UP-C8505	Canadair Challenger 850	8054	Comlux KZ
☐ UR-ICD	Canadair Challenger 850	8072	ISD Avia
☐ UR-RUS	Canadair CRJ-200LR	7990	ISD Avia
☐ VP-BSD	Canadair Challenger 850	8051	GAMA Aviation
☐ VP-CON	Canadair Challenger 850	8083	Flight Test Consultants

☐ VP-CPP	Canadair CRJ-200LR	7625	Peak Pacific Global
☐ VT-ARE	Canadair CRJ-100ER	7163	Club One Air
☐ VT-IBP	Canadair Challenger 850	8070	Airmid Aviation Services
☐ 4L-GAA	Canadair Challenger 850	8046	Government of Georgia
☐ 5A-UAD	Canadair Challenger 850	8087	United Aviation
☐ 5Y-CAR	Canadair CRJ-200ER	7186	Government of South Sudan
☐ 9H-BVJ	Canadair Challenger 850	8071	Blue Square Aviation
☐ 9H-CLG	Canadair Challenger 850	8063	Common Sky
☐ B-4060	Canadair CRJ-701ER	10164	Government of PRC
☐ B-4061	Canadair CRJ-701ER	10183	Government of PRC
☐ B-4062	Canadair CRJ-701ER	10187	Government of PRC
☐ B-4063	Canadair CRJ-701ER	10204	Government of PRC
☐ B-4064	Canadair CRJ-701ER	10206	Government of PRC
☐ B-4661	Canadair CRJ-702	10337	Chinese Air Force
☐ B-4662	Canadair CRJ-702	10338	Chinese Air Force
☐ B-	Canadair CRJ-702	10339	Chinese Air Force
☐ N804X	Canadair CRJ-701	10002	Northrop Grumman Systems Corp (Delaware)
☐ N870DC	Canadair Challenger 870	10314	Dow Chemical
☐ N872DC	Canadair Challenger 870	10322	Dow Chemical
☐ UP-CL001	Canadair Challenger 870	10289	Euro-Asia Air
☐ VP-BCL	Canadair Challenger 870	10247	S & K Bermuda
☐ C-GSUA	Canadair Challenger 890	15182	Suncor Energy Oil Sands
☐ C-GSUM	Canadair Challenger 890	15158	Suncor Energy Oil Sands
☐ C-FNXG	Canadair CRJ-1000	19001	Bombardier
☐ C-FRJX	Canadair CRJ-1000	19991	Bombardier
☐ AMT-230	de Havilland DHC-8-202Q	572	Mexican Navy
☐ A6-ADD	de Havilland DHC-8-315Q	627	UAE Air Force
☐ A6-ADE	de Havilland DHC-8-315Q	628	UAE Air Force
☐ C-FJJA	de Havilland DHC-8-401Q	4001	Bombardier
☐ C-GPAB	de Havilland DHC-8-106	275	Netherlands Coast Guard
☐ C-GRNN	de Havilland DHC-8-106	314	Netherlands Coast Guard
☐ C-GULN	de Havilland DHC-8-202Q	536	
☐ D2-EEA	de Havilland DHC-8-402Q	4294	Government of Angola
☐ D2-EEB	de Havilland DHC-8-402Q	4305	Government of Angola
☐ D2-EYU	de Havilland DHC-8-315	645	Government of Angola
☐ JA007G	de Havilland DHC-8-315Q	619	Japanese Civil Aviation Bureau
☐ N560WK	de Havilland DHC-8-315Q	560	US Department of State
☐ N563AW	de Havilland DHC-8-315Q	563	US Department of State
☐ N567WK	de Havilland DHC-8-315Q	567	US Department of State
☐ N568AW	de Havilland DHC-8-315Q	568	US Department of State
☐ N569AW	de Havilland DHC-8-315Q	569	US Department of State
☐ N500AW	de Havilland DHC-8-315Q	570	US Department of State
☐ N589AW	de Havilland DHC-8-315Q	589	US Department of State
☐ N637CC	de Havilland DHC-8-202	637	Northrop Grumman Systems
☐ N646CC	de Havilland DHC-8-202	646	Northrop Grumman Systems
☐ N649CC	de Havilland DHC-8-202	649	Northrop Grumman Systems
☐ N713M	de Havilland DHC-8-102	030	Gary & Diane Heavin Community Fund
☐ N721AL	de Havilland DHC-8-402Q	4235	US Department of Justice
☐ N556PM	de Havilland DHC-8-202B	413	US Air Force
☐ N800AW	de Havilland DHC-8-315Q	573	US Department of State
☐ N801MR	de Havilland DHC-8-202Q	606	US Department of Homeland Security
☐ N802MR	de Havilland DHC-8-202Q	612	US Department of Homeland Security
☐ N803MR	de Havilland DHC-8-202Q	626	US Department of Homeland Security
☐ N805MR	de Havilland DHC-8-202Q	655	US Department of Homeland Security
☐ N806MR	de Havilland DHC-8-315Q	662	US Department of Homeland Security
☐ N807MR	de Havilland DHC-8-315Q	663	US Department of Homeland Security
☐ N808MR	de Havilland DHC-8-315Q	667	US Department of Homeland Security
☐ PNC-0259	de Havilland DHC-8-311	224	Colombian National Police
☐ P4-MCO	de Havilland DHC-8-315Q	549	Prime Aviation
☐ P4-TCO	de Havilland DHC-8-202	484	Prime Aviation
☐ SE-MAA	de Havilland DHC-8-311Q	622	Swedish Coast Guard
☐ SE-MAB	de Havilland DHC-8-311Q	631	Swedish Coast Guard
☐ SE-MAC	de Havilland DHC-8-311Q	638	Swedish Coast Guard
☐ TF-SIF	de Havilland DHC-8-314Q	660	Icelandic Coast Guard
☐ VH-DNU	de Havilland DHC-8-311B	571	Hawker Pacific
☐ VH-LCL	de Havilland DHC-8-202	492	Royal Australian Navy
☐ XA-UQY	de Havilland DHC-8-102	160	Mexican Air Force
☐ XA-URH	de Havilland DHC-8-102	155	Mexican Air Force
☐ 5N-GRS	de Havilland DHC-8-201Q	547	Cross River State Government
☐ 304	de Havilland DHC-8-103	189	Kenyan Air Force
☐ 305	de Havilland DHC-8-103	219	Kenyan Air Force
☐ 306	de Havilland DHC-8-103	223	Kenyan Air Force
☐ 1320	de Havilland DHC-8-315MPA	610	United Arab Emirates Air Force
☐ D-CNEU	Dornier 228-200NG	8206	RUAG Aerospace
☐ D4-CBK	Dornier 228-212	8222	Cape Verde Coast Guard
☐ EP-TCC	Dornier 228-212	8195	Iranian National Cartographic Centre
☐ EP-THA	Dornier 228-212	8207	Iranian National Cartographic Centre
☐ EP-TKH	Dornier 228-212	8204	Iranian National Cartographic Centre

☐ EP-TZA	Dornier 228-212	8208	Iranian National Cartographic Centre
☐ G-ENVR	Dornier 228-101	7051	Natural Environment Research Council
☐ OH-MVN	Dornier 228-212	8233	Finnish Border Guard
☐ OH-MVO	Dornier 228-212	8232	Finnish Border Guard
☐ PH-CGC	Dornier 228-212	8183	Netherlands Coast Guard
☐ PH-CGN	Dornier 229-212	5191	Netherlands Coast Guard
☐ YV2980	Dornier 228-212	8212	Venezuelan Air Force
☐ YV3000	Dornier 228-212	8211	Venezuelan Air Force
☐ 5N-AUV	Dornier 228-101	7011	Nigerian Air Border Patrol
☐ 5N-AUW	Dornier 228-101	7018	Nigerian Air Border Patrol
☐ 5N-AUX	Dornier 228-101	7095	Nigerian Air Border Patrol
☐ 5N-AUY	Dornier 228-101	7116	Nigerian Air Border Patrol
☐ 5N-AUZ	Dornier 228-101	7167	Nigerian Air Border Patrol
☐ 5Y-CES	Dornier 228-202	8094	
☐ N28CG	Dornier 328-100	3024	Corning
☐ N38CG	Dornier 328-100	3034	Corning
☐ N338PH	Dornier 328-120	3029	Katanga Wings
☐ N900LH	Dornier 328-120	3014	Northpark Aviation
☐ N929EF	Dornier 328-110	3026	US Air Force
☐ N953EF	Dornier 328-110	3075	US Air Force
☐ OB2	Dornier 328-100	3083	Botswana Defence Force
☐ OE-GBB	Dornier 328-110	3078	Tyrol Air Ambulance
☐ PF-801	Dornier 328-310	3220	Mexican Federal Police
☐ 11-3016	Dornier 328-110	3016	US Air Force
☐ 10 3068	Dornier 328-110	3068	US Air Force
☐ 10-3077	Dornier 328-120	3077	US Air Force
☐ 11-3031	Dornier 328-110	3031	US Air Force
☐ 11-3097	Dornier 328-110	3097	US Air Force
☐ 11-3104	Dornier 328-120	3104	US Air Force
☐ 12-3040	Dornier 328-120	3040	US Air Force
☐ 12-3050	Dornier 328-120	3050	US Air Force
☐ 12-3060	Dornier 328-110	3060	US Air Force
☐ 95-3058	Dornier 328-110	3058	US Air Force
☐ 97-3091	Dornier 328-110	3091	US Air Force
☐ C-GCPW	Dornier 328JET	3129	Pratt & Whitney Canada
☐ D-BADC	Dornier 328JET Envoy 3	3216	Aero Dienst
☐ D-BGAS	Dornier 328JET	3139	DC Aviation
☐ N57TT	Dornier 328JET	3205	Thompson Tractor
☐ N131BC	Dornier 328JET	3168	International Bank of Commerce
☐ N304CE	Dornier 328JET	3184	Cummins
☐ N328LN	Dornier 328JET	3150	Comtran
☐ N430FJ	Dornier 328JET	3209	Aviando Services
☐ N901SJ	Dornier 328JET	3197	Comtran International
☐ OY-JJB	Dornier 328JET	3199	JoinJet
☐ PZ-TVE	Dornier 328JET	3114	Hi-Jet Helicopters
☐ UR-WOG	Dornier 328JET	3118	Aerostar
☐ XA-	Dornier 328JET	3220	Policia Federal Preventiva
☐ ZS-IOC	Dornier 328JET	3219	Anglo Aircraft
☐ 5N-BMH	Dornier 328JET Envoy 3	3120	SkyBird Air
☐ 5N-SPE	Dornier 328JET Envoy 3	3151	SkyBird Air
☐ 5N-SPM	Dornier 328JET Envoy 3	3141	SkyBird Air
☐ N817NA	Douglas DC-8-72	46082	NASA
☐ TR-LTZ	Douglas DC-8-73CF	46053	Government of Gabon
☐ VP-BHM	Douglas DC-8-62	46111	Brisair
☐ VP-BHS	Douglas DC-8-72	46067	Brisair
☐ 9T-TCN	Douglas DC-8-55F	45753	Democratic Republic of Congo Air Force
☐ 5V-TGF	Douglas DC-8-62	46071	Government of Togo
☐ N45NA	Douglas DC-9-33RC	47410	National Nuclear Security Adminstration
☐ N120NE	Douglas DC-9-15	45731	Jet Executive Charter
☐ N681AL	Douglas VC-9C	47668	US Department of State
☐ N697BJ	Douglas DC-9-32	47799	Blue Jackets Air
☐ N932ML	Douglas DC-9-31	47547	US Navy
☐ N8860	Douglas DC-9-15	45797	Scaife Flight Operations
☐ ZS-PYB	Douglas DC-9-14	45706	Mantuba Executive Jet
☐ N220AU	Douglas DC-10-10	46501	Orbis International
☐ N330AU	Douglas MD-10-30CF	46800	Orbis International
☐ D2-EUN	Embraer EMB-110P1A Bandeirante	110467	Government of Angola
☐ D2-EUT	Embraer EMB-110P1A Bandeirante	110468	Government of Angola
☐ N316AF	Embraer EMB-110P1 Bandeirante	110271	Agape Flights
☐ N766KM	Embraer EMB.110P1 Bandeirante	110212	KMR Aviation Services
☐ PP-EIX	Embraer EMB-110P1A Bandeirante	110468	State Government of Amapa
☐ PP-EMG	Embraer EMB-110E Bandeirante	110032	State Government of Minas Gerais
☐ PP-ERN	Embraer EMB-110P1 Bandeirante	110344	State Government of Rio Grande do Norte
☐ PP-FFV	Embraer EMB-110B1 Bandeirante	110284	Especiais
☐ PT-EDO	Embraer EMB-110C Bandeirante	110016	Extreme Taxi Aereo
☐ PT-SGM	Embraer EMB-110P1 Bandeirante	110420	Triton Taxi Aereo
☐ PT-SHO	Embraer EMB-110P1A Bandeirante	110461	Furnas Centrais Eletricas

☐ PT-SHP	Embraer EMB-110P1A Bandeirante	110462	Hidroeletrica de Sao Francisco
☐ PT-SHR	Embraer EMB-110P1A Bandeirante	110464	Furnas Centrais Eletricas
☐ PT-SHY	Embraer EMB-110P1A Bandeirante	110470	NHR Taxi Aereo
☐ PT-WCM	Embraer EMB-110C Bandeirante	110041	Leticia Simis Corp
☐ PT-WDM	Embraer EMB-110C Bandeirante	110094	Taxi Aereo Hercules
☐ ZS-CSI	Embraer EMB-110P1 Bandeirante	110383	Northlands Charters
☐ VH-BQB	Embraer EMB-110P1 Bandeirante	110298	Robert Keys
☐ N22BD	Embraer EMB-120RT Brasilia	120143	Bill Davis Racing
☐ N52AP	Embraer EMB-120ER Brasilia	120214	Air Providencia
☐ N120HL	Embraer EMB-120RT Brasilia	120111	Hammer Aircraft Leasing
☐ N365AS	Embraer EMB-120RT Brasilia	120172	Ronald J Cozad
☐ N405PA	Embraer EMB-120ER Brasilia	120160	Evernham Motorsports
☐ N410PA	Embraer EMB-120 Brasilia	120195	Evernham Motorsports
☐ N460PA	Embraer EMB-120 Brasilia	120190	MWR Racing
☐ N597M	Embraer EMB-120ER Brasilia	120306	Team Aero
☐ PP-ISB	Embraer EMB-120ER Brasilia	120232	Air Minas
☐ PT-SOK	Embraer EMB-120ER Brasilia	120358	Piquiatuba Taxi Aereo
☐ PT-SXP	Embraer EMB-120ER Brasilia	120323	Embraer
☐ TT-DAG	Embraer EMB-120RT Brasilia	120253	RJM Aviation
☐ ZS-STR	Embraer EMB-120ER Brasilia	120215	NAC Flight Services
☐ 9J-RYL	Embraer EMB-120ER Brasilia	120292	Royal Air Charters
☐ 2002	Embraer EMB-120RT Brasilia	120040	Brazilian Air Force
☐ 2003	Embraer EMB-120RT Brasilia	120055	Brazilian Air Force
☐ 2004	Embraer EMB-120RT Brasilia	120066	Brazilian Air Force
☐ 2017	Embraer EMB-120ER Brasilia	120357	Brazilian Air Force
☐ CE-01	Embraer ERJ-135LR	145449	Belgian Air Force
☐ CE-02	Embraer ERJ-135LR	145480	Belgian Air Force
☐ N89LD	Embraer ERJ-135SE	145648	McKee Foods Transportation
☐ N325JF	Embraer ERJ-135SE	145499	Intel Air Shuttle
☐ N386CH	Embraer ERJ-135SE	145467	RCR Air
☐ N548M	Embraer ERJ-135ER	145364	Menard
☐ N549M	Embraer ERJ-135ER	145450	Menard
☐ N704PG	Embraer ERJ-135LR	145174	Freeport Minerals
☐ N804CE	Embraer ERJ-135LR	145326	Cummins
☐ N829RN	Embraer ERJ-135SE	145361	Executive Jet Management
☐ N926FM	Embraer ERJ-135ER	145466	RVR Air Charter
☐ N983JC	Embraer ERJ-135LR	14500977	Johnson Controls
☐ N1023C	Embraer ERJ-135LR	145550	ConocoPhillips
☐ PP-VVA	Embraer ERJ-135LR	145702	Vale SA
☐ VT-JSI	Embraer ERJ-135LR	14500893	Jindal Steel & Power
☐ VT-JMN	Embraer ERJ-135ER	145233	Reliance Industries
☐ 5N-BJM	Embraer ERJ-135BJ	14500983	Government of Nigeria
☐ 5N-RSG	Embraer ERJ-135BJ	14500891	Government of River State of Nigeria
☐ 7Q-WPB	Embraer ERJ-135LR	145676	Paladin Energy
☐ 209	Embraer ERJ-135ER	145209	Greek Air Force
☐ 1124	Embraer ERJ-135LR	14501124	Royal Thai Army
☐ 1084/HS-AMP	Embraer ERJ-135LR	14501084	Royal Thai Army
☐ 2112/HS-NVA	Embraer ERJ-135LR	14501077	Royal Thai Army
☐ 2113/HS-NVB	Embraer ERJ-135LR	14501125	Royal Thai Navy
☐ 2560	Embraer ERJ-135LR	145600	Brazilian Air Force
☐ 2561	Embraer ERJ-135LR	145608	Brazilian Air Force
☐ CE-03	Embraer ERJ-145LR	145526	Belgian Air Force
☐ CE-04	Embraer ERJ-145LR	145548	Belgian Air Force
☐ C9-SPM	Embraer ERJ-145EP	145114	Vale
☐ F-HAFS	Embraer ERJ-145EP	145177	Enhance Aero
☐ F-HFKC	Embraer ERJ-145LR	145282	Enhance Aero
☐ G-OWTN	Embraer ERJ-145EU	145010	BAE Systems Corporate Travel
☐ HC-CGO	Embraer ERJ-145LR	14500987	Petroecuador
☐ N286CH	Embraer ERJ-145XR	14501185	Intel Air Shuttle
☐ N286FM	Embraer ERJ-145XR	14501186	Intel Air Shuttle
☐ N859MJ	Embraer ERJ-145ER	145769	Hendrick Motorsports
☐ N978RP	Embraer ERJ-145EP	145169	Aerodynamics
☐ PR-DPF	Embraer ERJ-145EP	145127	Brazilian Federal Police Force
☐ PR-PFN	Embraer ERJ-145LR	145002	Brazilian Federal Police Force
☐ 3C-QQH	Embraer ERJ-145EP	145076	Government of Equatorial Guinea
☐ 5N-BOZ	Embraer ERJ-145EU	145617	Government of Nigeria
☐ ZS-	Embraer ERJ-145EP	145040	Titan Helicopters
☐ 2520	Embraer ERJ-145EP	145023	Brazilian Air Force
☐ 2521	Embraer ERJ-145EP	145020	Brazilian Air Force
☐ 2522	Embraer ERJ-145EP	145027	Brazilian Air Force
☐ 2523	Embraer ERJ-145EP	145028	Brazilian Air Force
☐ 2524	Embraer ERJ-145EP	145034	Brazilian Air Force
☐ 2525	Embraer ERJ-145EP	145038	Brazilian Air Force
☐ 2526	Embraer ERJ-145EP	145137	Brazilian Air Force
☐ 2550	Embraer ERJ-145LR	145350	Brazilian Air Force
☐ 4101	Embraer ERJ-145SA	145190	Government of Mexico
☐ AP-SSH	Embraer Legacy 600	14501029	KK Aviation
☐ A6-CPC	Embraer Legacy 600	14500960	Gama Aviation
☐ A6-DPW	Embraer Legacy 600	14500955	ExecuJet Middle East

☐ A6-GCC	Embraer Legacy 600	14500972	Gama Aviation
☐ A6-NKL	Embraer Legacy 600	14500944	Empire Aviation Group
☐ A6-SSV	Embraer Legacy 650	14501156	Empire Aviation
☐ A6-UGH	Embraer Legacy 600	14500993	DAS Holding
☐ A9C-MTC	Embraer Legacy 600	14500975	MAE Aircraft Management
☐ B-3096	Embraer Legacy 650	14501145	Minsheng Financial Leasing
☐ B-3097	Embraer Legacy 650	14501151	China Eastern Business Aviation
☐ B-3098	Embraer Legacy 650	14501155	China Eastern Business Aviation
☐ B-3096	Embraer Legacy 650	14501145	Minsheng Financial Leasing
☐ B-3098	Embraer Legacy 650	14501155	China Eastern Airlines Executive Air
☐ B-3099	Embraer Legacy 650	14501173	China Eastern Airlines Executive Air
☐ B-3290	Embraer Legacy 650	14501206	Minsheng Financial Leasing
☐ B-3291	Embraer Legacy 650	14501207	Minsheng Financial Leasing
☐ B-3292	Embraer Legacy 650	14501175	CITIC General Aviation
☐ B-3293	Embraer Legacy 650	14501180	China Eastern Airlines Executive Air
☐ B-3295	Embraer Legacy 650	14501203	China Eastern Airlines Executive Air
☐ B-3296	Embraer Legacy 650	14501174	Minsheng Jet
☐ B-3799	Embraer Legacy 650	14501173	China Eastern Airlines Executive Air
☐ B-99999	Embraer Legacy 600	145644	Executive Aviation Taiwan
☐ CN-MBP	Embraer Legacy 600	14501117	Dalia Air
☐ CN-SSH	Embraer Legacy 600	14501114	Dalia Air
☐ D-ADCP	Embraer Legacy 600	14501067	Baden Aircraft Operations
☐ D-AKAT	Embraer Legacy 600	14501038	KamAvia Handels
☐ D-AVAN	Embraer Legacy 600	14501092	Baden Aircraft Operations
☐ ER-KKL	Embraer Legacy 650	14501191	Nobil Air
☐ F-HFKD	Embraer Legacy 600	14500933	Enhance Aero
☐ FAC1215	Embraer Legacy 600	14501095	Colombian Air Force
☐ FAE051	Embraer Legacy 600	14501082	Ecuadorian Air Force
☐ FAH-001	Embraer Legacy 600	14501041	Honduras Air Force
☐ G-CJMD	Embraer Legacy 600	14500994	Hangar 8
☐ G-CMAS	Embraer Legacy 600	14501142	Execujet (UK)
☐ G-HUBY	Embraer Legacy 600	14500854	London Executive Aviation
☐ G-LALE	Embraer Legacy 600	14501017	London Executive Aviation
☐ G-LEGC	Embraer Legacy 600	14501025	London Executive Aviation
☐ G-OTGL	Embraer Legacy 650	14501162	Aravco
☐ G-PEPI	Embraer Legacy 600	14500873	London Executive Aviation
☐ G-PPBA	Embraer Legacy 650	14501160	London Executive Aviation
☐ G-RHMS	Embraer Legacy 600	14501072	TAG Aviation
☐ G-SYLJ	Embraer Legacy 600	14500937	TAG Aviation
☐ G-SYNA	Embraer Legacy 650	14501127	London Executive Aviation
☐ G-THFC	Embraer Legacy 600	14500954	London Executive Aviation
☐ G-XCJM	Embraer Legacy 600	14500998	Corporate Jet Management
☐ HB-JFL	Embraer Legacy 600	14501057	Nomad Aviation
☐ HP-1A	Embraer Legacy 600	14501066	Government of Panama
☐ HZ-IAM	Embraer Legacy 600	14501055	Al Musa
☐ K3601	Embraer Legacy 600	14500867	Indian Air Force
☐ K3602	Embraer Legacy 600	14500880	Indian Air Force
☐ K3603	Embraer Legacy 600	14500910	Indian Air Force
☐ K3604	Embraer Legacy 600	14500919	Indian Air Force
☐ LX-MOI	Embraer Legacy 600	14500841	Luxaviation
☐ LX-NVB	Embraer Legacy 600	14501002	Luxaviation
☐ LX-OLA	Embraer Legacy 600	14500995	LuxAviation
☐ LX-RLG	Embraer Legacy 600	14500967	Global Jet Concept
☐ M-AAKV	Embraer Legacy 650	14501183	AAK Company
☐ M-ALEN	Embraer Legacy 650	14501119	Execujet South Africa
☐ M-ANGA	Embraer Legacy 600	14501086	Maxair
☐ M-ARSL	Embraer Legacy 600	14500802	RB Sports International
☐ M-DSCL	Embraer Legacy 600	14500851	Legacy Aviation
☐ M-ESGR	Embraer Legacy 600	14501016	Hermes Executive Aviation
☐ M-IMAK	Embraer Legacy 600	14501140	Donard Trading
☐ M-INTS	Embraer Legacy 600	14501048	Swissport Systems
☐ M-IRON	Embraer Legacy 600	14501176	Rubio
☐ M-JCCA	Embraer Legacy 650	14501182	Jeju China Castle
☐ M-KPCO	Embraer Legacy 600	14500973	National Legacy for Aircraft Management
☐ M-MHFZ	Embraer Legacy 650	14501150	Arabian Jets
☐ M-OLEG	Embraer Legacy 600	14500991	Hermitage Air
☐ M-NJSS	Embraer Legacy 600	145686	Saby Finance
☐ M-RCCG	Embraer Legacy 600	14501113	RMK Group
☐ M-RRBK	Embraer Legacy 650	14501136	Delino Investments
☐ N6GD	Embraer Legacy 600	14500983	Elite Air
☐ N53NA	Embraer Legacy 600	145770	BD Advisors
☐ N63AG	Embraer Legacy 600	14501061	ACM Aviation
☐ N89FE	Embraer Legacy 600	14501058	FirstEnergy Solutions
☐ N106EC	Embraer Legacy 600	14501106	Aurogold Aviation
☐ N124LS	Embraer Legacy 600	14500948	Executive Jet Management
☐ N127BG	Embraer Legacy 600	14501064	Viewpoint Management
☐ N135SK	Embraer Legacy 600	14500989	United Aviation
☐ N135SL	Embraer Legacy 600	145711	United Aviation
☐ N188JT	Embraer Legacy 600	145699	Crystal Air Aviation
☐ N226HY	Embraer Legacy 600	14501014	Clay Lacy Aviation
☐ N227WE	Embraer Legacy 600	14501018	United States Aviation
☐ N286DP	Embraer Legacy 600	14501178	JP Morgan Trust
☐ N286HF	Embraer Legacy 650	14501177	Intel Air Shuttle

☐ N286SJ	Embraer Legacy 650	14501153	Intel Air Shuttle
☐ N317LL	Embraer Legacy 600	14501007	JRK Property Holdings
☐ N333BH	Embraer Legacy 650	14501167	Swift Air
☐ N373RB	Embraer Legacy 600	14500957	RBGT
☐ N386AZ	Embraer Legacy 650	14501159	Intel
☐ N419LP	Embraer Legacy 600	145555	Peed Aviation
☐ N470DC	Embraer Legacy 600	14500946	AVN Air
☐ N494TG	Embraer Legacy 600	145678	Sentient Flight Group
☐ N503JT	Embraer Legacy 600	14501032	ExcelAire Service
☐ N515JT	Embraer Legacy 600	14500950	Excelaire
☐ N580ML	Embraer Legacy 600	14500990	Stone Tower Air
☐ N597CJ	Embraer Legacy 600	14501015	C&J Spec-Rent Services
☐ N598SG	Embraer Legacy 600	14501098	
☐ N600LP	Embraer Legacy 600	14500863	Peed Aviation
☐ N600TN	Embraer Legacy 600	145505	WRI 1000
☐ N600YC	Embraer Legacy 600	14501069	Fortune Gold
☐ N605WG	Embraer Legacy 600	14500980	Northeastern Aviation
☐ N608EC	Embraer Legacy 650	14501128	Embraer Executive Aircraft
☐ N615PG	Embraer Legacy 600	14501004	Pacific Gas & Electric
☐ N650JV	Embraer Legacy 650	14501181	JSV Leasing III
☐ N660JM	Embraer Legacy 600	145642	SAS Aviation
☐ N661EC	Embraer Legacy 600	14501001	Embraer Executive Aircraft
☐ N665PF	Embraer Legacy 650	14501165	Vitesse Aviation Services
☐ N671EE	Embraer Legacy 600	14501171	Embraer Executive Aircraft
☐ N688JC	Embraer Legacy 650	14501139	JC Jet
☐ N698EE	Embraer Legacy 650	14501198	Embraer Executive Aircraft
☐ N725BD	Embraer Legacy 600	14501034	BDG AirCharter
☐ N728PH	Embraer Legacy 600	14500985	ExcelAire Service
☐ N730BH	Embraer Legacy 600	145730	SAS Aviation Holdings
☐ N742SP	Embraer Legacy 600	14500884	Insperity
☐ N747AG	Embraer Legacy 650	14501132	TWC Aviation
☐ N752SP	Embraer Legacy 600	14500903	Insperity
☐ N809TD	Embraer Legacy 600	14500809	Swift Air
☐ N810TD	Embraer Legacy 650	14501194	Meadow Lane Air Partners
☐ N818HR	Embraer Legacy 600	14501105	HR INV
☐ N827TV	Embraer Legacy 600	14500971	Pinnacle Aviation
☐ N865LS	Embraer Legacy 600	14501080	Leon Advertising and Public Relations
☐ N867VP	Embraer Legacy 600	14501035	
☐ N888ML	Embraer Legacy 600	14500818	New Macau Landmark Management
☐ N894JW	Embraer Legacy 600	145789	GSM Assets
☐ N898JS	Embraer Legacy 600	14501071	Bharat Hotels
☐ N900EM	Embraer Legacy 600	14500976	JetSource
☐ N904FL	Embraer Legacy 600	145780	Nextant Aircraft
☐ N905FL	Embraer Legacy 600	145775	Nextant Aircraft
☐ N908FL	Embraer Legacy 600	14500942	Flight Options
☐ N909MT	Embraer Legacy 600	14501011	HSMM
☐ N909TT	Embraer Legacy 600	14501044	Transcon International
☐ N910FL	Embraer Legacy 600	14500952	Flight Options
☐ N925FL	Embraer Legacy 600	14500825	Flight Options
☐ N939AJ	Embraer Legacy 600	14500939	Orfro
☐ N966JS	Embraer Legacy 600	14500966	Pebuny
☐ N974EC	Embraer Legacy 600	14500974	Sky Reality Holdings
☐ N8587	Embraer Legacy 650	14501175	UP Management
☐ OE-IBK	Embraer Legacy 600	14501110	Avcon Jet
☐ OE-IDB	Embraer Legacy 600	14500999	Avcon Jet
☐ OE-IDH	Embraer Legacy 600	14501026	Europ Star Aircraft
☐ OE-IML	Embraer Legacy 650	14501143	Avcon Jet
☐ OE-IMW	Embraer Legacy 600	14501029	Avcon Jet
☐ OE-IRK	Embraer Legacy 600	14500916	Europ Star Aircraft
☐ OE-ITA	Embraer Legacy 650	14501133	Avcon Jet
☐ OE-ITS	Embraer Legacy 650	14501133	Avcon Jet
☐ OE-LPV	Embraer Legacy 650	14501192	MJet
☐ OK-AEG	Embraer Legacy 600	14501111	ABS Jets
☐ OK-GGG	Embraer Legacy 600	14500986	ABS Jets
☐ OK-JNT	Embraer Legacy 600	14501087	ABS Jets
☐ OK-OWN	Embraer Legacy 650	14501200	ABS Jets
☐ OK-ROM	Embraer Legacy 600	14501039	ABS Jets
☐ OK-SLN	Embraer Legacy 600	145796	ABS Jets
☐ OK-SUN	Embraer Legacy 600	14500963	ABS Jets
☐ OK-SYN	Embraer Legacy 600	14501189	ABS Jets
☐ PH-ARO	Embraer Legacy 600	14500979	ASL
☐ PK-TFS	Embraer Legacy 600	145625	
☐ PP-FJA	Embraer Legacy 600	14501138	Neo Taxi Aereo
☐ PP-JLO	Embraer Legacy 600	14501090	Malibu Confin de Bovinos
☐ PP-INC	Embraer Legacy 650	14501179	Banco Bradesco
☐ PP-LEG	Embraer Legacy 650	14501170	Sumatera Participacoes
☐ PP-NLR	Embraer Legacy 650	14501149	Lojas Riachuelo
☐ PP-VVV	Embraer Legacy 600	14501099	JBS
☐ PR-AVX	Embraer Legacy 600	14501037	Grupo EBX Participacoes
☐ PR-CBY	Embraer Legacy 650	14501187	Brasil Warrant Administração de Bens
☐ PR-CRG	Embraer Legacy 650	14501169	Construtora Estrutural
☐ PR-FPS	Embraer Legacy 650	14601118	Cristalia Prod Farmaceuticos
☐ PR-IUH	Embraer Legacy 600	145717	Itau Unibanco

☐ PR-NIO	Embraer Legacy 600	14501012	CBMM-Compania Brasileira de Metalurgia e Mineracao
☐ PR-ODF	Embraer Legacy 600	14501054	Global Taxi Aereo
☐ PR-TLC	Embraer Legacy 650	14501164	Macbens Patrimonial
☐ PT-FKK	Embraer Legacy 650	14501188	546 Participacoes
☐ PT-LEG	Embraer Legacy 650	14501197	Soc Administradora e Gestao Patrimonial
☐ PT-SKW	Embraer Legacy 600	14501006	Sao Conrado Taxi Aereo
☐ PT-TKI	Embraer Legacy 650	14501115	Embraer
☐ PT-TKV	Embraer Legacy 650	14501119	Embraer
☐ P4-KUL	Embraer Legacy 600	14500978	Premier Avia
☐ P4-MIV	Embraer Legacy 600	14501031	RusJet
☐ P4-MSG	Embraer Legacy 600	14500913	Premier Avia
☐ P4-PAM	Embraer Legacy 600	14500982	Petroff Air
☐ P4-RYY	Embraer Legacy 600	14500941	Whitetail Aviation
☐ P4-SLK	Embraer Legacy 650	14501147	Comlux Aviation Kazakhstan
☐ P4-SMS	Embraer Legacy 650	14501123	Petroff Air
☐ P4-SUN	Embraer Legacy 600	14501074	Hyperion Aviation
☐ P4-SVM	Embraer Legacy 600	14501060	Petroff Air
☐ RA-02777	Embraer Legacy 650	14501163	Premier Avia
☐ RA-02857	Embraer Legacy 600	145549	RusJet
☐ RA-02858	Embraer Legacy 600	145586	Jet Air
☐ SP-DLB	Embraer Legacy 600	14501100	Blue Jet
☐ SP-FMG	Embraer Legacy 600	14501102	FM Group World Artur Trawinski
☐ SE-DJG	Embraer Legacy 600	14501042	EFS European Flight Service
☐ S5-ABL	Embraer Legacy 600	14501008	SiAvia
☐ T-501	Embraer Legacy 600	14500981	Angolan Peoples Air Force
☐ TC-DIA	Embraer Legacy 650	14501148	Tarkim Air
☐ T7-KAS	Embraer Legacy 600	14501079	Skyjet Aviation Services
☐ T7-LRK	Embraer Legacy 600	14501021	Skyjet Aviation Services
☐ T7-UBS	Embraer Legacy 650	14501122	Skyjet Aviation Services
☐ UP-EM007	Embraer Legacy 650	14501146	Comlux Aviation Kazakhstan
☐ UP-EM010	Embraer Legacy 650	14501154	Comlux Aviation Kazakhstan
☐ VH-VLT	Embraer Legacy 600	14501107	Southern Cross Jets
☐ VP-BGL	Embraer Legacy 600	14500961	Rusjet
☐ VP-CAA	Embraer Legacy 600	14501091	NasJet
☐ VP-CAN	Embraer Legacy 600	14501075	AlNahla Aviation
☐ VP-CFA	Embraer Legacy 650	14501120	FAL Aviation
☐ VP-CFB	Embraer Legacy 600	145637	SAMCO Aviation
☐ VP-CLL	Embraer Legacy 600	14501052	Titan Aviation
☐ VP-CMK	Embraer Legacy 600	14501083	Comoro Gulf Aviation
☐ VP-CRA	Embraer Legacy 650	14501196	
☐ VP-CTB	Embraer Legacy 650	14501193	Seeb
☐ VP-CWJ	Embraer Legacy 650	14501152	Anhui Foreign Economic Construction
☐ VQ-BFP	Embraer Legacy 600	14501049	Planair
☐ VQ-BFQ	Embraer Legacy 600	14501062	Planair
☐ VQ-BFR	Embraer Legacy 600	14501121	Planair
☐ VT-AML	Embraer Legacy 650	14501144	Kamavati Aviation
☐ VT-AOK	Embraer Legacy 650	14501157	Air One Aviation
☐ VT-AOL	Embraer Legacy 650	14501158	Air One Aviation
☐ VT-BSF	Embraer Legacy 600	14500901	Indian Border Security Force
☐ VT-CKP	Embraer Legacy 600	14501094	Krishnapatnam Port Company
☐ VT-KJG	Embraer Legacy 650	14501202	Kalyan Jewellers
☐ XA-LBO	Embraer Legacy 600	14500970	Transpais
☐ XA-RWS	Embraer Legacy 600	14500969	Redwings
☐ 484	Embraer Legacy 600	145484	Greek Air Force
☐ 2580	Embraer Legacy 600	145412	Brazilian Air Force
☐ 2581	Embraer Legacy 600	145462	Brazilian Air Force
☐ 2582	Embraer Legacy 600	145495	Brazilian Air Force
☐ 2583	Embraer Legacy 600	145528	Brazilian Air Force
☐ 2584	Embraer Legacy 600	14500997	Brazilian Air Force
☐ 2585	Embraer Legacy 600	14501078	Brazilian Air Force
☐ C-GSCL	Embraer 175LR	17000241	Shell Canada
☐ N170EH	Embraer 170LR	17000059	Honeywell
☐ N734A	Embraer 170LR	17000318	Saudi Aramco
☐ N735A	Embraer 170LR	17000319	Saudi Aramco
☐ N736A	Embraer 170LR	17000320	Saudi Aramco
☐ PP-XJB	Embraer 170	17000003	Embraer
☐ PP-XJD	Embraer 175	17000014	Embraer
☐ PP-XMA	Embraer 190	19000001	Embraer
☐ PP-XMI	Embraer 190	19000003	Embraer
☐ 2590	Embraer 190LR	19000214	Brazilian Air Force
☐ 2591	Embraer 190LR	19000277	Brazilian Air Force
☐ A6-AJH	Embraer Lineage 1000	19000140	AJA - Al Jaber Aviation
☐ A6-AJI	Embraer Lineage 1000	19000261	AJA - Al Jaber Aviation
☐ A6-ARK	Embraer Lineage 1000	19000109	Prestige Jet
☐ A6-KAH	Embraer Lineage 1000	19000236	ExecuJet Middle East
☐ B-3203	Embraer Lineage 1000	19000453	Zhuhai Helicopters
☐ B-3219	Embraer Lineage 1000	19000534	Minsheng Financial Leasing
☐ B-3220	Embraer Lineage 1000	19000641	Minsheng Financial Leasing
☐ CN-SHS	Embraer Lineage 1000	19000307	Dalia Air

☐ M-SBAH	Embraer Lineage 1000	19000225	Flemming House
☐ N666GL	Embraer Lineage 1000	19000317	Yu Heng International Investments
☐ N889ML	Embraer Lineage 1000	19000438	New Macau Landmark Management
☐ N966MS	Embraer Lineage 1000	19000683	Minghao Li
☐ N981EE	Embraer Lineage 1000	19000559	Embraer
☐ N28888	Embraer Lineage 1000	19000571	Sky Realty Holdings
☐ OO-NGI	Embraer Lineage 1000	19000611	Flying Services
☐ PP-ADV	Embraer Lineage 1000	19000568	Vale
☐ PP-XTF	Embraer Lineage 1000	19000159	Embraer
☐ VT-AOP	Embraer Lineage 1000	19000203	Air One Aviation
☐ XA-AYJ	Embraer Lineage 1000	19000243	Omni Flys
☐ PH-NLZ	Fairchild (Swearingen) Metro II	TC-277	Stichting Nationaal Lucht en Ruimtevaart Lab.
☐ AP-BHZ	Fokker F.27-500	10686	Aircraft Sales & Services
☐ A-2701	Fokker F.27-400M	10536	Indonesian Air Force
☐ G-525	Fokker F.27-400M	10520	Ghana Air Force
☐ T-41	Fokker F.27-600	10345	Argentine Air Force
☐ T-44	Fokker F.27-600	10454	Argentine Air Force
☐ TC-71	Fokker F.27-400M	10403	Argentine Air Force
☐ TC-74	Fokker F.27-400M	10408	Argentine Air Force
☐ TC-75	Fokker F.27-400M	10621	Argentine Air Force
☐ TC-79	Fokker F.27-400M	10575	Argentine Air Force
☐ 9Q-CNH	Fokker F.27 500	10550	XL Trading
☐ 10669	Fokker F.27-500RF	10669	Philippine Air Force
☐ 59-0259	Fokker F.27-200	10115	Philippine Air Force
☐ EP-PAZ	Fokker F.28-1000	11104	Government of Iran
☐ 5H-CCM	Fokker F.28-3000	11137	Government of Tanzania
☐ 5V-TAI	Fokker F.28-1000	11079	Government of Togo
☐ A-2801	Fokker F.28-1000	11042	Indonesian Air Force
☐ A-2802	Fokker F.28-3000	11113	Indonesian Air Force
☐ A-2803	Fokker F.28-3000	11117	Indonesian Air Force
☐ A-2804	Fokker F.28-4000	11234	Indonesian Air Force
☐ FAC0002	Fokker F.28-1000	11992	Colombian Air Force
☐ FAC1041	Fokker F.28-3000C	11162	Colombian Air Force
☐ G-530	Fokker F.28-3000	11125	Ghana Air Force
☐ M28-01	Fokker F.28-1000	11088	Royal Malaysian Air Force
☐ T-02	Fokker F.28-3000	11203	Argentine Air Force
☐ T-03	Fokker F.28-1000	11028	Argentine Air Force
☐ TC-52	Fokker F.28-1000C	11074	Argentine Air Force
☐ TC-53	Fokker F.28-1000C	11020	Argentine Air Force
☐ TC-54	Fokker F.28-1000C	11018	Argentine Air Force
☐ 1250	Fokker F.28-3000	11153	Government of the Philippines
☐ AE567	Fokker 50	20253	Peruvian Navy
☐ AE568	Fokker 50	20287	Peruvian Navy
☐ 5H-TGF	Fokker 50	20231	Government of Tanzania
☐ 5001	Fokker 50	20229	Republic of China Air Force
☐ 5002	Fokker 50	20238	Republic of China Air Force
☐ 5003	Fokker 50	20242	Republic of China Air Force
☐ 27228	Fokker 50	20228	Royal Thai Police
☐ KAF308	Fokker 70	11557	Government of Kenya
☐ PH-KBX	Fokker 70	11547	Dutch Royal Flight
☐ OE-IIB	Fokker 100	11403	MJet
☐ OE-IIC	Fokker 100	11406	MJet
☐ OE-IID	Fokker 100	11368	MJet
☐ N49	General Dynamics (Convair) 580	479	FAA / US DoT
☐ N580HW	General Dynamics (Convair) 580	2	Honeywell
☐ N730RS	Gulfstream Aerospace Mallard	J-50	Richard Sugden
☐ VP-CLK	Gulfstream Aerospace Mallard	J-34	Mallard Aviation Corporation
☐ B-3826	Harbin Y-12 IV	H5005	Harbin Aircraft Manufacturing Corporation
☐ B-610L	Harbin Y-12 E	YUN12E001	Harbin Aircraft Manufacturing Corporation
☐ VT-XSD	Hindustan Aeronautics Saras	PT-1	National Aerospace Laboratories
☐ RA-75939	Ilyushin Il-18D	187010104	Rossiya Special Flight Detachment
☐ 74296	Ilyushin Il-18D	188010603	NPP
☐ 75713	Ilyushin Il-18D	186009403	NPP
☐ C5-RTG	Ilyushin Il-62M	1356234	Government of The Gambia
☐ P-883	Ilyushin Il-62M	2546624	Government of North Korea
☐ RA-86495	Ilyushin Il-62M	2726628	223rd State Airline Flying Unit
☐ RA-86496	Ilyushin Il-62M	3829859	223rd State Airline Flying Unit
☐ RA-86538	Ilyushin Il-62M	2241758	223rd State Airline Flying Unit
☐ RA-86539	Ilyushin Il-62M	2344615	223rd State Airline Flight Unit
☐ RA-86555	Ilyushin Il-62M	4547315	223rd State Airline Flight Unit
☐ RA-86561	Ilyushin Il-62M	4154842	223rd State Airline Flight Unit

| ☐ | RA-86572 | Ilyushin Il-62M | 3154624 | 223rd State Airline Flying Unit |
| ☐ | ST-PRA | Ilyushin Il-62M | 2357711 | Government of Sudan |

☐	EW-004DE	Ilyushin Il-76MD	0093490721	Government of Belarus
☐	EW-005DE	Ilyushin Il-76MD	0093492771	Belarus Air Force
☐	RA-76635	Ilyushin Il-76MD	0053459775	223rd State Airline Flying Unit
☐	RA-78830	Ilyushin Il-76MD	1003401010	223rd State Airline Flying Unit
☐	RA-78850	Ilyushin Il-76MD	1013405196	223rd State Airline Flying Unit
☐	RF-75351	Ilyushin Il-76MDK	0083481431	Roscosmos
☐	RF-75352	Ilyushin Il-76MDK-2	0083487617	Roscosmos
☐	RF-75353	Ilyushin Il-76MDK-2	0093495871	Roscosmos
☐	RF-76325	Ilyushin Il-76TD	0093493810	FSB
☐	RF-76326	Ilyushin Il-76TD	1023411370	FSB
☐	RF-76327	Ilyushin Il-76MD	1013401006	FSB
☐	TN-AFS	Ilyushin Il-76TD	1033415504	Conga (Brazzaville) Government
☐	76454	Ilyushin Il-76LL	0073469074	LII Zhukovski
☐	76492	Ilyushin Il-76LL3	0043452549	LII Zhukovski
☐	76900	Ilyushin Il-76MF	1053417563	Ilyushin OKB

| ☐ | RA-76450 | Ilyushin Il-82 | 0053463900 | LII Zhukovski |

☐	5501	Kawasaki Heavy Industries P-1	PROTO001	Japan Maritime SDF
☐	5502	Kawasaki Heavy Industries P-1	PROTO002	Japan Maritime SDF
☐	08-1201	Kawasaki Heavy Industries XC-2 (C-X)	001	Japan Air Self Defence Force

☐	D6-NHD	LET L-410UVP-E20	072640	Government of the Comores
☐	ES-PLW	LET L-410UVP	810726	Estonian Border Guard
☐	ES-PLY	LET L-410UVP	810727	Estonian Border Guard
☐	HA-KDZ	LET L-410UVP-T	820929	
☐	HL5236	LET L-410UVP-E9	012638	Korean Forest Service
☐	J2-MBE	LET L-410UVP-E20	2732	Djibouti Air Force
☐	LY-AVA	LET L-410UVP-E3	880236	
☐	LY-AVZ	LET L-410UVP-E3	892336	
☐	OK-DZA	LET L-410MA	730207	Slovacky Aeroklub
☐	OK-JUM	LET L-410UVP	851401	Jump Tandem
☐	OK-LAZ	LET L-410UVP-E	902504	Aeroservis
☐	OK-LEK	LET L-410UVP-E20	851428	Aircraft Industry
☐	OM-VAV	LET L-410UVP-E3	892335	Aviation Alliance
☐	OK-WYI	LET L-410UVP-E	912616	Czech CAA
☐	RA-0152G	LET L-410UVP-E	892328	
☐	RA-3131K	LET L-410UVP	820736	
☐	RA-67001	LET L-410UVP-E20	092716	Sasovo Flying School of Civil Aviation
☐	RA-67002	LET L-410UVP-E20	092717	Sasovo Flying School of Civil Aviation
☐	RA-67004	LET L-410UVP-E20	092622	Arkayim
☐	RA-67012	LET L-410UVP-E20	2733	Urals Mining and Metallurgical Co.
☐	RA-67014	LET L-410UVP-E20	2806	Sasovo Flying School of Civil Aviation
☐	UR-ASM	LET L-410UVP	820832	Avia Soyuz
☐	UR-CJG	LET L-410UVP	810605	
☐	UR-GNG	LET L-410UVP-E3	872005	Universal Investments
☐	UR-LAA	LET L-410UVP	851425	Aviaexpress
☐	UR-MAK	LET L-410UVP	820924	
☐	UR-NPO	LET L-410UVP-E3	871932	
☐	UR-VTV	LET L-410UVP	810705	Ukrainian Pilot School
☐	UR-67439	LET L-410UVP	841204	Avia Soyuz
☐	UR-67449	LET L-410UVP	841214	Avia Soyuz
☐	UR-67472	LET L-410UVP	841237	SBA
☐	3C-LLP	LET L-410UVP-E20	092713	Government of Equatorial Guinea
☐	3C-REA	LET L-410UVP-E20	892316	Government of Equatorial Guinea
☐	4O-OO1	LET 410UVP	892335	Montenegro Ministry of Interior
☐	9U-BHT	LET L-410UVP	851432	

| ☐ | HZ-AFAS | McDonnell-Douglas MD-11 | 48533 | Asasco Aviation |
| ☐ | HZ-HM7 | McDonnell-Douglas MD-11 | 48532 | Government of Saudi Arabia |

☐	M-SFAM	McDonnell-Douglas MD-87	53042	ExecuJet Europe
☐	N168CF	McDonnell-Douglas MD-87	49670	Sunrider International
☐	N204AM	McDonnell-Douglas MD-87	49404	Wallace Holdings
☐	N287KB	McDonnell-Douglas MD-87	49768	KEB Aircraft
☐	N682RW	McDonnell-Douglas MD-81	48006	Olympia Aviation
☐	N880DP	McDonnell-Douglas MD-83	49504	Detroit Pistons
☐	N987GC	McDonnell-Douglas MD-87	53040	Genesis Custom Jetliners
☐	N14810	McDonnell-Douglas MD-82	49264	Evergreen Maintenance Center
☐	P4-AIR	McDonnell-Douglas MD-87ER	49412	Sistema
☐	SX-IFA	McDonnell-Douglas MD-83	49809	Amjet Executive
☐	TT-ABC	McDonnell-Douglas MD-87	49888	Government of Tchad
☐	VP-CBH	McDonnell-Douglas MD-82	53577	Mineralogy
☐	VP-CBI	McDonnell-Douglas MD-82	53581	Mineralogy
☐	VP-CKN	McDonnell-Douglas MD-83	49458	FC Mazembe
☐	VP-CNI	McDonnell-Douglas MD-87	49767	Corporate Aviation Holdings
☐	VP-CTF	McDonnell-Douglas MD-87	49777	AMAC Aerospace
☐	3DC-SWZ	McDonnell-Douglas MD-87	53041	Government of Swaziland

| ☐ | N9CJ | SAAB SF.340B | 340B-224 | Pentastar Aviation |

☐	N44KS	SAAB SF.340A	340A-050	JMJ Flight Services
☐	N632RF	SAAB SF.340A	340A-042	Pegasus Air
☐	N727DL	SAAB SF.340A	340A-036	Napleton Aviation
☐	SE-KSI	SAAB SF.340B	340B-223	SAAB Aircraft
☐	SE-MSA	SAAB SF.340B MSA	340B-441	SAAB Aircraft
☐	1335	SAAB SF.340B	340B-429	United Arab Emirates Air Force
☐	J-019	SAAB 2000	2000-019	Pakistan Air Force
☐	N509RH	SAAB 2000	2000-030	Hendrick Motorsports
☐	N511RH	SAAB 2000	2000-020	Hendrick Motorsports
☐	N517JG	SAAB 2000	2000-021	Joe Gibbs Racing
☐	N519JG	SAAB 2000	2000-017	Joe Gibbs Racing
☐	N813BB	SAAB 2000	2000-044	Meregrass
☐	N814BB	SAAB 2000	2000-034	Meregrass
☐	N92225	SAAB 2000	2000-028	US Department of Justice
☐	10-045	SAAB2000AEW	2000-045	Pakistan Air Force
☐	6001	SAAB 2000 AEW&C	2000-050	Royal Saudi Air Force
☐	6002	SAAB 2000 AEW&C	2000-052	Royal Saudi Air Force
☐	82911	Sukhoi SU-80GP	0102	Sukhoi Design Bureau
☐	RF-89151	Sukhoi SSJ 100-95B	95011	Ministry of Internal Affairs
☐	UP-SJ001	Sukhoi SSJ 100-95LR	95060	Comlux KZ
☐	97003	Sukhoi SSJ 100-95LR	95003	Sukhoi Design Bureau
☐	97005	Sukhoi SSJ 100-95LR	95005	Sukhoi Design Bureau
☐	97006	Sukhoi SSJ 100-95LR	95032	Sukhoi Design Bureau
☐	RA-64454	Tupolev Tu-134IK	64454	MAP LII Ramenskoye
☐	RA-65689	Tupolev Tu-134AK	62655	223 State Airline Flight Unit
☐	RA-65690	Tupolev Tu-134A-3	62895	223 State Airline Flight Unit
☐	RA-65931	Tupolev Tu-134BV	66185	VNIIRA
☐	RA-65979	Tupolev Tu-134A	63158	FSB
☐	RA-65984	Tupolev Tu-134A-3	63400	223 State Airline Flight Unit
☐	RA-65994	Tupolev Tu-134A-3	66207	FSB
☐	RA-65995	Tupolev Tu-134A-3	66400	FSB
☐	RA-65996	Tupolev Tu-134AK	63825	223 State Airline Flight Unit
☐	RA-65996	Tupolev Tu-134AK	63825	223 State Airline Flight Unit
☐	RF-65150	Tupolev Tu-134A-3	60650	Roscosmos
☐	RF-65153	Tupolev Tu-134AK	66198	Russian Customs
☐	UN-65120	Tupolev Tu-134A	93551025?	Government of Kazakhstan
☐	UN-65683	Tupolev Tu-134AK	62199	Government of Kazakhstan
☐	4K-65496	Tupolev Tu-134A-3	63468	Government of Azerbaijan
☐	65606	Tupolev Tu-134A	46300	Tupolev Design Bureau
☐	65721	Tupolev Tu-134A-3M	66170	SibNIa
☐	B-4016	Tupolev Tu-154M	91A872	People's Liberation Army Air Force
☐	B-4017	Tupolev Tu-154M	91A873	People's Liberation Army Air Force
☐	B-4138	Tupolev Tu-154M	85A712	People's Liberation Army Air Force
☐	RA-85001	Tupolev Tu-154M	89A820	Russian State Transport
☐	RA-85019	Tupolev Tu-154M	05A1019	Federal Security Service
☐	RA-85084	Tupolev Tu-154M	08A1004	Federal Security Service
☐	RA-85360	Tupolev Tu-154B-2	79A360	223 State Airline Flight Unit
☐	RA-85426	Tupolev Tu-154B-2	80A426	223 State Airline Flight Unit
☐	RA-85534	Tupolev Tu-154B-2	82A534	223 State Airline Flight Unit
☐	RA-85554	Tupolev Tu-154B-2	82A554	223 State Airline Flight Unit
☐	RA-85555	Tupolev Tu-154B-2	82A555	223 State Airline Flight Unit
☐	RA-85559	Tupolev Tu-154B-2	82A559	223 State Airline Flight Unit
☐	RA-85563	Tupolev Tu-154B-2	82A563	223 State Airline Flight Unit
☐	RA-85586	Tupolev Tu-154B-2	83A586	223 State Airline Flight Unit
☐	RA-85587	Tupolev Tu-154B-2	83A587	223 State Airline Flight Unit
☐	RA-85594	Tupolev Tu-154B-2	84A594	223 State Airline Flight Unit
☐	RF-85565	Tupolev Tu-154B-2	82A565	Russian Ministry of the Interior
☐	UP-T5401	Tupolev Tu-154M	889	Government of Kazakhstan
☐	RA-64010	Tupolev Tu-204-300A	1450743164010	Biznes Aero VIP
☐	RA-64014	Tupolev Tu-204	1450744364014	
☐	RA-64015	Tupolev Tu-204	1450741464015	
☐	RA-64150	Tupolev Tu-204SM	64150	OAK-United Aircraft Corp
☐	RA-64151	Tupolev Tu-204SM	145074..641511	OAK-United Aircraft Corp
☐	RA-64523	Tupolev Tu-214VPU	023	FSB
☐	94001	Tupolev Tu-334-100	01001	Tupolev Design Bureau
☐	94005	Tupolev Tu-334-100OAO	01005	Tupolev Design Bureau
☐	B-3489	Xian Y-7-100	07708	Peoples Republic of China Navy
☐	B-3493	Xian Y-7-100	08704	Peoples Republic of China Navy
☐	RA-88265	Yakovlev Yak-40	9722052	LII im. Gromova
☐	RA-88293	Yakovlev Yak-40	9510138	
☐	RA-88297	Yakovlev Yak-40	9530142	Lukoil Avia
☐	RF-88301	Yakovlev Yak-40K	9641251	Russian Ministry of the Interior
☐	UN-87488	Yakovlev Yak-40	9441638	Government of Kazakhstan

☐ UN-87816	Yakovlev Yak-40	9230724	Government of Kazakhstan
☐ UP-Y4007	Yakovlev Yak-40	9431435	
☐ UP-Y4015	Yakovlev Yak-40	9530842	Irtysh Air
☐ UP-Y4033	Yakovlev Yak-40K	9641050	Kazzinc
☐ UP-87850	Yakovlev Yak-40	9441738	Kazakhstan Border Guards
☐ YK-SQG	Yakovlev Yak-40K	9941959	Government of Syria
☐ 48112	Yakovlev Yak-40	9211520	RSK MiG
☐ 87200	Yakovlev Yak-40K	9811956	TANTK im. GM Berieva
☐ 87229	Yakovlev Yak-40	9841759	Sukhoi Aircraft
☐ 87659	Yakovlev Yak-40	9240325	Yakovlev OKB
☐ 87974	Yakovlev Yak-40	9041960	Aviaspetsnabkontrol
☐ 98111	Yakovlev Yak-40K	9741656	Sukhoi Aircraft
☐ RA-42412	Yakovlev Yak-42D	4520422219055	United Aircraft Corporation
☐ RA-42424	Yakovlev Yak-42D-100 (Yak-142)	4520421502016	Lukoil Avia
☐ RA-42427	Yakovlev Yak-42D	4520422305016	JetAlliance East
☐ UP-42721	Yakovlev Yak-42D	4520423310017	Kazakhstan Government
☐ UP-Y4204	Yakovlev Yak-42D	4520423408016	Kazzinc
☐ 42440	Yakovlev Yak-42D	4520424210018	Roshydromet

AIRLINES REMOVED FROM AIRLINE FLEETS 2014

AP	Rayyan Air – ceased ops Oct14
A6	Dolphin Air – status uncertain
	Sayegh Group Aviation – aircraft sold
B	China Southern Helicopters – part of China Southern Airlines
B-H	Jetstar Hong Kong – regulatory approval still not received
C	Abitibi Helicopters – renamed Opsmobil
	Alta Flights – aircraft sold
	Aviation Mauricie – aircraft sold
	Clearwater Airways – aircraft sold
	Fugro Aviation Canada – renamed CGG Aviation Canada
	Kimsquit Air – aircraft no longer registered
	Kelowna Flightcraft Air Charter – renamed KF Cargo
	Lakeland Airways – aircraft no longer registered
	MaxAvia – see EX-
	Melaire – aircraft sold
	Nadeau Air Service – flying school only
	Ootsa Air – aircraft no longer registered
	Ram Air Services – see USA (N)
	Selkirk Air – see Enterlake Air Services
CC	Inaer Helicopter Chile – AOC revoked Jly14
	Principal Airlines – ops suspended May14
CP	TAM-Tptes Aereo Militar and TAM Bolivia believed to be one and the same
CS	Windavia Airlines – ceased ops 2014
C2	Our Airline – renamed Nauru Airlines
C5	Gambia Bird – ops suspended Dec14
D	Condor Berlin – merged into Condor May13
	FlyNext – renamed Germania Express
	Hamburg Airways – ceased ops Dec14
DQ	Pacific Sun Airways – renamed Fiji Link
D4	Halcyon Air – ceased ops 2013
EC	Air Pack Express – status uncertain
	Calima Aviacion – ceased ops Jly14
	Helitt Lineas Aereas – ceased ops Sep14
	Melilla Airlines – status uncertain
	Pullmantur Air – renamed Wamos Air
EI	Aer Arann – renamed Stobart Air
EK	Air Highnesses – no current AOC
	Taron Avia – aircraft sold
	Vertir – no current AOC
EP	AriaTour – ceased ops Nov14
	Sahand Airlines – ceased ops 2013
ER	Grixona – no current AOC
	Jet Star – ceased ops 2014
	Moldavian Airlines – status uncertain
	Sky One – renamed MEGAviation
ES	Estonian Air Regional – aircraft sold
EY	East Air – AOC revoked Oct14
	Par Air – aircraft sold
E3	Nasair – ceased ops May14
E7	Elafly – moved to Italy I-
G	Global Supply Systems – ceased ops 2014
HA	Solyom Hungarian Airlines – ops never started
HB	Darwin Airlines – renamed Etihad Regional
	Swiss European Air Lines – renamed Swiss Global Air Lines
HC	Aerogal – renamed Avianca Ecuador
HK	Cosmos Air Cargo – status uncertain
HS	SGA Airlines – AOC cancelled Jly14
HZ	Al Khayala – status uncertain
	Almousa VIP Fly – aircraft sold
I	Air Europe Italy – does not operate aircraft
	Italiatour – ceased ops 2009
	Jetcom – not an airline
	Meridiana Fly – renamed Alisarda
	MiniLiner – AOC revoked Jan15
	New Livingston – ceased ops Oct14
JA	JAL Express – merged into Japan Airlines 01Oct14
	JALways – merged into Japan Airlines Dec10
JU	Eznis Airways – ceased ops May14
JY	Meelad Air – ceased ops 2008
	Petra Airlines – renamed Air Arabia Jordan
	Solitaire Air – status uncertain
J2	Djibouti Airlines – ceased ops 2010
LN	Norwegian Air Norway – aircraft transferred to Norwegian Air International (EI-)
LX	Westair Luxembourg – renamed Smart Cargo
N	AEX Air – ceased ops
	Alaska Island Air – aircraft sold
	American Connection – ceased ops Aug14
	American Eagle – renamed Envoy Air
	Brooks Fuel – aircraft no longer registered
	California Pacific Airlines – ceased ops Apr15
	Caribbean Cargo Carriers – status uncertain
	CDF Aviation – listed under USDA Forest Service (qv)
	Century Airlines – status uncertain
	Channel Island Aviation – only ops light aircraft
	Chautauqua Airlines – absorbed into Shuttle America Jan15
	Epps Air Service – now aircraft dealer only
	ERA Aviation – renamed Ravn Alaska
	Evergreen International Airlines – ceased ops Nov13
	Florida West International Airlines – aircraft sold
	Focus Air – status uncertain
	Hageland Aviation Services – aircraft sold
	Inter Island Airways – airline services licence expired
	Mid-Atlantic Freight/Atlantic Aero – status uncertain
	North American Airlines – ceased ops Jun14
	North South Airlines – aircraft sold
	Omniflight Helicopters – aircraft sold or deregistered
	Pacific Air Express/Leis Air – see Leis Air
	Paragon Air Express – status uncertain
	Paramount Jet – status uncertain
	Red Line Air – ops bizjets only
	Rhoades International – status uncertain
	Tepper Aviation – status uncertain
	Twin Cities Air Service – status uncertain
	Union Flights – status uncertain
	World Airways – ceased ops Jun14
OB	Coyotair Peru – aircraft sold
	Transportes Generales Aereos – aircraft cancelled
OD	Berytos Airlines – ceased ops 2008
	Imperial Jet – status uncertain
	TMA – ceased ops Nov14
OE	Air Alps Aviation – ceased ops Feb14
	Lauda Air – ceased ops Apr13
	Tyrolean Airways – merged into Austrian 01Apr15
OM	SamAir – ceased ops 2014
PK	Aero Nusantara – MRO only
	Dirgantara Air Service – declared bankrupt Mar13
	Merpati – ceased ops Feb14
	TigerAir Mandala – ceased ops Jly14
	Top Air – AOC suspended Feb07
PP	Aero Star Taxi Aereo – status uncertain
	Air Amazonia – aircraft sold
	Arizona Taxi Aereo – CofA suspended
	Atlantico Transporte Aereo – aircraft sold
	Axe Taxi Aereo – status uncertain
	Brava Linhas Aereas – aircraft sold or wfs
	Cruiser Taxi Aereo Brasil – declared bankrupt Aug10
	Flex Linhas Aereas – aircraft sold
	Gensa – status uncertain
	Interavia Taxi Aereo – now a bizjet operator
	Irmaos Passaura – aircraft cancelled
	Mais Linhas Aereas – aircraft sold
	META – aircraft sold or cancelled
	NHT Linhas Aereas – aircraft sold
	Nordeste Linhas Aereas Regionais – declared bankrupt
	Rico Taxi Aereo – merged into Rico Linhas Aereas
	Santa BarbaraTaxi Aereo – operator not in Brazil Register

	Skylift Taxi Aereo – aircraft no longer registered
	TAF Linhas Aereas – licence revoked Feb13
	TAM Jatos Executivos Marilia – aircraft sold or transferred to Two Taxi Aereo
	Taxi Aereo Itaituba – status uncertain
	Taxi Aereo Weiss – renamed Taxi Aereo Ribeiro
	Team Airlines – licence revoked Oct14
	TRIP Linhas Aereas - merged into Azul May14
P4	FlyAruba – aircraft transferred to Aruba Airlines
RA	Abakan-Avia – renamed Royal Flight
	Bylina – status uncertain
	Dobrolet – ops suspended Aug14 due EU sanctions
	Estar Avia – ceased ops
	KAPO S P Gorbunova – AOC revoked Feb15
	Moskovia – AOC revoked Dec14
	Polet Airlines – AOC revoked Jan15
	RusJet – AOC revoked Feb15
	Russian Sky Airlines – AOC revoked Jan15
	Ryazanaviatrans – ceased ops Oct12
	Vityaz Avia – not an airline
RP-C	Asian Spirit – aircraft cancelled
	Astro Air – status uncertain
	Chemtrad Aviation – aircraft cancelled
	Tigerair Philippines – renamed CebGo
	Transglobal Airways – aircraft cancelled
	Victoria Air – aircraft cancelled
SE	Direktflyg – a "virtual" airline
	Flyglinjen – a "virtual" airline
SP	Bingo Airways – ceased ops Jun14
	Eurolot – ceased ops Mar15
	Exin – AOC revoked Nov14
	LOT Charters – aircraft reintegrated into LOT
ST	Marsland Aviation – status uncertain
SU	Air Memphis – status uncertain
SX	Aerospace One – ceased ops 2014
	Hellenic Imperial Airways – ceased ops Jan12
	Sky Wings Airlines – ceased ops Nov14
S2	Sky Capital Airlines – renamed Sky Air
	Voyager Airlines – status uncertain
TC	AtlasJet Airlines – renamed AtlasGlobal
	Izair – flights now op by Pegasus Airlines
	Saga Airlines – status uncertain
TN	Equajet – status uncertain
TS	Nouvelair – delete Tunisie
TT	CHC Tchad – renamed Avmax Tchad
TY	Aero Benin – inactive since Jun12
UR	Aero-Charter Airlines – aircraft cx
	Business Aviation Centre – aircraft cx
	Wizz Air Ukraine – ceased ops Apr15
VH	Heavylift Cargo Airlines – status uncertain
	Slingair – renamed Aviair
	Vincent Aviation (Australia) – ceased ops May14
VT	Spirit Air – aircraft cancelled
XA	Hawk de Mexico/Helivan – aircraft sold
XU	Skywings Asia Airlines – renamed Sky Angkor Airlines

YI	Zagros Air – renamed Zagrosjet
YL	Alpha Express Airlines – aircraft returned to lessor
YR	United European Airlines – AOC suspended Jun14
YS	VECA Airlines – renamed Vuela Airlines
ZK	Anatoki Helicopters – aircraft sold
	Golden Wings – status uncertain
	Heli Hunt 'n' Fish – aircraft sold
	Helipro – ceased ops Nov14
	Heliventures New Zealand – aircraft too small for inclusion
	Rangitikei Helicopters – aircraft too small for inclusion
	Tuawhenua Helicopters – aircraft too small for inclusion
	Vincent Aviation – ceased ops Oct14
ZS	Allegiance Air – aircraft sold
	Summerset Charters – status uncertain
4L	Air Caucasus – renamed Air Georgia; status uncertain
5A	Alajnihah Airways – status uncertain
	Libo Air Cargo – merged into Afriqiyah Airways
5B	Cyprus Airways – suspended ops Jan15
5H	Fly Tanzania – aircraft sold
5N	Dominion Air – aircraft sold
	Tradecraft – never started ops
	Wings Aviation Nigeria – renamed JedAir
5T	Compagnie Mauritanienne de Transports – status uncertain
5X	Air Uganda – AOC suspended Jun14, ceased ops Jly14
	Sky Jet Aviation – status uncertain
5Y	Air Shuttle – renamed Starbow Airlines (9G-)
	Atlas Aviation – status uncertain
	DAC Aviation – see DAC East Africa
	D-Connection – aircraft sold
	Ken Air – see Yellow Wings Air Services
	Sky Relief – aircraft w/o
6O	Jubba Airways – see 5Y-
	Star African Air – status uncertain
6Y	Air Jamaica – merged into Caribbean Airlines
	Exec Direct Aviation – status uncertain
7O	Barash Aviation – aircraft destroyed
9G	Fly540 Ghana – ops suspended May14; aircraft sold
9H	MiniLiner Malta – status uncertain
9M	Berjaya Air – ceased scheduled ops Oct14; current status uncertain
	Transmile Air Services – renamed Raya Airways Oct14
	Weststar Aviation Services – not an airline
9Q	African Air Commuter – aircraft w/o
	FlyCongo – merged into Compagnie Africaine d'Aviation Oct12
	Goma Express – AOC revoked Mar14
	Lubumbashi Air Service – AOC revoked Mar14

IATA TWO-LETTER DESIGNATORS

0B	Blue Air	YR
0G	Ghadames Air Transport	5A
2B	Ak Bars Aero	RA
2E	Smokey Bay Air	N
2F	Frontier Flying Services	N
2F	Payam	EP
2G	Angara Airlines	RA
2G	San Juan Airlnes	N
2I	Star Peru	OB
2J	Air Burkina	XT
2K	Avianca Ecuador	HC
2L	Helvetic Airways	HB
2L	TAB Cargo	CP
2N	Nex Time Jet	SE
2P	PAL Express	RP
2Q	Air Cargo Carriers	N
2S	Sunny Airways	HS
2W	Welcome Air	OE
2Z	Chang An Airlines	B
2Z	TTA-Soc de Transporte e Trabalho	C9
2Z	Passaredo Transportes Aereos	PP
3B	Central Connect Airlines	OK
3F	Pacific Airways	N
3G	Gading Sari Aviation Services	9M
3H	Air Inuit	C
3K	Jetstar Asia Airways	9V
3L	InterSky	OE
3M	Silver Airways	N
3N	Air Urga	UR
3O	Air Arabia Maroc	CN
3P	Tiara Air	P4
3R	Trigana Air Service	PK
3S	Air Antilles Express	F
3S	Air Guyane Express	F
3S	AeroLogic	D
3U	Sichuan Airlines	B
3U	Chanchangi Airlines	5N
3V	TNT Airways	OO
3W	Malawian Airlines	7Q
3Z	Travel Service Poland	SP
4A	Air Kiribati	T3
4B	Aviastar - Tupolev	RA
4C	LAN Airlines Colombia	HK
4D	Air Sinai	SU
4E	Tanana Air Service	N
4G	Gazpromavia	RA
4H	United Airways	S2
4J	Somon Air	EY
4K	Kenn Borek Air	C
4L	Georgian International Airlines	4L
4M	LAN Argentina	LV
4N	Air North	C
6O	Orbest	CS
4O	Interjet	XA
4P	Travel Air	P2
4Q	Safi Airways	YA
4S	Solar Cargo	YV
4T	Belair Airlines	HB
4U	Germanwings	D
4W	Warbelows Air	N
4W	Allied Air Cargo	5N
4Y	Airbus Transport Intl	F
4Z	Airlink	ZS
5A	Alpine Air Express	N
5B	Bassaka Air	XU
5C	Natureair	TI
5C	Cargo Airlines	4X
5D	Aeromexico Connect	XA
5E	Equaflight Service	TN
5F	Arctic Circle Air Service	N
5G	Fly540 Ghana	9G
5H	Fly540	5Y
5J	Cebu Pacific Air	RP
5K	Hi Fly	CS
5K	Sky King	N
5M	Hi Fly Malta	9H
5N	Nordavia Regional Airlines	RA
5O	Europe Airpost	F
5Q	BQB Lineas Aereas	CX
5R	RUTACA	YV
5S	Sapair	HI
5T	Canadian North	C
5U	LADE	LV
5U	Transportes Aereos Guatemaltecos	TG
5X	UPS Airlines	N
5Y	Atlas Air	N
5Z	Bismillah Airlines	S2
5Z	Cemair	ZS
6B	Tuifly Nordic	SE
6D	Pelita Air	PK
6E	IndiGo	VT
6F	Falcon Air Express	N
6F	uFly Airways	N
6F	Primera Air Nordic	YL
6H	Israir	4X
6I	Alsie Express	OY
6J	Solaseed Air	JA
6J	Jubba Airways	5Y
6N	Al-Naser Airlines	YI
6N	Niger Airlines	5U
6P	Gryphon Airlines	ZS
6P	Rovos Air	ZS
6Q	Cham Wings Airlines	YK
6R	Alrosa Aviation	RA
6R	Aerounion	XA
6S	Star Air Aviation	AP
6T	Air Mandalay	XY
6U	Air Cargo Germany	D
6V	MRK Airlines	UR
6W	Saratov Airlines	RA
6Y	Smartlynx	YL
7C	Jeju Air	HL
7E	Evergreen Helicopters	N
7F	First Air	C
7G	Star Flyer	JA
7H	Ravn Alaska	N
7I	InselAir	PJ
7J	Swiftair	EC
7J	Tajik Air	EY
7L	Silk Way West Airlines	4K
7K	Kolavia	RA
7M	Mistral Air	I
7M	Mayair	XA
7P	Air Panama	HP
7Q	PAWA Dominicana	HI
7Q	Air Libya	5A
7R	RusLine	RA
7S	Ryan Air	N
7T	Trans Am Aero Express	HC
7T	Tobruk Air	5A
7W	Wind Rose	UR
7Y	Mann Yadanarpon Airlines	XY
8B	Business Air	HS
8C	ATI - Air Transport International	N
8D	Expo Aviation	4R
8E	Bering Air	N
8E	Easy Fly Express	S2
8F	Cardig Air	PK
8G	Instone Air Services	G
8H	BH Air	LZ
8I	Insel Air Aruba	P4

8J	Jet4You	CN		BB	Seaborne Airlines	N
8K	K-Mile Air	HS		BC	Skymark Airlines	JA
8L	Lucky Airlines	B		BD	Servant Air	N
8M	Myanmar Airways International	XY		BD	Cambodia Bayon Airlines	XU
8N	Barents Airlink	SE		BE	FlyBe	G
8N	Regional Air Services	5H		BF	Bluebird Cargo	TF
8O	West Coast Air	C		BG	Biman Bangladesh Airlines	S2
8P	Pacific Coastal Airlines	C		BH	Hawkair Aviation Service	C
8Q	Onur Air	TC		BI	Royal Brunei Airlines	V8
8R	Sol Lineas Aereas	LV		BJ	Nouvelair	TS
8T	Air Tindi	C		BK	Okay Airways	B
8U	Afriqiyah Airways	5A		BL	Jetstar Pacific Airlines	VN
8V	Astral Aviation	5Y		BM	BMI Regional	G
8W	Private Wings	D		BN	Bahrain Air	A9C
8Y	China Postal Airlines	B		BP	Air Botswana	A2
8Z	Wizz Air Bulgaria	LZ		BQ	Bukovyna Airlines	UR
				BR	EVA Air	B
9A	Eaglexpress Air	9M		BS	British International	G
9C	Spring Airlines	B		BT	AirBaltic	YL
9D	Toumaï Air Tchad	TT		BU	Compagnie Africaine d'Aviation	9Q
9I	Helitrans	LN		BV	Blu-Express	I
9I	Alliance Air	VT		BV	Blue Panorama Airlines	I
9J	Dana Airlines	5N		BW	Caribbean Airlines	9Y
9K	Cape Air	N		BX	Air Busan	HL
9L	Colgan Air	N		RY	Thomsonfly	G
9M	Central Mountain Air	C		BZ	Blue Dart Aviation	VT
9N	Tropic Air	V3		BZ	Blue Bird Airways	SX
9O	National Airways Cameroon	TJ				
9P	Air Arabia Jordan	JY		C2	Mountain Air Cargo	N
9Q	Caicos Express Airways	VQ-T		C2	Ceiba Intercontinental	3C
9R	SATENA	HK		C3	Sky Capital Airways	S2
9S	Southern Air	N		C3	Trade Air	9A
9T	myCARGO Airlines	TC		C4	Zimex Aviation	HB
9U	Air Moldova	ER		C6	Canjet	C
9V	Avior Airlines	YV		C7	Rico Linhas Aereas	PP
9W	Jet Airways	VT		C8	Cargolux Italia	I
				C8	Cronos Airlines	3C
A2	Astra Airlines	SX		CA	Air China	B
A3	Aegean Airlines	SX		CA	Air China Cargo	B
A4	Aerocon	CP		CB	ScotAirways	G
A5	HOP! Airlinair	F		CC	Air Atlanta Icelandic	TF
A6	Asia Pacific Airlines	P2		CE	Chalair Aviation	F
A8	Ameriflight	N		CF	City Airline	SE
A9	Georgian Airways	4L		CG	Airlines of Papua New Guinea	P2
AA	American Airlines	N		CH	Bemidji Airlines	N
AB	AirBerlin	D		CI	China Airlines	B
AC	Air Canada	C		CJ	BA Cityflyer	G
AD	Azul	PP		CK	China Cargo Airlines	B
AE	Mandarin Airlines	B		CL	Lufthansa Cityline	D
AF	Air France	F		CM	COPA Airlines	HP
AG	Air Contractors	EI		CN	Grand China Air	B
AG	Aruba Airlines	P4		CP	Chathams Pacific	A3
AH	Air Algerie	7T		CS	CSA Czech Airlines	OK
AI	Air India	VT		CT	Alitalia Cityliner	I
AK	Atrak Air	EP		CU	Cubana de Aviacion	CU
AK	AirAsia	9M		CV	Cargolux Airlines Intl	LX
AL	Midwest Connect	N		CV	Air Chathams	ZK
AM	Aeromexico	XA		CX	Cathay Pacific Airways	B
AP	Air One	I		CZ	China Southern Airlines	B
AQ	9 Air	B				
AR	Aerolineas Argentinas	LV		D0	DHL Air	G
AS	Alaska Airlines	N		D2	Severstal	RA
AT	Royal Air Maroc	CN		D3	Daallo Airlines	J2
AU	Austral Lineas Aereas	LV		D4	Alidaunia	I
AV	Avianca	HK		D5	DHL Aero Expreso	HP
AW	Africa World Airlines	9G		D6	Interair	ZS
AY	Finnair	OH		D9	Donavia	RA
AZ	Alitalia	I		DB	HOP! Brit'Air	F
				DC	Braathens Regional	SE
B0	La Compagnie	F		DD	Nok Air	HS
B2	Belavia	EW		DE	Condor	D
B4	Zanair	5H		DF	Center-South Airlines	RA
B5	Fly SAX	5Y		DG	CebGo	PR
B6	Jetblue Airways	N		DK	Thomas Cook Airlines Scandinavia	OY
B7	UNI Air	B		DL	Delta Airlines	N
B8	Eritrean Airlines	E3		DL	Delta Connection	N
B9	Iran Air Tours	EP		DM	Asian Air	HS
BA	British Airways	G		DN	Senegal Airlines	6V

DO	Discovery Air	5N		G9	Air Arabia	A6
DP	Pobeda	RA		GA	Garuda Indonesia	PK
DR	Ruili Airlines	B		GB	ABX Air	N
DS	Easyjet Switzerland	HB		GD	Grandstar Cargo Airlines	B
DT	TAAG Angola Airlines	D2		GE	Transasia Airways	B
DV	Scat Air	UP		GF	Gulf Air	A9C
DX	Danish Air Transport	OY		GG	Sky Lease Cargo	N
DY	Norwegian	LN		GH	Globus	RA
DY	Norwegian Long Haul	LN		GJ	Zhejiang Loong Airlines	B
				GK	JetStar Japan	JA
E3	NewGen Airways	HS		GL	Air Greenland	OY
E3	Domodedovo Airlines	RA		GM	Tri-MG Intra-Asia Airlines	PK
E4	Enter Air	SP		GO	ULS Cargo	TC
E4	Elysian Airlines	TJ		GP	Pantanal Linhas Aereas	PP
E5	Samara Airlines	RA		GQ	Sky Express	SX
E5	Air Arabia Egypt	SU		GR	Aurigny Air Services	G
E7	Estafeta Carga Aerea	XA		GS	Tianjin Airlines	B
E8	City Airways	HS		GU	AVIATECA Guatemala	TG
E9	Evelop Airlines	EC		GV	Grant Aviation	N
EA	Eastern Airlines	N		GW	Kuban Airlines	RA
EB	Wamos Air	EC		GW	SkyGreece	SX
ED	AirExplore	OM		GX	Guangxi Beibu Gulf Airlines	B
EE	Eastern Skyjets	A6		GX	Pacificair	RP
EE	East Horizon Airlines	YA		GY	Sky Bishkek	EX
EG	Enerjet	C		GZ	Air Rarotonga	E5
EH	ANA Wings	JA		GZ	Grozny-Avia	RA
EI	Aer Lingus	EI				
EJ	New England Airlines	N		H2	Sky Airline	CC
EK	Emirates	A6		H3	Hermes Airlines	SX
EL	Ellinair	SX		H4	Aero4M	S5
EN	Air Dolomiti	I		H5	I Fly	RA
EP	Iran Aseman Airlines	EP		H6	Bulgarian Air Charter	LZ
EQ	TAME	HC		H7	Eagle Air	5X
ER	Astar Air Cargo	N		H8	Sepahan Airlines	EP
ES	DHL Intl Aviation	A9C		HA	Hawaiian Airlines	N
ET	Ethiopian Airlines	ET		HB	Asia Atlantic Airways	HB
EU	Chengdu Airlines	B		HD	Air Do	JA
EV	Atlantic Southeast Airlines	N		HE	LGW - Luftfahrtgesellschaft Walter	D
EV	Expressjet Airlines	N		HF	Air Cote d'Ivoire	TU
EW	Eurowings	D		HG	Niki	
EX	Air Santo Domingo	HI			OE	
EY	Etihad Airways	A6		HH	Taban Airlines	EP
EZ	Sun Air of Scandinavia	OY		HI	Papillon Grand Canyon Airways	N
				HJ	Tasman Cargo Airlines	VH
F0	Felix Airways	7O		HM	Air Seychelles	S7
F4	Air Flamenco	N		HN	Afghan Jet International	YA
F7	Etihad Regional	HB		HO	Juneyao Airlines	B
F9	Frontier Airlines	N		HP	Amapola Flyg	SE
FA	FlySafair	ZS		HQ	Thomas Cook Airline Belgium	OO
FB	Bulgaria Air	LZ		HR	Hahn Air	D
FC	Falcon Express Cargo Airlines	A6		HU	Hainan Airlines	B
FC	Flybe Nordic	OH		HV	Transavia	PH
FD	Thai AirAsia	HS		HW	North-Wright Airways	C
FG	Ariana Afghan Airlines	YA		HX	HongKong Airlines	B
FH	Freebird Airlines	TC		HY	Uzbekistan Airways	UK
FI	Icelandair	TF		HZ	Aurora Airlines	RA
FJ	Fiji Airways	DQ				
FK	Keewatin Air	C		I3	ATA Airlines	EP
FM	Shanghai Airlines	B		I5	Nouvel Air Mali	TZ
FN	Regional Air Lines	CN		I5	AirAsia India	VT
FP	Freedom Air	N		I6	Air Indus	AP
FR	Ryanair	EI		I8	Indonesia Air Transport	PK
FS	Syphax Airlines	TS		I8	Izhavia	RA
FT	Farnair Switzerland	HB		I9	Air Italy	I
FU	Fuzhou Airlines	B		IA	Iraqi Airways	YI
FV	Rossiya Airlines	RA		IB	Iberia	EC
FW	Ibex Airlines	JA		ID	Batik Air	PK
FX	Federal Express	N		IE	Solomon Airlines	H4
FY	Firefly	9M		IG	Alisarda	I
FZ	FlyDubai	A6		II	IBC Airways	N
				IK	Kaya Airlines	C9
G2	Albatros Airlines	YV		IK	Ikar	
G3	Gol Transportes Aereos	PP			RA	
G4	Allegiant Air	N		IO	IrAero	RA
G4	Guizhou Airlines	B		IP	Atyrau Aue Joly	UP
G5	China Express Airlines	B		IP	Orbest Orizonia	EC
G7	GoJet Airlines	N		IR	Iran Air	EP
G8	Go Air	VT		IS	AIS Airlines	PH

IT	Tigerair Taiwan	B		KV	Asian Express Airlines	EY
IU	Hevi-Lift	P2		KW	KF Aerospace	C
IV	Caspian Airlines	EP		KW	Kharkiv Airlines	UR
IV	Investavia	UP		KX	Cayman Airways	VP-C
IW	Wings Abadi Air	PK		KY	Kunming Airlines	B
IX	Air India Express	VT		KZ	Nippon Cargo Airlines	JA
IY	Yemenia	7O				
IZ	Arkia Israeli Airlines	4X		L2	Lynden Air Cargo	N
				L3	DHL de Guatemala	TG
J2	Azerbaijan Airlines	4K		L4	Linea Turistica Aereotuy	YV
J3	Northwestern Air	C		L5	LAC – Linea Aerea Cuencana	HC
J4	Badr Airlines	ST		L6	Mauritania Airlines International	5T
J5	Donghai Airlines	B		L7	Lineas Aereas Carguera de	
J5	Alaska Seaplane Service	N			Colombia	HK
J7	Centre-Avia	RA		L8	Lynden Air Cargo	P2
J7	Denim Air ACMI	PH		L8	Afric Aviation	TR
J9	Jazeera Airways	9K		L9	Bristow US	N
JA	BH Air	E9		LA	LAN Airlines	CC
JA	Jagson Airlines	VT		LB	LAB Airlines	CP
JB	HeliJet International	C		LB	Air Costa	VT
JC	Japan Air Commuter	JA		LC	EC Air	TN
JD	Capital Airlines	B		LD	Air Hong Kong	B
JE	Mango	ZS		LF	Lao Central Airlines	RDPL
JF	Jet Asia Airways	HS		LG	Luxair	LX
JF	LAB Flying Service	N		LH	Lufthansa	D
JG	JetGo	VH		LH	Lufthansa Cargo	D
JH	Fuji Dream Airlines	JA		LI	LIAT - The Caribbean Airline	V2
JI	Meraj Air	EP		LJ	Jin Air	HL
JJ	TAM Linhas Aereas	PP		LL	Miami Air International	N
JL	J-Air	JA		LN	Libyan Airlines	5A
JL	Japan Airlines	JA		LO	LOT - Polish Airlines	SP
JO	JetTime	OY		LP	LAN Peru	OB
JP	Adria Airways	S5		LQ	Solaseed Air	JA
JR	Joy Air/Happy Airlines	B		LS	Jet2	G
JQ	Alba Star	EC		LT	Air Lituanica	LY
JQ	Jetstar Airways	VH		LU	LAN Express	CC
JS	Air Koryo	P		LV	Mega Global Maldives	8Q
JT	Lion Airlines	PK		LW	Pacific Wings	N
JU	Air Serbia	YU		LX	Swiss	HB
JV	Bearskin Airlines	C		LY	El Al Israel Airlines	4X
JW	Vanilla Air	JA				
JY	interCaribbean Airways	VQ-T		M0	Aero Mongolia	JU
				M2	MHS Aviation	D
				M2	Rhein-Neckar Air	D
K3	Taquan Air Service	N		M3	North Flying	OY
K3	Safe Air Kenya	5Y		M3	TAM Cargo	PP
K4	Kalitta Air	N		M4	Smart Aviation	SU
K4	ALS/Compion Aviation	5Y		M5	Kenmore Air	N
K5	Seaport Airlines	N		M6	Amerijet International	N
K5	Wings of Alaska	N		M7	MASair	XA
K6	Cambodia Angkor Air	XU		M8	Transnusa Aviation Mandiri	PK
K7	Air Almaty	UP		M8	Skyjet	RP
K7	Air KBZ	XY		M9	Motor Sich Airlines	UR
K8	Kan Air	HS		MA	Malev	HA
K8	World Atlantic Airlines	N		MB	MNG Cargo Airlines	TC
K9	Kalitta Charters	N		MD	Air Madagscar	5R
KA	Dragonair	B		ME	Middle East Airlines	OD
KB	Druk Air	A5		MF	Xiamen Airlines	B
KC	Air Astana	UP		MG	Midex Airlines	A6
KD	KalStar Aviation	PK		MG	Miami Air Lease	N
KE	Korean Air	HL		MH	Malaysia Airlines	9M
KF	Blue1	OH		MI	SilkAir	9V
KG	Aerogaviota	CU		MJ	Mihin Lanka	4R
KI	Slyway Enterprises	N		MJ	M&N Aviation	N
KJ	Air Incheon	HL		MK	Air Mauritius	3B
KK	AtlasGlobal	TC		ML	Air Mediterranée	F
KL	KLM Royal Dutch Airlines	PH		MM	Peach	JA
KM	Air Malta	9H		MM	Myanmar National Airlines	XY
KN	China United Airlines	B		MN	Comair	ZS
KN	Maroomba Airlines	VH		MO	Calm Air	C
KO	Alaska Central Express	N		MP	Martinair Holland	PH
KO	Khors Air	UR		MQ	American Eagle	N
KP	Asialink Cargo Express	PK		MR	Hunnu Air	JU
KP	ASKY	5V		MS	Egyptair	SU
KQ	Kenya Airways	5Y		MT	Thomas Cook Airlines	G
KR	Air Bishkek	EX		MU	China Eastern Airlines	B
KS	Penair	N		MU	China Eastern Yunnan	B
KT	Katmai Air	N		MV	Aviastar Mandiri	PK
KU	Kuwait Airways	9K				

MW	Mokulele Airlines/Go! Express	N
MY	Maya Island Air	V3
MZ	SAEREO	HC
MZ	AMC Airlines	SU
N3	Aerolineas MAS	HI
N4	Nordwind	RA
N5	Medavia	9H
N7	Neptune Air	9M
N8	National Airlines	N
N9	Kabo Air	5N
N9	Nova Airlines	SE
NC	Northern Air Cargo	N
NC	Cobham Aviation Services Australia	VH
ND	FMI Air	XY
NE	Nesma Airlines	SU
NF	Air Vanuatu	YJ
NG	Aero Contractors	5N
NH	ANA - All Nippon Network	JA
NI	Portugalia Airlines	CS
NJ	Nordic Global Airlines	OH
NK	Spirit Airlines	N
NL	Shaheen Air International	AP
NM	Nam Air	PK
NM	Mount Cook Airline	ZK
NN	VIM Airlines	RA
NO	Neos	I
NP	Nile Air	SU
NQ	Air Japan	JA
NR	MaxAir	5N
NS	Hebei Airlines	B
NT	Binter Canarias	EC
NU	Japan Transocean Air	JA
NX	Air Macau	B
NZ	Air New Zealand	ZK
O3	SF Airlines	B
O4	Antrak Air	9G
O5	Comores Aviation	D6
O6	Avianca Brazil	PP
O8	Siam Air Transport	HS
O9	Nova Airways	ST
OA	Olympic Airways	SX
OB	Boliviana de Aviacion	CP
OC	PGA Express	CS
OC	Oriental Air Bridge	JA
OI	Hinterland Aviation	VH
OI	Aspiring Air	ZK
OJ	Overland Airways	5N
OK	CSA Czech Airlines	OK
OJ	Fly Jamaica	6Y
OL	OFT - Ostfriesische Lufttransport	D
OM	MIAT - Mongolian Airlines	JU
ON	Nauru Airlines	C2
OO	Skywest Airlines	N
OQ	Chongqing Airlines	B
OQ	Hydro-Quebec (Service Tpt Aerien)	C
OR	Arkefly	PH
OS	Austrian Airlines	OE
OU	Croatia Airlines	9A
OV	Estonian Air	ES
OX	Orient Thai Airlines	HS
OY	Andes Lineas Aereas	LV
OY	Omni Air International	N
OZ	Asiana Airlines	HL
P0	Proflight Commuter Services	9J
P2	Airkenya Express	5Y
P3	AVE.com	A6
P5	COPA Airlines Colombia	HK
P6	Pascan Aviation	C
P7	Small Planet Airlines Polska	SP
P7	Palau Pacific Airways	T8A
P8	Sierra West Airlines	N
P9	Asia Pacific Airlines	N
P9	Peruvian Air Lines	OB
PA	AirBlue	AP
PB	Provincial Airlines	C

PC	Pegasus Airlines	TC
PD	Porter Airlines	C
PE	People's Viennaline	HB
PE	Phoebus Apollo Aviation	ZS
PF	Primera Air Scandinavia	OY
PG	Bangkok Airways	HS
PH	Phoenix Air	N
PH	Polynesian Airlines	5W
PI	Fiji Link	DQ
PI	Polar Airlines	RA
PJ	Air St Pierre	F
PK	Pakistan International Airlines	AP
PM	Canary Fly	EC
PN	West Air	B
PO	Polar Air Cargo	N
PQ	AirAsia Philippines	RP
PR	Philippine Airlines	RP
PS	Ukraine International Airlines	UR
PT	Piedmont Airlines	N
PT	West Air Sweden	SE
PU	Pluna Lineas Aereas Uruguayas	CX
PV	Pan Air	EC
PW	Precision Air	5H
PX	Air Niugini	P2
PX	Link PNG	P2
PY	Surinam Airways	PZ
PZ	TAM Mercosur	ZP
Q3	Anguilla Air Services	VP-A
Q4	Aviation Starlink	C
Q5	40 Mile Air	N
Q6	Skytrans Regional	VH
Q7	Sky Bahamas	C6
Q7	Swift Air	N
Q8	Trans Air Congo	TN
QA	Cimber	OY
QB	Qeshm Air	EP
QB	Sky Georgia	4L
QC	Camair	TJ
QF	QANTAS Airways	VH
QF	JetConnect	ZK
QG	Citilink	PK
QH	Air Kyrgyzstan	EX
QK	Air Canada Jazz	C
QL	Laser	YV
QL	Aero Lanka	4R
QN	Air Armenia	EK
QQ	Alliance Airlines	VH
QR	Qatar Airways	A7
QS	Smartwings	OK
QS	Travel Service	OK
QT	Avianca Cargo	HK
QU	UTair Ukraine	UR
QV	Lao Airlines	RDPL
QW	Qingdao Airlines	B
QX	Horizon Air	N
QZ	Indonesia Airasia	PK
R2	Orenair	RA
R3	Yakutia Airlines	RA
R4	Rus Aviation	EK
R5	Jordan Aviation	JY
R6	DOT/Danu Oro Transportas	LY
R7	Aserca Airlines	YV
RA	Nepal Airlines	9N
RB	Syrianair	YK
RC	Atlantic Airways	OY
RE	Stobart Air	EI
RG	Varig	PP
RH	RPX Airlines	PK
RJ	Royal Jordanian	JY
RK	R Airlines	HS
RL	Royal Falcon	JY
RO	Tarom	YR
RQ	Kam Air	YA
RS	Sky Regional Airlines	C
RT	Real Tonga Airlines	A3
RU	Airbridge Cargo	RA

RV	Air Canada Rouge	C		U4	Buddha Air	9N
RX	Regent Airways	S2		U5	Karinou Airlines	TL
RY	Royal Wings	JY		U6	Ural Airlines	RA
RZ	SANSA	TI		U8	Armavia	EK
				UA	United Air Lines	N
S2	JetKonnect	VT		UA	United Express	N
S3	SBA – Santa Barbara Airlines	YV		UB	Air Cargo Global	OM
S4	SATA International	CS		UC	LAN Cargo	CC
S5	Shuttle America	N		UD	Hex'Air	F
S5	Small Planet Airlines	LY		UF	UM Air	UR
S6	Salmon Air	N		UG	Tunisair Express	TS
S6	Star Air	OY		UH	AtlasJet Ukraine	UR
S6	Sunr Air	ST		UJ	Almasria Universal Airlines	SU
S7	S7 Airlines	RA		UJ	USA Jet Airlines	N
S8	Skywise	ZS		UK	Vistara	VT
S8	Shovkoviy Shlyah	UR		UL	Srilankan	4R
S9	Silk Road Cargo Business	UK		UM	Air Zimbabwe	Z
S9	Starbow	9G		UN	Transaero Airlines	RA
SA	South African Airways	ZS		UO	Hong Kong Express Airways	B
SB	AirCalin	F		UP	Bahamasair	C6
SC	Shandong Airlines	B		UQ	Urumqi Airlines	B
SD	Sudan Airways	ST		UR	UTair Express	RA
SE	XL Airways France	F		US	US Airways	N
SF	Tassili Airlines	7T		UT	Turukhan Aviakompania	RA
SG	Spicejet	VT		UT	UTair Airlines	RA
SI	Blue Islands	GI		UU	Air Austral	F
SI	Sierra Pacific Airlines	N		UV	Helisureste	EC
SJ	Sriwijaya Air	PK		UW	Uni-Top Airlines	B
SK	Scandinavian Airline System	SE		UX	Air Europa	EC
SL	Thai Lion Air	HS		UY	Cameroon Airlines	TJ
SM	Air Cairo	SU		UZ	Buraq Air	5A
SN	Brussels Airlines	OO				
SP	SATA Air Acores	CS		V0	Conviasa	YV
SQ	Singapore Airlines	9V		V2	Citywing	G
SQ	Singapore Airlines Cargo	9V		V2	Vision Air	N
SS	Corsair	F		V2	Avialeasing	UK
ST	Germania	D		V3	Carpatair	YR
SU	Aeroflot Russian Airlines	RA		V4	Vieques Air Link	N
SV	Saudia	HZ		V4	Vensecar Internacional	YV
SW	Air Namibia	V5		V4	Lignes Aeriennes Congolaises	9Q
SX	Skywork Airlines	HB		V7	Volotea Airlines	EC
SY	Sun Country Airlines	N		V8	Iliamna Air Taxi	N
				V8	ATRAN - Aviatrans Cargo Airlines	RA
T0	TACA Peru	OB		V8	TAPSA	LV
T2	Nakina Outpost Camps and Air	C		V9	Van Air Europe	OK
T3	Eastern Airways	G		VA	Virgin Australia	VH
T5	Turkmenistan Airlines	EZ		VA	Virgin Australia Regional Airlines	VH
T7	Twin Jet	F		VB	Veteran Avia	EK
T7	Transcarga International Airways	YV		VC	Voyageur Airways	C
TA	TACA International Airlines	YS		VC	Charter Air Transport	N
TB	Jetairfly	OO		VD	Henan Airlines	B
TB	Tara Air	9N		VF	Valuair	9V
TC	Air Tanzania	5H		VG	VLM Airlines	OO
TD	Atlantis European Airways	EK		VI	Volga-Dnepr Airlines	RA
TE	SkyTaxi	SP		VJ	VietJet	VN
TF	Tahi Flying Service	HS		VK	Air Vallée	I
TF	Malmo Aviation	SE		VL	VIA - Air Via	LZ
TG	Thai Airways International	HS		VN	Vietnam Airlines	VN
TH	Raya Airways	9M		VP	Flyme/Villa Air	8Q
TI	TACA Costa Rica	TI		VQ	Novoair	S2
TI	Tailwind Airlines	TC		VR	TACV – Transp. Aer. de Cabo Verde	D4
TK	Turkish Airlines	TC		VS	Virgin Atlantic Airways	G
TL	Airnorth Regional	VH		VT	Air Tahiti	F
TM	LAM - Linhas Aereas de Mocambique	C9		VW	Aeromar	XA
TN	Air Tahiti Nui	F		VX	Virgin America	N
TO	Transavia France	F		VY	Vueling Airlines	EC
TP	TAP Air Portugal	CS		VZ	Air Class	CX
TR	Tigerair	9V				
TS	Air Transat	C		W3	Arik Air	5N
TT	Tigerair Australia	VH		W4	LC Busre	OB
TU	Tunisair	TS		W5	Mahan Airlines	EP
TV	Tibet Airlines	B		W6	Wizz Air	HA
TW	T'Way Air	HL		W7	Sayakhat	UP
TY	Air Caledonie	F		W8	Cargojet Airways	C
TZ	Scoot	9V		W9	Air Bagan	XY
				WA	KLM Cityhopper	PH
U2	easyJet	G		WB	Rwandair	9XR
U3	Avies	ES		WC	Islena Airlines	HR

WE	Centurion Air Cargo	N
WE	Thai Smile Airways	HS
WF	Wideroe's Flyveselskap	LN
WG	Sunwing Airlines	C
WH	West Air Benin	TY
WI	White Airways	CS
WJ	Air Labrador	C
WK	Edelweiss Air	HB
WM	Winair	PJ
WN	Southwest Airlines	N
WR	Westjet Encore	C
WS	Westjet	C
WT	Wasaya Airways	C
WV	Aero VIP	CS
WW	WOW Air	TF
WX	City Jet	EI
WY	Oman Air	A4O
WZ	Red Wings Airlines	RA
X3	Tuifly	D
X5	Ten Airways	YR
X9	Avion Express	LY
XC	Corendon Air	TC
XE	Korea Express Air	HL
XG	Cygnus Air	EC
XH	Alexandria Airlines	SU
XK	Air Corsica	F
XL	LAN Ecuador	HC
XM	Qantas Freight	VH
XP	XTRAAirways	N
XQ	SunExpress	TC
XT	Indonesia AirAsia X	PK
XU	African Express Airways	5Y
XW	China Xinhua Airlines	B
XW	NokScoot Airlines	HS
XY	Flynas	HZ
XZ	SA Express	ZS
Y4	Volaris	XA
Y5	Golden Myanmar Airlines	XY
Y7	ADI Charter	N
Y7	Nordstar	RA
Y8	Yangtze River Express	B
Y9	Kish Air	EP
YB	Bora Jet	TC
YC	Yamal Airlines	RA
YE	Yan Air	UR

YG	South Airlines	UR
YH	Yangon Airways	XY
YI	Air Sunshine	N
YJ	Asian Wings	XY
YK	Avia Traffic Company	EX
YL	Yamal Airlines	RA
YM	Montenegro Airlines	4O
YN	Air Creebec	C
YO	Heli Air Monaco	3A
YR	Scenic Airlines	N
YS	HOP! Régional	F
YT	Yeti Airlines	9N
YU	EuroAtlantic Airways	CS
YV	Mesa Airlines	N
YW	Air Nostrum	EC
Z2	AirAsia Zest	PR
Z3	Promech Air	N
Z4	Puma Air	PP
Z4	Zagrosjet	YI
Z5	GMG Airlines	S2
Z6	Dniproavia	UR
Z7	FlyAfrica	Z
Z8	Amaszonas Transportes Aereos	CP
Z9	Bek Air	UP
ZA	Sky Angkor Airlines	XU
ZB	Monarch Airlines	G
ZC	Korongo Airlines	9Q
ZD	EWA Air	F
ZE	Eastar Jet	HL
ZF	Katekavia	RA
ZH	Shenzhen Airlines	B
ZI	Aigle Azur	F
ZK	Great Lakes Airlines	N
ZK	Zetavia	UR
ZL	REX - Regional Express	VH
ZM	Air Manas	EX
ZM	Cityline Hungary	HA
ZN	Naysa Aerotaxis	EC
ZP	Silk Way Airlines	4K
ZR	Aviacon Zitotrans	RA
ZS	Punto Azul	3C
ZT	Titan Airways	G
ZV	V Air	B
ZV	Zagros Airlines	EP
ZW	Air Wisconsin	N
ZX	Air Georgian	C

ICAO THREE-LETTER DESIGNATORS

AAF	Aigle Azur	F		AKA	Air Korea	HL
AAH	Aloha Air Cargo	N		AKC	AsiaLink Cargo Express	PK
AAJ	Alfa Airlines	ST		AKL	Air Kiribati	T3
AAL	American Airlines	N		AKN	Alkan Air	C
AAQ	Asia Atlantic Airlines	HS		AKX	ANA Wings	JA
AAQ	Copterline	OH		ALD	Air Leisure	SU
AAR	Asiana Airlines	HL		ALK	Srilankan	4R
AAW	Afriqiyah Airways	5A		ALM	Alfa Air	CN
AAY	Allegiant Air	N		ALV	Aeropostal	YV
AAZ	Aeolus Air	C5		ALW	ALS/Compion Aviation	5Y
ABD	Air Atlanta Icelandic	TF		ALX	Compagnie Africaine d'Aviation	9Q
ABF	Scanwings	OH		ALY	ALAS Uruguay	CX
ABG	Royal Flight	RA		AMC	Air Malta	9H
ABJ	Abaete Linhas Aereas	PP		AMF	Ameriflight	N
ABL	Air Busan	HL		AMI	Air America, PR	N
ABQ	AirBlue	AP		AMM	Aeroportul Intl Marculesti/AIM Air	ER
ABR	Air Contractors	EI		AMO	Angel Martinez Ridao	EC
ABS	Transwest Air	C		AMP	Aero Transporte - ATSA	OB
ABV	Antrak Air	9G		AMT	Amazon Sky	OB
ABW	Airbridge Cargo	RA		AMU	Air Macau	B
ABX	ABX Air	N		AMV	AMC Airlines	SU
ABY	Air Arabia	A6		AMY	Air Mandalay	XY
ACA	Air Canada	C		AMX	Aeromexico	XA
ACH	Africa's Connection	S9		ANA	Air Nippon Network	JA
ACI	AirCalin	F		ANA	ANA - All Nippon Network	JA
ACJ	AC Aviation Company	HS		AND	Servicios Aereos de los Andes	OB
ACP	Astral Aviation	5Y		ANE	Air Nostrum	EC
ACX	Air Cargo Germany	D		ANG	Air Niugini	P2
ADB	Antonov Airlines	UR		ANG	Link PNG	P2
ADH	Air One	I		ANK	Air Nippon	JA
ADO	Air Do	JA		ANO	Airnorth Regional	VH
ADR	Adria Airways	S5		ANQ	ADA - Aerolineas de Antioquia	HK
ADZ	Chukotavia	RA		ANR	Yan Air	UR
AEA	Air Europa	EC		ANS	Andes Lineas Aereas	LV
AEE	Aegean Airlines	SX		ANT	Air North	C
AEG	Airest	ES		ANZ	Air New Zealand	ZK
AEH	Aero4M	S5		AOA	Alcon Servicios Aereos	XA
AEK	Aerocon	CP		APC	Airpac Airlines	N
AEL	Aer Caribe	HK		APF	Amapola Flyg	SE
AER	Alaska Central Express	N		APG	AirAsia Philippines	RP
AEY	Air Italy	I		APJ	Peach	JA
AFE	Airfast Indonesia	PK		APK	Air Peace	5N
AFG	Ariana Afghan Airlines	YA		APP	Aeroperlas	HP
AFL	Aeroflot Russian Airlines	RA		AQU	Airquarius Aviation	ZS
AFN	Air Freight NZ	ZK		ARA	Arik Air	5N
AFR	Air France	F		ARE	LAN Airlines Colombia	HK
AFW	Africa World Airlines	9G		ARG	Aerolineas Argentinas	LV
AGU	Angara Airlines	RA		ARL	Airlec Air Espace	F
AGV	Air Glaciers	HB		ARM	MEGAviation	ER
AGX	Aviogenex	YU		ARR	Air Armenia	EK
AGY	Air Go Egypt	SU		ART	Smartlynx	YL
AHC	Azal Avia Cargo	4K		ARW	Airways Intl /Jamaica Air Shuttle	6Y
AHF	Aspen Helicopters	N		ASA	Alaska Airlines	N
AHK	Air Hong Kong	B		ASB	Air Spray	C
AHO	Air Hamburg	D		ASD	Air Sinai	SU
AHS	AHS Air International	AP		ASH	Mesa Airlines	N
AHU	ABC Air Hungary	HA		ASL	Air Serbia	YU
AHX	Amakusa Airlines	JA		ASM	Awesome Flight Services	ZS
AHY	Azerbaijan Airlines	4K		ASQ	Atlantic Southeast Airlines	N
AIA	Avies	ES		ATC	Air Tanzania	5H
AIC	Air India	VT		ATG	Aerotranscargo	ER
AIE	Air Inuit	C		ATG	Allegiance Air Gabon	TR
AIH	Air Incheon	HL		ATN	ATI - Air Transport International	N
AIJ	Interjet	XA		ATQ	CHC Helicopters Nigeria	5N
AIP	Alpine Air Express	N		ATR	Atrak Air	EP
AIQ	Thai AirAsia	HS		ATS	Aviacon Zitotrans	RA
AIZ	Arkia Israeli Airlines	4X		ATV	Avanti Air	D
AJA	Anadolu Jet	TC		ATY	Airtraffic	5Y
AJB	Aero JBR	XA		AUA	Austrian Airlines	OE
AJD	Vista Georgia	4L		AUI	Ukraine International Airlines	UR
AJI	Ameristar Jet Charter	N		AUL	Nordavia Regional Airlines	RA
AJI	Afghan Jet International	YA		AUR	Aurigny Air Services	G
AJK	Allied Air Cargo	5N		AUT	Austral Lineas Aereas	LV
AJT	Amerijet International	N		AVA	Avianca	HK
AJX	Air Japan	JA		AVE	Avex Air	ZS

AVJ	Avia Traffic Company	EX	BJN	Beijing Airlines	B
AVN	Air Vanuatu	YJ	BJU	Aerojet	UR
AVV	Aviator	SU	BKO	Briko Air Service	9Y
AVW	Aviator Airways	SX	BKP	Bangkok Airways	HS
AVX	Avirex	TR	BKV	Bukovyna Airlines	UR
AWC	Titan Airways	G	BLB	Blue Bird Airlines	ST
AWD	Aeroworld Pakistan	AP	BLF	Blue1	OH
AWK	Airwork New Zealand	ZK	BLJ	Bluelink Jets	SE
AWM	Asian Wings	XY	BLJ	Petter Solberg Aviation	SE
AWQ	Indonesia Airasia	PK	BLS	Bearskin Airlines	C
AWS	Arab Wings	JY	BLX	Tuifly Nordic	SE
AWU	Aeroline	D	BMJ	Bemidji Airlines	N
AXB	Air India Express	VT	BML	Bismillah Airlines	S2
AXE	AirExplore	OM	BMR	BMI Regional	G
AXK	African Express Airways	5Y	BMS	Blue Air	YR
AXL	Anguilla Air Services	VP-A	BND	Bond Helicopters	G
AXM	AirAsia	9M	BNJ	Air Service Liege	OO
AXU	Abu Dhabi Aviation	A6	BNT	Bentiu Air Transport	ST
AXY	Air X Charter	9H	BOL	TAB Cargo	CP
AYD	AB Aviation	D6	BON	BH Air	E9
AYG	Yangon Airways	XY	BOS	OpenSkies	F
AYK	Ayk Avia	EK	BOT	Air Botswana	A2
AYT	Ayit Aviation	4X	BOV	Boliviana de Aviacion	CP
AZA	Alitalia	I	BOX	Aerologic	D
AZE	Arcus Air	D	BPA	Blu Express	I
AZF	Air Zermatt	HB	BPA	Blue Panorama Airlines	I
AZG	Silk Way West Airlines	4K	BPS	Budapest Air Service	HA
AZI	Astra Airlines	SX	BQB	BQB Lineas Aereas	CX
AZM	Azman Air	5N	BRG	Bering Air	N
AZQ	Silk Way Airlines	4K	BRH	Star Air Cargo	ZS
AZS	Aviacon Zitotrans	RA	BRJ	Bora Jet	TC
AZU	Azul	PP	BRL	Topbrass Aviation	5N
AZW	Air Zimbabwe	Z	BRP	Aerobratsk	RA
AZZ	Azza Transport	ST	BRQ	Buraq Air	5A
			BRU	Belavia	EW
BAB	Bahrain Air	A9C	BRX	Braathens Regional	SE
BAN	British Antarctic Survey	VP-F	BRZ	Samara Airlines	RA
BAW	British Airways	G	BRZ	Bravo Air	4L
BAY	Bravo Airways	UR	BSK	Miami Air International	N
BAY	Cambodia Bayon Airlines	XU	BSL	Air Brasil	PP
BBC	Biman Bangladesh Airlines	S2	BST	Best Air	TC
BBD	Bluebird Cargo	TF	BSX	Bassaka Air	XU
BBG	Blue Bird Airways	SX	BTI	Air Baltic	YL
BBR	SBA – Santa Barbara Airlines	YV	BTK	Batik Air	PK
BBZ	Blue Bird Aviation	5Y	BTL	Baltia Air Lines	N
BCC	Business Air	HS	BTN	Bhutan Airlines / Tashi Air	A5
BCI	Blue Islands	G	BTZ	Bristow US	N
BCS	EAT Leipzig	D	BUC	Bulgarian Air Charter	LZ
BCY	City Jet	EI	BUL	Blue Airlines	9Q
BDA	Blue Dart Aviation	VT	BUN	Buryat Airlines	RA
BDI	Benair Air Service	OY	BUR	Air Bucharest	YR
BDR	Badr Airlines	ST	BVN	Baron Aviation Services	N
BDV	Aberdair Aviation	5Y	BWA	Caribbean Airlines	9Y
BEC	Berkut State Air Company	UP	BWD	Blue West Helicopters	OY
BEE	FlyBe	G	BWI	Blue Wing Airlines	PZ
BEK	Bek Air	UP	BXH	Bar XH Air	C
BEL	Brussels Airlines	OO	BXR	Redding Aero Enterprises	N
BER	AirBerlin	D	BYA	Berry Aviation	N
BEU	Bateleur Air Charter	ZS	BZH	HOP! Brit'Air	F
BFC	Basler Airlines	N	BZS	Aero Biniza	XA
BFF	Air Nunavut	C			
BFL	Buffalo Airways	C	CAD	Cardig Air	PK
BGA	Airbus Transport International	F	CAI	Corendon Airlines	TC
BGH	BH Air	LZ	CAJ	Air Caraibes Atlantique	F
BGM	Ak Bars Aero	RA	CAL	China Airlines	B
BGT	Bergen Air Transport	LN	CAO	Air China Cargo	B
BHA	Hawkair Aviation Service	C	CAT	Copenhagen Airtaxi	OY
BHA	Buddha Air	9N	CAV	Calm Air	C
BHL	Bristow Helicopters	G	CAW	Comair	ZS
BHN	Bristow Helicopters (Nigeria)	5N	CAY	Cayman Airways	VP-C
BHP	Belair Airlines	HB	CBC	Caribair	HI
BHR	Bighorn Airways	N	CBG	GX Airlines	B
BHS	Bahamasair	C6	CBJ	Capital Airlines	B
BID	Bin Air	D	CBL	Colombe Airlines	XT
BIE	Air Mediterrannée	F	CBT	Catalina Air Transport	N
BIG	Big Island Air	N	CCA	Air China	B
BIH	British International	G	CCC	Air Cargo Global	OM
BIS	Sky Bishkek	EX	CCD	Dalian Airlines	B

CCE	Cairo Aviation	SU		CSN	China Southern Airlines	B
CCM	Air Corsica	F		CSQ	IBC Airways	N
CCT	Connect Air	C		CSS	SF Airlines	B
CCY	Tailwind International	N		CSW	SW Italia	I
CDC	Zhejiang Loong Airlines	B		CSY	Shuangyang Aviation	B
CDG	Shandong Airlines	B		CSZ	Shenzhen Airlines	B
CDN	Canadian Helicopters	C		CTN	Croatia Airlines	9A
CDV	Skol Aviakompania	RA		CTQ	Citylink	9G
CEB	Cebu Pacific Air	RP		CTR	Aerolineas Centauro	XA
CEL	Ceiba Intercontinental	3C		CTS	Center-South Airlines	RA
CEM	Central Mongolian Airlines	JU		CTV	Citilink	PK
CES	China Eastern Airlines	B		CTW	Panair Cargo	HP
CEY	ACSA	HI		CUA	China United Airlines	B
CFA	China Flying Dragon Aviation	B		CUB	Cubana de Aviacion	CU
CFE	BA Cityflyer	G		CUH	Urumqi Airlines	B
CFG	Condor	D		CUO	Aero Cuahonte	XA
CHF	Care Flight	VH		CVA	Air Chathams	ZK
CFV	Aereo Calafia	XA		CVC	Centre-Avia Airlines	RA
CFZ	Zhongfei Airlines	B		CVE	Cabo Verde Express	D4
CGI	Atlas Jet	RA		CVK	Cavok Airlines	UR
CGF	Cargo Air	LZ		CVU	Grand Canyon Airlines	N
CGH	Guizhou Airlines	B		CVV	Comeravia	YV
CGK	Click Airways	EX		CWC	Centurion Air Cargo	N
CGN	Chang An Airlines	B		CWM	Air Marshalls	V7
CHB	West Air	B		CXA	Xiamen Airlines	B
CHC	CITIC Offshore Helicopters	B		CXB	Comlux Aruba	P4
CHH	Hainan Airlines	B		CXE	Caicos Express Airways	VQ-T
CHI	Cougar Helicopters	C		CXH	China Xinhua Airlines	B
CHN	Channel Island Aviation	N		CXI	Shan Xi Airlines	B
CID	Asia Continental Airlines	UP		CXP	XTRAAirways	N
CIF	Caribbean Flights	YV		CXT	Coastal Air Transport	N
CIG	Sirius Aero	RA		CYL	Alitalia Cityliner	I
CII	Cityfly	I		CYZ	China Postal Airlines	B
CIK	Comoros Islands Airways	D6				
CIM	Cimber	OY		DAE	DHL Aero Expreso	HP
CIR	Arctic Circle Air Service	N		DAG	Daghestan Airlines	RA
CIS	Cat Island Air	C6		DAH	Air Algerie	7T
CJA	Canjet	C		DAL	Delta Airlines	N
CJC	Colgan Air	N		DAL	Delta Connection	N
CJM	Corporate Jet Management	G		DAN	Dana Airlines	5N
CJR	Caverton Helicopters	5N		DAO	Daallo Airlines	J2
CJT	Cargojet Airways	C		DAP	Aerovias DAP	CC
CKK	China Cargo Airlines	B		DAT	Dart Airlines	UR
CKM	BKS Air	EC		DBK	Dubrovnik Airline	9A
CKS	Kalitta Air	N		DCD	Air 26	D2
CLG	Chalair Aviation	F		DCT	Direct Flight	G
CLH	Lufthansa Cityline	D		DCV	Discovery Air	5N
CLL	Aerovias Castillo	XA		DES	CC Helicopters	C
CLX	Cargolux Airlines Intl	LX		DEX	Asian Air	HS
CMJ	Comfort Jet Services	5V		DHE	DAP Helicopteros	CC
CMM	Air Mali	TZ		DHK	DHL Air	G
CMP	COPA Airlines	HP		DHL	Astar Air Cargo	N
CNB	Cityline Hungary	HA		DHV	DHL Aviation	ZS
CND	Corendon Dutch Airlines	PH		DHX	DHL International Aviation	A9C
CNF	Canaryfly	EC		DJT	La Compagnie	F
CNK	Sunwest Aviation	C		DKH	Juneyao Airlines	B
CNM	Air China Inner Mongolia	B		DKT	Business Aviation Courier	N
CNW	Continental	ER		DLA	Air Dolomiti	I
COT	Costa Airlines	YV		DLH	Lufthansa	D
COX	Compion Aviation	V5		DLT	DAT Lite	LY
CPA	Cathay Pacific Airways	B		DMJ	Global Air	XA
CPD	Capital Airlines	5Y		DMO	Domodedovo Airlines	RA
CPN	Caspian Airlines	EP		DNM	Denim Air ACMI	PH
CPT	Corporate Air	N		DNU	DAT/Danu Oro Transportas	LY
CQH	Spring Airlines	B		DNV	Donavia	RA
CQN	Chongqing Airlines	B		DOC	Norsk Luftambulance	LN
CRA	Cronos Airlines	3C		DOK	Nordic Air Ambulance	OY
CRC	Camair	TJ		DOP	Dancopter	OY
CRK	HongKong Airlines	B		DOV	Dove Air	ST
CRL	Corsair	F		DQA	Maldivian	8Q
CRN	Aerocaribbean	CU		DRK	Druk Air	A5
CRQ	Air Creebec	C		DRU	Alrosa Aviation	RA
CRS	Comercial Aerea	XA		DRY	Deraya Air Taxi	PK
CRT	Caribintair	HH		DSM	LAN Argentina	LV
CSA	CSA Czech Airlines	OK		DTA	TAAG Angola Airlines	D2
CSC	Sichuan Airlines	B		DTH	Tassili Airlines	7T
CSH	Shanghai Airlines	B		DTR	Danish Air Transport	OY
CSJ	Castle Aviation	N		DVI	Aero Davinci Internacional	XA

DVR	Divi Divi Air	PJ
DWI	Dominican Wings	HI
DWT	Etihad Regional	HB
DYA	Dynamic Aviation	N
DYL	Seair Airways	C6
DYN	ADI Charter	N
EAA	Air Bishkek	EX
EAG	Eagle Airways	ZK
EAL	Eastern Airlines	N
EAN	Skypower Express Airways	5N
EAQ	Eastern Australia Airlines	VH
EAS	Executive Aerospace	ZS
ECO	EcoJet	CP
EDC	Air Charter Scotland	G
EDO	Elidolomiti	I
EDR	Fly Allways	PZ
EDW	Edelweiss Air	HB
EFA	Express Freighters Australia	VH
EFG	Elifriula	I
EFX	Easy Fly Express	S2
EFY	Easyfly	HK
EGU	Eagle Air	5X
EHN	East Horizon Airlines	YA
EIN	Aer Lingus	EI
EKA	Equaflight Service	TN
EKG	Afric Aviation	TR
EKY	EasySky	HR
ELH	Elilario Italia	I
ELL	Estonian Air	ES
ELN	EllinAir	SX
ELY	El Al Israel Airlines	4X
EMO	Empire Airlines	N
EMT	Emetebe Taxi Aereo	HC
ENJ	Enerjet	C
ENT	Enter Air	SP
ENY	Envoy Airlines	N
EOA	Elilombarda	I
EPA	Donghai Airlines	B
ERH	Ravn Alaska	N
ERT	Eritrean Airlines	E3
ESD	Eastindo	PK
ESF	Estafeta Carga Aerea	XA
ESJ	Eastern Skyjets	A6
ESR	Eastar Jet	HL
ESW	SW Business Aviation	4K
ETC	Trans Attico	ST
ETD	Etihad Airways	A6
ETH	Ethiopian Airlines	ET
ETR	Estelar Latinoamerica	YV
EVA	EVA Airways	B
EVE	Evelop Airline	EC
EWG	Eurowings	D
EWR	EWA Air	F
EXK	American Eagle Executive	N
EXS	Jet2	G
EXT	Nightexpress	D
EXV	Expo Aviation	4R
EXY	SA Express	ZS
EXZ	Fly SAX	5Y
EZD	Air Asia Zest	RP
EZE	Eastern Airways	G
EZS	Easyjet Switzerland	HB
EZX	Eaglexpress Air	9M
EZY	Easyjet	G
FAB	First Air	C
FAH	Farnair Hungary	HA
FAO	Falcon Air Express	N
FAO	uFly Airways	N
FAT	Farnair Switzerland	HB
FAV	Fair Aviation	ZS
FBN	Florida Air Transport	N
FCM	Flybe Nordic	OH
FCX	Falcon Express Cargo Airlines	A6
FDA	Fuji Dream Airlines	JA
FDB	FlyDubai	A6
FDE	Federico Helicopters	N

FDR	Federal Air	ZS
FDX	Fedex Express	N
FEG	FlyAgypt	SU
FEI	Eagle Air Iceland	TF
FFM	Firefly	9M
FFT	Frontier Airlines	N
FFV	Fly540	5Y
FFX	Flex Linhas Aereas	PP
FGD	Conair Aviation	C
FHE	Hello	HB
FHY	Freebird Airlines	TC
FIN	Finnair	OH
FJI	Fiji Airways	DQ
FJM	Fly Jamaica	6Y
FKI	FLM Aviation	D
FLE	Flair Airlines	C
FLI	Atlantic Airways	OY
FMI	FMI Air	XY
FPO	Europe Airpost	F
FRE	Freedom Air	N
FRG	Freight Runners Express	N
FRI	Freedom Air	ZA
FRN	First Nation Airlines	5N
FSK	Africa Sky Airline	ZS
FTA	Frontier Flying Services	N
FTL	Flightline	EC
FTR	Finist'Air	F
FTZ	Fastjet	5H
FVS	Falcon Aviation Services	A6
FWI	Air Caraibes	F
FXI	Air Iceland	TF
FXX	Felix Airways	7O
FYE	East Link	5N
FZA	Fuzhou Airlines	B
FZW	flyAfrica.com	Z
GAA	Global Africa Aviation	Z
GAK	Global Aviation	5A
GAL	Albatros Airlines	YV
GAP	PAL Express	RP
GBA	Great Barrier Airlines	ZK
GBB	Global Aviation Leasing	ZS
GBG	Global Jet Airlines	A6
GBX	GB Airlink	N
GCA	Grand Cru Airlines	LY
GCR	Tianjin Airlines	B
GCW	Hevi Lift	P2
GDC	Grand China Air	B
GEA	Geasa	3C
GEC	Lufthansa Cargo	D
GFA	Gulf Air	A9C
GFG	Sky Georgia	4L
GGL	Gira Globo	D2
GGN	Air Georgian	C
GHN	Air Ghana	9G
GHS	Gatari Air Service	PK
GHT	Ghadames Air Transport	5A
GIA	Garuda Indonesia	PK
GIE	Elysian Airlines	TJ
GIL	Georgian International Airlines	4L
GJS	GpJet Airlines	N
GLA	Great Lakes Airlines	N
GLG	Avianca Ecuador	HC
GLO	Gol Transportes Aereos	PP
GLP	Globus	RA
GLR	Central Mountain Air	C
GMI	Germania	D
GMR	Golden Myanmar Airlines	XY
GMT	Magnicharters	XA
GNJ	GainJet	SX
GNX	Genex	EW
GOA	Province of Alberta	C
GOS	Goldfields Air Services	VH
GOT	Waltair Europe	SE
GOW	Go Air	VT
GOZ	Grozny-Avia	RA
GZQ	Zagrosjet	YI
GRF	Gryphon Airlines	ZS

GRL	Air Greenland	OY		IDA	Indonesia Air Transport	PK
GRV	Epsilon Aviation	SX		IDX	Indonesia AirAsia X	PK
GSB	Gading Sari Aviation Services	9M		IGA	SkyTaxi	SP
GSC	Grandstar Cargo Airlines	B		IGO	IndiGo	VT
GST	Georgian Star International	4L		IKM	Starbow	9G
GSW	HolidayJet	HB		ILF	Island Air Charters	N
GTA	City Airways	HS		ILN	Interair	ZS
GTI	Atlas Air	N		IMX	Zimex Aviation	HB
GTV	Aerogaviota	CU		INC	Insel Air	PJ
GUG	AVIATECA Guatemala	TG		IND	S Group International	EX
GUM	Gum Air	PZ		IOS	Isles of Scilly Skybus	G
GUN	Grant Aviation	N		IRA	Iran Air	EP
GUY	Air Guyane Express	F		IRB	Iran Airtours	EP
GWI	Germanwings	D		IRC	Iran Aseman Airlines	EP
GZA	Excellent Air	D		IRG	Naft Air Lines	EP
GZP	Gazpromavia	RA		IRM	Mahan Airlines	EP
GZQ	Zagros Airlines	YI		IRO	CSA Air	N
				IRP	Payam	EP
HAL	Hawaiian Airlines	N		IRQ	Qeshm Air	EP
HAU	Skyhaul	ZS		ISD	ISD Avia	UR
HAX	Benair	LN		ISK	Intersky	OE
HBH	Hebei Airlines	B		ISN	Interisland Airlines	RP
HBI	CHC Denmark	OY		ISR	Israir	4X
HBR	Hebridean Air Services	G		ISS	Alisarda	I
HBU	Universal Avia	UR		ISV	Islena Airlines	HR
HCC	Holidays Czech Airlines	OK		ISW	Islas Airways	EC
HDA	Dragonair	B		ITI	Island Transvoyager	RP-C
HDR	Helitrans	LN		IVJ	L-3 Flight International Aviation	N
HEC	Heli Campeche	XA		IVN	Ivoirienne de Transports Aeriens	TU
HEL	Helicol	HK		IWD	Orbest Orizonia Airlines	EC
HEM	CHC Helicopters (Australia)	VH		IWY	interCaribbean Airways	VQ-T
HER	Hex'Air	F		IYE	Yemenia	7O
HET	TAF Helicopters	EC		IZA	Izhavia	RA
HFM	Hi Fly Malta	9H		IZG	Zagros Airlines	EP
HFY	Hi Fly	CS				
HHH	Helicsa Helicopteros	EC		JAA	Jet Asia Airways	HS
HHK	Sky Shuttle Helicopters	B		JAB	Air Bagan	XY
HHN	Hahn Air	D		JAC	Japan Air Commuter	JA
HIB	Helibravo Aviacao	CS		JAF	Jetairfly	OO
HIS	Heliswiss	HB		JAI	Jet Airways	VT
HKE	Hong Kong Express Airways	B		JAL	J-Air	JA
HKL	Hak Air	5N		JAL	Japan Airlines	JA
HKN	Jim Hankins Air Service	N		JAV	Jordan Aviation	JY
HKR	Hawk Air	LV		JBA	HeliJet International	C
HKS	CHC Helikopter Service	LN		JBR	Central Connect Airlines	OK
HLG	Helog	HB		JBU	Jetblue Airways	N
HLR	Heli Air Services	LZ		JBW	Jubba Airways	5Y
HLU	Heli-Union	F		JCK	Jackson Air Services	C
HLW	Heliworks	CC		JGL	Jagson Airlines	VT
HMF	Norrlandsflyg Ambulans	SE		JGO	Jetgo Australia	VH
HMS	Hemus Air	LZ		JIA	PSA Airlines	N
HND	Hinterland Aviation	VH		JJA	Jeju Air	HL
HNL	CHC Helicopters Netherlands	PH		JJP	Jetstar Japan	JA
HPL	Heliportugal	CS		JLB	Jhonlin Air Transport	PK
HPR	Helipro	ZK		JLL	JetKonnect	VT
HPY	Happy Air	HS		JMP	BusinessWings	D
HRM	Hermes Airlines	SX		JNA	Jin Air	HL
HSE	Heliscan	LN		JNH	M&N Aviation	N
HSO	Heliservice International	D		JOL	Atyrau Air Ways	UP
HSU	Helisul	CS		JON	Johnsons Air	9G
HSW	Heliswiss Iberica	EC		JOS	DHL de Guatemala	TG
HVN	Vietnam Airlines	VN		JOY	Joy Air/Happy Airlines	B
HXA	China Express Airlines	B		JSA	Jetstar Asia Airways	9V
HYD	Hydro-Quebec	C		JSI	Jet Air Group	RA
HYP	Hyperion	9H		JSJ	JS Air Charter	AP
				JST	Jetstar Airways	VH
IAD	AirAsia India	VT		JTA	Japan Transocean Air	JA
IAE	IrAero	RA		JTB	Jet Budget	PJ
IAR	Iliamna Air Taxi	N		JTF	JetTime Finland	OH
IAW	Iraqi Airways	YI		JTG	JetTime	OY
IAX	Island Express Air	C		JTT	Jet-2000	RA
IBB	Binter Canarias	EC		JUA	South Supreme Airlines	ST
IBE	Iberia	EC		JUS	USA Jet Airlines	N
IBS	Iberia Express	EC		JWD	Jayawijaya Dirgantara	PK
IBX	Ibex Airlines	JA		JYH	9 Air	B
ICE	Icelandair	TF		JZA	Air Canada Jazz	C
ICL	Cargo Airlines	4X		JZR	Jazeera Airways	9K
ICV	Cargolux Italia	I				

KAC	Kuwait Airways	9K	LAP	TAM Mercosur	ZP
KAI	KaiserAir	N	LAU	Lineas Aéreas Sudamericanas	HK
KAL	Korean Air	HL	LAV	AlbaStar	EC
KAP	Cape Air	N	LAY	Layang-Layang Aerospace	9M
KAR	Ikar	UR	LBT	Nouvelair	TS
KAT	Kato Airline	LN	LCB	LC Busre	OB
KAV	Air Kurfa	5A	LCG	Lignes Aeriennes Congolaises	9Q
KAW	Kazair West	UP	LGC	Legacy Air	HS
KBA	Kenn Borek Air	C	LCI	Lao Central Airlines	RDPL
KBL	Kabul Air	YA	LCM	Lineas Aereas Comerciales	XA
KBZ	Air KBZ	XY	LCN	Lineas Aereas Canedo	CP
KCR	Kolob Canyons Air Services	N	LCO	LAN Cargo	CC
KDC	KD Air	C	LCR	Libyan Air Cargo	5A
KEA	Korea Express Air	HL	LCT	TAR-Transportes Aereos Regionales	XA
KEE	Keystone Air Service	C	LDE	LADE	LV
KEM	Cemair	ZS	LEP	Air Costa	VT
KEN	Kenmore Air	N	LER	Laser	YV
KEW	Keewatin Air	C	LGL	Luxair	LX
KFA	KF Aerospace	C	LGW	LGW - Luftfahrtgesellschaft Walter	D
KFS	Kalitta Charters	N	LIA	LIAT - The Caribbean Airline	V2
KFS	Kalitta Flying Services	N	LID	Alidaunia	I
KGL	Kolavia	RA	LID	Lider Taxi Aereo	PR
KGO	Korongo Airlines	9Q	LIM	Limitless Airways	9A
KHH	Alexandria Airlines	SU	LIN	Aerolimousine	RA
KHK	Kharkiv Airlines	UR	LIS	Luk Aero Airlines	RA
KHO	Khors Air	UR	LIX	Linxair	S9
KHT	Khatlon Air	EY	LKE	Lucky Airlines	B
KIR	Skiva Air	EK	LKV	Lukiaviatrans	RA
KIS	Kish Air	EP	LLB	LAB Airlines	CP
KKK	AtlasGlobal	TC	LLC	Small Planet Airlines	LY
KLC	KLM Cityhopper	PH	LLI	Small Planet Airlines Italy	I
KLM	KLM Royal Dutch Airlines	PH	LLL	Lao Skyway	RDPL
KLS	KalStar Aviation	PK	LLM	Yamal Airlines	RA
KMA	Komiaviatrans	RA	LLP	Small Planet Airlines Polska	SP
KMF	Kam Air	YA	LLR	Alliance Air	VT
KMI	K-Mile Air	HS	LMU	Almasria Universal Airlines	SU
KMZ	Comores Aviation	D6	LMY	Air Almaty	UP
KNA	Kunming Airlines	B	LNE	LAN Ecuador	HC
KND	Kan Air	HS	LHN	LANHSA	HR
KNE	Flynas	HZ	LNI	Lion Airlines	PK
KNM	GB Helicopters	G	LNQ	Links Air	G
KOM	Cosmo Lineas Aereas	EC	LOD	Fly Logic/North Express	SE
KOP	Copters	CC	LOG	Loganair	G
KOR	Air Koryo	P	LOK	Alok Air	ST
KPA	Henan Airlines	B	LOT	LOT - Polish Airlines	SP
KPM	Sky Prim Air	ER	LPE	LAN Peru	OB
KQA	Kenya Airways	5Y	LRA	Little Red Air Service	C
KRE	Aerosucre	HK	LRB	LR Airlines	OK
KRN	Karinou Airlines	TL	LRK	Skyjet Aviation Services	5N
KRP	Carpatair	YR	LRS	SANSA	TI
KRT	Kokshetau Airlines	UP	LSE	Lassa - Lineas de Aeroservicios	CC
KSA	KS Avia	YL	LSR	Alsair	F
KSM	Kosmos	RA	LTR	Lufttransport	LN
KSZ	Sunrise Airways	HH	LTS	Flight Inspections & Systems	RA
KTB	Transaviabaltika	LY	LTU	Air Lituanica	LY
KTK	Katekavia	RA	LUJ	Lukoil Avia	RA
KTV	Kata Transportation	ST	LUR	Atlantis European Airways	EK
KUH	Kush Air	ST	LVB	IRS Airlines	5N
KVA	Kavok Airlines	YV	LVS	Aviavilsa	LY
KYN	Skybridge Airops	I	LWA	Libyan Wings	5A
KYC	Skybird Air	5N	LXP	LAN Express	CC
KYE	Sky Lease Cargo	N	LYB	Lynden Air Cargo	P2
KYY	Kaya Airlines	C9	LYC	Lynden Air Cargo	N
KZE	Euro-Asia Air International	UP	LYM	Key Lime Air	N
KHZ	Zhez Air	UP	LYN	Air Kyrgyzstan	EX
KZR	Air Astana	UP	LZB	Bulgaria Air	LZ
KZS	Kazaviaspas	UP	LZF	Lease Fly	CS
KZU	ULS Cargo	TC			
			MAA	MASAir	XA
LAA	Libyan Airlines	5A	MAC	Air Arabia Maroc	CN
LAB	LAB Flying Service	N	MAF	Aerolineas MAS	HI
LAE	Lineas Aereas Carguera de		MAG	Meridian Airways	9G
	Colombia	HK	MAI	MaxAvia	EX
LAE	North Coast Aviation	P2	MAI	Mauritania Airlines International	5T
LAL	Air Labrador	C	MAL	Morningstar Air Express	C
LAM	LAM - Linhas Aereas de Mocambique	C9	MAS	Malaysia Airlines	9M
LAN	LAN Airlines	CC	MAU	Air Mauritius	3B
LAO	Lao Airlines	RDPL	MAV	Minoan Air	SX

MAW	Mustique Airways	J8		MWT	Midwest Aviation	N
MAX	Max Aviation	C		MXD	Malindo Air	9M
MBB	Air Manas	EX		MXE	Mocambique Expresso	C9
MBC	Aerojet	D2		MXU	Maximus Air Cargo	A6
MBI	Salmon Air	N		MYA	Myflug	TF
MCC	MCC Aviation	ZS		MYD	Maya Island Air	V3
MCJ	Macair Jet	LV		MYI	Mayair	XA
MCM	Heli Air Monaco	3A		MYP	Mann Yadanarpon Airlines	XY
MCR	Monacair	3A		MY	My Indo Airlines	PK
MDA	Mandarin Airlines	B		MYX	SmartLynx Estonian	ES
MDF	Swiftair Hellas	SX				
MDG	Air Madagascar	5R		NAC	Northern Air Cargo	N
MDM	Medavia	9H		NAI	Norwegian Air International	EI
MDS	McNeely Charter Service	N		NAL	Northway Aviation	C
MDT	Sundt Air	LN		NAM	Nam Air	PK
MEA	Middle East Airlines	OD		NAU	Danaus Lineas Aereas	XA
MED	Med Airways	OD		NAX	Norwegian	LN
MEG	Mega Global Maldives	8Q		NAY	Naysa Aerotaxis	EC
MEI	Merlin Airways	N		NCA	Nippon Cargo Airlines	JA
MEM	Meridian	UR		NCB	North Cariboo Air	C
MEN	Mena Aerospace	A9C		NCH	Chanchangi Airlines	5N
MEV	Med-View Airlines	5N		NCS	Simpson Air	C
MGD	Miami Air Lease	N		NCT	NokScoot	HS
MGE	Asia Pacific Airlines	N		NEA	New England Airlines	N
MGL	MIAT - Mongolian Airlines	JU		NFP	Neptune Air	9M
MGX	Montenegro Airlines	4O		NFA	North Flying	OY
MHK	Al-Naser Airlines	YI		NGB	Nordic Global Airlines	OH
MHV	MHS Aviation	D		NGL	MaxAir	5N
MIF	Miras Air	UP		NHV	Nordzee Helicopters	OO
MIX	Midex Airlines	A6		NIA	Nile Air	SU
MJA	Almajara Aviation	ST		NIG	Aero Contractors	5N
MJP	Air Majoro	OB		NIN	Niger Airlines	5U
MKU	Island Air	N		NJA	New Japan Aviation	JA
MLA	40 Mile Air	N		NJS	Cobham Aviation Services Australia	VH
MLC	Malift Air	9Q		NKF	Barents Airlink	SE
MLD	Air Moldova	ER		NKS	Spirit Airlines	N
MLG	Malagasy Airlines	5R		NKZ	Aerokuzbass	RA
MLN	Corporate Air, PA	N		NLC	Nelair Charter	ZS
MLP	Asia Pacific Airlines	P2		NLH	Norwegian Long Haul	LN
MLR	Mihin Lanka	4R		NLU	Insel Air Aruba	P4
MLT	Maleth-Aero	9H		NLY	Niki	OE
MMA	Myanmar Airways International	XY		NMB	Air Namibia	V5
MMD	Alsie Express	OY		NMD	Bay Air Aviation	V5
MMG	Aereo Ruta Maya	TG		NME	Nesma Airlines	SU
MML	Hunnu Air	JU		NMI	Pacific Wings	N
MMM	Meridian Air	UR		NOA	Olympic Airways	SX
MMZ	Euro Atlantic Airways	CS		NOF	Fonnafly	LN
MNB	MNG Cargo Airlines	TC		NOK	Nok Air	HS
MNG	Aero Mongolia	JU		NOR	Norsky Helikopter	LN
MNO	Mango	ZS		NOS	Neos	I
MNS	Manunggal Air Service	PK		NOT	Linea Aerea Costa Norte	CC
MNU	Elite Airways	N		NOV	Nova Airlines	ST
MON	Monarch Airlines	G		NOX	FlyLogic/North Express	SE
MOO	Moonair	4X		NPR	Air Napier	ZK
MOV	VIM Airlines	RA		NPT	Atlantic Airlines/West Atlantic	G
MPE	Canadian North	C		NRG	US Department of Energy	N
MPH	Martinair Holland	PH		NRK	Naturelink Charter	ZS
MPK	Air Indus	AP		NRL	Nolinor Aviation	C
MRA	Martinaire	N		NRO	Aero Rent	RA
MRE	Namibia Commercial Airways	V5		NRR	Natureair	TI
MRJ	Meraj Air	EP		NSE	Satena	HK
MRM	Murmansk Aviation Enterprise	RA		NSO	Aerolineas Sosa	HR
MRR	San Juan Airlines	N		NTA	NT Air	C
MRW	MRK Airlines	UR		NTG	FlyMex	XA
MSA	Mistral Air	I		NTH	Hokkaido Air System	JA
MSC	Air Cairo	SU		NTJ	Nex Time Jet	SE
MSI	Motor Sich Airlines	UR		NTN	National Airways Corp	ZS
MSJ	Skyjet	RP		NTV	Air Inter Ivoire	TU
MSM	Aeromas	CX		NUK	Strait Air	C
MSR	Egyptair	SU		NVD	Avion Express	LY
MTL	RAF-Avia	YL		NVR	Nova Airlines	SE
MTN	Mountain Air Cargo	N		NVS	Nouvelles Air Affaires Gabon	TR
MUA	National Airlines	N		NWG	Airwing	LN
MUI	Transair	N		NWL	North-Wright Airways	C
MUL	Mokulele Airlines/Go! Express	N		NWS	Nordwind	RA
MWG	Maswings	9M		NYL	Mid Airlines	ST
MWI	Malawian Airlines	7Q		NYT	Yeti Airlines	9N
MWM	Modern Logistics	PP		NZM	Mount Cook Airline	ZK

OAC	PGA Express	CS	PNR	Panair Lineas Aereas	EC
OAE	Omni Air International	N	PNS	Penas	PK
OAT	Omni AirTransport	N	PNW	Palestine Airlines	SU-Y
OAV	Omni - Aviacao e Tecnologia	CS	PNX	AIS Airlines	PH
OAW	Helvetic Airways	HB	POE	Porter Airlines	C
OBS	Orbest	CS	PPG	Phoenix Air	N
OCA	Aserca Airlines	YV	PPL	Air Pegasus	VT
OEA	Orient Thai Airlines	HS	PRF	Precisionair	5H
OHY	Onur Air	TC	PRI	Primera Air Scandinavia	OY
OKA	Okay Airways	B	PRN	Pirinair Express	EC
OLA	Overland Airways	5N	PRO	Propair	C
OLC	Solar Cargo	YV	PRY	Priority Air Charter	N
OLS	SOL Lineas Aereas	LV	PSC	Pascan Aviation	C
OLT	OFD – Ostfriesische Flugdienst	D	PSS	TSSKB Progress Aviakompania	RA
OMA	Oman Air	A4O	PST	Air Panama	HP
OMR	Minair	TL	PSV	Sapair	HI
ONE	Avianca Brazil	PP	PSW	Pskovavia	RA
ONS	One Airlines	CC	PTB	Passaredo Transportes Aereos	PP
ORB	Orenair	RA	PTG	Privatair	D
ORC	Oriental Air Bridge	JA	PTI	Privatair	HB
ORZ	Zorex	EC	PTK	Petropavlovsk-Kamchatsky Air	
OST	Alania Airlines	RA		Enterprise	RA
OTJ	Ten Airways	YR	PTN	Pantanal	PP
OTL	South Airlines	UR	PTR	Air Arabia Jordan	JY
OVA	Aeronova	EC	PUA	Pluna Lineas Aereas Uruguayas	CX
OWT	Two Taxi Aereo	PP	PUE	Air Plus Ultra	EC
			PVG	Privilege Style	EC
PAC	Polar Air Cargo	N	PVN	Peruvian Air Line	OB
PAG	Perimeter Aviation	C	PWD	PAWA Dominicana	HI
PAL	Philippine Airlines	RP	PWF	Private Wings	D
PAM	Mas Linhas Aereas	PP	PXA	Pecotox Air	ER
PAO	Polynesian Airlines	5W	PYA	Pouya Airlines	EP
PAQ	Pacific Air Express	H4	PVL	PAL Airlines	C
PAS	Pelita Air	PK			
PAU	Palau Pacific Airways	T8A	QCL	Air Class	CX
PAY	Aerolineas Paraguayas	ZP	QDA	Qingdao Airlines	B
PBD	Pobeda	RA	QFA	QANTAS Airways	VH
PBL	Virgin Samoa	ZK	QJE	Cobham Aviation Services Australia	VH
PBR	Fast Air	C	QLK	Qantaslink	VH
PBU	Air Burundi	9U	QNK	Kabo Air	5N
PCG	Aeropostal de Mexico	XA	QNZ	Jetconnect	ZK
PCM	West Air	N	QTR	Qatar Airways	A7
PCO	Pacific Coastal Airlines	C	QUE	Government of Quebec	C
PDA	Podilia Avia	UR	QWA	Pel-Air Aviation	VH
PDG	PDG Helicopters	G	QXE	Horizon Air	N
PDT	Piedmont Airlines	N			
PEA	Pan Européenne Air Service	F	RAC	Icar Air	E7
PEN	Penair	N	RAD	Alada	D2
PEO	Petro Air	5A	RAE	HOP! Régional	F
PER	Petroleum Air Services	SU	RAG	Regio-Air	D
PEV	People's Viennaline	HB	RAM	Royal Air Maroc	CN
PFR	Pacificair	RP	RAX	Royal Air Freight	N
PFY	Pel-Air	VH	RBA	Royal Brunei Airlines	V8
PFZ	Profilight Commuter Services	9J	RBD	CHC Helicopters International	C
PGA	Portugalia Airlines	CS	RBG	Air Arabia Egypt	SU
PGG	Praga Aviation	OK	RBI	Air Bright	YL
PGL	Premiair Aviation Services	G	RBV	Air Roberval	C
PGP	Perm Airlines	RA	RBY	Vision Air	N
PGT	Pegasus Airlines	TC	RCT	R Airlines	HS
PHA	Phoenix Air	N	REG	Regional Air Services	5H
PHB	Phoebus Apollo Aviation	ZS	REU	Air Austral	F
PHE	Pawan Hans Helicopters	VT	RFJ	Royal Falcon	JY
PHM	PHI - Petroleum Helicopters	N	RFS	Rossair Charter	VH
PHW	AVE.com	A6	RGB	Regional Air	C6
PHY	Phoenix Avia	EK	RGE	Regent Airways	S2
PIA	Pakistan International Airlines	AP	RGL	Regional Air Lines	CN
PIC	Jetstar Pacific Airlines	VN	RGN	Cygnus Air	EC
PKW	Sierra West Airlines	N	RHD	Bond Air Services	G
PLC	Police Aviation Services	G	RHL	Air Archipels	F
PLM	Wamos Air	EC	RJA	Royal Jordanian	JY
PLR	Northwestern Air	C	RJC	Richmor Aviation	N
PLV	Perla Airlines	YV	RJD	Rotana Jet	A6
PLY	Puma Air	PP	RKA	Polar Airlines	RA
PMA	Pan Malaysian Air Transport	9M	RKT	R Airlines	HS
PMM	Paradigm Air	N	RLA	HOP! Airlinair	F
PMS	Planemasters	N	RLB	Rus Aviation	EK
PNA	Universal Airlines	N	RLE	Rico Linhas Aereas	PP
PNP	Pineapple Air	C6	RLH	Ruili Airlines	B

RLK	Air Nelson/Airlink	ZS		SDM	Rossiya Airlines	RA
RLN	Lankan Cargo	4R		SDO	Air Santo Domingo	HI
RLT	Real Tonga Airlines	A3		SDP	Aero Sudpacifico	XA
RLU	RusLine	RA		SDV	Selva Colombia	HK
RLX	Go2Sky	OM		SEH	Sky Express	SX
RMK	Simrik Airlines	9N		SEN	Tunisair Express	TS
RMX	Air Max	LZ		SEJ	Spicejet	VT
RMY	Raya Airways	9M		SET	Solenta Aviation	ZS
RNA	Nepal Airlines	9N		SEV	Serair	EC
RNB	Rosneft-Baltika	RA		SEW	Skyward International Aviation	5Y
RNL	Aero Lanka	4R		SEY	Air Seychelles	S7
RNV	Armavia	EK		SFJ	Star Flyer	JA
ROA	Atom Airways	YR		SFR	FlySafair	ZS
ROD	Aerodan	XA		SFW	Safi Airways	YA
ROE	Aeroeste	CP		SGB	Sky King	N
ROI	Avior Airlines	YV		SGD	CebGo	RP
RON	Nauru Airlines	C2		SGG	Senegal Airlines	6V
ROR	Roraima Airways	8R		SGS	Saskatchewan Government	
ROT	Tarom	YR			Northern Air Operations	C
ROU	Air Canada Rouge	C		SGR	SkyGreece Airlines	SX
RPA	Republic Airways	N		SHU	Aurora Airlines	RA
RPB	Copa Airlines Colombia	HK		SIA	Singapore Airlines	9V
RPC	Aeropacsa	HC		SIB	Sibaviatrans	RA
RPH	RPX Airlines	PK		SID	Sideral Air Cargo	PT
RPX	HD Air	G		SIL	Silver Airways	N
RRN	Ararat International Airlines	EK		SJK	Nusantara Air Charter	PK
RRV	Mombasa Air Safari	5Y		SJO	Spring Airlines Japan	JA
RSB	Ruby star	EW		SJY	Sriwijaya Air	PK
RSC	CanariasAeronautica	EC		SKA	Skylink Arabia	A6
RSE	SNAS Aviation	HZ		SKA	Skyland Airways	6Y
RSG	Aero Services	6V		SKG	Sky Gabon	TR
RSI	Air Sunshine	N		SKI	Skyking Airlines	VQ-T
RSR	Aeroservice	TN		SKJ	Sky Net Airline	EK
RSS	Rossair	ZS		SKK	ASKY	5V
RSY	I Fly	RA		SKP	Skytrans Regional	VH
RTM	Trans Am Aero Express	HC		SKU	Sky Airline	CC
RTR	Air Trust	UP		SKW	Skywest Airlines	N
RUC	RUTACA	YV		SKY	Skymark Airlines	JA
RUM	Air Rum	9L		SKZ	Skyway Enterprises	N
RUN	myCARGO	TC		SLD	Silver Air	OK
RVL	Air Vallée	I		SLE	NAC Charter	ZS
RVL	Reconnaissance Ventures	G		SLI	Aeromexico Connect	XA
RVP	Aero VIP	CS		SLK	SilkAir	9V
RVT	Veteran Airline	EK		SLM	Surinam Airways	PZ
RWD	Rwandair	9XR		SLQ	Skylink Express	C
RWS	Air Whitsunday Seaplanes	VH		SMC	Sabang Merauke Raya Air Charter	PK
RWZ	Red Wings Airlines	RA		SME	Smart Aviation	SU
RXA	REX - Regional Express	VH		SMK	Semeyavia	UP
RYA	Ryan Air	N		SMR	Somon Air	EY
RYW	Royal Wings	JY		SNC	Air Cargo Carriers	N
RZO	SATA International	CS		SNJ	Solaseed Air	JA
				SNR	Sun Air	ST
SAA	South African Airways	ZS		SOL	Solomon Airlines	H4
SAB	Sky Way Air	EX		SON	Sepahan Airlines	EP
SAH	Sayakhat	UP		SOO	Southern Air	N
SAI	Shaheen Air Intl	AP		SOP	Solinair	S5
SAQ	Safe Air	5Y		SOR	Sonair	D2
SAS	Scandinavian Airline System	SE		SOV	Saratov Airlines	RA
SAT	SATA Air Acores	CS		SOY	Soriano Aviation	PR
SAV	Samal Air	UP		SPA	Sierra Pacific Airlines	N
SAW	Cham Wings Airlines	YK		SPB	Springbok Classic Air	ZS
SAX	Sabah Air	9M		SPM	Air St Pierre	F
SAY	Suckling Airways	G		SPR	Provincial Airlines/PAL Airlines	C
SBI	S7 Airlines	RA		SQC	Singapore Airlines Cargo	9V
SBK	Blue Sky Aviation	5Y		SQH	SeaPort Airlines	N
SBM	Sky Bahamas	C6		SQM	Siam Air Transport	HS
SBS	Seaborne Airlines	N		SQS	Susi Air	PK
Sbt	Taftan Air	EP		SRC	SEARCA	HK
SBU	St Barth Commuter	F		SRE	Serami	YV
SBX	North Star Air Cargo	N		SRI	Air Safaris & Services	ZK
SCD	Associated Aviation	5N		SRK	Skywork Airlines	HB
SCE	Scenic Airlines	N		SRN	SprintAir	SP
SCH	CHC Airways	PH		SRO	SAEREO	HC
SCO	Scoot	9V		SRR	Star Air	OY
SCU	Air Scorpio	LZ		SRU	Star Peru	OB
SCW	Malmo Aviation	SE		SRY	Charter Air Transport	N
SCX	Sun Country Airlines	N		SSC	Southern Seaplane	N
SDK	SADELCA	HK		SSF	Severstal	RA

Code	Airline	
SSG	Sloval Government Flying Service	OM
SSQ	Sunstate Airlines	VH
SSU	SASCA – Servicios Aereos Sucre	YV
STH	South Airlines	EK
STI	Sontair	C
STR	Solitaire Air	JY
SSJ	Krasavia	RA
STK	Stobart Air	EI
STT	Alpha Star Aviation Services	HZ
STX	Stars Away Aviation	ZS
SUB	Suburban Air Freight	N
SUA	Silesia Air	OK
SUD	Sudan Airways	ST
SUF	Fiji Link	DQ
SUK	Superior Aviation Services	5Y
SUL	America do Sul Taxi Aereo	PP
SUS	Sun Air of Scandinavia	OY
SUV	Sundance Air	YV
SUW	Interavia Airlines	RA
SVA	Saudia	HZ
SVD	SVG Air	J8
SVR	Ural Airlines	RA
SVT	748 Air Services	5Y
SWA	Southwest Airlines	N
SWC	Heliair Sweden	SE
SWG	Sunwing Airlines	C
SWM	Sky Angkor Airlines	XU
SWN	West Air Sweden	SE
SWQ	Swift Air	N
SWR	Swiss International Airlines	HB
SWT	Swiftair	EC
SWU	Swiss European Air Lines	HB
SWW	Shovkoviy Shlyah	UR
SWZ	Skywise	ZS
SXD	SunExpress Deutschland	D
SXR	SkyExpress	RA
SXS	SunExpress	TC
SYA	Sky Aviation	PK
SYA	Syphax Airlines	TS
SYB	Skyservice Business Aviation	C
SYJ	Slate Falls Airways	C
SYL	Yakutia Airlines	RA
SYR	Syrian Arab Airlines	YK
SYX	Midwest Connect	N
SZF	Skyforce Aviation	VH
TAE	TAME	HC
TAH	Air Moorea	F
TAI	TACA International Airlines	YS
TAJ	Tunisavia	TS
TAM	TAM Linhas Aereas	PP
TAN	Zanair	5H
TAO	Aeromar	XA
TAP	TAP Air Portugal	CS
TAR	Tunisair	TS
TAT	TACA Costa Rica	TI
TAY	TNT Airways	OO
TBA	Tibet Airlines	B
TBN	Taban Airlines	EP
TBQ	Tobruk Air	5A
TBT	Tombouctou Aviation	TZ
TBZ	ATA Airlines	EP
TCB	Transporte Aereo de Colombia	HK
TCF	Shuttle America	N
TCI	Air Turks & Caicos	VQ-T
TCU	Transglobal Airways	PR
TCV	TACV - Transportes Aereos de Cabo Verde	D4
TCW	Thomas Cook Airline Belgium	OO
TCX	Thomas Cook Airlines	G
TCY	Twin Cities Air Service	N
TDR	Trade Air	9A
TEB	Tenir Airlines	EX
TEZ	TezJet	EX
TFF	Talon Air Service	N
TFK	Transafrik International	S9
TFL	Arkefly	PH
TFO	Aeropacifico	XA

Code	Airline	
TFT	Thai Flying Service	HS
TFX	Toll Aviation	VH
TGN	Trigana Air Service	PK
TGO	Transport Canada	C
TGU	Transportes Aereos Guatemaltecos	TG
TGW	Tigerair	9V
TGY	Trans Guyana Airways	8R
TGZ	Georgian Airlines	4L
THA	Thai Airways International	HS
THD	Thai Smile Airways	HS
THE	Toumaï Air Tchad	TT
THK	THK - Turk Hava Kurumu	TC
THT	Air Tahiti Nui	F
THU	Thunder Airlines	C
THY	Turkish Airlines	TC
TID	Air Tindi	C
TIG	Tiger Helicopters	G
TIM	Team Airlines	PP
TIV	Alternative Air	XA
TIW	Transcarga	YV
TJK	Tajik Air	EY
TJS	Tyrolean Jet Service	OE
TJT	Trast Aero	EX
TJT	Twin Jet	F
TLB	Atlantique Air Assistance	F
TLG	Caspiy	UP
TLK	Starlink Aviation	C
TLM	Thai Lion Air	HS
TLR	Air Libya	5A
TLT	Turtle Airways	DQ
TMD	Transmandu	YV
TME	Thornas Air	JU
TMG	Tri-MG Intra-Asia Airlines	PK
TMI	Tamir Aviation	4X
TMN	Tasman Cargo Airlines	VH
TMS	Temsco Helicopters	N
TMW	Trans Maldivian Airways	8Q
TMX	Tramon Air	ZS
TNA	Transasia Airways	B
TNL	Sky Horse Aviation	JU
TNM	Tiara Air	P4
TNO	Aerounion	XA
TNR	Tanana Air Service	N
TNT	Trans North Helicopters	C
TNU	Transnusa Aviation Mandiri	PK
TNW	Trans Nation Airways	ET
TOK	Airlines of Papua New Guinea	P2
TOM	Thomsonfly	G
TOS	Tropic Air	V3
TOW	Airtanker Services	G
TPA	Avianca Cargo	HK
TPC	Air Caledonie	F
TPK	Air Horizon	TT
TPS	Tapsa	LV
TPU	TACA Peru	OB
TQB	Tobruk Air	5A
TRA	Transavia	PH
TRD	Trans Island Air 2000	8P
TRI	Ontario Ministry of Natural Resources Aviation Services	C
TRQ	Tarco Air	ST
TMG	Tri-MG Intra-Asia Airlines	PK
TRN	Aerotron	XA
TSB	Tusheti	4L
TSC	Air Transat	C
TSG	Trans Air Congo	TN
TSH	R1 Airlines	C
TSK	Tomskavia	RA
TSL	Thai Aviation Services	HS
TSO	Transaero Airlines	RA
TSP	Tonle Sap Airlines	XU
TSU	Gulf & Caribbean Air	N
TSY	Tristar Air	SU
TTA	TTA - Sociedade de Transportes e Trabalho Aereo	C9
TTJ	Tatra Jet	OM
TTL	Total Linhas Aereas	PP
TTW	Tigerair Taiwan	B

TUA	Turkmenistan Airlines	EZ	VGO	NewGen Airways	HS
TUD	Flight Alaska	N	VGV	Vologda Air Enterprise	RA
TUI	Tuifly	D	VIM	Air VIA	LZ
TUP	Aviastar - Tupolev	RA	VIR	Virgin Atlantic Airways	G
TUS	TAM Cargo	PP	VIS	Vision Air International	AP
TUY	Linea Turistica Aereotuy	YV	VIT	Aviastar Mandiri	PK
TVF	Transavia France	F	VIV	Viva Aerobus	XA
TVJ	Thai Vietjet Air	HS	VIZ	Aerovis Airlines	UR
TVL	Travel Service Hungary	HA	VJC	Vietjet	VN
TVP	Travel Service Poland	SP	VKG	Thomas Cook Airlines Scandinavia	OY
TVQ	Travel Service Slovakia	OM	VKY	Vent Airlines	N
TVR	Tavrey Aircompany	UR	VLA	Valan International Cargo	ZS
TVS	Smartwings	OK	VLG	Vueling Airlines	EC
TVS	Travel Service	OK	VLM	VLM Airlines	OO
TVV	Travira Air	PK	VLN	Valan International Cargo	ER
TWB	T'Way Air	HL	VLO	Varig Log	PP
TWI	Tailwind Airlines	TC	VLU	Valuair	9V
TWN	Avialeasing	UK	VNE	Venezolana	YV
TWT	Transwisata Air	PK	VNL	Vanilla Air	JA
TXC	Transavia Export	EW	VNX	Venexcargo	YV
TXZ	Thai Express Air	HS	VOE	Volotea Airlines	EC
TYA	Nordstar	RA	VOI	Volaris	XA
TZS	THE Cargo Airlines	4L	VOS	Rovos Air	ZS
			VPB	Veteran Airlines	UR
UAC	United Air Charters	Z	VQI	Flyme/Villa Air	8Q
UAE	Emirates	A6	VRB	Silverback Cargo Freighters	9XR
UAL	United Air Lines	N	VRD	Virgin America	N
UAR	Aerostar	UR	VRE	Air Côte d'Ivoire	TU
UBA	Myanmar National Airlines	XY	VRN	VARIG	PR
UBD	United Airways	S2	VSR	Aviostart	LZ
UCC	Uganda Air Cargo	5X	VSV	SCAT Air	UP
UDN	Dniproavia	UR	VTA	Air Tahiti	F
UEA	Chengdu Airlines	B	VTE	Corporate Flight Management	N
UGC	Urgemer Canarias	EC	VTF	Veteran Avia	EK
UGP	Shar Ink	RA	VTI	Vistara	VT
UHS	Uvauga	RA	VTK	Vostok Airlines	RA
UIA	UNI Air	B	VTM	Aeronaves VTM	XA
UJC	Ultimate JetCharters	N	VTS	Everts Air Cargo	N
UJX	Atlasjet Ukraine	UR	VTS	Everts Air Alaska	N
UKL	Ukraine Airalliance	UR	VUR	VIP - Vuelos Internos Privados	HC
UKM	UM Air	UR	VXP	Avion Express	TZ
UKU	Sverdlovsk 2nd Air Enterprise	RA	VXX	Aviaexpress Company	UR
UNF	Union Flights	N	VZR	Air Loyaute	F-O
UNS	Unsped Paket Servisi / UPS	TC			
UPL	Ukrainian Pilot School	UR	WAA	Westair Aviation	V5
UPS	UPS Airlines	N	WAE	Western Air Express	N
URG	Air Urga	UR	WAJ	Vanilla Air	JA
URJ	Star Air Aviation	AP	WAK	Wings of Alaska	N
URP	ARP 410 Airlines	UR	WAL	World Atlantic Airlines	N
URS	Silk Road Cargo Business	UK	WAM	Air Taxi	ST
USA	US Airways	N	WAV	Warbelows Air	N
USX	US Airways Express	N	WCO	Columbia Helicopters	N
UTA	UTair Airlines	RA	WDA	Wimbi Dira Airways	9Q
UTN	UTair Ukraine	UR	WDL	WDL Aviation	D
UTP	Uni-Top Airlines	B	WEN	Westjet Encore	C
UTX	UTair Express	RA	WEW	Express Air	C
UTY	Alliance Airlines	VH	WEW	West Wind Aviation	C
UZA	Constanta Airlines	UR	WGN	Western Global Airlines	N
UZB	Uzbekistan Airways	UK	WHT	White Airways	CS
			WIA	Winair	PJ
VAA	Van Air Europe	OK	WIF	Wideroe's Flyveselskap	LN
VAL	Voyageur Airways	C	WIG	Wiggins Airways	N
VAR	Vuela Airlines	YS	WJA	Westjet	C
VAS	ATRAN - Aviatrans Cargo Airlines	RA	WLA	Airwaves Airlink	9J
VAU	Virgin Australia	VH	WLB	Wings of Lebanon Aviation	OD
VAU	Virgin Australia Regional Airlines	VH	WLC	Welcome Air	OE
VAV	Cambodia Angkor Air	XU	WLX	Smart Cargo	LX
Vax	V Air	B	WOL	Air Guyana	8R
VBW	Air Burkina	XT	WON	Wings Air	PK
VCG	Fly Vectra	G	WOW	WOW Air	TF
VCV	Conviasa	YV	WRA	White River Air Services	C
VDA	Volga-Dnepr Airlines	RA	WRC	Wind Rose	UR
VEC	Vensecar Internacional	YV	WRF	Wright Air Service	N
VEJ	Aero Ejecutivos	YV	WSC	Westair Cargo Airlines	TU
VEN	Transaven	YV	WSF	Westair Benin	TY
VES	Vieques Air Link	N	WSG	Wasaya Airways	C
VFC	Vasco	VN	WSN	Air Wisconsin	N
VGJ	Vigo Jet	XA	WST	Western Air	C6

WVL	Wizz Air Bulgaria	LZ
WZZ	Wizz Air	HA
XAK	Airkenya Express	5Y
XAR	Express Air	PK
XAU	Aerolink Uganda	5X
XCA	Colt Transportes Aereos	XA
XKX	ASECNA	6V
XLF	XL Airways France	F
XLK	Safarilink Aviation	5Y
XLL	Air Excel	5H

XLR	Texel Air	A9C
XME	Qantas Freight	VH
XSA	Spectrum Air Services	N
XTH	Xinjiang General Aviation	B
YMR	Golden Myanmar Airlines	XY
YZR	Yangtze River Express	B
ZAV	Zetavia	UR
ZBA	ZB Air	5Y

AIRPORT THREE-LETTER IATA CODES

Airport locations are followed by the country's registration prefix, except in the cases of Australia (state), Canada (province) and USA (state)

AAC	Al-Arish, SU	
AAH	Aachen-Merzbrück, D	
AAL	Aalborg, OY	
AAN	Al Ain, A6	
AAR	Aarhus-Tirstrup, OY	
ABA	Abakan,RA	
ABD	Abadan- Boigny Intl, EP	
ABI	Abilene Regional, TX	
ABJ	Abidjan-Felix Houphouet Boigirly, TU	
ABQ	Albuquerque Intl, NM	
ABS	Abu Simbel, SU	
ABV	Abuja-Intl, 5N	
ABX	Albury, NSW	
ABZ	Aberdeen-Dyce, G	
ACA	Acapulco-Gen.Alvarez Intl, XA	
ACC	Accra-Kotoka Intl, 9G	
ACE	Arrecife, Lanzarote, EC	
ACH	Altenrhein, HB	
ACI	Alderney-The Blaye, G	
ACK	Nantucket Memorial, MA	
ACO	Ascona, HB	
ACS	Achinsk, RA	
ACT	Waco Regional, TX	
ACY	Atlantic City Intl, NJ	
ADA	Adana-Sakirpasa, TC	
ADB	Izmir-Adnan Menderes, TC	
ADD	Addis Ababa-Bole Intl, ET	
ADE	Aden Intl, 7O	
ADL	Adelaide, SA	
ADM	Ardmore Municipal, OK	
ADQ	Kodiak, AK	
ADS	Dallas-Addison, TX	
ADZ	San Andres-Sesquicentenario, HK	
AEH	Abecher, TT	
AEP	Buenos Aires Aeroparque Jorge Newbery, LV	
AER	Sochi-Adler, RA	
AES	Aalesund-Vigra, LN	
AET	Allakaiket, AK	
AEX	Alexandria-Intl, LA	
AEY	Akureyri, TF	
AFW	Fort Worth Alliance, TX	
AGA	Agadir-Inezgane, CN	
AGB	Augsburg-Mühlhausen, D	
AGC	Pittsburgh-Allegheny Co, PA	
AGF	Agen-La Gareenne, F	
AGP	Malaga, EC	
AGR	Agra-Kheria, VT	
AGV	Acarigua Oswaldo Guevara Mujica, YV	
AID	Anderson Municipal, IN	
AJA	Ajaccio-Campo Dell'Oro, F	
AKC	Akron-Fulton Intl, OH	
AKL	Auckland Intl, ZK	
AKN	King Salmon, AK	
AKT	Akrotiri, 5B	
AKX	Aktobe/Aktyubinsk, UN	
ALA	Almaty, UN	
ALB	Albany-County, NY	
ALC	Alicante, EC	
ALF	Alta, LN	
ALG	Algiers-Houari Boumediene, 7T	
ALW	Walla Walla Regional, WA	
ALY	Alexandria, SU	
AMA	Amarillo Intl, TX	
AMD	Ahmedabad, VT	
AMM	Amman-Queen Alia Intl, JY	

AMS	Amsterdam-Schiphol, PH	
AMZ	Auckland-Ardmore, NZ	
ANC	Anchorage Intl, AK	
ANE	Angers-Marce, F	
ANF	Antofagasta-Cerro Moreno Intl, CC	
ANG	Angouleme / Brie-Champniers, F	
ANI	Aniak, AK	
ANK	Ankara-Etimesgut, TC	
ANR	Antwerp-Deurne, OO	
ANU	Saint Johns/VC Bird, V2	
AOC	Altenburg-Nobitz, D	
AOG	Anshun, B	
AOI	Ancona-Falconara, I	
AOR	Alor Setar, 9M	
AOT	Aosta-Corrado Gex, I	
APA	Denver-Centennial, CO	
APF	Naples-Municipal, FL	
APS	Anapolis, PP	
APV	Apple Valley, CA	
APW	Apia-Faleolo, 5W	
AQJ	Aqaba, JY	
ARA	New Iberia-Acadiana, LA	
ARG	Walnut Ridge, AR	
ARH	Arkhangelsk-Talagi, RA	
ARK	Arusha, 5H	
ARN	Stockholm-Arlanda, SE	
ASB	Ashgabat/Ashkhabad, EZ	
ASF	Astrakhan-Narimanovo, RA	
ASH	Nashua-Boise Field, NH	
ASJ	Amami O Shima, JA	
ASM	Asmara Intl, E3	
ASP	Alice Springs, NWT	
ASU	Asuncion-Silvio Pettirossi, ZP	
ASW	Aswan, SU	
ATH	Athens-Eleftherios Venizelos Intl, SX	
ATL	Atlanta-William B Hartsfield Intl, GA	
ATW	Appleton-Outagamie Co, WI	
AUA	Oranjestad-Reina Beatrix, P4	
AUF	Auxerre-Branches, F	
AUH	Abu Dhabi Intl, A6	
AUR	Aurillac, F	
AUS	Austin-Bergstrom Intl, TX	
AUZ	Aurora-Municipal, IL	
AVB	Aviano, I	
AVN	Avignon-Caumont, F	
AVP	Scranton-Wilkes Barre Intl, PA	
AVV	Avalon, VIC	
AVW	Marana-Regional, AZ	
AWK	Wake Island, V6	
AWM	West Memphis-Municipal, AR	
AWZ	Ahwaz, EP	
AXA	Anguilla-Wallblake, VP-A	
AYK	Arkalyk, UN	
AYT	Antalya, TC	
AYU	Aiyura, P2	
AZI	Abu Dhabi-Bateen, A6	
AZP	Mexico City-Atizapan, XA	
BAH	Bahrain Intl, A9C	
BAK	Baku-Geidar Aliev Intl, 4K	
BAQ	Barranquilla-Ernisto Cortissoz, HK	
BAX	Barnaul-Mikhailovka, RA	
BBF	Burlington, MA	
BBJ	Bitburg, D	
BBP	Bembridge, G	
BBU	Bucharest-Baneasa, YR	
BBX	Blue Bell-Wing Field, PA	
BBZ	Zambezi, 9J	
BCN	Barcelona-le Prat, EC	
BCS	Belle Chase, LA	

BCT	Boca Raton, FL	
BDA	Bermuda Intl Hamilton, VP-B	
BDB	Bundaberg, QLD	
BDG	Blanding-Municipal, UT	
BDJ	Banjarmasin-Syamsuddin Noor, PK	
BDL	Windsor Locks-Bradley Intl, CT	
BDO	Bandung-Husein Sastranega-ra, PK	
BDQ	Vadodora, VT	
BDR	Bridgeport-Sikorsky Memorial, CT	
BDS	Brindisi-Papola Casale, I	
BDU	Bardufoss, LN	
BEB	Benbecula, G	
BEC	Wichita-Beech Field, KS	
BED	Bedford-Hanscom Field, MA	
BEG	Belgrade Intl, YU	
BEL	Belem-Val de Caes, PP	
BEN	Benghazi-Benina, 5A	
BEO	Newcastle-Belmont, NSW	
BER	Berlin-Brandenburg, D	
BES	Brest-Guipavas, F	
BET	Bethel, AK	
BEV	Beer-Sheba-Teyman, 4X	
BEW	Beira, C9	
BEY	Beirut Intl, OD	
BFE	Bielefeld, D	
BFF	Scottsbluff-Western Nebraska Regional, NE	
BFI	Seattle-Boeing Field, WA	
BFM	Mobile Downtown, AL	
BFN	Bloemfontein-JBM Hertzog, ZS	
BFP	Beaver Falls, PA	
BFS	Belfast-Intl, G	
BGA	Bucaramanga, HK	
BGF	Bangui-M'Poko, TL	
BGI	Bridgetown-Grantley Adams Intl, VP-B	
BGO	Bergen-Flesland, LN	
BGR	Bangor, ME	
BGW	Baghdad-Al Muthana, YI	
BGY	Bergamo-Orio al Serio, I	
BHB	Bar Harbor-Hancock Co, ME	
BHD	Belfast-City, G	
BHE	Blenheim, ZK	
BHM	Birmingham ,AL	
BHQ	Broken Hill, SA	
BHX	Birmingham Intl, G	
BIA	Bastia-Poretta, F	
BIK	Biak-Frans Kaiieppo, PK	
BIL	Billings-Logan Intl, MT	
BIM	Bimini Intl, C6	
BIO	Bilbao, EC	
BIQ	Biarritz-Parme, F	
BIR	Biratnagar, 9N	
BJI	Bemidji, MN	
BJL	Banjul-Yundum Intl, C5	
BJM	Bujumbura Intl, 9U	
BJS	Beijing-Metropolitan, B	
BJY	Belgrade-Batajnica, YU	
BKA	Moscow-Bykovo, RA	
BKI	Kota Kinabalu Intl, 9M	
BKK	Bangkok Suvarnabhumi, HS	
BKO	Bamako-Senou, TZ	
BKV	Brooksville-Pilot Co, FL	
BKY	Bukavu-Kavumu, 9Q	
BLA	Barcelona-Gen Anzoategui Intl, YV	
BLD	Boulder City, NV	
BLI	Bellingham-Intl, WA	
BLK	Blackpool, G	
BLL	Billund, OY	
BLQ	Bologna-Guglielmo Marconi, I	
BLR	Bangalore-Hindustan, VT	

BLX	Belluno, I
BLZ	Blantyre-Chileka, 7Q
BMA	Stockholm-Bromma, SE
BME	Broome, WA
BNA	Nashville Intl, TN
BND	Bandar Abbas, EP
BNE	Brisbane Intl, QLD
BNI	Benin City, TY
BNK	Ballina, NSW
BNS	Barinas, YV
BNX	Banja Luka, T9
BOD	Bordeaux-Merignac, F
BOG	Bogota-Eldorado, HK
BOH	Bournemouth Intl, G
BOI	Boise Air Terminal (Gowen Field), ID
BOM	Mumbai Intl, VT
BON	Kralendijk-Flamingo Int, Bonaire, PJ
BOO	Bodo, LN
BOS	Boston-Logan Intl, MA
BPN	Balikpapan-Sepinggan, PK
BQH	Biggin Hill, UK
BQK	Brunswick-Glynco Jetport, GA
BQN	Aguadilla-Rafael Hernandez, PR
BQS	Blagoveschensk-Ignatyevo, RA
BRE	Bremen, D
BRN	Bern-Belp, HB
BRO	Brownsville, TX
BRQ	Brno-Turany, OK
BRS	Bristol-Lulsgate, G
BRU	Brussels-National, OO
BRV	Bremerhaven, D
BRW	Barrow-Wiley Post / Will Rogers Memorial, AK
BSB	Brasilia Intl, PP
BSG	Bata, 3C
BSL	Basle-Mulhouse EuroAirport, HB
BSR	Basrah Intl, YI
BTK	Bratsk, RA
BTR	Baton Rouge, LA
BTS	Bratislava-MR Stefanik, OM
BTV	Burlington Intl, VT
BTZ	Bursa, TC
BUD	Budapest-Ferihegy, HA
BUF	Buffalo-Greater Buffalo Intl, NY
BUG	Benguela, D2
BUQ	Bulawayo, Z
BUR	Burbank-Glendale Pasadena, CA
BUS	Batumi-Chorokh, 4L
BVA	Beauvais-Tille, F
BVB	Boa Vista Intl, PP
BVO	Bartlesville, OK
BVX	Batesville-Municipal, AR
BWB	Barrow Island, WA
BWE	Braunschweig, D
BWI	Baltimore-Washington Intl, MD
BWN	Bandar Seri Begawan / Brunei Intl, V8
BWO	Balakovo, RA
BWS	Blaine, WA
BWU	Sydney-Bankstown, NSW
BXJ	Burundai, UN
BYG	Buffalo-Municipal, WY
BZE	Belize City-Philip SW Goldson Intl, V3
BZG	Bydgoszcz, SP
BZK	Bryansk, RA
BZV	Brazzaville Maya-Maya, TN
BZZ	Brize Norton, G
CAE	Columbia Metropolitan, SC
CAG	Cagliari-Elmas, I
CAI	Cairo Intl, SU
CAK	Akron-Canton Regional, OH

CAN	Guangzhou-Baiyun, B
CAP	Cap Haitien Intl, HH
CAS	Casablanca-Anfa, CN
CAY	Cayenne-Rochambeau, F-O
CBB	Cochabamba-Jorge Wilsterman, CP
CBG	Cambridge, G
CBL	Cuidad Bolivar, YV
CBQ	Calabar, 5N
CBR	Canberra, ACT
CCL	Chinchilla, QLD
CCP	Concepcion-Carriel Sur, CC
CCS	Caracas-Simon Bolivar Intl, YV
CCU	Calcutta-Chadra Bose Intl, VT
CDB	Cold Bay, AK
CDC	Cedar City-Municipal, UT
CDG	Paris-Charles de Gaulle, F
CDU	Camden, NSW
CDW	Caldwell-Essex Co, NJ
CEB	Cebu-Lahug, RP
CEE	Cherepovets, RA
CEJ	Chernigov-Shestovitsa, UR
CEK	Chelyabinsk-Balandino, RA
CEQ	Cannes-Mandelieu, F
CER	Cherbourg-Maupertun, F
CEW	Crestview-Bob Sikes, FL
CFE	Clermont-Ferrand, F
CFN	Donegal-Carrickfin, EI
CFR	Caen-Carpiquet, F
CFS	Coffs Harbour, NSW
CFU	Corfu: Kerkira-Ioannis Kapodidtrias, SX
CGH	Sao Paulo-Congonhas, PP
CGK	Jakarta-Soekarno Hatta Intl, PK
CGN	Cologne-Bonn, D
CGO	Zhengzhou, B
CGP	Chittagong Intl, S2
CGQ	Changchun, B
CGR	Campo Grande Intl, PP
CHA	Chattanooga, TN
CHC	Christchurch Intl, ZK
CHD	Chandler-Williams AFB, AZ
CHR	Chateauroux-Deols, F
CHS	Charleston Intl, SC
CHT	Chathams Island-Karewa, ZK
CIA	Rome-Ciampino, I
CIC	Chico, CA
CIH	Changzhi, B
CIX	Chiclayo-Cornel Ruiz, OB
CJB	Coimbatore-Peelamedu, VT
CJJ	Cheongju City, HL
CJN	El Cajun, CA
CJU	Cheju Intl, HL
CKC	Cherkassy, UR
CKG	Chongqing, B
CKY	Conakry-Gbessia, 3X
CLD	Carlsbad, CA
CLE	Cleveland-Hopkins Intl, OH
CLO	Cali-Alfonso Bonilla Aragon, HK
CLQ	Colima, XA
CLT	Charlotte-Douglas Intl, NC
CLU	Columbus-Municipal, IN
CMB	Colombo-Bandaranaike Intl, 4R
CMD	Cootamundra, NSW
CME	Cuidad del Carmen, XA
CMF	Chambery/Aix les Bains, F
CMH	Columbus-Port Intl, OH
CMN	Casablanca-Mohammed V, CN
CMR	Colmar-Houssen, F
CMU	Kundiawa-Chimbu, P2
CMV	Coromandel, ZK
CND	Constanta-Kogalniceanu, YR
CNF	Belo Horizonte-Neves Intl, PP
CNI	Shanghai, B
CNL	Sindal, OY

CNS	Cairns, QLD
CNW	Waco-James Connolly, TX
COA	Columbia, CA
COE	Coeur d'Alene, ID
CON	Concord-Municipal, NH
COO	Cotonou-Cadjehoun, TY
COR	Cordoba-Pajas Blancas, LV
COS	Colorado Springs Memorial, CO
COU	Columbia Regional, MO
CPE	Campeche-Intl, XA
CPH	Copenhagen-Kastrup, OY
CPQ	Campinhas-Viracopos Intl, PP
CPR	Casper-Natrona County Intl, WY
CPT	Cape Town-DF Malan Intl, ZS
CRD	Comodoro Rivadavia / Gen Mosconi, LV
CRE	Myrtle Beach-Grand Strand, SC
CRK	Diosdado Macapagal Intl, RP
CRL	Brussels-Charleroi, OO
CRU	Carriacou Island, J3
CRZ	Chardzhev, EZ
CSE	Crested Butte, CO
CSL	San Luis Obispo-O'Sullivan, CA
CSM	Clinton, OK
CSN	Carson City, NV
CSY	Cheboksary, RA
CTA	Catania-Fontanarossa, I
CTC	Catamarca, LV
CTG	Cartagena-Rafael Nunez, HK
CTM	Chetumal, XA
CTN	Cooktown, Qld
CTS	Sapporo-New Chitose, JA
CTU	Chengdu-Shuangliu, B
CUB	Columbus-Owens Field, SC
CUD	Caloundra, QLD
CUE	Cuenca, EC
CUG	Cudal, NSW
CUH	Cushing-Municipal, OK
CUM	Cumana-Antonio Jose de Sucre, YV
CUN	Cancun Intl, XA
CUR	Curacao-Willemstadt, YV
CUU	Chihuahua / Gen Villalobos Intl, XA
CUZ	Cuzco-Velaazco Astete, OB
CVF	Courchevel, F
CVG	Cincinnati-Covington Intl, OH
CVJ	Cuernavaca, XA
CVN	Clovis-Municipal, NM
CVQ	Carnarvon, G
CVR	Culver City, CA
CVT	Coventry-Baginton, G
CWA	Mosinee Central, WI
CWB	Curitiba-Alfonso Pena, PP
CWC	Chernovtsy, UR
CWF	Chenault Airpark, AK
CWL	Cardiff-Wales, G
CXH	Vancouver-Coal Harbour, BC
CYM	Chatham SPB, AK
CYS	Cheyenne, WY
CZM	Cozumel Intl, XA
CZS	Cruzeiro do Sul-Campo Intl, PP
CZX	Changzhou, B
DAB	Daytona Beach-Regional, FL
DAC	Dhaka-Zia Intl, S2
DAL	Dallas-Love Field, TX
DAM	Damascus Intl, YK
DAR	Dar-es-Salaam Intl, 5H
DAY	Dayton-James M Cox Intl, OH
DBO	Dubbo, NSW
DBV	Dubrovnik, 9A

DCA Washington-Reagan National, DC
DCF Dominica-Cane Field, HI
DCS Doncaster-Robin Hood, G
DEL Delhi-Indira Gandhi Intl, VT
DEN Denver Intl, CO
DET Detroit City, MI
DFW Dallas-Forth Worth Intl, TX
DGO Durango-Guadelupe Victoria, XA
DGX St Athan, G
DHA Dhahran Intl, HZ
DHF Abu Dhabi-Al Dhaffra, A6
DHN Dothan, AL
DHR Den Holder/de Kooy, PH
DIJ Dijon-Longvic, F
DIL Dili-Comoro, PK
DJE Djerba-Zarziz, TS
DJJ Jayapura, PK
DJN Delta Junction-Allen AFB, AK
DKR Dakar-Yoff, 6V
DKS Dikson, RA
DLA Douala, TJ
DLC Dalian, B
DLG Dillingham-Municipal, AK
DLH Duluth-Intl, MN
DLU Dali City, B
DMA Davis-Monthan AFB, AZ
DMB Taraz-Zhambyl, UN
DME Moscow-Domodedovo, RA
DMK Bangkok-Don Muang, HS
DNA Okinawa-Kadena, JA
DND Dundee-Riverside Park, G
DNJ ADI Charter Services, N
DNK Dnepropetrovsk-Kodaki, UR
DNQ Deniliquin, NSW
DNR Dinard-Pleurtuit, F
DNV Dannville-Vermillion County, IL
DOH Doha Intl, A7
DOK Donetsk, UR
DPA Chicago-du Page, IL
DPS Denpasar-Ngurah Rai, PK
DQH Douglas-Municipal, GA
DRS Dresden-Klotzsche, D
DRT Del Rio Intl, TX
DRW Darwin, NT
DSM Des Moines Intl, IA
DTM Dortmund-Wickede, D
DTN Shreveport-Downtown, LA
DTW Detroit Metropolitan, MI
DUB Dublin, EI
DUD Dunedin, ZK
DUJ DuBois-Jefferson County, PA
DUQ Duncan, BC
DUR Durban-Louis Botha Intl, ZS
DUS Dusseldorf, D
DUT Dutch Harbor, AK
DVT Phoenix-Deer Valley, AZ
DXB Dubai Intl, A6
DYR Anadyr-Ugolny, RA
DYU Dushanbe, EY
DZN Zhezkazgan, UN

EAT Wenatchee-Pangborn, WA
EAU Eau-Claire County, WI
EBA Elba Island de Campo, I
EBB Entebbe Intl, 5X
EBJ Esbjerg, OY
EBL Erbil Intl, YI
ECN Ercan-Leskofa, 5B
EDF Anchorage-Elmendorf AFB, AK
EDI Edinburgh, G
EDM La Roche-sur-Yon, F
EFD Houston-Ellington Field, TX
EGO Belgorod, RA
EGS Egilsstadir, TF
EGV Eagle River, WI
EIN Eindhoven, PH

EIS Beef Island, VP-L
EKO Elko Municipal, NV
EKT Eskilstuna-Ekeby, SE
EKX Elizabethtown, KY
ELC Elcho Island, NT
ELM Elmira-Corning Regional, NY
ELP El Paso Intl, TX
ELS East London-Ben Schoeman, ZS
EMA East Midlands-Nottingham, G
EME Emden, D
EMK Emmonak, AK
ENA Kenai Municipal, AK
ENS Twente-Enschede, PH
ENU Enugu, 5N
EOR El Dorado, YV
EPH Ephrata, WA
EPL Epinal-Mirecourt, F
EPZ Santa Teresa-Dona Ana Co, NM
ERF Erfurt, D
ERI Erie Intl, CO
ERS Windhoek-Eros, V5
ESB Ankara-Esenboga, TC
ESE Ensenada, XA
ESF Alexandria-Regional, LA
ESL Elista, RA
ESS Essen-Mülheim, D
ETH Eilat-Hozman, 4X
EUG Eugene-Mahlon Sweet, OR
EVE Harstad-Norvik, LN
EVG Sveg, SE
EVN Yerevan-Zvartnots, EK
EWR Newark Liberty Intl, NJ
EXT Exeter, G
EYP El Yopal, HK
EYW Key West Intl, FL
EZE Buenos Aires-Ezeiza, LV

FAB Farnborough, G
FAE Vagar-Faroe Island, OY
FAI Fairbanks Intl, AK
FAM Farmington Regional, MO
FAO Faro, CS
FAT Fresno Air Terminal, CA
FBK Fairbanks-Fort Wainwright, AK
FBM Lubumbashi-Luano, 9Q
FCM Minneapolis-Flying Cloud, MN
FCO Rome-Fiumicino, I
FDE Forde-Bringeland, LN
FDF Fort de France-le Lamentin, F-O
FDH Friedrichshafen, D
FEW Cheyenne/Warren AFB, WY
FGI Apia-Faqali'i, 5W
FGL Fox Glacier, ZK
FIH Kinshasa-N'Djili, 9Q
FJR Fujairah Intl, A6
FKB Karlsruhe-Baden Baden, D
FKI Kisangani, 9Q
FLF Flensburg, D
FLG Flagstaff-Pullman Field, AZ
FLL Fort Lauderdale-Hollywood Intl, FL
FLN Florianopolis-Hercilio Luz, PP
FLR Florence-Peretola, I
FLS Flinders Island, TAS
FMN Farmington-Four Counties Regional, NM
FMO Munster / Osnabruck, D
FNA Freetown-Lungi Intl, 9L
FNC Funchal-Madeira, CS
FNI Nimes-Garons, F
FNJ Pyongyang-Sunan, P
FNT Flint-Bishop Intl, MI
FOC Fuzhou, B
FOG Foggia-Gino Lisa, I
FOR Fortaleza-Pinto Martins, PP

FPO Freeport Intl, C6
FPR Fort Pierce / St Lucie Co, FL
FRA Frankfurt Intl, D
FRD Friday Harbor, WA
FRG Farmingdale-Republic Field, NY
FRJ Frejus-Saint Raphael, F
FRL Forli-Luigi Ridolfi, I
FRU Bishkek-Manas, EX
FSD Sioux Falls-Joe Foss Field, SD
FSP St Pierre et Miquelon, F-O
FTW Fort Worth-Meacham, TX
FTY Atlanta-Fulton Co, GA
FUK Fukuoka, JA
FWA Fort Wayne Intl, IN
FXE Fort Lauderdale Executive, FL
FZO Bristol-Filton, G

GAJ Yamaguchi, JA
GBE Gaborone-Sir Seretse Khama Intl, A2
GBI Grand Bahama Island, C6
GBL Goulburn Island, NT
GCI Guernsey, 2
GCJ Johannesburg-Grand Central, ZS
GCM Georgetown-Owen Roberts Intl, VP-C
GCN Grand Canyon National Park, AZ
GCO Zhengzhou, B
GDL Guadalajara-Costilla Intl, XA
GDN Gdansk, SP
GDT Grand Turk, VQ-T
GDX Magadan-Sokol, RA
GEA Noumea-Magenta, F-O
GEG Spokane Intl, WA
GEO Georgetown-Cheddi Jagan, 8R
GET Geraldtown, VIC
GEV Gallivare, SE
GEX Geelong, VIC
GEY Greybull-South Big Horn, WY
GHN Guanghan, B
GIB Gibraltar, G
GIG Rio de Janeiro-Galeao, PP
GIS Gisborne, ZK
GJT Grand Junction-Walker Field, CO
GKA Goroka, P2
GKH Gorkha, 9N
GLA Glasgow, G
GLE Gainsville-Municipal, TX
GLH Greenville, MI
GLO Gloucester, G
GLS Galveston-Scholes Field, TX
GLZ Gilze-Rijen, PH
GME Gomel-Pokalubishi, EW
GMN Greymouth, ZK
GNB Grenoble-St Geoirs, F
GOA Genoa-Cristoforo Colombo, I
GOH Godthaab-Nuuk, OY
GOI Goa-Dabolim, VT
GOJ Nizhny Novogorod-Streigino, RA
GOM Goma, 9Q
GON Groton-New London, CT
GOT Gothenburg-Landvetter, SE
GOV Gove-Nhulunbuy, NWT
GPT Gulfport-Biloxi Regional, MS
GRO Gerona-Costa Brava, EC
GRQ Groningen-Eelde, OY
GRR Grand Rapids-Kent County, MI
GRU Sao Paulo-Guarulhos, PP
GRV Grozny, RA
GRZ Graz-Thalerhof, OE
GSE Gothenburg-Save, SE
GSO Greensboro-Piedmont Triad Intl, SC

GTR	Columbus-Golden Triangle Regional, GA	
GUA	Guatemala City-La Aurora, TG	
GUB	Guerrero Negro, XA	
GUM	Guam-Ab Won Pat Intl, N	
GUP	Gallup-Sen Clark Municipal, NM	
GUW	Akyrau, UN	
GVA	Geneva-Cointrin, HB	
GVL	Gainsville, GA	
GVQ	Coyhaique-Teniente Vidal, CC	
GVT	Greenville-Majors Field, TX	
GWO	Greenwood-le Floor, MS	
GWT	Westerland-Sylt, D	
GWY	Galway-Carnmore, EI	
GXQ	Coyhaique-Teniente Vidal, CC	
GYE	Guayaquil-Simon Bolivar, HK	
GYN	Goiania-Santa Genovena, PP	
GYR	Goodyear-Litchfield, AZ	
GZA	Gaza-Yasser Arafat Intl, SU-Y	
GZM	Gozo, 9H	

HAH	Moroni-Prince Said Ibrahim, D6
HAJ	Hannover, D
HAK	Haikou-Dayingshan, B
HAM	Hamburg-Fuhlsbüttel. D
HAN	Hanoi-Gialam, VN
HAO	Hamilton, OH
HAU	Haugesund, LN
HAV	Havana-Jose Marti Intl, CU
HBA	Hobart, TAS
HDD	Hyderabad, VT
HEL	Helsinki-Vantaa, OH
HEM	Helsinki-Malmi, OH
HER	Heraklion, SX
HEX	Santo Domingo-la Herrara, HI
HFA	Haifa U Michaeli, 4X
HGH	Hangzhou-Jianqio, B
HGL	Helgoland-Dune, D
HGR	Hagerstown, MD
HGU	Mount Hagen-Kagamuga, P2
HHN	Hahn, D
HHR	Hawthorne, CA
HID	Horn Island, QLD
HIG	Highbury, QLD
HII	Lake Havasu City-Municipal, AZ
HIK	Honolulu-Oahu Island, HI
HIR	Honiara-Henderson, H4
HKD	Hakodate, JA
HKG	Hong Kong Intl, B-H
HKT	Phuket Intl, HS
HLA	Lanseria, ZS
HLF	Hultsfred, SE
HLP	Jakarta-Halim Perdanakusu-ma, PK
HLT	Hamilton, VIC
HLZ	Hamilton, ZK
HME	Hassi Messaoud, 7T
HMJ	Khmelnitsky-Ruzichnaya, UR
HMO	Hermosillo-Gen Garcia Intl, XA
HMT	Hemet-Ryan Field, CA
HND	Tokyo-Haneda Intl, JA
HNL	Honolulu Intl, HI
HNS	Haines Municipal, AK
HOH	Hohenems-Dornbirn, OE
HOM	Homer, AK
HOT	East Hampton, NY
HOU	Houston-Hobby, TX
HRB	Harbin-Yanjiagang, B
HRE	Harare Intl, Z
HRG	Hurghada, SU
HRK	Kharkiv-Osnova, UR
HSH	Las Vegas-Henderson, NV
HSM	Horsham, VIC
HST	Homestead, FL
HTA	Chita-Kadala, RA

HTI	Hamilton Island, QLD
HTO	East Hampton, NY
HUF	Terre Haute-Hulman Regional, IN
HUM	Houma-Terrebonne, LA
HUV	Hudiksvall, SE
HUY	Humberside, G
HVB	Hervey Bay, QLD
HVN	New Haven-Tweed, CT
HWO	Hollywood-North Perry, FL
HYA	Hyannis-Barnstable Municipal, MA
HZB	Mervilel-Calonnel, F

IAB	Wichita-McConnell AFB, KS
IAD	Washington-Dulles Intl, DC
IAG	Niagara Falls-Intl, NY
IAH	Houston-George Bush Intl, TX
IBA	Ibadan, 5N
IBE	Ibague-Perales, HK
IBZ	Ibiza, EC
ICN	Seoul-Incheon, HL
ICT	Wichita-Mid Continent, KS
IEV	Kiev-Zhulyany, UR
IFJ	Isafjordur, TF
IFN	Isfahan, EP
IFO	Ivano-Frankivsk, UR
IFP	Laughlin-Bullhead Intl, AZ
IGM	Kingman, AZ
IJK	Izhevsk, RA
IKI	Iki, JA
IKT	Irkutsk, RA
ILG	Wilmington-Newcastle, DE
ILI	Iliamna, AK
ILN	Wilmington-Airborne Airpark, OH
ILR	Ilorin, 5N
IMT	Iron Mountain-Ford, MI
IND	Indianapolis Intl, IN
INI	Nis, YU
INN	Innsbruck-Kranebitten, OE
INT	Winston-Salem-Smith Reynolds, NC
INU	Nauru Island Intl, C2
INV	Inverness-Dalcross, G
IOM	Ronaldsway, M
IQQ	Iquique-Diego Aracena, CC
IQT	Iquitos-Coronel Vignetta, OB
IRK	Kirksville-Regional, MO
ISA	Mount Isa, QLD
ISB	Islamabad-Chaklala, AP
ISM	Kissimmee Municipal, FL
ISO	Kinston-Stalling Field, NC
IST	Istanbul-Ataturk, TC
ITB	Itaituba, PP
ITM	Osaka-Itami Intl, JA
ITO	Hilo Intl, HI
IVC	Invercargill, ZK
IWA	Ivanovo-Zhukovka, RA

JAA	Jalalabad, YA
JAB	Jabiru, NT
JAN	Jackson Intl, MS
JAV	Ilulissat-Jakobshavn, OY
JAX	Jacksonville Intl, FL
JDP	Paris-Heliport, F
JED	Jeddah-King Abdul Aziz Intl, HZ
JER	Jersey, ZJ
JFK	New York-JFK Intl, NY
JGC	Grand Canyon Heliport, AZ
JHB	Johor Bahru-Sultan Ismail Intl, 9M
JHE	Helsingborg Heliport, SE
JHW	Jamestown-Chautauqua Co, NY
JIB	Djibouti-Ambouli, J2
JIL	Jilin, B

JJN	Jinjiang, B
JKG	Jonkoping-Axamo, SE
JNB	Johannesburg-OR Tambo Intl, ZS
JNU	Juneau Intl, AK
JST	Johnstown-Cambria County, PA
JUB	Juba, ST
JVL	Janesville-Rock County, WI

KAD	Kaduna, 5N
KAN	Kano Mallam Aminu Intl, 5N
KBL	Kabul-Khwaja Rawash, YA
KBP	Kiev-Borispol, UR
KCH	Koching, 9M
KDH	Kandahar, YA
KDK	Kodiak Municipal, AK
KEF	Keflavik Intl, TF
KEH	Kenmore Air Harbor, WA
KEJ	Kemorovo, RA
KEP	Nepalgunj, 9N
KER	Kerman, EP
KGC	Kingscote, SA
KGD	Kaliningrad-Khrabovo, RA
KGF	Qaragandy-Sary Arka, UN
KGI	Kalgoorlie, WA
KGL	Kigali-Gregoire Kayibanda, 9XR
KGO	Kirovograd-Khmelyovoye, UR
KGP	Kogalym, RA
KHH	Kaoshiung Intl, B
KHI	Karachi Jinnah Intl, AP
KHV	Khabarovsk-Novy, RA
KIH	Kish Island, EP
KIN	Kingston-Norman Manley Internatonal, 6Y
KIV	Kishinev-Chisinau, ER
KIW	Kitwe-Southdowns, 9J
KIX	Osaka-Kansai Intl, JA
KJA	Krasnoyarsk-Yemelyanovo, RA
KJK	Kortrijk-Wevelgem, OO
KKJ	Kitakyushu-Kokura, JA
KLF	Kaluga, RA
KLU	Klagenfurt, OE
KMG	Kunming-Wujiaba, B
KMI	Miyazaki, JA
KMJ	Kumamoto, JA
KMW	Kostroma, RA
KNX	Kununurra, WA
KOA	Kailua Kona, HI
KOV	Kokhshetan, UN
KOW	Ganzhou, B
KRB	Karumba, QLD
KRH	Redhill, G
KRK	Krakow Intl, SP
KRN	Kiruna, SE
KRO	Kurgan, RA
KRP	Karup, OY
KRR	Krasnodar-Pashkovskaya, RA
KRS	Kristiansand-Kjevik, LN
KRT	Khartoum-Civil, ST
KSC	Kosice-Barca, OM
KSD	Karlstad, SE
KSF	Kassel-Calden, D
KSK	Karlskoga, SE
KSM	St Mary's Bethel, AK
KSN	Kustanay, UN
KSZ	Kotlas, RA
KTA	Karratha, WA
KTE	Kerteh-Petronas, 9M
KTM	Kathmandu-Tribhuvan Intl, 9N
KTN	Ketchikan Intl, AK
KTP	Kingston-Tinson Peninsula, 6Y
KTR	Katherine-Tindal, NWT
KTW	Katowice-Pyrzowice, SP
KUF	Samara-Kurumoch, RA
KUL	Kuala Lumpur Intl, 9M
KUN	Kaunus-Karlelava Intl, LY

KUT   Kutaisi, 4L
KVB   Skovde, SE
KVX   Kirov, RA
KWE   Guiyang, B
KWI   Kuwait Intl, 9K
KXK   Komsomolsk, RA
KYZ   Kyzyi, RA
KZN   Kazan-Bonsoglebskow, RA
KZO   Kzyl-Orda, UN

LAD   Luanda-4 de Fevereiro, D2
LAE   Lae-Nadzab, P2
LAF   Lafayette-Purdue University, IN
LAJ   Lages, PP
LAL   Lakeland Regional, FL
LAO   Laoag Intl, RP
LAP   La Paz Gen Leon Intl, XA
LAS   Las Vegas-McCarran Intl, NV
LAW   Lawton, OK
LAX   Los Angeles Intl, CA
LBA   Leeds-Bradford, G
LBB   Lubbock, TX
LBD   Khudzhand, EY
LBE   Latrobe-Westmoreland Co, PA
LBG   Paris-le Bourget. F
LBH   Sydney-Palm Beach SPB, NSW
LBV   Libreville-Leon M'Ba, TR
LCA   Larnaca Intl, 5B
LCE   La Ceibe-Goloson Intl, TG
LCH   Lake Charles-Regional, LA
LCK   Columbus-Rickenbacker, OH
LCY   London-City, G
LDB   Londrina, PP
LDE   Tarbes-Ossun-Lourdes, F
LDH   Lord Howe Island, NSW
LDK   Lidkoping-Hovby, SE
LED   St Petersburg-Pulkovo, RA
LEH   le Havre-Octeville, F
LEJ   Leipzig-Halle, D
LEN   Leon, EC
LEQ   Lands End-St Just, G
LEW   Lewiston-Auburn Municipal, ME
LEY   Lelystad, PH
LFT   Lafayette-Regional, AL
LFW   Lome-Tokoin, 5V
LGA   New York-La Guardia, NY
LGB   Long Beach-Daugherty Field, CA
LGG   Liege-Bierset, OO
LGW   London Gatwick, G
LGY   Lagunillas, YV
LHD   Anchorage-Lake Hood SPB, AK
LHE   Lahore Allama Iqbal Intl, AP
LHR   London-Heathrow, G
LHW   Lanzhou, B
LIG   Limoges-Bellegarde, F
LIL   Lille-Lesquin, F
LIM   Lima-Jorge Chavez Intl, OB
LIN   Milan-Linate, I
LIS   Lisbon, CS
LIT   Little Rock-Adams Field, AR
LJU   Ljubljana-Brnik, S5
LKE   Seattle-Lake Union, WA
LKO   Lucknow-Amausi, VT
LKP   Lake Placid, NY
LLA   Lulea-Kallax, SE
LLC   Valdez, AK
LLW   Lilongwe-Tilange Intl, 7Q
LME   Le Mans-Arnage, F
LMM   Los Mochis, XA
LNA   West Palm Beach-Lantana Co Park, FL
LNX   Smolensk, RA
LNZ   Linz-Hoersching, OE
LOS   Lagos-Murtala Mohammed, 5N

LPA   Las Palmas-Gran Canaria, EC
LPB   La Paz-El Alto, CP
LPI   Linkoping-Malmen, SE
LPK   Lipetsk, RA
LPL   Liverpool-John Lennon Intl, G
LPP   Lappeenranta, OH
LPY   Le Puy-Loudes, F
LRD   Laredo Intl, TX
LRE   Longreach, QLD
LRH   La Rochelle-Laleu, F
LRR   Lar, EP
LSI   Sumburgh, G
LST   Launceston, TAS
LTN   London-Luton, G
LTX   Latacunga, HC
LUG   Lugano, I
LUK   Cincinatti Municipal, OH
LUN   Lusaka Intl, 9J
LUX   Luxembourg, LX
LWB   Lewisburg-Greenbrier Valley, WV
LWO   Lviv-Snilow, UR
LWR   Leeuwarden, PH
LXA   Lhasa, B
LXR   Luxor, SU
LXT   Latacunga, HC
LYN   Lyon-Bron, F
LYP   Faisalabad, AP
LYS   Lyon-Satolas, F
LYT   Lady Elliott Island, QLD
LYX   Lydd Intl, G

MAA   Chennai, VT
MAC   Macon-Smart, GA
MAD   Madrid-Barajas, EC
MAG   Madang, P2
MAH   Menorca-Mahon, EC
MAJ   Majuro-Amata Kabua Intl, V7
MAN   Manchester Intl, G
MAO   Manaus-Eduardo Gomes, PP
MAR   Maracaibo-La Chinita Internatonal, YV
MAW   Malden, MO
MBA   Mombasa-Moi Intl, 5Y
MBD   Mmbatho Intl, ZS
MBH   Maryborough, QLD
MBJ   Montego Bay-Sangster International, 6Y
MBW   Melbourne-Moorabin, VIC
MBX   Maribor, S5
MCI   Kansas City Intl, MO
MCM   Monte Carlo Heliport, 3A
MCO   Orlando Intl, FL
MCP   Macapa-Intl, PP
MCT   Muscat-Seeb Intl, A4O
MCW   Mason City Municipal, IA
MCX   Makhachkala-Uytash, RA
MCY   Sunshine Coast, QLD
MDE   Medellin-Olaya Herrera, HK
MDL   Mandalay, XY
MDT   Harrisburg Intl, PA
MDU   Mendi, P2
MDW   Chicago-Midway, IL
MEA   Macae & Sao Tome, PP
MEB   Melbourne-Essendon, VIC
MEL   Melbourne-Tullamarine, VIC
MEM   Memphis Intl, TN
MER   Merced-Castle AFB, CA
MES   Medan-Polonia, PK
MEV   Minden-Douglas Co, NV
MEX   Mexico City-Juarez Intl, XA
MFE   McAllen-Miller, TX
MFM   Macau Intl, B-M
MFN   Milford Sound, ZK
MGA   Managua-Sandino, YN
MGB   Mount Gambier, VIC
MGL   Mönchengladbach, D
MGQ   Mogadishu Intl, 6O

MHB   Auckland-Mechanics Bay, ZK
MHD   Mashad-Shahid Hashemi Nejad Intl, EP
MHG   Mannheim-Neu Ostheim, D
MHH   Marsh Harnour, C6
MHP   Minsk 1 Intl, EW
MHQ   Mariehamn, OH
MHR   Sacramento-Mather, CA
MHV   Mojave-Kern Co, CA
MIA   Miami Intl, FL
MID   Merida, XA
MIE   Newcastle, IN
MIR   Monastir-Habib Bourguiba Intl, TS
MIU   Maiduguri, 5N
MJI   Mitiga, 5A
MJM   Mbuji Mayi, 9Q
MJZ   Mirny, RA
MKC   Kansas City Downtown, MO
MKE   Milwaukee-Mitchell Field, WI
MKY   MacKay, QLD
MLA   Malta-Luqa, 9H
MLB   Melbourne-Cape Kennedy, FL
MLC   McAlester-Regional, OK
MLE   Male Intl, 8Q
MLH   Basle-Mulhouse EuroAirport, F
MLU   Monroe-Regional, LA
MLW   Monrovia-Spriggs Payne. A8
MMK   Murmansk, RA
MML   Marshall-Ryan Field, MN
MMX   Malmo-Sturup, SE
MNI   Plymouth-WH Bramble, VP-M
MNL   Manila-Nino Aquino Intl, RP
MNZ   Manassas, VA
MOB   Mobile-Regional, AL
MOL   Molde, LN
MON   Mount Cook, ZK
MOR   Morristown, TN
MPB   Miami-Watson Island SPB, FL
MPL   Montpellier-Mediterranean, F
MPM   Maputo, C9
MPR   McPherson, KS
MPW   Marlupol, UR
MQF   Magnitogorsk, RA
MQL   Mildura, VIC
MQS   Mustique Intl, J8
MQT   Marquette-Sawyer, MI
MQY   Smyrna, TN
MRI   Anchorage-Merrill Field, AK
MRO   Masterton, ZK
MRS   Marseille-Marignane, F
MRU   Plaisance Intl, 3B
MRV   Mineralnye Vody, RA
MRX   Morristown Nexrad, TN
MSC   Mesa-Falcon Field, AZ
MSE   Manston-Kent Intl, G
MSO   Missoula Johnson-Bell Field, MT
MSP   Minneapolis-St Paul Intl, MN
MSQ   Minsk 2 Intl, EW
MST   Maastricht-Aachen, PH
MSU   Maseru-Moshoeshoe, 7P
MSY   New Orleans Intl, LA
MTM   Metlakatla, AK
MTN   Baltimore-Glenn L Martin, MD
MTS   Manzini-Matsapha, 3D
MTY   Monterey-Gen Escobedo Intl, XA
MUB   Maun, A2
MUC   Munich-Franz Joseph Straus, D
MUN   Maturin, YV
MVA   Myvatn-Rykiahlid, TF
MVD   Montevideo-Carrasco Intl, CX
MVQ   Mogilev, EW
MVY   Martha's Vineyard, MA
MWO   Middletown-Hook Field Memorial, OH

MWZ	Mwanza, 5H	
MXE	Maxton, NC	
MXN	Morlaix-Ploujean, F	
MXP	Milan-Malpensa, I	
MXX	Mora-Siljan, SE	
MYD	Malindi, 5Y	
MYL	McCall, ID	
MYR	Myrtle Beach, SC	
MYV	Marysville-Yuba Co, CA	
MYY	Miri, 9M	
MZJ	Marana-Pinal Airpark, AZ	
NAG	Nagpur-Sonegaon, VT	
NAL	Nalchik, RA	
NAN	Nadi Intl, DQ	
NAP	Naples-Capodichino, I	
NAS	Nassau Intl, C6	
NAY	Beijing-Nan Yuan, B	
NBO	Nairobi-Jomo Kenyatta Intl, 5Y	
NCE	Nice-Cote d'Azur, F	
NCL	Newcastle, G	
NDJ	N'djamena, TT	
NEV	Nevis-Newcastle, V4	
NEW	New Orleans-Lakefront, LA	
NFG	Nefteyugansk, RA	
NGO	Nagoya-Chubu, JA	
NGS	Nagasaki, JA	
NHT	RAF Northolt, G	
NIC	Nicosia, 5B	
NIM	Niamey-Diori Hamani, 5U	
NKC	Nouakchott, 5T	
NKG	Nanjing, B	
NKM	Nagoya-Komaki AFB, JA	
NLK	Norfolk Island, NSW	
NLO	Kinshasa-N'dolo, 9Q	
NLP	Nelspruit, ZS	
NNK	Naknek, AK	
NNR	Connemara, EI	
NOA	Nowra, NSW	
NOE	Norden-Norddeich, D	
NOU	Noumea-La Tontouta, F-O	
NOZ	Novokuznetsk, RA	
NPE	Napier, ZK	
NQA	Millington, TN	
NQN	Neuquen, LV	
NQY	Newquay-St Mawgan, G	
NRK	Norrkoping, SE	
NRT	Tokyo-Narita Intl, JA	
NSI	Yaounde, TJ	
NSK	Norilsk, RA	
NSN	Nelson, ZK	
NSO	Scone, NSW	
NTB	Notodden, LN	
NTE	Nantes-Atlantique, F	
NTL	Newcastle-Williamstown, NSW	
NTY	Sun City-Pilansberg, ZS	
NUE	Nurenburg, D	
NVA	Neiva-la Marquita, HK	
NVR	Novgorod, RA	
NWI	Norwich, G	
NYM	Nadym, RA	
NYO	Nykoping-Skavsta, SE	
NZC	Jackonsville Cecil Field, FL	
OAG	Orange, NSW	
OAJ	Jacksonville, NC	
OAK	Oakland Intl, CA	
OAX	Oaxaca-Xoxocotlan, XA	
OBF	Oberpfaffenhofen, D	
OBN	Oban, G	
OBO	Obihiro, JA	
OCF	Ocala-Taylor Field, FL	
ODB	Cordoba-Palma del Rio, EC	
ODE	Odense-Beldringe, OY	
ODS	Odessa-Tsentralny, UR	
ODW	Oak Harbor, WA	
OEL	Orel, RA	
OGG	Kahului-Intl, HI	

OGL	Georgetown-Ogle, 8R	
OGZ	Vladivkavkaz-Beslan, RA	
OKA	Okinawa-Naha, JA	
OKC	Oklahoma City-Will Roger, OK	
OKD	Sapporo-Okadama, JA	
OLB	Olbia-Costa Smeralda, I	
OLM	Olympia, WA	
OMA	Omaha-Eppley Field, NE	
OME	Nome, AK	
OMS	Omsk-Severny, RA	
ONT	Ontario Intl, CA	
OOL	Coolangatta, QLD	
OPF	Opa Locka, FL	
OPO	Porto, CS	
ORB	Orebro-Bofors, SE	
ORD	Chicago-O'Hare Intl, IL	
ORG	Paramaribo-Zorg en Hoop, PZ	
ORK	Cork, EI	
ORL	Orlando-Executive, FL	
ORY	Paris-Orly, F	
OSC	Oscoda-Wurtsmith AFB, MI	
OSH	Oshkosh-Wittman Field, WI	
OSL	Oslo Intl, LN	
OSR	Ostrava-Mosnov, OK	
OSS	Osh, EX	
OST	Ostend, OO	
OTP	Bucharest-Otopeni Intl, YR	
OTS	Anacortes, WA	
OTZ	Kotzebue-Wien Memorial, AK	
OUA	Ouagadougou, XT	
OUL	Oulu, OH	
OVB	Novosibirsk-Tolmachevo, RA	
OVD	Castrillón-Asturias, EC	
OWD	Norwood Memorial, MA	
OXB	Bissau Vierira Intl, J5	
OXC	Oxford-Waterbury, CT	
OXR	Oxnard, CA	
OYS	Mariposa-Yosemite, CA	
OZH	Zaporozhye-Mokraya, UR	
PAC	Albrook-Marcos A Gelabert Panama City, HP	
PAD	Paderborn-Lippstadt, D	
PAE	Everett-Paine Field, WA	
PAP	Port-au-Prince Intl, HH	
PAQ	Palmer Municipal, AK	
PAZ	Poza Rica, XA	
PBG	Plattsburgh, NY	
PBH	Paro, A5	
PBI	Palm Beach Intl, FL	
PBM	Paramaribo-Pengel Interntional, PZ	
PCB	Pondok Cabe, PK	
PCL	Pucalipa-Rolden, OB	
PCM	Playa del Carmen, XA	
PDC	La Verne-Bracketts Field, CA	
PDK	Atlanta-Peachtree, GA	
PDL	Ponta Delgada, CS	
PDV	Plovdiv, LZ	
PDX	Portland Intl, OR	
PEE	Perm-Bolshoe-Savino, RA	
PEK	Beijing-Capital, B	
PEN	Penang-Intl, 9M	
PER	Perth Intl, WA	
PEZ	Penza, RA	
PFO	Paphos Intl, 5B	
PGA	Page, AZ	
PGD	Punta Gorda-Charlotte Co, FL	
PGF	Perpignan-Rivesaltes, F	
PGX	Periguex-Brassillac, F	
PHC	Port Harcourt, 5N	
PHE	Port Hedland, WA	
PHF	Newport News, VA	
PHL	Philadelphia Intl, PA	
PHS	Phitsanulok-Sarit Sena, HS	
PHX	Phoenix-Sky Harbor Intl, AZ	
PHY	Phetchabun, HS	

PIE	St Petersburg-Clearwater Intl, FL	
PIK	Prestwick, G	
PIR	Pierre-Regional, SD	
PIT	Pittsburgh Intl, PA	
PKC	Petropavlovsk Kam-chatsky-Yelizovo, RA	
PKR	Pokhara, 9N	
PKU	Pekanbaru-Simpang Tiga, PK	
PKV	Pskov, RA	
PLB	Plattsburg-Clinton Co, NY	
PLH	Plymouth, G	
PLL	Manaus-Ponta Pelada, PP	
PLS	Providenciales Intl, VQ-T	
PLU	Belo Horizonte-Pampulha, PP	
PLV	Poltava, UR	
PLX	Semipalatisnk, UN	
PMB	Pembina, ND	
PMC	Puerto Montt, CC	
PMD	Palmdale, CA	
PMF	Parma, I	
PMI	Palma de Mallorca, EC	
PMO	Palermo-Punta Raisi, I	
PMR	Palmerston-North, ZK	
PNA	Pamplona, EC	
PNE	Philadelphia-Northern, PA	
PNH	Phnom Penh-Pochentong, XU	
PNI	Pohnpei-Caroline Islands, V6	
PNK	Pontianak-Supadio, PK	
PNR	Pointe Noire, TN	
PNS	Pensacola-Regional, FL	
PNX	Sherman-Denison, TX	
POA	Porto Alegre-Canoas, PP	
POC	La Verne-Brackett Field, CA	
POG	Port Gentil, TR	
POM	Port Moresby, P2	
POP	Puerto Plata Intl, HI	
POS	Port of Spain-Piarco, 9Y	
POW	Portoroz, S5	
POX	Pontoise-Cormeilles, F	
PPB	Presidente Prudente, PP	
PPG	Pago Pago Intl, N	
PPK	Petropavlovsk, UN	
PPQ	Paraparaumu, ZK	
PPT	Papeete-Faaa, , F-O	
PQQ	Port Macquarie, NSW	
PRA	Parana, LV	
PRC	Prescott-Ernest A Love Field, AZ	
PRG	Prague-Ruzyne, OK	
PRN	Pristina, YU	
PRV	Prerov, OK	
PRY	Pretoria-Wonderboom, ZS	
PSA	Pisa-Galileo, I	
PSM	Portsmouth-Pease Intl, NH	
PSR	Pescara, I	
PSY	Port Stanley, VP-F	
PTA	Port Alsworth, AK	
PTG	Pietersburg-Gateway, ZS	
PTI	Port Douglas, QLD	
PTK	Pontiac-Oakland, MI	
PTN	Ptterson-HPW Memorial, LA	
PTP	Pointe a Pitre-Le Raizet, F-O	
PTY	Panama City-Tocumen Intl, HP	
PUF	Pau-Pyrenees, F	
PUG	Port Agusta, SA	
PUQ	Punta Arenas, CC	
PUU	Puerto Asi, HK	
PUY	Pula, 9A	
PVG	Shanghai-Pu Dong Intl, B	
PVH	Porto Velho, PP	
PVR	Puerto Vallarta-Lic Gustavo Dias Ordaz Intl, XA	
PVU	Provo-Municipal. UT	
PWK	Chicago-Pal Waukee, IL	
PWM	Portland Intl Jetport, ME	
PWQ	Pavlodar, UN	
PYL	Perry Island SPB, AK	

PZE	Penzance, G	
QKC	Karaj-Payam, EP	
QLA	Lasham, G	
QPG	Paya Lebar, 9V	
QPI	Palmira, CP	
QRA	Johannesburg-Rand, ZS	
QRC	Rancagua-de la Independence, CC	
QSC	San Carlos, PP	
QSM	Utersen, D	
QTK	Rothenburg, D	
RAB	Rabaul, P2	
RAI	Praia-Mendes, D4	
RAK	Marrakesh-Menara, CN	
RAO	Ribeirao Preto, PP	
RAR	Rarotonga, E5	
RAS	Rasht, EP	
RBA	Rabat-Sale, CN	
RBR	Rio Branco-Medici, PP	
RBY	Ruby-Municipal, AK	
RCM	Richmond, QLD	
RDD	Redding-Municipal, CA	
RDG	Reading-Gen Spaatz Field, PA	
RDM	Redmond-Roberts Field, OR	
RDU	Raleigh-Durham Intl, NC	
REC	Recife-Gararapes, PP	
REK	Reykjavik, TF	
REN	Orenburg-Tsentralny, RA	
REP	Siem Reap, XU	
REX	Reynosa-Gen Lucio Blanco Intl, XA	
RFD	Rockford, IL	
RGN	Yangon Intl, XY	
RHE	Reims Champagne, F	
RHI	Rhinelander-Oneida Co, WI	
RHO	Rhodes-Diagoras, SX	
RIC	Richmond-Byrd Intl, VA	
RIX	Riga-Skulte Intl, YL	
RJK	Rijeka, 9A	
RKD	Rockland-Knox County, ME	
RKE	Roskilde, OY	
RKT	Ras al Khaimah Intl, A6	
RLG	Rostock-Laage, D	
RMA	Roma, QLD	
RMI	Rimini, I	
RML	Colombo-Ratmalana, 4R	
RNC	McMinnville-Warren Co, OR	
RNO	Reno-Cannon Intl, NV	
RNS	Rennes-St Jacques, F	
RNT	Seattle-Renton, WA	
ROB	Monrovia Roberts Intl, A8	
ROK	Rockhampton, IL	
ROM	Rome Urbe, I	
ROR	Koror-Airai, T8A	
ROS	Rosario-Fisherton, LV	
ROT	Rotorua, ZK	
ROV	Rostov-on-Don, RA	
ROW	Roswell-Industrial Air Center, NM	
RPM	Ngukurr, NT	
RSE	Sydney-Au Rose, NSW	
RTM	Rotterdam, PH	
RTW	Saratov-Tsentrainy, RA	
RUH	Riyadh-King Khalid Intl, HZ	
RUN	St Denis-Gilot, F-O	
RVH	St Petersburg-Rzhevka, RA	
RWN	Rivnu, UR	
RYB	Rybinsk-Staroselye, RA	
RZN	Ryazan, RA	
SAH	Sana'a Intl, 7O	
SAL	San Salvador-Comalapa Intl, YS	
SAN	San Diego-Lindbergh Intl, CA	
SAT	San Antonio Intl, TX	

SAW	Instanbul-Sabiha Gokcen Intl, TC	
SBA	Santa Barbara Municipal, CA	
SBD	San Bernadino-Norton AFB, CA	
SBH	St Barthelemy, F-O	
SBP	San Luis Obispo, CA	
SBY	Salisbury-Wicomico, MD	
SCC	Prudhoe Bay, AK	
SCH	Schenectady County, NY	
SCI	San Cristobal-Paramilio, YV	
SCK	Stockton Metropolitan, CA	
SCL	Santiago-Merino Benitez Intl, CC	
SCN	Saarbrucken-Ensheim, D	
SCU	Santiago de Cuba, CU	
SCW	Syktyvkov, RA	
SDA	Damascus- Intl, YK	
SDF	Louisville-Standiford Field, KY	
SDJ	Sendai, JA	
SDQ	Santo Domingo Intl, HI	
SDU	Rio de Janeiro-Santos Dumont, PP	
SDV	Tel Aviv-Sde Dov, 4X	
SEA	Seattle-Tacoma Intl, WA	
SEL	Seoul-Kimpo Intl, HL	
SEN	Southend, G	
SEZ	Mahe-Seychelles Intl, S7	
SFB	Sanford Regional, FL	
SFC	St Francois, F-O	
SFD	San Fernando de Apure, YV	
SFG	St Martin-Esperance, F-O	
SFJ	Kangerlussuaq-Sondre Stromfjord, OY	
SFO	San Francisco Intl, CA	
SFS	Subic Bay Intl, PR	
SFT	Skelleftea, SE	
SGC	Surgut, RA	
SGD	Sondeberg, OY	
SGF	Springfield-Branson Regional, MO	
SGH	Springfield-Beckley, OH	
SGL	Manila-Sangley Point, RP	
SGN	Ho Chi Minh City-Tansonnhat, VN	
SGU	St George Municipal UT	
SGW	Saginaw Bay, AK	
SGY	Skagway Municipal, AK	
SGZ	Songkhla, HS	
SHA	Shanghai-Hongqiao, B	
SHE	Shenyang, B	
SHJ	Sharjah Intl, A6	
SHR	Sheridan County, WY	
SIA	Xi'an-Xiguan, B	
SID	Sal-Amilcar Cabral Intl, D4	
SIG	San Juan-Isla Grande, PR	
SIN	Singapore-Changi, 9V	
SIP	Simferopol, UR	
SIR	Sion, HB	
SIT	Sitka, AK	
SIX	Singleton, NSW	
SJC	San Jose Intl, CA	
SJJ	Sarajevo-Butmir, T9	
SJK	Sao Jose dos Campos, PP	
SJO	San Jose-Juan Santamaria Intl, YS	
SJU	San Juan-Luis Munoz Marin Intl, PR	
SJY	Deinajoki-Ilmajoki, OH	
SKB	Basseterre-Golden Rock, V4	
SKD	Samarkand, UK	
SKE	Skien-Geiteryggen, LN	
SKF	San Antonio-Kelly AFB, TX	
SKH	Surkhet, 9N	
SKP	Skopje, Z3	
SKX	Saransk, RA	
SKY	Sandusky, OH	
SLA	Salta Intl, LV	

SLC	Salt Lake City Intl, UT	
SLM	Salamanca Matacan, EC	
SLU	Castries, J6	
SLW	Saltillo, XA	
SLY	Salekhard, RA	
SMA	Santa Maria-Vila do Porto, CS	
SMF	Sacramento-Metropolitan, CA	
SML	Stella Maris, C6	
SMN	Salmon, ID	
SMO	Santa Monica, CA	
SMX	Santa Maria-Public, CA	
SNA	John Wayne-Orange Co, CA	
SNN	Shannon, EI	
SNR	St Nazaire-Montoir, F	
SOD	Sorocaba, PP	
SOF	Sofia-Vrazhdebna Intl, LZ	
SOU	Southampton Intl, G	
SOW	Show Low-Municipal, AZ	
SPB	St Thomas Seaplane, VI	
SPI	Springfield Capital, IL	
SPN	Saipan Island Intl, N	
SPR	San Pedro, V3	
SPU	Split, 9A	
SPW	Spencer Municipal, IA	
SPZ	Springdale, AR	
SRG	Senerang, PK	
SRN	Strahan, Tas	
SRQ	Sarasota-Bradenton Intl, FL	
SRZ	Santa Cruz-El Trompillo, CP	
SSA	Salvador-Dois de Julho, PP	
SSG	Malabo, 3C	
SSH	Sharm el Sheikh, SU	
SSQ	La Sarre, QU	
STA	Stauning, OY	
STI	Santiago Intl, HI	
STL	St Louis-Lambert Intl, MO	
STM	Santarem-Gomez Intl, PP	
STN	London-Stansted, G	
STR	Stuttgart, D	
STS	Santa Rosa-Sonoma, CA	
STT	St Thomas-Cyril E King, VI	
STU	Santa Cruz, V3	
STW	Stavropol-Shpakovskoye, RA	
STX	St Croix -Hamilton Airport, VI	
SUA	Stuart-Witham Field, FL	
SUB	Surabaya-Juanda, PK	
SUI	Sukhumi, 4L	
SUS	St Louis-Spirit of St Louis, MO	
SUV	Suva-Nausori, DQ	
SVD	Kingstown-ET Joshua, V8	
SVG	Stavanger-Sola, LN	
SVH	Statesville Municipal, NC	
SVO	Moscow-Sheremetyevo, RA	
SVQ	Seville-San Pablo, EC	
SVU	SavuSavu, DQ	
SVX	Yekaterinburg-Koltsovo, RA	
SWA	Shantou, B	
SWF	Newburgh-Steward-Hudson Valley Intl, NY	
SWH	Swan Hill, VIC	
SXM	St Maarten-Philipsburg, PJ	
SXQ	Soldotna, AK	
SYD	Sydney-Kingsford Smith Intl, NSW	
SYR	Syracuse-Hancock Intl, NY	
SYQ	San Jose-Tobias Bolanos Intl, YS	
SYX	Sanya-Fenghuang, B	
SYY	Stornoway, G	
SYZ	Shiraz Intl, EP	
SZB	Subang-Sultan Abdul Aziz Shah Intl, 9M	
SZG	Salzburg, OE	
SZO	Shanzhou, B	
SZX	Shenzhen-Huangtian, B	
SZZ	Szczecin-Goleniow, SP	
TAB	Scarborough-Crown Point, 9Y	

TAM	Tampico-Gen Francisco Javier Mina Intl, XA
TAR	Taranto-Grottaglie, I
TAS	Tashkent-Yuzhny, UK
TAT	Tatry-Poprad, OM
TBG	Tabubil, P2
TBS	Tbilisi-Novo Alexeyevka, 4L
TBU	Tongatapu-Fua'Amotu Intl, A3
TBZ	Tabriz, EP
TBW	Tambov, RA
TEB	Teterboro, NJ
TED	Thisted, OY
TER	Lajes-Terceira Island, CS
TFN	Tenerife-Norte los Rodeos, EC
TFS	Tenerife-Sur Reine Sofia, EC
TGD	Podgorica, YU
TGR	Touggourt, 7T
TGU	Tegucigalpa-Toncontin Intl, HR
TGZ	Tuxtla-Gutierrez, XA
THE	Terresina, PP
THN	Trolhattan-Vanersborg, SE
THR	Teheran-Mehrabad Intl, EP
TIA	Tirana-Rinas, ZA
TIF	Taif, HZ
TIJ	Tijuana-Rodriguez Intl, XA
TIP	Tripoli Intl, 5A
TIS	Thursday Island, Qld
TIV	Tivat, YU
TJM	Tyumen-Roschino, RA
TKA	Talkeetna, AK
TKJ	Tok, AK
TKU	Turku, OH
TLC	Toluca-Alfonso Lopez, XA
TLL	Tallinn-Ylemiste, ES
TLR	Tulare-Mefford Field, CA
TLS	Toulouse-Blagnac, F
TLV	Tel Aviv-Ben Gurion Intl, 4X
TMB	Miami-New Tamiami, FL
TML	Tamale, 9G
TMO	Tumeremo, YV
TMP	Tampere-Pirkkala, OH
TMS	Sao Tome Intl, 9L
TMW	Tamworth-Westdale, NSW
TNA	Jinan, B
TNF	Toussus-le-Noble, F
TNN	Tainan, B
TNR	Antananarivo, 5R
TOA	Torrance, CA
TOE	Tozeur-Nefta, TS
TOF	Tomsk, RA
TOL	Toledo-Express, OH
TOM	Tombouctou, TZ
TPA	Tampa Intl, FL
TPE	Taipei-Chiang Kai Shek Intl, B
TPQ	Tepic, XA
TPS	Trapani, I
TRD	Trondheim-Vaernes, LN
TRG	Tauranga, ZK
TRN	Turin-Caselle, I
TRS	Trieste, I
TRW	Tarawa, T3
TSA	Taipei-Sung Shan, B
TSE	Astana, UN
TSM	Taos-Municipal, NM
TSN	Tianjin, B
TSR	Timisoara-Giarmata, YR
TSV	Townsville, QLD
TTD	Portland-Troutdale, OR
TTN	Mercer-County, Trenton, NJ
TUL	Tulsa Intl, OK
TUN	Tunis-Carthage, TS
TUO	Taupo, ZK
TUS	Tucson Intl, AZ
TWB	Toowomba, QLD
TWF	Twin Falls, Joslin Field-Sun Valley Regional, ID
TXK	Texarkana Municipal, AR
TXL	Berlin-Tegel, D
TYA	Tula, RA
TYF	Torsby-Frylanda, SE
TYN	Taiyuan-Wusu, B
TYS	Knoxville-McGhee Tyson, TN
TYZ	Taylor, AZ
TZA	Belize-Municipal, V3
UAO	Aurora-State, OR
UBS	Columbus-Lowndes Co, MS
UCT	Ukhta, RA
UES	Waukesha, WI
UFA	Ufa, RA
UIK	Ust-Ilimsk, RA
UIO	Quito-Mariscal Sucre, HC
UKK	Ust-Kamenogorsk, UN
UKX	Ust-Kut, RA
ULN	Ulan Bator, JU
ULY	Ulyanovsk, RA
UME	Umea, SE
UNK	Unalakleet Municipal, AK
UNU	Juneau-Dodge Co, AK
UPG	Ujang Pendang, PK
UPN	Uruapan, XA
URA	Uratsk, UN
URC	Urumqi-Diwopou, B
URS	Kursk, RA
UTN	Upington, ZS
UTP	Utapao, HS
UTT	Umtata, ZS
UUA	Bugulma, RA
UUD	Ulan Ude-Mukhino, RA
UUS	Yuzhno-Sakhalinsk, RA
VAI	Vanimo, P2
VAR	Varna Intl, LZ
VBS	Brescia, I
VCE	Venice-Marco Polo, I
VCP	Sao Paulo-Viracopos, PP
VCT	Victoria-Regional, TX
VCV	Victorville, CA
VDM	Viedma-Castello, LV
VDZ	Valdez-Municipal, AK
VER	Vera Cruz-Jara Intl, XA
VFA	Victoria Falls, Z
VGD	Vologda, RA
VGT	Las Vegas-North, NV
VIE	Vienna-Schwechat, OE
VIH	Vichy-Rolla National, MO
VIR	Durban-Virginia, ZS
VIS	Visalia-Municipal, CA
VKO	Moscow-Vnukovo, RA
VLC	Valencia, EC
VLE	Valle-J Robidoux , AZ
VLI	Port Vila-Bauerfield, YJ
VLK	Volgodonsk, RA
VLL	Volladolid, EC
VLN	Valencia Intl, YV
VLU	Velikie Linki, RA
VNC	Venice, FL
VNE	Vannes-Meucon, F
VNO	Vilnius Intl, LY
VNY	Van Nuys, CA
VOG	Volgograd-Gumrak, RA
VOZ	Voronezh-Chertovtskye, RA
VPC	Cartersville, GA
VQS	Vieques, PR
VRN	Verona-Villafranca, I
VSG	Lugansk, UR
VTE	Vientiane-Wattay, RDPL
VTG	Vung Tau, VN
VVC	Villavicencio-La Vanguardia, HK
VVI	Santa Cruz-Viru Viru Intl, CP
VVO	Vladivostock-Knevichi, RA
WAG	Wanganui, ZK
WAT	Waterford, EI
WAW	Warsaw-Okecie, SP
WDH	Windhoek-Hosea Kutako Intl, V5
WDR	Winder-Barrow Co, GA
WFB	Ketchikan Waterfront SPB, AK
WGA	Wagga Wagga, NSW
WHO	Franz Josef Glacier, ZK
WHP	Los Angeles-Whiteman Field, CA
WIL	Nairobi-Wilson, 5Y
WIR	Wairoa, ZK
WKA	Wanaka, ZK
WLG	Wellington Intl, ZK
WMX	Wamena, PK
WOE	Woensdrecht, PH
WOW	Willow, AK
WRO	Wroclaw-Strachowice, SP
WST	Westerly State, RI
WSY	Airlie Beach-Whitsunday, QLD
WUH	Wuhan, B
WVB	Walvis Bay, V5
WVL	Waterville-Lafleur, ME
WVN	Wilhelmshaven-Mariensiel, D
WWA	Wasilla, AK
WYA	Whyalla, SA
WYN	Wyndham, WA
XBE	Bearskin Lake, ON
XCM	Chatham, ON
XCR	Vatry, F
XFW	Hamburg-Finkenwerder, D
XIY	Xi'an Xianyang, B
XLS	Saint Louis, 6V
XLW	Lemwerder, D
XMN	Xiamen-Gaoqi, B
XPK	Pukatawagan, MB
XSP	Singapore-Seletar, 9V
YAG	Fort Frances Municipal, QC
YAM	Sault Ste Marie, ON
YAO	Yaounde, TJ
YAW	Halifax-Shearwater CFB, NS
YBC	Baie Comeau, QC
YBL	Campbell River, BC
YBW	Calgary Springbank, AL
YBX	Lourdes-de-Blanc Sablon, QC
YCA	Courtenay, BC
YCB	Cambridge Bay, NT
YCD	Nanaimo-Cassidy, BC
YCE	Centralia, ON
YCH	Miramichi, NB
YCL	Charlo, NB
YCN	Cochrane-Lillabelle Lake, ON
YCR	Cross Lake-Sinclair Memorial, MB
YCW	Chilliwack, BC
YDF	Deer Lake, NL
YDL	Dease Lake, BC
YDQ	Dawson Creek, BC
YDT	Vancouver-Boundary Bay, BC
YDU	Kasba Lake, NT
YEG	Edmonton-Intl, AB
YEL	Elliott Lake-Municipal, ON
YEV	Inuvik-Mike Zubko, NT
YFB	Iqaluit, NT
YFC	Fredericton, NB
YFO	Flin Flon, MB
YFS	Fort Simpson, NT
YGG	Ganges Harbour, AK
YGH	Fort Good Hope, NT
YGL	La Grande Riviere, QC
YGM	Gimli, MB
YGR	Iles de la Madelaine, QC
YGV	Havre St Pierre, QC
YGX	Gillam, MB
YHF	Hearst, ON
YHM	Hamilton, ON
YHN	Homepayne, ON
YHR	Chevery, QC

YHS	Sechelt-Gibson, BC	
YHT	Haines Junction, YK	
YHU	Montreal-St Hubert, QC	
YHY	Hay River, NT	
YHZ	Halifax Intl, NS	
YIB	Atikokan Municipal, ON	
YIP	Detroit-Willow Run, MI	
YJF	Fort Liard, NT	
YJN	St Jean, QC	
YKA	Kamloops, BC	
YKE	Knee Lake, MB	
YKF	Kitchener-Waterloo, ON	
YKL	Schefferville, QC	
YKS	Yakutsk, RA	
YKZ	Toronto-Buttonville, ON	
YLB	Lac la Biche, AB	
YLJ	Meadow Lake, SK	
YLL	Lloydminster, AB	
YLP	Mingan, QC	
YLQ	La Tuque, QC	
YLT	Alert, NT	
YLW	Kelowna, BC	
YMM	Fort McMurray, AB	
YMO	Moosonee, ON	
YMP	Port McNeil, BC	
YMT	Chibougamau-Chapais, QC	
YMX	Montreal-Mirabel Intl, QC	
YNA	Natashquan, QC	
YNC	Wemindji, QC	
YND	Ottawa-Gatineau, QC	
YNF	Corner Brook, NL	
YNR	Arnes, MB	
YOJ	High Level/Footner Lake, AB	
YOO	Oshawa, ON	
YOW	Ottawa-McDonald Cartier Intl, QC	
YPA	Prince Albert, SK	
YPB	Port Alberni-Sproat Lake, BC	
YPD	Parry Sound, ON	
YPE	Peace River, AB	
YPL	Pickle Lake, ON	
YPQ	Peterborough	
YPR	Prince Rupert-Digby Island, BC	
YPZ	Burns Lake, BC	
YQA	Muskoka, ON	
YQB	Quebec-Jean Lesage Intl, QC	
YQD	The Pas, MB	
YQF	Red Deer, AB	
YQH	Watson Lake, YT	

YQK	Kenora, ON
YQN	Nakina, ON
YQR	Regina, SK
YQS	St Thomas, ON
YQT	Thunder Bay, ON
YQU	Grande Prairie, AB
YQV	Yorkton, SK
YQX	Gander Intl, NL
YRB	Resolute Bay, NT
YRJ	Roberval, QC
YRL	Red Lake, ON
YRO	Ottawa-Rockcliffe, ON
YRP	Carp, ON
YRT	Rankin Inket, NU
YSB	Sudbury, ON
YSE	Squamish, BC
YSF	Stony Rapids, SK
YSJ	Saint John, NB
YSM	Fort Smith, NT
YSN	Salmon Arm, BC
YSQ	Atlin-Spring Island, BC
YTA	Pembroke, ON
YTF	Alma, QC
YTH	Thompson, MB
YTP	Tofino SPB, BC
YTZ	Toronto-City Centre, ON
YUL	Montreal-Pierre Elliot Trudeau, QC
YUY	Rouyn-Noranda, QC
YVA	Moroni-Iconi, D6
YVC	La Ronge, SK
YVG	Vermillion Bay, AB
YVO	Val d'Or/La Grande, QC
YVP	Kuujjuaq, QC
YVQ	Norman Wells, NT
YVR	Vancouver Intl, BC
YVT	Buffalo Narrows, SK
YVV	Wiarton, ON
YWF	Halifax-Waterfront Heliport, NS
YWG	Winnipeg Intl, MB
YWH	Victoria-Inner Harbour, BC
YWJ	Deline, NT
YWK	Wabush, NL
YWR	White River, ON
YWS	Whistler, BC
YXD	Edmonton Municipal, AB
YXE	Saskatoon-John D Diefenbacker, SK
YXH	Medicine Hat, AB
YXJ	Fort St John, BC

YXK	Rimouski, QC
YXL	Sioux Lookout, ON
YXS	Prince George, BC
YXT	Terrace, BC
YXU	London, ON
YXX	Abbotsford, BC
YXY	Whitehorse, YT
YXZ	Wawa-Hawk Junction, ON
YYB	North Bay, ON
YYC	Calgary-Intl, AB
YYD	Smithers, BC
YYE	Fort Nelson, BC
YYF	Penticton, BC
YYG	Charlottetown, PE
YYJ	Victoria-Intl, BC
YYL	Lynn Lake, MB
YYQ	Churchill, MB
YYR	Goose Bay, NL
YYT	St Johns, NL
YYW	Armstrong, ON
YYZ	Toronto-Lester B Pearson Intl, ON
YZF	Yellowknife, NT
YZH	Slave Lake, AB
YZT	Port Hardy, BC
YZU	Whitecourt, AB
YZV	Sept-Iles, QC
ZAG	Zagreb-Pleso, 9A
ZAM	Zamboanga Intl, RP
ZAZ	Zaragoza, EC
ZFD	Fond du Lac, SK
ZFM	Fort McPherson, NT
ZIH	Ixtapa-Zihuatenejo Intl, XA
ZJN	Swan River, MB
ZNQ	Ingolstadt, D
ZNZ	Zanzibar-Kisuani, 5H
ZPB	Sachigo Lake , ON
ZQN	Queenstown-Frankston, NZ
ZQS	Queen Charlotte, BC
ZRH	Zurich-Kloten, HB
ZRJ	Weagqmow-Round Lake, ON
ZSJ	Sandy Lake, ON
ZSW	Price Rupert-Seal Cove, BC
ZTH	Zante-Zakinthos, SX
ZTR	Zhitomyr, UR
ZUC	Ignace, ON
ZUH	Zhuhai-Jiuzhou, B

NATIONALITY INDEX

YA	Afghanistan	572	TR	Gabon	517
ZA	Albania	–	C5	Gambia	132
7T	Algeria	625	4L	Georgia	604
C3	Andorra	132	D	Germany	134
D2	Angola	147	9G	Ghana	628
VP-A	Anguilla	551	VP-G	Gibraltar	–
V2	Antigua	559	SX	Greece	501
LV	Argentina	264	J3	Grenada	–
EK	Armenia	169	TG	Guatemala	514
P4	Aruba	461	2	Guernsey	–
VH	Australia	528	3X	Guinea	–
OE	Austria	415	J5	Guinea-Bissau	–
4K	Azerbaijan	603	8R	Guyana	627
C6	Bahamas	132	HH	Haiti	217
A9C	Bahrain	22	HR	Honduras	232
S2	Bangladesh	503	B-H/K/L	Hong Kong	63
8P	Barbados	626	HA	Hungary	211
EW	Belarus	178			
OO	Belgium	421	TF	Iceland	513
V3	Belize	560	VT	India	553
TY	Benin	520	PK	Indonesia	431
VP-B	Bermuda	–	EP	Iran	170
A5	Bhutan	10	YI	Iraq	573
CP	Bolivia	126	EI /J	Ireland	163
E7	Bosnia-Herzegovina	182	M	Isle of Man	–
A2	Botswana	8	4X	Israel	606
PP/R/T	Brazil	444	I	Italy	242
VP-L	British Virgin Islands	552	TU	Ivory Coast	519
V8	Brunei	561			
LZ	Bulgaria	268	6Y	Jamaica	624
XT	Burkina Faso	570	JA	Japan	247
9U	Burundi	639	JY	Jordan	258
XU	Cambodia	570	UP	Kazakhstan	521
TJ	Cameroon	516	5Y	Kenya	617
C	Canada	71	T3	Kiribati	520
D4	Cape Verde Islands	150	P	Korea (North)	426
VP-C	Cayman Islands	552	HL	Korea (South)	226
TL	Central African Republic	516	Z6	Kosovo	–
CC	Chile	122	9K	Kuwait	630
B	China (People's Republic)	22	EX	Kyrgyzstan	179
B	China (Republic of)	67			
HK	Colombia	219	RDPL	Laos	485
D6	Comoros	150	YL	Latvia	574
9Q	Congo (Democratic Republic)	637	OD	Lebanon	414
TN	Congo (People's Republic)	516	7P	Lesotho	–
E5	Cook Islands	182	A8	Liberia	–
TI	Costa Rica	515	5A	Libya	607
9A	Croatia	628	LY	Lithuania	267
CU	Cuba	130	LX	Luxembourg	267
5B	Cyprus	–			
OK	Czech Republic	419	B-M	Macau	67
			Z3	Macedonia	601
OY	Denmark	423	5R	Madagascar	616
J2	Djibouti	259	7Q	Malawi	624
J7	Dominica	–	9M	Malaysia	631
HI	Dominican Republic	218	8Q	Maldives	626
			TZ	Mali	520
4W	East Timor	–	9H	Malta	629
HC	Ecuador	216	V7	Marshall Islands	561
SU	Egypt	498	5T	Mauritania	616
EI/J	Eire	163	3B	Mauritius	602
YS	El Salvador	576	XA/B/C	Mexico	562
3C	Equatorial Guinea	602	V6	Micronesia	561
E3	Eritrea	182	ER	Moldova	175
ES	Estonia	176	3A	Monaco	601
ET	Ethiopia	177	JU	Mongolia	257
			4O	Montenegro	605
VP-F	Falkland Islands	552	VP-M	Montserrat	552
DQ	Fiji	146	CN	Morocco	125
OH	Finland	417	C9	Mozambique	133
F	France	182	XY	Myanmar	570
F-O	French Overseas Territories	190			

V5	Namibia	560		South Sudan	497
C2	Nauru	132	EC	Spain	150
9N	Nepal	636	4R	Sri Lanka	605
PH	Netherlands	426	VQ-H	St Helena	–
PJ	Netherlands Antilles	431	V4	St Kitts & Nevis	560
ZK	New Zealand	583	J6	St Lucia	259
YN	Nicaragua	575	J8	St Vincent & Grenadines	259
5U	Niger	617	ST	Sudan	496
5N	Nigeria	612	PZ	Suriname	457
LN	Norway	260	3D	Swaziland	603
			SE	Sweden	489
A4O	Oman	10	HB	Switzerland & Liechtenstein	212
			YK	Syria	574
AP	Pakistan	7			
T8A	Palau	520	EY	Tajikistan	180
SU-Y	Palestine	501	5H	Tanzania	609
HP	Panama	231	TT	Tchad	519
P2	Papua New Guinea	458	HS	Thailand	234
ZP	Paraguay	593	5V	Togo	617
OB	Peru	412	A3	Tonga	10
RP	Philippines	486	9Y	Trinidad & Tobago	642
SP	Poland	494	TS	Tunisia	518
CS	Portugal	127	TC	Turkey	505
			EZ	Turkmenistan	181
A7	Qatar	19	VQ-T	Turks & Caicos Islands	552
			T2	Tuvalu	–
YR	Romania	575			
RA	Russia	462	5X	Uganda	617
9XR	Rwanda	642	UR	Ukraine	523
			A6	United Arab Emirates	11
5W	Samoa	617	G	United Kingdom	192
T7	San Marino	–	N	United States of America	270
S9	Sao Tome	505	CX	Uruguay	131
HZ	Saudi Arabia	239	UK	Uzbekistan	520
6V	Senegal	623			
YU	Serbia	577	YJ	Vanuatu	573
S7	Seychelles	504	YV	Venezuela	577
9L	Sierra Leone	–	VN	Vietnam	549
9V	Singapore	639			
OM	Slovakia	420	7O	Yemen	624
S5	Slovenia	504			
H4	Solomon Islands	242	9J	Zambia	629
6O	Somalia	623	Z	Zimbabwe	582
ZS/U	South Africa	593			

OPERATOR INDEX

10 Tanker Air Carrier	N	Aerogaviota	CU
21 Air	N	Aerogulf Dubai	A6
40 Mile Air	N	Aerojet Angola	D2
748 Air Services	5Y	Aerokuzbass	RA
7th Sky	UP	Aerolamsa	XA
9 Air	B	Aeroland Airways	SX
AAR Airlift	N	Aeroleo Taxi Aero	PR
AB Aviation	D6	Aerolimousine	RA
Abaco Air	C6	Aeroline	D
Abaete Linhas Aereas	PR	Aerolineas Alas de Colombia	HK
ABC Air Hungary	HA	Aerolineas Andinas	HK
Aberdair Aviation	5Y	Aerolineas Argentinas	LV
Abu Dhabi Aviation	A6	Aerolineas Centauro	XA
ABX Air	N	Aerolineas de la Paz	HK
Abyssinian Flight Services	ET	Aerolineas del Occidente	HK
Ace Air Cargo	N	Aerolineas Federal Argentina	LV
ACSA	HI	Aerolineas Mas	HI
ADA – Aerolineas de Antioquia	HK	Aerolineas Paraguayas	ZP
Adagold Aviation	VH	Aerolineas Sosa	HR
Ad-Astral Aviation Services	VH	Aerolink Air Services	VH
ADI Charter	N	Aerologic	D
Adlair Aviation	C	Aeromar	XA
Adria Airways	S5	Aeromarine	5R
Advance Aviation	VH	Aeromas	CX
Advanced Aviation	D	Aeromaster Airways	HC
Adventure Air	C	Aeromaster del Peru	OB
Adventure Services	5H	Aeromed	YV
Aegean Airlines	SX	Aeromexico Connect	XA
Aeolus Air	C5	Aeromexico	XA
Aer Arann Islands	EI	Aeronaves TSM	XA
Aer Caribe	HK	Aeronaves Vive Peru	OB
Aer Lingus	EI	Aeronova	EC
Aereo Calafia	XA	Aeropacifico	XA
Aereo Owen	XA	Aeropacsa	HC
Aereo Ruta Maya	TG	Aeroportul International Marculesti	ER
Aerius Helicopters	ZK	Aeropostal	YV
Aero Air	N	Aeropostal de Mexico	XA
Aero Biniza	XA	Aerorelease	HC
Aero Centro Guatemala	TG	Aeroservice	TN
Aero Contractors	5N	Aeroservicio	CC
Aero Cuahonte	XA	Aeroservicios Ranger	YV
Aero Davinci Internacional	XA	Aerostar	UR
Aero Ejecutivos	YV	Aerosucre	HK
Aero Fret Business	TN	Aerotaxi del Upia	HK
Aero JBR	XA	Aerotaxi	CU
Aero Lanka	4R	Aerotrans Cargo	ER
Aero Mongolia	JU	Aerotrans Flugcharter	D
Aero Rio Taxi Aereo	PR	Aerotron Air Adventure	XA
Aero Services	6V	Aerotucan	XA
Aero Sotravia	F	Aerounion	XA
Aero Sudpacifico	XA	Aerovias Bolivar	YV
Aero Transporte - ATSA	OB	Aerovias Caribe Express	YV
Aero VIP	CS	Aerovias Centroamericas - AVIAC	HR
Aero4M	S5	Aerovias DAP	CC
Aeroandinas	YV	Aerovic	HC
Aerobell Air Charters	TI	Aerovis Airlines	UR
Aerobol	YV	AVFL Logistics	UR
Aerobratsk	RA	Aerupia	HK
Aerocarda	CC	Afghan Jet International	YA
Aerocaribbean	CU	Afric Aviation	TR
Aerocaribe de Honduras	HR	Africa Charter Airline	ZS
Aerocedros	XA	Africa Connection	TR
Aerocon	CP	Africa World Airlines	9G
Aerodan	XA	Africa's Connection	S9
Aerodesierto	CC	African Express Airways	5Y
Aerodiana	OB	Afrijet Business Service	TR
Aerodiva	TI	Afriqiyah Airways	5A
Aerodomca	HI	AG Air	4L
Aeroeste	CP	Aigle Azur	F
Aeroexpresso de la Frontera	HK	AIM Air	ER
Aero-Flite	N	Air 26	D2
Aeroflot Russian Airlines	RA	Air Algerie	7T
Aerofuturo	XA	Air Alliance	C

Air Almaty	UP	Air Greenland	OY
Air America	N	Air Guyana	8R
Air Annobon	3C	Air Guyane Express	F-O
Air Antilles Express	F-O	Air Hamburg	D
Air Arabia Egypt	SU	Air Hong Kong	B-H
Air Arabia Jordan	JY	Air Horizon	TT
Air Arabia Maroc	CN	Air Horizont	EC
Air Arabia	A6	Air Iceland	TF
Air Archipels	F-O	Air Incheon	HL
Air Arctic	N	Air India	VT
Air Armenia Cargo	EK	Air India Express	VT
Air Armenia	EK	Air India Regional	VT
Air Astana	UP	Air Indus	AP
Air Atlanta Icelandic	TF	Air Inter Island	HI
Air Austral	F-O	Air Inter Ivoire	TU
Air Bagan	XY	Air Inter Transport	HS
Air Baltic	YL	Air Intersalonika	SX
Air Bellevue	C	Air Inuit	C
Air Bishkek	EX	Air Italy	I
Air Bohemia	OK	Air Ivanhoe	C
Air Born	PK	Air J Michel	D2
Air Botswana	A2	Air Japan	JA
Air Brasil	PR	Air Juan	RP
Air Bravo	C	Air Kaibu	DQ
Air Bright	LZ	Air Kasa	9Q
Air Bucharest	YR	Air Kasthamandap	9N
Air Burkina	XT	Air Katanga	9Q
Air Burundi	9U	Air KBZ	XY
Air Busan	HL	Air Key West	N
Air Cab	C	Air Kiribati	T3
Air Cairo	SU	Air Korea	HL
Air Calédonie International	F-O	Air Koryo	P
Air Canada Express	C	Air Kurfa	5A
Air Canada Rouge	C	Air Kyrgyzstan	EX
Air Canada	C	Air Labrador	C
Air Caraibes Atlantique	F-O	Air Leasing Cameroon	TJ
Air Caraibes	F-O	Air Leisure	SU
Air Cargo Carriers	N	Air Libya	5A
Air Cargo Global	OM	Air Link International Airways	RP
Air Caribe International	HK	Air Link	VH
Air Charter Botswana	A2	Air Lituanica	LY
Air Charter Scotland	G	Air Loyauté	F-O
Air Charters Europe	PH	Air Macau	B-M
Air Chathams	ZK	Air Madagascar	5R
Air China Cargo	B	Air Majoro	OB
Air China Inner Mongolia	B	Air Maleo	PK
Air China	B	Air Mali	TZ
Air Class/Aero VIP	CX	Air Malta	9H
Air Colombia	HK	Air Manas	EX
Air Congo International	TN	Air Manawatu	ZK
Air Contractors	EI	Air Mandalay	XY
Air Corsica	F	Air Marshall Islands	V7
Air Costa	VT	Air Mauritius	3B
Air Côte d'Ivoire	TU	Air Max	LZ
Air Creebec	C	Air Mediterranée	F
Air Direct	N	Air Melancon	C
Air Do	JA	Air Melbourne	VH
Air Dolomiti	I	Air Milford	ZK
Air Dolphin	JA	Air Moldova	ER
Air East	N	Air Mont-Laurier	C
Air Europa	EC	Air Montmagny/Montmagny Air Service	C
Air Excel	5H	Air Montserrat	VP-M
Air Express Algeria	7T	Air Moorea	F-O
Air Fast Congo	9Q	Air Namibia	V5
Air Flamenco/Air Charter	N	Air Napier	ZK
Air France Regional	F	Air Nelson	ZK
Air France	F	Air New Zealand Link	ZK
Air Fraser Island	VH	Air New Zealand	ZK
Air Freight NZ	ZK	Air Niugini	P2
Air Frontier	VH	Air Nootka	C
Air Gaspesie	C	Air North	C
Air Georgian	C	Air Nostrum	EC
Air Ghana	9G	Air Nunavut	C
Air Gisborne	ZK	Air One	I
Air Glaciers	HB	Air Panama	HP
Air Go Egypt	SU	Air Peace	5N

Air Pegasus	VT	AirExpress Ontario	C
Air Peru Express	OB	Airfast Indonesia	PK
Air Plus Ultra	EC	AirKenya Express	5Y
Air Prague	OK	Airlec Air Espace	F
Air Rarotonga	E5	Airlift International	9G
Air Roberval	C	Airlines Of Papua New Guinea	P2
Air Safaris & Services	ZK	Airlines Of Tasmania	VH
Air Safaris	YJ	Airlink	ZS
Air Saguenay	C	Airmark Singapore	9V
Air Sanga	P2	Airnet Systems	N
Air Santo Domingo	HI	Airnor - Aeronaves del Noreste	EC
Air Scorpio	LZ	Airnorth Regional	VH
Air Serbia	YU	Airpac Airlines	N
Air Service Berlin	D	Airscapade	ZK
Air Service Liege	OO	Air-Tec Africa	ZS
Air Service Wildgruber	D	Airtraffic	5Y
Air Services Guyana	8R	Airwaves Airlink	9J
Air Seychelles	S7	Airways International	6Y
Air Sinai	SU	Airways Montenegro	4O
Air Sirin	UR	Airwing	LN
Air South Regional	VH	Airwork New Zealand	ZK
Air Spa	EC	Airworks Kenya	5Y
Air Spray	C	AIS Airlines	PH
Air St Kitts & Nevis	V4	Ak Bars Aero	RA
Air St-Pierre	F-O	Al Maha Airways	HZ
Air Sunshine	N	Alada	D2
Air Tahiti Nui	F-O	Alandia Air	OH
Air Tahiti	F-O	Alas de Columbia	HK
Air Tamarac	C	Alas Uruguay	CX
Air Tanzania	5H	Alaska Air Fuel	N
Air Taraba	5N	Alaska Air Taxi	N
Air Taxi Benin	TY	Alaska Airlines	N
Air Taxi	ST	Alaska Central Express	N
Air Taxi	YJ	Alaska Seaplane Service	N
Air Tec	OM	Alaska West Air	N
Air Teti'aroa	F-O	Albastar	EC
Air Tindi	C	Albatros Airlines	YV
Air Tractor Europe	EC	Alberta Central Airways	C
Air Transat	C	Alcon Servicios Aereos	XA
Air Transport Europe	OM	Alexandria Airlines	SU
Air Tribe	XA	Alfa Air	CN
Air Tropique	9Q	Alfa Airlines	ST
Air Trust	UP	Alfa Trans Dirgantara	PK
Air Tunilik	C	Algar Aviation Taxi Aereo	PR
Air Urga	UR	Aliansa	HK
Air Vallée	I	Alidaunia	I
Air Vanuatu	YJ	Alisarda	I
Air Venezuela	YV	Alitalia Cityliner	I
Air Via	LZ	Alitalia	I
Air Wakaya	DQ	Alkan Air	C
Air Wanganui Commuter	ZK	Allegiance Airways Gabon	TR
Air West Coast	ZK	Allegiant Air	N
Air Whitsunday Seaplanes	VH	Allen Airways	C
Air Wisconsin	N	Alliance Airlines	VH
Air X Charter	9H	Allied Air Cargo	5N
Air Zermatt	HB	Almasria Universal Airlines	SU
Air Zimbabwe	Z	Al-Naser Airlines	YI
Air2there	ZK	Aloha Air Cargo	N
AirAsia India	VT	Alok Air	ST
AirAsia Japan	JA	Alp Aereo Taxi	PR
AirAsia Philippines	RP	Alpha Star Aviation Services	HZ
AirAsia X	9M	Alpine Air Express	N
AirAsia Zest	RP	Alpine Aviation	C
AirAsia	9M	Alpine Helicopters	C
Airawak	F-O	Alpine Helicopters	ZK
Airberlin	D	Alrosa Aviation	RA
Airblue	AP	ALS	5Y
Airborne Support	N	Alsair	F
Airbridge Cargo	RA	Alsie Express	OY
Airbus Transport International	F	Alternative Air	XA
AirCalin	F-O	Amakusa Airlines	JA
Airco Aircraft Charters	C	Amapola Flyg	SE
Aircraft Systems SA	ZS	Amaszonas Transportes Aereos	CP
Air-Dale Flying Service	C	Amazon Sky	OB
Airest	ES	Amazonaves Taxi Aereo	PR
AirExplore	OM	Ambler Air Service	N

AMC Airlines	SU	Atlantic Airways	OY
America do Sul Taxi Aereo – ASTA	PR	Atlantic Aviation	5N
America–Asia Travel Air	B	Atlantic Southeast Airlines	N
American Air Freight	N	Atlantique Air Assistance	F
American Airlines	N	Atlantis European Airways	EK
American Jet	LV	Atlas Air	N
Ameriflight	N	Atlas Air	PR
Amerijet International	N	AtlasGlobal	TC
Ameristar Jet Charter	N	Atlasjet Ukraine	UR
Amur Artel Staratelei Aviakompania	RA	Atleo River Air Service	C
ANA - All Nippon Airways	JA	Atlin Air Charters	C
ANA Wings	JA	Atrak Air	EP
Anadolu Jet	TC	Atran	RA
Anderson Helicopters	ZK	Auckland Regional Health Trust	ZK
Andes Lineas Aereas	LV	Auckland Seaplanes`	ZK
Andrew Airways	N	Auric Air Services	5H
Angara Airlines	RA	Aurigny Air Services	G
Angel Air	C6	Aurora Airlines	RA
Angel Martinez Ridao	EC	Austral Lineas Aereas	LV
Angola Air Services	D2	Australian Helicopters	VH
Anguilla Air Services	VP-A	Austrian	OE
Antes	HK	AV Cargo Airlines	G
Antonov Airlines	UR	Avanti Air	D
Antrak Air	9G	Avcom	TG
Anyang General Aviation	B	Ave.com	A6
Aoraki Mount Cook Skiplanes	ZK	Avex Air	ZS
Apex Airlines	XY	Avia Air Charters	ZK
Appalachian Air	N	Avia Express	UR
Apui Taxi Aereo	PR	Avia Traffic Company	EX
Aquarius Aviation	ET	Aviacon Zitotrans	RA
Arab Wings	JY	Aviaexport	4L
Ararat International Airlines	EK	Aviair	VH
Arctic Air	SE	Aviakompaniya Panh	RA
Arctic Airlink	SE	Avialeasing	UK
Arctic Circle Air Service	N	Avialift	RA
Arctic Circle Air	N	AVIALSA – Aviación Agricola del Levante	EC
Arctic Transportation Services	N	Avianca Brazil	PR
Arcus Air Logisti	D	Avianca Cargo	HK
Ardmore Helicopters	ZK	Avianca Central America	YS
Ariana Afghan Airlines	YA	Avianca Ecuador	HC
Arik Air	5N	Avianca	HK
Arjet Airlines	LV	Aviaservice	4L
Arkefly	PH	Aviastar – Tupolev	RA
Arkhangelsk 2nd Aviation Enterprise	RA	Aviastar Mandiri	PK
Arkia Israeli Airlines	4X	Aviateca Guatemala	TG
Arnhem Land Community Airlines	VH	Aviation Horizons	HZ
Aruba Airlines	P4	Aviation Starlink	C
As Salaam Air	5H	Aviator Airways	SX
Asecna	6V	Aviator	SU
Aserca Airlines	YV	Aviatrans Cargo Airlines	RA
ASESA	XA	Aviavilsa	LY
Ashworth Helicopters	ZK	Avies	ES
Asi Pudjiastuti Aviation	PK	Aviheco Colombia	HK
Asia Airways	EY	Aviogenex	YU
Asia Atlantic Airways	HS	Avion Express	LY
Asia Pacific Airlines	N	Avion Express	TZ
Asia Pacific Airlines	P2	Aviones Taxi Aereo	TI
Asialink Cargo Express	PK	Avior Airlines/Avior Express	YV
Asian Air	HS	Aviostart	LZ
Asian Express Airlines	EY	Avirex	TR
Asian One Air	PK	Avmax Tchad	TT
Asian Wings	XY	Avro Express	5Y
Asiana Airlines	HL	Avtex Aviation	VH
ASky	5V	Awan Inspirasi	9M
Aspen Helicopters	N	Awesome Flight Services	ZS
Aspiring Air/Aspiring Helicopters	ZK	Ayit Aviation	4X
Associated Aviation	5N	Ayk Avia	EK
Astra Airlines	SX	Azerbaijan Airlines	4K
Astral Aviation	5Y	Azman Air	5N
Astral Cargo	5Y	Azul	PR
ATA Airlines	EP	Azza Transport	ST
ATA	PR		
ATI - Air Transport Internationa	N	BA Cityflyer	G
Atikokan Aero Service	C	Badr Airlines	ST
Atlantic Air Cargo	N	Bahamasair	C6
Atlantic Airlines	G	Baires Fly	LV

Bald Mountain Air Service	N	Briko Air Service	9Y
Balkan Holidays	LZ	Bristow Caribbean	9Y
Baltia Air Lines	N	Bristow Helicopters (Australia)	VH
Bamaji Air	C	Bristow Helicopters	5N
Bangkok Airways	HS	Bristow Helicopters	G
Bangla International Airlines	S2	Bristow Norway	LN
Bar XH Air	C	Bristow US	N
Barkol Aviakompania	RA	British Airways	G
Baron Aviation Services	N	British Antarctic Survey	VP-F
Barq Aviation	JY	British International	G
Barrick Servicios Mineros	CC	Brooks Aviation	N
Bassaka Air	XU	Broome Air Services	VH
Bateleur Air Charter	ZS	Broome Aviation	VH
Batik Air	PK	Brunei Shell	V8
Bay Air Aviation	V5	Brussels Airlines	OO
Bay Air	N	Budapest Air Service	HA
Bearskin Airlines/Bearskin Lake Air Service	C	Buddha Air	9N
Beaver Air Services	C	Buffalo Airways	C
Beck Helicopters	ZK	Bukovyna Airlines	UR
Beijing Airlines	B	Bulgaria Air	LZ
Bek Air	UP	Bulgarian Air Charter	LZ
Belair Airlines	HB	Buraq Air	5A
Belavia	EW	Buryat Airlines	RA
Bemidji Airlines	N	Business Air	HS
Benair Air Service	OY	Business Air	Z3
Bentiu Air Transport	ST	Business Aviation Courier	N
Bergen Air Transport	LN	Business Aviation Of Congo	9Q
Bering Air	N	Businesswings	D
Berkut State Air Company	UP	Busy Bee Congo	9Q
Berry Aviation	N	Bvi Airways	VP-L
BH Air	E7		
BH Air	LZ	CAA–Compagnie Africaine d'Aviation	9Q
BHS - Brazilian Helicopter Services	PR	Cabo Verde Express	D4
Bhutan Airlines	A5	Caicos Express Airways	VQ-T
Big Island Air	N	Cairns Seaplanes	VH
Bighorn Airways	N	Cairo Aviation	SU
Biman Bangladesh Airlines	S2	Calm Air	C
Bin Air	D	Camair	TJ
Binter Group	EC	Cambodia Angkor Air	XU
Bismillah Airlines	S2	Cambodia Bayon Airlines	XU
Bizcharters	N	Cameron Air Service	C
Black Sheep Aviation	C	Canadian Airways Congo	TN
Blue Air	YR	Canadian Helicopters Philippines	RP
Blue Airlines	9Q	Canadian Helicopters	C
Blue Bird Airlines	ST	Canadian North	C
Blue Bird Airways	SX	Canarias Aeronáutica	EC
Blue Bird Aviation	5Y	Canaryfly	EC
Blue Bird Aviation	7O	Canjet	C
Blue Dart Aviation	VT	Can-West Corporate Air Charters	C
Blue Islands	G	Cape Air (Hyannis Air Service)	N
Blue Panorama Airlines	I	Cape Verde Airlines	D4
Blue Sky Airways	A2	Capital Airlines	5Y
Blue Sky Aviation Services	A6	Capital Airlines	B
Blue Sky Aviation	5Y	Caravan Air	V5
Blue Sky Aviation	JU	Cardig Air	PK
Blue Water Aviation Services	C	Care Flight	VH
Blue West Helicopters Greenland	OY	Cargo Air Chartering	UR
Blue Wing Airlines	PZ	Cargo Air	LZ
Blue1	OH	Cargo Airlines	4X
Bluebird Cargo	TF	Cargo Three	HP
Bluesky Airlines	9Q	Cargo2fly	5Y
Bluewave Aviation	5Y	Cargohouse	RP
Blueway Offshore Norge	LN	Cargojet Airways	C
Blu-Express	I	Cargolux International Airlines	LX
BMI Regional	G	Cargolux Italia	I
Boliviana de Aviacion	CP	Caribair	HI
Bond Air Services	G	Caribbean Airlines	9Y
Bond Helicopters Australia	VH	Caribbean Commuter Airways	PZ
Bond Helicopters	G	Caribbean Flights	YV
Bora Jet	TC	Caribe Air Charters	VP-A
BQB Lineas Aéreas	CX	Caribe Rico	N
Braathens Regional	SE	Caribintair/Caribair	HH
Bradley Air Services	C	Caroline Island Air	V6
Bravo Air	4L	Carpatair	YR
Bravo Airways	UR	Carson Air	C
Bright Flight	LZ	Carson Helicopters	N

Casair	VH	City Airways	HS
Caspian Airlines	EP	Cityfly	I
Caspiy	UP	Cityjet	EI
Castle Aviation	N	Cityline Hungary	HA
Cat Helicopters	EC	Citylink	9G
Cat Island Air	C6	Citywing	G
Catalina Air Transport	N	Cleiton Taxi Aereo	PR
Catalina Airlines	VH	Click Airways	EX
Cathay Pacific Airways	B-H	CM Airlines	HR
Catovair	F	Coastal Air Transport	N
Caverton Helicopters	5N	Coastal Aviation	5H
Cavok Airlines	UR	Cobham Aviation Services Australia	VH
Cayman Airways Express	VP-C	Cochrane Air Services	C
Cayman Airways	VP-C	Colombe Airlines	XT
CebGo	RP	Colt Transportes Aereo	PR
Cebu Pacific Air	RP	Columbia Helicopters	N
Ceiba Intercontinental	3C	Columbia Helicopters	P2
Cemair	ZS	Comair	ZS
Center-South Airlines	RA	Comeravia	YV
Central Asian	EX	Comercial Aerea	XA
Central Aviation Services	P2	Commutai	N
Central Connect Airlines	OK	Comores Aviation	D6
Central Mongolian Airways	JU	Comoros Islands Airways	D6
Central Mountain Air	C	Compass Airlines	N
Central South Island Helicopters	ZK	Compion Aviation	5Y
Centurion Air Cargo	N	Compion Aviation	V5
Cezanne Air Express	5Y	Comunidad Autónoma de Euskadi – Erzaintza	EC
CGG Aviation Canada	C	Conair Aviation	C
Chalair Aviation	F	Condor	D
Challenge Aero	UR	Congo Airways	TN
Cham Wings Airlines	YK	Connect Air	C
Champion Air	N	Constanta Airlines	UR
Chanchangi Airlines	5N	Continental	ER
Chang An Airlines	B	Conveyor Express	HK
Chapi Air	YV	Conviasa	YV
Chapleau Air Services	C	Copa Airlines Colombia	HK
Chartair	VH	Copa Airlines	HP
Charter Air Transport	N	Copenhagen Airtaxi	OY
Charter del Caribe	HK	Corendon Airlines	TC
Charter Express	HK	Corendon Dutch Airlines	PH
Chartright Air	C	Corilair Charters	C
Chathams Pacific	A3	Corpflite	CC
CHC Airways	PH	Corpo Forestale dello Stato	I
CHC Cameroon	TJ	Corporate Air	N
CHC Helicopters (Africa)	ZS	Corporate Air	VH
CHC Helicopters (Australia)	VH	Corporate Flight Management	N
CHC Helicopters International	C	Corsair	F
CHC Helicopters Netherlands	PH	Costa Airlines	YV
CHC Helicopters	VP-C	Cotair	TU
CHC Helikopter Service	LN	Cougar Helicopters	C
CHC Ireland	EI	Coulson Aircrane	C
CHC Nigeria	5N	Courtesy Air	C
CHC Scotia Helicopters	G	Coyot Air	EC
Chengdu Airlines	B	Coyotair Peru	OB
Cherokee Air	C6	Croatia Airlines	9A
Chilejet	CC	Croman Corp	N
Chimo Air Service (Peter Hagedorn Investments)	C	Cronos Airlines	3C
China Airlines	B	CSA Air	N
China Cargo Airlines	B	CSA Czech Airlines	OK
China Eastern Airlines Jiangsu	B	CTA – Cleiton Taxi Aereo	PR
China Eastern Airlines	B	Cubana de Aviacion	CU
China Eastern Yunnan	B	Custom Helicopters	C
China Express Airlines	B	Cybrair	LN
China Flying Dragon Aviation Co	B	Cygnus Air	EC
China Postal Airlines	B		
China Southern Airlines	B	Daallo Airlines	J2
China United Airlines	B	Dac East Africa/Dac Aviation	5Y
China West Air	B	Daily Air	B
China Xinhua Airlines	B	Dalian Airlines	B
Chongqing Airlines	B	Dana Airlines	5N
Christian Aviation	ZK	Danaus Lineas Aereas	XA
Chukotavia	RA	Dancopter	OY
Cimber	OY	Danish Air Transport	OY
Cinnamon Air	4R	DAP Helicopteros	CC
Citic Offshore Helicopters	B	Dart Airlines	UR
Citilink	PK	De Bruin Air	VH

Delta Air Company	ST
Delta Air Lines	N
Delta Air	A2
Delta Connection	N
Denim Air ACMI	PH
Deraya Air Taxi	PK
Desert Air Transport	N
Desert Air	V5
Dexter Air Taxi	RA
DGP Cuerpo Nacional De Policia	EC
DGT - Direccion General de Trafico	EC
DHL Aero Expreso	HP
DHL Air	G
DHL Aviation (Zimbabwe)	Z
DHL Aviation	ZS
DHL de Guatemala	TG
DHL International Aviation	A9C
Diexim Express	D2
Dimonim Air	PK
Direct Flight	G
Dirgantara Air Service	PK
Discovery Air	5N
Divi Divi Air	PJ
Dniproavia	UR
Dodson International Charter	ZS
Dolphin Airlines	N
Dominican Wings	HI
Donavia	RA
Donghai Airlines	B
Donghua Airlines	B
DOT - Danu Oro Transportas	LY
Dove Air	ST
Dragonair	B-H
Druk Air	A5
Dubnica Air	OM
Dynamic Airways/Aviation	N
Eagle Air Iceland	TF
Eagle Air Transport	N
Eagle Air Uganda	5X
Eagle Airways	ZK
Eagle Copters	C
Eaglexpress Air	9M
East African Air Charter	5Y
East Clipper	UR
East Horizon Airlines	YA
Eastar Jet	HL
Eastern Airlines	N
Eastern Airways	3DC
Eastern Airways	G
Eastern Australia Airlines	VH
Eastern Skyjets	A6
Eastindo	PK
Easy Fly Express	S2
Easy Link	5N
Easyfly`	HK
easyJet Switzerland	HB
easyJet	G
EasySky	HR
EAT Leipzig	D
EC Air	TN
Eco Express	CP
Ecojet	CP
Edelweiss Air	HB
EG & G	N
Egyptair Express	SU
Egyptair	SU
El Al Israel Airlines	4X
El Dinder	ST
El Magal Aviation	ST
Elbafly	I
Elbow River Helicopters	C
Elidolomiti	I
Elifriulia	I
Elilario Italia	I
Elilombarda	I

Elitaliana	I
Elite Airways	N
Elk Island Air	C
Ellinair	SX
Elysian Airlines	TJ
Emerald Coast Air	N
Emetebe Taxi Aereo	HC
Emirates International Air Cargo	A6
Emirates	A6
Empire Airlines	N
Endeavor Air	N
Enerjet	C
Enggang Air Service	PK
Enter Air	SP
Enter Lake Air Services	C
Envoy	N
EP Aviation	N
Epsilon Aviation	SX
Equaflight Service	TN
ERA Helicopters	N
Erickson Aero Tanker	N
Erickson Air Crane	N
Eritrean Airlines	E3
Erojet	UR
Estafeta Carga Aerea	XA
Estelar	YV
Estonian Air	ES
Ethiopian Airlines	ET
Etihad Airways	A6
Etihad Regional	HB
Euro-Asia Air International	UP
EuroAtlantic Airways	CS
Europe Air	UR
Europe AirPost	F
European Air Crane	I
Eurowings	D
Eva Airways	B
EVAS Air	C
Evelop Airline	EC
Everett Aviation	5H
Evergreen Helicopters	N
Everts Air Alaska	N
Everts Air Cargo	N
Everts Air Fuel	N
Ewa Air	F-O
Excellent Adventures Outposts	C
Excellent Air	D
Executive Turbine Air Charter	ZS
Executive Turbine Kenya	5Y
Exin	SP
Exploits Valley Air Services	C
Express Caribbean Airlines	9Y
Express Freighters Australia	VH
Expressair	C
Expressair	PK
Expressjet Airlines	N
FAASA – Fumigación Aérea Andaluza	EC
Fair Aviation	ZS
Falcon Air Charters	5Y
Falcon Air Express	N
Falcon Air Service	N
Falcon Aviation Services	A6
Far Eastern Air Transport	B
Farnair Hungary	HA
Farnair Switzerland	HB
Fast Air	C
Fastjet	5H
Fazza Sky/Dubai Skydive	A6
Federal Air	5Y
Federal Air	ZS
Fedex Express	N
Felix Airways	7O
FIGAS - Falkland Islands Government Air Services	VP-F
Fiji Airways	DQ

Fiji Link	DQ	Garuda Indonesia	PK
Fil-Asian Airways	RP	Gatari Air Service	PK
Finist'air	F	Gateway Canyons Air Tours	N
Finnair	OH	Gazpromavia	RA
Firefly	9M	GB Airlink	N
First Air	C	GEASA	3C
First Flying Co	JA	General Works Aviacion	3C
First Nation Airlines	5N	Genex	EW
Fits Aviation	4R	Georgian Airways	4L
Flair Airlines	C	Georgian International Airlines	4L
Fleet Air International	HA	Georgian Star International	4L
Fleet Management Airways	F	Germania	D
Flex Air Cargo	5Y	Germanwings	D
Flight 2000	ZK	Ghadames Air Transport	5A
Flight Alaska	N	Gianair	9G
Flight Inspections & Systems	RA	Gillam Air Services	C
Flightcare	ZK	Gira Globo	D2
Flightline	EC	Gisborne Helicopters	ZK
Flightlink Air Charters	5H	Glacier Southern Lake Helicopters	ZK
FLM Aviation	D	Glacier	C
Florida Air Transport	N	Glenorchy Air Services	ZK
Fly Adjara	4L	Global Africa Aviation	Z
Fly Allways	PZ	Global Air	XA
Fly Bvi	VP-L	Global Airways	VQ-T
Fly Jamaica	6Y	Global Aviation Leasing	ZS
Fly Logic	SE	Global Aviation	5A
Fly My Skyisland	ZK	Global Jet Airlines	A6
Fly Safari Air Link	5H	Globus	RA
Fly Sax	5Y	Go Air	VT
Fly Wales	G	Go! Express	N
Fly540	5Y	Go2Sky	OM
Fly540 Angola	D2	Gogal Air Services	C
FlyAfrica	9G	GoJet Airlines	N
FlyAfrica.com	Z	GOL Transportes Aereos	PR
Flybe Nordic	OH	Gold Coast Seaplanes	VH
Flybe	G	Goldak Airborne Surveys	C
FlyDubai	A6	Golden Bay Air	ZK
FlyEgypt	SU	Golden Eagle Airlines	VH
FlyExall	ZS	Golden Myanmar Airlines	XY
Flying America	LV	Golden Wings Aviation	ST
Flying Bulls	OE	Goldfields Air Services	VH
Flyme	8Q	Goma Air	9N
FlyMex	XA	Gomair	9Q
FlyNas	HZ	Government Of Quebec	C
FlySafair	ZS	Gozen Air Service	TC
Flyvista	4L	Grand Canyon Airlines	N
Flyways Linhas Aéreas	PR	Grand China Air	B
FMI Air	XY	Grand Cru Airlines	LY
Fonnafly	LN	Grant Aviation	N
Forde Lake Air Services	C	Great Barrier Airlines	ZK
Forest Protection	C	Great Lakes Airlines	N
Fort Frances Sportsmen Airways	C	Great Southern Airways	N
Fox Glacier Helicopters	ZK	Great Western Aviation	VH
FR Aviation	G	Great Wing Airlines	B
Freebird Airlines	TC	Green Airways	C
Freedom Air	N	Green Flag Aviation	ST
Freedom Air	ZS	Greenlandcopter	OY
Freedom Airlines Express	5Y	Grenadine Airways	J8
Freight Runners Express	N	Griffings Island Airlines	N
Fretax Taxi Aereo	PR	Grixona	ER
Frisia Luftverkehr	D	Grodno Air	EW
Frontier Airlines	N	Grondair/Grondin Transport	C
Frontier Flying Services	N	Grozny-Avia	RA
Fuga Air Charter	N	Grupo Inaer Aviones Anfibios	EC
Fugro Airborne Surveys	ZS	Gryphon Airlines	ZS
Fugro Malta	9H	GT Air	PK
Fuji Dream Airlines	JA	Guangdong Province General Aviation	B
Futura Travels	VT	Guicango	D2
Fuzhou Airlines	B	Guinea Equatorial Airlines	3C
		Guizhou Airlines	B
Gading Sari Aviation Services	9M	Gulf & Caribbean Air	N
Gainjet	SX	Gulf Air	A9C
Galeyr Airline	6O	Gulf Atlantic Airways	N
Gallup Flying Service	N	Gulf Helicopters	A7
Gam Air Services	VH	Gum Air	PZ
Garden City Helicopters	ZK	GX Airlines	B

Haajara Airline	6O	Helitrips	ZK
Hahn Air	D	Heli-Union	F
Hai Au Aviation	VN	Heliview Helicopter Flights	ZK
Hainan Airlines	B	Heliwest	VH
Hainan Asia Pacific General Aviation	B	Heliworks Queenstown	ZK
Hak Air	5N	Heliworks	CC
Hanair	HH	Helvetic Airways	HB
Hangar Uno	LV	Hermes Airlines	SX
Hankyu Airlines	JA	Hevilift Aviation Indonesia	PK
Happy Air	HS	Hevilift	9M
Happy Airlines	B	Hevi-Lift	P2
Harbour Air Seaplanes	C	Hex'air	F
Hardy Aviation	VH	Hi Fly Malta	9H
Harlequin Air	J8	Hi Fly	CS
Havana Air	N	Hibiscus Air	DQ
Hawaiian Airlines	N	High Country Helicopters	ZK
Hawk Air	C	Highland Helicopters	C
Hawk Air	LV	Himalaya Airways	9N
Hawk Airlines	AP	Hinterland Aviation	VH
Hawkair Aviation Service	C	HM Airways	D2
Hearst Air Service	C	HNZ Australia	VH
Hebei Airlines	B	HNZ/Helicopters New Zealand	ZK
Hebei Avic General Aviation	B	Hokkaido Air System	JA
Hebridean Air Services	G	Holidayjet	HB
Heletranz	ZK	Holidays Czech Airlines	OK
Heli 7	ZK	Hong Kong Express Airways	B-H
Heli A1	ZK	HongKong Airlines	B-H
Heli Air Monaco	3A	Hop! Airlinair	F
Heli Air Services	LZ	Hop! Brit'air	F
Heli Campeche	XA	Hop! Régional	F
Heli Dubai	A6	Horizon Air	N
Heli Harvest	ZK	Hornbill Skyways	9M
Heli Holland	PH	Hulunbeier Avic General Aviation	B
Heli Niugini	P2	Hunnu Air	JU
Heli Sika	ZK	Huron Air And Outfitters	C
Heli Sky	EX	Hydro-Quebec (Service Transport Aerien)	C
Heli South	ZK		
Heli Tours	ZK	I Fly	RA
Helibravo Aviación	EC	IAS Helicopters	TU
Helicol	HK	IBC Airways	N
Heliconia Offshore Helicopters	CN	Iberia Express	EC
Helicopter Services	EP	Iberia Lineas Aereas de Espana	EC
Helicopter Services (Bay Of Plenty)	ZK	Ibex Airlines	JA
Helicopter Seychelles	S7	Icar Air	E7
Helicopteros del Pacifico	OB	Icarus Flying Service	C
Helicopteros del Sur	OB	Icelandair	TF
Helicópteros Insulares	EC	IDC Aircraft	S7
Helicopters Hawkes Bay	ZK	Ignace Airways	C
Helicopters Otago	ZK	Ikar	RA
Helicorp	ZK	Iliamna Air Taxi	N
Heliduero	EC	Ilin Aviakompania	RA
Heliexpress	C	Inaer Aviation Italia	I
Helifix Operations	P2	Inaer Helicopter Peru	OB
Helifly	HK	Inaer Helicoptères	F
Helifor Industries	C	Inaer Helicopters	EC
Heligo Charters	VT	IndiGo	VT
Heligolfo	HK	Indonesia Air Transport	PK
Heli-Italia	I	Indonesia AirAsia X	PK
Helijet International	C	Indonesia AirAsia	PK
Heli-Lift International	C	Infinity Heliline	ZK
Helilink	ZK	Inland Air Charters	C
Heli-Malongo	D2	Insel Air Aruba	P4
Helimar - Helicopters del Mare Nostrum	EC	Insel Air	PJ
Helipistas	EC	Instone Air Services	G
Heliportugal	CS	Integra Air	C
Heliservicio	XA	Inter Caribbean Express	J6
Helistar Cambodia	XU	Inter Coastal Air	N
Helistar Colombia	HK	Inter Regional Express	F-O
Helisul Taxi Aereo	PR	Interair	ZS
Helisur	OB	Interandes	HK
Heliswiss Iberica	EC	Inter-Archipelago Airways	N
Helitec	YV	Intercaribbean Airways	VQ-T
Helitours	4R	Intercopters	EC
Helitrans Pyrinees	EC	InterIsland Airlines	RP
Helitrans	C3	Interjet	XA
Helitrans	LN	International Air Response	N

International Airlink	6Y	Jungle Flying	TG
Intersky	OE		
Interstate Airways	ST	Kabeelo Airways	C
Iraero	RA	Kabo Air	5N
Iran Air	EP	Kaikoura Helicopters	ZK
Iran Airtours	EP	Kaiserair	N
Iran Aseman Airlines	EP	Kakadu Air Services	VH
Iranian Air Transport	EP	Kalahari Air Services And Charter	A2
Iraqi Airways	YI	Kalitta Air	N
Irs Airlines	5N	Kalitta Charters	N
Island Air Charters	N	Kalitta Flying Services	N
Island Air Charters	ZK	Kalstar Aviation	PK
Island Air Service	N	Kam Air	YA
Island Air Transport	N	Kamaka Air	N
Island Air	N	Kampala Executive Aviation	5X
Island Airlines	N	Kan Air	HS
Island Airways	N	Kanimanbo	C9
Island Aviation Services	8Q	Kannithi Aviation	HS
Island Express Air	C	Kapiti Heliworks	ZK
Island Hoppers	DQ	Karinou Airlines	TL
Island Nationair	P2	Karratha Flying Services	VH
Island Seaplane Service	N	Kasas	5Y
Island Transvoyager	RP	Kasba Air Service/Lake Lodge	C
Island Wings Air Service	N	Kata Transportation	ST
Islcna Airlines	HR	Katekavia	RA
Isles Of Scilly Skybus	G	Katherine Aviation	VH
Israir	4X	Katmai Air	N
Itab – International Trans Air Business	9Q	Kavok Airlines	YV
Ivoirienne de Transports Aeriens	TU	Kaya Airlines	C9
Izhavia	RA	Kayair Service	C
		Kazairjet	UP
Jackson Air Services	C	Kazan Air Enterprises	RA
Jagson Airlines	VT	Kazaviaspas	UP
J-Air	JA	KD Air	C
Jamaica Air Shuttle	6Y	Keewatin Air	C
Jambojet	5Y	Ken Air	5Y
Japan Air Commuter	JA	Kenai River Xpress	N
Japan Airlines International	JA	Kenair	5Y
Japan Transocean Air	JA	Kenmore Air Express	N
Jayawijaya Dirgantara	PK	Kenmore Air	N
Jazeera Airways	9K	Kenn Borek Air	C
Jedair	5N	Kenora Air Service	C
Jeju Air	HL	Kenya Airways	5Y
Jet 4 Now	ZS	Kenya Forest Service	5Y
Jet Air Group	RA	Key Lime Air	N
Jet Airways	VT	Keystone Air Service	C
Jet Asia Airways	HS	KF Cargo	C
Jet Eagle International	RP	Khabarovsk Airlines	RA
Jet Time	OY	Kharkiv Airlines	UR
Jet2	G	Khatlon Air	EY
Jet-2000	RA	Khors Air	UR
Jetairfly	OO	Kilwa Air	5H
Jetblue Airways	N	Kimberley Air	VH
Jetconnect	ZK	Kin Avia	9Q
Jetfly.com	TJ	King Air Charter	ZS
Jetgo Australia	VH	King Air	N
JetKonnect	VT	King Island Airlines	VH
Jetstar Airways	VH	Kirland Aviation	N
Jetstar Asia Airways	9V	Kish Air	EP
Jetstar Japan	JA	Kivalliq Air Nunavut Lifeline	C
Jetstar Pacific Airlines	VN	KJM Air	VH
Jettime Finland	OH	KLM Cityhopper	PH
Jhonlin Air Transport	PK	KLM Royal Dutch Airlines	PH
Jiangnan Universal Aviation	B	Kluane Airways	C
Jilin Province General Aviation	B	K-Mile Air	HS
Jim Hankins Air Service	N	KNAAPO	RA
Jin Air	HL	Kolavia	RA
Johnny May's Air Charters	C	Kolob Canyons Air Services	N
Johnsons Air	9G	Komavia Trans	RA
Jordan Aviation	JY	Korea Express Air	HL
Jordan International Air Cargo	JY	Korean Air Express	HL
Joy Air	B	Korean Air	HL
JP Air Cargo	ES	Korean Business Air Service/KBAS	HL
JS Air Charter	AP	Korongo Airlines	9Q
Jubba Airways	5Y	Kosmos	RA
Juneyao Airlines	B	Kostroma Air Enterprise	RA

Krasavia	RA	Lloyd Helicopter	RP
Kulula.com	ZS	Loch Lomond Seaplanes	G
Kunming Airlines	B	Loftleidir Icelandic	TF
Kura-Kura Aviation	PK	Loganair	G
Kush Air	ST	Logistic Air	N
Kuwait Airways	9K	LOT - Polish Airlines	SP
		LR Airlines	OK
L and A Aviation	C	Lucky Airlines	B
L-3 Flight International Aviation	N	Lufthansa Cargo	D
La Compagnie	F	Lufthansa Cityline	D
La Costena	YN	Lufthansa	D
LAB Flying Service	N	Lufttransport	LN
Labrador Air Safari	C	Luftverkehr Friesland Harle	D
Labrador Airways	C	Lukiaviatrans	RA
LAC – Linea Aérea Cuencana	HC	Lukoil Avia	RA
Lac La Croix Quetico Air Service	C	Luxair	LX
Lac Seul Airways	C	Lynden Air Cargo	N
LADE - Lineas Aereas del Estado	LV	Lynden Air Cargo	P4
Lake & Peninsula Airlines	N	Lynx Aviacao Taxi Aereo	PR
Lake Clark Air	N		
Lake Victoria Flying Safaris	5H	M & N Aviation	N
Lakeland Helicopters	ZK	Macair Jet	LV
Lakelse Air	C	Machjet	VH
Lakes District Air Services	C	Mack Air	A2
LAM - Linhas Aereas de Mocambique	C9	Madagascar Trans Air	5R
Lamia	P4	Magnicharters	XA
LAN Airlines Colombia	HK	MAGRAMA–Ministerio de Agricultura,	
LAN Airlines	CC	Alimentacion y Medio Ambiente	EC
LAN Argentina	LV	Mahan Air	EP
LAN Cargo	CC	Mainland Air Services	ZK
LAN Ecuador	HC	Majestic Air Cargo	RP
LAN Express	CC	Major Blue Air	A2
LAN Peru	OB	Makalu Air	9N
LANHSA	HR	Makond Air-Link	C9
Lankan Cargo	4R	Malagasy Airlines	5R
Lao Airlines	RDPL	Malawian Airlines	7Q
Lao Central Airlines	RDPL	Malaysia Airlines	9M
Lao Skyways	RDPL	Malaysian Helicopter Services	9M
Laser Aereo	HK	Maldivian Air Taxi	8Q
Laser	YV	Maldivian	8Q
LASSA- Linea de Aeroservicios	CC	Maleth-Aero	9H
Latin Air Cargo	PR	Malindo Airways	9M
Latina de Aviacion	HK	Malmö Aviation	SE
Lauzon Aviation	C	Malu Aviation	9Q
Lawrence Bay Airways	C	Manaus Aerotaxi	PR
Layang-Layang Aerospace	9M	Mandarin Airlines	B
Laynha Air	VH	Mango	ZS
LC Busre	OB	Manitoba Government Air Services	C
Leair Charter Services	C6	Mann Yadanarpon Airlines	XY
Lease Fly	CS	Manunggal Air Service	PK
Legacy Air	HS	MAP Linhas Aereas	PR
Leis Air	N	Marianas Air Transfer	N
Leuenberger Air Service	C	Marin Air	TC
LGQ - Luftfahrtgesellschaft Walter	D	Maritime Air Charter	C
Liat - The Caribbean Airline	V2	Marlborough Helicopters	ZK
Libyan Air Cargo	5A	Maroomba Airlines	VH
Libyan Airlines	5A	Martinair Holland	PH
Libyan Wings	5A	Martinaire	N
Lider Taxi Aereo	PR	Martini Aviation	C
Lignes Aeriennes Congolaises	9Q	Masair	XA
Lijing Helicopters	B	Massawa Airways	E3
Limitless Airways	9A	MASwings	9M
Linea Aerea Costa Norte	CC	Mauritania Airlines International	5T
Linea Aerea Cuencana	HC	Maverick Helicopters	N
Linea Turistica Aereotuy	YV	Max Aviation	C
Lineas Aereas Canedo	CP	Maxair	5N
Lineas Aereas Carguera de Colombia	HK	Maxair	TU
Lineas Aereas Comerciales	XA	Maxavia	EX
Lineas Aéreas Suramericanas	HK	Maximus Air Cargo	A6
Link Airs	JA	Maya Island Air	V3
Link PNG	P2	Mayair	XA
Links Air	G	MCC Aviation	ZS
Linxair	S5	McDermott Aviation	P2
Lion Airlines	PK	MCHS Rossii	RA
Little Red Air Service	C	McMurray Aviation	C
Little Red	G	Mcneely Charter Service	N

MCS Aerocarga	XA
MDLR Airlines	VT
Med Airways	OD
Medavia	9H
Med-View Airlines	5N
Mega Global Maldives	8Q
Megaviation	ER
Meiya Airways	B
Mena Aerospace	A9C
Menard	N
Meraj Air	EP
Meridian Air	RA
Meridian Airways	9G
Meridian	UR
Merlin Airways	N
Mesa Airlines	N
Mesoamerica Air Services	TG
MGC Airlines	ZS
MHS Aviation	D
MHS Aviation/Malaysian Helicopter Services	9M
Miami Air International	N
Miami Air Lease	N
MIAT Mongolian Airlines	JU
Mid Airlines	ST
Middle East Airlines	OD
Midex Airlines	A6
Midwest Connect	N
Mihin Lanka	4R
Milford Sound Flights	ZK
Milford Sound Helicopters	ZK
Military Support Services	VH
Millenium Aviation Transportes	TG
Mimika Air	PK
Minair	TL
Minden Air	N
Minipi Aviation	C
Ministerio de Hacienca Servicio de Vigilanica Aduenera	EC
Minoan Air	SX
Missionary Aviation Fellowship	P2
Mississippi Air Express	N
Mistral Air	I
Mistral Aviation	TN
Misty Fjords Air	N
MNG Cargo Airlines	TC
Mocambique Expresso	C9
Modern Logistics	PR
Mokulele Airlines	N
Molson Air	C
Mombasa Air Safari	5Y
MonacAir	3A
Monarch Airlines	G
Montenegro Airline	4O
Moonair	4X
Moremi Air Services	A2
Morningstar Air Express	C
Motor Sich Airlines	UR
Mount Cook Airline	ZK
Mount Hutt Helicopters	ZK
Mountain Air Cargo	N
Mountain Air	ZK
Mountain Helicopters	9N
Mountain Helicopters	ZK
Movil Air Tours	OB
MRK Airlines	UR
Mustang Helicopters	C
Mustique Airways	J8
My Indo Airlines	PK
Myanmar Airways International	XY
Myanmar National Airlines	XY
MyCargo Airlines	TC
Myflug	TF
NAC Charter	ZS
Nac Executive Charter	A2
Nacional de Aviacion Colombia	HK
Naft Air Lines	EP
Nakina Outpost Camps and Air Service	C
Nam Air	PK
Namibia Commercial Airways	V5
Nation Air	HH
National Airlines	N
National Airways Cameroon	TJ
National Airways Corp	ZS
National Aviation Services	P2
National Helicopter Services	9Y
National Helicopters	C
National Utility Helicopters	PK
Nationale Gabon	3C
Native American Air Service	N
Nature Air	TF
Natureair	TI
NaturelinkCharter	ZS
Nauru Airlines	C2
Nelair Charter	ZS
Neos	I
Nepal Airlines	9N
Neptune Air	9M
Neptune Aviation Services	N
Nesma Airlines	SU
Nestoil	5N
Nestor Falls Fly-In Outposts	C
Network Aviation Australia	VH
New Central Air Service	JA
New England Airlines	N
New Japan Aviation	JA
Newfoundland & Labrador Air Services	C
Newgen Airlines	HS
Next Jet	SE
Niger Airlines	5U
Nightexpress	D
Niigaani Air	C
Niki	OE
Nile Air	SU
Nippon Cargo Airlines	JA
NK Air	RA
Nok Air	HS
Nokomai Helicopters	ZK
NokScoot	HS
Nolinor Aviation	C
Nomad Air	C
Nomad Aviation	5H
Noordzee Helikopters	OO
Nord Aviation	N
Nord Helikopter	LN
Nordavia Regional Airlines	RA
Nordflyg Air Logistics	SE
Nordic Global Airlines	OH
Nordlandsfly	LN
Nordplus	C
Nordstar	RA
Nordwind	RA
Norlandair	TF
Norrlandsflyg Ambulans	SE
Norsk Helikopter	LN
Norsk Luftambulanse	LN
North Cariboo Air/Flying Service	C
North Coast Aviation	P2
North Express	SE
North Flying	OY
North Shore Helicopters	ZK
North Star Air Cargo	N
North Star Air	C
Northeast Shuttle	VT
Northern Air Cargo	N
Northern Air Charter	A2
Northern Air Charter	C
Northern Air Services Charter	DQ
Northern Air Solutions	C
Northern Air	5H
Northern Rockies Air Charter	C

Northern Thunderbird Air	C	Panair Cargo	HP
Northern Thunderbird Air	C	Pantanal	PR
Northland Emergeny Services Trust	ZK	Papillon Grand Canyon Airways	N
Northsky Air	RP	Paradigm Air Carriers	N
Northward Air	C	Paradise Air	TI
Northway Aviation	C	Parsa	HP
Northwest Flying	C	Pascan Aviation	C
Northwestern Air	C	Passaredo Transportes Aereos	PR
North-Wright Airways	C	Pawa Dominicana	HI
Norwegian Air International	EI	Payam	EP
Norwegian Long Haul	LN	Peach	JA
Norwegian	LN	Pearl Aviation	VH
Nouvelair	TS	Peau Vava'u Air	A3
Nouvelle Air Congo	TN	Pec Taxi Aereo	PR
Nouvelles Air Affaires Gabon	TR	Pecotax-Air	ER
Nova Airways	ST	Pegasus Air Services	PK
Novair	SE	Pegasus Airlines	TC
Novoair	S2	Pel-Air	VH
NT Air	C	Pelican Air	VH
Nusantara Air Charter	PK	Pelican Aviation & Tours	5H
Nusantara Buana Air	PK	Pelican Narrows Air Services	C
Nyaman Air	PK	Pelita Air	PK
		Penair/Peninsula Airways	N
Ocean Pacific Air Services	C	People's Viennaline	OE
Ohana	N	Perimeter Aviation	C
Oil Spill Response	G	Perla Airlines	YV
Okay Airways	B	Peruvian Airlines	OB
Olympic Air	SX	Petro Air	5A
Oman Air	A4O	Petrokam	RA
Omega Aerial Refuelling	N	Petroleos de Venezuela	YV
Omega Air	N	Petroleum Air Service	HK
Omni - Aviacao e Tecnologia	CS	Petroleum Air Services	SU
Omni Air International	N	Petroleum Helicopters	9G
Omni Taxi Aereo	PR	Petroleum Helicopters	N
One Airlines	CC	Petropavlovsk-Kamchatsky Air Enterprise	RA
Ontario Ministry of Natural Resources Aviation		PGA Express	CS
Services	C	PHI - Petroleum Helicopters	N
Onur Air	TC	PHI Helicopters	4X
OpenSkies	F	Philips Search & Rescue Services	ZK
Opsmobil	C	Phoebus Apollo Aviation	ZS
Orange Air	N	Phoenix Air	N
Orbest	CS	Phoenix Aviation	5Y
Orca Airways	C	Picton Float Plane	ZK
Orenair	RA	Piedmont Airlines	N
Orenburzhye	RA	Pineapple Air	C6
Orient Thai Airlines	HS	Pink Aviation	OE
Oriental Air Bridge	JA	Pinnacle Air	VT
Ornge Global Air	C	Piquiatuba Taxi Aereo	PR
Ortiz Taxi Aereo	PR	Planemasters	N
Osnaburgh Airways	C	Pobeda	RA
Osprey Express	N	Polar Air Cargo	N
Osprey Wings	C	Polar Airlines	RA
Over The Top	ZK	Polar Aviation	VH
Overland Airways	5N	Police Aviation Service	G
Oyonnair	F	Polynesian Airlines	5W
		Porter Airlines	C
Pacific Air Express	H4	Portugalia Airlines	CS
Pacific Airways	N	Pouya Airlines	EP
Pacific Coastal Airlines	C	Precision Air	5H
Pacific Helicopters	P2	Precision Helicopters	ZK
Pacific Helicopters	ZK	Premiair Aviation Services	G
Pacific Helicoptor Tours	N	Premiair	PK
Pacific Island Air	DQ	Prime Air Services	5N
Pacific Sky Aviation	C	Primera Air Nordic	YL
Pacific Wings	N	Primera Air Scandinavia	OY
Pacificair	RP	Priority Air Charter	N
Pakistan International Airlines	AP	Priority Air	N
PAL Airlines	C	Privatair	D
PAL Express	RP	Privatair	HB
Philippine Airlines	RP	Private Airways	HB
Palau Pacific Airways	T8A	Private Wings	D
Palestinian Airlines	SU-Y	Privilege Style	EC
Pan African Airways	5Y	Pro Aire Cargo	N
Pan Air	EC	Proflight Commuter Services	9J
Pan Européenne Air Service	F	Proflight Venezuela	YV
Pan Malaysian Air Transport	9M	Proflight-Zambia	9J

Promech Air	N	Royal Brunei Airlines	V8
Pronto Airways	C	Royal Falcon	JY
Propair	C	Royal Flight	RA
Proservicios	HI	Royal Flying Doctor Service	VH
Province Of Alberta Air Transportation Services	C	Royal Jordanian Xpress	JY
Provincial Airlines	C	Royal Jordanian	JY
PSA Airlines	N	Royal Star Aviation	RP
Pskovavia	RA	Royal Wing	JY
Ptarmigan Air	N	RPX Republic Express	PK
PTL Luftfahrtunternehmen	D	Ruby Star	EW
Puma Air	PR	Ruili Airlines	B
Punto Azul	3C	Ruraima Taxi Aereo	PR
		Rus Aviation	EK
Qantas Airways	VH	Rusline	RA
Qantas Freight	VH	Russian State Transport	RA
Qantaslink	VH	Rust's Flying Service/Rustair	N
Qatar Airways	A7	Rusty Myers Flying Service	C
Qeshm Air	EP	Rutaca	YV
Qingdao Airlines	B	Rvr Aviation	N
Qinghai Dragon General Aviation	B	Rwandair	9XR
Quantum Helicopters	C	Ryan Air	N
Queensway Air Services	5Y	Ryan Air	N
Qwila Air	ZS	Ryanair	EI
R Airlines	HS	S Group International	EX
R1 Airlines	C	S7 Airlines	RA
Rabbit Wings Airways	HS	SA Express	ZS
RAC - Ryukyu Air Commuter	JA	Sabah Air	9M
Raf-Avia	YL	Sabang Merauke Raya Air Charter	PK
Rainbow Airways	C	Sabourin Lake Lodge	C
Rainbow Jet	B	Sadelca	HK
Ram Air Services	N	Saereo	HC
Ravn Alaska	N	Safari Air	A2
Raya Airways	9M	Safari Express Airways	5H
RCMP-GRC Air Services (Royal Canadian Mounted Police)	C	Safarilink Aviation	5Y
Real Tonga Airlines	A3	Safe Air Kenya	5Y
Reconnaissance Ventures	G	Saffron Aviation	4R
Red Sea Air	E3	Safi Airways	YA
Red Sucker Lake Air Services	C	Sahand Airlines	EP
Red Wings Airlines	RA	Sahara African Aviation	ZS
Redding Aero Enterprises	N	SAL - Sociedade de Aviacao Ligeira	D2
Reeve Air Alaska	N	Salamis Aviation	C6
Regent Airways	S2	Salt Air	ZK
Regio-Air	D	Salt Spring Island Air	C
Regional Air Lines	CN	Saltwater West Enterprises	C
Regional Air Services	5H	Samoa Air	5W
Regional Air	C6	San Juan Airlines	N
Regourd Aviation	F	Sandbar Air	N
Reid Helicopters Nelson	ZK	Sandy Lake Seaplane Service	C
Republic Airways	N	SANSA	TI
REX – Regional Express	VH	Santa Barbara Airlines	YV
Rhein-Neckar Air	D	SAP – Sociedad Aeronáutica Peninsular	EC
Ribway Cargo Airlines	5Y	Sapair	HI
Rico Linhas Aereas	PR	Sapawe Air	C
Rico Taxi Aereo	PR	Saratov Airlines	RA
Ridge Air	ZK	Sarpa – Rent Air/Servicios Aereos Panamericanos	HK
Rio Branco Aerotaxi	PR	SAS Taxi Aereo	CX
Rio Linhas Aereas	PR	SASCA	YV
Rio Madeira Aerotaxi - RIMA	PR	SASEMAR– Sociedad de Salvamento y Seguridad Maritima	EC
River Air	C	Saskatchewan Government Northern Air Operations	C
RJM Aviation	TT		
ROC Aviation	B		
Roraima Airways	8R	SATA Air Acores	CS
Ross Air Service	C	SATA International	CS
Ross Air	C	Satena	HK
Rossair Charter	VH	Saudi Gulf Airlines	HZ
Rossair Kenya	5Y	Saudi Medevac	HZ
Rossair	ZS	Saudia	HZ
Rossiya Airlines	RA	Saurya Airlines	9N
Rotana Jet	A6	Savannah Air Services	5Y
Rotorsun	EC	Sazma Aviation	9M
Rovos Air	ZS	SBA	YV
Royal Air Charters	9J	Scandinavian Airambulance	SE
Royal Air Freight	N	Scandinavian Airline System	SE
Royal Air Maroc	CN	Scandinavian Airline System	LN

Scandinavian Airline System	OY	Sichuan West General Aviation	B
Scanwings	OH	Sideral Air Cargo	PR
SCAT	UP	Sierra Pacific Airlines	N
SCD Aviation	TR	Sierra West Airlines	N
Scenic Airlines	N	Sifton Air Yukon	C
Scoot	9V	Siga Taxi Aereo	PR
Scott Air	N	Sil Aviation	P2
SEAA	D2	Silesia Air	OK
Seabird Airlines	TC	Silk Road Cargo Business	UK
Seaborne Airlines	N	Silk Way Airlines	4K
Seair Airways	C6	Silk Way Helicopters	4K
Seair Pacific Gold Coast	VH	Silk Way West Airlines	4K
Seair Seaplanes	C	Silkair	9V
Seaplanes Africa	5H	Siller Helicopters	N
Seaport Airlines	N	Silver Air	OK
Searca	HK	Silver Airways	N
Seawing Airways	VH	Silver Fern Helicopters	ZK
Seawings	A6	Silverback Cargo Freighters	9XR
Securité Civile	F	Simplifly	4R
Sefofane Air Charter	A2	Simpson Air	C
Sefofane Air	V5	Simrik Airlines	9N
Seguridad Maritima	EC	Singapore Airlines Cargo	9V
Selva Colombia	HK	Singapore Airlines	9V
Semeyavia	UP	Sioux Narrows Airways	C
Senegal Airlines	6V	Sirius Aero	RA
Senegalair	6V	Sita Airlines	9N
Sepahan Airlines	EP	SJL Aeronáutica	D2
Sepehran Airlines	EP	Skagway Air Service	N
Serair Transworld Press	EC	Skippers Aviation	VH
Serami	YV	Skiva Air	EK
Servant Air	N	Skol	RA
Servicaribe Express	HK	Sky Air	OK
Services Air	9Q	Sky Air	S2
Services	C	Sky Airline	CC
Servicio Aereo Regional	HC	Sky Angkor Airlines	XU
Servicios Aereos Aeroconexos	HC	Sky Aviation Tanzania	5H
Servicios Aereos de los Andes	OB	Sky Aviation	PK
Servicios Aereos del Sur	CX	Sky Bahamas	C6
Servicios Aereos MTT	XA	Sky Bishkek	EX
Servicios Aereos Patagonicos	LV	Sky Express	SX
Servicios Aereos Profesionales	HI	Sky Gabon	TR
Servicios Aereps Sucre	YV	Sky Georgia	4L
Servis Air	D2	Sky Helicopteros	EC
SETCO	HR	Sky High Aviation	HI
Sete Linhas Aereas	PR	Sky Horse Aviation	JU
Seven Stars Air Cargo	N	Sky KG Airlines	EX
Severin Air Safaris	5Y	Sky King	N
Severstal	RA	Sky Lease Cargo	N
SF Airlines	B	Sky Net Airline	EK
Shaheen Air Cargo	AP	Sky Prim Air	ER
Shaheen Air International	AP	Sky Regional Airlines	C
Shan Xi Airlines	B	Sky Shuttle Helicopters	B-H
Shandong Airlines	B	Sky Way Air	EX
Shandong General Aviation	B	Sky Wind	4K
Shanghai Airlines	B	Skybird Air	5N
Shanxi General Aviation	B	Skybridge Airops	I
Shar Ink	RA	Skybus Jet Cargo	N
Sharp Airlines	VH	Skyforce Aviation	VH
Sharp Wings	C	SkyGreece Airlines	SX
Shenzhen Airlines	B	Skyhaul	ZS
Shenzhen Grand Sea Aviation	B	Skyjet	RP
Shin Chuo Koku	JA	Skylan Airways	6Y
Shine Air	5H	Skyline Aviation	ZK
Shine Aviation Services	VH	Skylink Arabia	A6
Shoal Air	VH	Skylink Express	C
Shortstop Air Charter	VH	Skymark Airlines	JA
Shovkoviy Shlyah	UR	Skynorth Air	C
Showalter's Fly-In Service	C	Skypower Express Airways	5N
Shree Airlines	9N	Skyservice Business Aviation	C
Shuangyang Aviation	B	Skysouth	G
Shuttle America	N	Skytaxi	SP
Siam Air Transport	HS	Skytraders	VH
Siberian Light Aviation	RA	Skytrails	5Y
Sibnia	RA	Skytrans Regional	VH
Sichuan Airlines	B	Skyward International Aviation	5Y
Sichuan Aolin General Aviation	B	Skyway Enterprises	N

Skyways Kenya	5Y
Skywest Airlines	N
Skywise	ZS
Skywork Airlines	HB
Skywork Helicopters	ZK
Slate Falls Airways	C
Slingair	VH
Slovak Government Flying Service	OM
SMA Helicopter Rescue	SE
Small Planet Airlines	LY
Small Planet Airlines	SP
Smart Aviation	SU
Smart Cargo	LX
Smartlynx Estonia	ES
Smartlynx	YL
Smartwings	OK
Smokey Bay Air	N
SNAS Aviation	HZ
Soc Beninoise des Hydrocarbures	TY
Sociedad Aeronáutica Peninsular	EC
Sol Lineas Aereas	LV
Sol Linhas Aereas	PR
Solar Cargo	YV
Solaseed Air	JA
Solenta Aviation (Kenya)	5Y
Solenta Aviation	5H
Solenta Aviation	ZS
Solinair	S5
Solitaire Air	JY
Solomon Airlines	H4
Som-Air	6O
Somon Air	EY
Sonair	D2
Sophia Airlines	TU
Sorem/Protezione Civile	I
Soriano Aviation	RP
Soundsair Travel & Tourism	ZK
South Aero	N
South African Airways	ZS
South Airlines	EK
South Airlines	UR
South China Sea Rescue Aviation	B
South East Air	ZK
South Nahanni Airways	C
South Supreme Airlines	ST
South Western Helicopters	G
Southern Air Charters	C6
Southern Air	N
Southern Alps Air	ZK
Southern Lakes Helicopters	ZK
Southern Seaplane	N
Southern Star Airways	ST
Southwest Air	P2
Southwest Airlines	N
Spectrum Air Services	N
Speedstar Express	N
Spernak Airways	N
Spicejet	VT
Spirit Air	N
Spirit Airlines	N
Spring Airlines Japan	JA
Spring Airlines	B
Springbok Classic	ZS
Sprintair	SP
Spruce Air	C
Srilankan	4R
Srilankan Air Taxi	4R
Sriwijaya Air	PK
St Barth Commuter	F-O
St Lucia Helicopters	J8
STA-Sociedade de Transports Aéreos	C9
Star Air Aviation	AP
Star Air Cargo	ZS
Star Air	OY
Star Aviation	7T
Star Flyer	JA

Star Peru	OB
Starbow	9G
Stars Away Aviation	ZS
State Airline 224 Flight Unit	RA
State Aviation Enterprise Ukraine	UR
Stellavia	9Q
Stobart Air	EI
Strait Air	C
Suburban Air Freight	N
Sudamericana	HC
Sudan Airways	ST
Sudbury Aviation	C
Summit Air (Charters)	C
Summit Helicopters	C
Sun Air Express	N
Sun Air Of Scandinavia	OY
Sun Air	ST
Sun Country Airlines	N
Sunair Aviation	ZK
Sunbird Aviation	P2
Sundance Air	YV
Sundance Helicopters	N
Sunday Airlines	UP
Sundt Air	LN
Sunexpress Deutschland	D
SunExpress	TC
Sunrise Airways	HH
Sunshine Helicopters	N
Sunstate Airlines	VH
Sunwest Aviation	C
Sunwing Airlines	C
Superior Airways	C
Superior Aviation Services	5Y
Supreme Aviation	EX
Surf Airlines	N
Surinam Airways Commuter	PZ
Surinam Airways	PZ
Susi Air	PK
Sverdlovsk 2nd Air Enterprise	RA
SVG Air	J8
SW Business Aviation	4K
SW Italia	I
Swala Airlines	9Q
Sweden Rescue	SE
Swedish Maritime Administration	SE
Swift Air	N
Swift Aircargo	9V
Swift Flite	ZS
Swiftair Hellas	SX
Swiftair	EC
Swiss Global Air Lines	HB
Swiss	HB
Sydney Seaplanes	VH
Syphax Airlines	TS
Syrian Arab Airlines	YK
T'way Air	HL
T2 Aviation	G
TAAG Angola Airlines	D2
Tab Air Charter	ZS
TAB Cargo	CP
Taban Airlines	EP
TAC Airlines	S2
TACA Costa Rica	TI
TACA Peru	OB
TACV - Transportes Aereos de Cabo Verde	D4
TAF Helicopters	EC
Taftan Airlines	EP
Tailwind Airlines	TC
Tailwind International	N
Tajik Air	EY
Talkeetna Air Taxi	N
Talon Air Service	N
TAM - Transportes Aereo Militar	CP
TAM Cargo	PR
TAM Linhas Aereas	PR

TAM Mercosur	ZP	Trabajos Aéreos Espejo	EC
TAME Amazonia	HC	Trackmark Cargo	5Y
TAME	HC	Trade Air	9A
TAMExpress	HC	Tradewind Aviation	N
Tanana Air Service	N	Tramon Air	ZS
Tanzanair - Tanzanian Air Services	5H	Trans Air Benin	TY
TAP Air Portugal	CS	Trans Air Cargo Services	9Q
TAPSA	LV	Trans Air Congo	TN
Taquan Air Service	N	Trans Am Aero Express	HC
TAR - Transportes Aereos Regionales	XA	Trans Anguilla Airlines	VP-A
Tara Air	9N	Trans Capital Air	C
Taranaki Air Ambulance	ZK	Trans Executive Airlines of Hawaii	N
Tarco Air	ST	Trans Guyana Airways	8R
Tarom	YR	Trans Island Air 2000	8P
TAS - Transporte Aereo de Santander	HK	Trans Maldivian Airways	8Q
Tasfast Air Freight	VH	Trans Nation Airways	ET
Tashi Air	A5	Trans Oriente	HK
Tasman Cargo Airlines	VH	Trans States Airlines	N
Tasman Helicopters	ZK	Transaer	OB
Tassili Airlines	7T	Transaero Airlines	RA
Tatarstan Air	RA	Transafricaine Air Cargo	XT
Taupo's Floatplane	ZK	Transafrik International	D2
Taxi Aérea de Caldas	HK	Transair	6V
Taxi Aéreo Caribeno	HK	Transair	N
Taxi Aéreo Cusiana	HK	Transasia Airways	B
Taxi Aéreo de Ibague	HK	Transaven – Transporte Aereo Venezuela	YV
Taxi Aéreo de la Costa - Taxco	HK	Transavia Export	EW
Taxi Aereo Ribeiro	PR	Transavia France	F
TBM	N	Transavia	PH
Teddy Air	ET	Transaviabaltika	LY
Teebah Airlines	JY	Transcarga	YV
Temsco Helicopters	N	Transmandu	YV
Ten Airways	YR	TransNiugini Airways	P2
Tengerin Elch	JU	Transnorthern Aviation	N
Tessel Air	PH	Transnusa Aviation Mandiri	PK
Texel Air	A9C	Transport Canada	C
Tezjet	EX	Transporte Aereo de Colombia	HK
Thai AirAsia X	HS	Transportes Aereos Bolivianos	CP
Thai AirAsia	HS	Transportes Aereos Cielos Andinos	OB
Thai Airways International	HS	Transportes Aereos Corporativos	CC
Thai Aviation Services	HS	Transportes Aereos Guatemaltecos	TG
Thai Express Air	HS	Transportes Aereos Pegaso	XA
Thai Flying Service	HS	Transportes Aereos Regionales	XA
Thai Lion Air	HS	Transportes Aereos Terrestres	XA
Thai Smile Airways	HS	Transportes Bragado	LV
Thai Vietjet Air	HS	Transwest Air	C
The Cargo Airlines	4L	Transwisata Air	PK
The Helicopter Line	ZK	Transworld Safaris	5Y
THK - Turk Hava Kurumu	TC	Travel Air	P2
Thomas Air	JU	Travel Express	PK
Thomas Cook Airline Belgium	OO	Travel Service Hungary	HA
Thomas Cook Airlines Scandinavia	OY	Travel Service Poland	SP
Thomas Cook Airlines	G	Travel Service Slovakia	OM
Thomson	G	Travel Service	OK
Thunder Airlines	C	Travira Air	PK
Thunderbird Aviation	C	Trident Aviation/Enterprises	5Y
Tianjin Airlines	B	Trigana Air Service	PK
Tiara Air	P4	Tri-Mg Intra-Asia Airlines	PK
Tibet Airlines	B	Tristar Air	SU
Tigerair Australia	VH	Tropic Air Charters	N
Tigerair Taiwan	B	Tropic Air Commuter	P2
Tigerair	9V	Tropic Air	5Y
Tiko Air	5R	Tropic Air	V3
Timair	6Y	Tropical Air (Zanzibar)	5H
Tintina Air	C	Tropical Airways	HH
Titan Airways	G	Tropical Transport Services	N
TNT Airways	OO	Tropicana	D2
Tobruk Air	5A	True Aviation	S2
Tofino Air Lines	C	Tsayta Aviation	C
Toll Aviation	VH	TSSKB Progress Aviakompania	RA
Tombouctou Aviation	TZ	TTA – Sociedade de Transporte e Trabalho	
Tomskavia	RA	Aereos	C9
Topbrass Aviation	5N	Tudhope Airways	C
Tortug'air	HH	TUI Netherland	PH
Total Linhas Aereas	PR	Tuifly Nordic	SE
Toumaï Air Tchad	TT	Tuifly	D

Airline	Code
Tunisair Express	TS
Tunisair	TS
Tunisavia	TS
Turbo Flite Aviation	N
Turkish Airlines	TC
Turkmenistan Airlines	EZ
Turtle Airways	DQ
Turukhan Aviakompania	RA
Tusheti	4L
Tweedsmuir Air Services	C
Twin Coast Helicopters	ZK
Twin Jet	F
Two Taxi Aero	PR
Tyax Air Service	C
Tyrolean Jet Service	OE
UB Air	HL
Ufly Airways	N
Uganda Air Cargo	5X
Ukraine Airalliance	UR
Ukraine International Airlines	UR
ULS Cargo	TC
Ultimate Jetcharters dba Ultimate Air Shuttle	N
UM Air	UR
Unapu Freight Services	P2
Uni Air	B
Unindo Aircharter	PK
Union Air	LV
United Air Charters	Z
United Air Lines	N
United Airways	S2
United Express	N
United Offshore Helicopters	HS
Uni-Top Airlines	B
Unity Airlines	YJ
Universal Airlines	B
Universal Airlines	N
Universal Avia	UR
Universal Helicopters	C
Uniworld Air Cargo	5Y
Unsped Paket Servisi	TC
Up	4X
UPS Airlines	N
Ural Airlines	RA
Urgemer Canarias	EC
Urumqi Airlines	B
US Airways Express	N
US Airways	N
US Department Of Energy	N
US Helicopters	N
USA Jet Airlines	N
US-Bangla Airlines	S2
USDA Forest Service	N
UTair Airlines	RA
UTair Cargo	RA
UTair Europe	OM
UTair Express	RA
UTair South Africa	ZS
UTair Ukraine	UR
Utin Lento	OH
Uvauga	RA
Uzbekistan Airways	UK
V Air	B
Valan International Cargo	ER
Van Air	OK
Van City Seaplanes	C
Vancouver Island Air	C
Vanilla Air	JA
Varig	PR
VASCO	VN
Vee Neal Aviation	N
Vega Offshore	YR
Venexcargo	YV
Venezolana	YV
Vensecar Internacional	YV
Vent Airlines	N
Ventura Airconnect	VT
Vera Cruz Taxi Aereo	PR
Vertical de Aviacion – Airfreight Aviation	HK
Veteran Avia	EK
Vi Air Link	VP-L
Via	LZ
Viarco	HK
Vias Aereas Nacionales	HK
Vieques Air Link	N
Vietjet	VN
Vietnam Airlines	VN
Vietnam Seaplane Shuttle	VN
Vigo Jet	XA
VIH Helicopters	C
Viking Outpost Air	C
Villa Air	8Q
Villers Air Services	C
Vim Airlines	RA
VIP - Vuelos Internos Privados	HC
Virgin America	N
Virgin Atlantic Airways	G
Virgin Australia	VH
Virgin Australia Regional Airlines	VH
Virgin Samoa	ZK
Vision Air International	AP
Vision Air	C6
Vision Air	HH
Vision Air	N
Vista Georgia	4L
Vistara	VT
Viva Aerobus	XA
Viva Colombia	HK
Vizion Air	PH
VLM Airlines	OO
Vol Air	HI
Volaris	XA
Volcanic Air	ZK
Volga-Dnepr Airlines	RA
Vologda Air Enterprise	RA
Volotea Airlines	EC
Vostok Airlines	RA
Voyage Air	C
Voyageur Airways	C
Vuela Airlines	YS
Vueling Airlines	EC
Waasheshkun Airways	C
Wabakimi Air	C
Wahkash Contracting	C
Wairarapa Helicopters	ZK
Wamair Service & Outfitting	C
Wamos Air	EC
Wanair	F-O
Warbelows Air	N
Ward Air	N
Wasaya Airways	C
Watermakers Air	N
Watson's Skyways	C
Way To Go Heliservices	ZK
WDL Aviation	D
Weagamow Air	C
Welcome Air	OE
West Air Sweden	SE
West Airpac	N
West Atlantic	G
West Caribbean Airways	HK
West Caribou Air Service	C
West Coast Air	C
West Wind Aviation	C
West Wing Aviation	VH
Westair Aviation	V5
Westair Benin	TY
Westair Cargo Airlines	TU
Westair de Mexico	XA
Westair Wings Charters	ZS

Western Air Express	N	Xiamen Airlines	B
Western Air	C6	Xinjiang General Aviation	B
Western Airways	N	XI Airways France	F
Western Global Airlines	N	XP Taxi Aereo	PR
Westjet Encore	C	Xtra Airways	N
Westjet	C	Xugana Air	A2
Westmann Islands Airlines	TF		
Westwind Air	N	YAK-Servis	RA
Westwind Aviation	N	Yakutia Airlines	RA
Westwind Aviation	TL	Yamal Airlines	RA
Wettenhall Air Services	VH	Yan Air	UR
White Airways	CS	Yangon Airways	XY
White River Air Services	C	Yangtze River Express	B
White River Helicopters	C	Yellow Wings Air Services	5Y
Whitsunday Air Services	VH	Yellowhead Helicopters	C
Widerøe's Flyveselskap	LN	Yemenia Yemen Airways	7O
Wiggins Airways	N	Yeti Airlines	9N
Wildcat Helicopters	C	Ying'an Airlines	B
Wilderness Air	A2	YoungOne	S2
Wilderness Air	C	Yukon Aviation	N
Wilderness Air	V5	Yuzmashavia	UR
Wilderness North Air	C		
Will Airlift	9Q	Zagros Airlines	EP
Wimbi Dira Airways	9Q	Zagrosjet	YI
Winair	PJ	Zambia Flying Doctor	9J
Windrose Air	UR	Zanair	5H
Windward Express Airways	PJ	Zantas Air Service	5H
Windward Islands Airways	PJ	ZB Air	5Y
Wings & Water	ZK	Zetavia	UR
Wings Abadi Air	PK	Zhejiang Donghua General Aviation	B
Wings of Alaska	N	Zhejiang Loong Airlines	B
Wings of Lebanon Aviation	OD	Zhez Air	UP
Wings over Kississing - Kississing Lake Lodge	C	Zhongfei General Aviation	B
Wings Over Whales	ZK	Zhongshan Eagle	B
Wizz Air	HA	Zhoushan AVIC General Aviation	B
Woodgate Executive Air Services	G	Zhuhai General Aviation	B
World Atlantic Airlines	N	Zil Air	S7
Wow Air	TF	Zimex Aviation	HB
Wright Air Service	N	Zorex	EC
Wuhan Helicopters General Aviation	B		
Wyngs Aviation	YV		

ALLIANCES

ONEWORLD

	AFFILIATES
airberlin	NIKI
American Airlines	Envoy, US Airways Express
British Airways	BA Cityflyer, Comair, Sun-Air of Scandinavia
Cathay Pacific Airways	Dragonair
Finnair	Flybe Finland
Iberia	Air Nostrum, Iberia Express
Japan Airlines	J-AIR, Japan Transocean Air
LAN Airlines	LAN Argentina, LAN Colombia, LAN Ecuador, LAN Express, LAN Peru
Malaysia Airlines	
QANTAS Airways	QantasLink, JetConnect
Qatar Airways	
Royal Jordanian	
S7 Airlines	Globus
TAM Linhas Aereas	

SKYTEAM

Aeroflot Russian Airlines	
Aerolineas Argentinas	Austral Lineas Aereas
AeroMexico	AeroMexico Connect
Air Europa	
Air France	CityJet
Alitalia	
China Airlines	Mandarin Airlines
China Eastern Airlines	Shanghai Airlines
China Southern Airlines	
CSA Czech Airlines	
Delta Air Lines	Delta Connection, Delta Shuttle
Garuda Indonesia	
Kenya Airways	
KLM Royal Dutch Airlines	KLM Cityhopper
Korean Air	
Middle East Airlines	
Saudia	
TAROM	
Vietnam Airlines	
Xiamen Airlines	

STAR ALLIANCE

Adria Airways	
Aegean Airlines	Olympic Air
Air Canada	Air Canada Express, Rouge
Air China	Dalian Airlines
Air India	Air India Regional
Air New Zealand	Air New Zealand Link
ANA-All Nippon Airways	Air Japan, ANA Wings
Asiana Airlines	
Austrian Airlines	
Avianca/TACA	Avianca Brasil, Avianca Costa Rica, Avianca Ecuador, Avianca El Salvador, Avianca Guatemala, Avianca Honduras, Avianca Nicaragua, Avianca Peru
Brussels Airlines	
Copa Airlines	Copa Airlines Colombia
Croatia Airlines	
Egyptair	Air Sinai, Egyptair Express
Ethiopian Airlines	
EVA Airways	Uni Air
LOT Polish Airlines	
Lufthansa	Air Dolomiti, Eurowings, Germanwings, Lufthansa Cityline
SAS-Scandinavian Airlines System	Blue1
Shenzhen Airlines	
Singapore Airlines	Scoot, SilkAir
South African Airways	Airlink, Mango, South African Express
SWISS	Edelweiss Air, Swiss European Air Lines
TAP Portugal	GA Express, Portugalia
Thai Airways International	Thai Smile
Turkish Airlines	Anadolu Jet, SunExpress
United	United Express

NOTES

NOTES

NOTES